THE ROUGH GUIDE TO

Europe

2002 EDITION

There are more than two hundred Rough Guide titles
covering destinations from Alaska to Zimbabwe
and subjects from Acoustic Guitar to Travel Health

Forthcoming travel guides include

The Algarve • The Bahamas • Cambodia • The Caribbean
Costa Brava • New York Restaurants • South America • Zanzibar

Forthcoming reference guides include

Children's Books • Online Travel • Weather

Rough Guides Online
www.roughguides.com

ROUGH GUIDE CREDITS

Text editor: Lucy Ratcliffe
Series editor: Mark Ellingham
Editorial: Martin Dunford, Jonathan Buckley, Jo Mead, Kate Berens, Ann-Marie Shaw, Helena Smith, Judith Bamber, Orla Duane, Olivia Eccleshall, Ruth Blackmore, Geoff Howard, Claire Saunders, Gavin Thomas, Alexander Mark Rogers, Polly Thomas, Joe Staines, Richard Lim, Duncan Clark, Peter Buckley, Lucy Ratcliffe, Clifton Wilkinson, Alison Murchie, Matthew Teller (UK); Andrew Rosenberg, Stephen Timblin, Yuki Takagaki, Richard Koss (US)
Production: Susanne Hillen, Andy Hilliard, Link Hall, Helen Prior, Julia Bovis, Michelle Draycott, Katie Pringle, Mike Hancock, Zoë Nobes, Rachel Holmes, Andy Turner

Cartography: Melissa Baker, Maxine Repath, Ed Wright, Katie Lloyd-Jones
Picture research: Louise Boulton, Sharon Martins, Mark Thomas
Online: Kelly Cross, Anja Mutig-Blessing, Jennifer Gold, Audra Epstein, Suzanne Welles (US)
Finance: John Fisher, Gary Singh, Edward Downey, Mark Hall, Tim Bill
Marketing & Publicity: Richard Trillo, Niki Smith, David Wearn, Chloë Roberts, Claire Southern, Demelza Dallow, (UK); Simon Carloss, David Wechsler, Kathleen Rushforth (US)
Administration: Tania Hummel, Julie Sanderson

CONTRIBUTORS

Rob Andrews (Italy); Jon Bousfield (Austria, Estonia, Latvia, Lithuania, Poland); Brian Catlos (Spain); Lance Chilton (Greece); Marc Dubin (Greece); Rupert Eden (Portugal); Nick Edwards (Greece); Bernadette Fallon (Ireland); Tracey Gambarotta (Italy); Geoff Garvey (Greece); Jon Gorvett (Turkey); Sharon Harris (Belgium & Luxembourg); Charles Hebbert (Hungary); Justin Holmes (Turkey); Rob Humphries (Austria); Daniel Jacobs (Basics, Morocco); Francisca Kellett (France); Jeffrey Kennedy (Italy); Susie Lunt (Czech Republic, Slovakia); Norm Longley (Croatia, Hungary, Slovenia); Malijn Maake (Netherlands); Gordon McLachlan (Germany); Lone Mouritsen (Denmark); David O'Byrne (Turkey); Catherine Phillips (Russia); Josephine Quintero (Spain); Neil Roland (Sweden); Paul Sentobe (Britain); Alexander Sirbu (Romania); Annette Slettbakk (Norway); Paul Smith (Spain); Andrew Spooner (Finland); Matthew Teller (Switzerland); Richard Watkins (Bulgaria).

ACKNOWLEDGEMENTS

Thanks on this edition due to Judith Bamber, Matthew Teller and Sam Thorne for their invaluable help with the text editing; Maxine Burke for cartography; Rachel Holmes for her heroic feats with the typesetting; Laurence Larroche and David Price for proofreading; and Helena Smith for indexing.

READERS' LETTERS

Many thanks to all those readers who wrote in with comments and updates on the previous edition including Mark Doser, Alan Hickey, Julie Lepsetz, Carl Schoenfeld, Keith Tester, Niklas Tunley and Toni Vorobyova.

HELP US UPDATE

We've gone to a lot of effort to ensure that *The Rough Guide to Europe* is thoroughly up to date and accurate. However, things in Europe do change with alarming rapidity, and we'd very much appreciate any comments, corrections or additions for the next edition of the book. For the best letters, we'll send a copy of the new edition or any other Rough Guide.

Please mark letters: "Rough Guide Europe Update" and send to: Rough Guides Ltd, 62–70 Shorts Gardens, London WC2H 9AH, or Rough Guides, 4th floor, 375 Hudson St, New York, NY 10014. Or send email to: mail@roughguides.co.uk
Online updates about this book can be found on Rough Guides' Web site at www.roughguides.com

THE ROUGH GUIDE TO

Europe

2002 EDITION

**ROUGH
GUIDES**

THE ROUGH GUIDES

TRAVEL GUIDES • PHRASEBOOKS • MUSIC AND REFERENCE GUIDES

 We set out to do something different when the first Rough Guide was published in 1982. Mark Ellingham, just out of university, was travelling in Greece. He brought along the popular guides of the day, but found they were all lacking in some way. They were either strong on ruins and museums but went on for pages without mentioning a beach or taverna. Or they were so conscious of the need to save money that they lost sight of Greece's cultural and historical significance. Also, none of the books told him anything about Greece's contemporary life – its politics, its culture, its people, and how they lived.

So with no job in prospect, Mark decided to write his own guidebook, one which aimed to provide practical information that was second to none, detailing the best beaches and the hottest clubs and restaurants, while also giving hard-hitting accounts of every sight, both famous and obscure, and providing up-to-the-minute information on contemporary culture. It was a guide that encouraged independent travellers to find the best of Greece, and was a great success, getting shortlisted for the Thomas Cook travel guide award,

and encouraging Mark, along with three friends, to expand the series.

The Rough Guide list grew rapidly and the letters flooded in, indicating a much broader readership than had been anticipated, but one which uniformly appreciated the Rough Guide mix of practical detail and humour, irreverence and enthusiasm. Things haven't changed. The same four friends who began the series are still the caretakers of the Rough Guide mission today: to provide the most reliable, up-to-date and entertaining information to independent-minded travellers of all ages, on all budgets.

We now publish more than 150 titles and have offices in London and New York. The travel guides are written and researched by a dedicated team of more than 100 authors, based in Britain, Europe, the USA and Australia. We have also created a unique series of phrasebooks to accompany the travel series, along with an acclaimed series of music guides, and a best-selling pocket guide to the Internet and World Wide Web. We also publish comprehensive travel information on our Web site:

www.roughguides.com

PUBLISHING INFORMATION

This eighth edition published November 2002 by
  Rough Guides Ltd, 62–70 Shorts Gardens, London
  WC2H 9AH.
  Distributed by the Penguin Group:
Penguin Books Ltd, 80 Strand, London WC2R ORL
Penguin Putnam, Inc., 375 Hudson Street, New York,
  NY 10014, USA
Penguin Books Australia Ltd, 487 Maroondah Highway,
  PO Box 257, Ringwood, Victoria 3134, Australia
Penguin Books Canada Ltd, 10 Alcorn Avenue, Toronto,
  Ontario, Canada M4V 1E4
Penguin Books (NZ) Ltd, 182–190 Wairau Road,
  Auckland 10, New Zealand
Typeset in Linotron Univers and Century Old Style to an
  original design by Andrew Oliver.
Printed in England by Clays Ltd, St Ives Plc. and in the
  United States by R.R.Donnelly & Son's Ltd.

Montages on p.1 & p.67 by Katie Pringle and Rob Evers
© Jonathan Buckley and Martin Dunford, 2001
No part of this book may be reproduced in any form
  without permission from the publisher except for the
  quotation of brief passages in reviews.
1424pp - Includes index
A catalogue record for this book is available from the
  British Library
ISBN 1-85828-737-5

CONTENTS

LIST OF MAPS

MAP SYMBOLS

▬ ▬ ▬	National boundary	♟	Museum
═══	Road	▪	Building
▬▬▬	Pedestrianized street	✝	Church
- - - -	Path	✡	Synagogue
▥▥▥	Steps	⛪	Monastery
▬▬▬	Railway	☪	Mosque
— —	Ferry route	⊞	Hospital
▓▓▓	River/canal	✉	Post office
▪▪▪▪	Wall	*i*	Information office
▒▒	Park	ℭ	Telephone
⊹⁺⊹⁺	Christian cemetery	✇	Swimming pool
ʸʸʸ	Muslim cemetery	Ⓜ	Metro station
⌐⌐	Jewish cemetery	◆	Barcelona metro station
▒▒▒	Forest	Ⓢ	S-Bahn
▒▒	Beach	Ⓤ	U-Bahn
⌒	Mountains	Ⓣ	Tram stop
▲	Peak	⊖	London Underground Station
※	Hill	🅿	Parking
⭣	Viewpoint	★	Bus stop
♦	Point of interest	⊠	Gate

PART ONE

THE
BASICS

INTRODUCTION

The collapse of the division between eastern and western **Europe** at the end of the 1980s, and the ever closer ties among the fifteen countries of the European Union – increasingly a political and cultural as well as economic union – made Europe a buzzword in the early 1990s, implying shared values and, despite all the wrangling, a broad consensus of political beliefs. Some of this is inevitably a superficial analysis, but although true European unity still remains a distant dream, developments such as the introduction of the euro, the creation of the frontier-free Schengen Group and the opening of the Channel Tunnel have done much to bring it closer.

Conventionally, the **geographical boundaries** of Europe are the Ural Mountains in the east, the Atlantic Coast in the north and west, and the Mediterranean in the south. However, within these rough parameters Europe is massively diverse. The environment changes radically within very short distances, with bleak mountain ranges never far from broad, fertile plains, and deep, ancient forests close to scattered lake systems or river gorges. Politically and ethnically, too, it is an extraordinary patchwork: Slavic peoples are scattered through central Europe from Poland in the north to Serbia and Bulgaria in the south; the Finnish and Estonian languages bear no resemblance to the tongues of their Baltic and Scandinavian neighbours, but more to that of Hungary, over 1000km south; meanwhile Romansch, akin to ancient Latin, is spoken in the valleys of southeastern Switzerland, while the Basques of the Western Pyrenees have a language unrelated to any others known. These differences have become more political of late with the rise of nationalism that coincided with the fall of Communism, and borders are even now being redrawn, not always peacefully, and usually along ethnic lines defined by language, race or religion.

Where you head for obviously depends on your tastes and the kind of vacation you want: you can sample mountain air and winter sports in the Alps of France, Austria or Switzerland, lie on a beach in the swanky resorts of the south of France or Italy, or view architecture and works of art in the great cities of London, Paris, Florence or Amsterdam. Suffice to say, the lifting of restrictions on travel in eastern Europe, with only a handful of countries still requiring visas and nothing like the bureaucratic regulations there were before, means that the Continent really is there for the travelling – something manifest in the increasingly good-value rail passes (see pp.20–23) which cover most of the countries in this book. Although you may want to make a long hop or two by air, **rail** is indeed the way to see the Continent, highlighting the diversity of the place when you travel in a few hours from the cool temperatures of northern Europe to the rich and sultry climes of the Mediterranean. In fact, with the richness and diversity of its culture, climate, landscapes and peoples, there is no more exciting place to travel.

This book is a little eccentric in its **definition of Europe**. We have excluded countries such as Albania, Belarus, Moldova and Ukraine, which are too far off the beaten track to be on most people's European "grand tour", while of the war-torn and strife-riven republics that have been carved out of the former Yugoslavia, only Slovenia and Croatia have been included as easily accessible and currently safe to visit.

On the other hand, we cover the British Isles and countries like Morocco and Turkey that are not strictly part of Europe, in the main because they are easy to reach on a European tour and are included by the InterRail pass. We also have chapters on Russia, Estonia, Latvia and Lithuania, though these countries are not covered by the InterRail pass.

CLIMATE AND WHEN TO GO

Europe's **climate** is as variable as everything else about the Continent. In **northwestern Europe** – Benelux, Denmark, southwestern Norway, most of France and parts of Germany, as well as the British Isles – the climate is basically a cool temperate one, with the chance of rain all year round and no great extremes of either cold or hot weather. There is no bad time to travel in most of this part of the Continent, although the winter months between November and March can be damp and miserable – especially in the upland regions – and obviously the summer period between May and September sees the most reliable and driest weather.

In **eastern Europe**, on the other hand, basically to the right of a north–south line drawn roughly through the heart of Germany and extending down as far as the western edge of Bulgaria (taking in eastern Germany, Poland, central Russia, the Baltic states, southern Sweden, the Czech and Slovak republics, Austria, Switzerland, Hungary and Romania), the climatic conditions are more extreme, with freezing winters and sometimes sweltering summers. Here the transitional spring and autumn seasons are the most pleasant time to travel; deep midwinter, especially, can be very unpleasant, although it doesn't have the dampness you associate with the northwestern European climate.

Southern Europe, principally the countries that border the Mediterranean and associated seas – southern France, Italy, Spain, Portugal, Greece and western Turkey – has the most hospitable climate in Europe, with a general pattern of warm, dry summers and mild winters. Travel is possible at any time of year here, although the peak summer months can be very hot and very busy and the deep winter ones can see some rain.

There are, too, marked regional variations within these three broad groupings. As they're such large countries, inland Spain and France can, for example, see a **continental** type of weather as extreme as any in central Europe, and the Alpine areas of Italy, Austria and Switzerland – and other **mountain areas** like the Pyrenees, Apennines and parts of the Balkans – have a climate mainly influenced by altitude, which means extremes of cold, short summers, and long winters that always see snow. There are also, of course, the northern regions of Russia and Scandinavia, which have an **Arctic climate** – again, bitterly cold, though with some surprisingly warm temperatures during the short summer when much of the region is warmed by the Gulf Stream. Winter sees the sun barely rise at all in these areas, while high summer can mean almost perpetual daylight.

There are obviously other considerations when deciding **when to go**. If you're planning to visit fairly touristed areas, especially beach resorts in the Mediterranean, avoid July and August, when the weather can be too hot and the crowds at their most congested. Bear in mind, also, that in a number of countries in Europe everyone takes their **vacation** at the same time (this is certainly true in France, Spain and Italy where everyone goes away in August). Find out the holiday month beforehand for the countries where you intend to travel, since you can expect the crush to be especially bad in the resorts; in the cities the only other people around will be fellow tourists, which can be miserable. In northern Scandinavia the climatic extremes are such that you'll find opening times severely restricted, even road and rail lines closed, outside the May–September period, making travel futile and sometimes impossible outside these months. In mountainous areas things stay open for the winter sports season, which lasts from December through to April, though outside the main resorts you'll again find many things closed. Mid-April to mid-June can be a quiet period in many mountain resorts, and you may have much of the mountains to yourselves.

TEMPERATURE CHART

	Jan	Feb	March	April	May	June	July	Aug	Sept	Oct	Nov	Dec
Amsterdam	4/40	5/42	9/49	13/56	18/64	21/70	22/72	22/71	19/67	14/57	9/48	6/42
Ankara	4/40	6/42	11/51	17/63	23/73	26/78	30/86	31/87	26/78	21/69	14/57	6/43
Athens	13/55	14/57	16/60	20/68	25/77	30/86	33/92	33/92	29/84	24/75	19/66	15/58
Berlin	2/35	3/37	8/46	13/56	19/66	22/72	24/75	23/74	20/68	13/56	7/45	3/38
Brussels	4/40	7/42	10/51	14/58	18/65	22/72	23/73	22/72	21/69	15/60	9/48	6/42
Bratislava	-1/30	0/30	5/41	10/50	13/58	12/54	20/68	19/67	16/61	10/50	4/40	0/32
Bucharest	1/34	4/40	10/50	18/64	23/74	27/81	30/86	30/85	25/78	18/65	10/49	4/40
Budapest	1/34	4/40	10/50	17/62	22/71	26/78	28/82	27/81	23/74	16/61	8/47	4/40
Copenhagen	2/36	2/36	5/41	10/51	16/61	19/67	22/71	21/70	18/64	12/54	7/45	4/40
Dublin	8/46	8/47	10/50	13/55	15/60	18/65	20/67	19/67	17/63	14/57	10/51	8/47
Helsinki	-3/26	-4/25	0/32	6/44	14/56	19/66	22/71	20/68	15/59	8/47	3/37	-1/31
Istanbul	8/46	9/47	11/51	16/60	21/69	25/77	28/82	28/82	24/76	20/68	15/59	11/51
Lisbon	14/57	15/59	17/63	20/67	21/71	25/77	27/81	28/82	26/79	22/72	17/63	15/58
London	6/43	7/44	10/50	13/56	17/62	20/69	22/71	22/71	19/65	14/58	10/50	7/45
Luxembourg	3/37	4/40	10/49	14/57	18/65	21/70	23/73	22/71	19/66	13/56	7/44	4/40
Madrid	9/47	11/52	15/59	18/65	21/70	27/80	31/87	30/85	25/77	19/65	13/55	9/48
Moscow	-9/15	-6/22	0/32	10/50	19/66	21/70	23/73	22/72	16/61	9/48	2/35	-5/24
Oslo	-2/28	-1/30	4/40	10/50	16/61	20/68	22/72	21/70	16/60	9/48	3/38	0/32
Paris	6/43	7/45	12/54	16/60	20/68	23/73	25/76	24/75	21/70	16/60	10/50	7/44
Prague	0/31	1/34	7/44	12/54	18/64	21/70	23/73	22/72	18/65	12/53	5/42	1/34
Rabat	17/63	18/65	20/68	22/71	23/73	26/78	28/82	30/83	27/81	25/77	21/70	18/65
Riga	-4/25	-3/27	2/35	10/50	16/61	21/69	22/71	21/70	17/63	11/52	4/40	-2/29
Rome	11/52	13/55	15/59	19/66	23/74	28/82	30/87	30/86	26/79	22/71	16/61	13/55
Sofia	2/35	4/40	10/50	16/60	21/69	24/76	27/81	26/79	22/70	17/63	9/48	4/40
Stockholm	-1/30	-1/30	3/37	8/47	14/58	19/67	22/71	20/68	15/60	9/49	5/40	2/35
Tallinn	-4/25	-4/25	0/32	7/45	14/57	19/66	20/68	19/66	15/59	10/50	3/38	-1/30
Vienna	1/34	3/38	8/47	15/58	19/67	23/73	25/76	24/75	20/68	14/56	7/45	3/37
Vilnius	-5/25	-3/26	1/34	12/54	18/65	21/71	23/74	22/71	17/62	11/52	4/40	-3/26
Warsaw	0/32	0/32	6/42	12/53	20/67	23/73	24/75	23/73	19/66	13/55	6/42	2/35
Zürich	2/36	5/41	10/51	15/59	19/67	23/73	25/76	24/75	20/69	14/57	7/45	3/39

Figures are average daily maximum in °C /°F

TRAVELLING FROM NORTH AMERICA

The air space between North America and Europe is one of the most heavily travelled in the world. It is served by literally dozens of airlines, both US carriers and the national airlines of almost every European country, and there is consequently a huge range of seats at a huge range of prices. It all depends on when and from where you're travelling, and, of course, where you want to go. There are, however, a number of "gateway" cities into which you'll find a greater – and cheaper – choice of options.

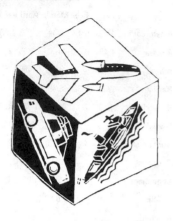

SHOPPING FOR TICKETS

Barring special offers, the cheapest of the airlines' published fares is usually an **Apex** ticket, although this will carry certain restrictions: you have to book – and pay – at least 21 days before departure, spend at least 7 days abroad (maximum stay 3 months), and you tend to get penalized if you change your schedule. There are also winter **Super Apex** tickets, sometimes known as "Eurosavers" – slightly cheaper than an ordinary Apex, but limiting your stay to between 7 and 21 days. Some airlines also issue **Special Apex** tickets to people younger than 24, often extending the maximum stay to a year. Many airlines offer youth or student fares to **under 25s**; a passport or driving licence is sufficient proof of age, though these tickets are subject to availability and can have eccentric booking conditions. It's worth remembering that most cheap return fares involve spending at least one Saturday night away and that many will only give a percentage refund if you need to cancel or alter your journey, so make sure you check the restrictions carefully before buying a ticket.

Most of the airlines maintain a fare structure which peaks between mid-June and early September and over the Christmas period, with cheaper deals available for the rest of the year, particulary during the winter months (November and March), when fewer people are travelling. You'll often find the cheapest fare by leaving from the airline's "hub" – New York, Atlanta, Dallas, Chicago, Los Angeles, San Francisco, Seattle, Vancouver, Toronto and Montréal are the main ones; hub cities also tend to have nonstop flights, with no changes at all. You do, however, need to be flexible: London, Paris, and Amsterdam are usually the cheapest "gateway cities" in Europe, simply because they are served by more flights; Milan, Rome and Frankfurt run a close second in some cases. Flying midweek rather than at the weekend is also a few dollars cheaper.

You can normally cut costs further by going through a **specialist flight agent** – either a **consolidator**, who buys up blocks of tickets from the airlines and sells them at a discount, or a **discount agent**, who in addition to dealing with discounted flights may also offer special student and youth fares and a range of other travel-related services such as travel insurance, rail passes, car rentals, tours and the like. Bear in mind, though, that penalties for changing your plans can be stiff (check the refund policy, and pay with a credit card if possible: then if you do change your mind there's a chance you can stop the payment going through). Some agents specialize in **charter flights**, which may be cheaper than anything available on a scheduled flight, but again departure dates are fixed and withdrawal penalties are high. If you travel a lot, **discount travel clubs** are another option – the annual membership fee may be worth it for benefits such as cut-price air tickets and car rental.

Remember that these companies make their money by dealing in bulk – don't expect them to answer lots of questions, and don't automatically assume that tickets from a travel specialist will be cheapest – once you get a quote, check with the airlines and you may turn up an even better deal. Be advised also that the pool of travel companies is swimming with sharks – exercise caution and never deal with a company that demands cash up front or refuses to accept payment by credit card.

A further possibility is to see if you can arrange a **courier flight**, although the hit-or-miss nature of these makes them most suitable for the single traveller who travels light and has a very flexible schedule. In return for shepherding a parcel through customs and possibly giving up your baggage allowance, you can expect to get a deeply discounted ticket. For more information on courier outfits, consult *A Simple Guide to Courier Travel* (New York: Pacific Data Sales Publishing).

If Europe is only one stop on a longer journey, you might want to consider buying a **Round-the-World (RTW) ticket**. Some travel agents can sell you an "off-the-shelf" RTW ticket that will have you touching down in about half-a-dozen cities (almost all include at least one in Europe); others will have to assemble a route for you, which can be more tailored to your needs but is apt to be more expensive. At the cheapest end of the scale, a low season RTW ticket with an itinerary of New York–Bangkok–Katmandu–London–New York could cost as little as $1365.

FLIGHTS FROM EASTERN AND CENTRAL USA

There are lots of options from most of the **eastern hub cities**, though most of the best deals are out of New York and Chicago to London. The official Apex 90-day advance round-trip fare from New York to London with the major carriers (British Airways, Virgin, American, etc) is, at the time of writing, $403 in low season, $733 in high season, plus taxes. If you don't want to book 3 months in advance, or be limited to a stay of just a few weeks, you should be able to find discounted fares, especially if you're a student or under-26, for around $360/$550. From Chicago, official Apex 90-day advance fares to London are $600/$780 depending on the season, with more flexible discounted tickets at around $395/$685. To give an idea of other alternatives, discounted tickets from New York can be found for $460/$740 to Paris ($509/$825 from Chicago), $530/$740 to Frankfurt ($530/$835 from Chicago), $595/$840 to Madrid ($630/$940 from Chicago), and $575/$840 to Athens ($685/$1135 from Chicago). There may also be Special Limited promotional offers which appear from time to time, especially in the off-peak seasons; each winter, for example, Virgin Atlantic have New York–London fares, with no advance purchase necessary, for $99 each way.

FLIGHTS FROM THE WEST COAST

From the **West Coast** it's much the same story. The big airlines fly at least three times a week (sometimes daily) from Los Angeles, San Francisco and Seattle to main European cities. The major carriers have plenty of flights, with round-trip 90-day-advance Apex fares from LA starting at $600 to London. Again, you can avoid the 3-month advance booking and length of stay restrictions and still find a comparatively inexpensive fare by going to a discount agent or youth travel specialist, where you can find tickets for $540/$762 (depending on the time of year) for a round trip to London, $530/$865 to Paris, $695/$955 to Frankfurt, $695/1085 to Madrid, and $715/$1220 to Athens.

FLIGHTS FROM CANADA

Most of the big airlines fly to the major European hubs from **Montreal** and **Toronto** at least once daily (3 times a week for the smaller airlines). From Toronto, London is your cheapest option, with the lowest official round-trip fares, as bought directly from the airline, currently at around CDN$900/CDN$1200 (depending on the time of year). From Montreal to Paris you can expect to pay CDN$1000/CDN$1100. Once again, a discount/student specialist such as Travel CUTS should be able to find a fare that's more flexible and, possibly, cheaper; current examples of discounted fares include CDN$529 from Toronto to London and CDN$689 from Montreal to Paris.

Flights from **Vancouver** have become more convenient since the expansion of the airport, with daily flights to London and other European cities now on offer. Round-trip fares to London can be had for around CDN$1000/CDN$1150, depending on the season.

PACKAGES AND ORGANIZED TOURS

Although you may want to see Europe in your own time, at your own pace, you shouldn't entirely write off the idea of a **package deal**. Many agents and airlines can put together very flexible deals, sometimes amounting to no more than a flight plus car and accommodation, and they can work out a great deal cheaper than organizing things when you arrive, especially as regards car rental, which in Europe can be very expensive on the spot. They are also great for peace of mind, even if all you're doing is taking care of the first week's accommodation on a longer tour.

There are literally hundreds – perhaps thousands – of different package operators, offering everything from fly-drive deals, sun-and-sea packages and coach tours to special-interest holidays. It shouldn't be too hard,

AIRLINES IN NORTH AMERICA

Aer Lingus ☎1-800/223 6537, *www.aerlingus.ie*

Aeroflot in US, ☎1-888/340 6400; in Canada, ☎514/288 2125; *www.aeroflot.com*

Air Canada ☎1-888/247 2262, *www.aircanada.ca*

Air France in US, ☎1-800/237 2747; in Canada, ☎1-800/667-2747; *www.airfrance.com*

Alitalia in US, ☎1-800/223 5730; in Canada, ☎1-800/361-8336; *www.alitalia.com*

American Airlines ☎1-800/433 7300, *www.aa.com*

Austrian Airlines ☎1-800/843 0002, *www.aua.com*

Balkan Bulgarian Airlines ☎1-800/852 0944 or 212/371 2047, *www.balkanair.com*

British Airways ☎1-800/2747 9297, *www.british-airways.com*

British Midland ☎1-800/788 0555, *www.flybmi.com*

Canadian Airlines ☎1-888/247 2262, *www.aircanada.ca*

Continental Airlines ☎1-800/231 0856, *www.continental.com*

Czech Airlines in US, ☎212/765 6022; in Canada, ☎416/363 3174; *www.czechairlines.com*

Delta Air Lines ☎1-800-221 1212, *www.delta.com*

Finnair ☎1-800/950-5000, *www.finnair.com*

Iberia ☎1-800/772-4642, *www.iberia.com*

KLM/Northwest in US, ☎1-800/447 4747; in Canada, ☎514/397 0775; *www.klm.com*

Lauda Air ☎1-800/588 8399, *www.laudaair.com*

LOT Polish Airlines in US, ☎1-800/223 0593; in Canada, ☎1-800/668 5928; *www.lot.com*

Lufthansa in US, ☎1-800/645 3880; in Canada, ☎1-800/563 5954; *www.lufthansa-ca.com*

Malév Hungarian Airlines ☎1-800/223 6884 or 212/757-6446, *www.malev.hu*

Martinair Holland ☎1-800/627 8462, *www.martinairusa.com*

Northwest/KLM Airlines ☎1-800/447 4747, *www.nwa.com*

Olympic Airways ☎1-800/223 1226 or 212/735 0200, *www.olympic-airways.gr*

Royal Air Maroc ☎1-800/344 6726 or 212/750 6071, *www.royalairmaroc.com*

Sabena ☎1-800/955-2000, *www.sabena.com*

SAS (Scandinavian Airlines) ☎1-800/221 2350, *www.flysas.com*

Swissair in US, ☎1-800/221 4750, *www.swissair.com*

TAP Air Portugal ☎1-800/221 7370, *www.tap-airportugal.pt*

Tarom Romanian Air ☎212/687 6013, *www.tarom.ro*

Tower Air ☎1-800/458 6937 or 718/553 8500, *www.towerair.com*

Turkish Airlines ☎1-800/874 8875, *www.thy.com*

TWA ☎1-800/892 4141, *www.twa.com*

United Airlines ☎1-800/538 2929, *www.ual.com*

US Airways ☎1-800/622 1015, *www.usairways.com*

with the help of a travel agent, to find something to suit, but be sure to examine the small print of any deal (Europe's a long way from home if you end up with something you don't want), and to remember that everything in a brochure always sounds great, but doesn't always live up to the promise. Also, try only to use an operator that is a member of the United States Tour Operator Association (USTOA) or approved by the American Society of Travel Agents (ASTA).

DISCOUNT FLIGHT AGENTS, TRAVEL CLUBS AND CONSOLIDATORS

Air Brokers International (☎1-800/883 3273 or 415/397 1383, *www.airbrokers.com*). Consolidator and specialist in RTW and Circle-Pacific tickets.

Air Courier Association (☎1-800/282 1202, *www.aircourier .org*). US Courier flight broker.

Council Travel (☎1-800/226 8624 or 212/822 2700, *www .counciltravel.com*). Nationwide organization that mostly, but by no means exclusively, specializes in student/budget travel.

Educational Travel Center (☎1-800/747 5551 or 608/256 5551, *www.edtrav.com*). Student/youth discount agent.

High Adventure Travel (☎1-800/350 0612 or 415/912 5600, *www.airtreks.com*). Round-the-world and Circle Pacific tickets. The website features an interactive database that lets you build and price your own RTW itinerary.

Moment's Notice, 7301 New Utrecht Ave, Brooklyn, NY 11204 (☎212/486 0500, *www.moment-notice.com*). Discount travel club.

New Frontiers/Nouvelles Frontières (☎1-800/677 0720 or 212/986 6006, *www.NewFrontiers.com*). French discount-travel firm. Other branches in LA, San Francisco and Quebec City.

Now Voyager (☎212/431 1616, *www.nowvoyagertravel .com*). Courier flight broker and consolidator.

Skylink (in US, ☎1-800/AIR ONLY or 212/573 8980; in Canada, ☎1-800/SKY LINK; *www.skylinkus.com*). Consolidator.

STA Travel (☎1-800/777 0112 or 1-800/781 4040, *www.sta.com*), and branches in other major North American cities. Worldwide specialist in independent and student travel.

Travac (☎1-800/872 8800, *www.thetravelsite.com*). Consolidator and charter broker.

Travel Avenue (☎1-800/333 3335, *www.travelavenue.com*). Full-service travel agent that offers discounts in the form of rebates.

Travel CUTS (in Canada, ☎1-800/667 2887; in US, ☎416/979 2406; *www.travelcuts.com*). Other branches across Canada (mostly on, or near, university campuses). Student travel specialists, with discounted fares for non-students too.

UniTravel (☎1-800/325 2222 or 314/569-2501, *www.unitravel.com*). Consolidator.

Whole Earth Travel (☎1-800/326 2009 or 212/864 2000, *www.airhitch.org*). Stand-by seat broker: for a set price, they guarantee to get you on a flight as close to your preferred destination as possible, within a week. Western Europe only.

Worldtek Travel (☎1/800-243-1723, *www.worldtek.com*) Discount travel agency for worldwide travel.

RAIL CONTACTS IN NORTH AMERICA

BritRail Travel (in US, ☎1-877/456-RAIL; in Canada, ☎1-800/361-RAIL; *www.raileurope.com*). UK passes.

CIT Tours (☎1-800/248 7245, *www.cit-rail.com*). Eurail, German and Italian passes.

DER Tours/GermanRail (☎1-800/421 2929 or 416/695 1209, *www.dertravel.com*). Eurail, Europass and many individual country passes.

Orbis Polish Travel Bureau (☎1-800/223 6037 or 212/867 5011, *www.orbistravel.com*). Passes for Poland.

RailEurope (in US, ☎1-800/438 7245; in Canada, ☎1-800/361 7245; *www.raileurope.com*). Official Eurail agent in North America; sells the widest range of regional and individual country passes.

ScanTours (☎1-800/223 7226 or 310/636 4656, *www.scantours.com*). Eurail, Scandinavian and other European country passes.

TOUR OPERATORS IN NORTH AMERICA

Adventure Center ☎1-800/227-8747 or 510/654 1879, *www.adventurecenter.com*

Adventures Abroad ☎1-800/665 3998, *www.adventures-abroad.com*

AESU Travel ☎1-800/638 7640, *www.aesu.com*

American Express Vacations ☎1-800/241 1700, *www.americanexpress.com/travel*.

Backroads ☎1-800/462 2848 or 510/527 1555, *www.backroads.com*

BCT Scenic Walking ☎1-800/473 1210, *www.bctwalk.com*

CBT Bicycle Tours ☎1-800/736-2453

Classic Journeys ☎1-800/200-3887, *www.classicjourneys.com*

CIT Tours in US, ☎1-800/CIT TOUR; in Canada, ☎1-800/387 0711; *www.cittours.com*

Contiki Holidays ☎1-800/CONTIKI, *www.contiki.com*

Delta Vacations ☎1-800/654 6559, *www.deltavacations.com*

Eastern Europe Tours ☎1-800/441 1339 or 206/448 8400, *www.imp-world-tours.com*

EC Tours ☎1-800/388 0877, *www.ectours.com*

Euro-Bike/Euro-Walking Tours ☎1-800/321 6060, *www.eurobike.com*

Euro Cruises ☎1-800/688 3876 or 212/691 2099, *www.eurocruises.com*

Europe Through the Back Door Inc. ☎425/771 8303, *www.ricksteves.com*

Europe Train Tours ☎1-800/551 2085 or 914/758 1777, *www.etttours.com*

Insight International Tours ☎1-800/582 8380, *www.insightvacations.com*

IST Cultural Tours ☎1-800/833 2111, *www.ist-tours.com*

Journeyworld International ☎1-800/255-8735, *www.journeys-intl.com*

Trafalgar Tours ☎1-800/854 0103, *www.trafalgartours.com*

Wilderness Travel ☎1-800/368 2794, *www.wildernesstravel.com*

SPECIALISTS IN TRAVEL FOR SENIOR TRAVELLERS

Elderhostel ☎1-877/426 8056, *www.elderhostel.org*

Saga Holidays ☎1-877/265 6862, *www.sagaholidays.com*

Vantage Travel ☎1-800/322 6677, *www.vantagetravel.com*

TRAVELLING FROM BRITAIN

Since the opening of the Channel Tunnel, it has been possible to travel to the Continent without using a plane or boat, though these may still be your cheapest and easiest, options. For destinations in northwestern Europe, train, long-distance bus and crossing the Channel by ferry tend to be best value for money, but the further you go the cheaper air travel becomes, and it's normally cheaper to fly than take the train to most parts of southern Europe, although special deals on rail passes can bring prices down considerably.

BY AIR

As ever, the best way to find the cheapest **flight** is to shop around: air travel in Europe is still highly regulated, which means that the prices quoted by the airlines can usually be undercut considerably, even on Apex fares, by going to an agent. In London, check the ads in the *Evening Standard, Time Out* or the free Australasian magazines such as *TNT*, available outside many tube stations; elswhere look in local listings magazines or the travel sections of the Sunday broadsheets. During the summer you can reach most of the countries of southern Europe – Portugal, Spain, Italy, Greece – on **charter flights**, block-booked by package holiday firms and usually having a few seats left over which they sell off cheap through selected **agents**, sometimes known as "bucket shops". Though they are inevitably rather restricted, with fixed return dates, a maximum validity of a month, and no chance of cancelling or changing your ticket once you've bought it, they can be very cheap – so much so in some cases that it's actually worth just using the outward portion if the return date doesn't suit. There are also flight agents who specialize in low-cost, discounted flights (charter and scheduled), some of them – like STA and Usit Campus – concentrating on deals for youths and students, though they can be a good source of bargains for everyone. In addition, there are agents specializing in offers to a specific country or group of countries on both charters and regular scheduled departures. To give a rough idea of prices booked through agents on scheduled flights in high season, reckon on paying, not including departure taxes, £55–100 to Paris, Brussels or Amsterdam; £75–200 to Scandinavia; £90–250 to the major cities of Spain or Italy; £165–210 to Athens, £180–270 to Istanbul; £70–220 to the major cities of eastern Europe. Many agents also do "open jaw" tickets, flying you into one city and out from another, not necessarily even in the same country. **One-way tickets** are normally very bad value, but some of the new "no-nonsense" airlines such as Ryanair and EasyJet charge single fares each way and are often much cheaper than other airlines for return fares too. Excellent deals can also be found on Ceefax or Teletext, or on the **Internet**: try *www.cheapflights.co.uk* and *www.ebookers.com*, with last-minute offers at *www.lastminute.com, www.deckchair.com* and *www.bargainholidays.com*.

BY TRAIN

There are now direct **trains** for foot passengers from London to Paris (16 daily, 3hr) and Brussels (9 daily, 3hr 15min) operated by Eurostar through the Channel Tunnel. Tickets for under-26s to Paris start at £45 one-way, £75 return, £40/75 to Brussels. For over-26s, the cheapest ticket is a weekend day return, which costs less than a single fare at £70 to Paris or Brussels. Through-ticket combinations for Eurostar, plus onward connections from Brussels and Paris, can be booked through Trainseurope, International Rail and European Rail.

Other rail journeys from Britain involve some kind of **sea crossing**, by ferry or, sometimes, catamaran. Current return fares from London (which include the crossing) are £58 to Paris, £65 to Brussels, £79 to Amsterdam, and £180 to Berlin. They can be bought at Charing Cross and some other stations, or from International Rail or Trainseurope. For some destinations, there are cheaper APEX fares (£49 to Amsterdam, £159 to Berlin, for example) requiring advance booking and subject to greater restrictions. 5-day return tickets to Paris and Brussels are also available, priced £49. Otherwise, international tickets are valid for two months and allow for stopovers on the way, providing you stick to the prescribed route (there may be a choice, with different fares applicable). One-way fares are generally around two-thirds the price of a return fare. If you're **under 26** you are entitled to all sorts of special deals, not least youth fares, which offer cut-price rail fares to European destinations. Also issued by International Rail and Trainseurope, youth tickets are also valid for two months with stopovers permitted en route. Examples of under-26 return ticket prices are: £48 to Paris, £43 to Brussels, £64 to Amsterdam and £160 to Berlin.

Whatever your age, however, and whether you cross the Channel by ferry or through the tunnel, **through tickets** to European destinations beyond France and Germany are becoming harder to find, largely because most intercity routes in Europe are now covered by super-fast, deluxe services with "special" (high, in other words) fares which cannot be paid as part of a through ticket. You could, for example, buy a ticket from London to Rome for £168 return, but you wouldn't be able to use it on any through train from Paris to Italy, so you'd have to travel by local services, changing along the way. Trainseurope and International Railways are the best people to contact for through tickets.

During the summer, especially if you're travelling at night or a long distance, it's best to make reservations on most legs of your journey, and on some trains (most French TGV services for example) it is compulsory. At night, couchettes in six-berth compartments cost around £6–15 per person, sleeper cars cost around £20–60, depending on the train, and may be 2-, 3- or 4-bed.

For **rail passes** and other types of discounted rail travel, see "Travelling in Europe", pp.20–31.

BY LONG-DISTANCE BUS

A long-distance **bus**, although much less comfortable than the train, is at least a little cheaper. The main operator based in Britain is **Eurolines**, who have a network of routes spanning the Continent – north as far as Scandinavia, east to Poland and the Baltic states, and south to Spain, Portugal and Morocco. Prices can be up to a third less than the equivalent train fare, and there are marginally cheaper fares on most services for those under 26 or over 60, which undercut BIJ rail rates for the same journey. Current Eurolines fares from London's Victoria Coach Station to Paris, Brussels or Amsterdam start at £23 one-way, £33 return (£25/36 without a youth or senior reduction). Berlin is £47/76 (£53/84); Nice £57/89 (£64/97); Madrid £76/116 (£90/137); and Stockholm £87/129 (£97/143). For many destinations, there is a cheaper APEX fare for return journeys booked at least a week in advance (£69 to Berlin, Nice or Madrid, for example). Slightly higher fares apply at Easter, in July and August and from mid-December to the beginning of January. Add-on return (but not one-way) fares of £10–20 are available for connecting services from other British cities. German-based firm **Gullivers** offer an alternative service to Amsterdam, Brussels, Berlin, Hamburg and Hanover, via the Channel Tunnel, and **Anglia International** serve all of those, plus Prague, Košice (Slovakia), Copenhagen, Oslo, Gothenburg (Sweden) and Moscow. Eurolines also have Explorer tickets from London to two or more European cities and back, valid for 90 days: for example, London–Amsterdam–Brussels–Paris–London costs £62, London–Cologne–Paris–London costs £69. Alternatively, you might consider Eurolines's 30- and 60-day passes, or one of the various passes offered by **Busabout** for their services around the Continent (see "Travelling in Europe", p.21), with a "London Link" to take you across the channel.

BY CAR

Taking a **vehicle** to Europe, you have a choice between a sea crossing or the train service through the Channel Tunnel operated by Eurotunnel.

Eurotunnel's **trains** run round-the-clock between Folkestone and Calais, carrying cars, motorcycles, coaches and their passengers, from coast-to-coast in 35–45 minutes. For daytime summer trips, advance bookings are a good idea. There are three to five departures hourly during the day (6am–midnight), and one every hour at night. One-way fares cost between £134.50 and £149.50 per car, including passengers, depending on the time of day, the day, and the season of travel; five-day returns cost between £159 and £185, with special offers for fixed-date bookings made in advance sometimes available for £89–99. Motorbikes cost £74.50–82.50 one-way, £89–99 for a five-day return. Bicycles are carried on two trains a day between May and October only (seats must be booked at least 14 days in advance) for £29.50 one-way (a day-trip costs £15, but Eurotunnel say they'll invoice you for the difference if you use it as a one-way ticket and don't return on it – also, it doesn't allow you to take baggage).

SEA CROSSING FROM BRITAIN

Route BRITAIN – EUROPE	Company	Frequency	Crossing time	Car +2 (min o/w fare incl hidden supps)	Foot passenger (min adult o/w fare)
Dover–Calais	SeaFrance	15 daily	1hr 30min	£134.50–187.50	£17
Dover–Calais	P&O Stena	27–35 daily	1hr 15min	£135–200	£26
Dover–Calais (fast ferry)[1]	Hoverspeed	6–10 daily	40min	£110–185	£24
Dover–Ostend (fast ferry)[1]	Hoverspeed	2–3 daily	2hr	£110–185	£24
Dover–Zeebrugge	P&O Stena	1–5 daily Mar–Dec	4hr 30min	£95–125	not allowed
Harwich–Esjberg	DFDS Seaways	3–4 weekly	19hr	£133–233	£49–89
Harwich–Hamburg	DFDS Seaways	3–4 weekly	20hr	£113–213	£39–79
Harwich–Hook of Holland	Stena	1 daily	6hr 15min–8hr	£97–147	£25
Harwich–Hook of Holland (fast ferry)	Stena	2 daily	3hr 40min	£97–147	£25
Hull–Rotterdam	P&O North Sea Ferries	1 daily	12hr 30min	£121–197[2]	£33–61[2]
Hull–Zeebrugge	P&O North Sea Ferries	1 daily	13hr 15min	£121–197[2]	£33–61[2]
Lerwick[3]–Bergen	Smyril Line	1 weekly May–Sept	12hr 30min	£110–157	£48–68
Newcastle–Amsterdam	DFDS Seaways	3–7 weekly	15hr	£93–183	£29–64
Newcastle–Gothenburg	DFDS Seaways	2 weekly	25hr	£173–323	£64–129
Newcastle–Haugesund, Stavanger, Bergen	Fjord Line	2–3 weekly	17hr 30min–25hr 45min	£178–350	£52–108
Newcastle–Kristiansand	DFDS Seaways	2 weekly	17hr	£173–293	£64–114
Newhaven–Dieppe (catamaran)	Hoverspeed	1–3 daily	2hr	£155–209	£28
Plymouth–Roscoff[4]	Brittany Ferries	2–12 weekly	6hr–7hr 30min	£79–237	£18–56
Plymouth–Santander[5]	Brittany Ferries	2 weekly March–Nov	24hr	£187–413	£33–204
Poole–Cherbourg	Brittany Ferries	1–2 daily	4hr 15min–5hr 45min	£75–220	£17–52
Poole–Cherbourg (catamaran)	Brittany Ferries/Condor	1 daily May–Sept	2hr 15min	£75–220	£17–52
Poole–St Malo[6]	Condor Ferries	1 daily May–Sept	4hr 35min	£100–196	£27–28
Portsmouth–Bilbao	P&O Portsmouth	1–2 weekly	35hr	£294–545	£126–207
Portsmouth–Caen	Brittany Ferries	2–3 daily	6hr	£75–201	£17–94
Portsmouth–Cherbourg	P&O Portsmouth	1–4 daily	5hr–7hr 30min	£105–220	£18–53
Portsmouth–Cherbourg (catamaran)	P&O Portsmouth	2 daily Apr–Sept	2hr 45min	£110–279	£22–53
Portsmouth–Le Havre	P&O Portsmouth	2–3 daily	5hr 30min–7hr 30min	£105–295	£20–61
Portsmouth–St Malo	Brittany Ferries	7 weekly	9hr–10hr 30min	£86–250	£19–59

1 sometimes catamaran
2 plus fuel surcharge
3 connecting service from Aberdeen – cheapest through fare for car plus two: £311–358
4 a few Jan & Feb sailings serve St Malo instead, taking 8hr
5 occasional winter sailings leave from Portsmouth, taking 30hr
6 via Jersey or Guernsey

Routes across the Channel or the North Sea by **ferry and catamaran** are numerous, and the fare struc- tures confusing. Most travel agents carry brochures of the various ferry companies, giving details of fares and frequencies. Prices vary with the month, day or even hour at certain times of the year, not to mention how long you're staying and the size of your car, and some firms' Web sites make it difficult to find the cheapest jour- ney by insisting you choose a departure date and time before they will quote any fares. Basically, the more convenient or popular the time of travel, the greater the cost; obligatory sleeping accommodation on longer crossings made at night also pushes the price way above the basic rate. Although those going for a short time benefit from well-priced five-day returns and the like, price structures tend to be geared to one-way rather than round-trip travel, one benefit of which is you don't necessarily have to use the same port in both directions. On some lines students qualify for a discount; on others the cheapest fares only apply if booked in advance – sometimes only via the Internet.

Obviously, the crossing you decide to take depends on where you are based in Britain and where you're plan- ning to head once across the water. The Brittany crossings are a bit out of the way for most of Europe, and are really only useful if you're planning to visit western France and perhaps drive down to Spain; Dieppe is more cen- tral, especially if you're intending to visit Paris, since it's closer than the French ports further north – Boulogne, Calais, Dunkerque. These three do, however, have the benefit of a much shorter crossing, and also leave you bet- ter placed for travelling through the heart of Europe, either through eastern France and down to Italy or into Belgium, Germany and eastern Europe. The same is true of Belgian Channel ports, though the crossings them- selves are a little longer. The Dutch ports, principally the Hook of Holland, might be worth choosing if you're specifically travelling to the Netherlands, northern Germany or perhaps northeastern Europe or Scandinavia, but the crossings are much longer than those to France. The Hull–Rotterdam service is a useful one if you live in the north of England, but the journey from Newcastle to the Danish and Norwegian ports is long and pricey, though it may save time and be worth the money if Scandinavia is your first stop. Links to timetables for various ferry services in the British Isles and elsewhere can be found online at *www.ex.ac.uk/~mspunter/ifg*.

HITCHING

It is possible to get a lift all the way from London to Istanbul if you happen to meet the right lorry, but in gen- eral it's a question of getting across the Channel and hitching from there. Getting across the Channel is cheap: Eurotunnel charge per car regardless of how many passengers are carried, and some ferries have flat rates for cars with certain numbers of passengers (3–9 on Hoverspeed services, other Dover–Calais services, and P&O Portsmouth Channel crossings for example), so you may even be able to get over for free. Otherwise, there's usually plenty of traffic heading south from the Channel ports – note that Belgium is somewhat better for lifts than France, with Calais notoriously bad for hitching out of.

PACKAGES AND INCLUSIVE TOURS

If you're sure of where you want to go, how long you want to spend there, and what you want to do during your time there, it's an odds-on bet there'll be a **package holiday** to suit you. Travelling this way isn't every- body's cup of tea, but it can work out cheaper, and it can also be a good idea if you're nervous of travelling alone. You can lie on a beach, take a short break in a major city, or there are any number of special-interest packages available, from hiking trips to cycling deals, although perhaps the most popular choice for young peo- ple, especially those coming from Australasia or North America for the first time, is an all-in coach tour of the major sights and cities with an operator like Top Deck or Contiki, who cater for the 18–35 age range.

DISCOUNT FLIGHT AGENTS

North South Travel (☎01245/608291, *www.northsouthtravel .co.uk*). Friendly, competitive travel agency, offering discounted fares worldwide – profits are used to support projects in the developing world, especially the promotion of sustainable tourism.

STA Travel (☎0870/160 6070, *www.statravel.co.uk*). Worldwide specialists in low-cost flights and tours for stu- dents and under-26s, though other customers welcome. Branches on university campuses and in town centres throughout the country.

Trailfinders (☎020/7628 7628, *www.trailfinders.co.uk*). One of the best-informed and most efficient agents. Branches nationwide.

Travel Bug (☎0870/900 1350, *www.flynow.com*). Large range of discounted tickets.

Travel CUTS (☎020/7255 2082, *www.travelcuts.co.uk*). British branch of Canada's main youth and student travel specialist.

usitCAMPUS (☎0870/240 1010, *www.usitcampus.co.uk*). Student/youth travel specialists, with branches in YHA shops and on university campuses all over Britain.

TOUR OPERATORS

Bike Tours (☎01225/310859, *www.biketours.co.uk*). Cycling tours of 1–2 weeks in eight European countries.

Contiki (☎020/8290 6777, *www.contiki.com*). Coach tours of Europe for 18–35s.

Eurocamp (☎01606/787000, *www.eurocamp.co.uk*). Flexible packages for campers and caravanners, plus self-drive vacations to fixed-site tents and mobile homes.

Exodus (☎020/8675 5550, *www.exodus.co.uk*). Walking, biking, hiking and touring holidays by local transport in several European countries.

Explore Worldwide (☎01252/760000, *www.exploreworldwide.com*). Adventure holidays in eighteen European countries, plus Morocco and Turkey.

Sunvil Holidays (☎020/8758 4722, *www.sunvil.co.uk*). Flexible packages and tailor-made holidays off the beaten track in Greece, Hungary, Italy, Portugal and Spain.

Thomas Cook Holidays (☎0870/566 6222, *www.thomascook.com*). High street specialists in European city breaks.

Time Off (☎0845/733 6622). Flexible city breaks in various price ranges.

Top Deck Travel (☎020/7370 4555, *www.topdecktravel.co.uk*). Coach tours around Europe for young people (camping or in hotels).

Tracks (☎020/7937 3028, *www.tracks-travel.com*). Youth-oriented bus tours.

Travelscene (☎0870/777 4445, *www.travelscene.co.uk*). European city breaks.

FERRY OPERATORS

Brittany Ferries (☎0870/536 0360, *www.brittanyferries.com*). Portsmouth to Caen and St Malo; Poole to Cherbourg; Plymouth to Roscoff and Santander.

Condor Ferries (☎01305/761551, *www.condorferries.co.uk*). Poole to St Malo via Jersey or Guernsey.

DFDS Seaways (☎0870/533 3000, *www.dfdsseaways.co.uk*). Harwich to Esbjerg and Hamburg; Newcastle to Amsterdam, Gothenburg and Kristiansand.

Fjord Line (☎0191/296 1313, *www.fjordline.com*). Newcastle to Stavanger, Haugesund and Bergen.

Hoverspeed (☎0870/240 8070, *www.hoverspeed.co.uk*). Dover to Calais and Ostend; Newhaven to Dieppe.

P&O Portsmouth (☎0870/242 4999, *www.poportsmouth.com*). Portsmouth to Bilbao, Cherbourg and Le Havre.

P&O North Sea Ferries (☎0870/129 6002, *www.ponsf.com*). Hull to Zeebrugge and Rotterdam.

AIRLINES IN BRITAIN

Adria ☎020/7437 0143, *www.adria.si*

Aer Lingus ☎0845/973 7747, *www.flyaerlingus.com*

Aeroflot ☎020/7355 2233, *www.aeroflot.com*

Air France ☎0845/084 5111, *www.airfrance.com*

Alitalia ☎0870/544 8259, *www.alitalia.it*

Austrian Airlines ☎020/7434 7350, *www.austrianairlines.co.uk*

Balkan Bulgarian Airlines ☎020/7637 7637, *balkanairlines@cs.com*

Britannia ☎0800/000747, *www.britanniaairways.com*

British Airways ☎0845/773 3377, *www.british-airways.com*

British Midland Airways ☎0870/607 0555, *www.flybmi.com*

Buzz ☎0870/240 7070, *www.buzzaway.com*

Croatia Airlines ☎020/8563 0022, *www.croatiaairlines.hr*

CSA Czech Airlines ☎020/7255 1898, *www.czechairlines.co.uk*

EasyJet ☎0870/600 0000, *www.eayjet.com*

Estonian Air ☎020/7333 0196, *www.estonian-air.ee*

Finnair ☎0870/241 4411, *www.finnair.co.uk*

Go ☎0870/607 6543, *www.go-fly.com*

Iberia ☎0845/601 2854, *www.iberia.com*

KLM uk ☎0870/507 4074, *www.klmuk.com*

Lauda Air ☎0845/601 0934, *www.laudaair.com*

Lithuanian Airlines ☎020/8759 7323, *www.lal.lt*

LOT Polish Airlines ☎020/7580 5037, *www.lot.com*

Lufthansa ☎0845/773 7747, *www.lufthansa.co.uk*

Maersk Air ☎020/7333 0066, *www.maersk-air.com*

Malév Hungarian Airlines ☎020/7439 0577, *www.malev.hu*

Olympic Airways ☎020/7409 3400, *www.olympicairways.com*

Royal Air Maroc ☎020/7439 4361, *www.royalairmaroc.com*

Ryanair ☎0870/156 9569, *www.ryanair.com*

Sabena ☎0845/601 0933, *www.sabena.com*

SAS Scandinavian Airlines ☎0845/607 2772, *www.sas.se*

Swissair ☎0845/601 0956, *www.swissair.com*

TAP Air Portugal ☎0845/601 0932, *www.tap-airportugal.pt*

Tarom ☎020/7224 3693, *www.tarom.ro*

Turkish Airlines ☎020/7766 9300, *www.turkishairlines.com*

Virgin Express ☎0800/891199, *www.virginexpress.com*

P&O Stena (☎0870/600 0600, *www.posl.com*). Dover to Calais and Zeebrugge.

SeaFrance (☎0870/571 1711, *www.seafrance.com*). Dover to Calais.

SMS Travel (☎020/7373 6548, *www.sms.com.mt*). Agent for Adriatica and a number of other ferry lines operating out of Italy.

Smyril Line (☎01224/572615, *www.smyril-line.fo*). Lerwick to Bergen, with connecting P&O Scottish service from Aberdeen.

Southern Ferries (☎020/7491 4968). Agent for a number of ferries operating out of France.

Stena Line (☎0870/570 7070, *www.stenaline.co.uk*). Parkeston Quay, Harwich, Essex CO12 4SR (☎01255/243333). Harwich to Hook of Holland.

Viamare Travel (☎020/7431 4560, *www.viamare.com*). Agent for several European ferry lines.

TRAIN TICKETS AND INFORMATION

European Rail ☎020/7387 0444, fax 7387 0888

Eurostar ☎0870/518 6186, *www.eurostar.com*

Eurotunnel ☎0870/535 3535, *www.eurotunnel.com*

International Rail (☎01962/773646). Agents for Dutch and Belgian railways.

RailEurope (☎0870/584 8848). SNCF French Railways.

Trainseurope ☎020/8699 3654, *www.trainseurope.co.uk*

Most national rail companies can be contacted through their national tourist organization.

BUS TICKETS AND INFORMATION

Anglia International ☎0870/608 8806, *www.anglia-lines .co.uk*

Busabout ☎020/7950 1661, *www.busabout.com*

Eurolines ☎0870/514 3219, *www.eurolines.co.uk*

Gullivers ☎00800/4855 4837, *www.gullivers.de*

TRAVELLING FROM IRELAND

There are direct flights **from Dublin** to most major cities in mainland Europe, and connections from those or from London to practically any airport you want to fly to. There are also one or two direct flights to the Continent **from Shannon and Cork**. You may save a little money travelling by land, sea or even air to London and buying your flight there, but the small amount you'd save hardly makes it worthwhile, and if you're going to London by surface routes, you may as well go the whole hog and carry on that way into Europe.

 From Belfast, there are direct flights with Sabena to Brussels, British Airways to Paris and Copenhagen, British Midland to Paris, and Jersey European to Toulouse. For other destinations, you'll have to change at Brussels, London or Manchester.

 Although Britain is the most obvious first stop if you are **going by land and sea**, it is possible to avoid it altogether by taking a ferry direct from Cork or Rosslare to Brittany. For routes via Britain, most firms do combination "landbridge" fares for both ferries if you're driving (€235–420 for a car and two people to France, €370–600 to Spain, other fares available to the Netherlands and Scandinavia), while **direct rail tickets** generally include both boat connections anyway. The latter are available from Irish Rail's Continental Rail Desk in the Republic, or NIR Travel in the North, with discounted **under-26 tickets** available from these, or from UsitNOW. International rail tickets can be booked up to two months in advance, are valid for two months, and allow stopovers en route.

RAIL PASSES AND INTERNATIONAL TRAIN TICKETS

Continental Rail Desk ☎01/836 6222, *www.irishrail.ie*

Iarnród Éireann ☎01/8366 6222, *www.irishrail.ie*

NIR Travel ☎028/9023 0671, *www.nirailways.co.uk*

SEA CROSSINGS FROM IRELAND

Route	Company	Frequency	Crossing time	Car +2 (min[1] o/w fare incl hidden supps)	Foot passenger (min full adult o/w fare including hidden supps)
IRELAND–BRITAIN					
Belfast–Heysham (catamaran)	Seacat	1–2 daily Mar–Nov	4hr	£113–143[1]	£17–26[1]
Belfast–Liverpool	NorseMerchant Ferries	1–2 daily	8hr 30min	£85–220	£25–45
Belfast–Stranraer	Stena	3–4 daily	3hr 15min	£69–104[1]	£18–24
Belfast–Stranraer (fast ferry)	Stena	4–5 daily	1hr 45min	£69–114[1]	£18–24
Belfast–Troon (catamaran)	Seacat	2–3 daily	2hr 15min	£83–133[1]	£17–21[1]
Larne–Cairnryan	P&O Irish Sea	3–6 daily	1hr	£68–103[1]	£18–21
Larne–Cairnryan (fast ferry)	P&O Irish Sea	5 daily March–Oct	2hr 15min	£68–113[1]	£18–25
Larne–Fleetwood	P&O Irish Sea	1–3 daily	8hr	£60–120	not allowed
Dublin–Holyhead	Irish Ferries	2 daily	3hr 15min	€150–255	€23–28
Dublin–Holyhead (fast ferry)	Irish Ferries	3–4 daily	1hr 50min	€192–276	€28–36
Dublin–Holyhead	Stena	1–2 daily	3hr 45min	€132–221	not allowed
Dublin–Liverpool	NorseMerchant Ferries	12 weekly	7hr 45min–8hr 30min	€100–235	€25–45
Dublin–Liverpool	P&O Irish Sea	6 weekly	8hr	€113–189	not allowed
Dublin–Liverpool (catamaran)	Seacat	1 daily Mar–Nov	3hr 45min	€102–180[1]	€22–33[1]
Dun Laoghaire–Holyhead (fast ferry)	Stena	3–4 daily	1hr 40min	€152–227	€28–36
Rosslare–Fishguard	Stena	1–2 daily	3hr 30min	€107–196	€22
Rosslare–Fishguard (catamaran)	Stena	2–4 daily Apr–Sept	1hr 50min	€120–227	€28–38
Rosslare–Pembroke	Irish Ferries	2 daily	3hr 45min	€123–230	€23–28
Cork–Swansea	Swansea–Cork Ferries	4–6 weekly March–Nov	10hr	€126–227	€30–43
IRELAND–EUROPE					
Cork–Roscoff	Brittany Ferries	1 weekly April–Sept	14hr	€189–442	€98–187
Rosslare–Cherbourg	Irish Ferries	2–3 weekly March–Oct	16hr	€189–455	€57–107
Rosslare–Cherbourg	P&O Irish Sea	3 weekly	18hr	€159–362	not allowed
Rosslare–Roscoff	Irish Ferries	1–3 weekly April–Sept	15hr	€189–438	€57–107

[1] On these routes the minimum car fare is an Apex, bookable at least 28 days in advance.
Fares on sailings from the Republic are quoted in euros, from Northern Ireland in sterling.

AIRLINES IN IRELAND

Aer Lingus Dublin ☎01/886 8888; Cork ☎021/432 7155; Limerick ☎061/474239; in Northern Ireland ☎0845/973 7747; *www.aerlingus.ie*

Aeroflot ☎01/844 6166, *www.aeroflot.com*

Air France ☎01/605 0383, *www.airfrance.com*

Alitalia ☎01/677 5171, *www.alitalia.it*

Austrian Airlines ☎01/608 0099, *www.austrianair.com*

British Airways in the Republic, ☎1800/626747; in Northern Ireland, ☎0845/722 2111; *www.british -airways.com*

British Midland in the Republic, ☎01/07 3036; in Northern Ireland, ☎0845/755 4554; *www.flybmi.com*

City Jet ☎01/844 5566, *www.airfrance.ie*

CSA Czech Airlines ☎01/814 4626

Finnair ☎01/844 6565, *www.finnair.co.uk*

Iberia ☎01/407 3017, *www.iberia.com*

Jersey European in Northern Ireland, ☎0870/567 6676, in the Republic, ☎1890/925532; *www.jersey -european.co.uk*

KLM in the Republic, ☎01/284 3823; in Northern Ireland ☎0870/507 4074; *www.klm.com*

Lauda Air ☎01/608 0055, *www.laudaair.com*

Lithuanian Airlines ☎01/890 0122, *www.lal.lt*

Lufthansa in the Republic, ☎01/844 5544; in Northern Ireland, ☎0845/773 7747; *www.lufthansa.com*

Maersk Air ☎01/608 0222, *www.maersk-air.com*

Malév Hungarian Airlines ☎01/814 5830, *www.malev.hu*

Olympic Airways ☎01/608 0090, *www.olympicairways.com*

Ryanair in the Republic, ☎01/609 7800; in Northern Ireland, ☎0870/156 9569; *www.ryanair.com*

Sabena in the Republic, ☎1890/200520; in Northern Ireland, ☎0845/601 0933; *www.sabena.com*

SAS Scandinavian Airlines ☎01/844 5888, *www.sas.se*

Swissair in the Republic, ☎1800/200512; in Northern Ireland, ☎0845/601 0956, *www.swissair.com*

TAP Air Portugal ☎01/679 8844, *www.tap -airportugal.pt*

TRAVEL AGENTS AND TOUR OPERATORS IN IRELAND

Exodus (☎01/677 1147, *cptravel@indigo.ie*). Walking, biking, hiking and touring holidays by local transport in several European countries.

Explore (☎01/677 9479). Adventure holidays in eighteen European countries, plus Morocco and Turkey.

Joe Walsh Tours (Dublin ☎01/872 2555 or 01/676 3053; Cork ☎021/427 7959; *www.joewalshtours.ie*). General budget fares agent.

Neenan Travel (☎01/676 5181, *www.neenantrav.ie*). European city breaks.

Student & Group Travel (☎01/677 7834). Student specialists.

Thomas Cook (Dublin ☎01/677 0469; Belfast ☎028/9055 0232; *www.thomascook.com*) Package holiday and flight agent, with occasional discount offers.

Trailfinders (☎01/677 7888, *www.trailfinders.ie*). Competitive fares, plus deals on hotels, insurance, tours and car rental.

usitNOW (Dublin ☎01/602 1777; Belfast ☎028/9032 7111; Cork ☎021/427 0900; Derry ☎028/7137 1888; Galway ☎091/565177; Limerick ☎061/415064; Waterford ☎051/872601; *www.usitnow.ie*). Ireland's main student and youth travel specialists.

FERRY OPERATORS

Brittany Ferries in the Republic, ☎021/277 705; in Northern Ireland, ☎0870/901 2400; *www.brittanyferries.co.uk*. Cork to Roscoff (March–Oct only).

Irish Ferries in the Republic, ☎01/661 0511; in Northern Ireland, ☎0875/171 717; *www.irishferries.com*. Dublin to Holyhead; Rosslare to Pembroke, Cherbourg and Roscoff. Continental services March to end Sept.

NorseMerchant Ferries in the Republic, ☎01/819 2999; in Northern Ireland, ☎0870/600 4321; *www.norsemerchant.com*. Belfast and Dublin to Liverpool.

P&O Irish Sea in the Republic, ☎01/800 406 049; in Northern Ireland, ☎0870/ 242 4777; *www.poirishsea.com*.

Larne to Cairnryan and to Fleetwood; Dublin to Liverpool; Rosslare to Cherbourg.

Sea Cat in Northern Ireland, ☎08705/523 523; in the Republic, ☎1800/551743; *www.steam-packet.com*. Belfast to Stranraer, to Heysham, to Troon, to Isle of Man; Dublin to Liverpool and to Isle of Man.

Stena Line in the Republic, ☎01/204 7777; in Northern Ireland, ☎0870/570 7070; *www.stenaline.co.uk*. Fishguard to Rosslare; Holyhead to Dun Laoghaire and Dublin; Stranraer to Belfast.

Swansea–Cork Ferries in the Republic, ☎021/427 1166; in Northern Ireland, ☎01792/456116; *www.swansea-cork.ie*. Cork to Swansea (no sailings Nov 7 to March 11).

TRAVELLING FROM AUSTRALIA AND NEW ZEALAND

There are flights from Melbourne, Sydney, Adelaide, Brisbane and Perth to most European capitals, and there really is not a great deal of difference in the fares to the busiest destinations – a scheduled return airfare from Sydney to London, Paris, Rome, Madrid, Athens or Frankfurt should be available through travel agents for around A$1450 in low season, rising to A$1850 or more in winter (European summer). A one-way ticket will cost slightly more than half that, while a return flight from Auckland to Europe will cost approximately NZ$2000 in low season, rising to NZ$2500 in high season. Asian airlines often work out cheapest, and may throw in a stopover, while the extremely large Greek population of Melbourne means there are often bargain deals to be had to Athens on Olympic Airways – ring around first.

Another option is to take in Europe on a **Round-the-World (RTW)** ticket. The route you choose determines the fare, depending on the airline, mileage and the number of continents covered, with a typical itinerary having six stops. A "no-frills" basic routing stopping in Asia on the way out and North America on the way back starts at A$1500/NZ$1800; for more stops be prepared to pay upwards of A$1900/NZ$2300. You can also get good deals with the "One World" and "Star Alliance" consortiums, which group a number of airlines together on one ticket – of the two, Star Alliance offer a much wider choice of routes.

For these and other **low-price tickets**, the most reliable operator is STA, who also supply packages with companies such as Contiki and Busabout and can issue rail passes. STA can also advise on visa regulations for Australian and New Zealand citizens – and for a fee will do all the paperwork for you. Bear in mind that to enter most countries your passport must be valid for at least six months after the end of your visit.

Popular **tour packages** around Europe include Busabout's 15-day pass starting at A$439, which covers up to seventy cities from Lisbon to Vienna – the advantage of Busabout being that you just jump on and off in whatever city you choose. More structured, and for frenetic party animals, are Contiki's European tours for 18–35-year-olds; their nine-day tour of seven countries, from the UK to Italy, starts at A$1149, including bus, accommodation and meals.

TRAVEL AGENTS IN AUSTRALIA AND NEW ZEALAND

Anywhere Travel, 345 Anzac Parade, Kingsford, Sydney, NSW 2032 (☎02/9663 0411, *anywhere@ozemail.com.au*).

Budget Travel, 16 Fort St, Auckland (☎09/366 0061) plus branches nationwide (call ☎0800/808 040 for nearest branch); *www.budgettravel.co.nz*

Destinations Unlimited, 7th floor, 220 Queen St, Auckland (☎09/373 4033).

Flight Centres, 82 Elizabeth St, Sydney, NSW 2000 (☎02/9235 3522), plus branches throughout Australia (call ☎13/1600 for nearest branch); 350 Queen St, Auckland (☎09/358 4310), plus branches throughout New Zealand; *www.flightcentre.com*

Northern Gateway, 22 Cavenagh St, Darwin, NT 0800 (☎08/8941 1394, *oztravel@norgate.com.au*).

STA Travel, 855 George St, Sydney, NSW 2000; 240 Flinders St, Melbourne, Vic 3000, plus branches nationwide (call ☎13/1776 for nearest branch, ☎1300/360960 for fastfare telesales, *www.statravel.com.au*); 10 High St, Auckland (☎09/309 0458, fastfare telesales ☎09/366 6673, *www.statravel.co.nz*) plus branches in Wellington, Christchurch, Dunedin, Palmerston North, Hamilton and at major universities.

Thomas Cook Branches throughout Australia (call ☎13/1771 for nearest branch, ☎1800/801002 for direct telesales); 191 Queen St, Auckland (☎09/379 3920); *www.thomascook.com.au*

Trailfinders, 8 Spring St, Sydney, NSW 2000 (☎02/9247 7666); 91 Elizabeth St, Brisbane, Qld 4000 (☎07/3229 0887); Hides corner, Shield St, Cairns, Qld 4870 (☎07/4041 1199); *www.trailfinders.com.au*

Travel.com, Australia: 76–80 Clarence St, Sydney, NSW 2000 (☎02/9249 5444 or 1800/000 447, *www.travel.com.au*). New Zealand: 52, Emily Place, Aukland (☎09/358 8200, *www.travel.co.nz*).

Usit Beyond, Shortland St/Jean Batten Place, Auckland (☎0800/788336 or 09/379 4224, *www.usitbeyond.co.nz*), plus branches in Christchurch, Dunedin, Palmerston North, Hamilton and Wellington.

YHA Travel Australia: 422 Kent St, Sydney, NSW 2000 (☎02/9261 1111); 83–85 Hardware Lane, Melbourne, Vic 3000 (☎03/9670 9611); 154 Roma St, Brisbane, Qld 4000 (☎07/3236 1680), plus branches in state capitals; *www.yha.com.au*

AIRLINES IN AUSTRALIA AND NEW ZEALAND

Aer Lingus in Australia, ☎02/9244 2123; in NZ, ☎09/308 3351; *www.aerlingus.ie*

Aeroflot in Australia, ☎02/9262 2233, *www.aeroflot.com*

Air France in Australia, ☎02/9244 2100; in NZ, ☎09/308 3352; *www.airfrance.fr*

Air New Zealand in Australia, ☎13/2476; in NZ, ☎0800/737000 or 09/357 3000; *www.airnz.co.nz*

Alitalia in Australia, ☎02/9244 2400); in NZ, ☎09/302 1452; *www.alitalia.it*

British Airways in Australia, ☎02/8904 8800; in NZ, ☎09/356 8690; *www.british-airways.com*

Cathay Pacific in Australia, ☎13/1747 or 02/9931 5500; in NZ, ☎09/379 0861; *www.cathaypacific.com*

Czech Airlines in Australia, ☎02/9247 6196, *www.csa.cz*

Egypt Air in Australia, ☎02/9267 6979, *www.egyptair.com*

Finnair in Australia, ☎02/9244 2299; in NZ, ☎09/308 3365; *www.finnair.com*

Garuda in Australia, ☎13/1223 or 02/9334 9900; in NZ, ☎1800/128 510 or 09/366 1862; *www.garuda.co.id*

Gulf Air in Australia, ☎02/9244 2199; in NZ, ☎09/308 3366; *www.gulfairco.com*

JAL in Australia, ☎02/9272 1111; in NZ, ☎09/379 9906; *www.japanair.com*.

KLM in Australia, ☎1300/303 747; in NZ, ☎09/302 1782; *www.klm.com*

Lauda Air in Australia, ☎1800/642 438 or 02/9251 6155; in NZ, ☎09/308 3368; *www.laudaair.com*

LOT Polish Airlines in Australia, ☎02/9299 5900; in NZ, ☎09/308 3369; *www.lot.com*

Lufthansa in Australia, ☎1300/655 727 or 02/9367 3887; in NZ, ☎008/945 220 or 09/303 1529; *www.lufthansa.com*

Malaysia Airlines in Australia, ☎13/2627; in NZ, ☎008/657472 or 09/373 2741, *www.malaysia-airlines.com*

Olympic Airways in Australia, ☎1800/221 663 or 02/9251 2044; *www.olympic-airways.gr*

Qantas in Australia, ☎13/1313; in NZ, ☎0800/808767 or 09/357 8900; *www.qantas.com.au*

Royal Jordanian Airlines in Australia, ☎02/9244 2701; in NZ, c/o Innovative Travel, ☎03/365 3910; *www.rja.com.jo*

SAS Scandinavian Airlines in Australia, ☎1800/251157 or 02/9299 9800; in NZ, c/o Air New Zealand, ☎0800/737000 or 09/357 3000; *www.flysas.com*

Singapore Airlines in Australia, ☎13/1011; in NZ, ☎0800/808 909 or 09/303 2129; *www.singaporeair.com*

Swissair in Australia, ☎1800/221339 or 02/9232 1744; in NZ, ☎09/358 3216; *www.swissair.com*

Tap Air Portugal in Australia, ☎02/9244 2344; in NZ, ☎09/308 3373; *www.tap-airportugal.pt*

Tarom Romanian Airlines in Australia, ☎02/9262 1144; *www.tarom.ro*

Thai Airways in Australia, ☎1300/651960; in NZ, ☎09/377 3886, *www.thaiair.com*

Turkish Airlines in Australia, ☎02/9299 8400, *www.turkishairlines.com*

Virgin Atlantic in Australia, ☎02/9244 2747; in NZ, ☎09/308 3377; *www.virgin-atlantic.com*

SPECIALIST AGENTS AND TOUR OPERATORS IN AUSTRALIA AND NEW ZEALAND

Adventure World (in Australia, ☎1300/363055 or 02/9956 7766, *www.adventureworld.com.au*; in NZ, ☎09/524 5118, *www.adventureworld.co.nz*). Agents for many adventure tour operators, including Contiki, Explore Worldwide and Top Deck. Branches in Adelaide, Brisbane, Melbourne, Perth and Sydney.

Bentours (☎02/9241 1353, *www.bentours.com.au*). Scandinavian and Russian specialist agents, including rail passes covering these countries.

Best of Britain (☎02/9909 1055). Flights, accommodation, car rental, tours, canal boats and B&Bs throughout the British Isles.

Blue Sky Travel (☎09/525 2363). Ireland specialists based in New Zealand.

CIT (☎02/9267 1255, *www.cittravel.com.au*). Agents specializing in all things Italian; also deal with Europe-wide rail and bus passes. Offices in Adelaide, Brisbane, Melbourne, Perth and Sydney.

Contiki Holidays for 18–35s (☎1300/301835 or 02/9511 2200; *www.contiki.com*). Frenetic tours for party animals.

Danube Travel (☎03/9530 0888). Cruises and specialist tours including birdwatching to Eastern Europe.

Eastern Europe Travel Bureau (☎02/9262 1144, *www.eetb.citysearch.com.au*). Branches in Brisbane, Melbourne and Sydney. Can book accommodation, cruises, train and bus travel, spa visits and tours throughout Eastern Europe and Russia.

European Travel Office (Melbourne ☎03/9329 8844; Sydney ☎02/9267 7714; Auckland ☎09/525 3074). All European travel arrangements.

French Travel Connection (☎02/9966 8600). Travel and tours across France.

Grecian Tours Travel (☎03/9663 3711, *www.greciantours.com.au*). Package tours, discounted flights, rail passes and car rental.

Iber Tours (☎1800/500016 or 03/9670 8388, *www.iber-tours.com.au*). Escorted and solo tours to rural and city areas of Spain, Portugal & Morocco, plus help organising study trips.

Snow Bookings Only (☎03/9809 2699). Skiing holidays in France, Switzerland and Austria.

TRAVELLING IN EUROPE

It's easy enough to travel in Europe, and a number of special deals and passes can make it fairly economical too. Air links are extensive, but
also expensive, give or take the odd charter
deal in season, and with the exception of
Britain, where flying is the cheapest way to
reach much of the Continent (see "Travelling
from Britain" p.10). In any case, you really
appreciate the diversity of Europe best at
ground level, by way of the enormous and generally efficient web of rail, road and ferry connections that covers the Continent.

BY TRAIN

Though to some extent it depends on where you intend to spend most of your time, **train** is without doubt
the best way to make a tour of Europe. The rail network in most countries is comprehensive, in some cases
exceptionally so, and the Continent boasts some of the most scenic rail journeys you could make anywhere
in the world. Train travel is relatively cheap, too, even in the richer parts of northwest Europe, where, apart
from Britain (whose rail system is in a state of virtual collapse following privatization), trains are heavily
subsidized, and prices are brought down further by the multiplicity of passes and discount cards available,
both Europe-wide (**InterRail** for those based in Europe or the British Isles, **Eurail** for anyone based elsewhere) and on an individual country basis. In some countries you'll find it makes more sense to travel by
bus, but if you're travelling further afield buying a rail pass may still pay dividends. We've covered the various passes here, as well as the most important international routes and most useful addresses; supplementary details, including frequencies and journey times of domestic services, are given throughout the
guide in each country's "Travel details" section.

If you intend to do a lot of rail travel, the *Thomas Cook European Timetable* is an essential investment,
detailing the main lines throughout Europe, as well as ferry connections, and is updated monthly. *Thomas
Cook* also publish a rail map of Europe, which may be a good supplement to our own train map on pp.24–25.

Finally, whenever you board an international train in Europe, check the route of the car you are in, since
trains frequently split, with different carriages going to different destinations.

EUROPE-WIDE RAIL PASSES

For young Europeans, probably the most popular of all the ways of travelling around the Continent is the
InterRail pass, a ticket for unlimited travel on rail lines the length and breadth of Europe. InterRail passes
are available from main stations and international rail agents (see p.9 & p.15) in Britain, Ireland and all other
countries covered by the scheme. A zoning system applies for the European countries valid under the pass,
as follows:

Zone A Britain and Ireland

Zone B Sweden, Norway and Finland

Zone C Denmark, Germany, Switzerland and Austria

Zone D Poland, the Czech Republic, Slovakia, Hungary and Croatia

Zone E France, Belgium, the Netherlands and Luxembourg

Zone F Spain, Portugal and Morocco

Zone G Italy, Slovenia, Greece and Turkey

Zone H Bulgaria, Romania, Yugoslavia and the Republic of Macedonia

The zones you want to travel in determine the price, which starts at £129 for under-26-year-olds (£179 over-26) for a one-zone card valid for 22 days; cards for more than one zone are valid for a month and cost £169/235 for two zones, £195/269 for three zones, and £219/309 for all the zones. To qualify, you need to have been resident in one of the participating countries for six months or more; you also need a valid passport. For further details, and price updates, see RailEurope's Web site at *www.raileurope.co.uk*.

Increasingly with InterRail passes, you need to pay **supplements** on most European express trains, all of them on some routes, and certainly all the most convenient ones (17 of the 18 daily trains between Paris and Brussels carry a supplement, for example, and the remaining service takes more than three times as long to cover the distance). Even where there is in theory no supplement, there is often a compulsory reservation fee, which may cost you double if you only find out about it once you're on the train.

Non-European residents aren't eligible for InterRail passes, though many agents don't in fact check residential qualifications. Better still, a **Eurail pass**, which should be bought outside Europe (but can be obtained from Usit Campus and RailEurope in London by non-residents who were unable to get it at home), gives unlimited travel in 17 countries – Austria, Belgium, Denmark, Finland, France, Germany, Greece, Hungary, Ireland, Italy, Luxembourg, the Netherlands, Norway, Portugal, Spain, Sweden and Switzerland – fewer than InterRail, but valid for more express trains, thus saving money on supplements. The **Eurail Youthpass** (for under-26s) costs US$388 for 15 days, US$499 for 21 days, US$623 for one month, US$882 for two months, or US$1089 for three months; if you're 26 or over you'll have to buy a first-class pass, available in 15-day (US$554), 21-day (US$718), one-month (US$890), two-month (US$1260) and three-month (US$1558) increments. If there are 2–5 of you, the **Eurail Saverpass** (first class only) can knock about 15 percent off the cost of the standard Eurail offerings. You stand a better chance of getting your money's worth out of a **Eurail Flexipass**, which is good for a certain number of travel days in a two-month period. This, too, comes in under-26 and first-class versions: 10 days cost US$458 for under-26s or US$654 for first-class travel; and 15 days, US$599 or US$862. There's also a **Saver Flexipass** for 2–5 people travelling together. A scaled-down version of the Flexipass, the **Europass** allows travel in France, Germany, Italy, Spain and Switzerland for US$233 under-26, or US$348 1st class, for 5 days in 2 months, rising to US$513 or US$728 for 15 days, with prices in between for 6, 8 or 10 days; there is also the option of adding adjacent "associate" countries. Eurail passes are available from the agents listed on p.22 and p.23.

BY BUS

For most people on a tour of Europe, a **bus** is something you take when there is no train. There are some countries (Greece, Turkey and Morocco are the most obvious examples) where the trains are slow or infrequent, and the bus network more widespread. In other countries, Spain and Portugal for example, the buses are cheaper, more efficient and genereally a more comfortable option. But on the whole in Europe you'll find yourself using buses for the odd trip here and there, usually locally, since on long-distance journeys between major European cities it's generally slower, more uncomfortable and not particularly cheap, especially if you have a rail pass. If you have a limited itinerary, however, a **bus pass** or **circular bus ticket** can undercut a rail pass, especially for over-26s. The **Eurolines** pass is valid for unlimited travel between 47 cities in Europe and the British Isles (though, with certain exceptions, it is not supposed to be used for journeys that do not cross international frontiers). It costs £90 (£109 for over-26s) for 15 days between 16 September and 31 May, and £120/145 between 1 June and 15 September. For 30-day passes, those prices are £129/162 and £179/222, and for a 60-day pass they are £162/205 and £195/259. Alternatively, **Busabout** run services for their own pass holders every two or four days between April and October (May to September in Spain and Portugal), taking in the major cities of nine European countries, with add-on connections to two more, plus a link to London and through tickets from elsewhere in Britain and Ireland. Two-week Busabout passes are £149 for youth or student card-holders, £169 for others, rising to £209/229 for 21 days, £279/309 for a month, £429/479 for two months, £529/589 for three, and £629/699 for the whole season. There are also Flexipasses for any 10 or 15 days in two months (£229/255 and £329/369 respectively), 20 days in 3 months (£429/479), or 30 days in 4 months (£599/659), with additional days at £25/30. Busabout passes are available at travel agents in Britain, North America or Australasia (for further enquiries call: in the US ☎1-800/664 4046, in Canada ☎416/322 8468, in the UK ☎020/7950 1661, in Australia ☎02/9657 3333 and in New Zealand ☎09/309 8824, or check Busabout's Web site at *www.busabout.com*).

NATIONAL RAIL PASSES

Some European countries provide a **national rail pass**, which can be good value if you're doing a lot of travelling within one country, or a EuroDomino (also called a Freedom Pass), which you buy before you leave. Main options are listed below: in general those quoted in pounds or dollars need to be bought before you leave home, either from the office of the national rail company or national tourist office, or in North America, from RailEurope, the general sales agent for most European railroads (they can be ordered online at *www.raileurope.com/us*). There is no pass as such for Russia.

Austria The VORTEILSCard rail pass gives a year's half-price travel throughout Austria for €94. A EuroDomino pass costs from £51 (£67 for over-26s) for 3 days up to £81/107 for 8 days. An Austrian Railpass gives 3 days' free travel in a 15-day period for $107, plus up to five additional days at $15 each.

Belgium A Belgian Tourrail gives 5 days' unlimited travel within a 1-month period for €57, and the Go Pass allows under-26s 10 single journeys of any length in 6 months for €38 (the over-26 version, Rail Pass, costs €57) but on weekdays it is only valid after 9am. A EuroDomino pass costs from £26 (£34 for over-26s) for 3 days up to £41/59 for 8 days. Also covered by Benelux passes.

Benelux A Benelux Tourrail card gives 5 days' travel in a month on the Netherlands, Belgium and Luxembourg railways, and Luxembourg CRL buses, for £56 (£76 for over-26s).

Britain The BritRail pass, available from British Rail agents outside Britain, qualifies you for unlimited rail travel throughout England, Wales and Scotland for 8 days at $215 ($265 for over-26s), 15 at $299 ($399), 22 at $355 ($505), or a month at $420 ($499). It also gives a discount of around 12 percent on Eurostar Channel Tunnel services, and can be bought as a package with the discounted cross-Channel ticket. Alternatively, the BritRail Flexipass gives unlimited travel on any 4 days in two months for $185 ($235 for over-26s), 8 for $239 ($339); or 15 for $359 ($515). Other passes include the Freedom of Scotland Pass, giving 4 days' travel in Scotland in an 8-day period at $134, 8 days in 15 at $168, 12 days in 20 at $219, the Freedom of Wales pass, which gives unlimited bus travel in Wales for 8 days with unlimited rail travel on any 4 of them for $85, or unlimited bus travel for 15 days with unlimited rail travel on any 8 of them for $154, and the BritRail SouthEast Pass, which gives 3 days' free travel in southeast England in an 8-day period for $73, 4 days for $106, or 7 days in 15 for $142. With a BritRail pass plus Ireland, you get 5 days' travel in a month throughout Britain and Ireland (plus a round trip on Stena Line Irish Sea ferries) for $399, or 10 days for $569. Available in Britain, the Young Person's Railcard costs $18 and gives 33 percent reductions to full-time students and under-26s for a year.

Bulgaria A EuroDomino pass costs from £21 (£26 for over-26s) for 3 days up to £41/51 for 8 days.

Croatia A EuroDomino pass costs from £32 (the same for over-26s) for 3 days up to £52/57 for 8 days.

Czech Republic A EuroDomino pass costs from £21 (£28 for over-26s) for 3 days up to £46/58 for 8 days.

Denmark A EuroDomino pass costs from £38 (£51 for over-26s) for 3 days up to £78/101 for 8 days. For ScanRail passes see Scandinavia.

Finland Finnrail passes are valid for unlimited rail travel on 3, 5 or 10 days in a month and cost €110, €146 and €198 respectively. A EuroDomino pass costs from £53 (£71 for over-26s) for 3 days up to £103/131 for 8 days. For ScanRail passes see Scandinavia.

France A EuroDomino pass costs from £80 (£109 for over-26s) for 3 days up to £155/204 for 8 days. The Carte 12–25 gives 12–25-year-olds 25–50 percent off all train journeys for a year for £29, while the France Railpass costs $180 for any 3 days' travel in a month ($146 each for 2–5 people travelling together), with up to 6 additional rail days at $30 each. For under-26s, the France Youthpass gives 3 days' travel in a month for $130, with up to 6 additional days at $20 each.

Germany The German Rail BahnCard gives a year of unlimited half-price travel on all trains in Germany and costs €138 (under-23s, students, senior citizens and spouses of holders €68). A EuroDomino pass costs from £85 (£112 for over-26s) for 3 days up to £125/167 for 8 days. A German Rail Pass costs $138 ($174 for over-26s, $261 for two travelling together) for any 4 days' travel in a month, rising to $210 ($306, $459) for 10 (with prices in between for 5–9 days).

Greece A EuroDomino pass costs from £30 (£38 for over-26s) for 3 days up to £55/73 for 8 days.

Hungary A EuroDomino pass costs from £24 (£31 for over-26s) for 3 days up to £54/71 for 8 days.

Ireland Irish Rail's Rover ticket buys unlimited rail travel in the Republic and the North on any 5 days out of 15 for €105, with an Irish Explorer Rail Ticket (the same deal in the Republic only) at €85. Use the Emerald Card on rail and bus in the Republic and the North at €146 for 8 days in 15 and €255 for 15 days in 30, or the Irish Explorer Rail and Bus Ticket for 8 days in 15 in the Republic only at €127. A EuroDomino pass costs from £37 sterling (£41 for over-26s) for 3 days up to £72/81 for 8 days and is valid only in the Republic. See Britain for details of the BritRail Pass plus Ireland (not available in Britain or Ireland).

Italy A 2-month Chilometrico ticket is valid for 3000km of travel, or 20 journeys if shorter, for up to five people within 2 months for $147 each. A EuroDomino pass costs from £67 (£89 for over-26s) for 3 days up to £107/139 for 8 days. The Italy Railcard gives unlimited rail travel for 8 days at $199, 15 at $249, 21 at $289, or 30 at $348. A Flexi RailCard gives 4 days in a month for $159, 8 days for $223, or 12 days for $286.

Luxembourg One-day rail passes are €4 each, €15 for a book of 5. A EuroDomino pass costs from £10 (£13 for over-26s) for 3 days up to £15/18 for 8 days. A Luxembourg Card covering buses too costs €9 for one day, €15 for any 2 days in a week, and €21 for any 3 days in a week, with free entry to numerous sights as well. See also Benelux.

Morocco A EuroDomino pass costs from £21 (£22 for over-26s) for 3 days up to £46/52 for 8 days.

Netherlands Rover tickets give a day's unlimited travel for £29. A Summer Tour Rover giving free travel on any 3 days in 10 during July and August costs £30 for one person, £39.50 for two travelling together, £36.50/48 for one covering bus services too. A HollandRail Pass gives 3 days' free travel in a month at $52 for one person, $75 for two travelling together (over-26s $65/98), or 5 days for $79/119 ($98/147). A EuroDomino pass costs from £24 (£32 for over-26s) for 3 days up to £59/77 for 8 days. See also Benelux.

Norway A Norway Rail Flexipass gives 3 days free travel in a month for $139, 4 days for $172, or 5 days for $192. A EuroDomino pass costs from £82 (£109 for over-26s) for 3 days up to £157/204 for 8 days. For ScanRail passes see Scandinavia.

Poland Polrail passes cost £45 (£65 for over-26s) for 8 days travel, £52/74 for 15, £58/84 for 21, and £76/109 for a month. A EuroDomino pass costs from £29 (£34 for over-26s) for 3 days up to £59/69 for 8 days.

Portugal A Bilhete Turistico pass, which costs €95 for a week's rail travel, €159 for 2 weeks, and €222 for 3, is not really worth it. A EuroDomino pass costs from £26 (£38 for over-26s) for 3 days up to £51/68 for 8 days.

Romania A EuroDomino pass costs from £24 (£32 for over-26s) for 3 days up to £54/77 for 8 days.

Scandinavia The ScanRail pass is valid on the rail networks of Denmark, Norway, Sweden and Finland and costs £97 (£129 for over-26s) for 5 days' travel in 2 months, £129 (£172) for 10 days in 2 months, and £150 (£199) for 21 days unlimited.

Slovakia A EuroDomino pass costs from £19 (£24 for over-26s) for 3 days up to £34/44 for 8 days.

Slovenia A EuroDomino pass costs from £24 (£32 for over-26s) for 3 days up to £39/52 for 8 days.

Spain A EuroDomino pass costs from £52 (£69 for over-26s) for 3 days up to £122/159 for 8 days. The Spain Flexipass gives 3 days' free travel in a 2-month period for $155, plus $30 each for up to 7 additional days.

Sweden EuroDomino passes for Sweden cost from £80 (£99 for over-26s) for 3 days up to £130/164 for 8 days. The Sweden Railpass gives 3 days' free travel in a month for $159, 4 days for $181, 5 for $202. ScanRail passes are also valid (see Scandinavia).

Switzerland The Swiss Pass, valid for unlimited travel on rail, bus and ferry routes, costs $160 for 4 days ($136 each for two or more people travelling together), $220 ($187) for 8 days, $265 ($225) for 15, $305 ($260) for 21, and $345 ($294) for a month. Alternatives are the Swiss Flexipass (giving 3–9 days in a month at $156–303, or $132–258 each for two or more travelling together), the Swiss Half-Fare Card (50 percent discount on rail travel for a month for £38), and the Swiss Card (free travel between border or airport and your main resort plus 50 percent discount on other tickets for a month at £67). A EuroDomino pass costs from £49 (£65 for over-26s) for 3 days up to £79/100 for 8 days.

Turkey A EuroDomino pass costs from £13 (£17 for over-26s) for 3 days up to £28/37 for 8 days.

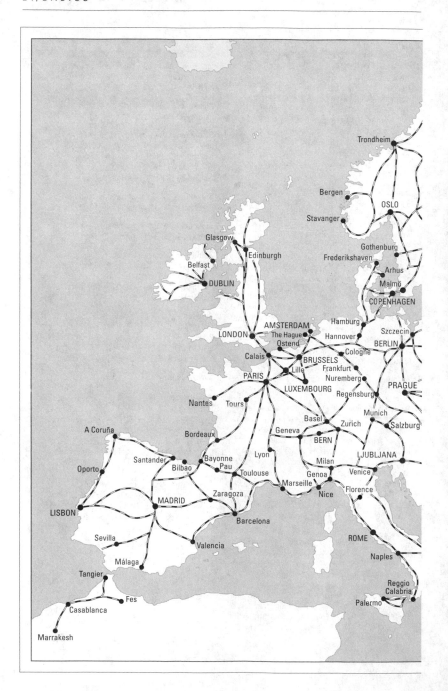

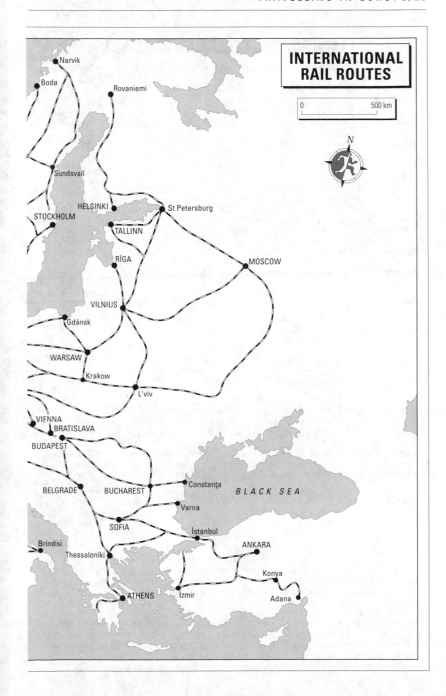

INTERNATIONAL RAIL ROUTES

0   500 km

N

Narvik
Bodø
Rovaniemi
Sundsvall
HELSINKI
St Petersburg
STOCKHOLM
TALLINN
RĪGA
MOSCOW
VILNIUS
Gdánsk
WARSAW
Krakow
L'viv
VIENNA
BRATISLAVA
BUDAPEST
BELGRADE
BUCHAREST
Constanţa
BLACK SEA
Varna
SOFIA
Bríndisi
İstanbul
ANKARA
Thessaloníki
Konya
ATHENS
İzmir
Adana

INTERNATIONAL TRAIN ROUTES

TO FROM	Amsterdam	Berlin	Bratislava	Brussels	Bucharest
Amsterdam	–	4 (6hr 20min)	Berlin	22 (2hr 55min)	Vienna
Berlin	4 (6hr 20min)	–	1 (9hr 20min)	1 (8hr 45min)	Budapest
Bratislava	Berlin	1 (9hr 15min)	–	Vienna	1 (16hr 50min)
Brussels	22 (3hr 05min)	1 (8hr 15min)	Vienna	–	Vienna
Bucharest	Vienna	Budapest	1 (17hr 50min)	Vienna	–
Budapest	Vienna	2 (12hr)	9 (2hr 35min)[2]	Vienna	6 (13hr 40min)
Copenhagen	Duisburg	Malmö	Hamburg & Breclav	Cologne	Munich
Ljubljana	Munich	Munich	Vienna	Munich	Budapest
Luxembourg	Brussels	Cologne	Cologne & Prague	25 (3hr)	Strasbourg & Munich
Milan	6 weekly (14hr 30min)	Munich	Vienna	2 (11hr 55min)	Munich
Moscow	Hanover[b]	3–7 weekly (27hr)[b]	1 (35hr 05min)[b]	Cologne [b]	1 (47hr 50min)[U]
Munich	1 (10hr 50min)	8 (8hr 45min)	Vienna	1 (10hr 50min)	1 (23hr)
Paris	6 (7hr 55min)	1 (11hr)	Vienna	21 (4hr 45min)[3]	2 weekly (35hr 20min)[1]
Prague	1 (14hr 30min)	5 (5hr 20min)	7 (5hr 15min)	Frankfurt & Cologne	1 (23hr)
Rome	Milan	Munich	Vienna	Milan	Vienna
Vienna	1 (14hr 25min)	2 (9hr 50min)	10 (1hr 15min)[2]	1 (14hr 20min)	2 (17hr 30min)
Vilnius	Warsaw & Berlin[5]	Warsaw[5]	Warsaw[5]	Warsaw & Cologne[5]	Warsaw[5]
Warsaw	Berlin	4 (7hr)	2 (8hr 45min)	Cologne	1 (28hr 20min)
Zagreb	Munich	Munich	Vienna	Munich	Budapest
Zurich	1 (9hr)	1 (11hr 50min)	Vienna	2 (7hr 45min)	Vienna

This chart shows the number of direct daily trains between European capitals and the fastest scheduled time by ordinary services where practical (those with a supplement will be faster, and may be your only choice). Where there is no direct service, a suggested interchange point is given instead, but note that you may have to pick up your connecting service from a different terminal, and that you may have to wait several hours for your connection: you could take it as an opportunity to wander round town, with your bags at the left luggage deposit in the meantime, or to freshen up – many major stations have washing facilities. Depending on the time of day, or day of the week, you may be able to get to your destination more quickly or conveniently with one or two extra changes of train. Note too that most trains to Russia and the Baltic states pass through Belarus or Ukraine, and that you may therefore need a transit visa to use them (see p.32). Direct services to Athens, Istanbul and Sofia pass through Belgrade and sometimes Skopje, so you may wish to check on the current political situation in Yugoslavia, the republic of Macedonia and the neighbouring countries before deciding to use them.

Budapest	Copenhagen	Ljubljana	Luxembourg	Milan
Vienna	Duisburg	Munich	Brussels	6 weekly (13hr 55min)
2 (12hr)	Malmö	Munich	Cologne	Munich
9 (2hr 40min)[2]	Breclav & Hamburg	Vienna	Prague & Cologne	Vienna
Vienna	Cologne	Munich	25 (3hr)	2 (11hr 50min)
7 (13hr 15min)	Munich	Budapest	Munich & Strasbourg	Munich
–	Munich	2 (8hr)	Zurich	Venice (Mestre)
Munich	–	Munich	Cologne	Stuttgart
2 (7hr 55min)	Munich	–	Zurich	Venice (Mestre)
Zurich	Cologne	Zurich	–	2 (8hr 55min)
Venice (Mestre)	Stuttgart	Venice (Mestre)	2 (8hr 50min)	–
1–2 (33hr 45min)[u]	Hanover & Hamburg[b]	Zagreb[1u]	Cologne[b]	Vienna[4b]
3 (8hr 10min)	1 (14hr 35min)	3 (6hr 35min)	Strasbourg	3 (8hr 50min)
1 (18hr 15min)	Cologne	Munich	6 (3hr 40min)	3 (7hr)
5 (7hr 05min)	Hamburg	Munich	Frankfurt & Cologne	Munich
Venice (Mestre)	Munich	Venice (Mestre)	Milan	22–27 (5hr 55min)
10 (3hr)[2]	Munich	2 (6hr)	Zurich	1 (12hr 45min)
Warsaw[5]	Warsaw, Berlin & Malmö[5]	Warsaw & Vienna[5]	Warsaw & Cologne[5]	Warsaw & Vienna[5]
2 (11hr 25min)	Berlin & Malmö	Vienna	Cologne	Vienna
4 (6hr 30min)	Munich	6 (2hr 20min)	Zurich	Venice (Mestre)
1 (12hr 55min)	Frankfurt	1 (11hr)	2 (5hr)	9 (4hr 30min)

[1] On days when there is no direct connection, change (also) at Budapest.
[2] There is also a hydrofoil service in summer.
[3] Journey time by the one ordinary daily train; 1hr 25min on the remaining 20 special-fare trains.
[4] On days when there is no direct Moscow–Vienna service, change (also) at Warsaw.
[5] The Warsaw–Vilnius train should not be routed via Belarus, but check before travelling. On days when there is no direct connection, change (also) at Šeštokai.
[b] via Belarus – transit visa needed.
[u] via Ukraine – transit visa needed.

INTERNATIONAL TRAIN ROUTES

FROM \ TO	Moscow	Munich	Paris	Prague	Rome
Amsterdam	Hanover[b]	1 (11hr)	6 (8hr 30min)	1 (14hr 10min)	Milan
Berlin	3–7 weekly (27hr 30min)[b]	8 (8hr 45min)	1 (11hr 45min)	5 (4hr 45min)	Munich
Bratislava	1 (31hr 10min)[b]	Vienna	Vienna	7 (5hr 20min)	Vienna
Brussels	Cologne [b]	1 (10hr 25min)	21 (5hr 30min)[3]	Cologne & Frankfurt	Milan
Bucharest	1 (46hr)[u]	1 (24hr)	2 weekly (35hr)[1]	1 (23hr 20min)	Vienna
Budapest	1–2 (34hr 15min)[u]	3 (8hr 25min)	1 (17hr 20min)	5 (7hr)	Venice (Mestre)
Copenhagen	Hamburg & Hanover[b]	1 (14hr 40min)	Cologne	Hamburg	Munich
Ljubljana	Zagreb[1u]	3 (6hr 50min)	Munich	Munich	Venice (Mestre)
Luxembourg	Cologne[b]	Strasbourg	6 (3hr 40min)	Cologne & Frankfurt	Milan
Milan	Vienna[4b]	3 (8hr 20min)	3 (6hr 55min)	Munich	22–27 (6hr 40min)
Moscow	–	Prague[b]	Cologne[b]	1 (33hr 30min)[b]	Vienna[4b]
Munich	Prague[b]	–	4 (10hr 05min)	3 (8hr 20min)	2 (11hr 50min)
Paris	Cologne[b]	4 (10hr 25min)	–	Frankfurt	1 (14hr 25min)
Prague	1 (30hr 15min)[b]	3 (9hr)	Frankfurt	–	Munich
Rome	Vienna[4b]	2 (11hr 15min)	1 (14hr 25min)	Munich	–
Vienna	3 weekly (31hr 30min)[4b]	4 (5 hr)	2 (13hr 35min)	3 (4hr 25min)	2 (13hr 35min)
Vilnius	2–3 (16hr)[b]	Warsaw & Prague[5]	Warsaw & Berlin[5]	Warsaw[5]	Vienna & Warsaw[5]
Warsaw	3 (19hr 35min)[b]	Prague	Cologne	3 (10hr 20min)	Vienna
Zagreb	3 weekly (49hr)[1u]	3(9hr 20)	Munich	Budapest	Venice (Mestre)
Zurich	Prague	4 (4hr 15min)	3 (7hr 45min)	1 (11hr 25min)	1 (11hr)

This chart shows the number of direct daily trains between European capitals and the fastest scheduled time by ordinary services where practical (those with a supplement will be faster, and may be your only choice). Where there is no direct service, a suggested interchange point is given instead, but note that you may have to pick up your connecting service from a different terminal, and that you may have to wait several hours for your connection: you could take it as an opportunity to wander round town, with your bags at the left luggage deposit in the meantime, or to freshen up – many major stations have washing facilities. Depending on the time of day, or day of the week, you may be able to get to your destination more quickly or conveniently with one or two extra changes of train. Note too that most trains to Russia and the Baltic states pass through Belarus or Ukraine, and that you may therefore need a transit visa to use them (see p.32). Direct services to Athens, Istanbul and Sofia pass through Belgrade and sometimes Skopje, so you may wish to check on the current political situation in Yugoslavia, the republic of Macedonia and the neighbouring countries before deciding to use them.

Vienna	Vilnius	Warsaw	Zagreb	Zurich
1 (14hr 30min)	Berlin & Warsaw[5]	Berlin	Munich	1 (9hr 10min)
2 (9hr 20min)	Warsaw[5]	4 (7hr 25min)	Munich	1 (11hr 40min)
10 (3hr)[2]	Warsaw[5]	2 (8hr 30min)	Vienna	Vienna
1 (14hr 40min)	Cologne & Warsaw[5]	Cologne	Munich	2 (7hr 45min)
1 (17hr 50min)	Warsaw[5]	1 (27hr 35min)	Budapest	Vienna
10 (3hr)[2]	Warsaw[5]	2 (11hr 15min)	4 (5hr 55min)	1 (12hr 45min)
Munich	Malmö, Berlin & Warsaw[5]	Malmö & Berlin	Munich	Frankfurt
2 (6hr)	Vienna & Warsaw[5]	Vienna	6 (2hr 20min)	1 (11hr 55min)
Zurich	Cologne & Warsaw[5]	Cologne	Zurich	2 (5hr)
1 (12hr 30min)	Vienna & Warsaw[5]	Vienna	Venice (Mestre)	9 (4hr 30min)
3 weekly (33hr)[4][b]	2–3 (13hr 55min)[b]	3 (19hr 05min)[b]	3 weekly (51hr)[1][u]	Prague[b]
4 (5hr 25min)	Prague & Warsaw[5]	Prague	3 (9hr 20min)	4 (4hr 10min)
2 (13hr 30min)	Berlin & Warsaw[5]	Cologne	Munich	3 (7hr 40min)
2 (4hr 25min)	Warsaw[5]	3 (10hr 40min)	Budapest	1 (11hr 30min)
2 (13hr 40min)	Vienna & Warsaw[5]	Vienna	Venice (Mestre)	1 (11hr 30min)
–	Warsaw[5]	2 (10hr)	2 (6hr 55min)	3 (9hr 15min)
Warsaw[5]	–	every two days (9hr 55min)[5]	Warsaw & Budapest[5]	Warsaw & Vienna[5]
2 (10hr)	every two days (10hr 05min)[5]	–	Budapest	Vienna
2 (6hr 40min)	Budapest & Warsaw[5]	Budapest	–	1 (14hr 25min)
3 (9hr 35min)	Vienna & Warsaw[5]	Vienna	1 (13hr 30min)	–

[1] On days when there is no direct connection, change (also) at Budapest.
[2] There is also a hydrofoil service in summer.
[3] Journey time by the one ordinary daily train; 1hr 25min on the remaining 20 special-fare trains.
[4] On days when there is no direct Moscow–Vienna service, change (also) at Warsaw.
[5] The Warsaw–Vilnius train should not be routed via Belarus, but check before travelling. On days when there is no direct connection, change (also) at Šeštokai.
[b] via Belarus – transit visa needed.
[u] via Ukraine – transit visa needed.

DRIVING

In order to drive in Europe you need a full and up-to-date **driver's licence**. EC-approved licences, such as those now issued in Britain and Ireland, are valid throughout the EU, and in theory elsewhere in Europe too. North American and Australasian licences are also in theory valid for driving in most of Europe (in Italy, Austria and Spain you need to carry a translation of this, available from your national motoring organization), but it is better to carry an International Driving Licence, especially if you want to rent a car. These are required in some East European countries and are available from national motoring organizations for a small fee; you'll need to show your driver's licence, passport, one passport photo and proof of age (18 or over). You should also carry your vehicle registration document at all times (if the named owner is not present on the trip you'll need a letter from them authorizing use of the vehicle) and, if taking your own vehicle, be insured. Your existing insurance policy may already provide third-party cover for a certain period in Europe (this is frequently the case with British policies), but for some countries you will need to take out a supplementary policy. As proof of insurance cover, it's sensible to get hold of an International Green Card from your insurers – and it's obligatory in certain countries anyway. In case of breakdown, you can take out, at extra cost, extended cover with automobile associations, although the motoring organizations of most countries operate some kind of reciprocal **breakdown** agreement with members of most foreign motoring organizations, so if you are a member it's wise to have your membership documents with you as well. Your national organization can provide a list of countries with reciprocal arrangements. A nationality plate should be displayed on the rear of your vehicle, and a warning triangle (which must be displayed if you stop on the road) and first-aid kit are either required or advised throughout Europe. A fire extinguisher is obligatory in Estonia, Lithuania, Greece and Turkey. All the countries of mainland Europe drive on the right-hand side of the road, so your headlights should be adjusted accordingly, and priority to traffic coming from the right is a common rule of the road. Pretty much every country included in this book has a decent network of main roads; only when you get onto minor roads do the differences between southern, eastern and northwestern Europe become really apparent. In most of Europe motorways are free, but in some countries **tolls** are levied: in Greece, Spain and Portugal these are fairly cheap; in France they cost more but the primary roads there are invariably excellent; in Italy the cost can be substantial if you're travel-

---

MOTORING ORGANIZATIONS

American Automobile Association (AAA)
☎407/444 7000, *www.aaa.com*
Australian Automobile Association ☎02/6247 7311, *www.aaa.asn.au*
Automobile Association (AA) ☎0870/ 550 0600, *www.theaa.co.uk*
Automobile Association of Ireland (AA)
☎01/617 9999, *www.theaa.ie*

Canadian Automobile Association (CAA)
☎613/247 0117, *www.caa.ca*
New Zealand Automobile Association ☎09/377 4660, *www.nzaa.co.nz*
Royal Automobile Club (RAC) ☎0800/550055, *www.rac.co.uk*

CAR RENTAL RESERVATION NUMBERS

Avis US ☎1-800/331 1212; Canada ☎1-800/879 2847; UK ☎0870/606 0100; Ireland ☎01/605 7555; Australia ☎1800/225 533; New Zealand ☎0800/655 111 or 09/526 2847; *www.avis.com*
Budget US & Canada ☎1-800/527 0700; UK ☎0800/973159; Ireland ☎1850/575767; Australia ☎1300/362 848; New Zealand ☎0800/652 227 or 09/375 2222; *www.budgetrentacar.com*
Europcar US & Canada ☎1-877/940 6900; UK ☎0870/607 5000; Ireland ☎01/614 2800; Australia ☎03/9330 6161; *www.europcar.com*

Hertz US ☎1-800/654 3131; Canada ☎1-800/263 0600; UK ☎0870/848 4848; Ireland ☎01/676 7476; Australia ☎1800/550 067; New Zealand ☎0800/654321; *www.hertz.com*
National US & Canada ☎1-800/CAR RENT; UK ☎0870/400 4502; Ireland ☎021/432 0755; Australia ☎02/8255 9039; New Zealand ☎0800/800115 or 09/3379 5080; *www.nationalcar.com*
Thrifty US & Canada ☎1-800/847 4389; UK ☎01494/751600; Ireland ☎1800/515800; Australia ☎02/9331 1385; New Zealand ☎0800/737070; *www.thrifty.com*

ling long distances. Fuel prices vary from around 52¢/36p for a litre of unleaded in Poland, or 75¢/52p in Greece, Spain, Poland and the Czech Republic, to a hefty $1.20/84p in the UK and almost as much in Norway and Finland; petrol is also pricey in the Netherlands, France, Belgium, Italy, Sweden, Denmark and Germany, while in Eastern Europe it is generally cheaper. Leaded petrol is being withdrawn in most European countries, and is already unavailable in a few. Diesel is usually only slightly cheaper than gasoline; in Britain, amazingly, it actually costs more.

The alternative to taking your own car is to rent one on the spot. Compared to rates in North America, this can be expensive, and you may find it cheaper to arrange things in advance through one of the multinational chains, or by opting for some kind of fly-drive deal. If you do rent a car in Europe, rates for a small hatchback start at £140/$200 a week (depending on the country and the time of year) if you book in advance, usually more if you rent on the spot; we've given more precise details in the relevant sections of the guide but in general costs are higher in Scandinavia and northern Europe, lower in eastern and southern Europe. Unlimited mileage deals (as opposed to those where you pay a charge per kilometre) work out better value and give more flexibility. To rent a car you'll need to present your driving licence, sometimes an international driver's permit, and should be at least 21 years of age with more than one year's driving experience, though these regulations can vary some countries like Italy will not rent out a car if you don't have a credit card to put down a returnable deposit; if in doubt, check in advance with the car rental company or your home motoring organization. Note also that some firms don't allow you to take their cars across country borders.

BY FERRY

Travelling by **ferry** is often the most practical way to get from one part of Europe to another, the obvious routes being from the mainland to the Mediterranean islands, as well as moving between the countries bordering the Baltic and Adriatic Seas. There are countless routes across the whole of Europe serving a huge range of destinations, too numerous to outline here, so where possible we've given the details of ferries to other countries within individual Guide accounts. For further details of schedules and operators, see the *Thomas Cook European Timetable*, or visit the Web site *www.ex.ac.uk/~mspunter/ifg*.

HITCHING

If you're not sticking to a definite itinerary – and, in some countries, even if you are – **hitching** can be as good a way to get around as any, with the added advantages of being cheaper and much more sociable. When hitching, it's important to choose a place where a car can see you in good time and preferably has a place to pull over if they decide to pick you up. Hitching on motorways is illegal pretty much throughout Europe, in which case you should try motorway service stations or slip roads – though success at these can be patchy. Travel as light as possible – enormous backpacks tend to put drivers off – and carry a decent road map. Always look clean and presentable, and always, even if you have been waiting several hours for a lift, smile. Whether you use a sign or not is up to you: opinions differ about whether it helps, but it may put off drivers who could take you part of the way. Hitching is of course always a risky business – you never know quite who will pick you up – and women in particular should be wary of hitching alone. As for when to hitch, generally it's better to make an early start during the week, when you'll pick up most long-distance traffic. Germany is by far the best country in Europe to hitch in, though the Netherlands and Belgium are good, as in general are Britain and Ireland. Southern Europe can be patchy, while Scandinavia is notoriously bad. Though it might seem like cheating, there are a few countries (France and Germany most notably) which have hitchhiking organizations that for a fee will put you in touch with a driver going your way who wants to share petrol costs. This may seem to take the excitement out of hitching, but if you've been waiting several days for a lift it can be a godsend.

RED TAPE AND VISAS

Since the lifting of many immigration restrictions for European Union members in January 1993, border-crossing for most EU nationals has become a much less formal procedure, with holders of most passports just having to wave their documents at border officials. Border controls between some countries, Scandinavian states in particular, are virtually nonexistent, and ten EU states (Austria, Belgium, France, Germany, Greece, Italy, Luxembourg, the Netherlands, Portugal and Spain), known as the Schengen Group, now have joint visas valid for travel in all of them, and in theory no border immigration controls between them – though this may mean more ID checks within those countries. There is talk of other EU states joining the group, though two have left and others seem to be holding back.

Citizens of the UK (but not other British passport holders), Ireland, Australia, New Zealand, Canada and the USA do not need a **visa** to enter most European countries (exceptions are listed in the next paragraph), and can usually stay for one to three months, depending on your nationality; for some countries, your passport must be valid at least six months beyond the end of your stay. Always check on visa requirements before travelling, as they can and do change, though EU countries should never require visas from British or Irish citizens.

Everyone needs a visa to visit Russia. UK and Irish citizens need them for Turkey (available at the border). Americans need visas for Turkey (available at the border); Canadians also need them for the Czech Republic, Estonia, Latvia, Poland, Romania and Turkey (last two available at the border). Australians require visas to visit the Czech Republic, Hungary, Latvia, Poland, Portugal, Romania and Turkey (last two available at the border); New Zealanders need them for Latvia, Poland, Romania and Turkey (Romanian visas available at the border). Note that the three Baltic states (Lithuania, Latvia and Estonia) all allow entry to Canadians and certain other nationalities who have a visa for any one of them. Note also that you will need transit visas to cross the Ukraine and Belarus (if travelling for example from Poland, Slovakia, Hungary or Romania to Moscow).

When **crossing a border**, it pays to look reasonably well turned-out, and to be polite at all times, even in the face of the most overweening officialdom. On entering some countries you may be asked to show an onward ticket or sufficient funds to support yourself. Remember that governments are eager for rich tourists

PASSPORT OFFICES

USA Passport Office, 1111 19th St NW, Washington, DC 20005 (☎1-900/225 5674 or 202/647 0518); others in Boston, Chicago, Honolulu, Houston, Los Angeles, Miami, New Orleans, New York, Philadelphia, San Francisco, Seattle and Stamford. Free information and application forms available online at *travel.state.gov/passport_services.html*.

Canada Passport Office, Suite 209, West Tower, Guy Farreau Complex, 200 René Lévesque Blvd West, Montreal, PQ H2Z 1X4 (☎1-800/567-6868); others in major cities.

UK Passport Office, 70–78 Petty France, London SW1H 9HD (☎0870/521 0410); others in Belfast, Durham, Glasgow, Liverpool, Newport and Peterborough. Applications can be made at any post office. Information on line at *www.ukpa.gov.uk*.

Ireland Passport Office, Setanta Centre, Molesworth St, Dublin 2 (☎1890/426888) and 1a South Mall, Cork (☎1890/426900).

Australia There are offices in Canberra, Sydney, Newcastle, Melbourne, Brisbane, Adelaide, Perth, Hobart and Darwin; for information, call ☎13/1232.

New Zealand Passport Office, Dept of Internal Affairs, PO Box 10 526, Wellington (☎0800/225050 or 0800-PASSPORT).

CUSTOMS

Customs and duty-free restrictions vary throughout Europe, but are standard for travellers arriving in the EU at one litre of spirits, plus two litres of table wine, plus 200 cigarettes (or 250g tobacco, or fifty cigars). Since the inauguration of the Single Market, there is no longer any duty-free allowance for travel within the EU, but travellers between EU countries can effectively carry as much in the way of duty-paid goods as they want (so long as they are for personal use). Remember that carrying contraband such as controlled drugs, firearms or pornography is illegal, not to mention foolhardy in the extreme. If you are carrying prescribed drugs of any kind, it might be a good idea to have a copy of the prescription to flash at suspicious customs officers. If in doubt consult the relevant embassy.

---

with lots of money to spend, but accept poor, scruffy backpackers under sufferance. Non-Whites may also get the feeling that they are only accepted under sufferance by border officials in some countries, and will often be subjected to much greater scrutiny than their white fellow travellers.

Finally, don't leave it too late to get a passport before leaving home, since by post this can take four weeks or longer in the summer and is rather irksome to do in person.

EUROPEAN EMBASSIES

AUSTRIA USA 3524 International Court, NW, Washington, DC 20008–3022 (☎202/895 6700); **Canada** 445 Wilbrod St, Ottowa, ON K1N 6M7 (☎613/789 1444); **UK** 18 Belgrave Mews West, London SW1X 8HU (☎020/7235 3731); **Ireland** 15 Ailesbury Ct, 93 Ailesbury Rd, Dublin 4 (☎01/269 4577); **Australia** PO Box 375, Manuka, Canberra, ACT 2603 (☎06/6295 1533); **New Zealand** 58 Willis St, Wellington (☎04/499 6393).

BELGIUM USA 3330 Garfield St, NW, Washington, DC 20008 (☎202/333 6900); **Canada** 80 Elgin St, 4th floor, Ottawa, ON K1P 1B7 (☎613/236 7267); **UK** 103–105 Eaton Sq, London SW1W 9AB (☎020/7470 3700); **Ireland** 2 Shrewsbury Rd, Dublin 4 (☎01/269 2082); **Australia** 19 Arkana St, Yarralumla, Canberra, ACT 2600 (☎06/6273 2501); **New Zealand** 12th floor, Axon House, 1–3 Willeston St, PO Box 3379, Wellington (☎04/472 9558).

BRITAIN USA 3100 Massachusetts Ave, NW, Washington, DC 20008 (☎202/588 6500); **Canada** 80 Elgin St, Ottawa, ON K1P 5K7 (☎613/237 1530); **Ireland** 29 Merrion Rd, Dublin 4 (☎01/205 3700); **Australia** Commonwealth Ave, Canberra, ACT 2600 (☎06/6270 6666); **New Zealand** 44 Hill St, PO Box 1812, Wellington (☎04/472 6049).

BULGARIA USA 1621 22nd St, NW, Washington, DC 20008 (☎202/387 7969); **Canada** 325 Stewart St, Ottawa, ON K1N 6K5 (☎613/789 3215); **UK** 186–188 Queens Gate, London SW7 5HL (☎020/7584 9400); **Ireland** 22 Burlington Rd, Dublin 4 (☎01/660 3293); **Australia** 4 Carlotta St, Double Bay, NSW 2028 (☎02/9327 7581).

CROATIA USA 2343 Massachusetts Ave, NW, Washington, DC 20008 (☎202/588 5899); **Canada** 229 Chapel St, Ottawa, ON K1N 7Y6 (☎613/562 7820); **UK** 21 Conway St, London W1P 5HL (☎020/7387 2022); **Australia** 14 Jindalee Cres, O'Malley, Canberra, ACT 2606 (☎06/6286 6988); **New Zealand** 131 Lincoln Rd, Henderson, Auckland (☎09/836 5581).

CZECH REPUBLIC USA 3900 Spring of Freedom St, NW, Washington, DC 20008 (☎202/274 9100); **Canada** 541 Sussex Drive, Ottawa, ON K1N 6Z6 (☎613/562 3875); **UK** 26 Kensington Palace Gdns, London W8 4QY (☎020/7243 1115);

Ireland 57 Northumberland Rd, Ballsbridge, Dublin 4 (☎01/668 1135); **Australia** 38 Culgoa Circuit, O'Malley, Canberra, ACT 2606 (☎06/6290 1386).

DENMARK USA 3200 Whitehaven St, NW, Washington, DC 20008–3683 (☎202/234 4300); **Canada** 47 Clarence St, Suite 450, Ottawa, ON K1N 9K1 (☎613/562 1811); **UK** 55 Sloane St, London SW1X 9SR (☎020/7333 0200); **Ireland** 121–122 St Stephen's Green, Dublin 2 (☎01/475 6404); **Australia** 15 Hunter St, Yarralumla, Canberra, ACT 2600 (☎06/6273 2195); **New Zealand** Level 1, 45 Johnston St, PO Box 10874, Wellington (☎04/471 0520).

ESTONIA USA 2131 Massachusetts Ave, NW, Washington, DC 20008 (☎202/588 0101); **Canada** 958 Broadview Ave, Toronto, ON M4K 2R6 (☎416/461 0764); **UK** 16 Hyde Park Gate, London SW7 5DG (☎020/7589 3428); **Ireland** 24 Merlyn Park, Dublin 4 (☎01/269 1552); **Australia** 86 Louisa Rd, Birchgrove, Sydney, NSW 2041 (☎02/9810 7468).

FINLAND USA 3301 Massachusetts Ave, NW, Washington, DC 20008 (☎202/298 5800); **Canada** 55 Metcalfe St, Suite 850, Ottawa, ON K1P 6L5 (☎613/236 2389); **UK** 38 Chesham Pl, London SW1W 8HW (☎020/7838 6200); **Ireland** Russell House, Stokes Pl, St Stephen's Green, Dublin 2 (☎01/478 1344); **Australia** 10 Darwin Ave, Yarralumla, Canberra, ACT 2600 (☎06/6273 3800); **New Zealand** 44–52 The Terrace, 6th floor, PO Box 2402, Wellington (☎04/499 4599).

FRANCE USA 4101 Reservoir Rd, NW, Washington, DC 20007 (☎202/944 6000); **Canada** 42 Sussex Drive, Ottawa, ON K1M 2C9 (☎613/789 1795); **UK** 58 Knightsbridge, London SW1X 7JT (☎020/7201 1000); **Ireland** 36 Ailesbury Rd, Ballsbridge, Dublin 4 (☎01/260 1666); **Australia** 6 Perth Ave, Yarralumla, Canberra, ACT 2600 (☎06/6216 0100); **New Zealand** Rural Bank House, 34–42 Manners St, 12th floor, PO Box 11–343, Wellington (☎04/384 2555).

GERMANY USA 4645 Reservoir Rd, NW, Washington, DC 20007–1998 (☎202/298 4000); **Canada** 1 Waverley St, 14th floor, Ottawa, ON K2P 0T8 (☎613/232 1101); **UK** 23 Belgrave Square, London SW1X 8PZ (☎020/7824 1300); **Ireland** 31 Trimleston Ave, Booterstown, Blackrock, Co Dublin (☎01/269

3011); **Australia** 119 Empire Circuit, Yarralumla, Canberra, ACT 2600 (☎06/6270 1911); **New Zealand** 90–92 Hobson St, PO Box 1687, Thorndon, Wellington (☎04/473 6063).

GREECE USA 2221 Massachusetts Ave, NW, Washington, DC 20008 (☎202/939 5800); **Canada** 76–80 MacLaren St, Ottawa, ON K2P 0K6 (☎613/238 6271); **UK** 1a Holland Park, London W11 3TP (☎020/7229 3850); **Ireland** 1 Upper Pembroke St, Dublin 2 (☎01/676 7254); **Australia** 9 Turrana St, Yarralumla, Canberra, ACT 2600 (☎06/6273 3011); **New Zealand** 10th floor, 5–7 Willeston St, PO Box 24–066, Wellington (☎04/473 7775).

HUNGARY USA 3910 Shoemaker St, NW, Washington, DC 20008 (☎202/362 6730); **Canada** 299 Waverley St, Ottawa, ON K2P 0V9 (☎613/230 2717); **UK** 35 Eaton Pl, London SW1X 8BY (☎020/7235 5218); **Ireland** 2 Fitzwilliam Pl, Dublin 2 (☎01/661 2902); **Australia** 17 Beale Cres, Deakin, Canberra, ACT 2600 (☎06/6282 3226); **New Zealand** 7/1a Picton St, Ponsonby, Auckland (☎09/376 3609).

IRELAND USA 2234 Massachusetts Ave, NW, Washington, DC 20008 (☎202/462 3939); **Canada** 130 Albert St, Suite 1105, Ottawa, ON K1P 5G4 (☎613/233 6281); **UK** 17 Grosvenor Pl, London SW1X 7HR (☎020/7235 2171); **Australia** 20 Arkana St, Yarralumla, Canberra, ACT 2600 (☎06/6273 3022).

ITALY USA 1601 Fuller St, NW, Washington, DC 20009 (☎202/328 5500); **Canada** 275 Slater St, 21st floor, Ottawa, ON K1P 5H9 (☎613/232 2401); **UK** 14 Three Kings Yard, Davies St, London W1Y 2EH (☎020/7312 2200); **Ireland** 63–65 Northumberland Rd, Dublin 4 (☎01/660 1744); **Australia** 12 Grey St, Deakin, Canberra, ACT 2600 (☎06/6273 3333); **New Zealand** 34–38 Grant Rd, Thorndon, PO Box 463, Wellington (☎04/473 5339).

LATVIA USA 4325 17th St, NW, Washington, DC 20011 (☎202/726 8213); **Canada** Place de Ville, Tower B, 112 Kent St, Suite 208, Ottawa, ON K1P 5P2 (☎613/238 6014); **UK** 45 Nottingham Pl, London W1M 3FE (☎020/7312 0040); **Australia** 32 Parnell St, Strathfield, Sydney (☎02/9745 5981).

LITHUANIA USA 2622 16th St, NW, Washington, DC 20009 (☎202/234 5860); **Canada** 130 Albert St, Suite 204, Ottawa, ON K1P 5G4 (☎613/567 5458); **UK** 84 Gloucester Pl, London W1H 3HN (☎020/7486 6401).

LUXEMBOURG USA 2200 Massachusetts Ave, NW, Washington, DC 20008 (☎202/265 4171); **UK** 27 Wilton Crescent, London SW1X 8SD (☎020/7235 6961).

MOROCCO USA 1601 21st St, NW, Washington, DC 20009 (☎202/462 7979); **Canada** 38 Range Rd, Ottawa, ON K1N 8J4 (☎613/236 7391); **UK** 49 Queen's Gate Gdns, London SW7 5NE (☎020/7581 5001); **Ireland** 53 Raglan Rd, Ballsbridge, Dublin 4 (☎01/660 9449).

NETHERLANDS USA 4200 Linnean Ave, NW, Washington, DC 20008 (☎202/244 5300); **Canada** 350 Albert St, Suite 2020, Ottawa, ON K1R 1A4 (☎613/237 5030); **UK** 38 Hyde Park Gate, London SW7 5DP (☎020/7580 3200); **Ireland** 160 Merrion Rd, Dublin 4 (☎01/269 3444); **Australia** 120 Empire Circuit, Yarralumla, Canberra, ACT 2600 (☎06/6273 3111); **New Zealand** Investment Centre, 10th Floor, Ballance St/Featherstone St, PO Box 840, Wellington (☎04/471 6390).

NORWAY USA 2720 34th St, NW, Washington, DC 20008–2714 (☎202/333 6000); **Canada** 90 Sparks St, Suite 532, Ottawa, ON K1P 5B4 (☎613/238 6571); **UK** 25 Belgrave Sq, London SW1X 8QD (☎020/7591 5500); **Ireland** 34

Molesworth St, Dublin 2 (☎01/662 1800); **Australia** 17 Hunter St, Yarralumla, Canberra, ACT 2600 (☎06/6273 3444); **New Zealand** 61 Molesworth St, Wellington (☎04/471 2503).

POLAND USA 2640 16th St, NW, Washington, DC 20009 (☎202/234 3800); **Canada** 443 Daly Ave, Ottawa, ON K1N 6H3 (☎613/789 0468); **UK** 47 Portland Pl, London W1N 4JH (☎020/7580 4324); **Ireland** 5 Ailesbury Rd, Dublin 4 (☎01/283 0855); **Australia** 7 Turrana St, Yarralumla, Canberra, ACT 2600 (☎06/6273 1208); **New Zealand** 17 Upland Rd, PO Box 10211, Kelburn, Wellington (☎04/475 9453).

PORTUGAL USA 2125 Kalorama Rd, NW, Washington, DC 20008 (☎202/328 8610); **Canada** 645 Island Park Drive, Ottawa, ON K1Y 0B8 (☎613/729 0883); **UK** 11 Belgrave Sq, London SW1X 8PP (☎020/7235 5331); **Ireland** Knocksinna House, Foxrock, Dublin 18 (☎01/289 4416); **Australia** 23 Culgoa Circuit, O'Malley, Canberra, ACT 2606 (☎06/6290 1733).

ROMANIA USA 1607 23rd St, NW, Washington, DC 20008 (☎202/232 3694); **Canada** 655 Rideau St, Ottawa, ON K1N 6A3 (☎613/789 3709); **UK** Arundel House, 4 Palace Green, London W8 4QD (☎020/7937 9666); **Ireland** 47 Ailesbury Rd, Dublin 4 (☎01/269 2852); **Australia** 4 Dalman Cres, O'Malley, Canberra, ACT 2606 (☎06/6286 2343).

RUSSIA USA 2650 Wisconsin Ave, NW, Washington, DC 20007 (☎202/298 5700), visa section 1825 Phelps Place NW, Washington, DC 20008 (☎202/939 8907); **Canada** 285 Charlotte St, Ottawa ON K1N 8L5 (☎613/235 4341; visa enquiries ☎613/236 7220); **UK** 13 Kensington Palace Gdns, London W8 4QX (☎020/7229 3628); **Ireland** 186 Orwell Rd, Rathgar, Dublin 14 (☎01/492 2048); **Australia** 78 Canberra Ave, Griffith, Canberra, ACT 2603 (☎06/6295 9033); **New Zealand** 57 Messines Rd, Karori, Wellington (☎04/476 6113).

SLOVAKIA USA 2201 Wisconsin Ave, Suite 250, NW, Washington, DC 20007 (☎202/965 5160); **Canada** 50 Rideau Terr, Ottawa, ON K1M 2A1 (☎613/749 4442); **UK** 25 Kensington Palace Gdns, London W8 4QY (☎020/7243 0803); **Ireland** 20 Clyde Rd, Ballsbridge, Dublin 4 (☎01/660 0012); **Australia** 47 Culgoa Circuit, O'Malley, Canberra, ACT 2606 (☎06/6290 1516).

SLOVENIA USA 1525 New Hampshire Ave, NW, Washington, DC 20036–1203 (☎202/667 5363); **Canada** 150 Metcalfe St, Suite 2101, Ottawa, ON K2P 1P1 (☎613/565 5781); **UK** Suite 1, Cavendish Ct, 11–15 Wigmore St, London W1H 9LA (☎020/7495 7775); **Australia** PO Box 284, Civic Sq, Canberra, ACT 2608 (☎06/6243 4830).

SPAIN USA 2375 Pennsylvania Ave, NW, Washington, DC 20037 (☎202/452 0100); **Canada** 74 Stanley Ave, Ottawa, ON K1M 1P4 (☎613/747 2252); **UK** 39 Chesham Pl, London SW1X 8SB (☎020/7235 5555), visa section 20 Draycott Place, London SW3 2SB (☎0891/600123 premium-rate charge); **Ireland** 17a Merlyn Park, Dublin 4 (☎01/269 1640); **Australia** PO Box 976, Deakin, Canberra, ACT 2600 (☎06/6273 3555).

SWEDEN USA 1501 M St, NW, Washington, DC 20005–1702 (☎202/467 2600); **Canada** Mercury Ct, 377 Dalhousie St, Ottawa, ON K1N 9N8 (☎613/241 8553); **UK** 11 Montagu Place, London W1H 2AL (☎020/7917 6400); **Ireland** Sun Alliance House, 13–17 Dawson St, Dublin 2 (☎01/671 5822); **Australia** 5 Turrana St, Yarralumla, Canberra, ACT 2600 (☎06/6270 2700); **New Zealand** 13th floor, Vogel Bldg, Aitken St, Thorndon, PO Box 12538, Wellington (☎04/499 9895).

SWITZERLAND USA 2900 Cathedral Ave, NW, Washington, DC 20008–3499 (☎202/745 7900); **Canada** 5 Marlborough Ave, Ottawa, ON K1N 8E6 (☎613/235 1837); **UK** 16–18 Montagu Place, London W1H 2BQ (☎020/7616 6000); **Ireland** 6 Ailesbury Rd, Ballsbridge, Dublin 4 (☎01/218 6382); **Australia** 7 Melbourne Ave, Forrest, Canberra, ACT 2603 (☎06/6273 3977); **New Zealand** Panama House, 22 Panama St, Wellington (☎04/472 1593).

TURKEY USA 2525 Massachusetts Ave, NW, Washington, DC 20008 (☎202/612 6700); **Canada** 197 Wurtemburg St, Ottawa, ON K1N 8L9 (☎613/789 4044); **UK** 43 Belgrave Sq, London SW1X 8PA (☎020/7393 0202); **Ireland** 11 Clyde Rd, Ballsbridge, Dublin 4 (☎01/668 5240); **Australia** 60 Mugga Way, Red Hill, Canberra, ACT 2603 (☎06/6295 0227); **New Zealand** 15–17 Murphy St, Level 8, PO Box 12–248, Wellington (☎04/472 1292).

HEALTH AND INSURANCE

EU citizens resident in the UK or Ireland are covered by reciprocal health agreements for free or reduced-cost emergency treatment in many of the countries in this book (main exceptions are the Baltic states, Switzerland, Slovenia, Morocco and Turkey). To claim this, you will often need only your passport, but you may also be asked for your NHS card or proof of residence. In EU countries and Norway, far from it being simpler, you'll also need form E111, available from post offices, DSS offices and travel agents, which you must get before you leave. Without an E111 you won't be turned away from hospitals but you will almost certainly have to pay for any treatment or medicines. Also, in practice, some countries' doctors and hospitals charge anyway and it's up to you to claim reimbursement when you return home. Make sure you are insured for potential medical expenses, and keep copies of receipts and prescriptions.

There aren't many particular **health problems** you'll encounter travelling in most parts of Europe. You don't need to have any inoculations for any of the countries covered in this book, although for Morocco and Turkey typhoid jabs are advised, and for some parts of Turkey, even malaria pills are a good idea for much of the year. When travelling, remember to be up to date with your polio and tetanus boosters.

Tap water in most countries is drinkable, though you may prefer bottled mineral water, either for the taste (mains supply in some places can be very hard or heavily chlorinated), or to be on the safe side, though you only need to avoid tap water altogether in southern Morocco and parts of Turkey. Diarrhoea and sickness from tap water or – in southern Europe – food, are reasonably likely, if only in a mild form. The best thing to do is carry anti-diarrhoea tablets with you at all times. One of the biggest problems you may face if travelling in southern Europe is the sun: don't spend too much time in direct sunlight if you're not used to it, and certainly not without any kind of sun block cream; just half an hour on your first day's sunbathing is probably the limit – more than this can leave you beetroot-red and nauseated. Mosquitoes, too, are a problem Europe-wide, especially in the south and places where there's a lot of water around; the Netherlands, for example, harbours particularly virulent species. It's hard to know what to do about them: most people develop an immunity to bites after a few days' exposure; until then an antihistamine cream like Phenergan can ease the itching. As for repellants, citronella oil is excellent, though not long-lasting, and some people swear by Avon Skin So Soft bath oil too. Finally, AIDS is as much of a problem in Europe as it is in the rest of the world, and it hardly needs saying that unprotected casual sex is highly inadvisable.

For minor health problems it's easiest to go to the local pharmacy. You'll find these pretty much everywhere and we've detailed out-of-hours ones in the text. In more serious cases your nearest consulate will have a list of English-speaking doctors, as will the local tourist office, and in the larger cities we've listed the most convenient casualty departments (emergency rooms).

INSURANCE

Wherever you're travelling from, it's a very good idea to have some kind of **travel insurance**. A typical travel insurance policy usually provides cover for the loss of baggage, tickets and – up to a certain limit – cash or cheques, as well as cancellation or curtailment of your journey. Most of them exclude so-called dangerous sports unless an extra premium is paid: in Europe this can mean anything from scuba-diving to mountaineering, skiing and even bungee-jumping. Read the small print and benefits tables of prospective policies carefully; coverage can vary wildly for roughly similar premiums. Many policies can be chopped and changed to exclude coverage you don't need – for example, sickness and accident benefits can often be excluded or included at will. If you do take medical coverage, ascertain whether benefits will be paid as treatment proceeds or only after returning home, and whether there is a 24-hour medical emergency number. When securing baggage cover, make sure that the per-article limit – typically under £500 equivalent – will cover your most valuable possession. If you need to make a claim, you should keep receipts for medicines and medical treatment, and in the event you have anything stolen, you must obtain an official statement from the police. Bank and credit cards often have certain levels of medical or other insurance included and you may automatically get travel insurance if you use a major credit card to pay for your trip.

Despite EU health care privileges, **British and Irish** residents would do well to take out an insurance policy before travelling to cover against theft, loss and illness or injury. Travel agents and tour operators are likely to require some sort of insurance when you book a package holiday, though according to UK law they can't make you buy their own (other than a £1 premium for "schedule airline failure"). If you have a good all-risks home insurance policy it may cover your possessions against loss or theft even when overseas. Many private medical schemes such as BUPA or PPP also offer coverage plans for abroad, including baggage loss, cancellation or curtailment and cash replacement as well as sickness or accident.

Americans and Canadians should also check that they're not already covered. Canadian provincial health plans usually provide partial cover for medical mishaps overseas. Holders of official student/teacher/youth cards are entitled to meagre accident coverage and hospital in-patient benefits. Students will often find that their student health coverage extends during the vacations and for one term beyond the date of last enrollment. Homeowners' or renters' insurance often covers theft or loss of documents, money and valuables while overseas, though conditions and maximum amounts vary from company to company.

ROUGH GUIDES TRAVEL INSURANCE

Rough Guides now offer their own **travel insurance**, customized for our readers by a leading UK broker and backed by a Lloyds underwriter. It's available for anyone, of any nationality, travelling anywhere in the world, and we are convinced that it's the best-value scheme you'll find.

There are two main Rough Guide insurance plans: Essential, for effective, no-frills cover, starting at £13.40/$21.44 for fifteen days; and Premier – more expensive but with more generous and extensive benefits. Each offers European or Worldwide cover, and can be supplemented with a "Hazardous Activities Premium" if you plan to indulge in sports considered dangerous, such as skiing, scuba-diving or trekking. A European policy covers all the places in this book (including Morocco, Turkey, Russia west of the Urals, and, if bought elsewhere, the UK). Unlike many policies, the Rough Guides schemes are calculated by the day, so if you're travelling for 27 days rather than a month, that's all you pay for. You can alternatively take out annual multi-trip insurance, which covers you for all your travel throughout the year (with a maximum of 60 days for any one trip).

For a policy quote in the UK, call the Rough Guides Insurance Line toll-free on ☎0800 015 0906; from outside Britain call +44-1243/621046. Alternatively, you can get an online quote and buy your cover at *www.roughguides.com/insurance*.

INFORMATION AND MAPS

Before you leave, it's worth contacting the tourist offices of the countries you're intending to visit, since most produce copious quantities of free leaflets, maps and brochures, some of which can be quite useful, both in planning your trip and when you're travelling. This is especially true for parts of central and eastern Europe, where up-to-date maps in particular are often scarcer in the country than in their tourist offices abroad. Also note that Estonia, Latvia, Lithuania and Russia do not have official tourist offices, so it may help to contact their embassies for more information. For the rest of Europe go easy, though: much of the information these places pump out can be picked up just as easily on your travels, and it can weigh a ton. Note that in Britain, far from encouraging potential visitors to call for information, national tourist boards of certain countries see this as an opportunity to fleece the punter even before arrival with 09-code premium-rate numbers and drawn-out taped messages – in fact it is cheaper in such cases to make an international call to their US offices.

TOURIST INFORMATION WEB SITES AND OFFICES ABROAD

AUSTRIA www.austria-tourism.at; **USA** 500 5th Ave, Suite 800, New York, NY 10110 (☎212/944 6885); **Canada** 2 Bloor St East, Suite 3330, Toronto, ON M4W 1A8 (416/967 3381); **UK** 14 Cork St, London W1S 3NS (☎020/7629 0461); **Ireland** Merrion Centre, Nutley Lane, Ballsbridge, Dublin 4 (☎01/283 0488); **Australia** 36 Carrington St, 1st Floor, Sydney, NSW 2000 (☎02/9299 3621).

BELGIUM www.visitbelgium.com; **USA** 789 3rd Ave, Suite 1501, New York, NY 10017–7076 (☎212/758 8130); **Canada** PO Box 760, Succursale NDG, Montreal, PQ H4A 3S2 (☎514/484 3594); **UK** (for Brussels and Wallonia) 225 Marsh Wall, London E14 9FW (☎020/7531 0393), (for Flanders) 31 Pepper St, E14 9RW (☎020/7458 0045).

BRITAIN www.visitbritain.com; **USA** 551 5th Ave, 7th floor, New York, NY 10176–0799 (☎212/986 2266), or 625 North Michigan Ave, Suite 1001, Chicago IL 60611-1977 (☎312/787 0464), or 10880 Wilshire Blvd, Suite 570, Los Angeles, CA 90024 (☎310/470 2782); **Canada** 5915 Airport Rd, Suite 120, Mississauga, ON L4V 1T1 (☎905/405 1720); **Ireland** 18–19 College Green, Dublin 2 (☎01/670 8000); **Australia** Level 16, Gateway, 1 Macquaire Pl, Sydney, NSW 2000 (☎02/9377 4400); **New Zealand** Fay Richwhite Bldg, 151 Queen St, Auckland 1 (☎09/303 1446).

BULGARIA USA c/o Balkantourist, 181 E 86th St, New York, NY 10028 (☎212/722 1110). Be warned: it is very difficult to get through by phone.

CROATIA www.htz.hr; **USA** 350 5th Ave, Suite 4003, New York, NY 10118 (☎1-800/829 4416); **UK** 2 The Lanchesters, 162–164 Fulham Palace Rd, London W6 9ER (☎020/8563 7979).

CZECH REPUBLIC www.visitczech.cz; **USA** 1109 Madison Ave, New York, NY 10028 (☎212/288 0830); **Canada** c/o

CSA, 401 Bay St, Suite 1510, Toronto, ON M5H 2Y4 (☎416/363 9928); **UK** 95 Great Portland St, London W1W 7NY (☎020/7291 9925).

DENMARK www.dt.dk; **USA** 655 3rd Ave, New York, NY 10017–5617 (☎212/885 9700); **UK** 55 Sloane St, London SW1X 9SY (☎020/7259 5959); **Australia** c/o Finnesse Communications, Level 4, York Street, Sydney, NSW 2000 (☎02/9290 1980).

ESTONIA www.tourism.ee

FINLAND www.mek.fi; **USA** 655 3rd Ave, 18th floor, New York, NY 10017 (☎212/885 9700); **UK** PO Box 33213, London W6 8JX (☎020/7365 2512).

FRANCE www.francetourism.com; **USA** 444 Madison Ave, 16th floor, New York, NY 10022 (☎212/838 7800), or 676 N Michigan Ave, Suite 3360, Chicago, IL 60611 (☎312/751 7800), or 9454 Wilshire Blvd, Suite 715, Beverly Hills, Los Angeles, CA 90212-2967 (☎310/271 6665); **Canada** 1981 av McGill College, Suite 490, Montreal, PQ H3A 2W9 (☎514/876 9880); **UK** 178 Piccadilly, London W1V 0AL (☎0906/824 4123 – premium rates charged for calls); **Ireland** 10 Suffolk St, Dublin 2 (☎01/679 0813); **Australia** 25 Bligh St, Level 22, Sydney, NSW 2000 (☎02/9231 5244).

GERMANY www.germany-tourism.de; **USA** 122 E 42nd St, 52nd floor, New York, NY 10168–0072 (☎212/661 7200); **Canada** PO Box 65162, Toronto, ON M4K 3Z2 (☎1-877/315 6237); **UK** PO Box 2695, London W1A 3TN (☎020/7317 0908); **Australia** c/o German-Australian Chamber of Industry and Commerce, PO Box A980, South Sydney, NSW 1235 (☎02/9267 8148).

GREECE www.gnto.gr; **USA** Olympic Tower, 645 5th Ave, New York, NY 10022 (☎212/421 5777); **Canada** 1300 Bay St,

TRAVEL BOOK AND MAP OUTLETS

NORTH AMERICA

Chicago: Rand McNally, 444 N Michigan Ave, IL 60611 (☎312/321 1751, www.randmcnally.com).

Montreal: Ulysses Travel Bookshop, 4176 St-Denis, PQ H2W 2M5 (☎514/843 9447, www.ulysses.ca).

New York The Complete Traveler Bookstore, 199 Madison Ave, NY 10016 (☎212/685 9007); Rand McNally, 150 E 52nd St, NY 10022 (☎212/758 7488, www.randmcnally.com); Traveler's Choice Bookstore, 22 W 52nd St, NY 10019 (☎212/941 1535, tvlchoice@aol.com).

Ottawa: World of Maps, 1235 Wellington St, ON K1Y 3A3 (☎613/724 6776, www.worldofmaps.com).

Palo Alto: Phileas Fogg's Books & Maps, #87 Stanford Shopping Center, CA 94304 (☎1-800/533-FOGG, www.foggs.com).

San Francisco: The Complete Traveler Bookstore, 3207 Filmore St, CA 92123 (☎415/923 1511); Rand McNally, 595 Market St, CA 94105 (☎415/777 3131, www.randmcnally.com); Sierra Club Bookstore, 730 Polk St, CA 94110 (☎415/977-5653, www.sierraclub-bookstore.com).

Santa Barbara: Map Link, 30 S La Petera Lane, Unit #5, CA 93117 (☎805/692-6777, www.maplink.com).

Seattle: Elliott Bay Book Company, 101 S Main St, WA 98104 (☎206/624 6600, www.elliottbaybook.com).

Toronto: Open Air Books and Maps, 25 Toronto St, ON M5R 2C1 (☎416/363 0719).

Vancouver: World Wide Books and Maps, 552 Seymour St, BC V6B 3J5 (☎604/687 3320, www.itmb.com).

Vermont: Adventurous Traveler Bookstore, PO Box 64769, Burlington, VT 05406 (☎1-800/282 3963, www.adventuroustraveler.com).

Washington DC: ADC Map and Travel Center, 1636 I St NW, DC 20006 (☎202/628 2608); Travel Books & Language Center, 4437 Wisconsin Ave NW, DC 20016 (☎1-800/220 2665).

Rand McNally has stores across the US; call ☎1-800/333 0136 (ext 2111) for the address of your nearest store, or for direct mail maps.

UK AND IRELAND

Belfast: Waterstone's, Queens Bldg, 8 Royal Ave, BT1 1DA (☎028/9024 7355, s1.waterstones.co.uk).

Bristol: Stanfords, 29 Corn St, BS1 1HT (☎0117/929 9966, www.stanfords.co.uk).

Cambridge: Heffer's Map Shop, 3rd floor, 19 Sydney St, CB2 3HL (☎01223/568467, www.heffers.co.uk).

Cardiff: Blackwell's, 13–17 Royal Arcade, CF1 2PR (☎029/2039 5036, www.bookshop.blackwell.co.uk).

Toronto, ON M5R 3K8 (☎416/968 2220) or 1170 pl Frère André, 3rd Floor, Montreal, PQ H3B 3C6 (☎514/871 1535); **UK** 4 Conduit St, London W1R ODJ (☎020/7499 9758); **Australia** 51 Pitt St, Sydney, NSW 2000 (☎02/9241 1663).

HUNGARY www.hungarytourism.hu; **USA** 150 E 58th St, 33rd Floor, New York, NY 10155–3398 (☎212/355 0240); **UK** 46 Eaton Place, London SW1X 8AL (☎020/7823 1055).

IRELAND www.ireland.travel.ie; **USA** 345 Park Ave, 17th Floor, New York, NY 10154 (☎212/418 0800); **UK** Ireland Desk, BTA, 1 Lower Regent St, London SW1Y 4NR (☎0800/039 7000); **Australia** 5th Level, 36 Carrington St, Sydney, NSW 2000 (☎02/9299 6177); **New Zealand** Dingwall Bldg, 2nd floor, 87 Queen St, Auckland 1 (☎09/379 8720).

ITALY www.enit.it; **USA** 630 5th Ave, Suite 1565, New York, NY 10111 (☎212/245 5095), or 500 N Michigan Ave, Suite 2240, Chicago, IL 60611 (☎312/644 0996), or 12400, Wilshire Bvd, Suite 550, Los Angeles, CA 90025 (☎310/820 1898); **Canada** 17 Bloor Street East, Suite 907, South Tower, Toronto, ON M4W 3R8 (☎416/925 4882); **UK** 1 Princes St, London W1R 9AY (☎020/7355 1557); **Australia** Level 26–44 Market St, Sydney, NSW 2000 (☎02/9262 1666).

LUXEMBOURG www.luxembourg.co.uk; **USA** 17 Beekman Pl, New York, NY 10022 (☎212/935 8888); **UK** 122–124 Regent St, London W1B 5SA (☎020/7434 2800).

MOROCCO www.tourism-in-morocco.com; **USA** 20 E 46th St, Suite 1201, New York, NY 10017 (☎212/557 2520); **Canada** 1800 Av McGill College, Suite 2450, Montreal, PQ H3A 2J6 (☎514/842 8111/8112); **UK** 205 Regent St, London W1R 7DE (☎020/7437 0073); **Australia** 11 West St, North Sydney, NSW 2060 (☎02/9922 4999).

NETHERLANDS www.visitholland.com; **USA** 355 Lexington Ave, 19th floor, New York, NY 10017 (☎1-888/464 6552); **UK** 18 Buckingham Gate, London SW1E 6NT (☎020/7828 7900).

NORWAY www.visitnorway.com; **USA** 655 3rd Ave, Suite 1810, New York, NY 10017 (☎212/885 9700); **UK** 5th floor, Charles House, 5 Lower Regent St, London SW1Y 4LR (☎020/7839 6255).

POLAND www.polandtour.org; **USA** 275 Madison Ave, Suite 1711, New York, NY 10016 (☎212/338 9412); **UK** 310–312 Regent St, 1st floor, London W1R 5AJ (☎020/7580 8811).

PORTUGAL www.portugal-insite.pt; **USA** 590 5th Ave, New York, 4th floor, NY 10036–4785 (☎212/719 3985); **Canada** 60 Bloor St W, Suite 1005, Toronto, ON M4W 3B8 (☎416/921 7376); **UK** 22–25a Sackville St, London W1X 1DE (☎020/7494 1441); **Ireland** 54 Dawson St, Dublin 2 (☎01/670 9133).

ROMANIA www.rezq.com/ronto; **USA** 14 E 38th St, 12th floor, New York, NY 10016 (☎212/545 8484); **UK** 22 New Cavendish St, London (☎☎020/7224 3692).

Cork: Waterstone's, 69 Patrick St (☎021/276 522).

Dublin: Easons Bookshop, 40 O'Connell St, Dublin 1 (☎01/873 3811, *www.eason.ie*); Fred Hanna's Bookshop, 27–29 Nassau St, Dublin 2 (☎01/677 1255); Hodges Figgis Bookshop, 56–58 Dawson St, Dublin 2 (☎01/677 4754, *www.hodgesfiggis.com*); Waterstone's, 7 Dawson St, Dublin 2 (☎01/679 1415).

Inverness: James Thin Melven's Bookshop, 29 Union St, IV1 1QA (☎01463/233500, *www.jthin.co.uk*).

Leicester: The Map Shop, 30a Belvoir St, LE1 6QH (☎0116/247 1400).

London: Daunt Books, 83 Marylebone High St, W1M 3DE (☎020/7224 2295), 193 Haverstock Hill, NW3 4QL (☎020/7794 4006); National Map Centre, 22–24 Caxton St, SW1H 0QU (☎020/7222 2466, *www.mapsworld.com*), Stanfords, 12–14 Long Acre, WC2E 9LP (☎020/7836 1321, *www.stanfords.co.uk*), in the USIT Campus shop at 52

Grosvenor Gardens, SW1W 0AG (☎020/7730 1314), and in the British Airways shop at 156 Regent St, W1R 5TA (☎020/7434 4744); The Travel Bookshop, 13–15 Blenheim Crescent, W11 2EE (☎020/7229 5260, *www.thetravelbookshop.co.uk*).

Manchester: Waterstone's, 91 Deansgate, M3 2BW (☎0161/837 3000; *s1.waterstones.co.uk*).

Newcastle: Newcastle Map Centre, 55 Grey St, NE1 6EF (☎0191/261 5622, *www.traveller.com*).

Oxford: Blackwell's Map and Travel Shop, 53 Broad St, OX1 3BQ (☎01865/792792, *www.bookshop.blackwell.co.uk*).

Worcestershire: The Map Shop, 15 High St, Upton-upon-Severn, WR8 0HJ (☎01684/593146, *www.themapshop.co.uk*).

Maps by **mail or phone order** are available from Stanfords (☎020/7836 1321, *sales@stanfords.co.uk*) and several of the other listed suppliers.

AUSTRALIA AND NEW ZEALAND

Adelaide: The Map Shop, 6 Peel St, SA 5000 (☎08/8231 2033, *www.mapshop.net.au*).

Auckland: Specialty Maps, 46 Albert St (☎09/307 2217).

Brisbane: Worldwide Maps and Guides, 187 George St, Qld 4000 (☎07/3221 4330, *www.worldmaps.com.au*).

Christchurch: Mapworld, 173 Gloucester St, (☎03/374 5399, *www.mapworld.co.nz*).

Melbourne: Mapland, 372 Little Bourke St, Vic 3000 (☎03/9670 4383, *www.mapland.com.au*).

Perth: Perth Map Centre, 884 Hay St, WA 6000 (☎09/9322 5733, *perthmap.com.au*).

Sydney: Travel Bookshop, Shop 3, 175 Liverpool St, NSW 2000 (☎02/9261 8200).

RUSSIA *www.russia-travel.com*; **USA** 130 West 42nd Street, Suite 412, New York, NY 10036 (☎877/221 7120).

SLOVENIA *www.slovenia-tourism.si*; **USA** 345 E 12th St, New York, NY 10003 (☎212/358 9686); **UK** 49 Conduit St, London W1R 9FB (☎020/7287 7133).

SPAIN *www.tourspain.es*; **USA** 666 5th Ave, New York, NY 10103 (☎212/265 8822), or 845 N Michigan Ave, Suite 915E, Chicago IL 60611 (☎312/642 7188), or 8383 Wilshire Blvd, Suite 960, Beverley Hills, CA 90211 (☎213/658 7188); **Canada** 2 Bloor St W, 34th floor, Toronto, ON M4W 3E2 (☎416/961 3131); **UK** 22–23 Manchester Sq, London W1U 3PX (☎020/7486 8077).

SWEDEN *www.visit-sweden.com*; **USA** 655 3rd Ave, New York, NY 10017-5617 (☎212/885 9700); **UK** 11 Montagu Pl, London W1H 2AL (☎020/7724 5869).

SWITZERLAND *www.myswitzerland.com*; **USA** 608 5th Ave, New York, NY 10020 (☎011-800/1002 0030); **UK** Swiss Centre, Swiss Court, Leicester Sq, London W1V 8EE (☎00-800/1002 0030); **Australia** c/o Swissair, 33 Pitt St, Level 8, Sydney, NSW 2000 (☎0011-800/1002 0030). Worldwide toll-free number: ☎+800/1002 0030.

TURKEY *www.turizm.gov.tr*; **USA** 821 UN Plaza, New York, NY 10017 (☎212/687 2194), or 2525 Massachusetts Ave, Washington, DC 20008 (☎202/612 6800); **Canada** 360 Albert St, Suite 801, Ottawa, ON K1R 7X7 (☎613/230 8654); **UK** 170–173 Piccadilly, London W1V 9DD (☎020/7629 7771); **Australia** Unit 17, Level 3, 428 George St, Sydney, NSW 2000 (☎02/9223 3055).

If no office in your home country is listed here, apply to the embassy.

INFORMATION ON THE ROAD

Once you're travelling in Europe, you'll find on-the-spot information easy enough to pick up. Most countries have a well-equipped and widespread network of tourist offices that answer queries, dole out a range of (sometimes free) maps and brochures, and can often book accommodation, or at least advise you on the best-value places if you're stuck. Tourist offices are, as you might expect, better organized in northern Europe – Scandinavia, the Netherlands, France – with branches in all but the smallest village, and mounds of information; in Greece, Turkey and eastern Europe you'll find tourist offices more infrequent and less helpful on the whole, sometimes offering no more than a couple of dog-eared brochures and a photocopied map. We've given further details, including a broad idea of opening hours, in "Practicalities" for each country.

MAPS

Whether you're doing a grand tour or confining yourself to one or two countries you will need a decent **map**. Though you can often buy these (or sometimes better, locally produced alternatives) on the spot, you may want to get them in advance to plan your trip – if you know what you want, Stanfords in London (perhaps the world's best map shop) and Rand McNally in the US both do maps by mail order.

Geo-Center's 1:1,250,000 double-sided Europe map is one of the best covering the entire Continent, clear, with a large scale, showing roads, railways and relief. Other good road maps covering the whole of Europe include Lascelles's 1:2,600,000 map, Phillip's 1:3,500,000 version, and Hallwag's at 1:3,600,000, all of which show the road networks pretty well, though they omit most of Turkey and Morocco; of the three, only Hallwag shows railways, and not very clearly. Michelin's (1:3,000,000) is cheaper but less clear and doesn't show road numbers; nor does Kümmerley and Frey's (1:5,000,000), though it does cover Turkey and Morocco. A good compromise is the Collins 2000 map (1:4,500,000), which is clear, shows the main road and rail routes, and covers Turkey as well as the most important part of Morocco, as does the Marco Polo map (also 1:4,500,000). For extensive motoring, it is better to get a large-page road atlas such as Michelin's Tourism and Road Atlas. If you intend to travel mainly by rail, on the other hand, it might be worth getting the Thomas Cook Rail Map of Europe or Geo-Center's Euro-Map Rail Map of Europe. We've recommended the best maps of individual countries throughout the book. In general, though, you'll find the best series to be Bartholomew/RV, Kümmerley & Frey or Hallwag, or, in North America, those published by Rand McNally. For plans of over fifty European cities, the Falk series of detailed, indexed maps are excellent, and easy to use.

COSTS, MONEY AND BANKS

It's hard to generalize about what you're likely to spend travelling around Europe. Some countries – Norway, Switzerland and the UK – are among the priciest places to be in the world, while in others you can live like a lord on next to nothing – Turkey, for example. The collapse of the eastern European economy means that many of the countries there appear very inexpensive if you're coming from the west. However, the absorption of a number of the previously inexpensive countries of southern Europe into the EU means their costs are becoming much more in tune with the European mainstream.

THE EURO

On 1 January 1999, eleven EU countries – Austria, Belgium, Finland, France, Germany, Ireland, Italy, Luxembourg, the Netherlands, Portugal and Spain, subsequently joined by Greece – fixed their exchange rates to a new currency, **the euro (€)**, which will gradually take over as the single currency for all of them. Euro notes and coins replace francs, Deutschmarks, lire and the like from 1 January 2002 onward. The remaining three EU countries (the UK, Denmark and Sweden) are expected to join Euroland eventually, though their politicians may have a hard time convincing voters that this is a good idea, especially if the new currency continues to perform badly against the dollar, the yen or the pound sterling. The British government has promised a referendum before joining; Denmark had one and voted against; but attitudes in those countries are expected to change as the euro becomes established.

Accommodation will be the largest single cost, and can really determine where you decide to travel. For example, it's hard to find a double hotel room anywhere in Scandinavia – perhaps the most expensive part of the Continent – for much under £40/$65 a night, whereas in most parts of southern Europe, and even in France, you might be paying under half that on average. Everywhere, though, even in Scandinavia, there is some form of bottom-line accommodation available, and there's always a youth hostel on hand. In general, reckon on a minimum budget of around £10/$15 a night per person in most parts of Europe.

Food and drink costs also vary wildly, although again in most parts of Europe you can assume that a restaurant meal will cost on average £5–10/$8–15 a head, with prices at the top end of the scale in Scandinavia, at the bottom end in eastern and southern Europe. **Transport** costs are something you can pin down more exactly if you have a rail pass or are renting a car. Nowhere, though, are transport costs a major burden, except perhaps in Britain where public transport is less heavily subsidized than elsewhere. Local city transport, too, is usually good, clean and efficient, and is normally fairly cheap, even in the pricier countries of northern Europe. It's hard to pinpoint an average daily budget for touring the Continent, but a bottom-line survival figure – camping, self-catering, hitching, etc – might be around £15/$25 a day per person; building in an investment for a rail pass, staying in hostels and eating out occasionally would bring this up to perhaps £20/$30 a day; while staying in private rooms or hotels and eating out once a day would mean a personal daily budget of at least £25/$40. Obviously in the more expensive countries of northern Europe you might be spending more than this, but on a wide tour this would be balanced out by spending less in southern and eastern Europe, where everything is that much cheaper.

When and where you are travelling also makes a difference. Accommodation rates tend to go up across the board in July and August, when everyone is on vacation – although paradoxically there are good deals in Scandinavia during these months. Also bear in mind that in capital cities and major resorts in the peak season everything will be a grade more expensive than anywhere else, especially if you're there when something special is going on, for example in Munich during the Beer Festival, Pamplona for the running of the bulls, Siena during the Palio. These are, in any case, times when you will be lucky to find a room at all without having booked.

As for ways of **cutting costs**, there are plenty. It makes sense, obviously, to spend less on transport by investing in some kind of rail pass, and if you're renting a car to do so for a week or more, thereby qualifying for cheaper rates. Always try to plan in advance. Although it's good to be flexible, buying one-off rail tickets and renting cars by the day can add a huge amount to your travel budget. The most obvious way to save on accommodation is to use hostels and/or camp; you can also save by planning to make some of your longer trips at night, when the cost of a couchette may undercut the cost of a night's accommodation. It's best not to be too spartan when it comes to food costs, but doing a certain amount of self-catering, especially at lunchtime when it's just as easy (and probably nicer) to have a picnic lunch rather than eat in a restaurant or café, will save money. Bear in mind, also, that if you're a student an **ISIC card** is well worth investing in. It can get you reduced (usually 50 percent, sometimes free) entry to museums and other sights – costs which can eat their way into your budget alarmingly if you're doing a lot of sightseeing – as well as qualifying you for other discounts in certain cities; it can also save you money on some transport costs, notably ferries, and especially if you are over 26. For Americans there's also a health benefit, providing up to $3000 in emergency medical coverage and $100 a day for 60 days in hospital, plus a 24-hour hotline to call in the event of a medical, legal or financial emergency. If you are not a student but under 26, the **Go-25 Card** (or FIYTO) costs the same as the ISIC and can in some countries give much the same sort of reductions. Teachers qualify for the International **Teacher Identity Card**, offering similar discounts. All these cards are available from youth travel specialists such as Council Travel, STA, Usit and Travel CUTS. Basically, it's worth flashing one or the other at every opportunity to see what you can get.

PRICES

In the Guide we've quoted **prices** in local currency wherever possible, except in those countries where the weakness of the currency and the inflation rate combine to make this a meaningless exercise. In these cases – parts of eastern Europe and Turkey – we've used either US dollars, pounds sterling or Deutschmarks, depending on which hard currency is most commonly used within that country.
For accommodation prices, we've used a standard coding system throughout the Guide: see p.46 for details.

TRAVELLERS' CHEQUES AND EXCHANGE

The easiest and safest way to carry your money is in **travellers' cheques**, in either dollars, euros or pounds sterling. These are available for a small commission from any bank. You should, strictly speaking, order them in advance but this isn't always necessary in larger branches, or if you get them direct from offices of the issuing companies. The usual fee for travellers' cheque sales is one or two percent, though this may be waived if you buy the cheques through a bank where you have an account. It pays to get a selection of denominations. Make sure to keep the purchase agreement and a record of cheque serial numbers safe and separate from the cheques themselves. In the event that cheques are lost or stolen, the issuing company will expect you to report the loss forthwith to their local office; most companies claim to replace lost or stolen cheques within 24 hours. The most commonly accepted travellers' cheques are American Express, with Visa a close second, and Thomas Cook/Mastercard trailing third. Most cheques issued by banks will be one of these three brands. You'll usually pay commission again when you cash each cheque; this varies from country to country but is normally another 1 percent or so, or a flat rate, in which case it makes sense to cash as many as possible at once, though in some countries it's a flat rate per cheque. Keep a record of the cheques as you cash them, and you can get the value of all uncashed cheques refunded immediately if you lose them (though in practice most firms drag their feet if they can, especially when dealing with backpackers, or if fraud is suspected).

An alternative now available from Visa (and their competitors will no doubt soon be offering the same) is **travel money**, a disposable pre-paid debit card that you can use in ATM machines worldwide. It's a sort of electronic version of travellers' cheques, where you can buy as much credit as you think you'll need, throw the card away when it runs out and carry up to eight spare cards in case you lose one (or for a family or group with a common pool of money). The card is available from, among other places, Colombus Bank in the US and Thomas Cook in the UK. For further information, ring Visa's 24hr toll-free customer services line on 1-410/581-9091 or check out their Web site at *www.visa.com.*

APPROXIMATE EXCHANGE RATES

Current market rates (bank rates will not be as good) can be found on Oanda's universal currency converter at *www.oanda.com/converter/classic.* The countries that now use the euro as their currency are Austria, Belgium, Finland, France, Germany, Ireland, Italy, Luxembourg, the Netherlands, Portugal and Spain, and Greece. The European Bank's Web site – *www.ecb.de* – provides a useful currency convertor. Bear in mind that in the case of certain less stable currencies, the rates quoted below may fluctuate considerably.

currency	£1	$1	€1	currency	£1	$1	€1
Austrian Schilling	22.80	14.40	13.7603*	Lithuanian Litas	5.75	4.00	3.55
Belgian Franc	66.80	42.25	40.3399*	Moroccan Dirham	16.70	10.90	9.70
Bulgarian Lev	3.15	2.20	1.95	Netherlands Guilder	3.56	2.50	2.20371*
Croatian Kuna	12.25	8.55	7.55	Norwegian Kroner	13.10	9.10	8.10
Czech Koruna	55.80	38.80	34.45	Polish Zloty	5.76	4.00	3.56
Danish Kroner	12.00	8.40	7.50	Portuguese Escudo	330	210	200.482*
Estonian Kroon	25.30	17.60	15.65	Romanian Leu	40,045	27,850	27,730
Euro	1.65	1.05	1	Russian Rouble	41.38	28.80	25.55
Finnish Markka	9.85	6.25	5.94573*	Slovakian Koruna	70.05	48.70	43.25
French Franc	10.85	6.85	6.55957*	Slovenian Tolar	348	242	215
German Mark	3.25	2.05	1.95583*	Spanish Peseta	275	175	166.386*
Greek Drachma	555	350	335	Swedish Krona	14.60	10.17	9.05
Hungarian Forint	430	300	267	Swiss Franc	2.45	1.70	1.52
Irish Pound (Punt)	1.30	0.83	0.78756*	Turkish Lira	1,610,000	1,120,000	995,000
Italian Lira	3200	2030	1936.27*	UK Pound Sterling	1	0.70	0.62
Latvian Lat	0.90	0.63	0.56	*exact fixed rate			

You'll find that most hotels, shops and restaurants in Europe accept the major **credit cards** – Access/Mastercard, Visa, American Express and Diners Club – although they're less useful in eastern Europe, where you shouldn't depend on being able to use one. Credit cards can also come in handy as a backup source of funds, and can even save on exchange-rate commissions; just be sure someone back home is taking care of the bills if you're away for more than a month. Your card will also enable you to get cash advances from certain ATMs, mostly in western Europe, but remember that all cash advances are treated as loans, with interest accruing daily from the date of withdrawal; there may be a transaction fee on top of this, and there will invariably be a minimum amount you can draw. This varies from one country to the next, but it's usually at least the equivalent of £50–100/$80–150 in local currency. Bear in mind though that you can always use your credit or debit card to withdraw money from ATMs across the whole of Europe.

In many countries **banks** are the only places where you can legally change money, and they often offer the best exchange rates and lowest commission. They can also mess you around a lot, be annoyingly bureaucratic, and sting you for hidden charges, though this is improving and banks in most countries are much better in this respect than they once were. Bank opening hours are given in the text. Outside these times there are normally bureaux de change, often at train stations and airports, though rates and/or commissions may well be less favourable (always check the rate of commission first – it is sometimes as high as ten percent), and even automatic money-changing machines. Try to avoid changing money or cheques in hotels, where the rates are generally rock-bottom.

WIRING MONEY

Having **money wired** from home is never cheap, and should be considered as a last resort. Funds can be sent to most countries via MoneyGram or Western Union. Both companies' fees depend on the amount being transferred, but as an example, wiring £700/$1000 will cost around £40/$60. The funds should be available for collection (usually in local currency) from the company's local agent within minutes of being sent; you can do this in person at the company's nearest office (in the UK all post offices are agents for MoneyGram), or over the phone using your credit card with Western Union. It's also possible, and slightly cheaper, to have money wired from a bank in your home country to one in Europe, but this is much slower (a couple of weeks is not unheard of) and less reliable; if you go down this route, the person wiring the funds will need to know the routing number of the destination bank. From the UK, a compromise option is Thomas Cook's Telegraphic Transfer service, available through their high street branches, which costs £15 plus one percent of the amount to be sent (minimum charge £25), and takes 1–2 days to arrive.

If you have no money in your account, and there is no one you can persuade to send you any, then the options are inevitably limited. You can either find some casual, cash-in-hand work (see p.54), sell blood (not possible in all European countries), or, as a last resort, throw yourself on the mercy of your nearest consulate. They won't be very sympathetic or even helpful, but they may cash a cheque drawn on a home bank and supported by a cheque card. They might, if there's nothing else for it, repatriate you, though bear in mind your passport will be confiscated as soon as you set foot in your home country and you'll have to pay back all costs incurred (at top-whack rates). They never lend money.

WIRING MONEY

To find the location of your nearest agent or branch call:

MONEYGRAM (*www.moneygram.com*)

Australia ☎1800/955 1230
Ireland ☎1850/205800
New Zealand ☎0800/444630
UK ☎0800/8971 8971
USA and Canada ☎1-800/926 9400

WESTERN UNION (*www.westernunion.com*)

Australia ☎1800/501 500
Canada ☎1-800/235 0000
Ireland ☎1800/395395
New Zealand ☎0800/270000 or 09/270 9173
UK ☎0800/833833
USA ☎1-800/325 6000 or 1-888/PAY 3773

COMMUNICATIONS

Communications throughout northwestern Europe are invariably excellent: public phones are readily available and normally work, and the postal system is reasonably efficient and easy to use. In southern Europe, services are sometimes less impressive, notably in Italy and Spain where the post is still not overly reliable, though it has improved a lot in recent years; and in eastern Europe the infrastructure is still very poor and services consequently unpredictable.

POST

For buying stamps and, sometimes, making telephone calls, we've listed the **central post offices** in major cities and given an idea of opening hours. Bear in mind, though, that throughout much of Europe you can avoid the queues in post offices by buying **stamps** from newsagents and the like. If you know in advance where you're going to be and when, it is possible to receive mail through the **poste restante** (general delivery) system, whereby letters addressed "poste restante" and sent to the main post office in any town or city will be kept under your name at the relevant counter to be picked up. When collecting mail, make sure you take your passport for identification, and bear in mind, in some countries, the possibility of letters being misfiled by someone unfamiliar with your language; if there is nothing under your surname it may have been filed under your first name. If you are using American Express travellers' cheques, or have an American Express card, you can also have mail kept for you at the city centre office; again, where appropriate, we've given addresses throughout the text.

PHONES

It is often possible, especially in western Europe, to make **international calls** from a public call box; this can often be more trouble than it's worth due to the constant need to feed in change, although most countries now have phone cards, making the whole process much easier. Otherwise, you can go to a **post office**, or a **special telephone bureau**, where you can make a call from a private booth and pay afterwards. Most countries have these in one form or another, and we've listed their whereabouts in the text. Wherever possible, avoid using the telephone in your **hotel room** – it costs the earth.

To dial any country in this book from Britain, Ireland or New Zealand, dial ☎00, then the country code, then the city/area code, if there is one, less the initial zero (except in Italy, Russia and the Baltics, where it must be dialled; from the US and most of Canada, the international access code is ☎011, from Australia ☎0011 – otherwise the procedure is the same. To call home from most European countries, dial ☎00, then the country code, then the city code (less the initial zero if there is one), then the subscriber number. The exception is Russia, where you dial ☎8, wait for a continuous dialling tone and then dial ☎10 followed by the country code etc; and in Estonia, it's ☎8-00 – you need to wait for a new tone after the 8 only on old phones. For collect calls, Home Country Direct services are available in most of the places covered in this book. In Britain and some other countries, international calling cards available from newsagents enable you to call North America and Australasia very cheaply. Most North American, British, Irish and Australasian phone companies either allow you to call home from abroad on a credit card, or billed to your home number (call your company's customer service line before you leave to find out their toll-free access codes from the countries you will be visiting), or else issue an international calling card which can be used worldwide, and for which you will be billed on your return. If you want a calling card and do not already have one, leave yourself a few weeks to arrange it before leaving.

Mobile phones from North America are unlikely to work in Europe – for details of which phones will work outside the US and Canada, contact your provider. Mobiles from the British Isles or Australasia can be used in most parts of Europe, and a lot of countries – certainly in western Europe – have nearly universal coverage, but for all bar the very top-of-the-range packages, you'll have to inform your provider before leaving home to get international access switched on. Also note that it will not always be possible to charge up or replace your firm's pre-paid cards, so again check beforehand and if necessary remember to bring enough credit with you. A standard two-pin socket is used on the Continent so you may need an adaptor for charging up.

INTERNET AND EMAIL

Europe still lags some way behind the US in terms of **Internet** access, and surfing the Web is rather more expensive due to the high rates charged for local phone calls. Nonetheless, things are improving all the time: more and more Internet cafés and locales are opening up, and it is becoming increasingly easy to access the Web and send and receive **email**. That being the case, a good way to keep in touch is to open up an account with one of the free Internet email sites that can be accessed from anywhere, for example YahooMail and Hotmail – accessible through *www.yahoo.com* and *www.hotmail.com*, so that you can receive emails while on the road.

THE MEDIA

British **newspapers and magazines** are fairly widely available in Europe, sometimes – in the Netherlands and Belgium, for example – on the day of publication, more often the day after. They do, however, cost around three times as much as they do at home. Exceptions are the *Guardian* and *Financial Times*, which print special European editions that are cheaper and available on the day of issue. You can also find the terminally dull and self-righteous *International Herald Tribune* just about everywhere, as well as the uninspiring *USA Today*, if you're lucky you may come across the odd *New York Times* or *Washington Post*, but don't count on it outside the major centres. What you will find are *Time*, *Newsweek*, and *The Economist* pretty much everywhere, as well as a host of British and American glossies.

It's cheaper to get your news by tuning a **radio** into the BBC World Service (still considered to have the most reliable news of all the media), Radio Canada, the Voice of America, or one of the many local news broadcasts in English. In northern France, the Netherlands and Belgium you can pick up BBC domestic services as well. BBC World Service frequencies include: 6195kHz, 9410kHz, 12,095kHz and 15,485kHz on shortwave, or in western Europe 648kHz MW, and in southeastern Europe 1323kHz MW (programme details at *www.bbc.co.uk/worldservice*). Radio Canada can be picked up at 5–5.30am GMT on 13,755kHz, and at 6–6.30pm on 21,570kHz (details at *www.rcinet.ca*). The Voice of America can be found during the day on 1197kHz, at night on 15,205kHz, also afternoons on 1548kHz, and evenings on 9760KHz, among other frequencies – further details and full schedules on their website on *www.voa.gov*.

With the advent of cable and satellite channels, **television** has become more of a pan-European medium than radio. Sky TV, Superchannel, CNN, Eurosport and the European version of MTV are all popular across the Continent and normally available in the better hotels. In many parts of Europe there is, in any case, a reasonably wide choice of channels (by British, if not by American, standards), since a border is never far away and you can often pick up at least one other country's TV stations. This is at its most extreme in Belgium and the southern Netherlands, where as well as all the satellite and cable channels you can pick up Dutch and Belgian TV, French TV, BBC1 and BBC2, all the German stations, and even the state Italian channel.

INTERNATIONAL DIALLING CODES

Andorra ☎376	Finland ☎358	Lithuania ☎370	Russia ☎7
Australia ☎61	France ☎33	Luxembourg ☎352	San Marino ☎378
Austria ☎43	Germany ☎49	Monaco ☎377	Slovakia ☎421
Belgium ☎32	Gibraltar ☎350	Morocco ☎212	Slovenia ☎386
Bulgaria ☎359	Greece ☎30	Netherlands ☎31	Spain ☎34
Canada ☎1	Hungary ☎36	New Zealand ☎64	Sweden ☎46
Croatia ☎385	Ireland ☎353	Norway ☎47	Switzerland ☎41
Czech Republic ☎420	Italy ☎39	Poland ☎48	Turkey ☎90
Denmark ☎45	Latvia ☎371	Portugal ☎351	UK ☎44
Estonia ☎372	Liechtenstein ☎423	Romania ☎40	USA ☎1

ACCOMMODATION

Although it is obviously one of the more crucial costs to consider when planning your trip, accommodation needn't be a stumbling block to a budget-conscious tour of Europe. Indeed, even in Europe's pricier reaches the hostel system means there is always an affordable place to stay, and if you're prepared to camp you can get by on very little while staying at some excellently equipped sites. The one thing you should bear in mind is that in the more popular cities and resorts – Florence, Venice, Amsterdam, Prague, Barcelona, the Algarve – things can get chock-a-block during the peak summer months, and even if you've got plenty of money to throw around you should book in advance.

HOSTELS

The cheapest way for young people to travel around Europe is by using the extensive network of youth hostels that covers the Continent. Some of these are **private** places, run on a one-off basis in the major cities and resorts, but by far the majority are **official hostels**, members of Hostelling International (**HI**), which incorporates the national youth hostel associations of each country in the world. Youth hostelling isn't the hearty, up-at-the-crack-of-dawn and early-to-bed business it once was; indeed, hostels have been keen to shed this image of late and now appeal to a wider public, and in many countries they simply represent the best-value overnight accommodation available. Most are clean, well-run places, always offering dormitory accommodation, some – especially in Scandinavia and other parts of northern Europe – offering a range of private single and double rooms, or rooms with 4–6 beds. Many hostels also either have self-catering facilities or provide low-cost meals, and the larger ones have a range of other facilities – a swimming pool, games room, common room, etc. There is no age limit (except in Bavaria), but where there is limited space, priority is given to those under 26 years of age.

Strictly speaking, to use an HI hostel you have to be a member, although if there is room you can stay at most hostels by simply paying extra – and you can often join the HI on the spot. If you do intend to do a lot of hostelling, however, it is certainly worth joining, which you can do by becoming a member of your home country's hostelling association. Annual membership costs are low everywhere. We've detailed the hostelling situation in each country in the text, as well as giving the name and address of the relevant national hostelling organization if you want further information. The HI Guide to Europe, available from bookstores or national hostelling associations, is a good investment at £8/$11.50, detailing every official hostel in Europe (but not Morocco, which is covered by the HI Guide to Africa, the Americas, Asia and the Pacific).

ACCOMMODATION PRICE CODES

Throughout this guide, accommodation is coded on a scale of ① to ⑨, the code indicating the lowest price per person per night you could expect to pay in each establishment in high season. With hostels this is the nightly rate per person; with hotels, the price is arrived at by dividing the cost of the cheapest double room by two. The prices indicated by the codes are as follows:

① under £5/$8 (€9)
② £5–10/$8–16 (€9–18)
③ £10–15/$16–24 (€18–27)

④ £15–20/$24–32 (€27–36)
⑤ £20–25/$32–40 (€36–45)
⑥ £25–30/$40–48 (€45–54)

⑦ £30–35/$48–56 (€54–63)
⑧ £35–40/$56–64 (€63–72)
⑨ £40/$64 (€72) and over

HOTELS AND PENSIONS

If you've got a bit more money to spend, you may want to upgrade from hostel accommodation to something a little more comfortable and private. With **hotels** you can really spend as much or as little as you like. Most hotels in Europe are graded on some kind of star system. One- or two-star category hotels are plain and simple on the whole, usually family-run, with a number of rooms without private facilities; sometimes breakfast won't be included. In three-star hotels all the rooms will have private facilities, prices will normally include breakfast and there may well be a phone or TV in the room; while four- and five-star places will certainly have all these, perhaps on a plusher, roomier basis, perhaps also including access to other facilities – sauna, swimming pool, etc. In the really top-level places breakfast, oddly enough, isn't always included. When it is, in the Netherlands, Britain or Germany, it's fairly sumptuous; in France it wouldn't amount to much anyway and it's no hardship to grab a croissant and coffee in the nearest café. We've only detailed one- and two-star hotels in the text, since for most people on a tour of Europe these are usually perfectly acceptable; in any case, it's not hard to find places above this level. The prices quoted in the text are for the cheapest option in peak season for one person – which usually works out as being the price of half a basic double room, generally without a private bathroom. Single rooms tend to be at least 75 percent of the price of a double, and for private facilities you can expect to pay around 25 percent extra in most countries. For information on the accommodation pricing codes we've used throughout the text, see box opposite.

Obviously prices vary greatly, but you're rarely going to be paying less than £10/$15 for a double room even in southern Europe, while in the Netherlands the average price is around £25/$40, and in Scandinavia somewhat higher than that. In some countries **pensions** or **bed and breakfasts** (variously known as guesthouses, pensão, gasthausen or numerous other names) – smaller, simpler affairs, usually with just a few rooms, that are sometimes part of a larger family house – are a cheaper alternative. In some countries these advertise with a sign in the window; in others they are bookable through the tourist office, which may demand a booking fee. There are various other kinds of accommodation – apartments, farmhouses, cottages, paradors (in Spain), gîtes (in France), etc – but most are geared to longer-term stays and we have only detailed them where relevant.

CAMPING

The cheapest form of accommodation is, of course, the **campsite**, either pitching your own tent or parking your caravan or camper van. Most sites make a charge per person, plus a charge per plot and another per vehicle. Obviously you'll pay less if you're travelling on foot – maybe just a couple of pounds per night between two people – but parking a car or camper van doesn't add a lot to the cost. Bear in mind also, especially in countries like France where camping is very popular, that facilities can be excellent – though the better the facilities, the pricier the site. If you're on foot you should add in the cost and inconvenience of getting to the site, since most are on the outskirts of towns, sometimes further. Although some sites can be congested and noisy, you do, however, benefit from what can sometimes be a relatively bucolic location – often a bonus after a hard day's sightseeing. Some sites have cabins, which you can stay in for a little extra, although these are usually fairly basic affairs, only really worth considering in regions like Scandinavia where budget options are thin on the ground. In Britain, the AA issue a *Caravan and Camping Europe* guide (£8.99), which lists campsites in eleven west European countries.

If you're planning to do a lot of camping, an **international camping carnet** is a good investment. The carnet gives discounts at member sites, serves as useful identification, and is obligatory on some sites in Portugal and some Scandinavian countries. Many campsites will take it instead of making you surrender your passport during your stay, and it covers you for third-party insurance when camping. However, the carnet is not recognized in Sweden, where you may have to join their own carnet scheme. In the US and Canada, the carnet is available from home motoring organizations, or from Family Campers and RVers (FCRV), 4804 Transit Rd, Building 2, Depew, NY 14043 (☎1-800/245-9755, *www.fcrv.org*). FCRV annual membership costs $25, and the carnet an additional $10. In the UK and Ireland, the carnet costs £4.50, and is available to members of the AA or the RAC, or for members only from either of the following: the Camping and Caravanning Club, Greenfields House, Westwood Way, Coventry, CV4 8JH (☎024/76694995, *www.campingandcaravanningclub .co.uk*), or the foreign touring arm of the same company, the Carefree Travel Service (☎024/76422024), which provides the CCI free if you take out insurance with them; they also book ferry crossings and inspect camping sites in Europe.

As for **camping rough**, it's a fine idea if you can get away with it – though perhaps an entire trip of rough camping is in reality too gruelling to be truly enjoyable. In some countries it's easy – indeed in parts of Scandinavia it is a legal right, and in Greece and other southern European countries you can usually find a bit of beach to pitch down on – but in others it's almost a nonstarter and can get you into trouble with the law.

POLICE, TROUBLE AND SEXUAL HARASSMENT

Travelling around Europe should be relatively trouble-free, but, as in any part of the world, there is always the chance of petty theft. However, conditions do vary greatly from, say, Scandinavia, where you're unlikely to encounter much trouble of any kind, to poorer and potentially more troublesome regions like Morocco, Turkey, or southern Italy. In order to minimize the risk of having your stuff ripped off, you should take some obvious precautions.

First and perhaps most important, you should try not to look too much like a tourist: appearing lost, even if you are, is to be avoided if you can; neither is it a good idea, especially in southern Europe, to walk around draped with cameras or expensive jewellery – the professional bag-snatchers who tour train stations can have your watch or camera off in seconds. If you're waiting for a train, keep your eyes (and hands if necessary) on your bags at all times; if you want to sleep, put everything valuable under your head as a pillow. You should be cautious when choosing a train compartment, and if you're a woman travelling alone, you should try and avoid situations which make you feel uncomfortable. If staying in a hostel, take your valuables out with you unless there's a very secure store for them on the premises; some people even make photocopies of their more crucial documentation and leave them at home; a copy of your address book, certainly, can be a good idea.

If the worst happens and you do have something stolen, inform the police immediately (we've included details of the main city police stations in the text); get a statement from them detailing exactly what has been lost, which you'll need for your insurance claim back home. Generally you'll find the police sympathetic enough, sometimes able to speak English, though unwilling to do much more than make out a report for you.

As for **offences** you might commit, it's hardly necessary to state that drugs like cocaine, amphetamines, heroin, LSD and ecstasy are illegal all over Europe, and although use of cannabis is widespread in most countries, and legally tolerated in some (famously in the Netherlands, for example), you are never allowed to possess more than a small amount for personal use, and unlicensed sale remains illegal. Penalties for possession of hard drugs and psychedelics can be severe; in certain countries, such as Turkey, even possession of cannabis can result in a hefty prison sentence, and your consulate is unlikely to plead any kind of case for you. Other, more minor, misdemeanours you should be wary of committing include sleeping rough, which is more tolerated in some parts of Europe than others and should be undertaken everywhere with a certain amount of circumspection, and topless sunbathing, which is now fairly common throughout southern Europe but still often frowned upon, especially in parts of Greece, Turkey and Italy. As always, be sensitive, and err on the side of caution. If you're arrested for any kind of motoring offence, again don't expect your consulate to be very sympathetic; in any case, unless it's something really serious you'll probably get off with a spot-fine. The same goes for fare avoidance on public transport. It's also worth remembering that, in theory, it is illegal to be on the streets without an official ID card or passport throughout most of mainland Europe (except the Netherlands and Scandinavia). Finally, although it's much less of an issue than it once was, avoid photography around sensitive military sites or installations – you may be arrested as a spy.

One of the major irritants for women travelling through Europe is **sexual harassment**, which in Italy, Greece, Turkey, Spain and Morocco especially can be almost constant for women travelling alone or with another woman, and can put certain areas completely out of bounds. Southern European coastal areas, especially, can be a real problem, where women tourists are often regarded as being on the lookout for sex. By far the most common kind of harassment you'll come across simply consists of street whistles and cat-calls; occasionally it's more sinister and very occasionally it can be dangerous. Indifference is often the best policy, avoiding eye contact with men and at the same time appearing as confident and purposeful as possible. If this doesn't make you feel any more comfortable, shouting a few choice phrases in the local language is a good idea;

don't, however, shout in English, which often seems to encourage them. You may also come across gropers on crowded buses and trains, in which case you should complain as loudly as possible in any language – the ensuing scene should be enough to deter your assailant. The best way of avoiding more dangerous situations is to simply be as suspicious as possible: if you're hitching, don't get into a car if you've even a hint of doubt about the driver (always ask where they are going before volunteering the information yourself); indeed, don't ever get yourself into a situation where you're alone with a man you don't know. In the larger European cities we've detailed contact points and women-only bars and cafés, so if all else fails, or you just get fed up with avoiding would-be lotharios, you can always seek out a completely male-free environment.

FESTIVALS AND ANNUAL EVENTS

There is always some annual event or other happening in Europe, and some of the bigger shindigs can be reason enough alone for visiting a place, some even worth planning your entire trip around. Be warned, though, that if you're intending to visit a place during its annual festival you need to plan well in advance, since accommodation can be booked up months beforehand, especially for the larger, more internationally known events.

RELIGIOUS AND TRADITIONAL FESTIVALS

Many of the festivals and annual events you'll come across were – and in many cases still are – **religion-inspired affairs**, centring on a local miracle or saint's day. **Easter**, certainly, is celebrated throughout Europe, with most verve and ceremony in Catholic and Orthodox Europe, where Easter Sunday or Monday is usually marked with some sort of procession; it's especially enthusiastically celebrated in Greece, where it is more important even than Christmas, though be aware that the Orthodox Church's Easter can in fact fall a week or two either side of the Western festival. Earlier in the year, traditionally at the beginning of **Lent** in February, **Carnival** (or Mardi Gras) is celebrated, most conspicuously (and perhaps most stagily) in Venice, which explodes in a riot of posing and colour to become one of Italy's major tourist draws at this time of year. There are smaller, perhaps more authentic carnivals in **Viareggio**, also in Italy, and in Germany, Belgium and the Netherlands, most notably in **Cologne**, **Maastricht** and tiny **Binche** in the Ardennes, where you can view some 1500 costumed *Gilles* or dancers in the streets. Also in Belgium, in mid-Lent, catch if you can the procession of white-clad *Blanc Moussis* through the streets of Stavelot in the Ardennes – one of Europe's oddest sights. Other religious festivals you might base a trip around include the Festa di San Gennaro three times a year in **Naples**, when the dried blood of the city's patron saint is supposed to liquefy to prevent disaster befalling the place – it rarely fails; the Ommegang procession through the heart of **Brussels** city centre to commemorate a medieval miracle; the Heilig Bloed procession in **Bruges**, when a much-venerated relic of Christ's blood is carried shoulder-high through the town; and, in Italy, the annual procession across **Venice**'s Grand Canal to the church of the Madonna della Salute to recall the deliverance of the city from a seventeenth-century plague. In Morocco and Turkey, where the predominant religion is Islam, and in the Muslim areas of Bulgaria, **Ramadan**, commemorating the revelation of the Koran to Muhammad, is observed. The most important Muslim festival, it lasts a month, during which time Muslims are supposed to fast from sunrise until sunset – although otherwise, as far as is possible, life carries on as normal.

There are, of course, other, equally long-established events which have a less obvious foundation. One of the best-known is the April Feria in **Seville**, a week's worth of flamenco music and dancing, parades and bullfights, in a frenziedly enthusiastic atmosphere. Also in Spain, for a week in early July, the San Fermín festival in **Pamplona** is if anything even more famous, its centrepiece – the running of the bulls along with local macho men, through the streets of the city – drawing tourists from all over the world, though there is much more to the festival than that. Also in July, at the beginning of the month (and again in mid-August), the Palio in **Siena** is perhaps the most spectacular annual event in Italy, a bareback horse race between representatives of the different quarters of the city around the main square, its origins dating back to medieval times. It's a brutal affair, with few rules and a great sense of deeply felt rivalry, and, although there are other Palio events in Italy, it's like no other horse race you'll ever see. At least as big a deal as the Palio and San Fermín is the **Munich** Oktoberfest, a huge beer festival and fair that goes on throughout the last two weeks in September. Unlike most events of its size in Europe it's less than two hundred years old, but it attracts vast numbers of people to consume gluttonous quantities of beer and food. **London**'s Notting Hill Carnival, held at the end of August, is also a recent phenomenon, a predominantly Black and Caribbean celebration that's become the world's second biggest street carnival after Rio. Other, smaller events include the great Venice Regata Storica, each September, a trial of skill for the city's gondoliers, and the gorgeous annual displays and processions of flowers in the **Dutch bulbfield towns** in April and May.

ARTS FESTIVALS

Festivals celebrating all or one specific aspect of the **arts** are held all over Europe throughout the year, though particularly in summer, when the weather is better suited to outdoor events. Of general international arts festivals, the **Edinburgh Arts Festival** held every August is perhaps the best known and most enjoyable, not to mention one of the most innovative, with a mass of topnotch and fringe events in every medium, from rock to cabaret to modern experimental music, dance and drama. For three weeks every year the whole city is given over to the festival and it's a wonderful time to be around if you don't mind the crowds and have booked somewhere to stay in advance. There is another major general arts festival in **Spoleto**, the Festival dei Due Mondi, held over two months each summer, which is Italy's leading international arts festival, though on a somewhat smaller scale than Edinburgh, while the midsummer **Avignon** festival in southern France is slanted towards drama but hosts plenty of other events besides and is again a great time to be in town. Smaller general arts festivals, though still attracting a variety of international names, include the **Holland Festival**, held in Amsterdam in June; the **Flanders Festival**, an umbrella title for all sorts of dramatic and musical events held mainly in the medieval buildings of Bruges and Ghent in July and August; and the **Dubrovnik Summer Festival**, with a host of musical events and theatre performances against the backdrop of the town's beautiful Renaissance centre.

As regards more specialist gatherings, the **Montreux Jazz Festival** in July and the **North Sea Jazz Festival** in The Hague in mid-July are the Continent's premier jazz jamborees, while the same month sees the beginning of the **Salzburg Music Festival**, perhaps the foremost – if also the most conservative – serious music festival in Europe, though **London's Prom** season (July–Sept) maintains very high standards at egalitarian prices. Florence's **Maggio Musicale** is also worth catching, a festival of opera and classical music that runs from late April until early July. Less highbrow musical forms – rock, folk, etc – are celebrated, most conspicuously at the huge **Glastonbury** festival in Britain; at the **Pink Pop Festival**, held every June in Geleen near Maastricht in the Netherlands; and the **Roskilde Festival** in Denmark. Look out also for the **Womad** gettogethers, a number of which are usually held each year at a variety of sites all over Europe, celebrating World, folk and roots music, and the excellent and still relatively small **Cambridge Folk Festival** in late July. For **films**, there is, of course, **Cannes**, though this is more of an industry affair than anything else, and the **Venice** and **Berlin** film festivals, which are more geared to the general public.

GAY TRAVELLERS

Gay men and lesbians will find most of Europe a tolerant part of the world in which to travel, the west rather more so than the east. Most countries have at least in part legalized homosexual relationships, and the only part of Europe covered in this guide where homosexual acts are still against the law is Romania. Laws still in the main apply to male homosexuality; lesbianism, it would seem, doesn't officially exist, so it is in theory legal everywhere. The homosexual age of consent is, however, usually different from the heterosexual one – on average 18 years of age as opposed to 15 or 16 years. In general, the Netherlands and Scandinavia (except Finland) are the most tolerant parts of the Continent, with anti-discrimination legislation and official recognition of lesbian and gay partnerships. Reactionary laws against "outraging public decency" or "promotion" of homosexuality exist in Russia, Turkey and the UK.

Most cities of any size, at least in northern Europe, have a few bars or cafés frequented by **gay men**, and it's not hard to make contact with other gay people. In the major northern capitals, certainly, the gay scene is usually fairly sophisticated, with any number of bars, bookshops, clubs and gay organizations and switchboards, though things are usually firmly slanted towards gay men. The gay capital of Europe is perhaps Amsterdam, but there is plenty of interest for gay men in London, Paris, Copenhagen, and, to a lesser extent, Madrid and Barcelona. In southern Europe, things are less developed: the main cities may have the odd gay bar, but it may not advertise itself as such, and outside of the capitals there won't be many obvious places to meet at all. **Lesbians** can likewise usually find somewhere to meet with other gay women in northern Europe, albeit on a much smaller scale than gay men, while elsewhere, in southern and eastern Europe, word-of-mouth is about the only course open. We've detailed the best of the gay scenes of the major cities in the text; for further information, contact the organizations listed below.

INTERNATIONAL GAY AND LESBIAN CONTACTS

Damron Company, PO Box 422458, San Francisco, CA 94142 (☎1-800/462 6654 or 415/255 0404, *www.damron.com*). Publishes a men's and a women's guide, and an accommodation guide and gay road atlas, all mainly on North America but covering major European cities too.

Ferrari Publications, PO Box 37887, Phoenix, AZ 85069 (☎1-800/962 2912 or 602/863 2408, *www.ferrariguides.com*). Publishes *Ferrari Gay Travel A to Z*, a worldwide gay and lesbian guide; *Inn Places*, a worldwide accommodation guide; the worldwide guides *Men's Travel in Your Pocket* and *Women's Travel in Your Pocket*.

International Gay Travel Association, 4331 N Federal Hwy, Suite 304, Ft Lauderdale, FL 33308 (☎1-800/448 8550, *www.iglta.org*). Trade group that can provide a list of gay-owned or gay-friendly accommodation, travel agents, etc.

Madison Travel, 118 Western Rd, Hove, East Sussex NN3 1DB (☎01273/202532, *www.madison travel.co.uk*). Established travel agents specializing in packages to gay- and lesbian-friendly mainstream destinations, and also to gay/lesbian destinations.

Pinkstay *www.pinkstay.com*. Austalian-based organization with information on everything from visa information to finding accommodation and work around the world.

Silke's Travel, PO Box 1099, Sydney, NSW 1300 (☎02/8837 2000, *www.silkes.com.au*). Long-established gay and lesbian specialist, with the emphasis on women's travel.

Spartacus Gay Guide, Bruno Gmünder Verlag, Wrangelstrasse 100, 109977 Berlin (☎49-30/6100 1120); at Bookazine Co, 75 Hook Rd, Bayonne, NJ 07002 (☎1-800/548 3855); at Turnaround, Unit 3, Olympia Trading Estate, Coburg Rd, London N22 6TZ (☎020/8829 3009); at Bulldog Books, PO Box 300, Beaconsfield, NSW 2014 (☎02/9699 3507). International gay guide with information on meeting and cruising spots for gay men, but nothing much for lesbians.

www.gaytravel.co.uk Online gay and lesbian travel agent, offering good deals on all types of holiday. Also lists gay- and lesbian-friendly hotels around the world.

TRAVELLERS WITH DISABILITIES

It's easier for disabled people to get around in northern Europe than in the south and east, which is not surprising given the fact that this part of the Continent is more developed in every other way. Wheelchair access to public buildings is, however, far from easy in many countries, as is wheelchair accessibility to public transport – indeed, the only big-city underground systems that are accessible are those in Berlin, Amsterdam, Stockholm and Helsinki, with the rest lagging far behind; buses, too, are in general out of bounds to wheelchair users, although airport facilities are improving, as are those on the cross-Channel ferries. As for rail services, these vary greatly: France, for example, has very good facilities for disabled passengers, as have Belgium, Denmark and Austria, but many other countries make little, if any, provision.

CONTACTS FOR TRAVELLERS WITH DISABILITIES

BRITISH ISLES

Disability Action Group, 2 Annadale Ave, Belfast BT7 3JH (☎028/9049 1011).

Holiday Care Service, 2nd Floor, Imperial Building, Victoria Rd, Horley, Surrey RH6 7PZ (☎01293/ 774535, Minicom ☎776943, www.holidaycare.org.uk). Provides an information sheet on North Africa including a short list of accessible accommodation in Tunisia. Information on financial help for holidays available.

Irish Wheelchair Association, Blackheath Drive, Clontarf, Dublin 3 (☎01/833 8241, iwa@iol.ie). National voluntary organization for people with disabilities, including services for holidaymakers.

Tripscope, The Vassal Centre, Gill Ave, Fishponds, Bristol BS16 2QQ (☎08457/585641, www.justmobility.co.uk). A national telephone information service offering free transport and travel advice for those with mobility problems.

www.everybody.co.uk Provides information on accommodation suitable for disabled travellers throughout the UK, including Northern Ireland.

NORTH AMERICA

Access First, 239 Commercial St, Malden, MA 02148 (☎1/800-557-2047 or 781/322-1610). Current information for disabled travelers.

Directions Unlimited, 123 Green Lane, Bedford Hills, NY 10507 (☎1-800/533-5343 or 914/241-1700, cruisesusa@aol.com). Tour operator specializing in custom tours, packages and cruises for people with disabilities.

Jewish Rehabilitation Hospital, 3205 Place Alton Goldbloom, Chomedy Laval, Quebec H7V 1RT (☎450/688-9550, ext. 226). Guidebooks and travel information.

Mobility International USA, PO Box 10767, Eugene, OR 97440 (☎541/343-1284, www.miusa.org). Information and referral services, access guides, tours and exchange programs. Annual membership $35 (includes quarterly newsletter).

Society for the Advancement of Travel for the Handicapped (SATH), 347 5th Ave, Suite 610, New York, NY 10016 (☎212/447-7284, www.sath.org). Non-profit travel-industry referral service that passes queries on to its members as appropriate; allow plenty of time for a response.

Travel Information Service Moss Rehabilitation Hospital, 1200 West Tabor Rd, Philadelphia, PA 19141 (☎215/456-9603). Telephone information and referral service.

Twin Peaks Press, Box 129, Vancouver, WA 98666 (☎1-800/637-2256 or 360/694-2462, www.pacifier.com/twinpeak). Publisher of the Directory of Travel Agencies for the Disabled, listing more than 370 agencies worldwide; Travel for the Disabled; the Directory of Accessible Van Rentals and Wheelchair Vagabond, loaded with personal tips.

Wheels Up!, (☎1-888/389-4335, www.wheelsup.com). Provides discounted airfare, tour and cruise prices for disabled travellers, also publishes a free monthly newsletter and has a comprehensive website.

AUSTRALIA AND NEW ZEALAND

ACROD (Australian Council for Rehabilitation of the Disabled), PO Box 60, Curtin ACT 2605 (☎02/6282 4333); 24 Cabarita Road, Cabarita NSW 2137 (☎02/9743 2699). Provides lists of travel agencies and tour operators for people with disabilities.

Barrier Free Travel, 36 Wheatley St, North Bellingen, NSW 2454 (☎02/6655 1733). Consultancy service for disabled travellers; can draw up individual itineraries for a fee.

Disabled Persons Assembly, 4/173–175 Victoria St, Wellington (☎04/801 9100). Resource centre with lists of travel agencies and tour operators for people with disabilities.

Your particular disability may govern whether you decide to see Europe on a **package tour** or **independently**. There are any number of specialist tour operators, mostly catering for physically disabled travellers, and the number of nonspecialist operators who cater for disabled clients is increasing. It's also perfectly possible to go it alone, either with your own helper or by hiring one if you require assistance while away, or by joining some kind of group tour for disabled travellers.

Pressure on space means that it is impossible for us to detail wheelchair access arrangements for everywhere we list in the guide; neither can we detail the best and worst of the operators, and for more **information on disabled travel abroad** you should get in touch with the organizations listed on p.53. As well as their publications, look out for *Access London* and *Access Paris*, with information specific to those cities, published by Access Project in the UK.

WORK AND STUDY

The opportunities for working or studying your way around Europe are almost unlimited, especially for citizens of EU nations, who benefit from the easing of restrictions on the movement of labour. You can either fix something up before you leave home and build your trip around that, or simply look out for casual labour on your travels, treating it as a way of topping up your vacation cash. Certainly the best way of discovering a country properly is to work there, learning the language if you can and discovering something about the culture. Study opportunities are also a good way of absorbing yourself in the local culture, but they invariably need to be fixed up in advance; check the newspapers for ads or contact one of the main organizations (listed opposite) direct.

If you're just looking to supplement your spending money while you're travelling, there are any number of jobs you can pick up on the road. It's normally not hard to find **bar or restaurant work**, especially in large resort areas during the summer, and your chances will be greater if you can speak the local language – although being able to speak English may be your greatest asset in the more touristy areas; you may be asked for documentation, in which case you're better off in an EU member-state, but it's unlikely. Don't be afraid to march straight in and ask, or check the noticeboards in local bars, hostels or colleges, or the local newspapers, particularly the English-language ones. Cleaning jobs, nannying and **au pair** work are also common, if not spectacularly well paid, often just providing room and board plus pocket money, and are something you can either fix up on the spot or before you leave home. If you're staying in a place for a while, you can always place an ad or a notice yourself offering your services. The other big casual earner is farmwork, particularly **grape-picking**, which is an option in the August–October period when the vines are being harvested. The best country for this is easily France, but there's sometimes work in Germany too. Once again, you're unlikely to be asked for any kind of documentation. Also in France, along the Côte d'Azur, and in other yacht-havens like Greece and parts of southern Spain, there is sometimes **crewing** work available, though you'll obviously need some sailing experience. If this isn't up your street but you want something active to last the whole summer, tour operators are often on the lookout for **travel couriers**, though this is something better arranged from home. If you're really serious, get in touch with the companies that run bus tours for young people around Europe, who are often keen to take on new blood.

Rather better paid, and equally widespread, if only during the September to June period, is **teaching English as a foreign language** (TEFL), which is something you normally (though not exclusively) need to fix up from home. Everyone is desperate to learn English right now, all over Europe, but it is becoming harder to find English-teaching jobs without some kind of TEFL qualification. If you do organize work on the spot you may have to leave the country while your employers apply for a work permit. You'll normally be paid a liveable local salary, sometimes with somewhere to live thrown in as well, and you can often supplement your income with much more lucrative private lessons. Incidentally, North Americans and Australasians might be interested to know that the TEFL teaching season is reversed in Britain, with plenty of work available during the summer in London and on the south coast (but again, some kind of TEFL qualification is pretty well indispensable).

If you want to know more about working in Europe, there are several handy publications. The publishers Vacation Work (☎01865/241978, *www.vacationwork.co.uk*) produce the useful *Work your Way around the World* by Susan Griffiths, and David Woodworth's *Summer Jobs Abroad* (Vacation Work), which has details of places you could try before leaving home, while Mark Hempshell's *Working Holidays Abroad – A Practical Guide* (Kuperard) also has some good leads for short-term work. For more on TEFL possibilities, check out *Teaching English Abroad* by Sue Griffiths (Vacation Work). Travel magazines like the reliable *Wanderlust* (every two months; £2.80) have a Job Shop section which often advertises job opportunities with tour companies.

Studying abroad invariably means learning a language, doing an intensive course that lasts between two weeks and three months and staying with a local family. There are plenty of places you can do this, and you should reckon on paying around £200/$300 a week including room and board – though there are lots of options; contact the Central Bureau for full details. If you know a language well, you could also apply to do a short course in another subject at a local university; once again, scan the classified sections of the newspapers back home, and keep an eye out when you're on the spot. The Web site *www.studyabroad.com* has useful listings and links to study and work programmes worldwide. The EU runs a programme called Erasmus (part of a wider project called Socrates) in which university students from Britain and Ireland can obtain mobility grants to study in one of 26 European countries (including the other EU countries, Bulgaria, the Czech Republic, Estonia, Hungary, Latvia, Lithuania, Norway, Poland, Romania, Slovakia and Slovenia) for three months to a full academic year if their university participates in the programme. Anyone interested should check with their university's international relations office, or on the Erasmus/Socrates Web site at *europa.eu.int/comm/education/socrates/erasmus/home.html*.

USEFUL ADDRESSES

AFS Intercultural Programs, 310 SW 4th Ave, Suite 630, Portland OR 97204–2608 (☎1-800/AFS INFO); 1290, rue St-Denis, 6th floor, Montreal, PQ H2X 3J7 (☎514/288 3282); Leeming House, Vicar Lane, Leeds LS2 7JF (☎0113/242 6136); c/o Interculture Ireland, 10a Lower Camden St, Dublin 2 (☎01/478 2046); Level 5, 418 Elizabeth St, Surry Hills, NSW 2010 (☎02/9215 0077); PO Box 5562, Level 3, 125 Featherston St, Wellington (☎04/494 6020); *www.afs.org*. Worldwide, UN-recognized organization running summer experiential programmes to foster international understanding.

American Institute for Foreign Study, River Plaza, 9 W Broad St, Stamford, CT 06902–3788 (☎1-800/727 2437, *www.aifs.com*). Language study and cultural immersion for the summer or school year in Austria, Britain, the Czech Republic, France, Ireland, Italy, Poland, Russia and Spain.

ASSE International, 228 North Coast Highway, Laguna Beach, CA 92651 (☎714/494 4100); 7 Rue De La Commune Ouest, Suite 204, Montreal, PQ H2Y 2C5 (☎514/287 1814); PO Box 20, Harwich, Essex CO12 4DQ (☎01255/ 506 347); c/o Southern Cross Cultural Exchange, Locked Bag 1200, Mt Eliza, Vic 3930 (☎03/9776 4711); PO Box 340, Te Puke, New Zealand (☎07/573 5717 or 0800/488 884); *www.asse.com*. International student exchanges to Scandinavia, Germany, Switzerland, the Netherlands, France, Spain, Italy, the Czech Republic, Slovakia, Poland and the UK; also offers summer language programmes in France, Spain and Germany.

Association for International Practical Training, 10400 Little Patuxent Pkwy, Suite 250, Columbia, MD 21044–3510 (☎410/997 2200, *www.aipt.org*). Summer internships in various European countries for students who have completed at least two years of college in science, agriculture, engineering or architecture.

Australians Studying Abroad, 1st Floor, 970 High St, Armadale, Vic 3143 (☎03/9509 1955, *www.asatravinfo.com.au*). Study tours focusing on art and culture.

British Council Central Bureau for Educational Visits and Exchanges, 10 Spring Gdns, London SW1A 2BN (☎020/7930 8466; publications ☎020/7389 4880; *www.britishcouncil.org/cbeve*). Enables teachers to find out about development programmes abroad, or gap year students to take part in foreign language assistant programmes in France and Germany. Also recruits qualified EFL teachers for schools in Europe and elsewhere (to check vacancies call ☎020/7389 4931, or look up *www.britishcouncil.org/work/jobs.htm*).

Council on International Educational Exchange (CIEE), 633 3rd Ave, 20th floor, New York, NY 10017–6706 (☎800/40-STUDY, *www.ciee.org*); 52 Poland St, London W1V 4JQ (☎020/7478 2000); Level 3, 91 York St, Sydney, NSW 2000 (☎02/8235 7000, *www. ciee.org.au*). An international organization worth contacting for advice on studying, working and volunteering in Europe. They run summer semester and one-year study programmes, and volunteer projects, in Belgium, the Czech Republic, Denmark, France, Germany, Hungary, Ireland, the Netherlands, Poland, Russia, Spain, Sweden, Turkey, and the UK.

School for International Training, Kipling Rd, PO Box 676, Brattleboro, VT 05302 (☎802/257 7751, *www.sit.edu/studyabroad*). Accredited college semesters abroad, comprising language and cultural studies, homestay and other academic work in the Czech Republic, France, Germany, Greece, the Netherlands, Ireland, Morocco, Spain, Switzerland and Russia.

DIRECTORY

Baggage deposit (Left luggage) Almost every train station of any size has facilities for left luggage, either lockers or a desk that's open long hours every day. We've given details in the major capital accounts.

Bargaining The only places where you need really do any bargaining when shopping are in Turkey – in the bazaars and carpet shops – and in the souks of Morocco. Everywhere else, even in the less developed parts of southern Italy and Greece, people would think it odd if you tried to haggle.

Children Travelling with kids is easy enough everywhere, although you'll find a marked difference in attitudes to them between northern and southern Europe.

In the north you'll find people rather indifferent to children, sometimes worse – an attitude epitomized in Britain where they're regarded as something of a nuisance in public places, and barred from entry altogether to many pubs, some restaurants, even hotels. In the southern European nations, however – such as Italy, Spain and Turkey – children are by contrast much revered and made a fuss of in public, and, although you'll sometimes pay extra for them in hotels, they are never refused, even in restaurants or cafés. Indeed, the only problem with travelling with kids in southern Europe may be the summer heat and sun.

Contraceptives Condoms are available everywhere, and are normally reliable international brands like Durex, at least in northwestern Europe; the condoms in eastern European countries, Morocco and Turkey are of uncertain quality, however – so it's best to stock up in advance. The pill is available everywhere, too, though often only on prescription; again, bring a sufficient supply.

Electric current The supply in Europe is 220v (240v in the British Isles), which means that anything on North American voltage normally needs a transformer. However, one or two countries (notably Spain and Morocco) still have a few places on 110v or 120v, so check before plugging in. Continental, Moroccan and Turkish sockets take two round pins, British and Irish ones take three square pins. A travel plug which adapts to all these systems is useful to carry.

Shops Opening hours vary from northern to southern Europe. Those in the north are usually open Monday–Friday all day without a break (sometimes opening late one evening midweek), opening for at least half a day on Saturday and closing on Sunday almost everywhere. In the south they tend to take a break at lunchtime, during the hottest part of the day, and open again around 4pm until perhaps 8pm. They are again generally open until at least Saturday lunchtime and closed on Sunday.

Tampons In western and southern Europe you can buy tampons in all chemists and supermarkets, although in parts of eastern Europe they can still be hard to come by. If you're travelling in the east for any length of time, best to bring a supply.

Time The places covered in this book are in four time zones. Britain, Ireland, Portugal and Morocco are in principle on GMT (or UTC), which is five hours ahead of Eastern Standard Time, eight hours ahead of Pacific Standard Time, eight hours behind West Australia, ten hours behind eastern Australia, and twelve hours behind New Zealand. Most of the Continent is an hour ahead of that, with Finland, Estonia, Latvia, Lithuania, Romania, Bulgaria, Greece, Turkey and the Baltic Russian enclave of Kaliningrad two hours ahead, and Moscow and St Petersburg on GMT+3. All of these countries except the three Baltic states and Morocco have daylight saving time in summer, but don't necessarily change over at the same time (though EU countries do, and the others try to) – this, plus daylight saving in North America and Australasia, can mean a further hour or two's difference.

Tipping Although it varies from one country to the next, tipping is not really the serious business it is in North America, but in many countries it is customary to leave at least something in most restaurants and cafés, if only rounding the bill up to the next major denomination. Even in swankier establishments, a ten percent tip is sufficient, and you shouldn't feel obliged to tip at all if the service was bad, certainly not if service has been included in the bill. In smarter hotels you should tip hall porters, etc. Cab drivers expect a tip in Britain and Ireland, but not necessarily on the Continent.

CLOTHING AND SHOE SIZES

Dresses

Continental	42	44	46	48	50	52
American	8	10	12	14	16	18
British	10	12	14	16	18	20

Men's suits

Continental	46	48	50	52	54	56
American	36	38	40	42	44	46
British	36	38	40	42	44	46

Men's shirts

Continental	36	38	41	43	45
American	14	15	16	17	18
British	14	15	16	17	18

Women's shoes

Continental	36	37	38	39	40	41
American	5	5	6	7	8	8$^1/_2$
British	3	4	5	5	6$^1/_2$	7

Men's shoes

Continental	41	42	43	44	45	46
American	8	8$^1/_2$	9$^1/_2$	10$^1/_2$	11$^1/_2$	12
British		7	7$^1/_2$	8$^1/_2$	9$^1/_2$	10$^1/_2$

METRIC MEASURES

1 centimetre = approx 0.394 inches; 1 inch = approx 2.5cm; 1 foot = approx 30cm.
1 metre = approx 1.094 yards or 39 inches; 1 yard = approx 0.914m.
1 hectare = aprox 2.47 acres; 1 acre = approx 0.405 ha.
1 kilometre = approx 0.621 miles; 1 mile = approx 1.609km; 5 miles = approx 8km.
1 kilo = approx 0.551lb; 1lb = approx 454g/0.454kg; 1oz = approx 28.3g.
1 litre = approx 2.11 US pints; 1 US pint = approx 0.473 litres; 1 US quart = approx 0.946 litres.
1 litre = approx 0.264 US gallons; 1 US gallon = approx 3.785 litres.
1 litre = approx 1.76 UK pints; 1 UK pint = approx 0.568 litres; 1 UK gallon = approx 4.54litres.
1 US pint = approx 0.834 UK pint; 1 UK pint = approx 1.2 US pints; 6 US pints = approx 5 UK pints.

TEMPERATURE

To convert Celsius to Fahrenheit, multiply by nine, divide by five and add 32.
To convert Fahrenheit to Celsius, take away 32, multiply by five and divide by nine.

Celsius	0	10	20	30	40
Fahrenheit	32	50	68	86	104

LANGUAGE

If you're making a general tour of Europe you can't hope always to speak the language of the country you're travelling in, and in any case in Germany, Scandinavia, and especially the Netherlands and Switzerland, many people, particularly the young, speak reasonable English. That said, it is polite to know at least a few very basic words and phrases wherever you happen to be, which is why we've included the chart on the following pages, and a smattering of French, German or Russian is handy everywhere as a common language if English fails.

Rough Guides phrasebooks are now available for Czech, Dutch, French, German, Greek, Hungarian, Italian, Polish, Portuguese, Russian, Spanish and Turkish, and there's also a European Languages phrasebook. Pocket **dictionaries** can easily be bought for most European languages in the countries where they are spoken, and usually at home too. If you want to get to grips further with any of the languages, Routledge's "Colloquial" series is the best place you could start.

BULGARIAN, CROATIAN AND CZECH

	Bulgarian	Croatian	Czech
Yes	Da	Da	Ano
No	Ne	Ne	Ne
Please	Molya	Molim	Prosím
Thank you	Blagodarya	Hvala	Děkuju
Hello/Good day	Dobâr den	Bog/Dobar dan	Dobrý den/ahoj
Goodbye	Dovizhdane	Bog/Do vidjenja	Na shledanou
Excuse me	Izvinyavaïte	Izvinite	Promiňte
Where	Kude	Gdje	Kde
When	Koga	Kada	Kdy
How	Kak	Kako	Jak
Left	Lyavo	Lijevo	Vlevo
Right	Dyasno	Desno	Vpravo
Large	Golyama	Veliko	Velký
Small	Malko	Malo	Malý
Good	Dobro	Dobro	Dobrý
Bad	Plosho	Loše	Spatný
Near	Blizo	Blizu	Blízko
Far	Daleche	Daleko	Daleko
Cheap	Eftino	Jeftino	Levný
Expensive	Skupo	Skupo	Drahý
Open	Otvoreno	Otvoreno	Otevřeno
Closed	Zatvoreno	Zatvoreno	Zavřeno
Today	Dnes	Danas	Dnes
Yesterday	Vechera	Juče	Včera
Tomorrow	Utre	Sutra	Zítra
Day	Den	Dan	Den
Week	Sedmitza	Tjedan	Týden
Month	Mesetz	Mjesec	Měsíc
Year	Godina	Godina	Rok
How much is....?	Kolko stroova?	Koliko stoji...?	Kolík stojí...?
What time is it?	Kolko e chasut?	Koliko je sati?	Kolík je hodin?
Where is...?	Kude e...?	Gdje je...?	Kde je...?
I don't understand	Ne razbiram	Ne razumijem	Nerozumím
Do you speak English?	Govorite li Angliski?	Govorite li engleski?	Miuvíte Anglicky?
Please write it down	Molya napishete go	Napišite ga molim	Prosím, napište to
One	Edin/edna	Jedan	Jeden
Two	Dve	Dva	Dva
Three	Tri	Tri	Tři
Four	Chetiri	Četiri	Čtyři
Five	Pet	Pet	Pět
Six	Shest	Šest	Šest
Seven	Sedem	Sedam	Sedm
Eight	Osem	Osam	Osum
Nine	Devet	Devet	Devět
Ten	Deset	Deset	Deset

DANISH, DUTCH AND ESTONIAN

	Danish	Dutch	Estonian
Yes	Ja	Ja	Jah
No	Nej	Nee	Ei
Please	Vaer så venlig	Alstublieft	Palun
Thank you	Tak	Dank u/Bedankt	Aitäh/tänan
Hello/Good day	Goddag	Hallo	Tere
Goodbye	Farvel	Dag/Tot ziens	Head aega
Excuse me	Undskyld	Pardon	Vabandage
Where	Hvor	Waar	Kus
When	Hvornår	Wanneer	Millal
How	Hvordan	Hoe	Kuidas
Left	Venstre	Links	Vasak
Right	Højre	Rechts	Parem
Large	Stor	Groot	Suur
Small	Lille	Klein	Väike
Good	God	Goed	Hea
Bad	Dårlig	Slecht	Halb
Near	Naer	Dichtbij	Lähedal
Far	Fjern	Ver	Kaugel
Cheap	Billig	Goedkoop	Odav
Expensive	Dyr	Duur	Kallis
Open	Åben	Open	Avatud
Closed	Lukket	Dicht	Suletud
Today	I dag	Vandaag	Täna
Yesterday	I går	Gisteren	Eile
Tomorrow	I morgen	Morgen	Homme
Day	Dag	Dag	Päev
Week	Uge	Week	Nädal
Month	Måned	Maand	Kuu
Year	År	Jaar	Aasta
How much is....?	Hvor meget koster...?	Wat kost...?	Kui palju maksab...?
What time is it?	Hvad er klokken?	Hoe laat is het?	Mis kell praegu on?
Where is...?	Hvor er...?	Waar is...?	Kus on...?
I don't understand	Jeg forstår ikke	Ik begrijp het niet	Ma ei saa aru
Do you speak English?	Taler de Engelsk?	Spreekt u Engels?	Kas te räägite inglise keelt?
Please write it down	Vaer venlig at skrive det	Wilt u het opschrijven, alstublieft	Palun kirjutage see üles
One	En	Een	Uks
Two	To	Twee	Tkaks
Three	Tre	Drie	Kolm
Four	Fire	Vier	Neli
Five	Fem	Vijf	Viis
Six	Seks	Zes	Kuus
Seven	Syv	Zeven	Seitse
Eight	Otte	Acht	Kaheksa
Nine	Ni	Negen	Uheksa
Ten	Ti	Tien	Kümme

FINNISH, FRENCH, AND GERMAN

	Finnish	French	German
Yes	Kyllä	Oui	Ja
No	Ei	Non	Nein
Please	Olkaa hyvä	S'il vous plaît	Bitte
Thank you	Kiitos	Merci	Danke
Hello/Good day	Hyvää	Bonjour	Güten Tag
Goodbye	Hyvästi	Au revoir/à bientôt	Auf Wiedersehen
Excuse me	Anteeksi	Pardon	Entschuldigen Sie, bitte
Where	Missä	Où	Wo
When	Milloin	Quand	Wann
How	Kuinka	Comment	Wie
Left	Vasen	Gauche	Links
Right	Oikea	Droite	Rechts
Large	Suuri	Grand	Gross
Small	Pieni	Petit	Klein
Good	Hyvä	Bon	Gut
Bad	Paha	Mauvais	Schlecht
Near	Lähellä	Près	Nah
Far	Kaukana	Loin	Weit
Cheap	Halpa	Bon marché	Billig
Expensive	Kallis	Cher	Teuer
Open	Avoin	Ouvert	Offen
Closed	Suljettu	Fermé	Geschlossen
Today	Tänään	Aujourd'hui	Heute
Yesterday	Eilen	Hier	Gestern
Tomorrow	Huomenna	Demain	Morgen
Day	Päivä	Jour	Tag
Week	Viikko	Semaine	Woche
Month	Kuukausi	Mois	Monat
Year	Vuosi	Année	Jahr
How much is....?	Kuinka paljon on...?	Combien coûte...?	Wieviel kostet...?
What time is it?	Paljonko kello on?	Quelle heure est-il?	Wieviel Uhr ist es?
Where is...?	Missä on...?	Où est...?	Wo ist...?
I don't understand	En ymmärrä	Je ne comprends pas	Ich verstehe nicht
Do you speak English?	Puhutteko Englantia?	Parlez-vous anglais?	Sprechen Sie Englisch?
Please write it down	Olkaa hyvä ja kiarjoit-takaa se	Veuillez me l'écrire	Bitte schreiben Sie es
One	Yksi	Un	Eins
Two	Kaksi	Deux	Zwei
Three	Kolme	Trois	Drei
Four	Neljä	Quatre	Vier
Five	Viisi	Cinq	Fünf
Six	Kuusi	Six	Sechs
Seven	Seitsemän	Sept	Sieben
Eight	Kahdeksan	Huit	Acht
Nine	Yhdeksän	Neuf	Neun
Ten	Kymmenen	Dix	Zehn

GREEK, HUNGARIAN, AND ITALIAN

	Greek	Hungarian	Italian
Yes	Néh	Igen	Sì
No	Óhi	Nem	No
Please	Parakaló	Kérem	Per favore
Thank you	Efharistó	Köszönöm	Grazie
Hello/Good day	Yássas/hérete	Jó napot	Ciao/buon giorno
Goodbye	Adío	Viszontlá-tásta	Ciao/arriverderci
Excuse me	Signómi	Bocsánat	Mi scusi/prego
Where	Pou	Hol	Dove
When	Póte	Mikor	Quando
How	Pos	Hogyan	Come
Left	Aristerá	Balra	Sinistra
Right	Dheksiá	Jobbra	Destra
Large	Megálo	Nagy	Grande
Small	Mikró	Kicsi	Piccolo
Good	Kaló	Jó	Buono
Bad	Kakó	Rossz	Cattivo
Near	Kondá	Közel	Vicino
Far	Makriá	Távol	Lontano
Cheap	Fthinós	Olcsó	Buon mercato
Expensive	Akrivós	Drága	Caro
Open	Aniktós	Nyitva	Aperto
Closed	Klistós	Zárva	Chiuso
Today	Símera	Ma	Oggi
Yesterday	Khthés	Tegnap	Ieri
Tomorrow	Ávrio	Holnap	Domani
Day	Méra	Nap	Giorno
Week	Iméra	Hét	Settimana
Month	Evdomáda	Hónap	Mese
Year	Chrónos	Ev	Anno
How much is....?	Póso káni...?	Mennyibe Kerül...?	Quanto è...?
What time is it?	Ti óra inai...?	Hány óra?	Che ore sono?
Where is...?	Pou íne...?	Hol van?	Dov'è...?
I don't understand	Dhen katalavéno	Nem értem	Non ho capito
Do you speak English?	Ksérite Angliká?	Beszél Angolul?	Parla Inglese?
Please write it down	Parakaló grápiste to	Legyen szives, irja le	Lo scriva, per favore
One	Éna/mía	Egy	Uno
Two	Dhío	Kettö	Due
Three	Tría	Három	Tre
Four	Tésera	Négy	Quattro
Five	Pénde	Ot	Cinque
Six	Éksi	Hayt	Sei
Seven	Eftá	Hét	Sette
Eight	Októ	Nyolc	Otto
Nine	Enyá	Kilenc	Nove
Ten	Dhéka	Tíz	Dieci

LATVIAN, LITHUANIAN, AND NORWEGIAN

	Latvian	Lithuanian	Norwegian
Yes	Jā	Taip	Ja
No	Nē	Ne	Nei
Please	Lūdzu	Prašau	Vaer så god
Thank you	Paldies	Ačiu	Takk
Hello/Good day	Labdien	Labas	God dag
Goodbye	Uz redzēšanos	Viso gero	Adjø
Excuse me	Atvainojiet	Atsiprašau	Unnskyld
Where	Kur	Kur	Hvor
When	Kad	Kada	Når
How	Cik	Kaip	Hvordan
Left	Kreisi	Kairė	Venstre
Right	Labi	Deyinė	Høyre
Large	Liels	Didelis	Stor
Small	Mazs	Mažas	Liten
Good	Labs	Geras	God
Bad	Slikts	Blogas	Dårlig
Near	Tuvs	Artimas	I naerheten
Far	Tāls	Tolimas	Langt Borte
Cheap	Lēts	Pigus	Billig
Expensive	Dārgs	Brangus	Dyr
Open	Atvērts	Atidarytas	Åpen
Closed	Slēgts	Uždarytas	Lukket
Today	Šodien	Šiandien	I dag
Yesterday	Vakar	Vakar	I går
Tomorrow	Rīt	Rytdiena	I morgen
Day	Diena	Diena	Dag
Week	Nedela	Savaitė	Uke
Month	Menesis	Mėnuo	Måned
Year	Gads	Metai	År
How much is....?	Cik tas maksā...?	Kiek kainuoja ...?	Hvor mye er...?
What time is it?	Cik ir pulkstenis?	Kiek valandū?	Hvor mange er klokken?
Where is...?	Kur ir...?	Kur yra...?	Hvor er...?
I don't understand	Es nesaprotu	Nesuprantu	Jeg forstår ikke
Do you speak English?	Vai jūs runājat Angliski?	Ar jūs kalbate angliškai?	Snakker de Englesk?
Please write it down	Lūdzu uzrakstiet	Prašau užrašyti	Vennligst skriv det ned
One	Viens	Vienas	En
Two	Divi	Du/dvi	To
Three	Trīs	Trys	Tre
Four	Četri	Keturi	Fire
Five	Pieci	Penki	Fem
Six	Seši	Šeši	Seks
Seven	Septiņi	Septyni	Sju
Eight	Astoņi	Aštuoni	Åtte
Nine	Deviņi	Devyni	Ni
Ten	Desmit	Dešimt	Ti

POLISH, PORTUGUESE, AND ROMANIAN

	Polish	Portuguese	Romanian
Yes	Tak	Sim	Da
No	Nie	Não	Nu
Please	Proszę	Por favor	Vă rog
Thank you	Dziękuję	Obrigado	Mulmumesc
Hello/Good day	Dzień dobry	Olá	Salut/buna ziua
Goodbye	Do widzenia	Adeus	La revedere
Excuse me	Przepraszam	Desculpe	Permitemi-mi
Where	Gdzie	Onde	Unde
When	Kiedy	Quando	Când
How	Jak	Como	Cum
Left	Na lewo	Esquerda	Stânga
Right	Na prawo	Direita	Dreapta
Large	Duży	Grande	Mare
Small	Mały	Pequeno	Mic
Good	Dobry	Bom	Bun/bine
Bad	Zły	Mau	Rău
Near	Bliski	Perto	Apropriat
Far	Daleko	Longe	Departe
Cheap	Tani	Barato	Ieftin
Expensive	Drogi	Caro	Scump
Open	Otwarty	Aberto	Închis
Closed	Zamknięty	Fechado	Deschis
Today	Dziś	Hoje	Azi
Yesterday	Wczoraj	Ontem	Ieri
Tomorrow	Jutro	Amanhã	Mâine
Day	Dzień	Dia	Zi
Week	Tydzień	Semana	Săptămână
Month	Miesiąc	Mês	Lund
Year	Rok	Ano	An
How much is....?	Ile kosztuje...?	Quanto é... ?	Cât costa...?
What time is it?	Która godzina?	Que horas são?	Ce ora este?
Where is...?	Gdzie jest...?	Onde é...?	Unde este...?
I don't understand	Nie rozemiem	Não comprendo	Nu înţeleg
Do you speak English?	Pan(i) mówi po Angielsku?	Fala Inglés?	Vorbiţi Englezeşte?
Please write it down	Proszę to napisać	Escreva-mo, por favor	Vă rog scriemi
One	Jeden	Um	Unu
Two	Dwa	Dois	Doi
Three	Trzy	Três	Trei
Four	Cztery	Quatro	Patru
Five	Pięć	Cinco	Cinci
Six	Sześć	Seis	Şase
Seven	Siedem	Sete	Şapte
Eight	Osiem	Oito	Opt
Nine	Dziewięć	Nove	Noua
Ten	Dziesięć	Dez	Zece

RUSSIAN, SLOVENE AND SPANISH

	Russian	Slovene	Spanish
Yes	Da	Ja	Sí
No	Net	Ne	No
Please	Pozháluysta	Prosim	Por favor
Thank you	Spasíbo	Hvala	Gracias
Hello/Good day	Zdrávstvuyte	Živjo/dober dan	Hola
Goodbye	Do svidániya	Nasvidenje	Adiós
Excuse me	Izvinite	Oprostite	Con permiso
Where	Gde	Kje	¿Dónde?
When	Kogdá	Kdaj	¿Cuándo?
How	Kak	Kako	¿Cómo?
Left	Nalévo	Levo	Izquierda
Right	Naprávo	Desno	Derecha
Large	Bolshóy	Veliko	Gran
Small	Málenkiy	Majhno	Pequeño
Good	Khoróshiy	Dobro	Buen
Bad	Plokhóy	Slabo	Mal
Near	Bleezkiy	Blizu	Próximo
Far	Da-lyiko	Daleč	Lejos
Cheap	Dyi-shovee	Poceni	Barato
Expensive	Daragoy	Drago	Caro
Open	Otkryto	Odprto	Abierto
Closed	Zakryto	Zaprto	Cerrado
Today	Syivo-dnya	Danes	Hoy
Yesterday	Vcherá	Včeraj	Ayer
Tomorrow	Závtra	Jutri	Mañana
Day	Dyin	Dan	Día
Week	Nyi-dyel-ya	Teden	Semana
Month	Mye-syats	Mesec	Mes
Year	Got	Leto	Año
How much is....?	Skólko stóit?	Koliko stane?	¿Cuánto cuesta...?
What time is it?	Katoree chass?	Koliko je ura?	¿Tiene la hora?
Where is...?	Gde...?	Kje je	¿Dónde está...?
I don't understand	Ya ne ponimáyu	Ne razumem	No entiendo
Do you speak English?	Vy govoríte po-anglíyski?	Govorite angleško?	¿Habla inglés?
Please write it down	Zapishíte éto pozháluysta?	Prosim, če mi napišete	Escríbamelo, por favor
One	Odín	Ena	Un/Una
Two	Dva	Dve	Dos
Three	Tri	Tri	Tres
Four	Chetyre	Štiri	Cuatro
Five	Pyat	Pet	Cinco
Six	Shest	Šest	Seis
Seven	Sem	Sedem	Siete
Eight	Vósem	Osem	Ocho
Nine	Dévyat	Devet	Nueve
Ten	Désyat	Deset	Diez

SWEDISH AND TURKISH

	Swedish	Turkish
Yes	Ja	Evet
No	Nej	Hayır/yok
Please	Var så god	Lütfen
Thank you	Tack	Teşekküler/mersi/sağol
Hello/Good day	Hej	Merhaba
Goodbye	Adjö	Qxyi günler/görüşürüz
Excuse me	Ursäkta mig	Pardon
Where	Var	...nereye
When	När	Ne zaman
How	Hur	Nasıl
Left	Vänster	Sol
Right	Höger	Sağ
Large	Stor	Büyuk
Small	Liten	Kücük
Good	Bra	İyi
Bad	Dalig	Kötü
Near	Nära	Yakın
Far	Avläqsen	Uzak
Cheap	Billig	Ucuz
Expensive	Dyr	Pahalı
Open	Öppen	Açık
Closed	Stängd	Kapalı
Today	I dag	Bugün
Yesterday	I går	Dün
Tomorrow	I morgon	Yarın
Day	Dag	Gün
Week	Vecka	Hafta
Month	Månad	Ay
Year	Är	Sene
How much is....?	Vad kostar det...?	Ne kadar...?
What time is it?	Hur mycket är klockan?	Saatınız var mi?
Where is...?	Var är...?	Nerede...?
I don't understand	Jag förstår int	Anlamadım Qxngilizce
Do you speak English?	Talar ni Engelska?	Biliyormusunuz?
Please write it down	Skulle ni kunna skriva det?	Onu yazarmqxsqxnqxz
One	Ett	Bir
Two	Två	İki
Three	Tre	Uç
Four	Fyra	Dört
Five	Fem	Beş
Six	Sex	Altı
Seven	Sju	Yedi
Eight	Ätta	Sekiz
Nine	Nio	Dokuz
Ten	Tio	On

PART TWO

THE

GUIDE

CHAPTER ONE

AUSTRIA

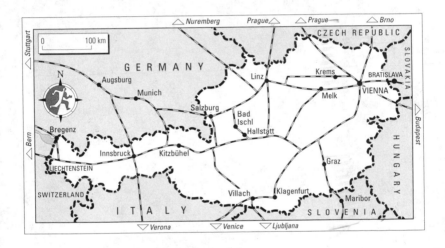

Introduction

For centuries the heart of an empire which played a pivotal role in the political and cultural destiny of Europe, Austria underwent several decades of change and uncertainty in the twentieth century. The interwar state, shorn of its empire and racked by economic problems and political strife, fell prey to the promise of a greater Germany. After World War II, denazification was pretty desultory, since most Austrians preferred to forget their wartime role. Postwar economic stability encouraged an almost Scandinavian emphasis on social policy as the guiding principle of national life, and the growth of a low-key but genuine patriotism. With the end of the Cold War, the country returned to the heart of Europe, finally joining the EU in 1995.

From time to time, however, Austria's reactionary past has come back to haunt it, most notably in 1986 during the **Waldheim affair**, when the president's wartime record was called into question. Then, in February 2000, the right-wing People's Party (ÖVP) formed a coalition with the far-right **Freedom Party** (FPÖ). The EU immediately froze bilateral relations with Austria, but the protest eventually petered out. The ÖVP/FPÖ coalition may turn out to be a short-term exercise in political pragmatism rather than the opening of a new dark age, but the persistence of xenophobic attitudes in Austria – and their exploitation by the populist right – continue to be a source of concern.

Despite the PR disaster of the Waldheim affair and the rise of xenophobic politics, Austria is still primarily known for two contrasting attractions – the fading imperial glories of Vienna, and the variety of its Alpine hinterland. **Vienna** is the gateway to much of central Europe and a good place to soak up the culture of *Mitteleuropa* before heading towards the Magyar and Slav lands over which the city once held sway. Less renowned provincial capitals like **Graz** and **Linz** provide a similar level of culture and vitality. The most dramatic of Austria's Alpine scenery is west of here, in and around the **Tyrol**, whose capital, **Innsbruck**, provides the best base for exploration. **Salzburg**, however, between Innsbruck and Vienna, represents urban Austria at its most picturesque, an intoxicating Baroque city within easy striking distance of the mountains and lakes of the **Salzkammergut** to the east.

Information and maps

Tourist offices are plentiful and come under an assortment of names, often just *Information, Tourismusverband, Verkehrsamt, Fremdenverkehrsverein* or other variants. All are helpful and well orga-

nized, often hand out free maps and almost always book accommodation, sometimes for a small fee, a deposit, or both. They are open all day, every day, in the larger cities during the summer; outside this period, and in smaller towns and remote areas, times may be restricted to a few hours on weekday mornings.

There are plenty of good general **maps** of Austria; one of the best is the 1:500,000 Freytag & Berndt. The 1:200,000 Generalkarte series of regional maps are useful for lengthier touring, as are the more detailed 1:50,000 Freytag & Berndt Wanderkarten and rival Kompass Wanderkarten, both covering all the Alpine districts and many rural eastern areas as well.

Money and banks

Austria is one of twelve European Union countries which have changed over to a single currency, the **euro** (€). Euro notes and coins are scheduled to be issued from the beginning of 2002, with Austrian Schillings (öS) remaining in circulation during a transition period, at a fixed rate of öS13.7603 to 1 euro, until they are scrapped entirely at the end of February 2002. After this date you will still be able to exchange your Schillings for euros in banks for at least a year. Euro notes are issued in **denominations** of 5, 10, 20, 50, 100, 200 and 500 euros, and coins in denominations of 1, 2, 5, 10, 20 and 50 cents and 1 and 2 euros.

All prices in this chapter are given in euros correct at the time of going to press. There will no doubt be some rounding off or, more probably, up of prices in the first few months after the introduction of the euro.

Banking hours tend to be Mon–Fri 8am–12.30pm and 1.30–3pm; in Vienna they're Mon–Wed and Fri 8am–3pm, Thurs 8am–5.30pm (smaller Viennese branches take an hour for lunch). Post offices charge slightly less commission on exchange transactions than banks do, and in larger cities they are open longer hours.

Communications

Most **post offices** are open Mon–Fri 8am–noon and 2–6pm; in larger cities they do without the lunch break and open Sat 8–10am as well; some are open 24 hours. You can also buy stamps at tobacconists (*Tabak-Trafik*).

At the time of writing, the smallest coin accepted in public call boxes is öS1 and a couple of these should suffice for a local call; insert öS10 and upwards if calling long distance, or buy a phone card (*Telefonkarte*), available from tobacconists, and seek out a card phone. You can make **international calls** from all public telephones, but it's easier from larger post offices, which have booths. The operator number is ☎1611 for domestic calls, ☎1616 for international.

Generally **Internet access** is limited to the larger cities – smaller, more conservative towns are unlikely to have cybercafés. Expect to pay around €7/hr spent online.

Getting around

Austria's public transport system is fast, efficient and pretty comprehensive, with trains covering the country, supplemented in remoter regions by buses.

■ Trains and buses

Austrian Federal Railways (Österreichische Bundesbahnen or ÖBB; *www.oebb.at*) run a punctual, clean and comfortable network, which includes most towns of any size. **Trains** marked "EC" or "EN" (EuroCity and EuroNight international expresses), "ICE" or "IC" (Austrian InterCity expresses) are the fastest. Those designated "D" (*Schnellzug*) or "E" (*Eilzug*) are the next fastest, stopping at most intermediate points, while the *Regionalzug* is the slowest form of service, stopping at all stations. **Fares** are calculated according to distance, with the first 100km costing €13; 200km costing €23; 500km, about €42. In terms of **passes** a EuroDomino (see Basics p.22) is the only real option: these range from around €100 for three days (€80 for under 26s) to €160 for eight days (€125 for under 26s). The national timetable (*Kursbuch*), detailing the whole network, complete with lake and Danube transport, costs €7.50; timetable leaflets covering major routes are free at stations.

Austria's **Bahn- and Postbus** system fills the gaps in the network, serving the remoter villages and otherwise inaccessible Alpine valleys. Where there is a choice, you will find trains easier and quicker, and bus fares are only slightly cheaper at around €9.50 per 100km. As a general rule, *Bahnbus* services, operated by ÖBB, depart from outside train stations; the *Postbus* tends to stop outside the post office. Twenty-four-hour or seven-day regional **travelcards** (*Netzkarte*), covering both trains and buses, are avail-

able in many regions of Austria, but prices – and areas of coverage – vary widely from place to place.

■ Driving, hitching and cycling

Given the deals available on Austria's trains, driving is not a budget option. National **speed limits** are 50kph in built-up areas, 100kph on normal roads and 130kph on motorways. All Austria's Autobahns are subject to a single **motorway toll**, which basically involves buying a windscreen sticker (*Vignette*) from the petrol stations or shops found at border posts when entering the country (information on *www.vignette.at*). You can also buy them from post offices and tobacconists once inside the country. A ten-day *Vignette* costs €7.60 (and you'll need to buy a ten-day one even if you're merely passing straight through the country); a two-month *Vignette* €21.80. Motorbikers get a discount on all *Vignettes*. You don't need a *Vignette* at all, of course, if you intend to stick to normal main roads; however, those caught driving on Austria's Autobahns without displaying a valid *Vignette* will be subject up to a maximum of €218 fine.

If you break down, the *Österreichischer Automobile, Motorrad und Touring Club* (ÖAMTC, ☎120, *www.oemtc.at*), and the Auto-, Motor- und Radfahrerbund Österreichs (ARBÖ, ☎123, *www.arboe.or.at*) both offer **breakdown services**. Call-out charges hover around the €70 mark. **Car rental** charges start at around €70 per day or €230 per week for a small car with unlimited mileage, although you may land something cheaper with smaller local firms. You need to be over 25 to rent a car.

Hitching can be difficult away from the main east–west routes, and many locals make use of the Mitfahrzentrale (☎01/408 22 10), a telephone-only agency that puts potential hitchers in touch with drivers willing to take passengers for a fee – usually significantly cheaper than public transport.

Austria is very **bicycle**-friendly, with cycle lanes in all major towns. All except the smallest train stations rent out bikes for €13 per day (€8.70 if you have a valid rail ticket). You can return them to any station for an extra fee of €6.50 (€3.30 if you have a ticket).

Accommodation

Despite profiteering in tourist centres like Vienna and Salzburg, accommodation need not be expensive,

---

ACCOMMODATION PRICE CODES

Throughout this guide, accommodation is coded on a scale of ① to ⑨, the code indicating the lowest price per person per night you could expect to pay in each establishment in high season. With hostels this is the nightly rate per person; with hotels, the price is arrived at by dividing the cost of the cheapest double room by two. The prices indicated by the codes are as follows:

① under £5/$8 (€9)	④ £15–20/$24–32 (€27–36)	⑦ £30–35/$48–56 (€54–63)
② £5–10/$8–16 (€9–18)	⑤ £20–25/$32–40 (€36–45)	⑧ £35–40/$56–64 (€63–72)
③ £10–15/$16–24 (€18–27)	⑥ £25–30/$40–48 (€45–54)	⑨ £40/$64 (€72) and over

and, although it can be a scramble in July and August, finding a room doesn't present too many problems. Most tourist offices book accommodation with little fuss, usually for a fee (€2–3) and/or a deposit.

■ Hotels, pensions and private rooms

A high standard of cleanliness and comfort can usually be taken for granted in Austrian **hotels**, although in resorts and larger towns prices can be high. Outside of Vienna, expect to pay a minimum of €35 for a double with bathroom, slightly less for rooms with shared facilities. Good-value **bed and breakfast** accommodation is usually available in the many small family-run hotels known as *Gasthöfe* and *Gasthäuser*, with prices starting at €35 for a double. In the larger towns and cities a **pension** or **Frühstückspension** situated in large apartment blocks, will offer similar prices. Most (though not all) tourist offices also have a stock of **private rooms**, although in well-travelled rural areas where the locals depend a great deal on tourism, roadside signs offering *Zimmer Frei* are fairly ubiquitous anyway. Prices for a double room are usually somewhere between €30 and €45.

■ Hostels and student accommodation

Hostels (*Jugendherberge* or *Jugendgästehaus*) are fairly widespread in Austria, with around a hundred in all. They're run by two separate national organizations, the Österreichischer Jugendherbergsverband (ÖJHV; ☎01/533 5353, *www.oejhv.or.at*) and the Österreichischer Jugendherbergswerk (ÖJHW; ☎01/533 1833, *www.oejhw.or.at*), although both are affiliated to HI (Hostelling International; *www.iyhf.org*). Standards vary from the hearty, basic rural variety to the well-appointed (but crowded) hostels of the larger cities. **Rates** hover between €10 and €18, normally including a nominal breakfast. Sheet sleeping bags are obligatory, although the cost of renting one is often included in the charge. Many hostels serve other meals besides breakfast for €3.50–5.50.

■ Camping

Austria's high standards of accommodation are reflected in the country's **campsites**, the vast majority of which have laundry facilities, shops and snack bars, as well as the standard necessities. Most are open May–Sept, although in the winter-sports resorts of western Austria many never close. Prices vary enormously depending on the facilities available and the season. In general, you can expect to pay about €4–6 per person, €3–9 per pitch, plus €1.50–3.50 per vehicle.

Food and drink

Foodstuffs in Austria are expensive, which makes eating out marginally cheaper than self-catering. Drinking is remarkably affordable, especially wine, and the country's bars and cafés are among its real joys.

■ Food

For ready-made snacks, try a bakery (*Bäckerei*) or confectioner's (*Konditorei*), which sell sweet pastries and cakes, as well as sandwiches. **Street food** centres around the ubiquitous *Würstelstand*, which sells hot dogs, *Bratwurst* (grilled sausage), *Käsekrainer* (spicy sausage with cheese), *Bosna* (spicy, thin Balkan sausage) or *Currywurst*, usually chopped up and served with a *Semmel* or bread roll, along with a dollop of *Senf* (mustard) and *Dose* (can) of beer. *Schnell-Imbiss* or *Bufet* establishments serve similar fare, augmented by hamburgers and simple grills.

It's difficult to make hard distinctions between places to eat and places to drink – most establishments offer **snacks and meals** of some kind. Similarly, it's possible just to have a drink in most restaurants. Food served up in town-centre *Kaffeehäuser* or cafés and bars can actually be great value, with light meals and snacks starting at about €5; all restaurant and café menus have filling central European standbys such as spicy *Serbische Bohnensuppe* (Serbian bean soup) and *Gulaschsuppe* (goulash soup) for less than €4. Main dishes (*Hauptspeisen*) are dominated by veal – *Schnitzel* –

often accompanied by potatoes and a vegetable or salad: *Wienerschnitzel* is fried in breadcrumbs, *Pariser* in batter, *Natur* served on its own or with a creamy sauce. In general you can expect to pay €6.50–9.50 for a standard main course, though set lunchtime menus (*Mittagsmenü*) always offer a wide range of cheaper dishes. Desserts (*Mehlspeisen*) include sweets and pastries: various types of *Torte* (including the famous rich chocolate *Sachertorte*); strudel, cheesecake; and *Palatschinken* (or pancake, with various nut or jam fillings) are all common.

■ Drink

For urban Austrians, daytime drinking traditionally centres around the *Kaffeehaus* or **café** – relaxed places furnished with a stock of the day's newspapers. They serve alcoholic and soft drinks, snacks and cakes, alongside a wide range of different coffees: a *Schwarzer* is small and black, a *Brauner* comes with a little milk, while a *Melange* is half-coffee and half-milk; a *Kurzer* is a small espresso; an *Einspänner* is a glass of black coffee topped with *Schlag*, the ubiquitous whipped cream that is offered with most pastries and cakes. A cup of coffee in one of these places is, however, pricey at around €2.50–3, and numerous stand-up **coffee bars** (many part of the Anker or Eduscho chains) are a much cheaper alternative at €1.50 a cup.

Night-time drinking centres around a growing number of youthful **bars** and cafés, although more traditional *Bierstuben* and *Weinstuben* are still thick on the ground, especially in rural areas. Austrian **beers**, while of a high standard, don't come in the infinite variety found in Germany. Most establishments serve the local brew on tap, either by the *Krügerl* (half-litre, for around €2.50–3), *Seidel* (third-litre, €1.80) or *Pfiff* (fifth of a litre, €0.80–1.30), while also keeping a few international speciality beers in bottles. Wine, drunk by the *Viertel* (a 25cl mug) or the *Achterl* (a 12.5cl glass), is often cheaper than other alcoholic drinks and is widely consumed. The *Weinkeller* is a regular sight in Austrian towns and cities; in the vine-producing areas wine is also consumed in a *Heuriger* or a *Buschenshenk*, a traditional tavern, customarily serving cold food as well. In autumn a lot of establishments serve *Sturm*, a misty, part-fermented concoction made from newly harvested grapes.

Opening hours and holidays

Until very recently, all shops used to conform to the following **opening hours**: Monday to Friday 9am to noon and 2 to 6pm, with late shopping on Thursdays, and Saturday 8am to noon – except on the first Saturday of the month (known as the *Langersamstag*, or "long Saturday"), when hours are 8am to 5pm. Shops may now open all day on every Saturday, but many shops still stick to the old *Langersamstag* routine; some shops in the larger towns and cities also stay open at lunchtimes. The only shops you're likely to find open after hours and on Sundays and public holidays, however, are the small general stores at the main train stations and airports. Many cafés and restaurants also have a weekly *Ruhetag* (closing day). All shops and banks will be closed, and most museums will at least have reduced hours, on the following **public holidays**: Jan 1; Jan 6; Easter Monday; May 1; Ascension Day; Whit Monday; Corpus Christi; Aug 15; Oct 26; Nov 1; Dec 8; Dec 25 & 26.

Emergencies

Although the traditionally laid-back Austrians lack quite the same reverence for rules and regulations as the Germans and Swiss, the country is still extremely law-abiding, and is a reasonably safe place to travel. This doesn't prevent the tabloids from complaining about the increase in urban **crime**, which the political right attributes to East Europeans. Austrian **police** are armed, and are not renowned for their friendliness especially towards other races. There are few places where female travellers will feel ill at ease, except for some outer districts of Vienna and Graz. Hitting children is illegal in Austria, though the law is practically unenforceable.

As for **health**, city hospital casualty departments will treat you and ask questions later. For prescriptions, pharmacies or *Apotheke* tend to follow normal shopping hours. A rota system covers night-time and weekend opening; each pharmacy has details of those open posted up in the window.

EMERGENCY NUMBERS

Police ☎133; Ambulance ☎144; Fire ☎122.

VIENNA

Most people visit **VIENNA** with a vivid image in their minds: a romantic place full of Habsburg nostalgia and musical resonances. Visually it's unlikely to disappoint: an eclectic feast of architectural styles, from High Baroque through monumental imperial projects from the late nineteenth century to modernist experiments and enlightened municipal planning. However, the capital often seems aloof from the rest of the country; Alpine Austrians look on it as an alien eastern metropolis with an impenetrable dialect, staffed by an army of fund-draining bureaucrats. The former imperial city had a tough time of it in the twentieth century, deprived of its hinterland by World War I, then washed up on the edge of western Europe by the Cold War. Its population has dropped by a quarter since 1910, and its image is one of melancholy and decay, though the latter is perhaps more a romantic affectation than a realistic portrait of the city today.

The first settlement of any substance here, Roman Vindobona, was never much more than a garrison town, and it was only with the rise of the Babenberg dynasty in the tenth century that Vienna became an important centre. In 1278 the city fell to Rudolf of Habsburg, but had to compete for centuries with Prague, Linz and Graz as the imperial residence on account of its vulnerability to attack from the Turks, who first laid siege to it in 1529. It was only with the removal of the Turkish threat in 1683 that the court based itself here permanently. The great aristocratic families, grown fat on the profits of the Turkish wars, flooded in to build palaces and summer residences in a frenzy of construction that gave Vienna its Baroque character.

Imperial Vienna was never a wholly German city; as the capital of a cosmopolitan empire, it attracted great minds from all over central Europe. By the end of the Habsburg era it had become a breeding ground for the ideological movements of the age: nationalism, socialism, Zionism and anti-Semitism all flourished here. This turbulence was reflected in the cultural sphere, and the ghosts of Freud, Klimt, Schiele, Mahler and Schönberg are nowadays bigger tourist draws than old stand-bys like the Lipizzaner horses and the Vienna Boys' Choir. There is more to Vienna than *fin-de-siècle* decadence, however; a strong, home-grown, youthful culture, coupled with new influences from former Eastern Bloc neighbours, has placed the city at the heart of European cultural life once again.

Arrival and information

Trains from the west and from Hungary terminate at the **Westbahnhof**, five U-Bahn stops (U3) from the city centre, close to Mariahilferstrasse, Vienna's brashest shopping street. Trains from eastern Europe, Italy and the Balkans arrive at the **Südbahnhof**, to the south of the city centre; you can either walk five minutes west to Südtiroler Platz U-Bahn station, or hop on tram #D into town. Of Vienna's other stations, **Franz-Josefs-Bahnhof**, north of the centre, serves as arrival point for services from Lower Austria and the odd train from Prague (take tram #D), while **Wien-Nord** (U-Bahn Praterstern), in the northeast, is used exclusively by local and regional trains, including the S-Bahn to the airport (see below).

International, long-distance buses arrive at Vienna's **main bus terminal** beside the City Air Terminal and Hilton Hotel, east of the city centre (U-Bahn Wien-Mitte/Landstrasse). If you arrive on one of the **DDSG boat** services (*www.ddsg-blue-danube.at*) from further up the Danube, or from Bratislava or Budapest, you'll find yourself disembarking at the Schiffahrtszentrum by the Reichsbrücke, some way northeast of the city centre; the nearest station (U-Bahn Vorgartenstrasse) is five minutes' walk away, one block west of Mexicoplatz.

The city's **international airport**, Flughafen Wien-Schwechat (*www.viennaairport.com*), lies around 20km southeast of the city. It's connected to the centre by S-Bahn line S7; **trains** (every 30min; €2.80 for a single ticket, or €1.40 plus the price of a travel pass) taking thirty minutes to reach Wien-Mitte. **Buses** (every 20min) from the airport take twenty minutes to reach the City Air Terminal (adjacent to Wien-Mitte) and cost €5.10 one way. There are also

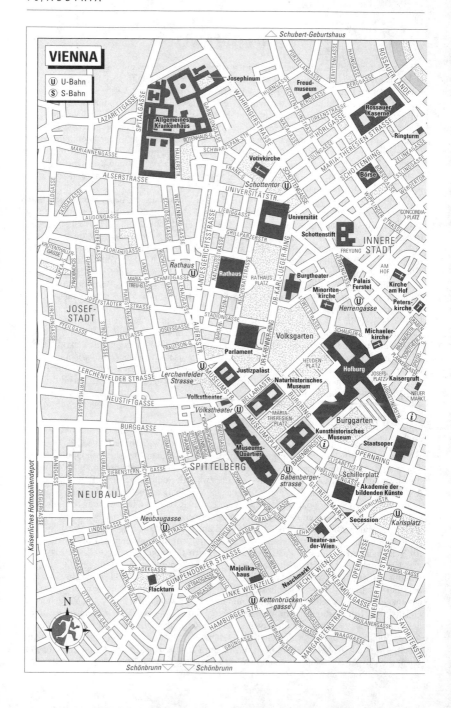

△ *Schubert-Geburtshaus*

VIENNA

Ⓤ U-Bahn
Ⓢ S-Bahn

Josephinum
Allgemeines Krankenhaus
Freud-museum
Rossauer Kaserne
Ringturm
Votivkirche
Schottentor Ⓤ
Börse
Universität
Schottenstift
INNERE STADT
FREYUNG
Rathaus
Rathaus
RATHAUS PLATZ
Burgtheater
Minoriten-kirche
Palais Ferstel
AM HOF
Kirche am Hof
Peters-kirche
Herrengasse Ⓤ
JOSEF-STADT
Michaeler-kirche
Volksgarten
Parlament
HELDEN-PLATZ
Hofburg
JOSEFS-PLATZ
Kaisergruft
NEUER MARKT
Justizpalast
Naturhistorisches Museum
Volkstheater
Volkstheater Ⓤ
MARIA-THERESIEN-PLATZ
Burggarten
Kunsthistorisches Museum
Museums-Quartier
SPITTELBERG
Babenberger strasse
Staatsoper
Schillerplatz
Akademie der bildenden Künste
NEUBAU
Neubaugasse Ⓤ
Secession
Karlsplatz Ⓤ
Theater-an-der-Wien
Majolika-haus
Flackturm
Naschmarkt
Kettenbrücken-gasse Ⓤ

△ *Kaiserliches Hofmobiliendepot*

N

Schönbrunn ▽   ▽ *Schönbrunn*

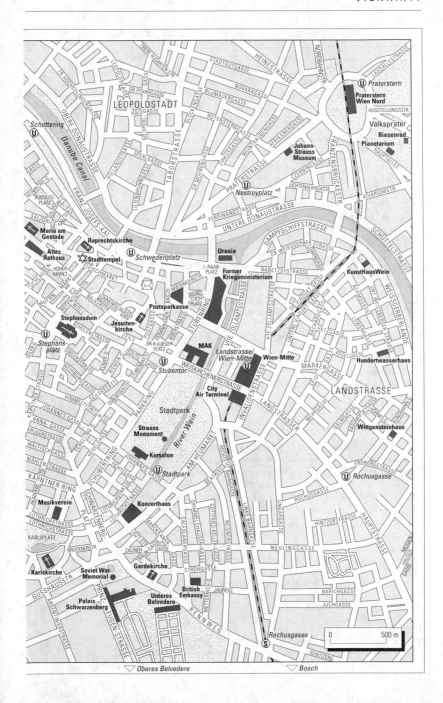

hourly buses to the Südbahnhof and Westbahnhof (see below). **Taxis** to the centre take twenty minutes or so and charge around €30.

All points of arrival have **tourist kiosks** with accommodation booking facilities. In the city centre, the main **tourist office** is behind the opera house on Albertinaplatz (daily 9am–7pm; ☎211 14-222, *www.info.wien.at*), and has maps, brochures and a room booking service (€3). There's an **information centre** for young people, *Jugendinfo*, at Babenbergerstrasse 1 (Mon–Sat noon–7pm; *www.jugendinfowien.at*), on the corner of the Ringstrasse, which also sells tickets for gigs.

City transport

Vienna is divided into numbered **districts** (*Bezirke*). District 1 is the Innere Stadt, the area enclosed by the Ringstrasse; districts 2–9 are arranged clockwise around it; beyond here, districts 10–23 are a fair way out from the city centre. All Viennese **addresses** begin with the number of the district, followed by the name of the street, and then the number of the house or building, occasionally followed by the number of the apartment. So many of Vienna's attractions are within the Innere Stadt that you can do and see a great deal on foot. Otherwise **public transport** consists of a combination of **trams** (*Strassenbahn*, colloquially known as *Bim*) **buses**; and the ultra-clean **U-Bahn** or metro, which has five lines; complemented the **S-Bahn** (*Schnellbahn*) network of fast commuter trains. You're expected to buy your ticket in advance from the ticket booths or machines at U-Bahn stations and from tobacconists, and punch it on board buses and trams or before entering the U- or S-Bahn. Fares are calculated on a zonal basis: tickets for the central zone (covering most of Vienna) cost €1.40 and allow any number of changes, on any mode of transport. If you're going to be using public transport a fair bit, invest in a **travel pass** (*Netzkarte*): a 24-hour ticket (€4.40) or a 72-hour ticket (€10.90). The much-touted *Wien-Karte* or **Vienna Card** (€15.30; *www.wienkarte.at*) gives various minor discounts at local attractions, as well as being a 72-hour *Netzkarte*. Be warned that the penalty for fare-dodging is €40, plus the fare. Public transport runs between 5am and midnight; at other times half-hourly **night buses** radiate out from Schwedenplatz. You can catch a **taxi** at one of the cab ranks around town, or phone ☎31330, 40100 or 60160.

Accommodation

There's an abundance of **accommodation** in Vienna for those prepared to splash out. However, extreme pressure on the cheaper end of the market means that booking ahead is essential in summer, and advisable during the rest of the year. It's hard to find anything very affordable in the central area, and the cheapest double rooms within reach of it will set you back at least €25 a head. The likeliest hunting grounds are in the western districts between the Ring and the Gürtel (districts 5–9); places here are often located on the upper floors of nineteenth-century apartment buildings, and have undeniable character. Vienna's hostels are clean and efficient, but often full – the official HI hostels all have daytime lock-outs.

The tourist offices have a limited number of **private rooms** for upwards of €22 per person (☎01/2111 4444; minimum three nights), but these go quickly and are often in distant suburbs. You could also try the Mitwohnzentrale, 8, Laudongasse 7 (Mon–Fri 10am–2pm & 3–6pm; ☎01/402 60 61), which tends to have cheaper properties and also offers weekly rates; or the nearby youth travel specialists ÖKISTA, at 9, Türkenstrasse 8 (Mon–Wed & Fri 9.30am–4pm, Thurs 9.30am–5.30pm; ☎01/401 48).

Hostels

Believe It or Not, 7, Myrthengasse 10 (☎526 46 58). Friendly, cheap crash pad opposite the HI hostel; no breakfast, but kitchen facilities available. No curfew. Bus #48A or 10min walk from U-Bahn Volkstheater. ②.

Hostel Ruthensteiner, 15, Robert-Hamerling-Gasse 24 (☎893 4202, *hostel.ruthensteiner@telecom.at*). Excellent hostel, with a nice courtyard, within easy walking distance of the Westbahnhof, with dorm beds, doubles and triples (discounts for HI members). Open all year. Breakfast is extra. No curfew. U-Bahn Westbahnhof. ②.

Jugendgästehaus Brigittenau, 20, Friedrich-Engels-Platz 24 (☎332 8294, *oejhv-wien-jgh-brigittenau@oejhv.or.at*). Huge modern HI hostel in a dour working-class suburb, with dorms and en-suite bunk-bed doubles. Curfew 1am; 24hr reception. Tram #N from U-Bahn Schwedenplatz or Dresdner Strasse. ②.

Jugendgästehaus Hütteldorf-Hacking, 13, Schlossberggasse 8 (☎877 0263, *jgh@wigast.com*). A 220-bed dorm-only hostel, out in the sticks, but convenient for those who wish to explore the wilds of the Lainzer Tiergarten and Schönbrunn. 11.45pm curfew, but night key available for a small fee. S- and U-Bahn Hütteldorf. ②.

Jugendherberge Myrthengasse/Neustiftgasse, 7, Myrthengasse 7/Neustiftgasse 85 (☎523 6316, *oejhv-wien-jgh-neustiftg.@oejhv.or.at*). The most central of all the official hostels, with 200-plus dorm beds divided between two addresses, round the corner from each other. Book well in advance and go to the Myrthengasse reception on arrival. Curfew 1am. Bus #48A or short walk up Neustiftgasse from U-Bahn Volkstheater. ②.

Wombat's, 15, Grangasse 6 (☎897 2336, *wombats@chello.at*). Plain dorm beds and bunk-bed doubles, but a party atmosphere at this laid-back hostel, within easy walking distance of U-Bahn Westbahnhof. 24hr reception. ②.

Hotels and pensions

Pension Dr. Geissler, 1, Postgasse 14 (☎533 28 03). Modern central pension; rooms with shared facilities are among the cheapest in the Innere Stadt. U-Bahn Schwedenplatz. ④.

Pension Kraml, 6, Brauergasse 5 (☎587 8588). Smart, clean, modern, friendly, reliable and cheap pension off Mariahilferstrasse. U-Bahn Zieglergasse/Neubaugasse. ④.

Hotel Kugel, 7, Siebensterngasse 43 (☎523 3355, *www.hotelkugel.at*). Within spitting distance of Spittelberg's numerous restaurants and bars. Plain but clean rooms; continental breakfast. U-Bahn Neubaugasse. ④.

Pension Lerner, 1, Wipplingerstrasse 23 (☎533 5219, *www.pensionlerner.com*). Small pension with just seven bright, simple ensuite rooms. Big buffet breakfasts served until 11am. U-Bahn Schottentor/Herrengasse. ⑤.

Pension Lindenhof, 7, Lindengasse 4 (☎523 04 98). Appealing rooms with creaky parquet flooring in a lugubrious building off Mariahilferstrasse. U-Bahn Neubaugasse. ④.

Pension Nossek, 1, Graben 17 (☎533 7041, *pensions.nossek@faxvia.net*). Large family-run pension on the pedestrianised Graben – it's popular, so book in advance. U-Bahn Stephansplatz. ⑦.

Hotel Orient, 1, Tiefer Graben 30 (☎533 73 07). Vienna's equivalent of a Tokyo "love hotel", with mind-bogglingly exotic rooms rented by the hour and per night. U-Bahn Herrengasse. ⑤–⑨.

Hotel Post, 1, Fleischmarkt 24 (☎515 83, *www.hotel-post-wien.at*). A civilized, very large central hotel with big old rooms and modern furnishings. U-Bahn Schwedenplatz. ⑤.

Pension Riedl, 1, Georg-Coch-Platz 3 (☎512 79 19). Bright, cheerful pension just off the Ring. The rooms are small, though most have shower and toilet, and you get breakfast in bed. Closed mid-Jan to mid-Feb. U-Bahn Schwedenplatz/Wien Mitte. ⑤.

St Stephan Appartement-Pension, 1, Spiegelgasse 1 (☎512 2990). Incredible location overlooking Graben. Just six doubles, with lovely period furnishings, TV, shower, toilet, fridge and cooking facilities. No breakfast. U-Bahn Stephansplatz. ⑦.

Pension Wild, 8, Lange Gasse 10 (☎406 5174, *www.pension-wild.com*). Laid-back pension, a short walk from the Ring, popular with backpackers and gay travellers. Booking essential. U-Bahn Lerchenfelder Strasse. ④.

Campsites

Camping Rodaun, 23, An der Au 2 (☎888 4154). Nice location by a stream in the very southwestern outskirts, near the Wienerwald. Tram #60 from U-Bahn Hietzing to its terminus, then 5min walk. April to mid-Nov.

Wien West, 14, Hüttelbergstrasse 80 (☎914 2314). In the plush, far-western suburbs of Vienna, close to the Wienerwald, with 4-people bungalows to rent between April and October (€29). Bus #151 from U-Bahn Hütteldorf, or a 15min walk from tram #49 terminus. Closed Feb.

The City

For all its grandiosity, Vienna is surprisingly compact: the historical centre or **Innere Stadt**, bound to the northeast by the Danube canal and surrounded on all other sides by the majestic sweep of the **Ringstrasse**, is just a kilometre across at its broadest point. From the Ringstrasse, the main arteries of communication radiate outwards before reaching another ring road, the **Gürtel** (literally "belt"), further west. Most of the important sights are concentrated in the tourist-clogged central district and along the Ring, but a lot of the essential Vienna lies beyond it, in the initially forbidding grid of barracks-like nineteenth-century apartment blocks; and there are outlying sights such as the imperial palace at **Schönbrunn**, or the funfair and parklands of the **Prater**. With judicious use of public transport, which enables you to travel from one side of the city to the other in less than thirty minutes, you should be able see a great deal in a couple of days.

Stephansplatz

The obvious place to begin is the central **Stephansplatz**, a lively pedestrianized square overlooked by the hoary Gothic bulk of the **Stephansdom** (Mon–Sat 9am–noon & 1–5pm, Sun 12.30–5pm; free), whose spire, nicknamed *Steffl* ("Little Stephen") by the locals, together with the multicoloured chevrons on its roof, still dominates the Vienna skyline. The first thing that strikes you as you enter the gloomy, high-vaulted interior is that, despite the tourists, Stephansdom is still very much a place of worship. The highlight in the nave is the early sixteenth-century carved stone pulpit with portraits of the four fathers of the Christian church, and a self-portrait by the sculptor who peers from a window below the pulpit stairs. The area beyond the transepts is roped off, so to get a good look at the Wiener Neustädter Altar, a masterpiece of late Gothic art, and, to its right, the tomb of the Holy Roman Emperor Friedrich III, you must sign up for a guided tour (Mon–Sat 10.30am & 3pm, Sunday 3pm, with English tours April–Oct daily 3.45pm; €2.90).

Other features of interest include the **catacombs** (guided tours every 30min Mon–Sat 10–11.30am & 1.30–4.30pm, Sun 1.30–4.30pm; €2.90), where, among other macabre remains, the entrails of illustrious Habsburgs are housed in bronze caskets; the north tower or Eagle Tower, which can be ascended by lift (daily: April, June, Sept & Oct 9am–6pm; July & Aug 9am–6.30pm; Nov–March 8.30am–5pm; €2.90) for a look at the *Pummerin*, or great bell; and the 137-metre-high *Steffl* (daily 9am–5.30pm; €2.20), a blind scramble up intestinal stairways, which has better views. Finally, the seventeenth-century Archbishop's Palace, on the north side of the cathedal at Stephansplatz 6, contains the **Dom-** and **Diözesanmuseum** (Tues–Sat 10am–5pm; €5.10), in which the church silver is outshone by a collection of marvellous fifteenth-century devotional paintings.

East of Stephansplatz

The warren of alleyways to the north and east of the cathedral preserves something of the medieval character of the city, although the architecture reflects centuries of continuous rebuilding. The medieval house on Raubensteingasse 8 where **Mozart** died while at work on his **Requiem** has long since disappeared, but is commemorated by a small memorial on the ground floor of the *Steffl* department store that now occupies the site. The only one of the composer's residences to survive is the so-called **Figarohaus**, immediately east of the cathedral at Domgasse 5 (Tues–Sun 9am–6pm; €1.80), though there's little to see inside. A much more intriguing find is the **Treasury of the Order of Teutonic Knights** (Schatzkammer des Deutschen Ordens), around the corner at Singerstrasse 7 (May–Oct Mon, Thurs & Sun 10am–noon, Wed 3–5pm, Fri & Sat 10am–noon & 3–5pm; Nov–April closed Fri am & Sun; €3.60), where you can view ceremonial regalia and domestic trinkets assembled by seven centuries of Grand Masters.

To the north of Stephansdom, one of the prettiest little squares in Vienna, **Judenplatz**, is now totally dominated by a bleak concrete mausoleum designed by British sculptor Rachel Whiteread as a **Holocaust Memorial**, and unveiled in 2000. Judenplatz was originally the site of the city's medieval Jewish ghetto, and you can view the foundations of an old synagogue, plus an interactive multimedia exhibition and short video on medieval Jewish life, at the **Museum Judenplatz** (Mon–Thurs & Sun 10am–6pm, Fri 10am–2pm; €3), whose entrance is at no. 8.

Further eastward, the seventeenth-century **Jesuitenkirche** (also known as the Universitätskirche), on Dr.-Ignaz-Seipel-Platz, is by far the most awesome High Baroque church in Vienna. Inside, the most striking features are the red and green barley-sugar spiral columns, the exquisitely carved pews and the clever trompe l'oeil dome. Further in this direction is the early modernist **Postsparkasse** (Postal Savings Bank) on Georg-Coch-Platz (Mon–Wed & Fri 8am–3pm, Thurs 8am–5.30pm; free), completed in 1912 by the doyen of Vienna's turn-of-the-twentieth-century architects, Otto Wagner.

Not far away, on the other side of Stubenring is perhaps Vienna's most enjoyable museum, known simply as the **MAK** (Tues 10am–midnight, Wed–Sun 10am–6pm; €6.50; *www.mak.at*). The highlights of its superlative, highly eclectic collection, stretching from the Romanesque period to the twentieth century, are Klimt's *Stoclet Frieze* and the unrivalled collection of Wiener Werkstätte products. But what really sets it apart is the museum's provocative early 1990s makeover, which gave some of Austria's leading designers free rein to create a unique series of rooms, each one individually designed.

Kärntnerstrasse, Graben and Kohlmarkt

From Stephansplatz, **Kärntnerstrasse** leads off southwest, a continuous pedestrianized ribbon lined with street entertainers and elegant shops that ends at the city's illustrious **Staatsoper** (*www.wiener-staatsoper.at*), opened in 1869 as the first phase of the development of the Ringstrasse. You can visit the opera house on a guided tour (€4.40), but a more unusual tribute to the city's musical genius can be found down Annagasse at the new **Haus der Musik** (daily 10am–10pm; *www.haus-der-musik-wien.at*; €8), a hugely enjoyable, state-of-the-art exhibition on the nature of sound, filled with high-tech installations.

Halfway along Kärntnerstrasse and one block to the west lies **Neuer Markt**, centred on the writhing figures of the Donnerbrunnen, a copy of an eighteenth-century fountain in which animated nudes symbolize four of the rivers feeding into the Danube. At the southwest exit of the square, the Kapuzinerkirche houses the **Kaisergruft** (daily 9.30am–4pm; €2.90), where Habsburg family members were interred from 1633. Maria Theresia reputedly came here on the eighteenth of every month to commune with the remains of her late husband Franz Stephan, and was eventually placed beside him in a riotously ornamented sarcophagus of stunning proportions – a stark contrast to the humble, unadorned coffin of her enlightened successor, Josef II.

The prime shopping streets of **Graben** and **Kohlmarkt**, which lead northwest off Stephansplatz, retain an air of exclusivity that Kärntnerstrasse has lost. Just off Graben, at Dorotheergasse 11, is the city's intriguing **Jüdisches Museum** (daily except Sat 10am–6pm, Thurs 10am–9pm; €5; *www.jmw.at*). On the whole, the curators have rejected the usual static display cabinets and newsreel photos of past atrocities. Instead, the emphasis of the museum's excellent temporary exhibitions on the first floor is on contemporary Jewish life, while on the second floor, visitors are confronted with a series of free-standing glass panels imprinted with holograms, ghostly images of the city's once vast Jewish population.

At the far end of Kohlmarkt is Michaelerplatz, site of the **Looshaus**. Built as a department store in 1911 by pioneering modernist Adolf Loos, it marked a total break with the Jugendstil (literally "youth style") confections of Otto Wagner. Its initial unpopularity was largely due to the fact that it was constructed directly opposite the statue-laden nineteenth-century Michaelertor, entrance to the Habsburgs' city residence, the Hofburg.

The Hofburg

The **Hofburg** (Court Palace) is a real hotchpotch of a place, with no natural centre, no symmetry and no obvious main entrance. Apart from being the seat of the Austrian president (*www.hofburg.at*), it now contains a range of museums with imperial connections, beginning with the rather dull parade of **Kaiserappartements** (daily 9am–4.30pm; €5.80) on the north side of the main courtyard. To the southeast is the brightly painted entrance to the Schweizerhof, a smaller courtyard where you'll find the much more impressive **Schatzkammer** or Imperial Treasury (daily except Tues 10am–6pm; €7.30), which holds some of the finest medieval craftsmanship and jewellery in Europe, including the imperial regalia and relics of the Holy Roman Empire, not to mention the Habsburgs' own crown jewels. Steps beside the Schatzkammer lead up to the **Burgkapelle** (guided tours Jan–June & mid-Sept to Dec Mon–Thurs 11am–3pm, Fri 11am–1pm; €1.10), primarily known as the venue for Mass in the company of the *Wiener Sängerknaben* (*www.wsk.at*) or **Vienna Boys' Choir** (mid-Sept to June Sun 9.15am), for which you can obtain free standing-room only tickets from 8.30am.

Another monument to the Habsburgs' hoarding instincts is the ornate Baroque **Prunksaal** (mid-May to Oct Mon–Wed, Fri & Sat 10am–4pm, Thurs 10am–7pm, Sun 10am–1pm; Nov to mid-May Mon–Sat 10am–2pm; closed for the first three weeks of Sept; €4.40; *www.onb.ac.at*), overlooking Josefsplatz, worth a glimpse for its frescoes, globes and gold-bound volumes. On the other side of Josefsplatz, a door leads to the Stallburg imperial stables, home to the performing white horses of the **Spanish Riding School** (Spanische Reitschule; *www.spanische-reitschule.com*). Tickets for performances (March–June & Sept–Dec) are expensive (standing room: €14.50; seats: €22–65) and difficult to obtain; **check the Web site** and then email *tickets@srs.at* if you're serious. Training sessions are open to the public (Tues–Sat 10am–noon; €7.30) and tickets are sold at the Josefsplatz entrance box office; the queue for tickets is at its worst early on, but by 11am it's usually easy enough to get in. The cheapest option of all is to visit the **Lipizzaner Museum** (daily 9am–5pm; €5.10; combined ticket with a training session €10.20; *www.lipizzaner.at*), which is housed in part of the *Stallburg* (stables). Josefsplatz also contains a **Dalí-Ausstellung** (daily 10am–6pm; €6.50), a paltry exhibition of works by the Catalan surrealist.

South of Josefsplatz, down Augustinerstrasse, lies the **Albertina** (*www.albertina.at*), home to one of the largest collections of **graphic arts** in the world, with works by the likes of Raphael, Rembrandt, Dürer, Leonardo, Michelangelo, Rubens, Bosch, Picasso, Klimt, Schiele and Kokoschka. The Albertina is due to open once more in 2002, with newly expanded exhibition halls, an international study centre, a winter garden, and a restaurant on the terrace, and whatever the exhibition, it'll be worth a look.

To the west of the Hofburg is Heldenplatz, an enormous open space partially enclosed by the great curve of the palace's **Neue Burg**, a bombastic neo-Renaissance edifice completed only in 1913. Steps lead up to a series of **museums** (daily except Tues 10am–6pm; €4.40), all of which are covered by one ticket. The exhibits include musical instruments, arms and armour, and finds of Austrian archeologists from Ephesus in Asia Minor. A separate entrance leads to the **Museum für Volkerkünde** (daily except Tues: Jan–March 10am–6pm; April–Dec 10am–4pm; €4.40), which features the collections of Captain Cook, Aztec treasures and other ethnographical exhibits.

The Kunsthistorisches and the MuseumsQuartier

Across the Ring from Heldenplatz, Maria-Theresien-Platz is framed by two pompous neo-Renaissance museums designed to accommodate the vast imperial collections. On the right is the **Naturhistorisches Museum** (daily except Tues 9am–6pm, Wed until 9pm; €2.20; *www.nhm.at*), which has changed little since it was opened by Franz-Josef over a hundred years ago. Basically a depository for rocks and stuffed fauna, it also boasts seventh-century-BC Celtic grave finds from the Salzkammergut village of Hallstatt, plus a copy of the *Venus of Willendorf*, a small stone figure carved by Paleolithic inhabitants of the Danube valley 25,000 years ago.

On the left is one of the richest fine arts museums in the world, the **Kunsthistorisches Museum** (Tues–Sun 10am–6pm; €7.30; *www.khm.at*). Its ground floor is largely given over to decorative arts and the ancient world, with impressive Egyptian, Greek and Roman collections, while the fine arts section (also open Thurs till 9pm) upstairs is a good place to gain a perspective on the German Renaissance – the Gothic-infused canvases of Danubian painters like Altdorfer and the two Cranachs providing a link between the medieval world and the perfection of Dürer. Rubens, Caravaggio and Velázquez are well represented, along with two fine Rembrandt self-portraits and a portrait of the artist's mother. However, it's the unparalleled collection of Pieter Bruegel the Elder that attracts most visitors, pictures such as *The Meeting of Lent and Carnival* and the famous winter scenery of the *Return of the Hunters* portraying the seasons and peasant festivities of the sixteenth-century Netherlands (then Habsburg dominions).

If you stand between the two big museums with your back to the Hofburg, you will find yourself confronted with Vienna's new **MuseumsQuartier** (*www.mqw.at*), which was due to open as this book went to print. Housed in the former imperial stables, the MuseumsQuartier hopes to do for Vienna what the Tate Modern has done for London. It is the new home of, among other things, the city's chief permanent collection of modern art, and the Leopold Museum (*www.leopoldmuseum.org*), containing the world's biggest collection of works by Egon Schiele. To service the needs of the MuseumsQuartier's visitors, numerous restaurants and bars will stay open until the early hours.

Rathausplatz and around

By now you will have crossed the **Ringstrasse**, built to fill the gap created when the last of the city's fortifications were demolished in 1857 and subsequently lined with monumental civic buildings – "Ringstrasse Historicism" became a byword for the bombastic taste of the late Habsburg bourgeoisie. The broad sweep of the Ring wasn't just a symbol of imperial and municipal prestige: it was designed to facilitate the mobility of cannons in the event of any rebellious incursions from the proletarian districts beyond.

Rathausplatz, to the northwest of the Hofburg, is the Ringstrasse's showpiece square, framed by no fewer than four monumental public buildings – the Rathaus, the Burgtheater, Parliament and the University – all completed in the 1880s. The most imposing building of the four is the cathedralesque **Rathaus**, parts of which are accessible on guided tours (Mon, Wed & Fri 1pm; free). Directly opposite the Rathaus stands the **Burgtheater** (*www.burgtheater.at*), flanked by two grandiose staircases decorated with frescoes by, among others, Gustav Klimt (guided tours Tues, Thurs & Fri 9am & 3pm, Sat 3pm, Sun 11am & 3pm; €3.60). The **Parlament** (*www.parlament.gv.at*) is an imposing pastiche of Greco-Roman styles fronted by a monumental statue of Pallas Athene (guided tours mid-Sept to June Mon–Thurs 11am and 3pm, Fri 11am, 1, 2 & 3pm; July to mid-Sept Mon–Fri 9, 10 & 11am and 1, 2 & 3pm; free).

Not far north of Rathausplatz is the former home of Sigmund Freud, who moved to the second floor of Berggasse 19, six blocks north of the Ring, in 1891 and stayed here until June 4, 1938, when he and his family fled to London. His apartment, now the **Freud Museum** (daily: July–Sept 9am–6pm; Oct–June 9am–5pm; €5.10; *www.freud-museum.at*; tram #D to Schlickgasse), is a place of pilgrimage, even though Freud took almost all his possessions with him into exile. His hat, coat and walking stick are still here, however, and there's home-movie footage from the 1930s, but the only room with any original decor is the waiting room.

Karlsplatz

Karlsplatz should be one of Vienna's showpiece squares. Instead, the western half is little more than a vast traffic interchange, with pedestrians relegated to a set of seedy subways that give access to the U-Bahn and stretch north as far as the Staatsoper. Immediately above the subway are Otto Wagner's elegant Jugendstil **Station Karlsplatz** pavilions, now used as a café (daily 10am–7pm) and exhibition space (April–Oct Tues–Sun 1–4.30pm; €1.80). Rising majestically above everything around it, the **Karlskirche** (Mon–Sat 9–11.30am & 1–5pm, Sun 1–5pm; €2.90), designed by Fischer von Erlach, is, without doubt, the city's finest Baroque church. A huge Italianate dome with a Neoclassical portico, flanked by two giant pillars modelled on Trajan's Column, it's an eclectic and rather self-conscious mixture of styles, built to impress. The modernist **Historisches Museum der Stadt Wien** (Tues–Sun 9am–6pm; €3.60) next door includes three floors of medieval sculpture and painting, arms and armour recalling the city's struggles against the Turks, a reconstruction of Adolf Loos's ascetic living quarters, several works by Klimt and Schiele, and a model of the city as it was before the Ring was built.

Over on the west side of Karlsplatz, stands the **Secession** (*www.secession.at*) building, completed in 1898 as the headquarters of Vienna's Art Nouveau movement. Led by Gustav Klimt, this younger generation rebelled against academic historicism in favour of something more modern, although the Jugendstil they initiated was in many ways equally nostalgic. The building itself is a case in point, though the "gilded cabbage" that crowns it is in a league of its own. One of Klimt's most characteristic works, the **Beethoven Frieze**, created for an exhibition of 1902, remains on permanent display in the basement, while the rest of the building is used for contemporary exhibitions (Tues–Sun 10am–6pm, Thurs until 8pm; €4.40). Immediately behind the Secession, on Schillerplatz, is the **Akademie der bildenden Künste** (Tues–Sun 10am–4pm; €3.60; *www.akbild.ac.at*), which has an often overlooked collection, strong on Flemish works, including Bosch's triptych, *The Last Judgement*.

South of the Ring

Immediately south of the Ring, beyond the Soviet war memorial and fountain on Schwarzenbergplatz (one stop on tram #71 or walk up Rennweg) lies the **Belvedere** (*www.belvedere.at*), the finest palace complex in the whole of Vienna, at least from the outside. Two magnificent Baroque mansions, designed by Lukas von Hildebrandt for Prince Eugene of Savoy, face each other across a sloping formal garden, commanding a superb view over central Vienna. Today, the loftier of the two palaces, the **Oberes Belvedere** (Tues–Sun 10am–6pm; €8.70), houses one of the most popular art galleries in Vienna, with an unrivalled collection of paintings by Gustav Klimt, plus a few choice works by Egon Schiele and Oskar Kokoschka. The same ticket lets you into the **Unteres Belvedere**, which preserves more of its original, lavish decor than the Oberes Belvedere, and for that reason alone it's worth exploring the **Barock-Museum** now installed in its rooms.

Beyond the Belvedere, the area around the Südbahnhof has a distinctly Balkan feel, with scattered ethnic bars and restaurants providing a meeting place for emigrants from the former Yugoslavia and Turkey. Heading southeast from the Südbahnhof through the Schweizer Garten brings you to the city's former **Arsenal**, a huge complex of barracks and munitions factories, that also houses the **Heeresgeschichtliches Museum** (daily except Fri 9am–5pm; €5.10; *www.bmlv.gv.at/hgm*), built in 1856 to glorify the imperial army. One of the highlights is the Gräf & Stift open-top car in which Archduke Ferdinand and his wife Sophie Chotek were assassinated in Sarajevo in June 1914; his bloodstained uniform lies nearby.

Ten minutes' walk from here (or tram #71 from Schwarzenbergplatz) is the **St Marxer Friedhof**, on Leberstrasse (daily 7am–dusk), Vienna's principal cemetery from 1784 to 1874. Planted with a rather lovely selection of trees, the cemetery today gives little indication of the bleak and forbidding place it must have been when, on a rainy night in December 1791, **Mozart** was given a pauper's burial, in an unmarked mass grave with no one present but the grave-diggers. A memorial marking the area in which the composer was interred – a broken column accompanied by a cherub – was first raised in 1859. The original, however, now stands in Vienna's greatest necropolis, the **Zentralfriedhof** (Central Cemetery) on Simmeringer Hauptstrasse, further down the #71 tram line (daily: March, April, Sept & Oct 7am–6pm; May–Aug 7am–7pm; Nov–Feb 8am–5pm), in which graves of eminent Viennese are grouped by profession. The musicians, principally Mozart, Beethoven, Schubert, Brahms and the Strauss family, lie a short way beyond Gate 2, to the left of the central avenue.

East of the Ring

One of Vienna's most popular tourist attractions, the brightly-coloured kitsch **Hundertwasserhaus** (tram #N to Hetzgasse from Schwedenplatz U-Bahn), lies in the unassuming residential area of Landstrasse, east of the Ring. Following his philosophy that "the straight line is godless", the Austrian artist Friedensreich Hundertwasser (1928–2000) transformed some dour council housing on the corner of Löwengasse and Kegelgasse into a higgledy-piggledy, childlike ensemble that caught the popular imagination. Understandably, the residents were none too happy when hordes of pilgrims began ringing on their doorbells, asking to be shown round, so Hundertwasser obliged with a shopping arcade opposite, called **Kalke Village**, the most disconcerting aspect of which is his penchant for uneven floors. There's another of Hundertwasser's Gaudi-esque conversions, **KunstHausWien** (daily 10am–7pm; €6.90, Mon half-price; *www.kunsthauswien.com*), three blocks north up Untere Weissgerberstrasse, featuring a gallery devoted to Hundertwasser's own paintings and inventions, and temporary exhibitions by other headline-grabbing contemporary artists.

On the other side of the Danube canal, which runs east of the centre, is **Leopoldstadt**, home to a thriving Jewish community until the Nazi Holocaust. The district's main attraction is the **Prater** (U-Bahn Praterstern), a large expanse of parkland that stretches for miles between the Danube canal and the river itself. Formerly the royal hunting grounds, the public were allowed access to the Prater by Josef II, who often walked here himself, quixotically ordering passing members of the public not to salute him. The funfair at the northern end is renowned for the **Riesenrad** (daily: March & April 10am–10pm; May–Sept 9am–midnight; Oct 10am–10pm; Nov to early Jan 10am–6pm; €3.30), the giant Ferris wheel featured in Carol Reed's film *The Third Man*. You can take U1 east from Praterstern to the **Donauinsel**, an island in the middle of the Danube crisscrossed with cycle paths, which becomes the city's most popular bathing area throughout the summer.

Schönbrunn

The biggest attraction in the west of the city is the imperial summer palace of **Schönbrunn** (*www.schoenbrunn.at*), reachable by U4 to Schönbrunn or Hietzing. This was originally a royal hunting lodge until Leopold I commissioned Fischer von Erlach to draw up plans for a palace on the model of residences like Versailles. The plans proved too expensive, however, and what was eventually completed during the reign of Maria Theresia, was, for all its size and elegance, far more modest. To visit the palace rooms or **Prunkräume** (daily: April–Oct 8.30am–5pm; Nov–March until 4.30pm; €6.90–9.10; bookings ☎01/8111 3239), there's a choice of two tours: the "Imperial Tour" (€6.90), which takes in 22 state rooms, and the "Grand Tour" (€9.10), which includes all 40 rooms. For both tours, you're given a hand-held audioguide in English. There are also hour-long guided visits of the "Grand Tour" in English (€10.90). There's little point in opting for the shorter (cheaper) tour, since it misses out the best rooms – such as the Millions Room, a rosewood-panelled room covered from floor to ceiling with wildly irregular Rococo cartouches, each holding a Persian miniature watercolour.

There are coaches and carriages to see in the **Wagenburg** (April–Oct daily 9am–6pm; Nov–March Tues–Sun 10am–4pm; €2) in the right wing, but you'd do better to concentrate on strolling through the **Schlosspark** (daily 6am–dusk; free), with its frolicking fountain statuary, its maze (Irrgarten; daily: April–Sept 9am–5.30pm; Oct 9am–4.30pm) and Gloriette, a hilltop colonnaded monument, now a café (daily 9am–dusk), from which you can enjoy splendid views back towards the city. The park also holds Vienna's Tiergarten or **Zoo** (daily 9am–dusk; €6.90) and **Palmenhaus** (daily: May–Sept 9.30am–6pm; Oct–April 9.30am–5pm; €3.30), a glasshouse full of tropical ferns.

Eating and drinking

More so than anywhere else in Austria, Vienna has a huge variety of places to **eat and drink**, from *Beisln*, the Viennese version of a local pub, to upmarket restaurants, as well as a wide range of cuisines, from Balkan to South American. Vienna is, of course, also home of the *Kaffeehaus*, and has by far the largest selection in the country. While the rest of the world queues up for fast food, the Viennese *Kaffeehaus* implores you to slow down. For the not insignificant price of a coffee (€2.50), you can sit for as long as you like without being asked to move on or buy another drink. In summer a visit to a wine tavern (*Heuriger*), to sample their produce along with traditional fare, is also extremely popular; you'll find *Heurigen* in Vienna's outlying districts such as Grinzing (tram #38) or Stammersdorf (tram #31).

For **food on the move**, the *Wurstelstand* is as big an institution in Vienna as anywhere else in Austria (note that *Wurst* tend to be priced according to weight); look out for *Leberkäse*, a slice of spicy meat sandwiched between two halves of a *Semmel*. There are plenty of lunchtime stand-up snack bars and places selling bite-size open-topped sandwiches, *Brötchen*, in the city centre, one of the most famous being *Trzesniewski*, Dorotheergasse 1, off Graben. *Zum schwarzen Kameel*, Bognergasse 5, has sandwiches and a good delicatessen, while if you want to sit down, the *Naschmarkt* chain of **self-service restaurants** has branches at Schottengasse 1 and Mariahilferstrasse 85. The **Naschmarkt** itself – the city's main fruit and veg market off Karlsplatz – is a great place to assemble a picnic or grab a tasty take-away, and also home to numerous cheap cafés attached to the various stalls. Finally, another budget option are the student **Mensas**, which serve subsidized three-course lunches; ask for the details from the tourist office. You don't actually have to be a student, and some, like the Technical University *Mensa* on Resselgasse, behind Karlsplatz, are even open during the holidays.

Cafés

Aera, 1, Gonzagagasse 11. Relaxing café upstairs serving tasty food; live bands in dimly lit cellar downstairs. Open until 2am. U-Bahn Schwedenplatz.

Alt Wien, 1, Bäckerstrasse 9. Dark, smoky, Bohemian Kaffeehaus atmosphere, open until 2am. Good food if you can find a table. U-Bahn Stephansplatz.

Berg, 9, Berggasse 8. Trendy modern café, with good food and relaxed, mostly gay, clientele. Open until 1am. U-Bahn Schottentor.

Central, 1, Herrengasse 14. Traditional meeting place of Vienna's intelligentsia, and Trotsky's favourite café, this is probably the most ornate of Vienna's cafés. Closes 8pm. U-Bahn Herrengasse.

Demel, 1, Kohlmarkt 14. Vienna's most prestigious and priciest café/patisserie. U-Bahn Herrengasse.

Drechsler, 6, Linke Wienzeile 22. Opens at 4am for the stallholders of the Naschmarkt. A good place for breakfast after the bars and clubs have closed. Closed Sun. U-Bahn Kettenbrückengasse.

Europa, 7, Zollergasse 8. Lively, spacious café that attracts a trendy crowd; food is a tasty mixture of Viennese and Italian. Open until 5am. U-Bahn Neubaugasse.

Hawelka, 1, Dorotheegasse 6. Famed for its smoky, Bohemian atmosphere, this is a popular night-time drinking venue, open until 2am. Closed Tues. U-Bahn Stephansplatz.

Landtmann, 1, Dr.-Karl-Lueger-Ring 4. One of the poshest of the Kaffeehäuser – and a favourite with Freud – with a high quota of politicians and Burgtheater actors. U-Bahn Herrengasse/Schottentor.

Palmenhaus, 1, Burggarten. Stylish modern café set amidst the palms of the greenhouse in the Burggarten behind the Hofburg. Open until 2am. U-Bahn Karlsplatz.

Prückel, 1, Stubenring 24. Great original 1950s decor; opposite the MAK. U-Bahn Stubentor.

Savoy, 6, Linke Wienzeile 36. Wonderfully scruffy, but ornate fin-de-siècle decor, packed with bohemian bargain-hunters during Saturday flea market. Closed Sun. U-Bahn Kettenbrückengasse.

Sperl, 6, Gumpendorferstrasse 11. The *fin-de-siècle* interior is one of the set pieces of the Vienna coffeehouse scene. July & Aug closed Sun. U-Bahn Karlsplatz/Babenbergerstrasse.

Stein, 9, Währingerstrasse 6; *www.café-stein.com*. Big, trendy, designer café, with funky music, online facilities and decent food. Open until 1am. U-Bahn Schottentor.

Restaurants

Beim Czaak, 1, Postgasse 15. Cosy, yet smart Beisl, with lovely dark green wood panelling and low-lighting. Closed Sun. U-Bahn Schwedenplatz.

Figlmüller, 1, Wollzeile 5. So popular they don't need to make much effort, but this is the place in the city centre to eat Wienerschnitzel. U-Bahn Stephansplatz.

Fischer Bräu, 19, Billrothstrasse 17. Very civilized micro-brewery pub near the Gürtel, serving lots of tasty food. Open until 1am. U-Bahn Nussdorferstrasse.

Hunger-Künstler, 6, Gumpendorferstrasse 48. Candle-lit restaurant serving Vorarlberg specialities and plenty of veggie options. Open until 2am. U-Bahn Kettenbrückengasse.

Margherita, 1, Wallnerstrasse 4. Smart, bustling Neapolitan pizza and pasta joint in the inner court of the Palais Esterházy. Closed Sun. U-Bahn Herrengasse.

Osteria Venexiana, 3, Rennweg 11/corner of Marokkanergasse. Genuinely delicious Venetian menu in this small, attractive restaurant, just round the corner from the Unteres Belvedere. Tram #71.

Reinthaler, 1, Gluckgasse 5. Genuine, no nonsense busy Viennese Beisl. No concessions to modern cooking and certainly none to veggies. Closed Sat & Sun. U-Bahn Karlsplatz.

Schnitzelwirt, 7, Neubaugasse 52. Another great place to eat Wienerschnitzel – and cheaper than Figlmüller. Closed Sun. Tram #49.

Schweizerhaus, 2, Strasse des 1 Mai 116. Czech-owned restaurant in the Prater; known for its draught beer and grilled pigs' trotters (Steltzen). March–Oct only. U-Bahn Praterstern.

Siebenstern Bräu, 7, Siebensterngasse 19. Popular modern Bierkeller, which brews its own beer and serves solid Viennese food. U-Bahn Volkstheater/Neubaugasse.

Spatzennest, 7, Ullrichsplatz 1. Traditional, inexpensive food, beer and ambience, near the Spittelberg area. Closed Fri & Sat. Bus #13A and #48A.

Wrenkh, 1, Bauernmarkt 10. Fashionable vegetarian restaurant just north of Stephansplatz. Closed Sun.

Nightlife

Vienna's late-night **bars** are concentrated in three main areas: the central **Bermuda Triangle** of Rabensteig, Seitenstetten-gasse, Ruprechtsplatz where you're bound to find somewhere that appeals; the **Naschmarkt**, where late-night licences abound, and the **Spittelberg** area, between Burggasse and Siebensterngasse. At clubs, you may have to pay an entrance fee, though it's rarely more than €7.50; for the latest, visit the Web site *www.club.at*. For details of what's on, the local listings magazine, *Falter* (*www.falter.at*), has comprehensive details of the week's cultural programme, and is pretty easy to decipher even if you have scant German. The tourist office also publishes a free monthly *Programm*.

Musikcafés, live venues and clubs

American Bar, 1, Kärntnerstrasse 59. Small, dark late-night bar with a rich interior designed by Adolf Loos. Open until 2am. U-Bahn Stephansplatz.

B72, 8, Stadtbahnbögen 72, Hernalser Gürtel. Dark, designer club underneath the U-Bahn arches – features a mixture of DJs and live indie bands. Open until 4am. U-Bahn Alserstrasse.

Blue Box, 7, Richtergasse 8. *Musikcafé* with resident DJs and a good snack menu. Open until 2am or later. U-Bahn Neubaugasse.

Chelsea, 8, U-Bahnbögen 29–31, Lerchenfelder Gürtel. Favourite venue with up-and-coming Brit guitar bands; situated underneath the U-Bahn. U-Bahn Thaliastrasse.

Flex, Donaukanal; *www.flex.at*. A popular club that also has live bands, as well as the odd art installation. Open until 4am. U-Bahn Schottenring.

Porgy & Bess, 1, Riemergasse 11; *www.porgy.or.at*. A converted porn cinema provides the new home for Vienna's top jazz venue, attracting serious jazz acts from all over the world. U-Bahn Stubentor.

Rhiz, 8, Stadtbahnbögen 37–38, Lerchenfelder Gürtel; *www.rhiz.org*. A modish cross between a bar, a café and a club, with several DJs spinning everything from dance to trance. Open until 4am. U-Bahn Lerchenfelder Strasse.

Rosa-Lila-Villa, 6, Linke Wienzeile 102. Gay and lesbian centre housing a café-restaurant with a nice leafy courtyard. A good place to pick up information about events. Open until 2am. U-Bahn Pilgramgasse.

Shultz, 7, Siebensterngasse. Large, trendy bar with outdoor seating and good cocktails.

Szene Wien, 11, Hauffgasse 26. Live music venue, with a good café run by a radical bunch of rockers from Simmering. U-Bahn Enkplatz.

Tunnel, 8, Florianigasse 39. Large, clean-living student establishment with café upstairs and frequent live bands down in the cellar. Open until 2am. Tram #5.

U4, 12, Schönbrunnerstrasse 222; *www.u4club.com*. Dark, cavernous disco, mostly break beats and house, with frequent gigs; a Mecca of the alternative crowd. Gay and lesbian night. Open until 4am. U-Bahn Meidling-Hauptstrasse.

Volksgarten, 1, Burgring 1; *www.volksgarten.at*. Situated in the park of the same name, Vienna's longest-running club. A firm favourite with the dance crowd. Open until 5am. U-Bahn Volkstheater.

w.u.k., 9, Währingerstrasse 59; *www.wuk.at*. Old school now an arts venue run by a sprinkling of anarchists and others. Café, live music and much more. Open until 2am. Tram #40, #41 or #42.

Opera, ballet and classical music

You can catch high-class international **opera** and **ballet** at the Staatsoper, 1, Opernring 2 (*www.wiener-staatsoper.at*), and opera and operetta at the Volksoper, 9, Währingerstrasse 78 (*www.volksoper.at*). There's a huge number of **classical music** venues, of which the principal ones are the Musikverein, 1, Karlsplatz 6 (*www.musikverein-wien.at*), home of the Vienna Philharmonic, and the Konzerthaus, 3, Lothringerstrasse 20 (*www.konzerthaus.at*). Bookings can be made for the above venues at Bundestheaterkassen, 1, Hanuschgasse 3 (☎01/51444 2960; *www.oebthv.gv.at*) though you can get cheap standing-room tickets (*Stehplätze*) at the venues by queuing up an hour before the performance.

Listings

Airlines Austrian Airlines, 1, Kärntner Ring 18 (☎517 66); British Airways, 1, Kärntner Ring 10 (☎505 7691).

Bike rental The cheapest place to rent bicycles is at one of the mainline stations: Westbahnhof, Südbahnhof and Wien-Nord. The charges are reduced on production of a valid train ticket.

Books and newspapers Shakespeare & Co, 1, Sterngasse 2, for English-language books; Morawa, 1, Wollzeile 11, for international newspapers and magazines.

Car rental Avis, 1, Opernring 5 (U-Bahn Karlsplatz); Europcar, 3, Erdbergstrasse 202 (U-Bahn Erdbergstrasse); Hertz, 1, Kärntner Ring 17 (U-Bahn Karlsplatz).

Cinema Full listings appear in *Falter*. "OF" or "OmU" after the title means that the film is not dubbed; "Omengu" means it's got English subtitles. Burg, 1, Opernring 19, and English Cinema Haydn, 6, Mariahilferstrasse 57, both have regular showings of original-language films. The Burgkino has a weekly showing of *The Third Man*.

Embassies Australia, 4, Mattiellistrasse 2–4 (☎512 85 80); Canada, 1. Laurenzerberg 2 (☎531 38 30); Ireland, 3, Hilton Centre, Landstrasse Hauptstrasse 2 (☎715 42 46); UK, 3, Jauresgasse 12 (☎71 61 30); USA, 9, Boltzmanngasse 16 (☎313 39).

Exchange Outside banking hours, try the offices at the Westbahnhof (daily 7am–10pm), or the Südbahnhof (daily 6.30am–9pm) train stations.

Hospital Allgemeines Krankenhaus, 9, Währinger Gürtel 18–20; U-Bahn Michelbeuern-AKH.

Internet Free Internet access at Amadeus, fourth floor of Steffl department store, 1, Kärntnerstrasse 19 and in the basement of their flagship store at Mariahilferstrasse 99; *www.amadeusbuch.co.at*.

Laundry 8, Josefstädter Strasse 59; tram #J. Mon–Fri 7.30am–7.30pm.

Post office and telephones at 1, Fleischmarkt 19 (24hr).

Travel agent ÖKISTA, 9, Türkenstrasse 8, is best for discount flights and train tickets.

THE DANUBE VALLEY

Heading west from Vienna, there are two alternative routes for onward travel: to Salzburg, around three hours away, and then on to Munich or Innsbruck; or a more leisurely route following the Danube through the **Wachau**, a tortuously winding stretch of water where vine-bearing, ruin-encrusted hills roll down to the river from the north. Wachau is an Austria decidedly different from either cosmopolitan Vienna or the Alpine southwest, and accommodation here is generally cheaper than in either place. At the eastern entrance to the region, within easy reach of Vienna by train, is the historic town of **Krems**, with its older, medieval suburb of Stein; further on lies **Melk**, with its superb Benedictine monastery overlooking the river. Transport to Salzburg from Melk is pretty straightforward, although the industrialized, but culturally vibrant, northern city of **Linz** has enough of interest to make a further stopoff worthwhile. Note that trains to Krems leave from Vienna's Franz-Josefs-Bahnhof (FJB), while Melk is reached on the main line from Westbahnhof.

The most stylish way to travel is by **boat**. The DDSG line (*www.ddsg-blue-danube.at*) operates weekend services between Vienna, Linz and Passau during the summer and year-round services (four daily in summer) between Krems and Melk, the most scenic stretch. The journey takes about three hours upstream, two in the opposite direction, and costs about €18 each way; making your way along the river by shorter hops will work out more expensive, although Eurail holders can travel free and those with an InterRail get a fifty percent reduction.

Krems

KREMS, which clings to the hilly north bank of the Danube, is actually made up of three previously separate settlements: Krems, Und and Stein. Krems' main thoroughfare, **Landstrasse**, three blocks north of the train station, is a busy, pedestrianized shopping street studded with old buildings, including a sixteenth-century **Rathaus**. To the north, a series of small squares preserves the late medieval character of this provincial wine-growing town. One of these, Pfarrplatz, is dominated by the **Pfarrkirche**, with an interior rich in High Baroque furnishings. A covered stairway behind it leads up to the imposing Gothic **Piaristenkirche**, with several altarpieces by Baroque artist Johann Martin Schmidt, who is also celebrated in the town's **Wienstadt Museum** in Körnermarkt, west of Pfarrplatz (March–Nov Tues 9am–6pm, Wed–Sun 1–6pm; €2.90), atmospherically located in a dour thirteenth-century Dominican church. Born in nearby Grafenwörth in 1718, Schmidt trained under local artisans and set up his own workshop in Krems, eschewing the cosmopolitan art scene of the capital, and it's this attachment to provincial roots that sets his work apart from the more academic painters of the Austrian Baroque.

At the western end of Landstrasse, the **Steiner Tor**, a monstrously belfried fifteenth-century town gate, confusingly marks the end of Krems' old town, while Kremsor Tor (a ten-minute walk along Kasernstrasse) signals the beginning of **Stein** – a sequence of Renaissance town houses and crumbling old facades, opening out every hundred metres or so into small cobbled squares. Just before you pass under Stein's Kremsor Tor, check out the **Kunst-Halle-Krems** (daily 10am–6pm; entrance fee varies; *www.kunsthalle.at*), the town's arts venue, which hosts major modern art exhibitions, both here and in the impressive shell of the thirteenth-century **Minoritenkirche**, halfway along Steinerlandstrasse. Further along, steps climb up to the fourteenth-century **Frauenbergkirche**, now a chapel commemorating Austrian war dead. Traces of faded medieval frescoes can still be made out on the walls.

Practicalities

The local **tourist office** is situated in the former Und monastery, halfway between Krems and Stein at Undstrasse 6 (May–Oct Mon–Fri 9am–6pm, Sat 10am–noon & 1–6pm, Sun 10am–2pm; Nov–April Mon–Fri 8.30am–noon & 1.30–5pm; ☎02732/85620, *www.tiscover.com/krems*). If you're planning on staying in town, there's a **HI hostel**, Ringstrasse 77 (☎02732/83452, *oejhv-noe@oejhv.or.at;* April–Oct; ②), while the nearest **campsite** (☎02732/84455; April–Oct) is just a few minutes' walk south of town over the railway lines by the river bank. Both *Gästehaus Einzinger*, Steiner Landstrasse 82 (☎02732/823 16; ④), in Stein, and *Hotel Alte Post*, Obere Landstrasse 32 (☎02732/822 76; ⑤), in Krems, have doubles overlooking arcaded courtyards. Without doubt, one of the best places to **eat** is at *Jell*, Hoher Markt 8–9 (closed Sat & Sun lunch & Mon), a seriously *gemütlich* rustic place; the stylish, minimalist, sushi *Soho*, Obere Landstrasse 36, makes for a pleasant change from Austrian cuisine.

Dürnstein and Melk

The tiny, walled town of **DÜRNSTEIN**, 9km upstream from Krems, is probably the most photographed spot in the Wachau, thanks to the beautiful ice-blue and white Baroque tower that overlooks the river. Its one other great claim to fame is that the English king Richard the Lionheart was imprisoned in the castle above the town in the winter of 1192–93, after being kidnapped by Duke Leopold V of Austria, and escaped thanks to the perseverance of his minstrel, Blondel.

For real High Baroque excess, head for the Benedictine monastery at **MELK** – a pilgrimage centre associated with the Irish missionary Saint Coloman – designed by the local architect Jakob Prandtauer in the first half of the eighteenth century. The monumental coffee-cake monastery, perched on a bluff over the river, dominates the town. Highlights of the interior (mid-April to mid-Nov daily 9am–6pm; mid-Nov to mid-April guided tours only 11am & 2pm; €7.30; €2.20 extra with a guided tour; *www.stiftmelk.at*) are the exquisite library, with a cherub-infested ceiling by Troger, and the monastery church, with similarly impressive work by Rottmayr.

Melk's **river station** is situated about ten minutes' walk north of town. The **train station** is to be found at the head of Bahnhofstrasse, which leads directly into the old town. The **tourist office**, on Abbe-Stadler-Gasse (April–Oct Mon–Sat 9am–7pm, Sun 10am–2pm; Nov–March Mon–Fri 9am–noon & 1–4pm; ☎02752/52307, *www.tiscover.com/melk*), has a substantial stock of **private rooms**, though most are out of the centre. Melk's **HI hostel** is just ten minutes' walk east of the tourist office, at Abt Karl Strasse 42 (☎02752/52681, *oejhw-wien-noe@telecom.at*; March–Oct; ②). A similar distance in the opposite direction is the town's **campsite**, *Melker Camping* (☎02752/53291; March–Nov), adjacent to the Schiffsstation on the Danube.

Linz and Around

Away from its heavy industrial suburbs, the Upper Austrian capital of **LINZ** (*www.linz.at*) is a pleasant Baroque city straddling the Danube. However, the city's greatest claim to fame is as the childhood home of Adolf Hitler, something about which the local tourist board is understandably coy. Inspired by nostalgic memories of schooldays spent here, Hitler spent his last days in his Berlin bunker poring over a model of the city planning its lavish reconstruction.

The City
A tour of the city should perhaps start at the rectangular expanse of the **Hauptplatz** or main square, with its tall, pastel-coloured facades, and central Trinity Column, crowned by a gilded sunburst. The pea-green **Alter Dom** (daily 7am–noon & 3–7pm) to the southeast of the square is an unusually stern piece of seventeenth-century architecture. In the **Pfarrkirche** round the corner to the north, a gargantuan marble slab contains Emperor Friedrich III's heart (the rest of him is in Vienna's Stephansdom). To the west of Hauptplatz lies a pedestrianized quarter rich in Baroque houses leading up to the fifteenth-century **Schloss**, Tummelplatz 10 (Tues–Fri 9am–5pm, Sat & Sun 10am–4pm; €3.70), two blocks west of Hauptplatz, the former residence of Emperor Friedrich III, who made Linz the imperial capital for four years from 1489. Inside, there's little to see save for a good view across the Danube. The castle's museum is particularly strong on medieval weaponry, musical instruments and folk art – it also contains a large but uneven art collection with a smattering of works by Klimt, Schiele and Kokoschka plus a wonderful room of exquisite *fin-de-siècle* glassware and accessories.

The streets east of Hauptplatz contain a few more museums: the **Stadtmuseum Nordico**, Bethlehemstrasse 7 (Mon–Fri 9am–6pm, Sat & Sun 2–5pm; €3.70; *www.nordicomag.linz.at*), which hosts modern art exhibitions and contains a model of the town from 1740; and the **Landesmuseum**, Museumstrasse 14 (Mon, Tues & Thur 9am–noon & 2–5pm, Wed & Fri 9am–noon; €3.70), which likewise plays host to temporary shows – usually prestigious selections from Austrian art history as well as natural history exhibitions.

However, you're better off strolling across to the suburb of **Urfahr**, on the north bank of the river, where you'll find Linz's most recent attraction, the **Ars Electronica Center**, Hauptstrasse 2 (Wed–Sun 10am–6pm; €5.80; *www.aec.at*), a museum dedicated to new technology, immediately on your right after you've crossed the bridge. Even if you're barely computer-literate, this place is fun, and though most of the instructions are in German, the helpful staff speak English. You can play around with various pieces of state-of-the-art computer equipment, but the highlight is a visit to the "CAVE", a virtual reality room with 3D projections on three walls and the floor – you need to get here early to book a ticket for this (no extra charge).

Also in Urfahr, on the first floor of the supremely unattractive Lentia 2000 shopping centre on Blütenstrasse, is the **Neue Galerie** (daily 10am–6pm, Thur until 10pm; €4.40; *www.neuegalerie.linz.at*), which has a small, permanent collection of modern art, including a few works by Klimt, Kokoschka, Schiele and their lesser-known contemporaries. The only other reason to visit Urfahr is to take a ride on the **Pöstlingbergbahn**, a narrow-gauge railway which climbs to the eighteenth-century pilgrimage church of Pöstlingberg – a good vantage point for sweeping views of the valley; trains leave from a twee station at the end of the #3 tram line every twenty minutes (Mon–Sat 6am–8pm, Sun 7.15am–7pm; €3.20).

Practicalities

Linz's **train station** is 2km south of the centre, on the other side of the city's main artery, Landstrasse, and connected with the central Hauptplatz by tram #3. To get into the centre, you can buy a single tram ticket (Midi; €1.50), or a day ticket (Maxi; €2.90). There's a **tourist office** in the Altes Rathaus on Hauptplatz (May–Oct Mon–Fri 8am–7pm, Sat 9am–7pm, Sun 10am–7pm; Nov–April Mon–Fri 8am–6pm, Sat 9am–6pm, Sun 10am–6pm; ☎0732/7070 2939). Affordable central **accommodation** is thin on the ground, the only feasible options the *Wilder Mann*, ten minutes' walk from the station off Landstrasse at Goethestrasse 14 (☎0732/65 60 78; ③), whose rooms come with ensuite showers but shared hallway WCs; the similarly equipped *Goldenes Dachl*, Hafnerstrasse 27 (☎0732/77 58 97; ④), one block south of the neo-Gothic city cathedral, west of Landstrasse; or the *Goldener Anker*, just off the main square at Hofgasse 5 (☎0732/77 10 88), which has some ensuite rooms (⑤) and some with shared bathrooms (④). There's a small but pleasant **hostel** ten minutes west of Hauptplatz at Kapuzinerstrasse 14 (☎0732/78 27 20, *zentrale@ooe-jugendherbergswerk.at*; ②; no curfew; March to mid-Nov), offering simple dorm accommodation; and two bigger **hostels**, both with self-contained double rooms, at Stanglhofweg 3 (☎0732/66 44 34; ②; mid-Jan to mid-Dec; bus #27 from the train station), off Roseggerstrasse near the botanical gardens, and at Blütenstrasse 23 (☎0732/73 70 78; ②) in the Lentia 2000 shopping centre across the river in Urfahr. The city's main **campsite** is 5km southeast of the centre on the Pichlinger See (☎0732/30 53 14; March–Nov), reached by hourly bus or local train from the Hauptbahnhof, but it's too close to the autobahn for comfort. For a more peaceful site (tents only) head to the Pleschinger See (☎0732/24 78 70; May–Sept), 3km northeast of the centre, on the north bank of the Danube; take bus #33 or #33a from Reindlstrasse in Urfahr.

There are plenty of **bars and restaurants** around the Hauptplatz and in the largely pedestrianized streets immediately to the west. *Mangolds*, Hauptplatz 6, is a self-service vegetarian café with cheap but tasty food and a great salad bar; while *Klosterhof*, Landstrasse 30, serves solid Austrian food in the labyrinthine rooms of a former monastery – it also boasts the city's largest beer garden. *Gelbes Krokodil* (closed Sat & Sun lunch), Dametzstrasse 30, is a superb, stylish café inside the city's Moviemento arts cinema, with an excellent selection of Med-influenced food and good wine. *Traxlmayr*, Promenade 16, southwest of

Hauptplatz, a traditional coffee house and local institution, is a good place to treat yourself to a slice of *Linzer Torte*, the local chocolate cake, washed down with excellent coffee. *Alte Welt*, Hauptplatz 4 (closed Sun), is a trendy **wine bar** that features regular live jazz, folk- and world-music bands; alternatively try one of the *Weinkellers* along the river front in Urfahr, all good places to sample the white wines of the Mühlviertel, the vine-covered hills north of the city. Otherwise, most characterful of the downtown drinking dives is *Café Ex-Blatt*, Waltherstrasse 15, a popular studenty pub decked out with nostalgic posters and adverts. *Posthof*, 2km east of the centre at Posthofgasse 43 (*www.posthof.at*; bus #21 from the train station), organizes regular gigs and **club nights**; while *Cembranikeller*, 500m northwest of the station at Kellergasse 4, organizes regular rave parties – look out for posters advertising both. There's free **Internet access** at Ars Electronica (see p.91) but you have to buy a ticket to the museum first.

Around Linz

Of a couple of worthwhile excursions from Linz, one of the most popular is to the Augustinian **Monastery of St Florian**, 7km southeast and accessible by the occasional bus (#2040 or #2042). Local-born composer Anton Bruckner was a choirboy here in the 1830s, and returned in later life to become the monastery's organist. The complex was rebuilt by Prandtauer, fresh from supervising similar work at Melk. For much of the year access is restricted to the abbey church, in whose crypt Bruckner is buried directly underneath the organ. From April to October you can take a guided tour of the interior (daily 10am, 11am, 1pm, 2pm & 3pm; €4.40); highlights include Prince Eugene's four-poster bed, an over-the-top half-Turkish, half-Rococo confection. There's also an excellent collection of paintings by Albrecht Altdorfer, a prolific early-sixteenth-century master whose work blends the German Gothic and Italian Renaissance styles.

The former granite quarry at **Mauthausen** (daily: Feb, March & Oct to mid-Dec 8am–4pm; April–Sept 8am–6pm; €1.83), 20km east of Linz, was used by the Nazis as a concentration camp from 1938. Personal memorials to loved ones are interspersed throughout the huge granite fortress, along with numerous official national war memorials. Getting there by public transport is not easy: take the train towards Vienna and change at St Valentin. Mauthausen train station is a good 5km from the camp, so your best option is to rent a bike from the station.

SOUTHEAST AUSTRIA

The **southeastern** corner of Austria, despite the subalpine terrain of the central province of Styria and the sun-baked plains of the Burgenland, is bypassed by most visitors. The area contains a wealth of diffuse attractions, though these demand leisurely exploration, and the only obvious focus of concentrated interest is the Styrian provincial capital of **Graz**.

Graz

Austria's second largest city, **GRAZ** (*www.graztourismus.at*) owes its importance to the defence of central Europe against the Turks. From the fifteenth century, Graz was constantly under arms, rendering it far more secure than Vienna. This led to a modest seventeenth-century flowering of the arts; the Baroque style appeared in Graz before its adoption elsewhere in Austria. During the last years of the empire, the city's mild climate made it a popular retirement choice for ageing officers and civil servants, and its reputation as a conservative town swarming with pensioners has proved almost impossible to shake off. Nowadays, however, it is a rich and culturally varied city, with plentiful night-time diversions, partly due to its 42,000-strong student population.

Arrival and accommodation

Graz's **train station** is on the western edge of town, a fifteen-minute walk or short tram ride (#1, #3 #6 or #7) from the central Hauptplatz. There's a **tourist office** at the station (Mon–Fri 9am–6pm, Sat 9am–3pm; ☎0316/80750) and a bigger one a couple of hundred metres from Hauptplatz at Herrengasse 16 (same hours plus Sun 10am–3pm), which can book private rooms from around €18.30 per person, although these are almost all a lengthy bus ride from the centre. More convenient are *Pension Iris*, Bergmanngasse 10 (☎0316/32 20 81; ⑤), north of the Stadtpark; and *Pension Rückert*, Rückertgasse 4 (☎316/32 30 31; tram #1 from the train station to Teggethofplatz; ⑤), in a leafy suburb 2km east of the centre. The town's **HI youth hostel** is four blocks south of the station at Idlhofgasse 74 (☎0316/71 48 76) and offers simple dorms (③) and comfy ensuite doubles (④) – it's justifiably popular so book in advance. *Camping Central* is the only **campsite**, south of the centre at Martinhof-strasse 3 (☎0316/28 13 31, *www.tiscover.com/campingcentral*; bus #32 from Jakominiplatz).

The City

Graz is compact and easy to explore, most sights being within striking distance of **Hauptplatz**, a broad market square in the centre of which is a statue of the Habsburg Archduke Johann, a popular nineteenth-century benefactor. Herrengasse leads off to the south towards the **Landhaus**, a sixteenth-century town hall with Italianate arcading in the courtyard. Next door **Zeughaus**, Herrengasse 16 (March–Oct Tues–Sun 9am–5pm; Nov–Jan Tues–Sun 10am–3pm; €4.40) is an armoury whose galleries bristle with weaponry used to keep the Turks at bay. The main attraction west of Herrengasse is the **Landesmuseum Joanneum** (*www.museum-joanneum.at*), founded by Archduke Johann, a vast collection housed in different locations; entrance to the natural history section (Tues–Sun 9am–4pm; €4.40) is at Raubergasse 10, while the more interesting **Alte Galerie** (Tues–Sun 10am–5pm; €4.40) at Neutorgasse 45, houses a collection rich in Gothic devotional paintings. A fifteenth-century altarpiece by the illustrious Tyrolean Michael Pacher depicts the martyrdom of Thomas à Becket, and, among other Flemish paintings, there's a grippingly macabre *Triumph of Death* by Brueghel.

On the other side of Herrengasse, Stempfergasse leads into a neighbourhood of narrow alleyways that dog-leg their way up the hill towards the **Mausoleum of Ferdinand II** (Mon–Sat: May–Oct 11am–noon & 2–3pm; Nov–April: 11am only; €0.70). It's a fine example of the early Baroque style, begun in 1614 when its intended incumbent was a healthy 36-year-old. Next door is the **Domkirche**, immediately north of which is the **Burg**, an erstwhile imperial residence now given over to local government offices; peer through the archway at the end of the first courtyard to view the unique double spiral of a fifteenth-century Gothic staircase. From here Hofgasse descends to the bustling shopping street of **Sporgasse**, where the Saurau palace at no. 25 features a Turkish figure throwing himself from a small window.

A short way north of Hauptplatz, down Sackstrasse, the **Neue Galerie** (Tues–Sun 10am–6pm; €4.40), housed in the seventeenth-century Herberstein Palace, displays nineteenth- and twentieth-century works including a sprinkling of Klimts and Schieles. From Schlossbergplatz a balustraded stone staircase zigzags up to the **Schlossberg**, a wooded hill overlooking the town; both the Schlossberg lift (daily 8am–9pm; €1.50 one way), and the Schlossbergbahn funicular, a little further along Sackstrasse, make the same trip (every 15min 9am–10pm; €2.20 one way). The Schloss from which its name derives was destroyed by Napoleon in 1809; only two prominent features survive – the sixteenth-century **Uhrturm** or clock tower, whose steep overhanging roof figures prominently in the town's tourist literature, and the more distant **Glockenturm** or bell tower of the same period. Paths descend south from the Schlossberg to the elegant sweep of the **Stadtpark**, a leafy barrier between the city and the residential suburbs beyond.

Some 4km west of the town centre, at the end of tram line #1, are the luxurious state rooms of **Schloss Eggenburg**, Eggenberger Allee 90 (May–Oct: daily 9am–5pm; €5.81), built in 1625 for Hans Ulrich of Eggenburg, Ferdinand II's First Minister. Tickets include a guided tour of the state rooms as well as the Schloss's museums. The archeological collection is strong on prehistory, its most valued exhibit being the Strettweg chariot – a remarkable eighth-century-BC wheeled platform peopled by small, weapon-wielding figures.

Eating, drinking and entertainment

Graz is foremost among Austria's provincial cities in preserving the culture of the *Kaffeehaus*. *Hofcafé Edegger Tax*, Hofgasse 8, is the refuge of the city's more sedate citizens; the modern *Operncafé*, Opernring 22, attracts a youthful crowd and is equally popular in the evening; whilst *Café Promenade*, Erzherzog-Johann-Allee, is an attractive pavilion in the Stadtpark.

For something more substantial than munching a *Wurst* on Hauptplatz or visiting the fishy *Nordsee* outlet on Herrenstrasse, try *Gambrinuskeller*, Farbergasse 6–8 (closed Fri & Sun), which has a wide choice of reasonably priced **food**, including kebabs, stuffed peppers and other Balkan dishes; or *Glockenspielkeller*, Mehlplatz 3, with more standard Austrian fare and pleasant outdoor seating. *Pizzeria Catharina*, Sporgasse 32, has a wide range of inexpensive pizzas and *Zu den 3 goldenen Kugeln*, east of the centre in the University district, on the corner of Goethestrasse and Heinrichstrasse, doles out dirt-cheap Schnitzel-and-chips fare. Many of the best places to **drink** are in the alleys around the Hauptplatz – *MI*, Färberplatz, is a swish designer bar, while the lively *Flann O'Brien's*, Paradiesgasse, is the best of the Irish pubs. It's also worth venturing out to the cafés and bars which cluster in the streets around the university, east of the Stadtpark: *Café Harrach*, Harrachgasse 26, is good and *Bier Baron*, Heinrichstrasse 56, is a student favourite, serving inexpensive food. *Park House*, a pavilion in the Stadtpark, is a late bar with resident DJs. Other **clubbing venues** include the Kulturhauskeller, a studenty dive at Elisabethstrasse 31 (*www.kulturhauskeller.com*); and *Arcadium*, Griesgasse 25 (*www.arcadium.at*), which organizes themed nights with guest DJs. Graz also has a summer classical **music festival**, with various concerts held all over the city from late June to late July (information on ☎0316/825 000, *www.styriarte.com*).

SALZBURG AND THE SALZKAMMERGUT

Salzburg, straddling the border with Germany, is Austria's most heavily touristed city after Vienna – a magnet for those seeking the best of Austria's Baroque heritage and a taste of sub-alpine scenery. The most accessible and popular of these mountain areas is the **Salzkammergut**, a region of glacier-carved lakes and craggy peaks a couple of hours to the east by bus or train.

Salzburg

The Austrian writer Thomas Bernhard, an acerbic critic of the postwar state who spent his formative years in **SALZBURG**, called his home town "a fatal illness", whose Catholicism, conservatism and sheer snobbery drove its citizens to a miserable end. Yet for many visitors Salzburg represents the quintessential Austria, offering the best of the country's Baroque architecture, subalpine air, and a musical heritage largely provided by the city's most famous son, Wolfgang Amadeus Mozart, whose bright-eyed visage peers from every box of the city's ubiquitous chocolate delicacy, the *Mozartkügel*.

Despite this, for much of its history Salzburg either belonged to the Bavarian sphere or was an independent city-state, only becoming part of the Habsburg domain in 1816. In the Middle Ages the city looked west, its powerful archbishops serving a see which extended over much of southern Germany, prosperous on the proceeds of the Salzkammergut salt trade. The city's High Baroque appearance is largely due to the ambition of sixteenth- and seventeenth-century Prince-Archbishops Wolf Dietrich and Paris Lodron, who hired artists and craftsmen from south of the Alps to recast Salzburg on the model of Rome.

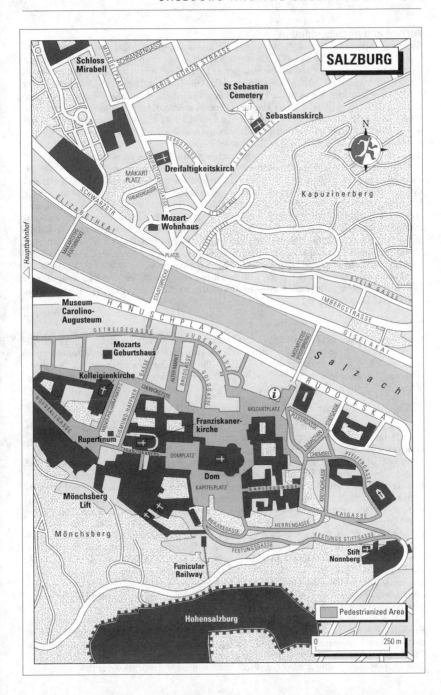

Arrival and accommodation

Salzburg's **airport** is 5km west of town on the Innsbrucker Bundesstrasse and is linked to the city's train station by bus #77. It's over a kilometre into town from the train station, but there are regular buses covering the distance (#1, #2, #5, #6, #51 & #55 all go to Ferdinand-Hanusch-Platz or Rudolfskai on the fringes of the Old Town); a 24-hr pass (*Netzkarte*) costs €3. There's a **tourist kiosk** at the train station (platform 2a; daily: May–Sept 8.30am–9pm, Oct–April 9am–8pm), and a larger **tourist office** is at Mozartplatz 5 in the old town centre (May–Sept daily 9am–8pm; Oct–April Mon–Sat 9am–6pm; ☎0662/889 8133). Both offices sell maps, have accommodation details and book rooms for a €2.60 fee; they also sell the Salzburg card (€16.80 for 24hrs, €23.40 for 48hrs), which gives you unlimited use of public transport and free entry to many of the top sights. Of the **hostels**, most conveniently placed are the *YO-HO International Youth Hotel Obermair*, Paracelsusstrasse 9 (☎0662/87 96 49, *www.yoho.at*; ②), a lively place nicely poised between the train station and main sights; and the HI-affiliated *Haunspergstrasse* hostel, three blocks west of the train station at Haunspergstrasse 27 (☎0662/87 50 30; ②; midnight curfew; July & Aug). As for **hotels**, rooms fill quickly in summer and can be pricey. The *Schwarzes Rössl*, Priesterhausgasse 6 (☎0662/87 44 26, *www.academia-hotels.at*; ③; July–Sept), is a marvellous, creaky old building in a good location; *Bergland*, Rupertgasse 15 (☎0662/87 23 18, *pkuhn@sol.at*; ⑤), is a friendly place on the right bank, 1km northeast of the centre – handy for both sightseeing and the train station. *Goldener Krone*, also on the left bank at Linzergasse 48 (☎0662/87 23 00; ⑤), is an old-fashioned pension-style place with small but comfortable ensuites. *Camping Gnigl*, Parscher Strasse 4, is the most convenient campsite, bus #29 from Mirabellplatz (☎0662/64 30 60; mid-May to mid-Sept).

The City

Salzburg has a compact centre and an easily walkable concentration of sights. The ensemble of archiepiscopal buildings in the centre, on the **west bank** of the river, forms a tight-knit network of alleys and squares, overlooked by the brooding presence of the medieval Hohensalzburg castle. From here it's a short hop over the River Salzach to a narrow ribbon of essential sights on the **east bank**.

THE WEST BANK

From the Staatsbrücke, the main bridge across the River Salzach, **Judengasse** funnels tourists up into **Mozartplatz**, home to a statue of the composer and overlooked by the **Glockenspiel**, a seventeenth-century musical clock whose chimes attract crowds at 7am, 11am and 6pm. The complex of Baroque buildings on the right exudes the ecclesiastical and temporal power wielded by Salzburg's archbishops, whose erstwhile living quarters – the **Residenz** – dominate the west side of the adjacent **Residenzplatz**. You can guide yourself round the lavish state rooms (daily 10am–5pm; €6.60) with the accompanying audio commentary; while one floor above, the **Residenzgalerie** (April–Sept daily 10am–5pm; Oct–March Mon, Tues & Thurs–Sun 10am–5pm; €3.60) offers a fine display of archiepiscopal acquisitions, including works by Rembrandt and Caravaggio, and a fairly comprehensive collection of Flemish works. From here arches lead through to **Domplatz**, dominated by the pale marble facade of the **Dom** – an impressively cavernous Renaissance structure put up by Archbishop Wolf Dietrich in 1628, and decorated with dazzling ceiling frescoes. The cathedral **museum** (mid-May to mid-Oct Mon–Sat 10am–5pm, Sun 1–6pm; €4.40; *www.dommuseum.salzbergkirchen.net*) holds the collection of artworks and curiosities assembled by seventeenth-century Archbishop Guidobaldo Thun.

At the opposite end of the Domplatz an archway leads through to the Gothic **Franziskanerkirche**, a thirteenth-century reconstruction of an eighth-century edifice that houses a fine Baroque altar by Fischer von Erlach around an earlier, Gothic Madonna and Child sculpted by the Tyrolean master Michael Pacher. The altar is enclosed by an arc of nine chapels, adorned in a frenzy of stucco ornamentation. Look, also, for the twelfth-century marble lion which guards the stairway to the pulpit. Around the corner is the **Rupertinum**, Wiener-Philharmonikergasse 9 (mid-July to Sept Mon & Thurs–Sun 10am–5pm, Wed until 9pm; Oct to mid-July Tues & Thurs–Sun 10am–5pm, Wed 10am–9pm; €2.90), a picture gallery devoted to twentieth-century work, particularly Kirchner and other German well-knowns, which hosts worthwhile touring exhibitions; it also has a nice secluded café. Art exhibitions often grace the cavernous interior of Fischer von Erlach's sizeable if graceless **Kollegienkirche** or University Church, on the adjacent Universitätsplatz. Around the back of the church, Hofstallgasse is dominated by the modern **Festspielhaus**, a principal venue for the Salzburg festival. Northeast of here, the **Museum Carolino-Augusteum**, Museumplatz 1 (Tues–Sun: July–Sept 10am–6pm; Oct–June 9am–5pm; €2.90), contains Roman finds from the town centre, including reconstructed mosaics retrieved from beneath Mozartplatz, more Gothic religious art, and a room devoted to moralistic works by the late-nineteenth-century local painter Hans Makart. On the other side of the square from the Carolino-Augusteum, the **Haus der Natur** (daily 9am–5pm; €4) crams in five floors of science and natural history, with exhibits ranging from live piranha fish to space rockets. From here Getreidegasse leads east back towards the centre, lined with opulent boutiques, painted facades and wrought-iron shop signs. At no. 9 is **Mozart's Geburtshaus** or birthplace (daily: July & Aug 9am–7pm; Sept–June 9am–5.30pm; €5). Born in 1756, the musical prodigy spent his first seventeen years in this house. Now a rather overcrowded place of pilgrimage, it harbours some fascinating period instruments, including a baby-sized violin used by the composer as a child.

You can get up to the **Höhensalzburg**, which commands excellent views across town from Mönchberg, by funicular from Kapitelplatz behind the cathedral, although the journey on foot isn't as hard or as time-consuming as it looks. Begun around 1070 to provide the archbishops with a refuge from belligerent German princes, the fortress (daily: July–Sept 8am–7pm; April–June & Oct 9am–6pm; Nov–March 9am–5pm; €3.10) was gradually transformed into a more salubrious courtly seat. State rooms can be visited by guided tour (€3.10), or with a CD audio guide, although a roam around the ramparts and passageways of the castle is enough to gain a feel for the place. Paths lead east from the fortress to another piece of pre-Baroque Salzburg, the **Stift Nonnberg**, whose church is a largely fifteenth-century Gothic rebuilding of an earlier Romanesque structure.

THE EAST BANK

Streets on the eastern bank of the river radiate out from **Platzl**, a small square at the foot of the **Kapuzinerberg**, named after a Capuchin monastery at the summit. It can be scaled in five minutes: the climb is rewarded with excellent views of Salzburg's domes and spires. Linzergasse heads east from Platz towards the **Sebastianskirche** and its fascinating graveyard, last resting place of the Renaissance humanist and alchemist Paracelsus and home to the mausoleum of Wolf Dietrich, tiled with an almost Islamic delicacy. Two blocks northwest of Platzl is Makartplatz, where **Mozart's Gewohnhaus** or family home (1773–87) is located (daily: July & Aug 9am–7pm; Sept–June 9am–5.30pm; €4.70), containing an engrossing multimedia history of the composer and his times. Fischer von Erlach's **Dreifaltigkeitskirche** or Church of the Holy Trinity stands nearby, notable for the elegant curve of its exterior and murky frescoes by Rottmayr inside. Dreifaltigkeitsgasse brings you shortly to the **Schloss Mirabell**, on the site of a previous palace built by Wolf Dietrich for his mistress Salome, with whom the energetic prelate was rumoured to have sired a dozen children. Completely rebuilt by Lukas von Hildebrandt in the early eighteenth century, and further reconstructed after a fire in the nineteenth, it now houses local government buildings and a prestigious concert hall. Its most outstanding features are the cherub-lined staircase by Baroque master George Raphael Donner and the ornate gardens, the rose-filled high ground of the adjoining Kurgarten which offers a much-photographed view back across the city towards the Höhensalzburg.

Eating, drinking and nightlife

If you're just after a **snack**, there are plenty of outlets around the Old Town offering sandwiches and suchlike; *Fischkrieg*, Ferdinand-Hanusch-Platz, is a renowned riverside snackbar serving up everything from fishburgers to grilled squid. Salzburg is full of elegant **cafés**; the most renowned are *Tomasselli*, Alte Markt 9, and *Bazar*, Schwarzstrasse 3, on the east bank with a nice terrace overlooking the Salzach. For more substantial eating, *Resch & Lieblich*, next to the Festspielhaus at Toscaninihof 1, offers good-value Austrian cuisine in dining rooms carved out of the cliff of the Hohensalzburg hill. *Bio Terra*, in the Rupertinum art gallery at Wiener-Philharmoniker-Gasse 9, is an arty and informal café-restaurant with some good vegetarian choices. *Gablerbräu*, Linzergasse 9, serves good Austrian grub and has several vegetarian options, as does *Stieglkeller*, Festungsgasse 10 (May–Sept only), which provides pleasant outdoor seating on the way up to the Burg – it's also a good place for drinking beer on warm evenings. *Sternbrau* is a massive beer garden and restaurant complex occupying two courtyards between Griesgasse and Getriedegasse. *Zur Glocke*, Schanzlgasse 2, is a smaller establishment just east of the old town with homely Austrian cooking; as has *Gasthof Alterfuchs*, Linzergasse 47–49. There are numerous raucous night-time **drinking** venues along Rudolfskai on the left bank – *O'Malley's* and *Shamrock* are two of the best – and Giselakai opposite on the right bank. *Zwettlers Gastwirtschaft*, just off Mozartplatz at Kaigasse 3, is a relaxing pub with good food and blues music; while *Stadtkino*, Anton-Neumayr-Platz 2, is an arty café which draws in crowds with resident DJs at night. Further afield, *Augustiner Bräu*, Augustinerstrasse 4–6, is a vast open-air courtyard fifteen minutes northeast of the centre serving huge mugs of locally brewed beer; while *Shakespeare*, Hubert-Sattler-Gasse 12, is a jazzy east-bank café-restaurant which often has themed DJ nights in the back room. **Club events** also take place in *Arge Nonntal*, also a venue for theatre and live gigs, 15 minutes' southwest of the Old Town at Mühlbacherhofweg 5.

The Salzburg Festival

The **Salzburg Festival** (*www.salzburgfestival.at*) has been running since 1920 and is one of Europe's premier festivals of classical music, opera and theatre – running from the last week of July and continuing throughout August. Tickets are hard to come by: write to Salzburger Festspiele, Postfach 140, A-5020 Salzburg, for programme and booking details. Some standing places for the outdoor performances are available on a stand-by basis; check with the box office on Hofstallgasse (☎0662/844 5579).

Numerous other classical music concerts – many of them Mozart-related – take place in Salzburg all year round. The Salzburg Ticket Service (*www.salzburgticket.com*) located inside the tourist office on Mozartplatz is the best place for info and bookings.

Listings

Airlines Austrian Airlines (also serving Lauda Air and Tyrolean Airways), at the airport (☎0662/85 45 11); British Airways, Griesgasse 29 (☎0662/84 21 08); Lufthansa, Rainbergstrasse 3a (☎0800/90 08 00).

Car rental Avis, F-Porsche-Strasse 7 (☎0662/87 72 78); Budget, at the airport (☎0662/85 50 38); Hertz, Rainerstrasse 17 (☎0662/873452), and at the airport (☎0662/852094).

Consulates Great Britain, Alter Markt 4 (Mon–Fri 9am–noon; ☎0662/848133); USA, Alter Markt 1–3 (Mon, Wed & Fri 9am–noon; ☎0662/848776, fax 849777).

Exchange Banks are open Mon–Fri 8.30am–12.30pm & 2–4.30pm. Outside these hours, you can try the exchange counter at the main train station (May–Sept 7am–9pm; Oct–April 7.30am–8.30pm); Salzburger Sparkasse at the airport (daily 8am–4pm); or the exchange counter on Alte Markt (July–Oct Mon–Fri 8.30am–4.30pm, Sat 9.30am–1pm; Nov–June Mon–Fri only).

Hospital Müllner Hauptstrasse 48 (☎0662/4482).

Internet access Internet Café, Mozartplatz (daily 10am–10pm; €4.40/30min); Piterfun, diagonally opposite the railway station at Ferdinand-Porsche-Strasse 7 (daily 11am–11pm; €3/30min).

Post office The main office is at Residenzplatz 9 (Mon–Fri 7am–7pm, Sat 8am–10am); also the best place to find phone booths.

Taxis ☎81 11; ☎1715.
Travel agents ÖKISTA, Wolf-Dietrich-Strasse 31 (☎883252, fax 883 25 220, *www.oekista.co.at*); Young Austria, Alpenstrasse 108a (☎625758-0, fax 625758-2, *www.youngaustria.at*).

The Salzkammergut

Straddling the border between Land Salzburg and Upper Austria, the peaks of the **Salzkammergut** (*www.salzkammergut.at*) may not be as lofty as those further south, but the glacier-carved troughs that separate them make for some spectacular scenery. Most of the towns and villages in the area are modest places, quiet throughout much of the year until the annual summer influx of visitors. It's a good area for making use of plentiful private rooms and *Gasthöfe*. The natural transport and commercial hub of the region is the nineteenth-century spa town of **Bad Ischl**, 60km east of Salzburg, close by two of the most scenic Salzkammergut lakes – the **Wolfgangersee** and **Hallstättersee**. You can reach Bad Ischl by train by way of a branch line off the main Salzburg–Vienna route from Attnang-Puchheim – or from Stainach-Irdning on the Graz–Salzburg route to the south. From Salzburg, a bus is the most direct route.

St Wolfgang

Hourly buses from Salzburg to Bad Ischl run east along the southern shores of the Wolfgangersee, though they bypass the lake's main attraction, the village of **ST WOLFGANG**, on the opposite shore. Get off the bus at the village of Strobl, at the lake's eastern end, and pick up a connecting bus to the village from there. A traditional stomping ground of lakes-and-mountains package-tourists, St Wolfgang can be crowded in summer, but you should make a point of stopping off, if only to visit the **Pfarrkirche**, just above the lake shore, which contains a high altar by Michael Pacher. An extravagantly pinnacled structure measuring some 12m high, the altar was probably built with the help of the artist's brother Friedrich, and was completed sometime between 1471 and 1481 in Pacher's home town of Bruneck before being carted over the Alps to St Wolfgang. Brightly gilded, sculpted scenes of the *Coronation of the Virgin* form the altar's centrepiece, while the outer panels of the altar wings depict scenes from the Life of St Wolfgang. From Ash Wednesday to the day before Palm Sunday the wings are opened further to allow a glimpse of the eight richly coloured paintings from the Life of Christ. Ascents of the local peak, the **Schafberg**, by mountain railway (May–Oct; return €19; InterRail/Eurail concessions), are possible from a station on the western edge of town. There are two **tourist offices**: the chief one is at the eastern entrance to the tunnel (Mon–Fri 9am–8pm, Sat 9am–noon & 2–8pm, Sun ☎2–8pm; ☎06138/2239, *www.salzkammergut.at/wolfgangsee*), with a subsidiary one at the western end of the tunnel in the Michael-Pacher-Haus (Mon–Fri 9am–noon & 2–5pm); either will fix you up with a private room if you want to stay.

Bad Ischl

The elegant town houses, fountains and gardens of **BAD ISCHL** have an air of bourgeois repose. The soothing properties of the waters here prompted the penultimate Habsburg emperor, Franz Josef, to spend each summer here in the **Kaiservilla** (April Sat & Sun 9–11.15am & 1–4.45pm; May to mid-Oct daily 9–11.15am & 1–4.45pm; €9.50; park only €3), across the River Ischl from the centre. Beyond the villa (which is crammed with victims of the emperor's hunting expeditions) stretches a park containing the **Marmorschlössel** (April–Oct daily 9.30am–5pm; €1), an exquisite neo-Gothic garden retreat built for the Empress Elizabeth; it now houses a small museum of photography. Both the **bus** and **train station** are on the eastern fringe of the town centre, a few steps away from the **tourist office**, at Bahnhofstrasse 6 (Mon–Fri 9am–7pm, Sat 9am–3pm, Sun 10am–1pm; ☎06132/27757, *www.badischl.at*), who will direct you to the town's numerous **private rooms**. There's a modern, functional **HI hostel** near the swimming pool at Am Rechensteg 5 (☎06132/26577, *jgh.badischl@oejhv.or.at*; ②); and a clean and comfy **pension**, *Eglmoos*, at Eglmoosgasse 14 (☎06132/23154; ③).

Hallstatt

The real jewel of the Salzkammergut is **HALLSTATT**, occupying a dramatic position 20km south of Bad Ischl on the western shores of Hallstättersee, jutting out into the lake at the base of a precipitous cliff. Before the building of the road along the western side of the lake, local transport was provided by a sharp-prowed boat known as a *Fuhr*, propelled by a single paddle at the stern, rather like a punt; a few still ply the lake, emerging from the characteristic wooden boathouses that line the shore.

Hallstatt gave its name to a distinct period of Iron Age culture after Celtic remains were discovered in the salt mines above the town. Many of the finds which made the town famous date back to the ninth century BC, and can now be seen in the **Prehistoric Museum** (April & Oct daily 10am–4pm; May–Sept daily 10am–6pm; Nov–March Wed 2–4pm; €3.60) – they include wooden mining implements, pit props and hide rucksacks used by Iron Age miners, alongside more ornamental objects such as jewellery and ornate dagger handles. The same ticket is valid for the nearby **Heimat Museum** (as above, but closed Nov–March), full of the natural historical and anthropological collections of Friedrich Morton, the archeologist who worked on the sites in the 1930s. Tableaux on the history of salt mining illustrate working conditions through the centuries.

Hallstatt's **Pfarrkirche**, uphill from the water's edge, has a south portal adorned with Calvary scenes painted around 1500. Inside, the most interesting of the winged altars is the late-Gothic one on the right, with its heavily gilded statuettes of the Madonna and Child flanked by St Catherine (the patron of woodcutters, on the left) and St Barbara (the patron of miners); high relief scenes from the lives of Mary and Christ are depicted on the wings. In the graveyard outside stands a small stone structure known as the **Beinhaus** (daily 10am–6pm; €1), traditionally the repository for the skulls of villagers, with their bones neatly stacked below like firewood. The skulls, some of them quite recent, are inscribed with the names of the deceased and date of their death, and are often decorated with finely painted floral patterns. Steep paths behind the graveyard lead up to a highland valley, the Salzachtal, where the **salt mines** that provided the area's prosperity are viewable on regular guided tours (daily: May to mid-Sept 9.30am–4.30pm; mid-Sept to Oct 9.30am–3pm; €10.20). Between May and mid-October you can also take the **funicular** (€7.60 return) up here from the nearby suburb of Lahn.

Hallstatt's **train station** is on the opposite side of the lake to the town, a local ferry meeting all incoming trains. However, after about 6pm trains don't stop here and instead continue on to the village of Obertraun, a five-kilometre walk away along the shores of the lake. Hallstatt's **tourist office** is centrally located at Postfach 7 (July & Aug Mon–Fri 8am–6pm, Sat 10am–6pm, Sun 10am–2pm; Sept–June Mon–Fri 9am–noon & 1–5pm; ☎06134/8208, *www.hallstatt.net*), and can arrange **accommodation** in private rooms or guest houses. The family-run *Seethaler*, Dr F. Mortonweg 22 (☎06134/8421; ②), is on a quiet backstreet with lake views from every room, while *Gasthaus zur Mühle*, set back from the landing stage at Kirchenweg 36 (☎06134/8318; ②), has dorm beds, as well as some doubles. *Bräugasthof*, Seestrasse 120, is a very pleasant **place to eat** with a lakeside terrace and a competitively priced range of fresh fish, which you can also buy smoked from the fishmonger's round the corner from the tourist office.

WESTERN AUSTRIA

West of Salzburg towards the mountain province of the **Tirol**, the grandiose scenery of Austria's Alpine heartland begins to unfold in earnest. Most of the trains from Vienna and Salzburg travel through a corner of Bavaria before joining the Inn valley and climbing back into Austria to the Tirolean capital, **Innsbruck**. A less direct but more scenic route (and one you will be more likely to follow if coming from Graz and the southeast) cuts between the

Kitzbühler Alpen and the majestic **Hoher Tauern** (site of Austria's highest peak, the Grossglockner), before joining the River Inn at Wörgl. Settlements such as the exclusive resort-town of **Kitzbühel** provide potential stopoffs on the way, although it's Innsbruck which offers the most convenient mix of urban sights and Alpine splendour. Further west towards Switzerland, the **Vorarlberg** is a distant, isolated extremity of Austria, though its capital, **Bregenz**, on the shores of Lake Constance (or *Bodensee* in German), makes for a tranquil stop before pressing on.

Kitzbühel

KITZBÜHEL began life as a sixteenth-century copper- and silver-mining town, and preserves an exceedingly pretty medieval centre, despite the suburbs that clutter the valley below. From the train station, head down Bahnhofstrasse and turn left at the end; the town centre is a dull fifteen-minute stroll from here. Downtown Kitzbühel revolves around two squares, **Vorderstadt** and **Hinterstadt**. A twelfth-century pile at the southern end of Hinterstadt contains a small **museum** of local history (Mon–Sat 9am–noon; €2.20), offering a jumble of folk crafts and mining implements which reveal some of the industrial grit behind the tinseltown that Kitzbühel has since become. Some of the mining wealth no doubt went into the brightly coloured facades of the town houses lining Vorderstadt, now the backdrop to a promenade of tourists ambling endlessly up and down. Perched above are two worth while churches, the fifteenth-century Gothic **Pfarrkirche**, whose overhanging roof covers some medieval frescoes in the choir, and, immediately above it, the **Liebfrauenkirche**, with a monumental tower and more frescoes in the graveyard chapel.

However the main reason to come to Kitzbühel is to escape into the beautiful highland scenery close by. Ten minutes' west of Hinterstadt, the **Hahnehkammbahn** gondola at the end of Heroldstrasse (June to mid-Oct & mid-Dec to April; €13 return) leads up to the summit of the Hahnenkamm, where you can pick up numerous hiking trails and admire stupendous views of the jagged Wilder Kaiser mountains over to the northeast. Over on the eastern side of town, the **Kitzbüheler Hornbahn** gondola (mid-May to late Oct & mid-Dec to April; €13 return) offers access to yet more high-altitude walking, and sumptuous views back into the valley.

The **tourist office** is at Hinterstadt 18 (July–Sept & mid-Dec to mid-April Mon–Fri 8am–6pm, Sat 8am–noon & 4–6pm, Sun 10am–noon; mid-April to June & Oct to mid-Dec Mon–Fri 8am–noon & 2–6pm; ☎05356/62 15 50), and can arrange **accommodation** either in private homes or in any number of inexpensive pensions. *Hörl*, Josef-Pirchler-Strasse 60 (☎05356/63144; ③), is a cosy pension between the train station and the centre; while *Kaiser*, Bahnhofstrasse 2 (☎05356/64708; ③), is a backpacker-friendly hotel which offers a mixture of ensuite doubles and hostel-style dorms. For **food**, *Huberbräu Stüberl*, Vorderstadt 18, is a cosy central place offering solid Austrian fare; and *Chizzo*, Josef-Herold-Strasse 2, has an affordable range of Tirolean specialities. For **drinking**, try the numerous bars around Vorderstadt and Hinterstadt, or head for *The Londoner* at Franz-Reisch-Strasse 4, a legendary drinking den popular with locals and tourists alike.

Innsbruck

Located high in the Alps, with ski resorts within easy reach, **INNSBRUCK** is as rich in history as any other Austrian city: Maximilian I based the imperial court here in the 1490s, suddenly placing this provincial Alpine town at the heart of European politics and culture. It remained an imperial residence for a century and a half, so it's perhaps not surprising that its incorporation into Bavaria (a move precipitated by the Napoleonic carve-up of Europe) produced an insurrectionary movement under the local hero after whom so many streets and squares are named – Andreas Hofer.

Arrival and accommodation

The **tourist kiosk** in the forecourt of Innsbruck's **train station** (daily: June–Sept 8am–10pm, Oct–May 9am–9pm) offers a speedy room-booking service for a small fee and a refundable deposit. The main **tourist office** is centrally located at Burggraben 3 (MonSat 8am–7pm, Sun 9am–6pm; ☎0512/5356, *www.tiscover.com/innsbruck*). Both offices sell the "Innsbruck Card" (€16.70 for 24hrs; €21.80 for 48hrs) which allows you free travel in the centre and entry to all the sights. Best of the **hostels** is the HI-affiliated *Jugendherberge Innsbruck*, 4km east of the centre at Reichenauerstrasse 147 (☎0512/346179, *yhibk@tirol.com*; ③), which has both dorm rooms and ensuite doubles – bus O from Museumstrasse trundles past. Other options include: *Paula*, Weiherburggasse 15 (☎0512/29 22 62; ④), a friendly **pension** with fine views across the city from a hillside spot north of the Inn; the *Gasthof Innrain*, Innrain 38 (☎0512/58 89 81; ⑤), a small *Gasthof* on the south bank of the river; and *Hotel-Pension Binder*, Dr-Glatz-Strasse 20 (☎0512/33 43 6, *www.info.hotelbinder.at*; ④), clean and friendly, in a suburban street twenty minutes south of the centre. The only **campsite** is *Innsbruck Kranebitten*, Kranebitnner Allee 214, 5km west of the city centre (April–Oct; ☎0512/28 41 50, *campinnsbruck@hotmailcom*); take bus #LK from Boznerplatz, a block west of the station.

The City

Most of what you will want to see in Innsbruck is confined to the central precincts of the **Altstadt**, a small area bounded by the river and the Graben, following the course of the moat which used to surround the medieval town. Leading up to this, Innsbruck's main artery is **Maria-Theresien-Strasse**, famed for the view north towards the great rock wall of the Nordkette, the mountain which dominates the city. At its southern end, three blocks west of the train station down Salurnerstrasse, the triumphal arch, **Triumphpforte**, was built in advance of celebrations marking the marriage of Maria Theresia's son Leopold in 1756. Halfway along, the **Annasäule**, a column supporting a statue of the Virgin, but named after St Anne, who appears at the base, was erected to commemorate the retreat of the Bavarians, who had been menacing the Tirol, on St Anne's day (July 26), 1703.

North of here, Herzog-Friedrich-Strasse leads into the centre, opening out into a plaza lined with arcaded medieval buildings. Commanding attention at the plaza's southern end is the **Goldenes Dachl**, or golden roof (though the tiles which give the roof its name are actually copper), built in the 1490s to cover an oriel window from which the court of Kaiser Maximilian could observe the square below. Inside is the **Maximilianeum** (May–Oct: daily 10am–6pm, Nov–April Tues–Sun 10am–noon & 2–5pm; €3.70), a flashy and insubstantial museum of Maximilian's life and times, although it does include an entertaining video-style documentary about the man in English. An alley to the right leads down to Domplatz and the **Domkirche St Jakob**, home to a valuable *Madonna and Child* by German master Lucas Cranach the Elder, although it is buried in the fussy Baroque detail of the altar. The adjacent **Hofburg**, entered from Rennweg, at the end of Hofgasse around the corner, has late medieval roots but was remodelled in the eighteenth century, its Rococo state apartments crammed with imperial portraits and opulent furniture (daily: May–Oct 9am–5pm; Nov–April 10am–5pm; €5.10; *www.tirol.com/hofburg-ibk*).

At the head of the Rennweg is the **Hofkirche**, an outwardly unassuming building which nevertheless contains the most impressive of Innsbruck's imperial monuments, the **Cenotaph of Emperor Maximilian** (Mon–Sat: July–Aug 9am–5.30pm; Nov–April 10am–5pm; €2.20, combined ticket with the Tiroler Volkskunstmuseum €4.40). This extraordinary project was originally envisaged as a series of 40 larger-than-life statues, 100 statuettes and 32 busts of Roman emperors, representing both the real and the spiritual ancestors of Maximilian, but in the end only 32 of the statuettes and 20 of the busts were completed. The resulting ensemble is still impressive, though the effect is dulled slightly by the knowledge that the emperor is actually buried at the other end of Austria in Wiener Neustadt. Upstairs is the Silberkapelle or silver chapel, named after the silver Madonna that adorns the far wall. The chapel was built by sixteenth-century Archduke Ferdinand II (one of Maximilian's grandsons) in honour of his beloved first wife Philippine Welser – whose grave, and relief, lies against one wall.

Entrance to the Hofkirche is through the same door as the **Tiroler Volkskunstmuseum** (Mon–Sat 9am–5pm, Sun 9am–noon; €4.38; price includes entrance to the Hofkirche), which features wonderful recreations of traditional wood-panelled Tirolean peasant interiors, and models of Tirolean village architecture. The **Tiroler Landesmuseum Ferdinandeum**, a short walk south at Museumstrasse 15 (May–Sept: daily 10am–5pm; Oct–April Tues–Sat 10am–noon & 2–5pm, Sun 9am–noon; €4.38; *www.tiroler-landesmuseum.at*), contains one of the best collections of Gothic paintings in the country. Most originate from the churches of the South Tirol (now Alto-Adige in Italy), although some are by the "Pustertal painters" based around Bruneck (now Brunico in Italy) in the East Tirol, pre-eminent among whom were Michael and Friedrich Pacher, who imported Italian Renaissance techniques into German painting and sculpture.

Also worth a visit is **Schloss Ambras** (April–Oct daily 10am–5pm; Nov–March daily except Tues 2–5pm; €6.57), 2km southeast of the centre and accessible by tram #6. It was the home of the above-mentioned **Archduke Ferdinand** of Tirol, and still houses his cabinet of curiosities, a wondrously wide-ranging collection of artworks and objects from around the globe.

The quickest route to higher altitudes is the **Hungerburgbahn** (daily: Jul–Sept 8am–6pm, April–June & Oct 8.30am–5.30pm, Nov–March 8.30am–5pm; €4.02 return), which leaves from a station at the end of Rennweg (end of tram lines #1 and #6), calling at an intermediate station for the **Alpenzoo** (daily: May–Sept 9am–6pm; Oct–April 9am–5pm; €5.10) before reaching the Hungerburg plateau itself, a good base for hikes. A three-stage sequence of cable cars continues from here to just below the summit of the **Nordkette**, where you can enjoy stupendous views of the high alps to the south.

Eating, drinking and nightlife

The streets around the Goldenes Dachl are a good source of **places to eat**, packed with old coaching inns transformed into restaurants; one of the more atmospheric is the *Ottoburg* at Herzog-Friedrich-Strasse 1, with solid Austrian fare and at least one **vegetarian** main dish. Other central options include: *Stiftskeller*, Stiftgasse 1, offering a good choice of fresh fish; and *La Cucina*, Museumstrasse 26, with a wide range of reasonably priced pizza and pasta. *Philippine*, ten minutes south of the centre at Müllerstrasse 9, is an eccentrically decorated restaurant with plenty of vegetarian dishes. There are plenty of convivial **drinking venues** in Innsbruck's old town, many of which also do decent food: *Café Central*, Gilmstrasse 5, is a venerable old coffeehouse serving up excellent pastries and cakes as well as decent breakfasts; while *Elferhaus*, on Herzog-Friedrich-Strasse, is a perenially popular beer bar that also does decent pub grub. *Prometheus*, Hofgasse 2, has an intimate student bar upstairs and a disco in the cellar; while *Weli*, under the railway arches just east of the centre at Viaduktbogen 26, is an informal café/bar with good food. *Innkeller*, on the other side of the river at Innstrasse 1, is another popular late-night haunt. *Treibhaus*, Angerzellgasse 8, is the place to look for live jazz, folk and alternative theatre.

Listings

Car rental Avis, Salurnerstrasse 15 (☎0512/57 17 54); Budget, Leopoldstrasse 15 (☎0512/588468); Hertz, Südtirolerplatz 1 (☎0512/58 09 01).

Consulates UK, Matthias-Schmid-Strasse 12 (Mon–Fri 9am–noon; ☎0512/58 83 20).

Exchange Banks are generally open Mon–Thur 7.45am–12.30pm & 2.15–4pm, Fri 7.45am–3pm. Outside these hours, try bureaus in the train station (daily 9am–8pm); at the tourist office, Burggraben 3 (Mon–Sat 8am–7pm, Sun 9am–6pm); or the main post office (24hr), Maximilianstrasse 2.

Hiking tours Hiking tours depart daily at 8.30am (June–Sept) from Innsbruck Congress Centre, and are free to those staying in town for three nights or more; check with the tourist office for details of this and other numerous adventure activities.

Hospital Universitätklinik, Anichstrasse 35 (☎0512/50 40).

Internet access Café-bar Piccolo, Maria-Theresien-Strasse 16; and Internet Café, Brunecker Strasse 12, opposite the train station.

Post office The office at Maximilianstrasse 2 is open 24hr.

Telephones At the post office.

Travel agents Tiroler Landesreisebüro, Wilhelm-Griel-Strasse (☎0512/59885).

Bregenz

Stretched along the southern shores of Lake Constance, **BREGENZ** (*www.bregenz.at*) is an obvious staging post on journeys into neighbouring Bavaria to the north, as well as Liechtenstein and Switzerland. The Vorarlbergers who live here speak a dialect close to Swiss German, and have always considered themselves separate from the rest of Austria. In November 1918 they declared independence and requested union with Switzerland, but this was denied by the Great Powers.

The Town

At first sight Bregenz is a curiously disjointed town, the tranquil lakeside parks cut off from the main body of the town by the main road and rail links along the shore of Lake Constance. Most points of interest are located in the old town, up the hill from the lake, around **St Martinsturm**, an early seventeenth-century tower crowned by a bulbous wooden dome. The small **Militarmuseum** inside (May–Sept Tues–Sun 9am–6pm; €2.20) contains arms and armour, and views down towards the lake. Up the street from here is the seventeenth-century **town hall**, an immense half-timbered construction with a steeply inclined roof. Down in the modern town nearest the lake on Kornmarkt, the **Kunsthaus Bregenz** (Tues–Sun 10am–6pm; €4.38; *www.kunsthaus-brengenz.at*) is a cooly modernist green cube that hosts high-profile modern art exhibitions. The **Vorarlberger Landesmuseum**, Kornmarkt 1 (Tues–Sun 9am–noon & 2–5pm; €1.50; *www.vlm.at*), has some outstanding paintings by sixteenth-century artists like Wolf Huber and Jörg Frosch and a selection of portraits and Classical scenes by Angelika Kauffmann, the Vorarlberg painter who achieved success in late eighteenth-century London. Beyond here, leafy **parklands** line the lake, at the western end of which stands the **Festspielhaus**, a modern concert hall built to accommodate the operatic and orchestral concerts of the Bregenz Festival, which usually runs from the last week in July to mid-August (information on ☎05574/4076, *www.festspiele.com*). The most popular excursion from Bregenz, however, is by cable car from a station at the eastern end of town to the **Pfänder** (July–Sept daily 9am–7pm; shorter hours rest of year; €9.10 return; *www.pfaenderbahn.at*;), a wooded hill commanding an excellent panorama of the lake. An alternative route is via the **Pfänderweg**, a worthwhile hour-and-a-half walk that takes you to the top through the wooded hillside.

Practicalities

The **tourist office**, Bahnhofstrasse 14 (July–Sept Mon–Sat 9am–7pm; Oct–June Mon–Fri 9am–6pm, Sat 9am–noon; ☎05574/49590), can book **rooms** for €18.30 a head plus a €2.20 fee. *Gästehaus Tannenbach*, im Gehren 1 (May–Sept only; ☎05574/44174; ④), is the friendliest of the smaller pensions, in a quiet street east of the centre; *Pension Sonne*, Kaiserstrasse 8 (☎05574/642572, *www.bregenz.at/sonne*; ④), is the best of the cheap central hotels. The brand-new HI **hostel** west of the train station at Mehrerauerstrasse 5 (☎05574/42867, *bregenz@jgh.at*; ②) offers dorms as well as swanky doubles; while *Seecamping*, Bodengasse 7, is a large **campsite** by the lake, 2km west of town. *Günz*, Anton-Schneider-Strasse 38, is one of the cheapest sources of traditional Austrian **food** in town; *Zum Goldener Hirschen*, Kirchstrasse 8, is a more atmospheric, pub-like venue with slightly more expensive eats. Best of the central **bars** are *1 Akt*, Kornmarktstrasse 24, and the stylish but cosy *Flexibel*, Rathausgasse 27. *S'logo*, at Kirchstrasse 47 (*www.slogo.at*) is an **Internet** café.

travel details

Trains

Vienna (Franz-Josefs Bahnhof) to Krems (hourly; 1hr–1hr 15min).

Vienna (Südbahnhof) to: Graz (every 2hr; 2hr 40min).

Vienna (Westbahnhof) to: Attnang-Pucheim (hourly; 2hr 30min); Bregenz (8 daily; 10hr); Innsbruck (every 2hr; 5hr 20min); Linz (1–2 hourly; 2hr); Melk (every 1–2hr; 1hr); Salzburg (1–2 hourly; 3hr–3hr 20min).

Attnang-Pucheim to: Bad Ischl (hourly; 1hr); Gmunden (hourly; 20min); Hallstatt (hourly; 1hr 30 min).

Bad Ischl to: St Wolfgang (hourly; 40min).

Graz to: Innsbruck (7 daily; 6hr); Linz (every 2hr; 3hr 30min); Salzburg (8 daily; 4hr 30min).

Innsbruck to: Bregenz (10 daily; 3hr); Kitzbühel (10 daily; 1hr 10min).

Salzburg to: Attnang-Pucheim (hourly; 45min); Innsbruck (8 daily; 2hr 30min); Kitzbühel (hourly; 1hr 45min); Linz (hourly; 1hr 20min).

Buses

Bad Ischl to: Hallstatt (5–7 daily; 40min); Salzburg (hourly; 1hr 40min); St Wolfgang (hourly; 45min).

Krems to: Melk (3–4 daily; 1hr).

Linz to: St Florian (Mon–Fri every 2hr; 35min).

Salzburg to: Bad Ischl (hourly; 1hr 30min); Ströbl (hourly; 1hr).

CHAPTER 2

BELGIUM AND LUXEMBOURG

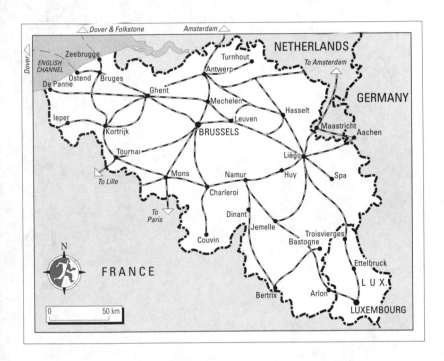

Introduction

A federal country, with three official languages and an intense regional rivalry, Belgium has a cultural diversity that belies its rather dull reputation among travellers. Its population of around ten million is divided between Flemish-speakers (about sixty percent) and French-speaking Walloons (forty percent), with a few pockets of German-speakers in the east. Prosperity has shifted back and forth between the two communities over the centuries, and relations remain acrimonious. The constitution was redrawn in 1980 on a federal basis, with three separate entities: the Flemish North, Walloon South, and Brussels, which is officially bilingual (although its population is eighty percent French-speaking).

The north and south of **Belgium** are visually very different. Marking the meeting of the two, **Brussels**, the capital, is a culturally varied city at the heart of the European Union. The **north**, made up of the provinces of West and East Flanders, Antwerp, Limburg and much of Brabant, is mainly flat, with a landscape and architecture not unlike Holland. **Antwerp** is the second city, a bustling old port with doses of high art, redolent of its sixteenth-century golden age. Further south and west are the great historic cities, **Bruges** and **Ghent**, with a stunning concentration of Flemish art and architecture. Another enjoyable inland Flanders town is the cathedral city of **Mechelen**, halfway between Brussels and Antwerp. The southern reaches of **Brabant** are French-speaking, and merge into the Walloon province of **Hainaut** – rich agricultural country, scarred by pockets of industry and boasting the historic city of **Tournai**. East of here lies Belgium's most scenically rewarding region, the **Ardennes**, an area of deep, wooded valleys, high elevations and dark caverns.

The Ardennes reach across the border into the northern part of the **Grand Duchy of Luxembourg**, a verdant landscape of rushing rivers and high hills topped with crumbling castles. **Diekirch**, **Vianden** and **Echternach** are perhaps the three best centres for touring the countryside, and **Luxembourg City** itself is at least worth a stop, although its population of around 80,000 is tiny by capital-city standards.

Information and maps

In both Belgium and Luxembourg there are **tourist offices** in all but the smallest villages. They usually provide free maps, and in the larger towns offer an accommodation booking service. As for **maps**, the Belgian Tourist Office gives out a decent free map of the country that indicates the most important highways as well as provincial and international boundaries. Otherwise, the best-value general road map is the clear and easy-to-use Baedeker & AA Belgium and Luxembourg (1:250,000) map.

Money and banks

Belgium is one of twelve European Union countries who have changed over to a single currency, the **euro** (€). Euro notes and coins will be issued from the beginning of 2002, with Belgian francs remaining in place for cash transactions, at a fixed rate of F40.3399 to 1 euro, until they are scrapped entirely at the end of February 2002. Euro notes will be issued in **denominations** of 5, 10, 20, 50, 100, 200 and 500 euros, and coins in denominations of 1, 2, 5, 10, 20 and 50 cents and 1 and 2 euros.

Until it is superseded by the euro, the **currency** in both Belgium and Luxembourg is the franc (abbreviated as F, or BEF and LUF). The Belgian and Luxembourg francs are interchangeable, though, while Belgian francs can be used without difficulty in Luxembourg, the reverse is not always the case. All prices in this chapter are given in euros correct at the time of going to press. There will no doubt be some rounding off or, more probably, up of prices in the first few months after the introduction of the euro.

Banks are the best places to change money. In Belgium they are open Mon–Fri 9am–4pm, in Luxembourg 9am–4.30pm, some with a one-hour lunch break between noon and 2pm. You can also change money in larger cities at train stations, some hotels, and **bureaux de change**, though the rates are less favourable; you can obtain cash through ATMs in Brussels and elsewhere if you have an appropriate card with a PIN number.

Communications

In Belgium **post offices** are open Mon–Fri 9am–noon & 2–4pm, and in Luxembourg Mon–Fri 9am–noon & 1.30–5pm. Some open Saturday mornings, too. Many public **phones,** in both Belgium and Luxembourg, only take phonecards which are available from newsagents and post offices. There are no area phone codes in Belgium or Luxembourg. The international operator numbers are ☎1324 (or ☎1405 for an English-language service) in Belgium,

☎0010 in Luxembourg, and they handle collect calls. Mobile phone usage is widespread in both countries. In Belgium the networks are Mobistar, Orange and Proximus while in Luxembourg LuxGSM and Tango are the service providers. **Internet access** is extremely limited in Luxembourg, but in Belgium is much more widespread and you shouldn't have too many problems in tracking down a terminal, either in Internet cafés or in libraries and shops.

Getting around

Travelling around Belgium is rarely a problem. Distances are short, and an efficient, reasonably priced train service links the major centres. Luxembourg, on the other hand, can be problematic: the train network is not extensive, and bus timetables demand careful study.

■ Trains and buses

Run by the Société Nationale des Chemins de Fer de Belgique/Belgische Spoorwegen (Belgian Railways; *www.sncb.be*), **Belgium**'s rail system is comprehensive and efficient, and fares are comparatively low. InterRail and Eurail passes are valid throughout the network, as is the **Belgian Tourrail pass**, which gives entitlement to five days' unlimited rail travel within a month for €56.50. There is also the so-called **Fixed-price reduction card** (Carte de réduction à prix fixe/Reduktiekaart), which costs €15.90 and allows you to purchase tickets at half-price during a specified monthly period, or the under-26 **Go Pass**, valid for ten second-class, single journeys within six months (€38.40). Consider also the **Benelux Tourrail Card**, which gives five days' train travel in a month for €81.80 (over-26s €109.10) throughout Belgium, Luxembourg and the Netherlands. Belgian Railways publish **information** on their various offers and services, and all are

detailed in their comprehensive national and international timetable book, Indicateur/Spoorboekje, which has an English-language section and is available for €4.50 from major train stations. As so much of Belgium is covered by the rail network, **buses** are only really used for travelling short distances, or in parts of the Ardennes where there are fewer rail lines.

In Luxembourg trains are run by Chemins de Fer Luxembourgeois (CFL; *www.cfl.lu*). There's one main north–south route down the middle of the country to Luxembourg City, but apart from that only a few lines branch out from the capital, and the system is mainly supplemented by buses. Fares are comparable with those in Belgium, and there are a number of passes available, giving unlimited train and bus travel for periods lasting from one day to one month: the price for a **one-day pass** is €4.50, €17.90 for a pack of five.

■ Driving

Both countries are well covered by networks of main **roads** and (toll-free) **motorways**, and congestion is normally tolerable outside the major cities. The **speed limit** in built-up areas is 50kph, on main roads 90kph and on motorways 120kph. Seat belts are compulsory in both countries and penalties for drunken driving stiff. Spot fines are common for some offences, and in Luxembourg it's obligatory always to carry cash on you for payment of fines – although fines can range between €12 and €75. The leading national motoring organization in Belgium is the Touring Club de Belgique (TCB), rue de la Loi 25, Brussels 1040 (☎02223 2211, *www.touring.be*). In Luxembourg there's the Automobile Club of Luxembourg (ACL), route de Longwy 54, L-8007 Bertrange (☎45 00 45, *www.acl.lu/*). Both organizations can be called upon in case of breakdown – and most major roads are dotted with phones – but only if your insurance grants you affiliated membership;

check this out before departure. **Car rental** in both countries is quite pricey, about €250 a week with unlimited mileage, though there are cheaper weekend rates.

■ Cycling

Cycling is something of a national sport in **Belgium**, and the distances and flat terrain make it a fairly effortless way of getting around. You have to be selective, however; cycling in most big cities and on the majority of trunk roads – where cycle lanes are unusual – is precarious. Once you've reached the countryside, though, there are dozens of clearly signposted cycle routes to follow. Fortunately, you can rent a bike from around 30 train stations during the summer. Rates are economical: reckon on €8.50 a day, though note that some train excursion tickets include the cost of **bike rental**. Non-Belgians have to stump up a refundable deposit of €12.50. For a list of train stations offering this service, get a copy of Belgian Railways' Train & Vélo (Trein & Fiets) leaflet. It is possible to take your bike on the train for about €4.50 per journey.

In **Luxembourg** you can rent bikes throughout the country for around €10 a day, and you can take your bike on trains for €1.50 per journey. The Luxembourg Tourist Office has leaflets showing cycle routes and also sells guides.

Accommodation

Inevitably, hotel **accommodation** is one of the major expenses you will incur on a trip to Belgium and Luxembourg – indeed, if you're after a degree of comfort, it's going to be the costliest item by far. There are, however, budget alternatives, principally the no-frills end of the hotel market, private rooms arranged via the local tourist office and unofficial and HI-registered youth hostels, though these are largely confined to the larger, tourist-oriented cities.

■ Hotels and private rooms

In both countries prices range from €37–50 for a double room in the cheapest one-star **hotel** to €100 in big city hotels – more if you go for somewhere really luxurious; in cheaper establishments breakfast isn't always included. During the summer you'd be well advised to **book ahead** by phoning or emailing the hotel direct. Hotel reservations can be made through most tourist offices on the day itself, though they'll often require a deposit. The Belgian Tourist Office produces two comprehensive accommodation guides, one for the north and one for the south – the latter including Brussels. In Belgium, Belgium Tourist Reservations (BTR), blvd Anspach 111/4, Brussels 1000 (☎02513 7484, *btr@boreca.be*) offers a hotel booking service while the Luxembourg Tourist Office produces a booklet of approved hotels.

Private rooms, bookable through local tourist offices for a fee of around €0.50, are slightly cheaper (around €25–€37 a night for a double) but they are often inconveniently situated.

■ Hostels and student rooms

Belgium has more than thirty **HI hostels**, run by two separate organizations, one for Flanders – Vlaamse Jeugdherbergcentrale, Van Stralenstraat 40, B-2060 Antwerp (☎03232 72 18, *www.vjh.be*) – another for Wallonia – Les Auberges de Jeunesse de Wallonie, rue de la Sablonnière 28, B-1000 Brussels (☎02219 5676, *www.planet.be/aubjeun*). Most Belgian hostels charge a flat rate per person of around €10 for members; breakfast is included. Many hostels also offer meals for €5.00–7.50. During the summer you should book in advance wherever possible.

Some of the larger cities – Antwerp and Brussels, for example – have a number of **unofficial hostels**. These normally charge about €12.50 for a dormitory bed and are often just as comfortable. You'll also find some universities offering **student rooms** for rent during the summer vacation, Ghent being a good example. Rooms are frugal and rates are rea-

---

ACCOMMODATION PRICE CODES

Throughout this guide, accommodation is coded on a scale of ① to ⑨, the code indicating the lowest price per person per night you could expect to pay in each establishment in high season. With hostels this is the nightly rate per person; with hotels, the price is arrived at by dividing the cost of the cheapest double room by two. The prices indicated by the codes are as follows:

① under £5/$8 (€9)
② £5–10/$8–16 (€9–18)
③ £10–15/$16–24 (€18–27)
④ £15–20/$24–32 (€27–36)
⑤ £20–25/$32–40 (€36–45)
⑥ £25–30/$40–48 (€45–54)
⑦ £30–35/$48–56 (€54–63)
⑧ £35–40/$56–64 (€63–72)
⑨ £40/$64 (€72) and over

sonable – reckon on about €12.50 per person per night.

There are fourteen HI hostels in **Luxembourg**, all of which are members of the Auberges de Jeunesse Luxembourgeoises (AJL), rue du Fort Olisy 2, L-2261 Luxembourg (☎22 55 88, *www.youthhostels.lu*). Rates for HI members are €9.50–21.50 per person, with the Luxembourg City hostel at the top end of the price range. Breakfast is always included; lunch or dinner is an extra €3–6.50. Sheets can also be rented for an extra €3.

■ Camping

Camping is a popular pastime in both Belgium and Luxembourg, but many sites are located with the motorist in mind. There are around five hundred sites in **Belgium**, most of them well-equipped and listed in the Belgian Tourist Office's Camping leaflet, broadly classified on a one- to five-star basis. The vast majority are one-star establishments, for which a family of two adults, two children, a car and a tent can expect to pay between €12.50–25 per night; surprisingly most four-star sites don't cost much, if any, more – add about €2.50 – though the occasional five-star campsite is more like a recreation park and here the price can reach around €40. **Luxembourg** has a little over one hundred campsites, all detailed in the free booklet available from the national tourist board. They are classified into three broad bands with each category having minimum standards. The majority are in Category 1, the best-equipped and most expensive classification. Prices vary considerably even within each category, but are usually between €1.50 and €3.50 per person, plus €2.50–4 for a site.

In both countries during peak season, it can be a good idea to **reserve ahead** if you have a car and large tent or trailer; phone numbers are listed in the free camping booklets, and in Luxembourg the national tourist board will gladly make a campsite reservation on your behalf – phone ☎00352/42 82 82 20.

Food and drink

Belgian cuisine is held in high regard, second only – if not equal – to French, and the country also offers a wide range of ethnic food. Luxembourg's food is less varied, more Germanic – but you can still eat out extremely well. As for drink, beer is one of the real delights of Belgium, and Luxembourg produces some very drinkable white wines along its side of the Moselle.

■ Food

Southern Belgian cuisine is not unlike traditional French, retaining the fondness for rich sauces and ingredients that the latter has to some extent lost of late. In **Flanders** the food is more akin to that of Holland, with many interesting traditional dishes. Pork, beef, game, fish and seafood, especially mussels, are staple items, often cooked with butter, cream and herbs, or sometimes beer. Soups, too, are common: hearty affairs, especially in the south and the **Ardennes**, a region also renowned for its smoked ham and pâté.

In most parts of Belgium and Luxembourg you'll start the day in routine Continental fashion with a cup of coffee and a roll or croissant. Later in the day, the most obvious snack is a portion of frites – served everywhere in Belgium from *friture* stalls, with just salt or mayonnaise, or, as in Holland, with more exotic dressings. Other street stalls, especially in the north, sell various sausages, and everywhere there are stands selling waffles (*gaufres*), piping hot with jam and honey. There are also the usual burger joints, including the Belgian Quick chain, and Panos, which specializes in bakery products.

Many **bars** do meals, at least at lunchtimes, and a host of **cafés** serve basic dishes – omelettes, steak or mussels with chips (virtually the Belgian national dish). The distinction between the two is, however, becoming increasingly blurred with **café/bars** often the most fashionable place to be, especially in the city. You can expect to pay about €5 for an omelette; anything more substantial will cost F8–13, though most places have a dish of the day for €10–12.00. Though they serve very similar food, restaurants are more expensive, and sometimes only open in the evening. A main course will rarely cost under €8.50, with €12.50 being a more usual price, particularly in Luxembourg.

Belgium is also renowned for its **chocolate**. The big Belgian chocolatiers, Godiva and Leonidas, have shops in all the main towns and cities, and their pralines and truffles are almost worth the trip alone. Of the two, Leonidas is the cheaper; reckon on spending €12.50 or so for 500g of their chocolates.

■ Drink

The price of food in Belgium and Luxembourg is compensated for by the low cost of **drinking**, especially if you like **beer**, which is always good and comes in numerous varieties. Ask for a *bière* in a bar and you'll be served a half-litre glass of whatever the bar has on tap. The most common Belgian brands are Stella

Artois, Jupiler and Maes. In Luxembourg the most widespread brands are Diekirch, Mousel and Bofferding. There are also any number of **speciality beers**, usually served by the bottle but occasionally on draught. The most famous is perhaps *lambic*, the generic title for beer brewed in the Brussels area which is fermented by contact with the yeast in the air. A blend of old and young *lambic* beers is known as *gueuze*, a cidery concoction sold in all Brussels bars. There's also *kriek–lambic* with cherries added – and *faro*, given a distinctive and refreshing flavour by adding candy sugar. Try also some of the strong ales brewed by the country's five Trappist monasteries; the most widely available being Chimay, brewed in Hainaut. **Bar prices** don't vary greatly: in Belgium you'll pay around €1.50 for a glass of beer, while in Luxembourg, €1.40 is the usual price. In the swankiest places, you'll pay around €3.50 for beers like Duvel and Chimay.

French **wines** are the most commonly drunk, although Luxembourg is a wine producer, and its white and sparkling wines, produced along the north bank of the Moselle, are very drinkable: in the shops they go for around €6–9 a bottle of sparkling stuff, €6 for ordinary white wine. In restaurants they'll cost two or three times as much.

There's no national Belgian **spirit**, but all the usual kinds are widely available, at about €1.50 a glass in a bar. You will also find Dutch-style *jenever* in most bars in the north. In Luxembourg spirits are cheaper than elsewhere in Europe. You'll also come across home-produced *eau de vie*, distilled from various fruits and around fifty percent alcohol by volume.

Opening hours and holidays

In both Belgium and Luxembourg, the weekend fades painlessly into the week with some shops staying closed till late on Monday morning, even in major cities. Nonetheless, normal **shopping hours** are Monday through Saturday 9/10am to 6pm or 7pm, with most supermarkets staying open on Fridays till 8pm or 9pm and many smaller places shutting down a little earlier on Saturday. In the big cities, a smattering of convenience stores (*magasins de nuit/avondwinkels*) stay open either all night or until around 1 or 2am every day including Sundays, and some souvenir shops open late or on Sunday. At the other extreme, some shops close for the half-day on Wednesday or Thursday afternoon, though this tradition has died out in all but the smaller towns and villages. Most museums are open Tues–Sat 10am–4/5pm, and often on Sunday. Outside the April–Sept period, many sightseeing places close unless they're of prime touristic importance.

Shops, banks and many museums are closed on the following **public holidays**: Jan 1; Easter Monday; May 1; Ascension (around mid-May); Whit Monday; Assumption (mid-Aug); Nov 1; Nov 11 (Belgium only); Dec 25. In addition, the Luxembourg national day is June 23, Belgium's is July 21.

Emergencies

The Belgian **police** force is not quite the friendly bunch you find in the Netherlands, but the country is relatively free of street crime and you shouldn't have much cause to come into contact with them. As far as **personal safety** goes, it's fairly safe to walk anywhere in the centres of the larger cities at any time of day, though you should obviously be wary of badly lit or empty streets; parts of Brussels and Antwerp especially can be intimidating and are best avoided after dark. If you are unlucky enough to have something stolen, report it immediately to the nearest police station. Get a police report number, or better still a copy of the statement itself, for your insurance claim when you get home.

With regard to **medical emergencies**, if you're reliant on free treatment within the EU health scheme, try to remember to make this clear to the ambulance staff, and, if you're whisked off to hospital, to the medic you subsequently encounter. It's a good idea to hand over a photocopy of your E111 on arrival at hospital to ensure your non-private status is clearly understood. In terms of describing symptoms, you can anticipate that someone will speak English in Flemish Belgium and in Brussels and Luxembourg, though in parts of Wallonia you'll be struggling unless you have some rudimentary grasp of French.

Outside normal working hours, all **pharmacies** are expected to display a list of open alternatives on their windows. Weekend rotas are also listed in local newspapers.

Emergency Numbers

Belgium
Ambulance & Fire ☎100; Police ☎101.

Luxembourg
Police ☎113; all other services, including late-opening chemists, doctors & dentists ☎112.

BRUSSELS

Wherever else you go in Belgium, it's likely that at some point you'll wind up in **BRUSSELS**. The city is the major air gateway for the country; it's on the main routes heading inland from the Channel ports via the Flemish art towns; trains arrive here direct from London via the Channel Tunnel; and, in addition, it's a convenient stopover on the train between France and the Netherlands.

Brussels takes its name from Broekzele, or "village of the marsh", which grew up in the sixth century on the trade route between Cologne and the towns of Bruges and Ghent. Under the Habsburgs, the town flourished, eventually becoming capital of the Spanish Netherlands; later Brussels took turns with The Hague as capital of the new United Kingdom of the Netherlands. In the nineteenth century it became the capital of newly-independent Belgium, and was kitted out with all the attributes of a modern European capital. Since World War II, the city's appointment as headquarters of both NATO and the EU has instigated many major development projects, not least a rudimentary metro system.

It's true that the city has a reputation as a dull centre of commerce and bureaucracy, but this is thoroughly unfair. Brussels has architecture and museums to rank with the best of Europe, a well-preserved medieval centre, and an energetic street- and nightlife. It's also very much an international city with European civil servants and business people, together with immigrants from Africa, Turkey and the Mediterranean, constituting a quarter of the population.

Arrival and information

Brussels has three main **train stations** – Bruxelles-Nord, Bruxelles-Centrale and Bruxelles-Midi, each a few minutes apart; almost all **domestic** trains stop at all three. The majority of **international** services only stop at Bruxelles-Midi, including Eurostar trains from London via the Channel Tunnel and Thalys express trains from Amsterdam, Paris, Cologne and Aachen.

Bruxelles-Centrale is, as its name suggests, the most central of the city's three main stations, a five-minute walk from the Grand-Place; **Bruxelles-Nord** lies amongst the bristling tower blocks of the business area just north of the main ring road; and **Bruxelles-Midi** is located in a depressed immigrant area to the south of the city centre. Note that on bus timetables and the city transit system, Bruxelles-Nord appears as *Gare du Nord*; Bruxelles-Centrale as *Gare Centrale*; and Bruxelles-Midi as *Gare du Midi*. The former is the name of the mainline train station, while the latter signifies the métro stop. You can travel between the three by both rail and métro. Eurolines **buses** drop off (and pick up) from the Gare du Nord complex. The **airport** is in Zaventem – 14km northeast of the city centre – and from here there are three trains an hour to the city's three main train stations (30min; €2.40). Trains run from 4.44am until 11.12pm; after that you'll need to take a **taxi**: reckon on paying around €35 to the centre.

LANGUAGE

In Brussels, the **languages** of the French- and Flemish-speaking communities have parity. This means that every instance of the written word, from road signs to the yellow pages, has to appear in both languages. Visitors soon adjust, but on arrival this can be confusing, especially in the names of the city's three main **train stations**: Bruxelles-Nord (in Flemish it's Brussel-Noord), Bruxelles-Centrale (Brussel-Centraal), and, most bewildering of the lot, Bruxelles-Midi (Brussel-Zuid). Note that for simplicity we've used the French version of street names, sights, etc.

There's a **tourist information desk** at the airport: it has a reasonable range of information on Belgium as a whole, though it's much better equipped to deal with enquiries about Brussels and the Flemish-speaking region than it is about Wallonia. It also offers a free hotel reservation service. There are two **tourist offices** in the city centre. The main one, the **TIB** in the Hôtel de Ville on the Grand Place (Mon–Sat 9am–6pm; Sun: April–Oct 9am–6pm, Nov–March 10am–2pm, closed Jan–Easter; ☎02513 8940, *www.tib.be*), has information on the city and hotel booking in Brussels itself, and can also sell you a Tourist Passport (€7.40) which is valid for a year and offers reductions on a variety of attractions and services along with two one-day travel cards. The **Tourism Centre**, nearby at rue du Marché aux Herbes 63 (May–Oct Mon–Fri 9am–6pm, Sat & Sun 9am–1pm and 2–6pm; until 7pm in July & Aug; Nov–April Mon–Fri 9am–6pm, Sat 9am–1pm & 2–6pm, Sun 9am–1pm; ☎02504 03 90, *www.belgique-touristique.net* and *www.toervl.be*), has information on the rest of Belgium, and will make hotel reservations for areas outside the city.

City transport

The easiest way to get around central Brussels is to **walk**, but to get from one side of the centre to the other, or to reach some of the more widely dispersed attractions, you'll need to use **public transport**. Operated by STIB (☎02515 2000, *www.stib.irisnet.be*), the system runs on a mixture of bus, tram and metro lines and covers the city comprehensively. A single flat-fare **ticket** costs €1.40, a strip of five €6, and a strip of ten €8.90 – all available from tram drivers, bus drivers, metro kiosks and ticket machines, the STIB information offices in the Port de Namur, Midi and Rogier stations, and some newsagents. A go-as-you-please **day-pass** (*carte d'un jour*) allows 24 hours of travel on public transport for €3.60. Spot fines for fare-dodging are heavy. Services run from 6am until midnight; route maps are available free from the tourist office and from STIB information kiosks. **Taxis** don't cruise the streets but can be picked up from the ranks spread around the city – notably on Bourse, Brouckère, Grand Sablon and Porte de Namur – and outside leading hotels and at train stations. Prices start at €2.40 during the day and €4.20 at night. To book, phone Taxis Verts (☎02349 4949) or Taxis Orange (☎02349 4343).

Accommodation

Brussels has no shortage of **places to stay**, but given the number of visitors, finding a room can be hard, particularly in summer, and it's best to book ahead at least for your first night. Tourist offices can book hotel rooms on arrival. Staying in a hotel on or around the narrow lanes near the Grand Place is an attractive and central option. Bed & Brussels, rue Kindermans 9, 1050 Brussels (☎02646 0737, *www.BnB-brussels.be*) provides a B&B reservation service.

Hostels

Bruegel, rue du Saint Esprit 2 (☎02511 0436, *www.vjh.be*). Housed in a modern building, this official HI hostel is centrally located – a ten-minute walk south from the Gare Centrale. Some doubles, but mostly 4- to 12-bed dorms with shared showers. Internet access. Closed 10am–2pm. Dorms ②, doubles ③.

CHAB, rue Traversière 8 (☎02217 0158, *www.ping.be/chab*). Spacious independent hostel. Price includes breakfast. Sinks in all rooms, but shared showers and toilets. Kitchen facilities and Internet access. Open until 2am. Métro Botanique. No curfew or lock-out. Dorm beds, triples or quads ②, doubles ③.

Jacques Brel, rue de la Sablonnière 30 (☎02218 0187, *www.planet.be/aubjeun*). Official HI hostel with excellent facilities including showers in every room. Own laundry, bar, restaurant and Internet facility. Wheelchair accessible. Métro Madou or Botanique. No curfew or lock-out. Dorms ②, doubles ③.

New Sleep Well, rue du Damier 23 (☎02218 5050, *www.sleepwell.be*). Conveniently located hostel, in a smart, clean new building with its own bar and Internet access. Lock-out 10am–4pm and 3am curfew. Métro Rogier. Triples or quads ②, doubles ③.

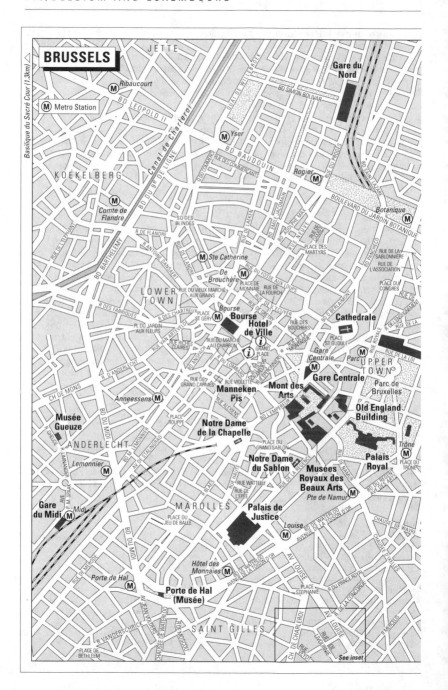

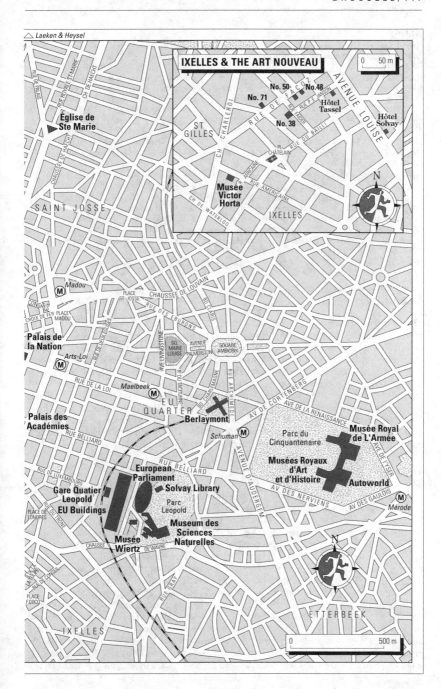

△ *Laeken & Heysel*

IXELLES & THE ART NOUVEAU

0   50 m

ST GILLES

No. 71
No. 50   No. 48
No. 38
Hôtel Tassel
Hôtel Solvay

RUE DE FACQZ
CH CHARLEROI
RUE DE LA COZ
RUE P.E. JANSON
RUE DU BAILLI
AVENUE LOUISE

PL. CHÂTELAIN

RUE DE L'ARDENNE
RUE AMÉRICAINE

Musée Victor Horta

CH DE WATERLOO

IXELLES

N

SAINT JOSSE

Église de Ste Marie

RUE ROYAL ST-MARIE
CH DE HAECHT
RUE DE PALAIS
CHAUSSÉE DE HAECHT

Ⓜ Madou

PLACE ST JOSSE
CHAUSSÉE DE LOUVAIN
RUE DES EBURONS
BD CHARLS

CONGRÈS
CROIX DE FER
PLACE MADOU

Palais de la Nation

Arts-Loi
Ⓜ

RUE DES COLONIES

SQ. MARIE LOUISE
AVENUE PALMERSTON
SQUARE AMBIORIX

AVE LIVINGSTONE
RU DU TACITURNE

RUE DE LA LOI

Maelbeek Ⓜ

BD CLAIRE FONTAINE
RUE ARCHIMÈDE

E.U. QUARTER
Berlaymont

Palais des Académies

RUE BELLIARD

Schuman Ⓜ

AV DE CORTENBERG
AVE DE LA RENAISSANCE

Parc du Cinquantenaire

Musée Royal de L'Armée

AVE DE L'YSER

RUE DE LUXEMBOURG

RUE BELLIARD

AVENUE D'AUDERGEM

Musées Royaux d'Art et d'Histoire

European Parliament

Solvay Library

Gare Quatier Leopold
EU Buildings

Parc Leopold

AV DES NERVIENS

Autoworld

AV DES GAULOIS

Ⓜ *Mérode*

PLACE DE LONDRES

Museum des Sciences Naturelles

Musée Wiertz

CHAUSSÉE DE WAVRE

RUE SKAY

N

LA GODIE
RUE DE CONSEIL
PLACE F. COCO

IXELLES

ETTERBEEK

0   500 m

Hotels

Astrid Centre Hotel, place du Samedi 11 (☎02219 3119, *www.astridhotel.be*). Crisp modern hotel with smart, comfortable rooms in the fashionable Ste Catherine area. Substantial weekend discounts. Métro Ste Catherine. ⑨.

Comfort Hotel Siru, place Rogier 1 (☎02203 3580, *www.comforthotelsiru.com*). It may not look like much from the outside, but the interior of this hotel is the most original in town. Each room was individually decorated by an art student in a modernistic style, and figurines, mini-polystyrene effigies, murals and cartoon strips – everything from Tintin to Marilyn Monroe – pop up all over the place. It's delightful. Métro Rogier. ⑨.

Hôtel du Congrès, rue du Congrès 42 (☎02217 1890, *www.hotelducongress.com*). Three-star hotel in a good-looking, turn-of-the-century mansion about five minutes' walk from the cathedral. A popular hotel with pleasant rooms, so advance booking is advised. Discounts at the weekend. Métro Madou. ⑥.

Eperonniers, rue des Eperonniers 1 (☎02513 5366). No frills, but excellent position near Grand Place. Métro Gare Centrale. ③.

Georges V, rue 't Kint 23 (☎02513 5093, *www.george5.com*). Ramshackle period hotel in a quiet neighbourhood of big, old, balconied and grilled town houses. Breakfast included. Métro Bourse. ⑤.

La Légende, rue du Lombard 35 (☎02512 8290, *www.hotellalegende.com*). Pleasant if frugal accommodation in an old building set around a courtyard in the heart of the city, just metres from the Grand Place. Half the rooms have sinks but not showers – en-suite rooms cost about €25 extra. Métro Bourse. ⑥.

Sabina, rue du Nord 78 (☎02218 2637). Spruce, pretty rooms in a turn-of-the-century house in a quiet residential area that was once a favourite haunt of the city's nineteenth-century bourgeoisie, with a beamed and panelled breakfast room. Good value. Métro Madou. ⑤.

Windsor, place Rouppe 13 (☎02511 2014, *www.hotel-windsor.com*). Clean, simple and cheerful rooms with breakfast included. Métro Anneessens. ⑤.

The City

The centre of Brussels is enclosed within a rough pentagon of boulevards following the former course of the medieval city walls. It is divided between the Upper and Lower Towns, the neighbourhoods generally becoming more bourgeois the higher you go. The greater part of the centre is occupied by the **Lower Town**, of which the Grand Place – perhaps the best-preserved city square in Europe – is the unquestionable focus. South of here, the busy centre fades into the old working-class streets of the Marolles district and Gare du Midi, now a relatively depressed, predominantly immigrant area; north, the shopping street of rue Neuve leads up to place Rogier and the office blocks which surround the Gare du Nord. The **Upper Town** is quite different in feel from the rest of the centre, with statuesque buildings lining wide, classical boulevards and squares. Appropriately, it's the home of the Belgian parliament and government departments, some of the major museums and the swishest shops.

The Lower Town

The obvious place to begin any tour of the **Lower Town** is the **Grand Place**, the commercial hub of the city since the Middle Ages – though only the Hôtel de Ville and one guildhouse survived a 36-hour bombardment by the French in 1695. The **Hôtel de Ville** (tours in English April–Sept Tues & Wed 3.15pm, Sun 12.15pm; Oct–March Tues and Wed only; €2.50) still dominates, and inside you can view various official rooms; most dazzling is the sixteenth-century council chamber, decorated with gilt moulding, faded tapestries and an oak floor inlaid with ebony. But the real glory of the Grand Place lies in the **guildhouses**, rebuilt in the early eighteenth century, their slender facades swirling with exuberant carving and sculpture. The western side of the square is perhaps the most impressive. At no. 1, the **Roi d'Espagne** was once the headquarters of the guild of bakers and is named after its bust of Charles II, the last of the Spanish Habsburgs, which is flanked by Moorish and Native American prisoners to symbolize his mastery of a vast empire. At no. 4 comes the **Maison de Sac**, the headquarters of the carpenters and coopers – the upper storeys were appropriately designed by a cabinet-maker, and feature pilasters and caryatids which resemble the ornate legs of Baroque furniture. Next door, the **Maison de la Louve**, at no. 5, is the only guildhouse to have survived the French bombardment intact, its elegant pilastered facade fronting the former home of the archers' guild, studded with pious representations of concepts like Peace and Discord, together with a pediment relief of Apollo firing at a python. Adjoining it, at no. 6, the **Maison du Cornet** was the headquarters of the boatsmen's guild, a fanciful creation of 1697 whose top storey resembles the stern of a ship. The adjacent **Maison du Renard** was the house of the haberdashers' guild: on the ground floor animated cherubs in bas-relief play at haberdashery, while a scrawny, gilded fox – after which the house is named – squats above the door.

Most of the northern side of the square is taken up by the sturdy neo-Gothic **Maison du Roi**, a reconstruction of a sixteenth-century building that now houses the **Musée de la Ville de Bruxelles** (Tues–Fri 10am–5pm, Sat & Sun 10am–1pm; €2.50), where you'll find an eclectic collection of locally manufactured tapestries, ceramics, pewterware and porcelain. To the south, rue de l'Etuve leads down to the **Manneken Pis**, a diminutive statue of a little boy pissing that's supposed to embody the "irreverent spirit" of the city and is today one of Brussels' biggest tourist draws. Jerome Duquesnoy cast the original statue in the 1600s, but it was stolen several times and the current one is a copy.

Northwest of the Grand Place

To the northwest of the Grand Place, at the end of rue au Beurre, the **Bourse** (or Stock Exchange), a Neoclassical structure of 1873, caked with fruit, fronds, languishing nudes and frolicking *putti*, hides the view of busy boulevard Anspach beyond. Right up the boulevard is **place de Brouckère**, Brussels' modern centre, a busy traffic-choked junction surrounded by advertising hoardings, and, close by, **place de la Monnaie** an uninteresting modern square that's home to the **Théâtre de la Monnaie**, the city opera house. From here, **rue Neuve** forges north, a mundane pedestrianized shopping street meeting the inner ring at the junction of **place Rogier**, beyond which lies the Gare du Nord and ultimately the seedy redlight area. About a third of the way up rue Neuve, **place des Martyrs** is a cool, rational square imposed on the city by the Habsburgs that is nowadays one of its most haunting sights, a forlorn, abandoned open space, with many of the buildings around it being redeveloped into apartments. Beyond the square, at 20 rue des Sables, the **Grand Magasin Waucquez**, one-time department store designed at the turn of the century by Victor Horta, now houses the **Centre Belge de la Bande Dessinée** (Tues–Sun 10am–6pm; €6.20), whose various displays are devoted to the history of the Belgian comic strip, focusing on a wide range of cartoonists, with specific sections on animation and, of course, Hergé's Tintin.

The Quartier Marolles

In the opposite direction from the Grand Place, **Notre Dame de la Chapelle**, a sprawling Gothic structure, is the city's oldest church, founded in 1134. Its main claim to fame is the memorial plaque over the tomb of Pieter Bruegel the Elder in the third chapel of the south aisle – Bruegel is supposed to have lived and died down the street at rue Haute 132. With parallel rue Blaes, rue Haute forms the spine of the **Quartier Marolles** – an earthy neighbourhood of cheap restaurants, shops and bars that grew up in the seventeenth century as a centre for artisans working on the nearby mansions of Sablon. Today, gentrification is creeping into the district, but it's got some way to go, and **place du Jeu de Balle**, the heart of Marolles, is still the scene of the city's best **flea market** (daily from 7am), which is at its busiest on Sundays. Beyond, the area around the **Gare du Midi** is home to the city's many North African immigrants, a depressed quarter with an uneasy undertow by day and sometimes overtly threatening at night. However, it's well worth venturing down here on a Sunday morning, when a vibrant souk-like **market** is held under the arches of the station.

The Upper Town

The steep slope that marks the start of the **Upper Town** rises just a couple of minutes' walk from the Grand Place at the east end of rue d'Arenberg. Here you'll find the city's **Cathedral** (daily 8am–6pm; free), a Brabantine-Gothic building begun in 1220 and dedicated jointly to

St Michael and Ste Gudule, the patrons of Brussels. The cathedral sports a striking twin-towered, whitestone facade, with the central doorway trimmed by fanciful tracery and statues of the Three Wise Men and the Apostles. However, the intensity of the decoration fades away inside, where the triple-aisled nave is an airy affair supported by plain, heavy-duty columns topped with capitals carved with curled leaves – or crockets. The interior is also short on furnishings and fittings, reflecting the combined efforts of the Protestants, who ransacked the church (and stole the shrine of Ste Gudule) in the seventeenth century, and the French Republican army, who wrecked the place one hundred or so years later. Two survivors are the massive oak pulpit, an extravagant chunk of frippery by the Antwerp sculptor Hendrik Verbruggen, and the superb sixteenth-century **stained glass** windows in the transepts and above the main doors.

Five minutes' walk south of the cathedral, the so-called **Mont des Arts** also occupies the slopes of the Upper Town, its collection of severe geometric buildings given over to a variety of government- and arts-related activities. In the middle, a wide stairway climbs up towards **place Royale** and **rue Royale**, the grandiose backbone of the Upper Town. On the way up to place Royale on the left is the **Old England** building, one of the finest examples of Art Nouveau in the city. It is now home to the **Musée des Instruments de Musique**, rue Montagne de la Cour 2 (Tues–Fri 9.30am–5pm, Thurs until 8pm, Sat & Sun 10am–5pm; €3.70; *www.mimfgov.be*), which contains around 1500 instruments and some interactive displays. Around the corner, the **Palais du Roi** (end July to Aug Tues–Sun 10.30am-4.30pm; free) is something of a disappointment, a sombre conversion of some eighteenth-century town houses that isn't actually lived in by the Belgian royals; sumptuous rooms, especially the Throne Room, and tapestries designed by Goya, are the highlights of a visit. Opposite is the **Parc de Bruxelles**, the most central of the city's parks.

Musées Royaux des Beaux Arts

Just off place Royale, the **Musées Royaux des Beaux Arts**, rue de la Régence 3, comprises Belgium's most satisfying collection of fine art, with the outstanding permanent collection featuring examples of the work of every major Belgian artist, supplemented by internationally acclaimed exhibitions. Though they share the same entrance, there are actually two museums here – the **Musée d'Art Ancien** (Tues–Sun 10am–5pm) and the adjacent **Musée d'Art Moderne** (Tues–Sun 10am–5pm; *www.fine-arts-museum.be*), the former displaying works from up to the late eighteenth century, the latter more modern works through to contemporary art. The admission fee of €3.70 covers both museums, but not necessarily the temporary exhibitions. The permanent collection is much too big to absorb in one go – and it's best to see the two museums on separate visits. The organization is made more comprehensible by a system of colour-coded areas.

In the **Musée d'Art Ancien**, the **blue area** takes in paintings of the fifteenth and sixteenth centuries, including the sharply observed nudes of *Adam and Eve* by Lucas Cranach; a marvellous *Triptych of the Holy Kindred* by Quentin Matsys; several delicately realistic paintings by Rogier van der Weyden, including an exquisite *Lamentation;* Jan Mostaert's wonderfully busy *Passion*; and Pieter Bruegel the Elder's most haunting work, *The Fall of Icarus*. The **brown area** concentrates on work of the seventeenth and eighteenth centuries, notably some glorious canvases by Rubens and his contemporaries Jacob Jordaen and Antony van Dyck. Moving on into the **Musée d'Art Moderne**, the **yellow area** begins with the Neoclassicism of Jacques Louis David, whose famous *Death of Marat* is here, and continues with the dramatic Romantic canvases of Géricault and Delacroix. Then comes the Realism of Courbet, Charles de Groux and Constantin Meunier, plus a sample of Symbolist paintings, including those of Fernand Khnopff. French painters are represented by the likes of Bonnard, Gauguin and Monet, though the highlight of the late nineteenth century works on display are the disconcerting canvases of the Belgian James Ensor. The **green area** boasts an extremely varied collection of modern art and sculpture, laid out on six subterranean levels. There are fine examples of Fauvism, Cubism, Futurism, Expressionism, and, above all, Surrealism, with the oddly erotic works of Paul Delvaux; a small show of paintings by Magritte; a fine Dali, *The Temptation of St Anthony*, and an eerie Francis Bacon, *The Pope with the Owls*.

The Sablon Neighbourhood

From the Beaux Arts it's a short walk south to the **place du Petit Sablon**, a small rectangular area off to the left of rue de la Régence that's decorated with 48 statues representing the medieval guilds, and a fountain surmounted by the Counts Egmont and Hoorn, beheaded on the Grand Place for their opposition to Spanish tyranny in the 1500s. On the opposite side of rue de la Régence stands the fifteenth-century church of **Notre Dame du Sablon**, which began life as a chapel for the medieval guild of archers; the present church was built after a statue of Mary with powers of healing was brought by boat from Antwerp, an event still celebrated each July by the Ommegang procession. Behind the church, the sloping wedge of **place du Grand Sablon** is the centre of one of the city's wealthiest districts and scene of a lively weekend antiques market. At the southern end of rue de la Régence is the immense **Palais de Justice**. Built in 1883, it is actually larger than St Peter's in Rome.

Outside the petit ring: the parks and outer boroughs

Brussels by no means ends with the *petit* ring. East of this inner ring road, the **Quartier Leopold** takes its name from the late nineteenth-century king of Belgium, who laid out much of the area with wide boulevards, monuments and statues. More recently, the district has been colonized by the huge concrete and glass high-rises of the EU, notably the winged **Berlaymont** building (Métro Schuman), whose main claim to fame is the money and time it's taken to remove the asbestos put in during its construction in the 1960s. The latest addition to the sprawling EU complex is the lavish **Hémicycle européen**, an imposing series of structures culminating with the spectacular curved glass roof of the brand new EU Parliament building. If you want to take a look, the parliament building is a couple of minutes' walk from place du Luxembourg, behind the Gare Quartier Leopold train station.

Just south of the ring road is **St Gilles**, a gritty multiracial borough that stretches from the refinement of ave Louise in the east to the solidly immigrant quarters around the Gare du Midi. The main reason to trek out here is the **Musée Victor Horta**, the former home of the Belgian Art Nouveau architect at rue Américaine 25 (Tues–Sun 2–5.30pm; €5), accessible by tram #92, in the direction of Fort JACO, from place Louise. The exterior is modest, but inside are all the architect's trademarks: crisp, bright rooms spiralling around a superbly worked staircase, stained glass, sculpture, and ornate furniture and panelling.

West of the city centre, **Anderlecht** is a dull, grimy quarter most famous for its football team. That said, it's worth making the effort to see the mustily evocative **Musée Bruxellois de la Gueuze**, in the Cantillon Brewery, at rue Gheude 56 (Mon–Fri 9am–5pm, Sat 10am–5pm; €3), ten minutes' walk from Midi station. This friendly, family-run brewery is the last in Brussels still brewing *gueuze* beer according to traditional methods. The self-guided tour (using an excellent English-language leaflet) shows how the beer is allowed to ferment naturally, reacting with yeasts peculiar to the Brussels air. The result is unique, as you can find out during the tasting at the end.

North of the ring road, **Laeken** is the royal suburb of Brussels. Its large public **park** is best known for the **Atomium** (daily: April–Aug 9am–7.30pm; Sept–March 10am–5.30pm; €5.50; *www.atomium.be*), a hugely magnified model of a molecule built for the 1958 World Fair (Métro Heysel). Something of a symbol of the city, it provides a panoramic view of Brussels and its surroundings and contains an unremarkable exhibition of cartoons and photographs of the Atomium.

Eating and drinking

Brussels has an international reputation for the quality of its cuisine, which is richly deserved. Even at the dowdiest snack bar, you'll almost always find that the food is well-prepared and generously seasoned – and then there are the city's **restaurants**, many of which equal anywhere in Paris. Traditional Bruxellois dishes feature on many restaurant menus, canny amalgamations of Walloon and Flemish ingredients and cooking styles – whether it be rabbit cooked in *gueuze* beer or steamed pigs' feet. The city is also among Europe's best for sampling a wide range of different cuisines – from the ubiquitous Italian places and the Turkish restaurants of St Josse through to Spanish, Vietnamese, Japanese, and even Buddhist vegetarian restaurants. You can also eat magnificent fish and seafood, especially in and around the fashionable district of Ste Catherine.

For the most part, eating out is rarely inexpensive, but the **prices** are almost universally justified by the quality. As a general rule the less formal the restaurant, the less expensive the meal – and indeed it's hard to distinguish between the less expensive restaurants and the city's **cafés**, some of which provide some of the tastiest food in town. In addition, many **bars** serve food, often just spaghetti, sandwiches and *croque monsieurs*, but many have wider ranging menus, taking in traditional Brussels cuisine.

For **fast food**, aside from the multinational burger and pizza chains, there are plenty of *frites* stands and kebab places around the Grand Place, notably on rue du Marché aux Fromages and near the beginning of rue des Bouchers. Pitta is also popular, stuffed with a wide range of fillings – though vegetarian ones are rare – along with the more substantial thin Turkish pizzas, or *pide*, topped with combinations of cheese, ground meat or even a fried egg, sold at any number of cafés along the chaussée de Haecht and rue du Méridien in St Josse.

For straight **drinking**, the enormous variety of bars and cafés is one of the city's real joys – sumptuous Art Nouveau cafés, traditional bars with ceilings stained brown by a century's smoke, speciality-beer bars with literally hundreds of different varieties of ale, and, of course, more modern hangouts. Many of the centrally located bars are much frequented by tourists and expats, but outside the centre, and even tucked away off the Grand Place, there are places which remain refreshingly local. Bars also stay open late – most until 2 or 3am, some until dawn.

Restaurants

Bij den Boer, quai aux Briques 60. There's nothing pretentious here in this excellent neighbourhood café/bar with its tiled floor and bygones on the wall. A great place for a drink or a meal in the traditional Belgian manner. Closed Sun.

Chez Léon, rue des Bouchers 18. Touristy but good-value restaurant near the Grand Place serving traditional Belgian fare. Most famous for its mussel dishes.

Brasserie Horta, rue des Sables 20. The café of the Centre Belge de la Bande Dessinée, serving imaginative snacks and light meals in a delightful Horta-designed Art Nouveau setting. Popular drinking spot with a young crowd.

La Grande Porte, rue Notre–Seigneur 9. Cosy and crowded place serving good traditional food. Closed Sun.

Katja's Kitchen, rue Marché au Charbon 87. Small homely place off the tourist trail serving a variety of unpretentious meals from a limited set menu which varies every day (vegetarian options). €14 fixed price for starter and main course. Closed Mon.

't Kelderke, Grand Place 15. Boisterous, excellent-value cellar restaurant on the Grand Place. No reservations, so you might have to queue. The new *'t Kelderke estaminet* next door has regular live music.

Le Pré Salé, rue de Flandre 16. Friendly, old-fashioned neighbourhood restaurant just off place Ste-Catherine, and a nice alternative to the swankier eateries of the district. Great mussels and other Belgian specialities. Closed Mon.

Sahbaz, chaussée de Haecht 102. Reckoned to be the city's best Turkish restaurant; friendly atmosphere and cheap too.

In't Spinnekopke, place du Jardin-aux-Fleurs 1. Ancient restaurant and bar near the Bourse that serves many traditional Bruxellois dishes cooked in beer as well as lots of fish and mussels. Not especially cheap – dish of the day from about €12.40. Closed Sun.

Au Stekerlapatte, rue des Prêtres 6. On the far side of the Palais de Justice, a wonderful old brasserie, usually packed with a youngish crowd, serving main meals for around €12.40.

Bars and cafés

À la Bécasse, rue de Tabora 11. Spartan, old-fashioned bar right near the Bourse that is one of the few remaining venues for sampling *lambic* – which can be bought by the jug and shared – along with simple bar snacks.

Le Cirio, rue de la Bourse 18. One of Brussels' oldest café/bars, sumptuously decorated in *fin-de-siècle* style.

Le Falstaff, rue Henri Maus 17–23. Art Nouveau café/brasserie next to the Bourse. Full of atmosphere and usually packed, though fairly impersonal. Also serves snacks and full meals.

La Fleur en Papier Doré, rue des Alexiens 53-55. Cluttered, cosy locals' bar, with walls covered with doodles and poems and a couple of cats prowling around the place. Once a watering hole of René Magritte.

Le Greenwich, rue des Chartreux 7. Brussels' traditional chess café with a lovely old wood-panelled and mirrored interior. Laid-back atmosphere. Close to place St Géry.

À l'Image de Notre-Dame, rue du Marché aux Herbes 6. A welcoming if extremely quiet bar at the end of a long alley, decorated like an old Dutch kitchen. Good range of speciality beers. Near the Grand Place.

À la Mort Subite, rue Montagne-aux-Herbes-Potagères 7. Popular bar with a wonderful 1920s interior. Snacks served, or just order a plate of nibbles – cheese-cubes, salami, chips – to accompany your Mort Subite beer.

Rick's, ave Louise 344. A gathering place of resident English-speakers for close on thirty years. Full menu available, though it's most famous for its ribs.

Au Soleil, rue Marché au Charbon 86. Popular bar with a wide choice of beer, crowded until late every night with a young and trendy crowd.

Toone VII, down an alley off petite rue des Bouchers 21. Cosy, largely undiscovered bar belonging to the Toone puppet theatre. One of the centre's most congenial watering holes.

L'Ultime Atome, rue Saint Boniface 14, Ixelles. Affable café serving a range of 75 beers and an excellent and varied menu to a youngish clientele. Out in the suburb of Ixelles.

Wittamer, place du Grand Sablon 12–13. Brussels' most famous patisserie, established in 1910 and still run by the Wittamer family. Gorgeous, if pricey, pastries and cakes. Tables outside are for coffee and drinks only.

Nightlife

As far as **nightlife** goes, you may be perfectly happy to while away the evenings in one of the city's restaurants or bars, but Brussels is also a reasonably good place to catch **live bands** with nightspots scattered across the city centre and the suburbs. **Clubs** are less impressive, but entry **prices** are low: you rarely have to pay more than €10 and many of the smaller clubs have no cover at all, though you will have to tip the bouncer a nominal fee (€0.50) on the way in. As a general rule, clubs **open** Thursday to Saturday from 11pm to 5/6am. The best English-language source of **listings** is the weekly magazine *The Bulletin* (out on Wednesdays; €2.20). *What's On Magazine* – a supplement of *The Bulletin* – is available (free) from the tourist office. The Wednesday pull-out in the newspaper *Le Soir* is also useful. **Tickets** for most things are available from FNAC in City 2, a shopping centre on rue Neuve.

Concert halls

Forest National, ave du Globe 36 (☎02340 2211). Brussels' main venue for big-name international concerts, holding around 10,500 people.

Palais des Beaux Arts, rue Ravenstein 23 (☎02507 8200). With a concert hall holding around 2000, the Palais is used for anything from contemporary dance to Tom Jones, though the main slant is on classical music.

Live music bars

L'Archiduc, rue Antoine Dansaert 6. Small and tasteful bar with regular live jazz on the weekend. Near place St Géry.

Le Cercle, rue Sainte-Anne 20-22, just off place du Grand Sablon. Live music three or four times a week – everything from jazz and Latino through to Chanson Française. A relaxed and easy atmosphere and the bands are usually very good.

Magasin 4, rue du Magasin 4 (☎02223 3474). This small converted warehouse is a great place for catching up-and-coming rock and indie bands. Only open when there's a gig, so check listings – or phone – before you set out. Entrance around €7.50. Métro Yser.

Sounds Jazz Club, rue de la Tulipe 28. Earthy bar in the suburb of Ixelles serving up Latin jazz and R&B.

Travers, rue de Vergnies 25 (☎02217 4800, *www.cyclone.be/travers*). Informal jazz club with a reputation for showcasing up-and-coming Belgian musicians.

Clubs

Le Bazaar, rue des Capucins 63. In the Marolles, off rue Haute. Split-level club with a dimly lit restaurant upstairs and a dance floor below playing funk, soul, rock and indie.

Cartagena, rue du Marché au Charbon 70. Enjoyable downtown club offering arguably the best and certainly the widest range of South American and Latin sounds in town. Attracts a late-twenties age group, and gets going around midnight. Open Friday and Saturday nights only.

The Fuse, rue Blaes 208. Large, young, and vibrant techno, jungle and house club in the Marolles district. Big-name, international DJs are a regular feature. Chill-out rooms and visuals. Saturday nights only.

Pitt's Bar, rue des Minimes 53. Near the Palais de Justice, the music here is techno, garage, bangra and house. Popular with students. Open Tues to Sun.

Listings

Airlines Aer Lingus, rue du Trône 98 (☎02548 9848); British Airways, rue du Trône 98 (☎02548 2122); British Midland, avenue des Pléiades 15 (☎02772 9400); KLM, at the airport (☎02717 2070); Sabena, at the airport (☎02723 2323).

Airport information 24hr information line ☎02723 3913, *www.brusselsairport.be*.

American Express blvd du Souverain 100 (Mon–Fri 9am–5.30pm; ☎02676 2111).

Books Waterstones, blvd Adolphe Max 71–75, is the best central source of English-language books and magazines.

Car rental Avis, blvd du Midi 41 (☎02513 6969) and at the airport (☎02720 0944); Budget, at the airport (☎02753 2170); Europcar-Interrent, Gare du Midi (☎02522 9573) and at the airport (☎02721 0592); Hertz, at the airport (☎02720 6044).

Embassies Australia, rue Guimard 6-8 (☎02286 0500); Canada, ave de Tervueren 2 (☎02741 0611); Ireland, rue Froissart 89–93 (☎02230 53 37); New Zealand, blvd de Régent 47–48 (☎02512 1040); UK, rue d'Arlon 85 (☎02287 6211); USA, blvd du Régent 27 (☎02508 2111).

Exchange Outside bank hours you can change money and travellers' cheques at bureaux de change in the Gare du Nord (daily 8am–8pm), Gare du Midi (daily 7am–10pm), and the Gare Centrale (daily 8am–9pm), though none of these places give cash advances on credit cards. Otherwise there's Goffin, rue du Marché aux Herbes 88 (daily 9am–9pm), and Change Centre, rue du Marché aux Herbes 18 (daily 9am–11.30pm). There are also bureaux de change at the airport. There are ATMs dotted throughout the city centre.

Gay and lesbian scene For the most up-to-date information on the Brussels gay scene, contact Tels Quels, rue du Marché au Charbon 81 (daily 5pm–2am; ☎02512 4587, *www.telsquels.be*) – something of a city institution, a social centre with a political slant that welcomes both lesbians and gay men. The tourist office can provide a gay and lesbian map (free).

Hospital Medical emergencies and ambulances on ☎100.

Internet access easyEverything, Place de Brouckere 9–13. From €2.50/hr; price depends on how many of the 450 terminals are in use (daily 24hrs). Avenue Cyber Theatre, ave de la Toison d'Or 4–5 (☎02500 7811).

Laundry Quick Wash, rue de Flandre 129.

Left luggage All the main train stations have left-luggage facilities, as well as coin-operated lockers (€2, €2.70, €3.20).

Post office The main central post office is on the first floor of the Centre Monnaie, place de la Monnaie (Mon–Fri 8am–8pm, Sat 9am–3pm).

Train enquiries Belgian Rail ☎02555 2525; British Rail International, rue de la Montagne 50 (☎02717 4500); Le Shuttle (☎02717 4500); Eurostar, Gare du Midi (☎02224 8856, *www.eurostar.com*)

Women's contacts Artemys, Galerie Bortier 8–10 (☎02512 0347), off rue St Jean, is Brussels' largest feminist bookstore with English-speaking staff and a notice-board upstairs. Amazone, rue du Méridien 10 (☎02229 3800), brings together under one roof many different women's organizations, and has a café too.

NORTHERN BELGIUM

North of Brussels, Belgium is entirely Flemish-speaking. The provinces of East and West Flanders, Antwerp, Limburg and North Brabant represent one-third of the Belgian federation, and their people have maintained a distinctive cultural and linguistic identity. It's dull countryside on the whole, but a string of fine historic cities more than compensates. **Antwerp**, a large old port with many reminders of its sixteenth-century golden age, is due north of Brussels. Between the two is the ecclesiastical capital of the country, **Mechelen**, which merits a brief stop, while to the west is the heartland of Flemish-speaking Belgium, a stupendously prosperous region in the Middle Ages and home to much of the country's industrial base. There are many reminders of the area's medieval greatness, but the most vivid lie to the west in the ancient cloth cities of **Ghent** and **Bruges**, whose well-preserved old centres hold marvellous collections of early Flemish art.

Mechelen

Home of the Primate of Belgium, **MECHELEN** was one of the more powerful cities of medieval Flanders, even overshadowing Brussels when the Burgundian prince Charles the Bold decided to base his administration here in 1473. Nowadays, Mechelen has a surprisingly provincial atmosphere, a likeably low-key contrast to Antwerp and Brussels.

The centre of town, **Grote Markt**, is flanked on the eastern side by the **Stadhuis**, whose incoherent appearance is the result of a half-finished sixteenth-century rebuilding: the plan was to replace the dour medieval original with a delicately fluted Renaissance edifice, but the money ran out halfway through. In front of the Stadhuis, just outside the tourist office, is a modern sculpture showing the town's grotesque mascot, **Op Signoorke**, being tossed in a blanket. A little way west, the **Cathedral of St Rombout** (daily: April–Oct 9.30am–5pm; Nov–March 9.30am–4.30pm; free), a gigantic church completed in 1546, dominates the centre of town. The thirteenth-century nave has all the cloistered elegance of the Brabantine Gothic style, and in the south transept hangs Van Dyck's muscular *Crucifixion*, while the elaborate doors at the rear of the high altar hide the remains of St Rombout himself. The tower contains Belgium's finest carillon, a fifteenth-century affair of 49 bells, which resounds over the town on high days and holidays. There are also regular, hour-long performances on Mondays and Saturdays (11.30am), Sundays (3pm), and from June through to mid-September on Monday evenings (8.30pm).

A short walk north at the end of St Jansstraat, the **Museum Hof van Busleyden** (Tues–Sun 10am–5pm, Sat & Sun 2–6pm; €2) is housed in a splendid sixteenth-century mansion and includes a display of miscellaneous bells, a room devoted to Mechelen's guilds, a range of Gallo-Roman artefacts, and an unusual assortment of unattributed paintings. Biest leads southeast from here to Veemarkt where the church of **St Pieter en St Paulus** (daily: Apr–Oct 1–5pm; Nov–March noon–4pm; free) was built for the Jesuits in the seventeenth century. The interior has an oak pulpit that pays tribute to the order's missionary work, carved in 1701 by Hendrik Verbruggen, with a globe near its base attached to representations of the four continents known at the time.

Practicalities

From Mechelen's **train station** it's about fifteen minutes' walk north to the centre, straight down Hendrik Consciencestraat. The **tourist office**, in the Stadhuis on the east side of the Grote Markt (March–Oct Mon–Fri 8am–6pm, Nov–Feb Mon–Fri 8am–5pm; March–Sept also Sat & Sun 9.30am–12.30pm & 1.30–5pm, Oct–Feb Sat & Sun 10am–noon & 2–4.30pm; ☎01529 7655, *www.mechelen.be*), can arrange **accommodation** in one of the few private rooms (€37–50 per double). The town has just one recommendable, central hotel, the four-star *Golden Tulip Alfa Alba*, Korenmarkt 24 (☎01542 0303; ⑨). For **hostel** accommodation try the brand new *Jeughotel Zandpoort*, Zandpoortvest (☎03232 7218, *www.vjh.be*; ②). There are plenty of places to **eat** on and around Grote Markt, but the best places are down by the river Dijle – try the vegetarian fare on offer at *Eetcafe De Grasport* at Begijnestraat 28–30 or the good-value Spanish food at *Madrid*, off Ijzerenleen at Lange Schipstraat 4 (closed Tues). **Bars** worth trying include the lively *Lord Nelson* and the *Arms of York*, on Wollemarkt, or the fashionable *De Cirque* on Nauwstraat, a narrow sidestreet off Ijzerenleen. There is **Internet access** at *'t Metkot*, Leopoldstraat 81 (☎01543 1444).

Antwerp

Belgium's second city, **ANTWERP**, fans out from the east bank of the Scheldt about 50km north of Brussels. Many people prefer it to the capital: though not an immediately likeable place, it has a denser concentration of things to see, not least some fine churches and distinguished museums – reminders of its auspicious past as centre of a wide trading empire. It also has a more focused character: in recent years, the city has become the effective capital of Flemish Belgium, a lively cultural centre with a spirited nightlife. On the surface it's not a wealthy city – the area around the docks especially is run-down and seedy – but its diamond industry (centred behind the dusty facades around Centraal Station) is the world's largest. On a less contemporary note, there is also the enormous legacy of Rubens, some of whose finest works adorn Antwerp's galleries and churches.

Arrival, information and accommodation

Most trains stop at **Centraal Station**, about 2km east of Grote Markt and connected with the centre by tram #2 or #15 to Groenplaats (direction Linkeroever) from the Diamant underground station. A useful **tram and bus system** serves the city and its suburbs from a number of points around Centraal Station, principally Pelikaanstraat and Koningin Astridplein. The city **transport information** office in Diamant underground station (Mon–Fri 8am–12.30pm & 1.30–4pm; ☎03218 1411) sells tickets and has free maps of the transport system. A standard single fare costs €1, a ten-strip *Rittenkaart* €2.90, a 24-hour unlimited travel tourist card €7.40. Tickets (but not the 24-hour pass or *Rittenkaart*) are also available from bus and tram drivers. Antwerp's **tourist office** is at Grote Markt 15 (Mon–Sat 9am–5.45pm, Sun 9am–4.45pm; ☎03232 0103, *www.visitantwerpen.be*); it has detailed city maps, and will make accommodation reservations for free. It's worth noting that admission to all the city's museums is free on a Friday. **Internet access** can be found at *Cybercafé*, Centrale Openbare Bibliotheek, Lange Nieuwstraat 105 (☎03231 1805) and *easyEverything*, Century Center, De Keyserlei 58–60 (daily: 24hrs, from €1.20).

The city has a range of accommodation to suit all pockets, although they are on the whole rather characterless places. Two of the cheapest **hostels** are the *New International Youth Hotel*, Provinciestraat 256 (☎03230 0522; ③), just a ten-minute walk south from Centraal Station; and the nearby *Scoutel Jeugdverblifcentrum*, Stoomstraat 3–7 (☎03226 4606, *www.vvksm.be*; ③). Another possibility is the *International Zeemanshuis* (Seamen's House), a ten-minute walk north of the Grote Markt at Falconrui 21 (☎03227 5433, *www.zeemanshuis.be*; ④). There is a **HI hostel**, *Op Sinjoorke* (closed 10am–4pm), 5km south of the centre at Eric Sasselaan 2 (☎03238 0273, *www.vjh.be*; ②) – take tram #2 from Centraal Station (direction Hoboken). Among moderately priced and reasonably central **hotels**, the options include: *Eden*, Lange Herentalsestraat 25 (☎03233 0608, *www.diamond-hotels.com*; ⑤), a modern, medium-sized hotel in the diamond district near the station; *Ibis Antwerpen Centrum*, Meistraat 39 (☎03231 8830, *www.ibishotels.com*; ⑥), a standard chain-hotel in a decent location close to the Rubenshuis; *Prinse*, Keizerstraat 63 (☎03226 4050, *hotel-prinse@skynet.be*; ⑦), a smart if slightly characterless hotel whose modern furnishings and fittings occupy a big old house in a good, quiet location just five minutes' walk north of the Rubenshuis; and *Cammerpoorte*, Nationalestraat 38 (☎03231 9736; ④), a frugal one-star hotel in a handy location, just five minutes' walk south of Groenplaats.

The City

The centre of Antwerp is **Grote Markt**, at the heart of which stands the **Brabo Fountain**, a haphazard pile of rocks surmounted by a bronze of Silvius Brabo, depicted flinging the hand of the giant Antigonus – who terrorized passing ships – into the Scheldt. The north side of Grote Markt is lined with daintily restored sixteenth-century **guildhouses**, though they are overshadowed by the **Stadhuis**, completed in 1566 to a design by Cornelis Floris (tours Mon, Tues, Wed & Fri 11am, 2pm, 3pm, Sat 2pm, 3pm; €0.70) and one of the most important buildings of the Northern Renaissance. Among rooms you can visit are the Leys Room, named after Baron Hendrik Leys, who painted the frescoes in the 1860s, and the Wedding Room, which has a chimneypiece decorated with two caryatids by Floris.

Southeast of Grote Markt, the **Onze Lieve Vrouwe Cathedral** (Mon–Fri 10am–5pm, Sat 10am–3pm, Sun 1–4pm; €2) is one of the finest Gothic churches in Belgium, mostly the work of Jan and Pieter Appelmans in the middle of the fifteenth century. The broad nave is notable primarily for its paintings by Rubens, of which the *Descent from the Cross*, to the right of the central crossing, is the most beautiful. In the ambulatory – the second chapel down the right hand side – is a *Resurrection* triptych by Rubens, painted for the tomb of his friend Jan Moretus in 1612. Moretus is also remembered by the **Plantin-Moretus Museum** on Vrijdagmarkt, south of Grote Markt (Tues–Sun 10am–4.45pm; €3.70), housed in the mansion of his father-in-law, the printer Christopher Plantin. One of Antwerp's most interesting museums, it provides a marvellous insight into how Plantin and his family conducted their business. Highlights include a delightful seventeenth-century bookshop, the old print room, and examples of Plantin's work. There are also sketches by Rubens, who occasionally worked for the family as an illustrator.

Fifteen minutes' walk south (or tram #8 from Groenplaats), the **Museum voor Schone Kunsten** (Tues–Sun 10am–5pm; €3.70) has one of the country's finest art collections. Its early Flemish section includes two charming works by Jan van Eyck – a tiny *Madonna at the Fountain* and a *St Barbara* – along with works by Memling, Rogier van der Weyden and Quentin Matsys, whose triptych of the *Lamentation* was commissioned for Antwerp Cathedral in 1511. Rubens has two large rooms to himself, in which one very large canvas stands out: the *Adoration of the Magi*, a beautifully human work apparently completed in a fortnight. The museum also has a comprehensive collection of modern Belgian art, including the paintings of Paul Delvaux and James Ensor.

North, back towards the city centre, the **Mayer van den Bergh Museum**, Lange Gasthuisstraat 19 (Tues–Sun 10am–4.45pm; €3.70), contains delightful examples of the applied arts, from tapestries to ceramics, silverware, illuminated manuscripts and furniture, in a crowded reconstruction of a sixteenth-century town house. There are also some excellent paintings, including a *Crucifixion* triptych by Quentin Matsys and a *St Christopher* by Jan Mostaert – though the museum's best-known work is Bruegel's *Dulle Griet* or "Mad Meg", a misogynistic allegory in which a woman, loaded down with possessions, stalks the gates of Hell. It's a ten-minute walk northeast from here to the **Rubenshuis** at Wapper 9 (Tues–Sun 10am–4.30pm; €5), the former home and studio of the artist, now restored as a museum. Unfortunately, there are only one or two of his less distinguished paintings here, but the restoration of the rooms is convincing; behind the house, the garden is laid out in the formal style of his day. Rubens died in 1640 and was buried in the **St Jacobskerk**, just north of here on Lange Nieuwstraat 73 (April–Oct Mon–Sat noon–5pm; Nov–March Mon–Sat 9am–noon; €1.70). Rubens and his immediate family are buried in the chapel behind the high altar, where, in one of his last works, *Our Lady Surrounded by Saints*, he painted himself as St George, his two wives as Martha and Mary, and his father as St Jerome.

Back in the centre of the town, on the waterfront at the far end of Suikerrui from Grote Markt, is the **Steen**, the remaining gatehouse of what was once an impressive medieval fortress. Today the Steen houses the **National Maritime Museum** (Tues–Sun 10am–4.45pm; €3.70), whose cramped rooms feature exhibits on inland navigation, shipbuilding and waterfront life. The open-air section has a long line of tugs and barges under a

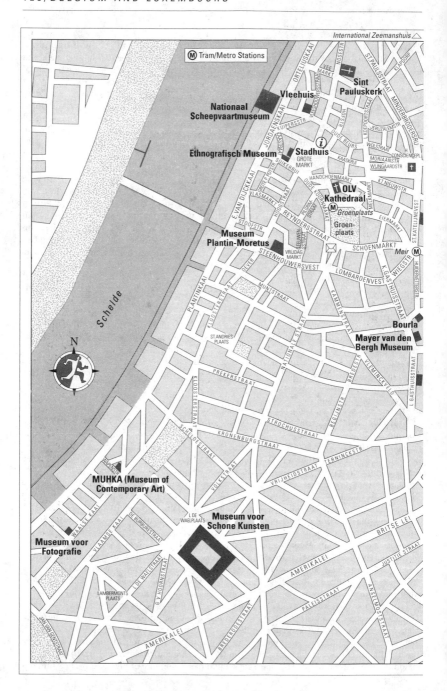

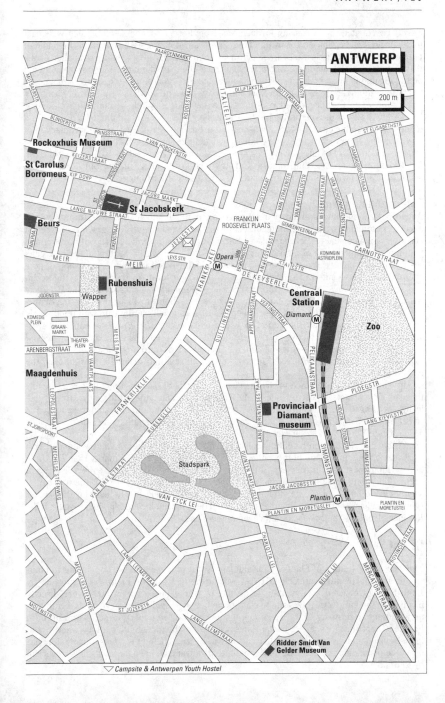

rickety corrugated roof. Crossing Jordaenskaai from here, it's a couple of minutes' walk east to the impressively gabled **Vleeshuis** (Tues–Sun 10am–4.45pm; €2.50), built for the guild of butchers in 1503 and today used to display a large but incoherent collection of applied arts – there are several fine medieval woodcarvings and a good set of antique musical instruments on the ground floor and period rooms up above. The streets around here, badly damaged by wartime bombing, have been redeveloped in a cosy pastiche of what went before, forming a stark contrast to the dilapidated **red-light area** beyond. A couple of minutes' walk along Vleeshouwersstraat on Veemarkt, the **St Pauluskerk** (Easter–Sept daily 2–5pm; free) is a dignified late-Gothic church of 1517 whose most prominent feature is the extraordinary mid-seventeenth-century carving of the confessionals and choir stalls. Rubens' *Scourging at the Pillar* is among a set of fifteen canvases hung on the north aisle wall in 1617 to illustrate the Mysteries of the Rosary. Outside, the **Calvaryberg** grotto clings to the buttresses of the south transept, eerily adorned with statues of Christ and other figures.

Eating and drinking

Antwerp is an enjoyable and inexpensive place to **eat**, full of informal café-restaurants, which excel at combining traditional Flemish techniques and dishes with Mediterranean, French and vegetarian cuisines. There are places serving delicious food all over the city centre, and you don't even pay much of a premium on or around Grote Markt. Several of the best café-restaurants are clustered on Suikerrui and Grote Pieter Potstraat, and there's another concentration in the vicinity of Hendrik Conscienceplein. For **food on the run**, try the kebab and falafel takeaways on Oude Koornmark. Recommended restaurants include *Het Elfde Gebod*, on the north side of the cathedral, which serves light meals in an eccentric, statue-filled interior; *Facade*, Hendrik Conscienceplein 18, a laid-back, funky café with good music and inexpensive vegetarian, meat and fish dishes; and *Het Dagelijks Brood*, Steenhouwersvest 48, an enjoyable and distinctive café where the variety of breads is the main event, served with delicious, wholesome soups and light meals (daily 7am–7pm). For something a tad more expensive, try *Hoorn des Overloed*, Melkmarkt 1, an outstanding seafood restaurant near the cathedral.

Antwerp is also a fine place to **drink**. There are loads of bars in the city centre, notably those on Groenplaats, whose terraces make a nice spot to watch the world go by. More specifically, *Den Engel*, on the northwest corner of the Grote Markt at no.3, is an agreeable venue as is *Den Billekletser*, across Grote Markt at Hoogstraat 22. Just south, you could try *De Volle Maan*, Oude Koornmarkt 7, or *Het Miniatuurke*, on the same street at Oude Koornmarkt 11, in an atmospheric thirteenth-century cellar. Failing that, there's the wild and wonderful *Café Pelikaan*, on the north side of the cathedral at Melkmarkt 14. At Melkmarkt 15 is *De Muze*, one of the hippest bars in Antwerp, with a young and trendy crowd and frequent live jazz at night. The long-established *Kulminator*, five minutes' walk south of the centre at Vleminckveld 32–34, claims to stock 500 speciality beers; alternatively head for the *jenever* (gin) specialists, *De Vagrant*, Reyndersstraat 21. The favourite local tipple, incidentally, is *De Koninck*, drunk by the *bolleke*, or small, stemmed glass.

Ghent

The seat of the Counts of Flanders and the largest town in western Europe during the thirteenth and fourteenth centuries, **GHENT** was at the heart of the Flemish cloth trade. By 1350, the city boasted a population of 50,000, of whom no less than 5000 were directly involved in the industry. However, the cloth trade began to decline in the early sixteenth century and although many of the city's merchants switched to exporting surplus grain from France, Ghent slowly declined. Better times returned in the nineteenth century when Ghent industrialized and it's now the third largest city in Belgium. Ghent is a less immediately picturesque place than Bruges, but this is much to its advantage in so far as it's never overrun by tourists.

Arrival, information and accommodation

Of Ghent's two **train stations**, the most useful is **St Pieters**, 2km south of the centre and connected by **trams** #1, #10, #11, #12 and #13. The **tourist office** is in the crypt of the old belfry, the Belfort, right in the centre on the Botermarkt (daily: April–Oct 9.30am–6.30pm; Nov–March 9.30am–4.30pm; ☎09266 5232, *www.gent.be*). The best way of seeing the sights is on foot, but Ghent is a large city and you may find you have to use a **tram** or **bus** at some point. Standard single fares cost €1, a ten-journey *Rittenkaart* €7.40 and a day pass €2.90. Single tickets can be bought direct from the driver; passes are sold at shops and kiosks all over town. For **Internet access**, try Internet Café, Sportcentrum Stadium Coupure, Coupure Links 625 (☎09266 1893) or The Globetrotter, Kortrijksepoortstraat 180 (☎09269 0860, €3.70/hr).

The plush, modern *De Draecke* **HI hostel** is a few minutes' walk from the castle at Sint-Widostraat 11, just off Braderijstraat (☎09233 7050, *youthhostel.gent@skynet.be*; ②). Between mid-July and the end of September, **student rooms** are let for €15 per person including breakfast; ask at the tourist office for further details. Among several reasonably priced, central **hotels** there's *Ibis Gent Centrum Kathedraal*, Limburgstraat 2 (☎09233 0000, *www.hotelibis.be*; ⑤), a handily situated hotel with comfortable modern rooms opposite the cathedral; *Ibis Gent Centrum Opera*, Nederkouter 24–26 (☎09225 0707, *www.hotelibis.com*; ⑤), a spick-and-span, five-storey block five minutes' walk south of the Korenmarkt; and *Erasmus*, Poel 25 (☎09224 2195, *www.bbb.proximedia.com*; ⑤), a charming, family-run hotel located in an old and commodious town house just off the Korenlei. The best **campsite** is *Camping Blaarmeersen* at Zuiderlaan 12, west of the centre (March to mid-Oct; ☎09221 5399, *camping.blaarmeersen@gent.be*) – take bus #38 from Korenmarkt.

The City

The best place to start exploring is at the mainly Gothic **St Baaf's Cathedral**, squeezed into the corner of St Baafsplein (daily: April–Oct 8.30am–6pm, Nov–March 8.30am–5pm; free). Inside, a small chapel (April–Oct Mon–Sat 9.30am–5pm, Sun 1–6pm; Nov–March Mon–Sat 10.30am–4pm, Sun 2–5pm; €2.50 includes the crypt) holds Ghent's greatest treasure, the altarpiece of the *Adoration of the Mystic Lamb*, an early fifteenth-century work believed to be by Jan van Eyck. The cover screens display an *Annunciation* scene with the archangel Gabriel's wings reaching up to the timbered ceiling of a Flemish house; on the inside – only revealed when the shutters were opened on Sundays and feast days – the upper level shows God the Father, the Virgin and John the Baptist, while in the lower panel is the Lamb, approached by various figures in paradise, seen as a sort of idealized Low Countries – look closely and you can see the cathedrals of Bruges, Utrecht and Maastricht. The twelfth-century crypt (same times) preserves features of the earlier Romanesque church of St John, along with murals painted between 1480 and 1540.

Just west of St Baaf's, the fifteenth-century **Lakenhalle** (Cloth Hall) is little more than an empty shell, whose first-floor entrance leads to the adjoining **Belfry** (tours daily; €2.50), a much-amended edifice from the fourteenth century. A glass-sided lift climbs up to the roof for excellent views over the city centre. A few strides away to the north is the **Stadhuis** (tours May–Oct Mon–Thurs 3pm; €2.50), whose long facade was erected in two phases – the earlier and more flamboyant section was designed by Rombout Keldermans. Each ornate niche was intended to hold a statuette, but the money ran out; the present carvings, representing the powerful and famous – including Keldermans himself rubbing his chin and studying his plans for the building – were only inserted at the end of the last century.

A couple of minutes' walk from the Stadhuis, **Korenlei** forms the western side of the old city harbour, home to a series of expansive, high-gabled merchants' houses dating from the eighteenth century. In architectural contrast, the **Graslei**, opposite, holds the squat, gabled guild- and warehouses of the town's medieval boatmen and grain-weighers. A few minutes north of here is the sinister-looking **'s Gravensteen** (daily: April–Sept 9am–6pm, Oct–March

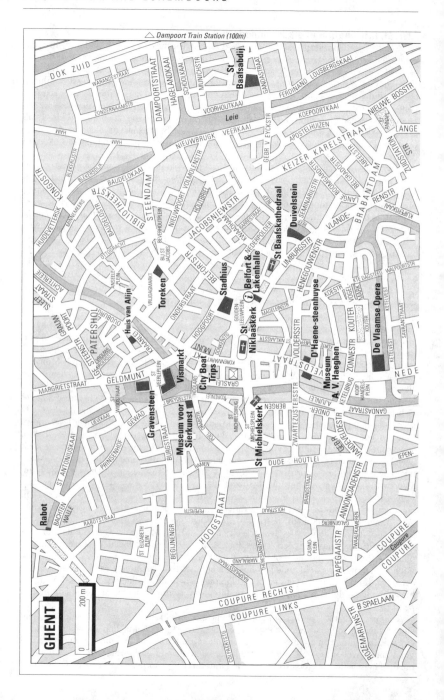

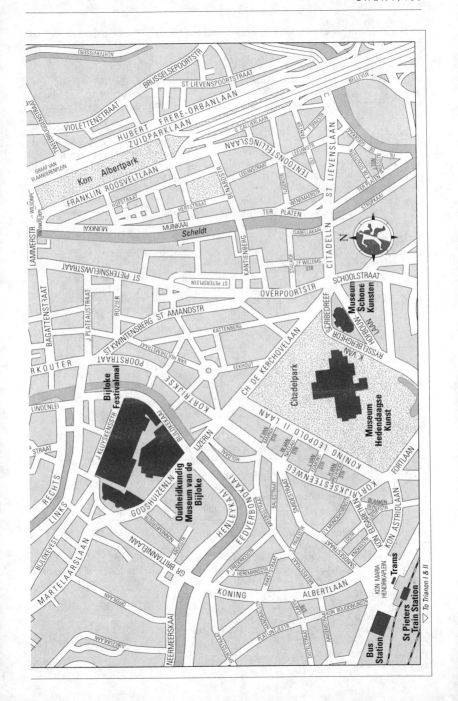

9am–5pm, last ticket 45 minutes before closing; €5) or Castle of the Counts, whose interior holds an assembly room with a magnificent stone fireplace and a gruesome collection of torture instruments. North of here, Braderijstraat leads to **Lievekaai**, Ghent's second oldest harbour, while east of the castle are the part-gentrified, seventeenth-century lanes and alleys of the **Patershol**, home to the **Huis van Alijn Volkskunde**, Kraanlei 65 (Tues–Sun 9am–12.30pm & 1.30–5.30pm; €2.50; *www.aijn.gent.be*), a series of restored almshouses where a delightful chain of period rooms depicts local life and work in the eighteenth and nineteenth centuries.

South of the centre, Ghent's main shopping street, **Veldstraat**, heads off towards the impressive **Museum voor Schone Kunsten**, fifteen minutes' walk away at Nicolaas de Liemaeckereplein 3, Citadelpark (Tues–Sun 9.30am–5pm; €2.50; *www.finearts .museum.gent.be*). Here, there's a first-rate sample of old masters including Bosch's *Carrying of the Cross* and the smaller, less well-known *St Jerome at Prayer*, along with work by Pieter Bruegel the Younger, Jordaens, Van Dyck and Frans Hals. Opposite, the old casino has been turned into **SMAK** (Tues–Sun 10am–6pm; €5; *www.smak.be*), a museum of contemporary art, which illustrates every major artistic movement since 1945.

Eating and drinking

Ghent is as fine a place to **eat** as any other Belgian city: its numerous cafés and restaurants offer the very best of Flemish and French cuisines, with a sprinkling of Italian, Chinese and Arab places. The more deluxe restaurants are concentrated in and around the Patershol, while less expensive spots, including a rash of fast food joints, cluster the Korenmarkt. Options include the central *Auberge de Fonteyne*, Gouden Leeuwplein 7, a large café/restaurant with kitsch Art Nouveau decor serving Flemish food at very reasonable prices; *Café Leffe*, Botermarkt 11, a straightforward, inexpensive café offering snacks and filling meals of good quality until late every night; and the *Brooderie*, Jan Breydelstraat 8, a café with a healthfood slant near the castle and open till 6pm. Ghent has great **bars** too: try the dark and mysterious *De Tap en de Tepel* ("Tap and Nipple") on Gewad 7, with its vast and expensive wine list; or the packed *Tolhuisje Tavern* on Graslei 11. *Het Waterhuis*, near the castle at Groentenmarkt 9, serves over one hundred sorts of beer in pleasant surroundings.

Bruges

"Somewhere within the dingy casing lay the ancient city", wrote Graham Greene of **BRUGES**, "like a notorious jewel, too stared at, talked of, trafficked over." And it's true that Bruges' reputation as one of the most perfectly preserved medieval cities in western Europe has made it the most popular tourist destination in Belgium, packed with visitors throughout the summer. Inevitably, the crowds tend to overwhelm the town's charms, but you would be mad to come to Flanders and miss the place: its museums, to name just one attraction, hold some of the country's finest collections of Flemish art; and its intimate, winding streets, woven around a pattern of narrow canals and lined with gorgeous ancient buildings, live up to even the most inflated hype.

By the fourteenth century Bruges shared effective control of the cloth trade with its two great rivals, Ghent and Ypres, turning high-quality English wool into thousands of items of clothing that were exported all over the known world. It was an immensely profitable business, and made the city a centre of international trade: at its height, the town was a key member of the Hanseatic League, the most powerful economic alliance in medieval Europe. By the end of the fifteenth century, though, Bruges was in decline, partly because of a recession in the cloth trade, but principally because the Zwin river – the city's vital link to the North Sea – was silting up. By the 1530s the town's sea trade had collapsed completely, and Bruges simply withered away. Frozen in time, Bruges escaped damage in both world wars to emerge the perfect tourist attraction.

Arrival, information and accommodation

Bruges' **train station** is twenty minutes' walk or a short bus ride southwest of the town centre. There is a **hotel booking** service, operated by the tourist office, just outside the station (April–Sept Mon–Sat 10.30am–1.15pm & 2–6.30pm; Oct–March Mon–Sat 9.30am–1.15pm & 2–5.30pm; ☎05038 8083). You can also book accommodation at the **tourist office** in the city centre at Burg 11 (April–Sept Mon–Fri 9.30am–6.30pm, Sat & Sun 10am–noon & 2–6.30pm; Oct–March Mon–Fri 9.30am–5pm, Sat & Sun 9.30am–1pm & 2–5.30pm; ☎05044 8686, *www.brugge.be*), where there's also a bureau de change, useful maps and bus timetables. You can access the **Internet** at The Coffee Link, Mariastraat 38 (Mon–Sat 10am–9.30pm, Sun 1.30–6.30pm, *www.thecoffeelink.com*; €5/hr). There are several **unofficial hostels** with dormitory beds and limited supplies of smaller rooms, including the *Bauhaus International Youth Hotel*, fifteen minutes' walk east of Burg at Langestraat 135–137 (☎05034 1093, *info@bauhaus.be*; ②), and the first-rate *Passage*, Dweersstraat 24 (☎05034 0232; ②). A laid-back option in the old town is the *Snuffel Sleep In*, Ezelstraat 47–49 (☎05033 31 33, *www.snuffel.be*; ②; take bus #3 or #13 from the station to the first stop after the market place). There's a **HI hostel**, *Europa*, 2km south of the centre at Baron Ruzettelaan 143 (☎05035 2679; ②; take bus #2 from the train station) and a cluster of routine but reasonably priced **hotels** west of Markt around 't Zand: try the *Speelmanshuys*, 't Zand 3 (☎05033 9552; ④). Alternatively, try the cosy *Cordoeanier*, Cordoeaniersstraat 18 (☎05033 9051, *www.cordoeanier.be*; ④), or the tiny *Het Gheestelic Hof*, just west of the Burg at Heilige Geeststraat 2 (☎05034 25 94; ⑤). There's an all-year **campsite**, *St Michiel*, 3km southwest of the train station at Tillegemstraat 55 (☎05038 0819); take bus #7 from the train station and get off at the junction of St Michielslaan and Rijselstraat.

The City

The older sections of Bruges fan out from two central squares, Markt and Burg. **Markt**, edged on three sides by nineteenth-century gabled buildings, is the larger of the two, an impressive open space, on the south side of which the octagonal **Belfry** (daily 9.30am–5pm; €2.50) was built in the thirteenth century when the town was at its richest and most extravagant. Inside, the staircase passes the room where the town charters were locked for safekeeping, and an eighteenth-century carillon, before emerging onto the roof. At the foot of the belfry, the rectangular **Hallen** is a much-restored edifice dating from the thirteenth century, its style and structure modelled on the cloth hall at Ieper (Ypres). From the Markt, Breidelstraat leads through to **Burg**, whose southern half is fringed by the city's finest group of buildings. One of the best is the **Heilig Bloed Basiliek** (Basilica of the Holy Blood; April–Sept daily 9.30am–noon & 2–6pm; Oct–March 10am–noon & 2–4pm, closed Wed pm; free), named after a phial of the blood of Christ that dried out soon after it was brought here in 1150 and then miraculously liquefied every Friday at 6pm until 1325. The twelfth-century basilica divides into a shadowy Lower Chapel, built to house a relic of St Basil, and an Upper Chapel where the rock-crystal phial is stored in a grandiose silver tabernacle given by Albert and Isabella of Spain in 1611. The Holy Blood is still venerated here on Fridays at 8am and 3pm, and on Ascension Day (mid-May) is carried through the town in a colourful but solemn procession, the *Helig-Bloedprocessie*. In the tiny **Treasury** (€1) you'll find the jewel-encrusted reliquary that holds the Holy Blood during the procession.

To the left of the basilica, the **Stadhuis** has a beautiful, turreted sandstone facade, a much-copied exterior that dates from 1376, though its statues of the counts and countesses of Flanders are replacements. Inside, the magnificent Gothic Hall of 1400 (daily 9.30am–5pm; €3.70) is well worth a look, with vault-keys depicting New Testament scenes and paintings commissioned in 1895 to illustrate the history of the town. The price of admission covers entry to the former alderman's house, the **Renaissancezaal Brugse Vrije** (daily 9.30am–12.30pm & 1.30–5pm), also on the square, where there's just one exhibit, an enormous marble and oak chimney piece located in the old Magistrates' Hall. A fine example of Renaissance carving, it was completed in 1531 to celebrate the defeat of the French at Pavia

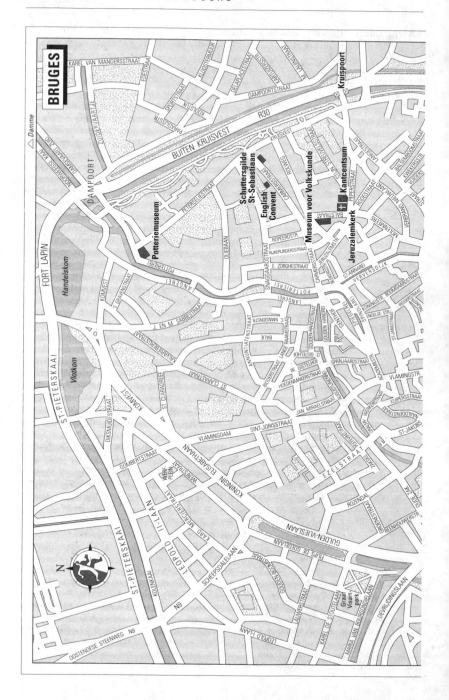

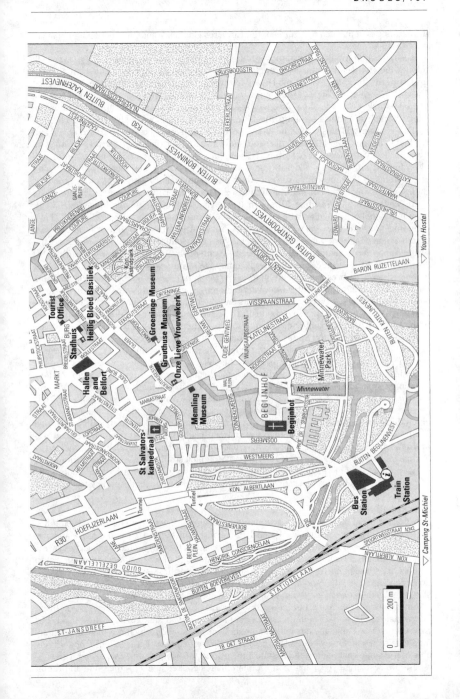

in 1525, and is dominated by figures of the Emperor Charles V and his Austrian and Spanish relatives.

Heading south from the Burg, through the archway next to the Stadhuis, it's a brief walk to both the eighteenth-century **Vismarkt**, and the huddle of picturesque houses that make up **Huidenvettersplein**. Close by, **Dijver** follows the canal to the **Groeninge Museum** at Dijver 12 (April–Sept daily 9.30am–5pm; Oct–March Mon & Wed–Sun 9.30am–5pm; €6.20, combined ticket with Memling, Arentshuis & Gruuthuse museums €9.90), which houses a superb sample of Flemish paintings from the fourteenth to the twentieth centuries. The best section is of early Flemish work, including several canvases by Jan van Eyck, who lived and worked in Bruges from 1430 until his death eleven years later, and the *Judgement of Cambyses* by Gerard David. There's also work by Hieronymus Bosch, his *Last Judgement* a trio of panels crammed with mysterious beasts and scenes of awful cruelty, and the *Moreel Triptych* by Hans Memling. The museum's selection of seventeenth-century paintings is more modest, though there's a delightfully naturalistic *Peasant Lawyer* after Pieter Bruegel the Younger.

At Dijver 17 the **Gruuthuse Museum** (same times as the Groeninge Museum; €3.20), sited in a rambling fifteenth-century mansion, has a varied collection of fine and applied art, including fine intricately carved altar pieces, musical instruments, sixteenth- and seventeenth-century tapestries and many different types of furniture. Beyond the Gruuthuse, the **Onze Lieve Vrouwekerk** (daily April–Sept 10am–noon & 2–5pm; Oct–March Mon–Fri 10–noon, Sat 10am–noon & 2–4pm; free) is a massive shambles of different dates and styles, among whose treasures is a delicate marble *Madonna and Child* by Michelangelo, an influential early work brought from Tuscany by a Flemish merchant. It is also home to the mausoleums (€1.80) of Charles the Bold and his daughter Mary of Burgundy, striking examples of Renaissance carving. The earth beneath the mausoleums has been dug out and mirrors now reveal the frescoes painted on the tomb walls at the start of the sixteenth century.

Opposite the church, the **St Jans Hospitaal** complex contains a well-preserved fifteenth-century dispensary and the small but important **Memling Museum**. At the time of writing the museum was closed for rennovation, but the collection of paintings are being held in the Groeninge Museum – ask at the tourist office for details. Born near Frankfurt in 1433, Hans Memling spent most of his working life in Bruges. Of his six paintings on display, the *Mystical Marriage of St Catherine*, the middle panel of an altarpiece painted between 1475 and 1479, is perhaps the most notable. There's also the unusual *Reliquary of St Ursula*, a miniature wooden Gothic church painted with the story of St Ursula and the 11,000 martyred virgins. Just north of the St Jans Hospitaal, Heilige Geeststraat heads northwest to the **Sint Salvatorskathedraal** (St Saviour's Cathedral), a replacement for the cathedral destroyed by the French in the eighteenth century. From here, it's a quick stroll down to the **Begijnhof** (daily 9am–6pm), a circle of whitewashed houses around a tidy green. Nearby, the picturesque **Minnewater** was once used as a town harbour, and still has a fifteenth-century lock gate.

Eating and drinking

Inevitably, most of the **cafés** and **restaurants** in Bruges are geared up for the tourist industry, with the majority working from a fairly uniform Flemish menu. By and large, standards are high, portions substantial and prices quite reasonable, the only problem being the crowds that make many city-centre places unbearable in the height of summer. Several of the youth hostels offer **inexpensive meals**, the best of which are those served up by the *Passage*, Dweersstraat 26, and the *Bauhaus*, Langestraat 135. For fresh **seafood** snacks, the fish shops along the Vismarkt are a good bet, with delicious specialities for around €7.

Among Bruges's many **eateries**, try *Taverne Curiosa*, Vlamingstraat 22, a lively bar/restaurant in an old vaulted cellar a couple of minutes' walk north of the Markt; *Het Dagelijks Brood*, Philipstockstraat 21, an excellent bread shop which doubles as a wholefood café with one, long wooden table; *La Dentellière*, Wijngaardstraat 33, the most agreeable of the somewhat overpriced restaurants around the Minnewater; *Den Dyver*, Dijver 5, a first-rate restaurant specializing in Flemish dishes cooked in beer – the quail and rabbit are magnificent; *Erasmus*, Wollestraat 35, a straightforward, brightly-lit café with reasonably priced, mostly Flemish dishes; or *Beethoven*, St Amandsstraat 6, a cosy family-run restaurant serving top-notch Belgian dishes at expensive prices. As for **bars**, *'t Brugs Beertje*, Kemelstraat 5, is a small and friendly speciality beer bar that claims a stock of two hundred ales; *'t Dreupelhuisje*, Kemelstraat 9, is a tiny place specializing in *jenevers* and *advocaats*, of which it has an excellent range; and the *Oude Vlissinghe*, Blekerstraat 2, is – with its wood panelling, old paintings and long wooden tables – one of the oldest and most distinctive bars in town. The *Cactusclub*, in the city centre at St Jakobsstraat 33 (☎05034 8643), hosts quality touring DJ's and bands – everything from rock through to R&B and jazz.

SOUTHERN BELGIUM

South of Brussels, the western reaches of Wallonia are given over mainly to the French-speaking province of Hainaut, whose rolling farmland is marked by pockets of industrialization, which coalesce between Mons and Charleroi. The highlight of the province is **Tournai**, a vibrant, unpretentious city with a number of decent museums and the finest Romanesque-Gothic cathedral in the country. East of Charleroi lie the high wooded hills of the **Ardennes**, covered by the three provinces of Namur in the west, Luxembourg in the south and Liège in the east. The best gateway towns for the Ardennes, which are well worth exploring on the way south into Luxembourg and Germany, are the lively provincial centre of **Namur**, an hour from Brussels by train, and **Dinant** – a small but much visited town beside the Meuse a further thirty-minute train journey south.

Tournai

TOURNAI is the nearest southern Belgium has to the Flemish "art towns" of Flanders and the north, and is a pleasant spot to spend a couple of nights. The town was badly damaged by Allied bombing during World War II, but the cathedral, arguably the finest in the country, survived pretty much unscathed, as did the narrow lanes and alleys of the medieval street plan.

Most things of interest are on the southern side of the river, grouped around or within easy walking distance of the sprawling **Grand Place**. Dominating the skyline with its distinctive five towers is Tournai's Romanesque **Cathédrale Notre-Dame** (daily 10am–noon & 2–4/6pm; free), built out of the local slate-coloured marble. The most unusual feature of the exterior is the fascinating Porte Mantile, a Romanesque doorway on its north side, adorned with forceful, almost pagan carvings of the virtues and vices. Inside, the nave was erected in 1171, its intricately carved capitals leading down to a choir that was the first manifestation of the Gothic style in Belgium. Be sure to visit the treasury (€0.50), which houses two important thirteenth-century gilt reliquaries – the Romanesque-Gothic *châsse de Notre-Dame* (1205) by Nicolas de Verdun, and the *châsse de Saint Eleuthère* (1247) – as well as a stunning *Ecce Homo* by Quentin Matsys.

Close to the cathedral, virtually on the corner of the Grand Place, the **Belfry** is the oldest in Belgium, its lower portion dating from 1200. Close by, on place Reine Astrid, is the **Musée de la Tapisserie** (daily except Tues 10am–noon & 2–5.30pm; €2), which features old tapestries on the ground floor and modern works above – Tournai was among the most important pictorial tapestry centres in Belgium in the fifteenth and sixteenth centuries. Just along the street, cut up through the gardens to the **Hôtel de Ville**, the grandest of several municipal buildings that share the same compound. Behind here, the **Musée des Beaux Arts** (daily except Tues 10am–noon & 2–5.30pm; €3), housed in an elegant late-1920s building by Victor Horta, has a well-displayed collection of mainly Belgian painting from the Flemish primitives to the twentieth century.

Practicalities

Tournai's **train station** is on the northern edge of the town about 600m from the river. The **tourist office** at Vieux Marché-aux-Poteries 14, opposite the Belfry (Mon–Fri 9am–6pm, Sat 10am–1pm & 3–6pm & Sun 10am–noon & 2–6pm; ☎06922 2045, *www.tournai.be*), has a list of **hotels**. The cheapest are on or around the Grand Place: the *De la Tour St-Georges*, Place de Nédonchel 2 (☎06922 5035; ③) has dowdy but perfectly adequate rooms and is located just behind the Halle aux Draps. Much better – and much more expensive – is the *Hôtel d'Alcantara*, rue des Bouchers St-Jacques 2 (☎06921 2648; ⑥), a delightful and chic modern hotel slotted in behind an old facade about 400m northwest of the Grand Place. There's also a first-rate **HI hostel**, centrally placed, about five minutes' walk from the Belfry at rue St-Martin 64 (☎06921 6136, *ajtournai@skynet.be*; ②; Feb–Dec).

As for **food**, the *Bistro de la Cathédrale*, next door to the tourist office at rue Vieux Marché-aux-Poteries 15, serves a number of excellent daily specials and is a good spot to try the local speciality, *lapin à la Tournaissienne* (rabbit cooked with prunes); *La Strada*, rue de l'Yser 2, is an extremely popular Italian place serving an inexpensive range of tasty pizzas and pastas; and *A la Bonne Franquette*, quai Marché au Poisson 13a, is a good restaurant serving French food and local specialities (closed Mon). The best **bars** are strung out along the river on quai Marché au Poisson. Try *Fabrique* at no. 13b for drinks with the local crowd. There's **Internet access** at *CyberCenter*, rue Soil de Morialme 6 (Mon–Thurs 11am–11pm, Fri & Sat 11am–late, Sun 2–10.30pm; €5/hr).

Namur

Known as the "Gateway to the Ardennes", **NAMUR** is a logical first stop if you're heading into the region from the north or west, though without a car the dark forests and hills are still a long way off. That said, the town feels refreshingly free of the industrial belt of Hainaut, and its elegant, mansion-filled centre is the backdrop of a night scene lent vigour by the university.

Cutting through the centre of town, **rue de l'Ange** is Namur's main shopping street, running north into the rue de Fer, where the **Musée des Arts Anciens du Namurois** (Tues–Sun 10am–6pm; €1.20) has displays of the work of Mosan goldsmiths and silversmiths of the eleventh to thirteenth centuries. Leaving the museum, it's a short stroll southwest to the finest of Namur's churches, the **Église Saint Loup**, a Baroque extravagance that overshadows a narrow pedestrianized street, rue du Collège. Built for the Jesuits between 1621 and 1645, the church boasts a breezy, flowing facade and a sumptuous interior of marble walls and sandstone vaulting. At the west end of rue du Collège, on place St-Aubain, the **Cathédrale St-Aubain** might well be the ugliest church in Belgium, a monstrous Neoclassical pile remarkably devoid of any charm. The interior isn't much better, acres of creamy white paint and a choir decorated with melodramatic paintings by Jacques Nicolai, one of Rubens' less talented pupils.

Heading south from the cathedral towards the river, turn left along rue des Brasseurs and then first left for the **Musée Félicien Rops**, rue Fumal 12 (daily 10am–6pm, closed Mon except during July & Aug; €2.50; *www.ciger.be/rops/*), devoted to the life and work of the eponymous painter, graphic artist and illustrator, who is best-known for his erotic drawings, which reveal an obsession with the macabre and perverse – characteristically skeletons, nuns and priests depicted in compromising poses. The museum possesses a large collection of his works and is currently being extended to provide enough space to display it all. East of here, the **Trésor d'Oignies**, rue Julie Billiart 17 (Tues–Sat 10am–noon & 2–5pm, Sun 2–5pm; ring for entry; €1.20), is Namur's best museum, located in a nunnery and holding a unique collection of the beautiful gold and silver reliquaries and devotional pieces created by local craftsman Hugo d'Oignies in the first half of the thirteenth century; the nuns give the guided tour in English.

Across the Sambre River Bridge, Namur's **Citadel** (June–Sept & Easter daily 11am–5pm; April–May, except Easter, Sat & Sun only 11am–5pm; €6) is inevitably the city's major attraction, and deservedly so. Originally constructed in medieval times to defend Namur's strategic position at the junction of the Sambre and Meuse rivers, it was later turned into one of the most impregnable fortresses in Europe by Vauban and the Dutchman Coheoorn. It's a huge, sprawling place, and the entrance fee includes an audiovisual display, a miniature train ride around the grounds, and a guided tour of the deepest underground passages, as well as access to the fortress's wildlife and armaments museums.

Practicalities

Namur's **train station** is on the northern edge of the city centre, on place de la Station, close to the **tourist office** on square Léopold (daily 9.30am–6pm; ☎08124 6449, *www.ville .namur.be*). From here, it's a ten-minute walk along rue de Fer to the town centre, situated on the north bank of the Sambre River near its confluence with the Meuse. Both the tourist office and the seasonal **information chalet** (April–Sept daily 9.30am–6pm), over the bridge on the south bank of the Sambre, sell combined tickets for town sights, including the citadel and major museums. Namur's cheapest recommendable **hotel** is *L'Excelsior*, avenue de la Gare 4 (☎08123 1813; ③), a mundane budget place a few metres from the train station. Down by the Meuse, the *Beauregard*, avenue Baron Moreau 1 (☎08123 0028, *www.diamond-hotels.com*; ⑦), is much more enticing, a swish hotel adjoining the casino and with attractive, large and modern rooms. Alternatively there's a **HI hostel**, *Félicien Rops*, on the far edge of town beyond the casino, twenty minutes' walk from the centre, at ave Félicien Rops 8 (☎08122 3688, *namur@laj.be*; ②) – take bus #3 or #4 from the station.

Namur is a great place to **eat and drink**, and there are lots of spots to do both in the narrow streets around rue de l'Ange. Down near the river, at rue des Brasseurs 61, is *Aux Petits Brasseurs*, a smart little bistro serving excellent Franco-Belgian cuisine with prices to match, or you could try *Chez Guigoz*, rue St Jean 19, a medium-sized restaurant serving excellent fondues and steaks for around €15 a head; it's just off place Marché-aux-Légumes. Not far away is *L'Ecailler des Halles*, rue de la Halle 5, an upmarket deli with a small restaurant serving excellent seafood. For dinner it's hard to beat *La Petite Fugue*, on place Chanoine Descamps – an outstanding restaurant with mouth-watering Franco-Belgian dishes at around €30 for a three-course feast. *Brasserie Henry*, by the cathedral at place St-Aubain 3, is a bustling brasserie with a simple French menu and plenty of good Belgian beer; close by, behind the cathedral at rue du Séminaire 4, is *Le Chapitre*, with an excellent selection of domestic beers. The *Piano Bar*, on place Marché-aux-Légumes, is one of the town's trendiest bars with live jazz on the weekend. To access the **Internet**, try *Cybermedia*, Rue Rogier 46 (Mon & Wed–Sat 10am–6pm; ☎08126 0870).

Dinant

At the centre of the Meuse Valley tourist industry, **DINANT** is a pretty little town slung along the river beneath craggy green cliffs about 30km south of Namur. A handy base for venturing into the surrounding countryside either by boat, bike or on foot, its only drawback is its popularity – on summer weekends the place literally heaves with visitors. The town also has a couple of minor attractions of its own, the Gothic church of **Notre-Dame** (daily 9am–6pm; free), topped with the bulbous spire that features on all the brochures, and the mainly nineteenth-century **citadel** (daily 10am–6pm; July & Aug until 7pm), right behind the church and reached either by cable car (€5.20) or by a long flight of steps; the fortress is, however, a bit dull if you've already been to the one in Namur.

Practicalities

Dinant's **train station** is on the opposite side of the river and five minutes' walk from the town centre: head right then turn left across the central bridge. The **tourist office**, Ave Cadoux 8 (July–Aug daily 8.30am–7pm, Sept–June daily 8.30am–5/6pm; ☎08222 2870, *www.maison-du-tourisme.net*), is a five minute walk from the station just before the bridge.

For **Internet** access, try Adam's Computer Dinant, place Cardinal Mercier 16 (☎08222 4498). There's surprisingly little choice when it comes to **accommodation**, but the *Au Fil De L'Eau* (☎08222 7606; ③), at ave Cadoux 88, has modern facilities in a house on the banks of the Meuse, whilst the *Hôtel de la Couronne*, in the middle of town by the church at rue Adolphe Sax 1 (☎08222 2441, *www.lacouronne.be*; ④), has comfortable rooms with routine modern fittings. There's no hostel, but there are plenty of **campsites**, the closest being *Camping de Bouvignes* (☎08222 4002; March–Oct), a kilometre or so west out of town.

For **food**, most of the town's cafés and restaurants are geared up for the day-trippers, but there are still several good spots including the water's edge *Villa Casanova*, ave Churchill 9, which has tasty pasta and pizza dishes from around €7.40, and *Chez Léon*, place Reine Astrid 15, where fish and mussels are on offer. *Le Sax*, place Reine Astrid 13, is an unpretentious **bar** with a good beer selection – sit outside and watch the floodlit citadel.

As for **hiking** and **biking**, the Dinant tourist office sells the *Dinant et ses anciennes communes* map, which shows fifteen circular walks, five mountain-bike routes and one cycling circuit in the area. Each of the walks has a designated starting point in or near town. The bike routes range from five to forty kilometres, though to see the most attractive scenery you need to get out on the longer trails. You can **rent mountain bikes** from the canoe operators in nearby Anseremme, Kayaks Ansiaux (☎08222 2325), or in Dinant at Adnet Cycles, rue Saint-Roch 17 (☎08222 3243).

LUXEMBOURG

Across the border from the Belgian province of Luxembourg, the **Grand Duchy of Luxembourg** is one of Europe's smallest sovereign states, a tiny independent principality with a population of around 420,000. As a country, it's relatively neglected by travellers, most people tending to write it off as a dull and expensive financial centre, but this is a mistake. Compared to much of Europe, its attractions are indeed fairly low-key, and it is pricey, but it does have marvellous scenery in abundance: the green hills of the Ardennes spreading over the border to form a glorious heartland of deep wooded valleys spiked with sharp craggy hilltops crowned with castles.

The capital, dramatically-sited **Luxembourg City**, is almost impossible to avoid if you're not travelling by car. Home to something like a fifth of the population, it is the country's only genuinely urban environment, and well worth one or two nights' stay. The **central** part of Luxembourg is, however, even more spectacular, rucking up into rich green hills and valleys that reach their climax in the narrowing **north** of the country around **Echternach**, a tiny town dominated by its ancient abbey, and **Vianden**, with its magnificent castle.

Once part of the Spanish and later Austrian Netherlands, Luxembourg today is an independent constitutional monarchy. Although everyone speaks the indigenous language, Letzebuergesch – a dialect of German that sounds a bit like Dutch – most also speak French and German and many speak English too. Indeed, multilingualism is one of Luxembourg's most admirable features and different languages are favoured for different purposes – French is the official language of the government and judiciary, the one you'll see on street signs and suchlike, whilst German is the language most used by the press.

Luxembourg City

The city of **LUXEMBOURG** is one of the most spectacularly sited capitals in Europe, the deep canyons of its two rivers, the Alzette and Pétrusse, lending it an almost perfect strategic location. It's a tiny place by capital city standards, and broadly divides into three distinct sections. The **old town**, on the northern side of the Pétrusse valley, is not noticeably very ancient, but its tight grid of streets, home to most of the city's sights, makes for a pleasant, lively area by day. On the opposite side of the Pétrusse, connected by two bridges, the Pont

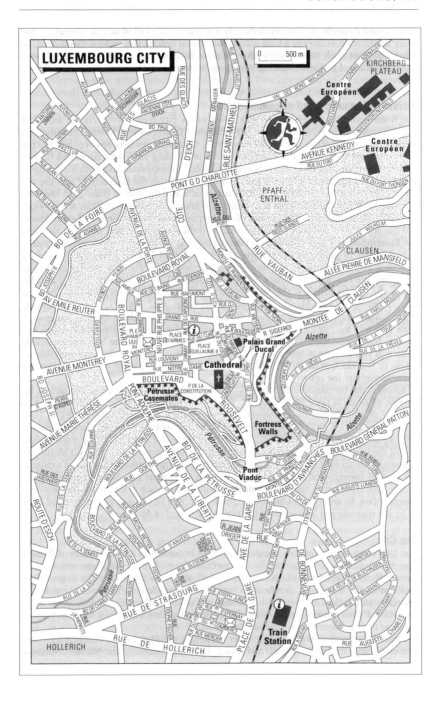

LUXEMBOURG CITY

0   500 m

N

KIRCHBERG
PLATEAU

Centre
Européen

Centre
Européen

AVENUE KENNEDY

PFAFF
ENTHAL

CLAUSEN

ALLÉE PIERRE DE MANSFELD

RUE VAUBAN

Alzette

Palais Grand
Ducal

Cathedral

Pétrusse
Casemates

Fortress
Walls

Pétrusse

Pont
Viaduc

Alzette

BOULEVARD GENERAL PATTON

BOULEVARD D'AVRANCHES

AV CH DE GALLE

Train
Station

HOLLERICH

RUE DE HOLLERICH

PLACE DE LA GARE

clubs mostly west of the train station in Hollerich. Opening hours are fairly elastic, but bars usually stay open till around 1am, clubs till 3am. While you're out on the tiles, try one of the local pilsener ales such as Mousel or the tasty *Bofferding* brews, which are the most widely available. Good **bars** to try include the funky *Chiggeri*, rue du Nord 11, which attracts a lively, youthful crowd to its groovy Old Town premises and – catering for a slightly older crowd – the *Café des Artistes*, Montée du Grund 2, a charming café-bar close to the bridge in Grund with piano accompaniment and Luxembourg singalongs. For clubs, there's *Didjeridoo*, rue Bouillon 31, Hollerich, a boisterous club west of the train station offering a wide range of sounds (Wed, Fri & Sat) and *Melusina*, rue de la Tour Jacob 145, Clausen, with varied sounds plus live jazz and folk music nights.

Listings

Airlines British Airways, at the airport (☎0800 2000); Luxair, at the airport (☎47 98 42 42); Sabena, at the airport (☎43 24 24 1).

Airport enquiries ☎47 98 50 50.

Bike rental rue Bisserwe 8, Grund (Mon–Fri 1–8pm, Sat & Sun 9am–noon & 1–8pm; ☎47 96 23 83); €2.50 an hour, €6.20 for a half-day, €9.90 a day, €18.60 for a weekend and €49.60 for a week. Discounts of 20 percent available for groups and under-26s. Advance booking is advised, and a repair service is also available. A cycle trail encircles the city – details here or at the tourist office.

Car rental Avis, place de la Gare 17 (☎48 95 95), and at the airport (☎43 51 71); Europcar, route de Thionville 84 (☎40 42 28), and at the airport (☎43 45 88); Hertz, at the airport (☎43 46 45); Thrifty, blvd Prince Henri 33 (☎22 11 81) and at the airport (☎43 52 43).

Embassies Belgium, rue des Girondins 4 (☎44 27 46); Ireland, route d'Arlon 28 (☎45 06 10); Netherlands, rue C M Spoo 5 (☎22 75 70); UK, Boulevard Roosevelt 14 (☎22 98 64); USA, Boulevard E Servais 22 (☎46 01 23).

Festivals The city's main knees-up is the Schueberfouer, three weeks of jollity beginning in late August and with one of the biggest funfairs in Europe.

Internet access There are only two places in the city for use by non-residents: Chiggeri, rue du Nord 15 (☎22 99 36; €5/hr); Sparky's, ave Monterey 11a (☎26 20 12 23; €7.40/hr).

Laundry Quick-Wash, rue de Strasbourg 31.

Left luggage There are coin-operated lockers and a luggage office at the train station (€1.20/2.00/2.50).

Newspapers English-language newspapers are available from most newsagents from about 11am on the day of publication.

Pharmacies Molitor, place d'Armes 5 and Mortier, avenue de la Gare 11. Duty rotas are displayed in pharmacy windows.

Police Main station: rue Glesener 58–60. Emergencies: ☎113.

Post office The main post office is on place Emile Hamilius (Mon–Fri 7am–7pm, Sat 7am–5/7pm). There's also an office opposite the train station (Mon–Fri 9am–noon & 1-5pm, Sat 9am–noon).

Train enquiries The CFL office in the station is open daily 7am–8pm (☎49 90 49 90).

Walking tours The city tourist office in place d'Armes coordinates a first-rate programme of guided walking tours. Options include a City Promenade (Easter–Oct 1 daily, Nov–Easter 3 weekly; 2hr; €6); and the Wenzel Walk (May–Oct 1 weekly; 2hr; €6.90) – touted as 1000 years in 100 minutes – which starts from the Bock casemates, and takes you right around the fortifications on the east side of the Old Town.

The Grand Duchy

Having explored Luxembourg City, you may want to get out to see something of the rest of the **Grand Duchy**, about two-thirds of which is feasibly visited on day-trips, especially with a car. To the north, the first major rail junction is **Ettelbruck**, within easy striking distance by bus of some of the country's finest scenery. Here, confined by the Sûre River, which forms the border between Luxembourg and Germany, is an area of thickly wooded hills and rocky valleys known optimistically as **Petite Suisse** or "Little Switzerland". **Echternach** has long been the main centre of this region and, along with picturesque **Vianden** further north, is the best base for nosing round the Luxembourg Ardennes.

Echternach

Now a town of some 4000 people, **ECHTERNACH** grew up around an abbey founded here in 698 by the English missionary St Willibrord. The centre is the wedge-shaped **place du Marché**, an elegant conglomeration of ancient buildings, notably the fifteenth-century turreted **Town Hall**, with its Gothic loggia of 1520. The town's real attraction is, however, the **abbey** itself, just north of place du Marché, signalled by the spires of its enormous **church**, rebuilt to a former eleventh-century plan after heavy bomb damage in 1944. The most diverting part of the interior is the crypt dating from around 900, its walls bearing some antique frescoes and the primitive coffin of the saint himself, covered by an ornate, modern canopy. The huge abbey complex spreads out beyond the church to a set of formal gardens by the river, its mainly eighteenth-century buildings now given over to secular activities. One houses the **Musée de l'Abbaye** (daily: April–June & Sept–Nov 10am–noon & 2–5pm; July & Aug 10am–6pm; €2), with stone fragments from St Willibrord's original foundation and the eleventh-century *Codex Aureus* of Echternach, whose superb jewelled cover, from 990, was the work of a Trier craftsman.

The **bus station** is five minutes from the centre, at the end of rue de la Gare. The **tourist office**, opposite the abbey church (Mon–Fri 9am–noon & 2–5pm, also June-Aug Sat & Sun 9am–noon & 2–5pm; ☎72 02 30), has maps and information on **accommodation**. There are plenty of **hotels** along rue de la Gare: try the *Régine* at no. 53 (☎72 74 52; ④); the *Pavillon* at no. 2 (☎72 98 09, *www.lepavillion.lu*; ⑤); or the *Petit Poèt*, very central on place du Marché 13 (☎72 00 72; ⑤). There's a **campsite**, *Camping Officiel* (☎72 02 72; mid-April to mid-Oct), 300m beyond the bus station following the river out of town, and a **HI hostel** at rue André Duchscher 9 (☎72 01 58, *echternach@youthhostels.lu*; ②; mid-March to mid-Nov), south from the corner of place du Marché and rue de la Gare. The *Benelux* **restaurant**, on the same corner, offers good quality and reasonably priced meals.

Vianden

Probably the most strikingly sited of all Luxembourg's provincial towns, **VIANDEN** is still surrounded by ramparts and dominated by its hilltop **castle** (daily 10am–4/6pm; €4.50; *www.castle-vianden.lu*), a mostly eleventh-century edifice garnished with everything from Romanesque to Renaissance features. Inside, some rooms have been partly furnished in period style – the Banqueting Hall and the huge Counts' Hall decorated with seventeenth-century tapestries – but much has been left empty, notably the long Byzantine Room and the octagonal upper chapel, surrounded by a narrow defensive walkway. For more authentic mustiness, peek down the well just off the old kitchen, and leave through the Gothic dungeon. You can survey the castle from the hill above by taking the chair lift to its 450-metre-high summit (Easter–Oct daily 10am–5/6pm; €4.50 return) from rue du Sanatorium, just off rue Victor Hugo. At the top there's a restaurant with a terrace, and you can walk down to the castle by way of a footpath.

Buses to Vianden stop on the far eastern edge of town on the route de la Frontière, about five minutes' walk from the **tourist office** (June–Aug daily 8am–noon & 1.30–5.30pm, Sept–May Mon–Fri 9.30am–noon & 1.30–5.30pm; ☎83 42 57, *www.tourist-info-vianden.lu*), on the main street, rue du Vieux Marché, by the bridge. For somewhere to stay, try the **hotel**-lined Grand Rue where the best of the budget options include the *Hôtel Collette*, at no. 68–70 (April–Nov; ☎83 40 04; ③), and the *Hôtel Heintz*, no. 55 (☎83 41 55, *www.hotelheintz.lu*; ④), a comfortable, friendly place with a first-rate restaurant. On the other side of the river is the equally pleasant *Auberge de l'Our*, rue de la Gare 35 (☎83 46 75; ④). There's also a **HI hostel** at the top of Grand Rue at Montée du Château 3, a strenuous twenty-minute walk uphill from the bus station (☎83 41 77; ②; mid-March to mid-Nov). The nearest **campsite** is *Op dem Deich* (☎83 43 75; mid-April to early Oct) by the river near the bus station. For **food**, the restaurant of the *Auberge de l'Our* serves a good range of local specialities, though its riverside terrace means it gets very busy; alternatively head for the *Café de la Poste* on Grand Rue.

travel details

Trains

Antwerp to: Bruges (hourly; 1hr 20min); Ghent (every 30min; 50min).

Bruges to: Ostend (every 20min; 15min); Zeebrugge (hourly; 15min).

Brussels to: Antwerp (every 30min; 40min); Bruges (every 30min; 1hr); Ghent (every 30min; 40min); Luxembourg (every 2hr; 2hr 30min); Mechelen (every 30min; 20min); Namur (hourly; 50min); Ostend (hourly; 1hr 20min); Tournai (hourly; 1hr).

Luxembourg to: Brussels (hourly; 2hr 30min); Ettelbruck (hourly; 1hr); Liège for Maastricht (7 daily; 2hr 30min); Namur (hourly; 1hr 50min).

Namur to: Dinant (hourly; 30min); Luxembourg (hourly; 1hr 50min).

Buses

Diekirch to: Echternach (10 daily; 35min); Vianden (hourly; 20min).

Ettelbruck to: Echternach (10 daily; 45min); Vianden (12 daily; 30min).

Luxembourg to: Echternach (10 daily; 1hr 05min); Vianden (2 daily; 55min).

BRITAIN

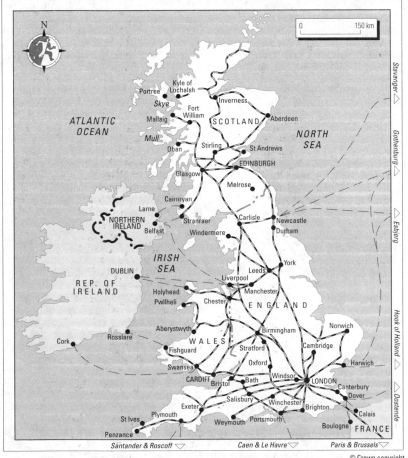

Introduction

Though detached from the continent of Europe by just a few miles of water, **Britain** is permeated by a strong sense of its cultural separateness. From extravagant ceremonies of state to such humble institutions as the village pub, life for the British retains a continuity with a past that bears little resemblance to that of its economic partners across the Channel. Yet social and political changes of the last few years have brought on a sense that this insular stability is collapsing: many Britons have difficulty reconciling themselves to ever-closer ties with the EU, but just as many have problems identifying with an Anglocentric United Kingdom. Wales and Scotland, with long traditions of independent nationhood, have their own distinct cultures, while Northern Ireland, politically joined to Britain but culturally affiliated to Ireland, embodies the most intractable problem thrown up by the deconstruction of national identity. The re-elected Labour government has brought the issue to the fore, moving closer towards acceptance of European unity whilst (belatedly) acknowledging the desire for regionally devolved power by setting up political assemblies in Edinburgh and Cardiff. Even within England itself – which missed out on the rush into devolution – regional differences remain more pronounced than you might expect in a country of this size.

Yet the complexity of Britain is not always obvious. The high streets of British towns and cities now resemble each other more than ever, with nationwide shops and businesses – many of them multinationals – driving out locally based firms. The tourist infrastructure is very well developed but the growth of a nostalgia-obsessed heritage industry has produced a plethora of attractions which conjure a rose-tinted simulation of the nation's past. However, to discover the variety of Britain is an immensely satisfying experience. The country is rich in monuments that attest to its intricate history, from ancient hill forts and Roman villas, through a host of medieval cathedrals, to the ambitious civic projects of the Industrial Revolution. In addition, many of the national museums and art galleries are the equal of any in Europe.

For cultural sightseeing as for nightlife, **London** is a ceaselessly entertaining city, and inevitably it's the one place that features on everyone's itinerary. Within the heavily built-up southeast, **Brighton** and **Canterbury** offer contrasting diversions – the former an appealing seaside resort, the latter one of Britain's finest medieval cities. The southwest of England, with the rugged moorlands of **Devon** and the rocky coastline of **Cornwall**, is an altogether wilder region, albeit one that pulls in droves of visitors in the height of summer. The chief attractions of central England are the university cities of **Oxford** and **Cambridge**, and Shakespeare's home town, **Stratford-upon-Avon**. Further north, the industrial cities of **Manchester, Liverpool** and **Newcastle** are gritty and lively places, and **York** and **Durham** have splendid historical treasures, but the landscape is again the real magnet, especially the uplands of the **Lake District** and the dales of **Yorkshire**. For true wilderness, however, you're better off heading to the **Welsh mountains** or **Scottish Highlands**. The finest of Scotland's lochs, glens and peaks, and the magnificent scenery of the west coast islands, can be reached easily from the contrasting cities of **Glasgow** and **Edinburgh** – the latter perhaps the most attractive urban landscape in Britain.

Information and maps

Tourist offices (usually called Tourist Information Centres) exist in virtually every British town. In high season, the average opening hours are much the same as standard shop hours, with the difference that they'll be open on a Sunday; in winter, it's usual for a tourist office to close a couple of hours earlier every day, with some rural offices closing altogether. All offer a basic range of information on accommodation, local public transport, and maps. In many cases this is free, but a growing number of offices make a small charge for an accommodation list or a town guide with an accompanying street plan. Check *www.visitbritain.com* for stacks of useful material. Areas designated as National Parks (such as the Lake District, Exmoor and Dartmoor) also have a fair sprinkling of National Park Information Centres, which are generally more expert in giving guidance on local walks and outdoor pursuits.

The most comprehensive series of **maps** is produced by the Ordnance Survey (*www.ordsvy.gov.uk*). Their 1:50,000 Landranger series covers the whole country, while the more detailed 1:25,000 Explorer series is invaluable for serious walking. The Outdoor Leisure series (also 1:25,000) is devoted to Britain's National Parks and Areas of Outstanding Natural Beauty. The best **road maps** are by Collins or the OS.

Money and banks

The British **pound** (£) is divided into 100 pence; there are coins of 1p, 2p, 5p, 10p, 20p, 50p, £1 and £2; and notes of £5, £10, £20 and £50. Banknotes issued by Scottish banks (among them a £1 note) are legal tender throughout the UK, but businesses outside Scotland may be unwilling to accept them.

Normal **banking hours** are Mon–Fri 9.30am–4.30pm. Some branches also stay open for a few hours on Saturday mornings, but times can vary. Most banks have cash-machines (ATMs) which accept a wide range of debit and credit cards.

Communications

Post offices are usually open Mon–Fri 9am–5.30pm, Sat 9am–12.30/1pm, though some town-centre offices may have extended hours. Individual **stamps** can be bought at post office counters; many newsagents and vending machines outside post offices also sell books of four or ten stamps.

Most public **payphones** are operated by British Telecom (BT), though you'll also see other companies' phone boxes in a variety of designs, especially in London. Most BT phones take all coins from 10p upwards, as well as **phonecards**, available from post offices and most newsagents in denominations of £3, £5, £10 and £20. An increasing number of public phones accept credit cards too. Newsagents can also sell you good-value cards from other phone companies for making international calls – you generally call a toll-free ☎0800 or ☎0808 number and then key in a PIN number printed on the card to access their cut-price rates. Domestic calls are cheapest between 6pm and 8am and at weekends; ☎0845 numbers are charged at local rate; ☎0870 at long-distance rate; ☎07 and ☎09 are very expensive. For the operator (domestic/international) call ☎100/☎155; for directory enquiries ☎192/☎153.

Cybercafés providing **email** and **Internet** access are common in the major cities, and you'll also find access at some hostels, main train stations, and in London, some public telephones. Prices vary, but £1 should be enough for you to reply to your email.

Getting around

Most significant places in the country are accessible by train or by coach (bus), usually by both. **Public transport** in Britain has been shaken up by large-scale privatization in recent years but promised price-cuts have failed to materialize, leaving costs still among the highest in Europe. In many cases it can be cheaper to fly than to take the train (see London listings for budget airlines), although tiresome coach travel is generally best value.

■ Planes

It's often worth looking into the numerous budget airlines such as Easyjet, Ryanair, Go and Buzz (see p.180) when planning a trip to the north of England or Scotland. Although you miss the views of the countryside, flights (which leave from London's Luton and Stansted airports) are frequent and often very competitively priced. Most are bookable via the Internet using a ticketless system, making it an extremely quick, hassle-free method of covering longer distances.

■ Trains

The **rail** network covers most of the country, but it's a London-centric system: travelling out from London is usually extremely quick, but traversing the country from east to west can be less easy. Trains are run by 25 companies that sometimes compete on popular routes.

Following privatization, standard **fares** have become extremely expensive; more affordable fares do exist, but the bafflingly complicated pricing system makes them hard to find. **Saver** and **Supersaver returns** are the cheapest options, often less expensive than a one-way ticket. On certain intercity routes you also get massively reduced **Advance**, **Superadvance**, **Apex** and **Bargain Return** tickets, which have to be booked a week or two in advance; book as early as you can, since there's only a limited number available on each train. The price of an ordinary return depends on the day of travel, Fridays being more expensive than the rest of the week, and weekends in general being pricier than weekdays. On several mainline routes it also depends on the time of day: mornings and evenings (the rush hour) tend to be expensive. If travelling on routes between London and other major cities during public holidays or around Christmas you should **book a seat** as far in advance as possible. Seat reservations are usually free if made at the same time as ticket purchase, although on some routes you'll have to pay an extra £1.

The only feasible way to get around by train in Britain is to buy a special pass. Although Eurail passes aren't valid in Britain and InterRail only gives thirty-percent discounts there's a series of **Britrail** passes available outside the country – see Basics, p.22 for a rundown of the options or visit *www. britrail.com* and *www.raileurope.com* for details. These also give a discount of around 12 percent on Eurostar's Channel Tunnel services (*www.eurostar. com*). A **Young Person's Railcard** (*www.youngpersons-railcard.co.uk*), available from all UK station ticket offices for £18, gives thirty percent reductions on travel for full-time students or under-26s, with discounts on ferries to Ireland. There are also regional passes, like the seven-day "Freedom of Wales" and "Highlands and Islands" tickets, but these are attractive only if you're exploring these particular areas intensively.

For details of all UK train services, consult *www. rail.co.uk* or *www.thetrainline.com* or call ☎0845/ 748 4950.

■ Buses

The long-distance **coach** (bus) services run by **National Express** (☎0870/580 8080, *www.gobycoach.com*) duplicate many intercity rail routes, very often at half the price or less. The frequency of service is often comparable to rail, and in some instances the difference in journey time is minimal.

Coaches are comfortable, and some have drinks and sandwiches available on board. If you're a student or under 26 you can buy a **Coachcard** (£8), which gives a quarter off standard fares. The **Tourist Trail Pass**, only available within the UK, offers unlimited travel for 2 days within 3 (£49/£39 with a Coachcard), 5 days within 30 (£85/£69), 8 days within 30 (£135/£99) or 15 days within 30 (£190/£145). These are valid on National Express through-routes to Scotland, but not on services within Scotland itself, provided by the sister company Scottish Citylink (☎0870/550 5050, *www.citylink. co.uk*), which has its own Explorer Pass for 3 days (£33), 5 days within 10 (£55) or 8 days within 10 (£85) – this also lets you travel free on Inverness-Aberdeen trains and half-price on some island ferries.

Local bus services are run by a bewildering array of companies, some private, some not. As a rule, the further away from urban areas you get, the less frequent and more expensive bus services become, but there are very few rural areas which aren't served by at least the occasional privately owned minibus.

■ Driving and hitching

Unlike continental Europe, Britain drives on the left, a situation which makes the roads around the Channel ports particularly hazardous. **Speed limits** are 30 or 40mph in built-up areas, 70mph on motorways and 60mph on dual carriageways. **Car rental** costs from around £130 per week with unlimited mileage; many towns have small companies whose rates can undercut the big names, but you'll have to return the car to the place from which you rented it. The Automobile Association and the Royal Automobile Club (see box on p.30) both operate 24-hour emergency **breakdown** services. On motorways they can be called from roadside booths; elsewhere ring toll-free on ☎0800/887766 (AA) or ☎0800/828282 (RAC).

The extensive motorway network and the density of traffic makes long-distance **hitching** relatively easy, though in rural areas you might be left hanging around a long time. As in the rest of Europe, it's not advisable to hitch alone.

Accommodation

Budget **accommodation** isn't hard to come by in Britain – the Web site *www.visitbritain.com* gives some idea of the wealth of options covering virtually every town in the country. Many tourist offices will book local rooms for you, but you should expect to pay at least a ten percent deposit. Most also operate a "Book a Bed Ahead" service for accommodation in other towns, which usually costs £3 and/or 10 percent of one night's stay.

■ Hotels and B&Bs

Hotel accommodation in Britain is generally of a high quality but it's also expensive – in tourist cities it's hard to find a double for less than £50, although higher-class places sometimes have cut-price deals at weekends. Fortunately, there's a wide range of budget accommodation in the form of **guest houses** or **bed and breakfasts** – often a comfortable room in a family home, followed by a substantial breakfast, from around £15 a head (a bit more in the affluent south, and a lot more in London). Many B&Bs have only a few rooms so several days' advance booking is advisable in summer and holiday periods.

■ Hostels and camping

Britain has an extensive network of **HI hostels**, operated by the separate associations for Scotland and for England and Wales; all of the HI hostels listed in the Guide can be contacted by email via their respective **Web sites** (see below). In Scotland a bed for the night can cost as little as £4, except in the cities, where you can pay more than twice that. In England and Wales the charge for under-18s is generally nearer the £10 mark (considerably higher in London); over-18s pay around fifty percent more. Catering varies with the size of the hostel, from a set meal at a set time in the smaller ones to a cafeteria system in the bigger ones. Some of the more basic hostels – and most rural ones in Scotland – still retain a duty roster where you may be set a few cleaning chores, but generally hostels are shedding this old-fashioned image in an attempt to attract a wider public. The YHA for England and Wales is at Trevelyan House, 8 St Stephen's Hill, St Albans, AL1 2DY (☎01727/845047; *www.yha.org.uk*); the Scottish

YHA is at 7 Glebe Crescent, Stirling, FK8 2JA (☎01786/891400; *www.syha.org.uk*).

There are more than 750 official **campsites** in Britain, charging from £8 per tent per night. In the countryside farmers will let you camp in a field if you ask, sometimes charging a couple of pounds for the privilege. Camping rough is illegal in designated parkland and nature reserves.

Food and drink

British **food** has long had a justifiably poor reputation, but things have been changing in recent years and it's now possible to eat well and cheaply, thanks chiefly to the inspiration of Britain's various ethnic communities. Social life, however, has always focused more on **drinking** than eating, and a pub is often the best introduction to a town.

■ Food

In many B&Bs you'll be offered an "**English breakfast**" – basically sausage, bacon and fried eggs – although these days the British are a nation of cereal eaters, and most places will give you this option as well. Every major town will have its upmarket restaurant specializing in classic meat-based British food, but for most people the quintessential British meal is **fish and chips**, a dish that can vary from the succulently fresh to the indigestibly greasy. However, the once ubiquitous fish-and-chip shop ("chippy") is now outnumbered on Britain's high streets by pizza, kebab and burger joints. Less threatened is the so-called "greasy spoon" **café**, generally a down-at-heel diner where the average menu will include bacon sandwiches and high-cholesterol variations on sausages, fried eggs, bacon and chips.

Most mid-range menus consist of meat-and-vegetable dishes such as steak-and-kidney pie, shepherd's pie (minced lamb topped with potato), chops or steaks, accompanied by boiled potatoes and plain veg. Many **pubs** also serve food, usually at lunchtime only; less the range and quality is improving and can sometimes be excellent. There's also an increasing number of **vegetarian** restaurants, especially in the larger towns; most restaurants will make some attempt to cater for vegetarians anyway.

For sit-down dining, though, the innumerable outlets for **non-British cuisine** offer the best-value meals. In every town of any size you'll find Chinese, Indian (the "curry house" has become a national institution to rival the chippy) and Italian eateries, and more – from Caribbean to Thai – with London and the industrial cities of the north holding the widest choice and the finest quality.

■ Drink

Drinking traditionally takes place in a public house, or **pub**, where a standard range of draught **beers** – sold by the pint or half-pint – generates most of the business, although imported bottled beers are also fashionable. Beers fall into two distinct groups: cold, blond, fizzy lager and the very different darker ale, or bitter, which is flat, served at room temperature and varies considerably in flavour according to the idiosyncracies of each region's local brands. Many pubs also serve tea and coffee, and all have soft drinks. In England pubs are generally open Mon–Sat 11am–11pm, Sun noon–10.30pm (some close daily 3–5.30pm), although 24hr licensing is still being mooted. Hours are often longer in Scotland, while Sunday closing is common in Wales. In bigger towns there's an increasing number of wine bars, European-style cafés and brasseries, which also serve food.

In Scotland, the national drink is of course **whisky**, a spirit of far greater subtlety than bland mass-marketed blended whiskies might lead you to believe. The best are the single malts, produced by often very small distilleries from local spring water. Most English and Welsh pubs sell only two or three whiskies (invariably blends); you'll generally find the best malt selections in pubs in Scotland.

Opening hours, holidays and heritage sites

Throughout Britain many places have set summer and winter **opening hours**, switching from one set of times (but not days) to the other according to the season. Where this is the case, we've separated the times with a slash: the summer hours are the longer ones and the winter hours the shorter. As a rule, sum-

mer times apply from Easter to October, and winter times the rest of the year. In the case of tourist offices, if you think you'll be arriving late it's best to ring in advance to check which set of times they're operating to.

General **shop hours** are Mon–Sat 9am–5.30/6pm, although there's an increasing amount of Sunday and late-night shopping in big towns. In Scotland you'll find more places open on a Sunday than in England, but Welsh Sundays are infamous for their calm. Many small towns still have an "early closing day" when shops close at 1pm – Wednesday is the favourite.

Public holidays (or "bank holidays") in England and Wales are: Jan 1; Good Friday and Easter Monday; first Mon after May 1 and last Mon in May; last Mon in August; Christmas Day and Boxing Day (Dec 25 and 26). In Scotland Jan 1, Jan 2 and Dec 25 are the only fixed public holidays – otherwise towns are left to pick their own holidays.

Many of Britain's national museums are free, but stately homes and monuments are often administered by the state-run **English Heritage** (*www.english-heritage.org.uk*) and **Historic Scotland** (*www.historic-scotland.gov.uk*). Wales is famous for its dramatic ruined castles and churches, many of them cared for by **Cadw**, Welsh Historic Monuments (*www.cadw.wales.gov.uk*). The trio run a joint membership scheme whereby if you join one, admission to the other two's properties is half-price – good value if you intend to visit more than half-a-dozen, since entry fees can be high. EH's Overseas Visitor Pass is cheapest, at £13 for 7 days or £17 for 14 days. Annual fees to join EH/HS/Cadw are £31/£26/£22. You can join EH/Cadw for £18/15 if you're under 21, or HS for £20 if you're a full-time student. The private **National Trust** (*www.nationaltrust.org.uk*) and **National Trust for Scotland** (*www.nts.org.uk*) also run a large number of gardens and stately homes nationwide; annual membership of NT/NTS costs £30/£27 (£15/£12 for under-25s), and is recognized by both, as well as by EH, HS and Cadw. All these let you join online or at any of their properties. The **Great British Heritage Pass**, which covers entry to sites administered by all the organizations above and many others too is worth considering; it's available from the British Travel Centre and Tourist Information Centres (7 days £35, 15 days £46, 1 month £60), as well as worldwide agents. All but the biggest churches and cathedrals are free, although most charge for access to towers, museums, cloisters and the like, and nearly all request donations.

Emergencies

Although the traditional image of the friendly British bobby has become tarnished by recent exposés of racism and corruption, **police** remain approachable and helpful. Tourists aren't a particular target for criminals except perhaps in the crowds of central London, where you should be on your guard against pickpockets. Britain's bigger conurbations all contain inner-city areas where you may feel uneasy after dark, but these are usually away from tourist sights.

Pharmacists can dispense only a limited range of drugs without a doctor's prescription. Most pharmacies are open standard shop hours, though in large towns some may stay open as late as 10pm. Local newspapers carry lists of late-opening pharmacies. Opening times of doctors' surgeries vary greatly from the once common average of 9am to noon and a couple of hours in the evenings; in any case, you can always turn up at the accident and emergency (A&E) department of a local hospital for complaints that require immediate attention.

Emergency Numbers

Police, Fire & Ambulance ☎999.

LONDON

With a population of well over seven million, **LONDON** is by far Europe's biggest city, spreading over an area of more than 1500 square kilometres from its core on the River Thames. This is where the country's news and money are made, and if Londoners' sense of superiority causes some resentment in the regions, it's undeniable that the city has a unique aura of excitement and success. However, all this comes at a price; with high accommodation and transport costs, the cost of living in London exceeds almost every other world city.

London is both a thrilling and a contrasting city, where ostentatious private affluence lives uncomfortably close to poverty and public neglect. Its central thoroughfares, buzzing late into the night, are interspersed with quiet squares and explorable alleyways. It's a green city too, with sizeable parks right in the centre – Hyde Park, Green Park and St James's – and the vast open spaces of Hampstead Heath, Greenwich and Kew on the periphery. Its museums and galleries are as rich and varied as you'll find anywhere, and many are still free, even if others are very expensive. And, of course, the city is replete with monuments of the capital's past, from its Roman origins to its role at the centre of the British Empire.

The **Romans** founded the town of Londinium on the north bank of the Thames soon after invading Britain in 43 AD, but the city's expansion didn't really begin until the eleventh century, when the last successful invader of Britain, **William of Normandy**, became in 1066 the first king of England to be crowned in Westminster Abbey. Subsequent monarchs left their imprint, but many of the city's finest structures were destroyed in a few hours in 1666, when the **Great Fire of London** razed over 13,000 houses and nearly ninety churches. Sir Christopher Wren was commissioned to replace much of the lost architecture, and rose to the challenge by designing such masterpieces as St Paul's Cathedral. Unfortunately, only a portion of the post-Fire splendours has survived, due partly to the German bombing raids of the **Blitz** of 1940–41 and partly to some equally disfiguring postwar development, which has lumbered London with more than its fair share of concrete-and-glass architectural mediocrity. However, the special atmosphere comes less from the look of the streets than from the people. This has been a multicultural city since at least the seventeenth century, when it was a haven for Huguenot (French Protestant) refugees. The last century saw waves of **immigration** from – at various times – Eastern Europe, the Caribbean, the Indian subcontinent and Africa, along with a steady, ongoing trickle from all corners of the globe, and this influx has played a large part in defining the character of a metropolis that is not so much a single organism as a patchwork of sub-cities.

Arrival

Flying into London, you'll arrive at one of the capital's five international airports – Heathrow, Gatwick, Stansted, Luton or City – all of which are less than an hour from the city centre. From **Heathrow**, twelve miles west of the city, the Piccadilly Line **underground** runs to central London in about an hour (£3.60), or there's the smart, fast and expensive Heathrow Express **rail** link to Paddington Station (every 15min; 15min; £12). For both underground and Heathrow Express trains Terminals 1, 2 and 3 share one station while Terminal 4 has its own. There's also an **Airbus** service #A2 which runs to King's Cross Station throughout the day, picking up from outside all terminals (every 20min; 1hr; £7); it can drop you at Notting Hill Gate, Marble Arch, Baker St, Euston or Russell Square. After midnight, **night bus** #N97 runs every half-hour from Heathrow to Trafalgar Square.

Gatwick Airport is thirty miles south of the city. **Trains** run from the South terminal: the Gatwick Express speeds to Victoria Station (every 15min; 30min; £10.50), although Connex trains on the same route are cheaper (every 20min; 40min; £8.20); Thameslink trains run to Blackfriars and King's Cross (every 15min; 30–45min; £9.50). **Airbus** #A5 serves Victoria Coach Station from both terminals (hourly 6.30am–11.30pm; 1hr 15min; £7).

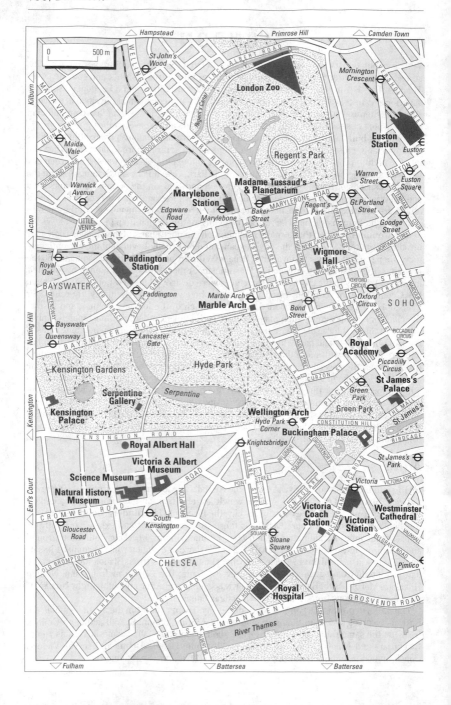

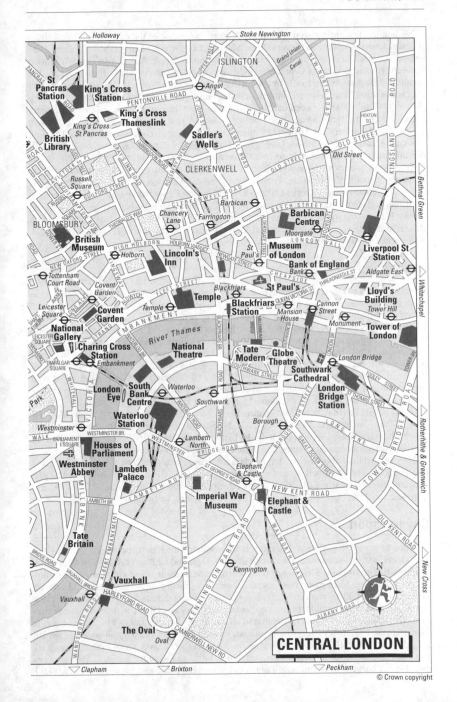

CENTRAL LONDON

© Crown copyright

Slick and efficient **Stansted Airport** is 34 miles northeast of the city, served by Skytrain trains to Liverpool St Station (every 30min; 50min; £13), which also stop at Tottenham Hale should you wish to switch onto the Victoria Line underground. Airbus #A6 and #A7 run on different routes to Victoria Coach Station, dropping off at central points (every 30min; 1hr 40min; £7). **Luton Airport** is 37 miles north of the city; free buses shuttle to Luton Airport Parkway station, from where Thameslink trains run to King's Cross and Blackfriars (every 20min; 30–50min; £9.60). Green Line bus #757 runs from the airport terminal to Buckingham Palace Rd beside Victoria Station, via Baker St and Marble Arch (every 30min; 1hr 15min; £7.50). Tiny **London City Airport** is 9 miles east of the centre, connected by bus to Canning Town tube station on the Jubilee Line (every 10min; 10min; £2) and Liverpool St (25min; £5). For information on all airport buses, visit *www.airlinks.co.uk* or call ☎0870/574 7777.

Overland journeys have a variety of arrival points. Eurostar **trains** from Paris or Brussels through the Channel Tunnel terminate at Waterloo. Trains from the English Channel ports arrive at Victoria, Liverpool St or Charing Cross, while those from elsewhere in Britain come into one of London's numerous mainline termini (see Listings on p.181), all of which have underground stations that link into the tube network. **Buses** from around Britain and continental Europe arrive at Victoria Coach Station on Buckingham Palace Rd, 500m south of Victoria Station.

Information

London Tourist Board (LTB, *www.londontown.com*) has desks at Heathrow Airport – in the underground station for terminals 1, 2 and 3 (daily 8am–6/7pm), and in the Terminal 3 arrivals hall (daily 6am–11pm). The best of their city-centre offices is in the **British Visitor Centre**, just off Piccadilly Circus at 1 Lower Regent St (Mon–Fri 9.30am–6.30pm, Sat & Sun 9/10am–4/5pm); others are at Waterloo Station's international arrivals hall (daily 8.30am–10.30pm), Liverpool St tube station (daily 8am–6/7pm), and the newly refurbished office in the forecourt of Victoria Station (Mon–Sat 8am–7/10pm, Sun 8am–6/7pm). None of these offices accept telephone queries but LTB's well-designed Web site is crammed with useful material. Handy local tourist information centres include one beside London Bridge station at 6 Tooley St (Mon–Sat 10am–4/6pm, Sun 10.30am–4/5.30pm; ☎020/7403 8299); another in St Paul's Churchyard (April–Sept daily 9am–5.30pm; Oct–March Mon–Fri 9am–5.30pm, Sat 9am–12.30pm; ☎020/7332 1456); and an office near the *Cutty Sark* at 2 Cutty Sark Gardens (April–Sept daily 10.15am–4.45pm; ☎0870/608 2000). The **British Tourist Authority** has an enquiry line for specific queries (☎020/8846 9000).

Museum addicts should consider the London Pass (*www.londonpass.com*), which gives free entry to over 60 attractions and many other discounts. The one-day card costs £22, the two- and three-day cards £39 and £49 respectively – buy them at the British Visitor Centre, from London Transport information centres (see opposite), or by phone (☎020/72332300).

City transport

The quickest way to get around London is by **underground**, or **tube**, as it's known to all Londoners, which operates daily between about 5.30am and 12.30am on thirteen lines criss-crossing the metropolis. Tickets are bought from machines or ticket counters in all station entrance halls, or from many newsagents. A one-way journey anywhere in central London (zone 1) costs £1.50, or you can buy a carnet of ten one-way tickets for £11.50. A better-value option is a **travelcard**, valid for buses and suburban trains as well as the tube. A one-day travelcard, valid on weekdays after 9.30am and all day at weekends, costs £4 for zones 1 and 2, enough to cover virtually everything you'll want to see, rising to £4.90 for all six zones, which includes Heathrow. (If you're travelling on weekdays *before* 9.30am, you'll have to buy an LT card instead, valid all day on buses and tubes only, and costing £5.10/£7.70 for zones 1–2/1–6.) A bargain weekend travelcard, valid all day Saturday and Sunday, costs £6/£7.30.

Weekly travelcards are more economical, at £15.70 for zone 1, or £18.90 for zones 1 and 2; to buy these and passes for longer periods you need a **photocard**, which you can get free from tube station ticket counters (you'll need ID and a passport-sized photo). **Visitor travelcards**, which come packaged with discount vouchers for city attractions, are only available outside the UK (see Web site).

The network of **buses** is comprehensive, but the city's dire traffic problems mean you'll find the tube quicker, especially in the summer when central London regularly suffers grid-lock. Without a travelcard, any bus journey in the central zone costs £1; normally you pay the driver on entering, although older buses with an open rear platform are staffed by a fare-collecting conductor. A lot of bus stops are **request stops**, so if you don't hold your arm out the bus will drive past. Regular buses operate daily between about 6am and midnight; after this, **night buses** (prefixed with the letter "N") take over, with services radiating out from Trafalgar Square at approximately hourly intervals all night. Cash fares are more expensive than usual on night buses, but all travelcards are valid.

In 2000 long-neglected **river-boat** services also resumed on the Thames. Westminster Pier, beside Westminster Bridge, and Embankment Pier are the main central embarkation points. Among the many routings are boats east to the Tower of London (every 20–30min; 30min; £4.80) and Greenwich (50min; £8), and west to Kew (3 daily; 1hr 30min; £7) and Hampton Court (3hr 30min; £10).

The principal **London Transport information office** (*www.londontransport.co.uk*), providing excellent free maps and details of bus, tube and boat services, is at Victoria station (daily 8am–7pm), with desks at all Heathrow Airport terminals, and at Euston, King's Cross, Liverpool St, Oxford Circus, Piccadilly Circus, St James's Park and Hammersmith tube stations. There's also a 24-hour phone line for information on all bus, tube and boat services (☎020/7222 1234).

If you're in a group of three or more, London's metered **black cabs** (taxis) can be an economical way of getting around: a ride across the centre, from Euston to Victoria, should cost around £10. A yellow light over the windscreen tells you if the cab is available – just wave to hail it. To book in advance, call ☎020/7272 0272. London's cabbies are the best-trained in Europe, and every one of them knows the shortest route between any two points; they won't rip you off by going the long way round. **Minicabs** are less reliable than black cabs, since their drivers are private individuals rather than trained professionals, but they can be a lot cheaper (especially at night, so useful after clubbing). There are hundreds of minicab firms all over London – you'd do best to get the number of a local outfit from the pub or club you're at (unless you want to be certain of a woman driver, in which case call Ladycabs on ☎020/7254 3501). Although nearly all minicabs are metered, you should always check the fare before you get going.

Accommodation

London is extremely expensive, and lower-cost **accommodation** in the centre tends to be poor quality. However, the sheer size of the place means you'll have little trouble finding a room, even in midsummer, and the tube network makes staying outside the centre a feasible option. The capital also has plenty of **hostel** space, both in HI properties and student halls. As well as our listings, you'll find a huge accommodation database on LTB's Web site *www.londontown.com*, but if you can't find a bed you could always pay someone else to do the phoning round for you. All the LTB offices listed above operate a **room booking service**, which costs £5 (plus the first night's room charge in advance), or you can book by phone with a credit card through the LTB (Mon–Fri 9am–6pm, Sat 9am–1pm; ☎020/7604 2900).

The best-value accommodation in the centre is in **Bloomsbury**, a genteel area centred on the British Museum and the nearby B&B-filled Gower St which is less than ten minutes' walk from Oxford St and Covent Garden. **Earl's Court** on the southwest edge of the centre has long been favoured by budget travellers – streets around the tube station are packed with backpacker-oriented establishments. Further north, beside Paddington station, elegant **Bayswater** is also crammed with options, and sits on the doorstep of tranquil Hyde Park and the vibrant Notting Hill area. The grey streets around **Victoria station** harbour dozens of inexpensive B&Bs, but the area itself lacks much character and falls pretty quiet after the office-workers have gone home.

Hotels and B&Bs

You should phone **hotels** as far in advance as you can if you want to stay within easy reach of the West End during high season; expect to pay around £40 for an unexceptional double room without a private bathroom. If three or more of you are travelling together, it's always worth asking the price of the family rooms, which generally sleep four and can save you a few pounds.

BLOOMSBURY, WC1

Arosfa Hotel, 83 Gower St (☎020/7636 2115). Simple, well-maintained historical house with a small garden. Goodge Street tube. ⑦.

Cavendish, 75 Gower St (☎020/7636 9079). Clean, tastefully decorated guest house, one of the best in the area. Goodge St tube. ⑤.

Crescent, 49 Cartwright Gardens (☎020/7387 1515). En-suite doubles in a beautiful Regency house that are a cut above the rest. Euston tube. ⑨.

Jenkins, 45 Cartwright Gardens (☎020/7837 4654). Small, well-kept B&B overseen by a houseproud black labrador. Euston tube. ⑤.

Ridgemount Hotel, 65-67 Gower St (☎020/7636 1141). Old fashioned family-run place with small rooms with shared facilities, a garden and a laundry room. Goodge Street tube. ⑥.

EARL'S COURT, SW5

Half Moon Hotel, 10 Earl's Court Sq (☎020/7373 9956). Small, friendly B&B with clean rooms, some with en-suite facilities, at good prices. ⑤.

Kensington Court Hotel, 33 Nevern Place (☎020/7370 5151). Modern hotel with comfortable en-suite rooms. Breakfast included. ⑨.

Merlyn Court, 2 Barkston Gardens (☎020/7370 1640, *www.smoothhound.co.uk/hotels*). Plain but serviceable, mostly en-suite rooms on a quiet garden square. Earl's Court tube. ⑥.

Philbeach, 30 Philbeach Gardens (☎020/7373 1244). Friendly gay hotel, with a nice restaurant. Earl's Court tube. ⑦.

Windsor House, 12 Penywern Rd (☎020/7373 9087). Simple rooms in a large old Victorian terrace; use of garden and kitchen facilities. Earl's Court tube. ⑥.

BAYSWATER, W2

Ashley Hotel, 15 Norfolk Sq (☎020/7723 3375). Three long-established hotels joined into one, a couple of minute's walk from Paddington Station. Breakfast included. ⑨.

Garden Court, 30 Kensington Gardens Sq (☎020/7229 2553). Popular family-run hotel off cosmopolitan Westbourne Grove. Bayswater tube. ⑥.

Porchester, 33 Princes Sq (☎020/7221 2101, *www.vienna-group.co.uk*). Friendly but antiseptic budget hotel on a quiet square, with an excellent-value restaurant and bar. Bayswater or Queensway tube. Dorms ④, doubles ⑥.

St David's & Norfolk Court, 16 Norfolk Sq (☎020/7723 3856). Pleasant, well-appointed B&B in a quiet, attractive square. Serves big breakfasts. Paddington tube. ⑥.

VICTORIA, SW1

Dover, 44 Belgrave Rd (☎020/7821 9085, *www.rooms.demon.co.uk*). Best in the area, with nice decor and en-suite rooms. Victoria tube. ⑥.

Goring, 15 Beeston Place (☎020/7396 9000). Elegant Edwardian pile still in the Goring family, with class and character. Victoria tube. ⑨.

Luna & Simone Hotel, 47–49 Belgrave Rd (☎020/7834 5897). B&B with a welcoming owner and plain but very well-maintained rooms, some with shared facilities. Victoria tube. ⑦.

Oxford House, 92 Cambridge St (☎020/7834 6467). Very friendly B&B with marvellous food, so booking essential. Victoria tube. ⑤.

Woodville House & Morgan House, 107 & 120 Ebury St (☎020/7730 1048). Jointly run above-average B&B's, some en-suite rooms. Patio garden and great breakfasts. Victoria tube. ⑥.

Hostels

Most **HI hostels** in London are slightly less basic and significantly more expensive than those in the rest of Britain, but in summer you'll have to arrive as early as possible to stand a chance of getting a room, and you're usually limited to a maximum stay of four consecutive nights. Consulting the YHA's booking service (☎020/7373 3400, *www.yha.org.uk*) can save time and shoe leather. A handful of **other hostels** fill out the options, including a number of Astor's hostels (all of which can be contacted via *www.scoot.co.uk/astorhostels*).

HI HOSTELS

City of London, 36 Carter Lane (☎020/7236 4965). In the City – a desolate area at night – with crowded dorms or private rooms. St Paul's or Blackfriars tube. ⑤.

Earl's Court, 38 Bolton Gardens (☎020/7373 7083). Comfortable and fairly capacious, with good-value meals. Earl's Court tube. ④.

Hampstead Heath, 4 Wellgarth Rd (☎020/8458 9054). One of the biggest and best-appointed, near the wilds of Hampstead Heath. Golders Green tube. ④.

Holland House, Holland Walk, Kensington (☎020/7937 0748). Fairly convenient for the centre, with a nice location overlooking parkland, and large dorms. Holland Park or High St Kensington tube. ④.

Oxford St, 14 Noel St, Soho (☎020/7734 1618). In the heart of the West End, but with only 75 beds, it fills up very fast. Discounts for weekly stays. Oxford Circus or Tottenham Court Rd tube. ⑤.

Rotherhithe, Island Yard, Salter Rd (☎020/7232 2114). Rather far out to the east, but a viable option in peak season, with 320 beds. Canada Water tube or bus #381 from Waterloo. ⑤.

St Pancras, 79 Euston Rd (☎020/7388 9998). Sparkling new hostel in a good location opposite St Pancras station and within walking distance of both the West End and Camden Town, with small dorms and twins. King's Cross tube. ⑤.

OTHER HOSTELS

Astor's Hyde Park, 2 Inverness Terrace, Bayswater (☎020/7229 5101). Clean, well-kept hostel just off buzzing Queensway and yards from Hyde Park. Bayswater or Queensway tube. ③.

Astor's Leinster Inn, 7 Leinster Sq, Bayswater (☎020/7229 9641). Huge, noisy backpacker hostel close to Notting Hill, with a variety of rooms from singles to 8-bed dorms and various facilities including a canteen, all-night bar and Internet access. Bayswater tube. ③.

Astor's Museum Inn, 27 Montague St, Bloomsbury (☎020/7580 5360). Right opposite the British Museum, with the usual friendly young crowd. Russell Sq or Holborn tube. ③.

Astor's Quest, 45 Queensborough Terrace, Bayswater (☎020/7229 7782). Small backpacker den just north of Hyde Park, with wacky paintwork and loud music. Bayswater or Queensway tube. ③.

Generator, Compton Place, Bloomsbury (☎020/7388 7666, *www.the-generator.co.uk*). Huge former police barracks, with neon-lit post-industrial decor, a self-service cafeteria, cheap bar until 2am, Internet access and a selection of dorms and rooms. Russell Sq tube. ⑤.

St Christopher's Inn, 121 Borough High St (☎020/7407 1856, *www.interpub.co.uk/st.christophers*). New hostel in a listed building near London Bridge, with a café and late bar onsite and cosmopolitan clientele. Borough tube. ③.

Student halls and campsites

Spartan singles and doubles in **student halls of residence** are available outside term-time, and can slightly undercut B&B prices. London's **campsites** are out on the edges of the city, offering pitches for around £4, plus £3 per person per night (reductions for children and in low season).

STUDENT HALLS

City University (☎020/7477 8811, *www.city.ac.uk/ems*). Various halls near Angel tube (July–Sept). ④.

Institute of Education, 15 Endsleigh St (☎020/7387 4086, *jah@ioe.ac.uk*). In the heart of Bloomsbury (Jan, March, April, July–Sept & Dec). Euston tube. ⑤.

International Students House, 229 Great Portland St (☎020/7631 8300, *www.ish.org.uk*). Vast hall near Regent's Park, open all year. Gt Portland St tube. ⑤.

King's College (☎020/7848 1700, *vac.bureau@kcl.ac.uk*). Halls in Westminster and Denmark Hill (both Jan, April, June–Sept & Dec) and leafy Hampstead (June–Sept). ④.

University of Westminster (☎020/7911 5799, *comserv@westminster.ac.uk*). Locations all over town. ④–⑤.

CAMPSITES

Abbey Wood, Federation Rd, SE2 (☎020/8311 7708). Enormous site east of Greenwich, closed for redevelopment until May 2002.

Crystal Palace, Crystal Palace Parade (☎020/8778 7155). All-year site, maximum 14 days stay in summer, 21 days in winter. Train from London Bridge to Crystal Palace.

Tent City Hackney, Millfields Rd, Hackney Marshes (☎020/8985 7656, *www.tentcity.co.uk*). Big, cheap campsite beside a canal which also has tented dorm-beds. Inconveniently sited though, way over in the east of the city. Open June–Aug. Bus #38 from King's Cross to Hackney Central, then walk down Millfields Rd.

The City

London is too big to have a single centre. The heaviest consumer spending is done on and around Oxford St, while the financial district is a couple of miles to the east (in the area known, confusingly for first-time visitors, as the City of London), and the hubs of political and royal London – Parliament and Buckingham Palace – lie just under two miles to the south. But the area that feels like the fulcrum is the **West End**, lying between all these points and centred roughly around the neighbouring spaces of Piccadilly Circus, Leicester Square and Trafalgar Square. **Leicester Square** is liveliest at night, heaving with people on their way to its cinemas or to the clubs and restaurants of Soho immediately to the north. **Piccadilly Circus**, just beyond the west side of Leicester Square, is hectic throughout the day, choked with traffic, its facades lurid with the famous but rather disappointing colossal neon advertisements – opposite the billboards there's always a gang of sightseers and rather shiftier street-drinkers gathered on the steps of a statue entitled the Angel of Christian Charity, but commonly known as "Eros". From here, Shaftesbury Avenue storms northeast into London's Theatreland, chic Piccadilly makes its way west to the famous *Ritz Hotel*, while the elegant curve of Regent St leads north to shop-strewn Oxford Circus.

Trafalgar Square and the National Gallery

Some 300m south of Piccadilly Circus and Leicester Square is **Trafalgar Square**. Dominating the large traffic island is the 51m-high Nelson's Column, surmounted by a statue of Admiral Horatio Nelson, who died in the defeat of the French navy at the Battle of Trafalgar in 1805. Four lions designed by Victorian painter Edwin Landseer guard the column's base, and two adjacent fountains are a magnet for overheating sightseers during the summer. At the south of the square, a small statue of Charles I marks the original site of **Charing Cross**, the name of which derives from the last of twelve crosses erected by Edward I to mark the funeral procession of his wife Eleanor (it also remains the point from which all distances from the capital are measured). A nineteenth-century replica now stands in the forecourt of Charing Cross train station, just to the east.

Extending across the north side of the square is the bulk of the **National Gallery** (Mon–Sat 10am–6pm, Wed until 9pm, Sun noon–6pm; free; *www.nationalgallery.org.uk*), one of the world's great art collections. A quick tally of the National's Italian masterpieces includes works by Piero della Francesca, Raphael, Botticelli, Michelangelo, Caravaggio, Titian, Veronese and Mantegna. From Spain there are dazzling pieces by Velázquez (including the *Rokeby Venus*), El Greco and Goya. From the Low Countries there's Memlinck, van Eyck (the *Arnolfini Marriage*), van der Weyden and Rubens, and some of Rembrandt's most searching portraits. Poussin, Lorrain, Watteau and the only David paintings in the country are the earlier highlights of a French contingent that comes up to the twentieth century with Seurat, Cézanne and Monet.

If you want to take the art chronologically, you should start in the Sainsbury Wing, a mildly postmodern annexe on the west side. The compactness of its rooms makes it difficult to get a clear view of many of the pictures at peak times (Sunday afternoon is often hellish), and there's nearly always a snarl-up created by people queueing to pay reverence to the Leonardo cartoon, installed in a bullet-proof chapel behind his *Virgin of the Rocks*. High Renaissance and later works are displayed in the main building – don't overlook the basement galleries, which are crammed with excellent pictures.

The northeastern corner of Trafalgar Square is occupied by **St Martin-in-the-Fields** (*www.stmartin-in-the-fields.org*), James Gibbs' stately early-eighteenth-century church, which combines classical columns and pediment with a distinctly un-classical spire and is a popular place for evening and lunchtime concerts. Opposite here, around the side of the National Gallery in St Martin's Place, is the **National Portrait Gallery** (Sat–Wed 10am–6pm, Thur & Fri 10am–9pm, Sun noon–6pm; free; *www.npg.org.uk*), founded in 1856 to house uplifting depictions of the great and good. Despite some fine pieces such as Hans Holbein's larger-than-life drawing of Henry VIII, many of the portraits are of less intrinsic interest than their subjects. An airy new wing opened in 2000, holding both the earliest Tudor portraits and the latest depictions of pop stars, sports personalities, politicians and royalty; the older wing holds the rest, including an array of eminent Victorians grouped by profession. From time to time a part of the building is given over to a special exhibition – the photography shows are often excellent.

Covent Garden and the British Museum

Northeast of Trafalgar Square, cheek-by-jowl with Leicester Square, lies the attractive area of **Covent Garden**, centred on the splendid nineteenth-century market hall which housed London's principal fruit and vegetable market until the 1970s. The structure now shelters a gaggle of tasteful shops, arty stalls and popular watering holes. The surrounding cobbled piazza, laid out by Inigo Jones in the seventeenth century and dominated on the western side by Jones's classical St Paul's Church, is a semi-institutionalized venue for buskers and more ambitious street performers. On the piazza's southeast corner is the **London Transport Museum** (Sat–Wed 10am–5.30pm, Thu & Fri 10am–8.30pm; £5.50; *www.ltmuseum.co.uk*), a fun scamper through the history – and possible future – of public transport in the city.

From here it's a short walk northwards up fashionable Neal St and across New Oxford St into the district of Bloomsbury, home to the **British Museum** on Great Russell St (Mon–Sat 10am–5pm, Sun noon–6pm; free; *www.british-museum.ac.uk*). It's far too big to be seen in one go – the best advice is to check the floor plans as you go in, and make for the two or three displays that interest you most. Whichever sections you pick, the exhibits will include some breathtaking items. Archeological treasures of the ancient world dominate the ground floor, where the heaviest flow of visitors winds towards the Elgin Marbles, taken from the Parthenon in Athens by Lord Elgin in 1801 and still the cause of discord between the British and Greek governments. A whole room is devoted to these glorious sculptures, the main series of which depicts scenes probably from a procession in honour of the goddess Athena.

A wander through the surrounding areas will take you past Roman mosaics and the exquisite Portland Vase; amazing Assyrian finds, including huge winged beasts with human heads from a royal palace near Nineveh in modern Iraq; and a hoard of Egyptian antiquities that features the Rosetta Stone, bearing a trilingual inscription that enabled scholars to decode hieroglyphs for the first time. A huge Egyptian mummy collection is located on the first floor, where a couple of preserved corpses come in for some ghoulish scrutiny – a sand-desiccated Egyptian and the 2000-year-old Lindow Man, preserved in a Cheshire bog after his sacrificial death. On the same floor, various treasure troves display some extraordinary craftwork: two of the most remarkable were found in East Anglia – Saxon pieces from Sutton Hoo, and the Roman silverwork known as the Mildenhall Treasure.

The building once also housed the British Library, centred around the famous circular **Reading Room** where Karl Marx sat and studied. With the transfer of the library collections in 2000 to a new building beside St Pancras station, space was freed up and the newly restored Reading Room opened to the public, along with the adjacent, long-hidden Great Court, housing the ethnographic collection, the African galleries and virtual reality displays beneath an ultra-modern glass roof designed by the renowned architect Norman Foster.

Whitehall and Parliament Square

Heading south from Trafalgar Square is the broad sweep of **Whitehall**, which holds the main concentration of government buildings and civil service offices. The original Whitehall was a palace built for King Henry VIII and subsequently extended, but little of it survived a 1698 fire. The only remnant is the supremely elegant **Banqueting House** (Mon–Sat 10am–5pm, sometimes closed for functions; £3.80), built by Inigo Jones for James I in the Palladian style and decorated with vast ceiling paintings by Rubens, glorifying the Stuart dynasty. They were commissioned by James' son Charles I – who on January 30, 1649, stepped onto the executioner's scaffold from one of the building's front windows.

Current monarchical tradition is displayed at the **Horse Guards** building on the opposite side of the road. Mounted sentries of the Queen's Life Guard, in ceremonial uniform, are posted daily here from 10am to 4pm, after which they are replaced by horseless colleagues. Try to time your visit to coincide with the changing of the guard (Mon–Sat 11am, Sun 10am), when a squad of mounted troops in full livery arrives from the Parade Ground to the rear.

Further down this west side of Whitehall is the most famous street in London, **Downing Street**. Number 10 has been the residence of the Prime Minister since the house was presented to Sir Robert Walpole by King George II in 1732. Nowadays you can only gaze at the famous black doorway from afar: public access has been denied since 1990, when Margaret Thatcher ordered wrought-iron gates to be installed at the head of the street. During the 1940 Blitz, the Cabinet was forced to vacate Downing Street in favour of a bunker in nearby King Charles St, which runs between the Home Office and the Foreign Office. The **Cabinet War Rooms** (daily 9.30/10am–6pm; £5; *www.iwm.org.uk*) – left more or less as they were in 1945 – provide a glimpse of the claustrophobic suites from which Churchill directed wartime operations. Whitehall ends at **Parliament Square**, dominated by two of the city's most historic buildings – the Houses of Parliament and Westminster Abbey.

THE HOUSES OF PARLIAMENT

The **Houses of Parliament** (or Palace of Westminster, to give it its proper title; *www.parliament.uk*) stand on the site of the palace that was the seat of the English kings for five centuries before Henry VIII moved the court to Whitehall. Following Henry's death, the House of Commons, previously ensconced in the chapterhouse of Westminster Abbey, moved into the Palace – a jumble of buildings which burned down in 1834. Save for a few pieces of the original structure buried deep inside the current edifice, what one sees today is entirely nineteenth century. The architect Charles Barry was told to construct something which expressed national greatness through the use of Gothic or Elizabethan styles. The resulting orgy of pinnacles and tracery is restrained only by the building's blocky symmetry. Although the angular Victoria Tower at the south end is higher, the ornate clock tower to the north is more famous; "**Big Ben**", the title given to this iconic structure, is in fact the name of its main bell.

The Victorian love of pseudo-Gothic detail shines through in the interior warren of committee rooms and offices, which were largely the responsibility of Barry's assistant on the project, Augustus Pugin, who was to become the leading ideologue of the Gothic revival. Both the House of Commons and the House of Lords have public galleries – the Commons is the livelier of the two (Commons: Mon & Tues from 2.30pm, Wed & Fri 9.30am–2/3pm, Thurs 11.30am–7pm; Lords: Mon–Thurs from about 2.30pm, Fri from 11am; free). Queues are long, numbers restricted and security procedures lengthy. To avoid the crush, simply turn up after 6pm, when most tourists have gone home (parliament sits Mon–Thurs until at least 10pm). However, to join a guided tour or get to see Prime Minister's Question Time (Wed 3–3.30pm) you must obtain tickets from your local MP or embassy in London several weeks in advance. Note that parliament doesn't sit at Christmas, Easter, or from August to mid-October. The public entrance leads into one of the few remaining parts of the original Palace of Westminster, the eleventh-century **Westminster Hall**, a cavernous space with a magnificent fourteenth-century oak-beamed roof.

WESTMINSTER ABBEY

On the southwestern side of Parliament Square soars **Westminster Abbey** (Mon–Fri 9.30am–4.45pm, Sat 9am–2.45pm, last entry 1hr before closing; £6; *www.westminsterabbey.org*), founded in the eighth century, rebuilt in the eleventh century by Edward the Confessor and again in the thirteenth by Henry III. Since 1066, when William the Conqueror was crowned here, the abbey has been the venue for all but two coronations and – for the half-millennium between Henry III and George II – the site of all royal burials; in 1997, famously, it was also the location of the memorial service for Diana, Princess of Wales. Many of the nation's most celebrated citizens are honoured here, too, and the interior is crowded with monuments, reliefs and statuary. The north transept, traditionally reserved for statesmen, includes monuments to the nineteenth-century prime ministers Peel, Palmerston and Gladstone; Poet's Corner, in the south transept, contains the graves or memorials of Chaucer, Tennyson, T.S. Eliot and many others. Behind the high altar is the chapel of Edward the Confessor, who, canonized in the twelfth century, is still venerated by pilgrims for his powers of healing. In front of Edward's tomb is the Coronation Chair, an oak monstrosity dating from around 1300 which used to squat above the Stone of Scone – the semi-mystical Scottish coronation stone pilfered by Edward I in 1297 and returned to Edinburgh in 1996. Many of the nearby royal tombs are surmounted by superb effigies; one of the finest is the black marble sarcophagus of Henry VII and his wife, housed at the rear of the abbey below the elaborate fan-vaulted ceiling of Henry's chapel. The ambulatory is the dual resting place of his granddaughters, Queen Elizabeth I and Queen Mary.

Doors on the south side of the nave lead to the **Great Cloister**, at the eastern end of which are entrances to the Chapter House (daily 10am–4/5.30pm), with its thirteenth-century paving stones, the Pyx Chamber (daily 10.30am–4pm), sacristy of Edward the Confessor's church and subsequently the royal treasury, and the Norman Undercroft, now housing the abbey museum (daily 10.30am–4pm), in which several generations of royal death-masks are displayed (entrance £2.50; free with £2 audioguide, or £1 in addition to the abbey entry ticket).

The Tate Britain

From Parliament Square traffic speeds south on riverside Millbank past the **Tate Britain** (daily 10am–5.50pm; free; *www.tate.org.uk*; Pimlico tube), which holds the national collection of British art from 1500 onwards. With the opening of the new Tate Modern at Bankside, which is devoted to international contemporary art (see p.168), this gallery has been freed up to concentrate solely on British artists, placing works on show that have spent years languishing in storage. Whole rooms are given over to Blake, Spencer, Bacon and others, with the main highlights being the quintessentially English landscapes of John Constable, plenty of glutinous Pre-Raphaelite canvases, and dozens of works by Turner in the adjoining postmodern Clore Gallery. There's nearly always a good temporary exhibition in progress – ranging from modest one-artist shows to surveys of entire movements. The gallery also runs contemporary art's prestigious, and often controversial, Turner prize. Every autumn the finalists' works are displayed for a month or two prior to the prize-giving. As with the National Gallery, weekends can be a real crush, and Sunday afternoon is a favourite slot for coach parties. Go-ahead has been given for a river ferry connection linking both Tates, completion is due in Spring 2002. In the meantime the galleries are linked by a free bus service.

Along the South Bank

Traffic-heavy Westminster Bridge crosses from Parliament Square to the **south bank** of the Thames and the unmistakeable **London Eye**, a giant 135m-tall observation wheel on Jubilee Gardens (daily 9/10am–6/10pm or dusk; £8.50; *www.ba-londoneye.com*). The stately 25-minute round-trip provides unrivalled views over London. A delightful riverside footpath leads north from the Eye past the shabby Hungerford Bridge (new pedestrian walkways are under construction) to London's "culture bunker", the **South Bank Centre** (*www.sbc.org.uk*). This sprawl of concrete near Waterloo station embraces the Royal National Theatre, the National Film Theatre and a trio of concert halls, the largest of which is the Royal Festival Hall. The onsite **Hayward Gallery** (daily 10am–6pm, Tues & Wed until 8pm; £6) hosts prestigious, mostly contemporary, art exhibitions, but the adjacent Museum of the Moving Image, or MOMI, is currently closed.

The riverfront stretching eastward from the South Bank Centre to London Bridge is defined by Bankside Power Station, a characterful, long-derelict brick building designed by Sir Giles Gilbert Scott and transformed by the Swiss architects Herzog & de Meuron into the **Tate Modern** (Sun–Thurs 10am–6pm, Fri & Sat 10am–10pm; free; *www.tate.org.uk*). It displays a vast collection of international modern art from 1900 to the present, and is sister gallery to the Tate Britain (see p.167). The Tate Modern has a great deal more space than the old gallery on Millbank, and so has dusted off a large quantity of works that had spent most of their lives under wraps. The collection is arranged thematically, and takes in key works by such luminaries as Picasso, Dali, Matisse, Warhol, Bacon, Rothko and Pollock, to select just a few. Comprehensive assemblies of Constructivism, Surrealism, Minimal Art, Pop Art, Dada and Expressionism (both Abstract and Germanic) are regular attractions, along with more contemporary works and excellent temporary exhibitions. As with all London's big galleries, avoid weekends if possible; they can be a real crush. Norman Foster's supremely elegant **Millennium Bridge**, intended as a pedestrian link between the gallery and St Paul's Cathedral, has remained closed since its inaugural weekend in 2000 when it swung dangerously as people tried to cross. While engineers puzzle over how to make the structure workable the folorn bridge remains an attractive, if rather costly piece of sculpture.

The Bankside area was the pleasure quarter of Tudor and Stuart London, beyond the jurisdiction of the city authorities and thus a place in which brothels and other disreputable institutions (notably theatres associated with Shakespeare and his contemporaries) could flourish. Beside the Tate Modern, the circular **Globe Theatre** (*www.shakespeares-globe.org*) has been rebuilt in its original form with an accompanying exhibition on Shakespeare and the history of the locality. You can take a guided tour of the theatre (daily: May–Sept 9am–12.30pm; Oct–April 10am–5pm; £7.50) or, better still, go to a live performance in the timber-built thatched arena (summer only; ☎020/7401 9919). Some 400m east you'll come to Clink St, home of the **Clink** (daily 10am–6pm; £4; *www.clink.co.uk*), a small museum on the site of a former prison devoted to the riverside lowlife who often ended up incarcerated there. **Southwark Cathedral** – London's finest Gothic church after Westminster Abbey (*www.dswark.org*) – stands nearby at the southern end of London Bridge, its most conspicuous interior feature being the brightly painted tomb of poet John Gower, a contemporary of Chaucer's.

One other national institution on the south bank is the **Imperial War Museum**, on Lambeth Rd, half a mile south of Waterloo station (daily 10am–6pm; £5.50, free after 4.30pm; *www.iwm.org.uk*; Lambeth North tube). Though it does feature galleries of uniforms and weaponry, this is not the celebration of imperialistic bloodletting its name might suggest. The museum houses some incisive examples of war art, and uses stagecraft to convey the miseries of combat, with re-creations of World War I trenches and a simulation of bomb-ravaged wartime London. The **Holocaust Exhibition** (☎020/74165439; free), on the third floor, is an intelligent and well measured exhibition that pulls few punches. Including archive footage and personal accounts from survivors, the centrepiece is a vast scale model of Auschwitz-Birkenau with survivors describing their attempts to come to terms with the past.

The Mall and Buckingham Palace

The southwestern exit of Trafalgar Square is marked by the imposing Admiralty Arch, built in 1910 as the eastern half of a memorial to Queen Victoria; the rest is half a mile away down the tree-lined avenue of **The Mall** in the shape of the statue of Victory in front of Buckingham Palace. Just beyond Admiralty Arch, ranged above the Mall, is Carlton House Terrace, a stretch of impressive Regency town houses built by John Nash and now partly occupied by the Institute of Contemporary Arts, or **ICA** (Mon noon–11pm, Tues–Sat noon–1am, Sun noon–10.30pm; *www.ica.org.uk*), the city's main forum for the avant-garde, with frequently changing art exhibitions (daily noon–7.30pm; day pass Mon–Fri £1.50, Sat & Sun £2.50), films and performances.

Nash was also responsible for landscaping **St James's Park**, which stretches south of the Mall, its lake providing an inner-city reserve for wildfowl and a recreation area for the employees of Whitehall. Continuing towards Buckingham Palace, the Mall runs behind St James's Palace, a grand Tudor pile built on the site of a leper hospital by bon viveur Henry VIII. Foreign ambassadors in London are still officially titled "Ambassador to the Court of St James", although the court itself has long since moved down the road. The palace – now Prince Charles's pad – is closed to visitors, as is Clarence House (residence of the Queen Mother) at the end of the Mall.

Buckingham Palace has served as the monarch's permanent residence since the accession of Queen Victoria in 1837. The building's exterior, remodelled in 1913, is as bland as could be, but there are a few rooms open to a clamouring public in summer (Aug & Sept daily 9.30am–4pm; £10.50; *www.royal.gov.uk*). At other times there's not much to do save wait for the **Changing of the Guard**, when mounted troops ride down the Mall from St James's Palace (April–July daily 11.30am; Aug–March alternate days only; no band if it rains). **The Queen's Picture Gallery**, around the south side on Buckingham Gate, has been substantially revamped and will open again in the Spring of 2002.

Hyde Park and west to Notting Hill

Following Constitution Hill along the north side of Buckingham Palace brings you to **Hyde Park Corner**, at the southeastern angle of the park, where a Triumphal Arch celebrates Wellington's victory at Waterloo in 1815. Below is Wellington himself, mounted on his favourite horse and facing his former residence, Apsley House, on the northern corner of Piccadilly. Known during the Iron Duke's lifetime as Number One, London, the house is now the **Wellington Museum** (Tues–Sun 11am–5pm; £4.50), which holds, in addition to Wellington's effects, a curious nude statue of the vanquished Napoleon, sculpted by Italian Neoclassicist Canova. Traffic rushes north on Park Lane past a clutch of luxury hotels to **Marble Arch**, built by Nash in imitation of the arch of Constantine in Rome, and shifted here from in front of Buckingham Palace in 1851. This patch of the park is known as **Speakers' Corner**, after the Sunday free-for-all held here since 1866, when riots persuaded the government to give the hotheads their unfettered say. Nowadays it's a place to go and enjoy a little soapbox theatre, both from the cranks who expound their views and from the often more inventive hecklers. In the middle of Hyde Park is the **Serpentine** lake, with a popular lido towards its centre; the nearby **Serpentine Gallery** (daily 10am–6pm; free; *www.serpentine-gallery.org*) hosts excellent contemporary art exhibitions. To the west the park merges into Kensington Gardens, leading to **Kensington Palace** (daily 10am–5pm; £8.50; *www.hrp.org.uk*), Diana's London residence following her separation from Prince Charles; in the days after her death in 1997, the gardens in front of the Palace were buried under truckloads of flowers sent by mourners. Until a decision is made whether to convert the palace into a permanent memorial to Diana, some rooms are open (by guided tour only), including the State Apartments, a gallery of seventeenth-century paintings and a display of court costume.

A short walk north from Kensington Palace takes you into the trendy Notting Hill district worth visiting on the last weekend in August for the riotous **Notting Hill Carnival**, Europe's biggest street-party, and on any Saturday of the year for one of London's best markets along **Portobello Road**, where hundreds of stalls sell everything from antiques to ethnic food.

The South Kensington museums

At the southern end of Kensington Gardens is the **Albert Memorial**, an over-decorated Gothic canopy covering a statue of Queen Victoria's much-mourned consort, who died in 1861, which has recently been stunningly regilded after being painted black during the Blitz. Albert is also the dedicatee of the Royal Albert Hall across the road, completed in 1871 on the model of the Pantheon in Rome and home of the famous "Proms" concerts. To the east of the Albert Hall, Exhibition Road heads south into South Kensington and London's richest concentration of museums. Biggest is the **Victoria and Albert Museum** (daily 10am–5.45pm; Wed 10am-10pm; free; *www.vam.ac.uk*), the world's finest collection of decorative arts. All historic periods and civilizations are represented in the V&A's eleven-kilometre maze of halls and corridors, with especially strong collections of Byzantine and medieval reliquaries, religious sculpture and other devotional items. The Raphael cartoons, a series of designs for tapestries now in the Vatican, are another highlight, while the Nehru Gallery holds one of the world's biggest assemblies of Indian sculpture. The museum's Cast Rooms are worth an afternoon in themselves, with their full-scale replicas of Michelangelo's *David*, Trajan's Column and scores of other sculptural masterpieces. In addition, the V&A's temporary shows are among the best to be seen in Britain.

The innovative **Natural History Museum**, across the way on Cromwell Rd (Mon–Sat 10am–5.50pm, Sun 11am–5.50pm; £7.50, free Mon–Fri after 4.30pm, Sat & Sun after 5pm; *www.nhm.ac.uk*), is enthralling, with its massive-jawed skeletons and models of tyrannosaurus rex and even an animated tableau of the more grisly of its prehistoric colleagues. Inventive displays on human biology and ecology delve a little deeper, though there are plenty of buttons to press if your concentration flags. The same ticket gets you into the neighbouring Earth Galleries, partially refurbished with a Kobe earthquake simulator and other spectacular new galleries explaining volcanic eruptions, tectonic plates and other acts of God. The worthy **Science Museum** in Exhibition Rd (daily 10am–6pm; £6.95, free after 4.30pm; *www.sciencemuseum.org.uk*) gives a lot of space to British technology in the era of the Industrial Revolution, featuring eighteenth-century steam engines, George Stephenson's 1813 *Puffing Billy*, and the achievements of the likes of Humphry Davy, Michael Faraday and Isambard Kingdom Brunel. There are also plenty of stimulating interactive displays roaming through every conceivable area of experimental science, including medicine and space travel, concentrated in the new Wellcome Wing, and houses an IMAX cinema too.

North of Oxford Street

The grid of streets north of Oxford Street holds little of interest, save for a cluster of sights along the Marylebone Rd, near Baker St tube station. **Madame Tussauds** (daily 9.30/10am–5.30pm; £11.50, joint ticket with Planetarium £13.75; *www.madame-tussauds.com*) has been renowned for its waxworks of the rich and famous ever since the good lady arrived in London in 1802, bearing sculpted heads of the guillotined from revolutionary France. These days, though, regardless of which celeb dummy is currently in the spotlight, the place is a shocking waste of money. Next door, the equally poor-value **London Planetarium** (daily 10.20am/12.20pm–5pm; shows every 40min; £6.30) features clunky displays of the heavens projected onto the inner surface of a dome.

The road circling nearby **Regent's Park** is flanked by more of Nash's Regency terraces, some of the most elegant residential buildings in London. At the northern end of this attractive park is **London Zoo** (daily 10am–4/5.30pm; £9.50; *www.londonzoo.co.uk*), one of the world's oldest and most varied collections of animals.

Just five minutes' walk from the north side of the park lies bustling **Camden Town**, host to a vast **weekend market** – centred on Camden Lock, beside the canal, but spilling over several locations either side of the main street – that is now less of a genuine street mart than a hand-over-fist grab for your cash. The number of stalls multiplies each month, even if the range of stuff on offer doesn't – it's mostly clothes, jewellery, music and smokers' paraphernalia. Camden gets so crowded that the tube station is deemed exit-only on Sunday (1.30–5.30pm).

North of here, several residential neighbourhoods repay exploration. The affluent suburb of **Hampstead** retains a small-town atmosphere and excellent walking opportunities on Hampstead Heath, one of the few wild areas left within reach of central London. One major attraction east of Hampstead is **Highgate Cemetery**, ranged on both sides of Swains Lane (Highgate or Archway tube, or bus #214 from Camden Town). Opened in 1838 as a private venture, Highgate was the preferred resting place of wealthy Victorian families and the cemetery is full of monuments to their vanity; the older, more atmospheric western side can only be seen on a guided tour (April–Oct Mon–Fri noon, 2pm & 4pm, Sat & Sun hourly 11am–4pm; Nov–March Sat & Sun hourly 11am–3pm; £3), while the eastern side, whose most famous denizen is Karl Marx, is usually open for a general wander (Mon–Fri 10am–4/5pm, Sat & Sun 11am–4/5pm; £3). Times and prices do change, phone ☎020/83401834 to check.

The City of London

Once the fortified heart of the capital, the **City of London** is now its financial district, also known as the Square Mile. Few people live here, making it a desolate place after nightfall. The area suffered more in the Blitz than anywhere bar the East End, and soulless postwar buildings further detract from its appeal. An earlier conflagration, the 1666 Great Fire of London, led to an era of much more dignified rebuilding and produced the area's finest structure, **St Paul's Cathedral** (Mon–Sat 8.30am–4pm; £5; *www.stpaulslondon.anglican.org*) – just one of over fifty church commissions Sir Christopher Wren received in the wake of the blaze. His Baroque design is fronted by a double-storey colonnaded portico flanked by towers, but the most distinctive feature is the dome, second in size only to St Peter's in Rome, and still a dominating presence on the London skyline. In fact it's a triple dome, its interior cupola separated from the wooden, lead-covered outer skin by a funnel-shaped brick structure. The interior of the church is filled with funerary monuments, predominantly military figures and obscure statesmen – the only memorial to have survived from the original cathedral is an effigy of the poet John Donne, once Dean of St Paul's, in the south aisle of the choir.

A staircase in the south transept leads up to a series of galleries in the dome (10am–4pm). The internal **Whispering Gallery** is the first, so called because of its acoustic properties – words whispered to the wall on one side are distinctly audible on the other. The broad exterior Stone Gallery and the uppermost Golden Gallery both offer good panoramas over London. The **crypt** is the resting place of Wren himself; his son composed the inscription that graces his tomb – *Lector, si monumentum requiris, circumspice* ("Reader, if you seek his monument, look around"). The architect is joined by Turner, Reynolds and other artists, but the most imposing sarcophagi are the twin black monstrosities occupied by the Duke of Wellington and Lord Nelson.

A few minutes north of St Paul's is the **Barbican**, a millionaire's residential complex that incorporates a multi-level arts centre intended to be London's answer to the Pompidou Centre. It remains largely unloved but, as the home of both the Royal Shakespeare Company and the London Symphony Orchestra, it nonetheless figures high on the city's cultural agenda. The excellent **Museum of London** (Mon–Sat 10am–5.50pm, Sun noon–5.50pm; £5, free after 4.30pm; *www.museumoflondon.org.uk*) occupies its southwestern corner, offering a lot of relics from Roman London and an educative trot through subsequent epochs; the models of London in previous centuries are particularly interesting.

The eastern extent of the old city is marked by the **Tower of London** (daily 9/10am–4/6pm; £11; *www.hrp.org.uk*), on the river a mile southeast of St Paul's. It's usually thought of as a place of imprisonment and death, but has variously been used as an armoury, royal residence and repository of the Crown's treasure. The Tower's oldest feature is the central **White Tower**, built by William the Conqueror, although the ubiquitous Christopher Wren adorned each corner with cupolas. The inner wall, with its numerous towers, was built in the time of Henry III, and a further line of fortifications was added by Edward I, so that much of what's visible today was already in place by the end of the thirteenth century. Once inside, you can explore the complex on your own, although decent free tours of the Tower are given every half-hour by Yeomen of the Guard, better known as "Beefeaters" – actually ex-servicemen in Tudor costume. The White Tower itself holds part of the **Royal Armouries** collection (the rest resides in Leeds), and, on the second floor, the Norman Chapel of St John, London's oldest church. Surrounding the White Tower is the Tower Green, where the executions took place of those lucky enough to be spared the public executions on nearby Tower Hill. A stone marks the spot where Lady Jane Grey, Anne Boleyn, Catherine Howard and four others met their end. The Waterloo Barracks contain the **Crown Jewels**, the majority of which postdate the period of the Commonwealth (1649–60), when most were melted down. The three largest cut diamonds in the world are on display here; the most famous of them, the Koh-i-noor, is set into a crown made for the Queen Mother in 1937. On the south side of the complex, the **Bloody Tower** contains the room thought to have seen the murder of the "Princes in the Tower", Edward V and his brother, as well as the quarters where Walter Raleigh spent thirteen years of captivity writing his *History of the World*. Below lies **Traitor's Gate**, through which prisoners arrived after having been ferried down the Thames from the courts of justice at Westminster.

River views from here are dominated by the twin towers of **Tower Bridge**, built in the 1880s and featuring a roadway which is raised to allow ships access further up the Thames. The main attraction of the "Tower Bridge Experience" tour is a wander across the walkways linking the summits of the towers (daily 9.30/10am–6/6.30pm; £6.25; *www.towerbridge. org.uk*). Intended for public use when the bridge was first built, the walkways were closed in 1909 due to their popularity with prostitutes and the suicidal.

Greenwich

Some nine miles east of central London, **GREENWICH** (pronounced "gren-itch") is steeped in naval history; it is also the site of the Greenwich Meridian and housed the controversial Millennium Dome. Transport links are good: boats run regularly from Westminster Pier, and the Docklands Light Railway (*www.dlr.co.uk*) scoots east from the City into the redeveloped Docklands, beneath the towering Canary Wharf and south to the **Cutty Sark**, which stands in a dry dock next to Greenwich pier (daily 10am–5pm; £3.50, combined ticket with Maritime Museum and Royal Observatory £12; *www.cuttysark.org.uk*). The majestic vessel was one of the last of the clippers, sail-powered cargo ships built for speed and used on long-distance routes to bring wool, tea and other produce to London from the far-flung corners of the Empire – until rendered obsolete by the arrival of steam. Hugging the riverfront to the east is the extraordinary Baroque facade of the **Royal Naval College** (Mon–Sat 10am–5pm, Sun 12.30–5pm; £5; *www.greenwichfoundation.org.uk*), probably Wren's finest work after St Paul's. Across the road the interesting **National Maritime Museum** (daily 10am–5pm; £7.50, combined ticket with *Cutty Sark* and Royal Observatory £12; *www.nmm.ac.uk*), exhibits model ships, charts and globes, and has been rejuvenated with some inventive new galleries under an enormous glazed roof. The next-door **Queen's House** (same times; £7.50) is an impressively simple classical villa built for Henrietta Maria by Inigo Jones, the first example of domestic Palladian architecture in Britain. From here Greenwich Park stretches up the hill, crowned by the **Royal Observatory** (same times; £6, combined ticket with *Cutty Sark* and Maritime Museum £12), another largely Wren-inspired structure. The museum houses a brain-stretching display of timepieces, telescopes and navigational equipment, but if grappling with the complexities of longitude doesn't take your fancy, you can straddle the world instead; the Greenwich Meridian, which marks 0° longitude, runs through the centre of the building.

Squatting on reclaimed wasteland two miles north, the **Millennium Dome** sits awaiting its outcome after a life as the subject of wrangling and controversy. Plans muted for the future of the huge structure range from development as a theme park or a sports centre to being taken down and the land sold for luxury riverside housing.

The western outskirts: Kew to Windsor

Boats ply westwards from Westminster Pier, upstream to **KEW** where you'll find the wonderful **Royal Botanic Gardens** (daily 9.30am–dusk; £5; *www.kew.org*; Kew Gardens tube), home to over 50,000 species grown in the plantations and glasshouses of a 300-acre site.

Further upstream, thirteen miles southwest of the centre and also served by riverboat, is the finest of Tudor mansions, **Hampton Court Palace** (Mon 10.15am–4.30/6pm, Tues–Sun 9.30am–4.30/6pm; £10.80; train from Waterloo; *www.hrp.org.uk*). Cardinal Wolsey commissioned this immense house in 1516, then handed it to Henry VIII in a vain attempt to win back his favour. Henry enlarged and improved the palace, but it was William III who made the most radical alterations, hiring Sir Christopher Wren to remodel the buildings. William and Mary's Apartments are chock-full of treasures, while the highlight of Henry VIII's State Apartments is the Great Hall with its astonishing hammerbeam roof. There's plenty more to see in the sixty-acre grounds (open dawn–dusk; free): the Great Vine, grown from a cutting in 1768 and still averaging about 300kg of black grapes per year; William III's Banqueting House; and the Lower Orangery, a gallery for Mantegna's heroic canvases, *The Triumphs of Caesar*. The famous **maze**, laid out in 1714, lies just north of the palace.

WINDSOR, 21 miles west of central London, is dominated by **Windsor Castle** (daily 10am–4/5.15pm; Mon–Sat £10.50, Sun £8.50; train from Waterloo; *www.royalresidence.com*), which began its days as a wooden fortress built by William the Conqueror, with numerous later monarchs having had a hand in its evolution. Some of their work was undone by a huge fire in November 1992, but the magnificent **State Apartments** have re-opened after meticulous restoration. Highlights include Van Dyck's triptych of Charles I in the King's Drawing Room; the Queen's Ballroom, dominated by an enormous silver mirror and table, and more Van Dyck paintings; and the vast array of crested helmets and sixteenth-century armour in the Queen's Guard Chamber, which includes an etched gold suit made for Prince Hal. A separate gallery to the left of the main entrance holds exhibitions of the royal art collection – Windsor possesses the world's finest collection of drawings and notebooks by Leonardo da Vinci. A visit to the castle should take in **St George's Chapel** (closed Sun); a glorious fan-vaulted perpendicular structure, ranking with King's College Chapel in Cambridge, that contains the tombs of numerous kings and queens.

Eating

London is renowned as one of the best cities in the world for **eating**, with new restaurants opening almost daily. The cosmopolitan population means you can find a restaurant representing almost any nationality or culture you can think of and, despite the city's reputation for expense, there are affordable places to be found, even in the buzzing West End districts of **Soho** and **Covent Garden**. London's tiny **Chinatown**, comprising the alleys between Leicester Square and Shaftesbury Avenue, offers value-for-money eating right in the centre. But to sample the full range of possibilities you need to get out of the West End – to the Indian restaurants of **Brick Lane** in the East End or **Drummond Street** near Euston, or to the eateries of the trendy neighbourhoods of **Camden Town**, **Shoreditch** and **Islington**, north and east of King's Cross. There are also plenty of spots to pick up a street **snack** or cheap **lunch** – and some of these places are good stand-bys for an evening filler. The usual burger and pizza chains are on every corner, and there are any number of sandwich shops, which – if they have seating – may well serve hot meals too, from omelettes and fry-ups to meat-and-two-veg daily specials, normally for around £3.

For details of London's post-code system, see Listings on p.180.

Snacks and quick meals

Bagel Bakery, Brick Lane north end, E1. A 24hr stand-up café offering filled bagels for mere pennies. Fresh bread, cakes and hot salt beef too. Aldgate East tube.

Bar Italia, 22 Frith St, Soho. A tiny café that's a Soho institution, serving coffee, sandwiches, pizza and the like. Popular with clubbers and those here to watch the Italian football on the big screen. Open 24hr Fri & Sat, until 4am Sun–Thurs. Leicester Sq tube.

Beach Café, 13 Neal's Yard. Best of the excellent cafés on this atmospheric cobbled courtyard, a former hippy hangout off Monmouth St. Good lunchtime specials and outdoor seating. Covent Garden tube.

Café in the Crypt, St Martin-in-the-Fields church, Trafalgar Sq. Good-quality buffet food makes this an ideal spot to fill up at before hitting the West End, or after touring the National Gallery. Charing Cross tube.

Carrie Awaze II, 27 Endell St. Experience a range of weird-and-wonderful sandwiches, curries and salads while the charismatic owner serenades customers on the sitar. Covent Garden tube.

Crazy Salads, 128 Wardour St, Soho. Bargain takeaway pasta and salad bar for healthy lunchtime meals.

Food For Thought, 31 Neal St. Very small vegetarian restaurant – the inexpensive food is delicious, but there are long queues at peak times. Covent Garden tube.

Lee Ho Fook, 4 Macclesfield St, cnr Dansey Place, Chinatown. No English sign. An authentic Chinese barbecue house, tiny, bright and fast-paced. Leicester Sq tube.

Maison Bertaux, 28 Greek St, Soho. Founded in 1871 this old school French café has a dazzling array of some of the best pastries in London. Leicester Sq tube.

Mildred's, 58 Greek St, Soho. Very tasty wholefood in this relaxed restaurant with organic drinks and a young, down-to-earth crowd. Tottenham Court Rd tube.

Pollo, 20 Old Compton St, Soho. The best-value Italian food in town. Always packed, though the queues move quickly. Leicester Sq tube.

Stockpot, 18 Old Compton St, Soho (Leicester Sq tube); 40 Panton St (Piccadilly Circus); 50 James St (Bond St); 6 Basil St (Knightsbridge); 273 King's Rd (Sloane Sq). Filling bistro-style grub at rock-bottom prices.

Yo! Sushi, 52 Poland St, Soho. Over-priced but fun conveyor-belt sushi bar, with a robotic drinks trolley. Oxford Circus tube.

Restaurants

Afghan Kitchen, 35 Islington Green. Quality Afghan food for budget prices – expect to share a table. Angel tube.

Belgo Centraal, 50 Earlham St. Hugely popular Belgian restaurant serving heaps of mussels and other hearty fare, as well as beer of course. The lunchtime deals are hard to beat. Covent Garden tube. Also Belgo Noord at 72 Chalk Farm Rd (Camden Town tube), and Belgo Zuid at 124 Ladbroke Grove (Ladbroke Grove tube).

Café Delancey, 3 Delancey St. Comfortable Camden brasserie that's good for both a quick coffee and a snack, and reasonably priced full lunches and dinners. Camden Town tube.

Café Pacifico, 5 Langley St. Rated as the best Mexican in central London, though that isn't saying much. Fairly quiet during the day, unbelievably noisy in the evening. Good bar. Covent Garden tube.

Churchill Arms, Church St, Notting Hill. Excellent quality Thai dining at the rear of this colourful lively pub with a landlord to match. Notting Hill Gate Tube.

Chutneys, 124 Drummond St. Superb vegetarian Bangladeshi food, especially attractive on a Sunday (all you can eat for £5). Euston Sq tube.

Daquise, 20 Thurloe St. Something of a cult, with its gloomy Eastern Bloc decor, long-suffering staff and heartily utilitarian Polish food. Good place for a quick bite and a shot of vodka after the museums. South Kensington tube.

Duke of Cambridge, 30 St Peter's St, Islington. Award-winning gastro-pub serving very tasty organic fare in the comfortable bar and restaurant. Outside tables in summer. Angel tube.

Fakhreldine Express, 92 Queensway. Outpost of the expensive West End restaurant of the same name, this bright little spot is the many Arabic diners on Queensway. Bayswater tube.

Gallipoli's, 102 & 120 Upper St, Islington. Superb value, always packed Turkish café/bistro. Wonderful mixed meze. Tables outside in the summer. Angel tube.

India Club, 143 Strand. Faded canteen-style diner above the Strand Continental Hotel serving homely Indian food that's authentic enough for the discerning staff of the Indian High Commission opposite. Temple tube.

Jimmy's, 23 Frith St, Soho. Basement Greek-Cypriot eatery that's long been part of Soho's cheap-eating scene. Leicester Sq tube.

Kastoori, 188 Upper Tooting Rd. Thoroughly authentic, aromatic Gujarati cooking that's well worth the journey south. Tooting Broadway tube.

Kettner's, 29 Romilly St, Soho. Grand old place with high ceilings and a pianist, that's actually part of the Pizza Express chain and consequently cheaper than it looks. Leicester Sq tube.

Lorelei, 21 Bateman St, Soho. Tiny pizza/pasta joint offering one of Soho's cheapest routes to a full stomach. Tottenham Court Rd tube.

Nazrul II, 49 Hanbury St, E1. Massive curry palace off Brick Lane, with over fifty great-value balti dishes on offer, plus biryanis, tandooris, and the rest. Excellent Sunday set meals. Aldgate East tube.

New Tayyab, 83 Fieldgate St, E1. Very tasty Pakistani food at unbelievably cheap prices. It's unlicensed but you can bring your own. Cash only. Aldgate East or Whitechapel tube.

Nontas, 14 Camden High St. Archetypal boisterous Greek taverna, doing all the basics well. Camden Town tube.

Pizza Express, 10 Dean St, Soho; 30 Coptic St, Bloomsbury (both Tottenham Court Rd tube); and other branches all over London. Does a good line in thin-crust pizzas at reasonable prices. The Dean St branch houses one of London's leading jazz venues in the basement.

Poons, 27 Lisle St, Chinatown. A tatty Chinese diner quite unlike its smarter offspring nearby at 4 Leicester St, but with better food. Leicester Sq tube. Branches in Whiteley's mall on Queensway, and 50 Woburn Place (Russell Sq tube).

La Quercia d'Oro, 16a Endell St. Shabby, cheerful, basic Italian eatery, with big rustic portions. Covent Garden tube.

Ravi Shankar, 133 Drummond St. Another cracking South Indian restaurant on this street – great value, as is its competition. Euston Sq tube.

Royal China, 13 Queensway. Dim sum that beats Chinatown's best hands-down, and is still very cheap. Queensway tube.

Smiths, 67–77 Charterhouse St, Smithfield. Housed in a former warehouse, this lively place runs two restaurants and two bars on different floors. Good British cooking with dishes strongly influenced by the nearby meat market, all at fair prices. Farringdon tube.

Tokyo Diner, 2 Newport Place, Chinatown. Excellent Japanese diner, with quality service and authentic food at a fraction of the cost of its rivals. Leicester Sq tube.

Wagamama, 4 Streatham St, Bloomsbury. Popular noodle/sushi joint with a hi-tech interior, bench seating and waiters who take orders on palmtop PCs. Filling and cheap, but expect to queue. Tottenham Court Rd tube. Branches all across town.

Wong Kei, 27 Wardour St, Chinatown. Five-storey newly renovated, Cantonese place boasting London's rudest waiters, along with food that's good and fast. Open 5pm–4.30am. Leicester Sq tube.

Drinking

Central London is full of **pubs**, and, although you'll find much pleasanter places in the neighbourhoods further out, there are one or two watering holes that retain an element of character. Expect prices to be well above what you might have been used to paying anywhere else in Britain, but on the plus side, pub food in London is often more adventurous than outside the capital. As for modern **bars**, there are countless numbers of them, from cocktail places to subterranean salsa joints, mostly with a young, hip clientele and high prices.

Albert, 52 Victoria St, Westminster. Handily situated pub serving good food, including hearty breakfasts in the upstairs restaurant. St James's Park tube.

Alphabet Bar, 61 Beak St, W1. Ultra-trendy cocktail bar serving the infamous absinthe. Piccadilly Circus tube.

Blackfriar, 174 Queen Victoria St, City. Art Nouveau landmark, handy for the City sights. Closed Sat & Sun. Blackfriars tube.

Camden Head, 2 Camden Walk, Islington. A popular local pub, handy for the Camden Passage antiques trade. Reasonable lunchtime food too. Angel tube.

Coach & Horses, 29 Greek St, Soho. Long-standing and little changed haunt of the ghosts of old Soho, popular with nightclubbers and art students from nearby St Martin's College. Leicester Sq tube.

Cubana Bar, 36 Southwick St, Paddington. Newly opened authentic Cuban bar with live bands on Fridays and Saturdays. Wide choice of South American food and good cocktails.

Cutty Sark, Ballast Quay off Lassell St, Greenwich. Ancient riverside pub with a nautical theme, outside tables and fine views of Docklands and the Dome. Cutty Sark tube, then walk downstream.

Dog & Duck, 18 Bateman St, Soho. Tiny pub that retains much of its old character and a loyal clientele. Leicester Sq tube.

Dragon Bar, Leonard St, Shoreditch. A small lounge-bar with large sofas, minimal decor, and an admirable no suit policy. Old Street tube.

Electricity Showrooms, 39a Hoxton Sq, Shoreditch. The epitome of the chic regeneration of the East End. With an enormous bar; restaurant and club downstairs. Old Street Tube.

Embassy Bar, Essex Rd, Islington. A huge oval bar and minimalist yet somehow warming interior ensure that this bar, on the edges of Islington, is always packed. Angel tube.

Flask, 14 Flask Walk, Hampstead. Convivial local, close to the station and serving good food and real ale. Hampstead tube.

Freedom Brewing Co., 41 Earlham St. Basement bar with post-industrial decor, microbrewery and good food. Pricey though. Covent Garden tube.

French House, 49 Dean St, Soho. Only wine, spirits and half-pints are served at this tiny, characterful pub, home to the French Resistance during the war and to arty Soho types today. Leicester Sq tube.

George Inn, 77 Borough High St. Magnificent seventeenth-century coaching inn, now owned by the National Trust. 10 min walk from the Tate Modern. Borough tube.

Gordon's, Villiers St, off Trafalgar Sq. Cellar wine bar that looks like it hasn't seen a lick of paint since World War II. Excellent wine list, decent buffet food and genial atmosphere. Closed Sat & Sun. Charing Cross tube.

King's Head, 115 Upper St, Islington. Busy pub in the heart of Islington that has regular live music and fringe theatre. For some reason the bar staff quote prices in "old money". Angel tube.

Lamb, 94 Lamb's Conduit St, Bloomsbury. Pleasant pub with a marvellously well-preserved Victorian interior of mirrors, old wood and "snob" screens. Russell Sq tube.

Lamb & Flag, 33 Rose St. Busy, historic pub tucked away down an alley between Garrick St and Floral St. Decent food. Covent Garden tube.

Lux Bar, Hoxton Sq, Old Street. Attached to the cutting-edge cinema next door, this large, airy, bright lounge-restaurant attracts a young, ultra stylish media crowd. Old Street tube.

Moon Under Water, 105 Charing Cross Rd. Part of the Wetherspoon's chain and therefore very cheap; housed in a cavernous ex-gig venue. Tottenham Court Rd tube.

Museum Tavern, 49 Great Russell St, Bloomsbury. Large old pub, right opposite the main entrance to the British Museum. Holborn tube.

Old Queen's Head, 44 Essex Rd, Islington. Cool minimalist decor and an original Elizabethan fireplace – go early, it gets packed. Angel tube.

Orange Brewery, 37 Pimlico Rd, Victoria. Pleasant cosy pub that brews its own beer – powerful stuff. Sloane Sq tube.

Paviour's Arms, Page St, Westminster. Untouched Art Deco pub, close to Tate Britain. Pimlico tube.

Salisbury, 90 St Martin's Lane, off Trafalgar Sq. One of the most beautifully preserved Victorian pubs in the capital. Leicester Sq tube.

Sevilla Mia, 22 Hanway St. Tiny, back-alley joint that serves until 1am, and so is jammed with drinkers. As is the Troy Club upstairs. Tottenham Court Rd tube.

Warrington, 93 Warrington Crescent, Maida Vale. Yet another architectural gem – flamboyant Art Nouveau – in an area replete with them. Excellent Thai food upstairs. Warwick Ave tube.

Nightlife

No matter what your taste, you'll find what you're looking for in London, a city that in many ways becomes a more appealing place after dark. The capital's rich ethnic mix and concentration of creative talent gives it a diversity and energy that no other town in England comes close to matching – Birmingham might have a better concert hall, Manchester might have a couple of hot clubs, but nowhere can match the capital's consistent quality and choice. The array of gigs, movies, plays and other events is charted most completely in the main weekly **listings magazine**, *Time Out (www.timeout.com)*.

As for **clubs**, London continues to maintain its status as dance-music capital of Europe and favourite destination of visiting DJs from all over the world. Late-night licences allow many venues to keep serving alcohol until 6am or later, although the club scene is most heavily fuelled by ever-popular proscribed chemicals including Ecstasy, speed and cocaine. At weekends you'll find most of the major venues playing the latest dance sounds – house, garage and drum'n'bass – while "alternative" nights, playing funk, Seventies, indie or R&B, tend to feature on weekdays; check *Time Out* or dance magazines such as *DJ*, *Eternity* or *Mixmag*. Prices vary enormously, with small midweek nights starting at under £5 and large weekend events charging around £10 on average, but even as much as £25 – and bear in mind that the mark-up on drinks is phenomenal. Most venues open their doors between 10pm and midnight and host a different club on each night of the week.

The **live music** scene is amazingly diverse, encompassing all variations of rock music, from big names on tour at the huge arenas, through to a network of indie and pub bands in more intimate surroundings. There's a fair slice of World Music too, especially African, Latin and Caribbean bands. Entry prices for gigs run much the same as clubs, though bar prices tend to be lower; for pub gigs, admission is often free.

Though a stroll through the West End can create the impression that Lloyd-Webber musicals and revivals of clapped-out plays have a stranglehold on London's **theatres**, the scene is less staid than it might appear. Apart from the classic productions of the major repertory companies, there's a large fringe circuit, staging often provocative pieces in venues that range from proper independent auditoriums to back-rooms in pubs. **Cinema** is not as adventurous as it is in some European capitals, with the number of repertory houses diminishing steadily, but there's a decent spread of screenings of general-release and re-run films each night of the week. With two opera houses and several well-equipped concert halls, London's programme of **classical music** is excellent, and the annual Proms season represents Europe's most accessible festival of highbrow music. For most plays and concerts you should be able to get a seat for under £15 in the West End, or less at venues off the main circuit.

Clubs and discos

Bagley's, King's Cross Goods Yard, off York Way. Vast warehouse-style venue, with a different DJ or ambience in each room. King's Cross tube.

Bar Rumba, 36 Shaftesbury Ave. Maintains a Latin flavour with pre-club dance classes, but you'll find anything from drum'n'bass to R&B at this friendly club. Live shows too. Piccadilly Circus tube.

Camden Palace, 1a Camden High St. Big old cavern of a place, studentish and much-loved. Mornington Crescent tube.

Cargo, 83 Rivington St, EC2. Set within three old railway arches this medium club packs it all in, from world food, afro-beat and hi-life, nu jazz and future funk. Farringdon Tube.

Elbow Room, 89 Chapel Market, Islington. Well-appointed club-bar and lounge in a trendy area. Angel tube.

The End, 16a West Central St, Bloomsbury. Big beat house meets techno in London's best-looking club. Tottenham Court Rd tube.

Fabric, 77 Charterhouse St, EC1. A vast converted factory complex that boasts a 'body sonic dancefloor'. With three stages ranging from hard house, drum'n'bass, to hip-hop and live sets. Queue early. Farringdon tube.

Fridge, Town Hall Parade, Brixton. Popular South London club and venue, specializing in techno and house. Brixton tube.

Gossips, 69 Dean St, Soho. Dingy basement that seems to have been running forever, with an alternative flavour. Tottenham Court Rd tube.

Heaven, Under the Arches, Craven St. Smiley, dressy club with two large floors and a big gay presence, although the music and atmosphere also attract a mixed crowd. Charing Cross tube.

Mass, St Matthew's Church, Brixton. Serious techno and cutting-edge sounds. Brixton tube.

Ministry of Sound, 103 Gaunt St. Large, long-running club on three floors that has become an institution; one of the best sound systems around. Elephant & Castle tube.

Subterania, 12 Acklam Rd. Worth a visit for its diverse (but dressy) club nights on Fridays and Saturdays – if you can get in. Ladbroke Grove tube.

Turnmills, 63 Clerkenwell Rd. Home to Trade and other gay – though not exclusively so – nights. Farringdon tube.

Velvet Room, 143 Charing Cross Rd. Very cool, velvet-dripping interior; happy-house tunes. Tottenham Court Rd tube.

Wag, 35 Wardour St, Chinatown. A hot spot in the mid-1980s, now hugely popular for its retro night on Saturday, and still going strong through the week. Leicester Sq tube.

Live music venues

100 Club, 100 Oxford St. Unpretentious and inexpensive jazz venue that moonlights as a venue for fairly big rock and mainstream acts. Tottenham Court Rd tube.

12-Bar Club, 23 Denmark Place. Atmospheric small club up an alley behind Andy's Guitar Workshop on Charing Cross Rd. Blues, new songwriters, acoustic bands. Tottenham Court Rd tube.

606 Club, 90 Lots Rd. Jazz restaurant, off the untrendy part of the King's Rd. Fulham Broadway tube.

Astoria, 157 Charing Cross Rd. One of London's best-used venues – a large balconied theatre that has live bands and clubs. Tottenham Court Rd tube.

Blues Bar, 20 Kingly St. A bona fide American blues bar in the heart of London, with live blues most nights of the week. Oxford Circus tube.

Borderline, Orange Yard, Manette St, Soho. Intimate venue with diverse musical policy, often focused on up-and-coming American acts. Tottenham Court Rd tube.

Brixton Academy, 211 Stockwell Rd. Massive Victorian hall used for gigs and club nights. Brixton tube.

Forum, 9 Highgate Rd. Perhaps the capital's best medium-sized venue – large enough to attract established bands, but also a prime spot for newer talent. Kentish Town tube.

Garage, 20 Highbury Corner. Eclectic indie-based mix with a more acoustic focus upstairs. Highbury & Islington tube.

Hope & Anchor, 207 Upper St. Originally a punk venue, this tiny basement below the pub is still preferred by new indie bands. Highbury & Islington tube.

Jazz Café, 5 Parkway. Slick, modern venue for excellent jazz, funk and occasional solo songwriters. Camden Town tube.

Ronnie Scott's, 47 Frith St, Soho. The most famous jazz club in London, small, smoky and rather precious, but featuring top-line names. Leicester Sq tube.

Salsa Club, 96 Charing Cross Rd. Quality Latino venue, with bands and club nights. Tottenham Court Rd tube.

Shepherds Bush Empire, Shepherds Bush Green. Lovely old theatre with great acoustics, featuring an eclectic, often excellent, choice of music. Shepherds Bush tube.

Swan, 215 Clapham Rd. Raucous late-opening Irish pub with rootsy gigs most nights. Stockwell tube.

ULU, Manning Hall, Malet St, Bloomsbury. The University of London Union (yoo-loo), with an exceptionally cheap bar and loud bands. Russell Sq tube.

Underworld, 174 Camden High St. New indie bands and occasional club nights. Camden Town tube.

Gay and lesbian nightlife

The **gay and lesbian** scenes in London are livelier than almost anywhere else in Europe, with a vast range of venues from quiet pubs to cruisy bars and frenetic clubs. Soho is the rising "gay village", focused on Old Compton St. Apart from *Time Out* and *The Pink Paper*, you should check the latest listings in *Boyz* and *QX*, available in all the places listed below. An excellent source of information on all aspects of gay life in the city is the 24hr London Lesbian and Gay Switchboard (☎020/7837 7324).

Black Cap, 171 Camden High St. North London gay institution – a big drag cabaret venue. Camden Town tube.

Brompton's, 294 Old Brompton Rd. Long-established gay bar, drawing in a mixture of tourists, local yuppies and clones. Earl's Court tube.

Candy Bar, 4 Carlisle St, Soho. Lesbian bar and club on three floors. Tottenham Court Rd tube.

Central Station, 37 Wharfdale Rd. Friendly, relaxed gay pub and cabaret, with sports bar and late-opening. King's Cross tube.

Compton's of Soho, 53 Old Compton St, Soho. Welcoming, long-standing loud gay pub that has seen a dozen or so new gay cafés, bars and shops grow up around it. Leicester Sq tube.

Freedom, 60 Wardour St, Soho. Trendy café-bar attracting a hip, mixed gay/straight crowd. Leicester Sq tube.

G.A.Y. at the Astoria, 157 Charing Cross Rd. London's biggest gay club of the moment, attracting an unpretentious, dance-happy bunch (Mon & Thurs–Sat). Tottenham Court Rd tube.

Heaven, Under the Arches, Craven St. Huge club playing glam, trash disco and soul/funk to a dressed-up crowd (Mon, Wed, Fri & Sat). Charing Cross tube.

King William IV, 75 Hampstead High St. Long-established, relaxed north London gay pub. Hampstead tube.

Liquid Lounge, 275 Pentonville Rd, N1. A cheap bar with a popular alternative pop, funk Saturday night. Geared more towards the girls. Kings Cross tube.

Theatre and cinema

London's big two **theatre** companies are the **National Theatre**, performing in three theatres on the South Bank (☎020/7452 3000, *www.nt-online.org*), and the **Royal Shakespeare Company**, whose productions launch in Stratford-upon-Avon and then transfer to the two houses in the Barbican (☎020/7638 8891, *www.rsc.org.uk*). For a show that's had good reviews, tickets under £10 are difficult to come by at either, but it's always worth ringing their box offices for details of stand-by deals, which can get you the best seat in the house for as little as £5 if you're a student, otherwise £10. During the summer months you can also see Shakespeare performed in the authentic setting of the reconstructed **Globe Theatre** (☎020/7401 9919, *www.shakespeares-globe.org*). Other venues with a reputation for staging challenging drama include the Almeida, Donmar Warehouse, ICA, Royal Court, Tricycle and Young Vic.

Many of London's theatres have cut-price deals for stand-by tickets on the day; otherwise head for the large booth in Leicester Square selling **half-price theatre tickets** (*www.officiallondontheatre.co.uk*) for that day's performances at all West End theatres (note that they specialize in the top end of the price range). Offices around Charing Cross Rd and Leicester Square can get tickets for any show, but at a huge mark-up – as high as two hundred percent. Don't buy from street touts: they ask outrageous amounts, and you have no guarantee that the tickets are genuine.

The main concentration of big-screen **cinemas** showing new releases is on Leicester Square, Piccadilly, Haymarket and Lower Regent St. Seats cost £8–12. The main repertory cinemas in the centre are the **National Film Theatre** (*www.bfi.org.uk*) and the **ICA** (*www.ica.org.uk*). After a spate of closures, London has very few other repertory cinemas: the Lux in Hoxton, the Riverside in Hammersmith, and the Rio in Dalston have perhaps the most interesting programmes. There are, however, several excellent independent cinemas for new art-house releases, including the Renoir (Russell Square), Gate (Notting Hill) and Metro (Rupert St, Soho). The **Prince Charles** off Leicester Sq is a cheap and cheerful institution on its own with its infamous Sing-Along-a-Sound-of-Music every weekend. The **BFI London IMAX** cinema in Waterloo (☎020/7902 1234, *www.bfi.org.uk*) has a ten-storey screen, the UK's largest, showing both ordinary and 3D films.

Classical music, opera and dance

For **classical concerts** the principal venue is the **South Bank Centre** (☎020/7960 4242, *www.sbc.org.uk*), where the biggest names (including the resident London Philharmonic) appear at the Festival Hall, with more specialized programmes in the Queen Elizabeth Hall and Purcell Room. Programmes in the concert hall of the **Barbican Centre** (☎020/7638 8891, *www.barbican.org.uk*) – home of the London Symphony Orchestra – are too often pitched at a corporate audience, though you can also find some affordable recitals; for chamber music and lieder, the intimate **Wigmore Hall**, 36 Wigmore St (☎020/7935 2141), is many people's favourite. Tickets for all these venues begin at about £5, with cheap stand-bys sometimes available to students on the day. There are free weekday lunchtime recitals at a clutch of **churches** in the City (information ☎020/7332 1456) and at St Martin-in-the-Fields church, Trafalgar Square, which also hosts inexpensive evening candlelit concerts. From July to September every year the **Proms** at the **Royal Albert Hall** in Kensington (☎020/7589 8212, *www.bbc.co.uk/proms*) feature at least one concert daily, with hundreds of standing places sold for just a couple of pounds on the night. The acoustics aren't the world's best, but the calibre of the performers is unbeatable, and the programme is a fascinating mix of standards and new or obscure works.

The **Royal Opera House** in Covent Garden (☎020/7304 4000, *www.royaloperahouse.org*) has undergone major restoration work and now stages world-class opera and dance (from the resident **Royal Ballet**) in a stunning setting, with tickets from £10. The **English National Opera** at the Coliseum, St Martin's Lane (☎020/7632 8300, *www.eno.org*), stages less traditional productions, all of which are sung in English, from £7 – any unsold seats are released on the day of the performance at discount prices. Smaller venues (often the Queen Elizabeth Hall) regularly stage innovative productions by touring companies such as Opera North. Rebuilt **Sadler's Wells**, Rosebery Avenue in Clerkenwell (☎020/7863 8000, *www.sadlerswells. com*), hosts world-class **contemporary and classical dance**, while adventurous contemporary dance programmes are staged at the South Bank, the ICA and The Place, 17 Duke's Rd, Bloomsbury (☎020/7387 0031, *www.theplace.org.uk*), as well as at numerous, more ad hoc venues.

Listings

Airlines American Airlines (☎0845/778 9789); British Airways (☎0845/773 3377); Buzz (☎0870/240 7070); EasyJet (☎0870/600 0000); Go (☎0845/605 4321); KLM (☎0870/507 4074); Lufthansa (☎0845/773 7747); Ryanair (☎0870/156 9569); Virgin Atlantic (☎01293/747747).

Airports City (☎020/7646 0000); Gatwick (☎0870/0002468); Heathrow (☎0870/000 0123); Luton (☎01582/405100); Stansted (☎01279/680500).

American Express 30 Haymarket, SW1 (☎020/7484 9600).

Bike and roller blade rental London Bicycle Touring Company, 1a Gabriels Wharf, 56 Upper Ground, SE1 (☎020/7928 6838, *www.londonbicycle.com*).

Books Along Charing Cross Rd, between Tottenham Court Rd and Leicester Sq tubes, you'll find every bookshop imaginable, including the labyrinthine Foyles, and departmental outlets of Waterstones, Blackwells and Borders. There are also multistorey Waterstones at 82 Gower St and 203 Piccadilly – the latter the largest bookshop in Europe and yards from Hatchards, the Queen's bookseller. For more radical publications call in at Compendium, 234 Camden High St. London's best map and travel bookshop is Stanford's, 12 Long Acre, Covent Garden.

Bus station Long-distance coach services depart from Victoria Coach Station, on Buckingham Palace Rd (Victoria tube). National Express ticket offices (☎0870/580 8080) can be found here and opposite Victoria train station at 52 Grosvenor Gdns, where you can also get Eurolines tickets for European services (☎08705/143219).

Car rental Avis (☎0870/606 0100); Budget (☎0800/181181); Europcar (☎0870/607 5000); Hertz (☎0870/844 8844); Holiday Autos (☎0870/530 0400); National (☎0870/400 4502).

Embassies Australia, The Strand, WC2 (☎020/7379 4334); Canada, 38 Grosvenor St, W1 (☎020/7258 6600); Ireland, 17 Grosvenor Pl, SW1 (☎020/7235 2171); New Zealand, 80 Haymarket, SW1 (☎020/7930 8422); USA, 24 Grosvenor Sq, W1 (☎020/7499 9000).

Exchange Shopping areas such as Oxford St and Covent Garden are littered with private exchange offices, and there are 24hr booths at the biggest central tube stations, but their rates are always worse than the banks. You'll find branches of all major banks around Oxford St, Regent St and Piccadilly.

Internet access No-frills EasyEverything is at 9 Tottenham Court Rd (junc. Oxford St), 358 Oxford St (Bond St tube), 9 Wilton Rd (opp. Victoria station), 7 The Strand (off Trafalgar Sq), and 160 Kensington High St. All are open 24hr with access starting from £1. More personable cybercafés include Buzzbar, 95 Portobello Rd (☎020/7460 9606; Notting Hill); the Vibe Bar, 91 Brick Lane, E1 (☎020/7247 3479); Cyberia, 39 Whitfield St (☎020/76814200; off Goodge St); Webshack, 15 Dean St (☎020/74398000; Soho).

Left luggage At all airport terminals and major train stations (daily, generally 7am–11pm); most offices are run by The Excess Baggage Company (☎0800/783 1085, *www.excess-baggage.com*).

London Transport For bus, tube and river-boat enquiries, call ☎020/7222 1234.

Lost property On a bus or tube, call ☎020/7486 2496; on a train ☎020/7928 5151; in a black taxi ☎020/7833 0996.

Medical facilities The Medical Advisory Service general helpline is ☎020/8994 9874 (Mon–Fri 6–9pm). Central hospitals with 24hr emergency units are: Charing Cross, Fulham Palace Rd, Fulham (☎020/8846 1234); St Mary's, Praed St, Paddington (☎020/7886 6666); St Thomas's, Lambeth Palace Rd, Southwark (☎020/7928 9292); University College, Grafton Way, Bloomsbury (☎020/7387 9300). For emergency dental service phone ☎020/7955 2185 (Mon–Fri) or ☎020/7737 4000 (Sat & Sun). The Rape Crisis Centre is on ☎020/7837 1600.

Pharmacies Every police station keeps a list of emergency pharmacies in its area; otherwise try Bliss, 5 Marble Arch, W1 (daily 9am–midnight), also at 50–56 Willesden Lane, NW6 (daily 9am–2am).

Police The most convenient West End station is at 27 Savile Row, W1 (☎020/7437 1212).

Postcodes London is carved up into postal areas, used by everyone to locate addresses. The whole of the West End from Soho to Marble Arch and north to Marylebone counts as W1; Bloomsbury is WC1; Leicester Sq and Covent Garden are WC2; Victoria and Westminster are SW1; Waterloo and Bankside are SE1; the City is EC1–EC4; Brick Lane is E1; King's Cross and Islington are N1; Euston, Regent's Park and Camden are NW1; Paddington and Bayswater are W2; South Kensington is SW7; Earl's Court is SW5.

Post offices The Trafalgar Square post office has the longest opening hours: Mon–Sat 8am–8pm. Poste restante mail should be addressed to this branch, at 24–28 William IV St, London WC2N 4DL.

Train information For all enquiries, call ☎0845/748 4950. Broadly, Euston handles services for northwest England, north Wales and Glasgow; King's Cross for the Northeast and Edinburgh; Liverpool St for eastern England; Paddington for the West Country and south Wales; Waterloo for southwest England, France and Belgium; and Victoria, London Bridge and Charing Cross for southeast England.

Travel agents STA Travel, 11 Goodge St, 38 Store St, 117 Euston Rd, 86 Old Brompton Rd (all ☎020/7361 6161); Trailfinders, 215 Kensington High St (☎020/7937 5400); Travel Cuts, 295a Regent St (☎020/7255 1944); Usit CAMPUS, 52 Grosvenor Gdns, Victoria (☎0870/240 1010).

SOUTHEAST ENGLAND

Nestling in self-satisfied prosperity, **southeast England** (*www.southeastengland.uk.com*) is the richest part of the country, due to its agricultural wealth and proximity to the capital. Swift, frequent rail and coach services make it ideal for day-trips from London. Medieval ecclesiastical power-bases such as **Canterbury** and **Winchester** offer an introduction to the nation's history; while on the coast you can choose between the upbeat hedonism of **Brighton**, London's playground by the sea, and **Dover**, an uninspiring but necessary stopover for those entering or leaving the country by this port.

Canterbury

CANTERBURY, one of the oldest centres of Christianity in England, was home to the country's most famous martyr, archbishop Thomas à Beckct, who fell victim to Church–State rivalry in 1170. It became one of northern Europe's great pilgrimage sites, as Chaucer's *Canterbury Tales* attest, until Henry VIII had the martyr's shrine demolished in 1538. The cathedral remains the focal point of a compact town centre, which is enclosed on three sides by medieval walls. Today, as well as hosting a sizeable student population, it's thronged with visitors, particularly in summer, but remains relatively free from tackiness.

Built in stages from the eleventh century onwards, the vast **Cathedral** (Mon–Fri 9am–6.30pm, Sat 9am–2.30pm, Sun 12.30–2.30pm & 4.30–5.30pm; £3.50, free on Sun; *www.canterbury-cathedral.org.uk*) derives its distinctive presence from the perpendicular thrust of the late Gothic towers, dominated by the central, fifteenth-century Bell Harry tower. Notable features of the high vaulted interior are the tombs of Henry IV and his wife, and the gilded effigy of the Black Prince, both in the Trinity chapel behind the main altar. The spot where Becket was killed in the northwest transept is marked by a modern shrine, with a crude sculpture of the murder weapons suspended above. Steps descend from here to the heavy Romanesque arches of the **crypt**, one of the few remaining visible relics of the Norman cathedral.

East of the cathedral, opposite the coach park, are the evocative ruins of **St Augustine's Abbey** (daily 10am–4/6pm; £2.60), on the site of a church built by St Augustine, who began the conversion of the English in 597. Most of the town's other sights are located on or near the High St. The **Eastbridge Hospital** (Mon–Sat 10am–5pm; £1), on the other side of the street from the library, was founded in the twelfth century to provide poor pilgrims with shelter, and a thirteenth-century wall painting of Jesus is still faintly visible in the refectory upstairs. The **West Gate**, at the far end of St Peter's St (a continuation of High St), is the only one of the town's medieval gates to survive; it houses a small museum (Mon–Sat 11am–12.30pm & 1.30–3.30pm; £1) containing weaponry used by the medieval city guard. For the best exposition of local history, bypass the lightweight "Canterbury Tales" in the centre of town in favour of the genuinely educational, interactive **Heritage Museum**, round the corner on Stour St (Mon–Sat 10.30am–5pm; June–Oct also Sun 1.30–5pm; £2.40).

Practicalities

Most **trains** on the main line between London Victoria and Dover stop at Canterbury East, from where it's a short walk north into the walled town; less frequent trains from London

on Old Ship Beach; and *BN1*, Preston Rd, for visiting DJs. *Escape*, 10 Marine Parade; and the predominantly gay *Revenge*, 32 Old Steine.

Winchester

WINCHESTER's rural tranquillity betrays little of its former importance as the political and ecclesiastical power base of southern England. A town of Roman foundation fifty miles south-west of London, Winchester rose to prominence in the ninth century as King Alfred the Great's capital, and remained an important locus of power well into the Middle Ages. The shrine of St Swithin, Alfred's tutor and Bishop of Winchester, made the town an important destination for pilgrims, and the flow of European merchants to the annual St Giles' fair kept the civic coffers full.

Alfred's statue stands at the eastern end of the Broadway, the town's main thoroughfare, which becomes High St as it progresses west towards the train station. Much of the exterior of the **Cathedral** (daily 8.30am–5pm; £2.50 donation requested; *www.winchester-cathedral.org.uk*), to the south, is twelfth century, although bits of earlier masonry show through here and there, in particular the Norman stonework of the south transept. Raised above a screen surrounding the high altar are mortuary chests holding the remains of the pre-Conquest kings of England. The Angel chapel contains sixteenth-century wall paintings of the miracles of the Virgin Mary, although a modern replica now covers the originals in order to protect them. Jane Austen is buried on the south side of the nave; the inscription on the floor slab remembers her merely as the daughter of a local clergyman, making no mention of her renown as a novelist.

Immediately outside are traces of the original Saxon cathedral, built by Cenwalh, king of Wessex, in the mid-seventh century. The true grandeur of this structure is shown by a model in the **City Museum** (Apr–Oct 10am–5pm, Sun 12–5pm; Nov–March 10am–4pm; closed Mon; free) on the western side of the cathedral close; other exhibits include mosaics and pottery from Roman Winchester. Continuing west along High St, you'll come to the thirteenth-century **Great Hall** (daily 10am–4/5pm; free), a banqueting chamber used by successive kings of England and renowned for what is alleged to be King Arthur's Round Table – but the piece, which now hangs from the wall, is probably fourteenth-century (and so about 500 years too young). It seems to have been repainted with portraits and the names of King Arthur's knights for the visit of Emperor Charles V, who was entertained here by Henry VIII in 1522.

South of the Cathedral is the fourteenth-century Pilgrims Hall, from where a signposted route leads through a medieval quarter to **Winchester College**, the oldest of Britain's public schools. It's then a 25-minute walk across the Water Meadow to the medieval almshouse of **St Cross** (April–Oct Mon–Sat 9.30am–5pm; Nov–March Mon–Sat 10.30am–3.30pm, closed Sun; £2), with fifteenth-century courtyards and a church containing a triptych by the Flemish painter Mabuse. Continuing a medieval tradition, needy wayfarers may still apply for the "dole" here – a tiny portion of bread and beer.

Practicalities

Winchester's **train station** is about a mile northwest of the cathedral. The **bus terminal** is on High St, just opposite the Guildhall, in which the **tourist office** is installed (Mon–Sat 10am–5/6pm; May–Sept also Sun 11am–2pm; ☎01962/840500, *www.winchester.gov.uk*). Winchester's affluence is reflected in both the style and prices of its **B&Bs**, most of which cluster in the streets between St Cross Rd and Christchurch Rd, south of town. *The Farells*, 5 Ranelagh Rd (☎01962/869555; ⑤), is a cosy option, or try the slightly cheaper *Sullivans*, 29 Stockbridge Rd beside the train station (☎01962/862027; ③). There's also a lovely **hostel** in the *City Mill*, just east of Alfred's statue (☎01962/853723; ②; March–Nov). For **food**, the fine old *Wykeham Arms* inn and B&B, 75 Kingsgate St, offers imaginative meals served in a labyrinthine interior, while the excellent *Lochfyne*, 18 Jewry St, has a growing reputation.

THE WEST COUNTRY

The West Country has never been a precise geographical term, and there will always be a certain amount of argument as to where it actually starts. But as a broad generalization, the cosmopolitan feel of the southeast begins to fade into a slower, rural pace of life from **Salisbury** onwards, becoming more pronounced the further west you travel. In Neolithic times a rich and powerful culture evolved here, as shown by monuments such as **Stonehenge** and **Avebury**, and the isolated moorland sites of inland **Cornwall**. Urban attractions of western England include **Bristol** and the well-preserved Regency spa town of **Bath**; those in search of rural peace and quiet should head for the compelling bleakness of **Dartmoor**. The southwestern extremities of Britain include some of the most beautiful stretches of coastline, its rugged, rocky shores battered by the Atlantic, although the excellent sandy beaches make it one of the country's busiest corners over the summer. All of the region's major centres can be reached fairly easily by train or coach from London. Local bus services cover most areas, although in the rural depths of Dartmoor they can be very sparse indeed. Consult the tourist office Web sites *www.westcountryholidays.com* and *www.swtourism.co.uk* for more.

Salisbury, Stonehenge and Avebury

SALISBURY's central feature is the elegant spire of its **Cathedral** (daily 7am–6.15/8.15pm; £3 donation; *www.salisburycathedral.org.uk*), the tallest in the country, rising over 400ft above the lawns of the cathedral close. With the exception of the spire, the cathedral was almost entirely completed in the thirteenth century, and is one of the few great English churches that is not a hotchpotch of different styles. Prominent among the features of the interior are the fourteenth-century clock just inside the north porch, one of the oldest working timepieces in the country, and an exceptional Tudor memorial to the Earl of Hertford, Lady Jane Grey's brother-in-law, in the Lady Chapel at the eastern end of the church. An octagonal **chapterhouse**, approached via the extensive **cloisters** (Mon–Sat 9.30am–5.30/7.45pm; free), holds a collection of precious manuscripts, among which is one of the four original copies of the Magna Carta.

Most of Salisbury's remaining sights are grouped in a sequence of historic houses around The Close, the old walled inner town around the cathedral. The **Salisbury and South Wiltshire Museum**, opposite the main portal of the cathedral on West Walk (Mon–Sat 10am–5pm; July & Aug also Sun 2–5pm; £3), is a good place to bone up on the Neolithic history of Wessex before heading out to Stonehenge and Avebury. The **Mompesson House** on The Close's North Walk (April–Oct Mon–Wed, Sat & Sun noon–5.30pm; £3.90) is a fine eighteenth-century house complete with Georgian furniture and fittings. For the postcard view of the cathedral immortalized by John Constable, wander across the meadows and over the River Avon to **HARNHAM**, where you can have lunch or a drink at the *Old Mill* pub.

A ten-minute hop on any Andover- or Amesbury-bound bus takes you to the ruins of **Old Sarum** (daily 9/10am–4/6pm; £2), abandoned in the fourteenth century when the bishopric moved to Salisbury. Traces of the medieval town are visible in the outlines of its Norman cathedral and castle mound, but the ditch-encircled site is far older, populated in Iron Age, Roman and Saxon times.

Practicalities

It's a short walk southeast from Salisbury's **train station** (served from London Waterloo) across the River Avon into town. **Buses** from nearby Winchester and elsewhere terminate behind Endless St, a block south of which is the **tourist office**, just off Market Sq (Mon–Sat 9.30am–5/7pm, Sun 10.30am–4.30/5pm; ☎01722/334956). There's an excellent **HI hostel** at Milford Hill House, Milford Hill, five minutes east of the city centre, which allows camping

(☎01722/327572; ②), and the smaller *Matt & Tiggy's* hostel in Salt Lane near the bus station (☎01722/327443; ②). Most **B&Bs** inhabit an arc north of town beyond the train station; try the *Clovelley* at 17 Mill Rd (☎01722/322055, *clovelly.hotel@virgin.net*; ⑥); *Farthings Guest House*, 9 Swaynes Close (☎01722/330749; ⑤); or the sixteenth-century *Old Bakery*, 35 Bedwin St (☎01722/320100; ④). Café culture has arrived in Salisbury including the ubiquitous *Costa Café*, Butcher Row. For **pub food**, try the *Coach and Horses* on Winchester St for an imaginative menu or the ancient *Haunch of Venison* for more traditional cuisine. The charmingly wonky fifteenth-century tavern *New Inn* on New St is no-smoking, and the friendly *Wyndham Arms*, Estcourt Rd, is a microbrewery.

Stonehenge

The uplands northwest of Salisbury were a thriving centre of Neolithic civilization, the greatest legacy of which is **Stonehenge** (daily: June–Aug 9am–7pm; Sept–May 9.30am–5/6pm; £4.20). It is served by five daily buses from Salisbury (8 daily June–Aug), three on Sundays. You can also take a tour – ask at the bus station for details – or get an Explorer pass, which costs £4 and is valid all day including travel to Avebury and Bath.

The monument's age is being constantly revised as research progresses, but it's known that it was built in several distinct stages and adapted to the needs of successive cultures. The first Stonehenge probably consisted of a circular ditch dug somewhere between 2600 and 2200 BC. This was followed by the construction within the ditch of two concentric circles of sixty bluestones, thought to have originated in the Presili Mountains of South Wales. At least two more centuries elapsed before the outer circle and inner horseshoe were put in place, made up of local Wiltshire sarsen stones, the twenty-foot uprights topped by horizontal slabs. The way in which the sun's rays penetrate the central enclosure at dawn on midsummer's day has led to speculation about Stonehenge's role as either an astronomical observatory or a place of sun worship, but knowledge of the cultures responsible for building it is too scanty to reach any firm conclusions. Overlooking the point where two main roads meet, the stones themselves are controversially fenced off to prevent the erosion caused by thousands of summer day-trippers, but it makes the visit a slightly disappointing experience. The only way to enter the circle itself is to take a guided tour at sunrise or sunset costing £25 per person – ask at Salisbury tourist office.

Avebury

Salisbury also serves as a base for visiting the equally important – and much more atmospheric – Neolithic site at **AVEBURY**. The #6 Salisbury–Swindon bus (2–3 daily) passes through Avebury village, making a day-trip more than feasible.

The Avebury monoliths were erected some time between 2600 and 2100 BC, and their main circle – with a diameter of some 400m – forms a monument bigger in scale than Stonehenge, albeit not as impressive in its architectural sophistication. Further lines of standing stones form the West Kennet Avenue, thought to be a processional way, running two miles south to the so-called Sanctuary, possibly a gathering place of religious significance, where a small circle of stones surrounds the site of a wooden hut constructed around 3000 BC. All this is best considered with a pint or two from the *Red Lion* village pub, set right beside the main stone circle. To walk off the beer, follow a section of the **Ridgeway**, a 4000-year-old prehistoric highway, which loops northeast from Overton Hill, just south of the village; it once ran the breadth of Britain and can still be walked or cycled (it is signposted as a National Trust trail) as far as London. Avebury's little **Archeological Museum** (daily 10am–4/6pm; Nov–March closed Sun; £2) has a display on it as well as the monoliths and other ancient sites in the vicinity. Among the most interesting and accessible are **Silbury Hill**, an enormous conical mound constructed around 2800 BC, two miles southeast of the village, and **West Kennet Long Barrow** just beyond, an impressive stone passage grave in use for over 1500 years from about 3700 BC.

Bath

Just twelve miles southeast of Bristol is the handsome town of **BATH**, an ancient Roman spa revived by eighteenth-century high society. It's the extensive reconstruction put into effect by neoclassicist architects John Wood and his son, John Wood the Younger, that gives the town its distinctive appearance, with endless terraces of weathered sandstone fringed by spindly black railings. In the Roman era, a hot spring sacred to the Celtic goddess of the waters, Sulis, provided the centrepiece of an extensive bath complex, now restored as the **Roman Baths and Museum** (daily: April–Sept 9am–6pm, Aug till 9.30pm; Oct–March 9.30am–5.30/6pm; £7.50, or combined ticket with Costume Museum £8.90; *www.romanbaths. co.uk*). The pools, pipes and underfloor heating are remarkable demonstrations of the ingenuity of Roman engineering. The **Pump Room** (free entry), built above the Roman site in the eighteenth century, is the place to sample the waters while listening to genteel tunes from the resident chamber ensemble, and from late 2002 you'll be able to bathe or receive any number of health treatments in the modern **Bath Millennium Spa** (daily 7am–10pm) a few blocks away. The neighbouring **Abbey** (daily 9am–4.30pm) is renowned for the lofty fifteenth-century vault of its choir and the dense carpet of gravestones and memorials which cover the floor. The Abbey's **Heritage Vaults** (Mon–Sat 10am–4pm; £2) house Saxon and Norman sculpture and a reconstruction of the original building.

The best of Bath's eighteenth-century architecture is on the high ground to the north of the town centre, where the well-proportioned urban planning of the Woods is best showcased by the elegant Circus and the adjacent **Royal Crescent**. The house at 1 Royal Crescent is now a museum (Tues–Sun 10am–4/5pm, closed Jan; £4), showing how the Crescent's houses would have looked in the Regency period. The social calendar of Bath's elite centred on John Wood the Younger's **Assembly Rooms** (daily 10am–5pm; free), just east of the Circus; recently renovated, it includes the interesting **Museum of Costume** in the basement (same times; £4.20, or combined ticket with Roman Baths £8.90; *www.museumofcostume.co.uk*).

The triple arches of Pulteney Bridge lead northeast from the town centre across the River Avon and up Great Pulteney St to the **Holburne Art Museum** (Mon–Sat 11am–5pm, Sun 2.30–5.30pm; Nov–Easter closed Mon & closed Jan; £3.50; *www.bath.ac.uk/holburne*), which contains silver, porcelain and furniture from the Regency period. Just south of the town centre at 19 New King St is the **Herschel House** (March–Oct daily 2–5pm; Nov–Feb Sat & Sun same times; £2.50; *www.bath-preservation-trust.org.uk*), another eighteenth-century interior, housing the home-made telescope with which astronomer William Herschel first spotted Uranus in 1781.

Practicalities

The **train** and **bus stations** are both on Manvers St, five minutes south of the centre. The **tourist office** is just off the Abbey churchyard (Mon–Sat 9.30am–5/6pm, Sun 10am–4pm; ☎01225/477101, *www.visitbath.co.uk*). The **HI hostel** is halfway up Bathwick Hill (☎01225/465674; ③), a mile and a half east of town (bus #18), while the more relaxed and central *Backpackers' Hostel* is at 13 Pierrepont St (☎01225/446787, *stayinbath@backpackers-uk. demon.co.uk*; ③), five minutes' walk north from the train and bus stations. Inexpensive **B&Bs** include the *Henry*, 6 Henry St, near the Abbey (☎01225/424052; ⑤), and the *Alderney*, 3 Pulteney Rd (☎01225/312365; ④). The main tourist thoroughfares and neighbouring backstreets provide more tearooms than you can handle. *RSVP*, 5 Edgar Buildings, is a popular bistro with students/workers alike, often hosting DJs, while *Demuth's*, 2 North Parade Passage off Abbey Green, is a stylish vegetarian restaurant. On nearby Monmouth St behind the theatre is the trendy *Raincheck* café-bar. The best **pubs** include *The Bell* on Walcot St, with live music; *The Porter* on 15 George St, with cheap lunches and a pre-club crowd in the evenings; and the sociable *Pig & Fiddle* on Saracen St. The eclectic *Bath International Music Festival* (*www.bathmusicfest.org.uk*) is held in late April-May. For **Internet** access and coffee try Click, 19 Broad St (☎01225/337711; £5/hr, student discount £3/hr).

Bristol

Situated on a succession of lumpy hills just inland from the mouth of the Avon, the thriving city of **BRISTOL** grew rich on transatlantic trade – slaving, in particular – in the early part of the nineteenth century. It doesn't have quite the status now that it did then, but the city remains a wealthy, commercial centre; home to tobacco and aviation industries, a major university and a thriving music culture. The ongoing millennial redevelopment of the docks area and parts of the centre aims to provide a more attractive centre for Bristol's vibrant, but still rather scattered, arts and nightlife scene.

The city centre – in so much as there is one – is an elongated oval traffic interchange, **The Centre**, well away from the stations. To the east, the intimate Old City has seen an influx of bars and restaurants, while on its south side is the **Floating Harbour**, an area of waterways which formed the commercial hub of the nineteenth-century town, now the scene of a good deal of renovation. A couple of important cultural institutions occupy converted warehouses here: the **Arnolfini** on Narrow Quay (exhibitions open Mon–Sat 10am–7pm, Sun noon–6pm; free; *www.arnolfini.demon.co.uk*), one of Britain's best contemporary arts venues, and the **Watershed Arts Centre**, directly opposite (*www.watershed.co.uk*); both have pleasant, reasonably priced cafés that stay open late. Directly across from here is the **Harbourside** area, focus of the millennium project, "at-Bristol" (*www.at-bristol.org.uk*), where two interactive centres – **Explore** (daily 10am–6pm; £6.50), a hands-on technology park, and **Wildscreen**, (same times and prices), a hi-tech wildlife museum – are overshadowed by a giant **IMAX cinema** (Thurs–Sun; £6.50). Across a swing bridge from the Arnolfini, on Prince's Wharf, is the imaginative **Bristol Industrial Museum** (April–Oct Sat–Wed 10am–5pm; Nov–March Sat & Sun only; free), with cars and ship models. Just east of here rises the Gothic **Church of St Mary Redcliffe** (daily 8am–5/8pm), described by Queen Elizabeth I as the "fairest, goodliest and most famous parish church in England". To the west of the Industrial Museum, ten minutes' walk along the quayside and a right onto Gas Ferry Rd (or a ferry from near the Watershed) brings you to the **Maritime Heritage Centre** (daily 10am–4.30/5.30pm; free), celebrating Bristol's shipbuilding past and providing access to a replica of the fifteenth-century *Matthew* and to Brunel's *SS Great Britain* (ticket for both ships £6; *www.ss-great-britain.com*), the first propeller-driven iron ship, launched from this very dock in 1843.

Uphill from The Centre, past College Green – flanked by the city's **Cathedral** (not a patch on St Mary's) – you can follow Park St to the university's Wills Memorial Building, a Victorian neo-Gothic monster, endowed by the local tobacco dynasty along with the adjacent **Bristol City Museum and Art Gallery** (daily 10am–5pm; free; *www.bristol-city.gov.uk/museums*), which, beyond its offerings of Egyptology, dinosaurs and giant elks, has a half-decent art collection, strongest on the Victorian Pre-Raphaelites. The street opposite leads to **Brandon Hill**, topped by a splendid folly, **Cabot Tower** (daily 8am–dusk; free), from where there are views over much of the city, with the old docks spread out below you to the south, the suburb of Clifton and its suspension bridge to the west.

The rest of your time is best spent wandering around **CLIFTON**, whose airy terraces, crescents and circuses are reminiscent of the Georgian splendours of nearby Bath. It's a somewhat genteel quarter, but full of enticing pubs and with a spectacular focus in the **Clifton Suspension Bridge**, a glorious creation by the indefatigable engineer and railway builder Isambard Kingdom Brunel, spanning the limestone abyss of the Avon Gorge. On a low ridge above the bridge is the **Observatory** (daily: April–Oct 10am–5pm; Nov–March 10am–4pm; closed when cloudy; 75p; *www.clifton-suspension-bridge.org.uk*), another Victorian job, in whose dome is a camera obscura, encompassing views of the gorge and bridge.

Practicalities

Bristol's Temple Meads **train station** is a five-minute bus ride southeast of the centre, although it is due to be linked to the centre via a pedestrian walkway. The **bus station** is 500m north of the centre on Marlborough St. There's a **tourist office** in St Nicholas' Church beside Bristol Bridge (Mon–Sat 9.30am–5.30pm, Sun 11am–4pm; ☎0117/926 0767, *www.visitbristol. co.uk*). The **HI hostel**, at 14 Narrow Quay (☎0117/922 1659; ③), is splendidly situated in an old wharfside building next to the Arnolfini. In the heart of the pub district is the friendly *Bristol Backpackers*, 17 St Stephen's St (☎0117/925 7900; ③). For **B&Bs**, Clifton is the most pleasant location; one option is the *Oakfield*, 52 Oakfield Rd (☎0117/973 5556; ④).

For **food and drink**, the stretch between Clifton and the city centre – from Park St up Queen's Rd to Whiteladies Rd – offers a vast choice of ethnic eats and late bars. In Clifton itself don't miss the *Coronation Tap* (on an obscure alley – ask for it by name), a classic scrumpy (cider) bar whose regulars show the effects. In the centre, on St Stephen's Avenue, *Bar Latino* is a small late licence funky bar. In the harbourside area, on The Grove, *The Severn Shed* restaurant serves middle eastern organic food and has a unique "hovering" bar that can be moved back to make room for bands; the *Riverstation* has a good-value deli-bar, while farther along, the *Mud Dock Cycleworks Café* is another trendy café-bar, with DJs. The café beneath St Mary's church has healthy snacks during the day. For **nightlife** listings galore check out the magazine *Venue* (*www.venue.co.uk*) available from most bars and clubs. There's usually a lot on, with art cinemas at the Arnolfini and Watershed, and a renowned theatre company at the Old Vic on King St. Bristol's vibrant **music** scene has produced a host of influential names (Tricky, Massive Attack, Portishead); top **clubs** include *Rock* on Frogmore St, with international Djs and one of the largest sound systems in Europe, *Thekla* on The Grove; the massive *Evolution* beside the Watershed. The *Bierkeller* on All Saints St is good for gigs as well as club nights. Bristol Life **Internet** Café, 27 Baldwin St. (☎0117/9459926; £4/hr, student discount £2/hr) has a full range of facilities.

Wells and Glastonbury

A small town dwarfed by its extraordinary cathedral, **WELLS** is served by shoals of buses from nearby Bath and Bristol, all arriving at Princes Rd bus station, five minutes from the centre. Follow Cuthbert St eastwards from here to the picturesque inn-lined Market Place, and the **tourist office** in the Town Hall (daily 9.30/10am–4/5.30pm; ☎01749/672552). From here a gateway leads through to the close, bringing you face to face with an intoxicating array of Gothic statuary, mostly from the 1230s and 1240s. Inside the majestic **Cathedral**, the great interlacing "scissor-arches" at the crossing were devised to support the unstable tower, while in the north transept a fourteenth-century clock strikes the quarter-hours. South of the cathedral, a drawbridge leads across a moat to the **Bishop's Palace** (Easter–Oct Tues–Fri 11am–6pm, Sun 2–6pm, Aug daily 10.30am–6pm; £3), where opulently furnished rooms are watched over by portraits of former bishops. On the other side of the cathedral close are the **town museum** (July & Aug daily 10am–8pm; Easter–June, Sept & Oct daily 10am–5.30pm; Nov–Easter Wed–Sun 11am–4pm; £2.50) and the **Vicar's Close**, a row of fourteenth-century terraced houses. The tourist office has a list of B&Bs, but the nearest **hostel** (☎01934/742494; ③) is six miles northwest in the village of **CHEDDAR**, reached on bus #126 or #826. The dramatic **Cheddar Gorge**, formed by the collapse of a cave system, is walkable from here.

Buses #163, #376 and #676 head southeast from Wells to **GLASTONBURY**, a small rural town whose associations with the Holy Grail and King Arthur have made it a magnet for those with a taste for the mystical – the **Tor**, a natural mound overlooking the town, is identified with the Isle of Avalon. Joseph of Arimathea, a relation of the Virgin Mary, is also said to have owned land nearby, and to have brought Mary and Jesus here; William Blake's poem *Jerusalem* replays the legend: "And did those feet in ancient time / Walk upon England's mountains green?" Glastonbury itself is not much more than a High Street, the lower end of which, around the Market Cross, is overrun by New Age book- and crystal-shops. The impressive ruins of the **Abbey** are approached around the corner from Magdalene St (daily: June–Aug 9am–6pm; Sept–May 10am–dusk; £3; *www.glastonburyabbey.com*); this was the oldest Christian establishment in continuous use in England until Henry VIII ordered its near-destruction. The choir is alleged to hold the tomb of King Arthur and Guinevere. A mile to the east is the Tor, at the base of which stands the natural spring known as **Chalice Well** (daily: April–Oct 10am–6pm; Nov–March noon–4pm; £2). The ferrous waters which flow from the hillside here were popularly thought to have gained their colour from the blood of Christ, supposedly flowing from the Holy Grail, buried here by Joseph of Arimathea. On top of the Tor stands a tower, all that remains of a fourteenth-century church; the views from here are spectacular, and the Tor is a popular place from which to observe the sunrise on the summer solstice.

By nightfall Glastonbury reverts to sleepy rural stillness – except over the summer solstice and during the **Glastonbury Festival**, which is held on a nearby farm over a weekend in mid-June and draws around 80,000 people to its binge of music, drugs and events – the **tourist office**, housed in the Tribunal on High St, sells tickets (daily 10am–4/5pm; ☎01458/832954, *www.somerset.gov.uk*). There's a friendly crowd at the *Glastonbury Backpackers* **hostel** on Market Place (☎01458/833353, *glastonbury@backpackers-online.com*; ②). The *Isle of Avalon* **campsite** is a short walk up Northload St from the centre (☎01458/833618). For **food and drink**, the *Backpackers* has cheap, filling meals and a lively bar with events, or you'll find well-priced veggie food at the *Spiral Gate* on the High St.

Dartmoor

Dartmoor (*www.dartmoor-npa.gov.uk*) is one of England's most beautiful wilderness areas, an expanse of wild uplands 75 miles southwest of Bristol that's home to an indigenous breed of wild pony and dotted with **tors**, characteristic wind-eroded pillars of granite. The main focus for visitors in the middle of the park is **POSTBRIDGE**, reached by local bus from the nearest city, Plymouth. Famous for its medieval bridge over the East Dart river, this is a good starting point for walks in the woodlands surrounding Bellever Tor to the south. Postbridge's **tourist office**, on the main road through the village (daily 10am–4/5pm; ☎01822/880272), can supply information on the national park. The nearest **hostel** is at Bellever, one mile south (☎01822/880227; ②; April–Oct).

The most untamed parts of the moor, around its highest points of High Willhays and Yes Tor, are above the market town of **OKEHAMPTON** – served by regular buses from Plymouth and Exeter. Despite the stark beauty of the terrain, this part of the moor is used by the Ministry of Defence as a firing range: details of times when it's safe to walk the moor are available from the **tourist office** on Fore St (daily 10am–4.30pm; ☎01837/53020), which also operates a room-booking service. Okehampton has a couple of attractions in its own right. The **Museum of Dartmoor Life** next to the tourist office (June–Sept daily 10am–5pm; Oct–May Mon–Sat 10am–4/5pm; £2) offers interesting anthropological insights, including a look at life in one of the Dartmoor longhouses, the stone and turf huts in which the moorland natives used to live. Surrounded by woods one mile southwest of town is the now crumbling Norman keep of **Okehampton Castle** (April–Oct daily 10am–5/6pm; £2.50).

Cornwall

England's westernmost county, **Cornwall** (*www.cornwall-online.co.uk*) includes some of the country's most scenic stretches of coastline. Largely a rocky, rugged area, the Cornish coast – parts of which are dubbed the "English Riviera" – also features some extensive sandy beaches, making it one of the country's busiest seaside destinations; beware of the summer crush in principal resorts like St Ives. One obvious place to gain access to the more dramatic stretches of the coast is Land's End, at the southwestern tip of the country; nearby Penzance provides a convenient base for exploration, served by direct trains from London and Bristol.

Penzance
The busy port of **PENZANCE** forms the natural gateway to England's westernmost extremity, the Penwith Peninsula, and all the major sights of the region can be reached by day-trips

from here. From the **train station** located at the northern end of town, Market Jew St threads its way through the town centre, culminating in the Neoclassical facade of Market House, fronted by a statue of local-born chemist and inventor Humphry Davy. A left turn into Chapel St brings you to the **Maritime Museum** (Easter–Oct Mon–Sat 10.30am–4.30pm; £2), which re-creates the interior of an eighteenth-century man-o'-war. West of here, a series of parks and gardens punctuate the quiet residential streets overlooking the promenade. The **Penlee House Gallery and Museum**, off Morrab Rd (Mon–Sat 10am–5pm; July & Aug also Sun 12.30–4.30pm; £2, free on Sat), features works by members of the Newlyn school, late nineteenth-century painters of local seascapes. There are paintings of a more modern bent in the **Newlyn Art Gallery** (Mon–Sat 10am–5pm; free), an eminently walkable mile and a half west along the coast road in the working fishing village of Newlyn. The view east across the bay from Penzance is dominated by **St Michael's Mount**, site of a fortified medieval monastery perched on an offshore pinnacle of rock. At low tide, the Mount is joined by a cobbled causeway to the mainland village of **Marazion** (with regular buses from Penzance); at high tide, a boat can ferry you over (£1). You can amble around part of the Mount's shoreline, but most of the rock lies within the grounds of the **abbey and castle**, now a stately home belonging to Lord St Levan (April–Oct Mon–Fri 10.30am–5pm, plus most weekends; Nov–March in good weather only; £4.50).

Penzance's **train** and **bus stations** are at the northeastern end of town, a step away from Market Jew St. The **tourist office** (Mon–Fri 9am–5pm, Sat 10am–4pm; June–Aug also Sun 10am–1pm; ☎01736/362207, *www.cornwall-online.co.uk/westcornwall*) is in the bus station. B&Bs congregate at the western end of town around Morrab Rd. The comfortable **HI hostel**, Castle Horneck, Alverton (☎01736/362666; ③), is a short walk along the Land's End road, or there's *Penzance Backpackers*, Alexandra Rd (☎01736/363836, *www.penzancebackpackers.ndirect.co.uk*; ②). *Co-Co's Tapas Bar*, Chapel St, has **snacks** and cakes as well as coffee and beer; *Dandelions*, on Causeway, is a veggie café. Town-centre **pubs** include the *Star* on Market Jew St, or the more touristy *Admiral Benbow* on Chapel St, a seventeenth-century house with maritime fittings. Over the summer, look out for live folk music at the *Acorn*, Parade St.

Land's End

Land's End exerts a hold over the popular imagination that the site itself can't always live up to – especially now that a small **theme park** has been built here (daily 10am–5/6pm; £2.50; *www.landsend-landmark.co.uk*). The coastal path, however, remains a public right of way, and, despite commercialization, a visit is really worthwhile, with beautiful clifftop walks overlooking some spectacular wave-carved rocks. One and a half miles north is the secluded village of **Sennen Cove**, overlooking the extensive sandy beaches of Whitesand Bay, where you'll find the *Land's End Backpacker's Hostel* at Whitesands Lodge (☎01736/871776; ③). Head a similar distance south for the more rugged beauty of Mill Bay. Four miles north of Land's End is an equally spectacular stretch of coast around **Cape Cornwall**, less crowded than its more famous neighbour, although a popular venue for observing dramatic sunsets. The cape itself is a mile west of the former tin-mining village of **St Just**; the walk here from Land's End is recommended, although it's also easily reached by bus from Penzance. St Just is also the site of a **hostel** at Letcha Vean, half a mile south of town (☎01736/788437; ③; various opening days during March–Oct – phone beforehand).

St Ives

Across the peninsula from Penzance on Cornwall's north coast, the fishing village of **ST IVES** is the quintessential Cornish resort, featuring a maze of narrow streets lined with whitewashed cottages, sandy beaches and lush subtropical flora. The village's erstwhile tranquillity attracted several major artists earlier this century – Ben Nicholson, Barbara Hepworth and Naum Gabo among them. Insipid sunsets now fill the small galleries cramming the streets, but there's more challenging work on show in the **Tate Gallery** which overlooks Porthmeor

Beach and features the work of the various St Ives schools (April–Sept Mon–Sat 11am–7pm, Sun 11am–5pm; Oct–March Tues–Sun 10.30am–5.30pm; £3.50; *www.tate.org.uk*). A combined ticket (£6) admits you to the **Barbara Hepworth Museum** (same hours), which preserves the studio of the modernist sculptor. Her photos of Cornwall quoits and landscapes provide clues to the inspiration behind her sleek monoliths, many splendid examples of which are displayed in the garden. Of the town's three beaches, the north-facing Porthmeor occasionally has good surf, and boards can be rented at the beach. The **tourist office** in the Guildhall, St An Pol (May–Sept Mon–Sat 9.30am–5.30pm; May–Aug also Sun 10am–1pm; Oct–April Mon–Fri 9.30am–5/5.30pm; ☎01736/796297), is a couple of minutes from both the bus and train stations, while *St Ives Backpackers* **hostel** is in the centre of town (☎01736/799444, *st-ivesbackpackers@dial.pipex.com*; ②).

CENTRAL AND EASTERN ENGLAND

Central England was the powerhouse of the Industrial Revolution, and although vast areas of the Midlands are greener than most people realize, it is still predominantly a region of unattractive manufacturing towns. There are however a couple of mandatory stops: the university town of **Oxford** and **Stratford-upon-Avon**, home of William Shakespeare; both are within easy reach of London. Close by is Britain's second largest city, Birmingham, at the hub of an industrial sprawl which encompasses some three million people; it may boast one of the best concert halls and orchestras in the country but is still unlikely to feature on a quickstop national tour.

Eastern England is primarily known for the endless flat expanses of East Anglia, long isolated by the Fens, areas of wetland which were substantially drained only in recent centuries. Of the many historical towns that dot the landscape, the university town of **Cambridge** is an obvious draw, although, further east, the workaday town of **Norwich** preserves a surprising amount of its medieval and Tudor heritage.

Oxford

Preconceptions about the aristocratic atmosphere of **OXFORD** are now slightly wide of the mark, for the city's university has lost some of its social exclusivity: the place is just as renowned for generating such successful bands as Radiohead and Supergrass as it is for future cabinet ministers. Yet the privileges of Oxford, embodied in its fine architecture and ambience of timeworn academia, are what make the place an unmissable stop.

Students were originally attracted here by the scholars attached to the Oxford monasteries, before their ranks were swelled by the expulsion of English students from Paris in 1167. By the sixteenth century the collegiate system began to take shape, with students and tutors living, working and taking their meals together in the same complex of buildings – usually a couple of quadrangles ("quads") with a chapel, library and dining hall. Most Oxford colleges follow this basic pattern, forming a dense maze of historic buildings in the heart of the city. Access to many of the colleges may be restricted during term-time, and they often close to visitors entirely in May and June, when exams are approaching. Nonetheless, wandering Oxford's streets is as good a way as any to imbibe the town's unique atmosphere.

The City

The main point of reference is **Carfax**, a central crossroads overlooked by the fourteenth-century **Carfax Tower** (April–Oct daily 10am–5.30pm; £1.20), last surviving remnant of a church of the same name and the first of many opportunities to enjoy a panorama of Oxford's "dreaming spires" skyline. Avoid the shopper-choked Cornmarket and head south down St Aldate's, which leads past Pembroke St – home to Oxford's world-class Museum of Modern

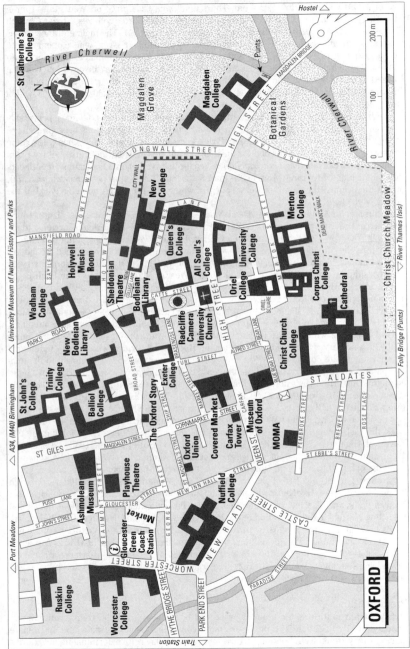

OXFORD

© Crown copyright

Art, or **MOMA** (Tues–Sun 11am–6pm, Thurs until 9pm; £2.50, free on Wed 11am–1pm & Thurs 6–9pm; *www.moma.org.uk*) – down to the biggest of Oxford's colleges, **Christ Church** (Mon–Sat 9.30am–5.30pm, Sun 9am–1pm; £4; *www.chch.ox.ac.uk*). The main entrance passes underneath the dome of Tom Tower, built in 1681 by Christopher Wren, before opening onto the vast expanse of Tom Quad, mostly dating from the college's foundation in the sixteenth century. It is an indication of the prestige and wealth of the college that the city's late Norman **Cathedral** also serves as the college chapel. From Oriel Sq you can enter the college's **Picture Gallery** (Mon–Sat 10.30am–1pm & 2–4.30/5.30pm, Sun 2–4.30/5.30pm; £1), with a strong collection of Old Masters.

South of the college, Christ Church Meadow leads down to the River Thames, perversely referred to hereabouts as the Isis. The narrow streets immediately east of Christ Church are occupied by a cluster of three colleges: **Oriel** (*www.oriel.ox.ac.uk*), which has a fearsome rowing reputation and is renowned for the gabled frontages of its seventeenth-century Front Quad; **Corpus Christi** (*www.ccc.ox.ac.uk*), noted for its paved Front Quad and sixteenth-century sundial; and **Merton** (Mon–Fri 2–4pm, Sat & Sun 10am–4pm; *www.merton.ox.ac.uk*), one of the original thirteenth-century colleges, which still preserves one courtyard of the period, Mob Quad.

At the rear of Merton College, Dead Man's Walk heads east to join Rose Lane, which emerges at the eastern end of "The High" (High St) beside the **Botanical Gardens** (daily 9am–4.30/5.30pm; £2.50) and the River Cherwell, where you can rent punts in summer. Opposite is the fifteenth-century bell tower of **Magdalen College** (pronounced "maudlin"; daily 2–6pm; £2.50; *www.magdalen.ox.ac.uk*); the Cloister Quad of the same period, lined with gargoyles, is the most striking of its courtyards. West of Magdalen along The High is the **University Church** (July & Aug daily 9am–7pm; Sept–June Mon–Sat 9am–5pm, Sun 11.30am–5pm; tower £1.60), scene of the trial of Cranmer, Ridley and Latimer, the "Oxford Martyrs" burned at the stake by Queen Mary's Catholic regime in 1555. Behind the church extends an area containing many of the university's most important and imposing buildings, most dramatic of which is the Italianate **Radcliffe Camera**. Built in the 1730s by James Gibbs, it is now used as a reading room for the **Bodleian Library**, whose main building is immediately to the north in the Old Schools Quad. Most of the library is closed to the general public, but you can see part of the immense collection of ancient manuscripts on a guided tour of Duke Humfrey's library (Mon–Fri 2pm & 3pm, Sat & Sun 10.30am & 11.30am; July & Aug also Mon–Fri 10.30am & 11.30am; £3.50). The adjacent **Sheldonian Theatre** (Mon–Sat 10am–12.30pm & 2–4.30pm; £1.50), a copy of the Theatre of Marcellus in Rome, was designed by Christopher Wren and is now a venue for concerts and university functions.

To the east, a copy of Venice's Bridge of Sighs spans New College Lane, joining the two halves of Hertford College. The Lane winds to **New College** itself (daily: Easter–Oct 11am–5pm; Nov–Easter 2–4pm; £2; *www.new.ox.ac.uk*), founded by William of Wykeham in 1379; the public entrance is on Holywell St. West from the Sheldonian, several colleges cluster around Turl St and Broad St. The **Ashmolean Museum** (Tues–Sat 10am–5pm, Sun 2–5pm; free; *www.ashmol.ox.ac.uk*) in Beaumont St is strong on Egyptian, classical and Minoan finds, and also has a broad-based fine art collection featuring excellent Italian and French works and a good selection of the English Pre-Raphaelites. North of the Sheldonian, on Parks Rd, the **University Museum of Natural History** is an odd Victorian-Gothic pile full of rocks and dinosaur bones, but further inside you'll find the fusty **Pitt-Rivers Museum** (Mon–Sat 1–4.30pm; free; *www.prm.ox.ac.uk*), housing case after case of bizarre archeological and anthropological finds in an impressive iron-vaulted gallery, including totem poles and some famous shrunken heads from Ecuador.

Practicalities

Oxford's **train station** is ten minutes' walk west of town, with regular trains from London Paddington (1hr). **Coaches**, though, are more convenient: services make the 100-minute journey every 10min from London Victoria for around £6 day return, terminating at Oxford's

Gloucester Green **coach station**, on the edge of the centre. Bus #X5 runs direct from Cambridge (3hr), a route without an equivalent train service. The **tourist office** is on the north side of the coach station (Mon–Sat 9.30am–5pm; June–Sept also Sun 10am–3.30pm; ☎01865/726871, *www.oxfordcity.co.uk*); they will book rooms for a £2.50 fee. You'll find **Internet** access at Internet Exchange, 10 George St, or *Mico's Café*, 118 High St. Bike Zone on Market St is the best place for **bike rental**.

There's an overloaded **HI hostel** three miles east at 32 Jack Straws Lane in Headington (☎01865/762997; ③; bus #13/#14a); the much more central *Backpackers' Hostel* at 9a Hythe Bridge St (☎01865/721761, *www.hostels.co.uk*; ③) also has a late bar and Internet facilities. Booking ahead is strongly advised for **B&Bs**. Good places include *Isis*, just beyond the Magdalen Bridge at 45 Iffley Rd (☎01865/741024; ④; June–Sept); *Becket House*, 5 Becket St near the train station (☎01865/724675; ④); and *St Michael's*, 26 St Michael's St (☎01865/242101; ⑤), most central of the lot but often booked solid. The nearest **campsite** is *Oxford Camping International*, 426 Abingdon Rd (☎01865/244088; bus #35/#36), 1–2 miles south of the centre.

For **eating**, the Covered Market between High St and Market St has loads of sandwich and snack bars, including the quirky *Georgina's*, or you could head to the atmospheric *Convocation Coffee House*, behind University Church. *Falafel House*, in the Market Sq, has unbeatable falafels for eating on the hoof; and there's a great fish-and-chip shop in Carfax Passage, just off High St. The laidback *Cock & Camel*, on Gloucester St, is one of the many popular and affordable restaurant/winebars, but you'd do just as well with "pub grub" from places like the *King's Arms*, a quintessential students' **pub** on Holywell St. Check out also the tiny, ramshackle *Bear* on Alfred St, Oxford's oldest pub (founded 1242); and the seventeenth-century *Turf Tavern*, hidden under the old city wall on Bath Place off Holywell St. *Que Pasa*, on Castle St, is a wine bar with a late licence.

For details of **concerts** have a look at *Daily Information* (pinned up in the tourist office and in colleges and pubs; *www.dailyinfo.co.uk*) and *Adhoc*. There's a fairly good art-house **cinema**, The Phoenix, on Walton St, and in summer look out for open-air **theatre**, often Shakespeare, in the college gardens. For **live music**, the *Philanderer & Firkin* pub on Walton St hosts good indie bands. *The Cricketers Arms*, 45 Iffley Rd, hosts everything from jazz to dub reggae. Both *Zodiac* and the *Old Fire Station* on George St have excellent indie **dance** nights.

Blenheim Palace

Half-hourly buses (#x50, #20 a,b,c) depart from the bus station or Cornmarket to the village of Woodstock, eight miles north and site of **Blenheim Palace** (mid-March to Oct daily 10.30am–5.30pm; £9.50; gardens only: £6 with car, £2 on foot; *www.blenheimpalace.com*). The palace was built by John Vanbrugh for John Churchill, the first Duke of Marlborough, whom the king wished to reward for defeating the army of Louis XIV at Blenheim in 1704. The stern Palladian exterior is an unambiguous expression of power; inside, things are marginally more homely, with opulently furnished period state rooms and a Churchill Exhibition, which includes a few of Winston's attempts at painting and a re-creation of the room in which he was born. Italianate **gardens** (daily 9am–4.45pm) are laid out to the rear of the palace, a contrast with the open spaces of Capability Brown's landscaped parkland.

Stratford-upon-Avon

Blessed with a higher-than-average sprinkling of attractive Tudor and Jacobean half-timbered houses and gorgeous riverside gardens, **STRATFORD-UPON-AVON** has put itself firmly on the tourist map by making the most of the five sights associated with William Shakespeare, who was born here on April 23, 1564. There are three restored properties linked with the Bard in the town itself, and two within easy reach of it. If you've time to visit them all, it's worth considering the combined tickets (£8.50 for the three town properties, £12 for all five; *www.shakespeare.org.uk*); otherwise save your money to hear the Bard's poetry performed at the Royal Shakespeare Company's theatres in the town.

Shakespeare's Birthplace (Mon–Sat 9/9.30am–4/5pm, Sun 9.30/10am–4/5pm; £6), a pale ochre, half-timbered structure on Henley St, is entered from the informative **Shakespeare Centre** just up the road, which has its own exhibition on Elizabethan life. Although a bit of a crush over summer, the house provides an evocative re-creation of Elizabethan life. John Shakespeare, William's father, was a glove-maker and wool dealer who served on the town council, and the rooms, although sparsely furnished, point to a life of relative comfort. Prominent among the Elizabethan facades of High St is that of the **Harvard House** (May–Oct Tues–Sat 10am–4.30pm; free), with its intricately carved timbers. Heading southwest, High St becomes Chapel St and leads to **New Place**, site of the home where Shakespeare died in 1616. Sadly, the house no longer stands, demolished by a subsequent owner in 1759, who was tired of all the visitors. The Elizabethan Garden, however, has been re-created and is entered via the adjacent **Nash's House** (Mon–Sat 9.30am–5pm, Sun 10am–5pm; £3.50), home of Thomas Nash, husband of Shakespeare's granddaughter Elizabeth Hall. The half-timbered frontage is a 1911 replica, with the Tudor interior re-creating the atmosphere of a middle-class seventeenth-century home, while upstairs is a small museum devoted to the town's history, with mementoes of the 1769 Shakespeare Jubilee mounted by the actor David Garrick, who did much to promote the town as a place of literary pilgrimage. Across the road on the corner of Chapel Lane and Church St is the medieval **Guild Chapel**, with some frescoes from around 1500. Behind the chapel is the half-timbered frontage of the King Edward VI Grammar School, supposedly attended by the Bard. Continuing along Church St, a left turn leads into Old Town and Stratford's most impressive medieval house, **Hall's Croft** (same hours as Nash's house; £3.50), home of Shakespeare's son-in-law Dr John Hall. The interior is furnished in period style, with a selection of antique medicines and herbal remedies from the doctor's dispensary. From here it's a five-minute walk to Shakespeare's last resting place, the **Holy Trinity Church** on the banks of the Avon.

About a half-hour's walk west of Stratford is the village of Shottery, where you'll find **Anne Hathaway's Cottage** (same hours as the Birthplace; £4.50), home of Shakespeare's wife; while **Mary Arden's House**, home of his mother, is three miles northwest of town in **Wilmcote** (same hours as the Birthplace; £5.50).

Practicalities

Stratford's **train station** is half a mile northwest of town. **Coaches** (including the #X50 direct from Oxford) terminate just east of the centre, two minutes from the **tourist office** at the junction of Bridgeway and Bridgefoot (Mon–Sat 9am–5/6pm; April–Oct also Sun 11am–5pm; ☎01789/293127, *www.shakespeare-country.co.uk*). There's an **HI hostel** two miles east in Hemmingford House, Alveston (☎01789/297093; ④; bus #18/X18/#618) and you'll find dorms, cheap meals and Internet access at the excellent *Backpackers* (☎01789/263838, *www.hostels.co.uk*; ③) on Greenhill St between the train station and the centre. You'll find a wealth of **B&Bs**, many to the west of the centre around Evesham Place, but rooms fill up speedily during the tourist season. Try *Chadwyn's*, 6 Broad Walk (☎01789/269077; ⑤) or *Parkfield*, 3 Broad Walk (☎01789/293313; ⑤), or simply ask the tourist office to book for you (£3 fee).

Stratford is an expensive place to **eat**, but the *Kingfisher*, 13 Ely St, is a traditional and affordable fish-and-chip shop in the town centre. Sheep St is lined with options, including the popular *Opposition*, or the Italian *De'Arto* on the waterside. Amongst Stratford's plentiful **pubs**, the most famous is the *Black Swan* (better known as the *Dirty Duck*) on Waterside.

Tickets from the **Royal Shakespeare Company**, which performs in three theatres on the banks of the Avon – the main house, the smaller Jacobean-style galleried Swan and the experimental Other Place studio – begin at around £6. Students can buy stand-by tickets on the day, and a hundred day-tickets for the main house are sold from 9am (prepare for long queues). Sell-outs are very common, so book seats well in advance (☎01789/403403, *www.rsc.org.uk*).

Cambridge

Tradition has it that the University of **CAMBRIDGE** was founded by refugees from Oxford, who fled the town after one of their number was lynched by hostile townsfolk in the 1220s. There's been rivalry between the two institutions ever since, but what distinguishes Cambridge are "the Backs" – the green swathe of land straddling the River Cam which overlooks the backs of the old colleges, and provides the town's most enduring image of grand academic architecture.

A logical place to begin a tour is the **Fitzwilliam Museum**, at the southern end of the centre on Trumpington St (Tues–Sat 10am–5pm, Sun 2.15–5pm; free; *www.fitzmuseum.cam.ac.uk*). The archeological collections on the ground floor contain an imposing relief of Assyrian King Ashurnasirpal II alongside strong Egyptian and Greek sections; upstairs, the art collection includes a couple of Titians, a Veronese, a Tintoretto, a good selection of Pre-Raphaelites and Impressionists, and a fine *Odalisque* by Delacroix, not to mention an eclectic selection of twentieth-century works.

The neighbouring **Peterhouse** (*www.pet.cam.ac.uk*) is Cambridge's oldest college, founded in 1284, but retaining little of its original architecture. The college's most interesting feature is the seventeenth-century chapel, a hybrid structure flanked by classical colonnades and sporting light-hearted Baroque gables. The fairy-tale Cloister Court of **Queens' College** just round the corner (daily 10am–4.30pm; £1.20; *www.quns.cam.ac.uk*) is original Tudor, but the timber-roofed college hall is nineteenth-century, decorated by William Morris. The neo-Gothic gatehouse of King's College, hogging the limelight on King's Parade, leads through to the extraordinary **King's College Chapel** (Mon–Sat 9.30am–3.30/4.30pm, Sun: out of term 10am–5pm, in term-time 1.15–2.15pm; £3.50; *www.kings.cam.ac.uk*), painted by Turner and Canaletto and eulogized in three sonnets by Wordsworth. Begun by the college founder Henry VI in the 1450s, it boasts an extravagantly fan-vaulted ceiling, supported by a wall of Flemish stained glass on each side (paid for by Henry VIII), an intricately carved choir screen added in the 1530s, and Rubens' *Adoration of the Magi* over the main altar.

Next door to King's is the **Senate House**, an exercise in Palladian classicism by James Gibbs, and the scene of graduation ceremonies in June. The nineteenth-century turreted monstrosity next door marks the southern entrance to **Gonville and Caius** (pronounced "keys") **College** (*www.cai.cam.ac.uk*), hiding a fascinating series of sixteenth-century courtyards. Caius Court bears much of the personality of the college's co-founder John Keys, a widely travelled philosopher and physician who latinized his name, as was the custom with men of learning. He placed a gate on each side of two courts – the Gates of Wisdom, Humility, Virtue and Honour – each representing a different stage on the path to academic enlightenment; the Gate of Honour on the south side of the court, capped with sundials, is the most ornate.

The Great Court of **Trinity College** (daily 10am–6pm; £2; *www.trin.cam.ac.uk*), the largest of Cambridge's colleges, is the finest ensemble of Tudor-period buildings in the city. Another Tudor gatehouse marks the entrance to **St John's** (daily 10am–5.30pm; £1.75; *www.joh.cam.ac.uk*) and more fine sixteenth-century courts. Standing on the corner where St John St meets Bridge St is the **Round Church**, built in the twelfth century on the model of the Church of the Holy Sepulchre in Jerusalem; the spire is a nineteenth-century addition, but Norman pillars remain inside. Just beyond here, Magdalene Bridge is a good place to rent boats for a leisurely punt down the river. Across the bridge, **Magdalene College** (as in Oxford, pronounced "maudlin"; *www.magd.cam.ac.uk*), the last of the colleges to admit women (in 1988), straddles both sides of the street, the older parts to the east. A couple of sixteenth-century courts lead through to the Pepys Library, named after the Magdalene alumnus whose collection of books has been on display here since 1742. His diary is on permanent view. **Jesus College** (*www.jesus.cam.ac.uk*), reached from Jesus Lane by a narrow alleyway known as the Chimney, holds a chapel which contains original medieval elements, but many of the Victorian architects engaged in the Gothic revival were involved in the

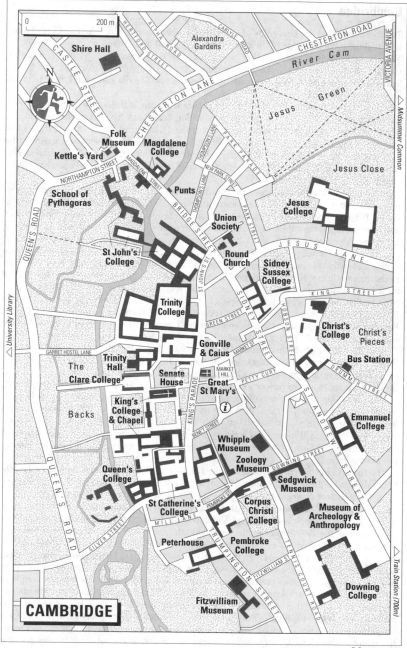

0   200 m

Shire Hall

Alexandra Gardens

CHESTERTON ROAD

River Cam

Jesus Green

Jesus Close

CASTLE STREET

HERTFORD STREET

ALPHA ROAD

CARLYLE ROAD

VICTORIA AVENUE

△ Midsummer Common

CHESTERTON LANE

Folk Museum

Kettle's Yard

Magdalene College

NORTHAMPTON STREET

MAGDALENE STREET

THOMPSON'S LANE

NEW PARK STREET

PARK PARADE

School of Pythagoras

Punts

BRIDGE STREET

THOMPSON'S LANE

PARK STREET

Jesus College

QUEEN'S ROAD

Union Society

Round Church

JESUS LANE

St John's College

ST JOHN'S ST

Sidney Sussex College

KING STREET

Trinity College

SIDNEY STREET

HOBSON STREET

Christ's College

Christ's Pieces

GREEN STREET

MARKET ST

△ University Library

GARRET HOSTEL LANE

Gonville & Caius

Bus Station

Trinity Hall

The

Clare College

Senate House

MARKET HILL

PETTY CURY

DRUMMER STREET

Great St Mary's

King's College & Chapel

Backs

KING'S PARADE

ST ANDREW'S STREET

Emmanuel College

BENE'T STREET

Whipple Museum

Zoology Museum

DOWNING STREET

Queen's College

Sedgwick Museum

QUEEN'S ROAD

St Catherine's College

PEMBROKE ST

MILL LANE

Corpus Christi College

Museum of Archeology & Anthropology

SILVER STREET

Peterhouse

Pembroke College

TRUMPINGTON STREET

TENNIS COURT ROAD

Downing College

FITZWILLIAM STREET

△ Train Station (700m)

Fitzwilliam Museum

CAMBRIDGE

© Crown copyright

chapel's reconstruction, making for an interesting hybrid. Ceiling paintings were provided by William Morris, who – together with Burne-Jones and Ford Madox Brown – also provided designs for the windows. **Christ's College** (*www.christs.cam.ac.uk*), south of Jesus on St Andrew's St, has one of Cambridge's finest Tudor gate towers, adorned with coats of arms of the Beaufort family and mythical, antelope-like beasts. The fifteenth-century stained glass in the college chapel depicts, among others, Henry VI and Henry VII.

Practicalities

Cambridge's **train station**, with services from London Liverpool St and Stansted Airport, is a dull, twenty-minute trudge south of the centre; alternatively, take shuttle bus #1 into town (every 10min; not Sun). There's no train line from Oxford – instead take bus #X5 into the **bus station** on Drummer St, a couple of blocks east of the **tourist office** on Wheeler St (Mon–Fri 10am–5.30/6pm, Sat 10am–5pm; Easter–Oct also Sun 11am–4pm; ☎01223/322640; *www.cambridge.gov.uk*) which can book rooms for a £3 fee. The busy **HI hostel** is close to the train station at 97 Tenison Rd (☎01223/354601; ③), while opposite the station is *Sleeperz*, Station Rd (☎01223/304050; *www.sleeperz.com*; ⑤). **B&Bs** are grouped around Tenison Rd and Chesterton Rd to the north, including *Benson House*, 24 Huntingdon Rd (☎01223/311594; ⑤); and *Netley Lodge*, 112 Chesterton Rd (☎01223/363845; ⑤). Cheaper but less central is *Abbey Guest House*, 588 Newmarket Rd (☎01223/241427; ④). The nearest **campsite** is *Cherry Hinton*, Lime Kiln Rd in Cherry Hinton, three miles east (☎01223/244088; ③)

For **food**, *The Copper Kettle* is a traditional café at 4 King's Parade, and there are plenty of places near the Magdalene Bridge offering cappuccino and ciabatta. *Brown's* is a vast, bustling brasserie opposite the Fitzwilliam Museum, while the Greek *Varsity*, 35 Regent St, has cosy upstairs tables. *Rainbow*, 9a Kings Parade, is the only vegetarian restaurant in town. As for **pubs**, the *Boathouse*, 14 Chesterton Rd, and the well-loved *Anchor*, Silver St, both overlook the Cam and are good places for a bar lunch or beery evening. Others to check out are the *Eagle*, Bene't St, a historic inn with an old cobbled courtyard. The Cambridge Arts **Cinema**, off Market St, and Cambridge Arts **Theatre**, off King's Parade, both excel in their fields. The Corn Exchange, Wheeler St, is the major venue for **gigs**. *The Fez Club*, 15 Market St, hosts various dance nights.*What's On*, a freesheet distributed by the tourist office, has listings, as does *ad hoc*, *Sticks* and *Varsity* (*www.varsity.cam.ac.uk*).

Norwich

NORWICH was England's second city in Tudor times, serving a vast hinterland of cloth producers in the eastern counties, whose work was exported from here to the Continent. Due to its isolated position beyond the Fens, the city often had closer cultural and trading links with the Low Countries than with London; the overland journey to the capital took far longer than the relatively simple North Sea crossing.

The twelfth-century **Castle Keep** (Mon–Sat 10am–5pm, Sun 2–5pm; July–Sept £3.40, Oct–June £2.50) includes an archaeology and Egyptian gallery and is replete with blind arcading, a rare piece of ornamentation on a military structure; stands in the centre of town. You can join a "battlements and dungeons" tour for an extra £1.50. The **Art Gallery** inside contains a representative selection of landscapes by painters of the nineteenth-century Norwich School, whose outstanding figures were John Sell Cotman and John Crome. West of the castle stretches the largely pedestrianized city centre, where you'll find the twelfth-century **Guildhall**, built from the Norfolk flint that gives a glass-like quality to many of the city's older buildings. Two blocks north of the castle, the **Bridewell Museum** (April–Sept Mon–Sat 10am–5pm; £2) has artefacts illustrating the town's trades and professions, including a steam-powered fire engine, while the fifteenth-century church of **St Peter Hungate** (April–Sept Mon–Sat 10am–5pm), two minutes' walk northeast, has been converted into a museum exhibiting medieval illustrated manuscripts and church brasses. Nearby, the descending cobbled lane of Elm Hill evokes something of the atmosphere of Tudor Norwich with a few half-timbered buildings. Immediately east of here, with a lofty 97m-high spire, is the **Cathedral** (daily 7.30am–6/7pm; donation; *www.cathedral.org.uk*), whose twelfth-century nave retains a couple of heavily ornamented Norman piers. Look out also for some fine examples of medieval art: the *Despenser Reredos* in St Luke's chapel, commemorating the 1381 Peasants' Revolt, and medieval frescoes in the treasury on the north side of the altar. Beyond the cathedral to the east are the best of Norwich's **riverside walks**, following the River Wensum past the ruined Cow Tower.

The University of East Anglia on the western outskirts of the city holds an unusual collection of sculpture and painting from all over the world in the amazing Foster-designed **Sainsbury Centre for Visual Arts** (Tues–Sun 11am–5pm; £2; *www.uea.ac.uk/scva*), where Picasso and Modigliani rub shoulders with Egyptian antiquities. To get to the university, take either bus #26, #27 or #35 from the centre to Constable Terrace.

Practicalities

Norwich's **train station** is ten minutes east of the centre. **Buses** terminate on Surrey St, 5min south of the centre. The **tourist office** is in the Guildhall (Mon–Sat 9.30am–4.30/5pm; ☎01603/666071, *www.norwich.gov.uk*). There's an **HI hostel** at 112 Turner Rd (☎01603/627647; ③; March–Oct) and a YMCA at 48 St Giles St (☎01603/620269; ③). **B&Bs** worth trying include the *Rosedale*, 145 Earlham Rd (☎01603/453743, *drcbac@aol.com*; ④) and the *Earlham* next door at no. 147 (☎01603/454169; ⑤); check also with the university for discount lodging year-round (☎01603/592092; ③–④). The nearest **campsite** is *Lakenham* (☎01603/620060; April–Sept), a mile south on Martineau Lane, off King St. Central places to **eat** include *St Andrew's Hall Crypt*, right in the centre on St Andrew's Plain, and the civilised *Ha Ha bar*, 1 Upper King St; a livelier place veggies should home in on is *Tree House*, above the *Rainbow* healthfood shop at 14 Dove St. The new Riverside Development at the bottom of King St houses all the newest **bars**, including the Norwegian Blue vodka bar. A pub popular with students is the *Plough* on St Benedicts St; but the *Adam & Eve* on Bishopgate (Norwich's oldest pub) has better beer. The *Waterfront*, 139 King's St, is the main student **club** and gig venue.

NORTHERN ENGLAND

The main draw of **northern England** is the **Lake District**, a scenic region taking in stone-built villages and sixteen major lakes within a compact area of Cumbria just thirty miles across, overlooked by the steeply pitched faces of England's highest mountains. However, to restrict yourself purely to the outdoors would be to do a great disservice to industrial cities such as **Manchester** and **Liverpool** on the northwest coast (*www.visitnorthwest.com*), and **Newcastle** on the northeast (*www.ntb.org.uk*), whose centres are alive with the ostentatious civic architecture of nineteenth-century capitalism. An entirely different angle on northern history is provided by the great medieval ecclesiastical centres of **Durham** and **York** (*www.ytb.org.uk*), where famous cathedrals provide a focus for extensive medieval remains.

Manchester

Whether you approach from the north or south, your first glimpse of **MANCHESTER** (*www.manchester.com*) is likely to include traditional images of a struggling post-industrial city – tower blocks and empty shells of mills and factories beside rows of back-to-back houses. However, Manchester is being treated to an urban facelift unequalled in Britain. After a massive IRA bomb destroyed much of the centre in 1996, quick and impressive rebuilding works have transformed the city, bringing in their wake a welter of shops, bars and restaurants. With a huge population of students, a lively Gay Village, and a venerable history churning out talent for the twin glories of British culture – music and football – Manchester today hosts one of the most vibrant social and cultural scenes in the country. Its crowning achievement of recent years was to be selected to host the **Commonwealth Games** in summer 2002 (25th July–4th August). The *Spirit of Friendship Festival* has been programmed to coincide with the games and will be hosted at various locations throughout the city. Check with the tourist office for more details and remember to book accommodation well in advance if you want to visit the city during the celebrations.

From the main Piccadilly train station, it's a few minutes' walk northwest to **Piccadilly Gardens**, an untidy square with a bus station in the middle. North of the gardens is what's been dubbed the **Northern Quarter**, full of trendy boutiques and cafés. West of the gardens is Market St, lined with more mainstream shops, on the way to the concrete horror of the Arndale shopping centre, which took the brunt of the 1996 bomb and is now thankfully overhauled. It sits alongside **St Ann's Square**, a sociably pedestrianized shopping, eating and entertainment area home to the **Royal Exchange** building, now restored as a theatre. Turning right onto Victoria St leads you north through more revamped areas to the demure fifteenth-century **Cathedral**, a fine Perpendicular structure renowned for the wood carving of its choir stalls and, just to the left of the choir, a small stone bearing an eighth-century carving of an angel. South again on drab Deansgate brings you to the Victorian Gothic **John Rylands Library** at no. 150 (Mon–Fri 10am–5.30pm, Sat 10am–1pm; free), which exhibits a small and changing selection of rare and ancient items, from Egyptian papyri to early examples of European printing. A short distance east is Albert Square and the **Town Hall** (Mon–Fri 9am–5pm), another, more overbearing example of Victorian Gothic. A block east again is the **City Art Gallery** on Mosley St, due to re-open in March 2002 after major expansion and restoration work, with Britain's largest **Chinatown**, centred on Faulkner St, spreading nearby. Southeast across Portland St, the area down to the waterside has been rejuvenated as a thriving **Gay Village**, full of cafés, clubs and bars.

South of the town hall is the Italianate **Free Trade Hall** on Peter St, a good venue for classical music and jazz and the original home of the Hallé Orchestra, northern England's best, now resident just to the south in the Bridgewater Hall alongside the G-Mex conference centre. For a celebration of the triumphs of industrialization, head a few minutes west from G-Mex, past the southern end of Deansgate, to the **Museum of Science and Industry** on Liverpool Rd (daily 10am–5pm; £6.50; *www.msim.org.uk*), where exhibits include working early steam engines, textile machinery and a glimpse of the Manchester sewer system.

Trams run from Piccadilly west to **Salford Quays**, scene of a massive urban renewal scheme in the old dock area. Centrepiece is the spectacular waterfront **Lowry Centre** (*www.thelowry.org.uk*), complete with two theatres and two art galleries, one of which is devoted to the work of the artist after whom the centre is named – L.S. Lowry, best-known for his "matchstick men" scenes of Manchester's mill workers in the 1920s and 1930s (Mon–Wed 11am–5pm, Thurs, Sat & Sun 11am–8pm, Fri 11am–10pm; free). Nearby, a new **Imperial War Museum and Holocaust Museum** (*www.iwm.org.uk*), housed in a strikingly designed broken-globe complex, is due to open in March 2002. Trams also run from Piccadilly to the **Manchester United Football Club Museum**, contained in the North Stand of the club's Old Trafford stadium (daily 9.30am–5pm; £8; booking essential on ☎0161/868 8631, *www.manutd.com*; Metrolink tram to Old Trafford, or bus #256/#257). As well as getting a tour around the ground, you can wallow in the team's past and present glories in the onsite museum of kits and trophies galore.

Practicalities

Most **trains** arrive at Piccadilly station, although services from the north come into Victoria station, a little way northwest and linked to Piccadilly by Metrolink tram. **Coaches** stop at Chorlton St, just west of Piccadilly. The **airport** is ten miles south, with direct trains to Piccadilly. The main **tourist office** is in the town hall extension on Lloyd St (Mon–Sat 10am–5.30pm, Sun 11am–4pm; ☎0906/470 0847, *www.manchester.gov.uk*), with branches in both airport terminals (☎0161/436 3344). There's a large **HI hostel** on Potato Wharf near the Science Museum (☎0161/839 9960; ③), as well as the holistically-run *Manchester Backpackers*, two miles out at 41 Greatstone Rd, Stretford, five minutes' walk from Old Trafford Metrolink (☎0161/872 3499, *www.manchesterbackpackers.co.uk*; ③). More central is *Monroe's Hotel*, 38 London Rd, opposite Piccadilly station (☎0161/236 0564; ④). In summer you should also be able to find rooms in a student hall of residence (☎0161/275 2888; ③). You can get **Internet** access at Cyberia, 12 Oxford St.

For budget **eating**, head a couple of blocks east of the town hall to Chinatown. Alternatively, Wilmslow Rd in the student quarter in Rusholme (buses #40–#49), otherwise known as "Curry Mile", has some of Britain's best Indian cooking on offer, veggie and not; try *Sangam*, no. 13, *Punjab Sweethouse*, no. 177, or just follow your nose. The *Fallen Angel*, 263 Upper Brook St, is an excellent vegetarian café in the centre. The trendiest places to **drink** are in the booming Castlefield area around Liverpool Rd; the Northern Quarter around Oldham St; and the Gay Village on the Rochdale Canal, although café-bars have sprung up all over the city. Favourites are *Metz*, 3 Brazil St on the canalside, and *Cord* on Dorsey St, decked out completely in corduroy.

For details of the city's **nightlife**, pick up a copy of the fortnightly *City Life*. Cyberia, 12 Oxford St, is a long-standing **club**. *Velvet Underground*, 111 Deansgate, and *Paradise Factory*, 112 Princess St, are two of the liveliest crop of dance clubs, with regular gay and lesbian nights. The newest gay club is *Essential Planet K* on Oldham St, which has lots of varied and cheap student nights. For **live music** catch up-and-coming bands at *The Roadhouse*, Newton St; bigger acts play the *Academy*, and the *Students' Union* on Oxford Rd.

Liverpool

Once Britain's main transatlantic port and the empire's second city, **LIVERPOOL** spent too many of the twentieth-century postwar years struggling against adversity. Things are looking up at last, as economic and social regeneration brightens the centre and the old docks on the River Mersey. Yet even at its nadir in the 1980s, when the city had record unemployment figures, Liverpool's extraordinary spirit of community persisted, and it remains a warm and invigorating place to visit. Acerbic wit and loyalty to one of the city's two great football teams are the linchpins of Liverpudlian "Scouse" culture, along with an underlying pride in the local musical heritage – fair enough from the city that produced the Beatles. Liverpool's central layout is easy to assimilate: a grid of downtown streets separates Lime Street train station in the east from the Mersey to the west. Behind the station, Mount Pleasant heads uphill towards the university and a lively student quarter. **Lime Street** itself is the scene of a fine ensemble of public buildings: immediately opposite the station, **St George's Hall** (Aug Mon–Sat 10.30am–4pm; £1.50) exemplifies the municipal classicism which spread throughout industrial Britain early last century. Just north of the hall is the **Walker Art Gallery** (Mon–Sat 10am–5pm, Sun noon–5pm; free), one of the richest collections outside London. The odd Rubens and Rembrandt counterpoint a fairly representative jaunt through British art history, with Turner, Gainsborough, Joseph Wright of Derby, and Stubbs all being well represented – as, inevitably, are the Pre-Raphaelites. Going down the hill from the Walker you'll pass the **Liverpool Museum** (same hours; free), five floors of varied exhibits featuring anthropology, stuffed beasts, Amazonian rain forests, a basement aquarium and a planetarium, along with a top-floor café.

From here it's an uneventful walk westwards to the **Pier Head** and Liverpool's waterfront, from where it's worth taking a ferry to Birkenhead for the views back towards the city (£1). A short stroll to the south is the **Albert Dock**, showpiece of the renovated docks area; its main focus is the **Tate Gallery** (Tues–Sun 10am–6pm; free; *www.tate.org.uk*), showing off choice modernist exhibits from the Tate's mostly London-based collection on four floors of well-designed, airy rooms. Occupying the other side of the dock is the excellent **Maritime Museum** (Mon–Sat 10am–5pm, Sun noon–5pm; NMGM), housing an exhibition entitled "Transatlantic Slavery: Against Human Dignity", which gives an honest and shocking account of the conditions forced upon African slaves in the eighteenth and nineteenth centuries, as well as Liverpool's key role in the slave trade. Other displays outline the city's more palatable function as a launching pad for British and Irish emigration to North America and Australia, with re-creations of conditions on board an emigrant ship. The Albert Dock is also home to **The Beatles Story** (daily 10am–5/6pm; £7.95), a concentrated multimedia attempt to capture the essence of the Fab Four's rise from Hamburg rags to Abbey Road riches. Continuing the theme, the area back in the town centre around Mathew St has been designated the "**Cavern Quarter**". On the street itself lies the **Liverpool Hall of Fame**, a trip down Liverpool's memory lane of number 1 hits since 1952. The current *Cavern Club* at no. 10 is a re-built version of the original – where the Beatles played in the Sixties – but its history and numerous souvenirs are exhibited in the pub of the same name opposite. You can take a "Magical Mystery Tour" of other sites associated with the band, such as Penny Lane and Strawberry Fields, on board a customized double-decker bus (daily 2.20pm, July & Aug also Sat 11.50am; £10.95; book on ☎0151/709 3285) – and join in with moptops galore at the **International Beatles Festival** on the last weekend of August (combination ticket with the Beatle's story £15). If your appetite is still unsated there is the tour of **20 Forthlin Road**, the terraced home of Paul McCartney (☎0151/427 7231; £5.50).

To the east and south of Lime St are the city's two cathedrals; both are twentieth-century but they could hardly differ more in style. The Roman Catholic **Metropolitan Cathedral of Christ the King** (daily 8am–6pm; free), ten minutes' walk up Mount Pleasant, is a vast inverted funnel of a building, whose fading modern architecture belies the beauty of its interior, with stained-glass windows bathing the nave in a surreal blue light. Hope St, opposite, runs to the Anglican **Liverpool Cathedral** (same times; £2 donation), the largest in the country. Designed by Sir Giles Gilbert Scott in 1903 while still in his early twenties, this neo-Gothic mass of pale-red stone wasn't completed until 1978. On a clear day, a trip up the 100m-tall **tower** (daily 11am–4pm; £2) is rewarded by views to the Welsh hills.

Liverpool FC, one of the world's most successful football teams, play at Anfield stadium, a few miles north (bus #17, #117 or #217 from Lime St station), and offer tours around the club museum, the trophy room and the dressing-rooms (daily 10am–5pm; £8; booking essential on ☎0151/260 6677; museum only £5; *www.liverpoolfc.net*).

Practicalities

Trains arrive at Lime St station, 500m east of the river; **coaches** stop on Norton St, northeast of the station. The **airport** is eight miles southeast (take bus #80/180, express bus #500 into the centre). From the station, a short walk down Elliott St brings you to the **tourist office** in Queen Sq (Mon–Sat 9am–5.30pm, Sun 10.30am–4.30pm; ☎0906/680 6886, *www.visitliverpool.com*); and there's another **tourist office** in the Albert Dock (daily 10am–5.30pm; ☎0151/708 8854). Both book accommodation without charge (☎0845/601 1125). The top-quality **HI hostel** is just south of Albert Dock, 25 Tabley St (☎0151/709 8888; ④); otherwise, head for the noisy but friendly YMCA, 56 Mount Pleasant (☎0151/709 9516; ③); the YWCA, 1 Rodney St (☎0151/709 7791; ③); or the cosy *Embassie Youth Hostel*, 1 Falkner Sq, 500m east of the Anglican cathedral (☎0151/707 1089; ③; bus #80). John Moores University also offers self-catering **student rooms** (☎0151/709 3197; ③; mid-June to Aug). The best of the **hotel** options on Mount Pleasant is the *Feathers Hotel* at no. 119 (☎0151/709 9655, *www.feathers.uk.com*; ⑥).

There's a wide range of inexpensive ethnic **food** around Mount Pleasant, Hardman St and the grid of streets in between. Otherwise, *Harry Ramsden's* on Brunswick Way cooks up excellent fish and chips; cafés within both cathedrals offer good-value lunches; the *Life Café* Bold St, has snacks and inexpensive lunches for students; and the solar-powered *Hub Café*, 9 Berry St, serves vegetarian cuisine. The *Philharmonic*, 36 Hope St, is Liverpool's most characteristic **pub**, with a carefully re-created Victorian interior. The *Pacific Bar & Grill*, Temple St, is the most stylish example of Liverpool's new crop of restaurant-bars. *Havana*, North John St, is a busy late night Cuban bar with a tiny club attached. For more **nightlife**, *Cream*, off Hanover St, and the *Cavern Club* on Mathew St are both popular clubs, while *Escape*, Paradise St, is a leading gay club. The *Picket*, 24 Hardman St, and the *L2*, Hotham St, have the best selection of bands, but *Zanzibar* and *Heebieejeebies*, both on Seel St, have a more varied programme, ranging from indie to jazz. The *Royal Court*, Roe St, is the main venue for touring bands.

If you wish to travel by **ferry** to the Irish Republic, Liverpool port is an alternative to Holyhead; the route is served by P&O Irish Sea (☎0870/598 0777) and Norse Merchant Ferries (☎0870/600 4321). Liverpool also links with Northern Ireland, served by Norse Irish Ferries (☎01232/779090). A faster Sea Cat service also goes to the Isle of Man and to Dublin (☎08705/523523). In either case the tourist office can book tickets (0151/236 0888).

The Lake District

The site of England's highest peaks and its biggest concentration of lakes, the glacier-carved **Lake District** (*www.golakes.co.uk*) is the nation's most popular walking and hiking area. The weather changes quickly here, but the sudden shifts of light on the bracken and moorland grasses, and on the slate of the local buildings, are part of the area's appeal. For a twice daily updated weather forecast of the region phone ☎017687/75757. The most direct way of reaching the Lake District is via the west coast main line **train** route from London Euston, Manchester or Liverpool towards Glasgow, disembarking at Lancaster, from where bus #555 (Mon–Sat hourly, Sun every 2hr) runs right through the Lake District, calling at Windermere, Ambleside, Grasmere and Keswick. Alternatively, you could get off at Oxenholme, connecting with a branch line to Windermere; or Penrith, where buses #105 and #X5 run to Keswick. Among long-distance **coach** services, National Express go daily from London Victoria to Kendal, near Windermere; local **buses** go everywhere in the region. Cumbria Journey Planner (☎01228/606000, *www.cumbria.gov.uk*) can advise about all the local bus, train, coach and ferry services, which tend to operate a skeleton service on Sundays.

Lake Windermere and around

Largest and southernmost of the lakes, **Lake Windermere** is also the most accessible – and so one of the most crowded in summer. The town of **WINDERMERE** itself is set back from the lake, and offers little to do other than to stroll a mile south to the sister town of **BOWNESS** on the lakeshore. The children's author Beatrix Potter was the most famous local resident, and both resorts groan with Peter Rabbit memorabilia. Windermere's **tourist office** is just outside the train station (daily 9am–5/7.30pm; ☎015394/46499), steps from the *Backpackers Hostel* in the Old Bakery (☎015394/46374; ③). The nearest **HI** hostel is a couple of miles north, just off Ullswater Rd (☎015394/43543; ③). Those wanting the quiet life can take a **ferry** on the lake: from Bowness (where there's another tourist office; ☎015394/42895), cruises (*www.marketsite.co.uk/lakes*) operate to, among other places, **Lakeside** in the south and **WATERHEAD** in the north. The latter has the Lake District National Park Visitor Centre (April–Oct daily 10am–5pm; ☎015394/46601, *www.lake-district.gov.uk*) as well as another **HI** **hostel** (☎015394/32304; ③). From Waterhead, it's a mile north to **AMBLESIDE** – also served by bus #555 from Windermere and Bowness. Thronged with visitors throughout the year, the pubs here are busier and the range of food wider than down the lake. Ambleside's most unlikely resident was German Dadaist Kurt Schwitters, who settled here in 1945; his gravestone can be seen in the cemetery. The **tourist office** is in the Central Buildings by the Market Cross, off Church St (daily 9am–5pm; ☎015394/32582).

Hawkshead and Coniston

Ferries shuttle from Bowness to Sawrey, from where it's a steep two-mile walk to the hamlet of **NEAR SAWREY** and Beatrix Potter's beloved **Hill Top** farm (April–Oct Mon–Wed, Sat & Sun 11am–4.30pm; £4), still crammed with her effects. It's another two miles to Hawkshead, and on to Coniston, both served by buses #505/ 506 from Ambleside, and both refreshingly peaceful after the hurly-burly of Windermere. Six miles southwest of Ambleside, the white-washed cottages of **HAWKSHEAD** harbour some marvellous village pubs and **Hawkshead Grammar School**, where Wordsworth was a pupil (Easter–Oct Mon–Sat 10am–12.30pm & 1.30–4.30pm, Sun 1–5pm; £2); it displays a desk carved with the young delinquent's name, and more ancient mementos of the school's long history, much more appealing than yet more Beatrix Potter gewgaws. A small **tourist office** next to the bus stop (Easter–Oct daily 9.30am–5.30/6pm; Nov–Easter Sat & Sun 10am–3.30pm; ☎015394/36525) handles a range of B&Bs and farmhouse stays, but the plush, family-oriented **HI hostel** at Esthwaite Lodge (☎015394/36293; ③), a mile south of town, is one of the best in the country. **Camping** is available at *Waterson Ground*, half a mile along the Ambleside Rd.

Four miles southwest of Hawkshead by bus #515 lies **Grizedale Forest**, an industrial plantation littered with intriguing wood sculptures. Straddling the only road into the forest, the Grizedale Forest Centre (daily 10am–5pm) sells trail maps for walkers and cyclists: you can rent mountain bikes from a booth across the road (reserve on ☎01229/860369). Walking through the forest from Hawkshead and descending towards the graceful **Coniston Water** is a good way of reaching **CONISTON** village, another elegant cluster of houses nestling beneath the craggy Old Man of Coniston. There's an **HI hostel** just north of the village at Holly How, Far End (☎015394/41323; ②), and another more peaceful one above Coniston on the slopes of Old Man, at Coppermines House (☎015394/41261; ②). The most popular walk from Coniston – and one which can also be approached from Hawkshead – is to **Tarn Hows**, three miles northeast, a lake surrounded by wooded high ground, with several vantage points across the hills.

Unlike on Windermere, speed-limits are enforced on Coniston Water, making a trip on the *Steam Yacht Gondola* a most stately experience (April–Oct 4–5 daily; £4.75 round-trip). This is the best means of getting to the elegant lakeside villa, **Brantwood** (March–Nov daily 11am–5.30pm; Dec–Feb Wed–Sun 11am–4.30pm; £4.50; *www.brantwood.org.uk*), once inhabited by the art historian John Ruskin, and also served by wooden motor-launches from Coniston (return ticket including entrance fee £7.10; *www.lakefell.co.uk*). Distressed by the effects of the Industrial Revolution, Ruskin saw the medieval era as a golden age of pre-capitalist harmony, providing the theoretical substance for the work of the Pre-Raphaelites. The house is full of Ruskin's own drawings and sketches, as well as items relating to the painters he inspired.

Rydal and Grasmere

The trusty #555 bus connects Ambleside with the heart of Wordsworth country, but it's an expedition which you could easily accomplish on foot. The hamlet of **RYDAL**, three miles northwest of Ambleside, was where Wordsworth made his home from 1813 until his death in 1850; his house, **Rydal Mount** (daily 9.30/10am–4/5pm; Jan closed Tues; £4), is famous largely for the gardens laid out by Wordsworth himself. Paths on either side of Rydal Water cover the two miles to **GRASMERE**, site of Wordsworth's more famous abode, **Dove Cottage** (daily 9.30am–5.30pm; closed Jan; £5; *www.wordsworth.org.uk*). The cottage is an austere, cramped farmhouse, and you may have to queue to get in. The adjoining museum has portraits and manuscripts relating to Wordsworth, Coleridge – who regularly hiked over from Keswick to visit him here – and De Quincey, author of *Confessions of an English Opium-Eater* and biographer of the Lake poets, who took over Dove Cottage after Wordsworth's move to Rydal. Wordsworth and his sister Dorothy lie in simple graves in the churchyard of St Oswald's, in the heart of the village. Grasmere's **tourist office** is on Redbank Rd just before the church (April–Oct daily 9.30am–5pm; ☎015394/35245). A host of tearooms and cafés cater for the tides of daytrippers. There are two co-owned **hostels**: *Butterlip How* (☎015394/35316; ③), ten minutes north of the village on Easedale Rd, and the more basic *Thorney How* (same number; ②) a mile further north on the same road, which was one of the first hostels opened in the country.

Keswick

Principal centre for the northern lakes, **KESWICK** (pronounced "kez-ick") lies on the northern fringes of **Derwentwater**, one of the few stretches of water in the area which can be walked all the way around – although there are also boats which make circular tours. The main hiking attraction is up **Latrigg Fell** to the north (2–3hr), rising sharply through coniferous forests to give splendid views; the trek up **Skiddaw** (5hr) is more demanding, but the easiest of the many (much tougher) true mountain hikes around and about. Keswick itself doesn't have a great many attractions; the best thing to do is to hike a mile and a half eastwards to **Castlerigg Stone Circle**, a Neolithic monument which commands a spectacular view of the amphitheatre of mountains surrounding Thirlmere. Keswick's **tourist office** is in the Moot Hall, Market Sq (daily 9.30/10am–4.30/5/7pm; ☎017687/72645). The nearest **HI hostel** is on Station Rd by the river (☎017687/72484; ③); the other is on the eastern shores of Derwentwater, two miles south, in Barrow House (☎017687/77246; ③), near a **campsite** (☎017687/72392; ②).

York

It's the spectacular Gothic Minster, alleyways and ancient stone walls that draw tourists to **YORK**, but the city's character-forming experiences go back a lot further than that. It was adopted by the Romans as a base for their operations against the Brigantes, a fearsome tribe holding sway over the north from around the Humber estuary. York became the principal northern headquarters of the Romans, and when Emperor Severus, over here on a Scot-bashing expedition in 208, decided to split the administration of Britain into two halves, he made it one of the capitals. The city's position as the north's spiritual capital dates from 627, when Edwin of Northumbria adopted Christianity (the faith of his Kentish wife). Northumbrian power crumbled in the face of a Danish invasion that swept through York in 866, destroying one of the finest libraries in western Europe in the process. By 876 one of the Danish leaders, Halfdan, had settled here with half the Viking army, beginning a century of Scandinavian rule in York and adding another layer to a tradition of northern independence.

Without doubt, one of the best introductions to York is a stroll along the city walls (open until dusk), a three-mile circuit that takes in the medieval Bars, or gates. **Bootham Bar**, adjacent to the tourist office, is as good a place as any to start, and progressing northeastwards from here will give you good views overlooking the Minster. Immediately opposite the tourist office, the **City Art Gallery** (Mon–Sat 10am–5pm, Sun 2.30–5pm; £2) includes portraits of local Tudor worthies and a room devoted to the sentimental, moralizing work of local-born nineteenth-century artist William Etty, plus displays devoted to other local art and artists. The next-door Museum Gardens lead to the ruins of the Benedictine abbey of St Mary and the **Yorkshire Museum** (daily 10am–5pm; £4.50), which contains much of the abbey's medieval sculpture, a Roman mosaic and a good selection of Saxon and Viking finds. In the same park are the remains of a tower built by Constantius at the end of the third century.

Ever since Edwin built a wooden chapel on the site in preparation for his baptism into the faith, **York Minster** (daily 7am–dusk; £2 donation; *yorkminster.org*) has been the centre of spiritual authority for the north of England. Most of what's visible now was built in stages between the 1220s and the 1470s, and today it ranks as the country's largest Gothic building, crammed with treasures. Inside, the apocalyptic scenes of the East Window, completed in 1405, and the abstract thirteenth-century *Five Sisters* window represent the finest collection of stained glass in the country, and there's a four-century-old wooden clock in the north transept, complete with oak knights. The **crypt** (70p) has sections from the Minster's Norman predecessor, while the **undercroft** (£2), down in the foundations, holds remnants and artefacts from the previous Roman and Norman buildings, set against the extraordinary steel and concrete engineering works which saved the tower from collapsing in the 1960s. The octagonal **chapter house** (£1) usually contains a few medieval manuscripts from the Minster's rich collection, while climbing the **central tower** (£3) gives views over the

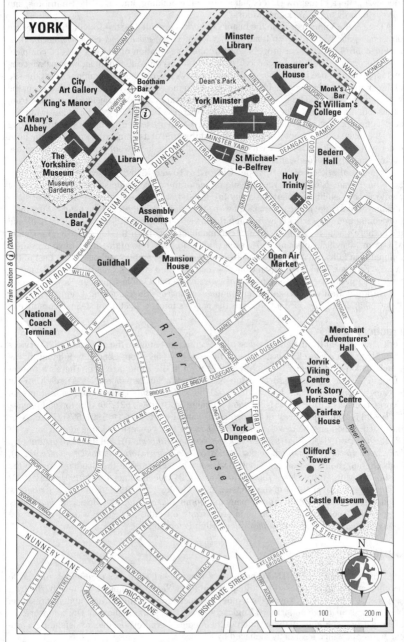

medieval pattern of narrow streets just south of the building, known as the **Shambles**, and out northwards to the Yorkshire Moors.

A taste of the Viking period in the history of York is provided by the **Jorvik Viking Centre** on Coppergate Walk (daily 9/10am–4.30/5.30pm; £6.95; *www.jorvik-viking-centre.co.uk*). A remote-control dodgem car propels you through a re-creation of Jorvik's streets, complete with appropriate smells and recorded sounds, to the accompaniment of an informative commentary. With an eye to archeological integrity, however, the journey continues past the site of the excavations themselves, blackened shapes in the earth showing the foundations of the wattle-and-daub huts. The faces of the wax dummies are careful reconstructions made from skulls found in the digs. The **Merchant Adventurers' Hall** nearby on Fossgate (Mon–Sat 9am–5pm; Apr–Oct also Sun noon–4pm; £2) is a well-preserved medieval guildhall dating from the fourteenth century. Despite the romantic sound of its name, this was in fact the head office of the middle-class businessmen who controlled the local wool export trade and whose portraits adorn the wood-panelled rooms.

Originally the keep of York castle, **Clifford's Tower** (daily: July & Aug 9.30am–7pm; Sept–June 10am–5/6pm; £2) was the site of one of the more tragic and bizarre episodes of medieval anti-Semitism. Following a city fire in 1190, which the Jews were accused of starting, they took refuge in the tower; faced with starvation or slaughter at the hands of the mob, they committed mass suicide by burning the tower to the ground. It was rebuilt in 1245, and today there's little to see other than a commanding view from the top. Nearby, the **Castle Museum** (daily 9.30am–5pm; £5.75; *www.york.gov.uk*) was one of the first British museums to indulge in full-scale re-creations of life in bygone times, and it's still one of the best of the genre; "Kirkgate" and "Half Moon Court" – reconstructed street scenes of the Victorian and Edwardian periods – are masterpieces of evocative detail. One last museum is worth a call: the **National Railway Museum**, ten minutes' walk from the station on Leeman Rd (daily 10am–6pm; £7.50; *www.nrm.org.uk*), has the nation's finest collection of steam locomotives.

Practicalities

York's magnificent **train** station is west of the centre, just outside the city walls, with services from Manchester, as well as fast trains on the east coast line from London to Edinburgh; the coach station is at Rougier St, slightly nearer town in the same direction. There's a **tourist office** in the train station (April–Oct Mon–Sat 9am–6pm, Sun 9am–5pm; Nov–March Mon–Sat 9.30am–5.30pm, Sun 10am–4pm; ☎01904/621756, *www.yorkshirevisitor.co.uk*), with others on George Hudson St (☎01904/554488) and Exhibition Sq (☎01904/621756). The top-of-the-range **HI hostel** is 20min northwest of the centre at Water End, Clifton (☎01904/653147; ④). Near the coach station are the excellent *York Backpackers*, in a converted Georgian mansion at 88 Micklegate (☎01904/627720, *www.yorkbackpackers.mcmail.com*; ③), and the more institutional *York Youth Hotel*, 11 Bishophill Senior (☎01904/625904, *www.yorkyouthhotel.demon.co.uk*; ②), both offering rooms and dorms. Good **B&Bs** are concentrated in the Bootham area, to the west of the Minster: try *Queen Anne's Guest House*, 24 Queen Annes Rd (☎01904/629389; ④) or *City Guesthouse*, just east of the Minster at 68 Monkgate (☎01904/622483; ⑤). *Crumble's*, Goodramgate, is the oldest of York's many **tearooms**. *Blake Head*, 104 Micklegate, is a quality veggie café. Good places for **pub** food are *Oscar's*, on Little Stovegate, with an impressive choice of menus and the *Hole in the Wall* on High Petergate.

Durham

Seen from the train, **DURHAM** presents a magnificent sight, with cathedral and castle perched atop a bluff enclosed by a loop of the River Wear, and linked to the suburbs by a series of sturdy bridges. Nowadays a quiet provincial town with a strong student presence, Durham was once one of northern England's power bases: the Bishops of Durham were virtual royal agents in the north for much of the medieval era, responsible for defending a crucial border province frequently menaced by the Scots.

The town initially owed its reputation to the possession of the remains of St Cuthbert, an early prior of Lindisfarne, which were evacuated to Durham in the ninth century because of Viking raids. His shrine has dominated the eastern end of the spectacular **Cathedral** (daily 9.30am–6/8pm; £3 donation; *www.durhamcathedral.co.uk*) ever since. The cathedral itself is the finest example of Norman architecture in England, with the nave, completed in 1128, the first to use pointed arches, raising the interior dimensions to dizzying heights. A series of intricately carved pillars, decorated with chevrons and other Moorish-influenced geometric designs, lines the nave, and medieval frescoes depicting St Cuthbert are just visible in the Galilee Chapel, inspired by the Great Mosque of Córdoba and containing the remains of the Venerable Bede, England's first historian, brought here in 1020. The original coffin of St Cuthbert and other antiquities can be seen in the **treasury** (Mon–Sat 10am–4.30pm, Sun 2–4.30pm; £2), adjacent to the cloisters, while the **tower** gives the usual breathtaking views (Mon–Sat 9.30/10am–3/4pm; £2).

On the opposite side of Palace Green is the Norman **Castle** (Easter & July–Sept daily 10-12am & 2-4.30pm; £3), now halls of residence for a few of Durham's luckier students, but preserving a solid twelfth-century chapel thought to have once served as a strongroom; look out for the naive carvings adorning the capitals of the pillars. Both the cathedral and castle are surrounded by North and South Bailey, a continuous street that curves around the hillside, lined with eighteenth- and nineteenth-century buildings that are now largely the preserve of the university. A pleasant half-hour stroll follows a pathway on the wooded river bank below, all the way around the cathedral's peninsula, passing a succession of elegant bridges with fine vantage points.

Practicalities

The **train station** is ten minutes' walk from the centre, via either of two bridges over the Wear. The **bus station** is just to the south on North Rd. **Minibuses** link the cathedral with the bus station. The **tourist office** is housed in the new Millenium Centre along Freemans Place (July & Aug Mon–Sat 9.30am–6pm, Sun 2–5pm; Sept–June Mon–Sat 9.30/10am–5/5.30pm; ☎0191/384 3720, *www.durham.gov.uk*). **B&Bs** are concentrated on Gilesgate, northeast of Market Place, and around Crossgate, south of the bus station. Good bets include *Green Grove*, 99 Gilesgate (☎0191/384 4361; ④), and the small *Koltai Guesthouse*, 10 Gilesgate (☎0191/3862026; ④). The cheapest beds in town are at the university – either dorms or rooms (☎0191/374 3863; ④; Easter, July–Sept & Christmas only). The nearest **campsite**, *Grange*, is three miles northeast of the city towards Sunderland on Meadow Lane, Carrville (☎0191/384 4778; ②; bus #220/222).

For good value **food**, *Vennel's Café*, Saddler's Yard, serves great snacks in a lovely little hidden courtyard off Saddler St, while *Chadwick's* in Saddler St is a chic, popular café/bistro. For **drinking**, try the *Market Tavern* on the marketplace for a traditional pub, or *Saints*, directly underneath the indoor market, a trendy bar overlooking the river with cheap meals, Internet access, DJ nights and confessional screens linking the ladies toilet cubicles!

Newcastle-upon-Tyne

Once a tough, industrial city with a proud shipbuilding heritage, **NEWCASTLE** has retained its undeniable raw vigour, which has served it well during the decimation of local industry. These days, it's streets ahead of its rivals in the northeast, and has a slew of good galleries and music venues. It also serves as a good base for explorations of **Hadrian's Wall**, a Roman-era barricade that stretches from coast to coast, cutting England off from Scotland and still serving as the border between the two today.

Arriving by train, your first view is of the River Tyne and its redeveloped quaysides, along with the five bridges that join Newcastle to the suburb of Gateshead. The single steel arch of the **Tyne Bridge**, built in 1929, and the high-tech 'winking' **Millenium Bridge**, completed in 2001, are world renowned trademarks. Newcastle's centre owes a lot of its character to

John Dobson, who remodelled the city along Neoclassical lines in the early nineteenth century. His most imposing legacy is the sweep of **Grey Street**, leading north from the cathedral – just east of the station – to the lofty Grecian column of Grey's Monument, the city's central landmark. Newcastle's status as a border stronghold is remembered in the **castle**, with its Norman keep (Tues–Sun 9.30am–4.30/5.30pm; £1.50), which offers good rooftop views and a succession of draughty rooms, including a Norman chapel in the basement. The city's main art collection is housed in the **Laing Art Gallery** on New Bridge St, east of the monument (Mon–Sat 10am–5pm, Sun 2–5pm; free). A venue for prestigious contemporary exhibitions, it also houses an excellent selection of Victorian painting, including the manic biblical works of local artist John Martin. The university campus on Haymarket, fifteen minutes' walk north of the city centre, contains a couple of worthwhile museums. The **Museum of Antiquities** (Mon–Sat 10am–5pm; free) is a good introduction to the frontier culture of Hadrian's Wall, including a reconstruction of a *Mithraeum* – a temple to the Middle Eastern deity Mithras, imported to the region by Roman soldiers serving on the Wall – which once stood in the nearby town of Carrawburgh. The **Hatton Gallery** (Mon–Sat 10am–4.30/5.30pm; free) contains the one surviving wall of Kurt Schwitters' barn studio in Ambleside; but has been dwarfed by the opening of the **Baltic Centre for Contemporary Art** (*www.balticmill.com*), on the southern banks of the Tyne opposite Quayside. The former Baltic Flour Mill opens in March 2002 and will house several galleries, a cinema and an interesting collection of contemporary European art.

Practicalities

Newcastle's **Central Station** is ten minutes' walk south of the centre; the **coach station**, on Gallowgate, is a couple of minutes west. The **ferry** port is in North Shields, seven miles east, with buses running to the centre (for details of crossings from Newcastle to Amsterdam and Scandinavia see Basics, p.12), and the **airport** is six miles north, linked by metro. There are **tourist offices** in Central Station (June–Sept Mon–Fri 10am–8pm, Sat 9am–5pm, Sun 10am–4pm; Oct–May Mon–Sat 10am–5pm; ☎0191/277 8000, *www.newcastle.gov.uk*) and at 132 Grainger St (same number). There's an **HI hostel** at 107 Jesmond Rd (☎0191/281 2570; ③). Jesmond – a mile north of the centre – is also the main location for **B&Bs**, which are clustered around Osborne Rd; try the *George* at no. 88 (☎0191/281 4442; ⑤), or the *Westland* round the corner at 27 Osborne Ave (☎0191/281 0412; ⑤).

A local institution for cheap **eats** is the *Quayside Café*, 1 Queen St, with more upmarket meals at *Panni's*, 61 High Bridge St. City-centre **pubs** and bars are clustered around Bigg Market, a block east of Grey St, although there are trendier (and pricier) options down on the quayside. Be sure to check out the *Crown Posada*, 31 The Side, a cosy quayside drinking den, or close by, the sleek and stylish *Pitcher & Piano* with fine views of the river. The city's foremost **dance club** venue is the *Foundation*, 57 Melbourne St; also look out for **live acts** performing at the university Students' Union on Haymarket. **Internet** access is available at *Coffee Trader* (☎0191/2612634; £3.50/hr) on Northumberland Place.

Hadrian's Wall

Preserving the *Pax Romana* amidst the troublesome tribes of Britain's wild north was always a difficult task when there were more important frontiers in Europe and Asia to defend, and the Emperor Hadrian opted for containment rather than outright conquest. The turf and stone **Hadrian's Wall** (*www.hadrians-wall.org*) which bears his name was the result, separating Roman England from barbarian Scotland; it was punctuated by **mile castles**, strong points spaced at one-mile intervals, and by sixteen more substantially garrisoned forts. Regular trains and hourly buses (#685) between Newcastle and Carlisle pass by many of the sites: a day-trip from Newcastle will suffice to see a little of the wall. The best base, however, is the market town of **HEXHAM**, on the train and bus route 45 minutes west of Newcastle; it has a central **tourist office** on Hallgate (☎01434/605225, *www.tynedale.gov.uk*) and plenty of accommodation including a basic **HI hostel** in nearby Acomb (☎01434/602864; ②) and the *Hadrian Lodge* hostel just west at Haydon Bridge (☎01434/688688, *www.hadrianlodge.co.uk*; ②). In summer a bus service (#880) links Hexham with Carlisle via all the main sites along Hadrian's Wall; on summer Sundays it sometimes links through to Newcastle, but check with the tourist office.

WALES

The relationship between England and **Wales** (Cymru in Welsh; *www.visitwales.com*) has never been entirely easy. Impatient with constant demarcation disputes, the eighth-century Saxon king Offa constructed a dyke to separate the two countries; today, a long-distance footpath follows its route from near Chepstow in the south to Prestatyn in the north, still marking the border to this day (*www.offa.demon.co.uk/offa.htm*). During Edward I's reign the last of the Welsh native princes, Llywelyn ap Gruffudd, was killed, and Wales passed uneasily under English rule. Trouble flared again with the rebellion of Owain Glyndŵr in the fifteenth century, but the Welsh prince Henry Tudor's defeat of Richard III at the Battle of Bosworth crowned him King Henry VII of England and paved the way for the 1536 Act of Union, which joined the English and Welsh in restless but perpetual partnership.

Contact with England has watered down indigenous Welsh culture: bricked-up, decaying chapels stand as reminders of the days when Sunday services and chapel choirs were central to community life. The **Eisteddfod** festivals of Welsh music, poetry and dance still take place throughout the country in summer – the *Llangollen International Musical Eisteddfod*, held on the first full week in July being the best-known example (*www.international-eisteddfod.co.uk*) – but harp-playing and the carving of lovespoons survive more or less solely courtesy of the tourism industry. Nevertheless, the Welsh language is undergoing a revival and you'll see it on bilingual road signs all over the country, although you're most likely to hear it spoken in the North, West and Mid-Wales. Some Welsh place-names have never been anglicized, but where alternative names do exist, we've given them in the text.

Much of the country, particularly the **Brecon Beacons** in the south and **Snowdonia** in the north, is relentlessly mountainous and offers wonderful walking and climbing terrain. **Pembrokeshire** to the west boasts a spectacular rugged coastline, dotted with offshore island nature reserves. The biggest towns, including the capital **Cardiff** in the south, **Aberystwyth** in the west, and **Caernarfon** in the north, all cling to the coastal lowlands, but even then the mountains are no more than a bus-ride away. **Holyhead**, on the island of **Anglesey**, is the main British port for ferry sailings to the Irish capital, Dublin.

South Wales

Main road and rail routes west from Bristol bypass the region's most spectacular historic monument, accessible from the old market town of **CHEPSTOW** (Cas-Gwent; *www.chepstow.co.uk*), itself ringed on three sides by thirteenth-century walls and on the fourth by the River Wye. Within the town, the Wye bridge gives stunning views of cliff-faces soaring above the river and of the first stone **castle** in Britain, built by the Normans in 1067, a year after William the Conqueror's victory at Hastings (April–Oct daily 9.30am–5/6pm; Nov–March Mon–Sat 9.30am–4pm, Sun 11am–4pm; £3). Opposite the castle is Gwy House, an eighteenth-century town house that now features the unassuming **Chepstow Museum** (Mon–Sat 11am–1pm & 2–5pm, Sun 2–5pm; £1). However, nothing within the town can match the six-mile stroll north along the Wye to the impossibly romantic ruins of **Tintern Abbey**, built by the Cistercians in 1131, rebuilt 150 years later and now in a state of majestic disrepair (same hours as Chepstow castle; £2.50). The nave walls rise to such a height that, from a distance, you might think the magnificent Gothic church still stood intact beneath the overhang of the wooded cliff – only when you get close do you find the roof is long gone. If you don't fancy walking, catch Red and white bus #69 (every 2hr), which runs from Chepstow to Tintern and on to Monmouth, eight miles north. You can top up for the return journey in the fourteenth-century *Moon and Sixpence* pub – almost a mile north of the Abbey by the river – which does excellent **food**. For information on Chepstow and the popular **Offas' Dyke Path** contact the **tourist office** on Bridge St (daily 9.30/10am–4/6pm; ☎01291/623772). The *Coach and Horses Inn* on Welsh St offers **B&B** accommodation (☎01291/622626; ⑤), or you could head one mile east across the Wye to the characterful *Upper Sedbury House* (☎01291/627173; ④). St Pier Caravan & **Camping**, at Port Skewett (☎01291/425114) is the only cheap option in the area. Take the Caldicote and Newport bus four miles west.

Newport and around

First stop in Wales for mainline trains from Bristol and London is **NEWPORT** (Casnewydd), also served by buses and local trains from Chepstow. An unexciting town, Newport never-theless does have its claim to fame: the legendary *TJ's* pub music venue, 14 Clarence Place (just over the river from the station), was where Kurt Cobain proposed to Courtney Love. Three miles northeast, and almost contiguous, is **CAERLEON**, a small, traffic-bedevilled town that preserves the extensive remains of its important Roman forebear, Isca. The state-of-the-art **Legionary Museum**, High St (Mon–Sat 10am–4.30/6pm, Sun 2–4.30/6pm; free; *www.nmgw.ac.uk/rlm*), contains finds from all the adjacent sites. The museum stands oppo-site the road leading to the less dramatic remains of the barracks and grassed-over amphithe-atre (free). Beside the museum is the **tourist office** (Mon–Sat 9.30am–5pm; ☎01633/842962), while further down the High St are the **Fortress Baths**, built on the site of a 75 AD bath-house (same hours as museum; £2). Caerleon is more amenable to stay in than Newport, and has three good **B&Bs**, including *Pendragon*, 18 Cross St (☎01633/430871; ⑤).

Bus #23 from Newport runs fourteen miles north to **BLAENAFON**, a town recently awarded UNESCO world-heritage status for its place in the Industrial Revolution. It is home to both a vast ironworks museum and, housed in a defunct coal-mine a mile west of town, the **Big Pit Mining Museum** (March–Nov daily 9.30am–5pm; free), which gives a revealing glimpse of working life in the South Wales valleys. The mine closed in 1980, and former min-ers are now employed as tour guides. The full tour involves descending 294ft in a miners' cage to inspect coalfaces, underground roadways and haulage engines dating back almost 200 years.

The Brecon Beacons

The **Brecon Beacons National Park** (*www.breconbeacons.org*) occupies a swathe of rocky uplands stretching from the English border to the remote moorlands above Swansea – per-fect walking territory. The Beacons themselves, a pair of hills 2900ft high accessed from Brecon town, share the limelight with the **Black Mountains** north of Crickhowell. Red and white bus #21 (every 2hr, not Sun) runs from Newport to Brecon, passing through Abergavenny and Crickhowell, but trains from Newport veer off into England after Abergavenny.

The market town of **ABERGAVENNY** (Y Fenni) sits in a fold between seven green hills at the eastern edge of the park, about fifteen miles north of Newport. Before setting out for the mountains, pick up maps from the combined **tourist office** and **national park infor-mation office** (daily 9.30/10am–4.30/6pm; ☎01873/857588) at Swan Meadow beside the bus station – and check what sort of weather you can expect, as sudden mists can play havoc. The most accessible walking areas are the **Sugar Loaf** (1955ft), four miles northwest, and **Holy Mountain** (Skirrid Fawr; 1595ft), three miles north. The *Black Sheep* **hostel** opposite the train station offers dorm beds (☎01873/859125; ③). Plenty of **B&Bs** line Monmouth Rd on the five-minute walk between the train station and the town centre; *Maes Glas* on Raglan

Terrace is best (☎01873/854494; ④). For good value eating try the *Greyhound Vaults* on Market St or for excellent Chinese but terrible service head for the *Peking Chef* on Cross St.

CRICKHOWELL (Crughywel), a friendly village with a fine seventeenth-century bridge five miles west of Abergavenny, is a more picturesque point to begin your explorations. A six-mile hike into the Black Mountains from Crickhowell takes you through remote and occasionally bleak countryside to tiny **Partrishow Church**; inside, you'll find a rare carved fifteenth-century rood screen complete with dragon, and an ancient mural of the grim reaper. Beaufort St in Crickhowell holds both the **tourist office** (April–Oct daily 9am–5pm; ☎01873/812105), and *Greenhill Villas* **B&B** (☎01873/811177; ④).

The largest central Brecon Beacons rise just south of **BRECON** (Aberhonddu), a lively little town eight miles west of Crickhowell which springs to life in mid-August for the huge international Brecon Jazz Festival. For details of the numerous trekking routes into the Beacons and an extensive programme of guided walks, call in at the park's **information office**, which shares premises with the **tourist office** in the Cattle Market car park beside Safeway (daily 9/10am–5/6pm; ☎01874/622485, *www.brecon.co.uk*). **B&Bs** abound, including *Tirbach*, 13 Alexandra Rd (☎01874/624551; ④); both *Pickwick House*, St John's Rd (☎01874/624322; ④), and *Beacons*, in a rambling town house at 16 Bridge St (☎01874/623339, *www.beacons.brecon.co.uk*; ④), also cook excellent evening meals. The *Ty'n-y-Caeau* **hostel** is two miles east of Brecon at Groesfford (☎01874/665270; ②), a mile off the Abergavenny bus route, while the *Held Bunkhouse* hostel is in Cantref (☎01874/624646; ③), a mile southwest of town.

Cardiff and around

The Welsh capital **CARDIFF** (Caerdydd; *www.virtualcardiff.co.uk*) is rapidly picking itself up after the collapse of the coal-mining industry, and in the last couple of years has gained added status as the home of the Welsh Assembly, wielding powers newly devolved from London. The city's narrow Victorian arcades are interspersed with spanking new shopping centres and wide pedestrian precincts, seemingly sprung up at random. Long-distance coaches, and buses from the airport, arrive at the **bus terminal**, right beside Cardiff Central **train station**, south of the city centre off Penarth Rd (local trains use Queen St station instead, east of the centre). You can pick up free maps and information at the Visitor Centre **tourist office** in Wood St (daily 10am–2/4pm; ☎029/2022 7281).

The geographical and historical heart of the city is **Cardiff Castle** (daily 9.30am–4.30/6pm; £5; tours every 20min; ☎029/2087 8110). Standing on a Roman site developed by the Normans, the castle was embellished by William Burges in the 1860s, and each room is now a wonderful example of Victorian "medieval" decoration; best of all are the Chaucer Room, the Banqueting Hall, the Arab Room and the Fairy-tale Nursery. Five minutes' walk northeast, the **National Museum and Gallery** in Cathays Park (Tues–Sun 10am–5pm; free; *www.nmgw.ac.uk/nmgc*) houses a version of Rodin's *The Kiss*, a fine collection of Impressionist paintings, and natural history and archeological exhibits. A half-hour walk south of the centre is the **Cardiff Bay** area, also reached by bus #8 from Central Station, or a train from Queen St. Once known as Tiger Bay, the long-derelict area (birthplace of singer Shirley Bassey) has seen massive redevelopment since the opening of the Welsh Assembly in 1999; now you'll find waterfront walks, glittering new architecture and an old Norwegian seamen's chapel, converted into a cosy café.

Attractions near Cardiff include the **Museum of Welsh Life** at St Fagans, four miles west of the centre on bus #32. This 100-acre open-air museum is packed with reconstructed rural and industrial heritage buildings from all over Wales (daily 10am–5/6pm; free; *www.nmgw.ac.uk/mwl*); every May Day, a huge fair is held here. Fans of William Burges' elaborate interiors shouldn't miss the fairy-tale **Castell Coch** ("Red Castle") at Tongwynlais, five miles north of town on bus #136 (April–Oct daily 9.30am–5/6pm; Nov–March Mon–Sat 9.30am–4pm, Sun 11am–4pm; £2.50). Built on the site of a thirteenth-century castle and perched dramatically on a steep, forested hillside, Burges' lavish Victorian showpiece was commissioned by the third Lord Bute as a country retreat. The outside has turrets, a fully-operational portcullis and drawbridge, while inside you'll find vaulted ceilings and astonishing decorations and furnishings.

Cardiff's **HI hostel** is a couple of miles north of the centre at 2 Wedal Rd (☎029/2046 2303; ③), or you could try the excellent *Cardiff International Backpacker*, just west of the centre across the River Taff at 98 Neville St (☎029/2034 5577; ③). **B&Bs** include *Rosanna*, at 175 Cathedral Rd (☎029/2022 9780; ③), a 15min walk west of the centre, and the *Georgian*, 179 Cathedral Rd (☎029/2325194; ⑤). To **eat** laver bread and other Welsh delicacies, head for *Celtic Cauldron* in the shopping arcade opposite the castle. *Cibo*, 83 Pontcanna St, is a small Italian trattoria serving sandwiches and more substantial fare, while the café in the Norwegian church by Cardiff Bay is great for salads and snacks. Ale-lovers can sample the local bitter surrounded by rugby memorabilia in the *Old Arcade* pub, Church St. **Internet** access is available from *Cardiff Cybercafé*, 9 Duke St.

Pembroke and the southwest

PEMBROKE (Penfro), birthplace of Henry VII, is a sleepy town at the southwestern extremity of the country, lying at the heart of the Pembrokeshire Coast National Park and easily accessible by train from Cardiff. Centrepiece of the town is the magnificent water-surrounded **Castle** (daily 9.30/10am–4/6pm; £3), whose circular keep, dating from 1200, offers fine views of the countryside. The castle overshadows the high street where shops are shoehorned into an assortment of Tudor and Georgian buildings, one of them housing the **Museum of the Home**, an eclectic collection of exhibits ranging from toys and games to fashion accessories (May–Sept Mon–Thurs 11am–5pm; £1.20). The Visitor Centre on Commons Rd includes the tourist office (daily 10am–5.30pm; ☎01646/622388). *Beech House* is the best-value **B&B** in town, 78 Main St (☎01646/683746; ③). The nearest **HI hostel** is six miles east at Manorbier (☎01834/871803; ②), accessible by train. Regular **ferries** to Rosslare in Ireland (4hr) leave from Pembroke Dock, two miles north of the town.

The **Pembrokeshire Coast National Park** (*www.pembrokeshirecoast.org*) sweeps all the way around the edge of the southwestern peninsula of Wales, and the coastal path includes some of the country's most stunning and remote scenery, offering sheer cliff-faces, panoramic sea views and excellent seabird-watching. Tricky though it may be without a car, it's worth trying to get to **St Govan's Head** – directly south of Pembroke near Bosherston – where a thousand-year-old chapel clings, barely credibly, to the rock face.

From Pembroke, bus #359 runs north to Haverfordwest where you can catch bus #411 sixteen miles west to **ST DAVID'S** (Tyddewi), one of the most enchanting spots in Britain, where a breathtakingly beautiful **Cathedral** (*www.stdavidscathedral.org.uk*), delicately tinted purple, green and yellow by a combination of lichen and geology, hides in a dip below the High St. Constructed between 1180 and 1522, but heavily restored in the last century, the cathedral hosts a prestigious classical music festival each May. Across a thin trickle of river thousands of jackdaws congregate around the extensive remains of the magnificent fourteenth-century **Bishop's Palace** (Easter–Oct daily 9.30am–5/6pm; Nov–Easter Mon–Sat 9.30am–4pm, Sun noon–2pm; £2), which adds to the beauty of the setting. There's a **hostel** at Llaethdy, two miles west of town (☎01437/720345; ②), and bus 411 takes you to the **HI hostel** off the St Davids Rd, near the attractive little village of Solva (☎01437/721940; ③). For central **B&Bs**: try *Pen Albro*, 18 Goat St (☎01437/721865; ④), or *Y Glennydd*, 51 Nun St (☎01437/720576; ④). The **tourist office** is 200m east of the bus station on the High St (Easter–Oct daily 9.30am–5.30pm; Nov–Easter Mon–Sat 10am–4pm; ☎01437/720392, *www.stdavids.co.uk*).

Seventeen miles further north on bus #411 – and at the end of the main train line from Cardiff and London – is **FISHGUARD** (Abergwaun), an attractive fishing port that's another embarkation point for Rosslare, with ferries and catamarans departing daily from alongside the train station. *Hamilton Backpackers Lodge*, a **hostel** near the tourist office at 21 Hamilton St (☎01348/874797; dorms ②, twins ③), and *Glanmoy Lodge*, ten minutes from the port on Tref-Wrgi Rd (☎01348/874333; ⑤), are used to people arriving late or departing early.

Mid-Wales

Mid-Wales (*www.mid-wales-tourism.org.uk*), an area of wild mountain roads, hidden valleys and genteel ex-spa towns, is the least visited part of the country, perhaps because access is a little trickier than elsewhere. Nevertheless, it's worth making the effort, because it's here that you'll discover the traditional rural Wales, in quiet towns where the pub conversation takes place in Welsh rather than English. But this is also Wales at its most "alternative" – look out for healthfood shops and trendy bookshops, their English-speaking owners often escapees from the industrial Midlands and other English urban centres.

Central Trains operate on a line which penetrates mid-Wales from Shrewsbury, accessible on the main line north from Cardiff. Three miles inside Wales is **WELSHPOOL** (Y Trallwng), a market town full of the distinctive black-and-white half-timbered houses typical of the *Marches*, the Welsh–English borders. It's worth a stop simply to visit the thirteenth-century **Powis Castle**, a gorgeous red limestone building that's been continuously inhabited for five hundred years (April–Oct Wed–Sun 1–5pm; July & Aug also Tues 1–5pm; £7.50). The castle houses Wales' best collection of furniture, tapestries and pictures, as well as the Clive of India collection of Indian treasures. Capability Brown designed the lovely terraced **gardens** (same days 11am–6pm; free with castle ticket, or £5). The **tourist office** is on Church St (daily 10am–5/6pm; ☎01938/552043). If you decide to stay, one of the many **B&Bs** on Salop Rd is *Montgomery House* (☎01938/552693; ③).

Aberystwyth and around

Trains terminate at **ABERYSTWYTH**, a lively, thoroughly Welsh seaside resort of neat Victorian terraces and a thriving student culture. The train station is ten minutes' east of the seafront, but if you walk north up Terrace Rd, you'll come to the **tourist office** (daily 10am–5/6pm; ☎01970/612125); upstairs, the **Ceredigion Museum** (£1) contains coracles once used by local fishermen as well as a reconstructed cottage interior. The flavour of the town is best appreciated on the seafront, where one of Edward I's castles bestrides a windy headland to the south. There's also a Victorian camera obscura further north, which can be reached via a clanking cliff train (Easter–Oct daily 10am–6pm; £2 return). For a more extended rail trip, you could take the very popular **Vale of Rheidol** narrow-gauge steam train to **Devil's Bridge**, a canyon where three bridges of assorted ages and in assorted conditions span a dramatic waterfall (April–Oct; 3hr return trip, 1hr to Devil's Bridge; £10.50).

The seafront is lined with genteel **guest houses**, all much of a muchness; try *Yr Hafod*, 1 Marine Terrace (☎01970/617579; ④). Out of term-time, contact University College about B&B in **student halls** (☎01970/621960; ④). *Y-Graig*, 34 Pier St, is a great place to eat vegetarian **food**, and the owner is a mine of information on what's going on locally. Check out the university's Arts Centre on Penglais Hill for films, plays, exhibitions and other events.

North of Aberystwyth the train passes through a succession of seaside resorts, some small and discreet, others large and upfront, before reaching **HARLECH**, where one of the best of Edward I's great castles, later Owen Glyndûr's residence, towers above everything else on a rocky crag overlooking the sea (April–Oct daily 9.30am–4/6pm; Nov–March Mon–Sat 9.30am–4pm, Sun 11am–4pm; £3); the ramparts offer panoramic views over the mountains of Snowdonia on one side and Tremadog Bay on the other. The town itself huddles apologetically behind the castle with little to say for itself, but if you want **to stay**, try the *Aris Guesthouse*, 4 Pen-y-Bryn (☎01766/780409; ⑤) or the *Plas Newydd* hostel, three miles south by bus #38 or train in Llanbedr (☎01341/241287; ②). The **tourist office** is on the High St in town (Easter–Oct daily 10am–6pm; ☎01766/780658).

Midway between Aberystwyth and Harlech is down-at-heel **Barmouth**, from where you can catch bus #94 inland to **DOLGELLAU**, a base for exploring **Cadair Idris** (2930ft). The mountain looms over the southern side of town, its summit accessible via a tough six-mile, five-hour trek along the Pony Path starting three miles south of Dolgellau at Ty Nant – just one of the many walks in the area. The **tourist office** is on central Eldon Sq, right by the bus stop (Easter–Oct daily 10am–5/6pm; Nov–Easter closed Tues & Wed; ☎01341/422888). *Aber Cottage Tearooms,* centrally placed on Smithfield St (☎01341/422460; ④), has good **B&B** accommodation, or you could make for *Kings* **hostel** at Penmaenpool, four miles west, off the #28 bus route (☎01341/422392; ②).

North Wales

Snowdonia National Park is the glory of **North Wales** (*www.nwi.co.uk*), with some of the most dramatic mountain scenery Britain has to offer – jagged peaks, towering waterfalls and glacial lakes decorating every roadside. Not surprisingly, walkers congregate here in strength, and the villages around the area's highest peak, Snowdon (3650ft), see steady tourist traffic even in the bleakest months of the year. Whatever season you're here, make sure you're equipped with suitable shoes, warm clothing, and food and drink to see you through any unexpected hitches. For daily weather updates on Snowdonia phone ☎0891/500449 or weekly regional updates ☎0891/500415.

There are two main routes into North Wales. From Porthmadog, a few miles north of Harlech, **buses** skirt the base of Snowdon west to Caernarfon and Llanberis, and east to Blaenau Ffestiniog; while mainline **trains** from Crewe and Chester hug the north coast through Conwy and Bangor to Holyhead, with a branch line heading south to Betws-y-Coed and Blaenau Ffestiniog.

Blaenau Ffestiniog and Betws-y-Coed

A private train (call for times; 01766/512340, *www.festrail.co.uk*) twists and loops inland from Porthmadog up to the slate-quarrying town of **BLAENAU FFESTINIOG**, a fourteen-mile journey through a corner of the Snowdonia National Park. On a grey day, Blaenau Ffestiniog can look particularly desolate, but it's worth a call for the **Llechwedd Slate Caverns** a mile north, reached by bus. A train takes visitors into the side of the mountain, past an underground lake and spectacular caverns to the very bottom of the mine, on Britain's steepest train incline (daily 10am–4.15/5.15pm; £6.95; *www.llechwedd.co.uk*). Should the brooding scenery have cast its spell over you, **B&B** can be had at *Afallon,* Manod Rd (01766/830468; ④).

Most people push on to **BETWS-Y-COED**, ten miles northeast by ordinary train. A popular base for Snowdonia National Park – though no serious walks start here – the town has one of the prettiest settings in Wales but is overrun with visitors in summer, many coming here just to see the **Swallow Falls** in the wooded Llugwy Valley, two miles west of town. If you want to stay to appreciate the wood-and-water setting after the day-trippers have moved on, try the **B&B** above the *Riverside Restaurant,* Holyhead Rd (☎01690/710650; ③), though keen walkers would be better catered for at the **hostel** at Capel Curig, six miles west by bus #19 (☎01690/720225; ②). In Betws-y-Coed the *Glan Aber* pub and *Pont-y-Pair,* both on Holyhead Rd, do reasonable bar meals and are the liveliest places for a drink. Beside the station sits the **tourist office** (daily 9/10am–4/6pm; ☎01690/710426, *www.betws-y-coed.co.uk*). From Betws-y-Coed there are trains and buses to Llandudno Junction, on the main Chester–Holyhead line.

Conwy and Caernarfon

A mile or two west of Llandudno Junction is **CONWY**, where Edward I's magnificent **Castle** (April–Oct daily 9.30am–5/6pm; Nov–March Mon–Sat 9.30am–4pm, Sun 11am–4pm; £3.60) and the town walls have been listed by UNESCO as a World Heritage Site. Inside you'll also find the **tourist office** (same times; ☎01492/592248). The ramparts offer fine views of Thomas Telford's recently restored 1826 **suspension bridge** (July & Aug daily 10am–5pm;

April–June, Sept & Oct closed Tues; £1) over the River Conwy. For **B&B** try *Gwynedd Guesthouse*, 10 Upper Gate St (☎01492/596537; ③), or, if it's full (as it often is), the *Pen-y-Bryn*, 28 High St (☎01492/596445; ④). Otherwise, there's the *Larkhill* **HI hostel**, Sychnant Pass Rd, ten minutes west of the centre (☎01492/593571; ③).

West of Conwy, trains pass through Bangor on the way to Holyhead. To get to **CAERNAR-FON** – the springboard for trips into Snowdonia from the north – you'll need bus #5, #5A or #5B from the bus station off Bangor High St. Every Prince of Wales since 1301 has been invested in doughty **Caernarfon Castle** (April–Oct daily 9.30am–5/6pm; Nov–March Mon–Sat 9.30am–4pm, Sun 11am–4pm; £4.20), built in 1283 and arguably the most splendid castle in Britain. The walls completely dominate the town, but form only a shell enclosing a three-acre space.

Buses to Penllyn St stop on Castle Sq, a few metres from the **tourist office** on Castle St (Easter–Oct daily 10am–6pm; Nov–Easter closed Wed; ☎01286/672232). In town, the cheapest place **to stay** is *Totters*, an excellent backpacker hostel at 2 High St (☎01286/672963; ①); *Isfryn Guesthouse*, 11 Church St (☎01286/675628; ③) is another good bet. There is a **cyber-café** at Dimension 4 (☎01286/678777; daily; £3/hr) on Bangor St.

Llanberis and Snowdon

Regular buses run the seven miles northeast from Caernarfon to **LLANBERIS**, a lakeside village bursting to grow into a town in the shadow of **Snowdon**, at 3560ft the highest mountain in England and Wales. With the biggest concentration of guest houses, hostels and restaurants in Snowdonia, Llanberis offers the perfect base for even the most tentative mountain exploration. The longest but easiest ascent of the mountain is the Llanberis Path, a signposted five-mile hike (3hr) that is manageable by anyone reasonably fit, although the final stretch up to the Yr Wyddfa summit involves a bit of a scramble. Alternatively, you can cop out and take the generally steam-hauled **Snowdon Mountain Railway** (daily mid-March to October; £15) which operates from Llanberis to the summit café, pub and post office, weather permitting (note that in adverse conditions trains may terminate at Clogwyn, three-quarters of the way up the mountain). Return tickets permit half an hour's viewing from the summit. The slate quarries which seared Llanberis's surroundings now lie idle, with the **Welsh Slate Museum** (daily 9.30/10am–4.30/5.30pm; free; *www.nmgw.ac.uk/wsm*) remaining as a memorial to the workers' tough lives. Nearby, the Dinorwig Pumped Storage Hydro Station is carved out of the mountain and can be visited on underground tours starting at the **Electric Mountain Museum** (Easter–Dec daily 9.30/10.30am–4.30/5.30pm; Feb–Easter Thurs–Sun only; £5), whose displays take a Disney approach to the complexities of Welsh history.

Buses stop near the **tourist office**, 41a High St (daily 10am–4/6pm; Nov–March closed Mon & Tues; ☎01286/870765). Walkers have a good choice of **accommodation**. There are several different **HI hostels**, all served by Gwynedd bus #11 from Llanberis, and each at the base of a footpath up Snowdon: *Llanberis*, Llwyn Celyn (☎01286/870280; ②); *Snowdon Ranger*, Rhyd Ddu (☎01286/650391; ②); *Bryn Gwynant*, Nantgwynant (☎01766/890251; ②); and *Pen-y-Pass*, Nantgwynant (☎01286/870428; ②). Llanberis's High St is lined with small **hotels**: try *The Heights* at no. 74 (☎01286/871179; ⑤), which also has eight-bed dorms (②), or *Dolafon*, another pleasant B&B (☎01286/870933; ⑤). The enduringly popular *Pete's Eats*, 40 High St, satisfies walkers' appetites.

Holyhead, Anglesey

The Menai Bridge was built by Thomas Telford in 1826 to connect North Wales with the island of **Anglesey** (Ynys Môn) across the Menai Straits, and it's one of the two chief sights on the little island (*www.anglesey.gov.uk*), even though it's been superseded by a newer rival alongside. The other draw is the last of Edward I's masterpieces, **Beaumaris Castle** (April–Oct daily 9.30am–5/6pm; Nov–March Mon–Sat 9.30am–4pm, Sun 11am–4pm; £2.50), reached by bus #53, #57 or #58 from Bangor. The giant castle was built in 1295 to guard the straits and has a fairy-tale moat enclosing its twelve sturdy towers. Nonetheless, most tourist traffic in this direction speeds past to **HOLYHEAD** (Caergybi), the busiest Welsh ferry-port, with several daily ferry and catamaran sailings with Irish Ferries (☎0870/517 1717) to **Dublin**, and Stena Line (☎0870/570 7070) to both Dublin and Dún Laoghaire a little south, as well as some bargain day-trips. **B&Bs** galore are within a few minutes' walk of the combined bus, train and ferry terminal, including *Glan Ifor*, 8 Walthew Ave (☎01407/764238; ③) and many more on the same street. The **tourist office** is on Penrhos Beach Rd (daily 10am–4.30/5.30pm; ☎01407/762622, *www.holyhead.com*).

SCOTLAND

Scotland (*www.holiday.scotland.net*) presents a model example of how a small nation can retain its identity within the confines of a larger one. Unlike the Welsh, the Scots successfully repulsed the expansionist designs of England, and when the "old enemies" first formed a union in 1603, it was because King James VI of Scotland inherited the English throne, though the parliaments were not united for another hundred years. Even then, Scotland retained many of its own institutions, notably distinctive legal and educational systems, and in 1997 the Scots voted to re-establish a parliament; elections were held in May 1999, and by 2000 it was taking a full and active role in day-by-day affairs. It is unlikely that this will lead to full Scottish independence, but in the meantime the country is imbued with a newfound energy and optimism.

Most of the population clusters in the narrow central belt between the two principal cities: stately **Edinburgh**, the national capital, with its magnificent architecture and imperious natural setting, and earthy **Glasgow**, a powerhouse of the Industrial Revolution and still a hard-working, hard-playing place. The third city, **Aberdeen**, set in one of the rare strips of lowland in the north, is now fabulously wealthy from the proceeds of offshore oil, and its pristine granite buildings and abundant parks and gardens look even more immaculate than ever. Yet it's the **Highlands**, severely depopulated but comprising over two-thirds of the total area, which provide most people's enduring image of Scotland. The dramatic landscapes are further enhanced by the volatile climate, producing an extraordinary variety of moods and colours. Here you'll find some of the last wildernesses in Europe, though even the highest mountain, **Ben Nevis**, is an uncomplicated ascent for the average walker, while much of the finest scenery – such as the famous **Loch Lomond** and **Loch Ness**, and the islands of the **Hebrides** – can be enjoyed without too much effort.

ScotRail (*www.scotrail.co.uk*) runs Scotland's **trains**, and also offers discount passes covering ferries and buses; Caledonian MacBrayne (*www.calmac.co.uk*) is the main **ferry** company for the islands, and has many special offers; and in addition to the Scottish YHA, there are several rival **hostelling** groups (*www.hostel-scotland.co.uk*; *www.highland-hostels.co.uk*; *www.haggis-backpackers.com*; and *www.scotlands-top-hostels.com*), some of which operate private buses between their hostels.

Edinburgh

EDINBURGH is the showcase capital of Scotland, a well-heeled, cosmopolitan and cultured place which regularly tops the polls as Britain's best place to live. Its natural contours, stone-built houses and monuments make it visually stunning: the fairy-tale castle, perched on the summit of an extinct volcano, looks over the rooftops towards the 823-foot rise of Arthur's Seat, from where there are breathtaking vistas of hills and water. Inevitably, the city is suffering from the increasingly intrusive trappings of the tourist trade. The 430,000 population swells massively in high season, peaking in mid-August during Festival time, when an estimated one million visitors come to town for the biggest arts event in Europe. Yet despite this annual invasion, and despite its proximity to the border, Edinburgh is emphatically Scottish – and is now building a parliament to prove it.

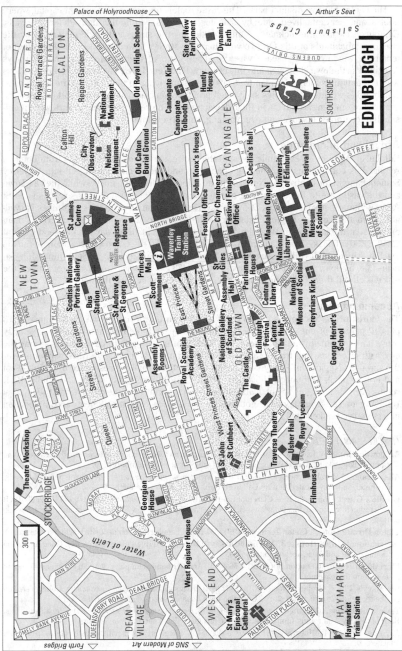

EDINBURGH

Palace of Holyroodhouse △

△ Arthur's Seat

Salisbury Crags

QUEENS DRIVE

SOUTHSIDE

N

LONDON ROAD

LEOPOLD PLACE

Royal Terrace Gardens

CALTON

Regent Gardens

ROYAL TERRACE

REGENT TERRACE

REGENT ROAD

Site of New Parliament

Dynamic Earth

Huntly House

Canongate Kirk

Old Royal High School

Calton Hill

National Monument

Nelson Monument

City Observatory

Old Calton Burial Ground

Canongate Tolbooth

CANONGATE

St Cecilia's Hall

PLEASANCE

NICOLSON STREET

BROUGHTON STREET

PICARDY PL

LEITH WALK

LEITH STREET

WATERLOO PLACE

CARLTON ROAD

John Knox's House

Festival Office

City Chambers

Festival Fringe Office

Magdalen Chapel

University of Edinburgh

Festival Theatre

SOUTH BR.

St James Centre

York Place

ALBANY STREET

YORK PLACE

ELDER ST

Register House

NORTH BRIDGE

Waverley Train Station

Central Library

National Library of Scotland

Royal Museum of Scotland

GEORGE IV BRIDGE

BRISTO SQUARE

GEORGE SQUARE

FORREST RD

NEW TOWN

ABERCROMBY PLACE

DUBLIN ST

Scottish National Portrait Gallery

Bus Station

St Andrew & St George

Princes Mall

Scott Monument

i

East Princes Street Gardens

National Gallery of Scotland

St Giles

Assembly Hall

St Parliament

COWGATE

National Museum of Scotland

Greyfriars Kirk

George Heriot's School

LAURISTON PLACE

DRUMMOND PLACE

GREAT KING STREET

DUNDAS STREET

ST ANDREW SQUARE

THISTLE ST

HANOVER STREET

Assembly Rooms

FREDERICK STREET

Royal Scottish Academy

THE MOUND

OLD TOWN

Edinburgh Festival Centre "The Hub"

JOHNSTON TERRACE

WEST PORT

HERIOT ROW

Queen Street Gardens

Queen Street

CASTLE STREET

GEORGE STREET

HILL STREET

ROSE STREET

West Princes Street Gardens

PRINCES STREET

The Castle

GRASSMARKET

COWGATE

HOWE STREET

FREDERICK STREET

YOUNG STREET

CASTLE STREET

CHARLOTTE SQUARE

HOPE ST

St John

St Cuthbert

KING'S STABLES

Traverse Theatre

Usher Hall

Royal Lyceum

LOTHIAN ROAD

GRINDLAY ST

BREAD STREET

Filmhouse

MORRISON STREET

ROYAL CIRCUS

GLOUCESTER LANE

Theatre Workshop

STOCKBRIDGE

MORAY PLACE

GLENFINLAS ST

Georgian House

AINSLIE PLACE

GREAT STUART ST

DARNAWAY ST

Water of Leith

DEAN BRIDGE

300 m

0

West Register House

QUEENSFERRY ST

QUEENSFERRY PL

SHANDWICK PL

WEST END

WILLIAM STREET

COATES CRES

ATHOLL CRESCENT

MELVILLE STREET

WEST MAITLAND ST

PALMERSTON PLACE

St Mary's Episcopal Cathedral

WEST APPROACH ROAD

HAYMARKET

Haymarket Train Station

COMELY BANK AVENUE

QUEENSFERRY ROAD

ANN STREET

DEAN VILLAGE

DEAN BRIDGE

BELFORD ROAD

DEAN BRIDGE

GLENOGLE RD

△ Forth Bridges

△ SNG of Modern Art

© Crown copyright

The centre has two distinct parts. The castle rock is the core of the ancient capital, where nobles and servants lived side by side for centuries within the tight defensive walls. Edinburgh earned the nickname "Auld Reekie" for the smog and smell generated by the cramped inhabitants of this **Old Town**, where the streets flowed with sewage tipped out of tenement windows and disease was rife. The riddle of medieval streets and alleyways remained a rundown slum well into this century. The **New Town** was begun in the late 1700s with the announcement of a plan to develop farmland lying to the north of the castle rock. Edinburgh's wealthier worthies speculated profitably on tracts of this land and engaged the services of eminent architects in their development. The result of their labours was an outstanding example of Georgian town planning, still largely intact.

Arrival and information

Edinburgh **airport** is seven miles west of the centre, served by cheap flights from London; regular bus connections into the city operate around the clock. **Trains** pull into Waverley Station, bang in the centre; the New Town and Princes St lie to the north, while the Old Town and the castle are to the south. The **bus** terminal for local and inter-city services is on St Andrew Square, across Princes St from Waverley; information on routes and times is available from the Lothian Region Transport office, 100m to the left of the Waverley's main entrance, at the junction of Waverley Bridge and Market St (their day-pass is good value at £2.40, £1.50 off-peak). The main **tourist office** is at 3 Princes St, above the station on the top level of Princes Mall (July & Aug Mon–Sat 9am–6/7pm, Sun 9am–5pm; Sept–June Mon–Sat 9am–4.30/5.30pm, Sun 9.30am–2.30pm; ☎0131/473 3800, *www.edinburgh.org*). When the office is closed there is a 24hr touch-screen information service at the door.

Accommodation

The tourist office has details of all grades of **accommodation**, and will book rooms for £3 plus 10 percent of one night's stay (free online). Space in central hotels and hostels may prove hard to come by in peak season, but **B&B** is offered in hundreds of houses around the city, with prices starting from £15 per person. In addition, you can get **student rooms** over the summer; Napier University (☎0131/445 4291; ③) has halls of residence open July–Sept and Pollock Hall, Edinburgh University (☎0131/651 2011; ⑥), has single and double B&B rooms over Easter & July–Sept. **Campsites** are on the fringes of the city. During the Festival (mid-Aug to early Sept) you've got virtually no chance of getting cheap accommodation unless you've booked well ahead.

HOTELS AND B&BS

Ardgowan House, 1 Lady Road (☎0131/6677774, *ardgowan@sol.co.uk*). Private or small dorm-rooms in this immaculately kept, non-smoking B&B: one of the best deals in Edinburgh. ③.

Ailsa Craig, 24 Royal Terrace (☎0131/556 1022, *www.townhousehotels.co.uk*). Well-furnished and friendly family hotel, superbly located behind Calton Hill with views across the Firth. ⑦.

Brodie's Guest House, 22 East Claremont St (☎0131/556 4032, *rose.olbert@saqnet.co.uk*). Friendly B&B in a Victorian town house, ideally located on the eastern edge of the New Town. Rates include a good breakfast. ⑥.

Clifton Private Hotel, 1 Clifton Terrace (☎0131/337 1002). Family-run hotel opposite Haymarket station. ④.

International Guest House, 37 Mayfield Gdns (☎0131/667 2511, *intergh@easynet.co.uk*). Good reputation for comfortable and clean accommodation. ⑥.

Marrakech Hotel, 30 London St (☎0131/556 4444). Another family-run place, with an excellent Moroccan restaurant in the basement. ⑥.

Six Mary's Place, Raeburn Place (☎0131/332 8965, *www.socialfirms.org.uk/guesthouse*). Collectively run smoke-free guest house in a restored Georgian town house. Quality vegetarian meals. ⑥.

Teviotdale House, 53 Grange Loan (☎0131/667 4376, *teviotdale.house@btinternet.com*). Probably the best B&B in the city – all rooms (non-smoking) have private facilities and the food is glorious. ⑥.

Thrums Hotel, 14 Minto St (☎0131/667 5545/8545). Excellent hotel with equally classy restaurant attached. ⑧.

HOSTELS

Belford, 6 Douglas Gardens (☎0131/225 6209, *www.hoppo.com*). Housed in a redundant Arts and Crafts church near the West End of the city centre. Dorms ③; doubles ④.

Brodies Backpacker, 12 High St (☎0131/556 6770, *www.brodieshostels.co.uk*). Small, homely and well-situated towards the foot of the Royal Mile. ④.

Bruntsfield, 7 Bruntsfield Crescent (☎0131/255 9666). Large, strictly-run HI hostel a mile south of Princes St – bus #11, #15 or #16. Curfew 2am. ②.

Castle Rock, 15 Johnstone Terrace (☎0131/225 9666, *www.scotlands-top-hostels.com*). Busy hostel tucked below the castle ramparts. No curfew. ③.

Cowgate, 94 Cowgate (☎0131/226 2153). A large backpackers hostel half given over to students in the winter months. ③.

Edinburgh Backpackers, 65 Cockburn St (☎0131/220 1717, *www.hoppo.com*). Superior, well-thought-out hostel – right down to the tartan bedspreads. Dorms ③; doubles ④.

Eglinton, 18 Eglinton Crescent (☎0131/337 1120). To the west of the centre, near Haymarket train station, the last stop before Waverley. More easy-going HI than the Bruntsfield place. Curfew 2am. ③.

High Street Hostel, 8 Blackfriars St (☎0131/557 3984, *www.scotlands-top-hostels.com*). Large lively, if slightly scruffy, hostel just off the Royal Mile. No curfew. ③.

Princes Street West Backpackers, 3 Queensferry St (☎0131/226 2939). A cosmopolitan hostel in a historic court building at the east end of Princes St, but rooms are shabby. Partner hostel at 5 West Register St (☎0131/556 6894). Dorms ②; doubles ③.

Royal Mile Backpackers, 105 High St (☎0131/557 6120, *www.scotlands-top-hostels.com*). Small friendly place, linked with High St and Castle Rock hostels. ③.

CAMPSITES

Mortonhall Park, 38 Mortonhall Gate, Frogston Rd East (☎0131/664 1533, *mhallcp@aol.com*). A well-equipped site five miles out of town, convenient for walking the nearby Braid Hills. Includes an onsite restaurant and games room – bus #11 from Princes St. April–Oct; £9.80 per night.

Edinburgh Caravan Club Site, Marine Drive, Silverknowes (☎0131/312 6874). Immaculate and friendly year-round site close to the shore four miles north; a 20min ride on bus #14, #8a and #10 from North Bridge and Princes St. £7.50 per night.

The City

The cobbled **Royal Mile** – composed of Castlehill, Lawnmarket, High St and Canongate – is the busiest stretch of the tourist itinerary and the central thoroughfare of the Old Town, connecting the Palace of Holyroodhouse (see p.222) to the **Castle** (daily 9.30am–5/6pm; £7.50). For centuries the seat of kings, the castle is thought to have evolved from an Iron Age fort, the sheer volcanic rock on which it stands providing formidable defence on three sides. Within its precincts is St Margaret's Chapel, a Norman church that's probably the oldest building in the city. Also open to the public are the state apartments, including the room in which James VI of Scotland was born, the Great Hall with its magnificent hammerbeam roof, the ancient crown jewels of Scotland and the even older Stone of Destiny, the coronation stone of the kings of Scotland returned north of the border in 1996 after a 700-year stay in London. There's a large military museum here, too, and the castle esplanade provided a dramatic setting for the world-famous Military Tattoo, formerly staged every year during the Festival.

Descending the Lawnmarket from the castle, you'll pass **Gladstone's Land** (April–Oct Mon–Sat 10am–5pm, Sun 2–5pm; £3.50), a magnificent six-storey mansion named after the merchant who set up shop there in 1617. Inside, the National Trust for Scotland has restored the painted ceilings and furnished the upper floors as they would have been during his day. Behind Gladstone's Land, the **Writers' Museum** (or Lady Stair's House; Mon–Sat 10am–5pm, during Festival also Sun 2–5pm; free), is dedicated to Sir Walter Scott, Robert Burns and Robert Louis Stevenson, with memorabilia of the trio housed on three floors of the building.

The High St section of the Royal Mile starts at the **High Kirk of St Giles** (daily 9am–5/7pm), whose beautiful crown-shaped spire is an Edinburgh landmark. In all likelihood there's been a church here since the eighth century, but the existing building is chiefly late fourteenth and early fifteenth century, with large-scale alterations carried out in the nineteenth. At the east end of the simple and impressive interior, the Thistle Chapel, designed in 1911, is an amazing display of mock-Gothic woodcarving. The heart-shaped cobble pattern set outside the west door is known as the Heart of Midlothian – passers-by traditionally spit on it for luck. To the rear are the Neoclassical law courts, which incorporate the seventeenth-century **Parliament House**, under whose spectacular hammerbeam roof the Scottish parliament met until the 1707 Union with England. Heading south across George IV Bridge, you come to Chambers St, home of the highly acclaimed **National Museum of Scotland** (Mon–Sat 10am–5pm, Tues until 8pm, Sun noon–5pm; free; *www.nms.ac.uk*), which tells the history of Scotland through its many artefacts, culminating in a thought-provoking gallery on the top floor; the objects it contains, ranging from a football shirt to a Saab convertible, are the result of a range of Scots being asked to pick a single representative object. In the same complex, but with its own entrance, is the **Royal Museum** (same times), which houses a typically rich collection of colonial acquisitions.

Canongate starts at the junction of St Mary's and Jeffrey streets, the original city boundary. Before the New Town was built, Canongate was the chic end of the Royal Mile, where nobles and merchants established their homes. Moray House, with its balcony jutting out over the pavement, is a rare survivor, as is sixteenth-century **Huntly House** (Mon–Sat 10am–5pm, during Festival also Sun 2–5pm; free), now a museum focusing on the history of the city. Across the road is **Canongate Tolbooth** (same hours; free), once a prison, now a museum dedicated to Edinburgh's social history; it features reconstructed interiors such as a wartime kitchen and a washhouse. Nearby **Canongate Kirk**, set back from the street, was built in the late 1600s after the parish church in Holyrood Abbey was converted into a Catholic chapel. The simple church is used by the Royal Family whenever they are at Holyrood, as the coat of arms on one of the pews indicates. Just south of Canongate is the site of the new Scottish **Parliament**, sure to be a major draw whenever it finally opens. South again, backing onto Holyrood Park, is the futuristic tented structure of **Our Dynamic Earth** (April–Oct daily 10am–6pm; Nov–March Wed–Sat 10am–5pm; £6.50), a trendy exhibition on the earth and the environment using hi-tech audio-visual-tactile displays.

The **Palace of Holyroodhouse** (Apr–Oct tours daily 9.30am–3.15/5.15pm; £6.5), the Royal Family's official residence in Scotland, looks out over the Queen's Park, 650 acres of wilderness in the heart of the city. Except when the royals are in residence or when there are garden parties, the public are admitted to the sumptuous state rooms and historic apartments, which include the chamber where Mary Queen of Scots, pregnant with her son James VI, witnessed the murder of her courtier David Rizzio by associates of her husband. The gaunt, roofless ruins of Holyrood Abbey stand within the palace grounds; dating mainly from the turn of the thirteenth century, they were the inspiration for Mendelssohn's *Scottish Symphony*. From the palace, fine walks lead across parkland up to the arc of the **Salisbury Crags** and **Arthur's Seat** beyond, where a fairly stiff climb is rewarded with magnificent views of the city and out over the Firth of Forth towards Fife.

THE NEW TOWN

The most pleasant route from the Old Town to the Georgian grid of the New Town is to descend the Mound to the **National Gallery of Scotland**, just west of Waverley Station (Mon–Sat 10am–5pm, Sun 2–5pm; free) and one of the best small collections in Europe. Arranged chronologically, it includes representative or important works from a large number of major European artists, including Raphael, Titian, Rembrandt, Rubens and El Greco, and of course an unrivalled show of Scottish works, including David Wilkie's *Pitlessie Fair*, Henry Raeburn's *The Reverend Robert Walker Skating* – a postcard favourite – and Allan Ramsay's *Portrait of Rousseau*. Opposite, the **Royal Scottish Academy** is the grandest exhibition space in the city, usually hosting a major international show during the Festival.

The Academy looks onto the broad avenue of **Princes Street**, the main shopping area, with chain stores crammed in cheek-by-jowl. About 100m to the east is the spire of the **Scott Monument**, decorated with figures from Sir Walter's novels and now oddly piebald following restoration work. Equally conspicuous is the **National Monument** atop Calton Hill at the far eastern end of Princes St; it would have been a copy of the Parthenon had money not run out in 1829. Built along a ridge parallel to Princes St, George St capitalizes on the views to the north: standing at its junction with Hanover St you look down across the New Town and out beyond the city. The **Assembly Rooms**, 54 George St, are a glorious confection of ornate plasterwork and extravagant chandeliers; one of the most prestigious theatre venues during the Festival, at other times they're used for a variety of purposes, from tea dances to craft fairs. At its western end George St runs into suave Charlotte Sq, the most elegant square in the New Town. The National Trust for Scotland has restored no. 7 – the **Georgian House** (Mar–Oct Mon–Sat 10am–5pm, Sun 2–5pm; £5) – to a state of pristine perfection, stocking it with magnificent specimens from the workshops of Hepplewhite, Sheraton and Chippendale, the great names of eighteenth-century furniture. North of George St is the broad avenue of Queen St, at whose eastern end stands the **Scottish National Portrait Gallery** (Mon–Sat 10am–5pm, Sun 2–5pm; free). As well as a collection of portraits of prominent Scots – many of them outstanding examples of the genre – it contains a collection of photographic works from the beginnings of the art to the present day.

In the northwest corner of the New Town, beyond Queen St Gardens, lies **Stockbridge**, a smart residential suburb with bohemian pretensions – especially noticeable around the atmospheric huddle of old mill buildings known as Dean Village. From here Belford Rd leads up to the **Scottish National Gallery of Modern Art** and its **Dean Gallery** extension opposite (Mon–Sat 10am–5pm, Sun 2–5pm; free) where the likes of Matisse, Picasso, Giacometti and Mondrian share space with modern Scottish artists such as Paolozzi and Ian Hamilton Finlay in a reasonably broad-ranging display of examples from most of the significant artistic movements of the twentieth century, while the wooded grounds make a fine setting for the sculptures of Moore, Epstein and many others.

Another luscious retreat from the city is offered by the **Royal Botanic Garden** (daily 9.30am–dusk; free) on the north side of Stockbridge, entered from either Arboretum Place or Inverleith Row; it's served by buses #23, #27 or #37 from the city centre. Covering seventy acres, the gardens support a vast array of rare plants from around the world in their landscaped grounds and magnificent hothouses.

Eating and drinking

Edinburgh is well served with **restaurants** to suit most tastes, but – as with accommodation – there's a lot of pressure on space. Whatever you plump for, be sure to book in advance at the ones for which we've given phone numbers. Unless specified otherwise, you can eat well at all our recommendations for under £10. Edinburgh's **cafés** are among the most enjoyable spots in the city – serving coffee, food and most often alcohol too, and sometimes doubling as exhibition and performance spaces during the Festival. The city's multitudinous **bars** are among the most congenial in the country, with live music a frequent bonus.

CAFÉS AND RESTAURANTS

Blue Moon, 36 Broughton St. Coffee and snacks at this friendly lesbian/gay café; all welcome.

Café 9, 9a Castle St. Self-service basement café with more healthy food than the usual; one of the few cheap places anywhere near Princes St.

Chinese Home Cooking, 34 West Preston St (☎0131/668 4946). Plain, straightforward café, with a three-course lunch for £5.

Elephant & Bagels, Nicolson Sq. Scotland's only genuine bagel café that is cheap, filling yet healthy.

Elephant House, 21 George IV Bridge. An enduringly popular and cosy café, much loved by locals and students alike.

Good Year, 21 Argyle Place (☎0131/229 4404). Cantonese and Peking style. Good family atmosphere and inexpensive food (average dish £3).

Kalpna, 2 St Patrick Sq (☎0131/667 9890) Prize-winning vegetarian Indian; lunchtime all-you-can-eat buffet for £5. Closed Sun.

Khushi's, 16 Drummond St. Popular and very cheap curries in the former university canteen. Closed Sun.

Henderson's, 94 Hanover St. Well-known self-service restaurant with a lively atmosphere, good-value vegetarian food and occasional live music.

Ndebele, 57 Home St (☎0131/221 1141). Colourful African café offering snacks and juices.

Pierre Victoire, 10 Victoria St (☎0131/225 1721). Excellent bargain menus presented with Gallic dash.

Le Sept, 7 Old Fishmarket Close (☎0131/225 5428). Upstairs gets busy early, serving filling crepes and a good vegetarian selection. Downstairs is posher and pricier.

Susie's Diner, 51 West Nicolson St (☎0131/667 8729). Popular student veggie/vegan café.

Tampopo, 25a Thistle St (☎0131/220 5254). Excellent noodle bar. Closed Sun.

Tinelli, 139 Easter Rd (☎0131/652 1932). A well-kept secret: small and efficient dining room serving the real North Italian thing. Closed Sun.

Viva Mexico, 41 Cockburn St (☎0131/226 5145) and 50 East Fountainbridge (☎0131/228 4005). Run by Mexican–Scot husband and wife team. Lavish portions and great margaritas.

PUBS AND BARS

Bannerman's Bar, 212 Cowgate. The best pub on the street, with an old-world atmosphere and a good range of real ales and food.

Bar Kohl, 54 George IV Bridge. Trendy Hip-Hop vodka bar, with a huge choice of bevvies.

Café Royal, 17a West Register St, off Princes St. Beautiful horseshoe-shaped bar, original Victorian decor, frequented after office hours by city professionals. Open Thurs–Sat.

City Café 2, 19 Blair St. A stylish yet inviting café/bar that is popular with the pre-club crowd.

Garibaldi's, 97a Hanover St. A basement Mexican bar serving authentic dishes and cocktails alongside a dancefloor.

Last Drop Tavern, 74 Grassmarket. A late-closing studenty pub with an admirable range of healthy pub food.

Malt Shovel, 11 Cockburn St. Good beer, plenty of local colour and a wide choice of single malt whiskies; live jazz some evenings.

Rose St Brewery, 55 Rose St. Edinburgh's only microbrewery.

NIGHTLIFE

Edinburgh's **nightlife** is as lively as that of any city in Britain, and venues change name and location with such speed that the only way to keep up with what's going on is to get hold of *The List* magazine, a comprehensive source of information published fortnightly. The Playhouse theatre generally has long-running musicals, with occasional rock bands. *Canon's Gait*, 232 Canongate, hosts local indie and rock bands. Visiting bands and Dj's play the *Venue*, 15 Calton Rd, and *La Belle Angèle*, Cowgate. There is a lively **club** scene: currently most popular are *Wilkie House*, Cowgate, the *Honeycomb*, 15–17 Niddry St, the *Cavendish* at West Tollcross with a long-running reggae/ragga and R'n'B night on Saturdays, and the *Liquid Room*, 9c Victoria St. There are a number of mainstream discos on Lothian Rd, the largest being *Revolution*. **Gay** nightlife is centred round the top of Leith Walk, notably at *CC Bloom's* next to the Playhouse on Greenside Place.

The Edinburgh Festival

The hugely entertaining **Edinburgh Festival** (*www.edinburghfestival.co.uk*), billed as the world's largest arts jamboree, was founded in 1947, and now attracts artists of all kinds for three weeks in August and September. The show is, in fact, a multiplicity of festivals, with the official programme traditionally presenting highbrow fare, while the frenetic **Fringe** – run by a separate organization – offers a melange of just about everything else in the field of the performing and visual arts. In addition, there's a Film Festival focusing on the latest movies, a Jazz Festival, and a Book Festival. A Folk Festival takes place in early April. Tickets are available at the venues and from the International Festival Office, 21 Market St (☎0131/473 2000) or the Fringe Office, 180 High St (☎0131/226 5257).

Listings

Airport enquiries ☎0131/333 1000.

Bike rental Central Cycles, 13 Lochrin Place (☎0131/228 6333); Scottish Cycle Safaris, 29 Blackfriars St (☎0131/556 5560).

Car rental Avis (☎0131/337 6363); Europcar (☎0131/557 3456); Hertz (☎0131/557 5272).

Consulates Australia, 37 George St (☎0131/624 3333); Canada, 30 Lothian Rd (☎0131/220 4333); USA, 3 Regent Terrace (☎0131/556 8315).

Internet access EasyEverything, 58 Rose St; Tourist Information Centre, Princes Mall (£3/hr).

Medical facilities Royal Infirmary, Lauriston Place (☎0131/536 1000), has a 24hr A&E department. Boots pharmacy, 48 Shandwick Place, is open Mon–Fri 8am–9pm, Sat 8am–7pm, Sun 10am–5pm.

Police HQ is on Fettes Ave (☎0131/311 3131).

Post office The central post office is in St James' Shopping Centre, off Leith St near the bus station (Mon 9am–5.30pm, Tues–Fri 8.30am–5.30pm, Sat 8.30am–6pm).

Taxis Central Taxis (☎0131/229 2468); City Cabs (☎0131/228 1211).

Glasgow

GLASGOW is the largest city in Scotland, home to 750,000 people. It once thrived on the tobacco trade with the American colonies, on cotton production and, most famously, on the shipbuilding on the River Clyde. The civic architecture of Victorian Glasgow was as grand as any in Britain, and the West End suburbs were regarded as among the best designed in the country. Since its heyday, however, it has not enjoyed the best of reputations. The Gorbals area became notorious as one of the worst slums in Europe, and the city's association with violence and heavy drinking stuck to it like a curse. However, like many British cities, rejuvenated Glasgow has undergone another change of image, symbolized by its selection as the European City of Culture in 1990 and City of Architecture and Design in 1999, and by extensive urban renewal programmes. This is set to continue with the completion of the **IMAX** Cinema and the development of the futuristic **Science Centre** (*www.gsc.org.uk*) on the South Bank. Glasgow's remarkable overhaul as a dynamic cultural centre has firmly imbued it with a buzz and sophistication that sets it apart from Edinburgh's stuffier image.

Arrival and accommodation

Budget flights from London and the south serve both **Glasgow airport** (☎0141/887 1111), eight miles west, with regular buses shuttling to the central Buchanan St **bus station**; and **Prestwick airport** (☎01292/479822), thirty miles south, with trains into the centre. Glasgow has two main **train stations**, Central (which serves all points south) and Queen St (which serves Edinburgh and the north). It's an easy city to explore on foot – you can walk from the city centre to Kelvingrove Park in about thirty minutes. Should you tire of the pavements, the **Underground** is cheap and easy, operating on a circular chain of fifteen stations with a flat fare of 85p (day-pass £3.50). The **Strathclyde Travel Centre**, above St Enoch underground station (Mon–Sat 8.30am–5.30pm), has information on all public transport, as well as discount passes. The helpful **tourist office** is on the south side of George Sq, near the top of Queen St (Mon–Sat 9am–6/8pm, May–Sept also Sun 10am–6pm; ☎0141/204 4400, *www.seeglasgow.com*) and a smaller office is open at the airport (Mon–Sat 7.30am–5pm; 0141/8484440).

Park Terrace, near Kelvingrove Park, holds the **HI hostel** at no. 7 (☎0141/332 3004; ③) and *Glasgow Backpackers* at no. 17 (☎0141/332 9099; ③; July–Sept). *Berkeley Globetrotters Hostel* is more central at 63 Berkeley St (☎0141/221 7880, *www.geocities.com/globeberkeley*; ②) and the enormous *Euro Hostel* along the northern shore at 318 Clyde St (☎0141/222 2828; ③). Near Kelvingrove are a number of inexpensive **B&Bs**, including the *Alamo*, 46 Gray St (☎0141/339 2395; ④); the busy *Sandyford* **Hotel**, 904 Sauchiehall St (☎0141/334 0000; ⑥); and *Scott*, 417 Woodside Rd, beside Kelvingrove underground (☎0141/339 3750; ④). During summer, the universities of Glasgow (☎0800/027 2030) and Strathclyde (☎0141/553 4148) have inexpensive rooms. *Craigendmuir Park*, Campsie View (☎0141/779 4159), is a **campsite** four miles northeast, 15min walk from Stepps train station.

The City

Glasgow's centre lies on the north bank of the Clyde, around the grandiose and frenetic **George Square**, a little way east of Central Station. Just south of the square, down Queen St, is the **Gallery of Modern Art** (Mon–Sat 10am–5pm, Sun 11am–5pm; free). Formerly a "temple of commerce" built by one of the eighteenth-century tobacco lords, it now houses an exciting collection of contemporary Scots art, notably works by Ken Currie and John Bellay. Down by the river, southeast of George Square, is Glasgow Green, site of the **People's Palace** (Mon–Sat 10am–5pm, Sun 11am–5pm; free), opened in 1898 as a cultural centre for the area. It now records the social history of the city, giving most of its space to memorabilia of Victorian Glasgow. No visit to Glasgow would be complete without a trip to the **Barras**, a huge weekend market selling bric-a-brac, clothes, furniture and food just to the north of Glasgow Green, that invariably draws a crowd. Northeast of George Square is the **Cathedral** on Castle St (Mon–Sat 9.30am–4/6pm, Sun 2–4/5pm). Built in 1136, destroyed in 1192 and rebuilt soon after, it's the only Scottish mainland cathedral to have escaped the hands of the country's sixteenth-century religious reformers, whose hatred of anything that smacked of idolatry wrecked many of Scotland's ancient churches. This one survived chiefly thanks to the intervention of the city guilds. The magnificent vaulted crypt – the Laigh Kirk – is the principal remnant of the twelfth century, and contains the tomb of St Mungo, the city's patron. Compared to many English cathedrals, it's a modest-sized building, dominated by the adjacent **Necropolis**, resting place of the magnates who made Glasgow rich. Opened in 1832, and including a colossal figure of arch-reformer John Knox, the Necropolis is a compendium of jumbled pastiche architecture, its vaults mimicking every style from Byzantine to Gothic and Ottoman. On the other side of the cathedral is the **Provand's Lordship** (Mon–Sat 10am–5pm, Sun 11am–5pm; free), the oldest house in Glasgow. Built late in the fifteenth century as a priest's dwelling, it's now furnished with items mostly dating from later centuries, complete with waxwork occupants.

Follow Cathedral St west to Buchanan St and then turn right to reach **The Lighthouse** (Mon–Sat 10.30am–6pm, Thurs until 8pm, Sun noon–5pm), the first commission of Glasgow's famous architect Charles Rennie Mackintosh, whose distinctively streamlined Art Nouveau designs appear in shops all over the city; within is an exhibition devoted to the man (£2.55). From here, Glasgow's most famous thoroughfare, **Sauchiehall Street**, heads west. About halfway along, one block to the north, is the **Glasgow School of Art**, 167 Renfrew St, a remarkable building by Mackintosh that is a fusion of Scottish manor house solidity and modernist refinement. The interior, making maximum use of natural light, was also furnished and fitted entirely by the architect, and can be seen on a guided tour (Mon–Fri 11am & 2pm, Sat 10.30am & 11.30am; £5; booking advised ☎0141/353 4526). A short distance north is the **Tenement House**, 145 Buccleuch St (March–Oct daily 2–5pm; £3.50), which was occupied from 1911 to 1965 by the obsessive Agnes Toward, who seems to have been incapable of throwing anything away. Her home is full of nineteenth-century furniture and bric-a-brac, from box beds and gas lamps to bars of soap – an intriguing if sanitized vision of working-class life. About fifteen minutes' walk west, past the salubrious crescents of the West End, **Kelvingrove Park** is home to the **Glasgow Art Gallery and Museum** (Mon–Sat 10am–5pm, Sun 11am–5pm; free), a first-rate collection founded on donations from various captains of industry. Its particular strengths are pictures from Italy, the Low Countries and nineteenth-century France: Rembrandt's *Man in Armour* is perhaps the single most arresting painting, and there are notable pieces from Jordaens, Millet, van Gogh and Monet. Across the road in the Kelvin Hall, Argyle St, the **Transport Museum** (Mon–Sat 10am–5pm, Sun 11am–5pm; free) boasts fleets of trams, cars and motorbikes, with models and photos celebrating the Clyde shipyards and a reconstruction of a Glasgow street of 1938. On the northern edge of the park the campus of Glasgow University houses the **Hunterian Art Gallery** (Mon–Sat 9.30am–5pm; free), with works by Chardin, Stubbs and Rembrandt, plus a display of nineteenth- and twentieth-century Scottish art, but the highlights are a comprehensive survey of the output of James Abbott McNeill Whistler, and the reconstructed interior of Charles Rennie Mackintosh's house – an astonishingly fresh creation, even decades after his death.

About four miles south of the centre, in **Pollok Country Park** (bus #45, #48 or #57 from Union St, or train to Pollokshaws West), is the astonishing **Burrell Collection**, housed in a custom-built gallery (Mon–Sat 10am–5pm, Sun 11am–5pm; free). Sir William Burrell began collecting at the age of 15 and kept going until his death at 96, buying an average of two pieces a week. Works by Memling, Cézanne, Degas, Bellini and Géricault feature among the paintings, while in adjoining galleries there are pieces from ancient Rome and Greece, medieval European arts and crafts, and a massive selection of Chinese artefacts, with outstanding ceramics, jades and bronzes. Somewhat overshadowed, the nearby **Pollok House** (daily 10/11am–4/5pm; April–Oct; £4, rest of year free) is a lovely eighteenth-century mansion containing paintings by El Greco, Goya and Murillo, and works by William Blake.

Eating, drinking and nightlife

For **snacks**, one of the best and cheapest places is the *Grosvenor Café*, Ashton Lane, just off Byres Rd in the West End. On the same street, *Ashoka* does excellent-value Indian **meals**, while on Byres Rd itself the *University Café* serves up cheap, filling fare to students. The Mackintosh-designed *Willow Tea Rooms*, 217 Sauchiehall St, is good for a light meal, while the ultra-ornate *Corinthian,* 191 Ingram Rd, is worth a visit for the decor alone. For innovative organic food, try the bright and airy *Grassroots Café*, 97 St Georges Rd. *Insomnia*, 38 Woodlands Rd, is a cheap 24hr café packed with the post-club crowd.

Of the huge number of **pubs**, *The Horseshoe Bar*, 17 Drury St, has the longest bar in the UK and plenty of atmosphere. *Arta* on 13 Walls St has a sumptuous velvet curtain interior, while the *Halt Bar*, 106 Woodlands Rd, often has live music; *Bargo*, Albion Rd, is a trendy pre-club DJ-bar; the *Scotia*, 112 Stockwell St, has live folk music; and *Del Monica's*, 68 Virginia St, is the liveliest gay bar. *King Tut's Wah Wah Hut*, 272a Vincent St, is famous as the place where Oasis were discovered, and still hosts excellent **gigs**. The fortnightly magazine *The List* is the best source of **club** listings. Pick of the crop include: *The Arches*, on Midland St; and *The Tunnel*, 84 Mitchell St with soul, funk and house nights. For big name touring DJs head for *Privilege*, 69 Hope St. The **Centre for Contemporary Arts**, 346 Sauchiehall St, has a reputation for a programme of controversial performances and exhibitions. The wonderful Glasgow Film Theatre, Rose St, shows art films and old favourites.

The Scottish Borders

Scotland's **Border Country** (*www.scot-borders.co.uk*), an upland region of rich farmland, secluded valleys, quiet villages and bustling little market towns, was for centuries the frontline between Scotland and England, and its history became an inspiration for its most famous resident, Sir Walter Scott, whose writings were to create the enduring romanticized image of Scotland. During the twelfth-century reign of King David I, four magnificent abbeys were built in the region as showpieces of the independent Scottish state, and these now rank among the most evocative ruins in Europe. The defensive towers which were their secular counterparts were often replaced in more peaceful times by magnificent stately homes. The Border towns are connected to each other and to Edinburgh by plentiful bus services; contact local tourist offices or visit the Web site for information, and to book accommodation – although they're easy to visit on a day-trip from Edinburgh.

Melrose and around

If you've only time to visit one Border town, **MELROSE**, 37 miles south of Edinburgh, is the obvious choice. The town is very pretty, and superbly set between the triple-peaked Eildon Hills and the supremely beautiful **Abbey** (April–Sept daily 9.30am–6.30pm; Oct–March Mon–Sat 9.30am–4.30pm, Sun 2–4.30pm; £3.80). It's best seen on a bright morning, with the sun streaming through the tracery of the exquisite east and south windows and illuminating the richly sculpted capitals and cornices of the nave.

Scott's custom-built home, **Abbotsford House** (June–Sept daily 10am–5pm; March–May & Oct Mon–Sat 10am–5pm, Sun 2–5pm; £3.80), lies a couple of miles west of Melrose, just off the road to Galashiels. Self-consciously over-the-top, it attempts to give a physical presence to the mythical world of his novels. Details from Scotland's great ruined or unfinished buildings are aped in the architecture, while the rooms overflow with souvenirs of the military heroes of the nation's past. Even more aesthetically pleasing is Scott's burial place, **Dryburgh Abbey** (same times as Melrose Abbey; £2.70), near the village of St Boswells, five miles southeast of Melrose. The early Gothic transept housing the writer's grave is the only part of the church to have survived, but the monastic buildings are partly intact. Best of all is the secluded setting by the River Tweed, all gentle hills and ancient woodland.

Buses to Melrose stop in Market Sq, a short walk from the **tourist office** (July & Aug Mon–Sat 9.30am–6.30pm, Sun 10am–6pm; March–June & Sept Mon–Sat 10am–5pm, Sun 10am–2pm; Oct Mon–Sat 10am–1pm; ☎01896/822555). The **HI hostel** is in an old Victorian villa overlooking the abbey (☎01896/822521; ②). There's a plentiful supply of **B&Bs**, including one on High St and a couple each on Buccleuch and Abbey streets. The old coaching inns in the village offer quality **meals**: *Burt's* is excellent, but *The Ship* is even better.

Kelso and around

KELSO, twelve miles east of Melrose, lies at the point where the Tweed is joined by its main tributary, the Teviot. Here the **Abbey** (Mon–Sat 9.30am–4/6pm, Sun 2–4/6pm; free) was the grandest in the Borders but is now the most ruined by far: the magnificent fragment represents only the western transept and tower. Across the park to the northwest is the eccentric octagonal **Old Parish Church**; further west is the spacious Georgian **Market Square**, the largest in Scotland, dominated by the town hall and the *Cross Keys Hotel*, once the most celebrated of the town's several coaching inns. At the northern edge of town is **Floors Castle** (April–Oct daily 10am–4.30pm; £5.50), the largest inhabited house in Scotland. William Adam's original construction was given its overloaded Romantic look by William Playfair in the 1840s, and the interior is no less rich, containing a superb set of Gobelin tapestries. An even more impressive stately home, **Mellerstain House** (May–Sept Sun–Fri 12.30–5pm; £5), lies six miles northwest of Kelso. Here Robert Adam created a stunning sequence of luxuriant interiors, including some dazzling plasterwork ceilings – the library's is outstanding. Kelso's **tourist office** is on Market Square (July & Aug Mon–Sat 9.30am–6.30pm, Sun 10am–6pm; March–June & Sept Mon–Sat 10am–5pm, Sun 10am–2pm; Oct Mon–Sat 10am–1pm; ☎01573/223464).

St Andrews

Well-groomed **ST ANDREWS**, situated on the coast 56 miles northeast of Edinburgh, has the air of a place of importance. Retaining memories of its days as medieval Scotland's metropolis, it is the country's oldest university town, the Scottish answer to Oxford or Cambridge with a snob-appeal to match. The upper-class English accents that you hear everywhere in term time are only set to increase as the university plays host to Prince William's undergraduate years.

St Andrews has an exalted place in Scottish sporting history too. Entering the town from the Edinburgh road, you pass no fewer than four golf links, the last of which is the **Old Course**, the most famous and – in the opinion of Jack Nicklaus – the best in the world. At the southern end of the Old Course, down towards the waterfront, is the award-winning **British Golf Museum** (April–Oct daily 9.30am–5.30pm; Nov–March Thurs–Mon 11am–3pm; £3.75). Immediately south of the Old Course begins North St, one of St Andrews' two main arteries. Much of it is taken up by university buildings, with the tower of **St Salvator's College** rising proudly above all else. Together with the adjoining chapel, this dates from 1450 and is the earliest surviving part of the university. Further east, you can reach the ruined **Castle** on North Castle St (April–Sept Mon–Sat 9.30am–6pm, Sun 9.30am–4pm; Oct–March Mon–Sat same times, Sun 2–4pm; £2.80, or combined ticket with cathedral £4). Commanding a prominent headland, it began as a fortress, but was partly transformed by the local archbishops into a Renaissance palace, of which little more than the facade survives. A short distance further along the coast is the equally ruined Gothic **Cathedral** (same times), the mother church of medieval Scotland and the largest and grandest ever built in the country. Even though little more then the cemetery survives, the intact east wall and the exposed foundations give an idea of the vast scale of what has been lost. The **visitor centre** (same times; £2, or £4 with castle) contains the *St Andrews Sarcophagus*, probably ninth-century, one of the most refined products of the so-called Dark Ages. With the entrance ticket you can get a token to ascend the austere Romanesque **St Rule's Tower** – part of the priory that the cathedral replaced – for superb views over the sea and town.

Outside the cathedral enclosure and now forming an entrance to the coastal road southwards are **the Pends**, huge fourteenth-century arches which served as the main gateway to the priory. Running westwards from the Pends is South St, site of more historic university buildings and, further along, the elegant ruins of Blackfriars monastery, while the street terminates at the **West Port**, a well-preserved, late sixteenth-century gateway that now creates a traffic bottleneck.

Practicalities

You can reach St Andrews by **bus** on a day-trip from Edinburgh or Stirling. There are no direct trains, though frequent buses connect with the train station five miles away in Leuchars (where the parish church incorporates the most beautiful and intact piece of Norman architecture in Scotland). St Andrews' **tourist office**, 70 Market St (summer Mon–Sat 9.30am–8pm, Sun 11am–6pm; shorter hours rest of year; ☎01334/472021, *www.standrews.com/fife*) will book **rooms** for a 10 percent charge – worth paying in the summer and during big golf tournaments when **accommodation** is in short supply. The only **hostel** in the area is *Inchape House Backpackers* on St Mary's Pl (☎01334/479911; ③). *Aedel House*, 72 Murray Place (☎01334/472315; ④), and *Bell Craig*, 8 Murray Park (☎01334/472962, *bellcraig@eidosnet.co.uk*; ④), are two options of the many on those streets. For **eating**, student favourites are *Brambles*, 5 College St; *Ma Belle's*, 40 The Scores; and the Mexican *La Pasada* on St Mary's Place. Most **pubs** are concentrated on Market St and South St; best of the bunch are *Central*, 1 Market St, and *Victoria Café* on St Mary's Place off the west end of Market St, both popular student joints. Sports fans head for *Ogstons* on South St.

Stirling

Occupying a key strategic position between the Highlands and Lowlands at the easiest crossing of the River Forth, **STIRLING** has played a major role throughout Scottish history. Imperiously set on a rocky crag, its **Castle** (daily 9.30am–5/6.30pm; £6.50 includes Argyll's Lodging) combined the functions of a fortress with those of a royal palace. Highlights within the complex are the **Royal Palace**, dating from the late Renaissance, and the earlier **Great Hall**, where recent restoration, including a complete rebuilding of the vast hammerbeam roof, has revealed the original form and scale.

The oldest part of Stirling is grouped around the streets leading up to the castle. Just downhill, on Castle Wynd, stands a richly decorated facade, all that remains of **Mar's Wark**, one of two imposing Renaissance town houses. The other, **Argyll's Lodging**, is intact, with some rooms furnished in period style (same times and ticket as castle). Beyond stands the Gothic **Church of the Holy Rude** (May–Sept Mon–Fri 10am–5pm), which boasts a fine timber roof. Here the infant James VI – later James I of the United Kingdom – was crowned King of Scotland in 1567. From here, Broad St slopes down to the lower town. If you continue north along Upper Bridge St then Union St, you'll come to the fifteenth-century **Old Bridge**, a replacement for the wooden construction that was the scene of Sir William Wallace's victory over the English in 1297, a crucial episode in the Wars of Independence (as portrayed in the film *Braveheart*). The Scottish hero was commemorated in Victorian times by the **Wallace Monument** (daily 10am–5/6.30pm; £3.95), about a mile further north. Though the refurbished building seems ugly close up, compensation comes in the stupendous views – finer even than those from the castle. In the foreground can be seen **Stirling University**, the youngest in Scotland and sometimes claimed as the most beautiful campus in the world.

The train and bus stations are both five minutes' walk from the **tourist office**, 41 Dumbarton Rd in the lower part of town (July & Aug Mon–Sat 9am–7.30pm, Sun 9.30am–6.30pm; Sept–June Mon–Sat 9/10am–5/6pm; ☎01786/475019, *www.scottish.heartlands.org*). The quality **HI hostel**, St John St at the top of town, occupies a converted church (☎01786/473442; ②) and *Willy Wallace backpackers*, 77 Murray Place, is a competent **hostel** (☎01786/446773; ③). Of the many guest houses, *No.10*, 10 Gladstone Place, is especially friendly (☎01786/472681; ⑤). The picturesque *Witches' Craig* **campsite** is three miles east of town on bus #62, off the St Andrews road (☎01786/474947; April–Oct). Try the lively *Barnton Bar and Bistro*, Barton St, or the traditional *Porter's* **pub**, on Port St, for cheap **meals**.

Loch Lomond

The name of **Loch Lomond** (*www.stayatlochlomond.com*) – the largest stretch of fresh water in Britain – is almost as famous as Loch Ness, thanks to the ballad about its "bonnie, bonnie banks". The easiest way to get to the loch is to take one of the frequent buses from Glasgow to **BALLOCH** at its southern tip, from where you can take a cruise around the 33 islands nearby. The **western shore** is very developed, and the road seldom strays far from its banks. The West Highland train – from Glasgow to Mallaig, with a branch line to Oban – joins the loch seventeen miles north of Balloch at Tarbet, and has one other station on the loch eight miles further at Ardlui (which is handy for some of the trails), at its mountain-framed head. There are, however, plenty of buses along this shore from Balloch. No buses run on the **eastern shore**, much of which can only be traversed by the footpath which forms part of the West Highland Way. The easiest access to the graceful peak of **Ben Lomond** (3192ft) is by ferry from Inverbeg (south of Tarbet) to Rowardennan, from where it's a straightforward three-hour hike to the summit.

Above Balloch marina is Loch Lomond's main **tourist office** (daily: July & Aug 9.30am–7.30pm; April–June, Sept & Oct 10am–5pm; ☎01389/753533, *www.scottish.heartlands.org*); they'll find you a **B&B** – of which there's a plentiful supply – without charge. A couple of miles up the west side of the loch is Scotland's most beautiful **HI hostel**, complete with resident ghost (☎01389/850226; ②); and there's another alluringly sited HI hostel at Rowardennan (☎01360/870259; ②). There are **campsites** in all the villages.

Oban and the southern Hebrides

The southernmost of the Hebrides – notably the large island of **Mull**, the tiny sacred isle of **Iona** and the spectacular rock of **Staffa** – are among the most compelling of the entire archipelago and the easiest to reach from central Scotland. Their main point of access is **Oban**, seventy miles northwest of Glasgow. Approaching Oban from the south, take the West Highland train from Glasgow to the hill-walking resort of Crianlarich, where the train divides, one part continuing north through Fort William to Mallaig, the other branching west to Oban. Coming from the north, a scenic **bus** running along Loch Linnhe provides the quicker and cheaper approach from Fort William, and it can also be picked up at Ballachulish, about a mile west of Glencoe Village.

Oban

Solidly Victorian in appearance, **OBAN** is an attractive enough place, if uncomfortably crowded for at least five months a year. It has a superb setting, the island of Kerrera providing its bay with a natural shelter, and a further distinctive note is struck by the huge circular **McCaig's Tower** on a hilltop above the town. Imitating the Colosseum in Rome, it was the brainchild of a local banker a century ago, who had the twin aims of alleviating local unemployment and creating a family mausoleum. Work never progressed further than the exterior walls, but the folly provides a wonderful seaward panorama, particularly at sunset. Equally beautiful evening views can be had by walking along the northern shore of the bay, either from or below the medieval ruins of **Dunollie Castle**. Another attraction is the **Oban Distillery** (Mon–Sat 9.30am–5pm, July–Sept Sat until 8.30pm; £3) on Stafford St in the town centre, the tour of which ends with a dram of the strong stuff. Caledonian MacBrayne's **ferry terminal** for services to the Hebrides (information on ☎01475/650100) is a stone's throw from the train station, which has the bus terminus on its other side. There's also a host of private boat operators in the harbour area; their excursions – to the castles of Mull, to the seal colonies, or to Staffa – are worth considering, particularly if you're pushed for time.

Oban's **tourist office** (Mon–Fri 9am–5.30pm, Sat & Sun 10am–5pm; longer hours in the summer season ☎01631/563122) is on Argyll Sq east of the bus terminus. There are dozens of **B&Bs** in town, as well as an **HI hostel** on the Esplanade (☎01631/562025; ③) just beyond the cathedral, *Jeremy Inglis'* hostel at 21 Airds Crescent (☎01631/565065; ②), and *Oban Backpackers* on Breadalbane St (☎01631/562107, *www.scotlands-top-hostels.com*; ③). The nearest **campsite** is about two miles north at Ganavan Sands (☎01631/562179). **Eating** is predictably sea-based, Oban's fish-and-chip shops are better than average, especially *Onorio's* on George St, as is the seafood counter by the ferry terminal. More upmarket options are available from *Ee-Usk* and *Mondo* both on George St. The best pubs in town are: *O'Donnell's*, Breadalbane St, for that complete Celtic vibe, and *Aulays*, 8 Airds Place, a local bar of character with a vast selection of whiskies. For the **Internet** and veggie snacks head for *Cafe Na Lusan*, 9 Craigard Rd (☎01631/567268; £3.50/hr).

The island of Mull

The chief appeal of the island of **Mull** is its remarkably undulating coastline – three hundred miles of it in total. Despite its proximity to the mainland, the slower pace of life is clearly apparent: most roads are single lane, with only a handful of (very cheap) buses linking the main settlements. **CRAIGNURE** is the main entry point, linked to Oban by ferries (6 daily; 45min; £6.10 return). The village itself is fairly nondescript, but it offers a few guest houses, a campsite, bike hire and the island's main tourist office (☎01680/812377). Both of Mull's most important historic monuments lie in the immediate vicinity. **Torosay Castle** (April–Oct daily 10.30am–5.30pm; £4.50) is in the full-blown Victorian Baronial style, set in a magnificent garden (open dawn to dusk) complete with eighteenth-century statues. The mile-and-a-half between Craignure and the castle is covered by the narrow-gauge Mull Rail (April–Oct daily 11am–5pm; £3.30 return). A further 15min walk along the bay is **Duart Castle** (May–Oct daily 10.30am–6pm; £3.50), the thirteenth-century stronghold of the MacLean clan – you can peek in the dungeons and ascend to the rooftops. Mull's longest road, served by three daily buses (Mon–Sat), extends 35 miles west from Craignure to **FIONNPHORT**, the port for Iona. This cuts through Glen More and past the island's highest peak, the extinct volcano of **Ben More** (3169ft). Both Fionnphort and Bunessan, five miles before it, have a few B&B options; worth considering for an overnight stop, given the accommodation shortage on Iona and the beauty of the coastline to the south. **Camping** is possible at Fidden Farm (☎01681/700427), a mile south of town beside the beach.

TOBERMORY, Mull's picturesque "capital", is 22 miles northwest of Craignure and served by up to five buses a day; though be warned the buses leave fairly swiftly after the ferry docks at Craignure. For a list of the local **B&Bs** the **tourist office** (April–Oct daily 9/10am–5/6pm; ☎01688/302182) is in the Cal-Mac ticket office at the northern end of the harbour. Accommodation is in short supply during the annual music festival in late April, so book ahead if possible. The island's sole bank and **HI hostel** (☎01688/302481; ②) are both on Main St, near *Fàilte*, the best of the many guest houses (☎01688/302495; ④). Also on Main St is the *Mishnish Hotel* **pub**, popular for the live folk music at the weekends and during the festival.

The isles of Iona and Staffa

Just three miles long and no more than a mile wide, **Iona** nevertheless manages to encapsulate all the enchantment and mystique of the Hebrides. Its chief claim to fame is as one of the cradles of British Christianity: St Columba arrived here from Ireland in 563 and established a monastery which was responsible for the conversion of more or less all of Scotland and northern England. Reached in a few minutes by regular ferry from Fionnphort, Iona is a feasible day-trip from Oban in summer, and in high season the island is often overrun by organized tours from the mainland. To appreciate its special atmosphere and to have time to see the whole island, including the usually overlooked west coast, you should spend at least one night either here or in Fionnphort. The two hotels are fairly expensive, but **B&B** is available in a few houses near the harbour; try *Iona Cottage* (☎01681/700569; ④; Easter to October) right near the pier; or the more remote *Kilona* in Sithean (☎01681/700362; ④).

No buildings remain from Columba's time: the present **Abbey**, which dominates all views of the island, dates from a re-establishment of monasticism here by the Benedictines in around 1200. Extensively rebuilt in the fifteenth and sixteenth centuries, it fell into decay after the Reformation and was only restored in the last century, with the latest revival of religious life – the now-flourishing multidenominational Iona Community. Adjoining the facade is a small chamber, traditionally assumed to be St Columba's grave. In front stand three delicately carved **crosses** from the eighth and ninth centuries, among the masterpieces of European sculpture of the Dark Ages. The finest of these is now represented by a copy, the original having been moved to the Abbey **Museum** housed in the monastic infirmary behind the abbey. South of the church is the oldest building on the island, **St Oran's Chapel**, with a Norman door dating from the eleventh century. It stands at the centre of the sacred burial ground, Reilig Odhrain, which is said to contain the graves of sixty kings of Norway, Ireland and Scotland, including the two immortalized by Shakespeare – Duncan and Macbeth. Walking back to the harbour, you pass **MacLean's Cross**, a fifteenth-century interpretation of those in the abbey grounds, and the ruins of a nunnery founded around the same time as the Benedictine abbey.

A basaltic mass rising direct from the sea, **Staffa** is the northern end of Ireland's Giant's Causeway, and is the most romantic and dramatic of Scotland's plethora of uninhabited islands. On one side, its perpendicular rockface has been cut into caverns of cathedral-like dimensions, notably **Fingal's Cave**, whose haunting noises inspired Mendelssohn's *Hebrides Overture*. To get to Staffa, join one of the many boat-trips from Oban, Fionnphort or Dervaig (on Mull's northern coast near Tobermory), which start from around £12.50 return. The MB Iolaire is one outfit based at Fionnphort (☎01681/700358); for others, consult with tourist offices.

Lochaber

As the **Lochaber** district contains **Ben Nevis**, Britain's highest mountain, and **Glencoe**, its most famous glen, it's small wonder that it has become one of the most popular parts of the Highlands. The hub of the area is **Fort William**, which is served by buses from Glasgow and Inverness but is better approached on the **West Highland railway**, Scotland's most scenic train route, crossing countryside which can otherwise only be seen from long-distance footpaths. From the junction at Crianlarich, the line climbs around Beinn Odhar on a unique horseshoe-shaped loop of viaducts, then crosses the desolate peat bogs of Rannoch Moor. Skirting Loch Ossian, the train descends steeply along the entire length of Loch Treig, then circumnavigates Ben Nevis to approach Fort William from the northeast, through the dramatic Monessie Gorge. Consult the **Highlands of Scotland tourist office** Web site, *www.host.co.uk*, for more.

Fort William and Ben Nevis

Nothing remains of the fort which gave **FORT WILLIAM** its name, nor is there anything much in the way of conventional sights – the town is chiefly of use as a base for the countryside and for having the only decent shops within a radius of fifty miles. Its setting, just beyond the point where Loch Eil merges with the huge Loch Linnhe, is its strongest feature. Top attraction, however, is the ascent of **Ben Nevis** (4406ft/1356m) itself. Although it gives the impression of being a brute of a mountain – particularly when seen from its precipitous northern side – it's actually rather a gentle climb, with a well-defined path carved out of the whaleback south side from the bridge opposite the youth hostel. Reckon on about four hours for the ascent, two for the descent and plenty of time for the vast plateau-like summit; you may have to do a fair amount of trudging through snow towards the end. The views are all you'd expect, though they might be better from halfway up, as the top is often shrouded in mist.

Fort William's bus and train stations are beside each other at the east end of High St. The **tourist office** (July & Aug Mon–Sat 9am–8.30pm, Sun 9am–6pm; Sept–June Mon–Sat 9am–5pm, Sun 10am–4pm; ☎01397/703781) is on Cameron Sq, about halfway down High St. Aside from the dozens of **B&Bs** – many of them on and around Fassifern Rd, uphill from the train station – the best of the scenery can be viewed from one of the three **campsites** in the area; *Glen Nevis Caravan and Camping* (☎01397/702191; March–Oct), take the direction signposted from the entrance to **Glen Nevis** and walk for 2 1/2 miles, and the nearby **HI hostel** (☎01397/702336; ③). Occasional buses follow this lovely route, departing from Middle St, between High St and the loch, and terminating at the hostel. Also in Glen Nevis is the *Ben Nevis* **Bunkhouse** at Achinke Farm (☎01397/702240; ②). The easiest **walk** in the area is to continue up the glen on the road or accompanying footpath; there are constantly changing views of Ben Nevis on one side and the peaks of Mamore Forest on the other, with the additional bonus of several waterfalls.

Glencoe

Easily reached by buses running between Glasgow and Fort William, **Glencoe** stretches southeast from the shore of Loch Leven, some fifteen miles south of Fort William. Its name translates as "the Vale of Weeping", a doubly appropriate title: not only was it the site of the infamous massacre in 1692 of the MacDonalds by the Campbells, it can be drenched by rain at all seasons of the year, making its untamed scenery look all the more dramatic and menacing. The massacre, ordered by King William III as punishment for the failure of the MacDonald chief to take his oath of loyalty, took place in the vicinity of **GLENCOE VILLAGE**, which is set back from Loch Leven and in the shadow of the Pap of Glencoe, with its distinctively head-shaped summit. Here you'll find several B&Bs, whereas the **HI hostel** (☎01855/811219; ②) and the *Leacantuim Farm* **bunkhouse** and **campsite** (both ☎01855/811256; ②) are down the old road southeast along the banks of the River Coe. At the point where the old road rejoins the main highway is a **visitor centre** (April–Oct daily 9.30am–5.30pm; 50p) run by the National Trust for Scotland, which owns most of Glencoe. Ask here for detailed hiking information: the ridges to the east are among the finest on mainland Britain, but are for experienced hill-walkers only.

From Fort William to Mallaig

For the 47-mile journey from Fort William to Mallaig (departure point for ferries to Skye), the **train** just has the edge on the bus: in summer, you can occasionally be hitched up to a steam engine. At Banavie, just a couple of miles after Fort William, the line crosses the Caledonian Canal and passes the spectacular flight of locks known as Neptune's Staircase. Wonderful views back towards the mass of Ben Nevis come before the line reaches the northern shore of Loch Sheil, after which it passes over a mighty curved viaduct. Approaching Mallaig, the train proceeds past the rock-strewn Sound of Arisaig and along the length of Loch Eilt before passing between Loch Morar – the deepest in the country at over 1000ft – and the silver sands.

The little fishing port of **MALLAIG** is linked by ferry to Armadale on Skye, as well as by two or three sailings a week to the "Small Isles" nearby – Muck, Eigg, Rhum and Canna. Mallaig makes a pleasant base for exploring the area, boasting a good hostel, *Sheena's Bunkhouse*, just above the harbour (☎01687/462764; ②), as well as plenty of inexpensive guest houses. The **tourist office** is by the harbour (June–Aug Mon–Sat 9am–8pm, Sun 10am–4pm; shorter hours at other times; ☎01687/462170).

The Isle of Skye

The closest Hebridean island to the mainland, **Skye** (*www.skye.co.uk*) is also the most beguiling, its richly varied scenery taking in Britain's most daunting mountain range, lush stretches of greenery and a coastline indented with majestic sea lochs. The tranquil present is the mirror opposite of the island's turbulent past. Throughout the Middle Ages, it was fiercely disputed by the rival MacLeods and MacDonalds, and the later conversion of the chiefs to landlords led to impoverishment for the majority of the population, provoking an armed uprising – the last in British history – in 1881.

For all its beauties, some words of warning are in order for visitors to Skye. Not for nothing is it nicknamed the "Misty Isle": the scenery is often covered from sight for days on end, even in summer – though the atmospheric light is part of Skye's charm, and the island is at its most magical when a spell of bad weather suddenly clears. Secondly, Skye isn't a place which can be seen in a hurry: many of the most beautiful spots are only accessible on foot, and are often far from the villages. Thirdly, bus services, other than on the main north–south route, are sparse as well as being the most expensive in Scotland.

Southern Skye

Two ferries make the crossing to Skye from the mainland. The first is from Mallaig to **ARMADALE**, where there's an **HI hostel** (☎01471/844260; ②; March–Sept) along the shore from the harbour and a few guest houses in the adjacent village of Ardvasar. The shorter crossing is the more picturesque trip from Glenelg to Kylerhea (Easter–Oct Mon–Sat, mid-May to Aug also Sun; 15min). Buses and trains also make the crossing to Kyleakin from the **KYLE OF LOCHALSH** (at the end of a train line from Inverness) over the controversial Skye Bridge, the most expensive toll bridge in Europe. **KYLEAKIN** itself has a picturesque harbour, dominated by the ruined Castle Moil. The island's official **HI hostel** is a few minutes' walk from the dock (☎01599/534585; ②) as is *Skye Backpackers* nearby (☎01599/534510, *www.scotlands-top-hostels.com*; ②); there are also plenty of guest houses, but you'd do better to push on to **BROADFORD**, eight miles north at the island's crossroads, which makes a much better base for touring the island. It has a small **tourist office** (July & Aug Mon–Sat 9am–7pm, Sun 10am–5pm; shorter hours at other times; ☎01471/822361).

There's another **HI hostel** on the west shore of the bay, which rents bikes (☎01471/822442; ②), as well as the much more beautiful and simple *Fossil Bothy* hostel (☎01471/822297; ②), on the east side of the bay. A popular choice for **eating** and **drinking** is the *King Haakon Bar* on the Main Rd; there's decent pub fare and a small restaurant next door.

The Cuillin mountains

The **Cuillin mountains** in western Skye are among the great natural wonders of Europe, and although some of the peaks do require climbing skills there are other summits well within the capability of normal walkers; while wonderful views of the range can be had without expending any energy at all. One of the classic views is across the dark waters of Loch Scavaig from the beach of **ELGOL**, fourteen miles west of Broadford via the most beautiful road in Skye; the return trip can be made by post-bus on working days and there are **boat trips** from Elgol to Loch Coruisk on the *Bella Jane* (☎0800/731 3089). The northern starting point for exploration is **SLIGACHAN**, sixteen miles north of Broadford; there's little more to this hamlet than the *Sligachan* hotel (☎01478/650204; ⑦), and a **campsite** (April–Oct). The most rewarding hike is down Glen Sligachan by the path to Loch Coruisk: the full return trip is a very long day's walk, though there's no need to proceed further than the Druim Hain ridge, five miles away, from which the whole of the Cuillin can be seen. Serious hill-walkers head for **GLEN BRITTLE**, fifteen miles southwest of Sligachan by road (daily bus each way), or eight miles by footpath. The **HI hostel** here (☎01478/640278; ②; March–Oct) also offers guided hikes into the mountains (advance reservations obligatory; ☎08701/553255). There's also a **campsite** not far away by the beach (☎01478/640404; April–Sept).

Northern Skye

Skye's largest peninsula is **Trotternish**, which forms the northeastern part of the island. The gateway to this is the "capital" of **PORTREE**, which has the shops and banks that are otherwise a rare commodity on Skye. Here also is the main **tourist office** on Bayfield Rd (July & Aug Mon–Sat 9am–8pm, Sun 10am–4pm; shorter hours at other times; ☎01478/612137). The town has dozens of **B&Bs**, as well as the smart *Portree Independent Hostel* (☎01478/613737, *portreeindhostel@hotmail.co.uk*; ②), and the smaller *Portree Backpackers* (☎01478/613641; ②), at 6 Woodpark. The most imposing scenery is to be found on the east coast of the peninsula, north of Portree – most buses from Glasgow to Portree go on around the peninsula to Uig, seventeen miles north on the west coast, duplicating the route of some local buses. Some nine miles from Portree, at the edge of the Storr ridge, is a 165-foot obelisk known as **the Old Man of Storr**, while a further ten miles north, rising above Staffin Bay, are the **Quiraing** – a forest of jagged pinnacles including the Needle, the Prison and the Table, where Victorian ramblers used to picnic and play cricket. The straggling village of **UIG** has ferries to the islands of the Outer Hebrides, including Harris and North Uist, as well as an **HI hostel** (☎01470/542211; ②) off the Portree road at the southern end. 10mins along the Staffin Rd lies the nearest **campsite**, *Torvaig Caravan and Camping* (☎01478/612209).

The main centre of the remote northwestern corner of Skye is **DUNVEGAN**, set on a sea loch between the peninsulas of Vaternish and Duirnish, some 22 miles west of Portree. Just north of the village is the **Castle** (April–Oct daily 10am–5.30pm; £5.30), the stronghold of the MacLeods and by far the most notable monument on Skye. Although prettified by the Victorians, the outlines of the medieval fortress are still apparent. Inside, you can see the rather tatty Fairy Flag, a Byzantine cloth allegedly given to a chief by his fairy wife and possessing the magic to save the clan on three occasions, two of which have already been used up. Also on show is the Dunvegan Horn, which each heir-apparent must, at the time of coming of age, fill with claret and drain in one gul There's the added bonus of well-tended gardens, while summer excursion boats sail from the harbour to the nearby seal colonies. The best budget **guest house** is the beautifully situated *Silverdale*, out towards Cobust (☎01470/521251; ⑤). The nearest **campsite** is halfway towards Portree on the A850 at *Greshornish Camping* (☎01470/582230).

Inverness and around

Capital of the Highlands, **INVERNESS** is 160 miles north of Edinburgh, the train line between the two traversing the gentle countryside of Perthshire before skirting the stark Cairngorm mountains. Approaching from Skye in the west, there's the magnificent eighty-mile train journey from Kyle of Lochalsh. If you're using this approach, try to travel on *The Clansman* (mid-June to Aug departs Kyle 3.10pm), a train whose tourist provisions include an observation car. Inverness **airport** (☎01463/232471) is seven miles east of town, with some budget flights to London.

Inverness has a fine setting astride the River Ness at the head of the Beauly Firth, but despite having been a place of importance for a millennium – it was probably the capital of the Pictish kingdom and the site of Macbeth's castle – there's nothing remarkable to see, nor any particularly strong sense of character. The chief attractions of historical interest lie some six miles east of town, reached by regular buses. **Culloden Moor** was the scene in 1746 of the last pitched battle on British soil, when the troops of "Butcher" Cumberland crushed Bonnie Prince Charlie's army of volunteers in just forty minutes. This ended forever Stuart ambitions of maintaining the monarchy, and marked the beginning of the break-up of the clan system which had ruled Highland society for centuries. A **visitor centre** (daily 9/10am–4/6pm; closed Jan; £4) has displays describing the action. About a mile below the battlefield are the **Clava Cairns**, a late-Neolithic burial site comprising three stone cairns. Six miles further east is **Cawdor Castle** (May–Oct daily 10am–5.30pm; £5.60), immortalized by Shakespeare as the setting for *Macbeth*, and now set in lovely gardens and parkland. The original fourteenth-century keep has grown towers, turrets and battlements over the years, and approached over its drawbridge it's real fairy-tale stuff.

As well as the only big choice of shops, restaurants and nightlife in the Highlands, you'll find **B&Bs** by the score in Inverness. These tend to fill up in summer, and the **tourist office** on Castle Wynd (Mon–Fri 9am–5pm, Sat & Sun 9.30am–5pm; ☎01463/234353, *www.host.co.uk*) charges £3 to find a room. The **HI hostel** is on Victoria Drive, off Milburn Rd (☎01463/231771; ③); there are plenty of independent hostels, including the non-smoking *Bazpackers*, at the top of Castle St (☎01463/717663; ②). Also try the *Eastgate Backpackers*, 98 Eastgate (☎01463/718756; ③), which has a wide range of facilities including Internet, bike rental and laundry. There are **campsites** at Culloden (March–Oct), on the road to Loch Ness, and within Inverness at Bught Parl, west of the river. Inverness and around is best explored by bike; *Highland Cycles*, 16a Telford St (☎01463/234789) hire out bikes.

Loch Ness

Loch Ness forms part of the natural fault line known as the Great Glen, which slices across the Highlands between Inverness and Fort William. In the early 1800s, Thomas Telford linked the glen's lochs by means of the **Caledonian Canal**, which enabled ships to pass between the North Sea and the Atlantic without having to navigate Scotland's treacherous northern coast. Pleasure craft galore now ply the canal and its lochs, the link having long lost its commercial significance. Summer **cruises** from Inverness (book at the tourist office) provide the most straightforward way of seeing the terrain; they depart from Tomnahurich Bridge, just over a mile south of the centre. The most popular trip is to Castle Urquhart; alternatively, try Forbes' backpacker-oriented minibus tour of the loch (also bookable at the tourist office) – it's a sociable way to take in the area's most impressive landscape. Most visitors are eager to catch a glimpse of the elusive Loch Ness Monster, **"Nessie"**. Tales of the monster date back at least as far as the seventh century, when it came out second best in an altercation with St Columba. However, the possibility that a mysterious prehistoric creature might be living in the loch only attracted worldwide attention in the 1930s, when sightings were reported during the construction of the road along its western shore. Numerous appearances have been reported since, but even the most hi-tech surveys of the loch have failed to come up with conclusive evidence. To find out the whole story, take a bus to

DRUMNADROCHIT, fourteen miles southwest of Inverness, where you can visit the **Official Loch Ness Monster Exhibition Centre** (daily: July & Aug 9am–8pm; shorter hours at other times; £5.95). There are also cruises from here, predictably focusing on "Nessie" lore. Most photographs allegedly showing the monster have been taken a couple of miles further south, around the ruined **Castle Urquhart** (Mon–Sat 10am–5pm, Sun 2–5pm; £3.80), once one of Scotland's largest, most beautifully sited fortresses.

Aberdeen

Set on the eastern coast some 120 miles north of Edinburgh, **ABERDEEN** is the third city of Scotland and Europe's boom town of the last two decades. Solid and hard-wearing like the distinctively-coloured granite used for so many of its buildings, it has been nicknamed the "Silver City", although its wealth is built on black gold – North Sea oil – and the local stone is more grey than anything else.

Until a hundred years ago, Aberdeen was two separate towns a couple of miles apart. While Old Aberdeen slumbered in academic and ecclesiastical tranquillity, the newer town became a major port and commercial centre, and was subject to grandiose planning schemes. The most ambitious of these, in the early nineteenth century, included the layout of spacious **Union Street**, a block north of the bus and train stations, which runs for more than a mile east–west across the centre. At its eastern end is Castlegate, the square which fronted the long-vanished castle, where you can see the richly carved seventeenth-century **Mercat Cross**. A short way down King St is **St Andrew's Cathedral** (May–Sept Mon–Sat 10am–4pm), mother-church of the American Episcopal Church, the first American bishop having been consecrated in Aberdeen in 1784.

Proceeding along Union St, then left down Shiprow, brings you to Provost Ross's House, a sixteenth-century mansion now containing the award-winning **Maritime Museum** (Mon–Sat 10am–5pm, Sun noon–3pm; free), which describes Aberdeen's relationship with the sea through imaginative displays, films and models, including a thirty-foot oil rig. A further short walk downhill is the bustling **harbour** area, seen at its best in the early morning, before the daily fish market winds down at 8am. Across Union St from Shiprow is Broad St, dominated by **Marischal College**, the younger half of Aberdeen University. Its facade, a century-old historicist extravaganza, is probably the most spectacular piece of granite architecture in existence. Nestling in stranded isolation behind the hideous municipal offices opposite is the oldest surviving residential building in the city, **Provost Skene's House** (Mon–Sat 10am–5pm, Sun 1–4pm; free). Highlight of the interior is the sixteenth-century Painted Gallery, whose wooden ceiling is covered with depictions of religious scenes. Just west of here, on the north side of Union St, is the weird **St Nicholas church** (May–Sept Mon–Fri noon–4pm, Sat 1–3pm; Oct–April Mon–Fri 10am–1pm), known as the "Mither Kirk" for being the main pre-Reformation church in Aberdeen. Tellingly, four separate churches now nestle in the shell of the original. Less than a mile east of Union St is perhaps one of Britain's best **beaches**, a great two-mile sweep of clean sand, very popular in summer.

Twenty minutes north of the centre by bus #20, **Old Aberdeen** preserves the atmosphere of a cloistered academic community. Dominating High St is **King's College**, the university's older half. The chapel (Mon–Fri 9am–5pm), founded just a few years after the college at the end of the fifteenth century, boasts an outstanding crown spire; inside is a remarkably complete set of flamboyant late medieval furnishings. Over St Machar Drive lie the **Chanonry**, formerly a walled precinct and still with many fine houses, and, at the end, the former cathedral, **St Machar's** (daily 9am–5pm), Aberdeen's first great granite construction. Its early fifteenth-century facade is a highly original, fortress-like design; equally impressive is the huge sixteenth-century heraldic ceiling covering the nave, which bears the coats of arms of the royal houses of Europe and the bishops and nobles of Scotland. A walk of about a mile through Seaton Park leads to Bridgend of Balgownie, a cluster of restored houses, beyond which is the **Brig o' Balgownie**, a graceful, single-arched, fourteenth-century bridge.

Practicalities

Aberdeen **airport** (☎01224/722331) is seven miles northwest, with plenty of budget flights to London. Both **bus** and **train** stations are on Guild St, 200m south of Union St. The **tourist office** (June–Sept Mon–Sat 9am–5/7pm, Sun 10am–2/4pm; Oct–May Mon–Fri 9am–5pm, Sat 10am–2pm; ☎01224/88828) is in Provos Ross' House on Shiproy St. **Guest houses** are on Bon Accord St (south from Union St) and on the Great Western Rd. The **HI hostel** is at 8 Queen's Rd (☎01224/646988; ③), west of the centre by buses #14, #15, # 210, #215, and #27; the **campsite** is five miles west by the same buses in Hazlehead Park (☎01224/321268; April–Sept).

Top of the list for **eating** is *Ashvale*, 46 Great Western Rd, long rated as one of Britain's best fish-and-chip shops. Decent pub grub is available in most of the city's hostelries, including the *Blue Lamp* on Gallowgate and the *Howff* on Union St. Belmont St holds the busy *Wild Boar*, which transforms into a DJ-bar at night. For **drinking**, just down Belmont St the *Wodka Bar* serves a range of bizarre home-made flavoured vodkas while round the corner in Little Belmont St, *Ma Cameron's* is Aberdeen's oldest pub. In Old Aberdeen, the *St Machar Bar*, 97 High St, is a popular student hangout. Opposite lies the bizarre *Slaines Castle* bar, a converted church complete with piped torture sounds!

travel details

Trains

London to: Aberdeen (6 daily; 7hr 30min); Aberystwyth (change at Birmingham; 14 daily; 5hr); Bath (every 15min; 1hr 20min); Brighton (every 15min; 50mins); Bristol (every 30min; 1hr 45mins); Cambridge (every 15min; 45min); Canterbury (every 30min; 1hr 20min–2hr 10min); Cardiff (hourly; 2hr–2hr 20min); Dover (every 30min; 1hr 45min); Durham (hourly; 2hr 45min); Edinburgh (every 30min; 4hr–4hr 30min); Glasgow (15 daily; 5hr 30min); Liverpool (hourly; 2hr 50min); Manchester (20 daily; 2hr 40min); Newcastle (every 30min; 2hr 50min); Newport (every 30min; 1hr 45min); Norwich (every 30min; 1hr 50min); Oxford (every 20–30min; 1hr); Penzance (8 daily; 5hr 30min–6hr); Stratford-upon-Avon (5 daily; 2hr 15min); Winchester (every 15min; 1hr); York (every 30min; 2hr 15min).

Bristol to: Bath (24 daily; 15min); Cardiff (every 30min; 50min–1hr); Manchester (5 daily; 3hr 30min); Oxford (11 daily; 1hr 20min); Salisbury (hourly; 1hr 10min); York (6 daily; 4hr).

Edinburgh to: Aberdeen (hourly; 2hr 30min); Durham (hourly; 2hr); Glasgow (every 15min; 1hr); Inverness (6 daily; 3hr 30min); Newcastle (every 30min; 1hr 30min); Leuchars for St Andrews (hourly; 1hr 20min); Stirling (every hour; 1hr); York (hourly; 2hr 30min).

Glasgow to: Aberdeen (hourly; 2hr 20min); Fort William (5 daily; 3hr 45min); Inverness (some change at Perth; 8 daily; 4hr); Mallaig (5 daily; 5hr 20min); Preston for Liverpool and Manchester (13 daily; 1hr 30min); Newcastle (every 2hr; 2hr 30min);

Oban (8 daily; 3hr); Stirling (every 30min; 30min).

Inverness to: Aberdeen (10 daily; 2hr 15min); Stirling (some change at Perth; 9 daily; 2hr 30min).

Liverpool to: Cardiff (some change at Crewe; 13 daily; 4hr); Manchester (every 20min; 1hr); Preston for Glasgow and Edinburgh (hourly; 1hr); York (hourly; 2hr 20min).

Manchester to: Newcastle (12 daily; 2hr 50min); York (every 30min; 1hr 40min); Preston for Glasgow (every 20min; 1hr); Windermere (5 daily; 2hr 10min).

Buses

London to: Aberdeen (2 daily; 12hr); Aberystwyth (1 daily; 6hr 45min); Bangor (for Holyhead; 1 daily; 8hr 35min); Bath (13 daily; 2hr 20min); Brighton (hourly; 2hr); Bristol (hourly; 2hr 50min); Cambridge (hourly; 1hr 50min); Canterbury (hourly; 1hr 50min); Cardiff (6 daily; 3hr 10min); Dover (hourly; 2hr 15min–2hr 45min); Durham (5 daily; 5hr 30min); Edinburgh (4 daily; 8hr 30min–9hr 10min); Fort William (2 daily; 13hr); Glasgow (5 daily; 7hr 45min–8hr 50 min); Inverness (2 daily; 12hr 20min–13hr 10min); Lancaster (2 daily; 5hr 50min–7hr 30min); Liverpool (5 daily; 4hr 45min); Manchester (7 daily; 4hr 35min); Newcastle (5 daily; 6hr); Newport (6 daily; 2hr 45min); Norwich (6 daily; 2hr 45min–3hr); Oxford (every 12min; 1hr 30min–2hr); Penzance (5 daily; 7hr 45min–9hr 15min); Salisbury (2–3 daily; 2hr 45min); Stirling (2 daily; 9hr); Stratford (3 daily; 2hr 45min–3hr 15min); Winchester (9 daily; 2hr); York (3 daily; 4hr 30min).

Bristol to: Bath (every 30min; 50min); Cardiff (hourly; 1hr 10min); Manchester (2 daily; 6hr); Oxford (4 daily; 2hr 30min); Salisbury (1 daily; 3hr); Wells (1 daily; 1hr 20min).

Edinburgh to: Aberdeen (change at Perth or Dundee; hourly; 3hr 20min); Durham (1 daily; 4hr 30min); Fort William (1 daily; 3hr 50min); Glasgow (every 20min; 1hr 10min); Inverness (hourly; 4hr); Kyle of Lochalsh for Skye (1 daily 2hr 15min); Manchester (3 daily; 5hr 30min); Melrose (every 30min; 2hr 15min); Newcastle (3 daily; 3hr); St Andrews (every 30min; 2hr–3hr); Stirling (every 30min; 1hr 50min).

Fort William to: Inverness (7 daily; 1hr 50min); Mallaig (2 daily; 1hr 30min); Oban (2 daily; 1hr 30min); Portree (3 daily; 3hr); Stirling (2 daily; 2hr 50min).

Glasgow to: Aberdeen (hourly; 3hr 30min); Fort William (3 daily; 3hr 45min); Glencoe (4 daily; 2hr 30min); Inverness (every 15mins; 4hr 5min); Kyle of Lochalsh for Skye (3 daily; 5hr–5hr 50min); Lancaster (2 daily; 3hr 15min); Liverpool (2 daily; 4hr 40min–5hr 15min); Manchester (3 daily; 5hr 30min); Newcastle (every 2hr; 2hr 30min); Oban (3 daily; 3hr); Portree (3 daily; 6hr 15min–7hr); St Andrews (12 daily; 2hr 20min); Stirling (every 30min; 30min).

Inverness to: Aberdeen (10 daily; 2hr 15min); Portree (2 daily; 3hr 10min); Stirling (2 daily; 3hr 20min).

Liverpool to: Cardiff (4 daily; 5hr 40min–6hr 40min); Manchester (hourly; 50min); Newcastle (3 daily; 4hr 30min–7hr 30min); Oxford (4 daily; 5hr 30min); Stratford (1 daily; 4hr 35min); Windermere (2 daily; 4hr 30min–5hr 45min); York (2 daily; 3hr 40min–5hr).

Manchester to: Durham (3 daily; 4hr 15min–4hr 45min); Glasgow (2 daily; 4hr 30min–5hr); Leeds (14 daily; 2hr); Newcastle (5 daily; 4hr 50min); Windermere (2 daily; 2hr 45min–4hr); York (3 daily; 3hr 20min).

CHAPTER 4

BULGARIA

Introduction

If Westerners have an image of **Bulgaria**, it tends to be coloured by the murky intrigues of Balkan politics, exemplified by the infamous tales of poisoned umbrellas and plots to kill the pope. From the Bulgarians' standpoint, though, the nation has come a long way since it threw off the 500-year-old yoke of the Ottoman Empire in the 1870s, and is now struggling to cope with the aftermath of Communist misrule. The Socialists retained power through the early 1990's and moves towards free-market reforms were slow, to say the least. The election of a right-of-centre government in April 1997 brought some measure of stability, while in 2001, the former King, Simeon II, was democratically elected as prime minister and pledged to fight institutional corruption. In the meantime, low wages and high unemployment remain ever-present features of life here; the growing number of beggars, including young children, on the city streets bear testimony to the economic malaise. Recent war in neighbouring Serbia, and unrest in Macedonia have also taken their toll.

Independent travel here is not common, but there are relatively few restrictions, the costs are low, and for the committed there is much to take in. The main attractions are the mountainous scenery, and the web of towns and villages with a crafts tradition, where you'll find the wonderfully romantic architecture of the National Revival era. Foremost among these are **Koprivshtitsa** in the Sredna Gora range; **Bansko** in the Pirin mountains; **Plovdiv**, the second largest city; and **Veliko Târnovo**, the medieval capital. The monasteries can be stunning, too – the finest, **Rila**, is on every tourist's itinerary. For city life, the bustling, if rather faded capital, **Sofia**, and the cosmopolitan coastal resort of **Varna** are the places to aim for.

Information and maps

The lack of publicly funded **tourist offices** in Bulgaria means that it is almost impossible to get impartial travel advice. Most main towns have agencies, working on commission, responsible for handling private rooms, hotel accommodation and transport, although they're usually pretty hopeless at giving other information. While hotel and travel agency staff in Sofia and the main resorts generally speak some English, knowledge of foreign languages elsewhere in the country is patchy; Russian is more widely understood, and some Bulgarians speak a little

French. Wherever you go, street signs, public signs and menus will almost invariably be written in the **Cyrillic** alphabet.

Increasingly, the Internet is becoming a useful resource for finding out information on Bulgaria. Among the most comprehensive tourism **Web sites** are *www.online.bg*, *http://tourist.cjb.net* and *www.travel-bulgaria.com*.

The best **maps** currently available are those produced by Datamap (*datamap@mail.techno-link.com*), covering the Sofia region and Bulgaria as a whole. It's best to get hold of those before you leave home. Once in the country, you're limited to much less detailed and often out-of-date maps. Street plans of Sofia, Plovdiv and Varna are widely available, but plans for other cities are harder to come by.

Money and banks

Bulgaria's national currency is the **lev**, which is divided into 100 stotinki. The currency was reformed in 1999, since when it has been pegged to the Deutschmark, and comes in 1, 2, 5, 10, 20, and 50 leva notes, as well as coins of 1, 2, 5, 10, 20 and 50 stotinki. For the moment, the lev is fairly stable, although hotels, travel agencies, car rental firms and so on, still quote prices in US dollars; you can pay in the local currency, but at a disadvantageous exchange rate. Tourist sights like museums and galleries normally charge in leva, although as prices fluctuate, prices have been given in US dollars in text. A supply of dollar bills may be useful, particularly for using some taxi firms, and for bartering at markets.

Cash machines (ATM's) are becoming a familiar sight in the cities, while exchange bureaux, offering variable but generally fair rates, are widespread. Be careful, though, as some bureaux may try and give you a lower rate for older banknotes, or may refuse to change them altogether. Many smaller banks and offices won't accept travellers' cheques, and while Visa and Mastercard are gaining greater acceptance, their use is generally restricted to the more expensive shops and hotels.

Be sure to keep a ready supply of coins and 1 lev notes on you for small purchases, as shops are often unable to change larger denomination notes.

Communications

Stamps (*marki*) can be bought from some street kiosks or from **post offices**, usually open Mon–Sat 8.30am– 7.30pm. The main *Poshta* will have a **poste** restante, but postal officers tend to return mail to sender if not claimed immediately.

Coin-operated public telephones (which accept 5 stotinki tokens, available from kiosks) rarely work, and it's usually better to use one of the card phones operated by Mobikom or Bulfon – Mobikom (whose cards also work in the older Betkom phones) are marginally more reliable. **Phonecards** (*fonkarta*) for both systems are available from post offices and some street kiosks and shops. For international calls, it's easier to go to a post office or telephone exchange. The **operator number** for domestic calls is ☎121, for international calls ☎0123.

Internet cafés are beginning to appear in the larger towns and cities, but access is still scanty in smaller towns, and connection times can be slow. Costs are variable, but you will rarely pay more than 70c/hr.

■ Body language

Bulgarians shake their heads when they mean "yes" and nod when they mean "no". Sometimes they reverse these gestures if they know they're speaking to foreigners, thereby complicating the issue further. Emphatic use of the words *da* (yes) and *ne* (no) should be enough to avoid misunderstandings.

Getting around

Public transport in Bulgaria is inexpensive, although vehicles and carriages tend to be outmoded and dirty. Bear in mind that bus and train journeys are notoriously slow – a product of mountainous terrain and badly maintained routes.

■ Trains

Bulgarian State Railways (BDZh) can get you to most towns; trains are punctual, if slow, and fares low – to the coast from Sofia for as little as £6/$9 first class; it is always worth paying the extra £2/$3 or so to travel first class (*purva klassa*) – if nothing else, at least you will have more room. Express services (*Ekspresen*) are restricted to trunk routes, but on all except the humblest branch lines you'll find so-called Rapid (*bârz vlak*) trains. Use these rather than the snail-like *pâtnicheski* services unless you're planning to alight at some particularly minor halt. Long-distance/overnight trains have reasonably priced couchettes (*kushet*) and/or sleepers (*spalen vagon*). For these, on all expresses and many rapids, you need seat **reservations** (*zapazeni mesta*) as well as **tickets** (*bileti*). In large towns, it's usually easier to obtain tickets and reservations from **railway booking offices** (*byuro za bileti*) or **transport service bureaux** (*kompleksni transportni uslugi*) rather than the station, and wise to book a day in advance. Tickets can only be bought on the day of travel at the station. Advance bookings are required for **international tickets**, handled by a separate organization, the Rila Agency. Most stations have **left-luggage offices** (*garderob*). Both InterRail and Eurail passes are valid in Bulgaria.

■ Buses

Practically everywhere is accessible by **bus** (*avtobus*), though in remoter areas there may only be two or three services a day. Generally, you can buy a ticket at least an hour in advance when travelling between towns, but on some routes they're only sold when the bus arrives. On rural routes, tickets are often sold by the driver rather than at the terminal.

■ Driving and hitching

To drive in Bulgaria you'll need a current **driving licence**, third-party insurance plus a Green Card – which can be bought at the border. Entering Bulgaria, your vehicle will be registered with a special "visa tag" which must be presented on leaving the country. **Speed limits** are 50–60kph in towns, 120kph on express roads, and 80kph on all other roads. **Car rental** is arranged by major travel agents in the bigger towns, who reckon payment in US dollars – expect to pay around $70 per day with unlimited mileage.

You'll find filling stations spaced every 30–40km along the highways, but queues are common. **Breakdown assistance** is available only on the principal highways – the emergency number is ☎146.

Hitching is possible in parts of Bulgaria where public transport is sparse; otherwise, people expect you to catch the bus. Hitching alone is not advised.

Accommodation

Although foreigners are required to pay five to ten times the rate charged to Bulgarians, **accommodation** in Bulgaria is still very cheap by Western standards. Though prices are normally quoted in dollars, you can pay in local currency, but it will cost you slightly more.

■ Hotels

Most one- or two-star **hotels** (for the most part uninspiring high-rise blocks) rent doubles for

---

ACCOMMODATION PRICE CODES

Throughout this guide, accommodation is coded on a scale of ① to ⑨, the code indicating the lowest price per person per night you could expect to pay in each establishment in high season. With hostels this is the nightly rate per person; with hotels, the price is arrived at by dividing the cost of the cheapest double room by two. The prices indicated by the codes are as follows:

① under £5/$8 (€9)	④ £15–20/$24–32 (€27–36)	⑦ £30–35/$48–56 (€54–63)
② £5–10/$8–16 (€9–18)	⑤ £20–25/$32–40 (€36–45)	⑧ £35–40/$56–64 (€63–72)
③ £10–15/$16–24 (€18–27)	⑥ £25–30/$40–48 (€45–54)	⑨ £40/$64 (€72) and over

---

£10–15/$16–24 a head, a little more in Sofia and Plovdiv. Cosier family-run hotels are beginning to appear on the coast and in village resorts like Koprivshtitsa, Bansko and Melnik, offering a higher level of service often for a much lower price.

■ Private rooms

Private rooms (*chastni kvartiri*) are available in most large towns, and are usually administered by accommodation agencies, although in the smaller resorts you can usually find a room by asking around – expect to pay around £10–15/$16–24 for a double, more in Sofia and Plovdiv. Single travellers usually get a small reduction on the price of a double. The quality varies enormously (it's rarely possible to inspect the place first), but as a rule, private rooms in big cities will be in large residential blocks, while those in village resorts can often be in atmospheric, traditional-style houses.

■ Campsites and hostels

Some towns of interest have a **campsite** (*Kamping*) on the outskirts, although these are few and far between, and can be unkempt affairs with bad connections to the town centre. The majority have two-person chalets (£5–10/$8–16 per night). **Camping rough** is illegal and punishable with a fine. **Hostels** (*Turisticheska spalnya*) are thin on the ground, although those that exist (in Plovdiv or Sofia, for example) are well run and accustomed to foreigners.

Food and drink

Fresh fruit and vegetables have long formed the basis of Bulgarian cuisine, a tradition rarely reflected in restaurants, where menus have become pretty standardized and uninspiring. Grilled meats are the backbone of most Bulgarian restaurant meals, although

you'll sometimes find more traditional roasted or stewed dishes.

■ Food

Sit-down food is eaten in either a **restorant** (restaurant) or a **mehana** (taverna). There's little difference between the two, save for the fact that a *mehana* is likely to offer folksy decor and a wider range of traditional Bulgarian dishes – wherever you go, you're unlikely to spend more than £6/$9 for a main course, salad and drink.

Foremost among **snacks** are *kebapcheta*, grilled mincemeat served with a chunk of bread, or variations on the theme like *shishche* (shish kebab) or *kebap*. Another favourite is the *banitsa*, a flaky-pastry envelope with a filling – usually cheese; it's sold by street vendors in the morning and evening, to people going to and from work. Elsewhere, *hamburgeri* (basically anything placed between two halves of a bun), *sandvichi* (sandwiches) and *pitsi* (pizzas) dominate the fast-food repertoire. Bulgarians consider their **yoghurt** (*kiselo mlyako*) the world's finest, and hardly miss a day without consuming a glass.

Mainstay of any Bulgarian restaurant menu are the **grilled meats**, of which *kebapcheta* and *kyofte* (meatballs) are the most common. More substantial are chops (*pârzhola* or *kotlet*) or fillets (*file*), invariably *teleshko* (veal) or *svinsko* (pork); offal, in various forms, also makes a strong appearance on menus. In the grander restaurants the main course will be accompanied by potatoes (*kartofi*) and a couple of vegetables, as well as bread: sometimes a *pitka* or small bread bun. Lower down the scale, you may just get chips (*pârzheni kartofi*) and a couple of slices of a stale loaf.

The most characteristic **traditional Bulgarian dishes** are those baked and served in earthenware pots. The best-known dish is *gyuvech* (which literally means "earthenware dish"), a rich stew comprising peppers, aubergines and beans, to which is added either meat or meat stock. *Kavarma*, a spicy meat stew (often pork), is prepared in a similar fashion.

Finally, along the coast and around the highland lakes and reservoirs, there's **fish** (*riba*) – most often fried or grilled, but sometimes in a soup or stew.

Vegetarian meals (*yastia bez meso*) are hard to obtain, although *gyuveche* (a variety of *gyuvech* featuring baked vegetables) and *kachkaval pane* (cheese fried in breadcrumbs) are worth trying.

Pancakes – sweet or savoury – are sold in **patisseries** or *Sladkarnitsa*, alongside various cakes (*torta*) and the occasional gooey oriental treat, such as *baklava*.

■ Drink

From having an insular **wine** industry before World War II, Bulgaria has muscled its way into the forefront of the world's export market. Among the **reds** are full-bodied Cabernet, heavier, mellower Melnik and Gâmza, rich, dark Mavrud, and the smooth, strawberry-flavoured Haskovski Merlot. Dimyat is a good, dry **white** wine, though if you prefer the sweeter variety, try Karlovski Misket (Muscatel) or Tamyanka. The **web site** *http://members.tripod.com/~POCEH* is a good source of information on Bulgarian wines.

Cheap native **spirits** are highly potent, drunk diluted with water in the case of *mastika* (like ouzo in Greece) or downed in one, Balkan-style, in the case of *rakiya* – brandy made from either plums (*slivova*) or grapes (*grozdova*). Bulgarian **beer** has improved immeasurably in recent years, and brands such as Kamenitza, Zagorka and Astika are infinitely preferable to pricey imported alternatives.

Coke, Pepsi and the like are sold everywhere, as is fresh fruit juice. Cafés serve **coffee** (*kafe*), which if you don't specify will probably come *espresso*, though you will also encounter *kapuchino*, *viensko* (Viennese) or *kafe sâs smetana* (coffee with cream). **Tea** (*chai*) is nearly always herbal – ask for *cheren chai* (literally "black tea") if you want the real stuff, normally served with lemon.

Opening hours and holidays

Big-city shops and supermarkets are generally **open** Mon–Sat 8.30am–6pm or later. In rural areas and small towns, a kind of unofficial siesta may prevail between noon and 3pm. Most shops, offices and banks, and many museums, are closed on the following days: Jan 1; March 3; Easter Sunday; Easter Monday; May 1; May 24; Dec 25 and 26. Additional public holidays may occasionally be called by the government. Museum entry charges are usually higher for foreigners than for the locals, although producing a student card will secure a discount.

Emergencies

Petty theft is a danger on the coast, and the Bulgarian **police** can be slow in filling out insurance reports unless you're insistent. If you're driving on roads near the Turkish (or Serbian) border, watch out for traffic cops charging foreign drivers spot fines for spurious offences. **Consulates** may be helpful in some respects, but they never lend cash to nationals who've run out or been robbed. **Women** travelling alone can expect to encounter stares, comments and sometimes worse from macho types, and discos on the coast are pretty much seen as cattle-markets, but a firm response should be enough to cope with most situations.

If you need a **doctor** (*lekar*) or dentist (*zâbolekar*), go to the nearest *Poliklinika* (health centre), whose staff might well speak English or German. Emergency treatment is free of charge although you must pay for **medicines** – larger towns will have at least one 24-hour pharmacy.

Emergency Numbers

Police ☎166; Ambulance ☎150; Fire ☎160.

Belvedere Palace, Vienna, Austria

Salzburger Land mountainscape, Austria

Dubrovnik, Croatia

Rila Monastery, Bulgaria

Bridges over the Vltava, Prague, Czech Republic

Aleksandâr Nevski Cathedral, Sofia, Bulgaria   The Vismarkt, Bruges, Belgium

Nyhavn, Copenhagen, Denmark

Landscape in Finland

Flower shop, Ile St-Louis, Paris, France

Louvre pyramid, Paris, France

SOFIA

Gone are the days when **SOFIA** resembled a kind of communist Geneva, with fresh wreaths stacked against its monuments and a police force that one could imagine clubbing litterbugs and jaywalkers. Although much has been done in recent years to revitalize the heart of the city, some of Sofia's older buildings are still in need of renovation, while many of the roads and pavements are in a dreadful state. In fact, the mixture of chaos and decay which characterizes most of Sofia's points of arrival makes it an unwelcoming city for first-time visitors, but once you've settled in and begun to explore, you'll find it surprisingly laid-back for a capital city. Though it's hardly a great European metropolis brimming with fine sights, the place comes into its own on fine spring and summer days, when the downtown streets and their pavement cafés buzz with life. Urban pursuits can be combined with the outdoor recreational possibilities offered by verdant **Mount Vitosha**, an easily-accessible 12km to the south. Despite occasional concerts and a few discos, entertainment still revolves around the evening promenade or *korso*, followed by a drink in one of the cafés, bars or beer halls.

The city was founded by a Thracian tribe some 3000 years ago, and various **Byzantine ruins** attest to its zenith as the regional Imperial capital of **Serdica** under Constantine (306–337). The Bulgars didn't arrive on the scene until the ninth century, and with the notable exception of the thirteenth-century Boyana Church, their cultural monuments largely disappeared during the Turkish occupation (1381–1878), of which the sole visible legacy is a couple of stately **mosques**. Sofia's finest architecture postdates Bulgaria's liberation from the Turks: handsome public buildings and parks, and the magnificent Aleksandâr Nevski Cathedral.

Arrival and information

Trains arrive at **Central Station** (*Tsentralna Gara*), a concrete hive harbouring a couple of exchange bureaux and snack bars, but little else to welcome the visitor. Five minutes' ride along bul Knyaginya Mariya Luiza (tram #1 or #7 or minibus #2) is Sveta Nedelya Square, within walking distance of several hotels and the main accommodation bureaux (see below). Most national **buses** arrive in the various bus parks situated around the *Hotel Princess* (still known to locals by its former name, *Novotel Europa*), just opposite the train station, although some Bansko services and Blagoevgrad buses (for connections to Rila monastery) use the Ovcha Kupel terminal, 5km southwest of the centre along bul Tsar Boris III (tram #5 from behind the Law Courts). International buses (daily connections with Istanbul, Salonika, Athens and Skopje) arrive either near the *Hotel Princess* or at a small terminal at Damian Gruev 38, ten minutes walk west of the centre. Bus #84, running every ten to twenty minutes, connects **Sofia Airport** (*www.sofia-airport.bg*) with the Orlov Most, from where you can walk into the city centre; the last bus leaves the airport at around 11.30pm. Minibus #30, which runs every twelve minutes, and operates like a shared taxi, will take you from the airport to the city centre for 50c. Ignore the misleading **Tourist Service** office in the foyer – they might well try to charge you $20 for a taxi.

There is no official tourist office in Sofia: the closest approximation to one is the friendly **Odysseia-In**, at bul Stamboliiski 20, entrance on ul Lavele (Mon–Fri 9am–6.30pm; ☎02/989-0538, *www.newtravel.com*). They can give practical advice and arrange accommodation and tours throughout Bulgaria, and also have their own en-suite room to rent (②). You could also try the sombre, government-run **National Information and Advertising Centre**, Sveta Sofia 1 (Mon–Fri 9am–5pm; 02/987-9778, *www.bulgariatravel.org.*), which provides general information and has a few timetables and glossy brochures (often out of date) but otherwise is of limited use. Otherwise the **Web site** *www.sofia.com* is a useful starting point for finding

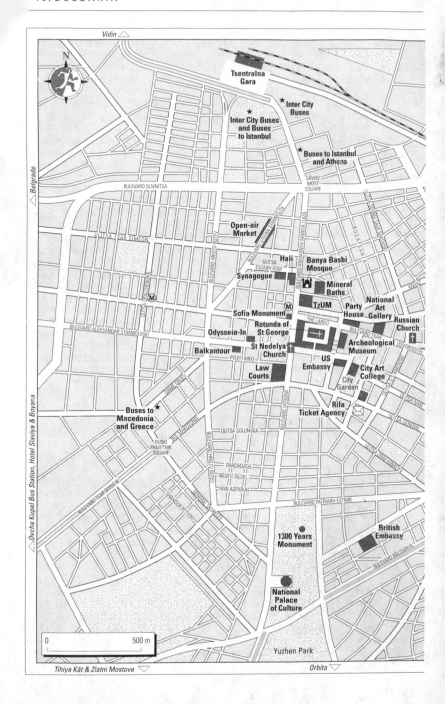

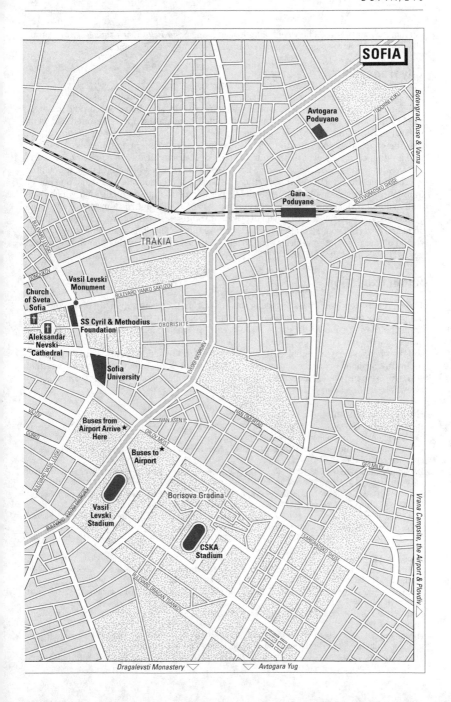

SOFIA

Avtogara
Poduyane

Gara
Poduyane

BOTEVGRADSKO SHOSE

Botevgrad, Ruse & Varna

TODORINI KUKLI

TRAKIA

Vasil Levski
Monument

BULEVARD LOSM

PODUNYKOV

Church
of Sveta
Sofia

SS Cyril & Methodius
Foundation

BULEVARD YANKO SAKUZOV

OBORISHTE

GEORGI GEORGIEV

Aleksandâr
Nevski
Cathedral

Sofia
University

VAZOV

GURKO

Buses from
Airport Arrive ★
Here

IVAN ASEN II

JAN OM IRIAC

BULEVARD VASIL LEVSKI

Buses to
Airport ★

ORLOV MOST

GEO MILEV

Vasil
Levski
Stadium

BULEVARD HRISTO SMIRNENSKI

Borisova Gradina

SARIGADSKO SHOSE

Vitana Campsite, the Airport & Plovdiv

CSKA
Stadium

BULEVARD DRAGAN TSANKOV

out more about the city. The weekly English-language *Sofia Echo* (*www.sofiaecho.com*), available from some newsstands, is a good source for local news and listings.

City transport

The **public transport** network – consisting of buses (*avtobus*), trolleybuses (*troleibus*), a one-line metro system, and, slowest of all, trams (*tramvai*) – runs between 5am and midnight and is ridiculously cheap and reasonably efficient. There's a **flat fare** of around 20c on all urban routes; tickets (*bileti*) are sold from street kiosks, and, occasionally, on board, and must be punched as you enter the vehicle (inspections are frequent and there are spot fines for fare-dodgers). Kiosks at the main tram stops sell one-day tickets (*karta za edin den*; $1) and five-day tickets (*karta za pet dena*; $4.50). Metro tickets must be bought from the station; a 'combination ticket' (*kombiniran bilet*) costs 25c and is valid for one metro and one bus or tram journey. **Taxis** should charge about 50c per kilometre until nightfall, after which rates tend to double. Make sure the driver has his clock running, though, as tourists are prime rip-off targets. Additionally, there's a fleet of private **minibuses** (*marshrutka*), acting like shared taxis and covering some 37 different routes across the city. Destinations and routes are displayed on the front of the vehicles – in Cyrillic – and passengers flag them down like normal taxis. There's a flat fare of 50c.

Accommodation

The budget **hotels** you'll pass if walking into town from the train station are the kind of flop houses it's prudent to avoid, and most of central Sofia's older hotels are overpriced considering the level of comfort they are able to offer. The smaller family-run hotels are the best bases for a few days in the city, although advance bookings are advisable. A **private room** is still the cheapest way of getting a decent place close to the action. Centrally located private rooms are available from Balkantour (see p.254) for $16 per person depending on length of stay. Odysseia-In (see p.247) can book rooms in the smaller private hotels both in Sofia and elsewhere in the country.

Hotels and hostels

Baldzhieva, ul Tsar Asen 23 (☎02/981-1257). Small hotel in a nicely refurbished town house just one block west of bul Vitosha. Rooms are clean and cosy, all with phone, fridge, TV and WC. ⑤.

Central, bul Hristo Botev 52 (☎02/981-2364). Smart, modern hotel catering largely for business travellers, in a fairly central spot. ⑧.

Deva-Spartak, bul Arsenalski (☎02/661-261). Small, modern place with tidy en-suite rooms, 2km south of the centre beyond Yuzhen Park, next to the Spartak swimming pool. Tram #6 from the station. ⑤.

Enny, Pop Bogomil 46 (☎02/833-002). Small and simple downtown hotel just off bul Knyaginya Mariya Luiza, with cramped but clean rooms, and shared facilities in the hallway. ③.

Ganesha, Al von Humboldt 26 (☎02/707-936 or 718-798). A converted apartment block on a suburban street, midway between the city centre and the airport. Neat rooms have en-suite shower, satellite TV and small balcony. Bus #213 or #313 from the train station, or bus #84 from the airport to the *Hotel Pliska* stop. ③.

Hostel Sofia, Pozitano 16 (☎02 989-8582, *hostelsofia@usa.net*). Despite the grubby external appearance, this friendly, 2-dorm, 13-bed hostel, just west of Sveta Nedelya Square, is a clean and well-run establishment, with shared kitchen, bathroom and cable TV. Breakfast included. ②.

Maya, Trapezitsa 4 (☎02/894-611). Small, family-run place in an apartment block bang in the centre, just opposite the Largo. Rooms have TV. ④.

Niky, Neofit Rilski 16 (☎02/511-915). Small hotel just off bul Vitosha. Tiny rooms with shared bathrooms, but most have TV. ③.

Orbita, bul Dzheimz Bauchâr 76 (☎02/657-447). Characterless postwar block with plain en-suites, handy for the foothills of Mount Vitosha and Yuzhen Park. Tram #9 from the station. ④.

Slavyanska Beseseda, ul Slavyanska 3 (☎02/880-441). Gloomy Communist-era hotel, with sullen staff. Fairly central, but a last resort. ④.

The City

The heart of Sofia fits compactly between two rivers, the Perlovets and Vladaya, whose modest width didn't deter architects from designing a fancy bridge for both of them during the 1890s. Crowned with four ferocious-looking statues and set amidst weeping willows, the **Orlov Most** (Eagle Bridge), to the east of the centre, marks the spot where liberated prisoners of war were greeted by their victorious Russian allies and compatriots in 1878. Popular regard for the "Slav elder brother" stems from Russian support for Bulgarian liberation in the nineteenth century, and has little or no parallel in most other parts of the former eastern bloc.

From the bridge it's a brief stroll up bul Tsar Osvoboditel to **Sofia University**, the country's most prestigious seat of learning. In the distance, across the park, a glint of gold betrays the proximity of the **Aleksandâr Nevski Cathedral**, one of the finest pieces of architecture in the Balkans. Financed by public subscription and built between 1882 and 1924 to honour the 200,000 Russian casualties of the 1877–78 War of Liberation, it's a magnificent structure, bulging with domes and semi-domes and glittering with gold leaf. Within the cavernous interior, a white-bearded God glowers down from the main cupola, an angelic sunburst covers the central vault, and as a parting shot, Vasnetsov's *Day of Judgement* looms above the exit. The modern crypt, entered from outside (daily except Tuesday 9.30am–12.30pm & 2–5.30pm; free), contains a superb collection of **icons** from all over the country, mostly eighteenth- and nineteenth-century pieces – though look out for some medieval gems from the coastal towns of Nesebâr and Sozopol.

On the north-eastern edge of the cathedral square an imposing gallery houses the **SS Cyril and Methodius Foundation** (Tue–Sun 11am–6.30pm; $1), an international art collection which devotes a lot of space to Indian wood-carvings and second-division French artists, though there are a few sketches by the likes of Millet and Renoir, and a couple of Rodin busts. Heading west across the square, you'll pass two recumbent lions flanking the Tomb of the Unknown Soldier, set beside the wall of the brown-brick **Church of Sveta Sofia**. Raised during the sixth-century reign of Justinian, it follows the classic Byzantine plan of a regular cross with a dome at the intersection.

The best route from here is to cut down past the building housing the National Assembly on to **Bulevard Tsar Osvoboditel**, an attractive thoroughfare surfaced with yellow stone and partly lined with chestnut trees. West along the boulevard is the **Russian Church**, a stunning golden-domed confection, with an emerald spire and an exuberant mosaic-tiled exterior, concealing a dark, candle-scented interior. Close by is the **Natural Science Museum** (daily 10am–6.30pm; $1), containing a dull collection of rocks, minerals and threadbare stuffed animals, as well as live specimens – including pythons and baby crocodiles – housed extremely uncomfortably in tiny glass tanks.

At its western end bul Tsar Osvoboditel opens into **ploshtad Alexander Battenberg**, named after the German aristocrat chosen to be the newly independent country's first monarch in 1878. The square was once the scene of Communist rallies and parades, and until its demolition in 1999, was dominated by the mausoleum of Georgi Dimitrov, first leader of the People's Republic of Bulgaria. On the north side of the square, the dilapidated former royal palace houses the uninspiring **National Art Gallery** (Tues–Sun 10.30am–6.30pm; $1.50), currently only staging small temporary exhibitions, and the slightly more interesting **Ethnographic Museum** (Tues–Sun 10am–5.30pm; $1.50), where a range of ecclesiastical and folk art from around Bulgaria is on display. Far better than either is the **City Art Gallery** (Tue–Sat 10am–6pm, Sun 11am–5pm; free) immediately south of here in the City Garden, home to an excellent collection of nineteenth and twentieth century Bulgarian paintings.

Since World War II the seat of power has shifted westwards to the **Largo**. Flanked on three sides by severe monumental buildings, this elongated plaza was built on the ruins of central Sofia, pulverized by British and American bombers in the autumn of 1944. Of the complex, the white, colonnaded supertanker of the former **Party House**, originally the home of the

Communist hierarchy, and now serving as government offices, is the most arresting structure. Protesters set fire to it in the summer of 1990, but the Party wasn't ejected from the building until early 1992. In front of the Party House, a pedestrian subway provides glimpses of the Roman walls built to protect the eastern entrance to the city. Just south of the Party House, a fifteenth-century mosque now holds the **Archaeological Museum** (Tues–Sun 10.30am–4.30pm; free), with a fine but poorly labelled collection of Thracian and Roman artefacts, including numerous tombstones and grave-goods, as well as some early Christian art.

Immediately to the west is the **Presidency**, guarded by soldiers in colourful nineteenth-century garb (Changing of the Guard hourly). Alongside, the *Sheraton Hotel*'s sombre wings run round a courtyard containing Sofia's oldest church, the fourth-century **Rotunda of St George**. It houses frescoes from the eighth century onwards, although most eyes are drawn to the fourteenth-century Christ the Pantokrator, surrounded by a frieze of 22 prophets, in the dome. On the northern side of the Largo, an equally large structure houses the Council of Ministers (Bulgaria's cabinet) and Sofia's upmarket shopping mall, **Tzum**. Another underpass gives access to a sunken shop-lined plaza, with the tiny **Church of Sveta Petka Samardzhiiska** (daily 8am–7pm; $2.50) at its centre. Dating back to the twelfth century, it contains fragmentary and much-restored frescoes, while national hero Vasil Levsky is rumoured to lie buried beneath the crypt. The plaza extends westwards to the Serdica metro station, watched over by the towering **Sofia Monument**, representing the eponymous Goddess of Wisdom – the city's new symbol.

The square elongates northwards to join **Bulevard Knyaginya Mariya Luiza**. Here the **Banya Bashi Mosque** catches the eye, built in 1576 by Hadzhi Mimar Sonah, who also designed the great mosque at Edirne in Turkey. Behind stand Sofia's **mineral baths**, housed in a yellow and red-striped fin-de-siècle building, presently undergoing restoration – its ultimate function has yet to be decided. Locals still gather to bottle the hot, sulphurous water, which gushes into the long stone troughs outside. Right opposite the mosque is the **Hali**, Sofia's old market hall, housing three floors of shops and restaurants. The **Church of St Nedelya**, marking the southern boundary of pl Sveta Nedelya, was constructed after the liberation as the successor to a number of churches that have stood here since medieval times. South of St Nedelya, the silhouette of Mount Vitosha surmounts the rooftops of **Vitosha Bulevard**, Sofia's main shopping street, dominated at its northern end by the brooding columned bulk of the **Law Courts**.

Heading east from bul Vitosha, the shop-flanked **Graf** meanders to the **Friendship Bridge** (Most na Druzhba), one of the approaches to **Borisova Gradina** ("Boris's Garden", after Bulgaria's inter-war monarch, Boris III). The park itself is the oldest and largest in Sofia, with a rich variety of flowers and trees and two huge football stadiums. As an evening parade ground for the city's burgeoning youth culture, though, it's outshone by **Yuzhen Park**, at the southern end of bul Vitosha, which is dominated by the **National Palace of Culture** (NDK), a cavernous concert and exhibition centre.

Mount Vitosha

A wooded mass of granite 20km long and 16km wide, **Mount Vitosha** is where Sofians come for picnics, views and skiing, and the ascent of its highest peak, the 2290m **Cherni Vrâh**, has become a traditional test of stamina. Public transport to the mountain is straightforward, although there are fewer buses on weekdays than at weekends.

One approach is to take tram #5 from behind the Law Courts to Ovcha Kupel bus station, then change to bus #61, which climbs through the forests towards **ZLATNI MOSTOVE**, a beauty spot on the western shoulder of Mount Vitosha beside the so-called **Stone River**. Beneath the large boulders running down the mountainside is a rivulet which once attracted gold-panners. Trails lead up beside the rivulet towards the mountain's upper reaches: Cherni Vrâh is about two to three hours' walk from here.

Another route up Vitosha is on tram #12 from Graf Ignatiev to the Hladilnika terminus on bul Cherni Vrâh, and then bus #66 to the resort centre of **ALEKO**. Aleko can also be reached by taking bus #64 or #93 from Hladilnika to the suburb of **Dragalevtsi**, where there's a **chair-lift** (*lifta*; daily in winter season; rest of year weekends only; 50c); or taking bus #122 from Hladilnika to **Simeonovo**, starting point for the Aleko-bound **gondola** (daily in winter season; rest of year weekends only; 50c. However you get there, Aleko is well-served with snack bars, restaurants and innumerable walking trails. The peak of Cherni Vrăh is an easy forty-metre walk from here. From November to late spring Aleko is a thriving winter sports centre, with pistes to suit all grades of skiers and a couple of ski schools that rent out gear.

Two km northwest of Dragalevtsi lies the suburb of **Boyana**, chiefly famed for its thirteenth century **church**, which is disappointingly rarely open. The nearby **museum** (Tue–Sun 9am–5pm; $1) houses photographs of the church's murals. Take bus #64 to the Boyansko Hanche stop. The **National History Museum** (Daily 9.30am-5.30pm; $5) has recently relocated to the modern but remote Residence Boyana – take trolleybus #2 from outside Sofia University. The star attraction is the Thracian Panagyurishte gold treasure, but there's little else to cause excitement. Other exhibits include pottery, ecclesiastical art and nineteenth century costumes, all labelled only in Bulgarian.

Eating, drinking and entertainment

Market economics and creeping westernization have made big changes in the range of food, drink and nightlife, ensuring that the Bulgarian capital is no longer the stern and joyless place it was before 1989. Indigenous grilled **snack foods** have been largely replaced by hamburgers, sandwiches and pizzas, served at kiosks and fast-food joints throughout the city. *Kenar*, with numerous branches around Sofia, including those at bul Vitosha 19 and bul Stamboliiski 55, offers take-away sandwiches and salads made from traditional Bulgarian ingredients. Sofia's **restaurants** have undergone a facelift, with many dingy, unprofitable places closing down to be replaced by rather more garish, cosmopolitan haunts, some featuring live music. Menus continue to be rather one-dimensional, but if you tire of the standard Bulgarian meal of grilled meat plus salad, there are plenty of restaurants offering foreign cuisine.

Daytime **drinking** takes place in the cafés around bul Vitosha or around the numerous kiosks which dot the city's open spaces. **Bars** are on the increase, and come and go with alarming rapidity. If you're renting a room in suburban Sofia, you'll probably find a couple of these small and intimate drinking venues on your block: otherwise, the streets either side of bul Vitosha are the best places to look in the city centre.

Restaurants

Art Club Museum, ul Gogol 4a. Lunch amid the Thracian tombstones, in this very pleasant patio café at the back of the Archaeological Museum. Salads, pasta and other light meals are on the menu.

Baalbek, Vasil Levski 4. Highly-regarded Lebanese establishment, with sit-down restaurant upstairs and fast food counter (offering kebabs, shawarma and falafel) on the ground floor.

Camelot, Graf Ignatiev 1. Subterranean medieval-themed restaurant, with an emphasis on heavy meat dishes and low lighting.

Chen, Rakovski 86. Popular Chinese restaurant with authentic food, just opposite the opera house.

The Friends, corner of Graf Ignatiev and Rakovski. Smart self-service restaurant offering a range of Bulgarian dishes. Also has a bar and take-away burger counter.

Happy Bar and Grill, corner of Stamboliiski and pl Sveta Nedelya. Home-grown fast-food chain, with fairly standardised Bulgarian and 'Western' options.

Perfect, in the sunken plaza beneath Tzum. 'Western' style restaurant right in front of the Church of Sveta Petka Samardzhiiska, offering Bulgarian staples and international fare, including a reasonable stab at 'English breakfast'.

Pizza Palace, Vitosha 34. Popular restaurant, with a large selection of pizza and pasta dishes at very reasonable prices.

Ramayana, Hristo Belchev 32. Pretty authentic Indian restaurant one block east of bul Vitosha, with a range of vegetarian options.

Rancho Ribs, Stamboliiski 33. American-style ribs and hot-dogs, with a fair selection of moderately priced drinks.

Trops-kâshta, Sâborna 11. Excellent value self-service restaurant offering tasty Bulgarian standards. There's another branch in the basement of the Hali, on bul Knyaginya Mariya Luiza.

Cafés, bars and discos

Background Pub, Vitosha 14. Small courtyard pub, which also serves decent food. Occasional live music in the evenings.

Biblioteka, Vasil Levski 88. Busy, youthful, rock & pop-orientated disco beneath the National Library building, one block north of Sofia university. Cover charge $1.

Café Rene, Dondukov 29. Typical local bar, with a terrace, in a quiet location not far from the centre.

Chervilo, Tsar Osvoboditel. Bar and disco with a different style of music every night.

El Corazón, Graf Ignatiev 12. Trendy bar and disco attracting a largely youthful crowd.

The French Café, Makedonia 48. Coffee and French-style pastries in an elegant three-storey town house on Ruski Pametnik Square.

Indigo, Yuzhen Park. Large club venue behind the National soccer stadium. Events range from commercial disco to rave.

The Irish Harp, Sveta Sofia 7. Dimly lit 'Irish' pub just off pl Sveta Nedelya, with regular live music.

Miss Kapriz, Angel Kunchev 2. Bright and airy café and bar near the National Library, serving a range of light meals, coffee and cakes.

Pri Kmeta, Parizhka. Roomy basement beer hall near the Aleksandâr Nevsky church. Good food, and occasional noisy disco.

Quo Vadis, Moskovska, near the Levski Monument. Late night beer and dance hall with live music ranging from local folk acts to tango. Open till 4am.

Schweik, Vitosha 1A. International beers (including excellent Czech ones) and sausagey snacks in a basement just off Vitosha.

Swingin' Hall, Dragan Tsankov 8. Modern suburban bar serving imported drinks at Western prices. Live music (usually pop/rock or jazz) on two stages. Open well after midnight. Cover charge.

Listings

Airlines Aeroflot, Oborishte 23 (☎02/943-4489); Air France, ul Sâborna 2 (☎02/981-7830); Alitalia, Graf Ignatiev 40 (☎02/981-6702); Austrian Airlines, bul Vitosha 41 (☎02/980-2323); British Airways, Alabin 56 (☎02/981-7000); KLM, Uzundjovska 14 (☎02/981-9910); Lufthansa, ul Sâborna 9a (☎02/980-4101); Malev, Patriarh Evtimii 19 (☎02/981-5091); Olympic, bul Stamboliiski 46 (☎02/981-4545); Swissair, Angel Kunchev 1 (☎02/980-4459).

Airport information ☎02/72 0672 or 02/79 8035.

Car rental Avis, Kaloyan 8 (☎02/981-4960); Hertz, bul Vasil Levski 47 (☎02/980-0461), and at the airport (☎02/79-1477); National, Acsakov 11 (☎02/980-6290).

Embassies and consulates Britain, bul Levski 38 (☎02/980-1220); USA, ul Sâborna 1 (☎02/980-5241); Australia, ul Trakia 37 (☎02 946-1334).

Internet access Ultima Internet Centre, Lavele 16 (daily 9am–11.30pm); Infocafe, Graf Ignatiev 32 (daily 9am–10.30pm); Internet Agency at the NDK (daily 9.30am-11.30pm); Cyberzone, Rakovski 149.

Libraries American Center, Kârnigradska 18 (daily 1–5pm); British Council, Tulovo 7 (Mon–Fri 9am–noon & 2–5pm).

Medical emergencies The main accident and emergency department is at the Pirogov hospital, bul Totleben 21 (☎51531).

Pharmacies 24hr service at pl Sveta Nedelya 5.

Post office ul General Gurko (daily 7am–9pm).

Taxis Okay ☎2121; Express ☎1280; Yes ☎91119.

Telephones On ul Stefan Karadzha, behind the post office; open 24 hrs.

Train tickets International tickets can be bought at the station (Tsentralna Gara) on the day of travel or from the Rila Bureau, General Gurko 5 (Mon-Fri 8am-7pm, Sat 9am-2pm), in advance.

Travel agents Pandion, bul Cherni Vrâh 20a (☎02/963-0436, *www.birdwatchingholidays*), organize guided wildlife and archaeology tours around the country; USIT Colours (Travel Byte), bul Levski 35 (☎02/981-1900), handle discount international air tickets; Balkantourist, bul Vitosha1 (☎02/9802324, *baltour@mail.tecno-link.com*), arrange accommodation and tours across Bulgaria. Balkantour, bul

Stamboliiski 27 (☎02/987-7233 or 986-5691, *balkantour@hotmail.com*), and at the airport (☎02/796-293), can organize private accommodation.

SOUTHERN BULGARIA

Trains heading from Bulgaria to Greece follow the Struma Valley south from Sofia, skirting some of the country's most grandiose mountains on the way. Formerly noted for their bandits and hermits, the Rila and Pirin Mountains contain Bulgaria's highest, stormiest peaks, swathed in forests and dotted with alpine lakes awaiting anyone prepared to hike or risk their car's suspension on the backroads. If time is short, the two spots to select are the most revered of Bulgarian monasteries, **Rila**, lying some 30km east of the main southbound route, and the village of **Melnik**, known both for its wine and its vernacular architecture. More traditional architecture is to be found in the village of **Bansko** on the eastern side of the Pirin range, a small detour from the main north–south route. As well as being one of the country's newest **skiing** resorts, Bansko also makes a good base for **hiking**.

Another much-travelled route heads southeast from Sofia towards Istanbul, through the Plain of Thrace, a fertile region that was the heartland of the ancient Thracians, whose culture began to emerge during the third millennium BC. The main road and rail lines now linking Istanbul and Sofia essentially follow the course of the Roman Serdica–Constantinople road, past towns ruled by the Ottomans for so long that foreigners used to call this "European Turkey". Of these, the most important is **Plovdiv**, Bulgaria's second city, whose old quarter is a wonderful melange of Renaissance mansions, mosques and classical remains, spread over three hills. Thirty kilometres south of Plovdiv is **Bachkovo Monastery**, whose churches and courtyards contain some of Bulgaria's most vivid frescoes.

The Rila Monastery

The best-known of Bulgaria's monasteries, famed for its architecture and mountainous setting, **RILA** receives a steady stream of visitors, many of whom come on excursions from Sofia. You can treat Rila as a day-trip from the capital if you book a tour with a travel agent in Sofia (such as Odysseia-In; around $30 per day), or travel with the (summer-only) daily bus service, which leaves Sofia's Ovcha Kupel terminal at 6.30am. Otherwise, public transport is so meagre that you'll have to stay the night: catch a bus or train from Sofia to Blagoevgrad in the Struma Valley, where you can catch local buses to Rila village, 27km short of Rila Monastery. Here, you can change to one of three daily buses to the monastery itself.

The single road to the **Rila Monastery** runs above the foaming River Rilska, fed by innumerable springs from the surrounding mountains, which are covered with pine and beech trees beneath peaks flecked with snow. Even today there's a palpable sense of isolation, and it's easy to see why Ivan Rilski – or **John of Rila** – chose this valley to escape the savagery of feudal life and the laxity of the established monasteries at the end of the ninth century. The current foundation, 4km from John's original hermitage, was plundered during the eighteenth century and repairs had hardly begun when the whole structure burned down in 1833. Its resurrection was presented as a religious and patriotic duty: public donations poured in throughout the last century, and the east wing was built as recently as 1961 to display the treasury.

Ringed by mighty walls, the monastery has the outward appearance of a fortress, but past the west gate this impression is negated by the beauty of the interior, which even the crowds can't mar. Graceful arches above the flag-stoned courtyard support tiers of monastic cells, and stairways ascend to top-floor balconies, which – viewed from below – resemble outstretched flower petals. Bold red stripes and black-and-white check patterns enliven the facade, contrasting with the sombre mountains behind and creating a harmony between the cloisters and the **Church** within. Richly coloured frescoes shelter beneath the porch of the monastery church and cover much of its interior. The iconostasis is particularly splendid, almost 10m wide and covered by a mass of intricate carvings and gold leaf.

Beside the church is **Hrelyo's Tower**, the sole remaining building from the fourteenth century. Cauldrons, which were once used to prepare food for pilgrims, occupy the kitchen on the ground floor of the north wing, where the soot-encrusted ceiling has the shape and texture of a huge termite's nest. Things are more salubrious on the floors above, where the spartan refectory and some of the panelled guest rooms are open for inspection. The **ethnographic collection** (daily 8am–5pm; free) is notable for its carpets and silverware, while beneath the east wing there's a wealth of objects in the **treasury** (same hours). These include icons and medieval Gospels, Rila's charter from Tsar Ivan Shishman, written on leather and sealed with gold in 1378, and a miniature cross made by the monk Raphael during the 1970s. Containing more than 1500 human figures, each the size of a grain of rice, the cross took Raphael twelve years to carve with a needle, and cost him his eyesight.

It's possible to **stay** (both men and women) in the monastery cells for about $10 a night if you don't mind the lack of hot water and the curfew (10pm or earlier; check before going out for the evening). Otherwise, try the *Turisticheska spalnya* (②) just outside the monastery's eastern gate, the three-star *Hotel Tsarev Vrah* (☎07054/2280; ④), about 200m further on, or the older but still agreeable *Hotel Rilets* (☎07054/2106; ④), 2km further east. Near the *Rilets* the primitive *Bor* **campsite** occupies an attractive riverside site. The more comfortable *Camping Zodiac* (☎07054/2291), another 200m east, rents out four-person chalets (②).

For **snacks**, delicious bread can be obtained at the bakery (which is run by monks), just outside the monastery's east gate. For more substantial meals, the **restaurants** at the hotels *Tsarev Vrah* and *Rilets* are preferable to the outlets near the monastery gates, which sometimes overcharge stray foreigners. **Nightlife** is limited to the plush bar of the *Rilets*, where there's sometimes a disco.

Melnik and around

Approaching the village of **MELNIK** on the bus from Sandanski, the nearest major town, 15km away, you catch glimpses of the wall of mountains, which allowed the townsfolk to thumb their noses at Byzantium during the eleventh century. The village hides until the last moment, encircled by hard-edged crags, scree slopes and rounded sandstone cones. With its whitewashed stone houses on timber props festooned with flowers, its cobbled alleys and its narrow courtyards, Melnik is stunning – but socially and economically it's fast becoming a fossil. In 1880 the village had 20,000 inhabitants, 75 churches and a thriving market on the Charshiya, the main street. The economy waned towards the end of the last century, and the Balkan War of 1913 saw Melnik burned to the ground and its trade routes sundered. Nowadays there are only a few hundred inhabitants and the village survives on **wine making** – the traditional stand-by – and tourism.

Melnik's backstreets invite aimless wandering and guarantee a succession of eye-catching details. Its oldest ruin – known as the Byzantine or **Bolyar House** is sited on the high ground immediately east of the centre, and was clearly built with defence in mind. It was probably the residence of Melnik's thirteenth-century overlord, Alexei Slav, who invited rich Greeks to settle here. Southeast of the Bolyar House you'll see the balustraded tower of the **Church of Sveti Nikolai**. Inside, a wooden bishop's throne decorated with light-blue floral patterns offsets a fine iconostasis, on which white-bearded St Nicholas himself is prominently featured.

The houses that belonged to the village's Greek entrepreneurs, rebuilt during the National Revival, are now Melnik's most impressive buildings, and none more so than the old **Kordopulov Mansion** (Tues–Sun 8am–noon & 1.30–6pm; $1.50) situated on the eastern outskirts. The stone-walled house protrudes from the hillside, its windows surveying every approach. The spacious rooms are intimate, the reception room a superb fusion of

Greek and Bulgarian crafts, with an intricate latticework ceiling and a multitude of stained-glass windows.

Several steep and slippery tracks lead up the hillside immediately south of the Kordopulov house onto the **Nikolova Gora**, a wooded plateau bearing the ruins of a couple of monasteries and, at its western end, a medieval fortress. The view from the latter – with pyramidal sandstone formations rearing to the left and right – is spectacular.

A more strenuous walk heads northeast towards **Rozhen monastery**. You can either take the asphalt road to Rozhen from the west end of Melnik village (1hr 30min), or the more direct path over the mountains (1hr). For the latter, follow the gulley at the eastern end of Melnik village, take the right-hand fork after a kilometre and a half, and look for a steep path which ascends the hillside to your left. Views of rippling mountains reward the effort, although the subsequent descent to the monastery has been narrowed by soil erosion, and can be unsuitable for those who don't have a head for heights. The monastery itself has a beautiful, balconied courtyard, and the village of Rozhen below is just as pretty as Melnik, although less developed.

Practicalities

There's one **bus** a day from Sofia to Melnik (leaving at 2pm from behind the *Hotel Princess*) – otherwise take one of the more frequent buses from Sofia to Sandanski, and change to one of the local minibuses (5 daily). Try and avoid travelling to Sandanski by rail – the train station is miles away from the town centre. The **tourist office** in Sandanski, on the main square just down from the bus stop (Mon–Fri 9am–6pm; ☎0746/22549, *bicc@omega.bg*), can arrange **rooms** for you in Melnik – otherwise just head for the village and ask around. There are plenty of small bed-and-breakfast hotels, such as *Uzunova Kâshta* (☎07437/270; ②), a traditional-style house at the eastern end of the village, or the *Melnik* (☎07437/272; ②), a more modern establishment in the centre. Of the half-dozen **places to eat**, the best are *Loznitsite* on the main street, offering traditional meat-based dishes in a stone-built house; and *Menchevata Kashta* further east, which offers a broad range of Bulgarian food and a few vegetarian options: try *gyuveche po makedonski*, local vegetables baked in a pot.

Bansko and around

Lying some 40km east of the main Struma valley route, **BANSKO** is the main centre for walking and skiing on the eastern slopes of the Pirin mountains. It's a traditional agricultural centre and a growing tourist resort, boasting a wealth of stone-built nineteenth-century farmhouses and a growing number of small, B&B-style hotels. Though connected to Sofia and other towns by bus (see p.258), Bansko can also be reached by a narrow-gauge railway which leaves the main Sofia–Plovdiv line at **Septemvri** and forges its way across the highlands. It's one of the most scenic trips in the Balkans, but also one of the slowest, taking five hours to cover a distance of just over 100km.

Bansko centres around the modern pedestrianized pl Nikola Vaptsarov, where the **Nikola Vaptsarov Museum** (Mon–Fri 9am–6pm, Sat & Sun 9am–noon & 2–6pm; $1) contains a display relating to the local-born poet and socialist martyr, as well as housing a crafts exhibition where you can purchase distinctive local rugs. Immediately north of here, pl Vâzrazhdane is watched over by the solid stone tower of the **Church of Sveta Troitsa**, whose interior contains exquisite nineteenth-century frescos and icons. On the opposite side of the square, the **Rilski Convent** contains an **Icon Museum** (Mon–Fri 9am–noon & 2–5pm; $1) devoted to the achievements of Bansko's nineteenth-century icon painters – a school largely centred around the Vienna-educated Toma Vishanov, who, with pupils Dimitâr and Simeon Molerov, travelled from village to village decorating local churches.

The easiest way of getting into the **Pirin mountains** from Bansko is to walk (or take a taxi) west to the Vihren hut (where dorm accommodation is available; ②), a steep 14km uphill. This is the main trail-head for hikes towards the 2914m summit of **Mt Vihren** (Bulgaria's second-highest peak), or gentler rambles around the meadows and lakes nearby.

Practicalities

There are five buses a day to Bansko from Sofia, although if you're approaching the area from Rila or Melnik, it's far easier to head for Blagoevgrad in the Struma valley and change buses there. Bansko's **bus and train stations** are on the northern fringes of town, ten minutes' walk from the central pl Vaptsarov. The **Pirin Tourist Forum**, Stefan Milenkov 3, Blagoevgrad (☎07365/458, *www.pirin-tourism.bg*), is the best source of information on hiking and accommodation in the region, while the Web site *www.ewpnet.com/bulgardos* gives an idea of local hiking routes. Best of the family-run **hotels** are *Albert*, ul Byalo More 12 (☎07443/4264; ④), a cosy place with en-suite rooms just off pl Vâzrazhdane; *Dzhangal*, Gotse Delchev 24 (☎07443/2661; ③), in a quiet area ten minutes' walk from the centre and featuring a garden, barbecue and sauna; *Hadzipopov*, Tsar Boris III 3 (☎07443/2131; ③), and the friendly *Karol*, Kaloyan 21 (☎07443/3902; ④). For **eating**, there are over forty tavernas offering traditional specialities: *Sirleshtova Kâshta*, *Bayrakovata Mehana* and *Dyado Pene*, all grouped around the centre, are among the most atmospheric.

Plovdiv

Bulgaria's second largest city, **PLOVDIV** is, in many ways, a more attractive and affluent place than Sofia. The old town embodies Plovdiv's long history – Thracian fortifications subsumed by Macedonian masonry, overlaid with Byzantine walls and by great timber-framed mansions erected during the Bulgarian renaissance, symbolically looking down upon the derelict Ottoman mosques and artisans' dwellings of the lower town. But Plovdiv isn't merely a parade of antiquities: the city's arts festivals and trade fairs are the biggest in the country, and its restaurants and promenades are equal to those of the capital. The **Web sites** *www.plovdivcityguide.com* and *www.plovdiv.org* are a good source of information on the city.

Arrival and accommodation

Trains arrive at Tsentralna Gara on the southern fringe of the centre, and the two **bus terminals** are nearby. Rodopi, serving the mountain resorts to the south, is just on the other side of the tracks, while Avtogara Yug, serving the southeast, is one block east. Private **rooms** are available from Esperansa, Ivan Vazov 14 (on leaving the station, go anticlockwise round the square and it's the second street on the right; daily 11am–5pm; ☎032/260653), which has centrally located rooms for around $10. Try also *Pâldin Tours*, bul Bâlgariya 106 (daily 9am–5.30pm; ☎032/555120; take bus #2 or #102 from the station and alight once you've crossed the river). Basic **hostel** accommodation is available in the atmospheric but over-subscribed *Turisticheski Dom* (☎032/633211; ②) in the old town at ul Slaveikov 5; or *Ucheben Tsentar*, Konstantin Nunkov 13a (☎032/772847; ②), a tower-block postgrad hostel in a residential district south of the train station – take the underpass to the far side of the tracks, pass through the Rodopi bus station, continue past the Spartak football stadium and take the fourth right. **Hotel** prices in Plovdiv tend to be relatively high; the friendly *Elit*, ul Daskalov 53 (☎032/624537; ④), is the best of the mid-range choices, while the *Bulgaria*, Patriarh Evtimii 13 (☎032/633599; ⑤) is a more luxurious, and very central option. The *Gorski Kat* **campsite** (☎032/551360) is located some 4km west of the city, and can be reached by bus #222 from outside the train station.

The City

Central Plovdiv revolves around the large **Tsentralen** square, dominated by the monolithic *Hotel Trimontium Princess*. Heading north from here, the pedestrianized Knyaz Aleksandâr Battenberg is lined with shops, cafés and bars, with terraces from which people watch life going by. Off to the right, Gavril Genov and Stanislav Dospevski streets lead up past the lovely church of **Sveta Marina**, which has boldly coloured murals beneath its porch and beguiling creatures peeping out from the wooden foliage of its iconostasis.

Further north, Al Battenberg gives onto the arresting **ploshtad Dzhumaya**, surrounded by small cafés packed with students and bewhiskered elders. The ruins of a **Roman Stadium**, visible in a pit beneath the square, are just a fragment of the arena where up to 30,000 spectators watched gladiatorial spectacles. Among the variously styled buildings around here, the **Dzhumaya Mosque** (open for noon prayers on Friday), with its diamond-patterned minaret and lead-sheathed domes, steals the show. It's believed that the mosque dates back to the reign of Sultan Murad II (1359–85), and its thick walls and the configuration of the prayer hall — divided by four columns into nine squares – are typical of mosques of that period. From the square, ul Raiko Daskalov continues north to meet bul Hristo Danov and two further relics of Turkish rule: the leaden domes and sturdy masonry identify the *Chifte Hamam* as an original **Turkish bath**, while the zigzag brickwork on the minaret of the **Imaret Mosque** livens up the ponderous bulk of the building.

With its cobbled streets and orieled mansions covering one of Plovdiv's three hills, Plovdiv's **Old Quarter** is a painter's dream and a cartographer's nightmare. As good a route as any is to start from pl Dzhumaya and head east up ul Sâborna. Blackened **fortress walls** dating from Byzantine times can be seen around Sâborna and other streets such as Knyaz Tsertelov, sometimes incorporated into the dozens of **National Revival-style houses** that are Plovdiv's speciality. Typically, these rest upon an incline and expand with each storey by means of timber-framed oriels – cleverly resolving the problem posed by the scarcity of groundspace. Outside and inside, the walls are frequently decorated with niches, floral motifs or false columns painted in the style known as *alafranga*, executed by itinerant artists. At the top of Sâborna, the **Church of SS Constantine and Elena** contains a fine gilt iconostasis by Ivan Pashkula, partly decorated by the prolific nineteenth-century artist Zahari Zograf, whose work also appears in the adjacent **Museum of Icons** (Mon 1–6pm, Tue–Fri 9.30am–12.30pm & 1–6pm, Sat 10am–6pm; $1). A little further uphill is the **Hisar Gate**, just north of which stands Plovdiv's most photographed building, the **Kuyumdzhioglu House**. Named for the Greek who commissioned it in 1847, the house graces a garden which you enter from ul Dr Chomakov, and combines Baroque and native folk motifs in its richly decorated facade, with its undulating pediment echoing the line of the carrying-yoke. The **Ethnographic Museum** (Tues–Sun 9am–noon & 2–5pm; $1.50) in the mansion's lower rooms is mundane, but upstairs the elegant rooms are furnished with objects reflecting the owner's taste for Viennese and French Baroque, and filled with showcases of exquisite jewellery and traditional peasant costumes. Heading west from the Hisar Gate, a road leads downhill to ul Artin Gidikov, where the **Hindlian House** at no. 4 (daily: summer 9am–5.15pm; winter 9am–noon; $1.50), former home of an Armenian merchant, harbours some of Plovdiv's most evocative nineteenth-century interiors.

Eating and drinking

Several **restaurants** in the old town serve good Bulgarian food in elegant surroundings. The *Alafrangite*, ul Nektariev 15, and the *Trakiiski Stan*, ul Pâldin 7, occupy the nicest nineteenth-century buildings, but food and service can sometimes be pretty average. Far superior is the excellent *Philipopol*, Konstantin Stoilov 56b, which specializes in authentic Bulgarian fare such as *kavarma*. In the new town, *Gremi*, just off Tsentralen on bul Vâzrazhdane, has a palm-filled garden and good grills and fish, while the rather sombre restaurant of the *Hotel Trimontium Princess*, open to non-guests, offers Bulgarian and international dishes at reasonable prices. Al Battenberg - awash with hamburger, doner kebab and pizza outlets - is the place to look for cheaper **snack** fare, though most of it is pretty mediocre.

Drinking takes place in the pavement cafés of Al Battenberg and pl Stamboliiski. *Murphy's*, at ul 11 Avgust 2, is typical of the trendy bars just off the main drag, while the

Caligula Club, Al Battenberg 30, is a good central spot for an alfresco beer. Several clubs and discos, including *Dive* and *Karamba*, huddle together on ul Lady Strangford, immediately west of ploshtad Dzhumaya. For **Internet** access, try Stratus Internet Studio, Al Battenberg 26, Internet Savage, Ivan Vasov 38a, or Club 12, ul Bresovcka 12, just north of the river.

Bachkovo Monastery

The most attractive destination to the south of Plovdiv is **Bachkovo Monastery** (daily dawn–dusk; free), around 30km away and an easy day-trip from the city (hourly buses from Plovdiv's Rodopi station, destination Smolyan). Alternatively, take a bus from Plovdiv-Yug to the town of Asenovgrad (every 30min), and pick up a local bus from there. The fortress-like stone houses of **BACHKOVO** village, overgrown with flowers, give no indication of the exuberance of the monastery, a kilometre or so further up the road. Founded in 1038 by two Georgians in the service of the Byzantine Empire, this is Bulgaria's second largest monastery and, like Rila, has been declared a UNESCO World Heritage Site.

A great iron-studded door admits visitors to the cobblestoned courtyard, surrounded by wooden galleries and kept free of grass by a solitary goat. Along one wall of the courtyard, frescoes provide a pictorial narrative of the monastery's history, showing Bachkovo roughly as it appears today, but watched over by God's eye and a celestial Madonna and Child. Beneath the vaulted porch of Bachkovo's principal church, **Sveta Bogoroditsa**, are frescoes depicting the horrors in store for sinners, but the entrance itself is more cheerful, overseen by the Holy Trinity. Floral motifs in a naive style decorate the beams of the interior, where the iconostasis bears a fourteenth-century Georgian icon of the Virgin.

The church of **St Nicholas**, originally founded during the nineteenth century and recently restored, features a fine *Last Judgement* covering the porch exterior, which includes portraits of the artist, Zahari Zograf, and of two of his colleagues in the upper left-hand corner. In the old refectory – only sporadically open to visitors – you can see *The Procession of the Miraculous Icon,* executed by Zograf's pupils, which repeats the pilgrimage scene portrayed on the wall of the courtyard. Finally, **Sveta Troitsa**, standing 300m from the main gate, contains a number of early medieval frescoes and life-sized portraits of Tsar Ivan Aleksandâr and the royal family, who lavishly endowed the monastery in the fourteenth century.

You can **stay** in the monastery for $7 a night, although there's no hot water. There are three **restaurants** outside the monastery - *Vodopada*, with its mini waterfall, is the best.

Travelling on from Plovdiv

There's a daily **train** to Istanbul (the overnight *Balkan Express,* which leaves Plovdiv at 11pm); Turkish visas can be purchased for £10 sterling (British citizens), $45 (American citizens), or US$5 (Australian citizens) at the Kapikule frontier – have the exact sum ready in cash, as they don't always have change and won't let you in without it. There's a wider choice of **international buses**, which leave from Tsentralen Square in front of the *Hotel Trimontium Princess.* There are three daily buses to Thessaloniki, one to Istanbul and one to Athens. Tickets are available from the Tourist Service office, in the pedestrian underpass beneath Tsentralen Square, or from the Plovdiv City Transport Office in the building of the State Philarmonic Orchestra, next door to the *Hotel Trimontium Princess.*

NORTHERN BULGARIA

Routes from Sofia to the Black Sea coast take you through the mountainous terrain of central and northern Bulgaria – a gruelling eight- or nine-hour ride that's worth interrupting to savour something of the country's heartland. For over a thousand years, the "Old Mountain" (Stara Planina) – known to foreigners as the **Balkan range** – has been the cradle of the

Bulgarian nation. It was here that the Khans established and ruled over the feudal realm known as the "First Kingdom". Here, too, after a period of Byzantine control, the Boyars proclaimed the "Second Kingdom" and created a magnificent capital at **Veliko Târnovo** – which remains one of Bulgaria's most impressive cities. Closer to the capital, the **Sredna Gora** (Central Range) was inhabited as early as the fifth millennium BC, but for Bulgarians this forested region is best known as the "land of the April Rising", the nineteenth-century rebellion for which the highly picturesque town of **Koprivshtitsa** will always be remembered.

Although they lie some way off the main rail lines from Sofia, neither Veliko Târnovo nor Koprivshtitsa is difficult to reach. The former lies just south of Gorna Oryahovitsa, a major rail junction midway between Varna and Sofia, from where you can pick up a local train or bus; the latter is served by a stop on the Sofia–Burgas line, whose three daily trains in each direction are met by local buses to ferry you the 12km to the village itself.

Koprivshtitsa

Seen from a distance, **KOPRIVSHTITSA** looks almost too lovely to be real, its half-timbered houses lying in a valley amid wooded hills. It would be an oasis of rural calm if not for the tourists drawn by the superb architecture and Bulgarians paying homage to a landmark in their nation's history. From the Place of the Scimitar Charge to the Street of the Counter Attack, there's hardly a part of Koprivshtitsa that isn't named for an episode or participant in the **April Rising of 1876**. As neighbouring towns were burned by the Bashibazouks – the irregular troops recruited by the Turks to put the rebels in their place – refugees flooded into Koprivshtitsa, spreading panic. The rebels eventually took to the hills while local traders bribed the Bashibazouks to spare the village – and so Koprivshtitsa survived unscathed to be admired by subsequent generations as a symbol of heroism.

You arrive at a small bus station 100m south of the main square, where a street running off to the west leads down to the **Oslekov House** (Wed–Sun 9am–noon & 1.30–5.30pm; $1.50), the finest building in Koprivshtitsa, with pillars of cedar wood imported from Lebanon supporting the facade. Its Red Room is particularly impressive, with a vast wooden ceiling carved with geometric motifs. One of the medallions painted on the wall shows the original, symmetrical plan of the house, never realized as Oslekov's neighbours refused to sell him the necessary land. Further along, the street joins ul Debelyanov, which straddles a hill between two bridges and boasts some more lovely buildings. Near the Surlya Bridge is the birthplace of the poet **Dimcho Debelyanov** (no. 6), who is buried in the yard of the hilltop **Church of the Holy Virgin**. Built in 1817 and partly sunk into the ground to comply with Ottoman restrictions, the church contains icons by nineteenth-century artist Zahari Zograf.

A gate at the rear of the churchyard leads to the birthplace of **Todor Kableshkov** (same times as Oslekov House), leader of the local rebels. Kableshkov's house now displays the insurgents' silk banner embroidered with the Bulgarian Lion and "Liberty or Death!", and one of the twenty **cherry-tree cannons** secretly manufactured by the rebels. Although one bore the engraved slogan "End of the Turkish Empire, 1876", the cannons soon became a liability, as they tended to blow up.

On the opposite side of the river at the southern end of the village, steps lead up to the birthplace of another major figure in the uprising, **George Benkovski** (same times as Oslekov House). A tailor by profession, he made the insurgents' banner and uniforms and commanded a rebel band on Mount Eledzhik, which fought its way north until it was wiped out near Teteven.

Practicalities

A **tourist office** (daily 9am–6pm; ☎07184/2191, *koprivshitza@hotmail.com*) on the main square books private **rooms** in charming village houses for around $10, and there are plenty of small bed-and-breakfast places scattered around the village; the nearby **museum centre**

(☎07184/2180) also provides information about accommodation as well as the museum houses. The *Byaloto Konche* (☎07184/2250; ②), across the road from the Oslekov House, has delightful rooms in the National Revival style; while the *Panorama*, at the south end of the village near the Benkovski House (☎07184/2035; ②), has neat modern rooms with en-suite facilities. For **eating and drinking**, the best places to sample traditional food are the *Dyado Liben Inn*, in a fine nineteenth-century mansion opposite the main square; and *Lomeva Kashta*, a folk-style restaurant just north of the square.

Veliko Târnovo

Even the dour Prussian Field-Marshal Von Moltke was moved to remark that he had "never seen a town of more romantic location" than **VELIKO TÂRNOVO**, which seems poised to leap into the chasms that divide the city. Medieval fortifications add melodrama to the scene, and the huddles of antique houses seem bound to the rocks by wild lilac and vines. But for Bulgarians the city has a deeper significance. When the National Assembly met here to draft Bulgaria's first constitution in 1879, it did so in the former capital of the Second Kingdom (1185–1396), whose civilization was snuffed out by the Turks.

The Town

Modern Târnovo revolves around the **Mother Bulgaria** (Mayka Bâlgariya) **monument:** from here bul Nezavisimost (which becomes ul Stefan Stambolov after a few hundred metres) heads northeast into the network of narrow streets which curve around the heights above the River Yantra and mark out the old town, with its photogenic houses teetering over limited ground space. From the old bazaar at the junction of ul Rakovski and pl Georgi Kirkov, alleyways climb from Stefan Stambolov to the peaceful old **Varosh Quarter**, where a couple of nineteenth-century churches are verging on decrepitude.

Continuing along Stefan Stambolov, you'll notice steps leading off downhill to **ulitsa General Gurko**, a street lined with picturesque nineteenth-century houses perched along the curve of the ravine. Don't miss the **Sarafina House** at no. 88 (Mon–Fri 9am–noon & 1–6pm; $1), which is arranged so that only two floors are visible from General Gurko though a further three overhang the river. The interior is notable for the splendid octagonal vestibule with wrought-iron fixtures and a panelled rosette-ceiling. Rejoining Stefan Stambolov and continuing downhill, you can't miss the spacious blue-and-white edifice where the first Bulgarian parliament assembled in 1878. It's now occupied by a **Museum of the National Revival** and the Constituent Assembly (daily 8am–6pm; $2), which has an excellent display of icons in the basement.

From here, Ivan Vazov leads directly to the medieval fortress, **Tsarevets** (daily 8am–7pm; $2). Approaching it along the stone causeway, you appreciate how the boyars Petâr and Asen were emboldened by possession of this citadel to lead a rebellion against Byzantium in 1185. Byzantine attempts to retake Târnovo were successfully beaten off, and Tsarevets remained the centre of Bulgarian power until 1393, when the Ottoman Turks plundered it after a three-month siege. The partially restored fortress is entered via the **Asenova Gate** halfway along the western ramparts; to the right, paths lead round to a bastion known as **Baldwin's Tower**, where the Latin Emperor of the East, Baldwin of Flanders, was incarcerated by Asen's successor Kaloyan. Above lie the scrappy ruins of the royal palace and a replica of the thirteenth-century **Church of the Blessed Saviour**, ribbed with red brick and inset with green and orange ceramics.

Downhill to the west of Tsarevets lies the **Asenova Quarter**, where chickens strut and children fish beside the river. The only one of its medieval churches currently open is the **Church of SS Peter and Paul** (Easter–Sept only), which contains several capitals carved with vine leaves and some well-preserved frescoes of which the oldest – dating back to the fourteenth century – is the Pietà opposite the altar.

Practicalities

All **trains** between Sofia and Varna stop at Gorna Oryahovitsa, from where local trains (8 daily) cover the remaining 12km to Veliko Târnovo **train station**, which stands 2km south of the city centre – buses #4 and #13 run to the Mother Bulgaria monument.

The *Etura* **hotel**, just downhill from here at ul Ivailo 2 (☎062/621838; ③), is an unkempt high-rise with good views of the old town. In the heart of the old town the *Turistichni Dom Trapezitsa*, Stefan Stambolov 79 (☎062/22061; ②), is a cheap option, or you could try the traditional-style *Gurko*, near the river on ul Gurko 33 (☎062/627838; ④). The *Bolyarski Stan* **camping site** can be found on the western outskirts of the town, and is served by bus #110. The terrace of the *Voennen Klub* (Officers' Club) opposite the Mother Bulgaria monument is popular for its simple grilled **food**. Otherwise, best of the **restaurants** are the small family-run places just off Stefan Stambolov – follow signs pointing down the steps to find *Mehana Belite Brezi* and the nearby *Starata Mehana*, both serving good home-cooked meals. Further towards Tsarevets, *Lâv*, Chitalishtna 3, serves the best trad Bulgarian fare in town. For **drinking**, there are numerous cafés along the main drag, with *Café Aqua* at Nezavisimost 3 being a pleasant spot for coffee and cakes. The most central **Internet café** is Internet Prolink, at ul Dondukov 17.

THE COAST

It was the Soviet leader Khrushchev who first suggested that the Black Sea coastline be developed for tourism, and since then have mushroomed, growing increasingly sophisticated as the prototype mega-complexes have been followed by "holiday villages". With fine weather and safe bathing practically guaranteed, the selling of the coast has been a success in economic terms, but with the exception of ancient **Sozopol** and touristy **Nesebâr**, there's little to please the eye. Of the coast's two main towns – **Varna** and **Burgas** – the former is by far preferable as a base for getting to the less-developed spots.

Varna

VARNA's origins go back almost five millennia, but it wasn't until seafaring Greeks founded a colony here in 585 BC that the town became a port. The modern city is both a shipyard and port for commercial freighters and the navy, and a riviera town visited by tourists of every nationality. It's a cosmopolitan place and a nice one to stroll through: Baroque, nineteenth century and contemporary architecture pleasantly blended with shady promenades and a handsome seaside garden.

Social life revolves around **ploshtad Nezavisimost**, where the opera house and theatre provide a backdrop for an ensemble of restaurants and cafés. The square is the starting point of Varna's evening promenade, which flows eastward from here along bul Knyaz Boris I towards bul Slivnitsa and the seaside gardens. Beyond the opera house, Varna's main lateral boulevard cuts through pl Mitropolit Simeon to the domed **Cathedral of the Assumption**. Constructed in 1886 along the lines of St Petersburg's cathedral, it contains a splendid iconostasis and carved bishop's throne, and murals painted after the last war.

Exhibits in the **Archaeology Museum** on the corner of Mariya Luiza and Slivnitsa (Tues–Sat 10am–5pm; $1) fill forty halls, three of them devoted to skeletons and artefacts from a necropolis where a hoard of 4500-year-old gold objects was discovered in 1972. Other halls display Greek and Roman antiquities, medieval weaponry and ecclesiastical art, while upstairs there's an excellent icon gallery.

South of the centre, on ul Han Krum, you'll stumble upon the impressive second-century **Roman baths** complex (Mon–Fri 9am–5pm, Sat 10am–5pm; $1.50). Ten minutes' west of here on ul Panagyurishte, the **Ethnographic Museum** (closed at the time of writing), which occupies an old house, contains a fine display of folk costumes and jewellery. The boat responsible for the Bulgarian Navy's only victory - the *Drazki* (Intrepid) – is honourably embedded on the waterfront outside the **Navy Museum** (daily 10am–5pm; $1); it sank the Turkish cruiser *Hamidie* off Cape Kaliakra in 1912. The museum houses a musty collection of nineteenth and twentieth century naval relics, with some rusting armaments in the gardens, including a helicopter.

Practicalities

Each of the main points of arrival has good bus connections with the centre. You'll approach the centre from the northwest if you come in from the **bus terminal** (bus #1, #22 or #41) on bul Vladislav Varnenchik or Varna **airport** (#409), whereas travellers coming in at the **train station** can walk up ul Tsar Simeon into the centre in ten minutes.

Private rooms in central Varna (②) can be obtained from the small accommodation bureau (daily 7am–10.30pm) inside the train station or CM92 (daily 7am–7pm; ☎052/630776, *smtouristagency@yahoo.com*) across the road at Tsar Simeon 36b. Interservice Travel, ten minutes further uphill at ul Devnya 14 (Mon-Fri 9am–12.30pm & 1.30–6pm; ☎052/630100), can organize hotel accommodation and tours. Best of the cheap **hotels** are the slightly decrepit but very reasonable *Voennomorski Klub*, opposite the cathedral at bul Varnenchik 2 (☎052/238312; ②), and the rather more modern *Trite Delfina*, near the train station at ul Gabrovo 27 (☎052/600911, *three_dolphins@abv.bg*; ②). *Akropolis*, 500m east of the train station at Tsar Ivan Shishman 3 (☎052/603108; ④), is another modern, well-furnished hotel, with air-conditioned, en-suite rooms, though it is a little overpriced.

Most of Varna's **eating and drinking** venues are to be found along bul Knyaz Boris I and bul Slivnitsa. For the best food and service, stick to the backstreets; *Staviko*, near the Roman baths at ul osmi Noemvri 11, has good quality Bulgarian standards; *Shanghai*, at Tsar Osvoboditel 25, is an excellent Chinese restaurant with generous portions; and *Chuchirite*, right opposite the Ethnographic Museum, serves authentic Bulgarian food in an atmospheric old wooden house, with a tiny flag-stoned coffee bar attached. *Club Stage*, Knyaz Boris 24, is the place to head for live jazz, though it gets crowded early on (cover charge $3). The municipal **beach**, reached by pathways descending from the seaside gardens, is lined with open-air bars and fish restaurants, such as *Tonga* and *Zharta*, and a couple of **discos**, including *Epsylon Beach*. For **Internet access**, try Doom Internet Café, at ul 27 July 13 (daily 9am–11pm) or Internet Club at ul Voden 19 (daily 9.30am–10pm).

The southern coast

BURGAS, the south coast's prime urban centre, can be reached by train from Sofia and Plovdiv, or by bus from Varna. The town provides easy access to the museum town of **Nesebâr** to the north or the attractive fishing village of **Sozopol** to the south. There are regular buses from the airport into town, and other points of arrival are clustered near the port. If it's necessary to stay, private **accommodation** can be arranged by **Primovets Travel** opposite the train station (☎056/842727), which offers rooms from around $8.

Nesebâr

Founded by the Greeks, **NESEBÂR** – 35km northeast of Burgas and served by buses every 45 minutes – was later used by the Byzantines as a base from which to assail the Bulgarian First Kingdom, provoking Khan Krum to seize it in 812. Thereafter ownership alternated between Bulgaria and Byzantium until the Ottomans captured it in 1453. The town's decline to a humble fishing port under Turkish rule left Nesebâr's **Byzantine churches** reasonably intact, and nowadays the town depends on them for its tourist appeal, ably demonstrated by the stream of summer visitors crossing the slender isthmus that connects the old town with the mainland. Outside the hectic summer season, though, the place is much more relaxed, with little open other than a few sleepy cafés.

Buses arrive at the harbour at the western end of town, above which lies an **Archaeological Museum** (Summer: Mon–Fri 9am–7pm, Sat & Sun 9am–1.30pm & 2–7pm; $1.50) containing ancient Greek tombstones and a feast of medieval icons. Immediately beyond this is the first of Nesebâr's churches, the **Church of Christ the Pantokrator**. Completed during the fourteenth-century reign of Tsar Aleksandâr, its blind niches, turquoise ceramic inlays and red-brick motifs are characteristic of latter-day Byzantine architecture, although the frieze of swastikas – a symbol of the sun and continual change – is rather disturbing at first sight. Slightly downhill on ul Mitropolitska, **St John the Baptist** (now an art gallery) also has a cruciform plan, but its undressed stone exterior dates it as a tenth- or eleventh-century building.

Overhung by half-timbered houses carved with sun-signs, fish and other symbols, ul Aheloi branches off from ul Mitropolitska towards the **Church of Sveti Spas** (Summer only: Mon–Fri 9am–1.30pm & 2–5.30pm, Sat & Sun 9.30am–1.30pm; $1), outwardly unremarkable but filled with seventeenth-century frescoes. Diagonally opposite is the now ruined **Church of the Archangels Michael and Gabriel**, patterned not unlike the Pantokrator. A few steps to the east lies the ruined **Old Metropolitan Church**, dominating a plaza filled with pavement cafés, street traders and hawkers. The church itself dates back to the fifth or sixth century, and it was here that bishops officiated during the city's heyday. South of the town's main street, down ul Ribarska, lies the **New Metropolitan Church** (also known as *Sveti Stefan*; daily 9am–1pm & 2–6pm; $1), whose interior fresco of the *Forty Martyrs*, on the west wall, gives pride of place to the patron who financed the church's enlargement during the fifteenth century. Just downhill from here there's the ruined **Church of St John Aliturgetos**, standing in splendid isolation beside the shore and representing the zenith of Byzantine architecture in Bulgaria. Its exterior decoration is strikingly varied, employing limestone, red bricks, crosses, mussel shells and ceramic plaques, with a representation of a human figure composed of limestone blocks incorporated into the north wall.

Private rooms (②–③), many in fine old houses, are available from several agencies; you'll see signs along the main street directing you towards two of the longest established: Mesambria-93 and Stoyanovi-94. The **Web** site *www.nesebar.com* is also useful for finding lodgings. The *Morska Perla*, behind the post office (☎0554/45606; ③), is a family-run **hotel** with large, clean en-suites, most with TV and balconies. There are plenty of places to get **food**. Around the harbour are kiosks serving fresh mackerel and chips during the summer. The old town is crammed with restaurants; the sea-facing *Neptun*, towards the far end of town, is reasonably reliable, while the *Plakamo*, just downhill from the New Metropolitan Church at Ivan Aleksandâr 8, is family-run and relatively sheltered. *Bar Burgas*, Mena 10, is one of the better places to enjoy an evening **drink**.

Sozopol

SOZOPOL, the oldest settlement on the coast, was founded in the seventh century BC by Ionian colonists from Miletus, who called the town Apollonia and prospered by trading Greek textiles and wine for honey and corn. Today it's a busy fishing port and the favoured resort of Bulgaria's literary and artistic set. The **Church of the Holy Virgin** (for opening times enquire at the Archaeological Museum, see below), built in the nineteenth century, features a finely carved iconostasis and bishop's throne, but it's the old houses that give Sozopol its charm. With space at a premium, their upper storeys project so far out that houses on opposite sides of the narrow, cobbled streets almost meet. Sozopol's **Archaeological Museum** (Mon–Fri 9am–5pm, Sat & Sun 10am–2pm), hidden behind the library, should not be missed for its collection of amphoras dredged from the surrounding waters and its display of exquisitely decorated Greek vases called *kraters*.

The hourly **buses** from Burgas arrive at the southern edge of the old town opposite the main beach. The nearby *Sozopol Hotel* (☎05514/2362; ②) is a reasonable option; otherwise, try the Lotos **accommodation** bureau on ul Apoloniya 22 (daily 8am–9pm), which offers atmospheric rooms in the old town or more roomy apartments in the new town from about $10. You could also just ask around – everyone in Sozopol rents out rooms over the summer. The *Mehana Sozopol*, ul Apoloniya, and the *Vyatarna Melnitsa*, ul Morski Skali, are a couple of good, if touristy, **restaurants** – both featuring occasional live music. The Italian-influenced food at *Cazanova*, on the cliffside path on the east side of the old town, attracts a trendier crowd.

travel details

Trains

Sofia to: Blagoevgrad (5 daily; 2hr 30min–3hr 30min); Burgas (4 daily; 6–8hr); Gorna Oryahovitsa (6 daily; 4hr 30min); Koprivshtitsa (4 daily; 1hr 40min–2hr 20min); Plovdiv (11 daily; 2hr 30min–3hr 30min); Sandanski (5 daily; 3hr 30min–4hr 30min); Varna (5 daily; 8–9hr).

Gorna Oryahovitsa to: Veliko Târnovo (8 daily; 20min).

Plovdiv to: Burgas (4 daily; 5hr); Sofia (13 daily; 2hr 30min–3hr 30min); Varna (3 daily; 5 hr).

Buses

Sofia to: Bansko (5 daily; 3hr); Koprivshtitsa (1 daily; 2hr); Plovdiv (5 daily; 2hr); Rila monastery (summer only: 1 daily; 3hr); Sandanski (5 daily; 3hr); Veliko Târnovo (2 daily; 4hr).

Blagoevgrad to: Bansko (8 daily; 1hr); Rila village (hourly; 35min).

Burgas to: Nesebâr (every 45min; 50min); Sozopol (hourly; 40min); Varna (4 daily; 3hr).

Dupnitsa to: Rila monastery (2 daily; 1hr); Rila village (4 daily; 30min).

Gorna Oryahovitsa to: Veliko Târnovo (every 30min; 30min).

Plovdiv to: Bachkovo (13 daily; 40min).

Rila village to: Rila monastery (3 daily; 30min).

Sandanski to: Melnik (3 daily; 40min).

CHAPTER 5

CROATIA

Introduction

Croatia (Hrvatska) has come a long way since the summer of 1991, when foreign tourists fled from a region standing on the verge of war. Now that stability has returned, visitors are steadily coming back to a country which boasts one of the most outstanding stretches of coastline that Europe has to offer. This return to normality has been keenly awaited by Croats, but patriotism – and a sense of the nation's place in history – remains a serious business here. Croatia was an independent kingdom in the tenth century, fell under the rule of Hungary in the eleventh, and was subsequently absorbed by the Austro-Hungarian Empire before becoming part of the new state of Yugoslavia in 1918. Croatian aspirations were frustrated by a Yugoslav state which was initially dominated by Serbs, and then (after 1945) ruled by Communists. Croatia's declaration of independence on June 25, 1991 was fiercely contested by a Serb-dominated Yugoslav army eager to preserve their control over portions of Croatia in which groups of ethnic Serbs lived. The period of war – and fragile, UN-supervised ceasefire that followed – was finally brought to a close by Croatian offensives during the summer of 1995.

Croatia's capital, **Zagreb**, is a typical central-European metropolis, combining elegant nineteenth-century architecture with plenty of cultural diversions and a vibrant café life. At the northern end of the Adriatic coast, the peninsula of **Istria** contains many of the country's most developed resorts, with old Venetian towns like **Poreč** and **Rovinj** rubbing shoulders with the raffish port of **Pula**. Further south lies **Dalmatia**, a dramatic, mountain-fringed stretch of coastline studded with islands. Dalmatia's main town is **Split**, an ancient Roman settlement and modern port which provides a jumping-off point to the most enchanting of Croatia's islands, **Brač**, **Hvar**, **Vis** and **Korčula**, where you'll find lively fishing villages and the best of the beaches. South of Split lies the walled medieval city of **Dubrovnik**, site of an important festival in the summer and a magical place to be whatever the season.

Information and maps

Most towns of any size have a **tourist office** (*turistički ured*) run by the local authority, who will happily give out brochures and local maps if they have any available; English is widely spoken in these places. Many offices will also book private rooms, or at least direct you to an agency that does. Freytag & Berndt produce a good 1:600,000 **map** of Croatia, Slovenia and Bosnia-Hercegovina; as well as 1:100,000 regional maps of Istria and the Dalmatian coast.

Money and banks

Croatia's unit of currency is the **kuna** (kn), which is divided into 100 lipa. Coins come in denominations of 1, 2, 5, 10, 20 and 50 lipa, and 1, 2, and 5 kuna; and there are notes of 5, 10, 20, 50, 100, 200, 500 and 1000 kuna. The exchange rate is currently around 12kn to £1, 8.50kn to $1 Although accommodation and ferry prices are often quoted in Deutschmarks, you pay in kuna.

Banks (*banka*) are generally open Monday to Friday 7.30am. Money can also be changed in post offices, travel agencies and exchange bureaux (*mjenjačnica*), which have more flexible hours. Credit cards are only accepted in the bigger hotels and more expensive restaurants, although you can use them to get cash from ATMs and the bigger banks.

Communications

Most **post offices** (*pošta* or HPT) are open Monday to Friday 7/8am–8pm and Saturday 8am–1pm. In big towns and resorts, some offices are open daily, sometimes until 10pm. Stamps (*marke*) can also be bought at newsstands.

Public **telephones** use magnetic cards (*telekarta*), which come in denominations of 12kn, 23kn, 37kn and 67kn; you can buy these from post offices or newspaper kiosks. When making long-distance and international calls, it's usually easier to go to the post office, where you're assigned a cabin and given the bill afterwards.

CROATIA ON THE NET

www.htz.hr – Croatia's tourist board site

www.zagreb-touristinfo.hr – The capital's main web site

www.istra.com – One of the better regional sites

www.dalmacija.net – Comprehensive coverage of the Dalmatian islands and online accommodation booking service

Zagreb is the only place where **Internet access** has really caught on, although you should be able to find at least one place in most towns; expect to pay around 15kn per hour online.

Getting around

Trains are of limited value in a country with such a small rail network, although they do connect Zagreb with the coastal towns of Rijeka and Split. Elsewhere, Croatia is well served by an extensive and reliable bus network. Ferries offer a leisurely way of getting up and down the coast, and provide the only transport to Croatia's many Adriatic islands.

■ Trains and buses

Croatian railways (Hrvatske željeznice) run a smooth and efficient service. **Trains** (*vlak*, plural *vlakovi*) are divided into *putnički* (slow ones which stop at every halt) and *IC* (inter-city trains which are faster and more expensive). There's an overnight service from Zagreb to Split, for which places in couchettes (*kušet*) and sleeping cars (*spalnica*) are best booked in advance. Timetables (*vozni red*) are usually displayed on boards in stations – *odlazak* means departure, *dolazak* means arrival.

Croatia's **bus network** is run by a confusing array of small local companies, but services are well integrated and bus stations tend to be well-organized affairs with clearly listed departure times and efficient booking facilities. If you're at a big city bus station, tickets (*karta*) must be obtained from ticket windows before boarding the bus. Elsewhere, they can be bought from the driver. It's a good idea to buy tickets well in advance in summer if you can, especially for any services running to, or along, the coast. You'll be charged around 5kn for items of baggage to be stored in the hold.

■ Driving and hitching

The **road system** is comprehensive, but not always of good quality once you get beyond the main highways. Stretches of the Zagreb–Rijeka and Zagreb–Split routes are classified as motorway (*autocesta*) and are subject to a modest toll, although elsewhere the main routes (especially the main road down the Adriatic coast) are single-lane roads, often clogged by traffic – especially in summer, when movement up and down the coast can be time-consuming. Off the beaten track, roads can be badly maintained. **Speed limits** in Croatia are 60kph in built-up areas, 80kph on normal roads, 100kph on

highways and 120kph on motorways. If you break down, the Croatian automobile club (HAK) has a 24-hour emergency service (☎987). **Car rental** charges are expensive at around £75/$110 a day for a reliable car with unlimited mileage.

Hitching on the main routes between Zagreb and the coast is fairly common – but be prepared to wait a long time for a lift. Anywhere else in the country, prospects for hitching are fairly bad.

■ Ferries

Jadrolinija (*www.jadrolinija.tel.hr*) operate **ferry services** down the coast on the Rijeka–Zadar–Split–Korčula–Dubrovnik route at least once a day in both directions between June and August, and two or three times weekly for the rest of the year. Rijeka to Dubrovnik is a 22-hour journey, involving one night on the boat. In addition, ferries link Split with the islands of Brač, Hvar, Vis and Korčula. Ferries are also a good way of moving on from Croatia, with connections to Italy (Split and Zadar to Ancona, Pula and Brioni to Trieste and Dubrovnik to Bari) and Greece (Dubrovnik to Igoumenitsa).

Prices (often quoted in dollars or Deutschmarks, but payable in kuna) are reasonable for short trips: for example, Split to Hvar costs around $4. For longer journeys, prices vary greatly according to the level of comfort you require. The cheapest Rijeka–Dubrovnik fare, in high season (July–Sept), is $29, while you'll pay double that for a couchette-style bunk bed, and three times more for a bed in a well-appointed cabin (breakfast included); taking a car on the same journey costs an extra $88, $29 for a motorbike, but bicycles travel free of charge. Book in advance for longer journeys wherever possible; addresses and phone numbers are provided in the text where relevant.

Accommodation

Private rooms have long been the mainstay of Croatian tourism, especially on the coast, and represent an inexpensive way of finding a bed for the night. There are well-appointed campsites all along the Adriatic coast, although Croatian hotels tend to be bland and overpriced.

■ Hotels and private rooms

Croatian **hotels** tend to be modern multi-storey affairs providing modern comforts but little atmosphere. Although the international five-star grading system is being introduced, most Croatian hotels are

ACCOMMODATION PRICE CODES

Throughout this guide, accommodation is coded on a scale of ① to ⑨, the code indicating the lowest price per person per night you could expect to pay in each establishment in high season. With hostels this is the nightly rate per person; with hotels, the price is arrived at by dividing the cost of the cheapest double room by two. The prices indicated by the codes are as follows:

① under £5/$8 (€9)
② £5–10/$8–16 (€9–18)
③ £10–15/$16–24 (€18–27)

④ £15–20/$24–32 (€27–36)
⑤ £20–25/$32–40 (€36–45)
⑥ £25–30/$40–48 (€45–54)

⑦ £30–35/$48–56 (€54–63)
⑧ £35–40/$56–64 (€63–72)
⑨ £40/$64 (€72) and over

still classified by letter: generally speaking, C-class (one-star) hotels have rooms with shared WC and bathroom; B-class (two- to three-star) have rooms with en-suite facilities; A-class (four-star) is business class; and L-class (five-star) are in the international luxury bracket. A double room in a C-class establishment will cost around £30/$45, although these tend to be in very short supply, and in most places you'll be dependent on B-class hotels, where you should expect to pay £40/$60 a double.

Private rooms (*privatne sobe*) are available just about everywhere in Croatia. Bookings are administered either by the local tourist office or by private travel agencies. Agencies are usually open daily 8am–8/9pm in summer, although they may take a long break on Sunday afternoons. Prices hover around £8/$12 per person for a simple double sharing your host's WC and bathroom, rising to around £10/$14 per person for a double with en-suite facilities; stays of less than three nights are often subject to a surcharge of thirty percent or over. Places fill up quickly in July and August, when it's a good idea to arrive in town early in order to begin your search. Single travellers sometimes find it difficult to get a room in high season unless they're prepared to pay the price of a double. It is quite likely that you will be offered rooms by people waiting outside train, bus and ferry stations, particularly in Southern Dalmatia. Don't be afraid to take a room offered in this manner, but be sure to establish the location of the room and agree a price before setting off – and if anything makes you feel uncomfortable about the situation, don't go. If taking a room this way expect to pay 10–20% less than you would with an agency. However you find a room, you can usually examine it before committing yourself to paying for it.

■ Hostels and campsites

HI-affiliated **hostels** are thin on the ground, although those that exist – mostly in the big cities – are on the whole clean and well run. You can get details from Hrvatski Ferijalni i Hostelski Savez, De manova 9, Zagreb (☎01/48-47-474, *hfhs-cms@zg.tel.hr*). In addition, **student halls of residence** are often let out cheap to travellers during the summer vacation – usually mid-July to the end of August. For both, expect to pay £10–15/$15–$22 for a bed.

Campsites abound on the Adriatic coast, and tend to be large-scale, well-appointed affairs with plentiful facilities, restaurants and shops. Most of them are open from May to September. Two people travelling with a tent can expect to pay around £8/$12 per night; add about £2/$3 for a vehicle.

Food and drink

There's a varied and distinctive range of cuisine on offer in Croatia, largely because the country straddles two culinary cultures: the fish-and-seafood-dominated cuisine of the Mediterranean, and the hearty meat-oriented fare of central Europe.

■ Food

Basic **self-catering** and picnic ingredients like cheese (*sir*), vegetables (*povrće*) and fruit (*voće*) can be bought at a supermarket (*samoposluga*) or open-air market (*tržnica*). Bread (*kruh*) is bought from either a supermarket or a *pekara* (bakery). For breakfasts and fast food, look out for street stalls or snack-food outlets selling *burek*, a flaky pastry filled with cheese; or grilled meats such as *ćevapčići* (rissoles of minced beef, pork or lamb), and *pljeskavica* (a hamburger-like mixture of the same meats).

For a more relaxed, sit-down meal, a **restaurant** menu (*jelovnik*) will usually include Croatian speciality starters like *pršut* (home-cured ham) and *paški sir* (piquant hard cheese), as well as a range of soups (*juha*). Typical main courses include *punjene paprike* (peppers stuffed with rice and meat), *gulaš* (goulasch), or some kind of *odrezak* (fillet of meat, often pan-fried), usually either *svinjski* (pork) or *teleški* (veal). *Mješano meso* is a mixed grill. Lamb, often roasted, is *jagnjetina*. Traditional dishes from the area around Zagreb include *purica z mlincima* (turkey with pasta noodles), and *strukli* (ravioli-like blobs of pasta dough with a cheese filling). One typically Dalmatian dish is *pašticada* (beef and bacon cooked in vinegar and wine). On the coast, you'll be regaled with every kind of seafood. *Riba* (fish) can come either *na žaru* (grilled) or *u pečnici* (baked). *Brodet* is a hot peppery fish stew. Otherwise, the main menu items to look out for on the coast are *lignje* (squid), *škampi* (unpeeled prawns eaten with the hands), *rakovica* (crab), *oštrige* (oysters), *kalamari* (squid), *školjke* (mussels) and *jastog* (lobster); *crni rizoto* is risotto with squid. No Croatian town is without at least one pizzeria, often the cheapest place to eat and the easiest, if not the most imaginative, source of a **vegetarian** meal.

Typical **desserts** include *palačinke* (pancakes), *voćna salata* (fruit salad) and *sladoled* (ice cream).

■ Drink

Daytime drinking takes place in a *kavana* (café) or a *slastičarnica* (patisserie). **Coffee** (*kava*) is usually served black unless specified otherwise – ask for *mlijeko* (milk) or *šlag* (cream). Tea (*čaj*) is widely available, but is drunk without milk.

Night-time drinking takes place in a growing number of small *kafići* or café/bars. Croatian **beer** (*pivo*) is of the light lager variety; Karlovačko and Ožujsko are two good local brands to look out for. The local wine (*vino*) is consistently good and reasonably cheap. In Dalmatia there are some pleasant whites, crisp dry wines like Kastelet, Grk and Posip, as well as reds like the dark heady Dingač and Babić. In Istria, Semion is a bone-dry white, and Teran a light fresh red. Local spirits include *loza*, a clear grape-based spirit; *travarica*, herbal brandy; *vinjak*, locally produced cognac, and *Maraskino*, a cherry liqueur from Dalmatia.

Opening hours and holidays

Most **shops** open Monday to Friday 8am–8pm and Saturday 8am–1pm, although many food shops, supermarkets and outdoor markets are open daily 7am–7pm. **Museum and gallery** times vary from one place to another, although most are closed on Monday.

All shops and banks will be closed on the following **public holidays**: January 1; January 6; Easter Monday; May 1 (Labour Day); May 30 (Day of Croatian Statehood); June 22 (Day of the 1941 Anti-Fascist Uprising); August 5 (National Thanksgiving Day); August 15 (Assumption); November 1 (All Saints' Day); and December 25 and 26.

Emergencies

The crime rate in Croatia is low by European standards. Croatian **police** (*policija*) are generally helpful when dealing with holidaymakers, although they can be slow when filling out reports. Police often make routine checks on identity cards and other documents; always carry your **passport**.

Hospital treatment is free to EU citizens. **Pharmacies** (*ljekarna*) tend to follow normal shopping hours, and a rota system covers night-time and weekend opening; details are posted in the window of each pharmacy.

You're unlikely to see too many reminders of the **war** during your travels round Croatia. Apart from Dubrovnik, which was heavily shelled by Serb and Montenegrin troops in 1991 and 1992, none of the places featured in this chapter were part of a war zone. Most of the fighting took place in areas well away from the tourist spots – and at the time of writing it is safe to travel anywhere in the country.

Emergency Numbers

Police ☎92; Ambulance ☎94; Fire ☎93.

ZAGREB

Capital of an independent state since 1991, **ZAGREB** has served as the cultural and political focus of the nation since the Middle Ages. The city grew out of two medieval communities, **Kaptol**, to the east, and **Gradec**, to the west, each sited on a hill and divided by a river long since dried up but nowadays marked by a street known as Tkalčićeva. Kaptol (meaning "Cathedral Chapter") was a religious centre and the seat of an archbishop; Gradec was ruled by a group of Croatian nobles. The two communities became bitter rivals, and remained so until the sixteenth century, when the threat of Turkish invasion caused them to unite against the common enemy; they took the name Zagreb, which means, literally, "behind the hill". Zagreb grew rapidly in the nineteenth century, and the majority of its buildings are relatively well-preserved, grand, peach-coloured monuments to the self-esteem of the Austro-Hungarian Empire. Nowadays, with a population topping one million, Zagreb is the boisterous capital of a newly self-confident nation. A handful of good museums and a vibrant nightlife ensure that a few days here will be well spent.

Arrival, information and city transport

Zagreb's central **train station**, or Glavni Kolodvor, is on Tomislavov Trg, on the southern edge of the city centre, a ten-minute walk from Trg bana Jelačića, the main square. The main **bus station** is a fifteen-minute walk east of the railway station, at the junction of Branimirova and Držićeva – trams #2, #3 and #6 run to the railway station from here. Zagreb's **airport** is about 10km southeast of the city, connected with the main bus station by a half-hourly Croatia Airways bus (6am–8pm, at other times services run to connect with flights; 25kn).

There are two **tourist offices** in central Zagreb; the main one is at Trg bana Jelačića 11 (Mon–Fri 8.30am–8pm, Sat 9am–5pm, Sun 10am–2pm; ☎01/48-14-051, *www.zagreb-touristinfo.hr*) and the other is at Trg N. Zrinskog 14 (Mon, Wed & Fri 9am–5pm, Tues & Thu 9am–6pm; ☎01/49-21-645). Both have maps, up-to-date leaflets on events, and can help out with general queries, though neither arrange accommodation.

Zagreb has an efficient and comprehensive **public transport** network of trams and, to a lesser extent, buses, though much of the city centre can easily be seen on foot. For both buses and trams within the central zone, there's a flat fare per journey of 5.50kn; **tickets** (*karte*) are sold from cigarette and newspaper kiosks. Day tickets (*dnevne karte*) cost 15kn. Validate your ticket by punching it in the machines on board the trams. The train station and Trg bana Jelačića are the two main hubs of the city transport system.

Accommodation

It's difficult to find cheap **accommodation** in Zagreb, especially during the summer. **Hotels** are relatively expensive and **hostel beds** are often reserved way in advance. **Private rooms** can be arranged through the accommodation agency Evistas, midway between the train and bus stations at Šenoina 28 (Mon–Fri 9am–8pm, Sat 9.30am–5pm; ☎01/48-39-546, *evistas@zg.tel.hr*). The grubby **hostel**, soon to be completely renovated, is conveniently placed at Petrinjska 77 (☎01/48-41-261; ② dorm bed, ③ room), five minutes' walk from the railway station. The nearest **campsite** (☎01/65-30-444) is 10km southeast of town at the *Plitvice Motel* beside the main Zagreb–Ljubljana motorway – there's no public transport.

In addition, **student rooms** (④) in halls of residence are made available to tourists from mid-July to late September. You can book them through the student travel office at Odranska 8 (Mon–Fri 9am–4pm; ☎01/61-91-241; tram #17 or #14 from Trg bana Jelačića), and will be located in either the Cvijetno naselje (at the same address) or Stjepan Radić, Jarunska 2 (tram #17 from Trg bana Jelačića).

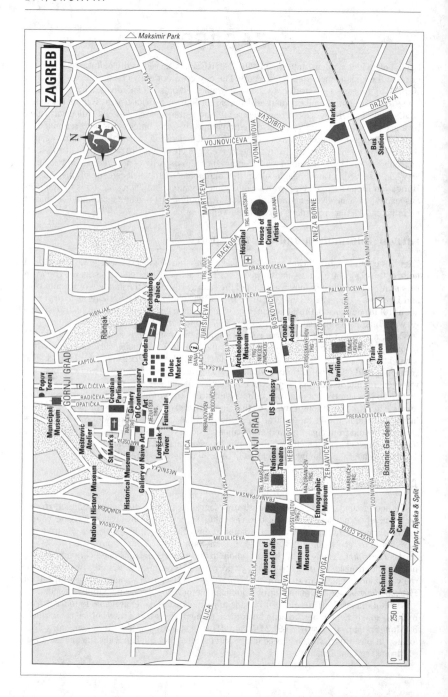

ZAGREB

Maksimir Park

Market

Bus Station

DRŽIĆEVA

VOJNOVIĆEVA

ZVONIMIROVA

SUBIĆEVA

MARTIĆEVA

VLAŠKA

House of Croatian Artists

Hospital

TRG. HRVATSKIH VELIKANA

KNEZA BORNE

RAČKOGA

BRANIMIROVA

TRG. JOZE VLANOVICA

DRAŠKOVIĆEVA

PALMOTIĆEVA

PALMOTIĆEVA

SENOINA

PETRINJSKA

RIBNJAK

Archbishop's Palace

VLAŠKA

JURIŠIĆEVA

Archeological Museum

BOŠKOVIĆEVA

Croatian Academy

HATZOVA

TOMIS-LAVOV TRG

Train Station

Cathedral

GORNJI GRAD

KAPTOL

Dolac Market

TRG BANA JELAČIĆA

TESLINA

PRAŠKA

TRG NIKOLE ZRINSKOG

STROSSMAYEROV TRG

GAJEVA

Art Pavilion

Popov Toranj

Municipal Museum

KALČIĆEVA

RADIĆEVA

OPATIČKA

Croatian Parliament

Gallery Of Contemporary Art

RADIĆEVA TRG

ĆIRILO-METODSKA TRG

Funicular

PRERADOVIĆEV TRG

BOGOVIĆEVA

GAJEVA

US Embassy

MASARYKOVA

PRERADOVIĆEVA

Meštrović Atelier

St Mark's

Historical Museum

Gallery of Naive Art

MATOŠEVA

Lotrščak Tower

ILICA

MESNIČKA

GUNDULIĆA

DONJI GRAD

HEBRANGOVA

Botanic Gardens

National History Museum

NAZOROVA

KOVAČIĆEVA

VARŠAVSKA

FRANKOPANSKA

National Theatre

TRG MARŠALA TITA

MAZURANIĆEV TRG

Ethnographic Museum

ŽERJAVIĆEVA

MARULIĆEV TRG

VODNIKOVA

MIHANOVIĆEVA

Student Centre

Airport, Rijeka & Split

GJURE DEŽELIĆA

MEDULIĆEVA

ROOSEVELTOV TRG

Museum of Art and Crafts

Mimara Museum

KLAIĆEVA

KRŠNJAVOGA

SAVSKA CESTA

Technical Museum

ILICA

250 m

0

Hotels

Astoria, Petrinjska 71 (☎01/48-41-222, *hotel-astoria@zg.tel.hr*). Slightly careworn though clean en-suites with TV. Convenient for the train and bus stations. ⑤.

Central, Branimirova 3 (☎01/48-41-122, *www.hotel-central.hr*). Small, recently renovated rooms with ensuite facilities and TV opposite the railway station. ⑥.

Ilica, Ilica 102 (☎01/37-77-522, *www.hotel-ilica.hr*). Modern, smart and friendly B&B with en-suite rooms 1.5km west of the main square. Only twelve rooms, so ring in advance. ⑤.

Jadran, Vlaška 50 (☎01/45-53-777). Cheapest of the downtown hotels offering en-suite rooms. Just east of the city centre and fifteen minutes' walk from the train station at the top end of Draskovićeva. ④.

Lido, Jarun (☎01/38-32-839). Small hotel at the eastern end of Lake Jarun, 4km southwest of the centre. Attractive loft rooms with en-suite facilities. Tram #17 from Trg bana Jelačića. ⑦.

Pension Jägerhorn, Ilica 14 (☎01/48-33-877). In a courtyard just off the main shopping street. Comfortable, central and soon fills up. ⑦.

The City

Modern Zagreb splits neatly into three parts. **Donji Grad** or "Lower Town", which extends north from the train station to the main square (Trg bana Jelačića), is the bustling centre of the modern city. Uphill from here, to the northeast and the northwest, are the older quarters of **Kaptol** (the "Cathedral Chapter") and **Gradec** (the "Upper Town"), both peaceful districts of ancient mansions, quiet squares and leafy parks.

Donji Grad

The **railway station** is as good a place as any to start an exploration of the city. **Tomislavov Trg**, opposite the station, is the first in a series of three shady, green squares which form the backbone of the lower town. Taking its name from the tenth-century Croatian king – there's a horseback-statue of him in the centre of the square – Tomislavov Trg's main attraction is the **Art Pavilion** (Umjetnički Paviljon; Mon–Sat 11am–7pm, Sun 10am–1pm; 20kn), built in 1898 and now hosting art exhibitions in its gilded stucco and mock-marble interior. Behind the pavilion lies the second of the three squares, **Strossmayerov Trg**, at the end of which stands another palatial nineteenth-century building, the brick-built **Croatian Academy of Science and Arts**, founded as the Yugoslavian Academy of Science and Arts by the nineteenth-century Bishop Strossmayer, a Croatian patriot and keen supporter of the Yugoslav ideal. His statue, the work of Croatia's greatest sculptor, Ivan Meštrović (1883–1962), sits among the trees in front of the building. The **Archeological Museum** (Arheološki muzej; Tues–Fri 10am–5pm, Sat & Sun 10am–1pm; 20kn) lies to the north of here, in the last of the three squares, **Trg Nikole Zrinskog** (marked on some maps as "Zrinjevac"); the museum has pieces from prehistoric times to the Middle Ages, including jazzily designed pottery fragments from the fourth century BC Vučedol culture, ancient Roman and Greek artefacts, and a selection of Egyptian antiquities.

Walk up from here and you're on Zagreb's main square, **Trg bana Jelačića**, flanked by cafés, hotels and department stores, and hectic with the whizz of trams and hurrying pedestrians. The statue in the centre of the square is of the nineteenth-century governor of Croatia, ban Josip Jelačić (*ban* means "governor"); the tall clock to the east where half the city seems to agree to meet in the evenings. From here, Jurišićeva runs east towards Trg hrvatskih velikana and the **House of Croatian Artists** (Dom Hrvatskih Likovnih Umjetnika; Tues–Sat 11am–7pm, Sun 10am–2pm; 10kn), housed in a pavilion designed by Meštrović in the 1930s and containing displays of contemporary painting and sculpture. There's not much else to tempt you further east from here except for the **Maksimir Park**, which is Zagreb's largest open space, reachable by tram #4, #7, #11 or #12. The park was founded in 1794, and is a carefully landscaped enclosure containing a belvedere, an eighteenth-century mock Swiss-chalet (now a café), and five lakes – the city's **zoo** (daily 9am–6pm; 20kn) stands on an islet in one of them.

Pod Grčkim Topom, Zakmardijeve stube 5 (☎01/48-33-607). Good Croatian food in a small restaurant on the steps leading down from Strossmayerovo Šetalise to Trg bana Jelačića, with a terrace overlooking the lower town. Daily 11am–midnight.

Rubelj, Dolac market. Cheapest central place for simple but tasty grilled-meat standards. Daily 9am–11pm.

Stari Fijaker, Mesnička 6. A dimly lit, intimate restaurant serving local cuisine. Mon–Sat 8am–11pm, Sun 10am–10pm.

Cafés and bars

Atrij, Teslina 7. One of several café/bars in a courtyard just south of the main square, heaving with bright young things at weekends.

@VIP, Preradovičev Trg. Breezy new café with a few super sleek screens for Internet access.

Bulldog Pub, Bogovićeva. A typically elegant Zagreb bar and pavement café, this is one of the most popular meeting places in the town centre.

Dobar Zvuk, Gajeva 18. Popular, pub-style café-bar with moderately bohemian clientele.

Kolding, Berislavićeva 8. Civilized cellar bar with turn-of-the-century furnishings. Nice place for an intimate drink.

Melin, Košarska 19. Opposite the Oliver Twist, this energetic pub is a terrific alternative to the posier establishments nearby.

Oliver Twist, Tkalčićeva 60. Three floors of lively, solid beer (mainly Irish) drinking.

Tolkein, Vranicanijeva. Relaxed Gradec bar, with a pleasant leafy courtyard.

Music, theatre and festivals

Zagreb offers a rich and varied diet of high culture, with the Croatian National Theatre at Trg maršala Tita 15 (Hrvatsko narodno kazalište; ticket office Mon–Fri 10am–1pm & 5–7.30pm, Sat 10am–1pm & 90min before each performance, Sun 30min before each performance; ☎01/48-28-532), providing the focus for serious, Croatian-language **drama**, as well as **opera** and **ballet**. The city's main **orchestral-music** venue is the Lisinski Concert Hall south of the train station at Trg Stjepana Radića 4 (Dvorana Vatroslav Lisinski; ticket office Mon–Fri 9am–8pm, Sat 9am–2pm; ☎01/61-21-166). Intimate **chamber-music** concerts take place at the Croatian Musical Institute (Hrvatski glazbeni zavod), Gundulićeva 6 (☎01/48-30-822). The free monthly English-language pamphlet *Events and Performances*, available from the Zagreb tourist office, contains **listings** of all forthcoming events.

Zagreb's annual **folklore festival**, held at the end of July, is one of the city's biggest events, with performances of ethnic music and dance from all over the world, usually taking place on an outdoor stage in the upper town, just off Jezuitski Trg. Advance information is available from the tourist office or from the Festival Organizers (☎01/46-11-808).

Discos and clubs

Nightlife centres around a moderate selection of discos and clubs, many of which present the best opportunities for catching live rock and jazz.

Aquarius, Jarun. Popular venue at the eastern end of Lake Jarun, 4km southwest of the centre, specializing in techno and drum 'n' bass. Occasional host to live bands.

BP Club, Teslina 7. Jazz club and relaxed late-night drinking haunt, although it can be difficult to get in when live bands are playing.

Gjuro II, Medveščak 58. Relaxed cellar club with varied programme of dance music and alternative rock, with regular live music.

Močvara, Tvornica Jedinstvo building, Trnjanski nasip. Unpretentious cultural centre in an old factory on the banks of the River Sava. Live gigs (usually alternative rock), film shows and club nights – something happening every night. Take any bus heading for Novi Zagreb and alight just before the bridge – the club is on your right.

Saloon, Tuškanac 1a. Legendary Zagreb meeting place in a leafy corner of town 500m west of the centre. Dressy, showbizzy clientele, but it's not dishearteningly exclusive by any means. Music is an enjoyable mish-mash of commercial disco.

Tvornica, Šubićeva 1. Former ballroom just north of the bus station now hosting live rock, club nights and theatre.

Listings

Airlines British Airways, Sheraton Hotel, Kneza Borne 2 (☎01/45-53-336, *www.britishairways.com/croatia*); Croatia Airlines, Trg N. Zrinskog 17 (☎01/48-19-633, *www.croatiaairlines.hr*).

Airport enquiries ☎01/45-62-182.

American Express Lastovska 23 (☎01/61-24-422).

British Council Ilica 12 (Mon, Tues, Thurs & Fri 10am–4pm, Wed 1.30–6.30pm; ☎01/48-13-700, *www.britishcouncil.hr*). Library, newspapers, reading room and Internet access.

Bus enquiries ☎060/313-333.

Car rental Avis, Hotel Intercontinental, Kršnjavoga 1 (☎01/48-36-006); Budget, Sheraton Hotel, Kneza Borne 2 (☎01/45-54-936); Hertz, Kačićeva 9a (☎01/48-46-777); Unirent, Gajeva 29a (☎01/49-22-382).

Embassies Australia, Hotel Intercontinental, Kršnjavoga 1 (☎01/48-36-600); Canada, Prilaz Gjure Deūelića 4 (☎01/48-81-200); UK, Vlaška 121 (☎01/45-55-310); US, Hebrangova 2 (☎01/66-12-200).

Exchange 24hr exchange facilities in the post office at Branimirova 4.

Ferry tickets Jadrolinija, Trg N. Zrinskog 20 (☎01/48-73-307).

Hospital The main casualty department is at Draskovićeva 19.

Internet access Aquarius, Kralja Držislavova 4 (Mon–Sat 9am–4am, Sun noon–2am; 24kn/hr); Art Net Club, Preradovičeva 25 (daily 9am–11pm; 20kn/hr); Charlies, Gajeva 4 (Mon–Sat 8am–10pm; 15kn/hr); Sublink, Teslina 12 (Mon–Sat 9am–10pm, Sun 3–10pm; 15kn/hr).

Laundry Predom, Draškovićeva 31 (Mon–Fri 7.30am–7pm, Sat 8am–noon).

Left luggage At the train station (24hr) and the bus station (6am–10pm).

Pharmacy 24-hour pharmacy at Ilica 43.

Post offices Jurišićeva 13 (Mon–Fri 7am–9pm, Sat 8am–6pm, Sun 8am–2pm) and Branimirova 4 (24hr).

Taxis Ranks on Trg maršala Tita and Gajeva. To book, call ☎01/66-82-505, 66-82-558.

Telephones International telephone calls can be made at either of the main post offices listed above.

Train station Information on ☎9830 (domestic services), ☎01/45-73-238 (international).

Travel agents Croatia Express, Teslina 4 (☎01/48-11-842, *www.croatiaexpress.com*); Generaltourist, Praška 5 (☎01/48 05-652, *www.generaltourist.com*); Kvarner Express, Praška 4 (☎01/48-10-522).

ISTRIA

A large peninsula jutting into the northern Adriatic, **Istria** (*Istra*) is Croatian tourism at its most developed. Many of the towns here were tourist resorts back in the last century, and in recent years their proximity to northern Europe has ensured an annual influx of sun-seekers from Germany, Austria and the Netherlands. Yet the growth of modern hotel complexes, sprawling campsites and (mainly concrete) beaches has done little to detract from the essential charm of the region. This stretch of the coast was under Venetian rule for 400 years and there's still a fair-sized Italian community, with Italian very much the second language. Regular trains and buses from Zagreb (and the Slovene capital Ljubljana, another good gateway to the region) arrive at Istria's largest centre, the port city of **Pula**. With its Roman amphitheatre and other relics of Roman occupation, it's a rewarding place to spend a couple of days – rooms are relatively easy to come by and most of Istria's interesting spots are only a bus ride away. On the western side of the Istrian peninsula, resort towns like **Poreč** and **Rovinj**, with their cobbled piazzas and shuttered houses, are almost overwhelmingly pretty.

Pula

Once the chief port of the Austro-Hungarian Empire, **PULA** is an engaging combination of working port, naval base and brash riviera town. The Romans put the city squarely on the map when they arrived in 177 BC, transforming it into an important commercial centre. The most obvious relic of their rule is the first century BC **Amphitheatre** (*amfiteatar*; daily: June–Sept 8am–9pm; Oct–May 9am–5pm; 16kn) just north of the centre, a great grey elliptical skein of connecting arches, silhouetted against the skyline from wherever you stand in the city. It's the sixth largest in the world, and once had space for over 23,000 spectators. The outer shell is fairly complete, as is one of the towers, up which a slightly hair-raising climb gives a good sense of the enormity of the structure and a view of Pula's industrious harbour. You can also explore some of the cavernous rooms underneath, which would have been used for keeping wild animals and Christians before they met their death. They're now given over to piles of crusty amphora, and reconstructed olive presses.

South of the amphitheatre, central Pula circles a pyramidal hill, scaled by secluded streets and topped with a star-shaped Venetian fortress. On the eastern side of the hill, Istarska (which subsequently becomes Giardini) leads down to the first-century BC **Triumphal Arch of the Sergians** (Slavoluk obitelja Sergijevaca), through which ul Sergijevaca, a lively pedestrianized thoroughfare, leads in turn to a square known as **Forum** – site of the ancient Roman forum and these days the centre of Pula's old quarter. On the far side of here, the slim form of the **Temple of Augustus** was built between 2 BC and 14 AD to celebrate the cult of the emperor; the high Corinthian columns of its frontage intact and imposing, this is one of the best examples of a Roman temple outside Italy.

Heading north from Forum along Kandlerova leads to Pula's **Cathedral** (daily 7am–noon & 4–6pm), a broad, simple and very spacious structure that is another mixture of periods and styles: a fifteenth-century renovation of a Romanesque basilica built on the foundations of a Roman temple. Inside, the high altar consists of a third-century marble Roman sarcophagus, said to have once contained the remains of the eleventh-century Hungarian King Solomon. From the cathedral, you can follow streets up to the top of the hill, the site of the original Roman Capitol and now the home of a mossy seventeenth-century **fortress**, built by the Venetians and now housing the pretty inessential **Historical Museum of Istria** (daily: summer 8am–7pm; winter 9am–6pm; 10kn). You're better off following tracks to the far side of the fortress where there are the remains of a small **Roman Theatre**, and the **Archeological Museum** (Arheološki muzej; May–Sept Mon–Sat 9am–8pm, Sun 10am–3pm; Oct–April Mon–Fri 9am–3pm; 12kn), which hides in the trees next to the second-century AD Porta Gemina. Inside the museum are pillars and toga-clad statues mingling haphazardly with ceramics, jewellery and trinkets from all over Istria, some dating back to prehistoric times.

Practicalities

Pula's **train station** is a ten-minute walk north of the town centre, at the far end of Kolodvorska; the **bus station** is along Istarska, just south of the amphitheatre. The **tourist office**, located in the Forum (Jun–Sept daily 9am–10pm; Oct–May Mon–Sat 9am–8pm; ☎052/219-197, www.gradpula.com), can provide information and useful maps, but does not offer a private room booking service. For this, you need to go to Arenatours, just down from the bus station at Giardini 4 (summer daily 8am–8pm; winter Mon–Fri 8am–5pm; ☎052/218-696, arenaturist@pu.tel.hr), or head for Istra Way on the seafront at Riva 14 (summer daily 9am–10pm; winter Mon–Fri 9am–4pm, Sat 9am–1pm; ☎052/214-613). Of the **hotels**, Omir, slightly uphill from Giardini at Sergia Dobrića 6 (☎052/210-614; ④), is small and friendly, but rather plain. Much more comfortable and only slightly more expensive, Scaletta, a stone's throw from the amphitheatre at Flavijevska 26 (☎052/541-599; ⑤), is one of the best family-run hotels in Croatia. There's also a **HI hostel**, at Valsaline bay, 4km south of the centre (☎052/391-133, www.whereisthebeach.com; ②); take bus #2 or #7 from Giardini to Vila Idola and then bear right towards the bay. The nearest **campsite** is Stoja, on a rocky wooded peninsula 3km southeast of town (☎052/387-144); take bus #1 from Giardini.

Most **eating and drinking** venues are concentrated around the arena, Forum and Kandlerova. Delfin, opposite the cathedral at Kandlerova 17, offers inexpensive fish dishes; Jupiter, below the fortress at Castropola 38, is the best of the pizzerias; Pompei, Clarissova 1, does good pasta dishes and salads; while the restaurant of the Scaletta hotel (see above) is the place to go for expensive seafood. Best of the drinking haunts are Cvajner, a people-watching café next to the tourist office; Ulix, an elegant bar next to the triumphal arch; and

Bounty Pub, an animated place with plenty of outdoor seating two blocks east of the arch at Veronska 8. In the summer, the amphitheatre is used to stage pop events and world-class opera; details can be obtained from the tourist office.

Rovinj and around

There are few more pleasant towns in Istria than **ROVINJ**, which lies forty kilometres north of Pula. Its harbour is a likeable mix of fishing boats and swanky yachts, its quaysides a blend of sunshaded café-tables and the thick orange of fishermen's nets. Rovinj is the most Italian town on this coast: there's an Italian high school, street-names are in Italian, and the language is widely spoken in the town. From the main square, **Trg maršala Tita**, the Baroque **Vrata svetog Križa** leads up to Grisia Ulica, which is lined with ateliers and galleries selling local art. It climbs steeply through the heart of the old town to **St Euphemia's Church** (Crkva svete Eufemije; daily 10am–noon & 4–7pm), dominating Rovinj from the top of its stumpy peninsula. This eighteenth-century church, Baroque in style, has the sixth-century sarcophagus of the saint inside, and offers the chance to climb its 58-metre-high tower (same times; 10kn). Back on maršala Tita, the **Town Museum** (Zavičajni muzej Rovinj; May–Sept Mon–Sat 9am–12.30pm & 6–9pm; Oct–April Tues–Sat 10am–1.30pm; 10kn) has the usual collection of archeological oddments, antique furniture and exhibitions of Croatian art. North of here is **Trg Valdibora**, home to a small fruit and vegetable market, from where Obala palih boraca leads along the waterfront to the Marine Biological Institute at Obala Giordano Paliaga 5; the institute's **aquarium** (Easter–Oct daily 9am–9pm; 10kn) has tanks of Adriatic flora and marine life.

Paths on the south side of Rovinj's busy harbour lead beyond the *Hotel Park* towards **Zlatni rt**, a densely-forested cape, crisscrossed by numerous tracks and fringed by rocky **beaches**. Other spots for bathing can be found on the two islands just offshore from Rovinj – **Sveta Katerina**, the nearer of the two, and **Crveni otok**, just outside Rovinj's bay; both are linked every thirty minutes by boats from the harbour and are home to a couple of hotels, a handful of pebbly beaches and some reasonable places to swim.

Practicalities

Rovinj's **bus station** is five minutes' walk southeast of the town centre, just off Trg na lokvi, at the junction of Carrera and Carducci. The **tourist office** is located at Obula Pina Budicin 12 (Jun–Sep daily 8am–9pm; rest of year Mon–Sat 8am–3pm; ☎052/811-566, *www.istra.com/rovinj*). **Private rooms** can be obtained from Natale, opposite the bus station at Carducci 4 (☎052/813-365, *www.natale.hr*); and Onio, also near the bus station at Aldo Rismondo 19 (☎052/811-155). Of the **hotels**, the *Adriatic*, Trg maršala Tita (☎052/815-088, *hotel-adriatic@jadran-turist.tel.hr*; ⑤) is a venerable establishment by the port; while the *Katarina* on the island of Sveta Katarina (☎052/811-233; ④) is a comfortable off-shore alternative. The nearest **campsite** is the *Polari* (☎052/801-501), 3km south and reached by regular bus. For **eating**, *da Sergio*, at Grisia 11, is the best place for pizza; while *Konoba Veli Jože*, near the tourist office at Sveti Križ 1, has top-notch seafood.

Poreč and around

Regular buses head north from Rovinj towards **POREČ**, Istria's largest and busiest resort. Another peninsula town with an ordered mesh of streets that dates from its days as a Roman encampment, Poreč's star historic turn is the **Basilica of Euphrasius** (Eufrazijeva basilika; daily 7am–8pm; free), a sixth-century Byzantine structure harbouring mosaics claimed by some experts to be comparable with those at Ravenna. Situated just off Ljubljanska, in the centre of Poreč, the basilica is at the heart of a religious complex, established by Bishop

Euphrasius in 543, which includes a bishop's palace, atrium, baptistry and campanile. Entry is through the **Atrium**, an arcaded courtyard that was heavily restored in the nineteenth century but still has ancient bits of masonry incorporated in its walls. Beyond lies the **Bishop's Palace** (daily 10am–6.30pm; 10kn), a seventeenth-century building harbouring a display of mosaic fragments which once adorned the basilica floor. To the left of here is the octagonal Baptistry. The basilica itself is a rather bare structure, save for the wall **mosaics** above the altar which are studded with semi-precious gems, encrusted with mother-of-pearl and emblazoned everywhere with Euphrasius's personal monogram: he was, it's said, a notoriously arrogant man. The central part of the composition shows the Virgin enthroned with Child, flanked by a worldly Euphrasius holding a model of his church. Underneath are scenes of the *Annunciation* and *Visitation*, the latter surprisingly realistic, with the imaginative invention of a doltish eavesdropping servant.

Due east of the basilica is ul Dekumanska, which follows the line of the ancient Roman *decumanus* (main street) and opens out into a square busy with street artists and tourist traffic. The **Poreč Museum** at ul Dekumanska 9 (daily 9am–noon & 4–7pm; 10kn), housed in the Baroque Sinčić Palace, displays Greek and Roman finds from the surrounding area. Heading south, towards the end of the peninsula, you'll find the distinctive thirteenth-century **Romanesque House**, with an unusual projecting wooden balcony – a venue for art shows. Further on is **Trg Marafor**, with its remains of Roman temples to Mars and Neptune. Little is known about these and they're not much more than heaps of rubble really, the interesting parts having found their way into the town museum.

The **beaches** around the old town can get crowded. As an alternative, take a boat from the jetty next to the Marina (7am–midnight every 30min; 14kn) to the island of **Sveti Nikola** across the water, or walk south beyond the marina where pathways head along a rocky coastline shaded by gnarled pines.

Practicalities

Poreč's **bus station** is just outside the town centre, behind the marina. From here, it's a five-minute walk to the **tourist office** at Zagrebačka 11 (Jun–Sep daily 8am–10pm; Oct–May daily 8am–3pm & 4.30–7.30pm; ☎052/451-458, *www.istra.com/porec*), which provides information and will point you in the direction of agencies offering **rooms**: Atlas, Bože Milanovića 11 (☎052/432-273), is probably the easiest to find. For **hotels**, try the friendly and central *Poreč*, just behind the bus station on Rade Končara 1 (☎052/451-811, *www.tel.hr/duga*; ④). The closest **campsites** are at the Zelena Laguna complex, a few kilometres south – *Zelena Laguna* (☎052/ 410-541) and, further south, *Bijela Uvala* (☎052/410-551) – reachable by hourly bus from the bus station.

As for **food**, there's a good sprinkling of places in the old town. *Amicus*, at Eufrazijeva 45, offers good-quality and good-value pizza, grilled meat and seafood; the *Sarajevo Grill*, just off Dekumanska on Matije Vlačiča, has a good array of meat dishes; while *Istra*, on the corner of Obala maršala Tita and Bože Milanovića, is one of the best places to eat fish. Central Poreč is full of cafés and bars with outdoor seating; it's really a question of deciding which brand of blaring music you're happy to tolerate.

Moving on from Istria: Rijeka

Travelling on from Istria towards Zagreb or Dalmatia, most routes lead through the brusque port city of **RIJEKA**, hardly worth a stopoff in its own right but an important transport hub for onward travel. Regular buses run from Rijeka to Zagreb, Split and Dubrovnik; and it's also the starting point for the once-daily Jadrolinija coastal ferry, which calls in at Split and Dubrovnik on its way south. Rijeka is easy to get in and out of. Train and bus stations are about 400m apart; the former at the western end of Trpimirova, the latter at the eastern end of the same street on Trg Žabica. The **Jadrolinija ferry office** (daily 7am–6pm, Wed & Sun till 8pm; ☎051/211-444) is just along the waterfront from the bus station at Riva 16.

DALMATIA

Stretching from Zadar in the north to the Montenegrin border in the south, the region of **Dalmatia** (Dalmacija) possesses one of Europe's most dramatic shorelines, the sheer wall of Croatia's mountain ranges sweeping down to the sea from stark, grey heights, scattering islands in their path. For centuries, the region was ruled by Venice, spawning towns, churches and an architecture that wouldn't look out of place on the other side of the water. All along, well-preserved medieval towns sit on tiny islands or just above the sea on slim peninsulas, beneath a grizzled karst landscape that drops precipitously into some of the clearest – and cleanest – water anywhere. The main centres to aim for are in southern Dalmatia: the provincial capital **Split** is served by buses and trains from Zagreb and provides onward bus connections with the walled city of **Dubrovnik**. Ferry connections with the best of the islands – **Brač**, **Hvar**, **Vis** and **Korčula** – are also made from Split.

Split

By far the largest city in Dalmatia, and its major transit point, **SPLIT** is one of the most enticing spots on the Dalmatian coast; a hectic city, full of shouting stall-owners and travellers on the move. At the heart of all this, hemmed in by the sprawling estates and a modern harbour, lies a crumbling old town built within the precincts of Diocletian's Palace, one of the most outstanding classical remains in Europe. The palace was built as a retirement home by Dalmatian-born Roman Emperor Diocletian in AD 305, and although it fell into disrepair soon after his death, the palace's shell was used as a refuge by those fleeing the Byzantine city of Salona (6km inland), sacked by the Avars in 614. Modified and built-onto over the centuries, Diocletian's Palace has remained the core of Split ever since.

Arrival, information and accommodation

The main **bus and railway stations** are next door to each other on Obala Kneza Domagoja, five minutes' walk from the centre, just around the harbour; the **ferry terminal** for both domestic and international ferries, together with the Jadrolinija booking office, is a few hundred metres south of here. Split's **airport** is some 16km west of town. Croatia Airlines buses (25kn) connect with scheduled flights and run into central Split, dropping you right on the waterfront; alternatively, a taxi will set you back about 200kn.

Split's new **tourist office** is located in the Peristil of the Palace (Mon–Sat 8am–8pm, Sun 8am–1pm; ☎021/355-088, *www.visitsplit.com*). Turist Biro, on the waterfront at Obala narodnog preporoda 12 (July–Sept Mon–Fri 7.30am–9pm, Sat 8am–8pm, Sun 8am–1pm; rest of year Mon–Fri 7.30am–8pm, Sat 8am–2pm; ☎021/342-142), arranges accommodation in **private rooms** (②); it's quite likely that you'll be accosted by landladies offering rooms at both the train and bus stations – particularly worth considering if arriving late at night. Most reasonable of the **hotels** are the *Slavija*, which has basic rooms (some with shower, some without) in the old town at Buvinova 3 (☎021/347-053; ③); the more comfortable *Bellevue* on the western fringes of the old town at bana Jelačića 2 (☎021/585-701; ④); and the *Marjan*, (☎021/342-866, *www.hotel-marjan.com*; ⑤), a more business-oriented place five minutes' further west at Obala kneza Branimira 8.

The City

Most of Split's attractions are concentrated in the compact **old centre** behind the waterfront, largely made up of the remains of Diocletian's Palace. The palace was begun in AD 295 and finished ten years later, when the emperor came back to his native Dalmatia to escape the cares of the empire, cure his rheumatism and grow cabbages. However Diocletian continued to maintain an elaborate court here, in a building that mixed luxurious palatial apartments with the infrastructure of a Roman garrison. The best place to start a tour of the palace area is on the seaward side, through the **Bronze Gate** (Mjedena vrata), a functional gateway giving access to the sea that once came right up to the palace itself. Inside, you find yourself in a vaulted hall, from which imposing steps lead through the now domeless vestibule to the Peristil. Little remains of the imperial apartments to the left, but you can get some idea of their grandeur and floor-plan by visiting the **subterranean halls** (Podrum; daily: July & Aug 8am–8pm; Sept–June 8am–noon & 4–7pm; 6kn) beneath the houses which now stand on the site; the entrance is to the left of the Mjedena vrata. Through the vaulted hall, which is usually full of stalls selling arts and crafts, and up the steps, is the **Peristyle** (Peristil), once the central courtyard of the palace complex. These days it serves as the main town square, crowded with cafés and surrounded by remnants of the stately arches that framed the square. At the southern end, steps lead up to the **vestibule**, a round, formerly domed building that is the only part of the imperial apartment area of the palace that's anything like complete. It was here that subjects would wait in apprehension before being admitted to Diocletian himself.

On the east side of the Peristyle stands one of two black granite Egyptian sphinxes, dating from around 15 BC, which originally flanked the entrance to Diocletian's mausoleum, an octagonal building surrounded by an arcade of Corinthian columns that's since been converted into Split's **Cathedral** (Katedrala; Mon–Sat 7am–noon & 4–7pm). Diocletian's body is known to have rested here for 170 years until one day it disappeared – no one knows why or where. On the right of the entrance is the **campanile** (same hours; 5kn), a Romanesque structure much restored in the late nineteenth century. The haul up is worth the effort for the panoramic view over the city and beyond. As for the cathedral itself, its most immediate feature is the walnut and oak main **doorway**, carved with an inspired comic strip showing scenes from the life of Christ – the work of local artist Andrija Buvina in 1214. Inside the cathedral is an odd hotchpotch of styles, the dome ringed by two series of decorative Corinthian columns and a frieze which contains portraits of Diocletian and his wife. The **pulpit** is a beautifully proportioned example of Romanesque art, sitting on capitals tangled with snakes, strange beasts and foliage. But the church's finest feature is the Altar of St Anastasius, on which a cruelly realistic *Flagellation of Christ* – completed by local artist Juraj Dalmatinac in 1448 – shows Jesus pawed and brutalized by some peculiarly oafish persecutors.

Opposite the cathedral, a narrow alley runs from a gap in the arched arcade down to the **Baptistry** (opening times vary, check at the cathedral). Another pre-Christian edifice, variously attributed to the cults of Janus and Jupiter, this is an attractive building with a richly coffered ceiling and well-preserved figures of Hercules and Apollo on the eastern portal. Later Christian additions include a skinny *John the Baptist* by Meštrović (a late work of 1954), and, more famously, an eleventh-century baptismal font with a relief popularly believed to be a grovelling subject paying homage to a Croatian king.

A block north of the cathedral on Papalićeva, the flowery Gothic Papalić Palace now houses the **City Museum** (Gradski muzej; June–Sept Tues–Fri 9am–noon & 5–8pm, Sat & Sun 10am–noon; Oct–May Tues–Fri 9am–2pm, Sat & Sun 10am–noon; 10kn), which displays city documents, weaponry and fragments of sculpture. Just north of here, reached by following Dioklecijanova, is the grandest and best preserved of the palace gates, the **Golden Gate** or Zlatna vrata. Just outside there's another Mestrović, a gigantic statue of the fourth-century Bishop **Grgur Ninski**. Ninski is an important historical character for the Croats since he fought Rome for the right of his people to use their own language in the liturgy.

Fifteen minutes' walk northwest of here, the **Archeological Museum** at Zrinsko Frankopanska 25 (Arheoloski muzej; June–Sept Tues–Fri 9am–1pm & 5–8pm, Sat & Sun 10am–noon; Oct–May Tues–Fri 9am–2pm, Sat & Sun 10am–1pm; 10kn) contains comprehensive displays of Illyrian, Greek, medieval and Roman artefacts that conjure up a picture of life for the average noble of the time. Outside, the arcaded courtyard is crammed with a wonderful array of Greek, Roman and early Christian gravestones, sarcophagi and decorative sculpture.

Crisscrossed by footpaths and minor roads, the woods of the **Marjan peninsula** west of the old town are the best place to head for if you want to exchange central Split's turmoil for some peace and quiet. On foot, the peninsula is accessible from Obala hrvatskog narodnog preporoda via Sperun and then Senjska, which cuts up through the slopes of the **Varoš** district. Most of Marjan's visitors stick to the road around the edge of the promontory with its infrequent, tiny rocky **beaches**; the Bene beach, on the far northern side, is especially popular. From the road, tracks lead up into the heart of the Marjan Park, which is thickly wooded with pines, rising to its peak at 175m. The main historical attractions of Marjan are on the lower, southern edge, along Šetalište Ivana Meštrovića. First of these is the **Museum of Croatian Archeological Monuments** (Muzej Hrvatskih arheoloskih spomenika; Tues–Sat 9am–4pm, Sun 9am–noon; 20kn), fifteen minutes' walk west of the centre or bus #12 from the seafront, an oversized modern pavilion housing a disappointing collection of jewellery, weapons and fragmentary reconstructions of chancel screens and ciboria from ninth- and tenth-century Croat churches. A couple of minutes' walk away, the **Meštrović Gallery**, Ivana Meštrovića 46 (Galerija Ivana Meštrovića; Tues–Sat 10am–4/6pm, Sun 10am–2/3pm; 15kn), is another Croatian shrine, housed in the ostentatious Neoclassical building that was built – and lived in – by Croatia's most famous twentieth-century artist, Ivan Meštrović (1883–1962). The gallery displays many of his smaller statues – boldly fashioned bodies curled into elegant poses and greatly influenced by Croatian folk art. Mestrović's former workshop, **Kaštelet**, (check at the Meštrović Gallery first) is 300m up the same road, and contains a chapel decorated with one of the sculptor's most important set-piece works, a series of wood-carved reliefs showing scenes from the Stations of the Cross.

Beaches

The main city beach is **Bačvice**, a few minutes' walk south past the railway station, a small stretch of shingle backed by a high-tech pavilion packed with cafés and eateries. **Bene**, on the northern side of the Marjan peninsula (bus #12 from the seafront), occupies a rockier shore backed by pine forest.

Eating and drinking

For **eating**, the daily market at the eastern edge of the old town is an excellent place to shop for fruit, veg and local cheeses, while the 24-hour bakery directly opposite the market on Zagrebačka is something of a late-night Split institution. There are few restaurants in the old town, although *Sarajevo*, Domaldova 6, has a good range of Croatian meat and fish dishes. Further afield, *Galija* at Matošića 2 on the western fringes of the old town, is the best of the pizzerias; while *Konoba kod Jože* at Sredmanuška 4, ten minutes' northeast of the old town, is an atmospheric place specializing in seafood. *Konoba Varo*, up behind the *Bellevue Hotel* at ban Mladenova 7, is another traditional Dalmatian restaurant.

There are plenty of pavement cafés along the seafront for daytime and evening **drinking**, though they are usually packed. The best of the rest are the bars within the old town: try *Planet Jazz*, a bohemian hangout on Grgura Ninskog; the similar *Jazz III* on Vukičovićeva; or *Song* on Mihovilova širina, a slightly dressier place which is crowded on summer evenings. *Shakespeare*, Uvala Zente 3, is a popular disco just east of Bačvice beach with an outdoor terrace overlooking the shore. *Obojena Svjetlost*, on the beach beneath the Meštrović gallery, is an animated open-air disco/bar that stays open until the early hours. **Internet access** is available at *Internet, Games & Books*, 200m north of the train station on Obala kneza domagoja.

Brač

The third largest island on the Adriatic coast, **BRAČ** is famous for its milk-white marble, which has been used in places as diverse as Berlin's Reichstag, the high altar of Liverpool's Metropolitan Cathedral, the White House in Washington – and, of course, Diocletian's Palace. In addition to the marble, a great many islanders were once dependent on the grape harvest, though the phylloxera (vine lice) epidemics of the late nineteenth century and early twentieth century forced many of them to emigrate. Even today, as you cross Brač's interior, the signs of this depopulation are all around in the tumbledown walls and overgrown fields.

The easiest way to reach Brač is by **ferry** from Split to **Supetar**, an engagingly laid-back fishing port on the north side of the island, from where it's a straightforward bus journey to **Bol**, a major windsurfing centre on the island's south coast and site of one of the Adriatic's most famous beaches.

Supetar

Though the largest town on the island, **SUPETAR** is a rather sleepy village onto which package tourism has been painlessly grafted. There's little of specific interest, save for several attractive shingle **beaches** which stretch away westwards from the town's harbour, and the **Petrinović Mausoleum**, a neo-Byzantine confection on a wooded promontory 1km west of town, built by sculptor Toma Rosandić to honour a local businessman.

Supetar's **tourist office** beside the ferry dock at Porat 1 (mid-June–mid-Sept daily 8am–10pm; rest of year Mon–Fri 10am–4pm; ☎021/630-551, *www.supetar.hr*) has information on the whole island. **Private rooms** are available from Supetar Tours (☎021/630-022) near the bus station, or Atlas (☎021/631-105) on the harbourfront. There's also the *Palute*, 1.5km west of the harbour at Put pašike 16 (☎021/631-541; ③), a friendly and agreeable **pension** offering bed-and-breakfast accommodation. The **Hotel** *Britanida*, 200m east of the ferry dock at Hrvatskih velikana 26 (☎021/631-038; ④), is a step up in comfort; but avoid the line of overpriced package hotels behind the beaches. There are two **campsites** just east of the ferry dock. Best of the places to **eat** on the harbourfront is *Palute* at Porat 4, which serves good grilled fish. *Vinotoka*, just inland from the harbour at Dobova 6, has a wide range of traditional Croatian food and an extensive choice of local wines. The clear waters around Supetar are perfect for **scuba diving**; the Dive Center Kaktus in the *Kaktus Hotel* complex (☎021/630-421; April–Oct) rents out gear and arranges scuba and snorkelling crash courses from around 200kn, as well as renting out mountain bikes. **Ferry tickets** can be purchased from the Jadrolinija office inside the bus station.

Bol

Stranded on the far side of the Vidova Gora mountains, there's no denying the beauty of **BOL**'s setting, or the charm of its old stone houses. The main attraction of the village is its beach, **Zlatni rat** (Golden Cape), which lies to the west of the centre along the wooded shoreline. Unusually sandy and unusually beautiful, the cape juts into the sea in the form of an extended finger, changing shape from season to season as the wind plays across it. It does, however, get very crowded during summer. When you're through with the beach, look in at the late-fifteenth-century **Dominican Monastery** (Dominikanski samostan; daily 10am–noon & 5–9pm; 10kn), perched on a bluff just east of Bol's centre. Its location is dramatic, and the monastery museum holds among its small collection a *Madonna with Child* by Tintoretto.

Buses from Supetar stop just west of Bol's harbour, at the far end of which stands the **tourist office** (June–Aug daily 8am–10pm; Sept–May Mon–Fri 8.30am–3pm; ☎021/635-638, *www.bol.hr*) which has free leaflets and maps. **Private rooms** can be obtained from Boltours, 100m west of the bus stop at Vladimira Nazora 18 (daily June–Aug 8.30am–10pm; rest of year 9am–1pm & 5–8pm; ☎021/635-693, *www.boltours.com*) and there are several **campsites** in the new part of town uphill from the centre. For **eating**, there are numerous places along the waterfront, although *Gust*, above the harbour at F. Radića 14, has the widest range of traditional food. There are a couple of **windsurfing** centres on the shoreline west of town, on the way to Zlatni rat, which offer board rental and a range of courses for beginners. Big Blue (☎021/306-222, *www.big-blue-sport.hr*), with offices next to the tourist office and in front of the *Hotel Borak*, is one of the most reliable and also rents out sea kayaks (20kn per hr) and **mountain bikes** (75kn per day) – useful if you want to get to Blaca.

Blaca

One way to escape Bol's crowds is to make for the hermitage of **Blaca**, tucked away at the head of a valley about 12km to the west of the town. You can walk there by following the road, subsequently a track, which heads west from Bol, before heading inland at Blaca bay – the route is well signposted, but the trip takes three hours each way. If you have your own transport on the other hand, follow the signposted track (just about passable for cars, but rough on the suspension) which leaves the main road from Bol to Supetar. At the track's end, head on foot along the path downhill, which leads to the monastery in about forty minutes. The **hermitage** (Tues–Sun 10am–5pm, but check in the tourist office at Bol or Supetar as times can vary; 10kn) was founded in 1588 by monks fleeing the Turks; the last resident was an enthusiastic astronomer who left all sorts of bits and bobs, including an assortment of old clocks and a stock of lithographs by Poussin. But the principal attraction is the hermitage's setting, hugging the sides of a narrow, scrub-covered ravine.

Hvar

One of the most hyped of all the Croatian islands, **HVAR** is undeniably beautiful – a slim, green slice of land punctured by jagged inlets and cloaked with hills of spongy lavender. Tourist development hasn't been too crass, and the island's main centre, **Hvar town**, retains much of its old Venetian charm. **Ferries** run between here and Split twice daily, and to **Stari Grad**, farther east, roughly four times daily. The Dubrovnik–Rijeka coastal ferry stops at Hvar town once a day in summer, less frequently through the rest of the year. Buses make the 30 minute trip from the terminal, 4km east of Stari Grad itself, to Hvar Town.

Hvar Town

The best view of **HVAR TOWN** is from the sea, the tiny town centre contoured around the bay, grainy-white and brown with green splashes of palms and pines bursting from every crack and cranny. At the centre, the creamy brown main square cuts its way in, flanked by the arcaded bulk of the Venetian arsenal. The upper storey of the arsenal was added in 1612 to house the city **theatre** (*kazalite*; daily: summer 10am–noon & 8–11pm; winter 10am–noon; 10kn), the oldest in Croatia and one of the first in Europe. It's since been converted to a cinema, but the painted Baroque interior has survived pretty much intact. The square culminates in the skeletal campanile of Hvar's **Cathedral** (no fixed opening times, but usually open mornings), a sixteenth-century construction with an eighteenth-century facade that's a characteristic mixture of Gothic and Renaissance styles. Inside is routine enough, but the **Bishop's Treasury** (Riznica; daily: summer 9am–noon & 5–7pm; winter 10am–noon; 10kn) is worth the entry fee for its small but fine selection of chalices, reliquaries and embroidery. Look out for a nicely worked sixteenth-century crozier, carved into a serpent, encrusted with saints and embossed with a figure of the Virgin attended by Moses and an Archangel.

The rest of the old town backs away from the piazza in an elegant confusion of twisting lanes and alleys. Up above, the **Fortress** (Kaštil; June–Sept daily 8am–8pm; 10kn) is a good example of sixteenth-century military architecture. The views over Hvar and the islands beyond are well worth the trek to the top. From the fort you can pick out the fifteenth-century **Franciscan Monastery** (Franjevački samostan; Mon–Fri 10am–noon & 5–7pm; 10kn), to the left of the harbour, a sliver of white against the blue of the sea. The monastery has a small collection of paintings, mostly obscure Venetian, which includes a tender, dark and modernistic *Ecce Homo* by Leandro Bassano and, stretching right across one wall, a melodramatic, almost life-size *Last Supper* attributed to Matteo Ingoli. Next door, the monastic **church** is pleasingly simple, with beautifully carved choir stalls and a fanciful partition dating from 1583; look out for the extravagant dragon candle-holders.

The **beaches** nearest to Hvar town are rocky and crowded, and it's best to make your way towards the **Pakleni otoci** (the Islands of Hell), just to the west of Hvar. Easily reached by water taxi from the harbour (about 15kn each way), the Pakleni are a chain of eleven wooded islands, only three of which have any facilities (simple bars and restaurants): Jerolim island, the nearest, offers nudist bathing; next is Marinkovac – partly nudist, but with a main beach, U Stipanska; then Sv Klement, the largest of the islands – here, most people head for Palmižana, one of its most attractive coves with a fine shingle beach. Bear in mind that **camping** is forbidden throughout Pakleni.

PRACTICALITIES
Hvar town's **tourist office** (June–Sept daily 8am–2pm & 4–10pm; Oct–May Mon–Fri 8am–3pm; ☎021/741-059, *www.hvar.hr*) is on the waterfront below the theatre; for assistance in booking **private rooms**, however, you should head for the Mengola agency, also on the harbour (☎021/742-099, *www.mengola.hr*); or Pelegrin, by the ferry dock (☎021/742-250). The local **hotels** are not cheap, and are often full in July and August. The characterless but acceptable *Dalmacija*, on the eastern side of the harbour (☎021/741-120; ⑤), and the *Delfin*, over on the western side (☎021/741-168; ⑤), are as reasonable as you'll get.

There are dozens of **restaurants** in Hvar town, none of which are too expensive. *Kod Kapetana*, next to the *Delfin hotel*, dishes up splendid seafood, with terrific terrace views to boot; while *Hanibal*, on the main square, has a slightly pricier, but more wide-ranging menu. *Macondo*, signposted in a backstreet uphill from the harbour, is another good place for meat and fish. For **drinking**, there are several cafés and bars around the harbour: *Sidro*, *Atelier* and *Carpe Diem* are three of the best.

The **Jadrolinija ferry office** (☎021/741-132) is along the quay, opposite the ferry dock.

Vis

Compact, humpy, and at first glance a little forbidding, **Vis** is situated further offshore than any other of Croatia's inhabited Adriatic islands. Closed to foreigners for military reasons until 1989, the island has never been overrun by tourists, and even now depends much more heavily on independent travellers than its package-oriented neighbours Brač and Hvar. Croatia's bohemian youth seem to have fallen in love with the place over the last decade, drawn by its wild mountainous scenery, two good-looking towns, **Vis town** and **Komiža**, and a brace of fine wines, including the white Vugava and the red Viški plavac.

Ferries leave Split for the two-and-a-half-hour journey to Vis town once or twice daily all year, though in winter the trip can get mighty rough. From mid-May to mid-September there are daily **hydrofoils** from Split and Hvar Town. From Vis town, **buses** depart for Komiža on the western side of the island.

Vis Town
VIS TOWN is attractively sited, a sedate arc of grey-brown houses stretching around a deeply indented bay, above which looms a steep escarpment covered with the remains of abandoned agricultural terraces. The most attractive parts of town are east of the ferry landing in the suburb of **Kut**, a largely sixteenth-century tangle of narrow cobbled streets overlooked by the summer houses built by nobles from Hvar. There are no specific buildings to visit, although the stone balconies and staircases give the place an undeniably aristocratic air. Heading west around the bay soon brings you to a small peninsula, from which the campanile of the **Franciscan monastery of St Hieronymous** (Sveti Jere) rises gracefully alongside a huddle of cypresses. The town's small pebbly **beach** is just beyond.

Just to the right of the ferry dock are the **tourist office** (June–Sept Mon–Sat 8am–1pm & 4–8pm, Sun 8am–1pm; Oct–May Mon–Fri 9am–1pm; ☎021/717-017, *www.tz-vis.hr*) and the Darlić & Darlić agency (☎021/713-760), which has **rooms** (①–②). Best of the **hotels** are the stately turn-of-the-century *Tamaris*, on the waterfront at Šetalište Apolonija Zanelle 5 (☎021/711-350; ④), and the smaller, pension-like *Paula*, Petra Hektorovića 2 (☎021/711-362, *paula-hotel@st.tel.hr*; ③) in Kut. Also in Kut, the **restaurants** *Paula*, *Val* and *Vatrica* are worth trying.

Komiža

Three times a day the bus leaves Vis harbour for the 25-minute drive to **KOMIŽA**, the island's main fishing port – a compact and intimate town with a palm-fringed seafront on one side and a ring of mountains on the other. Dominating the southern end of the harbour is the **Kaštel**, a stubby sixteenth-century fortress which now holds a **Fishing Museum** (Ribarski muzej; daily: July & Aug 9am–noon & 6–10pm; June & Sept 9–10am & 7–10pm; 15kn), whose worthy display of nets and knots is enlivened by the presence of a reconstructed *falkuša*, one of the traditional, triangular-sailed fishing boats common to these waters until the early twentieth century. You can walk out to the seventeenth-century **Benedictine Monastery** (Mušter), about a kilometre behind the town on a vineyard-cloaked hillock. Most of the island's population congregate beneath the monastery every year on St Nicholas's Day (Sveti Nikola, December 6), when an old fishing boat is hauled here by hand and then set alight.

Rearing up above Komiža to the southeast is **Mount Hum**, at 587m Vis's highest point. To climb it you can either scramble up a series of tracks which ascend steeply from behind the Benedictine monastery, or follow the road as it works its way round the southern side of the island, and turn left to the hamlet of Žena Glava (about 10km in all). There's a wonderful view of the Adriatic from the top, with the pale grey stripe of the Italian coastline far away to the west, and the mountains of the Croatian mainland to the east.

Buses from Vis Town terminate about 100m behind the harbour, from where it's a short walk southwards to the **tourist office** (July & Aug daily 8am–10pm; rest of year Mon–Fri 8am–1pm; ☎021/713-455), on the Riva just beyond the Kaštel. There's a comfy modern **hotel**, the *Biševo* (☎021/713-095 or 713-279; ⑤), and plenty of **rooms** available from a number of agencies in the centre, such as Darlić & Darlić (☎021/713 760, *ines.darlic@st.tel.hr*) on the harbourfront, and Srebrnatours (☎021/713 668, *sandra.vitaljic@st.tel.hr*) on Ribarska just to the north. There are a couple of pizzerias on the harbour, and one good seafood **restaurant** just off Ribarska, *Bako*, which has a vine-shaded terrace right on the beach. For **drinking**, head for the tiny main square, which is ringed by lively café-bars.

Around Vis: Biševo and the Blue Cave

Each morning small boats leave Komiža harbour for the short crossing to **BIŠEVO**, a tiny islet just to the southwest of Vis. There's a seasonally inhabited hamlet just up from Biševo's small harbour, and a couple of attractive coves, but the main attraction here is the **Blue Cave** (Modra špilja; 25kn) on the island's east coast, a grotto which can only be reached by sea, so-named because water-filtered sunlight shines in through a submerged side entrance to bathe everything in the cavern in an eerie shimmering blueness. Due to the narrowness of the entrance, the cave can't be entered when the sea is choppy, so you should ask the tourist office in either Komiža or Vis Town about weather forecasts as soon as you arrive on the island. There are two ways to visit the cave: the easiest is to take one of the many advertised excursions from either Komiža or Vis Town (price of about 60–80kn per person includes the cave entrance fee); although it's also possible to take a taxi boat from Komiža harbour to the island itself (10kn), from where you can walk to a spot near the cave entrance. Whichever way you come, you'll be transferred to a small boat before being ferried inside. If you come clad in swimming costume you're allowed to take a dip in the water – although be warned that the volume of tourist traffic often means that you're hurried along by the boatman and never get to spend as much time in the cave as you would wish.

Korčula

Like so many islands along this coast, **KORČULA** was first settled by the Greeks, who gave it the name Korkyra Melaina or "Black Corfu" for its dark and densely wooded appearance. Even now, it's one of the greenest of the Adriatic islands, and one of the most popular. The island's main settlement is **Korčula town**, and the rest of the island, although beautifully wild and untouched, lacks any real centres. The main coastal **ferry** drops you right in the harbour of Korčula town. In addition, local ferries travel daily between Split and Vela Luka at the western end of Korčula island, from where there's a connecting bus service to Korčula town. There's also a **direct bus service** (1 daily) from Dubrovnik, which crosses the narrow stretch of water dividing the island from the mainland via car ferry from Orebić.

Korčula Town

KORČULA TOWN sits on a beetle-shaped hump of land, a medieval walled city ribbed with a series of narrow streets that branch off the spine of the main street like the veins of a leaf. The Venetians first arrived here in the eleventh century, and stayed, on and off, for nearly eight centuries. Their influence is particularly in evidence in Korčula's old town, which huddles around the **Cathedral of St Mark** (Katedrala svetog Marka), squeezed into a space between the buildings that roughly passes for a main square. The cathedral facade is decorated with a gorgeous fluted rose window and a bizarre cornice frilled with strange beasts. The interior, reached through a door framed by statues of Adam and Eve, is one of the loveliest in the region – a curious mixture of styles which range from the Gothic forms of the nave to the Renaissance northern aisle, tacked on some time in the sixteenth century, the whole appealingly squashed into a space quite obviously too small for it. The clutter of artefacts ranges from pikes used against sixteenth-century Algerian corsair Uliz Ali, to paintings that include an altarpiece by Leandro Bassano, in the south aisle, and an early Tintoretto, behind the high altar and difficult to make out. However, the best of the church's treasures have been removed to the **Bishop's Treasury** (summer only Mon–Sat 10am–noon & 5–9pm; 10kn), a couple of doors down. This is one of the best small collections of fine and sacral art in the country, with an exquisite set of paintings, including a striking *Portrait of a Man* by Carpaccio, a perceptive *Virgin and Child* by Bassano, some Tiepolo studies of hands and some Raphael drawings, and a tiny *Madonna* by a local Renaissance artist, Blaž Jurjev of Trogir. There is also a Leonardo da Vinci sketch of a soldier wearing a costume that bears a striking resemblance to that of the Moreška dancers (see opposite). Oddities include an ivory statuette of Mary Queen of Scots, whose skirts open to reveal kneeling figures in doublet and hose. How this got here, no one knows. Opposite the treasury, a former Venetian palace holds the **Town Museum** (Gradski muzej; summer Mon–Sat 9am–noon & 5–9pm; winter Mon–Fri 9am–1pm; 8kn), whose more modest display contains a plaster cast of a fourth-century BC Greek tablet from Lumbarda – the earliest evidence of civilization on Korčula.

Close by the main square, down a turning to the right, is another remnant from Venetian times, the so-called **House of Marco Polo** (daily: summer only 10am–1pm & 5–7pm; 5kn). Korčula claims to be the birthplace of Marco Polo – a claim not as extravagant as it might first appear. The Venetians recruited many of their sea captains from their colonies, and Polo was indeed captured by the Genoese off the island in 1298, after which he used his time in prison to write his *Travels*. Whatever the truth of the matter, it seems unlikely that he had any connection with this seventeenth-century house, which is these days little more than an empty shell with some terrible twentieth-century prints on the walls.

Back down the main street, follow the signs to the **Icon Gallery** (summer only Mon–Sat 10am–1pm & 5–7pm; 5kn), where there's a permanent display of icons in the rooms of the All Saints' Brotherhood. Most of the exhibits were looted from the Cretans in the seventeenth century, and the best is the fifteenth-century triptych of *The Passion*.

The nearest **beaches** to the old town are on the headland southeast of town around the *Hotel Marko Polo*, though they're crowded, rocky and uncomfortable. A better bet is to head off by **water taxi** from the old harbour to one of the **Skoji** islands just offshore. The largest and nearest of these is **Badija**, where there are some secluded rocky beaches, a couple of snack bars and a naturist section. There's also a sandy beach just beyond the village of **Lumbarda**, 8km south of Korčula (reached by hourly bus in the summer).

Practicalities

Korčula's **bus station** is 400m southeast of the old town. Work your way round to the north-western side of the peninsula to find the **tourist office** (June–Sept Mon–Sat 8am–9pm, Sun 8am–3pm; Oct–May Mon–Sat 8am–3pm; ☎021/715-701), although **rooms** are handled by Marko Polo (☎020/715-400, *marko-polo-tours@du.tel.hr*) between the bus station and the entrance to the old town. Cheapest of the **hotels** is the *Badija*, accessible by taxi boat from the harbour (☎020/711-115; ③); a spartan but idyllically situated place in a former Franciscan monastery on the island of Badija. The *Park* is a package-tour-orientated place in a bay south-east of the centre (☎020/726-004; ⑤); while the stately *Korčula* (☎050/711-078; ⑥) is a grander affair on the western side of the old town. The nearest **campsite** is *Autocamp Kalac* (☎020/711-182), about 3km southeast of town and reached by hourly buses for Lumbarda. The **Jadrolinija ferry office** (☎020/715-410) is 100m west of Marko Polo Tours at Plokata 19 Travnja.

Not surprisingly, most **restaurants** in the old town tend to be expensive. One exception is the excellent *Adio Mare*, near Marco Polo's House, one of the best restaurants on the coast and justifiably popular; arrive early to make sure of a table. Another worthy choice is *Gradski Podrum*, just inside the main gate of the old town. A cheaper and more functional alternative is *Planjak*, next to the ferry office at Plokata 21. Wherever you eat, do try some of the **local wines**, some of which are excellent: look out for the delicious dry white Grk from Lumbarda, Posip from Smokvica, or the headache-inducing red Dingač from Postup on Peljesac.

Performances of Korčula's famous **folk dance**, the **Moreška**, take place outside the main gate to the old town every Thursday evening (tickets from Marko Polo tours; 50kn) during the summer. The dance is the story of a conflict between the Christians (in red) and the Moors (in black): the heroine, Bula (literally "veiled woman"), is kidnapped by the evil foreign king and his army, and her betrothed tries to win her back in a ritualized sword fight which takes place within a shifting circle of dancers. The dance gets gradually more and more frantic, the swords clashing furiously, rising to a climax in which the evil king is forced to surrender while his adversary unchains Bula and carries her off, triumphant.

Dubrovnik

DUBROVNIK is a beautifully preserved fortified town pressed against the sea within magnificent medieval walls. Considered the jewel in the crown of Croatian tourism, Dubrovnik was the subject of a largely spiteful attack by Yugoslav forces in autumn 1991. Bombarding the town from the rocky heights above, and aided by a blockade by the Yugoslav navy, they subjected Dubrovnik to an eight-month siege that was only broken by the UN-mediated ceasefire of May 1992. Now almost totally rebuilt and restored, the town is back on the tourist map with a vengeance.

Dubrovnik was first settled by Roman refugees in the early seventh century, when the nearby city of Epidaurus (now Cavtat) was sacked by the Slavs. They took up residence on the southern part of what is now the old town, then an island, and gave their settlement the name Ragusa. The Slavs, meanwhile, settled on the wooded mainland opposite, from which the name Dubrovnik (from *dubrava*, meaning a "glade") came. Before long the slim channel between the two was filled in and the two merged, producing a Latin-Slav culture unique to the region. Sandwiched between Muslim and Christian powers, Ragusa exploited its favourable position on the Adriatic with a maritime and commercial genius unmatched anywhere else in Europe at the time, and by the mid-fourteenth century, having shaken off the yoke of first the Byzantines and then the Venetians, had become a successful and self-contained city state, its merchants trading far and wide. Dubrovnik fended off the attentions of the Ottoman Empire with cunning and pragmatic obsequiousness – and regular payment of enormous tributes. It continued to prosper until 1667, when an earthquake killed around 5000 people and destroyed many of the city's buildings. Though the city-state survived, it fell into decline and, in 1808, it was formally dissolved by Napoleon.

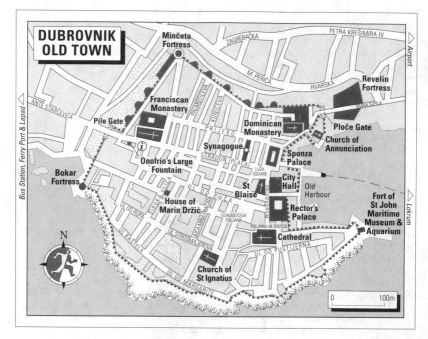

Arrival, information and accommodation

Both **ferry and bus terminals** are located in the port suburb of Gruž, 3km west of the old town. The main western entrance to the old town, the Pile Gate, is a thirty-minute slog along ul Ante Starčevića and you'd be better off catching a bus – #1a and #3 from the ferry terminal, #1a, #3 or #6 from behind the bus station. Flat-fare tickets for local buses are bought from the driver (exact change only; 10kn) or from newspaper kiosks (7kn). Dubrovnik's **airport** is situated some 20km south of the city, close to the resort town of Cavtat; Croatia Airways buses meet all arrivals and run to the town bus station, returning from there ninety minutes before each departure.

Plans are afoot for a couple of official **tourist offices** in the old town. In the meantime you'll have to make do with the unimpressive, privately-run information office just inside the Pile Gate (summer daily 9am–10pm; winter Mon–Sat 8am–7.30pm; ☎020/426-354); as well as selling city maps they can book **private rooms**. There are numerous other accommodation agencies, too: Gulliver, Obala Stjepana Radića 32 (☎020/419-109, *www.gulliver.hr*) is conveniently located opposite the ferry terminal; and Atlas has an office downhill from the Pile Gate at Svetog Djurdja 1 (☎020/442-585, *atlas-pile@atlas.tel.hr*), and another just off Luža square in the old town at Lučarica 1 (☎020/442-591). You'll probably be approached by a scrum of landladies offering rooms at both the bus station and the ferry terminal – they're worth considering if you arrive late at night, and will probably work out cheaper than those obtained through agencies. There's a basic, well-run **HI hostel** at bana Jelačića 15/17 (☎020/423-241; ②) – head up Ante Starčevića from the bus station and turn uphill to the right after five minutes. There's a dearth of affordable **hotels** near the old town, and you're restricted to staying a walk or bus ride away. *Lero*, 1.5km west of Pile Gate at Iva Vojnovića 14 (☎020/332-122, *hotel-lero@du.tel.hr*, ⑤), has modern en suites with TV; while *Petka*, Obala Stjepan Radića 38 (020/418-008; ④), has smaller rooms but the advantage of being opposite the ferry terminal. Most of the big package hotels are on the Lapad peninsula 5km west of the Pile Gate (bus #6). *Zagreb*, Šetalište Kralja Zvonimira 27 (☎020/436-146; ④), is a pleasant, turn-of-the-century building near Lapad beach; the nearby *Vis*, Masarykov Put 4 (April–Nov ☎020/437-303; ⑤), is a modern place with simple en suites and a generous stretch of private beach. The free, monthly *Dubrovnik Riviera*, available from hotels and the tourist office, is a tremendous little **pocket guide** incorporating bus and ferry timetables and comprehensive listings of events for that month.

The City

The main entrance to Dubrovnik's old town (*stari grad*) is the **Pile Gate**, a fifteenth-century construction decorated with a statue of St Blaise (Sv Vlaho), the city's protector, set in a niche above the arch. Inside, and accessible from the Pile Gate, the best way to get your bearings is by making a tour of the **city walls** (*gradske zidine*; daily: summer 9am–9pm; winter 9am–4pm; 15kn), 25m high and with all its towers intact. Some parts date back to the tenth century, but most of the original construction was undertaken in the twelfth and thirteenth centuries, with subsequent rebuildings (and reinforcements) being carried out over the years. Of the various towers and bastions that punctuate the walls, the **Minčeta fortress**, which marks the northeastern side, is perhaps the most impressive, built in 1455 to plans drawn up by Dalmatian architect Juraj Dalmatinac and the Italian Michelozzi.

Within the walls, Dubrovnik is a sea of roofs faded into a pastel patchwork, punctured now and then by a sculpted dome or tower. At ground level, just inside the Pile Gate, **Onofrio's Large Fountain**, built in 1444, is a bulbous-domed affair at which visitors to this hygiene-conscious city had to wash themselves before they were admitted any further. Across the street is the fourteenth-century **Franciscan Monastery** complex (Franjevački samostan; free access); its treasury (daily 9am–4/5pm; 5kn) holds some fine Gothic reliquaries and manuscripts tracing the development of musical scoring, together with relics from the apothecary's shop, dating from 1317, which claims to be the oldest in Europe.

From outside the monastery church, **Stradun** (also known as Placa), the city's main street, runs dead straight across the old town, its limestone surface polished to a slippery shine by the tramping of thousands of feet. Its far end broadens into the pigeon-choked **Luža Square**, the centre of the medieval town and even today hub of much of its activity. On the left, the **Sponza Palace** was once the customs house and mint, a building which grew in storeys as Dubrovnik grew in wealth, with a facade that's an elegant weld of florid Venetian Gothic and quieter Renaissance forms; dating from 1522, its majestic courtyard is given over to contemporary art exhibitions (opening times and prices variable). Across the square, the Baroque-style **Church of St Blaise** (Crkva svetog Vlaha), built in 1714 to replace an earlier church, serves as a graceful counterpoint to the palace. Outside the church stands the carved figure of an armoured knight, usually referred to as **Orlando's Column**. Surprisingly for such an insignificant-looking object, this was the focal point of the city-state: erected in 1428 as a morale-boosting monument to freedom, it was here that government ordinances were promulgated and punishments executed. Orlando's right arm was also the standard measurement of length (the Ragusan cubit); at the base of the column you can still see a line of the same length cut in the stone. On the eastern side of the square a Gothic arch leads through to an alley which winds past the **Dominican monastery** (Dominikanski samostan). Here, an arcaded courtyard filled with palms and orange trees leads to a small **museum** (daily 9am–5/6pm; 10kn), displaying outstanding examples of local sixteenth-century religious art.

Back on Luža, a street leads round the back of Sv Vlaho towards the fifteenth-century **Rector's Palace** (Knežev dvor), the seat of the Ragusan government, in which the incumbent Rector sat out his month's term of office. The building was, effectively, a prison: the Rector had no real power and could only leave with the say-so of the nobles who elected him.

From the palace atrium an imposing staircase leads up to the balcony; the former state rooms lead off here, including the rooms of the city council, the Rector's study and the quarters of the palace guard. Today these are given over to the **City Museum** (Gradski muzej; summer daily 9am–6pm; winter Mon–Sat 9am–2pm; 10kn), though for the most part it's a rather paltry collection, with mediocre sixteenth-century paintings and dull furniture. The highlight is the work of the fifteenth-century Dalmatian artist, Blaž Jurjev, notably a polyptych of *Our Lady*.

Immediately south of the palace, Dubrovnik's seventeenth-century **Cathedral** is a rather plain building, although there's an impressive Titian polyptych of *The Assumption* inside. The **Treasury** (Riznica; daily: summer 9am–8pm; winter 9am–noon & 3–6pm; 5kn) boasts a twelfth-century skull reliquary of St Blaise, an exquisite piece in the shape of a Byzantine crown, stuck with portraits of saints and frosted with delicate gold and enamel filigree work. Even more eye-catching is a bizarre fifteenth-century *Allegory of the Flora and Fauna of Dubrovnik* in the form of a jug and basin festooned with snakes, fish and lizards clambering over thick clumps of seaweed.

From the cathedral, it's a short walk through to the small town harbour, dominated by the monolithic hulk of the **Fort of St John** (Tvrdjava svetog Ivana). The fort has been refurbished to house a downstairs **aquarium** (Akvarium; summer daily 9am–9pm; winter Mon–Sat 9am–1pm; 15kn), full of local marine life; upstairs is the **maritime museum** (Pomorski muzej; summer daily 9am–6pm; winter Tues–Sun 9am–1pm; 10kn), which traces the history of Ragusan sea power through a display of naval artefacts and model boats.

Walking back east from here, you skirt one of the city's oldest quarters, **Pustijerna**, much of which predates the seventeenth-century earthquake. On the far side, the **church of St Ignatius**, Dubrovnik's largest, is a Jesuit confection, modelled, like most Jesuit places of worship, on the enormous church of Gesù in Rome. The steps that lead down from here also had a Roman model – the Spanish Steps – and they sweep down to **Gunduliceva Poljana**, the square behind the cathedral which is the site of the city's morning fruit and vegetable market. The statue in the middle is of Ivan Gundulić, the early seventeenth-century poet and native of Dubrovnik who wrote a long poem, *Osman*, on the battles between the Turks and Christian Slavs, and after whom the square is named. From here, Od Puča leads west through the maze of streets that make up the city centre, stepped alleys branching right to meet the southern sea-walls. One of these, Široka Ulica, leads to the **house of Marin Držić** at no. 7 (Mon–Sat 9am–2pm; 10kn). Dubrovnik's greatest sixteenth-century playwright is remembered here in an imaginative display (featuring English headphone commentary and a short video), which manages to conjure up something of the city's Renaissance past.

The main city **beach** is a short walk east of the old town – noisy and crowded with radios and flirting adolescents. There's an equally crowded, but somewhat cleaner, beach on the Lapad peninsula 5km to the west. The best bet is to catch one of the **boats** from the old city jetty (April–Oct 9am–6pm, every 30min, journey time 10min; 25kn return) to the wooded island of **Lokrum**. Reputedly the island where Richard the Lionheart was shipwrecked, Lokrum is crisscrossed by shady paths overhung by pines. Extensive rocky beaches run along the eastern end of the island, and there's a nudist section (FKK) at the far eastern tip.

Eating and drinking

For self-catering, there are regular fruit and vegetable **markets** (Mon–Sat mornings) on Gundulićeva Poljana and on the waterfront at Gruž you can also buy fresh fish as soon as the boats come in. For **snacks**, try the sandwich bars lining the alleys running uphill from Stradun, notably *Kaktus* on Vetranovićeva. There's no shortage of **restaurants** in the old town. Prijeko, the street running parallel to Stradun to the north, is especially stacked with eateries, although beware of the hard sell – each waiter invariably has the biggest fish caught that day. *Rozarij*, tucked away on the corner of Prijeko and Zlatarska, is cosy, intimate and good for fresh fish; while *Kamenica*, Gundulićeva poljana 8, is an unpretentious place serving up cheap portions of *girice* (tiny deep-fried fish) and *kamenice* (oysters). Similarly informal is *Baracuda*, a tiny pizzeria on Božidarevičeva. *Konoba Posat*, uz Posat 1, is a large garden terrace just outside the Pile Gate which is good for grilled meats.

The pavement cafés at the eastern end of Stradun are the places for daytime and evening **drinking**, although none of them have much atmosphere if the weather's not suitable for sitting outside. On such occasions it's best to head for the smaller café/bars in the backstreets: *Mirage*, Bunićeva Poljana, is a popular meeting point for Dubrovnik youth; while *Hard Jazz Café Troubadur* on the same square has live jazz most nights. *Otok*, Pobijana 8, is an alternative cultural centre whose café-bar attracts bohemian types. For a more beery evening, head for *Pivnica Karaka*, Izme Đu Polaća 5. Outside the centre, ulica bana Jelačića, just above the bus station, is lined with bars buzzing until late on summer evenings – although none stand out individually. For clubbing, *Arsenal*, outside the Pile Gate, and *Esperanza*, near the bus station at Put Republike 30, are mainstream places. Gigs or themed disco nights take place at the Karantena, a cultural centre just beyond Pile Gate on Frana Supila.

The Dubrovnik Festival

Dubrovnik's **Summer Festival** (early July to late Aug) is a good, if crowded, time to be in town, with classical concerts and theatre performances in most of Dubrovnik's courtyards, squares and bastions – sometimes the only chance to see the inside of them. Seats can be pricey and are often booked well in advance. For further details contact *Dubrovački ljetni festival*, Od Sigurate 1 (☎020/412-288, *www.dubrovnik-festival.hr*).

Listings

Airlines Croatia Airlines, Brsalje 9 (☎020/413-777; Mon–Fri 8am–4pm, Sat 9am–noon).

Bus station Put Republike 19 (☎020/357-088).

Car rental Budget, Obala S. Radića 34 (☎020/418-998); Gulliver, Obala S. Radića 31 (☎020/313-061); Hertz, F. Supila 5 (☎020/425-000).

Exchange Dubrovačka Banka, Stradun (Mon–Fri 7.30am–1pm & 2–8pm, Sat 7.30am–1pm); Gospodarsko-Kreditna Banka, Pile Gate (daily 8am–8pm).

Ferries Tickets from Jadrolinija, Obala S. Radića 40 (☎020/418-000); and Globetour, Stradun (☎020/428-992).

Internet access Dubrovnik Internet Centar, Brsalje 1 (daily 8am–midnight; 20kn/hr); DuNet Club, Put Republike 7 (daily 9am–10pm; 20kn/hr).

Left luggage At the bus station (daily 4.50am–9.00pm).

Post office/telephone Put Republike 28 (Mon–Fri 8am–8pm, Sat 8am–7pm, Sun 8am–noon); A. Starčevića 2 (Mon–Fri 8am–3pm).

Taxis Ranks outside the bus station and the Pile Gate. To book, call ☎424-343 or 357-044.

Travel agents Atlas, Lučarica 1 (☎020/442-591); Generalturist, F. Supila 9 (☎020/432-974).

travel details

Trains

Zagreb to: Pula (2 daily; 6hr 40min); Rijeka (6 daily; 4hr); Split (2 daily; 8hr–9hr).

Pula to: Zagreb (2 daily; 6hr 40min).

Buses

Zagreb to: Dubrovnik (8 daily; 11hr); Poreč (7 daily; 5hr); Pula (11 daily; 6hr); Rijeka (hourly; 4hr); Rovinj (5 daily; 9hr); Split (hourly; 7-9hr).

Dubrovnik to: Korčula (1 daily; 3hr 30min); Rijeka (5 daily); Split (14 daily; 4hr 30min); Zagreb (7 daily; 11hr).

Hvar town to: Starigrad (7 daily; 35min).

Poreč to: Rijeka (7 daily; 2hr 30min); Pula (10 daily; 2hr); Zagreb (5 daily; 7hr).

Pula to: Dubrovnik (1 daily); Opatija (hourly; 2hr); Poreč (10 daily; 2hr); Rijeka (hourly; 2hr 30min); Rovinj (hourly; 1hr); Split (3 daily; 10hr); Zagreb (13 daily; 6hr).

Rijeka to: Dubrovnik (4 daily; 13hr); Pula (hourly; 2hr 30min); Split (4 daily; 8hr); Zagreb (hourly; 4hr).

Rovinj to: Poreč (8 daily; 45min); Pula (hourly; 1hr); Rijeka (8 daily; 5hr).

Split to: Dubrovnik (15 daily; 4hr 30min); Pula (3 daily; 10hr); Rijeka (3 daily; 8hr); Zagreb (hourly; 7-9hr).

Supetar to: Bol (5 daily; 1hr).

Ferries

Dubrovnik to: Stari Grad, Hvar (1 daily in summer; twice weekly in winter; 7hr); Korčula (1 daily in summer; twice weekly in winter; 4hr); Rijeka (1 daily in summer; twice weekly in winter; 21hr); Split (1 daily in summer; twice weekly in winter; 8hr).

Rijeka to: Dubrovnik (1 daily in summer; twice weekly in winter; 20hr); Korčula (1 daily in summer; twice weekly in winter; 18hr); Split (1 daily in summer; twice weekly in winter; 12hr); Hvar (1 daily in summer; twice weekly in winter; 14hr).

Split to: Dubrovnik (1 daily; 8hr); Hvar (1 daily; 2hr); Korčula (1–2 daily; 4hr); Rijeka (1 daily; 12hr); Stari Grad, Hvar (3–4 daily; 2hr); Supetar, Brač (7 daily; 1hr); Vis (1–2 daily; 2hr 30min).

CHAPTER 6

CZECH REPUBLIC

Introduction

Czechoslovakia's "Velvet Revolution" in November 1989 was probably the most unequivocably positive of eastern Europe's anti-Communist upheavals, as the Czechs and Slovaks shrugged off 41 years of Communist rule without a shot being fired. But the euphoria and unity of those first few months evaporated more quickly than anyone could have imagined. Just three years on, the country split into two separate states: the Czech Republic and Slovakia. The Czechs – always the most urbane, agnostic and liberal of the Slav nations – have fared well, although they are now having to contend with growing unemployment and an increasing cost of living.

Almost untouched by the wars of the twentieth century, the capital, **Prague**, is justifiably one of the most popular destinations in Europe. An incredibly beautiful city with a wealth of architecture, from Gothic cathedrals and Baroque palaces to Art Nouveau cafés and Cubist villas, it's also a lively meeting place for young people from all over Europe. The rolling countryside of **Bohemia** is swathed in forests and studded with well-preserved medieval towns and castles, especially in the south around **České Budějovice**. In the west, you'll find the old watering-holes of the European aristocracy, the spa towns of **Karlovy Vary** and **Mariánské Lázně**. The country's eastern province, **Moravia**, is every bit as beautiful, only less touristed. **Olomouc** is the most attractive town here, but **Brno**, the regional capital, has its own peculiar pleasures.

Information and maps

Prague has an excellent chain of **tourist offices** specifically set up to give information to foreign visitors (look for the "PIS" sign). Most other cities and towns have their own tourist offices (*informační centrum*). A comprehensive range of **maps** is available You can buy them, often very cheaply, from book-

shops, petrol stations and some hotels – ask for a *plán města* (town plan) or *mapa okolí* (regional map). For road maps, the 1:100,000 *Euroatlas* produced by Kartografie Praha is still the best, marking all camp-sites and petrol stations. For hiking, the 1:100,000 *turistická mapa* series details the country's complex network of marked footpaths. You can find great maps **online** at *www.mapy.cz* or *mapy.atlas.cz*, which, though in Czech, are pretty straightforward to use.

Money and banks

The **currency** in the Czech Republic is the Czech crown, or *koruna česká* (kč), which is divided into one hundred hellers or *haléř* (h). Coins come in 10h, 20h, 50h, 1kč, 2kč, 5kč, 10kč, 20kč and 50kč; notes as 20kč, 50kč, 100kč, 200kč, 500kč, 1000kč, 2000kč and 5000kč. The crown is now fully convertible, though you may find problems getting hold of any in foreign banks.

Banks are the best places to change money; they're open Mon–Fri 8am–6pm, although some close early on Fridays. Assistants are generally more helpful and likely to speak English at branches of foreign banks, although charges can be a bit higher. **Travellers' cheques** in US dollars, Sterling or Deutschmarks are undoubtedly the safest way of carrying money, though it's a good idea to keep some hard currency in cash for emergencies. **Credit cards** are accepted in most hotels, upmarket restaurants and some shops; you can also use them to get cash from the extensive network of ATMs.

Communications

Most **post offices** (*pošta*) are open Mon–Fri 7am–6pm (larger ones until 8pm), Sat 7am–noon. Look for the right sign to avoid queueing unnecessarily: *známky* (stamps), *dopisy* (letters) or *obalky* (parcels). You can also buy stamps from tobacconists

CZECH REPUBLIC ON THE NET

www.czech-tourism.com
eclectic site, from ecotourism to women's issues

www.gurman.cz
reviews of Prague's restaurants

www. pis.cz
superb background and cultural info, accommodation and ticket services

www.regioninfo.cz
regional information

travelguide.cpress.cz
Czech accommodation

www.radio.cz – the site of Radio Prague, with latest news and reviews

www.visitczech.cz
the official site of the Czech Tourist Board

and kiosks, though often only for domestic mail. **Poste restante** services are available in major towns, but remember to write *Pošta 1* (the main office), followed by the name of the town.

The majority of **public phones** only take phone cards (*telefonní karty*), costing 175kč and 320kč and available from post offices, tobacconists and some shops. You can make local calls (costing 4kč a minute) or international calls from all card phones, all of which have instructions in English. International calls are charged at a rate of about 10kč a minute to the UK, and 17kč a minute to the US, Canada and Australia. Off-peak calls are cheaper (between 7pm and 7am, dial 052 instead of 00 for significantly cheaper international calls).

Internet cafés are booming in Prague, where you'll pay 60–100kč/hr, but access gets harder outside the capital and major cities.

Getting around

The most pleasant way of travelling around the Czech Republic is by train – it's scenic, safe and inexpensive, although fares are gradually creeping up. If you're in a hurry, however, buses are nearly always quicker and more frequent. **Car-sharing** is also a good option; for more information try the Town-to-Town agency at Národní 9, Nové Město (☎ 02/22 07 54 07).

■ Trains

The Czech Republic has one of the most comprehensive rail networks in Europe. Czech Railways (České dráhy or ČD), run two main types of **trains**: *rychlík* trains are faster, stopping only at major towns, while *osobní* trains stop at just about every station and stagger along as slowly as 30kph. In addition, there are InterCity (IC), and EuroCity (EC) expresses, for which you must pay a supplement. **Tickets** (*jízdenky*) for domestic journeys can be bought at the station (*nádraží*) before or on the day of departure. Fares are still cheap – a second-class single from Prague to Brno costs around £9/$13 – but they're rising. ČD runs reasonably priced **sleepers** to and from a number of cities in neighbouring countries. You must, however, book as far in advance as possible and in any case no later than six hours before departure. InterRail passes are valid; Eurail passes are not.

■ Buses

Regional **buses** (*autobus*) – mostly run by the state bus company, Česká státní automobilová doprava

(ČSAD) – travel to most destinations, with private companies like ČEBUS providing an alternative on most inter-city routes. Bus stations are usually next to the train station, and if there's no separate terminal you'll have to buy your ticket from the driver. It's essential to book your ticket at least day in advance if you're travelling at the weekend, on a public holiday or early in the morning on one of the main routes. A useful Web site for times and information is *www.vlak-bus.cz*.

■ Driving and motorcycling

Travelling by **car** is not the most relaxing way to tour the country; increased vehicle ownership in the Republic has made major roads fast and busy, plus signposting is poor and potholes ubiquitous. **Speed limits** are 130kph on motorways, 90kph on other roads, and 50kph in all cities, towns and villages. Seat belts are compulsory at all times, and you are not allowed to drink any alcohol if you're driving. If you want to travel on any motorway within the Czech Republic, you'll need a **motorway tax sticker** (*dálniční známka*). This currently costs 800kč a year for a car (buses, caravans and lorries are much more expensive) and is available from all border crossings, post offices and petrol stations. **Fuel** is fairly cheap by European standards; *natural* is the word used for lead-free petrol. If you break down, dial ☎154. The major **car rental** firms currently charge around £250/$400 per week for a small car with unlimited mileage, though local firms offer much more reasonable rates.

Accommodation

Accommodation remains the most expensive aspect of travelling in the Czech Republic. There is no organized hostel system, as such, though some places are now affiliated with Hostelling International. Private rooms are available all over the country, and more often than not the local tourist office will help to book a room. To book accommodation online try *www.avetravel.cz* or *www.accomgroup.cz*

■ Hotels and private rooms

Hotels are still occasionally priced up for foreigners and are in any case fairly expensive, especially in Prague. Most old state hotels have been refurbished by their new owners, and many new hotels and pensions have opened, particularly in the more heavily touristed areas. In the newer places, continental or

---

ACCOMMODATION PRICE CODES

Throughout this guide, accommodation is coded on a scale of ① to ⑨, the code indicating the lowest price per person per night you could expect to pay in each establishment in high season. With hostels this is the nightly rate per person; with hotels, the price is arrived at by dividing the cost of the cheapest double room by two. The prices indicated by the codes are as follows:

① under £5/$8 (€9)	④ £15–20/$24–32 (€27–36)	⑦ £30–35/$48–56 (€54–63)
② £5–10/$8–16 (€9–18)	⑤ £20–25/$32–40 (€36–45)	⑧ £35–40/$56–64 (€63–72)
③ £10–15/$16–24 (€18–27)	⑥ £25–30/$40–48 (€45–54)	⑨ £40/$64 (€72) and over

---

buffet-style breakfast is normally included. Ignore the star system outside Prague – this only refers to room number, not quality, service or atmosphere. With ongoing privatisation, refurbishment and renovation work, make it a rule to check hotel prices before you book.

Private rooms are available in Prague, Brno and several other towns on the tourist trail, and are often the best bet. Elsewhere, just keep your eyes peeled for signs saying *Zimmer Frei*. Prices start at around 300kč per person per night, but expect to pay far more in Prague.

■ Hostels and campsites

Prague now has a number of **hostels**, which offer varying degrees of discomfort; some, known as *turistická ubytovna*, are mostly occupied by migrant workers or sports groups. The student travel organization CKM can arrange cheap **student accommodation** in the big university towns during July and August and usually charge 200kč per person for dorm beds. The KMC (Club of Young Travellers), at Karolíny Světlé 30, Prague - Staré Město (☎02/22 22 03 47) is an umbrella organization for youth hostels throughout the republic who can help organise accommodation for you.

Campsites, known as *autokemp*, are plentiful all over the Republic; the facilities are often basic and the ones known as *tábořiště* are even more rudimentary. Most have simple **chalets** (*chata*) for anything upwards of 500kč for two people. Very few sites remain open all year, and most don't open until May, closing mid- to late September. Even though prices are sometimes inflated for foreigners, camping charges remain minimal.

Food and drink

Forty years of culinary isolation under the Communists introduced few innovations to the Germanic-influenced **Czech cuisine**, with its predilection for slabs of meat served with lashings of gravy, dumplings and sauerkraut, although pizza is swiftly turning into a national dish.

■ Food

For Czechs, the days of starting at 5am with a cup of Turkish coffee are disappearing – these days they're as likely to breakfast on cereal as salami and rolls. Popular **snacks** include *bramburák*, a potato pancake with flecks of bacon, *párek*, a frankfurter dipped in mustard or ketchup and shoved in a white roll, and *smažený sýr* – a slab of melted Edam fried in breadcrumbs and served in a roll (*v housce*) with tartar sauce.

Coffee (*káva*) is drunk thick and black and described rather hopefully as "Turkish" or *turecká*. However nowadays filter coffee, latte and espresso are common on the tourist track. The **cake shop** (*cukrárna*) is an important part of the country's social life, particularly on Sundays when it's often the only place that's open, although the cakes aren't up to Austrian standards.

In and outside of Prague, eating out is inexpensive; **restaurants** (*restaurace*) always display their menus and prices outside. They serve hot meals nonstop from about 11am until 11pm (10pm outside Prague). Most **pubs** (*pivnice*) also serve basic hot dishes, as do **wine cellars** (*vinárna*) – often the most stylish places around.

Most lunchtime menus start with **soup** (*polévka*), one of the country's culinary strong points. **Main courses** are overwhelmingly based on pork or beef, but one treat is carp (*kapr*), traditional at Christmas and cheaply and widely offered just about everywhere, along with trout (*pstruh*). Goose (*husa*), duck (*kachna*) and wild boar (*kanci maso*) dishes are also generally delicious. Main courses are served with different varieties of **dumpling** (*knedlíky*) or **vegetables**, most commonly potatoes and sauerkraut. With the exception of *palačinky* (pancakes) filled with chocolate or fruit, cream, delicious fruit dumplings (*ovocné knedlíky*) and ice cream, **desserts**, where they exist at all, can be pretty uninspiring.

■ Drink

Even the most simple *bufet* in the Czech Lands almost invariably has draught beer (*pivo*). The *pivnice* (which close around 10 or 11pm) is still a predominantly male affair, with heavy drinking; **wine bars** and restaurants (*vinárna*) are generally far more upmarket and **cocktail bars** have now opened up in most main towns.

The Czech Republic tops the world league table of **beer** consumption, even beating the Germans – hardly surprising since its beer ranks among the best in the world. The most natural starting point for any beer tour is the Bohemian city of **Plzeň** (Pilsen), whose local lager is the original Pils. The other big brewing town is **České Budějovice** (Budweis), home to Budvar, a mild beer by Bohemian standards but still leagues ahead of the American Budweiser. The burgeoning in-house breweries offer some great brews, as do the hundreds of small breweries dotted around the country.

The republic also produces a modest selection of medium-quality **wines**; the largest wine-producing region is southern Moravia. The home-production of firewater is a national pastime, resulting in some almost terminally strong concoctions, most famously a plum brandy called Slivovice. The most well-known Czech **spirit** is Becherovka, a medicinal herbal tipple from Karlovy Vary, known as a *beton* when ordered with ice and tonic.

Opening hours and holidays

Shops in the Czech Republic are open Mon–Fri 9am–5pm, with some shops and most supermarkets staying open till 6pm or later. Smaller shops close for lunch for an hour or so sometime between noon and 2pm, while others stay open late on Thursdays. In larger towns, shops stay open all day Saturday and Sunday, and the **midnight shop** (*večerka*) stays open daily until 11pm.

The basic opening hours for **castles** and **monasteries** are Tues–Sun 9am–noon, & 2–5pm; opening is often restricted to weekends and holidays in April and October; and most close for the rest of the year. In Prague the main museums open Tues–Sun 10am–6pm, though there are exceptions. Whatever the time of year, if you want to see the interior of a building, nine times out of ten you'll be forced to go on a **guided tour** that will last at least 45 minutes. Ask for an *anglický* text, an often unintentionally hilarious English resumé. **Entrance tickets** rarely cost more than 50–250kč, so prices are not quoted in the text except where the entrance fee is prohibitive; the last tour usually leaves an hour before the advertised closing time.

Public holidays include Jan 1; Easter Monday; May 1; May 8 (Liberation day in 1945); July 5 (the day saints Cyril and Methodius introduced Christianity into the Czech Lands); July 6 (the anniversary of the martyrdom of Jan Hus); Sept 28 (Czech State day); Oct 28 (the anniversary of the Foundation of the Republic); Nov 17 (The Battle for Freedom and Democracy Day); Dec 24, 25 and 26.

Emergencies

In the last decade, public confidence in the **police** (*policie*) has declined as the crime level has risen. For tourists, theft from cars is the biggest worry, although pickpockets are as rife as in any European capital in the centre of Prague, particularly in the Old Town Square, on the No. 22 tram, in the metro and in the main railway stations. Make sure you keep your cash and ID stowed away in a money belt. Report any thefts to the nearest police station immediately in order to get a statement detailing what you've lost for your insurance claim – although this will entail hours of mind-bending form filling. Likewise, although everyone is obliged to carry some form of ID and you should theoretically carry your **passport** with you at all times, you're highly unlikely to get stopped unless you're driving a car bearing foreign plates or if you are non-White, so you may choose to leave your ID in the hotel safe.

Minor ailments can be easily dealt with by the **chemist** (*lékárna*), but language is likely to be a problem outside the capital. If it's a repeat prescription you want, take any empty bottles or remaining pills along with you. If the chemist can't help, they'll be able to direct you to a **hospital** (*nemocnice*). If you do have to pay for any medication, keep the receipts for claiming on your insurance once you're home.

Emergency Numbers

Police ☎150; Ambulance ☎155; Fire ☎158.

PRAGUE

Prague (Praha) is one of the least "eastern" European cities you could imagine. Architecturally it is a revelation: few other cities anywhere in Europe look so good – and no other European capital can present six hundred years of architecture so completely untouched by natural disaster or war. Hardly surprising, then, that ninety percent of Western visitors spend all their time in and around the capital and that Praguers exude an air of confidence about their city.

Prague rose to prominence in the ninth century under Prince Bořivoj, its first Christian ruler and founder of the Přemyslid dynasty. His grandson, Prince Václav, became the Good "King" Wenceslas of the Christmas carol and the country's patron saint. The city prospered from its position on the central European trade routes, but it was after the dynasty died out in 1306 that Prague enjoyed its **golden age**. In just thirty years Charles IV of Luxembourg transformed it into one of the most important cities in fourteenth-century Europe, founding an entire new town, Nové Město, to accommodate the influx of students. Following the execution of the reformist preacher Jan Hus in 1415, the country became engulfed in **religious wars**, and trouble broke out again between the Protestant nobles and the Catholic Habsburgs in 1618. The full force of the Counter-Reformation was brought to bear on the city's people, though the spurt of Baroque rebuilding that went with it gave Prague its most striking architectural aspect.

After two centuries as little more than a provincial town in the Habsburg Empire, Prague was dragged out of the doldrums by the **Industrial Revolution** and the **národní obrození**, the Czech national revival that led to the foundation of the **First Republic** in 1918. After World War II, which it survived substantially unscathed, Prague disappeared completely behind the Iron Curtain. The city briefly re-emerged onto the world stage during the cultural blossoming of the **Prague Spring** in 1968, but the decisive break came in November 1989, when a peaceful student demonstration, brutally broken up by the police, triggered off the **Velvet Revolution** which eventually toppled the Communist government. The popular unity of that period is now history, but there is still a great sense of new-found potential in the capital, which has been transformed by restorations over the last decade.

Arrival and information

Prague's **airport**, Ruzyně, is 10km northwest of the city. The cheapest way of getting into town is by bus #119 (every 10–15min), a 30 min ride to the Dejvická metro station at the end of metro line A. Alternatively, there's the **express minibus** (every 30min), which stops first at Dejvická metro station, and ends up at náměstí Republiky (90kč) or 100 metres down the road at V Celnici (in front of the Hotel Marriot). The express minibuses will also take you straight to your hotel if you wish for around 350kč per drop-off – a bargain if there's a few of you. Avoid so-called "fixed price" taxis. Arriving by **train** from the west, you're most likely to end up at **Praha hlavní nádraží**, on the edge of Nové Město and Vinohrady. It's only a short walk to Wenceslas Square from here (though inadvisable at night), and there's also a metro station inside the station. International expresses, passing through Prague, often stop only at **Praha-Holešovice**, north of the city centre at the end of metro line C. Some trains from Moravia and Slovakia wind up at the central **Masarykovo nádraží**, on Hýbernská street near náměstí Republiky; and provincial trains from the south usually get no further than **Praha-Smíchov**, connected to the centre by metro line B. There are lockers and **left-luggage** offices (open 24hr) at all these stations. The main **bus station** is Praha-Florenc, on the eastern edge of Nové Město, on metro line B.

The best place to go for information is the **Prague Information Service**, or PIS (Pražská informačni služba), whose main branch is at Na příkopě 20 (Mon–Fri 8.30am–7pm, Sat & Sun 9am–5pm; ☎02/24 48 22 02, *www.pis.cz*). The staff speak English and will be able to answer

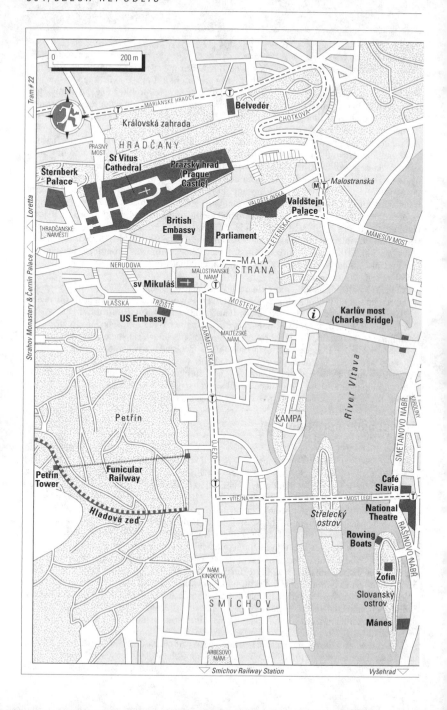

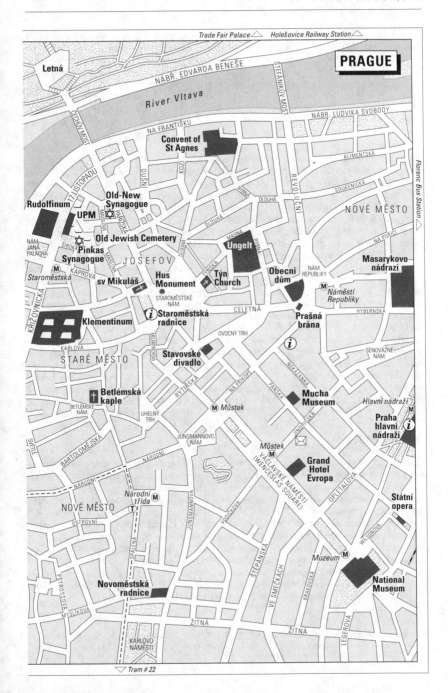

most inquiries, arrange private accommodation, sell maps and guides and act as a ticket agency. As for listings, it's worth getting hold of the free English-language monthly *Culture in Prague*, the fortnightly *Do města/ Downtown* (*www.downtown.cz*) or the monthly freebie *Think* magazine for trendy clubs and hang-outs. The English-language newspaper *Prague Post* (*www.praguepost.cz*), which comes out every Wednesday, also has a good selective listings section. There are additional PIS offices in the main train station, underneath the astronomical clock at Staroměstské náměsti 1 and in the tower (Mostecká věz) at the west end of the Charles Bridge (the latter is only open April to October).

City transport

Prague is reasonably small, but to cross the city quickly, or reach some of the more widely dispersed attractions, you'll need to use the public transport system. There are two main types of **ticket**: the 12kč *přestupní jízdenka*, which is valid for an hour (ninety minutes off-peak), during which time you may change metro lines, trams and buses as often as you like, and the 8kč *nepřestupní jízdenka*, which allows you to travel for up to fifteen minutes on a single tram or bus, or up to four stops on the metro (not including the one you start at). Tickets must be bought in advance from a tobacconist, kiosk or from one of the extraordinarily complicated ticket machines inside all metro stations and at some tram stops; basically, you want to hit the "8" or "12" button, followed by the *výdej/enter* button. You must validate your ticket on board or at the metro entrance. Alternatively, if you're going to be using the public transport system a lot, it's worth getting hold of a **travel pass** (*denní jízdenka*), available for 24 hours (70kč), three days (200kč), seven days (250kč) or fifteen days (280kč); write your name and date of birth on the reverse of the ticket, and validate it when you first use it. Plain-clothes inspectors, who will show you a red and yellow star-shaped badge plus ID, check tickets – it's a fine of 400kč on the spot if it's not valid. The fast Soviet-built **metro** (daily 5am–midnight) is the most useful form of city transport. The **trams** navigate Prague's hills and cobbles with remarkable dexterity, and run every ten or twenty minutes throughout the day. Tram #22, which runs from Vinohrady to Hradčany, is a good way to sightsee. Night trams #51–58 run every forty minutes between midnight and 4.30 am, and all pass by Lazarská in Nové Město. The horror stories about Prague **taxi** drivers ripping off tourists are too numerous to mention, so your best bet is to flag a taxi down or call the English-speaking AAA (☎02/14014), rather than go to the mafia-controlled ranks on Václavské náměstí, Národní and outside Obecní dům.

Accommodation

Prague's **hotels** are exorbitant for what you get and booking ahead is absolutely essential. As a result, most tourists on a budget now stay in private accommodation or hostels, both of which are easy to organize on arrival. At both the main international train stations and at the airport, there are numerous accommodation agencies dealing with **private rooms** (② and upwards): the largest and best is AVE (☎02/51 55 10 11/21 29, *www.avetravel.cz*), which also has 350 hotels on its books, where prices start at 600kč per person. Prague's university, the Karolinum, rents out over a thousand **student rooms** from June to mid-September, starting at 220kč for a bed – contact the booking office at Terronská 28 (☎02/24 31 12 58; metro Dejvická). Another organization specializing in summer-only dorms is Traveller's Hostels, a chain of centrally located hostels which are very popular with US students, from 350kč to 550kč per person; their main booking office is also the site of one of the hostels at Dlouhá 33 (☎02/24 82 66 64, *hostel@travellers.cz*; metro Náměstí Republiky) and features a bar and Internet access.

Hostels

Clown and Bard, Bořivojova 102, Žižkov (☎02/22 71 64 53). Clean hostel with laid-back atmosphere and loads of staged events. Laundry facilities, open 24 hours and rents out doubles as well as dorm beds. Tram #5 or #9, Lipanská stop, from metro Hlavní nádraží. ②.

Club Habitat, Na Zderace 10, Nové Město (☎02/24 91 82 52). Friendly hostel in a good location south of Národní. Metro Karlovo náměstí. ②.

Domov Mládeže, Haštalská 20, Staré Město (☎02/24 82 67 51, *jana.drysmidova@telecom.cz*). Clean, dormitory-style accommodation in the centre of town. ①–②.

Imperial Kavarna A-B, Na Poříčí 15/1072, Nové Město (☎02/231 6012). Friendly, atmospheric and spotless hostel in a former Art Nouveau hotel on the edge of the old town, with its own jazz café. ②.

Sokol, Újezd 40, Malá Strana (☎02/57 00 73 97). Shambolic student hostel in Sokol sports centre right in the heart of Malá Strana. ①.

Traveller's Hostel, Dlouhá 33, Staré Město (☎02/24 82 66 62-3, *www.travellers.cz*). Three minutes from Old Town Square; facilities include laundry, kitchen, Internet access, even its own night club. ①–②.

Hotels and pensions

Betlem Club, Betlemské náměstí 9, Staré Město (☎02/22 22 15 75). Cheerful pension just west of Národní. Metro Národní třída. ③–④.

City, Belgická 28, Vinohrady (☎02/22 52 16 06, *hotel.city@telecom.cz*). Pretty basic but clean and close to the city centre in leafy Vinohrady. Metro Naměstí Míru. ③–④.

Cloister Inn/Pension Unitas, Bartolomějská 9, Staré Město (☎02/24 21 10 20). Hotel and hostel in a very centrally located former nunnery, with rooms ranging from the clean and bright to claustrophobic converted secret-police prison cells (where Havel was once detained). Metro Národní třída. ④–⑨.

Dum U velké boty, Vlašská 30, Malá Strana (☎02/57 53 32 34). The most delightful, tastefully decorated pension, run by a very welcoming couple. Metro Malostranská. ⑤.

Expres, Skořepka 5, Staré Město (☎02/24 21 18 01). Simple, central hotel with friendly staff, breakfast included. Metro Staroměstká. ④.

Hotel a hostel Junior, Senovažné náměstí 21, Staré Město (☎02/22 10 51 18). Plain, clean, and friendly, 3 minutes walk from Wenceslas Square. Metro: Můstek. ①.

U krále Jiřího, Liliová 10, Staré Město (☎02/22 22 09 25). Eight slightly kitsch rooms above an "Irish" pub, deep in the heart of the old town. Metro Staroměstská. ⑥–⑧.

U medvídků, Na Perstýně 7, Staré Město (☎02/24 21 19 16). Eight simple rooms over a pub in the centre of the old town; booking ahead essential. Metro Národní třída. ⑧.

Campsites

Autocamp Žižkov, Koněvová 141, Žižkov. Reasonably central space for tents and caravans. Trams #1, 19, 16. Open all year.

Intercamp Kotva, U ledáren 55, Braník (☎02/44 46 17 12). The oldest, and nicest, site, with a riverside location 6km south of the city. Tram #3 or #17 from metro Karlovo náměstí. Open April–Oct.

Trojská, Trojská 375, Troja (☎02/83 85 04 87). One of a whole host of back garden sites, 3km north of the centre, on the road to the Troja château. Bus #112 or tram #14 from metro Nádraží Holešovice. Open all year.

The City

The **River Vltava** (Moldau in German) divides the capital into two unequal halves: the steeply inclined left bank, which accommodates the quarters of Hradčany and Malá Strana, and the more gentle, sprawling right bank, which includes Staré Město, Josefov and Nové Město. **Hradčany**, on the hill, contains the most obvious sights – the castle itself, the cathedral and the former palaces of the aristocracy. Below Hradčany, **Malá Strana** (Little Quarter), with its narrow eighteenth-century streets, is the city's ministerial and diplomatic quarter, though its Baroque gardens are there for all to enjoy. Over the river, on the right bank, **Staré Město** (Old Town) is a web of alleys and passageways centred on the city's most beautiful square, Staroměstské náměsti. Enclosed within the boundaries of Staré Město is **Josefov**, the old Jewish quarter, now down to a handful of synagogues and a cemetery. **Nové Město** (New Town), the focus of the modern city, covers the largest area, laid out in long wide boulevards – most famously Wenceslas Square – stretching south and east of the old town.

Hradčany

Hradčany's raison d'être is its **Castle**, or *Hrad*, built on the site of one of the original hill settlements of the Slav tribes who migrated here in the seventh or eighth century. Viewed from the Charles Bridge (Karlův most), Prague Castle stands aloof from the rest of the city, protected by a sheer wall that's breached only by the great mass of **St Vitus Cathedral** (daily 9am–4/5pm). Building started under Charles IV, who summoned the precocious 23-year-old German mason **Peter Parler** to work on the church. But only the choir and the south transept were finished when Charles died in 1399, and the whole structure wasn't completed until 1929. The eastern section recalls the building's authentic Gothic roots and the south door, or **Golden Gate** (Zlatá brána), is also pure Parler in style.

The Cathedral is the country's largest church, and, once inside, it's difficult not to be impressed by its sheer height. The grand chapel of **sv Václav**, by the south door, is easily the main attraction. Built by Parler, its rich decoration resembles the inside of a jewel casket: the gilded walls are inlaid with over 1300 semiprecious stones, set around ethereal fourteenth-century Biblical frescoes, while above, the tragedy of Wenceslas unfolds in later paintings. A door in the south wall leads to the coronation chamber which houses the Bohemian crown jewels, including the gold crown of St Wenceslas. At the centre of the choir, within a fine Renaissance grill, cherubs lark about on the sixteenth-century marble **Imperial Mausoleum**, commissioned by Rudolf II for his grandfather, Ferdinand I, and father, Maximilian II.

If you want to see the choir or the ambulatory, you'll need to buy a ticket (250kč), valid for three days, which also gives you entry into a handful of other sights in the castle, including the **Old Royal Palace** (Starý královský palác), just across the courtyard from the south door of the cathedral, and home to the princes and kings of Bohemia from the eleventh to the seventeenth centuries. It's a sandwich of royal apartments built by successive generations – these days you enter at the third and top floor, built at the end of the fifteenth century. The massive Vladislav Hall (Vladislavský sál) is where the early Bohemian kings were elected, and where every president since Masaryk has been sworn into office – including Havel on December 29, 1989.

Don't be fooled by the uninspiring red facade of the **Basilica of sv Jiří** (Basilica of St George) – this is Prague's most beautiful Romanesque monument (and a popular venue for events), its inside meticulously restored to re-create the crumble-coloured basilica which replaced the original tenth-century church in 1173. Next door, the **Convent of sv Jiří** (Jiřské Klášter), founded in 973, now houses the National Gallery's **Old Bohemian art collection** (Tues–Sun 10am–6pm), incorporating a remarkable collection of Gothic art – including the original of the bronze equestrian figure of St George that stands in the central courtyard. Round the corner from the convent is the **Golden Lane** (Zlatá ulička), a blind and crowded alley of miniature sixteenth-century cottages in dolly-mixture colours. A plaque at no. 22 commemorates Franz Kafka's brief sojourn here during World War I.

North of the castle walls, across the Powder Bridge (Prasný most), is the entrance to the **Královská zahrada** (May–Oct Tues–Sun 10am–5.45pm), founded by Ferdinand I and still the best-kept gardens in the country, with functioning fountains and immaculately cropped lawns. At the end of the gardens is Prague's most celebrated Renaissance legacy, the **Belvedér** (Tues–Sun 10am–6pm), a delicately arcaded summer house, now an art gallery.

TO THE STRAHOV MONASTERY

Hradčanské náměstí (Castle Square) fans out from the castle's main gates, surrounded by the oversized palaces of the old nobility. A passage down the side of the Archbishop's Palace leads to the early eighteenth-century **Šternberk Palace** (Šternberský palác; Tues–Sun 10am–6pm), housing the National Gallery's relatively modest **Old European art collection** (ie non-Czech), which primarily consists of works from the fifteenth to the eighteenth centuries, the most significant of which is the *Festival of the Rosary* by Dürer.

Nestling in a shallow dip to the northwest, **Nový Svět** is all that is left of the medieval slums, painted up and sanitized in the nineteenth century. Uphill from Nový Svět, Loretánské náměstí is dominated by the brutal 150-metre-long facade of the **Černín Palace**. The facade of the **Loretto** (Tues–Sun 9am–12.15pm & 1–4.30pm), immediately opposite, is a perfect antidote, all hot flourishes and twirls, topped by a tower which lights up like a Chinese lantern at night – and which by day clanks out a tuneless version of the hymn *We Greet Thee a Thousand Times* on its 27 Dutch bells. However, the two-storey cloisters and chapels are just the outer casing for the main focus of the complex, the Santa Casa, a shrine that was built in 1626–31. You can get some idea of the shrine's popularity with the Bohemian nobility in the **treasury**; its padded ceilings and low lighting create a kind of giant jewellery box for the master exhibit, a ghastly Viennese silver monstrance studded with 6,222 diamonds and standing over three feet high.

A short way west up Pohořelec from Loretánské náměstí, the chunky remnants of the eighteenth-century fortifications mark the edge of the old city. Close by sits the **Strahov Monastery** (Strahovský klášter), which managed to escape the 1783 dissolution of the monasteries and continued to function until the Communists closed down all religious orders in 1948. Through the cobbled courtyard, past a small church and chapel, is the monastery proper, famous for its rich collection of manuscripts and its ornate **libraries** (daily 9am–noon & 1–5pm). Leaving through a narrow doorway in the eastern wall, you enter the gardens and orchards of the **Strahovská zahrada**, from where you can see the whole city in perspective.

Malá Strana

More than anywhere else, **Malá Strana**, the "Little Quarter", conforms to the image of Prague as the quintessential Baroque city. Its focus is the sloping, cobbled **Malostranské náměstí**, a busy square split in two by the former Jesuit seminary and church of **sv Mikuláš** (daily 9am–4pm; tower daily April–Oct 10am-6pm, Nov–March weekends only, 10am–5pm), possibly the most magnificent Baroque building in the city. Nothing of the plain west facade prepares you for the overwhelming High Baroque interior – the fresco in the nave alone covers over 1500 square metres, and portrays some of the more fanciful feats of St Nicholas.

Follow Tomášská north from the square and you'll arrive at the **Valdštejn Palace**. The largest palace complex in the city after the castle, it was built by Albrecht von Waldstein, who demolished 21 houses to make space for a palace befitting the most powerful man in central Europe. It currently houses the Czech Senate and is only rarely open to the public. You'll have to make do with the view from the formal gardens (daily: April & Oct 10am–6pm; May–Sept 9am–7pm), access to which is from a concealed entrance off Letenská.

South of the main square, a continuation of Karmelitská brings you to the funicular railway up **Petřín** hill (daily 9.15am–8.45pm, every 10–15 minutes; 8kč, or included in travel pass), a better green space than most in Prague, and a good place for a picnic and views from the 60-metre Petřín tower (June–Oct, 10am–6pm).

Staré Město

Staré Město, the "Old Town", founded in the early thirteenth century, is where most of the capital's markets, shops, restaurants and pubs are located. It is linked to Malá Strana by the city's most familiar monument, the **Charles Bridge** (Karlův most), begun in 1357. The statues that line it – brilliant pieces of Jesuit propaganda added during the Counter-Reformation – have made it renowned throughout Europe and choked during the summer. Cross to Staré Město and you're in busy **Křížovnické náměstí**, from where the narrow, crowded **Karlova** winds past the massive **Klementinum**, the former Jesuit College, completed just before the order were turfed out of the country in 1773. It now serves as the national library and state technical library, though the first floor has temporary exhibitions of some of the library's prize possessions, and there are regular concerts in the **Mirrored Chapel** (Zrcadlová kaple) and hourly tours at weekends (30 kč).

At the end of the street lies **Staroměstské náměstí**, the most spectacular square in Prague and the city's main marketplace from the eleventh century. At its centre is the dramatic Art Nouveau **Jan Hus Monument**. When John of Luxembourg gave Prague the right to have a town hall in 1338, the community bought a corner house on the square, gradually incorporating neighbouring buildings to form the **Old Town Hall** (Staroměstská radnice). Over the next century, the east wing was added, but only its graceful Gothic oriel and wedge-tower survived the arson of retreating Nazis. On the south facade, the central powder-red building now forms the entrance to the whole complex (Mon 11am–6pm, Tues–Sun 9am–5/6pm). You can also climb the tower – one of the few with access for the disabled – and get a close-up view of the figures of Christ and the Apostles which take part in a mechanical performance on the town hall's **Astronomical Clock** every hour (daily 8am–8pm).

Staré Město's most impressive Gothic structure is the mighty **Týn Church**, whose twin towers rise like giant antennae above the two arcaded houses which otherwise obscure its facade. It was completed during the reign of George of Poděbrady (1436–1471), the one and only Hussite King of Bohemia, but little of the interior survived its ferocious Catholicization. Behind, at the end of Týnská, lies Ungelt, a stunning fortified courtyard where customs used to be collected; it houses the Renaissance Granovský palace plus some very upmarket shops and cafés.

JOSEFOV

Within Staré Město lies **Josefov**, the Jewish quarter of the city until the end of the nineteenth century, when this ghetto area was demolished in order to create a beautiful bourgeois district on Parisian lines. Kafka spent most of his life in and around Josefov, and the destruction of the Jewish quarter, which continued throughout his childhood, had a profound effect on his psyche.

The "sights" of Josefov are covered by one 280kč ticket, or 480kč including the Old-New Synagogue, available from any of the quarter's box offices (daily except Sat and Jewish holidays 9am–4.30/6pm). The best place to begin is the **Pinkas Synagogue** on Široká, which contains a chilling memorial to the 77,297 Czechoslovak Jews who were killed during the Holocaust – the names of all the victims cover the walls, while children's drawings from the Theresienstadt (Terezín) camp are displayed in the women's gallery. From here, you enter the **Old Jewish Cemetery** (Starý Židovský hřbitov), established in the fifteenth century and in use until 1787, by which time there were some 100,000 graves piled on top of one another. Get there before the crowds, and the jumble of 12,000 Gothic, Renaissance and Baroque tombstones are a poignant reminder of the ghetto, its inhabitants subjected to over-crowding even in death.

Pařížská, Prague's most glamorous shopping street, now runs through the heart of the old ghetto in a riot of turn-of-the-century sculpturing, balconies and turrets. Halfway down here, on the left, is the steep brick gable of the **Old-New Synagogue** (Staronová synagóga; 200kč), completed in the fourteenth century and still the religious centre of Prague's Jewish community. Originally it was known simply as the New Synagogue, but after several fires gutted the ghetto it became the oldest synagogue building in the quarter – hence its name.

Opposite the synagogue is the **Jewish Town Hall** (Židovská radnice), founded in the sixteenth century and later turned into a creamy-pink Baroque house crowned by a wooden clocktower. In addition to the four main clocks, there's one on the north gable, which (like the Hebrew script) goes "backwards". The nearby Baroque **Klaus Synagogue** at U Starého hřbitová 4 and the neo-Gothic **Maisel Synagogue** at Maiselova 10 display some beautiful religious objects and portray the history of the Jews in the Czech lands until the eighteenth century, while the highly ornate neo-Byzantine **Spanish Synagogue**, at Věženská 1, on the other side of Pařížská, contains an exhibition on the history of the city's Jewish community since 1791 (after Emperor Joseph I's Toleration Edict).

Nové Město

Nové Město, the "New Town", now a sprawling late nineteenth-century bourgeois quarter, was actually founded in 1348 by Charles IV. The borderline between Staré and Nové Město is made up by the continuous boulevards of **Národní** and **Na příkopě**, a boomerang curve which follows the course of the old moat. The latter is Prague's busiest shopping street and the former the unlikely setting for the November 17 demonstration that sparked off the Velvet Revolution.

At the river end of Národní is the gold-crested **National Theatre** (Národní divadlo), a proud symbol of the Czech nation. Refused money by the Austrian state, Czechs of all classes dug deep into their pockets to raise funds for the venture themselves. Construction work commenced in 1868, but in 1881 the theatre was gutted by fire; once again, people emptied their pockets and it finally opened in 1883. In the summer, you'll get the best views of Prague from one of the rowing boats for rent on **Slovanský ostrov** (40kč/hr; Easter–Oct), the island opposite the theatre. Halfway along Na příkopě you can visit the **Mucha Museum**, at Panská 7 (daily 10am–6pm; 120kč), dedicated to the country's best-known artist, Alfons Mucha.

At the far end of Na příkopě, on náměstí Republiky, stands the **Municipal House** (Obecní dům), where you can see more of Mucha's work. Begun in 1903, it was decorated inside and out with the help of almost every artist connected with the Czech Secession and superbly renovated a few years ago. The easiest way of soaking up the dramatic interior, covered with Art Nouveau mosaics and pendulous chandeliers, is to have a reasonably pricey but delicious meal in the French restaurant to the right or a coffee in the equally dazzling café to the left.

Cross the boulevard at its central point and you're into the pivot of modern Prague and the political focus of the events of November 1989 – the wide, gently sloping **Wenceslas Square** (**Václavské náměstí**). The square's history of protest goes back to the Prague Spring of 1968: towards the top end, there's a small memorial to the victims of Communism, the most famous of whom, the 21-year-old student Jan Palach, set himself alight on this very spot in January 1969 in protest against the Soviet occupation. A six-lane freeway effectively cuts off the square from the **National Museum** (daily: May–Sept 10am–6pm; Oct–April 9am–5pm), one of the great symbols of the nineteenth-century Czech national revival, with its monumental glass cupola, sculptural decoration and frescoes from Czech history. However, unless you're a geologist or a zoologist you're likely to be unmoved by the exhibits.

Trade Fair Palace: Museum of Modern Art

One reason to hop on a tram is to visit the city's modern-art museum, housed in a vast functionalist 1920s building known as the **Trade Fair Palace** (Veletržní palác; Tues–Sun 10am–6pm, Thurs until 9pm), on Dukelských hrdinu 47 (tram #5 from náměstí Republiky). The museum's raison d'être is its unrivalled permanent collection of twentieth-century Czech art, but it also houses the National Gallery's modest collection of nineteenth- and twentieth-century European art, including works by Klimt, Schiele, Picasso and the French Impressionists, as well as temporary exhibitions of contemporary Czech and foreign art.

Eating

There are three main types of establishment in Prague and elsewhere in the country where you can get something to eat: a **restaurant** (*restaurace*), where eating is ostensibly the main activity; a **wine restaurant** (*vinárna*), which tends to think of itself as a touch more exclusive; and, that most typical of Czech institutions, the **pub** (*pivnice*), though these are largely concerned with serious drinking – and are covered in the next section. In practice, these definitions are blurred, with some places having *restaurace* and *pivnice* sections under the same roof, some *vinárna* offering food, some only wine, and so on.

Angel Café, Opatovicka 3, Nové Město. Sunny decor, friendly service, home-made cakes and imaginative meals make this a trendy eatery. Metro Národní.

Bar Bar, Všehrdova 17, Malá Strana. Arty crêperie with big, cheap salads and sweet and savoury pancakes. Metro Malostranská.

Bazaar Mediterranée, Nerudova 40, Malá Strana. Sprawling wine cellar with a great terrace and French cooking – understandably popular with folk heading to and from the castle. Metro Malostranská.

Bohemia Bagel, Újezd 16, Malá Strana (tram #22) and Masná 2, Staré Město (Metro Staroměstská). Internet café serving endless bagel variations, bottomless coffee and American cakes, quiche and cookies.

Country Life, Melantrichova 15, Staré Město. Popular, sit-down vegan place with a health food shop attached. Closed Sat. Metro Můstek.

U Góvindy, Soukenická 27, Nové Město. Self-service veggie slop from the local Hare Krishna posse. Closed evenings and Sundays. Metro náměstí Republiky.

Hogo Fogo, Salvátorská 4, Staré Město. Monochrome decor and cheap, filling Czech food at this popular student hangout. Metro Staroměstská.

Klášterní restaurace, Stráhovské nád. 302, Hradčany. In-house brewery serving South Bohemian specialities at reasonable prices in a twelfth century monastery. Tram #22.

Le Café Colonial, Široká 6, Staré Město. Pricey French brasserie-style cuisine, located right by Josefov, and very popular with locals. Metro Staroměstská.

Pizzeria Kmotra, V jirchářích 12, Nové Město. Hugely popular basement pizza place in the backstreets behind Národní. Metro Národní třída.

Radost FX Café, Bělehradská 120, Vinohrady (*www.radostfx.cz*). Outstanding veggie food attracts ultra-fashionable crowd; open till very late, brunch at weekends. Metro I.P. Pavlova.

Drinking

The choice of Prague **cafés** is pretty varied – from Art Nouveau relics and swish espresso bars (both of which are called *kavárna* and are licensed), to simple sugar and caffeine joints (*cukrárna*). For no-nonsense boozing you need to head for a **pub** (*pivnice*), which invariably serves excellent beer by the half-litre, but many of which close around 11pm. For late-night drinking, head for one of the clubs or all-night bars.

Café Slavia, Národní 1, Nové Město. Famous café, opposite the National Theatre. Metro Národní třída.

Dobrá čajovna, Boršov 2, Staré Město. Buddhist tea house off Karoliny Světlé; no smoking, no alcohol, just chilling out. Metro Staroměstská.

Evropa café, Václavské náměstí 25, Nové Město. Although now deeply touristy, the Art Nouveau decor is well worth a peek. Metro Můstek.

Jo's Bar, Malostranské náměstí 7, Malá Strana. Narrow bar serving hot Tex-Mex food – something of a backpacker institution. Metro Malostranská.

Kavarna Obecní dům, náměstí Republiky 5, Nové Město. Glorious Art Nouveau decor, impeccable service, good cake trolley and even a few Internet terminals. Metro náměstí Republiky.

Louvre, Národní 20. With high ceiling, mirrors, daily papers and a billiard hall, this first-floor café is a fair approximation of a typical Viennese *Kaffeehaus*. Metro Národní třída.

Marquis de Sade, Templová 8, Staré Město. High ceilings, comfy sofas, dubious live music and crap beer, but a great atmosphere till early in the morning. Metro náměstí Republiky.

Molly Malone's, U obecního dvora 4, Staré Město. One of the best of Prague's Irish pubs with an open fire and draught Guinness. Metro Staroměstská.

Novoměstské pivovar, Vodičkova 20, Nové Město. Micro-brewery, which serves up its own misty brew along with solid Czech food. Metro Můstek.

Restaurace Pivovarský dům, Lipova 15, Nové Město. In-house brewery offering everything from wheat to banana beer – along with excellent Czech pub grub and good service. Metro I.P. Pavlová.

Terminal Bar, Soukenická 6, Nové Město. Prague's trendiest Internet café is also a great place to chill out, especially in the downstairs retro bar. Metro náměstí Republiky.

Velryba, Opatovická 24, Nové Město. Smoky and studenty café, with cheap Czech food. Metro Národní třída.

Nightlife

As far as **live music** is concerned, the classical scene still has the edge in Prague, though more new jazz clubs have livened up the scene. Some better **discos and nightclubs** have sprouted up around Wenceslas Square – although others still act as mini red-light districts. Predictably enough, with a playwright as president, **theatre** in Prague is thriving; without knowing the language, however, your scope is limited, though there's a tradition of innovative mime, puppetry and "black light" theatre in the city. **Tickets** are cheap and available from any Ticketpro outlet (there's one in each PIS office) as well as from the venues themselves. As for particular areas, in the summer Hradčany hosts many open-air concerts and plays.

Classical music and opera

Classical concerts take place throughout the year in concert halls and churches, the biggest event being the Prague Spring (*Pražské jaro*) **international music festival**, which traditionally begins on May 12, the day of Smetana's death, with a performance of *Má vlast*, and finishes on June 2 with a rendition of Beethoven's Ninth. As well as the main venues, watch out for concerts in the churches and palaces, especially in summer.

Rudolfinum, Alsovo nábřeží 12, Staré Město. Stunning Neo-Renaissance concert hall and home to the Czech Philharmonic. Metro Staroměstská.

Státní opera Praha, Wilsonova 4, Nové Město. The former German opera house, and the city's second-choice venue for opera and ballet. Metro Muzeum.

Stavovské divadlo, Ovocný trh 1, Staré Město. Prague's main opera house, which witnessed the première of Mozart's *Don Giovanni*. Metro Můstek.

Jazz and rock

AghaRTA Jazz Centrum, Krakovská 5, Nové Město. Prague's best jazz club with a good mix of top-name foreigners and locals. Open until 1am. Metro Muzeum.

Akropolis, Kubelíkova 27, Žižkov (*www.spinet.cz/akropolis*). Decent live arts/gig venue in the backstreets of Žižkov, renowned for Romany and other ethnic music festivals. Doors open 5.30pm. Tram #5, #9 or #26.

Lucerna Music Bar, Vodičkova 36, Nové Město. Central, small dance space, live music, occasionally jazz. Open 9pm–6am. Metro Můstek/Muzeum.

Radost FX, Bělehradská 120, Vinohrady (*www.radostfx.cz*). By far the best dance club in Prague, with a great veggie café attached. Open until 5am. Metro I.P. Pavlova.

Reduta, Národní 20, Nové Město. Prague's oldest-established jazz club, serving up anything from trad to modern. Open daily 9pm onwards.

The Roxy, Dlouhá 33, Staré Město (*roxy@roxy.cz*). Good mix of trendy café and experimental clubby venue – worth checking out. Open Tues–Fri 9pm–2.30am, bar open Mon–Sat noon–midnight, Sun 5pm–midnight. Metro náměstí Republiky.

Listings

Airlines British Airways (☎02/22 11 44 44, *www.britishairways.cz*); ČSA (☎02/20 10 41 11, *www.csa.cz*).

American Express, Václavské náměstí 56, Nové Město (☎02/22 80 04 44).

Books The Globe, Pštrossova 6, Nové Město;(☎02/24 91 62 64; metro Karlovo náměstí).

Car rental Avis, Klimentská 46, Nové Město (☎02/21 85 12 25); Budget, Čistovická 100, Dejvice (☎02/302 57 13).

Embassies Australia, Na Ořechovce 38, Střešovice (☎02/24 31 00 71); Canada, Mickiewiczova 6, Hradčany (☎02/72 10 18 00); Great Britain, Thunovská 14, Malá Strana (☎02/57 32 03 55); Ireland, Tržiště 15, Malá Strana (☎02/57 53 00 61); USA, Tržiště 15, Malá Strana (☎02/57 53 06 63). Nationals of New Zealand should contact the Australian Embassy.

Exchange There's a 24-hour exchange service at the airport but banks and ATMs are your best bet.

Gay Prague For up-to-date information try the Gay Information Centre (☎02/26 44 08).

Internet access Cybeteria, Štěpánská 18 (Mon–Fri 10am–8pm, Sat & Sun noon–6pm; 100kč/hr); Terminal Bar, Soukenická 6 (Mon–Sun 11am–1am, 90kc/hr); KávaKávaKáva, Národní 37 - Platýz passage, (Mon–Fri 7am–8pm, Sat & Sun 9am–8pm; 25–30kc/15 mins). All in Nové Město.

Laundry Laundry Kings, Dejvická 16, Dejvice; metro Hradčanská (Mon–Fri 10am–10pm).

Pharmacy 24-hour service at U sv Ludmilly, Belgická 37, Vinohrady (☎02/24 23 72 07; metro náměstí Míru).

Post office The main post office is at Jindřišská 14, Nové Město, open daily 7am–8pm; there's a 24-hour service for parcels, telegrams and telephones at Hybernská 15.

BOHEMIA

Prague is the natural centre and capital of Bohemia; the rest divides easily into four geographical districts. **South Bohemia**, bordered by the Šumava Mountains, is the least spoilt; its largest town by far is the brewing centre of **České Budějovice**, and its chief attraction, aside from the thickly forested hills, is a series of well-preserved medieval towns, whose undisputed gem is **Český Krumlov**. Neighbouring **West Bohemia** has a similar mix of rolling woods and hills, despite the industrial nature of its capital **Plzeň**, home of Pilsen beer and the Škoda empire. Beyond here, as you approach the German border, Bohemia's famous **Spa Region** unfolds, with magnificent resorts such as **Mariánské Lázně** and **Karlovy Vary** enjoying sparkling reputations. **North Bohemia** has real problems: devastated by industrialization, many parts are virtually uninhabitable. **East Bohemia** has suffered indirectly from the polluting industries of its neighbour, but remains relatively blight-free. There's some great walking and climbing country here, but the only essential stop on a quick tour is the silver-mining centre of **Kutná Hora**.

České Budějovice

Since its foundation in 1265, **ČESKÉ BUDĚJOVICE** (Budweis) – just two hours by train from Prague – has been a self-assured place, convinced of its own importance. Its wealth, based on medieval silver mines and its position on the salt route from Linz to Prague, was wiped out in the seventeenth century by war and fire, but the Habsburgs lavishly reconstructed most of České Budějovice in the eighteenth century. Its real renown, however, is for its local brew Budvar, better known abroad under its original German name, Budweiser.

České Budějovice has a compact old town that's only a five-minute walk from the **train** and **bus stations**, both situated to the east of the city centre, along the pedestrianized Lannova tpída. The medieval grid plan leads inevitably to the magnificent central **náměstí Přemysla Otakara II**, one of Europe's largest market squares. Its buildings are elegant enough, but it's the arcades and the octagonal **Samson's Fountain** – once the only tap in town – that make the greatest impression. The 72-metre status symbol, the **Black Tower** (Černá věž), one of the few survivors of the 1641 fire, leans gently to one side of the square; its roof gallery (daily: March–June 10am–6pm; July & Aug 10am–7pm; Sept–Nov 9am–5pm) provides superb views.

When the weather's fine, people tend to promenade by the banks of the Malše, where parts of the original town walls have survived along with some of České Budějovice's oldest buildings. All that is left of the bishop's palace is the serene **garden** (May–Sept daily 8am–6pm), accessible through a small gateway in the walls. Round the corner, on Piaristické náměstí, stands the thoroughly medieval **zbrojnice** (one-time arsenal), once the centre of the town's all-important salt trade. The Budvar **brewery**, Karoliny světlé 4, is on the road to Prague (guided tour daily at 2pm; call ☎038/770 53 40; bus #2 or #4).

České Budějovice's popularity with neighbouring Austrians and Germans means that **hotels** tend to charge over the odds. The best-value options are *Penzion JV* (☎038/53 47 5; ③), off Kanovnická at Na mlýnské stoce 7; or *Hotel Malý pivovar*, Karla IV 8–10 (☎038/731 32 85; ⑧). There's a friendly **tourist office** (May–Sept daily 8.30am–6pm; Oct–March Mon–Fri 9am–5.30pm, Sat 9am–noon; ☎038/63 59 48 0, *www.budnet.cz*) at no. 2 on the main square, too, where you can book accommodation. You can also stay in cheap private **rooms** at *Privat Petera* at Panská 23 (☎038/73 18 36 1; ①–②). From July to September rooms are available in **student halls**, located at Studentská 13–19 (☎038/77 74 20 1; ①–②). There's also a good **campsite**, *Dlouhá louka* at Stromovká 8 (☎038/72 10 60 1; bus #16 from station;

May–Sept). The most famous hostelry in town is *Masné krámy* at Krajinská 29, which serves huge quantities of Budvar all day. The *Hotel Malý pivovar* is widely recommended for great pub **food** and **beer**, as is the *Hotel Zvon* on the main square – head for the pub section, rather than the more expensive restaurant.

Český Krumlov

Squeezed into a tight S-bend of the River Vltava, **ČESKÝ KRUMLOV** (Krumau) is undoubtedly one of the most picturesque towns in the country, having hardly changed in the last three hundred years. This, however, is no secret, and the crowds are getting increasingly thick throughout the summer.

The **train station** is twenty minutes' walk north of the old town, up a precipitous set of steps, while the **bus station** is just outside the old town. The twisting River Vltava divides the town into two: the circular staré město (old town) on the right bank and the Latrán quarter on the hillier left. For centuries, the focal point has been the **Castle**, the Krumlovský zámek (April–Oct Tues–Sun 9am–noon & 1–4/5/6pm; 70kč per tour in Czech, 140kč per tour in another language) in the Latrán quarter, as good a place as any to begin a roam. There's a choice of two hour-long guided tours: one concentrating on feudal opulence, the other peaking at the castle's eighteenth-century Rococo ballroom. Another covered walkway puts you high above the town in the unexpectedly expansive **terraced gardens** (open all year; free).

The shabby houses leaning in on Latrán lead to a wooden ramp-like bridge which connects with the staré město. Head straight up the soft incline of Radniční to the main square, where a long, white Renaissance entablature connects two-and-a-half Gothic houses to create the **town hall** (radnice). On the other side, the high lancet windows of the church of **St Vitus** rise above the ramshackle rooftops. Continuing east off the square, down Horní, the beautiful sixteenth-century Jesuit college now provides space for the *Hotel Růže*. Opposite, the local **Museum** (Tues–Fri 9am–noon & 12.30pm–5pm, Sat & Sun 1–4pm) includes a reconstructed seventeenth-century shop interior among its exhibits. While you're there ask for directions to the **Schiele International Cultural Center** (daily 10am–6pm; 120kč), on Široká, a whole series of galleries and exhibition halls housed in a fifteenth-century former brewery in the staré město. The centre is devoted to the Austrian painter Egon Schiele, who moved here briefly in 1911, and contains many of his drawings and paintings, as well as featuring contemporary artists.

There's a helpful **tourist office** (Mon–Fri 9am–6pm, Sat & Sun 10am–4pm; ☎0337/71 16 50, *www.ckrumlov.cz*) at nám. Svornosti in the staré město, which can organize accommodation for you. *Hotel Růže*, Horní 24 (☎0337/77 21 00, *www.hotelruze.cz*; ⑨), is the town's most beautiful and grand old **hotel**, bar the occasional dodgy bit of Seventies decor; the friendly **pub/pension**, *Na louži*, Kájovská 66 (☎0337/71 12 80, *www.ck.ipex.cz/hotlouze*; ②) is a good bet. The central *Travellers Hostel* at Soukenická 43 (☎0337/71 13 45; ①–②) is a safe bet, with bike rental, a barbecue and other amenities. An even cheaper option is the **hostel** *Krumlov House* (☎0337/71 19 35; ①); to get there follow Horní out of the old town and turn right towards Rooseveltova 68. There's also a primitive **campsite** (May–Sept), 2km south on road 160 to Nové Spolí. As far as **eating** goes, there's a wide choice: *Papa's Living Restaurant*, Latrán 13, offers funky Mexican, Italian and veggie dishes, while the fish restaurant *Rybařská bašta*, off Široká, is good value. A cheaper option still is to head for the basic stand-up *Krumlovská fontána*, on náměstí Svornosti. **Drinking** is best done at the *Krumovské pivnice*, off Latrán next to the brewery, or at the aforementioned *Na louži* which offers local Eggenberg beer.

Plzeň

PLZEŇ (Pilsen) is Bohemia's second city, with a population of 170,000. Despite its industrial character, there are compensations – a large number of students, eclectic architecture (including the recently-restored Great Synagogue) and an unending supply of (probably) the best **beer** in the world. All of which make Plzeň a popular stopoff on the main rail line between Prague and the west. Plzeň's **train stations** are works of art in themselves: your likeliest point of arrival is the Hlavní nádraží, just a little east of the city centre. The **bus terminal** is on the west side of town. From both stations, the city centre is only a short walk away.

The main square, **náměstí Republiky**, presents a full range of architectural styles, starting with the exalted heights of the Gothic cathedral of **sv Bartoloměj**, its green spire (daily 10am–6pm) reaching up almost 103m. Over the way rises the sgraffitoed Renaissance **Old Town Hall** (Stará radnice), self-importantly one storey higher than the rest of the square. Here and there other old buildings survive, but the vast majority of Plzeň's buildings hail from the city's heyday during the industrial expansion around the turn of the century. In the old town, this produced some wonderful variations on neohistorical themes and Art Nouveau motifs, particularly to the north and west of the main square.

But the reason most people come to Plzeň is to sample its famous 12° Plzeňský Prazdroj, or **Pilsner Urquell** (its Germanized export name; *www.pilsner-urquell.cz*). Beer has been brewed in the town since it was founded in 1295, but it wasn't until 1842 that the famous Bürgerliches Brauhaus was built, after a near-riot by the townsfolk over the declining quality of their brew. The **brewery** is at U prazdroje 7; a **guided tour** (Mon–Fri 12.30pm; 1hr) leaves from the historical gate, but you'll have to pay extra for a tasting. You could, of course, just settle for a half-litre of the stuff at the vast *Na stílce* pub (daily from 11am), beyond the brewery's triumphal arch, or try out the smaller theme restaurant to the left. The truly dedicated can then head for the **Brewery Museum** (Pivovarské muzeum; daily 10am–6pm) at Veleslavínova 6.

Finding a vacancy in one of Plzeň's **hotels** presents few problems, though rooms don't come cheap. There are some reasonable rooms at the faded *Slovan*, Smetanovy sady 1 (☎019/722 72 56; ②–④), and better ones at the *Continental*, Zbrojnická 8 (☎019/723 52 92; ②), and a decent pension at Solní 8 (☎019/723 6652; ②). **Private rooms** and other accommodation are available at the **tourist office** (daily 9/10am–3.30/5/6pm; ☎019/703 27 50, *www.plzen-city.cz*), at nám. Republiky 41. Alternatively, you can stay at the **hostel** at Bolevecká 30 (☎019/725 98 14; ①; tram #4 north along Karlovarská). Bus #20 from the train station will drop you at the *Bílá hora* **campsite** (April–Sept), at 28. pijna 55/59 (☎019/53 49 05) in the northern suburb of the same name.

All the hotels have **restaurants** attached but for cheap meals you might as well combine your **eating** with your **drinking**. Apart from *Na stílce*, you can get Pilsner Urquell (and cheap grub) at the wood-panelled *U Salzmannů* at Pražská 6. Gambrinus, Plzeň's other main beer, is best at *U Žumbery* at Bezručova 14 or you could try the garden restaurant at *Zach's pub*, Palackého náměsti.

The Spa Region

The big West Bohemian spas – especially **Mariánské Lázně** and **Karlovy Vary** – were the Côte d'Azur of Habsburg Europe in the nineteenth century, attracting the great names of *Mitteleuropa*. What was the prerogative of the mega-wealthy became the right of the toiling masses after the postwar nationalization of the entire spa industry enabled every factory worker and trade union member to receive three weeks' annual holiday at a spa pension. Nowadays, the wealthy Germans and Russians are back, though the area has still a long way to go before it catches up with the likes of Baden-Baden.

Mariánské Lázně

Once one of the most fashionable European spas – and a regular haunt of King Edward VII, who also came for the golf – **MARIÁNSKÉ LÁZNĚ** (Marienbad) is far less exclusive today. The riotous, turn-of-the-century architecture is gradually being restored and the spa now surveys busloads of elderly Germans getting the full works. Buses and trains stop 3km from the spa, from where trolley bus #5 runs the remaining distance, up Hlavní třída to the *Hotel Excelsior*. Sumptuous, regal buildings, most dating from the second half of the nineteenth century, rise up from the pine-clad surroundings – an appropriate backdrop for the genteel classical music festivals hosted annually here.

The focal point of the spa is the **Kolonáda**. This beautiful wrought-iron colonnade gently curves like a whale-ribbed railway station, the atmosphere relentlessly genteel and sober, although the view has been marred by a functionless concrete splat left by Communist developers. In summer, Bohemian bands and orchestras give daily concerts here, while tourists buy up the Bohemian crystal in the upstairs gallery. Access to the colonnade's life-giving faucets is restricted (daily 6am–noon & 4–6pm), though the spa's first and foremost **spring**, Křížový pramen, is accessible all day and night. Mariánské Lázně's altitude lends an almost subalpine freshness to the air, and **walking** is as important to "the cure" as the various specialized treatments. At the end of the Kolonáda, by the new "singing fountain", there's a map showing the marked walks around the spa. However, don't miss trying out the spa itself: you can book treatments, which include various massages, mineral baths in the gorgeously colonnaded indoor pool and mud treatment, through the spa organization (☎0165/65 55 55, *marienbad.thc@.plz.pvtnet.cz*) at Masarykova 22.

If you want to **stay**, rooms are getting increasingly pricey, but try the pleasant family pension, *Villa Rožemberg* (☎0165/62 58 30; ②), at Dobrovského 154/5 south east of the centre. The *Kossuth*, Ruská 77 (☎0165/62 28 61; ②), parallel to the main street, is pretty basic, but the *Bohemia,* Hlavní třída 100 (☎0165/62 32 51; ⑤), is central and classy. Accommodation is also available from the **tourist office** at Hlavní 47 (Mon–Fri 9am–6pm, Sat & Sun 9am–5pm; ☎0165/62 24 74, *www.marienbad.com*). Hlavní třída is punctuated with **cafés**, shops and **restaurants**, some hinting at bygone opulence; *Café Polonia*, Hlavní třída 50, offers chocolate cakes and Viennese coffee as rich as its stucco decoration. *The Golden Globe*, Nehrová 26, is a stylish **pub** offering live classical music, or you can really splurge at the elegant *Villa Romano*, Anglická 62.

Karlovy Vary

KARLOVY VARY (Karlsbad), king of the Bohemian spas, is one of the most cosmopolitan Czech towns. Its international clientele annually doubles the local population, which is further supplemented by thousands of able-bodied tourists in summer, when the narrow valley resounds with German and the multifarious languages of central Europe.

There are two **train stations**, one by the bus station and one by the River Ohře (Eger). Don't get off from the Prague bus at the **bus station**; along with almost everyone else, hop off at Tržnice, one stop before, which is far more central. Half a kilometre south, the pedestrianized **spa quarter** stretches along the winding Teplá Valley. Unfortunately, many visitors' first impressions are marred by the inexcusable concrete scab of *Hotel Thermal*, for whose sake a large slice of the old town bit the dust. However, its open-air spring-water **swimming pool** is superb and offers unbeatable views. As the valley narrows, the river disappears under a wide terrace in front of the graceful **Mlýnská kolonáda**, each of whose four springs is more scalding than the last.

Most powerful of the town's twelve springs is the **Sprudel** (*Vřídlo* to the Czechs), which belches out over 2500 gallons every hour. The smooth marble floor of the modern **Vřídelní kolonáda** (the old fountain was melted down for armaments by the Nazis) allows patients to shuffle up and down contentedly, while inside the glass rotunda the geyser shoots hot water forty feet upwards. Clouds of steam obscure a view of Dientzenhofer's Baroque masterpiece, the **church of sv Maria Magdaléna**, pitched nearby on a precipitous site. South of the Sprudel is Karlovy Vary's most famous shopping street, the **Stará louka** (Alte Wiese). Its shops exude little of the snobbery of former days, and the tea and cakes served on marble tables at the *Café Elefant* are among the few reminders of the halcyon era. At Stará louka 30 is the **Grand Hotel Pupp**. Founded in 1701 as the greatest hotel in the world it still has a certain snooty grandeur, and now hosts the annual Karlovy Vary International Film Festival in July.

It's best to start looking for **accommodation** early in the day – Karlovy Vary is a very fashionable spa town so nothing comes dirt cheap. The Vřídelní Kolonáda (☎017/32 24 09 7 or 32 29 31 2, *www.karlovyvary.cz*), can organize private and long-term spa accommodation, as will ČEDOK (☎017/322 29 94), on the corner of Moskevská and dr. Bechera. Moderately priced **hotels** include the *Adria*, Západní 1 (☎017/322 37 65; ③); the *Kavalerie*, T.G. Masaryka 43 (☎017/322 96 13; ③), the best value in this range; and the modern *Pension Holiday*, Ondříčkova 26 (☎017/322 06 49; ③). Karlovy Vary's most central **campsite** is *Gézi* (☎017/322 5101; May–Sept; bus #7), at Slovenská 9; take the Brezova shuttle bus from the main station. The best place **to eat** has to be the splendid *Hotel Imperial* at Libusina 16 (if you're interested in splashing out and staying the night). Otherwise, try the various hotel restaurants or go for *Pizzeria Palermo* at Moskevska 44.

Kutná Hora

Undisputed gem of the region east of Prague and UNESCO World Heritage site is **KUTNÁ HORA** (Kuttenberg), 60km from the capital and once one of the most important towns in this neck of the Habsburg Empire. In 1308 Václav II founded the royal mint here, and the town's sudden wealth allowed it to underwrite the construction of one of the most magnificent churches in central Europe, plus a number of other prestigious monuments. By the late Middle Ages its population was equal to that of London, its shantytown suburbs straggling across what are now green fields. When the silver mines dried up at the end of the sixteenth century, Kutná Hora's importance came to an abrupt end.

The easiest way to get here from Prague is by bus, as the main train station is several kilometres from the centre, whereas the buses stop just across the ring road. The small houses which line the town's medieval lanes give little idea of its former glories, and the same goes for **Palackého náměstí**, nominally the main square though it's no showpiece. A narrow alleyway on the south side of the square leads to the leafy Havlíčkovo náměstí, off of which is the **Italian Court** (Vlašský dvůr), where Florentine workers produced Prague's silver *Groschen*, a coin used throughout central Europe until the nineteenth century. The building itself has been mucked about over the centuries, though the short guided tour (daily 9/10am–4/5/6pm) is interesting enough. Better still, head for the **Mining Museum** (April–Oct Tues–Sun 9am–5/6pm), the other side of sv Jakub, the town's oldest church. Here, you can visit some of the medieval mines that were discovered beneath an old fort in the 1960s.

The Jesuits arrived too late to exploit the town's silver stocks, but with their own funds they built a **Jesuit College** on the ridge to the southwest of town. With its gallery of saints and holy men, it was a crude attempt to eclipse the astounding achievement of the neighbouring Gothic **Cathedral of sv Barbora** (Tues–Sun: May–Sept 9am–5.30pm; Oct–April 9am–11.30am & 1/2–3.30pm). Not to be outdone by the St Vitus Cathedral in Prague, the miners of Kutná Hora financed the construction of a great cathedral of their own, dedicated to Barbara, the patron saint of miners and gunners. The foundations were probably laid by Peter Parler himself in the 1380s, but work was interrupted by the Hussite wars, and the church remained unfinished until the late 1800s. From the outside it's an incredible sight, bristling with pinnacles, finials and flying buttresses supporting a roof of three tent-like towers and unequal needle-sharp spires. Inside, cold light streams through the plain glass, lighting up a vaulted nave whose ribs form branches and petals stamped with coats of arms belonging to Václav II and the miners' guilds.

While you're in Kutná Hora, don't miss the weird subterranean *kostnice* or **ossuary** (daily: 8/9am–noon & 1–4/5pm), overflowing with 40,000 complete sets of bones, moulded into sculptures and decorations by František Rint in the nineteenth century. To get there, take bus #1 or #4 to the giant tobacco factory; you'll find the ossuary behind a Baroque church.

The **tourist office** at Palackeho náměstí 377 (Mon–Fri 9am–6.30pm; April–Oct also Sat & Sun 9am–5pm; ☎0327/51 55 56, *www.kutnahora.cz*) can arrange **accommodation** in private rooms. Follow signs to the *turistická ubytovna* or **hostel** (☎0327/51 34 63; ①) for the cheapest accommodation in town; reception is open only 5–6pm. There are numerous pensions: the *U hrnčíře*, Barborská 24 (☎0327/51 21 13; ②), and the comfortable *U vlašského dvora*, just off Palackého náměstí on 28 října (☎0327/51 46 18; ③) are both good. The nearest **campsite** is the unlikely sounding *Santa Barbara* on Česká (April–Oct, ☎0327/51 20 51, 800m from the cathedral, with hot showers and a restaurant).

MORAVIA

Wedged between Bohemia and Slovakia, **Moravia** (Morava) is the smallest of the three provinces which once made up Czechoslovakia, but possibly the prettiest, friendliest and most bucolic. Although the North Moravian corridor is heavily industrialized and has suffered from increasingly high unemployment over the past decade, much of the region is rural and the folk roots, traditions and religion here are strongly felt. The Moravian capital, **Brno**, a once-grand nineteenth-century city, is within easy striking distance of Moravia's spectacular **karst region**. In the northern half of the province, the Baroque riches of the Moravian prince-bishopric have left their mark on the old capital, **Olomouc**, now a thriving university town and one of the region's main attractions.

Brno

BRNO (Brünn) "welcomes the visitor with new constructions", as the Communist-era travel brochures used to euphemistically put it. In fact, the high-rise tenements that surround the city play a major part in discouraging travellers from stopping here. But as the second largest city in the Czech Republic, with a couple of really good museums and galleries plus a handful of other sights and a fair bit of nightlife, it's worth a day or two of anyone's time.

Brno was a late developer, the first cloth factory being founded in 1766, but by the end of the nineteenth century this was easily the largest city in Moravia. Between the wars Brno enjoyed a cultural boom, heralded by the 1928 Exhibition of Contemporary Culture which provided an impetus for much of the city's modernist architecture. After the war, Brno's German-speakers (one quarter of the population) were sent packing on foot to Vienna. Capital fled with the capitalists and centralized state funds were diverted to Prague and Bratislava, pushing Brno firmly into third (now second) place.

Arrival and accommodation

Brno's main **train station** and **bus station** sit closely together, on the edge of the city centre; the train station has lockers and a 24-hour left-luggage office. Most of Brno's sights are within easy walking distance of the train station, although **trams** will take you almost anywhere in the city within minutes. You need to buy either a 11kč ticket for half an hour's travel or a 15kč ticket, valid for an hour and allowing changes between trams or buses. Tickets must be bought beforehand from kiosks, hotel lobbies or yellow ticket machines, and validated on board.

The main **tourist office** is in the Old Town Hall (Stará radnice) at Radnická 8 (Mon–Fri 8am–6pm, Sat & Sun 9am–5pm; ☎05/42 32 07 58 or 05/42 21 10 90, *www.brno.cz*) and there's also a smaller bureau in the train station (☎05/42 22 14 50) and another in Mendlovo nám (☎05/43 24 22 36). They can sell you a map and various guides and will also book you a private or hotel room, as will the Synergie Agency (☎05/43 23 32 72, *pselucky@iol.cz*). These days Brno is host to many trade fairs, so it's wise to book ahead. **Hostel** accommodation is theoretically available all year round, but you're better off trying cheap hotels outside the summer season. However, you'll find summer accommodation in the student dorms at

where Protestantism had spread like wildfire in the sixteenth century. Jutting out into the road, it signals the gateway to the less hectic part of town. The great mass of the former Jesuit College, now the **Palacký University**, dominates the first square, náměstí Republiky, opposite which is the dull town museum and, next door, the vastly superior **art museum** (muzeum umění; Tues–Sun 10am–6pm); the top floor houses a fascinating selection of twentieth-century works by local-born artists and features a viewing tower.

Three blocks east of náměstí Republiky, the **Cathedral**, or Dóm, of sv Václav comes into view. Though it started life as a Romanesque basilica, the current structure is mostly nineteenth-century neo-Gothic. However, the walls and pillars of the nave are prettily painted in Romanesque style, and the crypt (Mon–Thurs & Sat 9am–5pm, Fri 1–5pm, Sun 11am–5pm) has a wonderful display of gory reliquaries and priestly sartorial wealth.

Practicalities

The **tourist office** (Mon–Fri 8.30am–5pm; ☎068/551 33 92/85, *www.olomoucko.cz*) in the town hall, at Horní nám. 1 to the right of the astronomical clock, will book **private rooms** for you. Cheap rooms are hard to come by in Olomouc – the only bargain is the *Sigma* (☎068/52 32 07 6; ③–④), opposite the train station at Jeremenkova 36, or the centrally located pension *U Dómu garni*, Dómská 4 (☎068/522 05 02; ④), near the cathedral. Rooms can be even harder to come by in May when the Spring Music Festival follows the Flower Festival. **Hostels** aren't much of an option either – but you can try *Správa kolejí a menz* for summer dorm accommodation (☎068/52 26 05 7).

For **restaurants**, the *U červeného volka* on Dolní náměstí is a cheap place with a wide range of veggie dishes, but *Caesar Pizzeria* in the cobbled vaults under the town hall is by far the most popular joint in town. A good range of cakes can be found in the *Maruška cukrárna* at 28 října or the *Café Mahler*, at Horní náměstí 11. In the evenings, head for a backstreet pub like the reasonably priced *U bakaláre*, on Žerotinovo náměstí. The *Depo no. 8* at náměstí Republiky 1, has occasional DJs and bands, as does the *U-Klub* at the Studentcentrum at the far end of Křížovského, and the *LTC Club* is a cheap, studenty bar at U rozária 9.

travel details

Trains

Prague to: Brno (hourly; 2hr 30 min–3hr 30min); České Budějovice (11 daily; 2hr 20min–4hr 50min); Karlovy Vary (8 daily; 3hr 20min–5hr 30min); Mariánské Lázně (9 daily; 2hr 30min–3hr 20min); Olomouc (every 1–2hr; 2hr 50 min–3hr); Plzeň (every 45 mins; 1hr 25min–2hr 35min).

Brno to: Olomouc (hourly; 1hr 30min–2hr 30min).

České Budějovice to: Brno (3–5 daily; 4hr 20min–5hr 30min); Český Krumlov (up to 9 daily; 1hr); Plzeň (hourly; 1hr 50min–3hr 15min).

Mariánské Lázně to: Karlovy Vary (8–10 daily; 1hr 30min–2hr 30min).

Buses

Prague to: Brno (hourly; 2hr); České Budějovice (up to 20 daily; 2hr 20min–3hr 45min); Český Krumlov (up to 14 daily; 3hr–5hr); Karlovy Vary (30 daily; 2hr 20min–4hr 10min); Kutná Hora (32 daily; 55min–1hr 40min).

CHAPTER 7

DENMARK

Introduction

Delicately balanced between Scandinavia proper and mainland Europe, **Denmark** is a difficult country to pin down. In many ways it shares the characteristics of both regions: it's an EU member, and has prices and drinking laws that are broadly in line with those in the rest of Europe. But Denmark's social policies and its style of government are distinctly Scandinavian: social benefits and the standard of living are high, and its politics are very much that of consensus.

Denmark is the easiest Scandinavian country in which to travel, both in terms of cost and distance, but its landscape is the region's least dramatic: very green and flat, largely farmland interrupted by innumerable pretty villages. Apart from a scattering of small islands, three main landmasses make up the country – the islands of Zealand and Funen and the peninsula of Jutland, which extends northwards from Germany.

The vast majority of visitors make for **Zealand** (Sjælland), and, more specifically, **Copenhagen**, the country's one large city and an exciting focal point, with a beautiful old centre, a good array of museums and a boisterous nightlife. Zealand's smaller neighbour, **Funen** (Fyn), has only one positive urban draw in **Odense**, and otherwise is a sedate place, renowned for its cute villages and the sandy beaches of its fragmented southern coast. Only **Jutland** (Jylland) is far enough away from Copenhagen to enjoy a truly individual flavour, as well as Denmark's most varied scenery, ranging from soft green hills to desolate heathlands. **Århus** and **Aalborg** are two of the liveliest cities outside the capital.

Information and maps

All towns and some villages will have a **tourist office**, giving out free maps and sometimes able to book accommodation and change money. Most railway and motorway service stations also offer a hotel booking service. In large cities tourist offices sell useful **discount cards** giving reductions on public transport, museum entry and the like. They're open long hours every day in the most popular places, but have much reduced times outside the April to September period. The best general **map** of Denmark is the Hallwag one.

Money and banks

Coming from any of the other Scandinavian countries, Denmark seems remarkably cheap, with prices roughly only 10–20 percent higher than other western European countries. **Danish currency** is the krone (plural kroner), made up of 100 øre, and it comes in notes of 50kr, 100kr, 200kr, 500kr, 1000kr, and coins of 25øre, 50øre, 1kr, 2kr, 5kr, 10kr, 20kr. **Banks** are the best places to change travellers' cheques and foreign cash; there's a uniform commission of 30kr per transaction, so change as much as possible in one go. Banking hours are Mon–Fri 10am–4pm, Thurs until 6pm. Most airports and ferry terminals have late-opening exchange facilities, and automatic cash machines are everywhere.

Communications

Most **post offices** are open Mon–Fri 9.30am–5pm, Sat 9am–noon, with reduced hours in smaller communities. You can buy stamps either there or from most newsagents; mail to other parts of Europe under 20g costs 4.50kr and to the rest of the world 5.50kr. Danish **public telephones** come in two forms. Coin-operated ones are red and require a minimum of 2 x 1kr for a local call (the machines irritatingly swallow one of the coins if the number is engaged), and 5kr to go international; plastic for the blue card phones comes in denominations of 30kr,

50kr and 100kr and works out a little cheaper. One thing to remember when dialling Danish numbers is always to use the area code. Danish directory enquiries (10kr) is on ☎118, international directory enquiries (also 10kr) on ☎113, with almost all operators speaking English.

Internet access is available for free at most libraries and some tourist offices. Alternatively some sleep-ins will offer access for 25–35kr/hr, and Internet cafés can be found in most towns.

Getting around

Despite being an island country, Denmark is a swift and easy place in which to travel. All types of public transport – trains, buses and ferries – are punctual and efficient, and the timetables are well integrated.

■ Trains, buses and ferries

Trains are easily the best way to get about. Danske Statsbaner (DSB; ☎70.13.14.15, *www.dsb.dk*) – Danish State Railways – run an exhaustive and reliable network. Train types range from the large intercity expresses (*ICs*) to smaller local trains (*regionaltog*). **Tickets** should be bought in advance from the station, and fares are calculated on a zonal system: Copenhagen to Århus – probably the longest single trip you'll make – costs 275kr including a 15kr seat reservation, and your train ticket will get you around on the local buses in the departure and arrival town of your journey. Buying a return offers no savings over two singles. InterRail and Eurail passes are valid on all DSB trains, as is the **ScanRail pass**, which costs £129/US$204 (£97/$153 for under-26s) for five days of travel within two months; £172/$310 (£129/$233) for ten days within two months; and £199/$360 (£150/$270) for 21 consecutive days. This gives you unlimited travel in the four main Scandinavian countries, plus large discounts on many ferry crossings and bus journeys; tickets can be bought in Scandinavia, but this is more expensive and limits you to just three days' travel in the country you buy it in, so it's best to get one before you go. The newly opened Øresund Link means train travel between Denmark and Sweden is now possible.

DSB's *Køreplan* (free) details all train, bus and ferry services, including the S-train system in Copenhagen and all private services; smaller timetables detailing specific routes are available free at tourist offices and station booking counters.

There are a few out-of-the-way regions trains fail to penetrate, and these can easily be crossed by **buses**, which often run in conjunction with the trains, some operated privately, some by DSB – on which railcards are valid. Much of Funen and the northeast of Jutland is barely touched by trains, and you can save several hours by taking the bus. **Abildskous Rutebiler** (☎70.21.08.88, *www.abildskou.dk*) run from Århus to Copenhagen (200kr) and connections to the airport (20kr), and **Thinggaard Rutebiler** (☎70.10.00.30) provide a service from Ålborg to Copenhagen (220kr), Nykøbing to Copenhagen (255kr) and Frederikshavn to Esbjerg (230kr). The quickest and most convenient way to travel by bus around Jutland is to take one of the X-busser. You can get information about routes and destinations by calling their office (☎98.90.09.00, *www.xbus.dk*) – ask for a timetable (*køreplan*), which the staff will be happy to send you free of charge.

Ferries link all the Danish islands, and where applicable train and bus fares include the cost of crossings (although you can also pay at the terminal and walk on); the smaller ferry crossings normally cost 30–60kr for foot passengers.

■ Driving and hitching

Given the excellence of the Danish public transport system, the size of the country and the comparatively high price of petrol, **driving** isn't really economical unless you're travelling in a group. Danes drive on the right, and there's a speed limit in towns of 50kph, 80kph in open country and 110kph on motorways – speed traps lead to hefty fines. Like the other Scandinavian countries, dipped headlights have to be used during daylight hours. There are random breath tests, and the penalties for drunk driving are severe. When parking unmetered in a town, a parking-time disc must be displayed; you'll be able to get one from a tourist office, police station or bank. The national motoring organization, Forenede Danske Motorejere, operates a breakdown service Mon–Fri 9am–5pm, Sat 10am–1pm (☎45.88.00.25) for AA members; if you find yourself stranded outside those hours or you are not an AA member Dansk Autohjælp (☎70.10.80.90) and Falck (☎44.92.22.22) can be summoned from call boxes by the road – although a standard call-out fee will be charged. **Car rental** in Denmark starts at around 3000kr a week for a small hatchback with unlimited mileage (you'll need your driving licence). **Hitching** is illegal on motorways but fairly easy elsewhere.

■ Cycling

Cycling is the best way to appreciate Denmark's mostly flat landscape. Most country roads have sparse vehicle traffic and all large towns have cycle tracks. Bikes can be **rented** at nearly all youth hostels, bike shops and tourist offices and some train stations from 40kr per day, 200–225kr per week, although there's often a 200–500kr deposit. IC and certain regional trains (marked on timetables) won't accept bikes; on those that do, you'll have to pay according to the zonal system used to calculate passenger tickets – 50kr to take your bike from Copenhagen to Århus with 15kr on top if you want to reserve a space in advance.

Accommodation

While much less costly than it can be in other Scandinavian countries, **accommodation** is still going to be your major daily expense in Denmark. Hotels, however, are by no means off-limits if you are prepared to seek out the better offers, and both the youth hostels and campsites that you'll come across are plentiful and of a uniformly high standard.

■ Hotels and private rooms

Most Danish **hotel** rooms include phone, TV and bathroom, for which you'll pay around 700kr for a double, although in most large towns you'll also find hotels offering rooms without bathrooms for as little as 450kr for a double. One advantage of staying in most hotels is the inclusive all-you-can-eat breakfast – so large you won't need to buy lunch. Danish tourist offices overseas can provide a free list of hotels throughout the country, though much more accurate and extensive information can be found at local tourist offices; it's a good idea to book in advance, especially in peak season. Tourist offices can also supply details of **private rooms** in someone's home, for which you should reckon on paying 400–500kr a double. Alternatively, staying on farms (*Bondegårdsferie*) is becoming increasingly popular in Denmark, with many offering accommodation and the chance to watch a farm at work. Information and

catalogues can be obtained from Ferie på Landet, Ceresvej 2, 8410 Rønde (☎86.37.39.00, *www.bondegaardsferie.dk*).

■ Hostels and sleep-ins

Hostels are the cheapest option under a roof. Every town has one, they're much less pricey than hotels and they have a high degree of comfort, most offering a choice of private rooms, often with toilets and showers, or dorm accommodation; nearly all have cooking facilities. Rates are around 100kr per person for a dorm bed; non-HI members pay an extra 30kr a night. An **IYHF card** will cost you 160kr. It's rare for hostels other than those in major towns or ferry ports to be full, but during the summer it's still wise to phone ahead. If you're doing a lot of hostelling, it's worth contacting Danhostel Danmarks Vandrerhjem, Vesterbrogade 39, 1620 Copenhagen V (☎33.31.36.12, *www.danhostel.dk*), for their free hostel guide.

Sometimes cheaper still, and occasionally free, are **sleep-ins**, usually open in the main towns during the summer (June–Aug). You need your own sleeping bag, sometimes only one night's stay is permitted and there may be an age restriction. Sleep-ins come and go, however; check the current situation at a tourist office.

■ Campsites and cabins

If you don't have an International Camping Card from a camping organization at home, you'll need to get hold of a Camping Card Scandinavia to **camp** in Denmark, which costs 75kr for both individuals and families and can be bought from any campsite and is valid on all official sites in Scandinavia until the year's end. A Transit Pass can be used for a single overnight stay and costs 20kr per person. Campsites are virtually everywhere. All sites open through the three summer months, many from April to September, while a few stay open all year. There's a rigid grading system: one-star sites have drinking water and toilets; two-stars have, in addition, showers, laundry and a food shop within a kilometre; three-stars, by far the majority, have all the above plus a TV-room, shop, cafeteria, etc. Prices vary only slightly, three-stars charging 52–62kr per person, others a few kroner less.

Many sites also have **cabin accommodation**, usually with cooking facilities, for around 2500kr–4000kr for a six-berth affair, although these are often booked up in summer. Any tourist office will give you a free leaflet listing all the sites. **Camping rough** without permission is illegal, and an on-the-spot fine may be imposed.

Food and drink

There are plenty of ways to eat affordably and healthily in Denmark, and with plenty of variety, too. Much the same applies to drink: the only Scandinavian country free of social drinking taboos, Denmark is an imbiber's delight – both for its choice of tipples and the number of places they can be sampled.

■ Food

Traditional Danish **food** centres on meat and fish, served with potatoes and another, usually boiled, vegetable. **Breakfast** (*morgenmad*) can be the tastiest Danish meal, and almost all hotels offer a sumptuous breakfast as a matter of course, as do youth hostels: a table laden with cereals, bread, cheese, boiled eggs, fruit juice, milk, coffee and tea for around 40kr. Breakfast elsewhere is less substantial, although **brunch**, served from 11am until early afternoon, is a filling option for late starters consisting of variations of American, English, French or Australian breakfasts for 40–70kr. Later in the day, a tight budget may leave you dependent on self-catering. As for **snacks**, you can buy *smørrebrød* – open sandwiches heaped with meat, fish or cheese, and assorted trimmings – for 15-45kr from special shops, at least one of which will be open until 10pm. There are also fast-food stands (*pølsevogn*) in all main streets and at train stations, serving various hot sausages (*pølser*), toasted sandwiches (*parisertoast*) and chips (*pommes frites*). If you just want a cup of coffee or tea, cafés serve both; help it down with a Danish pastry (*wienerbrød*), tastier and much less sweet than the imitations sold elsewhere.

You can find an excellent-value **lunch** (*frokost*) simply by walking around at lunchtime and choosing from the signs chalked up outside a café, restaurant or bodega (a bar which sells no-frills food). You'll often see the word *tilbud*, which refers to the "special" priced dish, or *dagens ret*, "dish of the day" – a plate of chilli con carne or lasagne for around 50kr. A three-course set lunch will cost you about 80–100kr and open buffets where you can help yourself to as much as you like will set you back 60–80kr. You can also usually get a choice of three or four *smørrebrød* for about 75kr. Elsewhere, the American burger franchises are commonplace, as are pizzerias, many of which offer special deals such as all-you-can-eat-salad with a basic pizza for 50kr. You can also get a filling but ordinary self-service meat, fish or omelette lunch in a supermarket cafeteria for 50–90kr.

Dinner (*aftensmad*) presents as much choice as does lunch, but the cost is likely to be much higher, although many youth hostels serve filling evening meals for 50–60kr. For 70–90kr you can fill up in an **ethnic restaurant**, most commonly Chinese and Middle Eastern, many of which, besides à la carte dishes, have a help-yourself table. Sadly, the same **Danish restaurants** that are promising for lunch turn into expense-account affairs at night although many still will have good-value buffets. If you plan to save money by eating in, head for Netto supermarkets, where the food and drink is cheap and of excellent quality.

■ Drink

Although you can buy booze much more cheaply from supermarkets, the most sociable places to drink are pubs and cafés, where the emphasis is on beer. There are also bars and bodegas, in which, as a very general rule, the mood tends to favour wines and spirits and the customers are a bit older. The cheapest beer is draught beer (*Fadøl*), half a litre of which costs 30–45kr. Draught is a touch weaker than bottled beer, which costs 20–30kr for a third of a litre, and is a great deal less potent than the export beers (*Guldøl* or *Eksport-Øl*) costing 25–35kr a bottle. The most common brands are Carlsberg and Tuborg; Lys Pilsner is a very low alcohol lager, more like a soft drink. Most international wines and spirits are widely available, a shot of the hard stuff costing 20–30kr in a bar, a glass of wine upwards of 20kr. You should also investigate the many varieties of the schnapps-like Akvavit, which Danes consume as eagerly as beer; a tasty relative is the hot and strong Gammel Dansk Bitter Dram – Akvavit-based but made with bitters and drunk occasionally at breakfast time.

Opening hours and holidays

Standard shopping hours are Mon–Fri 9.30/ 10am–5.30/7pm, Sat 9/9.30am–2/4pm. All shops and banks are closed, and public transport and many museums run to Sunday schedules on the following days: Jan 1; Maundy Thursday; Good Friday; Easter Day; Easter Monday; Prayer Day (fourth Friday after Easter); Ascension (around mid-May); Whit Sunday; Whit Monday; Constitution Day (June 5); Dec 24 (afternoon only); Dec 25 and Dec 26. On International Workers' Day, which falls on May 1, many offices and shops close at noon.

Emergencies

You're likely to have little cause to trouble the Danish **police**, as street crime and hassle is minimal in Denmark – but if you do, you'll find them helpful and almost certainly able to speak English. For prescriptions, **doctors'** consultations and dental work – but not hospital visits – you have to pay on the spot, but to get a full refund, take your receipt, E111 and passport to the local health office.

Emergency Numbers

All emergencies ☎112.

COPENHAGEN AND AROUND

COPENHAGEN, as any Dane will tell you, is no introduction to Denmark; indeed, a greater contrast with the sleepy provincialism of the rest of the country would be hard to find. Despite that, the city completely dominates Denmark: it is the seat of all the nation's institutions – politics, finance and the arts. Copenhagen is also easily Scandinavia's most affordable capital, and one of Europe's most user-friendly cities, welcoming and fairly small, with a compact, strollable centre largely given over to pedestrians. In summer, there's a varied range of lively street entertainment, while at night there's a plethora of cosy bars and an intimate club and live-music network that can hardly be bettered. For daytime sights the city has first-rate galleries housing collections of Danish and international art, as well as a worthy batch of smaller museums.

There was no more than a tiny fishing settlement here until the twelfth century, when Bishop Absalon oversaw the building of a castle on the site of the present Christiansborg. The settlement's prosperity grew after Erik of Pomerania granted special privileges and imposed the Sound Toll on vessels passing through the Øresund, then under Danish control, which gave the expanding city tidy profits and enabled a self-confident trading centre to flourish. Following the demise of the Hanseatic ports, the city became the Baltic's principal harbour, earning the name København ("merchant's port"), and in 1443 it was made the Danish capital. A century later, Christian IV began the building programme that was the basis of the modern city: up went Rosenborg Slot, Børsen, Rundetårn, and the districts of Nyboder and Christianshavn; and in 1669, Frederik III graced the city with its first royal palace, Amalienborg, for his queen, Sophie Amalie.

Arrival and information

However you get to Copenhagen you'll find yourself within easy reach of the centre. Trains pull into the **Central Station**, near Vesterbrogade, and **long-distance buses** from other parts of Denmark stop at the Central Station or a short bus or S-train ride from the centre: buses from Århus stop at Valby; from Aalborg at the Central Station; and those from Hanstholm on Hans Knudsens Plads. **Ferries** and catamarans from Norway and Sweden dock close to Nyhavn, a few minutes' walk from the inner city. **Planes** use Kastrup Airport, 8km from the city, which is connected with the Central Station in Copenhagen by the Øresund Link train (every 20min 4.30am–12.30am; journey time 13min; 19kr).

Across the road from the Central Station is the **tourist office** at Bernstorffsgade 1 (May–Aug Mon–Sat 10am–8pm, July & Aug also Sun 11am–6pm; rest of year Mon–Fri 10am–4.30pm, Sat 10am–1pm; ☎33.11.13.25, *www.visitcopenhagen.dk*), where you can pick up maps, general information and accommodation reservations in hotels and hostels (booking fee 25kr for camping and hostels, 50kr for hotels). You can also buy a **Copenhagen Card** here, valid for the entire metropolitan transport system (which includes much of eastern Zealand) and giving entry to virtually every museum in the area. A 24-hour card costs 175kr, those for 48 hours and 72 hours cost 295kr and 395kr respectively. Cards are also sold in other tourist offices, hotels and travel agents and at the train station.

Far better for youth and budget-oriented help is **Use-It**, centrally placed in the Huset complex at Rådhusstræde 13 (mid-June to mid-Sept daily 9am–7pm; rest of year Mon–Wed 11am–4pm, Thurs 11am–6pm, Fri 11am–2pm; ☎33.73.06.20, *www.useit.dk*). It provides a wide range of help for travellers, including poste restante and email services, accommodation and entertainment information, luggage storage facilities and a very useful free magazine called *Playtime*. The staff fall over themselves to help you find a room in the busy summer period and, if you are willing to queue, use of the Internet is free.

City transport

An integrated network of **buses** and electric **S-trains** (S-tog) covers a zonal system over the whole of Copenhagen and the surrounding areas between 5am and 1am, after which a night bus (Natbus) system comes into operation; route maps can be picked up free of charge from stations. You can use InterRail or Eurail cards on the S-trains, but otherwise the best option after a Copenhagen Card (see above) or the *24-timer* ticket (75kr) – which covers the same transportation area but without admission to museums – is a two- (85kr) or three-zone (115kr) *Klippekort*, which has ten stamps you cancel individually; one stamp gives unlimited transfers within one hour in two or three zones respectively. For a single journey of less than an hour, use a *Billet* (13kr), valid for unlimited transfers within two zones in that time. *Billets* and *24-timers* can be bought on board buses or at train stations, *Klippekort* only at stations and HT Kortsalg kiosks; they should be stamped when boarding the bus or in machines on station platforms. A passenger without a valid ticket faces an instant fine of 500kr. The basic **taxi** fare is 22kr plus 10kr per kilometre (11kr after 3pm and at weekends) – only worthwhile if several people are sharing. Under the **City Bike scheme** (summer only) you can borrow bikes from racks spread throughout the city for a 20kr deposit which is returned when the bike is locked back into any other city rack after use.

Accommodation

Accommodation is not as easy to come by in Copenhagen as it used to be, especially if you're going to be arriving late, or during July and August, in which case it's essential to book in advance. Most of the cheaper **hotels** are just outside the main centre, around Istedgade, a slightly seedy area on the far side of the train station, while there is also a good range of mid-priced hotels around Nyhavn, on the opposite side of the Indre By. Enquire at the tourist office early in the day and you may get a double room for as little as 450kr; **private rooms**, most of which are in the inner suburbs, are also mainly within this price range. Copenhagen has a great, though less central, selection of **hostel accommodation**, and space is only likely to be a problem in the peak summer months, when you should phone ahead or turn up as early as possible to be sure of a place. Breakfast is not included in the prices given unless otherwise stated.

Hostels and sleep-ins

Bellahøj Vandrehjem, Herbergsvejen 8, Brønshøj (☎38.28.97.15, *www.danhostel.dk/bellahoej*). IYHF hostel with large dorms, but more cosy than its rivals, and just fifteen minutes from the city centre on buses #2 and #11. No curfew. Open from March to mid-Jan. ②.

City Public Hostel, Absalonsgade 8, Vesterbro (☎32.31.20.70). Noisy 60-bed dormitory on the lower floor, and less crowded conditions on other levels. Handily ten minutes' walk from the train station. Buses #6 and #16 stop close by. No curfew. Open May–Aug. ③ incl. breakfast.

Copenhagen Hostel, Vejlands allé 200, Amager (☎32.52.29.08, *www.danhostel.dk/copenhagen*). IYHF hostel with fairly frugal 2- and 5-bed rooms. Bus #46 (daytime only), or take the E or A line S-train to Sjælør, then a #100S bus towards Sundbyvester Plads; in all a 30–60min journey. No curfew. Open mid-Jan to Nov. ②.

ACCOMMODATION PRICE CODES

Throughout this guide, accommodation is coded on a scale of ① to ⑨, the code indicating the lowest price per person per night you could expect to pay in each establishment in high season. With hostels this is the nightly rate per person; with hotels, the price is arrived at by dividing the cost of the cheapest double room by two. The prices indicated by the codes are as follows:

① under £5/$8 (€9)
② £5–10/$8–16 (€9–18)
③ £10–15/$16–24 (€18–27)
④ £15–20/$24–32 (€27–36)
⑤ £20–25/$32–40 (€36–45)
⑥ £25–30/$40–48 (€45–54)
⑦ £30–35/$48–56 (€54–63)
⑧ £35–40/$56–64 (€63–72)
⑨ £40/$64 (€72) and over

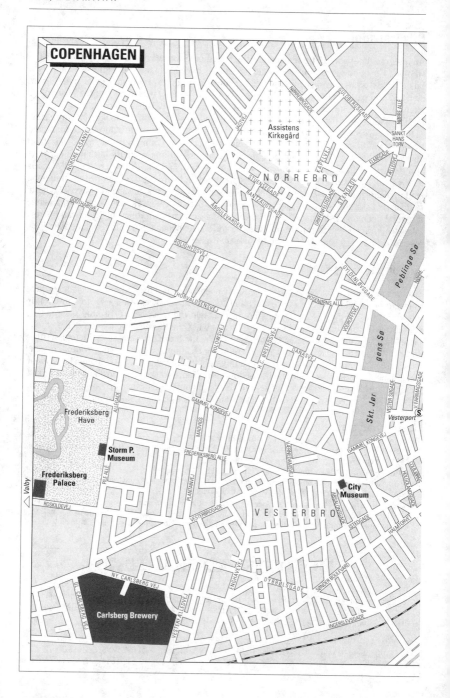

COPENHAGEN

Assistens
Kirkegård

NØRREBRO

Peblinge Sø

gens Sø

Skt. Jør

Vesterport

Frederiksberg
Have

Storm P.
Museum

Frederiksberg
Palace

City
Museum

VESTERBRO

Carlsberg Brewery

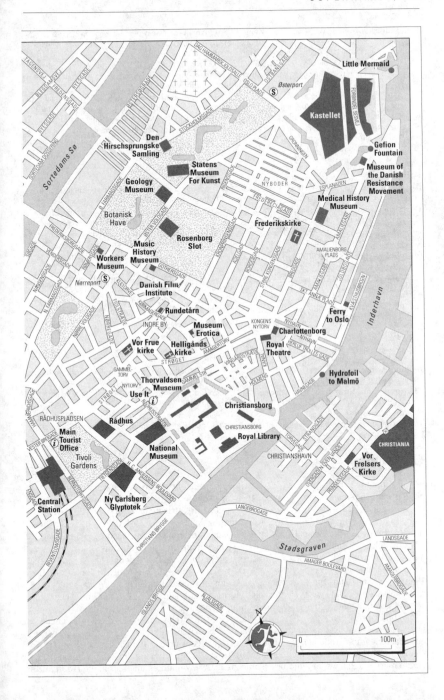

Hotel Jørgensens, Rømersgade 11 (☎33.13.81.86). North of Nørreport station on Isreals Plads. Predominantly dorm accommodation in 6-, 9- and 12-bed rooms, with a few cheap, newly decorated doubles. Popular with gay travellers. Open all year. ② incl. breakfast.

Sleep-in-Fact, Valdemarsgade 14 (☎33.79.67.79, *www.sleep-in-fact.dk*). In the heart of Vesterbro, Sleep-in-fact is a sports centre out of season and and has all sorts of sport facilities for hire. Fifteen minutes' walk from the Central Station or take bus #6. Open mid-June to mid-Aug. ②.

Sleep in Heaven, Struensegade 7, Nørrebro (☎35.35.46.48, *www.sleepinheaven.com*). Two vast halls, the largest with 76 beds divided into 4-bed and 8-bed compartments. Nice atmosphere, with young staff and sporadic free gigs. Ten minutes from the centre by bus #8, #12 or #13. No curfew. Open mid-Feb to Dec. ②.

YWCA/Interpoint, Valdemarsgade 15, Vesterbro (☎33.31.15.74). 4-, 6- and 10-bed rooms. Fifteen minutes' walk from Central Station or take bus #3, #6 or #16. Open July to mid-Aug; reception open only 8–11.30am, 3.30–5.30pm and 8pm–12.30am. ②.

Hotels

Absalon Hotel, Helgolandsgade 15–19 (☎33.24.22.11, *www.absalon-hotel.dk*). Very large family-run hotel, near the Central Station. Vast range of rooms to suit all budgets. ⑤/⑥/⑦.

Bertrams Hotel, Vesterbrogade 107a (☎33.25.04.05). Relaxed and cosy, modelled on Agatha Christie's *Bertrams* in London, a quiet haven in the lively area of Vesterbro. Fairly large rooms, some self-contained. ⑤.

Hotel Cab Inn, Vodroffsvej 55, Frederiksberg (☎35.36.11.11, *www.cab-inn.dk*). Inspired by the Oslo ferry, 200 small self-contained cabins with everything you need folded away. ⑥.

Missionhotellet Nebo, Istedgade 6 (☎33.21.12.17, *www.nebo.dk*). Small, friendly, and one of the best deals in the tame red light area of the city. ⑤.

Saga Hotel, Colbjørnsensgade 18–20 (☎33.24.49.44). Cheap, central hotel, a stone's throw from Central Station (head out the back exit of the station). On the edge of the red light district. ④.

71 Nyhavn Hotel, Nyhavn 71 (☎33.43.62.00, *www.71nyhavnhotelcopenhagen.dk*). Beautifully restored woodbeamed warehouse with small but immaculate rooms, close to trendy Nyhavn. ⑨.

Campsites

Absalon, Korsdalsvej 132, Rødovre (☎36.41.06.00). Reasonable site about 9km southwest of the city and open all year. S-train line B to Brøndbyøster, then a fifteen-minute walk or bus #550S.

Bellahøj Camping, Hvidkildevej 66 (☎38.10.11.50), near the Bellahøj hostel. Central but grim, with long queues for the showers. Bus #11 or S-train line F or M to Fuglebakken. June–Aug.

Charlottenlund Strandpark, Strandvejen 144, Charlottenlund (☎39.62.36.88). Beautifully situated at Charlottenlund Beach. Reached by bus #6. Mid-May to mid-Sept.

Nærum Camping, on Ravnebakken (☎45.80.19.57). A long way out from the centre but very pleasant. Take an S-train to Jægersborg (line A and B), then private train (InterRail and Eurail not valid; Copenhagen Card valid) to Nærum. April–Sept.

The City

Seeing Copenhagen is a doddle. Most of what you're likely to want to see can be found in the city's relatively small centre, between the long scythe of the harbour and a semicircular series of lakes. **Indre By** forms the city's inner core, an intricate maze of streets, squares and alleys. The main way into Indre By is from the buzzing open space of Rådhuspladsen, where the **Rådhus** (open to the public Mon–Fri 10am–3pm, guided tours Mon–Fri 3pm, Sat 10 &11am; 30kr) has an elegant main hall that retains many of its original fin-de-siècle features and a **bell tower** (tours June–Sept Mon–Fri 10am, noon & 2pm, Sat noon; Oct–May Mon–Sat noon; 20kr) that gives wonderful views over the city. **Jens Olsen's World Clock** (Mon–Fri 10am–4pm, Sat 10am–1pm; 10kr), in a room close to the entrance, took 27 years to perfect and contains a 570,000-year calendar plotting moon and sun eclipses, solar time, local time and various planetary orbits – all with astounding accuracy.

Beyond here, **Strøget** leads into the heart of the city, a pedestrianized street lined by pricey stores and fast-food dives, whose appeal is in the walkers, roller-skaters and street entertainers who parade along it. The liveliest part is around Gammeltorv and Nytorv, two squares ("old" and "new") on either side of Strøget, where there's a morning fruit and vegetable market and jewellery and bric-a-brac stalls. A few minutes further on, the **Helligånds**

Kirke (daily noon–4pm) is one of the oldest churches in the city, founded in the fourteenth century and largely rebuilt from 1728 onwards. Its summer café and the art shows and exhibitions held inside provide a good excuse for a peek at the church's vaulted ceiling and slender granite columns. At the end of Strøget, **Kongens Nytorv** is the city's largest square, with an equestrian statue of its creator, Christian V, in the centre and a couple of grandly ageing structures around two of its shallow angles, most notably **Charlottenborg** – finished in 1683, at the same time as the square itself, for a son of Frederik III. Since 1754 it has been the home of the **Royal Academy of Art**, which uses some of the spacious rooms for decidedly eclectic art exhibitions.

There's more to see among the tangle of buildings and streets **west of Strøget**, not least the old university area, sometimes called the Latin Quarter, where the **Vor Frue Kirke** (Daily 8am–5pm, Fri–Sun also 8pm–0.30am), Copenhagen's cathedral, dates from 1829. The weighty figure of Christ behind the altar and the solemn statues of the Apostles, some crafted by Bertel Thorvaldsen, others by his pupils, merit a quick call. Northeast, the **Rundetårn** (June–Aug Mon–Sat 10am–8pm, Sun noon–8pm; Sept–May Mon–Sat 10am–5pm, Sun noon–5pm; 15kr), whose summit is reached by a spiral ramp, was built by Christian IV as an observatory. Close by, the **Music History Museum**, just off Kultorvet at Åbenrå 30 (May–Sept Mon–Wed & Fri–Sun 1–3.50pm; Oct–April Mon, Wed, Sat & Sun 1–3.50pm; 30kr) holds an impressive quantity of musical instruments and sound-making devices, spanning the globe and the last thousand years. Many musical recordings can be listened to through headphones, and guided tours take place every Wednesday at 11am. The **Museum Erotica** at Købmagergarde 24 (May–Sept daily 10am–11pm; Oct–April Mon–Fri & Sun 11am–8pm, Sat 10am–10pm; 69kr) has been moved from its former home in the red-light district and exhibits a mixture of titillating historical photos, sex toys and waxworks. Over Nørre Voldgade, the **Workers Museum** at Rømersgade 22 (July–Oct daily 10am–4pm; rest of year Tues–Sun 10am–4pm; 50kr) is an engrossing guide to working-class life in Copenhagen from the Thirties to the Fifties using reconstructions and authentic period materials.

Nørrebro, northwest of the train station, has shed its crime-related reputation and is now a lively, young area that buzzes right through the night. Directly behind the station is **Vesterbro**, the city's slightly seedy though unthreatening red light district.

North of Gothersgade

Gothersgade, the road marking the northern perimeter of Indre By, is home to the **Danish Film Institute, Film Museum and Cinematek** (Tues–Fri 9.30am–midnight, Sat & Sun 1.30–midnight; *www.cinemateket.dk*; free). It houses a cinema, a section with free showings of children's films, documentaries and short films, and a museum which displays cameras, props and other remnants of an early film industry that before Hollywood and the talkies was among the world's best. There's a profound change of mood once you cross Gothersgade: the congenial alleys of the old city give way to long, broad streets and proud, aristocratic structures. Running from Kongens Nytorv, a slender canal divides the two sides of **Nyhavn**, picturesquely lined by eighteenth-century houses – now bars and cafés – that were until recently frequented by docked sailors; they earned the area a racy reputation, but it's now in the advanced stages of gentrification and is *the* place to be seen enjoying a beer in the summer season. Just north, the cobbled Amalienborg Plads focuses on a statue of Frederik V flanked by four identical Rococo palaces. Two serve as royal residences, and there's a changing of the guard each day at noon when the monarch is at home. Between the square and the harbour are the lavish gardens of Amaliehaven, while in the opposite direction the great marble dome of **Frederikskirke**, also known as "Marmorkirken", meaning marble church (Mon–Sat 10.30am–4.30pm, Wed until 6pm, Sun noon–4.30pm), was modelled on St Peter's in Rome. It was begun in 1749 but because of its enormous cost remained unfinished until a century and a half later. The reward of joining a guided tour (mid-June to Aug Mon–Fri 1pm & 3pm; rest of the year Sat & Sun 1pm & 3pm; 20kr) is the chance to climb to the whispering gallery and step out onto the rim of the dome itself. Further along Bredgade, a German armoured car commandeered by Danes to bring news of the Nazi surrender marks the entrance to the **Museum of the Danish Resistance Movement** (Frihedsmuseet; May to mid-Sept Tues–Sat 10am–4pm, Sun 10am–5pm; rest of year Tues–Sat 11am–3pm, Sun 11am–4pm; 30kr, free on Wed).

The road behind the museum crosses into the grounds of the **Kastellet** (daily 6am–sunset; free), a fortress built by Christian IV and expanded by his successors through the seventeenth century. It's now occupied by the Danish army and closed to the public, but on a nearby corner the **Little Mermaid** has, since its unveiling in 1913, been one of the city's most massive tourist targets, a bronze statue of a Hans Christian Andersen character, sculpted by Edvard Erichsen and paid for by the founder of the Carlsberg brewery. It's worth enduring the crowds for the more spectacular **Gefion Fountain**, a short walk to the south, which shows the goddess Gefion with her four sons, whom she's turned into oxen having been promised, in return, as much land as she can plough in a single night.

Still north of Gothersgade, but away from the harbour across Store Kongensgade, lies **Nyboder**, a curious area of narrow streets lined with rows of compact yellow dwellings, originally built by Christian IV to encourage his sailors to live in the city. The area declined into a slum, but a recent overhaul has made it increasingly sought after. The oldest (and cutest) houses can be found along Skt. Pauls Gade; Baron Bolton's Court, tucked behind the corner of Gothersgade and Store Kongensgade, is a revamped precinct of eighteenth-century town houses, holding shops and restaurants and hosting live jazz in summer. Across Sølvgade from Nyboder is the main entrance to **Rosenborg Slot** (May–June daily 10am–4pm; July–Sept daily 10am–5pm, Oct daily 11am–3pm; Nov–April Tues–Sun 11am–2pm; 50kr). This Dutch-Renaissance-style palace served as the main residence of Christian IV and, until the end of the nineteenth century, of the monarchs who succeeded him. The main building displays the rooms and furnishings used by the regal occupants, although the highlight is the downstairs treasury, which displays the crown jewels and rich accessories worn by Christian IV. Adjacent to Rosenborg Slot is **Kongens Have**, the city's oldest public park and a popular place for picnics, while on the west side is the **Botanical Garden** (Botanisk Have; summer daily 8.30am–6pm; winter Tues–Sun 8.30am–4pm; free).

The neighbouring **Statens Museum for Kunst** (State Museum of Fine Arts; Tues & Thurs–Sun 10am–5pm, Wed 10am–8pm; *www.smk.dk*; 40kr, Wed free to view the permanent collection), was recently extended with a modern flavour that complements the grand old building and almost doubles its capacity. The mammoth collection of art (*kunst*) embraces some minor Picassos and more major works by Matisse and Braque, Cranach, El Greco, Titian, Rubens, Poussin and Claude Lorrain – although it's Emil Nolde, with his grotesque pieces showing bloated ravens, hunched figures and manic children, who manages to steal the show. The new section houses mostly contemporary Danish art. The Skagen artists (see p.356), known for their interesting use of light, are amongst a nearby collection of twentieth-century Danish art across the park, behind the museum, at **Den Hirschsprungske Samling** on Stockholmsgade (Mon & Thurs–Sun 11am–4pm, Wed 11am–9pm; *www.hirschsprung.dk*; 25kr, free on Wed).

Christiansborg

Christiansborg sits on the island of Slotsholmen, tenuously connected to Indre By by several short bridges. It was here, in the twelfth century, that Bishop Absalon built the castle that instigated the city. The drab royal palace completed in 1916 that now occupies the site is today primarily given over to government offices and the state parliament or **Folketinget** (guided tours in English at 2pm: July–mid-Aug daily, mid-Aug to Sept closed Sat, rest of the year Sun only; free). Close to the bus stop on Christiansborg Slotsplads is the doorway to the **Ruins under Christiansborg** (May–Sept daily 9.30am–3.30pm; Oct–April Tues, Thurs, Sat & Sun 9.30am–3.30pm; 20kr), where a staircase leads down to the remains of Absalon's original building; it's surprisingly absorbing, the mood enhanced by the semi-darkness and lack of external noise. **The Royal Reception Rooms** (Guided tours in English: May–Sept daily at 11am & 3pm, rest of the year Tues, Thurs, Sat & Sun at 11am & 3pm; 40kr), in the palace's north wing, are used by the royal family to entertain important visitors and worth a peek. In and around Christiansborg's courtyard there are a number of other, less captivating museums, including the **Royal Stables** (May–Sept Fri–Sun 2–4pm; Oct–April Sat & Sun 2–4pm; 20kr); a **Theatre Museum** (Wed 2–4pm, Sat & Sun noon–4pm; 20kr), housed in what was the eighteenth-century Court Theatre; and an **Armoury Museum** (Tues–Sun noon–4pm; 30kr).

On the far side of Slotsholmen, the **Thorvaldsens Museum** (Tues–Sun 10am–5pm; 20kr, Wed free) is the home of an enormous collection of work and memorabilia (and the body) of Denmark's most famous sculptor, who lived from 1770 to 1844. The labels of the great, hulking statues read like a roll call of the famous and infamous: Vulcan, Adonis, Gutenberg, Pius VII and Maximilian; and the Christ Hall contains the huge casts of the Christ and Apostles statues that can be seen in Vor Frue Kirke. There's another major collection a short walk away over the Slotsholmen moat, in the **National Museum** (Tues–Sun 10am–5pm; *www.natmus.dk*; 40kr, Wed free), which has excellent displays on Denmark's prehistory and Viking days – jewellery, sacrificial gifts, bones and even bodies, all remarkably well preserved by Danish peat bogs.

Christianshavn and Christiania

From Christiansborg, a bridge crosses to **Christianshavn**, built by Christian IV as an autonomous new town in the early sixteenth century as housing for shipbuilding workers. It was given features more common to Dutch ports of the time, even down to a small canal, and in parts is more redolent of Amsterdam than Copenhagen. Reaching skywards on the other side of Torvegade is the blue-and-gold spire of **Vor Frelsers Kirke** (church: April–Oct daily 11am–4.30pm, rest of year daily 11am–3.30pm, free; tower: April–Oct only, 20kr), which, with its helter-skelter-like outside staircase, was added to the otherwise plain church in the mid-eighteenth century, instantly becoming one of the more recognizable features on the city's horizon.

A few streets from Vor Frelsers Kirke, **Christiania** is a former barracks area that was colonized by hippies after declaring itself a "**free city**" in 1971. A pseudo-Statue of Liberty greets visitors as they pass under the little arched entrance and head for the open hash market, where smoking is tolerated by the government. Bob Marley and John Lennon blare out from the bars and the area is awash with psychedelic painting. Christiania's population is currently around a thousand, but it swells in summer when curious tourists flood in to take in the scene, browse the market and perhaps rent a pony to ride around the beautiful lake. Residents ask visitors not to camp or point cameras directly at them. The craft shops and restaurants are fairly cheap, and nearly all are good, with a couple of innovative music and performance art venues. If you are hungry, head for *Morgenstedet*, a clean and friendly restaurant close to the market, with the option of outside seats (12pm–9pm; closed Tues). For information, call in to Galopperiet (Tues–Sun noon–5pm), to the right of the main entrance on Prinsessegade, which also has an interesting gallery. For the really keen, there are guided tours of the area during the summer which take in Pusherstreet (named after the open dealing and smoking of hashish that goes on there), but you have to book at least one day in advance (☎32.57.96.70, fax 32.57.60.05; 25kr per person, minimum 6 people per tour; 1.30hr).

Along Vesterbrogade

Hectic **Vesterbrogade** begins on the far side of Rådhuspladsen, and its first attraction is perhaps Copenhagen's most famous, the **Tivoli Gardens** (mid-June to mid-Aug Mon–Thurs & Sun 11am–midnight, Fri & Sat 11am–1am, mid-April to mid-June & mid-Aug to Sept Mon, Tues & Sun 11am–11pm, Wed & Thurs 11am–midnight, Fri & Sat 11am–1am; 45kr; 50kr if you take advantage of late opening until 1am), whose opening each year marks the beginning of summer. Throughout the season, the gardens feature fairground rides, fireworks, fountains, and a variety of nightly entertainment in the central arena, which can include every-thing from acrobats and jugglers to the mid-Atlantic tones of various fixed-grin crooners. It's rather overrated and expensive, but you can still have an enjoyable evening wandering among the revellers of all ages. On the other side of Tietgensgade, the **Ny Carlsberg Glyptotek** (Tues–Sun 10am–4pm; 30kr, free on Wed & Sun), is Copenhagen's finest gallery, with a stirring array of Greek, Roman and Egyptian art and artefacts, as well as what is reck-oned to be the biggest and best collection of Etruscan art outside Italy. There are, too, excel-lent examples of modern European art, including a complete collection of Degas casts, Manet's *Absinthe Drinker* and an antechamber with early work by Man Ray, some Chagall sketches and a Picasso plate.

In the narrow streets between Vesterbrogade and Istedgade, a few pornography shops remain as evidence of this increasingly respectable area's former role as Copenhagen's red-light district. At Vesterbrogade 59, the **City Museum** (May–Sept Mon & Wed–Sun 10am–4pm; Oct–April Mon & Wed–Sun 1–4pm; 20kr) has reconstructed ramshackle house exteriors and tradesmen's signs from early Copenhagen, a large room recording the form Christian IV gave the city, and a collection of memorabilia concerning the nineteenth-centu-ry Danish philosopher Søren Kierkegaard. Further along Vesterbrogade, down Pile Allé and along Gamle Carlsberg Vej (buses #6 and #18), the exhibition at **Carlsberg Brewery Visitors Center** (Tues–Sun 10am–4pm; free) is well worth seeing, if only for the free booze provided at the end.

Eating and drinking

Whatever you feel like **eating** you'll find a wider choice and lower prices in Copenhagen than in any other Scandinavian capital. In the city centre, the areas around Kultorvet and along Studiestræde are loaded with great places to eat. Farther afield, Nørrebro across Peblinge Søen draws the trendy set, and Vesterbrogade turns up a number of lower-key places, better the further you venture. An almost unchartable network of **cafés** and bars serving drinks and snacks covers Copenhagen. The best are in or close to Indre By, and it's no hardship to sam-ple several on the same night, though bear in mind that on Fridays and Saturdays you'll prob-ably need to queue.

If you're **self-catering**, there are numerous *smørrebrød* outlets – Smørrebrødsforretningen, on Sankt Peders Stræde 26, and Centrum Smørrebrød, Vesterbrogade 6C, are two of the most central. For more general food shopping Netto and Fakta are by far the cheapest supermar-kets. You'll find Netto at Nørre Voldgade 94, Nørregade 12 and Store Kongensgade 47, Fakta is on Havnegade 37, opposite the ferries to Sweden, and on Borgergade 27.

Snacks and fast food

Bang & Jensen, Istedgade 130. At the quieter end of Istedgade, a popular café that serves snacks daily until 6pm for up to 65kr, sandwiches start at 40kr.

Base Camp, Halvtolv bygningen 148, Holmen. Located in the old navy artillery hall on Holmen island off Christianshavn (take bus #8), this gigantic hip café/eatery/music venue offers fantastic all-you-can eat Sunday brunches for 80kr.

Café au Lait, Nørre Voldgade 27. Opposite the Nørreport S-train station, a pleasantly unflustered place for a coffee or snack. Also branches at Gothersgade 11, Vesterbrogade 16 and Værnedamsvej 16.

Café Sommersko, Kronprinsensgade 6. Off the Købmagergade pedestrian street. A popular café visited both for its food and drinks. The Sunday brunch is especially recommended.

Husets Café, Rådhusstræde 13. Located in the Huset complex, this is a popular sandwich spot; sandwich-es from 25kr and lunch buffet for 39kr. Open Mon–Fri.

Klaptræet, Kultorvet 11. Renowned for the largest and most filling sandwiches in town, from 41kr. Brunch, salads and soup of the day also on the menu.

Sebastopol, Sankt Hans Torv 2. Trendy brunch spot in the centre of the Nørrebro café quarter. Brunch (from 42kr) is served outdoors on the square.

Restaurants

Atlas Bar, Larsbjørnstræde 18. Global eco-restaurant/café serving tasty Asian and South American dishes. The salad platter at 80kr is good value.

Bali, Lille Kongen Nytorv 19. Indonesian restaurant that does a good rice *tafel* for around 170kr.

Den Grønne Kælder, Pilestræde 48. A simple tiled-floor vegetarian eatery with a very filling *grøn platte* for 65kr. Mon–Sat until 10pm.

Hackenbusch, Vesterbrogade 124. Colourful café/bar with an inventive blackboard menu. Dishes (always one vegetarian) from 70kr. Tuesdays bargain burgers for 25kr.

Morgenstedet, Langgade in Christiania. Generous, inexpensive portions. Vegetarian options. Smoking and alcohol prohibited. Closed Tues.

Nyhavns Færgekro, Nyhavn 5. Unpretentious and very tasty traditional food, available either from the lunchtime fish-laden open table or the à la carte restaurant upstairs.

Pasta Basta, Valkensdorfsgade 22. Help yourself from the nine cold pasta bowls for 69kr. Fri & Sat open until 5am.

Peder Oxe, Gråbrødretorv 11. Three hunks of *smørrebrød* for 78kr, at lunchtimes only. Also magnificent organic burgers for 89kr.

Sala Thai, Vesterbrogade 107. Thai food cooked in the authentic manner.

Shezan, Viktoriagarde 22. The first Pakistani restaurant in Copenhagen and still going strong.

Spiseloppen, Christiania. Award-winning restaurant with reasonable prices. Meals from 65kr.

Thai Esan, Lille Istedgade 7. Bargain Thai eating in this cramped but authentic restaurant.

Bars

Barcelona, Fælledvej 21. This swanky hangout is very much the place to be seen. Fri & Sat renamed *Bar'Cuda* and becomes a sweaty cavern of funk and soul that closes at 5am (free).

Café Ludvigsen, Sundevedsgade 2. Vesterbro's most popular pool bar, complete with jukebox and inexpensive beer.

Café Sommersko, Kronprinsensgade 6. Sizeable bar, crowded most nights. Free live music on Sun afternoons.

Dan Turell, Store Regnegade 3. Something of an institution with the artier student crowd and a fine place for a sociable tipple. Open 11–2am.

Hviids Vinstue, Kongens Nytorv 19. Old-fashioned bar with crowded rooms patrolled by uniformed waiters. Outdoor seating in the summer.

Krasnapolsky, Vestergade 10. The Danish avant-garde art hanging on the wall reflects the trend-setting reputation of this ultramodern watering hole. DJs Thurs, Fri & Sat. Tasty food too.

Kulkafeen, Teglgårdsstræde 5. Cosy multi-cultural café that gets going in the evening and has live music on Sat.

The Moose, Sværtegade 5. Tiny-looking bar that stretches back into a spacious room with pool tables. Special feature is the 9pm till 2am happy-hour which ensures a big happy crowd.

Peder Hvitfeldt, P. Hvitfeldtsstræde 15. Immensely popular spit-and-sawdust place. Come early if you want to sit down.

Universitetscaféen, Fiolstræde 2. A prime central location and long hours (until 5am).

Nightlife

The city is a pretty good place for **live music**. Major international names visit regularly, and there are always plenty of minor gigs in cafés and bars, often free early in the week. You can get the latest on who's playing where by reading *Neon Guiden*, or *Gaffa* (free from cafés, music and record shops). If you get a craving for the dance floor, you'll find clubs and discos much like those in any major city, busy between midnight and 5am. Dress codes are fairly easy-going; drink prices are seldom hiked-up and admission is fairly cheap at 30–60kr.

Live music, clubs and discos

Annabell's, Lille Kongensgade 16. Comparatively upmarket full-on disco. Brash young crowd at the weekend.

Copenhagen Jazz House, Niels Hemmingsensgade 10 (*www.jazzhouse*). Laid-back jazz concerts, followed by a jazz, funk and mainstream disco.

Distotek In, Nørregade 1. Cavernous disco playing mainstream hits. Thurs until 6am and Fri & Sat until 10am the following day.

Femøren and **Tiøren**, Amager. Two open-air rock concert venues from June to Aug on the beach at Amager. Get there by bus #12 or #13.

Huset i Magstræde, Rådhusstræde 13. In the same building as *Use-It* (see opposite) with regular live bands: Mon–Thurs Beebop, Fri & Sat old-fashioned danceable jazz.

Loppen, Bådsmandsstræde 43, Christiania. Regular rock, jazz and performance artists. Discos Fri & Sat after live music events.

Mojo, Løngangstræde 21 (*www.mojo.dk*). Renowned for its jazz and blues evenings – live music every night. Happy hour 8–10pm.

Pavillonen, Fælledparken, near Borgmester Jensens Allé (*www.pavillonen.dk*). Open-air venue serving barbecued food. Thurs–Sat Latin/jazz/rock concerts followed by a disco. May–Sept.

Park Café, Østerbrogade 79 (*www.parkcafe.dk*). Popular café/restaurant/music venue with mainstream disco and live music Thurs (free), Fri & Sat (50kr). Gets packed at weekends.

Pumpehuset, Studiestræde 52. A broad sweep of middle-strata rock, hip-hop and funk from Denmark and around the world about three times a month.

Rust, Guldbergsgade 8, Nørrebro (*www.rust.dk*). Huge complex catering for all: rock bands play on a main stage, and 3 dancefloors offer a range from Break Beat to Latin jazz. Closed Mon.

Stengade 30, Stengade 18 (*www.subcity.dk/stengade30*). Alternative scene with a mixed bag of live music and dance events. Popular hardcore metal venue.

Stereo Bar, Linnégade 16A. This once trendy bar has mellowed with age, becoming a sociable hangout with a dancefloor in the basement and open till 3am.

Vega, Enghavevej 40 (*www.vega.dk*). A large multi-levelled centre with DJ music at Lille Vega and concerts at Store Vega. Lille Vega: Thurs & Fri soul and funk, Sat hardcore techno.

Gay Copenhagen

Denmark has a very liberal attitude to gay men and lesbians. The age of consent is fifteen and for over a decade homosexuals have enjoyed the same inheritance rights as heterosexuals and can marry at registry offices, as long as one of the partners is Danish. Copenhagen itself has a lively **gay scene**, which includes a couple of hotels at which gays are especially welcome – *Copenhagen Rainbow*, Frederiksberggade 25C (☎33.14.10.20), and the *Hotel Windsor*, Frederiksborggade 30 (☎33.11.08.30) are exclusively gay. For **information**, contact the National Organization for Gay Men and Women, Teglgårdstræde 13 (☎33.13.19.48, *www.lbl.dk*) – which also has a bookshop, disco and café – or get hold of a copy of *Pan* magazine. As for gay bars, the *Cosy Bar*, Studiestræde 24, is frequented by gay men of all ages, while *Sebastian*, Hyskenstræde 10, draws a predominantly young trendy crowd. *Pan Club*, Knabrostræde 3, part of the largest gay centre in the country, has a great disco, Thursdays women only. *Masken*, Studiestræde 33, has a great bar and disco often featuring drag shows. Of primarily lesbian places *Kvindehuset*, Gothersgade 37 (☎33.14.28.04), has a café and a disco every third Friday of the month as well as other regular events. *Jeppes Club*, Allégade 25, is a lesbian meeting place open every first and last Friday of the month 9pm–3am.

Listings

Airlines British Airways, Rådhuspladsen 16 (☎80.20.80.22); SAS, Hammerischgade 1–5 (☎70.10.20.00).

American Express Nørregade 7A third floor (☎33.12.23.01).

Books The Book Trader, Skindergade 23, has old and new books in English.

Car rental Avis, Kampmannsgade 1 (☎33.15.22.99); Hertz, Ved Vesterport 3 (☎33.17.90.20); InterRent/Europcar, Gl. Kongevej (☎33.55.99.00).

Cycle hire Københavns Cykelbørs, Gothersgade 157 (Mon–Fri 8.30am–5.30pm, Sat 10am–1.30pm); Københavns Cykler, Reventlowsgade 11 (Mon–Fri 8am–6pm, Sat 9am–1pm); Østerport Cykler, Oslo Plads 9 (Mon–Fri 8am–6pm, Sat 9am–1pm).

Doctor ☎33.93.63.00 (8am–4pm). Outside hours ☎38.88.60.41. Emergencies ☎112.

Embassies Australia, Strandboulevarden 122 (☎70.26.36.76); Britain, Kastelsvej 40 (☎35.44.52.00); Canada, Kristen Bernikowsgade 1 (☎33.48.32.00); Ireland, Østbanegade 21 (☎35.42.32.33); Netherlands, Toldbodgade 33 (☎33.70.72.02); New Zealand, use the British Embassy; USA, Dag Hammerskjölds Allé 24 (☎35.55.31.44).

Exchange Arbejdernes Landsbank, Vestrebrogade 5, has a 24-hour service. Otherwise change money at Den Danske Bank at the Central Station (daily 8am–8pm).

Ferries Reservations and information: DFDS ☎33.42.30.00, *www.dfds.dk*; Pilen ☎33.32.12.60; Scanlines ☎33.12.80.88, *www.scanlines.dk*.

Hospital Rigshospitalet, Blegdamsvej 9 (☎35.45.35.45).

Internet cafés Cyber Space Net Café, Jagtvej 55, Nørrebro (daily 24hrs; ☎35.83.11.45; 15kr/hr); MåneBase Alpha, Elmegade 20, Nørrebro (Mon–Fri 1pm–midnight, Sat–Sun 24hr; ☎35.36.34.41; 25kr/hr); Gamestation, Vesterbrogade 115, Vesterbro (Sun–Thurs noon–midnight, Fri & Sat noon–8am; 25kr/hr); free Internet access is available at Usit, Rådhusstræde 13, and at the Royal Library, Søren Kirkegaard Plads 1, but in both cases you may have to wait.

Left luggage Lockers at Central Station (5.30–1am; 25kr); larger ones are free for a day at Use-It, Rådhusstræde 13.

Pharmacies Steno Apotek, Vesterbrogade 6, and Sønderbro Apotek, Amagerbrogade 158, are both open 24hr.

Police ☎33.25.14.48. Emergencies ☎112.

Post office Main office at Tietgensgade 37 (Mon–Fri 11am–6pm, Sat 10am–1pm). Also at Central Station (Mon–Fri 8am–9pm, Sat 9am–4pm, Sun 10am–4pm).

Travel agents Wasteels Rejser, Skoubogade 6 (☎33.14.46.33, *www.wasteels.dk*); Kilroy Travels, Skindergade 28 (☎70.15.40.15, *www.kilroytravels.com*); STA travel, Fiolstræde 18 (☎33.14.15.01, *www.statravel.dk*); Inter-travel, Frederiks Holms Kanal 2 (☎33.15.00.77, *www.inter-travel.dk*).

Women Copenhagen's main centre for women in crises is Dannerhuset, Nansensgade 1 (☎33.14.16.76), with a café (Mon–Wed 5–8pm) and bookshop (Mon–Fri 5–10.30pm).

Day-trips from Copenhagen

If the weather's good, take a trip to the Amager **beaches** on bus #12 along Øresundsvej. On the other side of the airport from the beaches lies **DRAGØR**, an atmospheric cobbled fishing village which has good local history collections in the **Dragør Museum** (May–Sept Tues–Sun noon–4pm; 20kr), by the harbour, and the **Amager Museum** (May–Sept Tues–Sun noon–4pm; rest of the year Wed & Sun noon–4pm; 20kr), just off the Copenhagen road at the extreme western edge of the village. From the city, take buses #30, #36 or #350S. Failing that, if you're in the mood for an amusement park but can't afford Tivoli, venture out to **BAKKEN** (end March to Aug daily noon–midnight; free), close to the Klampenborg stop at the end of line C on the S-train network, which has been an amusement park since the sixteenth century. Besides swings and rollercoasters, it offers pleasant walks through woods of oak and beech, which were once royal hunting grounds.

The most noteworthy attractions are a little further away from Copenhagen. A fifteen-minute walk from Rungsted Kyst train station, the **Karen Blixen Museum** (May–Sept Tues–Sun 10am–5pm; Oct–April Wed–Fri 1–4pm, Sat & Sun 11am–4pm; 35kr) is housed in what used to be the home of the author of *Out of Africa*, who wrote under the name of Isak Dinesen. In **HUMLEBÆK**, 10km further north and a short walk from the train station, you'll find **Louisiana**, an excellent modern art gallery on the northern edge of the village at Gammel Strandvej 13 (daily 10am–5pm, Wed until 10pm; 60kr); its setting alone is worth the journey, harmoniously combining art, architecture and the natural landscape. The museum's American section, sited in the south corridor, stands out, with its collection of pieces by Edward Kienholz and Malcolm Morley's scintillatingly gross *Pacific Telephone Los Angeles Yellow Pages*. In addition you'll find some of Giacometti's gangly figures haunting a room of their own off the north corridor, and an equally affecting handful of sculptures by Max Ernst, squatting outside the windows, leering in.

Also feasible as a day-trip is the short hop to **Sweden** on the new Øresund Link, a part-tunnel part-bridge that has recently opened. Both the Danish and Swedish governments have invested heavily in the project, which carries a railway and road from Copenhagen to Malmø (train crossing: 35min).

THE REST OF ZEALAND

You will discover how different the rest of Denmark is when you venture outside Copenhagen – worthwhile even if you're just passing through. As home to the capital, **Zealand** is Denmark's most important and most visited region, and, with a swift metropolitan transport network covering almost half of the island, you can always make it back to the capital in time for an evening drink. North of Copenhagen, **Helsingør**, the departure point for ferries to Sweden, is the site of the renowned fortification Kronborg Slot – though Frederiksborg Slot, at nearby **Hillerød**, is if anything more impressive. West of Copenhagen, and on the main route to Funen, is **Roskilde**, a former capital with an extravagant cathedral that's still the last resting place for Danish monarchs, and with a gorgeous location on the Roskilde fjord – from where five Viking boats were salvaged and are now restored and displayed in a specially built museum.

Hillerød

Last stop on lines A and E of the S-train network from Copenhagen, **HILLERØD** has a castle which pushes the more famous Kronborg into second place: **Frederiksborg Slot**, which houses Denmark's National Portrait Gallery (daily: April–Oct 10am–5pm; Nov–March 11am–3pm; 50kr), lies decorously across three small islands on an artificial lake. The Frederiksborg ferry crosses the castle lake (June–Aug Mon–Sat 11am–5pm, Sun 1–5pm; rest of the year Sat 11am–5pm, Sun 1–5pm; 45kr). Buses #701, #702 and #703 run from the train station to the castle but walking only takes about twenty minutes, following the signs through town.

The castle was the home of Frederik II and birthplace of his son Christian IV. At the turn of the seventeenth century, under the auspices of Christian, rebuilding began in an unorthodox Dutch Renaissance style. It's the unusual aspects of the monarch's design – prolific use of towers and spires, pointed Gothic arches and flowery window ornamentation – which still stand out, despite the changes wrought by fire and restoration. Inside, the National Portrait Gallery was largely funded by the Carlsberg brewery magnate Carl Jacobsen. The illustrated guide to the museum costs 40kr, but most rooms have detailed descriptions in English pasted up on the walls. Two rooms deserve special mention: the exquisite chapel, where monarchs were anointed between 1671 and 1840, and the Great Hall above, a reconstruction but still beautiful, bare but for the staggering wall and ceiling decorations: tapestries, wall-reliefs, portraits and a glistening black marble fireplace.

The **tourist office** at Slangenrupsgade 2 (☎48.24.26.26; June to Aug Mon–Fri 10am–6pm, Sat 10am–3pm; rest of year Mon–Fri 10am–5pm, Sat 10am–1pm) offers **private rooms** for around 150kr per person (25kr booking fee). Few of Hillerød's **hotels** can match the prices you might find in Copenhagen but you could try *Hotel Hillerød*, Milnersvej 41 (☎48.24.08.00, *www.hotelhillerod.dk*; ⑥). Less expensive are beds at the *Nordiske Lejerskole og Kursuscenter*, Lejerskolevej 4 (☎48.26.19.86, *www.nordlejr.dk*; ③). The only budget accommodation is the **campsite** on Blytækkervej 18 by the agricultural showground 1km from the centre (☎48.26.48.54, *www.hillerodcamping.dk*) which also has cabins (Easter to mid-Sept). If you're up for a splurge, the *Slotsherrens Kro*, in one of the castle's gatehouses, serves fantastic *smørrebrød* at 70kr a piece, one should suffice if you're not too famished. Otherwise the *Engelhardt's Cafe*, at Slotsarkaderne 112, serves good value sandwiches and light snacks.

Helsingør

First impressions of **HELSINGØR**, 30min north of Hillerød, are none too enticing, but away from the hustle of its terminals it is a quiet and likeable town. Its position on the four-kilometre strip of water linking the North Sea and the Baltic brought the town prosperity when, in 1429, the Sound Toll was imposed on passing vessels – an upturn only matched in magnitude by the severe decline following the abolition of the toll in the nineteenth century. Shipbuilding brought back some of the town's self-assurance, but today it's once again the whisker of water between Denmark and Sweden, and the ferries across it to Helsingborg, which account for most of Helsingør's through-traffic.

The town's other great tourist draw is **Kronborg Slot** (April & Oct Tues–Sun 11am–4pm; May–Sept daily 10.30am–5pm; Nov–March Tues–Sun 11am–3pm; 40kr, Copenhagen Card not valid), principally because of its literary associations as Elsinore Castle, whose ramparts Shakespeare's Prince Hamlet supposedly strode. Actually, the playwright never visited Helsingør, and the tenth-century character Amleth on whom his hero was based long predates the castle. Nevertheless, there is a thriving Hamlet souvenir business, and during the summer the numbers visiting the place make guided tours impossible. The present castle dates from the sixteenth century; Frederik II commissioned the Dutch architects van Opbergen and van Paaschen to construct it on the site of an earlier fortress. Various bits have been destroyed and rebuilt since, but it remains a grand affair, enhanced immeasurably by its setting; and the interior, particularly the royal chapel, is spectacularly ornate. The castle also houses the national **Maritime Museum** (30kr, 60kr for a joint ticket with the castle itself), an uninteresting collection of model ships and nautical knick-knacks.

Moving away from Kronborg and the harbour area, Helsingør has a well-preserved medieval quarter, worth a stroll through. **Stengade** is the main pedestrianized street, linked by a number of narrow alleyways to Axeltorv, the town's small market square and usually a good spot to linger over a beer. Near the corner of Stengade and Skt. Annagade, the spired **Skt. Olai's Kirke** is now Helsingør's cathedral. Just beyond is the **Karmeliterklostret**, the best-preserved medieval monastic complex in Scandinavia (Mid-May to mid-Sept Mon–Fri 10am–3pm, rest of the year Mon–Fri 10am–2pm; guided tours mid-May to mid-Sept at 2pm; 20kr). Its former hospital contains the **Town Museum** (daily noon–4pm; 10kr), which prided itself on brain operations – the unnerving tools of which are still here, together with diagrams of the corrective insertions made into patients' heads.

Practicalities

Buses stop outside the noisy combined **train station** and **ferry terminal**. You can pick up a free map from the **tourist office** on Havnepladsen 3 (mid-June to Aug Mon–Fri 9am–5pm, Sat 10am–1pm; Sept to mid-June Mon–Fri 9am–4pm, Sat 10am–1pm; ☎49.21.13.33, *www.helsingorturist.dk*), and you can also book **private rooms** for 400kr a double (50kr booking fee). The closest thing to a cheap **hotel** is *Hotel Skandia*, Bramstræde 1 (☎49.21.09.02; ⑤). More affordably, there is a **youth hostel** (☎49.21.16.40, *www.helsingorhostel.dk*; ②) on the beach, a twenty-minute walk to the north along the coastal road (Ndr. Strandvej), or accessible on bus #340 from the station. The **campsite** (☎49.28.12.12) at Campingvej 1, is closer to town and also by a beach, between the main road and the sea; take the private train – Hornbæk banen (Copenhagen Card valid, rail passes not) – to Marienlyst or bus #340. For **food**, *Rådmands Davids Hus*, Strandgade 70, is a prime lunchtime spot for its daily specials; *Møllers Conditori*, Stengade 39, Denmark's oldest bakery, has sizable sandwiches and Danish pastries to follow; or try the varied delights of *Færgegården*, Stengade 81b, three ethnic restaurants in one building – Chinese, Mexican and Greek – all with good value help-yourself buffets starting at 50kr.

Three **ferry lines** make the twenty-minute crossing from Helsingør to Helsingborg in Sweden. The main one, and probably the best option, is the Scandlines boat leaving every 20 minutes from 6am to 11.30pm and every 30 minutes at night from the main terminal by the train station and costing 16kr one way. The alternative options are Sundbusserne, costing 32kr for a return and 19kr one way, who operate small craft, often heavily buffeted by the choppy waters, every 20 minutes between 7am and 7pm, and HH Ferries which has the cheapest off-peak prices: 8kr one way and 16kr, but docks a good walk from the centre of

Helsingborg. For all three companies rail passes are valid and a Copenhagen Card gives a fifty percent discount.

Roskilde

There's very little between Copenhagen and the west Zealand coast in the way of things to explore, except for the ancient former Danish capital of **ROSKILDE**, less than half an hour by train from the capital. The arrival of Bishop Absalon in the twelfth century made the place the base of the Danish church, and as a consequence the national capital. Importance waned after the Reformation, and Roskilde came to function mainly as a market for the neighbouring rural communities – which it still is, as well as being dormitory territory for Copenhagen commuters. Its ancient centre is one of Denmark's most appealing – well worth a look on your way west to Odense.

The major pointer to the town's former status is the fabulous **Roskilde Domkirke** (April–Sept Mon–Fri 9am–4.45pm, Sat 9am–noon, Sun 12.30–4.45pm; rest of the year Tues–Fri 10am–3.45pm, Sat 11.30am–3.45pm, Sun 12.30am–3.45pm; *www.roskildedomkirke.dk*; 15kr), founded in 1170 and finished during the fourteenth century, although portions have been added since. Four royal chapels house a claustrophobic collection of coffins containing the regal remains of twenty kings and seventeen queens. The most richly endowed chapel is that of Christian IV, a previously austere resting place jazzed up in the early nineteenth century with bronze statues, wall-length frescoes and vast paintings of scenes from his reign. From one end of the cathedral, a roofed passageway, the **Arch of Absalon**, feeds into the **Roskilde Palace**, housing the **Palace Collections** (mid-May to mid-Sept daily 11am–4pm; rest of the year Sat & Sun 2–4pm; 25kr), made up of paintings, furniture and other artefacts belonging to the wealthiest Roskilde families of the eighteenth and nineteenth centuries. In the same building is the **Museum of Contemporary Art** (Tues–Fri 11am–5pm, Sat & Sun noon–4pm; 20kr, Wed free), hosting high-standard temporary exhibitions and a charming small sculpture garden.

The history of the town recorded in the **Roskilde Museum** at Skt. Ols Gade 18 (daily 11am–4pm; 25kr) is an enticing collection, with strong sections on medieval pottery and toys, although time is really better spent at the absorbing **Viking Ship Museum** (May–Sept daily 9am–5pm; 54kr; Oct–April daily 10am–4pm; 45kr), in Strandengen on the banks of the fjord. Inside, five excellent specimens of Viking shipbuilding are proudly displayed: there's a deep-sea trader, a merchant ship, a warship, a ferry and a longship, each one retrieved from the fjord where they had been sunk to block invading forces. The museum also includes the newly built Museum Island where you can watch new Viking ships being built.

The **tourist office** (April–June Mon–Fri 9am–5pm, Sat 10am–1pm; July–Aug Mon–Fri 9am–6pm, Sat 10am–2pm; Sept–March Mon–Thurs 9am–5pm, Fri 9am–4pm, Sat 10am–1pm; ☎46.35.27.00, *www.visitroskilde.dk*), is at Gullandsstræde 15, a short walk from the main square. If you decide to stay, there's a **campsite** (☎46.75.79.96) on the wooded edge of the fjord 4km away – an appealing setting which makes it very crowded at peak times; it's open from mid-April to mid-September, and linked to the town centre by bus #603, Veddelev direction. The new **youth hostel** on Vindeboder 7 is near the harbour (☎46.35.21.84, *www.danhostel.dk/roskilde*; ②); to get there take bus #605 towards Boserup. Neither the hostel nor campsite are worth bothering with if you're here for the **Roskilde Festival** (*www.roskilde-festival.dk*), one of the largest open-air rock events in Europe, attracting around ninety thousand people annually. The festival takes place late June/early July and there's a special, free camping ground beside the festival site, to which shuttle buses run from the train station every ten minutes. For **lunch**, coffee or a game of backgammon, head for *Café Satchmo*, signposted off Algade; for a beer try the informal *Café Grunk* on Store Gråbrødrestræde.

FUNEN

Known as "the Garden of Denmark", partly for the lawn-like neatness of its fields, partly for the immense amounts of fruit and vegetables which come from them, **Funen** is the smaller of the two main Danish islands. The pastoral outlook of the place and the coastline draw many visitors, but its attractions are mainly low-profile cultural sights, such as the various collections of the "Funen painters" and the birthplaces of writer Hans Christian Andersen and composer Carl Nielsen. **Odense**, Denmark's third city, is easily the island's main urban attraction. Close to this, the former fishing town of **Kerteminde** retains some faded charm, and is near the Ladby Boat, an important Viking relic.

Odense

ODENSE is proud to be the birthplace of Denmark's best-loved writer, Hans Christian Andersen, as well as the childhood home of composer Carl Nielsen. Named after Odin, chief of the pagan gods, Odense is one of the oldest settlements in the country and was even home to King Knud II, canonized after his murder here in 1086. Much of the pleasantly sleepy city is pedestrianized, making it a perfect place to saunter about. You can also cycle along the old rail tracks, which have been converted into bicycle paths, or along the canal's edge past the elegant Danish mansions painted in mustard, terracotta and sky blue. The city has a range of good museums and a nightlife that's surprisingly lively, with the focus on live music and jazz.

Arrival, accommodation and information

Long-distance buses and trains both terminate at the **train station**, a ten-minute walk from the city centre, where you'll find the **tourist office** (mid-June to Aug Mon–Sat 9am–7pm, Sun 10am–5pm; rest of year Mon–Fri 9.30am–4.30pm, Sat 10am–1pm; *www.odenseturist.dk*) on the Vestergade side of the Rådhus – follow the signs. They sell the useful **Adventure Pass** (one day 85kr, two days 125kr), which gets you discounts on entrance to all of Odense's museums and gives unlimited travel on local buses. The only cheap options among Odense's **hotels** are *Det Lille Hotel*, Dronningensgade 5 (☎66.12.28.21; ④), and *Ydes*, Hans Tausens Gade 11 (☎66.12.11.31, *www.ydes.dk*; ④). A **youth hostel** has recently opened next to the train station, Østre Stationsvej 31 (☎66.11.04.25, *www.cityhostel.dk*; ②; open year round) and there's another at Kragsbjergvej 121 (☎66.13.04.25, *www.odense-danhostel.dk*; ②; mid-Feb to Nov) – take buses #61, #62, #63 or #64 south to Tornbjerg or Fraugde and get out along Munkebjergvej at the junction with Vissenbjergvej. The closest **campsite** (☎66.11.47.02) has cabins and is at Odensevej 102, near the Funen Village; take buses #21, #22 or #23 from the Rådhus or station to Højby. For **Internet** use, head for Game Play Net-cafe, Kongensgade 70 first floor (daily noon–midnight; 20kr/hr); Net Cafe 5000, Vindegade 43 (daily until midnight; 20kr/hr); or the large local library in the train station.

The Town

Save for an outlying museum, Odense is easily seen on foot, and you may as well start with the city's major collection: the **Hans Christian Andersen Museum** at Hans Jensen Stræde 37–45 (mid-June to Aug daily 9am–7pm; rest of the year Tues–Sun 10am–4pm; *www.odmus.dk*; 35kr), in the house where the writer was born in 1805. The son of a hard-up cobbler, Andersen was only really accepted in his own country towards the end of his life, which was perhaps why he travelled widely and often, and left Odense at the first opportunity. The museum is stuffed with intriguing items – bits of school reports, early notes and manuscripts of his books, illustrations from the tales, an invitation from Charles Dickens to stay in England and paraphernalia from his travels. A separate gallery has headphones for listening to some of Andersen's best-known tales and screens a sloppy slide-show, though plans for renovating the museum and making more of Andersen's fabulous imagination are under way.

The area around the museum, despite being all half-timbered houses and clean, car-free cobbled streets, lacks character; indeed, if Andersen were around he'd hardly recognize the neighbourhood, which is now one of Odense's most expensive. For far more realistic local history, head to **Bymuseet Møntergården**, a few streets away at Overgade 48–50 (Tues–Sun 10am–4pm; 15kr), where there's an engrossing assemblage of artefacts dating from the city's earliest settlements to the Nazi occupation, plus an immense coin collection. There's more about Andersen at Munkemøllestræde 3–5, between Skt. Knud Kirkestræde and Klosterbakken, in the tiny **Hans Christian Andersen's Childhood Home** (mid-Jun to Aug daily 10am–4pm; rest of year Tues–Sun 11am–3pm; 10kr), where Andersen lived from 1807 to 1819. More interesting, though, is the nearby **Skt. Knud's Kirke** (April–Oct Mon–Sat 9am–5pm, Sun noon–3pm; rest of the year Mon–Sat 10am–4pm, Sun noon–3pm; free), whose crypt holds one of the most unusual and ancient finds Denmark has to offer: the skeletons of King Knud II and his brother Benedikt, both slain in 1086 by Jutish farmers angry at the taxes Knud imposed on them – Knud was canonized soon after. The cathedral is the only example of pure Gothic church architecture in the country; its finely detailed sixteenth-century wooden altarpiece, saturated with gold leaf, is one of the greatest works of the Lübeck master, Claus Berg.

The **Funen Art Gallery** at Jernbanegade 13 (Tues–Sun 10am–4pm; *www.odmus.dk*; 30kr), just a few minutes' walk away, will give you a good idea of the region's importance to the Danish art world during the late nineteenth century, when a number of Funen-based painters abandoned portraiture for impressionistic landscapes and studies recording the lives of the peasantry. The collection contains some stirring works by Vilhelm Hammershøi, P.S. Krøyer, Michael and Anne Ancher, and H.A. Brændekilde's enormously emotive *Udslidt* ("worn out"). A short walk to the east, at Claus Bergs Gade 11, is the **Carl Nielsen Museum** (July–Aug Tues–Sun noon–4pm; rest of the year Thurs–Sun noon–4pm; 15kr). Born in a village just outside Odense, Nielsen is best remembered in Denmark for his popular songs, though it was his operas, choral pieces and symphonies that established him as a major international composer. The exhibits, detailing Nielsen's life and achievements, are enlivened by the accomplished sculptures of his wife, Anne Marie, and you can listen to some of his work on headphones.

Well worth a visit to the west of the centre is the Brandts Klædefabrik, on Brandts Passage just off Vestergade, an old cloth-weaving factory which now contains four museums (July–Aug daily 10am–5pm, Sept–June Tues–Sun 10am–5pm; *www.brandts.dk*; 50kr for ticket to all exhibitions). In the large halls that once housed the huge machinery are the Brandts Art Gallery (30kr), which holds national and international exhibitions, mostly of contemporary art, and the Museum of Photographic Art (25kr), featuring a permanent collection of fine art photography unique in Denmark. On the third floor the Danish Museum of Printing (25kr) illustrates the development of the printing trade in Denmark over the last three centuries. Further down Brandts Passage on the second floor of no 27 is the Tidens Samling (the "Time Collection"; 25kr); it gives a fascinating insight into the development of fashion and housing interiors since the turn of the last century.

To the south of the Odense centre at Sejerskovvej 20 is **Funen Village** (April to mid-June & mid-Aug to Oct Tues–Sun 10am–5pm; mid-June to mid-Aug daily 9.30am–7pm; Nov–March Sun 11am–3pm; 35kr), an open-air museum made up of a reconstructed nineteenth-century country village of original buildings taken from all over Funen, painstakingly reassembled and refurnished. In summer, some of the old trades are revived in the former workshops and crafthouses, and free shows are regularly staged at the open-air theatre. Though often crowded, it's well worth a call, and you should watch out for the village-brewed beer, handed out free on special occasions. Bus #42 runs to the village from the city centre (get off at the sign Den Fynske Landsby), or you can do what the locals do and take the Odense Åfart boat from Munke Mose (May to mid-Aug; seven times daily; ☎65.95.79.96; 30–45kr), stopping on the way at **Odense Zoo** (March–April & Sept–Oct Mon–Fri 9am–5pm, Sat & Sun 9am–6pm;

May–June & Aug Mon–Fri 9am–6pm, Sat & Sun 9am–7pm; July daily 9am–7pm; Nov–March daily 9am–4pm; *www.odensezoo.dk*; 65kr).

Eating, drinking and nightlife

There are plenty of **restaurants** and **snack bars** in the city centre, and some good bargains to be had. *Den Gyldne ovn* on Fisketorvet is a reliable spot for freshly made sandwiches from the in-house bakery, while for more substantial eating, the best and oldest of the many pizzerias is *Pizzeria Ristorante Italiano*, Vesterbrogade 9. You might also try the Thai food all-you-can-eat buffet of the *Oriental Barbeque House*, Slotsgade 20, Mexican dishes at *Tortilla Flat*, Frederiksgade 38, or the only vegetarian option, *Kærnehuset* on the first floor of Nedergade 6, where the meal of the day costs 40kr and is served promptly between 6 and 7pm – bring your own wine. If you'd prefer a steak or spareribs, head for *Edyes Kælder*, Kongensgade 31A. For evening **drinking**, try *Carlsen's Kvarter*, an inexpensive Irish pub on Læssøgade which serves fine beers; otherwise drop into the fashionable *Café Biografen*, one of many eating and drinking spots in Brandts Passage, which has a little three-screen cinema that tends to show more arty films than the seven-screen complex in the train station. At the passage entrance, *Cuckoo's Nest* is a favourite for drinks or a light snack before moving on to *Jazzhus Dexter*, Vindegade 65, for swing to fusion **jazz** until early morning. The *Badstuen* cultural centre, Østre Stationsvej 26, has a café that occasionally hosts raucous live **bands**, as does *Rytmeposten* across the road at Østre Stationsvej 27a. There's bluesier fare to be found in the likeably scruffy *Musikkælderen*, Dronningsgengade 2B, and easier rock at *Rådhuskælderen*, Vestergade 15-17.

Kerteminde and around

A thirty-minute bus ride (#890) northeast from Odense takes you to **KERTEMINDE**, a sailing and holiday centre that has a prettily preserved nucleus of shops and houses around its fifteenth-century Skt. Laurentius Kirke. Across the road from the bus station on Magrethes Plads 1, **Fjord & Bæltcentret** (July to mid-Aug daily 10am–6pm, mid-Feb to June & mid-Aug to Nov Mon–Fri 10am–4pm, Sat & Sun 10am–5pm; *www.fjord-baelt.dk*; 65kr) is a state-of-the-art aquarium with a 50m long underwater tunnel from where you can watch and learn about the sea's environment. On Strandgade, the **Town Museum – Farvergården** (Tues–Sun 10am–4pm; 15kr) has five reconstructed craft workshops and a collection of local fishing equipment. Kerteminde was home to the "birdman of Funen", the late-nineteenth-century ornithological painter Johannes Larsen and a fairly lengthy stroll around the marina and along Møllebakken brings you to the **Johannes Larsen Museum** (June–Aug daily 10am–5pm; Sept–Oct & March–May Tues–Sun 10am–4pm; Nov–Feb Tues–Sun 11am–4pm; 40kr) – the painter's house, kept as it was when he lived there, with his furnishings, knick-knacks, canvases and, in the dining room, his astonishing wall-paintings.

Kerteminde's **tourist office** on Strandgade is opposite the Skt. Laurentius Kirke, across a small alleyway (mid-June to Aug Mon–Sat 9am–5pm, rest of year Mon–Fri 9am–4pm, Sat 9.30am–12.30pm; ☎65.32.11.21, *www.kerteminde-turist.dk*). The only low-cost accommodation option is the **youth hostel** at Skovvej 46 (☎65.32.39.29, *www.danhostel.dk/kerteminde*; ②), a twenty-minute walk from the centre (cross the Kerteminde Fjord by the road bridge and take the first major road left and immediately right). There's also a **campsite** (☎65.32.19.71; mid-April to mid-Sept) with cabins, at Hindsholmvej 80, not far from the Larsen Museum, on the main road along the seafront – a thirty-minute walk from the centre.

About 4km from Kerteminde, along the banks of the fjord at Vikingvej 123, is the **Ladby Boat** (March–May & Sept–Oct Tues–Sun 10am–4pm; June–Aug daily 10am–5pm; Nov–Feb Wed–Sun 11am–3pm; 25kr), a vessel dredged up from the fjord and found to be the burial place of a Viking chieftain. The craft, along with the weapons, hunting dogs and horses which accompanied the deceased on his journey to Valhalla, is kept in a small purpose-built museum, and is well worth the trip out. The infrequent bus #482 stops here and motorboats make the run out in summer, although it's a pleasant enough walk or cycle.

JUTLAND

Long ago, the people of **Jutland**, the Jutes, were a separate tribe from the more warlike Danes who occupied the eastern islands. In pagan times, the peninsula had its own rulers and much power, and it was here that the legendary ninth-century monarch Harald Bluetooth began the process that turned the two tribes into a unified Christian nation. By the dawn of the Viking era, however, the battling Danes had spread west, absorbing the Jutes, and real power gradually shifted towards Zealand. This is where it has largely stayed, making unhurried lifestyles and rural calm the overriding impression of Jutland for most visitors; indeed, its distance from Copenhagen makes it perhaps the most distinct and interesting area in the country. In the south, Schleswig is a territory long battled over by Denmark and Germany, though beyond the immaculately restored town of **Ribe** it holds little of abiding interest. **Esbjerg**, further north, is dull too, but as a major ferry port you might well pass through. The old military stronghold of **Fredericia** is worth a brief stop before reaching **Århus** halfway up the eastern coast, Jutland's main urban centre and Denmark's second city. Further inland, the landscape is the country's most dramatic – stark heather-clad moors, dense forests and swooping gorges. Ancient **Viborg** is the best base for this, from where you can head north to vibrant **Aalborg**, on the southern bank of the Limfjord, which cuts deep into Jutland this far north – across which the landscape reaches a crescendo of storm-lashed savagery around **Skagen**, on the very tip of the peninsula. **Frederikshavn**, on the way, is the port for boats to Norway and Sweden.

Fredericia

FREDERICIA – junction of all the rail routes in east Jutland and those connecting the peninsula with Funen – has one of the oddest histories (and layouts) in Denmark. It was founded in 1650 by Frederik III, who envisaged a strategically placed reserve capital and a base from which to defend Jutland. Three nearby villages were demolished and their inhabitants forced to assist in the building of the new town. Military criteria resulted in wide streets that followed a strict grid system and low buildings enclosed by high earthen ramparts, making the town invisible to approaching armies. The train age made Fredericia a transport centre and its harbour expanded as a consequence. But it still retains a soldiering air, full of memorials to heroes and victories, and is the venue of the only military tattoo in Denmark.

The twenty-minute walk from the **train station** along Vesterbrogade toward the town centre takes you past the most impressive section of the old ramparts. They stretch for 4km and rise 15m above the streets, and walking along the top gives a good view of the layout of the town. But it's the **Landsoldaten** statue, opposite Princes Port, which best exemplifies the local spirit. The bronze figure holds a rifle in its left hand, a sprig of leaves in the right, and its left foot rests on a captured cannon. The inscription on the statue reads "6 July 1849", the day the town's battalion made a momentous sortie against German troops in the first Schleswig war – an anniversary celebrated as Fredericia Day. The downside of the battle was the 500 Danes who were killed and who lie in a mass grave in the grounds of Trinitatis Kirke in Kongensgade. Predictably, 300 years of armed conflict also form the core of the displays at the **Fredericia Museum**, Jernbanegade 10 (daily noon–4pm, Sept to mid-June closed Mon; ☎72.10.69.80; 20kr), along with local house interiors from the seventeenth and eighteenth centuries.

Fredericia's **tourist office** (June–Aug Mon–Fri 9am–6pm, Sat 9am–2pm; rest of year Mon–Fri 9.30am–5pm, Sat 10am–1pm; ☎75.92.13.77, *www.visitfredericia.dk*) is on the corner of Danmarksgade and Norgesgade. Unless you want to laze on Fredericia's fine **beaches**, which begin at the eastern end of the ramparts, there's little reason to hang around very long. If you do want to stay, however, try the **youth hostel** at Vester Ringvej 98 (☎75.92.12.87, *www.fredericia-danhostel.dk*; ③), a short ride on bus #6 from the train station, or the **campsite** (☎75.95.71.83; April–Oct), on the Vejle fjord, adjacent to a public beach, also reached by bus #6.

Esbjerg

The only large city in southern Jutland is **ESBJERG**, which was purpose-built as a deep-water harbour during the nineteenth century and has generally been thought of as being gloomy and run-down. However, it is in the process of massive redevelopment and its environment and cultural life are being dramatically improved.

The best way to get a sense of the city's newness is by dropping into the **Esbjerg Museum** (daily 10am–4pm, from Sept to May closed Mon; ☎75.12.78.11; 30kr) at Torvegade 45, with its gallery devoted to amber along with a display recalling the so-called "American period" from the 1890s, when Esbjerg's rapid growth matched that of the US gold-rush towns. Also within easy reach of the centre is the **Museum of Art** (daily 10am–4pm; ☎75.13.02.11; 30kr), although its modern Danish artworks are fairly limp affairs; you'd do better to visit the art displays in the recently refurbished **Watertower** next door (April–May & mid-Sept to Oct Sat & Sun 10am–4pm; June to mid-Sept daily 10am–4pm; 15kr), or the **Museum of Printing** at Borgergade 6 (June to mid-Sept daily noon–4pm; rest of the year Tues–Sun 1–4pm; 15kr), which has an entertaining assortment of hand-, foot- and steam-operated presses, as well as more recent printing machines. With more time to spare, take a bus (#1, #3, #8 or #40 from Skolegade) to the large **Fisheries and Maritime Museum and Sealarium** on Tarphagevej (daily: July–Aug 10am–6pm; Sept–June 10am–5pm; ☎76.12.20.00, *www.fimus.dk*; 60kr), where you can cast an eye over the vestiges of the early Esbjerg fishing fleet and clamber around inside a spooky wartime bunker built by the Germans. The Sealarium is part of a seal research centre, which often rescues pups marooned on sandbanks, then feeds them for the public's entertainment at 11am & 2.30pm daily. Opposite is Svend Wiig Hansen's nine-metre-high *Man meets the Sea*, an austere, blandly modernist sculpture of four white seated figures.

Esbjerg's **tourist office** is at Skolegade 33 (mid-June to Aug Mon–Fri 9am–5pm, Sat 9.30am–3.30pm; rest of the year Mon–Fri 10am–5pm, Sat 10am–1pm; ☎75.12.55.99, *www.esbjerg-tourist.dk*), on a corner of the main square. The passenger harbour is a twenty-minute well-signposted walk from the city centre, and **trains** to and from Copenhagen connect directly with the **ferries**, using the harbour station. The main **train station** is at the end of Skolegade. The cheapest central **hotels** are *Palads Hotel Cab Inn*, Skolegade 14 (☎75.18.16.00, *www.cab-inn.dk;* ⑤) and the *Park Hotel* at Torvegade 31 (☎75.12.08.68; ④, not including breakfast). A little more upmarket is the *Hotel Ansgar*, Skolegade 36 (☎75.12.82.44, *www.hotelansgar.dk*; ⑦). The **youth hostel** is at Gammel Vardevej 80 (☎75.12.42.58, *www.sima.dk/esbjerg*; ②; closed Dec–Feb), 25 minutes' walk, or buses #1, #4, #12, #40 or #41 from Skolegade. There is also an excellent **campsite**, Ådalens Camping, with cabins at Gudenåvej 20 (☎75.15.88.22, *www.adal.dk*), reached by buses #1, #14 and #7. The Esbjerg **eating** options are fairly limited if you're on a tight budget, although you can get a decent two-course lunch for around 70kr at the *Park Hotel*, while inexpensive, but mainly meat, dishes can be found at *Jensens Bøfhus*, Kongensgade 9. A good place to **drink** is *Café Christian IX*, overlooking Torvet, and Skolegade in general is flooded with places to go after dark.

Ribe

Just under an hour south by train from Esbjerg, the exquisitely preserved town of **RIBE** was once a major stopover point for pilgrims on their way to Rome, as well as a significant port, until thwarted by the Reformation and the sanding-up of the harbour. Since then, not much appears to have changed. The surrounding marshlands, which have prevented the development of any large-scale industry, and a long-standing preservation programme, have enabled Ribe to keep the appearance and size of medieval times, making it a delight to wander in.

From Ribe's train station, Dagmarsgade leads to Torvet and the towering **Domkirke** (April & Oct Mon–Sat 11am–4pm, Sun noon–4pm; May–June & mid-Aug to Sept Mon–Sat

10am–5pm, Sun noon–5pm; July to mid-Aug Mon–Sat 10am–5.30pm, Sun noon–5.30pm; Nov–March Mon–Sat 11am–3pm, Sun noon–3pm; 12kr; 1-hour tours from July to mid-Aug at 11.30am; 45kr), begun around 1150. Only the "Cat's Head Door" on the south side remains from the original construction and the church's interior is not as spectacular as either its size or long history might suggest, though you can normally climb the red-brick tower and peer out over the town. Behind the cathedral, the **Weis' Stue** is a tiny inn built around 1600, from which the nightwatchman of Ribe makes his rounds (May–Sept 10pm, June–Aug 8pm & 10pm) – a throwback to the days when Danish towns were patrolled by guards looking for unattended candles, though these days he stops at points of interest to explain the town's history to tourists. It's free and can be fun. The **Viking Museum** (July & Aug Wed 10am–6pm, Thurs–Tues 10am–4pm; rest of the year daily 10am–4pm, Nov–March closed Mon; 50kr), nearby on Odins Plads, offers an informative display on Ribe's past, including archeological finds and interactive computer exhibits. If you haven't had enough of Vikings, you can watch their daily life in action at the **Ribe Vikingecenter** (July & Aug daily 11am–4.30pm; May, June & Sept Mon–Fri 11am–4pm; 50kr), 2km south of the town centre at Lustrupvej, where staff in Viking dress give pottery demonstrations and cook over open fires.

The **tourist office** (April–June & Sept–Oct Mon–Fri 9am–5pm, Sat 10am–1pm; July–Aug Mon–Fri 9.30am–5.30pm, Sat 9am–5pm; Nov–March Mon–Fri 9.30am–4.30pm, Sat 10am–1pm; ☎75.42.15.00, *www.ribetourist.dk*) is behind the cathedral, opposite the Weis' Stue; it has a full list of **private homes** with rooms to rent. There's also a **youth hostel** (☎75.42.06.20, *www.danhostel.dk/ribe*; ②; Feb–Nov), on the opposite side of the river from Skibbroen: cross the river bridge and turn left into Sct. Peders Gade. Failing that, there are several moderately priced places such as the *Weis' Stue* (☎75.42.07.00; ⑤), which is opposite the atmospheric but expensive *Hotel Dagmar* (☎75.42.00.33, *www.hoteldagmar.dk*; ⑨), the oldest hotel in Denmark. The nearest **campsite**, which also has cabins, is 1.5km from Ribe, along Farupvej (☎75.41.07.77; bus #715; open Easter to late October). A daytime and evening alternative with **food** and excellent coffee is *Valdemar Sejr* next to the art gallery on Sct. Nicolaj Gade. For an evening **drink** try *Stenbohus* on Stenbogade, which attracts artists, students and musicians and has live blues, folk or rock bands at least once a week.

Århus

Geographically at the heart of the country and often regarded as Denmark's cultural capital, **ÅRHUS** typifies all that's good about Danish cities: it's small enough to get to know in a few hours, yet big and lively enough to fill both days and nights. Despite Viking-era origins, the city's present-day prosperity is due to its long, sheltered bay, on which the first harbour was constructed during the fifteenth century, and the more recent advent of railways, which made Århus a nationally important trade and transport centre. Easily reached by train from all the country's bigger towns, and by ferry from Zealand, Århus also receives nonstop flights from London. There's certainly no better place for a first taste of Denmark.

Arrival and accommodation

Trains, **buses** and **ferries** all stop on the southern edge of the city centre, a short walk from the **tourist office** in Park Allé (May to mid-June Mon–Fri 9.30am–5pm, Sat 10am–1pm; mid-June to mid-Sept Mon–Fri 9.30am–6pm, Sat 9.30am–5pm, Sun 9.30am–1pm; mid-Sept to April Mon–Fri 9.30am–4.30pm, Sat 10am–1pm; ☎89.40.67.00, *www.visitaarhus.dk*), on the first floor of the city's Rådhus. **Airport** buses from Tirstrup connect regularly with the train station (50min; 60kr). Buses form the city's public transport system, which is divided into four zones: zones one and two cover the centre; zones three and four reach into the country; a basic ticket costs 13kr from machines on board and is valid for any number of journeys for two hours from the time stamped on it. However, getting around is best done on foot: Århus has a compact centre and you'll seldom need to use the buses unless you're venturing out to the beaches or woods on the outskirts. An **Århus Pass** (88kr for a 24-hour pass, 110kr for

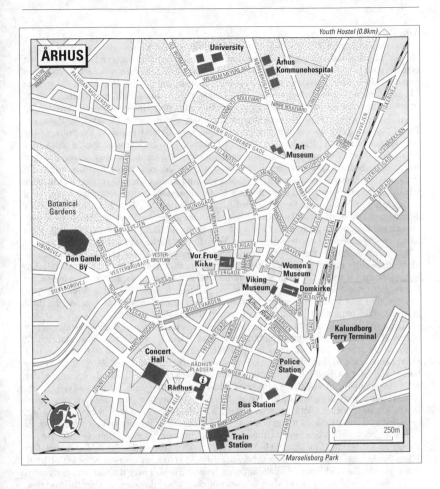

Marselisborg Park

48 hours, 155kr for a week) covers unlimited bus travel and entrance to most museums and sightseeing tours (though you must book these at the tourist office first).

The **tourist office** can arrange accommodation in **private rooms** for 150kr a night plus a 25kr booking fee. The Århus **youth hostel**, 4km from the centre at Marienlundsvej 10 (☎86.16.72.98, *www.hostel-aarhus.dk*; ②; bus #1, #6, #8, #9, #16, #56 or #58), is beautifully situated in the middle of Risskov wood and close to Den Permanente beach, to which locals flock in summer. The *Århus City Sleep-In*, Havnegade 20 (☎86.19.20.55, *www.citysleep-in.dk*; ②), is more central and has an impressive range of facilities for travellers. There are just three reasonably priced central **hotels**: *Hotel Guldsmeden* at Guldsmedegade 40 (☎86.13.45.56; ⑥), *Get In*, Jens Baggesensvej 43 (☎86.10.86.14; ③) and the new *Hotel Cab Inn Århus*, Kannikegade 14 (☎70.21.62.00, *www.cab-inn.dk*; ⑤). Of a number of **campsites**, the two most useful are *Blommehaven* (*www.blommehaven.dk*; April to early Sept; bus #6 or #19), overlooking the bay 3km south of the city centre, and *Århus Nord* (*www.dk-camping.dk/aarhusnord*), 8km north, open year round – take bus #117 or #118 from the bus station; both have cabins.

The City

Århus divides into two clearly defined parts: the old section, close to the cathedral, a tight cluster of medieval streets, and, surrounding this, a less characterful modern sector. **Søndergade** is the city's main street, a pedestrianized strip that leads down into Bispetorvet and the old centre, the streets of which form a web around the **Domkirke** (May–Sept Mon–Sat 9.30am–4pm; Oct–April Mon–Sat 10am–3pm), a massive if plain Gothic church, most of which dates from the fifteenth century, the original twelfth-century structure having been destroyed by fire. At the eastern end, the altarpiece is a grand triptych by the noted Bernt Notkes. Look also at the painted glass window behind the altar, the work of the Norwegian Emmanuel Vigeland (brother of Gustav). The area around the cathedral is a leisurely district of browsable shops and enticing cafés. On Clements Torv, across the road from the cathedral in the basement under Unibank, the **Viking Museum** (Mon–Wed & Fri 9.30am–4pm, Thurs 9.30am–6pm; free) displays Viking finds, including sections of the original ramparts and some Viking craftsmen's tools, alongside some informative accounts of early Århus. Close by, at Domkirkeplads 5, the **Women's Museum** (June–Aug daily 10am–5pm; rest of the year Tues–Sun 10am–4pm; *www.kvindemuseet.dk*; 25kr) stages temporary exhibitions on many aspects of women's lives and lifestyles past and present. West along Vestergade, the thirteenth-century **Vor Frue Kirke** (Mon–Fri 10am–2pm, Sat 10am–noon) is actually the site of three churches, most notable of which is the atmospheric eleventh-century crypt church, discovered beneath several centuries-worth of rubbish during restoration work on the main church in the 1950s. Look in, also, at the main church, for Claus Berg's detailed altarpiece, and, through the cloister remaining from the pre-Reformation monastery, now an old folks' home, for the medieval frescoes inside the third church, which depict local working people rather than biblical scenes.

If you've visited the tourist office, you've already been inside the least interesting section of one of the modern city's major sights, the **Århus Rådhus**, a controversial structure built in the 1940s. You're free to walk in and look for yourself, but it's best to take a guided tour (10kr) conducted in English at 11am on weekdays during the summer. Above the entrance hangs Hagedorn Olsen's huge mural, *A Human Society*, symbolically depicting the city emerging from World War II. Perhaps most interesting are the walls of the small civic room; Albert Naur, who designed them during the Nazi occupation, concealed various Allied insignia in their intricate floral patterns. Finally, a lift (late June to early Sept noon & 2pm; 5kr, included in the tour) climbs to the bell tower and a view over the city and across the bay.

It's a short walk from here to the city's best-known attraction, **Den Gamle By**, on Viborgvej (daily: Jan 11am–3pm; Feb–March & Nov–Dec 10am–4pm; April–May & Sept–Oct 10am–5pm; June–Aug 9am–6pm; *www.dengamleby.dk*; 60kr), an open-air museum of traditional Danish life, with sixty-odd half-timbered houses from all over the country, dismantled and moved here piece by piece. Many of the craftsmen's buildings are used for their original purpose, the overall aim of the place being to give an impression of an old Danish market town, something it does very effectively. Fans of Danish art may well prefer to visit the **Århus Art Museum** (Tues–Sun 10am–5pm, Wed until 8pm; *www.aarhuskunstmuseum.dk*; 40kr) in Vennelystparken, a little way north, with works from the late eighteenth century to the modern day, including the radiant canvases of Asger Jorn and Richard Mortensen, and Bjørn Nørgaard's sculptured version of Christian IV's tomb: the original, in Roskilde Cathedral (see p.344), is stacked with riches; this one features a coffee cup, an egg and a ballpoint pen.

The outskirts

On Sundays Århus resembles a ghost town, with most locals spending the day in the parks or beaches on the city's outskirts. The closest beaches are just north of the city at Riis Skov, easily reached with buses #6, #12 or #16. Otherwise, the Marselisborg Skov is the city's largest park, home to the Marselisborg Slot, summer residence of the Danish royals, the landscaped grounds of which can be visited when the monarch isn't staying. Further east paths run down to rarely crowded pebbly beaches, and, near the junction of Ørneredevej and Thorsmøllevej, to the Dyrehaven or Deer Park. A few kilometres further on, the **Moesgård Prehistoric Museum** (April–Sept daily 10am–5pm; rest of the year Tues–Sun 10am–4pm; *www.moesmus.dk*; 35kr), reached direct on bus #6, details Danish civilizations from the Stone Age onwards with copious finds and easy-to-follow illustrations. Its most notable exhibit is the "Grauballe Man", a body dated 80 BC discovered to the west of Århus in a peat bog and thus amazingly well preserved. From the museum, a "prehistoric tramway" runs 3km to the sea, past a scattering of reassembled prehistoric dwellings, monuments and burial places. If you don't have the energy for any more walking, you can take a #19 bus back to the city from here; the stop is a hundred metres to the north.

Eating, drinking and nightlife

If cash is tight, or you're stocking up for a picnic, use the *Special Smørrebrød* outlet at Nybanegårdsgade 53, or the late-opening supermarket (8am–midnight) at the train station. Cruising the old-town **cafés** and **restaurants** will turn up plenty of lunchtime specials for around 55kr; for instance the theatrical *Pind's Café* at Skolegade 11, which often looks shut but does excellent *smørrebrød*. For something quick and inexpensive try the tasty burgers at *Karls* on Klostergade or the bagel burgers at *Rhodes* on Frederiks Allé. At *Dragen*, Åboulevarden 64, you can, for 99kr, choose your ingredients from the wok buffet and have them stir-fried in front of you. *Italia*, at Åboulevarden 9, is good value, as are the highly rated **vegetarian** meals at *Kulturgyngen*, Fronthuset Mejlgade 53. On Åboulevarden, along the northern bank of a newly uncovered section of the Århus River (previously covered by pavement), a string of trendy eating and drinking venues have recently popped up; try *Cross Café* for their generous brunch platters at 67kr or their over-sized salmon sandwiches. If you can afford a bit more, try visiting the beautiful Marselisborg Havn harbour, which has a number of pricey restaurants including the superb *Seafood*. For superb Danish pastry, *Emmerys*, the city's oldest patisserie in Guldsmedegade 24-26 is worth a visit; the bakery is organic and the cakes to die for.

Århus, along with Aalborg further north, is the only place in Denmark with a **nightlife** to match that of Copenhagen. The city has particularly wonderful **bars**, many situated in the streets close to the cathedral, including the movie-themed *Casablanca* at Rosensgade 12, the pricey *Carlton* nearby at no. 23, and *Englen* and *Kindrødt* both on Studsgade. Around the corner, *Masken* on Store Torv is also a worthwhile stop with impressive masks from around the globe decorating the walls. The cream of Danish and international rock acts can be found at *Voxhall*, Vester Allé 15, with its restaurant and cinema, and *Train*, Toldbodgade 6, with a slightly older clientele; *Fatter Eskil*, Skolegade 25, and *Kulturgyngen*, Fronthuset, Mejlgade 53, have more run-of-the-mill blues bands. *New Clear*, Klostergade 34, currently hosts the hottest **club scene**, while the leading **jazz** venue is the smoky, atmospheric *Bent J*, at Nørre Allé 66.

Listings

Airlines SAS ☎70.10.20.00; for domestic ☎70.10.30.00.

Car rental Avis, Jens Baggesens Vej 27 (☎86.16.10.99) and Spanien 63 (☎86.19.23.99); Europcar, Sønder Allé 35 (☎89.33.11.11).

Cycle rental Cycle Sports Centre, Gunnar Asmussen, Fredensgade 54 (☎86 19 57 00) 50kr a day, 250kr a week.

Hospitals Århus Kommunehospital, on Nørrebrogade. For a doctor, call ☎86.20.10.22 (4pm–8am).

Internet cafés Gate 58, Vestergade 58 (☎87.30.02.80; Mon–Thurs noon–midnight, Sat & Sun noon–8am; 25kr/hr); Net House Computercafé, Nørre Allé 66A (☎87.30.00.96; daily noon to midnight; 25kr/hr).

Pharmacy Løve Apoteket, Store Torv 5 (☎86.12.00.22) is open 24hr.

Police Århus Politistation, Ridderstræde 1 (☎87.31.14.48).

Post office On Banegårdpladsen, by the station (Mon–Fri 9.30am–6pm, Sat 10am–1pm).

Viborg

For a long time the junction of the major roads across Jutland, **VIBORG** was once one of the most important communities in the country. From Knud in 1027 to Christian V in 1655, all Danish kings were crowned here, and until the early nineteenth century the town was the seat of a provincial assembly. As the national administrative axis shifted towards Zealand, however, Viborg's importance waned, and although it still has the high court of West Denmark, it's now primarily a market town for the local farming community.

The twin towers of the **Domkirke** (April–May & Sept Mon–Sat 11am–4pm, Sun noon–4pm; June–Aug Mon–Sat 10am–5pm, Sun noon–5pm; Oct–March Mon–Sat 11am–3pm, Sun noon–3pm) are the most visible feature of the compact town centre, and the most compelling reminder of Viborg's former glories. The interior is dominated by the brilliant frescoes of Joakim Skovgaard, whose work can also be seen in the **Skovgaard Museum** (daily: May–Sept 10am–12.30pm & 1.30–5pm; Oct–April 1.30–5pm; June–Aug 10kr, rest of the year free), inside the former Rådhus across Gammel Torv. For a broader perspective of Viborg's past, keep an hour spare for exploring the **Viborgs Stiftsmuseum** (District Museum) on the northern side of Hjultorvet between Vestergade and Skt. Mathias Gade (mid-June to Aug daily 11am–5pm; Sept to mid-June Mon–Fri 2–5pm, Sat & Sun 11am–5pm; 20kr), which has everything from prehistoric artifacts to clothes, furniture and household appliances.

The **tourist office** on Nytorv (mid-June to Aug Mon–Fri 9am–5pm, Sat 9am–3pm; mid-May–mid-June Mon–Fri 9am–5pm, Sat 9am–12.30pm; rest of the year Mon–Fri 9am–4pm, Sat 9.30am–12.30pm; ☎86.61.16.66, *www.viborg.dk*) can supply a handy map for exploring old Viborg and advise on **accommodation**. In town, *Palads Hotel*, 5 Sct. Mathias Gade (☎86.62.37.00, *www.hotelpalads.dk*; ⑨), often has reduced rates. The more affordable **youth hostel** (☎86.67.17.81, *www.danhostel.dk/viborg*; ②, closed Dec–March) and **campsite** (with cabins), are both 2km across the lake from the town centre, along Vinkelvej (bus #707).

Aalborg

The main city of north Jutland and the fourth largest in Denmark, **AALBORG** hugs the southern bank of the Limfjord and boasts a nightlife and music scene to rival Copenhagen's. The most obvious place to spend a night or two before venturing into the wilder countryside beyond, Aalborg is the main transport terminus for the region, and boasts a well-preserved old centre dating from its seventeenth-century trading heyday. The era is perhaps best exemplified by the Jens Bangs Stenhus opposite the tourist office, a grandiose five stories in the Dutch Renaissance style, which has functioned as a pharmacy since it was built. The commercial roots of the city are further evidenced by the collection of portraits of the town's merchants that hang inside the **Budolfi Domkirke** (May–Sept Mon–Fri 9am–4pm, Sat 9am–2pm; Oct–April Mon–Fri 9am–3pm, Sat 9am–noon), behind: a small but elegant specimen of sixteenth-century Gothic, built on the site of an eleventh-century wooden church, from which a few tombs remain, embedded in the walls close to the altar. Outside, across the square, the **Aalborg Historical Museum** at Algade 48 (Tues–Sun 10am–5pm; *www.aahm.dk;* 20kr) has fairly routine displays, apart from an impressive glasswork collection. Behind here, just off Gammel Torv, the fifteenth-century **Monastery of the Holy Ghost** can be viewed by way of guided tours (mid-June to late Aug Mon–Fri at 1.30pm; 25kr), which take in the monks' refectory, kept largely unchanged since the last monk left, and the small Friar's room, the only part of the monastery in which nuns (from the adjoining nunnery) were permitted. Most interesting, however, are the frescoes that cover the entire ceiling of the chapel.

On the other side of Østerågade, the sixteenth-century **Aalborghus Slot** is worth visiting for a trip round its severely gloomy **dungeon** (May–Oct Mon–Fri 8am–3pm; free). Outside the centre of town, the **North Jutland Art Museum** located on Kong Christians Allé (July & Aug daily 10am–5pm; Sept–June closed Mon; ☎98.13.80.88, *www.nordjyllandskunst-*

musem.dk; 30kr), close to the junction with Vesterbro (buses #5, #8, #10 and #11 or a fifteen-minute walk), and housed in a building designed by the Finnish architect Alvar Aalto, is one of the country's better modern art collections, featuring, alongside numerous Danish contributions, works by Max Ernst, Andy Warhol, Le Corbusier and Claes Oldenburg. After leaving the museum, you can get a grand view over the city and the Limfjord by ascending the **Aalborg Tower** (daily: July to mid-Aug 10am–7pm; April–June & mid-Aug to Sept 11am–5pm; 20kr), on the hill just behind. The **Aalborg Maritime Museum** (daily: May–Aug 10am–6pm; rest of the year 10am–4pm; *www.aalborgmarinemuseum.dk*; 60kr), 2km west of the centre at Vestrefjordvej 81 (buses #2 and #8), recalls the city's time as an important shipbuilding port. The highlight is inspecting the tight working and living conditions in "Springeren", the 54-metre-long submarine which now forms the museum's centrepiece.

Practicalities

The **tourist office** is centrally placed at Østerågade 8 (mid-June to Sept Mon–Fri 9am–5.30pm, Sat 10am–1pm; rest of year Mon–Fri 9am–4.30pm, Sat 10am–1pm; ☎98.12.60.22, *www.visitaalborg.dk*). The cheapest **hotels** are the traditional *Aalborg Sømandshjem*, Østerbro 27 (☎98.12.19.00, *www.hotel-aalborg.com*; ⑤) and the slightly cosier *Hotellet Krogen*, Skibstedsvej 4 (☎98.12.17.05, *www.krogen.dk*; ⑤). There's a large **youth hostel** (Fjordparken: ☎98.11.60.44, *www.danhostelnord.dk/aalborg*; ②; reservations necessary) 3km west of the town on the Limfjord bank beside the marina – take bus #8 from the centre to the end of its route – and, about 300m away, a **campsite**, *Strandparken* (☎89.12.76.29, *www.strandparken.dk*; mid-April to mid-Sept). For a little more adventure, catch the half-hourly **ferry** (☎98.11.78.23; 6.30am–11.15pm; 12kr) from near the campsite to Egholm, an island in Limfjord with free camping under open-sided shelters. In pursuit of **food and drink**, almost everybody heads for Jomfru Ane Gade, a small street close to the harbour between Bispensgade and Borgergade, on which a number of restaurants/bars advertise daily specials: the most reliable are *Fyrtøjet* at no.7, and *Dirch's Regensen* at no.16, which generally offer lunch for 50–60kr. Aalborg Kongres & Kultur Center at Europa Pads 4 (☎99.35.55.65, *www.akkc.dk*) is the city's new theatre and concert venue.

Frederikshavn

FREDERIKSHAVN is neither pretty nor particularly interesting, and as a ferry port it's usually full of Swedes and Norwegians taking advantage of Denmark's liberal boozing laws. But the town is virtually unavoidable if you're heading north, being at the end of the rail route from Aalborg. If you've an international ferry to meet at Hirtshals, change to the private train (InterRail fifty percent reduction, Eurail not valid) at Hjørring.

If you have half an hour to spare, visit the squat white tower, **Krudttårnet** (June to mid-Sept daily 10.30am–5pm; 10kr), near the station, which has maps detailing the harbour's seventeenth-century fortifications and a collection of military paraphernalia from the seventeenth to the nineteenth centuries. With more time, take bus #3 to Møllehuset and walk on through Bangsboparken to the **Bangsbo Museet** (June to mid-Sept daily 10.30am–5pm; winter closed Mon; 35kr), where displays chart the development of Frederikshavn from the 1600s, alongside the grotesque but engrossing "Collection of Human Hairwork" and an assortment of maritime exhibits, distinguished only by the twelfth-century Ellingå Ship and an exhibition covering the German occupation during World War II and the Danish resistance movement.

Buses and trains into Frederikshavn both stop at the **train station**, a short walk along Skippergade and Denmarksgade from the town centre. Some continue to the **ferry terminal** near Havnepladsen, also close to the centre where Color Line ferries leave for Larvik, Stena Line ferries for Oslo and boats (InterRail fifty percent reduction) and the cheaper and much quicker sea catamarans make for Gothenburg. The **tourist office** is close by at Skandiatorv 1 (mid-June to Aug Mon–Sat 8.30am–7pm, Sun 11am–7pm; rest of year Mon–Fri

9am–4pm, Sat 11am–2pm; ☎98.42.32.66, *www.frederikshavn-tourist.dk*). The cheapest **hotels** are both central: *Discount Logi Teglgården*, Teglgårdsvej 3 (☎98.42.04.44; ③), and *Hotel Herman Bang* at Tordenskjoldsgade 3 (☎98.42.21.66; ④). There's also a **youth hostel** at Buhlsvej 6 (☎98.42.14.75, *www.danhostel.dk/frederikshavn*; ②), 1500m north of the train station, and a cabin-equipped **campsite**, Nordstrand, at Apholmenvej 40 (☎98.42.93.50; April to late Oct; bus #4), 3km north of the centre off Nordre Strandvej.

Skagen

If you have the option, skip Frederikshavn altogether in favour of **SKAGEN**, 40km north, which perches almost at the very top of Jutland amid a breathtaking landscape of heather-topped sand dunes. It can be reached by private bus or train (Eurail not valid, Scanrail and InterRail fifty percent reduction on both) roughly once an hour. The bus is the best choice if you're planning to stay at the Skagen youth hostel, as it stops outside.

Sunlight seems to gain extra brightness as it bounces off the two seas which collide off Skagen's coast, something which attracted the **Skagen artists** in the late nineteenth century. They arrived in the small fishing community during 1873 and 1874 and often met in the bar of *Brøndum's Hotel*, off Brøndumsvej, the grounds of which now house the **Skagen Museum** (April & Oct Tues–Sun 11am–4pm; May & Sept daily 10am–5pm; June–Aug daily 10am–6pm; Nov–March Wed–Fri 1–4pm, Sat 11am–4pm, Sun 11am–3pm; 50kr). Many of the canvases depict local scenes, using the town's strong natural light to capture subtleties of colour. The hotel owner's stepsister, Anna, herself a skillful painter, married one of the group's leading lights, Michael Ancher. Nearby, at Markvej 2–4, is **Michael and Anna Anchers' Hus** (daily: July to mid-Aug 10am–6pm; May–June & mid-Aug to Sept 10am–5pm; April & Oct 11am–3pm; rest of the year Sat & Sun 11am–3pm; 40kr), evoking the atmosphere of the time through an assortment of squeezed tubes of paint, sketches, paintings, piles of canvases, books and ornaments.

The artists made Skagen fashionable, and the town continues to be a popular holiday destination. But it still bears many marks of its tough past as a fishing community, the history of which is excellently documented in **Skagens By og Egnsmuseum** on P.K. Nielsensvej 8–10, a fifteen-minute walk south along Skt. Laurentii Vej from the centre (July daily 10am–6pm; May–June & Aug–Sept Mon–Fri 10am–4pm, Sat & Sun 11am–4pm; March–April & Oct Mon–Fri 10am–4pm; rest of the year Mon–Fri 11am–3pm; 30kr). Amid the dunes south of town, a further twenty minutes' walk along Skt. Laurentii Vej, Damstedvej and Gammel Kirkesti, is **Den Tilsandede Kirke** (The Buried Church; June–Sept 11am–5pm; 8kr). This fourteenth-century church was swallowed by sandstorms during the eighteenth century. Part of the tower is open to the public, while the floor and cemetery lie beneath the sands. The impressive new **Skagen Odde Naturcenter** (daily: June–Aug 10am–10pm; Sept–May 10am–4pm; *www.skagen-natur.dk*; 65kr) is designed by the world-famous architect Jørn Utzon (author of the Sydney Opera House) and centred around the themes of sand, water, wind and light. The forces of nature can be further appreciated at Grenen, a lighthouse and restaurant 4km north of Skagen (hourly bus #79 during the summer), along Skt. Laurentii Vej, Fyrvej and the beach, where two seas – the Kattegat and Skagerrak – meet with a powerful clashing of waves. You can also get there by a tractor-drawn bus (April–Oct; 15kr return) aptly named the *Sandormen* (lugworm) – although it's an enjoyable walk as the scenery is beautiful.

Practicalities

The combined **bus and train station** is on Skt. Laurentii Vej, and plays host to the **tourist office** (mid-June to early-Aug Mon–Sat 9am–7pm, Sun 10am–4pm; rest of year reduced hours; ☎98.44.13.77, *www.skagen-tourist.dk*); check here for details of the summer sleep-in, whose location is liable to change. Otherwise, for its artistic associations *Brøndum's Hotel*, Anchervej 3 (☎98.44.15.55, *www.broendumshotel.dk*; ⑧), is by far the most atmospheric spot to stay – book well ahead in summer. A little cheaper is *Skagen Sømandshjem*, Østre Strandvej

2 (☎98.44.25.88, *www.skaw.dk/soemandshjem*; ⑥), which also serves up bargain meals. Or try *Den Gamle Skibssmedie*, Vestre Standvej 28 (☎98.44.67.16; ⑨); or *Clausens Hotel*, Skt. Laurentii Vej 35 (☎98.45.01.66, *www.clausenshotel.dk*; ⑦). There are two **youth hostels**: one at Rolighedsvej 2 (☎98.44.22.00, *www.danhostelnord.dk/skagen*; ②) and one at Højensvej 32 in Gammel Skagen (☎98.44.13.56, *www.skaw.dk/hostel*; ②; late March to late Oct; bus #79 to Frederikshaven), 3km west of Skagen. Of a number of **campsites**, the most accessible are *Grenen* (☎98.44.25.46, *www.grenencamping.dk*; May to early Sept), to the north along Fyrvej, which has cabins, and *Poul Eeg's* (☎98.44.14.70; mid-May to early Sept), on Batterivej, left off Oddenvej just before the town centre.

travel details

Trains

Copenhagen to: Aalborg (hourly; 4hr 40min); Århus (30 daily; 3hr 10min); Esbjerg (12 daily; 3hr 15min); Helsingør (every 20 min; 1hr); Odense (45 daily; 1hr 30min); Ringsted (every 15min; 45min); Roskilde (every 12min; 22min).

Århus to: Aalborg (34 daily; 1hr 25min); Frederikshavn (every 2hr; 3hr); Viborg (every 30min; 1hr).

Esbjerg to: Århus (hourly, change at Fredericia; 2hr 10min); Fredericia (hourly; 1hr); Ribe (hourly; 35min).

Fredericia to: Århus (38 daily; 1hr 10min).

Frederikshavn to: Aalborg (23 daily; 1hr 10min); Skagen (12 daily; 1hr 15min).

Helsingør to: Hillerød (hourly; 30min).

Odense to: Århus (30 daily; 1hr 30min); Esbjerg (30 daily; 2hr).

Roskilde to: Kalundborg (hourly; 1hr 15min)

Buses

Copenhagen to: Aalborg (3 daily; 4hr 45min); Århus (6 daily; 3hr 30min); Hanstholm (1 daily; 8hr 45min); Helsingør (30 daily; 1hr).

Aalborg to: Esbjerg (3 daily; 4hr 45min).

Århus to: Copenhagen (6 daily; 3hr 30min).

Frederikshavn to: Esbjerg (3 daily; 5hr); Skagen (8 daily; 1hr).

Kerteminde to: Nyborg (23 daily; 30min).

Odense to: Kerteminde (46 daily; 40min); Nyborg (39 daily; 50min).

Ferries

Kalundborg to: Århus (ferry 2–8 daily; 3hr; catamaran 3–5 daily; 1hr 40min).

CHAPTER 8

ESTONIA

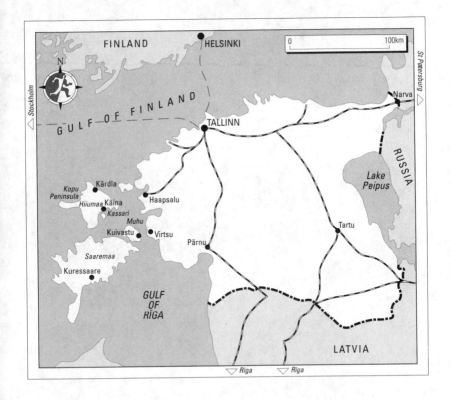

Introduction

It's a tribute to the resilience of the **Estonians** that during the ten years since the Declaration of Independence in August 1991 they've transformed their country from a dour outpost of the former Soviet Union into a viable nation with the most stable economy in the Baltic region. This is even more impressive in the light of the fact that Estonians have ruled their own country for barely thirty years out of the past eight hundred. A Finno-Ugric people related to the Finns, the Estonians have had the misfortune to be surrounded by powerful, warlike neighbours. The first to conquer Estonia were the Danes, who arrived at the start of the thirteenth century; they were succeeded in turn by German crusading knights, Swedes and then Russians. Following a mid-nineteenth-century cultural and linguistic revival known as the National Awakening, the collapse of Germany and Tsarist Russia allowed the Estonians to snatch their independence in 1918. Their brief freedom between the two world wars was extinguished by the Soviets in 1940 and Estonia disappeared from view again. When the country re-emerged from the Soviet shadow in 1991, some forty percent of its population were Russians who had been encouraged to settle there during the Soviet era.

The capital **Tallinn** is an atmospheric city with a magnificent medieval centre and lively nightlife. Two other major cities, **Tartu**, a historic university town, and **Pärnu**, a major seaside resort, are worth a day or so each. Estonia's low population means that the countryside – around forty percent of which is covered by forest and much of the rest by lakes – is generally empty and unspoilt. To get a feel for it at its best, head for the Baltic islands of **Saaremaa** and **Hiiumaa**. **Kuressaare**, capital of the former, is home to one of the finest castles in the Baltics.

Spring and summer are the best times to visit, with the warm weather bringing colour to the countryside and a rash of outdoor pavement-cafe drinking to the cities. In winter the temperature can fall below zero for weeks at a time, although it's worth bearing in mind that public transport continues to function normally, and the sight of both countryside and townscapes decked out in deep snow can be a magical one.

Information and maps

The Estonian national tourist association (*www.tourism.ee*) operates **tourist offices** in all the places covered in this chapter, which can be useful for booking bed-and-breakfast accommodation and hotel rooms. Most will also have a few **maps**, brochures and limited information on specific sights. The useful Kümmerly & Frey 1:1,000,000 map of the Baltic States covers Estonia and includes a rudimentary street plan of central Tallinn. Once in the country, you'll find the range of regional maps and city plans published by local firms Regio and Eomap readily available in bookshops. The best detailed street map of Tallinn is the *Falk Plan* which includes enlarged Inner and Old Town sections and also covers public transport routes. For other destinations, local tourist offices and bookshops will usually have reasonably priced maps and plans.

The following terms or their abbreviations are commonly encountered in Estonian **addresses**: *mantee* (mnt.) – road; *puistee* (pst.) – avenue; *tänav* (tn.) – street. Normally when giving an address or naming a street in Estonia *tänav* is not actually used – the street's name alone is enough.

Money and banks

The unit of currency is the **kroon**, normally abbreviated to EEK (Eesti kroon – Estonian Crown), and is divided into 100 sents. Notes come in 1, 2, 5, 10, 25, 50, 100 and 500EEK denominations and coins in 0.05, 0.10, 0.20, 0.50, 1 and 5 EEK denominations. The kroon's value is determined by the value of the German Mark and the current exchange rate is approximately 24EEK to £1 and 16EEK to $1.

Bank (*pank*) **opening hours** in large towns are usually Monday to Friday 9am–4pm, many staying open until 6pm, and most major banks also open on Saturdays 9am–2/4pm. As well as exchanging cash, major banks such as the Tallinna Pank and Hansapank will also cash travellers' cheques (Thomas Cook and American Express preferred) and give you an advance on your Visa card for a commission of around three percent. All banks charge commission. Outside banking hours cash can be exchanged in **exchange offices** (*Valuutavahetus*), and in Tallinn some of the big hotels accept travellers' cheques. ATM machines taking all the usual international cards are now widespread throughout the country. **Credit cards** can be used in some of the more expensive hotels, restaurants and stores, and in some petrol stations in Tallinn, and although you will find places that accept cards outside Tallinn, don't rely on being able to use them.

Communications

Most **post offices** (*postkontor*) are open Monday to Friday 9am–7pm and Saturday 9am–3pm. You can buy stamps here and at some shops, hotels, and kiosks. You can use **public telephones**, most of which now operate on magnetic cards (available in denominations of 30, 50 and 100EEK), for both local and long-distance calls. You can also phone long-distance from a post office or telephone centre where you'll be assigned a phone and asked to pay up front for the number of minutes you expect to talk – don't underestimate because they cut you off automatically. You'll find **Internet cafés** in Tallinn and Tartu, but they're still rare elsewhere. Expect to pay around 40–60EEK per hour.

Getting around

The destinations covered in this chapter are all easily reached by bus. Estonia's rail network has been cut back so drastically in recent years that you're unlikely to use those parts of it that still survive, save perhaps for international services.

■ Trains and buses

Bus tickets can either be bought from the **bus** station ticket office or direct from the driver. It's best to buy long-distance bus tickets in advance if you're travelling at the height of summer or at weekends, especially to the islands. Opt for an express (*ekspress*) bus if possible to avoid frequent stops. Normally **luggage** is taken on board – if you have a large bag you may have to pay a nominal fee to have it stowed in the luggage compartment. Buses are also useful for travelling to the other Baltic countries with services linking Tallinn, Vilnius and Rīga.

Train tickets should also be bought in advance – ticket windows are usually marked *piletite müük*: international lines are *rahvusvaheline*, suburban lines *linnalähedane*. Long-distance services are divided into the following categories: *reisirong* (passenger) and *kiir* (fast). Both are slow but the latter, usually requiring a reservation, won't stop at every second village.

Both train and bus information is available from station timetable boards – the Estonian for departure is *väljub*, and arrival is *saabub*. A Baltic Explorer **rail pass** gives you unlimited travel throughout Estonia and other Baltic Republics; it's available to ISIC-card holders, under-26s, and ITIC-card holders and their

accompanying spouses. For further information on the latest conditions of use and prices contact the RailEurope or Usit CAMPUS branches before leaving home.

■ Driving, hitching and cycling

Driving in Estonia is not too nerve-racking, with main roads in reasonable condition and traffic fairly light outside the towns. Reckless driving is the exception rather than the rule, but watch out for people showing off in BMWs and four-wheel drives. There's no motorway to speak of – just a few stretches of two-lane highway either side of Tallinn and another near Pärnu. **Petrol stations** can be a little thin on the ground in rural areas, so carry a spare can. Speed limits are 50kph in built-up areas and 70 to 100kph on the open road. In towns it's forbidden to overtake stationary trams so that passengers can alight in safety, and it's against the law to drive after drinking any alcohol.

Car rental costs around $60 per day from one of the international companies, as little as half that from some local firms – though it's worth double-checking both the contract and the quality of the car before going for one of the cheaper deals. If you are not the car owner a valid driving licence, plus another form of ID with a photo is required, along with proof of insurance, the car's registration and a letter of authorization. **Hitching** is fairly common between major centres and holiday destinations, and you'll be expected to make a contribution towards petrol. Estonia, being predominantly flat, is reasonable for **cycling** but there aren't any cycle lanes and you can't expect much consideration from other road users. In summer it's reasonable easy to find bike hire outlets in the major tourist centres on the islands, although they're pretty rare elsewhere.

Accommodation

Though cheaper than in western Europe, **accommodation** in Estonia is still going to take a large chunk out of most budgets. However, it is possible to keep costs down by staying in private rooms, and most towns have one or two reasonable budget hotels. If money isn't an issue you'll have few problems finding a decent place to stay.

■ Private rooms and hotels

For budget travellers **private room** accommodation is often the best option, usually costing between

ACCOMMODATION PRICE CODES

Throughout this guide, accommodation is coded on a scale of ① to ⑨, the code indicating the lowest price per person per night you could expect to pay in each establishment in high season. With hostels this is the nightly rate per person; with hotels, the price is arrived at by dividing the cost of the cheapest double room by two. The prices indicated by the codes are as follows:

① under £5/$8 (€9)　　　④ £15–20/$24–32 (€27–36)　　　⑦ £30–35/$48–56 (€54–63)
② £5–10/$8–16 (€9–18)　　⑤ £20–25/$32–40 (€36–45)　　　⑧ £35–40/$56–64 (€63–72)
③ £10–15/$16–24 (€18–27)　⑥ £25–30/$40–48 (€45–54)　　　⑨ £40/$64 (€72) and over

200–400EEK per person. This can be arranged through local tourist offices or private agencies. You should be able to find plain but clean **hotel** rooms for between 300–500EEK per person, often in converted student hostels or apartment buildings, and better value for money than the purpose-built Soviet-era places. There's a growing number of small **guest-houses** and mid-range pension-type establishments in the more popular destinations – expect to pay between 200–350EEK per night. Prices for mid-range and expensive places usually include breakfast, and many places accept credit cards. In all but the very cheapest hotels there will usually be at least one English-speaking member of staff.

■ Hostels and campsites

Estonia has a network of **hostels**, though these are often merely student dorms converted during the summer. Contact the Estonian Youth Hostel Association (EYHA), Tatari 39, room 310, Tallinn (Mon–Fri 9am–6pm; ☎2/6461 455, *www.baltichostels.net*) for the latest details. Hostel accommodation, where available, costs around 100–200EEK per person. An ex-Soviet phenomenon is the cabin **campsite** (*kämping*), usually offering accommodation in 3- to 4-bed cabins (shared facilities) for around 180–260EEK per person. Many of these places will also let you pitch a tent, an option which works out slightly cheaper than sleeping under a roof.

Food and drink

Elderly expats aside, not too many people come to Estonia for the food. The national cuisine consists mainly of pig by-products teamed with potatoes and other home vegetable-patch produce. Note that you're very likely to encounter indigenous recipes in Estonian restaurants where, in true post-Soviet style, stodgy meat and two veg dishes dominate most menus.

■ Food

Soup (*supp*), dark bread (*leib*), sour cream (*hapukoor*) and herring (*heeringas*) figure prominently in the Estonian diet, a culinary legacy of the country's largely peasant past, and if you like your food without frills you can eat very well here. A typical **national dish** is *verevorst* and *mulgikapsad* (blood sausage and sauerkraut), and you're also likely to encounter various kinds of smoked fish, particularly eel (*angerjas*), perch (*ahven*) and pike (*haug*).

You'll really have to be invited into a local home to enjoy Estonian food at its best as, unfortunately, the average **restaurant** (*restoran*) tends to serve up hearty international meat dishes – the most common of which is *karbonaad*, basically pork chop (sometimes fried in batter) – with potatoes and seasonal vegetables. You might occasionally encounter game, and several ethnic restaurants break the culinary monotony in Tallinn. **Vegetarianism** is not a widely understood concept. When eating out you're often better off heading for bars and cafés, many of which serve snack dishes and even full meals, and where the bill is likely to be less than in a restaurant. By and large you should be able to have a decent meal (two courses and a drink) for less than 130EEK and you'd have to really push the boat out for the bill to come to more than 200EEK.

If you really want to keep costs down there are various **fast-food** options. Some establishments going under the name of café (*kohvik*) are essentially canteen-style restaurants where you can pick up main courses and dishes-of-the-day for as little as 30EEK, as well as basic soups, salads and sweets. There's also a growing number of pizzerias, many of which offer a range of pasta dishes. For self-catering, **food shopping** poses no major problems with staples like bread, cheese, smoked meat and tinned fish all available in supermarkets, and fresh fruit and vegetables available in markets.

◼ Drink

Estonians are enthusiastic drinkers with **beer** (õlu) being the most popular tipple. The principal local brands are Saku and A. Le Coq, both of which are rather tame light lager-style brews, although both companies also produce stronger, Guinness-like porters. The strongest beers are found on the islands – Saaremaa õlu is the best known. In bars a lot of people favour **vodka** (viin) with mixers which, thanks to generous measures, is a more cost-effective route to oblivion. **Local alcoholic specialities** include hõõgvein (mulled wine) and Vana Tallinn, a pungent dark liqueur which some suicidal souls mix with vodka.

An ever-increasing range of pubs and bars – most of which imitate Irish or American models – are beginning to take over the Estonian drinking scene, especially in Tallinn and other major centres. If you're not boozing, head for a kohvik (café), where, although alcohol is usually served, getting drunk is not a priority. In Estonia **coffee** (kohv) is usually of the filter variety, and **tea** (tee) is served without milk.

Opening hours and holidays

Most **shops** are open Monday to Friday 9/10am–6/7pm and Saturday 10am–2/3pm. Some food shops stay open until 10pm or later and are also open on Sundays. **Public holidays** when most shops and all banks will be closed are as follows: Jan 1; Feb 24 (Independence Day); March 14 (Language Day); Good Friday; Easter Monday; May 1; Whitsun; June 23 (Victory Day); June 24 (St John's Day); August 20 (Day of Restoration of Independence); Dec 25 & 26.

Emergencies

Estonians claim that their country is a hotbed of crime and that visitors run a routine risk of being robbed and murdered, particularly in Tallinn. The truth is that while there are problems with theft and street crime they're still at lower levels than in western Europe, and if you keep your wits about you and avoid staggering around the backstreets drunk after dark you should come to no harm. The Estonian **police** (politsei) are mostly very young and some may speak a little English, but don't bank on it. As far as **health** goes, though emergency health care is free in Estonia, the country's hospitals are underequipped and if you fall seriously ill it's best to head for home if possible. No immunizations are required for Estonia.

> **Emergency Numbers**
> Police, Ambulance and Fire ☎112.

TALLINN

The port city of **TALLINN**, Estonia's compact, human-scale capital, has been shaped by nearly a millennium of outside influence. Its name, derived from *taani linnus*, meaning "Danish Fort", is a reminder of the fact that the city was founded by the Danes at the beginning of the thirteenth century, and since that time political control has nearly always been in the hands of foreigners – Germans, Swedes and Russians. The Germans have undoubtedly had the most lasting influence on the city; Tallinn was one of the leading cities of the Hanseatic League, the German-dominated association of Baltic trading cities, and for centuries it was known to the outside world by its German name, Reval. Even when Estonia was ruled by the kings of Sweden or the tsars of Russia, the city's public life was controlled by the German nobility, and its commerce run by German merchants. Today reminders of foreign rule abound in the streets of Tallinn, where each of the city's one-time rulers have left their mark. Everything about Tallinn, from the fortress of the Germanic knights above the Old Town to the grimmest Soviet-era satellite suburbs, reveals something of its past, making it a fascinating place to explore.

Arrival, information and city transport

Tallinn's international **train station** is the Balti jaam at Toompuiestee 35, just northwest of the Old Town, while the city's **bus terminal** (*Autobussijaam*) is at Lastekodu 46, a couple of kilometres southeast of the centre – trams #2 and #4 run from nearby Tartu mnt. to Viru väljak, right on the eastern fringes of the old town. For those coming in by **sea** the passenger port (*Reisisadam*) is just northeast of the centre at the end of Sadama. The **airport** (*Lennujaam*) is 3km southeast of the city centre and linked to Viru väljak by bus #2 (every 20–30min, journey time 10min; 15EEK). Tallinn's **tourist office** at Raekoja Plats 10 (April–Oct Mon–Fri 9am–6pm, Sat & Sun 10am–4pm, Nov–March Mon–Fri 9am–5pm, Sat 10am–4pm; ☎2/645 7777, *www.tallinn.ee*) sells various maps and city guides and has limited information about other destinations in Estonia. You can also buy a **Tallinn Card** here, which entitles you to unlimited use of public transport, entrance to museums, a tour of the city, discounts on car rental and savings in some shops and cafés. A 24-hour card costs 195EEK, a 48-hour one 270EEK, and a 72-hour one 325EEK – it's worth doing a few sums to work out if a card will actually give any savings on your planned itinerary. Good sources of up-to-the-minute listings and what's on in the city are *Tallinn This Week* (free) and the very good *City Paper* (29EEK; *www.BalticsWorldwide.com*), available from most newsstands, which also contains information about Rīga and Vilnius. The excellent *Tallinn In Your Pocket* city guide (19EEK; *www.inyourpocket.com*) is available from shops and hotels.

Though most of Tallinn's sights can be covered on foot, the city has an extensive **tram**, **bus** and **trolleybus** network should you need to travel further afield. Services are frequent and cheap, though usually crowded, with tickets (*talongid*) common to all three systems available from kiosks near stops for 10EEK or from the driver for 15EEK. Tickets should be validated using the on-board punches. **Taxis** are reasonably cheap (around 10EEK per km, slightly more after 10pm) though as a foreigner you may occasionally find your meter running faster than it should. Try to ensure that you're not charged the evening rate during the day. Most companies have a minimum charge of 25EEK, but a taxi from one point in the city centre to another should never exceed 50EEK.

Accommodation

There's a shortage of cheap and mid-range hotels in central Tallinn, making **private rooms** the best value for money if you want to be close to the heart of things. *Bed & Breakfast Rasastra*, a few steps north of Viru väljak at Mere 4 (daily 9.30am–6pm; ☎2/6412 291, *rasas-*

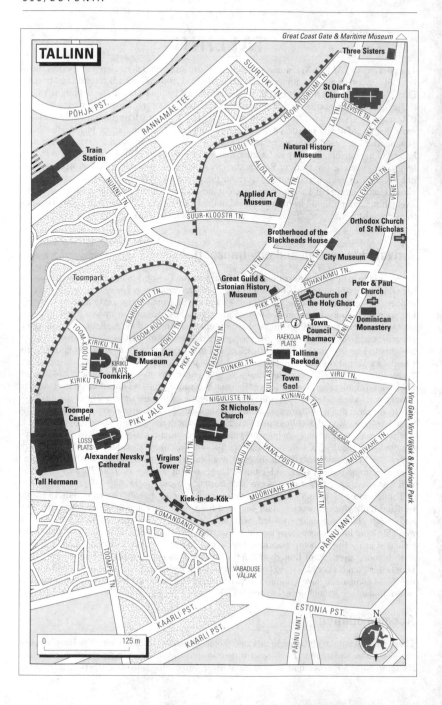

TALLINN

Great Coast Gate & Maritime Museum

Three Sisters

St Olaf's Church

SUURTÜKI TN.

LABORATOORIUMI TN.

PÕHJA PST.

RANNAMÄE TEE

OLEVISTE TN.

LAI TN.

PIKK TN.

Train Station

KOOLI TN.

Natural History Museum

OLEVIMÄGI TN.

VENE TN.

NUNNE TN.

ALDA TN.

LAI TN.

Applied Art Museum

SUUR-KLOOSTR TN.

Orthodox Church of St Nicholas

Brotherhood of the Blackheads House

LAI TN.

PIKK TN.

City Museum

Toompark

Great Guild & Estonian History Museum

PUHAVAIMU TN.

Peter & Paul Church

RAHUKOHTU TN.

TOOM-RÜÜTLI TN.

KOHTU TN.

PIKK TN.

NUNNE TN.

SAIAKANG TN.

Church of the Holy Ghost

VENE TN.

Dominican Monastery

TOOM-KOOLI TN.

KIRIKU TN.

PIKK JALG

RATASKAEVU TN.

Town Council Pharmacy

RAEKOJA PLATS

Estonian Art Museum

KIRIKU PLATS

Toomkirik

DUNKRI TN.

KÜLLASSEPA TN.

Tallinna Raekoda

KIRIKU TN.

VIRU TN.

Toompea Castle

PIKK JALG

NIGULISTE TN.

Town Gaol

KUNINGA TN.

Viru Gate, Viru Väljak & Kadriorg Park

LOSSI PLATS

St Nicholas Church

Alexander Nevsky Cathedral

Virgins' Tower

RÜÜTLI TN.

HARJU TN.

VANA-POSTI TN.

VÄIKE-KARJA

MÜÜRIVAHE TN.

SUUR-KARJA TN.

Tall Hermann

Kiek-in-de-Kök

MÜÜRIVAHE TN.

KOMANDANDI TEE

TOOMPEA TN.

PÄRNU MNT.

VABADUSE VÄLJAK

ESTONIA PST.

N

KAARLI PST.

PÄRNU MNT.

KAARLI PST.

0   125 m

tra@online.ee), offers the widest range of central rooms (②). Best of the **hostels** is the cosy *Vana Tom*, bang in the Old Town at Väike-Karja 1 (☎2/631 3252), with spotless dorms (②) and some double rooms (③), and ten percent discount for HI and Peace Corps members. Of the hostels outside the centre you could do worse than opt for *Merevaik*, Sopruse 182 (☎02/655 3767; ②; 10 percent discount for HI and ISIC cardholders), which has faded but clean singles, doubles and triples in a red-brick block 3km southwest of the Old Town (trolleybus #2 or #3 from Vabaduse väljak to the Linnu stop).

Hotels

Bed & Breakfast, Uus 22 (☎2/641 1464). Small and friendly six-room guesthouse in the old town. Shared facilities. ③.

Central, Narva mnt. 7 (☎2/633 9800, *www.revalhotels.com*). Friendly, English-speaking staff and 3-star comforts. ⑥.

Dorell, Karu 39 (☎2/626 1200). Entrance is through a passage on Narva mnt. A 10min walk from the Old Town, this place is pretty basic but still good value. Shared facilities or rooms to yourself. Parking available. ②.

Eeslitall, Dunkri 4/6 (☎2/631 3755, *www.eeslitall.ee*). Small, simple but central pension. Facilities in corridor. ③.

Kelluka, Kelluka tee 11 (☎2/623 8811, *www.kelluka.ee*). Quiet, pension-type place on the northeastern edge of town. Facilities include a sauna and pool – recommended if your funds stretch that far. Bus #5 from the centre to the Helmiku stop. ④.

Kristiine, Luha 16 (☎2/646 4600, *www.kristiine.ee*). Quiet, friendly place occupying two floors of a grey office block, around 15 minutes' walk from the centre. The rooms are plain but have en-suite facilities and TV. Bus #5, #18, #36 from Vabaduse väljak or tram #3, #4 from Pärnu mnt. to the Luha stop. ③.

Mihkli, Endla 23 (☎2/6664800, *www.mihkli.ee*). Fifteen minutes from the centre on foot, this is a peaceful business-class hotel with small, modern en-suites with TV. ⑤.

PÄÄSU, Söpruse 182 (☎6542013, *paasu@mail.ee*). Unpretentious place occupying the same building as the *Merevaik* hostel (see above). Rooms have dated furnishings but all are clean and with TV. WC and shower shared between every 2 rooms. ②

TKTK Üliopilashotell, Nomme tee 47 (☎2/655 2679). Hotel attached to a student hostel some 3km southwest of the centre, offering plain but neat rooms at good rates. One bathroom for every two rooms. No breakfast. Take bus #17 or #17a from Vabaduse väljak to Koolimaja, or trolleybus #4 from the train station to Tedre. ②.

The City

The heart of Tallinn and location of most of its sights is the Old Town (Vanalinn), once enclosed by the city's medieval walls. At its centre is the **Town Hall Square**, the medieval marketplace, above which looms **Toompea**, the hilltop stronghold of the German Knights who controlled the city during the Middle Ages. There's little to do or see in the streets outside the Old Town, and Tallinn's remaining attractions are located in outlying districts.

Around Town Hall Square

Town Hall Square (Raekoja plats), the cobbled and gently sloping market square at the heart of the Old Town, is as old as the city itself. On its southern side stands an imposing reminder of the Hanseatic past: the fifteenth-century **Town Hall** (Tallinna Raekoda), which boasts an elegant arcade of gothic arches at ground level, and a delicate, slender steeple at its northern end. Look out for the water-spouts in the shape of green-painted dragons just below roof level. Near the summit of the slender steeple you'll spy Vana Toomas (Old Thomas), a sixteenth-century weather vane depicting a medieval mercenary, which has become Tallinn's city emblem. Inside, the two main chambers – the Citizens' Hall and the Council Hall – are almost devoid of ornamentation, except for the latter's elaborately carved benches, the oldest surviving woodcarvings in the country.

Of the other old buildings which line the square, the most venerable is the **Town Council Pharmacy** (Raeapteek) in the northeastern corner, whose dull grey facade dates from the seventeenth century, though the building is known to have existed in 1422 and may be much older. If the Raeapteek leaves you underwhelmed, head for the former Town Gaol (Raevangla) behind the town hall at Raekoja 4/6, which now houses the **Town Hall Museum** (Raemuuseum; Thurs–Tue 10.30am–5.30pm; 10EEK), an entertaining little photographic collection with views of Tallinn from the days when it was still known as Reval, and portraits of Estonians in traditional costume (captions in English).

Close to Raekoja plats are a couple of churches that neatly underline the social divisions of medieval Tallinn. The fourteenth-century **Church of the Holy Ghost** (Pühavaimu kirik; daily 10am–2pm) tucked away on Pühavaimu – reached via a small passage called Saiakang tänav next to the Raeapteek – is the city's most appealing church, a small Gothic building with stuccoed limestone walls, stepped gables and a tall, verdigris-coated spire. Originally the Town Hall chapel, this later became the place where the native Estonian population worshipped, and in 1535 priests from here compiled an Estonian-language Lutheran catechism, an important affirmation of identity at a time when most Estonians had been reduced to serf status. The ornate clock set into the wall above the entrance dates from 1680 and is the oldest public timepiece in Tallinn. The interior of the church – all dark-veneered wood and cream-painted walls – has an intimate beauty, and contains one of the city's most significant pieces of religious art, an extraordinary triptych altar depicting the *Descent of the Holy Ghost* (1483) by the Lübeck master Bernt Notke.

Contrasting sharply is **St Nicholas Church** (Niguliste kirik), sitting on raised open ground just southwest of Raekoja plats. This late-Gothic edifice with its huge limestone basilica and vast white tower was originally built by German merchants. Most of what can be seen today dates from the fifteenth century, and has been extensively restored following Soviet bombing raids at the end of World War II. These days the church is a **museum** (Wed–Fri 10am–6pm, Sat & Sun 11.30am–6pm; 15EEK; English-language pamphlets available) of religious art, its dominating exhibit a spectacular double-winged altar by Herman Rode of Lübeck from 1481, and a largish fragment from a fifteenth-century *danse macabre* frieze by Bernt Notke.

Toompea

From the environs of Town Hall Square the most obvious goal is **Toompea** (from the German, Domberg, meaning "Cathedral Hill"), the hill where the Danes built their fortress after conquering what is now Tallinn in 1219. According to legend Toompea is also the grave of Kalev, the mythical ancestor of the Estonians. The most atmospheric approach is through the sturdy gate tower – built by the Teutonic Knights to contain the Old Town's inhabitants in times of unrest – at the foot of Pikk jalg (Long Leg). This is the cobbled continuation of Pikk, the Old Town's main street, and climbs up to Lossi plats (Castle Square), dominated by the incongruous-looking **Alexander Nevsky Cathedral** (Aleksander Nevski Katedraal; daily 8am–7pm). This gaudy, onion-domed concoction, complete with tacky souvenir shop, built at the turn of the last century for the city's Orthodox population, is an enduring reminder of the two centuries Tallinn spent under the rule of the Russian tsars.

At the head of Lossi plats is **Toompea Castle** (Toompea Loss), on the site of the original Danish fortification. Today's castle is the descendant of a stone fortress built by the Knights of the Sword, the Germanic crusaders who kicked out the Danes in 1227 and controlled the city until 1238 (when the Danes returned). The castle has been altered by every conqueror who raised their flag above it since then; these days it wears a shocking-pink Baroque facade, the result of an eighteenth-century rebuild under Catherine the Great. The northern and western walls are the most original part of the castle, and include three defensive towers, the most impressive of which is the fifty-metre **Tall Hermann** (Pikk Hermann) at the southwestern corner, which dates from 1371.

Toompea Castle is now home to the Riigikogu, Estonia's parliament, and is therefore out of bounds to the public, but nearby a couple of towers that formed part of the Old Town fortifications are accessible. A narrow archway in the medieval walls just south of the Alexander

Nevsky Cathedral leads to the ironically named **Virgins' Tower** (Neitsitorn) which was once a prison for prostitutes and is now home to a café/bar. A little south of here on Komandandi tee is the impregnable-looking **Kiek-in-de-Kök tower** dating from 1475, whose name means "look in the kitchen" in Low German. Kiek-in-de-Kök now contains a **museum** (Tues–Fri 10.30am–5.30pm, Sat & Sun 11am–4.30pm; 10EEK) devoted to the history of Tallinn fortifications, with all exhibits labelled in English.

From Lossi plats Toom Kooli leads north to the **Toomkirik/St Mary's Church** (Tues–Sun 9am–5pm; English-language leaflet 10EEK), the city's understated Lutheran cathedral, originally a wooden church built here by the Danes soon after their arrival in Tallinn. This was replaced by a stone building and named a cathedral in 1240, though the church's present appearance is the result of a 1686 rebuild. Consequently, the cathedral's exterior is hard to pin down stylistically, the Gothic lines of the nave and tower softened by the addition of Baroque side chapels and a spire. The interior is worth dropping in on to admire the fine tombs and the ornate seventeenth-century pulpit by Christian Ackerman, who also carved many of the 107 coats of arms of noble families which adorn the white walls of the vaulted nave and choir. The interior also offers an interesting insight into the social divisions of the church's original congregation; while normal people sat in the pale green pews, local notables had glass-enclosed family boxes to enable them to keep their distance from the hoi polloi.

A stone's throw from the Toomkirik, in a peppermint green neo-Renaissance palace, is the **Estonian Art Museum**, Kiriku plats 1 (Eesti Kunstimuuseum; Wed–Sun 11am–6pm; 10EEK), housed here temporarily pending the construction of a new building in Kadriorg park. This small museum, tracing the development of art in Estonia, displays a range of works from conventional nineteenth-century studies of Tallinn and portraits of peasants in traditional costume to twentieth-century paintings heavily influenced by European artistic trends like Expressionism.

Elsewhere in the Old Town

The remainder of the Old Town contains the commercial streets of medieval Tallinn, lined by merchants' residences and warehouses. Pikk tänav (Long Street), running northeast from Pikk jalg gate and linking Toompea with the port area, has some of the city's most important secular buildings from the Hanseatic period, kicking off with the **Great Guild** (Suur Gild) at Pikk 17. Completed in 1430 this was the city's main guild, meeting place of the German merchants who controlled the city's wealth. Its gloomy Gothic facade now fronts the **Estonian History Museum** (Ajaloomuuseum; 11am–6pm; closed Wed; 10EEK) where a predictable array of weapons, domestic objects and jewellery offers an uninspiring history of Estonia from the Stone Age to the eighteenth century. A side room has more interesting displays of traditional costumes. Exhibits are labelled in Estonian and Russian but there are also English summaries.

If the appearance of their headquarters is anything to go by, the guild who occupied the **House of the Brotherhood of the Blackheads** (Mustpeade Maja), Pikk 26, were a more exuberant bunch than the merchants of the Great Guild. The Renaissance facade of their building, inset with an elaborate stone portal and richly decorated door, cuts a bit of dash amid the stolidity of Pikk. According to legend the guild was founded to defend Tallinn during the Estonian uprising of St George's Day in 1343, though in later years it seems to have degenerated into a drinking club for bachelor merchants. The Brotherhood moved here in 1531 and remained until the guild was abolished by the Soviets in 1940. These days their building houses a concert hall – you can look inside for 10EEK.

Continuing along Pikk brings you to the **St Olaf's Church** (Oleviste kirik), first mentioned in 1267 and named in honour of King Olaf II of Norway, who was canonized for battling against pagans in Scandinavia. Were it not for its size this slab-towered Gothic structure would not be particularly eye-catching, and extensive renovation between 1829 and 1840 has left it with an unexceptional nineteenth-century interior. The church is chiefly famous for the height of its spire which reaches 124 metres today and was even taller in the past. According to local legend the citizens of Tallinn wanted the church to have the highest spire in the world in order to attract passing ships and bring trade into the city. Whether Tallinn's prosperity during the Middle Ages had anything to do with the visibility of the church spire is not known, but between 1625 and 1820 the church burned down eight times as a result of lightning striking the tower.

Bearing witness to the city's medieval wealth are the Old Town's merchants' houses. The best example are the **Three Sisters** (Kolm Õde), a gabled group at Pikk 71. Supremely functional with loading hatches and winch-arms set into their facades, these would have served as combined dwelling places, warehouses and offices, and are among the city's best-preserved Hanseatic buildings. At its far end Pikk is straddled by the **Great Coast Gate** (Suur Rannavärav), a sixteenth-century city gate flanked by two towers. The larger of these, the aptly named "Fat Margaret Tower" (Paks Margareeta) has walls four metres thick and now houses the **Estonian Maritime Museum** (Mere Museum; Wed–Sun 10am–6pm; 10EEK; Estonian, Russian and some English captions), a surprisingly diverting collection of model boats and nautical ephemera spread out over several floors.

West of Lai is one of the longest-surviving sections of Tallinn's medieval city wall, complete with nine towers – to reach it, head down Suur-Kloostri. The walls that surrounded the Old Town were largely constructed during the fourteenth century, but they were added to and enhanced over succeeding centuries until improvements in artillery rendered them obsolete during the eighteenth century. Today just under two kilometres of city wall survive, along with eighteen towers.

The eastern outskirts

Kadriorg Park, a large, heavily wooded park a couple of kilometres east from the Old Town, is closely associated with the Russian Tsar Peter the Great, who first visited Tallinn in 1711, the year after Russia conquered Livonia and Estonia from Sweden. The main entrance to the park is at the junction of Weizenbergi tänav and J. Poska (tram #1 or #3 from Viru väljak). Weizenbergi cuts through the park, running straight past **Kadriorg Palace** (Kadrioru Loss), a Baroque residence designed by the Italian architect Niccolò Michetti, which Peter had built for his wife Catherine (Kadriorg is Estonian for "Catherine's Valley"). These days the palace is the official home of the **Museum of Foreign Art** (Tues–Sun 11am–6pm; 25EEK), with a highly recommended selection of European art through the centuries. The smaller palace behind it is now home to Estonia's president. While waiting for the palace to be completed Peter lived in a small cottage in the grounds of the park. Today this simple building at the junction of Weizenbergi and Mäekalda houses the **Peter the Great House Museum** (Peeter Esimese Majamuuseum; Mon–Fri 11.30am–5pm, Sat & Sun noon–5.30pm; 6EEK) with furniture from the time Peter lived there, along with a few objects from the palace.

Walking down Mäekalda from Peter's cottage leads, after around fifteen minutes, to Narva mnt. On the other side of this busy road is the **Song Bowl** (Lauluväljak), a vast amphitheatre that's the venue for Estonia's Song Festivals. These gatherings, featuring massed choirs thousands strong, have been an important form of national expression in Estonia since the first all-Estonia Song Festival was held in Tartu in 1869, and are held every two years. The present structure, which can accommodate 15,000 singers (with room for a further 30,000 or so on the platform in front of the stage), went up in 1960. The Song Bowl grounds were filled to capacity for the September 1988 festival which was a significant public expression of longing for independence from Soviet rule, and gave rise to the epithet "Singing Revolution".

A tree-lined avenue runs downhill from the amphitheatre to Pirita tee, which runs along the seashore. Turn right here and continue north for 750m to reach **Maarjamäe Palace** (Maarjamae Loss), a neo-Gothic residence built for a Russian count in the 1870s, which looks out over Tallinn Bay at Pirita tee. The building now houses a branch of the **History Museum** (Ajaloomuuseum; Wed–Sun 11am–5.30pm; 5EEK), covering the mid-nineteenth century onwards, and is far more interesting and imaginative than its city-centre counterpart. The display starts with a section on urban and rural life in nineteenth-century Estonia which includes a few re-created domestic interiors, before moving on to the political and social upheavals of the early twentieth century. Later sections have information on the Molotov-Ribbentrop "secret protocols" which effectively handed the Baltic Republics to Stalin, leading into material about the fate of Estonia during World War II, and the activities of the "Forest Brothers", Estonian partisans who carried on the battle against Soviet occupation into the 1950s. Most exhibits have English captions but the earlier sections are in Estonian and Russian only.

The western outskirts

At the other end of Tallinn on the western outskirts of the town is the **Open-Air Museum** (Vabaōhumuuseum; daily: May–Aug 10am–8pm; Sept 10am–6pm; Oct 10am–5pm; Nov–April 10am–4pm; 30EEK), a collection of eighteenth- and nineteenth-century village buildings gathered here from different parts of the country. The exhibits illustrate how Estonian farms developed, from all-timber structures with humans and animals living cheek by jowl, to more sophisticated stone buildings. The museum also includes an appealing wooden church and a windmill, though for many visitors the biggest attraction is the Kolu Kõrts café which serves up traditional bean soup and beer. The museum site slopes down to the sea and is known by the Italian name Rocca al Mare (Rock by the Sea), having been thus christened by a merchant who built himself a mansion here during the late nineteenth century. Get there by bus #21 from the train station or trolleybus #6 from Vabaduse väljak.

Eating, drinking and nightlife

Meat and potatoes figure heavily on most **restaurant** menus in Tallinn, with alternatives available in a handful of ethnic places. Vegetarians are not well catered for, though a few places make a token effort. Many **cafés** and **bars** do **snacks** or even full meals, an option which will usually work out cheaper than eating in a restaurant.

Bars and cafés are your best bet for a good time, with many featuring live music and/or dancing. Most of Tallinn's discos cater for a mainstream techno-loving crowd. More underground, cutting-edge dance music events tend to change location frequently and are advertised by flyposters – if you can't spot any try asking around in the city's hipper bars. Expect to pay 50–70EEK admission for discos and clubs.

Cafés and snacks

Café Anglais, Raekoja plats 14. Excellent coffee and hot chocolate, and sumptuous range of salads and sweets. More expensive than average. Daily 11am–11pm.

Coffe, Vanaturu Kael 8. Good place for a breakfast pastry or a pasta-based lunch, just off the main square. Mon–Sat 9am–6pm, Sun 10am–6pm.

E-köök, Nunne 9. Bakery with takeaway or sit-down cakes, pastries and salad bar. Mon–Sat 7.30am–10pm, Sun 7.30am–6pm.

Elsbet, Viru 2. Old-fashioned café above the *Gnoom* restaurant with a genteel atmosphere, and cakes and snack dishes on the menu. Mon–Sat 8am–9pm, Sun 9am–6pm.

Maiasmokk, Pikk 16. Tallinn's most venerable café – founded in 1864 – with a beautiful wood-panelled interior. You may have to queue for a seat as it's popular with elderly ladies taking a coffee-and-pastries break from shopping. Mon–Sat 8am–7pm, Sun 10am–6pm.

Stockmann Department Store, Liiva laia 53. Self-service restaurant on the fifth floor with excellent sandwiches and salads. Mon–Fri 10am–9pm, Sat & Sun 10am–8pm.

Tristan ja Isolde, Raekoja plats 1. Dark, poky and atmospheric café in the town hall with a full range of drinks and tasty salads and cakes. Daily 8am–11pm.

Restaurants

Buon Giorno, Muurivahe 17. Good place for soups, pasta dishes and cheap specials. Daily 10am–11pm.

Controvento, Vene 12 (☎2/644 0470). Tasteful and authentic Italian restaurant in a fourteenth-century granary. Good selection of pizza and pasta dishes and a decent wine list. Main courses from around 90EEK.

Reservations recommended. Daily 12.30–11pm. Café open for drinks and sandwiches Sun–Thurs 11am–midnight, Fri & Sat 11am–1am.

Eeslitall Restoran, Dunkri 4/6. Probably Tallinn's most famous restaurant, with a formal dining room on the ground floor and a more relaxed cellar downstairs. Pasta and chicken dishes augment the basic pork and potatoes selection. Sun–Thurs 9am–midnight, Fri & Sat 9am–1am.

Egeri Kelder, Roosikrantsi 6. Hungarian, spicy meals. Mon–Sat 11am–10pm.

Elevant, Vene 5. Chic Indian restaurant with affordable range of dishes, including plenty of vegetarian choices. Daily noon–midnight.

Ganga, Tartu mnt. 23. Small but highly recommended Indian vegetarian restaurant serving excellent food at reasonable prices. Mon–Sat 11am–10pm.

Golden Dragon, Pikk 37. Highly recommended Chinese place with a large variety of fish and vegetarian options. Daily noon–11pm.

Mõõkkala, Rüütli 16/18. Excellent, if a little pricey, seafood place in the cellar of what used to be the Tallinn executioner's house. Daily noon–midnight.

Pappa Pizza, Dunkri 6. Comfortable pizzeria with good thin-crust pizzas. Open daily 11am–11pm.

Pizza Americana, Pikk 1–3. Excellent deep-pan pizzas and a range of inexpensive pasta dishes. Mon–Sat noon–10pm, Sun noon–9pm.

Pudru ja Pasta, Pikk 35. Cellar bar-restaurant with small but imaginative range of inexpensive pasta and meat-and-potato standards. Mon–Sat noon–11pm, Sun noon–9pm.

Roosikrantsi, Vabaduse väljak 7. Smart, expensive but not over-formal place dishing up credible French and Belgian cuisine. Mon–Fri 8am–11pm, Sat & Sun noon–11pm.

Vanaema Juures, Rataskaevu 12 (☎2/626 9080). Cosy, elegant cellar restaurant with a country theme and local dishes such as pork, trout and wild boar with wine sauce. Meals average 150EEK. Reservations necessary. Mon–Sat noon–10pm, Sun noon–6pm.

Bars

Diesel Boots, Lai 25. "Genuine American Bar" packed with ephemera that draws a *Saku*-swilling local crowd. Daily noon–2am.

George Browne's, Harju 6. A busy "Irish pub" popular with expats and locals alike. A pint of Guinness will set you back 45EEK – local beer is cheaper. Fill up on spaghetti, burgers and fries if you get hungry. Live music some nights. Daily 11am–2am.

Guitar Safari, Muurivahe 22. Popular venue for live cover-bands and dancing, open until 3am.

Hell Hunt, Pikk 39. The name means "Gentle Wolf" and this is the most congenial and perhaps most authentic of Tallinn's Irish bars. A basement and outside seating to the rear. Vaguely Irish food available. Sun & Mon 11am–11pm, Tues–Thurs 11am–1am, Fri & Sat 11am–3am.

Kloostri Ait, Vene 14. With its enormous open fire and intellectual-ish crowd this is quieter than most beer-swilling places. Also serves coffee and snacks. Occasional live folk music, poetry readings or jazz. Sun–Thurs 11am–midnight, Fri & Sat 11am–1am.

Molly Malone's, Möndi 2. Large pub just off town hall square – a mixture of ex-pat haunt, tourist pub, and meeting-place for local yuppies. Frequent live music by cover bands and trad pub-grub menu. Daily 10am–2am.

Nimega Baar (The Pub with a Name), Suur-Karja 13. Scottish-owned bar serving British food. DJs at weekends. Mon–Thur 11am–2am, Fri & Sat 11am–4pm, Sun noon–2pm.

Nimeta Baar (The Pub with no Name), Suur-Karja 4/6, where international boy meets international girl, and live soccer matches are often screened. Sun–Thurs 11am–2am, Fri & Sat 11am–4am or later.

Spirit, Mere pst. 6E. Ultra-cool designer bar patronized by fans of alternative dance music and chill-out beats. Daily 11am–midnight. Stays open later at weekends when there are club nights, and an admission charge.

Von Krahli Theatre Bar, Rataskaevu 10/12. Hip hangout that's always packed with a bohemian crowd. The atmosphere is friendly and there's frequent live music and dancing. Beer costs 25EEK, though locals favour vodka with orange juice. Sun–Thurs noon–1am, Fri & Sat noon–3am.

VS, Pärnu mnt. 28. Hip new addition to the bar scene featuring industrial decor, late-night DJs in the basement, and restaurant-quality food. Daily noon–2am.

Live music and discos

Bonnie & Clyde, in the *Olümpia Hotel*, Liivalaia 33. Live bands usually on Saturdays and a dance floor occupied by a young, beautiful dressed-up crowd. Closed Mon.

Café Amigo, in the Viru Hotel, Viru väljak 4. Heaving but likeable disco playing mainstream dance music for locals and tourists into the early hours. Frequent appearances by Estonian bands. Open daily.

Hollywood Club, Vana-Posti 8. Popular Old Town dance club specializing in commercial techno. Trendy and busy. No trainers. Closed Sun, Mon & Tues.

Von Krahli, Rataskaevu 10/12. Live music a couple of times a week and regular club nights, including the monthly "Mutant Disco", when UK DJs play.

Classical music, opera and ballet

The Estonia Theatre and the Estonia Concert Hall, both at Estonia pst. 4 (box office Mon–Fri noon–7pm, Sat noon–5pm, Sun one hour before performance; ☎2/614 7700, www.concert.ee and www.opera.ee), are reliable venues, the former for ballet, opera and musicals, the latter for classical music and choral works including performances by the Estonian National Symphony Orchestra. Other venues for concerts include the Niguliste Church, the Town Hall, the House of the Brotherhood of Blackheads and the Dominican Monastery on Vene.

Listings

Airlines Estonian Air, Vabaduse väljak 10 (☎2/631 3302); Finnair, Roosikrantsi 2 (☎2/611 0950); SAS, Rävala 2 (☎2/627 9399).

Airport information (☎2/605 8888).

Books Kupar, Harju 1 (Mon–Fri 10am–7pm, Sat 11am–5pm); and Apollo, Viru 23 (Mon–Fri 10am–7pm, Sat 11am–6pm, Sun 11am–3pm), sell maps and locally produced English guides.

Car rental Avis, airport (☎2/631 5930, www.avis.ee); Europcar, airport (☎2/638 8031); Budget, airport, (☎2/605 8600); Hertz, airport (☎2/605 8923).

Embassies United Kingdom, Wismari 6 (☎2/667 4700); USA, Kentmanni 20 (☎2/668 8100).

Exchange Outside banking hours, try the Monex exchange offices in the ferry dock, or the Kaubamaja or Stockmann department stores (all daily 9am–8pm).

Ferries Most travel agents in the old town sell tickets to Helsinki and Stockholm and the main operators have offices in the harbour-front terminals; terminals A, B and C are on the south side of the harbour at the end of Sadama, and terminal D is on the north side at the end of Lootsi. The main operators for Helsinki are Eckerö Lines at terminal B (☎2/631 8606, www.eckeroline.ee); Nordic Jet Line at terminal C (☎2/613 7000, www.njl.ee); Silja Line at terminal A (☎2/611 6661, www.silja.ee); and Tallink, also at terminal A (☎2/640 9808, www.hansatee.ee). The main operator for Stockholm is Estline at terminal D (☎2/644 8348, www.estline.ee). It's worth bearing in mind also that getting an onward connection from Helsinki to Stockholm may be quicker than going direct from Tallinn. For crossing details see p.379.

Hospital Ravi 18 (☎2/602 7000).

Internet access Enter, Gonsiori 4 (daily 10am–8pm; 1EEK/min); 5th floor, Kaubamaja Department Store, Gonsiori 2 (2 (Mon–Fri 9am–9pm, Sat 9am–8pm, Sun 10am–6pm; 40EEK/hr).

Laundry Vendlus, Pärnu 48. Self and full-service available. Mon–Sat 8am–8pm, Sun 8am–5pm.

Left luggage Try the main train station at Toompuiestee 35 (5am–midnight; 10EEK), or the bus station at Lastekodu 46 (4–10EEK).

Pharmacies Tonismae Apteek, Tõnismägi 5; Tallinna Linna Apteek, Pä Apteek, Pärnu mnt. 10.

Police On Pärnu mnt. 11 (☎2/6123 523).

Post office Narva mnt. 1, opposite the Viru Hotel (Mon–Fri 8am–8pm, Sat 8am–6pm).

Taxis Ranks on Vabaduse väljak or just outside the Viru gate. Otherwise call Tulika (☎2/612 000); Linnatakso (☎2/644 2442).

Telephones Next to the post office on Narva mnt. 1 (Mon–Fri 8am–7pm, Sat 9am–4pm).

THE REST OF ESTONIA

The islands of **Saaremaa** and **Hiiumaa**, off the west coast of Estonia, are both easily reached from Tallinn and immensely popular as holiday and weekend home destinations. Saaremaa, at 2922 square kilometres the largest of Estonia's 1500 islands, is the more developed of the two, with tourist facilities already well established. Hiiumaa, smaller at 1024 square kilometres, remains remarkably unspoilt, its forests and coastline ripe for exploration. Elsewhere on the mainland, **Tartu**, the former Hansa city of Dorpat 190km southeast of Tallinn, is regarded by many Estonians as the spiritual capital of Estonia, thanks to its role in the nineteenth-century National Awakening. These days it's a laid-back university town with a population of 95,500 and a small and easily walkable Old Town. **Pärnu**, west of Tartu, is Estonia's fifth largest city with a population of 55,000, and has grown up around the nucleus of a castle built by the Livonian Order in the thirteenth century. There are a handful of sights in the Old Town but Pärnu's main claim to fame is as Estonia's major mainland resort, and its sandy beach still draws thousands of visitors every summer – particularly during the jazz festival in July.

Saaremaa

Cloaked with pine trees and juniper bushes, and littered with glacial boulders, the island of **SAAREMAA** is a tranquil place with Kuressaare as its major town. It was the last part of Estonia to come under foreign control (when the Knights of the Sword captured it in 1227) and the locals have always maintained a strong-minded indifference to the influence of foreign occupiers, leading many to claim that the island is one of the most authentically Estonian parts of the country.

To get to Saaremaa take the ferry from Virtsu on the mainland to Kuivastu on Muhu island. If you're travelling by car try and book a ferry ticket in advance, otherwise you may end up queuing for hours. A causeway links Muhu with Saaremaa.

Kuressaare

Approaching **KURESSAARE**, Saaremaa's main town, don't be put off by the ugly Soviet-era industrial zone that surrounds it – the centre remains much as it was before World War II and is home to one of the finest castles in the Baltic region. From the bus station on Pihtla turn left onto Tallinna in order to reach the central **Square** (Kesk väljak). Here you'll find Kuressaare's oldest building (after the castle), the yellow-painted **Town Hall** (Raekoda) dating from 1670, its door guarded by stone lions, and, facing it, the **Weigh House** (Vaekoda), another yellow building with a stepped gable. From the square Lossi runs south past a monument to the dead of the 1918–20 War of Independence, when the Estonians beat off Soviet and German forces, recently restored to pride of place after a lengthy Soviet-era absence. Continuing, the street runs past the eighteenth-century **Nikolai kirik**, a white Orthodox church with green onion domes. The church has an Estonian rather than Russian congregation, a reminder of the fact that an estimated twenty percent of Estonia's population joined the Orthodox Church when the country belonged to the Russian Empire. The interior, with icons set in white-painted frames, is noticeably plainer than in Orthodox churches with predominantly Russian congregations.

Lossi leads to the magnificent **Kuressaare Castle** (Kuressaare Kindlus), a vast fortress built from locally quarried dolomite. Set on an artificial island surrounded by a moat, the castle was founded during the 1260s as a stronghold for the bishop of Ösel-Wiek who controlled western Estonia from his base on mainland Haapsalu. The castle as it stands today dates largely from the fourteenth century and is a formidable structure, protected by huge seventeenth-century ramparts. The labyrinthine keep houses the **Saaremaa Regional Museum** (Saaremaa Koduloomuuseum; Wed–Sun 11am–6pm; 30EEK), an interesting but confusingly laid-out collection that covers the history and culture of the island from prehistoric times to date. The various sections are summarized in English but detailed labelling is in Estonian and Russian only. It's also possible to view the spartan living quarters of the bishops on the ground floor and climb the watchtowers. **Pikk Hermann**, the eastern (and thinner) corner tower is linked to the rest of the keep only by a wooden drawbridge. In the park surrounding the castle moat you'll find the wooden Kuursaal building from 1889, which makes a decent place for a drink or meal.

The **tourist office** (mid-May to mid-Sept daily 9am–7pm; mid-Sept to mid-May Mon–Fri 9am–5pm; ☎245/33120) is in the town hall on Kesk valjak, and can give details on bike rental and book **private rooms** in Kuressaare and across the island for around 150EEK per person. About the cheapest **hotel** in town is the *Hotel Mardi*, Vallimaa 5a (☎245/33285; ②), which is actually part-hotel and part-hostel – it has a cheap but excellent restaurant too; hostel beds are only available May to August. For a bit more comfort head for *Repo*, Vallimaa 1a (☎245/55111; ③), a friendly, pension-type establishment that's about the best in town, though it's often fully booked. Nearest campsite is the *Mändjala* (☎245/75193; May–Sept), 11km west of town just beyond the village of Nasva (Kuressaare–Järve buses pass by), which also has places in cabins (150EEK per person, including breakfast).

The smartest *restaurant* in town is the *Vannallin*, Kauba 8, while the next-door *Vannalinna Kohvipood* café is the best place for pastries, sandwiches and salads. *Veski*, Pärna 19, dishes up pork and potato variations in an old windmill. Another atmospheric venue is the *Kohvik Kuursaal* in the Kuursaal building in the castle park, offering soup, sandwiches and fish dishes – open daily until 10pm with terrace seating. *Budweiser Pub*, Kauba 6, has Czech and German beers on tap, a pool table and pub grub Estonian-style. *Nimeta*, in the old weigh house at Tallinna 3, is a convivial bar which also offers rather stylish food, featuring plenty of local fish. While in town don't forget to try Saaremaa-brewed beer, which packs a bit more of a punch than *Saku*.

Elsewhere on Saaremaa

Exploring the rest of Saaremaa is one way of getting acquainted with the unspoilt Estonian countryside. The places described below are all within easy reach of Kuressaare – if you want to explore further afield the island tourist office has information about more far-flung attractions and on how best to get around Saaremaa by public transport. Thanks to its largely flat terrain, though, exploring the island by bike is also a viable option.

KAARMA, just over 10km north of Kuressaare, is a small village that's the centre of the local dolomite-mining industry. More interestingly, it's also the location of the thirteenth-century **Kaarma kirik**, a large, red-roofed church containing a christening stone from the same period, and a pulpit supported by a wooden Joseph figure from 1450. The church's graveyard is littered with ancient stone crosses – the oldest are the so-called "sun crosses" – crosses set within a circle carved in stone. In woods at the edge of the village of **KAALI**, 10km northeast of Kaarma, is a murky green pool about 100m in diameter, created by the impact of a meteorite during the eighth century BC. Though not particularly spectacular, it is one of the world's few easily accessible meteorite craters, and the locals are very proud of it. Around 15km north of Kaali is **ANGLA**, with five much-photographed wooden windmills by the roadside. A right turn just past the windmills leads to the thirteenth-century **Karja kirik**, a plain white village church with an unusual crucifixion carving above its side door. Inside the church are more stone carvings, depicting religious figures and scenes from village life.

Hiiumaa

Most of **HIIUMAA** island is forested (elk, wild boar and lynx are among the local fauna) with swathes of peat moor and swamp at its heart. The sandy, rocky soil is of little agricultural use and supports a permanent population of just 12,000 but, like Saaremaa, Hiiumaa is a very popular holiday destination and weekend/summer-house location. Places to head for are the smaller island of **Kassari**, linked to southern Hiiumaa by a causeway, and the **Kõpu peninsula** at the western end of the island. Mainland ferries arrive in Hiiumaa at Heltermaa from Rohuküla near Haapsalu and there's also a ferry service (summer only) to Hiiumaa from Triigi on Saaremaa, although it's not met by any buses.

Hiiumaa's capital is **KÄRDLA**, an uneventful little town that nevertheless serves as the island's main transport hub. The centre of the town is just south of the bus station at **Kesk**

väljak, where the **tourist office** (mid-April to mid-May Mon–Fri 9am–5pm, Sat 10am–2pm; mid-May to mid-Sept Mon–Fri 9am–6pm, Sat & Sun 10am–2pm; mid–Sept to mid-April Mon–Fri 10am–4pm; ☎246/22233, *www.hiiumaa.ee*) can arrange both private room and hotel accommodation. Other **accommodation** possibilities include Sõnajala, at the western end of the village on Leigri väljak (☎246/31220), with simple rooms with shared facilities (②) or comfier ensuites (③); the Nuutri, a pleasant bed and breakfast just east of the main square at Nuutri 4 (☎250/98023; ②); or the more stylish *Padu*, at the eastern entrance to Kärdla at Heltermaa mnt. 22 (☎246/33037; ③). You can pick up **food** from shops and cafés on the main square.

Regular buses head 20km south from Kärdla to the village of **KÄINA**, a useful jumping-off point for the small island of **KASSARI**, joined to the rest of Hiiumaa by a causeway, and containing some of the most unspoilt juniper-covered heathland in the region. The road to Kassari leaves the Käina–Heltermaa road 3km east of Käina, passing after a further 3km a turn-off to **Kassari Kabel**, the only reed-roofed church in the country. A couple more kilometres beyond the turn-off is Kassari village, where a signpost points the way to Sääre Tirp, a promontory jutting out into the sea at the southern end of the island. After 2km the track to the promontory terminates in a car park, and a path flanked by juniper bushes leads to the foot of Sääre Tirp, ending in a shingle spit that peters out into the sea after a couple of hundred metres.

All of Kassari can be covered on foot if you make a day of it, and it also makes a good place to explore by bike; ask at the Kärdla tourist office for information on places to rent bikes. If you want to **stay** overnight head for the well-appointed hotel in Käina, *Liilia*, Hiiu mnt. 22 (☎246/36146; ④) which also has a reasonable **restaurant**. The Kärdla tourist office has information about private rooms in the area.

Forty kilometres or so west of Kärdla the **Kõpu peninsula** juts out into the sea. The main sight here is the **Kõpu Lighthouse** (Kõpu Tuletorn), one of the oldest continuously operating lighthouses in the world. The heavily buttressed lower part dates back to 1531 and was built at the request of the Hanseatic League to warn ships away from the Hiiu Madal sandbank and the pirate-infested coastline. Initially a pyre was burned at the top, but in 1845 a properly enclosed light was built. You can climb to the top for a view of trees and sea (admission 5EEK).

Tartu

Major city of south-central Estonia, and only two and a half hours away from Tallinn by bus, **TARTU**'s main sights lie between **Cathedral Hill** (Toomemägi), right in the centre of Tartu, and the Emajõgi river. The train station is about 500m southwest of the city centre at Vaksali 6, and the bus station is just east of the centre at Turu 2.

Tartu's focal point is its cobbled **Town Hall Square** (Raekoja plats) lined by prim Neoclassical buildings, the most eye-catching of which is the **Town Hall** (Raekoda), a toy-town edifice at the head of the square, painted lilac and purple and topped by a spire. The Neoclassical architectural theme continues in the yellow and white stucco facade of the main **Tartu University** (Tartu Ülikooli) building at Ülikooli 18, a couple of hundred metres north of Raekoja plats. The university was founded by the Swedish king Gustaf Adolphus in 1632 but closed by the Russians and not reopened again until the start of the nineteenth century (the present building dates from then). It wasn't until the country achieved independence after World War I, however, that Estonians finally supplanted Germans in the lecture hall.

A hundred metres or so beyond the university is the red-brick shell of the Gothic **St John's Church** (Jaani kirik), founded in 1330, bombed out in 1944 and now undergoing extensive restoration. The building is inaccessible, but from the street you can admire the unusual terracotta sculptures in niches that surround the main entrance. From behind the

Town Hall, Lossi climbs **Cathedral Hill** (Toomemägi), now a pleasant park with a few historic buildings dotted among its trees. On the way up, the street passes beneath **Angel's Bridge** (Inglisild), a brightly painted wooden bridge dating from the nineteenth century. At the top of the hill you'll find the remains of the red-brick **Cathedral** (Toomkirik), built by the Knights of the Sword during the thirteenth century. The cathedral was ruined during the Reformation and subsequently used as a barn. Tacked onto the end of the cathedral is a new building housing the **University History Museum** (Wed–Sun 11am–5pm; 10EEK), with three floors of ancient-looking text books, scientific instruments, and the sabres and flags brandished by nineteenth-century student fraternities.

Within a few minutes' walk of Toomemägi is the **Estonian National Museum**, J. Kuperjanovi 9 (Eesti Rahva Muuseum; Wed–Sun 11am–6pm; 10EEK, free on Fri). Devoted to peasant life and the development of agriculture in Estonia, it includes some imaginatively re-created farmhouse interiors, good English labelling, and a thorough display of folk costume from all over the country.

Practicalities

Tartu's **tourist office** is at Raekoja plats 14 (Mon–Fri 10am–6pm, Sat 10am–3pm; ☎27/432 141, *www.tartu.ee*) and can provide you with town plans. There are a number of small guesthouses in Tartu's suburbs offering **accommodation** in the ② range, although few of the hosts speak English and you're best off making reservations through the tourist office. Of Tartu's hotels the pleasant *Park Hotel*, Vallikraavi 23 (☎27/427 000, *www.parkhotell.ee*; ④), is centrally located in the leafy shadow of Toomemägi. Another possibility is *Carolina*, a comfy B&B 4km north of the centre at Kreuzwaldi 15 (you'll see it on the left as you enter town from the Tallinn direction; ☎27/422 070; ③); to get there, take bus #6 from the station to the Teemeistri stop. The hotel *Tartu*, Soola 3 (☎27/432 091, *tarhotel@server.ee*; ③), the long yellow building behind the bus station, is overpriced but offers discounts to HI cardholders.

For fast **food** try the *Pronto Pizzeria*, Küütri 3. *Tsink Plekk Pang*, Küütri 6, does a reasonable line in Chinese food, while you can get soups, sandwiches and meat-and-potato main courses at *Zum Zum*, Küüni 2; or the *Wilde Irish Pub*, Vallikraavi 4. The latter two places are also good for **drinking**, as is *Zavood*, a more bohemian dive just north of the centre at Lai 3. *Atlantis*, on the opposite bank of the river from the centre at Narva mnt 2, is a large and lively mainstream disco; and the basement bar at *Tsink Plekk Pang* has themed DJ nights at weekends. **Club** nights also take place at Varjend 2000, a graffiti-covered bunker 500m south of the centre on Pargi; or at Illusioon, a cinema 1km east of the centre at Raatuse 97 – check posters advertising what's on before heading out. There's an **Internet café**: Virtuaal (daily 11am–midnight; 40EEK/hr) at Pikk 40, east of the centre on the other side of the Emajõgi river.

Pärnu

Main town of the southwestern coast, down towards the border with Latvia, **PÄRNU**'s sights are mostly clustered in the **Old Town**, on and around Rüütli and Kuninga. The town's bus station is on Pikk at the northeastern edge of the Old Town (information & ticket office is round the corner at Ringi 3), and the **train station** is about 5km east of the centre at Riia mnt. 116.

Rüütli, lined with two-storey wooden houses, is the Old Town's main thoroughfare, cutting east–west through the centre. Near the junction with Aia is the **Pärnu Museum** (Linnamuuseum), Rüütli 53 (Tues–Fri 11am–6pm, Sat 11am–5pm; 30EEK), devoted to local history, and housing some of Estonia's oldest archeological finds – dating back to 8000 BC – and examples of local traditional costume. The oldest building in town is the **Red Tower** (Punane Torn), a fifteenth-century remnant of the medieval city walls on Hommiku, running north from Rüütli a few blocks west of the museum. Despite its name the tower is actually white – only the roof and window frames are red – and it now houses an antique shop.

Pühavaimu, a few blocks to the west, has a pair of respectable-looking seventeenth-century houses near the junction with Malmö, one in lemon yellow, the other in washed-out green with a large gabled vestibule. Moving west from Pühavaimu along Uus leads to the **Catherine Church** (Jekateriina kirik), a green-domed and multi-spired Orthodox church from 1760 named after the Russian empress Catherine the Great. The interior is abundantly furnished with icons but is open for services only.

From the Catherine Church, Vee runs down to **Kuninga**, the Old Town's other major street. At the western end of Kuninga is the seventeenth-century **Tallinn Gate** (Tallinna värav), a rather elegant relic of the Swedish occupation, set into the remains of the city ramparts and now home to a bar. To see the gate at its best head into the park on its outer side from where, with its massive gable and decorative pillars, it looks more like a Baroque chapel. Heading east along Kuninga leads to the Lutheran **Elizabeth Church** (Elisabethi kirik; Mon–Fri 10am–2pm) dating from 1747, with a maroon and ochre Baroque exterior and plain, wood-panelled interior. From here, Nikolai leads south to Esplanaadi, where the **Pärnu New Art Museum** (Pärnu Uue Kunsti Muuseum; daily 9am–9pm; 20EEK) occupies the former communist party headquarters at no. 10. Taken over by local artists in the post-independence years (when it was briefly renamed the Charlie Chaplin House), it's now a cultural centre with a collection of twentieth-century Estonian paintings, and contemporary works donated by international artists, including Yoko Ono. South of here Nikolai joins Supeluse, which runs down to the city's **resort area**, passing beneath the trees of the Rannapark, a shady park separating the town from the beach. At the southern end of Supeluse are the grand, colonnaded Neoclassical **Pärnu Mud-Baths** (Pärnu Mudaravila), built in 1926, and painted in the familiar ochre. Nearby is Pärnu's sandy, white beach, immensely busy at weekends and on public holidays. To escape the crowds make for the dunes east of the Mud Baths, but if you want to mingle with the masses head in the opposite direction, where you'll find a stretch of open sand backed by kiosks, bars, cafés and ice-cream places.

Practicalities

Pärnu **tourist office** is at Rüütli 16 (June–Aug Mon–Sat 9am–6pm, Sun 10am–3pm; Sept–May Mon–Fri 9am–5pm; ☎244/73000, *www.parnu.ee*). English-speaking staff have maps and can provide accommodation price lists. **Private rooms** (①) are available from Tanni Vakoma, a block east of the bus station at Hommiku 5 (☎244/43913). Best of the **hotels** are grouped between the town centre and the beach: the *Vesiroos*, Esplanaadi 42a (☎244/43350; ③), has sparse en-suites; while the *Leharu*, Pärna 12 (☎244/45895; ③), has functional but cosy rooms on the fourth floor of a high-rise sanatorium. If it's full, the *Monate*, on the next floor up (☎244/41472; ③), offers similar standards. The *Lootos*, opposite the Vesiroos at Muru 1 (☎244/31030; ④), has rooms with TV. *Linnakamping Green*, 3km east of the centre, has cabins for 100EEK a bed, and tent pitches for 60EEK (May–Sept).

For **food**, *Kohvik Georg*, Rüütli 43, is an inexpensive but civilized self-service restaurant open until 7.30pm; while *Steffani*, Nikolai 24, has a big choice of pizza and pasta dishes. *Mõnus Margarita*, Akadeemia 5, is a lively Tex-Mex joint with reasonable prices. The best of the **drinking** venues also do good food – try *Väike Klaus*, a pub-style venue at Supeluse 3 with a meaty Estonian menu; or the nearby *Texas Honky Tonk* at Supeluse 14, an eye-catching place decked out in kitschy Americana and offering a good line in TexMex snacks. UP, 100m west of the bus station on Pikk, is the principal venue for mainstream-techno clubbing. You can log onto the **Internet** at the New Art Museum (daily 9am–9pm; 30EEK/hr).

travel details

Trains

Tallinn to Moscow (1 daily; 15hr 30min); Pärnu (2 daily; 3hr); Rīga (1 daily; 9hr); St Petersburg (1 daily; 11hr); Tartu (3 daily; 3hr 20min).

Buses

Tallinn to: Haapsalu (7 daily; 2hr); Kaina (1 daily; 5hr); Kärdla (3 daily; 5hr); Kuressaare (6 daily; 4hr 30min); Pärnu (12 daily; 2hr); Rīga (4 daily; 5hr); St Petersburg (2 daily; 9hr); Tartu (every 30min; 2hr 30min); Vilnius (2 daily; 10hr).

Kuressaare to: Tallinn (6 daily; 4hr 30min).

Pärnu to: Tallinn (12 daily; 2hr).

Tartu to: Tallinn (every 30min; 2hr 30min)

Ferries

Tallinn to: Helsinki (around 17 daily; 1hr 30min–3hr); Stockholm (1 daily; 15hr).

Rohuküla to: Heltermaa for Hiiumaa (12 daily; 2hr).

Triigi to: Orjaku (summer only; 5 daily; 1hr 30min).

Virtsu to: Kuivastu for Saaremaa (12-20 daily; 30min).

Introduction

Mainland Scandinavia's most culturally isolated and least understood country, **Finland** has been independent only since 1917, having been ruled for hundreds of years by first the Swedes and then the Tsarist Russians. Much of its history involves a struggle for recognition and survival, and it's not surprising that modern-day Finns have a well-developed sense of their own culture, manifest in the widely popular Golden Age paintings of Gallen-Kallela and others, the music of Sibelius, the National Romantic style of architecture, and the deeply ingrained values of rural life.

Finland is mostly flat and punctuated by huge forests and lakes, but has wide regional variations. The South contains the least dramatic scenery, but the capital, Helsinki, more than compensates, with its brilliant architecture and superb collections of national history and art. Stretching from the Russian border in the east to the industrial city of Tampere, the vast waters of the Lake Region provide a natural means of transport for the timber industry – indeed, water here is a more common sight than land. Towns lie on narrow ridges between lakes, giving even major manufacturing centres green and easily accessible surrounds. North of here, Finland ranges from the flat western coast of Ostrobothnia to the thickly forested heartland of Kainuu and gradually rising fells of Lapland, Finland's most alluring terrain and home to the Sami, the semi-nomadic reindeer herders found all over northern Scandinavia.

Information and maps

Most towns have some sort of **tourist office**, with free maps and information, which sometimes book accommodation. In summer they open daily, usually for long hours in more popular centres; in winter, opening hours will be much reduced, if they open at all. Specific opening hours are given in the text. The best general **map** of Finland is the *Daily Telegraph* one; there is also an excellent map in the *Finland: Budget Accommodation* booklet, available from tourist offices.

Finland is very Internet-friendly. The best starting point is to check out the tourist office **Web sites** of the place you are visiting (listed in the guide) and browse for local links. Useful general sites include *www.mek.fi*, the official Finnish Tourist Board site, and *www.finland.org*, the Finnish embassy in USA site.

Money and banks

Finland has a reputation for high expense. This still rings true if you want a modicum of luxury but it's easily the cheapest of the Scandinavian countries, particularly for food, accommodation and public transport.

Finland is one of twelve European Union countries which have changed over to a single currency, the **euro** (€). Euro notes and coins are scheduled to be issued from the beginning of 2002, with Finnish markka (mk) remaining in circulation during a transition period, at a fixed rate of 5.94573 mk to 1 euro, until they are scrapped entirely at the end of February 2002. After this date you will still be able to exchange your markka for euros in banks for at least a year. Euro notes are issued in **denominations** of 5, 10, 20, 50, 100, 200 and 500 euros, and coins in denominations of 1, 2, 5, 10, 20 and 50 cents and 1 and 2 euros.

All prices in this chapter are given in euros correct at the time of going to press. There will no doubt be some rounding off or, more probably, up of prices in the first few months after the introduction of the euro.

Travellers' cheques and currency can be changed at most **banks** (Mon–Fri 9.15am–4.15pm); the commission charge is usually €2.50, though several people changing money together need only pay the charge once. You can also change money at hotels, but normally at a worse rate. Some banks have exchange desks at transport terminals, and you can also withdraw cash from ATM machines across the country.

Communications

In general, communications in Finland are dependable and quick, although in the far north and parts of the east minor delays arise due to geographical remoteness. An out-of-order **public phone** is virtually unheard of in Finland, although many of them have a dilapidated look – 80 percent of Finns own mobile phones so have little need for them. Coin phones are gradually being phased out to be replaced with card phones. Cards (*kortti*) are available at post offices *R-kioski* and other official outlets like tourist offices – denominations vary from roughly €5–15. If you are planning to use the telephone regularly stock up on phonecards as they can be very hard to come by out of hours or in remote areas. Some phones do accept major credit cards. **International calls** are cheapest between 10pm and 8am but calls from hotels can be frighteningly expensive. The operator numbers are ☎118 for domestic calls and ☎92020 for international calls. The international access code is ☎00.

Free **Internet access** is easy to find even in the most out-of-the-way place. The first place to look is the local library where you should be able to find at least one online terminal, though you may need to book a few hours in advance. Municipal and tourist offices often have online access too.

Getting around

You'll have few headaches getting around the more populated parts of Finland. The chief forms of public transport are trains, backed up, particularly on east–west journeys, by long-distance buses. For the most part trains and buses integrate well, and you'll only need to plan with care when travelling through the remoter areas of the far north and east.

■ Trains and buses

The swiftest land link between Finland's major cities is invariably **trains**, operated by **VR**, Finnish State Railways (☎0100121, *www.vr.fi*). Large, comfortable express trains (and a growing number of super-smooth Inter-city and EP, or special express, trains) serve the principal **north–south** routes several times a day. Elsewhere, especially on east–west hauls through sparsely populated regions, rail services tend to be skeletal and trains are often tiny or replaced by buses on which rail passes are still valid.

InterRail and **ScanRail** passes (see p.22-23) are valid on all trains. If you don't have one of these and are planning a lot of travelling, get a **Finnrail Pass** before arriving in Finland, from either the Finnish Tourist Board or a travel agent. This costs £67/$105 for 3 days' travel in a month, £97/$140 for 5 days and £129/$190 for 10 days. The pass is valid for travel on the entire rail network. Ordinary fares are surprisingly reasonable. One-way tickets are valid for 8 days, returns for a month and you can break your journey once in each direction, provided the ticket is stamped at the station where you stop and the total distance covered is over 80km. If there are three or more of you travelling together, group tickets, available from a train station or travel agent, can cut fares by at least 20 percent. **Seat reservations**, costing €6, are a good idea at weekends and holidays; on EP and IC trains, a supplement of between €6 and €13.50 must be paid, which includes (compulsory) seat reservation. **Sleeping berths** are also available on a number of routes, for €10 sharing a three-berth, €20 sharing a twin. The complete **timetable** (*Suomen Kulkuneuvot*) of Finnish rail, bus, ferry and air routes costs €16 from bookshops and kiosks, though the *Taskuaikataulu* booklet (€0.85) from any tourist office or station covers the major connections.

Buses – run by local private companies but with a common ticket system – cover the whole country, and are often quicker and more frequent than trains over the shorter east–west hops. **Fares** are approximately €14 for 100km, €36 for a 400km journey; seat reservations cost €2. All types of ticket can be purchased at a bus station or at most travel agents; only ordinary one-way tickets can be bought when boarding the bus. Of the **discount tickets** available, return fares are ten percent less than two one-ways, three or more people travelling 80km or more qualify for a **group reduction** of 20 percent; holders of YIEE/FIYTO and GO-25 (€10 for those under 26) cards get a 30 percent reduction on trips of similar length. A €17 supplement is charged on express buses. **Students** can also buy a bus travel discount card for €8.50 (certificate from school or college and photo required), giving 35–50 percent reductions on journeys of 80km or more. If you're going to travel a lot by bus, get a **Coach Holiday Ticket**, which gives 1000km of travel over any two-week period for about €60, from any long-distance bus station. The **timetable** (*Pikavuoroaikataulut*), available at all main bus stations, lists all bus routes.

■ Driving, hitching and cycling

If you **bring your own car** to Finland, it's advisable to have a Green Card as proof of insurance. More detailed information about driving in Finland can be obtained from the Automobile and Touring Club of Finland, Hameentie 105a, FIN-00550, Helsinki (☎09/7258 4400, fax 09/7258 4460). Though **roads** are generally good, there can be problems with melting snows, usually during April and May in the south and during June in the far north. The speed limit is 40–60kph in built up areas, 100kph on major roads, 120kph on motorways. If not signposted, the basic limit is 80kph. Other rules of the road include using headlights when driving outside built-up areas and the compulsory wearing of seatbelts by drivers and all passengers; as elsewhere in Scandinavia, there are severe penalties for drunk driving. **Car rental** is expensive, at €40–100 per day. You need a valid driving licence, at least a year's driving experience, and to be aged at least between 19 and 25, depending on the company.

Hitching is generally easy, and sometimes the quickest means of transport between two spots. Finland's large student population has helped accustom drivers to the practice, and you shouldn't have to wait too long for a ride. For information about **cycling**, contact Mountain Bike Club Finland (☎09/611052, fax 09/454 6466) or ask for their special booklet at the tourist office. Most of the bigger towns have at least one cycle hire option; prices are around €25 per day.

■ Flying

With a range of discounts aimed particularly at under-26s, domestic flights can be comparatively cheap as well as time-saving. However, the only time you'll find flying a truly economic option is if you are planning to visit Lapland and the far north of the country. If you're flying into Finland check out Finnair's very reasonable through fare deals. The company also offer a variety of off-peak summer reductions which can be checked at travel agents or tourist offices once you're in the country.

Accommodation

Although **accommodation** prices are high in Finland, if you are aware of the special offers which tend to run throughout the summer months, you will be able to sleep well on a budget. Note that prices can go up quite a bit out of season, a reverse situation to normal. **Bookings** all over Finland can be made through Hotel Booking Centre (☎09/22881400), situated inside the City Tourist Office in Helsinki. The free *Finland: Budget Accommodation* booklet, available from any tourist office, contains a comprehensive list of hostels and campsites, and an excellent map of the country.

■ Hotels

Most Finnish **hotels** come with all facilities: TV, phone and private bathrooms are standard, some rooms include private sauna, and large eat-as-much-as-you-can buffet breakfasts are invariably included in the price. Costs can be formidable – sometimes in excess of €100 – but planning ahead and taking advantage of various discount schemes and summer reductions can cut prices to around €35 per person in double rooms. Expense can also be trimmed under the **Finncheque** system, available outside Finland from the Finnish Tourist Board or a specialist travel agent, which offers an unlimited number of vouchers, costing €35 each per person per night, entitling the holder to a room in hotels in participating chains between mid-May and September – there's often a surcharge of €13.50 in more expensive hotels, though in cheaper places lunch is thrown in. The Scanhotel chain offers a similar and slightly more expensive cheque system costing about €75 for a double room including breakfast, but once again look out for surcharges. In many towns you'll also find **tourist hotels** (*matkustajakoti*), a more basic type of hotel usually charging €35–50 per person, although they are often full during summer. **Summer hotels** (*kesähotelli*) are another possibility, offering pretty decent accommodation, normally with breakfast, in student blocks from June to the end of August. Bookable in Finland through travel agents and by telephoning in person, they cost €25–45 per person.

■ Hostels

The cheapest option, and always spotlessly clean, are **hostels** (*retkeilymaja*). There are around 150 throughout the country and each city has at least one. It's always advisable to book ahead, especially between June and August. Many hostels close altogether after mid-August until the following June. Hostels cost between €17 and €25 per person, and range from the basic dormitory type to those with two-bedded rooms and a bathroom betweeen three.

ACCOMMODATION PRICE CODES

Throughout this guide, accommodation is coded on a scale of ① to ⑨, the code indicating the lowest price per person per night you could expect to pay in each establishment in high season. With hostels this is the nightly rate per person; with hotels, the price is arrived at by dividing the cost of the cheapest double room by two. The prices indicated by the codes are as follows:

① under £5/$8 (€9)
② £5–10/$8–16 (€9–18)
③ £10–15/$16–24 (€18–27)

④ £15–20/$24–32 (€27–36)
⑤ £20–25/$32–40 (€36–45)
⑥ £25–30/$40–48 (€45–54)

⑦ £30–35/$48–56 (€54–63)
⑧ £35–40/$56–64 (€63–72)
⑨ £40/$64 (€72) and over

Bedlinen, if not included, costs an extra €3.50–5; Finnish health regulations prohibit the use of sleeping bags in hostels. HI cards, while not obligatory, reduce an overnight stay by €2.50. Alternatively, you can get a similar reduction by buying an International Guest card for €15 at the Finnish Hostel Association at Yrjönkatu 38b, 00100 Helsinki (☎09/6940377).

■ Campsites and camping cottages

Official **campsites** (*leirintäalue*) are plentiful in Finland. Most open from May or June until August or September, although some stay open longer and a few all year. Sites are **graded** on a star system: one-star sites are in rural areas and are fairly basic; two-star sites have running water, toilets and showers; three-star sites, often on the outskirts of major towns, have hot water and full cooking and laundry facilities. The cost for two people sharing is €5–15 depending on the rating. Many three-star sites also have **camping cottages**, from simple sleeping accommodation for two to six people, to luxury places equipped with TV, sauna and kitchen. The cabins cost €100–500 per week; it's advisable to book as far ahead as possible during July or August. Without an International Camping Card you'll need a National Camping Card, available at every site for €3.40 and valid for a year.

Food and drink

Finnish food can be pricey, but you can keep a rein on the expense by self-catering. Though tempered by many regulations, alcohol is more widely available than in much of the rest of Scandinavia.

■ Food

Though it may at first seem a stodgy, unsophisticated cuisine, **Finnish food** is an interesting mix of Western and Eastern influences, with Scandinavian-style fish specialities and exotic meats like reindeer and elk alongside dishes that bear a Russian stamp – pastries, and casseroles strong on cabbage and pork. If you're staying in a hotel, **breakfast** (*aamiainen*) is a sumptuous affair, a buffet of herring, eggs, cereals, cheese, salami and bread. Later in the day you can lunch on the economical **snacks** sold in ubiquitous market halls (*kauppahalli*) or in their adjoining cafeterias, where you are charged by the weight of food on your plate. Most train stations and some bus stations and supermarkets also have cafeterias proffering a selection of snacks and light meals, and the

Grilli and Nakkikioski street stands turn out burgers and hot dogs for €2.50–3.50. Otherwise, campus cafeterias or **mensas** are the cheapest places to get a hot dish, with a choice of three menus, with bread and coffee, for €2–3.40. Theoretically you have to be a student but you are unlikely to be asked for ID, though if you can prove you're a student, a discount is in order. In a regular restaurant, or *ravintola*, **lunch** (*lounas*) is the cheapest option, many places offering a lunchtime buffet table (*voileipäpöytä* or *seisova pöytä*) stacked with a choice of traditional goodies for a set price of around €8.50–13. A *baari*, an unlicensed restaurant with a range of Finnish dishes and snacks, is another low-cost option, although most close early – at 5 or 6pm. Pizzerias, too, are widespread, serving "lunch specials" for €6–9.

For **evening meals** you'll always have a couple of options. In smaller towns there will no doubt be cheap pizzerias or *grillis* or bars and *ravintolas* often serve standard plates of meat and two veg. In Helsinki and the big towns there are usually a range of options from Chinese to reindeer steak. Prices will vary from €6 for a cheap pizza to €100 for a slap up meal in a top restaurant.

■ Drink

Whilst the attitude to **drinking** can seem austere Finland has a truly staggering problem with alcoholism and in some of the smaller towns bars can be quite depressing places. In Helsinki and the bigger towns, however, the drinking culture is more sophisticated and you'll be able to find numerous appealing places to have a jar or two.

Beer (*olut*) falls into three categories: "light beer" (I-Olut), like a soft drink; "medium strength beer" (*Keskiolut*, III-Olut), perceptibly alcoholic, sold in shops and cafés; and "strong beer" (A-Olut or IV-Olut), on a par with the stronger European beers, and only available at fully licensed restaurants, clubs and ALKO shops. Even the smallest town will have one, and prices don't vary. Strong beers, like Lapin Kulta Export, Karjala, Lahden A, Olvi Export and Koff porter, cost about €1.35 for a 300ml bottle. Imported beers go for €1.50–2 a bottle. As for **spirits**, Finlandia vodka is €27 and Koskenkorva, a popular rough form of vodka, €25 per litre.

Most restaurants have a full licence, and some are actually frequented more for drinking than eating. To add to the confusion, some so-called "pubs" are not licensed. **Bars** are usually open until midnight or 1am and service stops half an hour before closing. You have to be 18 to buy beer and wine, and 20 for spirits. Expect to queue for entry into popular bars as you'll only be allowed in if there's a seat free – no standing allowed. There's always either a doorman (*portsari*) – whom some tip (usually €1) on leaving – or an obligatory cloakroom (again usually €1).

The main – and cheapest – outlet for alcohol of any kind is the government-run **ALKO** shops (Mon–Thurs 10am–5pm, Fri 10am–6pm, Sat 9am–2pm; closed Sat May–Sept). Even the smallest town will have one and prices don't vary.

Opening hours and holidays

Shops are usually open Mon–Fri 9am–6pm, Sat 9am–4pm. Shops and banks will be closed on the following **public holidays**, when most public transport and museums operate to a Sunday schedule: Jan 1; Jan 6 (Epiphany); Good Friday and Easter weekend; May 1; Midsummer's Eve and Day; All Saints' Day

(the Sat between Oct 31 and Nov 6); Dec 6; Dec 24, 25 and 26.

Emergencies

You probably won't have much cause to come into contact with the Finnish **police**, though if you do they are likely to speak English. As for **health problems**, if you're insured, you'll save time by seeing a doctor at a private health centre (*Lääkäriasema*) rather than queuing at a national health centre (*Terveyskeskus*). Medicines must be paid for at a **pharmacy** (*apteekki*), generally open daily 9am–6pm.

> **Emergency Numbers**
> All emergencies ☎112.

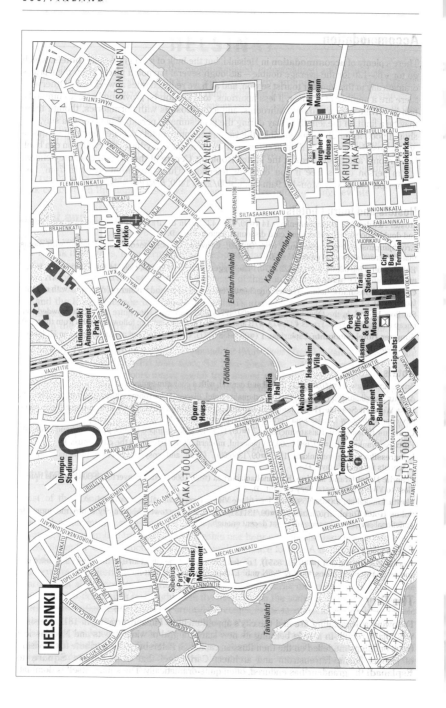

HELSINKI

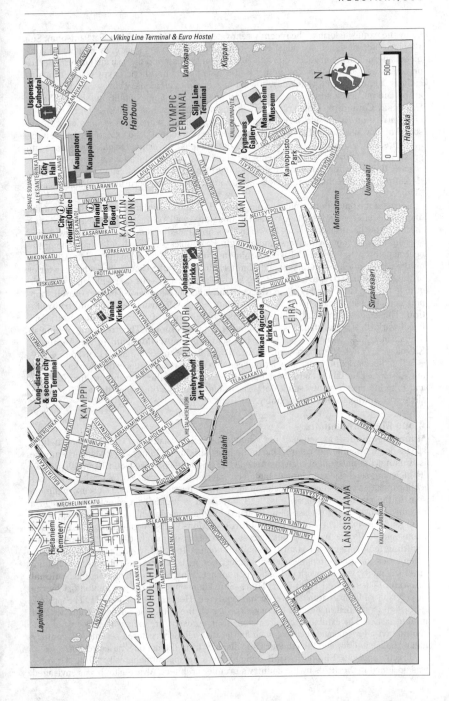

ed by the exquisite form of the recently renovated **Tuomiokirkko** (Mon–Sat 9am–6pm, Sun 12noon–6pm), designed, like most of the other buildings on the square, by Engel, and completed after his death in 1852. After the elegance of the exterior, the spartan Lutheran interior comes as a disappointment; better is the gloomily atmospheric **crypt** (same times as cathedral; entrance on Kirkkokatu), now often used for exhibitions. Walking east, the square at the end of Aleksanterinkatu is overlooked by the onion domes of the Russian Orthodox **Uspenski Cathedral** (Mon–Fri 9.30am–6pm, Sat 9am–2pm, Sun 12noon–3pm, closed Mon Oct–April; tram #3). Inside, a rich display of icons glitters while incense mingles with the sound of Slavonic choirs. Beyond it is Katajanokka, a wedge of land extending between the harbours, where a dockland development programme is converting the old warehouses into pricey new restaurants and apartments for Helsinki's yuppies. Just a block south of Senate Square, the new **City Museum** at Sofiankatu 4 (Mon–Fri 9am–5pm, Sat & Sun 11am–5pm; €4.20) offers a hi-tech record of Helsinki life in an impressive permanent exhibition called "Time".

Across a mishmash of tramlines from South Harbour is **Esplanadi**. At the height of the mid-nineteenth-century language conflict, Finns would walk on the south side and Swedes on the north of this neat boulevard. Nowadays it's dominated at lunchtime by office workers, later in the afternoon by buskers, and at night by couples strolling hand-in-hand along the central pathway to free musical accompaniment from the bandstand in the middle. Close by, on the corner of Aleksanterinkatu and Mannerheimintie, is the Constructivist brick exterior of the **Stockmann Department Store**. Europe's largest, it sells everything from bubble gum to Persian rugs. Further along Mannerheimintie, steps head down to the **Tunneli** shopping complex which leads to one of the city's most enjoyable structures, **Helsinki train station**. This solid yet graceful 1914 building is often thought of as architect Eliel Saarinen's finest work. Beside the station is the imposing granite **National Theatre**, home of Finnish drama since 1872. Directly opposite the bus station is the **Art Museum of the Ateneum**, Kaivokatu 2 (Tues & Fri 9am–6pm, Wed & Thurs 9am–8pm, Sat & Sun 11am–5pm; €4.20, €7.60 for special exhibitions). Its stirring selection of late-nineteenth-century works – including Akseli Gallén-Kallela and Albert Edelfelt's scenes from the Finnish epic, the *Kalevala*, and Juho Rissanen's moody studies of peasant life – recalls a time when the spirit of nationalism was surging through the country.

Along Mannerheimintie

Mannerheimintie – named after the Finnish soldier and statesman C.G.E. Mannerheim – spears north from the city centre. One of the most striking buildings along Mannerheimintie is **Kiasma**, the museum of contemporary art (Tues 9am–5pm, Wed–Sun 10am–10pm; €5). Its gleaming steel-clad exterior and high-tech interior make it well worth a visit, and its collection includes installations in which sound, moving images and smell add a sensory dimension to the experience. Opposite is the **Lasipalatsi**, a multimedia complex situated in a recently renovated 1930s classic Functionalist building, inside which are trendy shops and cafés and the excellent **Cable Book Library** (Mon–Thurs 10am–midnight, Sat & Sun noon–6pm), offering free Internet access. Further along on the left, the **Parliament Building** (guided tours Sat 11am & noon, Sun noon & 1pm; July & Aug also Mon–Fri 2pm; when in session access to public galleries only; free), with its pompous columns and choking air of solemnity, was the work of J.S. Sirén, completed in 1931. North of here, the **National Museum** (Tues & Wed 11am–8pm, Thurs–Sun 11am–6pm; €4.20) is a joint effort by the three giants of Finnish architecture, Armas Lindgren, Herman Gesellius and Eliel Saarinen. Its design is steeped in Finnish history, drawing on the country's medieval churches and granite castles. The exhibits, from prehistory to the present, are exhaustive; it's best to concentrate on a few specific sections, such as the marvellously restored seventeenth-century manor house interior and the ethnographic displays from the nation's varied regions.

Directly opposite, **Finlandia Hall** (guided tours by appointment, call ☎09/40241; free) was designed in the 1970s by the country's premier architect, Alvar Aalto. It was envisaged as part of a grand plan, begun by Eliel Saarinen and still under discussion, to rearrange the city centre. Inside, Aalto's characteristic asymmetry and hallmark wave pattern (the architect's surname means "wave") are everywhere, from the walls and ceilings through to the lamps and vases. A little further up Mannerheimintie is Finland's new **Opera House** (Mon–Fri 9am–6pm, Sat 3–6pm); like so much contemporary Finnish architecture, it's a white, Lego-like expanse, but the interior is enlivened by displays of colourful costume. A little way north, the **Olympic Stadium** is clearly visible; originally intended for the 1940 Olympics, it hosted the second postwar games in 1952. Its **tower** (Mon–Fri 9am–8pm, Sat & Sun 9am–6pm; €17) gives an unsurpassed view over the city and a chunk of the southern coast. Back towards the city centre, the **Hietaniemi Cemetery** houses the graves of some of the big names of Finnish history – Mannerheim, Engel and Alvar Aalto, whose witty little tombstone, with its chopped Neoclassical column, stands beside the main entrance. East of here, at Lutherinkatu 3, is the late-1960s **Temppeliaukio kirkko** (Rock Church; Mon–Fri 10am–8pm, Sat 10am–6pm, Sun noon–1.45pm & 3.15–5.45pm; closed Tues 1–2pm and during services; tram #3B). Blasted from a single lump of granite beneath a domed copper roof, it's a thrill to be inside.

South of Esplanadi

South of Esplanadi on Korkeavourenkatu, the excellent **Museum of Art & Design** (Mon–Fri noon–7pm, Sat & Sun noon–6pm; €8.50) traces the relationship between art and industry in Finnish history, with explanatory texts and period exhibits. Northwest of here is the **Vanha kirkko** (Old Church). Engel's humble wooden structure was the first Lutheran church to be erected after Helsinki became the capital. A few blocks from the end of Kasarminkatu is the large and rocky **Kaivopuisto** park, where nobility from St Petersburg came to sample the waters at its 1830s spa house. The park also contains the **Mannerheim Museum** (Fri–Sun 11am–4pm; €6.80, includes guided tour), the house where the famous Finnish commander spent his later years. Mannerheim led the Whites during the Russian Civil War of 1918, and two decades later the Finnish campaigns in the Winter and Continuation Wars. His political influence was considerable, including a brief spell as president. The interior – cluttered with the plunder of his travels – is much as it was when he died in 1951. Close by is the yellow-turreted house of another famous Finn, the nineteenth century philanthropist Frederik Cygnaeus. Inside, the beautifully laid-out **Cygnaeus Gallery** (Wed 11am–7pm, Thurs–Sun 11am–4pm; €2.50), displays his collection of bird and nature studies by the von Wright brothers.

Suomenlinna and Seurasaari

Built by the Swedes in 1748 to protect Helsinki from seaborne attack, the fortress of **Suomenlinna** stands on five interconnected islands and is the biggest sea fortress in the world. Reachable by ferry every thirty minutes from the South Harbour, it makes a rewarding break from the city. You can visit independently, or take one of the hour-long summer **guided walking tours**, beginning close to the ferry stage and conducted in English (June–Aug daily 10.30am, 1pm & 3pm; €3.40). Suomenlinna has a few museums, though none is particularly riveting. The **Suomenlinna Museum** (March, April & Oct Sat & Sun 11am–5pm, May–Sept 10am–5pm; €5) contains a permanent exhibition on the island as well as a multi-vision show that is played in several languages. The **Ehrensvärd Museum** (summer daily 10am–5pm; Sept daily 10am–4.30pm; Oct–April Sat & Sun 11am–4.30pm; €1.70) is the residence used by the first commander of the fortress, Augustin Ehrensvärd, who oversaw the building of Suomenlinna and now lies in an elaborate tomb in the grounds; his personal effects remain inside the house alongside displays on the fort's construction. Finally, the **Coastal Artillery Museum** (May–Aug daily 10am–4.45pm; Sept daily 11am–3pm, April and Oct Sat & Sun 11am–3pm; €3.40) records Suomenlinna's defensive actions and, for another €2, lets visitors clamber around the claustrophobic World War II submarine *Vesikko*.

There are more museums close by the small wooded island of **Seurasaari**, a fifteen-minute tram (#4) or bus (#24) ride from the city centre. The tram stops a few hundred metres north, at the junction of Tamminiementie and Meilahdentie, conveniently close to the **Helsinki City Art Museum** (Wed–Sun 11am–6.30pm; €2.50–7.60) which hosts temporary exhibits of a broad range of art from fifteenth Century Japanese through to contemporary Finnish works. A few minutes' walk away, towards the Seurasaari bridge, is the long drive-way leading to the **Urho Kekkonen Museum** (mid-May to mid-Aug daily 11am–5pm; rest of year closed Mon; €3.40), the villa where the former president lived from 1956 until his death in 1986, and the former official home of all Finnish presidents. Kekkonen played a vital role in the establishment of Finnish neutrality after World War II, gaining the favour of Soviet leaders, legend has it, by taking them to a sauna. Close by, on Seurasaari itself, is the **Seurasaari Open Air Museum** (June–Aug daily 11am–5pm, Wed until 7pm; Sept–May Mon–Fri 9am–3pm, Sat & Sun 11am–5pm; €3.40), a collection of vernacular buildings from all over Finland.

Eating and drinking

Eating in Helsinki, as in the rest of Finland, isn't cheap, but there is a lot of choice, and, with planning, a number of ways to stretch funds – many places offer good-value lunchtime deals, and there are plenty of affordable ethnic restaurants and fastfood *grillis*. At the end of Eteläesplanadi the **Old Market Hall** (Kauppahalli; Mon–Fri 8am–5pm, Sat 8am–3pm) is good for snacks and reindeer kebabs. Helsinki has several **student mensas**, two of which are centrally located at Aleksanterinkatu 5 and Yliopistonkatu 3. One or the other will be open in summer; both will be open during term time.

Drinking can be enjoyed in the city's many pub-like restaurants; on Fridays and Saturdays it's best to arrive as early as possible to get a seat without having to queue. Most drinking dives also serve food, although the grub is seldom at its best in the evening. If you want a drink but are hard-up, self-service ALKO shops are located at Fabianinkatu 9–11 and Kaivokatu 10.

Restaurants and Cafés

Café Ekberg, Bulevardi 9. Nineteenth-century fixtures and a deliberately fin-de-siècle atmosphere, with starched waitresses bringing expensive open sandwiches and pastries to marble tables.

Café Fazer, Kluuvikatu 3. Owned and named after Finland's biggest chocolate company, it's justly celebrated for its pastries.

Café Tamminiementie, Tamminiementie 8. On the way to Seurasaari this is one of Helsinki's nicest cafés, with excellent home-made cakes and countless varieties of tea.

Kasakka, Meritullinkatu 13. Great atmosphere and food in this old-style Russian restaurant.

Lappi, Annankatu 22. Great Lapland food in a restaurant done out in tacky log cabin style. Lunchtime specials are good value though in the evening prices escalate and the place is usually full. If there are two of you try the smoked fish – hot smoked while you wait – at €15 per head.

Lasipalatsi – Mannerheimintie 22–24. Decent modern Finnish food served in a classic Functionalist style building with great views of Kiasma and the street life below.

Mama Rosa, Runeberginkatu 55. A classic pizzeria also serving fish steaks and pasta. A decent mid-priced restaurant (daily 11am–midnight).

Namaskar, Mannerheimintie 100. Popular evening buffet (€16) and plenty of vegetarian options.

Saslik, Neitystpolku 12. Pricey but delicious authentic Russian grub which you can eat to the sound of traditional troubadours in the evening.

Sipuli Kanavarantu 3. Taste-bud thrilling, formal and glamorous – a perfect splash-out, at about €30 a head.

Strindberg, Pohjoisesplanadi 33. The upstairs restaurant serves contemporary Scandic cuisine combines while the street level café is one of *the* places in town to see and be seen.

Ursula, Kaivopuisto. On the beach at the edge of the Kaivopuisto park, with a wonderful view from the out-door terrace. There's a new *Ursula* at Pohjoisesplanadi 21, which is good for cakes too.

Zucchini, Fabianinkatu 4. Though only open on weekdays 11am–4pm and closed in July this place serves excellent veggie food; lunch specials start at about €8–10.

Bars

Ateljee Bar, on the roof of *Hotel Torni*, Yrjönkatu 26. Offers the best views of Helsinki in a stylish atmosphere.

Bar Nº9, Uudenmaankatu 9. A popular hangout for professionals at lunchtime and bohemians in the evening, it has a beer list and menu as cosmopolitan as its staff. Food is reasonably cheap and filling and there is always a vegetarian option.

Bulevardia, Bulevardi 34. Art Deco fittings by 1930s architect Kaisa Blomstedt; reasonably priced special lunch deals.

Elite, Eteläinen Hesperiankatu 22. Once the haunt of the city's artists, many of whom settled their bill with the paintings that line the walls. Especially good in summer, when you can drink on the terrace.

O'Malley's, *Hotel Torni*, Yrjönkatu. Guinness on tap and live music.

St Urho's Pub, Museokatu 10. One of the most popular student pubs. Guitars, a piano, etc, available for spontaneous jam sessions.

Vanha, Mannerheimintie 3. A self-service and comparatively cheap café/bar. Arrive early for a seat on the balcony overlooking the bustle of the streets below. The cellar is given over to a smoky beerhall whilst other parts of the building serve as an indie/rock concert venue.

Nightlife

Helsinki has a vibrant night scene, with several venues putting on a steady diet of **live music** (€6–13) and free gigs almost every summer Sunday in Kaivopuisto park. There is also a wide range of **clubs and discos**, which charge a small admission fee (around €6). For details of **what's on**, read the entertainments page of *Helsingin Sanomat*, or the free fortnightly paper, *City*, found in record shops, bookshops, department stores and tourist offices. Advance **tickets** can be bought at Tiketti, Yrjönkatu 29c (Mon–Fri 9–5pm; ☎0600/11 616 premium rate call).

Clubs and venues

Botta, Museokatu 10. Vibrant dance music of various hues most nights.

DTM (Don't Tell Mama), Annankatu 32. Helsinki's legendary gay night club which occasionally hosts classy drag shows.

Kerma, Erottaja 7. One of the grooviest places in town. Seventies-style decor and funky Latin rhythms abound. Open till 4am at weekends.

KY-Exit, Pohjoinen Rautatiekatu 21. Sometimes has foreign bands; more often lively disco nights.

Saunabar, Eerikinkatu 27. With a sauna (€7) attached and a legendary Sunday night DJ spot this is one the most idiosyncratic places in town.

Soda, Uudenmaankatu 16–20. Losing its edge a little but still a good night out. Dance music downstairs; bar and guest DJs upstairs.

Storyville, Museokatu 8. Popular venue for nightly live jazz. Good food, too.

Tavastia, Urho Kekkosenkatu 4–6. Major showcase for Finnish and Swedish bands.

Listings

Airlines British Airways, Aleksanterinkatu 21a (☎09/650677) opposite the Stockman Department Store; Finnair, Töölönkatu 21 (☎09/818800); SAS, Keskuskatu 7a (☎09/228021).

Books Academic Bookstore, Keskuskatu 1, has a good stock of English paperbacks.

Car rental Avis, Pohjoinen Rautatiekatu (☎09/441155); Budget, Malminkatu 24 (☎09/6866500); Europcar/InterRent, Mannerheimintie 50 (☎09/47802220).

Embassies Canada, Pohjoisesplanadi 25b (☎09/171141); Ireland, Erottajankatu 7A (☎09/646006); UK, Itäinen Puistotie 17 (☎09/22865100); USA, Itäinen Puistotie 14a (☎09/171931). Australian citizens should contact their embassy in Stockholm (see p.1274).

Exchange Best done at banks, otherwise try the airport (6.30am–11pm); Katajanokka harbour, where Viking and Finnjet dock (daily 9–11.30am & 3.45–6pm); or Forex at the train station (daily 8am–9pm).

Ferries Reservations and information: Silja Line ☎9800/74 552, *www.silja.fi*; Tallink ☎09/2282 1277, *www.tallink.fi*; Viking Line ☎09/123 577, *www.vikingline.fi*.

Gay Helsinki See *Z* magazine, widely available in larger newsagents or drop into Lost and Found, Annankatu 6, a relaxed café/bar-cum-restaurant-and-disco whose staff are friendly, helpful and speak excellent English. SETA, Heitalahdenkatu 2b 16, is the state-supported gay organization (☎09/6123233, *www.seta.fi*).

Hospital Töölö Hospital, Topeliuksenkatu 5 has a first-aid unit; Meilahti Hospital, Haartmaninkatu 4, has an emergency department. Both ☎09/4711.

Laundry Runeberginkatu 47 (Mon–Thur 10am–8pm, Fri 10am–6pm, Sat 10am–4pm).

Left luggage Long-distance bus station (Mon–Fri 9am–8pm, Sat 7am–6pm, Sun 9am–6pm); lockers at train station (daily 6.30am–10pm).

Pharmacies Yliopiston Apteekki, Mannerheimintie 96 (24hr); Mannerheimintie 5 (daily 7am–midnight).

Police Pieni Roobertinkatu 1–3 (☎1891).

Post office The main office, with poste restante services, is at Mannerheimaukio 1a (Mon–Fri 9am–5pm).

Saunas & Swimming Pools Yrjo/nkatu 21b. Stunning recently renovated Art Deco pool and sauna complex in city centre (daily 6.30am–9pm though some sessions are women/men only; €4–10).

Around Helsinki

There's little in Helsinki's outlying area that's worth venturing out for. But a couple of places a little further afield, both an easy day-trip from the city, merit a visit: the home of the composer Sibelius at **Järvenpää** and the evocative old town of **Porvoo**.

Järvenpää

About 40km north of Helsinki, and easy to get to by bus or train, **JÄRVENPÄÄ** is the site of **Ainola** (June–Aug Tues–Sun 11am–5pm; May & Sept Wed–Sun 11am–5pm; €3.40), the house where Jean Sibelius lived from 1904 with his wife, Aino, after whom the place is named. Long seen as the authentic voice of Finnish national identity, Sibelius is now also considered one of the world's great composers. His early pieces, inspired by the Finnish folk epic, the *Kalevala*, and the nationalist mood of the times, incurred the wrath of the country's Russian rulers. In 1899 they banned performances of his rousing *Finlandia* under any name which suggested its patriotic sentiment, and the piece was published as "Opus 26, No. 7". He is still revered in Finland, despite his notorious bouts of heavy drinking and angst-ridden last years that became known as "the silence from Järvenpää". This tranquil place, close to lakes and forests, is an object of pilgrimage for devotees, although there is little to see other than books, furnishings and a few paintings. The composer's simple grave is in the grounds.

Porvoo

One of the oldest towns on the south coast, **PORVOO**, 50km east of Helsinki, with its narrow cobbled streets lined by small wooden buildings, gives a sense of the Finnish life which predated the capital's bold squares and Neoclassical geometry – although its elegant riverside setting and unhurried mood mean it's inevitably popular with tourists.

Close to the station, visit the preserved **Johan Ludwig Runeberg House**, Aleksanterinkatu 3 (May–Aug Mon–Sat 10am–4pm, Sun 11am–5pm; Sept–April closed Mon & Tues; €4), where the famed Finnish poet lived from 1852 while a teacher at the town school. Despite writing in Swedish, he greatly aided the nation's sense of self-esteem, and one of his poems provided the lyrics for the Finnish national anthem. Across the road, the **Walter Runeberg Gallery** (May–Aug Mon–Sat 10am–4pm, Sun 11am–5pm; Sept–April Wed–Sun 11am–3pm; €2.50) has a collection of sculpture by Johan Runeberg's third son, one of Finland's more celebrated sculptors. The old town is built around the hill on the other side of Mannerheimkatu, crowned by the fifteenth-century **Tuomiokirkko** (May–Sept Mon–Fri 10am–6pm, Sat 10am–2pm, Sun 2–5pm; Oct–April Tues–Sat 10am–2pm, Sun 2–4pm), where Alexander I proclaimed Finland a Russian Grand Duchy and convened the first Finnish Diet. This, and other aspects of the town's past, can be explored in the **Porvoo Museum** (May–Aug daily 10am–4pm; Sept–April Wed–Sun noon–4pm; €2.50) at the foot of the hill in

the main square, by way of a selection of furnishings, musical instruments and oddities largely dating from the days of Russian rule.

Buses run all day taking about 90 minutes from Helsinki to Porvoo, and a one-way trip
costs around €25. There's also a **boat**, the *J. L. Runeberg*, which sails through the summer
(June–Aug Tues, Wed, Sat & Sun, also Mon in July, Fri July to mid-Aug) from Helsinki's
South Harbour at 10am, arriving in Porvoo at 1.15pm and leaving at 4pm; a return fare is €25
with tickets available from a booth at the quayside by Helsinki's market square (*kauppatori*).
The **tourist office** is opposite the **bus station**, at Rihkamakatu 4 (July & Aug Mon–Fri
10am–6pm, Sat & Sun 10am–4pm; rest of year Mon–Fri 10am–4.30pm, Sat 10am–2pm;
☎019/5202316, *www.porvoo.fi*), and has free maps of the town. **Spending a night** in Porvoo
leaves you well-placed to continue into Finland's southeastern corner, though rates are steep.
There is, however, a **hostel**, open all year, at Linnankoskenkatu 1–3 (☎019/5230012; ③), and
a **campsite** (☎019/581967; June to mid-Aug), 2km from the town centre. For something **to
eat** check out *La Carte* at Kirkkokatu 1, which serves French-Scandic cuisine for about €15
a head, and has a good wine list.

THE SOUTHWEST

The area immediately west of Helsinki is probably the blandest section of the country, endless forests interrupted only by modest-sized patches of water and virtually identical villages
and small towns. The far southwestern corner, however, is more interesting, with islands and
inlets around a jagged shoreline and some of the country's distinctive Finnish-Swedish
coastal communities. The country's former capital, **Turku**, is the main target, historically and
visually one of Finland's most enticing cities.

Turku

TURKU was once the national capital but lost its status in 1812 and most of its buildings in a
ferocious fire in 1827. These days it's a small and highly sociable city, bristling with history
and culture and with a sparkling nightlife, thanks to the boom years under Swedish rule and
the students from its two universities. Many of its Swedish-speaking contingent still consider Åbo – the Swedish name for Turku – the real capital and Helsinki just an upstart.

Arrival, accommodation and information

The river Aura splits the city, its tree-lined banks forming a natural promenade as well as a
useful landmark. On the northern side of the river is Turku's central grid, where you'll find
the **tourist office** at Aurakatu 4 (Mon–Fri 8.30am–6pm, Sat & Sun 10am–3pm; ☎02/2627444,
www.turku.fi); here you can pick up the excellent value **Turku Card** (24hrs €22; 48hrs €30),
which includes bus travel and entrance to most museums, and the free comprehensive
English-language listings brochure, *Fun Times*. Both the **train** and **bus station** are within
easy walking distance of the river, just north of the centre. If you are making for the
Stockholm ferry, you can stay on the train to the terminal 2km west or catch bus #1 on
Linnankatu. The **InterRail Centre** is currently at Eerikinkatu 7 (mid-July to mid-Aug), right
by the river, where you can shower, leave luggage, rent bicycles and eat cheaply. **Bikes** can
also be rented from T. Saario, Tuureporinkatu 19 (☎02/316356).

There are some good deals to be had at Turku's mid-range **hotels**, especially if you make
an early reservation and pick a weekend. Try *Hotel Julia*, Eerikinkatu 4 (☎02/336311; ⑧) or
for a real slice of luxury and character try *Park Hotel*, Rauhankatu 1 (☎02/273 2555; ⑨). Alvar
Aalto fans should stay at *Good Morning Hotel Ateljee* (☎02/336 111; ⑦), Humalistonkatu 7,
housed in a building designed by Finland's most famous architect; ask for room 422 or 534.
Cheaper options include the excellent **hostel**, *Hostel Turku* by the river at Linnankatu 39

(☎02/262 7680; ③; buses #1 and #30). The nearest **campsite** (☎02/2589100; June to mid-Aug; bus #8) is on the island of Ruissalo, which has two sandy beaches and overlooks Turku harbour. For free **Internet access** try the central library at Linnankatu 2 (Mon–Fri 10am–8pm, Sat 10am–3pm) which has bookable and walk-up terminals.

The City

To get to grips with Turku and its pivotal place in Finnish history, cut through the centre to the river. This tree-framed space was, before the great fire of 1827, the bustling heart of the community, and is overlooked by Turku's cathedral or **Tuomiokirkko** (9am–7pm daily except during services; free guided tours in English available), which was erected in the thirteenth century and is still the centre of the Finnish Church. Despite repeated fires, a number of features survive, notably the deliriously ornate seventeenth-century tomb of Torsten Stålhandske, commander of the Finnish cavalry during the Thirty Years' War. On top of a small hill near the cathedral, you'll see the wooden dome of the **Engel Observatory**, which currently houses the **Turku Art Museum** (Tues–Sat 10am–4pm, Thurs closes 7pm, Sun 11am–6pm; €5–8 according to the exhibition) while its usual home, a granite Art Nouveau structure close to the train station, is being renovated. The museum contains one of the better collections of Finnish art, with works by all the great names of the country's golden age plus a commendable stock of moderns. Steps away on the bank of the Aurajoki river is Turku's newest and most splendid museum, the combined **Aboa Vetus and Ars Nova** (May–Aug daily 11am–7pm, Sept–April Thurs–Sun 11am–7pm, July–Aug daily guided tours in English at 2.30pm; €6 or €9 including tour). Digging the foundations of the modern art gallery revealed a warren of medieval lanes which are now on view beneath the glass floor of the building. The gallery itself comprises 350 striking works plus temporary exhibitions, and there's a great café too.

Just north of the cathedral is the sleek low form of the **Sibelius Museum** (Tues–Sun 11am–4pm, Wed 6–8pm; €3), which – although Sibelius had no direct connection with Turku – displays family photo albums and original manuscripts, the great man's hat, walking stick and even his final half-smoked cigar, alongside exhibits covering the musical history of the country. There is also a concert hall where you can listen to recorded requests. South of here, the engrossing **Luostarinmäki Handicrafts Museum** on Vartiovuorenkatu (mid-April to mid-Sept 10am–6pm; rest of the year Tues–Sun 10am–3pm; €2.50; guided tours in English, with demonstrations, from June to Aug) is one of the best and most authentic open-air museums in Finland, and as true a record of old Turku as exists. The wooden houses here were built by local working people in traditional style and they became a museum as descendants of the original owners died and the town bought them up.

A short walk away, on the southern bank of the river Itäinen Rantakatu 38, is another worthwhile indoor collection: the **Wäinö Aaltonen Museum** (Tues–Sun 11am–7pm; €4, more for special exhibitions), devoted to the best-known modern Finnish sculptor, who grew up close to Turku and studied at the local art school. Aaltonen dominated his field throughout the 1920s and 1930s, and his influence is still felt today; his imaginative and sensitive work turns up in every major Finnish town. Crossing back over Aurajoki and down Linnankatu and then towards the mouth of the river will bring you to **Turku Castle** (mid-April to mid-Sept daily 10am–6pm; rest of the year Tues–Sun 10am–3pm; €3.75). The featureless exterior conceals a maze of cobbled courtyards, corridors and staircases, with a bewildering array of intriguing finds and displays. The castle probably went up around 1280; the seat of government for centuries, its gradual expansion accounts for the patchwork architecture.

Eating and drinking

If money's tight, *Gadolinia*, a **student mensa**, part of Åbo Akademi on Henrikenkatu, offers Turku's cheapest **food**. The *Italia*, Linnankatu 3, produces sizeable and affordably-priced pizzas. For excellent food at sensible prices, it's worth trekking out to *Turun Hotelli Ravintola*

Oppilaitos in the Data Centre, close to Turku hospital (take the train one stop to Kupittaa); run by the catering college, the food and service are excellent. Near the tourist office **Market Square** (Kauppatori) sells fresh produce, and in summer is full of open-air cafés, whilst nearby, the effervescent **Market Hall** (Kauppahalli; Mon–Fri 8am–5pm, Sat 8am–2pm) offers a slightly more upmarket choice of delis and other eateries. There are two decent riverside restaurants, *Pinella*, in Porthaninkatupuisto, or *Herman*, Läntinen Rantakatu 37, set in a bright, airy storehouse dating from 1849, with main courses costing around €10–25. Floating restaurants change each summer, but look out for *Papa Joe* and *Svarte Rudolph*. Popular **drinking** venues are *Uusi Apteekki*, Kaskenkatu 1, which, true to its name, is an old pharmacy complete with ancient fittings; and the atmospheric *Koulu Brewery Restaurant*, Eerikinkatu 18.

THE LAKE REGION

About a third of Finland is consumed by the **Lake Region**, a huge area of bays, inlets and islands, interspersed with dense forests. Despite holding much of Finland's industry, it's a tranquil, verdant region, and even **Tampere**, Finland's major industrial city, enjoys a peaceful lakeside setting, as well as being easily accessible from Helsinki by train. The eastern part of the Lake Region is the most atmospheric, slender ridges furred with conifers linking the few sizeable landmasses, reached from Tampere via **Jyväskylä**, whose wealth of buildings by Alvar Aalto make it a worthwhile break. Direct from Helsinki, the route goes via dull Lahti to the lakes' regional centre, **Savonlinna**, which stretches delectably across several islands and boasts a superb medieval castle. Further north, **Kuopio**, where many displaced Karelians settled after World War II, makes a decent break on the way up to Kajaani.

Tampere

TAMPERE, a leafy place of parks and lakes, is Finland's biggest manufacturing centre and Scandinavia's largest inland city. Its rapid growth began just over a century ago, when Tsar Alexander I abolished taxes on local trade, encouraging the Scotsman James Finlayson to open a textile factory, drawing labour from rural areas where traditional crafts were in decline. Metalwork and shoe factories soon followed, their owners paternally supplying culture to the workforce by promoting a vigorous local arts scene. Free outdoor rock and jazz concerts, lavish theatrical productions and one of the best modern art collections in Finland maintain such traditions to this day.

The City

Almost everything of consequence is within the central section, a thin strip of land bordered on two sides by lakes Näsijärvi and Pyhäjärvi. The main streets run off either side of Hämeenkatu, which leads directly from the train station across Hämeensilta. Left off Hämeenkatu, up the Tampere Workers' Theatre and **Lenin Museum** (Mon–Fri 9am–6pm, Sat & Sun 11am–4pm; €2.50) remembers the time when, after the abortive 1905 revolution in Russia, Lenin lived in Finland and attended the Tampere conferences, held in what is now the museum. Northwest of here there's more labour history, where some thirty homes have been preserved as the **Workers' Museum of Amuri** at Makasiininkatu 12 (mid-May to mid-Sept Tues–Sun 10am–6pm; €3.40), a simple but affecting place which records the family life of working people over a hundred-year period. In each home there's a description of the inhabitants and their jobs, and authentic articles from relevant periods – from tables to family photos and newspapers. Around the corner at Puutarhakatu 34, the **Art Museum of Tampere** (Tues–Sun 10am–6pm; €3.40–6.80) holds powerful if staid temporary exhibitions. If you're looking for Finnish art you might be better off visiting the **Hiekka Art Gallery**, a few minutes' walk away at Pirkankatu 6 (Wed & Thurs

3–6pm, Sun noon–3pm; €3.40), which has sketches by Gallén-Kallela and Helene Schjerfbeck. Better still is the tremendous **Sara Hildén Art Museum** (daily 11am–6pm; €3.50 combined ticket with Särkänniemi), built on the shores of Näsijärvi (bus #16 from the bus station or the central square), a quirky collection of Finnish and foreign modern works. Occupying the same waterside strip as the Hildén collection is **Särkänniemi**, Finland's most popular theme park with dolphinarium, aquarium, planetarium, a smattering of white knuckle rollercoasters and an observation tower – at 168m the highest free standing building in Scandinavia – which affords fantastic views (daily 11am–midnight; park entry fee €3.50, all-in ticket costs €22, though rollercoasters and aquarium are closed from Sept–April. Each other attraction then costs an extra €3.50–5)

Practicalities

The city's **tourist office** is by the river, 500m from the **train station** at Verkatehtaankatu 2 (June–Aug Mon–Fri 8.30am–8pm, Sat 8.30am–6pm, Sun 11.30am–6pm; Sept–May Mon–Fri 8.30am–5pm; ☎03/31466800, *www.tampere.fi*), and a similar distance along Hatanpään from the **bus station**: it offers free **Internet access** and hands out an excellent free Tampere guide. **Bicycles** can be rented from Sportia-10, Sammonkatu 60 (☎03/225 0000). Central, moderately priced **hotels** include the *Victoria*, Itsenäisyydenkatu 1 (☎03/2425111; ⑥), and *Sokos Hotel Villa*, Sumeliuksenkatu 14 (☎03/2626267; ⑦). There are various **hostels**, the best being the *Uimahallin maja*, an HI hostel centrally located at Pirkankatu 10–12 (☎03/2229460; ②), and the *NNKY* opposite the cathedral at Tuomiokirkonkatu 12a (☎03/2524020; ②; June–Aug). The nearest **campsite** is *Härmälä*, 5km south (☎03/2651355; mid-May to late Aug; bus #1), which also has three-person cabins for €30.

The cheapest places to eat are the **student mensas** at the university at the end of Yliopistonkatu. Still cheap are the usual pizza joints such as *Paprika* on the second floor of the *Hostel Uimahallion Maja*, Pirkankatu 10–12 (nightly till 11.45pm), and for relaxed posing, *Café Strindberg*, opposite the train station, serves fine baguettes as well as full meals. For a local speciality, try *mustamakkara*, a type of black sausage, at the *Laukontori* open-air **market** by the rapids. For **drinking**, the *Plevna* is a German-style beer hall in Finlayson's converted factory on Kuninkaankatu, which is especially busy at weekends; for live music, head for *Tullikamari*, a **nightclub** in an old customs house on Itsenäisyydenkatu behind the train station. The observation tower at Särkänniemi has an excellent revolving restaurant, *Näsinneula*, which serves traditional Finnish delicacies for about €25.

Jyväskylä

JYVÄSKYLÄ is a pleasant low-key lake town which houses a big university – giving it a youthful feel - as well as being home to an array of buildings created by legendary Finnish architect **Alvar Aalto**. He grew up here and opened his first office in the town in 1923, and his handiwork – a collection of buildings spanning his entire career – provides an excellent showcase of his work.

Aalto left Jyväskylä in 1927 for fame, fortune and Helsinki, but returned in the 1950s to work on what by the 1970s had grown into the **Jyväskylä University**. Although Aalto died before his ambitious plan for an Administration and Cultural Centre was complete, the scheme is still under construction along Vapaudenkatu. Beside the uninspiring ex-police station – unveiled in 1970 – stands the **city theatre** that epitomises the style Aalto created.

On the hill running down from the university towards the lake, Jyväsjärvi, stands two of the towns most important museums. At the request of the town authorities rather than through vanity, Aalto built the **Alvar Aalto Museum** at Alvar Aallon Katu 7 (Tues–Sun 11am–6pm, Aug until 8pm; €5, free on Fri). The architect's best works are obviously out on the streets, but there is a reasonable collection of plans, photos and models interspersed with an interesting selection of Aalto-designed furniture. Aalto also contributed to the exterior of the nearby **Keski-Suomen Museo** (Museum of Central Finland; Tues–Sun 11am–6pm, Aug until 8pm; €3.40, free on Fri), which contains two exhibitions: one devoted to Middle Finland – well designed but with no English translations – and the other representing each decade of the twentieth century through various domestic artifacts.

Near the bus and train stations the **tourist office**, at Asemakatu 6 (mid-June–Aug Mon–Fri 9am–6pm, Sat & Sun 9am–3pm; Sept–May Mon–Fri 9am–5pm, Sat 9am–2pm; ☎014/624 903, *www.jyvaskyla.fi*) can supply a useful free leaflet on the local Aalto buildings. For free **Internet** access try the pubic library at Vapaudenkatu 39–41 (Mon–Fri 11am–8pm, Sat 10am–3pm; June-Aug Mon–Fri 11am–7pm) – bookings required. For **accommodation**, the central, family-run *Hotel Milton*, Hannikaisenkatu 27–29 (☎014/3377 900; ③), is a good choice, while for a bit more luxury, try the *Scandic Hotel Jyväskylä* at Vapaudenkatu 73 (☎014/330 3000; ⑥). The local **youth hostel**, *Laajari* (☎014/624 885; ③), is 4km from the centre, at Laajavuorentie 15 – take bus #25 from Vapaudenkatu.

For **eating** options try the pizza establishments along the main streets or *Kissanviikset* at Puistokatu 3, which serves good fish dishes at lunchtime. For **nightlife** check out the hard-drinking and hard-chess playing in the smoky *Ruthin ravintola*, Seminaarinkatu 19, or if you want your evening to swing try the *Jazz Bar* on Kavelakatu.

Savonlinna and around

Leisurely draped across islands, **SAVONLINNA** is one of the most relaxed towns in Finland, a woodworking centre that also makes a decent living from tourism and its renowned annual **opera festival** (*www.operafestival.fi*) in July. It's packed throughout summer and if you haven't booked well ahead don't expect to find somewhere to stay. However, out of peak season its streets and beaches are uncluttered, and the town's easy-going mood makes it a pleasant place to linger.

The best locations for soaking up the atmosphere are the **harbour** and **market square** (*kauppatori*) at the end of Olavinkatu, where you can cast an eye over the grand *Seurahuone Hotel*, with its Art Nouveau fripperies, facing the **market hall** (*kauppahalli*). Follow the harbour around Linnankatu, or better still around the sandy edge of Pihlajavesi, which brings you to atmospheric and surprisingly well-preserved **Olavinlinna Castle** (daily: June to mid-Aug 10am–5pm; rest of year 10am–3pm; visits by hourly guided tours only; €3.40), perched on a small island. After being founded in 1475, the castle witnessed a series of bloody conflicts until the Russians claimed possession of it in 1743 and relegated it to being the town jail. Nearby is the **Savonlinna Regional Museum** (July daily 10am–6pm; Aug daily 11am–5pm; Sept–June Tues–Sun 11am–5pm; €3.40), which occupies an old granary and displays an intriguing account of the evolution of local life, with rock paintings and ancient amber carved with human figures.

Practicalities

Of the two **train stations**, be sure to get off at Savonlinna-Kauppatori, just across the main bridge from the **tourist office** at Puistokatu 1 (June & Aug daily 8am–6pm; until 10pm during festival; Sept–May Mon–Fri 9am–4pm; ☎015/517 510, *www.travel.fi/fin/Savonlinna*). The **bus station** is off the main island but within easy walking distance of the town centre. **Bikes** can be rented at several places on Olavinkatu, including Koponen at no. 42 (☎015/533977). For information and tickets for the opera festival visit the **opera office** at Olavinkatu 27 (☎015/476 750, *www.operafestival.fi*).

The most central **accommodation** is at the *Perehotelli Hospits*, Linnankatu 20 (☎015/515661; ⑤, ⑧ during festival). There is a **hostel**, *Malakias*, Pihlajavedenkatu 6 (☎015/533 283; ③; July to early Aug), 2km west of the centre along Tulliportinkatu and then Savontie, and a summer hotel, the *Vuorilinna*, on Kasinonsaari (☎015/739 5494; ⑤), five minutes over the bridge from the marketplace. The nearest **campsite** is 7km from the centre at Vuohimäki (☎015/537 353; June–Aug; bus #4). Anything sold around the harbour is liable to be overpriced; you can find cheaper, better **food** in the pizza joints along Olavinkatu and Tulliportinkatu. *Majakka*, Satamakatu 11, offers good Finnish nosh at lunchtime, though the most adventurous place to try is *Paviljonki*, Rajalatiendenkatu 4, where Finland's top trainee chefs serve their latest creations.

Around Savonlinna

Deep in the heart of the Lake Region, Savonlinna boasts beautiful scenery all around, as well as being a jumping-off point for several striking places a little way beyond. Closest is the **Punkaharju Ridge**, a narrow strip of land between the Puruvesi and Pihlajavesi lakes, 28km from town. Locals say it has the healthiest air in the world, super-oxygenated by abundant conifers. With the water never more than a few metres away on either side, this is the Lake Region at its most breathtakingly beautiful. The ridge is traversable by road and rail, both running into the town of Punkaharju and passing the incredible **Retretti Arts Centre** (daily 10am–5pm/6pm; €11.80), situated in man-made caves gouged into three-billion-year-old rock, and with a large sculpture park outside, in which fibreglass human figures by Olavi Lanu are cunningly entwined with natural forms. Trains and buses make the short journey between Savonlinna and Retretti. A more expensive, but very pleasant, option is to go by **boat** from Savonlinna harbour (summer 1 daily; €22 return). In high summer some boats make the eleven hour journey north to Kuopio – for all transport timings check with the tourist office.

Kuopio

Superficially cosmopolitan, with smart broad streets and modern buildings, **KUOPIO** is the only city in a vast expanse of countryside, and its earthy peasant heritage is always felt: traditional dress is common, sophistication is rare, and everything takes a back seat to unbridled revelry when the night comes.

All the sights are within the immediate central area, with one exception: the wonderful **Orthodox Church Museum**, Karjalankatu 1 (May–Aug Tues–Sun 10am–4pm; Sept–April Mon–Fri noon–3pm, Sat & Sun noon–5pm; €3.40), set on the brow of the hill at Kuopio's northwest corner. The museum houses many objects from the nearby Valamo Monastery, and it's easy to spend several hours wandering around elaborate icons, gold-embossed Bibles and other extravagant items. Back in the centre, the block formed by Kirkkokatu and Kuninkaankatu holds the **Kuopio Open-Air Museum** (mid-May to mid-Sept daily 10am–5pm, Wed until 7pm; mid-Sept to mid-May Tues–Sun 10am–3pm; €2.50), whose buildings, still in their original locations, have interiors decked out to show housing conditions of ordinary townspeople from the late eighteenth century to the 1930s. Another interesting old building, **J.V. Snellman's Home**, is situated nearby at Snellmaninkatu 19 (mid-May to mid-Sept daily 10am–5pm, Wed till 7pm; rest of year by appointment, call ☎017/182624; €7). Snellman lived here after the Swedish-speaking ruling class expelled him from his university post in 1843; he became head of the local school and continued his struggle to have Finnish granted the status of official language.

Practicalities

During the summer months **ferries** run to Savonlinna (€42.50; 11 hours; check with the tourist office for times). The **bus station** is at one end of Puijonkatu, which leads past the **train station** into the **market square** (*kauppatori*). The **market hall** (*kauppahalli*; Mon–Fri 8am–5pm, Sat 8am–2pm) forms a colourful contrast with the glass fronts of the encircling department stores and is a good place to sample the local speciality, *kalakukko*, a kind of fish and pork pie. Opposite stands the nineteenth-century City Hall and, around its side, the **tourist office** is at Haapaniemenkatu 17 (June–Aug Mon–Fri 9am–6pm, Sat 9am–4pm; rest of year Mon–Fri 9am–5pm; ☎017/182584). **Bikes** can be rented at Puijon Pyöräpiste, Kauppakatu 26 (☎071/2633273).

The **youth hostel** *Rauhalahti* is at Katiskaniementie 8 (☎017/473473; ③), a thirty-minute walk or short bus-ride from the tourist office – here you'll also find what is claimed to be the **world's biggest wood smoke sauna** (€8.50), an enormous unisex affair which can hold up to sixty people. Its size is such that it takes 24 hours just to heat up – consequently, it's only open on Tuesdays and Fridays. For about €14.30 you can avail yourself of an inclusive deal combining sauna and a traditional Finnish feast – ask at the hostel for more details. Just 500m further south of the hostel is a **campsite** (☎017/312 244; May–Aug). There is also a more central, **private hostel** – *Puijo Hovi*, Vuorikatu 35 (☎017/2614943; ④), a short walk from the station. For more luxurious accommodation, *Puijonsarvi*, Minna Canthinkatu 16 (☎017/170111; ⑦), boasts private saunas and lake views. Away from the harbour-side market, **food** is less exotic: *Pamukkale* beside the market square serves decent pizza whilst *Henry's Pub*, Kauppakatu 18, does cheapish lunches. During the summer you might also try the vibrant *Wanha Satma*, a mid-priced, outdoor place ideal for soaking up the bustling harbour atmosphere.

NORTHERN FINLAND

The three northern regions of Ostrobothnia, Kainuu and Lapland take up by far the largest portion of Finland. Unlike the populous south or more industrialized sections of the Lake Region, they're predominantly rural, their small communities separated by long distances. The coast of **Ostrobothnia** is fairly affluent due to the flat and fertile farmlands; the busy and expanding **Oulu** is the region's major city as well as a centre of high-tech expertise, though it maintains a pleasing small town atmosphere. Further north, **Lapland** is a poor, remote territory, excitingly unexplored, whose wide open spaces are home to several thousand Sami, who have lived in harmony with this special, harsh environment for millennia. Here the long, harsh winters are eerily dark and the summers plagued by mosquitoes, making the splendid early Arctic autumn (Aug–Sept) the most popular time to explore. Moving around is fairly easy as there is an extensive bus service and regular flights to Helsinki. As well as enjoying the scenery, make sure you try the Lappish cuisine, with fresh cloudberries, cold-smoked reindeer and wild salmon being highlights. **Rovaniemi** is the rather bland gateway to the Arctic North; from here a road leads onwards towards **Sodankylä** and **Inari**, both convenient bases for further exploration.

Oulu

OULU with its renowned technical college is now a leading light in Finland's burgeoning computing and microchip industries. During the last century it was the centre of the world's tar industry and the city's affluence and vibrant cultural scene date from that time, though the old buildings clustered around the river bank are now somewhat overshadowed by the faceless office blocks of the past twenty years. In the centre of town on Kirkkokatu, the **City Hall** retains some of the grandeur of the late nineteenth century, when it was built as a luxury hotel, and you can peek in at the wall paintings and enclosed gardens. Further along Kirkkokatu, the copper-domed and stuccoed **Tuomiokirkko** (daily: summer 10am–7pm; rest of year noon–1pm), seems anachronistic amid the bulky blocks of modern Oulu. Inside the vestry, open on request, is a portrait of Johannes Messinius, the Swedish historian, supposedly painted by Cornelius Arenditz in 1611 and believed to be the oldest surviving oil portrait in Finland. Across the small canal just north of the cathedral, the **North Ostrobothnia Museum** (Mon, Tues & Thurs 10am–6pm, Wed 10am–8pm, Sat & Sun 11am–5pm; €17), packed with tar-stained remnants from Oulu's past, is a large regional collection with a good Sami section.

The connected **train and bus station** are linked to the city centre by several parallel streets feeding to the *kauppatori* and *kauppahalli* (**markets**) by the water beyond. The

tourist office is at Torikatu 10 (July Mon–Sat 9am–6pm, Sun 10am–4pm; rest of year Mon–Fri 9am–4pm; ☎08/5584 1330, *www.ouka.fi*). **Bikes** can be rented from Jussin Pyöräpiste, Albertinkatu 11 (☎08/3114983). Low-cost **accommodation** in the centre is available at the *Hotel Turisti*, opposite the train station at Rautatienkatu 9 (☎08/375233; ⑤), which provides hostel-type accommodation during summer, when it takes the overspill from the official **hostel** at Kajaanintie 36 (☎08/880 3311; ③; June–Aug), a fifteen-minute walk from the train station. There's a **campsite** (☎08/5586 1351) with cabins on Hietasaari Island, 4km from town; take bus #5 from outside the tourist office. Oulu boasts some charming **cafés** including *Sokeri Jussi* in an old salt warehouse on Pikisaanie just over the bridge from the mainland, while *Katri Antell* on Rotuaari (Mon–Fri 8.30am–5pm, Sat 9am–2.30pm) is justly famed for its luscious, but expensive, cakes. Cheapest **meals** are at the numerous pizzerias – *Fantasia* serves the best and also has a selection of Finnish dishes – while *Oskarin Kellari* just opposite the train station serves a stuff-your-face lunch buffet for about €7.50. For extravagant waterside dining, try *Neptunus* which serves fish and meat in a boat moored by the market square. For **nightlife** try the eclectic *Foxia*, Pakkohuoneenkatu 19, a nightclub with varying musical fare depending which evening you go.

Rovaniemi

Relatively easy to reach by rail from Ostrobothnia or Kainuu, **ROVANIEMI** is touted as the capital of Lapland, though it's more an administrative than cultural capital, and the tourists who arrive on day-trips from Helsinki expecting sleighs and tents are normally disappointed. The wooden huts of old Rovaniemi were razed by departing Germans at the close of World War II, and the town was completely rebuilt during the late 1940s. Alvar Aalto's bold but impractical design has the roads forming the shape of reindeer antlers – fine if you're travelling by helicopter but it makes journeys on foot far longer than they need be. Rovaniemi is a likeable enough town, though most visitors only use it as a short-term stopover, or to study Sami culture.

Aside from eating reindeer in the local restaurants, the best way to prepare yourself for what lies further north is to visit the 172m-long glass tunnel of **Arktikum**, Pohjoisranta 4 (May–Aug daily 10am–6pm; Sept–April closed Mon; €10), symbolically pointing north across Ounasjoki from its surrounding landscape of arctic flora. Subterranean galleries along one side house the **Provincial Museum of Lapland**, a thoughtful museum placing genuine Sami crafts and costumes alongside the imitations sold in souvenir shops to emphasize the romanticization of their culture. It also demonstrates the changes in the use of tools and clothing – anoraks and Wellington boots have replaced traditional apparel, which has caused a young generation of Sami to be plagued by rheumatism and foot trouble. Across the corridor is the **Arctic Centre**, which gives a thorough treatment of all things circumpolar, from Inuit and Aleut languages to mineral exploration and hunting from kayaks decked out in walrus-gut waterproofs.

The remaining sights are on the south side of town near the **bus** and **train stations**, where pristine Aalto-designed civic buildings line Hallituskatu. **Lappia House** (pre-booked guided tours only call ☎016/3562096) has a theatre and concert hall, and next door, the **library** (Mon–Thur 11am–8pm, Fri 11am–5pm, Sat 10am–4pm) has a **Lapland Department** with a staggering hoard of books in many languages covering every Sami-related subject. Most other things of interest are outside town, not least the **Arctic Circle**, 8km north and connected by the half hourly bus #8 from the bus station – though there's not much to see on arrival. Near the circle and served by the same buses, is **Santa Claus Village** (daily: Dec & June–Aug 9am–7pm; rest of the year 10am–5pm; free), a large log cabin where you can meet Father Christmas all year round and leave your name for a Christmas card from Santa himself. South of the Arctic Circle, the **Midnight Sun** is visible from town for a couple of weeks either side of midsummer, the best vantage points being the striking "Lumberjack's Candlestick" bridge or atop the conifer and mosquito-clad hill, Ounasvaara.

Practicalities

The main **tourist office** is at Koskikatu 1 (June–Aug Mon–Fri 8am–6pm, Sat & Sun 10am–4pm; rest of year Mon–Fri 8am–4pm & Dec Sat & Sun 10am–2pm; ☎016/346270, *www.rovaniemi.fi*). The **hostel**, *Tervashonka* at Hallituskatu 16 (☎016/344644; ③), is always crowded in summer – try to book in advance. Otherwise you can fall back on the **guest houses**, the best of which are within five minutes' walk of the train station: *Matka Borealis* is nearest at Asemieskatu 1 (☎016/3420130; ④) whilst *Matka Outa*, Ukkoherrantie 16 (☎016/312474; ④), is towards the town centre. The only other budget accommodation is the **campsite** (☎016/345 304; June–Aug) on the far bank of Ounasjoki, facing town, a thirty-minute walk from the station. For filling **food** at very reasonable prices try *Café Kisälli*, Korkalonkatu 35 (Mon–Fri 8.30am–5pm) or the neighbouring *Oppipoika* restaurant, which serves good evening meals.

Sodankylä

A two-hour bus ride north of Rovaniemi, **SODANKYLÄ** has enough of interest to warrant a stop-off on the road to the far north. The **bus station** is in the centre of the town where you'll find the helpful **tourist office** at Jäämerentie 7 (Mon–Fri 9am–5pm, July also Sat & Sun 9am–3pm; ☎016/618168). Next door is the **Andreas Alariesto Art Gallery** (Mon–Fri 10am–5pm; June–Aug Sat 10am–5pm, Sun noon–6pm; rest of year Sat 10am–4pm, Sun noon–6pm; €2.50), which has an engaging collection of Alariesto's early-twentieth century bold, colourful paintings, depicting the life, struggles and myths of the Sami. Just behind towards the Kitinen River is Lapland's **oldest surviving church**, dating from 1689, its plain roof of rough-hewn timbers crowding in on the narrowest of naves.

A good time to come to Sodankylä is in mid-June for Lapland's biggest annual cultural event, the **Midnight Sun Film Festival** (☎016/614 52, *www.msfilmfestival.fi*). During the festival, the town swarms with film buffs from Scandinavia and beyond who descend on this modest place to catch works by invited directors such as John Sayles, Jim Jarmusch, Terry Gilliam and Finnish regulars the Kaurismäki brothers, all of whom tend to mingle in with the festival crowd creating a unique atmosphere.

If you want **accommodation** during the festival, you'll need to book as far ahead as possible, but at other times there should be no problem in finding somewhere to stay. For comfort try *Hotel Sodankylä* (☎016/612181; ⑥) just opposite the bus station. There's a **campsite** (☎016/612181; June to mid-Aug) just across the river which also has cabins from 160mk. Places to **eat** can be found along Jäämerentie with good pizzas at number 52, *Poronsarvi*.

Inari

Situated about 230km north of Sodankylä, **INARI** lies along the fringes of Inarijärvi, one of Finland's largest lakes, and makes a rather attractive point from which to base further exploration of this part of Lapland. The bus stops off outside the helpful **tourist office** in Inari House (June–Sept Mon–Fri 9am–7pm, Sat & Sun 10am–3pm; Oct–May Mon–Fri 10am–4pm; ☎016/661666), which provides maps and fishing licences and can point you in the right direction for guided snow scooter trips in winter and fishing trips around the lake in summer. Close by is the recently renovated "Siida", the **Sami Museum** (June–Sept daily 9am–8pm; Oct–May Tue–Sun 10am–5pm; €5), which is one of the best museums in Lapland. An excellent outdoor section gives you an idea of how the Sami survived in Arctic conditions in their tepees, or *kota*, while the indoor section has a well-laid-out and easy-to-understand exhibition on all aspects of life in the arctic.

Towards the northern end of the village, pleasure cruises depart from under the bridge in summer (about €8.50–17). Most of these trips will take you out to an ancient Sami holy site on an island in the middle of Inarijärvi at **Ukkonkivi**, named after Ukko, the Sami equivalent of the Norse god of thunder, Thor; a plaque marks an ancient site of worship rumoured to have been a place of sacrifice. The views over the lake are stunning. If walking's your thing then check out the pretty **Pielpajärvi Wilderness Church**, normally a one- to two-hour well-signposted hike from the village. There was a church on this site as far back as 1646, and the present one dates from 1754; services are still held during mid-summer and for special occasions such as weddings.

Accommodation should not be too problematic, though Inari does get very busy during the summer months. A basic hotel is the *Inarin Kultahovi* (☎016/671221; ⑦), which also has a decent affordable **restaurant**. About 2km south of the village is the highly recommended *Uruniemi* campsite (☎016/671331; open all year Oct–April, advanced booking obligatory), set in a lovely location right by the lake.

travel details

Trains

Helsinki to: Jyväskylä (12 daily; 3hr 30mins); Oulu (8 daily; 7hr); Rovaniemi (5 daily; 9hr 45min); Tampere (22 daily; 2hr); Turku (12 daily; 2hr).

Jyväskylä to: Tampere (9 daily; 2hr).

Kuopio to: Jyväskylä (5 daily; 1hr 50min).

Oulu to: Rovaniemi (7 daily; 3hr); Tornio (4 daily; 2hr 15min).

Pori to: Tampere (7 daily; 1hr 30min).

Tampere to: Helsinki (22 daily; 2hr); Oulu (7 daily; 5hr); Pori (7 daily; 1hr 30min); Savonlinna (2 daily; 4hr); Turku (7 daily; 2hr 15min).

Turku to: Tampere (8 daily; 1hr 50min).

Flights

Helsinki to: Ivalo for Inari (1–3 daily; 1hr 30min–2hr 30min); Oulo (5–7 daily; 1hr), Rovaniemi (5–7daily; 1hr).

Buses

Helsinki to: Jyväskylä (8 daily; 5hr); Kotka (10 daily; 2hr 10min); Lahti (26 daily; 1hr 30min); Mikkeli (8 daily; 4hr); Porvoo (18 daily; 1hr); Savonlinna (3 daily; 5hr 30min); Tampere (20 daily; 2hr 30min); Turku (21 daily; 2hr 30min).

Kuopio to: Jyväskylä (3 daily; 2hr 15min).

Rovaniemi to: Sodankyla (6 daily; 2hr 30min); Inari (3 daily, 5hr).

Savonlinna to: Kuopio (4 daily; 3hr 40min).

Tampere to: Helsinki (12 daily; 2hr 15min–3hr); Turku (5 daily; 2hr 30min).

Ferries

Helsinki to: Stockholm (2daily; 13 hr); Tallinn (15–25 daily; 1hr 40 min–4 hr).

Turku to: Stockholm (4 daily 10hr–11hr)

CHAPTER 10

FRANCE

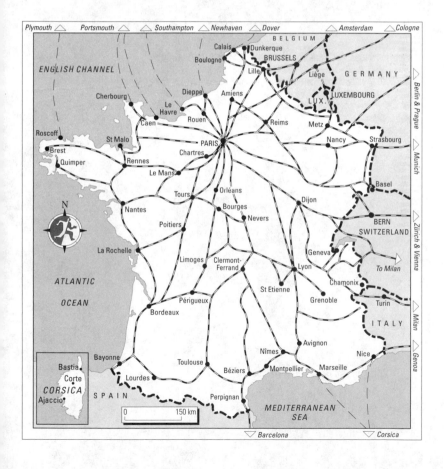

Introduction

Straddling the continent between the Iberian peninsula and the nations of central Europe, **France** is a core country on any European tour. It would be hard to exhaust its diversity in a lifetime of visits. Each area looks different, feels different, has its own style of architecture and food and often its own *patois* or dialect. There is an astonishing variety of things to see, whether it's the Gothic cathedrals of the north, the châteaux of the Loire or the Roman monuments of the south. The countryside, too, has its own appeal, seemingly little changed for hundreds of years.

Travelling in France is easy. Budget restaurants and hotels proliferate; the rail and road networks are efficient; and the tourist information service is highly organized. As for where to go, it's hard to know where to begin. If you arrive from the north, you may pass through the Channel ports – **Calais** or **Boulogne**, or those of **Normandy** – to **Paris**, one of Europe's most elegant and compelling capitals. To the west lie the rocky coasts of **Brittany** and, further south, the châteaux of the **Loire**, although most people push on south to the limestone hills of **Provence**, the canyons of the **Pyrenees** on the Spanish border, or the glorious Mediterranean coastline of the **Côte d'Azur** towards Italy. There are good reasons, however, for taking things more slowly, not least the Germanic towns of **Alsace** in the east, the gorgeous hills and valleys of the **Lot** and the **Dordogne**, and, more adventurously, the high and rugged French heartland of the **Massif Central**.

Information and maps

You'll find a Syndicat d'Initiative (SI) or Office du Tourisme in practically every town and in many villages, giving local **information**, listings of things to see, free maps and, occasionally, bike rental. Some can book accommodation anywhere in France. In larger cities and tourist resorts these will be open every day during the high season, often without a break, although times are greatly cut back in most places in the winter months.

The best **road map** of France is the Michelin no. 989 (1:1,000,000). A useful free map for car drivers, obtainable from filling stations and traffic information kiosks in France, is the *Bison Futé*, showing alternative back routes. For more **regional detail**, the Michelin yellow series (scale 1:200,000) is best for the motorist. If you're planning to **walk or cycle**, check out the IGN green (1:100,000 and 1:50,000) and blue (1:25,000) maps.

Money and banks

France is one of twelve European Union countries which have changed over to a single currency, the **euro** (€). Euro notes and coins will be issued from January 1, 2002, with French francs remaining in circulation during a transition period, at a fixed rate of F6.55957 to €1, until they are scrapped entirely on February 17. After this date you will be able to exchange your francs for euros in commercial banks until June 30. Euro notes are issued in **denominations** of 5, 10, 20, 50, 100, 200 and 500 euros, and coins in denominations of 1, 2, 5, 10, 20 and 50 cents and 1 and 2 euros.

All prices in this chapter are given in euros correct at the time of going to press. There will no doubt be some rounding off (or, more probably, up) of prices in the first few months after the introduction of the euro.

The best place to change money is a bank: standard **banking hours** are Mon–Fri 9am–noon & 2–4.30pm, some are also open on Saturdays. Rates of exchange and commissions vary greatly; the Banque Nationale de Paris often gives the best rate for the least commission. Outside banking hours, there are **exchange counters** at the train stations of all big cities, and usually one or two in the town centre as well, though normally they offer a much worse deal. You can also change money at post offices and tourist offices.

Communications

Post offices *(la Poste)* are generally open Mon–Fri 9am–7pm, Sat 8am–noon. To avoid the long queues at lunchtimes and in the late afternoon, buy **stamps** *(timbres)* from *tabacs* instead.

You can make international **phone calls** from any box *(cabine)*. Many post offices have metered booths from which you can make calls and pay afterwards. Phone boxes take only **phonecards** *(télécartes)*, available from post offices, *tabacs* and train station ticket counters. For calls within France – local or long distance – dial **all ten digits** of the number. The operator number is ☎12. To call Monaco from France, prefix the eight-digit number with ☎00377.

All towns have cybercafés offering **Internet access** for around €6/hr. Post offices also offer access: to use their terminals you need a pre-paid card costing €7.60 for the first hour. Street-side kiosks in major cities are operated by France Telecom *télécartes*.

Getting around

With the most extensive rail network in western Europe, run by the **SNCF** *(www.sncf.com)*, France is a country best travelled by train. The only areas not well served are the mountains, where rail routes are replaced by SNCF buses. Private bus services throughout the country tend to be confusing and uncoordinated.

■ Trains and buses

SNCF **trains** are generally clean, fast and frequent. **Fares** are reasonable, with a 300km journey costing around €30 and a 600km journey roughly €53 off-peak in second class. The numerous and ultrafast **TGV**s *(Trains à Grande Vitesse)* require compulsory reservation (€1.50–3) plus a supplement at peak times. The slowest trains are those marked *Autorail* in the timetable, stopping at all stations.

The under-26 InterRail and all Eurail **passes** are valid throughout France, as is the EuroDomino pass, though you have to buy it before you enter the country. SNCF also offer a whole range of **discount fares**, depending on colour-coded time periods, blue or white: *période bleue* covers most of the year and gives the largest discounts (50 percent). All tickets (not passes) must be stamped in the orange machines on station platforms. Rail journeys may be broken any time, anywhere, for up to 24 hours. On night trains, an extra €14 or so will buy you a **couchette**.

Regional **rail maps** and **timetables** are on sale at *tabacs*, and leaflet timetables are available free at every train station *(gare SNCF)*. All but the smallest stations have an information desk and most have *consignes automatiques* – coin-operated left-luggage lockers. Many also rent bicycles (see opposite).

The designation *Autocar* at the top of a timetable column means it's an **SNCF bus service**, on which rail tickets and passes are valid. Apart from these, the only time you'll need to take a **bus** is in cities; indeed the most frustrating thing about buses is that they rarely serve regions outside the SNCF network – which is precisely where you need them. In larger towns the bus station *(gare routière)* is normally next to the train station.

■ Driving, hitching and cycling

Taking a **car** gives you enormous advantages of access to remote areas, especially if you're camping. Overseas drivers' licences are valid in France; you should also carry your vehicle registration document and insurance papers. Motorways *(autoroutes)* are fast and fairly extensive, but the **tolls** are expensive; you might prefer to use the older "N" roads, which are fast enough, or "D" roads, the next grade down (both these are toll-free). An antiquated **rule of the road** which is still operative in some areas is that you must give way to traffic on your right *(priorité à droite)*, even from an incoming minor road – though on main roads there are nearly always yellow diamond roadsigns indicating the contrary. The same sign with a black diagonal slash, or a red-edged inverted triangle containing a sideways black cross means that you **must** give way to traffic coming from the right. (The triangle sign usually appears only before individual junctions.) **Speed limits** on motorways are 130kph (110kph in rain); on major roads 110kph (80kph in rain); on other roads 90kph; and in towns 50kph. Fines are exacted on the spot and only cash is accepted: the minimum for speeding is €200, and for exceeding the drink-driving level €400–800. For **information** on traffic and weather conditions on the motorways call Service d'Information des Autoroutes on ☎08.36.68.10.77 (24hr). In case of **breakdown**, there are emergency phones every 2km on the motorways. **Car rental** is about €300–400 a week for a small hatchback, with unlimited mileage.

Hitching, you'll have to rely almost exclusively on car drivers, and the French aren't renowned for their sympathy to hitchhikers. On motorways the toll-booths at each major junction are the best bet for picking up long lifts. You might be better off contacting Allostop Provoya, a national organization with offices in Paris (8 rue Rochambeau, on place Montholon; ☎01.53.20.42.42), and a few other major towns. In return for a registration fee, they'll match you up with a driver who is going your way and wants to share petrol costs.

Keen **cyclists** are much admired in France. Traffic keeps at a respectful distance (except in the big cities) and restaurants and hotels go out of their way to find a safe place for your bike. Bikes go free on some SNCF trains, though on others you have to pay €30 to send it to your destination – for details, consult the free leaflet *Train et Vélo*, available from most stations. Some SNCF stations also **rent bikes** for around €7.50 per day plus a €150 or €200 deposit (or a credit card number). You can return the bike to any other specified station.

Accommodation

For most of the year it's possible to turn up in any French town and find **accommodation**, whether a room or a place on a campsite. Booking a couple of nights in advance can, however, be reassuring, and is essential from mid-July to mid-Aug, when the French take their vacations. The first weekend of August is the busiest time of all, though campsites are still usually OK unless you're travelling with a caravan.

■ Hotels

All French **hotels** are officially graded, and prices are relatively uniform. Ungraded and single-star hotels go for €15–30 per double, and are often very good; for a private bath, reckon on paying around €5–7 more, plus sometimes €3–5 for breakfast – although there is no obligation to take this and you will nearly always do better at a café. For a room in a two-star place, which will normally always include a private bath, reckon on an average of €23–45. It is illegal for hotels to insist on your taking meals, but they often do, and in busy resorts you may not find a room unless you agree. In country areas you will come across **chambres d'hôte** – bed and breakfast accommodation in someone's house or farm. These

vary in standard and are rarely cheap, usually costing the equivalent of a two-star hotel.

Full **accommodation lists** for each province are available from any French Government Tourist Office or from local SIs. In peak season it is worth getting hold of these, together with a handbook for the **Logis de France** – independent hotels, promoted for their consistently good food and reasonably priced rooms, and recognizable by their green and yellow logo.

■ Hostels and foyers

France boasts a wide network of official **hostels**, or *auberges de jeunesse*, and most are of a high standard. However, at €6–14 for a dormitory bed (more in Paris), they are sometimes no less expensive for a couple than the cheapest hotel room – particularly if you take into account fares to their sometimes inaccessible locations. You can sometimes cut costs by preparing your own food in their kitchens, or eating in their cheap canteens. There are two rival youth hostel associations: the Fédération Unie des Auberges de Jeunesse, 27 rue Pajol, 75018 Paris (☎01.44.89.87.27, *www.fuaj.org*), and the Ligue Française pour les Auberges de Jeunesse, 67 rue Vergniaud, 75013 Paris (☎01.44.16.78.78). HI membership covers both organizations, although only the former's hostels are detailed in the HI handbook.

A few large towns provide a more luxurious standard of hostel accommodation in **Foyers des Jeunes Travailleurs/-euses**, residential hostels for young workers and students, charging around €11 for an individual room. They also normally have a good canteen. In rural areas, **gîtes d'étape** – often run by the local village or municipality and less formal than the hostels – provide bunk beds and simple kitchen facilities. Tourist offices can provide regional accommodation listings and sell guides to *gîtes* and *chambres d'hôte*.

■ Campsites

Practically every village and town in the country has at least one **campsite**: thousands of French people

---

ACCOMMODATION PRICE CODES

Throughout this guide, accommodation is coded on a scale of ① to ⑨, the code indicating the lowest price per person per night you could expect to pay in each establishment in high season. With hostels this is the nightly rate per person; with hotels, the price is arrived at by dividing the cost of the cheapest double room by two. The prices indicated by the codes are as follows:

① under £5/$8 (€9)	④ £15–20/$24–32 (€27–36)	⑦ £30–35/$48–56 (€54–63)
② £5–10/$8–16 (€9–18)	⑤ £20–25/$32–40 (€36–45)	⑧ £35–40/$56–64 (€63–72)
③ £10–15/$16–24 (€18–27)	⑥ £25–30/$40–48 (€45–54)	⑨ £40/$64 (€72) and over

choose to spend their holidays under canvas. The cheapest – starting at €4 per person per night – is usually the *Camping Municipal*, normally clean, well-equipped and in a prime location. On the coast especially, there are superior campsites where you'll pay amounts similar to a hotel room for what can be extensive facilities. Inland, camping on somebody's farm is another possibility. Lists of sites are available from tourist offices. Never **camp rough** *(camping sauvage)* on anyone's land without asking permission: farmers have been known to shoot first and ask questions later. Consult *www.campingfrance.com* for a list of sites.

Food and drink

French **food and drink** is as good a reason as any for a visit to France. Cooking has art status, the top chefs are stars, and dining out is a national pastime, whether it's at the local brasserie or a famed house of *haute cuisine*. It also doesn't have to cost much as long as you avoid tourist hot spots.

■ Food

Generally the best place to eat **breakfast** is in a bar or café. Most serve buttered *baguettes* (French bread) and have a basket of croissants on the counter to which you can help yourself; the waiter will keep an eye on how much you've eaten and bill you accordingly. **Coffee** is invariably espresso and strong. *Un café* or *un express* is black; *un crème* is with milk; *un grand café* is a large cup. In the morning, ask for *café au lait* – espresso in a large cup or bowl with plenty of hot milk. Ordinary **tea** *(thé)* is not as common; to have it with milk, ask for *un peu de lait frais*. Hot chocolate *(chocolat chaud)* can be had in any café. Every bar or café displays a full price list for taking drinks at the bar *(au comptoir)*, sitting down inside *(la salle)*, or outside *(la terrasse)* – each progressively more expensive.

Cafés are often the best option for **lunch** as well, serving omelettes, fried eggs and sandwiches (generally half-baguettes filled with cheese or meat), and *croque-monsieur* and *-madame* (variations on the grilled cheese sandwich). On street stalls you'll also find *frites* (chips/french fries), *crêpes*, *galettes* (wholewheat pancakes), *gaufres* (waffles) and Tunisian snacks like *brik à l'œuf* (fried pastry with egg) and *merguez* (spicy sausage). For **picnic and takeaway food**, there's nothing to beat the ready-made dishes – salads, meats and fully prepared main courses – from a *charcuterie* (delicatessen), which

are also available at supermarket *charcuterie* counters. You buy by weight, or you can ask for *une tranche* (a slice), *une barquette* (a carton) or *une part* (a portion).

You can also eat lunch at a **brasserie** – like a restaurant, only open all day and geared more to quicker meals; **restaurants** tend to stick to the traditional meal times of noon–2pm & 7–9.30/10.30pm. In major cities, town centre brasseries often serve until 11pm or midnight. Prices at both are posted outside. Normally there is a choice between one or more *menus fixes* and choosing from the menu (*à la carte*); the latter is more expensive but often the only option available after 9pm. Look out, at lunchtime and in the evening, for the **plat du jour** (daily special), which for €6–12 in a cheap restaurant will often be the most interesting and best-value thing on the menu. *Service compris* means the service charge is included; if not, you need to add fifteen percent. Wine *(vin)* or a drink *(boisson)* may be included in a *menu fixe*, but when ordering your own wine ask for *un quart*, *un demi-litre* or *une carafe* (a litre). You'll normally be given the house wine unless you specify otherwise.

■ Drink

Where you can eat you can usually **drink**, and vice versa. Drinking is done most often at a **café** and at a leisurely pace, whether taken as an *apéritif* before eating, a *digestif* after eating, or as a meal's accompaniment. **Wine** *(vin)* is drunk at just about every meal or social occasion. *Vin de table* or *vin ordinaire* (table wine) is generally drinkable and always cheap, and in wine-producing areas can be very good indeed. Wines marked *AOC (Appellation d'Origine Contrôlée)* are another matter. They can be excellent value at the lower end of the scale – favourable domestic taxes keep prices down to €1.50 or so a bottle – but serious wines command serious prices. In a café, a **glass of wine** is simply *un rouge* or *un blanc*. If you select an *AOC* wine you may have the choice of a round glass *(un ballon)* or a smaller glass *(un verre)*.

Most of the **beers** you'll find comprise the familiar Belgian and German names, plus home-grown brands from Alsace. Beer on tap *(à la pression)* is France's cheapest alcoholic drink, alongside wine – just ask for *une pression*. Stronger alcohol is drunk by some people from 5am as a pre-work fortifier, right through the day: **cognac** or **armagnac** brandies, dozens of *eaux-de-vie* (spirits distilled from fruit) and **liqueurs**. Measures are generous, but don't come cheap. *Pastis* is a refreshing and inexpensive aniseed-flavoured liquor (popular brands are Pernod and Ricard), drunk diluted with water and ice *(glaçons)*.

Top **soft drinks** include fresh orange/lemon juice *(orange pressée/citron pressé)* and bottled fruit juices such as apricot *(jus d'abricot)* or blackcurrant cordial *(sirop de cassis)*. Bottled **spring water** *(eau minérale)* – either sparkling *(gazeuse)* or still *(eau plate)* – is everywhere, but you're entitled to ask for tap water *(l'eau du robinet)*, which is free.

Opening hours and holidays

The basic **working hours** in France are 8am–noon & 2–7pm. Sunday and Monday are the standard **closing days**, though you'll always find at least one *boulangerie* (bakery) open. **Museums** open at around 10am and close between 5 and 6pm, with reduced hours outside mid-May to mid-September, sometimes even outside July and August. They also tend to close on Monday or Tuesday, usually the latter. Admission charges can be off-putting, though most state-owned museums give reductions to **students**, so always carry your ISIC card and check with tourist offices for passes that give access to all local museums and monuments.

All shops, museums and offices are closed on the following **national holidays**: Jan 1; Easter Sunday & Monday; May 1; May 8; Ascension Day; Whit Sunday & Monday; July 14; Aug 15; Nov 1; Nov 11; Dec 25.

Emergencies

There are two main types of French police – the **Police Nationale** and the **Gendarmerie Nationale** – which are, for all practical purposes, indistinguishable; you can report a theft, or other incident, to either. You can be stopped anywhere in France and asked to produce ID, so always carry your passport.

Under the French social security system every **hospital** visit, doctor's consultation and prescribed medicine is charged, though in an emergency not upfront. Although all employed French people are entitled to a refund of 70–75 percent of their medical expenses, this can still leave a hefty shortfall, especially after a stay in hospital. In **emergencies** you will always be admitted to the local hospital *(hôpital)*, whether under your own power or by ambulance. To find a **doctor**, stop at any *pharmacie* and ask for an address. Consultation fees for a visit should be €15–23 and in any case you'll be given a *Feuille de Soins* (Statement of Treatment) for documentation of your insurance claims when you get home. Prescriptions should be taken to a *pharmacie*, which is also equipped – and obliged – to give first aid (for a fee). For minor illnesses pharmacists will dispense free advice and a wide range of medication.

Emergency Numbers

Police ☎17; Ambulance ☎15; Fire ☎18.

PARIS

PARIS is the paragon of style – perhaps the most captivating city in Europe. Yet it is also deeply traditional, a village-like and, in parts, dilapidated metropolis. Famous names and events are instilled with a glamour that elevates the city and its people to a legendary realm, and it is still keen to preserve its status as an artistic, intellectual and literary pacesetter.

From a shaky start, the kings of France gradually extended their control from Paris over their feudal rivals, centralizing administrative, legal, financial and political power as they did so. The supremely autocratic Louis XIV made the city into a glorious symbol of the pre-eminence of the state, a tradition his successors have been happy to follow. Napoleon I added to the Louvre and built the Arc de Triomphe, the Madeleine and the Arc du Carrousel, while Napoleon III had Baron Haussmann redraw the city centre. The habit of breaking architectural moulds has continued with the Pompidou Centre's luridly-coloured tubing, the landmark steel-and-glass Louvre Pyramid, the enormous hollow cube of the Grande Arche de la Défense and the new L-shaped glass towers of the Bibliothèque Nationale.

The most tangible and immediate pleasures of Paris are to be found in its **street life** and along the lively banks of the river Seine. Few cities can compete with the cafés, bars and restaurants – trendy and traditional, local and cosmopolitan, humble and pretentious – that line every street and boulevard. And the city's compactness makes it possible to experience the individual feel of the different *quartiers*. You can move easily, even on foot, from the calm, almost small-town atmosphere of **Montmartre** and parts of the Latin Quarter to the busy commercial centres of the **Bourse** and **Opéra** or to the aristocratic mansions of the **Marais**. An imposing backdrop is provided by the monumental architecture of the **Arc de Triomphe**, the **Louvre**, the **Eiffel Tower**, the **Hôtel de Ville**, the bridges and the institutions of the state. As for entertainment, Paris is a real world **cinema** capital, while the best Parisian **music** encompasses jazz, avant-garde, salsa and, currently, Europe's most vibrant African music scene.

Paris is divided into twenty postal districts, known as **arrondissements**, which are used by everyone to locate addresses. The first, or *premier* (abbreviated as 1er) is centred on the Louvre, with the rest (abbreviated as 2e, 3e, 4e) spiralling outwards clockwise: the inner hub of the city, where most of the major sights and museums are located, is covered by the first six *arrondissements*.

Arrival and information

Paris's two main **airports** *(www.adp.fr)* are Roissy-Charles de Gaulle and Orly. **Charles de Gaulle**, or CDG for short, 23km northeast, is connected to the Gare du Nord by Roissyrail, a combination of free shuttle bus and the RER train line B (every 8min 5am–midnight; takes 35min; €7.30). There's also the Roissybus, which terminates at métro Opéra (every 15min 5.45am–11pm; takes 45min; €7.30), or the more expensive Air France bus, which departs from both terminals to métro Charles-de-Gaulle-Étoile (every 12min 6am–11pm; €9.20), métro Porte Maillot (same hours and price), and Gare Montparnasse (every 30min 7am–9pm; €10.50). Taxis cost from €31 (plus €1 for each piece of luggage) and take up to an hour. **Orly**, 14km south of Paris, has two bus–rail links; Orly-Rail to the Gare d'Austerlitz and other Left Bank stops (every 20min 5.50am–10.50pm; €4.80), and Orlyval, a fast train shuttle link to RER line B station Antony then métro connection to Denfert-Rochereau, St-Michel and Châtelet (every 10min 6.30/7am–10.30/11pm; €8.70). Air France buses go to the Gare des Invalides via Montparnasse (every 12min 5.45am–11pm; takes 30min; €7), and Orlybus goes to métro Denfert-Rochereau (every 15min 6am–11.30pm; takes 30min; €5.30). A taxi costs around €20. A door-to-door **shuttle** from either airport costs €14–19 (☎01.45.38.55.72, *www.airportshuttle.fr*).

Paris has six mainline **train** stations, all of which are served by the métro. You can buy national and international train tickets at any mainline station. Eurostar trains from London, as well as trains from northern France, Belgium, Holland, northern Germany and Scandinavia, arrive at the **Gare du Nord**; Eurostar have their own booking offices and departure lounge on a raised tier at one side of the station. The **Gare de l'Est** serves eastern France, Luxembourg, southern Germany, northern Switzerland, Austria and eastern Europe; **Gare St-Lazare** serves the Normandy coast; **Gare de Lyon** serves the south, the Alps, western Switzerland, Italy and Greece; **Gare Montparnasse** serves Chartres, Brittany and the Atlantic coast; **Gare d'Austerlitz** serves Versailles, the southwest and Spain. All long-distance **buses** except Gulliver's and Hoverspeed use the main *gare routière* at **Bagnolet** in eastern Paris (métro Gallieni, last stop on line 3); Gulliver's coaches arrive at the corner of rue Maubeuge and bd de La Chapelle near the Gare du Nord; Hoverspeed coaches arrive at 165 av de Clichy, 17e (métro Porte de Clichy or Brochant).

The main **tourist office** is at 127 av des Champs-Élysées, métro Georges V (daily 9am–8/9pm; recorded information on ☎08.36.68.31.12, *www.paris-touristoffice.com*). They have maps and leaflets, and can book last-minute accommodation for a €3–8.50 fee, depending on the category of hotel. There's an annexe of the tourist office at the Gare de Lyon (Mon–Sat 8am–8pm) and a seasonal office by the Eiffel Tower, métro Bir Hakeim (May–Sept daily 11am–6.40pm).

City transport

Getting around is easy: central Paris is relatively small, with a public transport system that is cheap, fast and meticulously signposted. The **métro** (abbreviated as M°) is the simplest way of getting around: stations are widespread, and the lines are colour-coded and numbered – within each station, lines are signposted with the names of the end-station. Every **bus** stop displays the numbers of the buses which stop there, as well as a map showing all the stops on the route and the times of the first and last buses. Generally speaking, buses run from 6.30am until around 8.30pm, while the métro operates from 5.30am to 12.30am, after which **night buses** *(Noctambus)* run on eighteen routes from place du Châtelet near the Hôtel de Ville hourly or half-hourly from 1am to 5.30am. Tickets are €2.30. Noctambus stops are marked with a black and yellow owl.

Free route **maps** are available at métro stations, bus terminals and tourist offices. Flat-fare **tickets** that are valid on buses, the métro and, within the city limits, the RER express rail lines cost €1.20 (the RER also extends further out into the suburbs). Single tickets can be bought in *carnets* of ten from any station or *tabac* for about €9. Be sure to keep your ticket until the end of the journey; you'll be fined on the spot if you can't produce one. If you're staying more than a day or two, the *Carte Orange*, buyable at all métro stations and *tabacs* (you need a passport photo), is better value, costing €13 (zones 1 and 2) for a week's travel (Mon–Sun) within the city centre. Alternatively, you can buy a one-day *Mobilis* pass for €6.40 (zones 1–3) or €11.30 (zones 1–5). Also available are *Paris Visites*, €18.30 for 3 days or €26.70 for 5 days (zones 1–3), valid for the funicular, Montmartrobus and Noctambus, with first-class travel on RER and short-distance mainline trains thrown in. Paris **taxis** are fairly reasonable (€6–11 within the city), though they'll usually only take a maximum of three passengers. However, you won't have much luck trying to hail one in the street; instead, you need to find one of the 470 taxi ranks dotted around the city.

Accommodation

Compared to other European capitals, Paris's **accommodation** is relatively cheap, and it is possible to find a double room without bath in a decent and centrally located **hotel** for under €38, and even as low as €27 – although you should always book in advance. There are also,

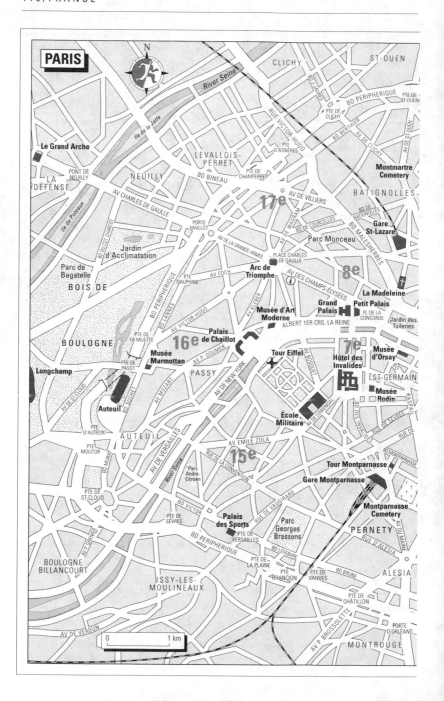

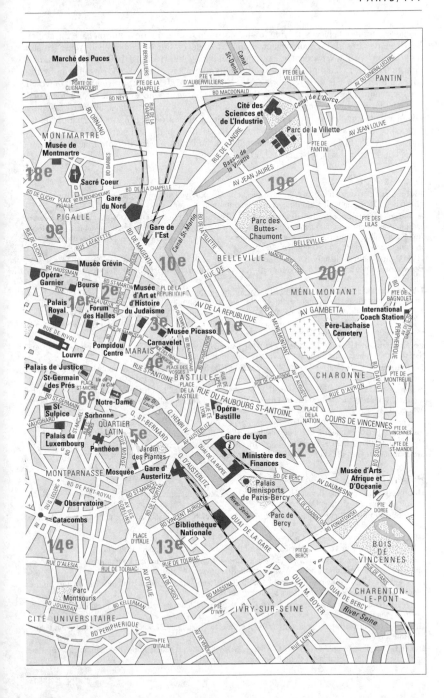

of course, numerous places offering **hostel** accommodation. In the main you have the choice between the hostels of four organizations. Hostels of the official French Youth Hostel Association (**FUAJ**; *www.fuaj.org*) require Hostelling International (HI) membership, and charge from €17.50 a night (usually with a maximum stay of five days). Hostels run by the Maison Internationale de la Jeunesse et des Étudiants (**MIJE**; *www.mije.com*), most of which are located in elegant old mansions in the Marais, charge around €21 a night for a dorm bed and €52 for a double room; they impose a maximum stay of seven days, but don't take any advance bookings. Hostels run by the Union des Centres de Rencontre Internationaux de France (**UCRIF**; *www.ucrif.asso.fr*) charge €18 for dorm beds, and some do canteen meals for around €8; but again there are no advance bookings accepted. Note that in summer, prices of dorm beds rise by about €1.50.

Hostels

Aloha, 1 rue Borromé, 15e (☎01.42.73.03.03, *www.aloha.fr*). A well-known bargain with its own bar serving cheap beer. Young and noisy atmosphere. M° Volontaires. ②.

Auberge Internationale des Jeunes, 10 rue Trousseau, 11e (☎01.47.00.62.00, *www.aijparis.com*). Despite the official-sounding name, this is a laid-back (but very noisy) independent hostel in a great location 5min walk from the Bastille. Clean and professionally run with 24hr reception, generous breakfast and free luggage storage. M° Ledru-Rollin. ②.

BVJ Centre, 20 rue Jean-Jacques-Rousseau, 1er (☎01.53.00.90.90; M° Louvre Rivoli); and 44 rue des Bernadins, 5e (☎01.43.29.34.80; M° Maubert Mutualité). Central, efficient UCRIF hostels with little to distinguish between them. Both ②.

D'Artagnan, 80 rue Vitruve, 20e (☎01.40.32.34.56). Enormous FUAJ/HI hostel, with lots of facilities, but a fair way out on the eastern fringes of the city. M° Porte de Bagnolet. ③.

Jules Ferry, 8 bd Jules-Ferry, 11e (☎01.43.57.55.60). The other FUAJ/HI hostel, smaller and more central – located in the lively area at the foot of the Belleville hill. Its location and popularity make it very difficult to get a bed. M° République. ③.

Le Fauconnier, 11 rue du Fauconnier, 4e (☎01.42.74.23.45). MIJE hostel in a superbly renovated seventeenth-century mansion with a courtyard. Breakfast included. M° St-Paul. ③.

Le Fourcy, 6 rue de Fourcy, 4e (☎01.42.74.23.45). MIJE place in a beautiful mansion with a small garden and restaurant with menus from €7.50. Small, 4–8-bed dorms only. M° St-Paul. ③.

Maubuisson, 12 rue des Barres, 4e (☎01.42.74.23.45). MIJE hostel in a magnificent medieval building in a quiet street. Restaurant meals from €6.40. Singles and doubles available. Breakfast included. M° Pont-Marie. ③.

3 Canards (Three Ducks), 6 place Étienne-Pernet, 15e (☎01.48.42.04.05, *www.3ducks.fr*). Independent hostel with bar, beer and use of kitchen facilities. Book ahead May–Oct. M° Félix Faure. ②.

Woodstock, 48 rue Rodier, 9e (☎01.48.78.87.76, *www.woodstock.fr*). Inexpensive hostel located in the heart of Montmartre. Friendly staff, cheap bar, courtyard and a lively atmosphere. M° Anvers. ②.

Hotels

Hôtel des Alliés, 20 rue Berthollet, 5e (☎01.43.31.47.52). Simple, cheap and clean, with some spacious ensuite options. M° Censier-Daubenton. ⑤.

Avenir-Jonquière, 23 rue de la Jonquière, 17e (☎01.46.27.83.41). Friendly place with clean, good-value rooms. M° Guy-Môquet. ④.

Hôtel des Carmes, 5 rue des Carmes, 5e (☎01.43.29.78.40). A long-established hotel offering modern, colourful ensuite rooms and an excellent view of the Panthéon. M° Maubert-Mutualité. ⑨.

Castex, 5 rue Castex, 4e (☎01.42.72.31.52, *www.castex-hotel.com*). Friendly, family-run hotel in a quiet street on the edge of the Marais. Spacious rooms with bath/shower. M° Bastille. ⑥.

Le Central, 6 rue Descartes, 5e (☎01.46.33.57.93). Clean and decent accommodation on top of the Montagne Ste-Geneviève. M° Maubert Mutualité. ④.

Hôtel du Dragon, 36 rue du Dragon, 6e (☎01.45.48.51.05). Clean, friendly and in a great location. M° St-Germain-des-Prés. ⑨.

Grand Hôtel du Loiret, 8 rue des Mauvais-Garçons, 4e (☎01.48.87.77.00). Simple place but good value. M° Hotel-de-Ville. ⑤.

Henri IV, 25 place Dauphine, 1er (☎01.43.54.44.53). Well-known cheapie in the beautiful place Dauphine on the Île de la Cité. Breakfast included. Booking essential. M° Pont-Neuf. ③.

Jeanne d'Arc, 3 rue de Jarente, 4e (☎01.48.87.62.11). Clean, quiet and attractive. Its Marais location – just by the lively Place du Marché Ste-Catherine – means you have to reserve. M° St-Paul. ⑦.

Lévèque, 29 rue Cler, 7e (☎01.47.05.49.15, *www.hotel-leveque.com*). Clean and decent, run by nice people who speak some English. Book one month ahead. M° École-Militaire. ⑤.

Marignan, 13 rue du Sommerard, 5e (☎01.43.54.63.81). One of the best bargains in town. You'll need to book a month ahead in summer. M° Maubert-Mutualité. ④.

Nouvelle France, 31 rue Keller, 11e (☎01.47.00.40.74). Cheap and ideally located in an arty street with a gay focus near the nightlife of rue de Lappe and rue de la Roquette. M° Bastille. ③.

Pratic, 20 rue de l'Ingénieur-Robert-Keller, 15e (☎01.45.77.70.58, *www.pratichotel.fr*). Clean and friendly, and close to the Eiffel Tower. M° Charles-Michels. ⑤.

Tiquetonne, 6 rue Tiquetonne, 2e (☎01.42.36.94.58). Good-value place in a small, attractive street. Closed Aug. M° Étienne-Marcel. ④.

Campsite

The closest **campsite** is on allée du Bord-de-l'Eau, 16e, by the river in the Bois de Boulogne (☎01.45.24.30.00, *www.mobilehome-paris.com*; Métro Porte-Maillot, then bus #244 to Route des Moulins). It's on pebbly ground, but is well-equipped and has a useful information office. Open all year, but usually booked out in summer.

The City

Paris is split into two halves by the Seine. On the north of the river, the **Right Bank** *(rive droite)* is home to the grand boulevards and most monumental buildings, many dating from Haussmann's nineteenth-century redevelopment, and is where you'll probably spend most time, during the day at least. The top museums are here – the Louvre and Beaubourg, to name just two – as well as the city's widest range of shops around rue de Rivoli and Les Halles; and there are also peaceful quarters like the Marais for idle strolling. The **Left Bank** *(rive gauche)* has a noticeably different feel, its very name conjuring Bohemian, dissident, intellectual connotations, and something of this atmosphere survives in the city's best range of bars and restaurants, and its most wanderable streets: the areas around St-Germain and St-Michel are full of nooks and crannies to explore. Parts of Paris, of course, don't sit easily in either category. **Montmartre**, rising up to the north of the centre, has managed to retain a village-like, almost rural atmosphere despite the daily influx of tourists, with its colourful mixture of locals and artists. The dilapidated working-class quarters of **eastern Paris**, undisturbed by tourism, offer a rich, ethnically diverse slice of Parisian streetlife; in direct contrast, the ground-breaking science museum constructed in the recently renovated **Parc de la Villette** celebrates technological wonder.

If you're planning to visit any **museums**, it's worth knowing that many have reduced fees for under-25s, are often free for children, reduce their fees by up to half on Sunday, and are free on the first Sunday of every month. They are often closed on Mondays or Tuesdays and, if you plan to see more than a few during your stay, it's a good idea to invest in a **museum pass** (one day €13, three consecutive days €26, five consecutive days €39). You can get a museum pass from participating museums, some tourist offices, the larger métro stations and FNAC ticket offices (there's one in Les Halles) and it'll encourage you to be more adventurous with the vast choice of museums and monuments in Paris.

The Arc de Triomphe, Champs-Élysées and place de la Concorde

As good a place as any to start exploring is along the **Voie Triomphale** (Triumphal Way), which stretches in a straight line from the Louvre to the corporate skyscrapers at La Défense, 9km northwest, and has some of the city's most famous landmarks. The best view is from the top of the **Arc de Triomphe**, Napoleon's homage to the armies of France and himself (daily 9.30/10am–10.30/11pm; €6.40, under-25s €4; métro Charles-de-Gaulle-Étoile), at the centre of **place Charles-de-Gaulle** – which is still better known as place de l'Étoile – where traffic swarms from the twelve avenues leading into it in a alarming display of horn-blaring and near-misses. From here, Paris's most famous street, the **Champs-Élysées**, sweeps gracefully southeast to the equally traffic-bound **place de la Concorde**, whose striking centrepiece, an obelisk from the temple of Luxor, was offered as a favour-currying gesture by the viceroy of Egypt in 1829. The symmetry continues beyond the square in the formal layout of the **Jardin des Tuileries** (daily 8/9am–7/8pm; métro Concorde) which stretches down to the Louvre. Towards the river, the **Orangerie** (undergoing renovation at the time of writing) displays Monet's largest water-lily paintings, as well as Cézanne's southern landscapes and portraits by van Dongen, Utrillo and Modigliani.

The Louvre

On the east side of the Jardin des Tuileries is the home of the *Mona Lisa*, the **Louvre** (Mon & Wed 9am–9.45pm, Thurs–Sun 9am–6pm; €7, after 3pm and all day Sun €4.60; audioguide in English €4.60; *www.louvre.com*; métro Palais Royal-Musée du Louvre/Louvre-Rivoli). The building was first opened to the public in 1793, during the Revolution, and within a decade Napoleon had made it the largest art collection on earth with the takings from his empire. It's a vast collection that would take months to cover in detail, but although the layout of the museum is at first overwhelming and seemingly nonsensical, it's a delight to explore. I.M. Pei's stunning **glass pyramid** is the main entrance to the Louvre, although alternative access directly from the métro or from rue de Rivoli (via passage Richelieu) avoids the queues for the pyramid. Beneath the pyramid, a subterranean concourse leads to the recently arranged sections of the museum: Sully (around the Cour Carrée), Denon (the south wing) and Richelieu (the north wing).

The **seven basic categories** of the museum's collections are Oriental antiquities; Egyptian antiquities; Greek, Etruscan and Roman antiquities; sculpture; decorative arts; painting; and graphic arts. Each category spreads out over more than one wing and several floors. Recent building work also allowed the excavation of what remains of the **medieval Louvre** under the Cour Carrée – Philippe-Auguste's twelfth-century fortress and Charles V's fourteenth-century palace conversion. The foundations and archeological findings are on show along with a permanent exhibition on the history of the Louvre on the *entresol* floor in the Sully wing. **Oriental Antiquities** – including the recently presented Islamic Art collection – covers the Sumerian, Babylonian, Assyrian and Phoenician civilizations, plus the art of ancient Persia. **Egyptian Antiquities** comprise jewellery, domestic objects, sandals, sarcophagi and dozens of examples of the delicate naturalism of Egyptian decorative technique, and statues like the pink granite *Mastaba Sphinx*. **Greek and Roman Antiquities**, divided between the Denon and Sully wings, include the *Winged Victory of Samothrace* and the famous *Venus de Milo*. The **Applied Arts** collection is heavily weighted on the side of imperial opulence, but also includes a great deal of impressive tapestry as well as smaller, less public items, such as the carved Parisian ivories of the thirteenth century and the Limoges enamels. **Sculpture** covers the entire development of the art in France from Romanesque to Rodin, all in the new Richelieu wing, plus Italian and northern European sculpture in Denon, including Michelangelo's *Slaves*, designed for the tomb of Pope Julius II.

The largest section by far is **Painting**: French from the year dot to mid-nineteenth century, along with Italian, Dutch, German, Flemish and Spanish. The *Mona Lisa* in Denon is the painting most people head for, and it is normally swamped with onlookers; no one pays the slightest attention to the other Leonardos nearby, such as the *Virgin of the Rocks*. There is a good selection of other Italian paintings, including works by Giotto, Botticelli, Titian, Tintoretto and Mantegna (a *Crucifixion*), one of Uccello's *Battle of San Romano* series and, most strikingly, Paolo Veronese's huge *Marriage at Cana*, painted in 1563. Among the Flemish and Dutch paintings in the Richelieu Wing are Quentin Matsys' moralistic *Moneychanger and his Wife*, Memling's *Mystic Marriage of St Catherine*, Rembrandt's masterful *Supper at Emmaus*, and several works by Rubens. The works of Caravaggio are also richly represented, and the two exquisite Vermeers in the last part of the Richelieu are certainly worth the wait. There are French paintings of all periods, notably works by Poussin and later canvases by the great nineteenth-century artists David, Ingres and Delacroix. Géricault's harrowing *Raft of Medusa* made his name as an artist.

The **north wing** of the Louvre, entered from rue de Rivoli, is given over to three related museums which all share the same hours and ticket (Tues, Thurs & Fri 11am–6pm, Wed 11am–9pm, Sat & Sun 10am–6pm; €5.30, under-25s €3.80; *www.ucad.fr*; métro Louvre). The **Musée des Arts Décoratifs** is devoted to interior design, with furnishings and fittings from the Middle Ages to the 1990s. The contemporary section is fairly meagre, but the rest of the twentieth century is fascinating, and includes a bedroom by Guimard, Jeanne Lanvin's Art Deco apartments and a salon created by Georges Hoentschel for the 1900 Expo. The smaller **Musée de la Mode et du Textile** pays homage to Paris fashion with a collection of haute couture from the seventeenth century to the present day. The entertaining **Musée de la Publicité** deals with the art of advertising, from nineteenth-century poster art to contemporary Internet campaigns.

The Opéra, Les Halles and the Pompidou Centre

A short walk north of the Louvre is the **Opéra-Garnier**, on place de l'Opéra, a preposterously ornate building designed by Charles Garnier and built in 1875 as the venue for opera in Paris, although since the completion of the Opéra-Bastille in 1989 it has been used chiefly for ballet. You can visit the splendid interior (daily 10am–5pm; €4.60; métro Opéra), including the auditorium, where the domed ceiling is the work of Chagall, and the entrance fee includes admission to the small museum. A short walk northeast brings you to the **Musée Grévin**, 10 bd Montmartre (undergoing renovation at the time of writing; *www.musee-grevin.com;* métro Richelieu-Drouot), a Paris institution since 1882 that displays around 500 wax statues of celebrities and historical figures. South of here is the area around the former **Les Halles** (a covered market) which was redeveloped in the 1970s amid widespread opposition and is now promoted as the heart of trendy Paris. In truth, the multi-layered shopping precinct at its core, the **Forum des Halles**, is a tacky affair, and it can be unsafe, too, especially at night – hence the high-profile police presence. During the day the main flow of feet is from here a little way east to the **Pompidou Centre**, or **Beaubourg** as it's known locally (métro Rambuteau; *www.centrepompidou.fr*). This seminal design by Renzo Piano and Richard Rogers was the first public structure to manifest the hi-tech notion of displaying its services on the outside, the tubing colour-coded according to function, leaving maximum space for the interior. Inside, the **Multimedia Library** (Mon & Wed–Fri noon–10pm, Sat & Sun 10am–10pm) remains hugely popular, as does the ever-growing exhibition of twentieth-century art from the late Impressionists to the 1980s, the **Musée National d'Art Moderne** (Mon & Wed–Sun 11am–9pm; €4.60, under-25s €3). Early paintings include canvases by Henri Rousseau such as *La Charmeuse de Serpent*. Picasso's *Femme Assise* of 1909 introduced Cubism, which was represented in its fuller development by Braque's *L'Homme à la Guitare* and Léger's *Les Acrobates en Gris*. Among abstracts, there's the sensuous rhythm of colour in Sonia Delaunay's *Prismes Électriques* and a good showing of Kandinsky at his most playful. Dalí disturbs, amuses or infuriates with *Six Apparitions de Lénine sur un Piano* and there are further Surreal images by Magritte and de Chirico. One of the most compulsive German pictures is the portrait of the journalist *Sylvia von Harden* by Otto Dix. Among the more recent canvases, Francis Bacon's work figures prominently, as do the provocative images of the Pop Art movement, not least Warhol's *Ten Lizes*.

The Marais, the Bastille and Île St-Louis

Just east of Beaubourg, the **Marais** is a formerly fashionable aristocratic district that until some 35 years ago was one of the city centre's poorer quarters. Regentrification has since turned the renovated mansions into museums, offices and chic apartments flanked by designer clothes shops. A little way down the neighbourhood's main drag, rue des Francs-Bourgeois, one of the grandest Marais mansions houses the **Musée Carnavalet** (entrance around the corner at 23 rue de Sévigné; Tues–Sun 10am–5.40pm; €4.60, under-25s €3; métro St-Paul), which presents the history of Paris from the reign of François I to the early twentieth century, with models, maps and plans, reconstructions of interiors and mementoes of the 1789 Revolution. Slightly further north, at 71 rue du Temple, the **Musée d'Art et d'Histoire du Judaïsme** (Mon–Fri 11am–6pm, Sun 10am–6pm; €6 including audioguide, under 26s €3.80; métro Rambuteau) has a fascinating display of Jewish artefacts and historical documents as well as some fine modern paintings by the likes of Chagall and Soutine.

A short walk east, another mansion, the proud seventeenth-century Hôtel Juigné Salé at 5 rue de Thorigny, is home to the **Musée Picasso** (Mon & Wed–Sun 9.30am–5.30/6pm, Thurs until 8pm; €4.60 (€3 on Sun), under-25s €3; métro St-Paul). It is an overwhelming collection, much of which was the artist's personal property, and comprises the largest number of his works anywhere. The broad range of work provides a valuable sense of Picasso's growth and the alarming ease with which he moved between media, from paint and pen to pottery and sculpture. Personal items serve to flesh out his persona, including his collection of works by Renoir, Cézane, Matisse and Braque, photographs and letters, and the tender drawings and paintings he made of his wives, lovers and family. There are references to the artist's political commitments, too, in his delegate credentials for the 1948 World Congress of Peace, and the pacifist painting *Massacre en Corée* from 1951.

At the far end of rue des Francs-Bourgeois, off to the right, **place des Vosges** (originally known as Place Royale) is a masterpiece of aristocratic urban planning, a vast square of stone and brick symmetry built for Henri IV and Louis XIII. It is one of the city's most charming squares and, unusually for Paris, the grass is fit for sprawling on, making the relaxing park a great spot for a picnic. You can check out the surrounding mansions in the form of the **Maison Victor Hugo**, 6 place des Vosges (Tues–Sun 10am–5.40pm; €3.40; métro Bastille), once home to the writer of the oft-adapted *Les Misérables*; not surprisingly, a whole room is devoted to posters of its various stage productions.

A short walk southeast, heading for the landmark column with the gilded "Spirit of Liberty", is **place de la Bastille**, the site of the storming of the Bastille in 1789. The column was erected not to commemorate the surrender in 1789 of the prison, which was subsequently demolished, but the July Revolution of 1830 – although it is the 1789 Bastille Day that France celebrates every July 14. The Bicentennial in 1989 was marked by the inauguration of the **Opéra-Bastille**, on the far side of the square, a bloated building that caused great controversy when it went up – a "hippopotamus in a bathtub", one critic called it.

Just south from here, across Henri IV bridge, the **Île St-Louis** is one of the centre's swankier quarters, with no monuments or museums, just high houses on single-lane streets. It's a peaceful and atmospheric route through to the Île de la Cité, either strolling down the centre along the shop-filled rue Île-St-Louis – a real levened promenade with pedestrians taking over the street, many intent on queuing for an ice-cream at the famous *Berthillon* – or along the tree-lined *quais* down by the Seine. It is particularly atmospheric at night as the lights from the *Bateaux Mouches* cast shadows of the trees over the buildings, whose lit-up windows offer a glimpse of their elegant interiors.

Île de la Cité

Île de la Cité is where Paris began, the original site of the Roman garrison and later of the palace of the Merovingian kings and the counts of Paris, who in 987 became kings of France. Nowadays the main lure, however, is the astounding **Cathédrale de Notre-Dame** (Mon–Fri 8am–6.45pm, Sat & Sun 8am–7.45pm; free; métro Cité), begun in 1163 under the auspices of Bishop de Sully and completed around 1345. In the nineteenth century, Viollet-le-Duc carried out extensive renovation work, remaking most of the statuary and adding the steeple and baleful-looking gargoyles, which you can see close up if you brave the 387-step ascent of the **towers** (daily: summer 9.30am–7.30pm (July & Aug until 10pm); rest of year 10am–5.30pm; €5.30). The sculpture of the west front portals is amazingly detailed, dating mainly from the twelfth and thirteenth centuries, while, inside, the immediately striking feature is the dramatic contrast between the darkness of the nave and the light falling on the first great clustered pillars of the choir. All this light is admitted by the end walls of the transepts, nearly two-thirds glass, including two magnificent rose windows in imperial purple that were added in 1267. In front of the cathedral, the **crypte archéologique** (Tues–Sun 10am–5.40pm; €5) holds the remains of the original cathedral, as well as of streets and houses of the Cité back as far as the Roman era. At weekends and during summer getting in to see the cathedral may involve queueing for a while, as this is the real tourist heart of Paris and things can get crowded.

At the other, western end of the island, the dull mass of the **Palais de Justice** swallowed up the palace that was home to the French kings until the bloody revolt of 1358 frightened them into the greater security of the Louvre. The only part of the older complex that remains in its entirety is Louis IX's **Sainte-Chapelle** at 4 bd du Palais (daily: April–Sept 9.30am–6.30pm; Oct–March 10am–5pm; €5.50, or €7.50 joint ticket with the Conciergerie; métro Cité). This was built to house a collection of holy relics and one of the finest achievements of French Gothic style, lent a fragility by its height and huge expanses of glorious stained glass, most of which is original. You should also visit the **Conciergerie**, Paris's oldest prison, whose entrance is around the corner facing the river on quai de l'Horloge (daily: April–Sept 9.30am–6.30pm; Oct–March 10am–5pm; €5.50, or €7.50 joint ticket with the Ste-Chapelle). This was where Marie-Antoinette and, in their turn, the leading figures of the Revolution were incarcerated before execution. Its chief interest is the enormous late-Gothic Salle des Gens d'Armes, canteen and recreation room of the royal household staff, as well as Marie-Antoinette's cell and various macabre mementoes of the guillotine's victims. Outside the Conciergerie is Paris's first public clock, the **Tour de l'Horloge**, built in 1370.

The Beaux Quartiers, Bois de Boulogne and La Défense

South and west of the Arc de Triomphe lie the so-called **Beaux Quartiers**, the 16e and 17e *arrondissements*, in turns aristocratic and rich, bourgeois and staid districts, mainly residential, which hold little of interest save the wonderful **Musée Marmottan**, 2 rue Louis-Boilly (Tues–Sun 10am–5.30pm; €6; métro La Muette), whose Monet paintings were bequeathed by the artist's son. Among them is the canvas entitled *Impression, Soleil Levant*, an 1872 rendering of a misty sunrise over Le Havre, whose title unwittingly gave the Impressionist movement its name. There's also a dazzling collection of almost abstract canvases from Monet's last years at Giverny. Beyond the museum, the **Bois de Boulogne** (open daily), running all down the west side of the 16e, is the city centre's largest open space, supposedly modelled on London's Hyde Park and offering all sorts of facilities – various museums, a children's amusement-park-cum-zoo, a formal garden with beautiful displays of flowers in the spring, a riding school, boating on the Lac Inférieur, wild walks in its southeast corner, and the racecourses of Longchamp and Auteuil, although it's long been known for its prodigious sexual pick-up activity after dark.

La Défense has been elevated to one of the top places of pilgrimage for visitors to Paris by the breathtaking **Grande Arche** (métro Grande-Arche-de-la-Défense), a 112m-high hollow cube clad in white marble. Suspended within its hollow are open lift shafts and a "cloud canopy". You can ride up to the roof (daily 10am–7pm; €7), but the views – right down the Voie Triomphale 6km to the Arc de Triomphe – are no more impressive than those gained from the series of steps which lead up to the Arch, and which provide a popular focus for just sitting about. Between the Grande Arche and the river is the business complex of La Défense, a perfect monument to late-twentieth-century capitalism that lacks any formal pattern to its dizzying arrangement of towers. Mercifully, bizarre artworks transform the nightmare into comic entertainment, with Joan Miró's giant wobbly creatures and Alexander Calder's red iron interspersed between a coloured plastic waterfall and concrete flower-beds.

The Eiffel Tower, Les Invalides and the Musée d'Orsay

A short walk south of place de l'Étoile is the **Musée d'Art Moderne de la Ville de Paris** in the Palais de Tokyo, 11 av du Président-Wilson (Tues–Fri 10am–5.45pm, Sat & Sun

10am–6.45pm; €4.60; métro Iéna). This displays examples of the schools and trends of twentieth-century art, as well as sculpture and painting by contemporary artists. Among the most spectacular works on show are Robert and Sonia Delaunay's huge whirling wheels and cogs of rainbow colour, the leaping figures of Matisse's *La Danse* and Dufy's enormous mural, *La Fée Électricité* (done for the electricity board), illustrating the story of electricity from Aristotle to the modern power station in 250 colourful panels. A short walk down the river, at **Trocadéro**, the terrace of the Palais de Chaillot – home to several uninteresting museums – gives splendid vistas across the river to the **Eiffel Tower**, especially at night. Though no conventional beauty, the tower (Tour Eiffel in French) is nonetheless an amazing structure, at 300m the tallest building in the world when it was completed by Gustave Eiffel in 1889. Reactions to it were violent, but it stole the show at the 1889 Exposition, for which it had been constructed. It's possible to go right to the top (daily: July & Aug 9am–midnight; rest of year 9.30am–11pm; *www.tour-eiffel.fr*; métro Bir Hakeim/RER Champ de Mars). By lift it's €10 to the top; if you're fit enough, you can cut costs by walking up the 704 stairs to the second level for €3, and then taking the (obligatory) lift for the final leg for an additional €3. Taking the lift partway costs €3.70 to the first level, or €6.90 to the second. Daytime queues for the final stage can be massive during high season, and the effort is only really worth it on an absolutely clear day. At night the queues are much shorter and the views often more impressive.

To the east, the **Esplanade des Invalides** strikes south from the river to the wide facade of the **Hôtel des Invalides**, built as a home for invalided soldiers on the orders of Louis XIV and topped by a distinctive gilded dome which is a real Paris landmark. One of its two churches was intended as a mausoleum for the king but now contains the mortal remains of Napoleon enclosed within a gallery decorated with friezes of execrable taste and captioned with quotations of awesome conceit from the great man (his tomb can be seen June–Sept 10am–7pm). The main part of the building houses the vast **Musée de l'Armée** (daily 10am–5/6pm; €5.80; métro La Tour Maubourg/Varenne). Immediately east, the **Musée Rodin**, at no. 77 on the corner of rue de Varenne, is housed in a beautiful eighteenth-century mansion which the sculptor leased from the State in return for the gift of all his work at his death (Tues–Sun: April–Sept 9.30am–5.45pm; rest of year 9.30am–4.45pm; €4.30, under-25s €2.70; métro Varenne; *www.musee-rodin.fr*). This represents the whole of Rodin's work, with larger projects like *The Burghers of Calais* and *The Thinker* exhibited in the garden, and works in marble like *The Kiss*, *The Hand of God* and *The Cathedral* indoors.

A little way northeast along the river, on the quai d'Orsay, the **Musée d'Orsay** (Tues–Sat 9/10am–6pm, Thurs until 9.45pm, Sun 9am–6pm; €6 (€4.60 on Sun), under-25s €4.60; *www.musee-orsay.fr*; RER Musée d'Orsay/métro Solférino) was converted from a disused train station in the mid-1980s and now houses an outstanding collection of painting and sculpture from the pre-modern period (1848–1914), bridging the gap between the collections of the Louvre and the Pompidou Centre. On the ground floor are a few canvases by Ingres and Delacroix, whose work serves to illustrate the transition from the early nineteenth century. The Symbolists and early Degas follow, while in the galleries to the left Daumier, Corot, Millet and the Realist school lead on to the first Impressionist works, including Manet's *Olympia* – controversial for its colour contrasts and sensual surfaces, as well as for its portrayal of Olympia as nothing more than a high-class whore. On the top floor are landscapes and outdoor scenes by Renoir, Sisley, Pissarro and Monet – including one of his water lilies, along with five of his Rouen cathedral series. Cézanne is also wonderfully represented, as is Van Gogh, with some of his most mesmerizing canvases. The rest of this level is given over to Gauguin pre- and post-Tahiti, a number of *pointilliste* works by Seurat and some of Toulouse-Lautrec's most intriguing nightclub pieces. The middle floor is dominated by sculpture with some amazing works by Rodin, and several rooms of Art Nouveau and Jugendstil furniture and objects.

The Latin Quarter, St-Germain and Montparnasse

The warren of medieval lanes around the boulevards St-Michel and St-Germain is known as the **Quartier Latin** because that was the language of the university sited there right up until 1789.

The pivotal point of the area is **place St-Michel**, where the tree-lined **boulevard St-Michel** begins, its cafés and shops jammed with people – mainly young and, in summer, largely foreign. **Rue de la Huchette**, gathering-place of beatniks and bums in the post-World War II years, is now a tourist trap given over to Greek restaurants of indifferent quality and suspect hygiene, as is the adjoining rue Xavier-Privas, with the odd couscous joint thrown in. Close to the St-Michel/St-Germain junction, the walls of the third-century Roman baths are visible in the garden of the **Hôtel de Cluny** on place Paul-Poinlevé. This sixteenth-century mansion, built by the abbots of the powerful Cluny monastery as their Paris pied-à-terre, now houses the **Musée National du Moyen Age – Thermes de Cluny** (Mon & Wed–Sun 9.15am–5.45pm; €4.60 (€3 on Sun), under-25s €3; métro Cluny-La Sorbonne), a treasure-house of medieval art that includes some wonderful, finely detailed tapestries. The real masterpiece is *La Dame à la Licorne* – six highly symbolic medieval scenes featuring a beautiful woman flanked by a lion and a unicorn, probably made in Brussels in the late fifteenth century.

Immediately south of here, the **Montagne Sainte-Geneviève** slopes up to the domed **Panthéon**, Louis XIV's thankyou to St Geneviève, patron saint of Paris, for curing him of illness, which was transformed during the Revolution into a mausoleum for the great: its incumbents include Voltaire, Rousseau, Zola and Hugo (daily 9.30/10am–6.15/6.30pm; €6.40, under-25s €4; métro Cardinal Lemoine/RER Luxembourg). Down rue Soufflot from here, across bd St-Michel, you might prefer to while away a few hours in the elegant surrounds of the **Jardin du Luxembourg** (daily 8/9am–7/8pm; métro Luxembourg), laid out by Marie de Médici, Henri IV's widow, to remind her of the Palazzo Pitti and Giardino di Bóboli of her native Florence. They are the chief recreation ground of the Left Bank, with tennis courts, a *boules* pitch, toy yachts to rent on the pond and, in the southeast corner, a miniature orchard of elaborately espaliered pear trees.

Beyond the Luxembourg gardens, the northern half of the 6e *arrondissement* is one of the most attractive parts of the city, full of bookshops, art galleries, antique shops, cafés and restaurants. It is also, perhaps, its most culturally historic: Picasso painted *Guernica* in rue des Grands-Augustins; in rue Visconti, Delacroix painted and Balzac's printing business went bust; and in the parallel rue des Beaux-Arts, Oscar Wilde died and the crazy poet Gérard de Nerval went walking with a lobster on a blue ribbon. **Place St-Germain-des-Prés**, the hub of the *quartier*, is the site of the *Deux Magots* café, renowned for the number of politico-literary backsides that have shined its seats. On the other side of the Luxembourg gardens, **Montparnasse** also trades on its association with the colourful characters of the interwar artistic and literary boom, many of whom were habitués of the cafés *Select, Coupole, Dôme* and *Rotonde* on bd du Montparnasse. Close by, the colossal 59-storey skyscraper **Tour Montparnasse** on av du Maine has become one of the city's principal landmarks since its construction in 1973; it can be climbed for less than the Eiffel Tower, but it is more than 100m shorter (daily 9.30am–10.30/11.30pm; €7.60; métro Montparnasse-Bienvenue). A short walk down bd Edgar-Quinet, the **Montparnasse cemetery** (daily 9/9.30am–5.30/6pm; free; métro Raspail) has plenty of illustrious names, from Baudelaire to Sartre and André Citroën to Serge Gainsbourg. Not far from the southeastern edge of the cemetery, on place Denfert Rochereau, are the much spookier **catacombs** (Tues–Fri 2–4pm, Sat & Sun 9–11am & 2–4pm; €5; métro Denfert-Rochereau), a series of damp underground tunnels dating from the Roman occupation that contain the skulls and bones from overflowing eighteenth-century churchyards.

Montmartre and eastern Paris

Montmartre lies in the middle of the largely petty bourgeois and working-class 18e *arrondissement*, a mixture of depressing slums towards the Gare du Nord and Gare de l'Est, and respectable, almost countrified pockets around its main focus on the hill, the **Butte Montmartre**. You can get up here by **funicular** from place Suzanne-Valadon or, for a quieter and prettier approach – though not for the unfit – climb stairs via place des Abbesses. The **place du Tertre** is the heart of touristic Montmartre, photogenic but totally bogus, jammed with day-trippers, overpriced restaurants and "artists" doing quick portraits while you wait. Crowning the Butte is the nineteenth-century **Sacré-Cœur** (daily 6am–11pm; free; métro Anvers/Abbesses), along with the Eiffel Tower one of the classics of the Paris skyline, although the best thing about it is the **view** from the top (dome and crypt daily 9am–6pm; €2.30).

North of place du Tertre, the house that holds the **Musée de Montmartre** at 12 rue Cortot (Tues–Sun 11am–5.30pm; €3.80; métro Lamarck-Caulaincourt) was rented at various times by Renoir, Dufy, Suzanne Valadon and her alcoholic son Utrillo, but its exhibits are disappointing. Close by, off rue Lepic, the **Moulin de la Galette** is the only survivor of Montmartre's forty-odd windmills, which were immortalized by Renoir. Down the hill from here the artistic associations continue in the **Moulin Rouge** on bd de Clichy, although these days it's a mere shadow of its former self. This stretch – known as **Pigalle** – has always been a sleazy neighbourhood, the centre of the boulevard occupied by funfair sideshows while the pavements are dotted with transvestite prostitutes on the lookout. At the western end, a little way up rue Caulaincourt, the **Montmartre cemetery** (daily 9/9.30am–5.30/6pm; métro Place de Clichy) holds the graves of Zola, Stendhal, Berlioz, Degas, Offenbach and François Truffaut among others. Way north, on the other side of the bd Périphérique from the porte de Clignancourt, the **puces de St-Ouen** (Sat, Sun & Mon 10am–6pm; métro Porte de Clignancourt) claims to be the largest flea market in the world. Although the core of the market still deals with expensive antiques and bric-à-brac, you can find just about everything here, along the further reaches of rue Fabre and rue Lécuyer, including secondhand clothes, records, ethnic accessories and army surplus.

East of Montmartre, the **Bassin de la Villette** and the **canals** at the northeastern gate of the city were for generations the centre of a densely populated working-class district but have recently become the subject of yet another big Paris redevelopment, whose major extravagance is the **Cité des Sciences et de l'Industrie** in the **Parc de la Villette**, built into the concrete hulk of the abandoned abattoirs on the north side of the canal de l'Ourcq (Tues–Sat 10am–6pm, Sun 10am–7pm; planetarium from 11am; €7.50 (€5.30 on Sat); métro Porte de la Villette; *www.cite-sciences.fr*). Three times the size of the Pompidou Centre, this is the most astounding monument to be added to the capital in the last two decades, and is worth visiting for the interior alone – all glass and stainless steel, cantilevered platforms and suspended walkways, the different levels linked by lifts and escalators around a huge central space. Its permanent exhibition, Explora, on the top two floors, is the science museum to end all science museums, covering everything from microbes and maths to outer space. You can intervene in stories acted out on videos, changing the behaviour of the characters to engineer a different outcome, steer robots through mazes and make music by your own movements.

South of La Villette, Paris' **eastern** districts – Belleville and Ménilmontant – are among the poorest of the city and not on most visitors' itineraries. However, the **Père-Lachaise cemetery**, on bd de Ménilmontant, draws a fair number of tourists (daily 7.30/9am–5.30/6pm; métro Père-Lachaise), most of them heading for Jim Morrison's small, guarded grave in the east of the cemetery or Oscar Wilde's more extravagant tomb. There are countless famous others buried here – Edith Piaf, Modigliani, Abélard and Héloïse, Sarah Bernhardt, Ingres and Corot, Delacroix and Balzac, to name only a few.

South of Père-Lachaise is the big open space of the **Bois de Vincennes**, where you can spend an afternoon boating on Lac Daumesnil or feeding the ducks on Lac des Minimes on the other side of the wood (bus #46 from Gare du Nord). To the north, the **Musée des Arts d'Afrique et d'Océanie**, 293 av Daumesnil (Mon & Wed–Fri 10am–5.30pm, Sat & Sun 12.30–6pm; €4.60; métro Porte-Dorée), is a rewarding museum, one of the least crowded in the city, with a gathering of pieces from the old French colonies – masks and statues, furniture, adornments and tools – but retaining a vague air of imperialism. Heading back towards the centre and across the Seine are the four L-shaped glass towers of the **Bibliothèque Nationale François Mitterrand** (Tues–Sat 10am–8pm, Sun noon–7pm; day-pass €3), more notable for its stunning architecture than for the general and specialist collections it holds.

Eating

Contrary to what you might expect, **eating out** in Paris need not be an enormous extravagance. There are numerous fixed-price menus under €12 providing simple but well-cooked fare; paying a little more than this gives you the chance to try out a greater range of dishes, and once over €23 you should be getting some gourmet satisfaction. There is a wide range of ethnic restaurants too – North and West African, Chinese, Japanese, Vietnamese, Greek and lots more, though they are not necessarily any cheaper. The number of vegetarian restaurants is on the increase, so although there's not exactly one in every street, being a veggie in Paris is now much easier than it used to be. Indian, Jewish and Italian restaurants are also a good bet for non-meat dishes. In general, the latest you can walk into a restaurant and order is about 10pm. Anyone in possession of an ISIC card is eligible to apply for tickets for the **university restaurants** run by CROUS, headquartered at 39 av Georges-Bernanos, 5e (☎01.40.55.55.55). You can get a list of addresses (which are near the universities) from CROUS, but you must buy your tickets from the restaurants themselves.

Snacks, sandwiches, cakes and ice cream

Angélina, 226 rue de Rivoli, 1er. A long-established gilded cage for the well-coiffed to sip the best hot chocolate in Paris, plus high-quality pastries and desserts. Open 9am–7pm; closed Tues. M° Palais Royal.

Berthillon, 31 rue St-Louis-en-l'Île, 4e. Long queues for superb ice creams and sorbets. Open Wed–Sun 10am–8pm. M° Pont Marie.

Café Martini, 11 rue du Pas-de-la-Mule, 4e. Italian café just down from place des Vosges; a relaxing place for a cappuccino or a generous warm Italian sandwich while listening to jazz. You can opt for takeaway and picnic on the grass of the place des Vosges. M° St-Paul.

Fauchon, 30 place de la Madeleine, 8e. Narrow counters at which to gobble wonderful *pâtisseries*, *plats du jour* and sandwiches – at a price. M° Madeleine.

Lina's Sandwiches, 7 av de l'Opéra, 1er. One of a number of branches around town offering excellent breakfasts, sandwiches and salads. Daily 9am–6pm.

Le Loir dans la Théière (The Dormouse in the Teapot), 3 rue des Rosiers, 4e. This peaceful retreat has a laid-back, quirky atmosphere with leather armchairs, big tables and naive paintings on the walls. Sunday brunch, superb midday *tartes* (from €7) and omelettes, fruit teas of every description and cakes served all day. M° St-Paul.

Mosquée de Paris, 39 rue Geoffroy St Hilaire, 5e. Drink sweet mint tea and eat even sweeter cakes in this oasis of calm, popular with women. The boisterous restaurant next door serves some of Paris's best couscous. Daily 8am–midnight. M° Jussieu.

A Priori Thé, 35 Galerie-Vivienne, 2e. Classy little *salon de thé* in a charming nineteenth-century gallery. Tea, cakes and more substantial dishes available. M° Pyramides/Sentier.

La Samaritaine, 19 rue de la Monnaie, 1er. Wonderful views over Paris – the Pont Neuf, la Monnaie and the Conciergerie – from the inexpensive self-service rooftop café of this Art Deco department store. M° Pont Neuf.

La Tartine, 24 rue de Rivoli, 4e. A good selection of affordable wines, plus excellent cheese and snacks. Closed Tues & Aug. M° St-Paul.

Restaurants and brasseries

Bistro de la Sorbonne, 4 rue Toullier, 5e. Large portions of traditional French and great North African dishes in a noisy, friendly ambience. Menus €10.50–21.50. Closed Sun. M° Place Monge.

Chardenoux, 1 rue Jules-Vallès, 11e. An authentic oldie, with engraved mirrors dating back to 1900, that still serves solid meaty fare at moderate prices. M° Charonne.

Chartier, 7 rue du Faubourg-Montmartre, 9e. Good cheap food served at a run in an original and quite splendid turn-of-the-century soup kitchen. Closes 10pm. Menus under €15.50, but expect to queue. M° Le Peletier.

La Chaumière, 46 av Secrétan, 19e. A superb gourmet restaurant at out-of-town prices. If you get the urge to splurge, this is the place to head for. M° Bolivar.

Chez Justine, 96 rue Oberkampf, 11e. Well recommended for traditional cooking at very reasonable prices. €9 for a main course. Closed Aug. M° Parmentier.

Chez Paul, 13 rue de Charonne, 11e. Lopsided corner building housing a small, popular restaurant which preserves the faded colours and furnishings of an older Bastille. Food is traditional and affordable. Main courses from €9.50. M° Bastille.

Le Commerce, 51 rue du Commerce, 15e. Long-established place serving nourishing, inexpensive food. Menus from €13. M° Commerce.

Drouot, 103 rue de Richelieu, 2e. Good budget food, served at a frantic pace, in an Art Nouveau setting. M° Bourse.

Flo, 7 cours des Petites-Écuries, 10e. Handsome old-time brasserie, where you eat elbow-to-elbow at long tables. Excellent food and thoroughly enjoyable atmosphere. Menus €18–29. M° Château d'Eau.

Le Fouta Djalon, 27 bd St-Martin, 3e. A crowded, family-run African restaurant. There's often a hefty delay between ordering and eating but the massive, spicy African specialities are well worth the wait. M° République/Strasbourg St Denis.

Goldenberg, 7 rue des Rosiers, 4e. Paris's best-known Jewish restaurant. Its borscht, blinis, strudels and other central European dishes are a treat, although the service can be somewhat surly. *Plat du jour* €12.50. M° St-Paul.

Higuma, 32 rue Ste-Anne, 1er. Authentic Japanese noodle bar serving cheap, filling ramen dishes and set menus. Open noon–10pm. M° Pyramides.

Lao Thai, 128 rue de Tolbiac, 13e. Spacious, glass-fronted restaurant on a busy corner. Serves spicy Thai and Laotian food at moderate prices. M° Tolbiac.

Little Havana, 5 rue de Sévigné, 4e. This cosy and fashionable Cuban restaurant serves delicious Caribbean dishes and great cocktails to the beats of salsa and merengue. M° St-Paul.

Le Muniche, 7 rue St-Benoît, 6e. An appealing old-style eatery with an oyster bar, mirrors and theatre posters, serving classic French brasserie fare. Can get crowded. Menus from €15. M° St-Germain-des-Prés.

Perraudin, 157 rue St-Jacques, 5e. Well-known traditional bistro with menus from about €9 at lunchtime, and €23 in the evening. M° Cluny La Sorbonne.

Le Petit Mabillon, 6 rue Mabillon, 6e. Small Italian restaurant, popular for good food at reasonable prices. Menus from €12. M° St-Germain des Prés.

Le Petit Prince, 12 rue Lanneau, 5e. Good food in a restaurant full of charm in one of the Latin Quarter's oldest lanes. Menus start around €20. M° Cardinal Lemoine.

Le Petit Saint-Benoît, 4 rue St-Benoît, 6e. A simple, genuine and very appealing local for the neighbourhood's chattering classes. Solid traditional fare. M° Mabillon.

La Petite Légume, 36 rue des Boulangers, 5e. Tiny homely vegetarian café with a mezzanine level and a serious macrobiotic and organic-only approach, though they do serve a bit of fish. Downstairs it feels like you're in someone's kitchen. Main dishes for around €9. Closed Sun. M° Jussieu.

Port de Pidjiguiti, 28 rue Etex, 18e. Pleasant atmosphere and excellent food. Run by a village in the West African state of Guinea-Bissau, whose inhabitants take turns in staffing the restaurant; the proceeds go to the village. Menus from €15. M° Guy Môcquet.

Le Quincampe, 70 rue Quincampe, 3e. Moroccan restaurant and *salon de thé* offering excellent tagines and mint tea. *Plat du jour* from €12. M° Etienne-Marcel/Rambuteau.

Au Rendez-vous des Camionneurs (At the Lorry Drivers' Meeting Place), 34 rue des Plantes, 14e. No lorry drivers anymore, but the good French cooking remains. Small, popular and good value. Closed Sat & Sun, and Aug. M° Alésia.

Le Temps des Cerises, 18–20 rue de la Butte-aux-Cailles, 13e. A well-established workers' co-op with elbow-to-elbow seating and menus under €18. M° Corvisart.

Thoumieux, 79 rue St-Dominique, 7e. Large and popular establishment in this rather smart district, with menus starting at €12.50. M° Invalides.

Le Vaudeville, 29 rue Vivienne, 2e. A lively late-night brasserie where it's often necessary to queue, with good food and an attractive marble-and-mosaic interior. Menu at €20. M° Bourse.

Drinking

Most of Paris's main squares and boulevards have **cafés** spreading out onto the pavements and, although these are usually the priciest places to drink, it can be worth shelling out for a coffee for the chance to observe the streetlife. Using the terrace or seating inside the café means you will pay around double the price you would pay at the bar (if you find a bar with stools, you can get the best of both worlds). The Left Bank harbours some of the city's best-known and longest-established cafés on boulevards Montparnasse and St-Germain, while the presence of the university means there are plenty of places to drink around place de la Sorbonne and rue Soufflot. The Bastille is now livelier than ever as the Opéra and rocketing property values bring headlong development, as is Les Halles – though the latter's trade is principally among out-of-towners up for the bright lights. The Marais offers small crowded watering holes and many gay bars; there are plenty of bars in Montmartre; while Ménilmontant and Belleville are popular but less obvious drinking haunts. You'll also find **wine bars** – revitalized, ironically, by the English – the best of which are long-established places serving food as well as decent wine by the glass. There are plenty of establishments more geared to **beer**, most inspired by Belgian or British watering holes.

Académie de la Bière, 88 bd Port-Royal, 5e. Large selection of beers from around the world, with a focus on Belgian varieties. Also food – good mussels and chips/french fries, plus Belgian cheeses and charcuterie. M° Gobelins.

Apparemment Café, 18 rue des Coutures-St-Gervais, 3e. Chic but cosy café resembling a series of comfortable sitting-rooms, with deep sofas and quiet corners. Popular Sunday brunch until 4pm. M° St-Paul.

Bar de la Fontaine, 1 rue de Charonne, 11e. Perfect corner spot for watching a slice of life from the pavement tables. An easygoing place where the clientele ranges from old characters in berets to a casual but hip twenty-something crowd, with a soundtrack of funk and soul. Open until 1 or 2am. M° Bastille.

Café Oz, 184 rue-St-Jacques, 5e. Australian-run bar, complete with kitsch souvenirs from down under. Parisians, not just tourists, consider the place a fun night out. Staff keep the jokes running and there's s a big range of Australian beers and wines. Daily 4pm–2am. M° Luxembourg.

Coolin, rue Clément, 6e. Anglophile pub with a friendly mixed crowd, serving pints, burgers and great salads. Gets very lively at weekends. M° Odéon.

Le Dépanneur, 27 rue Fontaine, 9e. Popular all-night bar on a busy corner just down from place Blanche and the Moulin Rouge. M° Blanche.

Les Deux Magots, 170 bd St-Germain, 6e. Former haunt of Sartre and numerous famous others from the postwar years. Touristy now, with a terrace often besieged by buskers. Open until 2am; closed one week in Jan. M° St-Germain des Pres.

La Fresque, 100 rue Rambuteau, 1er. Nicely dingy place, formerly a snail merchant's hall, and still retaining the original decor. Closed Sun lunch. M° Les Halles.

Au Général Lafayette, 52 rue Lafayette, 9e. Beer-drinking hangout with a dozen on tap, including Guinness, and many more bottled. Mixed clientele and a pleasant, quiet feel. M° Poissonnière.

La Gueuze, 19 rue Soufflot, 5e. Comfy surroundings, decent food and numerous Belgian bottles and several draughts, including cherry *kriek*. M° Cardinal Lemoine.

Café de l'Industrie, corner of rue Sedaine and rue St-Sabin, 11e. Rugs on the floor around solid old wooden tables, paintings and miscellaneous objects on the walls, and a young, unpretentious crowd. M° Bastille.

Café de la Mairie, 8 place St Sulpice, 6e. Famous yet unpretentious café which holds an enviable position overlooking the enormous St Sulpice church. M° St-Sulpice.

L'Oiseau Bariolé, 16 rue Ste-Croix-de-la-Bretonnerie, 4e. Small and friendly, surreal paintings on glass, and full of Americans. *Plats du jour*, omelettes and Breton cider. The place where the Marais drinkers inevitably end up as it's open until dawn. M° Hôtel de Ville.

Polly Magoo, 11 rue St-Jacques, 5e. A scruffy all-night bar frequented by chess addicts. M° Cluny La Sorbonne.

Pub St-Germain, 17 rue de l'Ancienne-Comédie, 6e. Hundreds of bottled beers plus 26 on tap. Spread over five floors, it's huge – and crowded. Hot food at mealtimes, otherwise cold snacks. Open 24hr. M° Odéon.

Le Rubis, 10 rue du Marché-St-Honoré, 1er. One of the oldest wine bars in Paris, with a reputation for having some of the best wines, plus excellent snacks and *plats du jour*. M° Tuileries.

Le Sancerre, 35 rue des Abbesses, 18e. The self-conscious hub of the Butte Montmartre, pumping out high-volume rock. The place is packed, pulsating and great for people-watching. Black leather jacket optional. M° Abbesses.

Le Sélect, 99 bd du Montparnasse, 6e. The least spoilt of the swanky Montparnasse cafés, still thriving since its 1920s heyday. M° Vavin.

Le Violon Dingue, 46 rue de la Montagne-Ste-Geneviève, 5e. A long, dark student pub, noisy and friendly. Happy hour 8–10pm; closed Sun & Mon. M° Maubert Mutualité.

Web Bar, 32 rue de Picardie, 3e. This Internet café is very Marais-chic, a multimedia centre that has films and videos on its menu, as well as offering low-tech storytelling and chess. Mon–Fri 8.30am–2am, Sat & Sun noon–2am. M° Temple.

Nightlife

Nightlife in Paris is as lively and diverse as you would expect. The city's reputation for **live music** is impeccable; Paris is a centre of world music second-to-none in Europe, and there is excellent live jazz in numerous St-Germain and Les Halles clubs. The tradition of *chansons* – epitomized by Edith Piaf and developed to its greatest heights by Leo Ferré, Georges Brassens and Jacques Brel – endures too, and there's an almost limitless choice of classical music and opera. Should you be after a place to dance, **clubs** come and go as rapidly as in any other large city, but there are one or two long-established places that won't let you down; most clubs open around 11pm, some stay open until sunrise. For **what's on** listings, there are two weekly guides, *Pariscope* (*www.pariscope.fr*; €0.50) and *L'Officiel des Spectacles* (€0.30), which both come out on Wednesdays; the former is easier to use and has a small *Time Out* section in English. The best places to get **tickets** are FNAC, main branch at Forum des Halles, 1–5 rue Pierre-Lescot, level 3 (métro Les Halles), and the Virgin Megastore, 56–60 av des Champs-Élysées (métro Franklin Roosevelt).

Live music venues

Le Bataclan, 50 bd Voltaire, 11e (bookings ☎01.43.14.35.35). One of the best larger rock venues. M° Oberkampf.

Le Caveau de la Bolée, 25 rue de l'Hirondelle, 6e. Ancient place where Parisian luminaries used to go to hear their favourite singers. Still mainly *chansons* with occasional jazz. M° St-Michel.

La Cigale, 120 bd de Rochechouart, 18e. Old-fashioned theatre with an eclectic programme of rock. Long a fixture on the Pigalle scene. M° Anvers.

Divan du Monde, 75 rue des Martyrs, 18e. Youthful venue in a café whose regulars once included Toulouse-Lautrec. An eclectic and exciting programme with a focus on world music. M° Pigalle.

L'Escale, 15 rue Monsieur-le-Prince, 6e. Hugely popular Latin American venue. M° Odéon.

L'Eustache, 37 rue Berger, 1er. Cheap beer and very good jazz by local musicians in this young and friendly Les Halles café. Music from 10pm. M° Les Halles.

La Guinguette Pirate, quai de la Gare, 13e. Beautiful Chinese barge, moored alongside the quay in front of the Bibliothèque Nationale, hosting funk, reggae, rock and folk concerts. M° Bibliothèque.

New Morning, 7–9 rue des Petites-Ecuries, 10e. Famed jazz venue where blues, Latin and world music now also hold sway. M° Château d'Eau.

Petit Journal St-Michel, 71 bd St-Michel, 5e. A small, smoky bar, long frequented by Left Bank student types, with good, mainly French, traditional and mainstream jazz. Music from 10pm. M° Luxembourg.

Rex Club, 5 bd Poissonnière, 2e. Live music early on and DJs from 11pm. Friday is techno night for a style-conscious crowd. Entrance €5–12. Open until 6am. M° Bonne Nouvelle.

Satellit' Café, 44 rue de la Folie-Méricourt, 11e. Multicultural acoustic evenings, anything from swing to folk, Brazilian to Balkan. Entry is reasonable (€6–7.50) when bands are playing. M° République.

Utopia, 79 rue de l'Ouest, 14e. Good French blues singers interspersed with jazz and blues tapes. M° Pernety.

Clubs and discos

Les Bains, 7 rue du Bourg-l'Abbé, 3e. A former Turkish bath-house, this is currently one of the hippest clubs in Paris playing house and garage with hip-hop on Wednesdays. If you can get past the door policy and afford the €15 entry, the spectacle of punters plunging into the pool by the dance floor awaits. Daily 11.30pm–5am. M° Etienne Marcel.

Balajo, 9 rue de Lappe, 11e. Old-style music hall or *bal musette* with extravagant 1930s decor and music ranging from mazurkas and tangos to slurpy *chansons*. Entry around €15. Closed Mon and Aug. M° Bastille.

La Java, 105 rue du Faubourg-du-Temple, 11e. Live Latin bands Thurs–Sat followed by DJs playing similar sounds. Older, energetic and friendly crowd. M° Goncourt.

La Locomotive, 90 bd de Clichy, 18e. Enormous hi-tech nightclub next to the legendary *Moulin Rouge* with two crowded dance floors and a very young crowd. Open until 6am. M° Place de Clichy.

Le Queen, 102 av des Champs-Élysées, 8e. Mainly gay club with women welcome except Thurs. Drag queens and model types dance to house music; Monday is "Disco inferno" night. Daily midnight–dawn. €12. M° Georges V.

Classical and contemporary music, opera and ballet

Paris is a stimulating environment for **classical music**, both established and **contemporary**. The Cité de la Musique project at La Villette (*www.cite-musique.fr*; métro Porte-de-Pantin) has given Paris two major concert venues: the Conservatoire, the national music academy, 209 av Jean-Jaurès (☎01.40.40.45.45), and, next door at no. 221, the Salle des Concerts (☎01.44.84.44.84) where ancient music, contemporary works, jazz, *chansons* and music from around the world are featured. Otherwise, the top auditorium is the Salle Pleyel, 252 rue du Faubourg-St-Honoré, 8e (☎01.45.61.53.00; métro Ternes), home to the Orchestre de Paris. There are also regular concerts at the Théâtre des Champs-Élysées, 15 av Montaigne, 8e (☎01.49.52.50.50; métro Alma Marceau), home of the Orchestre National de France, and the Châtelet Théâtre Musical de Paris, 2 rue Edouard Colonne, 1er (☎01.40.28.28.40; *www.chatelet-theatre.com*; métro Châtelet).

The ultra-modern **Opéra-Bastille**, 120 rue de Lyon, 12e, is the main place for **opera** (☎08.36.69.78.68, *www.opera-de-paris.fr*; métro Bastille). Tickets cost anything from €9 to €102, with the cheapest seats only available to personal callers; unfilled seats are sold at a discount to students five minutes before the curtain goes up. The original opera house, now known as **Opéra-Garnier** or Palais Garnier (☎08.36.69.78.68; métro Opéra), still has some small-scale operas, but its main feature now is **ballet** as home to the Ballet de l'Opéra National de Paris. Seats range from €5 to €58, and even if the cheapest provide a very restricted view, the splendid interior certainly makes for a memorable visit.

Film

There are over 350 **films** showing in Paris in any one week. Tickets cost around €7.50, or €5.30 for students; most cinemas have lower rates on Mondays and Wednesdays. Almost all of the huge selection of foreign films will be shown at some cinemas in their original language – *v.o.* in the listings (as opposed to *v.f.*, which means it's dubbed into French). Committed film freaks should head to the small *cinémathèques*, which show a choice of over fifty movies a week; tickets are only €4.60. The Vidéothèque de Paris in the Forum des Halles, 2 Grande Galerie, Porte Eustache (métro Les Halles), is an excellent-value venue for the bizarre or obscure on celluloid; its repertoires are always based around a Parisian theme. There is also the Géode, the mightily impressive mirrored globe at La Villette (métro Porte de la Villette), which shows documentaries at several screenings a day; tickets cost €8.70, or €14 as a combined ticket with the Cité des Sciences. Also look out for the Max Linder Panorama, 24 bd Poissonnière (métro Grands Boulevards), and the Pathé Wepler, 140 bd de Clichy (métro Place de Clichy).

Gay and lesbian Paris

Paris has a well-established **gay scene** concentrated in the Halles, Marais and Bastille areas, and there are numerous gay organizations. For **information** visit the main gay and lesbian bookshop, Les Mots à la Bouche, 6 rue Ste-Croix-de-la-Bretonnerie, 4e (☎01.42.78.88.30, *www.motalabouche.com*; métro Hôtel de Ville); or the handy drop-in information office Centre Gai et Lesbien, 3 rue Keller, 11e (☎01.43.57.21.47, *www.cglparis.org*; métro Bastille), which has its own café. The CGL also produces a free guide map to gay Paris and a monthly publication, *Le 3 Keller*.

Gay and lesbian bars and clubs

Banana Café, 13 rue de la Ferronnerie, 4e. Popular, expensive and very fashionable. Try and catch the cabaret and go-go dancing. Daily 5pm–dawn. M° Châtelet/Les-Halles.

Bar Hôtel Central, 33 rue Vieille-du-Temple, 4e. The oldest gay local in the Marais. Small, friendly and always crowded. Daily 2/4pm–dawn. M° Hôtel de Ville.

Le New Monocle, 60 bd Edgar-Quinet, 14e. Lesbian club with cabaret; some men also allowed in. M° Edgar-Quinet.

Le Piano Zinc, 49 rue des Blancs-Manteaux, 4e. A happy riot of songs, music-hall acts and dance, from 10pm onwards. One of the few venues patronized by both lesbians and gay men. Closed Mon. M° St-Paul.

Le Queen, 102 av des Champs-Élysées, 8e. Very trendy mainstream gay club, with a strict door policy. It's also one of the hippest spots in town for heterosexuals – if they can get in. Mainly house music with big-name guest DJs. €12. M° Georges V.

Le Quetzal, 10 rue de la Verrerie, 4e. A trendy gay bar crammed with a well-toned and stylish clientele, with space for dancing. Daily until 5am. M° Hôtel de Ville.

Les Scandaleuses, 8 rue des Ecouffes, 4e. Trendy women-only bar in the Marais. Lively atmosphere guaranteed. M° St-Paul.

Listings

Airlines Air France, 119 av des Champs-Élysées, 8e (☎08.02.80.28.02, *www.airfrance.fr*; M° Georges V); British Airways, 13–15 bd de Madeleine, 8e (☎08.25.82.54.00, *www.britishairways.com*; M° Madeleine).

Airport information CDG/Roissy-Charles de Gaulle (☎01.48.62.22.80); Orly (☎01.49.75.15.15); *www.adp.fr.*

Bike rental Paris Vélo, 4 rue du Fer-à-Moulin, 5e (☎01.43.37.59.22; M° Censier Daubenton); Paris à Vélo C'est Sympa, 37 bd Bourdon, 4e (☎01.48.87.60.01; M° Bastille).

Books English-language books from Shakespeare & Co, 37 rue de la Bûcherie, 5e (M° Maubert Mutualité); W.H. Smith, 248 rue de Rivoli, 1er (M° Palais Royal); Village Voice Bookshop, 6 rue Princesse, 6e (M° Mabillon).

Car rental Europcar, 145 av de Malakoff, 16e (☎01.45.00.08.06, *www.europcar.com*; M° Victor Hugo); Locabest, 104 bd de Magenta, 10e (☎01.44.72.08.05; M° Gare du Nord); Rent a Car, 79 rue de Bercy, 12e (☎01.43.45.98.99, *www.rentacar.fr*; M° Bercy).

Embassies Australia, 4 rue Jean-Rey, 15e (☎01.40.59.33.00; M° Bir Hakeim); Canada, 35 av Montaigne, 8e (☎01.44.43.29.00; M° Franklin Roosevelt); Ireland, 4 rue Rude, 16e (☎01.44.17.67.00; M° Iéna); New Zealand, 7 rue Léonard-de-Vinci, 16e (☎01.45.00.24.11; M° Victor Hugo); UK, 35 rue Faubourg-St-Honoré, 8e (☎01.44.51.31.00; M° St-Phillippe du Roule); USA, 2 av Gabriel, 8e (☎01.43.12.22.22; M° Concorde).

Exchange The Crédit Commercial de France is at 103 av des Champs-Élysées, 8e (M° Georges V), and there are counters at the main train stations (daily 8am–9pm).

Hitching Allostop Proyova, 8 rue Rochambeau, 9e (☎01.53.20.42.42; M° Cadet).

Hospital SOS-Médecins (☎01.47.07.77.77 or ☎01.43.37.77.77) for 24hr medical help.

Internet Café Orbital, 13 rue de Médicis, 6e (☎01.43.25.76.77, *www.cafeorbital.com*; M° Odéon); Cyber Café Latino, 13 rue de l'Ecole Polytechnique, 5e (☎01.40.51.86.94, *www.cybercafelatino.com*; M° Maubert-Mutualité); Cybersport, Forum des Halles, 4e (☎01.44.76.63.99, M° Les Halles); Easyeverything, 37 bld de Sébastopol, 1er (☎01.42.44.32.42; M° Châtelet/Les-Halles); Toyota, 79 av des Champs Elysées, 8e (☎01.56.89.29.79; M° Georges V).

Left luggage Lockers at all train stations and *consignes* for bigger items.

Pharmacies Dérhy, 84 av des Champs-Élysées, 8e (☎01.45.62.02.41; M° Georges V), has a 24hr service.

Police The main *Préfecture* is at 7 bd du Palais, 4e (☎01.53.71.53.71; M° Châtelet); ☎17 for emergencies.

Post office Main office at 52 rue du Louvre, 1er (open 24hr; M° Louvre). *Poste Restante*, 52 rue du Louvre, 75001 Paris; to avoid confusion your surname should be in capitals and underlined.

Telephones The main post office is open 24hr for phone calls. Phonecards are available at *tabacs*.

Train information SNCF ☎08.36.35.35.35; Eurostar ☎08.36.35.35.39.

Travel agent CTS Voyages, 20 rue des Carmes, 5e (☎01.43.25.00.76; M° Maubert Mutualité).

Around Paris

Like most Parisians, you may find there's enough in Paris to keep you from ever thinking about the world beyond. However, the city can get claustrophobic; there are one or two places in the countryside around that are worth making the trip out for. The most visited of these is undoubtedly **Versailles**, the most hyped **Disneyland Paris**, but the most rewarding is without doubt the cathedral at **Chartres**.

Versailles

The **Palace of Versailles** (Tues–Sun 9am–5.30/6.30pm; €7, or €5.30 after 3.30pm; *www.chateauversailles.com*) is one of the three most visited monuments in France. The palace, 16km west of Paris, is the apotheosis of French regal indulgence, its decor a grotesque homage to two of the greatest of all self-propagandists, Louis XIV (the "Sun King") and Napoleon. It's more impressive for its size than anything else, which, by any standards, is incredible. The most amazing room is perhaps the **Hall of Mirrors**, although the mirrors are not the originals; this is, more importantly, the room in which the Treaty of Versailles was signed, so bringing World War I to an end. You can also visit the state apartments of the king and queen, and the **royal chapel**, a grand structure that ranks among France's finest Baroque creations. Outside, the **park** is something of a relief, and you could wander for hours through its vast extent. It is inevitably a very ordered affair, although the catastrophic storms of 1999 razed an estimated ten thousand trees, devastating much of the scenery. The park is gradually returning to its former state, thanks to international donations. The scenery becomes less formal the further you go from the palace, especially around the **Grand** and **Petit Trianons** (Tues–Sun noon–5.30/6.30pm; €3.80 and €2.30 respectively, €4.60 for both). Beyond is **Le Hameau** (the hamlet), an area of thatched cottages, a mill and a dairy set around a lake where Marie Antoinette played at being a shepherdess, that was, sadly, decimated by the storm.

The easiest **transport** to Versailles is the half-hourly RER line C5 from Gare d'Austerlitz to Versailles-Rive Gauche (takes 30min; €4.40). Alternatively, take bus #171 from Pont de Sèvres at the end of métro line 9. You can get maps of the park from the Versailles **tourist office** at 2bis, rue de Paris, to the left of the palace.

Chartres

About 35km west of Versailles, an hour by train from Paris-Montparnasse, **CHARTRES** is a small and relatively undistinguished town. However, its **Cathédrale Notre-Dame** (daily 8am–7.15/8pm; *www.diocesechartres.com*) is one of the finest examples of Gothic architecture in Europe, and, built between 1134 and 1260, perhaps the quickest ever to be constructed. Its size and hilltop position are awe-inspiring, and there are more than enough visible wonders to enthral: the geometry of the building, unique in being almost unaltered since its consecration; the Renaissance choir screen and the hosts of sculpted figures above each transept door; and the shining symmetries of the stained glass, 130 windows in all, virtually all of which are original, dating from the twelfth and thirteenth centuries – the light coming through the rose windows is one of the wonders of Chartres. There's also a treasury and crypt, and it's possible to climb the north **tower** (check for opening times; €3.80).

Though the cathedral is the main reason for coming here, Chartres town is not entirely without appeal, with a small old quarter of mazey streets and a picturesque district of bridges and old houses down by the river Eure. The **Musée des Beaux-Arts** in the former episcopal palace just north of the cathedral (Mon & Wed–Sat 10am–noon & 2–5/6pm, Sun 2–5/6pm; €2.30) has some beautiful tapestries, a room full of Vlaminck paintings, and Zurbarán's *St Lucy*, as well as good temporary exhibitions. The **tourist office** is in front of the cathedral, at place de la Cathédrale, and can supply free maps and help with accommodation (April–Nov Mon–Sat 9am–7pm, Sun 9.30am–5.30pm; Dec–March Mon–Sat 10am–6pm, Sun 9.30am–1pm & 2.30–4.30pm; *www.ville-chartres.fr*). Rue du Cygne is a good place to look for **restaurants** or, if you want to splash out, have a meal at *À l'Escargot d'Or*, 13 rue du Soleil-d'Or; the name – "At the Golden Snail" – says it all.

Disneyland Paris

Around 32km east of Paris, **Disneyland Paris** (daily: July & Aug 9am–11pm; rest of year 9/10am–8pm; subject to change; *www.disneylandparis.com*) is a 5000-acre slice of the USA grafted onto a bleak tract of the Bassin Parisien. The ploy was to make the Disney empire more accessible to Europeans, but it seems that many Europeans are either not interested or would rather opt for the more reliable weather and better rides of Florida's version. But for all the jokes about "Disneybland", the theatricality and professionalism of the place elevate it head and shoulders above any other theme park in Europe.

Admission in peak season (April–Oct) costs €36 for a one-day pass (under-11s €28) or €70/97 for a two-/three-day pass (€54/75). The **Magic Kingdom** is divided into four "lands" radiating out from Main Street USA – Fantasyland, Frontierland, Discoveryland and Adventureland. The grand **parade** sallies down Main Street USA at 3pm sharp every day, and Snow White, Dumbo, Pinocchio, Mickey and the rest strut their stuff with insistent joviality. Night-time Electrical Parades and **firework displays** take place several times a week. The themed Disney **hotels** are out of many people's price range, the least expensive room off-season being €90 a night (2 adults, 2 children), rising to over €380 peak season for a room in the *Disneyland Hotel* inside the Magic Kingdom on Main Street.

Transport from Paris involves RER line A4 to Marne-la-Vallée/Chessy – about a forty-minute journey from Gare de Lyon (€11.60 return).

THE NORTH

When thinking up exotic holiday locations, **northern France** is unlikely to spring to mind, including as it does some of the most industrial and densely populated parts of the country. However, it is possible that you'll both arrive and leave France via this region, and there are curiosities within easy reach of the Channel ports – of which **Boulogne** is the nicest – and one of France's finest cathedrals at **Amiens**. Further south, the *maisons* and vineyards of the **Champagne** region are the main draw, for which the best bases are **Épernay** and **Reims**, the latter with another fine cathedral. Most of the champagne houses offer free visits and tastings, although beyond them the region is not the most enthralling. For information on the far north go to *www.pas-de-calais.com* and for Champagne *www.tourisme-champagne-ard.com*.

Calais

CALAIS is less than 40km from Dover in England – the Channel's narrowest crossing – and is the busiest French passenger port. The ferry business dominates the town, for there's not much else here. In the last war the British destroyed Calais to impede its use as a port, fearing a German invasion. Seized by Edward III after the battle of Crécy in 1346, it remained English until 1558, and the association has been maintained across the centuries. Today, nine million British travellers a year pass through, in addition to one million day-trippers.

Once you've checked out the shopping on the central place d'Armes and rue Royale, Calais-Nord's charms wear thin. Calais-Sud is scarcely more significant, its focus bring the extravagant **Hôtel de Ville**, outside which Rodin's famous bronze **Burghers of Calais** records the self-sacrifice of these local dignitaries who offered their lives to assuage the English conqueror. Across the street in the Parc St-Pierre, the **Musée de la Guerre** (Mon & Wed–Sun: May–Sept 10am–5.15pm; rest of year 11am–6.45pm; €3.80) records the town's wartime travails.

There is a **free bus service** during the day from the **ferry dock** alongside Calais-Maritime train station to place d'Armes and on to the central Calais-Ville train station in Calais-Sud; at night take a taxi, which will cost about €7.50. The **tourist office** is at 12 bd Clemenceau (Mon–Sat 9am–7pm, Sun 10am–1pm; *www.ot-calais.fr*) and has an accommodation service, for which there is a small charge. There is a **hostel** near the seafront on av de Lattre de Tassigny (☎03.21.34.70.20; ②), and a **campsite** at 26 av Poincaré (☎03.21.97.89.79), beyond the end of rue Royale. An affordable **hotel** is the seafront *Albert 1er*, 51–53 rue de la Mer (☎03.21.34.36.08; ④). The place d'Armes area is good for **restaurants**: *Le Touquet's*, 57 rue Royale, and *Le Channel*, 3 bd de la Résistance, are both recommended.

Boulogne

BOULOGNE is the one northern Channel port that might tempt you to stay. Its **Ville Basse**, centring on **place Dalton**, is home to some of the best *charcuteries* and *pâtisseries* in the north, as well as an impressive array of fish restaurants. Rising above, the **Ville Haute** is one of the gems of the northeast coast, flanked by grassy ramparts that give impressive views over the town and port. Inside the walls, the **Basilique Notre-Dame** is something of an oddity, raised by the town's vicar in the nineteenth century without any architectural knowledge or advice. Its **crypt** (Tues–Sun 2–5pm; €1.50) has frescoed remains of the previous Romanesque building and relics of a Roman temple to Diana, while the main part of the church has a curious statue of the Virgin and Child on a boat-chariot, drawn here on its own wheels from Lourdes. Also worth a visit is **Nausicaa**, bd St-Beuve (daily 9.30am–6.30/8pm; €10), claimed to be the largest marine complex in Europe, with 36 aquariums and over 10,000 animals.

Ferries from England dock within a few minutes' walk of the town centre. The **tourist office** (Mon–Sat 8.45am–12.30pm & 1.30–6.15pm, Sun 10am–12.30pm & 2.30–6pm; *boulogne@tourism.norsys.fr*), over the bridge as you leave the ferry terminal, can advise on availability of rooms, which in summer fill early. Your best bet is probably the friendly **hostel** in front of the train station, 56 place Rouget de l'Isle (☎03.21.99.15.30, *boulogne-sur-mer@fuaj.org*; ②). Most of the budget **hotels** enclose the port area and include the *Hamiot*, 1 rue Faidherbe (☎03.21.31.44.20; ③), and *Hôtel les Arts*, 102 bd Gambetta (☎03.21.31.53.31; ③). For **eating**, there are dozens of possibilities around place Dalton and the cathedral, but you need to be selective. The brasserie *Chez Jules*, 8 place Dalton, is always a good bet and serves food all day. Opposite the cathedral on rue de Lille, *Estaminet du Château* offers inexpensive menus in a pleasant setting. Near place Dalton is the *Hamiot* restaurant, a decent alternative, while *La Houblonnière*, 8 rue Monsigny, has a vast international selection of brews to wash down its *plats du jour*.

Lille

By far the largest city in the far north of France, **LILLE** is the very symbol of French industry and working-class politics, but suffers from some of the country's worst poverty and racial conflict, and a crime rate rivalled only by Paris and Marseille. There is regionalism – the Lillois sprinkle their speech with a French-Flemish patois and, to an extent, assert a Flemish identity – but there is also classic French affluence here: the city has a lovely old quarter, **Vieux Lille**, along with some vibrant and prosperous commercial areas, and it's a place that takes its culture and its restaurants very seriously. Though not a prime destination, Lille is now a stop for Eurostar trains between London and Paris, and is worth at least a night.

At the heart of the old quarter is the **Grand Place** (also known as place du Général de Gaulle, who was born here in 1890), a busy square dominated by the old exchange building, the lavishly ornate **Ancienne Bourse**. A couple of minutes' walk north of here is the **Hospice Comtesse** on rue de la Monnaie, which is perhaps the main thing to see in Lille, a twelfth-century hospital that served as such right through to World War II. Its old ward, the **Salle des Malades** (Mon & Wed–Sun 10am–12.30pm & 2–6pm; €2), has a selection of Dutch, Flemish and French paintings on loan from the Palais des Beaux-Arts. South of the old quarter lies the modern place Rihour, beyond which the stylish rue de Béthune leads into café-lined **place Béthune**, and on to bd de la Liberté and the city's **Palais des Beaux-Arts** on place de la République (Mon 2–6pm, Wed–Sun noon–6pm, Fri until 8pm; €4.60).

Arriving at the **train station**, you're only a few minutes' walk from Vieux Lille. The **tourist office** is in the old Palais Rihour on place Rihour (Mon–Sat 9.30am–6.30pm, Sun 9am–noon & 2–5pm; *www.lille.cci.fr*). Most of the inexpensive **hotels** are gathered around the train station. The *Hôtel des Voyageurs*, right opposite (☎03.20.06.43.14; ②), is basic but reasonable; you could also try the plusher *Hôtel de France* in the centre at 10 rue de Béthune (☎03.20.57.14.78; ④). A good fall-back is the **hostel** near the Hôtel de Ville at 12 rue Malpart (☎03.20.57.13.57; *lille@fuaj.org*; ②). The nearest **campsite** is *Les Ramiers*, 10km north of the centre in Bondues (☎03.20.23.13.42; bus #35/36). The main area for **restaurants** is around place Rihour and place Béthune. For mussels – a local speciality – the brasseries around the station are as good as any in town, and *La Galetière*, 4 place Louise-de-Bettignies, is a pleasant crêperie. For **drinking**, monied local students hang around *Café 'Imaginaire* on place Louise-de-Bettignies.

Amiens

Few travellers would stop at **AMIENS** unless they were visiting its cathedral. Badly scarred during both world wars, the city is not an immediately likeable place, but the **Cathédrale Notre-Dame** provides the city's focus as the largest Gothic building in France (daily: Easter–Oct 8.30am–6/6.45pm; rest of year 8.30am–noon & 2–5/6pm; free). Begun in 1220 it was virtually complete by the end of the century. The interior is a light, calm space, its only real embellishments the sixteenth-century choir stalls (viewable on guided tours only), and the sculpted panels depicting the life of St Firmin, Amiens' first bishop, on the right-hand side of the choir screen. Close by the cathedral, the seventeenth-century **Musée de l'Hôtel de Berny** on rue Victor Hugo (Easter–Oct Thurs–Sun 1–6pm; rest of year Sun 10am–12.30pm & 2–6pm; €1.50) has displays on local history, while another mansion five minutes' walk south of the central **place Gambetta** houses the **Musée de Picardie** (Tues–Sun 10am–12.30pm & 2–6pm; €0.50), the star exhibit of which is a collection of rare sixteenth-century paintings on wood, some in their original frames, carved by the same craftsmen who worked the cathedral's choir stalls. The **Maison de Jules Verne**, 2 rue Charles Dubois (Mon–Fri 9am–noon & 2–5.30pm, Sat–Sun 2–6pm; €3), is devoted to the author of *Around The World In Eighty Days* and *20,000 Leagues Under the Sea*, who spent most of his life in Amiens.

The **train station** is on place Alphonse Fiquet, five minutes' walk southeast of the cathedral. The **tourist office** is between the two, at 6bis rue Dusevel (Mon–Sat 9.30am–6/7pm, Sun 10am–noon & 2–5pm; *www.amiens.com*). The most affordable places to stay are the central **hotels**: *Hôtel Spatial*, 15 rue Alexandre-Fatton (☎03.22.91.53.23; ④) and *Victor Hugo*, 2 rue de l'Oratoire (☎03.22.91.57.91; ③). Good places to **eat** include a number of cheap brasseries in front of the station and around place Gambetta, of which *Au Bureau*, 15 place de l'Hôtel de Ville, is one of the best.

Épernay

Though **ÉPERNAY** is a pleasant enough town, the only real reason for coming here is to visit the **champagne** houses, whose tours could keep you fully occupied for a couple of days. The largest and most famous is **Moët et Chandon**, at 18 av de Champagne (daily 9.30–11.30am & 2–4pm; Dec–March closed Sat & Sun; €6, including tasting; *www.moet.com*), who own Mercier, Ruinart and a variety of other concerns. The cellars are adorned with mementos of Napoleon, a good friend of the original Monsieur Moët, and the vintage is named after the monastic hero of champagne history, Dom Pérignon. Of the other *maison* visits, the most rewarding are **Mercier**, up the road at no. 70 (daily 9.30–11.30am & 2–4.30pm; Dec–Feb closed Tues & Wed; €5.30, including tasting), and **Castellane**, over by the station at 57 rue de Verdun (April–Nov daily 10am–noon & 2–6pm; €5.30, including tasting; *www.castellane.com*). Mercier's glamour relic is a giant barrel that held 200,000 bottles, taken to the Paris Exposition of 1889 with the help of 24 oxen. Visits round the cellars here are by electric train, and climax with a *dégustation* (tasting). The Castellane tour is much less gimmicky than Mercier's or Moët's, and the *dégustation* a lot more generous.

The **tourist office** is a short walk from the train station at 7 av de Champagne (Mon–Sat 9.30am–noon/12.30pm & 1.30–5.30/7pm, Easter–Oct also Sun 11am–4pm; *www.tourisme-champagne-ardenne.com*). **Accommodation** does not generally come cheap in Épernay. Your best bet is the *Foyer des Jeunes Travailleurs*, 2 rue Pupin (☎03.26.51.62.51; ②), a few minutes' walk from the station, or there's a **hostel** 15km away in Verzy, 14 rue du Bassin (☎03.26.97.90.10; ②). As for **hotels**, the *St-Pierre*, 1 rue Jeanne d'Arc (☎03.26.54.40.80; ③), is probably the least pricey, followed by *Le Chapon Fin* at 2 place Mendès-France (☎03.26.55.40.03; *www.chaponfin.fr*; ④), and *Du Progrès*, 6 rue des Berceaux (☎03.26.55.24.75; ④). The **campsite** is just over 1km north in the Parc des Sports, on the south bank of the Marne along allée de Cumières (☎03.26.55.32.14; April–Sept). **Eating** is good and affordable at *La Terrasse*, 7 quai de Marne, across the river from the station, while *Le Messina*, 17 rue Gambetta, serves inexpensive pizzas and pasta. *La Table Kobus* at 3 rue du Dr-Rousseau is excellent but a bit more expensive, with a menu at €30.

Reims

Laid flat by World War I artillery, **REIMS** (pronounced like a nasal "Rance") is not the most inspiring of cities, although there are two good reasons for visiting: it's the best centre (along with Épernay) for the Champagne region, and it's home to one of the country's most impressive Gothic cathedrals, once scene of the coronations of French monarchs. The battered west front of the **Cathédrale** is still a rare delight, with an array of restored and remarkably expressive statuary – although many of the originals have been removed to the former bishops' palace (see below). Inside, the stained glass includes stunning designs by Marc Chagall in the east chapel and glorifications of the champagne making process in the south transept. Next door to the cathedral, the **Palais du Tau** (daily: July & Aug 9.30am–6.30pm; rest of year 9.30/10am–noon/12.30pm & 2 5/6pm; €5.30), in the bishops' palace, is worth a visit to see some of the dislodged west-front figures: there are grinning angels, friendly-looking gargoyles and a superb Eve. The building also preserves the paraphernalia of Charles X's coronation in 1824. Most of the early kings were buried in Reims's oldest building, sited 1km east of the cathedral – the eleventh-century **Basilique St-Rémi** (daily 8/9am–dusk/7pm; closed during services; free). Part of a former Benedictine abbey, it's an immensely spacious building, with side naves wide enough for a bus to drive through, and preserves its Romanesque choir and ambulatory chapels. You can also visit the adjacent monastic buildings, with more displays of stone sculpture and tapestries.

If you're in Reims for the **champagne**, head to place des Droits-de-l'Homme and place St-Niçaise, around which are most of the Reims *maisons*; most charge a small fee for their tours. If you're limiting yourself to one, the **Maison Veuve Clicquot**, 1 place des Droits-de-l'Homme (☎03.26.89.54.41; by appointment only; *www.veuve-clicquot.com*), is one of the least pompous and has the best video. The *caves*, with their horror-movie fungi, are old Gallo-Roman quarries. **Pommery**, at 5 place du Général-Gouraud (April–Oct daily 11am–5.30pm; Nov–March by appointment only; €6; *www.pommery.com*), also has excavated Roman quarries for cellars. At **Taittinger**, 9 place St-Niçaise (March–Nov Mon–Fri 9.30–11.50am & 2–4.30pm, Sat & Sun 9–11am & 2–5pm; rest of year closed Sat & Sun; €5.30; *www.taittinger.com*), there are still more ancient *caves*, plus statues of St Vincent and St Jean, patron saints respectively of *vignerons* and cellar hands.

Reims **train station** is on the northwest edge of the town centre, which focuses on place Drouet d'Erlon. The **tourist office** is beside the cathedral, 2 rue Guillaume de Machault (Mon–Sat 9am–6/8pm, Sun 10am–5/6pm, *www.tourisme.fr/reims*). Among central **hotels**, the *Thillois*, 17 rue de Thillois (☎03.26.40.65.65; ③), and the *Alsace*, 6 rue Général Sarrail (☎03.26.47.44.08; ④), are both affordable, and there's a *Centre International* with **dorm beds** south of the centre at Parc Léo Lagrange (☎03.26.40.52.60, *info@cis-reims.com*; ②), twenty minutes' walk from the station. For **food**, place Drouet d'Erlon is lined with cafés and restaurants: try *A Casa Mia* at no. 84 or the more upmarket *l'Apostrophe* at no. 59. There's **Internet** access at Clique et Croque, 27 rue de Vesle (Mon–Sat 10.30am–12.30am, Sun 2pm–12.30am).

NORMANDY

To the French, the essence of **Normandy** is its produce: this is the land of butter and cream, famous cheeses and seafood, cider and calvados. Yet parts of Normandy are among the most economically depressed of the whole country. The Normans themselves have a reputation for being insular and conservative, with a hatred of Parisians with weekend homes in the region. Normandy's Channel ports, **Dieppe** and **Le Havre**, provide a better introduction to France than their counterparts to the north; the white cliffs are impressive, and there are occasional surprises, notably the Benedictine distillery at **Fécamp** and the Beaux-Arts museum in Le Havre. Further along the coast, you may dock at either **Caen**, which gives good access to the town of **Bayeux** with its famous tapestry, or **Cherbourg**, to the south of which is the much-photographed monastic site of **Mont St-Michel**. Inland, it's hard to pin down specific highlights; the pleasures lie in the feel of particular landscapes – lush meadows and orchards, half-timbered houses, and the food and drink for which the region is famous. Of urban centres, **Rouen**, the Norman capital, is by far the most compelling. For excellent regional information go to *www.normandy-tourism.org*.

Dieppe

Crowded between high cliff headlands, **DIEPPE** is an enjoyably small-scale port, but an industrious one, its docks unloading half the bananas of the West Indies and forty percent of all shellfish destined to slither down French throats. The town was the place where Parisians used to take the sea air before fast cars took them further afield, and its restaurants provide a marvellous introduction to the delights of French cooking.

The liveliest part of town, particularly for its Saturday market, is the pedestrianized **Grande-Rue**, although the obvious place to start exploring is the medieval **castle** overlooking the seafront from the west, home of the **Musée de Dieppe** (June–Sept daily 9am–noon & 2–6pm; rest of year Mon & Wed–Sun 9am–noon & 2–5pm; €2) and two showpiece collections – a group of carved ivories plundered from Africa, and a hundred or so prints by the co-founder of Cubism, **Georges Braque**, who spent summers here and is buried just west of the town at Varangeville-sur-Mer.

The main **train station** is about 800m southwest of the ferry terminal; the **tourist office** is alongside the ferry terminal on Pont Ango (Mon–Sat 9am–noon/1pm & 2–6/8pm, Sun 10am–1pm & 3–6pm; winter closed Sun; *www.mairie-dieppe.fr*), and can supply maps. For a **room**, try *Les Arcades*, 1–3 Arcades de la Bourse, on the curve of the port towards the ferry terminal (☎02.35.84.14.12; ⑤), or *Hôtel Etap*, 6 rue Claude Groulard (☎02.32.14.06.37; ④). The **hostel** (☎02.35.84.85.73, *dieppe@fuaj.org*; ①; March–Oct) is 2km to the south, on rue Louis Fromager, accessible by bus #2 from bd Général-de-Gaulle by the train station. The nearest **campsite**, *Marqueval*, is 3km down the coastal road to Pourville (☎02.35.82.66.46; March–Oct; bus #11). The best area for **food** is along quai Henri IV – try the small and friendly *Écamias* at no. 129 for delicious seafood and good-value menus, or the *Port* at no. 99, one of the best for fresh fish. The *Arcades* hotel also has a good restaurant, while a great choice for some local colour is the popular *Bistrot du Pollet*, 23 rue Tête de Bœuf.

Fécamp

About 25km west of Dieppe, **FÉCAMP** is another serious fishing port, with a seafront promenade and a **Benedictine distillery** in the narrow strip of streets running parallel to the port towards the town centre, at 110 rue Alexandre-le-Grand (tours daily: July & Aug 9.30am–7pm; rest of year 10am–12.15/1pm & 2–6/6.30pm; closed Jan; €4.60 including tasting; *www.benedictine.fr*). Tours of the distillery last 90 minutes and start with a small **muse-

um, set in the Middle Ages beneath a nightmarish mock-Gothic roof with props of manuscripts, locks, testaments, lamps and religious paintings. The boxes of ingredients are a rare treat for the nose and there's further theatricality in the old distillery, where boxes of herbs are thrown with gusto into copper vats and alembics.

The **tourist office** is opposite the distillery at 113 rue Alexandre-Le-Grand (July & Aug daily 10am–6pm; rest of year Mon–Fri 9am–12.15pm & 1.45–6/7pm, Sat 10am–noon & 2–6.30pm; *www.fecamp.com*), with a seafront annexe on Quai du Vicomte open daily during July and August. The **train station** is between the port and the town centre on av Gambetta. If you plan to stay, try *Hôtel de l'Univers*, 5 place St-Étienne (☎02.35.28.05.88; ③), or *Angleterre*, 91–93 rue de la Plage (☎02.35.28.01.60; *www.hotelangleterre.com*; ④), but be warned that Fécamp is popular and can get booked out. There's a superb **campsite**, *Camping de Renneville* (☎02.35.28.20.97), a short walk away on the western cliffs. *Le Martin*, 18 place St-Étienne, behind the post office, does good basic Norman **food**, with menus at all prices.

Le Havre

On the whole, people arriving by ferry at **LE HAVRE** keep right on going. The port, the second largest in France after Marseille, takes up half the Seine estuary, extending far further than the town. **Avenue Foch**, the central street, runs east to west, looking onto the sea between the beach and the yacht harbour. On bd Clemenceau, overlooking the port entrance, is the recently renovated **Musée Malraux** (Mon & Wed–Fri 11am–6pm, Sat & Sun 11am–7pm; €3.80), one of France's best-designed art galleries, with fine collections of nineteenth- and twentieth-century painting, including fifty canvases by Eugène Boudin and works by Corot, Courbet, Monet and Dufy, the last a native of Le Havre who has a room to himself.

The **tourist office** (Mon–Sat 9am–6.30/7pm, Sun 10am–12.30/1pm; June–Sept also Sun 2.30–6pm; *www.lehavretourisme.com*) is on the seafront at 186 bd Clemenceau; bus #1 or #3 makes the 2km journey from the **train station**, which is on cours de la République. For **accommodation**, try *Séjour Fleuri*, 71 rue Émile-Zola (☎02.35.41.33.81; ③), or *Hôtel Suisse*, 3 rue Racine (☎02.35.42.37.05; ③). The **campsite** is in the Forêt de Montgeon (☎02.35.46.52.39), accessible on bus #1 from Hôtel de Ville. For food, try the reasonably priced **restaurant**, *Le Noosi Bé*, 50–52 quai Michel Féré.

Honfleur

HONFLEUR is the best-preserved of the Normandy ports and a near-perfect seaside town. The ancient port still functions and although only pleasure craft now make use of the moorings in the harbour basin, fishing boats tie up alongside the pier close by, and there are usually freshly caught fish for sale either directly from the boats or from stands on the pier. It's all highly picturesque, and not so different from the town that had such appeal to artists in the late nineteenth century.

It's this artistic past – and a present-day concentration of galleries and painters – which dominates Honfleur. The town owes most to Eugène Boudin, forerunner of Impressionism, who was born and worked in the town, trained the 15-year-old Monet, and was joined here for various periods by Pissarro, Renoir and Cézanne. There's a good selection of his work in the **Musée Eugène Boudin**, west of the port on place Erik-Satie (mid-March to Sept Mon & Wed–Sun 10am–noon & 2–6pm; rest of year Mon & Wed–Fri 2.30–5pm, Sat & Sun 10am–noon & 2.30–5pm; closed Jan to mid-Feb; €4.60, or €4 in winter) – quite appealing here in context, particularly the crayon seascapes, along with an impressive set of works by Dufy and Monet.

The **tourist office** is on place Arthur Boudin (July & Aug daily 9.30am–7pm; rest of year Mon–Sat 9.30am–12.30pm & 2–6.30pm, Sun 10am–5pm). Honfleur is on the direct **bus** route between Caen and Le Havre (4 buses daily); the town's nearest **train station** is at Pont-l'Évêque, connected by the Lisieux bus #50 (takes 20min). None of Honfleur's **hotels** are very affordable – the *Cascades*, 17 place Thiers (☎02.31.89.05.83; ④), is the best bet, or there's a **campsite**, *Du Phare*, at the west end of bd Charles V on place Jean de Vienne (☎02.31.89.10.26; April–Sept). The most reasonable **restaurants** and **bars** are on rue Haute, on the way up to the Boudin museum: try *Au P'tit Mareyeur* at no. 4. At the harbour itself, it's hard to beat *Le Vieux Honfleur*, 13 quai St Etienne.

Caen

CAEN, capital of Basse Normandie, is a largely mediocre sprawl due to its devastation during World War II. Its central feature is a ring of ramparts that no longer have a castle to protect, while roads and roundabouts fill the wide spaces where prewar houses once stood. Nonetheless, the favoured residence of William the Conqueror is still impressive. The **château** ramparts are dramatically exposed, having been cleared of their medieval houses by aerial bombardment. Within are two museums. The **Musée des Beaux Arts** (Mon & Wed–Sun 9.30am–6pm; €3) is a maze of halls dominated by sixteenth and seventeenth century Flemish, French and Italian paintings, and also has some engaging works by Monet, Bonnard and Boudin, amongst others. The **Musée de Normandie** (same days 9.30am–12.30pm & 2–6pm; €1.50) celebrates the history of the region, with interesting exhibits including prehistoric finds, the evolution of agriculture and examples of local crafts. Below the ramparts to the south is the fourteenth-century church of **St-Pierre**, its facade reconstructed since the war, which spared the magnificent Renaissance stonework of the apse. To the west and east of the town centre respectively stand two great Romanesque constructions, the **Abbaye aux Hommes** with its church of **St-Étienne**, and the **Abbaye aux Dames** with **La Trinité** church. The first was founded by William the Conqueror to hold his tomb; the other by his wife, Queen Matilda. Hers is the more starkly impressive, with a gloomy pillared crypt, wonderful stained glass behind the altar, and odd sculptural details like the fish curled up in the holy-water stoup.

To the north of the city, at the end of av Maréchal-Montgomery, is the new **Mémorial de Caen**, standing on a plateau beneath which the Germans had their HQ in June and July 1944 (daily 9am–6/8pm; *www.memorial-caen.fr*; €11.60). The museum is split into different sections, dealing with the rise of Nazism in Germany, resistance and collaboration in France, and the major battles of World War II. There's also a film documentary covering all the conflicts since 1945. Bus #17 goes directly to the museum from the Tour le Roi stop in the centre of town.

These days, most of the centre of Caen is taken up with busy new shopping developments and pedestrian precincts, and the **port**, at the end of the long canal which links Caen to the sea, is where most life goes on, at least during the summer. The **tourist office** is located on the central place St-Pierre (July & Aug Mon–Sat 9.30am–7pm, Sun 10am–1pm & 2–5pm; rest of year Mon–Sat 9.30am–1pm & 2–6pm, Sun 10am–1pm; *www.ville-caen.com*); it has an **Internet** access point, and is connected by regular bus with the **train station** and adjacent **bus station** on the south of the river. *L'Escapade*, 20 place de la Gare (Mon–Sat 5am–1am, Sat & Sun 8am–1am) also offers **Internet** access.

Most of the **hotels** are situated around the port, including the *Hôtel de l'Univers* at 12 quai Vendeuvre (☎02.31.85.46.14; ④) or *Rouen*, 8 place de la Gare (☎02.31.34.06.03; ③). Caen's **hostel** is a bit further out, southwest of the train station in the *Foyer Robert-Remé* at 68bis rue E-Restout (☎02.31.52.19.96; ②; June–Sept; bus #5 or #17 to Lycée Fresnel). Near the hostel is the town's **campsite** (☎02.31.73.60.92; May–Oct), down beside the River Orne on route de Louvigny. For **restaurants**, rue de Geôle, running alongside the western ramparts to place St-Pierre, is the most promising location, with some good Vietnamese and Chinese places as well as local. Another area worth trying is around the Abbaye aux Hommes. For a big traditional feast, go to *Le Lucaïn* at 14 rue Porte-au-Berger.

Bayeux

BAYEUX's perfectly preserved medieval ensemble, magnificent cathedral and world-famous tapestry depicting the 1066 invasion of England by William the Conqueror make it one of the high points of Normandy. However, it's only fifteen minutes by train from Caen, and receives an influx of summer tourists that can make its charms pall somewhat.

The **Bayeux Tapestry** is housed in the **Centre Guillaume le Conquérant**, clearly signposted on rue de Nesmond (daily: April–Oct 9am–6/7pm; rest of year 9.30am–12.30pm & 2–6pm; €6.25). Visits begin with a projection of slides on swathes of canvas, before moving on to an almost full-length reproduction of the original, complete with photographic extracts and detailed commentary. Upstairs in the theatre there's a film (in alternate French and English versions) on the general context and craft of the piece, and beyond this the tapestry itself, a 70m strip of linen embroidered over nine centuries ago with coloured wools. It records scenes from the Norman Conquest, as well as incidental details of domestic and daily life, which run along the bottom as a counterpoint. The tapestry was commissioned for the consecration of the nearby **Cathédrale Notre-Dame** in 1077 – and, despite some eighteenth-century vandalism, the Romanesque plan of the church is still intact. The **crypt**, entirely unaltered, is a beauty, its columns graced with frescoes of angels playing trumpets and bagpipes. Also well worth a visit while in Bayeux is the **Memorial Museum to the Battle of Normandy** on bd Fabian Ware (daily: May–Sept 9.30am–6.30pm; rest of year 10am–12.30pm & 2–6pm; €5.20). The numerous original documents, life-size models, equipment and videos dramatically capture the most decisive chapter in the battle to re-establish peace in Europe during the war.

Bayeux's **train station** is on the southern side of town, on bd Sadi Carnot. The **tourist office**, at Pont St Jean (July & Aug daily 9am–7pm, rest of year Mon–Sat 9.30am–noon & 2.30–6pm; *www.bayeux-tourism.com*), might be able to help you find reasonable **accommodation**. Most affordable of the **hotels** are the *Notre-Dame*, 44 rue des Cuisiniers (☎02.31.92.87.24; *hotel-notre-dame@welcome.to*; ④), and *la Gare*, 26 place de la Gare (☎02.31.92.10.70; ②). The *Family Home* at 39 rue du Général de Dais (☎02.31.92.15.22; ②), north of the cathedral, functions as a friendly and decent **hostel**, and serves good food too. The nearest **campsite** is on bd d'Eindhoven, a fifteen-minute walk from the centre (☎02.31.92.08.93). Most of the **restaurants** are on the pedestrianized rue St-Jean – *La Rapière* at no. 53 is the most popular. Failing that, try the *Le Petit Normand*, 35 rue Larcher.

Cherbourg

Situated at the top end of the Cotentin Peninsula, the mucky metropolis of **CHERBOURG** may be your port of arrival, in which case you should head straight for the **train station** on av François-Millet – a ten-minute walk from the ferry terminal behind the inner dock. The town itself is almost devoid of interest. If you're waiting for a boat, the most enjoyable way of killing time is to settle into one of the **restaurants** around quai Caligny. *Les Trois Capitaines*, 16 quai de Caligny and *Le Faitout* at no. 25 rue Tour-Carrée, are excellent. Should you need to **stay** overnight, *Hôtel de la Renaissance*, 4 rue de l'Eglise (☎02.33.43.23.90; ③), has a good selection of rooms and there's a **hostel** (☎02.33.78.15.15; ②) at 55–57 rue de l'Abbaye, 1km from the train station, near the town hall.

Mont St-Michel

One place many visitors to the area hurry to is the island of **Mont St-Michel**, site of a marvellous **Gothic abbey** on the far western edge of Normandy. The abbey church, long known as the Merveille, is visible from all around the bay, and it becomes more awe-inspiring the closer you get: as Maupassant said, it's "the most wonderful Gothic dwelling ever made for God on this earth." The abbey's granite was sculpted to match the exact contours of the hill, and though space was always limited, the building has grown through the centuries in ever more ingenious uses of geometry. To visit, it's a good idea to join an English-speaking **tour** (daily 9.30am–7pm; €6.40); these last for about an hour, and the guides are real experts, pointing out – amongst much other useful information – that the current dour state of the stone walls is a far cry from the way the monastery would have looked in medieval times, brightly painted and festooned with tapestries. The most famous **hotel**, *La Mère Poulard* (☎02.33.60.14.01; ⑥), uses the time-honoured legend of its fluffy omelettes to justify extortionate charges. Higher up the one twisting street is the *Croix Blanche* (☎02.33.60.14.04; ⑧), with excellent rooms and an exceptional **restaurant**. Near the causeway on the mainland is a **campsite** (☎02.33.60.09.33; Feb–Nov).

The nearest **train station** is at **PONTORSON**, 6km south, a forgettable town where you can rent a bike from the station or take an expensive bus to the Mont. There's an **HI hostel** on rue Général-Patton, near the town's cathedral (☎02.33.60.18.65; ①). The best budget **hotel** is *Le Grillon*, 37 rue Couesnon (☎02.33.60.17.80; ③). Otherwise, you could stay at **AVRANCHES**, where there are a number of reasonable **hotels**, including *du Jardin des Plantes* at 10 pl Carnot (☎02.33.58.03.68; *www.le-jardin-des-plantes.fr*; ④) and *Le Croix d'Or*, 83 rue de la Constitution (☎02.33.58.04.88; ⑤). Avranches town centre is an uphill walk from its **train station**, but the views make up for it.

Rouen

ROUEN is another city that was flattened during World War II, although a flood of money was spent on restoring it. The result is an attractive, if in parts fake, medieval centre complete with half-timbered houses, cobbled streets and impressive churches. A prominent point in the centre, between place du Vieux-Marché and the cathedral, is the **Gros Horloge**, a colourful one-handed clock which spans the street named after it. You can climb up the **belfry** and see the surrounding towers and spires arraying themselves in startling density. Just off here is the **Cathédrale de Notre-Dame** (Mon–Sat 9am–6/7pm, Sun 8am–6pm), a Gothic masterpiece built in the twelfth and thirteenth centuries, although various vertical extensions have since been added. The west facade, intricately sculpted like the rest of the exterior, was Monet's subject for his series of celebrated studies of changing light.

The church of **St-Ouen**, in a park a short walk northeast, is larger than the cathedral and has far less decoration, so that the Gothic proportions have a more instant impact. Close by, the church of St-Maclou is more flamboyant, although perhaps the real interest is in its adjacent **Aître St-Maclou**, once a cemetery for plague victims, which still has its original macabre decorations together with a mummified cat. The **Musée des Beaux-Arts** on place Vedrel (Mon & Wed–Sun 10am–6pm; €3), while not enthralling, does include a number of works by the Rouennais Géricault, Boudin, Sisley and Monet. Also worth a visit is the **Musée Flaubert et d'Histoire de la Médicine** in the Hôpital Hôtel-Dieu on the corner of rue de Lecat and rue du Contrat-Social (Tues 10am–6pm, Wed–Sat 10am–noon & 2–6pm; €1.80), dedicated to Rouen's most famous novelist, Gustave Flaubert, whose father was chief surgeon at the medical school here.

The main **train station**, Rouen Rive-Droite, is a ten-minute walk or one metro stop from the centre. The bus station is just off the southern end of the main rue Jeanne d'Arc. The **tourist office** is opposite the cathedral at 25 place de la Cathédrale (May–Sept Mon–Sat 9am–7pm, Sun 9.30am–12.30pm & 2–6pm; rest of year Mon–Sat 8am–6pm, Sun 10am–1pm; *www.mairie-rouen.fr*). Choice of the **hotels** are the *Sphinx*, 130 rue Beauvoisine (☎02.35.71.35.86; ②), the old and beautifully decorated *des Carmes*, 33 pl des Carmes (☎02.35.71.92.31; ⑤), or the centrally located *Le Palais*, 12 rue du Tambour (☎02.35.71.41.40; ③). The town's **campsite** is 5km northwest on rue Jules-Ferry in Déville-lès-Rouen (☎02.35.74.07.59; bus #2 from Théâtre des Arts).

Rouen has a reputation for good **food**, and its most famous dish, duckling (*caneton*), can be enjoyed quite affordably at *Pascaline*, 5 rue de la Poterne. For good basic meals, the south side of place du Vieux-Marché and the north side of St-Maclou church are both lined with good-quality restaurants. Some specific recommendations include the traditional *Au Temps des Cerises* at 4–6 rue des Basnages and *La Walsheim* at 260 rue Martainville, next to St-Maclou, with menus from around €9. Otherwise there's the *des Beaux-Arts*, 34 rue Damiette, which serves mountains of couscous and paella for very affordable prices or the *Jumbo*, 11 rue Guillaume-le-Conquérant, where you can pile up your own whopping salads. You can access the **Internet** at Cybernetics, 59 pl du Vieux-Marché (☎02.35.07.02.77), or Place Net, 37 rue de la République (☎02.32.76.02.22).

Giverny

For a complete shift of mood, the best place to head for near Rouen is **GIVERNY**, where you can visit **Monet's house and gardens**, complete with water-lily pond (April–Oct Tues–Sun 10am–6pm; *www.fondation-monet.com*; €5.30 for house and gardens, or €3.80 for gardens only). Monet lived here from 1883 until his death in 1926 and the gardens that he laid out were considered by many of his friends to be his masterpiece; the best months to visit are May and June, when the rhododendrons flower around the lily pond and the wisteria over the Japanese bridge is in bloom, but it is overwhelmingly beautiful at any time of year. While you do get to see his famous water lilies in real life, there aren't any paintings on show; the house is filled with Monet's collection of Japanese prints. It can get very busy, and the crowds and cameras can induce a feel that seems far removed from Monet's intentions, but really there's no place like it.

Giverny isn't easy to get to from Rouen by **public transport**. Your best bet is a train to **VERNON** and then either rent a bicycle or make the ten-minute ride on the *Gisor* bus from the station (Tues–Fri hourly; Sat 9.25am, 11.25am, 1pm, 3.10pm & 4.10pm; Sun hourly until 12.55pm, then 3.55pm; €4.40 return). **Accommodation** is not much easier, with the *Auberge La Musardiere*, 123 rue Claude Monet in Giverny (☎02.32.21.03.18; ⑤) or a **hostel** in Vernon at 28 av de l'Île-de-France (☎02.32.51.66.48; ②).

BRITTANY

For generations the people of **Brittany** risked their lives fishing and trading on the violent seas or struggling with the arid soil of the interior, and their resilience is tinged with Celtic culture: mystical, musical, sometimes morbid, sometimes vital and inspired. Unified with France in 1532, the Bretons have seen their language steadily eradicated, and the interior severely depopulated. Today, the people still tend to treat France as a separate country, even if few of them actively support Breton nationalism much beyond putting stickers on their cars reading *Breizh* (Breton for "Brittany"). The recent economic resurgence, helped partly by summer tourism, has largely been due to local initiatives; at the same time, a Celtic artistic identity has consciously been revived at festivals of traditional Breton music, poetry and dance.

For most visitors to Brittany, the **coast** is the dominant feature. After the Côte d'Azur, this is the most popular summer resort area in France, and the attractions are obvious – white sand beaches, towering cliffs and offshore islands. Whether you approach across the Channel by ferry, or along the coast from Normandy, the River Rance, guarded by **St-Malo** on its estuary and **Dinan** 20km upstream, makes a spectacular introduction to Brittany. To the **west** stretches a varied coastline culminating in one of the most seductive of the islands, the Île **de Bréhat**; inland, most roads curl eventually to **Rennes**, the Breton capital. Brittany's **southern coast** takes in Europe's most famous prehistoric site, the alignments of **Carnac**, and although the beaches are not as spectacular as Finistère's, the water is warmer. Of the cities, **Vannes** has one of the liveliest medieval town centres. For information on the region visit *www.brittanytourism.com*.

Rennes

Capital and power centre of Brittany, **RENNES**, with its Neoclassical layout and the pompous scale of its buildings, is at first glance uncharacteristic of the province. It was razed in a fire of 1720 and the task of remodelling it was handed out to Parisian architects – not in deference to the capital but to rival it. The city's one central building to survive the great fire was, symbolically enough, the **Palais de Justice**, on place du Parlement de Bretagne, home of the Brittany parliament, which fought battles with the French governor from the reign of Louis XIV up until the Revolution (tours must be booked in advance with the tourist office on ☎02.99.67.11.11; €6). This area is the most appealing in Rennes, with examples of the typical beamed, leaning houses of Brittany, and a lively outdoor café scene.

South of here, at 20 quai Émile-Zola, the interesting **Musée des Beaux-Arts** (Mon & Wed–Sun 10am–noon & 2–6pm; €3) has some early Picassos and a room dedicated to Brittany, with mythical and real-life scenes. The excellent **Musée de Bretagne** is currently being rehoused in what was the bus station on bd Magenta, and is due to reopen in 2003.

The **train station** is linked with the central place de la République by buses #1 and #17. The **tourist office** is at 11 rue St Yves (Mon–Sat 9am–6/7pm, Sun 11am–6pm; www.ville-rennes.fr). **Hotels** are heavily concentrated around the station; the *Riaval*, 9 rue de Riaval (☎02.99.50.65.58; ③), is reliable, as is the sometimes noisy *Le Magenta*, 35 bd Magenta (☎02.99.30.85.37; ③). If you'd prefer to stay in the medieval quarter of town, the attractive *Rocher de Cancale*, 10 rue St-Michel (☎02.99.79.20.83; ④), fits the bill. The **hostel** is 3km out at 10–12 Canal St-Martin (☎02.99.33.22.33; ②), on bus #18 to St-Malo. Bus #3 takes you northeast to Gayeulles, from where it's a short walk to the city's **campsite** (☎02.99.36.91.22). The old town is the liveliest part of Rennes and stays up late, particularly in the vicinity of St-Aubin church. For **food**, anywhere along the lovely rue St-Georges makes for pleasant dining; otherwise, for excellent Bretagne crepes and cider head to *Crêperie St-Anne* at 5 place St-Anne. For something a little more upmarket, try *Léon le Cochon* at 1 rue Maréchal-Joffre. Cybernet On Line offers **Internet** access on rue St-Georges (daily 10.30am–8pm). Rennes is at its best in the first week of July, when the **Festival des Tombées de la Nuit** takes over the city to celebrate Breton culture with music, theatre, film and poetry.

St-Malo

About 50km north of Rennes, **ST-MALO**, walled and built with the same grey granite as Mont St-Michel, presents its best face to the River Rance and the sea. Once within the old ramparts, St-Malo can seem a little grim and squat, and overrun by summer tourists. But away from the thoroughfares of the tiny **citadel**, with its high seventeenth-century houses, random exploration is fun and you can surface to the light on the ramparts or head through them to the nearby beaches. The **town museum**, in the castle to the right as you enter Porte St-Vincent (Tues–Sun 10am–noon & 2–6pm; summer also Mon same times; €4.30), glorifies, on several exhausting floors, St-Malo's sources of wealth and fame – colonialism, slave-trading and privateering among them.

Buses drop you at the main city gate, the **Porte St-Vincent**, while **trains** stop on the other side of the docks, a ten-minute walk away. The **tourist office** is on the corner of Esplanade St-Vincent and av Louis Martin beside the Bassin Duguay-Trouin (July & Aug Mon–Sat 8.30am–8pm, Sun 10am–7pm; rest of year Mon–Sat 9am–12.30pm & 1.30–6/7pm; April–June & Sept also Sun 10am–noon & 2.30–6pm; www.ville-saint-malo.fr). It's always more difficult to find **accommodation** in the old city, despite the extraordinary number of hotels, but rooms at *La Rotonde*, 1 place Châteaubriand (☎02.99.40.47.97; ③), or *Le Louvre*, 2 rue des Marins (☎02.99.40.86.62; ④), are worth trying. Otherwise, there's an array near the station. In the suburb of **Paramé**, 2km northeast of the train station, is an often-crowded hostel at 37 av R.P. Umbricht (☎02.99.40.29.80; ②; bus #2). There's a municipal **campsite**, *Cité d'Aleth*, on allée Gaston Buy (☎02.99.81.60.91), near some shops and the beach. Most of the citadel's **restaurants** are pricey tourist traps, so you're better off at the *crêperies* and *mouleries* such as *Chantal*, 2 place aux Herbes, and *Le Brick*, 5 rue Jacques-Cartier. You can access the **Internet** at Ultima, 75 bd des Talards (☎02.23.18.18.23).

Dinard and Dinan

Across the estuary from St-Malo, reachable by shuttle boat from below the southern wall of the citadel, **DINARD** was transformed last century from a simple fishing village to something along the lines of a Côte d'Azur resort, with a casino, shady villas and a glut of pricey hotels and restaurants. It's not a very welcoming place to stay, but is the start of some pleasant coastal walks. A short distance along the river Rance lies **DINAN**, in contrast one of the most enyoyable towns in Brittany. Its **citadel** has been preserved almost intact within a three-kilometre circuit of walls, inside which lies a warren of beautiful late-medieval houses. It's almost too good to be true and time is easily spent rambling from crêperie to café, admiring the houses on the way. Unfortunately, there's only one small stretch of the **ramparts** that you can walk along – from the gardens behind St-Sauveur to just short of the Tour Sillon – but you get a good general overview from the **Tour de l'Horloge** (daily: June–Sept 10am–6.30pm; April & May 2–6pm; €2.50). Another good view can be had from the **Château Duchesse Anne** (June–Sept daily 10am–5.45pm; March–May, Oct & Nov Mon & Wed–Sun 10am–noon & 2–6.45pm; rest of year Mon & Wed–Sun 1.30–6pm; €3.80). An inevitable target of any Dinan wanderings is the church of St-Sauveur, a real mix-up of periods, with a Romanesque porch and eighteenth-century steeple. Even its nine Gothic chapels have numerous and asymmetrical vaulting; the most complex pair, in the centre, are wonderful.

Dinan's **train station** is a ten-minute walk away from place Duclos. The **tourist office** (summer daily 9am–7.30pm; winter Mon–Sat 9am–12.30pm & 2–6.15pm; *www.dinan-tourisme.com*) is opposite the Tour de l'Horloge. The less pricey **hotels** are near the station: *De l'Océan*, 9 pl du 11 Novembre (☎02.96.39.21.51; ③), is as good as any. Within the walls there's *La Duchesse Anne* at 10 place Duguesclin (☎02.96.39.09.43; ④). Dinan's **hostel** (☎02.96.39.10.83, *dinan@fuaj.org*; ②) is attractively set in the Moulin de Méen near the port at Taden, about 3km away, while the closest **campsite** is at 103 rue Châteaubriand (☎02.96.39.11.96; late May to Sept), a street running parallel to the western ramparts. Among a wide choice of **eating places**, one of the best bets is *Crêperie Pizzéria d'Armor*, 15 place des Cordeliers. For **Internet** access, try @rospace on rue de la Chaux (Tues–Sat 10am–7pm).

Roscoff

The opening of the deep-water port at **ROSCOFF** in 1973 was part of a general attempt by the government to revitalize the Breton economy. The ferries to Plymouth and Cork are intended not just to bring tourists, but also to revive the traditional trading links that used to exist between the Celtic nations of Brittany, southwest England and Ireland. Roscoff itself has, however, remained a small resort with almost all activity confined to rue Gambetta and the old port. Until the last couple of centuries, the town – like many other ports along the Breton coast – made most of its money from piracy, and a few reminders of its past wealth remain in the ornate stone houses and the **church**, with its sculpted ships and protruding stone cannons, all dating from the sixteenth century.

To reach the town from the **ferry terminal**, follow the signs across the narrow promontory and down into the harbour. The **tourist office** is at 46 rue Gambetta (July & Aug Mon–Sat 9am–12.30pm & 1.30–7pm, Sun 10am–12.30pm; rest of year Mon–Sat 9am–noon & 2–6pm; *www.sb-roscoff.fr/Roscoff)*. Later than 9pm it may be difficult to find a **restaurant** still serving, but **hotels** are used to clients arriving on late sailings. The two most reasonable are both on rue Amiral-Réveillère: *Des Arcades* at no. 15 (☎02.98.69.70.45, *www.acdev.com*; ④), which has an unusually trendy bar and good food; and the quieter, more expensive *Les*

Chardons Bleus at no. 4 (☎02.98.69.72.03; ④). Access the **Internet** at System D Plus, 5 rue Gambetta (Tues–Fri 1.30–6pm, Sat 1.30–7pm).

Quimper and around

QUIMPER, capital of the ancient diocese and kingdom of Cornouaille, is the oldest Breton city, founded according to legend by the original bishop of the town, St Corentin, who came here across the channel to the place they named Little Britain some time between the fourth and seventh centuries. It's a laidback place, with old granite buildings, two rivers and the rising woods of Mont Frugy overlooking the centre of town.

The town focuses on the enormous Gothic **Cathédrale St-Corentin**. The **Musée des Beaux-Arts** is next to the Hôtel de Ville, 40 place St-Corentin (July & Aug daily 10am–7pm; rest of year Mon & Wed–Sat 10am–noon & 2–6pm, Sun 2–6pm; €3.80), and has an amazing collection of drawings by Cocteau, Max Jacob and Gustave Doré (shown in rotation) and nineteenth- and twentieth-century paintings of the famed Pont-Aven school. If you're interested in seeing pottery made on an industrial scale, and an exhibition of the changing styles since the first Quimper *ateliers* of the late seventeenth century, head for rue Jean-Baptiste Bosquet, where you'll find the worthwhile **Faïenceries de Quimper** (guided visits only Mon–Fri: March–Sept 9–11.15am & 1.30–4.15/4.45pm; rest of year 11am or 3.45pm; €3) and the **Musée de la Faïence** (April–Oct Mon–Sat 10am–6pm; €4).

A short walk west along the river brings you from the adjacent **train** and **bus stations** to the centre of town. The **tourist office** is on the south bank of the River Odet at 7 rue de la Déesse, place de la Résistance (July & Aug Mon–Sat 9am–7pm, Sun 10am–1pm & 3–6pm; rest of year Mon–Sat 9am–noon/12.30pm & 1.30–6pm, Sun 10am–1pm & 3–6pm; winter closed Sun; May & June closed Sun afternoon; *www.bretagne-4villes.com*). Budget **hotels** include the *Pascal*, near the station at 17 av de la Gare (☎02.98.90.00.81; ④), and the pleasant *de l'Ouest*, at 63 rue le Déan (☎02.98.90.28.35; ③). The **hostel** (☎02.98.64.97.97; ②) and **campsite** (☎02.98.55.61.09) are downstream on av des Oiseaux in the Bois du Séminaire – take bus #1 from place de la Résistance. In the week preceding the last Sunday in July there's the **Festival de Cornouaille**, a jamboree of Breton music, costume and dance; the town is packed, and every room booked.

Boats down the Odet to the coast leave from the end of quai de l'Odet, opposite the Faïenceries, a winding journey to the upmarket resort of **BÉNODET**, where there's a long sheltered beach; for times and prices call ☎02.98.57.00.58. **Hotels** are comparatively expensive, but you could try *Le Minaret* overlooking the beach on corniche de l'Estuaire (☎02.98.57.03.13; ⑥) or the *Bains de Mer*, 11 rue du Kerguéleu (☎02.98.57.03.41; ⑥), and there are several large **campsites**. There are more **beaches** along the coast between Penmarch and Loctudy and beyond, about an hour by bus from Quimper. Another possibility is a trip to the **Pointe du Raz**, the Land's End of France, a series of plummeting fissures, filling and draining with deafening force, above which you can walk on precarious paths.

Carnac and around

About 10km along the coast from the functional port of Lorient, **CARNAC** is home to one of the most important prehistoric sites in Europe, a congregation of some two thousand or so **menhirs** stretching for more than 4km to the north of the village, long predating the Pyramids or Stonehenge. The stones may have been part of an observatory for the motions of the moon, but no one really knows. Though many have been pillaged as ready-quarried stone, the megaliths remain an amazing site. The main alignments, fenced from the public, are viewed from a raised platform at one end of the plain. You can get plenty of information at the **Musée de la Préhistoire**, 10 place de la Chapelle, near rue du Tumulus in Carnac-Ville (June–Sept Mon–Fri 10am–6.30pm, Sat & Sun 10am–noon & 2–6.30pm; rest of year

Mon & Wed–Sun 10am–noon & 2–5pm; *www.museedecarnac.com*; €4.60), which entertainingly traces the area's history from about 450,000 years ago.

Carnac, divided between the original **Carnac-Ville** and the newer seaside resort of **Carnac-Plage**, is extremely popular. **Buses** to Quiberon and Vannes depart regularly from the main **tourist office** at 74 av des Druides in Carnac-Plage (July & Aug Mon–Sat 9am–7pm, Sun 3–7pm; rest of year Mon–Sat 9am–noon & 2–6pm; *www.ot-carnac.fr*). The office has an annexe on place de l'Eglise (April–Oct). Among the town's innumerable **hotels**, the *Ratelier*, 4 chemin du Douet (☎02.97.52.05.04; ④), is a good deal, and the *Chez Nous*, 5 pl de la Chapelle (☎02.97.52.07.28; ④), is central and convenient. The best of Carnac's many **beaches** is the smallest, the **Men Dû**, just off the road towards La Trinité. If you're set on **camping** by the sea, you should go to the *Men Dû* (☎02.97.52.04.23; *www.camping-du-mendu.com*); otherwise, the best site is *La Grande Métairie* (☎02.97.52.24.01), opposite the stones, which organizes horse-riding and rents out bicycles.

Quiberon

South of Carnac, the **Presqu'île de Quiberon** is well worth visiting on its own merits. The town of **QUIBERON** itself is a lively port, and provides a jumping-off point for boats out to the nearby islands or simply a base for the peninsula. The ocean-facing shore, known as the **Côte Sauvage**, is a wild and unswimmable stretch, but the sheltered eastern side has safe and calm sandy beaches, and offers plenty of **campsites**. In Quiberon, **Port Maria**, the fishing harbour, is the most active part of town and has the best concentration of **hotels**, though they're often full in high season – try *Le Neptune* at 4 quai de Houat (☎02.97.50.09.62; ④), or *Au Bon Accueil*, 6 quai de Houat (☎02.97.50.07.92; ③), which also has a very good fish restaurant. The **hostel**, *Les Filets Bleus*, 45 rue du Roch-Priol (☎02.97.50.15.54; ②; May–Oct), is set back from the sea about 1km southeast of the **train station**. A vast array of fish **restaurants** line the seafront, and **cafés** by the long bathing beach are also enjoyable. The **tourist office** is at 14 rue de Verdun (Mon–Sat 9am–12.30pm & 2–6pm; Sun 9am–12.30pm & 3–6pm; *www.quiberon.com*).

Vannes and the Golfe de Morbihan

VANNES is one of the most historic towns in Brittany, and it was here that the Breton assembly ratified the Act of Union with France in 1532. Its old centre is a chaotic web of streets crammed around the cathedral and enclosed by ramparts and gardens. The **Cathedral** itself is not the finest edifice in the town, but it does have one exquisite treasure, an early medieval wedding chest with beautifully painted figures (cathedral closed for renovation at time of writing). Close by, between rue des Halles and the cathedral square, the building where the Act of Union was ratified, **La Cohue**, is now the **Musée de Vannes** (July & Aug daily 10am–noon & 2–6pm; rest of year Mon & Wed–Sat 10am–noon & 2–6pm, Sun 2–6pm; €4), with what was the local Beaux-Arts museum on its top floor, and a gallery downstairs for temporary exhibitions.

Vannes' harbour is a channelled inlet of the ragged-edged **Golfe de Morbihan**, which lets in the tides through a narrow gap. By popular tradition, the **islands** scattered around this enclosure used to number the days of the year, though for centuries the waters have been rising and there are now fewer than one for each week. Of these, thirty are privately owned, while two – the Île aux Moines and Île d'Arz – have regular populations and ferry services, and end up being crowded in summer. You can take a **boat tour** around the rest, a compelling trip through a baffling muddle of channels, megalithic ruins, stone circles and solitary menhirs on small hillocks. Boat companies that organize tours include Navix (☎02.97.46.60.00) and Isle (☎02.97.46.18.19).

It's twenty minutes' walk south from the **train station** to the centre at place de la République. The **tourist office** is at 1 rue Thiers (July & Aug Mon–Sat 9am–6pm, Sun

9.30am–1pm & 2–6pm; rest of year Mon–Sat 9.30am–12.30pm & 2–6pm; *www.pays-de-vannes.com/tourisme*). Vannes has the best choice of **hotels** anywhere around the Golfe de Morbihan: two good ones are *Le Bretagne*, 36 rue du Mené, in the old town (☎02.97.47.20.21; ③), and *Le Marina* overlooking the port at 4 place Gambetta (☎02.97.47.22.81; ④). For **food**, the *Villa Romana*, 16 rue des Vierges, serves great pizzas, pasta and fresh fish.

Nantes

Though **NANTES**, the former capital, is these days not officially a part of Brittany, it remains to its inhabitants an integral part of the province. Crucial to its self-image is the **Château des Ducs**, subjected to a certain amount of damage over the centuries, but still preserving the form in which it was built by two of the last rulers of independent Brittany, François II and his daughter Duchess Anne, who was born here in 1477. The most significant act in the castle's history was the signing of the Edict of Nantes by Henri IV in 1598, which ended the Wars of Religion and granted Protestantism a certain degree of tolerance. You can walk into the courtyard and up onto the low ramparts for free, and visit temporary exhibitions in the Harnachement building, but the rest of the castle is undergoing a huge renovation in order to become the Museum of the History of Nantes and its Region, projected to open completely by 2008, although parts may open before that. In 1800 the castle's arsenal exploded, shattering the stained glass of the **Cathédrale de St-Pierre et St-Paul**, 200m away, just one of many disasters that have befallen the church. Newly restored, its soaring heights are home to the tomb of François II and his wife, Margaret. Back past the château, the so-called **Île Feydeau**, once an island, was the birthplace of **Jules Verne** and has a museum dedicated to him at 3 rue de l'Hermitage (Mon & Wed–Sat 10am–noon & 2–5pm, Sun 2–5pm; €3).

The **train station** is on the south side of the centre, a short way east of the castle. For **accommodation**, try the *Cœur du Loire*, 3 rue Anatole-le-Braz (☎02.40.74.35.61; ③), *Hôtel de l'Océan*, 11 rue du Maréchal-de-Lattre-de-Tassigny (☎02.40.69.73.51; ③), or *Fourcroy*, 11 rue Fourcroy (☎02.40.44.68.00; ③). The city's **hostel** is at 2 place de la Manu, and is reached by tram #1 to Beaujoire (☎02.40.29.29.20; ②). The **tourist office** is on place du Commerce (Mon–Sat 10am–7pm; *www.nantes-tourisme.com*) in an appealing, largely pedestrian area that is a good source of diverse **restaurants**. You can access the Internet at Virus.com, 22 rue Bellamé (☎02.40.35.53.51) or Planet Web, 4 rue de Héronnière (☎02.40.71.73.26).

THE LOIRE

Intimidated by the sheer density of **châteaux**, people tend to make bad use of their time spent in the **Loire**, which is a pity, for if you pick your castles selectively, this can be one of the most enjoyable of all French regions. The most salient features of the Loire itself are whirlpools, vicious currents and a propensity to flood. No one swims in or boats on the Loire, nor are any goods carried along it – it's just there, the longest river in France. The stretch above Saumur is the loveliest on the lower reaches, the land to the south planted with vines and sunflowers. Other than the châteaux, the best of which are those at **Chenonceaux**, **Azay-le-Rideau** and **Loches**, the region has few sights; of the towns, **Tours** is good for museums, while **Saumur** is perfect for indolence, but not hot on entertainment. For regional information, visit *www.loirevalley.org*.

Saumur and around

SAUMUR is a peaceful and pretty town, and a good place to base yourself for a while, with Angers and Chinon within easy reach and the vineyards of St-Hilaire-St-Florent, which produce Saumur's famous sparkling wines, just 4km south on the road to Angers. There is a **château** (July & Aug daily 9.30am–6pm, Wed & Sat also 8.30–10.30pm; June & Sept daily

9am–6pm; rest of year Mon & Wed–Sun 9.30am–noon & 2–5.30pm; €5.80), where you can visit dungeons and a watchtower, and be guided around two museums within its walls – the **Musée des Arts Décoratifs**, with its huge collection of European china, and the **Musée du Cheval**, with bridles, saddles and stirrups.

Arriving at the **train station** leaves you on the north bank of the river; from here cross over the bridge to the island, then over another bridge to the main part of the town on the south bank. Saumur's main street, rue d'Orléans, cuts back through the south-bank sector; the **tourist office** is unmissable at the foot of the second bridge, on place de la Bilange (summer Mon–Sat 9.15am–7pm, Sun 10.30am–7.30pm; winter Mon–Sat 9.15am–12.30pm & 2–6pm, Sun 10am–noon; *www.saumur-tourisme.com*). The best **hotel** is *Le Cristal*, 10 place de la République (☎02.41.51.09.54; ④), with river views from most rooms and very friendly proprietors; other options include the *de Bretagne*, 55 rue St-Nicolas (☎02.41.51.26.38; ③), and the *Central*, 23 rue Daillé (☎02.41.51.05.78; ⑤). On the Île d'Offard, connected by bridges to both banks of the town, there's a good **hostel** at the eastern end of rue de Verden (☎02.41.40.30.00; ②), offering bike rental, and a **campsite** next door. The best area for **eating** is around place St-Pierre: *Auberge St-Pierre*, at no. 6, has a fairly cheap menu, or try *Les Forges de St-Pierre*. The *Le Cristal* hotel offers **Internet** access with a phonecard (daily 7.30am–midnight).

Fontévraud

The **Abbaye de Fontévraud** (daily: June–Sept 9am–7pm; rest of year 9.30am–12.30pm & 2–6pm; €4.90), 13km southeast of Saumur on bus #16, was founded in 1099 as both a nunnery and a monastery with an abbess in charge – a radical move, even if the post was filled solely by queens and princesses. The premises had to be immense to house and separate not only nuns and monks but also the sick, lepers and repentant prostitutes. A prison from the Revolution until 1963, its most famous inmate was the writer Jean Genet, but its chief significance is as the burial ground of the Plantagenet kings. Four tombstone effigies remain, of Henry II, Eleanor of Aquitaine, Richard the Lionheart and Isabelle of Angoulême (King John's wife).

Chinon and around

The first of the big Loire **châteaux** is at **CHINON** (daily: July & Aug 9am–7pm; April–June, Sept & Oct 9.30am–6pm; Nov–March 9.30am–noon & 2–5pm; €4.40). This was one of the few places in which Charles VII could stay while Henry V of England held Paris and the title to the French throne. Charles' situation changed with the arrival here in 1429 of Joan of Arc, who persuaded him to give her an army. All that remains of the scene of this encounter, the Grande Salle, is a wall and first-floor fireplace. More interesting is the **Tour Coudray**, to the west, covered with intricate thirteenth-century graffiti carved by imprisoned and doomed Templar knights. Below the castle, the town is a tacky and rather sterile place, with very few **hotels** and everything closed up long before midnight. If you're looking for a room, the two least expensive alternatives are the *Point du Jour*, 102 quai Jeanne-d'Arc (☎02.47.93.07.20; ③), and the *Jeanne d'Arc*, 11 rue Voltaire (☎02.47.93.02.85; ③). The **campsite** (☎02.47.93.08.35) is across the river at Île-Auger. The **tourist office** is on place Hofheim (summer daily 9am–7pm; winter Mon–Sat 10am–noon & 2–6pm; *www.chinon.com*). The most reasonable **restaurant** is *Les Années 30* at 78 rue Voltaire. For **Internet** access, go to L'Astrol@b, 28 rue Ravelais (Tues–Sat 9.30am–12.30pm & 2pm–7pm).

Azay-le-Rideau

A few kilometres upstream from Chinon, **AZAY-LE-RIDEAU** is worth visiting for its serene setting and its **château** (daily: April–Oct 9.30am–6/7pm; Nov–March 9.30am–12.30pm & 2–5.30pm; €5.30), which is one of the Loire's loveliest, at least from the outside. Its interior, furnished in Renaissance style, doesn't add much to the experience, but the **portrait gallery** has the whole sixteenth-century royal Loire crew – François I, Catherine de Médici et al – and includes a fine semi-nude painting of Gabrielle d'Estrées, Henri IV's lover. There is a large **campsite**, *Le Sabot* (☎02.47.45.42.72) a little way upstream from the château, although **hotels** don't come cheap: one possibility if you're stuck is *Le Balzac*, 4–6 rue A-Richer (☎02.47.45.42.08; ⑤).

Tours and around

A little way upriver, **TOURS**, set on the Loire and a good base for seeing châteaux and enjoying the surrounding vineyards, has a delightful old town and a handful of decent museums. The town's main street is rue Nationale, a short walk down which is the **Musée du Compagnonnage** (daily 9am–noon/12.30pm & 2–6pm; Oct–May closed Tues; €3.80), which documents the origins and militant activity of the guilds that built the châteaux. Next door is the **Musée des Vins** (Mon & Wed–Sun 9am–noon & 2–6pm; €2.40), which provides a pretty comprehensive examination of the history, mythology and production of the wondrous liquid. More interesting perhaps is a trip to the surrounding vineyards; the tourist office organizes tours to cellars such as those at Vouvray, including tasting (April–Oct daily; ☎02.47.70.37.37). Over beside the **Cathédrale St-Gatien**, with its crumbling, Gothic frontage, the city's third museum, the **Musée des Beaux-Arts** on place François Sicard (Mon & Wed–Sun 9am–12.45pm & 2–6pm; €4.60), has some beauties in its rambling collection – *Christ in the Garden of Olives* and the *Resurrection* by Mantegna, and Frans Hals' portrait of Descartes. The museum's top treasure, however, Rembrandt's *Flight into Egypt*, is difficult to see through the security glass. In the opposite direction, west of rue Nationale, Tours' **Old Town** crowds around place St-Pierre-le-Puellier, whose medieval half-timbered houses and bulging stairway towers are the city's showpieces.

The **tourist office** is in front of the train station at 78–82 rue Bernard-Palissy (summer Mon–Sat 8.30am–7pm, Sun 10am–12.30pm & 2.30–5pm; winter Mon–Sat 9am–12.30pm & 1.30–6pm, Sun 10am–1pm; *www.ligeris.com*). Finding **accommodation** isn't a problem. The official **hostel** is on av d'Arsonval in Parc de Gramont (☎02.47.25.14.45; ②; bus #3 to Auberge de Jeunesse); a better choice is the **hostel** for under-25s, *Le Foyer*, 16 rue Bernard-Palissy (☎02.47.60.51.51; ②) – call first as they may be full. The nearest **campsite**, *Les Acacias* (☎02.47.44.08.16), is on the south bank of the Loire east of town. As for **hotels**, the *St-Éloi* is one of the cheapest options, at 79 bd Béranger (☎02.47.37.67.34; ③), as is *Mon Hôtel*, near the cathedral at 40 rue de la Préfecture (☎02.47.05.67.53; ③). The *Central Hôtel*, 21 rue Berthelot (☎02.47.05.46.44; ⑤), has good rooms in an excellent location close to the old town. Rue du Grand-Marché and rue de la Rôtisserie, on the periphery of old Tours, and rue Colbert – which runs down to the cathedral – are the most promising streets for **restaurants**. Try *Le Petit Patrimoine* at 58 rue Colbert for good French food. *Comme Autre Fouée* at 11 rue de la Monnaie serves good-value local specialities. *Les Trois Rois* and *Le Vieux Mûrier* in place Plumereaux stand out for late-night **drinking** and, for **dancing**, check out *Les Trois Orfèvres*, 6 rue des Orfèvres. Multimedia Point, in the station, offers **Internet** access (Mon 2–7.15pm, Tues–Fri 9am–1pm & 2–7.15pm, Sat 10.30am–1pm & 2–7pm).

Villandry, Chenonceaux and Loches

The most popular attraction close to Tours is the **château** of **VILLANDRY**, about 13km west, where there are some extraordinary Renaissance **gardens** set out on several terraces that give marvellous views over the river (château daily 9am–5/6.30pm; gardens daily 9am–5.30/7.30pm; €7 for both, €4.60 gardens only). The château holds Spanish paintings and a Moorish ceiling from Toledo. There's no public transport, but if you rent a bike it's a wonderful ride along the banks of the Cher.

Perhaps the finest of all the castles of the region is the river-straddling **château** at **CHENONCEAUX** (daily 9am–5/6.30pm; €7.60), about 15km away and accessible by train from Tours or Blois. The building went up in the 1520s and was the home of Diane de

Poitiers, the lover of Henry II. You're allowed to roam around the place and there is lots to see – floors of tapestries, paintings and furniture, not least Zurbarán's penetrating depiction of Archimedes in the Salle François I.

The **château** at **LOCHES**, an hour by train southeast of Tours, is visually the most impressive of the Loire fortresses, with ramparts and a huddle of houses below still partly enclosed by the outer wall of the medieval town (daily: July & Aug 9am–7pm; March–June & Sept 9.30am–6pm; rest of year 9.30am–noon & 2–5pm; €3.70). You can climb unescorted to the top of the keep, poke around in the dungeons and torture chamber and visit the royal lodgings in the northern end of the castle, where Charles VII and his three successors had their residence.

Blois and Chambord

The **château** at **BLOIS**, 40km or so upriver from Tours (March–Sept daily 9am–6.30/8pm; rest of year 9am–12.30pm & 2–5.30pm; €5.30), was another residence of Catherine de Médici, and she died here in 1589. All six French kings of the sixteenth century spent time at Blois; Henri III murdered the Duc de Guise and his brother here, shortly before being knocked off himself by a monk. The building is a strange mixture of architectural styles: the oldest parts date from the thirteenth century, and are viewable in the Salle des États or the main hall; Louis XII built the later east wing in flamboyant Gothic style, while the early sixteenth-century north wing shows the influence of the Italian Renaissance.

Blois is a modern, uninteresting town, the château girdled by a busy road. However, if you have to stay, the **tourist office** at 3 av Jean-Laigret (May–Sept Mon–Sat 9am–7pm, Sun 10am–7pm; rest of year Mon–Sat 9am–12.30pm & 2–6pm, Sun 9.30am–12.30pm; *www.loiredeschateaux.com*) organizes private rooms for a small fee, and there are a few inexpensive **hotels**, including the *St-Jacques*, 7 rue Ducoux (☎02.54.78.04.15; ③), and the *Hôtel du Bellay*, 12 rue des Minimes (☎02.54.78.23.62; ③). The closest **campsite** is 2km away across the river, on the Lac de Loire at Vineuil (☎02.54.78.82.05; April–Sept). There is a **hostel** 3km downstream at Les Grouets, 18 rue de l'Hôtel-Pasquier (☎02.54.78.27.21; ②; March–Nov); take bus #4 from the train station to Auberge de Jeunesse. Best bets for **food** are the many restaurants on rue Foulérie, rue St-Lubin and rue des Violettes.

A few kilometres southeast of Blois, the **château** at **CHAMBORD** (daily 9am–5.15/6.45pm; €6.10), François I's little "hunting lodge", was one of the most extravagant commissions of the age – its patron's principal object was to outdo the Holy Roman Emperor Charles V, and it would, he claimed, leave him renowned as "one of the greatest builders in the universe". It was begun in 1519 and the work was executed by French masons, so the overall result is essentially French Medieval, something particularly evident in the massive round towers with their conical tops and the forest of chimneys and turrets. The details, however, are pure Italian: for example the double spiral Great Staircase (attributed by some to Leonardo), panels of coloured marble, niches decorated with shell-like domes, and freestanding columns. Irregular **buses** run daily from Blois, and from May to September there's a special train service from Blois; otherwise, you'll have to use the expensive château tour buses from Blois or Tours (Touraine Evasion ☎06.07.39.13.31; Cars Millet ☎02.47.58.32.06).

Orléans

Directly below the turned-up nose of Paris, poor **ORLÉANS** feels compelled to recuperate its faded glory from 1429, when Joan of Arc delivered the city from the English. There is, however, enough to merit a stop. The **Cathédrale Ste-Croix** (daily 9am–noon & 2–4/6pm; free), battered for five and a half centuries, is wonderful. In the north transept, Joan's pedestal is supported by two golden leopards (representing the English) on an altar carved with the battle scene. The late nineteenth-century stained-glass windows in the nave tell the story of

Joan's life, with caricatures of the loutish Anglo-Saxons and snooty French nobles. There's more on Joan of Arc in the **Maison de Jeanne d'Arc** on place Général-de-Gaulle (May–Oct Tues–Sun 10am–noon & 2–6pm; Nov–April Tues–Sun 2–6pm; €3); it's fun for children, with good models and displays of the breaking of the Orléans siege. If you've had your fill of Joan, the best escape is the modern art collection in the basement of the **Musée des Beaux-Arts**, opposite the Hôtel de Ville (Tues & Sun 11am–6pm, Wed 10am–8pm, Thurs–Sat 10am–6pm; €3), with works by Picasso, Miró, Dufy, Renoir and Monet.

The **train station** and **tourist office** (Mon 10am–1pm & 2–7pm; Tues–Sun 9am–noon & 2–7pm; *www.ville-orleans.fr*) are beside each other on place Albert I, north of the town centre, connected by rue de la République to the central place du Martroi. There are cheap **hotels** near the station, including the pleasant *Hôtel de Paris*, 29 rue Faubourg-Bannier (☎02.38.53.39.58; ④), and in the centre, you could try the *Charles Sanglier*, 8 rue Charles Sanglier (☎02.38.53.38.50; ⑤). The **hostel** is at 14 rue Faubourg-Madeleine to the west of town, accessible on bus #4 from the train station (☎02.38.62.45.75; ①; closed Dec & Jan). Bus #6 goes to the nearest **campsite** at St-Jean-de-la-Ruelle, 2km out on the Blois road, rue de la Roche (☎02.38.88.39.39). Rue de Bourgogne, parallel to the river, has a good choice of **restaurants** of which *Le Dakar*, serving African food, is one of the best. For decent French cuisine head for *La Chancellerie*, 27 place Martroi.

Bourges

The capital of the *département* of Berry, **BOURGES**, about 50km south of Orléans, has strong medieval links and is an obvious stop-off if you're heading towards the Massif Central. There's not much to the town, but it's a pleasant enough place to spend the day, not least for its **Cathédrale St-Étienne** (daily 8am–6.30/7.30pm), which is one of the country's most distinctive cathedrals, with five great portals opening out of its west front, adorned by thirteenth-century sculpture. Beloved of Gothic purists, the interior is impressive too: light, large and airy, double-aisled with no transepts, setting off to best effect the marvellous stained glass in the choir and apsidal chapels – the finest in France after Chartres.

Old Bourges lies within a loop of roads northwest of the cathedral. On rue Jacques-Cœur stand the head office, the stock exchange, dealing rooms, safes and the home of Charles VII's finance minister, **Jacques Cœur**, a medieval shipping magnate, moneylender and arms dealer who dominates Bourges much as Joan of Arc does Orléans. The visit to his **palace** (tours daily 9am–noon & 2–6pm; €4.90) is fun and worthwhile, starting with the fake windows from which realistic sculpted figures look down. Though few furnishings remain, the decorations on the stonework, including numerous hearts and scallop shells (*cœurs* and *coquilles St-Jacques*), show the mark of the man who had it built.

The **train station** is 1km north of the centre on pl du G.Leclerc, just off av Pierre Sémard, across the river. The **tourist office** (April–Sept Mon–Sat 9am–7/7.30pm, Sun 10am–7/7.30pm; rest of year Mon–Sat 9am–6pm, Sun 2–5pm; *www.ville-bourges.fr*) is close to the cathedral, at 21 rue Victor-Hugo. There is a **hostel** a short walk out of town at 22 rue Henri-Sellier (☎02.48.24.58.09, *bourges@fuaj.org*; ②), and a **campsite** (☎02.48.20.16.85) across the stream from the hostel on bd de l'Industrie. Closer to the city centre and the train station is the *Centre International de Séjour*, 17 rue Felix-Chédin (☎02.48.70.25.59; ②). Bourges's least expensive **hotel** is *Au Rendez-vous des Amis*, 6 av Marx-Dormoy (☎02.48.70.81.80; ③), a short walk from the station up av P-Sémard and right, while in the middle of town there's *Le Central*, 6 rue du Docteur-Témoin (☎02.48.24.10.25; ③). The main centre for **restaurants** is place Gordaine, an attractive medieval square where *Le Comptoir de Paris* makes a reasonable option; the *Arôme de Vieux Bourges* is a coffee shop selling all manner of edible delicacies that make for a good lunch.

POITOU-CHARENTE AND
THE ATLANTIC COAST

The summer light, the warmth, the fields of sunflowers and the siesta-silent air of the farm-houses of **Poitou-Charente** give the first exciting promise of the south. The coast has great charm in places – it remains distinctly Atlantic, with dunes, pine forests and misty mud flats, certainly lacking much of the glitz and glamour of the Côte d'Azur. The principal port, **La Rochelle**, is one of the prettiest and most distinctive towns in France, and the islands of **Ré** and **Oléron**, out of season at least, are lovely, with kilometres of sandy beaches. **Poitiers** is a likely entry point to the region, a pleasant enough town with an attractive old centre. South of here, the valley of the Charente river, slow and green, epitomizes blue-overalled, peasant France, accessible on boat trips from **Cognac**, itself famous for the eponymous brandy. For regional information go to *www.cr-poitou-charentes.fr*.

Poitiers

POITIERS is no seething metropolis, but a country town with a certain charm that comes from a long and sometimes influential history as seat of the dukes of Aquitaine, discernible in the winding lines of the streets and the breadth of architectural fashions of its buildings.

The tree-lined **place Leclerc**, and **place de Gaulle** just a few streets north, are the two poles of communal life, flanked by cafés and bustling market stalls. Between is a web of streets, with rue Gambetta cutting north past the **Palais de Justice** (June–Sept daily 9am–6pm; rest of year Mon–Fri 9am–6pm; free), whose nineteenth-century facade hides the twelfth-century great hall of the dukes of Aquitaine. This magnificent room is where Jean, Duc de Berry, held his sumptuous court in the late fourteenth century, seated on the intricately carved dais at the far end of the room. In one corner, stairs give access to the **Maubergeon Tower**, the old castle keep. The stairs lead out onto the roof with a memorable view over the town.

Across from the Palais is one of the most idiosyncratic churches in France, **Notre-Dame-la-Grande** (daily 8am–7pm), whose west front is loaded with enthralling sculpture, typical of the Poitou brand of Romanesque. The interior, crudely overlaid with nineteenth-century frescoes, is not nearly as interesting. There is another unusual church a little way east, literally in the middle of rue Jean-Jaurès as you head towards the River Clain. This is the mid-fourth-century **Baptistère St-Jean** (July & Aug daily 10am–12.30pm & 2.30–6pm; April–June & Sept–Oct Mon & Wed–Sun 10.30am–12.30pm & 3–6pm; Nov–March Mon & Wed–Sun 2.30–4.30pm; €0.60), reputedly the oldest Christian building in France and until the seventeenth century the only place in town to conduct a proper baptism; the font was the octagonal pool sunk into the floor. There are also some ancient and faded **frescoes** on the walls, including the Emperor Constantine on horseback.

With giant spheres, cubes, crystals and planes of glass, **Futuroscope** (summer 9am–10pm; €32; rest of year 9am–6/7pm; €22), looks more like the set of a science fiction film than a tourist draw. Situated 7km north of Poitiers, it's an amusement area given over to science and technology, with an IMAX 3D cinema, and "La Cyber Avenue", a small street dedicated to every form of cyberculture. It's accessible on bus #16 or #17 from Poitiers, or 90min on the TGV from Paris.

Poitiers **train station** is a ten-minute walk from the centre at the foot of the hill which forms the kernel of the town. Among cheap **hotels** the *Victor Hugo*, east of the train station at 5 rue Victor Hugo (☎05.49.41.12.16; ②), is a real bargain or there's the *Petite Villette*, 14 bd de l'Abbé de Frémont (☎05.49.41.41.33; ②). It's only a short uphill walk to the town centre, where you'll pay a bit more at the attractive *Hôtel du Plat d'Étain*, 7–9 rue du Plat d'É-tain (☎05.49.41.04.80; ③). The **hostel** is at allée Roger Tagault (☎05.49.30.09.70; ②; bus #3) and there's a municipal **campsite** on rue du Porteau, 2km north of the town (☎05.49.41.44.88; bus #7; April–Sept). The **tourist office** is at 8 rue des Grandes-Écoles (June–Sept Mon–Sat 9.30am–7.30pm, Sun 10am–6pm; rest of year Mon–Sat 10am–6pm; *www.mairie-poitiers.fr*). As for **eating**, *Le St-Hubert*, 13 rue Cloche Perse, does regional food at reasonable prices, and *Le Cappuccino*, on rue de l'Université, is one of several good Italians in the area. Le Maillon, 20–22 rue de la Chaîne, offers **Internet** access (Mon–Thurs noon–6.30pm, Tues until 10pm, Fri 2–8pm).

La Rochelle and around

LA ROCHELLE is the most attractive seaside town in France, with a beautiful seventeenth- and eighteenth-century centre and waterfront and a lively, bustling air. The town has a long history. Eleanor of Aquitaine gave it a charter in 1199, and it rapidly became a port of major importance, trading in salt and wine, the principal terminus for trade with the French colonies in the West Indies and Canada. Indeed, many of the settlers, especially in Canada, came from this part of France.

From the visitor's point of view, most attractions lie in the area behind the waterfront, between the harbour and place de Verdun. The heavy Gothic gateway of the **Porte de la Grosse Horloge** straddles the entrance to the old town, dominating the pleasure-boat-filled inner harbour, overlooked by two towers. Through the Grosse Horloge, the main shopping street, **rue du Palais**, is lined by eighteenth-century houses and arcaded shop fronts. To the west, especially in rue de l'Escale, are the discreet residences of the eighteenth-century shipowners and chandlers, while to the east, rue du Temple leads to the **Hôtel de Ville**, begun in the reign of Henri IV, whose initials, intertwined with those of Marie de Médici, are carved on the ground-floor gallery. It's a beautiful specimen of frenchified Italian taste, adorned with niches and statues and coffered ceilings. There's more of this rich world in the **Musée du Nouveau Monde**, 10 rue Fleuriau (Mon & Wed–Sat 10.30am–12.30pm & 1.30–6pm, Sun 3–6pm; €3.50), which occupies the former residence of the Fleuriau family, who, like many of their fellow Rochelais, made fortunes from slaving and West Indian sugar, spices and coffee. The new, hugely enjoyable **aquarium** (daily: July & Aug 9am–11pm; rest of year 9/10am–8pm; €10), beside the marina towards the station, is also well worth a look, with impressive collections of indigenous and tropical species, albeit in a rather Disneyesque setting.

From the **train station**, it's ten minutes down av de Gaulle to the town centre. The **tourist office** is by the harbour on place de la Petite Sirène, Quai de Gabut (June–Sept Mon–Sat 9am–7/8pm, Sun 11am–5pm; May Mon–Sat 9am–6pm, Sun 10am–noon; rest of year Mon–Sat 9am–noon & 2–6pm; *www.ville-larochelle.fr*). Finding **accommodation** can be a problem in season. There's a **hostel** in av des Minimes to the west (☎05.46.44.43.11; ②; bus #10 from place de Verdun or the train station) and two **campsites**: the *Soleil* by the hostel (☎05.46.44.42.53; May–Sept) and a municipal site, *Port Neuf*, on the northwestern side of town on bd A. Rondeau (☎05.46.43.81.20; bus #6 from Grosse Horloge). Of the handful of budget **hotels** in the centre, the best bets are the *Bordeaux*, 45 rue St-Nicolas (☎05.46.41.31.22; ③), and friendly *Henri-IV*, 31 rue des Gentilshommes (☎05.46.41.25.79; ③). For **eating**, try the area around rue du Port and rue St-Sauveur just off the waterfront, and rue St-Nicolas. *À Côté de Chez Fred*, 34 rue St-Nicolas, has fresh fish and a down-to-earth atmosphere, while *Café de la Poste*, place de l'Hôtel de Ville, has decent menus. *Café Expo*, 18 rue des Dames, has **Internet** access from €5/hr and serves good pasta dishes. On the other side of town is the cybercafé AAT Web Conception, av Amérigo Vespucci (Mon–Sat 10.15am–1pm & 2–8.15pm; Sun 3–8pm).

For **beaches**, you're best off crossing over to the **Île de Ré**, a long narrow island immediately west of La Rochelle (buses from place de Verdun or pricey boat trips from the Vieux Port), which is surrounded by sandy strands. Out of season it has a slow, misty charm, with life in its little ports revolving around the cultivation of oysters and mussels.

Île d'Oléron

If you want to **swim**, head south of La Rochelle to the **ÎLE D'OLÉRON**, France's largest island after Corsica, which has kilometres of beautiful sandy beaches. It's joined to the mainland by a toll-free bridge. The little towns, inevitably, have been ruined by the development of hundreds of holiday homes, and it can be a real battle in the summer season to find a place to stay, but, for all that, it's a pretty and distinctive island. With its pines, tamarisks and evergreen oaks, the stretch from Boyardville to St-Pierre – the most attractive of the towns – takes the biscuit.

Cognac

COGNAC is a sunny, prosperous, little town, best-known for its brandy distilleries, which reveal themselves through the heady scent that pervades the air. The **tourist office**, close by the central place François I, 16 rue du 14-Juillet (summer Mon–Sat 9am–7pm, Sun 10.30am–4pm; rest of year Mon–Sat 9am–12.30pm & 2–6.15pm; *www.tourism-cognac.fr*), has information on visiting the various cognac *chais*, most of which are situated at the end of Grand-Rue, which winds through the old quarter of town. Perhaps the best for a visit are those of Hennessy (daily: July–Sept 10am–6pm; March–May & Oct–Dec 10am–5pm; Jan & Feb by appointment; €4.60; ☎05.45.35.72.68, *www.hennessy-cognac.com*), a seventh-generation family firm of Irish origin, where tours begin with a film explaining what's what in the world of cognac. Hennessy alone keeps 180,000 barrels in stock; all are regularly checked and various blends made from barrel to barrel. Only the best is kept, a choice which depends on the taste buds of the maître du chais. At Hennessy the job has been in the same family for six generations; the present heir apparent has already been nineteen years under his father's tutelage and is still said to be not yet fully qualified.

From the **train station**, take rue Mousnier, then rue Bayard, which leads you up rue du 14-Juillet to place François I. There are a couple of **cafés** and a reasonable **brasserie** on the square or try the excellent *La Boîte-à-Sel*, 68 av Victor-Hugo. Upstream from the bridge, the oak woods of the Parc François I stretch along the riverbank to the town **campsite** (☎05.42.32.13.32). The cheapest **rooms** are at *Le Cheval Blanc*, 6–8 place Bayard (☎05.45.82.09.55; ③); while the *Hotel d'Orléans* at 25 rue d'Angoulême (☎05.45.82.01.26; ③) is slightly more upmarket and characterful.

AQUITAINE, THE DORDOGNE AND THE LOT

Steamy, moist and green, the southwest of France can feel like a lower-latitude England. In the **Dordogne** heartlands, the country is certainly beautiful, but the more famous spots, especially in the Dordogne valley, have become oppressively crowded in season. **Bordeaux** is a possible entry point to the region and has an appealing air of faded glory, an especially stimulating base for those interested in wine.

East of Bordeaux, the northern half of the Dordogne *département*, the **Périgord Blanc**, is named for the light, white colour of its rock outcrops – undulating, fertile, wooded country, rising in the north and east to the edge of the Massif Central. The regional capital is **Périgueux** which, because of its central position and relative ease of access, makes the best base for the whole region, especially the cave paintings at **Les Eyzies** and around. The **Périgord Noir** is the stretch of territory from Bergerac to Brive. It's this area that people always think of when you say Dordogne, where most of the picture-book villages are, where the cuisine is at its richest and the prices at their highest. **Sarlat** is its capital and a good base for exploration. South from here lies the drier, poorer and more sparsely populated region through which the **Lot** river flows roughly parallel with the Dordogne, an ideal area to hike, bike and camp. Consult *www.cr-aquitaine.fr* for information on the entire region and links to the cities.

Bordeaux and around

Celebrated first and foremost for the **wines** of the surrounding countryside, **BORDEAUX** has clung onto its grand avenues and eighteenth-century architecture, allowing a glimpse of its former grandeur and making it an enjoyable stop in itself. Today the city remains affluent, yet outside its old centre is somewhat scruffy. Nevertheless, it is a vibrant centre with a large student body and an ethnically diverse population, and while sights are rather thin on the ground, it is a great base for exploring the area. The surrounding countryside is not the most enticing, and you definitely need your own transport to explore it; you go for the wines rather than the landscape. More interesting are the vast pine-covered expanses of **Les Landes** to the south, and the wild Atlantic **beaches**.

The centre of the city is the café-lined **place Gambetta**, a once majestic square conceived in the time of Louis XV. Its house fronts, arcaded at street level, are decorated with rows of carved masks and surround a beautifully tended garden in the centre. In one corner, the eighteenth-century arch of the **Porte Dijeaux** spans the street. East, cours de l'Intendance, full of chic shops, leads to the impeccably classical **Grand Théâtre** on place de la Comédie, built in 1780 and faced with an immense colonnaded portico topped by Muses and Graces. From here, smart streets radiate out. Sanded and tree-lined **allée de Tourny** leads to a statue of Tourny, the eighteenth-century administrator who was prime mover of the city's golden age. Cours du 30-juillet leads into the vast expanse of **Esplanade des Quinconces**, said to be Europe's largest municipal square, with an enormous memorial to the Girondins, the influential local deputies to the Revolutionary Assembly of 1789, purged by Robespierre as counter-revolutionaries.

Rue Ste-Catherine, the city's main shopping street, leads down from place de la Comédie towards the best of the city's museums, the **Musée d'Aquitaine** at 20 cours Pasteur (Tues–Sun 11am–6pm; €3.80), an imaginative collection that indicates why eighteenth-century Bordeaux was compared to Paris by contemporary writers. Take a look, too, at the section on the wine trade before venturing off on a vineyard tour. A couple of blocks east is the cathedral of **St-André**, whose most eye-catching feature is the great upward sweep of its twin steeples. The surrounding square is attractive, with enticing pavement cafés and the classical **Hôtel de Ville**. Just around the corner on cours d'Albret, the **Musée des Beaux-Arts** (Mon & Wed–Sun 11am–6pm; €3.80) has a small but commendable collection, including works by Rubens, Matisse and Kokoschka.

Practicalities

Bordeaux **airport**, west of the city, is connected by regular shuttle **buses** (daily 6am–10.45pm; takes 30–45min; €5.30) with the city (place Gambetta) and the train station. Arriving by **train**, you find yourself at the **gare St-Jean**, linked to the centre of town by bus #7 or #8, and in the heart of a convenient if insalubrious area for **accommodation**. Right outside the station, rue Charles-Domercq and cours de la Marne are full of one- and two-star **hotels** – try the *San Michel* at 32 rue Charles-Domercq (☎05.56.91.96.40; ③). More central is the *Clemenceau* at 4 cours Georges-Clemenceau (☎05.56.52.98.98; ④). The large **hostel** is near the station, to the left off cours de la Marne, at 22 cours Barbey (☎05.56.94.51.66; ②); watch out for its 11pm curfew. The main **tourist office** is in the centre of town, 12 cours du 30-juillet, just north of place de la Comédie (May–Oct Mon–Sat 9am–7/8pm, Sun 9am–7pm; Nov–April Mon–Sat 9am–7pm, Sun 9.45am–4.30pm; *www.bordeaux-tourisme.com*), with an annexe at the station. Though the city centre is walkable, you need to take **buses** to cover longer distances; €1.20 tickets, valid for one journey only, are available on board but it's cheaper to buy packs of ten from a *tabac*.

There are a lot of inexpensive **eating** places in the station quarter, and ethnic restaurants along the left bank of the river near the station. In the centre of town, wholesome meals and terrace drinks are available from the very popular *Café des Arts* on the corner of rue St-Catherine and cours Victor-Hugo. For typical French cooking try *Le Tire-Bouchon*, 15 rue des

Bahutiers, and for French Bordelais specialities *Le Bistro d'Édouard*, 16 place du Parlement. Bordeaux has an excellent reputation for seafood restaurants: head for *Chez Joël D*, 13 rue des Pilliers-de-Tutelle, for oysters. The city is home to a large university and has a good selection of studenty **bars**, such as *Chez Auguste*, place de la Victoire, *The Bus Stop*, 8 rue des Augustins, and the hip *Aviatic Café*, 41 rue des Augustins. You can check your **email** at Cyberstation, 23 cours Pasteur (Mon–Sat 11am–2am, Sun 2pm–midnight) or Arobas, 7 rue Maucoudenat (☎05.56.44.26.30).

Bordeaux's vineyards

Along with Burgundy and Champagne, the **wines** of Bordeaux form the Holy Trinity of French viticulture. The reds in particular – known as **claret** to the English – have graced the tables of the discerning for many a century. The countryside that produces them stretches north, east and south of the city, and is the largest quality wine district in the world. North along the west bank of the brown, island-spotted Gironde estuary are **Médoc** and **Haut-Médoc**, whose wines have a full-bodied, smoky taste and a reputation for improving with age. Across the Gironde – via seven or eight ferries a day from Lamarque to Vauban-fortified Blaye – the green slopes of the *côtes* of **Bourg** and **Blaye** are home to heavier, plummier reds, less pricey than anything found on the opposite side of the river. South of the city is the domain of the great whites, the super-dry **Graves** and the sweet dessert wines of **Sauternes**, which get their flavour from grapes left to rot on the vine. East, on the other side of the River Garonne, are the **Premières Côtes de Bordeaux**, which form the first slopes of the **Entre-Deux-Mers** (by far the prettiest countryside in the Bordeaux wine region), whose wines are regarded as good but less fine than the Médocs and Graves – less fine also than the superlative reds of **Pomerol**, **Fronsac** and **St-Émilion**, just to the north of the River Dordogne.

The Bordeaux tourist office has information detailing all the châteaux that allow **visits and wine-tasting**, as does the Maison du Vin de Bordeaux, opposite it at 3 cours du 30-Juillet. Getting to any of these places without your own transport is hard work. An exception is the pretty town of **ST-EMILION**, served by an infrequent daily train service from Bordeaux (takes 30min). The tourist office organizes generally interesting and informative wine **tours** (May–Oct daily 1.30pm; Nov–April Wed & Sat 1.30pm), which, at €24.40 including tasting, are well worth the money.

Around Bordeaux

On summer weekends the Bordelais escape to **ARCACHON** (*www.arcachon.com*), a smart seaside resort forty minutes' train ride away through sandy forest. The white-sand **beaches** are magnificent but inevitably get crowded. **Hotels** tend to be expensive and fully booked in season; a good bet is the *St Christaud*, 8 allée de la Chapelle (☎05.56.83.38.53; ④), though there's also a **campsite**, allée de la Galaxie (☎05.56.83.24.15). Arcachon's chief curiosity is the **dune du Pyla,** at 114m the highest sand dune in Europe, offering superb views of the coast and the stretches of Les Landes from its wind-swept summit, but becoming somewhat of a tourist trap in season. Buses run there from Arcachon **train station** (June–Sept every 30min; rest of year twice daily).

Travelling south from Bordeaux and Arcachon by road or rail, you pass for half a day through the unremitting, flat, sandy pine forest of **Les Landes**. Until the nineteenth century this was a vast, infertile swamp, steadily encroached upon by the shifting sand dunes of the coast; today it supports over 10,000 square kilometres of trees. At **SABRES**, 18km east of Labouheyre on the N10 road from Bordeaux to Bayonne, a resuscitated steam train runs to the **Éco-musée de Marquèze** (daily July–Sept 10.10am–12.10pm & 2–5pm; April, May & Oct 2–4.40pm; €7.30 including train fare) run by the **Parc Régional des Landes de Gascogne**. The museum illustrates the traditional *landais* way of life, where shepherds clomped around the scrub on long stilts because the terrain was too muddy and dangerous to cover by foot.

Périgueux

PÉRIGUEUX is a busy and prosperous market town which makes a good base for seeing the best of the Dordogne's prehistoric caves. The centre of town focuses on **place Bugeaud**, a ten-minute walk from the train station. Ahead, down rue Taillefer, the **Cathédrale de St-Front**, its square, pineapple-capped belfry surging above the roofs of the surrounding medieval houses, is one of the most distinctive Romanesque churches in France, modelled on the Holy Apostles in what was then Constantinople. Outside, place de la Clautre gives on to Périgueux's renovated **old quarter**, with a number of fine Renaissance houses, particularly along rue Limogeanne. The **Musée du Périgord**, at the end of rue St-Front on the cours de Tourny (Mon & Wed–Fri 10/11am–5/6pm, Sat & Sun 1–6pm; €3), has some beautiful Gallo-Roman mosaics from local sites. There are some exquisite Limoges enamels near the exit; look out especially for the portraits of the twelve Caesars.

There are some good inexpensive **hotels** in front of the train station: try the *Hôtel du Midi*, 18–20 rue Denis Papin (☎05.53.53.41.06; ③), whose good regional restaurant has menus for around €12. Alternatively, there is a **campsite** on the river Barnabé (☎05.53.53.41.45). The **tourist office** is at 26 place Francheville (Mon–Sat 9am–6/7pm; June–Sept also Sun 10am–6pm; *www.ville-perigueux.fr*), next to the Tour Mataguerre, the last remnant of the town's medieval defences. Surprisingly, Périgueux isn't greatly blessed with good **restaurants**, but *Hercule Poireau*, 2 rue de la Nation, and *Au Petit Chef*, 5 place du Coderc, both serve up decent French meals. Failing that, you could try one of the **brasseries** around bd Montaigne.

The Vézère valley caves

Half-an-hour or so by train from Périgueux is a luxuriant cliff-cut region riddled with **caves** and subterranean streams. Human skeletons were first unearthed here in 1868, and an incredible wealth of archeological evidence of the life of late Stone Age people has since been found. The paintings which adorn the caves – perhaps to aid fertility or hunting rituals – are remarkable not only for their age, but also for their exquisite colouring and the skill with which they are drawn. **Lascaux** is the most famous of a number of locations.

LES EYZIES is the centre of the region, a rambling, unattractive village given over to tourism. Three or four **trains** run daily to Les Eyzies from Périgueux, and the Périgueux tourist office issues a sheet detailing how to get there and back in a day. Worth a glance before or after visiting the caves is the **Musée National de la Préhistoire** (Mon & Wed–Sun: July & Aug 9.30am–7pm; rest of year 9.30am–noon & 2–5/6pm; €3.40), which exhibits prehistoric artefacts and art objects including copies of one of the most beautiful pieces of Stone Age art – two clay bison from the Tuc d'Audoubert cave in the Pyrenees. Just outside Les Eyzies, off the road to Sarlat, the tunnel-like **Grotte de Font de Gaume** (Mon, Tues & Thurs–Sun 9/10am–noon & 2–5/6pm; €5.50) contains dozens of polychrome paintings. Most miraculous of all is a frieze of five bison discovered in 1966 during cleaning operations, the colour remarkably preserved by a protective layer of calcite. Only twenty people are allowed in at any one time and **tickets** sell out fast. To be sure of a place in season, especially on a Sunday when they're half-price, get to the ticket office at least an hour before opening. Les Eyzies has a riverside **campsite**, *La Rivière* (☎05.53.06.97.14; April–Oct) but **hotels** are pricey and likely to ask for *demi-pension*. If you're not staying in Périgueux, try **LE BUGUE**, 10km down the River Vézère, where you'll find the friendly *Hôtel de Paris* at 14 rue Paris (☎05.53.07.28.16; ③). The Les Eyzies **tourist office** on place de la Mairie (July & Aug daily 9am–8pm; June & Sept Mon–Sat 9am–7pm, Sun 10am–noon & 2–5pm; rest of year Mon–Sat 9am–noon & 2–6pm, Sun 10am–noon & 2–6pm; Oct–Dec closed Sun) has information on private rooms in the area and rents out **bikes**.

Not a cave but a rock shelter, **Abri du Cap-Blanc** (daily: July & Aug 9.30am–7pm; April–June, Sept & Oct 10am–noon & 2–6pm; €5.20) is a steep but manageable 7km bike ride from Les Eyzies. Its sculpted frieze of horses and bison, dating from 12,000 BC, is polished and set off against a pockmarked background in extraordinary high relief. Of the ten surviving prehistoric sculptures in France, this is the best. The road up takes you past the **Grotte des Combarelles** (same hours & price as Grotte de Font de Gaume), whose engravings of humans, reindeer and mammoths dating from the Magdalanian period are also worth a visit.

Montignac and Lascaux

Heading up the valley of the Vézère river northeast of Les Eyzies, **MONTIGNAC** (linked to Sarlat by bus) is more attractive than Les Eyzies. The **tourist office**, on place Bertran de Born (July & Aug daily 9am–7pm; rest of year Mon–Sat 9am–noon & 2–6pm), is in the same building as a museum of local crafts and the ticket office for the nearby cave of **Lascaux** – or rather, for a tantalizing replica, Lascaux II (May–Nov daily 9am–7pm; Dec & Feb–April Tues–Sun 10am–noon & 1.30–5.30pm; €7.50); the original has been closed since 1963 due to deterioration caused by the breath and body heat of visitors. Executed 17,000 years ago, the paintings are said to be the finest prehistoric works in existence. There are five or six identifiable styles, and subjects include the bison, mammoth and horse, plus the biggest-known prehistoric drawing in existence, a 5.5-metre bull with astonishingly expressive head and face. The visit lasts forty minutes, and the commentary is in French, with English translations if requested. Montignac is short on even moderately priced **accommodation**, though *Auberge le Lascaux*, 109 av Jean Jaurès (☎05.53.51.82.81; ③), has a couple of inexpensive rooms and a good budget menu. There is also a three-star **campsite** a short walk away on the riverbank (☎05.53.51.83.95; April–Oct).

Bergerac and the Dordogne valley

Lying on the banks of the Dordogne southeast of Périgueux, **BERGERAC** is the main market centre for the surrounding maize, vine and tobacco farms. Devastated in the Wars of Religion, when most of its Protestant population fled overseas, it is essentially a modern town, yet it is still attractive. What's left of the old quarter has a lot of charm, with numerous late-medieval houses. In rue de l'Ancien-Pont, the seventeenth-century Maison Peyrarède houses a **tobacco museum** (Tues–Sat 10am–noon & 2–5/6pm, Sun 2.30–6.30pm; €2.50), detailing the history of the weed, with collections of pipes and tools of the trade. Bergerac is the mainstay of the French tobacco-growing industry, somewhat in the doldrums today since the traditional *brune* (brown cigarette tobacco) is gradually being superseded by the *blonde*, which is oven-cured and therefore a lot less labour-intensive to make. **Accommodation** isn't hard to find: there's a **campsite** (☎05.53.24.82.80) west of the centre by the river, and several small **hotels**, among them the *Pozzi*, 11–13 rue Pozzi (☎05.53.57.04.68; ②), and the *Family*, 3 rue du Dragon (☎05.53.57.80.90; ④), which has a good **restaurant**. The **tourist office** is at 97 rue Neuve-d'Argenson (July & Aug daily 9.30am–7pm; rest of year Mon–Sat 9.30am–1pm & 2–7pm; *www.bergerac-tourisme.com*).

To the east is **SARLAT**, capital of Périgord Noir, held in a hollow in the hills a few kilometres back from the Dordogne valley. It has an alluring medieval core, focusing on the central **place de la Liberté**, where you'll find the **tourist office** (summer daily 9am–8pm; winter Mon–Sat 9am–noon & 2–6pm; *www.sarlat-tourisme.com*). Although there's not much to see, it makes a good base for the surrounding countryside and trips further upstream: the tourist office has details of organized trips if you don't have your own transport. There is a **hostel** on the Périgueux road at 77 av de Selves (☎05.53.59.47.59; ②), and a prettily sited **campsite** 2km beyond the rail viaduct. **Hotels** include the *Marcel*, 50 av de Selves (☎05.53.59.21.98; ④), which has a good restaurant, and the *Hôtel de la Mairie*, 13 place de la Liberté (☎05.53.59.05.71; ③).

Among the places you might visit from Sarlat are **SOUILLAC**, further upstream, where the twelfth-century church of St-Marie has some marvellous Romanesque sculptures. **ROCAMADOUR**, about 10km southeast of there, is wonderfully sited tucked under a cliff in a deep canyon and has been visited by pilgrims for centuries for its miracle-working Black Madonna, housed in a votive-packed **Chapelle Miraculeuse**, to which the devout drag themselves on their knees. But be warned that it can sometimes get unbearably crowded these days, and is home to all manner of tourist junk.

THE PYRENEES

Basque-speaking and wet in the west, snowy and patois-speaking in the middle, dry and Catalan in the east, **the Pyrenees** are physically beautiful, culturally varied and a great deal less developed than the Alps. The whole range is marvellous walking country, especially the central region around the **Parc National des Pyrénées**, with its 3000-metre peaks, streams, forests, flowers and wildlife. If you're a serious hiker, it's possible to walk all the way across from Atlantic to Mediterranean between June and September, following the GR10 or the more difficult *Haute Randonnée Pyrénéenne* – although bear in mind that these are big mountains, and to cover any of the main walks you'll need hiking boots and, despite the southerly latitude, warm and windproof clothing. As for more conventional tourist attractions, the **Basque coast** is lovely but very popular, suffering from seaside sprawl and a massive surfeit of campsites: **St-Jean-de-Luz** is by far the prettiest of the resorts; **Bayonne** is the most attractive town, with an excellent Basque museum and art gallery; and **Biarritz** has the best surf. The foothill towns, on the whole, are dull, though **Pau** is worth a day or two, while **Lourdes** is a monster of kitsch that has to be seen to be believed.

Bayonne and Biarritz

Bayonne and Biarritz are virtual continuations of each other, but their characters are entirely different. **BIARRITZ** is a nineteenth-century resort once patronized by Queen Victoria; today it is upmarket and aloof, but its waves provide some of the best surfing in Europe and ensure a busy summer season. **BAYONNE** on the other hand is a sunny, southern town, workaday and very Basque: it stands some 6km from the Atlantic, a position that's protected it from any real exploitation by tourism. This is fortunate, for with its half-timbered houses, their shutters painted in the Basque tones of green and red, it is a distinctive and enjoyable town.

Bayonne is situated at the junction of the Nive and Adour rivers, with the centre grouped closely around the banks of the Nive. **Place de la Liberté** is the main town square, close to the confluence of the two rivers and full of cafés and *pâtisseries*; alongside the Hôtel de Ville on the square is a stop for bus #1 bound for Biarritz and the beaches, and the **tourist office** is a short way west on place des Basques (July & Aug Mon–Sat 9am–7pm, Sun 10am–1pm; rest of year Mon–Fri 9am–6.30pm, Sat 10am–6pm; *www.bayonne-tourisme.com*). The **quays** nearby along the Nive are fun to wander, and on the opposite side of the river – in the area known as "Petit Bayonne" – at the corner of the second bridge, is the excellent **Musée Basque** (Tues–Sun: May–Oct 10am–6.30pm; Nov–April 10.30am–12.30pm & 2–6pm; €5.30, free on first Sun of month). The city's second museum, the **Musée Bonnat** on nearby rue Jacques Lafitte (Mon & Wed–Sun 10am–12.30pm & 2–6pm; €3), is an unexpected treasury of art, with works by Rubens, Degas and Goya. Across the Nive, the **Cathédrale Ste-Marie** (Mon–Sat 7.30am–noon & 3–7pm, Sun 3.30–6.30pm; free) looks its best from a distance, its twin towers and steeple rising with airy grace above the houses.

Biarritz's **tourist office** is on place d'Ixelles (July & Aug daily 8am–8pm; rest of year Mon–Sat 9am–6pm, Sun 10am–5pm; *www.biarritz.tm.fr*), near the town's focal point, the restored **Casino Municipal** just behind the Grande-Plage. Biarritz's headline draw is its beautiful shoreline, with Atlantic breakers crashing on broad stretches of fine sand, fashion victims lounging cheek-by-jowl with suburban families and surf bums. Mid-July is the busiest time, when the **surf festival** attracts crowds for a week of longboard competitions, music and film. The **beaches** – served by STAB buses #4 and #9 from Biarritz centre – extend northwards in a long chain, but most of the action occurs on the sheltered and intimate **Plage du Port-Vieux**, **Grande-Plage** and **Plage Miramar**, all side-by-side, with the last of them overlooked by Napoleon III's huge *Hôtel du Palais*.

Practicalities

Bayonne's **train station** is in the quarter of St-Esprit on the opposite bank of the Adour from the centre, ten minutes' walk along the Pont St-Esprit. The finest budget **accommodation** is at the charming *Hôtel des Basques* with its floral wallpaper and uneven floorboards, at 4 rue des Lisses (☎05.59.59.08.02; ③). If that's full, try *Paris-Madrid* by the station (☎05.59.55.13.98; ③), or the more upmarket *Mercure*, av Jean Rostand (☎05.59.52.84.44; ⑤). The closest **campsite** is the well-equipped *La Chêneraie* (☎05.59.55.01.31; April–Sept), in the St-Frédéric quarter on the north bank of the Adour. There's a **hostel** between Bayonne and Biarritz at 19 route des Vignes, Anglet (☎05.59.58.70.00; ②); take bus #4 from the Hôtel de Ville to La Barre and change to bus #9, direction La Bourd, getting off at the Auberge de Jeunesse. The best area for **cafés and restaurants** in Bayonne is Petit Bayonne – cheerful *Le P'tit Pub*, on rue des Tonneliers, offers decent, simple fare, including the excellent local ham, while the *Auberge du Cheval Blanc*, 68 rue Bourgneuf, is good value considering it's been awarded a Michelin star. For **live music** and a pint of Guinness, head to *Katie Daly's* by pl Charles de Gaulle. You can surf the **Internet** at Cyber Net Café, 9 pl de la République.

Biarritz **train station** is 3km southeast of the centre at the end of avenue Foch/avenue Kennedy, in the *quartier* known as La Négresse (STAB bus #2 or #9 to place d'Ixelles). Biarritz **airport** (*www.biarritz.aeroport.fr*), 3km out, has shuttle buses running into town (€1.10). The friendly **hotel** *de la Marine*, corner rue des Goélands and rue du Port-Vieux (☎05.59.24.34.09; ④), is popular with backpackers and surfers. There's a **hostel** at 8 rue Chiquito de Cambo (☎05.59.41.76.00; ②), 2km southwest of the centre, just walkable from the train station (down towards the lake and away from the beach). For **food**, *Bistrot des Halles*, 1 rue du Centre, serves generously portioned, tasty fish dishes; for grills and *frites* head to *Le Surfing*, behind Plage de la Côte des Basques, which is festooned with antique boards. **Clubbers** prefer *Le Morgan*, 4 rue du Helder off place Clemenceau, open from evening until dawn. Just south of town on the Plage d'Ilbarritz is the hip *Blue Cargo*, which serves fish and salads on the terrace; its tent-bar gets packed after midnight.

St-Jean-de-Luz

ST-JEAN-DE-LUZ is by far the most attractive resort on the Basque coast. Although it gets crowded and its main seafront is undistinguished, it boasts a long curve of beautiful fine sand. It is also a thriving fishing port, the most important in France for catches of tuna and anchovies, and the old houses around the harbour, both in St-Jean and across the water in Ciboure (effectively the same town) are very picturesque.

The focus of life for visitors is **place Louis XIV** near the harbour, with its cafés, bandstand and plane trees. The seventeenth-century **mansion** (June–Sept Mon–Sat 10.30am–noon/12.30pm & 2.30–5.30/6.30pm, Sun 2.30–5.30/6.30pm; €3.80) on the harbour side of the square was built by a shipowner called Lohobiague in 1635 and still belongs to the same family. It is also where Louis XIV stayed at the time of his marriage to Maria Theresa, Infanta of Castile, which took place in the town – an extravagant event at which Cardinal Mazarin alone presented the queen with 12,000 pounds of pearls and diamonds, a gold dinner service and a pair of sumptuous carriages drawn by teams of six horses. Maria Theresa lodged just along the quay in an Italianate mansion of faded pink brick. A short distance up rue Gambetta, on the town side of the square, is the church of **St-Jean-Baptiste**, the largest of the Basque churches where Louis and Maria Theresa were married. It is a plain, fortress-like building from the outside; inside, the barn-like nave is roofed in wood and lined on three sides with tiers of dark oak galleries, a distinctive feature of Basque churches – they were reserved for the men, while the women sat in the nave.

The **train station** is on place de Verdun, close to the **tourist office** on place du Maréchal-Foch (July & Aug Mon–Sat 9am–8pm, Sun 10am–1pm & 3–7pm; rest of year Mon–Sat 9am–12.30pm & 2–7pm, Sun 10am–1pm; *www.saint-jean-de-luz.com*). ATCRB run 12 inexpensive **buses** a day to the town from Bayonne (buses leave from just behind the Bayonne tourist office). There are several **hotels** near the train station: *Le Verdun*, 13 av de Verdun (☎05.59.26.02.55; ④), is comfortable and has a good regional restaurant; alternatively try *Hôtel de Paris* at 1 bd du Commandant Passicot (☎05.59.85.20.20; ⑤). There are plenty of **campsites** in the vicinity, all grouped together a few kilometres northeast of the town; try the *Chibau Berria* (☎05.59.26.11.94), left off the N10. Aldin's, at 8 blvd Thiers, offers **Internet** access (Mon–Fri 9am–12.30pm & 2–7pm).

Pau and the mountains

Capital of the viscounty of Béarn, **PAU** has had a more than usually turbulent history, maintaining its separatist leanings well into the seventeenth century; even today many of the Béarnais speak *Occitan* rather than French. Pau is a university town, good-looking, lively and, partly thanks to tourism, fairly prosperous. It occupies a grand natural site on a steep scarp overlooking the Gave de Pau, and from its **boulevard des Pyrénées**, the promenade which runs along the rim of the scarp, there are superb **views** of the higher peaks. Not surprisingly, Pau has become the most popular starting point for the Parc National des Pyrénées, and it's well-equipped for the purpose. As for its own sights, Pau's **château** (daily 9.30–11.45am/12.15pm & 1.30/2–5/5.45pm; €3.80), at the west end of bd des Pyrénées, was done up by Louis-Philippe in the nineteenth century after standing empty for 200 years.

From the **train station** down by the river, a free funicular shuttles you up to bd des Pyrénées. The **bus station** (for non-SNCF buses) is off place Clemenceau, on rue Gachet. The **tourist office** is at the end of place Royale (July & Aug daily 9am–6pm; rest of year Mon–Fri 9am–12.30pm & 1.30–6pm, Sat 9am–noon & 2–6pm; *www.ville-pau.fr*). There's a **hostel** over the river in Gelos (☎05.59.06.53.02; ②), a *Foyer des jeunes travailleurs* at 30 rue Michel-Houneau (☎05.59.11.05.05, *www.ldpau.org*; ②), and a similar *Maison Léo-Lagrange* at 18 rue Bourbaki (☎05.59.62.50.50; ②). For **hotels**, try the quiet and hospitable *d'Albret*, 11 rue Jeanne d'Albret (☎05.59.27.81.58; ③), or *Le Matisse*, 17 rue Mathieu-Lalanne (☎05.59.27.73.80; ③). The municipal **campsite** is on bd du Cami-Salié (☎05.59.02.30.49), off av Sallenave on the northern edge of town. **Restaurants** are numerous, too, especially towards the château: *La Brochetterie*, 16 rue Henri-IV, has reasonably priced menus and a pleasant family atmosphere; *Le Berry* on place Clemenceau is a brasserie popular with local students.

The mountains above Pau

Pau is probably the best large base for launching into the highest parts of the Pyrenees, since the **Parc National des Pyrénées Occidentales** lies to the south of the town. It's possible to hitch-hike up to the spectacular main passes of **Col d'Aubisque** and **Col du Tourmalet**, though you may well find that you get left on the top by drivers coming up for the view and going back down the same way. The tourist office in Pau supplies walking information and will recommend local organizations that run **guided hikes**. More specialist knowledge can be gleaned from the Club Alpin Français, 5 rue René Fournets in Pau (☎05.59.27.71.81).

Lourdes

LOURDES, about 30km southeast of Pau, has just one function. Around five million Catholic **pilgrims** arrive here each year, and the town is totally given over to looking after and exploiting them. Before 1858, Lourdes was hardly more than a village, but in that year Bernadette

Soubirous, the 14-year-old daughter of an ex-miller, had the first of eighteen visions of the Virgin Mary in a spot called the Grotte de Massabielle, by the Gave de Pau. Since then Lourdes has grown a great deal, and it is now one of the biggest attractions in this part of France, many of its visitors hoping for a miraculous cure.

Practically every shop is given over to the sale of religious kitsch – Bernadette can be found in every shape and size adorning barometers, key rings, bottles and candles. The architecture of the **Cité Religieuse** has grown up around the Gave de Pau and is scarcely any better. The **grotto** is a moisture-blackened overhang by the riverside with a statue of the Virgin in waxwork white and baby blue. Suspended in front is a row of rusting crutches, *ex votos* offered by the hopeful. Up above is the first church built here, dating from 1871, and below this a massive subterranean **basilica**, reputedly able to hold twenty thousand people at one time.

The **train station** is on the northeastern edge of town. The **tourist office**, which can help with accommodation, is on place Peyramale; turn right outside the station and then left down Chaussée Maransin (Easter–Sept Mon–Sat 9am–7pm, Sun 10am–6pm; rest of year Mon–Sat 9am–noon & 2–7pm; *www.lourdes-france.com*). There's an abundance of inexpensive **hotels** on ave de la Gare, and more en route to the Grotte and around the castle. **Hostel** accommodation can be had on the western edge of town, ten minutes' walk from the centre, at the *Village des Jeunes*, Ferme Milhas, rue Monseigneur-Rodhain (☎05.62.42.79.95; ①; April–Nov), which has ultra-cheap dorm beds. There are several **campsites** – the nearest is *La Poste*, 26 rue de Langelle (☎05.62.94.40.35), east off the Chaussée Maransin and near the post office. If everything is full, consider staying in **TARBES**, twenty minutes from Lourdes by train, which has a **hostel** at 88 rue Alsace-Lorraine (☎05.62.38.91.20; ②), and cheap **hotels** around its train station.

LANGUEDOC AND ROUSSILLON

Languedoc is more an idea than a geographical entity. The modern region covers only a fraction of the lands which stretched south from Bordeaux and Lyon into Spain and northwest Italy where once *Occitan* or the *langue d'oc* was spoken. Although things are changing, the sense of being Occitanian remains strong, a regional identity that dates back to the Middle Ages, when its castles and fortified villages were the final refuges of the Cathars, a heretical religious sect. The old Roman town of **Nîmes** is an entry point; beyond, **Montpellier** is a good base, though otherwise the coast is not generally noteworthy, the beaches for the most part bleak strands, windswept and cut off from their hinterland by marshy lakes. They have the bonus of relatively unpolluted and uncrowded water, but even this is under threat from development. **Narbonne** and **Béziers** are enjoyable urban diversions, as is **Toulouse**, the cultural capital, though it lies some way west.

South of Languedoc, **Roussillon**, or French Catalonia, maintains much of its Catalan identity, though by contrast with the Basques there is little support nowadays for political independence or reunification with Spanish Catalunya, of which it was a part until the seventeenth century. Its countryside is its best feature, its hills and valleys providing some fine walking. The coast is again something of a disappointment, although the region's main town, **Perpignan**, provides an enjoyable diversion.

For information on the region, consult *www.cr-languedocroussillon.fr*.

Nîmes and around

NÎMES is inescapably linked to two things: Rome – whose influence is manifest in some of the most extensive Roman remains in Europe – and denim, a word corrupted from *de Nîmes*, from Nîmes. Denim was first manufactured as *serge* in the city's textile mills and exported by a certain Mr Levi-Strauss to the USA to clothe miners.

The old centre of Nîmes spreads northwards from place des Arènes, site of the magnificent first-century **Arena** (daily: May–Sept 9am–6.30pm; rest of year 9am–5.30pm; €4.30), one of the best-preserved Roman arenas in the world. The arcaded two-storey facade conceals massive interior vaulting that supports tiers giving a capacity of more than 20,000. When Rome's sway was broken by the barbarian invasions, the arena became a fortress and eventually a slum, home to some two thousand people until the early 1800s. Today it has recovered something of its former role: in summer it hosts bullfights, opera and an international jazz festival. Heading northeast along Boulevard Victor Hugo is the **Maison Carrée** (daily 9am–5/6.30pm; free), a compact temple built in 5 AD and celebrated for its harmony of proportion. It stands in a square opposite rue Auguste, former site of the Roman forum.

The **Cathedral** on place aux Herbes was mutilated in the Wars of Religion and significantly altered in the nineteenth century. Alphonse Daudet was born in its shadow, as was Jean Nicot, the doctor who introduced tobacco into France from Portugal in 1560, and gave his name to nicotine. Next to the cathedral in the Bishop's Palace, the **Musée du Vieux Nîmes** (Tues–Sun 11am–6pm; €4.30) has interesting displays of Renaissance furnishings and decor, while the **Musée Archéologique** (same hours and price), backing onto Grande Rue in a seventeenth-century Jesuit chapel, gives further background on Roman Nîmes. Further out, across rue de la Libération, the **Musée des Beaux-Arts** on rue Cité Foulc (same hours and price) prides itself on a huge Gallo-Roman mosaic showing the *Marriage of Admetus*. You can buy a €9 **museum pass** from the tourist office, which gives access to all sites for a day.

Practicalities

Nîmes **train station** is at the end of av Feuchères, and at the time of writing is expanding to allow for a new TGV line from Paris. The main **tourist office** is at 6 rue Auguste, by the Maison Carrée (Mon–Fri 8.30am–7/8pm, Sat 9am–7pm, Sun 10am–6pm; *www.ot-nimes.fr*). If you want to stay in the heart of things, try the welcoming and excellent value *Hôtel du Temple*, 1 rue Charles Babut (☎04.66.67.54.61, ④). Just opposite, at 2 place de Château, is the similarly appealing *Hôtel Central* (☎04.66.67.27.75; ④). There's a **hostel** on chemin de la Cigale (☎04.66.68.03.20, *nimes@fuaj.org*; ②) which also has tent space. The main **campsite** is the *Domaine de la Bastide* on route de Générac (☎04.66.38.09.21), 4km from the station. For superb regional **food** at low prices, you can do no better than *Le Ménestrel*, 6 rue de l'École. Place du Marché and place aux Herbes are home to several good cafés and brasseries, while bd Victor Hugo has plenty of lively spots for a drink. Netgames, noisy with local lads playing the latest computer games, offers **Internet** access just behind the temple, at place de la Maison Carrée (daily 10am–midnight).

Around Nîmes

Several buses a day head east from Nîmes bus station to Uzès via the **Pont du Gard**, the greatest surviving stretch of the Roman water supply system to the city and a supreme piece of engineering. Three tiers of arches span the river, with the covered water conduit on the top waterproofed with a paint based on fig juice. As long as the height doesn't bother you, feel free to walk across it.

UZÈS is another 17km on, an attractive old town perched on a hill above the River Alzon, a bit of a backwater until renovation put its half-dozen medieval towers and narrow lanes of Renaissance and classical houses on the tourist circuit. From **Le Portalet**, with its view out over the valley, walk past the classical church of St-Étienne into the medieval **place aux Herbes**, where there's a market on Wednesdays and Saturdays, and up the arcaded **rue de la République**. To the right, the castle of **Le Duché** (daily: June–Sept 10am–6pm; rest of year 10am–noon & 2–6pm; €7.50), still inhabited by the same family a thousand years on, is dominated by its original keep, the Tour Bermonde. Uzès **tourist office** is in av de la Libération, next to the bus station (June–Sept Mon–Fri 9am–6pm, Sat & Sun 10am–1pm & 2–5pm; rest of year Mon–Fri 9am–noon & 1.30–6pm, Sat 10am–1pm; *www.ville-uzes.fr*).

Montpellier

A thousand years of trade and intellect have made **MONTPELLIER** a teeming, energetic city. Benjamin of Tudela, the twelfth-century Jewish traveller, reported its streets crowded with traders – Christian and Saracen, Arabs, and merchants from Lombardy, Rome and every corner of the Mediterranean from Egypt to Spain. Little has dented this progress, and the reputation of its university, founded in the thirteenth century, has shone untarnished.

At the town's hub is **place de la Comédie** – *L'Oeuf* to the initiated – a grand oval square paved with cream-coloured marble and surrounded by cafés. The **Opéra**, an ornate nineteenth-century theatre, presides over one end, while the other end leads onto the similarly colossal tree-lined **Esplanade** and, to the right, the **Polygone** shopping complex. On the Esplanade, Montpellier's most trumpeted museum, the **Musée Fabre** (Tues–Fri 9am–5.30pm, Sat & Sun 9.30am–5pm; €3), has a vast collection of seventeenth- to nineteenth-century European painting, some Delacroix, Courbet, Impressionists and a few moderns. Behind the Opéra lie the tangled, hilly lanes of Montpellier's **old quarter**, full of seventeenth- and eighteenth-century mansions, a curious mix of chic restoration and dilapidated disorder. Rue de l'Argenterie forks up to **place Jean-Jaurès**, with its morning **market** and cafés, a short walk from two local-history museums on place Pétrarque: the **Musée du Vieux Montpellier** (Tues–Sat 9.30am–noon & 1.30–5pm; free), concentrating on the city's history, and the more interesting **Musée du Fougau** (Wed & Thurs 3–6pm; free), dealing with the folk history of Languedoc. On the western edge of the centre, at the end of rue Foch, are the formal gardens of the **Promenade du Peyrou** and a vainglorious triumphal arch showing Louis XIV/Hercules stomping on the Austrian eagle and the English lion. The **Jardin des Plantes**, just north of here, with its alleys of exotic trees, is France's oldest botanical garden (Tues–Sat 10/11am–6/7pm).

Practicalities

The **train station** is next to the **bus station** on the southeastern edge of the centre, a short walk down rue Maguelone. The main **tourist office** is in the passage du Tourisme, at the top end of place de la Comédie (Mon–Fri 9am–6.30/7.30pm, Sat 10am–6pm, Sun 9am–1pm & 2–5pm; *www.ot-montpellier.fr*); there's also a desk in the station during July & August. There are numerous **hotels** between the station and place de la Comédie: the *Majestic*, 4 rue du Cheval-Blanc (☎04.67.66.26.85; ③), and the *Central*, 3 rue Passage Bélugou (☎04.67.58.39.28; ③), are both clean and inexpensive, or there's the friendly if slightly overpriced *Mistral*, 25 rue Boussairolles (☎04.67.58.45.25; ④). The **hostel** is on rue des Écoles-Laïques (☎04.67.60.32.22; ②), and there's a municipal **campsite** 2km east of town on route de Mauguio (bus #15). The best general area for places to **eat** is around rue des Écoles-Laïques, and rue de l'Université. Try *Cellier Morel*, 27 rue de l'Aiguillerie, *Chez Marceau* or *Le Vieil Écu* in the delightful place de la Chapelle-Neuve, or *Crêperie des Deux Provinces*, 7 rue Jacques Cœur. For **Internet** access, make for Cybersurf, 22/24 place du Millénaire (Mon–Fri 8am–10pm, Sat & Sun 10am–6pm).

Béziers

Though no longer the rich city it was in its nineteenth-century heyday, **BÉZIERS** is the capital of the Languedoc **wine** country and consequently popular with visitors keen on wine-tasting. The first view of the old town as you come in from the west is spectacular. From the Pont-Neuf across the River Orb, you look upstream at the sturdy golden arches of the **Pont-Vieux**, with the **Cathedral** crowning the steep-banked hill behind, more like a castle than a church. The building is mainly Gothic, in the northern style, the original having been burned in 1209 when much of the city was destroyed and the population massacred for refusing to hand over about twenty Cathars. From the top of the cathedral's tower, there's a superb view out across the vine-dominated surrounding landscape. Next door, an ancient **cloister** gives access to a terraced garden above the river. The narrow medieval streets make for a pleasant stroll, with their mixture of sunny southern elegance and dilapidation. Centre of Béziers' life are the lively **allées Paul-Riquet**, a broad, leafy esplanade laid out in the nineteenth century and lined with cafés and restaurants; the *allées* run from an elaborate theatre in the north to the gorgeous little park of the **Plateau des Poètes**, designed by the creator of the Bois de Boulogne in Paris.

Arriving at Béziers **train station**, the best way into town is through the Plateau des Poètes. The **tourist office** is at 29 av Saint-Saëns (July & Aug daily 9am–7pm; rest of year Mon–Fri 9am–noon & 2–6/6.30pm, Sat 9am–noon & 3–6pm; *www.ville-beziers.fr*). For **hotels**, try the attractive *Hôtel des Poètes*, 80 allées Paul-Riquet (☎04.67.76.38.66; ③), the central *Angleterre*, 22 place Jean-Jaurès (☎04.67.28.48.42; ③), or the *Hôtel du Théâtre*, 13 rue de la Coquille (☎04.67.49.13.43; ④). The nearest **campsite** is on Route de Bessan (☎04.67.76.78.97; April–Oct). For **eating**, there are several places on allées Paul-Riquet, or try *Le Cep d'Or* at 7 rue Viennet, which specializes in seafood.

Carcassonne

CARCASSONNE couldn't be easier to reach, sited on the main Toulouse–Montpellier train link, and for anyone travelling through this region it is a must – one of the most dramatic (if also most visited) towns in the whole of Languedoc. It owes its division into two separate "towns", the **Cité** and **Ville Basse**, to the Cathar wars of the Middle Ages. Following Simon de Montfort's capture of the town in 1209, its people tried to restore their traditional ruling family, the Trencavels, in 1240. In reprisal King Louis IX expelled them, only permitting their return on condition they built on the low ground by the River Aude.

The Ville Basse is enticing, but the main attraction is without question the Cité, a double-walled and turreted **fortress-town** crowning the hill above the Aude. Viollet-le-Duc rescued it from ruin in 1844, and his "too-perfect" restoration has been furiously debated ever since. It is, as you would expect, a real tourist trap. There is no charge for admission to the main part of the city, or the grassy *lices* (moat) between the walls. However, to see the inner fortress of the **Château Comtal**, and to walk along the walls, you have to join a guided tour (daily: June–Sept 9.30am–7.30pm; rest of year 9.30am–5/6pm; €5.30). In addition to wandering the narrow streets, don't miss the beautiful church of **St-Nazaire** at the end of rue St-Louis (July & Aug daily 9am–7pm; rest of year Mon–Sat 9–11.45am & 1.45–5pm, Sun 9–10.45am & 2–5pm), a serene combination of Romanesque nave with carved capitals, and Gothic transepts and choir adorned with some of the loveliest stained glass.

From Carcassonne **airport**, bus #7 shuttles to the **train station** in the Ville Basse (takes 30min; €0.90). The **tourist office** is at 15 bd Camille-Pelletan, at the end of place Gambetta in the Ville Basse (July & Aug daily 9am–7pm; rest of year 9am–12.15pm & 1.45–6.30pm; *www.tourisme.fr/carcassonne*), with an annexe in the Tours Narbonnaises in the Cité (daily: June–Sept 9am–7pm; rest of year 9am–6/7pm). You can rent **bikes** at the train station. **Accommodation** in the Cité is pricey, apart from the **hostel** on rue Trencavel (☎04.68.25.23.16; ②; closed Dec & Jan), and you're better off at a **hotel** in the Ville Basse such as the reasonable *Le Cathare*, 53 rue Jean-Bringer (☎04.68.25.65.92; ③). The nearest **campsite**, *Camping de la Cité*, is off route de St-Hilaire (☎04.68.25.11.77) just west of the Cité. The only affordable **restaurant** in the Cité is the excellent *Auberge de Dame Carcas*, 3 place du Château, a traditional bistro with meals for less than €15.

Toulouse

TOULOUSE, with its historic, pink-coloured buildings, is one of the most vibrant provincial cities in France, a result of a deliberate policy to make it the centre of hi-tech industry. Always an aviation centre – St-Exupéry and Mermoz flew out from here on their pioneering flights over Africa in the 1920s – Toulouse is now home to Aérospatiale, the driving force behind Concorde, Airbus and the Ariane space rocket. Added zest comes from its 60,000 students, who make it second only to Paris as a university centre.

The centre of the city is a rough hexagon clamped around a bend in the wide, brown Garonne. At 21 rue de Metz, the **Musée des Augustins** (Mon & Wed–Sun 10am–6pm; €1.80) incorporates the two cloisters of an Augustinian priory and houses collections of outstanding Romanesque and Gothic sculpture, much of it saved from the now-vanished churches of Toulouse's golden age. Outside the museum, the main shopping street, **rue Alsace-Lorraine**, runs north. West of here are the cobbled streets of the **old city**, lined with the ornate *hôtels* of the merchants who grew rich on the woad trade, basis of the city's economy until the sixteenth century. The almost exclusive building material is the flat Toulousain brick, whose cheerful rosy colour gives the city its nickname of *ville rose*. Best known of these palaces is the **Hôtel Assézat**, towards the river end of rue de Metz, which houses the marvellous private art collection of the **Fondation Bemberg** (Tues–Sun 10am–6pm, Thurs until 9pm; €4.60), which includes an excellent room of works by Bonnard. Also for art lovers is the new modern art museum **Les Abattoirs**, housed in a vaulted nineteenth-century building at 76 allées Charles de Fitte (Tues–Sun noon–8pm; *www.lesabattoirs.org*; €3). It features inspiring and, at times, bizarre temporary exhibitions, but the highlight is the extraordinary *La dépouille de Minotaure en costume d'Arlequin*, an enormous theatre backdrop completed by Picasso with Luis Fernandez in 1936. The room which holds it offers several viewpoints of the magnificent canvas, and the sheer size of the thing, coupled with the intriguing subject matter and dream-like hues, makes it quite breathtaking.

The **place du Capitole** is the site of Toulouse's huge classical town hall and is today a great meeting-place, with numerous cafés and a weekday market. North, rue du Taur leads to **place St-Sernin** and the largest Romanesque church in France, the **basilica de St-Sernin**. Begun in 1080 to accommodate the passing hordes of pilgrims, it is one of the loveliest examples of its genre. To get into the ambulatory you have to pay €1.50, but it's worth it for the exceptional eleventh-century marble reliefs on the end wall of the choir. Right outside on Saturday and Sunday mornings is an impressively shambolic **flea market**. West of place du Capitole, on rue Lakanal, the church of **Les Jacobins** is another unmissable ecclesiastical building, started in 1230 by the Dominicans. It's a huge fortress-like rectangle of unadorned brick, with an interior divided by a central row of ultraslim pillars from whose capitals spring an elegant splay of vaulting ribs. Beneath the altar lie the bones of the philosopher St Thomas Aquinas, while on the north side is a calming cloister.

Practicalities

Trains and buses arrive at the **gare Matabiau**, twenty minutes' walk from the centre down allées Jean-Jaurès or a five-minute métro ride. The **tourist office** is just behind place du Capitole on pl Charles de Gaulle (May–Sept Mon–Sat 9am–7pm, Sun 10am–1pm & 2–6.30pm; rest of year Mon–Fri 9am–6pm, Sat 9am–12.30pm & 2–6pm, Sun 10am–12.30pm & 2–5pm; *www.toulouse.com*). Best of the city's budget **hotels** are the centrally placed *Hôtel du Grand Balcon*, 8 rue Romiguières (☎05.61.21.48.08; ④), the *Anatole France*, 46 pl A-France (☎05.61.23.19.96; ③) and *Hôtel de l'Université*, 26 rue Emile Cartailhac (☎05.61.21.35.69; ③). The closest **campsite** is on the chemin du Pont de Rupé, just north of the city (☎05.61.70.07.35); bus #59 from place Jeanne-d'Arc. When the time comes to **eat**, several excellent places in the food market on place Victor-Hugo open only for lunch. The cafés and brasseries on trendy pl St-Georges get busy in the evenings; alternatively, try around place Arnaud-Bernard in the rapidly gentrifying former Arab quarter on the north edge of the centre, where you'll find the lively jazz, blues and salsa bar *La Cav' Ragtime*. Beside the river, the chic brasserie *Des Beaux-Arts*, by Pont Neuf, is good for a gastronomic treat, while the nearby *Tantina de Burgos*, 27 av de la Garonnette, has great tapas. Cyber Copie, 5 pl du Peyrou, and Cyber Media, 10 rue de la Combette, offer **Internet** access.

Albi

Though not itself an important centre of Catharism, **ALBI** gave its name – Albigensian – to both the heresy and the crusade to suppress it. Today it is a small industrial town an hour's train ride northeast of Toulouse, with two unique sights. The first, the **cathedral** (daily: June–Sept 8.30am–7pm; rest of year 9am–noon & 2.30–6.30pm; €0.80 admission to the choir), is visible the moment you arrive at the train station, dwarfing the town. The brutal, fortress-like exterior expresses the power and authority the church had over the heretical townspeople. The vast hall-like nave is richly decorated with colourful Italian paintings. Opposite the east end of the cathedral, rue Mariès leads into the shopping streets of the **old town**, but the most interesting sight is next door in the powerful red-brick Palais de la Berbie, which houses Albi's other main attraction, the **Musée Toulouse-Lautrec** (Mon & Wed–Sun July & Aug 9am–6pm; rest of year 10am–noon & 2–6/6.30pm; €3.70). The artist was a native of the town, and the museum boasts a huge collection of his paintings, drawings, lithographs and posters, from the earliest work to his very last.

The **tourist office** is on the corner of Palais de la Berbie and place St-Cécile (July & Aug Mon–Sat 9am–7.30pm, Sun 10.30am–1pm & 3.30–6.30pm; rest of year Mon–Sat 9am–noon & 2–6pm, Sun 10.30am–12.30pm & 2.30–5.30pm; *www.mairie-albi.fr*). There's a scruffy *Maison des Jeunes* **hostel** at 13 rue de la République (☎05.63.54.53.65; ①), with very low-priced dorm beds; inexpensive **hotels** include the *Terminus*, by the station at 33 av Maréchal Joffre (☎05.63.54.00.99; ③), and the *Fouillade*, 12 place Pelloutier (☎05.63.54.21.86; ③). The nearest **campsite** is the *Parc du Caussels*, about 2km east on the D999 (☎05.63.60.37.06; April–Oct). For **eating**, try the *Casa Créole* or *Auberge Saint-Loup*, both on rue Castelviel at the west of the cathedral; the vegetarian *Le Tournesol*, in rue de l'Ort-en-Salvy, is also good.

Perpignan and around

This far south, climate and geography alone would ensure a palpable Spanish influence. But more than this, a good part of **PERPIGNAN**'s population is of Spanish origin – refugees from the Civil War and their descendants. The southern influence is further augmented by a substantial admixture of North Africans, including both Arabs and white French settlers repatriated after Algerian independence in 1962. While there are few memorable monuments, Perpignan is a pleasant city with a lively street life. Its heyday was during the thirteenth and fourteenth centuries, when the kings of Mallorca held their court here. For most of the Middle Ages its allegiance swung back and forth between France and Aragon, until finally it became part of the French state under Louis XIV in 1659.

The centre of Perpignan is marked by the palm trees and smart cafés of **place Arago**. From here rue Alsace-Lorraine and rue de la Loge lead past the massive iron gates of the classical Hôtel de Ville to the tiny **place de la Loge**, the focus of the renovated old core, dominated by the **Loge de Mer**, a late fourteenth-century Gothic building designed to hold the city's stock exchange and a maritime court. North up rue Louis-Blanc is one of the city's few remaining fortifications, the crenellated fourteenth-century gate of **Le Castillet**, now home to the **Casa Pairal**, a fascinating **museum** of Roussillon's Catalan folk culture (Mon & Wed–Sun: summer 10am–7pm; winter 11am–5.30pm; €3.80). In the gloomy nave of the fourteenth-century **Cathédrale St-Jean**, down rue St-Jean and across place Gambetta, are some elaborate Catalan altarpieces, while a side-chapel to the south, somewhat incongruously, houses a tortured Rhenish altarpiece dating from around 1400. Through place des Esplanades, crowning the hill which dominates the southern part of the old town, is the **Palais des Rois de Majorque** (daily: June–Sept 10am–6pm; Oct–May 9am–5pm; €3). Vauban's walls surround it now, but the two-storey palace and its great arcaded courtyard date from the late thirteenth century. The Spanish–Moorish influence lends sophistication and finesse to the architecture and detailing, particularly the beautiful marble porch to the lower of the two chapels.

To get to the centre from the **train station**, follow av Général-de-Gaulle to place de la Catalogne, and then continue along bd Clemenceau as far as Le Castillet. The **tourist office** is a short stroll from here, in the Palais des Congrès at the end of bd Wilson (June–Sept Mon–Sat 9am–7pm, Sun 10am–noon & 2–5pm; rest of year Mon–Fri 9am–6pm, Sat 9am–noon & 2–6pm; *www.little-france.com/perpignan*), with an annexe in the Hôtel de Ville (June–Sept Mon–Sat 9am–7pm). The **bus station** is beside Pont Arago, on av Général-Leclerc. The best place to look for **accommodation** is around the station: try the friendly, inexpensive *Hôtel le Berry*, 6 av Général-de-Gaulle (☎04.68.34.59.02; ②). The **hostel** (☎04.68.34.63.32; ②) is about 1km from the station in Parc de la Pépinière by the river. The **campsite**, *Le Catalan*, is on route de Bompas (☎04.68.63.16.92), signposted from the centre. The station is also a good area for inexpensive **food**, while *Bistro St Jean* in place Gambetta nearer the centre dishes up quality Catalan cuisine at low prices.

Around Perpignan

Regular **buses** from Perpignan's bus station follow the D115 inland up the **Tech valley** to the Spanish border, offering a wealth of possibilities for countryside walks. Just west of the first town, **CÉRET**, past the leaping single span of its fourteenth-century **Pont du Diable**, the view opens north towards the towering Canigou Massif. The GR10 hikers' footpath passes through **ARLES-SUR-TECH**, 4km up the valley, climbing north towards Canigou and south towards the Roc de France. A couple of kilometres out of Arles is the entrance to the spectacular **Gorges de la Fou**, some 2km in length, very narrow and up to 250m deep (Easter–Oct 10am–6pm; closed during bad weather; €4.60). The road climbs on, between valley sides thick with walnut, oak and sweet chestnut, to **PRATS-DE-MOLLO**, the last town in France, unspoiled, attractive and very Spanish, with an atmospheric cobbled old quarter. Hotel *Bellevue* (☎04.68.39.72.48; ③; April–Oct) overlooks the main square, **El Firal**.

THE MASSIF CENTRAL

Thickly forested, and sliced by numerous rivers and lakes, the **Massif Central**, occupying a huge swathe of the middle of France, is geologically the oldest part of the country, and culturally one of the most firmly rooted in the past. Industry and tourism have made few inroads here, and the people remain rural and taciturn, with an enduring sense of regional identity. The heart of the region is the **Auvergne**, a wild, inaccessible landscape dotted with extinct volcanic peaks known as *puys*, much of it now incorporated into the **Parc Naturel Régional des Volcans d'Auvergne**, France's largest regional park. To the southeast are the gentler wooded hills of the **Cévennes** that form part of the **Parc National des Cévennes**. Only a handful of towns have gained a foothold in this rugged terrain. **Le Puy**, spiked with jagged pinnacles of lava and with a majestic cathedral, is the most compelling, but there is appeal, too, in the elegant spa city of **Vichy** and in the provincial capital, **Clermont-Ferrand**. Surf to *www.crt-auvergne.fr* for information on the region.

Clermont-Ferrand and around

CLERMONT-FERRAND is an incongruous capital for rustic Auvergne – a lively, youthful city with a major university and a manufacturing base (it's the HQ of the Michelin organization). Although hardly resplendent with cultural treats, it has a well-preserved historic centre and is an ideal base for this side of the Massif and the nearby spectacle of **Puy de Dôme** and the Parc des Volcans.

Clermont and neighbouring Montferrand were united in 1631 to form a single city, but you're likely to spend most of your time in the former, since what is left of Vieux Montferrand stands out on a limb to the east. Clermont's most immediate feature is its *"ville-noire"* aspect – so-called after the local black volcanic rock used in the construction of many of its buildings: the town, dark and sombre, clusters untidily around the summit of a worn-away volcanic peak. On the edge of old Clermont, the huge and soulless **place de Jaude** is the hub of the city and its main shopping area. In the centre stands a rousing statue of the Gallic chieftain Vercingétorix, who in 53 BC led his people to their only – and indecisive – victory over Julius Caesar just south of the town. North from place de Jaude, **place St-Pierre** is the site of Clermont's principal market, with a morning food **market**, at its liveliest on Saturdays. The nearby **Musée du Ranquet**, in a sixteenth-century building at 34 rue des Gras (opening times vary due to ongoing renovations; €1.90), is one of the city's best museums, with displays on local history back to Roman times.

The streets gather up to the dark and soaring **Cathédrale Notre-Dame**, whose strong volcanic stone made it possible to build vaults and pillars of unheard-of slenderness and height; off the nave, the **Tour de la Bayette** (summer only Mon–Sat 2–6pm, Sun 3–6pm; €1.50) gives extensive views across the city. A short step northeast of the cathedral, on place Delille, stands Clermont's other great church, the **Basilique Notre-Dame du Port**, a beautiful building, pure Auvergnat Romanesque, that is on the UNESCO World Heritage list.

Practicalities

The **train station** is on av de l'URSS, east of the city centre, and is connected by frequent buses with place de Jaude. The main **tourist office** is on place de la Victoire (June–Sept Mon–Fri 9am–7pm, Sat & Sun 10am–6pm; rest of year Mon–Fri 9am–6pm, Sat 10am–1pm & 2–6pm, Sun 9.30am–12.30pm & 2–6pm; *www.clermont-fd.com*), with an additional office at the train station and a summer annexe in the Roger-Quillet Fine Arts Museum in the old centre of Montferrand. The main tourist office has an area devoted to local **hiking** and **mountain-biking** as well as a Romanesque Art Centre in the basement. Clermont's **hostel** is at 55 av de l'URSS (☎04.73.92.26.39; ②; March–Oct), two minutes' walk right of the station; the *Corum St-Jean*, 17 rue Gaultier-de-Biauzat (☎04.73.31.57.00; ②), charges a little more but is much nicer. There's a cluster of **hotels** outside the station, of which the *Grand Hôtel du Midi*, 39 av de l'URSS (☎04.73.92.44.98; ③), is one of the least expensive; nearer the centre is the *Foch*, 22 rue Maréchal-Foch (☎04.73.93.48.40; ④). The nearest **campsite** is at Royat to the west (☎04.73.35.97.05; April–Oct; bus #41). For **food**, the very popular *Crêperie 1513*, 3 rue des Chaussetiers, has a fine setting in a medieval mansion opposite the cathedral, and *Le Bistrot Vénitien*, 26 rue des Gras, dishes up good pizzas and pastas. The tiny place Renoux, off rue Maréchal-Joffre, and place de la Victoire make pleasant drinking spots. Check your **email** at the Internet Café, 34 rue Ballainvilliers (daily 8am–9.30pm).

Puy de Dôme

Puy de Dôme, a few kilometres west of Clermont-Ferrand, is one of the tallest of the *puys*, with sweeping views back towards the town and the Parc des Volcans. Getting there is tricky: there is no public transport and a **taxi** will set you back around €38. There are shuttle buses from the base to the summit (€3.20), but access is often blocked due to bad weather – make sure to call the site before you leave to check conditions (☎04.73.62.12.18). Close to the summit, ruins survive of a **Roman temple** to Mercury, in its time considered one of the marvels of the empire, fashioned from over fifty different kinds of marble and with an enormous bronze statue of Mercury where a TV antenna now stands. If you're walking here from Clermont, or even Royat, be sure to allow a good half-day, and take food. The **restaurant** on top enjoys a monopoly and makes full use of it. **Vulcania**, a park and museum dedicated to exploring the universe of volcanoes, is due to open in mid-2002 on a site just north of Puy de Dôme.

Vichy

VICHY is famous for two things: its World War II puppet government under the Nazi collaborationist Marshal Pétain and its curative sulphurous springs. The population is largely elderly and swells several-fold in summer. Life revolves around the **Parc des Sources**, a stately tree-shaded park that takes up most of the centre. At the north end stands the **Halle des Sources**, an enormous iron-framed greenhouse in which the various waters emerge from their spouts, people lining up to get their prescribed cupful. For a small fee you can join them, though bear in mind that only one of the five springs (the *Célestin*) is bottled and widely drunk; the others are progressively more foul and sulphurous, culminating in the Source de l'Hôpital, a truly despicable brew, which has its own building at the far end of the park. After the waters, Vichy's curiosities are limited. Marshal Pétain's own offices were at the *Pavillon*, while the Gestapo had their headquarters at the *Hôtel du Portugal*, but, unsurprisingly, there's nothing to commemorate either of them.

The **train station** is on the eastern edge of the centre, at the end of rue de Paris. The **tourist office** is housed in Pétain's government building, 19 rue du Parc (July & Aug Mon–Sat 9am–7.30pm, Sun 9.30am–12.30pm & 3–7pm; rest of year Mon–Sat 9am–noon/12.30pm & 1.30–6/7pm, Sun 9.30am–12.30pm & 3–7pm; Oct–March Sun 2.30–5.30pm only; *www.ville-vichy.fr*). *Villa Claudius Petit* offers student **accommodation** on av des Célestins (☎04.70.98.43.39; ②) and there's a **campsite** (☎04.70.32.36.22) across the pont de Bellerive from the Parc de l'Allier. Among **hotels**, try either the *Trianon*, 9 rue Desbrest (☎04.70.97.95.96; ④), or the *Azurea* down the street at no. 14 (☎04.70.98.33.88; ⑤). The junction of rue Clemenceau, rue de Pans, rue Lucas and rue Jean-Jaurès has plenty of **restaurants**.

Le Puy

A strange town in a strange setting, **LE PUY** sprawls across a broad basin in the mountains, a muddle of red roofs barbed with poles of volcanic rock. Both landscape and architecture are totally theatrical. In medieval times it was the assembly point for pilgrims heading for Santiago de Compostela in Spain, and amid the cobbled streets of the old town are some of the most richly endowed churches in the land. The odd surrounding countryside is an added attraction. And the town still produces its famous green *Le Puy* lentils.

The **old town**, reached by climbing the steep sequence of streets and steps that terrace the town's *puy* foundation, is dominated by the **Cathedral** – almost Byzantine in style, striped with alternate layers of light and dark stone and capped with a line of small cupolas. The Black Virgin inside is a copy of a revered original burned during the Revolution, and is still paraded through the town every August 15. Other, lesser treasures are displayed at the back of the church in the sacristy, beyond which is the entrance to the beautiful twelfth-century **cloister** (daily: July–Sept 9.30am–6.30pm; rest of year 9.30am–noon/12.30pm & 2–4.30/6.30pm; €4). At the highest point in the town is the giant crimson statue of the **Virgin and Child**, fashioned from the metal of guns captured in the Crimean War; you can pay €3 to climb to the top for some stunning views. The nearby church of **St-Michel** (daily: mid-June to mid-Sept 9am–7pm; rest of year 9/10am–noon & 2–5/7pm; €2), sitting on the peak of an even steeper *puy*, the Rocher d'Aiguilhe, is an eleventh-century construction that seems to grow out of the rock itself. It's a tough ascent, but one you should definitely make: St-Michel is a quirky little building decorated with mosaics, arabesques and trefoil arches, its bizarre shape following that of the available flat ground. Back down below, lace-makers – a traditional, though now commercialized industry – do a fine trade. Le Puy's old lanes form an uncluttered and wonderful maze, while in the new part of town, beyond the squat Tour Pannessac, **place de Breuil** and **place Michelet** form the social hub, with spacious public gardens.

Arriving by **bus or train** you'll find yourself on place du Maréchal-Leclerc, a ten-minute walk from place de Breuil and the **tourist office** (July & Aug daily 8.30am–7.30pm; rest of year daily 8.30am–noon & 1.30–6.15pm; Oct–Easter Sun 10am–noon only; *www.ot-lepuyenve-lay.fr*), and within easy striking distance of some reasonably priced **hotels**, including the *Régional*, 36 bd Maréchal-Fayolle (☎04.71.09.37.74; ③). There's a **hostel** at the Centre Pierre-Cardinal, 9 rue Jules-Vallès (☎04.71.05.52.40; ②), and a **campsite**, *Bouthézard*, half-an-hour's walk from the station along chemin de Roderie (☎04.71.09.55.09; bus #6). For **food**, the restaurants around place Breuil and place Michelet are decent.

BURGUNDY

Peaceful, rural **Burgundy** is one of the most prosperous regions of modern France and was for a long time independent from the French state. In the fifteenth century its dukes ruled an empire that embraced much of northeastern France, Belgium and the Netherlands, with revenues equalled only by Venice. Everywhere there is startling evidence of this former wealth and power, both secular and religious. **Dijon**, the dukes' capital, is a slick and prosperous town with plenty of remnants of old Burgundy; to the north, the town of **Sens** is a worthy stop-off on the way into the region, as is the great abbey of **Vézelay**. South, there are substantial Roman remains at **Autun** and the ruins of the monastery of **Cluny**, whose influence was second only to that of Rome for a time, though wine devotees may head straight for the **vineyards**, whose produce has been a major moneymaker since Louis XIV's doctor prescribed the stuff for the royal dyspepsia. **Beaune** is a good centre for sampling the best of the wine, washed down with rich local specialities like *escargots à la bourguignonne*, *bœuf bourguignon* and *coq au vin*. For regional information go to *www.burgundy-tourism.com*.

Sens

Only an hour by train from Paris, **SENS**, though never part of the Duchy of Burgundy, feels like a typically Burgundian town. Contained within a ring of tree-lined boulevards where the city walls once stood, its ancient centre, focusing on place de la République, is still dominated by the **Cathédrale de St-Étienne**. Begun around 1130, it was the first of the great French Gothic cathedrals and is a fine example of the space and weightlessness of the genre. The architect who completed it, William of Sens, was later to rebuild the choir of Canterbury Cathedral in England. Thomas à Becket spent several years in exile around Sens, and the story of his murder is told in the twelfth-century windows in the north aisle of the choir, just part of the cathedral's outstanding collection of stained glass. The **treasury** (June–Sept daily 10am–noon & 2–6pm; rest of year Mon, Thurs & Fri 2–6pm, Wed, Sat & Sun 10am–noon & 2–6pm; €3) is also uncommonly rich, containing Islamic, Byzantine and French vestments, jewels and embroideries. Just south is the thirteenth-century **Palais Synodal**, with its roof of Burgundian glazed tiles, restored like so many other buildings in this region by Viollet-le-Duc. Its vaulted halls, originally designed to accommodate the ecclesiastical courts, now house a small **museum** (same hours and ticket as treasury) of statuary from the cathedral and Gallo-Roman mosaics. Underneath is a medieval prison.

The **train station** is about ten minutes' walk from the cathedral, at the end of the main Grand Rue. The **tourist office** is on the north edge of the small centre, on place Jean-Jaurès (July & Aug Mon–Sat 9am–12.30pm & 1.30–7pm, Sun 10am–12.30pm & 1.30–5.30pm; rest of year Mon–Fri 9am–noon & 1.30–6.15pm, Sat 9am–noon & 1.30–5.30pm; *otsi.sens@wanadoo.fr*). For **accommodation**, try *Le Chemin de Fer* (✆03.86.65.10.27; ②) opposite the station or, in the centre, the *Esplanade*, 2 bd du Mail (✆03.86.83.14.71; ③). The nearest **campsite** is *d'Entre-deux-Vannes*, on av de Sénigallia (✆03.86.65.64.71; April–Nov; bus #6 from the centre). For **eating**, rue de la République is a safe bet: *La Cathédrale*, at no. 13, does good traditional fare. Alternatively, there's a good crêperie, *Au Petit Creux*, at 3 rue de Brennus.

Vézelay

The abbey church of **La Madeleine** at **VÉZELAY**, one of the seminal buildings of the Romanesque period, was saved from collapse by Viollet-le-Duc in 1840. The church was home, it was thought, to the bones of Mary Magdalene, and so was a major pilgrimage site and assembly point for pilgrims heading for Santiago de Compostela in Spain; today it is a UNESCO World Heritage site. Just inside, the colossal narthex was added to the nave around

1150 to accommodate the pilgrims, and is striking for the superb sculpture on its central doorway, while on the outer arch there are small-scale medallions of the zodiac signs and labours of the months. The long body of the church is vaulted by arches of alternating black and white stone, edged with fretted mouldings, and the supporting pillars are crowned with finely cut capitals depicting scenes from the Bible, classical mythology, allegories and morality stories, in complete contrast to the clean, soaring lines of the early Gothic choir beyond.

There's a small **tourist office** on the right in rue St-Pierre as you go up towards the abbey (summer daily 10am–1pm & 2–6pm; winter closed Thurs; *vezelay.otsi@ipoint.fr*). There are a number of reasonable **hotels**, including *Le Cheval Blanc* (☎03.86.33.22.12; ③) on place Champ-du-Foire, and an HI **hostel** with camping space, about 1km along route de l'Étang (☎03.86.33.24.18; ①; closed Jan).

Dijon

DIJON owes its origins to its strategic position in Celtic times on the merchant route from Britain up the Seine and across the Alps to the Adriatic. But it was as capital of the dukes of Burgundy from 1000 until the late 1400s that it knew its finest hour, under the auspices of dukes Philippe the Bold, Jean the Fearless, Philippe the Good and Charles the Rash. They used their tremendous wealth and power to make Dijon one of the greatest centres of art, learning and science in Europe. Though it lost some of this status with incorporation into the French kingdom in 1477, it has remained one of the pre-eminent provincial cities, especially since the industrial boom of the mid-nineteenth century.

You sense Dijon's former glory more in the lavish houses of its burghers than in the former seat of the dukes, the **Palais des Ducs**, an undistinguished building from the outside and one that has had many alterations, especially in the sixteenth and seventeenth centuries when it became the Parliament of Burgundy. In fact, the only outward reminders of the dukes' building are the fifteenth-century **Tour Philippe le Bon** (closed at the time of writing), from whose terrace on the clearest of days they say you can see Mont Blanc, and the fourteenth-century **Tour de Bar**, which now houses Dijon's **Musée des Beaux-Arts** (Mon & Wed–Sun 10am–6pm; €3.40, free on Sun), with a collection of paintings that represents many different schools and periods from Titian and Rubens to Monet, Manet and other Impressionists, as well as religious artefacts, ivories and tapestries. Visiting the museum also provides the opportunity to see the surviving portions of the ducal palace, including the vast kitchens, the magnificent Salle des Gardes, and the relocated tombs of Philippe the Bold and of Jean the Fearless and his wife, Marguerite de Bavière.

The palace looks onto **place de la Libération**, a gracious semicircular space designed in the late seventeenth century and bordered by houses of honey-coloured stone. Behind the palace is the tiny, enclosed **place des Ducs**, and a maze of lanes flanked by beautiful old houses, best of which are those on **rue des Forges**. Parallel to rue des Forges, **rue de la Chouette** passes the north side of the impressive thirteenth-century Gothic church of **Notre-Dame**, whose north wall holds a small sculpted owl (*chouette*) which people touch for luck and which gives the street its name. At the end of the street is the attractive **place François-Rude**, a favourite summer hangout, crowded with café tables. Just south of here, the **Musée Archéologique**, 5 rue Docteur-Maret (Mon & Wed–Sun 9.30am–6.30pm; €2, free on Sun), has interesting Gallo-Roman funerary bas-reliefs depicting the perennial Gallic preoccupation with food and wine, and a collection of *ex votos* from the source of the Seine, among them the little bronze of the goddess Sequana (Seine), upright in her bird-prowed boat. Back in the town centre at 4 rue des Bons-Enfants, the **Musée Magnin** (Tues–Sun 10am–noon & 2–6pm; €3.70, free on Sun) is a seventeenth-century *hôtel* with its original furnishings, more interesting than its paintings. Further south, the **Musée de la Vie Bourguignonne**, 17 rue St-Anne (Mon & Wed–Sun 9am–noon & 2–6pm; €3, free on Sun), documents Burgundian life in the nineteenth century and is housed in a stark modern setting inside a former convent. Being the mustard capital of France, Dijon of course has a museum dedicated to the stuff, the diverting **Musée de la Moutarde Amora** on Quai Nicolas Rohin (tours only: mid-June to mid-Sept Mon–Sat 3pm; rest of year Wed & Sat 3pm; €3; tickets in advance from tourist offices).

Practicalities

The **train station** is at the end of av Maréchal-Foch, beside the bus station and five minutes from place Darcy, site of the main **tourist office** (May to mid-Oct daily 9am–8pm; rest of year Mon–Sat 10am–5.30/6pm, Sun 10am–1pm; *www.ot-dijon.fr*). Another tourist office is at 34 rue des Forges (May to mid-Oct Mon–Sat 9.30am–1pm & 2–6pm; rest of year Mon–Fri 10am–noon & 2–5pm). Both sell a general **museum ticket** for Dijon museums for €7. The official **hostel** is 4km from the centre at 1 bd Champollion (☎03.80.72.95.20; ②) – take bus #5 from place Grangier. As for **hotels**, try the noisy but welcoming *Monge* at 20 rue Monge (☎03.80.30.55.41; ③), or on the same road, the *Hostellerie Sauvage*, at no. 64 (☎03.80.41.31.21; ⑤). The nearest **campsite** is by the lake off bd Chanoine Kir (☎03.80.43.54.72; April–Oct; bus #12).

There's no problem finding a good **restaurant** in this centre of *haute cuisine*, though locating affordable places is harder. A good bet is bustling rue Berbisey, crammed with cafés and restaurants. With a student card, you can eat in the very cheap university restaurant at 3 rue Docteur-Maret in the centre of town, while the *Coum' Chez Eux*, 68 rue J.J. Rousseau, is just a little more upmarket. If you're prepared to spend even more, *Le Clos des Capucines*, 3 rue Jeannin, serves excellent regional specialities. For a **drink**, *La Marina* and *Flannery's Pub*, in front of the cathedral, are lively bars popular with students, as is *Le Café des Grand Ducs*, 96 rue de la Liberté, open until 3am in summer. Multiresco, in the bus station, offers **Internet** access (Mon–Sat 10am–midnight, Sun 2pm–midnight).

Autun

AUTUN, today scarcely bigger than the circumference of its medieval walls, was one of the leading cities of Roman Gaul, founded by Augustus around 10 BC as part of his campaign to romanize the Celts. Two of the city's four **Roman gates** survive – **Porte St-André** spanning rue de la Croix-Blanche in the northeast and **Porte d'Arroux** in Faubourg d'Arroux in the northwest – while in a field just across the River Arroux stands the so-called **Temple of Janus**, a lofty section of brick wall that was probably part of the sanctuary of some Gallic deity. Off av du 2ème-Dragon are the few remains of the largest **Roman theatre** in Gaul – a measure of the importance of the settlement.

Autun's main street is av Charles-de-Gaulle, leading to the main square, **Champ de Mars**, from which the narrow streets of the **old town** spread, converging towards the **Cathédrale de St-Lazare** in the most southerly and best-fortified corner. Built in the twelfth century and much altered since, the church is uniquely important for its works by Gislebertus, one of the greatest of Romanesque sculptors. The tympanum of the Last Judgement above the west door bears his signature beneath the feet of Christ. The interior was also decorated by Gislebertus, who himself carved most of the capitals, some of the finest of which are now in the old chapter library. There are more pieces by Gislebertus outside the cathedral in the **Musée Rolin**, an old Renaissance *hôtel* on rue des Blancs (April–Sept Mon–Wed & Fri–Sun 9.30am–noon & 1.30–6pm; rest of year same days 10am–noon & 2/2.30–5pm; €3), including his unashamedly sensual portrayal of Eve.

The **train station** is on av de la République, at the far end of av Charles-de-Gaulle, on which you'll find the **tourist office** at no. 2 (June–Sept daily 9am–7pm; rest of year Mon–Sat 9am–noon & 2–6pm; *www.autun.com*). There's a cluster of **hotels** opposite the station: the *Hôtel de France* (☎03.85.52.14.00; ③) and *Commerce et Touring* (☎03.85.52.17.90; ③) are both decent and inexpensive, and the latter has a good, moderately priced **restaurant**. There's a **campsite** (☎03.85.52.10.82) just across the river beyond Porte d'Arroux. Of a number of places to **eat**, check out the *Auberge de la Bourgogne* and the brasserie *Morvandiau* on place

Champ de Mars, and *Le Châteaubriant*, 14 rue Jeannin. **Internet** access is available at Explorateur, 17 rue Guerin (daily 10am–7:30pm).

Cluny

The voice of the abbot of **CLUNY** once made monarchs tremble. His power in the Christian world was second only to that of the pope, his intellectual influence arguably greater. Founded in 910 around 50km south of Dijon, the **monastery** was also one of the richest in France, and it was its wealth and secular involvement that led to the decline of its spiritual influence in the wake of the reforming zeal of St Bernard and his Cistercians.

Sadly, practically nothing of the complex remains. The Revolution suppressed the monastery, and the eleventh-century **church**, the largest building in Christendom until St Peter's in Rome, was dismantled in 1810. All you can see now is an octagonal belfry, the south transept and, in the granary of the former **abbey** (daily: July–Sept 9am–7pm; rest of year 9.30/10am–noon & 2–4/6pm; €5.50), some capitals from its immense columns. The **Musée d'Art et d'Archéologie** (same hours; €2), in the fifteenth-century palace of the last abbot to be freely elected, helps flesh out the picture with reconstructions and sculpture fragments.

If staying in the village, the cheapest option for groups of three or more is *Cluny Séjour,* a municipal **hostel** on rue Porte-de-Paris (☎03.85.59.08.83; ②), though it has a 10pm curfew, or there's a **campsite** (☎03.85.59.08.34; May–Oct) on rue des Griottons across Pont de la Levée on the right. *Hôtel de l'Abbaye* on av Charles de Gaulle (☎03.85.59.11.14; ④) and *Hôtel du Commerce*, 8 place du Commerce (☎03.85.59.03.09; ③), have inexpensive double rooms. The **tourist office** at 6 rue Mercière (June–Sept daily 10am–7pm; rest of year Mon–Sat 10am–12.30pm & 2/2.30–6/7pm; *cluny@wanadoo.fr*) will reserve rooms for a small fee. *Les Marronniers* on av Charles de Gaulle is a reasonable **restaurant**, or you can sample the regional specialities at *Auberge du Cheval Blanc*, 1 rue Porte de Mâcon.

South towards Lyon – the Burgundy vineyards

Burgundy's best **wines** come from a narrow strip of hillside – the **Côte d'Or**, which runs southwest from Dijon to Santenay. It is divided into two regions – **Côte de Nuits** and **Côte de Beaune**. With few exceptions, the reds of the Côte de Nuits are considered the better: they are richer, age better and cost more. Côte de Beaune is known particularly for its whites, such as Meursault, Montrachet and Puligny. The countryside hereabouts is attractive: the steep scarp of the *côte*, wooded along the top, is cut by deep little valleys called *combes*, where local rock climbers hone their skills. The villages, strung along the N74 through the town of Beaune and beyond, are sleepy and exceedingly prosperous, full of houses inhabited by well-heeled *vignerons*. There are numerous *caves* at which to taste and buy, but as usual the former is meant to be a prelude to the latter. If you are buying, be aware that the *Hautes Côtes* (both Nuits and Beaune), from the top of the slope, are lower in price – and cachet.

Beaune

BEAUNE, the principal town of the Côte d'Or, has many charms, but it is totally devoted to tourism. The chief attraction is the fifteenth-century hospital, the **Hôtel-Dieu** on the corner of place de la Halle (daily: March–Nov 9am–6.30pm; rest of year 9–11.30am & 2–5.30pm; €5), whose vast stone-flagged hall has an impressive painted timber roof and until quite recently continued to serve its original purpose. It is here that the Hospices de Beaune's wines are auctioned during the annual *Trois Glorieuses*, the prices paid setting the pattern for the season. The private residence of the dukes of Burgundy on rue d'Enfer now contains the **Musée du Vin** (daily 9.30am–6pm; Dec–March closed Tues; €3.80), with giant winepresses and an interesting collection of tools of the trade. At the other end of rue d'Enfer, the church of **Notre-Dame** (Mon–Sat 9.30am–12.30pm & 2–7pm, Sun 2–7pm) has five tapestries from the fifteenth century depicting the Life of the Virgin, commissioned by the Rolin family.

From the **train station**, the town centre is 500m up av du 8-Septembre, across the boulevard, and left onto rue des Tonneliers. **Buses** leave from outside the walls at the end of rue Maufoux. The **tourist office** is opposite the Hôtel-Dieu on rue de l'Hôtel-Dieu (summer Mon–Sat 9.30am–7/8pm, Sun 9.30/10am–5/6pm; winter Mon–Sat 9.30/10am–5/6pm, Sun 10am–1pm & 2–6pm; *www.ot-beaune.fr*) and has information on wine tours. **Accommodation** is pricey: it's cheaper to use Dijon or Chalon as a base, as both are easily accessible by train and Transco buses, which service all the villages down the N74. Should you have to stay, *Hôtel Foch* (☎03.80.24.05.65; ③), just to the west of town at 24 bd Foch, has some midpriced rooms, or there may be space at the *Foyer des Jeunes Travailleurs* opposite the hospital on av Guigone-de-Salins (☎03.80.24.88.00; ②). There's a **campsite**, *Les Cent Vignes* (☎03.80.22.03.91), 1km out on rue Auguste Dubois off rue du Faubourg-St-Nicolas. **Eating** can also be expensive. The best places for budget meals are rue Monge, place Carnot and rue de Lorraine. *Le Carnot* at 18 rue Carnot is a good cafeteria, and menus at the *La Cave à Crêpes*, 21 bd St-Jacques, start at €7.50. The massive number of **wine** sellers trying to lure you in to sample their wares can leave you feeling overwhelmed, tipsy or both, but one or two of the centrally located vendors are well worth a visit: try the *Caves des Cordeliers* on 6 rue de l'Hôtel-Dieu (daily: June–Sept 9.30am–7pm; rest of year 9.30–11.45am & 2–5.45pm; €3.80 including tasting).

Chalon, Mâcon and the Beaujolais

CHALON, around 30km south of Beaune on the banks of the Saône, has long been a thriving port and industrial centre, and its old riverside quarter has an easy charm, though it is not a place you want to stay very long. The one thing you might want to see is the **Musée Niepce** (Mon & Wed–Sun: summer 10am–6pm; winter 9.30–11.30am & 2.30–5.30pm; €3), on the river quays just downstream from Pont St-Laurent. Local boy Niepce is credited with inventing photography in 1816, and the museum possesses a fascinating range of cameras, from the first-ever to those taken on the Apollo moon mission, plus a number of 007-type spy devices. There are numerous **hotels** and a riverbank **hostel** on rue d'Amsterdam (☎03.85.46.62.77; ②), about a ten-minute walk north of the Pont St-Laurent, the last bridge upstream; the nearest **campsite** (☎03.85.48.26.86) is 3km out of town in St Marcel. SNCF **buses** go south through some of the **Chalonnais** wine villages, best known for their whites, to the uninteresting modern town of **MÂCON**. South of here towards Lyon is the **Beaujolais**, a large area of terraced hills producing light, fruity red wines. Of the three categories of Beaujolais, the superior *crus*, including Morgon and Fleurie, come from the northern part of the region; *Beaujolais villages*, which produces the best *nouveau*, comes from the middle; and *Beaujolais supérieur* comes from vineyards southwest of **VILLEFRANCHE**, itself within spitting distance of Lyon. Villefranche's **tourist office** on rue de la Sous-Préfecture (Mon–Sat 9am–noon & 1.30/2.30–6/7pm, Sun 9am–noon) has detailed information about wine-tasting and cellar tours.

ALSACE-LORRAINE

France's eastern frontier provinces were for a thousand years a battleground. Disputed through the Middle Ages, in the last century they became the scene of some of the worst fighting of two world wars. The democratically minded burghers of **Alsace** created a plethora of well-heeled semi-autonomous towns for themselves centuries before their eighteenth-century incorporation into the French state: neat, well-ordered places full of Germanic fripperies on the houses – though the Alsatians remain fiercely and proudly French, despite their German dialect. The combination of cultures is at its most vivid in the numerous little wine towns that punctuate the *Route du Vin* along the eastern margin of the wet and woody **Vosges** mountains, at **Colmar** and in the great cathedral city of **Strasbourg**. By comparison, the province of **Lorraine**, though it has suffered much the same vicissitudes, is rather wan, apart from the elegant eighteenth-century provincial capital of **Nancy**. For regional information, visit *www.tourisme-alsace.com* and *www.cr-lorraine.fr*.

Nancy

NANCY, capital of Lorraine, is lighter and more southern in feel than its close neighbour Metz, with a relatively untouched eighteenth-century core that was the work of the last of the independent dukes of Lorraine, Stanislas Leczinski, dethroned King of Poland and father-in-law of Louis XV. During the twenty-odd years of his office in the middle of the eighteenth century he ordered some of the most successful urban redevelopment of the period in all France.

The centre of this is **place Stanislas**, a supremely elegant, partially enclosed square at the far end of rue Stanislas, the south side of which is taken up by the **Hôtel de Ville**, its roof line topped by florid urns and lozenge-shaped lanterns dangling from the beaks of gilded cocks. On the west side of the square, the excellent **Musée des Beaux-Arts** (Mon & Wed–Sun 10am–6pm; €4.60, joint ticket with Musée de l'École €7.50) boasts work by Bonnard, Dufy, Modigliani and Matisse. A little north, at 64 Grand Rue, is the **Musée Lorrain** (Mon & Wed–Sun: May–Sept 10am–6pm; Oct–April 10am–noon & 2–5/6pm; €3), devoted to Lorraine's history and with a room of etchings by the seventeenth-century artist, Jacques Callot, whose concern with social issues presaged much nineteenth- and twentieth-century art. You could also make the twenty-minute walk to the **Musée de l'École de Nancy**, 36–38 rue Sergent-Blandan (Mon 2–6pm, Wed–Sun 10.30am–6pm; €4.60, joint ticket with Musée des Beaux Arts €7.50). It holds a collection of Art Nouveau furniture and furnishings, arranged as if in a private house – evidence of Nancy's prominence in the movement, a branch of which was founded here by Émile Gallé, a local manufacturer of glass and ceramics.

The **train station** is at the end of rue Stanislas, a five-minute walk from place Stanislas, where you'll find the **tourist office** (April–Oct Mon–Sat 9am–7pm, Sun 10am–5pm; rest of year Mon–Sat 9am–6pm, Sun 10am–1pm; *www.ot-nancy.fr*). For cheap **hotels**, there's the *Poincaré*, 81 rue Raymond-Poincaré, west of the train station (☎03.83.40.25.99; ③), and the *Jean-Jaurès*, 14 bd Jean-Jaurès, south of the station (☎03.83.27.74.14, *jjaures.hotel@wanadoo.fr*, ④). There's a **hostel** out at the Centre d'Accueil, Château de Rémicourt, Villers-lès-Nancy (☎03.83.27.73.67; ②); bus #4, #16 or #26 to St-Fiacre. *Camping de Brabois* (☎03.83.27.18.28; *campeoles.brabois@wanadoo.fr*) is a nearby **campsite**. For **food**, Grande Rue and rue des Ponts offer the best choice. Try *Les Pissenlits*, at 25bis rue des Ponts. The ornate café *L'Excelsior*, across place Thiers from the train station, is a nice place for coffee and, if you can afford it, a light meal. For **Internet** access, head to Voyager, 57 rue St-Jean (☎03.83.32.71.07).

Strasbourg

The capital of Alsace on the Rhine, **STRASBOURG** is prosperous and beautiful, big enough to have a metropolitan air, but with a cheerful appeal that prevents if from being overwhelming. It has one of the loveliest cathedrals in France, an old and active university and is the current seat of the Council of Europe and the European Court of Human Rights, and part-time base of the European Parliament. You may not be planning to spend time in eastern France, but Strasbourg is a genuine highlight and well worth a detour.

Strasbourg focuses on two main squares, the busy **place Kléber**, and, to the south, **place Gutenberg**, named after the pioneer of type, who lived here in the early fifteenth century. Close by, the **Cathédrale de Notre-Dame** (daily: July & Aug 8.30am–7pm; rest of year 8.30/9am–4.30/6.30pm; free, but €3 to access the cathedral platform) soars from a square of crooked medieval houses, with a spire of such delicate, flaky lightness it seems the work of confectioners rather than masons. In the south transept the slender triple-tiered thirteenth-century column, the **Pilier des Anges**, is decorated with some of the most graceful and

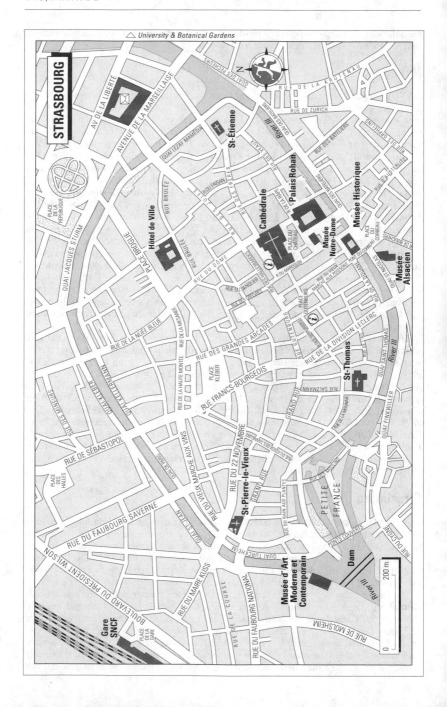

STRASBOURG

University & Botanical Gardens

AV DE LA LIBERTÉ

AVENUE DE LA MARSEILLAISE

QUATTEZAY MAMÉSIA

St-Étienne

RUE DE LA KRUTENAU

QUAI DES PÉCHEURS

RUE DE ZURICH

River III

RUE DES ORPHELINS

RUE DES BATELIERS

QUAI DES BATELIERS

QUAI DES VEAUX

Palais Rohan

Musée Historique

PLACE DE LA RÉPUBLIQUE

QUAI JACQUES STURM

Hôtel de Ville

PLACE BROGLIE

RUE BRÛLÉE

RUE BRÛLÉE

RUE BRÛLÉE

R DU FAISAN

RUE DES FRÈRES

RUE DU DÔME

Cathédrale

PLACE DU CHÂTEAU

Musée Notre-Dame

PLACE DU CORBEAU

RUE DE BOUCHERS

Musée Alsacien

R DU MAROQUIN

RUE DU SANGLIER

RUE DES HALLEBARDES

RUE DU VIEUX MARCHÉ AUX POISSONS

RUE DU VIEUX

PONT DU CORBEAU

R ST-NICOLAS

RUE DE LA NUÉE BLEUE

RUE DE LA MÉSANGE

RUE DES GRANDES ARCADES

PLACE GUTENBERG

RUE DES SERRURIERS

RUE GUTENBERG

RUE DE LA DIVISION LECLERC

QUAI KELLERMANN

QUAI KLÉBER

RUE DE LA HAUTE MONTÉE

PLACE KLÉBER

RUE FRANCS-BOURGEOIS

GRAND RUE

St-Thomas

QUAI SAINT-THOMAS

River III

RUE SALZMANN

RUE DES MINEURS

RUE DE SEBASTOPOL

QUAI DE PARIS

RUE DU VIEUX MARCHÉ AUX VINS

RUE DU 22 NOVEMBRE

GRAND'RUE

RUE DES TANNEURS

QUAI FINKWILLER

QUAI DE LA BRUCHE

PLACE DES HALLES

QUAI ST-JEAN

St-Pierre-le-Vieux

RUE DU BAIN AUX PLANTES

PETITE FRANCE

RUE DES MOULINS

PONTS COUVERTS

RUE DU CYGNE

RUE DU FAUBOURG SAVERNE

QUAI TURCKHEIM

RUE DE LA COURSE

Musée d'Art Moderne et Contemporain

Dam

River III

200 m

BOULEVARD DU PRÉSIDENT WILSON

RUE DU MAIRE KUSS

RUE DU FAUBOURG NATIONAL

RUE DE MOLSHEIM

Gare SNCF

PLACE DE LA GARE

0

expressive statuary of its age. Look also at the enormous and tremendously complicated **astrological clock** (visits 12.15–12.30pm; €0.80), built by Schwilgué of Strasbourg in 1842, a big hit with guided tours who roll up in droves to witness the clock's crowning performance of the day, striking the hour of noon with unerring accuracy at 12.30pm.

South of the cathedral the **Musée de l'Oeuvre Notre-Dame**, 2 place du Château (Mon & Wed–Sun 10am–6pm; €3), houses the original sculptures from the cathedral exterior, damaged in the Revolution and replaced today by copies. There's also the eleventh-century *Wissembourg Christ*, said to be the oldest representation of a human figure in stained glass, from the previous cathedral, as well as the present cathedral architect's original parchment drawings for the statuary, done in fascinating detail. Just north of the old centre, across the river, **place de la République** is surrounded by vast German-Gothic edifices erected during the Prussian occupation (1870–1918), a few hundred metres beyond which is the **Palais de l'Europe**, an imposing piece of contemporary architecture that is home to the European Parliament. The opposite edge of the city centre is much more picturesque, where, around **quai Turckheim**, four square towers guard the so-called **Ponts Couverts** over a series of canals. This beautiful area, known as **La Petite France**, has winding streets bordered by sixteenth- and seventeenth-century houses with carved woodwork and decked with flowers. The new **Musée d'Art Moderne et Contemporain**, 1 place Jean-Hans-Arp (Tues, Wed & Fri–Sun 11am–7pm, Thurs noon–10pm; €4.60), stands on the west bank of the river and houses an impressive collection featuring Monet, Klimt, Ernst, Klee and Jean Arp. Just upstream you can see a dam built by Vauban to protect the city from waterborne assault.

Practicalities

From the **train station** take rue du Maire-Kuss and cross the Rhine onto rue du 22-Novembre, which leads to place Kléber, from where rue des Grandes-Arcades heads south to place Gutenberg and the **tourist office** at 17 place de la Cathédrale (Mon–Sat 9am–7pm, Sun 9am–6pm; *www.strasbourg.com*). The tourist office also has annexes in the underground shopping centre in front of the train station and at the Pont de l'Europe. **Hotels** are expensive and often booked up: close to the station there's the *Weber*, 22 bd de Nancy (✆03.88.32.36.47; ③) and *Du Rhin*, 7–8 place de la Gare (✆03.88.32.35.00; *www.hotel-du-rhin.com*; ⑤). *Patricia*, 1a rue du Puits, is in the backstreets of the old town (✆03.88.32.14.60; ④). There's a modern **hostel** at 9 rue de l'Auberge-de-Jeunesse (✆03.88.30.26.46; ②; closed Jan; bus #2), an HI hostel on rue des Cavaliers, close to the Pont de l'Europe (✆03.88.45.54.20; ②; bus #21), and more central hostel beds at *CIARUS*, 7 rue de Finkmatt (✆03.88.15.27.88; ②), which has a 1am curfew. The nearest **campsite** is at 2 rue Robert Forrer (✆03.88.30.25.46). For **food**, the *FEC* student canteen on place St-Étienne has rock-bottom prices and good meals. Otherwise, eating out can be pricey. *Flam's*, 1 rue des l'Épine, serves the local speciality, *tarte flambée*, a pizza-like onion tart, and *St-Sépulcre*, 15 rue des Orfèvres, is a pleasant, traditional den. The city abounds in **wine bars** and **beer halls**: *L'Académie de la Bière*, 17 rue Adolphe Seyboth, is its most serious beer palace; *Le Java*, 6 rue Faisan, is a good place for live music, and is open until 1am. Access the **Internet** at the *Californian Coffee House*, 36 rue de la Krutenau (✆05.88.35.33.53) or *Midi Minuit*, 5 place du Corbeau (✆03.88.36.09.92).

Colmar

A fifty-minute train ride south of Strasbourg towards Bâle/Basel, **COLMAR** is at first sight an unattractive sprawl, but it merits a stop for its picturesque old centre and some remarkable paintings in its **Musée d'Unterlinden**, at the end of av de la République in a former Dominican convent (April–Oct daily 9am–6pm; Nov–March Mon & Wed–Sun 10am–5pm; €5.30). The most notable of these is Mathias Grünewald's altarpiece for St Anthony's monastery at Isenheim, one of the most extraordinary of all Gothic works. Although displayed "exploded", the **Isenheim altarpiece** was designed to form a single piece. On the front was the *Crucifixion*, with an emaciated, tortured Christ flanked by his pale fainting mother, St John and Mary Magdalene.

To get there from the **train station**, go straight ahead and turn left onto av de la République. There's a **tourist office** opposite the museum, 4 rue des Unterlinden (April–Sept Mon–Sat 9am–6/7pm, Sun 9.30/10am–2pm; rest of year Mon–Sat 9am–noon & 2–6pm, Sun 10am–2pm; *www.ot-colmar.fr*). Of the **hotels** on and around av de la République, *La Chaumière* at no. 74 (☎03.89.41.08.99; ③), and *Colbert*, 2 rue des Trois-Épis (☎03.89.41.31.05; ④), are about the least expensive. There's also an HI **hostel** at 2 rue Pasteur (☎03.89.80.57.39; ②; bus #4 from the station), and a reasonable and more central *Maison des Jeunes* at 17 rue Camille-Schlumberger (☎03.89.41.26.87; ②), although the latter tends to prefer groups. For **food**, *L'Amandine* on place de la Cathédrale has brasserie-type fare or, for a more upmarket Alsatian experience, try *Bartholdi* at 2 rue des Boulangers near the Dominican church. Le Poussin Vert, 37 route Neuf Brisach, offers cut-price **Internet** access (Mon–Sat 11am–1.30am, Sun 3pm–1.30am).

THE ALPS

Rousseau wrote in his *Confessions*, "I need torrents, rocks, pine trees, dark forests, mountains, rugged paths to go up and down, precipices at my elbow to give me a good fright." And these are, in essence, the principal joys of the French **Alps**. Along the mountains' western edge, **Grenoble** and **Annecy** are the gateways to the highest parts, although you really need to spend several days here to create time for anything more strenuous than viewing the peaks from your hotel window. There are four **national or regional parks** – Vanoise, Écrins, Queyras (the least busy) and Vercors (the gentlest) – each of which is ideal walking country, as is the professionals' **Grande Traversée des Alpes**, which crosses all the major massifs from Lake Geneva to Nice. But on a quick tour you're best off grabbing a taster at **Chamonix**, principal base for accessing **Mont Blanc** on the French–Italian border, or simply doing day walks from the main centres. All **routes** are clearly marked and equipped with refuge huts and *gîtes d'étape*. The CIMES office in Grenoble can provide detailed information on GR paths, and local tourist offices often produce detailed maps of walks in their areas. Bear in mind that anywhere above 2000m will be free of snow only from early July until mid-September. For regional information go to *www.cdt-hautesavoie.fr*.

Grenoble

The economic and intellectual capital of the French Alps, **GRENOBLE** is a lively, thriving city, beautifully situated on the Drac and Isère rivers. The old centre, south of the Isère, focuses on place Grenette and place Notre Dame, both popular with local students lounging in the many outdoor cafés. Grenoble celebrates local boy Stendhal, author of *The Black and the Red*, in the **Musée Stendhal**, 1 rue Hector Berlioz (Tues–Sun 2–6pm; free). The **Musée de Grenoble** on place de Lavalette (Mon & Wed–Sun 11am–7pm, Wed until 10pm; €3.80), boasts an excellent collection of representative works by the big names in twentieth-century art; it also has some good temporary exhibitions. For an insight into the region, visit the **Musée Dauphinois** (Mon & Wed–Sun 10am–6/7pm; €3), which occupies the former convent of St-Marie-d'en-Haut, up a cobbled path opposite the Isère footbridge by the Palais de Justice. The French Resistance were particularly active in the Vercors Massif near Grenoble during World War II, and are commemorated – along with victims of the Holocaust – in the **Musée de la Résistance et de la Déportation**, 14 rue Hébert (Mon & Wed–Sun 9/10am–6pm; €3). Finally, the one thing you shouldn't miss is the trip by **téléférique** from the riverside quai Stéphane Jay up to **Fort de la Bastille** on the steep slopes above the north bank of the Isère (July & Aug daily 9.15am–12:15am; June, Sept & Nov–Feb Mon–Sat 9.15am–11.25pm, Sun 9.15am–7.25pm; March–May & Oct daily 9.15am–7.25pm, Tues–Sat until 11.45pm; year-round Mon from 11am only; €5.30 return, €3.70 one-way). It's a hair-raising ride to an otherwise uninteresting fort, but the view over the surrounding mountains and valleys, and down onto the town, is stunning.

The **train station** and **bus station** are on the western edge of the centre, at the end of av Félix-Viallet. The **tourist office**, at 14 rue de la République, near place Grenette (daily 9am–7pm; *www.grenoble-isere-tourisme.com*), can book rooms and **rents bikes** for around €7 a day. The CIMES desk in the same office will provide detailed information on hiking and climbing. There are numerous **hotels** in the station area, among them the *Alize* at 1 place de la Gare (☎04.76.43.12.91; ③). Slightly closer to town is the scruffy but very friendly *Lakanal*, 26 rue des Bergers (☎04.76.46.03.42; ③). The *Bellevue* (☎04.76.46.69.34; ④), on the corner of quai Stéphane-Jay and rue Belgrade, has simple rooms with river views. There's a **hostel** in Echirolles (☎04.76.09.33.52, *grenoble-echirolles@fuaj.org*; ④; 10min by bus #1); and hostel rooms at *Le Foyer de l'Étudiante*, 4 rue Ste-Ursule (☎04.76.42.00.84; ②; women only Oct–May). You can **camp** 5km away in Seyssins (☎04.76.96.45.73). For **food**, try any of the cafés and brasseries between place St-André and place Notre Dame, especially the lively, excellent value *Le Tonneau de Diogène*. For **Internet** access go to Le New Age Cyber Café, 16 place Notre Dame (*www.lenewage.net*).

Annecy

ANNECY is undeniably pretty, perched at the edge of a turquoise lake with views of Alpine peaks. The town inevitably gets busy with tourists, although it also serves as a transit point for hikers seeking access to Mont Blanc and the Lake Geneva area.

The most interesting part of the city is a warren of seventeenth-century lanes and passages cut through by branches of the Canal du Thiou, which drains the Lac d'Annecy into the River Fier. Opposite the **Hôtel de Ville**, in the main square, is the fifteenth-century church of **St-Maurice**, originally built for a Dominican convent, with attractive Flamboyant windows and walls leaning outwards to an alarming degree. South of here, across the canal bridge, is the grand old **Palais de l'Île** and **rue St-Claire**, the main street of the old town, with arcaded shops and houses. From rue de l'Île the narrow Rampe du Château leads up to the **Musée-Château** (June–Sept daily 10am–6pm; rest of year Mon & Wed–Sun 10am–noon & 2–6pm; €4.60), the former home of the counts of Genevois which now houses various archeological finds, Savoyard popular art, furniture and woodcarving and, on the top floor, an excellent display illustrating the geology of the Alps.

The **train** and **bus** station complex is five minutes' walk northwest of the centre. The **tourist office** is on rue Jean Jaurès (July & Aug Mon–Sat 9am–7.30pm, Sun 9am–12.30pm & 1.45–6.30pm; rest of year Mon–Sat 9am–12.30pm & 1.45–6.30pm; *www.lac-annecy.com*). The **hostel**, 4 route du Semnoz (☎04.50.45.33.19; ②), is a 45-minute walk from the old town and often full; near it is the municipal **campsite**, 8 route du Semnoz (☎04.50.33.87.96; June–Sept). **Hotels** need to be booked in advance; Annecy is a popular place, especially at weekends. For somewhere close to the centre and the lake, try the *Hôtel des Alpes*, 12 rue de la Poste (☎04.50.45.04.56; ④). Failing that, head for the *Central*, 6 rue Royale (☎04.50.45.05.37; ③). A clutch of **eating places** can be found around the château: *Restaurant des Arts*, 4 passage de l'Île, occupies an especially pleasant position here. Also good are *Auberge de Savoie*, a fish restaurant at 1 place Saint-François, and *Taverne de Maître Kanter* at 2 quai Perrière. There are round-the-lake **boat trips** from €9.30, leaving from Compagnie des Bateaux (☎04.50.51.08.40) located by the mouth of the Thiou canal at 2 place aux Bois. The tourist office sells a 1:50,000 map of the Annecy area with **walking trails** marked, and **bikes** can be rented at Little Big Shop on rue Carnot.

Chamonix and Mont Blanc

At 4807m, **Mont Blanc** is both Europe's highest mountain and the biggest tourist draw in the Alps, but by walking you can soon get away from the worst of the crowds. The two approach routes come together at Le Fayet, where the **tramway du Mont-Blanc** begins its 75-minute haul to the **Nid d'Aigle**, a vantage point on the northwest slope. There's more exciting access 30km further on, at the resort of **CHAMONIX**, although there's little to recommend the town beyond its **Musée Alpin** off rue Whymper (June–Oct daily 2–7pm; €3). The best thing you can do is to take the expensive **téléférique** (return ticket €30) to the **Aiguille du Midi** (3842m), a terrifying granite pinnacle on which the *téléférique* station and a restaurant are precariously balanced. The view of Mont Blanc from here is incredible. At your feet is the snowy plateau of the **Col du Midi**, with the glaciers of the Vallée Blanche and Géant crawling off left at their millennial pace. To the right, a steep snowfield leads to the "easy" ridge route to the summit with its cap of ice. You must, however, go before 9am, because the summits usually cloud over towards midday and the crowds become intolerable. Be sure also to take warm clothes: even on a summer day it can be well below zero at the top.

Finding **accommodation** in the area can be a big problem. The best bet is the comfortable and welcoming **hostel** just west of Chamonix proper at 127 Montée Jean-Balmat in Les Pèlerins d'en Haut (☎04.50.53.14.52, *chamonix@fuaj.org*; ②); take a bus to Pèlerins-École, from where the hostel is signposted. For more dorm accommodation, ask at the Chamonix **tourist office**, near the church at 85 place du Triangle de l'Amitié (daily 8.30am–12.30pm & 2–7pm; *www.chamonix.com*). **Campsites** are numerous; most convenient are *Les Molliases* (☎04.50.53.16.81) on the left of the main road, going west from Chamonix towards the Mont Blanc tunnel entrance, and *Les Arolles* (☎04.50.53.14.30), on the opposite side of the road, fifteen minutes walk from the station.

RHÔNE VALLEY AND PROVENCE

Of all the regions of France, **Provence** is the most irresistible, with attractions that range from the high mountains of the southern Alps to the wild plains of the Camargue. Yet, apart from the coast, large areas remain remarkably unscathed by development. Its complete integration into France dates only from the nineteenth century and, although the Provençal language is rarely heard, the accent is distinctive even to a foreign ear. The main problem is choosing where to go. The **Rhône valley**, north–south route of ancient armies, medieval traders and modern rail and road, is nowadays fairly industrialized, and other than the big city delights of **Lyon** – not strictly in Provence but the main gateway for the region – there's not much to detain you before the Roman city of **Orange** and the old papal stronghold of **Avignon**, the latter with a wonderful summer festival. Deeper into Provence, on the edge of the flamingo-filled lagoons of the **Camargue**, **Arles** is another ancient Roman settlement, retaining a superb amphitheatre. For regional information visit *www.rhonealpes-tourisme.com*.

Lyon

LYON, the third-largest city in France, became a UNESCO World Heritage site in 1998, one of only five urban sites in the world. Its charms are manifold, not least its gastronomy: there are more restaurants per square metre here than anywhere else on earth. It also has a beautifully preserved old quarter and an impressive town centre of grand boulevards and public squares. With a population of around half-a-million, there is a vibrant nightlife and cultural scene, including one of the few national operas outside Paris and the famous Lyonnais puppets.

Arrival, information and accommodation

The centre of Lyon is the **Presqu'île**, a tongue of land between the rivers Saône and Rhône just before their confluence. To the west of Presqu'île is the old town, Vieux Lyon, at the foot of **Fourvière**, on which the Romans built their capital of Gaul; to the north is the old silk weavers' district, **La Croix-Rousse**. Modern Lyon lies east of the Rhône, the city at its most self-assertive in the cultural and commercial centre of **La Part-Dieu**, where TGV trains pull into the **TGV station**. Non-TGV **trains** and **buses** arrive at the **Gare de Perrache**, on what was once the tip of the peninsula. **Buses** arrive at one of several bus stations dotted around town. Lyon-St-Exupéry **airport** is off the Grenoble autoroute, half-an-hour from both stations by Satobus (daily 5am–9pm, every 20min; €7.50) or €38–53 in a **taxi**. The **tourist office** is on the southeast corner of place Bellecour (daily 9/10am–6/7pm; *www.lyon-france.com*), where you can pick up maps for the city métro, tram and bus system. City transport tickets cost a flat €1.20, or you can buy them in *carnets* of ten for €10.40; the tourist office's *liberté* ticket gives unlimited travel on trams, buses and métro for two hours (€1.50) or a day (€3.70). The Lyon **City Card**, also available at the tourist office, covers entry to all museums, monuments, tours and transport (1 day €14, 2 days €24.50, 3 days €30). For **accommodation** close to Gare de Perrache, try the clean and homely *Vaubecour*, one block back from the Saône quays at 28 rue Vaubecour (☎04.78.37.44.91; ③), or the *d'Ainay*, 14 rue des Remparts d'Ainay (☎04.78.42.43.42; ③), which has decent-sized rooms. In Croix-Rousse, the friendly *de la Poste*, 1 rue Victor Fort (☎04.78.28.62.67; ③) is a good bet. Vieux Lyon has a new **hostel** at 41–45 montée du Chemin Neuf (☎04.78.15.05.50; *www.fuaj.org/aj/lyon*; ②), with great city views; there is an alternative 4km southeast of the centre by métro D in Vénissieux, 51 rue Roger Salengro (☎04.78.76.39.23; ②). The closest **campsite** is the Porte de Lyon at Dardilly (☎04.78.35.64.55), a ten-minute ride by bus #89 from the bus station in Gare de Vaise, north of the city.

The City

Directly in front of Gare de Perrache is the green square of **place Carnot** which leads to the pedestrian rue Victor Hugo, in turn opening out onto the vast **place Bellecour**, where even the statue of Louis XIV in Roman garb looks small. On rue de la Charité, which runs parallel to rue Victor Hugo on the Rhône side, is the **Musée des Tissus** (Tues–Sun 10am–5.30pm; €4.60; métro Bellecour), a surprisingly interesting collection of fabrics, clothes and tapestries dating from ancient Egypt to the present. From here, push straight on up rue de la République, full of people jostling between cafés and shops, past place Bellecour. Turning left leads to quai St-Antoine, lined in the mornings with a colourful food market; a Sunday book market lies just upriver. Heading back to the centre of Presqu'île is **Place des Terreaux**, the centrepiece of which is an imposing nineteenth-century fountain sculpted by Bartholdi, more famously responsible for New York's Statue of Liberty. The square also features the splendidly ornate **Hôtel de Ville**, as well as the **Musée des Beaux-Arts** (Wed–Sun 10.30am–6pm; €3.80; métro Hôtel de Ville). This absorbing collection includes ancient Egyptian, Greek and Roman artefacts as well as works by Pissarro, Degas and Picasso, among others. The **Musée d'Art Contemporain** is 3km north of the city centre at Cité Internationale, 81 quai Charles de Gaulle (Mon & Wed–Sat noon–7pm; €3.80; bus #4 or #47).

North of Place des Terreaux, the old silk weavers' district of **La Croix-Rousse** is still a working-class area, but only twenty or so people work on the computerized looms that are kept in business by the restoration and maintenance of the palaces and châteaux. You can watch the traditional looms in action at **La Maison des Canuts** at 12 rue d'Ivry, one block north of place de la Croix-Rousse (Mon–Sat 8.30am–noon & 2–6.30pm; €2; métro Croix Rousse). From here, cut through the narrow streets of the district to the river and cross to **Vieux Lyon**. The tangled streets on the left bank of the Saône form an attractive muddle of cobbled alleyways and Renaissance facades, at night brightly lit and populated by well-dressed Lyonnais in search of supper. The **Musée Historique de Lyon** on place du Petit-Collège (Mon & Wed–Sun 10.45am–6pm; €3.80; métro Vieux Lyon) has a good collection of Nevers ceramics, although the **Musée de la Marionnette** (same hours and ticket) on an upper floor of the same fifteenth-century mansion is more engaging, containing the eighteenth-century Lyonnais creations *Guignol* and *Madelon* (the French Punch and Judy), which you can see in action at Théâtre Guignol, 2 rue Louis Carrand (☎04.78.28.92.57; *www.theatre-guignol.com*).

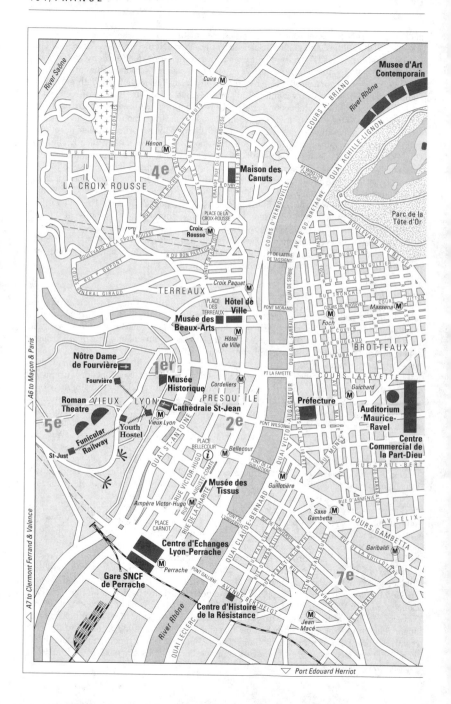

Musee d'Art
Contemporain

River Saône

River Rhône

Cuire Ⓜ

Ⓜ Hénon

4e

Maison des
Canuts

LA CROIX ROUSSE

PLACE DE LA
CROIX-ROUSSE

Parc de la
Tête d'Or

Croix
Rousse

PT DE
DE LATTRE
DE TASSIGNY

Croix Paquet Ⓜ

TERREAUX

PONT MORAND

PLACE
DES
TERREAUX

Hôtel de
Ville

BROTTEAUX

Musée des
Beaux-Arts

Massena Ⓜ

Hôtel
de Ville

PT LA FAYETTE

Nôtre Dame
de Fourvière

COURS LAFAYETTE

1er

Fourvière

Musée
Historique

Cordeliers Ⓜ

Guichard

LYON

PRESQU'ÎLE

Roman
Theatre

VIEUX

Préfecture Ⓜ

Cathédrale St-Jean

Auditorium
Maurice-
Ravel

5e

Vieux Lyon Ⓜ

2e

Youth
Hostel

PONT WILSON

Funicular
Railway

Centre
Commercial de
la Part-Dieu

St-Just

PLACE
BELLECOUR

Bellecour Ⓜ

ⓘ

Musée des
Tissus

Guillotière Ⓜ

Ampère Victor-Hugo Ⓜ

Saxe
Gambetta Ⓜ

COURS GAMBETTA

PLACE
CARNOT

AV FÉLIX-

Garibaldi Ⓜ

Centre d'Echanges
Lyon-Perrache

7e

Perrache Ⓜ

PONT GALLIENI

Gare SNCF
de Perrache

River Rhône

Centre d'Histoire
de la Résistance

Jean
Macé Ⓜ

A6 to Mâcon & Paris

A7 to Clermont Ferrand & Valence

QUAI LECLERC

▽ Port Edouard Herriot

Rue St-Jean ends at the **Cathédrale St-Jean**, a much-damaged twelfth- to fifteenth-century building, but one whose thirteenth-century stained glass above the altar and in the rose windows of the transepts is in perfect condition. Just beyond the cathedral, at métro Vieux Lyon on av Adolphe-Max, is a **funicular station**, from which you can ascend to a set of **Roman remains** on rue de l'Antiquaille, consisting of two theatres (free) and an underground museum of Lyonnais life from prehistoric times to 7 AD. There's a **Musée de la Civilisation Gallo-Romaine** at 17 rue Cléberg (Wed–Sun 9.30am–noon & 2–6pm; €3), from where it's a short walk to the late nineteenth-century **Basilique de Notre-Dame**, a commotion of multicoloured marble and mosaic. The belvedere behind the church affords an impressive view of Lyon and its curving rivers.

Reminders of the war are never far away in France and this is particularly true of Lyon where the **Centre d'Histoire de la Résistance et de la Déportation** at 14 av Berthelot (Wed–Sun 9am–5.30pm; €3.80; bus #11, #26, #32 or #39) tells of the immense courage and ingenuity of the French resistance, and also serves as a poignant memorial to the city's Jews who were deported to concentration camps.

Eating, drinking and nightlife

Lyon is the self-proclaimed gastronomic capital of France, and not without reason. It has hundreds of **restaurants** offering delicious, if somewhat heavy, Lyonnais fare. Vegetarians will be disappointed however, as its specialities focus on meat and offal, most famously in its *quenelles* (soufflé-like dumplings). Vieux Lyon is crammed with eateries, most claiming to be *"bouchons"*, typical Lyon wine bars serving food. *Les pavés de St-Jean*, 23 rue Saint-Jean, is open daily until midnight and offers good-value menus and local specialities. Around the corner on Place de la Baleine is *Maître Bœuf*, serving great steaks in quirky surroundings. *Café 203*, by the Opera House at 9 rue du Garet, is popular with Lyon's trendy youth and offers excellent-value menus. *L'Amphitryon*, 33 rue St-Jean on Presqu'île, is open daily until midnight and can get packed. The *Café des Fédérations*, 10 rue du Major Martin (closed weekends and Aug), is a typical *bouchon* in both food and surroundings. Lyon's most famous restaurant, *Paul Bocuse*, is 9km north of the city at 40 rue de la Plage, and is quite excellent. If you just want a **drink**, there's the *Albion Public House*, 12 rue Ste Catherine, where you can play pool and listen to jazz, or the popular *Smoking Dog*, 15 rue Lainerie, which hosts pub quizzes on Tuesdays. There are two **Internet** cafés worth trying: *Connectik*, 19 quai St Antoine (daily 11am–7pm), has a bar, while *Raconte-moi La Terre*, 38 rue Thomassin (Mon–Sat 10am–7.30pm), is a café and bookshop specializing in travel literature. Lyon also boasts a few **gay bars**, including *La Ruche* at 22 rue Gentil, which has 1930s-style decor, and *Le Village* at 8 rue St-Georges, which is women-only.

Orange

Around 100km south of Lyon, **ORANGE** is the first major stop in Provence proper, a pleasant town originally built by Julius Caesar for his troops as a reward for the successful conquest of Gaul. Aside from a **triumphal arch** on the north edge of town, friezed with celebrations of the campaign, the main feature of this period still left is the **Roman theatre** (daily: April–Sept 9am–6.30pm; rest of year 9am–noon & 1.30–5pm; joint ticket with the municipal museum €4.60), the best-preserved example in existence. The finest view of the theatre in its entirety is from the St-Eutrope hill, into which it is built, past the remains of the forum. At the top of the hill are the ruins of the short-lived seventeenth-century **castle** of the princes of Orange; Louis XIV had it destroyed and annexed the principality to France – a small price to pay for William of Orange, ruler of the Netherlands and, later, also king of England. The **municipal museum**, across the road from the theatre (daily: April–Sept 9.30am–7pm; rest of year 9.30am–noon & 1.30–5.30pm; joint ticket with Roman theatre €4.60), has various documents concerning the Orange dynasty.

The **train station** is about 1.5km east of the centre, at the end of av Frédéric-Mistral; the nearest bus stop is at the bottom of rue Jean-Reboul, first left out of the station. Bus #2, direction Nogent, takes you to the ancient theatre and – at the next stop – the **tourist office** on cours Aristide-Briand (April–Sept Mon–Sat 9am–7pm, Sun 10am–6pm; rest of year Mon–Sat 9am–1pm & 3–6pm; *www.provence-orange.com*); there's an annexe at place des Frères Mounet, close to the theatre (April–Sept Mon–Sat 10am–1pm & 2–7pm, Sun 10am–6pm). Of the **hotels**, the *Arcotel*, 8 place aux Herbes (☎04.90.34.09.23; ④), is central, appealing and good value. Orange's **campsite**, *Le Jonquier* (☎04.90.34.49.48; April–Oct), is northwest on rue Alexis-Carrel. For **food**, *La Fringale* on rue de Tourre does affordable *plats du jour*, and *Le Yaca*, 24 place Silvian, has a generous choice of dishes in an old vaulted hall. If it's full, try *La Roselière* at 4 rue du Renoyer, or *Le Parvis*, 3 cours des Pourtoules.

Avignon

AVIGNON, great city of the popes and for centuries one of the major artistic centres of France, can be daunting. The monuments and museums are huge, it's always crowded in summer and it can be stiflingly hot. But it is an immaculately preserved medieval town with endless impressively decorated buildings, ancient churches, chapels and convents, and plenty of places to eat and drink. During the **drama festival** in July, it's the only place to be.

Central Avignon is enclosed by medieval **walls**, built by one of the nine popes who based themselves here throughout most of the fourteenth century, away from the anarchic feuding and rival popes of Rome. Avignon was a lively place when the papacy was here. Every vice flourished in the overcrowded, plague-ridden town, full of hangers-on to the papal court, according to Petrarch it was "a sewer where all the filth of the universe has gathered". Centre of town is **place de l'Horloge**, lined with cafés and market stalls on summer evenings, just beyond which is the enormous **Palais des Papes** (daily: April–Oct 9am–7/9pm; Nov–March 9.30am–5.45pm; €6.80 with English audioguide, or €8.40 joint ticket with Pont d'Avignon). The denuded interior gives little indication of the richness of the papal court, although the building is impressive for sheer size alone. Visits take in the Consistoire, where sovereigns and ambassadors were received. The adjacent Chapelle St-Jean, and the Chapelle St-Martial upstairs, were decorated by the Sienese artist Matteo Giovannetti on the orders of Clement VI, whose secular concerns are evident in the wonderful food-oriented murals of his bedroom and study – part of Clement's New Palace, whose Grande Chapelle has the proportions of a cathedral.

The **Cathédrale Notre-Dame-des-Doms**, north of the palace, might have been a luminous Romanesque structure once, but the interior has had a bad attack of Baroque. You could bypass it and wander instead around the **Rocher des Doms** park, which gives great views over the river. Along the river is the famous **Pont d'Avignon** of the folk-song (daily: April–Nov 9am–7pm; Dec–March 9.30am–5.45pm; €2.40). The struggle to keep the bridge in good repair despite the ravages of the Rhône was finally abandoned in 1660, three-and-a-half centuries after it was built, and today just four of the original 22 arches survive.

Practicalities

Avignon's **train station** is beside porte de la République on bd St-Roch, on the southern edge of the centre. If you don't want to walk, you can take bus #4 from the main post office, on the left through porte de la République. A new TGV station is due to open in 2002, reducing journey time from Paris to two-and-a-half hours. The **tourist office** is a short walk from the station at 41 cours Jean-Jaurès (April–Sept Mon–Sat 9am–6pm, Sun 9am–1pm & 2–5pm; during festival Mon–Sat 10am–8pm, Sun 10am–5pm; rest of year Mon–Fri 9am–6pm, Sat 9am–1pm & 2–5pm; *www.avignon-tourisme.com*), and there's another office open daily at the Pont d'Avignon. Even outside festival time, finding **accommodation** can still be a problem. Off cours Jean-Jaurès between the station and the tourist office, rue Agricol Perdiguier has a couple of inexpensive **hotels**: *Le Parc* at no. 18 (☎04.90.82.71.55; ④) and the characterless *Splendid* at no. 17 (☎04.90.86.14.46; ④). The *Innova*, 100 rue Joseph-Vernet (☎04.90.82.54.10; ④), is nicer. There's a small **hostel**, the *Squash Club*, at 32 bd Limbert (☎04.90.85.27.78; ②). *Auberge Bagatelle* (☎04.90.86.30.39; ③), across the river on Île de la Barthelasse, is another hostel with a **campsite**; take bus #10 or #11 to the bridge, from where you can cross to the island.

Eating on a budget is easy. The big brasseries on place de l'Horloge all do well-priced meals and are pleasant places to sit outside – try *Le Venaissin* – and rue des Teinturiers is a good source of budget restaurants. *Le Mesclun*, 46 rue Balance, does good *plats du jour* for around €7.50. Place de l'Horloge is the liveliest place to sip an early evening **drink**, though place des Corps-Saints (near the tourist office) comes a close second. Surf the **Internet** at Cyberdrome, 68 rue Guillaume (☎04.90.16.05.15) or La Pomme Bleue, 5 place des Carmes (☎ 04.90.14.00.15).

The festival

Avignon's summer **festival**, every July, is a great time to be in town. Theatre dominates, but opera, classical music, film and street theatre are also featured. Much of it takes place in the Palais des Papes and other interesting locations, while the streets are given over to the fringe. Around 200,000 spectators come here for the show, so doing any normal sightseeing becomes virtually impossible. The **festival headquarters** is at 8 rue de Mons (☎04.90.14.14.26, *www.festival-avignon.com*; May–July), and, as well as providing the main festival programme and information, it shows videos and a collection of festival memorabilia dating back to the event's inception in 1947.

Arles

Around 25km south of Avignon, **ARLES** was one of the most important settlements of Gaul, providing grain for most of the western Roman empire, as well as being a crucial port and shipbuilding centre – indeed, in the fourth century it became the capital of Gaul, Britain and Spain. Today, Arles is a picturesque town with a laid-back Mediterranean atmosphere and well-preserved vestiges of its illustrious past – not least a marvellous Roman amphitheatre. Arles' most famous inhabitant, **Vincent van Gogh**, spent a fruitful, if turbulent, year here, producing some of his most famous works including the *Sunflowers* and his famous *Chair*, yet not one of his paintings remains in the town.

Boulevard des Lices is the main street, along with rue Jean-Jaurès and its continuation, rue Hôtel-de-Ville. The most obvious place to start exploring is the central **place de la République**, between rue Jean-Jaurès and rue Hôtel-de-Ville, highlight of which is the **Cathédrale St-Trophime**, whose doorway is one of the most famous bits of twelfth-century Provençal carving, depicting a *Last Judgement* trumpeted by angels playing with the enthusiasm of jazz musicians. Immediately east of the cathedral, the **Théâtre-Antique** (daily: May–Sept 9am–6.30pm; Oct 9–11.30am; Nov–April 9/10–11.30am & 2–4.30/5.30pm; €3) is fairly dilapidated, and you'd do better to stroll just beyond to the **Arènes** (daily: May–Sept 9am–6.30pm; Oct 9am–5.30pm; Nov–April 9/10am–4.30/5.30pm; €3), the town's most impressive imperial structure. Built in the first century AD, it originally seated 20,000, and is still used for bullfights.

For a better insight into Roman Arles, head for the **Musée de l'Arles Antique** (daily: March–Oct 9am–7pm; Nov–Feb 10am–5pm; €5.30), west of the town centre on the spit of land between the Rhône and the Canal du Rhône, where fabulous mosaics, sarcophagi and sculpture illuminate Arles' early history. If you feel that life in Arles stopped with the Romans, you will be reassured by the **Musée Réattu** (daily: April–Sept 9am–noon & 2–6.30pm; rest of year 9/10am–11.30am/12.30pm & 2–4/5pm; €3), opposite some Roman baths, which returns you to the twentieth century with a decent collection of modern paintings, not least a good array of work by Picasso, including sculpture and ink and crayon sketches he donated to the museum.

Practicalities

The **train station** is a few blocks north of the Arènes, close to the Porte de la Cavalerie. For **accommodation**, try the *Terminus & Van Gogh* at 5 place Lamartine (☎04.90.96.12.32; ④) and *Le Rhône*, 11 place Voltaire (☎04.90.96.43.70; ③). Perhaps the nicest choice is the *Gauguin*, also on place Voltaire (☎04.90.96.14.35; ④), which is comfortable and well-run. There's a **hostel** at 20 av Maréchal-Foch (☎04.90.96.18.25; ②; closed Jan), a five-minute walk from the tourist office (see below), and six **campsites** in the vicinity of Arles, of which the most pleasant is *La Bienheureuse* (☎04.90.98.48.06), 7km out on N453 at Rapheles-lès-Arles and with a restaurant; regular buses run there. Closer to town is *Camping City*, 67 route de Crau (☎04.90.93.08.86). The **tourist office** is opposite rue Jean-Jaurès on bd des Lices (April–Sept daily 9am–7pm; Oct–March Mon–Sat 9am–6pm, Sun 10am–2.30pm; *www.ville-arles.fr*), and provides a hotel booking service; there's an annexe at the train station. Both sell a €10 **museum pass**, which gives access to all museums and monuments for one day. **Bikes** can be rented from the *tabac* just next to the main tourist office from around €12 per day. For a special treat, the place to **eat** is the *Hostellerie des Arènes*, 62 rue du Refuge; otherwise there are plenty of affordable brasseries on the main boulevards and around place du Forum; try *L'Affenage*, 4 rue Molière, which serves Provençal specialities in a pleasant atmosphere. There's an **Internet** café, Connexion, at 10 rue du 4 septembre (Mon–Sat 8.30am–7.30pm).

The Camargue

The flat, marshy delta area immediately south of Arles – the **Camargue** – is a unique area that is used as a breeding-ground for the bulls used in *corridas* around here, along with the horses that their herdsmen ride. Neither they nor the bulls are wild, though they run in semi-liberty, and the true wildlife of the area is made up of flamingos, marsh- and seabirds, and a rich flora of reeds, wild flowers and juniper trees.

If you're interested in bird-watching or walking around the lagoons and have your own transport, your first stop should be the La Capelière **information centre** on the eastern side of the Étang du Vaccarès on the small road leading south off the D37 from Villeneuve (April–Sept 9am–1pm & 2–6pm; Oct–March 9am–1pm & 2–5pm; closed Tues). The imaginative **Musée Carmarguais**, halfway between Gimeaux and Albaron on the D570, documents the traditions and livelihoods of the Camarguais people and the region's main products, rice and salt (April–Sept daily 9.15am–5.45/6.45pm; Oct–March Mon & Wed–Sun 10.15am–4.45pm; €4.60).

The town that most people head for in the Camargue is **SAINTES-MARIES-DE-LA-MER**, on the western edge, where every May 24 and 25 gypsies gather to celebrate their patron saint, Sarah, who came to an island close by after being driven out of Palestine. There's a procession from the church to the sea, carrying the statue of Sarah, with the *gardiens* in full Camargue cowboy dress accompanying them. If you're in the area, it's not to be missed. The rest of the year Saintes-Maries is a very commercialized town, although its kilometres of beaches and good facilities makes it the best resort close to Arles. Exploring the region on **horseback** is a good way to get into the Camarguais spirit of things and the tourist office, 5 av Van-Gogh (daily 9am–5/6/8pm; *www.saint-mariesdelamer.com*), has a list of places where you can arrange a day or half-day excursion. **Bikes** can be rented from Le Vélo Saintois, 19 av de la République (☎04.90.97.74.56). The **bullfighting** season is March to November when a number of festivals take place – thankfully no animals are killed in Camargue bullfights. Of **hotels**, *Le Méditerranée*, 4 rue F-Mistral (☎04.90.97.82.09; ④), has some of the least pricey rooms in town, and the *Dauphin Bleu*, overlooking the sea at 31 av G-Leroy (☎04.90.97.80.21; ④), is also pleasant, and has a decent **restaurant**, although you may be obliged to take half-board. There's a **hostel** at Pioch-Badet 10km along the Arles road, open all year (☎04.90.97.51.72; ②). The closest **campsite** is *La Brise*, on the Vacharel road just outside the village (☎04.90.97.84.67). There's more budget accommodation along the coast at the more down-to-earth town of **Salin-de-Giraud**, and you can sleep on the beach near there at the **plage de Piémançon**.

MARSEILLE AND THE CÔTE D'AZUR

The **Côte d'Azur** is the most built-up, overpopulated, over-eulogized and expensive stretch of coast anywhere in the world. What's more, along with the Provence region, it's become a leading stronghold for the extreme right-wing party Le Front National, who have made significant gains in French regional elections. There are only two industries to speak of – tourism and construction, plus the related services of estate agents, yacht traffic wardens and Rolls-Royce valets. However, in every gap between the monstrous habitations, the remarkable beauty of the hills and coastline, the scent of the plant life and the strange synthesis of pollutants that make the Mediterranean so translucent all bombard the senses. The coast's eastern reaches are its most spectacular, the mountains breaking their fall just a few metres before levelling off to the shore. **St-Tropez** is an expensive high spot, though only **Nice** has real substance – a major city far enough away from Paris to preserve a distinctive character. At the opposite end of the coast, the squalid naval base of **Toulon** and vast, seedy sprawl of **Marseille** are quite different. There is no continuous *corniche*, few villas in the Grand Style, and work is geared to an annual rather than summer cycle. All the way along, the **months to avoid** are July and August, when the overflowing campsites become health hazards, all hotels are booked up, the people are overworked and the vegetation is at its most barren. Check *www.crt-riviera.fr* for regional information.

Marseille

France's most populous city after Paris, **MARSEILLE** has, like the capital, prospered and been ransacked over the centuries. It has suffered plagues, religious bigotry, republican and royalist terror and had its own Commune and Bastille-storming. It was the presence of so many revolutionaries from the city marching to Paris in 1792 that gave the name *Marseillaise* to the national anthem. Nowadays every social, economic and political conflict of the country is expressed in Marseille: it is a violent place, and racism, corruption and general lawlessness are rife. Certainly it is not a glamorous city and you might not choose to live there, but it's an invigorating place to visit – a real port with a trading history going back over 2500 years. It's as cosmopolitan as Paris, with a strong north African presence, and gritty, down-to-earth inhabitants that are at once welcoming and intimidating. Like Paris, Marseille is divided into *arrondissements*, sixteen in all, which spiral out from the focal point of the city, the Vieux Port.

Arrival and accommodation

Marseille's **airport**, de Marignane (*www.marseille.aeroport.fr*), is 25km northwest, connected by bus (daily 5.30am–9.50pm; every 20min; €7) with the main train station, **gare St-Charles**, centrally situated on the northern edge of the 1er *arrondissement*, round the corner from the **bus station** on place Victor-Hugo. The best way of getting around is to walk, although if you need to cover longer distances fast the **public transport** system – bus, tram and métro – is efficient enough; network details are available at *L'Espace Infos*, 6 rue des Fabres, and tickets cost €1.40 from métro stations and buses. The **tourist office** is at 4 La Canebière, down by the harbour (Mon–Sat 9am–7/8pm, Sun 10am–5pm; ☎04.91.13.89.00, *www.marseille-tourisme.com*), and offers a free **accommodation** booking service. Among the budget **hotels**, the *Caravelle*, 5 rue Guy-Mocquet, 1er (☎04.91.48.44.99; ③), is friendly, quiet and close to the action; *Pavillon*, 27 rue Pavillon (☎04.91.33.76.90; ④), is central and welcoming; and the *Edmond-Rostand*, 31 rue Dragon, 6e (☎04.91.37.74.95; ⑤), is further out but has great charm. Well worth the little extra money is *Le Corbusier* (☎04.91.16.78.00; *hotelcorbusier@wanadoo.fr*; ④), on the third floor of the architect's seminal tower block, Cité Radieuse, south of the city centre at 80 bd Michelet; take the métro to Rond-Point du Prado, then bus #21 or #22. There's only one **hostel**, the *Bois Luzy*, allée des Primevères, 12e

(☎04.91.49.06.18; ②), housed in an old château and easy to reach on bus #6 from Réformés, though it has an 11.30pm curfew. There are no campsites.

The City

The old harbour, or **Vieux Port**, is a good place to indulge in the sedentary pleasures of observing the city's streetlife. Two fortresses guard the entrance to the harbour, a little way south of which is the **Basilique St-Victor**, the city's oldest church. It looks and feels like a fortress – the walls of the choir are almost 3m thick – and you can visit the **crypt** and **catacombs** (daily 8.30am–6.30pm; €1.50). On the other, northern, side of the harbour is the former old town of Marseille, known as **Le Panier**, a densely populated area that was dynamited by the Nazis, who deported around 20,000 people from here. Nowadays it's a mainly Algerian quarter, especially over towards the train station, although it's becoming a fashionable area for the young and bohemian. After the war, archeologists reaped the benefits of the destruction by finding remains of the Roman docks equipped with vast storage jars for foodstuffs, now housed in the **Musée des Docks Romains** on place Vivaux (Tues–Sun: June–Sept 11am–6pm; rest of year 10am–5pm; €1.80). The **Musée d'Art Contemporain**, nearby at 69 bd de Haifa (same hours; €1.80), boasts a strong collection, including works by Warhol, Christo and Buren.

Below Le Panier is **La Canebière**, Marseille's main street, which cuts down to the Vieux Port. Just north, on busy cours Belsunce, the **Centre Bourse** is a giant mall, useful for mainstream shopping and also home to a museum of finds from Roman Marseille, the **Musée d'Histoire de Marseille** (Mon–Sat noon–7pm; €1.80), which includes a third-century wreck of a Roman trading vessel. At the far eastern end of La Canebière, the **Palais Longchamp** (bus #81) was the grandiose conclusion of an aqueduct bringing water from the outlying hills to the city. Water is still pumped into the middle of the central colonnade of the building, whose north wing houses the stuffy **Musée des Beaux-Arts** (Tues–Sun: June–Sept 11am–6pm; rest of year 10am–5pm; €1.80), with a fair share of goodies, most notably three beautiful paintings by Françoise Duparc, a room of political cartoons by the nineteenth-century Marseille satirist, Honoré Daumier, and a famous profile of Louis XIV by Pierre Puget. South of La Canebière are Marseille's main shopping streets, rue Paradis, rue St-Ferréol and rue de Rome, and the **Musée Cantini**, 19 rue Grignan (Tues–Sun: June–Sept 11am–6pm; rest of year 10am–5pm; €1.80), a collection of twentieth-century and contemporary art covering figures as diverse as Dufy, Léger, Bacon and Vasarely.

A short distance offshore is the **Château d'If**, the notorious island fortress that figured in Dumas' great adventure story, *The Count of Monte Cristo*. No one ever escaped from here: most prisoners, incarcerated for political or religious reasons, went mad or died (usually both) before reaching the end of their sentences. Boats leave for the island from the quai des Belges (roughly every two hours; takes 20min; €7.50 return, plus €3.80 admission to the château).

Eating, drinking and nightlife

Marseille's **markets** are a highlight. Some, such as the daily fish market at quai des Belges, are enjoyable but do little to whet your appetite; the morning markets (Mon–Sat only) at place Sébastopol near the Palais Longchamp and place Jean-Jaurès sell rather more tempting edibles. Marseille's speciality is *bouillabaisse*, a delicious fish stew served – to differing standards – in most **restaurants** around the Vieux Port; the finest place to try it is *Miramar*, 12 quai du Port (☎04.91.91.10.40), a local institution with correspondingly exorbitant prices. The best low-priced meals can be found around trendy cours Julien and place Jean-Jaurès, where you can sample various ethnic cuisines; *Ce Cher Arwell*, 96 cours Julien, is a popular place, serving good French food in generous portions. There is a branch of the vegetarian restaurant *Country Life* at 14 rue Venture, which has all-you-can-eat weekday lunchtime buffets.

As for **nightlife**, the clubs around cours d'Estienne-d'Orves and cours Julien are for trendy kids from the upper-crust *arrondissements*, with prices to match. *El Ache de Cuba*, 108 cours

Julien, is a lively **bar** popular with students. The deeply hip *Webbar*, a combined art gallery, **live music** venue, restaurant and **Internet** café, is on rue de la République. One of the best **clubs** is *Le Trolleybus*, 24 quai de Rive Neuve, a warren-like club complete with funk, techno and rock rooms and even a *boules* area. The *New Cancan*, 20 rue Sénac, is a camp **gay club**. The weekly *L'Hebdo* (€0.90) has comprehensive entertainment listings.

Listings

Airlines Air France, 14 La Canebière (☎08.20.82.08.20); British Airways, airport (☎04.42.14.21.24).

Beaches Best of the local beaches is the heavily landscaped plage du Prado, at the end of the Corniche du Président J.F. Kennedy (bus #83 from the Vieux Port).

Books Virgin Megastore, 75 rue St-Ferréol, 6e, stocks English books.

Embassies UK, 24 av du Prado, 6e (☎04.91.15.72.10); USA, 12 bd Peytral, 6e (☎04.91.54.92.00).

Exchange 22 La Canebière, 1er (Mon–Sat 9am–6pm).

Hospital La Conception, 147 bd Baille, 5e (☎04.91.38.36.52).

Internet Info-café, 1 quai de Rive Neuve, 1er (*www.info-cafe.com*); Webbar, rue de la République (*www.webbar.fr*).

Laundry Pressing Canebière, 73 allée Léon Gambetta, 1er.

Pharmacy 44 Quai du Port, 1er, is open on Sundays; for 24hr service check on pharmacy doors for the rota.

Police Commissariat, 2 rue Antoine Becker, 2e (☎04.91.39.80.00).

Post office 1 place de l'Hôtel des Postes, 1er (Mon–Fri 8am–7pm, Sat 8am–noon).

Travel agent Nouvelle Frontières, 11 rue Haxo, 1er (☎04.91.54.34.77).

Toulon

Home base to the French Mediterranean fleet and its arsenal, and until recently a major ship-building centre, the port of **TOULON** was half-destroyed in World War II and doesn't offer much joy today. But since it is a major transport hub you may well find yourself there, and it does have the advantage of being comparatively inexpensive for this coast. The **old town**, much besieged by bulldozers and planners intent on its gentrification, crams in between the main bd de Strasbourg and quai de Stalingrad, a pleasant enough place by day, though less appealing at night, especially towards the port. The **Musée d'Art**, 113 bd Maréchal-Leclerc (daily 1–7pm; free), has a good collection of paintings and sculpture including work by Brueghel, Carracci, Vlaminck, Rodin and Francis Bacon. The most impressive public artwork in the city is Pierre Puget's **Atlantes**, which hold up what's left of the old Town Hall on quai de Stalingrad. The best way to pass an afternoon is to take bus #40 to bd Amiral Vence, Super Toulon, and jump on the **funicular** (Tues–Sun 9am–noon & 2–6/8pm; closed Dec & Jan; €5.80 return) to the summit of **Mont Faron**, 542m above.

The **train station**, on place de l'Europe, and **bus station**, on place Albert-1er, lie northeast of the town centre. To reach the old town, head down rue Vauban, turn left onto av Mal-Leclerc, which becomes bd de Strasbourg, then right by the theatre and you'll arrive in place Victor-Hugo. The **tourist office** is near the harbour on place Raimu (Mon–Sat 9/9.30am–5.30/6pm; *www.toulon.com*). One of the least expensive and nicest **hotels** is *Hôtel des Allées* at 18 allée Amiral Courbet (☎04.94.91.10.02; ③). The pleasant *Little Palace*, close by at 6 rue Berthelot (☎04.94.92.26.62; ③), is also a bargain. For summer **hostel** accommodation, there's a *Foyer de la Jeunesse* at 12 place d'Armes, ten minutes from the station on the west side of town (☎04.94.22.62.00; ②; June–Aug only).

St-Tropez and around

The heart of **ST-TROPEZ** is surprisingly village-like, gathered around a port founded by the ancient Greeks and made up of a web of cobbled alleys and butter-coloured houses. Rustic it is not, however: while in the late nineteenth century it was a favoured haunt of artists, 1956 witnessed the arrival of Roger Vadim, who filmed **Brigitte Bardot** in *Et Dieu Créa La Femme (And God Created Woman)*, and the place has never looked back.

The road into St-Tropez splits in two as it enters the village, with the **bus station** between them; a short distance beyond on place Georges Grammont is the **Musée de l'Annonciade** (Mon & Wed–Sun 10am–noon & 2/3–6/7pm; €4.60) – a reason in itself for coming here, with works by Matisse, Signac and Derain. Beyond the museum, the **Vieux Port** is the centre of the town, the dockside café clientele face-to-face with the yacht-deck Martini-sippers, the latest fashions parading in between. Up from here, at the end of quai Jean-Jaurès, rue de la Mairie passes the **Town Hall**, with a street to the left leading down to the rocky Baie de la Glaye, and, along rue de la Ponche, the fishing port with a tiny **beach**. Both these spots are miraculously free from commercialization. Beyond the fishing port, roads lead up to the sixteenth-century **Citadelle**, which has a drab maritime museum but marvellous views from the ramparts, or along to Les Graniers and further **beaches** on Baie des Canoubiers – accessible by a coastal path and by frequent **bus** service.

St-Tropez has no train service. Sodetrav run **buses** from Toulon for €16.20 (7 daily; takes 2hr). The **tourist office**, on quai Jean-Jaurès, can help with reservations (daily: June–Sept 9.30am–1.30pm & 3.30–10pm; rest of year 9/9.30am–noon/1pm & 2–6/7pm; *www.nova.fr/saint-tropez*). The only vaguely affordable **hotels** are *Les Chimères*, Port du Pilon (☎04.94.97.02.90; ④), a short way back from the bus station towards La Foux – though it's likely to be booked out for the summer – and *La Méditerranée* on place Croix Fer (☎04.94.97.00.44; ⑤). **Camping** poses similar problems: the two sites on the plage du Pampelonne are closest to St-Tropez but cost a fortune. Better is *Les Tournels* on route de Camarat near Ramatuelle (☎04.94.55.90.90). For **eating**, try the takeaway places on rue G-Clemenceau and place des Lices, or for a prime people-watching seat, head to *Le Gorille* on quai Suffren, which serves *moules-frites* alongside its *plats du jour*.

St-Raphaël and Fréjus

There's a better choice of accommodation in **ST-RAPHAËL**, north of St-Tropez, and in the adjacent town of **FRÉJUS**, 3km inland. Both were established by the Romans and various remnants of this past lie scattered around the towns, including, in Fréjus, an **amphitheatre** on rue Henri-Vardon, used in its damaged state for bullfights and rock concerts, and a **theatre** on av du XV-Corps-d'Armées. Fréjus's **cathedral** (Tues–Sun: April–Sept 9am–7pm; rest of year 9am–noon & 2–5pm; free), on place Formigé, has superb twelfth-century Romanesque cloisters and a late-medieval fantasy ceiling, as well as a **museum** (same hours; €4) with a complete Roman mosaic of a leopard.

St-Raphaël's **hostel**, *Centre International Le Manoir*, is 5km east at Chemin de l'Escale, Boulouris (☎04.94.95.20.58; ②). Its **hotels** include *La Bonne Auberge*, close to the old port at 54 rue de la Garonne (☎04.94.95.69.72; ④), and the *Mistral*, 80 rue de la Garonne (☎04.94.95.38.82; ④). The nearest **campsite** is on RN98 (☎04.94.95.52.13; Mar–Nov). St-Raphaël's **tourist office** is at 210 rue W. Rousseau (July & Aug daily 8.30am–7pm; rest of year Mon–Sat 9am–12.30pm & 2–6.30pm; *www.saint-raphael.com*), by the **train** and **bus station**. Between here and the seafront you'll have no trouble finding **restaurants**.

In Fréjus, inexpensive **hotels** include *La Riviera*, 90 rue Grisolle (☎04.94.51.31.46; ③), and there's an HI **hostel** 2km northeast from the centre of town at Chemin du Counillier, where you can camp (☎04.94.53.18.75; ②); take bus #7 from St Raphael's bus station, which goes direct to the hostel twice a day (otherwise take bus #7 to Le Chênes, then walk 20min). **Campsites** are ubiquitous, with at least four on the Bagnols road and one close to the hostel. Fréjus's **tourist office** is at 325 rue Jean Jaurès (Mon–Sat 9am–noon & 2–6pm; *www.ville-frejus.fr*). Places to **eat** can be found on place Agricola, place de la Liberté and the main shopping streets.

Cannes and around

Fishing village turned millionaires' residence, **CANNES** is perhaps the most unpleasant town along the Côte d'Azur, with a fine sand beach that looks like an industrial production line for parasols. The seafront promenade, **La Croisette**, and the **Vieux Port** form the focus of Cannes life, especially during the frenzied two-week International Film Festival in May. The old town, **Le Suquet**, on the steep hill overlooking the bay from the west, masks its miserable passageways with quaint cosmetic streets. Beyond Le Suquet there's another **beach**.

Should you find yourself compelled to stay, aim for the centre, near the **train station** on rue Jean-Jaurès and around the main street of rue Antibes/Félix-Fauré, which holds the best concentration of **hotels**. Possibilities include the unappealing *Bourgogne*, 11 rue du 24-août (☎04.93.38.36.73; ④), the adequate *National*, 8 rue Maréchal Joffre (☎04.93.39.91.92; ④), or the *Chanteclair*, near the old town at 12 rue Forville (☎04.93.39.68.88; ③). More appealing is the excellent **hostel** at 35 av de Vallauris (☎04.93.99.26.79; ②), a ten-minute walk from the station, or take the bus towards Vallauris. The nearest **campsite** is *Parc Bellevue*, 67 av Maurice Chevalier (☎04.93.47.28.97; bus #2 or #9). There's a **tourist office** at the train station (daily 9am–noon & 2–5pm), with the main office in the Palais des Festivals on the waterfront (summer daily 9am–6.30pm, winter Mon–Sat 9am–6.30pm; *www.cannes-on-line.com*). Le Suquet is full of **restaurants**, which get cheaper as you reach the top. *Au Bec Fin*, at 12 rue du 24-août, has superb traditional cooking and good *plats du jour*; *Le Sevrina*, 3 rue Félix Faure, serves pizza, pasta and fondue; and *Le Bouchon d'Objectif*, 10 rue de Constantine, is an excellent, reasonably priced local bistro.

Vallauris and Antibes

Just east of Cannes, **VALLAURIS**, reached by half-hourly bus, was home to Picasso for a while, where he was inspired by the local craft of ceramics. The main street, av George-Clemenceau, sells nothing but pottery. The **Madoura** pottery, where Picasso worked, is off av Suzanne Ramie, and has the sole rights on reproducing his designs. At the top of the main street, Picasso's bronze *Man with a Sheep* stands in the marketplace right opposite an early medieval **chapel** painted by the artist as *La Guerre et la Paix* in 1952, which can be seen in the **Musée Picasso**, place de la Libération (Mon & Wed–Sun: June–Sept 10am–6pm; rest of year 10am–noon & 2–6pm; €3.80).

A few kilometres on lies **ANTIBES**, to which Picasso returned after the war; he worked in a studio that has since been converted into a museum. The artist left much of his output while here to what is now the **Musée Picasso**, place Mariejol (Tues–Sun 10am–noon & 2–6pm; €4.60), which displays numerous ceramics, still-lifes of sea urchins, the wonderful *Ulysse et ses Sirènes*, and a whole room full of drawings. Antibes's **tourist office** (summer daily 9am–7pm, winter Mon–Fri 9am–12.30pm & 2–6.30pm, Sat 9am–noon & 2–6pm; *www.antibes-juanlespins.com*) is at 11 place de Gaulle, to the right of the **train station**. The best accommodation option is the **hostel**, *Relais International de la Jeunesse*, by the sea on the corner of bd de la Garoupe and av de l'Antiquité (☎04.93.61.34.40; ②; March–Oct; bus #2A).

Cagnes and Vence

A little further east of Antibes, **CAGNES-SUR-MER** lies a short distance inland but is walkable from the Cannes–Nice bus stop, and was home to Renoir for the last eleven years of his life. His house, *Les Collettes*, is now a **museum** (Mon & Wed–Sun 10am–noon & 2–5/6pm; closed Nov; €3); his studio, north-facing to catch the late afternoon light, is arranged as if he had just popped out. On the other side of the town, to the north, is the ancient village of **HAUT-DE-CAGNES**, where the crenellated **château** (same hours; €3) houses a number of museums covering local history, fishing, the cultivation of olives and the **Musée d'Art Moderne Méditerranéen**. This contains changing exhibitions of the painters who have worked on the coast in the last hundred years, plus the Donation Suzy Solidor – wonderfully diverse portraits of the cabaret star from the 1920s to the 1960s by several great painters.

The next artistic treat, and one of the best in the region, is in **ST-PAUL-DE-VENCE**, reachable by taking the Nice–Vence bus from place de Gaulle in Cagnes-sur-Mer. The **Fondation Maeght** (daily 10am–12.30pm & 2.30–6pm; €7) is a wonderful collection of the early works of Miró, Léger, Chagall and their contemporaries, and has an outdoor sculpture garden featuring Giacometti at his best. **VENCE**, a few kilometres north, is the site of the **Chapelle du Rosaire** (Mon, Wed, Fri & Sat 2–5pm; Tues & Thurs 10–11.30am & 2–5.30pm; closed Nov; €2), built between 1949 and 1951 under the direction of Matisse, who painted the black outline figures on plain matt tiles with a brush fixed to a 180cm bamboo pole, specifically to remove his own signature from the lines. Colour comes from the sunlight diffused through green, blue and yellow windows. In Vence, *La Closerie des Genêts*, 4 impasse Marcellin Maurel (☎04.93.58.33.25; ④), is a reasonably priced **hotel**, and there's the *Camping la Bergerie* (☎04.93.58.09.36) about 3km west on the road to Tourettes-sur-Loup. The **tourist office** is near the main gate into the old town (July & Aug Mon–Sat 9am–12.30pm & 2–6pm, Sun 10am–noon; rest of year Mon–Fri 9am–12.30pm & 2–6pm; *www.ville-vence.fr*). For good Provençal **food**, try *La Fariguoule,* 15 av Henri-Isnard or, on the same street but for half the price, *La Vieille Douve.*

Nice

NICE, capital of the French Riviera and fifth-largest town in the country, should be a loathsome place. The population is largely made up of pensioners and fat-cat tycoons, and the place can't even boast a sandy beach. And yet it is delightful, its surprisingly affable inhabitants, beautiful location and attractive historical centre compensating for its sins. The city also makes the best base for visiting the 30km of the Riviera coast, which runs east to the Italian border and west to Cannes. The **Carnival of Nice** (held sometime in Feb or early March) packs out the town, with parades and music culminating at Mardi Gras, a city-wide party that takes up every street.

Arrival and accommodation

Nice **airport** is 6km southwest, connected to the city's train station by bus #23 (daily 6am–9pm; takes 30min; €1.30) and to the city's bus station by a special bus (every 20min; €3.50); a **taxi** costs €18–28. The main **train station**, Nice-Ville, is a ten-minute stroll from the centre, a couple of blocks left of the top of av Jean-Médecin. There's a **tourist office** next to the station on av Thiers (May–Sept daily 8am–8pm; rest of year Mon–Sat 8am–7pm, Sun 9am–6pm), with the main office at 5 promenade des Anglais (May–Sept Mon–Sat 8am–8pm, Sun 9am–6pm; rest of year Mon–Sat 9am–6pm; *www.nicetourism.com*), and an annexe at the airport (daily 8am–10pm). The tourist office and city museums sell a **museum pass** (€5.70), allowing one visit per museum over seven days. For **city transport**, single bus tickets cost €1 from the driver, or you can buy a bus pass for one/five/seven days (€3.80/€13/€17) from Sunbus, 10 av Félix-Faure. Sunbus, kiosks and *tabacs* also sell *carnets* of ten tickets (€8.50).

There are lots of affordable **hotels** around the train station, including *Les Orangers*, 10bis av Durante (☎04.93.87.51.41; ③; closed Nov), popular with American students. Nearer the sea is the charming *Les Mimosas,* 26 rue de la Buffa (☎04.93.88.05.59; ③), run by a jovial English–Belgian couple. *Hôtel du Danemark*, 3 av des Baumettes (☎04.93.44.12.04; ④), is quiet with well-kept rooms. The **hostel** is 4km out of town on route Forestière du Mont Alban (☎04.93.89.23.64; ②); take bus #14 from place Masséna. Further out, and with a 10.30pm curfew, is *R.I.J. Clairvallone*, north of Cimiez at 26 av Scudéri-Cimiez (☎04.93.81.27.63, *clajpaca@cote-dazur.com*; ③; bus #15). The only **campsite** is the tiny *Camping Terry*, 768 route de Grenoble (☎04.93.08.11.58), 6km north of the airport and off any bus routes, but the tourist office has a list of the many campsites in the area which can be reached by local train.

The City

It doesn't take long to get a feel for the layout of Nice. The **old town** nestles around the hill of Nice's former château, a rambling collection of narrow alleys lined with tall, rust-and-ochre houses that centres on place Rossetti and the Baroque **Cathédrale St-Réparate**. Nearby is the entrance to the **parc du Château** (also reachable by lift from the eastern end of rue des Ponchettes), decked out in a mock-Grecian style harking back to the original Greek settlement of Nikea. The point of climbing the stairs, apart from enjoying the perfumed greenery, is the view stretching west over the muddle of the old town's rooftops. Nearby, on Promenade des Arts, is the **Musée d'Art Moderne et d'Art Contemporain** (Mon & Wed–Sun 10am–6pm; €3.80), holding a collection of Pop Art and neo-Realist work, including pieces by Andy Warhol and Roy Lichtenstein. Lying to the south is the famous **promenade des Anglais** stretching along the pebble beach, laid out by nineteenth-century English residents to facilitate their afternoon stroll by the sea.

Up above the city centre, **Cimiez**, a posh suburb reached by bus #15 from av Thiers, was the social centre of the town's elite some seventeen centuries ago, when the city was capital of the Roman province of Alpes-Maritimae. Excavations of the Roman baths are housed, along with accompanying archeological finds, in the **Musée d'Archéologie**, 160 av des Arènes (Tues–Sun 10am–noon/1pm & 2–5/6pm; €3.80). Overlooking the baths is the wonderful **Musée Matisse** (Mon & Wed–Sun 10am–5/6pm; €3.80): Nice was the artist's home for much of his life, and the collection covers every period and includes models for the chapel in Vence, a near-complete set of the bronze sculptures, and a complete set of the books that Matisse illustrated. Among the paintings are a 1905 portrait of Madame Matisse, *A Tempest in Nice*, and the 1947 *Still Life with Pomegranates*. At the foot of the hill, just off bd Cimiez on av du Dr-Menard, there is more modern art in **Chagall's Biblical Message**, housed in a purpose-built museum opened by the artist in 1972 (Mon & Wed–Sun 10am–5/6pm; €4.60). The seventeen paintings, based on the Old Testament, are complemented by etchings, engravings, tapestries and mosaics, all perfectly set off by the light. Chagall himself contributed the stained-glass windows.

Eating, drinking and nightlife

Nice's Old Town stays up late and is full of **restaurants**. Marché aux Fleurs (not to be missed in the mornings for its colourful **market**) is lined with restaurants, their tables spilling outdoors, but they tend to be quite pricey. *Café de Turin*, on place Garibaldi, is a good, basic place for mussels and clams, while *Chez René Socca*, 2 rue Miralhéti, serves Niçois specialities at busy outdoor tables, including great *socca*, a pancake made from chickpea flour. *Passez à Table*, 30 rue Pertinax, serves vegetarian meals and organic produce. For **Internet** access, head to Cybercafé l'Arobas on rue Benoît Bunico in the old town, or Bar Masthome on rue de la Préfecture. *Wayne's* **bar** on rue de la Préfecture has **live music** and is popular with backpackers, as is *Thor's* on Marché aux Fleurs. *Scarlett O'Hara*, 22 rue Droite, is an Irish pub serving decent Guinness.

Monaco and Monte Carlo

Monstrosities are common on the Côte d'Azur, but nowhere, not even Cannes, can outdo **MONACO**. This tiny independent principality has lived off gambling and class for a century and is one of the greatest sites for property speculation in the world. Finding out about the workings of the regime is not easy, but it is clear that Prince Rainier is the one autocratic monarch left in Europe. A copy of every French law is sent to Monaco, reworded, and put to the Prince: if he likes it, it is passed; if not, it's not. There is a parliament of limited function elected by Monagesque nationals – who comprise about sixteen percent of the population – but there's no opposition to the ruling family. What the citizens and foreign residents like so much is that they pay no income tax.

The three-kilometre-long state consists of the old town of **Monaco-Ville** around the palace on a high promontory; the new suburb and marina of **Fontvieille** in its western shadow; **La Condamine** behind the harbour on the other side of the rock; **Larvotto**, a swimming resort to the east with artificial beaches of imported sand; and, in the middle, **MONTE CARLO**.

There's little in the way of conventional sights, only the toytown palace and assorted museums in the old town, where every other shop sells Prince Rainier mugs and other junk. The only real draw is the **Casino** (daily noon–dawn), with its riotously Rococo American Room and European Gaming Rooms that have an almost cathedral-like atmosphere; admission (€7.60) is for over 21s only – you may have to show your passport – and you'll be refused entry if you don't look enough like a gambler.

Monaco **train station** is on av Prince-Pierre in La Condamine, a short walk from the **bus station** on place d'Armes. Bus #4, direction Larvotto, takes you from the train station to the Casino-Tourism stop, near the **tourist office** at 2a bd des Moulins (Mon–Sat 9am–7pm, Sun 10am–noon; *www.monaco-congres.com*). Monaco's one good public service is the clean, efficient and free **lift system** for steep north–south journeys. Day-tripping is the way to go, but otherwise La Condamine is best for **hotels**: try *Cosmopolite*, 4 rue de la Turbie (☎93.30.16.95; ④), or its neighbour *Hôtel de France* (☎93.30.24.64; ⑤). If you arrive early enough, and you're under 26 or a student under 31, you may be able to get a **dorm bed** at the *Centre de Jeunesse Princesse Stéphanie*, near the station at 24 av Prince-Pierre (☎93.50.83.20; ②). La Condamine and the Old Town are the places to look for **restaurants**, but you'll struggle to find anything affordable; in Monte Carlo, try *Chérie's Café*, 9 av des Spélugues.

CORSICA

Despite two hundred years of French rule, the island of **Corsica** has more in common culturally with Italy than with its governing country, as testified by a profusion of Italianate churches and a language that's closely related to the Tuscan dialect. A history of repeated invasion has strengthened the cultural identity of an island whose reputation for violence and xenophobia has overshadowed the more hospitable nature of its inhabitants. The island, much of which is Regional Park, comprises an amazing diversity of landscapes: its magnificent rocky coastline is interspersed with outstanding beaches, while the inland mountains offer numerous opportunities for hiking. The extensive forests and sparkling rivers provide the locals with a rich supply of game and fresh fish: regional specialities include wild boar, blackbird pâté, cured hams and sausages.

Two French *départements* divide Corsica, each with its own capital: Napoleon's birthplace, **Ajaccio**, is a sunny elegant town on the southwest coast, while **Bastia** faces Italy in the north. The old capital of **Corte** is one of many fortress villages which characterize the interior. The coastal resorts are equally superbly sited: **Calvi** draws in the tourists with its massive citadel and long sandy beach, and strung out at the southernmost point facing Sardinia lies **Bonifacio**, perched on limestone cliffs that are buffeted by the clearest water in the Mediterranean. Ajaccio, Bastia, Corte and Calvi are connected by a slender **train** service; for Bonifacio you're reliant on **buses**. There's regional information at *www.corsica-online.com*.

FERRIES TO CORSICA

For details, go to *www.corsicaferries.com*,
www.corsicamarittima.com, *www.mobylines.it* or *www.sncm.fr*.

Genoa (Italy) to: Bastia (1 weekly; 9hr).

Livorno (Italy) to: Bastia (2–20 weekly; 4hr).

Marseille to: Ajaccio (1–8 weekly; 10hr); Bastia (1–10 weekly; 11hr).

Nice to: Ajaccio (1–8 weekly; 11hr 30min); Bastia (1–12 weekly; 3–6hr); Calvi (1–7 weekly; 3–5hr).

Toulon to: Ajaccio (June–Sept 1–4 weekly; 10hr); Bastia (June–Aug 1–3 weekly; 12hr).

Ajaccio

Set in a magnificent bay, **AJACCIO** combines all the ingredients of the archetypal Mediterranean resort with its palm trees, spacious squares, yachts and street cafés. There's not be a great deal to see, but Ajaccio is a pleasant place to spend some time. The town developed around a fifteenth-century Genoese citadel and the streets around it remain appealingly ancient. Napoleon, who was born here in 1769, gave the town fame but did little else for the place except to make it the island capital for the brief period of his empire. You can visit his family house, now a museum, and you'll find the town peppered with statues and streets named after the Bonaparte family.

Cours Napoléon is the main thoroughfare, running parallel to the sea and culminating in place Général-de-Gaulle, which in turn leads onto **place Foch**, a shady, palm-lined square bordered by cafés and restaurants and open to the sea. The most rewarding visit is to the **Musée Fesch** (July & Aug Mon 1.30–6.30pm, Tues–Sun 9am–6.30pm; rest of year Mon 1–5.15pm, Tues–Sun 9.15am–12.15pm & 2.15–5.15pm; €5.30), situated halfway down rue Cardinal-Fesch, an attractive winding shopping street that runs off place Foch. The building is home to an important collection of Italian paintings from the fifteenth and sixteenth centuries, the legacy of Napoléon's step-uncle Cardinal Joseph Fesch, as well as the **Chapelle Impériale** (€1.50 extra), where the Bonaparte family vaults have been gathered. Notable among the paintings is Botticelli's *Virgin and the Garland* and Veronese's startling *Leda and the Swan*. Place Letizia, off the west side of rue Napoléon in the heart of the old town, holds the **Maison Bonaparte** (April–Nov Mon 2–6pm, Tues–Sun 9am–noon & 2–6pm; rest of year Mon 2–4.45pm, Tues–Sun 10am–noon & 2–4.45pm; €3.40), a disappointingly sparse museum that displays Napoleon's bed and the chair his mother lay on when in labour. In the Hôtel de Ville is the **Salon Napoléonien** (Mon–Fri 8.30–11.30am & 2–6pm; €1.50), for dedicated fans only, which houses the Bonaparte family portraits and a gold replica of Napoleon's death-mask. The great man was baptized in Ajaccio's **Cathedral**, which dominates rue Forcioli-Conti, southwest of place Foch. Built in 1554, it boasts a Delacroix *Virgin* which hangs in the chapel to the left of the altar. Napoleon's dying words are inscribed on a plaque adorning the pillar to the left of the entrance, expressing his wish to be buried in Ajaccio if they wouldn't have him in Paris.

Tucked away behind place Général-de-Gaulle in rue Général-Levie is the **Musée a Bandera** (June–Sept daily 9am–7pm; July & Aug Fri until 10pm; rest of year Mon–Fri 9am–noon & 2–7pm; €3.80), offering a fascinating insight into Corsican military history. Displays include an impressive collection of vendetta daggers and a room dedicated to bandits, displaying photographs and life-size models of the most notorious *bandits d'honneur.*

Practicalities

Ajaccio's Campo dell'Oro **airport** is 6km southeast, connected to the town bus station by hourly bus #8. The **ferry port** is in the town centre, but the **train station** is a ten-minute walk north along the seafront. The **tourist office** (summer Mon–Sat 9am–8.30pm, Sun 9am–1pm; winter Mon–Fri 8am–6pm, Sat 8am–noon & 2–5pm; *www.tourisme.fr/ajaccio*) occupies the ground floor of the Hôtel de Ville in place Foch, directly opposite the port. There's not much affordable **accommodation**. The least expensive hotel is the tiny *Colomba*, 8 av de Paris (☎04.95.21.12.66; ③), but *Hotel Kalliste*, 51 cours Napoléon (☎04.95.51.34.45; ④), does a good deal whereby you can rent studios for one night. Otherwise there's the pleasant *Marengo*, 2 rue Marengo (☎04.95.21.43.66; ⑤; March–Nov); *San Carlu*, close to the beach at 8 bd Danielle-Casanova (☎04.95.21.13.84; ⑥); or *Bella Vista*, 20 bd Lantivy (☎04.95.21.07.97; ④). The nearest **campsite** is *Les Mimosas*, on route d'Alata (☎04.95.20.99.85; April–Oct).

Most **restaurants** are in and around the old town, east and west of place Foch. *Cantina*, just above place Foch at 3 bd du Roi-Jérôme, does inexpensive Corsican snacks, while *20123*, 2 rue Roi de Rome, offers true Corsican country cooking. *Le Menéstrel*, 5 rue Fesch, serves good food but its main attraction is the live local **music** most evenings. Young people hang out at *du Jetée* on the jetée de la Citadelle, overlooking the boats, or munch pizza at *Chez Paolo*, 8 rue Roi-du-Rome. **Bars and cafés** take up much pavement space, with cocktail bars and *glaciers* lining the seafront behind the beach. *Safari*, by the beach at 18 bd Lantivy, is popular, while the innovative *Café du Flore*, opposite Palais Fesch, plays jazz. The bookshop La Marge, 4 rue Emanuelle-Arène, offers **Internet** access, as does U Borgu, 52 rue Fesch (☎04.95.50.09.00).

Bastia

BASTIA is a charismatic harbour town, its crumbling golden-grey buildings set against a backdrop of fire-darkened hills. Now a thriving commercial port, it was the island capital under the Genoese and has remained an authentic working town with few concessions to tourism. The place has much to recommend it: the dilapidated Vieux Port, a sprinkling of Baroque churches, the imposing citadel, or bastion, from which the town gets its name, and the vast place Saint-Nicolas, lined with trees and cafés open to the sea.

The most appealing area is the **Vieux Port**, the site of the original fishing village around which the town grew, nowadays a tranquil backwater. Dominating the harbour are the twin towers of **Église St-Jean-Baptiste**, the largest but not the most interesting church in Bastia, which shoulders the place du Marché, where a half-hearted **market** takes place each morning. The narrow streets nearby, a flaking conglomeration of tenement blocks in attractive decay, are known as **Terra Vecchia**. Close by, in rue Napoléon, are two Baroque churches whose dull facades belie their interiors. Halfway up the street stands the little **Oratoire de l'Immaculée Conception**, dating from 1611, a Genoese showplace used for state occasions such as the inauguration of the Anglo-Corsican parliament in the 1760s.

Bastia's **airport**, Poretta, is 16km south of town off RN197. Shuttle **buses** into the centre (€7.50) stop opposite the **train station**, located above place St-Nicolas; other buses stop either at the top of boulevard Paoli, the main street, or outside the train station. **Ferries** use the Nouveau Port, five minutes' walk from the centre. The **tourist office** in place St-Nicolas (daily: June–Sept 8am–7pm; Oct–May Mon–Sat 8am–6pm) has lists of accommodation in the area. Rent **bikes** from Cycles 20, on rte du Fort La Croix by the Palais de Justice. **Accommodation** isn't a problem, even at the height of the season: try the *Riviera*, 1 rue du Nouveau Port (☎04.95.31.07.16; ④), a well-established place popular with travellers; *Central*, 3 rue Miot (☎04.95.31.71.12; ⑤); or *Voyageurs*, 9 av du Maréchal-Sébastiani (☎04.95.34.90.80; ⑤). Top **campsite** is *Les Orangers* (☎04.95.33.24.09; March–Oct), 4km north at Miomo; take the Erbalunga bus.

The best **restaurants** are in and around the Vieux Port. The emphasis is on Italian food; of the authentic Corsican places, the best is *U Tianu* in rue Monsignor-Rigo, off place du Marché – they do an excellent selection of *charcuterie*. Also in the Vieux Port is *A. Scaletta*, with good fish, the Moroccan *Le Zagora*, and *U Cantarettu*, where you can eat excellent pizzas to live music. For a **drink**, *Bar Corsica*, 2 rue Marine, features traditional Corsican singing, or try *L'Impériale*, 6 bd Général-de-Gaulle in place St-Nicolas.

Corte

Set amidst craggy mountains and gorges, the sleepy inland town of **CORTE** is known as the spiritual capital of Corsica, as this is where Pascal Paoli had his seat of government during the brief period of independence in the eighteenth century. Paoli founded a university here which was reopened in the early 1980s, but despite the weekly influx of students the town lacks much vibrancy: even its inhabitants call it a *trou perdu* (a lost hole).

The main street, **cours Paoli**, runs the whole length of the small town, culminating in place Paoli, a pleasant market square. A cobbled ramp leads from the square up to the Ville Haute, where in tiny **place Gaffori** you can still see the bullet marks that were made by

Genoese soldiers during the War of Independence. The vigorously pointing statue is of General Gaffori, one of Paoli's right-hand men, who led the independent army in 1756. Continuing north you'll soon come to the gates of the extraordinary **Citadelle**, whose ramparts remain intact, hiding within the **Museu di a Corsica** (June–Sept daily 10am–8pm; rest of year Tues–Sun 10am–6pm; Nov & Dec closed Sun; €7), which examines the island's heritage and tackles the issue of contemporary Corsican identity. Best views of the citadel, the town and its valley are from the **Belvédère**, a platform opposite the tower.

Corte's **train station** lies 1km out of town at the foot of the hill near the university. **Buses** stop at the north end of place Paoli. The **tourist office** is situated within the citadel (July & Aug daily 9am–8pm; rest of year Mon–Fri 9am–1pm & 2–6/7pm), with a summer-only annexe at the train station. Cheapest **hotel** is *de la Poste*, 2 place Padoue (☎04.95.46.01.37; ③), a gloomy, functional building without restaurant; it's preferable to head 1km out of town on the D623 to *Auberge de la Restonica* (☎04.95.46.20.13; ⑤), a sumptuous old-fashioned hunting-inn, set in the forest and overlooking a waterfall which provides its restaurant with fresh trout. There are also **campsites** along this road: *U Sognu* (☎04.95.46.09.07) lies at the foot of the Restonica valley, about 500m from the town centre. For **food**, try *U Montagnone* on place Paoli for local specialities, or *Le Gaffory* in place Gaffori de l'Église, for wild boar lasagne.

Calvi

Seen from the water, the great citadel of **CALVI** resembles a floating island, sharply defined against a hazy backdrop of snowcapped mountains. Calvi, home to the Foreign Legion, is the island's third port and draws in thousands of tourists for its 6km of sandy beach. It's a lighthearted holiday town, its marina packed with hundreds of boats, many of them huge yachts belonging to international glitterati. It became a Genoese stronghold in 1268, when its inhabitants were granted special privileges for being loyal citizens; their motto *Civitas Calvis Semper Fidelis* is inscribed above the gate into the *citadelle*, or **Haute Ville**, a labyrinth of cobbled lanes and stairways rising from **place Christophe Colomb**, the square linking the two parts of town. Shops, restaurants and hotels are all found in the **Basse Ville**, which backs onto the marina, and the **beach** starts just beyond the boats.

Ste-Catherine **airport** is 7km south, with only a **taxi** (€11–15) to get you into town. **Trains** stop behind the marina, and close by is the stop for **buses** from Bastia. The **ferry port** is at the far end of the quai Lantivy. The **tourist office** is on quai Landry (summer daily 9am–7pm; winter Mon–Fri 9–5/6pm, Sat 9am–noon & 2–5pm; *www.villedecalvi.fr*), with a summer annexe at the citadel gate. Among **hotels**, the *du Centre*, 14 rue Alsace-Lorraine (☎04.95.65.02.01; ⑤), is one of the cheapest and most central, but is closed in winter. There's a **hostel** at 43 av de la République (☎04.95.65.14.15; ②; April–Sept). The closest **campsite** is *La Pinède*, 2km along the N197 (☎04.95.65.17.80; summer only). **Restaurants** cram the streets of the Basse Ville. *U San Carlo*, place St-Charles, serves excellent seafood at reasonable prices. Lively but touristy *Le Santa Maria*, 14 rue Clemenceau, turns out some unusual Corsican specialities such as *stifatu*, a tasty blend of stuffed meats. The piano bar and restaurant *Chez Tao* is worth a visit for its impressive views of the bay.

Bonifacio

The port of **BONIFACIO** enjoys a superbly isolated situation on a narrow peninsula of dazzling white limestone at Corsica's southernmost point, only minutes by boat from Sardinia. For five hundred years Bonifacio was a virtually independent republic, and a sense of detachment from the rest of Corsica persists, with many Bonifaciens still speaking their own dialect. The town has become a chic holiday spot as well as a sailing centre, and gets unbearably overcrowded and expensive in midsummer.

The **Haute Ville** is connected to the marina by a steep flight of steps at the west end of the quay. Built within the massive fortifications of the *citadelle*, it's an alluring maze of dusty streets, its houses displaying pointed arches and closed arcades unique to Bonifacio. From the edge of the ramparts there's a glorious view across the straits to Sardinia. In rue de Palais de Garde, in front of the drawbridge at the top of the steps, is **Église Ste-Marie-Majeure**, its facade hidden by the loggia from where Genoese officers dispensed justice in the thirteenth century. Also in the Haute Ville is the **Cimetière Marin**, a captivating walled cemetery at the far end of the promontory filled with elaborate mausoleums. Down in the marina, a worthwhile **boat excursion** (€11.50) takes you round the base of the cliffs for a fantastic view of the town and also to the **sea-caves**, grottoes where the rock glitters with rainbow colours and the turquoise sea is deeply translucent. The tourist office has information on the five different tour companies. The closest **beach** is **plage de la Catena**, 1km west of the port, a ten-minute walk on the Ajaccio road then left down a track just before the *Araguina* campsite. Some outstanding beaches lie to the north of Bonifacio, most notably **Golfe de Santa Manza**, 5km north along the road to Porto Vecchio, and **plage de la Rondinara**, 5km further.

Ferries from Santa Teresa on Sardinia dock at the far end of the quay; **buses** from Ajaccio stop in the car park by the marina, close to most hotels. The **tourist office** is on Place de l'Europe (May–Oct daily 9am–8pm; Nov–April Mon–Fri 9am–noon & 2–6pm, Sat 9am–noon; *www.bonifacio.com*). Most affordable **hotel** is *Étrangers*, av Sylver Bohn (☎04.95.73.01.09; ⑥). **Campsites** include *L'Araguina*, 500m past the marina on the Ajaccio road (☎04.95.73.02.96), and *Campo di Leccia* (☎04.95.73.03.09), opposite the U Farniente building, which is more likely to have space in summer. For **food**, head up to the Haute Ville. *Le Rustic*, 16 rue Fred Scamaroni, offers good-value Corsican set menus for under €13, and *Café de la Poste*, at no. 6, is also very popular with the locals. For **Internet** access, head to Boni Boom on quai Comparetti (☎04.95.73.59.47).

travel details

Trains

Paris to: Amiens (14 daily; 1hr 10min); Bordeaux (hourly; 3hr); Boulogne (7 daily; 3hr); Caen (12 daily; 2hr); Calais (6 daily; 3hr 10min); Clermont-Ferrand (8 daily; 4hr); Dieppe (hourly; 2hr 20min); Dijon (hourly; 1hr 40min); Le Havre (10 daily; 2hr); Lille (hourly; 1hr); Lyon (hourly; 2hr); Marseille (13 daily; 4hr); Montpellier (14 daily; 4hr 30min); Nancy (14 daily; 2hr 30min); Nice (9 daily; 6hr 30min); Nîmes (14 daily; 4hr); Poitiers (hourly; 1hr 30min); Reims (11 daily; 1hr 40min); Rennes (hourly; 2hr 30min); Rouen (hourly; 1hr); Strasbourg (13 daily; 4hr); Toulouse (10 daily; 5hr 30min); Tours (hourly; 1hr).

Ajaccio to: Bastia (4 daily; 3hr 30min); Calvi (2 daily; 3hr 30min); Corte (4 daily; 2hr).

Bastia to: Ajaccio (4 daily; 3hr 30min); Calvi (2 daily; 3hr 30min); Corte (4 daily; 2hr).

Bergerac to: Sarlat (3 daily; 1hr 30min).

Bordeaux to: Bayonne-Biarritz (10 daily; 1hr 10min); Bergerac (4 daily; 1hr 20min); Marseille (8 daily; 6–7hr); Nice (8 daily; 9–10hr); Périgueux (13 daily; 1hr 20min); Toulouse (16 daily; 2hr).

Caen to: Rennes (4 daily; 2hr); Tours (3 daily; 3hr).

Calvi to: Ajaccio (2 daily; 3hr 30min); Bastia (2 daily; 3hr 30min); Corte (2 daily; 2hr 30min).

Clermont-Ferrand to: Marseille (7 daily; 6hr); Nîmes (3 daily; 4hr 50min); Toulouse (4 daily; 6hr); Vichy (12 daily; 35min).

Corte to: Ajaccio (4 daily; 2hr); Bastia (4 daily; 2hr); Calvi (2 daily; 2hr 30min).

Dijon to: Beaune (11 daily; 25min); Lyon (20 daily; 1hr 45min).

Le Puy to: Lyon (10 daily; 2hr 30min).

Lyon to: Avignon (19 daily; 2hr 30min); Grenoble (hourly; 1hr 45min); Marseille (11 daily; 3hr 30min); Orange (7 daily; 2hr).

Nancy to: Strasbourg (11 daily; 1hr 20min).

Nice to: Marseille (13 daily; 2hr 30min); St-Raphaël (hourly; 1hr 30min).

Nîmes to: Arles (10 daily; 20min); Avignon (hourly; 30min); Clermont-Ferrand (3 daily; 4hr 50min); Marseille (10 daily; 1hr 30min); Montpellier (hourly; 30min); Perpignan (hourly; 2hr 10min; change at Narbonne).

Périgueux to: Les Eyzies (5 daily; 30min).

Poitiers to: Bordeaux (14 daily; 1hr 50min); La Rochelle (8 daily; 1hr 30min).

Rennes to: Nantes (7 daily; 2hr); Quimper (7 daily; 2hr 30min); St-Malo (9 daily; 1hr 15min).

Rouen to: Amiens (4 daily; 1hr 30min); Caen (5 daily; 2hr); Fécamp (hourly; 1hr).

Sens to: Dijon (6 daily; 2hr).

Strasbourg to: Colmar (hourly; 30min); Mulhouse (hourly; 1hr).

Toulouse to: Albi (hourly; 1hr); Bayonne-Biarritz (3 daily; 4hr); Bordeaux (9 daily; 2hr); Clermont-Ferrand (2 daily; 7hr); Lourdes (12 daily; 2hr 20min); Lyon (5 daily; 5–6hr); Marseille (10 daily; 4hr 30min); Pau (6 daily; 2hr 30min).

Tours to: Azay-le-Rideau (8 daily; 30min); Bourges (6 daily; 2hr); Chinon (8 daily; 1hr); Lyon (5 daily; 5hr).

BUSES

Ajaccio to: Bastia (2 daily; 3hr); Bonifacio (2 daily; 3hr); Corte (2 daily; 3hr).

Corte to: Ajaccio (2 daily; 2hr); Bastia (2 daily; 2hr).

Ferries

For Channel crossings, see p.12; for Corsica crossings, see p.12.

- Searchable database of over **25,000 destinations** around the world, taken directly from the acclaimed Rough Guides books
- **Color maps** that get you right to the information you want
- Thousands of **color photographs** from every corner of the globe
- **Weekly Travel Spotlights** from Rough Guides authors, highlighting the world's hottest destinations
- **Travel resources** including airfare and hotel discounts, exclusive trips and tours, rail passes, travel insurance and much more
- **Interactive community** of Rough Guides readers, sharing opinions and advice on their travel experiences

Make sure to check out the Rough Guide Music section at **www.roughguides.com/music** where you'll find artist and performer biographies and discographies, and reviews of thousands of CDs across all kinds of music, straight from our music guidebook series.

TRAVEL IN STYLE

Experience the romance, adventure, convenience and reliability of Eurail.

O **HOP ON AND HOP OFF** - rail passes are the hassle-free way to go

O **UNLIMITED TRAVEL IN UP TO 17 COUNTRIES FOR THE DURATION OF YOUR PASS**

O **TRAVEL WITH THE LOCALS**

O **SAVE MONEY AND TIME**

O **OVER 5,000 DIFFERENT PASSES** - one for every possible itinerary

O **EASY, FAST CONVENIENT BOOKING** - just visit www.roughguides.com/rail

This chart outlines some of our most popular passes and their 2002 prices (passes purchased in 2001 will be cheaper than those listed below). Visit www.roughguides.com/rail for a complete list and description of our rail passes and point-to-point tickets including BritRail, individual country and regional passes.

EURAILPASS

	ADULT[1]	YOUTH[2]	SAVER[3]
15 DAYS	$572	$401	$486
21 DAYS	$740	$518	$630
1 MONTH	$918	$644	$780
2 MONTHS	$1,298	$910	$1,106
3 MONTHS	$1,606	$1,126	$1,366

Travel within 17 adjoining countries

EURAIL FLEXI PASS

10 DAYS in 2 MONTHS	$674	$473	$574
15 DAYS in 2 MONTHS	$888	$622	$766

Travel within 17 adjoining countries

EURAIL SELECTPASS

5 DAYS in 2 MONTHS	$346	$243	$294
6 DAYS in 2 MONTHS	$380	$266	$322
8 DAYS in 2 MONTHS	$444	$310	$378
10 DAYS in 2 MONTHS	$502	$352	$428

Travel within 3 adjoining countries

EUROPASS

5 DAYS in 2 MONTHS	$360	$253	$306
6 DAYS in 2 MONTHS	$400	$282	$340
8 DAYS in 2 MONTHS	$474	$332	$404
10 DAYS in 2 MONTHS	$544	$382	$464
15 DAYS in 2 MONTHS	$710	$497	$604

Travel within France, Germany, Italy, Spain, Switzerland

ADD 1 REGION	$62	$43	$54
ADD 2 REGIONS	$102	$72	$88

Choose from these regions; Austria/Hungary, Benelux, Greece, Portugal

ADULT[1] = 1st class travel

YOUTH[2] = 2nd class travel, must be under 26 on first day of travel

SAVER[3] = 1st class travel, must be 2-5 people traveling together

ROUGH GUIDES

 visit us at: **www.roughguides.com**

ROUGH GUIDES COMMUNITY: Join our community and share experiences, travel tips and photos. Earn valuable membership points and receive free books, frequent flier miles and other travel related rewards.

SHOP OUR STORE: We've partnered with the very best travel providers including airlines, hotels, tour companies and much more, who offer special deals and discounts to Rough Guide members. Of course, Rough Guides guidebooks, e-books and CDs are also available.

Get and share **ADVICE** from your fellow travelers – whether you're off to Albania or Zanzibar, contact a fellow Rough Guides reader and find out what's hot and what to avoid.

Add **PHOTOS** to the Photo Gallery and be automatically entered to win monthly prizes for Best Photo. Your pic may even be featured in an upcoming Rough Guide.

INTERACT with other users in Travel Talk – share info and advice about travel all over the world, or special-interest travel including Women Travelers, Gay and Lesbian Travel, Health and Safety and more.

Be **INVITED** to special, members-only discussions with Rough Guides authors sharing their tips and advice on adventurous and exotic travel around the world.

Get weekly **UPDATES** straight from our editors, with up-to-the-minute information about the site, our books and music, new deals and discounts available to Rough Guides members and more.

Don't miss the Rough Guides Music site, featuring new music reviews, artist bios and discographies, and our exclusive collection of world music. Visit us at www.roughguides.com/music

CHAPTER 11

GERMANY

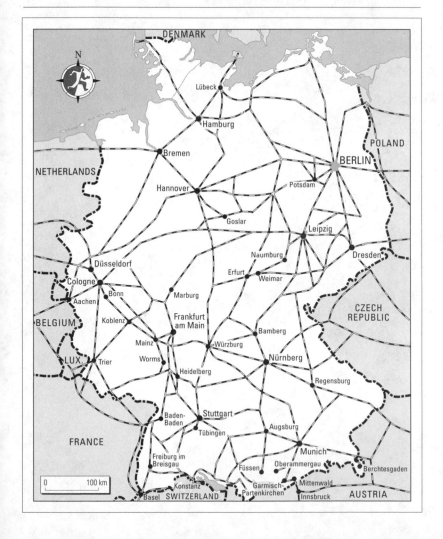

Introduction

The stereotype of **Germany** as the great monolith of western Europe has always been a long way from the truth. Regional characteristics are a strong feature of German life, and there are many hangovers from the days when the country was a patchwork of independent states. To travel from the ancient ports of the north, across the open fields of the German plain, down through the Ruhr conurbation and on to the forests, mountains and cosmopolitan cities of the south is to experience a variety as great as any continental country can offer.

Several of Germany's cities have the air of national capitals. **Cologne**, though enmeshed in one of Europe's most intensively industrialized regions, is rich in monuments. Bavaria's capital, **Munich**, is another star attraction, with great museums and galleries. **Berlin**, the nucleus of the turmoil of reunification, has an atmosphere at times electrifying, while **Nürnberg** retains more than a trace of its bygone glory. **Hamburg**, burned to the ground by a firestorm in 1943, is now a pleasant city with nightlife comparable to Berlin's. **Frankfurt**, the economic dynamo of postwar reconstruction, looks on itself as the "real" capital of the country, while **Stuttgart** and **Düsseldorf**, with their corporate skyscrapers and consumerist buzz, contest the title of champion of German economic success. In the east, as well as Berlin, there's the Baroque splendour of **Dresden**.

Engaging as they are, these cities suffered considerable damage in World War II and have been subjected to some heavy-handed redevelopment, so in many respects it's the smaller towns of Germany that offer the richer experience. There's nowhere as well-loved as the university city of **Heidelberg**, while **Trier, Bamberg, Regensburg, Rothenburg** and **Marburg** in the west and **Potsdam** and **Meissen** in the east are all attractive places that reward exploration.

Among the scenic highlights are the **Bavarian Alps** (on Munich's doorstep), the **Bodensee** (Lake Constance), the **Black Forest** and the valley of the **Rhine**, whose majestic sweep has spawned a rich fund of legends and folklore.

Information and maps

You'll find a **tourist office** (*Fremdenverkehrsamt*) in virtually every town in Germany. These are almost universally friendly and very efficient, providing large amounts of often useful literature and maps. The best general **maps** are those by RV or Kümmerly and Frey, whose 1:500,000 map is the most detailed single sheet of the country available. Specialist maps marking **cycling routes** or **alpine hikes** can be bought in the relevant regions.

Money and banks

Germany is one of twelve European Union countries which have changed over to a single currency, the **euro** (€). Euro notes and coins are scheduled to be issued from the beginning of 2002, with the German **Deutschmark** (DM) remaining in circulation during a transition period, at a fixed rate of 1.95583 to 1 euro, until they are scrapped entirely at the end of February 2002. After this date you will still be able to exchange your Deutschmarks for euros in banks for at least a year. Euro notes are issued in **denominations** of 5, 10, 20, 50, 100, 200 and 500 euros, and coins in denominations of 1, 2, 5, 10, 20 and 50 cents and 1 and 2 euros. All prices in this chapter are given in euros correct at the time of going to press. There will no doubt be some rounding off or, more probably, up of prices in the first few months after the introduction of the euro.

Exchange facilities can be found in most banks and in post offices and commercial exchange shops called *Wechselstuben*. The Deutsches Reisebank has branches in the train stations of most main cities, which are generally open seven days a week, until 10pm or 11pm. Basic **banking hours** are Mon–Fri 9am–noon & 1.30–3.30pm, with late opening on Thurs until 6pm, though these are often extended. Unusually, **credit cards** are used relatively infrequently, though they are becoming more popular.

Communications

Post offices are normally open Mon–Fri 8am–6pm & Sat 8am–noon. **Poste restante** services are available at the main post offices in any given town: collect mail from the counter marked *Postlagernde Sendungen*. Mail is usually only held for a couple of weeks.

In the west you can **telephone abroad** from all pay phones except those marked "National"; telephone cards (€6 or €25) are widely used. The **operator number** is ☎03.

Internet access in Germany is easy to find in larger towns and cities; although the institution of the cybercafé has limited popularity, many department stores (notably the Karstadt chain) offer the facility. Expect to pay around €2.50–3.50/hr.

Getting around

While it may not be cheap, getting around Germany is quick and easy. Barely an inch of the country is untouched by a reliable public transport system, and it's a simple matter to jump from train to bus on the integrated network.

■ Trains

By far the best form of public transport in **Germany** is the **train**, operated by the national company Deutsche Bahn (DB; www.bahn.de). **Fares** are €13.30 per 100km second class, exclusive of supplements, and a return costs the same as two one-way tickets. The most luxurious service is the 280kph **InterCityExpress** (**ICE**), where a supplement is charged according to the distance travelled up to a maximum cost of €25.50. Otherwise, the fastest and most comfortable trains are the **InterCity** (**IC**) and **EuroCity** (**EC**), with a supplement of €4.10, or €3.60 if bought before boarding. **InterRegio** (**IR**) trains offer a swift service along less heavily used routes (€2 supplement for journeys of under 50km). Around major cities, the **S-Bahn** is a commuter network on which InterRail and Eurail cards are valid, as they are on all other services.

If you're making a lot of rail journeys and don't have an InterRail or Eurail pass, it's sensible to buy one of the discount passes exclusively for foreigners. The broadest-ranging is the **EuroDomino**, which entitles the holder to unlimited travel on all trains in Germany, and many buses and boats. Other **passes** include the SchönesWochenende ticket, which costs €17.90 and allows up to five people travelling together to make unlimited journeys on local trains throughout the country on any given Saturday or Sunday.

The colossal national **timetable** (*Kursbuch*) can be bought from stations for €12.80, though it's too bulky to be easily portable.

■ Buses

If you must forsake the trains for **buses**, you'll find no decline in efficiency. Many are run by regional co-operatives in association with DB, although there are a few privately operated routes on which rail passes cannot be used. You're most likely to need buses in remote rural areas, or along designated "scenic routes" where scheduled buses take the form of luxury coaches that pause at major points of interest.

■ Driving and hitching

German traffic moves fast. There are no legally enforced **speed limits** on the Autobahnen (info on www.tank.rast.de), but there is a recommended limit of 100–130kph. The speed limit on country roads is 80–100kph, in towns it's generally 50kph. A national or international driving licence is valid for a year's driving. **Car rental** rates begin at around €200 per week. The Allgemeiner Deutscher Automobil Club (ADAC) runs a 24-hour **breakdown service**; they can be called from booths alongside the motorways or by dialling ☎1 92 11, with the prefix 0 13 08 if you're outside the city limits.

Hitching is common practice all over Germany and with the excellent Autobahn network it's usually quite easy to cover long distances in a short time – though hitching on them or their access roads is illegal. The Germans have also developed an institutionalized form called **Mitfahrzentralen**, agencies that put drivers and hitchers in touch with each other for a nominal fee.

■ Cycling

Cyclists are well catered for in Germany: many smaller roads have marked cycle paths, and bike-only lanes are a common sight in cities and towns. Between April and October, the best place to **rent a bike** is from a railway station participating in the **Fahrrad am Bahnhof** scheme (around €6 per day).

You can return it to any other participating station and holders of the various rail passes get a fifty percent discount.

Accommodation

Be it high-rise city hotels or half-timbered guesthouses in the country, **accommodation** of all types is easy to find in Germany, and it can often be good value.

■ Hotels

An immensely complicated grading system applies to German **hotels**, but they're all more or less the same: clean, comfortable and functional. Just take care not to turn up in a large town or city during a trade fair, or *Messe* – hotels often double their rates and still get booked solid. In country areas, prices start at about €17.50 for a single, €30 for a double; in cities, expect to pay an extra €5–10 extra for something similar. Hotels in eastern Germany are overwhelmingly geared to the business market, but the situation is much better for the budget traveller in holiday areas.

■ Pensions, guesthouses and private rooms

To escape the formality of a hotel, look for one of the plentiful **pensions**, which may be rooms above a bar or restaurant or simply space in a private house. In urban areas these cost roughly the same as hotels – they're usually a little cheaper in the countryside. An increasingly prevalent budget option is **bed & breakfast** accommodation in a private house (look for signs saying *Fremdenzimmer* or *Zimmer frei*). Prices vary but start at around €12.50–15 for a single, €22.50–25 for a double. Particularly plentiful along the main touring routes are **country inns** or **guesthouses** (*Gasthöfe* or *Gasthäuser*), charging

upwards of €25 per night for a double (more in popular areas).

The best budget option in the east is a room in a **private house**, of which thousands have now become available. Prices vary widely and may cost as much as €25 per person in the cities. Nearly all **tourist offices** will book you a room for a fee and there are also a number of private agencies that may give a better deal. Private rooms in the west are not as common, but there are some in rural areas.

■ Hostels

In Germany, you're never far away from an **HI hostel** (*Jugendherberge*), but at any time of the year (especially summer weekends) they're liable to be block-booked by school groups, so book as far in advance as possible. Most staff are courteous and helpful, but a minority insist on a regimented regime. Hostels divide into categories according to location and facilities. The most basic cost around €9; the most luxurious – which go under the youth guesthouse (*Jugendgästehaus*) designation – charge upwards of €20. Except in youth guesthouses, HI members over 27 pay around €1.25–2 more per night; non-members, if admitted at all, will be charged an extra €2 per night. Bavarian hostels are actually "youth", since over-27s can't use them unless accompanying children. The German YHA is DJH, Bismarckstr. 8, 32756 Detmold (☎00 49-52 31/7 40 10, *www.djh.de*); you can email any of the HI hostels through the Web site.

■ Campsites

Big, well-managed **campsites** are a feature all over Germany. Even the most basic have toilets, washing facilities and a shop, while the grandest are virtually open-air hotels with swimming pools and supermarkets. Prices are based on facilities and location, comprising a fee per person and per tent (each €2.50–5),

---

ACCOMMODATION PRICE CODES

Throughout this guide, accommodation is coded on a scale of ① to ⑨, the code indicating the lowest price per person per night you could expect to pay in each establishment in high season. With hostels this is the nightly rate per person; with hotels, the price is arrived at by dividing the cost of the cheapest double room by two. The prices indicated by the codes are as follows:

① under £5/$8 (€9)	④ £15–20/$24–32 (€27–36)	⑦ £30–35/$48–56 (€54–63)
② £5–10/$8–16 (€9–18)	⑤ £20–25/$32–40 (€36–45)	⑧ £35–40/$56–64 (€63–72)
③ £10–15/$16–24 (€18–27)	⑥ £25–30/$40–48 (€45–54)	⑨ £40/$64 (€72) and over

plus extra fees for vehicles. Many sites are full from June to September, so arrive early in the afternoon. Most close down in the winter, but those in popular skiing areas remain open all year.

Food and drink

German food is both good value and high quality, but it helps if you share the national penchant for solid, fatty fare accompanied by compensating fresh vegetables.

■ Food

The vast majority of German hotels and guesthouses include **breakfast** in the price of the room. Typically, you'll be offered a small platter of cold meats and cheeses, with a selection of breads, marmalades, jams and honey, and sometimes muesli. If breakfast isn't included, you can usually do quite well by going to a local bakery.

Elegant **cafés** are a popular institution in Germany, serving a choice of coffee to the accompaniment of cream cakes, pastries or handmade chocolates. More substantial food is available from **butcher's shops**; you can generally choose from a variety of freshly roasted meats to make up a hot sandwich. The easiest option for a snack is to head for the ubiquitous **Imbiss** stands and shops, serving a range of sausages, plus meatballs, hamburgers and chips; the better ones have soups, schnitzels, chops, spit-roasted chickens and salads too.

All **restaurants** display their menus and prices by the door. Hot meals are usually served throughout the day. Most of the *Gaststätte*, *Gasthaus*, *Gasthof*, *Brauhaus* or *Wirtschaft* establishments belong to a brewery and function as a meeting point, drinking haven and cheap restaurant. Their cuisine resembles hearty German home cooking, and portions are usually generous. Standards in west German restaurants are amazingly high, but this is not the case everywhere in the east. Main courses are overwhelmingly based on pork, served with a variety of sauces. Sausages feature regularly, and can be surprisingly tasty, with distinct regional varieties. **Vegetarians** will find east Germany extremely difficult – menus are almost exclusively for carnivores, though student towns and popular stopover points are slowly becoming more veggie-friendly.

Germany's multicultural society is mirrored in its wide variety of **ethnic** eateries. Italian restaurants are generally the most reliable, but there are also plenty offering Balkan, Greek, Turkish and Chinese cooking. In the largest cities, a host of other cuisines can be found as well.

■ Drink

For serious **beer** drinkers, Germany is paradise. The country has around forty percent of the world's breweries, with some 800 in Bavaria alone. It was in this province in 1516 that the Reinheitsgebot (Purity Law) was formulated, laying down stringent standards including a ban on chemical substitutes. A beer tour of Germany should really begin in **Munich**. The city's beer gardens and beer halls are the most famous drinking dens in the country, offering a wide variety of premier products, from dark lagers through tart *Weizens* to powerful *Bocks*. **Cologne** holds the world record for the number of city breweries, all of which produce the jealously guarded *Kölsch*. **Düsseldorf** has its own distinctive brew, the dark *Alt*, but wherever you go you can be fairly sure of getting a locally brewed beer.

Most people's knowledge of German **wine** starts and ends with Liebfraumilch, a medium sweet wine. Sadly, its success has obscured the quality of other German wines, especially those made from the Riesling grape, which many consider one of the world's great white grape varieties. The vast majority of German wine is white, since the northern climate doesn't ripen red grapes reliably. If, after a week or so, you're pining for a glass of red, try a *Spätburgunder*.

Apart from beer and wine, there's nothing very distinctive about German drink, save for *Apfelwein*, a variant of cider. The most popular **spirits** are the fiery *Korn* and after-dinner liqueurs, which are mostly fruit-based.

Opening hours and holidays

By law, **shops** in Germany close at 8pm on weekdays, at 4pm on Saturdays, and all day Sunday (except for bakers, which may open for a couple of hours between 11am and 3pm). Exceptions are pharmacies and shops in and around train stations, which stay open late and at weekends. **Museums** and **historic monuments** are, with few exceptions (mainly in Bavaria), closed on Mondays. Most museums offer half-price entry for students with valid ID.

Public holidays are: Jan 1; Jan 6 (regional); Good Friday; Easter Monday; May 1; Ascension Day; Whit Monday; Corpus Christi (regional); Aug 15 (regional); Oct 3; Nov 1 (regional); Dec 25 & 26.

Emergencies

The German **police** (*Polizei*) are not renowned for their friendliness, but they usually treat foreigners with courtesy. Reporting thefts at local police stations is straightforward, but inevitably there'll be a great deal of bureaucracy to wade through. The level of theft in the former GDR has increased dramatically with unemployment, but, provided you take the normal precautions, there's no real risk. All drugs are illegal in Germany, and anyone caught with them will face either prison or deportation: consulates will not be sympathetic towards those held on drug charges.

German **doctors** are likely to be able to speak English, but to be certain, ask your consulate for a list of English-speaking doctors in the major cities. **Pharmacies** (*Apotheken*) can deal with many minor complaints and again will often speak English. In the west you'll find international *Apotheken* in most large towns, who will be able to fill a prescription in any European language. All pharmacies display a rota of 24-hour *Apotheken*.

Emergency Numbers

Police ☎110; Ambulance & Fire ☎112.

NORTHERN GERMANY

The port of **Hamburg**, Germany's second city, is infamous for the sleaze of the Reeperbahn, but it has plenty more to offer, not least a sparkling nightlife and a city centre composed of enjoyably contrasting neighbourhoods. In this generally unprepossessing northernmost region of Germany, another maritime city, **Lübeck**, exerts the strongest pull, with the same sort of visual appeal as the finest mercantile towns of the Low Countries. To the north, Schleswig-Holstein's countryside mix of dyke-protected marsh, peat bog and farmland holds few rewarding sights, but to the south lies the diverse region of Lower Saxony. **Hannover**, its capital, demands a visit for its museums and magnificent gardens. The province's smaller towns present a fascinating contrast – **Goslar**, in particular, is a mining town quite unlike any other in the world. Near the centre of Lower Saxony sits the port of **Bremen**, the largest city of this region and, like Hamburg, a Land in its own right, a continuation of its age-long tradition as a free state.

Hamburg

A stylish media centre and the second largest port in Europe, **HAMBURG** has none of the sentimental folklore tradition of the Rhineland and the south – rather it has a certain coolness, solidity and sense of openness. Hamburg's skyline is dominated by the pale green of its copper spires and domes, but a few houses and the churches are just about all that's left from before the last century. The Great Fire of 1842 was a main cause of this loss, followed by demolition to make way for the warehouse area, and bombing during World War II. Much of the subsequent rebuilding might not be especially beautiful, but at least it has preserved the human scale of the city. Two-thirds of Hamburg is occupied by parks, lakes or tree-lined canals, giving a refreshing rural feel to one of the country's major industrial centres.

Arrival, information and accommodation

Ferries from Harwich and Newcastle dock at Fischerhafen on Grosse Elbstrasse from where buses run to Altona Station, west of town. Ferries from other destinations dock at St Pauli Landungsbrücken. Buses run from the **airport** to the train station (Hauptbahnhof) every twenty minutes, but it's a little cheaper to take the HVV airport bus to the U- and S-Bahn stop at Ohlsdorf, and then catch a train into town. The handiest **tourist office** is in the station (daily 7am–11pm; ☎0 40/30 05 13 00, *www.hamburg-tourism.de*); it has a full room-finding service. Rather than buy normal tickets or day passes for the integrated public transport network, it's best to invest in the Hamburg Card which also gives free or reduced admission to most of the city's museums. This costs €6.50 for a day (and can be used from 6pm the day before), or €13.50 for three days; a group card for five people costs €12.50, or €22 for three days.

Close to Sternschanze station (north of St Pauli; U-Bahn #3 or S-Bahn #21) are two **hostels**: *Backpacker Hostel Instant Sleep*, Max-Brauer-Allee 277 (☎0 40/4 31 82 31, *www.instantsleep.de*; ②), and *Schanzenstern*, Bartelsstr. 12 (☎0 40/4 39 84 41, *www.schanzenstern.de*; ③), which has a wholefood restaurant attached. **Hotels** are not cheap in Hamburg, though there's plenty of choice, particularly in the immediate vicinity of the train station. One of the best bargains in this area is *Annenhof*, Lange Reihe 23 (☎0 40/24 34 26; ③), which is clean and homely; more expensive alternatives include *Sarah Petersen*, just down the road at Lange Reihe 50 (☎0 40/24 98 26; ⑥), and *Steens*, Holzdamm 43 (☎0 40/24 46 42; ⑥). The nearest **campsite** is *Camping Buchholz* at Kieler Str. 374 (☎0 40/5 40 45 36; June–Sept); take S-Bahn #3 or #21 to Stellingen.

The City

Hamburg has no obvious centre, and it's probably best to begin an exploration in the oldest and liveliest area, the **harbour**. If you're arriving in Hamburg by ship, your landfall will be

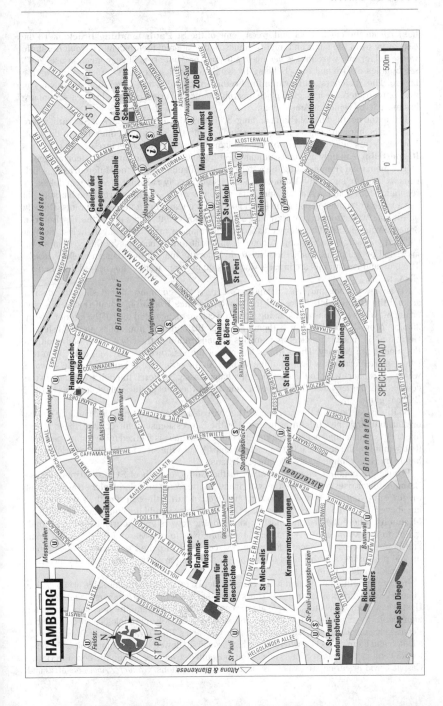

not far from the clock tower and green dome of the **St Pauli Landungsbrücken**. To the east, away from the ships and mighty cranes, is the late-nineteenth-century **Speicherstadt**, whose tall, ornate warehouses belong to a bygone era, but are still very much in use. You'll see bundles of Oriental carpets being hoisted, and smell spices and coffee wafting on the breeze. The Speicherstadt is within the **Freihafen** (customs-free zone), into which you can walk unrestricted. It's a magical place to stroll around and crisscross the bridges – Hamburg has more than Venice or Amsterdam.

Just to the north of the St Pauli Landungsbrücken is the nightlife centre of **St Pauli**, where music halls, bars and cafés sprang up in tandem with the growth of emigration to the USA. Nowadays this quarter is ruled by the sex industry, with its nerve centre on the notorious **Reeperbahn** – an ugly and unassuming street by day, ugly but sizzling with neon at night.

The main road running along the waterfront on St Pauli's edge is the **Hafenstrasse**, which runs west to the suburb of **Altona**, formerly a separate city ruled by the Holstein dukes. Its reputation for racial tolerance is one of the reasons it grew, and this part of the harbour still has a large Portuguese population – and good, very cheap Portuguese restaurants. Directly on Altona's waterfront one of Hamburg's main weekly events takes place: the **Fischmarkt**. Squeeze yourself out of bed early on a Sunday morning, or make Saturday night last, and you will find yourself in an amazing hubbub. If you want to buy bananas by the crate or a two-metre-tall potted palm, this is the place to do it, for the market by no means sells only fish. The bars and restaurants are in full swing by 6am; by 10am trading has ceased; by 11am it's all over.

To all intents and purposes, Hamburg's core is the commercial and shopping district around the **Binnenalster** lake and the neo-Renaissance **Rathaus**, seat of Hamburg's government. When sessions aren't taking place you can go on a guided tour of the interior (every 30min: Mon–Thurs 10.15am–3.15pm, Fri–Sun 10.15am–1.15pm; tours in English and German; €1); it's a magnificently pompous demonstration of the city's power and wealth in the nineteenth century. The Rathaus has one of the six towers, each well over 100m tall, whose spires form a key feature of the skyline. All the other five belong to churches, two of which are a short walk to the east along Rathausstrasse: **St Petri**, the oldest building in the centre, and the far more impressive **St Jakobi**, in the late Gothic hall style typical of the Baltic regions.

Southeast of here, at the junction of Burchardstrasse and Pumpen, is Hamburg's most original building, the **Chilehaus**, designed by the Expressionist architect Fritz Höger. Rising like the prow of a huge ocean liner, the end of the Chilehaus is flanked by two small pavilions that symbolize the sea breaking against the ship. Across the street is the huge Sprinkenhof, begun by Höger immediately after the Chilehaus.

From here continue along Dovenfleet to the Gothic church of **St Katharinen**, whose Baroque tower rises high above the waterfront. To the west you'll find **Deichstrasse**, one of the few surviving streets of old Hamburg and to the north is the tallest of the six towers, rising above **St Nicolai**. West of here, along Ost-West-Strasse and Ludwig-Erhard Strasse, is **St Michaelis**, where the last and most imposing of the towers gives a grandstand view (mid-march to Oct Mon–Sat 9am–6pm, Sun 11am–6pm; Nov to mid-March Mon–Sat 10am–5pm, Sun 11am–5pm; €2.60). Back at Rathausmarkt, continuing up the **Poststrasse** brings you to the old post office, and the heart of Hamburg's shopping area, the exclusivity of which puts London's Bond Street in the shade.

Just north of the train station is the **Kunsthalle**, Hamburg's one unmissable art collection (Tues, Wed & Fri–Sun 10am–6pm, Thurs 10am–9pm; €6.15; *www.hamburger-kunsthalle.de*). Upstairs, a room is devoted to three altarpieces by Master Bertram, the first German painter identifiable by name, and the layout continues in a broadly chronological order. After a Renaissance display in which the major work is Cranach's *The Three Electors of Saxony*, there's a Dutch and Flemish section where everything is overshadowed by two Rembrandts. The nineteenth-century German section is one of the museum's strengths: among the dozen works by Caspar David Friedrich are two of his most haunting creations, *Wanderer Above the Mists* and

Eismeer. Among the Expressionists, look out for two masterpieces by Munch: *Girls at the Seaside* and *Girls on the Bridge*. Pick of the twentieth-century paintings is Otto Dix's *War* triptych, a powerful antiwar statement. Next door to the Kunstalle is the **Galerie der Gegenwart** (Gallery of the Present; same times and ticket), where contemporary art is represented.

On the other side of the train station, the **Museum für Kunst und Gewerbe** (Tues, Wed & Fri–Sun 10am–6pm, Thurs 10am–9pm; €6.15; *www.mkg-hamburg.de*) has excellent collections of decorative art from ancient Egypt, Greece and Rome through to this century. The Jugendstil collection is extensive, and there are impressive sections dedicated to Chinese, Japanese and Islamic art, as well as photography through the ages, and a valuable collection of historic keyboard instruments in the new courtyard wing.

Eating, drinking and nightlife

Some of the best **places to eat** are northwest of the city centre, in the Univiertel or the Schanzenviertel around Schulterblatt and Schanzenstrasse (two minutes' walk south of Sternschanze station). For snacks, the stalls in front of the Rathaus are pricey but delicious, while most café-bars have food as well as drinks and sometimes music. Good choices include *Frank & Frei*, Schanzenstr. 93, and *Uma's Apotheke*, which is directly opposite at Schanzenstr. 85. Also worth trying is *Erika's Eck*, Sternstr. 98 (open 1am–2pm), which serves one of the best breakfasts in the city. For traditional German cuisine and fish dishes, the best-known addresses in the city centre include *Alt Hamburger Aalspeicher*, Deichstr. 43, *Nikolaikeller*, Cremon 36, and *Old Commercial Room*, Englische Planke 10. *Sagres*, Vorsetzen 42, is one of many good and inexpensive Portuguese restaurants in the vicinity of the harbour, while *Tre Fontane*, Mundsburger Damm 45, is a cosy and well-priced Italian.

Hamburg's **nightlife** is among the best the country has to offer – for up-to-the-minute **listings**, get hold of a copy of *Szene* magazine. Grosse Freiheit, Grosse Freiheit 36, St Pauli, is the city's main venue for live music, with big-name bands mostly playing at weekends. Logo, Grindelallee 5, hosts mainly English and American underground bands. For clubs try La Cage, Reeperbahn 136 (daily 10pm–9am). Rivals include the hard-rock Grünspan disco, Grosse Freiheit 58, and the massive Kaiserkeller, in the Grosse Freiheit basement.

Listings

American Express Ballindamm 39 (☎0 40/30 39 38 11).

Bike rental From the tourist office in the Hauptbahnhof.

Consulates Britain, Harvestehuder Weg 8a (☎0 40/4 48 03 20); Ireland, Feldbrunnenstr. 43 (☎0 40/44 18 62 13); USA, Alsterufer 28 (☎0 40/41 17 10).

Ferries From Hamburg there are ferry routes to Harwich in England with England Ferries (2 weekly; ☎0 40/3 89 03 71) and DFDS Seaways (3 weekly; ☎0 40/38 90 30).

Gay Hamburg The best way to find out what's on in the lively gay scene is through the magazine *Du und Ich* and the free sheet *Gay Express*.

Hitching Mitfahrzentrale at Ernst-Merck-Str. 8 (☎0 40/1 94 40) and Gotenstr. 19 (☎0 40/1 94 44).

Internet access Internet Café Fun Club, Fischersallee 78; at discount telecom shop, Int. Telecom, Kirchenallee 9.

Post office At the Kirchenallee exit from the train station.

Women's Hamburg There's a café in the women's bookshop Frauenbuchladen, Bismarckstr. 98, plus a pub for women, *Frauenkneipe*, Stresemannstr. 60.

Lübeck

LÜBECK is just over thirty minutes from Hamburg by train – but as many north and southbound trains depart from here, it's not necessary to return to Hamburg to continue your tour. What's more, Scandinavia-bound ships leave from nearby Travemünde.

Most things of interest to see are in the **Altstadt**, an egg-shaped island surrounded by the water defences of the Trave and the city moat. Left out of the train station it's only five minutes' walk to the old town, passing the twin-towered **Holstentor**, the city's emblem. Built in 1477, it leans horrifyingly these days, but that shouldn't put you off calling in at its small **Historical Museum** (Tues–Sun 10am–4/5pm; €2.60) – a useful introduction to the city and Hanseatic history. On the waterfront to the right of the Holstentor is a row of lovely gabled buildings – the **Salzspeicher** (salt warehouses).

Straight ahead over the bridge and up Holstenstrasse, the first church on the right is the Gothic **Petrikirche**, one of many buildings to suffer during the Allied bombing of March 1942. A lift goes fifty metres to the top of the spire (March–Dec daily 10am–4/6pm; €1.80) and a prime spot for an overview of the town's layout. Back across Holstenstrasse is the Markt and soaring above it the imposing **Rathaus**, or Town Hall (guided tours Mon–Fri at 11am, noon & 3pm; €2), displaying Lübeck's characteristic alternating rows of red unglazed and black glazed bricks. Opposite is the **Konditorei-Café Niederegger**, renowned for its vast display of marzipan, which the town began producing in the Middle Ages; its old-style first-floor café is surprisingly affordable. Behind the north wing of the town hall is the **Marienkirche**, the earliest brick-built Gothic church in Germany. It was severely damaged in 1942, but the restored interior now makes a light and lofty backdrop for the church's treasures: a magnificent 1518 carved altar, a life-size figure of John the Evangelist dating from 1505, a beautiful Gothic gilded tabernacle and some fourteenth-century murals.

The best feature of the **Katharinenkirche** on the corner of Königstrasse and Glockengiesserstrasse is its exterior. The first three sculptures on the left of the west facade are by Ernst Barlach, who was commissioned to make a series of nine in the early 1930s, but had completed only these when his work was banned by the Nazis. Just north of Glockengiesserstrasse, sharing an entrance in Breite Strasse, are the **Behnhaus** and the **Drägerhaus**, two patricians' houses now converted into a museum (Tues–Sun 10am–4/5pm; €2.60, free first Fri of the month). The former displays a good collection of paintings, including works by Kirchner and Munch, while in Drägerhaus it's the interiors that impress, along with nineteenth-century furniture, paintings and porcelain.

The nearby **Jakobikirche**, a sailors' church built in the thirteenth and fourteenth centuries, has Gothic wall paintings on its square pillars. On the other side of the Breite Strasse is a Renaissance house that used to belong to the sailors' guild, the **Haus der Schiffergesellschaft**. A tavern since 1535, it is decked out inside with all sorts of seagoing paraphernalia, and features on the programme of every tour group. East of here is the thirteenth-century **Heiligen-Geist-Hospital** (Tues–Sun 10am–4/5pm; free), one of the best-preserved hospices from this period, while if you carry on down Königstrasse you reach the Burgtor, an attractive square tower topped by a bell-shaped roof.

At the opposite end of the Altstadt are the **St-Annen-Museum** and the **Dom**. The museum (Tues–Sun 1–6pm; €2.60, free first Fri of the month) has a first-rate collection reflecting domestic, civic and church art and history from the thirteenth to the eighteenth century – including a magnificent *Passion* triptych by Memling. The large brick-built Dom, founded in 1173, contains an enormous triumphal cross by Bernt Notke, a celebrity throughout the Baltic in the late fifteenth century.

Practicalities

The **train station** is a few minutes west of the Altstadt, and houses one of the **tourist offices** (Mon–Fri 10am–6pm, Sat 10am–2pm; ☎04 51/86 46 75, *www.lübecker-verkehrsverein.de*); another can be found in the heart of the city at Breite Str. 62 (Mon–Fri 9.30am–7pm, Sat 10am–4pm, Sun 10am–2pm, *www.luebeck-tourismus.de*). A Lübeck Card, which can be used on **public transport** and for reduced entrance fees for museums and harbour-trips, costs €4.60 for one day or €9.20 for three days. The cheapest **hotel** in or near the centre is Stadt Lübeck, Am Bahnhof 21 (☎04 51/83 8 83; ④). A good **hostel** is *Rucksackhotel Backpackers* in the Werkhof complex at Kanalstr. 70 (☎04 51/70 68 92; ②). If that's full, try the **HI hostel** at Gertrudenkirchhof 4 (☎04 51/3 34 33; ②), close to the Burgtor, or its more luxurious counterpart at Mengstr. 33 (☎04 51/7 02 03 99; ③) in the historic centre. As a student town,

Lübeck has a good choice of **cafés** and eating places. The *Ratskeller*, Markt 13, offers tradi-tional German cuisine, while *Schmidt's*, Dr-Julius-Leber-Str. 60–62, has a highly eclectic menu and *Tipasa*, Schlumacherstr. 12–14, has cheap bistro-type dishes, highly popular with stu-dents. *Café Affenbrot*, part of the aforementioned Werkhof, has tasty veggie food and cakes. The Engelsgrube is the best street for bars.

From Lübeck **ferries** cross to Helsinki, Finland, with Farhre Helsinki (3 weekly; ☎04 51/5 89 90) and Fin-Lines (3 weekly; ☎04 51/1 50 74 43).

Bremen

Of the main north German cities, **BREMEN** is the most manageable, lacking the commer-cialism of Hamburg and the ugly redevelopment of Hannover. In 1949 Bremen was declared an autonomous Land, and since then it's had a reputation for being the most politically radi-cal part of the country, electing the first Green MPs in 1979.

Directly outside the train station, at Bahnhofplatz 13, is the **Übersee-Museum** (Tues–Sun 10am–6pm; €5.10), which, due to the city's historical overseas connections houses an exten-sive anthropology and natural history collection. The main area of historical interest, howev-er, is the **Altstadt**, on the Weser's northeast bank, reached by walking straight ahead from the train station. At the top of Sögestrasse, Bremen's main shopping street, is the **Liebfrauenkirche**, a Gothic hall church engulfed by a flower market.

The **Marktplatz** ahead of the church is relatively small but attractive, and dominated by the **Rathaus**, one of the most splendid buildings in northern Germany. You can only visit the main reception rooms as part of a guided tour (Mon–Sat 11am, noon, 3pm & 4pm, Sun 11am & noon; €3), but it's worth it to see the extremes of Bremen's civic pride: rooms awash with gilded wallpaper and ornate carving. On the left as you face the Rathaus is a vast **statue of Roland**, erected in 1404 as a symbol of Bremen's independence from its archbishop; he now stares at the modern Parliament building, one of the ugliest edifices to disgrace a German town.

On a small rise beyond the Rathaus stands the **Dom**, its brooding interior ranging from Romanesque to late Gothic. You can climb one of the twin towers (Easter–Oct Mon–Fri 10am–5pm, Sat 10am–2pm, Sun 2–5pm; €0.50). In the crypt are some fine works of art, notably an eleventh-century Enthroned Christ and a magnificent thirteenth-century font. Off the southeast corner is the **Bleikeller** (same hours; €1), where lead for the roofing was stored; a macabre attraction is provided by the corpses which were discovered here when the room was opened up, perfectly preserved as a result of the lack of air. Surviving buildings from Bremen's Hanseatic heyday are few – what's left include the line of restored patrician houses along the Marktplatz, and the Schütting, the ritzy, Flemish-inspired mansion where the guild of merchants convened.

Böttcherstrasse, off the south side of Marktplatz, was transformed in the 1920s by the Bremen coffee magnate Ludwig Roselius, who commissioned local artists to convert the alleyway into a Gothic-cum-Art Nouveau fantasy. Craft workshops are tucked in among the bronze reliefs, the arches and the turrets, and there's a musical clock depicting the history of transatlantic crossings. The only old house in the street is the **Roselius-Haus**, now a museum of art and furniture (Tues–Sun 11am–6pm; €4); the best works are paintings by the Cranachs and an alabaster statue of St Barbara by Riemenschneider. Adjacent is the **Paula-Becker-Modersohn-Haus** (same times and ticket), containing a number of paintings by the artist, who lived in nearby Worpswede.

Tucked away between the Dom and the river is a small, extraordinarily well-preserved area of medieval fishing houses known as the **Schnoorviertel**. Though prettified, it has man-aged to avoid soulless gentrification. Just east of the Schnoorviertel at Am Wall 207, the **Kunsthalle** (Tues 10am–8pm, Wed–Sun 10am–5pm; €4; *www.kunsthalle-bremen.de*) houses a superb array of mainly nineteenth- and early twentieth-century paintings, including some forty works by Modersohn-Becker.

Practicalities

The **train station** is just north of the city centre, and immediately outside is the **tourist office** (Mon–Wed 9.30am–6.30pm, Thurs & Fri 9.30am–8pm, Sat & Sun 9.30am–4pm; ☎04 21/30 80 00, *www.bremen-tourism.de*). Bremen's **HI hostel** is in the western part of the old town at Kalkstr. 6 (☎04 21/17 13 69; ②) and has an unparalleled view over the River Weser. The densest and most convenient cluster of hotels is also near the train station, where prices start at around €30 per person. Less costly but still fairly close to the centre is *Heinisch*, Wachmannstr. 26 (☎04 21/34 29 25; ④), ten minutes' walk from the train station and on the #5 tramline. *Weidmann*, Am Schwarzen Meer 35 (☎04 21/4 98 44 55; ③), is a small, busy pension in the Ostertorviertel, the heart of Bremen's nighlife, while *Weltevreden*, Am Dobben 62 (☎04 21/7 8015; ④), is excellently located about halfway between the city centre and the Ostertorviertel. There's a good **campsite**, *Campingplatz Bremen*, Am Stadtwaldsee 1 (☎04 21/21 20 02; year-round); take bus #28.

Bremen has a number of good **café-bars** and is also renowned for its fish specialities (particularly eel), best sampled in the gemütlich old restaurants of the Altstadt and Schnoorviertel. Try also *Café Engel*, Ostertorsteinweg 31, which offers inexpensive daily specials. Bremen is home of **Beck's**, one of the most heavily exported beers in the country, but the products of Haake-Beck are the ones to go for in the city itself; a good place to sample them is the *Kleiner Ratskeller*, Hinter dem Schütting 11.

Hannover

HANNOVER has a closer relationship with Britain than any other German city, a consequence of the 1701 Act of Settlement, which resulted in Georg Ludwig of Hannover becoming King George I of the United Kingdom in 1714. As well as a monarch, Britain gained a great composer: anticipating the accession, the court director of music, Georg Friedrich Händel, had already established himself in London by the time his employer arrived, and went on to write his finest works there. Hannover's showpiece is not a great cathedral, palace or town hall, but a series of gardens, which are among the most impressive in Europe. Add this to a number of first-class museums and there's plenty here to keep you occupied for a couple of days.

The City centre

Hannover has had to reconstruct itself after almost total demolition by World War II bombing, and the view on arrival at the train station isn't prepossessing, with a bland pedestrian precinct stretching ahead. Underneath runs the Passarelle, a sort of subterranean bazaar-cum-piazza that at night is a little disconcerting.

Standing at Hannover's most popular rendezvous, the **Café Kröpcke**, the most imposing building in view is the Neoclassical Opernhaus, perhaps the finest of the city's public buildings. A short distance southwest, a few streets of rebuilt half-timbered buildings convey some impression of the medieval town; most notable is the high-gabled fifteenth-century **Altes Rathaus**, its elaborate brickwork enlivened with colourful glazed tiles. Alongside is the fourteenth-century **Marktkirche**, whose bulky tower has long been the emblem of the city; inside, there's some miraculously preserved stained glass in the east windows. Close by, at Pferdestr. 6, the **Historisches Museum** (Tues 10am–8pm, Wed–Fri 10am–4pm, Sat & Sun 10am–6pm; €2.60) incorporates the sole remnant of the city walls. The displays include some state coaches, a section illustrating the changing face of Hannover, and several reconstructed interiors from farmhouses in the province.

Southwards, across the Friedrichswall, is the **Neues Rathaus**, a Baroque-cum-neo-Gothic extravaganza whose dome gives the best views of the city (April–Oct daily 10am–12.45pm & 1.30–4.45pm; €1.60). Next door, the **Kestner-Museum** (Tues & Thurs–Sun 11am–6pm, Wed 11am–8pm; €1.60 or €2.60 combined ticket with Rathaus, free Fri; *www.kestner-museum.de*) is a compact and eclectic decorative arts museum. Round the back of the Rathaus on Willy-Brandt-Allee is the **Niedersächsisches Landesmuseum** (Tues, Wed & Fri–Sun 10am–5pm, Thurs 10am–7pm; €3; *www.nlmh.de*), housing an excellent collection of paintings from the Middle Ages to the early twentieth century. Centre stage is taken by an exquisite Portrait of Philipp Melanchthon by Hans Holbein the Younger. A decent display of Italian Renaissance work includes pictures by Botticelli and Raphael, and there's a good cross-section of Dutch work, including one of Rembrandt's rare nature paintings. On the first floor, the archeology department's showpieces are the bodies of prehistoric men preserved in the peat bogs of Lower Saxony, along with the contents of several graves and an array of Bronze Age jewellery.

A bit further down the road, the **Sprengel-Museum** (Tues 10am–8pm, Wed–Sun 10am–6pm; €3.60; *www.sprengel-museum.de*) is one of the most exciting modern art galleries in Germany. Much of the display space is given over to changing exhibitions of photography, graphics and experimental art-forms, but there's also a first-rate permanent display of twentieth-century painting and sculpture. Focal point is a huge range of work by Hannover's own Kurt Schwitters, the landscapes and still lifes coming as a surprise if you're familiar only with the famous Dada collages. Also on show is a reconstruction of his *Merzbau*, the original of which was destroyed by the Nazis.

Herrenhausen

The royal gardens of **Herrenhausen**, summer residence of the Hannover court, can be reached by U Bahn #4 or #5, but it's better to pick up the free tourist office plan of the complex and walk through it. Proceeding north from town along Nienburgerstrasse, the least remarkable of the gardens – the **Welfengarten** – lies to the right, dominated by the huge neo-Gothic Welfenpalais, now occupied by the university.

To the left, the dead straight Herrenhäuser Allee cuts through the **Georgengarten**, an English-style landscaped garden with an artificial lake. This garden was created as a foil to the magnificent formal **Grosser Garten** (daily 8am–4.30/8pm; €2.60, free in winter), the city's pride and joy. If possible, time your visit to coincide with the playing of the fountains (May–Sept Mon–Fri 11am–noon & 3–5pm, Sat & Sun 11am–noon & 2–5pm) or when the illuminations are switched on (May–Sept Wed–Sun at about 9pm). Just inside the entrance gate is one of the most striking features, the Hedge Theatre, a permanent amphitheatre whose hedges double as scenery and changing rooms. Behind the Grande Parterre, eight small plots have been laid out to illustrate different styles of landscape gardening down the centuries, while the rear section of the Grosser Garten consists of a series of radiating avenues bounded by hedges and trees, each ending at a fountain. As a centrepiece, there's the Grosse Fontäne, which spurts a jet of water reaching 82m – Europe's highest garden fountain. In the adjoining **Georgengarten** is the **Wilhelm Busch Museum** (Tues–Sat 10am–5pm, Sun 10am–6pm; €4; *www.wilhelm-busch-museum.de*), which features a collection of works by the eponymous father of the comic-strip cartoon, and hosts shows of other caricaturists.

Across Herrenhäuser Strasse to the north of the Grosser Garten is the **Berggarten** (same times and ticket), set up to shelter rare and exotic plants. Some compensation for the loss of the palace in the last war is provided by a number of courtly buildings to the west along Herrenhäuser Strasse. One of these, the **Fürstenhaus**, is a sort of museum of the House of Hannover (Tues–Sun 10am–5/6pm; €2.60).

Practicalities

The **train station** is right in the centre of town; behind is the bus station for long-distance routes. The **tourist office** is to the right of the train station in the post office building at Ernst-August-Platz 2 (Mon–Fri 9am–7pm, Sat 9.30am–3pm; ☎05 11/30 14 25, *www.hannover.de*). A 24-hour Hannover Card, covering public transport and entrance to the main museums and sights, costs €7.15; a three-day one €11.75.

There's an **HI hostel** at Ferdinand-Wilhelm-Fricke-Weg 1 (☎05 11/1 31 76 74; ②); take U-Bahn #3 or #7 to Fischerhof, from where it's a five-minute walk to the left over the bridge, then right. For €5 the tourist office will book you into a **hotel**. As a centre of the trade fair industry (the April fair is Europe's largest), Hannover charges fancy prices – normally the lowest rates in the centre are at *Flora*, Heinrichstr. 36 (☎05 11/38 39 10; ④), and *Gildehof*, Joachimstr. 6 (☎05 11/36 36 80; ④); or you could try the pricier *Reverey*, Aegidiendamm 8 (☎05 11/88 37 11; ⑤).

Hannover's major find for **snacks** is the Markthalle, where German, Italian, Spanish and Turkish stallholders sell wonderful examples of their cooking. Alternatively, try the shops around Goetheplatz. Good **cafés** include the aforementioned *Kröpcke* and, outside the city centre, *Doppelkorn*, Limmerstr. 58. *Café Safran*, Königsworther Str. 39, *Weinloch*, Burgstr. 33, and *Hannen-Fass* on Knochenhauerstr. 36, are youthful bars serving food. **Internet access** is at Cyberbar, Bahnhofstr. 4–6.

Goslar

The stereotype of a mining town immediately conjures up images of grim terraced houses and louring machinery. **GOSLAR**, superbly located at the northern edge of the gentle wooded Harz mountains, could not be more different. For one thing, the mining here was always of a very superior nature – silver was discovered in the nearby Rammelsberg in the tenth century, and the town soon became the "treasure chest of the Holy Roman Empire". The presence of a POW hospital during World War II spared it from bombing, and Goslar can claim to have more old houses than any other town in Germany, ensuring its place as a UNESCO World Heritage site.

Although it hosts an attractive market every Tuesday and Friday morning, the central **Marktplatz** is best seen empty to fully appreciate its gorgeous visual variety, with its elegantly Gothic **Rathaus** (guided tours daily: April–Oct 9am–5pm; Nov–March 10am–4pm; €3) and roofs of bright red tiles and contrasting grey slate. The Huldigungssaal (Hall of Homage) in the Rathaus contains a dazzling array of medieval wall and ceiling paintings, with the most valuable items hidden in altar niches and closets behind the panelling.

Just behind the Rathaus is the **Marktkirche**, facing the sixteenth-century **Brusttuch**, with its top storey crammed with satirical carvings. Goslar's half-timbered beauty begins in earnest in the streets behind the church – the Frankenberg Quarter – the oldest houses lying in the Bergstrasse and Schreiberstrasse areas. An especially fine Baroque specimen is the **Siemenshaus** at their junction. Turning right into Bergstrasse, wind your way up to the roughly hewn **Frankenberger Kirche**, situated in tranquil solitude on the boundaries of the Altstadt. Some faint thirteenth-century frescoes compete in vain for attention against a Baroque pulpit.

Down Peterstrasse, past a variety of attractive buildings, lies the remarkable **Kaiserpfalz** (Imperial Palace). Built at the beginning of the eleventh century, the Kaiserpfalz continued to flourish until a fire gutted it in 1289 – it was rescued from disrepair by the future Kaiser Wilhelm I in 1868. Much of the interior (daily: April–Oct 9am–5pm; Nov–March 10am–4pm; €4) is occupied by the vast Reichssaal, decorated with romantic depictions of the emperors. Below the Kaiserpfalz, a large car park fills the former site of the **Dom**, pulled down in 1822 due to lack of funds for restoration. Only the entrance hall with its facade of thirteenth-century statues survived; you can peer at it through the glass doors. On Hoher Weg, which leads back to the Marktplatz, is the **Grosses Heiliges Kreuz** (daily 11am–4/5pm; free), a well-preserved thirteenth-century hospice. Down the Abzucht stream to the right is the **Goslarer Museum** (April–Oct Tues–Sun 9am–5pm; Nov–March Tues–Sun 10am–4pm; €2.60), which contains the bronze Krodo altar from the Dom and a section on mining.

A ten-minute walk northwest of Marktplatz brings you to the **Mönchehaus Museum** (Tues–Sat 10am–1pm & 3–5pm, Sun 10am–1pm; €2.60). A black-and-white half-timbered building over 450 years old, it's the curious home to Goslar's modern art collection. East of here, the **Jakobikirche** contains a moving Pietà by the great but elusive sixteenth-century sculptor, Hans Witten. A little to the north is the **Neuwerkkirche**, which has impressive Romanesque carvings both inside and out. Finally, the silver mine in the Rammelsberg hill on the southern edge of town – the spot where silver was first discovered in this vicinity – has been opened to the public as a mining museum (daily 9am–6pm; walking tours through the tunnels €4.60, rail trips €6.90, visit to ore processing equipment €4.60, combined ticket to all three sections €10.75; *www.rammelsburg.de*).

Practicalities

The **tourist office** is at Marktplatz 7 (May–Oct Mon–Fri 9.15am–6pm, Sat 9.30am–4pm, Sun 9.30am–2pm; Nov–April Mon–Fri 9.15am–5pm, Sat 9.30am–2pm; ☎0 53 21/7 80 60, *www.goslarinfo.de*). Just a few minutes' walk from the **train station** at the northern end of town is *Gästehaus Elisabeth Möller*, Schieferweg 6 (☎0 53 21/2 30 98; ③), an excellent **guesthouse** serving amazing breakfasts. The **HI hostel**, Rammelsberger Str. 25 (☎0 53 21/2 22 40; ②), is ten minutes' walk from the centre. Of the **hotels** in historic buildings the eighteenth-century *Zur Börse*, Bergstr. 53 (☎0 53 21/3 45 10; ④), is one of the prettiest. The nearest **campsite** is the well-equipped *Sennhütte*, Clausthaler Str. 28, several kilometres along the B241 to the south – take the bus for Clausthal-Zellerfeld. As for **restaurants**, *Bistro Filou*, Worthstr. 10, does salads and baguettes, and *Worthmühle*, Worthstr. 4, is good for provincial cooking.

CENTRAL GERMANY

Central Germany, the most populous region of the country, is the powerhouse of the economic miracle, and the zone of heaviest industrialization – the **Ruhrgebiet** – forms the most densely populated area in Europe. Within this conurbation, **Bonn**'s neighbour, **Cologne**, is the outstanding city, managing to preserve many of the splendours of its long centuries as a free state. The other city of top-class historical interest is **Aachen**, the original capital of the Holy Roman Empire. Swish, cosmopolitan **Düsseldorf** is the capital of present-day North Rhine-Westphalia (Nordrhein-Westfalen).

The adjoining province of Rhineland-Palatinate (Rheinland-Pfalz) is the land of the national epic, the Nibelungenlied, of the alluring Lorelei, of robber barons in their lofty fortresses, and of the traders who used the river routes to make the country rich. Nowadays pleasure cruisers run the length of the Rhine, through the **Rhine gorge**, past a wonderful landscape of rocks, vines, white-painted towns and ruined castles. Industry exists only in isolated pockets, and **Mainz**, the state capital, only just ranks among the forty largest cities in Germany. Its monuments, though, together with those of the two other imperial cathedral cities of **Worms** and **Speyer**, merit more than a passing glance, while **Trier** preserves the finest buildings of classical antiquity this side of the Alps.

Occupying the geographical centre of the Federal Republic, the province of Hesse (Hessen) is focused on the American-style dynamism of **Frankfurt**. Although heavy industry still exists around the confluence of the Rhine and the Main, it's the serious money generated by Frankfurt's banking and communications industries that provides the region's real economic base. Of the region's historical centres, the place of particular interest is the old university town of **Marburg**.

Düsseldorf

DÜSSELDORF, which disputes with Hamburg and Stuttgart the right to be regarded as the country's richest city, is the epitome of the economic miracle – orderly, prosperous and self-confident. Never as industrialized as its Ruhr neighbours, Düsseldorf has concentrated on its role as a financial and administrative centre: one of the country's largest stock exchanges is here, as are the headquarters and offices of innumerable multinationals. At least two of these, the Thyssen-Haus in the heart of the city and the Mannesmann-Haus on the banks of the Rhine, are dominant landmarks, in the way that towers of churches and town halls were in medieval cityscapes. Even for a short visit Düsseldorf is expensive, but on the plus side the nightlife is one of the most enjoyable in the country.

Arrival, information and accommodation

The **train station** is southeast of the city centre, with the shopping streets fanning out from it. S-Bahn trains #7 and #21 leave at twenty-minute intervals for the underground terminal at the airport, which also has a new main-line station. Düsseldorf's **tourist office** (Mon–Fri 8.30am–6pm, Sat 9am–12.30pm; room-booking counter Mon–Sat 8am–8pm, Sun 4–8pm; ☎02 11/17 20 20, *www.duesseldorf.de*) is at Immermannstr. 65b, facing the train station. The **HI hostel**, at Düsseldorfer Str. 1 in Oberkassel (☎02 11/55 73 10, *jgh-duesseldorf@t-online.de*; ③), has singles as well as dorm beds; from the station, take bus #835 or walk down Graf-Adolf-Strasse and continue over the Rheinkniebrücke – it's the first building on the other side. **Hotels** near the train station are about as reasonably priced as any in the city centre, especially on Graf-Adolf-Strasse with *Manhattan* at no. 39 (☎02 11/37 11 38; ④), and *CVJM*, at no. 102 (☎02 11/17 28 50; ⑤). Cheaper options can be found just to the south of the centre, including *Diana*, Jahnstr. 31 (☎ 02 11/37 50 71; ③), and *Haus Hillesheim*, Jahnstr. 19 (☎02 11/38 68 60, *www.hotel-hillesheim.de*; ③). There are two **campsites** (April–Sept): *Oberlörick*, Niederkasseler Deich 305 (☎02 11/59 14 01), is reached by U-Bahn #70, #74, #75, #76 or #77 to Belsenplatz, then bus #828; *Unterbacher See*, Kleiner Torfbruch 31 (☎02 11/9 20 38), by S-Bahn #7 to Eller, then bus #735.

The City

Though never one of Germany's great architectural attractions, Düsseldorf's **Altstadt** has a couple of churches to catch the eye: **St Lambertus**, a fourteenth-century brick building, is easily recognizable by its tall twisted spire, while a short walk to the east is the stuccoed **St Andreas**, mausoleum of the Electors Palatine – who were among the seven princes who elected the Holy Roman Emperor. The most popular of the Electors was Jan Wellem, commemorated in the huge open area named after him in the heart of the city, and by a masterly equestrian statue outside the Renaissance Rathaus. In the square immediately to the north is the **Schlossturm**, the only remnant of the old fortifications; it has been restored to house a small **Navigation Museum** (Wed & Sat 2–6pm, Sun 11am–6pm; €2.60), housing numerous models and charts.

Jan Wellem's successors employed French gardeners to transform their city with parks, canals and miscellaneous urban improvements. This culminated in the creation of the main thoroughfare, the famously chic **Königsallee**. Only the Jugendstil **Kaufhaus** has any merits as a building; diagonally opposite its rear entrance is **Wilhelm-Marx-Haus**, the earliest visible expression of Düsseldorf's infatuation with the New World, hailed as the first skyscraper in Germany when it went up in the 1920s.

The largest of the parks is the **Hofgarten**, shaped like a great stiletto-heeled shoe, now crossed by several busy streets. At its far end is **Schloss Jägerhof**, a Baroque palace which has been refitted as the **Goethe-Museum** (Tues–Fri & Sun 11am–5pm, Sat 1–5pm; €2) – though unless you're an avid fan the contents will not thrill. Düsseldorf's own favourite son is another of Germany's most celebrated writers, **Heinrich Heine**, in whose honour a research institute and **museum** have been set up at Bilkerstr. 14 (Tues–Fri & Sun 11am–5pm, Sat 1–5pm; €2).

The two large art museums each warrant a gentle browse. Housed in an ultramodern gallery in Grabbeplatz is the **Kunstsammlung Nordrhein-Westfalen** (Tues–Thurs, Sat & Sun 10am–6pm, Fri 10am–8pm; €2.60, or €6.15 when there's a loan exhibition on; *www.kunstsammlung.de*). The collection began with an act of contrition: in atonement for the dismissal of Paul Klee from his professorship at the Düsseldorf Academy in the Nazi purges of 1933, around ninety of his works were bought by the city in 1960. Klee remains the big attraction, but later acquisitions have turned the museum into a Who's Who of modern painting. The **Kunstmuseum** (Tues–Sun 11am–6pm; €2.60; *www.kunstmuseum-duesseldorf.de*), north of the Altstadt at Ehrenhof 5, has extensive displays on three floors. At ground level there's a fine collection of glass, much of it Art Nouveau and Art Deco. On the next floor, Rubens' altarpiece of *The Assumption* puts almost all its companions in the shade – exceptions being a *St Jerome* attributed to Ribera, and *St Francis in Meditation* by Zurbarán. Upstairs, there's a modern section that complements the Kunstsammlung, along with heavy stuff from the nineteenth-century Düsseldorf Academy.

Eating, drinking and nightlife

"The longest bar in Europe" is how the tourist office describes the Altstadt: the heart of the quarter – the parallel Kurze Strasse/Andreasstrasse and Bolkerstrasse, and streets perpendicular to them – is almost entirely given over to places of entertainment. **Eating** is one of the few things it's possible to do cheaply in Düsseldorf, thanks to the variety of the city's ethnic communities, with ubiquitous pizzerias leading the way. *Im Goldenen Kessel*, Bolkerstr. 44, is the flagship of the Schumacher **brewery**, and is equally renowned for its food. At no. 44 on the same street is *Zum Schlüssel*, a cavernous and popular bar-restaurant which brews its own beer on the premises. An even better-known boutique brewery is *Zum Uerige*, Bergerstr. 1. For something wilder, *Ratinger Hof*, Ratinger Str. 10, was the first punk bar in Germany and now attracts a housey crowd. *Café Bernstein*, Oststr. 158, is a genuine local, tucked away in the shopping district between the Altstadt and the train station. The huge Tor 3, Rosendorfer Str. 143 – south of the centre in the Bilk district – is an enduringly popular **disco**, while the small Unique Club, Bolkerstr. 30, is the main venue for top German House DJs.

Cologne

Currently the fourth largest city in Germany, with a population of just over a million, **COLOGNE** (Köln) is the colossus of the Rhine–Ruhr sprawl. The huge Gothic Dom is the country's most visited monument, Cologne's medieval buildings are unsurpassed, and its museums bettered only by those in Berlin, Munich and Dresden. The annual **Carnival** in the early spring is one of Europe's major popular celebrations, and the **Christmas markets** attract visitors from all over Europe. The city also ranks high as a **beer** centre, with some two dozen breweries, all of which produce the distinctive **Kölsch**.

Founded in 33 BC, Cologne owed much of its development to ecclesiastical affairs. A bishopric was established in the fourth century, and saints Severin, Gereon and Ursula were all martyred here. In the twelfth century Cologne acquired the relics of the Three Magi from Milan, thus increasing its standing as one of the greatest centres of pilgrimage in northern Europe. Situated on the intersection of the Rhine and several major trade routes, medieval Cologne became immensely rich – and the largest city in Germany. Later decline was partially reversed in the eighteenth century with the exploitation of an Italian recipe for distilling flower blossoms into almost pure alcohol. Originally created as an aphrodisiac, it was marketed here as a toilet water, achieving worldwide fame under its new name – **eau de Cologne**. In the twentieth century Cologne's great personality was Konrad Adenauer, deposed as mayor of the city by the Nazis, and the first Chancellor of the country after the war.

Arrival, information and accommodation

The **train station** is immediately below the Dom; moving on is never a problem, as around a thousand trains stop here daily. Directly behind is the **bus station**. For the **airport** take bus #170, which leaves every fifteen minutes or so, and takes twenty minutes. The **tourist office**, at Unter Fettenhennen 19, in front of the Dom (May–Oct Mon–Sat 8am–10.30pm, Sun 9am–10.30pm; Nov–April Mon–Sat 8am–9pm, Sun 9.30am–7pm; ☎02 21/22 12 33 45, *www.koeln.de* & *www.stadt-koeln.de*), publishes a monthly guide to what's on, *Köln-Monatsvorschau* (€1).

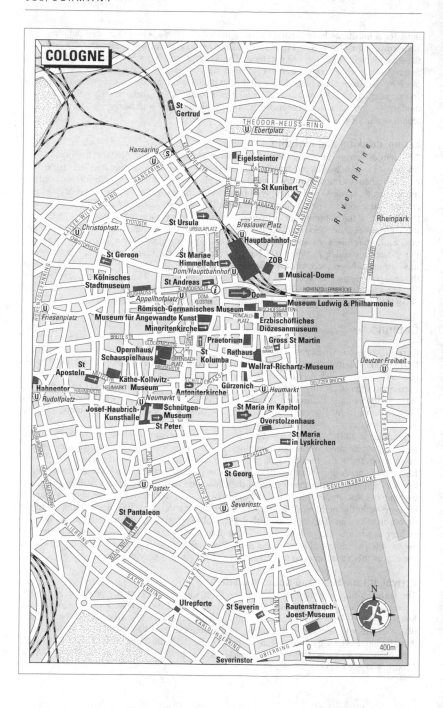

COLOGNE

St Gertrud

THEODOR-HEUSS-RING
Ebertplatz

Hansaring

Eigelsteintor

DAGOBERTSTR

St Kunibert

MACHABAERSTR

Christophstr.

St Ursula
URSULAPLATZ

Breslauer Platz

River Rhine

Rheinpark

St Gereon

Hauptbahnhof

ZOB

St Mariae
Himmelfahrt
Dom/Hauptbahnhof

Kölnisches
Stadtmuseum

St Andreas
KOMÖDIENSTR.

Musical-Dome

Appellhofplatz

DOM-
KLOSTER

Dom

Museum Ludwig & Philharmonie

Römisch-Germanisches Museum

BISCHOFSGARTEN-
STR.

Museum für Angewandte Kunst

RONCALLI-
PLATZ

Erzbischöfliches
Diözesanmuseum

Friesenplatz

Minoritenkirche

BREITE STR.

Praetorium

Gross St Martin

Opernhaus/
Schauspielhaus

GLOCKENGASS.

OFFENBACH-
PLATZ
BRÜDERSTR.

St
Kolumba

Rathaus

ALTER
MARKT

Deutzer Freiheit

St
Aposteln

Wallraf-Richartz-Museum

Hahnentor
HAHNENSTR.

Käthe-Kollwitz-
Museum
NEUMARKT

SCHILDERGASS.

Gürzenich

DEUTZER BRÜCKE

Rudolfplatz

Antoniterkirche

Neumarkt

Heumarkt

Josef-Haubrich-
Kunsthalle

Schnütgen-
Museum

St Maria im Kapitol

POSTSTR.

St Peter

Overstolzenhaus

St Maria
in Lyskirchen

GEORGSTR.

St Georg

SEVERINSBRÜCKE

Poststr.

Severinstr.

St Pantaleon

Ulrepforte

St Severin

Rautenstrauch-
Joest-Museum

N

KARL DER GROSSE RING

Severinstor

UBIERRING

0   400m

Cologne's **public transport** network, shared with Bonn, is a mixture of buses and trams, the latter becoming the U-Bahn around the centre. Fares are high, making it better to invest in a 24-hour ticket, which costs €4.90 for individuals, €6.90 for up to five people travelling together; there's also a three day version of the former (€12.25). Another option is the €15.35 KölnTourismus Card, which also covers entrance to many of the museums and sights.

Cologne has a good range of **hostel accommodation**. The most central is the privately run *Station Backpacker's Hostel*, Marzellenstr. 44–48 (☎02 21/9 12 53 01; *station@t-online.de*; ②) which also has a branch at Rheingasse 34-36 (☎02 21/23 02 47; ②). There are HI establishments at Siegesstr. 5a (☎0 2 21/81 47 11; ③) in Deutz, close to the station of the same name, directly across the Rhine from the Altstadt, and at An der Schanz 14 (☎02 21/76 70 81; ③) in the northern suburb of Riehl – take U-Bahn #5, #16 or #18 from the train station to Boltensternstrasse. For a hotel room, best advice is to pay the €2.60 the tourist office charges to find you a place, as they often offer special discounts. Accommodation is mainly geared to trade fairs, but it is plentifully scattered all over the city. If you prefer to look yourself, try the homely *Rossner*, Jakordenstr. 19 (☎02 21/12 27 03; ③), which is the pick of the cluster of hotels behind the station. Other bargain options with central locations include *Jansen*, Richard-Wagner-Str. 18 (☎02 21/25 18 75; ③); *Das Kleine Stapelhäuschen*, Fischmarkt 1–3 (☎02 21/2 57 78 62; ④); and *Im Kupferkessel*, Probsteigasse 6 (☎02 21/13 53 38; ④). The only all-year **campsite** is at Peter-Baum-Weg (☎02 21/60 33 15) in the northeastern suburb of Dünnwald.

The Dom

One of the most massive Gothic buildings ever constructed, the **Dom** is built on a scale that reflects its power – the archbishop was one of the seven Electors of the Holy Roman Empire, and the Dom remains the seat of the Primate of Germany. Impetus for its creation came with the arrival of the alleged relics of the Magi; when it came to commissioning a church of appropriate grandeur, it was decided to adopt the ethereal new Gothic style rather than the late Romanesque style still in vogue in the Rhineland.

The **chancel** was completed in 1322, but then the extravagant ambition of the plans began to take its toll. In 1560 the project was abandoned, to be resumed only in the nineteenth century. What you see today is substantially an act of homage from one age to another: taking guidance from recently discovered documents that showed the first designs for the facade, the masons continued the work in perfect imitation of the style of their precursors. Originally the **spires** were the tallest structures in the world, but were soon dwarfed by the Eiffel Tower and are no longer even the highest in Cologne. All the same, you need a fair bit of muscle to climb up the 509 steps of the south tower for the panorama over the city and the Rhine (daily 9am–4/6pm; €1.60); one of the bells passed on the way is the largest free-swinging church bell in the world.

From the west door your eye is immediately drawn down the length of the building to the **high altar**, with the spectacular golden shrine to the Magi, made in 1181. It's one of three masterpieces to be found here; the others are in the chapels at the entrance to the ambulatory. On the north side is the ninth-century **Gero crucifix**, the most important monumental sculpture of its period, while the corresponding chapel to the south has the greatest achievement of the fifteenth-century Cologne school of painters, the *Adoration of the Magi* by Stefan Lochner. Stained-glass windows are an essential component of a Gothic cathedral, and Cologne has a marvellously varied set. The oldest, dating from 1260, is in the furthest chapel of the ambulatory.

The new **Domschatzkammer** (daily 10am–5pm; €3) in the cellars, entered from the north side of the building, contains a really stunning array of treasury items, the original sculptures from the medieval south portal, and items excavated from Merovingian royal graves. Also well worth a visit is the **Diocesan Museum**, just outside on Roncalliplatz (11am–6pm, closed Thurs; free; *www.kolumba.de*). Another beautiful Lochner, *Madonna of the Violets*, forms the centrepiece of its displays.

The Museum Ludwig and the Römisch-Germanishes Museum

Housed in an modern building right next to the Dom, the **Museum Ludwig** (Tues 10am–8pm, Wed–Fri 10am–6pm, Sat & Sun 11am–6pm; €5; *www.museenkoeln.de*) is one of Germany's premier collections of modern art. Among German works there's a fine group of Kirchners, a room full of Beckmanns, three superb portraits by Dix and a number of sculptures by Barlach. Two rooms are devoted to Picasso, with sculptures, ceramics and paintings from most phases of his career. An extensive display of Pop Art is dominated by Andy Warhol's paintings of Brillo boxes and Campbell's cans. Part of the building is given over to the Agfa-Foto-Historama, which shows old photographic equipment and a selection of prints from the vast holdings of the company, whose headquarters are in nearby Leverkusen.

One of Germany's most important archeological museums, the neighbouring **Römisch-Germanisches Museum** (Tues–Sun 10am–5pm; €3.60; *www.museenkoeln.de*), was specially constructed around its star exhibit, the Dionysus Mosaic. The finest work of its kind in northern Europe, it was created for the dining room of a patrician villa in about 200 AD, and covers some 70 square metres. The other main item is the adjacent Tomb of Poblicius; dating from about 40 AD, it stands 15m high. The museum's collection of Roman glass is reckoned to be the world's finest, but of more general appeal is the dazzling array of jewellery on the first floor, mostly dating from the so-called Dark Ages.

The Altstadt

The vast Altstadt suffered grievous damage in the last war, and economic necessity meant that nondescript modern buildings were quickly raised to fill the bombsites. Where there wasn't a pressing need for reconstruction, as in the case of the churches, restoration projects were initiated, some of which are still going on. What has been achieved is so impressive that the Altstadt ideally requires two or three days' exploration.

For nearly 600 years, **Gross St Martin**'s tower, surrounded by four turrets, was the dominant feature of the Cologne skyline; the rest of the church seems rather truncated for such a splendid adornment, although the interior has a pleasing simplicity. A short distance beyond is the **Alter Markt**, one of three large squares in the heart of the city. From here, you can see the irregular octagonal tower of the **Rathaus**, a real fricassee of styles, the highlight being the graceful Renaissance loggia. Just in front of the entrance to the Rathaus, a door leads down into the **Mikwe** (ritual bathhouse), the only remnant of the Jewish ghetto, which was razed soon after the expulsion order of 1424 (Mon–Thurs 8am–4pm, Fri 8am–noon, Sat & Sun 11am–3pm; free). More subterranean sights can be found in nearby Kleine Budengasse, in the form of the **Praetorium**, the foundations of the Roman governor's palace, and the **Roman sewer**, a surprisingly elegant vaulted passageway some one hundred metres long (Tues–Fri 10am–4pm, Sat & Sun 11am–4pm; €1.60).

Proceeding south, you soon come to the strikingly angular new premises of the **Wallraf-Richartz-Museum** (Tues 10am–8pm, Wed–Fri 10am–6pm, Sat & Sun 11am–6pm; €5.10; *www.museenkoeln.de*), whose holdings are centred on the fifteenth-century Cologne school. Stefan Lochner's *Last Judgement* is an especially inventive work, but the gems of the whole display are the two large triptychs by the Master of St Bartholomew, representing the school's final flowering at the beginning of the sixteenth century. Displayed alongside these Cologne masters are other German paintings, including a small Dürer and several Cranach pieces. There are also a number of Flemish panels, while the rich show of seventeenth-century Dutch artists includes what is probably the last of Rembrandt's great self-portraits. The museum is joined onto the burned-out church of **Alt St Alban**, which has been left in this state as a war memorial. A little further south is the tower which is all that survives of **Klein St Martin**. Behind, hemmed in by modern houses, is the severe **St Maria im Kapitol**, with a majestic interior – look out for the wooden doors, contemporary with the eleventh-century architecture. Its cloisters, unusually placed adjoining the facade, are the only ones left in Cologne.

Continuing in a southerly direction, go down Rheingasse to see the step-gabled **Overstolzenhaus**, the finest mansion in the city. A short walk from here is **St Maria in Lyskirchen**, where the vaults are covered with thirteenth-century frescoes. From here, head up Grosse Witschgasse and Georgstrasse to the eleventh-century **St Georg**, whose spacious interior contrasts markedly with the stumpy exterior.

The most southerly of the churches are **St Severin**, which was much altered in the Gothic era, and – northwest of it – **St Pantaleon**, the oldest church in the city. North up Poststrasse and Peterstrasse is **St Peter**, a Gothic church with gleaming stained-glass windows. Rubens, whose childhood was spent in Cologne, painted its altarpiece of *The Crucifixion of St Peter*, though for the past few years this has been on display in the Dom.

Next door, the church of **St Cäcilien** now houses the **Schnütgen-Museum** (Tues, Thurs & Fri 10am–5pm, Wed 10am–8pm, Sat & Sun 11am–5pm; €2.60; *www.museenkoeln.de*), a collection of all kinds of Rhineland religious art except paintings. There are some wonderful ivories, but the museum's most famous possession is a painted bust of a woman, carved by one of the Parler family and thought to be the portrait of a relative. Across the road and down Antongasse is the tiny Gothic **Antoniterkirche**, housing one of the most famous twentieth-century sculptures, Barlach's *Memorial Angel*. Around the church is the main shopping centre; the streets follow the same plan as their Roman predecessors, but almost all the buildings are modern.

A short distance west lies **Neumarkt**, dominated at the far end by the superb apse of **St Aposteln**, due north of which is **St Gereon**, a church without parallel in European architecture. Its kernel is an oval fourth-century chapel which, after various additions, became the basis of a four-storey decagon in the early thirteenth century – which is also when the frescoed baptistery was built.

From here you can return towards the Dom, passing a fragment of Roman wall and the Arsenal en route to the stately **St Andreas**, worth a look for its frescoes and the Maccabees shrine, a notable piece of early sixteenth-century craftsmanship. If you then strike north you'll come to **St Ursula**, with its prominent sturdy tower; unless you're squeamish, try to get hold of the sexton, who will show you the **Goldene Kammer**, an ornate chamber gruesomely lined with reliquaries (Mon 9am–noon & 1–5pm, Wed–Sat 9.30am–noon & 1–5pm; €1). From here the **Eigelsteintor**, an impressive survival of the medieval fortifications, is reached via the street of the same name. Dagobertstrasse then leads east to **St Kunibert**, the final fling of the Romanesque in the early thirteenth century, completed just as work began on the Dom. It's also the last church to be restored after war damage, with the nave and massive facade not yet joined up. Inside, note the stained-glass windows in the apse, which are contemporary with the architecture.

Drinking, eating and entertainment

Cologne crams over three thousand pubs, bars and cafés into a relatively small area. Their ubiquitous feature is the city's unique beer, **Kölsch**. Light and aromatically bitter, it's served in a tall, thin glass (Stange) which holds only a fifth of a litre – hence its rather effete image among other German beer drinkers. Best places to try it are the **Brauhäuser**, brewery-owned beer halls which, although staffed by horribly matey waiters called Köbes, are definitely worth sampling, not least because they serve some of the cheapest and tastiest food in the city. Three are located very close to the Dom: *Alt-Köln* at Trankgasse 7–9, *Früh am Dom* at Am Hof 12–14, and *Brauhaus Sion* at Unter Taschenmacher 5. As these are sometimes overrun by tourists, it's worth sampling those a little further afield. Particularly worthwhile are *Zur Malzmühle* at Heumarkt 6 and *Päffgen* at Friesenstr. 64, both of which brew their Kölsch on the premises.

Cologne's **nightspots** are concentrated in several distinct quarters. Most obvious of these is the area around Gross St Martin in the Altstadt, which catches the tourists and businessmen, yet manages to create a distinctive atmosphere in places. *Papa Joe's Klimperkasten*, Alter Markt 50, is a deservedly popular Altstadt bar for traditional live jazz;

there's a cosier, smaller, equally good version called *Papa Joe's Em Streckstrumpf* at Buttermarkt 37. Down the road from the university, in the southwestern zone, the *Quartier Lateng* is more like the real thing as far as mingling with locals is concerned, particularly students. *Filmdose*, Zülpicher Str. 39, is one of the most original fun pubs in Cologne, particularly at weekends; it has a tiny cabaret stage and also shows films. *Gilberts Pinte*, Engelbertstr. 1 is a student bar with plenty of atmosphere, while *Peppermint Lounge*, Hohenstauffenring 23, is a popular late-night joint which springs into action around midnight. The Südstadt, the area beyond the church of St Severin, has plenty of stylish bars and cafés, including *Chlodwig-Eck*, Annostr. 1, and *Zaff*, Ubierring 22, as well as more youthfully oriented establishments, such as the garishly coloured *Opera*, Alteburger Str. 1. The more relaxed Belgisches Viertel, just to the west of the Altstadt, is nowhere near as packed or self-consciously trendy. Its best-known address is the *Stadtgarten*, Venloer Str. 40, which features modern and experimental live jazz, and uses the adjacent park as a summertime beer garden.

CARNIVAL

Though the **Carnival** season actually begins as early as November 11, the real business begins with Weiberfastnacht on the Thursday prior to the seventh Sunday before Easter. A ceremony at 10am in the Alter Markt leads to the official inauguration of the festival, with the mayor handing over the keys of the city to "Prinz Claus III", who assumes command for the duration. At 3pm there's the first of the great processions and in the evening the great series of costume balls begins – with singing and dancing in the streets and taverns as an authentic alternative. On the Saturday morning there's the Funkenbiwak, featuring the Rote und Blaue Funken, men dressed up in eighteenth-century military outfits who disobey every order. On Sunday the Schul- und Veedleszög, largely featuring children, forms a prelude to the more spectacular Rosenmontagzug (Rose Monday Parade). After this, the festival runs down, but there are numerous smaller parades in the suburbs on Shrove Tuesday, while the restaurants offer special fish menus on Ash Wednesday. The grandstand seats along the route are expensive for the Rose Monday Parade but good value on the Sunday.

Listings

Airlines Lufthansa, Am Hof 30 (☎02 21/2 05 05 30).

Car rental Avis, Clemensstr. 29 (☎02 21/23 43 33); Europ-Car, Christophstr. 24 (☎02 21/9 58 44 10); Hertz, Bismarckstr. 19–21 (☎02 21/51 50 84); Condor, Wilhelm-Mauser-Str. 53 (☎02 21/58 10 55).

Doctor ☎02 21/1 92 92.

Hitching Mitfahrzentrale, Saarstr. 22 (☎02 21/1 94 44); women-only branch at Moltkestr. 66 (☎02 21/52 31 20).

Post office The main office with poste restante is at Breite Str. 6–26.

Bonn

BONN, Cologne's neighbour, served as West Germany's capital from the time the country was set up in 1949 until the unification of 1990, when Berlin was restored to its former status. However, Bonn has managed to preserve an important administrative role, remaining the seat of seven ministries and a host of other governmental bodies. It is also a notable historic town in its own right, chiefly renowned, prior to its elevation as capital, as the birthplace of Beethoven.

The City

The small **Altstadt** is now predominantly a pedestrianized shopping area centred on two spacious squares. The square to the east is named after the huge Romanesque **Münster**, whose central octagonal tower with its soaring spire is the city's most prominent landmark. Below the chancel is a fine crypt, while there's an impressively severe and monumental cloister adjoining the southern side. The pink Rococo **Rathaus** adds a touch of colour to the other square, the Markt, which still hosts a market each weekday.

A couple of minutes' walk north of here, at Bonngasse 20, is the **Beethoven-Haus** (Mon–Sat 10am–5/6pm, Sun 11am–4pm; €4.10), one of the few old buildings in the centre to have escaped wartime devastation. Beethoven served his musical apprenticeship at the Electoral court of his home town, but left it for good at the age of 22, though this hasn't deterred Bonn from building up the best collection of memorabilia of its favourite son. The Altstadt's second dominant building is the Baroque **Schloss**, an enormously long construction which was formerly the seat of the Archbishop-Electors of Cologne and is now used by the university.

Branching out from the Schloss is the kilometre-long avenue of chestnut trees which leads to the suburb of **Poppelsdorf**, where a second Electoral palace is now occupied by university departments, the grounds serving as the **Botanical Gardens** (April–Sept Mon–Fri 9am–6pm, Sun 9am–1pm; Oct–March Mon–Fri 9am–4pm; free). Not far from Poppelsdorf's Schloss, at Sebastianstr. 182, is the **Robert-Schumann-Haus** (Mon & Fri 10am–noon & 4–7pm, Wed & Thurs 10am–noon & 3–6pm; free), containing a collection of memorabilia of the Romantic composer, who spent the last two years of his life in Bonn confined to the sanatorium adjoining his house.

Bonn's **government quarter** can be reached either by following Reuterstrasse from Poppelsdorf, or by taking Adenauerallee from the Hofgarten; the distance is about the same. Saddled with its "temporary status", it was not custom built, but utilized a series of existing structures, including the **Villa Hammerschmidt** and the **Palais Schaumburg** – pompous nineteenth-century buildings used nowadays as plush conference venues. Planned as a cultural accompaniment to the government quarter, the **Museumsmeile** (Museum Mile) contains a number of museums. The **Haus der Geschichte der Bundesrepublik Deutschland** (Tues–Sun 9am–7pm; free; *www.hdg.de*) has a wide range of exhibits detailing German history in depth. Further south, the **Kunstmuseum** (Tues & Thurs–Sun 10am–6pm, Wed 10am–9pm; €2.60), the municipal gallery of modern art, is especially strong in its representation of the Expressionists. To its rear is the most attention-seeking of the three, the **Kunst- und Ausstellungshalle der Bundesrepublik Deutschland** (Tues & Wed 10am–9pm, Thurs–Sun 10am–7pm; variable charges; *www.kah-bonn.de*), a monumental postmodern arts centre for temporary exhibitions, many of which are of international blockbuster status.

When Bonn was officially expanded in 1969, it annexed the old spa town of Bad Godesberg (U-Bahn #16 or #63, or main-line train) to the south. Rearing high over the town is the **Godesburg**, the most northerly of the great series of castles crowning promontories above the Rhine, built in the thirteenth and fourteenth centuries by the archbishops of Cologne and blown up in 1583. Today it's chiefly a hotel, but the cylindrical keep is still intact and can be ascended (April–Oct Wed–Sun 10am–6pm; €0.25) for a panoramic view.

Practicalities

The **train station** lies in the middle of the city; close by is the **bus station**, whose local services, along with the **trams** (which become the U-Bahn in the city centre), form part of a system integrated with that of Cologne. As the attractions are well spaced out, it's advisable to buy a public transport pass. For a 24-hour pass this costs €4.90 for individuals, €6.90 for up to five people travelling together; there's also a three-day version for individuals, costing €12.25. Alternatively, the one-day BonnCard (€12.25 for individuals, €16.40 for families) covers public transport plus entrance to the museums. The **tourist office** (Mon–Fri 9am–6.30pm, Sat 9am–4pm, Sun 10am–2pm; ☎02 28/77 50 00, *www.bonn.de*) is at Windeckstr. 9.

The city's **hostel** is at Haager Weg 42 (☎02 28/28 99 70; ③) in the suburb of Venusberg, served by bus #621. Good-value **hotels** in the centre of Bonn include: *Virneburg*, Sandkaule 3a (02 28/63 63 66; ③), *Deutsches Haus*, Kasernenstr. 19 (☎02 28/63 37 77; ④), *Mozart*, Mozartstr. 1 (☎02 28/65 90 71; ④), and *Savoy*, Berliner Freiheit 17 (☎02 28/72 59 70; ⑤). There's a **campsite** at Im Frankenkeller 49 (☎02 28/34 49 49) in Mehlem to the south of Bad Godesberg, to which it is linked by bus #613.

Bonn has a fairly eclectic range of **places to eat**. *Cassius Garten*, Maximilianstr. 28d, offers a mouth-watering choice of vegetarian food, which you pay for by weight, while *Don Quijote*, Oxfordstr. 18, is the most convenient of a surprising number of Spanish restaurants. *Grand' Italia*, Bischofsplatz 1, is the best of many Italian places; *Em Höttche*, Markt 4, is a good traditional Gaststätte; while *Im Bären*, Acherstr. 1–3, is an excellent brewery-owned establishment. Many of the best bars are conveniently located in the Altstadt. *Brauhaus Bönnsch*, Sterntorbrücke 4, produces a distinctive blond ale and does good-value meals, while *Zebulon*, Stockenstr. 19, is a big favourite with arts students, particularly for breakfast. Night owls should head south to *Zur Kerze*, Königstr. 25, which stays open until 5am.

Aachen

Now a frontier post – it borders both Belgium and the Netherlands – **AACHEN** once played a far grander role. Around the late eighth century the city became the hub of the great empire of Charlemagne, a choice made partly for strategic reasons but also because of the presence of hot springs – exercising in these waters was one of the emperor's favourite pastimes.

Aachen's centre is ten minutes from the train station – down Bahnhofstrasse then left into Theaterstrasse. Although the surviving architectural legacy of Charlemagne is small, Aachen retains its crowning jewel, the former **Palace chapel**. Now the heart of the **Dom**, the original octagon had to be enlarged by adding the Gothic chancel to accommodate the number of pilgrims that poured in. Some original furnishings – including the great bronze doors – survive, but these are overshadowed by the additions of Charlemagne's successors. Adorning the main altar is the **Pala d'Oro**, an eleventh-century altar front embossed with scenes of the Passion. Behind, and of similar date, is the ambo, a pulpit of gold-plated copper covered with precious stones. Suspended from the dome by a mighty iron chain is a massive twelfth-century chandelier. At the end of the chancel, the gilded **shrine of Charlemagne**, finished in 1215 after fifty years' work, contains the remains of the emperor. In the gallery is the imperial throne, which for long was thought to have been made for the coronation of Otto I, which initiated the tradition of emperors being crowned at Aachen. Recent tests, however, have all but conclusively proved that it actually dates back to the time of Charlemagne. In order to see the throne you have to join a guided tour (hourly in summer, at least twice daily for rest of year; €1.60).

The **Schatzkammer** (Mon 10am–1pm, Tues, Wed & Fri–Sun 10am–6pm, Thurs 10am–9pm; €2.60), housed in chambers off the cloisters, is the richest treasury in northern Europe. Prominent exhibits are the late-tenth-century Lothar cross, studded with jewels and bearing a cameo of Augustus, and the Roman Persephone sarcophagus, which served as Charlemagne's tomb for 400 years.

Charlemagne's palace once extended across the Katschhof, now lined with ugly modern buildings, to the site of the fourteenth-century **Rathaus**, which incorporates two of the palace's towers. Fronting the **Markt**, which boasts the finest of the medieval houses left in the city, its facade is lined with the figures of fifty Holy Roman Emperors, 31 of whom were crowned in Aachen. The glory of the interior (Mon–Fri 10am–5pm, Sat & Sun 10am–1pm & 2–5pm; €1.60) is the much-restored Kaisersaal, repository of the **crown jewels** – in reproduction. The originals have been in Vienna since the early nineteenth century, when they were commandeered by the Habsburgs for their new role as emperors of Austria.

Practicalities

The **tourist office** occupies the Atrium Elisenbrunnen on Friedrich-Wilhelm-Platz (Mon–Fri 9am–6pm, Sat 9am–2pm; ☎02 41/180 29 60, *www.aachen-tourist.de*). The HI **hostel** is in a suburban park to the southwest, at Maria-Theresia-Allee 260 (☎02 41/7 11 01; ②); take bus #2 as far as Brüsseler Ring or Ronheide. The cheaper **hotels** can be found near the train station: try *Dura*, Lagerhausstr. 5 (☎02 41/40 31 35; ③), *Hesse am Marschiertor*, Friedlandstr. 20 (☎02 41/47 05 40; ④), or *Marx*, Hubertusstr 33–35 (☎02 41/3 75 41, *www.hotel-marx.de*; ④). You'll find **places to eat and drink** in and around the Markt. A spiced gingerbread called **Printen** is the main local speciality, and the place to eat it is the old coffee house *Leo van den Daele* at Büchel 18, which still manages to retain its atmosphere. The most celebrated bar-restaurant is *Postwagen*, built onto the end of the Rathaus, with a cheerful Baroque exterior and wonderful cramped rooms inside. The student quarter centres on Pontstrasse, where *Tangente* and *Atlantis* – which share a terrace at no.141 – are popular haunts and *Labyrinth* at no. 156 is a large pub serving Greek-style food. *Café Kittel*, at no. 37, is a relaxed café-bar with garden.

Mainz

Situated by the confluence of the Rhine and Main, **MAINZ** developed in the eighth century, when St Boniface made it the main centre of the Church north of the Alps. Later, the local archbishop came to be one of the most powerful princes in the Holy Roman Empire, and further prestige came through **Johannes Gutenberg**, who revolutionized the art of printing here. Since the Napoleonic period it has never managed to recover its former status, and its strategic location inevitably made it a prime target of World War II bombers. Nonetheless, it's an agreeable mixture of old and new, and makes a good place to stay if you're flying in or out of Frankfurt, as the airport lies on the S-Bahn line linking the two cities.

Rearing high above the centre of Mainz is the red sandstone **Dom**, crowded in by eighteenth-century houses. Choirs at both ends of the building indicate its status as an imperial cathedral, with one area for the emperor and one for the clergy. A few years ago it celebrated its 1000th anniversary, but most of what can be seen today is twelfth-century Romanesque. The solemn and spacious interior makes a very superior cemetery for the archbishops, whose tombs form an unrivalled panorama of sculpture from the thirteenth century to the nineteenth. The **Diocesan Museum** (Tues–Sun 10am–5pm; free), off the cloisters, houses the best sculptures of all – fragments from the demolished rood screen carved by the mason known as the Master of Naumburg from his work in the eastern German city of that name.

On Tuesday, Friday and Saturday mornings the spacious **Markt**, with its riotously colourful fountain, is packed with market stalls and is unmissable. Dominating the adjoining Liebfrauenplatz, the resplendent pink Haus zum Römischen Kaiser houses the offices of the **Gutenberg Museum** (Tues–Sat 9am–5pm, Sun 10am–5pm; €3; *www.gutenberg.de*) – the actual displays are in a modern extension behind. It's a fitting tribute to one of the greatest inventors of all time, whose pioneering development of moveable type led to the mass-scale production of books. In 1978, the museum acquired the last Gutenberg **Bible** to still be in private hands – made in the 1450s, it's one of only forty-odd surviving examples.

Despite war damage, the centre of Mainz contains many fine old streets and squares, such as the magnificent **Knebelscher Hof** north of the Dom, and Kirschgarten and Augustinerstrasse to the south. Just off the end of Augustinerstrasse is the sumptuous church of **St Ignaz**, in front of which a monumental *Crucifixion* by Hans Backoffen stands over his own tomb, which is even more imposing than those he had made for the archbishops.

Across Schöfferstrasse from the Dom, Ludwigstrasse runs to Schillerplatz and Schillerstrasse, both lined with Renaissance and Baroque palaces. Up the hill by Gaustrasse is the Gothic **St Stephan** (daily 10am–noon & 2–5pm), whose priest persuaded Marc Chagall to make a series of stained-glass windows. Symbolizing the reconciliation between France and Germany, Christian and Jew, the nine windows were finished in November 1984, a few months before Chagall's death. Down Grosse Bleiche – which runs from the end of Schillerstrasse to the river – are the old imperial stables, now home of the **Landesmuseum Mainz** (Tues 10am–8pm, Wed–Sun 10am–5pm; €2.60, free Sat). The outstanding archeology department includes a hall of Roman sculptural remains, dominated by the Jupitersäule, the most important Roman triumphal column in Germany.

Further along is the Schloss, the enormous former palace of the Archbishop-Electors, a superbly swaggering Renaissance building. The interior had to be completely rebuilt after the war, and now contains the **Römisch-Germanisches Museum** (Tues–Sun 10am–6pm; free), a confusing mix of original antiquities and copies.

Practicalities

The **train station** is northwest of the city centre, while the **tourist office** (Mon–Fri 9am–6pm, Sat 9am–1pm; ☎0 61 31/28 62 10, *www.info-mainz.de*) is in the Brückenturm am Rathaus at the corner of Rheinstrasse. Near the station are some of the least expensive **hotels**, such as *Terminus*, Alicenstr. 4 (☎0 61 31/22 98 76; ④). *Stadt Coblenz*, Rheinstr. 49 (☎0 61 31/22 76 02; ④) has a more convenient location near the Dom, though the front rooms suffer from excessive street noise. Alternatively, there's the HI **hostel** (☎0 61 31/8 53 32; ②), situated in the wooded heights of Am Fort Weisenau and reached by buses #61 and #62. The nearest **campsite**, *Maarau* (☎0 61 31/43 83), is five minutes from the centre, across the river in the district of Kostheim.

Mainz boasts more vineyards than any other German city, and you don't need to stray far from the Dom if you fancy a **wine** crawl. Some Weinstuben are open in the evenings only, such as the oldest, *Alt Deutsche Weinstube*, Liebfrauenplatz 7, which offers cheap daily dishes. Even better **food** is available at *Weinhaus Schreiner*, Rheinstr. 38. Though Mainz is a wine rather than a beer city, it has an excellent home-brew **pub**, *Eisgrub-Bräu*, Weissliliengasse 4, which serves inexpensive buffet lunches. The hottest **nightspots** include KUZ, Dagobertstr. 20b, and Jazzid, in the Malakoff-Center, Rheinstr. 4.

The Rhine gorge

North of Mainz, the Rhine bends westwards and continues its hitherto stately but undramatic journey – then suddenly, at Bingen, the river widens and swings north into the spectacular 80km **Rhine gorge**. This waterway may have become one of Europe's major tourist magnets, but the pleasure steamers are still outnumbered by commercial barges – a reminder of the river's crucial role in the German economy.

In summer, inexpensive accommodation is scarce and heavily booked. Spring and autumn are undoubtedly the best times to visit, and you could easily spend several days meandering. Rail and road lines lie on each side of the river and, although there are no bridges between Bingen and Koblenz, there are fairly frequent ferries, enabling you to hop from one side of the river to the other. However, it's undeniably most fun by boat. **River cruises** from Mainz depart from in front of the Rathaus, where there's also a K-D Line office (☎0 61 31/23 28 00, *www.k-d.com*). Fares aren't cheap, but day returns cost only slightly more than one-way journeys – the respective rates for the Mainz to St Goar leg are €27.90 and €24.55. Eurail is valid; other rail passes should bring a discount.

At **BACHARACH**, 10km downstream from Bingen, the chunky castle of **Burg Stahleck** now houses the local **hostel** (☎0 67 43/12 66; ②), while moderately priced hotels are clustered in Blücherstrasse, Langstrasse and Oberstrasse. The local **campsite** is at Strandbadweg. From **KAUB**, a few kilometres on, you get a great view of the **Pfalz**, a whitewalled toll fortress standing on a mid-river island which has become a famous Rhineland symbol (Tues–Sun 9am–1pm & 2–5/6pm; €3.60 including ferry). This stronghold enabled the lords of **Burg Gutenfels** above Kaub to extract a toll from passing ships until well into the nineteenth century. Burg Gutenfels as you see it today is a late-nineteenth-century rebuild of the original thirteenth-century castle. There are **camping** facilities at Am Bacharach on Blücherstrasse.

Koblenz

Packed during the tourist season and deserted when it's over, **KOBLENZ** is a town that polarizes opinion – some enjoy its relaxed and faded charm, while others find it smug and boring. The Rhine and Mosel meet here, and nearby the Lahn flows in from the east, so the town lies close to the four scenic regions separated by these rivers – the Eifel, Hunsrück, Westerwald and Taunus – and thus makes an ideal touring base.

Central Koblenz is at its best in the area around the confluence at **Deutsches Eck**, close to which stands the fine Romanesque church of **St Kastor**. However, the most commanding sights are to be found across the Rhine in **Ehrenbreitstein**, where the Baroque **Residenz** of the Electors of Trier is overshadowed by the **Festung**. One of the largest fortresses in the world, it is now home to the **Landesmuseum Koblenz** (mid-March to Nov daily 9am–12.30pm & 1–5pm; €3) and to one of the best and most popular HI **hostels** in Germany (☎02 61/97 28 70; ②; bus #8, #9 or #10).

Koblenz's main **tourist office** (May–Sept Mon–Fri 9am–8pm, Sat & Sun 10am–8pm; Oct–April Mon–Fri 9am–6pm, Sat & Sun 10am–2pm; ☎02 61/3 13 04, *www.koblenz.de*) is located opposite the **train station** and **bus station**, which are a little to the southwest of the centre. **Hotel** rooms are reasonably priced, the cheapest being in Ehrenbreitstein, where you'll find *Sessellift*, Obertal 22 (☎02 61/7 52 56; ③). Slightly more expensive is *Jan van Werth* at Van-Werth-Str. 9, between the station and the centre (☎02 61/3 65 00; ④). The **campsite**, *Schartwiesenweg*, is at Lützel (☎02 61/80 34 89; April to mid-Oct), directly opposite Deutsches Eck; a ferry crosses the Mosel here in summer, while another crosses the Rhine further south.

Trier

The oldest city in Germany, **TRIER** was once the capital of the Western Roman Empire, and a residence of the Emperor Constantine. Nowadays, it has the less exalted role of regional centre for the upper Mosel valley, its relaxed air a world away from the status it formerly held. Despite a turbulent history, an amazing amount of the city's past has been preserved, in particular the most impressive group of **Roman monuments** north of the Alps (daily: April–Sept 9am–6pm; Oct, Nov & Jan–March 9am–5pm; Dec 10am–4pm; Barbarathermen closed Dec & Mon all year; ticket for individual sites €2; ticket for all sites €4.60).

The City

The centre of modern Trier corresponds roughly to the Roman city and can easily be covered on foot. From the train station, it's a few minutes' walk down Theodor-Heuss-Allee to the **Porta Nigra**, northern gateway to Roman Trier, and the biggest and best-preserved city gate of its period in the world. The Porta Nigra probably owes its survival to the fact that St Simeon chose the east tower as his refuge from the world. After his death in 1035, the gate was made into a church in his honour; the Romanesque choir and some Rococo carvings remain from post-Roman embellishments. Next door is the **Simeonstift**, a monastery built in 1037 as another memorial to Simeon; its Brunnenhof is the oldest monastery courtyard in Germany. Housed within is the **Städtisches Museum** (Easter–Oct daily 9am–5pm; rest of year Tues–Fri 9am–5pm, Sat & Sun 9am–1pm; €1.60), which contains some notable medieval sculptures plus a good ancient history section featuring Egyptian and Roman artefacts.

From the Porta Nigra, Simeonstrasse runs down to the **Hauptmarkt**, roughly following the route of an old Roman street. Today it's a busy pedestrian shopping area, with stalls selling fruit and flowers. The finest of the Hauptmarkt's medieval monuments is the thirteenth-century **Dreikönigshaus**, once a secure home in uncertain times for a rich merchant family.

At the southern end of the Hauptmarkt a Baroque portal leads to the Gothic **St Gangolf**, built by the burghers of Trier in an attempt to aggravate the archbishops, whose political power they resented.

If you go up Sternstr. from the Hauptmarkt you come to the magnificent Romanesque **Dom**, standing where Constantine had a huge church built in 325. The present building was started in 1030, and the facade has not changed significantly since then. Inside, the relative austerity is enlivened by devotional and decorative features added through the centuries. The **Schatzkammer** (April–Oct Mon–Sat 10am–5pm, Sun 1.30–5pm; Nov–March Mon–Sat 11am–4pm, Sun 1.30–4pm; €1) has many examples of the work of local goldsmiths, notably a tenth-century portable altar. From the cloisters there's a good view of the ensemble of the Dom and the adjacent **Liebfrauenkirche**, one of Germany's first Gothic churches. Facing the north side of the Dom on Windstrasse is the **Bischöfliches Museum** (April–Oct Mon–Sat 9am–5pm, Sun 1–5pm; Nov–March Tues–Sat 9am–1pm & 2–5pm, Sun 1–5pm; €2) with a fourth-century ceiling painting from the palace which preceded the Dom and some important sculptures, including most of the original statues from the facade of the Liebfrauenkirche.

From here, Liebfrauenstrasse goes past the ritzy Palais Kesselstadt to the **Konstantinbasilika**. Built as Constantine's throne hall, its dimensions are awe-inspiring: 30-metres high and 75-metres long, it has no pillars or buttresses and is completely self-supporting. It became a church for the local Protestant community in the nineteenth century, a role it still fills. Next door, the **Rokoko-Palais der Kurfürsten** was built in 1756 for an archbishop who felt that the adjoining old Schloss wasn't good enough for him. Its shocking pink facade overlooks the Palastgarten, setting for the **Rheinisches Landesmuseum** (Tues–Fri 9.30am–5pm, Sat & Sun 10.30am–5pm; €3.60). Easily the best of Trier's museums, its collection of Roman relics brings to life the sophistication and complexity of Roman civilization; prize exhibit is the famous Neumagener Weinschiff, a Roman sculpture of a wine ship.

At the southern end of the gardens are the **Kaiserthermen**, once one of the largest bath complexes in the Roman world. The extensive underground heating system has survived, and you can walk around the service channels and passages. From the Kaiserthermen the route to the **Amphitheatre** is well signposted. The oldest of Trier's surviving Roman buildings, it was built around 100 AD and had a capacity of 20,000. You can inspect some of the animal cages and take a look under the arena, which has an elaborate drainage system cut into its slate base.

If you go back towards the town centre down Olewiger Strasse and then head down Südallee, you'll eventually come to the **Barbarathermen**, Trier's second set of Roman baths. Built in the second century, they look more like Roman ruins should – piles of rock, vaguely defined foundations and ruined walls. Midway between the baths and the Hauptmarkt, at Brückenstr. 10, the **Karl-Marx-Haus** (April–Oct Mon 1–6pm, Tues–Sun 10am–6pm; Nov–March Mon 2–5pm, Tues–Sun 10am–1pm & 3–6pm; €1.60) explains the life and work of Trier's most influential son in detail that verges on the excruciating.

Practicalities

Trier's **tourist office** is at An der Porta Nigra (Jan & Feb Mon–Fri 9am–5pm, Sat 9am–3pm; March Mon–Sat 9am–6pm, Sun 9am–1pm; April–Oct Mon–Sat 9am–6.30pm, Sun 9am–3.30pm; Nov & Dec Mon–Sat 9am–6pm, Sun 9am–1pm; ☎97 80 80, *www.trier.de*). It sells the Trier-Card, which costs €9.70 for one person, €17.90 for two adults and three children, and covers entrance to the museums and various other discounts over a three-day period. There's a large HI **hostel** at An der Jugendherberge 4 (☎06 51/14 66 20; ②) on the banks of the Mosel. *Kolpinghaus Warsburger Hof*, Dietrichstr. 42 (☎06 51/97 52 50; ②), has dorm beds as well as individual rooms; otherwise the cheapest central **hotel** is *Zur Glocke*, Glockenstr. 12 (☎06 51/7 31 09; ③). The **campsite**, *Trier City* (☎0651/86921; Feb–Nov only), is on the western bank of the Mosel at Luxemburger Str. 81. There are plenty of places where you can get good and inexpensive **food**, thanks to the student population. The best bet is *Astarix*,

Karl-Marx-Str. 11, a big, relaxed student bar which stays open until 2am at weekends. *InFlagranti*, Viehmarkt 14, is another student favourite, while *Palais* on Stockplatz is a trendy bar cum disco. Trier's most innovative restaurant is *Zum Domstein*, Hauptmarkt 5, whose eclectic menu includes Roman-style dishes and some good vegetarian options. Among the many possibilities for tasting the local wines is the late-opening **bar** of the prestigious Reichsgraf von Kesselstatt estates, at Liebfrauenstr. 10.

Worms

Situated about 40km south of Mainz, **WORMS** achieved immense wealth during the Middle Ages and for a while was a venue for the Imperial Parliament. Terribly damaged in the Napoleonic Wars and the last war, it is now a medium-sized industrial town whose monuments stand out like oases amid modern rebuilding.

Foremost among the city's glories is the huge Romanesque **Dom**, with its distinctive pair of domes and four corner towers. These days the rich Gothic **Südportal** is the main entrance, but look out also for the **Kaiserportal**, on the north side of the building. As you enter the church, the sight of Balthasar Neumann's huge **high altar** – a tornado of technicolour marble and gilt – provokes a gasp. In marked contrast is the dank and eerie vault, where eight sinister sarcophagi sit in oppressive silence.

For over a millennium Worms had a large and influential **Jewish population** – so influential, in fact, that the city was long known as "Little Jerusalem". It all came to an end with the Nazis: in 1933 there were 1100 Jews in Worms, by 1945 all were either dead or had fled the country. The most famous and poignant reminder of the community is the **Heiliger Sand**, a short distance southwest of the Dom; the oldest Jewish cemetery in Europe, its crooked gravestones date as far back as 1076. To the southeast of the cemetery is the **Andreasstift**, comprising a Romanesque church and cloisters which now house the **Museum der Stadt Worms** (Tues–Sun 10am–5pm; €2). The most significant exhibits are in the Lutherzimmer, which includes some of Luther's original writings.

The **Heylshofgarten**, just to the north of the Dom, marks the site of the now-vanished imperial palace, where an Imperial Diet was convoked in 1521 by Emperor Charles V; Luther refused to renounce his views there, and was forced into exile, setting the Reformation in motion. Within the park is the **Kunsthaus Heylshof** (May–Sept Tues–Sun 11am–5pm; Oct–April Tues–Sat 2–4pm, Sun 11am–4pm; €2.60), a fine collection of paintings, porcelain, glassware and ceramics. Beyond here lies Lutherplatz, where you'll find the **Lutherdenkmal**, a gang of bronze figures with Luther at the centre. Keep going straight on and you'll come to the Romanesque **Martinskirche**; supposedly St Martin was once imprisoned in a dungeon underneath. Further north, around Judengasse, is the site of the old **Jewish quarter**. Here you'll find the Romanesque **Alte Synagoge** (daily: April–Oct 10am–12.30pm & 1.30–5pm; Nov–March 10am–noon & 2–4pm; free), re-inaugurated in 1961 following its destruction on Kristallnacht. In the Raschi-Haus, a former school and meeting house, is the **Jüdisches Museum** (Tues–Sun 10am–12.30pm & 1.30–5pm; €1.60), with an extensive collection detailing the history of the Jews of Worms.

Practicalities

Worms' **tourist office** is at Neumarkt 14 (Mon–Fri 9am–6pm; April–Oct also Sat 9am–noon; ☎0 62 41/2 50 45, *www.worms.de*). There's an HI **hostel** between the Dom and the Andreasstift at Dechaneigasse 1 (☎0 62 41/2 57 80; ②). Among the **hotels** in the town centre, try *Weinhaus Weis*, Färbergasse 19 (☎0 62 41/23 5 00; ②), or *Boos*, Mainzer Str. 5 (☎0 62 41/947 6 39; ③). **Camping** facilities are on the east bank of the Rhine near the Nibelungenbrücke. For typically hearty German food, head for *Kolb's* Biergarten or Hagenbräu, a boutique brewery, side-by-side on the west bank of the Rhine by the Nibelungenbrücke. There are also lively hangouts on Judengasse, such as *Café Jux* at no. 3 and *Kutscherschänke* at no. 2.

Speyer

SPEYER is an outstanding little city, well worth a day of anyone's time. Chief attraction is its Dom, one of the largest and finest Romanesque buildings in Germany. Speyer can be reached from Heidelberg or Worms by train, though it is sometimes necessary to change at Ludwigshafen. From the train station, head down Bahnhofstrasse and turn left into Maximilianstrasse, which leads into the centre.

The **Dom** was built in the mid-eleventh century and modified a generation later – the most significant alteration, the stone vault, was higher than any previously built. But even finer than the vaulting is the massive **crypt** – containing eight royal tombs, including that of Emperor Conrad II, who ordered the cathedral's construction; it has an almost Middle Eastern feel with its sandstone pillars and slabbed floor. Just to the south of the Dom, on Domplatz, is the palatial triple-towered **Historisches Museum der Pfalz** (Tues & Thurs–Sun 10am–6pm, Wed 10am–8pm; €4.10; *www.museum.speyer.de*). It includes objects found in the Dom's imperial graves, but the most celebrated exhibit is the Bronze Age Golden Hat of Schifferstadt, found in a nearby town. The same building also houses the **Weinmuseum**, featuring every conceivable kind of wine-related object and what is claimed to be the oldest bottle of wine in the world, dating from 300 AD. Not far from the museum, down Judengasse, is the **Judenbad**, a twelfth-century Jewish ritual bathhouse which is the oldest and best-preserved example in Germany (daily April–Oct 10am–noon & 2–5pm; €0.75).

The **tourist office** is at Maximilianstr. 11 (Mon–Fri 9am–5pm, Sat 10am–noon; ☎0 62 32/14 23 92, *www.speyer.de*). The HI **hostel** is at Geibstr. 5 (☎0 62 32/6 15 97; ②), on the Rhine south of the centre, while the cheapest conveniently located **hotel** is *Grüne Au*, Grüner Winkel 28 (☎0 62 32/7 21 96; ④). For **Kaffee und Küchen** try *Café Hindenburg*, Maximilianstr. 91; for something more substantial, go to the atmospheric old *Zum Alten Engel*, Mühlturmstr. 7.

Frankfurt

Straddling the Main not long before it meets the Rhine, **FRANKFURT** is a city with two faces. On the one hand it's the cut-throat financial capital of Germany, with its fulcrum in the Westend district, and on the other it's a civilized place which spends more per year on the arts than any other city in Europe. In fact, Frankfurt is a thriving recreational centre for the whole of Hesse, with a good selection of theatres and galleries, and an even better range of museums. Over half of the city, including almost all of the centre, was destroyed during the war and the rebuilders opted for innovation rather than restoration. The result is a skyline that smacks more of Chicago than of Germany.

Arrival, information and information

Frankfurt **airport**, one of the world's busiest, is a major point of entry into Germany, and there are regular rail links between the airport and most German cities. Trains leave the airport approximately every ten minutes for the city's main **train station**, from where there are even more comprehensive services. The airport is also linked to the train station by two S-Bahn lines, run by the regional transport company (RMV), which is also responsible for bus, tram and U-Bahn services. Ticket prices vary according to the time of travel, making it better to invest in the €4.20 24-hour ticket. Better still is the Frankfurt Card, which is available from tourist offices for €6.15 for one day, €9.70 for two days, and allows travel thoughout the city, plus reduced entry charges to most museums (bear in mind that these are free on Wed). From the train station you can walk to the centre in fifteen minutes, or take tram #11.

Frankfurt has two main **tourist offices**: one in the train station (Mon–Fri 8am–9pm, Sat & Sun 9am–6pm; ☎0 69/21 23 88 49, *www.frankfurt-tourismus.de*), the other at Römerberg 27

(Mon–Fri 9.30am–5.30pm, Sat & Sun 10am–4pm; ☎0 69/21 23 87 08). The free **listings magazines**, *Fritz* and *Strandgut*, are available at both.

Accommodation

Accommodation is pricey, thanks to the expense-account clientele. Best budget bet is the HI **hostel** at Deutschherrnufer 12 (☎0 69/61 90 58; ②), in Sachsenhausen, reached by bus #46 from the train station. As for cheap **hotels**, the majority of only a few reasonably priced options are in the sleazy environs of the train station, close to the Kaiserstrasse red-light district. The pick of the inexpensive hotels are listed below.

Atlas, Zimmerweg 1 (☎0 69/72 39 46). Within walking distance of the station but away from the sleazier streets. ④.

Backer, Mendelssohnstr. 92 (☎0 69/74 79 92). Pleasant place close to the university. U-Bahn to Westend or tram #19. ③.

Glockshuber, Mainzer Landstr. 120 (☎74 26 28). Pleasant budget hotel just north the Hauptbahnhof, away from the sleazier streets. ④

Gölz, Beethovenstr. 44 (☎0 69/74 67 35). Located on a quiet, tree-lined avenue in the Westend district. ④.

Royal, Wallstr. 17 (☎0 69/62 30 26). Good-value hotel in the heart of Sachsenhausen, close to some of the well-known apple wine taverns. ④.

The City

Almost all of the city's main sights lie within the bounds of the old city walls, which have now been transformed into a stretch of narrow parkland describing an approximate semicircle; from here it's an easy matter to cross the Main into Sachsenhausen, where most of the museums are located. As good a point as any to begin your explorations in the old city is the **Römerberg**, the historical and, roughly speaking, geographical centre of the city. Charlemagne built his fort on this low hill to protect the ford which gave Frankfurt its name – Frankonovurd (Ford of the Franks). At the start of this century the Römerberg was still the heart of the city, and an essentially medieval quarter. All this came to an end in March 1944 when two massive air raids flattened the historic core.

The most significant survivor was the thirteenth-century St Bartholomäus or **Dom**, and even that emerged with only its main walls intact. Before the construction of the skyscrapers it was the tallest building in the city, as befitted the venue for the election and coronation of the Holy Roman Emperors. Inside, to the right of the choir, is the restored **Wahlkapelle**, where the seven Electors used to make their final choice as to who would become emperor. The 95-metre tower (April–Oct daily 9am–1pm & 2.30–6pm; €1.60) commands a fine view over the city.

Slightly to the north, in Domstrasse, looms the **Museum für Moderne Kunst** (Tues & Thurs–Sun 10am–5pm, Wed 10am–8pm; €3.60, free Wed; *frankfurt-business.de/mmk*), its collection featuring some of the major names in postwar American and German art, with Joseph Beuys inevitably prominent. At the opposite end of the Römerberg is the building that gave the area its name – the **Römer**, formerly the Rathaus. Its distinctive facade, with its triple-stepped gables, fronts the Römerplatz market square, on whose southern side stands the former court chapel, the **Nikolaikirche**. The interior is refreshingly restrained, a real refuge from the noise and rampant commercialism of the Römerplatz; though the church was given a Gothic face-lift, the lines of the original Romanesque structure are visible on the inside.

For a long time the area between the Römer and the Dom remained little more than an ugly hole in the middle of the city. In 1978 the decision was taken to build replicas of some of the medieval buildings that had originally occupied the site, and fill the remaining space with an ultramodern complex. At its heart is the **Schirn Kunsthalle**, a general-purpose cultural centre known to the locals as the "Federal Bowling Alley".

The **Saalhof**, an amalgamation of imperial buildings now housing the Historisches Museum, is nearby on Mainkai, overlooking the river. Its twelfth-century chapel is all that remains of the old palace complex, which grew up in the Middle Ages. The **museum** (Tues & Thurs–Sat 10am–5pm, Wed 10am–8pm; €2.60, free Wed) contains an extensive local-history collection, with an eye-opening section on the devastation caused by the bombing.

A short distance to the west, on Untermainkai, is the **Karmeliterkloster** (Tues & Thurs–Sun 11am–6pm, Wed 11am–8pm; €2.60, free Wed), where Jerg Ratgeb's 80-metre-long fresco cycle of the life of Jesus occupies the cloister. The southern part of the complex houses the **Museum für Vor- and Frühgeschichte** (Tues & Thurs–Sun 10am–5pm, Wed 10am–8pm; €4, free Wed), a collection devoted to early and prehistory. Just north of here, at Grosser Hirschgraben 23, is the **Goethehaus und Goethe-Museum** (Mon–Fri 9am–4/6pm, Sat & Sun 10am–4pm; €2; *www.goethehaus-frankfurt.de*), the house where Goethe was born and raised. It has been made to look as much as possible like it did when Goethe lived here, and there are even a few objects which somehow survived the war.

A couple of minutes away on the Liebfrauenberg is the fifteenth-century **Liebfrauenkirche** – look inside for the unusual altar, a huge alabaster and gilt affair which sits well in the dusky pink interior. A little to the northwest of the **Hauptwache** (originally a guard house) is the **Börse**, Frankfurt's stock exchange. Appropriately enough, two of the most expensive shopping streets in the city are just around the corner. **Goethestrasse** is Frankfurt's Bond Street, all expensive jewellers and designer clothes shops, while **Grosse Bockenheimer Strasse** is home to upmarket delicatessens and smarter restaurants.

SACHSENHAUSEN

If you want to escape from the centre of Frankfurt, or have a laid-back evening out, then head for **Sachsenhausen**, the city-within-a-city on the south bank of the Main. Most people go here to eat, drink and be merry in the restaurants and bars of Alt Sachsenhausen, the network of streets around Affentorplatz, where the main attractions are the **apple wine** (Ebbelwei) houses. There's entertainment of a different sort to be had on the **Museumsufer** (or Schaumainkai), which runs between the Eiserner Steg and the Friedensbrücke.

Schaumainkai's biggest draw is the **Städel** located at no. 63 (Tues & Fri–Sun 10am–5pm, Wed 10am–8pm; €4, free Wed, *www.staedelmuseum.de*), one of the most comprehensive art galleries in Europe. The layout begins on the top floor, where virtually every big name in German art is represented, including Dürer, both Holbeins, Cranach and Altdorfer. Van Eyck's *Lucca Madonna* stands out amid the gallery's wealth of early Netherlandish paintings, while another *Madonna*, an ethereal image by Fra Angelico, and Botticelli's *Ideal Woman* dominate the Italian section. Pride of place among the seventeenth-century paintings goes to the *Altarpiece of the Cross* by Frankfurt's own Adam Elsheimer. Poussin, Claude and Rubens (all admirers of Elsheimer) are on display in the next section, which also includes Rembrandt's *Blinding of Samson* and a glorious Vermeer. Paintings from the late eighteenth century onwards occupy the first floor. Big French names such as Courbet, Degas and Monet appear, but German artists predominate – look out for Johann Heinrich Tischbein's celebrated portrayal of *Goethe in the Roman Campagna*.

The **Museum für Angewandte Kunst**, down at no. 15 (same times; €4, free Wed; *www.mak.frankfurt.de*), has a huge collection of applied art, divided into four sections: European, featuring a unique collection of furniture models, glassware and ceramics; Islamic, with some fine carpets; Far Eastern, with lots of jade and lacquer work plus a liberal sprinkling of porcelain and sculptures; and finally a section devoted to books and writing. Further along at no. 29, the **Museum für Völkerkunde** (same times; €3, free Wed; *www.voelkerkundemuseum.frankfurt.de*) is a small ethnographical museum with an extensive collection of masks and totems from all over the world. The **Deutsches Filmmuseum**, no. 41 (same times; €2.60, free Wed; *www.deutsches-filmmuseum.de*), is Germany's biggest and best film museum, with its own cinema and a good little café in the basement. The **Deutsches Architekturmuseum**, no. 43 (same times; €4, free Wed), is installed in a self-consciously avant-garde conversion of a nineteenth-century villa; the highpoint is the "house within a house" which dominates the museum like an oversized dolls' house. Finally, the

Liebieghaus, no. 71 (same times; €2.60, free Wed), is a step-by-step guide to the history of sculpture, going back to the third millennium BC; it also contains the best outdoor café of the museums.

Eating, drinking and nightlife

Not surprisingly, Frankfurt has a wealth of gastronomic possibilities, from the ultratrendy joints found in the Westend to the cheapo Italian restaurants of Bockenheim, the working-class/boho/student quarter. Whether it's vegan breakfast or Japanese afternoon tea you're after, you'll be able to find it somewhere in the city – though you might have to travel some distance to get it. Frankfurt's nightlife is pretty eclectic, too. Perhaps its best-known locale is Kleine Bockenheimer Strasse, aka Jazzgasse (Jazz Alley), the centre of Frankfurt's jazz scene.

APPLE WINE TAVERNS

Adolf Wagner, Schweizer Str. 71. One of the best of the taverns, with a lively clientele ranging from young to middle-aged. Frequently packed out.

Atschel, Wallstr. 7. This offers a more extensive menu than many of its counterparts, and has bargain set luches. Closed Mon.

Zum Eichkatzerl, Dreieichstr. 29. An excellent traditional tavern which is particularly popular on account of its low-priced food. Closed Mon.

Zum Gemalten Haus, Schweizer Str. 67. A bit kitschy with its oil-painted facade and stained-glass windows, yet quite intimate and lively, with long rows of tables outside. Closed Mon & Tues.

BARS, CAFÉS AND CAFÉ-BARS

Café Laumer, Bockenheimer Landstr. 67. One of Frankfurt's oldest cafés, halfway up the Westend's main thoroughfare.

Club Voltaire, Kleine Hochstr. 5. Tasty, good food with a Spanish bias, and a fairly eclectic clientele including left-wing political activists, artists and gays. One of the best-established meeting places in Frankfurt.

Gegenwart, Bergerstr. 6. Spacious and very trendy hangout whose walls are a forum for avant-garde art.

Harvey's, Bornheimer Landstr. 64. Slick, high-ceilinged colonnaded bar which in the evening hosts a mainly gay and lesbian crowd.

RESTAURANTS

Bistro Rosa, Grüneburgweg 25. The walls hung with pictures of pigs lend an element of kitsch, but the food is excellent. Closed Sun.

Iwase, Vibeler Str. 31. Reasonably priced Japanese, with seating at the counter or the few tables. Tues–Sun 6.30–10.30pm.

Knoblauch, Staufenstr. 39. Friendly, intimate little place where everything comes liberally laced with garlic.

Nibelungenschänke, Nibelungenallee 55. Typical Greek food at very reasonable prices. The clientele tends to be young and the place is usually open until 1am. U-Bahn line #5 to Nibelungenallee.

Stars und Starlet, Friedrich-Ebert-Anlage 49. Located in the basement of the Messeturm, this American-style restaurant has wonderful fantasy decor.

Tse Yang, Kaiserstr. 67. One of several good Chinese restaurants in the vicinity of the train station.

MUSIC AND DISCOS

Brotfabrik, Bachmannstr. 2–4. One of the most innovative venues in the city, featuring live and disco music from all over the world, with salsa, African and Asian sounds particularly popular. Also has a café and a Spanish restaurant.

Jazzkeller, Kleine Bockenheimer Str. 18a. This atmospheric cellar is Frankfurt's premier jazz venue. Open Tues–Sun 9pm–3am.

U60311, Rossmarkt Unterführung. Techno club that is always packed to the rafters; be prepared to queue.

Listings

Airlines Air Canada, Am Flughafen (☎0 69/27 11 51 11); Air New Zealand, Am Flughafen (☎0 69/9 71 40 30); British Airways, Am Flughafen (☎0 69/69 81 50); Lufthansa, Am Hauptbahnhof 2 (☎0 69/25 54 51 14).

Consulates Britain, Bockenheimer Landstr. 42 (☎0 69/1 70 00 20); US, Siesmayerstr. 21 (☎0 69/7 53 50).
Hitching Mitfahrzentrale at Baseler Platz 7 (☎0 69/1 94 40) and Homburger Str. 36 (☎0 69/1 94 44).
Internet access CyberRyder, Töngesgasse 31 (Mon–Thurs 10am–11pm, Fri & Sat 10am–1am, Sun 2–11pm).
Post office The main post office is at Goetheplatz 2-4.

Marburg

About 80km to the north of Frankfurt, **MARBURG**, the cradle of Hesse and its original capital, clusters up the slopes of the Lahn valley in a maze of narrow streets and medieval buildings, crowned by an impressive castle. Primarily a university town, Marburg has a relaxed and lively atmosphere, and has been touched by war less than almost any other city in the country.

The most important building is the **Elisabethkirche** (April–Sept Mon–Sat 9am–6pm, Sun 12.30–6pm; Oct Mon–Sat 9.30am–5pm, Sun 12.30–5pm; Nov–March Mon–Sat 10am–4pm, Sun 12.30–4pm; €1.60 for entry to chancel), reached from the train station by following Bahnhofstrasse. The first Gothic church in Germany, it was erected to house the remains of St Elisabeth, who died here in 1231. Inside, the church is like a museum of German religious art, full of statues and frescoes; Elisabeth's thirteenth-century shrine is in the sacristy. From the Elisabethkirche, the Steinweg, a stepped street hemmed in by half-timbered buildings, leads up to the **Marktplatz**, the centre of the **Altstadt**. During term time the square is the focal point of Marburg's nightlife, but out of term it's very peaceful. The **Rathaus**'s staircase tower features a statue of Elisabeth, holding a heraldic figure, said to be the arms of the count who financed the building.

From the Marktplatz make your way up Rittergasse to the thirteenth-century **Marienkirche**, just past which a flight of steps rises to the **Schloss** (April–Oct Tues–Sun 10am–6pm; Nov–March Tues–Sun 11am–5pm; €1.60), which towers 102 metres above the Lahn. The present structure was begun by Sophie, the daughter of St Elisabeth, but the bulk of what can be seen today dates from the fifteenth and sixteenth centuries. Look out for the Gothic Schlosskapelle and the Rittersaal, the largest secular Gothic hall in Germany.

Marburg's **train station** is on the right bank of the Lahn at the northern end of town. The **tourist office** is at Am Pilgrimstein 26 (Mon–Fri 9am–6pm; April–Sept also Sat 10am–2pm; ☎0 64 21/9 91 20, *www.marburg.de*). The HI **hostel** is at Jahnstr. 1 (☎0 64 21/2 34 61; ③), a little to the south of the Altstadt. Most central **hotels** are a little on the pricey side – *Gästehaus Müller*, Deutschhausstr. 29 (☎0 64 21/6 56 59; ④), is perhaps the best value. **Camping** facilities are over the river at Trojedamm 47 (☎0 64 21/2 13 31). For **eating and drinking**, two enduring student favourites are *Café Barfuss*, Barfüsserstr. 33, and *Hinkelstein*, Markt 18, while *Alter Ritter*, Steinweg 44, is a classy restaurant offering good-value set lunches.

SOUTHERN GERMANY

Theodor Heuss, the first Federal President, saw **Baden-Württemberg** as "the model of German possibilities", and it has remained the most prosperous part of the country. Weak in natural resources, the area has had to rely on ingenuity; the motor car was invented here in the late nineteenth century, and the region has stayed at the forefront of world technology ever since. Baden-Württemberg's largest city, **Stuttgart**, is the home of Mercedes and Porsche, and though extensively damaged in World War II it has plenty of good points. The historical centre of Freiburg im Breisgau was also bombed, but its Münster – one of Germany's greatest buildings – was spared. Germany's most famous university city, **Heidelberg**, was hardly touched, and the spa resort of **Baden-Baden** remains wonderfully evocative of its nineteenth-century heyday as the playground of Europe's aristocracy. The scenery of the province is wonderful too: its western and southern boundaries are defined by the Rhine and its bulge into Germany's largest lake, the **Bodensee** (Lake Constance); within the curve of the river lies the **Black Forest**, source of another of the continent's principal waterways, the Danube.

Bavaria (Bayern) is the home of all the German clichés: beer-swilling Lederhosen-clad men, sausage dogs, sauerkraut and Wurst. But that's only a small part of the picture, and almost entirely restricted to the Alpine region south of the magnificent state capital **Munich**. In the state's western region, around its pristine capital **Augsburg**, the food is less pork and sausages and more pasta and sauces, and the landscape gentle farming country ideal for camping and cycling holidays. To the north lies **Nürnberg**, centre of a region of vineyards and nature parks, while eastern Bavaria – apart from its capital **Regensburg** – is relatively poor; life in its highland forests revolves around logging and workshop industries such as glass production.

One practical note: **travellers over 27** are barred from using Bavarian youth hostels, but reasonable alternatives can usually be found, and you'll only be handicapped if you're on the tightest of budgets.

Heidelberg

Home to the oldest university on German soil, **HEIDELBERG** is a real-life fulfilment of the ideal German landscape, majestically set on the banks of the swift-flowing Neckar between ranges of wooded hills. Ever since the days of the Grand Tour it has seduced travellers to an extent no other German city comes close to matching.

Arrival, information and accommodation

First impressions of Heidelber are a let down: the **train station** and **bus station** are in an anonymous quarter fifteen minutes' walk west of the centre, with the dreary Kurfürsten-Anlage leading towards town. The harassed **tourist office** is on the square outside (mid-March to mid-Nov Mon–Sat 9am–7pm, Sun 10am–6pm; rest of year Mon–Sat 9am–6pm; ☎06221/14220, *www.cvb-heidelberg.de*).

The **hostel** is on the north bank of the Neckar, about 4km from the centre, at Tiergartenstr. 5 (☎0 62 21/412 0 66; ②); take bus #11. Although a large number of **hotels** are dotted all over the city, they are often booked solid; however, there's a chart outside the tourist office detailing vacancies. The only real budget option is *Jeske*, located in the heart of the city at Mittelbadgasse 2 (☎0 62 21/2 37 33; ②, without breakfast), which offers doubles and beds in small dorms. The few other conveniently sited inexpensive hotels are *Elite*, Bunsenstr. 15 (☎0 62 21/2 57 34; ④), *Schmitt*, Blumenstr. 54 (☎0 62 21/2 72 96; ④), and *Astoria*, Rahmengasse 30 (☎0 62 21/40 29 29; ④). Both **campsites** are east of the city by the river – *Heide* is between Ziegelhausen and Kleingemünd, *Neckertal* is in Schlierbach; both are served by local bus.

The City

Centrepiece of all the views of Heidelberg is the **Schloss**, a compendium of magnificent buildings, somehow increased in stature by its ruined condition. It was founded at the start of the thirteenth century, but its expansion gathered momentum in the middle of the sixteenth century, when the Electors converted to Protestantism, and began the construction of the most splendid Renaissance buildings in Germany. Friedrich V's ham-fisted attempt to establish a Protestant, anti-Habsburg majority in the Electoral college led to the Thirty Years' War, which devastated the country. However, it was French designs on the region in 1689 that led to the destruction of Heidelberg and its Schloss; after this, the Electorship passed to a Catholic branch of the family who, unable to establish a rapport with the locals, abandoned Heidelberg.

The Schloss can be reached by **funicular** from the Kornmarkt for €3 return, but it's more fun to walk up via the Burgweg. At the southeastern corner is the most romantic of the ruins,

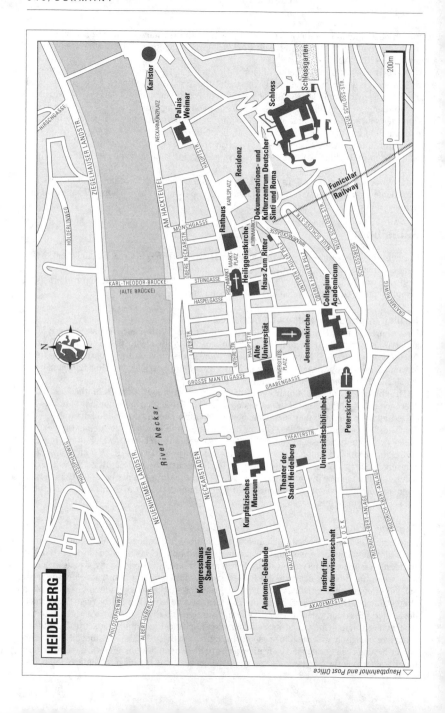

HEIDELBERG

Karlstor

Palais Weimar

Schloss

Schlossgarten

NECKARMÜNZPLATZ

HAUPTSTR

Residenz

KARLSPLATZ

Dokumentations- und
Kulturzentrum Deutscher
Sinti und Roma

AM HACKTEUFEL

Rathaus

MÖNCHGASSE

Funicular
Railway

OBERE NECKARSTR

Heiliggeistkirche

Haus Zum Ritter

KORNMARKT

NEUE SCHLOSS-STR

ZIEGELHAUSER LANDSTR

HIRSCHGASSE

HÖLDERLINWEG

KARL-THEODOR-BRÜCKE
(ALTE BRÜCKE)

STEINGASSE

FISCHMARKT
MARKT
PLATZ

HASPELGASSE

LAUERSTR

UNTERE STR

Alte
Universität

Collegium
Academicum

UNTERE FAULER PELZ

OBERE FAULER PELZ

HAUPTSTR

Jesuitenkirche

UNIVERSITÄTS
PLATZ

SCHLOSSBERG

GROSSE MANTELGASSE

GRABENGASSE

N

River Neckar

NEUENHEIMER LANDSTR

NECKARSTADEN

Universitätsbibliothek

Peterskirche

THEATERSTR

Theater der
Stadt Heidelberg

Kurpfälzisches
Museum

PHILOSOPHENWEG

ALBERT-UEBERLE-STR.

Kongresshaus
Stadthalle

HAUPTSTR

FRIEDRICH-EBERT-ANLAGE

FRIEDRICH-EBERT-ANLAGE

P L Ö C K

Institut für
Naturwissenschaft

Anatomie-Gebäude

AKADEMIESTR

GAISBERGWEG

NEUE SCHLOSS-STR.

0   200m

△ Hauptbahnhof and Post Office

now generally known as the **Gesprengter Turm** (Blown-up Tower); a collapsed section lies intact in the moat, leaving a clear view into the interior. In the **Schlosshof** (€2 8am–5.30pm, free access outside these hours; guided tours of interiors in English daily 11.30am, 2pm & 3.45pm; €3), what really catches your eye is the group of Renaissance palaces on the north and east sides. The triple loggia of the earlier **Saalbau** forms a link to the swaggering **Friedrichsbau**, which supports a pantheon of the House of Wittelsbach, beginning with Charlemagne, the alleged founder of the dynasty. The statues now on view are copies; the originals can be seen inside, along with a number of restored rooms which have been decked out in period style.

The finest surviving buildings in the **Altstadt** are grouped on **Marktplatz**, in the middle of which is the red sandstone **Heiliggeistkirche**, whose domed tower is one of the city's most prominent landmarks. Note the tiny shopping booths between its buttresses, a feature ever since the church was built. Inside, it's light, airy and uncluttered, but was not always so, as the church was built to house the mausoleum of the Palatinate Electors; only one tomb remains.

Facing the church is the only mansion to survive the seventeenth-century devastations, the **Haus zum Ritter**, so-called for the statue of St George on the pediment. The most striking Baroque building in Heidelberg is the **Alte Brücke**, reached from the Marktplatz down Steingasse; dating from the 1780s, it was blown up in the last war, but has been painstakingly rebuilt. The **Palais Rischer** on Untere Strasse was the most famous venue for one of the university's more risible traditions, the *Mensur*, or fencing match. Every vital organ was padded, but wounds were frequent and prized as badges of courage; for optimum prestige, salt was rubbed into them, leaving scars that would remain for life.

The **Jesuitenkirche**, across Hauptstrasse on Schulgasse, is in the sombre, Classically inspired style favoured by this evangelizing order, who came here with the ill-fated intention of recapturing Heidelberg for Catholicism. Housed in its gallery and the adjoining monastery is a moderate **Museum of Sacred Art** (Museum für Sakralkunst; June–Oct Tues–Sat 10am–5pm, Sun 1–5pm; Nov–May Sat 10am–5pm, Sun 1–5pm; €1.25).

One side of **Universitätsplatz**, the heart of the old town, is occupied by the **Alte Universität** (April–Oct Mon–Sat 10am–4pm; Nov–March Tues–Fri 10am–4pm; €2.60), which dates back to the first quarter of the eighteenth century, though its Aula or graduation hall is a grand example of nineteenth-century Romanticism. The rest of the square is occupied by the **Neue Universität**, erected in 1931 with American funding. The oddest of Heidelberg's traditions was that its students used not to be subject to civil jurisdiction: offenders were dealt with by the university authorities, and could serve their punishment at leisure. Now a protected monument, the **Students' Prison** (same hours and ticket as above) is at the back of the Alte Universität on Augustinergasse; used from 1712 to 1914, the otherwise spartan cells are covered with graffiti.

Eating and drinking

The **student taverns** in Heidelberg are a must: known for serving basic dishes at reasonable prices, they are still regularly patronized by the university fraternities, even if tourists these days make up most of the clientele. At the eastern end of Hauptstrasse are the two most famous of these hostelries – *Zum Sepp'l*, at no. 213, and *Roter Ochsen*, at no. 217. Less touristy is the oldest of all the **taverns**, *Schnookeloch*, at Haspelgasse 8. Among other traditional **restaurants**, and for cheaper eating, try *Essighaus*, Plöck 97, or *Goldener Hecht*, Steingasse 2.

The Biermuseum at Hauptstr. 143 has 101 varieties of **beer** to choose from, while *Vetters*, Steingasse 9, has its own small house brewery. The mid-nineteenth-century *Knösel*, Haspelgasse 20, is the oldest of Heidelberg's **cafés**; its speciality is Heidelberger Studentenkuss, a dark chocolate filled with praline and nougat. For something more like a **bistro** set-up, call in at the crowded *Café Journal*, Hauptstr. 162. There's an **Internet café** on Universitätsplatz.

Stuttgart

STUTTGART breathes success. Firms such as Bosch, Porsche and Daimler-Benz – whose three-pointed star beams down on the city – were in the vanguard of the German economic miracle, and have established the city at the forefront of European industry. Yet Stuttgart was slow to develop. Founded around 950 as a stud farm (Stutengarten), it became a town only in the fourteenth century, and lay in the shadow of its more venerable neighbours up to the early nineteenth century. Though not the comeliest of cities, Stuttgart has a range of superb museums, and a varied cultural and nightlife scene.

Arrival, information and accommodation

The **train station** is plumb in the centre of town; immediately behind is the **bus station**. S-Bahn #2 and #3 provide a link to the **airport** at approximately 20-minute intervals. There's a **tourist office** in front of the train station at Königstr. 1a (Mon–Fri 9.30am–8.30pm, Sat 9.30am–6pm, Sun 11am/1pm–6pm; ☎07 11/2 22 82 40, *www.stuttgart-tourist.de*). The integrated public transport network comprises buses, trams, the U-Bahn and main-line and S-Bahn trains; it's worth investing in a 24-hour ticket (€4.60 for individuals, €7.15 for up to five people travelling together). Alternatively, the €12.80 StuttCard, valid for three days, covers all public transport costs, plus admission to most museums and a range of reductions and numerous freebies, including drinks and food. There's a €7.65 variant called StuttCard Light giving the same benefits with the exception of public transport.

The **hostel** is about fifteen minutes' walk east of the train station at Haussmannstr. 27 (☎07 11/24 15 83; ②). There's also an unofficial hostel, the *Jugendgästehaus Stuttgart*, at Richard-Wagner-Str. 2–4a (☎07 11/24 11 32; ③). Though average **hotel** rates are high, there are some bargains, such as *Eckel*, Vorsteigstr. 10 (☎0711/29 09 95; ③), *Museum-Stube*, Hospitalstr. 9 (☎07 11/29 68 10; ③), and *Alte Mira*, Büchsenstr. 24 (☎07 11/2 22 95 02, ③). Alternatively, ask the tourist office to book a room; there's no charge. The **campsite** is on the banks of the Neckar in Bad Cannstatt – take a main-line train, or S-Bahn #1, #2 or #3.

The City

From the train station, Königstrasse passes the dull modern Dom and enters **Schlossplatz**, a welcome relief from the bustle, but favoured spot of Stuttgart's tramps and alcoholics. On the east side of the square, the colossal Baroque **Neues Schloss**, now used by the regional government, looks over at the Neoclassical **Königsbau**, its 135-metre facade lined with shops. At the south of the square is the **Altes Schloss**, which now houses the **Württembergisches Landesmuseum** (Tues 10am–1pm, Wed–Sun 10am–5pm; €2.60). Highlight of this richly varied museum is the Kunstkammer of the House of Württemberg, displayed in one of the corner towers: the first floor has small bronze sculptures of mainly Italian origin, while the second is laid out in the manner of a Renaissance curio cabinet. Upstairs, in the main part of the building, is a large collection of Swabian devotional sculptures, arranged thematically rather than chronologically. On the same floor, the archeology section includes excavations from Troy, Roman antiquities, the grave of a Celtic prince and Frankish jewellery. The top floor has musical instruments and a wonderful array of clocks. The nearby **Galerie der Stadt Stuttgart** (Tues & Thurs–Sun 11am–6pm, Wed 11am–8pm; free) is a poor relation of the Staatsgalerie, but does contain some superbly acerbic works by Otto Dix.

To the north of Schlossplatz, facing the straggling complex of the Staatstheater across Konrad-Adenauer-Strasse, is the **Staatsgalerie** (Tues, Wed & Fri–Sun 10am–6pm, Thurs 10am–9pm, first Sat in month 11am–midnight; €4.60). The most startling work in the entire gallery is the huge, violently expressive *Herrenberg Altar* by Jerg Ratgeb, whose reputation rests almost entirely on this work. The equally idiosyncratic Hans Baldung is represented by his *Man of Sorrows* and *Portrait of Hans Jacob*. After some good examples of Cranach, Bellini,

Carpaccio, Tintoretto and Tiepolo, Memling's sensual *Bathsheba at her Toilet* kicks off the Low Countries section, which also features Rembrandt's tender *Tobit Healing his Father's Blindness*. Nineteenth-century highpoints are *Bohemian Landscape* and *The Cross in the Woods* by Friedrich, and a decent cross-section of French Impressionism. The extension, a much-praised postmodern design by James Stirling, contains one of the two finest Picasso collections in Germany and traces the entire progress of German art in the twentieth century. Avant-garde works occupy the end halls, while major temporary exhibitions are regularly featured downstairs.

On the other side of Schlossplatz, the **Altes Schloss** overlooks **Schillerplatz**, Stuttgart's sole example of an old-world square. Presiding in the middle is a pensive statue of Schiller himself, erected the year after his death by the Danish sculptor Bertel Thorwaldsen. Also here are two more Renaissance buildings – the **Alte Kanzlei** and the gabled **Fruchtkasten**. The latter preserves its fourteenth-century core, now converted to house **Landesmuseum**'s musical instruments collection (times and prices as above). At the back of Schillerplatz is the **Stiftskirche**, the choir of which is lined with one of the most important pieces of German Renaissance sculpture, an ancestral gallery of the counts and dukes of Württemberg.

THE MERCEDES-BENZ MUSEUM
Set up in 1986 to celebrate the centenary of the invention of the motor car by Gottlieb Daimler and Carl Benz, the **Mercedes-Benz Museum** (Tues–Sun 9am–5pm; free) is an absolute must, unless you rue the day the car was invented. Even entering here is an experience – you take S-Bahn #1 to Neckarstadion, then walk; or take bus #56 to the works entrance, from where you're whisked in a sealed minibus to the museum doors. The earliest vehicle on display is the Daimler Reitwagen of 1885, the first ever motorbike, which was capable of 12kph. The Daimler company's first Mercedes dates from 1902, its Spanish-sounding name being taken from the daughter of the firm's principal foreign agent, Emil Jellinek. Other exhibits include fire engines, motorboats, aeroplanes and buses, but the show is stolen by the luxury cars and the machines specially designed for world record attempts: so futuristic it's hard to believe they were made more than half a century ago.

THE PORSCHE MUSEUM
The **Porsche Museum**, Porschestrasse 42, is right beside the Neuwirtshaus station on S-Bahn line #6 (Mon–Fri 9am–4pm, Sat & Sun 9am–5pm; free). Ferdinand Porsche made his name when Hitler commissioned him to create the original Volkswagen, precursor of the Beetle, the ultimate mass-market car. For his own enterprise, Porsche concentrated on the opposite end of the economic spectrum. The vehicles on show illustrate all the company's cars from the 356 Roadster of 1948 to current models.

Eating, drinking and nightlife
Though fancy **restaurants** abound in Stuttgart, there are a number of places offering traditional Swabian dishes at low cost, with plenty of ethnic eateries to stimulate the jaded palate. First recommendations for good-quality food and drink are the numerous **Weinstuben**, archetypally German establishments that are known for their solid cooking as well as for wine. *Zur Kiste*, Kanalstr. 2, is the best-known, but the widest choice of wines is at *Weinhaus Stetter*, Rosenstr. 32. The best restaurant in a **beer hall** setup is *Ketterer*, Marienstr. 3b; the best **pub** in the city with an adjoining house brewery is *Calwer-Eck-Bräu*, Calwer Str. 31; while the fullest range of vegetarian fare is at *Iden*, Eberhardstr. 1.

For **nightlife** details, pick up the tourist office's well-filled monthly programme, *Stuttgarter Monatsspiegel*, costing €1.80. Alternative listings can be found in both *Lift Stuttgart* and *Prinz Stuttgart*, available from newsagents. Schlesinger International, Schloss Str. 28, is a popular, youthful hangout; the former punk haunt of Exil, Filderstr. 61, now belongs to arty types, with jazz and blues in a laid-back atmosphere. Jazz also features at Laboratorium, Wagenburgerstr. 147, popular with the Green Party contingent. Occupying an old rail tunnel, Röhre, Neckarstr. 34, platforms live bands playing everything from jazz to punk, and is also a disco patronized by fashion-conscious locals. *Café Stella*, Haupstätter Str. 57, is a trendy **café-bar**.

Listings

Car rental Avis, Katharinenstr. 18 (☎07 11/23 93 20); Hertz, Im Hauptbahnhof (☎07 11/2 26 29 21).

Consulates Britain, Breite Str. 2 (☎07 11/1626 90); US, Urbanstr. 7 (☎07 11/21 02 21).

Hitching Mitfahrzentrale at Haupstätter Str. 154 (☎07 11/60 36 06) and Lerchenstr. 65 (☎07 11/6 36 80 36).

Post office Main office is at the rear of the Königsbau on Schillerplatz.

Tübingen

"We have a town on our campus" runs the saying in **TÜBINGEN**, which is sited above the willow-lined banks of the Neckar, some 55km upstream from Stuttgart. Over half the population of 70,000 is in some way connected with the university, and the current size of the town is due entirely to the twentieth-century boom in higher education.

The old town is a visual treat, a mixture of brightly painted half-timbered and gabled houses grouped into twisting and plunging alleys. Two large squares provide a setting for communal activities. The first, **Holzmarkt**, is dominated by the **Stiftskirche St Georg**, a gaunt, late-Gothic church with a fine interior. In the chancel (Easter–Oct Fri–Sun 11am–5pm, July & Aug daily; €1, including ascent of the tower) an outstanding series of stained-glass windows casts reflections on the pantheon of the House of Württemberg, the thirteen tombs showing the development of Swabian sculpture in the Gothic and Renaissance periods.

Overlooking the banks of the Neckar on Bursagasse, the street immediately below, is the **Hölderlinturm** (Tues–Fri 10am–noon & 3–5pm, Sat & Sun 2–5pm; €1.60). Originally part of the medieval fortifications, it's named after Friedrich Hölderlin, who lived here in the care of a carpenter's family, hopelessly but harmlessly insane, from 1807 until his death 36 years later. There's a collection of memorabilia of the poet, now regarded as one of the greatest Germany ever produced. At the end of the street is the Evangelisches Stift, a Protestant seminary established in a former Augustinian monastery in 1547.

The **Markt**, heart of old Tübingen, is just a short walk uphill from the Stift. It preserves many of its Renaissance mansions, along with a fountain dedicated to Neptune, around which markets are held on Mondays, Wednesdays and Fridays. Burgsteige, one of the oldest and handsomest streets in town, climbs steeply from the corner of the Markt to **Schloss Hohentübingen**, Renaissance successor to the original eleventh-century castle. One wing is now given over to the **Schausammlungen der Universität** (Wed–Sun 10am–5pm; €2), one of the largest university museums in the world, with archeology, history and ethnology displays. The northwestern part of town, lying immediately below the Schloss, has traditionally been the province of the non-academic community – especially the vine-growers. Here are some of the city's oldest and most spectacular half-timbered buildings, such as the old municipal **Kornhaus** on the alley of the same name, and the **Fruchtschranne**, formerly the storehouse for the yields of the ducal orchards, on Bachgasse.

The corresponding quarter northeast of the Markt is once more dominated by the university. Crossing Langegasse, and continuing along Metgergasse, you come to the **Nonnenhaus**, most photogenic of the half-timbered houses. Just outside the northeastern boundary of the old town are the former **Botanical Gardens**. These have been replaced by another complex, located amid most of the modern buildings of the university, 2km north by the ring road (Mon–Fri 7.30am–4.45pm, Sat & Sun 10–noon & 1.30–4.30pm).

Practicalities

The **train station** and **bus station** are side by side, just five minutes' walk from the old town. At the edge of Eberhardsbrücke is the **tourist office** (Mon–Fri 9am–7pm, Sat 9am–5pm;

May–Oct also Sun 2–5pm; ☎0 70 71/1 94 40, *www.tuebingen-info.de*). **Hotels** aren't plentiful and tend to be expensive; the best bet is *Am Schloss*, Burgsteige 18 (☎0 70 71/9 29 40; ④), or try the **hostel** on the banks of the Neckar, a short walk from the station at Gartenstr. 22/2 (☎0 70 71/2 30 02; ②); the tourist office also has a list of private rooms. To reach the **campsite**, also with a riverside setting at Rappenberghalde, turn left on leaving the train station, and cross at Alleenbrücke. The best **restaurant** in the centre is *Forelle*, a wine bar at Kronenstr. 8. Giant pancakes are the speciality of the *Ratskeller*, Haaggasse 4, while *Marktschenke*, Markt 11, is a lively student bar.

The Black Forest region

Stretching 170km north to south, and up to 60km east to west, the **Black Forest** (Schwarzwald) is the largest German forest and the most beautiful. As late as the 1920s, much of this area was an eerie wilderness, a refuge for boars and bandits. Nowadays most of the villages have been opened up as spa and health resorts, brimming with shops selling tacky souvenirs, while the old trails have become gravel paths smoothed down for easier walking. Yet by no means all the modernizations are drawbacks. Railway fans, for example, will find several of the most spectacular lines in Europe here. It should be noted, though, that the trains tend to stick to the valleys and that bus services are much reduced outside the tourist season.

Most of the Black Forest is associated with the Margravate of Baden, whose old capital of **Baden-Baden** is at the northern fringe of the forest, in a fertile orchard and vine-growing area. The only city actually surrounded by the forest is **Freiburg im Breisgau**, one of the most enticing in the country.

Baden-Baden

In the present century, the social class that made **BADEN-BADEN** the "summer capital of Europe" has almost disappeared, yet the town still has a style that no other spa in the country can quite match. Buoyed by the postwar economic prosperity, people flock here to enjoy a taste of a lifestyle their parents could only dream about. Baden-Baden is on the fast Karlsruhe–Freiburg line, but the station is 4km northwest of the centre in the suburb of Oos; take bus #201, #205 or #216 into the centre.

The therapeutic value of Baden's hot springs was discovered by the Romans, but the town's rise to international fame only came about as a result of Napoleon's creation of the buffer state of Baden in 1806. The Grand Dukes promoted their ancestors' old seat as a modern resort, and began embellishing it with handsome buildings such as the **Kurhaus** and its integral casino. The easiest way to see these is to take a guided tour (daily 9.30/10am–noon; €3); highlight is the **Winter Garden**, with its glass cupola, Chinese vases and solid gold roulette table. A day ticket, with no obligation to participate, is €2.60.

South of the Kurhaus runs Baden-Baden's most famous thoroughfare, the **Lichtentaler Allee**, landscaped with exotic trees and shrubs and flanked by buildings such as the Parisian-style theatre and the **Kunsthalle**, which often hosts major exhibitions of twentieth-century art. Immediately north of the Kurhaus is the **Trinkhalle**, whose arcades shelter vast frescoes illustrating legends of the town and the nearby countryside.

Little remains today of the old town, almost completely destroyed in a single day in 1689, the result of a fire started by French troops. However, halfway up the Florintinerberg is the **Marktplatz**, and the **Stiftskirche**, a Gothic hall church containing one of the masterpieces of European sculpture, an enormous sandstone *Crucifixion* by Nicolaus Gerhaert von Leyden. Hidden under the Stiftskirche are the remains of the Roman Imperial Baths; the more modest **Römerbad** (Easter–Oct daily 10am–noon & 1.30–4pm; €1.30), just east on Römerplatz, was probably for soldiers. Above the ruins is the **Friedrichsbad** (Mon–Sat 9am–10pm, Sun noon–8pm), begun in 1869 and grand as a Renaissance palace. Speciality of the house is a two-hour "Roman-Irish Bath", which will set you back upwards of €18.40, though the really broke need only fork out €0.05 for a glass of thermal water.

From here you can climb the steep steps to the **Neues Schloss**, a mixture of Renaissance and Baroque buildings. The main reception rooms are no longer open to the public, but one of the outbuildings houses a **local history museum** (Tues–Thurs noon–5pm, Fri–Sun 11am–5pm; €1). There's also the added attraction of the best view over Baden-Baden, a dramatic mix of rooftops, spires and the enveloping forest.

PRACTICALITIES

The **tourist office** is in the Trinkhalle on Kaiserallee (daily 10am–6.30pm; ☎0 72 21/27 52 00, *www.baden-baden.de*). A few **rooms** are available in private houses (②–④). Baden-Baden's **hostel** is between the train station and the centre at Hardbergstr. 34 (☎0 72 21/5 22 23; ②); take bus #201, #205 or #216 to Grosse-Dollen-Strasse, from where the way is signposted. The main group of cheap **hotels** is in Oos: try *Goldener Stern*, Ooser Hauptstr. 16 (☎0 72 21/6 15 09; ③), or *Adler*, Ooser Hauptstr. 1 (☎0 72 21/6 18 58; ④). The nearest **campsite** is in the Oberbruch park on the outskirts of Bühl, three stops by slow train. Among places to **eat and drink**, *Münchener Löwenbräu*, Gernsbacher Str. 9, is a good choice; complete with beer garden, it's like a little corner of Bavaria, and serves excellent meals. For a trendy atmosphere, try *Leo's*, Luisenstr. 10, while for solid, reasonably priced German food, there's *Rathausglöckel*, Steinstr. 7.

Freiburg im Breisgau

"Capital" of the Black Forest, **FREIBURG IM BREISGAU** basks in a laid-back atmosphere which seems completely un-German. A university town since 1457, its youthful presence is maintained all year round with the help of a varied programme of festivals. Furthermore, the sun shines here more often, and there are more vineyards within the municipal area than in any other city in the country.

Though it rivals any of the great European cathedrals, the dark red sandstone **Münster** was built as a mere parish church, the costs being met entirely by the local citizens. The transepts were begun in about 1200, after which one of the architects of Strasbourg Cathedral took over and created a masterly Gothic nave, resplendent with flying buttresses, gargoyles and statues. At around this time the magnificent sculptures of the west porch were created, the most important German works of their time – note the *Prince of Darkness*, carved where the natural light is weakest. More sculptures adorn the portals of the chancel, which was begun in the mid-fourteenth century – look out for the unusual depiction of God resting on the seventh day. From the **tower** (March–Nov Mon–Sat 9.30am–5pm, Sun 1–5pm; €1.25) you get a fine panorama over the city and the forest, and of the lacelike tracery of the spire, which rounds off the tower with a bravura flourish. Inside, the transept is lit by stained-glass windows of the early thirteenth century. Most of those in the nave date from a hundred years later, and were donated by the local trades and guilds, who incorporated their coats of arms. To get a decent look at Baldung's *Coronation of the Virgin* altarpiece, you have to take a guided tour of the ambulatory chapels (Mon–Fri 11am & 2.30pm; €1.60), which contain some wonderful pieces – including a retable by the two Holbeins, and a silver crucifix from the first Münster.

The spacious **Münsterplatz**, the north side of which was flattened in the last war, holds one of the most diverting daily markets in Germany. The south side of the square is dominated by the blood-red **Kaufhaus**, a sixteenth-century merchants' hall, flanked by handsome Baroque palaces.

A peculiarity of Freiburg is the system of rivulets known as the **Bächle**, which run in deep gulleys all over the city. Formerly used for watering animals, and as a fire-fighting provision, they have their purpose even today, helping to keep the city cool. Following the main channel of the Bächle southwards, you come to the **Schwaben Tor**, one of two surviving towers of the medieval fortifications. On Oberlinden, just in front, is **Zum Roten Bären**, which is generally considered to be Germany's oldest inn. Just to the west is Salzstrasse, where the **Augustinermuseum** (Tues–Sun 10am–5pm; €2, free first Sun of month) houses works of art from the Münster and a few top-class pictures, including the most important paintings by the mysterious draughtsman known as Master of the Housebook. South of here, on Marienstrasse, the **Museum of Modern Art** (same times; free) has a good cross-section of twentieth-century German painting. From here, follow Fischerau, the old fishermen's street, and you come to the other thirteenth-century tower, the **Martinstor**, in the middle of Freiburg's central axis, Kaiser-Josef-Strasse.

Back on the west side of the Münster, the **Neues Rathaus**, **Altes Rathaus** and the plain Franciscan friary church of **St Martin** stand around a shady chestnut-lined square. In the alley behind St Martin is the cheerful Gothic facade of the **Haus zum Wallfisch**, for two years the home of the great humanist Erasmus, who was forced to flee from Basel by the religious struggles there. A few minutes to the west, in the Columbipark opposite the tourist office, is the **Museum of Pre- and Early History** (same times; €1.75 donation requested), which has important archeological collections relating to the Black Forest region.

It's worth climbing one of the hills surrounding the city for the wonderful views. The **Schlossberg**, immediately to the east, is an easy ascent from the Schwaben Tor – or you could take the cable car. To the south, the **Lorettoberg** – where the stone for the Münster was quarried – makes a good afternoon or evening alternative.

PRACTICALITIES

The **train station**, with the bus station on its southern side, is about ten minutes' walk west from the city centre. Following Eisenbahnstrasse, you come to the **tourist office** on Rotteckring (Mon–Fri 9.30am–6/8pm, Sat 9.30am–2/5pm, Sun 10am–noon; ☎07 61/3 88 18 80, *www.freiburg.de*). For €1.60, they will find you a room; if you arrive after closing time, there's an electronic noticeboard equipped with a phone, which lists vacancies. Among **hotels** with a central location, the cheapest is *Schemmer*, Eschholzstr. 63 (☎07 61/20 74 90; ④). The **hostel** is at Karthäuserstr. 151 (☎07 61/6 76 56; ②), at the extreme western end of the city, reached by tram #1 to Hasemannstrasse. Nearby, slightly nearer town, is the *Hirzberg* **campsite** (open all year); *Mösle-Park* (mid-March to Oct) is on the opposite side of the river.

Freiburg has **restaurants** for all pockets. *Oberkirchs Weinstuben*, Münsterplatz 22, is a top-notch but not expensive wine cellar, and *Zur Traube* just behind at Schusterstr. 17 is equally good. Hearty South German cooking can be sampled at *Kleiner Meyerhof*, Rathausgasse 27 or *Grosser Meyerhof*, Grünwälderstr. 7. One of the trendiest places to be seen is *Uni-Café*, Niemensstr. 7, which serves a wide selection of coffees and has good snacks. Freiburg now ranks as one of the leading German cities for jazz, thanks to the Jazzhaus at Schnewlinstr. 1, which has concerts every evening.

Konstanz and the Bodensee

In the far south of the province, **KONSTANZ** lies at the tip of a tongue of land sticking out into the **Bodensee** (Lake Constance), which is really a swelling in the River Rhine. The town itself is split by the water: the **Altstadt** is a German enclave on the Swiss side of the lake, which is why it was never bombed by the Allies, who couldn't risk hitting neutral Switzerland. It's a cosy little place, with a convivial atmosphere in summer, when street cafés invite long pauses and the water is a bustle of sails.

The most prominent church is the **Münster**, set on the highest point of the Altstadt. It was here in 1417 that the papal court tried the reformer Johannes Hus for heresy – the spot on which he stood during his trial is marked in the central aisle. Konstanz's major museum is the **Rosgartenmuseum** on the street of the same name (Tues–Thurs 10am–5pm, Fri–Sun 10am–4pm; €1.60), which has a fine collection of local archeological finds, plus art and craft exhibits from the Middle Ages. Everything is as it was when the museum was designed in 1871, creating a pleasantly musty atmosphere.

The **tourist office** is located alongside the **train station** at Bahnhofplatz 13 (April–Oct Mon–Fri 9am–6.30pm, Sat 9am–4pm, Sun 10am–1pm; Nov–March Mon–Fri 9.30am–12.30pm & 2–6pm; ☎0 75 31/13 30 30, *www.konstanz.de*); they can book accommodation for you in private rooms (②–④). The **hostel** is at Zur Allmannshöhe 18 (☎0 75 31/3 22 60; ②); take bus #4 from the train station to Jugendherberge, or #1 to Post Allmannsdorf. If you'd prefer a **hotel**, however, try *Gretel* at Zollenstr. 6–8 (☎0 75 31/2 32 83; ③) or *Graf Zeppelin*, Am Stephansplatz 15 (☎0 75 31/2 37 80, *bashkin@t-online-de*; ④). Information on **cruises** and **ferries** is available from the Bodensee-Verkehrsdienst at Hafenstr. 6 (☎0 7531/28 13 98). Ferries regularly leave Konstanz for destinations all over the lake: perhaps the most worthwhile longer trip is to the Rheinfall in Switzerland – it costs €17.90, but it's worth it to travel up one of the Rhine's most scenic stretches and to see Europe's largest waterfall.

Munich

Founded in 1158, **MUNICH** (München) has been the sole capital of Bavaria since 1503, and as far as the locals are concerned it may as well be the centre of the universe. Münchener pride themselves on their special status; even people who have made Munich their home for most of their lives are still called *Zugereiste* (newcomers). Next to Berlin, Munich is Germany's most popular city, with everything you'd expect in a cosmopolitan capital. Yet it's small enough to be digestible in one visit, and it's got the added bonus of a great setting, with the mountains and Alpine lakes just an hour's drive away. The best time of year to come here is from June to early October, when the beer gardens, street cafés and bars are in full swing.

Arrival, information and city transport

Munich's **airport**, Franz Josef Strauss Flughafen, is connected to the **train station** (Hauptbahnhof) by S-Bahn #1 or #8. There are **tourist offices** at Bahnhofplatz 2 (Mon–Sat 9am–8pm, Sun 10am–6pm; ☎0 89/2 33 03 00, *www.muenchen-tourist.de*) and in the Rathaus on Marienplatz (Mon–Fri 10am–8pm, Sat 10am–4pm). They will book rooms, and provide brochures about the city and what's on. The bus station is a stone's throw from the train station.

Day tickets for all **public transport** in the city cost €4.60 (for the whole system €9.20); for up to five people travelling together they cost €7.15 and €14.30 respectively. A weekly pass covering the centre and most of Schwabing costs €8.50, but this is valid from Monday to Monday, so buying midweek means losing out. Tickets for a week upwards require ID and two photos; others can be bought from the automatic machines in all U-Bahn stations, at some bus and tram stops, and inside trams. If you're making several journeys across the city, it's far more economical to invest in a strip card (€8.20 for ten strips), and stamp two strips for every zone crossed – the zones are shown on maps at stations and tram and bus stops. For journeys of up to two S- or U-Bahn stops, or up to four bus or tram stops, only one strip needs to be cancelled. There's also a €3.30 children's strip card, for which it is only necessary to cancel one strip per trip. Tickets must be stamped before any journey – those without a validated ticket face an on-the-spot €30 fine.

Accommodation

Cheap accommodation can be hard to find, especially during the high season in the summer, though prices are fairly constant throughout the year. If you're going to be in town during the Oktoberfest, it's essential to book your room well in advance. Details of the pick of the hotels, hostels and campsites are given below. Many pensions offer rooms with three to six beds, a much more pleasant way of saving money than hostel-type accommodation.

HOSTELS

Burg Schwaneck, Burgweg 4–6 (☎0 89/7 93 06 43). HI hostel some way from the centre in an old castle on the river. Check-in 5pm–1am. S-Bahn #7 to Pullach, then follow signs to the Jugendherberge. ②.

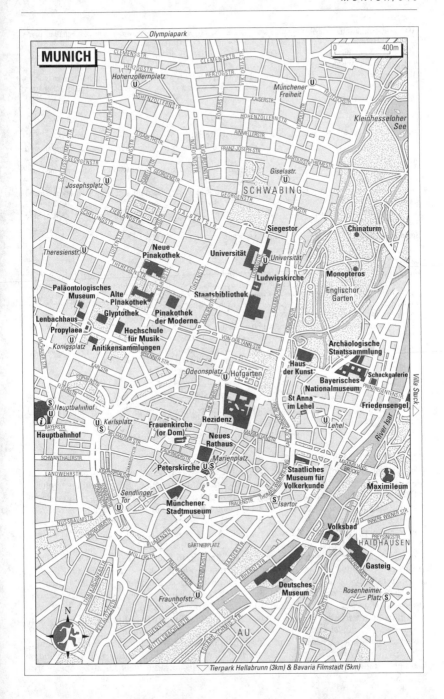

DJH Jugendgästehaus, Miesingstr. 4 (☎0 89/7 23 65 60, *JGHMuenchen@djh-bayern.de*). Smaller, more upmarket HI hostel with check-in 7am–11pm. U-Bahn to Harras, then tram #16 to Boschetsriederstr. ②.
DJH München, Wendl-Dietrich-Str. 20 (☎0 89/13 11 56, *JHMuenchen@djh-bayern.de*). The largest, most central and most basic HI hostel, with 535 beds. Check-in noon–1am. U-Bahn to Rotkreuzplatz. ②.
Haus International, Elisabethstr. 87 (☎0 89/12 00 60). Centrally located in Schwabing, rooms range from five beds to singles. No age limit, no need for HI card. U-Bahn to Hohenzollernplatz, then bus #33 or tram #12 to Barbarastrasse. ③.

HOTELS AND PENSIONS

Eder, Zweigstr. 8 (☎0 89/55 46 60). In a quiet road between the train station and Marienplatz. ③.
Frank, Schellingstr. 24 (☎0 89/28 14 51). A good choice for both price and atmosphere. Mainly frequented by young travellers. ③.
Haberstock, Schillerstr. 4 (☎0 89/55 78 55). Right beside the Hauptbahnhof with basic, no frills facilities, but it's good value nonetheless. ④.
Jedermann, Bayerstr. 95 (☎0 89/54 32 40, *www.hotel-jedermann.de*). Located well away from any noise and seediness, five minutes' walk from the Hauptbahnhof. ④.
Am Kaiserplatz, Kaiserplatz 12 (☎0 89/34 91 90). Very friendly, good location and big rooms, each done in a different style – from red satin to Bavarian rustic. ③.
Steinberg, Ohmstr. 9 (☎0 89/33 10 11). Friendly and in a good location. ④.

CAMPSITES

Kapuzinerhölzl Youth Camp. 500-berth tent with showers, canteen and information bureau. Price includes blankets, air mattress and morning tea. Check-in 5pm–9am. Officially for under-23s and for a maximum of three nights, but people in charge are very flexible. Open late June to Aug. U-Bahn to Rotkreuzplatz, then tram #12 to the Botanischer Garten. Check with the tourist office whether it's open before setting out, as its future is uncertain.
Obermenzing, Lochhausener Str. 59. In a posh suburb, close to Nymphenburg. Open mid-March to Oct. S-Bahn to Obermenzing, then bus #75 to Lochhausener Strasse.
Thalkirchen, Zentralländstr. 49. Most central site, in an attractive part of the Isar valley. Very popular during the Oktoberfest as it's close to the fairground. Open mid-March to Oct. U-Bahn to Thalkirchen.

The City

Almost nothing is left of Munich's medieval city, but three of the gates remain to mark today's city centre. Bounded by the Odeonsplatz and the Sendlinger Tor to the north and south, and the Isartor and Karlstor to the east and west, it's only a fifteen-minute walk across – but it is so tightly packed it needs two or three days to explore thoroughly.

MARIENPLATZ AND AROUND

The central **Marienplatz** – the heart of the U-Bahn system – is always thronged, with street musicians and artists entertaining the crowds, and with youths lounging around the fountain. At 11am and noon, the square fills with tourists as the tuneless carillon in the Rathaus tower jingles into action. The **Rathaus** itself is a late nineteenth-century neo-Gothic monstrosity whose only redeeming features are the café in its cool and breezy courtyard and the view from the **tower** (ascent by elevator May–Oct Mon–Fri 9am–7pm, Sat & Sun 10am–7pm; Nov–April Mon–Thurs 9am–4pm, Fri 9am–1pm, Sat & Sun 9am–5pm; €1.60). To the right is the plain Gothic tower of the Altes Rathaus, which was rebuilt in the fifteenth-century style after being destroyed by lightning; today it houses a **toy museum** (daily 10am–5.30pm; €2.60). Close by, the **Peterskirche** looks out across the busy Viktualienmarkt; the oldest church in Munich, it's notable for its grisly relics of St Munditia, patron saint of single women, and for the view from its **tower** (Mon–Sat 9am–5/8pm, Sun 10.15am–5/7pm according to season; €1.25).

Almost next to the Viktualienmarkt is the **Münchener Stadtmuseum** (Tues–Sun 10am–6pm; €2.60; *www.stadtmuseum-online.de*), the excellent local history museum, which also incorporates a Photo and Film Museum, a Museum of Brewing and a Puppet Museum. The last is highly recommended: it's one of the largest collections in the world, and includes puppets ranging from Indian and Chinese paper dolls to large mechanical European creations. Southwest of here, at Sendlinger Str. 62, stands the small **Asamkirche**, one of the most splendid Rococo churches in Bavaria.

Following the pedestrian Kaufingerstrasse west from Marienplatz, you walk with the mainstream of shoppers, overlooked by the Frauenkirche or **Dom**. The red-brick Gothic cathedral is seen to its best advantage from a distance, its twin onion-domed **towers** (ascent by elevator April–Oct Mon–Sat 10am–5pm; €2) forming the focus of the city's skyline. A little further up Kaufingerstrasse, the Renaissance facade of **St Michael** stands unassumingly in line with the street's other buildings. In the **crypt** (Mon–Fri 10am–1pm & 2–4.30pm, Sat 10am–3pm; €1) you'll find the coffins of the Wittelsbach dynasty – a candle is always burning at the foot of mad castle-builder Ludwig II's.

NORTH OF MARIENPLATZ – THE RESIDENZ

North of Marienplatz is the posh end of the city centre. **Maximilianstrasse**, the Champs-Elysées of Munich, is where the fashion houses have their shops, and the *Hotel Vierjahreszeiten* is one of the best addresses in town. When the refinement gets too much, the little Kosttor road leads straight to the **Hofbräuhaus**, Munich's largest and most famous drinking hall. Nearby, with its Baroque facade standing proud on the Odeonsplatz, is one of Munich's most regal churches, the **Theatinerkirche**, whose golden-yellow towers and green copper dome add a splash of colour to the roofscape.

The palace of the Wittelsbachs, the **Residenz** (April to mid-Oct Mon–Wed & Fri–Sun 9am–6pm, Thurs 9am–8pm; mid-Oct to March daily 10am–4pm; €4) stands across the square from the Theatinerkirche. One of Europe's finest Renaissance buildings, it was so badly damaged in the last war that it had to be almost totally rebuilt. To see the whole thing you have to go on two consecutive visits, as parts of the immense complex are shut in the morning and others in the afternoon. On the morning tour you see the Antiquarium, the oldest part of the palace; built in 1571 to house the ruling family's collection of antiquities, this cavernous chamber was transformed into a festive hall a generation later. The last stage of the morning tour – which can also be seen in the afternoon – includes the eight appropriately named Rich Rooms, and the Halls of the Nibelungs, in which medieval Germany's most famous epic is depicted in a series of paintings. The afternoon tour includes the two very contrasting chapels and the Baroque Golden Hall. A separate ticket is necessary to see the fabulous treasures of the **Schatzkammer** (same hours; €4, or combined ticket €7.15); star piece of the whole display, kept in a room of its own, is the dazzling stone-encrusted statuette of St George, made around 1590. Yet another ticket has to be bought for the glorious **Cuvilliés Theatre** (same hours; €2), the Wittelsbachs' private theatre.

ISARINSEL AND PRINZREGENTENSTRASSE

Munich's most overwhelming museum – the **Deutsches Museum** (daily 9am–5pm; €6.15; *www.deutsches-museum.de*) – occupies much of the mid-stream island called the Isarinsel. Covering every conceivable aspect of technical endeavour, from the first flint tools to the research labs of modern industry, this is the most compendious collection of its type in Germany. Another gargantuan collection – the **Bayerisches Nationalmuseum**, Prinzregentenstr. 3 (Tues–Sun 9.30am–5pm; €3, free Sun; *www.bayerisches-nationalmuseum. de*) – lies further north. This rambling decorative arts museum takes in arms and armour, ivories and sacred objects, with a superb display of German wood sculpture. The basement features Bavarian folk art, the first floor displays models of Bavarian towns as they appeared in the sixteenth century and the second floor has stained glass, crystal, ceramics and clocks. Close by, at Prinzregentenstr. 1, the Nazi-era **Haus der Kunst** (daily 10am–10pm; variable entrance charges) hosts important temporary exhibitions.

THE MUSEUM QUARTER

Tucked between the train station and Schwabing, the **museum quarter** contains enough treasures to keep you absorbed for days.

The **Alte Pinakothek**, Barerstr. 27 (Tues–Sun 10am–5pm, Thurs until 10pm; €4.60, free Sun; *www.pinakotheken-muenchen.de*), is one of the largest galleries in Europe and the world's finest assembly of German art. Among the collection are Dürer's Christ-like *Self-portrait* and panels of *SS Mark, John the Evangelist, Peter and Paul*; Lucas Cranach the Elder's *Lucretia* and *Venus and Cupid* (the first sensually explicit nudes in German art); and Albrecht Altdorfer's *Battle of Alexander*, a heaving mass of hundreds of soldiers, each painted in minute detail. In the Italian section works by Titian steal the show, notably the *Portrait of Charles V* and *Christ Crowned with Thorns*. Centrepiece of the entire museum is the collection of works by Rubens, with 62 paintings displaying the scope of the artist's prodigious output. There's also a haunting *Passion Cycle* by Rembrandt and, from an earlier period of Netherlandish art, Rogier van der Weyden's classic *Adoration of the Magi*.

The collection of eighteenth- and nineteenth-century European painting and sculpture in the **Neue Pinakothek** at Barerstr. 29 (Mon & Wed–Sun 10am–5pm, Thurs until 10pm; €4.60, free Sun; *www.pinakotheken-muenchen.de*) seems a little thin after the Alte Pinakothek, but it's nonetheless worth an hour or so. Neoclassicism, the preferred style of the age of rationalism, is beautifully embodied in the sober portrait of the *Marquise de Sourcy de Thélusson* by David, while Romanticism is represented by Carl Spitzweg, whose everyday scenes have a wry sense of humour. Of the works by French Impressionists, *Manet's Breakfast in the Studio* is probably the most famous. Turn-of-the-century art is represented by a few paintings by Cézanne, Van Gogh and Gauguin, and the museum rounds off with a small selection of Art Nouveau. A selection of the twentieth-century art works formerly displayed in the Haus der Kunst is currently on view on the Neue Pinakothek, pending the completion of the much-delayed **Pinakothek der Moderne** alongside, which is scheduled to open in the summer of 2002 (check with tourist office for latest details).

The meticulously restored **Glyptothek** (Tues, Wed & Fri–Sun 10am–5pm, Thurs 10am–8pm; €3, free Sun), the most striking structure on the majestically Neoclassical Königsplatz, contains a magnificent range of Classical sculpture, the most striking exhibits being the ancient statuary plundered from the temple on Aegina. Facing the Glyptothek is the **Staatliche Antikensammlungen** (Tues & Thurs–Sun 10am–5pm, Wed 10am–8pm; €3, joint ticket with Glyptothek €5.10, free Sun), displaying Greek vases from the fifth and sixth centuries BC, as well as beautiful jewellery and small statues from Greek, Etruscan and Roman antiquity.

Situated just off Königsplatz at Luisenstr. 30 is the **Lenbachhaus** (Tues–Sun 10am–6pm; €4), the nineteenth-century villa that belonged to the Bavarian painter Franz von Lenbach. It's a pleasant setting for some of German art's most interesting modern painters, the highlights coming with the group known as Der Blaue Reiter, whose members included Kandinsky, Klee, Marc and Macke. In recent years the museum has also concentrated on temporary exhibitions of contemporary German art.

SCHWABING

Marienplatz might be the geographical centre of town but **Schwabing** is its social hub. A large part of Munich's northern sector, with Leopoldstrasse forming a straight axis through the middle, Schwabing splits into three distinct areas. Around the university and left of Leopoldstrasse, residential streets mix with student bars and restaurants. Along the centre and to its right, trendy shops and café-bars ensure permanent crowds, day and night – nightclubs are thick on the ground here, especially around the Wedekindplatz, near Münchener Freiheit station. The far north is a tidy residential area, uninteresting apart from the **Olympiapark**, built for the 1972 Olympics, and now used for free open-air rock concerts in July and August.

One diversion that unites everyone is beer drinking, especially in summer, and one of the most famous beer gardens is around the Chinesischer Turm (or China Tower) in the **Englischer Garten**. Not far off by the Kleinhesseloher See are a couple of more peaceful gardens – the lakeside one is the more attractive. The Eisbach meadow is the city's main playground, where people come to sunbathe (often nude), picnic, swim or ride horses.

NYMPHENBURG

Schloss Nymphenburg (April to mid-Oct Mon & Wed–Sun 9am–6pm, Thurs until 8pm; mid-Oct to March daily 10am–4pm; €3.60; combined ticket with pavilions and Marstall €7.60), the summer residence of the Wittelsbachs, is reached by tram #17 from the train station. Its kernel is a small Italianate palace begun in 1664 for the Electress Adelaide, who dedicated it to the goddess Flora and her nymphs – hence the name. The Marstall, or stables, contain notable collections of historic coaches and porcelain, but more enticing than the palace itself are the wonderful park and its four pavilions – all of a markedly different character. Three were designed by Joseph Effner: the **Magdalenenklause**, built to resemble a ruined hermitage; the **Pagodenburg**, used for the most exclusive parties thrown by the court; and the **Badenburg**, which, like the **Pagodenburg**, reflects an interest in the art of China. For all their charm, Effner's pavilions are overshadowed by the stunning **Amalienburg**, the hunting lodge built behind the south wing of the Schloss by his successor as court architect, François Cuvilliés. This supreme expression of the Rococo style marries a cunning design – which makes the little building seem like a full-scale palace – with the most extravagant decoration imaginable.

To the north of the Schloss, the **Botanical Gardens** (daily 9am–4.30/7pm; hothouses closed 11.45am–1pm; €2) hide all manner of plants in their steamy hothouses, while the herbarium and other outdoor collections make a very fragrant landscape.

DACHAU

DACHAU, now reverted to a picturesque town on the northern edge of Munich, was site of Germany's first **concentration camp** (Tues–Sun 9am–5pm; free). The motto that greeted arrivals at the gates has taken its chilling place in the history of Third Reich brutality: Arbeit Macht Frei, "Work Brings Freedom". Of the original buildings, only the gas chambers, which were never used, remain. However, a replica hut gives an idea of the conditions under which prisoners were forced to live, and the permanent exhibition of photographs speaks volumes. Turn up at 11.30am or 3.30pm and you can also view the short, deeply disturbing, documentary *KZ-Dachau* in English. Get there by taking bus #724 or #726 from Dachau S-Bahn station.

Eating and drinking

It's not difficult to eat well for little money in Munich. **Mensas** are the cheapest places to get a good basic meal; you're supposed to have a valid student card to eat here, but no one seems to check. The most central one is at Leopoldstr. 15 (Mon–Thurs 9am–4.45pm, Fri 9am–3.30pm), and there are two more in the main building at Schellingstrasse and at the Technical University, Arcisstr. 17. Italian **restaurants** are especially cheap, and the Bavarian Gaststätten offer filling soups, salads and sandwich-type dishes. Not surprisingly, **drinking** is central to Munich social life and apart from the Gaststätten and beer gardens, Munich also has a lively café-bar culture, which carries on well into the early hours. The city's "alternative" district is the former working-class and immigrant quarter of Haidhausen, across the river to the southeast of the centre. Though tamer than Berlin's Kreuzberg and Prenzlauer Berg, it has a good mix of bars, cafés and restaurants, and makes a refreshing break from the glitz of the Schwabing nightspots.

CAFÉ/BARS, CAFÉS AND WINE BARS

Alter Simpl, Türkenstr. 57. Famous literary café-bar which spawned the satirical magazine *Simplicissimus*. Open daily 5pm–3am, 4am at weekends.

Café Kreutzkamm, Maffeistr. 4. One of the best (and most expensive) *Kaffee und Küchen* establishments.

Pfälzer Weinprobierstuben, Residenzstr. 1. Unpretentious place serving excellent wines from the Palatinate.

Weintrödler, Brienner Str. 10. Late-night wine bar (5pm–6am); the last boozer to close.

RESTAURANTS

Adria, Leopoldstr. 19. Popular late-night Italian, with good food at reasonable prices.

Bella Italia, Herzog-Wilhelm-Str. 8. One of a small chain of inexpensive Italian restaurants in Munich.

Bernard & Bernard, Innere Wiener Str. 32. Great place for crepes, in Haidhausen.

Donisl, Weinstr. 1. A fine old Munich Gaststätte, dating back to the early eighteenth century.

Haxnbauer, Munzstr. 6. Specializes in the delicious roasted pork knuckles that are such a high point of German cuisine; the lamb version is no less tasty.

Prinz Myshkin, Hackenstr, 2. Best vegetarian place in the centre.

Schelling Salon, Schellingstr. 54. Good for their large cheap breakfasts and also for playing pool.

BEER GARDENS AND BEER HALLS

Augustinerbräu, Neuhauser Str. 27. One of several beer halls and gardens on this central street, with an unusually long menu and wonderfully evocative turn-of-the-century decor.

Augustinerkeller, Arnulfstr. 52, near the Hackerbrücke S-Bahn stop. A shady island of green, hidden in one of Munich's grottier quarters.

Aumeister, Sondermeierstr. 1. At the northern end of the Englischer Garten; a good place for daytime breaks.

Hofbräuhaus, Platzl 9. The most famous, though nowadays, at least during the tourist season, it's by far the least authentic of any on this list.

Hofbräukeller, Innere Wiener Str. 19. Nestling under ancient chestnut trees; very popular in the evenings.

Weisses Bräuhaus, Im Tal 10. Famous for the favourite Munich snack of Weisswurst, a white sausage which should traditionally only be eaten before noon.

MUSIC, NIGHTLIFE AND FESTIVALS

Munich has a great deal to offer musically, from classical concerts to rock. Best sources for **information** on what's happening are the *Münchener Stadtzeitung* or *In München*, both available at any kiosk, or the monthly *Monatsprogram* from the tourist office or the English-language *Munich Found*. For **jazz concerts** – a major feature of Munich nightlife – check the monthly Münchener Jazz-Zeitung. Munich has three first-rate symphony orchestras – the Münchener Philharmonie, the Bayrisches Rundfunk Sinfonie Orchester and the Staatsorchester – as well as eleven major theatres and numerous fringe theatres. Advance tickets for plays and concerts can be bought at the relevant box offices or commercial ticket shops such as the one located in the Marienplatz U-Bahn station. Opera tickets can be bought at the advance sales office at Maximilianstr. 11, or from the box office in the Nationaltheater one hour before performances begin. As for **clubs**, a trendy new area, albeit one under an almost permanent threat of closure, is Kunstpark Ost (S- or U-Bahn to Ostbahnhof), a mini-city of clubs housed in a network of old factory buildings.

CLUBS AND LIVE MUSIC VENUES

Crash, Ainmillerstr. 10. Stage for heavy rock.

Kaffee Giesing, Bergstr. 5. Venue for small bands and solo artists.

Muffathalle, Zellstr. 4. Although not large, many well-known bands perform here.

Nachtwerk, Landsberger Str. 185. Draws a young crowd on Friday and Saturday.

Olympiapark. Free rock concerts by the lake in summer; they usually get going around 2pm at weekends.

Schwabinger Podium, Wagnerstr. 1. Chiefly Dixieland.

Sugar Shack, Herzogspitalstr. 6. A trendies' favourite.

Unterfahrt, Einsteinstr. 42. Showcase for avant-garde jazz.

CLASSICAL MUSIC, OPERA AND THEATRE

Cuvilliéstheater, in the Residenz. Premier venue for drama, plus the occasional chamber music recital.

Deutsches Theater, Schwanthalerstr. 13. Home-grown and visiting spectaculars.

Gasteig, Rosenheimer Str. 5. One of the two main venues for classical concerts.

Herkulessaal, in the Residenz. The other big classical concert hall.

Staatsoper or **Nationaltheater**, Max-Josef-Platz 1. Munich's answer to Covent Garden, with grand opera and ballet.

Residenztheater, Max-Josef-Platz 1. Traditional dramatic fare.
Staatstheater Am Gärtnerplatz, Am Gärtnerplatz. Mixed programme of operetta, musicals and popular operas.

THE OKTOBERFEST AND OTHER EVENTS

The **Oktoberfest**, held on the Theresienwiese fairground from the penultimate Saturday in September for the next sixteen days, is an orgy of beer drinking, spiced up by fairground rides that are so hairy they're banned in the USA. The proportions of the fair are so massive that the grounds are divided along four main avenues, creating a boisterous city of its own, heaving from morning till night. **Fasching**, Munich's carnival, is an excuse for parades, fancy-dress balls and general shenanigans from mid-January until the beginning of Lent. More sedate is **Auer Dult**, a traditional market that takes place on the Mariahilfplatz during the last weeks of April, July and October each year; there are stalls selling food, craftware and antiques, and there's also a fairground.

Listings

Airlines British Airways (☎0 18 05/26 65 22); Lufthansa, Lenbachplatz 1 (☎0 89/5 52 50 50).
Airport information ☎0 89/97 52 13 13.
Bike rental In the Hauptbahnhof, opposite platform 31.
Car rental Avis (☎0 89/5 50 22 51) and Europcar (☎0 89/5 50 13 41) both have offices at the train station.
Consulates Britain, Bürkleinstr 10 (☎0 89/21 10 90); Canada, Tal 29 (☎0 89/2 19 95 70); Ireland, Mauerkircherstr. 1a (☎0 89/98 57 23); US, Königinstr. 5 (☎0 89/2 88 80).
Exchange The bank at the train station is open daily 6am–11pm.
Gay Munich Despite Bavaria's deep conservatism, Munich has one of the most active and visible gay scenes in Germany. Cafés that cater predominantly for lesbians are *Inge's Karotte*, Baaderstr. 13, *Frauencafé im Kofra*, Baldestr. 8 and *Mädchenpower-Café*, Baldestr. 16. The following male gay bars are well known: *Colibri*, Utzschneiderstr. 8, *Juice*, Buttermelcherstr. 2a, and *Klimperkasten*, Maistr. 28.
Hitching Mitfahrzentrale at Adalbertstr. 10–12 (☎0 89/1 94 44) and Lämnerstr. 4 (☎0 89/1 94 40).
Internet access There's a cybercafé at Nymphenburger Str. 145.
Laundry Amalienstr. 61; Ismaninger Str. 45.
Medical emergencies ☎0 89/55 17 71.
Post office Bahnhofplatz 1, and Residenzstr. 2.

The Bavarian Alps

It's among the picture-book scenery of the **Alps** that you'll find the Bavarian folklore and customs that are the subject of so many tourist brochures, and the region also encompasses some of the most famous places in the province, such as the Olympic ski resort of **Garmisch-Partenkirchen**, and the fantasy castle of **Neuschwanstein**, just one of the lunatic palaces built for King Ludwig II of Bavaria. The western reaches are generally cheaper and less touristy, partly because they're not so easily accessible to Munich's weekend crowds. In contrast, much of the eastern region to **Berchtesgaden** is heavily geared to the tourist trade, but if you go outside the high season of July and August, you should have a good chance of avoiding the crowds and not straining your finances.

Hohenschwangau and Neuschwanstein

Lying between the Forggensee reservoir and the Ammer mountains, around 100km by rail from Munich, **FÜSSEN** and the adjacent town of **SCHWANGAU** are the bases for visiting Bavaria's two most popular castles. **Schloss Hohenschwangau** (daily: April–Sept 9am–6pm; Nov–March 10am–4pm; €7.15), originally built in the twelfth century but heavily restored in the nineteenth, was where Ludwig spent his youth. A mark of his individualism is left in the bedroom, where he had the ceiling painted with stars that were spotlit in the evenings. **Schloss Neuschwanstein** (same times; €7.15), the ultimate storybook castle, was built by

Ludwig a little higher up the mountain. The architectural hotchpotch ranges from a Byzantine throne hall to a Romanesque study and an artificial grotto. Left incomplete at Ludwig's death, it's a bizarre monument to a very sad and lonely man.

The nearest **hostel** is in Füssen, at Mariahilferstr. 5 (☎0 83 62/77 54; ②). An inexpensive guesthouse near the castles is *Pension Weiher*, Hofwiesenweg 11 (☎0 83 62/8 11 26; ③). The **tourist office** at Kaiser-Maximilian-Platz (Mon–Fri 8am–noon & 2–6pm, Sat 10am–noon; ☎0 83 62/70 77, *www.fuessen.de*) in Füssen can book accommodation. Füssen is also the end of the much-publicized **Romantic Road** from Würzburg via Augsburg, served by special **tour buses** in season.

Oberammergau and Schloss Linderhof

From Murnau, midway between Munich and Garmisch-Partenkirchen, a branch line runs to **OBERAMMERGAU**, world famous for its **Passion Play**, first performed in 1633 as thanks for being spared by a plague epidemic. The show takes place every ten years (next in 2010) between May and October, with a cast of local villagers. Many of Oberammergau's houses have traditional outside frescoes of religious or Alpine scenes, which you can see as either quaint or kitsch – that goes for the wood carvings in the local souvenir shops, too.

From here it's a short bus ride to **Schloss Linderhof** (April–Sept Mon–Wed & Fri–Sun 9am–6pm, Thurs 9am–8pm; Oct–March daily 10am–4pm; €5.60, €4 in winter), one of the architectural fantasies conjured for dotty King Ludwig. Though built as a discreet private residence, it has a reception room with intricate gold-painted carvings, stucco ornamentation, and a throne canopy draped in ermine curtains. The real attraction is the delightful **park**: Italianate terraces, cascades and manicured flowerbeds give way to an English garden design that gradually blends into the forests of the mountain beyond. A number of romantic little buildings are dotted around the park, the most remarkable of which is the Venus Grotto. Based on the set for Wagner's opera *Tannhäuser* (Ludwig was the composer's principal patron), it has an illuminated lake supporting a huge floating golden conch in which the king would sometimes take rides.

Garmisch-Partenkirchen and Mittenwald

GARMISCH-PARTENKIRCHEN is the most famous town in the German Alps, partly because it's at the foot of the highest mountain – the **Zugspitze** (2966m) – and partly because it hosted the Winter Olympics in 1936. It has excellent facilities for skiing, skating and other winter sports, as well as abundant accommodation, a full list of which can be obtained from the **tourist office** at Richard-Strauss-Platz 2 (Mon–Sat 8am–6pm, Sun 10am–noon; ☎0 88 21/18 06, *www.garmisch-partenkirchen.de*). The ascent of Zugspitze by **rack-railway** and cable car (both €32 in winter, €40 in summer) is the most memorable local excursion.

MITTENWALD, which remains a community rather than a resort, is just 15km down the road and the main rail line from Munich. The Karwendl mountain towering above Mittenwald is a highly popular climbing destination, and the view from the top is one of the most exhilarating and dramatic in Germany; a **cable car** goes there for €16.40 return. The **tourist office**, at Dammkarstr. 3 (Mon–Fri 8am–noon & 1–5pm, Sat 10am–noon; ☎0 88 23/3 39 81, *www.mittenwald.de*), will reserve rooms and provide free maps of the area. There are plenty of good **guesthouses** in the village, such as *Franziska*, Innsbrucker Str. 24 (☎0 88 23/9 20 30; ③) and *Bergfrühling*, Dammkarstr. 12 (☎0 88 23/80 89; ③). The nearest **campsite** is 3km north, on the road to Garmisch, and is open all year.

Berchtesgaden

Almost entirely surrounded by mountains at Bavaria's southeastern extremity, the area around **BERCHTESGADEN** has a magical atmosphere, especially in the mornings, when mists rise from the lakes and swirl around lush valleys and rocky mountainsides. The town is easily reached by rail from Munich and from Salzburg in Austria, which is just 23km to the north.

The town is famous for its **salt mine** (Salzbergwerk; May to mid-Oct daily 9am–5pm; mid-Oct to April Mon–Sat 12.30–3.30pm; €10.75), where a small train will take you deep into the mountainside; you have to don protective clothing and descend on wooden slides. The region's other star attraction is **Königssee**, Germany's highest lake, which bends around the foot of the spiky Watzmann 5km south of the town and can be reached by regular buses. There are **cruises** on the Königssee all year round (€11.50). You can also take a cable car up the Jenner, immediately above the lake (€17.40 return). There are some great mountain trails to take you out of the crowds – maps of suggested walking routes can be bought at the **tourist office** opposite the train station (late June to mid-Oct Mon–Fri 8am–6pm, Sat 8am–5pm, Sun 9am–3pm; rest of year Mon–Fri 8am–5pm, Sat 9am–noon; ☎0 86 52/96 70, *www.berchtesgaden.de*).

The area's main historical claim to fame is its connection with **Adolf Hitler**, who rented a house in the nearby village of **Obersalzberg**, which he later enlarged into the **Berghof**, a stately retreat where he could meet foreign dignitaries. It was blown up by the Allies, and the ruins are now overgrown. High above the village on the Kehlstein, the Kehlsteinhaus, Hitler's "**Eagle's Nest**", survives as a restaurant, and can reached by special bus from Obersalzberg (May–mid-Oct; €11.25 return).

Berchtesgaden has plenty of reasonable guesthouse **accommodation**. Options include *Haus am Hang*, Göllsteinbichl 3 (☎0 86 52/43 5 90; ②), *Hansererhäusl*, Hansererweg 8 (☎0 86 52/25 23; ②), *Gästehaus Alpina*, Ramsauer Str. 6 (☎0 86 52/25 17; ③), and *Haus Achental*, Ramsauer Str. 4 (☎0 86 52/45 49; ③). The tourist office can help with booking rooms and will direct you to any of the five campsites in the valley.

Augsburg

Innovations, both religious and secular, have found fertile ground in **AUGSBURG**, 70km from Munich. Luther's reforms found their earliest support here, and in 1514 the city built the world's first housing estate for the poor, the Fuggerei – an institution still in use today. The citizens of Augsburg have gone to great lengths to restore the city's appearance to that of its medieval heyday, yet this isn't just a museum piece. There's lively cultural action ranging from Mozart festivals to jazz and cabaret, and the university provides a thriving alternative scene to keep the place on its toes.

The City

Heart of the city is the spacious cobbled **Rathausplatz**, which turns into a massive open-air café during the summer and into a glittering market at Christmas. At the baseline of this great semicircle stands the massive **Rathaus**, perhaps Germany's finest secular Renaissance building. Inside, the spick-and-span **Goldener Saal** (daily 10am–6pm; €1.60), with its gold-leaf pillars and marble floor, recalls the period when the Fugger banking dynasty made Augsburg one of the financial centres of Europe. Next to the Rathaus stands the **Perlachturm** (May–Oct daily 10am–4/6pm; €1), a good vantage point.

To the south, **Maximilianstrasse** is lined by merchants' palaces and punctuated by fountains. Soon after the Mercury fountain, the **Fuggerhäuser** stand proudly to the right; built in 1515 by Jacob Fugger "the Rich", they still belong to his loaded descendants, but you can walk through the main door to see the luxurious arcaded courtyard. Opposite the Hercules fountain is the **Schaezler Palais** (Tues–Sun 10am–5pm; €2), through the courtyard of which is the Dominican nunnery of St Catherine and the **State Gallery** (same times and ticket, but currently closed for restoration), home of Dürer's portrait of Jacob Fugger. At the far end of Maximilianstrasse, Lutheran **St Ulrich** is dwarfed by the Catholic basilica of **St Ulrich-und-Afra**, resting place of the city's joint patron saints.

At the other end of the town's axis, the **Dom** stands in the grounds of the former episcopal palace, now the seat of the regional government. It was founded by St Ulrich in the tenth century, and preserves the oldest stained-glass windows still in position. There are also a number of altarpieces by Hans Holbein the Elder. The famous Romanesque bronze doors are now on view in the **Diocesan Museum St Afra** (Tues–Sat 10am–5pm, Sun 2–5pm, first Fri of the month 10am–9pm; €2) in the cloisters.

The town's historical museum, the **Maximilianmuseum** (Tues–Sun 10am–4pm; €2.60), is housed in a merchant's house at Philippine-Welser-Str. 24. In its courtyard, original figures from the city's three great Mannerist fountains are displayed under a specially designed glass roof. Prehistoric and Roman remains are shown separately in the **Römisches Museum** (same hours; €2.60), which occupies the old Dominican church at Dominikanergasse 15. The light and whitewashed interior makes an excellent setting for the Roman masonry and bronzes, and the uncluttered layout is a pleasure after the usual warehouse-like museums.

For a charge of one "Our Father", one "Hail Mary" and one Creed daily, plus €90 per annum, good Catholic paupers can retire to the **Fuggerei** at the age of 55. With an entrance in the Jacoberstrasse, it's a town within a town, and compared with modern housing estates is a real idyll, the cloister-like atmosphere disturbed only by the odd ringing doorbell. Number 13 (March–Dec daily 9am–6pm; €0.50) in the Mittlere Gasse is one of only two houses from the original foundation, and today it's full of furnishings that show how residents lived from the sixteenth to the eighteenth century.

On the other side of town, in Annastrasse, stands **St Anna**, where the **Fuggerkapelle** marks the belated German debut of the full-blooded Italian Renaissance style, a spin-off of the family's extensive business interests in Italy. An effect of overwhelming richness is created by the marble pavement, stained glass, choir stalls, a sculptural group of *The Lamentation over the Dead Christ*, and memorial tablets honouring the Fugger brothers made after woodcuts designed by Dürer. It was in St Anna that the final confrontation between the papal court and Luther took place in 1518. Luther found refuge with the Carmelites of St Anna when he was summoned to see the pope's legate, and today his room and several others in the old monastery have been turned into the **Lutherstiege** (Tues–Sun 10am–noon & 3–5pm; free), a museum of the reformer's life and times.

Practicalities

The **tourist office** (Mon–Fri 9am–6pm, Sat 10am–1pm; ☎08 21/50 207 0, *www.regio-augsburg.de* & *www.augsburg.de*) is a couple of minutes from the **train station** at Bahnhofstr. 7: there's also a branch on Rathausplatz (Mon–Fri 9am–6pm, Sat 10am–4pm; May–Sept also Sun 10am–1pm). Good **pensions** are to be found in the suburb of Lechhausen, 1.5km from the city centre and connected by three bus routes and tram #1: *Bayerische Löwe*, Linke Brandstr. 2 (☎08 21/70 28 70; ③), *Linderhof*, Aspernstr. 38 (☎08 21/71 30 16; ③), and *Märkl*, Schillerstr. 20 (☎08 21/79 14 99; ③). The **hostel** is three minutes' walk from the Dom, at Beim Pfaffenkeller 3 (☎08 21/3 39 09; ②). The nearest **campsite** is at motorway exit Augsburg-Ost, next to the Autobahnsee.

The cheapest places for **snacks** are the market and meat halls off Annastrasse, where you'll find several good Imbiss stands. Moving upmarket, excellent Swabian **meals** are served at the *Fuggerei-Stube*, Jakobergstr. 26. For **drinking**, *Kreslesmühle*, Barfüsserstr. 4, is a popular café-bar and arts centre; Striese, Kirchgasse 1, is also a theatre and music venue.

Regensburg

"Regensburg surpasses every German city with its outstanding and vast buildings," drooled Emperor Maximilian I in 1517. The centre of **REGENSBURG** has changed remarkably little since then; its undisturbed medieval panorama and its stunning location on the banks of the Danube make it a great place to spend a couple of days.

Maximilianstrasse leads straight from the train station to the centre. The best view of Regensburg's medieval skyline is from the twelfth-century **Steinerne Brücke**, which was the only safe and fortified crossing along the entire length of the Danube at the time it was built, and thus had tremendous value for the city as a trading centre. On the left, just past the medieval salt depot, the **Historische Wurstküche** (daily 8am–7pm) originally functioned as the bridge workers' kitchen. It's been run by the same family for generations and serves little else but delicious Regensburg sausages.

A short way south the **Dom** comes into full view. Bavaria's most magnificent Gothic building, it was begun around 1250, replacing a Romanesque church of which the **Eselsturm** is the only remaining part above ground. Highlights include the late thirteenth-century statues of the Annunciation and the fourteenth-century stained-glass windows in the south transept. In the cloisters – accessible only on guided tours (May–Oct Mon–Sat 10am, 11am & 2pm, Sun noon & 2pm; Nov–April Mon–Sat 11am, Sun noon; €2) – the **Allerheiligenkapelle** still has many Romanesque frescoes. Concerts and services are a musical treat in Regensburg, as the **Domspatzen** (Cathedral Sparrows) is one of the finest choirs in the country.

Perhaps the best of Regensburg's merchant and patrician houses are to be seen on the **Haidplatz**. The largest building on the square is the **Haus zum Goldenen Kreuz**, where Emperor Charles V used to meet a local girl called Barbara Blomberg: their son, John of Austria, was born here in 1547 and died Governor of the Netherlands in 1578. The nearby **Thon-Dittmer Palais** is one of the main cultural venues, concerts and plays being held in its courtyard in summer. A few minutes' walk away, the Neupfarrplatz is the centre of Regensburg's commercial life; the **Neupfarrkirche** occupies the site of the old synagogue, which was wrecked during the 1519 expulsion of the Jews.

Apart from the Dom, the town's most important Gothic structure is the **Altes Rathaus** on Kohlenmarkt. To appreciate its grand scale, you need to take a guided tour of the **Reichstagsmuseum** (tours in English May–Sept Mon–Sat 3.15pm; tours in German Mon–Sat 9.30am–noon & 2–4pm, Sun 10am–noon, also 2–4pm April–Oct; €2.60); the most significant room is the Imperial Diet Chamber, a parliamentary forum for the empire from 1663 to 1806.

On nearby Keplerstrasse, the **Kepler-Gedächtnishaus** (Tues–Sat 10am–noon & 2–4pm, Sun 10am–noon; April–Oct Sun also 2–4pm; €2) is dedicated to the great astronomer Johann Kepler, who died in Regensburg. Another museum worth looking into is the **Historical Museum on Dachauplatz** (Tues–Sun 10am–4pm; €2) – especially the section on Albrecht Altdorfer, who, apart from being one of Germany's greatest artists, was also a leading local politician.

Schloss Thurn und Taxis (tours: April–Oct Mon–Fri 11am, 2pm, 3pm & 4pm, Sat & Sun also 10am; Nov–March Sat & Sun only 10am, 11am, 2pm & 3pm; €6.15 combined entry to Schloss and cloisters), home of the Prince of Thurn und Taxis, is situated in the city's southern quarter, in the converted monastic buildings of the abbey of St Emmeram. The former cloisters represent some of the finest Gothic architecture to be found in Germany, while the nineteenth-century state rooms contain some wonderful Brussels tapestries recording the family's illustrious history. In the Neoclassical Marstall or stables are two museums that can be visited at leisure. The **Marstallmuseum** (April–Oct Mon–Fri 11am–5pm, Sat & Sun 10am–5pm; €3.60, or €4 combined ticket with Thurn and Taxis Museum) holds travelling and ceremonial coaches and winter sleighs; the **Thurn und Taxis Museum** (Mon–Fri 11am–5pm, Sat & Sun 10am–5pm; €3) has displays of decorative art.

Practicalities

The **tourist office** is bang in the middle, in the Altes Rathaus (Mon–Fri 8.30am–6pm, Sat 9am–4pm, Sun 9.30am–2.30/4pm; ☎09 41/5 07 44 10, *www.regensburg.de*). The **hostel**, Wöhrdstr. 60 (☎09 41/5 74 02; ②), is about five minutes' walk from the heart of things, on an island in the Danube. Cheapest **hotel** in the town centre is *Zum Fröhliche Türken*, Fröhliche-Türken-Str. 11 (☎09 41/5 36 51; ④). Just the other side of the Steinerne Brücke, *Spitalgarten*, St Katharinen-Platz 1 (☎09 41/8 47 74; ③), is conveniently sited next to the best beer garden. The **campsite** is about twenty minutes' walk from the centre, next to the Danube at Weinweg 40.

You're spoilt for **places to eat** in Regensburg. Two Gaststätten with good traditional and moderately priced Bavarian fare are *Alte Münz*, Fischmarkt 8, and *Kneitinger*, Arnulfsplatz 3. For more of a bar-type atmosphere, usually with good music, try *Rote Löwe*, Rote Löwengasse 10, or *Amopola*, Am Römling 1. Netzblick, Am Römling 9, is an **Internet café**. Popular student hangouts are *Schwedenkugel*, Haaggasse 15, and *Goldene Ente*, Badstr. 32. For a traditional **beer garden**, take bus #6 south to *Kneitinger-Keller*, at Galgenbergstr. 18 near the university, or for a great location on one of the Danube islands, try the aforementioned *Spitalgarten* on St Katharinen-Platz.

Nürnberg

Founded in the eleventh century, **NÜRNBERG** rapidly rose to become the unofficial capital of Germany, its position at the intersection of major trading routes leading to economic prosperity and political power. The arts flourished too, though the most brilliant period was not to come until the late fifteenth century, when the roll call of citizens was led by Albrecht Dürer. Like many other wealthy European cities, Nürnberg went into gradual economic and social decline once the sea routes to the Americas and Far East had been established; moreover, adoption of the Reformation cost the city the patronage of the Catholic emperors. It made a comeback in the nineteenth century, when it became the focus for the Pan-German movement, and the Germanisches Nationalmuseum – the most important collection of the country's arts and crafts – was founded at this time.

Nürnberg is especially enticing in the summer, when the historic centre – the Altstadt – is alive with street theatre and music, and open-air concerts liven up the parks and stadiums; but there's always a wide and varied range of nightlife.

Arrival, information and accommodation

The main **tourist office** (Mon–Sat 9am–7pm; ☎09 11/23 36 32, *www.nuernberg.de*) is currently situated in a kiosk in front of the train station, just outside the Altstadt. There's another office at Hauptmarkt 18, within the Altstadt (Mon–Sat 9am–6pm; May–Sept also Sun 10am–1pm & 2–4pm; ☎09 11/23 36 35). For €14.80, the Nürnberg KulTour Ticket covers two days' travel on the public transport network plus entrance to most of the museums and sights. The official **HI hostel** has a wonderful location within the Kaiserburg, overlooking the Altstadt (☎091 1/2 30 93 60; ②). There's also a privately run **youth hotel** to the north of the city at Rathsbergstr. 300 (☎09 11/5 21 60 92; ③; no age restriction). Cheapest reasonably central **pensions** include: *Vater Jahn*, Jahnstr. 13 (☎09 11/44 45 07; ③), *Melanchthon*, Melanchthonplatz 1 (☎09 11/41 26 26; ③), and *Altstadt*, Hintere Ledergasse 4 (☎09 11/2 22 61 02; ④). The **campsite** is in the Volkspark, near the Dutzendteich lakes; take tram #12.

The City

On January 2, 1945, a storm of bombs reduced ninety percent of Nürnberg's centre to ash and rubble, but you'd never guess it from the meticulous postwar rebuilding. Covering about 4 square kilometres, the reconstructed medieval core is surrounded by its ancient city walls and neatly spliced by the River Pegnitz. To walk from one end to the other takes about twenty minutes, but much of the centre, especially the area around the castle – known as the **Burgviertel** – is on a steep hill. It's not all medieval pictures, either. Significant areas of modern architecture and open spaces are nearby, ensuring a refreshing mix of old and new.

One of the highest points of the city is occupied by the **Kaiserburg** (April–Sept Mon–Wed & Fri–Sun 9am–6pm, Thurs 9am–8pm; Oct–March daily 10am–4pm; €5.10), whose earliest surviving part is the eastern **Fünfeckturm**, which dates back to the eleventh century. A century later, Frederick Barbarossa extended the castle to the west: his **Sinwellturm**, built directly on the rock, can be ascended for the best of all the views. Another survivor of this period is the **Kaiserkapelle**, whose upper level was reserved for the use of the emperor, with the courtiers confined to the lower tier. At the extreme east end of the complex is the **Luginslandturm**, erected by the city council in the fourteenth century. At the end of the fifteenth century, the Luginslandturm was joined to the Fünfeckturm by the vast Kaiserstallung – originally a cereal warehouse and later a stable, it's now a perfect home for the HI hostel.

The area around the **Tiergärtner Tor** next to the Kaiserburg is one of the most attractive parts of the old town centre, a meeting point for summertime street vendors, artists and musicians. Virtually next door, the **Dürer Haus** (Tues, Wed & Fri–Sun 10am–5pm, Thurs 10am–8pm; €4.10) is where the painter, engraver, scientist, writer, traveller and politician lived from 1509 to 1528, and is one of the very few original houses still standing. Don't come here looking for original Dürer paintings, though: there are only copies, plus works by artists paying homage to the great man. Dürer himself is buried in the St Johannisfriedhof, a few minutes' walk away, along Johannisstrasse.

Nürnberg's oldest and most important church, the twin-towered **Sebalduskirche**, is just down the road from the Fembohaus. Founded in the thirteenth century and altered a century later, it contains an astonishing array of works of art. Particularly striking are the bronze shrine of St Sebald and some pieces by Veit Stoss, Nürnberg's most famous sculptor: an expressive *Crucifixion* on the pillar behind the shrine and three stone reliefs in the chancel.

The **Hauptmarkt**, commercial heart of the city and the main venue for weekly markets (and the famous Christmas market), is a couple of minutes' walk away. Its east side is bounded by the **Frauenkirche**, on whose facade a clockwork mechanism known as the *Männleinlaufen* tinkles away at noon. Also on the Hauptmarkt is a replica of the famous **Schöner Brunnen**, looking like a lost church spire; the original parts are on display in the Germanisches Nationalmuseum.

Walking southwards from Hauptmarkt, you cross the river by Museumsbrücke, which gives you a good view of the **Fleischbrücke** to the right, and the **Heilig-Geist-Spital** – one of the largest hospitals built in the Middle Ages – on the left. Passing the oldest house in the city, the thirteenth-century **Nassauer Haus**, you shortly come to the **Lorenzkirche**, built about fifty years after the Sebalduskirche, its counterpart on the other side of the water. The nave has a resplendent rose window, while the chancel is lit by gleaming stained glass. The graceful late fifteenth-century tabernacle, some 20-metres high, was carved by Adam Kraft, who depicted himself as a pensive figure crouching at the base. Equally spectacular is the larger-than-life *Annunciation* by Veit Stoss, suspended above the high altar.

Further down Königstrasse in the direction of the train station is the massive and austere Renaissance **Mauthalle**, beyond which stands the Gothic **Marthakirche**, the hall of the *Meistersinger*. The distinctive form of lyric poetry known as *Meistergesang* flourished in Germany from the fourteenth century, and had a glorious final fling in Nürnberg, thanks above all to the shoemaker Hans Sachs, creator of some 6000 works.

West of the Mauthalle, the **Germanisches Nationalmuseum** occupies a fourteenth-century monastery on Kornmarkt (Tues & Thurs–Sun 10am–5pm, Wed 10am–9pm; €3, free Wed 6–9pm). On the ground floor the displays follow a roughly chronological layout, beginning with Bronze Age items and moving onto medieval sculptures and carvings, outstanding among which are *The Seven Stations of the Cross* by Adam Kraft and works by Tilman Riemenschneider and Veit Stoss. German painting at its Renaissance peak dominates the first floor, with pieces by Dürer, Altdorfer, Baldung and Cranach. The following rooms focus on the diversity of Nürnberg's achievements during the Renaissance. The strong tradition of gold- and silversmithing is shown to best effect in the superb model of a three-masted ship, while the city's leading role in the fast-developing science of geography is exemplified by the first globe of the earth, made by Martin Behaim in 1491 – just before the discovery of America. This floor's south wing is entirely devoted to German folklore, and in particular to Catholic worship, notably weird votive offerings – look out for the wax toads offered for help with women's complaints.

THE ZEPPELIN FIELD AND MARS FIELD

In virtually everyone's mind, "Nuremberg" conjures up thoughts of **Nazi rallies** and **war-crime trials**. As the city council is eager to point out, the Nazis' choice of Nürnberg had less to do with local support of Nazi ideology, and more to do with what the medieval city represented in German history. The rallies were held on the **Zeppelin and Mars fields** in the suburb of Luitpoldhain (tram #9 or bus #36 from the centre). The tourist board has put together a multimedia presentation called **Fascination and Force** (mid-May to Oct Tues–Sun 10am–6pm; €1), which was set to move from the Zeppelintribune to Albert Speer's gargantuan Congress Hall in the summer of 2001. The "**Nürnberg Laws**" of 1935 deprived Jews of their citizenship and forbade relations between Jews and Gentiles. It was through these laws that the Nazis justified their extermination of six million Jews, 10,000 of whom came from Nürnberg. Only ten remained here after the war. It was highly significant that the war criminals of the Nazi regime were tried in the city that saw their proudest demonstrations of power.

Eating, drinking and nightlife

Nürnberg is the liveliest Bavarian city after Munich, with a wealth of Studentenkneipen and café-bars catering for the students. The cheapest **meals** in town are to be found in the university **Mensa**, in the northeastern corner of the Altstadt. Otherwise there are plenty of Imbiss-type snack-joints in the pedestrian zone between St Lorenz and the Ehekarussel. In the Altstadt, good places to eat include *Bratwurst-Häusle*, Rathausplatz 1, the most celebrated of the city's sausage restaurants, and the excellent and reasonable *Nassauer Keller*, Karolinerstr. 2, installed in an atmospheric thirteenth-century cellar. In *Spitalgasse*, Heilig-Geist-Spital serves hearty fare in the setting of a medieval hospital building. At Bergstr. 19 is *Schwarzer Bauer*, the **pub** of the Altstadthof's celebrated house brewery. Another place which brews its own beer is *Barfüsser*, which occupies the cavernous cellars of the Mauthalle at Hallplatz 2. For a combination of beer haven and music bar, make for *Starclub*, Maxtorgraben 33. Ruhestörung, Tetzelgasse 21, is one of the most fashionable **café-bars**. The tiny, excellent café-bar *Meisengeige*, Am Laufer Schlagturm 3, caters for a mixed crowd, and its small cinema shows an offbeat selection of films. The trendiest **nightclub** in Nürnberg is Mach 1, Kaiserstr. 1–9, with four different bars and some good lighting effects (Wed–Sun 9pm–4am). To find out what else is going on, get either the *Monatsmagazin* from the tourist office, or the *Plärrer* magazine from any kiosk.

Rothenburg ob der Tauber

The tourist itinerary known as the **Romantic Road**, which winds its way along the length of western Bavaria, runs through the most visited medieval town in Germany: **ROTHENBURG OB DER TAUBER**, 50km west of Nürnberg. It is connected by a branch railway with Steinach, on the Augsburg–Würzburg line – and there are scores of special buses ferrying tourists along the chain of half-timbered villages that comprise the Romantic Road.

It takes about an hour to walk around the fourteenth-century walls of Rothenburg, the ultimate museum piece. The promontory on the western side of town is the site of the **Burgtor** watchtower – the oldest of all the 24 towers – and the **Blasiuskapelle**, with murals from the fourteenth century. The nearby Herrngasse leads up to the town centre, and is the widest street in Rothenburg, once home to the local nobs. Also on this street is the severe early Gothic **Franziskanerkirche**, which houses a startlingly realistic altarpiece showing *The Stigmatization of St Francis*.

The sloping **Marktplatz** is dominated by the arcaded front of the Renaissance Rathaus, which supplanted the Gothic building that stands behind it. The sixty-metre tower of the **Gotisches Rathaus** (April–Oct daily 9.30am–12.30pm & 1–5pm; Nov–March Sat & Sun noon–3pm; €1) is the highest point in Rothenburg and provides the best view of the town and surrounding countryside. The other main attractions on the Marktplatz are the figures on each side of the three clocks of the **Ratsherrntrinkstube**, which seven times daily re-enact an episode that occurred during the Thirty Years' War. The fearsome Johann Tilly agreed that Rothenburg should be spared if one of the councillors could drain in one draught a tankard holding over three litres of wine. A former burgomaster duly sank the contents of the so-called Meistertrunk, then needed three days to sleep off the effects. On the opposite side of the Marktplatz is Rothenburg's largest building, the Gothic **St Jakob-Kirche** (Easter–Oct daily 9am–5.30pm; Nov–Easter daily 10am–noon & 2–4pm; €1.30), rising above the sea of red roofs like a great ship; the entrance fee is worth paying purely to see Tilman Riemenschneider's exquisite limewood *Holy Blood Altar*.

Of the local museums, the most fascinating is the **Kriminalmuseum** at Burggasse 3 (daily: April–Oct 9.30am–6pm; Nov, Jan & Feb 2–3.30pm; Dec & March 10am–3.30pm; €3), which contains collections attesting to medieval inhumanity in the shape of torture instruments and related objects such as the beer barrels that drunks were forced to walk around in. The **Reichstadtmuseum** on Klosterhof (daily: April–Oct 10am–5pm; Nov–March 1–4pm; €2.60) is most interesting for its original medieval workrooms.

There are many cheap **pensions** and **inns** in Rothenburg; worth trying are *Pöschel*, Wenggasse 22 (☎0 98 61/34 30; ③), *Raidel*, on the same street at no. 3 (☎0 98 61/31 15; ③), and *Hofmann*, Stollengasse 29 (☎0 98 61/33 71; ③). The two **hostels** – *Rossmühle* and its annexe *Spitalhof* (☎0 98 61/45 10; ②) – are in beautifully restored houses off the bottom of the Spitalgasse. Private **rooms** are the next cheapest option(②–③): details from the highly efficient **tourist office** on Marktplatz (May–Oct Mon–Fri 9am–12.30pm & 1–6pm, Sat & Sun 10am–3pm; Nov–April Mon Fri 9am 12.30pm & 1 5pm, Sat 10am–1pm; ☎0 98 61/4 04 92, *www.rothenburg.de*).

Würzburg

Terminus of the Romantic Road, **WÜRZBURG** straddles the River Main some 60km north of Rothenburg, and can be reached either by bus from there or by train from Nürnberg, Augsburg or Munich. During the night of March 16, 1945, it got the same treatment from Allied bombers that Nürnberg had received two months earlier. Würzburg has been less successful in rebuilding itself, but a number of outstanding sights and the town's location among a landscape of vineyards easily justify a visit.

Bracketed by the river and the Residenz, the old town is focused on the **Marktplatz**, where a daily food market ensures a lively bustle. Just off the square, the **Haus zum Falken** is the city's prize example of a Rococo townhouse, perfectly restored to the very last stucco curl. Overlooking the Markt is the Gothic **Marienkapelle**, which has an intriguing *Annunciation* above the northern portal: a band leads from God to Mary's ear, a baby sliding towards her along its folds.

Halfway down the Kürschnerhof, leading off the Marktplatz, the **Neumünster's** dusky pink facade stands out among the postwar houses. The church was built over the graves of saints Kilian, Kolonat and Totnan, Irish missionaries martyred in 689 for trying to Christianize the region. The Kiliani festival, at the beginning of July, is the region's most important religious event, drawing thousands of pilgrims to the crypt where the saints are buried. The **Dom**, again consecrated to St Kilian, is virtually next door; it was burned out in 1945, so only the exterior is true to the original Romanesque.

The **Residenz** (April to mid-Oct Mon–Wed & Fri–Sun 10am–6pm, Thurs 9am–8pm; mid-Oct to March daily 10am–4pm; €4.10) was intended to show that the Würzburg bishops could hold their own among such great European courts as Versailles. Construction was left largely in the hands of the prolific Balthasar Neumann, whose famed staircase is covered by the largest fresco in the world. An allegory extolling the fame of the prince-bishops in the most immodest way imaginable, it was painted by the greatest decorator of the age, Giambattista Tiepolo. The tour of the palace goes through the plain stuccoed Weisser Saal, before plunging into the opulence of the Kaisersaal; once reserved for the use of the emperor, it now provides a glamorous setting for the June Mozart Festival. The marble, the gold-leaf stucco and the sparkling chandeliers produce an effect of dazzling magnificence, but finest of all are more frescoes by Tiepolo. Tucked discreetly into the southwest corner of the palace in order not to spoil the symmetry, the Hofkirche is a brilliant early example of Neumann's illusionism – the interior, based on a series of ovals, appears much larger than it really is. Both side altars are by Tiepolo.

On the other side of the Dom, the twelfth-century **Alte Mainbrücke** – the oldest bridge over the Main – leads towards the Festung Marienberg; if you don't fancy the climb to the castle, you can take bus #9 from the bridge. This was home to the ruling bishops from the thirteenth century until 1750, when they shifted to the Residenz. The devastations of foreign armies – the Swedes, the Prussians, the Allies in the last war – have been so great that although much of the original structure has been restored, the interiors are largely missing. The medieval core contains the round Marienkirche, one of Germany's oldest churches, as well as the Brunnenhaus, whose 105-metre well was chiselled through the rock in around 1200. Surrounding this are a number of other buildings, including the Renaissance **Fürstenbau** (April to mid-Oct Tues–Sun 9am–6pm; mid-Oct to March Tues–Sun 10am–4pm; €2.60). The **Mainfränkisches Museum** (Tues–Sun 10am–4/5pm; €2.60 or €4.10 combined ticket with Fürstenbau) in the former arsenal contains sculptures by Riemenschneider and examples of all genres of art across the ages, as well as an interesting display on Franconian wine.

During work on the Residenz, Neumann also took time to build the **Käppele**, a pilgrimage church imperiously perched on the heights to the south of the Marienberg. Apart from the opportunity to see the interior, lavishly covered with frescoes and stucco, it's worth visiting for the view from the terrace – the finest in Würzburg.

Practicalities

The **train station** is at the northern end of the city centre, while the **tourist office** is in the Haus zum Falken (Mon–Fri 10am–6pm, Sat 10am–2pm; April–Oct also Sun 10am–2pm; ☎09 31/3 73 98, *www.wuerzburg.de*). There are two reasonably priced **pensions** between the station and the centre: *Siegel*, Reisgrubengasse 7 (☎09 31/5 29 41; ④), and *Spehnkuch*, Röntgenring 7 (☎09 31/5 47 52; ④). The **hostel**, Burkarderstr. 44 (☎09 31/4 25 90; ②; tram #3), is situated below the Marienberg. The nearest **campsite** is about 4km south in Heidingsfeld (bus #16 from Barbarossaplatz).

Best places for Franconian **food** are *Bürgerspital*, Theaterstr. 19, and *Juliusspital*, Juliuspromenade 19. *Zur Stadt Mainz*, Semmelstr. 39, though excellent, is the tourist spot in town, printing its menus in five languages as well as Braille. For student **bars** go to Sanderstrasse in the south of town – *Till Eulenspiegel*, at no. 1a, is particularly good and a couple of doors down, at no. 5, is an **Internet café**, *H@ackm@c*.

Bamberg

The people of **BAMBERG**, a city which lies 60km north of Nürnberg and 95km east of Würzburg, knock back more beer per person than in any other town in the country: ten breweries produce thirty different kinds of ale, most notably the distinctive smoky **Rauchbier**. Bamberg's isolation has preserved it from the ravages of war, and today it is one of the most beautiful small towns in the world, where most European styles from the Romanesque onwards have left a mark.

Heart of the lower town is the **Maxplatz**, dominated by Balthasar Neumann's **Neues Rathaus**. A daily market is held here and on the adjoining Grüner Markt, which stands in the shadow of the huge Jesuit church of St Martin. On an islet anchoring the Obere Brücke to the Untere Brücke is the **Altes Rathaus**, almost too picturesque for its own good. Except for the half-timbered section overhanging the rapids, the original Gothic building was transformed into Rococo, and its walls are tattooed with exuberant frescoes. The famous **Klein-Venedig** (Little Venice) of medieval fishermen's houses is best seen from the Untere Brücke.

Uphill, the spacious, sloping **Domplatz** is lined with such a superb variety of buildings that it has no rival as Germany's finest square. The **Kaiserdom** was consecrated in 1012, but the present structure of golden sandstone is the result of a slow rebuilding that continued throughout the thirteenth century. The astonishing array of sculpture was initially executed in orthodox Romanesque style, best seen in the Fürstenportal on the north side of the nave, where figures of the Apostles are carved below a *Last Judgment*. The most famous sculpture is inside – the enigmatic **Bamberg Rider**, one of the first equestrian statues to be made since Classical antiquity. Focus of the nave is the white limestone tomb of the canonized imperial couple Heinrich II and Kunigunde; Tilman Riemenschneider laboured away for fourteen years on this sarcophagus, whose reliefs depict scenes taken from the life and times of the couple. The south transept contains a contemporaneous masterpiece, the *Nativity Altar* by Veit Stoss, made when the artist was about eighty years old.

The **Diocesan Museum** (Tues–Sun 10am–5pm; €2), entered from the square, houses some fascinating ecclesiastical vestments, notably the robes worn by Heinrich II and Kunigunde. Also here are statues of the ubiquitous emperor and his wife, in the company of the Dom's two patrons plus an erotic Adam and Eve.

Opposite the cathedral, the Ratstube is a Renaissance gem, now containing the **Historical Museum** (March–Oct Tues–Sun 9am–5pm; €2), which covers local history from the Stone Age to the twentieth century, as well as Bamberg's rich art history. Adjoining it is the **Reiche Tor**, where Heinrich and Kunigunde appear once more, leading into the huge courtyard of the Alte Hofhaltung, the former episcopal palace. Across the street is the building which supplanted it, the huge Baroque **Neue Residenz** (tours April–Sept Mon–Wed & Fri–Sun 9am–6pm, Thurs 9am–8pm; Oct–March daily 10am–4pm; €3). Inside are richly decorated state rooms, and the Staatsgalerie Bamberg, with medieval and Baroque paintings by German masters.

From the rose garden behind the Neue Residenz is a view of Michaelsburg, crowned by a huge **Abtei**. Much of the Romanesque shell of the church remains, but the interior is an awesome hotchpotch: lavish Rococo furnishings, tombs of Bamberg bishops and a ceiling depicting over 600 medicinal herbs. The cellars house the **Fränkisches Brauereimuseum** (April–Oct Thurs–Sun 1–4pm; €1.50) – even if you're not interested in beer, it's worth coming for the wonderful panorama of Bamberg's skyline and surrounding hills.

Another place for a great view is the path up to the **Altenburg**, a ruined castle at the end of the very steep Altenburger Strasse. En route, up Untere Kaulberg and past Karmelitenplatz, you'll find the **Karmelitenkloster**. The church is again Baroque, but the Romanesque cloister (daily 8–11am & 2.30–5.30pm; free), the largest in Germany, has been preserved.

Practicalities

The **train station** is fifteen minutes' walk northeast of the centre. The **tourist office** (Mon–Fri 9am–6pm, Sat 9am–3pm; May–Sept also Sun 10am–2pm; ☎09 51/87 11 61, *www.tourismus.bamberg.de*) is at Geyerswörthstr. 3. Among several inexpensive **hotels** are *Bamberger Weissbierhaus*, Obere Königstr 38 (☎09 51/2 55 03; ③), and *Zum Alten Goldenen Anker*, Untere Sandstr. 73 (☎09 51/6 65 05; ③). The hostel is 2km south of the centre at Oberer Leinritt 70 (☎09 51/5 60 02; ②), reached by buses #1, #7, #11 from the train station to ZOB Promenade, then bus #18 to Regnitzufer. The local **campsite** is another 2km downriver – also reached by bus #18.

Two **restaurants** worth trying are *Schlenkerla*, Dominikanerstr. 6, which is famous for its Rauchbier, and *Kaiserdom-Stuben*, Urbanstr. 18, which is good for vegetarian dishes. Three of the best **cafés** are *Am Dom*, Ringleinsgasse 2, *Michaelsberg*, Michaelsberg 10e, and the summer *Rosengarten* in the Neue Residenz. Good places to try the local **beers** are four beer cellar-cum-gardens: *Spezial*, on Obere Stephansberg 47; *Greiffenklau*, Laurenziplatz 20; *Keesmann*, Wunderburg 5; and *Mahr's-Bräu*, Oberer Stephansberg 36.

BERLIN

BERLIN is something of a weather-vane of modern European history, yet its rise to national prominence was a long and slow process. For five centuries, its fortunes were intimately tied to the fortunes of the hugely ambitious Hohenzollern dynasty, serving as capital of their ever-expanding state, which was successively known as Brandenburg, then Brandenburg-Prussia, and finally as the Kingdom of Prussia. As Prussia played the vanguard role in the belated achievement of national unity in 1871, Berlin duly became Imperial Germany's capital. It maintained that role in the Weimar Republic after World War I, and during the Nazis' Third Reich. Following defeat in World War II, however, the city was partitioned among the victorious Allies, and served as the frontline of the Cold War. In 1961, its division into two hostile sectors was given a very visible expression by the construction of the Berlin Wall, the most hated frontier the world has ever known.

After the Wall fell in 1989, Berlin's status as capital of Germany (which it had never officially lost, despite the relocation of the West German government to Bonn) was confirmed. However, although it narrowly won the bitter fight to become the main governmental seat, Bonn has been left with an important secondary role. This is a calculated measure designed to ensure that Berlin – with its deeply tainted historical record – does not become too powerful or dominant within Germany. Thus the vast rebuilding and re-development that the city is currently undergoing is something of a delicate balance. There is a clear need to increase the population (which had fallen by more than a million from its prewar level), and to create a city that is a worthy capital of Europe's most powerful nation, yet at the same time to ensure that it does not become a direct German counterpart of London or Paris.

The speed of change in the past few years has been astounding. Much of the new Berlin is already in place: parliament sits in the renovated Reichstag; Potsdamer Platz, formerly a field in the Wall's death strip, is now a bustling entertainment quarter; and some of the city's world-class museum collections have been put back together again. However, the transformation of the city will go on for another decade at least, ensuring that it will continue to be an exciting place to visit.

Arrival and information

Most flights to Berlin arrive at Tegel **airport**, from where frequent #X9 express or local #109 buses (€2.15) run to Zoo Station (Bahnhof Zoologischer Garten), central point for the western side of the city. The JetExpressBus TXL provides connection to Unter den Linden and the east, though tickets are more expensive (€5). Taxis are considerably faster and cost €15–20 to either destination. Most international coaches stop at the bus station near the Funkturm, linked to the centre by #149 buses or U-Bahn from Kaiserdamm.

Berlin's **tourist office** is in the Europa Center at Budapester Str. 45 (Mon–Sat 8.30am–8.30pm, Sun 10am–6.30pm; ☎0 30/25 00 25, *www.berlin-tourism.de*), with an additional office in the Brandenburg Gate (daily 9.30am–6pm) and smaller "Info Points" at Tegel Airport and the KaDeWe department store, Tauentzienstr. 21–24. Berlin has two **listings magazines**, *Zitty* (*www.zitty.de*; €2.20), *Tip* (*www.tip-berlin.de*; €2.40) published on alternate weeks, or alternatively, try the **Web sites** *www.berlin.de*, *www.berlinfo.com* and *www.globopolis.com*. Details of the city's state-owned museums and galleries can be found on *www.smb.spk-berlin.de*.

City transport

The **U-Bahn** (*www.bvg.de*) underground system is efficient and extensive; trains run from 4am to approximately 12.30am, an hour later on Friday and Saturday. The **S-Bahn** (*www.s-bahn-berlin.de*), whose stops are further apart, travels to the outer suburbs (such as Wannsee) and out of the city boundaries (to Potsdam, for instance). The city **bus network** – and the **tram system** in eastern Berlin – covers most of the gaps left by the U-Bahn: night buses run at intervals of around twenty minutes, although the routes often differ from daytime ones; agents in the U-Bahn stations can usually provide a map. **Tickets** can be bought from machines at U-Bahn station entrances, on trams, or from bus drivers; good for any mode of transport, they cost €2.15, allow you to travel in two of the three tariff zones, and are valid for two hours. Longer trips, from central Berlin to Potsdam for example, cost €2.40. An Einzelfahrschein Kurzstreckentarif, or short-trip ticket, costs €1.30 and allows you to travel up to three train or six bus stops. A day ticket (Tageskarte) is €6.15 for two tariff zones, €6.35 for all three. You can also buy a weekly ticket (7-Tage-Karte) for €22.50 (2 zones) or €28.15 (3 zones). There are on-the-spot fines of €30.70 for those without a valid ticket or pass.

Taxis are plentiful and can be hailed from the street or picked up at the taxi stands at major intersections, by U-Bahn stations, or in front of the larger hotels.

Accommodation

Accommodation in Berlin in high season can be very hard to find, and if booking your own place in the western part it's best to call at least a couple of weeks in advance. If you turn up with nothing arranged, head for the tourist office in the Europa Center as it offers a free hotel-**booking service**; most of the accommodation listed can be booked on their Web site. If you're planning on a longer stay, the best way to find a place is through one of the **Mitwohnzentrale** organizations, which can find a room, usually for a minimum of seven nights. Try the Home Company at Joachimstaler Str. 17 (Mon–Fri 9am–6pm, Sat 11am–2pm; ☎0 30/1 94 45, *www.homecompany.de*), an easy walk from the Zoo Station.

Hostels

The Circus, Rosa-Luxemburg-Str. 39–41 (☎0 30/28 39 14 33, *www.circus-berlin.de*). Rosa Luxemburg Platz U-Bahn. Internet access, breakfast service and near the action in the east. No curfew. ②.

Jugendherberge JGH Berlin, Kluckstr. 3 (☎0 30/2 61 10 98, *www.hostel.de*). Bus #129 to "Gedenkstätte Deutscher Widerstand". HI option in quiet location between the two city centres. No night curfew. ③.

Jugendgästehaus am Zoo, Hardenbergstr. 9a (☎0 30/3 12 94 10). Zoologischer Garten U- and S-Bahn. Excellent location in the western side of the city, extremely popular. No curfew. ③.

Mitte's Backpacker Hostel, Chausseestr. 102 (☎0 30/28 39 09 65, *www.backpacker.de*). Zinnowitzer Str. U-Bahn. A great location on the eastern side of the city in a renovated factory building. No curfew or lockout. ③.

Hotels

Acksel Haus, Belforter Str. 21 (☎0 30/44 33 76 33). Small and intimate hotel in the midst of the lively Prenzlauer Berg scene. ④.

Alpenland, Carmerstr. 8 (☎0 30/3 12 39 70). Well-situated and an excellent choice at this price. ⑤.

Altberlin am Potsdamer Platz, Potsdamer Str. 67 (☎0 30/2 61 29 99). Large pension just a few minutes' walk from the Tiergarten museums, recently refurbished with turn-of-the-century trappings. ⑥.

Artemisia, Brandenburgischestr. 18 (☎0 30/8 73 89 05). One of the city's women-only hotels. ⑦.

Artist Hotelpension Die Loge, Friedrichstr. 115 (☎0 30/2 80 75 13). Tiny hotel with flair. ④.

Bogota, Schlüterstr. 45 (☎0 30/8 81 50 01). Pleasant luxury at sensible prices. ⑤.

Bregenz, Bregenzer Str. 5 (☎0 30/8 81 43 07). A small family-run set-up only a 10-minute walk from the Ku'damm. Children are welcome. ⑥.

Charlot, Giesebrechtstr. 17 (☎0 30/3 27 96 60). Neatly restored, efficiently run hotel near Adenauerplatz. Excellent value for money. ⑤.

Hansablick, Flotowstr. 6 (☎0 30/3 90 48 00). A quiet location, on the far side of the Tiergarten, yet close to the city's western hub. ⑥.

Merkur, Torstr. 156 (☎0 30/2 82 82 97). Comfortable rooms within easy walking distance of city-centre attractions and local nightlife. Most rooms have showers. ④.

Unter den Linden, Unter den Linden 14 (☎030/23 81 10). Vintage East German hotel, now somewhat shopworn, located at the historic intersection of Unter den Linden and Friedrichstrasse. ⑥.

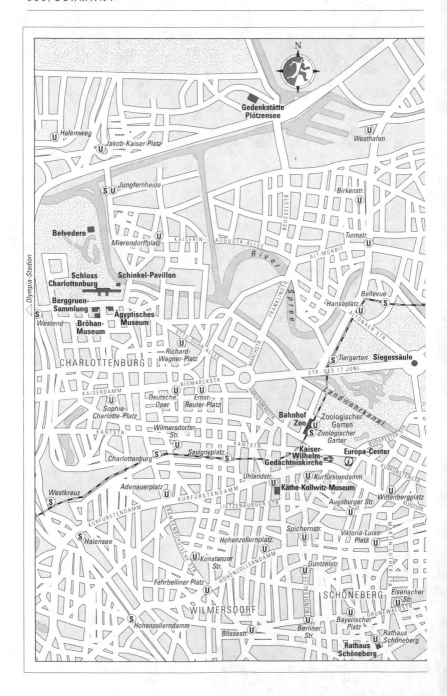

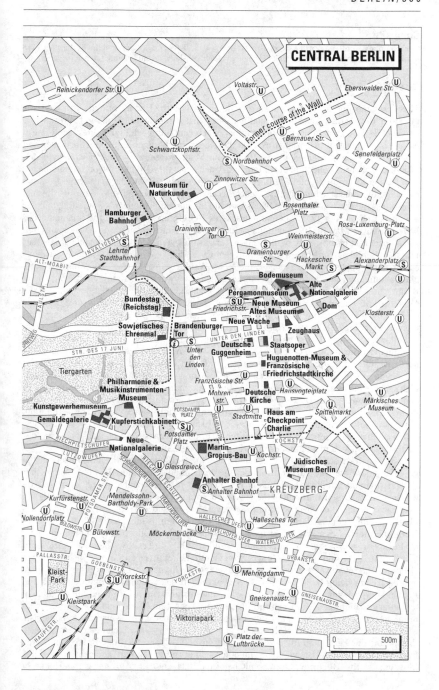

CENTRAL BERLIN

Reinickendorfer Str. Ⓤ

Voltastr. Ⓤ

Eberswalder Str. Ⓤ

Former course of the Wall

Schwartzkopffstr. Ⓤ

Bernauer Str.

Senefelderplatz Ⓤ

Ⓢ Nordbahnhof

Zinnowitzer Str. Ⓤ

Museum für Naturkunde

Rosenthaler Platz Ⓤ

Rosa-Luxemburg-Platz Ⓤ

Hamburger Bahnhof

Oranienburger Tor Ⓤ

Weinmeisterstr. Ⓤ

INVALIDENSTR.

Ⓢ Lehrter Stadtbahnhof

Oranienburger Str.

Hackescher Markt Ⓢ

Alexanderplatz Ⓢ

ALT-MOABIT

Ⓤ

PAULSTR

Bodemuseum

Pergamonmuseum

Alte Nationalgalerie

SPREEWEG

Bundestag (Reichstag)

Ⓢ Ⓤ **Neue Museum**

Friedrichstr. **Altes Museum**

Dom

Klosterstr. Ⓤ

Sowjetisches Ehrenmal

Brandenburger Tor

Neue Wache

Zeughaus

STR. DES 17 JUNI

ⓘ Ⓢ

UNTER DEN LINDEN

Deutsche Guggenheim

Staatsoper

Tiergarten

Unter den Linden

Huguenotten-Museum & Französische Friedrichstadtkirche

Philharmonie & Musikinstrumenten-Museum

Französische Str. Ⓤ

Mohrenstr. Ⓤ

Deutsche Kirche

Hausvogteiplatz Ⓤ

Märkisches Museum

Kunstgewerbemuseum

POTSDAMER PLATZ

Stadtmitte Ⓤ

Haus am Checkpoint Charlie

Spittelmarkt Ⓤ

Gemäldegalerie

Kupferstichkabinett

Ⓢ Ⓤ

WILHELMSTR.

RIEGPIETSCHUFER

Potsdamer Platz

KOCHSTR.

LÜTZOWUFER

Neue Nationalgalerie

Martin-Gropius-Bau

Ⓤ Kochstr.

Jüdisches Museum Berlin

SCHÖNEBERGER STR

SCHÖNEBERGER UFER

Gleisdreieck

POTSDAMER STR

TEMPELHOFER UFER

Anhalter Bahnhof

KREUZBERG

Kurfürstenstr. Ⓤ

Mendelssohn-Bartholdy-Park Ⓤ

Ⓢ Anhalter Bahnhof

Vollendorfplatz Ⓤ

HALLESCHES UFER

Hallesches Tor Ⓤ

BÜLOWSTR

Bülowstr. Ⓤ

Möckernbrücke Ⓤ

TEMPELHOFER UFER

WATERLOOUFER

PALLASSTR.

URBANSTR.

Kleist-Park

GOEBENSTR

Ⓢ Ⓤ Yorckstr.

Mehringdamm Ⓤ

Ⓤ Kleistpark

YORCKSTR.

Gneisenaustr. Ⓤ

GNEISENAUSTR

HAUPTSTR.

Viktoriapark

Platz der Luftbrücke Ⓤ

0   500m

Campsite

Campingplatz Kohlhasenbrück, Neue Kreiss Str. 36 (☎0 30/8 05 17 37). Closest of the Berlin sites. #118 bus in the direction of Drewitz. Facilities include a restaurant, showers and laundry room.

Eastern Berlin

The most atmospheric approach to eastern Berlin starts at the **Brandenburg Gate** and leads up **Unter den Linden**, a stately broad boulevard that is rapidly reassuming its prewar role as one of Berlin's most important thoroughfares. A recent fitting addition to the avenue, located just to the east of Friedrichstrasse, is the **Deutsche Guggenheim Berlin**, Unter den Linden 13–15 (daily 11am–8pm; €4.10, free on Mon; *www.deutsche-guggenheim-berlin.de*), which, as well as its collection of contemporary art, hosts three to four major exhibitions per year. Lining the wide promenade beyond are a host of historic buildings restored from the rubble of the war, starting with the Neoclassical Humboldt University, followed by the Alte Bibliothek, the flawless Deutsche Staatsoper and the domed St Hedwig's Cathedral, built for the city's Catholics in 1747. The cathedral faces **Bebelplatz**, the site of the infamous Nazi bookburning of May 10, 1933; an unusual memorial – an underground room visible through a glass panel set in the centre of the square – marks the event. More than anyone, it was Karl Friedrich Schinkel who shaped nineteenth-century Berlin. One of his most famous creations can be found opposite the Staatsoper: the **Neue Wache**, a former royal guardhouse resembling a Roman temple and now a memorial to victims of war and tyranny. Next door, one of Berlin's finest Baroque buildings, the old Prussian Zeughaus or Arsenal, is home to the **Museum of German History** (10am–6pm; closed Wed; free; *www.dhm.de*), currently closed for renovations until autumn 2002; until then, temporary exhibitions on historical themes are being held in the Kronprinzenpalais across the road.

Following Charlottenstrasse south from Unter den Linden leads to the **Gendarmenmarkt**, much of whose appeal is derived from the **Französische Kirche** on the northern side of the square. Built as a church for Berlin's influential Huguenot community at the beginning of the eighteenth century, it also now houses the **Hugenottenmuseum** (Tues–Sat noon–5pm, Sun 11am–5pm; €1.60), documenting their way of life. At the southern end of the square, the **Deutsche Kirche** was built around the same time for the city's Reformed community. It houses an engrossing though wordy historical exhibition, "Questions of German History" (Tues–Sun 10am–6pm; free). Schinkel's Neoclassical Schauspielhaus sits between the two churches. Friedrichstrasse, a high-class shopping district with an eclectic mix of modernist architecture, lies a block west of here.

At the eastern end of Unter den Linden lies the **Schlossplatz**, the former site of the imperial palace and the current home of the abandoned Palast der Republik, the former GDR parliament building. It stands at the midpoint of a city-centre island whose northwestern part, **Museumsinsel**, is the location of some of the best of Berlin's museums. An extensive reconstruction programme, however, has closed several of them: the Neues Museum will remain dark until 2008 and the Bodemuseum until 2004. The **Alte Nationalgalerie** (*www.smb.spk-berlin.de*), housing the city's collection of nineteenth-century European art, is set to reopen in December 2001. Currently, the **Altes Museum** (Tues–Sun 10am–6pm; €4, free first Sun on month; ticket gives admission on same day to all Berlin's state-owned museums; *www.smb.spk-berlin.de*), arguably Schinkel's most impressive surviving building, displays part of the city's excellent collection of Greek and Roman antiquities on the ground floor, while the upstairs rooms are used for all kinds of temporary exhibitions. The **Pergamonmuseum** (Tues–Sun 10am–6pm; €4, free first Sun of month; *www.smb.spk-berlin.de*) houses the treasure trove of the German archeologists who plundered the ancient world in the nineteenth century, and includes two must-sees: the spectacular Pergamon Altar, which dates from 160 BC, and the huge Processional Way from sixth-century BC Babylon. On the other side of the Pergamon, adjacent to the Altes Museum, is the **Berliner Dom**, built between 1894 and 1905 to serve the House of

Hohenzollern as a family church; its vault houses ninety sarcophagi containing the remains of various members of the line.

To reach **Alexanderplatz**, the commercial hub of eastern Berlin, head along Karl-Liebknecht-Strasse past the Neptunbrunnen fountain and the thirteenth-century Marienkirche, Berlin's oldest parish church. Like every other building in the vicinity, the church is overshadowed by the gigantic **Fernsehturm** or TV tower (March–Oct daily 9am–1am; Nov–Feb 10am–midnight; €6.15; *www.berlinerfernsehturm.de*), whose observation platform offers unbeatable views of the whole city on rare clear days. Southwest of here lies the **Nikolaiviertel**, a modern development that attempts to recreate the winding streets and small houses of this part of old prewar Berlin, which was razed overnight on June 16, 1944. At the centre of it all is the **Nikolaikirche** (Tues–Sun 10am–6pm; variable charge for temporary exhibitions), a rebuilt thirteenth-century structure that is Berlin's oldest parish church. Not far away on Mühlendamm is the rebuilt Rococo **Ephraim-Palais** (same times; €2), housing a collection of Berlin art from the reign of Frederick the Great to 1945.

Western Berlin

Zoo Station is at the centre of the city's western side: a short walk south and you're at the eastern end of the Kurfürstendamm or **Ku'damm**, a 3.5-kilometre strip of ritzy shops, cinemas, bars and cafés. The great landmark here is the **Kaiser-Wilhelm-Gedächtniskirche**, destroyed by British bombing in November 1943, and left as a reminder of the horrors of war. There's little to do on the Ku'damm other than spend money, and there's only one cultural attraction nearby, the **Käthe-Kollwitz-Museum** at Fasanenstr. 24 (11am–6pm; closed Tues; €4; *www.kaethe-kollwitz.de*), devoted to the drawings and prints of the left-wing and pacifist artist Käthe Kollwitz.

The **Zoologischer Garten** itself (daily 9am–sunset; €7.70; *www.zoo-berlin.de*) forms the beginning of the Tiergarten, a restful expanse of woodland and a good place to wander along the banks of the Landwehrkanal. At the centre of Strasse des 17 Juni, the broad avenue that cuts through the Tiergarten, rises the **Siegessäule** (daily 9.30am–5.30/6.30pm; €1), a victory column celebrating Prussia's military successes; its summit offers a good view of the surrounding area, but you'll have to climb 585 steps to get there. Strasse des 17 Juni comes to an end at the **Brandenburg Gate**, built as a city gate-cum-triumphal arch in 1791. A little way north stands the **Reichstag**, the nineteenth-century home of the German parliament – it was remodelled by Norman Foster for the resumption of its historic role in April 1999. Foster's glass cupola has become an instant landmark, and a trip to the top (daily 8am–10pm; free) affords a stunning view of the city. Immediately behind the Reichstag, it's now only just possible to make out the course of the **Berlin Wall**, which divided the city for 28 years until November 9, 1989.

The heart of prewar Berlin used to be to the south of the Brandenburg Gate, its core formed by **Potsdamer Platz**. A huge commercial project here, involving various eateries, theatres and a shopping mall, attempts to recreate the area's former liveliness but apart from the impressive tent-like Sony Center on the northern side, there is little that's original. Just to the east, near the corner of Wilhelmstrasse and An der Kolonnade, lies the site of **Hitler's bunker**, where the Führer spent his last days, issuing meaningless orders as the Battle of Berlin raged above.

West of Potsdamer Platz lies the Kulturforum, a series of museums centred on the unmissable **Gemäldegalerie**, Matthäikirchplatz 8 (Tues–Sun 10am–6pm; €4, free first Sun of month; *www.smb.spk-berlin.de*). In it the world-class collection of old masters, covering all the main European schools, ranges from the Middle Ages to the late eighteenth century. Highlights of the German section include Cranach's tongue-in-cheek *The Fountain of Youth* and Holbein's *The Danzig Merchant Georg Gisze*, celebrated for its virtuoso still-life background. The interconnected building to the north houses the **Kunstgewerbemuseum** (same times; €2 if visited separately, free first Sun of month; *www.smb.spk-berlin.de*), a sparkling collection of European arts and crafts from Byzantium to Bauhaus. Opposite are the Philharmonie, the home of the Berlin Philharmonic, and the **Musikinstrumenten-Museum** (Tues–Fri 9am–5pm, Sat & Sun 10am–5pm; €2), a collection of weird and wonderful musical instruments. At Potsdamer Str. 50, a couple of minutes' walk to the south, is the **Neue Nationalgalerie** (Tues–Fri 10am–6pm, Sat & Sun 11am–6pm; €4, free first Sun of month; *www.smb.spk-berlin.de*), which has a good collection of twentieth century German paintings, best of which are the Berlin portraits and cityscapes by George Grosz and Otto Dix.

Southeast of here, the **Martin-Gropius-Bau** at Niederkirchner Str. 7 (Tues–Sun 10am–8pm; admission varies) is now a venue for prestigious temporary art exhibitions. Next door an open-air exhibition, **The Topography of Terror** (daily 10am–6/8pm; free; *www.topographie.de*), occupies the former site of Gestapo and SS headquarters and documents their history. From here it's a ten-minute walk down Wilhelmstrasse and Kochstrasse to the site of the notorious Checkpoint Charlie; evidence of the trauma the Wall caused is still on hand in the **Haus am Checkpoint Charlie** at Friedrichstr. 44 (daily 9am–10pm; €6.15; *www.mauer-museum.com*), which tells the history of the Wall and the stories of those who tried to break through.

The checkpoint area marks the northern limit of **Kreuzberg**, famed for its large immigrant community, its self-styled "alternative" inhabitants and nightlife. Daniel Libeskind's striking new **Jewish Museum Berlin** (*www.jmberlin.de*), documenting the culture, achievements, and tragic history of Berlin's Jewish community, is finally due to open, after several postponements, in late 2001. Southwest is the slightly more upscale Schöneberg district, where the most famous attraction is the **Rathaus Schöneberg** on Martin-Luther-Strasse, where, in 1963, John F. Kennedy made his celebrated "Ich bin ein Berliner" speech.

Way over to the northwest of the Tiergarten stretches the district of **Charlottenburg**, its most significant target being the sumptuously restored **Schloss Charlottenburg** (Tues–Fri 10am–6pm, Sat & Sun 11am–6pm; inclusive ticket €8.20; *www.spsg.de*). Commissioned by the future Queen Sophie Charlotte in 1695, it was added to throughout the eighteenth and early nineteenth centuries. The inclusive ticket includes a guided tour of the main state apartments, self-guided visits to the private chambers (where the Prussian crown jewels can be seen), the Knobelsdorff-Flügel with its wonderful array of paintings by Watteau and other eighteenth-century French artists, and the Belvedere and Mausoleum in the park. Just to the south, at Schloss-Str. 70, is the **Ägyptisches Museum** (same times; €4; free first Sun of month; *www.smb.spk-berlin.de*), a fabulous collection of Egyptian antiquities; the famous bust of Nefertiti can be seen on the first floor. Also worth visiting is the **Berggruen Collection: Picasso and His Era** (same times; €4, free first Sun of month; *www.smb.spk-berlin.de*) directly opposite, which houses some seventy paintings of the Spanish artist.

The southwestern suburb of Dahlem, reached by U-Bahn line #1 to Dahlem-Dorf, is home to the **Dahlem Museums** (Tues–Fri 10am–6pm, Sat–Sun 11am–6pm; €4, free first Sun of month; *www.smb.spk-berlin.de*). Since the Gemäldegalerie moved to the Tiergarten, the Dahlem complex is no longer the must-see it once was, but it still impresses. Check out the rich and imaginatively laid out Museum of Ethnology, featuring treasures from Asia, the Pacific and South Sea Islands. The collections of the Museums for East Asian and Indian Art (the latter featuring a spectacular group of Buddhist cave paintings from the Silk Road) are also worth a visit.

West of Charlottenburg, U-Bahn line #2 runs to the Olympia Stadion station; a fifteen-minute, signposted walk brings you to the vast **Olympic Stadium** itself (daily 8am–sunset; €1), one of the few Nazi buildings left intact in the city.

For a break from the city pressure, you could take a trip to the **Grunewald** forest and beaches on the **Havel** lakes. To get to the beach, take S-Bahn #1 or #7 to Nikolassee station, from where it's a ten-minute walk to **Strandbad Wannsee** (April–Sept daily 10am–7pm; €3; *www.sensjs.berlin.de*), a 1km-long strip of pale sand that's the largest inland beach in Europe.

Eating, drinking and nightlife

The range and quality of **restaurants** in Berlin is unmatched in any other German city, and there's a wealth of **bars**, from Bavarian-style beer halls to sleek cocktail lounges. Cheapest way of warding off hunger is to use the **Imbiss** snack stands, or one of the **Mensas**, officially for German students but usually open to anyone who looks the part. Eating out in a restaurant won't break the bank, though, with prices for a main course usually between €6 and €16.

The **nightlife** in Berlin is worthy of any European capital. In Eastern Berlin there's a fast-developing scene: around Oranienburger Strasse, Rosenthaler Strasse, and Gipsstrasse in the Mitte neighbourhood are dozens of new bars and clubs that attract a young professional crowd as well as tourists, while further north, the streets around Käthe-Kollwitz-Platz and the Wasserturm in Prenzlauer Berg are a bit more "alternative" (to get there take the U-Bahn from Alexanderplatz to either Eberswalder Strasse or Schönhauser Allee). Western Berlin has four focal points for drinking: Savignyplatz is for conspicuous good-timers; Kreuzberg drinkers include political activists and punks; the area around Nollendorfplatz (northwestern Schönberg) and Winterfeldtplatz is the territory of sped-out all-nighters and the pushing-on-forty crew; central Schöneberg bars are on the whole more mixed and more relaxed. Unless you're into drunken businessmen, avoid the Ku'damm and the rip-off joints around the Europa Center. Berlin is very much a city that wakes up when others are going to sleep – don't bother turning up before midnight for the all-night clubs in Kreuzberg and Schöneberg. For more sedate nightlife there are a number of theatres and one of Europe's great orchestras. To find out what's on, buy one of the listings magazines *Tip*, *Zitty* or *Prinz*, get the Berlin *Programm* leaflet, or look for the flyposters about town.

Snacks

Al Rai, Grosse Hamburger Str. 20/21, Mitte. A spacious, informal place where you can linger long over your tea. It offers Arab specialities such as couscous and shish kebab.

Brooklyn, Oranienstr. 176, Kreuzberg. Wonderful, inexpensive American-style hero sandwiches, cheese-cake and brownies.

Soup Kultur, Kurfürstendamm 224. A closet-sized place that offers a selection of ten often exotic and always delicious soups. Mon–Fri noon–8pm, Sat noon–4pm.

Restaurants

Aroma, Hochkirchstr. 8 (☎0 30/7 82 58 21). Well above average, inexpensive Italian. One of the best places to eat in east Schöneberg; it's advisable to book after 8pm.

Astor, Oranienburger Str. 84. A snug and casual restaurant serving great fish and chips, passable sandwiches and other light meals.

Austria, Bergmannstr. 30. Delicious Austrian classics in a warm, woody atmosphere.

Carib, Motzstr. 30. Classical Caribbean cuisine, friendly service, lethal rum cocktails.

Chamisso, Willibald-Alexis-Str. 25. An intimate Italian restaurant with a reasonably priced menu; situated in a beautiful neighbourhood of restored prewar buildings.

Cour Carrée, Savignyplatz 5. Deservedly popular French restaurant with fin-de-siècle decor and garden seating.

Dachgarten, on the roof of the Reichstag, Platz der Republik (☎0 30/22 62 99 33). Fanciful German and continental nouvelle cuisine, not cheap, but in an unbeatable location. Booking recommended.

Gugelhof, Kollwitzstr. 59. Stylish and popular Alsatian restaurant in the trendy Kollwitzplatz neighbourhood.

Hardtke, Meinekestr. 27. Typical old-Berlin pub and restaurant with inexpensive German dishes such as Eisbein (boiled pork knuckle).

Henne, Leuschnerdamm 25 (☎0 30/6 14 77 30). Pub-style restaurant with the best oven-fried chicken in Berlin. Reservation advisable.

Historisches Weinstuben, Poststr. 23. Old-fashioned, but reasonably priced German restaurant in the basement of the historic Knoblauchhaus.

Kellerrestaurant im Brecht-Haus, Chausseestr. 125 (☎0 30/28 28 43). A cellar restaurant decorated with Brecht memorabilia in the basement of Brecht's old house. Viennese specialities supposedly dreamt up by Brecht's wife, Helen Weigel, make this a very popular place. Worth booking.

Maothai, Wörther Str. 30. Despite being rather pricey, this Thai place is a welcome addition to the Prenzlauer Berg restaurant scene. Great food and service.

Merhaba, Hasenheide 39. Highly rated Turkish restaurant that's usually packed with locals. A selection of the starters here can be more interesting than a main course.

Osteria No.1, Kreuzbergstr. 71 (☎030/786 9162). Excellent and imaginative Italian food made from organic ingredients and reasonably priced. Booking recommended.

Pasternak, Knaackstr. 24. Intimate Russian restaurant in the thick of the bustling scene in Prenzlauer Berg.

Publique, Yorckstr. 62 (☎030/786 9469). Friendly café-cum-restaurant serving superb food till 2am.

Restaurant am Wasserturm, Knaackstr. 22. Favourite old Eastern European Jewish dishes and surprises from Jewish cuisines of other regions.

Restauration 1900, Husemannstr. 1. An institution even before reunification. Excellent if unsurprising German food.

Schwarzenraben, Neue Schönhauser Str. 13. A bit pricey, but excellent Italian food in an enchanting, early twentieth-century interior. Plus a great cocktail bar in the basement.

Tuk-Tuk, Grossgörschenstr. 2 (☎030/781 1588). Amiable Indonesian near Kleistpark U-Bahn. Enquire about the heat of your dish before ordering. Booking advisable.

Vietnam, Suarezstr. 61. One of the city's most popular Vietnamese restaurants, quietly situated in a street of junk shops.

Bars and cafés

808 Bar & Lounge, Oranienburger Str. 42/43. Extremely hip cocktail lounge with upscale appointments and customers.

Akba Lounge, Sredzkistr. 64. Large bar with a healthy selection of cocktails and music – including house, funk, and soul – from 11pm.

Anderes Ufer, Hauptstr. 157. A casual gay café that's something of an institution in the city.

Bar am Lützowplatz, Lützowplatz 7. The longest bar in the city. A dangerously great place.

Begine, Potsdamer Str. 139. Stylishly decorated women-only bar-bistro/gallery with limited choice of inexpensive food.

Café Adler, Friedrichstr. 206. Small café next to the site of the Checkpoint Charlie border crossing. Moderately priced breakfasts and meals.

Café am Neuen See, Lichtensteinallee 2. A small café in winter, a huge, green and splendid beer garden in summer, in the middle of the Tiergarten park.

Café Einstein, Kurfürstenstr. 58. Housed in a seemingly ancient mansion, this is about as close as you'll get to the ambience of the prewar Berlin Kaffeehaus, with international newspapers and breakfast served daily till 2pm. Occasional live music plus a good garden. Expensive.

Café M, Goltzstr. 34. Berlin's favoured rendezvous for creative types and the conventionally unconventional. Usually packed, even for breakfast.

Obst & Gemuse, Oranienburger Str. 48. One of the anchors of the area's active nightlife; packed after 10pm.

Pinguin Club, Wartburgstr. 54. Tiny and cheerful Schöneberg bar with 1950–60s America supplying its theme and background music.

The Pips, Auguststr. 84. Very popular bar and dance club of bright colours and designer furnishings.

Schwarzes Café, Kantstr. 148. Kantstrasse's best hangout for the young and chic, with a relaxed atmosphere, good music and food. Open 24hr Wed–Sun, until 3am Mon, and from noon Tues.

Silberstein, Oranienburger Str. 27. One of eastern Berlin's trendiest bars, thanks to over-the-top designer furniture and fashion-conscious clientele.

VEB OZ, Auguststr. 92. A basement bar that attracts a crowd of punks and their admirers. Often loud but usually amiable nevertheless.

Zillemarkt, Bleibtreustr. 48a. Wonderful if shabby bar that attempts a fin-de-siècle feel.

Zum Nussbaum, Am Nussbaum 3. In the heart of the Nikolaiviertel and overshadowed by the Nikolaikirche, this is a convincing replica of a prewar Kneipe.

Zur Letzten Instanz, Waisenstr. 14–16. Near the old city wall, this claims to be the oldest bar in the city. Wine upstairs, beer downstairs, and in summer there's a beer garden.

Discos, clubs and rock venues

90 Grad, Dennewitzstr. 37. Practically an institution, this long-lived, predominantly gay club still maintains its cutting edge.

A-Trane, Pestalozzistr. 105. One of the city's top jazz venues, a comfortable, sophisticated, and intimate club featuring accomplished if not quite top-name, musicians.

ColumbiaFritz, Columbiadamm 9–11. A former movie theatre that now hosts moderately good rock groups.

Dunckerclub, Dunckerstr. 64. Indie gigs and frequent club evenings attract a youngish local crowd. A small but atmospheric venue with open-air gigs in the back yard in summer.

Junction Club, Gneisenaustr. 18. Basement club featuring local talent from jazz guitarists to soul singers.

Knaack Club, Greifswalder Str. 224. Multi-level club lacking style but featuring a generally solid line-up of local and touring bands.

Matrix, Warschauer Platz 18 (*www.matrix-berlin.de*). Famous disco, now in a new location, that attracts a young crowd. House and similar sounds.

Privat Club, Pücklerstr. 34. Tiny basement club with an eclectic and often unpredictable mix of house, disco, funk, and more.

SO 36, Oranienstr. 190. A dark and punky gay and lesbian club. Hosts the popular "Jane Bond" lesbian parties every third Friday in the month.

Soda, Schönhauser Allee 36. In the recently renovated Kulturbrauerei, an arts and entertainment complex in a former brewery, this Twenties-style dance club features house and funk. Wed–Sat.

Sophienclub, Sophienstr. 6. Crowded central club playing host to local bands and often putting on discos.

Classical music

Deutsche Oper, Bismarckstr. 35 (☎0 30/3 41 02 49, *www.deutsche-oper.berlin.de*). Good Classical concerts, plus opera and ballet in a large, modern venue.

Komische Oper, Behrenstr. 55–57 (☎0 30/47 99 74 00, *www.komische-oper-berlin.de*). The house orchestra performs classical and contemporary music, and some very good opera productions are staged here.

Konzerthaus Berlin, Schauspielhaus am Gendarmenmarkt, Gendarmenmarkt 2 (☎0 30/2 03 09 21 01, *www.konzerthaus.de*). Home to the Berlin Sinfonie Orchester and host to visiting orchestras.

Philharmonie, Herbert-von-Karajan-Str. 1 (☎0 30/25 48 80, *www.berlin-philharmonic.com*). Custom-built home of the world's most celebrated orchestra, the Berlin Philharmonic. In 2002 musical director Sir Simon Rattle takes over from Claudio Abbado.

Staatsoper, Unter den Linden 7 (☎0 30/20 35 45 55, *www.staatsoper-berlin.org*). Excellent operatic productions in one of central Berlin's most beautiful buildings.

Theatre

Berliner Ensemble, Bertolt-Brecht-Platz 1 (☎0 30/2 82 31 60, *www.berliner-ensemble.de*). The official Brecht theatre.

Maxim Gorki Theater, Am Festungsgraben 2 (☎0 30/20 22 11 15, *www.gorki.de*). Consistently good productions of modern works.

Schaubühne am Lehniner Platz, Kurfürstendamm 153 (☎0 30/89 00 23, *www.schaubuehne.de*). State-of-the-art theatre for performances of the classics and some experimental pieces.

Varieté Chamäleon, Rosenthaler Str. 40–41, Mitte (☎0 30/2 82 71 18). Cabaret and variety theatre in the beautiful early twentieth-century Hackescher Höfe complex.

Listings

Airlines British Airways, Europa Center (☎0 30/2 54 00 00, *www.britishairways.com*); Lufthansa, Kurfürstendamm 220 (☎0 30/88 75 88, *www.lhcc.de*).

Airport enquiries ☎0 18 05/00 01 86.

Bicycle rental Fahradstation, Rosenthaler Str. 40/41 (☎0 30/28 38 4848). From €10 per day, €35 per week; deposit, insurance payment and passport required.

Car rental Star Car (☎0 30/6 82 96 80, *www.starcar.de*); Allround (☎0 30/3 42 50 91).

Doctor ☎0 30/1 92 42.

Embassies and consulates Australia, Uhlandstr. 181–183 (☎0 30/8 80 08 80, *www.australian-embassy.de*); Britain, Wilhelmstr. 70/71 (☎0 30/20 18 40, *www.britischebotschaft.de*); Canada, Friedrichstr. 95 (☎0 30/20 31 20, *www.kanada-info.de*); Ireland, Friedrichstr. 200 (☎0 30/22 07 20); New Zealand, Friedrichstr. 60 (☎0 30/20 62 10); US, Neustadtische Kirchstr. 4–5 (☎0 30/2 38 51 74), visa section, Clayallee 170 (☎0 30/8 32 92 33, *www.usembassy.de*).

Exchange ReiseBank, at the main entrance to the Zoo Station (daily 7.30am–10pm) and in the Friedrichstrasse station (daily 7.30am–7.30pm).

Hitching Mitfahrzentrale, in Zoologischer Garten U-Bahn station (☎0 30/1 94 40). Frauen Unterwegs women's Mitfahrzentrale at Potsdamer Str. 139 (☎0 30/2 15 10 22).

Laundry Rosenthaler Str. 71 (7.30am–10pm); Hermannstr. 74-75 (7.30am–10.00pm). Other addresses are listed under Wäschereien in the Yellow Pages.

Pharmacies Europa-Apotheke, Tauentzienstr. 9 (daily 9am–8pm). A notice on the door of any Apotheke indicates the nearest one open outside normal hours.

Police Platz der Luftbrücke 6 (☎0 30/69 95).

Post office Joachimsthaler Str. 7 (Mon–Sat 8am–midnight, Sun 10am–midnight).

EASTERN GERMANY

By the time the former German Democratic Republic was fully incorporated into the Federal Republic of Germany, just one year after the peaceful revolution of autumn 1989 (the so-called Wende), most vestiges of the old political system had been swept away. Yet there is still a long way to go before the two parts of the country achieve parity, and the cities of eastern Germany remain in the process of social and economic change. While for visitors this transformation can be fascinating, for many citizens of the former GDR it is problematic.

Berlin stands apart from the rest of the east, but its sense of excitement finds an echo in the two other main cities – **Leipzig**, which provided the vanguard of the revolution, and **Dresden**, the beautiful Saxon capital so ruthlessly destroyed in 1945. Equally enticing are some of the smaller places, which retain more of the appearance and atmosphere of prewar Germany than anywhere in the west, notably **Erfurt**, capital of the ancient province of Thuringia, nearby **Weimar**, the small cathedral towns of **Naumburg** and **Meissen**, and the old Prussian royal seat of **Potsdam**. Although much of eastern Germany is monotonous – its heartland was once a vast swamp – it is by no means the drab industrial landscape you might imagine.

Potsdam

The favourite residence of Frederick the Great, **POTSDAM** is an easy and excellent day-trip from Berlin. From Alexanderplatz, Friedrichstrasse or Zoologischer Garten S-Bahn line #7 will take you directly to Potsdam's main station. This lies on the opposite side of the Havel from the historic centre, whose skyline is dominated by the huge dome of the Nikolaikirche, one of Schinkel's most admired designs, albeit one that was built posthumously.

Stretching for 2km west of the centre is **Park Sanssouci** (daily 9am until dusk; inclusive day ticket to all buildings €15; *www.spsg.de*), the fabled retreat of the Prussian kings. It's a beautiful spectacle in spring when trees are in fresh leaf and flowers in bloom – and even more so in autumn, when it is a riot of colour. These days it's too often overrun by visitors – to avoid the crowds, visit on a weekday. Frederick the Great worked closely with his court architect Georg Wenzeslaus von Knobelsdorff on designing **Schloss Sanssouci** (tours every 20min: April–Oct Tues–Sun 9am–5pm; Nov–March 9am–4pm; €8.20), which was to be a place where the king could escape Berlin and his wife Elizabeth Christine, neither of whom he cared for. Begun in 1744, it's a surprisingly modest one-storey Baroque affair, topped by an oxidized green dome and ornamental statues looking out over vine terraces. Frederick loved the Schloss so much that he intended to be buried here, and had a tomb excavated for himself in front of the eastern wing; in 1991 his body was finally moved here. Inside is a frenzy of Rococo, spread through the twelve rooms where Frederick lived and entertained his guests. The most eye-catching chambers are the opulent **Marble Hall** and the **Concert Room**, where the flute-playing king had eminent musicians play his own works on concert evenings.

West of the palace, overlooking the ornamental Holländischer Garten, is the **Bildergalerie** (mid-May to mid-Oct Tues–Sun 10am–12.30pm & 1–5pm; €2), a restrained

Baroque creation that contains paintings by Rubens, Van Dyck and Caravaggio. On the opposite side of the Schloss, steps lead down to the **Neue Kammern** (mid-May to mid-Oct Tues–Sun 10am–12.30pm & 1–5pm; April to mid-May Sat & Sun 10am–12.30pm & 1–5pm; €2), the architectural twin of the Bildergalerie, originally used as an orangery and later as a guest house. Immediately to the west of the Neue Kammern is the prim Sizilianischer Garten, crammed with coniferous trees and subtropical plants, complementing the Nordische Garten just to the north.

From the west of the Sizilianischer Garten, Maulbeerallee cuts through the park and ascends to the **Orangerie** (mid-May to mid-Oct Tues–Sun 10am–12.30pm & 1–5pm; €2.60), an Italianate Renaissance-style structure with belvedere towers. A series of terraces with curved retaining walls sporting water spouts in the shape of lions' heads leads to the sandy-coloured building, whose slightly down-at-heel appearance lends it added character.

To the west through the trees rises the **Neues Palais** (April–Oct Sat–Thurs 9am–12.30pm & 1–5pm; Nov–March Sat–Thurs 9am–12.30pm & 1–4pm; €6.15), another massive Rococo extravaganza from Frederick's time. The main entrance is on the western facade, approached via gates flanked by stone sentry boxes. The interior is predictably opulent, though a couple of highlights stand out: the vast and startling Grottensaal on the ground floor decorated entirely with shells and semi-precious stones to form images of lizards and dragons, and the equally huge Marmorsaal, with its beautiful floor of patterned marble slabs. The southern wing (which these days houses a small café) contains Frederick's apartments and the theatre where the king enjoyed Italian opera and French plays.

Leipzig

LEIPZIG has always been among the most dynamic of German cities. Its trade fairs have a tradition dating back to the Middle Ages and remained important during the Communist years, so that there was never the degree of isolation from outside influences experienced by so many cities behind the Iron Curtain.

Arrival, information and accommodation

The enormous **train station** – the largest dead-end terminal in Europe – is at the northeastern end of the Ring, which encircles the old part of the city. The **tourist office**, directly opposite at Richard-Wagner Str. 1 (Mon–Fri 9am–7pm, Sat 9am–4pm, Sun 9am–2pm; ☎03 41/7 10 42 60, *www.leipzig.de*), can book private rooms (③–④) and sells the Leipzig Card, which costs €5 for 24 hours, €10.75 for three days, and covers public transport costs plus entrance fees to the main museums and sights.

Other **accommodation** options include the privately owned *Hostel Sleepy Lion*, just west of the centre at Käthe Kollwitz-Str. 3 (☎03 41.9 93 94 80, *www.hostel-leipzig.de*; ②); the HI hostel at Volksgartenstr. 24 (☎03 41/2 45 70 11; ②; tram #1 to Löbauer Strasse); and the campsite, *Auensee*, at Gustav-Esche-Str 5 (☎03 41/4 65 16 00; tram #10). Most hotels are prohibitively priced: exceptions are *Weisses Ross*, Ross-Str. 20 (☎03 41/9 60 59 51; ④), and two pensions, *Am Nordplatz*, Nordstr. 58 (☎03 41/9 60 31 43; ⑤), a short walk west of the train station, and *Christin*, south of the centre at Kochstr. 4 (☎03 41/2 32 93 66; ④).

The City

Most points of interest are conveniently placed within the old centre. Following Nikolaistrasse due south from the train station brings you to the **Nikolaikirche**, one of the two main civic churches and a rallying point during the Wende. Although a sombre medieval structure from outside, the church's interior is a real eye-grabber, its coffered vault supported by fluted columns whose capitals sprout like palm trees. A couple of blocks to the west is the open space of the Markt, whose eastern side is entirely occupied by the **Altes Rathaus** (Tues–Sun 10am–6pm; €2.60, free first Sun in month), built in the grandest German Renaissance style with elaborate gables, an asymmetrical tower and the longest inscription to be found on any building in the world. The ground floor retains its traditional function as a covered walkway with shops; the upper storeys, long abandoned as the town hall, now house the local-history museum. However, the main reason for going in is to see the 53-metre-long Festsaal on the first floor, with its ornate chimneypieces and haughty portraits of the local mayors and Saxon dukes. On the north side of the square is another handsome public building from Renaissance times, the old weighing house or **Alte Waage**. To the rear of the Altes Rathaus, approached by a graceful double flight of steps, is the **Alte Handelsbörse**, a Baroque gem which was formerly the trade exchange headquarters. The nearby Handelshof at Grimmaische Str. 1–7 is the temporary home of the **Museum der Bildenden Künste** (Tues & Thurs 10am–6pm, Wed 1–9.30pm; €2.60), a distinguished collection of old masters, including works by van der Weyden, Cranach, Hals, Rubens and Böcklin. This is due to move into its new custom-built premises on Sachsenplatz in late 2002.

Following Barfussgässchen off the western side of the Markt brings you to Kleine Fleischergasse and the cheerful Baroque **Zum Coffe Baum**. One of the German pioneers in the craze for coffee which followed the Turkish invasion of central Europe in the late seventeeth century, it gained further fame courtesy of Robert Schumann, who came here regularly. On its second floor is the entrance to the **Museum Coffe Baum** (daily 11am–7pm; free), which illustrates the history of European coffee culture. Klostergasse leads southwards from here to the Thomaskirche, the senior of the two big civic churches, and the place where Johann Sebastian Bach served for the last 27 years of his life. Predominantly Gothic, the church has been altered down the centuries, notably by the addition of the galleries in line with the Protestant emphasis on preaching. However, the most remarkable feature remains its musical tradition: the **Thomanerchor**, which Bach once directed, can usually be heard on Fridays at 6pm, Saturdays at 3pm, and during the Sunday service at 9.30am. Directly across from the church is the **Bach-Museum** (daily 10am–5pm; €3; *www.bach-leipzig.de*), with an extensive show of mementos of the great composer. Close by, at Dittrichring 24, is another historically important museum, the Round Corner or **Runde Ecke** (Wed–Sun 2–6pm; free), which commemorates victims who suffered at the hands of the Stasi, East Germany's secret police.

The southeastern part of the Altstadt is the academic quarter. On Schillerstrasse, east of the Neues Rathaus, is a surprisingly good **Egyptian Museum** (Tues–Sat 1–5pm, Sun 10am–1pm; €1.60), containing finds from nineteenth-century excavations by archeologists from Leipzig University. Beyond is a fragment of the old fortifications, the **Moritzbastei**, beside which stands the **Gewandhaus**, the ultramodern home of the oldest orchestra in the world, and still one of the best.

Tram #15 runs southeast to the site of the **Battle of the Nations**, where Napoleon was defeated by a combined army of Prussians, Austrians, Russians and Swedes in 1813. A colossal and tasteless monument known as the **Völkerschlachtdenkmal** (daily May–Oct 10am–6pm; Nov–April 10am–4pm; €3) was erected to commemorate the centenary of the victory. It can be ascended for a sweeping view over the city and the flat countryside.

Eating and drinking

Leipzig offers mainly traditional German taverns with the occasional ethnic restaurant, giving a good choice when it comes to **eating**. Many of the best spots are conveniently close to the Markt. *Zum Coffe Baum*, Kleine Fleischergasse 4, is unmissable, whether for *Kaffee und Küchen* or a full meal. Tucked underneath the Mädler-Passage, one of the covered shopping malls off Grimmaischer Strasse at the southeastern end of the Markt, is *Auerbachs Keller*, an historic and quite formal restaurant that was the setting for a scene in Goethe's *Faust*. Good choices for a hearty, reasonably priced German meal are the rambling old *Thüringer Hof*, Burgstr. 19, and *Apels Garten*, Kolonnadenstr. 2, which uses recipes from a 300-year-old cookbook. *Varadero*, Barfussgässchen 8, is a popular Cuban restaurant – a hangover of the political allegiances of the recent past – specializing in grills and cocktails. *Spizz*, Markt 9, is a live music bar with regular jazz features. The city is also famous for its satirical **cabaret**: if your

German's up to it, try Pfeffermühle in the same building as the Bach-Museum, or SanftWut in the Mädler-Passage.

Naumburg

The old cathedral city of **NAUMBURG** is situated on the fast rail line between Leipzig and Weimar, and reachable from both in well under an hour. Rather neglected in recent decades, it has already made giant steps in scraping off the grime which had smothered its buildings, and is well on the way to reclaiming its former status as one of Germany's most distinctive towns.

The historic part of Naumburg, set on heights overlooking the Saale valley, is dominated by the **Dom**, which shows medieval German architecture and sculpture at their peak. Though it was built as the seat of the local prince-bishop, with choirs at both ends of the building to emphasize its status as an imperial cathedral, it has been no more than a Protestant parish church since the Reformation. The thirteenth-century builders began by erecting the eastern choir, complete with its almost Oriental towers, in a florid Romanesque style. However, by the time the west choir was finished – minus one of the towers, which was finally built to the original plans a century ago – Gothic had taken over completely. Pride of the **interior** (April–Sept Mon–Sat 9am–6pm, Sun noon–6pm; reduced hours out of season; €3) is the assemblage of sculptures by the so-called **Master of Naumburg**, one of the most original masons to have worked on a great European cathedral. His rood screen, illustrating the Passion, imbues the figures with a humanity and a realism previously absent from religious art, and the twelve life-size statues of the Dom's founders in the west choir are each given a distinctive characterization. Particularly outstanding are the couple Ekkehardt and Uta, who have come to symbolize the Germans' romantic view of their chivalric medieval past.

From the Dom, Steinweg and then Herrenstrasse – each with its fair share of fine houses often complete with wrought-iron identification signs – lead eastwards to the central **Markt**. The square is dominated by the Renaissance **Rathaus**, whose huge curved gables served as a model for other mansions in the city. Rising behind the south side of the Markt is the curiously elongated **Stadtkirche St Wenzel**, which was the burghers' answer to the prince-bishop's Dom. In the Baroque period, this late Gothic church was given an interior face-lift, including the provision of a magnificent organ; look out also for two paintings by Cranach.

More fine mansions are to be seen on Jakobstrasse, which leads eastwards from the Markt. Also well worth going to see is the **Marientor**, at the edge of the inner ring road directly to the north of the Markt. This double gateway, one of the best-preserved in the country, is the only significant reminder these days of the fifteenth-century fortifications.

Naumburg's **train station** is below and northwest of the historic centre. The **tourist office** at Markt 6 (March–Oct Mon–Fri 9am–1pm & 2–7pm, Sat 10am–4pm; Nov–Feb Mon–Fri 9am–1pm & 2–5pm; ☎0 34 45/20 16 14, *www.naumburg.de*), can book private rooms (②–③). Alternatively, there's a HI **hostel** way to the south of the centre at Am Tennisplatz 9 (☎0 34 45/70 34 22; ②). **Hotels** include *Zum Akten Krug*, Lindenring 44 (☎0 34 45/20 04 06; ④). Among **restaurants**, the *Ratskeller* in the Rathaus and *Café Kaffeklatsch*, Herrenstr. 9, are recommendable.

Weimar

Despite its modest size, **WEIMAR** has played a role in the development of German culture that is unmatched: Goethe, Schiller, Herder and Nietzsche all made it their home, as did the Cranachs and Bach, and the architects and designers of the Bauhaus school. Its part in the politics of Germany is scarcely less significant: Weimar was chosen as the seat of government of the democratic republic established after World War I, a regime whose failure ended with the Nazi accession. One of the most notorious concentration camps was to be built here, and its preservation is a shocking reminder of Germany's double-edged contribution to the history of modern Europe. It served as European City of Culture in 1999, and for the years prior to this was subject to a frantic programme of restoration which has once again established its immaculate appearance.

The Town

Weimar preserves the appearance and atmosphere of its heyday as the capital of the Duchy of Saxe-Weimar, whose population never rose much above 100,000. The seat of power was the **Schloss** (Tues–Sun 10am–6pm; €3; *www.kunstsammlungen-weimar.de*), set by the River Ilm at the eastern edge of the town centre, a Neoclassical complex of a size more appropriate for ruling a mighty empire. On the ground floor is a collection of old masters, including pieces by both the elder and younger Cranach, and Dürer's portraits of the Nürnberg patrician couple, Hans and Elspeth Tucher. Upstairs are some fine original interiors and German paintings from the Enlightenment era.

Just west of the Schloss on Herderplatz stands the **Stadtkirche St Peter und Paul** (April–Oct Mon–Sat 10am–noon & 2–4pm, Sun 11am–noon & 2–3pm; Nov–March daily 11am–noon & 2–3pm), usually known as the Herderkirche in honour of the poet who was its pastor for three decades. Inside are several impressive tombs plus a large triptych by the Cranachs. South of Herderplatz is the spacious **Markt**, lined by an unusually disparate jumble of buildings, of which the most eye-catching is the green and white gabled **Stadthaus** on the eastern side, opposite the neo-Gothic **Rathaus**. Schillerstrasse snakes away from the southwest corner of the Markt to the **Schillerhaus** (9am–4/5pm; closed Tues; €2.60), the home of the poet, dramatist and historian for the last three years of his life. Beyond lies Theaterplatz, in the centre of which is a large monument to Goethe and Schiller. The **Nationaltheater** on the west side of the square was founded and directed by Goethe, though the present building, for all its stern Neoclassical appearance, is a modern pastiche. Opposite is the **Wittumspalais** (Tues–Sun 9am–noon & 1–4/6/7pm; €3), a Baroque palace containing some of the finest interiors of Weimar plus mementos of the Enlightenment philosopher-poet, Christoph-Martin Wieland.

Last of the literary museums is **Goethewohnhaus und Nationalmuseum** (Tues–Sun 9am–4/6/7pm; €4), on Frauenplan south of the Markt, where Goethe lived for some fifty years until his death in 1832. In the adjoining museum his achievement is chronicled with typically Teutonic detail. From the Goethewohnhaus, Marienstrasse continues to the **Liszthaus** (Tues–Sun 9am–1pm & 2–4/6/7pm; €2), home of the Hungarian composer and virtuoso pianist for the last seventeen years of his life, when he was director of Weimar's orchestra and opera. A couple of minutes' walk west down Geschwister-Scholl-Strasse is the **Hochschule für Architektur und Bauwesen**, where in 1919 Walter Gropius established the original Bauhaus, which had a profound impact on architecture and design throughout Europe. Further to the west is the **Alter Friedhof** or Old Cemetery, site of the Neoclassical mausoleum of Goethe and Schiller (9am–1pm & 2–4/6/7pm; closed Tues; €2).

The **Park an der Ilm** stretches from the Schloss to the southern edge of town on both sides of the river. Almost due east of the Liszthaus, on the opposite bank, is **Goethes Gartenhaus** (9am–noon & 1–4/6/7pm, closed Tues; €2), where the writer stayed when he first came to Weimar in 1776 as a ducal administrator. Further south and back on the west bank is the ducal summer house, known as the **Römisches Haus** (Tues–Sun 9am–noon & 1–4/6/7pm; €2). At the south edge of town, in the suburb of Oberweimar, there's the full-blown summer palace of **Schloss Belvedere** (April–Oct Tues–Sun 10am–6pm; €2.60; *www.kunstsammlungen-weimar.de*), whose light and airy Rococo forms a refreshing contrast to the Neoclassical solemnity of so much of the town. The **orangery** (same hours; €0.50) contains a collection of historic coaches, while the surroundings were transformed under Goethe's supervision into a jardin anglais.

Finally, the **Konzentrationslager Buchenwald** (Tues–Sun 8.45/9.45am–5/6pm; free) is situated to the north of Weimar on the Ettersberg heights, and can be reached by buses which run every hour from just south of the train station. Over 240,000 prisoners were incarcerated in this concentration camp, with 65,000 dying here, among them the interwar leader of the German Communist Party, Ernst Thälmann. This gave the place a special significance for the GDR authorities, now tarnished by the emergence of evidence that the Russians used it after the war for their own political opponents.

Practicalities

Weimar's **train station**, on the main line between Leipzig and Erfurt, is a twenty-minute walk north of the main sights. One of the **tourist offices** (daily 10am–8pm) is to be found there; another, much larger one, is in the Stadthaus at Markt 10 (April–Oct Mon–Fri 9.30am–6pm, Sat 9.30am–5pm, Sun 9.30am–4pm; Nov–March Mon–Fri 10am–6pm, Sat & Sun 10am–2pm; ☎0 36 43/2 40 00, *www.weimar.de*). Both can arrange **accommodation** in private rooms (②–③) for €2.60. There are HI hostels at Humboldtstr. 17 (☎0 36 43/85 07 92; ②), Carl-August-Allee 13 (☎0 36 43/85 04 90; ②) and, 5km south of the centre, at Zum Wilden Graben 12 (☎0 36 43/85 07 50; ②). Reasonably priced pensions include *Am Berkaer Bahnhof*, Peter-Cornelius-Str. 7 (☎0 36 43/20 20 10; ③), and *Savina II*, Meyerstr. 60 (☎0 36 43/8 66 90; ③). *Residenz-Café* on Grüner Markt is recommended for coffee and cakes. For a more substantial meal, try the places on the Markt, such as the inevitable *Ratskeller* or the surprisingly affordable *Elephantenkeller* under the Hotel Elephant.

Erfurt

Of all Germany's major cities, it's **ERFURT**, twenty minutes from Weimar by train, which is most redolent of prewar Germany. Although it lost a couple of important monuments in bombing raids, it was otherwise little damaged in World War II, while its streets of grandiose fin-de-siècle shops were saved by the Communist authorities from the developers who would have demolished them had the city been on the other side of the Iron Curtain.

The vast open space of the Domplatz forms the heart of the protected city centre. Imperiously set on the hill above, and reached via a monumental stairway, the **Dom** perches on a mighty fortress-like crypt. It's entered by a magnificent fourteenth-century porch which bears statues of the Apostles on one side, the Wise and Foolish Virgins on the other. Inside, the richly carved stalls and gleaming windows in the choir stand out, and the nave is jam-packed with works of art, the most notable being the so-called Wolfram, a Romanesque candelabrum in the shape of a man, and a spectacular font. Alongside the Dom is the **Severikirche**, a pure early Gothic hall church containing the tomb of the saint after whom it's named, a fourteenth-century masterpiece by an anonymous sculptor whose work adorns several of the city's churches.

From Domplatz, Marktstrasse leads east to Fischmarkt, lined by handsome Renaissance mansions and the nineteenth-century **Rathaus**. Just beyond is Erfurt's most singular sight, the **Krämerbrücke**. Walking along, you have the illusion of entering a narrow medieval alley but it is actually a bridge lined with shops and galleries. On the west bank, to the north of the Krämerbrücke, is the imposing Gothic facade of the **University**; the rest of the building was a casualty of World War II. However, its outstanding collection of old manuscripts survived, as did the academic church, the **Michaeliskirche**, which has a fine late Gothic chapel.

Across the river is the **Augustinerkloster** (tours April–Oct Tues–Sat 10am–noon & 2–4pm, Sun 10.45am; Nov–March Tues–Sat 10am, noon & 2pm, Sun 10.45am; €3; *www.augustinerkloster.de*), one of a profusion of monasteries in Erfurt which earned it the nickname "little Rome". This one is best known – it was here that Luther served as a novice, then a monk, between 1505 and 1511. A visit to his cell forms part of the tour, which also includes the cloister and the typically austere church, which is enlivened by a fine stained-glass window depicting the life of St Augustine.

Of the other monastic churches, pride of place goes to the **Predigerkirche** just south of Fischmarkt. Built by the Dominicans, it's extremely plain on the outside, but the interior is a masterpiece of spatial harmony in the purest Gothic style, and has preserved its layout and furnishings intact. Bombing wrecked the nave of the Franciscan **Barfüsserkirche**, over the river to the south, but the choir has been restored to house a small museum of religious art (April–Oct Tues–Sun 10am–1pm & 2–6pm; €1.60). This is a branch of the **Angermuseum** (Tues–Sun 10am–6pm; €1.60), in a Baroque mansion at the intersection of two of the main shopping streets, Bahnhofstrasse and Anger. Highlight here is the display of medieval artefacts, including more sculptures by the master who carved the tomb in the Severikirche. A fine collection of German painting from the Renaissance to modern times is also featured.

Practicalities

Erfurt's **train station** is situated at the southeastern corner of the city centre. The **tourist office** (Mon–Fri 9am–6/7pm, Sat & Sun 10am–4pm; ☎03 61/6 64 00, *www.erfurt-tourist-info.de*) at Fischmarkt 27 can book **rooms** in private houses and small pensions (③–⑤) for €2.60. There's a HI hostel at Hochheimerstr. 12 (☎03 61/5 62 67 05; ②), southwest of the centre: take tram #5 to the Steigerstrasse terminus. Reasonably priced hotels include *Daberstedt*, Buddestr. 2 (☎03 61/3 73 34 61; ③) and *Haus zum Pfauen*, Marbacher Gasse 12–13 (☎03 61/2 11 11 00; ③). The latter has a restaurant and brews its own beer according to a sixteenth-century recipe.

Dresden

Generally regarded as Germany's most beautiful and culturally significant large city, **DRESDEN** survived World War II largely unscathed until the night of February 13, 1945. Then, in a matter of hours, it was reduced to ruins in the most savage saturation bombing ever mounted prior to Vietnam – according to official figures at least 35,000 civilians died (though the total was probably considerably higher), as the city was packed with people fleeing the advancing Red Army. With this background, it's all the more remarkable that Dresden is the one city in the former GDR which has slotted easily into the economic framework of the reunited Germany, and the post-Communist authorities are now brilliantly restoring all the historic buildings left as rubble. Today Dresden is a dynamic gateway between the East and West.

Arrival, information and accommodation

Dresden has two main **train stations** – the Hauptbahnhof is south of the Altstadt, while Neustadt is at the northwestern corner of the Neustadt district across the Elbe and only slightly further away from the main sights. One of the **tourist offices** (Mon–Fri 9am–7pm, Sat 9am–2pm; ☎03 51/49 19 20, *www.dresden-tourist.de*) is in a pavilion at Prager Str. 10, just a short walk from the Hauptbahnhof; the other is in the heart of the Altstadt, in the Schinkelwache on Theaterplatz (Mon–Fri 10am–6pm, Sat & Sun 10am–4pm). Both sell the Dresden Card (€13.80 for 48 hours), which covers public transport, entry to the main museums and sundry discounts. Otherwise, a 24-hour transport ticket costs €4, and a day ticket for the museums costs €6.15.

The tourist offices can book private **rooms** and **pensions** (③–④). There are two privately owned **hostels** in Neustadt, well placed for nightlife: the relaxed and friendly *Mondpalast*, Katharinenstr. 11–13 (☎03 51/8 04 60 61; ②, *www.mondpalast.de*), and close by the modern *Die Boofe*, Louisenstr. 20 (☎03 51/8 01 33 61; ②, *www.boofe.com*). The much larger HI **hostel** is just to the southwest of the Altstadt sights at Maternistr. 22 (☎03 51/49 26 20; ③). Among the budget **hotels** are *City-Herberge*, just to the east of the Altstadt at Lingnerallee 3 (☎03 51/4 85 99 00; ③), and *Am Birkenhain*, Barbarastr. 76 (☎03 51/8 51 40; ④), which lies close to the Pieschen S-Bahn station. Unless you're travelling alone, the three gargantuan Ibis hotels on Prager Str. are good value; try *Königstein* (☎03 51/48 56 66 62; ④). The *Mockritz* **campsite** is at Boderitzer Str. 30 (☎03 51/4 71 52 50; bus #76 from the Hauptbahnhof).

The City

If you arrive at the Hauptbahnhof, you see the worst of modern Dresden first: the **Prager Strasse**, a vast Stalinist pedestrian precinct with the standard cocktail of high-rise luxury hotels, public offices, boxlike flats and a few fountains and statues thrown in for relief. At the far end, beyond the inner ring road, is the **Altmarkt**, which was much extended after its wartime destruction; the only building of note which remains is the **Kreuzkirche**, a church which mixes a Baroque body with a Neoclassical tower. On Saturdays at 6pm, and at the 9.30am Sunday service, you can usually hear the **Kreuzchor**, one of the world's leading church choirs. Behind stands the **Rathaus**, built in the early twentieth century in a lumbering Historicist style.

North of here, the **Albertinum** (10am–6pm, closed Thurs; €3.60; *www.staatl-kunstsammlungen-dresden.de*) houses the Gemäldegalerie Neue Meister, whose highlights include one of the greatest of Romantic paintings, Friedrich's *Cross in the Mountains*. Works by most of the French Impressionists and their German contemporaries precede a section devoted to the Expressionists of the Brücke group, which was founded in Dresden. Of the later pictures, two pacifist works stand out: *War* by Otto Dix and *The Thousand Year Reich* by Hans Grundig, a local artist who spent four years in a concentration camp. For the time being, the Albertinum is also home to the major part of the **Grünes Gewölbe** or Green Vault, a dazzling array of treasury items including the Baroque fancies created by the Saxon Electors' own jeweller, Johann Melchior Dinglinger. His *Court of Delhi on the Birthday of the Great Moghul* is a real tour de force, featuring 137 gilded and enamelled figures studded with 3000 diamonds, emeralds, rubies and pearls.

West of the Albertinum is the **Neumarkt**, formerly dominated by the round, domed Frauenkirche. Only a fragment of wall was left standing after the war, and the Communists decided to leave it in this condition as a memorial. After fierce controversy, the decision was taken in 1991 to rebuild it completely, and you can now savour the slightly odd experience of watching a Baroque church rise from a modern building site.

The colossal **Residenzschloss** (Tues–Sun 10am–6pm; €2.60; *www.staatl-kunstsammlungen-dresden.de*) of the Electors of Saxony was also wrecked in the war, and the rebuilding programme now under way is a massive task, though the projected completion date of 2006 – the city's 800th anniversary – now looks achievable. Sooner or later, the miraculously preserved **Mirror Rooms** (currently closed) will re-house the entire Grünes Gewölbe collection; in the meantime, an exhibition on the history of the building in the Georgenbau includes reconstructed display cabinets in which some of the older items are displayed. The main tower, the **Hausmannsturm**, can be ascended (April–Oct only; included in entrance ticket) for a view over the complex and the city. At the end of nearby Augustusstrasse is the Baroque **Hofkirche** (or Dom). The existence of this Catholic church in a staunchly Protestant province is explained by the fact that the Saxon rulers converted in order to gain the Polish throne. In the gleaming white interior is an ornate pulpit by the great sculptor of Dresden Baroque, **Balthasar Permoser**. The plush **Staatsoper** (guided tours at times posted; €4.60) opposite was built by the leading architect of nineteenth-century Dresden, Gottfried Semper, and saw the first performances of Wagner's *The Flying Dutchman* and *Tannhäuser*, and Richard Strauss's *Der Rosenkavalier*.

THE ZWINGER

Baroque Dresden's great glory was the palace known as the **Zwinger**, which directly faces the Residenzschloss. Less severely damaged in the war, it was quickly restored, and is now undergoing further repairs. It's a daringly original building: a vast open space with fountains surrounded by a single-storey gallery linking two-storey pavilions, and entered by grandiose gateways. The effect is further enhanced by superbly expressive decoration by Permoser.

The Zwinger contains several museums. Beautifully displayed in the southeastern pavilion, entered from Sophienstrasse, is the **Porzellansammlung** (10am–6pm, closed Thurs and for the early part of 2002; €1.60; *www.staatl-kunstsammlungen-dresden.de*); products from the famous Meissen factory are extensively featured. A small natural history display, the **Tierkundemuseum** (July & Aug daily 9am–5pm; rest of year Tues–Sun 9am–4pm; €1), is housed in the southern gallery. The southwestern pavilion is known as the **Mathematisch-Physikalischer Salon** (10am–6pm, closed Thurs; €1.60), and offers a fascinating array of globes, clocks and scientific instruments. In the northeastern part of the nineteenth-century extension by Semper is the **Rüstkammer** (Armoury; Tues–Sun 10am–6pm; €1.60; *www.staatl-kunstsammlungen-dresden.de*), featuring various weapons (including the sword of Elector Frederick the Valiant) and the coronation robes of Augustus the Strong.

The extension also contains the **Gemäldegalerie Alte Meister** (Tues–Sun 10am–6pm; €3.60; *www.staatl-kunstsammlungen-dresden.de*). The Saxon Electors' collection of old masters ranks among the dozen best in the world, and includes some of the most familiar Italian Renaissance paintings: Raphael's *Sistine Madonna*, Titian's *Christ and the Pharisees* and Veronese's *Marriage at Cana*. The German section includes Dürer's *Dresden Altarpiece*, Holbein's *Le Sieur de Morette* and Cranach's *Duke Henry the Pious*. Van Eyck's *Madonna and Child* triptych, executed with miniaturist precision, kicks off a distinguished Low Countries section in which Rubens and Rembrandt are extensively featured. The great artists of seventeenth-century France and Spain are all represented, though the gem of this section is the set of *The Parables* by a short-lived Italian, Domenico Feti. Finally, look out for the brilliantly detailed set of views by Bernardo Bellotto showing Dresden in all its eighteenth-century splendour.

THE NEUSTADT AND SCHLOSS PILLNITZ

Across the Elbe, the Neustadt was a planned Baroque town and its layout is still obvious, even if few of the original buildings survive. In the centre of the Markt rises the **Goldener Reiter**, a gilded equestrian statue of the Elector Augustus the Strong. The Neustadt's central axis, Hauptstrasse, preserves several Baroque houses by Pöppelmann, along with the same architect's Dreikönigskirche, only recently restored following war damage. In the park overlooking the Elbe is the most esoteric creation of Dresden Baroque, the Japanisches Palais, which now contains archeological and ethnographic museums (Tues–Sun 10am–5.30pm; €2 each). You don't have to pay to see the courtyard, a fantasy inspired by the eighteenth-century infatuation with the Orient.

Schloss Pillnitz, which lies 10km up the Elbe at the extreme edge of the city boundary, is another Pöppelmann creation, completed in 1830 and inspired by the mystique of the East; it's also the only part of the city's Baroque heritage to escape war damage altogether. There are actually two summer palaces here: the **Wasserpalais** (May–Oct Mon & Wed–Sun 9.30am–5.30pm; €1.60; *www.staatl-kunstsammlungen-dresden.de*), directly above the river, contains a museum of applied arts; the **Bergpalais** (May–Oct Tues–Sun 9.30am–5pm; €1.60), across the courtyard, is an almost exact replica, whose apartments are themselves the main exhibits. Pillnitz can be reached directly by bus #85 from the villa suburbs of Blasewitz or Loschwitz; alternatively, take tram #9 or #14 from the city centre to the terminus at Kleinzschachwitz, then the ferry across the Elbe.

Eating, drinking and nightlife

There's a wide choice of **restaurants** in Dresden. Options in the Altstadt include the *Ratskeller*, Dr-Kulz-Ring 19, which serves hearty local dishes; *Szeged*, Wilsdruffer Str. 4, offering both Hungarian and German cuisine; and the three establishments in the Italienisches Dörfchen, Theaterplatz 3. In Neustadt, *Am Thor*, Hauptstr. 35, is a worthy survivor from GDR days; *Kügelgenhaus*, Hauptstr. 13, is an atmospheric restaurant-cum-beer cellar in a fine Baroque building; and *Pfund's*, Bautzner Str. 79, is a café-restaurant attached to a wonderful dairy shop with immaculately restored Jugendstil decor. At night, the liveliest areas are the outer fringes of the Neustadt, and the Univiertel to the south of the

Hauptbahnhof. Trendy **bars** in the former include *Raskolnikov*, Böhmische Str. 34, and *Plantwirtschaft*, Louisenstr. 20; in the latter, *Café B. liebig*, Liebigstr. 24, and *Müllers Café*, Bergstr. 78, are two enduring favourites. *Scheune*, Alaunstr. 36–40, is a Neustadt arts centre with a café, beer garden, live music and theatre and gay and lesbian nights, while *Internetcafé-Spielforum*, Leipziger Str. 172, offers a choice of games plus the opportunity to surf the Net.

Meissen

Reachable from Dresden by a cruise down the Elbe or by S-Bahn train, the porcelain-producing town of **MEISSEN** is one of the most photogenic cities in Germany. Unlike Dresden, it survived World War II almost unscathed. Walking towards the centre from the train station, lying on the other side of the Elbe, you can immediately see the commandingly sited castle. The present building, the **Albrechtsburg** (daily 10am–5/6pm, closed Jan; €3; *www.albrechtsburg-meissen.de*), is a late fifteenth-century combination of military fortress and residential palace. Cocooned within the castle precinct is the **Dom** (April–Oct Mon–Fri & Sun 9am–6pm, Sat 9am–5.30pm; Nov–March daily 10am–4pm; €1.80). For the most part it's a pure Gothic structure, but the distinctive openwork spires which dominate Meissen's skyline were added only in the first decade of the twentieth century. Inside, look out for the superb brass tomb plates of the Saxon dukes; the rood screen with its colourful altarpiece by Cranach; and the statues of the founders in the choir, made in the great Naumburg workshop.

Between the castle hill and the Elbe lies the atmospheric **Altstadt**, a series of twisting and meandering streets ideal for an aimless stroll. Centrepiece is the **Markt**, dominated by the Renaissance **Rathaus**. On its own small square to the side is the Flamboyant Gothic **Frauenkirche**, whose carillon, fashioned from local porcelain, can be heard six times daily. The church's tower (May–Oct daily 10am–12.30pm & 1–4pm; €1) commands a superb view of the city and the Elbe. On the terrace just above is the celebrated **Gasthaus Vinzenz Richter**, a half-timbered old tavern which preserves an eighteenth-century winepress. The wines served here have the reputation of being the best in eastern Germany.

The **Staatliche Porzellan-Manufaktur Meissen** (tours daily 9am–5/6pm; €2.60), about 1.5km south of the Markt, is most easily reached by going down Fleischer Gasse, then continuing straight down Neugasse; it's also close to the S-Bahn terminus, Meissen-Triebischtal. Alternatively, there's a city bus from the station (every 30min; 10am–5.30pm). This is the latest factory to manufacture Dresden china, whose invention came about when Augustus the Strong imprisoned the alchemist Johann Friedrich Böttger, ordering him to produce some gold. Instead, he invented the first true European porcelain, according to a formula which remains secret. In addition to seeing the works, you can also view the **museum** (same hours; €4.60), which displays many of the finest achievements of the factories, most notably some gloriously over-the-top Rococo fripperies made by the most talented artist ever employed here, Joachim Kaendler.

Practicalities

The **tourist office** at Markt 3 (May–Sept Mon–Fri 9am–6.30pm, Sat & Sun 9am–4pm; Oct–April Mon–Fri 10am–6pm, Sat & Sun 10am–3pm; ☎0 35 21/4 19 40, *www.meissen.de*) books private **rooms** (③). There are also a couple of reasonably priced pensions with a central location: *Burkhardt*, Neugasse 29 (☎0 35 21/45 81 98; ③) and *Im Kleinen Haus*, Leinewebergasse 3 (☎45 30 18). The youth hostel is at Wilsdruffer Str. 28 (☎0 35 21/45 30 65; ②). For **eating and drinking**, the one unmissable place is the aforementioned *Vinzenz Richter*; other possibilities include *Domkeller*, Domplatz 9, and *Bahrmanns Brauereikeller*, Webergasse 2.

travel details

Trains

Berlin to: Dresden (every 2hr; 2hr 15min); Erfurt (hourly; 4hr); Frankfurt (hourly; 4–6hr); Hamburg (hourly; 2hr 30min); Hannover (every 30min; 2–3hr); Leipzig (hourly; 2hr); Munich (hourly; 7–8hr); Weimar (every 2 hours; 3hr 10min).

Cologne to: Aachen (every 30min; 45min); Düsseldorf (frequent; 25min); Frankfurt (hourly; 2hr 15min); Heidelberg (hourly; 2hr 50min); Mainz (hourly; 1hr 45min); Stuttgart (hourly; 3hr 25min).

Dresden to: Meissen (every 30min; 40min).

Frankfurt to: Baden-Baden (hourly; 1hr 30min); Berlin (hourly; 7–8hr); Cologne (hourly; 2hr 15min); Hamburg (hourly; 3hr 30min); Hannover (hourly; 2hr 20min); Heidelberg (every 30min; 1hr); Munich (hourly; 4hr); Nürnberg (hourly; 2hr); Würzburg (hourly; 1hr).

Hamburg to: Bremen (hourly; 1hr); Hannover (every 30min; 1hr 25min); Lübeck (every 30min; 40min).

Hannover to: Goslar (hourly; 1hr 20min).

Koblenz to: Trier (hourly; 1hr 30min).

Leipzig to: Dresden (hourly; 1hr 30min); Erfurt (hourly; 50min); Meissen (hourly; 2hr–3hr 30min); Naumburg (hourly; 40min); Weimar (hourly; 1hr 20min).

Mainz to: Koblenz (frequent; 50min); Worms (every 30min; 40min).

Munich to: Augsburg (every 20min; 30min); Nürnberg (hourly; 1hr 30min); Regensburg (hourly; 2hr); Würzburg (hourly; 2hr 20min).

Nürnberg to: Bamberg (every 30min; 45min); Munich (hourly; 1hr 30min).

Stuttgart to: Freiburg (hourly; 45min); Heidelberg (every 30min; 1hr 10min); Konstanz (hourly; 2hr 40min).

CHAPTER 12

GREECE

Introduction

With 166 inhabited islands and a landscape that ranges from Mediterranean to Balkan, **Greece** has enough appeal to fill months of travel. The historic sites span four millennia of civilization, encompassing the renowned – such as Mycenae, Olympia, Delphi and the Parthenon in **Athens** – and the obscure, where a visit can still seem like a personal discovery. The **beaches** are distributed along a convoluted coastline equal in length to that of France, and they range from islands where the boat calls once or twice a week to hip, cosmopolitan resorts.

Modern Greece is the sum of an extraordinary diversity of **influences**. Romans, Arabs, Franks, Venetians, Slavs, Albanians, Turks, Italians, to say nothing of the great Byzantine Empire, have all been here and gone since the time of Alexander the Great. All have left their mark: the Byzantines in countless churches and monasteries, and in ghost towns like **Mystra**; the Venetians in impregnable fortifications such as **Monemvasía** in the Peloponnese; the Franks in crag-top castles, again in the Peloponnese but also in the east Aegean. Most obvious, perhaps, is the heritage of four hundred years of Ottoman Turkish rule which, while universally derided, exercised an inestimable influence on music, cuisine, language and the way of life. The contributions, and continued existence, of substantial minorities – Vlachs, Muslims, Jews, Gypsies – round out the list of those who have helped to make up the Hellenic identity.

From even before the fall of Byzantium, the Greek country people – peasants, fishermen, shepherds – created one of the most vigorous and truly **popular cultures** in Europe, which endured until quite recently in the songs and dances, costumes, embroidery, furniture and the white cubist houses of popular image. Since the 1970s most of this has disappeared under the impact of Western consumer values, and is now, at best, relegated to museums, but the architectural and musical heritage in particular have undergone a recent renaissance.

The **landscape** of Greece varies astonishingly, encompassing the stony deserts of the Máni, the drama of the Peloponnesian coastal hills, the poplar-studded plains of Macedonia, the fragrant uplands of Skiáthos and Sámos, and the weatherbeaten rockiness of the central Aegean. Landscapes, climate and **food** come together to make Greece special.

Information and maps

The National Tourist Organization of Greece (Ellinikós Organismós Tourismoú, or **EOT**; *www.gnto.gr*) publishes an impressive array of free regional pamphlets, a reasonable fold-out map of Greece and a large number of sheets on special interests. There are EOT offices in many of the larger towns and resorts; in other places, try **municipal tourist offices** – often much better than EOT. The usually helpful **tourist police**, a branch of the local police, can sometimes provide you with lists of rooms to let, and will assist if you have a serious complaint about a hotel or restaurant.

The most reliable road **maps** of Greece are at 1:250,000, published in Athens: Road Editions *(www.road.gr)* covers the entire country in a half-dozen folding sheets, while Emvelia Editions *(www.emvelia.gr)* does it all in seven sheets which include useful town plans; however neither is completely accurate. Geocenter's *Greece and the Islands* plus *Greek Islands/Aegean Sea* cover the whole country at 1:300,000, while the single-sheet Freytag-Berndt does so at 1:650,000. The best maps for mountainous regions and islands are published by Road Editions and tiny competitor Anavasi, the latter strongest on the mountain ranges of the central/north mainland.

Money and banks

Greece is one of twelve European Union countries which have changed over to a single currency, the **euro** (€). Euro notes and coins are scheduled to be issued from January 1, 2002, with Greek drachmas (dr) remaining in circulation during a transition period, at a fixed rate of 340.75dr to 1 euro, until they are scrapped entirely on February 28, 2002. After this date you will still be able to exchange your drachmas

---

GREECE ON THE NET

www.gnto.gr – national tourist board

www.gtpnet.com – Greek Travel Pages: useful, but with unreliable transport schedules

www.athensnews.gr – surprisingly useful and literate English-language daily

for euros in banks for at least a year. Euro notes are issued in **denominations** of 5, 10, 20, 50, 100, 200 and 500 euros, and coins in denominations of 1, 2, 5, 10, 20 and 50 cents and 1 and 2 euros.

All prices in this chapter are given in euros correct at the time of going to press. There will no doubt be some rounding off (or, more probably, up) of prices in the first few months after the introduction of the euro.

Greek **banks** are normally open Mon–Thurs 8am–2pm, Fri 8am–1.30pm. Certain branches in the major cities and tourist centres are open extra hours in the evenings and on Saturday mornings to change money. Be prepared for long queues. Banks usually charge a flat commission fee of about €2–3 per transaction, the National Bank usually being the cheapest; travel agencies and designated money-exchange booths may give a poorer rate, but often levy a sliding two-percent commission, meaning you'll come out ahead on small amounts compared with banks.

There are plenty of **ATMs** (cash machines) which accept foreign cards, especially in resort areas; this is always the easiest and cheapest way of obtaining routine amounts of cash. Only Alpha Bank machines accept Amex. **Travellers' cheques** can be cashed at all banks and most tourist agencies, but commissions – both to buy them and then get cash – are high. It's useful to carry a small amount of **foreign banknotes** (say £100 or US$200 in small notes), since they're more readily accepted by hotels, licensed exchange booths and tourist shops.

Communications

Post offices are open Mon–Fri 7.30am–2pm or thereabouts; in big towns and important tourist centres, hours may extend into the evening and even weekends. **Stamps** (grammatosímata) can also be purchased at a corner kiosk (periptero), though staff tend not to know correct rates; posting a postcard or standard letter costs roughly €0.59 within the EU, €0.73 to North America or Australasia. There are always several boxes outside post offices; the one marked exoterikó is for international. Poste restante is reasonably efficient, especially in larger towns. American Express holds mail for customers only at its offices in Athens, Thessaloníki, Iráklio, Rhodes and Corfu.

Public phones are almost always card-operated, either on countertops or pillar-mounted. But in a country with 6.5 million **mobile phones** for 11 million people, these are increasingly neglected; about a third of them are defective or torn out by the roots. You can buy phone cards from newsagents and kiosks in 4 price denominations, the priciest most economical. It is possible to make collect (reverse-charge) or charge-card calls from these phones, but you need credit on a Greek phone-card to begin. The **operator number** (domestic/international) is ☎151/☎161.

Internet access is good; all big towns have several places to connect, with the islands' offerings more thinly spread. Prices are around €4.50–6/hr.

Getting around

Buses are the standard means of **public transport**. They cover just about every route on the mainland and provide a basic service on the islands. To explore under your own steam, rent a **scooter** (50–100cc) or full-bore **motorbike** (over 100cc); any substantial town or resort, especially on the islands, has rental outlets. You'll need an ordinary driving licence for a scooter, and a motorcycle licence for anything bigger.

■ Buses

Bus services on the major routes – both on the mainland and islands – are highly efficient, with the national network run by a syndicate of bus companies known as the **KTEL**, charging about €0.06 per kilometre. However, even in medium-sized towns there can be several widely spaced termini for services in different directions, so make sure you have the right station (o stathmós leoforíon) for your departure. As a rule, buses are prompt, so be in good time for a scheduled departure. Ticketing is computerized for the major intercity lines, with assigned seating, so such buses often get fully booked. On smaller rural/island routes, tickets are generally dispensed on the spot, with some standing allowed. Even the most remote villages will be connected to the county town by a school or market bus, often leaving shortly after dawn and returning about 2pm. On the islands, buses usually run between the port and main town for ferry arrivals and departures.

■ Trains

The **rail** network, run by **OSE**, is limited to the mainland, and trains are slower than the equivalent buses – except on the growing number of showcase IC (intercity) lines, which cost more. However, most trains are cheaper than buses, and some of the routes are highlights in their own right. If you're starting a journey at the initial station of a run you can reserve a seat at no extra cost; at most intermediate points, it's first-come, first-served. **Timetables** are sporadically available, typically produced in May/June, but in Greek only; the best places to pick one up are the OSE offices in Athens and Thessaloníki. **Eurail** and **InterRail** are valid, though passholders must make reservations like other passengers.

■ Ferries and hydrofoils

Ferries and hydrofoils are of use primarily for travel to, and between, islands, though you may also want to make use of the routes between Athens and Monemvasiá in the Peloponnese, and between the Peloponnese and Crete. Routes and the speed of the boats vary enormously: before buying a ticket it's wise to establish how many stops there'll be before your destination, and the estimated time of arrival. Many agents act only for one specific boat, so you may have to ask around to uncover alternatives.

Schedules (see *www.ferries.gr* and *www.greek-islands.gr*) are notoriously erratic and out of season are severely reduced, with many islands served only once or twice a week. The most reliable, up-to-date information is available from the local **port police** *(limenarhío)*, which maintains offices at Pireás and on all larger islands.

Regular ferry tickets are, in general, best bought on the day of departure, unless you need to reserve a cabin, bunk or space for a car. There are only three periods of the year – March 23–25, Easter weekend and most of August – when ferries need to be booked several days in advance. The cheapest class of ticket, which you'll probably get by default, is **deck class**. Motorbikes and cars get issued extra tickets, in the latter case up to four times the price of a simple passenger fare.

"Flying Dolphin" **hydrofoils** are roughly twice as fast and twice as expensive as ordinary ferries. They operate mainly among the Argo-Saronic islands close to Athens, down the east coast of the Peloponnese to Monemvasiá and Kýthira, among the northern Sporades, and throughout the Dodecanese. There are also summer-only services in the Cyclades and between the northeast Aegean islands, and international hydrofoils between Turkey, Greece and Italy. You can only buy a hydrofoil ticket to go one-way; in summer, if you're on a tight schedule, it is worth buying your return (or onward) ticket as soon as you arrive, since certain departures can fill with tour groups. There's also a growing number of **high-speed catamarans**, priced the same as hydrofoils and equally fast, but which usually take a certain number of cars and scooters.

In season, **kaïkia** (caiques) sail between adjacent islands, and to a few of the more obscure ones. These are seldom cheaper than main services but can be useful and often very pleasant. The only firm information you'll get about them is on the quayside.

■ Scooter and bike rental

You can rent your own transport on many of the islands and in a few of the popular mainland resorts: **motorbikes** (usually 125cc) cost from around €16 a day (you'll need to show a driving licence); **scooters** from €10; **bikes** €3.50 for an ordinary model or €8 for a mountain-bike. Outside peak season, you can usually bargain these rates down; prices are lower if you rent for a longer period. Make sure your travel insurance covers spills and damage to the bike, since all-in rental insurance is almost always deficient.

■ Driving

Cars have obvious advantages for getting to the more inaccessible parts of mainland Greece and the larger islands such as Crete. Average cost for **rental** of the cheapest models is from €300 per week with unlimited mileage, VAT and CDW included. In Greece, Drive/Reliable, Kosmos, EuroDollar, Payless and Just are reliable medium-sized companies with branches in many towns. Note that initial prices quoted may not include tax and supplemental insurance premiums; check the fine print on your contract carefully. If you drive your own vehicle to Greece, check your insurance policy for the extent of cover. EU citizens are fine with their local driving licence, but North Americans require an international driver's licence. Greece has the highest **accident rate** in the EU after Portugal, and many of the roads can be quite perilous. Speed limits are 50kph in town, 80kph out of town and 100kph on motorways. The Automobile and Touring Club of Greece (ELPA; ☎104) operates a 24hr breakdown service on major roads, and a 7am–10pm service elsewhere, but trucks can take a long time to arrive; if you have a local breakdown number, use that instead.

Accommodation

Greece has a vast amount of tourist **accommodation**, and most of the year you can rely on turning up pretty much anywhere and finding a room. Only around Easter and in July and August are you likely to experience problems; at these times, it's worth striking off the standard tourist routes a little, and/or arriving at each new place early in the day.

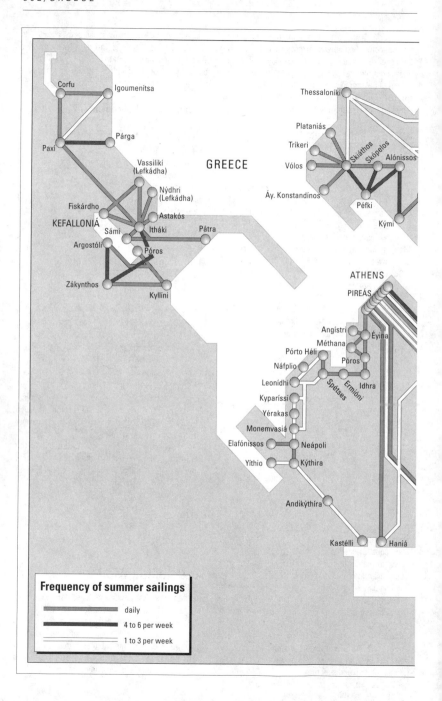

GREECE

KEFALLONIÁ

ATHENS

Frequency of summer sailings

daily
4 to 6 per week
1 to 3 per week

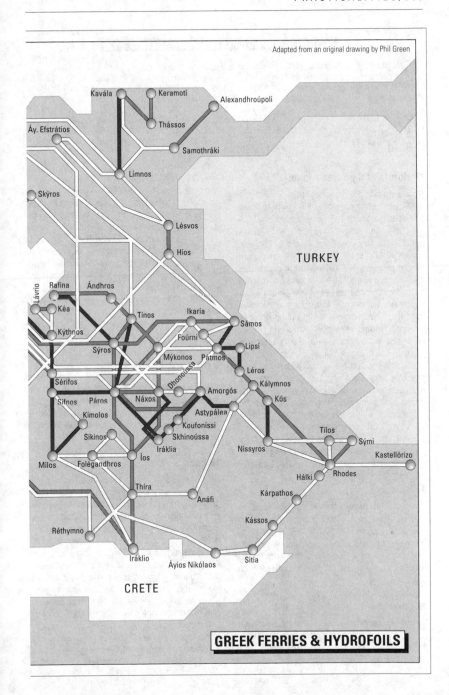

Adapted from an original drawing by Phil Green

GREEK FERRIES & HYDROFOILS

ACCOMMODATION PRICE CODES

Throughout this guide, accommodation is coded on a scale of ① to ⑨, the code indicating the lowest price per person per night you could expect to pay in each establishment in high season. With hostels this is the nightly rate per person; with hotels, the price is arrived at by dividing the cost of the cheapest double room by two. The prices indicated by the codes are as follows:

① under £5/$8 (€9)
② £5–10/$8–16 (€9–18)
③ £10–15/$16–24 (€18–27)

④ £15–20/$24–32 (€27–36)
⑤ £20–25/$32–40 (€36–45)
⑥ £25–30/$40–48 (€45–54)

⑦ £30–35/$48–56 (€54–63)
⑧ £35–40/$56–64 (€63–72)
⑨ £40/$64 (€72) and over

■ Hotels and private rooms

Hotels are officially categorized from "Luxury" down to "E-class", but these ratings have more to do with amenities and number of rooms than pricing; there are E-class hotels more comfortable and expensive than C-class. Outside Athens, D- and E-class hotels are a vanishing breed, but usually very reasonable, costing between €23 and €50 for a double room, €15–33 for a single. The better-value places tend to be in medium-sized resorts, where limited custom encourages competition. In resorts and throughout the islands, you have the additional option of privately let **rooms** *(dhomátia)*. These are officially divided into three classes (A–C), are often somewhat cheaper than hotels, and are kept spotlessly clean. These days the bulk are in new, purpose-built lowrises, but some are in people's homes, where you'll often be treated with disarming hospitality. As often as not, rooms find you: owners descend on ferry or bus arrivals to fill any space they have. In smaller places you'll often see rooms advertised, or you can just ask at the local taverna or café. Increasingly, rooms are being eclipsed by **self-catering** facilities, which can be good value; ask at travel agencies.

■ Hostels

Greece has few **hostels** *(xenón neotítos)* – and those that exist tend, with a few exceptions, to be rundown, filthy and non-IYHA-affiliated. Few ever ask for an HI card, and if they do you can usually buy one on the spot, or maybe just pay a little extra for your bed. Charges are around €8 a night, somewhat more in Athens.

■ Camping

Official **campsites** range from fairly basic compounds on the islands to highly organized EOT-run complexes, all generally **closed in winter** (open May–Oct only). Cheap, casual places rarely cost much above €2.50 a night per person; however, at the larger sites it's possible for two people and a tent to almost add up to the price of a basic room. Camping outside authorized campsites is such an established element of Greek travel that few people realize that it's officially forbidden. If you intend to do this, be aware of local sensibilities, especially near seaside resorts and villages; it's always best to ask the locals (they may suggest a better place), and make sure not to leave any rubbish behind. Once in a while the regulations get enforced. For further information contact the Greek Camping Association, Solonós 102, Athens (☎01/36 21 560), which publishes a handy booklet to all the official sites.

Food and drink

Food and **drink**, and Greek restaurants, are simple and straightforward. There's no snobbery about eating out; everyone does it, and it's reasonably priced – around €13 per person for a substantial meal with house wine.

■ Food

Greeks generally don't eat **breakfast**. The only egg-and-bacon diners are in resorts where foreigners congregate, and they're expensive compared to a taverna meal. The alternatives are bread-jam-yoghurt compromises, which you can get in some *zaharoplastía* or *galaktopolía* (cake- and milk-shops respectively).

Snacks can be one of the distinctive pleasures of Greek eating. *Souvlákia* (small kebabs) are on sale at bus stations, ferry crossings and everywhere in towns. The same goes for *tyrópites* (cheese pies), which can almost always be found at bakeries, as can *kouloúria* (crispy baked pretzel rings sprinkled with sesame seeds). Another city staple is *yíros* (doner kebab), served in *píta* bread with garnish.

In choosing a **restaurant**, the best strategy is to go where the Greeks go. An **estiatório** specializes in complicated, oven-baked casserole dishes, like *moussakás* and *pastítsio* (macaroni pie), stews like *kokinistó* and *stifádho*, *yemistá* (stuffed tomatoes or peppers), the oily vegetable casseroles called *ladherá*, and oven-baked meat and fish. **Tavernas** are now much more common. The primitive ones have a very limited menu, but the more established will offer some of the main *estiatório* dishes as well as standard taverna fare, which essentially means *mezédhes* (mixed hors d'œuvres) and *tis óras* (meat and fish fried or grilled to order). A **psistariá** has no ready dishes, but concentrates on salads, grilled meat (sometimes a bit of seafood) and a few hors d'œuvres.

The most common **mezédhes** are *tzatzíki* (yoghurt, garlic and cucumber dip), *melitzanosaláta* (aubergine dip), *kolokythákia tiganitá* and *melitzánes tiganités* (courgettes/aubergines fried in batter), *yígandes* (white haricot beans in a red sauce), *tyropitákia* and *spanakópites* (small cheese/spinach pies), *hórta* (steamed wild greens), *okhtapódhi* (octopus), *fáva* (fava-bean purée), and *mavromátika* (black-eyed peas). Of **meats**, *souvláki* (shish kebab) and *brizóles* (chops) are reliable standards. *Keftédhes* (meatballs), *biftékia* (a sort of mince rissole) and the spicy sausages called *loukánika* are cheap and good. Seaside tavernas also offer **fish** (*psári*): *kalamarákia* (fried baby squid) are a summer staple, but the choicer fish such as *tsipoúra* (gilt-head bream) and *lavráki* (sea bass) are expensive and usually farmed – you'd do best to stick with cheaper wild varieties such as *barboúnia* (red mullet), *marídhes* (picarel) and *gópes* (bogue), sold by the portion. For premium fish, the price is usually quoted by the kilo; the standard procedure is to go to the glass cooler, choose your fish and have it weighed in your presence.

Greeks eat **late**: 2.30–4pm and 9–11.30pm.

■ **Drink**

The **kafenío** is the traditional Greek coffee shop or café, and is the central pivot of life in the country villages – although like tavernas, they can range from the sophisticated to the old-fashioned. Its main business is Greek **coffee**, but it also serves spirits such as aniseed-flavoured **oúzo** and brandy, as well as beer, tea and soft drinks. Take your pre-dinner *oúzo* around 6pm, as the sun begins to sink and the heat of the day cools: you'll be served a glass of water alongside, to be tipped into your *oúzo* until it turns a milky white.

The **zaharoplastío**, a cross between café and patisserie, serves coffee, alcohol, yoghurt and a sometimes amazing variety of honey-soaked sweets.

In a **galaktopolío**, you'll often find *ryzógalo* (rice pudding), *kréma* (custard) and local *yiaoúrti* (yoghurt). There are also vast numbers of Western-style cafés, where you can get expensive cappuccinos, herbal teas, chocolate *Viennoise*, and all sorts of other fancy concoctions – at Western prices.

Bars *(barákia)* are a 1990s innovation, now ubiquitous in the largest towns and holiday resorts. They are often housed in buildings of historic interest, with the added enticements of a techno soundtrack and ultra-trendy clientele. Drinks, at about €4.90, are invariably more expensive than at a café.

Tavernas offer a better choice of **wines**. Boutari, Tsantali, Calliga and Afelia are good, low-priced bottles. If you want something better, the Lazaridhi, Spyropoulos, Papaïoannou and Skouras vintners are hard to beat, but be prepared to pay €13 and up per bottle. Otherwise, go for the local bulk wines: ask for *hýma* or *varelísia*, at around €4.50 per litre.

Opening hours and holidays

Shops generally open around 8.30 to 9.30am, then take a long break for the hottest part of the day before maybe reopening in the mid- to late afternoon. Tourist areas tend to adopt a more northern timetable, though, with shops and offices probably staying open right through the day. Shopping hours during the hottest months are theoretically Mon, Wed & Sat 9am–2pm and Tues, Thurs & Fri 9am–1.30pm & 5.30–8.30pm, but there are so many exceptions to the rule that you can't count on getting anything done except in the core hours of Mon–Fri 9.30am–1pm.

Opening hours for **museums** and **ancient sites** vary, and they change with exasperating frequency; we've given optimistic high-season hours, with winter hours where they are substantially different. Smaller sites generally close for a long lunch and siesta (even where they're not supposed to), as do **monasteries**, which are generally open 9am–1pm & 5–7pm for limited visits. Most state-owned museums and sites are closed on Mondays, and many of them – more so out of Athens – are free for students from EU countries (a valid card is required, but not necessarily an ISIC). Non-EU students, and all over-65s, are generally half-price.

There's a vast range of **public holidays** and festivals. The most important, when almost everything will be closed: Jan 1; Jan 6; the first Monday of Lent; March 25; May 1; Easter Sunday; Whit Monday; Aug 15; Oct 28; and Dec 24–27.

Emergencies

The most common causes of a run-in with the **police** are nude bathing or sunbathing, breaking into archeological sites after-hours, and camping outside an authorized site. Topless bathing may now be legal on virtually all Greek beaches but, especially in smaller places, you should be aware of local sensitivities before stripping off; if in doubt, cover up or find somewhere more isolated. The maximum penalty for drug offences is life imprisonment and a €30,000 fine but foreigners caught in possession even of a single joint have received jail sentences of up to a year. If you get arrested you have a right to contact your consulate who will arrange a lawyer for your defence. Beyond this, there is little they can, or in most cases will, do.

For **minor medical complaints** go to the local *farmakío* (pharmacy); in the larger towns, one will usually be English-speaking. If you regularly use any prescription drug you should bring along a copy of the prescription together with the generic name of the drug. For serious medical attention you'll find moderately priced English-speaking **doctors** in all the bigger towns or resorts; consult the tourist police, major hotels or your consulate for some names. Emergency treatment is free in state hospitals, though you'll only get the most basic level of nursing care. Even with an **E111** form, you may find that you'll have to pay up front for medications; keep all receipts in order to make later insurance claims.

Emergency Numbers

Police ☎110; Ambulance ☎166; Fire ☎199.

ATHENS AND AROUND

ATHENS (Athína) has been inhabited continuously for over 7000 years. Its acropolis, supplied with springwater, protected by a ring of mountains and commanding views of all approaches from the sea, was a natural choice for prehistoric settlement. Its development into a city-state and artistic centre reached its zenith in the Classical period of the fifth century BC with a flourish of art, architecture, literature and philosophy that pervaded Western culture forever after. Since World War II, the city's population has risen from 700,000 to four million – more than a third of Greece's total. The speed of this process is reflected in the city's chaotic mix of retro and contemporary: cutting-edge clothes shops and designer bars stand a few blocks away from the remnants of the Ottoman bazaar, and crumbling Neoclassic mansions are dwarfed by brutalist 1960s apartment blocks.

The ancient sites are only the most obvious of Athens' attractions. There are attractive cafés, landscaped stair-streets, and markets; startling views from the hills of Lykavitós and Filopáppou; and, around the foot of the Acropolis, scattered monuments of the Byzantine, medieval and nineteenth-century town. As you might expect, Athens also offers the best eating to be found in Greece, as well as the most varied nightlife.

Outside the city, the **Temple of Poseidon** at Sounion is the most popular trip, and rightly so, with its dramatic clifftop position. The port of **Pireás** (Piraeus), effectively an extension of Athens, is the main terminus for the island and international ferries, as well as being the hub of most Greek industry. The other port, **Rafína**, is on the east coast of the Attic peninsula, a useful departure point for many of the Cycladic and north Aegean islands, that is set for a massive increase in traffic as it's much closer to Athens' new airport than Pireás.

Arrival, orientation and information

Athens' vast new **airport**, Eletherios Venizelos (supposedly the third-largest in the world), 25km east at Spáta, opened in March 2001, replacing the more convenient little airport at Ellinikón. The **metro/light-rail** extension is due to reach the new airport in 2003; until then, the best you can do is take the E94 express **bus** (daily every 15min 6am–8.15pm, every 30min 8.30pm–midnight) from outside arrivals to the current last metro stop, Ethnikí Ámyna, and then continue into the centre. Alternatively, the E95 express bus runs all the way to central Sýndagma Square day and night (every 25/35min, 24hr), and the E96 express bus runs through the beach suburbs to Pireás port (every 20/40min, 24hr). A ticket on any of the three costs €3, and is valid on all Athens public transport for a day. A **taxi** is around €20, including a €1.20 airport surcharge and €0.15 for each bag, but but make sure the meter is working and visible from the start: overcharging of newcomers is the norm (flagfall €0.70, minimum fare €1.50).

International **trains** arrive at the Stathmós Laríssis in the northwest of the city centre, connected by metro to Sýndagma. The virtually adjacent Stathmós Peloponníssou handles traffic to and from the Peloponnese, and is connected to Sýndagma by bus #057. **Buses** from northern Greece or the Peloponnese arrive at Kifissoú 100, a ten-minute ride from the centre by bus #051 (roughly €3.25 by taxi). Buses from central Greece (not Delphi) arrive rather closer to the centre at Liossíon 260, north of the train stations (blue city bus #024 to Sýndagma). Most international buses drop off at the train station or Kifissoú 100; a few will drop you right in the city centre. Arriving by **boat** at Pireás, the simplest access to the centre is by metro to Monastiráki, Sýndagma, Omónia or Platía Viktorías stations; taxis cost around €4.70 at day rates (nearly double that between midnight and 5am).

Central Athens covers a mercifully small area: **Sýndagma Square** (Platía Sýndágmatos, "Constitution Square") is the main focus, and most sights are within twenty minutes' walk. The city's main EOT **tourist office** is at Amerikís 2, near Sýndagma Square (Mon–Fri 9am–4pm; ☎01/33 10 565).

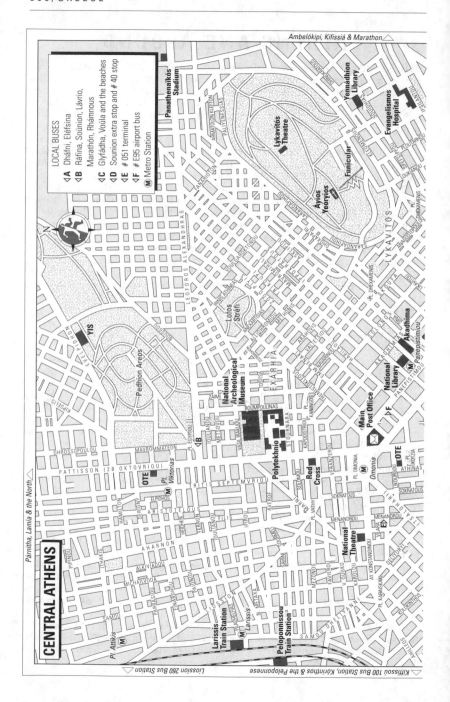

CENTRAL ATHENS

LOCAL BUSES
◁A Dháfni, Eléfsina
◁B Ráfina, Soúnion, Lávrio, Marathón, Rhamnous
◁C Glyfádha, Voúla and the beaches
◁D Soúnion extra stop and # 40 stop
◁E # 051 terminal
◁F # E95 airport bus
Ⓜ Metro Station

Ambelókipi, Kifissiá & Marathon △

Panathenaïkós Stadium

Yennádhion Library

Evangelismos Hospital

Lykavitós Theatre

Funicular

Ayios Yeóryios

LYKAVITOS

LEOFOROS ALEXANDHRAS

Lófos Stréfi

Akadhima

EXARHIA

National Archeological Museum

National Library

Panepistimíou

YIS

Pedhíon Áreos

Main Post Office

National Theatre

Polytekhnío

Red Cross

OTE

Omonia

OTE

Párnitha, Lamia & the North △

Laríssis Train Station

Peloponníssou Train Station

Kifíssou 100 Bus Station, Kórinthos & the Peloponnese

Liossíon 260 Bus Station △

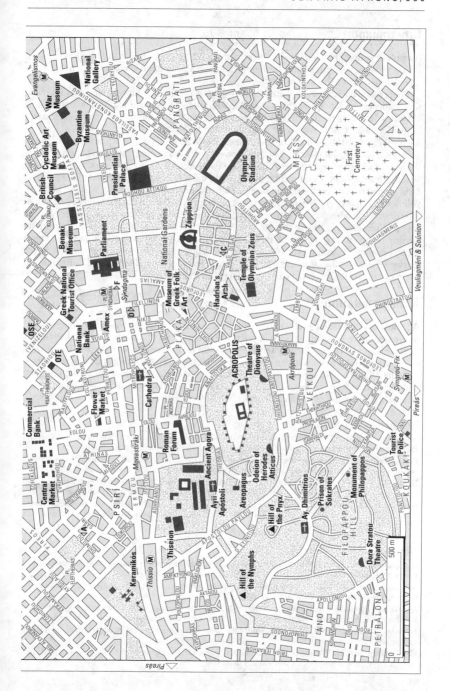

City transport

All **public transport** operates daily from around 5.30am to midnight. Athens' bus network is extensive but very crowded at peak times, though air-conditioned coaches are being introduced, especially on the trolley lines.

Overground-line extension work on the **metro** is continuing. Line 1 runs from Pireás in the southwest to Kifissiá in the northeast, with stops at Monastiráki, Omónia and Platía Viktorías; Line 2 currently runs from Dháfni to Sepólia via Sýndagma and a station at the foot of the Acropolis; Line 3 heads east from Monastiráki to Ethnikí Ámyna. Tickets, which cost a flat €0.75 (or €0.60 for line 1 only), are available at all stations from automatic coin-op dispensers or staffed windows. A €3 one-day travel card, buyable from metro stations, gives you the run of all buses and all metro lines. **Buses** cost a flat €0.45; you must buy tickets in advance from kiosks. **Taxis** can be surprisingly difficult to hail, but are very inexpensive: fares around the city centre should rarely come to more than €3 (officially licensed taxis are yellow with a special red-letter numberplate: beware of cowboys at the train and bus stations). Taxi drivers will often pick up a whole string of passengers along the way, each passenger (or group of passengers) paying the full fare for their journey – so if you're picked up by an already occupied taxi, memorize the meter reading; you'll pay from then on, including a €1.50 minimum. Luggage over 10kg costs €0.30 a piece extra; there are also surcharges for leaving or entering the airport or a ferry port, and bonuses around Easter and Christmas. All these extras should be set out clearly on a dashboard placard.

Accommodation

Accommodation can be packed to the gills in midsummer – August especially – but for most of the year there is enough choice in price and decor. Expect to pay from around €29 for a double room in a D- or E-class hotel; as little as €8 per person if you're prepared to share a three- to six-person room. You can reserve at the tourist office for hotels of C-class and above.

Many Athens hotels, especially around Pláka and Omónia, are prone to around-the-clock noise; our choices below are quieter, often on pedestrianized streets, or in neighbourhoods a little further out such as Koukáki or Exárhia.

Hostels

Aphrodite, Inárdhou 12, cnr Mihaíl Vódha 65 (☎01/88 10 589). Located between the main train station and Platía Viktorías, this friendly, clean hostel has a travel agency and a lively bar. Dorm €8, plus a few doubles (③).

Festos Youth and Student Guesthouse, Filellínon 18 (☎01/32 32 455). Centrally placed, if often overcrowded and noisy hostel on the edge of Pláka, with handy coffee and snack bar. Dorm €10; or two doubles (③).

Hostel #5, Dhamaréos 75, Pangráti (☎01/75 19 530). Friendly place in an appealing neighbourhood with cooking and laundry facilities, and no curfew, but a bit remote; trolley #2/#11 stops round the corner. ①.

International Youth Hostel, Victor Hugo 16 (☎01/52 34 170). Athens' cheapest option, an official HI hostel with a cheerful atmosphere, well-kept facilities and helpful staff, though location isn't wonderful. Bus #1/#12 to Karaïskáki Square nearby. ①.

Hotels

Acropolis House, Kódrou 6–8 (☎01/32 22 344). Clean, well-sited pension on a pedestrian street. Most rooms are en-suite and some have air-con, but the staff are notoriously snooty. ⑥.

Adonis, Kódrou 3 (☎01/324 9737). C-class hotel opposite *Acropolis House*, with plain, en-suite rooms and a stunning view of the Acropolis from the rooftop bar. ⑥.

Art Gallery Pension, Erekhthíou 5, Veïkoú (☎01/92 38 376). Variable en-suite rooms throughout (some with bathtubs), but not up to *Marble House* standard (see opposite). Management can be off-hand. ⑦.

Dryades, Dryádhon 4 (☎01/33 02 387). Under the same management as the adjacent *Orion*, but slightly quieter and with en-suite rooms. ⑥.

Elli, Heïdhen 29, Platía Viktorías (☎01/88 23 487). Characterful pension in a refurbished Neoclassical mansion on a tree-lined side street; TV and shower in all rooms. ⑤.

Erechtheion, Flammarion 8, corner Ayías Marínas, Thissíon (☎01/34 59 606). Rooms in better condition, better value and quieter than those at neighbouring annexe *Thission*; great Acropolis views from some, and from *Thission's* roof garden. ⑤.

Exarhion, Themistokléous 55, Exárhia (☎01/38 01 256). 1960s high-rise C-class hotel that's superbly placed (and priced) for the studenty nightlife, though noisy because of the adjacent plaza. ⑤.

John's Place, Patróöu 5, Pláka (☎01/32 29 719). Dark single/double/triple rooms with shared baths, but neat and well-kept. In a peaceful backstreet off Mitropóleos, with a functional, inexpensive restaurant on the ground floor. ④.

Kouros, Kódrou 11 (☎01/32 27 431). On the same pedestrianized street as *Adonis* and *Acropolis House*; recently had a light renovation, but shared bathrooms and breathtakingly rude management are drawbacks. ②.

Marble House, in a quiet alley off Anastasíou Zínni 35, Koukáki (☎01/92 34 058). The best-value outfit south of the Acropolis, this welcoming pension was completely overhauled in 2001; most rooms en suite and with balcony, all rooms with fans and fridge. Also two studios for long-term rental. Reserve a month in advance. ⑤.

Nefeli, Iperídhou 16, Pláka (☎01/32 25 800). Modern but salubrious and well-located bland C-class hotel free of tour groups. ⑥.

Orion, Emm. Benáki 105, corner Anexartisías, Exárhia (☎01/33 02 388). Quiet, well-run budget hotel across from the Lófos Stréfi park – a steep final walk to get there, yet close to many attractions. Rooftop kitchen and common area with an amazing view. ④.

Phaedra, Herefóndos 16, Pláka (☎01/32 38 641). Well-worn 1960s-vintage rooms with shared baths, but in a fine location overlooking a Byzantine church and the Acropolis. ④.

Student and Travellers' Inn, Kydhathinéon 16 (☎01/32 44 808). Right in the centre of Pláka, this popular, clean and well-run former hostel offers singles, doubles and triples, with shared bathrooms, as well as luggage storage and Internet. ⑤.

Tempi, Eólou 29 (☎01/32 13 175). Upgraded hotel, with helpful staff, fridge, book exchange and affiliated travel agency; well sited on a pedestrian street in the bazaar. ④.

Thisseus Inn, Thisséos 10 (☎01/32 45 960). Very central (three blocks west of Sýndagma). Small but brightly painted, parquet-floored singles and doubles, also quads run hostel-style; shared baths, self-catering kitchen. Dorm €12; rooms ④.

Campsites

Nea Kifissia, in the leafy suburb of Kifissiá, is open year-round and has a swimming pool. Bus #528 from near Omónia, or take the metro to its last stop, Kifissiá, and take bus #528 behind the station for the final stretch.

Várkiza, 27km south, in the beach suburb of Várkiza. Largish site on the beach, open year-round; access by blue city bus from Sýndagma.

The City

Pláka – roughly the area between Sýndagma, Odhós Ermoú and the Acropolis – is the best place to begin exploring. One of the few parts of Athens with charm and architectural merit, its narrow winding streets and stairs are lined with nineteenth-century Neoclassical houses, some grand, some humble. An attractive approach to Pláka is to follow **Odhós Kydhathinéon**, a pedestrian walkway starting near the Anglican and Russian Orthodox churches on Odhós Filellínon, south of Sýndagma. It leads gently downhill past the beautiful, small **Museum of Greek Folk Art** (Tues–Sun 10am–2pm; €1.50) at Kydhathinéon 17, the five floors of which are mostly devoted to collections of weaving, pottery and embroidery; most compelling of all are the third-floor murals by the primitive artist Theophilos (1873–1934). Odhós Kydhathinéon continues through café-crowded Platía Filomoússou Eterías to "Hadrian's Street", **Odhós Adhrianoú**, which runs nearly the whole east–west length of Pláka from Hadrian's Arch to the Thiseíon.

The downhill, northerly section of Adhrianoú is largely commercial – souvenir shops and sandals – as far as the Roman Forum (see p.603). But a few steps south from Kydhathinéon, there's a quiet and attractive sitting space around the fourth-century-BC **Monument of Lysikrates**, erected to celebrate the success of a prize-winning dramatic chorus. Continuing straight ahead from the Kydhathinéon–Adhriánou intersection up **Odhós Thespídhos**, you reach the edge of the Acropolis precinct. Up to the right, the whitewashed Cycladic houses of Anafiótika cheerfully proclaim an architect-free zone amidst the highest crags of the Acropolis rock.

The Acropolis

A rugged limestone plateau, watered by springs and rising an abrupt 100m out of the plain of Attica, the **Acropolis** (Mon 11am–6.30pm, Tues–Sun 8am–6.30pm; winter may close at 2.30pm; €6) was one of the earliest settlements in Greece, drawing a Neolithic community to its slopes around 5000 BC. In Mycenaean times it was fortified around a royal palace and temples where the cult of Athena was introduced. During the ninth century BC, the Acropolis became the heart of the first Greek city-state, and in the wake of Athenian military suprema-cy and a peace treaty with the Persians in 449 BC, Pericles had the complex reconstructed under the direction of architect and sculptor Pheidias, producing most of the monuments vis-ible today, including the **Parthenon**. Having survived more or less intact for over two thou-sand years, the Acropolis finally fell victim to the demands of war. In 1687 besieging Venetians ignited a Turkish gunpowder magazine in the Parthenon, blasting off the roof, and in 1801 Lord Elgin removed the frieze (the "Elgin Marbles"), which he later sold to the British Museum – though there is hope it will soon be restored to Greece. Meanwhile, gen-erations of visitors have slowly worn down the Parthenon's surfaces; and, more recently, smog has been turning the marble to dust. Since 1981, visitors have been barred from the Parthenon's precinct, and a major restoration programme is proceeding sporadically; scaf-folding and cranes may obscure the view.

The Acropolis's monumental entrance, or **Propylaia**, was constructed upon completion of the Parthenon in 437 BC, and its axis and proportions were aligned to balance the temple. The ancient Athenians, awed by the fact that such wealth and craftsmanship should be used for a purely secular building, ranked this as their most prestigious monument. In front of the Propylaia, the simple and elegant **Temple of Athena Nike** was begun late in the rebuilding scheme and stands on a precipitous platform overlooking Pireás and the Saronic Gulf. The temple's frieze, with more attention to realism than triumphalism, depicts the Athenians' vic-tory over the Persians at Plateia.

THE PARTHENON AND AROUND

The **Parthenon** was the first great building in Pericles's plan. Designed by Iktinos, it utilizes all the refinements available to the Doric order of architecture to achieve an extraordinary and unequalled harmony. Built on the site of earlier temples, it was intended as a new sanc-tuary for Athena and a house for her cult image, a colossal wooden statue decked in ivory and gold plate that was designed by Pheidias and considered one of the Seven Wonders of the Ancient World; the sculpture was lost in ancient times, but its characteristics are known through later copies – including a Roman one in the National Archeological Museum (see p.604). "Parthenon" means "virgins' chamber" and initially referred only to a room at the west end of the temple occupied by the priestesses of Athena. But the temple never rivalled the Erechtheion (see below) in sanctity and its role tended to remain that of treasury and artistic showcase. Its columns were originally painted, and the building was decorated by the finest frieze and pedimental sculpture of the Classical age, of which the best surviving exam-ples are in London.

To the north of the Parthenon, beyond the foundations of the Old Temple of Athena, stands the **Erechtheion**, the last of the great works of Pericles. Here, in symbolic reconcili-ation, Athena and the city's old patron Poseidon-Erechtheus were both worshipped. Its ele-gant Ionic porticoes are all worth close attention, particularly the north one with its fine dec-orated doorway and frieze of blue Eleusinian marble. On the south side, in the Porch of the Caryatids, the Ionic line is transformed into six maidens (caryatids) holding the entablature on their heads. These are replicas: four of the originals are in the Acropolis Museum, one is in storage, and a sixth was looted by Lord Elgin.

Placed discreetly on a level below that of the main monuments, the **Acropolis Museum** (admission included) contains nearly all of the portable objects removed from the Acropolis since 1834. In the first rooms to the left of the vestibule are fragments of pediment sculptures from the Old Temple of Athena, which give a good impression of the vivid colours that were used in temple decoration. Further on is the Moschophoros, a painted marble statue of a young man carrying a sacrificial calf, dated 570 BC and one of the earliest examples of Greek art in marble. Room 4 displays one of the chief treasures of the building, a unique collection of *korai*, or maidens, dedicated as votive offerings to Athena in the sixth century BC. The only pieces of Parthenon frieze left in Greece are in Room 8, while the same room contains the graceful and fluid sculpture of Athena Nike adjusting one sandal, known as *Iy Sandalízoussa*. Finally, in the last room are four authentic and semi-eroded caryatids from the Erechtheion, displayed in a vacuum chamber.

THE WEST AND SOUTH SLOPES
Rock-hewn stairs immediately below the entrance to the Acropolis ascend the low hill of the **Areopagus**, the site of the court of criminal justice. Following the road or path over the flank of the Acropolis, you come out onto pedestrianized Dhionysíou Areopayítou, by the Odeion of Herodes Atticus (see below). Turning right, a network of paths leads up **Filopáppou Hill**, its summit capped by a grandiose monument to a Roman senator and consul, Filopappos, who is depicted on its frieze, driving his chariot. Just north of the main path, which follows a line of truncated ancient walls, is the gingerbread-masoned church of **Áyios Dhimítrios**, with Byzantine frescoes. Above the church, further to the north, rises the **Hill of the Pnyx**, an area used in Classical Athens as the meeting place for the democratic assembly. All except the most serious political issues were aired here, the hill on the north side providing a semi-circular terrace from which to address the crowds of at least six thousand citizens that met more than forty times a year.

The second-century Roman **Odeion of Herodes Atticus**, restored for performances of music and Classical drama during the summer festival (the only time it's open), dominates the south slope of the Acropolis hill. The main interest hereabouts lies in the earlier Greek sites to the east, pre-eminent among which is the **Theatre of Dionysos**, beside the main site entrance on Dhionysíou Areopayítou (Tues–Sun 8.30am–2.30pm; July & Aug may close later; €1.50). One of the most evocative locations in the city, it was here that the masterpieces of Aeschylus, Sophocles, Euripides and Aristophanes were first performed. The ruins are impressive; the theatre, rebuilt in the fourth century BC, could hold some 17,000 spectators. To the west extend the ruins of the **Asclepion**, a sanctuary devoted to the healing god Asclepius and built around a sacred spring. The curative centre was probably incorporated into the Byzantine church of the doctor-saints, Kosmas and Damian, of which there are prominent remains. Nearer to the road are the foundations of the Roman **Stoa of Eumenes**, a colonnade of stalls which stretched to the Odeion of Herodes Atticus.

The Agora and Roman Forum
Northwest of the Acropolis, the **Agora** (Tues–Sun 8.30am–3pm; €3.50) was the nexus of ancient Athenian city life, where the various claims of administration, commerce, market and public assembly competed for space. The site is a confused jumble of ruins, dating from various stages of building between the sixth century BC and the fifth century AD. For some idea of what you are surveying, the place to head for is the **museum** (same hours), housed in the rebuilt Stoa of Attalos. The stoa itself is, in every respect bar one, a faithful reconstruction of the original; what's missing is colour: in Classical times the exterior would have been painted bright red and blue. In the far corner of the agora precinct sits the nearly intact but distinctly clunky Doric **Temple of Hephaistos**, otherwise known as the **Thiseion** from the exploits of Theseus depicted on its friezes.

The **Roman Forum**, or Roman agora (Tues–Sun 8am–3pm; €1.50), was built as an extension of the Hellenistic agora by Julius Caesar and Augustus, and its main entrance was through the relatively intact Gate of Athena Archegetis. The best-preserved and easily the most intriguing of the ruins, though, is the graceful, octagonal structure known as the **Tower of the Winds**. It was designed in the first century BC by a Syrian astronomer, and served as a compass, sundial, weather vane and water clock powered by a stream from one of the Acropolis springs. Each face of the tower is adorned with a relief of a figure floating through the air, personifying the eight winds.

Sýndagma Square, the National Gardens and Lykavitós

All roads lead to Platía Syndágmatos – **Sýndagma Square** – with its busy metro station. Geared to tourism, with a main post office, banks, luxury hotels, American Express, airline and travel offices grouped around, it has convenience but not much else to recommend it. Behind the parliament buildings on the square, the **National Gardens** provide the most refreshing spot in the whole city, a luxuriant tangle of trees, shrubs and creepers, whose shade, duck ponds, cafés and sparkling irrigation channels bring relief from the heat and pollution of summer. At the southern end of the park, beside one of the most hazardous road junctions in Athens, stands **Hadrian's Arch**, erected by the Roman emperor to mark the edge of the Classical city and the beginning of his own. Directly behind are the sixteen surviving columns of the 104 that originally comprised the **Temple of Olympian Zeus** (Tues–Sun 8.30am–3pm; €1.50) – the largest in Greece, dedicated by Hadrian in 131 AD.

At the northeast corner of the National Gardens, is the fascinating and much-overlooked **Benáki Museum**, Koumbári 1 (Mon & Wed–Sat 9am–5pm, Thurs until midnight, Sun 9am–3pm; €6), with a constantly surprising collection featuring Mycenaean jewellery, Greek costumes, rural tools and weapons, memorabilia of the Greek War of Independence and historical documents, engravings and paintings.

Taking the second left off Vassilísis Sofías after the Benáki Museum will bring you to the private **Museum of Cycladic and Ancient Greek Art**, Neofítou Dhouká 4 (Mon–Fri 10am–4pm, Sat 10am–3pm; €3), which in the quality of its display methods is streets ahead of anything else in Athens. Though the collections are restricted to covering the Cycladic civilization (third millennium BC), the pre-Minoan Bronze Age (second millennium BC), and the period from the fall of Mycenae to the beginning of historic times at around 700 BC (plus a selection of pottery), you come away having learned far more about these periods than from the equivalent sections of the National Museum.

North, past the posh shopping district of Kolonáki, a **funicular** at the corner of Dhorás Dhistría and Ploutárhou (Mon–Wed & Fri–Sun 8.45am–12.20am; Thurs 10.30am–12.20am; €1.50) begins its ascent to the summit of **Lykavitós**. The principal path up the hill begins here, too, rambling up through the woods. On top, the chapel of Áyios Yeóryios provides the main focus. There's a café on the adjacent terrace and another, more pleasant one, halfway down; both have views spectacular enough to excuse the high prices and unenthusiastic service.

The National Archeological Museum

The treasure house of the **National Archeological Museum** is due north of the central market at Patissíon 44 (summer Mon 12.30–7pm, Tues–Sun 8am–7pm; winter Mon 10.30am–5pm, Tues–Sun 8.30am–2.45pm; €6). To get the most out of the place, buy a detailed guide before you go in, as there's little in the way of explanatory captions. The biggest crowd-puller is the **Mycenaean hall** (Room 4), facing the main entrance, with all of Schliemann's gold finds from the grave circle at Mycenae, including the so-called Mask of Agamemnon, which is almost impossible to see in summer for the hordes surrounding it.

To the right of the Mycenaean hall, Room 6 houses a large collection of **Cycladic art** – pre-Mycenaean pieces from the islands; the most characteristic items are folded-arm figurines, among them a near full-sized nude. Most of the rest of the ground floor is occupied by **sculpture**. Beginning in Room 7, on the left of the main entrance, the exhibition evolves chronologically from the Archaic through the Classical and Hellenistic periods to the Roman-

and Egyptian-influenced. Room 15 heralds the Classical art collection, with the mid-fifth-century BC **Statue of Poseidon**, dredged from the sea off Évvia in the 1920s. Found in the same shipwreck was the virtuoso Little Jockey (Room 21). The most reproduced of all the sculptures is in Room 31: a first-century statue of a naked Aphrodite about to rap Pan's knuckles for getting too fresh. The many stelae (carved gravestones) offer fascinating glimpses of everyday life and changing styles of craftsmanship.

Keep a reserve of energy for the reconstructed **Thíra rooms** upstairs. Discovered at Akrotiri on the island of Santoríni, they date from around 1450 BC – contemporary with the Minoan civilization on Crete – and are frescoed with monkeys, antelopes and flowers, and furnished with painted wooden chairs and beds. The other upper rooms are occupied by a dizzying succession of pottery.

Eating, drinking and entertainment

As you'd expect, Athens has the best and the most varied **restaurants** and **tavernas** in the country. If it's character you're after, Pláka's hills and stepped lanes can still provide a pleasant evening's setting for a meal, despite the touts and tourist hype. But for good-value, good-quality fare, it's best to strike out into the ring of neighbourhoods around: Psyrrí, Pangráti, Exárhia, Neápoli, Veïkoú/Koukáki, or Áno Petrálona. None is more than a thirty-minute walk or bus ride from the centre. Quintessentially Greek **ouzerí** and **mezedhopolía** are bars selling oúzo, beer and wine, along with *mezédhes* (hors d'oeuvres). The more exciting of the city's **bars**, however, are music-oriented and tend to close down in the summer months. Bars, cinemas, exhibitions and nightlife venues change fast and often, so it's useful to have a copy of the weekly Greek-language *Athinorama* magazine and the English-language daily *Athens News* (*www.athensnews.gr*), which between them have full listings of the city's clubs, galleries, concerts and films.

Restaurants

Amvrosia, Dhrákou 3, beside Syngroú-Fix metro, Veïkoú. The best of several grills on this pedestrian street; always packed. Good takeaway *yíros*, or enjoy a whole roast chicken at the tables for about €3.

Barba Yannis, Emmanouíl Benáki 94. Vast menu of inexpensive home-style oven-cooked food, washed down by barrel wine. Equally varied clientele enjoying it, at indoor/outdoor tables most of year. Food is best at lunch, although it's open until 1.30am.

Eden, Lissíou 12. Athens' oldest vegetarian restaurant, hugely popular even though dishes tend to be soya this and soya that. Closed Tues.

Iy Gardhenia, Anastasíou Zínni 29, Koukáki. Extremely basic, but inexpensive (€7) oven-casserole food in a cool, cavernous setting. Closes 9pm, earlier in mid-summer.

Ikonomou, cnr Tróön & Kydhandídhon, Áno Petrálona. Simple, cheap *mayireftá* (casserole dishes) served to packed sidewalk tables in summer.

Iy Ipiros, Platía Ayíou Filíppou, Monastiráki. Long-established *mayireftá* taverna at the heart of the flea market; good value and great people-watching.

O Kostas, Ekális 7, Platía Varnáva, Pangráti. Among the oldest and least expensive tavernas in town; brief but lovingly cooked menu of a few bean dishes, meatballs and fried fish (€7), washed down by palatable bulk wine. Indoor/outdoor tables.

To Koutouki, Lakíou 9, Áno Petrálona. Excellent grills and vegetable starters like fáva or peppers served on an ever-popular roof terrace. Evenings only; indoor seating in winter. Around €13.

Iy Lefka, Mavromiháli 121, Neápoli. Traditional 1930s-style taverna with barrelled retsina (resinated wine), vegetable-based starters and *mayireftá*, plus a garden. Closed Sun.

O Megaritis, Ferekýdhou 2, corner Arátou. Cheap casserole food, barrel wine, indoor and outdoor seating.

O Pinaleon, Mavromihális 152, Neápoli. Rich starters, brought on the traditional *dhískos* or tray, precede hearty grills, all washed down by excellent bulk wine; allow €12. Open Oct–May in the evenings only; arrive before 9pm.

Rozalia, Valtetsíou 58, Exárhia. The best, and best-value all-round taverna near the triangular plaza: *mezédhes* on a *dhískos*, grills, seafood and *mayireftá*, plus excellent bulk wine and good service. Around €12. Garden open in summer.

Iy Taverna tou Psyrri, Eskhýlou, Psyrrí. The only straightforward taverna in a zone dominated by ouzerí, this excels at grilled/fried seafood, vegetable starters and wine from basement barrels. Arrive early or queue for a table. Maximum €13.

O Thanasis, Mitropóleos 69. Reckoned the best *souvláki* and kebab in this district, but watch out for the fiery-pepper side dish. Always packed with locals at lunchtime, worth the wait for either takeaway or sit-down service.

O Vyrinis, Arhimídhous 11, Pangráti. Traditional casserole-dish taverna, recently overhauled, still consistent in quality and price (€13). Oregano-baked lamb a speciality. Garden seating in summer. Closed Sun & Aug.

Ouzerí and mezedhopolía

To Athinaïkon, Themistokléous 2, corner Panepistimíou. Long-established ouzerí with marble tables and old posters, popular with local businessmen at lunch, and strongest on very fresh seafood. Allow €13. Closed Sun.

Avisynia Café, Platía Avissynías, Monastiráki. Furnished with antiques from the adjacent flea market, this upmarket ouzerí comes into its own at weekends when there's live, if slightly hokey, music. Specials include pork loin with prunes. €20. Closed Sun eve & Mon.

Kafenío Dhioskouri, Dhioskoúron, Pláka. Popular bar-café, where seafood snacks are served at tables with an unbeatable view of the ancient agora.

Ouzeri Evvia, Yeoryíou Olymbíou 8, Koukáki. Fresh dips and seafood titbits washed down by good bulk wine or ouzo; informal, inexpensive (€12), and with sidewalk seating on this pedestrian street. Closed Aug.

Filistron, Apostólou Pávlou 23, Thissío. Excellent all-round ouzeri; best in the evening when the roof terrace allows unimpeded views of the Acropolis. Allow €15.

Peri Fix, Yeoryíou Olymbíou 15, Koukáki. Mezedhopolío verging on conventional taverna: just a half-dozen daily casserole dishes, inexpensive and abundant, served at pleasant sidewalk tables under the trees. €10.

The Athens Festival

The summer **Athens Festival** has, over the years, come to encompass cultural events in just about every sphere: Classical Greek theatre most famously, but also established and contemporary dance, classical music, big-name jazz, traditional Greek music and a smattering of rock shows. As well as the Herodes Atticus theatre, which is memorable in itself on a warm summer's evening, the festival and its various satellite offshoots spread to the open-air theatre on Lykavitós hill, the Veákio amphitheatre in Pireás and (with special bus excursions) to the great ancient theatre at Epidaurus. The Festival runs from early June until late-September, and for theatre especially, you'll have to move fast to get tickets. The main **festival box office** is in the arcade at Stadhíou 4 (March–Sept Mon–Fri 8.30am–4pm, Sat 9am–2.30pm; ☎01/32 21 459); theatre box offices open early on the evening of performance.

Listings

Airlines Aegean/Cronus, Óthonos 10 (☎01/33 15 502); Alitalia, Vouliagmenis 577 (☎01/99 88 888); British Airways, Themistokléous 1, Glyfádha suburb (☎01/89 06 666); EasyJet (*www.easyjet.com*); Delta, Óthonos 4 (☎01/33 11 660); KLM, Vouliagménis 41, Glyfádha (☎01/96 05 000); Olympic, Andhréa Syngroú 96 (☎01/92 69 111); Virgin Atlantic, Panórmou 70, Ambelókipi (☎01/69 05 300).

Bookshops Compendium, Níkis 28 off Sýndagma, has a good stock of books on Greece, travel guides (including Rough Guides) and secondhands. Eleftheroudhakis, Panepistimíou 17 plus other branches, has the largest foreign-language stock in town, strong on art and cuisine. Iy Folia tou Vivlíou, arcade at Panepistimíou 25, has a good social science and fiction department upstairs, and a good travel guide/map shop on the ground floor, including most Rough Guides.

Car rental Most outlets line the top of Andhréa Syngroú, including Autorent, no. 11; Just, no. 43; Europcar/InterRent, no. 4; Hertz, no. 12; Holiday, no. 8; National/Alamo, no. 33; Budget, no. 6.

Embassies and consulates Australia, Tsóha 24 (☎01/64 50 404); Canada, I Yennadhíou 4 (☎01/72 73 400); Ireland, Vassiléos Konstandínou 7 (☎01/72 32 771); Netherlands, Vassiléos Konstandínou 5 (☎01/72 39 701); New Zealand, Xenías 24 (☎01/77 10 112); UK, Ploutárhou 1, Kolonáki (☎01/72 36 211); USA, Vassilísis Sofías av 91 (☎01/72 12 951).

Flight information ☎01/35 30 000. To get to the airport from town, leave plenty of time: from the Ethnikí Ámyna metro station, allow 40min on bus E94; from Sýndagma, bus E95 can take 1hr 20min. From Pireás, you'd do best to go as far as you can on the metro first, at least during the day; bus E96 can take up to 2hr.

Hospital Call the tourist police (☎171) for the address of the nearest hospital, and take a taxi to the address they give you. KAT, way out in Maroússi (with its own metro stop), is the designated Greater Athens emergency ward.

Internet Central cybercafés include Downtown Internet, Platía Omonía 10; Enydreion, Syngroú 13; Museum Internet Café, Patission 46; Sofokleous.com Internet Café, Stadhíou 5.

Laundry at Angélou Yerónda 10, off Platía Filomoússou Eterías, Pláka; at Dhidhótou 46, Exárhia; at Veïkoú 107 (below Platía Koukakíou).

Pharmacies Call ☎107 for details of after-hours pharmacies, or consult the rota schedule posted in the window of any pharmacy. Bakakos, on Platía Omonía, is the largest pharmacy in the city.

Post office Main offices at Eólou 100, just off Omónia (Mon–Fri 7.30am–8pm, Sat 7.30am–2pm) and on Sýndagma (same hours plus Sun 9am–1pm).

Tourist police Dhimitrakopoúlou 77, near corner Zínni (☎171).

Train tickets The OSE office by the university at Sína 6 (Mon–Sat 8am–3pm) has information and sells both domestic and international tickets. ISYTS, Nikis 11, sells train tickets and rail passes for under-26s.

Travel agents Discounted air tickets are sold by Magic Bus, Filellínon 20 (☎01/32 37 471, *magic@magic.gr*); Consolas, next door at no. 18; and Sotiriou, the Council Travel representatives, at Níkis 30 (☎01/32 20 503). Etos (USIT) at Filellínon 7, and Himalaya, Filellínon 7 upstairs, are also worth a look.

Around Athens

Attica (Attikí), the region encompassing the capital, is not much explored by tourists, except for the great romantic ruin of the Temple of Poseidon at Sounion. Otherwise, only the functional ports of Pireás and Rafína are of interest, to escape to the islands.

Pireás (Piraeus)

PIREÁS, port of Athens since Classical times, is today a municipality in its own right, containing much of Greater Athens' industries, as well as various commercial activities. Most visitors come for the **inter-island ferries**. The easiest way there is by metro: Pireás is the last stop heading southwest from Monastiráki.

Pireás has excellent **eating** options: you'll find several budget restaurants around the market area, back from the waterside Aktí Miaoúli/Ethnikís Andístasis. For more substantial meals, there is a string of ouzerí and seafood tavernas along Aktí Themistokléous, west of the Zéa Marina, most of them well priced. For a real blowout, *Vassilenas* at Etolikoú 72 provides enough *mezédhes* to defy all appetites (set menu €18; booking recommended ☎01/46 12 457).

It's worth picking up a schedule of **ferry** departures for the current week from an EOT office – in Athens near Sýndagma, or in Pireás in the Dhiikitirío Building on Zéa Marina (☎01/41 81 105). Most of the boats leave at set times: for the main Cycladic islands (8–9am); for the major Dodecanese islands (1–2pm); for the northeast Aegean islands (5–6pm); and for Crete (around 7pm). The best plan is to get to Pireás early and check with the various shipping companies around the metro station and along the quayside Platía Karaïskáki. The largest of these, Minoan Flying Dolphins, has an office at 26–28 Aktí Kondhýli (☎01/41 99 000, *www.mfd.gr*). Others are ANEK Lines, Aktí Possidhónos 32 (☎01/41 97 410, *www.anek.gr*) and NEL, which has no exclusive representation.

The Temple of Poseidon at Sounion

The 70km of coast south of Athens – dubbed the **Apollo Coast** – has some good but highly developed beaches. At weekends, when Athenians flee the city, the sands fill fast, as do the innumerable bars, restaurants and discos. If this is what you're after, then resorts like Glyfádha and Vouliagméni are functional enough. But for most visitors, the coast's attraction is at the end of the road. **Cape Sounion** (Akrí Soúnio) is one of the most imposing spots in Greece, and on its tip stands the fifth-century BC **Temple of Poseidon** (daily 10am–sunset;

€3), built in the time of Pericles as part of a sanctuary to the sea god. In summer there is faint hope of solitude unless you slip into the site before the tours arrive, but the temple is as evocative a ruin as Greece can offer. Doric in style, it preserves sixteen of its thirty-four columns, and the view from the temple takes in the islands of Kéa, Kýthnos and Sérifos to the southeast, Égina and the Peloponnese to the west. Below the promontory are several coves, the most sheltered of which is a five-minute walk east from the car park and site entrance. The main Soúnio **beach** is more crowded, but has a group of tavernas at the far end, which, considering the location, are reasonably priced. There's a single **campsite** about 5km short of the cape, the *Bacchus* (☎0292/39 262).

Buses to Soúnion leave every thirty minutes from the KTEL terminal on Mavromatéon at the southwest corner of the Pédhion Áreos park in central Athens. They alternate between coastal (*paraliakó*) and inland (*mesoyiakó*) services, the latter slightly longer and more expensive (the coastal route takes around 2hr).

Rafína

The port of **RAFÍNA** has ferries and hydrofoils to a dozen of the Cyclades, as well as to nearby Évvia and (seasonally) the northeast Aegean. It is connected regularly with Athens by a bus route from the Mavromatéon terminal through the "gap" in Mount Pendéli (takes 1hr or so). Much of the town has been spoilt by seaside development, but the little fishing harbour with its line of roof-terrace seafood restaurants remains one of the most attractive spots on the Attic coast. The town's handful of **hotels** are often full; the lowest-priced, the D-class *Corali* (☎0294/22 477; ④), is in Platiá Nikifórou Plastíra, but the beachside **campsite** at nearby Kókkino Limanáki is a good fall-back option.

THE PELOPONNESE

The appeal of the **Peloponnese** (Pelopónnisos) is hard to overstate. This southern peninsula, technically an island since the cutting of the Corinth Canal, seems to have the best of almost everything Greek. Its ancient sites include the Homeric palace of Agamemnon at **Mycenae**, the Greek theatre at **Epidaurus** and the sanctuary of **Olympia**, host of the Olympic Games for a millennium. The medieval remains are scarcely less rich, with the fabulous castle at **Acrocorinth**; the strange tower-houses and churches of the **Máni**; and the extraordinary Byzantine towns of **Mystra** and **Monemvasiá**. The Peloponnesian **beaches**, especially along the west coast, are among the finest and least developed in the country. And, last but by no means least, the landscape itself is inspiring, dominated by forested mountains, and cut by lush valleys and gorges.

The usual approach from Athens is via Kórinthos; buses and trains run this way at least every hour. A more attractive method is by hydrofoil, via the islands of the Argo-Saronic; the route runs from Pireás, through the islands and then south to Monemvasiá and the remote island of Kýthira.

Kórinthos (Corinth)

The modern city of **KÓRINTHOS** was levelled by earthquakes in 1858, 1928 and again in 1981. It's a hot and noisy industrial-agricultural centre, but it does have the attraction of easy access to its predecessor, ancient Corinth, 7km southwest and served by taxis and hourly buses (8am–9pm).

The centre of Kórinthos is its **park**, bordered on the longer sides by Ermoú and Ethnikís Andistásis streets. The **bus station** for Athens is opposite the **train station**, several blocks east towards the seafront, but bus stops for most local destinations are around the park. The few **hotels** are overpriced; probably the best value is *Ephira* at Ethnikís Andístásis 52

(☎0741/24 434; ④), conveniently near the most important bus terminus. There are also a couple of unenticing **campsites** along the gulf to the west: *Blue Dolphin* at Léheo (☎0741/25 766) is preferable. **Eating** options aren't spectacular; decent *Anaxagoras* and *Ekositesseres Ores*, both on waterfront Ayíou Nikoláou, are modestly priced. **Buses** to Mykínes, Árgos and Náfplio leave from a café at the corner of Ethnikís Andístasis and Arátou.

Ancient Corinth

The ruins of the **ancient city**, which displaced Athens as capital of the Greek province in Roman times, occupy a rambling site below the acropolis hill of **Acrocorinth**, itself littered with medieval remains. To explore both you really need a full day, or better still, to stay close by. The modern village of **ARHÉA KÓRINTHOS** spreads back around the main archeological zone, where you'll find good **accommodation** at, for instance, *Hotel Shadow* (☎0741/31 481; ④); there's also a scattering of **rooms** to rent in the backstreets.

Whoever possessed Corinth had control of trade between northern Greece and the Peloponnese, and a link between the Ionian and Aegean seas. It's not surprising, then, that the city's history is characterized by invasions and power struggles, but it nonetheless suffered only one break in its continuity, when the Romans razed it in 146 BC. The site lay in ruins for a century before being refounded, on a majestic scale, by Julius Caesar in 44 BC.

The main excavated **site** (daily 8am–5/7pm; €6), just behind the road where buses pull in, is dominated by the remains of the Roman city. You enter from the south side, which leads straight into the **Roman agora**, an enormous marketplace flanked by the foundations of a huge stoa, or covered walkway. To the north is a trace of the Greek city, a **sacred spring**, covered over by a grille at the base of a narrow flight of steps. More substantial is the elaborate Roman **Fountain of Peirene**, which stands below the level of the agora, to the side of a wide excavated stretch of what was the main approach to the city, the **Lechaion Way**; it exploits one of two natural springs in Corinth, and its cool water was channelled into a magnificent fountain and pool in the courtyard. The real focus, however, is a survival from the Classical Greek era: the fifth-century BC **Temple of Apollo**, whose seven austere Doric columns stand slightly above the level of the forum, and are flanked by the foundations of another marketplace and baths. To the west is the site **museum**, housing domestic pieces, some Roman mosaics and a frieze depicting the labours of Heracles.

Towering 575m above the lower town, **Acrocorinth** (Mon–Fri 8am–5/7pm, Sat & Sun 8.30am–3pm; €1.50) is an amazing mass of rock still largely encircled by 2km of wall. During the Middle Ages this ancient acropolis of Corinth became one of Greece's most powerful fortresses, besieged by successive waves of invaders. It's a 4km climb up (about 1hr), but unreservedly recommended. Amid the sixty-acre site, you wander through a jumble of semi-ruined chapels, mosques, houses and battlements, erected in turn by Greeks, Romans, Byzantines, Crusaders, Venetians and Ottomans.

Mykínes (Mycenae)

Tucked into a fold of the hills just east of the highway from Kórinthos to Árgos is Agamemnon's citadel, "well-built **Mycenae**, rich in gold", as Homer wrote. It was uncovered in 1874 by the German archeologist Heinrich Schliemann, whose work was impelled by his belief that there was a factual basis to Homer's epics; the brilliantly crafted gold and sophisticated architecture that he found bore out the accuracy of Homer's epithets. Unless you have your own transport, you might want to stay in the modern village of **MYKÍNES**, 2km east of both the highway and the **train station** at **Fíkhti**, and 2km southwest of the ancient site. Among the options are the *Rooms Dassis* (☎0751/76 123; ④), *Hotel Belle Hélène*, up the hill towards the site (☎0751/76 225; ⑤), and two fairly central **campsites**, *Mycenae* (☎0751/76 121) and *Atreus* (☎0751/76 221). The village has plenty of **restaurants**, all geared to the lunchtime bus-tour trade.

The buildings unearthed by Schliemann show signs of having been occupied from around 1950 BC to 1100 BC, when the town, though still prosperous, was abandoned. No coherent explanation has been found for this event, but war among rival kingdoms was probably a major factor. You enter the **Citadel of Mycenae** (daily 8am–5/7pm; €4.50) through the mighty **Lion Gate**; the motif of a pillar supported by two lions was probably the symbol of the Mycenaean royal house, for a seal found on the site bears a similar device.

Inside the walls to the right is **Grave Circle A**, the cemetery which Schliemann believed to contain the bodies of Agamemnon and his followers, murdered on their triumphant return from Troy. In fact the burials date from about three centuries before the Trojan war, but they were certainly royal, and the finds (now in Athens' National Archeological Museum) are among the richest yet unearthed. Schliemann took the extensive **South House**, beyond the grave circle, to be the Palace of Agamemnon. But a much grander building, which must have been the **Royal Palace**, was later discovered on the summit of the acropolis. Rebuilt in the thirteenth century BC, probably at the same time as the Lion Gate, like all Mycenaean palaces it is centred around a **Great Court**. The small rooms to the north are believed to have been royal apartments and in one of them the remains of a red stuccoed bath have led to its fanciful identification as the spot of Agamemnon's murder. Equally evocative are the ramparts and secret cistern at their east end, near the large, stately **House of Columns**.

Only the ruling elite were permitted to live within the citadel itself; outside its walls lay the main part of the town. The extensive remains of **merchants' houses** have been uncovered near to the road, beside a second grave circle. A few minutes walk down the road from the main site is the astonishing **Treasury of Atreus**, a royal burial vault entered through a majestic fifteen-metre corridor. Set above the chamber doorway is a lintel formed by two immense slabs of stone, one of which – a staggering 9m long – is estimated to weigh 118 tonnes.

Náfplio and around

NÁFPLIO – a lively, beautifully sited town with a fading elegance, inherited from when it was briefly the first capital of modern Greece – makes an attractive base for exploring the Argolídha area and resting up by the sea. **Buses** arrive on Odhós Syngroú, just south of the interlocking main squares, **Platía Trión Navárhon** and **Platía Kapodhístrias**, themselves just west of the **train station** for the service from Árgos. An alternative approach, or onward route, is by **hydrofoil**; there are summer connections to Spétses and the other Argo-Saronic islands, and to Pireás and Monemvasiá (details from Yannopoulos, Platía Syndágmatos 18; ☎0752/28 054).

The main fort, the **Palamídhi** (daily 8am–6.45pm; winter closes 3pm; €3), is most directly approached by 899 stone-hewn steps up from Polyzoïdhou street, by the side of a Venetian bastion. Within the walls are three self-contained castles, all built by the Venetians in the 1710s (hence the Lion of St Mark above the gateways). The **Íts Kalé** ("Inner Citadel" in Turkish), to the west, occupies the ancient acropolis, whose walls were adapted by successive medieval occupants. The third fort, the photogenic **Boúrtzi**, occupies the islet offshore from the harbour and allowed the Venetians to close the shallow shipping channel with a chain. In the town itself, **Platía Syndágmatos**, the main square, is the focus of most interest. On and around it survive three converted **Ottoman mosques**: one is now a cinema; another, near the southwest corner, is Greece's original parliament building; the third has been reconsecrated as the cathedral of Áyios Yeóryios.

The EOT **tourist office** is at 25-Martíou 2 (daily 9am–1pm & 4–8pm; ☎0752/24 444), but the verbal information provided is notoriously unreliable. **Hotels** are generally overpriced, the most reasonable being *Hotel Economou* at Argonaftón 22, located between the roads to Árgos and Toló a 15-minute walk from the centre (☎0752/23 955; ④), also with some dorm beds. *Hotel Dioscouri*, Výronos 6 (☎0752/28 550; ⑦) is another option. Private **rooms**, most of which cluster on the slope south of the main square, can be a better deal. For **eating**, try

Kakanarakis, Vassilísis Ólgas 18; the reliable *Omorfi Tavernaki* at no. 16; or *Byzantio*, Vasiléos Alexándrou 15.

Epídhavros (Epidaurus)

From the sixth century BC to Roman times, **EPÍDHAVROS**, 30km east of Náfplio, was a major spa and religious centre; its **Sanctuary of Asclepius** was the most famous of all shrines dedicated to the god of healing. The magnificently preserved 14,000-seat theatre (daily 8am–5pm; €4.50), built in the fourth century BC, merged so well into the landscape that it was rediscovered only last century. Constructed with mathematical precision, it has near-perfect acoustics: from the highest of the 54 tiers of seats you can hear coins dropped in the orchestra. Close by is a small **museum** (Mon noon–5pm, Tues–Sun 8am–5pm; admission included) containing various statuary and frieze fragments. The sanctuary itself encompasses hospitals, dwellings for the priest-physicians, and hotels and amusements for the fashionable visitors. Its circular **Tholos**, one of the best-preserved buildings on the site, was designed, like the theatre, by Polykleitos.

Most people take in Epídhavros as a day-trip (there are five buses daily from Náfplio), but you can **camp** near the car park or stay in **LYGOURIÓ**, 5km north, at *Hotel Koronis* (☎0753/22 267; ⑤) or *Hotel Alkyon* (☎0753/22 002; ④). The nearest **restaurant** to the site is *Oasis* on the Lygourió road, but *Leonides* in the village proper is better.

Trípoli

Uninspiring **TRÍPOLI** is a major crossroads of the Peloponnese, from where most travellers either head northwest towards Olympia, or south to Spárti and Mystra, or Kalamáta. Alternatives include more direct routes to the coast – west to Kyparissía, or east to Náfplio or Ástros/Leonídhi. On the outskirts, the Peloponnese **railway** continues its meandering course from Kórinthos and Árgos to Kyparissía or Kalamáta. The major **bus terminus**, serving all destinations in Arkadhía and the northern Peloponnese, is on Platía Kolokotróni, one of the main squares. All other buses, including those to Spárti, Kalamáta, and the Máni, leave from the café directly opposite the train station, ten minutes' walk away down Lagopáti at the southeastern edge of town. There's a good **hotel**, *Alex*, at Vassiléos Yeoryíou 26 (☎071/223 465; ⑤).

Mystra (Mystrás)

A glorious, airy place, hugging a steep flank of Taïyettos, **MYSTRA** is arguably the most exciting site that the Peloponnese can offer, an astonishingly complete Byzantine city which once sheltered a population of some 40,000. The castle on its summit was built in 1249 by Guillaume II de Villehardouin, fourth Frankish Prince of the Morea (as the Peloponnese was then known), and together with the fortresses of Monemvasiá and the Máni it guarded his territory. In 1262 the Byzantines drove out the Franks and established the Despotate of Mystra. This isolated triangle of land in the southeastern Peloponnese enjoyed considerable autonomy from Constantinople, flowering as a brilliant cultural centre in the fourteenth and early fifteenth centuries and only falling to the Ottomans in 1460, seven years after the Byzantine capital was conquered.

The site of the **Byzantine city** (daily: summer 8am–7pm; winter 8.30am–2pm; €6) has two entrances on the road up from Néos Mystrás: it makes sense to take the bus to the top entrance, then explore a leisurely downhill route. Following this course, the first identifiable building that you come to is the church of **Ayía Sofia**, erected in the fifteenth century as the burial place of the despot Manouil Cantacuzene and which served as the chapel for the Despots' Palace. The chapel's finest feature is its floor, made from polychrome marble; its frescoes have also survived reasonably well, protected until recently by whitewash applied by the Ottomans, who adapted the building as a mosque. The **Kástro**, reached by a path that climbs directly from the upper gate, maintains the Frankish design of its thirteenth-century construction, though modified by successive occupants.

Heading down from Ayía Sofía, there is a choice of routes. The right fork winds past the ruins of a Byzantine mansion, the **Palatáki** or Small Palace, and **Áyios Nikólaos**, originally a Turkish building. The left fork is more interesting, passing the massively fortified **Náfplio Gate**, which was the principal entrance to the upper town, and the vast, multi-storeyed complex of the **Despots' Palace**, parts of whose Gothic structures probably date to the Franks. At the **Monemvasiá Gate**, linking the upper and lower towns, turn right for the **Pandánassa convent** (closed for restoration at the time of writing), whose nuns were the only people allowed to stay among the ruins after the villagers were relocated in 1952. The church, whose name means "Queen of the World", is perhaps the finest that survives in the town, a perfectly proportioned blend of Byzantine and Gothic. Its frescoes date from various centuries, with some superb fifteenth-century work including scenes from the life of Christ in the gallery.

Further down on this side of the lower town stands the **House of Frangopoulos**, once the home of the Despotate's chief minister. Beyond it is the diminutive **Perívleptos monastery**, whose single-domed church, partly carved out of the rock, contains Mystra's most complete cycle of frescoes, almost all of which date from the fourteenth century. The **Mitrópolis**, or cathedral, immediately beyond the gateway, ranks as the oldest of Mystra's churches, built from 1270 onward. A marble slab set in its floor is carved with the symbol of the Paleologos dynasty, the double-headed eagle of Byzantium, commemorating the spot where Constantine XI Paleologos, the last emperor, was crowned in 1449. A short way uphill lies the **Vrondohión monastery**, the centre of intellectual life in the fifteenth-century town, serving as the usual burial place of the despots as well. There are a couple of churches attached; the further of the two, **Odhiyítria**, built in 1311, has been beautifully restored, revealing frescoes with startlingly bold juxtapositions of colour.

Practicalities

The modern village, **NÉOS MYSTRÁS**, is a small roadside community whose half-dozen tavernas are crowded with tour buses by day and revert to a low-key life at night. **Accommodation** is limited; one alternative to *Hotel Byzantion* (☎0731/83 309, *medotels@otenet.gr*; ⑤) are the more affordable rooms of *Khristina Vahaviolou* (☎0731/20 047; ④). Nearby **SPÁRTI** (ancient Sparta, though there's little left to see) is a good alternative base, with, near the top of Paleológou, the friendly *Cecil*, Paleológou 125 (☎0731/24 980; ④) and *Apollon*, Thermopýlon 84 (☎0731/22 491; ④). One **campsite**, 2.5km from Spárti, is *Mystras* (☎0741/22 724); closer to Mystra itself is *Castle View* (☎0731/93 303). There are a number of reasonable **restaurants** in Spárti, including *Averof*, Paleológou 77, and *Diethnes*, Paleológou 105. Spárti's bus station is at the far eastern end of Lykoúrgou, but buses for Mystra depart from the corner of Lykoúrgou and Leonídhou, on the west side of the central square.

Monemvasiá

Set impregnably on a great eruption of rock connected to the mainland by a kilometre-long causeway, the Byzantine seaport of **MONEMVASIÁ** is a place of grand, haunted atmosphere. At the outset of the thirteenth century it was the Byzantines' sole possession in the Morea, eventually being taken by the Franks in 1249 after three years of siege. Regained by the Byzantines as part of the ransom for the captured Guillaume de Villehardouin, it served as the chief commercial port of the Despotate of the Morea. The city was eventually liberated from the Ottomans in 1823. Mystra, despite the presence of the court, was never much more than a large village; Monemvasiá at its peak in the Byzantine era had a population of almost 60,000.

You can get there by road or, more enjoyably, by sea. There are more or less daily **hydrofoils** in season, linking it with Leonídhi, Spétses and Pireás to the north, and with Neápoli and the island of Kýthira to the south, dropping off midway along the causeway. **Buses** connect with Spárti and Athens three times daily, and with Yíthio twice daily in season only, arriving in the village of YÉFIRA on the mainland, where most **accommodation** is located. There are several reasonable hotels near the causeway – try the *Monemvassia* (☎0732/61 381; ④) – plus numerous pensions and rooms. The nearest **campsite**, *Kapsis Paradise*, is 3.5km south of Yéfira near a reasonable beach. Rooms on the rock are much more expensive, but worth the splurge: try the long-established *Malvasia* (☎0732/61 323; ⑤). The best **taverna** is *Matoula*.

The **Lower Town** once sheltered forty churches and over 800 homes, an incredible mass of building threaded by an intricate network of alleys. A single main street harbours most of the restored houses, plus cafés, tavernas and a scattering of shops. The foremost monument is the **Mitrópolis**, the cathedral built by Emperor Andronikos II Komnenos in 1293, and the largest medieval church in southern Greece. Across the square, the tenth-century domed church of **Áyios Pétros** was transformed by the Ottomans into a mosque and is now a small **museum** of local finds (unpredictable opening hours). Towards the sea is a third church, the **Khrysafítissa**, with its bell hanging from an old acacia tree in the courtyard. It was restored and adapted by the Venetians in the eighteenth century, when for twenty-odd years they took the Peloponnese from the Ottomans. The climb to the **Upper Town** is highly worthwhile, not least for the solitude. Its fortifications, like those of the lower town, are substantially intact; within, the site is a ruin, though infinitely larger than you could imagine from below. Close to the gateway is the beautiful thirteenth-century **Ayía Sofía**, the only relatively complete building. Beyond the church extend acres of ruins: the stumpy bases of Byzantine houses and public buildings, and, perhaps most striking, a vast **cistern** to ensure water in time of siege.

Yíthio and the Máni peninsula

YÍTHIO, Sparta's ancient port, is the gateway to the dramatic **Máni** peninsula and one of the south's most attractive seaside towns. Its somewhat low-key harbour, with occasional ferries, has a graceful nineteenth-century waterside. Out to sea, tethered by a long narrow causeway, is the islet of **Marathoníssi** (ancient Kranae), where Paris and Helen of Troy spent their first night after her abduction from Sparta. **Buses** drop you close to the centre of town, and finding **accommodation** should be a matter of a stroll along the waterfront Vassiléos Pávlou, where there is, amongst others, the *Kondogiannis* pension, no. 19 (☎0733/22 518; ④), and the French-run *Saga*, further round on Tzanetáki (☎0733/23 220; ⑤), with a **restaurant** on the ground floor and fine views of Marathoníssi. There are plenty more rooms along the front; others are up the steps from the waterside and then along streets parallel to the sea. There are several summer **campsites** along the huge Mavrovoúni beach, which begins 3km south of town off the Areópoli road. For **eating**, the *Iy Nautila* or *Korali* ouzeris, near the roundabout at the head of the port have more reasonable prices than the obviously touristy fish tavernas on the quay.

The Máni peninsula

The southernmost peninsula of Greece, the **Máni**, stretches from Yíthio in the east and Kalamáta in the west down to Cape Ténaro, mythical entrance to the underworld. It is a wild and arid landscape with an idiosyncratic culture and history: nowhere in Greece does a region seem so close to its medieval past. The quickest way into it is to take a bus from Yíthio to **AREÓPOLI**, gateway to the so-called Inner Máni. There are **rooms** at a number of tower-houses, including *Pyrgos Tsimova* (☎0733/51 301; ⑤), or there's the *Hotel Kouris* on the main square (☎0733/51 340; ⑤). You can rent a taxi here fairly easily, and there are daily **buses** in summer south to Yeroliménas (winter: 3 weekly). More regular buses running north to Stoúpa, Kardhamýli and Kalamáta usually involve a change in Ítylo, 10km north.

Some 8km south of Areópoli is the village of **PÝRGOS DHIROÚ**, where the road forks off for a further 4km to a set of **caves** (daily: summer 8am–6pm; winter 8am–2.30pm; €12). This is very much a packaged attraction, with long queues for admission, then a thirty-minute punt around the underground waterways of the Glyfádha caves and a tour on foot of the huge Alepótrypa caves, where recent excavation has unearthed evidence of prehistoric occupation. **YEROLIMÉNAS** has an end-of-the-world air, but despite appearances was only founded in the 1870s. There are a few shops, a couple of cafés and two **hotels**: *Akroyiali* (☎0733/54 204; ④) has a good taverna underneath. At the dock, occasional **boat trips** are offered around Cape Ténaro, passing the pebbly bay of **Asómati**, where a small cave is said to be the mythical gate to Hades.

North of Areópoli, the 80km of road to Kalamáta has views as dramatic and beautiful as any in Greece. A series of small **beaches** begins at **ÁYIOS NIKÓLAOS**, which has fish tavernas and rooms such as the *Skafidakia* (☎0721/77 698; ④), and extends more or less through to Kardhamýli. **STOÚPA**, which has possibly the best sands, is now geared very much to tourism, with several small hotels – friendliest and most reasonable of which is *Lefktron* (☎0721/77 322; ④) – a **campsite** five minutes' walk from Kalógria beach, a well-stocked supermarket and a fair number of tavernas. Doufexis Travel (☎0721/77 677) can arrange accommodation. **KARDHAMÝLI**, 8km north, remains a beautiful place despite its commercialization and busy road, with a long pebble beach and a restored tower-house quarter. Besides its ranks of prebooked self-catering apartments, there's the *Kardamýli Beach* hotel (☎0721/73 180; ⑦). Eating is best at *Kiki's* or *Lela's* (☎0721/73 541); the latter also has some good rooms (⑤).

Olymbía (Olympia)

The historic resonance of **OLYMPIA**, which for over a millennium hosted the Panhellenic Games, is rivalled only by Delphi or Mycenae. Its site, too, ranks with this company, for although the ruins are confusing, the setting is as perfect as could be imagined: a luxuriant valley of wild olive and plane trees beside the twin rivers of Alfiós and Kladhéos, overlooked by the pine-covered hill of Krónos. The contests at Olympia probably began around the eleventh century BC, slowly developing over the next two centuries from a local festival to a major quadrennial celebration attended by states from throughout the Greek world. From the very beginning, the main Olympic events were athletic, but the great gathering of people expanded the games' importance: nobles and ambassadors negotiated treaties here, while merchants chased contacts and sculptors and poets sought commissions. The games eventually fell victim to the Christian Emperor Theodosius's crackdown on pagan festivities in 391–2 AD, and his successor ordered the destruction of the temples, a process completed by invasion, earthquakes and, lastly, by the River Alfiós changing its course to cover the sanctuary site. There it remained, covered by seven metres of silt and sand, until the 1870s.

The entrance to the **ancient site** (daily 8am–5/7pm; €3.50; joint ticket including museum €6) leads along the west side of the sacred precinct wall past a group of public and official buildings, including a structure adapted to a Byzantine church. This was originally the studio of Pheidias, the fifth-century BC sculptor responsible for the great cult statue in the focus of the precinct, the great Doric **Temple of Zeus**. Built between 470 and 456 BC, it was as large as the Parthenon and its decoration rivalled the finest in Athens; partly recovered, its sculptures are now exhibited in the museum. In the cella was displayed the great gold and ivory cult statue by Pheidias, and here, too, the Olympian flame was kept alight from the time of the games until the following spring – a tradition continued at an altar for the modern games. The smaller **Temple of Hera**, behind, was the first built here; prior to its completion in the seventh century BC, the sanctuary had only open-air altars, dedicated to Zeus and a variety of other cult gods. Rebuilt in the Doric style in the sixth century BC, it's the most complete structure on the site. Finally, though, what makes sense of Olympia is the 200-metre track of the **Stadium** itself. The start and finish lines are still there, as are the judges' thrones in the middle and seating banked to each side. The tiers here eventually accommodated up to 30,000 spectators, with a smaller number on the southern slope overlooking the **Hippodrome** where chariot races were held.

In the **archeological museum**, about 200m north (summer Mon noon–7pm, Tues–Sun 8am–7pm; winter Mon 11am–5pm, Tues–Fri 8am–5pm, Sat & Sun 8am–2.30pm; €3.50; joint ticket including site €6), the centrepiece is the statuary from the Temple of Zeus, displayed in the vast main hall. Most famous of the individual sculptures is the **Hermes of Praxiteles**, dating from the fourth century BC; one of the best-preserved of all Classical sculptures, it retains traces of its original paint. The best of the smaller objects include several fine bronzes, among them the **helmet of Miltiades**, the Athenian general at the Battle of Marathon, and a superb terracotta miniature of *Zeus Abducting Ganymede*.

Practicalities

Most people arrive at Olympia **via Pýrgos**, which has frequent buses to the site, plus numerous connections to Pátra and a couple daily to Kalamáta/Kyparissía. The train line between Pýrgos and Olymbía is closed for renovation. The modern town of **OLYMBÍA** has grown up merely to serve the excavations and tourist trade. The not-always-helpful **tourist office** is on the south side of Praxiéous Kondhýli (Mon–Sat 9am–3pm; ☎0624/23 100). Among the **hotels**, the least expensive are *Hercules*, by the church (☎0624/22 696; ④), and *Hermes*, Kondhýli 63 (☎0624/22 577; ④). The closest **campsite**, *Diana*, just off the main road, has a pool and good facilities. For **eating**, most of the tavernas offer standard tourist meals at mildly inflated prices; honourable exceptions include *O Kladheos*, a beautiful and authentic grill near the river. Beware some cafés in town, which have positively Athenian prices.

Pátra (Patras)

PÁTRA is the largest town in the Peloponnese and the major port of Greece after Pireás. You can go from here to Italy, as well as to certain Ionian islands, and the city is a key to the transport network of the mainland too. It's not the ideal holiday retreat: there are no beaches, no particular sights, the hotels are on noisy streets and the restaurants are generally uninspired. Unless you arrive late in the day, you shouldn't need to spend more than a few hours in the city. The main concentration of budget **hotels** is on Ayíou Andhréou, a block back from the harbour road Óthonos & Amalías; *El Greco* at no. 145 is a good bargain (☎061/272 931; ④), but *Atlanta*, Zaïmi 10 (☎061/220 098; ④), is more central. For **eating**, try the affordable fish dishes at *Dinos*, Óthonos & Amalías 102.

Agents along the harbour road, Óthonos Ké Amalías, sell tickets for various **ferries to Italy**. En route to Italy, you can stopover at Kefaloniá (summer only), or, more easily, at Igoumenítsa or Corfu. There is a variety of journey times, routes and fares, so try Superfast Ferries, Óthonos Ké Amalías 12 (☎061/623 574, *www.superfast.com*), ANEK at no. 25 (☎061/226 053, *www.anek.gr*), Blue Star at no. 14 (☎061/622 602, *www.strintzis.gr*), or Minoan Lines, Athinón 2 (☎061/421 500, *www.minoan.gr*). The EOT **tourist office** (☎061/420 304), by the customs house at the harbour, can be helpful for information, but is closed at weekends. Kapa on Ayíou Andhréou charges no commission to change money.

The main **bus station**, midway along the waterside, has services to Athens, Kyllíni, Pýrgos, and to other towns in the Peloponnese, as well as north to Ioánnina. Buses to Zákynthos, Kefaloniá and Delphi go from *Snack-bar Sami*, Óthonos & Amalías 58.

CENTRAL AND NORTHERN GREECE

Central Greece has a slightly indeterminate character, consisting mostly of vast agricultural plains dotted with rather drab market and industrial towns. The highlights all lie at the fringes: **Delphi** above all, and further northeast the forested slopes of **Mount Pílion** with its magnificent villages and alluring beaches or northwest at the unworldly rock-monasteries of the **Metéora**. Access to these monasteries is through **Kalambáka**, from where the **Katára pass** over the Píndhos Mountains brings you into **Epirus** (Ípiros), the region with the strongest identity in mainland Greece. En route lies **Métsovo**, perhaps the easiest location for a taste of mountain life, though increasingly commercialized. Nearby **Ioánnina**, once the stronghold of the notorious Ali Pasha, remains a town of some character, and serves as the main transport hub for trips into the relatively unspoilt villages of the **Zagóri** and the **Vikos gorge**. The forested peaks, deep ravines and turbulent rivers of the Píndhos range which always protected Epirus also kept it isolated: the region's role in ancient Greek affairs was peripheral, so there are few significant archeological sites, the main exception being **Dodona**, where the sanctuary includes a spectacular Classical theatre. The Epirus coast is in general disappointing: **Igoumenítsa** is a functional ferry terminal with few admirers, while **Párga**, the region's major resort, is oversubscribed in peak season, when it's effectively off-limits to long-haul travellers.

The northern provinces of **Macedonia** and **Thrace** have only been part of the Greek state since 1913 and 1923 respectively. As such, the region stands slightly apart from the rest of the nation (it still is subject to a separate bureaucratic administration) – an impression reinforced for visitors by scenery and climate that are essentially Balkan, and a vigorous day-to-day life that proceeds independently of tourism. Macedonia is characterized by lake-speckled vistas to the west, and, to the east, moving towards Thrace, by heavily cultivated flood plains and the deltas of rivers finishing courses begun in the former Yugoslavia or Bulgaria. The only areas to draw more than a scattering of summer visitors are **Mount Olympus** and **Halkidhikí**, the latter providing the beach-playground for the relaxed Macedonian capital of **Thessaloníki** and also sheltering the "Monks' Republic" of **Mount Áthos**.

Delphi

Access to the extraordinary site of **DELPHI**, 150km northwest of Athens, is straightforward: a half-dozen buses run there from the capital daily, and services are as frequent from **Livádhia**, the nearest rail terminus. With its site raised on the slopes of a high mountain terrace and dwarfed by the ominous crags of Parnassós, it's easy to see why the ancients believed Delphi to be the centre of the earth. But what confirmed this status was the discovery of a chasm that exuded strange vapours and reduced all comers to frenzied, incoherent and obviously prophetic mutterings. For over a thousand years a steady stream of pilgrims worked their way up the dangerous mountain paths to seek divine direction in matters of war, worship, love or business, until the oracle eventually expired with the demise of paganism in the fourth century AD.

You enter the **Sacred Precinct of Apollo** (daily 7.30am–7pm; winter closes 5pm; €3.50) by way of a small agora, enclosed by ruins of Roman porticoes and shops for the sale of votive offerings. The paved **Sacred Way** begins after a few stairs, zigzaging uphill between the foundations of memorials and treasuries, to the **Temple of Apollo**. Of the main body of the temple only the foundations stood when it was uncovered by the French in the 1890s; they have, however, re-erected six Doric columns, giving a vertical line to the ruins and providing some idea of its former dominance over the sanctuary. In the innermost part of the temple was a dark cell where the priestess would officiate; no sign of cave or chasm has been found, but it is likely that it was closed by earthquakes. The theatre and stadium used for the main events of the Pythian games are on terraces above the temple. The **theatre**, built in the fourth century BC, was closely connected with Dionysos, god of the arts and wine, who reigned in Delphi over the winter months when Apollo was absent and the oracle was silent. A steep path leads up through cool pine groves to the stadium, which was banked with stone seats only in Roman times.

The **museum** (summer Mon–Fri 7.30am–6.45pm, Sat & Sun 8.30am–2.45pm; winter daily 8.30am–3pm; €3.50) contains a collection of archaic sculpture matched only by finds on the Acropolis in Athens. Its most famous exhibit is *The Charioteer*, one of the few surviving bronzes of the fifth century BC. The charioteer's eyes, made of onyx and set slightly askew, lend it a startling realism while the demure expression sets the scene as a victory lap. Other major pieces include two huge *kouroi* (archaic male figures) from the sixth century BC, and a group of three colossal dancing women, worshipping Dionysos.

Following the road east of the sanctuary towards Aráhova, you reach a sharp bend. To the left, marked by niches for votive offerings and the remains of an archaic fountain house, the celebrated **Castalian spring** still flows from a cleft in the cliffs. Visitors to Delphi were obliged to purify themselves in its waters, usually by washing their hair, though murderers had to take the full plunge. Across and below the road from the spring is the **Marmaria** or Sanctuary of Athena Pronoia (daily: summer 8am–7pm; winter closes 5pm; free), the "Guardian of the Temple". The precinct's most conspicuous building is the **Tholos**, a fourth-century BC rotunda whose purpose is a mystery. Outside the precinct on the northwest side, above the Marmaria, is a **gymnasium**, also built in the fourth century BC but later enlarged by the Romans.

Practicalities

The modern village of **DHELFÍ**, like most Greek site villages, has a quick turnaround of visitors, so finding a place to stay should present few problems. There are upwards of twenty **hotels** and pensions, plus a few rooms to let, though there is no low season: in winter, skiers throng the place. Best value of the budget hotels is the D-class *Athena*, Vassiléos Pávlou ké Frederíkis 55 (☎0265/82 239; ⑤), the E-class *Odysseus* at Iséa 1, corner Fillelínon (☎0265/82 235; ④) and – among pensions – the *Sun View*, Apóllonos 84 (☎0265/82 349; ④). The nearest official **campsite** is *Apollon* (☎0265/82 750), less than 1km west towards Ámfissa, with an acceptable **restaurant**. Other eating options aren't brilliant, the long-running *Taverna Vakchos* having lost out in recent ratings to the newish *Epikouros* at Pávlou ké Frederíkis 33. The helpful **tourist office** (Mon–Fri 8am–2.30pm; ☎0265/82 900), with up-to-date transport schedules, is in the town hall.

Vólos and around

Southeast of even bigger Lárissa, **VÓLOS** is a fast-growing industrial city, and not a pretty sight: a modern, concrete sprawl, rebuilt after various earthquakes between 1947 and 1957, and now edging to its natural limits against the Pílion foothills. That said, you may well be spending some time here, as Vólos is the gateway to the Pílion and the main port for **boats to the Sporades islands**. Ferries leave two to four times daily for **Skiáthos** and **Skópelos**, with at least one continuing to **Alónissos**; hydrofoils run up to five times daily to all three, continuing several times weekly to **Skýros**. The EOT's regional HQ on Platía Ríga Feréou (Mon–Fri 7.30am–2pm; ☎0421/23 500) provides information on ferry timetables, as well as accommodation. **Hotels** are fairly plentiful with a concentration of inexpensive places in the grid of streets behind the port. The *Iasson/Jason* near the sea at Pávlou Melá 1 (☎0421/26 075; ⑤), and the quieter *Roussas* at Iatroú Tzánou 1, towards the museum (☎0421/21 732; ③), are both en suite and decent value. Among several **ouzeris** lining the waterfront street of Argonaftón, *O Yiorgos* at no. 15 and *Naftilia* at no. 1 rate well for seafood platters. Vólos's **Archeological Museum** at the east end of the waterfront (Tues–Sun 8.30am–3pm; €3) has arguably the finest collection of Neolithic artefacts in Europe.

The Pílion (Mount Pelion)

There is something decidedly un-Mediterranean about the **Pílion peninsula**, with its lush fruit orchards and dense broadleaf forests. Water gurgles from crevices beside every road, and summers are a good deal cooler than in the rest of central Greece. Pílion villages are idiosyncratic too, sprawling affairs with sumptuous mansions and barn-like churches lining their cobbled streets. Add to the scenery and architecture a dozen or so excellent beaches, and easy access from Athens and Thessaloníki, and it's no wonder that this is a well-loved corner of Greece – especially by Greeks: avoid July, August, Easter and Christmas unless you wish to camp out.

The most visited part of the peninsula lies just north and east of Vólos, with bus services biased towards the twenty-plus villages here. If your time is limited, the best single targets are the recognized showcases of Makrinítsa and Vyzítsa. **MAKRINÍTSA** has become a bit commercialized, with fairly overpriced lodging in a bevy of restored mansions, though frequent connections to Vólos make day-trips easy. Remoter **VYZÍTSA** has equally good connections, with better possibilities of staying cheaply – try *Rooms Aphrodite* (☎0423/86 484; ③), west of the square – and eating cheaply, for instance at *Taverna O Yiorgaras* on the road east. The less homogeneous village of **MILIÉS**, 3km east, also has some accommodation and the *Korbas* bakery, down by the bus stop, cranking out every sort of pie, pastry and bread imaginable.

The largest village on the Pílion – almost a small town – is **ZAGORÁ**, destination of fairly regular buses across the peninsula's summit ridge. Unlike its seashore neighbours, it has a life independent of tourism, and is more appealing than first impressions suggest. You're also more likely to find a room here in season, for example at *Room Yiannis Halkias* (☎0426/22 159; ④), than down at **HOREFTÓ**, 8km below, where you might try the hotel *Erato* (☎0426/22 445; ④), and *Taverna O Petros*. There's also a good **campsite** at the south end of the main beach here; another cove beckons north of the resort.

Just before Zagorá, a junction funnels traffic southeast to **TSANGARÁDHA**, also the terminus of two daily buses from Miliés. Though nearly as large as Zagorá, it may not seem so, divided as it is into four distinct quarters along several kilometres of road. In the typical Pílion fashion, each is grouped around a parish church and plane-tree-shaded platía. Reasonable accommodation is difficult to come by, though you might enquire at *Villa ton Rodhon* (☎0426/49 340; ⑤) in Ayía Paraskeví. Eating out is generally uninviting; most people do so at **MOÚRESSI**, 3km northwest, where two adjacent tavernas dish out Pílion specialities at fairly moderate prices. **KISSÓS**, still further towards Zagorá, is another possibility for staying and dining, with its excellent, inexpensive *Xenonas Kissos* (☎0426/31 214; ④).

Most visitors, however, stay at one of several nearby beaches, the best on this shore of the peninsula. **ÁYIOS IOÁNNIS**, 6km below Kissós, is an overblown resort with plenty of accommodation – most reasonable are *Hotel Armonia* (☎0426/31 242; ④), also with a good restaurant, and *Hotel Evripidis* (☎0426/31 338; ⑤). If it's too busy for your tastes, head south along the sand, past the crowded campsite, to Papá Neró beach or further still to postcard-perfect **DAMOÚHARI** with its tiny ruined castle and fishing anchorage. The area's most scenic beach is reached by following a winding 7km road from the south end of Tsangarádha to **Mylopótamos**.

Kalambáka and the Metéora

There are few more exciting places to arrive at than **KALAMBÁKA**. The shabby town itself you hardly notice, for your eye is immediately drawn upwards to the weird grey cylinders of rock overhead. These are the outlying monoliths of the extraordinary valley of **the Metéora**. To the right you can make out the monastery of Ayíos Stefánou, firmly entrenched on a massive pedestal; beyond stretches a chaos of spikes, cones and stubbier, rounded cliffs, beaten into bizarre shapes by the action of the sea that covered the Plain of Thessaly around fifty million years ago. The earliest religious communities in the valley emerged during the late tenth century, when hermits made their homes in the caves that score many of the rocks. In 1336 they were joined by two monks from Mount Áthos, one of whom – Athanasios – established the first monastery here. Today, put firmly on the map by appearances in films, such as the James Bond *For Your Eyes Only*, the four most accessible monasteries are essentially museums. Only two, Ayías Triádhos and Ayíou Stefánou, continue to function with a primarily religious purpose.

If you want to see all six surviving Metéora monasteries in a day, start early to take in Varlaám, Megálou Meteórou and Roussánou before 1pm (when they close for two hours), leaving Ayíou Nikoláou for the afternoon as it's open continuously, and Ayías Triádhos for the late afternoon – but bear in mind the closing days for each place given below. Each monastery levies an **admission charge** of about €1.50 and operates a strict **dress code**: skirts for women, long trousers for men and covered arms for both sexes.

From Kastráki the road loops around between huge outcrops of rock, passing below the chapel-hermitage of **Doúpiani** before reaching a track to the left, which winds up a low rock to the fourteenth-century **Ayíou Nikoláou** (daily except Fri 9am–3.30pm). A small, recently restored monastery, this has some superb sixteenth-century frescoes in its *katholikón* (main chapel). Next to it on a needle-thin shaft is **Ayía Moní**, ruined and empty since an earthquake in 1858. Between Ayíou Nikoláou and Ayía Moní a clear path leads up a ravine between assorted monoliths; soon, at a fork, you've the option of bearing left for Megálou Meteórou or right to Varlaám, the two also linked by a higher access road. **Varlaám** (daily except Thurs 9am–2pm & 3–5pm) ranks as one of the oldest and most beautiful monasteries in the valley. The *katholikón* is small but glorious, supported by painted beams and with walls and pillars totally covered in sixteenth-century frescoes celebrating the desert ascetics, with a fine *Pandokrátor* (Christ in Majesty) in the dome. Varlaám also retains its old ascent tower; until 1923 the only way of reaching the monasteries was by being hauled up in a net drawn by rope and windlass, or by the equally perilous retractable ladders. Today, however, you can reach the monastery safely, if breathlessly, via the 195 steps cut into the side of the rock. From Varlaám the path system takes you northwest to **Megálou Meteórou** (daily except Tues 9am–1pm & 3–6pm). This is the grandest of the monasteries and also the highest, built 415m above the surrounding ground. Its *katholikón* is the most magnificent, a beautiful cross-in-square church surmounted by a lofty dome, though frescoes are not as compelling as elsewhere; enjoy instead the monastic museum in the former refectory, with fine wood-carved artefacts and icons.

Next you follow the main access road east, ignoring the turning back down for Kastráki, until you reach the signed access path for the tiny, compact convent of **Roussánou** (or Ayías Varváras) (daily: summer 9am–6pm, winter 9am–1pm & 3.20–6pm), approached in the final moment across a dizzying bridge from an adjacent rock. This has perhaps the most extraordinary site of all the monasteries, its walls built right on the edge of a sharp blade of rock. Its seventeenth-century frescoes include particularly bloody scenes of martyrdom and judgement. It's less than half-an-hour from Roussánou to the fourteenth-century **Ayías Triádhos** (Holy Trinity; daily except Thurs 9am–12.30pm & 3–5pm), approached up 130 steps carved into a tunnel in the rock. Although Ayías Triádhos teeters above a deep ravine and its little garden ends in a precipitous drop, there is a 3km, well-marked cobbled trail at the bottom of the monastery's steps back to Kalambáka, which saves a long trudge back around the circuit. **Ayíou Stefánou** (daily except Mon 9am–1pm & 3.20–6pm), the last and easternmost of the monasteries, is a further fifteen minutes' walk from Ayías Triádhos; bombed during World War II, it's the obvious one to omit if you've run out of time.

Practicalities

Visiting the Metéora demands a full day, which means staying at least one night in **Kalambáka** or at the village of **Kastráki**, right in the shadow of the rocks. Kalambáka is a characterless but pleasant enough base, with fairly plentiful **accommodation**. Arriving by bus or train, you should ignore any touts and make your own way into town, following numerous signs publicizing rooms and overpriced hotels. Good budget choices in the quieter, upper portion of town towards Kastráki, include *Hotel Meteora*, Ploutárhou 13 (☎0432/22 367; ⑤), and *Koka Roka Rooms*, Kanári 21 (☎0432/24 554; ④). **KASTRÁKI** is twenty minutes' walk out of Kalambáka; and there are regular buses in season. Along the way you pass the busy *Vrahos*, the first of two **campsites** here, offering rock-climbing lessons (☎0432/22 293); the other one, *Boufidhis/The Cave* (☎0432/24 802), is smaller but quieter, grassier and incomparably set under the pinnacles of the monasteries. Kastráki also has hundreds of rooms to rent, mostly better value than in Kalambáka (though avoid the main road); good examples include *Ziogas Rooms* (☎0432/24 037; ④), and the more basic ones at *The Cave* campsite (③). The best-value **eating** is at the tiny *Ziogas* grill (usually evenings only).

The Katára pass: Kalambáka to Ioánnina

West of Kalambáka, the **Katára pass** cuts across the central range of the Píndhos to link Thessaly and Epirus. The route is one of the most spectacular in the country, and is covered by two buses daily between **Tríkala** and **Ioánnina**. A tunnel has been bored through the mountains, and once local politics are sorted this may carry a much straighter road link between the two towns.

MÉTSOVO spreads just west of the Katára pass, a high mountain town built on two sides of a ravine and encircled by a mighty range of peaks. It is a startling site: from below the main road the eighteenth- and nineteenth-century stone houses, with their wooden balconies and modern tile roofs, wind down the ravine to the main platía, where a few old men still loiter after Sunday Mass, magnificent in full traditional dress. The town **museum** occupies the Arhondikó Tosítsa (group tours every 30min, daily except Thurs 9am–1.30pm & 4–6pm; €1.50), a mansion restored to the full glory of its eighteenth-century past, with panelled rooms, rugs and a fine collection of crafts and costumes. For **eating**, the restaurant of the *Athens/Athinai* is excellent for casserole dishes, while *Galaxias* around the corner, on the platía, offers some casserole-dish relief from the grills which dominate this pastoral village. Métsovo has quite a range of **accommodation**, most of it en suite, and apart from around July 26, date of the main local festival, and during the ski season, there's little difficulty getting a room. Ask at the friendly *Athens/Athinai* and they'll put you in their annexe the *Filoxenia* (☎0656/41 021; ④), below the platía with ravine views from some rooms. Otherwise, try the *Acropolis*, Triados 22 (☎0656/41 672; ③).

Ioánnina and around

Descending from Métsovo, you approach **IOÁNNINA** through more spectacular folds of the Píndhos Mountains, emerging high above the great lake of Pamvótidha (Pamvótis). Ioánnina's old town, once the capital of the Albanian Muslim chieftain Ali Pasha, covers a rocky promontory jutting out from the lake's southern edge, its fortifications punctuated by towers and minarets. From this base Ali, "the Lion of Ioannina", carved out of the Ottoman Empire a kingdom encompassing much of western Greece, an act of rebellion that foreshadowed wider defiance in the Greeks' own War of Independence.

Disappointingly, most of the city is modern and undistinguished – a testimony not so much to Ali, who did burn much of it to the ground when under siege in 1820, as to the developers of the 1950s and 1960s. However, the fortifications of his citadel, the **Kástro**, survive more or less intact, and this is an obvious point to stroll towards. Once within, signs direct you east to the **Byzantine Museum** (summer: Mon 12.30–7pm, Tues–Sun 8am–7pm; winter Tues–Sun 8.30am–5pm) inside the innermost citadel, a remarkably thin collection of coins, pottery and post-Byzantine fresco fragments; its annexe, devoted to the long-established local silver-smithing trade, is more worthwhile. At the northern apex of the Kástro, installed in the Aslan Pasha mosque, is the **Municipal (Popular Art) Museum** (daily: summer 8/9am-8pm, winter 8/9am–3pm), an elegantly arranged collection of costumes, antique guns and jewellery, as well as carpets and tapestries donated by the now all-but-vanished Jewish community of Ioánnina. Apart from the Kástro, the most enjoyable quarter is the old **bazaar** area, outside the citadel's main gate. This has a cluster of Ottoman-era buildings, as well as a scattering of copper- and tinsmiths, as well as a few surviving silversmiths, once a mainstay of the town's economy. The heart of town lies just south of the bazaar, grouped about the central platías of Pýrrou, Akadhimías and Dhimokratías. Just off the last, beside a small park and the town's modern cathedral, is the **Archeological Museum** (Tues–Sun 8.30am–2.30pm; €1.50), a must if you're planning a visit to Dodona; displayed here, along with some exceptionally crafted bronze seals, is a fascinating collection of lead tablets inscribed with questions to the Dodona oracle.

The island of **Nissí**, near the north shore of polluted Lake Pamvótidha, is served by waterbuses (every 30min) from the quay northwest of the Froúrio. Its village, founded during the sixteenth century by refugees from the Máni, is flanked by several beautiful, diminutive monasteries, providing the perfect focus for an afternoon's visit. Just south of the village, the churches of **Filanthropinón** and **Dilíou** contain vivid frescoes from the thirteenth and fourteenth centuries. The monastery of Pantelímonos, just east of the village, is where Ali Pasha was assassinated in January 1822, his hiding place having been revealed to troops of the sultan, who had finally lost patience with the wayward ruler. Stay on through the evening and you can eat at one of three waterfront restaurants (the simplest being the one under the Dellas inn), watching a superb sunset over the reed-beds.

If you arrive early enough in the day, it is worth heading straight out to Nissí, where the spotless, shared-bath rooms kept by Sotiris and Evangelos Dellas (☎0651/84 494; ④) offer the most attractive and quiet local **accommodation**. In Ioánnina, the best budget lodging is in the area between the bazaar and the central plazas; start hunting at *Metropolis/Metropole*, Krystálli 2 (☎0651/26 207; ④) or the nearby *Esperia*, Kaplání 3 (☎0651/24 111; ③). The pleasant, mosquito-free, lakeshore *Limnopoula* **campsite** is 2km out of town on the Pérama/airport road. Besides the island **tavernas**, more standard fare can be found immediately opposite the citadel gate, where the two rival grills *To Kourmanio* and *To Manteio* vie for your custom. The main **bus** station is at Zozimádhon 4, serving most points north and west; a smaller terminal at Bizaníou 19 connects Árta, Préveza, Dodona and villages south and east. (It is advisable to buy tickets the day before travelling, especially at weekends.) The **tourist office** at Dhódhoni 39, south of the centre (☎0651/25 086), can provide information on the whole Epirus region.

DODONA

At remote and mountainous **DODONA**, 22km southwest of Ioánnina, lie the ruins of the **Oracle of Zeus**, dominated by a vast amphitheatre which was meticulously restored at the end of the nineteenth century. This is the oldest oracle in Greece: worship of Zeus through his sacred oak tree at Dodona seems to have begun around 1900 BC. Entering the **ancient site** (daily 8am–7pm; winter closes 5pm; €1.50) you are immediately confronted by the massive western wall of the theatre. Able to seat 17,000, it is one of the largest on the Greek mainland, built during the time of Pyrrhus (297–272 BC); later the Romans made adaptations necessary for their blood sports, building a protective wall over the lower seating and also a drainage channel. Nowadays in summer, plays are sporadically but atmospherically performed: ask at the Ioánnina tourist office for the current programme. At the top of the auditorium, a grand entrance gate leads into the **acropolis**, an overgrown and largely unexcavated area. Beside the theatre are the foundations of a *bouleuterion* (council house), beyond which lie the complex ruins of the **Sanctuary of Zeus**, site of the ancient oracle. Worship centred upon the Sacred Oak, within which the god was thought to dwell, and which was hacked down by Christian zealots. Ruins of an early Christian **basilica**, constructed over a Sanctuary of Herakles, are prominent nearby.

Transport to Dodona is sparse, with at most two badly timed **buses** a day from Ioánnina (Mon, Wed & Fri only), but **hitching** back should be feasible in summer. A return trip by **taxi** from Ioánnina with an hour at the site costs around €18 – affordable in a group. There are some lovely spots to **camp**, and a friendly if basic **taverna** in the neighbouring modern village of **DHODHÓNI**, which also has rooms run by Stefanos Nastos (☎0651/71 106; ③). *Andromachi* near the ruins (☎0651/91 196; ④) is another option.

Zagóri and the Víkos Gorge

Few parts of Greece are more surprising, or more beguiling, than **Zagóri**, the wild, infertile region to the north of Ioánnina. This is the last place one would expect to find some of the most imposing architecture in Greece, yet the *Zagorohória*, as the 46 villages of Zagóri are called, are full of grand stone mansions, enclosed by semi-fortified walls and with deep-eaved gateways opening on to immaculately cobbled streets.

In the northwest corner of the region, the awesome trench of the **Víkos Gorge** – its walls nearly 1000m high in places – cuts through the limestone tablelands of Mount Gamíla, separating the villages of western and central Zagóri. A hike through or around Víkos is the highlight of any visit to the area, the usual starting point being the handsome village of **MONODHÉNDHRI**, perched right on the rim of the gorge near its south end. There are twice-daily buses from Ioánnina; if you arrive on the late-afternoon bus, you'll want to stay at *Katerina's Pension* (☎0653/71 300; ④), the only real budget option here. Much the clearest **path into the gorge**, marked as the long-distance O3, starts beside Áyios Athanásios church; the route is fairly straightforward and takes under five hours to reach the point where the gorge begins to open out. From here the best option is to follow the O3 path to **MEGÁLO PÁPINGO**, two hours further on. A hillside village of fifty or so houses along a tributary of the Voïdhomátis river, it offers abundant if pricey accommodation; most reasonable is *Xenonas Kalliopi* (☎0653/41 081; ⑤), also with a reliable taverna, and some cheaper rooms at no. 5 of the lane leading there. Around half the size of its neighbour, **MIKRÓ PÁPINGO** just uphill has one main inn, *Xenon O Dhias* (☎0653/41 257; ⑥), which provides both beds and meals, plus less expensive rooms through Evangelia Pantazi (☎0653/41 110; ④). Returning to Ioánnina, there are buses four days a week in summer from both the Pápingo villages; otherwise your best bet is to trail-walk west two and a half hours to the village of **Káto Klidhoniá**, where there are regular buses along the Kónitsa–Ioánnina highway.

Igoumenítsa and Párga

IGOUMENÍTSA is Greece's third passenger port after Pireás and Pátra, with almost hourly ferries to Corfu, and several daily to Italy, as well as daily ferry or hydrofoil connections to the Ionian island of Paxí, all departing from the south quay some way from the centre. Levelled during World War II and rebuilt in a concrete-laced, functional style, it's a place most travellers aim to pass through, a feasible enough strategy if you catch one of the Italy-bound ferries between 8.30pm and midnight (otherwise they leave between 6am and 11am). Shop around carefully for ferry tickets, as prices vary greatly on identical routings, generally due to boat quality and speed. **Brindisi** and **Bari** are the cheapest Italian destinations (and make the most sense if you're on a rail pass); **Ancona, Venice** and **Trieste** are vastly more expensive but popular with drivers. Unlike sailings from Pátra, ferries from Igoumenítsa are not allowed to sell tickets with a stopover on Corfu. You can, however, take the regular ferry to Corfu and then pick up most routes from there. Top-quality, durable, operators to Italy include Superfast Ferries, Ayíon Apostólon 61 (☎0665/28 150, *www.superfast.com*), which runs daily services to Bari and Ancona; Hellenic Mediterranean, Ethnikís Andístasis 30 (☎0665/25 682), to Brindisi via Corfu; and Minoan Lines, Ethnikís Antístasis 58A (☎0665/22 952, *www.minoan.gr*), to Ancona and Venice.

Budget **hotels** are plentiful if uninspiring; most are to be found either along, or just back from, the waterside. The two cheapest are generally the en-suite *Egnatia*, Eleftherías 1 (☎0665/23 648; ④), and *Stavrodhromi*, Souliou 14 (☎0665/22 343; ③). The beach villages of **Kalámi** and **Platariá**, respectively 10km and 12km south, both have campsites and tavernas. Further information can be had from the **tourist office** next to the customs house on the under-used central quay (daily 7am–2pm; ☎0665/22 227).

Some of the best nearby **beaches** are at **PÁRGA** (Mon–Fri 4 buses, 3 on Sat, 1 on Sun), a small resort with a crescent of tiered houses below a Norman-Venetian castle. Párga's beaches line three consecutive bays, split by the headland of the fortress hill. Váltos and Lýkhnos beaches both have **campsites**. Most rooms and hotels are block-booked by tour operators from June until August; an exception, up on the ridge leading inland from the castle, are the basic rooms kept by the incredibly friendly Kostas and Katerina Pappas (☎0684/31 171; ④). For **food**, the nearby *Panorama* is okay, and not as expensive as its location would suggest.

Thessaloníki and around

Second city of Greece and administrative centre for Macedonia and Thrace, **THESSA-LONÍKI** has a very different feel from Athens – more Balkan-European and modern, due largely to a disastrous 1917 fire which levelled most of the labyrinth of Ottoman lanes; the city was rebuilt over the next eight years on a grid plan with long central avenues running parallel to the sea. During the Byzantine era, **Salonica**, as it was then known, was the second city after Constantinople, remaining so until its sacking by Saracens in 904, Normans in 1185 and occupation by Latin crusaders in 1204. It was restored to the Byzantines in 1246, reaching a cultural "Golden Age" until the Ottoman conquest in 1430. As recently as the 1920s, the city's population was as mixed as any in the Balkans: besides the Ottomans, who had been in occupation for close on five centuries, there were Slavs, Albanians and the largest European **Jewish** community of the period – 80,000 at its peak. This had dropped to just under 60,000 by World War II when all but a fraction were deported to the concentration camps in one of the worst atrocities committed in the Balkans. You can get glimpses of "Old Salonica" in the walled **Kástra** quarter, on the hillside beyond the modern grid of streets. For most visitors, though, Thessaloníki's excellent archeological museum stands out, along with a unique array of churches dating from Roman times to the fifteenth century.

Arrival, information and accommodation

The **train station** on the west side of town is a short walk from the central grid of streets and the waterfront. If you're coming into Thessaloníki by **bus** you'll arrive at one of the scattered KTEL terminals nearby (buses to Kavála leave from Langadhá 59; to ancient Pella from Anayeníseos 22; to Litóhoro (for Mt Olympus) from Sapfoús 10; and for Halkidhikí (for Mt Áthos) from Karakássi 68, east of the centre. From the **airport**, 16km out at Mikrá, bus #78 runs hourly to the train station (6am–11pm; €0.40). The EOT **tourist office** is at Platía Aristotélous 8 (Mon–Fri 9am–9pm, Sat 10am–6pm, Sun 10am–5pm; ☎031/271 888).

Outside the fair-and-festival season (Sept–Nov), hotel vacancies are reasonably easy to find, though not, as a rule, very attractive or good value. Modest **hotels** tend to cluster along the noisy beginning of busy Egnatía, or in the more agreeable zone between Eleftherías and Aristotélous squares. Congenial ones on or just off Egnatía include the shared-bath *Atlantis*, no. 14 (☎031/540 131; ④), the *Acropol* at no. 10, corner Tantalídhou (☎031/536 170; ④), and *Nea Mitropolis*, Syngroú 22, just north of Egnatía (☎031/525 540; ④), also with pricier ensuite rooms. More pleasant downtown hotels include *Orestias Kastorias*, Agnóstou Stratiótou 14, corner Olýmbou (☎031/276 517; ④) and *Tourist*, Mitropóleos 21 (☎031/276 335; ⑤). The **hostel** at Svólou 44 (☎031/225 946; ①; March–Nov) is noisy, ill-equipped and poorly run. The closest **campsites** are at the beach resorts of Ayía Triádha (24km away) and Órmos Epanomís (33km); the latter is better, served by bus #69 from Platía Dhikastiríon.

The City

The obvious place to begin a wander is the **White Tower** (Lefkós Pýrgos), the last surviving bastion of the city's medieval walls; it now looks a little stagey, isolated on the seafront, but is a graceful symbol nonetheless. Today it contains a small but well-presented museum of Byzantine secular and sacred art (Tues–Sun 8am–2.30pm; free); you climb through its various galleries to the roof for the view. The tower is a couple of minutes' walk from the **Archeological Museum** (summer Mon 12.30–7pm, Tues–Sun 8am–7pm; winter Mon 10.30am–5pm, Tues–Sun 8.30am–3pm; €7), which contains many of the finds from the tombs of Philip II of Macedon and others at the ancient Macedonian capital of Aegae (modern Veryína). They include startling amounts of gold and silver – masks, crowns, necklaces, earrings, bracelets – all of extraordinary craftsmanship, although the exhibits are now slightly depleted following the transfer of many items back to a purpose-built underground gallery at Veryína itself. Thessaloníki's other main museum, the **Folklife (Ethnological) Museum** (visit by appointment only: ☎031/830 591), is a twenty-minute walk east at Vassilísis Ólgas 68,

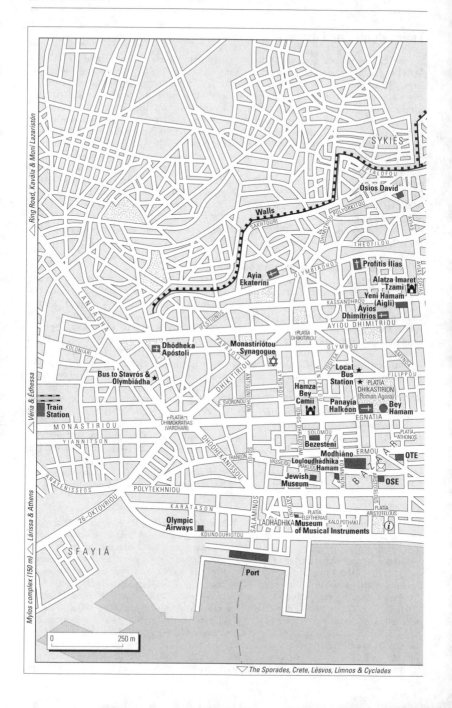

SYKIÉS

Ósios David

Walls

Ayia
Ekaterini

Profítis Ílias

Alatza Imaret
Tzami

Yeni Hamam
(Aígli)

Áyios
Dhimítrios

Dhódheka
Apóstoli

Monastirótou
Synagogue

Local
Bus
Station

PLATÍA
DHIKASTIRÍON
(Roman Agora)

Bus to Stavrós &
Olymbiádha

Hamza
Bey
Camii

Panayía
Halkéon

Bey
Hamam

Train
Station

PLATÍA
DHIMOKRATÍAS
(VARDHARI)

Bezesténi

Modhiáno

OTE

Louloudhádhika
Hamam

Jewish
Museum

OSE

Olympic
Airways

PLATÍA
ELEFTHERÍAS

Museum
of Musical Instruments

LADHÁDHIKA

PLATÍA
ARISTOTÉLOUS

SFAYIÁ

0   250 m

Port

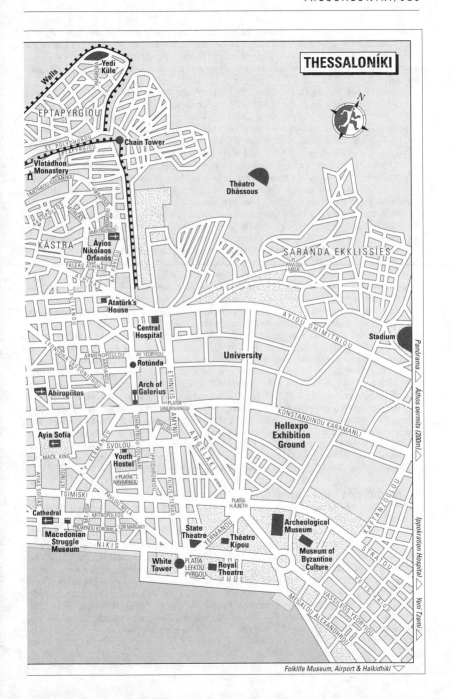

THESSALONÍKI

Walls
Yedi Küle
PAPARESKA
EPTAPYRGÍOU
ST. POLYOHOROU
EPTAPYRGÍOU
Chain Tower
Vlatádhon Monastery
TIMOTHEOU IGOUMENOU
Théatro Dhássous
AKROPOLEOS MEGA
AMFITRÍONOS
KÁSTRA
Áyios Nikólaos Orfanós
PALEAS ATHINAS
SARÁNDA EKKLISSÍES
PL. PAVLOU MELA
ATHINAS
IOULIANOU
AP. PAVLOU
Atatürk's House
AYÍOU DHIMITRÍOU
Central Hospital
Stadium
LEONTOS THASSONIDHOU
TASSONIDHOU
ARMENOPOULOU
AY. YEORYIOU
University
Rotúnda
ARRIANOU
Arch of Galerius
ETHNIKIS AMYNIS
PLATÍA SINDRIVANIOU
Ahiropíitos
DHIMITRÍOU GOUNARI
IPHIGENIAS
Hellexpo Exhibition Ground
KONSTANDINOU KARAMANLI
Ayía Sofía
MACK. KING
SVOLOU
IPPODHROMIOU
FILIKIS ETERIAS
AN. GELAKI
Youth Hostel
P. P. YERMANOU
DHIMITRÍOU GOUNARI
PLATÍA NAVARÍNOU
PLATÍA H.A.N.TH
AYÍAS SOFÍAS
IKTINOU
TSIMISKÍ
PAVLOU MELA
Cathedral
MET. JOSEF
MITROPOLEOS
YERMANOU
Archeological Museum
PROXENOU KOROMILA
LORI MARGARITI
Macedonian Struggle Museum
NIKIS
State Theatre
Théatro Kípou
Museum of Byzantine Culture
White Tower
PLATÍA LEFKOU PYRGOU
Royal Theatre
KAFTANZOGLOU
STRATOU
VELISSARIOU
VASSILÉOS YEORYIOU
MEGALOU ALEXANDHROU

Panórama △
Áthos permits (200m) △
Ippokration Hospital △
Yeni Tzami △

or a short ride on bus #5). It's perhaps the best museum of its kind in Greece, with well-written commentaries accompanying displays on housing, costumes, day-to-day work and crafts. There is a sharp, highly un-folkloric emphasis on context: on the role of women in the community, the clash between tradition and progress, and the cycle of agricultural and religious festivals.

The closest of the city's major churches to the White Tower is **Ayía Sofía**, built early in the eighth century on the model of its illustrious namesake in Istanbul. Its dome, ten metres in diameter, bears a splendid mosaic of *The Ascension*, currently obscured by scaffolding and requiring opera glasses to view at any time. Immediately northwest and across Egnatía stands Thessaloníki's oldest church, the fifth-century basilica of **Panayía Ahriopíitos**; its three aisles are divided by elaborate colonnades, with rich mosaics of birds, fruits and vegetation under the arches. Another basilica rises still further northwest: **Áyios Dhimítrios** (Mon 1.30–7.30pm, Tues–Sun 8am–7.30pm; free), the largest church in Greece. Conceived in the fifth century but completely rebuilt several times since, it's dedicated to the city's patron saint and stands on the site of his martyrdom. The church was nearly levelled by the 1917 fire, and following a 1950s reconstruction, just six small but brilliant mosaics remain from the building's early years. Five of these adorn the columns flanking the altar, and date back to the church's second reconstruction in the late seventh century; they include the celebrated *Áyios Dhimítrios with the Church's Founders* and a contrastingly humane scene of the saint with two young children. The crypt (same hours; free) contains the martyrion of the saint, and was probably adapted from the original Roman baths where he was imprisoned. Some 600m southwest of Áyios Dhimítrios along its namesake avenue is the church of **Dhódheka Apóstoli**, one of the last churches built in Thessaloníki. Its five domes rise in perfect symmetry above walls of fine brickwork, though as at Ayía Sofía you'll need opera glasses to appreciate fragmentary mosaics high up in the arches below the dome.

North of Ayía Sofía and Ahiropíitos, the church of Áyios Yeóryios, popularly known as the **Rotunda** (daily 8.30am–3pm; free), is the oldest and strangest of the churches. It was designed, but never used, as a Roman imperial mausoleum and converted to Christian use in the fourth century. Later it became one of the city's major mosques; the minaret remains. Following lengthy repairs in the wake of the 1978 earthquake, scaffolding obscures its highest and finest mosaics in the dome. Straight uphill and northwest, near the heart of the Kástra quarter, fourteenth-century **Áyios Nikólaos Orfanós** (Tues–Sun 8am–2.30pm) preserves its original frescoes, some of the finest in the city, mostly dealing with Christ's Passion. Ten minutes' walk west and uphill through a maze of lanes, **Ósios Davíd** (Mon–Sat 8am–noon & 5–6pm, Sun 8–10.30am) is a tiny late fifth-century church overzealously converted by the Ottomans that retains arguably Thessaloníki's single finest mosaic, depicting a clean-shaven Christ appearing in a vision to the prophets Ezekiel and Habakkuk.

Eating, drinking and nightlife

Since the mid-1990s there's been an explosion of interesting places to **eat** and **drink** in Thessaloníki, few of them as obvious as the fast-food outlets dominating the city centre. Most central are *O Loutros*, Koundourá 5, behind the Bezesténi or Ottoman valuables market, evicted from its long-time home in a Turkish bath but still purveying inexpensive food and good bulk wine; *Ta Koumbarakia*, Egnatía 140, behind the Byzantine chapel of the Transfiguration, a durable, low-priced ouzerí with grills, fish and *tursí* (pickled vegetables); *Platía Athonos* on Dhragoúmi, an alley off Platía Athonos, one of the more dependable of several ouzerís in this area; and *Kamares*, Ayíou Yeoryíou 11, just behind the Rotunda, a reliable source of reasonable seafood, meat and salads. Both *Tsarouhas*, Olýmbou 78, famous for local speciality *patsás* (tripe soup) and Anatolian puddings at slightly inflated prices, and *Hotpot*, Komninón 15, with pizzas, pasta, salads and omelette-based breakfasts, are open 24hr. Up in the medieval Eptapyrgíou quarter (bus #22/#28 if needed), *To Makedhoniko* by the Pórtara gate is cheap and popular with students for its no-nonsense, limited menu of grills and salads, while *To Yedi*, at the summit beside Yedi Kule fortress, is a popular evening-only ouzerí. For a gourmet splurge, *Ta Pringiponissia*, 600m past the Folklife Museum at Krítis 60, has Constantinopolitan-Greek delicacies which you select from the proffered *dhískos* (tray).

Bars and **clubs** tend to be concentrated in the rehabilitated warehouse area southeast of Platía Eleftherías known as Ladhádhika, especially pedestrianized Katoúni, Éyiptou and Platía Morihóvou; just stroll by and choose your favourite. *Zythos*, Platía Katoúni 5, is one of the best bars, with dozens of well-kept foreign beers. There's more beer to be had (as well as sausages and game) at *Kourdhisto Gourouni*, at Ayías Sofías 31, one of the few exceptions to the Ladhádhika concentration. The main indoor **music** venue is the multidisciplinary complex *Mylos*, out in an old flour mill at Andhréou Yeoryíou 56 (call ☎031/525 968 for what's on, or watch for posters in record stores); big Greek or international stars visit the open-air *Theatro Damari* in Triandhría district.

Listings

Bookshops Molho, Tsimiskí 10, has a good English-language stock.

Car rental Many are clustered near the fairgrounds and Archeological Museum on Angeláki, making comparison shopping easy; try Budget, Angeláki 15; Eurorent, Angeláki 3; Thrifty, Angeláki 5; Europcar/InterRent, Papandhréou 5.

Consulates UK and Commonwealth citizens are represented by the honorary consul, Venizélou 8 (☎031/278 006); Netherlands, Komnínon 26 (☎031/227 477); USA, Tsimiskí 43, Bldg A, 7th Floor (☎031/242 905). For onward travel in the Balkans, there's representation for Bulgaria at Mánou 12 (☎031/829 210), and Romania at Níkis 13, 4th Floor (☎031/225 481), but nothing for the FYROM (Former Yugoslav Republic of Macedonia); if you need a visa, get it in Athens rather than risk being turned back at the FYROM frontier.

Exchange For changing foreign notes, use the 24hr automatic machine at Platía Aristotélous 8.

Ferries All agents are down near the port entrance: Omikron Travel, Salamínos 4 (for DANE or G&A ferries to Sámos and the Dodecanese); Kriti Air Travel, Íonos Dhragoúmi 1, cnr Koundouriótou (for Minoan Lines or G&A to the Sporádhes, Cyclades and Crete, plus summer hydrofoils to the Sporádhes); Karacharisis, Koundouriótou 8 (for NEL Lines to Límnos, Lésvos and Híos).

Internet *Enterprise*, Goúnari 52; *The Link*, Goúnari 50 (both near the Rotunda); *Globus*, Amýnda 12, near Áyios Dhimítrious.

Laundry Bianca, Antoniádhou 3, and Freskádha, Filíppou 105, both near the Rotunda.

Mount Áthos permits Go with your passport to the Grafío Proskynitón Ayíou Órous (Mount Áthos Pilgrims' Office), Konstandínou Karamanlí 14, first floor (Mon–Sat 8.30am–1.30pm & certain evenings), to be issued an entry permit for a specific day. If you can't go in person, phone ☎031/861 611 (English-speaking) for instructions on faxing your details.

Post office Aristotélous 26 (Mon–Fri 7.30am–8pm, Sat 7.30am–2.15pm, Sun 9am–1.30pm).

Train tickets The OSE office at Aristotélous 18 is more central and more helpful than the main terminal.

Travel agents Flights out of Thessaloníki are usually not cheap, but student/youth travellers should try Nouvelles Frontières, Kalopotháki 8; Etos/USIT, Svólou 44; or Sunflight, Tsimiskí 144.

Pella

PELLA was the capital of Macedonia throughout its greatest period, and the first real capital of Greece after Philip II forcibly unified the country around 338 BC. It was founded some sixty years earlier by King Archelaos, and from its beginnings was a major centre of culture. The royal palace was said to be the greatest artistic showplace since Classical Athens: Euripides wrote and produced his last plays at the court, and Aristotle was tutor to the young Alexander the Great – born, like his father Philip II, in this city. The site, less than 50km from Thessaloníki, is an easy **day-trip**; take the Édhessa-bound **bus** (every 30min).

The **ruins** (summer Mon noon–7pm, Tues–Sun 8am–7pm; winter closes 3pm; €3) cover around four square kilometres and as yet only a few city blocks have been fully excavated. To the right of the road is a grand official building, probably a government office, divided into three open courtyards. The three main rooms of the first court have patterned geometric floors, in the centre of which were found superb, intricate pebble-mosaics depicting scenes of a lion hunt, a griffin attacking a deer, and Dionysos riding a panther. These are now in the **museum** across the road (same hours; €3 extra), but in the third court three mosaics have been left in situ; one of these, a stag hunt, is complete, and it is astounding in its dynamism and use of perspective.

Mount Olympus

Highest, most magical and most dramatic of all Greek mountains, **Mount Olympus** – the mythical seat of the gods – rears straight up nearly 3000m from the shores of the Thermaíkos gulf, south of Thessaloníki. Dense forests cover its lower slopes and its wild flowers are gorgeous. If you're equipped with decent boots and warm clothing, no special expertise is necessary to get to the top from mid-June until October, though it's a long hard pull, and at any time of year Olympus must be treated with respect: its weather is notoriously fickle and it regularly claims lives.

The best base for a walk up the mountain is the village of **LITÓHORO** on the eastern side. The station for trains from Thessaloníki is 9km from the village, with rare connecting buses; or you can get a bus direct from Thessaloníki. Cheapest **accommodation** is either *dhomátia* – for example those of Papanikoláou (☎0352/81 236; ③) – or *Hotel Markissa*, Dhionýsou 5 (☎0352/81 831; ③), just down from main street 28-Oktovríou. Otherwise, try *Hotel Enipeís* (☎0352/84 328; ④), on the main square near the National Bank, or *Hotel Myrto* (☎0352/81 398; ⑤), also near the main square – and significantly less pricey in spring or autumn. Best **eats** are at *Dhamaskinia*, uphill on Vassiléos Konstandínou, or *Psistaria Zeus*, at the start of the road up the mountain.

You'd do well to buy a proper **map** of the range in Athens or Thessaloníki (the 1:50,000 Road Editions one is adequate, as is the older Korfes/EOS product), since availability in Litóhoro is unreliable. Four to five hours' walking along the well-marked, scenic E4 long-distance path up the Mavrólongos canyon brings you to **Priónia**, also the end of the much longer road and with the last reliable water source. From Priónia there's a sharper three-hour climb along a trail to the *Spilios Agapitos* **refuge** (☎0352/81 800; ①; mid–May to mid-Oct), perched on the edge of an abrupt spur and surrounded by huge, storm-beaten trees. It's best to stay overnight here, as you need to make an early start for the three-hour ascent to **Mýtikas**, the highest peak at 2917m; the summit frequently clouds up towards midday, to say nothing of the danger of catching one of Zeus's thunderbolts. The path continues behind the refuge, reaching a signposted fork above the tree line in about an hour; straight on, then right, takes you to Mýtikas via the ridge known as Kakí Skála, while the abrupt right reaches the *Yiosos Apostolidhis* **hut** in one hour (☎0352/82 300; ①; July to mid-Sept), from where you can enjoyably loop down in another day's walk to the **Gortsiá** trailhead and from there back down into the Mavrólongos canyon, via the ancient monastery of Ayíou Dhionysíou.

Halkidhikí

The squid-shaped peninsula of **Halkidhikí** begins at a perforated edge of lakes east of Thessaloníki and extends into three prongs of land – Kassándhra, Sithonía and Áthos – trailing like tentacles into the Aegean Sea. **Kassándhra** and **Sithonía** are Thessaloníki's beach-playground, hosting some of the fastest-growing holiday resorts in Greece. Both are connected to Thessaloníki by bus, but neither peninsula is that easy to travel around if you are dependent on public transport. You really have to pick a place and stay there, perhaps renting a scooter for local excursions. Áfytos is by far the most attractive place on Kassándhra, with a few *dhomátia* that haven't been snapped up by tour companies, and a few genuine tavernas. Sithónia is marginally less packaged, with low-key resorts at Kalamítsi, Pórto Koufó and Toróni.

Mount Áthos

Mount Áthos, the easternmost peninsula, is in all ways separate: a "Holy Mountain" whose monastic population, semi-autonomous from the Greek state, excludes all women – even as visitors. For men who wish to experience Athonite life, all that's required is a visit to the pilgrims' office in Thessaloníki (see p.627) to arrange the necessary admission paperwork. You need to be over the age of eighteen, and demonstrate a religious or scholarly interest in Áthos, to be given an entry pass allowing up to four days' stay on the holy mountain, moving to a different monastery or monastic dependency each night. A visit is highly recommended, though you can't hope to see more than a fraction of the twenty main monasteries or their satellites in the time allotted. Choose between the "museum monasteries" of Meyístis Lávras, Vatopedhíou, Ivíron or Dhionysíou with their wealth of treasures and art, or the more modestly endowed cloisters where the brothers will make more time for you, such as Osíou Grigoríou, Pandokrátoros and the Serbian foundation of Hilandharíou.

Both Ierissós and Ouranópoli, villages at the top of the peninsula and the usual gateways to Áthos, are served by several daily buses from Thessaloníki. **IERISSÓS** has many rooms to let and the friendly if slightly noisy *Hotel Marcos* (☎0377/22 518; ③), but boats sail only three times weekly to the monasteries of Áthos's northeast shore (not in bad weather). It's often best to continue to **OURANÓPOLI**, the last settlement before you reach the monastic domains, a busy resort overrun by both Germans and Greeks in summer. **Accommodation** is plentiful, with numerous rooms and a few budget hotels, such as *Galini* (☎0377/71 217; ④) and *Akroyali* (☎0377/71 201; ④). It's from here that the most reliable ferries depart for the southwest shore of monastic Áthos, daily at 9.45am. You'll need the earliest bus of the day (6am) out of Thessaloníki to coincide. Allow time to queue up at the Grafío Proskynitón (Pilgrims' Bureau) to exchange your reservation chit from the Thessaloníki office for a full-fledged *dhiamonitírion* or pass (around €25) allowing overnighting at any of the major monasteries.

From the usual entry port of **DHÁFNI** on the southwest coast, there are more possibilities of moving about by boat, bus (and lately even taxi). But walking between the religious communities on a dwindling trail network is an integral part of the Athonite experience, so you should be reasonably fit and self-sufficient in dry snack food, as the two meals offered each day tend to be spartan. Most monks pay scant attention to foreigners, so you get more of an idea of the magnificent scenery and engaging architecture than of the religious life, though it's hard to avoid tangling with the disorientating daily schedule, dictated by the hours of sun and darkness. Also, some monasteries – in particular those with great ecclesiastical treasures or architecture – have become so visited that you must book a bed by phone in advance; the Pilgrim's Bureau provides a list of contact numbers.

Crossing into Turkey or Bulgaria

The border town and military garrison of **ALEXANDHROÚPOLI** has little to recommend it, but it can get very crowded in season, with overland travellers and Greek holidaymakers competing for space in the few hotels and gritty beach campsites. The most comfortable **accommodation** is away from the port area: the *Lido*, Paleológou 15 (☎0551/28 808; ③) offers best value, while for more luxury try the nearby *Hera*, Dhimokratías 179 (☎0551/34 222; ⑥). The municipal *Camping Alexandhroupoli* is a half-hour walk from the train station (or bus #5). Restaurants are limited in number and not wonderful; best is the evening-only *Psarotaverna Anesti*, Athanasíou Dhiákou 5. To **Turkey**, there's only one through **train** to Istanbul per day from Alexandhroúpoli, an eleven-hour pull with usually long halts at the frontier; trains are more frequent to Kastaniés, opposite the Turkish town of Edirne (but get an early departure to ensure arrival at the frontier before it shuts at 1pm). Once over – walking may be allowed here – buses cover the 8km to Edirne. Otherwise, there are several **buses** to Istanbul, but most start in Thessaloníki and by this stage are full. An alternative is to take a local bus to the border at **KÍPI** (6 daily). You're not allowed to cross the frontier here on foot, but it is generally no problem to get a driver to shuttle you the 500m across to the Turkish control post – and possibly to give you a lift beyond. The nearest town is Ipsala (5km), but if possible get as far as Keşan (30km), from where buses to Istanbul are much more frequent.

There is also one early-morning train daily into **Bulgaria**, reaching Svilengrad in three-and-a-half hours (typically with a change of trains at Orménio). From Svilengrad, it is best to move on immediately towards Plovdiv.

THE SOUTHERN AEGEAN ISLANDS

The rocky, partly volcanic chain of **Argo-Saronic** islands is the nearest archipelago to Athens and one of the busiest. **Égina** is most frenetic, but **Ídhra** and **Spétses** aren't far behind in summer: more than any other group, these islands are at their best outside peak season. To the east, the **Cyclades** is the most satisfying Greek archipelago for island-hopping. The majority of these islands are arid and rocky, with brilliant-white, cubist architecture. The impact of tourism is haphazard, and though some English is spoken in most places, a slight detour could have you groping for your Greek phrasebook. **Íos**, the original hippie island, is still a backpackers' paradise, while **Mýkonos** – with its teeming old town, nude beaches and highly sophisticated clubs and bars (many of them gay) – is by far the most visited of the group. After these, **Páros**, **Sífnos**, **Náxos** and **Santoríni** are currently most popular, their beaches and main towns drastically overcrowded in July and August. The one major ancient site worth making time for is **Delos**, the commercial and religious centre of the Classical Greek world. Almost all of the Cyclades are served by boats from Pireás, but there are also ferries from Rafína to Sýros, Mýkonos, Páros and Náxos, among others.

Further east still, the **Dodecanese** lie so close to the Turkish coast that some are almost within hailing distance of the shore. The islands were only included in the modern Greek state in 1948 after centuries of occupation by Crusaders, Ottomans and Italians. Medieval **Rhodes** is the most famous, but almost every Dodecanese has its Classical remains, its Crusaders' castle, its traditional villages and grandiose Art Deco public buildings. The dry limestone outcrop of **Sými** has always been forced to rely on the sea for its livelihood, while the sprawling, relatively fertile giants, Rhodes and **Kós**, have recently seen their traditional agricultural economies almost totally displaced by tourism. **Kárpathos** lies somewhere in between, with a partly forested north grafted onto a rocky limestone south. **Pátmos**, at the fringes of the archipelago, boasts architecture and landscapes more appropriate to the Cyclades. The main islands are connected almost daily with each other, and none is hard to reach. Rhodes is the main transport hub, with services to Turkey, Cyprus and Israel, as well as connections with Crete, the northeastern Aegean islands, the Cyclades and the mainland (Thessaloníki and Pireás).

Égina (Aegina)

It seems incredible today, but ancient **Égina** was a major power in Classical times, with trade carried on to the limits of the known world. Today the island is essentially regarded as a weekend suburb of Athens, and a solitary column of a Temple of Apollo beckons as your ferry steams around the point into the harbour at **ÉGINA TOWN**. The bus stop is at Platía Ethneyersías, while scooter rental is also handy for a one-day exploration of the island. There's some moderately priced **accommodation**, including *Electra Rooms* on Leonárdhou Ladhá (☎0297/23 360; ④). The helpful **tourist office** (☎0297/22 334) opposite the boat jetty will book hotels and private rooms. The **Temple of Aphaia** (Mon–Fri 8am–7pm, Sat & Sun 8am–3pm; €3), dating from the sixth century BC, and one of the most complete ancient buildings in Greece, stands 17km east of town among pines tapped to make the excellent local retsina. To get to the temple from Égina town you can go by bus, though the best approach is by bike on the inland road which passes deserted Paleohóra, the island's old capital.

Égina's only really sandy beach – and not very clean – is at the overdeveloped package resort of **AYÍA MARÍNA**, close to the temple and also mobbed due to its role as a stop-off for ferries. Otherwise, aim for **PÉRDHIKA**, a small resort twenty minutes by bus south of Égina town. Despite poor beaches, it has the *Hotel Hippocampus* (☎0297/61 363; ④) and a few rooms to rent. There's better swimming at Moní islet opposite, served by kaïki several times daily; bring a picnic as there are no facilities.

Ídhra (Hydra)

The port and town of **ÍDHRA**, with its tiers of stone mansions and tiled white houses climbing up from a perfect horseshoe harbour, forms a very beautiful spectacle. Unfortunately, from Easter to September it's packed to the gills, and the seafront becomes one uninterrupted outdoor café (there are no private cars on Ídhra). Dozens of mansions were built here, mostly during the eighteenth century, on the accumulated wealth of a merchant fleet which traded as far afield as America. By the 1820s the town's population stood at nearly 20,000, seven times what it is today. Ídhra is reputedly hallowed by no fewer than 365 churches, the most important being the cathedral of Panayía Mitropóleos, with its distinctive clock tower, down by the port. There's no lack of expensive cafés and **restaurants** on the waterfront, but better value is to be had inland, for example at *Xiri Elia* and the much-loved *Yeitoniko* (alias *Manolis & Christina's*). **Hotels** and pensions are overpriced; reasonable-value places include *Theresia Pension* (☎0298/53 984; ⑥), *Hotel Dina* (☎0298/52 248; ⑤), *Hotel Hydra* up on the hillside (☎0298/52 102; ⑥) and pleasant *Hotel Amarillis* (☎0298/53 611; ⑥).

The island's only sandy **beach** is the private one at Mandhráki, 2km east of town. On the opposite side of the harbour a coastal path leads to a pebbly but popular stretch, just before **KAMÍNI**, where there are a pair of reasonable pensions and a good year-round taverna, *Christina*. Thirty minutes' walk beyond Kamíni (or a boat ride from the port) will bring you to **VLYHÓS**, a small hamlet with pricier rooms and three tavernas. Camping is tolerated here, and the swimming between the pebble shore and an islet is good.

Spétses (Spetsai)

Spétses is very green, very small and alarmingly popular with well-to-do Athenians and foreigners, but it absorbs its visitors with grace. The port and town of **SPÉTSES** (or Kastélli) shares with Ídhra a history of nineteenth-century mercantile prosperity, and pebble-mosaic courtyards and streets sprawl between mansions whose architecture is quite distinct from the Peloponnesian styles across the channel. A few horse-drawn cabs still connect the various quarters of town, spread out along the waterfront, though noisy scooters and three-wheeled trucks make a mockery of a no-cars rule. All kinds of **accommodation** are available in Spétses town, including *Hotel Stelios* (☎0298/73 280; ④) and *Hotel Faros* (☎0298/72 613; ⑤). *Alasia Travel*, close to the Dápia quay (☎0298/74 098), can do bookings. Among cheaper places to **eat** are *Roussos*, 300m east of Dápia, and the traditional *Lazaros*, 400m inland and uphill from Dápia.

ÁYII ANÁRYIRI, on the south side of the island, is the best, if also the most popular, beach: a beautiful, long, sheltered bay of fine sand only about an hour's walk through the woods from the town. There's a taverna on the beach, and, just behind, the moderately priced *Tassos*, Spétses' most eccentric eating establishment.

Sífnos

Although **Sífnos** often gets crowded, its modest size means that wherever you stay, you can reach the rest of the island by the excellent bus service to all points or on foot over a network of old stone pathways. **KAMÁRES**, the port, is tucked at the base of high bare cliffs in the west. **Accommodation** can be expensive – the budget option are the rooms above the Katsoulakis Tourist Agency (☎0284/32 362; ④) close to the quay. There are other places behind the beach, including a mediocre **campsite**, and the reasonable *Hotel Stavros* (☎0284/31 641; ⑤), just past the church. The best **meals** are at the quayside *Meropi*.

A steep twenty-minute bus ride takes you up to **APOLLONÍA**, a rambling collage of flagstones, belfries and flowered courtyards. The island bank, post office and tourist police are all here, but rooms, though plentiful, are even more likely to be full than at Kamáres. Outside of high season, there will be vacancies along the road to Fáros; quieter, and pricier, digs are along the stair-street north of the main square, or you can apply to the travel agency Aegean

Thesaurus (☎0284/31 151). The **Folk Museum** (daily 9.30am–2pm & 6–10pm; €1.50) in the square by the bus stop is also well worth a look, since Sífnos once produced some of the finest pottery and fabrics in Greece. As an alternative base, head for **KÁSTRO**, a forty-minute trail walk or regular bus ride below Apollonía on the east coast; built on a rocky outcrop with an almost sheer drop to the sea on three sides, this medieval capital of the island retains much of its character.

At the southern end of the island, 12km from Apollonía by frequent bus, lies the busy beach resort of **PLATÝS YIALÓS**. It has a poor campsite and numerous rooms to let, as well as **tavernas**, best of which is *Sofía*. Far less crowded sand is to be found just to the northeast at **FÁROS**, which also has regular buses from Apollonía, rooms and good, cheap tavernas like *Zambelis*. Perhaps the finest walk is through the hills to **VATHÝ**, around three hours from Apollonía's Katavatí "suburb". A fishing and ex-pottery village on a stunning funnel-shaped bay, Vathý is the most attractive base on the island: there are rooms to let and summer tavernas, the cheapest being *Manolis* and *To Tsikali*. An alternative route here is by regular bus from Apollonía.

Mýkonos

Mýkonos has become the most popular and expensive of the Cyclades, visited by nearly a million tourists a year. But if you don't mind the crowds – or you come out of season – the upscale capital is one of the most beautiful of all island towns. Dazzlingly white, it's the archetypal island-postcard image, with sugar-cube buildings stacked around a cluster of seafront fishermen's dwellings. The labyrinthine design was intended to confuse the pirates who plagued Mýkonos during the eighteenth and early nineteenth centuries and it remains effective: everyone gets lost.

The **airport** is about 3km out of town, a short taxi ride away. **Ferries** and cruise ships dock at the northern jetty, where you'll be met by a horde of owners hustling hotels and rooms; you'd do better to proceed to the helpful Mýkonos **accommodation centre** in the village centre (☎0289/23 160) – be aware that a private room is likely to be cheaper than staying in a hotel on the nearby beaches. As for **hotels** in town, out of season you might consider *Delfines* on Mavroyénous (☎0289/24 505; ⑥); *Karbonis* on Matoyiánni (☎0289/22 217; ⑦); or *Philippi*, Kaloyéra 25 (☎0289/22 294; ⑥). *Zorzis* on Kaloyéra 25 (☎0289/22 167; ⑧) also offers rooms in nearby apartments and pensions. Otherwise there are very lively official **campsites** at Paradise (☎0289/22 852; *paradise@paradise.myk.forthnet.gr*) and Paránga beaches. Every other bay on the island has some sort of taverna. The harbour curves around past the dull, central Polykandhrióti beach, behind which is the **bus station** for Toúrlos, Áyios Stéfanos and Áno Méra. Continue along the seafront to the southern jetty for the **tourist police** (☎0289/22 482) and kaïkia to Delos. A second **bus terminus**, for beaches to the south of town, is right at the other end of Hóra, beyond the windmills.

Around Kaloyéra is a promising area for **food**: the *Edem* is a popular gay restaurant with an adventurous menu; *Sesame Kitchen* is also fairly reasonable, with vegetarian choices. Cheaper eats are at *Nikos*, behind the town hall. **Drinking** haunts are over in the Alefkándhra area in the south of the town (known as "Little Venice"); try *Kástro's* for an early-evening cocktail, moving on later to *Montparnasse*, which is fairly swanky. The **nightlife** in town is every bit as good – and expensive – as it's cracked up to be. It's impossible to list every hot spot, but among the most durable are *Remezzo*, with sunset views, or *Pierro's*, once the main draw for the island's substantial gay contingent, but now mixed. Just off K. Yiorgoúli, the *Skandinavian Bar-Disco* is a cheap, jovial and nonstop party bar. The mixed *Famous Mykonos Dance Bar* and *Rainbow* are also young and sweaty.

Mýkonos beaches

The closest decent beach is **ÁYIOS STÉFANOS** (4km north), connected by a very regular bus service. Other nearby, mainstream destinations are the resorts on the southwest peninsula, with fairly undistinguished beaches tucked into pretty bays at Áyios Ioánnis and Ornós. Better to make for **PLATÝS YIALÓS**, 4km south, though you won't be alone there. A kaïki service from Mýkonos town connects almost all the beaches east of Platýs Yialós: gorgeous, pale-sand **PARÁNGA** beach, popular with campers; **PARADISE**, well sheltered by its headland, predominantly nudist, with two tavernas; and **SUPER PARADISE**, which has a friendly atmosphere and another taverna. Probably the island's best beach (and its longest) is **ELIÁ**, the last port of call for the kaïkia; it's a broad sandy stretch with a verdant backdrop, split in two by a rocky area. Almost exclusively nudist, it boasts a few restaurants, including the excellent *Mattheos*.

Delos (Dhílos)

The remains of ancient **DELOS** (Tues–Sun 8am–2.30pm; €6), though skeletal and swarming now with lizards and tourists, give some idea of the past grandeur of this sacred isle a few sea-miles west of Mýkonos. The kaïki trip gives you three hours on the island – barely enough time to take in the main attractions, but it's no longer possible to stay the night.

Delos' ancient fame was due to the fact that Leto gave birth to the divine twins Artemis and Apollo on the island, and one of the first things you see is the **Sanctuary of Apollo**, while three Temples of Apollo stand in a row along the Sacred Way. To the east towards the museum you pass the **Sanctuary of Dionysos** with its marble phalli on tall pillars. To the north is the **Sacred Lake** where Leto gave birth: guarding it is a group of superb lean lions, masterfully executed in the seventh century BC. Set out in the other direction from the agora and you enter the residential area, known as the **Theatre Quarter**. Many of the walls and roads remain but there is none of the domestic detail that makes Pompeii, for example, so fascinating. Some colour is added by the mosaics: one in the **House of the Trident**, better ones in the **House of the Masks**, including a vigorous portrayal of Dionysos riding on a panther's back. The **Theatre** itself, though much ravaged, offers some fine views.

Páros and Andíparos

With a little of everything – old villages, monasteries, fishing harbour and a labyrinthine capital – **Páros** is a good point to begin your island wanderings, with boat connections to virtually the entire Aegean, though things have become nearly as expensive and commercialized here as on Mýkonos. **PARIKÍA**, the main town, sets the tone for the rest of Páros, with its ranks of white houses punctuated by the occasional Venetian-style building and church domes. All ferries dock here, and the waterfront is packed with bars, restaurants, hotels and ticket agencies. Just outside the central clutter, the town also has one of the most interesting churches in the Aegean – the **Ekatondapylianí**, or "Church of One Hundred Gates" (daily 9am–1pm & 5.30–9.30pm). The original construction was overseen in the sixth century by Isidore of Miletus but the work was carried out by his pupil Ignatius. Behind the Ekatondapylianí, the **Archeological Museum** (Tues–Sun 8.30am–2.30pm; €1.50) has a fair collection of antique pieces, its prize exhibit a portion of the Parian Chronicle, a social and cultural history of Greece up to 264 BC, engraved in marble.

Páros has long been the major hub of inter-island **ferry** services, eclipsing nearby Sýros, and the harbour is currently being extended. Boats dock by the windmill. The **bus stop** is 100m or so to the left; routes extend to Náoussa in the north, Alykí in the south, and Dhryós on the island's east coast (with another very useful service between Dhryós and Náoussa). You'll be met off the ferry by locals offering rooms; avoid offers of properties to the north as they're invariably a long walk away, though there is a crowded **campsite**, the *Koula*, at the northern end of the town beach. The better *Parasporos* campsite is 2km south of town (☎0284/21 100). Among pensions and hotels not block-booked by tour operators, try the *Pension Festos* (☎0284/21 635; ③); the family-run *Hotel Argonauta*, close to the National Bank (☎0284/21 440, *www.argonauta.gr*; ⑦) or the friendly *Hotel Dina* near Platía Veléntza on the main market street (☎0284/21 325; ⑥). For a touch of luxury, treat yourself to the friendly and comfortable *Sophia Rooms* (☎0284/22 085; ⑥), behind Cinema Paros. For **food**, *Trata* to the left of the cemetery of the ancient city is good for fish; *To Boundouraki*, overlooking the harbour, is another reasonable choice. Parikía has a wealth of pubs, bars and low-key discos, not as pretentious as on Mýkonos or as raucous as on Íos, but certainly everything in between. The most popular cocktail bars extend along the seafront, tucked into a series of open squares. For **Internet** access, try *Parosweb* on the main market street in the old town, or *Marina Internet Café* and *Memphisnet*, both on the harbourfront.

The second village of Páros, **NÁOUSSA** was until the early 1990s an unspoilt town, but a rash of new concrete hotels has all but swamped its character. Despite this development, the town is a good place to head for as soon as you reach Páros; there are some pleasant beaches nearby, while rooms are marginally cheaper than in Parikía – track them down with the help of the tourist office just over the bridge, west from the harbour. **Hotels** are more expensive; though out of season prices are reduced at the *Madaki* (☎0284/51 475; ⑥) and the *Stella* (☎0284/51 317; ⑦). There are two **campsites**, out of town towards **Kolymbíthres** and **Sánta María** beaches, both better than the mosquito-plagued one in Parikía, and various **tavernas**, all of which are pretty good, specializing in fresh fish and seafood: start with *Barbarossas* or *Vengera*.

There's little to stop for south of Parikía until **POÚNDA**, 6km away, and then only to catch the ferry to **Andíparos**. In recent years this islet has become something of an open secret, and in high season can be very full. Most of the population of 800 live in the single northern village, served by a barge-ferry from Poúnda and kaïkia from Parikía dock (daily every 30min 9.15am–12.15am). There are a dozen tavernas and some small **hotels** – the cheapest are *Korali* (☎0284/61 236; ⑤) and *Anargyros* (☎0284/61 237; ⑤) – and a very popular **campsite** with a nudist beach. The great cave in the south of the island is the chief attraction for day-trippers: in season hourly buses run there from the port, or it's a ninety-minute walk along the paved road.

Náxos

Náxos is the largest and most fertile of the Cyclades, and with its green and mountainous interior seems immediately distinct from many of its neighbours. The Venetian occupation left towers and fortified mansions scattered throughout the island, while medieval Cretan refugees bestowed a singular character upon the eastern settlements. A long causeway protecting the harbour connects **NÁXOS TOWN** with the islet of Palátia, where the huge stone portal of an unfinished **Temple of Apollo** still stands. Most of the town's life goes on down by the port or in the streets just behind it; stepped lanes behind lead up past crumbling balconies and through low arches to the fortified **kástro**, from where the Venetians ruled over the Cyclades. Other brooding relics survive in the same area: a seventeenth-century Ursuline convent, the Catholic cathedral and one of Ottoman Greece's first schools, now housing an excellent **Archeological Museum** (Tues–Sun 8am–2.30pm; €1.50), with an important early sculpture collection and a Hellenistic mosaic on the roof terrace.

Tourism has now reached such a level that an annexe of purpose-built **accommodation** extends south of the town centre, since rooms downtown are of a uniformly poor standard and overpriced. The helpful private **tourist office** near the jetty (☎0285/25 201) can book rooms around the island, and also provides a laundry service. In-town **hotels** are better on the cooler north slope of the *kástro*: best budget options are the *Panorama* on Amfitrítis (☎0285/24 404; ⑥) and the nearby *Anixis* (☎0285/26 475; ⑤). The air-conditioned *Chateau Zevgoli* (☎0285/26 123, *chateau-zevgoli@nax.forthnet.gr*; ⑨) is a luxury choice; *Yanios Rooms* (☎0285/22 816; ⑤), in a quiet residential street off the town square, is a clean and simple alternative. Along the quayside, cafés and **restaurants** are abundant enough, if a bit expensive; seaside *Psistaria tis Popis* doles out generous salads and cuts of roast meat, while the old-fashioned, durable *Iy Kali Kardhia*, also on the waterfront, is worth a visit. The only **Internet** café is Internet Naxos on the town square.

The island's best **beaches** line the southwest coast a few kilometres from town, and in season are regularly served by buses. **ÁYIOS YEÓRYIOS**, a lengthy sandy bay south of the hotel quarter, lies within walking distance. There are several tavernas here and you can camp officially just off the beach in the first of four organized sites on this coast; the second site, *Apollon*, has the best facilities, including a swimming pool, and offers free daily kung-fu classes. Access is south through the salt marshes near **ÁYIOS PROKÓPIOS** beach (cheapish hotels and basic tavernas), or you could follow the tracks a little further – an hour-plus walk from town – to **AYÍA ÁNNA**, a small port where there are plenty of rooms to let and a few modest tavernas (plus summer kaïkia to Píso Livádhi on Páros). Beyond the headland stretches less-developed **PLÁKA** beach, a 5km-long vegetation-fringed expanse of white sand which comfortably holds the summer crowds of nudists and campers from the two friendly campsites here.

Íos

No other island attracts the same vast crowds of young people as **Íos**, yet the island hasn't been commercialized in quite the same way as, say, Mýkonos, since many visitors are young and impecunious, though the island is being driven steadily more upmarket. You might be tempted to grab a room in **YIALÓS** as you arrive, though it's the most expensive place on the island to stay. A refurbished **campsite** is to the west of the harbour, although there are also two other remoter sites. Yialós beach, five minutes' walk from the harbour, is fringed by hotels and lodgings, but loud music seems to be accepted on the beach and obligatory in the tavernas. Most of the cheaper rooms are in **HÓRA**, a twenty-minute walk up the mountain behind the port, with dorms as well as the usual rooms and hotels. Every evening the streets throb to music from competing **clubs** (mostly free or with a nominal cover charge). Drinks tend to be expensive, although haggling can be rewarding, especially out of season. The *Ios Club* is an antidote to standard techno-pop. There are plenty of **restaurants** and fast-food places too, but the one most popular with savvy Greeks and non-Greeks alike is *Fiesta*, on the second bend of the road up from the harbour.

The most popular stop on the island's bus routes is **MYLOPÓTAMOS**, site of a magnificent beach and a mini-resort. By day, bodies cover every inch of the bus-stop end of the sand: for a bit more space head the other way, where there are dunes behind the beach. There are two decently equipped **campsites**, *Purple Pig/Stars* being preferable (☎0286/91 302); for **rooms**, try *Drakos Pension* (☎0286/91 281; ④) to the right of the bus stop, also with a well-respected taverna. From Yialós, daily day-trip boats depart at around 10am to **MANGANÁRI** on the south coast, the beach to go to for serious all-over tans. There's a better atmosphere, though, at **ÁYIOS THEODHÓTIS**, up on the northeast coast, served by daily buses from Yialós.

Santoríni (Thíra)

As the ferry manoeuvres into **Santoríni**, gaunt, sheer cliffs loom hundreds of feet above. Nothing grows to soften the view, and the only colours are the reddish-brown, black and grey pumice striations of the cliff face. As early as 3000 BC Santoríni developed as an outpost of Minoan civilization until, around 1450 BC, the volcano-island erupted; island and settlements were both destroyed and, it is thought, the great Minoan civilizations on Crete went with them.

Some small ferries and excursion boats dock at **SKÁLA FIRÁ**, but most vessels use the somewhat grim port of **ÓRMOS ATHINIÓS**. Half-rebuilt after a devastating earthquake in 1956, the island capital **FIRÁ** lurches demontedly at the cliff's edge. Besieged by day-trippers from cruise-ships, it's become incredibly tacky of late, the most grossly commercialized spot on what can – in summer, at least – seem a grossly commercialized island. There is no shortage of **rooms**, no matter what is shouted at you by the touts as you arrive, as well as three

hostels. The official hostel in the northern part of town (☎0286/22 387 or 23 864; ①) is a fair budget choice, also with doubles (④). The **campsite** is well-signposted 500m east of the bus terminal. Firá is not a place to linger, but the **Archeological Museum** (Tues–Sun 8am–2.30pm; €3) near the cable car to the north of town is excellent, including a curious set of autoerotic figures which may move to new premises in 2002. **Buses** are plentiful enough to get around between the town and beaches, but if you want to see the whole island in a couple of days, renting a scooter is useful – try any of the firms on the main road to Ía from the bus station square. **Internet** access is at *Lava*, on the main street close to Firá Square.

Near the northwest tip of the island is one of the most dramatic towns of the Cyclades, **ÍA**, a curious mix of pristine white reconstruction and tumbledown ruins clinging to the cliff face. It's also much the calmest place on Santoríni, and with the presence of a post office, travel agencies, scooter rental and an excellent **hostel** (☎0286/71 465; ②), there's no reason to feel stuck in Firá. However, conventional **rooms** aren't too easy to come by; the most reasonable choices are *Hotel Anemones* (☎0286/71 220; ⑤) or *Hotel Fregata* (☎0286/71 221; ⑤). Best-value **eating** is at *Anemomylos* and *Laokasti*, or for a fish treat scramble down the steps to *Kyra Katina* at Ammoúdhi harbour. **Beaches** on Santoríni are bizarre: long black stretches of volcanic sand which get blisteringly hot in the afternoon sun. There's little to choose between **KAMÁRI** and **PÉRISSA**, the two main resorts: both have long beaches and a mass of restaurants, rooms and apartments; neither is for those seeking solitude. Périssa gets more backpackers, and has the well-run hostel *Anna* (☎0286/82 182; ①), also with doubles (④). Camping rough is forbidden. Kamári and Périssa are separated by the **Mésa Vounó** headland, on which stood Classical (post-eruption) Thira (Tues–Sun 9am–2.30pm; free); most of the ruins are difficult to place, but the **theatre** is awesome: beyond the stage there's a sheer drop to the sea. Evidence of the Minoan colony was found at **AKROTÍRI** (summer Tues–Sun 8am–8pm; €6), a town buried under banks of volcanic ash at the southwest tip of the island, and reached by bus from Firá or Périssa. Tunnels through the ash uncovered structures two and three storeys high; lavish frescoes adorned the walls and Cretan pottery was found stored in a chamber. The frescoes are currently exhibited in Athens, but there are plans to bring them back once the new museum in Firá is operating.

Kárpathos

Though the third-largest of the Dodecanese, **Kárpathos** has always been something of a backwater, though its magnificent coastline of cliffs and rocky promontories constantly interrupted by little beaches has begun to attract significant tourism. **PIGÁDHIA**, the rather unsightly capital, curves around one side of Vróndi Bay, a long sickle of sandy beach stretching north. Even remoter **rooms** on the south hillside such as the welcoming *Rose Studios* (☎0245/22 284; ③) and *Elias Rooms* (☎0245/22 446; ③; June–Sept) often get full in midsummer, when you may have to head west to Arkássa or Finíki. Waterfront **tavernas** tend to improve in value and quality as you head for the ferry dock, for example *Orea Karpathos* and *To Perigiali*.

All ferries calling at Pigádhia stop also at **DHIAFÁNI**, the northern port, which is additionally served by a daily morning kaïki from Pigádhia. Although its popularity is growing, rooms in Dhiafáni are still easy to find and life slow outside August. The rugged, partly forested north of the island is favoured by walkers; paths lead north to the stony **Vanánda beach**, thirty minutes away, then west 90 minutes to **Avlóna**; or south in an hour to the better beach of **Papá Miná**. Both road and path climb to **ÓLYMBOS**, two hours' walk up from Dhiafáni and the one essential sight on the island. The older women in their magnificent traditional dress dominate the village, working in the gardens, carrying goods on their shoulders, or tending mountain sheep. The long-isolated villagers also speak a unique dialect, and **traditional music** is still heard regularly. There are several inexpensive places to stay, such as *Olympos* (☎0245/51 252; ②), and a couple of tavernas – but it is almost impossible to get a room around the dates of any festival.

Rhodes (Ródhos)

It's no surprise that **Rhodes** is among the most visited of Greek islands. Not only is its east coast lined with sandy beaches, but the core of the capital is a beautiful and remarkably preserved medieval city. **RÓDHOS TOWN** divides into two unequal parts: the compact old walled city, and the new town which sprawls around it in three directions. First thing to meet the eye, and dominating the northeast sector of the city's fortifications, is the **Palace of the Grand Masters** (Mon 2.30–9pm, Tues–Fri 8.30am–9pm; medieval walls Tues & Sat 2.45pm; palace €6, walls €6). Destroyed by an explosion in 1856, it was reconstructed by the Italians as a summer home for Mussolini and Victor Emmanuel III, neither of whom ever actually visited Rhodes. Inside, a marble staircase leads up to rooms paved with mosaics from Kós, and the furnishings rival many a grand northern European palace. Better than any of this, though, are two **museums** on the ground floor: one devoted to medieval Rhodes, the other to ancient Rhodes. The heavily restored **Street of the Knights** (Odhós Ippotón) leads due east from the front of the palace. The "Inns" lining it housed the Knights of St John for two centuries, and at the bottom of the slope the Knights' Hospital has been restored as the **Archeological Museum** (Tues–Sun 8.30am–3pm; €3), where the star exhibits are two statues of Aphrodite. Across the way is the recently restored **Byzantine Museum** (same hours; €1.50), housed in the knights' chapel and highlighting the island's icons and frescoes. Leaving the Palace and heading south, it's hard to miss the most conspicuous Ottoman monument in Rhodes, the candy-striped, recently restored **Süleymaniye Mosque**. Downhill and east from the mosque is **Odhós Sokrátous**, once the heart of the old bazaar, and now packed with souvenir shops and milling foreigners. The most enduring civic contribution of Rhodes's Muslims is the **bathhouse** on Platía Ariónos, up in the southwest corner of the old city; one of only a couple of working public baths in Greece, it's a great place to go on an off-season day (often shut for "repairs"; typical hours Tues 1–7pm, Wed–Fri 11am–7pm, Sat 8am–6pm; €1.50, or €0.90 on Wed & Sat).

Affordable **accommodation** abounds in the old town and is contained almost entirely in the quad bounded by Odhós Omírou on the south, Sokrátous on the north, Perikléos to the east and Ippodhámou to the west. At crowded times you may have to accept the offers of the persistent touts that meet the ferries, moving on the next day. Quiet, good value places include *Apollo Rooms*, Omírou 28C (☎0241/63 894; ③); *Pension Pink Elephant* on Timahídhas, off Irodhótou (☎0241/22 469; ④) and the modernized, ultra-clean, en-suite *Hotel Spot*, Perikleous 21 (☎0241/34 737; ④). There's a **hostel** at Eryíou 12, just off Ayíou Fanouríou (☎0241/30 491; ①). **Eating** cheaply can be more of a problem; try the little alleys and backstreets well south of Sokrátous. Here you'll find *Yiannis*, Apéllou 41, for oven casseroles; *Anthony's*, corner Pythagóra and Omírou, for fresh souvláki in characterful surroundings; and *Mikess* for affordable seafood, in the nameless alley behind Sokrátous 17. Better value can be had just outside the walls, for instance at *To Steno*, Ayíon Anaryíron 29, 400m southwest of the Ayíou Athanasíou gate, or *Vassilis (Kova)*, on Kolokotróni east of Kanadhá, near the Akándia commercial port.

The **post office**, most **banks** (there are just two in the old town), the EOT **tourist office** (Mon–Fri 7.40am–3pm; ☎0241/23 255) and the **police** are all in the new town, mostly northwest of the Italian-built New Market. **Buses** for the rest of the island leave from two terminals within sight of the market – one for the east coast, the other for the west. Most central **Internet** café is *Rock Style* at Dhimokratías 7, just southwest of the old town.

Around the island

Heading down the east coast from Ródhos, the giant promontory of **Tsambíka**, 26km south, is the first place to seriously consider stopping – there's an excellent eponymous beach just south of the headland, reached by a 1.5km slip road. The best overnight base on this stretch of coast is probably **HARÁKI**, a tiny port with rooms and tavernas overlooked by a very ruinous castle. **LÍNDHOS**, Rhodes's number-two tourist attraction, erupts 12km south of

Haráki. Like Ródhos town itself, its charm is undermined by commercialism and crowds, and there are relatively few self-catering houses that aren't block-booked through package companies – find vacancies through Pallas Travel (✆0244/31 494). Nevertheless, if you can arrive before or after the tours, Líndhos can still be a beautiful and atmospheric place. Its church is covered with eighteenth-century frescoes, and several of the older houses are open to the public; entrance is free but they tend to expect you to buy something. On the hill above the town, the scaffolding-swathed **Temple of Athena** stands inside the inevitable knights' castle (summer Mon 12.30–6.40pm, Tues–Fri 8am–6.40pm; €6). Líndhos' beaches are crowded and overrated, but you'll find better ones heading south past Lárdhos, the start of 15km of intermittent coarse-sand beach up to and beyond the growing resort of Yennádhi. Inland near here, the Byzantine frescoes in the village church of **ASKLIPIÓ** are the best on Rhodes.

On the west coast, the first place to stop would be the ruins of ancient **Kameiros** (Tues–Sun 8am–7pm; €3), which with Lindos and Ialyssos was one of the island's three Dorian city-states. The end of bus lines on this coast is the remote village of **MONÓLITHOS**, which can offer a castle, a superb beach at nearby Foúrni, and a single simple hotel, *Thomas* (✆0246/61 291; ④).

Sými

Sými's most pressing problem, lack of water, is in many ways also its saving grace, as the island can't hope to support more than two or three large luxury hotels. Instead, hundreds of people are shipped in daily from Rhodes, relieved of their money and sent back. The island's capital consists of **Yialós**, the port, and **Horió**, on the hillside above, collectively known as **SÝMI**. Until 1912 the town was richer and more populous than Rhodes, but now only about 2500 locals (and a large number of foreigners) inhabit the magnificent nineteenth-century mansions, some derelict with their windows gaping blankly across the harbour. There is an excellent island **museum** (Tues–Sun 10am–2pm; €1.50), which highlights Byzantine and medieval Sými, while at the very pinnacle of the hill a castle occupies the site of Sými's acropolis, surrounded by a dozen chapels. **Rooms** are outnumbered by studios and both are hard to come by in high season; best try a booking agency such as Sunny Land (✆0246/71 320) or Symi Visitor (✆0246/72 755). Otherwise, try *Katerina Tsakiris* (✆0241/71 813; ⑤) for rooms with shared kitchen, or *Rooms Titika* (✆0246/71 501; ⑤) for rooms with fridge and air-con. When **eating out**, shun the north quay in favour of *Dhimitris*, on the south quay; *To Amoni*, at the back of the square; or *Giorgios* up in Hório, a long-running, characterful supper venue.

Sými has only one sandy beach, but there are plenty of pebbly stretches at the heads of the coastline's deep narrow bays. **PÉDHI**, 45 minutes' walk or a ten-minute regular bus ride from Yialós, is a hamlet at the base of Sými's only farming valley, with an average beach but a better, sandy one at **ÁYIOS NIKÓLAOS**, twenty minutes' trail-walk beyond along the south shore. Further afield, taxi-boats take you to the southeasterly bays of **NANOÚ** (the best, with a decent taverna) and **ÁYIOS YEÓRYIOS DHYSSÁLONA**. Since the upgrading of the trans-island road, you can get a lift on the service van, or rent an expensive scooter, to reach the giant monastery of **Taxiárhis Mihaïl Panormítis** at the far south of the island.

Kós

Kós is the largest and most popular island in the Dodecanese after Rhodes, and there are superficial similarities between the two. Like its competitor, the harbour here is also guarded by a castle of the Knights of St John, the streets are lined with grandiose Italian public buildings, and minarets and palm trees punctuate extensive Greek and Roman remains. Except for Kós Town and Mastihári, there aren't many non-package travellers: in high season you'll be lucky to find any sort of room at all, except perhaps at the far west end of the island.

Mostly modern KÓS TOWN, levelled by a 1933 earthquake, spreads in all directions from the harbour. The helpful municipal tourist office (July & Aug daily 7am–9pm; spring & autumn Mon–Fri 7.30am–8pm, Sat 8am–3pm; winter Mon–Fri 8am–3pm), 500m south of the ferry dock on the shore road, offers maps and ferry schedules. Long-distance buses arrive at a park another 500m west of the tourist office. Among budget accommodation, the clean and friendly, co-managed *Pension Alexis*, Irodhótou 9 (☎0242/28 798; ③) and *Hotel Afendoulis*, 600m south at Evripýlou 1 (☎0242/25 321; ④), are long-running favourites, and deservedly so; if they're full, they tend to refer you to the good-value *Hotel Kamelia*, Artemissías 3 (☎0242/28 983; ⑤). The official campsite is thirty minutes' walk or a frequent city-bus ride along the scrappy beach to the southeast of town. Avoid the waterfront restaurants in favour of such inland outfits as *Frangoulis*, 1.5km inland in Kakó Prinári suburb; *Olympiadha*, Kleopátras 2; or *Australia-Sydney* on Vassiléos Pávlou. Internet access is at *Café del Mare*, Megálou Alexándhrou 4a.

Apart from the castle (Tues–Sun 8.30am–2.30pm; €3), the town's main attraction is its wealth of Hellenistic and Roman remains, the largest single section of which is the ancient agora, reached from the castle or the main square next to the Archeological Museum (same hours; €3). Next to the castle, scaffolding props up the branches of the so-called Hippocrates plane tree, which does have a fair claim as one of the oldest trees in Europe. The star exhibit in the museum is Hippocrates' statue, and he is also honoured by the Asklepion (Tues–Sun 8.30am–2.30pm; €3), a temple to Asclepius and renowned centre of Hippocratic teaching, 45 minutes on foot (or a short bus ride) from town. The road to the Asclepion passes through the bi-ethnic village of PLATÁNI (or Kermetés), where the island's ethnic Turkish minority run three tavernas; *Arap* and *Sherif*, in particular, serve excellent, affordable food, far better than you generally get in Kós town.

If you're looking for anything resembling a deserted beach near the capital, you'll need to ride the long-distance buses, or else find your own transport. Around 12km west of Kós town, TINGÁKI is easily accessible and thus oversubscribed, though the crowds thin out in the dunes between it and Marmári, another German-dominated resort 3km southwest. MAS-TIHÁRI, 30km from Kos town, is an actual village with a decent beach and non-package-tour rooms, as well as regular ferries to Kálymnos. KARDHÁMENA, halfway down the southeast coast, is the island's second-largest tourist playpen, and runaway development has banished whatever redeeming qualities it may once have had. Continuing west, buses run as far as KÉFALOS, which squats on a bluff looking back down the length of Kós. Well before Kéfalos are Áyios Stéfanos, where the exquisite remains of a mosaic-floored fifth-century basilica overlook tiny Kastrí islet, and KAMÁRI, the resort just below Kéfalos. Beaches begin at Kamári and extend east past Ayios Stéfanos for 7km, virtually without interruption; "Paradise" has the most facilities, but "Magic" or "Banana" are calmer and more scenic.

Pátmos

It was in a cave on Pátmos that St John the Divine wrote the Book of Revelation, and the monastery which commemorates him, founded here in 1088, dominates the island both physically and politically. While the monks no longer run Pátmos as they did for more than six centuries, their influence has stopped most of the island going the way of Rhodes or Kós. SKÁLA, the port and main town, is the chief exception, crowded on summer days with excursionists from Kós and Rhodes or cruise-ship shoppers, and by night with well-dressed cliques of French, Germans, Italians, Britons and Americans. Accommodation touts meet all ferries and hydrofoils, and their offerings tend to be a long walk inland – not necessarily a bad thing, as the waterfront is noisy. Hotels to book in advance include *Blue Bay* (☎0247/31 165; ⑥), just east of town, also with the town's main Internet café; the kindly *Australis* (☎0247/31 576; ⑤), in Netiá district; or *Diethnes* well inland (☎0247/31 357; ④). Among restaurants, try *Pantelis* one block inland, where excellent food offsets often grumpy service, or the seafood ouzerí *To Hiliomodhi*. The next bay north of the main harbour shelters MÉLOÏ BEACH, with a well-run campsite and an excellent *mayireftá* taverna, *Stefanos*. For swimming, the next beach, **AGRIOLIVÁDHI**, is usually less crowded.

The **Monastery of St John** (opening hours erratic, but at least daily 8am–2pm) shelters behind massive defences in the hilltop capital of **HÓRA**. There is a bus up, but the thirty-minute walk by a beautiful old cobbled path puts you in a more appropriate frame of mind. Just over halfway is the **Monastery of the Apocalypse**, built around the cave where St John heard the voice of God issuing from a cleft in the rock. This is merely a foretaste, however, of the main monastery, behind whose fortifications have been preserved a fantastic array of religious treasures dating back to medieval times (museum €3.50). Hóra itself is a beautiful little town whose antiquated alleys shelter over forty churches and monasteries, plus dozens of shipowners' mansions dating from the island's heyday in the seventeenth and eighteenth centuries. If you're determined to stay here – and there is a total of only about fifty beds – it's best to make morning enquiries at the recommended taverna *Vangelis*, on Platía Levías. From Hóra a good road runs above the forgettable package resort of Gríkou to the isthmus of **Stavrós**, from where a thirty-minute trail leads to the excellent beach, with one seasonal taverna, at **PSILÍ ÁMMOS** (there's also a summer kaïki service from Skála). There are more good beaches in the north of the island, particularly **LIVÁDHI YERÁNOU**, shaded by tamarisk groves and with a decent taverna, and **LÁMBI** with volcanic pebbles and another quality taverna.

THE NORTHERN AEGEAN ISLANDS

The seven scattered islands of the **northeastern Aegean** form a rather arbitrary archipelago and, despite their proximity to Turkey, bear few signs of an Ottoman heritage apart from the odd minaret. International tensions are high, and the resulting heavy military presence can be disconcerting. But, as in the Dodecanese, local tour operators do a thriving business shuttling passengers for absurdly high tariffs between the easternmost islands and the Turkish coast. **Sámos** is the most visited, and was – until a week-long forest fire in July 2000 devastated a fifth of the island – perhaps the most verdant and beautiful. **Híos** is culturally interesting, but its natural beauty has also been ravaged by fire and the development of tourism has, so far, been deliberately retarded. **Lésvos** is more of an acquired taste, though once you get a feel for the island you may find it hard to leave. The appeal of **Thássos** is rather broader, with a varied offering of sandy beaches, partly forested mountains (there have been fires here too) and minor archeological sites; cheaply accessible from the Greek mainland, it can, however, get rather overrun in high season. The **Sporades**, in the north-western Aegean, are a very easy group to island-hop and well connected with Athens by bus and ferry via Áyios Konstandínos or Kými (for Skýros only), and with Vólos.

Sámos

Sámos was the wealthiest island in the Aegean during the seventh century BC, but fell on hard times thereafter; today its economy is heavily dependent on package tourism, the eastern half of the island (as opposed to the more rugged western side) having surrendered to the onslaught of rather staid, Nordic, thirtysomething holidaymakers. It remains to be seen, however, whether arrival numbers will ever attain the levels of before the 2000 fire. Except for express boats, all main-line **ferries** to and from Pireás and the Cyclades call at both Karlóvassi in the west and Vathý in the east; additionally there are services to the Dodecanese out of Pythagório in the south. **VATHÝ**, the capital, lines the steep-sided shore of its namesake bay and is of minimal interest except for its hill quarter of tottering, tile-roofed houses, Áno Vathý, and an excellent **archeological museum** (Tues–Sun 9am–2.30pm; €3) which has a wealth of peculiar votive offerings and a huge, five-metre *kouros* (statue) of an idealized youth. The **tourist office**, 25-Martíou 4 (summer only

Mon–Fri 9am–2pm; ☎0273/28 530), is not very useful but keeps accommodation lists. **Accommodation** without tour-group allotment includes the welcoming *Pension Avli*, housed in a former convent at Áreos 2 (☎0273/22 939; ②); the basic *Pension Ionia*, Manóli Kalomíri 5 (☎0273/28 782; ②); and the noisier *Hotel Artemis* on the seafront "Lion Square" (☎0273/27 792; ③). When **eating out**, head inland to *Ta Kotopoula* at Plátanos junction, or the pricier but good-value *Ouzeri Apanemia*, at the far south end of the front. Bus services off the main corridors to Karlóvassi and Pythagório are skimpy; you're expected to rent a scooter or motorbike, for which there are a dozen outlets in town.

PYTHAGÓRIO by the airport is the island's main resort; its views across to Turkey are more attractive than the surroundings, though the village and its relentlessly commercialized harbour retain some charm. It's built atop the ancient capital of the island, of which evidence abounds: **Roman baths**; the **Evapalinio tunnel**, an ancient subterranean aqueduct (Tues–Sun 8.45am–2.30pm; €1.50); a heavily modified **amphitheatre**, and, 8km west, the **Sanctuary of Hera** (Tues–Sun 8.30am–2.45pm; €3), marked by a single standing column. There's no reason to stay or even eat in Pythagório; just show up for your onward ferry or hydrofoil.

Heading west from Vathý, the first place of any note is the busy resort of **KOKKÁRI**, enchantingly set between twin headlands at the base of still partly forested mountains. Nearby beaches are pebbly and exposed, prompting its role as a major windsurfers' resort. For **eating**, *Ta Adherfia/The Brothers* at the south end of the postcard-pretty seafront has fair-value grills and fish. Some 13km west is untouristed **ÁYIOS KONSTANDÍNOS**, with three modest pensions, including *Atlantis* (☎0273/94 239; ②).

Less than an hour's walk west from functional **Karlóvassi**, the island's second town, **POTÁMI** is a popular beach ringed by forest and weird rock formations; for more solitude you can continue another hour or so on foot to the two bays of **Mikró Seitáni** (pebbles) and **Megálo Seitáni** (sand). But for an actual amenitied beach resort in the west of the island, you'll need to shift south to **VOTSALÁKIA**, almost 2km of sand and pebbles lined with accommodation, under the shadow of brooding Mount Kérkis. *Emmanuel Dhespotakis* (☎0273/31 258; ④) has a few non-packaged **rooms** at the west end of the developed strip; *Loukoulos* is the most unique and interesting **taverna**.

Híos

Increasing numbers of foreigners are discovering **Híos** beyond its port city and single resort strip – fascinating villages, an important Byzantine monument and a healthy complement of beaches. In August there may not be enough beds to go around, but at other times you'll find the island blissfully tourist-free. **HÍOS TOWN** is always full of life, with a shambling old bazaar district, some excellent authentic tavernas, and a regular evening promenade along the waterfront. There's relatively cheap **accommodation** along and just behind the water-front; the helpful **tourist office**, Kanári 18 (summer Mon–Fri 7am–2.30pm & 7–10pm, Sat 10am–1pm, Sun 7–10pm; ☎0271/44 389), has comprehensive lists. The best-value and qui-etest include *Rooms Alex*, Mihaíl Livanoú 29 (☎0271/26 054; ③), and en-suite *Rooms Savvas*, Roïdhou 15 (☎0271/24 892; ④). **Eating out** is better than the glut of waterfront fast-food out-lets would suggest. Try *Ouzeri Theodhosiou*, right where the big ferries dock, or *O Hotzas* well inland at Yeoryíou Kondhýli 3. Green long-distance **buses** run from the terminal south of the central park to most of the villages on Híos, though services to the north are sparse. The closest decent beach is **KARFÁS** (7km; very frequent blue bus), a long if rather narrow sweep of sand unfortunately overwhelmed by package tours; the best independent option here is the delightful *Markos' Place* (☎0271/31 990; ④), installed in a disused monastery.

The monastery of **NÉA MONÍ** (daily 8am–1pm & 4–8pm; free), founded by Byzantine emperor Constantine IX in 1042, is the most beautiful and important medieval building on the Greek islands. Its mosaics rank among the finest artistic expressions of their age, and its set-ting, high in the mountains west of the port, is no less memorable. There are special KTEL bus excursions on Tuesday and Friday mornings; otherwise take a taxi or rent a scooter. Once a community of 600 monks, Néa Moní was pillaged during Ottoman atrocities in 1822 and most of its inmates put to the sword. Today the monastery, with its giant refectory and vaulted water cisterns, is deserted except for a few lay workers.

The hillsides of **southern Híos** are home to the mastic bush, whose resin – for centuries the base of paints and cosmetics – was the source of local wealth before petrochemicals came along. **PYRGÍ**, 24km from the port, is one of the liveliest and most colourful of the "mastic villages", its houses elaborately embossed with geometric patterns cut into the plaster and then outlined with paint. On the northeast corner of the central platía, the fresco-embellished Byzantine church of **Áyii Apóstoli** is tucked under an arcade (Tues–Thurs & Sat 10am–1pm). Pyrgí has a handful of rooms and some good beaches nearby, the closest being Emborió, 5km from Pyrgí and served by occasional buses in summer; eating is, however, better at equally impressive **MESTÁ**, 11km west, with two good tavernas on its square.

The villages of **northern Híos** never recovered from the Turkish massacres of the War of Independence, and many are now virtually deserted. The best target is **VOLISSÓS**, a large, half-inhabited village guarded by a castle, and with affordable restored **accommodation** through Stella Tsakiri (☎0274/21 421; ④). Just over 2km away is **LIMNIÁ**, a lively and authentic little fishing village with two good tavernas, plus a few more studios on the slopes inland. About 1km southeast, at **MANAGRÓS**, begins an almost boundless sand-and-pebble beach, while the more intimate cove of **LEFKÁTHIA** is just a ten-minute walk over the headland north of the harbour. **AYÍA MARKÉLLA**, 5km further north, stars in many of the local postcards: a long, stunning beach fronting the monastery of the same name, which has a summer taverna and lodging in the grounds.

Lésvos (Mytilíni)

Lésvos, birthplace of Sappho, the ancient world's foremost woman poet, may not at first strike the visitor as particularly beautiful, but the rocky volcanic landscape of pine and olive groves grows on you. Despite the inroads of tourism, this is still by and large a working island, with few large hotels outside the capital, Mytilíni, and the resorts of Skála Kallonís and Mólyvos. Moreover, buses from Mytilíni are run for the benefit of the locals, not tourists, and journeys are often slow and tortuous: it's wise to base yourself at one of the few resorts and explore its surroundings. **MYTILÍNI** itself has little to detain you, other than a good **archeological museum** (Tues–Sun 8.30am–3pm; €2). Rooms are fairly abundant – try *Pelayia Koumniotou*, Yeoryíou Tertséti 6 (☎0251/20 643; ③) – though most restaurants, apart from the *Averof*, are substandard. The EOT **tourist office** by the customs house (daily 8.30am–6pm; ☎0251/22 776) provides some good maps. Worth a detour at **VARIÁ**, 5km south, are the adjacent **Theophilos museum** (summer Tues–Sun 9am–2pm & 5–8pm; winter Tues–Sun 9am–2pm; €1.50) and **Thériade museum** (same hours; €1.50), with astonishing collections of naïve painting and modern art respectively.

MÓLYVOS, on the northwestern coast, is easily the most attractive spot on Lésvos. Tiers of sturdy, red-tiled houses mount the slopes between the picturesque harbour and the Genoese castle. Closer examination reveals a dozen weathered Ottoman fountains along stone-paved alleyways. There are plenty of rooms to let, a **tourist office** by the bus stop (summer daily 8am–3pm & 6.30–8.30pm) to help you find them if necessary, and a campsite east of town. The main lower road, straight past the tourist office, heads towards the picturesque harbour, where *The Captain's Table* is the best-value taverna. What with a bank, post office and abundant scooter rental, there's no need to move far. The island's best beach is at **SKÁLA ERESSOÚ** in the far southwest. There are rooms to let here, but sometimes not enough. Tavernas with wooden terraces line the beach – best of these are *Adonis* and *Blue Sardine*, at the far west end of the esplanade, with Canadian-run *Yamas* good for breakfasts and decadent cakes. Visitors to Skála Eressoú include substantial numbers of gay women paying homage to Sappho, who supposedly lived in ancient **Eressós**; all that remains of the old town crumbles away atop a bluff to the east. The southeastern peninsula also offers its share of attractions; foremost is the huge beach at **VATERÁ** – the equal of Skála Eressoú's, with a campsite and a sprinkling of shoreline tavernas.

Thássos

Just 12km from the mainland, almost circular **Thássos** has long been a popular resort for northern Greeks, and since the 1990s has been attracting considerable numbers of foreign tourists. Without being spectacular it is a very beautiful island, its low mountains hosting a few surviving groves of pine, olive and chestnut in the northeast which tumble down to a line of good sand beaches. **THÁSSOS TOWN** is the nexus of life, though not the main port: **ferries** from Kavála usually stop down the coast at **Órmos Prínou**, but a few each day continue to Thássos Town, as do all hydrofoils. The largely modern town is partly redeemed by its pretty harbour and popular sand beaches to either side, and the substantial remains of the ancient city. There are several inexpensive **hotels**, including *Athanasia* (☎0593/22 545; ③) and the welcoming, English co-run *Alkyon*, on the seafront (☎0593/22 148; ④), plus reasonably plentiful **rooms**, though in summer you should take the first offered on arrival. **Eating out**, menus tend to be expensive and bland, though *Iy Piyi*, at one corner of the inland square, has proven reliable over the years. The main excavated area of **ancient Thássos** (daylight hours; free) is the **agora**, entered beside the town museum (closed indefinitely for repairs), a little way back from the modern harbour. Prominent are two Roman stoas, but you can also make out shops, monuments, passageways and sanctuaries from the remodelled Classical city. Above the town, roughly in line with the smaller fishing port, steps spiral up to a recently restored **Hellenistic theatre**, fabulously positioned above a broad sweep of sea. Beyond the theatre, a path winds on to a **Genoese fort**, constructed out of stones from the acropolis. From here you can follow the circuit of **walls** to a high terrace supporting the foundations of a Temple of Apollo and onwards to a rock-hewn sanctuary of Pan. Below it, a precarious sixth-century BC "secret stairway" descends to the outer walls and back into town.

Several buses a day do the full island circuit in season, and there are several more buses to and from different villages, with a bias towards the west coast. The east- and south-facing coasts have most of the best beaches. Above the east coast, **PANAYÍA** village, with accommodation and proximity to Khryssí Amnoudhiá beach, makes the best base; **KÍNYRA**, 11km south, is quieter and right by "Paradise" beach. **ALYKÍ** faces a double bay which almost pinches off a headland; the mixed sand-and-pebble western strand gets too popular for its own good in high season, but the water is crystal-clear and the beachside *Glaros* taverna offers good food and the lowest-priced rooms among a half-dozen outfits here (☎0593/53 047; ③). At the south tip of Thássos, **ASTRÍS** has two excellent beaches and a few rooms, but the best-amenitied local resort – and virtually the only one to function outside of July and August – is German-dominated **POTÓS**, where there's the *Paradissos* campsite (☎0593/51 950) and a fine, kilometre-long sand beach facing the sunset.

The Sporades

The three northern **Sporades** – package-tourist haven Skiáthos, Alónissos and Skópelos, the pick of the trio – have good beaches, transparent waters and thick pine forests. Skýros, the fourth island, is slightly isolated from the others, less scenic, but with perhaps the most character; for a relatively uncommercialized island within a day's travel of Athens it is hard to beat.

Skópelos

More rugged and better cultivated than neighbouring Skiáthos, **Skópelos** is also very much more attractive. Most boats call first at the small port of Loutráki, below the western village of Glóssa, but it's best to stay on board until **SKÓPELOS TOWN**, which slopes down one corner of a huge, almost circular bay. Hotels here are ever-increasing in quantity, but occupied mainly by package tourists; tucked away on the far side of the bay, in the main body of the town there are dozens of places to let – take up one of the offers when you land. Nightlife is fairly subdued, with just one disco but a dozen or so late-hours bars. The most reliable waterfront **tavernas** are *To Aktaion* and *Spyros*. Within the town, spread below the oddly whitewashed ruins of a Venetian kástro, are an enormous number of churches – 123 reputedly, though some are small enough to be mistaken for houses. **Buses** cover the island's one asphalt road between Skópelos and Loutráki about seven times daily, stopping at the turn-offs to all the main beaches and villages. **STÁFYLOS** beach, 4km out of town, is the closest, but it's small, rocky and increasingly crowded; the overflow, much of it nudist, flees to **VELANIÓ**, just east. Much more promising, if you're after isolation and are content to walk, is **AGNÓNDAS** (with tavernas and rooms), a fifteen-minute walk or short kaïki ride from the sand beach at Limnonári. The large resort of **Pánormos** has become overdeveloped, and never had a really good beach, but slightly further on, **MILIÁ** offers a tremendous 1.5km sweep of tiny pebbles beneath a bank of pines.

Skýros

Skýros was until recently a very traditional and idiosyncratic island. Though it has definitely been "discovered" since the 1980s, it remains one of the most interesting places in the Aegean. The older men still wear the vaguely Cretan costume of cap, vest, baggy trousers, leggings and clogs, while the women favour yellow scarves and long embroidered skirts. Skýros also has some particularly lively **festivals** – notably the Apokriatiká (pre-Lenten) carnival's "Goat Dance", performed by masked revellers in the village streets. A **bus** connects Linariá – a functional little port with a few tourist facilities – to **SKÝROS TOWN**, perched on a high rock rising precipitously from the coast. Traces of Classical walls can still be made out among the ruins of the Venetian kástro; within the walls is the crumbling, tenth-century monastery of **Áyios Yeóryios**. At the north end of town, the **Memorial to Rupert Brooke** – a splendidly incongruous bronze nude of "Immortal Poetry" – commemorates the World War I poet who died on a hospital ship anchored offshore in 1915. There are several hotels and plenty of rooms to let in private houses; you'll be met with offers as you descend from the bus. Skyros Travel (☎0222/91 123) on the main street can help with accommodation. Eating out, you'll find most tavernas overpriced and mediocre, *Khristina's* and *Maryetis* being exceptions. The campsite is down the hill from the Rupert Brooke statue, at the fishing village of **MAGAZIÁ**, with rooms and tavernas fronting the best beach on the island. The only practical ways of getting around Skýros are on foot or by scooter (there are several rental places in the main town), though in summer the whimsical bus service also visits the more popular beaches. The most rewarding walk is a four-hour traverse of the island by rough jeep track to **ATSÍTSA** on the west coast.

THE IONIAN ISLANDS

The six **Ionian islands** are, both geographically and culturally, a mixture of Greece and Italy. Floating on the haze of the Adriatic, their green, even lush, silhouettes come as a shock to those more used to the stark outlines of the Aegean. The islands were the Homeric realm of Odysseus and here alone of all modern Greek territory (except for Lefkádha) the Ottomans never held sway. After the fall of Byzantium, possession passed to the Venetians, and the islands became a keystone in that city-state's maritime empire from 1386 until its collapse in 1797. Most of the population was immune to the establishment of Italian as the official language and the arrival of Roman Catholicism, but Venetian influence remains evident and beautiful despite a series of earthquakes. Tourism has hit **Corfu** in a big way – so much so that it's one of the few islands known to locals and foreigners by different names. None of the other islands has endured anything like Corfu's scale of development, although the process seems well advanced on parts of **Zákynthos**. For a less sullied experience, head for the trio of **Kefaloniá**, **Itháki** and **Lefkádha** (Lefkas).

Corfu (Kérkyra)

Corfu's natural appeal remains an intense experience, if sometimes a beleaguered one, for it has more package hotels and holiday villas than any other Greek island. The commercialism is apparent the moment you step ashore at the ferry dock, or cover the two kilometres from the airport to the city on foot, by taxi, or on local bus #2/#3, which depart from 500m north of the terminal gates. **KÉRKYRA TOWN**, the capital, has a lot more going for it than first exposure to the summer crowds might indicate. The cafés on the Spianádha (Esplanade) and in the arcaded Listón have a civilized air, and the **Palace of St Michael and St George** at the north end of the Spianádha is worth visiting for its Asiatic museum (Tues–Sun 8.30am–3pm; €2.50) and Municipal Art Gallery (daily 9am–9pm; €2.50). The **Byzantine Museum** (Tues–Sun 8.30am–3pm; €2.50) and the cathedral are both interesting, as is the **Archeological Museum**, Vraíla 3 (Tues–Sun 9am–3pm; €3), where the small but intriguing collection features a 2500-year-old Medusa pediment. The island's patron saint, Spirýdhon, is entombed in a silver-covered coffin in his own church on Vouthrótou, and four times a year, to the accompaniment of much celebration and feasting, the relics are paraded through the streets. Some 5km south of town lies one of Greece's most popular excursion targets, the picturesque island of **Vlahérna**, which is capped by a small monastery and joined to the plush mainland suburb of Kanóni by a short causeway, spoilt by airport noise.

There are several agencies along Vassiléos Konstandínou who can arrange your accommodation; the **tourist office** on the corner of Vouleftón and Mantazárou (Mon–Fri 8am–2pm; ☎0661/37 520) also has lists of **rooms**. Otherwise, try the least expensive old-town **hotel**, *Europa*, Yitsiáli 10, near the new port (☎0661/39 304; ③); the larger seafront *Hotel Ionion*, Xenofóndos Stratigoú 46 (☎0661/39 915; ③); or the refurbished *Hotel Hermes*, Markorá 14, behind the daily market in the old town (☎0661/39 321; ⑤). The nearest **campsite** is *Dionysos Camping Village* (☎0661/91 417) at Dhassiá, 8km north. For **eating out**, two authentic restaurants are *Faliraki*, at the jetty below the Palace of St Michael and St George, and the more expensive *Rex*, behind the Listón in Zavitsiánou.

There are two **bus terminals**: one on Platía San Rocco for the numbered blue-vehicle routes that run up to 10km from the town; the other on Platía Néou Frouríou, just below the fort, for green KTEL buses to more remote parts of the island as well as Thessaloníki and Athens. Scooters are also available to rent nearby, and at most other resorts on the island.

Around the island

The coast north of the port has been remorselessly developed as far as Pyrgí, and much of it is best written off. West of Kassiópi, the first attractive place to stay is **ÁYIOS SPYRÍDHON**, where there are restaurants and a few campers ignoring the "No camping" signs on the small beach. A little way on you'll see a sign to Almyrós beach, start of the continuous strand that sweeps around to **RÓDHA** – once a small village but now taken over by British travel companies. The best spot on this northern coast is beyond Sidhári at **PEROULÁDHES**, a genuine, somewhat run-down village with a spectacular beach of brick-red sand below wind-eroded cliffs.

On the west coast, **PALEOKASTRÍTSA** has gone the way of all package locations, though its coves are on a beautiful stretch of coast. Expensive villas and hotels are present in abundance, plus a few campsites, which are, however, some distance from the town. If you just want a **room**, search uphill in the villages of Lákones and Makrádhes, about 5km away. The tiny village of **VÁTOS**, just inland from west-coast Érmones, seems to be the one place within easy reach of Kérkyra Town that has an easy, relaxed feel to it. There are reasonable **rooms** and two **tavernas** here, both (as so often on Corfu) called *Spyro's*; the better is the one further from the road. Campers pitch tents down towards **Myrtiótissa Beach**, though they sometimes get encouraged to use the official site, *Vatos Camping*, near the village. The dirt track down to the sand is steep and has so far prevented development. Nearby **GLYFÁDHA** is dominated by a huge hotel, and adjacent **PÉLEKAS** is likewise busy, as the main crossroads in the west-centre of the island; but it's a good alternative base, with simple **tavernas**, a **hostel** and **rooms**. Continuing south, **ÁYIOS GÓRDHIS** beach is more remote but that hasn't spared it from the crowds who come to admire the cliff-girt setting or patronize the *Pink Palace* (☎0661/53 103; ②), a foreign-run combination holiday village/resort right on the sand.

Beyond Messongí stretches the flat, sandy southern tip of Corfu. **ÁYIOS YEÓRYIOS**, on the southwest coast, consists of a developed area just before its beautiful beach, which extends north alongside the peaceful Korissíon lagoon. **KÁVOS**, near the cape itself, rates with its many **clubs** and **discos** as the nightlife capital of the island; for daytime solitude and swimming, you can walk to beaches beyond the nearby hamlets of Spartêrá and Dhragotiná.

Kefalloniá (Kefallinía, Cephalonia)

Kefalloniá is the largest, and at first glance least glamorous, of the Ionian islands; the 1953 earthquake which rocked the archipelago was especially devastating here, with almost every town and village levelled. Couple that with the islanders' legendary eccentricity, and with poor infrastructure it's no wonder tourism didn't take off until the late 1980s. Already popular with the Italians, the island has, more recently, been attracting large numbers of British tourists, partly thanks to the success of Louis de Bernières' novel, *Captain Corelli's Mandolin*, which was set here; the big-budget film is already attracting even more. There's plenty of interest: beaches to compare with the best on Corfu or Zákynthos, good local wine, and the partly forested mass of Mount Énos (1632m). The island's size, skeletal bus service and persistent shortage of summer accommodation make **renting a motorbike** or **car** a must for exploration; scooters may not cope with some grades or surfaces. **Ferries** from Pátra, other Ionian islands and Astakós mostly dock at **SÁMI** on the east coast, which has returned to its functional role after the excitement of hosting the *Corelli* film set; few people linger, though the *Ionion* (☎0674/22 412; ④) has reasonable rooms and *To Karnayio* is the best of the many restaurants. **AYÍA EVFIMÍA**, 10km north, makes a far more attractive base, with the small but smart *Moustakis* hotel (☎0674/61 030; ④) and *Dendrinos*, arguably the best taverna on Kefalloniá. Between the two towns, 3km from Sámi, the **Melissáni cave** (daily 8am–8.30pm; €3.50), a partly submerged Capri-type "blue grotto", is well worth a stop. Southeast from Sámi you find the resorts of **PÓROS**, with ferries to Kyllíni on the Peloponnese, and **SKÁLA**, whose remains of a **Roman villa** boast fine mosaics. You may have to continue around the cape, past excellent beaches, to find accommodation in the coastal village of Lourdháta, about halfway between Skála and Argostóli. Just inland, detour to the Venetian **castle of Áyios Yeóryios** (daily 8am–3pm; free).

ARGOSTÓLI, with occasional ferries to Kyllíni and Zákynthos, is the bustling island capital: inevitably concrete, very Greek. The waterfront **tourist office** (Mon–Fri 7.30am–2.30pm; ☎0671/22 248) keeps comprehensive lists of **accommodation**; you're best off with private rooms as hotels are expensive. For eating out, a good if unromantically located fall-back is the *Kalafatis* on Andóni Trítsi, near the bus station; they also have rooms to rent. There are a dozen agencies on the waterfront renting out transport. The newly refurbished **Archeological Museum** (Tues–Sun 8.30am–3pm; €2.90) is second only to Corfu's in the archipelago. Heading north from Argostóli, there's little to stop for on the west coast until you emerge, along a dizzying corniche road, above **MÝRTOS**, considered the best beach on the island, although lacking in facilities; the closest place to **stay** is the almost busless **ÁSSOS**, a fishing port perched on a narrow isthmus linking it to a castellated headland. At the end of the line is **FISKÁRDHO**, with its eighteenth-century houses, notable mainly for having escaped damage in the earthquake. It's the most expensive place on the island; the main reason to come would be for the daily **ferry** to Lefkádha island, and sometimes to Itháki.

Itháki (Ithaka)

Despite its proximity to Kefalloniá, there's still very little tourist development to spoil **Itháki**, Odysseus's capital. There are no sandy beaches, but the island is good walking country, with a handful of small fishing villages and various coves to swim from. **Ferries** from Pátra, Kefallloniá, and Astakós (and, in peak season, also from Corfu, Igoumenítsa and Italy) land at the main port and the village-sized capital of **VATHÝ**, at the back of a deep bay within a bay. **Rooms** are fairly easy to come by except during the July music festival and the August–September theatre events; they tend, however, to be inconspicuous, and are best sought by nosing around the backstreets south of the ferry dock. There are two mid-range hotels at opposite ends of the long quay, *Odysseus* (☎0674/32 381; ④) and *Mentor* (☎0674/32 433; ⑤). There's more choice for **food**, with seven or eight tavernas, the seafront *To Kohyli* being the best of a remarkably similar bunch.

In season the usual small boats shuttle tourists from the harbour to a series of tiny coves along the peninsula northeast of Vathý. The pebble-and-sand **beaches** between Cape Skhinós and Sarakíniko Bay are excellent; most of those closer to town are little more than concrete diving platforms. Four daily **buses** run north along the main road out of Vathý to **STAVRÓS**, a fair-sized village with a couple of tavernas and some rooms. **FRÍKES**, a thirty-minute walk downhill beyond Stavrós, is smaller but has a handful of tavernas, rooms and a pebbly strip of beach. This is where the seasonal **ferries** dock, to and from Lefkádha and Fiskárdho on northern Kefalloniá; the port is linked to Vathý by the same bus as Stavrós. There are also five daily ferry crossings in summer (two in winter) from Pisaetós to Sámi on Kefalloniá.

Zákynthos (Zante)

Zákynthos, which once matched Corfu in architectural distinction, was hit hardest by the 1953 earthquake, and the island's grand old capital was completely destroyed. Although some of its beautiful Venetian churches have been restored, it's a town of limited appeal and the attraction for travellers lies more in the thick vineyards, orchards and olive groves of the interior, and some excellent beaches. Under two hours from Kyllíni on the mainland, Zákynthos now gets close to half a million visitors a year. Most tourists, though, are conveniently housed in one place, Laganás, on the south coast; if you avoid July and August, and steer clear of Laganás and the developing villages of Argási and Tsiliví, there is still a peaceful Zákynthos to be found. The most tangible hints of the former glory of **ZÁKYNTHOS TOWN** are in **Platía Solomoú**, the grand and spacious main square. At its waterside corner stands the beautiful fifteenth-century sandstone church of **Áyios Nikólaos**, whose paintings and icons, along with those from other island churches, are displayed in the imposing **Zákynthos Museum** (Tues–Sun 8am–2.30pm; €2.30) by the town hall. The large church of **Áyios Dhionýsios** was one of the few buildings left standing after the earthquake, and murals still cover the interior. If you've a couple of hours to fill, walk up the cobbled path to the town's massive **Venetian fortress** (Tues–Sun 8am–7.30pm, winter closes 2pm; €1.50) for great views across the town and sea. The **tourist police** on waterfront Lombárdhou have information about **accommodation** and **bus** services. Good-value places include *Egli* at the corner of Loútzi and Lombárdhou (☎0695/28 317; ④) and *Omonia*, Xanthopoúlou 4 (☎0695/22 113; ④). Restaurants or tavernas are a bit thin on the ground: *Taverna Arekia* is excellent and has authentic live music, but it's a 20-minute walk north along the east road. Places round the squares are pricey but two good options on the seafront are *Molos* and *Psaropoula*, which does great seafood *pikilíes*. To get to the **beaches**, buses depart from the station on Filitá (one block back from the Fina pump on the seafront), but since the island is fairly flat, apart from the north and west, this is an ideal place to rent a **bike** – available from Moto-Saki (which also has scooters and motorcycles) on Leofóros Dhimokratías, opposite the phone office.

CRETE

With its flourishing agricultural economy, **Crete** (*www.crete.tournet.gr*) is one of the few islands which could probably support itself without tourists. Nevertheless, tourism is heavily promoted. The northeast coast in particular is overdeveloped and, though there are parts of the south and west coasts that have not been spoiled, they are getting harder and harder to find. By contrast, the high mountains of the interior are still barely touched, and one of the best things to do is to rent a scooter and explore the remoter villages.

Crete is distinguished as the home of the **Minoan** civilization, Europe's earliest, which made the island the centre of a maritime trading empire as early as 2000 BC and produced artworks unsurpassed in the ancient world. Control of the island passed from Greeks to Romans to Saracens, through the Byzantine Empire to Venice, and finally to Turkey for more than two centuries. Almost wherever you go, you'll find some reminder of the island's history. The first priority is to get away from the capital **Iráklio** as quickly as possible, having first paid a visit to its superb archeological museum and the Minoan palace at nearby **Knossos**. There's another great Minoan site at **Mália** on the north coast, while to the south are Roman ruins at **Gortys**. For many people, unexpected highlights turn out to be Crete's **Venetian forts** (dominant at **Réthymno**) and its **Byzantine churches** (most famously near **Kritsá**). To get away from it all, head west towards **Haniá** and the smaller, less well-connected places along the south and west coasts; it is in this area that the mighty **White Mountains** rise, while below them yawns the famous **Samariá Gorge**, a magnet for trekkers.

Iráklio (Heraklion) and around

The best way to approach **IRÁKLIO** is by sea; that way you see the city as it should be seen, with Mount Ioúktas rising behind and the Psilorítis range to the west. As you get closer, it's the city walls which first stand out, still dominating and fully encircling the oldest part of town, and finally you sail in past the great fort defending the harbour entrance. Unfortunately, big ships no longer dock in the old port but at great modern concrete wharves alongside – which neatly sums up Iráklio itself: many of the old parts have been restored, but they're of no relevance to the dust and noise which characterize much of the city today. However, it has to be said that the city government has gone to great pains in recent years to upgrade Iráklion's image; the renovation and greening of many of the central areas have made a great improvement. **Platía Eleftherías** – the focus of a makeover a couple of years ago – is very much the traditional heart of the city, both in terms of its constant traffic and for the terraces of expensive cafés and restaurants which line it, jammed on summer evenings with strolling hordes. Most of Iráklio's more expensive shops are in the streets leading off the square. The **Archeological Museum** (Mon noon–7pm, Tues–Sun 8am–7pm; €4.50) also lies just off the north side of this square, with a fabulous if bewilderingly large collection that includes almost every important prehistoric and Minoan find on Crete (go early or late in the day to avoid tour groups). Remember to save some energy for the especially wonderful **Hall of the Frescoes** upstairs, with its intricately reconstructed fragments of wall paintings from Knossos and other sites. A major renovation is planned for 2002–3 and although the museum will remain open, some disruption is inevitable. Directly opposite the museum is the EOT **tourist office** (Mon–Fri 8.30am–5pm; ☎081/228 225), which can provide a useful city map.

Finding a **room** is usually not a problem except occasionally in August; the tourist office can help you find something. A good place to start looking is in the area below Platía Venizélou (named "Fountain Square" for its ancient Venetian fountain). *Vergina*, Hortátson 32 (☎081/242 739, *elikrp@her.forthnet.gr*; ③), and nearby *Rea*, Kalimeráki 1 (☎081/223 638; ③), are both good; not far away is *Mirabello*, Theotokopoúlou 20 (☎081/285 052, *mirabhot@otenet.gr*; ③), with decent rooms (some en-suite) in a quiet street. Clean, well-maintained *Rent Rooms Hellas*, Hándhakos 24, slightly west (☎081/280 858; dorms ①, rooms ③), is in competition with the friendly and comfortable non-HI *Youth Hostel*, Výronos 5 (☎081/286 281; dorms ①, rooms ②). The nearest **campsite**, *Creta Camping* at Káto Goúves (☎0897/41 400), lies an inconvenient 16km east; Hersónissos-bound buses will drop you off.

There are plenty of **places to eat**, but in general they're expensive. The inexpensive *Geroplatanos*, with a tranquil terrace in the small pedestrianized square fronting the church of Áyios Titos, just off Fountain Square, is good for a lunchtime treat. For plates of economical *mezédhes* the Marineli alleyway just to the south of the same square has a line of ouzeri (*Kapetanios* and *Katsina* are good). The best and cheapest fish in town is at *Ippokambos*, Sofoklí Venizélou, near the harbour at the foot of Odhós 25-Avgoústou. On the same square as *Geroplatanos* is a stylish **bar**, *Pagopoleion*, which has been imaginatively converted from an old ice factory. Students relax in the bars in and around Platía Koräï, a small square between Fountain Square and the Archeological Museum – *Flash*, *To Avgo* and the glittering new *Korais* are popular. **Internet** access is at Gallery Games, Korái 14, and Netc@fé (*www.the-netcafe.net*), Odós 1878, 4.

The **tourist police** are on Dhikeosýnis, halfway between Platía Eleftherías and the market, and the **post office** (Mon–Fri 7.30am–8pm) is just behind here, on Platía Dhaskaloyiánni. The 24-hour **OTE** office is next to El Greco Park, in the square immediately north of Venizélou. You can find several banks, plus shipping and travel agents, down 25-Avgoústou. You'll also find **motorbikes** and **cars to rent** down here, but places off the main road offer better prices; try the reliable Blue Sea, Kosmá Zótou 7 (☎081/241 097, *bluesea@hol.gr*; bikes and cars; 20-percent discount for Rough Guide readers), or Ritz, Kalimeráki 1 (inside the *Hotel Rea*; cars only). **Buses** for all points east along the coastal highway and to the **east** and **southeast** of the island (Hersónissos, Mália, Áyios Nikólaos, Sitía, Mýrtos, Árvi, Ierápetra and points en route) leave from the station near the ferry dock on the south (or town) side of the coast road. Main-road services **west** (Réthymno and Haniá) leave from the terminal opposite, on the north side of the coast road. Buses for the **southwest** (Festós, Mátala, Léndas and Ayía Galíni) operate out of a terminal just outside the Haniá Gate, beyond the walls in the west of the city (city buses go there from the centre).

Knossos

The largest of the Minoan palaces, **KNOSSOS** reached its cultural peak over 3500 years ago, though a town of some importance persisted here until well into the Roman era. It lies on a low, largely artificial hill some 5km southeast of Iráklio amid hillsides rich in lesser remains spanning 25 centuries, reached on local bus #2 from a city bus stand adjacent to the east and southeast station. As soon as you enter the **Palace of Knossos** (daily 8am–7pm; winter closes 5pm; €4.40) through the West Court, the ancient ceremonial entrance, it is clear how the legends of the Labyrinth of the Minotaur grew up around it. Even with a detailed plan, it's almost impossible to find your way around the site systematically – but wander around for long enough and you'll eventually stumble upon everything. Evidence of a luxurious lifestyle is plainest in the **Queen's Suite**, off the grand **Hall of the Colonnades** at the bottom of the stunningly impressive **Grand Staircase**. The main living room is decorated with a reproduction of the celebrated dolphin fresco, though the original, now in the Iráklio archeological museum, was actually found in the courtyard. Going up the Grand Staircase to the floor above the Queen's domain, you come to a set of rooms in a sterner vein, generally regarded as the **King's quarters**. The staircase opens into a grandiose reception chamber known as the **Hall of the Royal Guard**, its walls decorated in repeated shield patterns. Continuing to the top of the staircase you emerge onto the broad **Central Court**, which would once have been enclosed by the walls of the buildings all around. On the far side, in the northwestern corner of the courtyard, is the entrance to one of Knossos' most atmospheric survivals, the **Throne Room**, in all probability the seat of a priestess rather than a ruler.

Gortys, Phaestos and Mátala

The three major sites south of Iráklio – **Gortys**, **Phaestos** (Festós) and **Ayía Triádha** – can be visited on a day's tour from the city, probably with a lunchtime swim at Mátala thrown in. Public transport forces a more leisurely pace, but there's still no reason why you shouldn't get to all three sites and reach Mátala within the day; if necessary, it's easy enough to hitch the final stretch.

About 1km west of Áyii Dhéka, where the bus drops you off, **GORTYS** (daily 8am–6pm; €2.40) is the ruined capital of the Roman province of Cyrenaica which included not only Crete but also much of North Africa. Cutting across the fields to the south of the fenced site will give you some idea of the scale of this city at its zenith (approximately the third century AD); here, an enormous variety of other remains are strewn across your route, including an impressive **theatre**, a huge administrative complex and three temples. At the main entrance to the **fenced site**, alongside and to the north of the road, is the ruinous but still impressive basilica of **Áyios Títos**, the saint who converted Crete and was also its first bishop. Beyond this is the **Odeion**, which houses the most important discovery on the site, the Law Code – an inscription measuring about 10m by 3m.

Some 17km west of Gortys along the main highway lies the **Palace of Phaestos** (daily 8am–7pm; €3.50), another of the island's key Minoan sites. Unlike Knossós, the palace was not substantially reconstructed by its Italian excavators and requires a little more imagination. But the location is stunning, a hillside position giving a commanding view over the Messará plain spreading away to the south. The palace was constructed in the seventeenth century BC on the ruins of a previous palace, destroyed by a terrific earthquake. Merely following your nose will enable you to find the Theatral Area (some archeologists think there may have been some form of performances here) with an imposing staircase, royal apartments, storerooms with huge ceramic *pithoi* for storing oil, wine and grain, and a magnificent Central Court, the focus of all the Minoan palaces.

An easy 3km journey west of Phaestos is the smaller palace of **Ayía Triádha** (daily 8.30am–3pm; €1.50), thought to have been a summer residence for the royal occupants of Phaestos. The ruins are substantial and occupy another spectacular site, this time with views towards the coastal plain and the sea.

MÁTALA is the best-known beach hereabouts, widely promoted because of the famous **caves** cut into the cliffs above its beautiful beach. These ancient tombs used to be almost permanently inhabited by a sizeable hippie community; nowadays the town is full of package tourists and tries hard to present a respectable image. The cliffs were long ago cleared out and nowadays comprise a fenced-off **archeological site** (April–Sept daily 10am–4pm; €1.50). Should the crowds get too much, it's a twenty-minute clamber over the rocks to another excellent stretch of sand, known locally as "Red Beach". In the evening, when the trippers have gone, the waterside bars and restaurants look out over spectacular sunsets. However, rooms are both expensive (③) and oversubscribed, and food, though good, is also pricey.

Mália and Áyios Nikólaos

With its crowded sandy beach, the resort of **MÁLIA**, 31km east of Iráklio, lives for the holiday spirit: party all night, sleep all day. The raucous side of town lies along the snaking, 1km-long beach road, replete with supermarkets, souvenir shops, video bars and nightclubs which around midnight erupt into a pulsating cacophony. *Zoo* is one of the top choices along here, which really gets going after 2am when its body-piercing studio opens; others (mostly British-owned) include *Cloud*, *Cosmos* and a host of English-style pubs. **Eating** is of the pie-and-chips variety, but if you head into the **old town**, on the inland side of the main road, you'll find welcoming tavernas around Platía Ayíou Dhimitríou and rooms at *Esperia* (☎0897/31 086; ⑤).

Some 3km east are the thoroughly atmospheric ruins of the **Palace of Mália** (Tues–Sun 8.30am–3pm; €2.50), much less visited than Knossós or Phaestos, but with a virtually intact ground plan. Nothing stands more than a metre above ground apart from giant *píthoi* which have been left about the site; wandering between the various courts and halls – especially on the walkway above new excavations west of the main site – makes it easy to envisage this seaside palace in its days of glory.

About the same distance again east, **ÁYIOS NIKÓLAOS** (popularly abbreviated to "Ag Nik") is set around a supposedly bottomless salt lake, now connected to the sea to form an inner harbour. It is supremely picturesque, and exploits this fact to the full. Both the lake and the port are surrounded by restaurants and bars, all of which charge well above normal, and the town itself is permanently crammed with tourists, many of whom are distinctly surprised to find themselves in a place with no decent beach. If you're after clubs, crowds and souvenirs, though, this is the place for you. Finding a cheap **room**, however, is virtually impossible in season; among the more central options are *Rooms Aphrodite*, Koritsás 27 (☎0841/28 058; ②), and the backpackerish *Green House*, Modhátsou 15 (☎0841/22 025; ②). The helpful **tourist office** (April–Oct daily 8.30am–9.30pm; ☎0841/22 357), by the bridge dividing the lake and harbour, has accommodation lists. **Internet** access is at Café Peripou, 28-Oktovríou 25 (the first street leading uphill from the bridge).

Ag Nik's riviera set tends to hang out along the coast road north towards **ELOÚNDA**, a resort on a more acceptable scale. Buses cover the 8km regularly, and it's a spectacular ride with a series of impeccable views over a gulf dotted with islands and moored supertankers. From Eloúnda, kaïkia run to the fortress-rock of **SPINALÓNGA**. As a bastion of the Venetian defence, this tiny islet withstood the Turkish invaders for 45 years after the rest of Crete had fallen; in more recent decades it served as a leper colony. The other popular bus excursion goes 10km inland to **KRITSÁ**. Despite the rampant commercialization, the local crafts are fair value and there's the possibility of rooms. On the approach road some 2km before Kritsá stands the lovely Byzantine church of **Panayía Kyrá** (April–Oct daily 8.30am–2.30pm; €2.50), whose fourteenth- and fifteenth-century frescoes have been much retouched, but still make the visit worth the effort.

Sitía and Váï beach

The port and main town of the relatively unexploited eastern edge of Crete, **SITÍA** offers a plethora of waterside restaurants, a long sandy beach and a lazy lifestyle little affected even by the thousands of visitors in peak season. You pass the excellent **hostel** (☎0843/22 693; ②) as you come into Sitía from Áyios Nikólaos on the main road, and there are a few rooms between here and the town. More pleasant options can be found in the streets behind the northern stretch of the waterside, especially around the phone office where *Pension Venus*, Kondhilaki 60 (☎0843/24 307; ②), is a good bet. The **tourist office** on the seafront (daily 9am–9pm; ☎0843/28 300) has a complete accommodation list. For **food**, there are inexpensive options in the streets behind the waterfront, such as the ouzerí *Kali Kardia*, Foundalídhou 28, and *Mixos*, Kornárou 117, while *Itanos* **bar** at the start of the Beach Road does good *mezédhes*.

The superb **Váï beach** features on almost every Cretan travel agent's list of excursions and has become somewhat commercialized in recent years, with charges for parking and shower use. The beach itself is famous above all for its palm trees, creating an illusion of a Caribbean island. Now a fenced (and guarded) natural park, you will not be allowed to sleep on the main beach, but you should be able to get some peace at some of the smaller beaches north and south (watch your belongings – this seems to be the one place on Crete with crime on any scale). The trip to Váï is enjoyable, passing the **Monastery of Toploú**, which has a gorgeous flower-decked cloister and one of the masterpieces of Cretan art, the eighteenth-century icon *Lord Thou Art Great*.

Réthymno

Since the mid-1980s, **RÉTHYMNO** has seen a greater influx of tourists than perhaps anywhere else on the island, with the development of a whole series of large hotels extending almost 10km along the beach to the east. For once, though, the middle of town has been spared, so that at its heart Réthymno remains one of the most beautiful of Crete's major cities. A wide sandy beach and palm-lined promenade border a labyrinthine tangle of Venetian and Turkish houses lining streets where many of the old men still dress proudly in high boots, baggy trousers and black head-scarves. Medieval minarets lend an exotic air to the skyline, while dominating everything from the west is the superbly preserved outline of the fortress built by the Venetians after a series of pirate raids had devastated the town.

When you get off the bus, walk east, with the fortress to your left, to reach the beach and the centre; the seafront **tourist office** (April–Sept Mon–Fri 8am–7pm; ☎0831/56 350) can provide a town map. To explore, follow Arkadhíou, the street which curves around to the north immediately inland from the beach, and then continue towards the **fortress** (Tues–Sun 8am–7pm; €2.40). There are plenty of **rooms**, although you may struggle to find something if you turn up on spec in August; try *Olga's Rooms*, Soulíou 57, slightly west of the central Rimóndi Fountain (☎0831/54 896; ②). The **hostel**, Tombázi 45 (☎0831/22 848; ①), is a passable alternative, or there's a **campsite** – *Camping Elizabeth* (☎0831/28 694) – about 4km east along the beach, served by frequent buses from the main long-distance bus station. There's an unbroken line of **tavernas**, cafés and cocktail bars right around the waterside and into the area around the old port, but the sea view comes at a price. You'll find an assortment of better-value places around the focal seventeenth-century Venetian **Rimóndi Fountain**: tucked into an alley behind the fountain is *Kyria María*, a cosy taverna serving economical fare; after the meal, all diners get a couple of María's delicious *tyropitákia* (sweet cheese pies topped with honey) on the house. **Bars** and **nightlife** concentrate in the same general area, particularly towards the western end of the town beach.

Haniá

HANIÁ is the spiritual capital of Crete; for many it is also the island's most attractive city – especially if you can catch it in spring, when the Lefká Óri's snowcapped peaks seem to hover above the roofs. Although it is for the most part modern, the small outer harbour is surrounded by a wonderful jumble of half-derelict Venetian streets which survived the wartime bombardments. The **bus station** is on Odhós Kydhonías, within easy walking distance of the action: turn right, then left down the side of Platía 1866 and you'll emerge at a major road junction opposite the top of Halídhon, the main street of the old quarter. **Boats** dock about 10km away at the port of Soúdha: there are frequent city buses which will drop you by the market on the fringes of the old town.

The **port area** is the oldest and the most interesting part of town. The little hill which rises behind the landmark domes of the quayside **Mosque of the Janissaries** is called **Kastélli**, site of the earliest habitation and core of the Venetian and Turkish towns. Beneath the hill, on the inner harbour, the arches of sixteenth-century Venetian arsenals survive alongside remains of the outer walls. Following the esplanade around in the other direction leads to a hefty bastion which now houses Crete's **Maritime Museum** (daily 9am–4pm; €1.80; *www.forthnet.gr/mar-museum-crete*) – wander in for a look at the seaward fortifications. Walk around the back of these restored bulwarks to a street heading inland and you'll find the best-preserved stretch of the old city. Behind the harbour lie the less picturesque but more lively sections of the old city. A short way up Halídhon on the right is the **Archeological Museum** (Tues–Sun 8.30am–2.30pm; €1.45), housed in the Venetian-built church of San Francesco. Damaged as it is, this remains a beautiful building and a fine little display, even though there's nothing of outstanding interest. In the garden, a huge fountain and the base of a minaret survive from the period when the Ottomans converted the church into a mosque. Around the ordinary and relatively modern **cathedral** nearby are some of the more animated shopping areas, particularly leather-dominated **Odhós Skrídhlof**, with streets leading up to the back of the market beyond. In the direction of the Spiántza quarter are ancient alleys which have yet to feel much effect of the city's modern popularity, still with tumbledown Venetian stonework and overhanging wooden balconies.

Haniá's **beaches** all lie to the west: the packed **city beach** is a ten-minute walk beyond the Maritime Museum, but for good sand you're better off taking the local bus from the east side of Platía 1866 along the coast road to Kalamáki. In between you'll find emptier stretches if you're prepared to walk from Haniá.

Practicalities

The extremely helpful **tourist office** (Mon–Fri 8am–2.30pm; ☎0821/92 624) is in the new town at Kriári 40, just off Platía 1866. There seem to be thousands of **rooms** on offer but in season you may face a long search. *Pension Fidias*, Kalinikoú Sarpáki 8, behind the cathedral (☎0821/524 94; ②), is run along hostel lines, exceptionally friendly and comfortable, with dorms (①). Popular *Pension Lena*, Theotokopoúlou 60 (☎0821/86 860; *www.lena@travelling-crete.com*; ③), near the Maritime Museum, is a wonderfully restored house, and its owner is a mine of local information. Near Odhós Skrídlof is *To Dhiporto*, Betólo 41 (☎0821/53 430; ②), with very good value rooms, some en-suite. The **campsite**, *Camping Hania* (☎0821/31 138), lies on the coast 4km west, served by city bus from Platía 1866. Both the inner and outer harbours are circled by **cafés**, **tavernas** and **bars**, although most are overpriced. It's well worth seeking out the excellent restaurant *Tamam*, set in a former Turkish bathhouse at Zambelíou 49, behind the outer harbour; *Tasty Souvlaki*, Halídhon 80, does eat in or take away. Haniá's bustling and colourful **market**, inside a nineteenth-century steel-framed copy of the market at Marseilles, is not to be missed. There's a series of **bars** around the twin harbours, particularly along Odhós Sarpidhóna off the inner harbour. Along the inner harbour quayside *Prime Vision Ariadne* is a popular dance **club**, and the nearby *Four Seasons* bar has a popular terrace which allows drinkers to ogle the passing crowds. Haniá can also be a good place to catch local Cretan lyra **music**, especially at *Café Kriti*, Kallérgon 22, one block inland from the inner harbour. **Internet** access is at Café Vranas, adjoining Vranas Studios, opposite the cathedral's north flank.

The Samariá Gorge

It's easy to visit the beautiful **Gorge of Samariá** – Europe's longest – as a day-trip from Haniá. You should catch the early bus at 6.15am to avoid the full heat of the day while walking through the gorge, though be warned that you will not be alone: there are often as many as four coachloads setting off before dawn for the dramatic climb into the White Mountains. The **gorge** (May–Oct; €3.50; wardens' lodge ☎0821/67 179) begins at a stepped path descending steeply from the southern lip of the Omalós Plain through almost alpine scenery of pines, wild flowers and un-Cretan greenery. At an average pace with regular stops, the 18km walk down takes five to six hours; solid shoes are vital. There's plenty of water from springs and streams (except in a dry Sept & Oct), but nothing to eat. Small churches and viewpoints dot the route, and about halfway down you pass the abandoned village of Samariá, now home to a wardens' station, with picnic facilities and filthy toilets. Further down, the path levels out and the walls close in until at the narrowest point – the spectacular *Sidherespórtes* or **"Iron Gates"** – you can touch both rock faces at once where the gorge narrows to a mere three-metre width, and, looking up, see them rising sheer for over 300m.

When you finally get down to the sea, the village of **AYÍA ROÚMELI** is all but abandoned until you reach the beach, a mirage of iced drinks and a cluster of expensive tavernas with equally pricey rooms to let. If you aim to get back to Haniá, buy your **boat** ticket immediately, especially if you want an afternoon on the beach: the last boat tends to sell out first. Boats run west towards the pleasant resorts of Soúyia and Paleohóra, good beach stopovers to wait for a bus to Haniá; but most of your fellow gorge walkers will be taking boats east to the less desirable Hóra Sfakíon, where up to fifty daily buses congregate to take them back to Haniá and other places around the island.

travel details

BUSES

Athens to: Corfu (4 daily; 11hr); Delphi (6 daily; 3hr); Halkídha (every 30min; 1hr 30min); Igoumenítsa (4 daily; 8hr 30min); Ioánnina (8 daily; 7hr 30min); Kefallonía (3 daily; 7hr); Kými, for Skýros ferries (6 daily; 3hr 30min); Kórinthos (hourly; 1hr 30min); Lefkádha (4 daily; 5hr 30min); Mycenae (hourly; 2hr); Náfplio (hourly; 2hr 30min); Olympia (4 daily; 5hr 30min); Pátra (every 30min; 3hr); Pýlos (2 daily; 5hr 30min); Rafína (every 30min; 1hr 30min); Sounion (every 30min; 2hr); Spárti (10 daily; 4hr 30min); Thessaloníki (10 daily; 7hr 30min); Tríkala (9 daily; 5hr 30min); Trípoli (12 daily; 2hr 15min); Vólos (10 daily; 5hr 20min); Zákynthos (5 daily; 6hr).

Ioánnina to: Athens (9 daily; 7hr 30min); Igoumenítsa (9 daily; 2hr); Métsovo (2–3 daily, 1hr 30min); Dodona (3 weekly; 40min).

Igoumenítsa to: Párga (4 Mon–Fri, 3 on Sat, 1 on Sun; 1hr 30min); Préveza (2 daily; 3hr).

Kalamáta to: Areópoli (4 daily; 1hr 30min); Kóroni (8 daily; 1hr 30min); Methóni via Pýlos (5 daily; 1hr 30min); Pátra (2 daily; 4hr); Pýlos (8 daily; 1hr); Trípoli (8 daily; 1hr 45min).

Kórinthos to: Árgos (hourly; 1hr); Kalamáta (10 daily; 3hr–4hr); Mycenae-Fíkhti (hourly; 30min); Náfplio (hourly; 1hr 30min); Spárti (8 daily; 3hr–4hr); Tíryns (hourly; 15min); Trípoli (9 daily; 1hr 30min).

Lamía to: Lárissa (4 daily; 3hr 30min); Tríkala, via Kardhítsa (4 daily; 3hr); Vólos (2 daily; 3hr).

Lárissa to: Kalambáka (hourly; 30min); Litóhoro junction (hourly; 1hr 45min); Tríkala (every 30min; 1hr).

Náfplio to: Epidaurus (5 daily; 45min); Mycenae (3 daily; 30min); Trípoli (4 daily; 1hr 20min).

Pýrgos to: Kalamáta (2 daily; 2hr); Olympia (hourly; 45min); Pátra (10–11 daily; 2hr).

Thessaloníki to: Alexandhroúpoli (5 daily; 6hr); Ierissós (5–7 daily; 3hr 30min); Ioánnina (5 daily except Tues; 7hr); Kalambáka (7 daily; 4hr 30min); Litóhoro (7 daily; 1hr 30min); Ouranoúpoli (5–7 daily; 3hr 45min); Pella (hourly; 1hr); Vólos (4 daily; 4hr).

Tríkala to: Ioánnina (2 daily; 4hr); Kalambáka (hourly; 30min); Métsovo (2 daily; 2hr).

Trípoli to: Kalamáta (6 daily; 2hr); Olympia (2 daily; 5hr); Pýrgos (3 daily; 3hr); Spárti (10 daily; 1hr–1hr 30min).

Vólos to: Áyios Ioánnis (2 daily; 2hr 30min); Lárissa (hourly; 1hr 15min); Makrinítsa (10 daily; 50min); Miliés (6 daily; 1hr); Thessaloníki (4 daily; 3hr 20min); Tríkala (4 daily; 2hr 30min); Tsangarádha (2 daily; 2hr); Vyzítsa (6 daily; 1hr 10min); Zagorá (4 daily; 2hr).

TRAINS

Athens to: Halkídha (17 daily; 1hr 30min); Kalamáta (3 daily; 7hr); Kalambáka via Paleofársala (4 daily; 5–6hr 30min); Kórinthos (12 daily; 1hr 30min–2hr); Mykínes (5 daily; 2hr 45min); Náfplio (2 daily; 3hr–3hr 30min); Pátra (7 daily; 3hr 30min); Thessaloníki (9 daily, including 1 sleeper; 6–8hr); Vólos (6 daily; 4hr–6hr 30min).

Thessaloníki to: Alexandhroúpoli (2 daily; 7hr); Litóhoro (6 daily; 1hr 40min); Vólos (2 daily; 30min).

Vólos to: Athens (3 daily; 5hr); Kalambáka (2 daily; 2hr 45min); Lárissa (12 daily; 1hr).

FERRIES AND HYDROFOILS

Astakós to: Itháki (1 daily; 2hr 45min); Kefalloniá (peak season 1 daily; 3hr 30min).

Áyios Konstandínos to: Skópelos (2–5 daily; 1hr 45min–3hr 30min).

Híos to: Lésvos (6–10 weekly; 4hr); Sámos (2–5 weekly; 2hr–5hr).

Íos to: Náxos (3 daily; 3hr); Páros (2 daily; 5hr); Thíra (1–2 daily; 2hr).

Iráklio to: Pireás (3 daily; 12hr) also fast ferry (1 daily; 6hr); Páros & Cyclades (1 daily; 7hr); Rhodes (2–3 weekly; 11hr).

Kavála to: Lésvos/Híos (2–3 weekly; 10–12hr); Thássos (12–30 daily; 1hr 15min).

Kefalloniá to: Zákynthos/Porros (summer 2 daily; 1hr 30min).

Kós to: Pátmos (2–4 daily; 2hr 30min–5hr); Rhodes (2–4 daily; 2–4hr).

Kyllíni to: Kefalloniá (2 daily; 1hr 45min); Zákynthos (7 daily; 3 in winter; 1hr 30min).

Kými to: Skýros (1–2 daily; 2hr 30min).

Lésvos to: Híos (5–9 weekly; 4hr); Kavála (1–2 weekly; 10–12hr); Thessaloníki (2 weekly; 14hr).

Náxos to: Íos (3 daily; 3hr); Iráklio (3 weekly; 6hr); Páros (3 daily; 1hr); Thíra (3 daily; 4hr).

Pátra to: Corfu (3–5 daily; 8–10hr); Itháki (2 daily; 4hr 30min); Kefaloniá (2 daily; 2hr 30min).

Pireás to: Crete (2–4 daily; 12hr); Híos (6–7 weekly; 10hr); Íos (3–6 daily; 10hr); Kós (13 weekly; 12hr); Lésvos (6–7 weekly; 14hr); Mýkonos (2 daily; 5hr); Náxos (4 daily; 8hr); Páros (4 daily; 7hr); Rhodes (19 weekly; 18–23hr); Sámos (daily; 11–14hr); Sífnos (12 weekly; 6hr); Thíra (2–5 daily; 10–12hr).

Rafína to: Mýkonos, Sýros, Páros, Náxos, Íos, Santorini (all 1–2 daily; 3–7hr).

Rhodes to: Crete (Sitía/Áyios Nikólaos) (2–3 weekly; 13hr); Kárpathos (2–3 weekly; 5–6hr); Kós (2 daily; 4hr); Pátmos (2 daily; 8hr); Sými (1–3 daily; 50min–1hr 40min).

Sámos to: Kós (4–9 weekly; 3hr 45min); Pátmos (daily; 1hr 30min–3hr); Rhodes (1 weekly; 9hr).

Thessaloníki to: Híos (1–2 weekly; 15hr); Iráklio (2–5 weekly; 21hr); Lésvos (1–2 weekly; 15hr); Skýros (2–4 weekly; 3–7hr); Skópelos (summer daily; 3hr).

Thíra to: Íos (3 daily; 2hr); Iráklio (5 weekly; 5hr); Mýkonos (1 daily; 7hr); Náxos (3 daily; 4hr); Páros (3 daily; 5hr).

Vólos to: Skiáthos (2–4 daily; 1hr 30min–3hr); Skópelos (2–4 daily; 2hr 30min–5hr).

Zákynthos to: Kyllíni (7 daily, 3 in winter; 1hr 30min).

CHAPTER 13

HUNGARY

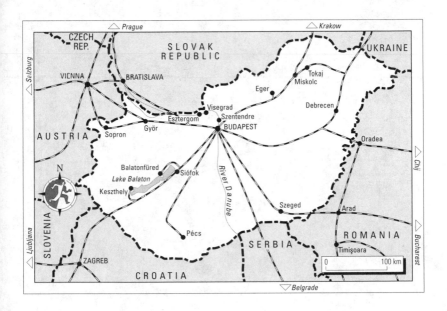

Introduction

Visitors who refer to **Hungary** as a Balkan country risk getting a lecture on how this small, landlocked nation of 10 million people differs from "all those Slavs": locals are strongly conscious of themselves as **Magyar** – a race that transplanted itself from Central Asia into the heart of Europe over a thousand years ago. Hungary was in the vanguard of the dissolution of communist hegemony in Eastern Europe. Its decision to open its borders in 1989 precipitated the fall of the repressive regimes in East Germany, Romania and Czechoslovakia.

The magnificent capital, **Budapest** (split into historic Buda and vibrant Pest), with its coffee houses, Turkish baths and fad for Habsburg bric-a-brac, has a strong whiff of Mitteleuropa – that ambient culture that welcomed Beethoven in Budapest and Hungarian-born Liszt in Vienna, a culture currently being revived in a new form by writers, film directors, artists and other media figures. But there is also an eager modern feel to the place, with international fashions snapped up and adapted to local tastes. North of Budapest, the **Danube Bend** region hugging the Slovakian border has plenty to offer in terms of scenery and historic architecture. In the west **Lake Balaton**, with its string of brash resorts, styles itself as the "Nation's Playground" and enjoys a fortuitous proximity to the Badacsony wine-producing region, while other highlights of **Transdanubia** include the historic towns of **Sopron**, within spitting distance of Vienna, and Turkish-flavoured **Pécs**. The forested **Northern Uplands** in the far northeast towards Ukraine are centred on the famous wine centres of **Tokaj** and **Eger**.

Information and maps

Tourinform, the Hungarian National Tourist Office's chain of offices that you'll find in Budapest and in larger towns across the country, has a large number of photo-packed brochures, maps and leaflets, with branches generally open Mon–Fri 9am–5pm (May–Sept open until 7 or 8pm, and at weekends). Tourinform staff have a reputation for being helpful and speaking English, but most branches don't book accommodation – though they do have information on where rooms and beds are available, including the small booklet *Hungarian Hotel Guide*, and *Camping* (both nationwide, and both complemented by increasingly well-produced leaflets on accommodation and events in each region). There are also **local tourist offices** in larger towns (Savariatourist, Balatontourist, etc, according to the region), where you can book rooms; opening hours are generally Mon–Fri 9am–6pm and Sat 8am–1pm, though in the winter months they may close on weekdays at 4pm and stay closed all weekend. It's cheapest to buy **maps** when you arrive: Cartographia does a good fold-out sheet (1:450,000) of the whole country for 400Ft.

Money and banks

The unit of currency is the **forint** (Ft), and they come in notes of 200, 500, 1000, 2000, 5000, 10,000 and 20,000Ft, and in coins of 1, 2, 5, 10, 20, 50 and 100Ft (the 50Ft coin is easily confused with the 10Ft coin). Changing money is best done at regional tourist offices or at a **bank**; these usually give the best rates. Standard banking hours are Mon–Thurs 8am–4pm, Fri 8am–3pm. Changing at large hotels, or at the growing number of exchange offices (including American Express), leaves you substantially worse off. Avoid the black market.

Budapest has a large number of **ATMs** (cash machines), and more are appearing in larger towns across the country, though you should not rely on finding one. Most brands of travellers' cheques are accepted. You can use a credit card to rent a car, buy an airline ticket or pay in many hotels, restaurants and tourist shops, but outside the main tourist centres their usefulness is more restricted.

Communications

Larger **post offices** *(posta)* are usually open Mon–Fri 8am–6pm, Sat 8am–1pm. Smaller branches close at 3pm and don't always open on Saturdays. Poste restante mail should be addressed "Poste restante, Posta", followed by the name of the town.

You can make local calls from public coin **phones**, where 20Ft is the minimum charge (40Ft if you are

---

calling a mobile phone number), or, better, from **cardphones** – they're increasingly common, and you have less chance of losing your money; cards come in 50 or 120 units, buyable from post offices and newsstands. To call elsewhere in Hungary, dial ☎06, wait for the buzzing tone, then dial the area code and number. Mobile phone numbers also begin ☎06, and have another nine digits. You can make **international calls** from most public phones: dial ☎00, wait for the buzzing tone, then carry on dialling the country code as usual. **Internet access** is widespread (usually 500–700Ft/hr): Budapest has several cybercafés, as do most larger towns.

Getting around

Although it doesn't break any speed records, **public transport** reaches most parts of Hungary, and fares are very low. The only problem is getting information, for staff rarely speak anything but Hungarian, although German is spoken around Lake Balaton.

■ Trains

The centralization of the MÁV rail network means that many cross-country journeys are easier if you travel via Budapest. The new network of Intercity **trains** is the fastest way of getting from Budapest to Eger, Esztergom, Keszthely, Miskolc, Pécs, Sopron, Tokaj and other destinations. Seat reservations, made at any MÁV office, are compulsory on Intercity trains (for an extra 360Ft) and on all international trains, but not for *személyvonat*, which stop at every hamlet en route. Most international, Intercity and some express trains have buffets, but it is best to take food and drink with you if you're embarking on a long trip. Except for some slower trains there is usually a first-class *(első osztály)* section; international services through Budapest have sleeping cars and couchettes *(hálókocsi* and *kusett)*. You can buy **tickets** *(jegy)* for domestic services at the station *(pályaudvar* or *vasútállomás)* on the day of departure,

but it's best to buy tickets for **international trains** *(nemzetközi gyorsvonat)* at least 36hr in advance. You're permitted to break your journey once. When buying your ticket, specify whether you want a one-way ticket *(egy útra)*, or a return *(retur* or *oda-vissza)*. **InterRail** and **Eurail** passes are both valid. If you don't have these, you'd need to travel intensively to make full use of a seven-day national **Runaround** pass (10,100Ft in 2nd class), which isn't valid on all trains from Budapest to Sopron, and which excludes paying for seat reservations on Intercity trains.

■ Buses

Regional **Volán** companies run the bulk of Hungary's **buses**, which are often the quickest way to travel between towns. Schedules are clearly displayed in bus terminals; arrive early to confirm the departure bay and ensure getting a seat. For long-distance services originating from Budapest or major towns, you can buy tickets with a seat booking up to 30min before departure; after that, you get them from the driver (and risk standing throughout the journey). In rural areas, tickets are only available on board and there may be only one bus a day.

■ Driving and hitching

To **drive** in Hungary you'll require an international driving licence, Green Card insurance and third-party insurance. Speed limits are 50kph in town, 80–100kph on main roads and 120kph on motorways. You can get 24hr breakdown assistance from the Magyar Autóklub (national breakdown service ☎188) provided you are insured. **Car rental** costs from 85,000Ft per week with unlimited mileage, and is available through Budget, Avis, Hertz and a number of others as well as from hotel reception desks, both terminals at Budapest airport and certain tourist offices.

Hitch-hiking is very common amongst young Magyars, but it's forbidden on motorways.

ACCOMMODATION PRICE CODES

Throughout this guide, accommodation is coded on a scale of ① to ⑨, the code indicating the lowest price per person per night you could expect to pay in each establishment in high season. With hostels this is the nightly rate per person; with hotels, the price is arrived at by dividing the cost of the cheapest double room by two. The prices indicated by the codes are as follows:

① under £5/$8	④ £15–20/$24–32	⑦ £30–35/$48–56
② £5–10/$8–16	⑤ £20–25/$32–40	⑧ £35–40/$56–64
③ £10–15/$16–24	⑥ £25–30/$40–48	⑨ £40/$64 and over

Accommodation

There's plenty of **accommodation** available, but costs have risen dramatically in recent years. More upmarket places tend to quote prices in euros (they'll usually accept US dollars or British pounds too); private rooms and hostels charge in forints. The cheapest places tend to fill up during high season (June–Sept), so it's wise to make bookings if you're heading somewhere that has limited accommodation.

■ Hostels and dormitories

Hostels go under various names: in provincial towns they're called *túristaszálló*, but in the highland areas they go by the name of *túristaház*. Local tourist offices can provide details and make bookings. They can also guide you to **college dormitories**, which are usually even cheaper: rooms are rented out in July and August, but can often also be taken at weekends year-round.

■ Private rooms

Private rooms *(fizetővendégszoba)* – B&B-style in a private home – are an inexpensive way of staying near town centres, and are often quite appealing. Such accommodation can be arranged by local tourist offices for a small fee; otherwise deal direct with the owner (who'll advertise with *szoba kiadó* or *Zimmer Frei*). Doubles range from 2000Ft in provincial towns to around 4000Ft in Budapest or around the Balaton, singles usually pay the full double rate, though there may be a small reduction. Rooms in a town's *belváros* (inner sector) are likely to be much better than those in outlying zones.

In some towns and resorts it's possible to rent whole apartments, while regional tourist offices can arrange home accommodation in villages through the village tourism *(falusi turizmus)* network, the central office of which is in Budapest at VII, Király utca 93 (☎1/352-1433, *budapest3@tourinform.hu*).

■ Hotels

Of **hotels** *(szálló* or *szálloda)*, three-star places have become most common; luxury four- and five-star establishments are still mainly confined to Budapest and major resorts, while humble one- and two-star joints are getting rarer. Outside Budapest and Lake Balaton (where prices are thirty percent higher), a three-star hotel will charge from around €45–60 for a double room with bath, TV, etc; solo travellers often have to pay this too, since singles are rare. The same goes for four-star or two-star hotel rooms, but luxury hotels in Budapest charge cheaper rates during winter. A similar rating system is used for **inns** *(fogadó)* and **pensions** *(panzió)*, which charge a little less than hotels, though prices in the middle range often turn out very similar.

■ Bungalows and campsites

Throughout Hungary, campsites and bungalows come together in complexes. **Bungalows** *(faház)* proliferate around resorts and on the larger campsites; prices depend on their amenities and size. The first-class bungalows – with well-equipped kitchens, hot water and a sitting room or terrace – are excellent, and will cost a few thousand forints, while the most primitive at least have clean bedding and don't leak. **Campsites** (usually signposted *Kemping*) likewise range across the spectrum from "de luxe" to third class. The more elaborate places include a restaurant and shops but tend to be overcrowded; second- or third-class sites often have a nicer ambience. In high season, expect to pay anything up to 2500Ft, more around Lake Balaton.

Food and drink

For foreigners the archetypal Hungarian **food** is goulash – historically a soup made of potatoes and whatever meat was available, which was later flavoured with paprika. Today, meat is still a central part of the Hungarian diet.

■ Food

As a nation of early risers, Hungarians like a calorific **breakfast** *(reggeli)* that includes cheese, eggs or salami, plus bread and jam. Though **coffee houses** *(kávéház)* are no longer at the centre of Budapest's cultural and political life, you'll still find plenty of them serving coffee with milk *(tejeskávé)* or whipped cream *(tejszínhabbal)*. Ask for a cappuccino in smaller towns and you may get funny looks: most Hungarians take their coffee short and strong *(eszpresszó)*.

A whole range of places sell **snacks**, including bakeries and delicatessens *(csemege)*, which display a tempting spread of salads, open sandwiches, pickles and cold meats. Numerous **patisseries** *(cukrászda)* pander to the Magyar fondness for sweet things. Pancakes *(palacsinta)* with fillings are very popular, as are strudels *(rétes)* and a staggering array of cakes and other sticky items. On the **streets** you can buy, in summer, corn-on-the-cob *(kukorica)* and in winter, roasted chestnuts *(gesztenye)*; while stalls selling fried fish *(sült hal)* are common in towns near rivers or lakes. Sandwich *(szendvics)* and hamburger stands are mushrooming in the larger towns, and in **markets** you'll also find various inexpensive diners.

Hungarians have a variety of words implying fine distinctions among **restaurants**. In theory an *étterem* is a proper restaurant, while a *vendéglő* approximates to the Western notion of a bistro; however, these distinctions are very thin now. The old word for a roadside inn, *csárda*, is often used today of folksy, touristy restaurants. Traditionally, the main meal of the day is lunch, when some eating places offer **set menus** *(napi menü)*, a basic meal at moderate prices. Keep an eye on prices: you can find yourself paying exorbitant amounts for not very much, and gone are the days when even the top restaurants were cheap; but there are still plenty of places where you can eat well and sink a few beers for 1000Ft. Always check your bill carefully as foreigners are a common target for being ripped off. (Recent scandals showed that foreigners had been lured into bars and restaurants in central Budapest and charged exorbitant rates, and then threatened when they refused to pay. Checking prices on the menu before you order is a good idea.)

Starters *(előételek)* range from soup *(leves)* to the popular *Hortobágyi palacsinta* (pancakes stuffed with mince and doused in a creamy paprika sauce) and the more extravagant *libamáj* (goose liver), though nobody will mind if you just have a **main course** *(főételek)*. Hungarians like most things fried in breadcrumbs, such as *rántott csirkecomb* (chicken drumstick), but they also have a taste for *marhapörkölt* (beef stew). The outlook for **vegetarians** is poor: aside from cooked vegetables (notably *rántott gomba* or *rántott sajt* – mushrooms or cheese in breadcrumbs), often the only meatless dishes are various permutations of eggs.

■ Drink

Hungary's mild climate and diversity of soils is perfect for **wine** *(bor)*, which is perennially cheap, whether you buy it by the bottle *(üveg)* or the glass *(pohár)*. Wine bars *(borozó)* are ubiquitous and generally far less pretentious than in the West; while true devotees of the grape make pilgrimages to the extensive **wine cellars** *(borpince)* around towns like Pécs, Tokaj and Eger. **Spirits** are inexpensive, if you stick to native brands; the best-known types of **brandy**

(pálinka) are distilled from apricots *(barack)* and plums *(szilva)*, the latter often available in private homes in a mouth-scorching home-distilled version. **Beer** *(sör)* of the **lager** type *(világos)* predominates, although you can also find **brown ale** *(barna)*: these come in draught form *(csapolt sör)* or in bottles *(üveges sör)*. Local brands to look out for are Pécsi Szalon sör and Soproni Ászok. Western brands are imported or brewed under licence.

Opening hours and holidays

Opening times for most public buildings are Mon–Fri 8.30am–4pm; smaller places usually close for an hour at lunchtime. Museums are generally open Tues–Sun 10am–6pm or 9am–5pm, and some have free admission over the weekends. **Public holidays** are: Jan 1; March 15; Easter Monday; May 1; Whit Monday; Aug 20; Oct 23; Dec 25 & 26.

Emergencies

The **police** *(rendőrség)* are badly paid and undertrained, which doesn't make for good policing. However, foreign tourists are treated with respect – unless they're suspected of black-marketeering, drug smuggling or driving under the influence of alcohol. Most police officers have at least a smattering of German, but rarely any other foreign language. Should you be arrested or need legal advice, ask to contact your embassy or consulate.

All towns and some villages have a **pharmacy** *(gyógyszertár* or *patika)*, with staff – often German-speaking – authorized to issue a wide range of drugs. (However, if you need specific medication, you should bring a supply with you.) Opening hours are normally Mon–Fri 9am–6pm, Sat 9am–noon or 1pm; signs in the window give the location or telephone number of all-night pharmacies *(ügyeletes gyógyszertár)*.

Tourist offices can direct you to local medical centres or doctors' surgeries *(orvosi rendelő)*, while your embassy in Budapest will have the addresses of **doctors** and **dentists**; these will probably be in private *(magán)* practice, so you should check on their charges.

Emergency Numbers

Police ☎107; Ambulance ☎104; Fire ☎105.

BUDAPEST

The importance of **BUDAPEST** to Hungary is difficult to overestimate. Around two million people – one-fifth of the population – live in the city, and everything converges here: wealth, political power, cultural life and transport. Surveying the city from Castle Hill, it's obvious why Budapest was dubbed the "Pearl of the Danube". Its grand buildings and sweeping bridges look magnificent, especially when floodlit or illuminated by the barrage of fireworks launched from **Gellért Hill** on St Stephen's Day. The inner city and the nineteenth-century boulevards have been swamped by Western fashions and advertising, but they retain a distinctively Hungarian character, which for visitors is highlighted by the sounds and appearance of the distinctive Magyar language.

Castle Hill (Várhegy) is the most prominent feature of the **Buda** district, a plateau one mile long laden with bastions, old mansions and a huge palace, commanding the **Watertown**. Its grandiosity and strategic utility have long gone hand-in-hand: Hungarian kings built their palaces here because it was easy to defend, a fact appreciated by the Turks, Habsburgs, and most recently the Nazis, so that the castle has had to be almost wholly reconstructed from the rubble of 1945.

Buda and its twin, **Pest**, have a surfeit of other fine sights, including museums and galleries, restaurants, bars and a wide variety of entertainments, accessible by efficient, inexpensive public transport. A host of new nightclubs and rave haunts mean that the city is making up for its dreary postwar past, though it is still true to say that many people get up early and then slope off at around 10pm, interrupting work with breaks in patisseries and *eszpresszó* bars. Perhaps the best way to ease yourself into Budapest life is to wallow away an afternoon in one of the city's **thermal baths** (*gyógyfürdő*), such as the Rudas, with its original sixteenth-century Ottoman dome, or the Art Nouveau Gellért. For 2000 years people have appreciated the relaxing and curative effects of the mineral water from the Buda Hills, currently gushing at a rate of about 70 million litres a day, at temperatures of up to 80°C. A basic ticket covers three hours in the pools, sauna and steamrooms (*gözfürdő*), while supplementary tickets are available for such delights as the mud baths (*iszapfürdő*) and massages (*masszázs*).

Arrival and information

Most points of arrival are fifteen to thirty minutes from the centre. There are three main **train stations**, all of which are directly connected by **metro** with the central **Deák tér** metro station in the Belváros, the city centre district of Pest: Keleti station handles most international trains, including those from Vienna (Südbahnhof), Belgrade, Bucharest, Zagreb and Bratislava, as well as domestic arrivals from Sopron and Eger; Nyugati station handles trains from Prague and Bratislava, some from Bucharest, and domestic ones from the Danube Bend; and Déli station has one train a day from Vienna (Westbahnhof), the odd train from Zagreb, and domestic services from Pécs and Lake Balaton. From Ferihegy **airport**, there's a half-hourly shuttle bus (800Ft from Terminals 2A and 2B) which stops in front of the *Kempinski Hotel* on Erzsébet tér, by Deák tér metro station, as well as an Airport Minibus, which will take you to wherever you're staying (1800Ft; book it in the terminal building). The airport taxi-drivers are notorious sharks. The central **bus station** is also at Erzsébet tér, serving international destinations and routes to Transdanubia. Out in Pest, Népstadion bus station (red metro) serves areas east of the Danube; and Árpád híd bus station (blue metro) serves the Danube Bend. **Hydrofoils** from Vienna dock alongside the Belváros embankment.

The best source of practical information is the friendly polyglot staff of **Tourinform** (daily 8am–8pm; ☎1/317-9800, *www.tourinform.hu*), just around the corner from Deák tér metro at Sütő utca 2, behind the big yellow Lutheran church; branches of Tourinform are on Liszt Ferenc tér, at Nyugati train station, and in the Castle District on Szentháromság tér. Other useful offices are the **Vista Tourist Center**, Paulay Ede utca 7 (Mon–Fri 8am–8pm, Sat &

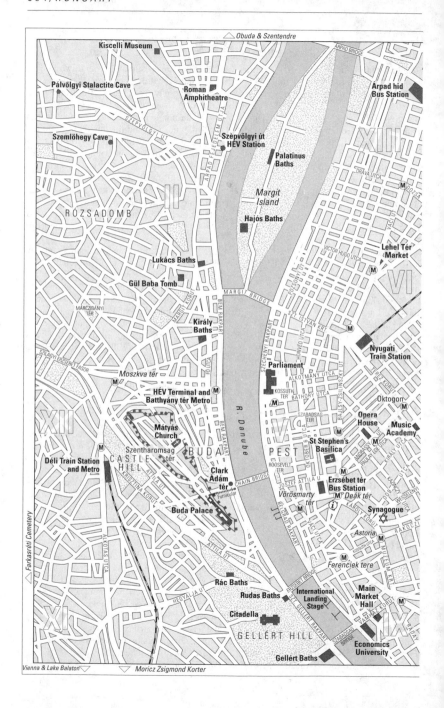

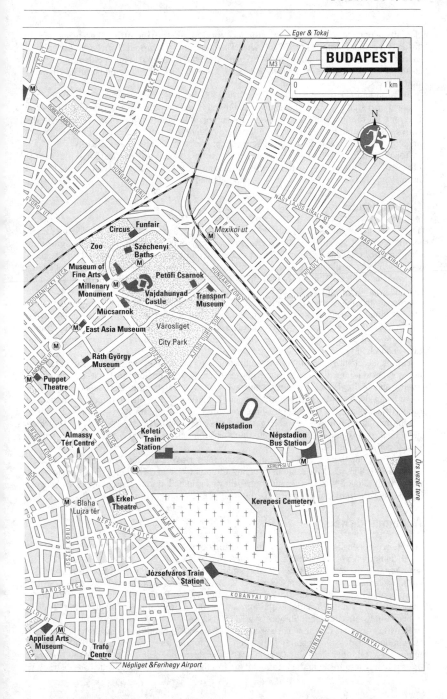

Sun 10am–6pm; ☎1/267-8603, *www.vista.hu*); the **IBUSZ tourist office**, Ferenciek tere 10 (Mon–Fri 8.15am–5pm; ☎1/485-2700, *www.ibusz.hu*); and **Budapest Tourist**, in the subway in front of Nyugati train station (Mon–Fri 9am–4pm; ☎1/332-6565). The weekly *Budapest Sun* has what's-on listings, as does *Where Budapest*, a free monthly events guide available in many hotel foyers.

A **Budapest Card** for two/three days (3400/4000Ft), buyable at tourist offices, hotels and major metro station ticket offices, gives unlimited travel on public transport, free admission to a long list of museums, reductions on the airport minibus (buying single tickets with the card gets you a bigger reduction than buying a return), car rental, certain sightseeing tours and cultural events, and discounts in some shops, restaurants and thermal baths.

You'd be well advised to pick up a proper **city map** as soon as possible; tourist offices supply small freebies, but far better is the wirebound 1:25,000 Budapest Atlas, available from newsstands in Deák tér metro and bookshops (1300Ft).

City transport

The **metro** is the easiest way of getting around (daily 4.30am–11.15pm). Its three lines intersect at Deák tér, and there's little risk of going astray once you've learned to recognize the signs: *bejárat* (entrance), *kijárat* (exit), *vonal* (line) and *felé* (towards). A basic 110Ft ticket is valid for a journey along one line, and is also valid for a single journey on buses, trolleybuses, trams and the **HÉV suburban train** as far as the city limits. On the metro you can also get 75Ft tickets for journeys of up to three stops, and combination tickets for transferring to another metro line. Rather than queueing at a metro station, it's quicker to buy tickets from street stands, tobacconists or newsagents. Note that tickets have to be punched in the machines at the entrances of metro stations, or on board buses, trolleybuses and trams: inspectors are increasingly common, often waiting at the bottom of the escalators to check tickets and hand out fines.

Buses (*busz*) with red numbers make limited stops, while those with the red suffix "E" run nonstop between termini. Buses run every ten minutes or so during the day, as do **trams** (*villamos*) and **trolleybuses** (*trolibusz*), and every thirty to sixty minutes between 11pm and dawn along those routes with a night service (denoted with the black suffix "É"). When the metro or trams are not running on a line, you'll find supplementary buses (*potlóbusz*) operating in their place. It might be worth getting a **pass** for one/three days (850/1750Ft) or buying a book of ten tickets (1100Ft) – but don't tear the tickets out, since they are only valid if kept together in the book.

Taxis are inexpensive, but are also a common rip-off. Go for Fötaxi (☎1/222-2222), Teletaxi (☎1/355-5555), or English-speaking Citytaxi (☎1/211-1111), charging a basic fee of up to 200Ft plus up to 200Ft per kilometre; they can be hailed in the street, but are cheapest if you order them by phone, giving the number you're calling from.

Accommodation

Hotels are generally expensive, and many of the better places expect payment in euros. For hotel bookings, you should contact HungarHotels, Petöfi Sándor utca 16 (☎1/318-3393, *www.danubiusgroup.com*); IBUSZ, V, Vörösmarty tér 6, facing the British Embassy (☎1/317-0532, *www.ibusz.hu*); American Express, V, Deák Ferenc utca 10 (☎1/235-4330), which charges a $20 service fee; or the Vista Visitor Center, VI, Paulay Ede utca 7 (☎1/267-8603, *www.vista.hu*). Another budget option is to book a **hostel** bed through the Tourist Information Centre in Keleti Station (☎1/343-0748).

Private rooms in downtown areas cost only 4000–6000Ft a night and are often the cheapest option. Besides the hotel-booking agencies, you can also try the small To-Ma Travel Agency at V, Október 6, utca 22 (☎1/353-0819, *www.tomatour.tsx.org*). A copy of the *Budapest Atlas* is handy for checking the location of prospective sites: preferable locales are districts V,

VI and VII in Pest, and the parts of Buda nearest Castle Hill. **Apartments**, rented out for 8000Ft a night, are perfect if you're in a group. They're not as common as rooms, but you should be able to find a tourist office with one on its books.

Each of Budapest's 23 districts (*kerületek*) is designated on maps, street signs and addresses by a Roman numeral; "V" is Belváros, "I" the Castle district.

Hostels

Some of the city's **hostels** tout for custom at the train stations, and will also transport you for free to the hostel.

Back Pack, XI, Takács Menyhért utca 33 (☎1/385-8946, *backpackguest@hotmail.com*). Tram #49 or bus #7 to Tétényi út stop, out in Buda. Charming, clean, with a shaded garden, and only 20min from the centre. Lots of city information, plus cave trips. Dorms ①, rooms ②.

Citadella, I, Citadella sétány (☎1/466-5794, *www.hotels.hu/hotelcitadella*). Breathtaking views of the city; get there early to get a bunk, but note that the weekend disco in the neighbouring nightclub sets the whole place shaking. Dorms ①, rooms ④.

Diáksport Szálló, XIII, Dózsa György út 152 (☎1/340-8585, *www.travellers-hostels.com*). Singles, doubles and dorms in a clean, lively but run-down hostel near the centre, with Internet access. ②.

Landler, XI, Bartók Béla út 17 (☎1/463-3621, *www.hotels.hu/hostellandler*). Tram #47 or #49 from Deák tér. An older hostel with high ceilings near the Gellért Baths, housed in the Baross Gábor Kollégium. July & Aug only. ②.

Museum Guest House, VIII, Mikszáth Kálmán tér 4, first floor (☎1/318-9508, *lotus@freemail.c3.hu*). In the streets behind the National Museum, handy for the bars and cafés of the centre. Three clean, spacious dorms, each sleeping seven or eight on mattresses on the floor. Free Internet access in the evening. ①.

Strawberry Youth Hostel, IX, Ráday utca 43–45 (☎1/218-4766, booking on ☎06-209/528-724, *www.strawberryhostel.com*). The blue metro line to Kálvin tér. The older of two *Strawberry Hostels* near Kálvin tér, with basic furniture but tall spacious rooms of two to six beds or dormitories. Internet access and discounts for HI members. July & Aug only. ②.

Hotels and pensions

ELTE Peregrinus Vendégház, V, Szerb utca 3 (☎1/266-4911). Located in a quiet backstreet in central Pest, this is a friendly, elegant place attached to the university; 25 rooms. ⑤.

Jager-Trio Panzió, XI, Ördögorom út 20 (☎1/246-4558, *jagertrio@ax.hu*). Small pension on the edge of the city in the Buda hills, close to the end of the bus #8 route. ③.

Medosz, VI, Jókai tér 6 (☎1/374-3000). Comfortable lodging in an ugly but well located building near the Oktogon. ④.

San Marcó Panzió, III, San Marcó utca 6 (☎1/388-9997). Small, friendly pension in northern Buda. ③.

Victoria, I, Bem rakpart 11 (☎1/457-8080, *www.victoria.hu*). Pleasant small hotel on the embankment directly below the Mátyás Church, with excellent views of the Chain Bridge and the river. Rooms have minibar, TV and air-conditioning. Sauna and garage facilities. ⑤.

Campsites

Csillebérci Camping, XII, Konkoly Thege M. út 21 (☎1/395-6537, *www.datanet.hu/csill*). A short walk from the last stop on bus #21 from Moszkva tér. Large, well-equipped site, open year-round, also with a range of bungalows.

Zugligeti Niche Camping, XII, Zugligeti út 101 (☎1/200-8346, *camping.niche@matavnet.hu*). Last stop on bus #158 from Moszkva tér. In a leafy cutting at the foot of a chair-lift in the hills that was once the end of a tram-line – the reception/restaurant at the far end of the site used to be the terminus.

The City

The **River Danube** (Duna) determines basic orientation, with **Pest** sprawled across the eastern plain and **Buda** reclining on the hilly west bank. Castle Hill is the historic focal point of Buda, home of the Royal Palace and for many years the government. Across the water, Pest has always been the commercial focus, with its hub around the Belváros, the old city centre. Construction of the first permanent bridge between the two in 1849 led to rapid expansion, and then unification in 1873.

Buda

Seen from the embankments, **Buda** looks irresistibly romantic with its palatial buildings, archaic spires and outsize statues rising from rugged hills. To experience its centre – Castle Hill – at its quasi-medieval best, come in the early morning before the crowds arrive. Then you can beat them to the museums, wander off for lunch or a Turkish bath, and return to catch streetlife in full swing during the afternoon.

CASTLE HILL

From the city centre, the best approach to **Castle Hill** starts with a breezy walk across the **Chain Bridge**, opened in 1849 and the first permanent bridge between Buda and Pest. The busy square on its western side, Clark Ádám tér, takes its name from Adam Clark, the engineer who completed the bridge. From here, you can ride up Castle Hill by the nineteenth-century funicular or **Sikló** (daily 7.30am–10pm; 400Ft up, 300Ft down). An alternative route is with the red metro line to Moszkva tér and the mini *Várbusz* from there.

By midday, **Trinity Square** (Szentháromság tér), the heart of the Castle district, is crammed with tourists, buskers, handicraft vendors and other entrepreneurs, a multilingual spectacle played out against the backdrop of the wildly asymmetrical **Mátyás Church** (Mátyás templom). The church is a riotous nineteenth-century re-creation of the medieval spirit, grafted onto those portions of the thirteenth-century structure that survived first 150 years of Ottoman rule – when the church was turned into a mosque – and then the siege of 1686, which brought to an end the Ottoman occupation. An equestrian statue of **King Stephen** stands just outside the church, commemorating this ruler who forced Catholicism onto his subjects, thus aligning Hungary with the culture of Western Europe. The **Fishermen's Bastion** or Halászbástya (daily: mid-March to end Oct 8.30am–11pm; 240Ft; same months 11pm–8.30am, plus Nov to mid-March 24hr; free) nearby is an undulating white rampart with gargoyle-lined cloisters and seven turrets, which frames the view of Parliament across the river.

Medieval architectural features have survived along **Országház utca** (Parliament Street), at the northern end of which the quasi-Gothic **Mary Magdalene Tower** still dominates Kapisztrán tér, albeit gutted and transformed into an art gallery. To the south of Szentháromság tér the street widens as it approaches the **Buda Palace**. The fortifications and dwellings built by Béla III after the thirteenth-century Mongol invasion were replaced by ever more luxurious palaces; the most recent reconstruction dates from after the devastation wrought in World War II. Grouped around two courtyards, the sombre wings of the palace contain a clutch of museums and portions of the medieval structures discovered in the course of excavation. The northern Wing A houses the **Museum of Contemporary Art (Ludwig Collection)** (Tues–Sun 10am–6pm; 400Ft), with a collection that includes well-known names such as Picasso, Hockney and Lichtenstein as well as pieces by younger Hungarian artists such as Attila Szűcs. The **National Gallery** (Tues–Sun 10am–4/6pm; 500Ft), occupying the central wings B, C and D, contains Hungarian art since the Middle Ages. Gothic stone-carvings, altars and painted panels fill the ground floor, while nineteenth-century painting, including major Hungarian artists such as Csontváry, Rippl-Rónai and Munkácsy, dominates upstairs. On the far side of the Lion Courtyard, the **Budapest History Museum** in Wing E (Mon & Wed–Sun 10am–4/6pm; 500Ft) gives the whole history of the territory that makes up the city, from its prehistory on the top floor down to the marbled and flagstoned halls of the Renaissance palace deep underground.

THE WATERTOWN AND GELLÉRT HILL

To the north of the Chain Bridge lies the **Watertown** (Víziváros) district, a wedge of narrow streets, some gas-lit, that was once a poor quarter housing fishermen, craftsmen and their families. Today it's a reclusive neighbourhood of old blocks and mansions meeting at odd angles on the hillside, reached by alleys which mostly consist of steps rising from the main street, Fő utca. North along Fő utca stand the **Király baths** (men only Mon, Wed & Fri

9am–8/9pm; women only Tues & Thurs 7am–7pm, Sat 7am–1pm; 600Ft), distinguishable by four copper cupolas shaped like tortoise shells.

South of Watertown rises **Gellért Hill** (Gellérthegy), named after Bishop Ghirardus, who converted the Magyars to Christianity at the behest of King Stephen. A statue of the bishop bestrides a waterfall facing the **Erzsébet Bridge**, marking the spot where he was murdered in 1064 by vengeful heathens following the demise of his royal protector. Near the foot of the bridge, puffs of steam and cute little cupolas surmount the men-only **Rudas baths** (Mon–Fri 6.30am–7pm, Sat 6am–1pm; 800Ft), Budapest's most atmospheric Turkish baths, whose interior has hardly changed since they were constructed in 1556. On the other side of the Hegyalja út flyover, the **Rác baths** (women only Mon, Wed & Fri 6am–6pm; men only Tues, Thurs & Sat 6am–6pm; 600Ft) were also built during the Turkish occupation, but largely modernized except for the pool. Crowning the summit of the hill is the **Liberation Monument**, a stark female figure holding aloft the palm of victory, and one of the few Soviet monuments to survive the fall of the Iron Curtain. Originally commissioned during World War II by Admiral Horthy in memory of his own son, it was adapted to suit the requirements of the Soviet liberators. Behind is the **Citadella**, a low fortress built by the Habsburgs to cow the population after the 1848–49 revolution. Nowadays the fort contains nothing more sinister than a few exhibits, a tourist hostel, a dismal disco/bar and an overpriced restaurant. Descending the southern slopes of the hill through the playgrounds of Jubileumi Park, you'll see rough-hewn stone figures seemingly writhing from the massive portal of the **Gellért baths**, at the side of *Hotel Gellért*. The best-publicized of the city's baths, they were built in 1913, and the grandeur of the entrance hall is continued in the main pool (daily 6am–7pm; Oct–April Sat & Sun closes 5pm; 1800Ft). You can get cheaper tickets just for the stunning thermal baths (close earlier at weekends), which are single-sex, but it's worth paying to enjoy the beauty of the whole complex. In summer the terrace and wave pool are packed.

Pest

Pest, busier and more vital than Buda, is the place where things are decided, made and sold. Much of the architecture and general layout dates from the late nineteenth century, when boulevards, public buildings and apartment houses were built on a scale appropriate to the Habsburg Empire's second city and the capital of Hungary, which celebrated its thousandth anniversary in 1896. The **Belváros** revels in its cosmopolitanism, with shops selling the latest Western fashions and French perfume, posters proclaiming the arrival of Western films and rock groups, and streets noisy with the sound of foreign cars and languages. The main **Vörösmarty tér**, haunt of portraitists, conjurers, violinists and other performers, is dominated by crowded café terraces. While children play in the square's fountains, their elders congregate around the statue of the poet and translator Mihály Vörösmarty (1800–55). Underfoot lies mainland Europe's first underground train system, opened in 1896, the **Millennial Railway** (metro line 1), which runs beneath Andrássy utca up to Heroes' Square. However, the most venerable institution on Vörösmarty tér is the *Gerbeaud* patisserie, the favourite of Budapest's high society since the late nineteenth century, and now packed with tourists. (Its rival on the square, the *Art Café*, has a reputation for being overpriced.) The city's most chic shopping street, **Váci utca**, runs south from the square parallel to the river and thronged with people strolling past its cafés and boutiques. Passing the Pesti Theatre, where twelve-year-old Liszt made his concert debut, the crowds flow down to **Ferenciek tere**, overlooking which is a slab of gilt-and-gingerbread architecture, the **Párisi udvar**, home to an ice-cream parlour and IBUSZ office, but chiefly known for its "Parisian arcade", adorned with arabesques and stained glass. Váci utca heads on south, via a subway by the twin Klothild palaces that flank the approach to Erzsébet Bridge, down to the **Main Market Hall** (Nagycsarnok), with its fancy ironwork, porcelain tiles and stalls festooned with strings of paprika and garlic. This has been a regular port of call for visiting statespersons ever since the visit of British prime minister Margaret Thatcher in 1984, who impressed the locals by haggling with the stallholders.

Peering over the rooftops to the north of Vörösmarty tér is the dome of **St Stephen's Basilica**, from the top of which in summer you can get a good view over the city (dome: April–Oct daily 10am–5/7pm; 500Ft). On his name day, August 20, St Stephen's mummified hand and other holy relics are paraded round the building; the rest of the year, the hand is on show on the righthand side of the church. Just north of the Basilica, dominating the banks of the Danube, is the large dome of the **Parliament** (Országház), a stupendous nineteenth-century creation befitting a small country with old longings for grandeur. Like that of the Basilica, its dome is 96m high – an allusion to 896, the year of the Magyar conquest. In 1999 the ambitious young prime minister Viktor Orbán displayed his nationalist leanings by transferring the old **Coronation Regalia** from the National Museum to the Parliament. Reputedly the very crown, orb and sceptre used by King Stephen, the regalia is now thought to be a combination of two crowns used by Stephen's successors, but nevertheless is still seen as a symbol of Hungarian statehood. There are hourly tours in Hungarian around the building and to the crown (Mon–Fri 8am–6pm, Sat 8am–4pm, Sun 8am–2pm; 1300Ft; tickets from Gate X half way along the east front), with tours in English daily at 10am and 2pm, if parliamentary business allows.

To the east of the Basilica, **Andrássy utca** runs dead straight for 2.5km, a parade of grand buildings laden with gold leaf, dryads and colonnades, including the magnificent Opera House at no. 22. Its shops and sidewalk cafés retain some of the style that made the avenue so fashionable in the 1890s. The boulevard culminates at **Heroes' Square** (Hősök tere), erected to mark the thousandth anniversary of the Magyar conquest. Its centrepiece is the **Millennary Monument**, portraying Prince Árpád and his chieftains grouped around a 36m-high column topped by the Archangel Gabriel, and half-encircled by a colonnade displaying statues of Hungary's most illustrious leaders, from King Stephen to Kossuth. The **Museum of Fine Arts** on the square (Tues–Sun 10am–4/6pm; 500Ft) contains Egyptian funerary relics, Greek and Roman ceramics, and paintings and drawings by European masters from the thirteenth to the twentieth century – including Dürer, El Greco, Velázquez and Bronzino. Behind the museum lies **Budapest Zoo** (daily 9am–4/6pm; 1000Ft), worth a visit for the architecture alone – the Palm House, the Elephant House and the Aviary in particular – although you can also feed the giraffes, tickle the rhinos behind the ears and coo at the baby white camel Jazmin. Under its new director the Zoo is improving conditions for its residents as well as taking an active role in conservation and returning animals to the wild.

Back towards the centre of the Belváros, on the corner of Wesselényi and Dohány utca, stands the dramatic main **Synagogue**, whose Byzantine-Moorish architecture has been undergoing much-needed restoration; the interior is now complete and utterly magnificent. In the **National Jewish Museum** next door (Mon–Fri 10am–2pm, Sun 10am–1pm; 600Ft), exhibits dating back to the Middle Ages are opposed by a harrowing Holocaust exhibition, which casts a chill over the third section, portraying Jewish cultural life today. In the streets behind the synagogue lies Pest's main **Jewish quarter**. In recent years the small Jewish community that survived the Holocaust has become much more visible in the city, although even here, where the community is strongest, it keeps a low profile. Along Dob utca there is the *Fröhlich* kosher coffee shop at no. 22, a wigmaker at no. 31, and at no. 35, by the entrance to the orthodox community buildings, a kosher butcher's (open Wed & Thurs), while further along in Klauzál tér you can buy excellent kosher *slivovitz* in the cellar of no. 16 (Thurs 2.30–4.30pm, Fri 11.30am–2pm).

Eating and drinking

Magyar cooking naturally predominates in Budapest's **restaurants**, but the capital has a growing number of places devoted to international cuisine. Prices by Western standards are very reasonable, and your budget should stretch to at least one binge in a top-flight place. The following categories – patisseries (for non-alcoholic drinks and sweet pastries), restaurants (for eating), and bars and beer halls (for drinking) – are to an extent arbitrary, since all restaurants serve alcohol and all bars serve some food, while *eszpresszós* (cafés) feature both, plus coffee and pastries.

Patisseries

Angelika, I, Batthyány tér 7. Quiet, but smoky atmosphere in a former convent, with a lively terrace. Daily 10am–midnight.

Central, V, Károlyi Mihály utca 9. Large old coffee house recently restored to its former grandeur, with a broad menu ranging from cheap to very expensive. Daily 8am–midnight/1am.

Eckermann, VI, Andrássy út 24. Big coffees and Internet access (from 2pm) in this popular café next to the Goethe Institute. Mon–Sat 8am–10pm.

Fröhlich, VII, Dob utca 22. A kosher patisserie five minutes' walk from the Dohány utca synagogue, presided over by the Fröhlich family. Specialities such as *flodni* (an apple, walnut and poppy-seed cake) are worth tasting. Mon–Thurs 9am–6pm, Fri 7.30am–3pm, Sun 10am–6pm; closed Sat & Jewish holidays.

Gerbeaud, V, Vörösmarty tér 7. A popular and very grand place in central Pest. A coffee and a torte will set you back around 500Ft; the same rich pastries are cheaper in *Kis Gerbeaud* around the corner. Gets unbearably full in summer. Daily 9am–9pm.

Múzeum Cukrászda, VIII, Múzeum körút 10. Friendly hangout by the National Museum. Fresh pastries arrive at dawn. Daily 24hr.

Müvész, VI, Andrássy út 29. Another grand old coffee house, less touristy and cheaper than *Gerbeaud*. Daily 8am–midnight.

Ruszwurm's, I, Szentháromság utca 7. Excellent cakes, served production-line fashion to those taking a break from sightseeing on Castle Hill, who crowd its diminutive interior. Daily 10am–8pm.

Fast food, self-service and snack bars

Duran Sandwich Bar, V, Október 6 utca 15. A sandwich and coffee bar – still, oddly enough, a rare combination in Budapest. Mon–Fri 8am–6pm, Sat 9am–1pm.

Falafel, VI, Paulay Ede utca 53. Best of the city's falafel joints. Mon–Fri 10am–8pm, Sat 10am–6pm.

Museum of Contemporary Art, I, Wing A, Buda Royal Palace. Excellent café on the museum's upper floor, with fast service and very tasty Hungarian food. Best value on Castle Hill – but you'll have to pay admission to the museum first! Tues–Sun 10am–4pm.

Marie Kristensen Sandwich Bar, IX, Ráday utca 7. The Danish flavour is hard to spot; this is just a decent regular sandwich bar behind Kálvin tér. Mon–Fri 8am–10pm.

Self-service canteen, V, Szende Pál utca 3. Very cheap lunches with the local office workers behind Vörösmarty tér. Nothing translated, so just point to what you want. Mon–Fri noon–3pm.

Tower Restaurant, 10th floor of the Central European University, V, Nádor utca 9. Excellent inexpensive university café open to all, run by the same people as the Ludwig Museum café. Mon–Fri 10am–8pm (university members only noon–2pm).

Restaurants

Al-Amir, VII, Király utca 17 (☎1/352-1422). Syrian restaurant serving excellent salads and hummus, making it a haven for vegetarians in a city of carnivores. If that isn't enough, the array of Arabic sweets is very enticing. No alcohol served. Cash only. Daily 11am–11pm.

Arcade, XII, Kiss János alt. utca 38 (☎1/225-1969). Excellent new restaurant just up the hill from Déli train station in Buda. International cuisine, the best Hungarian wines and good service make it relatively pricey, attracting a strongly foreign clientele. Tues–Sun 11am–11pm.

Bagolyvár, XIV, Állatkerti körút 20 (☎1/351-6395). Sister to the expensive top-bracket *Gundel* next door, but offering traditional Hungarian family-style cooking at lower prices. Daily noon–11pm.

Café Kör, V, Sas utca 17 (☎1/311-0053). Popular establishment near the Basilica with a continental feel, with excellent food and fine wines. Menu supplemented by specials written up on the wall. Booking essential. Mon–Sat 10am–10pm.

Chez Daniel, VI, Szív utca 32 (☎1/302-4039). Best French restaurant in town, run by idiosyncratic master chef. Booking recommended. Daily noon–3pm & 7–10.30pm.

Gandhi, V, Vigyázó Ferenc utca 4 (☎1/269-4944). An oasis of spiritual calm in the city serving a range of international vegetarian dishes. Daily noon–10.30pm.

Gundel, XIV, Állatkerti körút 2 (☎1/321-3550). Prides itself as the flagship of Hungarian cuisine and has prices that are high by Western standards. But on Sunday you can eat as much as you like for a mere 3600Ft at their bargain Sunday Brunch. Booking essential. Mon–Sat noon–4pm & 7pm–midnight, Sun 11.30am–3pm.

King's Hotel, VII Nagydiófa utca 25–27 (☎1/352-7675). Kosher food in the old Jewish quarter, ten minutes' walk from the Dohány utca synagogue. Daily noon–9.30pm.

Kiskacsa, VII, Dob utca 26. Small, friendly joint ten minutes up from the big synagogue, serving traditional Hungarian fare. You get three dice with your bill and if you roll three sixes your meal is on the house. Mon–Sat noon–midnight.

Márkus Vendéglő, II, Lövőház utca 17 (☎1/212-3153). Welcoming, inexpensive Hungarian restaurant near Moszkva tér. Daily 11am–1am.

Múzeum Kávéház, VIII, Múzeum körút 12 (☎1/338-4221). Excellent, pricey food in this beautiful nineteenth-century coffee house next to the National Museum. Booking essential. Mon–Sat 10am–1am.

Náncsi Néni, II, Ördögárok út 80 (☎1/397-2742). Large, popular garden restaurant in the leafy suburb of Hűvösvölgy, ten minutes' walk from the terminus of bus #56. Booking advisable. Daily noon–11pm.

Papageno, V, Semmelweis utca 10 (☎1/485-0161). Small, friendly new establishment with top chefs specializing in French and Italian cuisine. Good wines. Mon–Fri 11.30am–midnight, Sat 6.30pm–midnight.

Vörös és Fehér Borbar (Red and White Wine Bar), VI, Andrássy út 41 (☎1/413 1545). Restaurant serving top Hungarian vintages and very tasty food. Worth booking.

Bars, wine bars and beer halls

Bambi, I, Bem tér. Wonderful old bar from the socialist era serving breakfast, snack lunches, dry-looking cakes, and alcohol. Mon–Fri 7am–9pm, Sat & Sun 9am–8pm.

Buena Vista, VI, Liszt Ferenc tér 5. Popular new bar near the Music Academy on this square of cafés all spilling out under the trees. Good restaurant upstairs, plus tables with their own beer taps in the cellar bar. Daily 11am–2am.

Café Miro, I, Uri utca 30. A trendy bar in the Castle district which often has live music. Daily 9am–midnight.

Castro, IX, Ráday utca 35. A lively new place on Ráday utca, a popular street with students lined with cafés and bars. Internet access too. Daily 10am–midnight/1am.

Darshan Udvar, VIII, Krudy Gyula utca 7. The largest bar in a growing complex of bars, cafés and shops. Set at the back of the courtyard, with oriental/hippie decorations, good food and world music, but leisurely service. Mon–Wed 11am–midnight, Thurs & Fri 11am–2am, Sat 6pm–2am, Sun 6pm–midnight.

Gusto's, II, Frankel Leo utca 12 (☎1/316-3970). Tiny bar near Buda side of Margit Bridge, serving the best tiramisù in town. Mon–Sat 10am–10pm.

Libella, XI, Budafoki út 7. Friendly bar near the Gellért Baths with bar snacks, chess and draughts. Attracts a younger alternative crowd. Mon–Sat 8am–11pm, Sun 10am–11pm.

Móri Borozó, I, corner of Hattyú utca and Fiáth János utca. Typical inexpensive and cheerful neighbourhood wine-bar, in the backstreets north of Castle Hill. Mon–Sat 2–11pm, Sun 2–9pm (longer summer hours).

Old Man's Music Pub, VII, Akácfa utca 13. Large, popular joint in the centre of Pest, live local acts, and good food. Daily 3pm–dawn.

Ráczkert Söröző, I, Hadnagy utca 12, by the Rác Baths. This place on the edge of the Tabán is regularly packed. Live music at weekends. April–Oct daily 5pm–late.

Zöld Pardon, XI, by the Buda end of Petőfi Bridge, a large outdoor bar with live music sprawling across the grass near the university quarter, popular with students. March–Oct daily 6pm–2am.

Entertainment and nightlife

Star events in the capital's cultural year are the **Budapest Spring Festival** (two weeks in March or April) and the **Autumn Music Weeks** (late Sept to late Oct), both of which attract the cream of Hungary's artists and top international acts. There's hardly less in the way of concerts and the like during the summer. On **St Stephen's Day** (Aug 20) the area around the Royal Palace becomes one big folk and crafts fair, and in the evening the population lines the embankments to watch the fireworks.

You'll have to check the posters and listings publications for information on rock concerts. The **Petőfi Csarnok** in the Városliget (☎1/343-4327, *www.petoficsarnok.hu*), the **Almássy tér Cultural Centre** at VII, Almássy tér 6 (☎1/342-0387, *www.datanet.hu/~almassy*), the **Trafó** at IX, Liliom utca 41 (☎1/456-2040, *www.trafo.hu*), a revamped transformer station in Pest, and the **Fonó** at XI, Sztregova utca 3 (☎1/206-5300, *www.fono.hu*), in Buda, are four of the main venues for alternative concerts, folk music and modern dance events. **Tickets** for most events can be had through the Filharmonia Ticket office, Mérleg utca 10 (☎1/318-0281); Ticket Express for classical music, VI, Andrássy út 18 (☎1/312-0000); Music Mix at V, Váci utca 33 (☎1/266-7070); and Publika for rock and jazz at VII, Károly körút 9 (☎1/322-2010).

New **clubs and discos** are opening all the time, and the rave and floating party scene is growing constantly: check flyers and posters around town, or look in the "Könnyű" section of *Pesti Est*, the free listings magazine in cinema foyers. The old Turkish Rudas baths hosts monthly *Vizimozi* raves (*www.cinetrip.hu*). There's also a variety of cheap **student clubs**.

Nightclubs

Angyal, VII, Szövetség utca 33. Budapest's premier gay club: looks like an airport lounge but has an interesting crowd. Thurs–Sun 10pm–dawn; Sat men only.

Capella, V, Belgrád rakpart 23. Drag queens, jungle music and lots of tat: just the place for Friday night on the town. Tues 9pm–2am, Wed–Sun 9pm–5am.

Cha Cha Cha, IX, Kálvin tér subway. Despite its strange location, this attracts a big crowd spilling out into the concourse and has DJs at weekends. Mon–Fri 7am–2am, Sat 10am–2am.

Romkert, I, Döbrentei tér 9 (☎1/344-3155). Outside bar attracting a wealthy young crowd, that's one of the few places you can dance outside until the early hours. Good bar food; worth booking a table if you're eating. March–Oct Mon–Fri noon–2/3am, Sat 6pm–4/5am, Sun 6pm–2/3am.

Süss Fel Nap, V, Honvéd utca 40. Heaving, lively place attracting a young crowd. Daily 8pm–4am.

Trocadero Café, V, Szent István körút 15. Excellent Latin music and dancing just up from Nyugáti Station. Tues–Sat 9pm–2am.

Listings

Airport information Departures ☎1/296-7000; arrivals ☎1/296-8080. Call ☎1/296-8555 to book the Airport Minibus.

Books Bestsellers, V, Október 6 utca 11, near the Basilica. For maps, head for Cartographia, Pest VI, Bajcsy-Zsilinszky utca 37; or Térképkirály, Pest V, Sas utca 1.

Car rental All the main car rental companies have offices in both the airport terminals. Those also with offices in town include: Budget at *Hotel Mercure Buda*, I, Krisztina körút 41–43 (☎1/214-0420); Europcar at VIII, Üllői út 60–62 (☎1/477-1080); Avis at V, Szervita tér 8, beside the Jet petrol station (☎1/318-4240); Hertz at *Marriott Hotel*, V, Apáczai Csere János utca 4 (☎1/266 4361).

Embassies and consulates Australia, XII, Királyhágó tér 8–9 (☎1/457-9777); Canada, XII, Budakeszi út 32 (☎1/392-3360); Ireland, V, Szabadság tér 7, 7th floor, Bank Center (☎1/302-9600); New Zealand, VI, Teréz körút 38, 4th floor (☎1/331-4908); UK, V, Harmincad utca 6 (☎1/266-2888); USA, V, Szabadság tér 12 (☎1/475-4400).

Exchange You'll get better rates at banks than at exchange offices. Most banks offer similar rates; try the Gönc Szövetkezeti Takarékpénztár at V, Rákóczi út 5. Around Vörösmarty tér in central Pest, head for the Magyar Külkereskedelmi Bank at Türr István utca at the top of Váci utca. There is a 24hr service in the tourist office at V, Apáczai Csere János utca 1 by the *Marriott Hotel*.

Hospital 24hr casualty departments at V, Hold utca 19, behind the US embassy (☎1/311-6816), and at II, Ganz utca 13–15 (☎1/202-1370). Profident, VII, Károly körút 1, is a 24hr English-speaking dentist. Embassies can also recommend private English-speaking doctors and dentists.

Internet Eckermann Café, VI, Andrássy út 24, near the Opera House (Mon–Sat 2pm–10pm; 1hr free); Enternet at V, Deák Ferenc utca 15 on the corner of Vörösmarty tér, has stand-up terminals (15min free); Libri Könyvpalota, VII, Rákóczi út 12 (Mon–Fri 10am–7.30pm, Sat 10am–3pm); Vista Visitor Center, VI, Paulay Ede utca 7 (Mon–Fri 8am–8pm, Sat & Sun 10am–6pm).

Pharmacy Details of each district's 24-hour pharmacy are posted in every pharmacy's window. Central 24hr pharmacies are at Alkotás utca 2, opposite Déli station, and at Teréz körút 41, near Oktogon.

Post office Main office at V, Petőfi utca 13 (Mon–Fri 8am–8pm, Sat 8am–2pm); mail should be addressed to Poste Restante, Magyar Posta, 1364, Budapest. Also an office by Keleti Station at VII, Baross tér 11/c (daily 7am–9pm).

Travel agents Vista Travel, VI, Andrássy út 1 (entrance from Paulay Ede utca; ☎1/269-6032); Travel Unlimited, VIII, Rákóczi út 1–3 (☎1/266-8919).

THE DANUBE BEND

Entering the Carpathian Basin, the Danube widens hugely, only to be forced by hills and mountains through a narrow, twisting valley – almost a U-turn – before parting for the length of Szentendrei Island and flowing into Budapest. To escape Budapest's humid summers, people flock to this region, known as the **Danube Bend** (Dunakanyar), where there are historic attractions aplenty. **Szentendre**, forty minutes' journey by HÉV train from Batthyány tér in Budapest, is the logical place to start, though with hourly buses from the capital's Árpád híd terminal, you could travel directly to **Visegrád** or **Esztergom**, the heart of Hungarian Catholicism. Travelling **by boat** can be fun, but it takes five hours from Budapest to Esztergom; it's better to sail only part of the way, say between the capital and Szentendre (1hr 40min), or between Visegrád and Esztergom (1hr 30min) – or take the fast hydrofoil from Budapest to Esztergom (June–Aug weekends only; 1hr 20min).

Szentendre

Having cleared the bus and HÉV stations and found your way into its Baroque heart, you are unlikely to be disappointed by **SZENTENDRE**. Ignoring the outlying housing estates and the rash of Nosztalgia and Folklór boutiques in the centre, it's a friendly maze of houses painted in autumn colours, secretive gardens, and alleys leading to hilltop churches – the perfect spot for an artists' colony, which is what it became in the 1920s, when Budapest artists moved out to make the most of the superb natural light. Before the artists moved in, Szentendre's character was largely shaped by Serbs seeking refuge from the Ottomans. Their townhouses – now converted into galleries, shops and cafés – form a set piece around **Fő tér**, a stage for musicians, mime-artists and other performers.

The **Blagovestenska Church** (daily 10am–5pm; 100Ft) – whose iconostasis, painted by Mikhail Zivkovic (1776–1824), suggests the richness of the Serbs' artistry and faith – is the first stop on the heritage trail, while just around the corner at Vastagh György utca 1 stands the wonderful **Margit Kovács Museum** (Tues–Sun 10am–4/6pm; 300Ft), displaying the lifetime work of Hungary's best-known ceramicist, born in 1902. Above Fő tér there's a fine view of Szentendre's steeply banked rooftops and gardens from the hilltop **Templom tér**, where frequent craft fairs help finance the restoration of the Catholic parish church there. Opposite the church, paintings whose fierce brush strokes and sketching were a challenge to the canons of classicism during the 1890s hang in the **Béla Czóbel Museum** (Tues–Sun 10am–6pm; 100Ft), beyond which the spire of the **Serbian Orthodox Cathedral** pokes above a walled garden; tourists are generally not admitted, but you can see the cathedral iconostasis and treasury in the adjacent **museum** (Tues–Sun 10am–4/6pm; Jan & Feb closed Mon–Thurs; 120Ft). An hourly bus runs from the HÉV terminal out along Szabadságforrás út to Szentendre's fascinating **Village Museum** (Szabadtéri Múzeum; April–Oct Tues–Sun 9am–5pm; 500Ft; *www.sznm.hu*), which has reconstructed villages from five regions of Hungary (more are planned). The brochure on sale at the gate points out the finer distinctions between humble peasant dwellings such as the house from Kispalad and the cottage from Uszka, formerly occupied by petty squires. During the summer, on alternate weekends, there are demonstrations of traditional craft techniques like pottery, baking and basket-making.

The best place for **information**, both on the town and the Danube Bend, is Tourinform, Dumsta Jenő utca 22 (Mon–Fri 9am–5pm, Sat & Sun 10am–4pm; ☎26/317-965, *szentendre@tourinform.hu*). The friendly, English-speaking staff can provide information about **accommodation**, though they don't make bookings. The best budget options are the *Aradi Panzió*, Aradi utca 4 (☎26/314-274; ②), near the HÉV station; and *Ilona Panzió*, Rákóczi F. utca 11 (☎26/313-599; ②), in a pleasant location in the centre of town. IBUSZ, Bogdányi utca 11 (Mon–Fri 10am–5/6pm; summer also Sat & Sun 10am–1pm; ☎26/310-181) can arrange **private rooms**. A lot of people end up **camping**, either on Szentendre Island or on Pap Island north of town – accessible by ferry or bus respectively. Most **restaurants** are concentrated in and around Fő tér; the *Aranysárkány*, Alkotmány utca 1/a, and *Rab Ráby*, Péter-Pál utca 1, are two popular choices, and *Palapu*, Dumsta J 14/a, is an excellent Mexican bar/restaurant.

Visegrád

During the fifteenth-century reign of Mátyás and Beatrice the palace at **VISEGRÁD** was famed throughout Europe, but in the centuries that followed Visegrád declined, gradually becoming the humble village that it is today. However, the basic layout of the settlement – the stunning Citadel on the hill, and the ruins of the once-grand palace down by the river – hasn't altered significantly. The ruins of the **Palace** are spread over four levels behind the gate of 27 Fő utca (Tues–Sun 9am–4/5pm; 300Ft). Nothing remains of the building founded by the Angevin king Charles Robert, but the *cour d'honneur* built for his successor Louis can still be seen on the second terrace. Its chief features are a Renaissance **loggia** and two panels from its **Hercules Fountain**. From the decrepit **Water Bastion** just north of the main landing-stage – where boats from Budapest and Esztergom arrive – a rampart ascends the slope to **Solomon Tower**, a mighty hexagonal keep buttressed by concrete slabs. Inside, the tower's **Mátyás Museum** (May–Sept Tues–Sun 9am–5pm; 120Ft) houses finds from the excavated palace, including the white Anjou Fountain and the red marble *Visegrád Madonna*. Visegrád's most dramatic feature is the imposing **Citadel** on the mountain-top (mid-March to mid-Nov daily 9am–6pm; rest of year Sat & Sun 10am–4pm; closed when there is snow, as the battlements are too slippery; 250Ft). Though only partly restored, it is still mightily impressive, commanding a superb view of Nagymaros and the Börzsöny Mountains on the east bank. You can reach it by the Kálvária footpath which begins behind the church on Fő tér, or by catching a bus from the Mátyás statue on Fő utca, which follows the scenic Panorama út. From the car park on the summit, the road leads on up to the luxury *Hotel Silvanus*, and then to the Nagy-Villám **observation tower**, where you'll get a view that stretches into Slovakia.

During high summer you might have problems finding somewhere to **stay**: ask at the only **tourist office**, the rather unfriendly Visegrád Tours (May–Oct daily 9am–6pm; Nov–April Mon–Fri 10am–4pm; ☎26/398-160), beside the very touristy *Sirály* restaurant near the Nagymaros ferry pier in the centre of town; or organize rooms through Bauer Folk Art (May–Sept 10am–5pm; ☎26/316-469), Fő utca 46. If the grand *Mátyás tanya*, Fő utca 47, near the palace (☎26/398-309, *www.hotels.hu/matyas_tanya*; ②), does not appeal, try the more modern *Haus Honti*, Fő utca 66, which also rents bikes (☎26/398-120; ②) – or one of the many private rooms advertised everywhere. The best two central **restaurants** are *Gulyás Csárda*, Nagy Lajos utca 4 (just up from the church across the road), and *Renaissance*, opposite the landing stage at Fő utca 11.

Esztergom

Beautifully situated in a crook of the Danube facing Slovakia, enclosed by glinting water and soft hills, **ESZTERGOM** is dominated by its great Basilica, whose dome is visible for miles around. The sight is richly symbolic, for although the royal court abandoned Esztergom for Buda after the Mongol invasion, this has remained the centre of Hungarian Catholicism since 1000, when Stephen – who was born and crowned here – imposed Christianity. The **Basilica**, completed in 1869, is the largest in Hungary: 118m long and 40m wide, capped by a dome 71.5m high (daily 7am–5/6pm; Oct–Feb closed Mon). Its nave is on a massive scale, clad in marble, gilding and mosaics, with a collection of saintly relics in the chapel to the right as you enter. The **crypt** (daily 9am–4.45pm; 50Ft) resembles a set from an old horror movie, with giant stone women flanking the stairway that descends to gloomy vaults full of prelates' tombs, including that of the conservative Cardinal Mindszenty, whose politicking in the 1960s greatly embarrassed the compromise-seeking Vatican. The **treasury** (March–Oct daily 9am–4.30pm; Nov & Dec Tues–Sun 10am–3.30pm; 250Ft) has an entrance north of the altar; having viewed its overpowering collection of bejewelled crooks and chalices, it's almost a relief to climb the seemingly endless stairway to the bell tower and **cupola** (100Ft). On the same craggy plateau as the Basilica is the **Castle Museum**, where you'll find the ruins of the medieval palace (Tues–Sun 9am–4/5pm; 400Ft) once occupied by Béla III, the widowed Queen Beatrice and sundry archbishops. You can visit the remains of a chapel with its rose window and Byzantine-style frescoes, Beatrice's suite and the study of Archbishop Vítez – known as the Hall of Virtues after its allegorical murals. Below, the Baroque streets of the **Watertown** are connected by the sloping Bajcsy-Zsilinszky út to Rákóczi tér, the centre of downtown Esztergom. South of the Basilica, separated by a tributary of the Danube, is **Primás-Sziget**, where you'll find a couple of hotels, a restaurant, boats to Budapest, ferries across the river to Stúrovo in Slovakia, and the bridge across to Slovakia, which is currently being rebuilt.

The Gran Tours **tourist office** (Mon–Fri 8am–4/6pm, Sat 9am–noon; ☎33/413-756, *grantour@mail.holop.hu*) and the post office stand a short way south of the Basilica in Széchenyi tér. For **accommodation**, private rooms are probably the best budget option – ask at the tourist office or at IBUSZ, Kossuth utca 5 (Mon–Fri 8am–4/5pm; ☎33/411-643, *esztergom@mail.ibusz.hu*). There are also student hostels in summer and town pensions, of which *St Kristóf Panzió*, Dobozi Mihály utca 11 (☎33/416-255; ③), is the nicest and has a good restaurant attached, while the more basic *Platán Panzió*, Kis-Duna sétány 11 (☎33/411-355, *eurokt@mail.holop.hu*; ①) is attractively situated opposite Primás-Sziget. On Primás-Sziget itself is the bright, new *Szalma Csárda Panzió*, Nagy-Duna sétány 2 (☎83/315-336, *www.col.hu/szalmacsarda*; ②). The nearest **campsite** is *Gran Tours*, on the Primás-Sziget by the river (book through the Gran Tours office). There are some pleasant pavement cafés around Széchenyi tér; for **restaurants** try *St Kristóf Panzió*; *Hotel Esztergom* on Nagy Duna sétány on the northern tip of Primás-Sziget; *Csülök Csárda*, offering gargantuan portions on Batthyány utca; or *Szalma Csárda*, just along from the pension of the same name, which serves traditional Hungarian fare.

WESTERN HUNGARY

The major tourist attraction to the west of the capital is **Lake Balaton**, over-romantically labelled the "Hungarian sea". Despite the fact that rising prices are pushing out natives in favour of Austrians and Germans, this is still very much the nation's playground, with vacation resorts lining both shores. On the northern bank, development has been limited to some extent by reedbanks and cooler, deeper water, giving tourism a different slant. Historic **Tihany** and the wine-producing **Badacsony Hills** offer fine sightseeing, while anyone whose social life doesn't take off in **Keszthely** can go soak themselves in the thermal lake at **Hévíz**.

More than other regions in Hungary, the western region of **Transdanubia** (Dunántúl) is a patchwork land, an ethnic and social hybrid. Its valleys and hills, forests and mud flats have been a melting pot since Roman times: settled by Magyars, Serbs, Slovaks and Germans; torn asunder and occupied by Ottomans and Habsburgs; transformed from a state of near-feudalism into brutal collectives; and now operating under a modern capitalist form. All the main towns display evidence of this evolution, especially **Sopron**, with its well-preserved medieval centre, and **Pécs**, which boasts an Ottoman mosque and minaret.

Lake Balaton

Given the over-development of the southern shore, you'll get the best out of **Lake Balaton** by catching a **train** from Budapest's Déli station to the town of Balatonfüred; from there the route follows the northern shore to the Badacsony Hills, then north to Tapolca. Alternatively, catch a **bus** from Budapest's Erzsébet tér to the major lakeside towns. The shore is ringed with company holiday homes; it's worth asking about spare rooms at these places, as they are often rented out at a reasonable price. Out of season (Oct–March) the lake is pleasantly peaceful – since most places are shut.

Balatonfüred

The Romans were the first to imbibe the curative waters of **BALATONFÜRED**, and nowadays some 30,000 people come every year for treatment in its sanatoriums. A busy harbour and skyscraper hotels dominate approaches to the town, but the centre has a sedate, convalescent atmosphere, typified by the embankment promenade, Rabindranath Tagore sétány, named after the Bengali poet who came here in 1926. Above the tree-lined promenade lies Gyógy tér (Healing Square), where you can drink the Kossuth spring's carbonic water at a pagoda-like structure. Four other springs feed the mineral baths on the eastern side, but these are only open for patients at the adjoining hospital.

For **information** on the town and region there is a Tourinform office inconveniently located out by the *Füred* campsite on the road towards Tihany (Mon–Fri 9am–4/6pm; summer also Sat & Sun; ☎87/342-237, *balatonfured@tourinform.hu*) and a Balatontourist office at the *Füred* campsite (see below; ☎87/580-033). The least expensive **accommodation** includes the *Korona Panzió*, Vörösmarty utca 4 (☎87/343-278, *www.hotels.hu /korona_panzio*; ③), a decent pension open year-round; lakeside *Tagore*, Deák Ferenc utca 56 (☎87/343-173; ③; May–Oct); *Blaha Lujza*, Blaha Lujza utca 4 (☎87/581 210, *www.hotel-blaha.hu*; ③); and *Fortuna*, Honvéd utca 3 (☎87/343-037; ③; May–Sept). You can arrange better-value private rooms through Balatontourist, or IBUSZ in the Arany Csillag store, Zsigmond utca 1 (☎87/342-028). There are dorms at Széchenyi Ferenc Kollégium in Iskola utca, though those in the old town can be a long way from the water. The big lakeside *Füred* **campsite**, Szechenyi utca 24 (☎87/343-823), is west of town, beyond the *Füred* and *Marina* hotels.

Tihany

The historic centre of **TIHANY**, self-proclaimed "Pearl of the Balaton", sits above the harbour where the **ferries** from Siófok and Balatonfüred dock; you'll find it by following the winding steps up between a screen of trees, and you'll know you've arrived by the mass of tourist boutiques and stalls that crowd the streets. Since trains bypass the peninsula, the alternative method of arrival is by **bus** from Balatonfüred. Tihany's **Benedictine Abbey** was established in 1055 at the request of Andrew I, whose body now lies in the crypt. The church is embellished by the virtuoso woodcarvings of Sebestyén Stulhoff, who preserved the features of his fiancée in the face of the angel kneeling to the right of the altar of the Virgin. A few minutes' walk north from the abbey brings you to the **Open-Air Museum**, a collection of old cottages giving a feel of life in the village in the early twentieth century (May–Sept Tues–Sun 10am–6pm; 100Ft). Around Petőfi and Csokonai streets, houses are built of grey basalt tufa, with windows and doors outlined in white, and porticoed terraces. Even without a map it's easy to stumble upon **Belső-tó lake**, whose sunlit surface is visible from the abbey. From its southern bank, a path runs through vineyards, orchards and lavender fields past the Aranyház geyser cones and down to Tihanyi-rév.

There's a **Tourinform** office up by the abbey, Kossuth utca 20 (☎87/448-804, *tihany@tourinform.hu*). **Hotel** prices, like everything else in Tihany, are exorbitant by Hungarian standards. The neighbouring **campsite** or **private rooms** are the only affordable options; book at Balatontourist, Kossuth utca 12 (April–Oct Mon–Sat 8am–6.30pm, Sun 8am–1pm; Nov–March Mon–Fri 8am–4.30pm, Sat 8am–1pm; ☎87/448-519) or Tihany Tourist, Kossuth utca 11 (April–Oct Mon–Sat 9am–4/7pm; ☎87/448-481, *tihany.tourist @matavnet.hu*), both up in the village. The *Oazis* **restaurant**, Major utca 47, has good food and friendly staff.

The Badacsony

For 30km west of Tihany the shoreline is lined with holiday homes and small resorts. The next main stop is the **Badacsony**, a hulk of rock with four villages prostrated at its feet, backed by extinct volcanoes ranged across the Tapolca basin. A great semicircle of basalt columns, 210m high, forms the Badacsony's southeastern face, while Kőkapu (Stone Gate) cleaves the northeast side, its two natural towers flanking a precipitous drop. The rich volcanic soil of the mountain's lower slopes has supported vineyards since the Avars buried grape seeds with their dead to ensure that the afterlife wouldn't lack wine. The region's predominantly white wine is celebrated in the annual **wine festival** (second week of Sept), when there is a procession, lots of folk-dancing – and plenty to drink.

Developments are clustered around the southern tip of the hill where the crowds mill about in the summer. Maps and **information** are available from Tourinform, Park utca 6 (June–Aug daily 9am–7pm; May & Sept Mon–Fri 9am–5pm, Sat & Sun 9am–1pm; Oct–April Mon–Fri 9am–3pm; ☎87/431-046, *badacsonytomaj@tourinform.hu*). From mid-May you'll find two tourist offices in the Capitano Shopping centre by the quay: both Balatontourist (Mon–Fri 8.30am–4.30pm; ☎87/431-249) and IBUSZ (☎87/431-292) can help with private rooms, as can Miditourist, Park utca 6 and 53 (☎87/431-028) and Cooptourist, Egry sétány 1 (☎87/431-134). The cheapest central **accommodation** is *Neptun*, Szegedi Róza utca 1 (☎87/431-293; ①; April–Oct), while the flashier *Volán Panzió*, a neo-Baroque heap with a 1980s annexe, is five minutes' walk further on, Római út 168 (☎87/431-013, *www.hotels.hu/volan_badacsony*; ③; April–Nov). The **campsite** (☎87/431-091) is fifteen minutes' walk west of the pier. In **BADACSONYTOMAJ**, 1km east of Badacsony, are the friendly *Egry József Fogadó*, Római út 1, offering simple shared-bath rooms (☎87/471-057, *www.hotels.hu/egry-balaton*; ①; April–Sept), and the KSH pension, the holiday home of the Central Statistical Office, Római út 42–44 (☎87/471-245; ①; May–Sept). A little way along the same road at no. 78, smarter *Borbarátok* ("Wine Friends") pension (☎87/471-597; ②; Easter–Dec) also has a good **restaurant**.

Keszthely and around

Though you can change trains at Tapolca and ride back down to **KESZTHELY** – the Balaton's best hangout – it's easier to continue around the northern shore by bus. Absorbing thousands of visitors gracefully, Keszthely has some good bars and restaurants, a thermal lake at nearby Hévíz, and a university to give it some life of its own. The centre is roughly ten minutes' walk from the **dock** (follow Erzsébet királyné útja) or the **train station** at the bottom end of Mártirok útja, where some intercity **buses** terminate. Most buses drop off on Fő tér, halfway along Kossuth utca, the main drag. Walking up from the train station you'll pass the **Balaton Museum** (Tues–Sun 9/10am–5/6pm; 200Ft), with exhibits dating back to the first century AD. From Fő tér onwards, with its much-remodelled Gothic church, Kossuth utca is given over to cafés, vendors, buskers and strollers – a cheerful procession towards the **Festetics Palace**, founded in 1745 by Count György Festetics (July & Aug daily 9am–6pm; rest of year Tues–Sun 10am–5pm; 1400Ft), which attracted the leading lights of Magyar literature from the nineteenth century onwards. The building's highlights are its gilt, mirrored ballroom and the Helikon Library, a masterpiece of joinery and carving. It stages regular summer concerts.

Keszthely's waterfront has two moles (one for swimming, the other for ferries), a slew of parkland backed by plush hotels and miniature golf courses, and dozens of fast-food joints and bars. In the evening, action shifts to the centre, where the **bars and restaurants** work at full steam. The friendly *Oázis* restaurant, down Szalasztó utca from the palace at Rákóczi tér 3 (Mon–Fri 11am–4pm), has an excellent salad and vegetarian self-service bar, while the *Borház*, Helikon utca 4 (June–Aug only), offers Hungarian food cooked in the traditional way on an open fire. Local student hangouts are the trio of bars opposite the post office on Kossuth Lajos utca, whilst the smart *Pelzo Café*, next to the *Borház*, is ideal for a coffee stop.

The best source for **information** is Tourinform, Kossuth utca 28 (June–mid-Sept Mon–Fri 9am–8pm, Sat & Sun 9am–6pm; rest of year Mon–Fri 9am–5pm, Sat 10am–1pm; ☎83/314-144, *www.keszthely.hu*). For budget **accommodation**, private rooms are your best bet, available from the cluster of tourist offices around Kossuth utca, including Zalatour at no. 1 (☎83/312-560) and IBUSZ down the road at Fő tér (☎83/314-321). Ask at tourist offices about rooms in college dorms (July & Aug, plus weekends year-round). There are two **campsites** just south of the station and the big, expensive *Castrum* 1500m along the shore in the other direction (☎83/312-120). There's **Internet** access at Stones Café, on the corner of Bem utca and Kisfaludy utca.

HÉVÍZ

Half-hourly buses from Keszthely train station run to **HÉVÍZ**, a spa based around Europe's largest thermal lake. The wooden terraces surrounding the **Tófürdő** (Lake Baths; daily 8.30/9am–4.30/5.30pm; 550Ft) have a vaguely *fin-de-siècle* appearance, but the ambience is contemporary, with people sipping beer while bobbing on the lake in rented inner-tubes. Otherwise, Hévíz seems to consist of rest homes and costly hotels, with a late-night **bar** and **casino** in the *Hotel Thermál*. An inexpensive place to **stay** is *Pannon*, Széchenyi utca 23 (☎83/340-482, *pannonhotels@matavnet.hu*; ②), near the centre of town, or you could try the slightly smarter *Piroska Panzió*, Kossuth utca 10 (☎83/342-698; ②). Hévíz Tourist, Rákóczi utca 2 (☎83/341-348, *heviztour@matavnet.hu*), can book private rooms.

Sopron and around

SOPRON is the nearest big Hungarian town to Vienna – which is one reason why there are crowds of Austrians strolling around on summer weekends. The other is the town's 240 listed buildings, which allow it to claim to be "the most historic town in Hungary". The horseshoe-shaped Belváros (old town) is north of Széchenyi tér and the main train station. At the southern end, **Orsolya tér** features Renaissance edifices dripping with loggias and carved protrusions, and a Gothic church. For more atmosphere there's the *Cezár Borozó*, a cellar with oak butts and leather-aproned waiters, serving local wines and platters of wurst. Heading north towards the main square, **Új utca** (New Street – one of the town's oldest thoroughfares) is a gentle curve of arched dwellings painted in red, yellow and pink, with chunky cobblestones and pavements. At no. 22 stands one of the **synagogues** that flourished when the street was known as Zsidó utca (Jewish Street); its collection serves as a reminder that Sopron's Jewish community survived the expulsion of 1526 only to be all-but-annihilated during World War II. The main source of interest is up ahead on Fő tér, a parade of Gothic and Baroque architecture partly overshadowed by the **Goat Church** – so called, supposedly, because its construction was financed by a goatherd whose flock unearthed a cache of loot. The Renaissance **Storno House**, once visited by King Mátyás and Count Széchenyi, now exhibits Roman, Celtic and Avar relics, plus mementoes of Liszt. North of the square rises Sopron's symbol, the **Firewatch Tower** (Tues–Sat 10am–6pm; 300Ft), founded upon the stones of a fortress originally laid out by the Romans. From the top there's a stunning view of narrow streets and weathered rooftops. Offered the choice of Austrian citizenship in 1921, the townsfolk voted to remain Magyar subjects and erected a "Gate of Loyalty" at the base of the tower to commemorate this act of patriotism. Walk through it and you'll emerge onto Előkapu (outer gate), a short street where the houses are laid out in a saw-toothed pattern.

Information is at Tourinform, Előkapu 11 (May–Sept Mon–Sat 9am–6pm; Oct–April Mon–Fri 9am–4pm, Sat 9am–noon; ☎99/338-892, *sopron@tourinform.hu*). **Private rooms** can be arranged at Lokomotiv Tourist, Várkerület 90 (Mon–Fri 8.30am–4.30pm, Sat 8am–noon; ☎99/311-111, *loktur@gysev.hu*), who can also arrange student hotel accommodation in July and August, and Ciklámen Tourist, Ógabona tér 8 (Mon–Fri 8am–4pm, Sat

8am–1pm; ☎99/312-040). Of **hotels**, *Bástya Panzió*, Patak utca 40 (☎99/325-325; ②), and *Jégverem Panzió*, Jégverem utca 1 (☎99/510-113; ②), are good-value pensions just across the Ikva Stream to the northeast of town. The *Lövér* **campsite** (☎99/311-715), 4km south, is served by bus #12 hourly from Deák tér; you should book in advance through Ciklámen Tourist. There are some terrific places **to eat**, including *Várkerület Söröző*, Várkerület 83, and *Rókalyukhoz* opposite, which offers a prolific international and pizza menu. Up on Fövényverem utca, *Ameli* at no. 15 serves superb fish dishes (closed Mon), or try *Fekete Bárány* opposite. *Café Dakar*, Várkerület 86, is the place to go for cakes and coffees. To sample the local **wines**, head for the *Cezár* cellar, Orsolya tér, or *Gyógygödör Borozó*, Fő tér; both are open daily until 10pm. To Vienna, there are four **trains** a day, and a dozen Volán **buses** each week.

The Esterházy Palace

Some 27km from Sopron (hourly buses Mon–Sat) lies a monument to one of the country's most famous dynasties: the **Esterházy Palace** at Fertőd (guided tours: Tues–Sun hourly 9am–noon & 1–4/5pm; 700Ft). Originally of the minor nobility, the Esterházy family began its rise thanks to Miklós Esterházy I (1583–1645), who married two rich widows, sided with the Habsburgs, and got himself elevated to count. The palace itself was begun by his grandson, Miklós the Ostentatious, who inherited 600,000 acres and a dukedom in 1762. With its 126 rooms, fronted by a vast horseshoe courtyard where Hussars once pranced to the music of Haydn – Esterházy's resident maestro for many years – the palace was intended to rival Versailles. It now lies in a sad state of decaying splendour, but highlights of the **guided tour**, which only covers 26 of the rooms, include salons of blue and white chinoiserie, gilded rooms lined with mirrors, and a hall where concerts are held beneath a splendid fresco of Hermes, so contrived that from whichever angle you view it his chariot seems to be careering towards you across the sky. And, of course, there's also a room full of Haydn memorabilia.

The prospect of **staying in the palace** is almost irresistible – even if the accommodation is all in Socialist Realist style: rooms with shared showers are available in the east wing year-round (booking essential; ☎99/370-971; ①) and have delightful views over the neglected gardens. Alternatively, there's *Újvári Vendégház*, Kossuth utca 57/a (☎99/371-828, *www.hotels.hu/ujvari_fertod*; ②). There are a couple of **restaurants** outside the gates of the palace, but if you can arrange transport to the village of **FERTŐSZÉPLAK**, 2km west, you'll find the excellent *Polgármester Vendéglő* behind the church at Széchenyi utca 39. For **information** and a list of local accommodation, Tourinform is next to the palace at Madách sétány 1 (Mon–Fri 8am–4/6pm; June–Sept also Sat 8am–noon; ☎99/370-544, *fertod @tourinform.hu*).

Pécs

The town of **PÉCS** is one of Transdanubia's largest and most attractive towns; indeed, it lays claim to being the finest town in the country, with its tiled rooftops climbing the vine-laden slopes of the Mecsek range. And being so far south, it also tends to be a couple of degrees warmer than Budapest. Besides some fine museums, the fifth-oldest university in Europe (founded in 1367) and a great market, Pécs contains Hungary's best examples of **Islamic architecture**, a legacy of the long Ottoman occupation. Heading up Bajcsy-Zsilinszky út from the bus terminal, or by bus #30 from the train station towards the centre, you'll pass Kossuth tér and Pécs's **synagogue** (May–Oct Fri–Sun 10–11.30am & noon–4pm; 150Ft). The beautiful nineteenth-century interior is a haunting place, with Romantic frescoes swirling around space emptied by the murder of almost 4000 Jews – ten times the number that live in Pécs today. During the Ottoman occupation (1543–1686), a similar fate befell the Christian population, whose principal church was replaced by the **Mosque of Gazi Kasim Pasha** (mid-April to mid-Oct Mon–Sat 10am–4pm, Sun

12.30–4pm; rest of year Mon–Sat 10am–noon, Sun 12.30–2pm; donations) to the north on Széchenyi tér – an otherwise modern square, which is the focus for a good number of summer events and performances. Also on the square is a gallery of contemporary work by local artists and an **Archeological Museum** (Tues–Sun: April–Sept 10am–6pm; Oct–March 10am–2pm; 150Ft) displaying items testifying to a Roman presence between the first and fifth centuries. From here you can follow either Káptalan or Janus Pannonius utca towards the **Cathedral**. Though its architects have incorporated a crypt and sidechapels from eleventh- to fourteenth-century churches, the cathedral is predominantly nineteenth-century neo-Romanesque, with four spires, three naves and a lavish decor of blue and gold, with floral motifs. The site has been used for religious and funerary purposes since Roman times, and remnants of an early Christian basilica are sunk into the park-like square below Dóm tér. Behind the Bishop's Palace, a circular barbican occupies a gap in the decrepit **town walls** – once a massive rampart 5500 paces long, buttressed by 87 bastions erected after the Mongol invasion. South of the barbican, Szepessy Ignác utca slopes down to meet Rákóczi út, where grubby buildings almost conceal the sixteenth-century **Jakovali Hassan Mosque** (April–Sept daily except Wed 10am–6pm; 120Ft), with friezes and Turkish carpets adorning the cool white interior.

Practicalities

The best source of **information** is Tourinform, Széchenyi tér 9 (May–Oct Mon–Fri 8am–5.30pm, Sat & Sun 9am–2pm; Nov–April Mon–Fri 8am–4pm; ☎72/213-315, *baranyam@tourinform.hu*), with a complete list of hotels, dormitories and pensions, they don't book private rooms. Central **hotels** tend to be expensive – but see if there's space at *Fönix Hotel* just off Széchenyi tér, Hunyádi utca 2 (☎72/311-680; ②). **Private rooms** and student hostel beds from Mecsek Tours, Széchenyi tér 1 (☎72/513-370, *utir@mecsektours.hu*), or IBUSZ, Apáca utca 1 (☎72/212-157), are a better deal. Convenient for the station is the good-value *Vig Apát Hotel*, Mártirok utca 14 (☎72/313-340; ②). *Hotel Laterum* offers basic rooms west of the centre, Hajnóczy utca 37 (☎72/252-113; ①), while *Mandulás* **campsite** on the hill above town also has rooms, Ángyán János utca 2 (☎72/315-981; ②; mid-April to mid-Oct; bus #34). *Familia Privát Camping*, Gyöngyösi utca 6 (☎72/327-034), is the nearest campsite to the town centre. When it comes to eating, *Aranykacsa*, Teréz utca 4, is excellent, while wholesome Hungarian food is the order of the day at the magnificently decorated *Dóm Étterem*, Király utca 3. Similarly top-notch Hungarian cuisine is served at the classy *Fortuna Étterem*, Ferencesek utca 32. The very classy *Morik* café, on Jokai tér, is the place for coffee, and Király utca abounds with pizzerias and cafés. In summer, the beer garden of *Rózsakert* on Janus Pannonius utca is very pleasant; bars are more numerous in the western part of the Belváros, south of the centre. Pécs has its own **brewery** in Rókusalja utca, and the local beer is served up in the *Kiskorsó* restaurant there. Access the **Internet** in the relaxing café adjoining the *Fortuna* restaurant.

The **Pécs Fair**, held on the morning of the first Sunday of each month, sees some hard bargaining and hard drinking, and there are smaller flea markets on the same site every Sunday. Bus #50 runs to the market site from outside the Konzum store in Rákóczi utca; get a ticket from a newspaper stall or the train station before boarding. Pécs is also an excellent starting-point for heading to the nearby wine region of Villány to the south – for which the tourist offices can provide more information.

EASTERN HUNGARY

The hilly and forested northern region of **eastern Hungary** will not feature prominently in any hurried tour of the country, but nobody should overlook the famous wine-producing towns of **Eger** and **Tokaj**, mellow, historic places whose appeal goes beyond the local beverage.

Eger

Its colourful architecture suffused by sunshine, **EGER** seems a fitting place of origin for Egri Bikavér, the famous red wine marketed abroad as "Bull's Blood", which brings hordes of visitors to the town. Despite occasional problems with accommodation, it's a fine place to hang out and wander around, not to mention all the opportunities for drinking. There are five **trains** a day from Budapest; from the station, walk up the road to Deák Ferenc út, catch bus #10 or #12, and get off when you see the cupola of the Neoclassical **Cathedral** – József Hild's rehearsal for the still-larger basilica at Esztergom; inside the dome, the "City of God" rises triumphantly, while St Rita's shrine is cluttered with supplications and testimonials. The florid **Lyceum**, opposite the cathedral, was founded by two enlightened bishops whose proposal for a university was rejected by Maria Theresa. Now a teacher-training college (named after Ho Chi Minh during the communist era), the building is worth visiting for its **library** (April–Sept Tues–Sun 9.30am–3.30pm; Oct–March Sat & Sun 9.30–11.30am; 240Ft), whose beautiful floor and fittings are made of polished oak. There's also a huge trompe l'oeil ceiling fresco of the Council of Trent by Kracker and his son-in-law; the lightning bolt and book in one corner symbolize the Council's decision to establish an Index of forbidden books and suppress all heretical ideas. While in the building, it's definitely worth checking out the **observatory**, at the top of the tower in the east wing (same hours and ticket), where a nineteenth-century *camera obscura* projects a view of the entire town from a bird's-eye perspective: the monocled curator gleefully points out lovers kissing in the backstreets, unaware of surveillance. Close by, facing Széchenyi utca, stands the **Archbishop's Palace**, a U-shaped Baroque pile with fancy wrought-iron gates; in its right wing you'll find the treasury and a history of the bishopric of Eger (April–Oct Tues–Sat 9am–5pm; Nov–March Mon–Fri 8am–4pm; 120Ft).

Heading towards the centre you pass several tourist offices and restaurants before reaching **Dobó István tér**. With its wine bars and statues facing a stately Minorite church, the main square is a pleasant spot and the starting point for further sightseeing. Cross the bridge and head to the left to find Eger's most photographed structure, a slender fourteen-sided **minaret** (daily 9am–6pm; 100Ft), looking rather lonely without its mosque, which was demolished during a nineteenth-century building boom. Alternatively, head uphill from the square past the *Senator Ház Hotel* to the gates of the **Castle** (daily 8/9am–5/8pm; 400Ft; on Mon, admission is 300Ft, but only the underground galleries and the Hall of Heroes are open). From the bastion overlooking the main gate, a path leads up to the ticket office and the fifteenth-century Bishop's Palace. Tapestries, ceramics, Turkish handicrafts and weaponry fill the museum upstairs in the palace, while downstairs are temporary exhibits and a Hall of Heroes (Hősök terme), where a life-size marble István Dobó lies amid a bodyguard of heroes of the 1552 siege in which 2000 soldiers and Eger's women repulsed a Turkish force six times their number. From the ticket office a guide will take you into the Kazamata underground galleries, a labyrinth of sloping passageways, gun emplacements and mysterious chambers.

Practicalities and wine-tasting

For **information**, there's a Tourinform office at Dobó István tér 2 (mid-June to Aug Mon–Fri 9am–6pm, Sat & Sun 9am–1pm; rest of year Mon–Fri 9am–5pm, Sat 9am–1pm; ☎36/517-715, *www.ektf.hu/eger*). Cheapest **accommodation** is the summer student hostels; get details of these and private rooms from the tourist offices – Eger Tourist, Bajcsy-Zsilinszky utca 9 (☎36/510-270, *www.egertourist.hu*), IBUSZ, Széchenyi utca 9 (☎36/311-451, *eger@iroda.ibusz.hu*), and Express, Széchenyi utca 28 (☎36/427-757). Along from the castle is the *Tourist Motel*, Mekcsey utca 2 (☎36/429-014; ①). For more comfort, try *Hotel Minaret*, Harangöntő utca 5 (☎36/410-020, *hotelminaret@matavnet.hu*; ③), or the classier

Senator Ház Hotel, Dobó István tér 11 (☎36/320-466, *www.hotels.hu/senatorhaz*; ④). There are two **campsites**: *Autós Caraván Camping* to the north, Rákóczi út 79 (☎36/410-558; mid-April to mid-Oct; bus #10/#11), and *Tulipán* in the Szépasszony Valley (☎36/410-580). Two of the best **restaurants** are *Efendi*, Kossuth utca 19, and *Vadásztanya*, Klapka utca 8; *Kopcsik*, Kossuth utca 28, and *Dobos*, Széchenyi utca 6, are two elegant patisseries.

Local vineyards produce four types of **wine** – Muskotály (Muscatel), Bikavér (Bull's Blood), Leányka (medium-dry white with a hint of herbs) and Medoc Noir (rich, dark and sweet red), all of which can be sampled in the cellars of the **Szépasszony Valley** (Valley of Beautiful Women) just west of town (around 800Ft by taxi). Finding the right cellar is a matter of luck and taste; try Medoc Noir in Sándor Arvai's cellar at no. 31, and the old wines of János Birincsik at no. 32. Cellars tend to close by 8pm and getting a taxi back into town can be a challenge; tackling the twenty-minute walk is easier than arranging a pickup with a taxi. Later hours are kept in town, where the **Wine Museum**, Városfal utca 1, gives you the chance to sample the stuff (Tues–Sat until 10pm).

Tokaj

TOKAJ is to Hungary what Champagne is to France, and this small town has become a place of pilgrimage for wine lovers. Perched beside the confluence of the rivers Bodrog and Tisza, Tokaj is a place of sloping cobbled streets and faded ochre dwellings with nesting storks and wine cellars, overlooked by lush vineyards climbing the hillside towards the "Bald Peak" and its TV tower. The old town centre is fifteen minutes' walk left out of the station and left under the bridge. It has a few architectural sights – the old Town Hall and Rákóczi-Dessewffy mansion, the large half-restored synagogue and Jewish cemetery (reminders of the large Jewish population that lived here till the Holocaust), and a ruined castle by the river – but the wine is the big draw. **Tokaj wines** derive their character from the local soil, the prolonged sunlight and the wine-making techniques developed here. The two main grape varieties are Furmint and Hárslevelű (linden leaf). While these are used to make straight wines, what gets most of the attention are the special **golden wines** bottled in characteristic short, stubby bottles: Szamorodni (a word of Polish origin meaning "as it comes"), which can be dry or sweet, and the much sweeter Aszú. Heat is trapped by the volcanic soil, allowing a delayed harvest in October, when many over-ripe grapes have a sugar content approaching sixty percent. Their juice and pulp is added to barrels of ordinary grapes, the volume of the addition determining the qualities of the wine. The **Tokaj Museum**, Bethlen Gábor utca 7 (Tues–Sun 9am–3/5pm; 250Ft), has an excellent local history exhibition, recalling the strong Jewish and Greek presence that used to dominate the town. The favourite place for oenophiles is the **Rákóczi cellar** in the centre of the town at Kossuth tér 15 (daily 8am–noon & 12.30–7pm), but you can get more personal service in the small private cellars that line the hill, for example at the friendly Himesudvar, Bem utca 2, a former hunting lodge five minutes' walk up from the square.

All the **information** you need about Tokaj and the surrounding wine villages is at Tourinform, Serház utca 1 (☎47/353-390, *tokaj@tourinform.hu*). **Private rooms** are available through Tokaj Tours next door (☎47/353-323). Also worth trying are the *Kollégium*, Bajcsy-Zsilinszky utca 15–17 (☎47/352-355; June–Aug; ①); *Lux Panzió*, Serház utca 14 (☎47/352-533, *www.hotels.hu/lux_tokaj*; ②); and *Hotel Tokaj*, Rákóczi utca 5 (☎47/352-344; ②), a hideous building but with rooms offering an excellent view over the river. At the north end of the town, *Torkolat Panzió*, Vasvari utca 26 (☎47/352-827; ②), loans bikes and canoes to guests free of charge; for non-residents, bikes cost 1000Ft a day. There are two **campsites**, *Tisza* and *Pelsöczi*, opposite each other on the far side of the river, plus *Unió Vízitelep* up the river at Bodrogkeresztúri út 5. For **eating**, try *Róna Étterem* on Bethlen Gábor utca, or *Hotel Tokaj*, both of which serve up reasonable fare.

travel details

Trains

Budapest to: Balatonfüred (every 1–2hr; 2hr 15min); Esztergom (every 40min; 1hr 20min); Pécs (10 daily; 2hr 30min–3hr); Sopron (8 daily; 2hr 50min); Szentendre (every 15–30min; 45min); Tokaj (3 direct daily; 2hr 30min–3hr).

Buses

Budapest to: Balatonfüred (2 daily); Eger (hourly from the Népstadion bus station); Esztergom from the Árpád híd bus station via the Danube Bend (hourly) or via Dorog (every 30min); Hévíz (2 daily); Keszthely (2 daily); Sopron (4 daily); Szeged (5 daily); Szentendre from the Árpád híd bus station (every 30min–1hr); Visegrád from the Árpád híd bus station (hourly).

Badacsony to: Keszthely (hourly).

Balatonfüred to: Tihany (hourly).

Esztergom to: Visegrád (hourly).

Keszthely to: Hévíz (every 30min).

Szentendre to: Esztergom & Visegrád (hourly).

Visegrád to: Esztergom (hourly).

Ferries

(Operating April–Oct or Nov, as weather permits, with more running June–Aug.)

Budapest to: Esztergom (1–2 daily; 5hr 20min); Szentendre (1–3 daily; 1hr 40min); Visegrád (2–4 daily; 3hr 20min).

Esztergom to: Budapest (1–2 daily; 4hr); Szentendre (June–Aug 2 daily; 3hr).

Hydrofoils

Budapest to: Esztergom (June–Aug 2 at weekends; 1hr 20min); Vienna (April–Oct 1–2 daily; 6hr 20min); Visegrád (June–Aug 1 at weekends; 50min).

CHAPTER 14

IRELAND

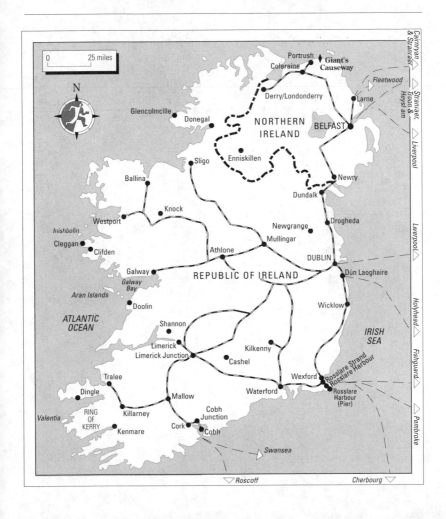

0 25 miles

N

Cairnryan & Stranraer ▷
Stranraer, Troon & Heysl am ▷
△ Fleetwood
▷ Liverpool

Portrush ◆ Giant's Causeway
Coleraine
Derry/Londonderry
Larne
Glencolmcille
Donegal
NORTHERN IRELAND
BELFAST
Sligo
Enniskillen
Ballina
Newry
Knock
Dundalk
Drogheda
Westport
Newgrange
Inishbofin
Mullingar
Cleggan
Clifden
Athlone
DUBLIN
Galway
REPUBLIC OF IRELAND
Dún Laoghaire
Galway Bay
Aran Islands
Doolin
Wicklow
ATLANTIC OCEAN
Shannon
IRISH SEA
Limerick
Kilkenny
Limerick Junction
Cashel
Tralee
Wexford
Dingle
Mallow
Waterford
Rosslare Strand
Rosslare Harbour
Valentia
RING OF KERRY
Killarney
Cobh Junction
Rosslare Harbour (Pier)
Kenmare
Cork
Cobh

△ Liverpool
Liverpool ▷
Holyhead ▷
Fishguard ▷
Pembroke ▷

Swansea ▷

▽ Roscoff   Cherbourg ▽

Introduction

Ireland's attractions are its landscape and people – both in the **Republic** (aka the South) and **Northern Ireland** (aka the North). Few visitors are disappointed by the reality of the stock Irish images: the green, rain-hazed loughs and wild, bluff coastlines, the inspired talent for conversation, the easy pace of life and wealth of traditional music. For although Ireland's urban centres, especially Dublin, have undergone a remarkable economic transformation based on high-tech industry in the last decade, the rural landscape remains unchanged. It's a place to explore slowly, roaming through agricultural pastures scattered with farmhouses, or along the endlessly indented coastline. In town, too, the pleasures are unhurried: evenings over Guinnesses in the snug of a pub, listening to the chat around a turf fire.

Especially in the Irish-speaking Gaeltacht areas, you'll be aware of the strength and continuity of the island's **oral tradition**. The speech of the country, moulded by the rhythms of the ancient tongue, has fired such twentieth-century greats as Yeats, Joyce, Beckett and Heaney. **Music**, too, has always been at the centre of Irish community life, and you can expect to find traditional music sessions in the pubs of all towns of any size and along the west coast. Side by side with this is a romping rock scene that has spawned Van Morrison, U2, Sinead O'Connor and The Corrs.

The area that draws most visitors is the **west coast**, whose northern reaches are characterized by the demonically daunting peninsulas and the mystical lakes and glens of **Donegal**. The midwest coastline and its offshore islands – especially the **Aran Islands** – are just as attractive, combining vertiginous cliffs, boulder-strewn wastes and violent mountains. In the south, the melodramatic peaks of the **Ring of Kerry** fall to lake-pools and seductive seascapes, while in the North the principal draw is the bizarre basalt formation of the **Giant's Causeway**. The **interior** is less spectacular, but the southern pastures and low wooded hills, and the wide peat bogs of the midlands, are the classic landscapes of Ireland. Of the **inland waterways**, the most alluring is the island-studded **Lough Erne**, easily reached from Enniskillen.

For anyone with strictly limited time, one of the best options is to combine a visit to **Dublin** with the mountains and monastic ruins of County Wicklow. Dublin is an extraordinary mix of youthfulness and tradition, of rejuvenated Georgian squares and vibrant pubs. **Belfast**, victim of a perennial bad press, vies with Dublin in the vitality of its nightlife, while the cities of **Cork** and **Galway** in particular have a rediscovered energy about them.

No introduction can cope with the complexities of Ireland's **politics**, which permeate every aspect of daily life, most visibly in the North. Suffice it to say that, regardless of partisan politics, Irish hospitality is as warm as the brochures say, on both sides of the border.

Information and maps

Tourist information in the Republic is handled by **Bord Fáilte**, in the North by the **Northern Ireland Tourist Board**. You'll find branches of one or the other almost anywhere that has a reasonable number of visitors, and they'll frequently be able to help in finding accommodation.

The best **road maps** are the Michelin 1:400,000 (#405) or the AA 1:350,000. The four Ordnance Survey 1:250,000 regional Holiday Maps are useful, but their 1:50,000 Discovery series are generally the best option for walkers. For areas high in archeological interest, it's worth buying locally produced specialist maps, such as the Folding Landscapes series for Connemara, the Burren and the Aran Islands.

Money and banks

The **Republic of Ireland** is one of twelve European Union countries which have changed over to a single currency, the **euro** (€). Euro notes and coins are

---

scheduled to be issued from January 1, 2002, with Irish pounds (or punts; £) remaining in circulation during a transition period, at a fixed rate of £0.787564 to €1, until they are scrapped entirely on February 9, 2002. After this date you will still be able to exchange your pounds for euros in banks for at least a year. Euro notes are issued in **denominations** of 5, 10, 20, 50, 100, 200 and 500 euros, and coins in denominations of 1, 2, 5, 10, 20 and 50 cents and 1 and 2 euros. Standard **bank hours** in the Republic are Mon–Fri 10am–4pm and most have late opening on Thursday until 5pm. In less populated areas banks may close for one hour at lunchtime and, in some cases, may only be open certain days of the week, so it makes sense to change money in the large towns. All prices in the section of this chapter dealing with the Republic are given in euros, correct at the time of going to press – but there will no doubt be some rounding off (or, more probably, up) of prices in the first few months after the introduction of the euro.

In **Northern Ireland** the currency is, and will remain for the foreseeable future, the British pound sterling (£), divided into 100 pence. In the main towns, most banks are open Mon–Fri 9.30am–4.30pm; some may open longer and on Saturdays. Elsewhere they may close 12.30–1.30pm, and in small villages the bank may not be open every day.

There are cash dispensers (**ATMs**) throughout the island – though not in all villages – and most accept a variety of cards.

Communications

Main **post offices** are open Mon–Fri 9am–5.30pm, Sat 9am–1pm. Stamps are sometimes available in newsagents and in shops selling postcards. You can make domestic and international calls from **pay phones** and **card phones** throughout Ireland (it's worth carrying a phonecard, since coin-operated phones are rare in rural areas). Off-peak rate for most international calls is after 6pm on weekdays, and all day at weekends. The **operator** in the Republic is ☎10 (domestic) or ☎114 (international); in Northern Ireland, it's ☎100/☎155. Expect a hefty price-hike for phoning from a hotel. All phone numbers in **Northern Ireland** comprise the UK area code ☎028 plus an eight-digit local number; if you're calling Northern Ireland from the Republic, you need to use a different ☎048 code as a prefix to the eight-digit number.

Internet access is widely available. All cities are well served by cybercafés, and smaller towns and villages have Internet booths in post offices, youth hostels, supermarkets and even a few pubs. Expect to pay around €8 or £4/hr. There's a list of Irish cybercafés at *www.iica.net*.

Getting around

Public transport in the Republic – run by state-supported train and bus companies – is reliable, but infrequent and slow; never assume that two nearby towns are necessarily going to be connected. Transport in the North is rather more efficient.

■ Trains and travel passes

In the **Republic**, Irish Rail *(Iarnród Éireann)* operates **trains** to most major towns and cities, and on direct lines it's by far the fastest way of covering long distances. In general, lines fan out from Dublin, with few routes running north–south across the country, so, although you can get to the west easily by train, you can't use the railways to explore the west coast. The Dublin–Belfast Enterprise trains comprise the only **cross-border service** between the Republic and the North.

Train travel is by no means cheap, so you should plump where possible for off-peak fares: the system is complicated, and it's always worth asking about any special deals. In the Republic, the **InterRail** pass entitles foreigners (including UK citizens) to unlimited free travel, while Irish citizens travel half-price; in Northern Ireland, InterRailing foreigners (except Irish citizens) travel free, while UK citizens get a 75-percent discount. ISIC card holders can buy a Travelsave stamp from any USIT office (€10.20 in the Republic, £6 in the North) giving discounts of up to a third off standard train and bus fares. The **Irish Explorer** pass covers rail travel in the Republic (€91.40 for five days' travel out of fifteen), while the **Rover** pass covers rail travel in all of Ireland (€114.30 for five days out of fifteen). The **Explorer** pass covers rail and bus travel in the Republic (€135.90 for eight days out of fifteen). The **Freedom of Northern Ireland** pass covers rail and bus travel in the province (£11 for one day; £40 for a week). The **Emerald Card** covers rail and bus services in all of Ireland (€157.50 for eight days out of fifteen). You can buy passes at all mainline stations; those which cover the whole island are available in the Republic and the North, while those specific to either region are only available in their home area.

For train timetables, check *www.irishrail.ie* for the Republic, *www.nirailways.co.uk* for the North.

■ Buses

Routings can be complex and slow on the Republic's national **bus** service – Dublin Bus in the capital *(www.dublinbus.ie)*, **Bus Éireann** elsewhere *(www.buseireann.ie)*. Fares are generally far lower than the train, especially in midweek. If you are going to be using buses a lot it makes sense to get a free **timetable** from any major bus station; remote villages may only have a couple of buses a week, so knowing when they run is essential. For buses within the Republic there are various **Rambler** passes (€40.60 for three days out of eight, for example), as well as **Rover** tickets that cover Northern Ireland as well (€53.30 for three days out of eight). **Private buses**, which operate on many major routes, are often cheaper than the national services, and sometimes faster – watch for local advertisements. They're very busy at weekends, so it makes sense to book ahead; during the week you can usually pay on the bus. Prices for parts of their journeys are often negotiable, and bikes can sometimes be carried if booked with your seat. Note that travel passes aren't valid on private buses.

In the North, **Ulsterbus** *(www.ulsterbus.co.uk)* runs regular and reliable services, particularly to towns not served by the rail network, with Citybus operating within Belfast.

■ Driving and hitching

Main roads in the **Republic**, especially around Dublin, can be busy at peak times. However, once in the countryside, roads are remarkably uncongested, making driving a very relaxing option – but watch out for unmarked junctions, appalling minor roads, and unlit cycles late at night. Beware for passing lanes or slow lanes, indicated by a broken yellow line: you are expected to pull over to the left to let someone overtake. As in Britain you drive **on the left**. The metric system is taken with a pinch of salt: while distances are usually marked in km, people will give you directions in miles, and speed limits are posted in mph: 30–40mph in town, 50mph outside and 70mph on motorways. All roadsigns, except in some *Gaeltacht* areas, are bilingual Irish–English. In case of breakdown, contact the Irish AA (☎1800/667788; members only).

Roads in the **North** are noticeably better-maintained than those in the Republic. Rules of the road are as in Britain, with speed limits and distances posted in miles. In case of breakdown, contact the AA (☎0800/887766) or RAC (☎0800/828282; both members only).

International **car rental** companies have outlets in the Republic at all major cities, airports and ferry terminals: costs are from around €220–285 a week, although smaller local firms can almost always offer better deals, and booking in advance can produce huge discounts. It's worth shopping round. In the North, expect to pay around £170–240 a week. Companies generally insist you have held a full, clean licence for two years, and most won't rent cars to under-21s or over-75s. Renting a car in the Republic and dropping it off in Northern Ireland will incur a hefty "drop-off" fee from most companies, but as long as you return it to the Republic, there's no extra fee for crossing the border in a rental car.

The **Republic** is one of the easiest European countries in which to **hitch**, though, as always, it's not advisable for women travelling alone. Men and women travelling together are at least in with a chance of a lift, but men travelling alone or in pairs may be viewed with suspicion, and may even find getting a ride impossible. Aside from this, the chief problem is the lack of traffic, especially off the main roads. If you are travelling around the tourist-swamped west you may come across a reluctance to pick up non-locals. In the **North**, by contrast, the best way to hitch is to make sure you look like a tourist – but even then, it's never easy. Getting a lift across the border can be difficult.

■ Cycling

If you're lucky enough to get decent weather, **cycling** is one of the most enjoyable ways to see Ireland. It's easy and relatively cheap to **rent a bike** in most towns in the Republic, and at a limited number of places in the North. You can't take a rental bike across the border. Raleigh is the biggest national operator (about €13 per day, €51 per week plus a deposit of around €50; for your nearest outlet call them in Dublin on ☎01/626 1333), but local dealers (including some hostels) are often less expensive. In the North, tourist offices have lists of local operators; prices are around £10 per day. If you arrive with your own bike, it costs you an extra €7.60 to carry it on each bus journey, or €2.50–7.60 on a one-way train journey in the Republic, though not all buses or trains have the capacity to carry bikes; check in advance. Taking a bike on a train in the North adds 25 percent to the price of each journey.

Accommodation

Though **camping** is obviously the cheapest way to sleep, in Ireland it can be hampered by tricky terrain and the possibility of continual rain. Next up in price,

hostels vary a lot, but all offer the essential basics, and some are very good indeed. Above these come bed and breakfasts (B&Bs), guest houses and **hotels**, usually registered with and graded by the tourist boards.

■ B&Bs and hotels

In the Republic, the least expensive form of comfortable accommodation is a **bed and breakfast**. They vary enormously, but most are welcoming, warm and clean, with huge breakfasts. Registered B&Bs are generally pretty good, though registration with a tourist board is not an absolute guarantee. Expect to pay from around €23 per person (€20 for non-registered houses); those with en-suite facilities are usually a little more expensive. For an extra €1–4/£1–3, you can book at a registered B&B through tourist offices or by phoning international toll-free ☎+800/668 668 66, or ☎1800/668 668 in the Republic, or ☎0800/783 5740 in the North. Even the lowliest regular **hotels** are generally pricier, though small village hotels can cost about the same as private B&Bs. B&B accommodation is expanding in the North, but you will probably need to ring ahead if you want to guarantee a bed during the summer months.

■ Hostels

Hostels run by **An Óige** (the Irish Youth Hostel Association) and **HINI** (Hostelling International Northern Ireland) are like youth hostels throughout Europe: some close during the daytime and have evening curfews. This is the official line, but in fact, you'll find many are more flexible than the rule book would suggest, particularly in out-of-the-way places. IYHA membership (€12.70) is required at all hostels, and overnight fees for members start at €7 in the country, €12 in Dublin and larger cities. In the North, HINI membership is £10; overnight costs are £8–12. Get full lists of places and prices from An Óige, 61

Mountjoy St, Dublin 7 (☎01/830 4555, *www.irelandyha.org*) and HINI, 22 Donegall Rd, Belfast BT12 5JN (☎028/9031 5435, *www.hini.org.uk*).

Across the island, **independent hostels** are often more interesting places to stay, as each reflects the character and interests of its owner, and some are tucked away in beautiful countryside. Very often the atmosphere is cosy and informal: you can stay in all day if you want and there are no curfews or chores, though some hostels cram people in to the point of discomfort. **Independent Holiday Hostels** (☎01/836 4700, *www.hostels-ireland.com*) has a list. It is worth using their book-ahead system during high season; although most won't let you book over the phone, some may reserve you a bed up to a certain time in the early evening. Other hostels may be members of the **Independent Hostels Ireland** network (☎073/30130, *www.holidayhound.com/ihi*). In tourist hot spots, you may be hassled by hostel touts at railway stations; there are a very small number of dangerous and disreputable hostels around, so it's a good idea to check the *Rough Guide* or ask around locally before booking in at a non-approved hostel. Expect to pay around €10 for a dorm bed (more in Galway, Cork and Dublin), €13–20 per person for private rooms where available; in the North, £8–12 for a dorm bed, £14–18 per person for a private room.

■ Camping

The cost of **camping** varies, but is usually about €4–8 a night in the Republic, £8 in the North. In out-of-the-way places nobody minds where you pitch; the only place in the Republic where you definitely can't camp is in state forests, though the North's forest parks contain some of its best campsites. Farmers in heavily touristed areas may ask for a small contribution to use their land, but other than this you can expect to camp for free in areas where there's no official site. Some hostels will also let you camp on their land for around €5/£4.

Food and drink

Although Ireland has no great tradition of **eating out**, the island has undergone a major transformation during the 1990s and you will now find a wide choice of sophisticated cuisine in most towns and resorts. In smaller, rural places, the food you'll find as a traveller will tend to be simple and hearty, though you'll often be surprised at the quality on offer, even in the remotest places.

■ Food

Irish **food** is highly meat-orientated. If you're staying in B&Bs you can expect a hearty "traditional" **Irish breakfast** of sausages, bacon and eggs, although a growing number of establishments now offer vegetarian alternatives. **Pub lunch** staples are usually meat or fish and two veg; in larger areas the menu will include a few veggie options. In cities and large towns there is generally a good variety of cuisine, with strong international influences – particularly Mediterranean – in much of the fare on offer, even in the simplest establishments, but wholefood and vegetarian restaurants or cafés are thin on the ground outside Dublin, Galway, Cork, Belfast and some of the more tourist-influenced areas in the west and southwest. The **fast-food** revolution has brought kebabs and burgers to every town of any size, but old-fashioned fish-and-chips are a better bet, especially in coastal towns. For the occasional binge, there are some very good **seafood** restaurants, particularly along the southwest and west coast, serving fresh catch-of-the-day, often with home-grown vegetables. Irish **oysters** are the country's most refined and celebrated culinary treat. Outside the urban centres, most towns have daytime **cafés** serving a selection of hot dishes, salads, soup, sandwiches and cakes. Hotels are usually a good bet for a sandwich and a cup of coffee at any reasonable hour; you can generally order a plate of sandwiches and a pot of tea in pubs, too.

■ Drink

To travel through Ireland without visiting a **pub** would be to miss out on a huge chunk of Irish life. Especially in rural areas, the pub is the social heart of the community, and often the political and cultural centre, too. Talking is an important business here, and drink is the great lubricant of social discourse. In major cities you'll find pubs heaving with life, and out in remote country villages it can be great fun drinking among the fig rolls and trifle sponges of the grocery-shops-cum-bars you'll find dotted around. It is in pubs that you'll most often find the proverbial **craic** (pronounced "crack"), a particular blend of Irish fun involving good company, witty conversation and laughter, frequently against a backdrop of drink and music. **Pub opening hours** in the Republic are Mon–Wed 10.30am–11.30pm, Thurs–Sat 10.30am–12.30am, Sun 12.30–11pm; and in the North Mon–Sat 11am–11pm, Sun 12.30–10pm. Many pubs, both North and South, have late licences on certain nights until 1am.

The classic Irish drink is, of course, **Guinness**, which, as anybody will tell you, is simply not the same as anything called Guinness you may have sampled outside Ireland. It's best in Dublin, home of the brewery. Ordering "a Guinness" means a pint; if you want a half-pint of any beer, ask for "a glass". Other local stouts, such as Beamish and Murphy's, make for interesting comparison: they all have their faithful adherents. If you want a pint of English-style keg alc, or **bitter**, try Smithwicks, which is not so different from what you'd get in an English pub. As everywhere, of course, fizzy **lager** is increasingly popular: most common are Carlsberg, Heineken and Budweiser, though more exotic continental brews are also available. Whatever your tipple, you're likely to find drinking in Ireland an expensive business at around €3.10 a pint, and up to €3.80 in Dublin. Irish **whiskeys** also seem expensive, but the measures are large: try Paddy's, Jameson, Powers or Bushmills (the last distilled in the North).

Opening hours and holidays

Business and shop **opening hours**, both North and South, are approximately Mon–Sat 9am–6pm, with a smattering of late openings (usually Thurs or Fri), half-days and Sunday opening. In the Republic, particularly away from the bigger towns, hours are much more flexible, with later closing times. There's no rigid pattern to the opening and closing of **museums** and the like, though most are closed at least one day a week, often Monday, and some close between 1 and 2pm. The bigger attractions will normally be open regular shop hours, while smaller places may open only in the afternoon. Many sites away from the main tourist trails are open only during the peak summer months.

Public holidays are: in the **Republic**, Jan 1; St Patrick's Day (March 17); Easter Monday; May 6; June 3; Aug 5; Oct 28; Dec 25 & 26. In the **North**, Jan

1; St Patrick's Day (March 17); Easter Monday; May 6 & 27; July 12; Aug 26; Dec 25 & 26.

Emergencies

In the Republic, people generally have a healthy indifference to law and red tape, perhaps in part a vestige of pre-Independence days, when any dealings with the police smacked of collusion with the British. The **police** – known as the **Gardaí** (pronounced "gar-dee") – accordingly have a low profile. If you have any dealings with them at all, you'll find them affable enough.

In Northern Ireland, the **RUC** (Royal Ulster Constabulary) deals with all general civic policing. The North is subject to UK law and is heavily policed, with several "emergency measures" permanently in effect. Despite a gradual relaxation in security measures you may occasionally find yourself being quizzed about where you are going, what you are doing, and so forth, especially in border areas. Be co-operative and polite and you should have no difficulties. Again, whatever their reputation, you'll find that the RUC are helpful enough in matters of everyday police activity.

Hospitals and medical facilities are of a high standard; you'll rarely be far from a hospital, and both Northern Ireland and the Republic are within the E111 scheme. Even the most remote rural areas will have a local doctor on 24-hour call. Most **pharmacies** are open standard shop hours, though in large towns some may stay open as late as 10pm, but pharmacists can dispense only a limited range of drugs without a doctor's prescription.

Emergency Numbers

☎999 for all emergencies, in North and South.

DUBLIN AND AROUND

Clustered on the banks of the River Liffey, **DUBLIN** is splendidly monumental, but it's also a youthful city. Of roughly one and a half million people in greater Dublin, about half are under 25, with the drift of population from the countryside continuing. The highly vibrant economy (referred to as the "Celtic Tiger") has resulted in extensive urban regeneration, but as well as seeing new buildings everywhere you're also likely to witness deprivation as bad as any in Europe. It's the collision of the old and the new, the slick and the tawdry, that makes Dublin the exciting, aggravating, energetic place it is.

Dublin really began as a Viking trading post called Dubh Linn (Dark Pool), which soon amalgamated with a Celtic settlement called **Baile Átha Cliath** (Town of the Hurdle Ford) – which is still the Irish name for the city. Because most of the early city was built of wood, only the two cathedrals, part of the castle and several churches have survived from before the seventeenth century. The fabric of the city dates essentially from the **Georgian** period, when the Anglo-Irish gentry began to invest their income in new townhouses. After the Act of Union Dublin entered a long economic decline, but it was the focus of much of the agitation that eventually led to independence. In 1829 Daniel O'Connell secured a limited role for Catholics in the administration of the city, and Dublin was later the birthplace of the Gaelic League, which encouraged the formation of an Irish national consciousness by nurturing the native language and culture. The long struggle for independence came to a head as open warfare hit the streets during the **Easter Rising** of 1916, a rebellion commemorated by a host of monuments in Dublin.

Arrival and information

Trains from Cork, Waterford, Limerick, Killarney, Tralee, Athlone, Galway, Westport and Ballina arrive at **Heuston Station** on the South Side of the city; trains from Belfast, Sligo, Wexford and Rosslare Harbour come into **Connolly Station** on the North Side. **Buses** from all parts of the Republic and Northern Ireland arrive at **Busáras**, the central bus station off Beresford Place, just behind the Customs House and within easy walking distance of O'Connell Street. From the **airport**, six miles north, the official airlink bus #747 or #748 (information ☎01/873 4222) runs to Busáras (every 10min; €4.40; takes 30min), and the privately run Aircoach serves the main shopping areas and hotels (every 15min; €5.10; ☎01/844 7118), or you can take a taxi (€19; takes 20min). **Boats** dock at either **Dún Laoghaire** (for Stena Line services), six miles south, connected to the centre by the **DART** (Dublin Area Rapid Transport; takes 20min), or at the closer **Dublin Port** (served by Irish Ferries; bus #53 into town) – although through-coaches from Britain usually drop you at Busáras.

Dublin's main **tourist office** is in a converted church on Suffolk St, off Dame St (July & Aug Mon–Sat 8.30am–6.30pm, Sun 10.30am–3pm; rest of year Mon–Sat 9.30am–5.30pm; *www.visitdublin.com*). There are other branches at 14 Upper O'Connell St; Dún Laoghaire; and the airport. Their accommodation service (☎1800/668 668) costs €3.80 per booking. The **USIT** office on Aston Quay, near O'Connell Bridge on the south side (Mon–Fri 9am–5.30pm, Sat 10am–1pm; ☎01/677 8117), also books B&Bs during the summer, and has its own hostel and a travel agency offering student discounts on ferries and flights. For what's-on **listings**, see the free *Dublin Event Guide* or *In Dublin* (€2.50, *www.indublin.ie*), or, for music events, *Hot Press* (€2.50, *www.hotpress.com*).

City transport

Dublin has an extensive and reasonably priced **bus** network that makes it easy to hop around – but without a pass, you'll need lots of change, as all buses are exact-fare-only. The maximum fare is €1.90, a one-day bus pass is €4.40, or there are bus and rail passes (including DART)

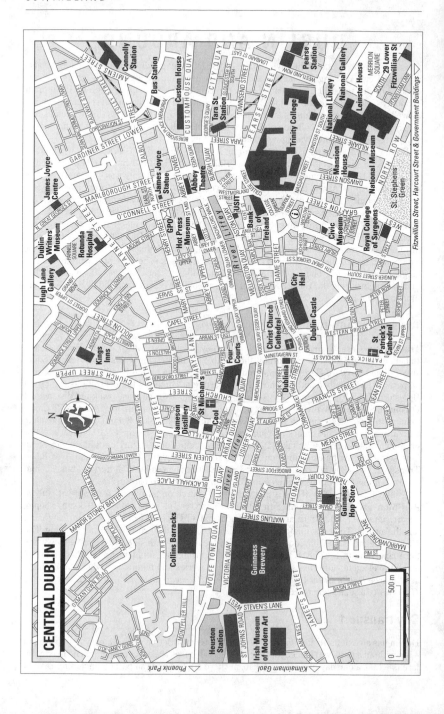

CENTRAL DUBLIN

for one day/four days (€6.60/€12.70). Students pay €12.70 for a seven-day travel pass. Orientation may prove a problem, as there's often no indication at the stops of where the buses go. Either ask an inspector – there usually seems to be one around – or invest in a bus timetable (€1.90 from Dublin Bus, 59 Upper O'Connell St). The **DART** links Howth to the north of the city with Bray to the south (maximum fare €3). **Taxis** wait at ranks in central locations, such as outside the Shelbourne Hotel on St Stephen's Green, or along the Quays near the O'Connell Bridge; however, demand far outstrips supply and it's virtually impossible to find one late at night. Many people resort to the network of **Nitelink** buses, which cost €3.80 or €5.70 depending on your destination.

Accommodation

Although Dublin has lots of **accommodation** in all price ranges, anywhere central is liable to be full at weekends year-round, and also full during the week over Easter and in high summer. Finding a bed may also be difficult around St Patrick's Day (March 17) and on the days of major sporting and musical events, so it's always wise to **book ahead** (at least two weeks). **Hotels** are generally expensive, and often no more comfortable than good **guesthouses**, but out-of-season reductions can be considerable; the tourist office in Suffolk St has a list of recommended accommodation. Most of the better **B&Bs** are in the suburbs, but this isn't such a problem, given the good public transport. The **hostel** booking service, *Irelandfound,* is at 10 Lower Abbey St (daily 9am–9pm; ☎01/856 1211; €1.90 booking fee).

Hostels

Abbey Court, O'Connell Bridge, 29 Bachelors Walk (☎01/878 0700, *info@abbey-court.com*). Close to the heart of the city, with all rooms ensuite. Breakfast is included. Dorms ③, doubles ④.

Abraham House, 82 Lower Gardiner St (☎01/855 0600). Large, well-run complex with en-suite and shared facilities. Kitchen and laundry. Dorms ③, doubles ④.

Ashfield House, 19–20 D'Olier St (☎01/679 7734, *ashfield@indigo.ie*). Handily located near Trinity College. Clean and spacious, all ensuite, plus a kitchen. Dorms ③, doubles ⑥.

Avalon House, 55 Aungier St (☎01/475 0001, *www.avalon-house.ie*). Impressive Victorian building 5min from St Stephen's Green. Cramped dorms and twin or four-bedded rooms, sharing unisex bathrooms. Friendly and noisy, with a good café. Dorms ③, doubles ⑤.

Barnacles Temple Bar House, 19 Temple Lane (☎01/671 6277, *www.barnacles.ie*). Modern place in the heart of Temple Bar. All rooms en-suite, continental breakfast included. Dorms ③, doubles ④.

Brewery Hostel, 22–23 Thomas St (☎01/453 8600, *brewery@indigo.ie*). Housed in a fine converted library not far from the Guinness Brewery – a less fashionable area, so often has space when other hostels are full. Also secure parking. Dorms ②, doubles ④.

Globetrotters Tourist Hotel, 46 Lower Gardiner St (☎01/874 0592, *gtrotter@indigo.ie*). Upmarket hostel where security-locked dorms and individual bed lights make for a peaceful night's sleep. Great breakfasts. Dorms ③, doubles ⑨.

Kinlay House, 2–12 Lord Edward St (☎01/679 6644, *kinlay_dublin@usitworld.com*). Bright and cheerful USIT hostel near Christ Church Cathedral. Doubles, quadruples and six-bed dorms with en-suite facilities. Café, laundry facilities and kitchen. Dorms ③, doubles ④.

Litton Lane, 2–4 Litton Lane (☎01/872 8389, *www.irish-hostel.com*). Situated off Bachelor's Walk on the north side, in a converted warehouse that was once a major recording studio. The showers are excellent and there are no problems with security. Open 24hr. Dorms ③, doubles ⑤.

Mount Eccles Court, 42 North Great George's St (☎01/873 0826, *info@eccleshostel.com*). A splendid converted house in what may be the North Side's finest Georgian street. Great kitchen, helpful staff, and breakfast included. Dorms ③, doubles ④.

Guesthouses, B&Bs and hotels

Bewley's Hotel, 19–20 Fleet St (☎01/670 8122, *www.bewleysprincipalhotel.com*). Comfy, cosy hotel on the edge of Temple Bar, bearing the name of Dublin's famous chain of cafés. Breakfast is extra. ⑨.

Carmel House, 16 Upper Gardiner St (☎01/874 1639). Modern guesthouse with nine en-suite rooms, close to all amenities. ⑥.

Clifden House, 32 Gardiner Place (☎01/874 6364). Friendly guesthouse in a slightly run-down Georgian street close to both the city centre and Busáras. Fourteen en-suite rooms, and a warm welcome. ⑥.

Harcourt Hotel, 60 Harcourt St (☎01/478 3677). In a Georgian terrace just off the southwest corner of St Stephen's Green, this comfortable hotel is famous for its regular Irish music sessions. Breakfast included. ⑨.

Harding Hotel, Copper Alley, Fishamble St (☎01/679 6500, *www.iol.ie/usitaccm*). Attractive USIT-run hotel beside the *Kinlay House* hostel. All rooms ensuite. Café, bar and pool tables. ⑨.

Marian Guesthouse, 21 Upper Gardiner St (☎01/874 4129). Friendly, good-value guesthouse. ④.

Campsites

Camac Valley Caravan and Camping Park, Corkegh Regional Park, off the Naas Rd, Clondalkin (☎01/464 0644). Pleasant site with views of the Dublin Mountains. Bus #68, #68A or #69.

Shankill (☎01/282 0011). Close to the DART stop at Shankill – or take bus #45, #45A or #84 from the city centre.

The City

A healthy rivalry exists between Dublin's North and South sides. The fashionable **South Side** can lay claim to the city's trendy bars, restaurants and shops, especially in the cobbled alleys of buzzing **Temple Bar** leading down to the river, and most of its historic monuments, centred on **Trinity College**, **Grafton Street** and **St Stephen's Green**. But the **North Side**, with its long-standing working-class neighbourhoods and inner-city communities, vaunts itself as the real heart of the city. Across the bridges from Temple Bar are the shopping districts around **O'Connell Street**, where you'll find a taste of the old Dublin, particularly along **Moore Street** where traders ply their wares in melodic tones. You'll also find here a fair amount of graceful – if slightly shabby – residential streets and squares, with plenty of interest in the museums and cultural centres around **Parnell Square**. In the North Side in particular, you should be wary of straying off the main streets after dark.

The South Side

The Vikings sited their assembly and burial ground near what is now **College Green**, where **Trinity College** is the most famous landmark. Founded in 1592, it played a major role in the development of a Protestant Anglo-Irish tradition: right up to 1966, Catholics had to obtain a special dispensation to study here, though nowadays roughly seventy percent of the students are Catholic. The stern grey and mellow red-brick buildings are ranged around cobbled quadrangles in a grander version of the quads at Oxford and Cambridge. **The Old Library** (Mon–Sat 9.30am–5pm, Sun noon–4.30pm; €5.70) owns numerous Irish manuscripts. Pride of place goes to the ninth-century **Book of Kells**, which totals 680 pages but was rebound in the 1950s into four volumes, of which two are on show at any one time, one open at a completely illuminated page, the other at a text page, itself adorned with patterns and fantastic animals intertwined with the capitals. The **Book of Durrow** is equally interesting: it is the first of the great Irish illuminated manuscripts, dating from between 650 and 680, and has, unusually, a whole page given over to abstract ornament. In summer there are guided tours of Trinity, and an audiovisual presentation of Dublin's history, the **Dublin Experience**, in the arts block (May–Oct daily 10am–5pm; €4.10).

Facing Trinity across the busy interchange, the imposing **Bank of Ireland** was built in 1729 originally as the parliament of independent Ireland. After the Act of Union in 1801, the building was sold to the bank, which still adheres to tradition by having a guard in a top hat and tailcoat, and a coal fire in the lobby. You can visit the former House of Lords (tours Tues 10.30am, 11.30am & 1.45pm) and the grand Cash Hall for free during working hours.

Just south of here, the streets around pedestrianized **Grafton Street** frame Dublin's quality shopping area – chic, sophisticated and expensive. After spotting the statue of Molly Malone (nicknamed "the tart with the cart"), drop into **Bewley's** coffee house, whose dark wood and marble-tabled interior is a great place to sit and watch people; there's even a small

museum tracing the history of this Dublin institution. Grafton Street's **buskers** are the best in town.

Walking south from Trinity you'll arrive at the northwest corner of **St Stephen's Green**, whose pleasant gardens with ponds and a lake are the focus of Georgian city planning. Running off beside the swanky *Shelbourne Hotel*, Kildare Street harbours the imposing Leinster House, built in 1745 as the Duke of Leinster's townhouse, and now the seat of the Irish parliament, the **Dáil** (open out of session; booking essential; ☎01/618 3333). Alongside are the rotundas of the **National Library** and the **National Museum** (Tues–Sat 10am–5pm, Sun 2–5pm; free), the repository of the treasures of ancient Ireland. Much of its prehistoric gold was found in peat-bogs, as were a sacrificed human and the Lurgan Longboat. The Treasury and the Viking exhibition display such masterpieces as the Ardagh Chalice and Tara Brooch, St Patrick's Bell and the Cross of Cong. The brooch is perhaps the greatest piece of Irish metalwork and is decorated both on the front and the back, where the intricate filigree could be seen only by the wearer.

Around the block, the other side of Leinster House overlooks **Merrion Square**, the finest Georgian plaza in Dublin. No. 1 was once the home of Oscar Wilde, and a flamboyant statue in the green opposite shows the artist draped insouciantly over a rock; on Sundays, the square's railings are used by artists flogging their wares. Here, the **National Gallery** (Mon–Sat 10am–5.30pm, Thurs until 8.30pm, Sun 2–5pm; free; *www.nationalgallery.ie*) owns a fair spread of European old masters and French Impressionists, but the real draw is the trove of Irish paintings, ranging from formal portraits and landscape paintings of the Anglo-Irish era to the modernist creations of Mainie Jellett, Evie Hone and Roderic O'Conor. Best of all is the new permanent exhibition devoted to the work of Ireland's best-known painter, Jack B. Yeats, tracing his development from Dublin illustrator to expressionist interpreter of Connemara sea- and landscapes.

Don't miss the guided tours of **29 Lower Fitzwilliam St** (Tues–Sat 10am–5pm, Sun 2–5pm; closed late Dec; €3.20), a sumptuously re-created Georgian household that includes a giant doll's house and an eighteenth-century exercise machine, or the **Government Buildings** on Merrion St Upper (Sat 10.30am–3.30pm; free; get tickets from 10am at the National Gallery), including the office of the Taoiseach (Prime Minister), complete with a private lift to a rooftop helipad or basement limo, and the Cabinet Room.

TEMPLE BAR AND WEST TO KILMAINHAM

Dame Street, the main thoroughfare leading west from College Green, marks the southern edge of the redeveloped **Temple Bar** quarter (*www.temple-bar.ie*), whose fashionable restaurants, pubs, boutiques and arts centres make this one of the liveliest parts of town. Dublin's **Viking Adventure** (Tues–Sat 10am–4.30pm; €7), on the corner of Essex St West and Exchange St Upper, beside Essex Quay, is an interactive exhibition on the Viking settlement that once existed on Wood Quay, where the Dublin Corporation has built its ugly Civic Offices.

Uphill, tucked away behind City Hall, **Dublin Castle** (Mon–Fri 10am–5pm, Sat & Sun 2–5pm) was founded by the Normans, and symbolized British power over Ireland for 700 years. Though parts date back to 1207, it was largely rebuilt in the eighteenth century. Tours of the State Apartments (€4) reveal much about the tastes and foibles of the viceroys and while you can see the lovely Chapel Royal, the real highlights are the excavations of Norman and Viking fortifications in the Lower Yard. Over the brow of Dublin Hill, **Christ Church Cathedral** (daily 9.45am–5.30pm; €2.50 donation) is a resonant monument built in 1190 by the Norman baron, Richard de Clare, "Strongbow." The north wall of the nave has leaned eighteen inches outwards since the roof collapsed in 1562. The former Synod Hall, connected to Christ Church by an overhead bridge, contains **Dvblinia** (daily 10/11am–4/5pm; €5, includes entry to Christ Church), an array of presentations, models and tableaux depicting Dublin's medieval past and Viking and Norman artefacts excavated at nearby Wood Quay. A small section of the old Norman city wall can be seen at Cook Street, further to the west.

Five minutes' walk south from Christ Church is Dublin's other great Norman edifice, **St Patrick's Cathedral** (daily 9am–5/6pm; Nov–Feb Sun closes 3pm; €2.90; *www.stpatrickscathedral.ie*). Founded in 1191, the cathedral is replete with relics of Jonathan Swift, its dean from 1713 to 1747. To the right of the entrance are memorials to both him and Esther Johnson, the "Stella" with whom he had a passionate though apparently platonic relationship, while the north pulpit contains Swift's writing table, chair, portrait and death mask. Handel's *Messiah* received its first performance here in 1742, and St Patrick's is the only cathedral in Ireland to sing two services every day.

A mile west of Christ Church, the **Guinness Brewery** covers 64 acres on either side of James's St. Founded in 1759, Guinness has the distinction of being the world's largest single beer-exporting company, dispatching some 300 million pints a year. Set in the centre of the brewery, the **Guinness Storehouse** (daily 9.30am–7pm; Oct–March closes 5pm; €11.40; *www.guinness.com*) presents a comprehensive exhibition detailing the history of this famous beer. The tour ends with reputedly the best glass of Guinness in Dublin, in the panoramic *Gravity* bar with superb views over the city.

Regular buses (#78A, #79 and #90) ply the road out to Heuston Station and the **Royal Hospital Kilmainham**, Ireland's first Neoclassical building, dating from 1680, which now houses the **Irish Museum of Modern Art** (Tues–Sat 10am–5.30pm, Sun noon–5.30pm; free; *www.modernart.ie*), with excellent permanent and visiting exhibitions. If you exit via the west wing and head towards the gateway at the end of the avenue, you'll emerge near **Kilmainham Gaol** (April–Sept daily 9.30am–4.45pm; Oct–March Mon–Fri 9.30am–4pm; €4.40; *www.heritageireland.ie*), where the British incarcerated patriots such as Charles Stewart Parnell, Pádraig Pearse and James Connolly (the last two were executed here). A superb museum on crime and punishment sets the tone for guided tours of the gaol.

The North Side

Crossing O'Connell Bridge from College Green, the view of the Georgian Custom House downstream is marred by a railway viaduct, and many of the handsome buildings on **O'Connell Street**, the main avenue on the North Side, have – with the exception of the General Post Office – been spoiled by tacky facades. A rejuvenation programme is currently underway to restore some of the boulevard's former glory and reduce the number of traffic lanes. Heading north from the bridge, just off O'Connell St on Middle Abbey St is the **Hot Press Museum** (daily 10am–6pm; €7.60; *www.imhf.com*), which traces Irish music from folk through to U2, Sinéad O'Connor and other contemporary artists. Further down O'Connell St looms the **General Post Office**, the insurgents' headquarters in the 1916 Easter Rising; only the facade survived the fighting, and its pillars are still scarred by bullets. Across the road on the corner of Essex St North is a **statue of James Joyce**. At the same junction, on the site of what was the city's most famous landmark, Nelson's Pillar (it was destroyed in an explosion in 1966), it's planned to erect an illuminated stainless-steel spike – the **Monument of Light** – representing the city's hopes for the new millennium.

At the northern end of O'Connell St lies Parnell Square, one of the first of Dublin's Georgian squares. Its plain red-brick houses are broken by the grey stone **Hugh Lane Municipal Art Gallery** (Tues–Thurs 9.30am–6pm, Fri & Sat 9.30am–5pm, Sun 11am–5pm; free; *www.hughlane.ie*), originally the townhouse of the Earl of Charlemont and the focus of fashionable Dublin before the city centre moved south of the river. The gallery exhibits work by nineteenth- and twentieth-century Irish and international masters, and features a reconstruction of Francis Bacon's working studio following a bequest from the artist's estate. Nearby at nos. 18–19, the **Dublin Writers Museum** (Mon–Sat 10am–6pm, Sept–May closes 5pm, Sun 11am–5pm; €5.10) whisks you through Irish literary history from early Christian writings up to Samuel Beckett and Brendan Behan. Especially worth visiting is the well-stocked bookshop and the summertime Zen garden. Two blocks east of Parnell Square, at 35 North Great George's St, the **James Joyce Centre** (Mon–Sat 9.30am–5pm, Sun 12.30pm–5pm; €3.80; *www.jamesjoyce.ie*) runs intriguing walking tours of the novelist's haunts (☎01/878 8547).

Half-a-mile to the west, on Church Street, you'll find **St Michan's Church** (March–Oct Mon–Fri 10am–12.30pm & 2–4.30pm, Sat 10am–12.45pm; rest of year Mon–Fri 12.30–3.30pm, Sat 10am–12.45pm; €2.50), the oldest on the North Side, founded in 1095. The crypt is famous for its "mummified" bodies, preserved by the constant temperature and dry air pervaded by methane gas. The oldest – thought to have been a Crusader – dates back 700 years. The church organ was played by Handel in 1742. At the bottom of Church Street, on the bank of the Liffey, stands the **Four Courts**. Like the Custom House downriver, it's a grand eighteenth-century edifice by James Gandon that has been restored after serious damage during the Civil War which followed the 1921 treaty.

One block west on Bow Street is the old **Jameson Distillery** (daily 9.30am–6pm; €6.30); tours cover the history and method of distilling what the Irish called *uisce beatha* ("water of life", anglicized to whiskey) – which differs from Scotch whisky by being thrice-distilled and lacking a peaty undertone – and end with a tasting session involving five different types of whiskey, Scotch and bourbon. Opposite the Distillery is **Ceol** ("Music") which tells the story of traditional Irish music through a visually arresting multimedia exhibition (Mon–Sat 10am–6pm, Sun 11am–6pm; €5; *www.ceol.ie*).

On the first Sunday of each month (9am–4pm; best at midday), the nearby cobbled **Smithfield** is the site of horse sales attended by Travellers who race their ponies bareback through the streets. Further west is the **Collins Barracks** (Tues–Sat 10am–5pm, Sun 2–5pm; free), an annexe of the National Museum housing its decorative arts collection and occasional special exhibitions. Finally, there's **Phoenix Park**, one of the largest urban parks in the world (bus #10 from O'Connell St or bus #37 from Middle Abbey St); originally priory land, it is now home to the Presidential Lodge, and attractions such as the medieval Ashtown Castle and **Dublin Zoo** (Mon–Sat 9.30am–5/6pm, Sun 10.30am–5/6pm; €8.90; *www.dublin-zoo.ie*). The visitor centre (daily 9.30/10am–5/6pm) has an exhibition on the park's history and wildlife.

Eating, drinking and entertainment

Thanks to a recent gastronomic revolution in Dublin, most kinds of **food** are now widely available, especially in the eateries of Temple Bar. Take advantage of the fact that many **cafés** and **restaurants** serve lunch at much lower prices than they'll charge in the evening (when it's wise to reserve a table); while Dublin's 800 **pubs** offer anything from soup and sandwiches to a full carvery at lunchtime. The **music** scene – much of which is based in the pubs – is volatile, so it's always best to check on the latest action by reading *In Dublin* or *Hot Press*. Nightclubs along Leeson Street (known as "The Strip"), at the southeastern corner of St Stephen's Green, are mostly pretty dire; the trendier clubs closer to Dame Street are a better bet. Dublin's **theatres** are among the best in Europe.

Restaurants and cafés

Alpha Café, Clarendon St. A well-kept secret just off Grafton Street with old-fashioned homely menu at great prices. Mon–Sat 9am–6pm.

Bewley's, 78 Grafton St; 11–12 Westmoreland St; 40 Mary St. An essential food experience in Dublin, serving everything from a sticky bun to a full meal. Check out the lunchtime theatre programme in Grafton St, with combined lunch and show ticket for €8.90. Open from 7.30am; closes Grafton St 11.30pm; Westmoreland St 7.30pm; Mary St 6pm.

Blazing Salads II, Powerscourt Townhouse Centre, off Grafton St. Delicious vegetarian food, on tables overlooking the atrium. Mon–Sat 9am–6pm.

Cornucopia, 51 Wicklow St. A wholefood shop with one of the city's few vegetarian cafés. Daily 8am–9pm.

Elephant and Castle, 18 Temple Bar (☎01/679 3121). Busy diner-cum-brasserie with burgers and Cajun-Creole dishes; classy without being posey. Mon–Fri 8am–11.30pm, Sat 10.30am–midnight, Sun noon–11.30pm.

Irish Film Centre, 6 Eustace St, Temple Bar (☎01/679 3477). Delicious, inventive food in elegantly minimal surroundings. Great all-day bar menu with excellent lunches and evening meals. Watch a film or just soak up the atmosphere. Daily 12.30–3pm & 5–9.30pm.

Leo Burdock's, 2 Werburgh St. Dublin's best fish-and-chips – takeaway only. Mon–Fri 12.30–11pm, Sat 2–11pm.

Mao Café and Bar, 2–3 Chatham Row (☎01/670 4899). Communist-chic themed restaurant serving reasonably priced rice- and noodle-based dishes with excellent service. Daily noon–11pm, Sun closes 10pm.

Pizza Stop, 6 Chatham Lane (☎01/679 6712). Tasty all-day Italian menu of pizza and pasta favourites, an economical option for evening dining. Daily noon–12.30am.

Steps of Rome, 1 Chatham Court. Limited seating area, though has great slabs of highly original pizza available to take away also. Good vegetarian options. Daily noon–11pm.

The Winding Stair, 40 Lower Ormond Quay. Quaint bookshop downstairs, wholefood café and coffee shop on two upper floors with great-value hearty lunches. Mon–Sat 9.30am–8pm.

Pubs

Chatham Lounge, 1 Chatham St. Plenty of bevelled glass and shiny wood, plus Liberty-print curtains to show some style appropriate for its theatrical clientele.

Davy Byrne's, 21 Duke St. An object of pilgrimage for *Ulysses* fans, since Leopold Bloom stopped by here for a snack. Despite the pastel-toned refit, it's still a good pub, and serves oysters at lunchtime.

The Duke, Duke St. The starting point for "Dublin's Literary Pub Crawl" (Mon–Sat 7.30pm, Sun noon; Nov–March not Mon–Wed; €8.30).

Fireworks, Pearse St. Converted fire station on three floors, where trendy Dubliners queue up to pose.

Kehoe's, South Anne St. Wonderful snugs for privacy to sip your pint.

The Long Hall, South Great George's St. Victorian pub encrusted with mirrors and antique clocks.

McDaid's, 3 Harry St. Excellent Guinness in Brendan Behan's former local. Often has traditional music.

Mulligan's, 8 Poolbeg St. Shabby and smoky, but always packed in the evenings; many claim that it serves the best Guinness in Dublin.

Ryan's, Parkgate St, near Heuston Station. Another pub famous for its wood-lined snugs.

Stag's Head, Dame Court, Dame St, almost opposite the Central Bank. Wonderfully intimate pub, all mahogany, stained glass and mirrors. Good lunches, too.

Music pubs and venues

Brazen Head, 20 Lower Bridge St. The oldest pub in Dublin, with traditional music most nights from 9.30pm.

The Cobblestone, 77 North King St, Smithfield. Popular old-fashioned bar with regular trad downstairs and a "listening venue" upstairs where chat is forbidden during sessions.

International Bar, 23 Wicklow St. Large smoke-filled saloon with gigs and comedy club upstairs – mostly rock bands, but also solo acts on Tuesdays.

The Kitchen, Essex St East. Curved walls, moat-surrounded dance floor and an occasionally strict entry policy for a club offering some of Dublin's best dance sounds.

The Globe, South Great George's St. Trendy hangout with loud music. Backs onto *RiRa*, an intimate but very lively club.

Mother Redcap's Tavern, Back Lane, off High St. Traditional and country music. Get some chips round the corner at *Leo Burdock's*, then come here for a great Friday night.

Oliver St John Gogarty's, 57/58 Fleet St. Lively tourist pub with Irish music upstairs, the starting point for "Dublin's Musical Pub Crawl" (May–Oct nightly; Nov–April weekends; €7.60). The adjoining *Left Bank Bar* often has live jazz and blues.

The Olympia, 74 Dame St. Hosts regular top-name gigs in an intimate theatre setting.

Slattery's, Grand Canal St. Great trad sessions every Sunday afternoon.

Temple Bar Music Centre, Curved St. Everything from traditional acts to salsa, with live recording of all gigs.

Whelans, 25 Wexford St. Very lively pub with nightly gigs and frequent bar extensions.

Theatres

Abbey Theatre, Lower Abbey St (☎01/878 7222, *www.abbeytheatre.ie*). Founded in 1904 by W.B. Yeats and Lady Gregory, the *Abbey* had its golden era in the days when writers like Yeats, J.M. Synge and later Sean O'Casey were its house playwrights. It's still known for its productions of older Irish plays, but does encourage younger writers. The building also houses the *Peacock Theatre*, which stages more experimental shows.

Gaiety Theatre, South King St (☎01/677 1717, *www.iom.com/gaietytheatre*). Dublin's oldest theatre stages a mix of musical comedy, revues and occasional opera, plus popular dance clubs on Fridays and Saturdays.

Gate Theatre, Cavendish Row, Parnell Square (☎01/874 4045, *www.gate-theatre.ie*). Another of Dublin's literary institutions, staging classic and modern Irish theatre.

Project Arts Centre, Essex St, Temple Bar (☎01/679 6622 or ☎1850/260027). Temple Bar's long-standing project continues to mount experimental and politically sensitive theatre.

Listings

Airlines Aer Lingus, 41 Upper O'Connell St & 42 Grafton St (☎01/876 6705); British Airways (☎1800/626747); British Midland (☎01/407 3036); Ryanair (☎01/609 7800).

Airport information ☎01/705 2222.

Bike rental Cycle Ways, 185 Parnell St, opposite Ilac shopping centre (☎01/873 4748; €12.70 per day, €50.80 per week).

Buses National services leave from around Busáras, local services from the Quays and Middle Abbey St. For information: Dublin Bus, 59 Upper O'Connell St (Mon–Fri 8.30/9am–5.30pm, Sat 9am–1pm; ☎01/836 6111); Bus Éireann, Busáras (☎01/873 4222).

Car rental Argus, in the tourist office on Suffolk St (☎01/605 7701); Budget, 151 Lower Drumcondra Rd (☎01/837 9802); Hertz, 149 Upper Leeson St (☎01/660 2255); Dan Dooley, 42 Westland Row (☎01/677 2723); Thrifty, 33 Batchelor's Walk (☎01/679 9420 or ☎1800/515800).

Embassies Australia, Fitzwilton House, Wilton Terrace (☎01/676 1517); Canada, 64–65 St Stephen's Green (☎01/478 1988); Netherlands, 160 Merrion Rd (☎01/269 3444); UK, 31–33 Merrion Rd (☎01/205 3700); US, 42 Elgin Rd, Ballsbridge (☎01/668 8777).

Exchange Thomas Cook, 118 Grafton St; or most city centre banks.

Ferry companies Irish Ferries, 2–4 Merrion Row (☎01/661 0715, *www.irishferries.ie*); Stena Line, 15 Westmoreland St (☎01/204 7777, *www.stenaline.com*); P&O Irish Sea (☎1800/409049, *www.poirishsea.com*); Super Seacat (☎1800/551743, *www.seacat.co.uk*).

Gay switchboard ☎01/872 1055 (Mon–Fri & Sun 8–10pm, Sat 3.30–6pm).

Hospital South Side: Meath Hospital, Heytesbury St (☎01/453 6555); North Side: Mater Misericordae Hospital, Eccles St (☎01/803 2000).

Internet *Planet Cyber Café*, St Andrew's St, beside Suffolk St tourist office (Mon–Wed 10am–10pm, Thurs & Fri 10am–11pm, Sat & Sun noon–10pm; €6.40/hr).

Laundry All American Laundrette, Wicklow Court, South Great George's St (☎01/677 2779).

Left luggage Busáras (Mon–Sat 8am–7.45pm, Sun 10am–5.45pm); Heuston (Mon–Sat 7.15am–8.35pm, Sun 8am–3pm & 5–9pm); Connolly (Mon–Sat 7.40am–9.30pm, Sun 9.15am–1pm & 5–9pm).

Pharmacy O'Connell's, 55 O'Connell St (Mon–Sat 7.30am–10pm, Sun 10am–10pm).

Police Pearse St, near Trinity College. The main Gardaí station is on Harcourt Terrace (☎01/666 9500).

Post office General Post Office, O'Connell St (Mon–Sat 8am–8pm, Sun 10.30am–6pm).

Taxis Taxi stands throughout central Dublin. Metro Cabs can be booked on ☎01/668 3333 (daily 24hr).

Trains Iarnród Éireann, 35 Abbey St Lower (☎01/836 6222).

Travel agents USIT, 19 Aston Quay (☎01/679 8833); World Travel Centre, 35 Pearse St (☎01/671 7155); Trailfinders, 4–5 Dawson St (☎01/677 7888).

Around Dublin

County Wicklow, easily accessible to the south of Dublin, has some of the wildest, most spectacular mountain scenery in Ireland, the impressive monastic monuments of **Glendalough**, and the Neoclassical splendour of **Russborough**. To the north of the city is the Brú na Bóinne complex of prehistoric remains, the most important and spectacular of which is **Newgrange**.

South of Dublin

The early Celtic monastery of **GLENDALOUGH**, eighteen miles south of Dublin, is one of the most important monastic sites in Ireland, with a tangible quality of peace and spirituality that's only marginally disturbed by coach parties. Transport is easy: the St Kevin's Bus

Service (☎01/281 8119; €12.70 return) runs twice daily from outside the Royal College of Surgeons on St Stephen's Green. The huge **visitors' centre** (daily: June–Aug 9am–6pm; rest of year 9.30am–5/6pm; €2.50) features an excellent exhibition and video show; entrance includes a guided tour of the site. The **Monastery** was founded by St Kevin in the sixth century, and became famous throughout Europe for its learning. The **Cathedral**, which dates from the early ninth century, has an impressive ornamental east window; the saint's burial spot is marked by the massive granite **St Kevin's Cross**, carved around 1150. The **round tower**, whose door is ten feet above the ground, was probably used as a refuge in times of trouble. Glendalough's most famous building is the solid barrel-vaulted stone oratory of **St Kevin's Church**; although it may well date from Saint Kevin's time, the round-tower belfry is eleventh-century, and the structure has clearly been altered many times. There are more monastic antiquities among the cliffs around the **Upper Lake**: the site of St Kevin's original church, the **Temple-na-Skellig**, is on a platform approached by a flight of stone steps, accessible only by boat, and **St Kevin's Bed**, a rocky ledge high up the cliff, is said to be where the holy man used to sleep in an attempt to escape the unwelcome advances of a young girl. Best accommodation in the area is the outstanding An Óige **hostel**, about half-a-mile up the valley (☎0404/45342; ②).

Forty minutes from Dublin on the Waterford bus is **Russborough House** (May–Sept daily 10.30am–5.30pm; rest of year Sun same times; main rooms €5.10, bedrooms €3.20), a classic Palladian building constructed for Joseph Leeson, MP for Rathcormack in the eighteenth century during the days of the semi-independent Irish parliament. No expense was spared: the fashionable architects of the day were employed, and the plasterwork is by the virtuoso Francini brothers. The chief reason to visit is the **art** collection, which includes works by Goya, Murillo, Velázquez, Gainsborough, Rubens and Frans Hals. You can stay at the An Óige *Baltyboys* **hostel** in a tranquil location on the wooded shore of the reservoir just outside Blessington (☎045/867266; ②; March–Nov).

North of Dublin

The main N1 Belfast road and the railway pass through **Drogheda**, from where it's a short bus hop to the great **NEWGRANGE** tumulus (daily 9/9.30am–5/7pm; €5.10; *www.knowth.com*); enter by the Brú na Bóinne visitor centre, but there is no advance booking and, since it's very popular, you may have a long wait. Raised around 5000 years ago and completely restored, the mound of earth and loose stone covers the chambers of a remarkable passage grave. The outer ring of **standing stones**, of which only twelve uprights now remain, was unique among passage grave tombs. Perhaps the most important feature is the unique **roof-box** several feet in from the tunnel mouth. This contains a slit through which, at the **winter solstice**, the light of the rising sun fills the chamber with a sudden blaze of orange light. The entry passage, about three feet wide, leads into the **central chamber**, where the stones are carved with intricate decoration.

SOUTHERN IRELAND

The southeast (*www.southeastireland.travel.ie*) is often Ireland's sunniest and driest corner, and the region's medieval and Anglo-Norman history is richly concentrated in **Kilkenny**, a bustling, quaint inland town, while on the coast there's **Waterford**, which preserves an ancient heart but is also a thriving commercial centre, young and enjoyably lively. To the west, County Tipperary consists largely of prosperous, contented farming country, with at its very heart the **Rock of Cashel**, a spectacular natural formation topped with Christian buildings from virtually every period. In the southwest, **Cork** manages to be relaxed as well as spirited, the perfect place to ease yourself into the exhilarations of the west coast.

Ferries to Rosslare

Ferries from Wales (Fishguard and Pembroke) and France (Cherbourg and Roscoff) arrive at **Rosslare Harbour/Europort**, on the southeastern tip of Ireland. Trains depart daily from the pier for Wexford, Waterford and Dublin, and there's also a daily bus service to Dublin and the west. There's a **tourist desk** in the terminal open for incoming sailings (May–Sept, except early mornings; ☎053/33622); otherwise, try the Kilrane tourist office, just over a mile from the dock along the N25 (May–Sept daily 11am–8pm; Oct–April Tues–Sun 2–8pm; ☎053/33232). There's an An Óige **hostel** a short walk from the ferry in Goulding St (☎053/33399; ②), though *Kirwan House Hostel*, 13 miles away in **WEXFORD**, 3 Mary St (☎053/21208; ②), is a more appealing place to spend your first night in Ireland.

Kilkenny

KILKENNY (*www.kilkenny.ie*) is Ireland's finest medieval city, its castle set above the broad sweep of the River Nore and its narrow streets laced with carefully maintained buildings. In the mid-seventeenth century, the city became virtually the capital of Ireland, with the founding of a parliament in 1641 known as the Confederation of Kilkenny. The power of this short-lived attempt to unite the resistance to English persecution of Catholicism had greatly diminished by the time Cromwell's wreckers arrived in 1650. Kilkenny never recovered its prosperity, but enough remains to attest to its former importance.

The **bus and train stations** are a short distance north of the city, at the top of John St. Following this road over the river and climbing Rose Inn St brings you to the **tourist office** (Mon–Sat 9am–5/6pm, May–Sept also Sun 11am–5pm; ☎056/51500), housed in the sixteenth-century **Shee Alms House**, one of the very few Tudor almshouses in Ireland. At the top of Rose Inn St to the left is the broad **Parade**, which leads up to the castle. To the right, the High St passes the eighteenth-century **Tholsel**, once the centre of the city's financial dealings and now the town hall. Beyond is **Parliament Street**, the main thoroughfare, where the **Rothe House** (April–Oct Mon–Sat 10/10.30am–5/6pm, Sun 3–5pm; Nov–March Mon–Sat 1–5pm, Sun 3–5pm; €2.50) provides a unique example of an Irish Tudor merchant's home, comprising three separate houses linked by cobbled courtyards. The highlight of this end of town is the thirteenth-century **St Canice's Cathedral** (Easter–Sept Mon–Sat 9am–1pm & 2–6pm, Sun 2–6pm; rest of year Mon–Sat 10am–1pm & 2–4pm, Sun 2–4pm; donations). Rich in carvings, it has a fine array of sixteenth-century monuments, many in black Kilkenny limestone (which looks remarkably like marble). The **round tower** next to the church (weather permitting; €1.30) is all that remains of the monastic settlement reputedly founded by St Canice in the sixth century; there are superb views from the top.

It's the **Castle**, though, that defines Kilkenny, an imposing building standing high and square above the river (guided tours: April–Sept daily 10/10.30am–5/7pm; Oct–March Tues–Sun 10.30/11am–12.45pm & 2–5pm; €4.40; *www.historic.irishcastles.com/kilkenny.htm*). Seat of the Butler family, the castle was founded in the twelfth century and radically altered by a nineteenth-century restoration – hence the folksy, pre-Raphaelite decoration on the flimsy wooden hammer-beam roof of the picture gallery. Within the castle the library, drawing room, bedrooms and Long Gallery of family portraits are open for viewing, as well as the **Butler Gallery**, housing an exhibition of modern art. The castle's kitchen is a tearoom in summer.

Practicalities

Kilkenny is well served by **B&Bs**, although in the summer the city can get crowded and during festival weeks in June and August you'll need to book in advance. *Bregagh* on Dean St (☎056/22315; ④) is very central; also within walking distance of the centre is *Celtic House* on Michael St (☎056/62249; ④). *Dempsey's* on James St (☎056/21954; ④) is also good. There's an An Óige **hostel**, *Foulksrath Castle*, at Jenkinstown (☎056/67674; ②), eight miles north along the N77; Buggy's buses (details ☎056/41264) run to the hostel three times a day from the Parade near the castle. The friendly *Kilkenny Tourist Hostel*, 35 Parliament St (☎056/63541, *kilkennyhostel@eircom.net*; ②), is a more central independent hostel. There's **camping** at *Tree Grove* (☎056/70302; ①), a mile outside the city, or further south near Bennettsbridge at *Nore Valley Park* (☎056/27229; ①).

Kilkenny has taken off in recent years: an influx of artists and craftspeople to the area in pursuit of the good life has boosted the town's restaurants and pubs. Among popular **eating** places are *Café Sol* on William St, great for lazy breakfasts, *Fl'éva* on High St, and *Pierre's* on Parliament St for authentic French food. The **café** in the Kilkenny Design Centre, opposite the castle, serves excellent home-cooked lunches; alternatively *The Gourmet Store* on High St has tasty sandwiches for a takeaway lunch. There are several good spots for **bar food**: *Kyteler's Inn*, St Kieran St, serves food in medieval surroundings, while *Lenehan's* on Barrack St has traditional Irish cooking popular with the locals. You won't be hard pushed to find **music**: try *Widow McGrath's* or *Cleere's*, both on Parliament St, or *Maggie's* on St Kieran St and *Ryan's* on Friary St. *Tynan's* on the Bridge is worth a visit for its cosy Victorian interior. Pick up a copy of the weekly *Kilkenny People* for information about what's on. The town is renowned for its "The Cat Laughs" comedy **festival** in June (*www.thecatlaughs.com*), and the Kilkenny Arts Festival in August (*www.kilkennyarts.ie*) when every music venue, theatre, pub and restaurant is packed to capacity.

Waterford

WATERFORD (*www.waterford.local.ie*) is a modern European port wrapped around an ancient Irish city. It's an important commercial centre and this, coupled with a large student population, makes it a fairly lively place. Alongside the city's modernity, though, there's plenty that is traditional, most obviously the place of the pub as a focal point of social activity, and the persistence of traditional music. The layout of the city, with its long quays and adjacent narrow lanes, dates back to its origin as a Viking settlement in the mid-ninth century. Waterford flourished as a European port into the eighteenth century – the period when the famous Waterford crystal was first produced – and there's plenty of architectural evidence of this prosperity.

The **train and bus stations** are just across the river from the city, a good twenty minutes' walk from Waterford's most historic building, **Reginald's Tower** (daily: June–Sept 9.30am–6.30pm; Easter–May & Oct 10am–5pm; €2.40), a large, cylindrical, late-twelfth-century tower at the far end of the quays. Built as a city defence on the site of an original Viking tower, the display inside illustrates its role in Viking and medieval periods. For a more thorough investigation of Waterford's lively past, head for the city's main visitor attraction, **Waterford Treasures** (daily 9.30/10am–5/6pm; June–Aug until 9pm; €5.10; *www.waterfordtreasures.com*), half-a-mile west along the quay in The Granary, a converted nineteenth-century warehouse. Here a series of excellent interactive and audio-visual presentations take you through a thousand years of the city's history, with a fascinating collection of artefacts from the Viking and Anglo-Norman periods. Also on show is the impressive collection of medieval, Tudor and Stuart royal charters showing the central role of Waterford's allegiance to the English Crown from the arrival of Henry II in 1171 onwards. The Granary also houses the **tourist office** (Mon–Sat 9am–5/6pm; July & Aug also Sun 11am–5pm; ☎051/875823).

Wander up Bailey's New St just off the quay and you'll immediately come to the ruined **French Church** on Greyfriars (key from Reginald's Tower). Founded by Franciscans in 1240, it was used as a place of worship by French Huguenot refugees from 1693 to 1815. Further up Bailey's New St, is **Christ Church Cathedral**, built in the 1770s by John Roberts, who did much work in Waterford for both Catholics and Protestants. It's a nicely proportioned building, with some fine monuments inside; look out for the tomb of James Rice (1482), an effigy of a corpse in an advanced state of decay. Roberts was also responsible for **Holy Trinity Cathedral** in Barronstrand St, originally built in 1793 and greatly altered during the nineteenth century to become the curvaceous extravaganza it is today. Christ Church Cathedral looks down over The Mall, where the **City Hall** – again by Roberts – was once used as a merchants' exchange. By far the finest eighteenth-century architectural detail in the city, though, is the beautiful oval staircase inside the former **Chamber of Commerce** in George St, yet again by John Roberts (check with the tourist office for access). Georgian housing continues down O'Connell St, where the **Garter Lane Arts Centre** has a gallery, a theatre and a good events noticeboard.

Practicalities

There is no shortage of **B&Bs**; good, central options include the *Portree Guest House* in Mary St (☎051/874574; ⑤); *Brown's Town House*, 29 South Parade (☎051/870594; ⑤); *Mayors Walk House*, 12 Mayors Walk (☎051/855427; ④; March–Nov); and *Avondale*, 2 Parnell St (☎051/852267; ⑤). Waterford's hostels have been off-limits for some time; consult the tourist office on the current situation.

There are plenty of **fast-food** joints down Michael St and John St. *Haricot's* on O'Connell St is a cosy, reasonably priced wholefood restaurant; *Café Luna*, John St, serves a good range of baguettes and hot lunches; *Moll's Tapas Bar* on Michael St is a trendy hangout for snacking. For **pub** food try the popular *Egan's*, Barronstrand St; *Dooley's Hotel*, The Quay; or *T.H. Doolan's*, George St. Two of the city's favourite pubs are *Geoff's* in the Apple Market off Barronstrand St and *The Pulpit* on John St; both lively, young places with a good social mix, and useful for keying into what's happening in the city. After hours head for *Preachers*, a wacky **club** behind *The Pulpit*. There are a couple of regular spots for **traditional music**: *T.H. Doolan's* again and *Muldoon's* on the corner of Manor St and Parnell St.

The Rock of Cashel

Approached from the north or west, **the Rock of Cashel** (daily: mid-June to mid-Sept 9am–7.30pm; rest of year 9am–5.30pm; €4.40; *www.historic.irishcastles.com*) appears as a mirage of crenellations rising bolt upright from the vast encircling plain. The rock, less than a quarter of a mile wide, is one of Ireland's most extraordinary architectural sites and is also the place where St Patrick is supposed to have picked a shamrock in order to explain the doctrine of the Trinity.

CASHEL, a ten-minute walk east of the Rock, is easily reached by bus from Waterford, changing at Cahir. Approaching from here, the first thing you'll encounter on the Rock is the fifteenth-century **Hall of the Vicars**, whose vaulted undercroft today contains the original **St Patrick's Cross**. Tradition has it that the cross's huge plinth was the coronation stone of the High Kings of Munster. **Cormac's Chapel**, built in the 1130s, is the earliest and most beautiful of Ireland's Romanesque churches; both north and south doors feature intricate carving, while inside, the alleged sarcophagus of King Cormac has an exquisite design of interlacing serpents and ribbon decoration. The graceful limestone **Cathedral**, begun a century after Cormac's chapel, is Anglo-Norman in conception, with its Gothic arches and lancet windows; a door in the south transept gives access to the tower, and in the north transept some panels from sixteenth-century altar-tombs survive, one with an intricately carved retinue of saints. The tapering **Round Tower** is the earliest building on the Rock, perhaps dating from the tenth century, though the officially accepted date is early twelfth century. From the grounds of the Rock you can look down at the thirteenth-century Hore Abbey on the plain below.

Cashel's **tourist office** (April–Sept Mon–Sat 9.15am–6pm; June & July also Sun 9am–6pm; ☎062/61333) is in the market house on Main St alongside the **Cashel of the Kings Heritage Centre** (July & Aug daily 9.30am–8pm; rest of year daily 9.30am–5.30/6pm; Sept–March closed Sat & Sun; free), where a small exhibition covers the history of the town. The **Bolton Library** (daily 9.30am–5.30pm; €2.40), up a lane opposite the Cashel Palace Hotel on Main Street, houses a fine collection of early manuscripts and rare maps. Cashel has two excellent **hostels**, both a short walk from the Rock: *O'Brien's Lodge*, off the Dundrun Rd (☎062/61003,

obriensholidayhostel@eircom.net; ②; also with camping), and *Cashel Holiday Hostel*, 6 John St
(☎062/62330, *cashelho@iol.ie*; ②). For **B&B**, try *Abbey House*, 1 Dominic St (☎062/61104; ④),
or *Maryville*, Bank Place (☎062/61098; ④).

Cork

Everywhere in **CORK** (*www.cork-guide.ie*) there's evidence of the city's history as a great
mercantile centre, with grey stone quaysides, old warehouses, and elegant, quirky bridges
spanning the River Lee to each side of the island core – but the city's lively, cosmopolitan
atmosphere and large student population, combined with a vibrant social and cultural scene,
are equally powerful draws. **St Finbarre** founded an abbey and school here in the seventh
century, but the Vikings wrecked both abbey and town in 820 before building a new settlement on one of the islands in the marshes, and eventually integrating with the native Celts.
Massive stone walls built by invading Normans in the twelfth century were destroyed by
Williamite forces at the **Siege of Cork** in 1690, after which waterborne trade brought increasing prosperity, as witnessed by the city's fine eighteenth-century bow-fronted houses and
ostentatious nineteenth-century churches.

The graceful arc of **St Patrick's Street** – which with **Grand Parade** forms the commercial heart of the centre – is crammed with major chain stores and modest traditional businesses. Just off Patrick's Street on Princes St, the sumptuous **English Market** offers the
chance to sample the local delicacies tripe and drisheen (the lining of a sheep's stomach
served with peppered blood-sausage). On the far side of Patrick's Street, chic Paul Street is
a gateway to the bijou environs of French Church Street and Carey's Lane. The downstream
end of the island, where many of the quays are still in use, gives the clearest sense of the old
port city. In the west the island is predominantly residential, though Fitzgerald Park is the
home of the **Cork Public Museum** (Mon–Sat 11am–1pm & 2.15–5/6pm, Sun 3–5pm; free),
which focuses on Republican history with side exhibits on the city trades and guilds, silver
and glassware and local natural history.

North of the River Lee is **Shandon**, a reminder of Cork's eighteenth-century status as the
most important port in Europe for dairy products. The most striking survival is the **Cork
Butter Exchange**, stout nineteenth-century Neoclassical buildings recently given over to
craft workshops. The old butter market itself, now renovated to house the Firkin Crane
Theatre, sits in a cobbled square. To the rear is the pleasant Georgian church of **St Anne
Shandon** (Mon–Sat 9am–6pm; *www.shandonsteeple.com*), easily recognizable from all over
the city by its weather vane – an eleven-foot salmon. The church tower (€4.40) gives excellent views and an opportunity to ring the famous bells: a good stock of sheet tunes is provided. West of here in Sunday's Well is the nineteenth-century **Cork City Gaol** (daily
9.30/10am–5/6pm; last admission 1hr before closing; €4.40), with an excellent taped tour
focusing on social history. From here, you can walk back to the town centre via the Shaky
Bridge and Fitzgerald Park.

Practicalities

The **bus station** (☎021/450 8188) is at Parnell Place alongside Merchant's Quay, while the
train station (☎021/450 6766) is about one mile out of the city centre on the Lower Glanmire
Road. **Ferries** from Swansea and Roscoff come in at Ringaskiddy, some ten miles out, from
where there's a bus into the centre.

The **tourist office** on Grand Parade (June–Sept Mon–Sat 9.30am–7pm; July & Aug also
Sun 10am–1pm; Oct–May Mon–Fri 9.30am–5.30pm, Sat 9.30am–4pm; ☎021/427 3251,
www.cork-kerry.travel.ie) will book **B&Bs**; try *Number Forty Eight*, 48 Lower Glanmire Rd
(☎021/450 5790; ⑤), *Westbourne House*, Western Rd (☎021/427 6153; ④), or the many along
Western Road near the university, and Lower Glanmire Road near the train station. For **hostels** try *Sheila's*, 4 Belgrave Place, Wellington Rd (☎021/450 5562, *info@sheilashostel.ie*; ②),
or the excellent *Isaac's*, 48 MacCurtain St (☎021/450 8388, *www.isaacs.ie*; ③). On the south

side of the city is *Kelly's Hostel*, 25 Summerhill South (☎021/431 5612; ②); and, to the west, the newly refurbished An Óige hostel, a 15min walk from the centre and just over a mile from the train station, at 1–2 Redclyffe along Western Rd (☎021/454 3289; ②; bus #8 to University College Cork). **Internet** access is at *webworkhouse*, 8a Winthrop St (daily 9.30am–3am).

For **food**, the *Quay Co-op*, 24 Sullivan's Quay, and *Café Paradiso*, on Lancaster Quay, are excellent vegetarian restaurants serving local produce; trendy *Pi* on Washington St is good for a reasonably priced pizza lunch; *Yumi Yucki* on Tobin St is another fashionable lunch option for sushi and seafood; *Wildways* on Princes St does healthy gourmet sandwiches; and *Farm Gate* upstairs in the English Market has great home-cooked breakfasts and lunches. There's plenty of **traditional Irish music**: two of the best spots are the *Corner Bar* on Coburg St and *Sin E* next door; also good are *An Spailpín Fánach*, South Main St; *The Lobby*, Union Quay (which has rock and indie too); *The Office*, Sullivan's Quay; and *Tom Barry's* on Barrack St which promotes young singer songwriters. Cork's best **club** is *The Savoy* on Patrick St, with DJs and live music; *The Bodega* on Coal Quay is a popular late café-bar with regular jazz sessions; and there's an international **jazz festival** in late October. For **theatre**, the *Granary Theatre* on the Mardyke (☎021/490 4275) has a year-round cutting-edge fringe programme, while *Triskel Arts Centre* in Tobin St (☎021/427 2022) is a lively spot with a cinema, exhibitions, readings and concerts. *Crawford Art Gallery* in Academy St is worth a visit for its permanent and visiting collections and excellent café. The *Kino Cinema* on Washington St screens independent films and is part-host for the excellent **film festival** in October (*www.corkfilmfest.org*). For what's-on details, buy the *Evening Echo*, or pick up the free *Cork List* (*www.thelist.ie*).

THE WEST COAST

If you've come to Ireland for mountainous scenery, sea and remoteness, you'll find them all in the southwestern County Kerry, miles of heather- and bracken-strewn mountain-moorland, a landscape whose smooth grassy hills and wildflowers fragment into jagged rocks as they near the ocean. By far the most visited area – indeed, the most visited in the whole of Ireland – is the town of **Killarney** and a scenic route around the perimeter of the Iveragh Peninsula known as the **Ring of Kerry**. Despite the region's touristic credentials, you'll have no difficulty losing all contact with modern civilization, whether you head for the mountains or the sea. The **Dingle Peninsula**, to the north, is on a smaller scale, but equally magical and peppered with ancient remains.

North across the Shannon estuary, beyond the busy city of Limerick, lies County Clare, with the massive Lough Derg to the east and the barren heights of the **Burren** to the north. The easiest approach to the Burren is from **Galway**, an exceptionally enjoyable, free-spirited sort of place, and a gathering point for young travellers. West of the city lies **Connemara**, a magnificently wild coastal terrain of wind, rock and water, with the nearby, elementally beautiful **Aran Islands**, in the mouth of Galway Bay, offering some of the most thrilling cliff scenery in Ireland. Further round the coast, the island of **Inishbofin** has a gentler landscape, slightly off the tourist trail. If you carry on up the coast the landscape softens around the historic town of **Westport**, while further north, around **Sligo**, the luscious scenery is marked by the beautiful mountain of **Benbulben** and the enchanting **Glencar Lough**.

Despite these attractions, not many people would disagree with the assertion that **County Donegal** in the far northwest has the richest scenery in the whole country, with a spectacular two-hundred-mile folded coastline whose highlight is **Slieve League** with its spectacular sea cliffs, the highest in Europe.

There are plenty of international **flights** directly into the region, to Shannon airport near Limerick (☎061/471444, *www.shannonairport.com*) or the smaller Knock airport near Westport (☎094/67222, *www.west-irl-holidays.ie*).

Killarney and around

Although **KILLARNEY** (*www.killarneyonline.ie*) has been commercialized to saturation point and has little in the way of architectural interest, its location amid some of the best lakes, mountains and woodland in Ireland more than compensates. The town is essentially one main street and a couple of side roads, full of souvenir shops, cafés, pubs, restaurants and B&Bs. Pony traps and jaunting cars line up while their owners talk visitors into taking trips through the surrounding country. It's all done with bags of charm, true to Killarney's long tradition of profitably hosting the visiting masses ever since its establishment as a resort in the mid-eighteenth century. Around the town, three spectacular lakes – Lough Leane, Muckross Lake and the Upper Lake – form an appetizer for MacGillycuddy's Reeks, the highest mountains in Ireland. **Cycling** is a great way of seeing the terrain, and makes good sense because local transport is sparse (David Sheehan at Market Cross and O'Sullivan's in Main St both offer **bike rental**).

The entrance gates to the **Knockreer Estate**, part of the Killarney National Park, are just over the road from Killarney's cathedral. A short walk through the grounds takes you to the banks of **Lough Leane**, where tall wooded hills plunge into the water, with the peaks rising behind to the highest, **Carrauntoohill** (3414ft). The main path through the estate leads to the restored fifteenth-century tower of **Ross Castle** (daily: June–Aug daily 9am–6.30pm; May, Sept & Oct 10am–5/6pm; €3.80; gardens free), the last place in the area to succumb to Cromwell's forces in 1652. From Ross Castle, you can tour the lake in large glassed-over boats, but these don't make stops; a fisherman will take you out in a little craft with an outboard motor (€5.10 per person), or you can simply rent a rowboat (€6.40/hr). This way, you can explore the island of **Inisfallen**, the biggest and the most enchanting of the thirty-odd islets that dot the lough, heavily wooded and scattered with monastic buildings, including a small Romanesque church and a ruined Augustinian priory.

A mile-and-a-half south of Killarney is the **Muckross Estate**; aim first for **Muckross Abbey**, not only for the ruin itself but also for its calm, contemplative location. Founded by the Franciscans in the mid-fifteenth century, it was suppressed by Henry VIII; the friars returned, but were finally driven out by Cromwell in 1652. Back at the main road, signposts direct you to **Muckross House** (daily 9am–6/7pm; €5.10), a solid nineteenth-century neo-Elizabethan mansion with wonderful gardens (free) and also a traditional working farm (€5.10; joint ticket with house €7.60). The estate gives access to well-trodden paths along the shores of the Muckross Lake, and it's here that you can see one of Killarney's celebrated beauty spots, the **Meeting of the Waters**. Actually a parting, it has a profusion of indigenous and flowering subtropical plants on the left of the Old Weir Bridge. Close by is the massive shoulder of Torc Mountain, shrugging off **Torc Waterfall**. The Upper Lake is beautiful, too, but still firmly on the tourist trail, with the main road running along one side up to Ladies' View, from where the view is truly amazing.

West of Killarney is the **Gap of Dunloe**, a natural defile formed by glacial overflow that cuts the mountains in two; this is one of Kerry's prime tourist locations. Rather than joining the continual stream of expensive jaunting cars, you'd do better to walk the four miles in the late afternoon, when the cars have gone home and the light is at its most magical. **Kate Kearney's Cottage**, a hamlet located six miles from Killarney at the foot of the track leading up to the Gap, is the last place for food and water before **Lord Brandon's Cottage**, a summer tearoom (Easter–Nov), seven miles away on the other side of the valley. The track winds its way up the desolate valley between high rock cliffs and waterfalls, past a chain of icy loughs and tarns, to the top, where you find yourself in what feels like one of the remotest places in the world: the **Black Valley**. Named after its entire population perished during the potato famine (1845–49), it's now inhabited by a mere handful of families, and was the very last valley in Ireland to get electricity. There's a wonderfully isolated An Óige **hostel** here too (☎064/34712; ②; March–Nov; booking advisable). From here, the quick way back to Killarney is to carry on down to Lord Brandon's Cottage and take the boat back across the Upper Lake.

Practicalities

B&Bs abound in Killarney, though in high season the town fills up and it's worth phoning to make advance bookings through the **tourist office**, on Beech Rd off New St (Mon–Sat 9/10am–5.30/6pm; June–Sept also Sun 9/10am–6pm; ☎064/31633, *www.cork-kerry.travel.ie*). The An Óige **hostel** (☎064/31240; ②) is three miles west of town along the Killorglin road at Aghadoe, but there are several independent hostels in Killarney itself: *Killarney Railway Hostel* is opposite the station (☎064/35299, *railwayhostel@eircom.net*;②); *Súgan Kitchen* is minutes away on Lewis Rd (☎064/33104; ②); bustling *Neptune's Hostel* is in the middle of town on New St (☎064/35255, *neptune@eircom.net*;②); and *Park Hostel* is up the hill off Cork Rd, opposite the petrol station (☎064/32119; ②). There's a **campsite** at the *Fossa Hostel and Caravan Park*, just past the Aghadoe hostel (☎064/31497, *fossaholidays@eircom.net*; ②; March–Oct). Places to **eat and drink** are thick on the ground: one of the best is *Bricín*, on High St, along with *The Flesk* on Main St for great seafood; or try *Celtic Cauldron* on High St, which creates innovative dishes from traditional Celtic recipes. *Café Internet* on New St (Mon–Sat 9.30am–10pm, Sun noon–9pm; ☎064/36711) serves sandwiches and drinks. Evening **entertainment** is everywhere as you walk the streets; pick up *The Kerryman* for up-to-date listings.

The Ring of Kerry

Most tourists view the spectacular scenery of the 110-mile **Ring of Kerry**, west of Killarney (*www.ringofkerryguide.com*), without ever leaving their coach or car. Consequently, anyone straying from the road or waiting until the buses stop running in the afternoon will be left to experience the slow twilights of the Atlantic seaboard in perfect seclusion. **Cycling** the Ring takes three days, and a bike will let you get onto the largely deserted mountain roads. Buses from Killarney (☎064/30011) go right around the Ring in summer (May–Sept 2 daily); for the rest of the year they travel along the northern coast as far as Caherciveen.

Valentia Island and around

Heading anticlockwise on the main N70 around the Ring of Kerry, at **Kells Bay** the road veers inland towards **CAHERCIVEEN**, a long, narrow street of a town and also the main shopping centre for the western part of the peninsula, giving itself over cheerfully to the tourist trade in summer. It has an independent **hostel**, *Sive*, 15 East End (☎066/947 2717; ②), with camping facilities. Beyond here, lanes lead out to **VALENTIA ISLAND**, Europe's most westerly harbour (*www.kerry.local.ie/valentiaisland*), its position on the Gulf Stream giving it a mild, balmy climate – hence the abundance of fuchsias on the intensively cultivated land. Access to the island is easiest by **ferry** from Reenard Point (two-and-a-half miles from Caherciveen) to **Knightstown**, the focal village, with about a thousand houses clustered around a slate church hidden within a dark rookery. The main street has a few well-stocked shops, a post office offering free maps of the island, and a couple of bars. The much-touted **Grotto** – Valentia's highest point – is a gaping slate cavern with a crude statue of the Virgin perched two hundred feet up amid dripping icy water. More exciting is the cliff scenery to the northwest, some of the most spectacular of the Kerry coast. You should book ahead for **accommodation** during the summer season. The Knightstown An Óige **hostel** (☎066/947 6154; ②; June–Sept) has space for forty at the Coastguard Station, though facilities are spartan. The *Royal Pier Bar* runs an independent hostel in the village (☎066/947 6144; ②) or for **B&B** try *Spring Acre* (☎066/947 6141; ④).

The stretch of coast south of Valentia is wild and almost deserted, apart from a scattering of farms and fishing villages. Sweet-smelling, tussocky grass dotted with wild flowers is raked by Atlantic winds, ending in abrupt cliffs or sandy beaches – a beguiling landscape where you can wander for days. The An Óige **hostel** (☎066/947 9229; ②; April–Sept) in **BALLINSKEL-LIGS** is pretty basic but sells supplies. Monks from the Skellig Islands retreated to Ballinskelligs Abbey in the thirteenth century; today, the village is a focus of the Kerry

Gaeltacht (Irish-speaking area), busy in summer with schoolchildren and students learning Irish. **WATERVILLE** may be touristy, but it does have a certain grace. Popular as a Victorian and Edwardian resort and angling centre, it still has an air of consequence that oddly contrasts with the wild Atlantic views. Its few bars and hotels aside, the town is chiefly notable as the best base on the Ring for exploring the coast and the mountainous country inland. For **B&B** try *Klondyke House*, New Line Rd (☎066/947 4119; ④), or *Ashling House* (☎066/947 4247; ④; March–Oct); and there's the independent *Charlie's Hostel* at Spunkane (☎066/947 4272, *swagman@esatclear.ie*; ②; April–Sept).

From Valentia there's a tantalizing view across a broad strip of sea to the **Skellig Islands**. Little Skellig is a bird sanctuary where landing isn't permitted, but you can visit the UNESCO world heritage site of Great Skellig, known as **Skellig Michael**, and climb up to its ancient monastic site. **Boat trips** depart from Ballinskelligs (contact Joe Roddy on ☎066/947 4268) and from Portmagee, seven miles off the main N70 opposite Valentia (contact Pat Joe Murphy on ☎066/947 7156, or Sean Murphy on ☎066/947 6214). Trips cost around €25, and as visitor numbers are limited for preservation purposes, it's wise to book in advance. From the sea there's no visible route to the summit, but from the tiny landing stage the cliff reveals steps cut into the rock that were formerly the monks' path. Nowadays there's also a path leading to Christ's Saddle, the only patch of green on this savage island. From here, a narrow path leads to the remains of the sixth-century **St Finian's Abbey** with its extraordinary cluster of beehive huts. If the weather is poor, pop into the **Skellig Experience Heritage Centre** (April to mid-Nov daily 10am–6.15pm; €3.80) on Valentia, just over the Maurice O'Neill Bridge from Portmagee, where you can see a short film of the experience.

Kenmare

With its delicatessens, designer boutiques and arty secondhand clothes shops, **KENMARE**, twenty miles south of Killarney, is something of a cosmopolitan anomaly, where you're more likely to hear English or German tones than Irish. Kenmare was established by Sir William Petty, Cromwell's surveyor general, who laid the foundations of the mining and smelting industries in this area, encouraged fishing and founded the enormous Lansdowne estate, many of whose buildings still surround the town. Evidence of much more ancient settlement is the stone circle just outside the centre, on the banks of the river. Kenmare's **hostel**, the *Fáilte*, is in Shelbourne St (☎064/42333; ②; April–Oct). There are plenty of **B&Bs**, both in and just outside town: try *Sunville* on Cork Rd (☎064/41169; ③) or the excellent *Druid Cottage*, a mile along Sneem Rd (☎064/41803; ④). Alternatively, check vacancies at the **tourist office** on The Square (July & Aug Mon–Sat 9am–7pm, Sun 9.15am–1pm & 2.15–5.30pm; April–June & Sept to mid-Oct Mon–Sat 9.15am–1pm & 2.15–5.30pm; ☎064/41233).

The Dingle Peninsula

The **Dingle Peninsula** (*www.dingle-peninsula.ie*) is a place of intense, shifting beauty. Spectacular mountains, long sandy beaches and the splinter-slatted mass of rocks that defines the extraordinary coast at Slea Head all conspire to ensure that, remote though it is, the peninsula is firmly on the tourist trail. There's plenty of myth and history too: here is one of the greatest concentration of Celtic ruins in Ireland, and the now uninhabited Blasket Islands once generated a wealth of Irish literature (the far west remains Irish-speaking to this day). As if all this were not enough, *Ryan's Daughter* was filmed here.

Served by several daily buses from Killarney via Tralee, **DINGLE** makes the best base for exploring the peninsula. Though little more than just a few streets by the side of **Dingle Bay**, the town has a solidity that suggests this was a place of some consequence, and Dingle was indeed Kerry's leading port in the fourteenth and fifteenth centuries. It later became a centre for smuggling, and even minted its own coinage during the eighteenth century when the revenue from contraband was at its height. There's no shortage of **accommodation**, and the

tourist office in Strand St (daily: July & Aug 9.30am–6pm; March–June, Sept & Oct 9am–1pm & 2.15–6pm; ☎066/915 1188) will book places. Although many of Dingle's **B&Bs** are fairly expensive, you'll find one of the most welcoming guest houses in the country at *Ocean View*, just a few minutes walk from the town at 133 The Wood (☎066/915 1659; ④). *Townhouse* on Main St (☎066/915 1147; ⑤) is another reasonable option. For **hostels**, try the *Grapevine*, Dykegate St (☎066/915 1434; ②); the haunted *Ballintaggart House*, one mile before Dingle Town (☎066/915 1454, *info@dingleaccommodation.com*; ③), which also offers camping; or the beautifully situated *Seacrest* (☎066/915 1390, *seacrest@indigo.ie*; ②), near Lispole. Dingle's top **restaurants** serve excellent seafood, landed just a few hundred yards away. Try *Doyle's* or the *Half Door* on John St for a good, if pricey, meal. *Greaney's*, on the corner of Dykegate and Strand streets, does good cheap lunches and dinners; *Nithe le n-ithe* deli on Main St does tasty gourmet sandwiches. **Internet** access is at *Johnny V's* on Main St (daily 9/10am–8pm). Many of Dingle's **pubs** run traditional music sessions; *An Droichead Beag* on Main St and *O'Flaherty's* on Bridge St are good places to start – there's music most nights, and advice on where to find it elsewhere.

West of Dingle town

Cycling is the best way to explore the area west of Dingle; there are bikes available at Foxy John's on Main St and Paddy's on Dykegate St. Public transport in the west of the peninsula amounts to a **bus** from Dingle to Dunquin (July & Aug daily; rest of year Mon & Thurs; call ☎066/712 3566 for a schedule).

The Irish-speaking area west of Dingle is rich with relics of the ancient Gaelic and early Christian cultures. **VENTRY**, now a small village, though once the main port of the peninsula, has the newly renovated *Ballybeag Hostel* (☎066/915 9876; ②), which sends a minibus to collect its guests from Dingle. The main concentration of ancient monuments lies between Ventry and Slea Head. First off there's the spectacular **Dun Beag** (€1.30), a scramble down from the road about four miles out from Ventry. A promontory fort, its defences include four earthen rings, with an underground escape route by the main entrance. It's a magical location, overlooking the open sea – into which some of the building has tumbled. West of here, the hillside above the road is studded with stone beehive huts, cave dwellings, souterrains, forts, churches, standing stones and crosses – over 500 of them in all. The beehive huts were being built and used for storing farm tools and produce until the late nineteenth century, but among ancient buildings like the **Fahan group** you're looking over a landscape that's remained essentially unchanged for centuries.

At **Slea Head** the view opens up to include the desolate, splintered masses of the **Blasket Islands**, which have been uninhabited since 1953, though there are some summer residents. In the summer, boats bound for **Great Blasket** depart from the pier just south of Dunquin (daily every 30min 11am–5.30pm, weather permitting; €17.80 return; *www.blasketferries.com*). Great Blasket's delights are simple ones: tramping the footpaths that crisscross the island, sitting on the beaches watching the seals and dolphins, or savouring the amazing spectacle of the sun sinking into the ocean. There is seasonal accommodation at the new *Great Blasket Hostel* on the island (☎087/852232; ②; April–Oct); you can camp for free and the café (noon–5pm) serves good, cheap vegetarian meals. At **DUNQUIN**, there's an An Óige **hostel** (☎066/915 6121; ②), and **B&B** in *Kruger's* pub (☎066/915 6127; ④).

A couple of miles north around the headland from Dunquin stands **BALLYFERRITER**, with the *Black Cat* hostel (☎066/915 6286; ②; May–Sept). From here, the little northward lanes lead to the 500-foot cliffs at Sybil Head or to Smerwick Harbour and **Dún án Óir** (Golden Fort). The single most impressive early Christian monument on the Dingle Peninsula is the **Gallarus oratory**, three miles further east, built sometime between the ninth and twelfth centuries of unmortared stone and still watertight. It's the best-preserved example of around twenty such oratories in Ireland, and represents a transition between the round beehive huts and the later rectangular churches, an example of which is to be found a mile to the north at **KILMALKEDAR**, with a nave dating from the mid-twelfth century and a corbelled stone roof which was an improvement on the unstable structure at Gallarus. From Gallarus, the **Pilgrim's Way**, dedicated to St Brendan, patron saint of Kerry (and so also known locally as the **Saint's Road**), leads to Brendan's shrine on the top of Brandon Mountain.

Galway and around

The city of **GALWAY** can be difficult to leave, since it continues to justify its reputation as the party capital of Ireland. University College Galway guarantees a high number of young people in term-time, but the energy is never more evident than during Galway's **festivals**, especially the Arts Festival in the last two weeks in July (*www.galwayartsfestival.ie*). For the locals, however, the most important event in the social calendar is the **Galway Races**, usually held in the last week of July. You'll have to pre-book accommodation during these weeks.

Galway originated as a crossing point on the River Corrib, and developed as a strong Anglo-Norman colony. Granted a charter and city status in 1484 by Richard III, it developed a flourishing trade with the Continent, especially Spain. When Cromwellian forces arrived in 1652, however, the city was besieged for ninety days and went into a decline from which it has only recently recovered. The prosperity of maritime Galway and its sense of civic dignity were expressed in the distinctive townhouses of the merchant class, remnants of which are littered around the city, even though recent development is rapidly destroying the character of the place. The **Browne doorway** in Eyre Square is one such monument, a bay window and doorway with the coats of arms of the Browne and Lynch families, dated 1627. Just about the finest medieval townhouse in Ireland is **Lynch's Castle** in Shop St – along with Quay St, the social hub of Galway. Now housing the Allied Irish Bank, it dates from the fifteenth century and has a stone façade decorated with carved panels, gargoyles and a lion devouring another animal. Joyceans may wish to take the short walk towards the river where, on Bowling Green, they can visit the home of Nora Barnacle, the author's wife, and peruse artefacts to do with their relationship (May–Sept 10am–1pm & 2–5pm; €1.30).

There are two churches of interest: the **Collegiate Church of St Nicholas** and the **Cathedral of Our Lady Assumed into Heaven and St Nicholas**. The former, founded in 1320, is the largest medieval church in Ireland. The Cathedral, in hideous contrast, sits on the banks of the river like a huge toad, its copper dome seeping green slime down the formica-bright limestone walls. Down by the river Corrib stands the **Spanish Arch**: more evocative in name than in reality, it's a sixteenth-century structure that was used to protect galleons unloading wine and rum. Cross the bridge over the river into the **Claddagh** district, the old fishing village that once stood outside the city walls and gave the world the Claddagh ring as a symbol of love and fidelity. Past the Claddagh the river widens out into **Galway Bay**; for a pleasant sea walk follow the road until it reaches **Salthill**, the city's seaside resort. Its cafes, restaurants, amusement arcades and seasonal fairground are packed to capacity during the summer months, but you'll find the locals taking the air along the promenade all year round. There are several beaches along the prom, though for the best you'll have to leave the city behind and head two miles past Salthill to **Silverstrand** on the Barna road. Once past Barna and into Connemara the beaches become quieter and more idyllic.

Practicalities

The **bus and train stations** are off Eyre Square, on the northern edge of the city centre. The **tourist office** (July & Aug daily 9am–7.45pm; May & June Mon–Sat 9am–5.45pm; rest of year Mon–Fri 9am–5.45pm, Sat 9am–12.45pm; ☎091/563081, *www.westireland.travel.ie*) is a short stroll away on Forster St, and has an accommodation service; it's best to ignore any hostel touts at the station. The best budget **accommodation** includes the *Galway Hostel* opposite the station (☎091/566959; ②), *Kinlay House*, Merchant's Rd (☎091/565244, *kinlay.galway@usitworld.com*; ③), and *Barnacles Quay Street House*, 10 Quay St (☎091/568644, *www.barnacles.ie*; ③). Other options include *Celtic Tourist Hostel*, Queen St

(☎091/566606; ③), and *Woodquay Hostel*, 23–24 Woodquay (☎091/562618; ②). For **B&B** head for *Joan Sullivan's*, 46 Prospect Hill (☎091/566324; ④), or *Villa Maria*, 94 Father Griffin Rd (☎091/589033; ⑤). There are **campsites** at *Ballyloughnane Caravan Park* on Dublin Rd (May–Sept), and several in Salthill, the most pleasant being *Hunter's* at Silver Strand, four miles west on the coast road (Easter–Sept). The Celtic e-centre beside Kinlay House on Merchant's Rd offers discounted international calls and **Internet** access (daily 9am–9pm).

If the "craic" has eluded you so far, this is where you're going to find it. The bars are the lungs of this town, and even the most abstemious travellers are going to find themselves sucked in. You're guaranteed to find music somewhere, and there's absolutely no problem finding places to eat. Good-value **pub food** is served around midday at *The Quays*, Quay St, *Busker Browne's*, Cross St, and *McSwiggan's* in Eyre St; for a more adventurous menu with a Latin influence, head for *BarCuba* on Eyre Square. In Quay St, *McDonagh's Seafood Bar* is a must for seafood at any time of day, *Fat Freddy's* is good for pizzas and people-watching (ask for a table outside), and *Café du Journal* is a coffee-head's heaven. On Dominick St the Italian owned *Pasta Paradiso* is popular locally for its tasty pizza. There's a good vegetarian restaurant, *Gabhar Orga*, opposite the university at Lower Newcastle, while the best noodle dishes in Ireland can be enjoyed at *Da Tang Noodle House*, Middle St. *Spud Murphy's* on Dominick St is the place to go for a huge Irish breakfast; fill up during the day on the sizeable baked potatoes at *Couch Potatas*, Abbeygate St. The best take-out sandwiches in town are just across the road in *Delight*, and to make a delicious picnic grab some filled bagels from *Bagelyn* on Edward Square.

The Quay Street area of the city leading down to the river is known as the "left bank" due to the proliferation of popular pubs, restaurants and cafes. *The Quays* bar remains one of the city's best-loved, along with the nearby *Front Door* on Cross St. **Traditional music** is plentiful; among the best places to hear music day and night are *Taaffes* on Shop St, the old fashioned *Tigh Neachtain* on Cross St and *The Crane* across the river on William St West. For nightly live music, *Róisín Dubh* in Dominick St attracts leading Irish and international names. Fashionable city bars include *Morgan's* on Forster St and *Massimo's*, William St West. Galway has its fair share of **clubs**: *Central Park* on Abbeygate St remains the perennial favourite; also popular is *ClubCuba*, Eyre Square, on three floors, and, for younger clubbers, the *Alley*, William St Upper, and *GPO*, Eglinton St. In Salthill, *Club Bogarts* and the *Warwick* attract the crowds. For **listings**, pick up a free copy of the *Galway Advertiser* (*www.galwayadvertiser.ie*) or *The List* (*www.thelist.ie*); the monthly *Magpie* (*www.magpie.ie*), on sale nationwide (€2.50), has listings for the entire west coast.

The Burren

A huge plateau of limestone and shale covering over a hundred square miles south of Galway Bay, the **Burren** will come as a shock to anyone associating Ireland with all things green. Barely capable of sustaining human habitation, it is bone white in sunshine, becoming dark and metallic in the rain, its cliffs and canyons blurred by mists. Yet this is a botanist's delight, with an astounding variety of Arctic, Alpine and Mediterranean **flora** – a mixture that nobody can account for. The area's lack of appeal to centuries of speculators and colonizers has meant that evidence of many of the Burren's earlier inhabitants remains. The place buzzes with the prehistoric and historic past, having over sixty Stone Age burial monuments, over four hundred Iron Age ring forts, and numerous Christian churches, monasteries, round towers and high crosses.

For a quick exploration, there's a **Bus Éireann** service from Galway to the lively if touristic village of **DOOLIN**, lodged beside a treacherous sandy beach and famed for a steady supply of **traditional music** in its three bars throughout the summer. There's plenty of **accommodation**, including *Paddy's Doolin Hostel* (☎065/707 4006, *doolinhostel@eircom.net*; ②); *Rainbow Hostel* (☎065/707 4415, *rainbowhostel@eircom.net*; ②); *Flanagan's Village Hostel* (☎065/707 4564; ②); and *Aille River Hostel* (☎065/707 4260, *ailleriver@esatclear.ie*; ②). The last two both offer **camping**; there's also a summer campsite by the pier, and *O'Connor's* campsite in the village by the *Aille River Hostel*. The *Rainbow* offers free **walking tours** of the Burren to guests. All of Doolin's pubs serve very good food; the *Lazy Lobster* and *Doolin Café* are two of the best restaurants. By the pier, from where a ferry runs to all three of the **Aran Islands**, bold shelves of limestone pavement step into the sea. The **Cliffs of Moher**, beginning four miles south of Doolin and stretching for five miles, are the area's most famous tourist spot, their great bands of shale and sandstone rising 660 feet above the waves.

The Aran Islands

The **Aran Islands** – Inishmore, Inishmaan and Inisheer (*www.aran-islands.com*) – lying thirty miles out across the mouth of Galway Bay, are spectacular settings for a wealth of pre-Christian and early Christian remains and some of the finest archeological sites in Europe. The islands are Irish-speaking, and their isolation allowed the continuation of a unique, ancient culture into the early twentieth century. There are daily **ferries** to Inishmore year-round, but less frequently to the other islands, departing from Galway city, Rossaveal (20 miles west by bus) and Doolin; the cost of a return trip ranges from €15.20 to €25.40, with some student reductions and some good-value accommodation packages, particularly during high season. Book through Island Ferries at Galway tourist office, or Victoria Place, Eyre Square in Galway (☎091/568903 or evenings 572273); O'Brien Shipping, New Docks, Galway city (☎091/567676); or Doolin Ferry Company (mid-April to Sept; ☎065/707 4455). You can also **fly** with Aer Árann (☎091/593034, *www.aerarann.ie*) for €44.40 return; book tickets and package tours at Galway tourist office. Buses leave for the airport one hour before flight time (€6.40 return).

Although **INISHMORE** is the most tourist-orientated of the Aran Islands, its wealth of dramatic ancient sites overrides such considerations. It's a long strip of an island, a great tilted plateau of limestone with a scattering of villages along the sheltered northerly coast. The land slants up to the southern edge, where tremendous cliffs rip along the entire shoreline. As far as the eye can see is a tremendous patterning of stone, some of it the bare pavementing of grey rock split in bold diagonal grooves, gridded by dry-stone walls that might be contemporary, or might be pre-Christian. The ferry comes in at **Kilronan**, where the cheapest place to stay is the *Kilronan Hostel* (☎099/61255; ②; April–Oct), though those wanting to enjoy the island's tranquillity should head to the relaxing *Mainistir House Hostel* (☎099/61318, *mainistirhouse@eircom.net*; ②), twenty minutes' walk from the pier. **B&Bs** can be booked through the Kilronan **tourist office** (daily 10am–6.45pm; winter closes 4pm; ☎099/61263), or when you buy your ferry ticket. Not surprisingly, seafood is the great speciality on the island, with most of the popular restaurants located in Kilronan: *Dún Aonghasa* has probably the most varied and reasonably priced menu; *Joe Watty's* bar serves good soups and stews; the *Aran Fisherman* has an extensive seafood menu; and *Café Pota Stoir*, based in the Heritage Centre, does delicious homemade soups and cakes. For **bike rental**, there's Aran Bicycle Hire beside the ferry dock, or Mullin & Burke, by the *Aran Islands Hostel*. Alternatively, take the minibus up through the island's villages and walk back from any point.

Most of Inishmore's sights are to the northwest of Kilronan; the first hamlet in this direction is Mainistir, from where it's a short signposted walk to the simple twelfth-century church of **Teampall Chiaráin**, the most interesting of the ecclesiastical sites on Inishmore. Back on the main road, three miles or so further is Kilmurvey, a fifteen-minute walk from the most spectacular of Aran's prehistoric sites, **Dún Aengus**. This massive ring fort, lodged on the edge of cliffs that plunge three hundred feet into the Atlantic, has an inner citadel of precise blocks of grey stone, their symmetry echoing the almost geometric regularity of the land's limestone pavementing. Nearby **Dún Eoghanachta** is a huge drum of a fort, a perfect circle of stone settled in a lonely field with the Connemara mountains as a backdrop. It's accessible by tiny lanes from Dún Aengus if you've a detailed map; otherwise retrace your steps to Kilmurvey and follow the road west for just over a mile. At the **seven churches**, just east of Eoghannacht, there are ancient slabs commemorating seven Romans who died here, testifying to the far-reaching influence of Aran's monasteries. The site is, in fact, that of two churches and several domestic buildings, dating from the eighth to the thirteenth centuries, and includes St Brendan's grave, adorned by an early cross with interlaced patterns.

From Inishmore, it's an easy hop by boat to the other two islands; all the ferry companies run daily services. In comparison with Inishmore, **INISHMAAN** is lush, its stone walls forming a maze that chequers off tiny fields of grass and clover. The island's main sight is **Dún Chonchubhair**: built some time between the first and seventh centuries, its massive oval wall is almost intact and commands great views. Inishmaan's indifference to tourism means that amenities for visitors are minimal; if you arrive on spec ask at the pub for information (☎099/73003) – it's a warm and friendly place which also serves snacks in summer. For **B&B** try *Ard Alainn* (☎099/73027; ④; April–Sept); or *An Dun* (☎099/73047; ⑤).

INISHEER, at just under two miles across, is the smallest of the Aran Islands. Tourism has a key role here; Inisheer doesn't have the archeological wealth of Inishmore, nor the wild solitude of Inishmaan, but regular day-trip ferry services from Doolin during the summer ensure a steady flow of visitors. A great plug of rock dominates the island, its rough, pale-grey stone dripping with greenery. At the top, the fifteenth-century **O'Brien's Castle** stands inside an ancient ring fort. Set around it are low fields, a small community of pubs and houses, and windswept sand dunes. The **tourist office** hut by the pier (June–Sept daily 10am–7pm) will give you a map and a list of **B&Bs**; try *Uí Chongaile's*, Lioseine, West Village (☎099/75025; ③). There's also a hotel, *Óstán Inis Oírr* (☎099/75020; ④; April–Sept), a **hostel**, *Brú Radharc na Mara* (☎099/75024; ②) and a **campsite** near the pier. Meals are available all day at *Radharc na Mara* (June–Sept) beside the hotel. For **live music**, head for the hotel bar or *Tigh Ned's*.

Connemara

The great asset of **CLIFDEN** – capital of the beautiful region of Connemara (*www.connemara.net*) – is its position, perched high above the deep sides of the boulder-strewn estuary of the Owenglin River, with the circling jumble of the Twelve Bens providing a magnificent backdrop. Clifden seems to be trying hard to cultivate the cosmopolitan atmosphere of Galway, and it attracts a fair number of young Dubliners, too, revving up the life of this rural town. The **tourist office** on Market St (Mon–Sat 9/10am–5/6pm; ☎095/21163, *www.westireland.travel.ie*) has lists of the plentiful **B&Bs** around Clifden, though these can be very busy in July and August and there are few budget options in the town itself. Just outside are *Winnowing Hill*, Ballyconneely Rd (☎095/21281; ④; March–Nov) and *Hyland's Bay View*, Westport Rd (☎095/21286; ④; Feb–Dec). Clifden has several **hostels**, best of which is the excellent *Clifden Town Hostel*, Market St (☎095/21076; ②). Two of the nicest **bars** for drink and music are *Mannion's* and *E.J. King's* on Market St, which also has a few good options for **food**: *Mitchell's* has a varied, reasonably priced menu, while for evening meals at €14 and upwards, try *O'Grady's Seafood Restaurant*. Clifden is a good base for getting out into the Connemara countryside, and to do this you really need your own transport; there are plenty of places for **bike rental**, including John Mannion on Bridge St.

Inishbofin

Located seven miles northwest from **Cleggan** village in Connemara, the lush island of **INISHBOFIN** (*www.inishbofin.com*) is a mellow, balmy place. Grassy slopes dotted with sheep rise sharply to jagged cliffs on the western shore; quiet winding lanes lead from the pier to the glorious golden beach on the island's north face. Inishbofin has several archeological treasures; the pier is guarded by the remains of a sixteenth-century **castle** built by the Spaniard pirate Don Bosco and later used by Cromwell's army as a garrison. The abbey, founded by St Colman, who arrived in Bofin in the seventh century, no longer exists but ruins of a thirteenth-century **church** stand on the original site towards the east end of the island. Two **ferry** companies run scheduled services from Cleggan: the modern Island Discovery

(☎095/44642; €12.70 return; April–Oct), and the slower mail boat Dun Aengus (☎095/45903; €12.70 return; year-round, weather permitting). There's a daily **bus** to Cleggan from Galway city and Clifden; contact Michael Nee (☎095/51082; €10.20 return). Inishbofin has plenty of **accommodation**: *Day's Hotel* (☎095/45809; ⑨) and Murray's *Doonmore Hotel* (☎095/45804, *info@doonmore.com*; ⑥) are both family-run and have sea views; both have excellent restaurants with seafood specialities, and bar food. The *Inishbofin Island* **hostel** (☎095/45855; ②; April-Oct) is extremely welcoming; for **B&B** try *Hybrazil* (☎095/45817; ③). You'll find **traditional music** in both hotel bars, as well as in *Day's Pub*, beside the hotel, which also serves good food.

Westport

Set on the shores of Clew Bay at the end of a rail line from Dublin, **WESTPORT** (*www .westport.mayo-ireland.ie*) is fast becoming one of the west's busiest spots, and while this ensures a lively atmosphere, the town is not the haven of tranquillity it once was. Planned by the eighteenth-century architect James Wyatt, its formal layout comes as quite a surprise in the midst of the west. The craggy **Croagh Patrick** makes an imposing background to the town, standing at 2510 feet above the bay; the climb is a strenuous one, but your reward after a short scramble up its steep slopes is spectacular views. It is said that St Patrick prayed on the mountain for forty days for the conversion of the Irish to Christianity, and on the last Sunday of July many tackle the pilgrimage to the summit barefoot. Another attraction is **Westport House** (summer Mon–Fri 11.30am–5.30pm, Sat & Sun 1.30–5.30pm; €7.60, joint ticket with zoo €15.20; *www.westporthouse.ie*), a mile or so out of town towards the bay. The house was beautifully designed in 1730 by the ubiquitous Richard Castle and is still in private hands: the present family are direct descendants of legendary pirate Grace O'Malley of Clew Bay. The grounds house a small **zoo** and amusement park, and offer accommodation in self-catering, horse caravan and camping parks (☎098/27766; ②). Inside the house is a *Holy Family* by Rubens and an upstairs room with intricate Chinese wallpaper dating from 1780.

Buses drop off on Mill St in the centre; the **train** station is on Altamount St (☎098/25253), ten minutes north of the centre. Westport's **hostel** is the enormous *Club Atlantic* on Altamount St (☎098/26644; ②; March–Oct), convenient for the train station and affiliated to both An Óige and IHH; plus, a little further out of town, the *Granary* on Quay Rd (☎098/25903; ②; April–Oct). There are plenty of **B&Bs** – check for availability at the **tourist office** in the Mall (July & Aug daily 9am–7pm; rest of year Mon–Sat 9am–5.45pm; ☎098/25711). *O'Malley's* on Bridge St is a popular **eating** choice while the Mediterranean-style *Sol Rio* on Bridge St is a good lunch option. For more formal Italian food, *La Bella Vita* on High St is excellent. The restaurant at *Quay Cottage*, the entrance to Westport House, serves enormous salmon salads and plenty of vegetarian food; the nearby complex of refurbished waterside buildings brims with people, pubs and more expensive restaurants. The best **music** pubs are on Bridge St – *The West* is hugely popular and *Matt Molloy's Bar*, owned by the eponymous Chieftains' flautist, occasionally features visiting celebrities and is a hive of activity during Westport's **Arts Festival** at the end of September.

Sligo and around

SLIGO (*www.sligo.local.ie*) is, after Derry, the biggest town in the northwest of Ireland and a focal point for the area. During the Famine its population fell by a third through death and emigration, but a recovery began at the end of the nineteenth century and the upswing has continued to the present day. Its appearance has changed dramatically in recent years with extensive building along the banks of the river Garavogue, bringing a new focal point and life to the town.

The legacy of **W.B. Yeats** – perhaps Ireland's best-loved poet – is still strongly felt in the town he loved so dearly: the **Yeats Building** on Hyde Bridge (Mon–Sat 10am–5pm; €2.50) features a photographic exhibition and film on his life, and houses a branch of the **tourist** office, the main branch of which is on Temple St (June–Aug daily 9am–8pm; May, Sept & Oct Mon–Sat 9am–6pm; rest of year Mon–Fri 9am–5pm; ☎071/61201, *www.northwestireland .travel.ie*). En route to see the poet's Nobel Prize for Literature and other memorabilia in the **Sligo County Museum** on Stephen St (Mon–Sat: June–Sept 10am–noon & 2–5pm; rest of year 2–5pm; free), admire his flamboyant bronze image outside the Ulster Bank. Further along the street, the **Model Arts Centre and Niland Gallery** on The Mall (Tues–Sat 10am–5.30pm; free) is home to a collection of paintings and drawings by the poet's brother Jack B. Yeats. His work has a strong local flavour, and his later efforts like *The Graveyard Wall* and *The Sea and the Lighthouse* are especially potent evocations of the life and atmosphere of the area. The gallery also houses a good representation of modern Irish art and regularly stages visiting exhibitions. Heading back towards the town centre, take a left onto Bridge St and cross the Garavogue to reach the thirteenth-century **Dominican Friary** on Abbey St. The modern visitor centre (April–Oct daily 10am–6pm; €1.90, guided tours on request) provides an informative introduction to many of its existing features, including the last remaining sculptured high altar in the country and an impressive cloistered arcade.

Buses (☎071/60066) and **trains** (☎071/69888) arrive at the station on Lord Edward St, five minutes west of the centre. For **bike rental**, try Gary's Cycles on Lower Quay St (☎071/45418). There are several **B&Bs** close to town: one of the most central is *Renaté House*, 9 Upper John St (☎071/62014; ④); or try *St Anne's* (☎071/43188; ⑤) or *St Theresa's* (☎071/62230; ④), two good choices from the many options on Pearse Rd. **Hostels** include the central and popular *White House* on Markievicz Rd (☎071/45160; ②), which gets overcrowded in the summer; *Eden Hill* on Pearse Rd (☎071/43204, *edenhill@iol.ie*; ②), where there's a cosy sitting-room, though the beds have seen better days; the *Yeats County Hostel*, Lord Edward St (☎071/46876; ②), clean, well-run, and handy for the train station; or the very comfortable *Harbour House*, Finisklin Rd (☎071/71547, *harbourhouse@eircom.net*; ②), a strangely exposed and desolate mile-long walk from the centre – women may feel uncomfortable doing this walk alone. There are **campsites** five miles from town at Rosses Point to the north (bus #473) and Strandhill to the west (bus #472); both have fine beaches and Strandhill, while unsafe for swimming, draws in plenty of surfers. Most pubs in Sligo serve a decent **bar lunch**: *Hargadon's* on O'Connell St is one of the best and has fine old traditional snugs; the *Garavogue* on Stephen St has a river terrace and serves excellent international food and bar snacks all day. For top pizza head for *Bistro Bianconni* restaurant on O'Connell St; *The Loft* on Lord Edward St has an extensive menu of world cuisine. Sligo does well for **pubs**: tiny *Shoot the Crows* on Castle St is popular with the arty set, and *Fiddler's Creek* along the river on Rockwood Parade is always lively. Best for **traditional music** are *Sheela na Gig* on Bridge St, owned by local trad stars Dervish, with nightly summer sessions; *Earley's* bar across the road also has regular sessions. A pre-club hangout is *The Belfry*, with adjoining nightclub *Toff's* on Kennedy Parade, the town's favourite night-spot. Check the weekly *Sligo Champion* or free *Sligo Weekender* for listings.

Drumcliff, Benbulben and Glencar Lough

Heading north from Sligo, the Derry bus will take you to **DRUMCLIFF**, a monastic site probably better known as the last resting place of **W.B. Yeats**. His grave is in the grounds of an austere nineteenth-century Protestant church, within sight of Benbulben, as the poet wished. In 575 St Columba founded a monastery here, and you can still see the remnants of a round tower on the left of the roadside and a tenth-century high cross – the only one in County Sligo – on the right. The attractive stone visitor centre (Mon–Fri 8.30am–6pm, Sat 10am–6pm, Sun 1–6pm) offers a visual presentation and guided tours of the grounds. The best **B&B** in the area is *Urlar House* (☎071/63110; ④; March–Oct), one mile north of Drumcliff graveyard. It makes the best base for the climb of **Benbulben**, which at 1730 feet is one of the most spectacular mountains in the country, its profile changing dramatically as you round it. Access to its slopes is easy, but avoid it after dark as there are a lot of dangerous clefts.

Just to the east of Drumcliff, set into the back of Benbulben, about ten miles from Sligo, is **Glencar Lough**. For the best of the lake, follow the road around its northern edge until you see the "Waterfall" signpost. From the nearby car park a path leads up to the waterfall itself, which is especially impressive after heavy rain. For an excellent mountain walk, continue along the road to the eastern end of the lake where a track rises steeply northwards to the **Swiss Valley**, a deep rift crowned with silver fir. Bus #64 from Sligo to Manorhamilton (info ☎071/60066) can drop you at the junction for the lake, from where it's a two-mile walk.

Donegal Town and around

Regular buses connect Sligo to **DONEGAL TOWN** (*www.donegal.ie*), a bustling place with traffic usually jammed around its old marketplace, the Diamond. Donegal is a fine base from which to explore the stunning coastal countryside and inland hills and loughs, though just about the only thing to see in the town itself is the well-preserved shell of **O'Donnell's Castle** on Tirchonaill St by the Diamond (Easter–Oct daily 10am–5.15pm; €3.80), a fine example of Jacobean architecture. On the left bank of the River Eske stand the few ruined remains of **Donegal Friary**, while on the opposite bank a woodland path known as Bank Walk offers wonderful views of **Donegal Bay** and towards the **Blue Stack Mountains**, which rise at the northern end of Lough Eske.

There are dozens of **B&Bs** in town, and to avoid a lot of walking it's simplest to call at the **tourist office** on the Quay (July & Aug daily 9am–8pm; Easter–June & Sept Mon–Sat 9am–5pm; ☎073/21148, *www.northwestireland.travel.ie*). There are two **hostels** off the Killybegs road just outside town: the nearest is *Donegal Town Independent Hostel* (☎073/22805; ②), with camping facilities, while An Óige *Ball Hill Hostel* is about three miles out on the north side of Donegal Bay (☎073/21174; ②; Easter–Sept). **Eating** places are plentiful. You'll find excellent burgers and pizza at the *Harbour*, opposite the tourist office; a substantial cheap meal at the *Atlantic Café* at the town end of Main St; and great fish-and-chips a few doors down at *The Errigal*. As for **pubs**, many do good lunches and are good evening watering holes. The *Olde Castle Bar*, next to the castle, is fine for a quiet daytime drink; *McGroarty's* on the Diamond has a good bar menu and weekly traditional session; while *The Scotsman* on Bridge St has regular open traditional sessions. The *Abbey Hotel* on the Diamond hosts a popular **disco** on Saturday and Sunday nights. For **bike rental** head for the Bike Shop on Waterloo St.

Slieve League and Glencolmcille

To the west of Donegal Town lies one of the most stupendous landscapes in Ireland – the stark and beautiful **Teelin Bay** and the awesome Slieve League cliffs. An ideal base for exploring the region is one of the most welcoming independent **hostels** in the country, the *Derrylahan Independent Hostel* (☎073/38079, *derrylahan@eircom.net*; ②), on the seaside road between **KILCAR** and **CARRICK**; it also has a **campsite**. If you're arriving by bus (daily from Donegal to Glencolmcille), ask to be put down at The Rock and the driver will direct you from there – otherwise it's two miles from Kilcar.

There are two routes up to the ridge of **Slieve League**: a back route following the signpost to Baile Mór just before you come into Teelin, and the road route from Teelin to Bunglass, which is one thousand sheer feet above the sea. The former path, which in places is only a few feet wide and can be extremely dangerous in windy weather, has you looking up continually at the ridge known as One Man's Path, on which walkers seem the size of pins, while the frontal approach swings you up to one of the most thrilling cliff scenes in the world, the **Amharc Mór** (Great View). On a good day it's possible to see one-third of Ireland from the summit.

Following One Man's Path across the summit it is possible to walk via Malinbeg and Malinmore to **GLENCOLMCILLE** – the Glen of St Columbcille, the name by which Columba was known after his conversion. Approaching it by road, you cross a landscape of desolate upland moor, after which the rich verdant beauty of Glen (as it's known) comes as a welcome shock. Glencolmcille has been a place of pilgrimage since the seventh century AD, following Columba's stay in the valley. Every June 9 at midnight the locals, holding flaming torches, commence a three-hour barefoot itinerary of the cross-inscribed slabs that stud the valley basin, finishing up with Mass at 3am in the small church. If you want to attempt *Turas Cholmcille* ("Columba's Journey") yourself, the **Folk Village Museum** (Easter–Sept Mon–Sat 10am–6pm, Sun noon–6pm; €2.50) has a map of the route, and is very informative about local history. Its primary business however is the guided tours through a cluster of replica thatched cottages, each decked out with appropriate period furniture and artefacts; there's a National School replica with a section on American artist Rockwell Kent, who painted marvellous landscapes of the area, and a Shebeen house and bakery producing seaweed wine, Guinness marmalade and other delicacies. A path up to the left from the Folk Village leads to the *Dooey Hostel* (☎073/30130, *www.holidayhound.com/dooeyhostel/htm*; ②), which has wheelchair access, a **campsite** and a staggering view; from behind the hostel, cliff walks steer off around the south side of the bay above a series of jagged drops. Rising from the opposite end of the valley mouth, the promontory of Glen Head is surmounted by a Martello tower. On the way out, you pass the ruins of **St Columbcille's Church**, with a "resting slab" where Columba lay down exhausted from prayer. The place to eat in Glencolmcille is *An Cistin*, part of the Foras Cultúir Uladh complex (Ulster Studies Centre), or there's the *Lace House Restaurant* on the main street above the **tourist office** (June–Aug daily 10am–6pm; ☎073/30116). **B&Bs** include *Brackendale* (☎073/30038; ④) and *Corner House* (☎073/30021; ④; April–Sept), both near *Biddy's Bar* in Cashel, the village centre.

NORTHERN IRELAND

Nowhere is the pace of political change more rapid, nor the future more uncertain, than in **Northern Ireland**. In May 1998, after thirty years of "The Troubles", its people overwhelmingly voted in support of a political settlement and, it was hoped, an end to political and sectarian violence. Although an assembly was elected and, in November 1999, an executive formed, deep mistrust and suspicion continues to exist on both sides, making the future of the executive extremely fragile. Despite the political instability the north remains a relatively safe place. **Belfast** and **Derry/Londonderry** – two lively cities that should be on every visitor's list of must-sees – have no obvious security presence beyond the occasional hovering army helicopter. Despite the fact that the North is generally more hospitable than the Republic, it's not as popular with tourists, even though the northern coastline – especially the weird geometry of the **Giant's Causeway** – is as spectacular as anything you will find in Ireland. In the southwest corner of the province is the great **Lough Erne**, a huge lake complex dotted with islands and surrounded by richly beautiful countryside, and **Enniskillen**, a town resonant with history.

Belfast

A quarter of Northern Ireland's population lives in the capital, **BELFAST**. While the legacy of "The Troubles" is clearly visible in the landscape of areas like West Belfast – the peace walls, derelict buildings and political murals – security measures have been considerably eased and the place buzzes with a tangible sense of optimism engendered by the peace process and economic rejuvenation.

Belfast began life as a cluster of forts guarding a ford across the River Farset, which nowadays runs beneath the High Street. However, the city was very slow to develop, and its history doesn't really begin until 1604, when Sir Arthur Chichester was "planted" in the area by James I. By the eighteenth century the cloth trade and shipbuilding had expanded tremendously, and the population increased ten-fold in a century. It was then noted for its liberalism, but in the nineteenth century the sectarian divide became wider and increasingly violent. Although Partition and the creation of Northern Ireland with Belfast as its capital inevitably boosted the city's status, the Troubles exacerbated the industrial decline which hit much of the British Isles during the 1980s. However, a massive programme of regeneration commenced in the 1990s at the first signs of peace, fuelled by the billions of pounds being pumped in from Britain, the European Union and the International Fund for Ireland in the hope that political stability would ensue. While a stable democracy has yet to be achieved and the city remains both physically and psychologically scarred from years of violence, there is a real sense of liveliness and hope.

Arrival, information and accommodation

Flights arrive at **Belfast International Airport** (☎028/9448 4848) in Aldergrove, nineteen miles west (buses every 30min to Europa bus station; £5), or **Belfast City Airport** (☎028/9045 7745), three miles northeast (bus #21 to city centre; £2). As for **ferries** from Britain, the Seacat catamarans from Heysham and Troon (☎0870/552 3523) use Donegall Quay (15min walk to centre, or £3 taxi-ride); Stena high-speed ferries from Stranraer (☎0870/570 7070) dock a little further north at Corry Road (taxi £4); Norse Irish Ferries from Liverpool (☎028/9077 9090) dock further north on West Bank Road (taxi £5); P&O ferries from Cairnryan and Fleetwood (☎0870/242 4777), as well as some Stena boats from Stranraer, dock at Larne, 20 miles north (bus or train into centre). Most **trains** call at Great Victoria Street Station in the centre, with the exception of trains from Dublin and Larne which terminate at Central Station on East Bridge St (☎028/9089 9411). **Buses** from Derry, the Republic, the airports and ferry docks arrive at Europa bus station beside Great Victoria St train station, while buses from the north coast use Laganside Buscentre in Queen's Square. A regular Centrelink bus connects all bus and train stations. The excellent **Citybus** company (☎028/9024 6485) covers nearly everywhere you'll want to go; it's worth buying a multi-journey ticket (£3.40) for four daily journeys, available from newsagents and the Citybus kiosk in Donegall Square West, which can also provide a free bus map. **Ulsterbus** (☎028/9033 3000) serves the outlying areas; and there are special weekend **late-night buses** from Donegall Square West (Fri & Sat 1–2am; £3). Full details of all buses and trains is at *www.translink.co.uk*. **Taxis**, based at ranks in Donegall Square and elsewhere, charge a minimum £2.

The **Belfast Welcome Centre** is at 47 Donegall Place (Mon–Fri 9am–5.30/7pm, Sat 9am–5.30pm; June–Sept also Sun noon–5pm; ☎028/9024 6609, *www.gotobelfast.com*), with information and an accommodation booking service as well as left-luggage facilities and an Internet café. **Bord Fáilte**, for information about the Republic, is at 52 Castle St (Mon–Fri 9am–5pm; June–Sept also Sat 9am–12.30pm; ☎028/9032 7888).

Many of Belfast's numerous **B&Bs** are on the south side of the city in the university area, and there are now a number of budget options.

The Ark, 18 University St (☎028/9032 9626, *www.harth.co.uk*). Friendly, comfortable hostel close to the university. ②.

Arnie's Backpackers, 63 Fitzwilliam St (☎028/9024 2867). Cheerful and relaxed independent hostel, also near the university. ②.

Belfast International Youth Hostel, 22 Donegall Rd (☎028/9031 5435, *www.hini.org.uk*). Large, well-equipped but characterless new hostel in the city centre. ②.

Botanic Lodge, 87 Botanic Ave (☎028/9032 7682). Popular, family-run B&B; 17 rooms, but only two ensuite. ⑤.

Eglantine, 21 Eglantine Ave (☎028/9066 7585). Seven cosy B&B rooms in a Victorian house. ⑤.

The Linen House, 18 Kent St (☎028/9058 6400, *www.belfasthostel.com*). Slightly shabby but very welcoming, centrally located hostel. ②.

Liserin, 17 Eglantine Ave (☎028/9066 0769). Another well-run seven-room B&B in the university area. ⑤.

The City

Belfast **City Hall**, presiding over central **Donegall Square**, is an austere building (guided tours June–Sept Mon–Fri 10.30am, 11.30am & 2.30pm, Sat 2.30pm; rest of year Mon–Sat

2.30pm; free), its civic purpose almost subservient to its role in propagating the ethics of Presbyterian power. At the northwest corner of the square stands **Linenhall Library** (Mon–Fri 9.30am–5.30pm, Sat 9.30am–4pm), where the Political Collection houses over 80,000 publications dealing with every aspect of Northern Ireland's political life since 1966. The streets leading north off Donegall Square North take you into the main shopping area. Towards the river, either side of Ann St, you're in the narrow alleyways known as the **Entries**, where you'll find some great old saloon bars. At the end of High Street the clock tower is a good position from which to view the world's second- and third-largest cranes, Goliath and Samson, across the river in the Harland & Wolff shipyard where the **Titanic** was built. North of the clock tower is a series of grand edifices which grew out of a similar civic vanity to that invested in the City Hall. The recently restored **Customs House**, a Corinthian-style building, is the first you'll see, but the most monolithic is the Protestant **Cathedral of St Anne** at the junction of Donegall and Talbot streets, a neo-Romanesque basilica started in 1899. Across the river from the Customs House is the face of a new Belfast, the ambitious **Odyssey** development (*www.theodyssey.co.uk*) housing a sports stadium, cinema complex, science exhibition centre, shopping malls and Ireland's first *Hard Rock Café*. Further along the waterside is the impressive Waterfront Hall concert venue.

The university area inhabits part of the stretch of **South Belfast** known as "The Golden Mile", starting at the **Grand Opera House** on Great Victoria St. The area is littered with eating places, pubs and bars, B&Bs and guest houses; dozens of restaurants have sprung up, triggered by the refurbishment of the grandiose, turn-of-the-century Opera House in 1980. Among the attractions is the **Crown Liquor Saloon**, one of the greatest of the old Victorian gin palaces and now a National Trust property, though still open for drinking. Before heading straight into the university quarter, sidestep off Great Victoria St into **Sandy Row**, which runs parallel to the west. A strong working-class, Protestant quarter, with the tribal pavement painting to prove it, it's one of the most glaring examples of Belfast's divided worlds, wildly different from the cosmopolitan Golden Mile. Just past the southern end of Sandy Row, three church steeples frame the entrance to the university quarter, of which **Queen's University** is the architectural centrepiece, flanked by the most satisfying Georgian terrace in Belfast, University Square. Just to the side of the university are the verdant **Botanic Gardens** whose Palm House (Mon–Fri 10am–4/5pm, Sat & Sun 2–4/5pm; free; *www.parks.belfastcity.gov.uk*) was the first of its kind in the world. Also in the Botanic Gardens you'll find the **Ulster Museum** (Mon–Fri 10am–5pm, Sat 1–5pm, Sun 2–5pm; free, except for some major exhibitions; bus #69/#70/#71; *www.ulstermuseum.org.uk*), with its collection of Irish art, history and natural sciences as well as an Early Ireland gallery, Living Sea interactive display and treasures salvaged from the Spanish Armada ships which foundered off the Giant's Causeway in 1588. Check the monthly *Arts Link*, available from the tourist office, for details of special exhibitions.

Eating, drinking and entertainment

It's never hard to keep yourself amused in the evenings. Many of the best places to **eat** and the liveliest **pubs** can be found around Great Victoria St and in the university area, and Belfast's best entertainment is **music** in the pubs. Some of the main sessions and venues are listed below; other good sources of information are *The Big List*, available free in pubs and record shops, and the *Belfast Evening Telegraph*.

RESTAURANTS AND CAFÉS

Archana, 53 Dublin Rd. Indian Balti house with *Little India*, reputedly the country's first vegetarian Indian restaurant, downstairs.

Bewley's, Donegall Arcade. Branch of the famous Dublin coffee house serving good-value breakfasts, lunches and snacks.

Café Conor, 11a Stranmillis Rd. Stylish café beside Botanic Gardens with chalkboard hot food specials and breakfasts.

Chez Delbart (aka **Frogities**), 10 Bradbury Place. French food at good prices, though you often have to queue.

Láziz, 99 Botanic Ave. Splendid Moroccan restaurant serving beautifully presented and extremely tasty specialities.

Maggie May's, 45 Botanic Ave. Huge, economically priced portions with lots of veggie choices.

Sun Kee, 38 Donegall Pass. No-frills decor, but superbly adventurous Chinese food, popular with the local Chinese community.

Villa Italia, 39 University Rd. Queues outside are the best indicator of this reasonably priced Italian restaurant's popularity.

PUBS AND MUSIC

The Apartment, Donegall Sq West. Trendy city centre hangout featuring two bars on three floors.

Bar Twelve, Lower Crescent. Fashionable spot in the university area, popular with young clubbers.

The Basement, Donegall Sq East. Basement bar with a stylish interior, cosmopolitan atmosphere and regular blues sessions (Fri).

Crown Liquor Saloon, 46 Great Victoria St. The city's most famous pub, decked out like a spa bath, with a good range of Ulster food and Strangford oysters in season.

The Empire, 42 Botanic Ave. Cellar bar in converted church with regular music and popular comedy club (Tues).

The John Hewitt, Donegall St. Owned by Belfast Unemployed Resource Centre, this popular bar is named after the Belfast poet, with all profits used to help the city's unemployed.

Kelly's Cellars, 30 Bank St. Traditional bar with live bands (Fri) and sessions (Sat).

Kitchen Bar, 16 Victoria Sq. Fine old bar, tucked away behind Ann St – great value lunches and traditional sessions (Fri & Sat).

Madden's, Smithfield. Unpretentious and atmospheric pub, with regular traditional sessions.

The Morning Star, 17 Pottinger's Entry. Old-fashioned bar serving great food in the restaurant upstairs, with a very cheap lunchtime buffet downstairs.

Morrison's Spirit Grocer's, 21 Bedford St. Retro bar with interesting lunchtime food.

The Rotterdam, 54 Pilot St. Names big and small play in this docklands venue. First-class sounds.

Listings

Airlines Aer Lingus, 46 Castle St (☎0845/973 7747); British Airways (☎0845/773 3377); British European (☎0870/567 6676); British Midland (☎0870/607 0555); EasyJet (☎0870/600 0000); Gill Airways (☎0191/214 6666).

Car rental Avis (☎028/9024 0404); Budget (☎028/9023 0700).

Exchange As well as banks, try Thomas Cook, 11 Donegall Place (Mon–Sat 9am–5.30pm; ☎028/9055 0030).

Hospitals Belfast City Hospital, Lisburn Rd (☎028/9032 9241); Royal Victoria, Grosvenor Rd (☎028/9024 0503).

Internet Broncos.web.net, Great Victoria St (Mon–Fri 8.30am–10pm, Sat 10am–10pm, Sun 11am–8pm; ☎028/9080 8081).

Left luggage Belfast Welcome Centre, 47 Donegall Place.

Police Main police station is in North Queen St (☎028/9065 0222).

Post office General Post Office, Castle Place (Mon–Sat 9am–5.30pm).

Travel agent USIT, Fountain Centre, College St (☎028/9032 4073).

The Giant's Causeway and around

Since 1693, when the Royal Geographical Society publicized it as one of the great wonders of the natural world, the **Giant's Causeway**, 65 miles north of Belfast on the coast (*www.giantscausewayofficialguide.com*), has been a major tourist attraction. Made up of an estimated 37,000 polygonal basalt columns, it's the result of a massive subterranean explosion some sixty million years ago, which stretched from here to Staffa in Scotland, where it was responsible for the formation of Fingal's Cave. A huge mass of molten basalt spewed out onto the surface and, as it cooled, solidified into what are, essentially, massive polygonal crystals. For sheer other-worldliness, it can't be beaten. Public transport is well-organized in summer. **Trains** from Belfast go to **COLERAINE**, and some go on to **PORTRUSH**; from either, you can catch the **"open-topper"** bus (July & Aug 4 daily) to the Causeway, or from Portrush there's bus #172. The scenic Antrim Coaster coach (Goldline Express #252) runs from both Belfast bus stations direct to the Causeway (June–Sept once daily). The Causeway's **visitor centre** (daily 10am–5pm, July & Aug until 7pm; ☎028/2073 1855; free; car parking £3) has information and a small exhibition. Taking the path down the cliffs from the visitor centre (or the shuttle bus; every 15min; £1 return) brings you to the most spectacular of the blocks where many people linger, but if you push on, you'll be rewarded with relative solitude and views of some of the more impressive formations high in the cliffs. One of these, **Chimney Point**, has an appearance so bizarre that it persuaded the ships of the Spanish Armada to open fire on it, believing that they were attacking Dunluce Castle, a few miles further west. An alternative two-mile circuit follows the spectacular clifftop path from the visitor centre, with views across to Scotland, to a flight of 162 steps leading down the cliff to a set of 40ft basalt columns known as the **Organ Pipes**, from where paths lead round to the shuttle-bus stop alongside the Causeway proper.

Seven miles west of the Causeway – just beyond **PORTBALLINTRAE**, a stop on the open-topper bus – sits sixteenth-century **Dunluce Castle** (Mon–Sat 10am–7pm, Sun 2–7pm; Oct–March closes 4pm; £1.50), the most impressive ruin along this entire coastline. Sited on a fine headland high above a cave, it looks as if it only needs a roof to be perfectly habitable once again. Its original owner, **Sorley Boy MacDonnell**, was driven from the castle by the English in 1584, but soon returned, using the salvage from a Spanish Armada wreck to finance the repairs. His son was made Viscount Dunluce and Earl of Antrim by James I, but in 1639 Dunluce Castle paid the penalty for its precarious position when the kitchen, complete with cooks and dinner, fell off during a storm. Shortly afterwards the MacDonnells moved to more comfortable lodgings in Glenarm.

Derry/Londonderry

DERRY lies at the foot of Lough Foyle, less than three miles from the border with the Republic. While many entrances to the city are marked by signs in Irish welcoming visitors to Derry, it appears as **"LONDONDERRY"** on Northern Ireland road-signs, a preference adhered to only by Unionists and the British government. The city presents a beguiling picture, its two hillsides terraced with pastel-shaded houses punctuated by stone spires, and, being two-thirds Catholic, has a very different atmosphere from Belfast. However, the reputation of the North's second city has more to do with its politics than its scenic appeal. Until recently Derry's Catholic majority was denied its civil rights by gerrymandering, which ensured that the Protestant minority maintained control of all important local institutions. The situation came to a head after the Protestant Apprentice Boys' March in August 1969, when the RUC attempted to storm the Catholic estates of the Bogside district. In the tension that ensued, British troops were for the first time widely deployed in Northern Ireland. On January 31, 1972, the crisis reached a new pitch when British paratroopers opened fire on civilians, killing thirteen unarmed demonstrators in what became known as **Bloody Sunday**. Derry is now greatly changed: tensions eased considerably here long before Belfast, thanks in part to a determinedly even-handed local council, although defiant murals remain and marching is still a contentious issue. The city centre has undergone significant regeneration too, with the construction of several new shopping malls, and Derry has gained a justifiable reputation for innovation in the arts.

The City

You can walk the entire circuit of Derry's **city walls** – some of the best-preserved defences left standing in Europe – and this makes the best starting point for exploration. A mile in length and never higher than a two-storey house, the walls are reinforced by bulwarks, bastions and a parapeted earth rampart as wide as a thoroughfare. Within their circuit, the medieval street pattern has remained, with four gateways – Shipquay, Butcher, Bishop and Ferryquay – surviving from the first construction, in slightly revised form.

You're more than likely to make your approach from the **Guildhall Square**, once the old quay. Most of the city's cannon are lined up here, between Shipquay and Magazine gates, their noses peering out above the ramparts. A reconstruction of the medieval **O'Doherty Tower** (Tues–Sat 10am–5pm, July & Aug also Sun 2–5pm; £4.20), houses an award-winning display outlining the turbulent historic development of the city including the recent Troubles. Turning left at **Shipquay Gate**, you follow the promenade as it doglegs at Water Bastion where the River Foyle once lapped the walls at high tide. Continue on to Newgate Bastion and **Ferryquay Gate**, where you can look out across the river to the Waterside area, once primarily Protestant, now almost half Catholic – further evidence of the lessening of the city's political tensions. Between Ferryquay and Bishop's Gate the major sight is the Protestant **St Columb's Cathedral** (Mon–Sat 9am–1pm & 2–4/5pm; £1 donation), just within the south section of the walls; it overlooks the Fountain, the Protestant enclave immediately outside the same stretch of walls, and offers one of the best views of the city. The cathedral was built in 1633, the first post-Reformation cathedral to be constructed in the British Isles. In 1688–89 Derry played a key part in the Williamite victory over the Catholic King James II by holding out against a fifteen-week siege that cost the lives of one-quarter of the city's population. The cathedral was used as a battery during the siege, its tower serving as a lookout post and in the entrance porch you'll find the cannonball shot into the grounds by the besieging army with proposals for the city's surrender. Inside, flags brought back from military expeditions give the interior a strong sense of British imperialism. Other things to look out for are the eighteenth-century bishop's throne, and the window panels showing scenes as diverse as the relief of the city on August 12, 1689, and St Columba's mission to Britain.

Back on the walls, you'll pass the white sandstone **courthouse** next to Bishop's Gate and you'll see, downhill to the left, the only remaining tower of the old Derry jail. At the **Double Bastion** sits the Roaring Meg cannon, used during the siege, while down in the valley below are the streets of the Bogside. This was once the undisputed preserve of the Republican IRA, and **Free Derry Corner** marks the site of the original barricades erected against the British army at the height of the Troubles. Nearby are the Bloody Sunday and Hunger Strikers' memorials, while several large murals commemorate victims of the fighting. Along the city wall to the right is the **Royal Bastion** lookout point, former site of the Rev. George Walker statue which was blown up in 1973. It is in Walker's and their predecessors' memory that the Protestant Apprentice Boys march round the walls every August 12.

Practicalities

Trains from Belfast arrive on the east bank of the Foyle; the old town is a short walk away across Craigavon Bridge. **Buses** (☎028/7126 2261) arrive at Foyle St beside Guildhall Square; Ulsterbus from Belfast and Dublin, and Bus Éireann from Galway and Dublin. City of Derry **airport** (☎028/7181 0784) is seven miles northeast, connected to the centre by bus. Good roads enter from all directions, making it easy to hitch. The **tourist office** is situated in a new building at 44 Foyle St (July–Sept Mon–Fri 9am–7pm, Sat 10am–6pm, Sun 10am–5pm; rest of year Mon–Thurs 9am–5.15pm, Fri 9am–5pm; ☎028/7126 7284) and contains both a Bord Fáilte office and a branch of the Northern Ireland Tourist Board. There's a 150-bed **hostel** in the city centre at Oakgrove Manor, 4 Magazine St (☎028/7137 2273; ②), which also has bikes for rent, and the independent *Steve's Backpackers* at 4 Asylum Rd, half-a-mile from town down Strand Rd (☎028/7137 7989; ②). **B&Bs** are springing up within the city; try the excellent-value *Saddler House*, 36 Great James St (☎028/7126 9691; ④), or *Clarence House*, 15 Northland Rd (☎028/7126 5342; ④). **Eating out** has recently improved dramatically, though the choice is still not great. Shipquay Street and Strand Rd have the widest variety, including *The Leprechaun*, 23 Strand Rd, which serves up delicious home-baking and hot meals, and *The Gallery* on Shipquay St, which offers tasty and reasonably priced meals. *Badger's Bar and Restaurant*, 16 Orchard Rd, is another good option. The **pubs** are the best bet for entertainment. Students congregate at *Café Rock* where Rock and Strand roads meet; upstairs *Club Earth* is hugely popular. *Sandinos* on the Foyle Road attracts an arty crowd with Tuesday night film screenings; *Metro* at the bottom of Shipquay St, *Mullans* on three floors at Little James St, and the central *Strand Bar*, leading into the trendy *Cosmopolitan*, are all lively drinking spots. **Traditional music** venues are mostly on Waterloo St just outside the northern walls: check out *Dungloe Bar* and the *Rocking Chair*. *Peadar O'Donnell's* also has regular sessions and a doorway through to the *Gweedore* with contemporary bands.

Enniskillen and around

South of Derry and Donegal, and a short distance east of Sligo, **ENNISKILLEN** – served by regular buses from Belfast, Derry and Dublin – sits on a lake island, a narrow ribbon of water passing each side of the town between the Lower and Upper **Lough Erne**. The water loops its way around the core of the town, its glassy surface lending Enniskillen a sense of calm and reflecting the mini-turrets of **Enniskillen Castle**. Rebuilt by William Cole, to whom the British gave Enniskillen in 1609, the castle houses the **Watergate History and Heritage Centre** and the **Regimental Museum of the Royal Inniskilling Fusiliers** in the keep (Mon 2–5pm, Tues–Fri 10am–5pm; May–Sept also Sat 2–5pm, July & Aug also Sun 2–5pm; £2), a proud, polished display of the uniforms, flags and paraphernalia of the town's historic regiments. A mile along the Belfast road stands **Castle Coole**, the eighteenth-century home of the Earls of Belmore (June–Aug Mon–Wed & Fri–Sun 1–6pm; April, May & Sept Sat & Sun 1–6pm; £3; gardens open all year for free; £2 per car). A perfect Palladian building of Portland stone, with an interior of fine plasterwork and superb furnishings, it sits in a beautiful land-scaped garden, whose cultivated naturalness reinforced its owners' belief that the harmony of God's creation mirrored that of society.

Opposite the **bus station** on Wellington Rd is the **tourist office** (Easter–Sept Mon–Fri 9am–5.30/7pm, Sat 10am–6pm, Sun 11am–5pm; rest of year Mon–Fri 9am–5.30pm; ☎028/6632 3110, *www.fermanaghlakelands.com*), which will book rooms for a small charge. **B&Bs** are across the town's western bridges, along the A46 Derrygonnelly road and along the Sligo road. For **eating out**, follow the locals to *Franco's* in Queen Elizabeth Rd, while the best Indian is *Kamal Mahal* in Water St, off High St. A lot of the **bars** along High St and its continuation, Townhall St, do decent pub food, particularly *The Vintage* and *Pat's Bar*; for fill-ing sandwiches, soups and hot meals head for the *Jolly Sandwich Bar* on Darling St. **Country music** is big in Enniskillen, but you'll find regular **traditional sessions** at the *Railway Hotel*, Forthill Rd every weekend; *The Vintage* has regular live music and DJs.

Lough Erne

The earliest people to settle in this region lived on and around the two lakes of **Lough Erne**, and many of the islands here are in fact *crannogs* (Celtic artificial islands). Its myriad water-ways were impenetrable to outsiders, protecting the settlers from invaders and creating an enduring cultural isolation. Evidence from stone carving suggests that Christianity was accepted far more slowly here than elsewhere: several pagan idols have been found on Christian sites, and the early Christian remains to be found on the islands strongly show the influence of pagan culture.

The easiest place to visit is **Devenish Island**, two miles northwest of Enniskillen in the south of the Lower Lough. A monastic settlement was founded here by St Molaise in the sixth century, and despite being plundered by Vikings in the ninth century and again in the twelfth, it continued to be an important religious centre up until the Plantations. It's a delight-ful setting, not far from the lough shore, and the considerable ruins span the entire medieval period. There are regular **ferries** (Easter–Sept) from Trory Point, four miles north of Enniskillen on the A32 road (£2.25; check times with tourist office; ☎028/6632 3110), as well as a two-hour **cruise** of Lough Erne, stopping at Devenish for half-an-hour, from the Round "O" pier off the Derrygonnelly road a short distance northwest of Enniskillen, by Erne Tours (May–Sept; £5; ☎028/6632 2882). To immerse yourself thoroughly in the beauty of the lough scenery, you could hardly do better than stay in the official **hostel** (☎028/6862 8118; ②) set in the **Castle Archdale** forest park near Lisnarrick on the eastern shore; buses from Enniskillen to Pettigo (4 daily) will put you down at the park gates, a mile from the hostel. From near the hostel you can get a ferry (June–Sept) to **White Island**, whose ruined abbey bears early Christian carvings that look eerily pagan. The most disconcerting is the lewd female figure known as a Sheila-na-Gig, with bulging cheeks, a big grin, open legs and arms pointing to her genitals. This could be a female fertility figure, a warning to monks of the sins of the flesh, or an expression of the demoniacal power of women, designed to ward off evil.

travel details

Trains

Details given below refer to weekday services; extra services may run on Mondays and Fridays, fewer on Sundays.

Dublin to: Belfast (8 daily; 2hr 10min); Cork (8 daily; 2hr 30min–3hr); Galway (5 daily; 2hr 45min); Killarney (5 daily; 3hr 30min); Limerick (11 daily; 2hr–2hr 30min); Rosslare (3 daily; 3hr); Sligo (3 daily; 3hr 15min); Waterford (4 daily; 2hr 40min); Westport (3 daily; 3hr 40min).

Belfast to: Derry/Londonderry (7 daily; 2hr 40min); Dublin (8 daily; 2hr 10min); Larne Harbour (15 daily; 55min).

Coleraine to: Portrush, for Giant's Causeway (7 daily; 15min).

Cork to: Dublin (8 daily; 2hr 30min–3hr); Killarney (5 daily; 2hr).

Derry/Londonderry to: Belfast (7 daily; 2hr 40min); Coleraine (7 daily; 40min).

Galway to: Dublin (5 daily; 2hr 45min).

Killarney to: Cork (5 daily; 2hr); Dublin (4 daily; 3hr 30min).

Sligo to: Dublin (3 daily; 3hr 15min).

Waterford to: Dublin (4 daily; 2hr 40min).

Westport to: Dublin (3 daily; 3hr 40min).

Buses

Details below cover Bus Éireann or Ulsterbus services on summer weekdays; extra services may run on Fridays, fewer in winter and on Sundays.

Dublin to: Belfast (7 daily; 3hr); Cork (6 daily; 4hr 30min); Derry (5 daily; 4hr 30min); Donegal (5 daily; 4hr 30min); Enniskillen (4 daily; 3hr 40min); Galway (13 daily; 3hr 30min); Killarney (5 daily; 6hr); Sligo (4 daily; 4hr); Waterford (7 daily; 2hr 45min); Westport (3 daily; 5hr).

Belfast to: Derry/Londonderry (6 daily; 1hr 40min); Dublin (7 daily; 3hr); Enniskillen (9 daily; 2hr 40min); Galway (1 daily; 7hr); Sligo (3 daily; 4hr).

Cork to: Dublin (6 daily; 4hr 30min); Killarney (7 daily; 2hr 30min).

Derry/Londonderry to: Donegal (4 daily; 1hr 30min); Dublin (5 daily; 4hr 15min); Enniskillen (6 daily; 1hr 30min); Sligo (3 daily; 2hr 45min).

Donegal to: Derry (4 daily; 1hr 30min); Dublin (5 daily; 4hr 30min); Galway (3 daily; 5hr); Glencolmcille (2 daily; 2hr); Sligo (3 daily; 1hr 30min).

Enniskillen to: Belfast (9 daily; 2hr 35min); Derry/Londonderry (6 daily; 1hr 30min); Dublin (4 daily; 3hr 40min).

Galway to: Clifden (2–5 daily; 1hr 45min–2hr 20min); Doolin (1–7 daily; 1hr 35min); Dublin (13 daily; 3hr 30min).

Killarney to: Dingle (5 daily; 2hr); Waterville via Caherciveen (1–2 daily; 2hr).

Sligo to: Belfast (3 daily; 4hr); Galway (5 daily; 2hr 45min).

CHAPTER 15

ITALY

Introduction

Of all the countries in Europe, **Italy** is perhaps the hardest to classify. It is a modern, industrialized nation; it is the harbinger of style, its designers leading the way with each season's fashions. But it is also a Mediterranean country, with all that that implies. Agricultural land covers much of the country, a lot of it, especially in the south, still owned under almost feudal conditions. In towns and villages all over the country, life stops during the middle of the day for a siesta. It is also strongly family-oriented, with an emphasis on the traditions and rituals of the Catholic Church. If there is a single national characteristic, it's to embrace life to the full, manifest in the hundreds of local festivals taking place on any given day; in the importance placed on good food; and above all in the daily domestic ritual of the collective evening stroll or *passeggiata*. There is also, of course, the country's enormous cultural legacy: Tuscany alone has more classified historical monuments than any country in the world and every region retains its own relics of an artistic tradition generally acknowledged to be the world's richest.

Italy wasn't a unified state until 1861, something borne out by the regional nature of the place today. The country breaks down into nineteen often very distinct *regione*, but the sharpest division is between north and south. The north is one of the most advanced industrial societies in the world; the south, known as *il mezzogiorno*, is by contrast one of the most economically depressed areas in Europe. In the northwest, the regions of Piemonte and Lombardy – and the two main centres of **Turin** and **Milan** – epitomize the wealthy north. Liguria, the small coastal province to the south, has long been known as the "Italian Riviera" and is accordingly crowded with sun-seeking holidaymakers for much of the summer season. But it's a beautiful stretch of coast, and its capital, **Genoa**, is a bustling port with a long seafaring tradition. The interest of the northeastern regions of the Veneto and Friuli-Venezia Giulia is of course **Venice** itself, a unique city, and every bit as beautiful as its reputation would suggest – though this means you won't be alone in appreciating it. If the crowds are too much, there's also the arc of historic towns outside the city – **Verona**, **Padua** and **Vicenza**. To the south, the region of Emilia-Romagna has been at the heart of Italy's postwar industrial boom. Its coast is popular among Italians, especially **Rimini**, Italy's brashest seaside resort; and there are also the ancient centres of **Ravenna**, **Parma** and **Bologna**, the capital – one of Italy's liveliest but least appreciated cities. Central Italy perhaps represents the most commonly perceived image of the country, and **Tuscany**, with its classic rolling countryside and the art-packed towns of **Florence**, **Pisa** and **Siena**, is one of its most visited regions. Neighbouring **Umbria** is similar in all but its relative emptiness, though it gets fuller every year, as visitors flock into towns such as Perugia, Spoleto and Assisi – and unspoilt Urbino in adjacent Marche. Lazio, to the south, is a poor and desolate region whose real focal point is **Rome**, Italy's capital, the one city in the country which owes allegiance neither to the north nor south. Beyond Rome, **Naples**, capital of Campania, a petulant, unforgettable city, is the spiritual heart of the Italian south, and is close to some of Italy's finest ancient sites in **Pompeii** and **Herculaneum**, not to mention its most spectacular stretch of coast around **Amalfi**. Puglia, the "heel" of Italy, has underrated pleasures, notably the souk-like quality of its capital, **Bari**. As for **Sicily**, the island is really a law unto itself, a wide mixture of attractions ranging from some of the finest preserved Hellenic treasures in Europe, to the drama of Mount Etna and one of the country's fanciest beach resorts in **Taormina**. **Sardinia**, too, feels far removed from the mainland, especially in its relatively undiscovered interior, though you may be content to just explore its fine beaches.

Information and maps

Most Italian towns, major train stations and airports have a **tourist office** – usually either an APT (Azienda Promozione Turistica), an EPT (Ente Provinciale per il Turismo), a provincial branch of the state organization, an IAT (Ufficio di Informazione e Accoglienza Turistica) or an AAST (Azienda

---

ITALY ON THE NET

www.enit.it – official Tourist Board site

www.virtualitalia.com – Italian culture and society

www.italytour.com – comprehensive site

www.thecity.it – excellent directory service

www.paginegialle.it – Italian Yellow Pages

Autonoma di Soggiorno e Turismo), a smaller local outfit. Very small or out-of-the-way villages may have a tiny office known as a Pro Loco. All offer much the same mix of general advice and bumph, free maps and accommodation lists, though rarely do they book accommodation. **Opening hours** vary, but larger city offices are likely to be open Mon–Sat 9am–1pm & 4–7pm, and sometimes for a short period on Sun mornings; smaller offices may open weekdays only.

Most tourist offices will give out **maps** of their local area for free, but if you want an indexed town plan, Studio FMB cover the country's towns and cities; Falk also sell decent plans of the major cities. For road maps, the Automobile Club d'Italia issue a reasonable free map, available from the State Tourist Office; the clearest and best-value large-scale commercial road map of Italy is the Michelin 1:1,000,000, or you have the choice between the TCI 1:800,000 North and South maps. Michelin also produce 1:400,000 maps of the north and south, as well as Sicily and Sardinia, and TCI do maps of the individual regions, scale 1:200,000.

Money and banks

Italy is one of twelve European Union countries which have changed over to a single currency, the **euro** (€). Euro notes and coins are scheduled to be issued from the beginning of 2002, with Lire (abbreviated as L or £) remaining in circulation during a transition period, at a fixed rate of 1936.27 lire to 1 euro, until they are scrapped entirely at the end of February 2002. After this date you will still be able to exchange your Lire for euros in banks for at least a year. Euro notes are issued in **denominations** of 5, 10, 20, 50, 100, 200 and 500 euros, and coins in denominations of 1, 2, 5, 10, 20 and 50 cents and 1 and 2 euros.

All prices in this chapter are given in euros correct at the time of going to press. There will no doubt be some rounding off or, more probably, up of prices in the first few months after the introduction of the euro.

If you have a debit or credit card with a PIN number, then the most convenient option for dealing with your money is to use the cash dispensers (bancomat) which are found everywhere, and often have the most favourable rate of exchange. If you must change money or travellers' cheques, an **exchange bureau** that charges no commission is a far better choice than a bank, which can add insult to injury by taking up at least an hour of your time. Otherwise, the larger hotels will change money and travellers' cheques,

but if you stay in a reasonably large city the rate is invariably better at the train station exchange bureau – normally open evenings and weekends.

Communications

Post office opening hours are usually Mon–Sat 8am–6.30pm (smaller towns have no service on Sat). If you want stamps, you can also buy them in *tabacchi*. Public **telephones** are run by several companies and come in various forms. For the most common type, you'll need a phonecard, available from *tabacchi* and news-stands for €2.50, €5 and €7.50. Coin phones have all but been phased out. If you can't find a call box, bars will often have a phone you can use. Alternatively, you'll find offices at the larger train stations and a few other areas where you can make a metered call from a kiosk. For calls within Italy – local, long-distance and international – dial all digits, including 0 and the area code. Note however, that **mobile** numbers no longer have the prefix 0 and you need to omit the 0 even when dialing any old numbers.

Italy is improving rapidly when it comes to **Internet access**. You'll find at least one cybercafé in most towns and increasing numbers in larger places. Hourly charges vary from €2 in the south to €7.75 in big cities, though some tourist offices and hostels offer the service for free.

Getting around

The easiest way of travelling around Italy is by train. The Italian train system is relatively inexpensive, reasonably comprehensive, and in the north of the country at least, fairly efficient – far preferable to the fragmented and sometimes grindingly slow buses.

■ Trains

Apart from a few private lines, Italian **trains** are operated by Italian State Railways (Ferrovie dello Stato or FS; *www.fs-on-line.com*). There are seven types of train. At the top of the range is the ETR 450 Pendolino, an exclusively first-class intercity service whose ticket prices include reservation, newspapers and a meal. EuroCity trains connect the major Italian cities with centres such as Paris, Vienna, Hamburg and Barcelona, while Eurostar Italia and Intercity/Intercity Notte trains link the major Italian centres; a supplement of around thirty percent of the ordinary fare is payable on all three services, while a reservation is obligatory only on Eurostar services.

Espresso, Diretto and Interregionale are long-distance expresses stopping at most major stations, and a Regionale stops just about everywhere and is usually worth avoiding. In summer it's often worth making a seat reservation on the main routes. Fares are very reasonable, calculated by the kilometre and thus easy to work out for each journey. The single second-class fare from Milan to Bari, one of the longest journeys you're ever likely to make, currently costs about €50.

As with most other European countries, you can cut costs greatly by using a **rail pass**. InterRail and Eurail passes give free travel on the whole FS network (though you'll be liable for supplements on the fast trains), and there are specific Italian passes available. For details of the EuroDomino pass, the Italy Railcard/Biglietto Turistico Libera Circolazione (which entitles you to unlimited travel on consecutive days on the entire network, including Intercity services) and Italy Flexi-Railcard (which allows travel for 24 hours, from midnight to midnight, on a number of days within a one-month period), see Basics, p.21. A Chilométrico ticket, valid for up to five people at once, gives 3000km worth of free travel on a maximum of twenty separate journeys and costs £88/$150 (€110 in Italy). Under-26s can also buy a Cartaverde, which for €20.70 entitles you to twenty percent off train fares for a year; it's available from any main train station in Italy. Children under four years old (not occupying a seat) travel free, while those aged four to twelve qualify for a fifty-percent discount on all journeys.

■ Buses

Almost everywhere is connected by some kind of **bus** service, but schedules can be sketchy, and are drastically reduced – sometimes nonexistent – at weekends. It's worth knowing that in rural areas timetables are often designed with the working or school day in mind, making for some frighteningly early starts and occasionally no buses at all during school holidays. Even if there are plentiful buses, anticipate

that the journey will be long and full of stops and starts. Bus terminals are often next door to the train station in larger towns. Tickets are bought on board, though on longer hauls you can try to buy them in advance direct from the bus company; seat reservations are, however, not possible.

■ Driving

Travelling by **car** in Italy is relatively painless. The roads are good, the highway (*autostrada*) network very comprehensive, and the notorious Italian drivers rather less erratic than their reputation suggests. Most highways are toll-roads, but rates aren't especially high: as a general reference, you'll pay about €10 for a small car from Milan to Bologna. As for documentation, if bringing your own car you need a valid **driving licence** and you're advised to get an International Green Card of insurance. You drive on the right, and at junctions give precedence to vehicles coming from the right. Speed limits are 50kph in built-up areas, 110kph on country roads, 130kph on highways. If you break down, dial ☎116 and the nearest office of the Automobile Club d'Italia (ACI) will be informed.

Car rental in Italy is pricey, currently around £260/$360 a week for a small car with unlimited mileage. Italy is also one of the more expensive countries in Europe in which to buy petrol. **Hitchhiking** is seldom practised, particularly not in the south, and is definitely not advisable for women travelling alone.

Accommodation in Italy is never especially cheap, but it is at least fairly reliable: hotels are star-rated and required to post their prices clearly in each room. Most tourist offices have details of hotel rates in their town or region, and you can usually expect them to be broadly accurate. In the major cities and resorts, booking ahead is often a good idea, particularly during the summer months.

One peculiar Italian institution is the confusingly named *albergo diurno* or day hotel, an establishment providing bathrooms, showers, hairdressers

---

ACCOMMODATION PRICE CODES

Throughout this guide, accommodation is coded on a scale of ① to ⑨, the code indicating the lowest price per person per night you could expect to pay in each establishment in high season. With hostels this is the nightly rate per person; with hotels, the price is arrived at by dividing the cost of the cheapest double room by two. The prices indicated by the codes are as follows:

① under £5/$8 (€9)	④ £15–20/$24–32 (€27–36)	⑦ £30–35/$48–56 (€54–63)
② £5–10/$8–16 (€9–18)	⑤ £20–25/$32–40 (€36–45)	⑧ £35–40/$56–64 (€63–72)
③ £10–15/$16–24 (€18–27)	⑥ £25–30/$40–48 (€45–54)	⑨ £40/$64 (€72) and over

and the like – but no accommodation. You'll find them at train stations and they're usually open daily 6am–midnight – useful for a fast clean-up if you're on the move.

■ Hotels

Hotels in Italy come with a confusing variety of names. *Locanda* are historically the most basic option, although the word is sometimes used to denote something quite fancy these days; *pensione* too can be little different from the regular *alberghi* or hotels. Prices do vary greatly between the poor south and the wealthy north, and between cities and the country, but on average, you can expect to pay about €35 for a double without private bathroom in a one-star hotel, and a minimum of about €75 for a double in a three-star. In very busy places it's not unusual to have to stay for a minimum of three nights, and many proprietors will add the price of breakfast to your bill whether you want it or not; try to resist this – you can eat more cheaply in a bar. Whatever happens, establish the full price of your room before you accept it. It is advisable to book ahead if you are travelling in high season or during holidays; many of the hotels listed are small and fill up quickly.

■ Hostels and student accommodation

There are around sixty **hostels** in Italy, charging between €7.50 and €15 for a dorm bed for HI members, and if you're two people travelling together, they don't represent a massive saving on the cheapest double hotel room. Whether or not you're a member, you'll need to book ahead in the summer months. You can get a full list of Italian hostels from the Associazione Italiana Alberghi per la Gioventù, Via Cavour 44, 00184 Roma (☎06.487.1152, *www.hostels-aig.org*); you can also email many of the HI hostels listed in the chapter via the Web site above. In some cities it's also possible to stay in **student accommodation** during the summer; accommodation is generally in individual rooms and can work out cheaper than a straight hotel room. Again, you'll need to book in advance.

■ Campsites

Camping is not really as popular in Italy as it is in some other European countries, but there are plenty of sites, and most of them are well equipped. The snag is that they're expensive, and, once you've added the cost of a tent and vehicle, don't always work out a great deal cheaper than staying in a hostel. Prices are around €3–5 per person daily, plus €3.50–8.50 for a caravan or tent, and around €3 for a vehicle. If you're camping extensively it might be worth investing in the *Guida Camping d'Italia* (€5.20 plus postage) from Federcampeggio, Via Vittorio Emanuele 11, 50041 Calenzano, Florence (☎055.882.391), or check out *www.camping.it* for campsite lists.

Food and drink

Though it has long been popular primarily for its cheapness and convenience, Italian **food** also gets its share of attention as one of the world's great cuisines. Indeed, there are few national cuisines that can boast so much variety in ingredients and cooking methods. Italian **wine**, too, is now more respected, as the Italian industry's devotion to fizzy pop and characterless plonk is replaced by a new pride and a better product.

■ Food

Most Italians start their day in a bar, their **breakfast** consisting of a cappuccino, and a *cornetto* – a jam, custard or chocolate-filled croissant. At other times of day, **sandwiches** (*panini*) can be pretty substantial. There are sandwich bars (*paninoteche*) in larger towns and cities, and in smaller places grocer's shops (*alimentari*) will normally make you up whatever you want for about €2–2.50 a sandwich. Bars may also offer *tramezzini*, ready-made sliced white bread with mixed fillings – less appetizing than the average panino but still tasty, and slightly cheaper at around €1.50 a time. You can get hot takeaway food in a *távola calda*, a snack bar that sometimes has limited seating. The bigger towns have these, and there's often one inside larger train stations. Try also a *rosticceria*, serving spit-roast chicken, slices of pizza, fries and burgers. Italian ice cream (*gelato*) is justifiably famous: a cone (*un cono*) is an indispensable accessory to the evening *passeggiata*. Most bars have a fairly good selection, but for real choice go to a *gelateria*.

As for sit-down food, the cheapest thing you can eat is **pizza**. This is now a worldwide phenomenon but Italy remains the best place to eat it – usually thin and flat, and, if you're lucky, cooked in the traditional way in wood-fired ovens. Pizzerias range from stand-up counters selling slices (*pizza al taglio*) to fully fledged restaurants. A basic cheese and tomato pizza (*margherita*) costs around €3–4, a fancier variety €4–8. Full meals are generally served in a trattoria or a ristorante. Traditionally, a **trattoria** is a cheaper purveyor of home-style cooking, a **ristorante** more upmarket, though these days there's a fine line between the two. In either, pasta dishes go for around €4–6, and there's usually not a problem just having this; the main fish or meat courses will normally be €5–8. Bear in mind that almost everywhere you'll pay about €1.50 per person extra for bread (*pane*), which is brought to your table automatically. Fish is generally either served whole or by weight: 250g is usually plenty for one person. Vegetables or salads – *contorni* – are ordered separately: potatoes will invariably be fried, salads either green (*verde*) or mixed (*mista*). Afterwards you nearly always get a choice of fresh fruit (*frutta*) or a selection of desserts (*dolci*). At the end of the meal ask for the bill (*il conto*). As well as the **cover charge** (*coperto*), service (*servizio*) will often be added, generally about ten percent. If service isn't included you should tip about the same amount, though trattorias outside the large cities won't necessarily expect this.

■ Drink

Although many Italian children are brought up on wine, there's not the same emphasis on dedicated drinking as there is in Britain or the US. Bars are less social centres than functional places for a quick coffee or beer. You pay first at the cash desk (*la cassa*), present your receipt (*scontrino*) and give your order. In the south of the country it's customary to leave a tip of about €0.05–0.10 on the counter, though no one will object if you don't. Bear in mind that sitting down sometimes costs twice as much, especially if you sit outside. Coffee is always excellent, small and black (*espresso*, or just *caffè*), or white and frothy (*cappuccino*); try also a *granita* – cold coffee with crushed ice, usually topped with cream. Tea (*te*) comes with lemon (*con limone*) unless you ask for milk (*con latte*); it's also served cold (*te freddo*). As for soft drinks, a *spremuta* is a fresh fruit juice; there's also crushed-ice fruit *granitas*, and the usual range of fizzy drinks and concentrated juices.

Beer (*birra*) usually comes in one-third or two-third litre bottles. Commonest and cheapest are the Italian brands, *Peroni* and *Dreher*, both of which are very drinkable; in most bars you have a choice of this or draught beer (*alla spina*). All the usual spirits are on sale and known mostly by their generic names, as well as Italian brandies like *Stock* and *Vecchia Romagna*. A generous shot of these costs about €1.50, more for imported stuff. There's also **grappa**, made from the leftovers from the wine-making process and something of an acquired taste. You'll

also find **fortified wines** like Martini, Cinzano and Campari and a daunting selection of liqueurs. Amaro is a bitter after-dinner drink, Amaretto much sweeter with a strong taste of marzipan, Sambuca a sticky-sweet aniseed concoction. Wine is invariably drunk with meals, and is still very cheap. If you're unsure about what to order, don't be afraid to try the local stuff: ask for *vino sfuso* or simply *un mezzo* (a half litre), or *un quarto* (a quarter), sometimes served straight from the barrel, particularly down south, and often very good for just €3.10 a litre. Bottled wine is pricier but still good value; expect to pay around €6.50 a bottle in a restaurant, less than half that from a shop or supermarket.

Opening hours and holidays

Most **shops and businesses** in Italy open Mon–Sat from 8 or 9am until around 1pm, and from about 4pm until 7pm or 8pm, though in the north offices work to a more standard European 9am–5pm day. Everything, except bars and restaurants, closes on Sunday, though you might find fish shops in some coastal towns and *pasticcerias* or bakers open until Sunday lunchtime. Closing days for restaurants and bars are given in the text wherever possible. Most **churches** (unless otherwise stated in the text) open early morning and close around noon, opening again at 4pm until 7pm or 8pm. **Museums** traditionally open Tues–Sat from 9am until 2pm, and from 9am to 1pm on Sunday, and are closed on Mondays, but many now have greatly extended hours – see individual accounts in the text. When opening hours change between summer and winter, we've separated the times with a slash: the summer hours are the longer ones. Be prepared to queue in Rome, Venice and Florence, where last tickets are usually issued 30–60min before closing. It's also worth checking out the main museums for late-night openings in summer. Most archeological sites open every day, 9am until late evening – usually one hour before sunset. Everything closes on the following **national holidays**: Jan 1; Jan 6; Easter Monday; April 25; May 1; Aug 15; Nov 1; Dec 8; Dec 25 and 26.

Emergencies

Despite what you hear about the mafia, most of the crime you're likely to come across in Italy is of the small-time variety, prevalent in the major cities and the south of the country, where gangs of *scippatori* operate, snatching handbags, wallets, jewellery, etc.

You can minimize the risk of this by being discreet, not flashing anything of value, keeping a firm hand on your camera and bag, and never leaving anything valuable in your car. If it comes to the worst, you'll be forced to have some dealings with the **police**. In Italy these come in many forms: the *Polizia Urbana/Vigili Urbani* are mainly concerned with directing the traffic and punishing parking offences; the *Polizia Stradale* patrol highways; the *Carabinieri*, with their military-style uniforms and white shoulder belts, deal with general crime, public order and drug control; and the *Polizia Statale* are the branch you'll perhaps have most chance of coming into contact with, since it's to them that thefts should generally be reported.

If you need medical treatment, Italian **pharmacies** (*farmacia*) are well qualified to give you advice on minor ailments, and to dispense prescriptions, and there's generally one open all night in the bigger towns and cities. They work on a rota system; you'll find the address of the nearest open one on any farmacia door. If you are more seriously ill, call an ambulance or go to the *Pronto Soccorso* (casualty) section of the nearest hospital.

Emergency Numbers

Police ☎112; Ambulance ☎113; Fire ☎115.

THE NORTHWEST

The **northwest** of Italy is many people's first experience of the country, and in many ways represents its least "Italian" corner, at least in the regions of **Piemonte** and **Val d'Aosta**, where French is still spoken by some as a first language. **Turin**, on the main rail and road route from France to Milan, is the obvious first stop, the first capital of Italy after the Unification in 1860 and a grand city with many remnants of its past as seat of the Savoy dukes, later the Italian royals. To the east, **Lombardy** was long viewed by northerners as the heart of Italy – emperors from Charlemagne to Napoleon came here to be crowned – and northern European business magnates continue to take its capital, Milan, more seriously than Rome, the region's big businesses and banks wielding political as well as economic power across the nation. Lombardy's landscape has paid the price for economic success: industry chokes the peripheries of towns and even spreads its polluting tentacles into the northern lakes and mountain valleys. Nonetheless, Lombardy has its attractions. **Milan** is a natural gateway to the region, an upbeat city with plenty to see, dominating the plain that forms the southern part of Lombardy, the towns of which – such as **Mantua** – flourished during the Middle Ages and Renaissance, and retain their historical character today. To the north, the lakes and low mountains shelter fewer historic towns, though **Brescia** is a notable exception. The region of **Liguria** to the south provides light relief, an unashamedly touristy strip, and perhaps the country's most spectacular stretch of coastline. Chief town of the province is the sprawling port of **Genoa**, west of which the **Riviera di Ponente** is one long ribbon of hotels, though **Finale Ligure** is a pleasant resort. Southeast, towards Tuscany, the **Riviera di Levante** is more rugged, its mix of mountains and fishing villages "discovered" by the Romantics in the late eighteenth century, preparing the way for the first package tourists in the early twentieth century. Now the whole area explodes into a ruck every July and August, with people coming to resorts like **Portofino** strictly for pose value – although stretches like the **Cinque Terre** are still well worth discovering.

Turin

"Do you know Turin?" wrote Nietzsche, "It is a city after my own heart…a princely residence of the seventeenth century, which has only one taste giving commands to everything, the court and its nobility. Aristocratic calm is preserved in everything: there are no nasty suburbs." Although **TURIN**'s traffic-choked streets are no longer calm, and its suburbs, built by the vast Fiat empire that virtually owns the city, are as nasty as any in Italy, the city centre's gracious Baroque avenues, opulent palaces, sumptuous churches and splendid collections of Egyptian antiquities and northern European paintings are still here – a pleasant surprise to those who might have been expecting satanic factories and little else.

Arrival and accommodation

Turin's main train station, Porta Nuova, is on Corso Vittorio Emanuele, at the foot of Via Roma, convenient for the city centre and hotels. There are two **tourist offices** – the main one at Piazza Castello 161 (Mon–Sat 9.30am–7.00pm, Sun 9.30am–3pm; ☎011.535.181, *www.turis-motorino.org*) and a smaller one at the train station (same hours). Many of Turin's **cheap hotels** are in the sleazy quarter off Via Nizza, convenient enough but not an advisable choice, particularly for solo women. Somewhat safer, but more expensive, are the streets opposite Porta Nuova, close to Piazza Carlo Felice. There are also a number of fairly reasonably priced hotels west of Piazza Castello. As for specific hotels, the *Paradiso*, Via Berthollet 3 (☎011.669.8678; ②), is extremely clean and does doubles without bath. The *Canelli*, Via San Dalmazzo 7, close to the pedestrian area of Via Garibaldi (☎011.537.166; ②), is the cheapest option and very central, while *Hotel Mobledor*, Via Accademia Albertina 1 (☎011.812.5805; ③), is a small friendly hotel and also in an excellent location. The HI hostel, *Ostello Torino*, is at Via Alby 1 (☎011.660.2939; ②) – take bus #52 from Porta Nuova. If you're camping, the Villa Rey is the most convenient site, on the far side of the river south of the hostel – take bus #61 from Porta Nuova, and then bus #56.

The City

The grid street-plan of Turin's Baroque centre makes finding your way about easy. **Via Roma** is the city's central spine, a grand affair lined with designer shops and ritzy cafés and punctuated by the city's most elegant piazzas, most notably **Piazza San Carlo**, a little way north of Porta Nuova station – known with some justification as the parlour of Turin. This is a grand and stylish open space, flanked with symmetrical porticoed buildings housing opulent cafés and centring on an equestrian statue of the Savoy duke, Emanuele Filiberto, its entrance guarded by the twin Baroque churches of **San Carlo** and **Santa Cristina**, whose languishing nude statues represent Turin's two rivers – the Po and the Dora. Around the corner, the **Museo Egizio** (Tues–Sat 8.30am–7.30pm, Sun 9am–2pm; €6.20) holds a superb collection of Egyptian antiquities, gathered together in the late eighteenth century under the aegis of Carlo Emanuele III. There are gorgeously decorated mummy cases, an intriguing assortment of everyday objects and, the undoubted highlight, the Tomb of Kha, the burial chamber of a 1400 BC architect, Kha, and his wife Merit, discovered in 1906 at Deir-el-Medina. Above the museum, the **Galleria Sabauda** (Tues–Wed & Fri–Sun 9am–2pm, Thurs 10am–7pm; €4.10) was built around the Savoys' private collection and is still firmly stamped with their taste – a miscellany of Italian paintings, supplemented by a fine Dutch and Flemish collection, including works by Memling, Brueghel, David Teniers Jnr and Van Dyck. Almost opposite, the **Museo del Risorgimento** (Tues–Sat 9am–7pm, Sun 9am–1pm; €4.10), housed in the double-fronted **Palazzo Carignano**, is worth a brief visit even if you usually give such things a miss.

Around the corner, the fifteenth-century **Duomo** (daily 8am–noon & 3–7pm) houses the **Turin Shroud**, which is usually kept under wraps and only on display to the public during holy years but a copy is on display by the altar. It's a piece of cloth imprinted with the image of a man's body that has been claimed as the shroud in which Christ was wrapped after his crucifixion. In 1989 it was announced that carbon-dating tests showed it to be a fake, made between 1260 and 1390 – although no one is any the wiser about how the medieval forgers actually managed to create the image. The shroud had a narrow escape in April 1997 when the church was gutted by fire. Beyond the Duomo, the massive **Piazza della Repubblica** was designed by the eighteenth century architect Juvarra, though his grand plan for it is marred nowadays by seedy market buildings.

The scruffy porticoes of Via Po lead down to the river, ending just before the bridge in the vast arcaded **Piazza Vittorio Veneto**. Turn off halfway down, along Via Montebello, to the **Mole Antonelliana**, which houses a new **Museo del Cinema** (Tues–Sun 9am–7pm; €6.70) that explores the development of cinema as a global phenomenon with exhibits including early moving pictures and twenty-first-century special effects. Along the river from here, the massive **Parco del Valentino** is one of Italy's largest parks, home to the Castello e Borgo Medioevale (daily 9am–7pm; castle closes at 6pm; €2.60), a synthesis of the best houses and castles of Piemonte and Val d'Aosta, built with the same materials and techniques as the originals. Further south still, the **Museo dell'Automobile** at Corso Unità d'Italia 40 (Tues–Sun 10am–6.30pm; ☎011.677.666; €5.16; bus #34 from Piazza Marconi) traces the development of the motor car, with one of the first Fiats, a bulky 1899 model, the gleaming Isotta Fraschini driven by Gloria Swanson in *Sunset Boulevard*, and, the pride of the collection, the 1907 Itala which won the Peking to Paris race in the same year.

Eating, drinking and nightlife

There are snack bars and takeaways on Via Nizza, some tempting delicatessens on Via Lagrange and a superb *rosticceria* on Corso Vittorio Emanuele for do-it-yourself lunches.

Cossolo, Via Roma 68, does great pastries, sandwiches and other snacks. *Frullati Varturi*, Piazza Castello 15, is in a good central location for sandwiches, and there are branches of the quality self-service chain, *Brek*, at Piazza Carlo Felice 22 and on Via Santa Teresa. For more substantial **meals** try *L'Arcimboldo*, Via Santa Chiara 54, a restaurant specializing in *pasta fresca* with a choice of a hundred different sauces (evenings only). *Pizza Cernaia*, on Via Cernaia, has a vast range of excellent pizzas, while *Porto di Savona*, Piazza Vittorio Veneto 2, is a popular, cheerful spot. Make sure you at least look in on one of the city's fin-de-siècle **cafés**, most of which have an atmosphere that more than compensates for the steep prices. In *Baratti* and *Milano*, Piazza Castello 29, genteel Torinese sip tea in a rarefied ambience of mirrors, chandeliers and carved wood. The glitzy *Caffè San Carlo*, Piazza San Carlo 156, is reputedly a favoured hang-out of politicians and industrialists, while *Fiorio*, Via Po 8, was once the haunt of Cavour, and is now visited mostly for its ice cream. There's also an **Internet** café, *@h!*, at Via Montebello 13 (daily 10am–1pm 2–7pm; €5.15/hr). Later on in the **evening**, Via Carlo Alberto and Via San Quintino are the areas to check out. Otherwise try *Doctor Sax*, Murazzi di Lungo Po Cadorna 4, a live-music bar (Afro, jazz and rock), or *Café des Arts* on Via Giolitti, which attracts a young, bohemian crowd. For something a bit more clubby, try *AEIOU*, Via Spanzotti 3, housed in a former warehouse with a wide selection of music.

Milan

The dynamo behind the country's economic miracle, **MILAN** is a city like no other in Italy. It's foggy in winter, muggy in summer, and is closer in outlook as well as distance to London than Palermo, a fast-paced business city in which consumerism and the work ethic rule. Because of this most people pass straight through, and if it's summer and you're keen for sun and sea this might well be best. But at any other time of year it's worth giving Milan a bit more of a chance. It's a historic city, with enough churches and museums to keep you busy for a week, much of the city a testament to the prestige-building of the Visconti dynasty and their successors, the Sforzas, who ruled here in Renaissance times; and the contemporary aspects of the place represent the leading edge of Italy's fashion and design industry, not to mention a nightlife scene which is perhaps Italy's most varied.

Arrival, information and city transport

Most international **trains** pull in at the monumental Stazione Centrale, northeast of the centre on Piazza Duca d'Aosta, on metro lines 2 and 3 (MM2 or MM3). International and long-distance **buses** arrive at and depart from Piazza Castello, in front of the Castello Sforzesco. Of Milan's two **airports,** Linate is the closer, 7km from the city centre, and connected with the airport bus terminal at Stazione Centrale every twenty minutes between 5.40am and 7pm and then every half-hour until 9pm; it's a twenty-minute journey (€2.30). There are also ordinary city buses (#73; €0.80) until around midnight from Linate to Piazza San Babila. The other airport, **Malpensa**, is 50km away towards Lago Maggiore. It's connected by train with Cadorna station (every 30min; €2.60; *www.malpensaexpress.com*) and by bus with Stazione Centrale to coincide with arrivals and departures (€6.70).

Information and city maps are available from Milan's main **tourist offices**, at the Stazione Centrale (Mon–Sat 8am–7pm, Sun 9am–12.30pm & 1.30–6pm; ☎02.725.24360) and at Via Marconi 1, off Piazza Duomo (summer Mon–Fri 8.30am–8pm, Sat 9am–1pm & 2–7pm, Sun 9am–1pm & 2–5pm; winter Mon–Fri 8am–7pm, Sat 9am–1pm & 2–6pm, Sun 9am–1pm & 2–5pm; ☎02.725.24300). There's also a good Web site on Milan at *www.vivimilano.it*. At some point you'll want to make use of the **public transport** system – an efficient network of trams, buses and metro. The metro is the most useful, made up of three lines, the red MM1, green MM2 and yellow MM3, converging at Duomo, Centrale FS, Loreto and Cadorna. Buses, trams and the metro run from around 6am to midnight, when night buses take over, following the metro routes until 1am. Tickets, valid for 75 minutes, cost a flat €0.80 from tobacconists, bars and metro station newsagents. The 75-minute ticket is valid for one journey only

CENTRAL MILAN

on the metro regardless of journey length. You can also buy a *blochetto* of ten tickets for €7.75, or a 24-hour ticket for €2.60, from the Centrale or Duomo metro stations.

Accommodation

Milan is more a business than a tourist city, and its **accommodation** is geared to the expense-account traveller. However, there are plenty of one-star hotels, mostly concentrated in the area around Stazione Centrale, and along Viale Vittorio Veneto and Corso Buenos Aires. Close to the station, the *Casa Mia*, Viale V. Veneto 30 (☎02.657.5249; ⑤), is the best option, while *San Tomaso*, at Viale Tunisia 6 (☎02.295.14747; ④), is another popular choice. Not far from Stazione Centrale off Viale Tunisia, the *Arno*, Via Lazzaretto 17 (☎02.670.5509; ④), gets packed from March to July, but you can always try the similar *Pensione Eva* (☎02.670.6093; ④) at the same address. *Siena*, on Via P. Castaldi 17 (entrance on Via Lazzaretto), has small, spotless rooms (☎02.295.16108; ⑤), and *Speronari*, Via Speronari 4 (☎02.864.61125; ⑤), is friendly, and very close to the cathedral; *Manzoni*, Via Senato 45, off Corso Venezia (☎02.760.21002; ⑤), is near the public gardens and also very central. *Trieste e Germania*, Via M. Polo 13 (02.65.54405; ⑤), is near Piazza della Repubblica. The official **HI** hostel, *Piero Rotta*, Via Salmoiraghi 2 (☎02.392.67095; ②), out in the northwest suburbs near the San Siro stadium, is perhaps the cheapest option but isn't especially welcoming and has a 12.30am curfew (MM QT8). Failing that, *ACISJF*, Corso Garibaldi 121 (☎02.290.00164; ③; MM Moscova), run by nuns, is a reasonable option for women under twenty-five; accommodation here is in four-bedded rooms. As for campsites, there's the *Autodromo* site (April–Sept) in Monza, in the park near the Formula One circuit; take a bus from Stazione Centrale.

The City

Historic Milan lies at the centre of a web of streets zeroing in on **Piazza del Duomo**, the city's main hub, a mostly pedestrianized square that's home to the best of Milan's streetlife, and, on its eastern side, the **Duomo**, the world's largest Gothic cathedral, begun in 1386 and taking nearly five centuries to complete. From the outside it's an incredible building, notable as much for its decoration as its size and with a front that's a strange mixture of Baroque and Gothic. The gloomy interior holds, among other things, a large crucifix which contains a nail from Christ's cross, crafted to become the bit for the bridle of Emperor Constantine's horse, while close by, beneath the presbytery, the **Scurolo di San Carlo** (daily 9am–noon & 2.30–6pm; €1.40) is an octagonal crypt designed to house the remains of Saint Charles Borromeo, a zealous sixteenth-century cardinal who was canonized for his work among the poor of the city. He lies here in a glass coffin, clothed and bejewelled, wearing a gold crown attributed to Cellini. Adjacent to Borromeo's resting place, the treasury has Byzantine ivory-work and heavily embroidered vestments, while, back towards the entrance, is the cathedral's fourth-century **Baptistry** (daily 9.45am–12.45pm & 2–5.45pm; €1.50) where St Ambrose baptized St Augustine in 387 AD. You can also get up to the cathedral **roof** (March–Nov 9am–5.45pm; Nov–Feb 9am–4.15pm; lift €4.65, on foot €3.10, combined ticket with the Duomo museum €6.20), whose you can sunbathe among a forest of pinnacles and statues with fine views of the city and, on clear days, even the Alps.

The **Museo del Duomo** (daily 9.30am–12.30pm & 3–6pm; €5.16; *www.internetlandia.com/duomo*), on the southern side of the piazza, holds casts of a good many of the three thousand or so statues and gargoyles that spike the Duomo. You can also see how it might have ended up, in a display of entries for a nineteenth-century competition for a new facade. South of Piazza del Duomo, the church of **San Satiro**, off the busy shopping street of Via Torino, is a study in ingenuity, commissioned from Milan's foremost Renaissance architect, Bramante, in 1476. Originally the oratory of the adjacent ninth-century church of San Satiro, Bramante transformed it into a long-naved basilica by converting the long oblong oratory into the transept and adding a trompe l'oeil apse to the back wall. Five minutes away, just off Via Torino at Piazza Pio XI 2, the **Pinacoteca Ambrosiana** (Tues–Sun 10am–5.30pm; €6.20, *www.ambrosiana.it*) was founded by another member of the Borromeo family, Cardinal Federico, and is one of the largest libraries in Europe – though what you come here for now is the art collection, stamped with his taste for Jan Brueghel, sixteenth-century Venetians and some of the more kitschy followers of Leonardo. Among many mediocre works, there is a rare painting by Leonardo himself, *Portrait of a Musician*.

On the opposite side of the piazza is the gaudily opulent **Galleria Vittorio Emanuele**, a cruciform glass-domed gallery designed in 1865 by Giuseppe Mengoni, who was killed when he fell from the roof a few days before the inaugural ceremony. Take a look at the circular mosaic beneath the cupola composed of the symbols of the cities of then newly unified Italy – it's considered good luck to spin round on the testicles of the bull (which represents Turin). The Galleria leads through to the world-famous **La Scala** opera house, opened in 1778 with an opera by Antonio Salieri. Its small **museum** (Mon–Sat 9am–noon & 2–5pm; €3.10), with composers' death masks, plaster casts of conductors' hands and a statue of Puccini in a capacious overcoat, may be the only chance you get to see the interior.

The shopping quarter to the northeast of La Scala – the few hundred square yards bordered by Via Monte Napoleone, Via Sant'Andrea, Via Spiga and Via Borgospesso, the so-called **Quadrilatero d'Oro** – is home to the shops of all the big designer names, along with design studios and contemporary art galleries. The area is well worth a stroll, if only to observe the better-heeled Milanese searching out the perfect objet d'art for their designer pads. Indeed, to leave Milan without looking in the windows of its designer boutiques would be to miss out on a crucial aspect of the city.

A couple of blocks east, **Via Brera** sets the tone for the city's arty quarter with its fancy galleries and art shops, and, at its far end, Milan's most prestigious gallery, the **Pinacoteca di Brera** (summer Tues–Fri 8.30am–7.30pm, Sat 8.30am–11pm, Sun 9am–8pm; winter Tues–Sat 9am–5pm, Sun 9am–midday; €4.14), filled with works looted from the churches and aristocratic collections of French-occupied Italy. There's a good representation of Venetian painters – works by Paolo Veronese, Tintoretto, Gentile Bellini and his follower, Carpaccio, and a *Pietà* by Gentile's more talented brother, Giovanni, deemed one of the most moving paintings in the history of art. Look out also for Mantegna's *The Dead Christ*, an ingenious painting of Christ on a wooden slab, viewed from the soles of his feet upwards; Piero della Francesca's chill *Madonna*, perhaps the most famous painting here; and Raphael's *Marriage of the Virgin*, whose languid Renaissance mood is in sharp contrast to the grim realism of Caravaggio's *Supper at Emmaus*, painted a century later.

West of the Via Accademia down Via Pontaccio, the **Castello Sforzesco** rises imperiously from the mayhem of Foro Buonaparte, laid out by Napoleon in self-tribute as part of a grand plan for the city. An arena and triumphal arch remain from the scheme, behind the castle in the **Parco Sempione**, a notorious hangout for junkies and prostitutes, but otherwise the red-brick castle is the main focus of interest, with its crenellated towers and fortified walls one of Milan's most striking landmarks. Begun by the Viscontis and rebuilt by their successors, the Sforzas, whose court was one of the most powerful and cultured of the Renaissance, the castle houses – along with a number of run-of-the-mill collections – the **Museo d'Arte Antica** and **Pinacoteca** (daily 9.30am–1pm & 2–5.30pm; free), the former including Michelangelo's *Rondanini Pietà*, which the artist worked on for the last nine years of his life. The latter contains a cycle of monochrome frescoes illustrating the Griselda story from Boccaccio's *Decameron*; one of Mantegna's last works, *Madonna in Glory among Angels and Saints*; and paintings by Vincenzo Foppa, the leading Milanese artist before Leonardo da Vinci.

South of the castle, the **Museo Archeologico** at Corso Magenta 15 (Tues–Sun 9.30am–5.30pm; free) is worth a visit for its displays of kitchen utensils and jewellery from Roman Milan, as well as a colossal head of Jove, found near the castle. But what really brings visitors into this part of town is the church of **Santa Maria delle Grazie**, an originally Gothic pile, partially rebuilt by Bramante (who added the massive dome), that is famous for its fresco of the **Last Supper** by Leonardo da Vinci, which covers one wall of the refectory. Advance booking is now essential to view the painting (Cenacolo Vinciano; reservations Mon–Fri 9am–7pm ☎02.8942.1146; viewing Tues–Sat 9am–6.30pm, Sun 9am–7.30pm; €6.20, plus €1 obligatory booking fee).

Eating, drinking and nightlife

Food in workaholic Milan, at lunchtime at least, is more of a necessity than a pleasure, with the city centre dominated by *paninoteche* and fast-food outlets. *Luini*, Via S. Radegonda 16, just east of the Duomo, is justifiably popular for delicious *panzerotti*; *Crota Piemunteisa*, Piazza Beccaria 10, has a vast array of chunky sandwiches for around €2.60, and a few tables; or try *Il Fornaio* on the opposite side of the piazza, for sandwiches and pizzas. Among restaurants, *Brek*, on Piazza Cavour, is a good-value and central self-service place, as is *Ciao*, a nationwide chain with branches on the corner of Via Dante and Via Meravigli and at Via Fabio Filzi 8, near Stazione Centrale. *Autogrill* is another chain, with self-service restaurants and good sandwiches; branches are located at Piazza Duomo and Piazza Cinque Fiornate amongst others. Moving upmarket a little, *Il Cantinone*, Via Agnello 19, is a famous old trattoria and bar, with home-made pasta and some choice wines; *La Bruschetta*, Piazza Beccaria 12, is one of the best city-centre pizzerias, though you'll have to wait for a table. *Grand Italia*, Via Palermo 5, is cheaper and just as good. On the other side of the centre, *Latteria Unione*, Via Unione 6, close to the Duomo, dishes up excellent and varied vegetarian food, with friendly service, though it closes at 8pm. Further out, there's *Da Abele*, Via della Temperenza 5 (MM Pasteur), a long-established, cosy and very popular haunt that specializes in risotto, and *La Stella d'Oro*, Via Donizetti 3, an institution among Milanese cheapo restaurants – take bus #60. In the Città Studi, *Lo Smeraldo*, Via Ajaccio 1, serves thirty types of pizza.

Milan's **nightlife** centres on two areas – the streets around the Brera gallery and the Navigli and Ticinese quarters, where there's a hip, late-night bar scene. *Bar Magenta*, Via Carducci 13, is timelessly posey and usually packed. As for live music, *Capolinea*, Via Lodovico Il Moro 119, named after its position at the terminal of tram #19, is a long-established jazz venue that hosts top-notch performers; *Scimmie*, Via Ascanio Sforza 49, is another popular stage, small and buzzy and mainly hosting jazz; while *Tunnel*, Via Sammartini, right by Stazione Centrale, puts on alternative rock. Among many clubs, *Plastic*, Viale Umbria 120, is a Gothic hangout; *SplashDown*, Via Natale Battaglia 12, plays a wide range of music, as does *Rolling Stone*, Corso XXII Marzo, an enormous place that sometime hosts big-name rock bands. *Hollywood*, Corso Como 15, is a long-established club with an airport theme. There's also, of course, *La Scala*, one of the world's most prestigious opera houses, whose season runs from December to July. Although seats are expensive and can sell out months in advance, there is often a reasonable chance of picking up a seat in the gods on the day – get there an hour or so before the performance. The English magazine *Milan Where, When, How* has comprehensive listings and the pull-outs in Wednesday's *Corriere della Sera* or Thursday's *La Repubblica* give the rundown on what's on. The city information office in the Galleria Vittorio Emanuele (Mon–Sat 8am–7pm; ☎02.869.0683) also has details of cultural events and can book tickets.

Listings

Airlines Air Canada, Viale Regina Giovanna (☎02.295.23943); Alitalia, Piazzale Cadorna 14 (☎02.249.92500 or 147.865.643); American Airlines, Via V. Pisani 19 (☎02.6791.41); British Airways, Corso Italia 8 (☎02.7241.6000 or 147.812.266); Qantas, Corso Italia 8 (☎02.864.53039).

Airport enquiries ☎02.748.52200.

American Express Via Brera 3 (Mon–Fri 9am–5pm; freephone ☎800.864.046 to report stolen cards).

Books A wide array of English-language books is available at the American Bookstore, Via Camperio ☎02.878.920.

Car rental Avis, Piazza Diaz 6 (☎02.8901.0645); Europcar, Piazza Armando Diaz 6 (☎02.8646.3454); Hertz, Via Gonzaga 5 (☎02.7200.4562).

Embassies Australia, Via Borgogna 2 (☎02.77.70421); Canada, Via V. Pisani 19 (☎02.67.581); UK, Via San Paolo 7 (☎02.723.001); USA, Via Principe Amedeo 2/10 (☎02.290.351).

Exchange The office in Stazione Centrale is your best bet: open daily 7am–9.30pm, it also has a 24hr automatic currency exchange machine.

Hospital 24hr casualty department at the Fatebenefratelli hospital, Corso Porta Nuova 23 (☎02.63.631), or Ospedale Maggiore Policlinico, Via Francesco Sforza 35 (☎02.55.031), a short walk from Piazza Duomo.

Internet access at Internet Corner, Centro Telecom, Galleria Vittorio Emmanuele. You'll need a standard phonecard; €0.25/minute.

Pharmacy 24hr service at Stazione Centrale.

Police Head office at Via Montebello (☎02.669.0935).

Post office Via Cordusio 4, off Piazza Cordusio (Mon–Fri 8.15am–7pm, Sat 8am–noon).

Telephones Telecom, Galleria V. Emanuele II (daily 8am–9.30pm), Stazione Centrale (daily 8am–8pm).

Train enquiries ☎02.63.711 or 147.888.088.

Mantua

Aldous Huxley called it the most romantic city in the world, and with an Arabian nights skyline rising above its three encircling lakes, **MANTUA** is undeniably evocative. It was the scene of Verdi's *Rigoletto*, and its history is one of equally operatic plots, most of them perpetuated by the Gonzagas, who ruled the town for three centuries and left two splendid palaces – the Palazzo Ducale, with Mantegna's stunning fresco of the Gonzaga court, and Palazzo Tè, whose frescoes have entertained generations of visitors with their combination of steamy erotica and illusionistic fantasy.

The City

Historic Mantua centres on four interlinking squares. Of these, **Piazza Mantegna** is dominated by the facade of Alberti's **Sant'Andrea**, an unfinished basilica commissioned by Lodovico II Gonzaga, who felt that the existing medieval church was neither impressive enough to represent the splendour of his state, nor large enough to hold the droves of people who flocked here to see the holy relic of Christ's blood that had been found on the site. Inside, an octagonal balustrade stands above the crypt where the holy relic is kept in two vases, copies of originals designed by Cellini and stolen by the Austrians in 1846. There are also wall-paintings designed by Mantegna and executed by his students, one of whom was Correggio; Mantegna himself is buried in the church, in one of the north aisle chapels, his tomb topped with a bust that's said to be a self-portrait. Opposite Sant'Andrea and sunk below the present level of the busy **Piazza dell'Erbe**, Mantua's oldest church, the eleventh-century **Rotonda**, narrowly escaped destruction under Lodovico's city-improvement plans, and still contains traces of twelfth- and thirteenth-century frescoes.

The dark underpassage beneath the red-brick **Broletto**, or medieval town hall, leads into **Piazza Broletto**, beyond which the sombre Piazza Sordello is flanked by the Baroque facade of the **Duomo**, which conceals a rich interior designed by Giulio Romano, and the **Palazzo Ducale** (Tues–Sun 8.45am–7.15pm, last ticket 6.30pm, June to September also 9pm–midnight; €6.20), an enormous complex that was once the largest palace in Europe, with a population of over a thousand. When it was sacked by the Habsburgs in 1630, eighty carriages were needed to carry the two thousand works of art contained in its five hundred rooms. Only a proportion of these are open to visitors, and to see them you have to take a guided tour. In the Salone del Fiume there's a trompe l'oeil garden complete with painted creepers and two ghastly fountains; the Sala degli Specchi, further on, has a notice outside signed by Monteverdi, who worked as court musician to Vincenzo I and gave frequent concerts of new works. Vincenzo also employed Rubens, whose *Adoration of the Magi* in the Salone degli Arcieri shows the Gonzaga family of 1604. However, the palace's real treasure is in the Castello di San Giorgio beyond, where you can see Mantegna's frescoes of the Gonzaga family, splendidly restored in the so-called Camera degli Sposi. In the main one Lodovico discusses a letter with a courtier while his wife looks on; their youngest daughter leans on her mother's lap, about to bite into an apple. The other fresco, *The Meeting*, shows Gonzagan retainers with dogs and a horse in attendance on Lodovico who is welcoming his son Francesco back from Rome, where he had just become the first Gonzaga to be made a cardinal.

Mantua's other main sight, the **Palazzo Tè**, on the opposite side of town (Mon 1–6pm, Tues–Sun 9am–6pm; €6.20), was designed for Federico Gonzaga and his mistress, Isabella Boschetta, by Giulio Romano, and a tour of it is like a voyage around Giulio's imagination, a sumptuous world where very little is what it seems. In the Sala dei Cavalli, portraits of horses stand before an illusionistic background in which simulated marble, fake pilasters and mock reliefs surround views of painted landscapes through nonexistent windows. The function of the Salotta di Psiche, further on, is undocumented, but the sultry frescoes, and its proximity to Federico's bedroom, might give a few clues, the ceiling paintings telling the story of Cupid and Psyche with some dizzying *sotto in su* (from the bottom up) works by Giulio. On the walls, too, are racy pieces, covered with orgiastic wedding-feast scenes, watched over by the giant Polyphemus, perched above the fireplace, while, beyond, the extraordinary Sala dei Giganti shows the destruction of the giants by the gods, with cracking pillars, toppling brickwork and screaming giants appearing to crash down into the room.

Practicalities

The city centre is a ten-minute walk from the **train station** down Via Solferino. Budget **accommodation** is almost nonexistent in Mantua. Of the less expensive hotels, you could try the *ABC*, Piazza Don Leoni 25 (☎0376.323347; ⑤) or the *Bianchi Stazione*, next door (☎0376.326.465; ⑤), both opposite the station, or the *Broletto* (☎0376.223.678; ⑥), a good-value three-star at Via Accademia 1. Otherwise, you'll have to stay outside the town – the *Marago* (☎0376.370.313; ③) in Virgiliana (3km away on bus #25) has cheap doubles. The **tourist office** (Mon–Sat 8.30am–12.30pm & 3–6pm, Sun 9am–noon; ☎0376.328.253, *www.mantovaoggi.com/apt*) is around the corner from Sant'Andrea, and has maps and accommodation lists. For inexpensive **food**, the cheapest place is the *Il Punto* self-service at Via Solferino 36, near the train station (closed Sun). Failing that, try the *Bella Napoli*, Piazza Cavalotti 14, which serves good pizza (closed Tues), or the atmospheric *Leoncino Rosso* Via Giustiziati 33, off Piazza Broletto (closed Sun). For tasty pasta try *Hosteria dei Canossa*, Vicolo Albergo 3 (closed Wed and Thur).

Genoa

GENOA is "a place that grows upon you every day…it abounds in the strangest contrasts; things that are picturesque, ugly, mean, magnificent, delightful and offensive break upon the view at every turn", wrote Dickens in 1844, and the description still fits. Genoa is a marvellously eclectic city, centring on the port that made it one of the five Italian maritime republics by the thirteenth century. Later, during the Unification era, the city was a base for radical thought. Mazzini, one of the main protagonists in Italy's unification, was born here, and in 1860 Garibaldi set sail for Sicily with his "Thousand" from the city's harbour.

After forty years of economic decline the city started reinvesting in the Nineties. State funding to celebrate the 500th anniversary of Columbus's 1492 voyage paid to renovate some of the city's late-Renaissance palaces and the old port area, with Genoa's most famous son of modern times, **Renzo Piano** (best known as the co-designer of Paris's Pompidou Centre), taking a leading role. The tidying-up hasn't sanitized the old town, a set of winding alleyways that forms the core of the city, between the two stations and the waterfront, and which is still dark and slightly threatening. But despite the sleaze, the overriding impression is of a buzzing hive of activity.

Arrival, information and accommodation

Trains from Ventimiglia and points west arrive at Stazione Principe in Piazza Acquaverde, just above the port; and trains from La Spezia, Rome and points south arrive at Stazione Brignole, Piazza Verdi, on the other side of the city centre; trains from Milan and Turin usually stop at both, but if you have to travel between the two, take bus #18 or #37. **Ferries** arrive at the Stazione Maríttima, ten minutes' walk downhill from Stazione Principe. **Getting around** is best done on foot; if you do need to take a bus, a basic ticket, available from *tabacchi* and newspaper stands, costs €0.80 and is valid for ninety minutes. There is a **tourist office** at Stazione Principe (Mon–Sat 8am–8pm, Sun 9am–noon; ☎010.246.2633, *www.apt.genova.it*), and another at Porto Antico, Palazzina S. Maria (Mon–Sat 8am–6.30pm, Sun 9am–noon; ☎010.248.711, *www.comune.genova.it*). If you plan on visiting several museums and other tourist attractions do some sums to see if the Museum Card (available from the train station or tourist office; seven day pass €15.49) is worth your while.

There are plenty of cheap **hotels** in the city centre, but many are grimy and depressing and you need to look hard to find the exceptions. Good areas to try are the roads bordering the old town, and Piazza Colombo and Via XX Settembre, near Stazione Brignole. The *Soana*, about ten minutes' walk from Stazione Brignole, at Via XX Settembre 23/8/a (☎010.562.814, *www.hotelsoana.it*; ⑤), is a very friendly place with a mixture of plain unmodernized rooms and others with TV and telephone; nearby, the *Carletto*, Via Colombo 16/4 (☎010.588.412, *www.paginegialle.it/h-carletto*; ④), is a good fallback option if the *Soana* is full. On the seaview walkway on Corso Italia try *Nettuno*, Via Mercantini 16 (☎010.628.106; ④), just ten minutes from the city centre. If you have a bit more money to spend, the *Cairoli*, Via Cairoli 14/4 (☎010.246.1454, *htlcairoli@tin.it*; ⑤), is a very pleasant option and is handy for the old town and Stazione Principe. Genoa's **HI hostel** is a clean and well-run place with great views up in the hills, north of the centre at Via Costanzi 120 (☎010.242.2457; ②) – take bus #40 from Stazione Brignole or bus #35 from Stazione Principe then #40 from Piazza Nunziata, three minutes downhill from Stazione Principe. Campers should try the *Villa Doria* **campsite** (☎010.696.9600, *www.camping.it/liguria/villadoria*). Take the train to Pegli and then the number 93 bus.

The City

Genoa spreads outwards from its **old town** around the port in a confusion of tiny alleyways and old palaces in which people speak the impenetrable Genoese dialect – a mixture of Neapolitan, Calabrese and Portuguese. From 1384 to 1515, except for brief periods of foreign domination, the doges ruled the city from the **Palazzo Ducale** in Piazza Matteotti (Tues–Sun 9am–9pm; prices vary; *www.palazzoducale.genova.it*), across from which the dour **Gesù** church, designed by Pellegrino Tibaldi at the end of the sixteenth century, contains Guido Reni's *Assumption* and two paintings by Rubens. Close by, the Gothic **Cattedrale di San Lorenzo** is home to the Renaissance chapel of St John the Baptist, whose remains once rested in the thirteenth-century sarcophagus. After a particularly bad storm, priests carried his casket through the city to placate the sea, and a commemorative procession takes place each June 24 to honour him. His reliquary is in the treasury (Mon–Sat 9am–noon & 3–6pm; €5.16), along with a polished quartz plate on which, legend says, Salome received his severed head. Also on display is a glass dish said to have been given to Solomon by the Queen of Sheba, and used at the Last Supper. East from the adjacent Piazza Ferrari, Via XX Settembre, Genoa's commercial nucleus, has big chain stores and pavement cafés in the arcades.

Heading south across **Via San Bernardo,** another busy street, the mosaic spire of the church of **Sant'Agostino** marks the adjacent **Museo dell'Architettura e Scultura Ligure** (Tues–Sat 9am–7pm, Sun 9am–12.30pm; €3.10), built around the cloister of a thirteenth-century monastery, with a collection of Roman and Romanesque fragments from other churches, as well as wood-carvings and ancient maps of Genoa. Down on the waterfront, the sea once came up to the vaulted arcades of **Piazza Caricamento**, a hive of activity, fringed by café-restaurants and the stalls of its market. Customs inspectors, and subsequently the city's elected governors, set up in the **Palazzo San Giorgio** on the edge of the square, some rooms of which are open to the public (Sat 10am–6pm; free). Beyond, the waterfront has been the subject of a massive restoration project manifest most obviously in the huge **Aquarium** (April–Sept Mon–Fri 9.30am–7pm, Sat & Sun 9.30am–8pm; Oct–March Tues–Fri 9.30am–6.30pm, Sat & Sun 9.30am–8pm; last ticket 1hr 30min before closing; €9.80; *www.acquario.ge.it*), which contains sea creatures from all the world's habitats. Behind Piazza Caricamento is a thriving commercial zone centred on **Piazza Banchi**, formerly the heart of the medieval city, off which the long Via San Luca leads to the **Galleria Nazionale di Palazzo Spinola** (Tues–Sat 9am–7pm, Sun 2–7pm; €4.10) whose collection includes work by the Sicilian master Antonello da Messina and an *Adoration of the Magi* by Joos van Cleve.

North of here, **Via Garibaldi** is lined with Renaissance palaces, two of which have been turned into art galleries. The **Palazzo Bianco** (Tues, Thurs, Fri 9am–1pm, Wed & Sat 9am–7pm, Sun 10am–6pm; €4.10) holds paintings by Genoese artists and others, including Van Dyck and Rubens, and a good general gathering of Flemish art. The paintings in the **Palazzo Rosso** across the road (same hours as Palazzo Bianco; €4.10) include works by Titian, Caravaggio and Dürer, but it's the decor which really impresses – fantastic chandeliers, mirrors, an excess of gilding, and frescoed ceilings. Behind, Genoa heaps up the hill like the steps of an amphitheatre, a part of town best seen by way of the **funicular** (bus tickets valid) from Piazza del Portello up to Sant'Anna. The view from up here is much hyped, but the trip is more absorbing than anything you'll see when you arrive.

Eating, drinking, nightlife and beaches

For cheap **lunches**, **snacks** and **picnic** ingredients, try the side streets around Stazione Brignole and Piazza Colombo, and the covered Mercato Orientale, halfway down Via XX Settembre in the old cloisters of an Augustinian monastery. There are also a lot of good cheap alternatives on Piazza Caricamento. For **full meals**, *Sâ Pesta*, Via Giustiniani 16, is a well-known source of good local cooking, including farinata, a thin chickpea-based pancake, but it closes early. The no-nonsense and endearingly chaotic *Trattoria da Maria*, Via Testadoro 14/b, just off Via XXV Aprile, also serves up simple Ligurian cooking at rock-bottom prices; the *Ostaja do Castello*, Salita Santa Maria di Castello 32, on the other side of the old town, closer to the water, is a similar small, family-run trattoria. If you've had enough of Italian food, try the *Circolo Latino Americano*, Via della Maddalena 50 (Wed–Sat only), which serves chilli, enchiladas, tacos, and above all lots of meat. Alternatively take bus #15 to Quarto, 15 minutes away along the sea. *Il Focone*, with an attractive seaview terrace, is the best place to go for pizza. For a **drink**, the *Britannia* in Vico Casana, just off Via XX Aprile, is a pseudo-English pub; for live music try *Sopraviaventi* – look for a staircase half way down on the main street of Via XX Settembre to get there.

As for **beaches**, you need to travel some way before you really feel free of the Genoa sprawl, and it's probably best to accept that sunbathing isn't part of the Genoese experience. If you fancy a swim, though, the small district of **Nervi**, on the eastern side of the city, is probably the most attractive spot that can be easily reached – take bus #15 from Piazza Caricamento; failing that take bus #3, also from Piazza Caricamento, to **Pegli**, on the opposite side of the city.

The Riviera di Ponente

You get the most positive impression of the coast west of Genoa – the **Riviera di Ponente** – as you speed along the autostrada, from where the marinas and resorts are mere specks in a panorama of glittering sea and acres of glasshouses. Close up, the seaside towns from Genoa to the French border are fairly functional places, yet they have their good points – chiefly the sandy beaches and an exceptionally mild climate, which means that flowering plants grow here all year round.

With nearly a hundred hotels in and around its centre, **FINALE LIGURE**, about 40km west of Genoa, is committed to tourism, yet manages to remain an attractive place. It is well known for its nearby Grotte delle Arene Candide, finds from which are on display at the **Museo Archeologico** (Tues–Sat 9am–noon & 2.30–4.30pm, Sun 9am–noon; €2.60) in the cloisters of Santa Caterina in the appealing old upper town – **Finale Borgo**; the main and tourist part of town, **Finale Marina**, is about a kilometre below here, along the seafront. Above all, it's a pleasant place to stay and see this part of the coast. There's a **hostel**, the *Wuillermin*, in a castle high above the train station at Via Generale Caviglia 46 (☎019.690.515, *hostelfinaleligure@libero.it*; ②; mid-March to mid-Oct), and a vast number of **hotels**, though many get booked up well in advance in high season and insist on you taking full board. Try the *San Marco* at Lungomare Concezione 22 (☎019.629.533; ③), which has cheap clean, if basic, rooms and is right across from the beach, or the more upmarket *Medusa* (☎019.692.545; ⑤), just the other side of the main square and tucked down the tiny Vico Bricchieri. The **tourist office**, on the seafront at Via San Pietro 14 (Mon–Sat 9am–12.30pm & 3.30–7pm, Sun 9am–noon; ☎019.681.019, *www.italianriviera.com*), has details of other possibilities, including **private rooms**. On the food side, there's a similarly wide range of **places to eat**, even if the quality isn't always high. In Finale Marina, the fairly typical *La Grotta*, on the seafront next to the tourist office, is a so-so lively *spaghetteria* serving pasta and pizza at reasonable prices. The pizzas at *Pizzeria da Tonino*, Via Bolla 5, are better – and you can sit outside – while if you want something a little more adventurous try the *Gnabbri Trattoria* up behind the church off Via Roma, bang in the centre of Finale Marina – its friendly neighbourhood atmosphere and regularly changing small menu of linguine specialities are excellent value.

One of the other main resorts of this stretch of coast is **SAN REMO**, a grand old place whose heyday was the early twentieth century, when wealthy Europeans paraded up and down the Corso Imperatrice and filled the large hotels overlooking the sea. There isn't a lot to see, and even the small beach by the train station is a bit mucky, but the place has a certain seedy charm and big-town feel that's refreshing after the resortiness of much of the rest of the coast. It also has an amazing old town – known as La Pigna – a kasbah-like maze of tunnels and blind alleys that makes for hours of happy clambering. The **train station** is right in the centre of town by the sea, just across the road from which is the tourist office, Via Nuvoloni 1 (Mon–Sat 8am–7pm, Sun 9am–1pm; ☎0184.571.571, *www.apt.rivieradeifiori.it*). There are loads of **places to stay**, including a number of handily placed budget hotels along the streets to the right as you come out of the station. Cheap options are the *Arenella*, Corso Raimondo 2 (☎0184.503.639; ④), or opposite the fish market, the *Saracena* at Via Francia 17 (☎0184.502.416; ③). Slightly pricier is the *Matuzia*, around the corner at Corso Matteotti 121 (☎0184.577.070; ④). For **food**, the *Cantine San Remo*, Via Palazzo 7, is a good place for lunch or an evening meal – it's a bar that serves snacks and has a few tables out back for more substantial fare; around the corner, Piazza Eroi San Remesi has a number of decent pizzerias – try the *Graziella*, on the left looking away from the sea. Up in the old town the tiny *Osteria della Costa* serves an excellent rabbit stew.

The Riviera di Levante

The stretch of coast east from Genoa, the **Riviera di Levante**, is not the place to come for a relaxing beach holiday. The ports which once survived on navigation, fishing and coral diving have now experienced thirty years of tourism; the coastline is still wild and beautiful in parts, but the sense of remoteness has gone. **PORTOFINO**, at the extremity of the Monte Portofino headland, manages to be both attractive and offputting at the same time, a wealthy resort but a beautiful one. The two-and-a-half-hour walk to San Fruttuoso's thirteenth-century Abbey (March, April & Oct daily 10am–4pm; May–Sept daily 10am–6pm; Jan, Feb & Dec Sat & Sun only 10am–4pm; €2.60) and beach is well worth doing. Boats go from San Fruttuoso to Camogli, Portofino, Santa Margherita and Rapallo. Three kilometres out of

Portofino, on the corniche road, the sparkling cove at **PARAGGI** is a good place for a swim, with a couple of bars set back from the beach, and you can take a bus to Ruta, from where you can either slog on foot to the summit of Monte Portofino or catch another bus to Portofino Vetta, from where it's twenty minutes' walk to the top. On very clear days the views are fantastic.

SANTA MARGHERITA LIGURE is a small, thoroughly attractive resort, with palm trees along the front and a minuscule pebble beach and concrete jetties to swim from; it also has plenty of cheapish accommodation, making it a convenient base for visiting Portofino and the other coastal towns. The hotels are friendly and pleasant: try *Albergo Annabella* at Via Costasecca 10, just off Piazza Mazzini (☎0185.286.531; ③), or the more expensive *Albergo Fasce*, a little further up the road at Via L. Bozzo 3 (☎0185.286.435, *www.hotelfasce.it*; ⑤), run by a friendly Anglo-Italian couple, and which has a dozen bikes guests may use free of charge. The **tourist office** on Via XXV Aprile (Mon–Sun 9am–12.30pm & 2.30/3.00–5.30/6.00pm; ☎018.287.485, *www.apttigullio.liguria.it*) has free footpath maps of the area. For **food**, either try *Trattoria Biacin*, just off the seafront square at Via Algeria 9, or the long-established *Da Pezzi*, around the corner at Via Cavour 21, a canteen-like locals' hangout serving a basic formula of pasta and grills, and takeaway snacks for lunch.

RAPALLO crowds around the first bay along in the gulf, a highly developed though still attractive resort that used to be patronized by a number of writers, drawn here by the bay's extraordinary beauty. Caricaturist and ferocious critic of British imperialism Max Beerbohm lived in Rapallo, attracting a vast coterie, and Ezra Pound wrote the first thirty of his Cantos here between 1925 and 1930. There are decent **places to stay** in the centre of town, most notably the extremely welcoming *Pensione Bandoni*, Via Marsala 24/3 (☎0185.50.423; ③); if it's full, try the *Fernanda*, along the front at Via Milite Ignoto 9 (☎0185.50.244; ④), cosy enough, but more expensive for less pleasant rooms. There are a couple of campsites, *Rapallo* (☎0185.262.018) at Via San Lazzaro 4 and the *Miraflores* (☎0185.263.000) at Via Savagna 10. Perhaps the least expensive and most authentic place to **eat** is *Bansin*, right in the heart of the old town at Via Venezia 49, though it closes early; if you have a little more money to spend, *Da Mario*, Piazza Garibaldi 23, is a good, moderately priced fish restaurant.

The Cinque Terre

If you're travelling on a fast train, you'll speed through the five villages of the Cinque Terre without seeing much more than a few tantalizing glimpses of sheer cliff as the train dashes from one tunnel to the next. However, the stopping services on the Genoa to La Spezia line call at each one, and there is a ferry service linking them with La Spezia. Their comparative remoteness, and the drama of their position on tiny cliff-bound inlets, make a visit to the area a real attraction. **RIOMAGGIORE**, closest to La Spezia and one of the larger villages, is the best place to head for, wedged impossibly into a hillside, with no two buildings on the same level. Along the cliff path which winds its way to charming **MANAROLA**, lemon trees flourish in every backyard, and in spring the cliffs are covered with wild flowers. From Manarola a spectacular path passes rock-cut steps leading down to the water all the way to **MONTEROSSO** (12km), largest and least charming of the villages, and the only one with a recognizable beach. **CORNIGLIA** and **VERNAZZA** are similar to Riomaggiore, but on a smaller scale. For **accommodation**, Manarola is a good option with the tiny *5 Terre* **hostel**, 300m up the hill from the station (☎0187.920.215, *www.cinqueterre.net/ostello*; ④), or the lovely, family-run *Ca' d'Andreana*, at Via Discovolo 101 (☎0187.920.040; ⑥). The only hotel in Riomaggiore is the smart, comfortable *Villa Argentina*, Via de Gasperi 37 (☎0187.920.213; ⑧). Be sure to book your room in advance if possible. You could base yourself in **LEVANTO**, a little way west, which has plentiful reasonable accommodation and food options, including a decent campsite, the *Aquadolce*, in the centre of town, plus a long stretch of sandy beach – and it's on the main rail line. If you do decide to stay, try the *Pensione Garden*, the cheapest hotel, located right by the sea at Corso Italia 8 (☎0187.808.173; ④); if that's full, or you have a little more money, try the slightly cosier atmosphere of the *Europa*, up the street at Via Dante 41 (☎0187.808.126; ⑨); half board obligatory in July and Aug). For food and late-night drinks, the *Caffè Roma*, on the square round the corner from the *Pensione Garden*, has a small, reasonably priced restaurant out the back.

THE NORTHEAST

Italy's **northeast** is one of the country's most appealing – and versatile – regions. The appeal of **Venice** hardly needs stating: it's one of Europe's truly unique urban landscapes, and, despite its equally unique huge number of visitors, really unmissable on any European – let alone Italian – tour. The region around Venice – the **Veneto** – is a prosperous one, where virtually every acre still bears the imprint of Venetian rule. **Padua** and **Verona** are the main attractions, with their masterpieces by Giotto, Donatello and Mantegna, and a profusion of great buildings from Roman times to the Renaissance. Much of the countryside is dull and flat, only perking up to the north with the high peaks of the Dolomite range. East, on the former Yugoslav border, **Trieste** is capital of the partly Slav region of **Friuli-Venezia Giulia**, a Habsburg city only united with Italy after World War II. South, between Lombardy and Tuscany, stretching from the Adriatic coast almost to the shores of the Mediterranean, **Emilia-Romagna** is the heartland of northern Italy, a patchwork of ducal territories formerly ruled by a handful of families, whose castles and fortresses remain in well-preserved medieval towns. Carving a straight route through the heart of the region, from Milan to Rimini on the coast, the Via Emilia is a central and obvious reference point, a Roman military road constructed in 187 BC that was part of the medieval pilgrim's route to Rome and the way east for crusaders to Ravenna and Venice. **Bologna**, the region's capital, is one of Italy's largest cities, but despite having one of the most beautifully preserved city centres in the country and some of its finest food, it's relatively neglected by tourists – definitely a mistake. Bologna also gives easy access to **Parma**, just an hour or so away by train, a wealthy provincial town that is worth visiting for its paintings by Parmigianino and Correggio. The coast is less interesting, and the water polluted, although **Rimini** provides a spark of interest, its oddly attractive seaside sleaze concealing a historic town centre, and, just south of the Po delta, **Ravenna** boasts probably the world's finest set of Byzantine mosaics in its churches and mausoleums.

Venice

The first-time visitor to **VENICE** arrives with a heavy freight of expectations, most of which turn out to have been well founded. It is an extraordinarily beautiful city, an urban landscape so rich that you can't walk for a minute without coming across something that's worth a stop; and the major sights like the basilica and piazza of San Marco are all they are cracked up to be, as are most of the lesser-known ones. The downside is that Venice is deluged with tourists, the annual influx exceeding the city's population two-hundredfold; and it is expensive – the price of a good meal anywhere else in Italy will get you a lousy one in Venice, and its hoteliers make the most of a situation where demand will always far outstrip supply. However, the crowds thin out beyond the magnetic field of San Marco, and in the off-season it's still possible to have parts of the centre virtually to yourself. As for keeping your costs down, there are a few inexpensive eating places, and it is still possible to find a bed for the night without spending a fortune.

Venice first rose to a kind of prominence when the traders of what was then a small settlement on the lagoon signalled their independence from Byzantium through a great symbolic act – the theft from Alexandria in 828 of the body of St Mark, who became the city's patron. Venice later exploited the trading networks and markets of Byzantium and the East, aided by the Crusades, by the twelfth century achieving unprecedented prosperity and benefiting especially from the Sack of Constantinople in 1204, which left much of the Roman Empire under the city's sway. Following the defeat of Genoa in 1380, Venice consolidated its position as the unrivalled trading power of the region, and by the middle of the fifteenth century was in possession of a mainland empire that was to survive virtually intact for several centuries – although its eastern dominions were increasingly encroached on by the Ottomans. Decline set in in the eighteenth century, when, politically moribund and constitutionally ossified, Venice became renowned as a playground of the rich, a position consolidated in the nineteenth century with the growth of tourism and the development of the Lido as Europe's most fashionable resort. This turns out to have been a wise move, despite the drawbacks. Nowadays some twenty million people visit the city each year, around half of whom don't even stay a night. Without them, however, Venice would barely exist at all.

Arrival and information

Flights arrive at the city's **Marco Polo** airport, on the edge of the lagoon, linked to the city centre by ACTV bus #5 (every 30min; €0.80); alternatively you can catch an ATVO bus (€2) or more expensive waterbus (€19.30). All road traffic comes into the city at **Piazzale Roma**, at the head of the Canal Grande, from where waterbus services run to the San Marco area, stopping off at Santa Lucia **train station**, the next stop along the Canal Grande. If you're coming right into Venice by **car**, you'll have to park in either the Piazzale Roma multistorey car park, or on the adjoining Tronchetto, a vast artificial island. The queues for both can be huge – a better option in summer is to park in Mestre's municipal car park, then take a bus over the causeway.

The main **tourist office** (daily 9.40am–3.20pm; ☎041.520.8964, *www.govenice.com*) is at San Marco 71/f, a couple of minutes' walk east of the square. There are also desks in the Casinò da Caffè by the San Marco waterbus stop, at the train station, and at the airport. Pick up their free map and English/Italian magazines, *Leo* and *Un Ospite di Venezia* (*www.aguestinvenice.com*) which give up-to-date what's-on information and waterbus timetables.

City transport

In most cases the speediest way of getting around Venice is on foot. Distances between major sights are short (you can cross the whole city in an hour), and once you've got your general bearings navigation is not as daunting a prospect as it seems. To get between two points quickly, however, it's sometimes faster to take a waterbus (*vaporetto*). **Tickets** are available from most landing stages and all shops displaying the ACTV sign. Flat-rate fares are €3.10 for any one continuous journey, except for most one-stop journeys, which cost €1.50. Tickets bought on board are subject to a surcharge, and the spot-fine for not having a valid ticket is €15.50, so it's a good idea to buy a block of ten (*un blochetto*) or a tourist ticket: a 24-hour ticket costs €9.30, a three-day pass is €18.80, and a weekly ticket costs €31. Timetables are posted at each stop and the tourist office's city map has a route plan. In addition, there are the **traghetti** that cross the Canal Grande, which cost €0.40 per trip and are the only cheap way of getting a ride on a gondola. In summer they run from early morning to around 7–9pm daily with a two-hour break for lunch. Otherwise the **gondola** is an adjunct of the tourist industry: to hire one costs €62 for 50 minutes, rising to €77.50 between 8pm and 8am, plus €31 for each additional 25 minutes – be sure to confirm the charge beforehand.

Accommodation

Accommodation is the major expense in Venice, although there are inexpensive options, not least a number of **hostels**, most owned by religious foundations, which are generally comfortable and well run. You should always book ahead; if you haven't, there are **booking offices** at the train station (daily 8am–9pm), on the Tronchetto (daily 9am–8pm), at Piazzale Roma (daily 9am–9pm), at Marco Polo airport (daily 9am/noon–7pm), and at the autostrada's Venice exit (8am–8pm). They only deal with hotels and take a deposit, deductable from your first night's bill.

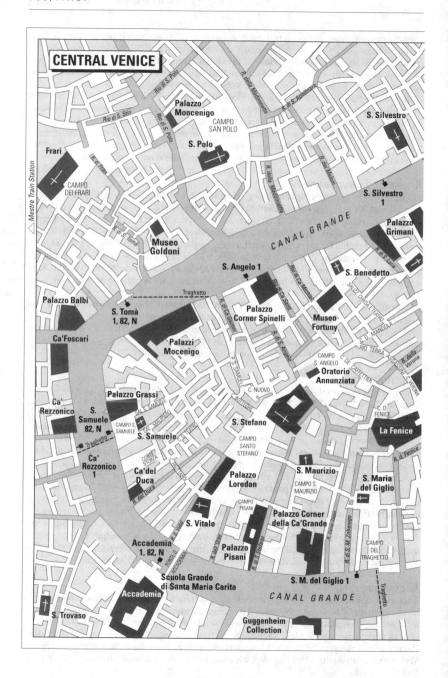

CENTRAL VENICE

Mestre Train Station

Rio di S. Stin

Rio di S. Polo

Palazzo Moncenigo

CAMPO SAN POLO

S. Polo

S. Silvestro

R. della Madonneta

R. di S. Agostin

Frari

R. di Fran.

CAMPO DEI FRARI

R. di S. Tomà

Museo Goldoni

CANAL GRANDE

S. Silvestro 1

Palazzo Grimani

R. di S. Luca

S. Angelo 1

Traghetto

Palazzo Balbi

S. Tomà 1, 82, N

Rio di Cà Garzoni

Palazzo Corner Spinelli

R. di Cà Michiel

S. Benedetto

SALIZ. CHIESA E TEATRO

Ca'Foscari

Palazzi Mocenigo

R. di S. Angelo

Museo Fortuny

R. TERRA ASSASSINI

C. DE' CALTETTIER

RIO TERRA

C. D. MANDOLA

R. della Verona

C. VERONA

P. S. SAMUEL

C. NUOVO

CAMPO S. ANGELO

Oratorio Annunziata

Ca' Rezzonico

Palazzo Grassi

SAL. S. SAMUELE

SAL. S. MAURIZIO

C. BOTTEGHE

C. D. FENICE

S. Samuele 82, N

CAMPO S. SAMUELE

S. Samuele

TEATRO

S. Stefano

La Fenice

Traghetto

CORTE STORTA

CANTIER

CAMPO SANTO STEFANO

R. d. Fenice

Ca' Rezzonico 1

Ca'del Duca

R. del Duca

Palazzo Loredan

S. Maurizio

CAMPO S. MAURIZIO

S. Maria del Giglio

R. di S. M. Zobenigo

CAMPO PISANI

Palazzo Corner della Ca'Grande

CAMPO DEL TRAGHETTO

S. Vitale

R. S. Vitale

Palazzo Pisani

R. del Orso

R. di S. Stefano

R. Corner Zaguri

Accademia 1, 82, N

PONTE D. ACCADEMIA

S. M. del Giglio 1

Traghetto

Scuola Grande di Santa Maria Carita

CANAL GRANDE

Accademia

S. Trovaso

Guggenheim Collection

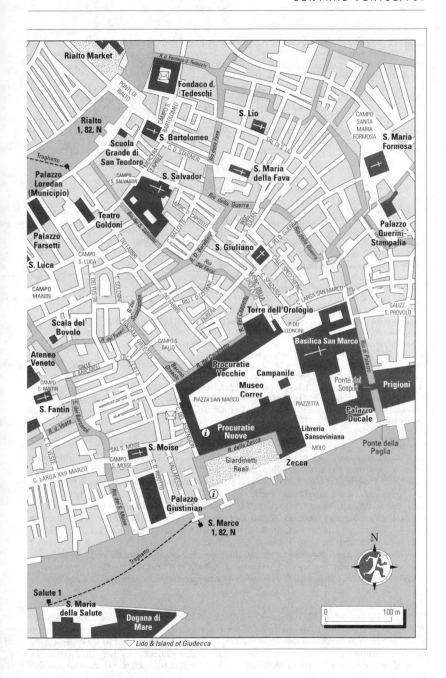

HOSTELS

Domus Cavanis, Rio Terrà Foscarini, Dorsoduro 896 (☎041.522.2826). Catholic-run, with separate rooms for men and women. ③.

Domus Civica, Calle Campazzo, San Polo 3082 (☎041.721.103). A student house in winter, open to women travellers only June–Sept. 11.30pm curfew. ③.

Foresteria Valdese, Santa Maria Formosa, Castello 5170 (☎041.528.6797). Difficult to find – go from Campo Santa Maria Formosa along Calle Lunga, and it's at the foot of the bridge at the far end. Three large dorms, and a few rooms for 2 to 4 people; open for registration 9am–1pm & 6–8pm. ③.

Ostello Venezia, Fondementa delle Zitelle, Giudecca 86 (☎041.523.8211). The official HI hostel, in a superb location looking at San Marco from the island of Giudecca (waterbus #82 from the station). Opens at 1.30pm for registration in summer, 4pm in winter, and it's a good idea to book ahead or get there early. 11pm curfew. ②.

HOTELS

Ai Do Mori, Calle Larga San Marco 658, San Marco (☎041.520.4817). Very friendly, recently renovated one-star, a few steps from the Piazza. ④.

Antica Casa Carettoni, Lista di Spagna, Cannaregio 130 (☎041.716.231). By a long way the most comfortable one-star in the vicinity of the train station, and newly refurbished. ⑤.

Antico Capon, Campo S. Margherita, Dorsoduro 3004/B (☎041.528.5292). Situated on one of the city's most atmospheric squares, in the heart of the student district. ④.

Bernardi Semenzato, Calle dell'Oca, Cannaregio 4366 (☎041.522.7257, *mtfepoli@tin.it*). Two-star place with very welcoming and helpful English-speaking owners. ⑤.

Ca' Fóscari, Calle della Frescada, Dorsoduro 3887B (☎041.710.401, *valtersc@tin.it*). Tucked away in a micro-alley near San Tomà, near the university. Quiet, well decorated and relaxed. ④.

Caneva, Ramo della Fava, Castello 5515 (☎041.522.8118). Overlooking the Rio della Fava on the approach to the busy Campo San Bartolomeo, yet very peaceful. ⑤.

Casa Gerotto Calderan, Campo S. Geremia 283, Cannaregio (☎041.715.361 or 041.715.562). Tremendous value, very welcoming and not far from the train station. Dormitory accommodation also available. ③.

Casa Petrarca, Calle delle Colonne, San Marco 4394 (☎041.520.0430). Friendly place, and the cheapest near the Piazza. Phone first, as they only have seven rooms. ④.

Fiorita, Campiello Nuovo, San Marco 3457/A (☎041.523.4754, *locafior@tin.it*). Just ten rooms, so it's important to book. Welcoming management. ④.

Sant'Anna, Corte del Bianco, Castello 269 (☎041.528.6466, *santanna@libero.it*). A fair way out from the centre but good for families, as it has rooms for 3–4 people and is near the Giardini Pubblici; book early. ④.

Toscana-Tofanelli, Calle Formenta, Castello 1650 (☎041.523.5722). Spartan hotel but a good location and excellent trattoria attached; midnight curfew. ③.

CAMPSITES

There are a number of fairly expensive **campsites** along the **Litorale del Cavallino**, accessible on waterbus #14 from the Riva degli Schiavoni, a forty-minute trip. Two to try are Marina di Venezia, Via Montello 6 (☎041.530.0955; April–Sept; minimum stay 3 nights; ④), and Miramare, Lungomare Dante Alighieri 29 (☎041.966.150; March–Oct; ③). There's an all-year site at **Fusina**, Mestre Fusina (☎041.547.005), on Via Moranzani – better in summer when there's a direct *vaporetto* (#16); at other times get the bus to Mestre and change there. The two sites out by the airport, the Marco Polo and the Alba d'Oro, are expensive and not particularly attractive.

Self-sufficient travellers used to spread their sleeping bags in front of the train station in summer, an expedient that was banned in 1987. Ask at the tourist office if there's a makeshift dormitory anywhere to absorb the overspill – there normally is somewhere in the city.

The City

The 118 islands of central Venice are divided into six districts known as *sestieri*. The *sestiere* of **San Marco** is home to the majority of the essential sights, and is accordingly the most expensive and most crowded district of the city. On the east it's bordered by **Castello**, on the north by **Cannaregio** – both of which become more residential the further you go from the centre. On the other side of the Canal Grande, the largest of the *sestieri* is **Dorsoduro**, which stretches from the fashionable quarter at the southern tip of the canal to the docks in the west. **Santa Croce**, named after a now demolished church, roughly follows the curve of the Canal Grande from Piazzale Roma to a point just short of the Rialto, where it joins the smartest and commercially most active of the districts on this bank – **San Polo**.

SAN MARCO

The section of Venice enclosed by the lower loop of the Canal Grande is, in essence, the Venice of the travel brochures. The **Piazza San Marco** is the hub of most activity, signalled from most parts of the city by the **Campanile** (daily 9.30am–4.15/6pm; €4.10), which began life as a lighthouse in the ninth century and was modified frequently up to the early sixteenth century. The present structure is in fact a reconstruction: the original tower collapsed on July 14, 1902. At 99m, it is the tallest structure in the city, and from the top you can make out virtually every building, but not a single canal; the other tower in the Piazza, the **Torre dell'Orologio**, was built between 1496 and 1506. Away to the left stretches the **Procuratie Vecchie**, an early-sixteenth-century structure that was converted into a palace by Napoleon, who connected the building with the other side of the piazza – the **Procuratie Nuove** – by way of a new wing for dancing. Generally known as the **Ala Napoleonica**, this short side of the Piazza is partly occupied by the **Museo Correr** (daily 9am–5/7pm; €9.30 combined ticket for Piazza San Marco museums), whose vast historical collection – coins, weapons, regalia, prints, mediocre paintings – is heavy going unless you have an intense interest in Venetian history. The **Quadreria** on the second floor is no rival for the Accademia's collection, but does set out clearly the evolution of painting in Venice from the thirteenth century to around 1500, and contains some gems – a *Pietà* by Cosmé Tura, the *Transfiguration* and *Dead Christ Supported by Angels* by Giovanni Bellini, along with a Carpaccio picture known as *The Courtesans*. There's also an appealing exhibition of applied arts, featuring a print of Jacopo de'Barbari's astonishing aerial view of Venice, engraved in 1500.

The **Basilica di San Marco** (Mon–Sat 10am–5.30pm, Sun 2–4pm; €1.50) is the most exotic of Europe's cathedrals, modelled on Constantinople's Church of the Twelve Apostles, finished in 1094 and embellished over the succeeding centuries with trophies brought back from abroad – proof of Venice's secular might and thus of the spiritual power of St Mark. The Romanesque carvings of the central door were begun around 1225 and finished in the early fourteenth century, while the mosaic above the doorway on the far left – *The Arrival of the Body of St Mark* – was made around 1260 (the only early mosaic left on the main facade) and includes the oldest-known image of the basilica. Inside, the narthex holds more mosaics, Old Testament scenes on the domes and arches, together with *The Madonna with Apostles and Evangelists* in the niches of the bay in front of the main door – dating from the 1060s, the oldest mosaics in San Marco. A steep staircase goes from the church's main door up to the **Museo Marciano** and the **Loggia dei Cavalli** (daily 10am–5.30pm; €1.50), where you can enjoy fine views of the city and the Gothic carvings along the apex of the facade, as well as the horses in question, replicas of Roman works thieved from the Hippodrome of Constantinople (the genuine articles are inside). Downstairs, beyond the narthex, the interior proper is covered with more mosaics, most dating from the middle of the thirteenth century, although the **Sanctuary**, off the south transept (Mon–Sat 10am–5.30pm, Sun 2–4pm; €1.50), holds the most precious of San Marco's treasures, the **Pala d'Oro** or golden altar panel, commissioned in 976 in Constantinople and studded with precious stones. The **Treasury** (same times; €4) nearby is a similarly dazzling warehouse of chalices, reliquaries and candelabra, a fair proportion pillaged from Constantinople in 1204. Back in the main body of the church, there's still more to see on the lower levels of the building. Don't overlook the **rood screen**'s marble figures of *The Virgin, St Mark and the Apostles*, carved in 1394 by the dominant sculptors in Venice at that time, Jacobello and Pietro Paolo Dalle Masegne. The **pulpits** on each side of the screen were assembled in the early fourteenth century from miscellaneous panels, some from Constantinople; the new doge was presented to the people from the right-hand one. The tenth-century *Icon of the Madonna of Nicopeia* (in the chapel on the east side of the north transept) is the most revered religious image in Venice, and was one of the most revered in Constantinople.

The adjacent **Palazzo Ducale** (daily 9am–5/7pm; €9.30 combined ticket for Piazza San Marco museums) was the residence of the doge, as well as housing Venice's governing councils, courts, a sizeable number of its civil servants and even its prisons. Like San Marco, the Palazzo Ducale has been rebuilt many times since its foundation in the first years of the ninth century, but the earliest parts of the current structure date from 1340. The principal entrance, the **Porta della Carta**, is one of the most ornate Gothic works in the city, commissioned in 1438 by Doge Francesco Fóscari; the figures of Fóscari and his lion are replicas – the originals were pulverized in 1797 by the head of the stonemasons' guild, as a favour to Napoleon. The passage inside ends under the **Arco Fóscari**, also commissioned by Doge Fóscari but finished a few years after his death. Parts of the Palazzo Ducale can be marched through fairly briskly, its walls covered with acres of wearisome canvas, although you should linger in the **Anticollegio**, one of the palace's finest rooms and home to four pictures by Tintoretto and Veronese's characteristically benign *Rape of Europa*. The cycle of paintings on the ceiling of the adjoining Sala del Collegio is also by Veronese, and he features strongly again in the most stupendous room in the building – the Sala del Maggior Consiglio, where his ceiling panel of the Apotheosis of Venice is suspended over the dais from which the doge oversaw the sessions of the city assembly. The backdrop is the immense *Paradiso* painted at the end of his life by Tintoretto, with the aid of his son, Domenico. From here you descend quickly to the underbelly of the Venetian state, crossing the **Ponte dei Sospiri** (Bridge of Sighs) to the prisons, and then back over the water to the Pozzi, the cells for the most hardened malefactors.

Facing the Palazzo Ducale across the Piazzetta is Sansovino's masterpiece and the most consistently admired Renaissance building in the city – the **Libreria Sansoviniana**, part of which is given over to the **Museo Archeologico** (daily 9am–7pm; €9.30 combined ticket for Piazza San Marco museums), a collection of Greek and Roman sculpture that's best left for a rainy day.

DORSODURO

Some of the finest architecture in Venice is in the *sestiere* of **Dorsoduro**, yet for all its attractions, not many visitors wander off the strip that runs between the main sights of the area, the first of which, the **Galleria dell'Accademia** (Tues–Sat 9am–7pm, Mon 9am–2pm, Sun 9am–noon; €6.20), is one of the finest specialist collections of European art, following the history of Venetian painting from the fourteenth to the eighteenth centuries. Housed in the church of Santa Maria della Carità and the incomplete Convento dei Canonici Lateranensi, partly built by Palladio in 1561, the gallery is laid out in roughly chronological order. The early sections include paintings by Paolo Veneziano, Carpaccio's strange and gruesome *Crucifixion* and *Glorification of the Ten Thousand Martyrs of Mount Ararat*, an exquisite *St George* by Mantegna, a series of Giovanni Bellini *Madonnas*, and one of the most mysterious of Italian paintings, Giorgione's *Tempest*. Tintoretto weighs in with three typically energetic pieces illustrating the legend of St Mark, and an entire wall is filled by Paolo Veronese's *Christ in the House of Levi* – called *The Last Supper* until the authorities objected to its lack of reverence. Among the most impressive pieces in the Accademia is the magnificent cycle of pictures painted around 1500 for the Scuola di San Giovanni Evangelista, of which Carpaccio's *Cure of a Lunatic* and Gentile Bellini's *Recovery of the Relic from the Canale di San Lorenzo* and *Procession of the Relic in the Piazza* stand out. There's also a cycle of pictures by Carpaccio illustrating the *Story of Saint Ursula*, painted for the Scuola di Sant'Orsola at San Zanipolo, which is one of the most unforgettable groups in the entire country. Finally, in room 24 there's Titian's *Presentation of the Virgin*, painted for the place where it hangs.

Five minutes' walk from the Accademia is the unfinished Palazzo Venier dei Leoni, home of the **Guggenheim Collection** (Mon & Wed–Sun 10am–6pm, Sat until 8pm; €6.20), and of Peggy Guggenheim for thirty years until her death in 1979. Her private collection is an eclectic choice of (mainly) excellent pieces from her favourite modernist movements and artists, including works by Brancusi, De Chirico, Max Ernst and Malevich. Continuing along the line of the Canal Grande, the church of Santa Maria della Salute, better known simply as the **Salute**, was built to fulfil a Senate decree of 1630 that a new church be dedicated to Mary if the city were delivered from plague. Every November 21 there's still a procession from San Marco to the church, over a specially constructed pontoon bridge, to give thanks for the city's good health, a major event on the Venetian calendar. In 1656, a hoard of Titian paintings were moved here and are now housed in the sacristy (€1.40), most prominent of which is the altarpiece of *St Mark Enthroned with Saints Cosmas, Damian, Sebastian and Rocco*. The *Marriage at Cana*, with its dramatic lighting and perspective, is by Tintoretto, featuring portraits of a number of the artist's friends.

SAN POLO

North of Dorsoduro is the *sestiere* of **San Polo**, on the northeastern edge of which the **Rialto** district was in former times the commercial zone of the city, home to the main Venetian banks and maritime businesses. It's the venue of the Rialto market on the far side of the Rialto Bridge, a lively affair and one of the few places in the city where it's possible to hear nothing but Italian spoken. The main reason people visit San Polo, however, is to see the mountainous brick church of the **Frari** west of here (Mon–Sat 10am–5.30pm, Sun 3–5.30pm; €1.50), whose collection of artworks includes a rare couple of paintings by Titian – most notably his *Assumption*, painted in 1518, a swirling piece of compositional bravura for which there was no precedent in Venetian art. Look also at the Renaissance tombs of the doges flanking the *Assumption*, dating from the late fifteenth century; the wooden *St John the Baptist*, in the chapel to the right, commissioned from Donatello in 1438; and, on the altar of the sacristy, a marvellous *Madonna and Child with Saints* by Giovanni Bellini. Titian is buried in the church, the spot marked by a bombastic nineteenth-century monument, opposite which the equally pompous mausoleum of Canova was erected by pupils of the sculptor, following a design he himself had made for the tomb of Titian.

At the rear of the Frari is the **Scuola Grande di San Rocco** (daily 9am–5.30pm; €4.70), a sixteenth-century building that is home to a cycle of more than fifty major paintings by Tintoretto. These fall into three main groups. The first, painted in 1564, adorns the upper Sala dell'Albergo – a *Glorification of St Roch*, painted for a competition, and a stupendous *Crucifixion*, which Ruskin claimed to be "above all praise". In the building's main hall, Tintoretto covered three large panels of the ceiling with Old Testament references to the alleviation of physical suffering – coded declarations of the Scuola's charitable activities – while around the walls are New Testament themes, an amazing feat of sustained inventiveness, in which every convention of perspective, lighting, colour and even anatomy is defied. The paintings on the ground floor were created between 1583 and 1587, when Tintoretto was in his late sixties, and include a turbulent *Annunciation*, a marvellous Renaissance landscape in *The Flight into Egypt* and two small paintings of *St Mary Magdalene* and *St Mary of Egypt*.

CANNAREGIO

In the northernmost section of Venice, **Cannaregio**, you can go from one extreme to another in a matter of minutes: it is a short distance from the bustle of the **train station** to areas which are among the quietest and prettiest parts of the whole city. The district also has the dubious distinction of containing the world's first **Ghetto**: in 1516, all the city's Jews were ordered to move to the island of the Ghetto Nuovo, an enclave which was sealed at night by Christian curfew guards. Even now it looks quite different from the rest of Venice, many of its buildings relatively high-rise due to the restrictions on the growth of the area. A couple of the oldest synagogues – the **Scola Levantina**, founded in 1538, and the **Scola Spagnola**, founded twenty years later – are still in use and can be viewed on an informative and multilingual guided tour that leaves on the half-hour, organized by the **Jewish Museum** in Campo Ghetto Nuovo (June–Sept 10am–7pm; Oct–May 10am–5.30pm; closed Sat and Jewish holidays; museum and synagogue €2.60; tours 10.30am–4.30pm; €6.20), where you can also see a collection of silverware and fabrics.

Northeast of the ghetto, the church of **Madonna dell'Orto** (Mon–Sat 10am–5.30pm, Sun 3–5.30pm; €1.50) contains several paintings by Tintoretto, including the colossal *Making of the Golden Calf* and *The Last Judgement* which flank the main altar; the artist is buried in the chapel to the right.

CASTELLO

Northeast of San Marco, **Castello** is home among other things to the **Miracoli** church, built in the 1480s to house a painting of the Madonna which was believed to have performed a number of miracles, such as reviving a man who'd spent half an hour lying at the bottom of the Giudecca canal. The church is thought to have been designed by Pietro Lombardo, who with his two sons Tullio and Antonio oversaw the building and executed much of the carving, which ranks as some of the most intricate decorative sculpture in Venice.

East of here, the **Campo San Zanipolo** (a contraction of Santi Giovanni e Paolo) is the most impressive open space in Venice after Piazza San Marco, dominated by the huge brick church of **San Zanipolo**, founded by the Dominicans in 1246, rebuilt and enlarged from 1333 and finally consecrated in 1430. The church is perhaps best known for the tombs and monuments around the walls, the memorials of some 25 doges, most impressive of which is the tomb of Doge Michele Morosini on the right of the chancel, selected by Ruskin as "the richest monument of the Gothic period in Venice". On the square outside the church, Verrochio's statue of the Venetian military hero **Bartolomeo Colleoni** is one of the finest Renaissance equestrian monuments in Italy, commissioned in 1481.

The other essential sight in this area is over to the east of San Marco – the **Scuola di San Giorgio degli Schiavoni** (Tues–Sat 10am–12.30pm & 3–6pm, Sun 10am–12.30pm; €2.60), set up by Venice's Slav population in 1451. The building dates from the early sixteenth century, and its interior looks more or less as it would have then, with a superb ground-floor room decorated with a cycle painted by Vittore Carpaccio between 1502 and 1509.

THE SOUTHERN ISLANDS

Immediately south of the Palazzo Ducale, Palladio's church of **San Giorgio Maggiore** stands on the island of the same name (Mon–Sat 10am–12.30pm & 2.30–4.30pm, Sun 9.30–10.30am & 2.30–4.30pm). This proved one of the most influential Renaissance church designs, and it has two pictures by Tintoretto in the chancel – *The Fall of Manna* and *The Last Supper*, perhaps the most famous of all his images, painted as a pair in 1592–94, the last years of the artist's life. On the left of the choir a corridor leads to the **Campanile**, rebuilt in 1791 after the collapse of its predecessor and one of the two best vantage points in the city.

The long island of **La Giudecca**, to the west, was where the wealthiest aristocrats of early Renaissance Venice built their villas, and in places you can still see traces of their gardens, although the present-day suburb is a strange mixture of decrepitude and vitality, boatyards and fishing quays interspersed with half-abandoned factories and sheds. Unless you're staying at the *Cipriani*, the most expensive hotel in Venice, the main reason to come is the Franciscan church of the **Redentore** (Mon–Sat 10am–5pm Sun 1–5pm; €1.50), designed by Palladio in 1577 in thanks for Venice's deliverance from a plague that killed a third of the population. Sadly, the church is in a bad state of repair, and a rope prevents visitors going beyond the nave, but you can see its best paintings, including a *Madonna with Child and Angels* by Alvise Vivarini, in the sacristy, as well as a curious gallery of eighteenth-century wax heads of illustrious Franciscans.

Sheltering Venice from the open sea, the thin strand of the **Lido** used to be the focus of the annual hullaballoo of Venice's "Marriage to the Sea", when the doge went out to the Porto di Lido to drop a gold ring into the brine and then disembarked for mass at San Nicolò al Lido. Later it became the smartest bathing resort in Italy, and although it's no longer as chic as it was when Thomas Mann set *Death in Venice* here, there's less room on its beaches now than ever before; indeed, unless you're staying at one of the flashy hotels on the seafront, or are prepared to pay a ludicrous fee to hire a beach hut, you won't even be allowed to get the choicest Lido sand between your toes. There are public beaches at the northern and southern ends of the island – though the water is, as you would expect, filthy.

The Northern Islands

The major islands lying to the north of Venice – **Murano**, **Burano** and **Torcello** – can be reached by waterbus from the **Fondamente Nuove**: the #40, #41 or #52, which run about every fifteen minutes, will take you to San Michele and Murano; for Burano and Torcello there is the #12 (roughly hourly), which takes forty minutes to Burano, from where it's a short hop to Torcello. This service can also be caught from Murano, at the Faro landing stage.

Chiefly famed as the home of Venice's glass-blowing industry, Murano's main *fondamente* are crowded with shops selling the mostly revolting products of the **furnaces**, but the process of manufacture is more interesting. There are numerous furnaces to visit, all free of charge on the assumption that you will then want to buy something, though you won't be pressed too hard to do so. Many of the workshops are along Fondamenta dei Vetrai. There's also the **Museo Vetrario** in the Palazzo Giustinian (daily except Wed 10am–4pm; €4.10), which displays Roman pieces and the earliest surviving examples of Murano glass from the fifteenth century. Other attractions include the church of **San Pietro Martire**, a Dominican Gothic church which houses an elegant *Madonna* by Giovanni Bellini, and the Veneto-Byzantine church of **Santi Maria e Donato**, founded in the seventh century and rebuilt in the twelfth, which has a beautiful mosaic floor.

Burano is still largely a fishing community, although there is also a thriving trade in **lace-making** here, and the main street is crammed with shops selling Burano-point and Venetian-point lace. The skills are taught at the **Scuola dei Merletti** in Piazza Baldessare Galuppi (10am–4pm; closed Mon; €2.60), which also houses a small museum with work dating back as far as the sixteenth century.

The island of **Torcello** was settled as early as the fifth century, and once had a population of some twenty thousand. Nowadays, however, the population is about one hundred, and there is little visible evidence of the island's prime except for Venice's first cathedral, **Santa Maria Assunta** (daily 10am–12.30pm & 2–5pm; €2). A Veneto-Byzantine building on the site of a seventh-century church (only the crypt of which survives), the cathedral has a stunning twelfth-century mosaic of the Madonna and Child in the apse. Look in also on the church of **Santa Fosca**, built in the eleventh and twelfth centuries to house the body of the saint, brought from Libya some time before 1011 and now resting under the altar. In the square outside sits the curious **chair of Attila**: sit in it and – local legend says – you will be wed within a year. Behind, the **Museo dell'Estuario** (Tues–Sun 10am–12.30pm & 2–4pm; €1.50) displays thirteenth-century beaten gold figures, sections of mosaic heads and pieces of jewellery.

Eating and drinking

Virtually every **restaurant** in Venice advertises a set-price *Menu Turistico*, which can be a cheap way of sampling Venetian specialities, but the quality and certainly the quantity won't be up to the mark of an *à la carte* meal. As a general rule, value for money tends to increase with the distance from San Marco; plenty of restaurants within a short radius of the Piazza offer menus that seem to be reasonable but you'll probably find the food unappetizing and the service abrupt. Most bars will also serve some kind of food, ranging from *tramezzini* through to more exotic tapas-style nibbles known as *cicheti*.

TAKEAWAYS AND PICNIC FOOD

Cip Ciap, close to the church of Santa Maria Formosa in Calle Mondo Nuovo, Castello, has perhaps the city's best range of takeaway pizzas, with a wonderfully tasty spinach and ricotta variety (closed Thurs). *Aliani Gastronomia*, Ruga Vecchia S. Giovanni, San Polo, is a good source of picnic fare, as are the fruit and veg **markets** at Santa Maria Formosa and Santa Margherita, and the general market at the Rialto, where you can buy everything you need for an impromptu feast – it's open Monday to Saturday from 8am to 1pm.

RESTAURANTS

Al Cugnai, Piscina del Forner, Dorsoduro. Good-value trattoria close to the Accademia – though the service can be brisk. Get there by 8pm or be prepared to queue. Closed Mon.

Alle Oche, Calle del Tintor (south side of Campo S. Giacomo dell'Orio), San Polo. Has about 80 varieties of inexpensive pizza to choose from.

Altanella, Calle dell'Erbe, Giudecca. Succulent fish dishes, and a terrace overlooking the island's central canal. Good for a treat. Closed Mon & Tues.

Antico Mola, Fondamenta degli Ormesini, Cannaregio. Originally a family-run, local place, but becoming trendier by the year. Good food, good value. Closed Wed.

Casa Mia, Calle dell' Oca, Castello. Very popular trattoria-pizzeria close to Santi Apostoli church. Closed Tues.

Paradiso Perduto, Fondamenta della Misericordia, Cannaregio. Fronted by a popular bar, with a lively relaxed atmosphere and sometimes live music. Full meals start at around €10. Closed Wed.

Rosticceria San Bartolomeo, Calle della Bissa, San Marco. A glorified snack bar serving low-priced full meals. Good if you need to refuel quickly and cheaply. Closed Mon.

BARS, CAFÉS AND PASTICCERIE

Al Volto, Calle Cavalli (near Campo S. Luca), San Marco. Stocks 1300 wines from Italy and elsewhere, some cheap, many not; good snacks, too; closed Sun.

Cantina del Vino gia Schiavi, Fondamenta Maravegie, Dorsoduro. Great wine shop and bar opposite San Trovaso church; closed Sun.

Do Mori, Calle Do Mori, San Polo. Narrow, standing-only bar, catering for the Rialto traders, office-workers, and locals just out for a stroll. One of the best of a number of bars in the market area, it serves delicious snacks; closed Wed afternoon & Sun.

Il Golosone, Salizzada San Lio, Castello. *Pasticceria* and bar with a glorious spread of cakes; does a delicious apple *spremuta*; closed Mon.

Marchini, Ponte San Maurizio, San Marco. The most delicious and expensive of Venetian pasticcerie, where people come on Sun morning to buy family treats.

Nico, Záttere ai Gesuati, Dorsoduro. High spot of a wander in the area, celebrated for an artery-clogging creation called a *gianduiotto* – a block of praline ice cream in whipped cream; closed Thurs.

Paolin, Campo Santo Stefano, San Marco. Thought by many to be the makers of the best ice cream in Venice; the outside tables also have one of the finest settings in the city; closed Fri.

VinoVino, Ponte delle Veste, San Marco. Slightly posey bar stocking over 100 wines; open until midnight; closed Tues.

The Carnevale, Regata Storica and Biennale

Perhaps the city's most famous annual event is the **Carnevale**, which occupies the ten days leading up to Lent, finishing on Shrove Tuesday with a masked ball for the glitterati and dancing in the Piazza for the plebs. It was revived in the late Seventies, and after three years gained support from the city authorities, who now organize various pageants and performances. It's also very much a time to see and be seen: people don costumes and in the evening congregate in the squares. Masks are on sale throughout the year in Venice, but new mask and costume shops suddenly appear during Carnevale, and Campo San Maurizio sprouts a marquee with mask-making demonstrations and a variety of designs for sale. Another big event is the **Regata Storica**, held on the first Sunday in September, an annual trial of strength and skill for the city's gondoliers which starts with a procession of richly decorated historic craft along the Canal Grande course, their crews all decked out in period dress. Bystanders are expected to join in the support for the contestants in the main event, and may even be issued with appropriate colours. There's also the **Venice Biennale**, set up in 1895 as a showpiece for international contemporary art and held every odd-numbered year from June to September. Its permanent site in the Giardini

Pubblici has pavilions for about forty countries, plus space for a thematic international exhibition. The *Aperto* ("Open") section, a mixed exhibition showing the work of younger or less-established artists, takes over spaces all over the city, and various sites throughout the city host fringe exhibitions, installations and performances, particularly in the opening weeks.

Listings

Airlines Alitalia, Via San Sovino 3, Mestre (☎041.258.1111); British Airways, Via Peschiera Vecchia 26, Mestre (☎041.971983).

Airport enquiries Marco Polo airport, ☎041.260.9260.

Books A good general bookshop is Goldoni, Calle dei Fabbri, San Marco.

Car rental All the major companies have desks at the airport and Piazzale Roma.

Consulates UK, Palazzo Querini, Accademia, Dorsoduro 1051 (☎041.522.7207). The nearest US consulate is in Milan; travellers from Canada, Australia, New Zealand and Ireland should contact the embassy in Rome.

Exchange American Express, Salizzada San Moisè, San Marco (Mon–Fri 9am–5.30pm, Sat 9am–12.30pm; ☎041.520.0844).

Hospital Ospedale Civili Riuniti di Venezia, Campo Santi Giovanni e Paolo (☎041.523.0000).

Internet access at Net House Venice, 2958–2976 Campo San Stefano (24-hr; €6.20/hour).

Laundry Ai Tre Ponti, Santa Croce 274; Salizzada del Pistor, Cannaregio 4553, near Santi Apostoli.

Left luggage Train station left-luggage desk open 24hr; €2.50 per item.

Pharmacies Consult Un Ospite di Venezia or get a list from ☎041.522.0573.

Police The Questura is on Via Nicoldi 24, Marghera (☎041.271.5511).

Post office Central office in the Fondaco dei Tedeschi, by the Rialto Bridge (Mon–Sat 8.15am–7pm, poste restante 8.15am–6.45pm); 24hr telegram service call ☎1795; international operator ☎176.

Train enquiries ☎147.888.088 toll free from Italy, ☎041.524.2303 for reservations, ☎041.238.1560 24 hour timetable.

Padua

Extensively rebuilt after damage caused by bombing during World War II, and hemmed in by the sprawl which accompanied its development as the Veneto's most important economic centre, **PADUA** is not immediately the most alluring city in northern Italy; however, it is one of the most ancient, and plentiful evidence remains of its lineage. A former Roman settlement, the city was a place of pilgrimage following the death of St Anthony here, and it later became an artistic and intellectual centre: Donatello and Mantegna both worked here, and in the seventeenth century Galileo researched at the university, where the medical faculty was one of the most ambitious in Europe.

The City

Just outside the city centre, through a gap in the Renaissance walls off Corso Garibaldi, the Giotto frescoes in the **Cappella degli Scrovegni** (daily 9am–6/7pm; by appointment only – ring ☎049.875.2077; €5.20 for joint ticket with Musei Civici) are for many the reason for coming to Padua. Commissioned in 1303 by Enrico Scrovegni in atonement for his father's usury, the chapel's walls are covered with illustrations of the life of Mary, Jesus and the story of the Passion – a cycle, arranged in three tiers and painted against a backdrop of saturated blue, that is one of the high points in the development of European art in its innovative attention to the inner nature of its subjects. Beneath the main pictures are shown the vices and virtues in human (usually female) form, while on the wall above the door is the *Last Judgement*. Directly above the door is a portrait of Scrovegni presenting the chapel; his tomb is at the far end, behind the altar with its statues by Giovanni Pisano. The adjacent **Musei Civici** (Tues–Sun 9am–5pm; free) contains an assembly of fourteenth- to nineteenth-century art from the Veneto and further afield, the high point being a *Crucifixion* by Giotto that was once in the Scrovegni chapel, a fine *Portrait of a Young Senator* by Bellini, and a sequence of devils overcoming angels by Guariento. In addition to the vast picture galleries, the museum complex also features a superbly presented archeological museum and one of the world's largest collections of coins and medals. Nearby, the church of the **Eremitani**, built at the turn of the fourteenth century but almost completely wrecked by bombing in 1944, has been fastidiously rebuilt, although the frescoes by Mantegna that used to be here were almost totally lost, and can now be assessed only from a few fuzzy photographs and some fragments on the right of the high altar.

South of here, on the other side of the centre, the main sight of the Piazza del Santo is Donatello's **Monument to Gattamelata**, as the *condottiere* Erasmo da Narni was known. He died in 1443 and this monument was raised ten years later, the earliest large bronze sculpture of the Renaissance, and a direct precursor to Verrocchio's monument to Colleoni in Venice. On one side of the square, the basilica of San Antonio or **Il Santo** (daily 6.30am–7/7.45pm) was built to house the body of St Anthony, and its Cappella del Santo has a sequence of panels showing scenes from his life, carved between 1505 and 1577. Take a look, too, at Padua's finest work by Pietro Lombardo, a monument to Antonio Roselli, and the high altar's sculptures and reliefs by Donatello. The **Cappella del Tesoro** (8am–noon & 2.30–7pm), off the ambulatory, houses the tongue and chin of St Anthony in a head-shaped reliquary.

From the basilica, Via Umberto leads you back towards the **University**, established in 1221, and older than any other in Italy except Bologna. The main block is the **Palazzo del Bò**, where Galileo taught physics from 1592 to 1610, declaiming from a lectern that is still on show, though the major sight is the sixteenth-century anatomy theatre (guided tours: March–Oct Tues & Thurs 9am, 10am & 11am, Mon, Wed & Fri 3pm, 4pm & 5pm; €2.60). The area west of here, around the **Piazza della Frutta** and **Piazza delle Erbe**, is effectively the hub of the city. Separating the two squares is the extraordinary **Palazzo della Ragione** (Tues–Sun 9am–6/7pm; €4.10), which, at the time of its construction in the early 1200s, sported frescoes by Giotto and his assistants. These were destroyed by fire in 1420 and most of the extant frescoes (1425–40) are by Nicola Miretto. Close by, Padua's **Duomo** (€1.50) is an unlovely church whose design was cribbed from drawings by Michelangelo, though the adjacent Romanesque **Baptistry** is one of the unproclaimed delights of Padua, lined with some fourteenth-century frescoes by Giusto de'Menabuoi – a cycle which makes a fascinating comparison with Giotto's in the Cappella degli Scrovegni.

Practicalities

The **train station** is at the far end of Corso del Popolo, a few minutes' walk north of the city walls. The main **tourist office** (Mon–Sat 9am–12.30pm & 3–7pm; ☎049.876.7927, *www.apt.padova.it*) is in Piazzetta Pedrocchio, just off Via 8 Febbraio. Of many affordable **hotels**, *Verdi*, Via Dondi dell'Orologio 7 (☎049.875.5774; ③), in particular is clean and friendly. Another good budget option is *Junior*, Via L. Faggin 2 (☎049.611.756; ③), just behind the station. The **HI hostel** is at Via A. Aleardi 30 (☎049.875.2219; ③), and has Internet access and an 11pm curfew – take bus #3, #8, #12, #18 or #22 from the station. The nearest **campsite** is 15km away in Montegrotto Terme (Via Roma 123), served by frequent trains – a fifteen-minute trip, or bus M. As for **food**, the *rosticceria* in Via Daniele Manin offers a wide variety of snacks, while *Pane e Foccaccia* on Via del Santo has excellent pizza slices. If you want to sit down, there's *La Mappa*, Via Matteotti 17, with decent self-service fare (closed Sat) or *Brek*, at the corner of Piazza Cavour. For a more relaxed session at only slightly greater expense, two good cheap restaurants are *Da Giovanni* at Via Maroncelli, and *Pago Pago* at Via Galilei 59. On Piazza Cavour, *Pe Pen* (closed Sun) has a wonderful range of pizzas, with seats on the square in summer. The *Dotto*, Via Randaccio 23, is a superb mid-range restaurant – allow around €25 per person.

Verona

The easy-going city of **VERONA** is the largest city of the Veneto, and, with its wealth of Roman sites and streets of pink-hued medieval buildings, one of its most interesting. First settled by the Romans, it later became an independent city-state, reaching its zenith in the thirteenth century under the Scaligeri family. Ruthless in the exercise of power, the Scaligeri were at the same time energetic patrons of the arts, and many of Verona's finest buildings date from the century of their rule. With their fall, the Viscontis of Milan assumed control of the city, which was later absorbed into the Venetian empire.

The City

The city centre clusters into a deep bend in the River Adige, the main sight of its southern reaches the central hub of **Piazza Brà** and its mighty Roman **Arena** (Tues–Sun 8am–7pm, July & Aug 9am–3pm; €3.10, first Sun of month €1.40). Dating from the first century AD, and originally with seating for some twenty thousand, this is the third-largest surviving Roman amphitheatre, and offers a tremendous panorama from the topmost of the 44 marble tiers. North, **Via Mazzini**, a narrow traffic-free street lined with expensive shops, leads to a grouping of squares, most noteworthy of which is the **Piazza dei Signori**, flanked by the medieval **Palazzo degli Scaligeri** – the residence of the Scaligeri. At right angles to this is the fifteenth-century **Loggia del Consiglio**, the former assembly hall of the city council and Verona's outstanding early Renaissance building, while, close by, the twelfth-century **Torre dei Lamberti** (Tues–Sun 9am–6pm; €2 by lift, €1.50 on foot) gives dizzying views of the city. Beyond the square, in front of the Romanesque church of Santa Maria Antica, the **Arche Scaligere** are the elaborate Gothic funerary monuments of Verona's first family, in a wrought-iron palisade decorated with ladder motifs, the emblem of the Scaligeri. Mastino I ("Mastiff"), founder of the dynasty, is buried in the simple tomb against the wall of the church; Mastino II is to the left of the entrance, opposite the most florid of the tombs, that of **Cansignorio** ("Top Dog"); while over the side entrance of the church is an equestrian statue of **Cangrande I** ("Big Dog") – a copy of the original now in Verona's Castelvecchio. Towards the river from here is the church of **Sant'Anastasia** (summer Tues–Sat 9am–6pm, Sun 1–6pm; winter Tues–Sat 10am–4pm, Sun 1–5pm; €1.50, combined ticket for all Verona churches €4.10), a mainly Gothic church, completed in the late fifteenth century, with Pisanello's delicately coloured fresco of *St George and the Princess* in the sacristy. Verona's **Duomo** (summer Tues–Sat 9am–6pm, Sun 1–6pm; winter Tues–Sat 10am–4pm, Sun 1–5pm; €1.50) lies just around the river's bend, a mixture of Romanesque and Gothic styles that houses an *Assumption* by Titian in an architectural frame by Sansovino, who also designed the choir.

In the opposite direction, off Piazza delle Erbe at Via Cappello 23, is the **Casa di Giulietta**, a fourteenth-century structure that's in a fine state of preservation, though there's no connection between this house and the historical character to whom Shakespeare's Juliet is distantly related (Tues–Sun 9am–6.30pm; €3.10). South of here, on the junction of Via Diaz and Corso Porta Borsari, the **Porta dei Borsari** is a fine Roman monument, with an inscription that dates it to 265 AD, though it's almost certainly older than that. Some way down Corso Cavour from here, the Arco dei Gavi is a first-century Roman triumphal arch, beyond which the **Castelvecchio** (Tues–Sun 8am–7pm; €3, first Sunday of the month free) houses a collection of paintings, jewellery and weapons, as well as the equestrian figure of Cangrande I, removed from his tomb, strikingly displayed on an outdoor pedestal. Outstanding among the paintings are works by Jacopo and Giovanni Bellini, a *Madonna* by Pisanello, Veronese's *Descent from the Cross*, a Tintoretto *Nativity*, and works by the two Tiepolos.

A kilometre or so northwest of here, the **Basilica di San Zeno Maggiore** (€1.50) is one of the most significant Romanesque churches in northern Italy, put up in the first half of the twelfth century. Its rose window, representing the Wheel of Fortune, dates from then, as does the magnificent portal, whose lintels bear sculptures representing the months while the door has bronze panels depicting scenes from the Bible and the miracles of San Zeno. The simple interior is covered with frescoes, although the church's most compulsive image is the altar's luminous *Madonna and Saints* by Mantegna.

Practicalities

The **train station** is twenty minutes outside the city centre, connected with Piazza Brà by a #1 or #8 bus. There's a **tourist office** at the train station (summer Mon–Sat 8am–7.30pm, Sun 9–noon; winter Mon–Sat 9am–6pm; ☎045.800.0861, *www.tourism.verona.it*) and at the Cortile del Tribunale, close to the Arche Scaligere (Tues–Sun 10am–7pm). Of **hotels**, the *Al Castello*, Corso Cavour 43 (☎045.800.4403; ④), has recently refurbished rooms, *Catullo*, Via Catullo 1 (☎045.800.2786, *locandacatullo@tiscalinet.it*; ④), is in a central position just off Via Mazzini, and the *Aurora*, Piazza delle Erbe 2 (☎045.594.717; ⑤), has many rooms overlooking the square itself. Verona's **HI hostel** is at Via Fontana del Ferro 15 (☎045.590.360; ②), on the north side of the river behind the Teatro Romano (bus #2), close to which there's a pleasant summer campsite. There's also the *Casa della Giovane*, Via Pigna 7 (☎045.596.880; ②), in the old centre, for women only. For **Internet access**, the stylish Cyber Club (Mon–Sat 8pm–midnight; €6.20/hr) is a couple of minutes' walk from Piazza Bra at Via Antonio 13.

Among **eating** options, *Alla Costa*, Via della Costa 2, serves good pizzas, as does *Pizzeria Arena*, Vicolo Tre Marchetti 1, which is open until 1am, and there's a *Brek* self-service on Piazza Brà. Otherwise, the most plentiful source of cheap places is over the river: especially good is the *Dal Ropeton* (closed Tues), below the hostel at Via S. Giovanni in Valle 46. On the other side of the Teatro Romano, *Pero d'Oro*, Via Ponte Pignolo 25, serves inexpensive but genuine Veronese dishes. For evening drinks, the ultra-friendly, but pricey, *Bottega del Vino* in Vicolo Scudo di Francia, just off the north end of Via Mazzini, is an old bar with a selection of wines from all over Italy. For a less touristy ambience, try *Al Carro Armato*, Vicolo Gatto 2a, or *Osteria Al Duomo*, Via Duomo 7a.

Trieste

Backed by a white limestone plateau and facing the blue Adriatic, **TRIESTE** is in a potentially idyllic setting – get close up, however, and you see that a lot of the place is run-down, and the water uninviting, which is why most vistors just pass through Trieste, and few actually stop. The city itself is a strange place, its massive Neoclassical architecture dating from the time when it was the Habsburg Empire's southern port. Lying as it does on the political and ethnic fault-line between the Latin and Slavic worlds, Trieste has long been a city of political extremes. Yugoslavia and the Allies fought over it until 1954, when the city and a connecting strip of coast were secured for Italy. The neo-Fascist MSI party has always done well here, and there's even a local anti-Slav party, Lista per Trieste.

The City

The social centre of Trieste is the huge **Piazza dell'Unità d'Italia**, opening onto the harbour and flanked by the vast bulks of the **Palazzo del Comune** and **Palazzo di Governo**. The focal point of the city's history, however, and its prime tourist site, is the hill of San Giusto, with its castle and cathedral, accessible on bus #24. The **Castello** (daily 9am–sunset; €1.50) is a fifteenth-century Venetian fortress, built near the site of the Roman forum, whose ramparts are worth a walk and whose museum (Tues–Sun 9am–1pm; €1.50) houses a collection of antique weaponry. The **Cattedrale di San Giusto** (daily 8am–noon & 3.30–7.30pm) is a typically Triestine synthesis of styles, with a predominantly Romanesque facade including five Roman columns and a Gothic rose window. Inside, between Byzantine pillars, there are fine thirteenth-century frescoes of St Justus, a Christian martyr killed during the persecutions of Diocletian. Trieste's principal museum, the **Museo Revoltella** at Via Diaz 27 (Mon

& Wed–Sun 10am–7pm; €2.60), is housed in a nineteenth-century Viennese-style palace and displays dull nineteenth-century and decent modern art collections. More disturbingly, on the southern side of the city, the **Risiera di San Sabba** at Rattodella Pileria 43 (Tues–Sun 9am–1pm; April & May Tues–Sat 9am– 6pm, Sun 9am–1pm; free), on the #10 bus route, was one of Italy's two concentration camps (the other is near Carpi in Emilia Romagna). A permanent exhibition serves as a reminder of Fascist crimes in the region.

Practicalities

The central **train station** is on Piazza Libertà, on the northern edge of the city centre. There's a **tourist information** desk here, and a main office at Via San Nicolo 20, by the seafront (Mon–Sat 9am–7pm, Sun 10am–1pm & 4–7pm; ☎040.679.6111, *www.triestetourism.it*). There are many reasonable **hotels**, nicest of which are the *Centro*, Via Roma 13 (☎040.371.116; ③); and the *Blaue Krone*, Via XXX Ottobre 12 (☎040.631.882; ③) or *Istria*, Via Timeus 5 (☎040 371343; ④). The **HI hostel** is 8km out of the city at Viale Miramare 331 (☎040.224.102; ②) – take bus #6 from the tourist office, then bus #36. The nearest **campsite** is in nearby Obelisco, on the #4 bus route.

For **snacks** and light meals, *Pepi Sciavo* in Via Cassa di Risparmio is a favourite student lunch-stop, with excellent sausages and sauerkraut. Another student hangout is *Notorious* in Via del Bosco – sandwiches and salads on the ground floor and a good cheap trattoria on the first floor. Decent pizzas can be had at *Il Barattolo* in Piazza Sant'Antonio Nuovo, and there are *Brek* self-service places in Via San Francesco and Via Campi Elisi. For more substantial food, try the excellent *Da Giovanni*, at Via Lazzaro 14, the popular *Galleria Fabris* at Piazza Dalmazia 4 which serves cheap pizzas and fish, or the *Arco di Riccardo* at Via del Trionfo 3. The city's favourite **café** is the *Caffè San Marco*, which has occupied its Liberty-style premises on Via G. Battisti for some eighty years. The *Caffè Tommaseo* on Piazza Tommaseo was a rendezvous for Italian nationalists in the last century and although refurbished still makes a pleasant, if pricey refuge in the summer heat. The *Caffe Walter* at Via San Niccolo 31 has fin-de-siècle decor and free nibbles in the afternoon, while among the bars, *Public House* at Via San Lazzaro 9, and *Osteria de Libero*, Via Risorta 8, are both atmospheric places.

Bologna

The capital of Emilia-Romagna, **BOLOGNA** is a boom town of the Eighties whose computer-associated industries have brought conspicuous wealth to the old brick palaces and porticoed squares. Previously, it was best known for its food, undeniably the richest in the country, and for its politics – up until the recent elections, when it fell to the right, "Red Bologna" was the Italian Communist Party's stronghold and spiritual home since World War II. The city centre is among the best-looking in the country, still startlingly medieval in plan, and has enough curiosities to warrant several days' exploration. However, Bologna is really enjoyable just for itself, with a busy cultural life and a café and bar scene that is one of the most convivial in northern Italy.

Arrival and accommodation

Bologna's **airport** is northwest of the centre, linked to the train station on Piazza delle Medaglie d'Oro, at the end of Via dell'Indipendenza, by the Airbus (*www.atc.bo.it*; €3.60). There are **tourist information** booths at the airport (daily 8am–8pm; ☎051.647.2036) and at the train station (Mon & Wed–Sat 9am–7pm, Tues 9am–2pm; ☎051.246.541), and a main office at Piazza Maggiore 6 (Mon–Sat 8.30am–7pm, Sun 9am–2pm; ☎051.239.660, *www.comune.bologna.it*), with leaflets, maps and a hotel-booking facility. In terms of **places to stay**, Bologna is not geared up for tourists, least of all for those travelling on a tight budget, and the trade fairs during high season make booking ahead imperative. The most inexpensive is the city's official **HI hostel**, *Due Torri*, 6km outside the centre of town at Via

Viadagola 5 (☎051.501.810; ②), with a midnight curfew. Bus #93 from Via Irnerio, a short walk southeast from the train station, takes you within 800m of the hostel. Among the few affordable **hotels** are the centrally positioned *Garisenda*, Via Rizzoli 9, Galleria del Leone 1 (☎051.224.369; ④), *Minerva*, Via De Monari 3 (☎051.239.652; ④), and the *Panorama*, Via Livraghi 1 (☎051.221.802; ④). More expensive is the *Accademia*, nicely situated at Via Belli Arti 6 (☎051.232.318; ⑤), and the popular *Orologio*, Via IV Novembre 10 (☎051.231.253; ⑧), which should be booked in advance. For **camping**, the *Camping Hotel and Residence* (☎051.325.016, *www.hotelcamping.com*), Via Romita 12/4a, near the exhibition centre, has a swimming pool.

The City

Bologna's city centre is quite compact, with most things of interest within the main ring road. **Piazza Maggiore** is the obvious place to make for first, buzzing with almost constant activity. On its western side, the **Palazzo Comunale** has two galleries: the **Museo Morandi** and the **Collezioni Comunali D'Arte** (Tues–Sun 10am–6pm; €4.10), and apartments open for public viewing when not in use for concerts and other events, and it is well worth visiting for the view over the square. On the square's south side, the church of San Petronio is the city's largest, intended originally to have been larger than St Peter's in Rome, and one of the finest Gothic brick buildings in Italy; money and land for the side aisle were diverted by the pope's man in Bologna towards a new university, and the architect Antonio di Vicenzo's plans had to be modified. You can see the beginnings of the planned side aisle on the left of the building and there are models of what the church was supposed to look like in the museum (10am–12.30pm; closed Tues); otherwise the most intriguing features are a beautiful carving of *Madonna and Child* by Jacopo della Quercia, above the central portal, and an astronomical clock – a long brass meridian line set at an angle across the floor, with a hole left in the roof for the sun to shine through on the right spot. The adjacent Piazza Nettuno has an extravagant statue of Neptune that was fashioned by Giambologna in 1566.

Across Via dell'Archiginnasio from here, the **Museo Civico Archeologico** (Tues–Fri 9am–2pm, Sat & Sun 9am–1pm & 3.30–7pm; €4.10) is a rather stuffy museum but its displays of Egyptian and Roman antiquities are good ones, and the Etruscan section is one of the best outside Lazio. Down the street, Bologna's university – the Archiginnasio – was founded at more or less the same time as the Piazza Maggiore was laid out, predating the rest of Europe's universities, though it didn't get a special building until 1565. The most interesting part is the recently renovated **Teatro Anatomico** (Mon–Sat 9am–1pm; free), the original medical faculty dissection theatre, whose tiers of seats surround an extraordinary professor's chair, covered with a canopy supported by figures known as *gli spellati* – the skinned ones. South, down Via Garibaldi, Piazza San Domenico, with its strange canopied tombs holding the bones of medieval law scholars, is the site of the church of **San Domenico**, built in 1251 to house the relics of St Dominic. The bones rest in the so-called *Arca di San Domenico*, a fifteenth-century work that was principally the creation of Nicola Pisano – though many artists contributed to it. Pisano and his pupils were responsible for the reliefs illustrating the saint's life; the statues on top were the work of Pisano himself; Nicola dell'Arca was responsible for the canopy; and the angel and figures of saints Proculus and Petronius were the work of a very young Michelangelo.

North of here, the eastern section of Bologna's centro storico preserves many of the older university departments, housed for the most part in large seventeenth- and eighteenth-century palaces. At Piazza di Porta Ravegnana, the **Torre degli Asinelli** (daily 9am–5/6pm; €2.60) and perilously leaning **Torre Garisenda** are together known as the *Due Torri*, the only survivors of literally hundreds of towers that were scattered across the city during the Middle Ages. From here, Via San Stefano leads down past a complex of four – but originally seven – churches, collectively known as **Santo Stefano**. The striking polygonal church of San Sepolcro, reached through the church of Crocifisso, is about the most interesting: the basin in its courtyard is by tradition the one used by Pilate to wash his hands after he condemned Christ to death, while, inside, the bones of St Petronius provide a pleasingly kitsch focus, held in a tomb modelled on the Church of the Holy Sepulchre in Jerusalem. A door-way leads from here through to **San Vitale e Agricola**, Bologna's oldest church, built from discarded Roman fragments in the fifth century; while the fourth church, the Trinitá, lies across the courtyard and is home to a small museum (daily 9am–noon & 3.30–6pm) con-taining a reliquary of St Petronius and a handful of dull paintings.

Eating, drinking and nightlife

Bologna is one of the best places in Italy to **eat**, and not just in restaurants. There are any number of places to put together delicious **picnics**, best of which is the Mercato delle Erbe, Via Ugo Bassi 2, biggest and liveliest of the city's markets, or the small but inviting market on Via Draperie. For **snacks**, the *Impero,* Via Indipendenza 39, does excellent croissants and pastries; *Altero,* at Via Indipendenza 33 or Via Ugo Bassi 10, is best for pizza by the slice; *La Torinese,* under the vaults of Palazzo del Podestà in Piazza Maggiore, does daily quiches and stuffed vegetables. Of **restaurants**, *C'entro,* Via Indipendenza 45 (open until 2am), and *Bassotto,* Via Ugo Bassi 8 (lunchtimes only), serve quality fast food in comfortable sur-roundings; *Boni,* Via Saragozza 88, has very good Emilian cuisine, likewise *Lamma* at Via dei Giudei 4 – a popular place with a pub atmosphere. For family-style Bolognese food, go to *Al Quindici,* south of the centre at Via Mirasole 13, an atmospheric place with wooden tables. *Nino's,* Via Volturno 9 (off Via dell'Independenza), serves inexpensive pizza and pasta; *Clorofilla,* Strada Maggiore 64, is a good place for vegetarians though it's expensive, and the self-service *Lazzarini,* Via Clavature 1 (Mon–Sat 7am–8pm), is cheap but more stylish than most.

To **drink**, there are plenty of good bars on Via Pratello and in the student quarter, and plenty of *osterie* all over town – pub-like places, that have been the mainstay of Bolognese **nightlife** for a few hundred years, and stay open till late. *Matusel,* at Via Bertolini 2, close to the university, is a lively and noisy example, with reasonably priced full meals; *Del Montesino,* at Via del Pratello 74b, is a convivial haunt, open until 2am; *Senzanome,* Via Senzanome 42, serves good meals and has a wide choice of beers and wines; and *Marione,* at Via San Felice 137, close to the city gate, is old and dark, with good wine and snacks. The tiny *Osteria dell'Infidele,* on Via Gerusalemme, has good economic food but is better for just drinking. For events, the excellent English-language listings magazine *Talkabout* (*www.talkabout.it*) has details of what's on in the city.

Parma

PARMA is about as comfortable a town as you could wish for. The measured pace of its streets, the abundance of its restaurants and the general air of provincial affluence are almost cloyingly pleasant, especially if you've arrived from the south. But it's a friendly enough place with plenty to see, not least the works of two key late Renaissance artists – Correggio and Parmigianino.

The Town

Piazza Garibaldi is the fulcrum of Parma, its packed-out cafés, along with the narrow streets and alleyways which wind south and west of the piazza, home to much of the town's nightlife. The mustard-coloured **Palazzo del Governatore** flanks the square, behind which the Renaissance church of the **Madonna della Steccata** stands, apparently using Bramante's original plan for St Peter's as a model. Inside there are frescoes by a number of sixteenth-cen-tury painters, notably Parmigianino, who spent the last ten years of his life on this work, even-tually being sacked for breach of contract by the disgruntled church authorities. Five min-utes' walk away, the beautiful Romanesque **Duomo** (daily 9am–12.30pm & 3–7pm), dating from the eleventh century, holds earlier work by Parmigianino in its south transept, painted when the artist was a pupil of Correggio – one of whose most famous works, a 1534 fresco of the *Assumption*, can be seen in the central cupola. There's more by Correggio in the cupola of **San Giovanni Evangelista** behind the Duomo – a fresco of the *Vision of St John*. You should also visit the Duomo's octagonal **Baptistry** (€2.60), considered to be Benedetto Antelami's finest work, built in 1196 and bridging the gap between the Romanesque and Gothic styles. Antelami sculpted the frieze which surrounds the building, and was also responsible for the reliefs inside, including a series of fourteen statues representing the months and seasons. Take the spiral staircase to the top for a closer view of the frescoes on the ceiling; they are by an unknown thirteenth-century artist. Correggio was also responsible for the frescoes in the **Camera di San Paolo** (daily 9am–1.45pm; €2.10) of the former Benedictine convent off Via Melloni, a few minutes north; he portrayed the abbess who commissioned the work as the goddess Diana, above the fireplace.

East of the cathedral square, the **Museo Glauco-Lombardi** at Via Garibaldi 15 (Tues–Sun 9.30am–6pm, €5.20) recalls later times, with a display of memorabilia relating to Marie-Louise of Austria, who reigned here after the defeat of her husband Napoleon at Waterloo, setting herself up with another suitor (much to the chagrin of her exiled spouse) and expanding the Parma violet perfume industry. Just across Piazza Marconi from here, it's hard to miss Parma's biggest monument, the **Palazzo della Pilotta**, begun for Alessandro Farnese in the sixteenth century and rebuilt after World War II bombing to house a number of Parma's museums, notably the city's main art gallery, the **Galleria Nazionale** (Tues–Sun 9am–1.30pm; €6.20, includes admission to Teatro Farnese). The hi-tech display includes more work by Correggio and Parmigianino, and the remarkable *Apostles at the Sepulchre* and *Funeral of the Virgin* by Caracci – massive canvases suspended each side of a gantry at the top of the building. The **Teatro Farnese**, which you pass through to get to the gallery, was almost entirely destroyed in 1944 and has been virtually rebuilt. An extended semicircle of seats three tiers high, made completely of wood, it's a copy of Palladio's Teatro Olimpico at Vicenza, and as well as being (temporarily) the biggest theatre of its kind, sported Italy's first revolving stage. Up a floor, the **Museo Archeologico Nazionale** (Tues–Sun 9am–6.30pm; €2.60) is less enticing but still worth a glance, with finds from the Etruscan city of Velleia and the prehistoric lake villages around Parma, as well as the tabletop on which the Emperor Trajan notched up a record of his gifts to the poor.

Practicalities

Parma's **train station** is fifteen minutes' walk from the central Piazza Garibaldi, or a short ride on bus #7, #8, #9 or #10. The main **tourist office** is on Strada Melloni (Mon–Sat 9am–7pm, Sun 9am–1pm; ☎0521.234.735, *www.parmaitaly.com*). Finding a **place to stay** can be tricky. There's an official **HI hostel** with **campsite** at Parco Cittadella 5 (☎0521.961.434; ②; April–Oct; 11pm curfew); take bus #9 or, after 8pm, #E. Among **hotels** near the station, the *Brozzi*, Via Trento 11 (☎0521.272.717; ③), is reasonable; the *Leon d'Oro*, a few minutes away at Viale A. Fratti 4 (☎0521.773.182; ③), has a **restaurant** attached. In the centre, the *Lazzaro*, Via XX Marzo 14 (☎0521.208.944; ④), is a small *locanda*. *Pizzeria Ristorante L'Artista*, Via Bruno Longhi 3/a, does good pizzas and has friendly English-speaking owners, and *Taverna San Ambrogio*, off Borgo Piero Torrigiani, has a meaty menu that leans towards game. At **night**, opera is the biggest deal; the Teatro Regio on Via Garibaldi (☎0521.218.678) is renowned for its discerning audiences.

Ravenna

When **RAVENNA** became capital of the Western Roman Empire 1500 years ago, it was more by quirk of fate than design. The Emperor Honorius, alarmed by armies invading from the north, moved his court from Rome to this obscure town on the Romagna coast because it was easy to defend, being surrounded by marshland, and situated close to the port of Classis – the biggest Roman naval base on the Adriatic. Honorius' anxiety proved well founded – Rome was sacked by the Goths in 410 – but Ravenna's days of glory were brief, and it, too, fell in

473. Yet the Ostrogoth king Theodoric continued to beautify the city, and it wasn't long before it was taken by the Byzantines, who were responsible for Ravenna's most glorious era – the city's mosaics are generally acknowledged to be one of the crowning achievements of Byzantine art.

The City

The best of the mosaics are in the basilica of **San Vitale**, ten minutes northwest of the centre (daily 9am–7pm; €9.70 combined ticket), a fairly typical Byzantine church, begun in 525 AD under Theodoric and finished in 548 under Justinian, which formed the basis for the great church of Aya Sofia in Constantinople fifteen years later. The mosaics are in the apse, arranged in a rigid hierachy, with Old Testament scenes across the semicircular lunettes of the choir, Christ, the Apostles and sons of San Vitale on the arch, and, on the semidome of the apse, a beardless Christ presenting a model of the church to San Vitale and Bishop Ecclesius. On the side walls of the apse are portraits of the Emperor Justinian and his wife Theodora, Justinian's foot resting on that of his general, Belisarius, who reclaimed the city from the Goths, while Theodora looks on, her expression giving some hint of the cruelty that she was apparently notorious for.

Across from the basilica is the tiny **Mausoleo di Galla Placidia** (same hours and ticket as San Vitale), named after the half-sister of Honorius, who later became regent of the Western Empire and was responsible for much of the grandeur of Ravenna's early days, though it's unlikely that the building ever held her bones. Inside, the mosaics glow with a deep blue lustre, most in an earlier style than San Vitale's, full of Roman and naturalistic motifs. Stars around a golden cross spread across the vaulted ceiling, while at each end are representations of St Lawrence, with the gridiron on which he was martyred, and the Good Shepherd, with one of his flock. Adjacent to San Vitale, housed in the former cloisters of the church, the **National Museum of Antiquities** (Tues–Sun 8.30am–7pm; €4.10) contains various items from this and later periods, most notably a sixth-century statue of Hercules capturing a stag, possibly a copy of a Greek original, and the so-called "Veil of Classis", decorated with portraits of Veronese bishops of the eighth and ninth centuries.

There are more fine mosaics east of here, on the busy Via di Roma, in the basilica of **Sant'Apollinare Nuovo** (daily 9.30am–7pm; same ticket as San Vitale), another building of the sixth century, again built by Theodoric. The mosaics run the length of the nave and depict ceremonial processions of martyrs bearing gifts for an enthroned Christ and the Virgin through an avenue of date palms. Some of the scenery is more specific to Ravenna: you can make out what used to be the harbour at nearby Classe against the city behind, out of which rises Theodoric's palace. Five minutes' walk up Via di Roma, the **Arian Baptistry** (8.30am–7pm; same ticket as San Vitale), also known as the Basilica dello Spirito Santo, has a fine mosaic ceiling showing the twelve Apostles and the baptism of Christ. Via Diaz leads from here down to Piazza del Popolo, the centre of Ravenna, a few blocks south of which the **Tomba di Dante** (9am–7pm; free) was put up in the eighteenth century to enclose a previous fifteenth-century tomb. Dante died here in exile from Florence in 1321 and was laid to rest in the adjoining church of San Francesco, a much-restored building, elements of which date from the fourth century.

A couple of minutes away on Piazza Duomo, the **Museo Arcivescovile** (daily 9.30am–7pm; same ticket as San Vitale) has mosaic fragments from around the city and the sixth-century Oratorio Sant'Andrea, adorned with mosaics of birds above a Christ dressed in the uniform of a Roman centurion. There are also fragments from the original cathedral (the present one is an uninteresting reconstruction), and an ornate ivory throne from Alexandria which belonged to Bishop Maximian in the sixth century. The **Neonian Baptistry** (daily 9.30am–7pm; same ticket as San Vitale), next door, is a conversion from a Roman bath-house. The original floor level has sunk into the marshy ground, and you can see the remains of the previous building, 3m below.

Note that you can't buy separate tickets for Ravenna's main monuments; the €9.70 **combined** ticket, valid for a year, covers all of them. Every Friday evening in July and August all of Ravenna's monuments are open to the public free until midnight.

Practicalities

Ravenna has a compact city centre, and it's only a short walk from the train station on Piazza Farini, along Viale Farini and Via A. Diaz, to the central Piazza del Popolo. The information office at Via Salara 8/12 (June–Sept daily 8.30am–7pm; Oct–May Mon–Sat 8.30am–6pm, Sun 10am–4pm; ☎544.35.404, *raiat1@alata.it*) has maps and accommodation lists. The slightly unsavoury district around the station is the best place for cheap **hotels** like the *Roma*, Via Candiano 26 (☎0544.421.515; ⑤), and *Al Giaciglio*, Via Rocca Brancaleone 42 (☎0544.39.403; ③), which has a decent restaurant, although it's further to walk. There's an **HI hostel**, the *Ostello Dante*, a ten-minute walk out of town at Via Aurelio Nicolodi 12 (☎0544.421.164; ②), or take bus #1 from outside the station. Ravenna's best places to **eat** are between the Duomo and Piazza San Francesco. *Ca' De Ven*, at Via C. Ricci 24, has a large selection of Emilia-Romagnan wine, and decent food. Back towards the square, on Via Mentana, *Da Renato*, and its sister restaurant next door, *Guidarello*, on Via R. Gessi, both do traditional local food. *Ristorante Scai*, Piazza Baracca 20, close to San Vitale, specializes in roast meat and game for those so inclined; it's reasonably priced and also serves pizzas in the evening. There are also mensas at the station and Via G. Oberdan 8, as well as a branch of the *Pizza Altero* chain on Via Camillo B. Cavour.

Rimini

RIMINI is the least pretentious town in Italy, the archetypal seaside city, with a reputation for good – if slightly sleazy – fun. Brash and high-rise, it's a traditional family resort, to which some Italians return year after year, but there's another, less savoury side to the town: Rimini is known across Italy for its fast-living and chancy nightlife, and there's a very active hetero- and transsexual prostitution scene.

In summer most activity is concentrated on the main seafront drag of souvenir shops, restaurants and video arcades, which stretches 9km north to the suburbs of Viserba and Torre Pedrera and 7km south to Miramare. Out of season, though, you'll find most life a little way inland in the older part of town, clustered around the main squares of **Piazza Tre Martiri** and **Piazza Cavour**. The latter is home to the Gothic **Palazzo del Podestà**; the square was rebuilt in the 1920s and bristles with fishtail battlements. Just inside the old town ramparts are the Roman Ponte di Tiberio and Arco d'Augusto. Rimini's best-known monument, however, is the strange-looking **Tempio Malatestiano** on Via 4 Novembre (Mon–Sat 8am–12.30pm & 3.30–6.30pm, Sun 9am–1pm & 3.30–7pm; free), one of the masterworks of the Italian Renaissance. Originally a Gothic Franciscan church, in 1450 it was transformed for the savage Sigismondo Malatesta by Leon Battista Alberti, and is an odd mixture of private chapel and personal monument. Sigismondo treated the church as a memorial chapel to his great love, Isotta degli Atti, and their initials are linked in emblems all over the building; the Malatesta armorial emblem – the elephant – appears almost as often, alongside chubby putti, nymphs and shepherds in a decidedly unchristian celebration of excess. There are some fine artworks – one by Piero della Francesca, and a *Crucifix* attributed to Giotto – although even now you get the feeling the authorities are slightly embarrassed by the place. It is, however, an appropriate attraction for a town that thrives on excess.

Practicalities

The **train station** is in the centre of Rimini, on Piazzale Cesare Battisti, ten minutes' walk from the sea and the old centre. There's a **tourist office** by the station and in Piazzale Fellini on the seafront (daily summer 8.30am–7pm; winter 9am–noon & 4–7pm; ☎0541.569.02, *www.riminiturismo.it*). They both provide **Internet** access (€2/hr) and can help with

accommodation, which can be a problem during the season, when you may have to take full or half board. Try *Nancy*, a lovely villa with garden five minutes' walk from the beach at Viale Leopardi 11 (☎0541.381.731; ⑤), or the cheaper *Alfieri* at Viale Alfieri 10 (☎0541.381.436; ④). You could also **camp** on sites next to the rail line at Viserba (Via Toscanelli), and Viserbella (off the main road), and south towards Miramare (Viale Principe di Piemonte).

The seafront is the best place **to eat** cheaply, with hundreds of takeaway pizza places. Most of the nicer restaurants are in the old town – try *Osteria dë Börg*, at Via Forzieri 12, just the other side of the old port from the town centre, or the *Rimini Key* at Piazzale Croce by the seafront. There's also a good student **mensa** by the train station at Via Roma 70. Rimini's lively **nightlife** also happens along the seafront, out towards Riccione.

CENTRAL ITALY

The Italian heartland region of **Tuscany** represents perhaps the most archetypal image of the country – its walled towns and rolling, vineyard-covered hills the classic backdrops of Renaissance art. Of Tuscany's urban centres, few people react entirely positively to **Florence**. But however unappealing some of the central streets might look, there are plentiful compensations – the Uffizi gallery's masterpieces, the great fresco cycles in the churches, the wealth of Florentine sculpture in the city's museums. Siena provokes less ambiguous reactions: one of the great medieval cities of Europe, it's also the scene of Tuscany's one unmissable festival – the Palio – which sees bareback horse riders careering around the cobbled central square. The other major cities, **Pisa** and **Lucca**, both have medieval splendours – Pisa has its Leaning Tower and cathedral ensemble, Lucca a string of Romanesque churches – and there are, of course, the smaller hill towns, of which **San Gimignano**, the "city of the towers", is the best known. The provincial capital of the upper Arno region, **Arezzo**, an hour's train ride from Florence, is also worth a stop, if only for its marvellous series of paintings by Piero della Francesca, while to the east lies **Umbria**, a beautiful region of rolling hills, woods and valleys – not unlike Tuscany but as yet less discovered. Most visitors head for the capital, **Perugia**, for **Assisi** – with its extraordinary frescoes by Giotto in the Basilica di San Francesco – or **Orvieto**, where the Duomo is one of the greatest Gothic buildings in the country, though lesser-known places like **Gubbio**, ranked as the most perfect medieval centre in Italy, and **Spoleto**, for many the outstanding Umbrian town, are worth taking in, too. Further east still, the **Marche** repeats much the same sort of pleasures, the town of **Urbino** in the north of the region, with its superb Renaissance ducal palace, providing a deserved highlight, and the port of **Ancona** useful ferry links to Greece.

Florence

Ever since the nineteenth-century revival of interest in the art of the Renaissance, **FLORENCE** has been a shrine to the cult of the beautiful. Close up, however, it does not immediately impress visitors as a beautiful city. The marble-clad Baptistry and Duomo are stupendous, of course, the architectural perfection of the latter's dome as celebrated now as it ever was. But these colourful monuments are not typical of the city as a whole: the streets of the historic centre are often narrow and dark, their palaces robust and intimidating, and few of the city's squares are places where you'd want to pass an idle hour. However, Florence is a city of incomparable indoor pleasures, its chapels, galleries and museums an inexhaustible treasure, embodying the complex, exhilarating and often elusive spirit of the Renaissance more fully than any other place in the country, and few leave completely disappointed.

Florence became the centre of artistic patronage in Italy under the Medici family, who made their fortune in banking and ruled the city as an independent state for some three centuries, most auspiciously during the years of Lorenzo de' Medici, tagged "Il Magnifico", who held fiercely onto Florentine independence in the face of papal resentment. Later, in the late

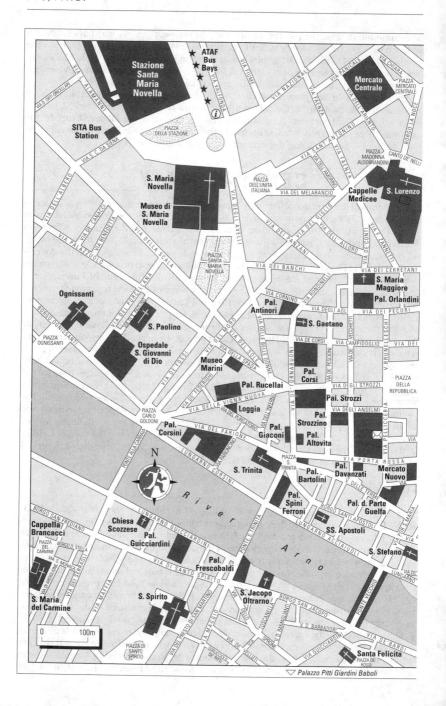

ATAF Bus Bays

Stazione Santa Maria Novella

Mercato Centrale

PIAZZA MERCATO CENTRALE

VIA CHIARA

VIA VALDONA

VIA FIUME

VIA NAZIONALE

VIA PANICALE

SITA Bus Station

PIAZZA DELLA STAZIONE

VIA S. C. DA SIENA

VIA D'OCILORCELLARI

VIA ALAMANNI

VIA SANT'ANTONINO

VIA FAENZA

VIA DELL'ARIENTO

PIAZZA MADONNA ALDOBRANDINI

CANTO DE NELLI

BORGO LA NOCE

S. Maria Novella

Museo di S. Maria Novella

PIAZZA DELL'UNITA ITALIANA

VIA DEL MELARANCIO

Cappelle Medicee

S. Lorenzo

VIA DELL'ALBERO

VIA DE' CANACCI

VIA BENEDETTA

VIA PALAZZUOLO

VIA DELLA SCALA

VIA DEGLI AVELLI

VIA DELL'AMORINO

VIA DEL GIGLIO

VIA DE' CONTI

VIA DEL' ZANNETTI

VIA DEI PANZANI

VIA DELL'ALLORO

PIAZZA SANTA MARIA NOVELLA

VIA DEI BANCHI

VIA DEI CERRETANI

S. Maria Maggiore

Pal. Orlandini

Ognissanti

VIA DEL PORCELLANA

VIA DEI FOSSI

VIA DELLA SPADA

VIA DEL SOLE

VIA DELLE BELLE DONNE

VIA CORNINO

VIA DEI BONDINELLI

Pal. Antinori

VIA DEGLI AGLI

VIA DEI PECORI

S. Gaetano

VIA DE' VECCHIETTI

BORGO OGNISSANTI

PIAZZA OGNISSANTI

S. Paolino

Ospedale S. Giovanni di Dio

VIA DELLA VIGNA NUOVA

VIA DE' FEDERIGHI

Museo Marini

Pal. Rucellai

VIA DE CORSI

VIA CAMPIDOGLIO

VIA DE'

VIA DE PESCIONI

Pal. Corsi

PIAZZA DELLA REPUBBLICA

V BRUNELLESCHI

VIA DELLA VIGNA NUOVA

VIA DELL'INFERNO

Loggia

Pal. Strozzi

VIA DEGLI STROZZI

VIA DEGLI ANSELMI

PIAZZA CARLO GOLDONI

VIA DEL PARIONE

Pal. Corsini

Pal. Giaconi

Pal. Strozzino

Pal. Altovita

VIA PELLICCERIA

VIA

PONTE ALLA CARRAIA

LUNGARNO CORSINI

N

S. Trinita

PIAZZA S. TRINITA

Pal. Bartolini

Pal. Davanzati

VIA PORTA ROSSA

Mercato Nuovo

VIA S. MARIA

River

Pal. Spini Ferroni

VIA DELLE TERME

Pal. d. Parte Guelfa

BORGO SAN FREDIANO

BORGO O. STELLA

Chiesa Scozzese

Pal. Guicciardini

LUNGARNO GUICCIARDINI

PONTE S. TRINITA

BORGO SANTI APOSTOLI

LUNGARNO ACCIAIUOLI

SS. Apostoli

S. Stefano

Cappella Brancacci

PIAZZA DEL CARMINE

VIA S. MONACA

Pal. Frescobaldi

Arno

VIA DEL PRESTO DI SAN MARTINO

VIA MAFFIA

S. Maria del Carmine

VIA DELL'ARDIGLIONE

VIA DEI SERRAGLI

S. Spirito

VIA DI SANTO SPIRITO

S. Jacopo Oltrarno

BORGO SAN JACOPO

VIA DE' RAMAGLIANTI

PONTE VECCHIO

VIA DEI

LUNGARNO

0   100m

PIAZZA DI SANTO SPIRITO

VIA MAGGIO

VIA DE' VELLUTI

SDRUCCIOLO DI PITTI

V. D. BARBADORI

VIA GUICCIARDINI

VIA DE' BARDI

Santa Felicita

PIAZZA DI ROSSI

▽ Palazzo Pitti Giardini Baboli

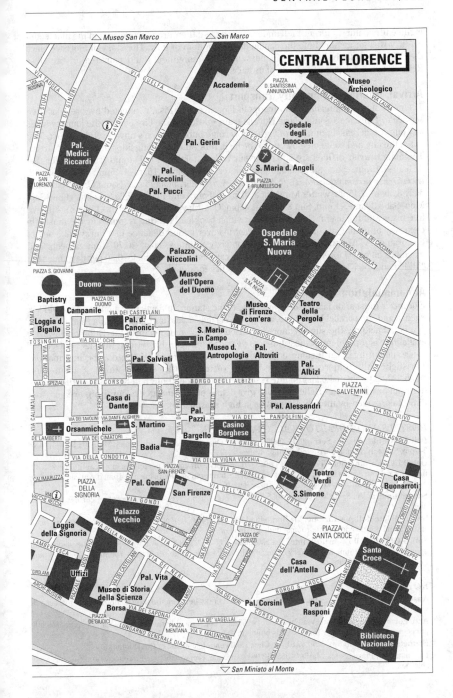

CENTRAL FLORENCE

eighteenth century, Florence fell under Austrian and then French rule, and in the nineteenth century was for a short time the capital of the kingdom of Italy. The story of Florence since then has been fairly low-key, and nowadays the monuments and paintings of the city's Renaissance heyday are the basis of its survival.

Arrival, information and city transport

The nearest major international **airport** to Florence is at Pisa, connected by a regular train service to Florence's Santa Maria Novella **train station** in the city centre; the journey takes an hour. An increasing number of flights now come into Florence's tiny Perètola airport, 5km out of the city and connected by bus to the main **bus station**, alongside Santa Maria Novella. The main **tourist offices** are at Via Cavour 7r, just north of the Duomo (summer Mon–Sat 8.15am–7.15pm, Sun 8.15am–1.45pm; winter Mon–Sat 8.15am–1.45pm; ☎055.290.832, *www.firenze.turismo.toscana.it*), at Borgo San Croce 29r, near Piazza Santa Croce (summer daily 8.30am–7.15pm; winter Mon–Sat 8.30am–1.45pm), and Piazza della Stazione (June–Sept Mon–Sat 8.30am–7.15pm, Sun 8.30am–1.45pm; Oct–May Mon–Sat 8.30am–1.45pm). All have free maps and the useful Concierge Information booklet. **Walking** is generally the most efficient way of getting around, but if you want to cover a long distance in a hurry, take one of the orange ATAF **buses**; tickets, valid for sixty minutes, cost €0.70 from tabacchi and machines all over Florence. Alternatively you can rent a bike for just €0.50 per day under the "Mille e una bici" scheme; ask at the tourist office for details.

Accommodation

Florence's most affordable **hotels** are close to the station, in particular along and around Via Faenza and the parallel Via Fiume, and along Via della Scala and Piazza Santa Maria Novella; you could also try the slightly more salubrious Via Cavour, north of the Duomo. However, availability is a problem at most times of year, and between Easter and the start of October you're taking a risk in turning up without a pre-booked room. If you do, the Informazioni Turistiche Alberghiere **accommodation office** at the station (daily 8.45am–8pm; ☎055.282.893) can make last-minute reservations for a fee, though in high season the queues here can be a nightmare. They will also give details of the emergency **camping area** or Area di Sosta provided by the city authorities in high season.

HOSTELS AND DORMITORY ACCOMMODATION

Istituto Gould, Via dei Serragli 49 (☎055.212.576). Over in Oltrarno, and open Mon–Fri 9am–1pm & 3–7pm, Sat 9am–1pm. It's wise to book in advance. ③.

Ostello Villa Camerata, Viale Righi 2 (☎055.601.451). The official HI hostel lies in a beautiful park, a 30-min outward journey on bus #17 (#17b back) from the train station. Doors open at 1pm; if you can't be there by then, ring ahead to make sure there's space left. ②.

Santa Monaca, Via Santa Monaca 6 (☎055.268.338). In Oltrarno. Free hot showers, 1am curfew. Very popular. ②.

Suore Oblate dell'Assunzione, Via Borgo Pinti 15 (☎055.248.0582). Not far from the Duomo, open to men and women. Single and double rooms; midnight curfew. ④.

Suore Oblate dello Spirito Santo, Via Nazionale 8 (☎055.239.8202). A few steps from the station, and open to women mid-June to Oct. Very clean and pleasant; single, double and triple rooms; 11pm curfew and minimum stay of 2 nights. ③.

HOTELS

Ausonia e Rimini, Via Nazionale 24 (☎055.496.547). Halfway between the train station and the market and welcoming. ⑤

Azzi/Locanda degli Artisti, Via Faenza 56 (☎055.213.806). Probably the most pleasant of six reasonably priced *pensioni* on the upper floors of this building. ④.

Brunetta, Borgo Pinti 5 (☎055.247.8134). Cheap and central, just east of the Duomo. ③.

La Casa Mia, Piazza Santa Maria (☎055.213.061). Clean and reasonable for Florence; some ensuites available. ④.

Concordia, Via dell'Amorino 14 (☎055.213.233). Extremely convenient, right in the heart of the market area and beautifuly decorated. ⑥.
Costantini, Via Calzaiuoli 13 (☎055.213.995). Friendly place on the city's main street ⑦.
Donatello, Via V. Alfieri 9 (☎055.245.870). In a quiet area between Piazzale Donatello and Piazza d'Azeglio; strongly recommended – smartly renovated, young and friendly – though they prefer you to pay in cash. ④.
Elite, Via della Scala 12 (☎055.215.395). Two-star hotel with very pleasant management in the Santa Maria Novella area. ⑤.
Firenze, Piazza dei Donati 4 (☎055.214203). Clean and comfortable rooms ensuite. No credit cards. ③.
La Romagnola (☎055.211.597) and **Gigliola** (☎055.287.981), both at Via della Scala 40. Best of the Via della Scala hotels – midnight curfews are the only drawback. Both ④.
Maxim, Via Dei Calzaiuoli 11 (☎055.217.474). A one-star hotel near the Duomo; most rooms have a bathroom. ②.

CAMPSITES

Italiani e Stranieri, Viale Michelangelo 80 (☎055.681.1977). Open April–Oct, and always crowded owing to its superb hillside location. Bus #13 from the train station.
Villa Camerata, Viale Righi 2 (☎055.600.315). Basic site in hostel grounds, open all year.

The City

Florence sprawls along both sides of the Arno and into the hills north and south of the city, but the major sights are contained within an area that can be crossed on foot in a little over half an hour. Perhaps the most obvious place to start exploring is the **Piazza della Signoria**, a rather charmless open space, fringed on one side by the graceful late-fourteenth-century **Loggia della Signoria**. Dotted with statuary, like Giambologna's equestrian statue of Cosimo I and copies of Donatello's *Judith and Holofernes* and Michelangelo's *David*, the square is dominated by the colossal **Palazzo Vecchio**, Florence's fortress-like town hall (summer Tues, Wed & Sat 9am–7pm, Mon & Fri 9am–11pm, Thurs & Sun 9am–2pm; winter Mon–Wed, Fri & Sat 9am–7pm, Thurs & Sun 9am–2pm; €5.20, last admission 45min before closing; a €5.20 carnet for 6 city museums gives you a 50 percent reduction on entrance fees plus a guidebook), begun in the last year of the thirteenth century as the home of the *Signoria*, the highest tier of the city's republican government. The Medici were only in residence here for nine years, but the layout of the palace owes much to them, notably Cosimo I, who decorated the state rooms with relentless eulogies to himself and his family. The huge Salone dei Cinquento, built at the end of the fifteenth century, is full of heroic murals by Vasari, though it is to some extent redeemed by the presence of Michelangelo's *Victory*, facing the entrance door, originally sculpted for Pope Julius II's tomb but donated to the Medici by the artist's nephew. The bizarre Studiolo di Francesco I was also created by Vasari, and decorated by several of Florence's prominent Mannerist artists as a retreat for the introverted son of Cosimo, most of the bronzes and paintings reflecting Francesco's interest in the sciences, though the best ones are those that don't fit the scheme – principally Bronzino's glacial portraits of the occupant's parents, Cosimo and Eleanor of Toledo. Bronzino also painted Eleanor's tiny chapel upstairs, and a Mannerist contemporary of Bronzino, Cecchino Salviati, produced what is widely held to be his masterpiece with the fresco cycle in the Sala d'Udienza, once the audience chamber of the Republic. The adjoining Sala dei Gigli was frescoed by Ghirlandaio, although the main focus is Donatello's restored *Judith and Holofernes*.

Immediately south of the piazza, the **Galleria degli Uffizi** (summer Mon–Fri 8.30am–9pm, Sat 8.30am–midnight, Sun 8.30am–8pm; winter daily 8.30am–6.50pm; €6.20, last admittance 30min before closing) is the greatest picture gallery in Italy, with a collection of masterpieces that is impossible to take in on a single visit. The early Renaissance is represented by three altarpieces of the *Madonna Enthroned* by Cimabue, Duccio and Giotto, and a luscious golden *Annunciation* by the fourteenth-century Sienese painter, Simone Martini. There's Uccello's *Battle of San Romano* – demonstrating the artist's obsessional interest in perspectival effects – which once hung in Lorenzo il Magnifico's bed chamber, in company with depictions of the skirmish now in the Louvre and London's National Gallery. Among plentiful works by Filippo Lippi is his *Madonna and Child with Two Angels*, one of the best-known Renaissance images of the Madonna. Close by, there's a fine *Madonna* by Botticelli, who in the next room is represented by some of his most famous works, notably *Primavera* and the *Birth of Venus*; look also at the huge *Portinari Altarpiece* by Botticelli's Flemish contemporary Hugo van der Goes, a work whose naturalism greatly influenced the artists of Florence. The Uffizi doesn't own a finished painting that's entirely by Leonardo da Vinci, but there's a celebrated *Annunciation* (mainly by him) and the angel in profile that he painted in Verrocchio's *Baptism*. Room 18, the octagonal Tribuna, houses the most important of the Medici sculptures, first among which is the *Medici Venus*, along with some chillingly precise portraits by Bronzino and Vasari's portrait of Lorenzo il Magnifico, painted long after the death of its subject. Michelangelo's *Doni Tondo* is his only completed easel painting, its contorted gestures and virulent colours studied and imitated by the Mannerist painters of the sixteenth century, as can be gauged from the nearby *Moses Defending the Daughters of Jethro* by Rosso Fiorentino, one of the pivotal figures of the movement. Separating the two Mannerist groups are a number of compositions by Raphael, including *Pope Leo X with Cardinals Giulio de' Medici and Luigi de' Rossi* – as shifty a group of ecclesiastics as ever was gathered in one frame – while Titian weighs in with his fleshily provocative *Venus of Urbino*. Later rooms include some large works by Rubens and Van Dyck; Caravaggio has a cluster of pieces, including a severed head of Medusa; while another room has portraiture by Rembrandt, notably his melancholic *Self-Portrait as an Old Man*, painted five years before his death.

To get a comprehensive idea of the Renaissance achievement in Florence, you need also to visit the **Museo Nazionale del Bargello** (Tues–Sat 8.30am–1.50pm, also second & fourth Sun and first, third & fifth Mon of each month; €4.10), a short step north in Via del Proconsolo, where there is a full collection of sculpture from the period, housed in a thirteenth-century palace that was formerly the HQ of the city's chief of police (the Bargello). The first part of the collection focuses on Michelangelo, represented by among others his first major sculpture, the lurching figure of *Bacchus*, carved at the age of 22. Beyond, the more flamboyant art of Cellini and Giambologna is exhibited, notably by a huge *Bust of Cosimo I*, Cellini's first work in bronze, a sort of technical trial for the casting of the Perseus nearby, and Giambologna's best-known creation, the nimble figure of *Mercury*. Out in the courtyard, at the top of its external staircase, the first-floor loggia has been turned into an aviary for Giambologna's bronze birds, imported from the Medici villa at Castello, while a nearby room displays work by Donatello – the mildly Gothic *David* and the alert figure of *St George*. His sexually ambiguous bronze *David*, the first freestanding nude figure since classical times, was cast in the early 1430s. Donatello's master, Ghiberti, is represented by his relief of *The Sacrifice of Isaac*, his successful entry in the competition for the Baptistry doors. The treatment of the theme submitted by Brunelleschi, the runner-up, is hung close by. Upstairs the Sala dei Bronzetti has Italy's best assembly of small Renaissance bronzes, with plentiful evidence of Giambologna's virtuosity, and a further room holds Renaissance portrait busts, including Mino da Fiesole's busts of *Giovanni de' Medici* and *Piero il Gottoso*, and a couple of pieces by Verrocchio, including a *David* clearly influenced by Donatello.

Parallel to Via del Proconsolo on the opposite side of Piazza della Signoria is **Via dei Calzaiuoli**, one of the city's more animated streets and home to the church of **Orsanmichele** (closed first and last Mon of the month). Its exterior is decorated by a number of early Renaissance sculptures, including a *John the Baptist* by Ghiberti, the first life-size bronze statue of the Renaissance, and an *Incredulity of St Thomas* by Verrocchio. Inside a vast tabernacle by Orcagna frames a *Madonna* painted by Bernardo Daddi in 1347 to replace a miraculous image of the Virgin destroyed by a 1304 fire.

The streets west of the Signoria retain a medieval character, lined with palaces like the fourteenth-century Palazzo Davanzati on Via Porta Rossa which houses the **Museo della Casa Fiorentina Antica** (presently closed for restoration). Inside, virtually every room of the reconstructed interior is furnished and decorated in medieval style. About 500m northwest, off Via della Scala, the partly Gothic church of **Santa Maria Novella** (Mon–Fri 7am–noon & 3–6pm, Sat & Sun 3–5pm) was the Florentine base of the Dominican order. Halfway down the left aisle of the nave is Masaccio's extraordinary fresco of *The Trinity*, one of the earliest works in which perspective and classical proportion were rigorously employed. The church's **cloisters** (daily 9am–2pm; €2.60) are richly decorated with frescoes by Uccello and his workshop.

THE DUOMO AND AROUND

North of the Signoria on **Piazza del Duomo**, the **Duomo** (Mon–Sat 10am–5pm, Sun 1–5pm) was built between the late thirteenth and mid-fifteenth centuries to an ambitious design, originally the brainchild of Arnolfo di Cambio and realized finally by Filippo Brunelleschi, who completed the majestic dome – the largest in existence until this century. The fourth largest church in the world, its ambience is more that of a great assembly hall than of a devotional building, its most conspicuous pieces of painted decoration two memorials to *condottieri* – Uccello's monument to Sir John Hawkwood, painted in 1436, and Castagno's monument to Niccolò da Tolentino, created twenty years later. Just beyond, Domenico do Michelino's *Dante Explaining the Divine Comedy*, painted in 1465, gives the recently completed dome a place only marginally less prominent than the Mountain of Purgatory. Above, the fresco of *The Last Judgement* in the dome is the work of Vasari and Zuccari, below which are seven stained-glass roundels designed by Uccello, Ghiberti, Castagno and Donatello – best inspected from a gallery which forms part of the route to the top of the dome (daily 10am–5.30pm daily; €5.20). The views at the very top are as stupendous as you would expect.

Next door to the Duomo, the **Campanile** (daily 9am–7.30pm; €5.20) was begun in 1334 by Giotto and continued after his death by Andrea Pisano and Francesco Talenti. The only part of the tower built exactly as Giotto designed it is the lower storey, studded with two rows of remarkable bas-reliefs, the lower one illustrating the *Creation of Man and the Arts and Industries* carved by Pisano. The figures of *Prophets and Sibyls* in the second-storey niches are by Donatello and others. Opposite, the **Baptistry** (Mon–Sat noon–6.30pm, until 4pm in winter; Sun 8.30am–1.30pm; €2.60), generally thought to date from the sixth or seventh century, is the oldest building in the city. Its most famous embellishments, the gilded bronze doors, were cast in the early fifteenth century by Lorenzo Ghiberti, and were described by Michelangelo as "so beautiful they are worthy to be the gates of Paradise". They're a primer of early Renaissance art, innovatively using perspective, gesture and sophisticated grouping of subjects to convey the human drama of each scene. Ghiberti included a self-portrait in the frame of the left-hand door – his is the fourth head from the top of the right-hand band. Inside, the Baptistry is equally stunning, with a thirteenth-century mosaic floor and ceiling and the tomb of Pope John XXIII, draped by a superb marble canopy, the work of Donatello and his pupil Michelozzo.

Since the early fifteenth century the maintenance of the Duomo has been supervised from the building at Piazza del Duomo 9, nowadays housing the **Museo dell'Opera del Duomo** (Mon–Sat 9am–6.30pm, Sun 8am–2pm; €5.20), the repository of the most precious and fragile works of art from the buildings around, including a series of sculptures by Arnolfo di Cambio; Brunelleschi's death mask; models of the dome and a variety of tools and machines devised by the architect; Michelangelo's anguished late *Pietà*; Pisano's bas-reliefs and Donatello's figures for the campanile; and four of Ghiberti's door panels and a dazzling silver-gilt altar from the Baptistry, completed in 1480.

NORTH OF THE DUOMO

The church of **San Lorenzo**, north of the Baptistry, has good claim to be the oldest church in Florence, and for the best part of three hundred years was the city's cathedral. Rebuilt by Brunelleschi in the mid-fifteenth century under the patronage of the Medici, the interior is a fine example of early Renaissance church design. Inside are two bronze pulpits by Donatello; close by, a large disc of multicoloured marble marks the grave of Cosimo il Vecchio, the artist's main patron, while further pieces by Donatello adorn the neighbouring Sagrestia Vecchia by Brunelleschi – the two pairs of bronze doors, the large reliefs of *SS Cosmas and Damian* and *SS Lawrence and Stephen*, and the eight terracotta tondi. At the top of the left aisle and through the cloisters, the **Biblioteca Medicea-Laurenziana** (Mon–Sat 9am–1pm; free) was designed by Michelangelo in 1524; its most startling feature is the vestibule, a room almost filled by a flight of steps resembling a solidified lava flow. Michelangelo's most celebrated contribution to the San Lorenzo buildings, however, is the Sagrestia Nuova, part of the **Cappelle Medicee** (Tues–Sun 8.30am–4.30pm, also second & fourth Mon of each month; €5.20). Begun in 1520, in part as a tribute to Sagrestia Vecchia, it contains the fabulous Medici tombs, carved between 1524 and 1533. To the left is the tomb of Lorenzo, duke of Urbino, the grandson of Lorenzo il Magnifico, bearing figures of *Dawn and Dusk* to sum up his contemplative nature. Opposite is the tomb of Lorenzo il Magnifico's youngest son, Giuliano, his supposedly more active character symbolized by *Day and Night*. Their effigies were intended to face the equally grand tombs of Lorenzo il Magnifico and his brother Giuliano, though the only part of this actually realized by Michelangelo is the serene *Madonna and Child*.

The **Museo di San Marco** (Tues–Sat 8.30am–1.50pm, also the first, third and fifth Mon & fourth Sun of the month same hours; €4.10), in a former convent in the piazza of the same name, is dedicated to the work of Fra Angelico. Just east of here, the **Galleria dell'Accademia** (Tues–Fri 8.30am–9pm, Sat 9am–12pm, Sun 9am–8pm; shorter hours in winter; €6.20) was Europe's first school of drawing. Its collection of paintings is impressive, but most people come to view the sculpture of Michelangelo, specifically his **David**. Finished in 1504, when Michelangelo was just 29, and carved from a gigantic block of marble, it's an incomparable show of technical bravura. The gallery also houses his remarkable unfinished *Slaves*.

THE SANTA CROCE DISTRICT

Down by the river, the Franciscan church of Florence, **Santa Croce** (summer Mon–Sat 8am–6.30pm, Sun 3–5.30pm; winter Mon–Sat 8am–12.30pm & 3–5.30pm, Sun 3–5.30pm), was begun in 1294, possibly by the architect of the Duomo, Arnolfo di Cambio, and is full of tombstones and commemorative monuments, including Vasari's monument to Michelangelo, and, on the opposite side of the church, is the tomb of Galileo, built in 1737 when it was finally agreed to give the great scientist a Christian burial; most visitors come to see the frescoes by Giotto in the Cappella Peruzzi and the Cappella Bardi (on the right of the chancel). The former shows scenes from the lives of St John the Baptist and St John the Evangelist; the latter, painted slightly earlier with some assistance, features the life of St Francis. Agnolo Gaddi was responsible for all the frescoes around and above the high altar and for the design of the stained glass in the lancet windows. At the end of the left chancel, a second Cappella Bardi houses a wooden *Crucifix* by Donatello. Also visit Brunelleschi's **Cappella dei Pazzi**, at the end of the first cloister (Mon & Wed–Sun 10am–6/7pm; €4.10), designed in the 1430s and completed in the 1470s, several years after the architect's death, with decorations by Luca della Robbia. The **Museo dell'Opera di Santa Croce**, off the first cloister (same times), also houses a miscellany of works of art, the best of which are Cimabue's flood-damaged *Crucifixion*, Gaddi's fresco of the *Last Supper and Crucifixion*, and Donatello's enormous gilded *St Louis of Toulouse*, made for Orsanmichele. North of Santa Croce at Via Ghibellina 70, the **Casa Buonarotti** (Mon & Wed–Sun 9.30am–1.30pm; €5.20) is enticing in name, but Michelangelo Buonarotti never actually lived here, and there is little to see of his work. The most exciting items are an early *Madonna of the Steps*, and the unfinished *Battle of the Centaurs*.

OLTRARNO AND SAN MINIATO

The thirteenth-century **Ponte Vecchio**, loaded with jewellers' shops which overhang the water, leads from the city centre across the river to **Oltrarno**. The district is dominated by the massive bulk of the **Palazzo Pitti**. Nowadays the fifteenth-century palace and its stupendous garden – the Giardino di Bóboli – contain six separate museums. The **Galleria Palatina** (Tues–Sun 9am–5.30/6.30pm; €6.20) has superb displays of the art of Raphael and Titian, including a number of Titian's most trenchant portraits. Andrea del Sarto is represented in strength, too, as is Rubens, whose *Consequences of War* packs more of a punch than most other Baroque allegories. Much of the rest of the first floor comprises the **Appartamenti Monumentali** (included in the Galleria Palatina ticket), the Pitti's state rooms, while on the floor above, the **Galleria d'Arte Moderna** (Tues–Sat 8.30am–2pm, also second & fourth Sun and first, third & fifth Mon of each month; €4.10) is a chronological survey of primarily Tuscan art from the mid-eighteenth century to 1945. The Pitti's enormous formal garden, the **Giardino di Bóboli** (April, May, Sept Tues–Sun 9am–6.30pm, also second & third Mon of each month; June–Aug closes 7.30pm; Oct closes 5.30pm, Nov–Feb 4.30pm; €2.10) is full of Mannerist embellishments including the Grotta del Buontalenti, close to the entrance to the left of the palace facade; among its fake stalactites are shepherds and sheep and replicas of Michelangelo's *Slaves*, replacing the originals that were here until 1908. In the deepest recesses of the cave stands Giambologna's *Venus*, leered at by attendant imps. In the eastern corner of the gardens is **Forte di Belvedere** (daily 9am–6/7pm; free), a star-shaped fortress built in 1590, which can only be entered through Porta San Giorgio at the top of the hill.

About 500m northwest of the Palazzo Pitti, the church of **Santa Maria del Carmine** is visited for the frescoes in its Cappella Brancacci (Mon & Wed–Sat 10am–5pm, Sun 1–5pm; €2.60) by Masaccio – recently, and controversially, restored. The cycle was completed by Filippino Lippi, his most distinctive contribution being the affecting *Release of St Peter* on the right-hand side of the entrance. In the opposite direction, the multicoloured facade of **San Miniato al Monte** lures troops of visitors up the hill. The interior is like no other in the city, and its general form has changed little since the mid-eleventh century. In the lower part of the church, don't overlook the intricately patterned panels of the pavement, from 1207, and the tabernacle between the choir stairs, designed in 1448 by Michelozzo.

Eating and drinking

Although Tuscan cuisine is distinguished by its simplicity, in recent years Florence's gastronomic reputation has suffered under the pressure of mass tourism. Certainly there's a dearth of good places to eat if you're on a limited budget, although a decent meal isn't hard to come by if you explore the remoter quarters. The best place to find **picnic food** and **snacks** is the **Mercato Centrale** (summer Mon–Sat 9am–7pm; winter Tues–Sat 9am–5pm), just east of the train station, which is full of greengrocers, pasta stalls and bars charging prices lower than elsewhere in the city. There are also plenty of city-centre **bars**, along Via de' Panzani, Via de' Cerretani, Via Por Santa Maria and Via Guicciardini, whose snacky food offers ample compensation for their lack of character. Otherwise, try a **vinaio**, a wine cellar/snack bar that serves *crostini* and other snacks. The *vinaio* at Via Cimatori 38 is a perfect example, as is the place at Via Alfani 70, in the university area, which serves stuffed tomatoes and a range of other vegetables in addition to the traditional *crostini*. For classier snacks, try the *panini* and pasta at *Fiaschetteria*, Via de' Neri 17, or the similar fare at *Fiaschetteria da 11 Latin*, Via del Palchetti 6r, behind Palazzo Rucellai. Another Florentine speciality is the **friggitoria**, serving polenta, potatoes and apple croquettes – try the one at Via Sant'Antonino 50, which also sells pizza, or *Antico Noê* at Volta di San Piero 6, which does burgers and salads and has a restaurant next door. *Giuliano* is a superb *rosticceria*, with seats, at Via de' Neri 74. For ice cream, leader of the pack is *Vivoli*, near Santa Croce at Via Isola delle Stinche 7r (closed Mon).

RESTAURANTS

Bar Santa Croce, Borgo Santa Croce 31r. Good lunchtime menu and marvellous pasta. Closed Sun.
Benvenuto, Via Mosca 16/5, off Via de' Neri. Looks more like a delicatessen than a trattoria from the street, but the groups waiting for a table give the game away; the *gnocchi* and *arista* are delicious. Closed Wed.

Dante, Piazza Nazario Sauro 10r. Friendly pizzeria with around a dozen types of spaghetti on the menu too. Closed Wed.

Da Mario, Via Rosina 2r. Popular with students and market workers – be prepared to queue and share a table. Closed Sun & evenings.

Palle d'Oro, Via Sant'Antonio 45r. Station area eatery that's halfway between a *rosticceria* and a trattoria. Besides full meals, they do sandwiches to take away. Closed Sun.

Trattoria Borgo Antico, Piazza Santo Spirito 6r. Busy trattoria on a quiet Oltrarno square, with excellent seafood, home-made pasta and tables outside in summer. Closed Sun.

Trattoria Casalinga, Via Michelozzi 9r. Oltrarno restaurant, off Via Maggio, that offers just about the best low-cost authentic Tuscan dishes in town. Always crowded. Closed Sun.

Za-Za, Piazza del Mercato Centrale 26r. A few tables on ground level, but a bigger canteen below. Closed Sun.

Nightlife

Florence enjoys a reasonably vibrant **nightlife** by Italian standards. Of **places to drink**, *Dolce Vita*, on Piazza del Carmine, is a trendy hangout that also stages small-scale art exhibitions; the nearby *Tiratoio*, on Piazza de' Nerli, is a large easy-going place, with a couple of video jukeboxes and a wide range of food. *Porfirio Rubirosa*, Viale Strozzi 38r, is where the *bella gente* drop in before heading for a late dinner or disco. In the Santa Croce district, *Rex*, Via Fiesolana 25r, has good music, a varied clientele, and serves snacks and cocktails, while in Oltrarno, *Zoe* on Borgo San Jacopo is a posey but atmospheric cocktail bar. For a quiet drink in a beautifully situated bar, try *Chalet Fontana* on Viale Michelangelo – pricey but worth it. *Tenax*, on Via Pratese 47, is the city's biggest disco and one of its leading venues for new and established bands. *Yab*, Via de' Sassetti 5r, is a city-centre disco playing the best of new dance music; and *Space Electronic*, Via Palazzuolo 37, is the favourite disco of young foreigners, open nightly. For information on what's on, call in at Box Office, Via Alamanni 39 (☎055.210.804), or consult the listings magazines *Firenze Spettacolo*, and *Informa Città*.

Listings

Airlines Alitalia, Piazza del Oro (☎055.27.881); British Airways, Via della Vigna Nuova 9r (☎055.215.174, ☎055.289.021 or ☎147.812.266).

Airport enquiries G. Galileo Airport, Pisa (☎050.500.707); A. Vespucci airport, Florence (☎055.373.498).

American Express Via Dante Alighieri 14r (Mon–Fri 9am–5.30pm, Sat 9am–12.30pm; ☎055.50.981).

Books Paperback Exchange, at Via Fiesolana 31r and Feltrinelli International, at Via Cavour 12–20r, stock a wide selection of English-language books.

Car rental Avis, Borgo Ognissanti 128r (☎055.213.629), airport (☎055.315.558); Hertz, Via Maso Finiguerra 23r (☎055.282.260); Maggiore, Via Maso Finiguerra 31r (☎055.210.238).

Consulates UK, Lungarno Corsini 2 (☎055.284.133); USA, Lungarno Vespucci 38 (☎055.239.8276).

Exchange Esercizio Promozione Turismo, Via Condotta 42 (☎055294.551; Mon–Sat 10am–7pm, Sun 10am–6pm).

Hospital Santa Maria Nuova, Piazza Santa Maria Nuova 1 (☎055.27.581). The Tourist Medical Service, Via Lorenzo il Magnifico 59 (☎055.475.411, *medserv@tin.it*), has English, French and German-speaking doctors on 24hr call.

Internet access Internet Train,Via Guelfa 24a, Via dell'oriuolo 40r, Borgo San Jacopo 30r (€4.10/hr, student discount).

Laundry Onda Blu, at Via degli Alfani 24r; Wash & Dry, at Via della Scala 52–54r.

Pharmacies All-night pharmacy at the train station, Molteni, Via dei Calzaiuoli 7r and All Insegna del Moro, Piazza San Giovanni 20r.

Police Main office at Via Zara 2 (☎055.49.771).

Post office Central office at Via Pellicceria 3 (Mon–Fri 8.20am–6pm, Sat 8.20am–12.30pm; ☎055.218.156).

Telephones Booths at the train station (24hr), Via San Piero Maggiore 10r (7–10pm) and Telecom Italia – which also has a fax service – at Via Cavour 21r (7am–11pm).

Train enquiries ☎055.288.785, ☎055.23.521 or ☎84.88.088.

Fiesole

A long-established Florentine retreat from the summer heat and crowds, **FIESOLE** spreads over a cluster of hilltops some 8km northeast of Florence. It rivalled its neighbour until the early twelfth century, when it became favoured as a semirural second home for Florence's wealthier citizens. The #7 ATAF bus runs there every fifteen minutes from Florence's train station, a twenty-minute journey that leaves you in piazza Mino. Fiesole's main square is home to the **Duomo**, in which the Cappella Salutati, right of the choir, contains two fine pieces carved by Mino da Fiesole in the mid-fifteenth century – an altar frontal of *The Madonna and Saints* and the tomb of Bishop Salutati. From here, Via San Francesco leads up to a terrace which gives a remarkable panorama of Florence, just above which the church of **Sant'Alessandro**, founded in the sixth century on the site of Etruscan and Roman temples, has a beautiful basilical interior with onion marble columns. Around the back of the Duomo, in Via Marini, is the entrance to the **Teatro Romano** and **Museo Archeologico** (daily: April–Sept 9am–6/7pm; Nov–Feb 9.30am–5pm; March & Oct 9.30am–6pm; €3.10). Built in the first century BC, the 3000-seat theatre is still used for performances during the *Estate Fiesolana* festival. Most of the museum exhibits were discovered in this area, and encompass pieces from the Bronze Age to the Roman occupation. The narrow Via Vecchia Fiesolana leads from just west of the main square to the hamlet of **SAN DOMENICO**, 1500m southwest. Fra Angelico was once prior of the Dominican monastery here, and the church retains a *Madonna and Angels* by him; the chapterhouse also has a Fra Angelico fresco of *The Crucifixion*. Five minutes' walk northwest from San Domenico brings you to the Badia Fiesolana, formerly Fiesole's cathedral and altered by Cosimo il Vecchio in the 1460s, who left the magnificent Romanesque facade intact while transforming the interior into a superb Renaissance building.

San Gimignano

SAN GIMIGNANO – "delle Belle Torri" – is one of the best-known towns in Tuscany. Its image as a "Medieval Manhattan", with its skyline of towers, has caught the tourist imagination, helped along, no doubt, by its convenience as a day-trip from Florence or Siena. However, from May through to October, San Gimignano is very busy, and to really get any feel for the place you need to come out of season. If you can't, aim to spend the night here – in the evenings the town takes on a very different pace and atmosphere.

Founded around the eighth century, San Gimignano was a force to be reckoned with in the Middle Ages, with a population of fifteen thousand (twice the present number). Nowadays it's not much more than a village: you could walk across it in fifteen minutes, around the walls in an hour. The main entrance gate, facing the bus terminal on the south side of town, is **Porta San Giovanni**, from where Via San Giovanni leads to the town's interlocking main squares, **Piazza della Cisterna** and Piazza del Duomo. You enter the Piazza della Cisterna through another majestic gateway, the **Arco dei Becci**, part of the original fortifications before the town expanded in the twelfth century. The more austere **Piazza Duomo**, off to the left, is flanked by the **Collegiata** church, frescoed with Old Testament scenes by Bartolo di Fredi on the left wall, from around 1367, and, opposite, slightly later New Testament scenes by Barna da Siena. Best, though, is the fresco cycle by Ghirlandaio in the Cappella di Santa Fina, depicting the trials of a local saint – a superb work, access to which is included on a **combined entrance ticket** (€9.30) for all the town's museums. There's more work by Ghirlandaio to the left of the cathedral – a fresco of the Annunciation on the courtyard loggia – while the **Palazzo del Popolo**, next door (Tues–Sun: summer 9.30am–7.20pm; winter 10.30am–4.20pm; €6.20), gives you the chance to climb the **Torre Grossa** (€4.10), the town's highest surviving tower and the only one you can ascend. The same building is home to a number of rooms given over to the **Museo Civico**, the first of which, frescoed with hunting scenes, is known as the Sala di Dante and houses Lippo Memmi's *Maestà*, modelled on that of Simone Martini in Siena. Search out also the delightful frescoes of wedding scenes in a small room off the stairs, completed early in the fourteenth century by the Sienese painter Memmo di Filipuccio. North from Piazza Duomo, **Via San Matteo** is one of the grandest and best preserved of the city streets, with quiet alleyways running down to the walls. The street ends at the **Porta San Matteo**, just inside which, in a corner of walls, is the large hall church of **Sant'Agostino**, with a much-damaged fresco series of the *Life of the Virgin* by Bartolo di Fredi and a cycle of seventeen scenes of the *Life of St Augustine* by Gozzoli, behind the high altar. At the **Museo Criminale Medioevale** (summer daily 10am–8pm; winter Mon–Sat 10am–5.30pm, Sun 10am–7pm; €7.80) at Via del Castello 1, you get a no-holds-barred exploration of the medieval torturer's mind, aided and abetted by explicit explanations in good English.

Practicalities

Accommodation lists are available from the **tourist office** on Piazza del Duomo (daily: April–Oct 9am–1pm & 3–7pm; Nov–March 9am–1pm & 2–6pm; ☎0577.940.008, *www.sangimignano.com*), but from May to September you'll save a lot of frustration by using the Associazione Extralberghiere at Piazza della Cisterna 6 (☎0577.943.111, *maurizio@temainf.it*; March–Oct daily 9.30am–7.30pm), which can arrange **private rooms** without commission, the Cooperativa Turistiche office, at Via San Giovanni 125 (summer Mon–Sat 9.30am–7pm, Sun 3–7pm; winter Mon–Sat 9.30am–12.30pm & 3–5.30pm), which arranges hotel accommodation for €1.50 commission, or the pro loco Association, Piazza del Duomo 1 (daily 9am–7pm; ☎0577.940.008, *prolococsg@tin.it*), who offers a similar service for free. San Gimignano's **hotels** are expensive, two of the cheapest being the three-star *Da Graziano* at Via Matteotti 39/a (☎0577.940.101, *hotelgraziano@cybermarket.it*; ④) and the beautifully situated *Leon Bianco*, Piazza della Cisterna 13 (☎0577.942.123; ⑦). The **hostel** is at Via delle Fonti 1 (☎0577.807.7009, *www.alfaweb.it/franchostel*; ②) and for **camping**, the nearest site is *Il Boschetto*, 3km downhill at Santa Lucia (☎0577.940.352). One of the most popular **restaurants**, and a fraction cheaper than most, is *Le Vecchie Mura* at Via Piandornella 15, off Via San Giovanni. The *Trattoria Chiribiri* in Piazza della Madonna 1 serves a good selection of pasta dishes for around €5.50. For **snacks**, tasty pizza is served by the slice at Via San Giovanni 38.

Arezzo

About 50km southeast of Florence, **AREZZO** was one of the most important settlements of the Etruscan federation and a prosperous independent republic in the Middle Ages, later falling under the sway of Florence. During the Renaissance, Petrarch, Pietro Aretino and Vasari brought lasting prestige to the city, yet it was an outsider – Piero della Francesca – who gave Arezzo its permanent Renaissance monument, the glorious fresco choir in the Basilica of **San Francesco** (daily 8.30am–noon & 2.30–6.30pm; reservation necessary to see restored part of frescoes; ☎0575.352.727, *www.pierodellafrancesca.it*; €5.16). Located to the left of Corso Italia, which leads from the **lower town** to the more interesting **older quarter** at the top of the hill, the church was built in the early fourteenth century. A century later Piero della Francesca was commissioned to paint the choir with a cycle depicting *The Legend of the True Cross*, one of the most radiant creations of the period.

Further up the Corso, the twelfth-century **Pieve di Santa Maria** is one of the finest Romanesque structures in Tuscany, with some wonderful early-thirteenth-century carvings of the months over the portal. The fourteenth-century campanile, known locally as "the tower of the hundred holes", has become the emblem of the town. On the other side of the church, the dramatically sloping Piazza Grande is bordered by the tiered facade of the **Palazzetto della Fraternità dei Laci**, with a Gothic ground floor and fifteenth-century upper storeys, and Vasari's **loggia**, occupied by shops that in some instances still have their original stone counters. At the highest point of the town, the large unfussy **Duomo**, begun in the late thirteenth century, has stained-glass windows from around 1520, terracottas by the della Robbia family, and a tiny fresco of the *Magdalene* by Piero della Francesca. A short distance in the opposite direction from the Duomo, the church of **San Domenico** has a dolorous *Crucifix* by Cimabue. Signs point the way to the nearby **Casa di Giorgio Vasari** at Via XX Settembre 55 (Mon & Wed–Sat 8.30am–7.30pm, Sun 9am–12.30pm; free), designed by the celebrated biographer-architect-painter for himself and coated with his own lurid frescoes.

Practicalities

The **tourist office** is in front of the train station (summer Mon–Sat 9am–1pm & 3–7pm, Sun 9am–1pm; winter Mon–Sat 9am–1pm & 3–6.30pm, also first Sun of the month 9am–1pm; ☎0575.208.39, *www.turismo.toscana.it*). **Rooms** are hard to come by on the first weekend of every month (because of the massive antiques fair), and at the end of August and beginning of September. The most convenient affordable **hotel** is *La Toscana*, Via M. Perennio 56 (☎0575.21.692; ③), on the main road coming in from the west. Alternatively try the centrally located, good-value *Astoria*, Via Guido Monaco 54 (☎0575.24.361; ③), or the *Cecco*, at Corso Italia 215 (☎0575.20.986; ④). Otherwise, there's a **hostel**, *Ostello Villa Severi*, Via Redi 13, some way out of town (☎0575.299.047; ②; reception open 8am–2pm & 6pm–midnight); take bus #4 from the train station. For **restaurants**, *Da Guido*, Via Madonna del Prato 85, is a basic local trattoria, and for more pricey but high-quality Tuscan cuisine, try *La Buca di San Francesco*, by San Francesco church.

Siena

During the Middle Ages **SIENA** was one of the major cities of Europe. Virtually the size of Paris, it controlled most of southern Tuscany and its flourishing wool industry dominated the trade routes from France to Rome. The city developed a highly sophisticated civic life, with its own written constitution and a quasi-democratic government. Nowadays it's the perfect antidote to Florence. Self-contained and still rural in parts behind its medieval walls, its great attraction is its own cityscape – a majestic Gothic whole that could be enjoyed without venturing into a single museum. To get the most from it you'll need to stay, especially if you want to see its spectacular horse race, the Palio – though you'll definitely need to book during this time (July & Aug).

Arrival and accommodation

Arriving by **bus**, you are dropped along Viale Curtatone, by the Basilica of San Domenico; the **train station** is less convenient, 2km northeast, connected with Piazza Matteotti, at the top end of Via Curtatone, by shuttle bus. **Accommodation** is less of a struggle than in Florence, though it still pays to phone ahead. If you haven't, make your way either to the Cooperativa Hotels Promotion booth opposite San Domenico on Via Curtatone (Mon–Sat 9am–7/8pm; ☎0577.288.084, *shpnet@novamedia.it*), which can book you a room in a hotel or at one of three *residenze turistico*; or to the **tourist office** at Piazza del Campo 56 (summer Mon–Sat 8.30am–7.30pm, Sun 8.30am–2pm; winter Mon–Fri 8.30am–1.30pm & 3.30–7pm, Sat 8.30am–1.30pm; ☎0577.280.551, *www.siena.turismo.toscana.it*), which provides an accommodation list including **private rooms** from €30 a double, and has good free maps. Otherwise, the *Tre Donzelle* (☎0577.280.358; ③), Via Donzelle 5, which has good clean rooms, and the small, smart *Piccolo Hotel Etruria* at Via Donzelle 3 (☎0577.280.358; ④), right in the heart of town, are good no-nonsense **locandas**. *La Perla*, Via delle Terme 25 (☎0577.47.144; ④), is a regular pensione in a very central location, just two blocks north of the Campo, and the *Bernini* (☎0577.289.047;④), at Via della Sapienza 15, has stunning views to the Duomo. The *Alma Domus*, Via di Camporegio 37 (☎0577.47.601; ⑤), is in a quiet spot, also with great views. Alternatively, you can try the **HI hostel** at Via Fiorentina 89

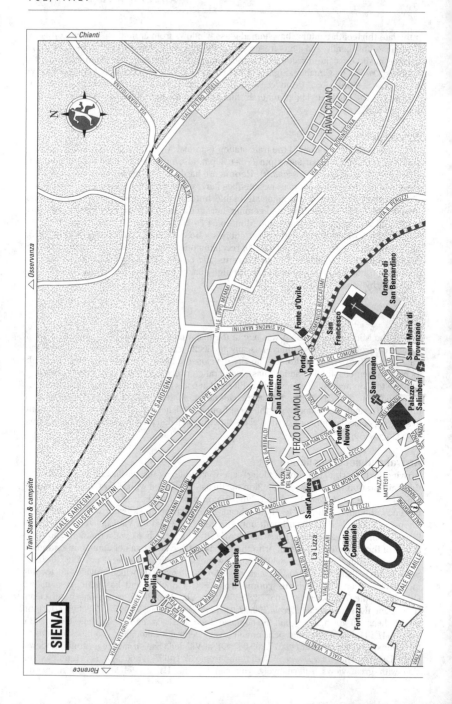

SIENA

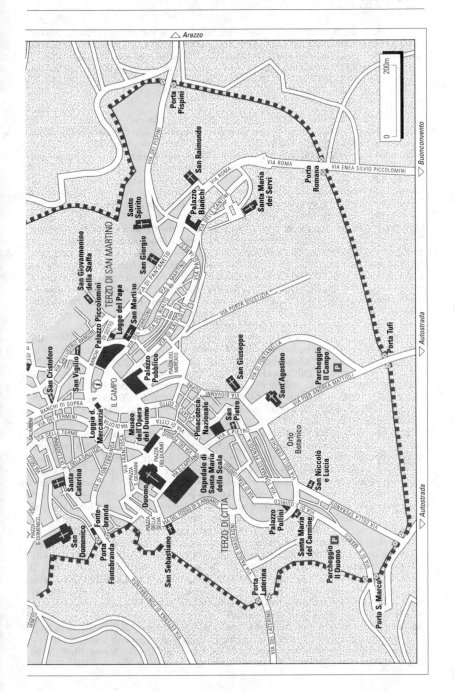

△ Arezzo

Porta Pispini

San Raimondo

VIA ROMA

VIA ENEA SILVIO PICCOLOMINI

▷ Buonconvento

Palazzo Bianchi

Santa Maria dei Servi

Porta Romana

VIA DEL PISPINI

Santo Spirito

San Giovamanino della Staffa

TERZO DI SAN MARTINO

San Giorgio

VIA DI PANTANETO

VIA ROMA

VIA DELLE CANTINE

Palazzo Piccolomini

Logge del Papa

San Martino

VIA DEL PORRIONE

VIA SAN MARTINO

VIA DEL RIALTO

VIA DELL'ORIOLO

VIA PAPA

VIA PORTA GIUSTIZIA

Porta Tufi

▷ Autostrada

San Cristoforo

BANCHI SALUSTRIO BANDINI

San Vigilio

Palazzo Bandini

VIA DEL CASATO DI SOPRA

Palazzo Pubblico

PIAZZA DEL MERCATO

San Giuseppe

VIA DI FONTANELLA

VIA GIOVANNI

Sant'Agostino

Parcheggio Il Campo P

BANCHI DI SOPRA

VIA DELLE TERME

VIA DI SALICOTTO

Loggia d. Mercanzia

IL CAMPO

i

Museo dell'Opera del Duomo

VIA DEL CASATO DI SOTTO

VIA DI CITTA

Pinacoteca Nazionale

San Pietro

VIA S. PIETRO

VIA GIAB ANDREA MATTIOLI

VIA DELLE TERME

VIA CATERINA

VIA DELLA GALLUZZA

VIA DI FONTEBRANDA

Santa Caterina

PIAZZA S. GIOVANNI

VIA FRANCIOSA

Duomo

PIAZZA DEL DUOMO

VIA DEL CAPITANO

VIA DEL POGGIO

Ospedale di Santa Maria della Scala

Orto Botanico

VIA TOMMASO PENDOLA

San Niccolò e Lucia

VIA DI STALLOREGGI

PIAZZA DELLA SELVA

VIA DEL FOSSO DI S. ANSANO

TERZO DI CITTA

Palazzo Pollini

VIA DI S. QUIRICO

VIA DELLA SPERANZE

Fonte-branda

San Domenico

PIAZZA S. DOMENICO

Porta Fontebranda

San Sebastiano

VIA PAOLO MASCAGNI

Santa Maria del Carmine

Parcheggio Il Duomo P

VIA DE S. MARCO

VENETO

VIA ESTERNA DI FONTEBRANDA

VIA DEL LATERINO

Porta Laterina

Porta S. Marco

△ Autostrada

0   200m

(☎0577.522.12; ②), 2km northwest of the centre; take bus #10 or #15 from Piazza Gramsci or, if you're coming from Florence, ask the bus driver to let you off at "Lo Stellino". The nearest **campsite** is the well-maintained *Campeggio Siena Colleverde*, Strada di Scacciapensieri 47, 2km north (☎0577.280.044, *campingsiena@siena.turismo.toscana.it*; mid-March to late-Nov); take bus #3 from Piazza Gramsci (last one at 11.45pm).

The City

The centre of Siena is almost entirely medieval in plan and appearance, and has been effectively pedestrianized since the 1960s. At its heart, the **Campo**, with its amphitheatre curve, is an almost organic piece of city planning, and is still the focus of city life. The **Palazzo Comunale**, with its 107-metre-tall bell tower, the **Torre del Mangia** (Mon–Sat 10am–7pm, Sun 10am–4pm; open till 11pm July & Aug; €5.20), occupies virtually the entire south side, and although it's still in use as Siena's town hall, its principal rooms have been converted into a **Museo Civico** of former public rooms, frescoed with themes integral to the secular life of the medieval city. Best of these are the Sala del Mappamondo, on the wall of which is the fabulous *Maestà* of Simone Martini, an acknowledged masterpiece of Sienese art, painted in 1315 and touched up (the site was damp) six years later, and the former Sale dei Nove, the "Room of the Nine", decorated with Lorenzetti's *Allegories of Good and Bad Government*, commissioned in 1377 to remind the councillors of their duties. Look, too, at the fine panel paintings by Lorenzetti's contemporaries, Guido da Siena and Matteo di Giovanni, in the adjacent Sala della Pace. At the top end of the Campo, the fifteenth-century **Loggia di Mercanzia**, built as a dealing room for merchants, marks the intersection of the city centre's principal streets. From here Via Banchi di Sotto leads up to the **Palazzo Piccolomini**, housing the state archive (Mon–Sat: summer 9am–7.30pm; winter 10am–1pm & 2.30–5.30pm; €1.50), which displays the painted covers of the *Tavolette di Biccherna*, the city accounts.

Further south, following Via di Pantaneto then Via Roma, the church of **Santa Maria dei Servi** houses two contrasting frescoes of the *Massacre of the Innocents* – a Gothic version by Lorenzetti, in the second chapel behind the high altar, and a Renaissance treatment by Matteo di Giovanni in the fifth chapel on the right. On the other side of the Campo, **Via di Città** cuts across the oldest, cathedral quarter of the city, fronted by some of Siena's finest private palazzi. At the end of the street, Via San Pietro leads to the **Pinacoteca Nazionale** (summer Mon 8.30am–1.30pm, Tues–Sat 8.15am–7.15pm, Sun 8am–1pm; winter Tues–Sat 8.30am–1.30pm; guided visits only at 2.30, 4 & 5.30pm; €4.14), a roll call of Sienese Gothic painting housed in a fourteenth-century palace. In the opposite direction Via di Capitano leads up to the **Duomo**, completed to virtually its present size around 1215; plans to enlarge the church withered with Siena's medieval prosperity, and the vast skeleton of an unfinished extension still stands at the north end of the cathedral square. The Duomo is in any case a delight, its style an amazing conglomeration of Romanesque and Gothic, delineated by bands of black and white marble on its facade. This theme is continued in the sgraffito marble pavement, which begins with geometric patterns outside the church and takes off into a startling sequence of 56 panels within, completed between 1349 and 1547; virtually every artist who worked in the city tried his hand on a design. The finest are reckoned to be Beccafumi's *Moses Striking Water from a Rock* and *Sacrifice of Isaac*, just beyond the dome area. The rest of the interior is equally arresting: among its greatest treasures are Nicola Pisano's font with its high-relief details of the *Life of Jesus* and *Last Judgement*, and a bronze Donatello statue of St John the Baptist in the north transept. Midway along the nave, the **Libreria Piccolomini** (daily: summer 9am–7.30pm; winter 10am–1pm & 2.30–5pm; €1.40), signalled by Pinturicchio's brilliantly coloured fresco of the *Coronation of Pius II*, has further frescoes by Pinturicchio and his pupils (including Raphael).

Behind the cathedral, the **Baptistry** (daily: April–Sept 9am–7.30pm, Oct 9am–6pm, Nov–March 10am–1pm & 2.30–5pm; €2) houses a Renaissance font with panels illustrating John the Baptist's life by della Quercia and Donatello. Visit also the **Museo dell'Opera Metropolitana** (daily: March–Sept 9am–7.30pm; Oct 9am–6pm; Nov–Feb 9am–1.30pm;

€5.20), which occupies part of the cathedral's planned extension and houses Pisano's original statues from the facade. Upstairs is a fine array of panels, including works by Simone Martini, Pietro Lorenzetti and Sano di Pietro, and the cathedral's original altarpiece, a haunting Byzantine icon known as the *Madonna dagli Occhi Grossi* ("Madonna of the Big Eyes"). The painting that repays a visit most, however, is the cathedral's second altarpiece, Duccio's *Maestà*, completed in 1311 and generally thought to be the climax of the Sienese style of painting. The church to the north of the cathedral is **San Domenico**, founded in 1125 and closely identified with St Catherine of Siena. Her chapel, on the south side of the church, has frescoes by Sodoma, and a reliquary containing her head.

Eating and drinking

Restaurants cost a bit over the odds in Siena, especially if you want to eat out in the Campo. If you just want a **snack**, there's pizza by weight at Via delle Terme 10, and an extravagantly stocked deli, the *Pizzicheria Morbidi*, at Via Banchi di Sotto 27. The cheapest **sit-down** alternative is the *Mensa Universitaria*, Via Sant'Agata 1 (Mon–Sat noon–2.30pm & 6.30–9pm; closed Aug), with meals for €6.20; there's another mensa at Via Bandini 47. *Gallo Nero*, Via del Porrione 65–67, dishes up medieval Sienese fare, with a set meal starting from €14.50, and the unpretentious café *Carlo e Franca*, Via di Pantaneto 138, serves pizza and pasta. Up a notch in price, the *Osteria Le Logge*, in an old *farmacia* in Via del Porrione 33, is a popular trattoria, while out towards San Lorenzo at Corso San Antonio 4, *Osteria Chiacchieria* is a rustic and welcoming option, where a plate of pasta will set you back less than €5.20. *Cane e Gatto*, Via Pagliaresi 6 (evenings only; closed Thurs), is just the place to go for the full works – €52 for seven sublime courses without drinks. For **ice cream**, try *Nannini Gelateria*, at the Piazza Matteotti end of Banchi di Sopra, or *La Costarella* just off the Campo near the corner of Via di Città and Via dei Pellegrini.

The Palio

The Siena **Palio** is the most spectacular festival event in Italy, a bareback horse race around the Campo contested twice a year (July 2 and Aug 16) between the ancient wards – or *contrade* – of the city. Each of the seventeen contrade has its own church, social centre and museum, and a heraldic animal motif, displayed in a modern fountain-sculpture in its individual piazza. Only ten *contrade* can take part in any one race, and these are chosen by lot with their horses and jockeys assigned at random. The only rule is that riders cannot interfere with each other's reins; everything else is accepted and practised. Each *contrada* has a traditional rival, and ensuring it loses is as important as winning. Jockeys may be bribed to throw the race, or whip a rival or his horse; and *contrade* have been known to drug horses and even ambush a jockey on his way to the race. Although there's a big build-up, the race itself lasts little more than a minute. Most spectators crowd into the centre of the Campo; for the best view, you need to have found a position on the inner rail by 2pm and to keep it for the next six hours.

Pisa

There's no escaping the Leaning Tower in **PISA**. The medieval bell tower is one of the world's most familiar images and yet its beauty still comes as a surprise, set in chessboard formation alongside the Duomo and Baptistry on the manicured grass of the **Campo dei Miracoli** where most of the buildings belong to the city's "Golden Age" of the twelfth and thirteenth centuries, when Pisa, then still a port, was one of the great Mediterranean powers (admission to all four museums on the Campo €9.30). Perhaps the strangest thing about the **Leaning Tower**, begun in 1173, is that it has always tilted; subsidence disrupted the foundations when it had reached just three of its eight storeys. For the next 180 years a succession of architects were brought in to try and correct the tilt, until around 1350 Tomasso di Andrea da Pontedera accepted the angle and completed the tower. Eight centuries on, it is thought to be nearing its limit: the overhang is over 5m, and the tower, supported by steel wires, is closed to the public at the time of writing – though following the success of recent attempts to stop the tilt increasing, restoration work has now been completed and the tower is scheduled to reopen in the near future. The entrance fee will be around €10 and a limited amount of people will be allowed to climb the tower, so booking in advance would be advisable. (☎050.560547). The **Duomo** (€1.50) was begun a century earlier, its facade – with its delicate balance of black and white marble, and tiers of arcades – setting the model for Pisa's highly distinctive brand of Romanesque. The interior continues the use of black and white marble, and with its long arcades of columns has an almost Oriental aspect. Most of the artworks are Renaissance or later, a notable exception being Cimabue's mosaic of *Christ in Majesty* in the apse. Its acknowledged highlight is the astonishingly detailed Gothic pulpit by Giovanni Pisano.

The third building of the Miracoli ensemble, the circular **Baptistry** (daily April–Sept 8am–7.40pm, March–Oct 9am–5.40pm, Nov–Feb 9am–4.40pm; €5.20 joint ticket), is a slightly bizarre mix of Romanesque and Gothic, embellished with statuary (now displayed in the museo) by Giovanni Pisano and his father Nicola, as well as another pulpit, sculpted by Nicola in 1260 – his first major commission. Along the north side of the Campo is the **Camposanto** (same hours as Baptistry; €5.20 joint ticket), a cloistered cemetery built towards the end of the thirteenth century. Most of the cloister's frescoes were destroyed by Allied incendiary bombs in World War II, but two masterpieces survived relatively unscathed – a fourteenth-century *Triumph of Death* and *Last Judgement* in the Cappella Ammanati, a ruthless catalogue of horrors painted around the time of the Black Death. It also has a number of sculptures and numerous Roman sarcophagi – Nicola Pisano's original sources of inspiration. At the southeast corner of the Campo, a vast array of pieces from the cathedral and Baptistry are displayed in the **Museo dell'Opera del Duomo** (daily same hours as Baptistry; €5.20 joint ticket), a huge collection which includes statuary by each of the Pisano family and examples of intarsia, the art of inlaid wood.

Away from the Campo dei Miracoli, Pisa takes on a very different character, as tourists give way to students at the still-thriving university. It's nonetheless a quiet place, eerily so at night, set about a series of erratic squares and arcaded streets, and with clusters of Romanesque churches and, along the banks of the Arno, a number of fine palazzi. The **Piazza dei Cavalieri** is an obvious first stop, a large square that was the centre of medieval Pisa, before being remodelled by Vasari as the headquarters of the Knights of St Stephen, whose palace, the curving **Palazzo dei Cavalieri**, topped with busts of the Medici, faces the order's church of **San Stefano**. A short walk east along the river, the **Museo Nazionale di San Matteo** (Tues–Sat 9am–7pm, Sun 9am–2pm; €4.10), housed in a twelfth-century convent, displays fourteenth-century panels by the Maestro di San Torpè, a Simon Martini polyptych and a panel of *San Paolo* by Masaccio. Also in the museum are the antique armour and wooden shields used in the annual *Gioco del Ponte* pageant (see opposite).

Practicalities

Pisa's **train station** is south of the centre on Piazza della Stazione, a ten-minute walk from the Campo dei Miracoli; or catch bus #3. From the **airport**, take the hourly Florence train, just a five minute journey. There are two **tourist offices**: one to the left of the station as you leave (Mon–Fri 8.30am–5.30/7pm, Sat & Sun 9am–5pm; ☎050.910.111, *www.pisa.turismo .toscana.it*) and another in the northeast corner of the Campo dei Miracoli (Mon–Sat 8.30am–5.30/7pm, Sun 10.30–4.30pm; ☎050.5650.464); both have maps and accommodation lists. The most attractive budget **hotels** are grouped around the Campo dei Miracoli, and the best of the lot is the elegant old *Albergo Gronchi* in Piazza Arcivescovado (☎050.561.823; ②). Others include the *Locanda Galileo*, Via Santa Maria (☎050.40.621; ③); the *Hotel Giardino*, behind a self-service restaurant on Via Cammeo (☎050.562.101; ③); and *Pensione Helvetia*, Via G. Boschi 31, off Piazza Arcivescovado (☎050.553.084; ③). You could also try the *Serena*, Via D. Cavalca 45 (☎050.580.809; ③); the *La Torre*, Via C. Battisti 17 (☎050.252.20; ④), or one of a number of places in the station area, best of which is the *Albergo Milano*, Via Mascagni 14, off Piazza della Stazione (☎050.23.162; ③). A good women-only alternative, five minutes' walk from the station (first right), is the *Casa della Giovane*, Via Corridoni 31 (☎050.43.061; ③). The nearest **hostel**, Via Pietrasantina 15 (☎050.890.622; ②), is 2.5km from the centre past the cemetery. The city **campsite**, *Campeggio Torre Pendente*, is 1km west of the Campo dei Miracoli at Viale delle Cascine 86 (☎050.561.704, *www.codekard.it/torrependente*; April–Oct) – a large, well-maintained site, with a restaurant and shop.

Restaurants in the environs of the Leaning Tower are not good value, but a few blocks south, around Piazza Cavalieri and Piazza Dante, are a number of reasonably priced places. One of the most popular is *Trattoria Stelio*, Piazza Dante 11, or there's a cheaper, unnamed pizzeria on the same square. Over to the west, *Pizzeria da Cassio*, Piazza Cavallotti 14, is a good *tavola calda*, and the university building on Via Martiri, off Piazza Cavalieri, houses a student **mensa** (mid-Sept to mid-July Mon–Fri noon–2.30pm & 7–9pm, Sat & Sun noon–2.30pm). The city's big traditional event is the **Gioco del Ponte**, held on the last Sunday in June, when teams from the north and south banks of the city stage a series of "battles", pushing a seven-tonne carriage over the Ponte di Mezzo. The event has taken place since Medici times and continues in Renaissance costume.

Lucca

LUCCA is as graceful a provincial capital as they come, set inside a thick swathe of Renaissance walls, and with a quiet, almost entirely medieval street plan. Palazzi and the odd tower dot the streets, at intervals overlooked by a brilliantly decorated Romanesque facade. It's not exactly undiscovered, but for once the number of tourists seems to fit.

The most enjoyable way to get your bearings is to follow the path around the top of the **Walls** – nearly 4km in extent and built with genuine defensive capability in the early sixteenth century, before being transformed to their present, garden aspect by the Bourbon ruler, Marie Louise. In the centre of town, just east of the main Piazza Napoleone on Piazza San Martino, the **Duomo of San Martino** (daily 7am–5/7pm) was in part sculpted by Nicola Pisano. The great hall-like interior includes paintings by Tintoretto, Ghirlandaio and Filippino Lippi. The most famous item, however, Jacopo della Quercia's **Tomb of Ilaria del Carretto** (summer daily 10am–6pm; winter Mon–Fri 10am–4.45pm, Sat 9.30am–6.45pm, Sun 9–10am & 3–5pm; €1.50), has been restored so vigorously that one expert declared it had been ruined – prompting a libel action from the restorer. Lucca's finest sculptor was perhaps Matteo Civitali, whose *Tempietto* in the north aisle was sculpted to house the city's most famous and lucrative relic, the *Volto Santo* – said to be the "true effigy of Christ" and the focus for international pilgrimage.

Northwest of the Duomo across Via Fililungo, the facade of **San Michele in Foro** church (daily 7.30am–8pm) is a triumph of eccentricity, each of its loggia columns different, some twisted, others sculpted or candy-striped. The interior is relatively plain, though there's a good Andrea della Robbia terracotta and a painting by Filippino Lippi. Giacomo Puccini was born almost opposite at Via di Poggio 30, and his home, the **Casa di Puccini** (Jan–Feb Tues–Fri 10am–1pm, Sat & Sun 10am–1pm & 3–6pm; March–June & Oct–Dec Tues–Sun 10am–1pm & 3–6pm; July–Sept Tues–Sun 10am–6pm; €2.60), is now a school of music with a small museum, featuring the Steinway piano on which he composed *Turandot*, along with original scores and photographs from premieres. At the end of the street in Via Galli Tassi is the seventeenth-century **Palazzo Mansi**, which houses a **Pinacoteca Nazionale** (Tues–Sat 9am–7pm, Sun 9am–2pm; €6.20), an indifferent collection of pictures, although the Rococo palace itself is a sight, at its most extreme in a spectacularly gilded bridal suite.

Northeast of here, the basilica of **San Frediano** has a facade with a brilliant thirteenth-century mosaic of *Christ in Majesty* and fine treasures inside, most enjoyable of which is the font carved with Romanesque scenes of Moses, the Good Shepherd and Apostles; set behind it is a ceramic *Annunciation* by Andrea della Robbia.

Be sure to visit the remarkable **Piazza Anfiteatro**, a circuit of medieval buildings whose foundations are the arches of the Roman amphitheatre. Just southeast, the strangest sight in Lucca is perhaps the **Casa-Torre Guinigi** (March–Sept daily 9am–7.30pm; Oct 10am–6pm; Nov–Feb 10am–4.30pm; €2.60), the fifteenth-century home of Lucca's leading family, with a battlemented tower surmounted by holm oaks whose roots have grown into the room below. Much of it is being restored, but from Via San Andrea you can climb it for one of the best views over the city. Across the narrow canal on Via della Quarquonia, the fifteenth-century **Villa Guinigi** is now the home of Lucca's major museum of art and sculpture, the **Museo Nazionale Guinigi** (Tues–Sat 9am–7pm; Sun 9am–2pm; €4.10), with a good deal of lively Romanesque sculpture from the city and some good work by the cathedral's maestro, Matteo Civitali.

Practicalities

The **train station** is just outside the city walls to the south, an easy walk or short bus ride to the centre. One of the most pleasant ways of exploring around Lucca is to rent a bike; try Barbetti in Via dell Anfiteatro 23 (0583.954.444; €2/hr) The **tourist office** is on the north side of Piazza Verdi (daily: summer 9am–7pm; winter 9.30am–5pm; ☎0583.419.689, *www.lucca.turismo.toscana.it*), a swish affair with plenty of information. Finding **accommodation** is a problem at almost any time of year, but of the hotels, the *Melecchi* at Via Romana 37 (☎0583.950.234; ③), *Stipino* at Via Romana 95 (☎0583.495.077; ③) and *Diana* at Via del Molinetto 11 (☎0583.492.202; ④) are all good. After these the best bet is the *Moderno*, in the centre at Via Civitali 38 (☎0583.558.40; ④). There's an **HI hostel** with **campsite** at Via del Brennero 673 (☎0583.341.811; ②), 3km north of the centre. For **food**, try the *Trattoria da Guido*, Via C. Battisti 28, the cheapest place in town, or *Trattoria da Leo*, Via Tegrimi 1. *Trattoria da Giulio*, Via delle Conce 47, is also good and very popular, as is *Ristorante all'Olivo*, Piazza S. Quirico 1. For excellent pizza, with good beer, try the *Gli Orti di Via Elisa*, Via Elisa 17; *Le Salette*, Piazza S. Maria 15, is another good pizzeria – a big friendly place with tables outside.

Perugia

The provincial capital, **PERUGIA** is the most obvious base to kick off a tour of Umbria. It's an oddly mixed town, with a medieval centre and not a little industry: Buitoni, the pasta people, are based here, and it's also where Italy's best chocolate, Perugini, is made. It can get very busy in summer, but there's a day's worth of good sightseeing to be done and the presence of the Italian University for Foreigners, set up by Mussolini to improve the image of Italy abroad, lends a dash of cosmopolitan style.

Perugia hinges on a single street, **Corso Vannucci**, a broad pedestrian thoroughfare constantly buzzing with action. At the far end, the austere **Piazza Quattro Novembre** is backed by the plain-faced **Duomo** (daily 8am–noon & 4pm–sunset), recently reopened after damage caused by the 1983 earthquake, although the interior, home to the so-called Virgin's "wedding ring", an unwieldy one-inch-diameter piece of agate that changes colour according to the character of the person wearing it, isn't especially interesting. The Perugians keep the ring locked up in fifteen boxes fitted into one another like Russian dolls, each opened with a key held by a different person; it's brought out for public viewing every July 30. The centrepiece of the piazza is the **Fontana Maggiore**, sculpted by the father-and-son team Nicola and Giovanni Pisano and describing episodes from the Old Testament, classical myth, Aesop's fables and the twelve months of the year. Opposite rises the gaunt mass of the **Palazzo dei Priori**, worth a glance inside for its frescoed **Sala dei Notari** (daily 9am–1pm & 3–7pm; free). A few doors down at Corso Vannucci 25 is the **Collegio di Cambio** (March–Oct Mon–Sat 9am–12.30pm & 2.30–5.30pm, Sun 9am–12.30pm; Nov–Feb Tues–Sat 8am–2pm, Sun 9am–12.30pm; €3.10 with the Collegio della Mercanzia), the town's medieval money-exchange, frescoed by Perugino. The palace also houses the **Galleria Nazionale di Umbria**

(Mon–Sat 9am–7pm, Sun 9am–1pm, closed first Mon of each month; €4.20), one of central Italy's best galleries – a twelve-room romp through the history of Umbrian painting, with works by Perugino and Pinturrichio along with one or two stunning Tuscan masterpieces (Fra Angelico, Piero della Francesca) and early Sienese works (Duccio).

The best streets to wander around to get a feel of the old city are either side of the Duomo. **Via dei Priori** is the most characteristic, leading down to Agostino di Duccio's colourful **Oratorio di San Bernardino**, whose richly embellished facade is by far the best piece of sculpture in the city. From here you can wander through the northern part of the centre, along Via A. Pascoli, to the **Arco di Augusto**, whose lowest section is now one of the few remaining monuments of Etruscan Perugia. The upper remnant was added by the Romans when they captured the city in 40 BC. On the other side of town, along **Corso Cavour**, is the large church of **San Domenico**, one of whose chapels holds a superb carved arch by Agostino di Duccio, and, to the right of the altar, the tomb of Pope Benedict XI, an elegant piece by one of the period's three leading sculptors: Pisano, Lorenzo Maitini or Arnolfo di Cambio – no one knows which. There are also some impressive stained-glass windows, the second biggest in Italy after those in Milan Cathedral. In the church's cloisters, the **Museo Archeologico Nazionale dell'Umbria** (Mon–Sat 9am–1.30pm & 2.30–7pm, Sun 9am–1pm; €2.10) has one of the most extensive Etruscan collections around. Further on down the Corso Cavour, advertised by a rocket-shaped bell tower, the tenth-century basilica of **San Pietro** is one of the most distinctive idiosyncratic of all the town's churches. Its choir has been called the best in Italy, and there is a host of works by Perugino and others.

Practicalities

Arriving by **train**, you'll find yourself well away from the centre of Perugia on Piazza V. Veneto; buses #6, #7, #9, #11, #13d, #13s or #15 run to Piazza Italia or Piazza Matteotti (15min journey) and you'd do well to take one rather than attempt the long walk. The **tourist office** is on Piazza IV Novembre 3 (Mon–Sat 8.30am–1.30pm & 3.30–6.30pm, Sun 9am–1pm; ☎075.572.3327 or ☎075.573.6458, *www.umbria2000.it*). There's an **HI hostel**, *Spagnoli*, near the station on Via Cortonese 4 (☎075.501.1366; ②). As for **hotels**, try *Rosalba*, at Via del Circo 7 (☎075.572.0626; ④); *Etruria*, just off the Corso at Via della Luna 21 (☎075.572.3730; ③); or *Anna*, centrally placed at Via dei Priori 48 (☎075.573.6304; ③). On the **food** front, *Osteria del Gambero*, Via Baldeschi 17(closed Mon), has healthy Umbrian specialities, and *Lo Scalino*, Via S. Ercolano 2, and *La Botte*, Via Volte della Pace 33 (closed Sun), are decent pizzerias, the latter with a tourist menu at €9.30. On Via dei Priori, *Papaia* is a good bar with plenty of seating and decent *panini*. The reasonably priced *Dal mì Cocco*, Corso Garibaldi 12, with a student clientele, offers traditional cuisine near the university (closed Mon). *Café del Cambio* at Corso Vannucci 29 is one of the trendiest **bars** in the centre, and does snacks and light meals at lunchtime. For evening **entertainment**, *Bratislava* at Via Fiorenzuola 12, near Corso Cavour, has live music on selected nights, and *Bar Morlacchi*, Piazza Morlacchi 6–8, offers live jazz. You can go **online** at Internet Point, Via Ulisse Rocchi 4 (Mon–Sat 10am–10pm, Sun 4–8pm; €3.60/hr).

Gubbio

GUBBIO is the most thoroughly medieval of the Umbrian towns, an immediately likeable place that's hanging onto its charm despite an ever-increasing influx of tourists. The first high peaks of the Apennines rising behind give the place the feel of a mountain outpost – something it's always been, in fact. The best (and most scenic) approach is by frequent bus from Perugia, or by train from Foligno to Fossato di Vico, 19km away but with an hourly connecting bus.

Centre-stage on the windswept Piazza della Signoria is the immense fourteenth-century **Palazzo dei Consoli** (daily: summer 10am–1pm & 3–6pm; winter 10am–1pm & 2–5pm), whose crenellated outline and campanile command your attention for miles around. Council officials and leading citizens met to discuss business here in the cavernous Salone dell'Arengo, from which the word "harangue" is derived. The building also holds the **Museo Civico** (Tues–Sun; same times; €3.70), unremarkable except for the famous Eugubine Tablets, Umbria's most important archeological find and the only extant record of the ancient Umbrian language. Admission to the museum also gets you into the five-roomed **Pinacoteca** upstairs, worth a look for works by the Gubbian School, notably Ottaviano Nelli, who painted seventeen frescoes on the life of the Virgin in the church of **San Francesco** on Piazza dei Quaranta Martiri. There's also an unusually lovely *Madonna del Belvedere* by him in the church of **Santa Maria Nuova**, off Corso Garibaldi. On the hillside above the town, the **Basilica of Sant'Ubaldo** is the place Gubbians drive to on Sunday mornings, a pleasant spot with a handy bar and great views, connected with the town's Porta Romana by a slightly scary funicular (€3.70 one way). There's not much to see in the basilica itself, except the body of the town's patron saint, Ubaldo, who's missing three fingers, hacked off by his manservant as a religious keepsake. You can't miss the big wooden pillars (*ceri*), though, featured in Gubbio's annual *Corsa dei Ceri* (May 15), a race to the basilica from the town that's second only to Siena's Palio in terms of its exuberance.

You shouldn't have any problem **staying** in Gubbio, though the place does get busy. The **tourist office**, Piazza Oderisi 6 (Mon–Sat 8.30am–1.30pm & 3–6pm, Sun 9am–12.30pm; ☎075.922.0790 or 075.922.0693, *www.umbria2000.it*), may be able to help; or try the *Locanda del Duca*, Via Piccardi 3 (☎075.927.7753; ③), or the *Grotta dell'Angelo*, Via Gioia 47 (☎075.927.1747; ③), which both have excellent restaurants. There's a good selection of additional eateries, including an excellent cheap pizzeria, *Il Bargello*, Via dei Consoli 37 (closed Mon), and if you want to be outdoors, try the *Trattoria di San Martino* at Via dei Consoli 8 (closed Tues). Failing that, you could try the classier *Taverna del Lupo*, Via Ansidei 21 (closed Mon). There are two **campsites** for Gubbio, both in Loc. Ortoguidone – 4-star *Villa Ortoguidone County Club* (☎075.927.2037) and 3-star *Città di Gùbbio* (both ☎075.927.2037, *www.agriturgubbio.com*), both open April–Sept. The Caffè Centrale offers the handiest **Internet** access, Piazza Oderisi 3 (daily 7am–midnight; €5.20/hr).

Assisi

Thanks to St Francis, Italy's premier saint and founder of the Franciscan order, **ASSISI** is Umbria's best-known town, and suffers as a result, crammed with people for ten months of the year. It quietens down in the evening, and does retain some medieval hill-town charm, but you may not want to hang around once you've seen all there is to see. An earthquake in September 1997 caused extensive damage to parts of the town, most notably to the Basilica di San Francesco, but restoration is now complete and the basilica is, mercifully, almost back to its original splendour.

The **Basilica di San Francesco** (daily 6.30am–7.30pm), at the end of Via San Francesco, is justly famed as Umbria's single greatest glory, and one of the most overwhelming collections of art outside a gallery anywhere in the world. Begun in 1228, two years after the saint's death, it was financed by donations that flooded in from all over Europe. The sombre **Lower Church** is the earlier of the two churches that make up the basilica, its complicated floor plan and claustrophobic vaults intended to create a mood of meditative introspection – an effect added to by brown-robed monks, strict rules on silence and no photography. Francis lies under the floor in a crypt only brought to light in 1818. Frescoes cover almost every available space, and span a century of continuous artistic development, from the anonymous early works above the altar, through Cimabue's over-restored *Madonna, Child and Angels with St Francis* in the right transept to work by the Sienese School painters, Simone Martini and Pietro Lorenzetti. Martini's frescoes are in the Cappella di San Martino, the first chapel on the left as you enter the nave, while Lorenzetti's works, dominated by a powerful *Crucifixion*, are in the transept and small chapel to the left of the main altar. The **Upper Church**, built to a light and airy Gothic plan, is richly decorated, too, with dazzling frescoes on the life of St

EDMUND NAGELE

St Paul's Cathedral, London, England

JOHN MORRISON

Judging sheep, Yorkshire dales, England

C. BOWMAN

Rathaus, Munich, Germany

NAGELE/KLAMMET

Burg Rheinstein, Trechtingshausen, Germany

Basalt columns, Staffa, Scotland

Erechtheion, Acropolis, Athens, Greece

Bay in Párga, Greece

Esterházy Palace, Fertőd, Hungary

Great Skellig, Co. Kerry, Ireland

White Island,
Co. Fermanagh, Ireland

Colosseum, Rome, Italy

The Canal Grande, Venice, Italy

PiEDi di MAiA
L.3000
L'UNO

Tripe stall in Quartieri Spagnoli, Naples, Italy

Francis, some of which at least, are considered to be the work of Giotto. The **treasury** contains a rich collection of paintings, reliquaries and religious clutter.

There's not a great deal worth seeing in Assisi's small centre – only a nondescript **Museo Civico** in the central Piazza del Comune (daily: summer 10am–1pm & 3–7pm; winter 10am–1pm & 2–5pm; €2.10), housed in the crypt of the now defunct church of San Nicolo, whose collection includes Etruscan fragments and the so-called **Tempio di Minerva**, six columns and a pediment from a Roman temple of the first century. A short trek up the steep Via di San Rufino from here, the thirteenth-century **Duomo** has the font used to baptize St Francis and St Clare, and close by is the **Basilica di Santa Chiara**, burial place of St Francis's devoted early companion. Consecrated in 1265, the church is a virtual facsimile of the basilica up the road, and is home to the macabrely blackened body of Clare herself and a Byzantine crucifix famous for having bowed to Francis and commanded him to embark on his sacred mission.

Practicalities

The **train station** is 5km south of Assisi, connected to the centre by half-hourly buses. The **tourist office** is at Piazza del Comune 12 (Mon–Sat 8am–2pm & 3.30–6.30pm, Sat 9am–1pm & 3.30–6.30pm, Sun 9am–1pm; ☎075.812.450, *www.umbria2000.it*) and has accommodation lists, including details of **private rooms**. There are plenty of cheap places to stay but they can get full. The functional *Italia*, off the central Piazza del Comune at Vicolo della Fortezza 2 (☎075.812.625, ③, March–Nov), is about the cheapest option; *La Rocca*, Via Porta Perlici 27 (☎075.812.284; ③), is also a fair bet, as is the *Anfiteatro Romano*, close by at Via Anfiteatro Romano 4 (☎075.813.025; ③). There are also pilgrim hostels (*Case Religiose di Ospitalità*) all over town, charging €10–25 depending on the type of accommodation; the *Suore del Giglio*, Via San Francesco 13 (☎075.812.267; ③), is perhaps the best as far as location goes. There's a big **campsite** and **hostel** at Fontemaggio (☎075.813.636; ②), 3km out on the road to the monastery of Eremo delle Carceri, and the official **HI hostel**, *Ostello della Pace*, is at Via di Valecchie (☎075.816.767; ②). For **food**, try the reasonably-priced pizzeria, *Il Pozzo Romano* (closed Thurs) on Via Sant'Agnese near Santa Chiara; *Pallotta*, Via San Rufino 4 (closed Tues), which is reasonable and friendly; or the excellent *I Monaci*, off Via Fontebella on the Scaletti del Metastasio (closed Wed), at Via A Fortini 10. The *La Rocca* hotel (see above) has a good no-frills restaurant, and *Medioevo*, Via dell'Arco dei Priori 4b Brizi 1, is busy and excellent but expensive (closed Wed, Jan & July 1–21). To use the **Internet**, try Bar del Corso, Via Corso Mazzini (daily 7am–midnight; €6.20/hr).

Spoleto

SPOLETO is Umbria's most compelling town, remarkable for its extremely pretty position and several of Italy's most ancient Romanesque churches. For several centuries it was among the most influential of Italian towns, the former capital of one of the Lombards' three Italian dukedoms, which at one time stretched as far as Rome. Barbarossa flattened the city in 1155, and in 1499 the nineteen-year-old Lucrezia Borgia was appointed governess by her father, Pope Alexander VI.

Spoleto's lower town, where you arrive, was badly damaged by World War II bombing, and doesn't hold much of interest, so it's best to take a bus straight to the upper town. There's no single, central piazza, but the place to head for is **Piazza Libertà**, site of a much-restored first-century **Roman Theatre**, visible at all times, but also visitable more closely in conjunction with the **Museo Archeologico** (Mon–Sat 9am–7pm, Sun 9am–1pm; €2.10). The adjoining **Piazza della Fontana** has more Roman remains, best of which is the **Arco di Druso**, built to honour the minor campaign victories of Drusus, son of Tiberius. The homely Piazza del Mercato, beyond, is a fine opportunity to take in some streetlife, and from there it's a short walk to the **Duomo**, whose facade of restrained elegance is one of the most memorable in the region. Inside, various Baroque embellishments are eclipsed by the superlative apse frescoes of the fifteenth-century Florentine artist Fra Lippo Lippi, dominated by his final masterpiece, a *Coronation of the Virgin*. He died shortly after their completion (amid rumours that he was poisoned for seducing the daughter of a local noble family) and was interred here in a tomb designed by his son, Filippino. You should also take the short walk out to the **Ponte delle Torri**, a picture-postcard favourite, and an astonishing piece of medieval engineering, best seen as part of a circular walk around the base of the **Rocca** – everyone's idea of a cartoon castle, with towers, crenellations and sheer walls; it served until recently as a high-security prison, home to Pope John Paul II's would-be assassin and leading members of the Red Brigades. The church of **San Pietro**, 1km or so beyond the bridge on a hillside, is also worth the walk for the splendid sculptures on its facade, among the best Romanesque carvings in Umbria.

Spoleto's **train station** is around 1km north of the town centre and the central Piazza della Libertà, where you'll find the **tourist office** (daily 9am–1pm & 4–7pm, Sat & Sun 10am–1pm & 4–7pm; ☎0743.220.311, *www.umbria2000.it*). There's an **Internet** café, Grizzly, on Corso Garibaldi 58 (☎0743.43.777). If you're planning on **staying** in town, there's the central and reasonably priced *Pensione dell'Angelo*, Via Arco del Druso 25 (☎0743.222.385; ④). If that's full, then the only other vaguely affordable place in the upper town is the *Pensione Aurora*, off Piazza Libertà at Via dell'Apollinare 3 (☎0743.220.315; ④). The lower town is very much a second choice, but there are more likely to be rooms available; try the *Anfiteatro*, Via dell'Anfiteatro 14 (☎0743.49.853; ③). The closest **campsite** is the small *Camping Monteluco*, behind San Pietro (☎0743.220.358; April–Sept); tiny but very pleasant. For **food**, the best basic trattoria, always full of locals, is the *Trattoria del Festival*, at Via Brignone 8 (closed Fri), *Il Panciolle*, Via del Duomo 3–4 (closed Wed), is also a popular choice and has a wonderful terrace. *Pecchiarda*, in Vicolo S. Giovanni off Via delle Postierno in the lower town, has a pleasant enclosed garden (closed Thurs), but if you want something really special, go to *Pentagramma*, off Piazza Libertà at Via T. Martani 4 (closed Mon).

In June and July Spoleto plays host to the country's leading international arts festival, the **Festival dei Due Mondi**. The jet-set audiences – and ticket prices to match – can be off-putting, but there's also an Edinburgh-type fringe with lots of film, jazz, buskers and so on. Tickets and information are available from the festival's information office at Via del Duomo 8 (☎0743.45.028).

Orvieto

Out on a limb from the rest of Umbria, **ORVIETO** is flooded with tourists in summer, most of whom are drawn by its **Duomo**, one of the greatest Gothic buildings in Italy, built, according to tradition, to celebrate the so-called Miracle of Bolsena (1263), in which a doubting priest celebrating Mass in a church on the nearby Lago di Bolsena noticed real blood dripping from the Host onto the altarcloth. The stained linen was whisked off to Pope Urban IV, who was in Orvieto to escape the heat and political hassle of Rome, and the building was constructed over the ensuing three centuries, in a surprisingly unified example of the Romanesque-Gothic style. The star turn is the facade, a riot of columns, spires, bas-reliefs, sculptures and dazzling colour, just about held together by four enormous fluted columns, the work of the master mason Lorenzo Maitini and his pupils, describing episodes from the Old and New Testaments in staggering detail. Inside, the church is surprisingly plain by comparison, mainly distinguished by the **Cappella di San Brizo** (Mon–Sat 10am–12.45pm & 2.30–5.15/7.15pm, Sun 2.30–5.45/6.45pm; €1.60; tickets from the tourist office), which holds Luca Signorelli's fresco of the *Last Judgement*, a realistic yet grotesque work, full of beautifully observed muscular figures which greatly influenced Michelangelo's celebrated cycle in the Vatican's Sistine Chapel. Signorelli, suitably clad in black, includes himself with Fra Angelico in the lower left-hand corner of *The Sermon of the Antichrist*, both calmly looking on as someone is garrotted at their feet. The twin Cappella del Corporale contains the sacred *corporale* (altar cloth) itself, locked away in a massive, jewel-encrusted casket (an accurate facsimile of the facade), and some appealing frescoes by local fourteenth-century painter Ugolino di Prete, describing the events of the miracle.

Next to the Duomo, the **Museo dell'Opera del Duomo** (closed for restoration at time of writing) has paintings by Martini, several important thirteenth-century sculptures by Arnolfo di Cambio and Andrea Pisano, and a lovely font filled with Escher-like carved fishes. Opposite, the **Museo Greco** (daily: summer 10.30am–1pm & 3–6.30pm; winter 10.30am–1pm & 2–5.30pm; €2.60, or €4.20 for the *Biglietto Cumulativo*) features a fairly predictable collection of vases and assorted fragments excavated from local tombs. Moving north up Via del Duomo, you come to **Corso Cavour**, the town's pedestrianized main drag, at the far end of which, across Piazza Cahen, is **Il Pozzo di San Patrizio** (daily 10am–6/7pm; €3.10 or €4.20 for the *Biglietto Cumulativo*), the novelty act of the town, a huge cylindrical well, commissioned in 1527 by Pope Clement VII to guarantee the town's water supply during an expected siege by the imperial army. It's a dank but striking piece of engineering, 62m deep, named after its alleged similarity to the Irish cave where St Patrick died in 493, supposedly aged 133 – though, apart from a small Etruscan tomb halfway down, it's really just an impressive hole in the ground.

Practicalities

Bus #1 makes a regular trip from the distant **train station** to Piazza XXIX Marzo, a short way north of the Duomo. A more charming alternative is the funicular up to Piazza Cahen, from where minibuses wind through the twisting streets to Piazza del Duomo. The **tourist office** at Piazza del Duomo 24 (Mon–Fri 8.15am–2pm & 4–7pm, Sat 10.30am–1pm & 4–7pm, Sun 10am–noon & 4–6pm, ☎0763.341.772, *www.umbria2000.it*) has plenty of information and an accommodation service. Of **hotels**, the *Duomo*, Via Vicolo di Maurizio 7 (☎0763.341.887; ③), is a good central option, as is the pleasant *Posta*, Via Luca Signorelli 18 (☎0763.341.909; ④). Slightly pricier, the *Corso*, Corso Cavour 343 (☎0763.342.020; ⑤), is the best hotel near Piazza Cahen. The nearest **campsite** is the *Orvieto*, 10km away on Lago di Corbara (take the bus to Baschi/Civitella). There's a group of cheap **restaurants** at the bottom of Corso Cavour, though the best-value eating is close to the Duomo, at Via Maitani 15, a canteen affair run by a co-operative, offering a choice between a restaurant and self-service trattoria (closed Sun). *La Grotta*, Via Signorelli 5, off Via del Duomo (closed Mon), is a standard, friendly trattoria, and the *Antico Bucchero*, Via de' Cartari 4, is a popular restaurant with reasonable prices (closed Wed). The *Bottega del Buon Vino*, Via della Cave 26, is a wine **bar** that's good for staples and has a few outside tables. For **Internet** access go to Caffé Montanucci, Corso Cavour 23 (daily 7am–10.30pm; €6.20/hr).

Urbino

For the second half of the fifteenth century, **URBINO** was one of the most prestigious courts in Europe, ruled by the remarkable Federico da Montefeltro, who employed a number of the greatest artists and architects of the time to build and decorate his palace in the town. At one time it was reckoned the most beautiful in all Italy, and it does seem from contemporary accounts that fifteenth-century Urbino was an extraordinarily civilized place, a measured and urbane society in which life was lived without indulgence.

In the centre of Urbino, the **Palazzo Ducale** is a fitting monument to Federico, home now to the **Galleria Nazionale delle Marche** (Mon 9am–2pm, Tues–Sat 9am–7pm, Sun 9am–7.30pm; €4.20), although it's the building itself that makes the biggest impression. Among the paintings in the Appartamento del Duca are Piero della Francesca's strange *Flagellation*, and the *Ideal City*, a famous perspective painting of a symmetrical and deserted cityscape long attributed to Piero but now thought to be by one of his followers. There's also Paolo Uccello's last work, the six-panelled *Profanation of the Host*, and, in the same room, a portrait of Federico da Montefeltro by the Spanish artist Pedro Berruguete. The most interesting and best preserved of the palazzo's rooms is Federico's Studiolo, a triumph of illusory perspective created by intarsia. Shelves appear to protrude from the walls, cupboard doors seem to swing open to reveal lines of books, a letter lies in an apparently half-open drawer. Even more remarkable are the delicately hued landscapes of Urbino as it might appear from one of the surrounding hills, and the life-like squirrel perching next to a bowl of fruit.

Urbino is a lively university town, and its bustling streets – a pleasant jumble of Renaissance and medieval houses – can be a welcome antidote to the rarefied atmosphere of the Palazzo Ducale. You can wind down in one of the many bars and trattorias, or take a picnic up to the gardens within the **Fortezza Albornoz**, from where you'll get great views of the town and the countryside, out to **San Bernardino**, a fine Renaissance church 2km away that is the resting place of the Montefeltros.

Urbino is notoriously difficult to reach – the best approach is by **bus** from Pésaro, about 30km away on the coast (last one leaves at around 8pm). Buses stop in Borgo Mercatale, at the foot of the Palazzo Ducale, which is reached either by lift or by Francesco di Giorgio Martini's spiral staircase. For **accommodation**, the cheapest options are **private rooms**, most of which are on Via Budassi – lists available from the **tourist office** on Piazza Rinascimento (summer Mon–Sat 9am–1pm & 3–7pm, Sun 9am–1pm; winter daily 9am–1pm; ☎0722.2613, *www.comune.urbino.ps.it*); you can also check the **Internet** for free. The most convenient **hotels** are the newly refurbished *Italia*, Corso Garibaldi 32 (☎0722.2701; ③), and the *San Giovanni*, Via Barocci 13 (☎0722.2827; ③; closed in July). The best deals for **food** are at the university mensa on Piazza San Filippo, or the *Self-Service Franco* on Via del Poggio (both closed Sun). If your budget's not too tight, *Il Girarrosto*, off Via Raffaello at Piazza San Francesco 3, serves good traditional food (open daily for lunch, Thurs–Sun only for dinner).

Ancona

ANCONA is a depressing place, severely damaged by war and earthquakes, with a modern centre of bland broad avenues and palm-shaded piazzas. However, it's the mid-Adriatic's largest **port**, with regular ferries to Greece and elsewhere, and you may well pass through. Regular buses run along the seafront from the train station to the port, so it's easy enough to miss the place altogether, but if you are hanging around between connections there are a couple of things to see. The port itself is headed by a well-preserved Roman arch, the **Arco di Traiano**, raised in honour of Emperor Trajan, under whose rule Ancona first became a major port. Behind it is the **Arco Clementino**, a piece of architectural self-congratulation by Pope Clement XII, who made Ancona a free port in the eighteenth century, and thus considered himself Trajan's equal. On Via Pizzecolli is the town's **art gallery** (Mon 9am–1pm, Tues–Sat 9am–7pm, Sun 3–7pm; €2.60), highlights of which are Titian's Apparition of the Virgin, a glorious *Sacra Conversazione* by Lotto and an exquisite *Madonna and Child* by Crivelli. Further up the hill is the **Museo Archeologico Nazionale delle Marche** (Tues–Sun 8.30am–7.30pm; €2.10), worth a visit for its frescoed ceilings by Tibaldi and a magnificent first-century gilded bronze sculpture of two Roman emperors on horseback.

The main **tourist office** for Ancona and the Marche region is at Via Thaon de Revel 4 (Mon–Fri 9am–2pm & 3–6pm, Sat 9am–1pm & 3–6pm, Sun 9am–1pm; July open til 7.30pm; ☎071.358.991, *www.marcheturismo.it*). Tickets for **ferries to Greece** are on sale at the Stazione Maríttima, as well as at the numerous agencies that line the road to the port; most operators run services to Igoumenitsa, Corfu and Patras. There are also three weekly **ferries to Croatia** (Split). The main operators are Superfast, whose offices are at Via XXIX Settembre 2 (☎071.202.033 or 071.202.805, *www.superfast.com*) and Minoan Lines at Via Astagno 1 (☎071.201.708 or 071.56.789, *www.ferries.gr/minoan*). In peak season ferries to Greece tend to run at least daily, two to four times a week at other times of the year. As most ferry departures are at night, you're unlikely to need to stay over in Ancona. However, if you do, the most convenient **hotels** are opposite the train station – the *Dorico*, Via Flaminia 8 (☎071.42.761; ③) and the *Gino*, Via Flaminia 4 (☎071.42.179; ④), the latter offering a good-value restaurant. **Bars** and **pizzerias** are plentiful along the port, otherwise *Osteria del Pozzo*, in the old town on Via Bonda (closed Sun), and *Osteria Teatro Strabacco* (closed Mon) at Via Oberdan 2, off Piazza Cavour, are both good for seafood dishes.

ROME

Of all Italy's historic cities, it's **ROME** that exerts the most compelling fascination. There's arguably more to see here than in any other city in the world, with the relics of more than two thousand years of continuous occupation packed into its sprawling urban area; and as a contemporary European capital, it has a feel that is quite unique. Rome is, in many ways, the ideal capital of Italy, perfectly placed between Italy's warring north and south factions and heartily despised by both. For the traveller, it is the sheer weight of history in the city that is most evident, its various eras crowding in on each other to an almost breathtaking degree. There are the classical features – the Colosseum, the rubbly Forum and Palatine Hill – and relics from the early Christian period in ancient basilicas; while the fountains and churches of the Baroque period go a long way to determining the look of the city centre. But these are just part of the picture, which is an almost continuous one right up to the present day, taking in Romanesque churches, Renaissance palazzi, Rococo fountains and the ponderous buildings of post-Unification, often all found within a few paces of each other.

Rome is not an easy place to absorb on one visit, and you need to approach things slowly, taking care not to try to see too much too quickly, even if you only have a few days here. On foot it's easy to lose a sense of direction in the twisting old streets, and in any case you're so likely to see something interesting that detours and stopoffs are inevitable. Stout, comfortable shoes and loose, cool clothes – Rome can get very sticky in summer – will be your greatest assets. Now is a good time to visit the Eternal City – after several years of neglect, many of Rome's monuments were finally restored in preparation for the *Giubileo* celebrations that took place in the year 2000. How long some of the more rushed renovations will last is anybody's guess – but in the meantime Rome looks better than ever.

Arrival and information

Travelling by train, you arrive at the central **Stazione Termini**, meeting-point of the metro lines and city bus routes. Rome has two **airports**: Leonardo da Vinci, better known as **Fiumicino**, which handles all scheduled flights, and Ciampino, where charter flights land. Two train services link Fiumicino to Rome: one leaves every hour and arrives at Termini (€9.30), the other leaves every twenty minutes and links Fiumicino with Trastevere, Ostiense and Tiburtina stations (€4.70). At night (1.15–5am) you can catch a train to Stazione Tiburtina (€4.40); nightbus #42 connects Tiburtina with Termini. A taxi will cost at least €40. From **Ciampino**, take a Cotral bus to Anagnina on metro line A (€0.80), from where it's a twenty-minute ride to Terminion on the metro (€0.80). Taxis cost around €30.

Rome's **Tourist Call Centre** (daily 9am–7pm; ☎06.3600.4399) is the best place to contact for up-to-the-minute information in five languages on anything from opening hours, prices to directions. There are **tourist information** booths at Fiumicino airport (Mon–Sat 8am–7pm; ☎06.65951) and at Termini (daily 9am–9pm), though heavy queues mean you're usually better off heading straight for the **main office** at Via Parigi 5 (Mon–Sat 9am–7pm; ☎06.4889.9253). They can help with accommodation, give out free maps, general information, and the *Musei e Monumenti* pamphlet which gives a listing of visitable sites. There are also information kiosks dotted around the city, open from 9am–6pm. The privately run and very helpful **Enjoy Rome** tourist information service near the station at Via Marghera 8a (Mon–Fri 8.30am–7pm, Sat 8.30am–2pm; ☎06.445.1843, *www.enjoyrome.com*) has a free hotel booking scheme, publishes a handy free guide and a monthly magazine, and runs bus, bike and walking tours which take in the essential sights of Rome. Two good **Web sites** on Rome are *www.romeguide.it* and *www.romaonline.net*.

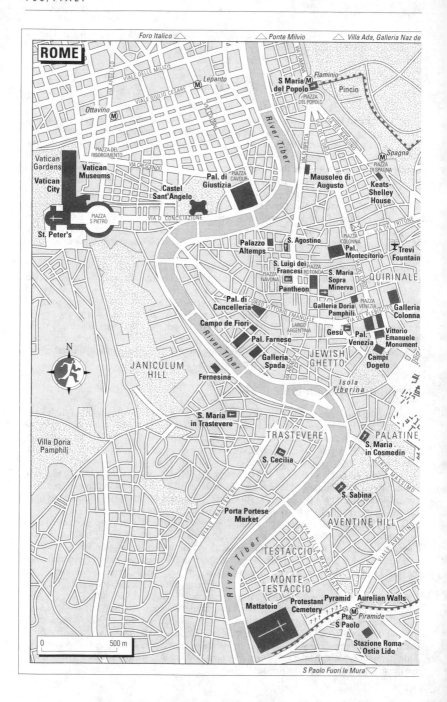

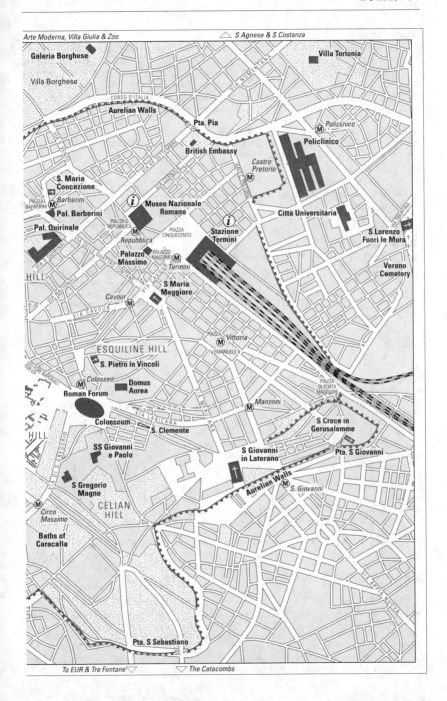

Galeria Borghese

Villa Torlonia

Villa Borghese

CORSO D'ITALIA

Aurelian Walls

Pta. Pia

Policlinico

Policlinico

British Embassy

Castro Pretorio

S. Maria Concezione

Barberini

Pal. Barberini

PIAZZA BARBERINI

Museo Nazionale Romano

Città Universitaria

Pal. Quirinale

PIAZZA D. REPUBBLICA

Repubblica

Stazione Termini

S Lorenzo Fuori le Mura

PIAZZA CINQUECENTO

Palazzo Massimo

PALAZZO MASSIMO

Verano Cemetery

HILL

Termini

S Maria Maggiore

Cavour

ESQUILINE HILL

PIAZZA Vittoria V. EMANUELE II

S. Pietro in Vincoli

VIA CAVOUR

VIA NAZIONALE

Colosseo

Domus Aurea

Roman Forum

PIAZZA DI PORTA MAGGIORE

Colosseum

Manzoni

S. Clemente

S Croce in Gerusalemme

SS Giovanni e Paolo

S Giovanni in Laterano

Pta. S Giovanni

S Gregorio Magno

Aurelian Walls

S. Giovanni

HILL

CELIAN HILL

Circo Massimo

Baths of Caracalla

Pta. S Sebastiano

City transport

As in most Italian cities, the best way to get around Rome is to **walk**. That said, its **bus** service, run by ATAC, is a good one – cheap, reliable and as quick as the clogged streets allow. Linking the major sites, there are also now the privately owned **J buses,** which cost more than the city buses (€1) but offer many advantages: less crowding, air-conditioning, and the ability to buy your ticket on board. Rome also has a **metro**, and although it is more directed at ferrying commuters out to the suburbs than transporting tourists around the city centre, there are a few useful stations. If you're planning to cover some ground, note that a single ticket includes all modes of public transport (ATAC bus, metro A and B and one-way urban trains), and is valid for 75 minutes and costs €0.80; a book of eleven tickets costs €7.80. A day pass (BIG) valid for 24 hours costs €3.10 and a weekly pass (CIS) costs €12.40. You can buy these from the ATAC booth on Piazza dei Cinquecento, where they also sell decent transport maps for €0.50. The buses and the metro stop around 11.30pm, after which a network of **night buses** clicks into service, serving most parts of the city until about 5.30am. **Taxis** are fairly costly; hail one in the street, or try the ranks at Termini, Piazza Venezia, Piazza San Silvestro; alternatively call ☎06.3570, 06.4494 or 06.6645 to book one. The meter should start at €2.40.

Accommodation

In summer Rome is as crowded as you might expect, and although the city's huge number of **hotels and hostels** offers a vast capacity for absorbing visitors, you should book in advance if you can; if you can't, make straight for the tourist office or Enjoy Rome (see p.795) to save your legs. Many of the city's cheaper hotels are handily located close to Stazione Termini, and you could do worse than hole up in one of these: the streets both sides of the station square are stacked full of cheap places. If you want to stay somewhere more central, there are hotels in the *centro storico*, some of them not that expensive, but again be warned that they might be full during the summer.

HOSTELS

Hostel Alessandro, Via Vicenza 42 (☎06.446.1958, *www.hostelalessandro.com*). Friendly, international staff, full use of kitchen, free beverages. In a pleasant area near Termini. No curfew. ②.

Colors, Via Boezio 31 (☎06.687.4030). Run by the Enjoy Rome crowd and located in Prati, near St Peter's. Clean, friendly and excellent value for money, offering Internet access and use of the kitchen and the terrace. No curfew, no lockout. Dorm beds, ③; rooms with bath, ⑤.

Fawlty Towers, Via Magenta 39 (☎06.445.4802). Near the station, efficient, clean, with all amenities, including Internet, kitchen use, satellite TV. No curfew, no lockout. ③.

Ostello del Foro Italico, Viale delle Olimpiadi 61 (☎06.324.2571). Rome's HI hostel is vast though not especially central. Take bus #492 or metro line A from Termini to Ottaviano, then bus #32. Breakfast included. Midnight curfew. ②.

M&J Place Hostel, Via Solferino 9 (☎06.446.2802, *www.mejplacehostel.com*). Just out of the station and to the right; facilities include kitchen, laundry and Internet access. No curfew. ②.

Hotel Ottaviano, Via Ottaviano 6 (☎06.3973.7253). Excellently situated private hotel/hostel, just outside the Vatican walls. Friendly, helpful staff, satellite TV and use of Internet. Take Metro line A from Termini to Ottaviano. No curfew. ②.

Hotel Sandy, Via Cavour 136 (☎06.488.4585). Young people's hotel/hostel accommodation. Good value central location between the station and the Colosseum. Internet use. No curfew. Metro Cavour. ②.

YWCA, Via C. Balbo 4 (☎06.488.3917). For all travellers, and much more conveniently situated than the HI hostel; ten minutes' walk from Termini. Breakfast included; midnight curfew. ⑤.

HOTELS

Abruzzi, Piazza della Rotonda 69 (☎06.679.2021). Bang in front of the Pantheon, and as such you pay for the location. ⑤.

Alimandi, Via Tunisi 8 (☎06.397.23941, *alimandi@tin.it*). Close to the Vatican with good facilities. Breakfast included. Metro Ottaviano or Cipro. ⑨.

Campo de' Fiori, Via del Biscione 6 (☎06.6880.6865). Friendly, clean, colourful, in a great location; the roof terrace has beautiful views over this medieval quarter. ⑥.

Capitol, Via G. Amendola 85 (☎06.488.2617, *h.capitol@inwind.it*). Comfortable hotel close to the station. Breakfast included. ⑥.

Della Lunetta, Piazza del Paradiso 68 (☎06.686.1080). Close to Campo dei Fiori, an unspectacular hotel in a great location. ⑤.

Di Rienzo, Via Principe Amedeo 79a (☎06.446.7131). Spacious clean rooms within spitting distance of the train station. ④.

Katty, Via Palestro 35 (☎06.490.079). One of the cheaper, pleasanter options east of the station. ④.

Kennedy, Via F. Turati 62–4 (☎06.446.5373, *hotelkennedy@micanet.it*). Well kept place, with young management, next to the sation. ⑦.

Marsala, Via Marsala 36 (☎06.444.1262, *hotelmarsala@iol.it*). Pleasant, clean hotel 50m from the station. ⑤.

Monaco, Via Flavia 84 (☎06.474.4335). Very welcoming and clean; between the station and Via Veneto. ④.

Navona, Via dei Sediari 8 (☎06.686.4203, *navona@posta2000.com*). Perfectly placed *pensione* run by a friendly Italian-Australian couple. Metro Colosseo. ⑥.

Perugia, Via del Colosseo 7 (☎06.679.7200). On a peaceful but central street. Breakfast included. Metro Colosseo. ⑤.

Prati, Via Crescenzio 89 (☎06.687.5357, *info@hotelprati-roma.com*). Two-star hotel across on the Vatican side of the river with a nice, family-run feel. Metro Ottaviano. ⑥.

Rosetta, Via Cavour 295 (☎06.4782.3069, *hotel_rosetta@iol.it*). Nice location close to the Colosseum. Metro Colosseo. ⑤.

Smeraldo, Via dei Chiodaroli 11 (☎06.687.5929). Popular place with lovely doubles. ⑦.

Sole, Via del Biscione 76 (☎06.6880.6873, *sole@italyhotel.com*). Near Piazza del Campo dei Fiori, one of the nicest city-centre locations. ④.

Trastevere, Via L. Manara 24a/25 (☎06.581.4713). In the heart of this busy medieval district; clean and inviting. ⑤. Apartments with kitchens also available. ⑨.

CAMPSITES

Camping Flaminio, Via Flaminia Nuova (☎06.333.2604). 8km north of the city; bus #202, #204 or #205 or the tram from Piazzale Flaminio (Metro line A) to Piazza Mancini, then take bus #200. March–Oct.

Camping Tiber, Via Tiburina Km1400 (☎06.3361.0733). Free shuttle service every 10 minutes with Prima Porta station which has train connections to Piazzale Flaminio Station (train F1; about 20 min). March–Oct.

The City

Piazza Venezia is a good central place to start your wanderings, flanked by the **Palazzo di Venezia** and overlooked by the hideous **Vittorio Emanuele Monument** or Altar of the Nation, erected at the turn of the twentieth century to commemorate Unification. Behind, the **Capitoline Hill**, formerly the spiritual and political centre of the Roman Empire, is home to one of Rome's most elegant squares, **Piazza del Campidoglio**, designed by Michelangelo in the 1550s for Pope Paul III, and flanked by the two branches of one of the city's most important museums of antique art – the **Capitoline Museums** (Mon–Fri & Sun 9.30am–7pm, Sat 9.30am–11pm; €7.80). On the left, the **Palazzo Nuovo** concentrates some of the best of the city's Roman and Greek sculpture into half a dozen or so rooms. There's a remarkable, controlled statue of the *Dying Gaul*, a Roman copy of a Hellenistic original; an original grappling depiction of *Eros and Psyche*; a *Satyr Resting*, after a piece by Praxiteles; and the red marble *Laughing Satyr*, another Roman copy of a Greek original. Walk through to the so-called Sala degli Imperatori, with its busts of Roman emperors and other famous names, and don't miss the coy *Capitoline Venus*, housed in a room on its own, again based on a work by Praxiteles. The same ticket will get you into the **Palazzo dei Conservatori** across the square, a larger, more varied collection, with more ancient sculpture, including the exquisite *Spinario* – a Hellenistic work from the first century BC showing a boy plucking a thorn from his foot – and the sacred Roman statue of the she-wolf suckling the twins, thought to be originally an Etruscan work. The second floor holds Renaissance painting – numerous works by Reni and Tintoretto, a vast picture by Guercino that used to hang in St Peter's, some nice small-scale work by Annibale Carracci, an early work by Ludovico Carracci, *Head of a Boy*, and Caravaggio's *St John the Baptist*. Behind the square, a road skirts the Forum down to the small church of **San Giuseppe dei Falegnami**, built above the prison where St Peter is said to have been held – you can see the bars to which he was chained, along with the spring the saint is said to have created to baptize other prisoners here, and, at the top of the staircase, an imprint claimed to be of St Peter's head as he was tumbled down the stairs.

Via del Plebiscito forges west from Piazza Venezia past the church of **Gesù**, a high, wide Baroque church of the Jesuit order that has served since as the model for Jesuit churches everywhere. Still well patronized, it's notable for its size (the left transept is surmounted by the largest single piece of lapis lazuli in existence) and the richness of its interior, especially the paintings of Baciccia in the dome and the ceiling's ingenious trompe l'oeil, which oozes out of its frame in a tangle of writhing bodies, flowing drapery and stucco angels. Crossing over, streets tangle down to **Piazza di Campo de' Fiori**, Rome's most appealing and unpretentious square, home to a morning market and surrounded by restaurants and bars. South of the Campo, at the end of Via dei Balestrari, the **Galleria Spada** (Tues–Sat 8.30am–7.30pm, Sun 8.30am–6.30pm; €5.20) is decorated in the manner of a Roman noble family and displays a small collection of paintings, best of which are a couple of portraits by Reni. To the left off the courtyard is a crafty trompe l'oeil tunnel by Borromini, whose trick perspective makes it appear to be about four times its actual length. Across Via Arenula through and beyond the Ghetto, the broad open space of **Piazza della Bocca di Verità** is home to two of the city's better-preserved Roman temples, the **Temple of Fortuna Virilis** and the circular **Temple of Hercules Victor**, both of which date from the end of the second century BC, though the church of **Santa Maria in Cosmedin**, on the far side of the square, is more interesting, a typically Roman medieval basilica with a huge marble altar and surround and a colourful and ingenious Cosmati mosaic floor – one of the city's finest. Outside in the portico, the **Bocca di Verità** ("Mouth of Truth") gives the square its name, an ancient Roman drain cover in the shape of an enormous face that in medieval times would apparently swallow the hand of anyone who hadn't told the truth.

The Centro Storico

You need to walk a little way northwest from the Capitoline Hill to find the real city centre of Rome, the **Centro Storico**, a roughly triangular knob of land that bulges into a bend in the Tiber, above Corso Vittorio Emanuele. The old Campus Martius of Roman times, it later became the heart of the Renaissance city, and is now an unruly knot of narrow streets holding some of the best of Rome's classical and Baroque heritage, and its street- and nightlife.

The boundary of the historic centre to the east, **Via del Corso**, is Rome's main street, holding some of its principal shops and cutting straight through the heart of the city centre. Walking north from Piazza Venezia, the first building on the left is the **Galleria Doria Pamphili** (10am–5pm; closed Thurs & Aug 15–31; €7.30), one of many galleries housed in palaces belonging to Roman patrician families. Its collection includes Rome's best cache of Dutch and Flemish paintings, canvases by Caravaggio and Velázquez's painting of Pope Innocent X. The second left after the palace leads into Piazza Sant'Ignazio, an odd little square dominated by the church of **Sant'Ignazio**, which has a marvellous ceiling by Pozzo showing the entry of St Ignatius into paradise, employing sledgehammer trompe l'oeil effects, notably in the mock cupola painted into the dome of the crossing. Stand on the disc in the centre of the nave for the truest sense of the ingenious rendering of perspective.

Through Via di Seminario from here and you're standing in front of the **Pantheon** (Mon–Sat 9am–6.30pm, Sun 9am–1pm; free) on Piazza della Rotonda, the most complete ancient Roman structure in the city, finished around 125 AD. A formidable architectural achievement even now, its dome still has the second widest diameter in Rome. Inside, the diameter of the dome and height of the building are precisely equal, and the hole in the dome's centre is a full 9m across; there are no visible arches or vaults to hold the whole thing up; instead, they're sunk into the concrete of the walls of the building. It would have been richly decorated, the coffered ceiling heavily stuccoed and the niches filled with statues of the gods. Now, apart from the sheer size of the place, the main thing of interest is the tomb of Raphael, inscribed by the writer and priest Bembo: "Living, great Nature feared he might outvie Her works, and dying, fears herself may die."

There's more artistic splendour on view behind the Pantheon, in the church of **Santa Maria sopra Minerva** (Mon–Sat 7am–7pm, Sun 8am–7pm), one of the city's art-treasure churches, crammed with the tombs and self-indulgences of wealthy Roman families. Of these, the Carafa chapel, in the south transept, is the best known, holding Filippino Lippi's fresco of *The Assumption*, below which one painting shows a hopeful Oliviero Carafa being presented to the Virgin Mary by Thomas Aquinas; another depicts Aquinas confounding the heretics in the sight of two beautiful young boys – the future Medici popes Leo X and Clement VII. You should look, too, at the figure of *Christ Bearing the Cross*, on the left-hand side of the main altar, a serene work that Michelangelo completed in 1521 especially for the church.

In the opposite direction from the Pantheon, **Piazza Navona** is in many ways the central square of Rome, an almost entirely enclosed space fringed with cafés and restaurants that follows the lines of the Emperor Domitian's chariot arena, whose overgrown ruins survived here until the mid-fifteenth century. The square was given a face-lift in the mid-seventeenth century by Pope Innocent X, who built most of the grandiose palaces that surround it and commissioned Borromini to design the church of **Sant'Agnese** on the west side. The church, typically squeezed into the tightest of spaces by Borromini, supposedly stands on the spot where St Agnes, exposed naked to the public in the stadium, miraculously grew hair to cover herself. The **Fontana dei Quattro Fiumi** opposite, one of three that punctuate the square, is by Borromini's arch-rival, Bernini; each figure represents one of the four great rivers of the world – the Nile, Danube, Ganges and Plate – though only the horse, symbolizing the Danube, was actually carved by Bernini himself.

Just out of the north end of the piazza, you'll find **Palazzo Altemps** (Tues–Sat 9am–7pm, Sun 9am–6pm; €5.20), functioning as part of the Museo Nazionale Romano and featuring the unmissable ancient statuary collected by the Ludovisi family. The highlight is the original fifth-century-BC Greek throne, embellished with a delicate relief of the birth of Aphrodite.

East of Altemps, the Renaissance facade of the church of **Sant'Agostino** is not much to look at but the church's handful of art treasures might draw you in – among them Raphael's vibrant *Isaiah*, on the third pillar on the left, Sansovino's craggy *St Anne, Virgin and Child*, and, in the first chapel on the left, a *Madonna and Pilgrims* by Caravaggio, which is badly lit, so come prepared with coins for the light box. There's more work by Caravaggio down Via della Scrofa, in the French national church of **San Luigi dei Francesi** (daily except Thurs afternoon 8.30am–12.30pm & 3.30–7pm), in the last chapel on the left: early works, describing the life and martyrdom of St Matthew, best of which is the *Calling of St Matthew* on the left wall – Matthew is the dissolute-looking youth on the far left, illuminated by a shaft of sunlight. A little way up Via della Ripetta from here, the **Ara Pacis Augustae** (closed for restoration) was built in 13 BC to celebrate Augustus' victory over Spain and Gaul. It supports a fragmented frieze showing Augustus himself, his wife Livia, Tiberius, Agrippa, and various children clutching the togas of the elders, the last of whom is said to be the young Claudius.

At the far end of Via di Ripetta the **Piazza del Popolo** provides an impressive entrance to the city, all symmetry and grand vistas, although its real attraction is the church of **Santa Maria del Popolo** (daily 7am–noon & 4–7pm), which holds some of the best Renaissance art of any Roman church, including frescoes by Pinturicchio in the south aisle and two fine tombs by Andrea Sansovino. The second chapel in the northern aisle, the Chigi chapel, was designed by Raphael for Antonio Chigi in 1516 – though most of the work was accomplished by other artists and not finished until the seventeenth century. Michelangelo's protégé, Sebastiano del Piombo, was responsible for the altarpiece; the two sculptures in the corner niches of Daniel and Habakkuk are by Bernini. Two pictures by Caravaggio get most attention – one, the *Conversion of St Paul*, showing Paul and horse bathed in a beatific radiance, the other, the *Crucifixion of St Peter*, showing Peter as an aged figure, dominated by the muscular figures hoisting him up.

Villa Borghese

At the northern edge of the city centre, the **Villa Borghese** (Metro Flaminio or Spagna), now beautifully restored, is made up of the grounds of the seventeenth-century palace of Cardinal Scipione Borghese – a vast area, whose woods, lakes and grass are about as near as you can get to a tranquil spot in Rome. Apart from the peace, the main attraction is the **Galleria Borghese** (Tues–Sat 9am–7pm, Sun 9am–5pm; €7.30), with an assortment of works collected by Scipione Borghese. The ground floor contains sculptures, where the work of Bernini, a protégé of Borghese, dominates: there's an *Aeneas and Anchises*, carved with his father when he was fifteen; an ingenious *Rape of Proserpine*, amid busts of Roman emperors; his dramatic *Apollo and Daphne*; and, in the next room, his *David* – a self-portrait.

The Villa Borghese's two other major museums are on the other side of the park, along the Viale delle Belle Arti. Of these, the **Galleria Nazionale d'Arte Moderna** (Tues–Sat 9am–10pm, Sun 9am–8pm; shorter winter hours; €5.20) is probably the least compelling, housing a wide selection of nineteenth- and twentieth-century Italian names, most undistinguished; artists you might recognize include Modigliani, Di Chirico, Boccione and other Futurists, along with the odd Cézanne, Mondrian and Klimt. The **Villa Giulia**, ten minutes away, is more of an essential stop, a collection of courtyards, loggias and gardens that is home to the **Museo Nazionale di Villa Giulia** (Tues–Sat 9am–7pm, Sun 9am–1.30pm; €4.20) – the world's primary collection of Etruscan treasures. Best among the sculpture is the group of *Apollo and Hercules*, from the site of Veio, north of Rome, and the remarkable *Sarcophagus of a Married Couple* from Cerveteri. Other highlights include the *Cistae* recovered from tombs around Praeneste – drum-like objects, engraved and adorned with figures, that were supposed to hold all the things needed for the care of the body after death – and marvellously intricate pieces of gold jewellery, delicately worked into tiny animals.

East of Via del Corso

The area immediately southeast of Piazza del Popolo is travellers' Rome, historically the artistic quarter of the city, for which eighteenth- and nineteenth-century Grand Tourists would make, lending the area a distinctly cosmopolitan air, even today. At the centre of the district, **Piazza di Spagna** is a long, thin square centring on the distinctive boat-shaped **Barcaccia** fountain, the last work of Bernini's father. Opposite, the Keats-Shelley Memorial House (Mon–Fri 9am–1pm & 3–6pm, Sat 11am–6pm; €2.60), where John Keats died in 1821, now serves as an archive of English-language literary and historical works and a museum of literary mementoes. Beside the house, the **Spanish Steps** – a venue for international posing and fast pick-ups late into the summer nights – sweep up to the **Trinità dei Monti**, a largely sixteenth-century church that holds a couple of works by Daniel da Volterra, notably a soft flowing fresco of *The Assumption* in the third chapel on the right, which includes a portrait of his teacher Michelangelo. His *Deposition*, across the nave, is also worth a glance; it was painted from a series of cartoons by Michelangelo.

From the church, follow Via Sistina to **Piazza Barberini**, a busy traffic junction, in the centre of which is Bernini's **Fontana del Tritone**. **Via Veneto** bends north from here, its pricey bars and restaurants once the haunt of Rome's Beautiful People but now home of high-class tack and overpriced sleaze. A little way up, the Capuchin **Church of the Immaculate Conception** is not particularly notable, but is worth visiting for its Cemetery (9am–noon & 3–6pm, closed Thurs; donation requested), one of the more macabre sights of Rome, somewhere between the chilling and the ludicrous; the bones of four thousand monks coat the walls of a series of chapels in rococo patterns or as fully clothed skeletons, their faces peering out of their cowls in expressions of agony.

Retracing your steps back across **Piazza Barberini**, the Palazzo Barberini is home to the **Galleria d'Arte Antica** (Tues–Sat 9am–7pm, Sun 9am–8pm; closes in winter; €6.20), which displays a rich patchwork of mainly Italian art from the early Renaissance to late Baroque period. In addition to canvases by Tintoretto, Titian and El Greco, highlights include Filippo Lippi's warmly maternal *Madonna and Child*, painted in 1437, and Raphael's beguiling

Fornarina. But perhaps the most impressive feature of the gallery is the building itself, the epitome of Baroque grandeur worked on at different times by the most favoured architects of the day: Bernini, Borromini and Maderno. The Salone is guaranteed to impress, its ceiling frescoed by Pietro da Cortona in one of the best examples of exuberant Baroque trompe l'oeil work, a manic rendering of *The Triumph of Divine Providence* that almost crawls down the walls.

East down Via del Tritone from Piazza Barberini, hidden among a tight web of narrow, apparently aimless streets, is one of Rome's more surprising sights, easy to stumble upon by accident – the **Fontane di Trevi**, a huge Baroque gush of water over statues and rocks built onto the backside of a Renaissance palace. Originally commissioned from Bernini by Pope Urban VIII, it wasn't begun until Niccolo Salvi took up the project in 1723. The Trevi fountain is now, of course, the place you come to chuck in a coin if you want to guarantee your return to Rome, and it's one of the city's most vigorous outdoor spots for visitors to hang out of an evening. A short stroll directly south from here brings you to the **Galleria Colonna**, Via della Pilotta 17 (Sat 9am–1pm; closed Aug; €5.20), worth forty minutes or so if only for the chandelier-decked Great Hall, where a display of paintings includes Carracci's early *Bean Eater*, a *Narcissus* by Tintoretto, and a *Portrait of a Venetian Gentleman* caught in supremely confident pose by Veronese.

Five minutes from the gallery, **Via Nazionale**, one of Rome's main shopping streets, lined with boutiques, leads up to **Piazza della Repubblica**, a stern but rather tawdry semicircle of buildings that occupies part of the site of Diocletian's Baths, the scanty remains of which lie across the square in the church of **Santa Maria degli Angeli**. This is a huge, open building, with an interior standardized after a couple of centuries of piecemeal adaptation (started by an aged Michelangelo) by Vanvitelli in a rich eighteenth-century confection. The pink granite pillars are, however, original, and the main transept formed the main hall of the baths – though only the crescent shape of the facade remains from the original caldarium. Michelangelo is also said to have had a hand in modifying another part of the baths, the courtyard that makes up part of the **Museo Nazionale Romano** behind the church (closed for restoration). The museum's collection of Greek and Roman antiquities is second only to the Vatican's and is now partly housed in the Palazzo Altemps (see p.801) and the **Palazzo Massimo** (Tues–Sat 9am–10pm, Sun 9am–8pm; €6.20), across the square at Piazza dei Cinquecento 68, a recently restored air-conditioned building featuring on the ground floor a series of Roman busts, mosaics and fresco fragments. The top floor gallery contains, among other treasures, stunning, sylvan frescoes from a country villa that belonged to the emperor Augustus's wife Livia, and some of the best examples of mosaics from Roman villas around the world. Close by on Via XX Settembre, the church of **Santa Maria della Vittoria** was built by Carlo Maderno and its interior is one of the most elaborate examples of Baroque decoration in Rome, its ceiling and walls pitted with carving, and statues crammed into remote corners like an overstuffed attic. The church's best-known feature is Bernini's melodramatic carving of the *Ecstasy of St Theresa*, the centrepiece of the sepulchral chapel of Cardinal Cornaro.

Southeast of Piazza Venezia

From Piazza Venezia **Via dei Fori Imperiali** cuts south, a soulless boulevard whose main pedestrians are tourists rooting about among the ancient sites. Just off Piazza Venezia, **Trajan's Column** was erected to celebrate the emperor's colonization of Dacia (modern-day Romania), and its reliefs illustrate the highlights of the Dacian campaign. Across the road is the main part of the **Roman Forum and Palatine Hill** (Tues–Sat 9am–3/6pm, Sun 9am–1pm; €6.20; forum area free; Metro Colosseo), in ancient times the centre of what was a very large city. Following the downfall of the city to various barbarian invaders, the area was left in ruin, its relics quarried for construction in other parts of Rome during medieval and Renaissance times. Excavation of the site didn't start until the beginning of the nineteenth century, since when it has been pretty much continuous: you'll notice a fair part of the site closed off for further digs.

Running through the core of the Forum, the **Via Sacra** was the best-known street of ancient Rome. At the bottom of the Capitoline hill, the **Arch of Septimus Severus** was built in the early third century AD to commemorate the emperor's tenth anniversary in power, and the grassy, wide-open scatter of paving and beached columns in front of it was the place where most of the life of the city was carried on. Nearby, the **Curia** is one of the few whole structures here, a huge barn-like building that was begun in 80 BC, restored by Julius Caesar soon after and rebuilt by Diocletian in the third century AD. The Senate met here during the Republican period, and augurs would come to announce the wishes of the gods. On the opposite side is the **House of the Vestal Virgins**, where the six women charged with the responsibility of keeping the sacred flame of Vesta alight lived: four floors of rooms around a central courtyard, with the round **Temple of Vesta** at the near end. On the far side of the site, the **Basilica of Constantine and Maxentius** is, in terms of size and ingenuity, probably the Forum's most impressive remains. It's said that Michelangelo studied the hexagonal coffered arches here when grappling with the dome of St Peter's. From the basilica, the Via Sacra climbs to the **Arch of Titus** on a low arm of the Palatine Hill – its reliefs showing the spoils of the sacking of Jerusalem being carried off by eager Romans. Just to the north left of the arch is the Forum Museum (Antiquarium Forense) – a small collection of Iron Age burial urns and pre-Roman artefacts.

Turning right at the Arch of Titus takes you up to the **Palatine Hill**, a pleasanter and greener site than the Forum. In the days of the Republic, the Palatine was the most desirable address in Rome (from it is derived our word "palace"), and the big names continued to colonize it during the imperial era, trying to outdo each other with ever larger and more magnificent dwellings. The gargantuan **Domus Augustana** spreads to the far brink of the hill. You can look down from here onto its vast central courtyard and maze-like fountain, and wander through a handful of its bare rooms. From close by, steps lead down to the **Cryptoporticus**, a passage built by Nero to link the Palatine with his palace on the far side of the Colosseum, and decorated along part of its length with well-preserved Roman stuccowork. A left turn leads to the **House of Livia**, originally believed to have been the residence of the wife of Augustus, whose courtyard and rooms are decorated with scanty frescoes. Turn right down the passage and up some steps and you're in the **Farnese Gardens**, among the first botanical gardens in Europe, laid out by Alessandro Farnese in the mid-sixteenth century and now a tidily planted refuge from the exposed heat of the ruins. The terrace here looks back over the Forum, while the terrace at the opposite end looks down on the real centre of Rome's ancient beginning – an Iron Age hut, known as the **House of Romulus**, that is the best preserved of a ninth-century Iron Age village discovered here, and the so-called **Lupercal**, beyond, which is traditionally believed to be the cave where Romulus and Remus were suckled by the she-wolf.

Immediately outside the Forum site, the fourth-century **Arch of Constantine** marks the end of the Via Sacra. Across from here, the **Colosseum** (Tues–Sat 9am–3/6pm, Sun 9am–7pm; €5.20) is Rome's most awe-inspiring ancient monument, begun by the Emperor Vespasian around 72 AD and finished by his son Titus about eight years later – an event celebrated by one hundred days of continuous games. The Romans flocked here for gladiatorial contests and other equally cruel spectacles that pitted man against animal, animal against animal – scenes recently dramatized in the film *Gladiator*. They even had mock sea battles – the arena could be flooded in minutes. After the games were outlawed in the fifth century, the Colosseum was pillaged over the centuries for building stone, and is now little more than a shell. But the basic structure of the place is easy to see, and has served as a model for stadia around the world ever since.

One of the **Esquiline Hill**'s most intriguing sights is Nero's **Domus Aurea** or "Golden House" (daily 9am–8pm, guided tours obligatory; €5.20, plus €3.10 for the tour, €1.10 reservation fee; booking recommended, ☎06.3974.9907). The entrance is opposite the Colosseum, off Via Labicana, a short walk up some steps on the Oppian Hill. The facade was said to have been coated in solid gold, the whole complex covered a full square mile, and its extravagant halls were decorated in the most lavish style: masterful frescoes and carved stucco painted in rich colours, and gold, everywhere gold. Much of the rich decoration is still intact and you can wander around the vast, vaulted rooms. When the site was first discovered, it was thought to be some sort of mystical cave, or grotto – giving us the word *grotesque*, originally meaning "grotto-like" in reference to the weird and wonderful images found here.

It's a short walk from here down Via San Giovanni in Laterano to the church of **San Clemente**, a light, twelfth-century basilica that encapsulates better than any other the continuity of history in the city. It's in fact a conglomeration of three places of worship. The ground-floor church is a superb example of a medieval basilica, with some fine mosaics in the apse. Downstairs (Mon–Sat 9am–12.30pm & 3–6pm, Sun opens 10am; €2.10), there's the nave of an earlier church, dated back to 392 AD. And at the eastern end and down another level of this church, are the remains of a Roman apartment building – a labyrinthine set of rooms including a Mithraic temple of the late second century standing next to a first-century imperial block. The same street leads to the basilica **of San Giovanni in Laterano** (daily 7am–7.30pm), Rome's cathedral and the seat of the pope until the Unification of Italy. There has been a church on this site since the fourth century, the first established by Constantine. The present building, reworked by Borromini in the mid-seventeenth century, evokes Rome's staggering wealth of history. The doors were taken from the Curia of the Roman Forum. Inside, the first pillar on the left of the right-hand aisle shows a fragment of Giotto's fresco of Boniface VIII, proclaiming the first Holy Year in 1300, while further on, a more recent monument commemorates Sylvester I, bishop of Rome during much of Constantine's reign, and incorporates part of his original tomb, said to sweat and rattle its bones when a pope is about to die. Kept secure behind the papal altar are the reliquaries for the heads of St Peter and St Paul, though the relics themselves are said to have been stolen in the early 1800s. Outside, the cloisters (€2.10) are one of the most pleasing parts of the complex, decorated with early thirteenth-century Cosmati work. Next door to the church, the **Baptistry** is the oldest surviving Baptistry in the Christian world, an octagonal structure built by Constantine, rebuilt during the fifth century, and now carefully restored after a 1993 car bomb damaged the stonework and some of the frescoes. On the other side of the church the **Scala Santa** is claimed to be the staircase from Pontius Pilate's house down which Christ walked after his trial. The 28 steps are protected by boards, and the only way you're allowed to climb them is on your knees – which pilgrims do regularly.

On the far side of the road from the Colosseum, the main feature of interest on the Esquiline Hill is the church of **San Pietro in Vincoli**, one of Rome's most delightfully plain churches, built to house an important relic: the chains of St Peter from his imprisonment in Jerusalem, along with those that bound him when a prisoner in Rome. These can still be seen in the glass case on the altar, but most people come for Michelangelo's unfinished Tomb of Pope Julius II in the southern aisle. The figure of Moses, pictured as descended from Sinai to find the Israelites worshipping the golden calf, and flanked by the gentle figures of Leah and Rachel, is one of the artist's most arresting works. Steps lead down from San Pietro to **Via Cavour**, a busy central thoroughfare which carves a route up to Termini past the basilica of **Santa Maria Maggiore** (daily 7am–6/7pm), one of the city's four great basilicas, with a broad nave fringed on both sides with strikingly well-kept mosaics, most of which date from the church's construction and tell of incidents from the Old Testament. The Sistine chapel, on the right, holds the elaborate tomb of Sixtus V, while the equally fancy Pauline chapel opposite has a venerated twelfth-century *Madonna* topped with a panel showing the legendary tracing of the church's plan after a miraculous August snowfall.

South of the centre

On its southern side, the Palatine Hill drops suddenly down to the **Circo Massimo**, a long green expanse that was the ancient city's main venue for chariot races. The arena could apparently hold a crowd of around two hundred thousand betting punters, and if it was still even half intact could no doubt have matched the Colosseum for grandeur. As it is, a litter of stones at the Viale Aventino end is all that remains. Across the far side of Piazza di Porta Capena, the **Baths of Caracalla** (Mon & Sun 9am–1pm, Tues–Sat 9am–3/6pm; €4.20) are better preserved, and give a much better sense of the scale of Roman architecture than most of the ruins in the city. It's a short walk from behind the baths down Via Gitto to the Protestant Cemetery (Tues–Sun, 9am–5pm; donations expected), accessible direct on metro line B (Piramide stop), the burial place of Keats and Shelley, along with a handful of other well-known names – a small, tranquil enclave, crouched behind the mossy pyramidal tomb of Caius Cestius.

Two kilometres or so south, **San Paolo fuori le Mura** (daily 7.30am–6.30pm) is one of the four patriarchal basilicas of Rome, occupying the supposed site of St Paul's tomb. Of the four, it has probably fared least well over the years, and the church you see is largely a nine-teenth-century reconstruction, which followed a devastating fire. It is a huge, impressive building, and home to a handful of ancient features: in the south transept, the Paschal Candlestick is a remarkable piece of Romanesque carving, supported by half-human beasts and rising through entwined tendrils and strangely human limbs and bodies to scenes from Christ's life; the bronze aisle doors date from 1070, and the Cosmati cloister, just behind here, is probably Rome's finest, its spiralling, mosaic-encrusted columns enclosing a peaceful rose garden.

Further south still, on the edge of the city, the **Via Appia** was the most important of all the Roman trade routes. Its sides are lined with the underground burial cemeteries or **Catacombs** of the first Christians. There are around five complexes in all, dating from the first to the fourth centuries, almost entirely emptied of bodies now but still decorated with the primitive signs and frescoes that were the hallmark of the then-burgeoning Christian movement. You can get to the main grouping on bus #218 from the Colosseum (Via San Gregorio in Laterano), but the only ones of any significance are the catacombs of **San Callisto** (Thurs–Tues 8.30am–noon & 2.30–5pm, closed Nov; €4.20), burial place of all the third-century popes, whose tombs are preserved in the papal crypt, and the site of some well-preserved seventh- and eighth-century frescoes; and those of **San Sebastiano** (daily except Thurs 9am–noon & 2.30–5pm; closed Nov; €4.20), 500m further on, situated under a basili-ca that was originally built by Constantine on the spot where the bodies of the Apostles Peter and Paul are said to have lain for a time. Thirty-minute tours take in paintings of doves and fish, a contemporary carved oil lamp and inscriptions dating the tombs themselves – although the most striking features are three pagan tombs discovered when archeologists were burrowing beneath the floor of the basilica upstairs. The nearby graffiti record the fact that this was indeed, albeit temporarily, where the Apostles Peter and Paul rested.

Trastevere

Across the Tiber from the centre of town, the district of **Trastevere** has traditionally been a place somewhat apart from the rest of the city centre, a small, tightly knit neighbourhood that was formerly the artisan quarter of the city and has since become rather gentrified, home to much of its most vibrant and youthful nightlife – and some of Rome's best and most affordable restaurants. The best time to come is on Sunday morning, when the **Porta Portese** flea market stretches down Via Portuense to Trastevere station in a congested med-ley of antiques, old motor spares, trendy clothing and assorted junk. Afterwards, stroll north up Via Anicia to the church of **Santa Cecilia in Trastevere**, built over the site of the second-century home of the patron saint of music. Locked in the hot chamber of her own baths for several days, she refused to die, singing her way through the ordeal until her head was hacked half off with an axe. At the back of the church you can descend to the excavations of the baths, though hints at restoration have robbed these of any atmosphere. If you get the chance, have a peek at the Singing Gallery's beautifully coloured and tender frescoes by Piero Cavallini (c.1293) (Tues–Thur 10am–noon, Sun 11.30am-12.15pm; donation expected).

Santa Cecilia is situated in the quieter part of Trastevere, on the southern side of Viale Trastevere, the wide boulevard which cuts through the centre of the district. There's more life on the other side centred around **Piazza Santa Maria in Trastevere**, named after the church of **Santa Maria in Trastevere** (daily 9.30am–12.30pm & 4–7pm) – held to be the first official church in Rome, built on a site where a fountain of oil is said to have sprung up on the day of Christ's birth and sporting some of the city's most impressive mosaics, also by Cavallini. North towards the Tiber, the **Villa Farnesina** is known for its Renaissance murals, including a Raphael-designed painting of *Cupid and Psyche*, completed in 1517 by the artist's assistants. Raphael did, however, manage to finish the *Galatea* next door. The other paintings in the room are by Sebastiano del Piombo and the architect of the building, Peruzzi, who also decorated the upstairs Salone delle Prospettive, which shows trompe l'oeil galleries with views of contemporary Rome – one of the earliest examples of the technique.

Castel Sant'Angelo, St Peter's and the Vatican Museums

Across the Tiber from Rome's old centre, the **Castel Sant'Angelo** (Tues–Sat 9am–10pm, Sun 9am–8pm; €6.20; Metro Lepanto) was the burial place of the Emperor Hadrian. In the sixteenth century, the papal authorities converted the building for use as a fortress and built a passageway to link it with the Vatican as a refuge in times of siege. Inside, rooms hold swords, armour, guns and the like, while below, dungeons and storerooms are testament to the castle's grisly past as the city's most notorious Renaissance prison. Upstairs, the official papal apartments, accessible from the terrace, are extravagantly decorated with lewd frescoes amid paintings by Poussin, Jordaens and others.

Via della Conciliazione leads up from here to the **Vatican City** (Metro Cipro), a tiny territory surrounded by high walls on its far side and on the near side opening its doors to the rest of the city and its pilgrims in the form of Bernini's **Piazza San Pietro**, whose two arms extend a symbolic welcome to the lap of the Catholic Church. The basilica of St Peter's (daily 7am–6/7pm; free) is the replacement of a basilica built during the time of Constantine, to a plan initially conceived at the turn of the fifteenth century by Bramante and finished off, heavily modified, over a century later by Carlo Maderno, making it something of a bridge between the Renaissance and Baroque eras. The inside is full of features from the Baroque period, although the first thing you see, on the right, is Michelangelo's *Pietà*, completed when he was just 24 and, following an attack in 1972, displayed behind glass. To the right is the Holy Door, opened by the pope on December 24, 1999 for the Jubilee year; in all other years it remains bricked up. On the right-hand side of the nave, the bronze statue of St Peter was cast in the thirteenth century by Arnolfo di Cambio and has its right foot polished smooth by the attentions of pilgrims. Bronze was also the material used in Bernini's massive 28m-high baldachino, the centrepiece of the sculptor's embellishment of the interior. Bernini's feverish sculpting decorates the apse, too, his *cattedra* enclosing the supposed chair of St Peter in a curvy marble and stucco throne. An entrance off the aisle leads to the **treasury** (daily 9am–5/6pm; €4.20), which, along with more recent additions, holds artefacts left from the earlier church – principally a wall-mounted tabernacle by Donatello, and the massive, though fairly ghastly, late-fifteenth-century bronze tomb of Sixtus IV by Pollaiuolo, which as a portrait is said to be very accurate. Back at the central crossing, steps lead down to the **Vatican Grottoes** (daily: summer 8am–6pm; winter 7am–5pm), where a number of popes are buried in grandiose tombs – in the main, those not distinguished enough to be buried up above. Under the portico, to the right of the main doors, you can ascend to the roof and dome (by lift €4.20) – though you'll probably need to queue – from where the views over the city are as glorious as you'd expect.

A five-minute walk out of the northern side of the piazza takes you up to the only part of the Vatican Palace you can visit independently, the **Vatican Museums** (March–Oct & Dec 20–30 Mon–Fri 8.45am–3.30pm, Sat 8.45am–12.30pm; rest of year Mon–Sat 8.45am–12.30pm; €9.30; also open last Sun of each month 8.45am–3.30pm; free; last ticket issued 1hr before closing) – quite simply the largest, richest, most compelling museum complex in the world, stuffed with booty from every period of the city's history. There's no point in trying to see everything on one visit; you'd do far better to select what you want to see and aim to return another time if you can. It's worth also taking account of the official, colour-coded routes which are constructed for varying amounts of time and interest and can take you anything from 45 minutes to the best part of a day. Bear in mind, too, that the queues are notorious.

Start off at the **Raphael Stanze**, at the opposite end of the building to the entrance, a set of rooms decorated for Pope Julius II by Raphael among others. Of the two most interesting rooms, the **Stanza Eliodoro** is home to the *Expulsion of Heliodorus from the Temple*, an allusion to the military success of Julius II, depicted on the left in portrait. Not to be outdone, Leo X, Julius's successor, in the *Meeting of Atilla and St Leo* opposite, ordered Raphael to substitute his head for that of Julius II, turning the painting into an allegory of the Battle of Ravenna at which he was present; thus he appears twice, as pope and as the equally portly Medici cardinal just behind. In the same room, the *Mass at Bolsena* shows Julius again on the right, pictured in attendance at a famous thirteenth-century miracle in Orvieto (see p.58). The next room, the **Stanza della Segnatura** or pope's study, was decorated between 1512 and 1514, and its *School of Athens*, on the near wall as you come in, is perhaps Raphael's most renowned work, a representation of the "Triumph of Scientific Truth" in which all the great minds from antiquity are present. Plato and Aristotle discuss philosophy in the background, and spread across the steps is Diogenes, lazily ignorant of all that is happening around him; to the right, Raphael cheekily added a solitary, sullen portrait of his rival Michelangelo, who was working practically next door on the Sistine Chapel at the time.

Steps lead down from the Raphael Stanze to the **Sistine Chapel**, a huge barn-like structure, built for Pope Sixtus IV in 1481, which serves as the pope's private chapel and is scene of the conclaves of cardinals for the election of each new pontiff. The **paintings** down each side wall are contemporary with the building, depictions of scenes from the lives of Moses and Christ by Perugino, Botticelli and Ghirlandaio among others. But it's the **ceiling frescoes** of Ghirlandaio's pupil, Michelangelo, depicting the *Creation*, that everyone comes to see, executed almost single-handed over a period of about four years, again for Pope Julius II. Whether the ceiling has been improved by the controversial recent restoration is a moot point, but the virtuosity of the work remains stunning. The *Last Judgement*, on the west wall of the chapel, was painted by Michelangelo over twenty years later, and is quite possibly the most inspired large-scale painting you'll ever see. The nudity caused controversy from the start, and the pope's zealous successor, Pius IV, would have had the painting removed had not Michelangelo's pupil, Daniele da Volterra, carefully added coverings – some of which have been left by the restorers – to the more obvious nudes, earning himself the nickname of the "breeches-maker".

Having seen the Raphael rooms and the Sistine Chapel, you've barely scratched the surface of the Vatican. At the opposite end of the Vatican Palace are grouped most of the other museums. In the main body of the palace, the small **Museo Pio-Clementino** holds some of the best of the Vatican's classical statuary, including the serene *Apollo Belvedere*, a Roman copy of a fourth-century BC original, and the second-century BC *Laöcoön*, which depicts the treacherous priest of Apollo being crushed with his sons by serpents. Near the Pio-Clementino museum, the **Museo Chiaramonti** and **Braccio Nuovo** hold more classical sculpture, the Museo Egizio has lots of mummies, and the **Museo Gregoriano Etrusco** offers sculpture, funerary art and applied art from the sites of southern Etruria. In a separate building, the **Pinacoteca** has works from the Early to High Renaissance: pieces by Crivelli, Lippi and Giotto; the rich backdrops and elegantly clad figures of the Umbrian painters Perugino and Pinturrichio; Raphael's unfinished *Transfiguration*, which hung above the artist as he lay in state; Leonardo's *St Jerome*; and Caravaggio's *Descent from the Cross* – a warts 'n' all canvas that is imitated successfully by Reni's *Crucifixion of St Peter* in the same room. Nearby, the **Museo Gregoriano Profano** holds more classical sculpture, mounted on scaffolds for all-round viewing, and mosaics of athletes from the Baths of Caracalla; the adjacent **Museo Pio Cristiano** has intricate early Christian sarcophagi, and, most famously, an expressive third-century statue of the Good Shepherd. Finally, the **Museo Missionario Etnologico** displays art and artefacts from all over the world, collected by Catholic missionaries.

Eating and drinking

It's relatively simple to **eat** cheaply and well in Rome, certainly easier than in Venice or Florence. Prices – even in the city centre – are reasonable, and the quality remains of a fair standard. You'll find a good array of places in the *centro storico*, not all of them tourist traps by any means, and Via Cavour and up around Stazione Termini is a good source of cheaply priced restaurants – though the area isn't renowned for its food quality rating. Similarly, you can eat cheaply in the Borgo district around the Vatican. Trastevere is Rome's traditional restaurant ghetto – touristy now, inevitably, but still the home of some fine and reasonably priced eateries, and Testaccio is also a popular evening place with a good selection of restaurants and pizzerias to choose from.

Snacks, cakes and ice cream

Il Delfino, Corso V. Emanuele 67. Central and very busy cafeteria with a huge choice of snacks and full meals. Good for a fast fill-up between sights.

Il Forno del Ghetto, Via del Portico d'Ottavia 1. Unmarked Jewish bakery with marvellous ricotta and dried fruit-filled cakes. Closed Sat.

Il Gelato di San Crispino, Via della Panetteria 42. Close to the Trevi fountain and considered Rome's best. Closed Tues.

Giolitti, Via Offici Uffici del Vicaro 40. An Italian institution which once had a reputation for the country's top ice cream. Still pretty good, however, with a choice of 70 flavours. Closed Mon.

Pascucci, Via di Torre Argentina 20. Just the thing after hours of hot sightseeing – a Roman *frullato*, the local version of a milkshake.

Sciam, Via del Pellegrino 56. A Middle Eastern-style tea room, done up in truly lavish style, offering exotic teas and treats.

Tre Scalini, Piazza Navona. Renowned for its absolutely remarkable *tartufo* – death by chocolate. Closed Wed.

Restaurants

Hosteria Africa, Via Gaeta 26. One of Rome's few African Eritrean/Ethiopian restaurants; very authentic. Closed Sat.

Ai Marmi, Viale Trastevere 53-59. Rome's most traditional pizzeria, with regional extras like deep-fried stuffed olives and batter-fried cod. Closed Wed.

Da Baffetto, Via Governo Vecchio 114. An old-fashioned pizzeria that has long been a Rome institution, though it now tends to be swamped by tourists. Amazingly, it's still good value – although service can be off-ish – but you'll always have to queue. Evenings only.

Ci Lin, Via Fonte d'Olio 6. A superb alternative choice – excellent Cantonese cooking in a welcoming atmosphere, and at very friendly prices.

Il Corallo, Via del Corallo 10. Friendly restaurant which attracts a lively crowd and serves way above average quality food – especially pizzas – though it isn't cheap. Open evenings only.

Filetti di Baccala, Largo dei Librari 88. Paper-covered Formica tables, cheap wine and beer, and fried fish dishes starting at €2.00. Evenings only; closed Sun and Aug.

Da Giggetto, Via del Portico d'Ottavia 21a. Much pricier than most, but worth it for genuine Roman–Jewish cooking. Closed Mon.

Grappola d'Oro, Piazza della Cancelleria 80. Curiously untouched place with genuine Roman cuisine and a timeless trattoria feel. Prices start at about €25 per person. Closed Sun.

L'Insalata Ricca, Largo di Chiavari 85. Relaxed and slightly out-of-the-ordinary place, with interesting salads and hearty pastas.

Al Leoncino, Via del Leoncino 28. Inexpensive and genuine city-centre pizzeria, little known to out-of-towners. Open daily; evenings only Sat & Sun.

Little India, Via Principe Amedeo 303/305. Wonderful Indian cuisine in a medieval Italian setting. Located between Termini and Piazza Vittorio.

Naturist Club – L'Isola, Via della Vite 14. Sublime vegetarian-Italian creations for lunch; reasonably priced, creative fish dishes at dinnertime. Closed Sun.

Dal Poeta, Vicolo del Bologna 45. One of the best pizzerias in Rome and with good salads and beer, too. Closed Mon.

Pizzeria San Callisto, Piazza San Callisto 9a. Probably Rome's cheapest pizzas – good and big enough to share. Always bustling and upbeat. Closed Mon.

Tram Tram, Via dei Reti 44–46. San Lorenzo district's top student favourite, featuring regional Pugliese cooking like seafood lasagna. Closed Mon.

Da Vittorio, Via San Cosimato 14a. Neapolitan pizza in the heart of Trastevere. Closed Mon.

Bars and birrerias

Bar della Pace, Via della Pace 5. Just off Piazza Navona, this is the summer bar to be seen in, with outside tables full of Rome's self-consciously beautiful people.

La Curia di Bacco, Via del Biscione 79. Near Campo de' Fiori, this lively, youthful place occupies rooms that were actually hollowed out of the ruins of the ancient Teatro di Pompeii.

The Dog and Duck, Via della Luce 70. A very cosy Irish-style pub, claiming to have the world's best Guinness.

Druid's Den, Via San Martino ai Monti 28. Appealing Irish pub with a mixed expat/Italian clientele. Cheap and lively, with occasional impromptu music.

Enoteca Cavour, Via Cavour 313. At the Forum end of Via Cavour, a handy retreat with an easy-going studenty feel, lots of wine and bottled beers and (slightly overpriced) snacks.

Jonathan's Angels, Via della Fossa 18. This colourful bar near Piazza Navona presents an explosion of kitschy décor; check out the bathroom.

Ombre Rosse, Piazza Sant'Egidio 12. Trastevere's liveliest venue, offering a huge menu of drinks and good light snacks, plus newspapers in several languages.

La Scala, Piazza della Scala. The most popular Trastevere *birreria* – big, bustling and crowded. Pub food, cheap beer and occasional (dire) music.

Trinity College, Via del Collegio Romano 6. A large, inviting space right in the centre of things, with traditional beers and international snacks.

Vineria, Campo de' Fiori 15. Small *vineria* which spills out into the square during the summer months.

Nightlife

Roman **nightlife** still retains some of the smart ethos satirized in Fellini's *Dolce Vita*. **Discos and clubs** cover the range: there are vast glittering palaces with stunning lights and sound systems, places that are not much more than upmarket bars with music, and other, more down-to-earth places to dance, playing a more interesting selection of music to a younger crowd, with the *centri sociali* (see below) offering an innovative alternative to the mainstream scene, usually on a "pay what you can" basis. Whichever you prefer, all tend to open and close late. Some charge a heavy entrance fee (€5–20) – though this usually includes one free drink. Rome's **rock scene** is a fairly limp affair, and the city is much more in its element with **jazz**, with lots of venues and a wide choice of styles performed by a healthy array of local talent. Most clubs close during July and August, or move to locations on the coast, but *Estate Romana* organizes many outdoor locations all over Rome for concerts, discos, bars and cinemas. Many top international groups participate. Bear in mind, too, that you may have to pay a membership fee on top of the admission price. Drinks, though, are generally no more expensive than you'd pay in the average bar.

The city's best source of **listings** is the magazine *Roma C'e* issued on Friday with a section in English, or the *TrovaRoma* supplement published with the Thursday edition of *La Repubblica*. For English-language information, there's *Wanted in Rome* or *Time Out*. First stop for **tickets** should be Orbis at Piazza Esquilino 37 (☎06.474.4776).

Centri sociali

In the suburbs of Rome, *centri sociali* have opened in abandoned public buildings, mostly by students, who offer a cheap, alternative programme of concerts, films and parties. The students are politically active, and work for and with newly arrived immigrants, the events they organize being among the more interesting that take place in Rome. The numerous *centri sociali* are listed in *Roma C'e* and *Il Manifesto*.

Forte Prenestino, Via F. del Pino. One of the most established *centri* situated in an abandoned nineteenth-century fortress. Offers two big arenas for concerts and a beehive of smaller spaces used for exhibitions, cinema, a disco and a bar.

Villaggio Globale, Ex-Mattatoio (☎06.573.00329) Located in the old slaughterhouse in Testaccio, this *centro* is partly run by the Senegalese community in Rome, which organizes concerts, parties and exhibitions, helped by a grant from local authorities.

Discos and clubs

L'Alibi, Via Monte Testaccio 44. Predominantly but not exclusively male venue that's one of Rome's best gay clubs. Downstairs cellar disco and upstairs open-air bar.

Alien, Via Velletri 13/19. Rome's trendiest club, this place is host to the best dance DJs.

Black Out Club, Via Saturnia 18. Popular disco playing a mix of house, punk and grunge.

Gilda, Via Mario de' Fiori 97. Slick, stylish club, the focus for the city's minor (and would-be) celebs.

Goa, Via Libetta 13. An ethnic feel to accentuate the house, techno and trance high-energy dance atmosphere.

Jam Session, Via del Cardello 13a. 1970's & 80's disco just off Via Cavour.

Piper, Via Tagliamento 9. One of the oldest discos in Rome, with live music, videos and different nightly events.

Rock Castle Café, Via B. Cenci 8. A fun foreign students' hangout, featuring lots of rock.

Live music: rock, jazz and Latin

Alexanderplatz, Via Ostia 9 (☎06.3974.2171). Rome's foremost jazz club/restaurant. Reservations recommended.

Alpheus, Via del Commercio 36–38. A four-roomed venue with simultaneous concerts, a disco, theatrical performances and a bar.

Berimbau, Via dei Fienaroli 30/b. Live Latin-American music and Brazilian drinks.

Big Mama, Vicolo San Francesco a Ripa 18. Trastevere-based jazz/blues club of long standing. Closed July–Sept.

Blue Knight, Via delle Fornaci 8–10. Ground level is a bar and gelateria; downstairs there's live music Thurs–Sat.

Caffè Latino, Via di Monte Testaccio 96. Multi-event club in the newly hip area near the Protestant cemetery. Best at weekends when it's crowded and more atmospheric.

Circolo degli Artisti, Via Casilina Vecchia 42. Huge bar and disco with more alternative live music. Cheap and fun.

Fonclea, Via Crescenzio 82a. Long running jazz/salsa outfit, with live music most nights. Metro Ottaviano.

Classical music, opera and film

During the summer there are also quite a few places you can hear **classical music**. The city's churches host a wide range of choral, chamber and organ recitals, many of them free. Year-round, the Accademia di Santa Cecilia (☎06.6880.1044) stages concerts by its own or visiting orchestras at Via delle Conciliazione 4 (☎06.678.0742) and in summer in the gardens of the Villa Giulia. Rome's **opera** scene concentrates on the Teatro dell'Opera, on the Via Firenze, Piazza B. Gigli, from November to May (box office Mon–Sat 10.45am–5pm; ☎06.481.601); check for information on outdoor summer venues. Purists should be prepared for a carnival atmosphere and plenty of unscheduled intervals. Rome's two **English-language cinemas** are the Pasquino, Piazza Sant'Egidio 10 on Vicolo del Piede in Trastevere (☎06.580.3622), which shows recent general releases, and the Quirinetta at Via Minghetti 4. Tickets are currently €6.20 for evening performances, €4.20 afternoons. Other cinemas show foreign-language films usually on Monday or Tuesday nights. Look in local papers for a list: the Nuovo Sacher, Largo Ascianghi 1 (☎06.581.8116), and Alcazar, Via Cardinal Merry del Val 14 (☎06.588.0099), are two.

Festivals

Much of Rome's nightlife moves outdoors during the summer, all part of the *Estate Romana* programme; festivals offer live music, movies, markets and munchies and may be a more appealing option than the clubs on a hot summer evening.

La Festa di Noantri, Viale Trastevere and around. Medieval Trastevere's traditional summer festival in honour of the Virgin, with street stalls selling all sorts of snacks and trinkets, and a grand finale of fireworks. The main event is the Virgin's effigy being hauled joyously from the church of Santa Agata to that of San Crisogono, and back again. Last two weeks of July.

La Festa del'Unità (venues change every year; ☎06.441.821 or check *RomaC'è* for details). Throughout the summer, this cheery hotchpotch of music, film, eateries, games and other attractions – much of it free – is the re-founded Communist Party's way of reminding people of what fun the Left can be.

Fiesta Capannelle, Via Appia Nuova 1245. Running from mid-June through to August, this festival based at Rome's racecourse in the southeast of the city has a Latin American flavour. Metro A to Subagosto, then bus #354 to Ippodromo Capannelle.

Testaccio Village, Viale del Campo Boario. Just behind the old Testaccio slaughterhouse, this nightly festival draws a young crowd for the bars and stalls, live bands (rock, Latin and jazz) and DJs. June–Sept. Metro B to Piramide, night bus 40N to return.

Tevere Expo, Tiber Embankment, main entrance by Castel Sant'Angelo. Atmospheric annual handicrafts fair along the river; nighttime stalls, bars and live entertainment. From mid-June until 31 July.

Listings

Airlines Alitalia, Via Bissolati 11 (☎06.65.643); British Airways, Via Bissolati 54 (☎848.812.266 or 147.812.266 or ☎06.6501.1513); Continental Airlines, Via Parigi 11 (☎06.6605.3030); TWA, Via Barberini 67 (☎06.47.241).

American Express Piazza di Spagna 38 (Mon–Fri 9am–5.30pm, Sat 9am–12.30pm; ☎06.67.641).

Books The Economy Book Center, Via Torino 136 (☎06.474.6877), has a good stock of new and used English-language paperbacks.

Car rental At Fiumicino Airport a shuttle bus takes you to the car-rental depot with all main firms. In the foyer at Termini there are car-rental booths. Avis, Via Sardegna 38a (☎06.4282.4728); Europcar, Via Lombardia 7 (☎06.481.9103); Hertz, Via Veneto 156 (☎06.321.6831); Maggiore, Via Po 8 (☎06.854.8698).

Embassies Australia, Via Alessandria 215 (☎06.852.721); Canada, Via G.b. de Rossi 27 (☎06.445.981); New Zealand, Via Zara 28 (☎06.441.7171440.2928); UK, Via XX Settembre 80 (☎06.482.5441); USA, Via V. Veneto 121 (☎06.46.741).

Exchange Two offices at Termini station operate out of banking hours; try also Thomas Cook, Via Barberini 21a (☎06.482.8082), Cambio Rosati, Via Nazionale 186 (☎06.488.5498), or look for booths which advertise no commission.

Hospital Call ☎06.884.0113 or ☎113 or ☎118 for 24hr assistance. The most central hospital is the Santo Spirito, Lungotevere in Sassia 1 (☎06.68.351). The International Medical Centre (☎06.488.2371) has an English speaker on hand.

Internet access Café, Via Cavour 213, between the forum and Termini (☎06.4782.3051; €3.10/hr) and Bibli, Via dei Fienaroli 28, in Trastevere (☎06.588.4097; €6.20/hr); both also serve snacks.

Left luggage At Stazione Termini 7am–midnight; per item: €3.10/5 hrs, plus €0.60 for each additional hour or fraction thereafter.

Pharmacies Try PIRAM at Via Nazionale 228 (☎06.488.0754) or at Stazione Termini (☎06.488.0019). A list of late-opening pharmacies is posted on pharmacists' doors.

Police The police station/foreign office is the Questura, Via Genova 3 (☎06.4686).

Post office The main office is on Piazza San Silvestro 18–20 (Mon–Fri 9am–6pm, Sat 9am–2pm; ☎06.160 for information).

Telephones Phone booths at Stazione Termini (Mon–Fri 9am–6pm & Sat 9am–2pm).

Train enquiries ☎848.888.088. The information booth at Stazione Termini is open daily 7am–11.30pm.

Travel agents CTS, Via Genova 16 (☎06.462.0431), and Corso Vittorio Emanuele II 297 (☎06.687.2672); Elsy Viaggi, Via di Torre Argentina 80 (☎06.689.6460).

Around Rome

You may find there's quite enough of interest in Rome to keep you occupied during your stay; but it can be a hot and oppressive city, and you really shouldn't feel any guilt about freeing yourself from its weighty history to see something of the countryside around. Two of the main attractions visitable on a day-trip are, it's true, Roman sites, but just the process of getting to them can be energizing.

Tivoli

Just 40km from Rome, **TIVOLI** has always been something of a retreat from the city. In classical days it was a retirement town for wealthy Romans; later, during Renaissance times, it again became the playground of the monied classes, attracting some of the city's most well-to-do families.

Most people head first for the **Villa d'Este** (Tues–Sun 9am–1hr before sunset; €4.20), the country villa of Cardinal Ippolito d'Este, across the main square of Largo Garibaldi. It's the gardens rather than the villa itself that they come to see, peeling away down the hill in a succession of terraces – probably the most contrived gardens in Italy, interrupted at decent intervals by one playful fountain after another, unfortunately not all in working order. In their day some of these were quite ingenious – one played the organ, another imitated the call of birds – though nowadays the emphasis is on the quieter creations. There's the central *Fontana del Bicchierone* by Bernini, one of the simplest and most elegant; on the far left, the *Rometta* or "Little Rome" has reproductions of the major buildings of the city; while the *Fontana del Ovato*, on the opposite side of the garden, has statues and an arcade in which you can walk. The town's other attraction, the **Villa Gregoriana** (daily 10am to 1hr before sunset; €1.80), is a park with waterfalls created when Pope Gregory XVI diverted the flow of the river here in 1831 to ease periodic flooding of the town. The lush, overgrown vegetation descends into a gorge over 60m deep. There are two main waterfalls – the *Grande Cascata* on the far side, and a small Bernini-designed one at the neck of the gorge. The path winds down to the bottom of the canyon, where you can get right up close to the pounding water, the dark shapes of the rock glowering overhead. From here the path leads up on the far side to an exit and the substantial remains of a **Temple of Vesta**, some say of the Sibyls, clinging to the side of the hill.

Once you've seen these two sights you've really seen Tivoli. But just outside at the bottom of the hill, fifteen minutes' walk off the main Rome road (CAT bus #4 from Largo Garibaldi), the **Villa Adriana** (daily 9am to 1hr 30min before sunset; €6.20) casts the inventions of the Tivoli popes and cardinals very much into the shade. This was probably the largest and most sumptuous villa in the Roman Empire, the retirement home of the Emperor Hadrian for a short while between 135 AD and his death three years later, and it is now one of the most soothing spots around Rome. Hadrian was a great traveller and a keen architect, and parts of the villa were inspired by buildings he had seen around the world. The massive Pecile for instance, through which you enter, is a reproduction of a building in Athens. And the Canopus, on the opposite side of the site, is a liberal copy of the sanctuary of Serapis near Alexandria, its long, elegant channel of water fringed by columns and statues. Nearby, a museum displays the latest finds from the excavations, though most of the extensive original discoveries have found their way back to Rome. Back towards the entrance, there's a fish pond with a *cryptoporticus* winding around underneath, and – perhaps the most photographed part of the site – the **Teatro Marittimo**, with its island in the middle of a circular pond, to which it's believed Hadrian would retire at siesta time.

Buses leave Rome for Tivoli frequently (every 20min) from Rebibbia Ponte Mammolo station, Metro B; tickets cost €3.10 return – journey time 50 minutes. In Tivoli they stop at and leave from the main Largo Garibaldi, opposite the **tourist office** (Mon–Sat 9am–1pm & 4–7pm; ☎0774.334.522), which has information on accommodation if you're planning to stay over.

Ostia

There are two **Ostias,** both reachable in around thirty minutes by regular train from Piramide (Metro line B; €0.80): one, Lido di Ostia, is an over-visited seaside resort that is well worth avoiding; if it's free **beach** you want, it's much better to go to the very last stop, Cristoforo Colombo, and take the local bus just 3 miles south, where the dunes are most inviting and there are excellent, good-value snack bars. The other important stop, the one just before the Lido, is for the excavations of the port of **OSTIA ANTICA**, is on a par with anything you'll see in Rome itself and easily merits a half-day's outing (Tues–Sun 9am to 1hr before sunset; €4.20). The site groups around the town's commercial centre, otherwise known as the **Piazzale di Corporazione** for the remains of shops and trading offices that still fringe it, the mosaics in front of which denote their trade. Flanking one side of the square, the **Theatre** has been much restored but is nonetheless impressive, enlarged in the second century to hold up to four thousand people. On the left of the square, the **House of Apulius** preserves mosaic floors and, beyond, a dark aisled mithraeum with more mosaics illustrating the cult. Behind here, the **Casa di Diana** is probably the best-preserved private house in Ostia, with a dark set of rooms around a central courtyard, and again with a mithraeum at the back. You can climb up to its roof for a fine view of the rest of the site, afterwards crossing the road to the **Thermopolium** – an ancient Roman café, complete with seats, counter, display shelves and even wall paintings of parts of the menu. North of the Casa di Diana, the **Museum** (Tues–Sat 9am–4.30pm, Sun 9am–1pm) holds a variety of articles from the site, including frescoes, and some fine sarcophagi and statuary. Left from here, the **Forum** centres on the Capitol building, reached by a wide flight of steps.

Anzio

About 40km south of Rome, **ANZIO** is much the best bet for a day by the sea if you're staying in Rome. Much of the town was damaged during a difficult Allied landing here on January 22, 1944, to which two military cemeteries (one British, the other, at nearby Nettuno, American) bear testimony. But despite a pretty thorough rebuilding it's a likeable resort, still depending as much on fish as tourists for its livelihood. The town's seafood **restaurants** are reason enough to come, crowding together along the harbour and not unreasonably priced, and the **beaches**, which edge the coast on either side, don't get unbearably stuffed outside August. Anzio is also a possible route onto the island of **Ponza**, for which hydrofoils leave daily in summer – ask for timings at the **tourist office** (daily 9am–1pm & 3.30–6pm; ☎06.984.5147) in the harbour.

THE SOUTH

The Italian south or *mezzogiorno* is quite a different experience from the north; indeed, few countries are more tangibly divided into two distinct, often antagonistic, regions. While the north is rich, the south is by contrast one of the most depressed areas in Europe. Its rate of unemployment (about 25 percent) is around twice that of the north, its gross regional product about a third. Its people are dark-skinned and speak with the cadences of the Mediterranean, the dialect down here sounding almost Arabic sometimes. Indeed the south's "capital", Naples, is often compared to Cairo.

For most people, **Naples**, regional capital of **Campania** and only a couple of hours south of Rome, is the obvious focus, an utterly compelling city, dominating the region in every way. The **Bay of Naples** is dense in interest, with the ancient sites of Pompeii and Herculaneum just half an hour outside – probably Italy's best-preserved and most revealing Roman remains – and the island of Capri, swarmed over by tourists these days but so beautiful that a day there is by no means time squandered. South of Naples, **Sorrento**, at the far east end of the bay, has all the beer 'n' chips trappings you'd expect from a major Brit package destination, but is a likeable place for all that; and the **Amalfi Coast**, across the peninsula, is probably Europe's most dramatic stretch of coastline, harbouring some enticing – if crowded – beach resorts. **Puglia** – the long strip of land that makes up the "heel" of Italy – was for centuries a strategic province, invaded and colonized by just about every major power of the day. There's no escaping these influences in the Saracenic kasbah-like quarters of cities such as Bari, and the Baroque exuberance of **Lecce**. All the same, **Puglia** is still very much a province you pass through on the way elsewhere, not least to Brindisi with its ferry connections with Greece. **Basilicata** and **Calabria** are also to some extent transit regions, although in many ways they represent the quintessence of the *mezzogiorno* – culturally impoverished, under-developed and – owing to emigration – sparsely populated. Artistically they are the most barren regions in Italy, but the combination of mountain grandeur and a relatively unspoilt coastline, often in close proximity, is a unique attraction, only now beginning to be exploited by the tourist industry.

Naples

Wherever else you travel south of Rome, the chances are that you'll wind up in **NAPLES** – de facto capital of the whole Italian south. It's the kind of city people visit with preconceptions, and it rarely disappoints: it is filthy, large and overbearing; it is crime-infested; and it is most definitely like nowhere else in Italy – something the inhabitants will be keener than anyone to tell you. In all these things lies the city's charm. Perhaps the feeling that you're somewhere unique makes it possible to endure the noise and constant harassment, perhaps it's the feeling that you've travelled from an ordinary part of Europe to somewhere that feels like an Arab bazaar in less than three hours. One thing, though, is certain: a couple of days here and you're likely to be as staunch a defender of the place as its most devoted inhabitants. No city on earth, except perhaps New York, excites fiercer loyalties.

Arrival and information

Naples' **Capodochino Airport** is northwest of the city centre at Viale Umberto Maddalena, connected with Piazza Garibaldi by buses #14 and #15 (every 15min, €0.80). The bus journey takes about thirty minutes – not much more than a taxi, for which you'll pay up to €25; there's also a blue official airport bus (every 30min 6am–midnight; €1.60) which will take you straight to the port, Piazza Municipio and Piazza Garibaldi. Arriving by **train**, Napoli Centrale is on Piazza Garibaldi, at the main hub of all transport services. The main **tourist office** is at Piazza Gesù Nuovo dei Martiri 58 (Mon–Sat 9am–8pm, Sun 9am–3pm; ☎081.551.2701, *www.ept.napoli.it*), and there are branches at Capodiochino Airport (daily 9am–7pm), and another on Piazza dei Martiri 58 (Mon–Fri 8.30am–3.30pm), but the most convenient is at the Stazione Centrale (Mon–Sat 9am–8pm, Sun 9am–1.30pm). All have free maps of the city, information on accommodation, and copies of the free monthly booklet *Qui Napoli*, handy for current events, ferry and bus times.

City transport

The only way to really get around Naples and stay sane is to walk. However, Naples is a large, sprawling city, and its transport services extend to the Bay as a whole, which means you'll definitely need to use some form of public transport sooner or later. City **buses** are much the best way of crossing the city centre: fares are a flat €0.80 per journey (valid for 90min); buy tickets in advance from tobacconists or the booth on Piazza Garibaldi; one-day tickets are also available for €2.30. The bus system is supplemented by the **metropolitana**, a small but expanding underground network which crosses the centre and runs around the Bay, and **funiculars** scaling the hill of the Vómero from stations at piazzas Montesanto, Amedeo and Augusto. For **trips around the bay** in either direction, there are three rail systems, the most useful of which is the **Circumvesuviana**, which runs from its station on Corso Garibaldi around the Bay of Naples about every half-hour as far as Sorrento, which it reaches in about an hour. The minimum **taxi** fare in the city is €3.10.

Accommodation

A good many of the city's cheaper **hotels** are situated around Piazza Garibaldi, within spitting distance of the train station and not badly placed for the rest of town. A word of warning: don't go with any of the touts inside or outside the station. One of the closest options, just to the right as you leave the station, is the sizeable and friendly *Hotel Eden*, Corso Novara 9

CENTRAL NAPLES

(☎081.285.690, *hotel_eden_napoli@libero.it*; ③); while the *Hotel Ginevra*, just across the street at Via Genova 116 (☎081.554.1757, *hginevra@tin.it*; ③), is slightly cheaper and just as friend-ly and helpful. Off the far end of Piazza Garibaldi to the right, is the very pleasant *Casanova*, with its own roof garden, Corso Garibaldi 333 (☎081.268.287, *hcasanova@tin.it*; ③); while straight across the piazza from the station is the small, welcoming *Hostel Pensione Mancini* (☎081.553.6731, *www.hostelpensionemancini.com*; ②, breakfast included), on the second floor at Via Mancini 33, whose proprietors will even meet you at the station if you call ahead. Another decent and appealing choice on the same street is the *Hotel Garibaldi*, Via Mancini 11 (☎081.563.0656; ③), a two-star hotel with good facilities, two minutes from the station. Several blocks further on, enjoying a nicer location right in the thick of the *centro storico*, the small *Soggiorno Imperia*, Piazza Luigi Miraglia 386 (☎081.459.347; ②, breakfast included), is a homey, clean hotel, offering kitchen and laundry facilities. Best of all in some respects is the welcoming *Bella Capri*, Via Melisurgo 4 (☎081.552.9494, *www.bellacapri.it*; ④), right on the main port, with nicely furnished rooms on the top sixth floor of a modern block, affording great views of Mt Vesuvius and Capri from your very own balcony. There's an **HI hostel**, *Ostello Mergellina*, Salita della Grotta 23 (☎081.761.2346; ②, including breakfast), in an attractive location, but a long way out and there's also an inconvenient 12.30am curfew and a three-day maximum stay during July and August; take the metro to the Mergellina metro stop, *not* to Mergellina train station, or bus #152 from Piazza Garibaldi. The closest **campsite** is *Vulcano Solfatara* in nearby Pozzuoli at Via Solfatara 161 (☎081.526.7413; April–Oct); bus #152 runs right there from Piazza Garibaldi, or take the metropolitana to Pozzuoli and walk ten minutes up the hill.

The City

Naples is a large city, with a centre that has many different focuses. The area between the vast and busy Piazza Garibaldi, where you will arrive, and Via Toledo, the main street a mile or so west, makes up the old part of the city – the **centro storico**. Buildings rise high on either side of the narrow, crowded streets, cobwebbed with washing; there's little light, not even much sense of the rest of the city outside – certainly not of the proximity of the sea. The two main drags of the *centro storico* are **Via dei Tribunali** and **Via San Biagio dei Librai** – two narrow streets, lined with old arcaded buildings, that are a maelstrom of hurrying pedestrians, revving cars and buzzing, dodging scooters. Via dei Tribunali cuts through to **Via Duomo**, where you'll find the tucked-away **Duomo**, a Gothic building from the early thirteenth century dedicated to San Gennaro, the patron saint of the city. San Gennaro was martyred in 305 AD. Two phials of his blood miraculously liquefy three times a year – on the first Saturday in May (when a procession leads from the church of Santa Chiara to the cathedral) and on September 19 and December 16. If the blood refuses to liquefy – which luckily is rare – disaster is supposed to befall the city. The first chapel on the right as you walk into the cathedral holds the precious phials and Gennaro's skull in a silver bust-reliquary from 1305. On the other side of the church, the basilica of **Santa Restituta** is officially the oldest structure in Naples, erected by Constantine in 324 and supported by columns taken from a temple to Apollo on this site. Downstairs, the **Crypt of San Gennaro** (€2.60) is one of the finest examples of Renaissance art in Naples, founded by Cardinal Carafa and holding the tombs of both San Gennaro and Pope Innocent IV.

Across Via Duomo, Via dei Tribunali continues on into the heart of the old city: the **Spaccanapoli** ("split-Naples"), the city's busiest and architecturally richest quarter. Cut down to its other main axis, **Via San Biagio dei Librai**, which leads west to **Piazza San Domenico Maggiore**, marked by the **Guglia di San Domenico** – one of the whimsical Baroque obelisks that pop up all over the city, built in 1737. The **church** of the same name flanks the north side of the square, an originally Gothic building from 1289, one of whose chapels holds a miraculous painting of the *Crucifixion* which is said to have spoken to St Thomas Aquinas during his time at the adjacent monastery. North, Via de Sanctis leads off right to one of the city's odder monuments, the **Cappella Sansevero** (Mon & Wed–Sat 10am–5pm, Sun 10am–1.30pm; €4.20), the tomb-chapel of the di Sangro family, decorated by the sculptor Giuseppe Sammartino in the mid-eighteenth century with some remarkable carving including a starkly realistic dead *Christ*. The chapel downstairs, commissioned by alchemist Prince Raimondo, contains the gruesome results of some of his experiments: two bodies under glass, their capillaries and organs preserved by a mysterious liquid developed by the prince.

Continuing west, the **Gesù Nuovo** church is most notable for its lava-stone facade. Originally part of a fifteenth-century palace which stood here, prickled with pyramids that give it an impregnable, prison-like air. The inside is in part decorated by the Neapolitan-Spanish painter Ribera. Facing the Gesù church, the church of **Santa Chiara** is quite different, a Provençal-Gothic structure built in 1328 and rebuilt after World War II with an austerity that's pleasing after the excesses opposite. The attached **cloister** (daily 8.30–12.30 & 4–6.30pm; €3.10 including entrance to museum), lushly planted and covered with colourful majolica tiles depicting bucolic scenes of life outside, is one of the gems of the city.

Piazza del Municipio is a busy traffic junction that stretches down to the waterfront, dominated by the brooding hulk of the **Castel Nuovo**. Built in 1282 by the Angevins and later the royal residence of the Aragon monarchs, it now contains the **Museo Civico** (Mon–Sat 9am–7pm; €5.20), which holds periodic exhibitions in a series of elaborate Gothic rooms. The entrance of the Castel incorporates a triumphal arch built in 1454 to commemorate the taking of the city by Alfonso I, the first Aragon ruler. Just beyond the castle, on the left, the **Teatro San Carlo** (guided tours Sept–June, Sat & Sun 2–4pm; €2.60) is still the largest opera house in Italy, and one of the most distinguished in the world. Beyond, at the bottom of the main shopping street of Via Toledo, the dignified **Palazzo Reale** (Mon, Tues, Thurs, Fri & Sun 9am–8pm, Sat 9am–11pm; €4.20) was built in 1602 to accommodate a visit by Philip III of Spain. Upstairs, the palace's first-floor rooms are decorated with gilded furniture, trompe l'oeil ceilings, overbearing tapestries and lots of undistinguished seventeenth- and eighteenth-century paintings. Best are the chapel, with its finely worked altarpiece, and the little theatre, which is refreshingly restrained after the rest of the palace. The original bronze doors of the palace, at the bottom of the main staircase, were cast in 1468 and show scenes from Ferdinand of Aragon's struggle against the local barons. The cannonball wedged in the bottom panel dates from a naval battle between the French and the Genoese.

Via Toledo leads north from Piazza Trieste e Trento to the **Museo Archeologico Nazionale** (Wed–Mon 9am–7.30pm; €6.20; bus #110 from Piazza Garibaldi) – perhaps Naples' most essential sight, home to the Farnese collection of antiquities from Lazio and Campania, and the best of the finds from the nearby Roman sites of Pompeii and Herculaneum. The ground floor concentrates on sculpture, including the *Farnese Bull* and *Farnese Hercules* from the Baths of Caracalla in Rome – the former the largest piece of classical sculpture ever found. The mezzanine floor at the back houses the museum's collection of mosaics, remarkably preserved works giving a superb insight into ordinary Roman customs, beliefs and humour. Upstairs, the wall paintings from the villas of Pompeii and Herculaneum are the museum's other major draw, rich in colour and invention. Look out for the group of four small pictures in the first main room, best of which is a depiction of a woman gathering flowers entitled *Primavera*. There are also everyday items from the Campanian cities – glass, silver, ceramics, charred pieces of rope, even foodstuffs – together with a model layout of Pompeii in cork. The other side of the first floor has sculptures in bronze from the **Villa dei Papiri** in Herculaneum, including a superb *Hermes at Rest*, a languid *Resting Satyr* and a convincingly woozy *Drunken Silenus*.

At the top of the hill is the city's other major museum, the **Palazzo Reale di Capodimonte** (Tues–Sun 8.30am–7.30pm; €7.30; bus #24 from Piazza Dante or #110 from Piazza Garibaldi), the former residence of the Bourbon King Charles III, built in 1738 and now housing the **Museo Nazionale di Capodimonte**. This has a superb collection of Renaissance paintings, including a couple of Brueghels, *The Misanthrope* and *The Blind*, canvases by Perugino and Pinturicchio, an elegant *Madonna and Child with Angels* by Botticelli and Lippi's soft, sensitive *Annunciation*. Later paintings include a room full of Titians, with a number of paintings of the shrewd Farnese Pope Paul III in various states of ageing, Raphael's austere portrait of *Leo X*, and Bellini's impressively composed *Transfiguration*.

Vómero, the district topping the hill immediately above the old city, can be reached on the Montesanto funicular. Go up to the star-shaped fortress of **Castel Sant'Elmo** (Tues–Sun 9am–7pm; €1.30), occupying Naples' highest point. Built in the fourteenth century, it now hosts exhibitions and concerts, and boasts the very best views of Naples.

Eating, drinking and nightlife

Neapolitan cuisine is among Italy's best – simple dishes cooked with fresh, healthy ingredients that have none of the richness or pretensions of the north. It's also the best place in the country to eat **pizza**, which originates from here. If you're just after a **snack**, you can pick something up from the city's **street markets** – the Forcella quarter market on the far side of Piazza Garibaldi or the fish market at Porta Nolana, off to the left. There are also plenty of snack places around Piazza Garibalidi, such as the *Gran Bar Chic*, Corso Garibaldi 353, an oasis of orderliness with very reasonable prices.

Restaurants in the station area tend to be of indifferent quality, but *Da Peppino Avellinese*, Via Spaventa 3135 (closed Sat in winter), is the most welcoming and best value of the many options on and around Piazza Garibaldi. A little farther on towards the historic centre, you'll find two of the most traditional pizzerias: *L'Antica Pizzeria "da Michele"*, Via Cesare Sersale 1–3 (on the corner of Via Colletta; closed Sun) is certainly the cheapest in town and possibly the most authentic; or alternatively, try the slightly more elegant and a little pricier, *La Trianon da Ciro*, across the street at Via Pietro Colletta 42–46. Pushing on into the depths of the old centre, *Pizzeria Sorbillo*, Via dei Tribunali 35 (closed Sun) is a tiny, old-fashioned treat, and *Da Carmine*, Via Tribunale 330 (closed Sun), is a simple trattoria with an extensive menu and low prices. *Bellini*, at Via Santa Maria di Constantinopoli 80 (closed Sun evening), is a good place for a splurge, one of the city's longest-established restaurants, also does great pizzas. On the other side of Via Toledo, *Brandi*, Salita Sant'Anna di Palazzo 1–2, off Via Chiaia (closed Mon), is possibly Naples' most famous pizzeria – very friendly, and serving pasta too. Near the port itself, *Da Antonio*, Via de Pretis 143 (closed Sat), is an unpretentious little place serving great regional specialities at moderate prices, while along the seafront closer to the City Park, *'a Taverna 'e zi Carmela*, Via Nicolò Tommaseo 11–12 (closed Mon), lays on special long pizzas and inventive seafood pastas.

As for **nightlife**, the beautiful Piazza Bellini is a trendy drinking spot, where tables spill out from the surrounding bars. Of these *Intra Moenia*, at number 70, offers snacks and salads as well as Internet access (€5/hr), and next door the *Libreria Caffè Ithaca* sells books and tasty organic snacks. Across the piazza, past the archeological site, check out the live music scene at *Tallioo*, Vicoletto Costantinopoli (closed Mon).

Listings

Airlines Alitalia, Via Medina 41–42 (☎081.542.5111); British Airways, Capodochino Airport (☎081.780.3087 or ☎848.812.266).

Car rental Avis, Via Piedigrotta 44 (☎081.761.1365); Europcar, Via Scarfoglio 10 (☎081.570.8426); Hertz, Via N. Sauro 21 (☎081.764.5323); Maggiore, Via Cervantes 92 (☎081.552.1900). All have desks at the airport and Stazione Centrale.

Consulates UK, Via Crispi 122 (☎081.663.511); USA, Piazza della Repubblica (☎081.583.8111).

Exchange Outside banking hours at Stazione Centrale (daily 7am–9pm).

Hospital ☎118 or go to the 24hr Guardia Medica Permanente in the Palazzo Municipio.

Internet access Internetbar By Tightrope, Piazza Bellini 74 (€5/hr); Internet Multimedia Napoli, Via Sapienza 43 (€1.50 per hr).

Laundry Bolle Blu at Corso Novara 62 (Mon–Sat 9am–8pm).

Pharmacy At Stazione Centrale (Mon–Sat 8am–8pm 24hr).

Police The main station is at Via Medina 75 (☎081.794.1111); for emergencies call ☎112.

Post office Main office on Piazza Matteotti, off Via Toledo (Mon–Sat 8.15am–7.20pm).

Telephones The Telecom Italia office at Via Depretis 40 (daily 24hr).

Train enquiries ☎848.888.088. Station booths are open daily 7am–10pm, but be prepared to queue.

Travel agents CTS, Via Mezzocannone 25 (☎081.552.7960).

The Bay of Naples

For the Romans, the **Bay of Naples** was the land of plenty, a blessed region of mild climate, gorgeous scenery and an accessible location that made it a favourite vacation and retirement area for the city's nobility. Later, when Naples became the final stop on northerners' Grand Tours, the relics of its heady Roman period only added to the charm for most travellers. However, these days it's hard to tell where Naples ends and the countryside begins, the city sprawling around the Bay in an industrial and residential mess that is quite at odds with the region's popular image. It's only when you reach **Sorrento** in the east, or the islands that dot the Bay, that you really feel free of it all. Of the islands, **Capri** is the best place to visit if you're here for a short time. There's also, of course, the ever-brooding presence of **Vesuvius**, and the incomparable Roman sites of **Herculaneum** and **Pompeii** – each of which is well worth extending your stay in the city for.

Herculaneum and Vesuvius

The first point of any interest travelling east is the town of **ERCOLANO**, the modern offshoot of the ancient site of Herculaneum, which was destroyed by the eruption of Vesuvius on August 2, 79 AD. It's worth stopping here for two reasons: to see the excavations of the site and to climb to the summit of Vesuvius – to which buses run from outside the train station. If you're planning to visit both Herculaneum and scale Vesuvius in one day, though, be sure to see Vesuvius first, and set off reasonably early – buses stop running up the mountain at lunchtime, leaving you the afternoon free to wander around the site.

Situated at the seaward end of Ercolano's main street, **Herculaneum** (daily 8.30am–7.30pm, last entry 6.30pm; €8.30) was a residential town in Roman times, much smaller than Pompeii, and as such it's a more manageable site, less architecturally impressive but better preserved and more easily taken in on a single visit. Because it wasn't a commercial town, there is no central open space or forum, just streets of villas and shops, cut as usual by two very straight main streets. The **House of the Mosaic Atrium** at the bottom end of the main street, Cardo IV, retains its mosaic-laid courtyard, corrugated by the force of the tufa, behind which the **House of the Deer** contains corridors decorated with richly coloured still lifes and a bawdy statue of a drunken Hercules seemingly about to piss all over the visitors. There's also a large **Thermae** or bath complex (sometimes partly closed) with a domed *frigidarium* decorated with frescoes of fish and a *caldarium* containing a plunge bath at one end and a scallop-shell apse complete with washbasin and water pipes. The women's bath complex has a mosaiced floor of Triton and sea creatures. Opposite, the **House of Neptune and Amphitrite**, holding a sparklingly preserved wall mosaic of the god and goddess, and frescoes of flowers and vegetables, served in lieu of a garden. Under the house is a wine shop, stocked with amphorae in wooden racks, left as they lay when disaster struck. Close by in the **Casa del Bel Cortile** are some skeletons poignantly lying in the same attitude as they were in 79 AD. Further down on the opposite side of the road in the **House of the Wooden Partition**, there's a room with the marital bed still intact, and in the house nearby a perfectly preserved coiled rope.

Since its first eruption in 79 AD, when it buried the towns and inhabitants of Pompeii and Herculaneum, **Vesuvius** has dominated the lives of those who live on the Bay of Naples. It's still an active volcano, the only one on mainland Europe, and there have been more than a hundred eruptions over the years, but only two of real significance: one in December 1631 that engulfed many nearby towns and killed three thousand people; and the last, in March 1944, which caused widespread devastation, though no one was actually killed. The people who live here still fear the reawakening of Vesuvius, and with good reason – scientists calculate it should erupt every thirty years or so, and it hasn't since 1944.

There are two ways to make the **ascent**. Trasporti Vesuviani run bus services (around 5 daily in summer; €3.10 return) from Ercolano train station to a car park and huddle of souvenir shops and cafés close to the crater; don't listen to the taxi drivers at the station who will try and persuade you there is no bus. If you've more energy, or have missed the bus, you can also take a local bus (#5) from the roundabout near the station to the end of the line and walk the couple of hours to the car park from there. The walk up to the crater from the car park where the bus stops takes about half an hour, across barren gravel on marked-out paths. At the top (admission €4.70), the crater is a deep, wide, jagged ashtray of red rock emitting the odd plume of smoke, though since the last eruption effectively sealed up the main crevice this is much less evident than it once was. You can walk most of the way around, but take it easy – the fences are old and rickety.

Pompeii

The other Roman town destroyed by Vesuvius, **Pompeii** (daily 8.30am–5/7.30pm; €8.30) was much larger than Herculaneum, and one of Campania's most important commercial centres. Out of a total population of twenty thousand, it's thought that only two thousand actually perished, asphyxiated by the toxic fumes of the volcanic debris, their homes buried in several metres of volcanic ash and pumice. In effect, the eruption froze the way of life in Pompeii as it stood at the time, and the excavations here have probably yielded more information about the life of Roman citizens during the imperial era than any other site. The full horror of their way of death is apparent in plaster casts made from the shapes their bodies left in the volcanic ash. Bear in mind, however, that most of the best mosaics and murals have found their way to the Archeological Museum in Naples.

The site covers a wide area, and seeing it properly takes half a day at least. Entering the site from the Pompeii-Villa dei Misteri side, the **Forum** is the first real feature of significance, a slim open space surrounded by the ruins of what would have been some of the town's most important official buildings. North from here, the **House of the Tragic Poet** is named after its mosaics of a theatrical production and a poet inside, though the "Cave Canem" (Beware of the Dog) mosaic by the main entrance is more eye-catching. Close by, the residents of the **House of the Faun** must have been a friendlier lot, its "Ave" (Welcome) mosaic outside beckoning you in to view the atrium and the copy of a tiny bronze dancing faun that gives the villa its name. On the street behind, the **House of the Vettii** is one of the most delightful houses in Pompeii, a merchant villa ranged around a lovely central peristyle that gives the best possible impression of the domestic environment of the city's upper middle classes. The first room on the right off the peristyle holds the best of Pompeii's murals viewable in situ: the one on the left shows the young Hercules struggling with serpents, while, through the villa's kitchen, a small room that's normally kept locked has erotic works showing various techniques of lovemaking, together with a potent-looking statue of Priapus from which women were supposed to drink to ensure fertility.

On the other side of the site, the **Grand Theatre** is very well preserved and still used for performances, as is the **Little Theatre** on its far left side. Walk up to the **Amphitheatre**, one of Italy's most intact and also its oldest, dating from 80 BC. Next door, the **Palestra** is a vast parade ground that was used by Pompeii's youth for sport and exercise. One last place you shouldn't miss is the **Villa dei Misteri**, outside the main site, a short walk from the Porta Ercolano and accessible on the same ticket. This is probably the best preserved of all Pompeii's palatial houses, and it derives its name from a series of excellently preserved paintings in one of its larger chambers: depictions of the initiation rites of a young woman into the Dionysiac Mysteries, an orgiastic cult transplanted to Italy from Greece in the Republican era and at times partially outlawed for its excesses.

To **reach Pompeii from Naples**, take the Circumvesuviana to Pompeii-Villa dei Misteri (direction Sorrento) for about thirty minutes; this leaves you right outside the western entrance to the site. The Circumvesuviana also runs to Pompeii-Santuario, outside the site's eastern entrance (direction Sarno), or you can take the roughly hourly main-line train (direction Salerno) to the main Pompeii FS station, on the south side of the modern town. It makes most sense to see the site from Naples, and there's really no need to stay overnight, though if you get stuck or are planning to move on south after seeing Pompeii, there are plenty of hotels in the modern town, and a large and well-equipped **campsite**, *Zeus*, right outside the Pompeii-Villa dei Misteri station. The **tourist office** on Piazza Esedra (Mon–Sat 9am–3pm; turn right outside Pompeii-Villa dei Misteri station) has full details and plans of the site.

Sorrento

Topping the rocky cliffs close to the end of its peninsula, **SORRENTO** is unashamedly a resort, its inspired location and mild climate having drawn foreigners from all over Europe for close on two hundred years. Nowadays it's strictly package-tour territory, but really none the worse for it, a bright, lively place that retains its southern Italian roots. Cheap restaurants aren't hard to find; neither is reasonably priced accommodation; and there's really no better place outside Naples itself from which to explore the rugged Amalfi shore and the islands of the Bay.

Sorrento's centre is **Piazza Tasso**, five minutes from the train station along the busy Corso Italia, the streets around which are pedestrianized for the lively evening *passeggiata*. Strange as it may seem, Sorrento isn't particularly well provided with beaches: most people make do with the rocks and a tiny, crowded strip of sand at **Marina Grande** – fifteen minutes' walk or a short bus ride from Piazza Tasso – or simply use the wooden jetties. If you don't fancy this, try the beaches further along, like the tiny **Regina Giovanna** at Punta del Capo, again connected by bus from Piazza Tasso, where the ruins of the Roman Villa Pollio Felix make a unique place to bathe. There's a **tourist office** in the large yellow Circolo dei Foresteri building at Via de Maio 35, just off Piazza Sant'Antonino (Mon–Sat 8.45am–2.15pm & 3.45–6.15pm; ☎081.807.4033, *www.sorrentotourism.com*), which has maps and details of accommodation. There's a **hostel** close to the station at Via degli Aranci 160 (☎081.807.2925; ②); walk out of the station, turn left on the main road and it's a little way down on your left. Among a number of centrally placed **hotels**, the cheapest are the *City*, Corso Italia 221 (☎081.877.2210; ③), and the *Astoria* on Via Santa Maria delle Grazie 24 (☎081.807.4030; ⑥, including breakfast). The cheapest and closest **campsite** is *Nube d'Argento* (April–Oct), ten minutes' walk from Piazza Tasso in the direction of Marina Grande at Via del Capo 12. For **eating**, the *Ristorante Sant'Antonino*, off Piazza Antonino, is good value. For late-night boozing and **nightlife**, there are the town's English-style pubs: try the *English Inn*, or *Chaplin's*, almost opposite, on Corso Italia.

Capri

Sheering out of the sea off the far end of the Sorrentine peninsula, the island of **Capri** has long been the most sought-after part of the Bay of Naples. During Roman times the emperor Tiberius retreated here to indulge in legendary debauchery until his death in 37 AD. Later, the discovery of the Blue Grotto and the island's remarkable natural landscape coincided with the rise of tourism; the island has attracted a steady flow of artists and writers and, more recently, inquisitive tourists, ever since. Inevitably, Capri is a crowded and expensive place, and in July and August it's perhaps sensible to give it a miss. But it would be hard to find a place with more inspiring views, and it's easy enough to visit on a day-trip.

From Naples, there are regular ferries to Capri from the Molo Beverello, at the bottom of Piazza Municipio (at least 6 daily in summer; journey time 1hr 15min). There are also regular hydrofoils from the Mergellina jetty a couple of miles north of here and from Sorrento; these are quicker, but are much more expensive. For more information, consult the daily newspaper, *Il Mattino*.

Ferries and hydrofoils dock at **MARINA GRANDE**, the waterside extension of Capri town, which perches on the hill above, connected by funicular (€1 one way). There's not much to actually see, but it's very pretty, its winding, hilly alleyways converging on the dinky main square of **Piazza Umberto**. The **Certosa San Giacomo** (Tues–Sat 9am–2pm, Sun 9am–1pm; free) on the far side of the town is a run-down old monastery with a handful of paintings, and the Giardini Augustos next door give tremendous views of the coast below and the towering jagged cliffs above. From here you can wind down to **MARINA PICCOLA**, a huddle of houses and restaurants around a few patches of pebble beach – pleasantly uncrowded out of season, though in season you might as well forget it. You can also reach the ruins of Tiberius' villa, the **Villa Jovis** (daily 9am to 1hr before sunset; €2.10), from Capri town, a steep thirty-minute trek east. The site is among Capri's most exhilarating, with incredible vistas of the Bay, although there's not much left of the villa.

The island's other main settlement, **ANACAPRI**, is less picturesque than Capri town, its tacky main square flanked by souvenir shops, boutiques and touristy restaurants. But during the season, a chair lift operates from here up **Monte Solaro**, at 596m the island's highest point, and you can also get to the island's most famous attraction, the **Blue Grotto** ("Grotta Azzurra"), from here – a good 45-minute trek down Via Lo Pozzo or reachable by bus every twenty minutes from the main square. This is a bit of a rip-off, with boatmen whisking visitors through the grotto in five minutes flat, but you may want to do it just to say you've been, despite the €7.80 fee. In the late afternoons after the tourists have gone you can swim into the cave for nothing – change at the bar next to the entrance. It's also possible to take a boat trip to the Grotto direct from Marina Grande, though at €4.20 a head, not including entrance to the cave, it's a pricey outing. Time is better spent walking in the opposite direction from Piazza Vittoria to Axel Munthe's **Villa San Michele** (daily 9am–6pm; €4.20), a light, airy house that was home to the Swedish writer for a number of years, and is filled with his furniture and knick-knacks, as well as Roman artefacts ingeniously incorporated into the villa's rooms and gardens.

There are **tourist offices** in Marina Grande, on Piazza Umberto in Capri town (Mon–Sat 8.30am–8.30pm, Sun 9am–1pm & 3.30–7pm; ☎081.837.0686), and on Via G. Orlandi in Anacapri (same times; ☎081.837.1524). If you're on a tight budget, you'd be advised not to **stay** overnight, but if keen you could try the centrally placed *Quattro Stagioni*, Via Marina Piccola 1 (☎081.837.0041; ⑦; March–Oct), *Stella Maris*, Via Roma 27 (☎081.837.0452; ⑤), or *Pensione Esperia*, Via Supramonte (☎081.837.0262; ⑧). The very best deal on the island, however, is the family-run *Villa Eva* in Anacapri, Via La Fabbrica 8 (☎081.837.1549; ⑤), a garden paradise with pool, breakfast included. Even if you don't stay, **eating** is an expense, and you might prefer to fix a picnic: in Capri town there is a supermarket and bakery a little way down Via Botteghe off Piazza Umberto, and well-stocked food stores at Via Roma 13 and 30. For inexpensive sit-down food, *Di Giorgio* in Via Roma (closed Tues) is your best bet. For seafood, try rather pricey *Da Gemma* in Via Madre Serafina 6 (closed Monday out of season), just off the south side of the piazza, up the steps, past the church and bearing right through the tunnel.

The Amalfi Coast

Occupying the southern side of Sorrento's peninsula, the **Amalfi Coast** lays claim to being Europe's most beautiful stretch of coast, its corniche road winding around the towering cliffs. It's an incredible ride, and if you're staying in Sorrento shouldn't be missed on any account; in any case, the towns along here hold the beaches that Sorrento lacks. It's become rather developed, but the cliffs are so steep and the towns' growth so constrained it seems unlikely that it can ever become completely spoilt.

Positano

There's not much to **POSITANO**, only a couple of decent beaches and a handful of clothing and souvenir shops. But its location, heaped up in a pyramid high above the water, has inspired a thousand picture postcards, and helped to make it a moneyed resort that runs a close second to Capri in the celebrity stakes. It's inevitably pricey – an overnight stay isn't recommended. But its beaches – a small one to the right of the pyramid, a larger one to the left, ringed with overpriced bars and restaurants – are rarely unpleasantly crammed. And if you can't bring yourself to get back on the bus, there are summer hydrofoil connections with Capri, Amalfi and Salerno. For food, try the *salumeria*, next to the *tabacchi*, which also sells hydrofoil tickets.

Amalfi

For affordable food and accommodation, you'd do better to push on to **AMALFI**, the largest town along this coast and an established seaside resort since Edwardian times, when the British upper classes spent their winters here. An independent republic in Byzantine times, Amalfi was one of the great naval powers with a population of some seventy thousand. Vanquished by the Normans in 1131, it was devastated by an earthquake in 1343. A few remnants of Amalfi's past glories survive, and the town has a crumbly attractiveness that makes it fun to wander through.

The **Duomo**, at the top of a steep flight of steps, dominates the town's main piazza, its decorated, almost gaudy facade topped by a glazed tiled cupola that's typical of the region. Inside, it's a mixture of Saracen and Romanesque styles, though now heavily restored, with a major relic in the body of St Andrew buried in its crypt. The most appealing part of the building is the cloister (daily 9am–9pm; €1.60) – oddly Arabic in feel, with its whitewashed arches and palms. Close by, the **Museo Civico** (same hours & ticket as the cloisters) displays the original *Tavoliere Amalfitane* – the book of maritime laws which governed the republic, and the rest of the Mediterranean, until 1570. Beyond these, the focus is along the busy seafront, where there's an acceptably crowded **beach**. There's a rather unhelpful **tourist office** (Mon–Fri 8.30am–1.30pm & 3–6pm, Sat 8.30–noon; ☎089.871.107, *www.amalficoast.it*) at Corso delle Repubbliche 27, next door to the **post office**. The cheapest **hotels** are the *Proto*, off Via Genova down Salita dei Curiali 4 (☎089.871.003; ⑤, including breakfast), and the *Lidomare*, just off the main square at Via Piccolomini 9 (☎089.871.332, *www.lidomare.it*; ⑥, including breakfast). Less than a kilometre outside town at Atrani, is the **hostel-cum-hotel** *A' Scalinatella*, Piazza Umberto I 5–6 (☎089.871.492, *www.amalficoast.it /hotel/scalinatella*; ②) with a free beach 150 metres away. For **eating**, try *La Taverna del Duca*, Piazza Spirito Santo 26 (closed Thurs), where you can sit outside; *Trattoria da Gemma* (closed Wed), back towards the sea on the opposite side, with a lovely terrace overlooking the street; or the inexpensive *Il Mulino* further up the hill on Via delle Cartiere.

Ravello

The best views of the coast can be had inland from Amalfi, in **RAVELLO**: another renowned spot, "closer to the sky than the seashore," wrote André Gide – with some justification. Ravello was also an independent republic for a while, and for a time an outpost of the Amalfi city-state; now it's not much more than a large village, but its unrivalled location, spread across the top of one of the coast's mountains, makes it more than worth the thirty-minute bus ride up from Amalfi.

Buses drop off on the main **Piazza Vescovado**, outside the **Duomo**: an eleventh-century church dedicated to St Pantaleone, a fourth-century saint whose blood – kept in a chapel on the left-hand side – is supposed to liquefy like that of Naples' San Gennaro, twice a year on May 19 and August 27. It's richly decorated, with a pair of twelfth-century bronze doors, cast with 54 scenes of the Passion; inside, attention focuses on a monumental ambo of 1272, adorned with mosaics of dragons and birds on spiral columns, and with the coat of arms and the vivacious profiles of the Rufolo family, the donors, on each side. The Rufolos figure again on the other side of the square, where various leftovers of their **Villa Rufolo** (daily 9.30–1pm & 3–5/7pm; €2.10) scatter among gardens overlooking the precipitous coastline. Ten minutes away, the gardens of the **Villa Cimbrone** (daily 9am–sunset; €2.58), laid out by a Yorkshire aristocrat earlier this century, spread across the furthest tip of Ravello's ridge. Most of the villa itself is not open to visitors, though it's worth peeking into the crumbly, flower-hung cloister as you go in, and the open crypt down the steps from here. Best bit of the gardens is the belvedere at the far end of the main path, giving marvellous views over the sea below.

Bari

Commercial and administrative capital of Puglia, and the second city of the *mezzogiorno*, **BARI** has its fair share of interest. But although an economically vibrant place, it harbours no pretensions about being a major tourist attraction. Primarily people come here to work, or to leave for Greece on its many ferries.

There's not a lot to the new part of the city so you should head straight for tree-lined **Corso Cavour**, Bari's main commercial street, which leads down to the waterfront and the old city, an entrancing labyrinth of seemingly endless passages weaving through courtyards and under arches that was originally designed to spare the inhabitants from the wind and throw invaders into a state of confusion. The **Basilica di San Nicola**, in the heart of the old city, was consecrated in 1197 to house the relics of the saint. Inside, its twelfth-century altar canopy is one of the finest in Italy, the motifs around the capitals the work of stonemasons from Como. The twelfth-century carved doorway and the simple, striking mosaic floor of the choir are lovely, and the twelfth-century episcopal throne behind the altar is a superb piece of work, supported by small figures wheezing beneath its weight. Close by, the **Cattedrale di San Sabino**, off Piazza Odegitria, was built at the end of the twelfth century, and is a plain church by contrast, home to an eighth-century icon known as the Madonna Odegitria that's said to be the most authentic likeness of the Madonna in existence, taken from an original sketch by Luke the Apostle. Across the piazza, the **Castello Normanno-Svevo** (Tues–Sat 8.30am–6.30pm, Sun 9am–1pm; €2.10) sits on the site of an earlier Roman fort. Built by Frederick II, much of it is closed to the public, but it has a vaulted hall that provides a cool escape from the afternoon sun.

Practicalities

The **tourist office** on Piazza Aldo Moro (Mon–Fri 8am–2pm; ☎080.524.2361, *www.puglia-turismo.com/aptbari*) by the train station, a kilometre south of the old city, has maps and a list of **private rooms** – probably the cheapest accommodation option. Otherwise, try *Pensione Giulia*, at Via Crisanzio 12 (☎080.521.6630 8271; ④, including breakfast). The nearest **campsite** is 6km south of the city on the SS16 – bus #12 from Teatro Petruzzelli. All **ferries** use the Stazione Maríttima, next to the old city. **Eating** out, *Le Travi e il Buco* (closed Mon), on Largo Chiurlia in the old part of town, is good, or the *Terranima*, Via Putignani 213–215 (closed Sun), specializing in regional cookery.

Ferries

For details of ferry services to **Greece**, contact Ventouris, c/o P. Lorusso, Via Piccini 133 (☎080.521.7699), who run services to Corfu or Igoumenitsa (€44 one way); there are four to seven sailings a week between May and September. Superfast, Corso di Tullio 6 (☎080.528.2828), run daily sailings, departing at 8pm, to Igoumenitsa and Patras (€42 one way). Travel agents around town often have a wide variety of offers on **tickets**, including CTS, Via Fornari 7 (☎080.521.3244; Mon–Fri 10am–1pm & 3–7pm; Sat 10am–1pm), who give a discount on student/youth fares; InterRail pass holders get discounts too. Once you've got your ticket, you must report to the Stazione Maríttima at least two hours before departure. There are also ferries from Bari to **Croatia** (Dubrovnik; four weekly) through P. Lorusso, Via Piccinni 133 (☎080.521.7643; €48 one way).

Bríndisi

BRÍNDISI, about 100km southeast of Bari, was once the main crossing point between the eastern and western empires, and later, under the Normans, on the route of pilgrims heading east towards the Holy Land – and it is still strictly a place for passing through, mainly for tourists on their way to Greece. It's not a particularly pleasant place, and there's not much to see, but the old centre has a pleasant, almost Oriental flavour, with a *passeggiata* that's one of the south's best.

Ferries dock at the **Stazione Maríttima** on Via del Mare, from where it's a few minutes' walk to the bottom of Corso Garibaldi, and another twenty minutes to the **train station** in Piazza Crispi. Lots of **buses** run down Corso Umberto and Corso Garibaldi (€0.80 a ride).

There's a **tourist office** on Viale Regina Margherita 43 (summer daily Mon–Fri 8.30am–2pm & 3–7pm; winter Sat 8.30am–1pm; ☎0831.523.072, *www.pugliaturismo.com/aptbrindisi*). As most ferries leave in the evening, **accommodation** isn't usually a problem: try the central and very basic *Venezia*, Via Pisanelli 4 (☎0831.527.511; ②). There's also a very friendly **hostel**, 2km out of town at Via Brandi 2 (☎0831.413.123; ②, including breakfast), with Internet access and lots of other amenities – call them and they'll send their shuttle to pick you up, or take bus #3 or #4 from the train station. It's not difficult **to eat** cheaply, the whole of Corso Umberto and Corso Garibaldi (particularly the port end) being smothered in bars and restaurants in which you should be able to grab a reasonably priced if average meal. Try *Pizzeria L'Angoletto*, Via Pergola 3, just off Corso Garibaldi, which has outdoor tables and cheap local wine.

Ferries to Greece

There is a huge array of **agents** selling ferry tickets to **Greece**, and you must take care to avoid getting ripped off. The most reliable are Grecian Travel, Corso Garibaldi 79 (☎0831.597.884), and UTAC Viaggi, Via Santa Lucia 11(☎0831.524.921). There's usually at least one daily service to the main Greek ports throughout the year; services increase between April and September, and mid-June to August is peak season, with several sailings a day to most destinations, though you still should book in advance if possible. The most reliable ferry companies are Hellenic Mediterranean Lines, Corso Garibaldi 8 (☎0831.528.531), who go to Corfu, Igoumenitsa, Patras and Cefalonia, and Fragline, Via Spalato 31 (☎0831.548.541), with sailings to Corfu and Igoumenitsa. In general the reliable companies, including those listed above, sail at night (between 9pm and 10.30pm); it's only the pirate companies that depart during the day. **Prices** vary according to season: you're looking at around €25–45 one way to Corfu/Igoumenitsa or Patras, though less than double that for returns, except in high season. Fragline is slightly cheaper. InterRail and Eurail passes are valid on the Corfu/Patras crossing with Hellenic Mediterranean lines. Everyone pays an **embarkation tax** – currently €6.20. Don't forget to stock up on **food and drink,** as there are serious mark-ups once on board.

SICILY

Coming from the Italian mainland, **Sicily** feels socially and culturally all but out of Europe. Occupying a strategically vital position, and as the largest island in the Mediterranean, Sicily's history and outlook is not that of its modern parent but of its erstwhile foreign rulers – from the Greeks who first settled the east coast in the eighth century BC, through a dazzling array of Romans, Arabs, Normans, French and Spanish, to the Bourbons seen off by Garibaldi in 1860. Substantial relics of these ages remain: temples, theatres and churches are scattered about the whole island. But there are other, more immediate hints of Sicily's unique past. A hybrid Sicilian language is still widely spoken in the countryside; the food is noticeably different, spicier; and there is, of course, the mafia – though this is not something which impinges upon the lives of tourists.

Inevitably perhaps, most points of interest are on the coast: the interior of the island is often mountainous, sparsely populated and relatively inaccessible. The capital, **Palermo**, is a memorable first stop, a bustling city with an unrivalled display of Norman art and architecture and Baroque churches. The most obvious other trips are to the chic resort of **Taormina** near to which you can skirt around the foothills and even up to the craters of **Mount Etna**, and to the ancient Greek centre of **Siracusa**, with its wonderful architecture and ancient remains. To the south, the greatest draw is the grouping of temples at **Agrigento**, the biggest concentration of the island's Greek remnants.

To **get to Sicily**, you can simply take a train from the mainland – they travel across the Straits of Messina on the ferries from Villa San Giovanni and continue on the other side. Travelling by car, there are also direct ferries from Reggio di Calabria, Naples, Genoa and Livorno.

Palermo and around

In its own wide bay underneath the limestone bulk of Monte Pellegrino, **PALERMO** is stupendously sited. Originally a Phoenician, then a Carthaginian colony, this remarkable city was long considered a prize worth capturing, and under Saracen and Norman rule in the ninth to twelfth centuries Palermo became the greatest city in Europe, famed for the wealth of its court and peerless as a centre of learning. Nowadays it's a brash and exciting city, a fascinating place to be as much for just strolling and consuming as for specific attractions. But Palermo's monuments, its unique series of Baroque and Arabo-Norman churches, the unparalleled mosaic work and excellent museums are also the equal of anything on the mainland.

Arrival, information and accommodation

Trains all pull in at the Stazione Centrale, at the southern end of Via Roma, connected with the modern centre by buses #101 and #102. **Ferry and hydrofoil** services dock at the Stazione Marittima, just off Via Francesco Crispi, from where it's a ten-minute walk up Via E. Amari to Piazza Castelnuovo. There are **tourist offices** at Stazione Centrale (Mon–Fri 8.30am–2pm & 2.30–6pm, Sat 8.30am–2pm) and the Stazione Marittima, and a main office at Piazza Castelnuovo 34 (same hours as station; ☎091.583.847, *www.aapit.pa.it*), with free maps, accommodation and entertainment guides. There are **Internet points** at Via Cala 64 (☎091.611.8483) and Via Candelai (☎091.327.151).

You'll find getting around exclusively on foot exhausting and impractical. **City buses** are easy to use, covering every corner of Palermo and stretching out to Monreale and Mondello. There's a flat fare of €0.80 (valid for 60min) or €2.60 (for a day) and you can buy tickets from the glass booths outside Stazione Centrale, at the southern end of Viale della Libertà, or from *tabacchi*.

Most of the budget hotel **accommodation** in Palermo is on and around the southern ends of Via Maqueda and Via Roma, in the area between Stazione Centrale and Corso Vittorio Emanuele. On Via Roma, there's the *Concordia* at no. 72 (☎091.617.1514; ③); or off to the right, just before Corso Vittorio Emanuele, the *Olimpia* (☎091.616.1276; ③) has rooms overlooking Piazza Cassa di Risparmio. At Via Maqueda 8, there's the *Vittoria* (☎091.616.2437; ③), and the atmospheric *Orientale* lies a little further up at no. 26 (☎091.616.5727; ③) in a marble-studded palazzo. Signposted left just before Corso Vittorio Emanuele, the *Cortese* (☎091.331.722; ③) has clean rooms in a murky neighbourhood, near the Ballarò market. Off Corso V. Emanuele, at Via Bottai 30, the *Letizia* (☎091.589.110; ④), is good, clean and safe. If you want to stay central and pay a little more, the *Grande Albergo Sole* (☎091.581.811; ⑤) offers plenty of old-fashioned comfort. If you're **camping**, take bus #616 from Piazza Vittorio Veneto (for which take any bus up Via Libertà from Piazza Castelnuovo) out to Sferracavallo, 13km northwest of the city, where there are two sites: the *Campeggio Internazionale Trinacria* on Via Barcarello (☎091.530.590), with two-bedded **cabins**, and the cheaper *degli Ulivi* (☎091.533.021), on Via Pegaso, both open all year.

The City

The heart of the old city is the Baroque crossroads of the Quattro Canti, erected in 1611, just around the corner from Piazza Pretoria and the church of **La Martorana** (Mon–Sat 9.30am–1pm & 3.30–7pm, Sun 8.30am–1pm), one of the finest survivors of the medieval city, with a slim twelfth-century campanile and a series of spectacular mosaics, animated twelfth-century Greek works. In the district southwest of here, the Albergheria, a warren of tiny streets, the deconsecrated church of **San Giovanni degli Eremiti** (Mon–Sat 9am–7pm, Sun 9am–1pm; €4) was built in 1148, and is the most obviously Arabic of the city's Norman relics, with five ochre domes topping a small church that was built upon the remains of an earlier mosque. A path leads up through citrus trees to the church, behind which lie its celebrated late-thirteenth-century cloisters. From here it's a few paces north to the **Palazzo dei Normanni** whose entrance is on Piazza Indipendenza; it was originally built by the Saracens and was enlarged considerably by the Normans, under whom it housed the most magnificent of medieval European courts. Sadly, there's little left from those times, and most of the interior is now taken up by the Sicilian parliament, but you can visit the beautiful **Cappella Palatina** (Mon–Fri 9–11.45am & 3–4.45pm, Sat 9–11.45am, Sun 9–10am & noon–1pm), the private royal chapel of Roger II, built between 1132 and 1143 and almost entirely covered in twelfth-century mosaics.

On the far side of Corso V. Emanuele from here, the **Cattedrale** (Mon–Sat 7am–7pm, Sun 8am–1.30pm & 4–7pm) is a more substantial Norman relic, an odd building mainly because of the eighteenth-century alterations which added the dome and spoiled the fine lines of the tawny stone. Still, the triple-apsed eastern end and the lovely matching towers are all original and date from 1185; the interior is cold and Neoclassical, the only items of interest the fine portal and wooden doors and the royal tombs, containing the remains of some of Sicily's most famous monarchs.

Across Via Roma, the **Museo Archeologico Regionale** (daily 9am–1.15pm, Tues, Wed & Fri also 3–6.15pm, Sun 9am–1pm; €4.10) is a magnificent collection of artefacts, mainly from the island's Greek and Roman sites. Two cloisters hold anchors and other retrieved hardware from the sea off the Sicilian coast, and there are rich stone carvings from the temple site of Selinunte. In the opposite direction from Santa Zita lies the depressed area around the old harbour, La Cala, and, across Corso V. Emanuele on Via Alloro, Sicily's **Galleria Regionale** (Mon–Sat 9am–1.30pm, Tues & Thurs also 3–7.30pm, Sun 9am–12.30pm; €4.10), a stunning medieval art collection that includes a magnificent fifteenth-century fresco of the *Triumph of Death*, work by the fifteenth-century sculptor Francesco Laurana and paintings by Antonello da Messina.

The third of Palermo's showpiece museums – the **Museo Etnografico Pitrè** (9am–8pm; closed Fri; €3.10) – lies on the edge of La Favorita, a large park around 3km from Piazza Castelnuovo (bus #106 or #806 from Piazza Sturzo, behind the Politeama, or from Viale della Libertà). This is the key exhibition of Sicilian folklore and culture on the island, with a wealth of carts painted with bright scenes from the story of the Paladins, a reconstructed puppet theatre and dozens of expressive puppets, and a whole series of intricately worked terracotta figures, dolls and games.

For real attention-grabbing stuff, take bus #327 from Piazza Indipendenza southwest to Via Pindemonte (a 20min walk), where the **Convento dei Cappuccini** (daily 9am–noon & 3–5pm; €1.30) has a warren of catacombs under its church that's home to some eight thousand bodies, preserved by various chemical processes and placed in niches along corridors, dressed in their best clothes. The bodies that aren't lined along the walls lie in stacked glass coffins, and – to say the least – it's an unnerving experience to walk among them.

Eating, drinking and nightlife

For authentic Sicilian **fast food**, the old-style *Antica Focacceria*, Via A. Paternostro 58, off Corso Vittorio Emanuele, is good: you can sample specialities like *panino* with *milze* (veal innards) and ricotta. If you're feeling less adventurous, try the busy *Pizzeria Italia* at Via Orologio 54, off Via Maqueda. For **full-blown meals**, the city's best bargain is *Trattoria-Pizzeria Enzo*, Via Maurolico 17/19, close to the station, while the *Trattoria Primavera* on Piazza Bologni has an excellent-value set meal. Nearby, you can eat **couscous** and other North African dishes at *Caffè d'Oriente*, hidden away on Piazza Cancellieri, at the top of Via Celso, an alley off Via Maqueda near Corso Vittorio Emanuele. During the day, the terrace cafés on Via Principe di Belmonte, leading east off Via Roma towards the Stazione Maríttima, are your best bet for a **drink**. On warm evenings a young crowd spills out onto the street from the *Bottiglieria del Mássimo*, a wine bar with pavement seating at Via Spinuzza 59, near the Teatro Mássimo and at the various bars and cafés behind the church of Sant'Ignazio All'Olivella.

Monreale

Sicily's most extraordinary medieval mosaics are to be seen in the Norman cathedral at Monreale, a small hill town 8km southwest of Palermo and accessible on bus #309 or #389 from Piazza dell'Indipendenza, a twenty-minute journey. The **Duomo** mosaics (daily 8am–6pm) represent the apex of Sicilian-Norman art, and were almost certainly executed by Greek and Byzantine craftsmen, revealing a unitary plan and inspiration: your eyes are drawn to the all-embracing figure of Christ in the central apse – an awesome and pivotal mosaic, the head and shoulders alone almost 20m high. Underneath sit an enthroned Virgin and Child, attendant angels and ranks of saints, each individually and subtly coloured and identified by name. No less remarkable are the nave mosaics, an animated series starting with the Creation to the right of the altar and running around the entire church. Ask at the desk by the entrance to climb the **tower** (€1) in the southwest corner of the cathedral – an unusual and precarious vantage point. The **cloisters** (Mon–Sat 9am–7pm, Sun 9am–1pm; €4.10), part of the original Benedictine monastery, form an elegant arcaded quadrangle, with some 216 twin columns that are a riot of detail and imagination.

Taormina and around

On Sicily's eastern coast, and dominating two grand sweeping bays below, **TAORMINA** is the island's best-known resort. The outstanding remains of its classical theatre, with Mount Etna as an unparalleled backdrop, arrested passing travellers when Taormina was no more than a medieval hill village, and these days it's virtually impossible to find anywhere to stay between June and August. Despite this, Taormina retains much of its small-town charm, the main traffic-free street, Corso V. Emanuele, an unbroken line of fifteenth- to nineteenth-century palazzi and small, intimate piazzas.

The **Teatro Greco** (daily 9am–1hr before sunset; €4.10) – signposted from just about everywhere – is the only real sight, founded by Greeks in the third century BC, though most of what's left is a Roman rebuilding from the first century AD, when the stage and lower seats were cut back to provide room and a deep trench dug in the orchestra to accommodate the animals and fighters used in gladiatorial contests.

Trains pull up at Taormina-Giardini station, way below town, from where it's a steep thirty-minute walk up or a short bus ride to the centre of town. The central **tourist office** (Mon–Sat 8.30am–2pm & 4–7pm; ☎0942.23.243, *www.taormina-ol.it*) in Palazzo Corvaja, Piazza Santa Caterina, has free maps. There are good **accommodation** possibilities along Via Bagnoli Croce, for example *Il Leone* at 124–126 (☎0942.23.878; ③), or try the tiny but cheap *Diana* (☎0942.23.898; ③), nearby, at Via di Giovanni 6. You could also try the *Pensione Svizzera*, at Via Pirandello 26 (☎0942.23.790; ⑥), just up from the bus terminal. If everywhere is full, you'll have to opt for nearby Giardini-Naxos. The **campsite**, *San Leo*, on the cape below town, is open all year, though it's not particularly good; take any bus running between Taormina and the station. **Eating** in Taormina is relatively pricey compared to the rest of Sicily – if money is tight, try the good **rosticceria** just up from Porta Messina, on the corner of Via Timeo and Via Patrizio. Among the less expensive **trattorias** are *La Botte*, Piazza Santa Domenica 4, and *Il Baccanale* in Piazza Filea, which has outdoor tables and similar prices – both close to Via Bagnoli Croce – or try *Trattoria Siciliana*, a quieter place outside Porta Catania at Salita Ospedale 9.

The closest beach to town is at **MAZZARO**, with its much-photographed islet. It's about a thirty-minute descent on foot but the preferable option is to use the cable car (€1.60) every fifteen minutes from Via Pirandello, and a steep path which starts just below the cable car station. The beach-bars and restaurants at **SPISONE**, a kilometre or so further north, are also reachable by path from Taormina, this time from below the cemetery in town. From Spisone, the coast opens out and the beach gets wider. Five kilometres north of Taormina, **LETO-JANNI** is a little resort in its own right, with a few fishing boats on a sandy beach, two campsites and regular buses and trains back to Taormina. Roomier and better for swimming are the sands south of Taormina at **GIARDINI-NAXOS**, which is an excellent alternative source of accommodation and food. Prices tend to be a good bit cheaper than in Taormina and in high season it's worth trying here first. Immobiliare Naxos, Via V. Emanuele 58 (☎0942.51.184), can arrange apartments – good value if you're a group of four or more – or provide lists of hotels. You could try *La Sirena*, Via Schisò 36 (☎0942.51.853; ③), by the pier with views over the bay. For eating, good pizzas and fresh fish can be had at *Fratelli Marano*, Via Naxos 181. *Da Angelina*, on Via Euboea by the pier, does marvellous well-priced pizzas and home-made pasta and has great views. Also good is *La Conchiglia*, Via Naxos 221, specializing in Sicilian meat dishes.

Mount Etna

Mount Etna's massive bulk looms over much of the coastal route south of Taormina, and, if you don't have the time to reach the summit, rail services provide some alternative volcanic thrills in a ride around the base of the volcano from **GIARRE-RIPOSTO**, thirty minutes by train or bus from Taormina; InterRail passes are not valid, and if you make the entire trip to Catania, allow four hours; tickets cost €5.20 one way. As for the ascent, this is a spectacular trip worth every effort to make – though without your own transport that effort can be considerable. At 3323m, Etna is a fairly substantial mountain, the fact that it's also one of the world's biggest volcanoes (and still active) only adding to the draw. Some of the eruptions have been disastrous: in 1669 Catania was wrecked; this century the Circumetnea rail line has been repeatedly ruptured by lava flows, and, in 1979, nine people were killed on the edge of the main crater. In 1997, 1998 and 2001 the eruptions were high, but not life-theatening. This is not to say you'll be in any danger, provided you heed the warnings as you get closer to the top. There are several approaches. On public transport, you'll need to come via **NICOLOSI**, an hour from Catania by frequent bus, one of which (8am from Catania train station) continues on to a huddle of souvenir shops and restaurants around the *Rifugio Sapienza* (☎095.911.062; ③), which provides simple food and lodging. Arriving on the early morning bus, you'll have enough time to make it to the top and get back for the return bus to Catania – it leaves around 4.45pm. To get up the volcano from the refuge, you can take the cable car up to about 2500m (€18.20 return) from where a guide can take you by jeep to the Torre del Filósofo (April–Oct; €35.40 for a return ticket including cable car, jeep and guide) or you can walk, following the rough minibus track (3–4hr each way). However you go, take warm clothes, good shoes and glasses to keep the flying grit out of your eyes. The highest you're allowed to get is 2900m, and though there's only a rope across the ground to prevent you from climbing further, it would be foolish to do so.

Siracusa

Further down Sicily's eastern seaboard, **SIRACUSA** (ancient Syracuse) was first colonized by Greeks in 733 BC and grew to become their main power base in Sicily. Today the city boasts some of the best Greek archeological remains anywhere, and also has a strong Baroque character in its old town, squeezed onto on the island of Ortygia, by the harbour.

    Ortygia makes a good place to start exploring the city. At the centre of the island, the most obvious attraction is the **Duomo**, set in an elongated piazza studded with Baroque architecture, and itself incorporating twelve fluted columns belonging to the temple which originally stood here. Round the corner from the piazza, the severe thirteenth-century Palazzo Bellomo houses the **Museo Regionale d'Arte Medioevale e Moderna** (Tues–Sun 9am–1.30pm, also Wed 3am–6pm; €2.60), an outstanding collection of medieval art, including a damaged fifteenth-century *Annunciation* by Antonello da Messina. Note that it's worth buying a **combined ticket** (valid over two days) if you're planning to see Siracusa's other major sights:

€5.20 for the Museo Regionale and the Museo Archeologico, €6.20 for the Museo Archeologico and Parco Archeologico, or €7.80 for all three.

North of the train station, the city is mainly new and commercial, though there are also the best of Siracusa's archeological sights here: take bus #4, #5, #12 or #15 from Ortygia's Largo XXV Luglio as far as Viale Teocrito where you should walk east for the **Museo Archeologico** (Tues–Sun 9am–1pm; Mon & Wed also 3.30–7.30/6.30pm; €4.10), which holds a wealth of material from the early Greek colonies. The most famous exhibit is the *Venus*, a headless figure arising from the sea.

Siracusa's extensive **Parco Archeologico** (daily 9am–2hr before sunset; €4.10) lies a twenty-minute walk to the west, reachable on bus #4, #5 or #6 from Largo XXV Luglio. Here, the **Ara di Ierone II**, an enormous altar of the third century BC, is the first thing you see, but the main highlight of the park is the **Teatro Greco**, cut out of the rock and looking down into trees below. It's much bigger than the one at Taormina, capable of holding around 15,000 people, though less impressive scenically. Look out for the set of carved names around the top of the middle gangway, which marked the various seat blocks occupied by the royal family. Aeschylus put on works here, and Greek dramas are still staged in even-numbered years.

Nearby, the **Latomia del Paradiso**, a leafy quarry, is best known for its unusually shaped cavern that Dionysius is supposed to have used as a prison, the **Orecchio di Dionigi** (or "Ear of Dionysius") – a high, S-shaped cave 65m long: Caravaggio, a visitor in 1586, coined the name after the shape of the entrance, but the acoustic properties are such that it's not impossible to imagine Dionysius eavesdropping on his prisoners from a vantage point above.

Just **out of Siracusa**, there are a few worthwhile excursions you can make to escape the summer crowds. Seven kilometres west of the city, the military and defensive works on the ridge of **Epipolae**, the ancient city's western limit, provide grand views over the coast (buses #9, #11 and #12 run here from Corso Gelone), while the nearest clean **beaches** lie about the same distance south of the city at **Arenella** and **Ognina** (reachable on buses #23 and #21 respectively), though the best sands are at **Fontane Bianche**, 20km south of Siracusa (bus #21, #22 or #24). Nearer at hand, you can take a shady riverside stroll along the banks of the **Ciane River**, thickly grown with papyrus. You can drive to the source of the river, 10km inland (follow signs from the Canicattini road) or else take bus #21, #22 or #23 to a stop where the SS115 crosses the river, from where a good path traces the course of the river, taking in the scant but evocative remains of the **Olympieion**, a Doric temple from the sixth century BC.

Practicalities

Siracusa's **train station** is on the mainland, about a twenty-minute walk from Ortygia. AST **buses** arrive either in Piazza della Poste, just over the bridge on Ortygia or else in Piazzale Marconi, in the modern town; SAIS buses stop in Via Trieste, close by Piazza della Poste. For maps, accommodation listings, details of performances in the Greek theatre, and other information, visit the **tourist office** at Via Maestranza 33 (Easter–Sept Mon–Fri 8.30am–2pm & 3–7.30pm, Sat 8.30am–2pm; Oct–Easter Mon–Fri 8.30am–2pm & 3–5.30pm, Sat 8.30am–2pm; ☎0931.464.255), or at Via San Sebastiano 43 (Mon–Fri 8.30am–1.30pm & 3.30–6.30pm, Sat 9am–1pm; ☎0931.481.200, *www.apt-siracusa.it*).

Accommodation choices aren't spectacular and in high season you must make an advance reservation. A popular choice on Ortygia is the *Gran Bretagna*, Via Savoia 21 (☎0931.68.765; ②), or there's a handful of cheaper hotels near the station: try the *Aretusa* at Via Francesco Crispi 75 (☎0931.24.211; ③), or the *Centrale*, Corso Umberto 141 (☎0931.60.528; ②), just off Piazzale Marconi. The nearest **campsite**, *Agriturist Rinaura* (☎0931.721.224), is 5km away – take bus #21, #22 or #23 from Corso Umberto or Piazza delle Poste.

Many of Siracusa's **restaurants** are overpriced, but there are some good-value places. *La Siciliana*, Via Savoia 17, has a wide range of pizzas, and the *Trattoria Archimede*, Via Gemmellaro 8, frequented by locals, is inexpensive and good for fish. *Spaghetteria do*

Scogghiu, Via Scina 11, has a huge selection of cheap pasta and is popular at night. Good **bars** and cafés are easy to come by, two of the best being the outdoor *Bar Ortygia*, at the Fonte Aretusa, and the *Bar Del Ponte*, at the end of the Ponte Nuovo on Ortygia, which is good for breakfasts.

Agrigento

Located halfway along Sicily's southern littoral, **AGRIGENTO** is primarily interesting for the substantial remains of Pindar's "most beautiful city of mortals", strung out along a ridge facing the sea a couple of kilometres below town. The series of Doric temples here, mostly dating from the fifth century BC, constitute the most evocative of Sicilian remains and are unique outside Greece. As such, they are the focus of a constant procession of tour buses which can overwhelm the site, and you should note that budget accommodation is often scarce and should be booked in advance.

A road winds down from the modern city to the Valle dei Templi, buses (#1, #2 or #3) dropping you at a car park between the two separate sections of archeological remains. The **eastern zone** (daily 8.30am–9pm; free) is home to the scattered remains of the oldest of the temples, the **Tempio di Ercole**, probably begun in the last decades of the sixth century BC, and the better-preserved **Tempio della Concordia**, dated to around 430 BC, with fine views of the city and sea. There's also the **Tempio di Giunone**, an engaging half-ruin standing at the very edge of the ridge. The **western zone** (daily: summer 8.30am–7pm; winter 8.30am–5.30pm; €2.10), back along the path and beyond the car park, is less impressive but fun to wander around the vast tangle of stone and fallen masonry from a variety of temples. Most notable is the mammoth construction that was the **Tempio di Giove**, or Temple of Olympian Zeus, the largest Doric temple ever known, though never completed, left in ruins by the Carthaginians and further damaged by earthquakes. Via dei Templi leads back to the town from the car park via the excellent **Museo Nazionale Archeologico** (Wed–Sat 9am–1.30pm & 2–6.30pm, Mon, Tues & Sun 9am–1.30pm; €4.10) – an extraordinarily rich collection devoted to finds from the city and the surrounding area.

Trains arrive at the edge of the old town, outside which – on Piazza Marconi – buses leave for the temples. The **tourist office** (Mon–Fri 8am–2pm; ☎0922.204.54) is nearby at Via Cesare Battisti 15, at the eastern end of Via Atenea, and has hotel listings and maps. Among **hotels** worth trying are the *Belvedere*, Via San Vito 20 (☎0922.20.051; ④), *Concordia*, at Piazza San Francesco 11 (☎0922.596.266; ④); and the *Bella Napoli*, Piazza Lena 6 (☎0922.20.435; ④). You can camp 5km away at the coastal resort of San Leone; take bus #2 or #2/ from outside the train station. You can **eat** cheaply and well at *Trattoria Atenea*, Via Ficani 12, an alley above Via Atenea, or at *La Forchetta*, next door to the *Concordia* hotel.

SARDINIA

A little under 200km from the Italian mainland, slightly more than that from the North African coast of Tunisia, Sardinia (*www.regione.sardegna.it*) is way off most tourist itineraries. Relatively free of large cities or heavy industry, the island boasts some of the country's cleanest, least crowded beaches, and, though not known for its cultural riches, holds some fascinating vestiges of the various civilizations that passed through. In addition to Roman and Carthaginian ruins, Genoan fortresses and a string of lovely Pisan churches, there are striking remnants of Sardinia's only significant native culture, known as the nuraghic civilization after the 7000 or so stone constructions which litter the landscape.

On the whole, Sardinia's smaller centres are the most attractive, but the capital, **Cágliari** – for many the arrival point – shouldn't be written off. With good facilities for eating and sleeping, it makes a useful base for exploring the southern third of the island. The other main ferry port and airport is **Olbia** in the north, little more than a transit town for visitors to the nearby Costa Smeralda, though budget travellers are unlikely to want to spend time in this uncomfortable mix of opulence and suburbia.

In the northwest of the island, **Sássari** and **Alghero** manifest the deepest imprint of the long Spanish presence in Sardinia, with the latter having developed into the chief package resort. Inland, **Nuoro** has impressive literary credentials and a good ethnographic museum. As Sardinia's biggest interior town, it also makes a useful stopover for visiting some of the remoter mountain areas, where you can find what remains of the island's traditional culture, best embodied in the numerous village **festivals**.

The island boasts a good network of **public transport** to get you round all but the remoter areas. On the roads there is the island-wide bus network run by ARST and the private PANI for longer hauls between towns, while trains connect the major towns of Cágliari, Sássari and Olbia, with smaller lines linking with Nuoro and Alghero (note that Interail/Eurail passes are not valid for these smaller private lines).

Getting to Sardinia

There are frequent daily **flights** from the Italian mainland to the island's three airports, at Cágliari, Olbia and Fertília (for Alghero and Sássari). The flights, which take about an hour, are run by Alitalia, and Sardinia's own Meridiana. Cheaper but slower are the overnight **ferries** to Cágliari, Arbatax (halfway up the island's eastern coast), Olbia, Golfo degli Aranci (near Olbia) and Porto Torres (on Sardinia's northwestern corner) from mainland Italy (Civitavecchia, Genoa, Livorno, Naples) – as well as from Sicily, Tunis, Corsica and France. In high summer, **fast ferries** connect Genova, Civitavecchia and Fiumicino to the island in 4–6 hours, though fares are higher than those on the regular ferries, and seats quickly get booked up. If you're travelling by car, it's essential to book well in advance: sailings in July and August can be fully booked by May. Prices on regular ferries range from €27.10 to €61.40 per person, depending on season and route taken: a berth costs a minimum of €12.50 extra. A vehicle will cost a minimum of €60.80 for a small car in low season. Note that some companies offer fifty percent discounts for vehicles on certain dates if you book your return when you buy your outward-bound ticket.

Cágliari

Rising up from its port and crowned by an old citadel squeezed within a protective ring of Pisan fortifications, **CÁGLIARI** has been Sardinia's capital at least since Roman times and is still the island's biggest town. Nonetheless, its centre is easily explored on foot, and offers sophistication and charm in its raggle-taggle of narrow lanes. The main attractions here are the museum with its unique collection of **nuraghic** statuettes, the city walls, with their two Pisan towers looking down over the port, and the cathedral.

Arrival, information and accommodation

Cágliari's **port** lies in the heart of the town, opposite Via Roma. The **airport** sits beside the Stagno di Cágliari, the city's largest lagoon, fifteen minutes' bus ride west of town. Tourist offices with maps and information on accommodation in Cágliari are at the port (Mon–Fri 8.30am–12.30pm & 4–6pm; ☎070.668.352), and opposite the train and bus stations on Piazza Matteotti (Mon–Fri 8.30am–1.30pm & 2.15–7.30pm, Sat 8.30am–1.30pm, also Sun in Aug 8.30am–1.30pm; ☎070.669.255), but the main office covering the whole of Sardinia is at Via Mameli 97 (mid-Feb to May Mon–Fri 9am–7pm, Sat 9am–1pm; June–Sept Mon–Sat 8am–8pm; Oct to mid-Feb Mon–Fri 9am–5.30pm, Sat 9am–1pm; ☎070.669.255, *www.regione .sardegna.it/eptca*). A bus service into town runs at least every ninety minutes from 6.15am until midnight to Piazza Matteotti; otherwise a taxi ride costs around €13. Piazza Matteotti also has the **bus and train stations** and an information kiosk (March–Oct Mon–Sat 8am–8pm, July to mid-Sept also Sun 9am–7pm; Nov–Feb Mon–Sat 8am–2pm; ☎070.669.255).

Cágliari has a good selection of budget **hotels**, though availability may be restricted in high season, and single rooms are always at a premium. Best choice is *Pensione Vittoria* at Via Roma 75 (☎070.657.970; ③); if this is full, nearby Via Sardegna has several basic choices, including *Palmas* at no. 14 (☎070.651.679; ③) and *La Perla* at no. 18 (☎070.669.446; ③). Away from the seafront, try the central *La Terrazza* at Via S. Margherita (☎070.668.652; ③). The nearest **campsite** is at Quartu Sant'Elena, a 45-minute bus ride east along the coast, where the *Pini e Mare* (☎070.803.103; July & Aug) has bungalows as well.

The City

Almost all the wandering you will want to do in Cágliari is encompassed within the old quarter. The most evocative entry to this is from the monumental **Bastione San Remy** on Piazza Costituzione. It's worth the haul up the grandiose flight of steps inside for Cágliari's best views over the port and the lagoons beyond – especially at sunset.

From the bastion, you can wander off in any direction to enter the intricate maze of Cágliari's citadel, traditionally the seat of the administration, aristocracy and highest ecclesiastical offices. It has been little altered since the Middle Ages, though the tidy Romanesque facade on the **Cattedrale** (daily 8am–12.30pm & 4–8pm) in Piazza Palazzo is in fact a fake, added in the twentieth century in the old Pisan style. The main structure dates originally from the thirteenth century but has gone through what D.H. Lawrence called "the mincing machine of the ages, and oozed out Baroque and sausagey."

Inside, a couple of massive stone pulpits flank the main doors: they were crafted as a single piece around 1160 to grace Pisa's cathedral, but were later presented to Cágliari along with the same sculptor's set of lions, now adorning the outside of the building. Other features of the cathedral include the ornate seventeenth-century tomb of Martin II of Aragon (left transept), a stunning portrait of Pope Clement VII by an unknown Flemish artist in the fifteenth century, usually displayed near the altar, and the **crypt**, hewn out of the solid rock beneath the altar. Little of this subterranean chamber has been left undecorated, and there are carvings by Sicilian artists of Sardinian saints.

At the opposite end of Piazza Palazzo a road leads into the smaller Piazza dell'Arsenale, site of the **Museo Archeologico Nazionale** (Tues–Sun 9am–7pm; €2.60), a must for anyone interested in Sardinia's past. The island's most important Phoenician, Carthaginian and Roman finds are gathered here, but everything pales beside the museum's greatest pieces, from Sardinia's **nuraghic** culture. Of these, the most eye-catching is a series of bronze statuettes, ranging from about 15 to 45cm in height, spindly and highly stylized, but packed with invention and quirky humour. The main source of information about this phase of the island's history, the figures were mostly votive offerings, made to decorate the inside of temples, later buried to protect them from the hands of foreign predators.

Off the piazza stands the **Torre San Pancrazio**, from which it's only a short walk to Via dell'Università and the **Torre dell'Elefante**, named after the small carving of an elephant on one side; the towers were erected by Pisa after it had wrested the city from the Genoans in 1305 and formed the main bulwarks of the city's defences. Both have a half-finished look about them, with the side facing the old town completely open, but they've been fitted with steps which you can climb for stupendous views over the city and coast (April–Sept Tues–Sun 9am–1pm and 3–7pm; Oct–March Tues–Sun 9am–4.30pm; free). Nearby, Viale Buon Cammino leads to the **Anfiteatro Romano** (Tues–Sun: April–Oct 9am–1pm & 3.30–7.30pm; Nov–March 9am–5pm; free). Cut out of solid rock in the second century AD, the amphitheatre could hold the entire city's population of twenty thousand.

The only item of interest in Cágliari's traffic-thronged modern quarters is the fifth-century church of **San Saturnino**, Sardinia's oldest and one of the most important surviving examples of early Christian architecture in the Mediterranean. Stranded on the busy Via Dante, and surrounded by various pieces of flotsam from the past, the basilica was erected on the spot where the Christian martyr Saturninus met his fate.

Eating and drinking

Most of Cágliari's **restaurants** are clustered around Via Sardegna. *Da Serafino*, at Via Sardegna 109, is extremely good value and popular with the locals. *Da Lillicu* at Via Sardegna 78 is plain but authentic, offering Sardinian specialities and delicious fish. Seafood-lovers will do well at the *Stella Marina di Montecristo*, at the end of Via Sardegna, where it meets Via Regina Margherita. Away from the port area, try *Il Gatto*, just off Piazza del Cármine at Viale Trieste 15, for seafood or meat dishes, all immaculately prepared.

For a **snack** and a beer, drop in on *Il Merlo Parlante* in Via Portascalas, an alley off Corso Vittorio Emanuele, where you can find drink, music and *panini* (open evenings only). Down by the port, the bars on Via Roma make good breakfast stops, while there are several decent pizza and sandwich joints in the alleys running off it.

Su Nuraxi

If you have no time to see any other of Sardinia's ancient stone *nuraghi*, make a point of visiting **Su Nuraxi**, the biggest and most famous of them and a good taste of the primitive grandeur of the island's only indigenous civilization. The snag is access: the site lies a kilometre outside the village of **BARÚMINI**, 50km north of Cágliari, to which there are only two daily ARST buses, which stop here en route to Désulo and Samugheo.

At Barúmini, turn left at the main crossroads and walk the last leg to Su Nuraxi (daily: April–Sept 9am–7.30pm; Oct–March 9am–5pm; €4.10). Its dialect name means simply "the *nuragh*" and not only is it the biggest *nuraghic* complex on the island, but it's also thought to be the oldest, dating probably from around 1500 BC. Comprising a bulky fortress surrounded by the remains of a village, Su Nuraxi was a palace complex at the very least – possibly a capital city. The central tower once reached 21m (now shrunk to less than 15m), and its outer defences and inner chambers are connected by passageways and stairs. The whole complex is thought to have been covered with earth by Sards and Carthaginians at the time of the Roman conquest, which may account for its excellent state of preservation.

Nuoro and around

Superbly sited beneath the soaring peak of Monte Ortobene opposite the stark heights of Sopramonte, **NUORO**, in Sardinia's eastern interior, is, in many respects, merely a bigger version of the other villages of the region. No place on the island, though, can match its extraordinary literary fame. The best-known Sard poet, **Sebastiano Satta** (1867–1914), was Nuorese, as was the author **Grazia Deledda** (1871–1936), who won the Nobel Prize for Literature in 1927. For **Salvatore Satta** (1902–75), "Nuoro was nothing but a perch for the crows," and the last century has done little to change this insular town, despite the unsightly apartment blocks, administrative buildings and banks.

Nuoro's **old quarter** is the most compelling part of town, spread around the pedestrianized hub of **Corso Garibaldi**, along which the *passeggiata* takes place. Otherwise the main attraction is the impressive **Museo Etnografico** (daily: mid-June to Sept 9am–8pm; Oct to mid-June 9am–1pm & 3–7pm; €2.60) on Via Mereu, a ten-minute walk from the Corso on the other side of Piazza Vittorio Emanuele, which contains Sardinia's most comprehensive range of local costumes, jewellery, masks, carpets and other handicrafts.

As many as three thousand of the costumes are aired at Nuoro's biggest annual **festival**, the **Festa del Redentore**, usually taking place on the penultimate Sunday of August and involving participants from all over the island, but especially the villages of the Barbágia. The religious festivities are held on August 29, when a procession from town weaves up to the 955-metre summit of **Monte Ortobene**, 8km away, where a bronze **statue** of the Redeemer stands, poised in an attitude of swirling motion with stunning views of the gorge separating Nuoro from the Sopramonte.

Practicalities

Nuoro's **train station** is a twenty-minute walk from the centre of town along Via Lamármora. ARST buses stop outside, while PANI buses stop at Via Brigata Sássari (parallel to Via Lamarmora). Nuoro's **tourist office** is on Piazza Italia (May–Sept daily 9am–1pm & 4–7pm; Oct–April Mon–Fri 10.30am–1pm, also Tues & Wed 4–6pm; ☎0784.30.083, *www.nuoro.com*) and is useful for a street-map. The few **hotels** are mostly antiquated and often full. Right opposite the station on Via Lamarmora, the *Grazia Deledda* (☎0784.31.257; ⑨) is grand but offers fairly good value, otherwise try the *Grillo*, a modern and characterless place, but centrally located at Via Monsignor Melas 14 (☎0784.38.668; ⑨). Nuoro's **restaurants** are equally hard to track down, but they offer good-quality fare at reasonable prices, for example the excellent *Tascusi* at Via Aspromonte 13, near the top end of the the Corso, where local dishes are served in simple white rooms decorated with Sard art. You'll find a more boisterous atmosphere at *Ciusa*, a plain pizzeria-restaurant popular with locals at Viale Ciusa 53, on the western end of town. For a lunch-time **snack**, there's a handy sit-down bar on Via Mereu, between the museum and the Duomo.

Sássari and around

Historically, while Cágliari was Pisa's base of operations during the Middle Ages, **SÁSSARI**, an inland town in northwestern Sardinia, was the Genoan capital, ruled by the Doria family, whose power reached throughout the Mediterranean. Under the Aragonese it became an important centre of Spanish hegemony, and the Spanish stamp is still strong.

The **old quarter**, a network of alleys and piazzas bisected by the main Corso Vittorio Emanuele, is a good area for aimless wandering, but take a look at the **Duomo**, whose florid facade is Sardinia's most imposing example of Baroque architecture, added to a simpler Aragonese-Gothic base from the fifteenth and sixteenth centuries. The only other item worth searching out is the late Renaissance **Fonte Rosello**, at the bottom of a flight of steps accessible from Corso Trinità, in the northern part of the old town. The fountain is elaborately carved with dolphins and four statues representing the seasons, the work of Genoese stonemasons.

Connected by a series of squares to the old quarter, the **newer town** is centred on the grandiose Piazza Italia. Leading off the piazza is Via Roma, site of the **Museo Sanna** (Tues–Sun: summer 9am–8pm, winter 9am–7pm; €4.10), Sardinia's second archeological museum; it's a good substitute if you've missed the main one at Cágliari, and like the Cágliari museum its most interesting exhibits are *nuraghic* sculptures.

Roughly 15km inland from Sássari, right on the main Sássari–Olbia road (the SS597), rises the tall bell tower of **Santa Trinità di Saccárgia**, its conspicuous zebra-striped facade marking its Pisan origins. Built in 1116, the church owes its remote location to a divine visitation, informing the wife of the *giudice* of Logudoro that she was pregnant. It has survived remarkably well, with lovely Gothic capitals at the top of the entrance porch.

Practicalities

The **train station** is at the bottom of the old town's Corso Vittorio Emanuele. All local and ARST **buses** arrive at and depart from the semicircular Emiciclo Garibaldi, south of the tourist office. PANI buses run from Via Bellini 5, just off Via Roma. Buses connect **Fert'lia airport** with the bus station (€1.80), scheduled to coincide with incoming and outgoing flights.

Sássari's **tourist office** is at Viale Umberto 72 (Mon–Thurs 9am–1pm & 4–6pm, Fri 9am–1pm; ☎079.231.777, *www.regione.sardegna.it/azstss.*), a couple of blocks up from the museum. **Staying** in Sássari can be a real problem, and you'd do well to ring ahead to ensure availability. The best budget option is the pleasant *Garden Hotel* (☎079.241.325; ③), a twenty-minute walk east of the train station at Via Pigliaru 10; otherwise try the *Giusy* (☎079.233.327;

③), conveniently near the station on Piazza Sant'Antonio. Among a range of **restaurants** in town try *Da Bruno*, a cheap pizzeria with tables outside on Piazza Matteotti, or *Fainé Sassu*, off Piazza Castello at Via Usai 17 (closed Sun & June–Sept), which specializes in *fainé*, a sort of pancake made of chickpea flour, either plain or cooked with onions, sausage or anchovies. For a full meal, try *Il Posto*, a friendly trattoria in the new town at Via Enrico Costa 16.

Alghero

Thirty-six kilometres southwest of Sássari, **ALGHERO** owes its predominantly Catalan flavour to a wholesale Hispanicization that followed the overthrow of the Genoese Doria family by Pedro IV of Aragon in 1354. The traces are still strong in the old town today, with its flamboyant churches, wrought-iron balconies and narrow cobbled streets named in both Italian and Catalan.

A walk around the old town should include the seven defensive **towers** which dominate Alghero's centre and surrounding walls. From the **Giardino Púbblico**, the **Porta Terra** is the first of the massive bulwarks: known as the Jewish Tower, it was erected at the expense of the prosperous Jewish community before their expulsion in 1492. Beyond is a puzzle of lanes, at the heart of which the pedestrianized Via Carlo Alberto, Via Principe Umberto and Via Roma have most of the bars and shops. At the bottom of Via Umberto stands Alghero's sixteenth-century **Cattedrale**, where Spanish viceroys stopped to take a preliminary oath before taking office in Cágliari. Its Neoclassical entrance is round the other side on Via Manno; inside, the lofty nave's alternating pillars and columns rise to an impressive octagonal dome. In fact, most of Alghero's finest architecture dates from the same period, and is built in a similar Catalan-Gothic style. Two of the best examples are a short walk away: the **Palazzo d'Albis** on Piazza Cívica and the elegantly austere Jewish palace **Palau Reial** in Via Sant'Erasmo.

The best of the excursions you can take from the port is to **Neptune's Grotto**, with hourly departures each day during summer: tickets cost €9.40, not counting the entry charge to the grotto. The ride takes you west along the coast past the long bay of Porto Conte as far as the point of **Capo Caccia**, where the spectacular sheer cliffs are riddled by deep marine caves. The most impressive is the **Grotta di Nettuno** (daily: April–Sept 9am–7pm; Oct 10am–5pm; Nov–March 9am–2pm; €7.80), a long snaking passage delving far into the rock, into which thirty-minute tours are led, single-file, on the hour every hour, past dramatically lit and fantastical stalagmites and stalactites. A cheaper alternative to the boat tour is by bus to Capo Caccia.

Practicalities

Trains to Alghero from Sássari arrive some way out of the centre, connected to the port by shuttle buses. **Buses** arrive in Via Catalogna, on the Giardino Púbblico. Alghero's efficient **tourist office** is on the corner of the Giardino Púbblico (Easter–June Mon–Sat 8am–1pm & 5–8pm, Sun 9am–1pm; July–Sept daily 8am–8pm; Oct–Easter Mon–Sat 8am–2pm; ☎079.979.054, *www.infoalghero.it*).

The best-value **hotel** in town is the *San Francesco* (☎079.980.330; ⑤), in the heart of the old town at Via Machin 2, just behind San Francesco church; each of its clean, quiet rooms has a bathroom. There's a cheaper alternative in the newer part of town: the *Normandie*, on Via Enrico Mattei, between Via Kennedy and Via Giovanni XXIII (☎079.975.302; ③), with shared bathrooms. Two kilometres out of town, *La Mariposa* **campsite** (☎079.950.360; April to mid-Oct) has direct access to the beach. Alghero's *Giuliani* **youth hostel** (☎079.930.353; ②) is actually 6km along the coast at Fert'lia, reachable by local bus. Ring first to check availability.

Alghero's **restaurants** are renowned for seafood, always fresh, inventively prepared and well presented – spring and winter are the best seasons. *La Lépanto* on Via Carlo Alberto, off

Piazza Sulis, is excellent (expect to pay at least €24 a head), as is *Da Pietro*, at Via Machin 20, with cheaper prices though less atmosphere. If you hanker for something meatier, *La Singular* on Via Arduino uses mostly land-based recipes, including kid and boar, while the best budget meals can be had in the right-angled streets of the new town, where the *Ristorante Mazzini* at Via Mazzini 59 has a wood-fired oven for pizzas. For **snacks**, the fast-food joints by the port aren't bad.

There is an abundant supply of decent **bars**: one of the most amenable is the *Café Latino*, with an entrance on Via Manno, which has parasols on the city wall overlooking the port, and serves ices and snacks as well as drinks.

travel details

Trains

Bari to: Bríndisi (hourly; 1hr 30min).

Bologna to: Ferrara (10 daily; 30min); Florence (7 daily; 1hr 30min); Milan (11 daily; 2hr–2hr 35min); Ravenna (15 daily; 1hr 25min); Rimini (hourly; 1hr 20min).

Cágliari to: Arbatax (1–2 daily; 7hr); Macomer (6 daily; 2–3hr); Olbia (4 daily; 4hr 30min); Oristano (hourly; 1hr–1hr 30 min); Sássari (3 daily; 3hr 40min).

Ferrara to: Rimini (2 daily; 2hr 15min).

Florence to: Arezzo (hourly; 1hr); Bologna (every 30min hourly; 1hr–1hr 30min); Genoa (hourly 6 daily; 3hr 10min–4hr 30min); Lucca (hourly; 1hr 5min–1hr 50min); Milan (18 daily; 2hr 50min–4hr 50min); Naples (9 daily; 4hr); Perugia (11 daily; 2hr 10min); Pisa (every 30min; 55min); Rome (hourly; 2hr 15min–3hr 30min); Venice (hourly; 3hr 25min–4hr 10min); Verona (14 daily; 2hr 40min–3hr 40min).

Genoa to: Bologna (3 daily; 3hr); Milan (hourly; 2hr); Naples (4 daily; 8hr); Pisa (every 2hr; 2hr 30min); Rome (every 2hr; 6hr).

Milan to: Bergamo (5 daily; 50min); Bologna (hourly; 2hr–2hr 35min); Brescia (every 15min; 45min–1hr 10min); Como (12 daily; 30min); Rome (10 daily; 4hr); Venice (hourly; 3hr).

Naples to: Bríndisi (1 daily; 6hr 30min); Palermo (4 daily; 9hr 30min).

Padua to: Bologna (34 daily; 1hr 25min); Milan (25 daily; 2hr 30min); Verona (hourly; 50min); Vicenza (25 daily; 55min).

Palermo to: Agrigento (11 daily; 2hr); Catania (5 daily; 3hr 10min).

Parma to: Brescia (8 daily; 1hr 45min).

Perugia to: Assisi (hourly; 20min); Florence (11 daily; 2hr 10min); Rome (14 daily; 2hr 5min–4hr).

Pisa to: Florence (hourly; 1hr); Livorno (every 30min; 15min); Lucca (hourly; 30min).

Rome to: Ancona (8 daily; 3hr 15min–6hr); Bologna (12 daily; 3hr 20min); Florence (hourly 10 daily; 2hr–3hr 30min); Milan (12 daily hourly; 3hr–5hr 40min); Naples (hourly; 2hr 30min).

Sássari to: Alghero (11 daily; 35min); Cágliari (3 daily; 3hr 40min); Macomer (4 daily; 1hr 35min); Olbia (4 daily; 2hr); Oristano (4 daily; 2hr 35min).

Turin to: Genoa (15 daily; 1hr 45min); Milan (hourly; 1hr 45min).

Venice to: Bologna (hourly; 2hr); Florence (hourly; 3hr 15min); Milan (hourly; 3hr); Padua (hourly; 30min); Trieste (hourly; 2hr 10min); Verona (hourly; 1hr 30min); Vicenza (hourly; 55min).

Verona to: Milan (hourly; 1hr 30min); Padua (hourly; 55min); Rome (6 daily; 6hr); Venice (hourly; 1hr 30min).

Vicenza to: Milan (hourly; 2hr); Verona (hourly; 30min).

Buses

Cágliari to: Macomer (5 daily; 2hr 30min); Nuoro (4 daily; 3hr 30min); Oristano (5 daily; 1hr 30min); Sássari (7 daily; 3hr 15min–4hr).

Sássari to: Alghero (hourly; 1hr); Bosa (1–4 daily; 2hr 15min); Cágliari (7 daily; 3hr 15min–3hr 45min); Olbia (2 daily; 1hr 45min); Stintino (2–6 daily; 1hr 15min).

Ferries

Arbatax to: Civitavécchia (2 weekly; 10hr 30min); Genoa (2 weekly; 19hr).

Cágliari to: Civitavécchia (1 daily; 14hr); Genoa (1 weekly in summer; 21hr); Naples (1 weekly; 16hr); Palermo (1 weekly; 13hr 30min); Trápani (1 weekly; 11hr); Tunis (1 weekly; 35hr 30min).

Genoa to: Bastia (1 weekly; 9hr); Cágliari (2 weekly in summer; 20 hr); Olbia (at least 7 weekly in summer; 13 hr); Palermo (6 weekly; 20 hr); Porto Torres (7 weekly; 12 hr).

Naples to: Capri (6 daily; 1hr 15min); Palermo (daily; 11hr); Sorrento (4 daily; 1hr 15min); Aeolian Islands (3–6 per week; 8 hrs overnight to Stromboli).

Olbia to: Civitavécchia (1daily; 8hr); Genoa (3–7 weekly in summer; 6hr); Livorno (1 daily; 10hr).

Porto Torres to: Genoa (June–Sept 1–2 daily; 12hr); Toulon, France (May–Sept 1 weekly; 9hr; Oct–Apr 1 weekly; 16hr).

Reggio di Calabria to: Messina (15–25 daily; 45min).

Santa Teresa di Gallura to: Bonifacio (2–12 daily; 50min).

Sorrento to: Capri (4 daily; 50min).

Villa San Giovanni to: Messina (every 15min; 45min).

Hydrofoils

Naples to: Capri (17 daily; 40min); Sorrento (7 daily; 40min); Aeolian Islands (2–4 per day; 4 hrs to Stromboli).

Olbia to: Civitavécchia (6–7 weekly; 4–6 hr)

Palermo to: Naples (daily; 4hr).

Reggio di Calabria to: Messina (12 daily; 20min); Naples (summer 1 daily; 6hr).

Sorrento to: Capri (12 daily; 20min).

CHAPTER 16

LATVIA

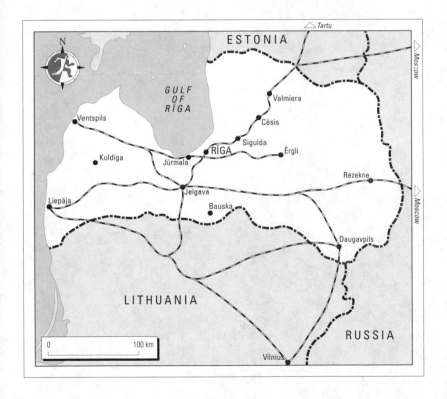

Introduction

The history of **Latvia**, like that of its neighbour Estonia, is largely one of foreign occupation. The indigenous Balts were overwhelmed at the start of the thirteenth century by German crusading knights, who massacred and enslaved them in the name of converting them to Christianity. The Germans continued to dominate both land and trade even after political control passed to the Polish-Lithuanian Commonwealth, then Sweden and finally Russia. During the second half of the nineteenth century the Latvians began to reassert their identity, achieving independence in 1918–20 after a war in which – with Estonian help – they beat off both the Soviets and the Germans. This hard-won independence was extinguished by Soviet annexation in 1940. As conditions in the Soviet Union relaxed during the late 1980s demands for increased autonomy turned into calls for outright independence, and on August 21, 1991, as the attempted coup against Gorbachev disintegrated in Moscow, Latvia declared its independence for the second time.

These days Latvia is engaged in turning over the economy to private ownership and struggling to put to rights the results of Soviet-era stagnation and neglect. Environmental damage aside, the most enduring legacy of Soviet occupation in Latvia is a Russian minority population of thirty percent.

The most obvious destination in Latvia is **Rīga**, a city whose architectural treasures have largely survived five decades of isolation. Places within easy reach of the capital include the resort area of **Jūrmala**, and the gently scenic **Gauja Valley** with the attractive small towns of Sigulda and **Cēsis**. The palace of **Rundāle**, 80km to the south of Rīga, also makes a great day-trip. These are just a few possibilities, with much more waiting to be discovered along Latvia's hundreds of miles of unspoilt coast and amid the forests of the countryside.

Information and maps

Tourist information centres run by the Latvian tourist board (*www.latviatravel.com*) are beginning to appear in major centres. The Kümmerly & Frey 1:1,000,000 **map** of the Baltic States includes Latvia, and has a basic street plan of Rīga. If you're planning to travel extensively in Latvia it's worth investing in the 1:300,000 Euromap map of Latvia. Jāņa Sēta, Elizabetes 83–85, Rīga, is well-stocked with maps

and guides, and also publishes its own excellent maps of the region. The Falk Plan of Rīga includes enlarged city-centre and old-town sections and also shows public transport routes. *Rīga in your Pocket* is an excellent English-language **listings** guide to the capital, with details on everything you could possibly need to know, and regular features on attractions elsewhere in the country.

Money and banks

Latvia's unit of currency is the **lat** (plural lati), normally abbreviated to Ls, which is divided into 100 santimi. Coins come in 0.01, 0.02, 0.05, 0.10, 0.20, 0.50, 1 and 2Ls and notes in 5, 10, 20, 50, 100 and 500Ls. At the time of writing £1 was worth 0.9Ls and $1 was worth 0.6Ls.

Bank (*banka*) opening times vary, but in Rīga you should be able to find ones that are open between 10am and 5pm, and some stay open later. Outside the capital many banks close at 1pm and all banks are closed on Saturday and Sunday. Most major banks like the Hansa Banka, Rīgas Komercbanka and Unibank will cash **travellers' cheques** (Thomas Cook and American Express preferred) and some give advances on major credit cards.

In Rīga some major hotels will also cash travellers' cheques and accept credit cards. **Exchanging cash** presents few problems, even outside banking hours, as Rīga is full of currency exchange offices (*valūtas apmaiņa*), many of which are little more than kiosks and often in unlikely locations like food shops. There are also **cash machines** throughout the country. **Credit cards** can be used in Rīga's more expensive restaurants and stores, and also in some petrol stations, but are not widely accepted outside the capital.

Communications

Post office (*pasts*) opening times are generally Monday to Friday 8am–7pm. For **telephone** calls there are modern digital call boxes operated using magnetic cards – which come in 2, 5 and 10Ls denominations and can be bought at the post office and most stores. As Latvia is in the process of switching from analogue to digital the whole telephone system, while good, is confusing and area codes are in flux. When in Latvia, for all calls to analogue phones (those with six-digit numbers) you should dial 2 before the six-digit number. If you're calling a digital phone (those with seven-digit numbers) from an analogue phone, dial 1 and wait for a tone before dialling the number. The Rīga city code (2) should be used if you're calling the capital from elsewhere in the country, but is omitted when you're calling from abroad. Direct international calls are only possible from digital phones – dial 00 followed by the country code, area code and number. Analogue users have to book international calls through the operator (dial 8 then 15).

Rīga is well served by an increasing number of **cafés**, although they are yet to appear in any of the regional centres. Prices are around 1L/hr.

Getting around

The destinations covered in this chapter are all easily reachable by bus and/or rail. Travelling by bus is generally slightly quicker, but also slightly more expensive, than by train.

■ Trains and buses

Train tickets should be bought in advance – stations have separate windows for long-distance (*starpilsetu*) and suburban (*pirpilsetu*) trains. Long-distance services are divided into the following categories: "passenger" (*pasažieru vilciens*) and fast (*ātrs*). Both are painfully slow but the latter, usually requiring a reservation, won't stop at every second village. Train information is available from station timetable boards – the Latvian for departure is *atiet*, and arrival is *pienāk*.

It's best to buy long-distance **bus** tickets in advance. Opt for an express (*ekspresis*) bus if possible to avoid frequent stops. You can also pay for your ticket on board, but this means you risk having to stand. Normally luggage is taken on board – if you have a particularly large bag you may have to pay extra to have it stowed in the luggage compartment. Buses are also useful for travelling to other Baltic countries, with services linking Rīga with Tallinn and Vilnius.

■ Driving and hitching

If you're **driving** in Latvia you'll soon notice that road conditions can vary dramatically. There's no highway apart from a brief stretch linking Rīga and Jūrmala. Roads linking major towns are usually in a reasonable state, but off the beaten track conditions deteriorate rapidly. The biggest hazard is reckless drivers – Latvia's road casualty rate is shocking. Though most towns are well provided with petrol stations, there are few in rural areas – carry a spare can. Speed limits are 50kph in built-up areas and 90kph on the open road. In towns it's forbidden to overtake stationary trams (allowing passengers to alight in safety) and it's against the law to drive after drinking any alcohol.

For **car rental**, Western rates apply, though you may get a better deal from small local firms – bear in mind though that with the latter contracts can be dubious, insurance coverage sketchy and the cars themselves not necessarily maintained properly.

Hitching is fairly common between major centres and holiday destinations; you should offer to make a contribution towards petrol.

Accommodation

Outside of Rīga and Jūrmala accommodation possibilities are fairly limited and even in tourist areas towns will often only have a couple of hotels and perhaps a campsite to their name.

■ Hotels and private rooms

Rīga has **hotels** at both the opulent and fleapit ends of the scale, but not much in between. Away from the capital, even in tourist areas like Jūrmala and the Gauja Valley, your only choice is likely to be either cheap Soviet-era dives with no facilities or overpriced Soviet-era places where higher rates are justified by leaky en-suite plumbing and the presence of

---

ACCOMMODATION PRICE CODES

Throughout this guide, accommodation is coded on a scale of ① to ⑨, the code indicating the lowest price per person per night you could expect to pay in each establishment in high season. With hostels this is the nightly rate per person; with hotels, the price is arrived at by dividing the cost of the cheapest double room by two. The prices indicated by the codes are as follows:

① under £5/$8	④ £15–20/$24–32	⑦ £30–35/$48–56
② £5–10/$8–16	⑤ £20–25/$32–40	⑧ £35–40/$56–64
③ £10–15/$16–24	⑥ £25–30/$40–48	⑨ £40/$64 and over

a broken TV in your room. Small, pension-type places are starting to appear but for the time being, they are few and far between. In Rīga there are also a number of private room agencies that generally represent good value for money.

■ Hostels, student accommodation and camping

Hostel accommodation exists in Rīga and in the capital it's also possible to find rooms in student halls of residence during college vacations – although non-Latvian speakers are often greeted by bemused staff who don't understand English. Such options don't really exist elsewhere in the country, where the only choice open to budget travellers is to head for a **campsite** (*kempings*), where accommodation consists of basic cabins with shared toilets and washing facilities. Most campsites also have space for tents.

Food and drink

Latvian cooking is based around meat, fish, potatoes and dairy products, with vegetables of the kind people can grow on their own plots. For drinking, Rīga has some excellent bars, and though some are expensive, you shouldn't have trouble finding somewhere affordable.

■ Food

Popular **starters** include cabbage soup (*svaigu kāpostu zupa*) – often almost a meal in itself – and sprats with onions (*šprotes ar sīpoliem*). Most **main courses** are meat- or fish-based – if you want to try something indigenous go for *cūkas galerts* (pork in aspic) or *rasols* (potato salad with herring, beetroot and apple). Popular fish dishes include herring (*siļķe*) and fried, smoked or salted eel (*zutis*). **Desserts** are normally based around forest berries – try *debess manna* (cranberry sauce and creamed wheat with vanilla sauce).

    Eating out in Latvia, particularly in Rīga, is often very expensive; two people can easily run up a bill of 20Ls. Keep costs down by dining in fast-food places serving indigenous snacks such as *pīrāgi* (blobs of dough with various stuffings) or *pelmeņi* (East-European ravioli). In Rīga you'll also find a few ethnic restaurants offering vegetarian options. Eating in cafès and bars is another cheap option, and self-catering should be no problem as food shops are well stocked with picnic staples.

■ Drink

The main alcoholic drink in Latvia is **beer** (*alus*). A lot of places serve imported beer but the local brews are fine, and usually cheaper – the most common brand is Aldaris. Worth trying once (and probably once only) is Rīgas Melnais Balzāms, or Rīga black balsam, a kind of bitter made according to a secret recipe that combines various roots, grasses and herbs.

    Outside the capital there isn't a great choice of watering-holes, but most places will have at least one bar, cafè or restaurant. If you want to sample local drinking culture head for a **beer bar**, though these are mostly male-only hangouts dedicated to serious imbibing. For something more civilized try **cafés** where, though alcohol is usually served, abstainers won't feel out of place. **Coffee** (*kafija*) and **tea** (*tēja*) are usually served black – if you want milk (*piens*) and/or sugar (*cukurs*) you'll have to ask.

Opening hours and holidays

Shops are usually open Monday to Friday 8/10am–6/8pm, though some close for an hour around lunchtime. A few food shops stay open until 10pm and also open on Sunday. Most shops and all banks will be closed on the following **public holidays**: Jan 1; Good Friday; Easter Day; May 1; Mothers' Day (second Sunday in May); June 23 (Midsummer); June 24 (St John's Day); Nov 18 (National Day); Dec 25 & 26; and Dec 31.

Emergencies

Latvia has a major organized crime problem, but though the mafia are highly visible in the smart bars and restaurants of Rīga, their activities are unlikely to impinge on the average visitor. **Theft** is the biggest hazard you're likely to face, and if you're staying in a cheap hotel it's better not to leave valuables in your room. Muggings and casual violence are not unknown in Rīga, but you can minimize the risks by avoiding the backstreets after dark. Latvian police (*policija*) are unlikely to speak much, if any, English.

    No **immunizations** are necessary for Latvia and emergency medical care is free, though if you fall ill it's best to head for home if you're able to do so as the country's medical facilities are run-down.

Emergency Numbers

Police ☎02; Ambulance ☎03; Fire ☎01.

RĪGA

RĪGA is the undisputed Baltic metropolis, a major port and industrial centre of nearly a million people. The city was founded by Albert von Buxhoeveden, a German canon who arrived in 1201 with twenty shiploads of crusaders to convert the Latvian tribes to Christianity. The main Hanseatic outpost in the region, Rīga was run by German nobles and merchants even when wider political control passed to other powers, starting with the Polish-Lithuanian Commonwealth in the late sixteenth century. After a subsequent period of Swedish rule Rīga became part of the Russian Empire in 1710 and during the second half of the nineteenth century it developed into a major manufacturing centre. Badly damaged during World War I, the city made a comeback during the first Latvian independence and remained a major centre after the country was swallowed up by the Soviet Union in 1940. Under the Soviets, the influx of Russian immigrants reduced the Latvians to a minority in their own capital – forty-seven percent of the city's population is now Russian, with a further sixteen percent made up of other non-Latvian nationalities. These days Rīga has a boom-town feel with a small but conspicuous section of the population making big bucks from the get-rich-quick opportunities thrown up by the switch to full-blown market economics.

Arrival, information and city transport

Rīga's main **train station** (Centrālā Stacija) and **bus station** (Autoosta) are just south of Old Rīga and within easy walking distance of the centre. The sea passenger terminal (Jūras pasažieru stacija) is to the north of the centre. **Trams** #5, #7 or #9 run from the stop in front of the terminal on Ausekļa iela into the centre of town (two stops). Rīga airport (Lidosta Rīga) is at Skulte, 8km southwest of the centre; bus #22 (0.20Ls) runs approximately every thirty minutes from the airport to the train station between 6am and 10.30pm; a taxi will set you back around 7Ls.

There are **tourist offices** at the airport (daily 9am–9pm; ☎2/720 7800), and on the Old Town's main square, Rātslaukums (daily 10am–7pm; ☎2/704 4377, *tourinfo@riga800.lv*), both of which have leaflets and hotel lists. They also sell the **Rīga Card** (8Ls for 24hrs, 12Ls for 48hrs, 16Ls for 72hrs) which allows unlimited use of public transport, entry to some museums, a guided tour of the city, and discounts in some restaurants – it's worth doing a few sums to see whether it will save you any money on your planned itinerary. Best advice to new arrivals is to purchase a copy of the excellent English-language guide *Rīga in Your Pocket* (0.60Ls; *www.inyourpocket.com*), which is available from newsstands and hotel foyers and contains all the information you could possibly require. *Rīga This Week*, available free from hotels, is also useful. Old Rīga is easily walkable, and you can cover the New Town on foot without much effort too. Outlying attractions are easily reached by bus, tram or trolleybus. Flat-fare single-journey **tickets** cost 0.20Ls and are purchased on board from the conductor. **Taxis** should cost 0.30Ls per kilometre during the day and 0.40Ls between 10pm and 6am, but watch out for rip-offs or non-functioning meters. The fleet of red Renaults operated by Rīga Taxi (☎2/739 1881) are usually reliable.

Accommodation

Rīga has no shortage of expensive hotels and there are a number of very basic budget places too. What's lacking are comfortable, reasonably priced mid-range places. If you're looking for something in this bracket you may want to consider bed and breakfast accommodation in a private apartment. Patricia Ltd, Elizabetes 22–6 (Mon–Fri 9.15am–6pm, Sat & Sun 10.15am–1pm; ☎2/728 4868, *tourism@parks.lv*), has private rooms from $20 per person, mostly within walking distance of the centre. The *Rīga Technical University* **student hostel**, in the

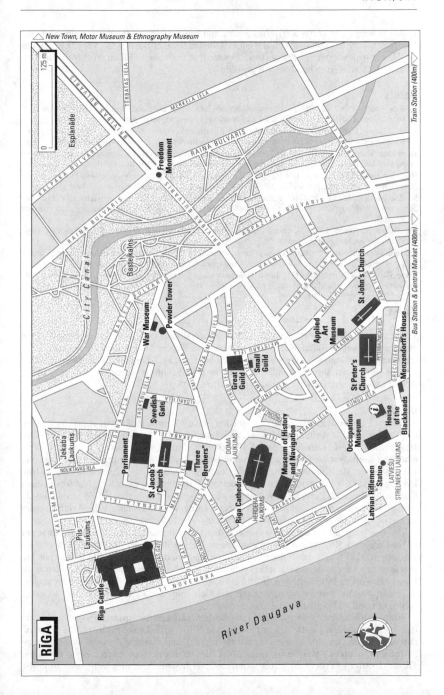

centre at Kaļķu 1 (☎2/708 9395), has double and triple rooms at 3Ls per person; while the *Studentu Kopmītne* hostel, just on the edge of the old town at Basteja 10 (☎2/721 6221), has doubles or triples from 6Ls per person – beware that both places fill up quickly due to their central location, so ring in advance if possible.

Hotels

Centra, Audēju 1 (☎2/722 6441, *hotel.centra@delfi.lv*). Newish business-standard hotel with chic modern en suites. Good value for what is essentially an upmarket city-centre establishment. ⑦.

Laine, Skolas 11 (☎2/728 9823, *laine@apollo.lv*). A friendly and comfortable mid-range hotel, ten minutes' walk northeast of the old town. Enter through the courtyard. Rooms with shared facilities (③) or ensuites (⑤).

Konventa Sēta, Kalēju 9/11 (☎2/708 7501, *www.derome.lv*). A charming, cosy upmarket hotel in restored monastery buildings, with a museum in the basement. Ideal location in the heart of the old town. ⑥.

Radi un Draugi, Mārstaļu 1/3 (☎2/722 0372, *radiundraugi@delfi.lv*). Comfy place with TV-equipped en suites bang in the centre, just off Grēcinieku iela. Often booked up weeks in advance, so ring ahead. ⑤.

Saulīte, Merķeļa 12 (☎2/722 4546). Rather basic place opposite the train station, acceptable for a short stay. Some renovated 'comfort' rooms have en-suite WC and showers, but are more expensive than standard doubles. ②.

Tia, Valdemāra 63 (☎2/733 3918, *www.tia.bkc.lv*). Modern hotel with sparsely-furnished but neat en suites, a 15-min walk northeast of the centre. ⑤.

Valdemārs, Valdemāra 23 (☎2/733 4462). En-suite rooms in this Art Nouveau building have dull brown colour schemes but are spacious and clean. A 10-min walk northeast of the centre. ④.

Viktorija, A Čaka 55 (☎2/701 4111). Reasonable place about 1km up the main road which heads east from the station. Renovated and unrenovated rooms available. ④.

The City

Vecrīga or **Old Rīga**, centred on Cathedral Square (Doma laukums) and neatly cut in two from east to west by Kaļķu iela, forms the nucleus of Rīga and is home to the majority of the city's historic buildings. To the east Old Rīga is bordered by Bastejkalns Park, beyond which lies the New Town, the nineteenth- and early twentieth-century extension of the city which contains some remarkable Jugendstil architecture.

Old Rīga

At the core of Old Rīga (Vecrīga) is Cathedral Square (Doma laukums), edged by government offices and a sprinkling of cafés, and dominated by the red-brick **Rīga Cathedral** (Rīgas Dome; Tues 11am–6pm, Wed–Fri 1–6pm, Sat 10am–2pm; 0.50Ls), a towering agglomeration of Romanesque, Gothic and Baroque architecture. The cathedral was established in 1211 by Albert von Buxhoeveden, the founder of Rīga, who became its first bishop. In true Lutheran style the interior is relatively unadorned, the most eye-catching features being a florid pulpit from 1641 and a magnificent nineteenth-century organ with 6768 pipes. The pillars of the nave are decorated with carved coats of arms while its walls are lined with German memorial slabs, mostly dating from the period after the Reformation.

The east wing of the cathedral was once a monastery but now houses the **Rīga Museum of History and Navigation** (Rīgas vestures un kuģniecības muzejs), Palasta 4 (Wed–Sun 10am–5pm; 1Ls). The ground floor has pictures, maps and postcards of Old Rīga, while the first floor has ship models and nautical ephemera. Of more general interest is the display on Jugendstil Rīga and the section on Rīga between the wars. The next floor houses archeological finds, with the usual array of weapons and tools enlivened by the remains of a longboat hauled out of the Daugava.

From the Cathedral Square Pils iela runs down to leafy **Castle Square** (Pils laukums) and the nondescript **Rīga Castle** (Rīgas pils), built in 1515 by the Livonian Order (the organization of crusading knights who conquered the region), and recently restored as a residence for the Latvian president. Heading along Mazā Pils iela from Pils laukums takes you past the **Three Brothers** (Trīs brāli), three plain medieval houses, one of which dates from the fifteenth century and is thought to be the oldest surviving house in Latvia. A left turn into Jēkaba iela at the end of Mazā Pils iela leads to the thirteenth-century red-brick **St Jacob's Church** (Jēkaba baznīca), the seat of Rīga's Roman Catholic archbishop. Next door at Jēkaba 11 is Latvia's **Parliament** (Latvijas augstākā padome), housed in a pompous Renaissance-style building. In January 1991 barricades were erected around the building to protect it from an expected Soviet attack and these remained in place for a year, even after the collapse of the Soviet Union and the recognition of Latvian independence by Russia.

Nearby on Torņa iela you'll find the seventeenth-century **Swedish Gate** (Zviedru vārti). This simple archway beneath a three-storey town house was built when Rīga was ruled by the Swedes, and is the sole surviving city gate. A more impressive relic can be found at the end of Torņa iela in the shape of the **Powder Tower** (Pulvertornis), a vast, fourteenth-century bastion whose red-brick walls are still embedded with cannonballs from various sieges. Today, it's home to the **Museum Of War** (Kara muzejs; Wed–Sun 10am–6pm; 0.50Ls; English-language leaflet 0.40Ls) with sections on the War of Liberation (1918–20) when the Latvians beat off the Soviets and the Germans, and on the Latvian Legion of volunteers who served with the German Waffen SS during World War II.

Though it's not readily apparent, **Bastion Hill** (Bastejkalns) – the park that slopes down to the city canal on the eastern edge of Old Rīga – is actually a vast earthworks built as part of the city's outer defences. It is also a reminder of Rīga's more recent history: on January 20, 1991 four people were killed here by sniper fire as Soviet OMON troops stormed the Latvian Ministry of the Interior on nearby Raiņa bulvaris during an attempted crackdown on Latvia's independence drive. Stones bearing the names of the victims mark where they fell near the Bastejas bulvaris entrance to the park.

From the Swedish Gate Meistaru iela runs down to the **Great Guild Hall** (Lielā Ģilde) at Amatu 6, once the centre of commercial life in Hanseatic Rīga. Though it dates from the fourteenth century the building owes its present neo-Gothic appearance to a nineteenth-century facelift and now houses the Latvia State Philharmonic. South of Kaļķu iela on Skārņu iela is **St Peter's Church** (Pēterbaznīca; Tues–Sun 10am–5pm), a large red-brick church with a graceful three-tiered spire, dedicated to the city's patron saint. Construction began in 1408 to replace a wooden church built two hundred years earlier. The new church boasted the highest wooden spire in Europe. This was rebuilt in 1746 after it was struck by lightning, only to be destroyed once more by German shelling in 1941. Today, the 123-metre spire is a steel replica, completed in 1973, with a lift (same times; 1.50Ls) taking visitors to a gallery in its upper reaches. A panoramic view of the city can be had from the observation platform.

More or less opposite the church, on Skārņu iela, are a clutch of restored medieval buildings. At nos. 10–16 a former chapel of the Knights of the Sword, built in 1208, now houses the **Museum of Decorative and Applied Arts** (Dekoratīvās mākslas muzejs; Tues–Sun 11am–5pm; 0.70Ls) with a collection of pottery, ceramics, glass and sculpture, while at no. 22 is the Ekes konvents, a fifteenth-century convent. Next door is the thirteenth-century **St John's Church** (Jāņa Baznīca), whose sober Gothic exterior conceals a fanciful Baroque altar.

Before World War II the late-Gothic **House of the Blackheads** (Melngalvju nams), headquarters of a guild of bachelor merchants and one of Rīga's most famous medieval buildings, stood to the west of St Peter's on what used to be the town hall square (Rātslaukums), which was destroyed in 1941, then totally rebuilt in celebration of Rīga's 800-year anniversary in 2001. These days the square, bereft of any other historic buildings, is known as **Latvian Riflemen's Square** (Latviešu Strēlnieku Laukums) in honour of the Latvian soldiers who fought with the Imperial Russian army during World War I, and then with the Bolsheviks, as the Latvian Red Riflemen, during the Russian Civil War. They are commemorated by a red marble statue depicting three stern figures clad in greatcoats and caps near the bridge at the western end of the square. Also on the square is the **Occupation Museum** of Latvia (Latvijas okupācijas muzejs; *www.occupationmuseum.lv*; daily 11am–5pm; free), formerly the Latvian Riflemen's Museum, but now devoted to Latvia's occupation by the Bolsheviks, Nazis and Soviets. Well presented and with some English-language texts, the display is an ideal introduction to Latvian contemporary history. Nearby at Grēcinieku 18 is **Menzendorff's House** (Mencendorfa nams; Wed–Sun 10am–5pm; 0.75Ls), an impeccably restored late-seventeenth-century merchant's house decorated in grand style and adorned with period furniture and artefacts.

The New Town

The boulevards of the **New Town**, rolling east from Old Rīga, bear witness to a period of rapid urban expansion that began in 1857, when the city's medieval walls were demolished, and lasted right up until World War I. As Rīga grew into a major industrial centre and country-dwellers flocked to the city, four- and five-storey apartment buildings – many of them decorated with extravagant Jugendstil motifs – were erected to house the expanding middle class.

As you head east out along Kaļķu, which widens out and becomes Brīvības bulvāris, the defiantly modernist **Freedom Monument** (Brīvības piemineklis) dominates the view. This stylized female figure, placed here in 1935 and known as "Milda", holds aloft three stars symbolizing the three regions of Latvia. Incredibly, the monument survived the Soviet era, and nowadays two soldiers stand guard here in symbolic protection of Latvia's independence.

Running north from Brīvības bulvāris to the east of the Freedom Monument is the formal **Esplanade Park** with the **Cathedral of Christ's Nativity** (Kristus dzimsanas katedrāle) just inside its grounds. This late nineteenth-century mock-Byzantine creation was recently returned to the city's Orthodox community after serving as a planetarium during the Soviet period. At the far end of the park is the **State Museum of Latvian Art** (Valsts mākslas muzejs), Valdemāra iela 10A (Mon & Wed–Sun 11am–5pm; 1.40Ls), housed in a grandiose Neoclassical building. Among the numerous nineteenth- and twentieth-century Latvian works inside, the odd street scenes and portraits of Jānis Tīdemanis (1897–1964) make the most lasting impression. Beyond the park it's worth continuing along Brīvības bulvāris as far as the **Alexander Nevsky Church** (Aleksandra Nevska Baznīca) at no. 56, an attractive little Orthodox church from the 1820s, partly concealed by trees on the southern side of the street.

Jugendstil architectural embellishments – florid stucco swirls surrounding doorways, stylized human faces incorporated into facades, and towers fancifully placed on top of buildings – can be seen on virtually every street of the New Town and, while walking through the area, it always pays to look up to catch details that might otherwise pass by unnoticed. One of the most famous Jugendstil creations in the city is at **Elizabetes 10a and 10b**, an apartment building adorned with plaster flourishes and gargoyles, and topped by two vast impassive faces. It was designed by Mikhail Eisenstein, the architect father of Sergei, director of the film *Battleship Potemkin*; more of Eisenstein's creations can be seen a block north of here at Alberta iela 2, 2a, 4, 6, 8 and 13.

Elsewhere in central Rīga

A few hundred metres south of Old Rīga, near the bus and train stations, is the bustling **Central Market** (Centrālais tirgus), housed in a couple of hulking 1930s Zeppelin-sized hangars. As well as being a useful source of fruit and vegetables, the market is an interesting place to wander round – but keep an eye on your possessions. Five run-down blocks southeast of the market on Elijas iela, the white-painted **Jesus Church** (Jēzus Baznīca), is surrounded by a neighbourhood of decaying timber houses. Dating back to 1635, this is Rīga's oldest wooden church, though it's been rebuilt following fires a couple of times since then. The interior is unusual, with a circular central hall supported by wooden pillars. The church is overshadowed by the **Academy of Sciences** (Latvijas Zinātņu Akedemija) at Turgeņeva 19, a Soviet-era pile built in monumental "wedding-cake" style during the early 1960s and nicknamed "Stalin's Birthday Cake".

Rīga's **Ghetto**, the area originally inhabited by the city's Jews and to which the Nazis later restricted Rīga's Jewish inhabitants, was located about 1km southeast of the train station, in an area now bounded by Lāčplēša iela, Maskvas iela, Lauvas iela and Kalna iela. Most of its original inhabitants were murdered at Salaspils concentration camp, outside the city, between November 30 and December 8, 1941. The ghetto remained in operation, occupied by Jews from elsewhere in Europe until 1943, when it was liquidated on the orders of Himmler after the Warsaw Ghetto uprising. Rīga still has a several-thousand-strong Jewish community and their synagogue is at Peitavas 6–8 in the old town.

On the edge of the former ghetto at Krasta 73, is the gold-domed **Grebenščikova Church** (Grebenščikova Baznīca), a wooden church dating from 1814 with a congregation of Old Believers, a dissenting sect which broke away from the Orthodox church during the seventeenth century, many of whose members had fled Russia to escape persecution. To the south of the former ghetto area on **Rabbit Island** (Zaķu sala; take bus #40 or #40A across the bridge) is Rīga's TV Tower, a 368-metre concrete tripod, with a viewing platform and restaurant halfway up, which ranks as one of the highest buildings in the world.

Eating, drinking and nightlife

You can **eat** very well in Rīga's restaurants, but at a price. If you're on a budget, many bars and cafés do food that is less expensive and often just as good as restaurant dishes. There are also plenty of inexpensive fast-food places. Many places have English-language menus. For **drinking**, most of the Old Town bars, particularly those around Cathedral Square, tend to be expensive and geared towards tourists and the local nouveaux riches. A number of cheaper and more off-beat places can be found in the New Town. The majority of locals can't afford Rīga bar prices so they buy beer from kiosks and wander the streets clutching bottles.

Rīga has a reasonable number of **live music** venues, a few discos and some excellent clubs. **Gambling** is very big in the city with a number of casinos and numerous bars devoted to gaming.

Cafés and snacks

Kirbis, Doma Laukums 1. Stylish vegetarian cafeteria next to the cathedral, with plenty of outdoor seating. Pick-and-mix from a wide range of dishes – the resulting plateful will be priced by weight. Mon–Fri 9am–11pm, Sat & Sun 10am–11pm.

Kolonāde, Brīvības 26. Central café in the shadow of the Freedom Monument, with outside seating to the rear. Excellent pastries and sweets – order from the counter. Daily 8am–10pm.

Lido, Elizabetes 65. Classy cafeteria serving all manner of tasty Latvian meat-and-potato dishes, with an interior decked out in country-cottage style. Daily 9am–11pm.

Monte Kristo, Ģertrūdes 27. Excellent little coffee house that also serves pastries. Sun noon–9pm, Mon–Sat 9am–9pm.

Pelmeņi XL, Kaļķu 7. Popular fast-food joint on the old town's main street offering ravioli-style blobs of dough (*pelmeņi*) filled with meat or cheese. Daily 9am–4am.

Pizza Lulū, Ģertrūdes 27. Fashionable little pizzeria where you can eat well at a reasonable price. Can get crowded. Daily 8am–midnight.

Sievasmātes Pirādzini, Kaļķu 12. No-nonsense cafeteria doling out cheap and tasty *pirādzini* – doughy balls with meat, cabbage and other fillings. Mon–Fri 9am–9pm, Sat & Sun 10am–9pm.

Šefpavārs Vilhelms, Sķūņu 6. Self-service, create your own pancake place near the Cathedral Square. Mon–Fri 8am–10pm, Sat & Sun 10am–10pm.

Restaurants

Arve, 12–14 Aldaru. Pleasant little restaurant near the Swedish Gate with a menu that's a little more varied than most. Good quality, but small portions. Daily noon–11pm.

Ļidojošā Varde, Elizabetes 31a. A New Town basement restaurant serving an eclectic international menu in Jugendstil-pastiche decor. Main courses from around 3Ls. Daily 10am–1am.

Mamma Mia, Torņa 4. Italian restaurant in cellar-like space near the Swedish Tower. Reasonable pizza and pasta dishes, generous risottos. Daily 11am–11pm.

Put Vējiņ!, Jauniela 18. Cheap burgers and pasta dishes on the ground floor, moderately-priced Latvian specialities in the low-key restaurant upstairs. Daily noon–midnight.

Rāma & Svāmīdži's Space Station, Barona 56. Hare-Krishna-run veggie place in the New Town with a tasty range of dirt-cheap Asian dishes. Daily 9am–9pm.

Rozamunde, Mazā Smilšu 8. The atmosphere of prewar Rīga, with live music from 7pm onwards. Daily 11am–11pm.

Saigona, Dzirnavu 87. Excellent and inexpensive little Vietnamese restaurant. Daily 10am–2am.

Senā Rīga, Aspazijas 22. Dine in rustic cabins while accordionists entertain you from on board a mocked-up pirate galleon, in a restaurant that forms part of the *Rīga Hotel*. The food is Latvian, portions are large and, if you choose carefully, the bill won't clean you out. Daily noon–midnight.

Slepenais Eksperiments, Šķūņu 15 (entrance on Amatu). Salads and other dishes during the day and techno at night. Sun–Thurs noon–5am, Fri & Sat 8pm–6am; 1–2Ls.

Staburags, Čaka 55. Traditional Latvian food served amidst old-fashioned oak rooms. Large portions at reasonable prices. Daily noon–1am.

Vincents, Elizabetes 19. The nouvelle-ish cuisine is excellent, but you're unlikely to escape with a bill of less than 12Ls per person. Daily noon–midnight.

Zilais Putns, Tirgoņu 4. Excellent Italian just off Cathedral Square. Reasonably expensive. Daily 11am–midnight.

Bars

Ala, Audēju 11. Popular with young locals. Good, inexpensive cocktails, but the steep stairs may prove to be an obstacle after a few drinks in "the cave". Open 1pm–2am.

Alus Sēta, Tirgotu iela 6. Justifiably popular pub with huge meals served from the grill. A good place to sample good, cheap Latvian ales accompanied by the national beer-snack – peas (*zirņi*) sprinkled with bacon bits. Outdoor seating in warm months. Daily 11am–1am.

Andalūzijas Suns, Elizabetes 83–85. Named after Dali and Buñuel's collaboration *Un Chien Andalou*, this arty café-bar is one of the most recommendable places in town. The menu lists some eclectic dishes, with main courses from around 3Ls and some good vegetarian options. Mon–Wed 8am–1am, Thur & Fri 8am–3am, Sat 11am–3am, Sun 11am–1am.

DECO Bars, Dzirnavu 84. Snacks, great cocktails, music, dancing and excellent service. Sun–Thur 11am–2am, Fri & Sat 11am–6am.

Dickens, Grēcinieku 11. Brit-pub with wide range of international beers, heaving with expats and locals every weekend. Top-notch pub grub in the restaurant section at the back. Sun–Thurs noon–midnight, Fri & Sat 11am–2pm.

M6, Mārstalu 6. Daily noon–11pm. Loungey bar attracting laid-back arty-intellectual crowd at the back of the Old-Town art gallery of the same name. Punk-goth-alternative misfits congregate in the cellar bar.

Možums, Šķūņu 19. Guinness on tap and reasonable, albeit pricey food. Attracts a business crowd. Sun noon–1am, Mon–Thurs 9am–1am, Fri 9am–3am, Sat noon–3am.

Paddy Whelan's Bar, Grēcinieku 4. Big, lively Irish pub popular with young locals and expats alike. Head upstairs to the laid-back *Paddy Go Easy* bar for a quiet pint. Sun–Thurs 10am–midnight, Fri 10am–2am, Sat 10am–1am.

Pulkvedim Neviens Neraksta, Peldu 26/28. Hip bar with industrial-chic decor and alternative-leaning crowd. Serves meat and pasta during the day, becomes a club at night (when there's an admission charge). Frequent live bands. Sun–Thurs noon–3am, Fri & Sat noon–5am.

Live music

Četri Balti Krekli, Vecpilsētas 12. Large upmarket cellar bar known for its Latvian-only music policy. Regular gigs by domestic rock-pop acts. Daily noon–2am.

Dizzi Music Club, Mārstaļu 10 (entrance round the corner on Alksnāja). Chic modern jazz bar in the old town with frequent live music and upscale food. Mon–Sat 5pm–3am.

Hamlet Club, Jāņa Sēta 5. Political cabaret and jazz. Daily 7pm–5am.

Kabata, Peldu 19. A basement club in Old Rīga, with a small dance floor and live bands. Daily 11am–5am; 2Ls.

Karakums, Lāčplēša 18. A popular café/bar with acoustic bands playing on the ground floor, and a dance floor upstairs with live bands or DJs providing the sounds. Daily 4pm–3am.

Saksofons, Stabu 43. Small rock, jazz and blues venue with a bohemian clientele. The cocktails are cheap and potent. Daily noon–2am.

Clubs and discos

Metro, Lāčplēša 5. Small and friendly cellar club 15min walk northeast of the centre, offering a much more cutting-edge menu of dance music than the bigger downtown clubs. Thur–Sat 9am–6pm. 2Ls.

Pepsi Forums, Kaļķu 24. Popular with Russian speakers, expats and beautiful young things. Bar, billiards and dancing. Daily 9pm–6am; 5Ls.

Slepenais Eksperiments, Šķūņu 15, entrance at Amatu 4. Hip techno-oriented club in town with great interior decor (check out the motif on the dance floor), live bands and DJs. Fri midnight–5am, Sat 8pm–6am. 2Ls, 1Ls after 4am.

Vernisāža, Tērbatas 2. Glitzy and glamorous mainstream disco in the park just east of the old town. Wed–Sun 9pm–6am. 5Ls.

Classical music, opera and ballet

The Philharmonic Concert Hall at Amatu iela 6 in the Lielā Ģilde is the home of the Latvian National Symphony Orchestra and is Rīga's main classical venue (☎2/721 3798). The lavishly – some would say tastelessly – refurbished National Opera House, Aspazijas bulvaris 3 (☎2/722 5803, *www.opera.lv*), stages classic operatic productions and is home to the Rīga Ballet (Rīgas Balets), where Mikhail Baryshnikov had his first break. There are regular organ and other recitals in the cathedral – tickets can be obtained from the office opposite the west door (☎2/721 3498). Another Rīga attraction is the celebrated Ave Sol, Citadeles 7, one of the best choral ensembles in the Baltic States.

Listings

Airlines Aeroflot, Ģertrūdes 6 (☎22/278 774, *www.aeroflot.ru*); Air Baltic, Kaļķu 15 (☎2/720 7777, *www.airbaltic.com*); British Airways, Torņa 4/IIIa (☎2/732 6737, *www.britishairways.com*); Estonian Air, Kaļķu 15 (☎2/721 4860); Finnair, Barona 36 (☎2/724 3008, *www.finnair.com*); LOT, Mazā Pils 5 (☎2/722 7234, *www.lot.com*); Lufthansa, at the airport (☎2/720 7183, *www.lufthansa.com*); SAS, Kaļķu 15 (☎2/720 7777).

Airport enquiries ☎2/720 7009.

Bike rental Gandrs Kalnciema 28 (☎2/7614 775).

Books Jāņa Rozes, Barona 5, has English-language paperbacks. For maps and travel guides, Jāna Sēta, Elizabetes 83/85. Mon–Fri 10am–7pm, Sat 11am–5pm.

Car rental Avis, at the airport (☎2/720 7353, *www.avis.com*); Europcar, Basteja 10 (☎2/722 2637, *www.europcar.lv*) and at the airport (☎2/922 2637); Hertz, at the airport (☎2/720 7980, *www.hertz.com*).

Embassies Canada, Doma laukums 4 (☎2/722 6315, *canembr@bkc.lv*); UK, Alunāna 5 (☎2/733 8126, *british.embassy@apollo.lv*); USA, Raiņa bulvaris 7 (☎2/703 6200).

Exchange Round-the-clock service at Marika, Basteja 14, Brīvības 30, Marijas 5, Merķeļa 10.

Hospital Ars, Skolas 5 (☎2/720 1001). Some English-speaking doctors.

Internet access Elektroniskā Kafejnīca, Elizabetes 83/85; Internet Kafejnīca, Jekaba 20.

Laundry Miele, Elizabetes 85a. Open 24hr.

Left Luggage at the bus station (daily 6.30am–9pm). There are also 24hr lockers at the left-luggage office (Rokas Bagāīas) in the basement of the long-distance section of the train station (0.50–1Ls per day).

Pharmacies 24hr service at Aptieka, Valdemāra 57/59.

Police Emergency number ☎02.

Post office 24hr service on Brīvības bulvāris 19.

Telephones Telephone Centre and fax-sending facilities at Brīvības bulvāris 19. Open 24hr.

Day-trips from Rīga

For a taste of the rest of Latvia, a number of destinations within easy reach of Rīga make feasible day-trips from the capital. Northeast of Rīga are the small towns of **Sigulda** and **Cēsis**, which lie at the heart of the **Gauja National Park** (Gaujas Nacionālais Parks), a 920-square-kilometre forested region, while **Rundāle Palace**, 80km to the south of the city, is one of the architectural highlights of Latvia.

Salaspils

The concentration camp at **SALASPILS**, 22km southeast of Rīga, is where most of Rīga's Jewish population perished during World War II. Around 100,000 people died here, including Jews from other countries who had been herded into the Rīga Ghetto after most of the indigenous Jewish population had been wiped out. Today the site is marked by monumental sculptures and a museum, with the former locations of the barrack buildings outlined by white stones. To get there take a suburban train in the direction of Ogre and alight at Dārziņi station from where a clearly signposted path leads to the memorial, a walk of about fifteen minutes.

Jūrmala

JŪRMALA or "Seashore" is the collective name for a string of small seaside resorts that straggle along the Baltic coast for about 20km west of Rīga. Originally favoured by the tsarist nobility, it became the haunt of Latvian intellectuals between the wars. Today, its sandy beaches backed by dunes and pine woods seethe with people at weekends and on public holidays. Despite the presence of a few decaying Soviet-era hotels, it's a delightfully low-rise area on the whole, with brightly painted wooden houses and more modern holiday homes nestling beneath the trees. The main centre is the small town of Majori, where a sprinkling of outdoor cafés and dance-til-dawn nightclubs cater for summertime hedonists; elsewhere Jūrmala is wonderfully underdeveloped and laid-back.

Trains to Jūrmala leave the suburban terminus of Rīga's central station (every 30min 5am–11pm) from platforms 3 and 4. Majori, about 10km beyond Rīga city limits, is the main stop and a service centre of sorts, with a number of restaurants and cafés along Jomas iela, the pedestrianized main street running east from the station square. Head north from here to Jūras iela, from where a few paths lead to the beach. The **tourist office** at Jomas 42 (daily 9am–9pm; ☎2/776 4276) can arrange accommodation in private rooms.

Sigulda and Cēsis

SIGULDA, dotted with parks and clustered above the southern bank of the River Gauja, around 50km northeast of Rīga, is the Gauja National Park's main centre and makes a good jumping-off point for exploring the rest of the Gauja Valley.

From the train station Raiņa iela runs north into town, passing the bus station on the way. After about 800m a right turn into Baznīca iela brings you to **Sigulda Church** (Siguldas Baznīca), built over seven hundred years ago, though much altered since. A left turn after the church leads, by way of **Sigulda New Castle** (Siguldas Jaunā Pils), a nineteenth-century manor house masquerading as a medieval castle, to the ruins of Sigulda Castle (Siguldas Pilsdrupas), a former stronghold of the Knights of the Sword. From here you can admire **Turaida Castle** (Turaidas Pils), perched on a bluff 3km away at the far side of the densely wooded Gauja Valley. To get there, you can catch one of the Turaida or Krimulda buses from Sigulda bus station, or walk there in about 45 minutes. Begin the walk by taking J. Poruka iela northwest from Sigulda church, and descending the wooden staircase at the end to the bridge across the Gauja river. On the far side of the bridge an asphalted path slopes down to the left, and runs past several sandstone caves before rejoining the main road just short of Turaida itself. Built on the site of an earlier stronghold by the bishop of Rīga in 1214, Turaida Castle was destroyed when lightning hit its gunpowder magazine during the eighteenth century. The pristine state of much of its brickwork attests to the fact that it has been extensively restored, and these days it houses a local history **museum** (Tues–Sun 10am–5/6pm; 0.80Ls). Just before the castle is the eighteenth-century **Turaidas Church** (Turaidas Baznīcas), an appealing little wooden church with a Baroque tower that's one of the best-preserved examples of Latvian native architecture in the country.

The well-preserved little town of **CĒSIS**, 35km northeast of Sigulda, is considered by many Latvians to have an atmosphere as close to that of prewar small-town Latvia as it's possible to get. One of the oldest towns in the country, it's the former seat of the master of the Livonian order and was also a member of the Hanseatic League. More recently Cēsis was the site of a crucial battle during the War of Independence, when a combined Latvian/Estonian force defeated the Iron Division of the German *Landeswehr* between June 19 and June 24, 1919.

From the **train** and **bus** stations walk down Raunas iela to Vienības Laukums, the town's main square. The attractive but run-down old town – a few narrow streets lined with flaking wooden buildings – lies to the south of here. On Rīgas iela just south of the square the remains of the old town gates have been excavated. Nearby, on Skolas iela, is the thirteenth-century **St John's Church** (Svēta Jāņa Baznīca), which contains the tombs of several masters of the Livonian order. East of the square are the remains of **Cēsis Castle** (Cēsu Pils) founded by the Knights of the Sword in 1209. Apart from a couple of towers, not much survives, but in the adjoining manor house you'll find a small regional history museum (Cēsu Vēstures; Tues–Sun 10am–4pm; 0.50Ls). More appealing perhaps are the grounds, with their small lake and Orthodox church.

Rundāle Palace

RUNDĀLE PALACE or Rundāles Pils (Wed–Sun: May–Oct 10am–6pm; Nov–April 10am–5pm; 1Ls), 77km south of Rīga, is one of the architectural wonders of Latvia. This 138-room Baroque palace, built in two phases during the 1730s and 1760s, was designed by Bartolomeo Rastrelli, the architect who created the Winter Palace in St Petersburg. It was privately owned until 1920 when it fell into disrepair, but meticulous restoration, begun in 1973, has largely returned it to its former glory. Highlight of the interior is the eastern wing, where a spectacular staircase leads to the most opulent rooms in the whole building – the Zelta zāle, or Gold Hall, throne room, and the Baltā zāle, or White Hall, ballroom featuring a dazzling stucco ceiling. To get there take the bus to **Bauska** and then a minibus for Rundāles Pils, from where it's a twenty-minute walk to the palace. Should you want to stay overnight try the *Viesnīca Bauska*, Slimnīcas 7, Bauska (☎239/23027; ②) adjacent to the bus station.

travel details

Trains

Rīga to: Cēsis (9 daily; 1hr 30min); Moscow (2 daily; 17hr 30min); Sigulda (14 daily; 1hr); St Petersburg (1 daily; 14hr); Tallinn (1 daily; 7hr); Vilnius (1 daily; 6hr).

Buses

Rīga to: Bauska (30 daily; 1hr 30min); Cēsis (14 daily; 2hr), Kaunas (3 daily; 4hr 30min); Sigulda (Mon–Fri 6 daily; Sat 4 daily; Sun 2 daily; 1hr), Tallinn (7 daily; 5hr 30min), Vilnius (5 daily; 6hr).

Sigulda to: Turaida (12 daily; 10min).

CHAPTER 17

LITHUANIA

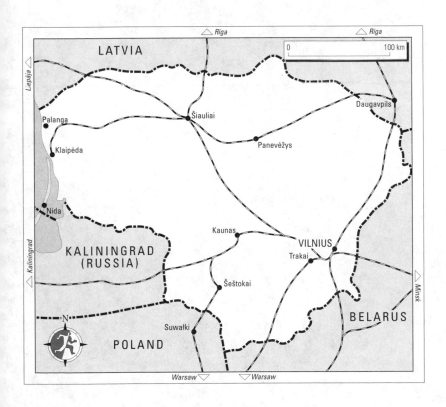

Introduction

Unlike its Baltic neighbours, **Lithuania** once enjoyed a period of sustained independence. Having driven off the German Knights of the Sword in 1236 at Šiauliai, the Lithuanians emerged as a unified state under Grand Duke Gediminas (1316–41). The 1569 Union of Lublin established a combined Polish-Lithuanian state which reached its zenith under King Stefan Bathory. But the Great Northern War of 1700–21, in which Poland-Lithuania, Russia and Sweden battled for control of the Baltics, left the country devastated, and by the end of the eighteenth century most of Lithuania had fallen into Russian hands. Uprisings in 1830 and 1863 presaged a rise in nationalist feeling, and Russia's collapse in World War I enabled the Lithuanians to re-establish their independence. In July 1940, however, the country was effectively annexed by the USSR. German occupation from 1941 to 1944 wiped out Lithuania's Jewish population and wrecked the country, and things scarcely improved when the return of the Soviets resulted in executions and deportations. When Moscow eventually relaxed its hard line in the late 1980s, demands for greater autonomy led to the declaration of independence on March 11, 1990, way ahead of the other Baltic States. A prolonged stand-off came to a head on January 11, 1991 when Soviet forces killed fourteen people at Vilnius TV Tower, but as the anti-Gorbachev coup foundered in August 1991, the world – soon followed by the disintegrating Soviet Union – recognized Lithuanian independence.

Travel in Lithuania presents no real hardships, and even in well-trodden destinations the volume of visitors is low, leaving you with the feeling that there's still much to discover here. **Vilnius**, with its Baroque old town, is the most architecturally beautiful of the Baltic capitals, with an easy-going charm all of its own. Lithuania's second city **Kaunas** also has an attractive old town and a couple of unique museums, along with a handful of surprisingly good restaurants and bars. The port city of **Klaipėda**, despite its restored old town, is more a stopping-off point en route to the low-key resorts of **Neringa**, a unique spit of sand dunes and forest that shields Lithuania from the Baltic.

Information and maps

Most of Lithuania's major towns now have **tourist offices** run by the state tourist board

(*www.tourism.lt*), often offering accommodation listings and events calendars in English. Otherwise the *In Your Pocket* guide series (available from bookshops, newsstands, tourist offices and some hotels; 4Lt) is the most indispensable source for practical information, with separate publications covering Vilnius, Kaunas and Klaipėda, each of which includes serviceable city maps. The Kümmerly & Frey 1:1,000,000 **map** of the Baltics includes Lithuania in some detail along with a basic street plan of Vilnius. If you're planning to travel extensively in Lithuania the Euromap 1:300,000 map of the country is a useful investment. Serviceable regional maps produced by local companies are available in bookshops and newspaper kiosks once you arrive. The Jāņa Sēta plan of Vilnius comes as either fold-out map or spiral-bound city atlas, and includes public transport.

Money and banks

Lithuania's unit of **currency** is the *litas* (usually abbreviated to Lt), which is divided into 100 *centai*. Coins come in denominations of 0.01, 0.02, 0.05, 0.10, 0.20, 0.50Lt and bank notes in 1, 2, 5, 10, 20, 50, 100 and 200Lt denominations. **Bank** (*bankas*) opening hours vary, though branches of the Vilniaus Bankas are usually open Monday to Friday 8am–3/4pm. They'll usually give you an advance on your Visa/Mastercard or American Express card and cash **travellers' cheques** (commission 2–3 percent). If you want to exchange cash outside banking hours, head for a **currency exchange** office (*valiutos keitykla*). **Credit cards** are most likely to be accepted in Vilnius, where big hotels, restaurants, luxury stores and petrol stations may let you pay with plastic. Outside the capital, apart from a handful of places in Kaunas and Klaipėda, you're unlikely to have much luck.

Communications

In major towns, **post offices** (*paštas*) are usually open Monday to Friday 8am–6pm, Saturday 8am–4pm; in smaller places hours are more restricted. Post offices are the best places to buy stamps, but it's also possible to obtain them from some newspaper kiosks and tourist offices. Lithuania has standard international rates for both airmail and surface letters and postcards. Virtually all public **telephones** now operate on cards (*telefono kortele*; 8.74Lt, 12.96Lt, 16.50Lt and 30.66Lt) from post offices and newspaper kiosks – the higher-denomination cards should sufffice for a short-duration international call. To make a long-distance call, first dial 82 before dialling the area code and phone number. When calling Lithuania from abroad, the initial 82 is omitted. For international calls from Lithuania, dial 8, wait for the tone, followed by 10, then the country code, area code and phone number.

There's a good choice of **Internet cafés** in Vilnius, but they're still pretty rare elsewhere.

Getting around

The destinations covered in this chapter are all easily reachable by bus and/or train. Travelling by bus is generally slightly quicker but also slightly more expensive than travelling by train.

■ Trains and buses

Train tickets should be bought in advance – stations have separate windows for long-distance and suburban (*priemiestinis* or *vietinis*) trains. Long-distance services are divided into the following categories: passenger (*keleivinis traukinys*) and fast (*greitas*). Both are painfully slow but the latter, usually requiring a reservation, won't stop at every second village. Train information is available from station timetable boards – the Lithuanian for departure is *išvyksta*, and arrival is *atvyksta*.

It's best to buy long-distance **bus** tickets in advance, and opt for an express (*ekspresas*) bus if possible to avoid frequent stops. You can also pay for your ticket on board, although this doesn't guarantee you a seat reservation and you may have to stand. Normally luggage is taken on board – if you have a large bag you may have to pay extra to have it stowed in the luggage compartment. As well as being a viable means of getting around Lithuania, buses are also useful for travelling to other Baltic countries, with services linking Vilnius, Rīga and Tallinn.

■ Driving and hitching

Driving in Lithuania throws up a number of hazards. Along with people showing off in high-powered Western cars and four-wheel drives there are also some spectacularly decrepit cars on the roads, and in country areas you may have to contend with slow-moving tractors, horses and carts, stray farm animals and the odd drunk wandering onto the road.

The road from Vilnius to Klaipėda via Kaunas is a fairly respectable two-lane highway for much of its length. Most other main roads are in reasonable repair, but many minor roads are little more than dirt tracks. Though most towns are well provided with petrol stations, there are few in rural areas – carry a spare can. Speed limits are 60kph in built-up areas and 90kph on the open road. The limit on highways is 100kph and the police are extremely vigilant. In towns it's forbidden to overtake stationary trams, allowing passengers to alight in safety, and it's against the law to drive after drinking any alcohol.

Car rental will be around $79 per day from one of the big companies, half that from some local firms – bear in mind though that with the latter contracts can be dubious, insurance coverage sketchy and the cars may not be well maintained. The car's registration papers and, if you don't own the car, a note of authorization should be carried at all times. **Hitching** is fairly common between major centres and it isn't necessary to make a contribution towards petrol. As in any country, women are advised not to hitch alone.

Accommodation

Accommodation in Lithuania is generally cheaper than in Western Europe, but it's still a good idea to look around first. The best way to keep costs down is by staying in private rooms, as budget hotels tend to be pretty grim. If money isn't a major issue, you'll have few problems finding a decent place to stay.

ACCOMMODATION PRICE CODES

Throughout this guide, accommodation is coded on a scale of ① to ⑨, the code indicating the lowest price per person per night you could expect to pay in each establishment in high season. With hostels this is the nightly rate per person; with hotels, the price is arrived at by dividing the cost of the cheapest double room by two. The prices indicated by the codes are as follows:

① under £5/$8	④ £15–20/$24–32	⑦ £30–35/$48–56
② £5–10/$8–16	⑤ £20–25/$32–40	⑧ £35–40/$56–64
③ £10–15/$16–24	⑥ £25–30/$40–48	⑨ £40/$64 and over

■ Private rooms and hotels

For budget travellers **private room** accommodation is often the best option, usually costing around 70Lt per person. The most ubiquitous and reliable agency is Litinterp, with offices in Vilnius, Klaipėda and Kaunas. Budget **hotels** tend to be fairly grim, though if you don't mind spartan conditions you may be able to find rooms in Soviet-era fleapits for as little as 40Lt for a double. Some cheap hotels can be dodgy – if things don't feel right (rooms show signs of past forced-entry, etc) don't stay. A few smaller, mid-range places are starting to appear, usually charging upwards of 280Lt a double, and where they exist they are usually preferable to similarly priced Soviet-era hotels which tend to be large and impersonal. In Vilnius and Kaunas you'll find innumerable international business-standard places charging 400Lt and upwards for a double; these are about as good as anything you'll find in Lithuania.

■ Hostels and camping

Lithuania has a few **hostels** where you'll pay 24–32Lt per night. Space is limited and it's best to try and ring individual establishments in advance. An ex-Soviet phenomenon is the cabin **campsite** (*kempingas*), offering accommodation in three- to four-bed cabins (WC and washing facilities, which can be on the primitive side, are shared with other cabins) for around 20Lt per person. Many of these places will also let you pitch a tent, an option which works out slightly cheaper than sleeping under a roof. The downside is that they're often located a long way out of town. You can also camp wild in the countryside, subject to the approval of the landowner (if there is one).

Food and drink

Lithuanian cuisine, based on traditional peasant dishes, is less bland than that of its Baltic neighbours, partly as a result of Polish influence. Typical **starters** include marinated mushrooms (*marinuoti grybai*), herring (*silkė*) and smoked sausage (*rukyta dešra*) along with cold beetroot soup (*šaltibarščiai*). Potatoes play a major role; one of the most commonly encountered dishes is *cepelinai*, or zeppelins – cylindrical potato dumplings stuffed with meat, mushrooms or cheese and topped with pieces of fried bacon. Also popular are potato pancakes (*bulviniai blynai*), and cabbage leaves stuffed with minced meat (*balandėliai* or *"pigeons"*). **Desserts** include stewed fruit (*kompotas*), sweet fruit sauce (*kisielius*),

and innumerable varieties of pancakes (*blynai*, *blyneliai* or *lietiniai* are synonyms for more or less the same thing) – a real treat.

Some **restaurants** serve indigenous cuisine, and even the ubiquitous post-Soviet chops (*karbonadas*) and roast meat (*kepsnys*), tend to be better than in the other Baltic States. Even in a fairly upmarket place a meal shouldn't work out much more expensive than in a mid-range restaurant in Western Europe, and it's possible to eat really well for much less if you head for simple self-service places. Western fast food is making inroads, and Vilnius has a few ethnic places. Although vegetarianism has yet to establish itself here, it is possible to find meat-free options on most menus – mushroom- or cheese-filled pancakes being the most widespread. As an alternative to restaurant dining most cafés and bars do reasonably priced food.

Beer (*alus*) is the most popular alcoholic drink. The biggest local brewers – Utenos, Švyturys and Kalnapilis – all produce eminently drinkable light lager-type beer (*šviesus*) as well as a dark porter (*tamsus*). The leading Lithuanian fire-waters are Starka, Trejos devynerios and Medziotoju – invigorating **spirits** flavoured with a variety of herbs and leaves.

Vilnius, Kaunas and Klaipėda can all muster a growing range of lively **bars** – many aping American or Irish models, although there are also plenty of folksy Lithuanian places. **Cafés** (*kavine*) come in all shapes and sizes: some are trendy and modern in style and have a wide food menu, others are chintzy places serving pastries and cakes. **Coffee** (*kava*) and **tea** (*arbata*) are usually served black.

Opening hours and holidays

Opening hours for shops are 9 or 10am until 6 or 7pm. Outside of Vilnius, some places take an hour off for lunch; most usually close on Sun (though some food shops stay open). Most shops and all banks will be closed on the following **public holidays**: Jan 1; Feb 16 (Old Independence Day); March 11 (New Independence Day); Easter Sunday; Easter Monday; July 6 (Statehood Day); Nov 1 (All Saints Day); Dec 25 and 26.

Emergencies

Though many Lithuanians claim that the streets are unsafe, you're unlikely to meet trouble if you're sensible. Nor is organized **crime** likely to affect the average visitor; you'll spot huddles of "mafia" types in bars and restaurants but you only need to think about going elsewhere if they're in the majority. Car theft and vandalism are the most common crimes.

The cash-starved Lithuanian **police** drive some of the most beaten-up squad cars in Europe, but they expect to be taken seriously – be polite if you have any dealings with them and you should have no problems. There's little chance that police officers will speak any language other than Lithuanian or Russian; a few of the younger ones may speak a little English. Emergency **health care** is free in Lithuania but if you get seriously ill it's best to head for home (or at least Western Europe) if you can.

Emergency Numbers

Police ☎02; Ambulance ☎03; Fire ☎01.

VILNIUS

"Narrow cobblestone streets and an orgy of Baroque: almost like a Jesuit city somewhere in the middle of Latin America," wrote the author Czesław Milosz of prewar **VILNIUS**. Soviet-era satellite suburbs aside, it's a description which still rings true today, though the city Milosz knew was, in many ways, a different one to modern Vilnius. Between the wars Vilnius, known as **Wilno**, belonged to Poland and was inhabited mainly by Poles and Jews, who played such a prominent role in the city's life that it was known as the "Northern Jerusalem". Though now firmly part of Lithuania, Vilnius is still a cosmopolitan place – around twenty percent of its population is Polish and another twenty percent is Russian – though with just 578,600 inhabitants it has an almost village-like atmosphere, making it an easy place to get to know.

Arrival, information and city transport

The main **train station** (*Stotis*) is at Geležinkelio 16, just south of the Old Town, and the main **bus station** (*Autobusų Stotis*) is just across the road. There are exchange facilities at both, although you'll get a better rate at banks in the town centre. Trolleybus #2 will take you from the square in front of the train station to the main Cathedral Square (Katedros aikstė). Walking into the Old Town is feasible too – avoid taxis as they tend to overcharge. The **airport** (*Oro uostas*) is around 5km south of the city centre at Rodūnės kelias (☎2/306 666) with exchange facilities in the arrival hall. From outside the main entrance bus #2 runs a couple of times an hour to Lukiškių aikstė in the city centre, and takes approximately 25 minutes. Bus #1 will take you to the train and bus station area. **Tickets** for both buses cost 1Lt from the driver. An honest taxi driver will charge 10–15Lt for the 5km journey to the Old Town – beware of rip-off merchants.

The **tourist offices** at Vilniaus 22 (May–Sept Mon–Fri 9am–7pm, Sat 12am–6pm; Oct–April Mon–Fri 9am–6pm; ☎2/629 660, *turizm.info@vilnius.lt*) and at Pilies 42 (Mon–Fri 10am–6pm; ☎2/626 470) offer maps, tours and information on hotels and museums, but your best bet is to pick up a copy of the excellent *Vilnius in Your Pocket* city guide (info also available on *www.inyourpocket.com*), which costs 4Lt from newspaper kiosks, tourist offices or hotels. It's also available from a special *Vilnius in Your Pocket* booth (open daily; times depend on flight arrivals) in the airport arrivals hall which, among other things, handles hotel and bed-and-breakfast bookings. Vilnius is well served for **public transport** with buses and trolleybuses covering most of the city. Tickets cost 0.80Lt from newspaper kiosks (*kioskas*) and 1Lt from the driver; remember to validate your ticket by punching it in the machine on board. Alternatively, hail a minibus at any bus stop in the direction you're going, pay the driver 2Lt and you'll be dropped off at the stop you require. **Taxi** prices are usually reasonable providing you stick to companies using newer cars and functioning meters, and fares should cost no more than around 1–2Lt per kilometre. Telephoning for a taxi is one way of ensuring a fair rate; try Vilniaus Taxi (☎006/228 888).

Accommodation

There's a shortage of good, cheap **accommodation** in Vilnius, and though there are a few very cheap hotels they're best avoided. Best value for money is offered by **private rooms**. *Litinterp*, Bernardinų 7/2 (Mon–Fri 8.30am–5.30pm, Sat 8.30am–3.30pm; ☎2/223 850, *www.litinterp.lt*), is the longest-established agency, offering rooms in the Old Town – either with a host family or in *Litinterp's* own self-contained guesthouse – with singles from 70Lt and doubles from 120Lt. Similar deals are offered by the two Vilnius tourist offices, and the *Vilnius In Your Pocket* office at the airport. Vilnius has two HI-affiliated **hostels**: the *Old Town Hostel*, near the train and bus stations at Aušros Vartų 20–15a (☎2/625 357; ②); reservations

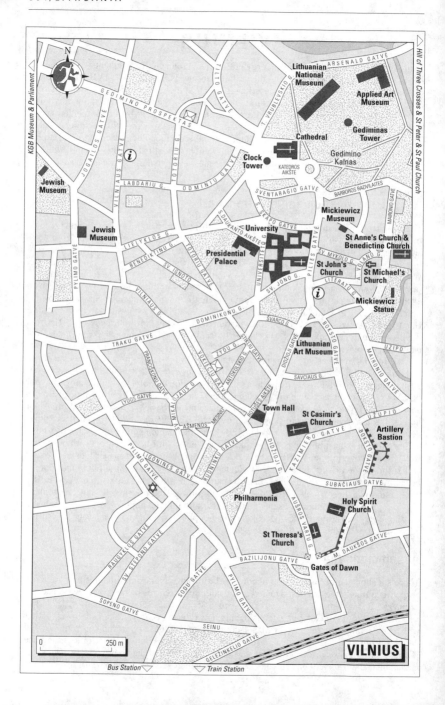

are essential due to the very limited number of beds), is cramped but comfortable; while *Filaretai*, fifteen minutes' walk east of the Old Town at Filaretų 17 (☎2/254 627; ①–②; bus #34 from the train station), is plainer, but just as friendly. The *Teacher's University Hotel* at Vivulskio 36 (☎2/230 509; dorms ①, rooms ②), is a twenty-minute walk west of the Old Town in a dull neighbourhood. The *JNN Hostel*, north of the river Neris at Ukmergės 25 (☎2/722 270, *centras@lvjc.lt*; ②; reductions for ISIC cardholders), is a slightly more upmarket place, with modern and clean rooms which come complete with their own showers and toilets – from the airport bus #2 or from the train station trolleybus #5 to Žaliasis Tiltas followed by bus #2 or #46.

Hotels

Apia, Šv Ignoto 12 (☎2/223426, *apia@takas.lt*). Friendly five-room guesthouse in superb Old Town location. ④.

Gintaras, Sodų 14 (☎2/738 011, *hotel.gintaras@tdd.lt*). Careworn but acceptable place near the station, with a mixture of unrenovated rooms with Soviet-era bathrooms and more expensive rooms with smarter facilities. ③.

Grybas House, Aušros Vartų 3A (☎2/608 420, *www.grybashouse.com*). Upmarket hotel with intimate guesthouse feel in the Old Town. Reserve in advance. ⑨.

Mabre Residence Hotel, Maironio 13 (☎2/222 087, *marbre@is.lt*). Fine courtyard and elegant quarters in a converted monastery, right in the centre. ⑧.

Mikotel, Pylimo 63 (☎2/609626, *mikotel@takas.lt*). Small-size hotel a few steps away from the train and bus stations, with pristine modern en suites and quirky paintings in the hallways. ⑤.

Naujasis Vilnius, Ukmergės 14 (☎2/726 756, *www.nvhotel.cjb.net*). Renovated Lithuanian-Swiss hotel, north of the river, with friendly service and comfortable rooms. ⑧.

Rudninkų Vartai, Rudninkų 15/46 (☎2/613916, fax 220507). Newish, medium-sized place on the fringe of the Old Town, occupying a couple of mazey town houses knocked together. Neat, tasteful and none-too cramped. ⑥.

Šauni Vietelė, Pranciškonų 3/6 (☎2/222 189, *sauni.vietele@takas.lt*). Tiny, cosy place in the Old Town with parquet floors. Excellent value; reservations essential. ⑤.

Victoria, Saltoniškių 56 (☎2/724 013, *www.victoria.lt*). Unprepossessing exterior but pleasant en suite rooms and friendly service inside. On the north side of the river, 20–25min walk from the town centre. From train or bus stations trolleybus #5 to žaliasis Tiltas followed by trolleybus #8, #9 or #19 to Pedagoginis Universitetas. ⑥.

Žemaitės, Žemaitės 15 (☎2/233187, *www.hotelzemaites.lt*). Modern block in an uninspiring area 2km west of the Old Town, accessible by trolleybus #15, #16 and bus #23 or #54 from the train and bus stations. Modernized doubles with TV and bath (⑤) or unrenovated rooms with shared facilities (②).

The City

At the centre of Vilnius, poised between the medieval and nineteenth-century parts of the city is **Cathedral Square** (Katedros aikštė). To the south of here along Pilies gatvė and Didžioji gatvė is the **Old Town**, containing perhaps the most impressive concentration of Baroque architecture in northern Europe. West of the square in the New Town is **Gedimino prospektas**, a nineteenth-century boulevard that's the focal point of the city's commercial and administrative life. Wedged between the Old Town and the Gedimino prospektas areas, the traditionally **Jewish areas** of Vilnius were shorn of their populations in the 1941–1945 period, but retain a sprinkling of worthwhile sights.

Cathedral Square and around

Cathedral Square (Katedros aikštė), dominated by the Neoclassical **Cathedral** (Arkikatedra bazilika; daily 7am–7pm), is the point where modern and old Vilnius meet. The cathedral belongs firmly in the old part, its origins going back to the thirteenth century, when a wooden church is thought to have been built here on the site of a temple dedicated to Perkūnas, the god of thunder. Today's structure is based on a more substantial stone building erected during the fifteenth century, and given a facelift over the next three hundred years that's left it looking more like a piece of grandiose Neoclassical civic architecture than a place of worship. The highlight of the airy, vaulted interior is the opulent **Chapel of St Kazimieras** (Kazimiero koplyčia), dedicated to the patron saint of Lithuania, whose remains lie in a silver casket in the chapel's main altar. Created between 1623 and 1636, the chapel is a riot of marble, stucco and statuary, with frescoes on the ceilings and side walls depicting episodes from the saint's life. Next to the cathedral on the square is the white **Belfry** (Varpine), once part of the fortifications of the vanished Lower Castle but now looking like a stranded Baroque lighthouse.

Rising behind the cathedral is the tree-clad **Gediminas Hill** (Gedimino kalnas), its summit crowned by the red-brick octagon of **Gediminas Tower** (Gedimino bokštas), one of the city's best-known landmarks. The first substantial fortification here was founded by Grand Duke Gediminas, the Lithuanian ruler who consolidated the country's independence. According to legend Gediminas dreamt of an iron wolf howling on a hill overlooking the River Vilnia and was told by a pagan priest to build a castle on the spot. These days the tower houses the **Vilnius Castle Museum** (Vilnius Pilies muziejus; May–Sept Wed–Sun 11am–6pm; Oct–April Tues–Sat 11am–5pm; 4Lt; free on Wed in winter), showing the former extent of the Vilnius fortifications.

A hundred metres or so north of the cathedral in a former arsenal building is the **Lithuanian National Museum** (Lietuvos Nacionalinis muziejus), Arsenalo 1 (Wed–Sun: May–Sept 11am–6pm; Oct–April 11am–5pm; *www.lnm.lt*; 4Lt; free Wed in winter), covering the history of Lithuania from prehistoric times to 1940. Though most items are labelled in Lithuanian and Russian only, the exhibits, ranging from a pair of mammoth tusks to re-created domestic interiors from the eighteenth and nineteenth centuries, are worth a visit. A separate department of the museum (entrance a little further north on Arsenalo) houses the Prehistoric Lithuania exhibition (same times; 4Lt), an extremely well-mounted display illustrating the history of Lithuania from the earliest times to the middle ages with grave finds and scale models of forts. Nearby is the **Applied Art Museum**, Arsenalo 3 (Taikomosios Dailės muziejus; Tues–Sun noon–5/6pm; 4Lt; free Wed in winter), home to a glittering array of ecclesiastical treasures, Baroque paintings and jewellery from the thirteenth to the nineteenth century.

The Old Town

The **Old Town** (Senamiestis), just south of Cathedral Square, is a network of narrow, often cobbled streets that forms the Baroque heart of Vilnius, with the theoretically pedestrianized **Pilies gatvė** (Castle Street) cutting into it from the southeastern corner of the square. To the right of this street is **Vilnius University** (Vilniaus Universitetas), a jumble of buildings constructed between the sixteenth and eighteenth centuries around nine linked courtyards that extend west as far as Universiteto gatvė. The university was founded by the Jesuits in 1579 at the behest of the Polish king, Stefan Bathory, and by the time Lithuania was annexed by tsarist Russia in 1795, it ranked as the oldest in the Russian Empire, though this didn't deter the Russians from closing it down in 1832. Reopened during the first independence, the university survived the Soviet era and now has fourteen thousand students.

Within its precincts you'll find the ornate **St John's Church** (Šv Jono bažnyčia), standing out from the crowd even in this city of beautiful churches – access from Šv Jono gatvė. Founded during the fourteenth century, St John's was taken over by the Jesuits in 1561 and given to the university in 1737. Reconstruction after a fire in the same year has left it with its present Baroque facade, and a no-holds-barred Baroque altar inside. The side-chapel dedicated to St Anne is comparatively restrained, with an unusual wooden altar showing Christ on the Cross with the disciples represented as bunches of grapes. Some recently uncovered ceiling frescoes depict the biblical story of Esther. St John's **bell tower**, separate from the main building, gives excellent views of the city.

The **Presidential Palace** (Prezidentūra), just west of the university on **Daukanto aikštė**, was originally built during the sixteenth century as a merchant's residence and remodelled into its present Neoclassical form at the end of the eighteenth century, going on to serve as the residence of the Russian governor-general during the Tsarist period. Napoleon Bonaparte stayed here briefly during his ill-fated campaign against Russia in 1812: the emperor's sojourn excited hopes that a French victory might bring a revival of Lithuanian independence, but in the event resulted in nothing more than a bout of plundering as his defeated army straggled westwards.

The emperor is said to have been so impressed by **St Anne's Church** (Šv Onos bažnyčia; Tues–Sat 10am–3pm & 5.30–9pm, Sun 8am–1pm & 5–7pm) on Maironio gatvė, to the east of Pilies gatvė, that he wanted to take it back to Paris on the palm of his hand. Studded with skeletal, finger-like towers, and its facade overlaid with intricate brick traceries and fluting, this late-sixteenth-century structure is the finest Gothic building in Vilnius. Rising behind St Anne's is the Gothic facade of the much larger **Bernardine Church** (Bernardinų vienuolyno bažničia) from 1520. Its once fine Baroque interior suffered during its Soviet-era incarnation as home to the Vilnius Art Academy, and the building is now undergoing a much-needed overhaul.

Just south of St Anne's and the Benedictine church is a **statue** commemorating the Polish Romantic poet Adam Mickiewicz (1798–1855), author of *Pan Tadeusz*, the Polish national epic. Nearby is the **A. Mickievičius Memorial Apartment** at Bernardinų 11 (A. Mickievičius Memorialinis butas; Tues–Fri 10am–5pm, Sat & Sun 10am–2pm; free), a small museum whose rather paltry exhibits include a couple of chairs and a desk owned by Mickiewicz and a number of Polish and Lithuanian first editions of his works. **Bernardinų gatvė** itself is one of the Old Town's more appealing back streets, a narrow lane lined by seventeenth- and eighteenth-century houses that runs back to Pilies.

Heading south Pilies becomes Main Street (Didžioji gatvė). The restored Baroque palace at no. 4 is the **Vilnius Picture Gallery**, which houses the Lithuanian Art Museum (Tues–Sat noon–6pm, Sun noon–5pm; 4Lt; free on Wed in winter), a marvellous collection of sixteenth- to nineteenth-century paintings and sculptures, gathered from around the country. The colonnaded Neoclassical building standing firmly at the end of **Town Hall Square** (Rotušės aikštė) has recently been restored to its original function as the town hall. The modern building behind it and to the right houses the **Contemporary Art Centre** (Šiuolaikinio Meno Centras; Tues–Sun 11am–7pm; 4Lt; free on Wed in winter), which hosts changing exhibitions of works by modern artists from Lithuania and elsewhere.

Just east of the square, **St Casimir's Church** (Šv Kazimiero bažnyčia; Mon–Fri 4–6.30pm, Sun 8am–2pm), dating from 1604 and the oldest Baroque church in the city, remains a striking building – its central cupola topped by an elaborate crown and cross symbolizing the royal ancestry of St Casimir, the son of King Casimir IV of Poland. The interior is, however, disappointingly ugly with a startlingly tacky-looking main altar, a legacy of a chequered history that saw the building remodelled as an Orthodox church in tsarist times and converted into a Museum of Atheism and the History of Religion under the Soviets.

South of here, Didžioji becomes **Aušros Vartų gatvė**, a short distance along which a gateway on the left-hand side leads to the seventeenth-century **Church of the Holy Spirit** (Šv Dvasios Cerkvė), Lithuania's main Orthodox church, a Baroque structure built on a low hill in the grounds of a monastery. The interior is surprisingly airy and in front of the large iconostasis stands a glass case in which the bodies of three fourteenth-century martyrs are displayed, their faces swathed in cloth.

A little further along Aušros Vartų gatvė the seventeenth-century **St Theresa's Church** (Šv Teresės Bažničia) rises to the left of the street, another soaring testimony to the city's dominating architectural style. The end of the street is marked by the **Gates of Dawn** (Aušros Vartai), the sole survivor of nine city gates that once studded the walls of Vilnius. A **Chapel** above the gate houses the city's most celebrated religious monument, the **White Madonna**, an image of the Virgin Mary said to have miraculous powers and revered by Polish Catholics. Only the Madonna's hands and face are visible, the rest of the likeness being overlaid by a gilt covering. Entrance to the chapel is via a small door in the walls of St Theresa's from where steps lead up to the room containing the White Madonna, which is usually surrounded by rapt worshippers. During the day the chapel windows are often left open and the Madonna is visible from the street below.

East of Aušros Vartų gatvė on Boksto 20/18 is the **Artillery Bastion** (Artilerijos Bastėja), a seventeenth-century bastion that was once part of the city's outer fortification ring and which now houses a **museum** (Wed–Sun 10am–5pm; 4Lt, free on Wed in winter) of weapons and armour. The museum is more interesting for its setting than its contents: exhibits are housed in a long brick passageway leading to the outer part of the bastion, where cannons similar to those used to defend the city have been placed in the embrasures. Labels are in Lithuanian and Russian, with some English.

Jewish Vilnius

Before World War II Vilnius was one of the most important centres of Jewish life in eastern Europe. The Jews – first invited to settle in 1410 by Grand Duke Vytautas – made up around a third of the city's population, mainly concentrated in the eastern fringes of the Old Town around present-day Vokiečių gatvė, Žydų gatvė and Antokolskio gatvė. The **Great Synagogue** was located just off Žydų gatvė, on a site now occupied by a kindergarten.

Massacres of the Jewish population began soon after the Germans occupied Vilnius on June 24, 1941, and those who survived the initial killings found themselves herded into two **ghettos**. The smaller of these ghettos centred around Žydų, Antokolskio, Stiklių and Gaono streets and was liquidated in October 1941, while the larger occupied an area between Pylimo, Vokiečių, Lydos, Mikalojaus, Karmelitų and Arklių streets and was liquidated in September 1943. Most of the Jews of Vilnius perished in Paneriai forest on the southwestern edge of the city (see p.872).

Today, the Jewish population of Vilnius numbers only a few thousand. The city has one surviving **synagogue** at Pylimo 39 (Mon–Thurs 8am–10am, Sun 7pm–9pm), out of the 96 that once existed. To find out about the history of Jewish Vilnius head for the **Lithuanian State Jewish Museum** (Lietuvos valstybinis žydų muziejus), housed in various parts of the labyrinthine Jewish community offices at Pylimo 4 (Mon–Thurs 10am–5.30pm, Fri 10am–4pm; 2Lt; free on Wed in winter). The display includes items salvaged from the Great Synagogue, including puppets used during the Purim festival and pictures of wooden synagogues from small towns in Lithuania. Some of the museum staff speak English and exhibits are captioned in English. A second branch of the museum, the Catastrophe Exhibition, occupies a small green house nearby at Pamenkalnio 12 (Mon–Thurs 9am–5pm, Fri 9am–4pm; donation requested). It contains a harrowing display about the fate of Vilnius Jews during the war – captions are in Lithuanian, Russian and English, but by and large the exhibits speak for themselves. The museum can also arrange "history of Jewish Vilnius" tours (☎2/620 730).

Gedimino prospektas

Gedimino prospektas, running west from Cathedral Square, was the main thoroughfare of nineteenth-century Vilnius, and remains the most important commercial street of the city centre. The city's largest department store and main post office, along with various government ministries and public buildings, are all situated here. Now bearing the name of the founder of the city, in the past this broad boulevard of flaking stuccoed buildings has been named after St George, Mickiewicz, Stalin and Lenin, reflecting the succession of foreign powers that have controlled the city.

Lukiškių aikštė, around 600m west of Cathedral Square, is the former location of the city's Lenin statue, removed after the failed 1991 coup which precipitated the final break-up of the Soviet Union. The square has long played an infamous role in city history. After the 1863–64 uprising against the Russians, a number of rebels were publicly hanged here, while Gedimino 40, on the southern side of the square, was Lithuania's **KGB headquarters**. The building also served as Gestapo headquarters during the German occupation and more recently the Soviets incarcerated political prisoners in the basement. It has now been turned into the **Genocide Museum** (Genocido Aukų Muziejus; mid-May to mid-Sept Tues–Sun

10am–6pm; mid-Sept to mid-May Tues–Sun 10am–4pm; 2Lt); the entrance is at Aukų 2a. The dank green cells and courtyard where some prisoners were tortured and executed are preserved in their pre-1991 state. The English-language cassette-tape commentary (8Lt) provides detailed background on the prison and its inmates.

At the far end of Gedimino prospektas stands Lithuania's graceless modern **Parliament Building** (Seimas). Thousands gathered here on January 13, 1991, when Soviet troops threatened to occupy it following the killing of a dozen people at the TV Tower (see below). On the side of the parliament facing the river some of the barricades built to defend the building have been preserved, complete with anti-Soviet graffiti; there's also a moving memorial of traditional wooden crosses commemorating those who died at the TV Tower and the seven border guards killed by Soviet special forces in July 1991. The 326-metre **TV Tower** (Televizijos bokštas; 10am–9pm; 12Lt) itself is around 3km west of the centre in the Karoliniskės district – trolleybus #16 from the train station or #11 from Lukiskių aikstė; alight at the Televizijos bokštas stop on Sausio 13-Osios gatvė. At the tower's base, wooden crosses commemorate those killed here in the bloodiest event of the struggle for Baltic independence, and there's a small photograph exhibition inside.

Eating, drinking and nightlife

There's a fast-growing range of **eateries** in Vilnius offering everything from Lithuanian to Lebanese cuisine – although the majority of places concentrate on the filling meat-and-potatoes fare common to much of northern Europe and the Baltics. There's often very little difference between eating and drinking venues: **bars** and **cafés** invariably serve snacks and meals and these often represent better value for money than white-tablecloth restaurants, where the expense is not always a guarantee of quality. Vilnius has a few **clubs** and **discos** that are worth investigating, though you may find you have a better (and cheaper) time in some of the bars mentioned below, where people tend to start dancing after a few beers. Cutting-edge DJ culture is limited to the monthly rave parties organized by hip magazine *Ore*, but venues change: look out for posters or check the Internet (*www.ore.lt*) for details

Cafés and snack bars

Afrika, Pilies 28. Popular lunchtime stop-off on the Old Town's main street, offering a tasty range of salads, sandwiches and soups. 10am–11pm.

Gabi, Šv Mykolo 6. Inexpensive drinks and good solid home-cooking in a relaxed, no-smoking atmosphere. 11am–10pm.

Greitai, corner of Gedimino and Totorių. Classy cafeteria with cheap main courses (peruse the choice at the counter and point to what you want) and goodish cakes. Daily 8am–10pm.

Literatų Svetainė, corner of Gedimino and Vrublevskio. Plush café conveniently located across from the Cathedral, with snooty restaurant attached. 11am–11pm.

Mano Kavinė, Bokšto 7. Stylish place in the Old Town with chic, modernist decor, trendy young clientele, wide range of snack dishes, and large choice of speciality teas. 10am–11pm.

Pilies Menė, Pilies 8. Flash modern café-bar with extensive menu of pancakes. Good place for a daytime coffee or night-time drink. Daily 10am–midnight.

Presto, Gedimino 32a. Bright modern coffee bar with an impressive range of brews, as well as salads and sumptuous cakes. Mon–Thurs 7am–10pm, Fri 7am–midnight, Sat 11am–midnight, Sun 11am–10pm.

Skonis ir Kvapas, Trakų 8. Relaxing café in barrel-vaulted rooms offering big pots of tea, excellent coffee, and an affordable range of hot meals. Daily 8am–midnight.

Užsuk, Vienuolio 4. Reasonable-quality cafeteria food in comfortable surroundings, just off Gedimino. Mon–Fri 7.30am–10pm, Sat 10am–10pm, Sun 10am–8pm.

Restaurants

Čili, Didžioji 5 (*www.cili.lt*). Popular place for a quick inexpensive bite, offering good choice of thin-crust and deep-pan pizzas in bright and breezy surroundings. There's another branch at Gedimino 23. Home delivery available on ☎2/333555. Daily 10am–midnight.

Finjan, Vokiečių 18. Middle-eastern place that looks like a fast-food café but charges restaurant prices. The kebabs, shawarma and falafel on offer taste good and the portions are reasonable. Daily 11am–midnight.

Freskos, Didžioji 31 (☎2/18133, *www.freskos.lt*). Imaginative, well-presented modern European cuisine in a barrel-vaulted chamber occupying the rear end of the Town Hall. Good value lunchtime salad buffet. Daily 11am–midnight.

Lokys, Stiklių 8/10. Reasonably priced and highly recommended Lithuanian cellar restaurant serving boar and elk alongside more traditional meat-and-potato favourites. Daily noon–midnight.

Po Saule, Labdarių 8. French bistro with superb food at very reasonable prices. Great place for a quick tarte á l'oignon or a more leisurely three-course meal. Daily 10am–10pm.

Ritos Slėptuvė, Goštauto 8 (*www.rita.lt*). Immensely popular pizza place run by a Lithuanian-American. The pizzas are excellent and they also do dishes like quiche and spaghetti and have a few vegetarian options. Order local beer to keep your bill manageable. Good place for breakfasts. Mon–Fri 2.30pm–2am, Fri & Sat 7.30am–6am, Sun 9am–midnight.

Stikliai, Gaono 7. French food in the posh restaurant upstairs, good Lithuanian fare in the beer-cellar-style restaurant downstairs. The latter hosts live Lithuanian folk music at weekends. Noon–midnight.

Sue's Indian Raja, Jogailos 11/2. Authentic Indian cuisine at slightly higher than average prices served up by attentive staff. Similarly good-quality Thai nosh is on offer at Sue Ka Thai, which occupies another section of the same restaurant. Mon–Sat noon–11pm, Sun noon–10pm.

Žemaičių Smuklė, Vokiečių 24. The top place for traditional Lithuanian cuisine. An excellent place to try *cepelinai* (potato dumplings stuffed with meat), or the similarly stuffed *žemaičių blynai* (potato pancakes). Great steaks and fish too. Warren of cellar rooms in winter; two tiers of outdoor courtyard seating in summer. 1pm–midnight.

Bars

Great new **bars** are opening up all over town. Check *Vilnius in Your Pocket* for a complete list but here are a few possibilities.

Amatininkų Užeiga, Didžioji 19/2. Atmospherically gloomy, faux-rustic café-bar right on Town Hall square. Decent food. Mon–Fri 8am–5am, Sat & Sun 11am–5am.

Amerika, Šv. Kazimiero 3. Saloon bar in a courtyard. Pool, cocktails and jazz nights. Mon–Fri noon–2am, Sat & Sun noon–5am.

Bix, Etmonų 6. Great bar with industrial decor, lively atmosphere and an enjoyable disco in the cellar – run by members of local rock band Bix. Serves meals too. Mon–Thurs & Sun 11am–2am, Fri & Sat 11am–5am.

Brodvėjaus Pubas (aka "Broadway"), Mėsinių 4. Deservedly popular drinking venue built around a long, galleried space packed with tables – with a stage at one end for live bands (Thurs–Sun) and bopping. Full menu of snacks and hot meals; lunchtime specials are chalked up on a board outside. Mon–Thurs noon–2am, Fri & Sat noon–5am.

Gero Viskio Baras, Pilies 34. Eternally popular Old-Town drinking joint both day and night. Aside from the main ground-floor bar there's a cocktail bar upstairs; cellar disco after 8pm. Mon–Thurs 10am–2am, Fri 10am–5am, Sat noon–5am, Sun noon–2am.

Prie Parlamento, Gedimino 46. Big, popular café-bar with restaurant-standard food and pub-style bar upstairs. The menu offers cooked breakfasts, salads and desserts and has an excellent vegetarian selection. Popular with expats. Sun 10am–2am, Mon–Thurs 8am–2am, Fri 8am–5am, Sat 10am–5am.

Ritos Slėptuvė, Goštauto 8. Lively bar to the rear of the pizza restaurant. Pulls in lots of expats and better-off locals, and there tends to be dancing here as the evening wears on. Mon–Thurs 7.30am–2am, Fri & Sat 8am–6am, Sun 8am–2am.

Savas Kampas, Vokiečių 4. The cosy wood-furnished interior sets a good mood in which to peruse the extensive list of alcohol available. Good pizzas too. Daily 11am–midnight.

Šuolaikinio Meno Centras (ŠMC), in the Contemporary Art Centre at Vokiečių 2. Dark, minimally decorated café-bar which has long been a prime meeting point for arty types and non-conformists of all ages. Ranges in atmosphere from cosy coffee bar to human zoo, depending on who's around. Daily 11am–midnight.

The PUB, Dominikonų 9. Popular bar with dark wooden interior and lots of seating in the covered courtyard. Frequent live music, big-screen sport and extensive pub-grub food menu. Mon–Thurs & Sun 11am–2am, Fri & Sat 11am–5pm.

Užupio Kavinė, Užupio 2. Relaxed, mildly bohemian place on the eastern fringes of the Old Town, with lime-tree-shaded outdoor terrace overlooking the Vilnia River. Good for eating or evening drinking. 11am–11pm.

Clubs and discos

Karolinos Klubas, Justiniškių 64. Hangar-sized nightclub specializing in frenetic mainstream techno-pop a good 5km northwest of the centre. Wed & Thurs 8pm–2am, Fri & Sat 8pm–5am. 5–10Lt.

Ministerija, Gedimino 46. Located in the cellar below Prie Parlimento. Newish dance stuff as well as popular classics. Favoured gathering point for ex-pats as well as local beautiful young things. Mon–Thurs & Sun 6pm–2am, Fri & Sat 8pm–5am. 5–15Lt.

Stiklių Tangomania, Gedimino 31. Stylish dicotheque with smart, older-than-teenage clientele.

Ultra, Goštauto 12. Trendy place catering for a younger age group. Pop during the week and techno on Sat. Thurs–Sat 8pm–5am. 5–15Lt.

Classical music, ballet and theatre

Lithuanian National Drama Theatre, Gedimino 4 (Lietuvos Nacionalinis Dramos Teatras; ☎2/629771, *www.teatras.lt*). Comfortable, modern auditorium hosting performances by the state drama company as well as prestigious independent drama troupes and high-profile groups from abroad.

National Philharmonic, Aušros Vartų 5 (Nacionalinė Filharmonija; ☎2/222290, *www.filharmonija.lt*). Home of the nation's top orchestra. A reliable venue for classical standards along with occasional forays into more unusual modern territory. Frequent guest appearances by international artists.

Opera and Ballet Theatre, Vienuolio 1 (Operos ir Baleto Teatras; ☎2/620636, *www.opera.lt*). Hugely popular venue, which stages excellent productions and is usually a sell-out, so book well in advance.

Russian Drama Theatre, Basanavičiaus (Rusų Dramos Teatras; ☎2/627133). Mixed programme of Russian-language classics and modern experimental work in a lovely 150-year-old building which is in sore need of renovation.

Vilnius Congress Hall, Vilniaus 6/14 (Vilniaus Kongresų rūmai; ☎2/618828). Modern venue hosting performances by Vulnius's second big orchestra, the Lithuanian State Philharmonic (as opposed to the National Philharmonic above; *www.lvso.lt*), as well as chamber concerts, and occasional musicals.

Listings

Airline offices Aeroflot, Pylimo 8/2 (☎2/224 189); Estonian Air at the airport (☎2/739 022, *www.estonianair.ee*); Lithuanian Airlines, Ukmergės 12 (☎2/752 588, *www.lal.lt*); LOT, room 104, Hotel Skrydis, Rodūnės Kelias 2 (☎2/739 020, *www.lot.com*); Lufthansa at the airport (☎2/262 222, *www.lufthansa.com*); SAS at the airport (☎2/395 500, *www.scandinavia.net*).

Airport information ☎2/306 666.

Bike rental Litinterp, Bernardinų 7–2 (☎2/223 850). Bikes for 20Lt per day.

Books and papers America Center, Pranciškonų 3/6, has American papers and magazines plus a well-stocked library (Tues–Thurs 2–5pm); the British Council, Vilniaus 39-6, also has books and papers (Tues & Thurs noon–6pm, Wed & Fri 11am–5pm, Sat 10am–3pm).

Car rental Cheapest is local company A & A Litinterp, Bernardinų 7–2 (☎2/223 850, *www.litinterp.lt*) with cars from around 190Lt per day. Otherwise try Avis, at the airport (☎2/306 820, *www.avis.lt*); Europcar, Stuokos-Gucevičiaus 9-1 (☎2/220 207, *www.europcar.lt*); Hertz, Kalvarijų 14 (☎2/726 940, *www.hertz.lt*).

Embassies and Consulates Australia, Totorių 15 (☎2/223 369); Canada, Gedimino 64 (☎2/220 853); USA, Akmenų 6 (☎2/223031); United Kingdom, Antakalnio 2 (☎2/222 070).

Exchange Main post office (see below); 24hr exchange facilities at Gelezinkelio 6.

Hospital Vilnius University Emergency Hospital, Šiltnamių 29 (☎2/269 069).

Internet access Bazė, Gedimino 50 (entrance round the corner on Rotundo; open 24hr; 10Lt/hr); Voo2 (pronounced "voodoo"), Ašmenos 8 (Mon–Fri 9am–midnight, Sat & Sun 11am–midnight; 8Lt/hour).

Pharmacies Gedimino Vaistinė, Gedimino 27 (24hr).

Police Jogailos 3 (☎2/616 208).

Post office Main office, Gedimino prospektas 7 (Mon–Fri 7am–7pm, Sat 9am–4pm). International phone calls and currency exchange facilities available.

Telephones Central Telegraph Office, Vilniaus 33 (daily 8am–9.30pm).

Around Vilnius

In the area surrounding Vilnius the two most accessible destinations are **Paneriai**, where the Jewish inhabitants of the city were murdered by Nazis during World War II, and **Trakai**, the medieval capital of Lithuania, now a recreation centre for the citizens of the present-day capital.

Paneriai

PANERIAI, the site where the Nazis and their Lithuanian accomplices murdered one hundred thousand people during World War II, lies within Vilnius city limits in a forest at the edge of a suburb 10km southwest of the centre. Seventy thousand of those killed here were Jews from Vilnius, who were systematically exterminated from the time the Germans arrived in June 1941 until they were driven out by the Soviet army in 1944.

The killing grounds are about 1km into the woods due west of Paneriai train station and marshalling yards. The entrance to the site is marked by the **Paneriai Memorial** (Panerių Memorialas). Here, two stone slabs with Russian and Lithuanian inscriptions commemorate the hundred thousand murdered "Soviet citizens", flanking a central slab with an inscription in Hebrew commemorating "seventy thousand Jewish men, women and children". From the memorial a path leads to the **Paneriai Museum**, Agrastų 15 (Panerių muziejus; officially Mon & Wed–Sat 11am–6pm; best to check times ☎2/620 730; donations requested), with a small display detailing what happened here. Nearby are two monuments, one with a Hebrew inscription (English on the obverse) honouring the seventy thousand Vilnius Jews, the other a Soviet obelisk recalling the "victims of fascist terror". From here paths lead to the pits in the woods where the Nazis burnt the bodies of their victims and to another eight-metre pit where the bones of the dead were crushed.

To get to Paneriai take a southwest-bound suburban train from Vilnius station and alight at Paneriai. From the station platform descend onto Agrastų gatvė, turn right and follow the road through the woods for about a kilometre.

Trakai

Founded during the fourteenth century and the site of two medieval castles, lakeside **TRAKAI**, 25km west of Vilnius, is the former capital of the Grand Duchy of Lithuania. The town's island castle, which was built by Grand Duke Vytautas, under whom Lithuania reached the pinnacle of its power during the fifteenth century, is one of Lithuania's most famous monuments, though for many Vilnius inhabitants boating and swimming in the town's lakes is as much of an attraction as reminders of past glories.

Trakai stands on a peninsula jutting out between two lakes. From the **train** and **bus stations** follow Vytauto gatvė to reach the main sights. After about 500m turn right down Kęstuaio gatvė to the remains of the **Peninsula Castle**, thought to have been built by Duke Kęstutis, son of Gediminas and father of Vytautas. These days only the walls and a couple of towers remain.

Trakai is home to the **Karaites**, members of a Judaic sect whose ancestors were brought here from the Crimea by Grand Duke Vytautas to serve him as bodyguards, and whose distinctive wooden cottages line Karaimų gatvė, the northern continuation of Vytauto gatvė. Around two hundred inhabitants of Trakai are Karaites; Lithuania's smallest ethnic minority, they recognize only the laws of the Old Testament. Down the street at no. 30 is their wooden **Kenessa**, or prayer house, built in the early nineteenth century.

A hundred metres or so beyond the Kenessa two wooden footbridges lead to the **Island Castle**, a cluster of red-brick towers built around 1400 on a small offshore island by Grand Duke Vytautas to provide stronger defences than those of the peninsula castle. Though it fell into ruin from the seventeenth century, a 1960s restoration has returned it to its former glory, and it now houses a **museum** (Tues–Sun: May–Sept 10am–7pm; Oct–April 10am–5pm; 7Lt). The main **tower**, built around a galleried courtyard, is separated from the outer buildings by a moat – you cross a footbridge to enter. Within are exhibits covering the history of the castle, plus examples of medieval weaponry and wooden carvings. Captions are in Lithuanian. The castle's outer buildings contain further exhibits, mostly furniture, including a bizarre table-and-chair set made from antlers in the "Hunters' Room". Some captions in this section are in English and German.

Trakai's main culinary claim to fame is the **kibinas**, a Cornish-pasty-like creation filled with grey meat that unleashes a deadly drip of hot fat after a few bites. Buy it from the cafés clustered around the footbridge leading to the Island Castle, or from *Kibininė*, a homely shack about 1km further on along Karaimų.

THE REST OF LITHUANIA

Outside Vilnius Lithuania is predominantly rural – a gently undulating, densely forested landscape scattered with lakes. However, it does boast at least one more major city in **Kaunas**, a genuine rival to Vilnius in terms of its historical importance to the Lithuanian nation. Further west, the main highlight of the Lithuanian coast is the holiday village of **Nida**, whose dramatic dunescapes and traditional timber architecture are reachable by ferry and bus from **Klaipėda**, the country's major port.

Kaunas

KAUNAS, 80km west of Vilnius and easily reached by bus or rail, is Lithuania's second city and seen by many Lithuanians as the true heart of their country. It served as provisional capital during the interwar period when Vilnius was part of Poland, and remains a major commercial and industrial centre. Nevertheless it's an attractive, easy-going city well served by road and rail, with enough sights to make it worth at least a full day's visit.

The Old Town

The most interesting part of town is predictably the **Old Town**, or **Senamiestis**, centred around **Town Hall Square** (Rotušės aikstė) on a spur of land between the Neris and Nemunas rivers. The square is lined with fifteenth- and sixteenth-century merchants' houses in pastel stucco shades, but the overpowering feature is the magnificent **Town Hall**, its tiered Baroque facade rising to a graceful 53-metre tower. Known as "White Swan" for its elegance, this building dates back to the sixteenth century and during its history has been used as an Orthodox church, a theatre and university department, though these days it houses a "Palace of Weddings" with a ceramics museum in the basement. After the town hall the most eye-catching structure on the square is the seventeenth century **Jesuit Church** (Jėzuitų bažnyčia) on the southern side. Originally part of a larger college and monastery complex, the church was built in 1666. In 1825 the Russians handed it over to the Orthodox church and later, the Soviets turned it into a trade school, but the Baroque interior remains intact, and the church has recently been reconsecrated.

Northeast of the square, the red-brick tower of Kaunas' austere **Cathedral** (Katedra Basilika) can be seen at the start of Vilniaus gatvė. Dating back to the reign of Vytautas the Great, the cathedral was much added to in subsequent centuries. After the plain exterior, the lavish gilt and marble interior comes as a surprise. There are nine altars in total, though the large, statue-adorned Baroque high altar (1775) steals the limelight.

Predating the cathedral by several centuries is **Kaunas Castle** (Kauno pilis), whose scant remains survive just northwest of the square. Little more than a restored tower and a couple of sections of wall are left, the rest having been washed away by the Neris, but in its day the fortification was a major obstacle to the Teutonic Knights.

South of the town square, the **Perkūnas House** (Perkūno namas) at Aleksoto 6 is an elaborately gabled red-brick structure, thought to have been built as a Hansa office or possibly a Jesuit chapel, standing on the reputed site of a temple to Perkūnas, the pagan god of thunder. From here Aleksoto descends to the banks of the Nemunas and the glowering **Vytautas Church** (Vytauto bažnyčia), built by Vytautas the Great in around 1399. During its long existence it has suffered various indignities, including use as a munitions magazine and potato store, and, like many other Lithuanian churches, it also had a stint as an Orthodox place of worship.

The New Town

The main thoroughfare of Kaunas' **New Town** (Naujamiestis) is **Freedom Avenue** (Laisvės alėja), a broad pedestrianized shopping street running east from the Old Town, which, bizarrely, was declared a no-smoking zone during the 1990s. At the junction with L. Sapiegos the street is enlivened by a bronze **statue of Vytautas the Great**, which faces the **City Garden** (Miesto sodas) where, on May 14, 1972, the 19-year-old student Romas Kalanta immolated himself in protest against Soviet rule. Kalanta's death sparked several days of anti-Soviet rioting, and today he is commemorated by a memorial stone in the gardens.

Towards the eastern end of Freedom Avenue the silver-domed **Church of St Michael the Archangel** (Igulos bažnyčia) looms over Independence Square (Nepriklausomybes aikštė). Originally an Orthodox church built for the tsarist garrison in the 1890s, this neo-Byzantine structure is now Catholic, its bare interior a reflection of the fact that it was an art gallery for most of the Soviet period. The striking modern building in the northeast corner of the square is one of the best art galleries in the country, the **Mykolas Žilinskas Art Museum** (Mykolo Žilinsko dailės muziejus; Tues–Sun: summer noon–6pm; winter 11am–5pm, closed last Tues of every month; 3Lt), which houses a fine collection of artifacts from Egypt, Renaissance paintings from Italy, Chinese porcelain, and Lithuania's only Rubens.

Kaunas celebrates its role in sustaining Lithuanian national identity on **Unity Square** (Vienybės aikštė), at the junction of S. Daukanto and K. Donelaičio, a block north of Laisvės. Here a **monument** depicting liberty as a female figure faces an eternal flame flanked by traditional wooden crosses, with busts of prominent Lithuanians from the nineteenth century between the two. Overlooking all this is the **Military Museum of Vytautas the Great** (Vytauto Didžiojo karo muziejus; Wed–Sun: summer 10am–6pm; winter 9am–5pm; closed last Thurs of every month; 3Lt; English leaflets available), with a display that covers local archeological finds and Lithuanian military history.

Behind the museum at Putvinskio 55 is the **M.K. Čiurlionis Art Museum** (M. K. Čiurlionio dailės muziejus; Tues–Sun: summer noon–6pm; winter 11am–5pm; closed last Tues of every month; 3Lt). The collection has a large display of pre-1940 Lithuanian art, but its raison d'être – and one of the highlights of Kaunas – is the section dedicated to **Mikalojus Konstantinas Čiurlionis** (1875–1911), Lithuania's best-known artist. During his short career (his most significant works were completed during the first decade of the twentieth century) Čiurlionis created a unique body of work, producing enigmatic mystical paintings influenced by the French Symbolists, many of them featuring Lithuanian folk motifs.

Kaunas has a second unique art collection nearby in the **A. Žmuidzinavičius Art Museum**, Putvinskio 64 (A. Žmuidzinavičius kūrinių ir rinkinių muziejus; Tues–Sun: summer noon–6pm; winter 11am–5pm; closed last Tues of every month; 4Lt). Better known as the **Devil's Museum** (Velnių muziejus), this houses a vast collection of devil figures put together by the artist Antanas Žmuidzinavičius. Though most of the images are comic, there's also a sinister representation of Hitler and Stalin as devils dancing on a Lithuania composed of skulls.

Heading east down Putvinskio brings you to the 1930s **funicular railway** (funikulierius) which climbs up to the **Žaliakalnis** district to the north of the city centre, allowing views across the rest of the city (0.50Lt). Near the upper terminal is the **Church of Christ's Resurrection** (Prisikėlimo bažnyčia), a striking 1930s modernist edifice with a very tall white tower. Used as a factory warehouse during Soviet times, the church is currently undergoing long-term restoration.

Before World War II Kaunas, like Vilnius, had a large **Jewish population**. Nearly all were killed during the war and little remains to remind of their presence. From medieval times, Kaunas' **ghetto** was in Viljampolė (then known as Slobodka) on the opposite side of the Neris to the Old Town. After 1858 restrictions on where Jews could live were eased, and many moved into other parts of the city. When the Nazis arrived the Jews were forced to return to Viljampolė. The city's sole surviving **synagogue** is at Ožeskienės 17 in the New Town and the ruins of two more are at Zamenhofo 7 and 9. To find out more about the fate of the Jews of Kaunas head out of town to the **Ninth Fort Museum** (Devintojo Forto Muziejus), Žemaičių plentas 73 (daily except Tues 10am–5/6pm; 14Lt to see all three parts), housed in the tsarist-era fortress where the Jews were kept while awaiting execution. You can get there by driving out of town on the Klaipėda road, or by taking bus #23 or #35 from Šv. Gertrūdos just north of the Old Town.

Practicalities

There's a helpful **tourist office** just off Laisvės alėja at Mickievičiaus 36 (April–Sept Mon–Fri 9am–7pm, Sat 9am–3pm; Oct–March Mon–Fri 9am–6pm; ☎27/323 436, *turizmas@takas.lt*) doling out English-language leaflets and a free map. You can also pick up a copy of *Kaunas in Your Pocket* here (*www.inyourpocket.com*; 4Lt), a very handy little publication produced by the *Vilnius in Your Pocket* people – also available from bookstores, newspaper kiosks and some hotel foyers. For **accommodation** the ever-reliable *Litinterp*, Kumelių 15–4 (☎27/228 718, *www.litinterp.lt*), can sort you out with a room in the centre for 60Lt single, 100Lt double. Central **hotels** include the unrenovated but tolerable *Monela*, Laisvės 35 (☎27/221 791; ③); the gloomy but charmingly olde-worlde *Lietuva I*, just north of Laisvės at Daukanto 21 (☎27/225 992, *metropol@takas.lt*; ③); and the hulking concrete *Takijoji Neris*, off Laisvės to the north at Donelaičio 27 (☎27/204 224, *takneris@takas.lt*; ④). Real comfort in Kaunas comes at a price: best of the upscale hotels is the friendly *Perkūno Namai*, in suburban streets east of the train and bus stations at Perkūno 61 (☎27/320 230, *hotel@perkuno-namai.lt*; ⑧).

To **eat** in style head for *Chez Eliza*, Vilniaus 30, with an international, French-influenced menu (main courses from 12Lt). For something a little more indigenous try the *Bernelių Užeiga*, Valančiaus 9, where you can dine on meat and potatoes in an attractive rustic interior. *Pizza Jazz*, Laisvės alėja 68, does delicious thin-crust pizzas and Mexican dishes at reasonable prices. **Cafés** and **bars** are often a good bet for eating too: *Avilys*,Vilniaus 9, is a chic cellar-bound establishment that has a full range of meals and brews its own beer; *Elfų Šėlsmas*, Laisvės 93, offers drinking, dining and dancing in faux-rustic surroundings. *Fortas*, Donelaičo 65, is an Irish pub just off Laisvės with bars on three levels. The *Skliautai*, Rotušės aikšte 26, and the nearby *B.O.*, Muitinės 9, are the best places to hook up with a young, arty, bohemian crowd. *Los Patrankos*, Savanorių 124, is the biggest and friendliest of the techno-oriented **clubs**. You can access the **Internet** at Kavinė Internetas, Daukšos 12 (8Lt per hour).

Klaipėda and around

KLAIPĖDA, Lithuania's third largest city and most important port, lies on the Baltic coast, a long and tedious 275km by road or rail northwest of Vilnius. Though it has a handful of sights the city is of more interest as a staging post en route to **Neringa**, the Lithuanian name for the Couronian Spit which shields much of Lithuania's coast from the open Baltic.

The City

Until 1919 Klaipėda was part of Germany and known as **Memel**, and its population remained largely German until 1945. The neatly restored Old Town draws quite a few visitors (mainly German), but there's not much to keep you here for more than a few hours.

Klaipėda is bisected by the River Danė and the main sights are in the **Old Town** (Senamiestis) on its southern bank, an area of half-timbered buildings and cobbled streets. At the heart of the Old Town is **Theatre Square** (Teatro aikštė) named after the ornate Neoclassical **Theatre** building on its northern side. Hitler spoke from the balcony in March 1939 after Germany annexed Klaipėda in its last act of territorial aggrandizement before the outbreak of war. In front of the theatre is **Anna's Fountain** (Anikės fontanas), a replica of a famous prewar monument to the German poet Simon Dach (1605–59), which depicts the heroine of his folksong *Ännchen von Tharau*.

Southeast of the square, the **History Museum of Lithuania Minor**, Didžioji vandens 6 (Mažosios Lietuvos istorijos muziejus; Wed–Sun 11am–7pm; 3Lt), has local archeological finds, national costumes and ancient domestic implements, while the nearby **Blacksmiths' Museum of Lithuania Minor**, Šaltaklvių 2 (Mažosios Lietuvos kalvystės muziejus; Wed–Sun 11am–7pm; 3Lt), has a display of wrought-iron work, a traditional Lithuanian folk art form, including some ornate grave memorials.

In the **New Town** (Naujamiestis), on the northern side of the Danė, at Liepų 16, is Klaipėda's splendid red-brick Gothic-revival **Post Office**. Built between 1883 and 1893, it is a vivid reminder of imperial German civic pride. A few doors along at Liepų 12, the **Clock Museum** (Laikrodžių muziejus; Tues–Sun noon–5pm; 4Lt) is stuffed with timepieces from the earliest candle clocks onwards, and includes some magnificent seventeenth- and eighteenth-century examples.

Practicalities

Klaipėda's **tourist office** is just off Teatro aikštė at Tomo 2 (summer Mon–Fri 9am–5pm, Sat 9am–3pm; winter Mon–Fri 9am–5pm; ☎26/412186, *kltic@takas.lt*). *Klaipėda in Your Pocket* (4Lt, from the tourist office or bookstores) is your best source of information about what's going on in town. *Litinterp*, Šimkaus 21/8 (Mon–Fri 9am–6pm, Sat 10am–4pm; ☎26/216 962, *www.litinterp.lt*), have central **private rooms** (②), and they can also help with rooms in Nida. *Klaipėda Travellers' Guesthouse*, Turgaus 3–4 (☎26/214 935, *oldtown@takas.lt*; ②), is a centrally located, friendly hostel. Reasonable mid-range **hotels** include the *Fortūna*, Poilsio 64 (☎26/348028; ④), a small pension 4km south of the centre best booked in advance. Nearer the centre and equally good is *Prūsija*, Šimkaus 6 (☎26/255 963; ④), a wonderful family-run pension with plenty of character. There's an unofficial **campsite** at Giruliai, 8km north of Klaipėda next to the *Pajūris* sanatorium on Slaito. There are no facilities at all but it's free (shuttle bus #8 from the centre).

Good places to **eat** in the Old Town are Galerija Pėda, Turgaus 10, whose tasty food looks as arty as the gallery it occupies; and *Būrų Užeiga*, Kepėjų 17, which serves up Lithuanian meat-and-potato favourites in homely wooden surroundings. For **drinking**, *Kurpiai*, Kurpių 1, is a pub-like place that also functions as the best jazz bar in the Baltics; while *Skandalas*, 10 minutes' northwest of the Old Town at Kanto 44, is an in-your-face American-themed bar.

Neringa

NERINGA, or the Kuršių Nerija, is the Lithuanian section of the Couronian Spit (known as Kurische Nehrung when the region was part of Germany), a 97-kilometre spit of land characterized by vast sand dunes and pine forests. Much of the spit can be seen as a day trip from Klaipėda, although you need to stay here for a day or two to soak up the unique atmosphere. To get there take a ferry from the quayside towards the end of Žvejų gatvė in Klaipėda (sailings every thirty minutes between 6am and 11pm; 1.40Lt return) to **SMILTYNE** on the northern tip of the spit. A road leads north from the landing stage, passing a re-created thatched wooden fishing village before reaching the **Maritime Museum and Aquarium** (Jūrų muziejus ir akvariumas; June–Aug Tues–Sun 11am–7pm; May & Sept Wed–Sun 11am–7pm; Oct–April Sat & Sun 11am–5pm; 6Lt), 1km away, where an engaging mixture of seals, penguins and model ships are assembled in a red-brick German fort. Nearby is a **dolphinarium** where captive Black Sea Dolphins are put through the hoops (May–Sept noon, 2pm & 4pm; 10Lt).

Back at the Smiltynė landing stage, frequent minibuses (7Lt) run south towards the more scenic, dune-dominated parts of the spit, terminating at Nida, 35km south. At the National Park Station 5km south of Smyltinė you will have to pay an entrance fee (2Lt per person, 10Lt per car without a trailer). Keep the receipt for your return journey. The speed limit is forty kilometres per hour.

NIDA is the most famous village on the spit – a small fishing village boasting several streets of attractive wooden houses, although there's some lumpen Soviet resort architecture at its heart. To get a feel for the old fishing settlement head for **Naglių gatvė** and **Lotmisko gatvė** (5min south of the village centre bus stop), lined by single-storey blue- and brown-painted wooden houses, many of which preserve their traditional thatched roofs. The **Etnografinė Žvejo Sodyba**, Naglių 4 (May–Sept Wed–Sun 11am–5pm; 3Lt), is a re-created nineteenth-century fisherman's cottage with simple wooden furnishings and explanations in Lithuanian, Russian and German of fishing-village development and architectural styles. Outside, between the building and the sea, are a couple of old fishing boats.

From the end of Naglių a shore path runs to a flight of wooden steps leading up to the top of the **dunes** south of the village. From the summit you can gaze out across a Saharan sand-scape to the Kaliningrad province, part of German East Prussia until 1945 but now belonging to the Russian Federation. At the northern end of the village is **Thomas Mann's House** (Tomo Mano Namelis; May–Sept Tues–Sun 11am–5pm; 3Lt), his summer residence from 1930 to 1932. An uneventful museum within contains a few photos of the man himself and various editions of his books. Nida's long, luxurious beach stretches along the western side of the spit, about 20min walk through the forest from the village.

The **tourist office**, bang in the centre of the village at Taikos 4 (Mon–Fri 9am–1pm & 2–6pm; ☎259/52345), will find you a **private room** (①–②). Litinterp back in Klaipėda can book rooms in advance, but for a slightly higher fee. Best of the numerous small **hotels** in town is the *Rasytė*, Lotmiskio 11 (☎259/52592; ④), a wooden house in the heart of the old fishing settlement, although it's essential to book in advance. The larger and less atmospheric *Nidos Smiltė*, Skruzdynės 2 (☎259/52221), offers simple doubles with shared facilities (③) and spartan cabins (②) in the Nidos Pušynas holiday settlement nearby. For **food** head for *Seklyčia*, Lotmiškio 1 (daily: summer 9am–3am; winter 9am–11pm), which does simple dishes like *cepelinai* as well as more sophisticated meat and fish dishes. *Reidas*, just behind the bus station at Naglių 20, is a good place to try the excellent local fish, and turns into an animated **bar** with live rock at night.

travel details

Trains

Vilnius to: Kaunas (12 daily; 1hr 15min–2hr), Klaipėda (3 daily; 5hr); Rīga (2 daily; 9hr); Šeštokai (2 daily; 3hr 30min); Warsaw (1 daily; 11hr). The only way to get from Vilnius to Warsaw by train without passing through Belarus, for which you will need an expensive visa, is to travel indirectly via Šeštokai and Suwałki.

Kaunas to: Klaipėda (3 daily; 3hr 30min); Rīga (1 daily; 7hr); Vilnius (12 daily; 1hr 15min–2hr).

Klaipėda to: Kaunas (3 daily; 3hr 30min); Vilnius (3 daily; 5hr).

Buses

Vilnius to: Kaunas (every 20–30min; 1hr 30min–2hr); Klaipėda (10–12 daily; 4hr); Rīga (5 daily; 6hr); Tallinn (2 daily; 11hr 40min); Warsaw (4 daily; 12hr).

Kaunas to: Klaipėda (10 daily; 3hr); Rīga (2 daily; 4hr 30min); Vilnius (every 20–30min; 1hr 30min–2hr).

Klaipėda to: Kaliningrad (2 daily; 3hr 50min); Kaunas (10 daily; 3hr); Nida (departures from Smiltynė; 8 daily; 50min); Vilnius (10–12 daily; 5hr).

Ferries

Kaunas to: Nida (hydrofoil service; June–Aug 1 daily; 4hr).

CHAPTER 18

MOROCCO

Note: This chapter covers only the most easily accessible towns in northern Morocco. The map therefore shows only the northern regions, not the whole of the country

Introduction

Though just an hour's ferry ride from Spain, **Morocco** seems very far from Europe, with a deeply traditional Islamic culture. Throughout the country, despite its 44 years of French and Spanish colonial rule, a more distant past constantly makes its presence felt. Travel here is an intense and rewarding – if not always easy – experience.

Contrary to general misconceptions, it is the **Berbers**, the indigenous population of the mountains, who make up over half of Morocco's population; only around ten percent of Moroccans claim to be "pure" Arabs, although with a recent shift of population to the industrialized cities, such distinctions are becoming less significant. More telling is the legacy of the **colonial** period: before Morocco reclaimed its independence in 1956, the country was divided into Spanish and French zones. The **French**, who ruled the main cities, had the most lasting effect, imposing their language, which is spoken today by all educated people (after Moroccan Arabic and/or one of the three local Berber languages). They built neat, ordered *Villes Nouvelles* (new towns) alongside the long-standing *Medinas* (old towns), created Casablanca – Morocco's commercial capital – in the image of Marseille, and chose Rabat, on the Atlantic coast, to be the new seat of government.

Most visitors' introduction to the country is **Tangier** in the north, a pleasant old town still shaped by its heyday of "international" port status in the 1950s. Inland lies the enthralling city of **Fes**, the greatest of the four imperial capitals of the country's various dynasties (the others are Meknes, Rabat and Marrakesh), and unique in the Arab world for the chance it offers to witness a city life that, in patterns and appearance at least, remains in large part medieval, with a dense Medina of tight, winding alleys taken up with rambling *souks* (bazaars) selling everything from mops to animal hides. The massive sprawl of **Meknes**, with its long ancient walls, makes an easy day-trip from Fes, but more than justifies a day or two of exploration on its own, while the elegant, orderly capital, **Rabat**, houses some of the greatest gems of Moroccan architecture. The

country's biggest city, **Casablanca**, has few tourist sights, but makes up for it with a cosmopolitan urbanism not found elsewhere in the country. Sensuous **Marrakesh**, the "beginning of the south", matches Fes for its fascinating *souks*, but tops it with the incomparable Djemaa el Fna, urban stage from noon 'til night for musicians, acrobats, poets and snake-charmers.

Information, guides and maps

There's a **tourist office** (Office National Marocain du Tourisme, or **ONMT**) in every major city. Each is correctly referred to as the Délégation du Tourisme, but locally it may be called the ONMT or just the **Tourisme**. In addition, there is sometimes a locally funded **Syndicat d'Initiative et de Tourisme**; in smaller towns, which do not justify a Délégation, there may be only a Syndicat. They stock nationally produced pamphlets on the four imperial capitals, the fortified towns of the coast and trekking, as well as leaflets with good maps of the other major cities and towns and, occasionally, local information sheets and lists of classified hotels and restaurants. Local offices can also put you in touch with an officially recognized **guide**. The ONMT booklet *Tourisme en Montagnes et au Désert* lists qualified **mountain guides** area by area, though it's difficult to find; the Rabat ONMT is your best bet, but the Marrakesh office, where it's most needed, always runs out of copies.

In addition to the guides trained by the government, there are scores of young Moroccans offering their services to show you around the *souks* (bazaars) and sights. Some of these "**unofficial guides**" are genuine students, who may want to earn a small fee but may equally be interested in practising their English. Others are out-and-out hustlers, and can be very hard to shake off. Even in the face of extreme provocation, deal with them politely at all times and don't let yourself be intimidated. In Marrakesh and Fes, "tourist police" operate to protect visitors from the worst of the hustlers.

Maps of Moroccan cities are hard to obtain locally or abroad. The most functional are those in the

Rough Guide to Morocco – beg, borrow or photocopy from travellers you meet. The best road map is the Michelin 1:1,000,000 sheet #959.

Money and banks

Morocco is inexpensive and generally offers excellent value, although you'll find the poverty demands some response – small **tips** can make a lot of difference to an individual's family life. The unit of currency is the **dirham** (dh), divided into 100 **centimes**; in markets, prices may well be in centimes rather than dirhams. There are **coins** of 10, 20 and 50 centimes, and 1, 5 and 10 dirhams, and **notes** of 10, 20, 50, 100 and 200 dirhams. You can't usually get dirhams outside Morocco. This can cause difficulties on arrival and departure. You can usually change foreign notes into dirhams on arrival at major sea- or airports, but you may find it difficult to change travellers' cheques until you reach a bank or *bureau de change* in the town centre. When you're nearing the end of your stay, it's best to get down to as little Moroccan money as possible, especially if you're flying or sailing out outside normal banking hours.

For **exchange** purposes, the most useful and efficient chain of banks is the **BMCE** (Banque Marocaine du Commerce Extérieur). They often have a separate *bureau de change* in the form of a small office or *guichet* next to the bank itself, open longer hours and at weekends. As for **travellers' cheques,** in theory they'll change them for a 10.70dh commission (only the state-run Bank al-Maghrib is commission-free) but in practice, you may well find that they'll invent all kinds of tactics to avoid doing so. Many banks will give **cash advances** on Visa and Mastercard, both of which can also be used in payment at most classified hotels (though rarely at *pensions*), restaurants, tourist shops, and for car rental.

Banking hours are, in summer, Mon–Fri 8am–2pm; in winter, Mon–Thurs 8.15–11.30am & 2.15–4.30pm, Fri 8.15–11.15am & 2.45–4.45pm. During the Muslim fasting month of Ramadan (currently in Nov), banks are open Mon–Fri 9am–2pm. In major resorts there's usually at least one bank that keeps flexible hours to meet tourist demand, or a travel agency that changes money. Large hotels may also change money outside banking hours, and a growing number of banks have 24-hour **ATMs** (cash machines) which accept Visa and Mastercard.

Communications

You can buy **stamps** at a post office (**PTT**), often at a postcard shop, and sometimes at tobacconists (look for the sign: three interlocking blue circles). Ignore boxes and always post items at a PTT. Most of the year, post offices are open Mon–Thurs 8.30am–12.15pm & 2.30–6.30pm, Fri 8.30–11.30am & 3–6.30pm; in July, August and during Ramadan, they may change to Mon–Fri 9am–3pm. Central post offices in large cities will be open longer hours (typically Mon–Fri 8am–6.30pm, Sat 8am–noon), except in summer and Ramadan. Receiving letters **poste restante** can be a bit of a lottery, as post office workers don't always file letters under the name you might expect. An alternative is to pick a big hotel (anything above three stars should be reliable). American Express will hold mail for customers sent to their agent Voyages Schwartz, with offices (open erratic hours) in Tangier, Rabat, Casablanca and Marrakesh.

Post offices' **public phone** sections often have separate entrances and are sometimes open longer – 24 hours in some of the main cities. However, in most towns you can make international calls more cheaply from **public phones** *(cabines)* in main streets and outside post offices, most of which work with a phonecard (buyable at post offices and some tobacconists). Alternatively, there are privately run **téléboutiques** that stay open late (often until midnight) where you can phone, and sometimes send faxes and make photocopies. You can also make calls through a hotel: even fairly small places will normally do this, but be sure to ask in advance about possible surcharges and the chargeable rate. Coin-operated **pay phones**, mostly in *téléboutiques*, accept 50c and 1dh coins, and usually the old, larger 5dh coins; a short call within the same town can cost only 50c, and a few dirhams is enough for a long-distance call. Moroccan **phone numbers** have nine digits; you must dial all nine, even within the same town.

Internet clubs and cybercafés are very common, and can be found easily in pretty much all Moroccan towns. Most of these are small places with very low prices (10–15dh/hr is typical).

Getting around

Public transport is, on the whole, good. There is an efficient rail network linking the main towns of the north, the coast and Marrakesh, and elsewhere you can travel easily enough by bus or collective *grand* *taxi* between towns and to outlying villages. Renting a car is a good idea, at least for part of your trip, opening up routes that are time-consuming or difficult on local transport.

Guidelines on **fares** are given below in each section, but as an example for comparison, the following options are available on the Marrakesh–Casablanca route. A train (3hr) costs 100dh/73dh for first/second class on an "express" or 84dh/54dh on an "ordinary". A CTM bus (3hr 30min) costs 65dh; an ordinary bus (4hr) costs 34dh. A seat in a shared *grand taxi* (2hr 30min) costs an unusually high 80dh (on most intercity routes, *grand taxi* fares are close to ordinary bus fares).

■ Trains

The **train** network is limited, but for travel between the major cities trains are the best option – comfortable, efficient and fairly fast. Major stations display (and/or give out) free **timetables**, printed by **ONCF** (*www.oncf.org.ma*), the national train company; they're updated from time to time but, over the years, the timing and frequency of trains have altered little. **InterRail** is valid, but **Eurail** is not. **Fares** follow a reasonably consistent pattern (around 2.50dh for each 10km in an ordinary train, 3dh for an express service), and second-class fares are comparable to what you'd pay for buses. In addition, there are **couchettes** (50dh extra) available in summer on trains from Tangier to Marrakesh (9hr 30min) and Fes (5hr 30min); these are worth the money for the extra comfort, though they also offer security, as passengers are locked into a carriage with a guard.

■ Grands taxis and petits taxis

Collective **grands taxis** are one of the best features of Moroccan transport. Usually big Peugeots or Mercedes, they operate on a variety of routes, are much quicker than the buses (often quicker than trains, too), and fares are very reasonable, though the drivers can be reckless; *grands taxis* are often involved in accidents. Most business is along specific routes, many served by almost continuous departures throughout the day. As soon as six (or, if you're willing to pay extra, five or even four) people are assembled, the taxi sets off; make sure you're clear about wanting only *une place* in a *collectif*, otherwise drivers may "assume" you want to charter the whole car (which means paying for all six places). On established routes *grands taxis* keep to fixed **fares** for each passenger – as a general guideline, around 2–4dh per person for each 10km. If you want to take

a non-standard route, or an excursion, it is possible to charter the whole car *(une course)* – bargain hard to get the price down to around 12–20dh per 10km.

Within towns **petits taxis** do short trips, carrying up to three people, with luggage on the roof. They queue in central locations and at stations and can be hailed on streets when they're empty. Payment – usually no more than 15dh – relates to distance travelled.

■ Buses

Buses are marginally cheaper than *grands taxis*, and run far more regularly, particularly over longer distances, but go much more slowly. Buses run by **CTM** (the national company) are usually most reliable, with numbered seats and fixed schedules. An additional service on certain major trainless routes is the express buses run by **Supratours**, on behalf of the train company ONCF. These are fast and comfortable – similar, both in terms of time and cost, to *grands taxis*. CTM and ONCF look after your **luggage** on routes to airports, at no extra cost – but bear in mind that they may insist that your luggage is locked, especially if it is deposited in left luggage *(consigne)*. On small private-line buses, you generally have to pay a standard 5dh for your bags to be loaded onto the roof or into the hold (this also covers unloading at your destination).

■ Driving, trucks and hitching

Car rental pays obvious dividends if you are pushed for time or want to explore the south, where getting to see anything can be quite an effort if you have to rely on public transport. For a week's unlimited mileage (excluding tax and insurance, which add another 20 percent), Budget and local Moroccan companies charge under 2000dh, other international companies 3000–4000dh. However, wherever buses are sporadic or nonexistent, it is standard practice for **vans, lorries** and **pick-up trucks** to carry and charge passengers. You may be asked to pay a little more than the locals, and you may also be expected to bargain.

Hitching is not very big in Morocco: most people, if they own any form of transport at all, have mopeds (which they use for journeys long and short). However, it is often easy to get rides from other **tourists**, particularly if you ask around at the campsites, and for **women travellers** this can be an effective and positive option for getting around. Out on the road, it's inevitably a different matter – and hitching is definitely not advisable for women travelling alone.

Accommodation

Accommodation is inexpensive, generally good value and usually pretty easy to find. The only times you might have any problems in getting a room are in the peak seasons (August, Christmas and Aïd el Kebir), and even then only in a handful of main cities and resorts.

Hotels are classified in accordance with national criteria which reflect the type and quality of accommodation, but the corresponding price scales are determined locally. **Unclassified hotels** and *pensions* charge according to market forces, which means there are seasonal variations. Note also that the exchange rate does fluctuate. Price codes given in this chapter are based on a rate of approximately 16dh to £1 (11dh to US$1; 10dh to €1). Almost everywhere quotes prices excluding breakfast, which typically costs an extra 20–30dh per person, although in Marrakesh breakfast tends to be included in the room price.

■ Unclassified hotels and pensions

Unclassified hotels and pensions (typically charging about 80dh for a double) are mainly to be found in the Medinas (the older, Arab-built city centres) and are almost always the cheapest options on offer. At their best, unclassified Medina hotels and *pensions* are beautiful, traditional houses with whitewashed rooms grouped around a central patio. On the down side, they regularly have a problem with **water**. Most of the Medinas remain substantially unmodernized – there are often no hot showers, and the toilets are occasionally nauseating. Local tourism officials prefer tourists not to use unclassified hotels, and will not accept responsibility for any problems encountered by tourists staying there.

■ Classified hotels

Classified hotels are almost always concentrated in a town's Ville Nouvelle – the "new" or adminis-trative quarter, built by the French and usually set apart from the Medina. Star-ratings are fairly self-explanatory and prices are reasonable for all except five-star places. At the lower end, there's often little difference between one-star B and one-star A, either of which will offer you a basic double room with a washbasin for around 145dh, depending on the local price scales which should be on display in the hotel; expect to pay a little more for an en-suite room. Going up to two- and three-star, there's a definite progression in comfort, and you can find a few elegant, old hotels in these categories. However, if you're in search of a touch of luxury, you'll most likely be looking for a room with access to a swimming pool – which generally means four stars.

■ Hostels and campsites

At the lower price levels – though often no cheaper than a shared room in the Medina – are ten **hostels**, or *auberges de jeunesse*. Most are in major cities, including Tangier, Meknes, Fes, Rabat, Casablanca and Marrakesh.

Campsites can be worth visiting in order to find a lift or people to share car costs. Most sites have limited facilities and are very cheap, at around 12dh per person, plus the same again per tent; the fancier places charge around double this, but offer swimming pools and better facilities.

Food and drink

Food falls into two basic categories: ordinary Moroccan meals served in the Medina cafés (or bought from stalls), and French-influenced tourist menus in most of the hotels and Ville Nouvelle restaurants. If funds are limited, it's best to stick to the Medina places (most are cleaner than they look), with an occasional splurge in the better restaurants. **Vegetarians** may have a hard time of it.

ACCOMMODATION PRICE CODES

Throughout this guide, accommodation is coded on a scale of ① to ⑨, the code indicating the lowest price per person per night you could expect to pay in each establishment in high season. With hostels this is the nightly rate per person; with hotels, the price is arrived at by dividing the cost of the cheapest double room by two. The prices indicated by the codes are as follows:

① under £5/$8	④ £15–20/$24–32	⑦ £30–35/$48–56
② £5–10/$8–16	⑤ £20–25/$32–40	⑧ £35–40/$56–64
③ £10–15/$16–24	⑥ £25–30/$40–48	⑨ £40/$64 and over

■ Food

For **breakfast** or a **snack**, you can always buy a half-**baguette** – plus packs of butter and jam, yoghurt, cheese or eggs, if you want – from many bread or grocery stores, and take it into a café to order a drink.

Basic Moroccan meals centre on a thick, very filling soup, most often the spicy, bean-based **harira**, which can be a meal in itself. To this you might add a plateful of kebabs and perhaps a salad, together with dates, or other fruit in season, bought at a market stall. Alternatively, you could go for a **tajine**, essentially a stew, steam-cooked slowly over a charcoal fire in a distinctive earthenware pot. Either alternative will set you back about 55dh for a hearty meal at a stall or simple Medina place.

More expensive dishes, available in some of the Medina cafés as well as in the pricier restaurants, include **fish** *(poisson)*, particularly on the coast, and **chicken** *(poulet)*, either spit-roasted *(rôti)* or with olives and lemon *(aux olives et citron)*. A particular speciality of Fes is **pastilla**, a succulent pigeon pie, made with filo pastry coated with sugar and cinnamon. The most famous Moroccan dish is **couscous**, a huge bowl of steamed semolina piled with vegetables and mutton, chicken, or occasionally fish. Tourist restaurants also have a few **French dishes** – steak, liver, various fish and fowl – and the ubiquitous **salade marocaine**, based on a few tomatoes, cucumbers and other greens. With a dessert of fruit or pastry, these meals usually come to around 100dh.

Excellent **cakes and desserts** are available in some cafés, but more often at pastry shops or street stalls. The most common are *cornes de gazelles*, sugar-coated pastries filled with a kind of marzipan, but there are infinite variations. **Yoghurt** *(yaourt)* is also delicious, and Morocco is surprisingly rich in seasonal **fruits**. In addition to the various kinds of **dates** – sold all year but at their best fresh from the October harvests – there are grapes, melons, strawberries, peaches and figs, all of which you should wash thoroughly before eating. For a real thirst-quencher (and a good cure for a bad stomach), you can have **prickly pear**, cactus fruit, peeled for you in the street for a couple of dirhams.

Eating in local cafés, or if invited to a home, you may find yourself using your hands rather than a knife and fork. Copy the locals and eat only with your **right hand**. When eating from a **communal bowl** at someone's home, it is polite to take only what is immediately in front of you, unless specifically offered a piece of meat by the host.

■ Drink

The national drink is **thé à la menthe** – green tea with a large bunch of mint and a massive amount of sugar. If you want them to hold back on the sugar, ask for it with *shweeya sukar* (a little) or *blé sukar* (none). You may also find *thé rouge* (black tea) or *thé au citron* (tea with lemon), which usually turn out to be *thé Lipton* (made with tea bags). **Coffee** *(café)* is best in French-style cafés – either *noir* (black), *cassé* (with a drop of milk), or *au lait* (white). Easily found at cafés or street stalls are wonderful fresh-squeezed **juices**: *jus d'orange, jus d'amande* (almond milk), *jus des bananes* and *jus de pomme* (apple); the last two are milk-based and served chilled. *Leben* – soured milk – is sold at most dairies, and is a lot tastier than it sounds. Though **water** is generally safe to drink, it's good to get accustomed to it slowly. **Mineral water**, available inexpensively throughout the country, is usually referred to by brand name: the ubiquitous Sidi Harazem, the much lauded Sidi Ali, or the naturally sparkling Oulmès.

As an Islamic nation, Morocco gives **alcohol** a low profile. It is not generally possible to buy any alcohol at all in the Medinas, and for beer or wine you always have to go to a tourist restaurant or hotel, or a bar in the Ville Nouvelle. Moroccan **wines**, however, can be very good, if a little heavy for drinking without a meal; most come from the area around Meknes and, generally speaking, reds are better than whites. Those Moroccans who drink in **bars** – a growing number in the major cities – tend to stick to **beer**, which costs around 12dh a bottle in ordinary bars. Bars are totally male domains, except in tourist hotels – but even then they can be a bit rowdy.

Opening hours and holidays

Shops and stalls in the *souk* areas stay open just about every hour of the day, though the shop owners might be found sleeping through the midday hours. The exception is Friday, when most vendors close at least for morning prayers, with some staying shut all day. **Museums** are generally open 9am–noon & 2–6pm, closing on Friday morning and sometimes all day Sunday, Monday or Tuesday as well. Admission to museums and to most secular buildings and historical sites is either free or a nominal 10dh. Bear in mind that non-Muslims are forbidden entry to virtually all **religious buildings**.

Islamic **religious holidays** are calculated on the lunar calendar, which is shorter than the solar calendar, meaning that the holidays move year-by-year through the seasons. **Aïd el Kebir** (aka **Aïd al Adha** or Fête des Moutons; February 22, 2002), a two-day break in celebration of Abraham's willingness to sacrifice his son Ishmael (not, as in the Old Testament, Isaac), is marked by ritual slaughter in the streets of thousands of sheep. The first day of the month of **Moharrem** marks the Muslim New Year (March 15, 2002) and **Mouloud** celebrates the birthday of the Prophet Muhammad (May 24, 2002).

During **Ramadan**, the ninth month of the Islamic calendar (currently falling in November), all Muslims observe a total fast lasting from sunrise to sunset. Non-Muslims are not expected to observe Ramadan, but you should be sensitive about not breaking the fast in public (particularly by smoking). After dark, everyone lets their hair down, with troupes of musicians, dancers and acrobats performing in Marrakesh's Djemaa el Fna, continuous promenading up and down main streets in Rabat and Fes until 3am, and plenty of celebration in rural villages. Ramadan begins on or near Nov 5, 2002 (the exact date depends on a clear sighting of the moon), and ends on Dec 5, 2002, with **Aïd es Seghir** (aka **Aïd el Fitr**), a two-day holiday with much festivity.

Secular holidays are considered less important, with most public services (except banks and offices) operating normally even during the two biggest ones – the Feast of the Throne (July 30), and Independence Day (Nov 18).

Emergencies

Keeping your luggage and money secure is an important consideration – it is obviously not wise to carry large sums of cash or valuables, especially in the main tourist cities. **Hotels** are generally secure for depositing money; **campsites** are considerably less secure, and many campers advise wearing a money belt even while sleeping.

There are two main types of **police**. The grey-clad **gendarmes**, who staff the road checkpoints, have authority outside city limits. The navy-clad **sûreté** have jurisdiction in towns, and sometimes have a brigade of specially designated "tourist police" (as in Fes and Marrakesh).

Moroccan **pharmacists** are well trained and dispense a wide range of drugs. If they feel you need a full diagnosis, they can usually recommend a **doctor**, or you can get a list of English-speaking doctors in major cities from consulates.

The smoking of marijuana (**kif**) and hashish (*"chocolaté"*) has for a long time been a regular pastime of Moroccans and tourists alike. There is no real effort to stop Moroccans from using *kif*, but it is nonetheless illegal. As a tourist you are extremely vulnerable to the rip-offs and scams of dealers. Some have developed aggressive tactics, such as selling hash and then turning their customers in to the police (or threatening to do so). Large fines and prison sentences do get levied, although you should be aware if arrested for cannabis that the police normally expect to be paid off, and that this should be done as quickly as possible while the minimum number of officers are involved.

Emergency Numbers

Police (Sûreté) ☎107; Gendarmes ☎177; Fire and Ambulance ☎15.

NORTHERN MOROCCO

The two chief cities of northern Morocco, Tangier and Tetouan, are by reputation difficult, known for hustlers (typically posing as "guides") who prey on new arrivals. However, their numbers and tenacity have diminished in recent years, and it doesn't take long to get the measure of them – and to enjoy the experience. **Tangier**, hybridized and slightly seedy from its long European contact, has a setting and skyline the equal of any Mediterranean resort, and is immediately compelling in its long-time role as the meeting point of Europe and Africa. **Tetouan**, in the shadow of the barren foothills of the Rif Mountains, feels more Moroccan, its Medina a glorious labyrinth dotted with squares and *souks*. Moving on from either city, the mountain town of **Chefchaouen** is a small-scale and enjoyably laid-back place in which to come to terms with being in Morocco. South from Tangier – which stands at the head of the train line to Fes and Meknes, and to Rabat, Casablanca and Marrakesh – the seaside resort of **Asilah** is another good place to get acclimatized.

Inland, **Fes** has for over a thousand years been at the heart of Moroccan history and is today unique in the Arab world, preserving the appearance and much of the life of a medieval Islamic city. **Meknes** is another city of bygone ages – its enduring impression being that of an endless series of high unbroken walls – though it is also a thriving market centre. There are, too, the local attractions of **Volubilis**, the best preserved of the country's Roman sites, and the hilltop town of **Moulay Idriss**, the oldest and most important Moroccan shrine.

Tangier

For the first half of the twentieth century **TANGIER** (*Tanja* in Arabic; *Tanger* in French) was one of the most stylish resorts of the Mediterranean – an "International City" with its own laws and administration, plus an eclectic community of exiles, expatriates and refugees. When Moroccan independence was gained in 1956, however, Tangier's special status was removed. Almost overnight, the finance and banking businesses shifted to Spain and Switzerland, and the expatriate colony dwindled as the new national government imposed bureaucratic controls. These days there's an air of decay about the city, most tangible in the older hotels and bars, and a somewhat uncertain overall identity: a city that seems halfway to becoming a mainstream tourist resort yet still retains hints of its decadent past amid the shambling 1930s architecture and the modern high-rise apartment blocks and tall, featureless four-star hotels.

Arrival and accommodation

Numerous **ferries** make short work of the journey from ports on the southern Spanish coast (principally Algeciras, Gibraltar and Cádiz), docking at the terminal immediately below the Medina. The **CTM bus terminal** is at the port entrance, but the *gare routière* **bus station** used by private long-distance buses and *grands taxis collectifs* is 1.5km inland near the Syrian Mosque. The Port and Ville **train stations** in town have now closed, and all trains use the new Tanger Morora (or Moghogha) station, 4km from the port on the Tetouan road (served by *petits taxis*). Tangier's **airport** is 15km out of town off the Asilah road, served by *grands taxis* to the *gare routière*. The **tourist office** is at 29 Bd Pasteur (Mon–Thurs 8.30am–noon & 2.30–6.30pm, Fri 8.30–11.30am & 3–6.30pm; July & Aug open over lunch and weekends; ☎039 94 80 50), just down from the Place de France opposite the *Hôtel de Paris*; despite its recent facelift, don't expect too much from it.

There are dozens of **hotels** and **pensions**, and finding a room is never much of a problem: if the first place you try is full, ask them to phone and reserve you a place elsewhere – most will be happy to do so. The city does, however, get crowded during July and August, when some places double their prices. In the **Medina**, *Mauretania*, 2 Rue des Almohades, aka Rue des Chrétiens (☎039 93 46 77; ①), is just off the Petit Socco; it has cold showers and shared toilets, but is clean. *Olid*, 12 Rue Mokhtar Ahardane, aka Rue des Postes (☎039 93 13 10; ①), has seen better days, and also has only cold water, but is still value for money, while *Palace*, 2 Rue Mokhtar Ahardane (☎039 93 61 28; ①), is more attractive with hot running water, balconies and a lovely courtyard – certainly one of the Medina's best cheapies. A good-value option in a slightly higher price bracket is *Mamora*, 19 Rue Mokhtar Ahardane (☎039 93 41 05; ②). In the **Ville Nouvelle** are *Magellan*, 16 Rue Magellan (☎039 37 23 19; ①), and *El*

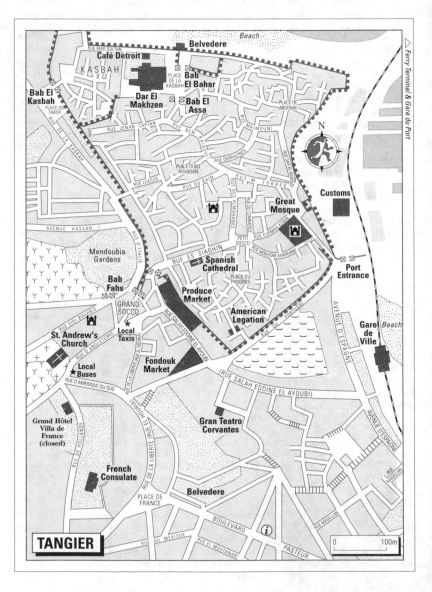

Muniria or *Tanger Inn*, 1 Rue Magellan (☎039 93 53 37; ①), the latter good-value and friendly as well as the star attraction of being where William Burroughs wrote his most famous
book, *The Naked Lunch*. On the main street opposite the tourist office is well-maintained
Hôtel de Paris, 42 Bd Pasteur (☎039 93 18 77; ②), best value in the area. Top choice on the
seafront are *Miramar*, 168 Av des FAR (☎039 94 17 15; ②), friendly, old and a little shabby
with a bar and restaurant; and *Marco Polo*, on the corner of Av d'Espagne and Rue El Antaki
(☎039 94 11 24; ②), well established and popular, with a bar and good restaurant. The **hostel**, 8 Rue El Antaki (☎039 94 61 27; ①; closed 10am–noon), near the seafront, is clean and
well run. The nearest reliable **campsite**, *Tingis* (☎039 94 01 91), is 6km east, beside the Oued
Moghogha lagoon.

The City

Together with the beach and the seafront **Avenue d'Espagne** and its continuation as
Avenue des FAR, the easiest reference points are the city's three main squares (the Grand
Socco, Petit Socco and Place de France). The **Grand Socco**, or Zoco Grande – once the main
market square (and, since Independence, officially Place du 9 avril 1947) – offers the most
straightforward approach to the **Medina**. The arch at the northwest corner of the square
opens onto Rue d'Italie, which becomes Rue de la Kasbah, the northern entrance to the
Kasbah quarter. To the right, there is an opening onto Rue es Siaghin, off which are most of
the *souks* and at the end of which is the memorably atmospheric **Petit Socco**, or Zoco Chico,
the Medina's principal landmark, a seedy square that is slightly conspiratorial in feel.
Heading past the Petit Socco towards the sea walls are two small streets straddled by the
Great Mosque, which, as throughout Morocco, is strictly closed to non-Muslims. If instead
you follow **Rue des Almohades** (aka Rue des Chrétiens) and its continuation **Rue Ben
Raisouli** you'll emerge, with luck, around the lower gate to the Kasbah.

The **Kasbah**, walled off from the Medina on the highest rise of the coast, has been the
palace and administrative quarter since Roman times. It is a strange, somewhat sparse area
of walled compounds, occasional colonnades and a number of luxurious villas built in the
1920s. The main point of interest is the former Sultanate Palace, or **Dar el Makhzen** (Mon
& Wed–Sun 9am–1pm & 3–6pm; 10dh), now converted into an excellent two-part museum of
crafts and antiquities. At the entrance to the main part of the palace is the **Bit el Mal**, the old
treasury, and adjoining it is a small private mosque, near to which is the the entrance to the
herb- and shrub-lined palace **gardens**, shaded by jacaranda trees. If you leave by Rue Riad
Sultan and Bab el Kasbah, you pass under the **Café-Restaurant Detroit** (up the stairs
through a doorway in the tunnel), set up in the 1960s by Beat writer Brion Gysin. The café is
now an overpriced tourist spot but worth the price of a mint tea for the views.

Eating, drinking and nightlife

As with most Moroccan cities, the cheapest places to **eat** are in the **Medina**, and an authentic
Tangier experience is to be had people-watching over a mint tea at one of the Petit Socco
cafés. There's also a choice of several basic cafés on Rue du Commerce and Rue des
Almohades (aka Rue des Chrétiens). *Andaluz*, 7 Rue du Commerce, off the Petit Socco, is
small and simple, and the food is good and cheap; try fried swordfish, grilled brochettes and
salad. *Ahlen*, 8 Rue des Postes, serves traditional Moroccan dishes. The cafés around the
Grand Socco are worth a look too; most stay open until midnight or later. Alcoholic drinks are
not served in the Medina or Grand Socco restaurants. In the **Ville Nouvelle**, *Africa*, 83 Rue
Salah Eddine el Ayoubi (aka Rue de la Plage) has a 50dh set menu and is licensed to serve
beer and wine with meals, while *Hassi Baida* next door offers a traditional Moroccan menu
(without alcohol). They are at the bottom of the hill, almost opposite *Hotel Valencia*; often
crowded, both offer generous portions of highly recommended food. *Agadir*, 21 Rue Prince
Héretier Sidi Mohammed, uphill from Place de France, is small and friendly, serving French
and Moroccan dishes, and *San Remo*, 15 Rue Ahmed Chaouki, opposite the terrace belvedere

on Bd Pasteur, specializes in Italian dishes and runs a takeaway pizzeria opposite. For Spanish seafood, including vast portions of fine paella, try the pricier *Romero*, 12 Rue Prince Moulay Abdallah, off Bd Pasteur around the corner from the tourist office. On the **seafront**, many of the hotels have reliable European restaurants, among which is the *Marco Polo* whose generous servings come at a fair price. As an alternative, try *L'Marsa*, 92 Av d'Espagne, with a roof terrace, open-air patio and indoor restaurant offering excellent pasta and pizzas, with homemade ice cream to follow. Finally, back in town, the long-established *Rubis Grill*, at 3 Rue Ibn Rochd off Rue Prince Moulay Abdallah, serves Spanish and other European dishes; the candlelit hacienda decor is a bit over the top but the food and service are exemplary.

For **drinking**, the *Tanger Inn*, the bar of the *Hôtel el Muniria* at 1 Rue Magellan (daily 9pm–1am), is quite an institution, serving expats since the days of the International Zone, and decorated with photos of the Beat Generation authors who used to stay at the hotel. *Hôtel Miramar* on Av des FAR is a hard-drinking seafront spot. *Scott's* on Rue El Moutanabi, traditionally a gay disco, is worth a look for its decor, although nothing much happens here before midnight; take care leaving late at night – the best idea is to tip the doorman 5dh to order you a taxi. *Morocco Palace*, Av du Prince Moulay Abdallah, is a strange, sometimes slightly manic place that puts on traditional Moroccan music and a belly-dancing floorshow until around 1am.

Listings

Airlines Royal Air Maroc, Place de France (☎039 37 95 03, 04, 05); British Airways, 83 Rue de la Liberté, aka Rue El Houria (☎039 93 58 77).

American Express Voyages Schwartz, 54 Bd Pasteur (Mon–Fri 9am–12.30pm & 3–7pm, Sat 9am–12.30pm; ☎039 33 03 72).

Car rental Most big companies – Avis, Europcar, Budget, Hertz – are along Bd Pasteur/Bd Mohammed V. For a more local and personal service visit Harris Rent-a-Car, 1 Rue Zerktouni, just off Bd Mohammed V (☎039 94 21 58).

Consulates UK, 41 Bd Mohammed V (☎039 94 15 57).

Exchange BMCE on Bd Pasteur is the most efficient and accessible; it has a separate **bureau de change** (daily 10am–1pm & 3–7pm) and an ATM, plus a branch in the Grand Socco. Bank al-Maghrib is at 80 Bd Mohammed V.

Internet Of the dozens in town, two to aim for are Cybercafé Adam, 4 Rue Ibn Rochd (off Bd Pasteur); or Futurescope, 8 Rue Youssoufia (off Bd Mohammed V).

Pharmacies There are several English-speaking pharmacies on Place de France and Bd Pasteur.

Post office Main PTT, 33 Bd Mohammed V.

Police Headquarters is on Rue Ibn Toumert near the Prefecture. There's also a station at 22 Rue Mountanabi, and a police post by the museum in the Kasbah.

Asilah

The first stop on the train south of Tangier, **ASILAH** is one of the most elegant of the old Portuguese Atlantic ports, with its square, stone ramparts flanked by palms. Its beach is also outstanding – the most popular stretches are to the north of the town. The **train station** is 2km north of the town – an easy enough walk if you can't hitch a lift. Arriving by **grand taxi** (1hr from Tangier), you're dropped in Place Mohammed V, a small square about 100m north of the ramparts and the northern entrance, Bab el Kasaba; buses drop you in an adjacent street. The circuit of **towers and ramparts**, built by the Portuguese in the sixteenth century, makes for a pleasant stroll. Along here, the main keep, **El Hamra**, has been restored as one of the venues for the **International Festival of the Arts** (usually mid-July to mid-Aug) and has occasional exhibitions at other times of year. The modern international arts centre is opposite the restored Great Mosque, just inside the Bab el Kasaba. Asilah's focal sight – stretching over the sea from the heart of the Medina – is the **Palais de Raisuli**, built in 1909 by one Er Raisuli, a local bandit who was eventually appointed governor over the tribes of northwest Morocco. It is closed outside festival times, but you may strike lucky with the caretaker. Failing that, and if you're keen, a note in Arabic from the town hall (*baladiya*) should do the trick.

Asilah can be packed full during the International Festival, but most of the year **accommodation** is easy enough to find and generally inexpensive. Small *Ennasr*, 3 Rue Ahmed M'dem (☎039 41 73 85; ②), is a basic but pleasant hotel on a side street just off Place Mohammed V. *Ouad el Makhazine*, Av Melilla (☎039 91 70 90; ②), close to the seafront, is pleasant and comfortable. *Las Palmas*, 7 Rue Imam Assili (☎039 41 87 56; ②), is modern but some distance from the seafront, albeit well signposted from the town centre. The refurbished *El Mansour*, 49 Av Mohammed V on the northern approach into town (☎039 91 73 90, *elmansourhotel@yahoo.fr*, ②), has a friendly and informative young proprietor and a good restaurant. There's a string of **campsites** north of the town but those between the train station and the centre are the most convenient. *Echrigui* (☎039 41 71 82) and *As Saada* (☎039 41 73 17) are well equipped; both have thatched bungalows (①).

The two most prominent **restaurants** are on Place Zallaka facing Bab el Kasaba: *Casa Pepe* (aka *El Oceano*), with a roof terrace overlooking the ramparts, is marginally better than its rival and neighbour, *Al Kasaba*; both have pavement tables and serve Spanish-style fried fish. *Sevilla*, nearby at 18 Av Imam Assili, also serves generous helpings of Spanish-style dishes. At the northern end of the seafront, and convenient for the campsites, *El Espignon* (☎039 41 71 57) has an extensive seafood menu and attentive staff; on high-season weekends it's worth booking in advance.

Ceuta

A Spanish enclave which dates back to the sixteenth century, the port of **CEUTA** (*Sebta* in Arabic) is a curious anomaly – politically and culturally a part of Spain – but since the ferries and hydrofoils from Algeciras are quicker than those going to Tangier, this drab outpost has become a popular point of entry. Try to arrive early in the day so that you have plenty of time to move on. The Moroccan border is 3km south of town at **FNIDEQ**, reached by local bus from the seafront. Once across, the easiest transport is a shared *grand taxi* to Tetouan; buses are infrequent, though a couple of dirhams cheaper. There are cash-only exchange places at the frontier.

It isn't easy to find a room in Ceuta – and not cheap when you do. You can get a complete list from the **tourist office** on Muelle Cañonero Dato by the ferry dock (daily 9am–8pm; ☎956 506 275), or another opposite the town hall (*ayuntamiento*) in Plaza de Africa (Mon–Fri 9am–8pm, Sat 9am–12.30pm; ☎956 501 410; *www.turiceuta.com*), which also has the list displayed in its window. The **hostel**, Plaza Rafael Gilbert 27 (☎956 515 148; ②), is open in July and August only and is often full. Alternatives include *Pensión Charito*, c/Arrabal 5 (☎956 513 982; ①), with other cheap *pensiones* nearby.

Departing by ferry from Ceuta to Algeciras, you can usually turn up at the port, buy tickets, and board within a couple of hours. The one time to avoid, as at Tangier, is the last week of August. For **hydrofoils**, book a day ahead in high season at travel agents around town or at the dockside office of Trasmediterranea, who run both ferries and hydrofoils, 6 Muelle Cañonero Dato (☎956 507 257).

Tetouan

If you're a new arrival coming from nearby Ceuta, **TETOUAN** can be intimidating. The Medina seems overwhelming, and the hustlers have the worst reputation in Morocco. Physically, though, Tetouan is strikingly beautiful, poised atop the slope of an enormous valley against a dark mass of rock. The town was hastily constructed by Andalusian refugees in the fifteenth century, and their houses, full of extravagant detail, seem more akin to the old Arab quarters of Córdoba and Seville than to other Moroccan towns.

Arriving by bus or grand taxi, you'll find yourself on the edge of the Ville Nouvelle, which follows a fairly straightforward grid. At its centre is **Place Moulay el Mehdi**, with the post office and main banks. From here, Av Mohammed V leads east towards **Place Hassan II**, the old meeting place and market square, recently remodelled with a pavement of Islamic motifs, minaret-like floodlights and a brand-new Royal Palace. The usual approach to the Medina is through **Bab el Rouah** (Gate of the Wind), the archway just south of the Royal Palace. You then find yourself on **Rue Terrafin**, a relatively wide lane which, with its continuations, cuts straight across to the east gate, **Bab Okla**. To the left of Rue Terrafin, a series of alleys gives access to most of the town's food and craft **souks**, packing the mass of alleys and passageways leading towards Bab Sebta, the northern gate. The quarter to the north of Bab Okla, below the Great Mosque, was the Medina's most exclusive residential area and contains some of its finest mansions. Just outside the gate is the **Museum of Moroccan Arts** (Mon–Thurs 8.30am–noon & 2.30–6.30pm, Fri 8.30–11.30am & 3–6.30pm; 10dh), a former arms bastion with one of the more impressive collections around of traditional crafts and ethnographic objects. Take a look particularly at the *zellij* (enamelled tile mosaics) and then cross the road to the **Crafts School** (Mon–Thurs & Sat 8.30am–noon & 2.30–5.30pm; 10dh), where you can see craftsmen producing them in ways essentially unchanged since the fifteenth century.

The **tourist office**, a few metres from Place Moulay el Mehdi, 30 Bd Mohammed V (Mon–Thurs 8.30am–noon & 2.30–6.30pm, Fri 8.30–11.30am & 3–6.30pm; ☎039 96 19 16), has lots of useful information about the province, including Chefchaouen (see below). Decent **hotels** include the friendly *Principe*, 20 Av Youssef Ibn Tachfine (no phone; ①), midway between the bus station and Place Moulay el Mehdi; *National*, 8 Rue Mohamed Ben Larbi Torres (☎039 96 32 90; ①), with some rooms en suite; the cold-water only *Trebol*, 3 Av Yacoub el Mansour (☎039 96 20 18; ①), behind the bus station; and *Paris*, 31 Rue Chakib Arssalane (☎039 96 67 50; ②), with small but clean en-suite rooms, central but sometimes noisy. The nearest **campsites** are on the coast at Martil, 11km to the east. As ever, the cheapest **food** is in the Medina, particularly the stalls inside Bab el Rouah and along Rue Luneta. For variety, try one of the many places on or around Bd Mohammed V/Bd Mohamed Ben Larbi Torres in the Ville Nouvelle, where good choices include *La Union* in Pasaje Achaach (off Rue Mohamed Ben Larbi Torres); *Saigon*, 2 Rue Mohamed Ben Larbi Torres, at the junction with Rue Abdelkrim el Kattabi (serving Spanish-Moroccan fish dishes, despite the name); and *Restinga*, 21 Bd Mohammed V, alongside Alcaraz bookshop, almost facing the tourist office, where you can eat outdoors or inside; either way the food and service are excellent (alcohol served).

For **moving on**, there are regular buses to Meknes and Fes, along with other destinations; for Tangier, Chefchaouen or Ceuta it's easiest to travel by *grand taxi*. The ONCF office on Av 10 Mai, alongside Place Al Adala, sells **train** tickets that include a shuttle bus to the train station at Tnine Sidi Lyamani, south of Asilah.

Chefchaouen

Shut in by a fold of the Rif mountains, **CHEFCHAOUEN** (sometimes abbreviated to Chaouen or Xaouen) becomes visible only once you have arrived – a dramatic approach to a town which, until the arrival of Spanish troops in 1920, had been visited by just three Europeans. The region is sacred to Muslims due to the presence of the tomb of Moulay Abdessalam Ben Mchich, one of the "four poles of Islam". These days, Chefchaouen is becoming a little over-concerned with tourism, but like Tetouan, its architecture has a strong Andalusian character, and it's a town of extraordinary light and colour, its whitewash tinted with blue and edged by golden stone walls. *Pensions* are among the friendliest and cheapest around, and to stay here a few days is one of the best possible introductions to Morocco.

With a population of around 25,000 – an eighth of Tetouan's – Chefchaouen is more like a large village, confusing only on arrival. **Buses** and **grands taxis** drop you outside the town walls; to reach the Medina, walk up across the old marketplace to the tiny arched entrance, **Bab el Ain**. Through the gate a dominant, but narrow lane winds up to the main square, the elongated **Place Outa el Hammam**. This is where most of the town's evening life takes place, its cafés overhung by upper rooms – some still the preserve of *kif* smokers. By day, the town's focus is the **Kasbah**, a quiet ruin with shady gardens which occupies one side of the square. Beyond, the smaller **Place El Makhzen** is in some ways a continuation of the downtown marketplace, an elegant clearing with an old fountain and pottery stalls set up for package tourists.

Along and just off the main route through the Medina is a series of small **hotels**, the quietest of which is *Abie Khancha*, 75 Rue Lala el Hora (☎039 98 68 79; ①), a converted house with an open courtyard, salon and high terrace. Outside the Medina, and nearer to transport, is the immaculate *Madrid*, Av Hassan II (☎039 98 74 96 or 97; ②). Nearby are two cheaper but still comfortable places: *Rif*, 29 Av Hassan II (☎039 98 69 82; ①) and the slightly better *Sevilla*, Av Allal Ben Abdallah (☎039 98 72 85; ①). The **campsite** (☎039 98 69 79) is up on the hill above the town, by the modern *Hôtel Asma*; it is inexpensive but can be crowded during summer. If there is nobody at the adjoining, very inexpensive but inconveniently located **hostel** (call via the campsite; ①), you can wait or leave things at the campsite until they return (which should be by 8pm). A few of the **cafés** in the Place Outa el Hammam serve regular Moroccan meals; the best is the *Ali Baba*. Better but pricier is *Tissemlal* (aka *Casa Hassan*), 22 Rue Targui, just up from Place Outa el Hammam, which serves delicious food in elegant surroundings. Outside the Medina, up from Bab el Ain on Rue Moulay Ali Ben Rachid, is *Zouar*, popular with local residents as much as with tourists.

Bus departures to Fes, and to a lesser degree Meknes, are quite often full, so try to buy tickets a day in advance. If you can't get on a direct bus, an alternative is to take a **grand taxi** or local bus to Ouezzane and another from there, or to return to Tetouan, where most of the buses originate. Buses head to Tetouan at least eight times a day, or you can share a *grand taxi*. There are also buses to the Ceuta border.

Meknes and around

Cut in two by the wide river valley of the Oued Boufekrane, **MEKNES**, on the main rail line south from Tangier, is a sprawling, prosperous provincial city. Monuments from its past well reward a day's exploration, as do the varied and busy *souks* of its Medina: getting a grasp of Meknes prepares you a little for the drama of Fes, and certainly helps give an idea of quality and prices for crafts shopping.

More than any other Moroccan town, Meknes is associated with a single figure, the **Sultan Moulay Ismail**, in whose reign (1672–1727) the city was built up from a provincial centre to a spectacular capital with over fifty palaces and some fifteen miles of exterior walls. The principal remains of Ismail's creation – the Imperial City of palaces and gardens, barracks, granaries and stables – sprawl below the Medina amid a confusing array of enclosures. **Place El Hedim** (the Square of Demolition and Renewal) originally formed the western corner of the Medina, but the sultan demolished the houses here to provide a grand approach to his palace quarter. Beyond the magnificent Bab Mansour, and straight ahead through a second gate, you will find yourself in an open square, on the right of which is the green-tiled dome of the **Koubba el Khayatine**, once a reception hall for ambassadors to the imperial court (daily 9am–noon & 3–6pm; 10dh). Below it, a stairway descends into a vast series of subterranean vaults, known as the **Prison of Christian Slaves**, though it was probably a storehouse or granary. Ahead of the Koubba, within the wall and at right angles to it, are two modest gates. The one on the left opens onto an apparently endless corridor of walls and, a few metres down, the entrance to **Moulay Ismail's Mausoleum** (daily 9am–noon & 3–6pm, closed Fri morning; free). The fact that this tyrannical ruler's tomb has remained a shrine might seem puzzling, but his extreme Islamic orthodoxy and success in driving the Spanish from Larache and the British from Tangier have conferred a kind of magic on him. Entering the mausoleum, you are allowed to approach the sanctuary; decorated in bright *zellij* tilework and spiralling stuccowork, it is a fine if unspectacular series of courts and chambers.

Past the mausoleum, a gate to your left gives access to the dilapidated quarter of **Dar el Kebira**, Ismail's palace complex. The imperial structures – the legendary fifty palaces – can still be made out between and above the houses here: ogre-like creations, whose scale is hard to believe. They were completed in 1677 and dedicated at an astonishing midnight celebration, when the sultan personally slaughtered a wolf so that its head might be displayed at the centre of the gateway. On the opposite side of the long-walled corridor, beyond the Royal Golf Gardens, more immense buildings are spread out, making up Ismail's last great palace, the **Dar el Makhzen**. At its end, and the principal "sight" of the Imperial City, is the **Heri as-Souani**, a series of storerooms and granaries that were filled with provisions for siege or drought. From the roof garden, with its café, you can gaze out across much of the Dar el Makhzen and the wonderfully still **Agdal Basin**, built as an irrigation reservoir and pleasure lake.

The **Medina**, although taking much of its present form and size under Moulay Ismail, bears less of his stamp. The **Dar Jamai** (Mon & Wed–Sun 9am–noon & 3–6pm; 10dh), at the back of Place El Hedim, is one of the best examples of a nineteenth-century Moroccan palace, and the museum inside is one of the best in Morocco. Its exhibits, some of which have been used to re-create the reception rooms, are predominantly of the same age, though some of the pieces of Fes and Meknes pottery date back to around Ismail's reign. The best display, however, is of Middle Atlas carpets, particularly those of the Beni Mguild tribe.

To get down into the **souks** from Place El Hedim, follow the lane immediately behind the Dar Jamai. You will come out right in the middle of the Medina's major market street: on your left is **Souk en Nejjarin**, the carpet souk; on your right, leading to the Great Mosque and Bou Inania Medersa, are the fancier goods offered in the **Souk es Sebbat**. The **Bou Inania Medersa** (daily 9am–noon & 3–6pm; 10dh) was constructed around 1340–50, and its most unusual feature is a ribbed dome over the entrance hall, an impressive piece of craftsmanship which extends right out into the *souk*. From the roof, to which there's usually access, you can look out to the tiled pyramids of the Great Mosque; the *souk* is mostly obscured from view, but you can get a good, general panorama of the town.

Practicalities

Meknes has two **train stations**, both of which are situated in the Ville Nouvelle on the east bank. The **Gare El Amir Abdelkader** is the more convenient, being only a couple of blocks from the centre; the **Gare de Ville** is further out, 500m east. All trains stop at both stations. Private **buses** and most **grands taxis** arrive west of the Medina by Bab el Khemis; **CTM buses** arrive at their terminal on Av de Fès, near the Gare de Ville, and some *grands taxis* from Fes may also drop you there. For bus connections onwards from Meknes, and other matters, check at the helpful **tourist office**, 27 Place Administrative (Mon–Thurs 8.30am–noon & 2.30–6.30pm, Fri 8.30–11.30am & 3–6.30pm; ☎055 52 44 26).

Hotels are concentrated in the Ville Nouvelle, and if you're looking for comfort and proximity to bars and restaurants, this is definitely the place to stay. However, it's a fairly long walk from the Ville Nouvelle to the Medina and, if you're here for only a short stay, there are some advantages in being close to the monuments and souks. Pick of the **Medina** hotels is *Maroc*, 7 Rue Rouamzine (☎055 53 00 75; ①), with hot showers; an alternative is *Paris* just up the street at no. 58 (no phone; ①). The best budget choice in the **Ville Nouvelle** is friendly *Bordeaux*, 64 Av de la Gare (☎055 52 25 63; ①), with a shaded garden, near the Gare de Ville and CTM bus station. *Touring*, 34 Av Allal Ben Abdallah (☎055 52 23 51; ①) is the best of the one-star places, followed by friendly, clean and comfortable *Nice*, 10 Rue Accra (☎055 52 03 18; ②), with en-suite rooms, and *Majestic*, 19 Av Mohammed V (☎055 52 20 35; ②), handy for the Gare El Amir Abdelkader, which includes breakfast. The **hostel**, Av Okba Ben Nafi (☎055 52 46 98; ①; closed 10am–noon & 3–7pm), is an easy 1.5km walk northwest of the city centre. Arguably the best **campsite** in Morocco is *Aguedal* (☎055 55 53 96), south of the Imperial City, a twenty-minute walk from Place El Hedim, opposite the Heri as-Souani.

For straight Moroccan **food** the *Economique*, 123 Rue Dar Smen, opposite Bab Mansour, is a top Medina café-restaurant. In the heart of the Medina is the lovely *Riad*, in a surviving section of Moulay Ismail's original palace at 79 Ksar Chaacha, where well-prepared Moroccan dishes are served in beautifully restored rooms or outdoors beside a sunken garden. *Collier de la Colombe*, 67 Rue Driba, is in an ornate mansion on the edge of the Medina;

the international cuisine is outstanding and the prices reasonable. In the Ville Nouvelle is the reasonably priced *La Coupole*, on the corner of Av Hassan II and Rue Ghana, serving Moroccan and European food (with a bar and nightclub). On Rue Atlas, near the *Hôtel Majestic*, off Av Mohammed V, is the reliable *Pizzeria Le Four* (pasta and pizzas). For excellent, cheap fresh fried fish in an unpretentious café-restaurant, try *Casse-Croute Driss*, 34 Rue Emir Abdelkader. *Diafa* serves great home cooking in what looks like a private house at 12 Rue Badr el Kobra (off Av Hassan II at its western end). There are also plenty of **bars**, several of them in Ville Nouvelle hotels, including the swing-doors-and-sawdust *Club de Nuit*, part of *Hôtel Excelsior* on Av des FAR.

Volubilis and Moulay Idriss

Volubilis and **Moulay Idriss** embody much of Morocco's early history – Volubilis as its Roman provincial capital, Moulay Idriss as the source of the country's first Arab dynasty. The sites stand 4km apart, at either side of a deep and very fertile valley, about 30km north of Meknes. You can take in both on a leisurely day-trip from Meknes by *grand taxi* or bus. It is simplest to visit Volubilis first, then go on to Moulay Idriss, where you can pick up a bus or *grand taxi* returning to Meknes.

Visible for miles from the bends in the approach road, **VOLUBILIS** occupies the ledge of a long, high plateau. It was the Roman Empire's most remote city, and direct Roman rule lasted little more than two centuries: the garrison withdrew in 285 AD to ease pressure elsewhere. The city remained active well into the eighteenth century, when its marble was carried away by slaves for the building of Meknes. What you are able to see today, well-excavated and maintained, are largely the ruins of second- and third-century AD buildings – impressive and affluent creations from its period as a colonial capital. The **entrance** (daily 9am–noon & 2.30–6pm; 20dh) is through a minor gate set into the city wall, built in 168 AD following a series of Berber insurrections. Just inside are the ticket office, a shaded café-bar and a small, open-air **museum** of sculpture and other fragments. The best of the finds made here – which include a superb collection of bronzes – have all been taken to the Rabat museum. Volubilis has, however, retained the great majority of its **mosaics**, some thirty or so in a good state of preservation.

MOULAY IDRISS takes its name from its founder, Morocco's most venerated saint and the creator of its first Arab dynasty. His tomb and *zaouia* (sanctuary) – the object of constant pilgrimage – lie right at the heart of the town. Even today, accessible to non-Muslims for several decades, it is still a place which feels closed and introspective. On arrival you find yourself below an elongated square near the base of the town; above you, almost directly ahead, stand the green-tiled pyramids of Moulay Idriss's **shrine** and **zaouia**. Rebuilt by Moulay Ismail, the shrine stands cordoned off from the street by a low, wooden bar to keep out Christians and beasts of burden. To get a true sense of it, you have to climb up towards one of the vantage points near the pinnacle of each quarter.

Fes

The most ancient of the imperial capitals, **FES** (anglicized to Fez) is a place that stimulates your senses with haunting and beautiful sounds, infinite visual details and unfiltered odours, and seems to exist suspended somewhere between the Middle Ages and the modern world. Some 200,000 of the city's approximately half-million inhabitants continue to live in an extraordinary Medina "city", **Fes el Bali**, an incredibly intricate web of lanes, blind alleys and *souks* with a culture and atmosphere quite different from anywhere in Europe. By building a new European-style city – the **Ville Nouvelle** – nearby, and then transferring Fes's economic and political functions to Rabat, the French ensured both the city's eclipse and the preservation of its Medina. The decline of the city notwithstanding, Fassis (the locals) have a reputation throughout Morocco for being successful and sophisticated.

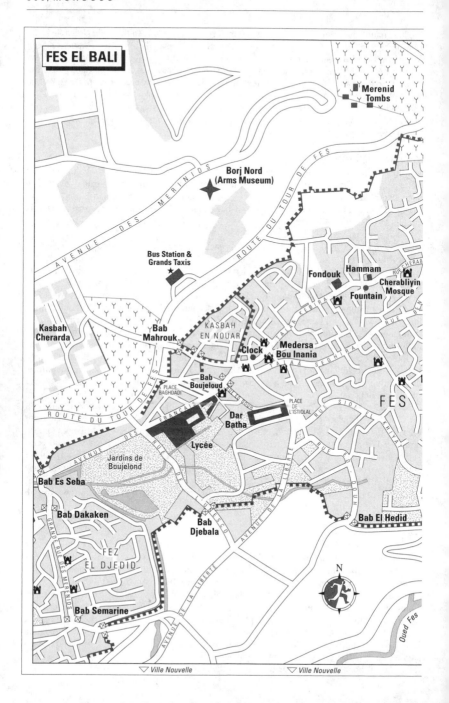

FES EL BALI

Merenid
Tombs

Borj Nord
(Arms Museum)

AVENUE DES MERINIDS

ROUTE DU TOUR DE FES

Bus Station &
Grands Taxis

Hammam

Fondouk

Cherabliyin
Mosque

Fountain

Kasbah
Cherarda

KASBAH
EN NOUAR

Bab
Mahrouk

TALAA KEBIRA

RUE BEIN

RUE CHERAB

Clock

Medersa
Bou Inania

TALAA SEGHIRA

ROUTE DU TOUR DE FES

Bab
Boujeloud

FES

PLACE
BAGHDADI

Dar
Batha

PLACE
DE
L'ISTIQLAL

RUE SIDI EL KHIYI

RUE DE FES

RUE DE

RUE BOU

Lycée

Jardins de
Boujelond

AVENUE DE LA LIBERTE

Bab Es Seba

Bab Dakaken

Bab
Djebala

Bab El Hedid

FRANÇAISE

GRANDE RUE DES MERINIDS

FEZ
EL DJEDID

N

Bab Semarine

AVENUE DE LA LIBERTE

Oued Fes

▽ *Ville Nouvelle*   ▽ *Ville Nouvelle*

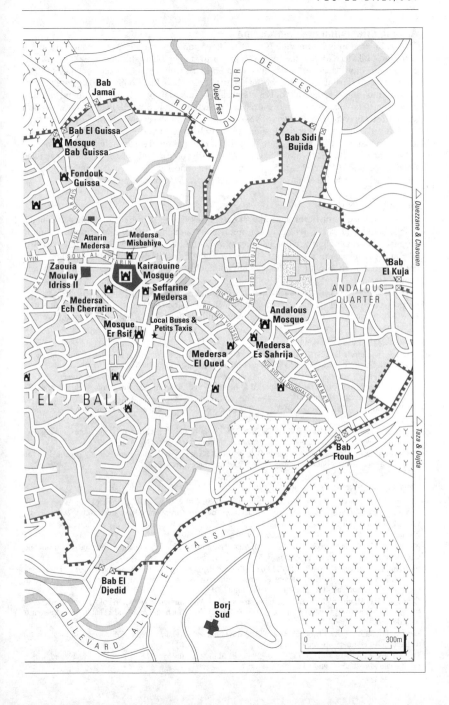

Arrival, orientation and information

The **train station** is in the Ville Nouvelle, fifteen minutes' walk from the concentration of hotels around Place Mohammed V. If you prefer to stay in the Medina, either take a *petit taxi* or walk down to Place de la Résistance (aka La Fiat), where you can pick up bus #9 to Dar Batha/Place de l'Istiqlal, near the western gate to Fes el Bali, Bab Boujeloud. The *gare routière* **bus station** is outside the walls of Fes el Bali, above Bab Mahrouk. The new terminal for CTM buses is off Rue Atlas, which links the far end of Av Mohammed V with Place d'Atlas. **Grands taxis** mostly operate from the *gare routière*, aside from those serving Meknes (from the train station) and one or two other destinations (from Bab Ftouh on the east side of the Medina, and just off La Fiat in the Ville Nouvelle). The **tourist office** is on Place de la Résistance (Mon–Fri 8.30am–noon & 2.30–6.30pm; ☎055 62 34 60), where you can find out about June's seven-day **Festival of World Sacred Music**, which includes concerts, films, lectures and exhibitions; more details from the secretariat (☎055 74 05 35, *www.fezfestival.org*).

Accommodation

There's a shortage of **hotel** space in all categories, so be prepared for higher-than-usual prices; booking ahead is advisable. For atmosphere and character, the **Medina** is definitely the place to be, although you'll need an easy-going attitude towards value or money and the size and cleanliness of your room. The less engaging **Ville Nouvelle** has a much wider choice of hotels, most of them adequate but unexciting, located close to restaurants, bars and transport.

One of Morocco's best **hostels** is at 18 Rue Abdeslam Seghrini (☎055 62 40 85; ①). The nearest **campsite** is *Camping International*, Route de Sefrou (☎055 61 80 61), 4km south (bus #38 from Place de l'Atlas), pricey but with full facilities including a pool in summer.

HOTELS IN THE MEDINA

Cascade, just inside Bab Boujeloud, Fes el Bali (☎055 63 84 42). An old building, with a useful public *hammam* (bath house) behind. Small rooms, but clean and friendly; this is the first place to fill. ①.

Du Commerce, Place des Alaouites, Fes el Djedid, facing the golden doors of the royal palace (☎055 62 22 31). Still owned by a Jewish family (this used to be the Jewish quarter); old, but comfortable and friendly, with a lively café at street level. ①.

Jardin Public, off Place Boujeloud, Fes el Bali (☎055 63 30 86). Cheapest and, for the price, reasonable enough. ①.

Lamrani, Talâa Seghira, Fes el Bali (☎055 63 44 11). Friendly with small but acceptable rooms, mostly doubles. No hot water, but stands opposite a *hammam*, right in the heart of the Medina. ①.

Pension Talaa, 14 Talâa Seghira, Fes el Bali (☎055 63 33 59). A small place and slightly pricier than the other Medina cheapies, but also newer, cleaner and more comfortable. ①.

HOTELS IN THE VILLE NOUVELLE

Amor, 31 Rue Arabie Saoudite, formerly Rue du Pakistan (☎055 62 27 24). One block from Av Hassan II, behind the Bank al-Maghrib. Attractive tiled frontage, bar, restaurant and reasonable rooms. ②.

Grand, Bd Abdallah Chefchaouni (☎055 93 20 26). Old colonial hotel opposite the sunken park on Place Mohammed V. Refurbished rooms, some very large and all en suite. ③.

Mounia, 60 Rue Asilah (☎055 65 07 71 or 72). Modern hotel with friendly management, plus restaurant and a popular bar (which can be noisy). ②.

Nouzha, 7 Av Hassan Dkhissi (☎055 64 00 02). Splendidly done-up hotel with mosaic tilework, rich carpeting and natural wood. In an out-of-centre district unknown to tourists but only twenty minutes' walk from the centre and convenient for the CTM bus terminal. ②.

Olympic, Rue Houman el Fetouaki (a small street off Av Mohammed V known in colonial days as Rue 3), facing one side of the Central Market (☎055 93 26 82). Refurbished, clean and reliable, with breakfast included. ②.

Du Pacha, 32 Av Hassan II (☎055 65 22 90). A downmarket hotel, favoured by Moroccans in town; useful as backup if the others are full or funds are low. ①.

De la Paix, 44 Av Hassan II (☎055 62 50 72). An established tour-group hotel, recently refurbished, with a good seafood restaurant and a bar. ③.

Rex, 32 Place Atlas (☎055 64 21 33). Built in 1910, this small, congenial hotel has been given a new lease of life by the nearby CTM terminal. ①.

Royal, 36 Rue es Soudan (☎055 62 46 56). Handy for the train station, and better than its near-neighbour, the *Kairouan*. All rooms have a shower (some have toilets too), but they vary in quality; look before you book. ①.

The City

The Medina is actually two separate cities: **Fes el Bali**, the oldest part, and **Fes el Djedid**, the "New Fes" established in the thirteenth century. Fes el Bali is where you'll want to spend most of your time, and a tour with an official guide is a useful introduction to the place, which is big, immensely confusing and disorientating at first; **hire a guide** from the tourist office or outside the upmarket hotels for about 120dh for half a day (look for the official guide medallion worn round their neck).

FES EL BALI

The area around **Bab Boujeloud** is today the principal entrance to Fes el Bali, a place with a great concentration of cafés and stalls where people come to talk and stare. Before heading into the Medina proper, take a look at the elegant Dar Batha palace, designed for the reception of ambassadors and now a **Museum of Moroccan Arts and Crafts** (Mon & Wed–Sun 8.30am–noon & 2.30–6pm; 10dh). The collections are probably the finest of their kind in Morocco, and the courtyards and gardens a good respite from the general exhaustion of the Medina.

Talâa Kebira (or Rue du Grand Talâa) is the major artery of the Medina, running (with its continuations) through to the Kairaouine Mosque; it's lined with shops and stalls for virtually its whole length. About 100m in is the most brilliant of Fes's monuments, the **Medersa Bou Inania** (closed for repairs at time of writing; normal hours: daily 8.30am–5.30pm; during Ramadan daily 9am–4pm; 10dh). Established as a rival to the Kairaouine university, and for a while the most important religious building in the city, it comes close to perfection in every aspect of its construction. In addition, it is the city's only building still in religious use that non-Muslims are allowed into; they cannot enter the prayer hall but can sit in the marble courtyard and gaze across to it.

Making your way down Talâa Kebira you will come to an arched gateway marked **Souk el Attarin** (Souk of the Spice Vendors); this is the formal heart of the city, and its richest and most sophisticated shopping district. The principal landmark south of Souk el Attarin is the **Zaouia Moulay Idriss II**, one of the holiest buildings in the city. As you look in from the doorway, the tomb of Moulay Idriss II is over on the left, and a scene of intense devotion is usually going on around it. Muslims may enter to check out the *zellij* tilework, original wooden *minbar* (pulpit) and collection of nineteenth-century clocks.

Standing at the women's entrance to the *zaouia*, you'll see a lane off to the left – **Rue du Bab Moulay Ismail** – full of stalls selling candles and silverware for devotional offerings. If you follow this lane around to the wooden bar, go under the bar (turning to the right), and then keep to your left, you should come out in the picturesque square of Place Nejjarin (Carpenters' Square). Here is the very imposing **Nejjarin Fondouk**, built in the early eighteenth century and now restored and opened as a woodwork museum (daily 10am–6pm, during Ramadan closes 4.30pm; 10dh), though the building is far more interesting than the exhibits. Next to it is the beautiful canopied **Nejjarin Fountain**. In the alleys off the square, you'll find the **Nejjarin Souk**, easily located by the sounds and smells of the carpenters chiselling away at cedar wood. The nearby **Souk el Henna**, a tree-shaded square adjoining what was once the largest mental asylum in the Merenid Empire, sells henna and cosmetics, as well as more esoteric ingredients for aphrodisiacs and other magic spells. Pottery stalls are gradually encroaching on the traditional pharmaceutical business.

All roads in Fes el Bali lead to the **Kairaouine Mosque**, the largest in the country until Casablanca's Grande Mosquée Hassan II went up, one of the oldest universities in the world, and the fountainhead of Moroccan religious life. The mosque was founded in 857 by a

Tunisian woman, a wealthy refugee from the city of Kairouan, but its present dimensions, with sixteen aisles and room for 20,000 worshippers, are essentially the product of tenth- and twelfth-century reconstructions. The mosque is enmeshed in houses and shops – the best point of reference is the fourteenth-century **Attarin Medersa** (daily 9am–5.30pm; during Ramadan closes 4pm; 10dh), whose fairly prominent bronze door is just to the north at the far end of Souk el Attarin. After the Bou Inania, this is the finest of the city's medieval colleges, with an incredible profusion and variety of patterning. Its lightness of feel is achieved by the relatively simple device of using pairs of symmetrical arches to join the pillars to a single lintel, a design repeated in the upper floors and mirrored in the courtyard basin. Near the east gate to the Kairaouine is **Place Seffarine**, almost wilfully picturesque with its faience fountain, gnarled fig trees and metalworkers hammering away. Just off the square is the entrance to the **Seffarine Medersa**. Built around 1285, the Seffarine is unlike all the other *medersas* in that it takes the exact form of a traditional Fassi house, with an arched balcony above its courtyard. It is also still in use as a hostel for students at the Kairouine, and you can pop in for a look at any reasonable hour without paying.

If you're beginning to find the medieval prettiness of the central *souks* and *medersas* slightly unreal, then the region beyond the Kairaouine, with its dyers' and tanners' souks, should provide the antidote. The dyers' market – **Souk Sabbighin** – is directly south of the Seffarine Medersa, and is draped with fantastically coloured yarn and cloth drying in the heat. Below, workers in grey, chimney-sweep's clothes toil over ancient cauldrons of multicoloured dyes. The tanneries quarter – the **Souk Dabbaghin** – is constantly being visited by groups of tourists, with whom you could discreetly tag along for a while if you get lost. Otherwise, follow your nose or accept a guide up from the Seffarine. Inside the **tanneries** (pay a tip to the *gardien*, usually 10dh, to enter), water deluges through holes that were once windows of houses, and hundreds of skins lie spread out on the rooftops, above vats of dye and the pigeon dung used to treat the leather.

FES EL DJEDID

Unlike Fes el Bali, whose development seems to have been almost organic, **Fes el Djedid** was an entirely planned city, begun around 1273 by Sultan Abou Youssef and completed in a manic three years. It was occupied largely by the **Dar el Makhzen**, a vast royal palace, and by a series of army garrisons. The French Protectorate left Fes el Djedid greatly changed and somewhat moribund: as a "government city" it had no obvious role after the transfer of power to Rabat. Walking down to Fes el Djedid from Bab Boujeloud involves a shift in scale. Gone are the labyrinthine alleyways and *souks*, to be replaced by a massive expanse of walls. Within them, to your left, are a series of gardens – the private **Jardins Beida**, behind the Lycée, and then the public **Jardins de Boujeloud**, a vital lung for the old city. If everything gets to be too much, wander in, lounge about on the grass and spend an hour or two at the tranquil café by an old waterwheel at their west corner.

Eating and drinking

Cafés are plentiful in the Ville Nouvelle, with some of the most popular along Av Mohammed es Slaoui and Av Mohammed V. Fes el Bali has two main areas for **budget eating**: around Bab Boujeloud and along Rue Hormis (which runs up from Souk el Attarin towards Bab Guissa), but for a cheap, solid option, it's best to try one of the café-restaurants near the municipal market in the Ville Nouvelle, on the left-hand side of Av Mohammed V as you walk from the post office.

For **bars**, you have to look a little harder. *Café Chope* on Av Mohammed V, south of Place Mohammed V, with its 1930s mock-classical interior, does good bar snacks, or try the hotel bars (the *Grand*, *Lamdaghri*, *Mounia*, *De la Paix* or *Splendid*).

Bouanania, Talâa Kebira, behind Bab Boujeloud. Rooftop or indoor eating, with *tajines* and other good food in large portions.

Chamonix, 5 Rue Moukhtar Soussi, off Av Mohammed V. A reliable restaurant serving Moroccan and

European dishes. Attracts a young crowd, and stays open late in summer.

La Cheminée, 6 Av Lalla Asma (aka Rue Chenguit) on the road to the train station. Small and friendly licensed restaurant, moderate prices.

Chez Vittorio Pizzeria, 21 Rue du Nador, opposite *Hôtel Central*. Pizza and pasta; reliable and good value, but not very exciting.

Fish Friture, 138 Av Mohammed V, at the far end of a short passageway off the main street. Fish dishes are the mainstay (the paella's great), but there is much else on offer. Courteous and quick.

Des Jeunes (aka Chez Hamid), inside Bab Boujeloud. Cheap and basic – soups, kebabs, couscous and *pastilla*.

Marrakesh, 11 Rue Abes Tazi (between *Hôtel Mounia* and the old CTM terminal). Small, but good and inexpensive, with a limited menu of tasty food.

Nautilus, in the basement of Hôtel de la Paix, 44 Av Hassan II. A classy place renowned for its seafood.

Zagora, 5 Av Mohammed V in a small arcade, behind the Derby shoe shop. New and a little pretentious, but the food and service are well above average.

Listings

Car rental Avis, 50 Bd Abdallah Chefchaouni (☎055 62 69 69); Budget, 6 Av Lalla Asma (aka Rue Chenguit) (☎055 94 00 92); Europcar, 45 Av Hassan II (☎055 62 65 45); Hertz, Bd Lalla Meryem, 1 Kissariat de la Foire (☎055 62 28 12); Tourvilles, 15 Rue Houman Fetouaki, off Bd Mohammed V (☎055 62 66 35).

Exchange BMCE, Place Mohammed V or Place Florence (also with ATMs).

Internet Plenty of places around town to connect, including Cyber Club, 70 Rue Bou Khessissat, Fes el Djedid (daily 10am–10pm) and Cyber Internet, 42 Rue des États-Unis (daily 8.30am–midnight).

Pharmacies Du Municipalité, in the *baladiya* (town hall) on Av Moulay Youssef (daily 24hr).

Police Commissariat Central is on Av Mohammed V behind the post office.

Post office Main PTT on the corner of avenues Mohammed V and Hassan II.

RABAT TO MARRAKESH

Rabat and **Casablanca** are the power axis of the nation – respectively the seats of government and of industry and commerce. They've acquired their pre-eminence almost entirely in the last sixty years, so French and post-colonial influences are dominant: "Casa" looks more like Marseille than anything you might imagine as Moroccan. Rabat is much the same, although it's one of the best places to make for as soon as you arrive in the country, well connected by train with Tangier, Fes and Marrakesh, and in addition an easy place in which to gain confidence in an unfamiliar culture. Rabat and the old port of **Salé**, facing it across the estuary, also have some of Morocco's finest and oldest monuments. Further south, and inland, **Marrakesh** has always been something of a pleasure city, a marketplace where the southern desert folk and Berber villagers bring their goods, spend their money and find entertainment. For tourists it's an enduring fantasy, given added allure by the proximity of the High Atlas, the grandest Moroccan mountain range, and **Essaouira**, the country's best resort.

Rabat and around

Capital of the nation since independence – and, before that, from 1912 to 1956, of the French Protectorate – **RABAT** is elegant, slightly self-conscious in its modern ways, and, as an administrative centre, a little bit dull. However, its monuments punctuate the span of Moroccan history, for both the Phoenicians and Carthaginians established trading posts here. The Arab city was largely the creation of the Almohad Caliph Yacoub el Mansour, whose twelfth-century legacy includes the superb Oudaïa Gate, the southwestern Bab er Rouah, and the early stages of the Hassan Mosque. After Mansour's death, Rabat fell into neglect until it was resettled by fifteenth-century Andalusian refugees, who rebuilt the Medina in a style reminiscent of their homes in Spanish Badajoz. Their pirate state survived until the time of Moulay Rashid, when Rabat finally reverted to government control.

Arrival and accommodation

Rabat Ville **train station** is at the heart of the Ville Nouvelle, with most of the classified hotels situated only a few minutes' walk away. Arriving from Casablanca, the train passes first through the smaller Rabat Agdal train station, which is 2km from the centre – don't get off here. The main **bus terminal** is 5km west of the centre, served by local bus #30 and *petits taxis*. It's easier, if you're arriving by bus from the north, to get off in Salé and take a *grand taxi* from there into Rabat. **Taxis** for non-local destinations operate from outside the main bus station; those to Casa cost only a couple of dirhams more than the bus and leave more or less continuously. **Local bus services** radiate from the corner of Rue Nador and Bd Hassan II, where *petits taxis* and local *grands taxis*, particularly for Salé, can also be found.

Accommodation can fill up in midsummer and during festivals; it's best to phone ahead. Unless stated otherwise, the places listed below are in the Ville Nouvelle. The adequate **hostel**, 43 Rue Marrassa (☎037 72 57 69; ①; closed 10am–noon & 3–6pm), is just outside the Medina walls north of Bd Hassan II; it's hard to find as the space between it and the boulevard has become a truck park and is overrun by shacks – if you arrive at night, don't come alone. The nearest **campsite** is *De la Plage* (no phone), across the river at Salé, but there are better campsites on the beaches at Erg Chiana, 24km south.

Berlin, 261 Av Mohammed V (☎037 72 34 35). Small hotel with hot showers. Centrally located above the Chinese restaurant *Hong Kong*. Good value. ①.

Central, 2 Rue Al Basra (☎037 70 73 56). Central position near train station and alongside better-known *Hôtel Balima* on Av Mohammed V. A good budget choice and, with 34 rooms, likely to have space. ①.

Dorhmi, 313 Av Mohammed V, Medina, just inside Bab Djedid (☎037 72 38 98). Above *Café Essalem* and Banque Populaire. Well furnished and maintained; highly recommended. ①.

Gaulois, corner of Rue Hims and Av Mohammed V (☎037 72 30 22). One of a cluster of budget hotels around the bottom end of Av Mohammed V; reasonable for the price. ①.

Majestic, 121 Av Hassan II (☎037 72 29 97, *majestic@welcom.net.ma*). Once an old hotel with fading charm, it has undergone a complete make-over and is still popular and good value; across the road from the Medina. ②.

D'Orsay, 11 Av Moulay Youssef, on Place de la Gare (☎037 70 13 19). Convenient for train station and café-restaurants, this is a friendly, helpful and efficient hotel, and a good mid-range alternative to the older *Hôtel Balima*. ②.

Splendid, 8 Rue Ghazza (☎037 72 32 83). A nice old hotel whose best rooms overlook a courtyard planted with palms and banana trees. Opposite is *Café-Restaurant Ghazza*, good for breakfast and a snack any time. ①.

Terminus, 384 Av Mohammed V (☎037 70 52 67). A good alternative to the *D'Orsay* round the corner. A large, featureless block, but the interior has been updated. ②.

Des Voyageurs, 8 Souk Semarine, Medina, near Bab Djedid (☎037 72 37 20). Very inexpensive, popular and often full. Clean, airy rooms but no showers. ①.

The City

Rabat's **Medina** – which comprised the whole city until the French arrived in 1912 – is a compact quarter, wedged on two sides by the sea and the river, on the others by the Almohad and Andalusian walls. From **Bd Hassan II**, a series of streets give access to the Medina, all of them leading more or less directly through the quarter, to emerge near the Kasbah and the old cemetery. At right angles to these run the main market street, **Rue Souika**, and its continuation **Souk es Sebbat**, behind which lies a residential area scattered with smaller *souks* and "parish" mosques.

North lies the **Kasbah des Oudaïas**, a striking quarter whose principal gateway – **Bab el Kasbah** or Oudaïa Gate – is one of the most ornate in the Moorish world. Built around 1195, the gate was the heart of the Kasbah, its chambers acting as a courthouse and state-rooms, with everything important taking place within its confines. It impresses not so much by its size as by the strength and simplicity of its decoration, based on a typically Islamic rhythm which establishes a tension between the exuberant, outward expansion of the arches and the heavy, enclosing rectangle of the gate itself.

You can get into the **Kasbah** proper through the Oudaïa Gate or by means of a lower, horseshoe arch that you'll find at the base of the ceremonial stairway. This latter approach leads directly to the **Palace** built by Moulay Ismail, now housing a **Museum of Moroccan Arts** (Mon & Wed–Sun 9.30am–noon & 3–5pm; 10dh), which features Berber and Arab jewellery from most regions of Morocco and traditional costumes which reveal the startling closeness of the medieval past. However, be warned that exhibits are often out on loan and collections described in the publicity are sometimes inexplicably absent. The adjoining **Andalusian Garden** – one of the most delightful spots in the city – was actually constructed by the French in the present century, though true to Spanish-Andalusian tradition, with deep, sunken beds of shrubs and flowering annuals. It has a pleasant Mauresque café.

The most ambitious of all Almohad buildings, the **Hassan Mosque** (daily 8.30am–6.30pm; free), with its vast minaret, dominates almost every view of the city. Designed by El Mansour as the centrepiece of the new capital, the mosque seems to have been more or less abandoned at his death in 1199. The minaret, despite its apparent simplicity, is among the most complex of all Almohad structures: each facade is different, with a distinct combination of patterning, yet the whole intricacy of blind arcades and interlacing curves is based on just two formal designs. Facing the tower are the **Mosque and Mausoleum of Mohammed V**, begun on the sultan's death in 1961 and dedicated six years later. The mosque, extending between a pair of stark white pavilions, gives a somewhat foreshortened idea of how the Hassan Mosque must once have appeared, roofed in its traditional green tiles. The Mausoleum, with its brilliantly surfaced marbles and spiralling designs, pays homage to traditional Moroccan techniques, though fails to capture their rhythms and unity. It is, nevertheless, an important shrine for Moroccans – and one which, unusually, non-Muslims are permitted to visit. On the opposite side of the Ville Nouvelle from the mausoleum is the **Archeological Museum**, Rue Brihi (Mon & Wed–Sun 9–11.30am & 2.30–6pm; 10dh), the most important in Morocco. Although small, it has an exceptional and beautiful collection of Roman-era bronzes, found mainly at Volubilis, including superb figures of a guard dog and a rider, and two magnificent portrait heads, reputedly the Roman politician Cato the Younger and Juba II, the last significant ruler of the Romanized Berber kingdoms of Mauretania and Numidia.

The most beautiful of Moroccan ruins, the royal burial ground called the **Chellah** (daily 8.30am–6pm; 10dh), is a startling sight as you emerge from the long avenues of the Ville Nouvelle, with its circuit of fourteenth-century walls, legacy of **Abou el Hassan** (1331–51), the greatest of Merenid rulers. Off to the left of the main gate – whose strange turreted bastions have an almost Gothic appearance – are the partly excavated ruins of the Roman city that preceded the necropolis. A set of Islamic ruins are further down to the right, situated within a second inner sanctuary which is approached along a broad path through half-wild gardens. You enter directly into the courtyard of Abou Youssef's Mosque, behind which is a series of scattered royal tombs, each aligned so that the dead, dressed in white and lying on their right-hand sides, may face Mecca to await the Call of Judgement. The nearby *zaouia* is in a much better state of preservation, its long, central court enclosed by cells, with a small oratory at the end.

Eating and drinking

Rabat has a wide range of good **restaurants** serving both Moroccan and international dishes. As ever, the cheapest ones are to be found in the Medina. Just on the edge of the quarter, down Rue Mohammed V and along Rue Souika, there is a string of good everyday café-restaurants, with *Jeunesse*, 305 Av Mohammed V, and *Taghazoute,* round the corner at 7 Rue Sebbahi among the better choices, the latter a good place for breakfast.

In the Ville Nouvelle restaurants are grouped around the train station, Place de la Gare and Av Moulay Youssef. Try *Brasserie Français*, 3 Av Moulay Youssef, with an upstairs restaurant that is one of the best places to eat around the train station. *La Clef*, alongside *Hôtel d'Orsay* on Rue Hatim, serves good French and Moroccan dishes upstairs, and has a small bar downstairs. Worthwhile, but more expensive, choices include *Saïdoune*, in the mall at 467 Av Mohammed V, opposite *Hôtel Terminus*, a good Iraqi-run Lebanese restaurant. *Hong Kong,*

261 Av Mohammed V, does a tasty range of Chinese and Vietnamese dishes. *La Bamba* on Rue Tanta, behind *Hôtel Balima* offers a choice of tourist, gastronomic and Moroccan set menus. For Italian specialities, go to *La Mamma* (with takeaway and home-delivery options), or the trendy *Equinox*, both also on Rue Tanta and with set and à-la-carte menus. Most of these serve beer and wine with meals.

Better suited for lunch is the alcohol-free *Café-Restaurant El Bahia*, set into the Andalusian wall on Bd Hassan II, with reasonably priced Moroccan dishes served in a pleasant courtyard, upstairs or on the street outside. If you're looking for a treat, get away from the city centre at *L'Entrecôte*, 74 Bd Al Amir Fal Ould Omar in Agdal (☎037 67 11 08) or the more expensive *Restaurant de la Plage* on the beach below the Kasbah des Oudaïas (☎037 72 31 48); both specialize in fish.

Avenues Mohammed V and Allal Ben Abdallah have some good **cafés**, but **bars** are few and far between outside the main hotels. The one at the *Hôtel Balima* is as good a place as any. Late-night options include a string of disco-bars around Place de Melilla and on Rue Patrice Lumumba.

Listings

Airlines Royal Air Maroc (☎037 70 97 66) is just across from the train station on the opposite side of Av Mohammed V; Air France (☎022 29 40 40) is on the same avenue at no. 281, just below *Hôtel Balima*.

Car rental Avis, 7 Rue Abou Faris Al Marini (☎037 72 18 18); Budget, Ville train station (☎037 70 57 89); Europcar, 25bis Rue Patrice Lumumba (☎037 72 23 28); Hertz, 467 Av Mohammed V (☎037 70 73 66); Visacar, Av Moulay Youssef, behind *Café Français* (☎037 70 13 58). Cheaper deals can be found in Casablanca.

Embassies Australia, at the Canadian embassy; Canada, 13bis Rue Jaafar as Sadiq, Agdal (☎037 67 28 80); New Zealand, at the UK embassy; UK, 17 Bd Tour Hassan (☎037 72 96 96); USA, 2 Av de Marrakesh (☎037 76 22 65). Irish citizens are covered by their embassy in Lisbon (see p.1042), but may get help from the UK embassy in cases of dire need.

Exchange Most banks are along Av Allal Ben Abdallah and Av Mohammed V. BMCE, 344 Av Mohammed V, also has a *bureau de change* in Ville train station.

Internet Student Cyber, 83 Av Hassan II (daily 8.30am–11.30pm); Int Plus, second floor, 279 Av Mohammed V (daily 9am–10pm).

Police Av Tripoli, near the Cathedral. Police post at Bab Djedid.

Post office Main PTT is halfway down Av Mohammed V.

Salé and around

Although it is now essentially a suburb of Rabat, **SALÉ** was the more prominent of the two right through the Middle Ages. Today, largely neglected since the French creation of a capital in Rabat, it looks and feels very distinct. The spread of a Ville Nouvelle outside its walls has been restricted to a small area around the bus station and the north gates, and the *souks* and life within its medieval limits remain surprisingly traditional. From Rabat you can cross to Salé on one of the **fishing boats** (1.5dh) that run from a departure point below Bab el Bahr, the riverside gate of Rabat's Medina, or take **bus** #12 to Bab Mrisa from Bd Hassan II. Salé's **Great Mosque** marks the most interesting part of town, its surrounding lanes fronting a concentration of aristocratic mansions and religious foundations. Almohad in origin, the mosque is one of the largest and oldest in Morocco, though all you can see if you are not Muslim (the gateway and minaret) are recent additions. Non-Muslims can, however, visit the **Medersa** (closed for renovation at the time of writing; normally daily 9am–6pm; 10dh), opposite the mosque's monumental main entrance. Salé's main monument, it was founded in 1341 by Sultan Abou el Hassan, and is intensely decorated in carved wood, stucco and *zellij* tilework. Close to its entrance there is a stairway up to the windowless student cells and to the roof, where, looking out across to Rabat, you sense the enormity of the Hassan Tower.

The best **beach** nearby is the **Plage des Nations**, 18km north (take bus #28 from Av Hassan II in Rabat to the village of **BOUKNADEL** and then follow the crowds). The beach is flanked by a couple of cafés and the refurbished four-star *Hôtel Firdaous* (☎037 82 21 31;

④), a slick modern complex with a freshwater pool that's open to all for a small charge. The waves are big and exciting, but there are dangerous currents, hence the lifeguards along the central strip.

Casablanca

Principal city of Morocco, and capital in all but administration, **CASABLANCA** is North Africa's largest port, busier even than Marseille, on which it was modelled by the French. Casa's westernized image – with the almost total absence of women wearing head-coverings, and its fancy beach clubs – masks what is still substantially a "first-generation" city and one which inevitably has some of Morocco's most intense social problems. Film buffs will be disappointed to learn that Bogart's *Casablanca* wasn't shot here, and that the legendary *Rick's Café Americain* – where Sam is told to "Play it!" – exists only as a gimmick in the luxury *Hyatt Regency* hotel on Place des Nations-Unies, where the waiters take your order dressed in trenchcoats and fedoras.

It used to be said that Casa didn't have a single "real" monument. This was never quite true, but the city did undoubtedly lack a great building: a situation that, in part, prompted King Hassan II's decision to construct on the waterfront here the world's second-largest mosque. The **Grande Mosquée Hassan II** (guided tours daily except Fri 9am, 10am, 11am & 2.30pm; 100dh, students 50dh) has space for 100,000 worshippers (80,000 in the courtyard and 20,000 indoors) and a minaret that soars to a record 172m. Equally extraordinary is its cost – an estimated £320m/US$500m, raised by not wholly voluntary public subscription. It's a twenty-minute walk northwest from the centre.

The French city centre and its formal colonial buildings already seem to belong to a different and distant age. Grouped around **Place Mohammed V**, they served as models for administrative architecture throughout the country. Their style, heavily influenced by Art Deco, is known as Mauresque, a French idealization of and "improvement" on Moorish design. The **Old Medina**, above the port and recently gentrified, is largely the product of the late nineteenth century, when Casa began its modest growth as a commercial centre. It has a fairly affluent air, and is said to be the place to go and look for any stolen goods you might want to buy back.

You can get out to the beach suburb of **Aïn Diab** by bus #9 from Place Oued el Makhzine (ex Place de la Concorde), by *petit taxi* from around Place des Nations-Unies, or on foot. The beach starts around 3km out from the port and Old Medina, past the Grande Mosquée, and continues for about the same distance. Aïn Diab's big attraction is not so much the sea as the **beach clubs** along its front. Each of these has one or more pools, usually filled with filtered seawater, a restaurant and a couple of snack bars.

Practicalities

Some trains terminate at the **Gare des Voyageurs** (2km southeast of the centre) rather than continuing on to the far better-situated **Gare du Port**, sandwiched between the town centre and the port. Bus #30 runs into town from the Voyageurs; otherwise, it's a twenty-minute walk or a *petit taxi* ride. The station for **CTM buses** is on Rue Léon l'Africain, behind *Hôtel Safir* on Av des FAR; other buses arrive at the *gare routière*, southeast of town on Route des Ouled Ziane. **Grands taxis** from Rabat arrive a block east of the CTM terminal, while those from points south come into a station south of town on the Route de Jadida (continuation of Bd Brahim Roudani) in Beauséjour. The **tourist office** is inconveniently located south of the centre at 55 Rue Omar Slaoui (Mon–Fri 8.30am–noon & 2.30–6pm; ☎022 27 11 77); more convenient is the **Syndicat d'Initiative**, 98 Bd Mohammed V (Mon–Fri 8.30am–noon & 3–6.30pm, Sat 8.30am–noon & 3–5pm, Sun 9am–noon; ☎022 22 15 24).

Hotels are plentiful, though they run near capacity for much of the year. There are some unclassified hotels in the Medina, but the ones in the centre are better and no pricier: for example, *Mon Rêve*, 7 Rue Chaouia (☎022 31 14 39; ①), is the best option in an area of cheap hotels, with *Colbert*, 38 Rue Chaouia (☎022 31 42 41; ③) a good fall-back option. *Du Centre*, 1 Rue Sidi Belyout, corner of Av des FAR (☎022 44 61 80 or 81; ②), is another golden oldie, with an antique lift and dicey wiring. *Terminus*, 184 Bd Ba Hamad (☎022 24 00 25; ③), is handy for the Gare des Voyageurs, and for eating places nearby. *Foucauld*, 52 Rue Araibi Jilali (☎022 22 26 66; ③), is great value and is near several good café-restaurants. Very central are two old places – *Excelsior*, 2 Rue El Amraoui Brahim, off Place des Nations-Unies (☎022 20 02 63; ②), which suffers from traffic noise, and *Plaza*, 18 Bd Houphouët Boigny (☎022 29 78 22; ②), which has good facilities and front rooms offering views of the Grande Mosquée. The **hostel**, 6 Place Ahmed Bidaoui (☎022 22 05 51; ③; closed 10am–noon), is a friendly, well-maintained, airy place just inside the Medina, facing a small leafy square and signposted from the nearby Gare du Port. The nearest **campsite**, *Oasis*, Av Jean Mermoz, Beauséjour (☎022 23 42 57), is 8km out on the P8 road to Azemmour and El Jadida (bus #31).

Casa has the reputation of being the best place to **eat** in Morocco, and if you can afford the fancier restaurant prices, this is certainly true. For anyone keeping to a budget, some of the best possibilities lie in the smaller streets off Bd Mohammed V. *L'Étoile Marocaine*, 107 Rue Allal Ben Abdallah, has an ambitious menu and a good atmosphere. There are grills across the street on Rue Chaouia (aka Rue Colbert), best of which is *Rotisserie Centrale*. *La Corrida*, 35 Rue El Haraar, near the main post office, is an informal tapas-style Spanish restaurant run by a Spanish-French couple; and the stylish *Petit Poucet*, 86 Bd Mohammed V, which still looks like a 1920s Parisian saloon, has a much cheaper snack bar next door – one of the best places for some serious drinking. Down near the port is *Centre 2000*, with five good ethnic restaurants serving Spanish, French, Italian and Moroccan food; nearby the *Chiang Mai* serves Chinese and Southeast Asian dishes. *Le Dauphin*, 115 Bd Houphouët Boigny, is a long-established and very popular fish restaurant, well worth queuing for. *Des Fleurs*, 42 Av des FAR, has a snack-bar/café, which is good for breakfast and serves meals upstairs.

Despite a scattering of more-or-less seedy **clubs** and **bars** on Bd Mohammed V and Bd Houphouët Boigny, nightlife in Casa is elusive. On the Aïn Diab coast road, Bd de la Corniche, from east to west are *Le Tube*, *La Notte*, *Balcon 33* and *Calypso*.

Marrakesh

MARRAKESH (*Marrakech* in French) is a city of immense beauty, low, pink and tent-like before a great shaft of mountains. It's an immediately exciting place, especially around the vast space of its central square, the **Djemaa el Fna**, the stage for a long-established ritual in which shifting circles of onlookers gather around groups of acrobats, drummers, pipe musicians, dancers, storytellers and comedians. Unlike Fes, for so long its rival as the nation's capital but these days stagnating, Marrakesh's population is growing and it has a thriving industrial area; the city remains the most important market and administrative centre of southern Morocco.

Arrival, orientation and information

The **Djemaa el Fna** (referred to simply as "el Djemaa", or even "la Place") lies right at the heart of the Medina, and almost everything of interest is concentrated in the web of alley-ways around it. Just to the west of the Djemaa, an unmistakable landmark is the minaret of the great **Koutoubia Mosque** (enchanting under floodlights at night), in the shadow of which begins **Avenue Mohammed V**, leading out of the Medina and up the length of the new city, **Gueliz**. It is a fairly long walk between Gueliz and the Medina, but there are plenty of taxis and the regular bus #1 between the two.

From the **train station**, alongside Gueliz, you should cross the street and take bus #3/#10 or a *petit taxi* (10–15dh) to get to the Djemaa. The **bus terminal** is just outside the north-western walls of the Medina by Bab Doukkala; from here it's a 20-minute walk to the Djemaa, or bus #4/#5/#6/#12 (across the street from the main entrance), or a *petit taxi* (8–10dh). The **airport** is 5km southwest; bus #11 terminates nearby and is supposed to run every half-hour to the Djemaa, but it is very erratic – *petits* or *grands taxis* (50–60dh) are a better option.

The tourist-friendly **GRIT** (*Groupement Régional d'Interêt Touristique*) is at 170 Av Mohammed V (July & Aug Mon–Fri 8.30am–3pm, Sat 8.30am–noon; rest of year Mon–Fri 8.30am–noon & 2.30–6.30pm, Sat 8.30am–noon; ☎044 43 08 86). There's not much at the **tourist office**, Place Abdelmoumen Ben Ali (July & Aug Mon–Sat 8.30am–6.30pm; rest of year Mon–Sat 8.30/9am–11.30am/noon & 2.30/3–6.30pm; during Ramadan Mon–Sat 9am–2.30pm; ☎044 43 61 79), or at its branch office at Place Venus by the Koutoubia (same hours). For an official **guide** you're best off asking at your hotel. Ask at GRIT or the tourist office for details of June's two-week long folklore and Moroccan music **Festival National des Arts Populaires**.

Accommodation

The Medina, as ever, has the main concentration of cheap places – most of them quite pleasant – and, unusually, has a fair number of classified hotels too. Given the attractions of the Djemaa el Fna and the *souks*, this is the first choice. The main advantages of Gueliz and Hivernage hotels are their convenience for the train station and their swimming pools, a major consideration in a city that swelters in the midday sun. Booking in advance is advisable. All our recommendations are in the Medina unless stated otherwise.

The immaculate **hostel** is on Rue El Jahid, Gueliz (☎044 44 77 13; ①; closed 9am–2pm), close to the train station. The nearest **campsite**, *Ferdaous* (☎044 30 23 11), is 13km out of town on the P7 towards Casablanca, a feasible option only if you have your own transport.

Ali, Rue Moulay Ismail (☎044 44 49 79, *hotelali@hotmail.com*). Near-legendary small hotel with showers in rooms, and dorms. ①.

CTM, Djemaa el Fna (☎044 44 23 25). Located above the old bus station overlooking the Djemaa. Decent-sized rooms, which are clean and relatively cheap; rooms 28–32 overlook the square. ①.

Farouk, 66 Av Hassan II, on the corner with Rue Mauretania, Gueliz (☎044 43 19 89). Excellent hotel with popular restaurant, within walking distance of the train station. ①.

De France, 197 Rue Zitoun el Kedim (☎044 44 30 67). One of the oldest and best of the cheapies, nothing special but friendly with decent rooms. ①.

Gallia, 30 Rue de la Recette (☎044 44 59 13, fax 044 44 48 53). Pleasant building in a quiet road; airy and spotless rooms (all en suite and with air-con) off two tiled courtyards. Highly recommended – reserve by fax well ahead if possible. ③.

La Gazelle, 12 Rue Bani Marine (☎044 44 11 12). Modern place with bright airy rooms and hot showers, on a street with a row of outdoor foodstalls. Reductions for long stays. ①.

Islane, 279 Av Mohammed V, facing the Koutoubia minaret (☎044 44 00 81 or 83). The view of Koutoubia and the comfortable modern rooms compensate for the traffic noise. ②.

Medina, 1 Derb Sidi Bouloukat (☎044 44 29 97). A real gem: small, clean, friendly and good value, with an English-speaking proprietor (who used to perform with a British circus) and breakfast on the roof terrace. ①.

Du Pacha, 33 Rue El Houria, aka de la Liberté, Gueliz (☎044 43 13 26), near the old covered market. An old hotel, renovated and extended, with a reliable restaurant. ①.

Sherazade, 3 Derb Djama, off Rue Zitoun Kadem (☎044 42 93 05, *sharazade@iam.net.ma*). Beautifully restored merchant's town house with a variety of rooms at different prices, most en suite, some with air-con. Seen as an overspill for the *Gallia*, but is generally more expensive. ③.

Souria, 17 Rue de la Recette (☎044 42 67 57). A deservedly popular family-run *pension*, spotlessly clean and very homely. ①.

Toulousain, 44 Rue Tariq Ben Ziad, Gueliz, near the old covered market (☎044 43 00 33). A bargain, famous locally as the hotel used by the Peace Corps. Some rooms en suite. ①.

Des Voyageurs, 40 Bd Mohammed Zerktouni, Gueliz (☎044 44 72 18). An old-fashioned respectable hotel; unexciting, but clean and good value. Some rooms en suite. ①.

The City

There's nowhere in the world like the **Djemaa el Fna**: by day it's basically a market, with a few snake charmers and an occasional troupe of acrobats; in the late afternoon it becomes a whole carnival of musicians, storytellers and other entertainers; and in the evening dozens of stalls set up to dispense hot food to crowds of locals, while the musicians and performers continue. If you get tired of the spectacle, or if things slow down, you can move over to the

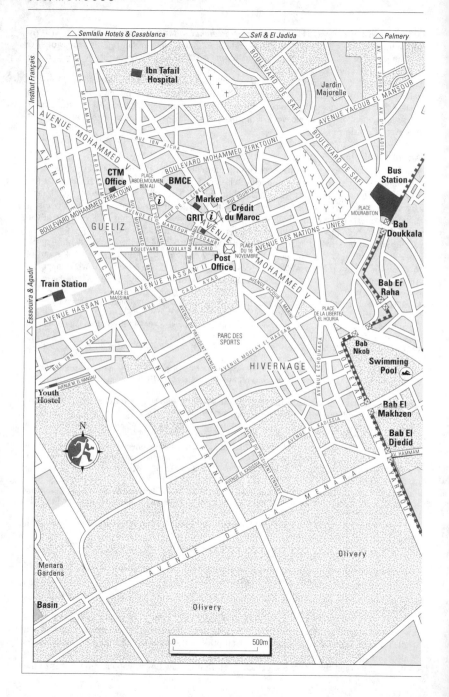

△ Semlalia Hotels & Casablanca   △ Safi & El Jadida   △ Palmery

△ Institut Français

Ibn Tafail
Hospital

Jardin
Majorelle

BOULEVARD DE SAFI

AVENUE MOHAMMED V

AVENUE YACOUB EL MANSOUR

RUE IBN AICHA

BOULEVARD MOHAMMED ZERKTOUNI

AVENUE DE FRANCE

BOULEVARD MOHAMMED ZERKTOUNI

CTM
Office

PLACE
ABDELMOUMEN
BEN ALI

BMCE

Market

Crédit
du Maroc

GRIT

GUELIZ

Bus
Station

PLACE
MOURABITON

Bab
Doukkala

AVENUE DES NATIONS - UNIES

BOULEVARD MOULAY RACHID

PLACE
DU 16
NOVEMBRE

Post
Office

Bab Er
Raha

△ Essaouira & Agadir

Train Station

PLACE EL
MASSIRA

AVENUE HASSAN II

AVENUE HASSAN II

AVENUE YACOUB EL MARIN

PLACE
DE LA LIBERTÉ
EL HOURIA

Bab
Nkob

PARC DES
SPORTS

AVENUE MOULAY EL HASSAN

HIVERNAGE

Swimming
Pool

AVENUE M. EL HANSALI

Bab El
Makhzen

Youth
Hostel

N

AVENUE DU PRESIDENT KENNEDY

Bab El
Djedid

AV. HAMMAM

AVENUE DE FRANCE

AVENUE EL KADISSIA

AVENUE DE LA MENARA

YARMOUK

Menara
Gardens

Olivery

Basin

Olivery

0   500m

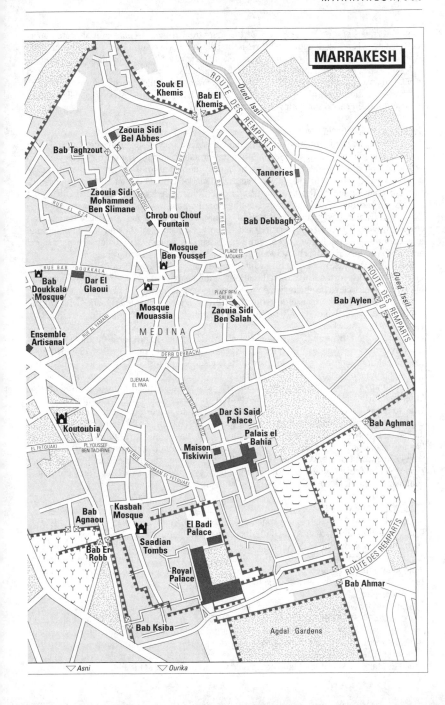

MARRAKESH

Souk El Khemis
Bab El Khemis
Zaouia Sidi Bel Abbes
Bab Taghzout
ROUTE DES REMPARTS
Oued Issil
Tanneries
RUE ASSOUEL
RUE DE BAB KHEMIS
Zaouia Sidi Mohammed Ben Slimane
Chrob ou Chouf Fountain
RUE EL GZA
Bab Debbagh
Mosque Ben Youssef
PLACE EL MOUKEF
RUE BAB DOUKKALA
Bab Doukkala Mosque
Dar El Glaoui
PLACE BEN SALAH
Mosque Mouassia
Zaouia Sidi Ben Salah
Bab Aylen
RUE AL YAMANI
MEDINA
Ensemble Artisanal
DERB DEBBACHI
ROUTE DES REMPARTS
Oued Issil
DJEMAA EL FNA
Dar Si Said Palace
Bab Aghmat
Koutoubia
Palais el Bahia
EL FETOUAKI
PL YOUSSEF BEN TACHFINE
Maison Tiskiwin
AVENUE HOUMAN EL FETOUAKI
Kasbah Mosque
Bab Agnaou
El Badi Palace
Bab Er Robb
Saadian Tombs
ROUTE DES REMPARTS
Royal Palace
Bab Ahmar
Bab Ksiba
Agdal Gardens

▽ Asni
▽ Ourika

rooftop terraces of the *Café de France* or the *Restaurant Argana* to gaze at it all from above. The absence of any architectural feature in the Djemaa serves to emphasize the drama of the **Koutoubia Minaret**, the focus of any approach to the city. Nearly 70m high and visible for miles on a clear morning, it was begun shortly after the Almohad conquest of the city, around 1150. It displays many of the features that were to become widespread in Moroccan architecture – the wide band of ceramic inlay near the top, the pyramid-shaped, castellated merlons, and the alternation of patterning on the facades.

THE NORTHERN MEDINA

On the northern corner of Djemaa el Fna itself there is a small potters' market, but the main **souk** area begins a little further beyond this. Its entrance is initially confusing – a fact exploited by the notorious hustlers who gather to "guide" tourists around. A lane opposite the *Café de France* will bring you to a stuccowork arch that marks the beginning of the crowded **Souk Smarine**, an important thoroughfare traditionally dominated by the sale of textiles. Just before the red ochre arch at its end, Souk Smarine narrows and you can get a glimpse through the passageways to its right of the **Rahba Kedima**, a small and fairly ramshackle square whose most interesting features are its apothecary stalls. At the end of Rahba Kedima, a passageway to the left gives access to another, smaller square – a bustling, carpet-draped area known as la **Criée Berbère**, which is where slave auctions used to be held.

Cutting back to **Souk el Kebir**, which by now has taken over from the Smarine, you emerge at the **kissarias**, the covered markets at the heart of the *souks*. Kissarias traditionally sell more expensive products, which today means a predominance of Western designs and imports. Off to their right is **Souk des Bijoutiers**, a modest jewellers' lane, while at the north end is a convoluted web of alleys comprising the **Souk Cherratin**, essentially a leatherworkers' market.

If you bear left through this area and then turn right, you should arrive at the open space in front of the Ben Youssef Mosque. The **Ben Youssef Medersa** (daily 9am–6pm; 10dh) – the annexe for students taking courses in the mosque – stands off a side street just to the east, distinguishable by a series of small, grilled windows. A Merenid foundation, it was almost completely rebuilt under the Saadians, and it is this dynasty's intricate, Andalusian-influenced art that has left its mark. Parts have exact parallels in the Alhambra Palace in Granada, and it seems likely that Muslim Spanish architects were employed in its construction. Next door, the **Marrakesh Museum** (daily 9am–6.30pm; 30dh) exhibits jewellery, art and sculpture, both old and new, in a beautifully restored nineteenth century palace. Almost facing it, just south of the Ben Youssef Mosque, the small **Almoravid Koubba** (daily 9am–5.30pm; 10dh) is easy to pass by, but this, the only intact Almoravid building, is at the root of all Moroccan architecture. The motifs you've just seen in the *medersa* – the pine cones, palms and acanthus leaves – were all carved here first.

THE SOUTHERN MEDINA

South of Djemaa el Fna there are two places not to be missed: the Saadian Tombs and El Badi Palace, the ruined palace of Ahmed el Mansour. For the tombs, the simplest route from the Djemaa is to follow Rue Bab Agnaou outside the ramparts, then aim for the conspicuous minaret of the **Kasbah Mosque** – the minaret looks gaudy and modern but is in fact contemporary with the Koutoubia and Hassan towers, and was restored to its original state in the 1960s. The narrow passageway to the tombs is well signposted at the near right-hand corner of the mosque.

Sealed up by Moulay Ismail after he had destroyed the adjoining El Badi Palace, the sixteenth-century **Saadian Tombs** (daily 8.30–11.45am & 2.30–5.45pm; 10dh) lay half-ruined and half-forgotten at the beginning of this century. Restored, they are today the city's main "sight" – overlavish, maybe, but dazzling nonetheless. There are two main mausoleums in the enclosure. The finer is on the left as you come in, a beautiful group of three rooms built to house El Mansour's own tomb and completed within his lifetime. Outside, around the garden and courtyard, are scattered the tombs of over a hundred more Saadian princes and members of the royal household. Like the privileged 66 given space within the mausoleums, their gravestones are brilliantly tiled and often elaborately inscribed.

Though substantially in ruins, enough remains of **El Badi Palace** (daily 8.30–11.45am & 2.30–5.45pm; 10dh) to suggest that its name – "The Incomparable" – was not entirely immodest. It took Moulay Ismail over ten years of systematic work to strip the palace of everything moveable or of value, and, even so, there's a lingering sense of luxury. The palace was begun shortly after Ahmed el Mansour's accession, its finance coming from the ransom paid out by the Portuguese after the Battle of the Three Kings at Ksar el Kebir in 1578. What you see today is essentially the ceremonial part of the palace complex, planned for the reception of ambassadors. To the rear extends the central court, over 130m long and nearly as wide, and built on a substructure of vaults in order to allow the circulation of water through the pools and gardens. When the pools are filled they are a majestic sight. In the southwest corner of the complex is an ancient *minbar* (pulpit) from the Dwiria, or Koutoubia mosque; both mosque and *minbar* have been lovingly restored (admission is an extra 10dh).

Heading north from El Badi Palace, **Rue Zitoun el Djedid** leads back to the Djemaa, flanked by various nineteenth-century mansions. Many of these have been converted into carpet shops or tourist restaurants, but one of them has been kept as a museum, the **Palais El Bahia** (daily 8.30–11.45am & 2.30/3–5.45pm; 10dh; guided tour compulsory, with a tip of at least 10dh expected), former residence of a grand vizier. The palace is still used by the royal family (usually over the Western New Year) and there is no public admission at these times. The name of the building means "The Brilliance", but after the guided tour around the rambling palace courts and apartments you might feel this a somewhat tall claim. There is reasonable craftsmanship in the main reception halls, and a pleasant arrangement of rooms in the harem quarter, but for the most part it is all fabulously vulgar. Also on this route is the **Dar Si Said** palace, which houses the **Museum of Moroccan Arts** (Mon, Wed, Thurs, Sat & Sun 9–11.45am & 2.30–5.45pm, Fri 9–11am & 3–5.45pm; 10dh), particularly strong on its collections of southern Berber jewellery and weapons – large, boldly designed objects of great beauty. There are also fine displays of eighteenth- and nineteenth-century carving, modern Berber rugs and a curious group of traditional wedding chairs, once widely used for carrying the bride, veiled and hidden, to her new home. A further superb collection of Moroccan art and artefacts is housed in the **Maison Tiskiwin** (daily 10am–12.30pm & 3–5.30pm; 15dh), which lies between the El Bahia and Dar Si Said palaces at 8 Rue de la Bahia; each room displays carpets, fabrics, clothes and jewellery from a different town or region.

If you're keen to buy the best in the *souks*, you should study the more-or-less fixed prices of the range of crafts in the excellent **Ensemble Artesenal** (Mon–Sat 7.30am–7pm), just inside the ramparts on Av Mohammed V.

THE GARDENS

With summer temperatures peaking in excess of 38°C it's best to devote the middle of a Marrakesh day to inactivity. If you want to do this in style, it means finding your way to one of the two **gardens** – Agdal and Menara – designed for just this purpose. Each rambles through acres of orchards and olive groves, and has, near its centre, an immense, lake-size pool. This is all: they are not flower gardens, but, cool and completely still, they are a luxurious contrast to the close and frenetic city streets. To get to either, walk or take a *petit taxi* or a horse-drawn calèche from El Badi Palace or the Koutoubia (3–5dh).

Perhaps Marrakesh's sole unmissable sight is the small but spectacular **Jardin Majorelle** (daily: summer 8am–noon & 3–7pm; winter 8am–noon & 2–6pm; 20dh), entered from a small cul-de-sac off Av Yacoub el Mansour, north of the bus station (*petit taxi* or calèche 3dh). Only twelve acres, this is the meticulously planned botanical haven created by the French painter Jacques Majorelle (1886–1962) and its combination of exotic flora, shady trees, pools of fish and stunning blue-plastered walls is one you won't forget in a hurry.

Eating and drinking

In the **Medina**, the most atmospheric place to eat is at the Djemaa el Fna foodstalls, which set up around sunset and serve up a range of hearty dishes, including *harira*, kebabs, fish and stews, to locals and visitors alike who crowd in side by side at the trestle tables. In addition, there's a fair range of inexpensive café-restaurants just off the Djemaa el Fna in Rue Bani Marine. Three popular hotels have restaurants; the best are *Ali*, with a lunchtime menu on the terrace and an excellent-value buffet in the evening, and *Foucauld*, on Av El Mouahidine, also with lunchtime menus and a sumptuous evening buffet – pricier, but worth the difference. *Tazi*, on nearby Rue Bab Agnaou has a restaurant and the only bar in the Medina, but recently the cuisine has disappointed. *Café Etoile de Marrakesh*, on Rue Bab Agnaou, is justifiably popular with the locals; eat upstairs on the balcony. The terrace café of the *Hôtel CTM* overlooks the Djemaa el Fna, as do two rooftop restaurants: *Argana*, with regular French-Moroccan food, and *Hôtel du Café de France*, where the restaurant is reasonable but the hotel itself is wretched (not to be confused with the *Hôtel de France* listed above). Better – and pricier – than these is *Al Baraka*, 1 Djemaa el Fna, by the Commissariat de Police, a French-Moroccan restaurant in a beautiful fountain courtyard. Not far away, facing the Koutoubia, is the restaurant on the roof terrace of the *Hôtel Islane*, 279 Av Mohammed V; the food and views can be superb.

Gueliz, naturally enough, is where you'll find French-style **cafés** and **restaurants**, and virtually all of the city's **bars**: Av Mohammed V is the busiest area, particularly around Place Abdelmoumen ben Ali, where Bd Mohammed Zerktouni crosses. *Le Jacaranda*, 32 Bd Zerktouni, is an upmarket French restaurant; *Chez Jack'Line*, 63 Av Mohammed V, serves Italian, French and Moroccan dishes at competitive prices; *L'Entrecôte*, 55 Bd Zerktouni, despite the Hollywood decor, has an international menu well worth checking out; and *Le Catanzaro*, behind the old covered market on Rue Tarik Ben Ziad, serves European fare and is very popular, particularly at weekends.

Listings

Airport information ☎044 44 78 65.

American Express Voyages Schwartz, Immeuble Moutaoukil, 1 Rue Mauritania (Mon–Fri: summer 8am–7pm, winter 8am–noon & 2.30–6.30pm; ☎044 43 30 22).

Car rental Best deals from local firms such as Najim Car, 9 Rue Loubnane (☎044 43 79 09), plus outlets in several hotels; Concorde Cars, 154 Av Mohammed V (☎044 43 11 16); Nomade Car, 112 Av Mohammed V (☎044 44 71 26). Pricier international firms such as Avis, Hertz, Budget, National and Europcar cluster at the junction of Av Mohammed V and Bd Zerktouni; all let you leave the car at an office elsewhere in Morocco.

Doctor Dr Abdelmajid Ben Tbib, 171 Av Mohammed V (☎044 43 10 30), is reliable and speaks English.

Exchange BMCE has branches with adjoining bureaux de change and ATMs in the Medina (Rue Moulay Ismail, facing Place de Foucauld) and Gueliz (114 Av Mohammed V).

Internet In the Medina, Ichbilia Internet off Rue Bani Marine by the *Hôtel Ichbilia* (daily 10am–11pm), with others nearby, including one in the *Hôtel Ali*; in Gueliz, Free Net, 55 Bd Zerktouni (daily 10.30am–1pm & 3pm–midnight).

Pharmacies Pharmacie Menara, Djemaa el Fna (daily 24hr). Also several along Av Mohammed V, including Pharmacie de la Liberté (daily 24hr), just off Place de la Liberté (or Houria), which has a doctor on call.

Post office Main PTT on Place du 16 Novembre, midway along Av Mohammed V; smaller branch on Djemaa el Fna.

Essaouira

ESSAOUIRA is Morocco's most congenial resort: an eighteenth-century town, enclosed by almost Gothic battlements, facing a cluster of rocky offshore islands, and fringed by a vast expanse of empty sands and dunes. Its whitewashed and blue-shuttered houses and colonnades, its wood workshops and art galleries, its boat-builders and sardine fishermen all provide a colourful and very pleasant backdrop to the beach. The life of the resort, too, is easy and uncomplicated, and very much in the image of the predominantly youthful Europeans and Marrakchis who come here on holiday – many of them for **surfing** and **windsurfing**, for which the town hosts international contests.

There are few formal "sights", but Essaouira is a great place just to walk around, exploring the ramparts, the harbour and the *souks* or wandering along the immense windswept beach. The **ramparts** are the obvious place to start. If you head north along the lane at the end of Place Prince Moulay el Hassan, you can gain access to the **Skala de la Ville**, the great sea bastion which runs along the northern cliffs. Along the top of it are a collection of European cannons, presented to Sultan Sidi Mohammed Ben Abdallah by ambitious nineteenth-century merchants, and at its end is the circular **North Bastion**, with panoramic views (closes at sunset). Along the Rue de Skala, built into the ramparts, are the **marquetry and wood-carving workshops**, long established in Essaouira. These artisans produce painstaking and beautiful work from thuja, a local mahogany-like hardwood. You will see their wares – boxes and chess sets – elsewhere in Morocco, but if you're thinking of buying this is the place to do it. There are further displays of marquetry, past and present, at the **Musée Sidi Mohammed Ben Abdallah** (daily except Tues 8.30am–7pm; Wed closed 12.30–2.30pm; 10dh), a nineteenth-century mansion on Rue Derb Laâlouj, the road running down from the ramparts to Av de l'Istiqlal. The museum also houses displays of carpets, costumes, jewellery and musical instruments, some of which are decorated with local marquetry, and there is an interesting gallery of old pictures of Essaouira. The town's other **souks** spread around and to the south of two arcades, on either side of Rue Mohammed Zerktouni, and up towards the Mellah district. Worth particular attention are the **Marché d'Épices** (spice market) and **Souk des Bijoutiers** (jewellers' market). The jewellery business was one of the traditional trades of Essaouira's Jewish community, who have long since deserted the Mellah, in the northwest corner of the ramparts.

At some point, perhaps around lunchtime or early evening, make your way down to the **harbour**, where fresh sardines (and all variety of other fish) are cooked on the quays. There is also an impressive sea bastion here, the **Skala du Port**, and a busy boatbuilding and repairs industry. The port is entered by a small gate to the left of its main Marine Gate. The northern **beach**, known as the Plage de Safi, is good in hot weather and with a calm sea, but unattractive and dangerous if the winds are up. The southern beach extends for miles, often backed by dunes, out towards Cap Sim. On its early reaches, the main activity, as ever, is football; it's also the better beach for surfing. Further along, you pass the riverbed of the Oued Ksob, and then the ruins of an old fort and royal summer pavilion known as the **Bordj el Berod** – the inspiration for Jimi Hendrix's *Castles Made of Sand* (Hendrix visited Essaouira in the late 1960s). The fort is an excellent viewing spot for the **Îles Purpuraires**, which are protected as a birdlife reserve. The **Île de Mogador**, the main island, topped with a ruined prison and mosque, can be visited but you need to get permission from the province authorities and the harbour master.

Practicalities

Still largely contained within its ramparts, Essaouira is a simple place to get to grips with. At the northeast end of town is the **Bab Doukkala**; at the southwest is the town's pedestrianized main square, **Place Prince Moulay el Hassan**, and the fishing **harbour**. Between them run two main parallel streets: Av de l'Istiqlal/Av Mohammed Zerktouni and Rue Sidi Mohammed Ben Abdallah. The **tourist office** is on Av du Caire (Mon–Thurs 9am–11.30am/noon & 3–6.30pm; ☎044 78 35 32).

Buses (both CTM and private lines) arrive at a new bus station, inconveniently sited on the outskirts of the town, about 500m (ten minutes' walk) northeast of Bab Doukkala. Especially at night, it's well worth taking a *petit taxi* (about 5dh) or horse-drawn calèche (about 10dh) into or out from town. **Grands taxis** also operate from the bus station, though they will drop arrivals at Bab Doukkala or Place Prince Moulay el Hassan. There is a *petit taxi* rank by the clocktower east of Place Prince Moulay el Hassan and calèches wait at Bab Doukkala.

Accommodation can be tight over Easter and in summer (when advance booking is recommended). A limited number of apartments, suitable for small groups, are available; enquire at Jack's Kiosk, a newspaper shop that displays plenty of ads for apartments, or *Restaurant Essalam*, both on Place Prince Moulay el Hassan. Of **hotels**, *Majestic*, opposite the museum, 40 Rue Laâlouj (☎044 47 49 09; ①) has good, clean rooms and hot showers, though is a little cheerless; *Souiri*, 37 Rue Latterine (☎044 47 53 39; ①) is a popular and colourful hotel in the Medina, good value and centrally located. *Beau Rivage*, Place Prince Moulay el Hassan (☎044 47 59 25; ②), is an attractive, long-established place above *Café de France*; some rooms are en suite, and some look out onto the main square. *Shahrazed*, 1 Rue Youssef el Fassi (☎044 47 29 77; ②) is new, spacious and very comfortable, alongside the tourist office and opposite police headquarters; and *Sahara*, Av Okba Ibn Nafia (☎044 47 52 92; ②), has big rooms around a central well, with en-suite hot showers – if the plumbing is in the mood. Top of the pile, and truly worth a splash, is the *Riad al Madina*, 9 Rue Latterine (☎044 47 57 27; *www.riadalmadina.com*; ④), a nineteenth century palace, now beautifully restored, which, in the 1960s as the *Hôtel du Pasha*, counted the likes of Jimi Hendrix, Frank Zappa, Cat Stevens and Jefferson Airplane among its guests. Hendrix's room was no. 24. There's also a **campsite**, *Sidi Magdoul*, 1km south of town behind the lighthouse (☎044 47 21 96).

For an informal **meal**, you can do no better than eat at the line of grills down at the port, an Essaouira institution. Among the regular restaurants, try the budget *Essalam*, on Place Prince Moulay el Hassan, or the pricier *Petite Perle*, just off the clocktower square, with well-prepared dishes in a traditional setting. For a seafood splurge, you can't beat the two fish restaurants by the port, the long-established *Chez Sam's* and upmarket newcomer *Le Coquillage*, which is the first you come to. Also good for seafood is *Chalet de la Plage* on the seafront. For Moroccan cuisine with a European twist, try *Dar Loubane*, signposted from the clocktower square, where there are also three rooms to let (☎044 47 62 96; ②).

Leaving for **Marrakesh**, there is a twice daily nonstop Supratours bus which leaves from Av Lalla Aicha, opposite Bab Marrakesh, at 6am and 4pm, arriving at Marrakesh train station; buy tickets from the kiosk here the day before. The best buses direct to **Casablanca** are the CTM Mumtaz Express (leaves Essaouira bus station daily at midnight, arrives 5am), or the cheaper 11.15am service both are fast, comfortable and take you to the centre of Casa.

travel details

Trains

Only direct trains listed here; for connections, consult *www.oncf.org.ma*.

Casablanca Port to: Mohammed V airport (9–12 daily; 45min); Rabat (9 daily; 1hr).

Casablanca Voyageurs to: Asilah (3 daily; 4hr 50min); Fes (8 daily; 4hr 45min); Marrakesh (8 daily; 3hr 30min); Meknes (8 daily; 3hr 45min); Mohammed V airport (9–12 daily; 35min); Rabat (13 daily; 1hr); Tangier (3 daily; 5hr 40min).

Fes to: Asilah (1 daily; 4hr); Casablanca Voyageurs (8 daily; 4hr 45min); Marrakesh (5 daily; 7hr 35min–10hr); Meknes (9 daily; 50min); Rabat (8 daily; 3hr 30min); Tangier (1 daily; 4hr 45min).

Marrakesh to: Casablanca Voyageurs (8 daily; 3hr 30min); Fes (5 daily; 7hr 35min–9hr 25min); Meknes

(5 daily; 6hr 45min–8hr 30min); Rabat (8 daily; 4hr 20min); Tangier (1 daily; 9hr).

Meknes to: Asilah (1 daily; 3hr 20min); Casablanca Voyageurs (8 daily; 4hr); Marrakesh (5 daily; 6hr 45min–9hr 15min); Fes (9 daily; 50min); Rabat (8 daily; 2hr 20min); Tangier (1 daily; 4hr 10min).

Rabat to: Asilah (3 daily; 3hr 50min); Casablanca Voyageurs (13 daily; 1hr); Casablanca Port (15–22 daily; 1hr); Fes (8 daily; 3hr 45min); Marrakesh (8 daily; 4hr 15min); Meknes (8 daily; 2hr 45min); Tangier (3 daily; 4hr 40min).

Tangier Moghogha to: Asilah (5 daily; 50min); Casablanca Voyageurs (3 daily; 5hr 45min–6hr 15min); Fes (1 daily; 5hr 40min); Meknes (1 daily; 3hr 50min); Marrakesh (3 daily; 9hr 30min); Rabat (3 daily; 4hr 45min–5hr 15min).

Buses

Asilah to: Casablanca (11 daily; 5hr 30min); Fes (8 daily; 6hr); Meknes (13 daily; 5hr); Rabat (11 daily; 4hr 30min); Tangier (8 daily; 1hr).

Casablanca to: Essaouira (20 daily; 5hr); Fes (25 daily; 5hr 30min); Fnideq (for Ceuta) (15 daily; 7hr); Marrakesh (36 daily; 4hr); Meknes (15 daily; 4hr 30min); Rabat (frequent; 1hr 20min); Tetouan (25 daily; 6hr); Tangier (40 daily; 6hr 30min).

Chefchaouen to: Fes (12 daily; 5hr); Meknes (5 daily; 5hr 30min); Rabat (5 daily; 8hr 30min); Tangier (11 daily; 3hr 30min); Tetouan (30 daily; 2hr).

Essaouira to: Casablanca (20 daily; 5hr); Rabat (6 daily; 6hr 30min); Marrakesh (12 daily; 3hr 30min).

Fes to: Casablanca (25 daily; 5hr 30min); Chefchaouen (12 daily; 5hr); Marrakesh (8 daily; 10hr); Meknes (hourly 7am–7pm; 50min); Rabat (30 daily; 4hr); Tangier (12 daily; 5hr 45min); Tetouan (10 daily; 5hr 20min).

Marrakesh to: Casablanca (36 daily; 4hr); Essaouira (12 daily; 3hr 30min); Fes (8 daily; 10hr); Meknes (5 daily; 9hr); Rabat (20 daily; 5hr 30min); Tangier (2 daily; 10hr).

Meknes to: Casablanca (15 daily; 4hr 30min); Chefchaouen (5 daily; 5hr 30min); Fes (hourly 7am–7pm; 50min); Marrakesh (5 daily; 9hr); Rabat (30 daily; 3hr); Tangier (14 daily; 8hr); Tetouan (7 daily; 6hr).

Rabat to: Casablanca (frequent; 1hr 20min); Fes (30 daily; 4hr); Marrakesh (20 daily; 5hr 30min); Meknes (30 daily; 3hr); Salé (frequent; 15min); Tangier (35 daily; 5hr).

Tangier to: Asilah (8 daily; 1hr); Casablanca (40 daily; 6hr 30min); Chefchaouen (11 daily; 3hr 30min); Fes (12 daily; 5hr 45min); Fnideq (for Ceuta) (20 daily; 1hr); Marrakesh (2 daily; 10hr); Meknes (14 daily; 8hr); Rabat (35 daily; 5hr); Tetouan (frequent; 1hr 30min).

Tetouan to: Casablanca (25 daily; 6hr); Chefchaouen (30 daily; 2hr); Fnideq (for Ceuta) (27 daily; 1hr); Fes (10 daily; 5hr 20min); Meknes (7 daily; 6hr); Rabat (32 daily; 5hr); Tangier (frequent; 1hr 30min).

Ferries and Hydrofoils

Ceuta to: Algeciras (20–36 daily; 35min–1hr 30min).

Tangier to: Algeciras (13–24 daily; 1hr 30min–2hr 30min); Cádiz (2 daily; 3hr); Gibraltar (6 weekly; 1hr 15min).

CHAPTER 19

THE NETHERLANDS

Introduction

The Netherlands is a country partly reclaimed from the waters of the North Sea, and around half of it lies at or below sea level. Land reclamation has been the dominant motif of its history, the result a country of resonant and unique images – flat, fertile landscapes punctured by windmills and church spires; ornately gabled terraces flanking peaceful canals; and mile upon mile of grassy dunes, backing onto stretches of pristine sandy beach.

A leading colonial power, its mercantile fleets once challenged the best in the world for supremacy, and the country enjoyed a so-called "Golden Age" of prosperity in the seventeenth century. These days, the Netherlands is one of the most developed countries in the world, with the highest population density in Europe, its sixteen million or so inhabitants (most of whom speak English) concentrated into an area about the size of southern England.

Most people travel only to the uniquely atmospheric capital, **Amsterdam**; the rest of the country, despite its accessibility, is comparatively untouched by tourism. The west of the country is the most populated and most historically interesting region – unrelentingly flat territory, much of it reclaimed, that is home to a grouping of towns known collectively as the **Randstad** (literally "rim town"). It's a good idea to forsake Amsterdam for a day or two and investigate places like **Haarlem**, **Leiden** and **Delft** with their old canal-girded centres, the gritty port city of **Rotterdam**, or **The Hague**, stately home of the government and the Dutch royals. Outside the Randstad, life moves more slowly. The province of **Zeeland**, in the southwest, is the country at its most remote, its inhabitants a sturdy, distant people, busy with farming and fishing and hardly connected to the mainland. In the north, **Groningen** is a busy cultural centre, lent verve by its large resident student population. To the south, around the town of **Arnhem**, the landscape undulates into heathy moorland, best experienced in the **Hoge Veluwe** national park. Further south still lies the compelling city of **Maastricht**, squeezed between the German and Belgian borders.

Though "Holland" is often used as a shorthand alternative name for the country, this is strictly speaking outdated; these days, although there are two Dutch provinces called North Holland and South Holland, they are separate entities. On the same note, it's common to call Belgium and the Netherlands "the Low Countries", and to use the abbreviation "Benelux" to refer to the neighbouring trio of Belgium, the Netherlands and Luxembourg.

Information and maps

"VVV" tourist offices are usually conveniently sited in the town centre or by the train station. They have plenty of information in English on the local area and the whole country, including maps and accommodation lists (usually for a small fee); they will also book rooms, again for a small charge. Most have ☎0900 premium-rate phone numbers, charged at €0.23–0.91/min from within the country, and normal international rates from outside. The best general **map** is Kümmerley and Frey's; the Dutch motoring organization ANWB publishes an excellent detailed 1:100,000 series that covers the whole country.

Money and banks

The Netherlands is one of twelve European Union countries which have changed over to a single currency, the **euro** (€). Euro notes and coins are scheduled to be issued from January 1, 2002, with Dutch guilders (*f*) remaining in circulation during a transition period, at a fixed rate of *f*2.20371 to €1, until they are scrapped entirely on January 28, 2002. After this date you will still be able to exchange your guilders for euros in banks for at least a year. Euro notes are issued in **denominations** of 5, 10, 20, 50, 100, 200 and 500 euros, and coins in denominations of 1, 2, 5, 10, 20 and 50 cents and 1 and 2 euros.

All prices in this chapter are given in euros correct at the time of going to press. There will no doubt be some rounding off (or, more probably, up) of prices in the first few months after the introduction of the euro.

Banking hours are Mon–Fri 9am–4/5pm; in larger cities some banks also open Thurs 7–9pm and occasionally on Saturday mornings. **GWK exchange offices**, usually at train stations, open late every day (24hr at Schiphol airport and Amsterdam Centraal

---

Station); they change money and travellers' cheques, and give cash advances on all the major credit cards, for similar rates – though there's normally a minimum charge of about €3.50. You can also change money at most VVV tourist offices, post offices and numerous *bureaux de change*, though the rates will be less favourable – many, such as Chequepoint, charge exorbitant commissions. **ATM**s dispense cash, though Visa card holders may have to search for a compatible machine. Only the more expensive shops and restaurants accept credit cards.

Communications

Dutch **post offices** open Mon–Fri 8.30am–5pm, plus Sat 8.30am–noon, or later in the big cities. All international post should go into the slot on postboxes marked "Overige".

Public phones are widespread but almost all take phonecards or credit cards only; post offices and VVVs sell phonecards, which can be used in Germany as well. Some train stations have a small number of coin-phones. The **operator** number is ☎0800/0410 (free); international directory enquiries is on ☎0900/8418 (premium rate).

Internet access is easy in most parts of the country, with plenty of cybercafés as well as terminals at public libraries.

Getting around

Distances are short, and the longest journey you'll ever make – say from Amsterdam to Maastricht – takes under three hours by train or car. Urban **public transport** is similarly efficient and cheap, running on an easy-to-understand ticketing system that covers the whole country. Networks link up together neatly, with bus terminals almost always beside train stations.

■ Trains

The best way to get around is by **train**. The system, run by Nederlandse Spoorwegen (Dutch Railways; *www.ns.nl*), is one of Europe's finest: trains are fast, modern and frequent, fares relatively low, and the network of lines extremely comprehensive. **InterRail** and **Eurail** are both valid. On production of a passport, you can buy a **Holland Rail Pass** for 3 days/5 days in a month (€60/€90; under-26s pay €48/€72). A **Daypass** (*Dagkaart*) gives unlimited travel nationwide for 1 day/5 days for €35/€169. An **Off-peak Pass** (*Dalurenkaart*) costs €45 and gives a forty-percent discount in off-peak hours for a year. Without a pass, reckon on spending about €14 to travel 50km, up to a maximum one-way fare of €35. A **day return** (*dagretour*), valid for 24hr, costs ten percent less than two one-ways. With any ticket, you're also free to stop off en route and continue your journey later that day.

Stations are well equipped and usually have a reasonably priced restaurant, left-luggage lockers (around €2 for 24hr), and a GWK change office. The NS **treintaxi** scheme (not valid in Amsterdam, Rotterdam or The Hague) means you pay €3 for a taxi to take you anywhere within the city limits from your destination train station, within a time span of 15min – very useful for smaller towns. Buy vouchers for *treintaxis* when you buy your train ticket. NS publish mounds of **information**, including a free intercity timetable.

■ Buses

For local transport you need to use **buses**, again very efficient, and almost always running from ranks of bus stops next to the train station. Ticketing is simple. The whole country is divided into zones, and you need buy just one kind of ticket, a **strippenkaart**, wherever you are. The bus driver will cancel one strip on your *strippenkaart* for your journey plus one for each zone you travel through: two strips will get you around the centre of most cities, three strips will take you out into the suburbs, travelling between towns will use up proportionately more strips. *Strippenkaarts* are not personal: any number of people can travel on the same *strippenkaart* by cancelling the requisite number of strips each. You can buy 2-, 3- or 8-strip *strippenkaarts* from bus drivers, or the better-value 15-strip (€6) or 45-strip (€17) *strippenkaarts* in advance from train stations, tobacconists, local public transport offices and some VVVs.

■ Driving and hitching

The **road** network is comprehensive. Drive on the right; **speed limits** are 50kph in built-up areas, 80kph outside and 120kph (or sometimes 100kph) on motorways. Drivers and passengers are required by law to wear seatbelts, and penalties for drink-driving are severe. There are no toll roads, but petrol isn't particularly cheap at around €1 a litre. If you break down, the ANWB (☎0800/0888) offers repair and breakdown services to members of foreign motoring organizations and have their own "tourist membership" (€84 for two months). **Car rental** is fairly expensive: reckon on paying upwards of €280 per week with unlimited mileage – though there are much cheaper weekend deals available.

Hitching is feasible throughout the country: the Dutch are usually well disposed towards giving lifts. Bear in mind, though, that motorways are hard to avoid, and that it's only legal to hitch on slip roads or at the special marked places you'll find on the outskirts of some larger cities, known as *liftplaatsen*.

■ Cycling

If you're not pushed for time, **cycling** is a lovely way to see the country. There's a nationwide system of well-signposted cycle paths, which often divert away from the main roads into the countryside; better bookshops sell cycling maps. You can **rent** a bike from all main train stations for €6/day or €27/week, plus ID and a €50 or €100 cash deposit – halved if you show a *treinfiets* voucher (obtainable when you buy your train ticket) The snag is that you must return the bike to the station from which you rented it, and in high season you may need to book ahead. You can also rent bikes from outlets in almost any town and village, some of which may accept a credit card imprint as a deposit. It's possible to take your bike on trains, but it isn't encouraged (and forbidden during the rush-hours); a bike ticket costs €4.50 one-way, €8 return – more for journeys over 80km. **Bike theft** is big business all round the country, and in Amsterdam in particular: never leave your bike unlocked, and don't leave it on the street overnight (even locked). Most stations have a storage area (around €1/day).

Accommodation

Accommodation can be a little pricey, though a wide network of hostels and well-equipped campsites can help to cut costs. Wherever you stay, you should book ahead during the summer and over holiday periods, especially Easter.

■ Hotels and private rooms

The cheapest one- or two-star **hotel** double room, not en suite, starts at around €54; reckon on a little more for en suite. Three-star hotel rooms average out at around €78. Prices usually include a reasonable **breakfast**. You can reserve at anywhere in the country for free through the Netherlands Reservation Centre (*www.hotelres.nl*), or for about €2 per person at VVV offices (plus a deposit of about one-third of the room rate, which is deducted from your final bill).

One way of cutting costs is to use **private accommodation** – rooms in private homes that are let out to visitors on a bed-and-breakfast basis. Prices are usually quoted per person and are normally about €15; if breakfast isn't included, it will cost about €2 extra. You can generally only book B&Bs through VVVs (who will sell you a list), although *www.bedandbreakfast.nl* is useful.

■ Hostels and student rooms

There are about 35 **HI hostels** nationwide (*www.njhc.org*), charging €11–18 per person per night including breakfast (plus €2 for non-members and €3 for bedding). Aside from dorms, some have single and double rooms. You can also often eat at hostels – about €7 for a filling meal – and some have kitchens where you can self-cater. The larger cities often have **independent hostels** with dorms at broadly similar prices, though standards are sometimes not as reliable and occasionally there are age limits and maximum lengths of stay. In a few cities, **student accommodation** is open during the holidays; ask at the local VVV.

■ Campsites and cabins

Camping is a serious option: there are plenty of sites, most well equipped, and they represent a good saving on other forms of accommodation. Prices vary greatly, but you can generally expect to pay around €3 per person, plus €2–4 for a tent (plus €3 for a

---

ACCOMMODATION PRICE CODES

Throughout this guide, accommodation is coded on a scale of ① to ⑨, the code indicating the lowest price per person per night you could expect to pay in each establishment in high season. With hostels this is the nightly rate per person; with hotels, the price is arrived at by dividing the cost of the cheapest double room by two. The prices indicated by the codes are as follows:

① under £5/$8 (€9)	④ £15–20/$24–32 (€27–36)	⑦ £30–35/$48–56 (€54–63)
② £5–10/$8–16 (€9–18)	⑤ £20–25/$32–40 (€36–45)	⑧ £35–40/$56–64 (€63–72)
③ £10–15/$16–24 (€18–27)	⑥ £25–30/$40–48 (€45–54)	⑨ £40/$64 (€72) and over

car or €2 for a motorbike). Some sites also have **cabins**, spartan affairs for up to four people, for around €34 a night. Both the VVV and ANWB can provide lists (the ANWB publishes an annual guide for €9), and you should normally book cabins in advance.

Food and drink

The Netherlands is not renowned for its **food**, with local cuisine drawing heavily on a sober, potato-eating culture. But, tempering this, there's an enormous variety of ethnic restaurants, especially Indonesian and Chinese, and if you're selective prices needn't break the bank. **Drinking**, too, is easily affordable: sampling the Dutch and Belgian beers on ready supply in every region is one of the country's real pleasures.

■ Food

Dutch food tends to be fairly plain, mainly consisting of steak, chicken or fish, along with filling soups and stews. In all but the very cheapest hostels or most expensive hotels **breakfast** (*ontbijt*) will be included in the room price. Though usually nothing fancy, it's generally very filling: rolls, cheese, ham, hard-boiled eggs, jam and honey, chocolate spread or peanut butter are the principal ingredients. Many bars and cafés also serve at least rolls and sandwiches, and some offer a set breakfast. The **coffee** is normally good and strong, around €1 a cup, served with a little tub of evaporated milk (*koffiemelk*). **Tea** generally comes with lemon if anything; if you want milk you have to ask for it. **Chocolate** (*chocomel*) is also popular, served hot or cold.

For the rest of the day, **fast-food** options include chips – *frites* or *patat* – sprinkled with salt and smothered with mayonnaise, curry, satay, goulash or tomato sauce. If you just want salt, ask for *patat zonder*, chips with salt and mayonnaise are *patat met*. Often chips are complemented with *kroketten* (meat goulash coated in breadcrumbs and deep fried) or *fricandel* (a frankfurter-like sausage). Tastier, and good both as a snack and a full lunch, are **fish** specialities sold from street kiosks: salted raw herrings, smoked eel (*gerookte paling*), mackerel in a roll (*broodje makreel*), mussels and various kinds of deep-fried fish. A nationwide chain of fish restaurants, *Noordzee*, serves good-value fish-based sandwiches and light fish lunches. Another common snack is *shoarma* (kebab), sold in numerous Middle Eastern restaurants and takeaways, which generally also have the chickpea-based falafel, a good vegetarian stand-by.

The majority of **bars** serve some kind of food; if they do a full menu, which many do, they may be known as an **eetcafé** instead. Most serve at least sandwiches and rolls (*boterham* and *broodjes* – *stokbrood* if made with baguette); in winter, they serve *erwtensoep*, a thick pea soup with smoked sausage, for about €3, and *uitsmijters* (literally "bouncers", traditionally served at the end of a long night to kick guests out), fried eggs on buttered bread, topped with ham or roast beef for about €6. **Restaurants** tend to open in the evenings only, until around 11pm; if you're on a tight budget, stick to the dish of the day (*dagschotels*) – €7–9 for a meat or fish dish with plenty of vegetables. À la carte meat dishes go for €10, fish for €12. **Train station** restaurants are a good stand-by, serving full meals for €7, and in university towns **student mensa** restaurants serve meals for under €9. **Vegetarians** will have few problems: many *eet-cafés* and restaurants have at least one meat-free item, and you'll find veggie restaurants in most towns offering full-course set meals for about €8, though they often close early. Colonial history has led to hundreds of Surinamese and especially **Indonesian** restaurants covering all budgets; at the former try *roti*, flat bread with spicy curry; at the latter (with may also do Chinese food), go for *nasi/bami goreng* (fried rice/noodles with meat), *loempia* (egg rolls), *ajam* (chicken) or *daging* (beef) with peanut satay sauce, or *gado gado* (vegetables in peanut sauce). A *rijsttafel* comprises rice or noodles served with a huge range of sampler side-dishes, pricey but delicious, usually ordered for two or more people (about €20 each).

■ Drink

Most drinking is done either in the cosy environs of a **brown café** (*bruine kroeg*) – so named because of the colour of the tobacco-stained walls – or in more modern-looking **bars**, usually catering to a younger crowd. Most bars are open till around 1am during the week, 2am at weekends. You may also come across *proeflokalen* or **tasting houses**, small, old-fashioned bars that once only served spirits – though most now serve beer and, usually, coffee – and close around 8pm. The most commonly consumed beverage is **beer**, usually served in small measures for about €1 (ask for *een pils*); a bigger glass is *een vaasje*. From a supermarket, you'll pay about the same for a half-litre bottle. The most common names are Heineken, Amstel, Oranjeboom and Grolsch, though there are other regional brews and you'll also come across plenty of Belgian brands. **Wine** is reasonably priced; expect to pay around €3 for an average bottle of French white or red. The indigenous firewater is **jenever** or Dutch gin, served in small glasses (€1) and traditionally drunk straight; *oud* (old) is smooth and mellow, *jong* (young) packs more of a punch, though neither is very strong.

Opening hours and holidays

The Dutch weekend fades painlessly into the working week with many **shops** staying closed on Monday morning, even in major cities, although markets do open early. Otherwise, opening hours tend to be 9am to 5.30 or 6pm, though certain shops stay open later on Thursday or Friday evenings, and city-centre supermarkets tend to close around 10pm. Night shops (*avondwinkels*) can be found in major cities, usually opening from 4pm to 1 or 2am. In general, shops shut a little earlier on Saturday.

Opening times of **museums** are fairly uniform, generally Tues–Sat 10am–5pm, Sun 1–5pm; admission to the more ordinary collections is €2, although the major museums can be around €7. If you're intending to visit more than a handful of museums, it's worth investing in a **museumcard** – available from VVVs or museums for €32 (under-24s €14) – which gives free or reduced access to all state and municipally run museums and galleries for a year. For under-26s, the **CJP** (€10), also available from VVVs, gives reductions for museum admission and theatre, film and concert tickets.

Shops and banks are closed, and museums adopt Sunday hours, on the **public holidays**: Jan 1; Good Fri; Easter Sun & Mon; Queen's Day; May 5; May 13; Whitsun & Monday; Dec 5; Dec 25 & Dec 26.

Emergencies and drugs

You're unlikely to come into contact with the **police force**. It's normally possible to walk anywhere in the larger cities at any time of day, though you should obviously be wary of pickpockets in busy places, and badly lit or empty streets at night. If you're detained by the police, you don't automatically have the right to a phone call, although they'll probably phone your embassy for you. As for **drugs**, people over the age of eighteen are legally allowed to buy five grammes of hashish or marijuana (less than one-fifth of one ounce) for personal use. Don't assume that the bar or café you're in permits dope-smoking; if in doubt, ask. Also bear in mind that the liberal attitude exists only in Amsterdam and the larger cities of the Randstad: elsewhere, public dope-smoking is frowned upon. Possession of amounts less than 28 grammes (one ounce) is ignored by police. All other narcotics – except fresh magic mushrooms – are illegal. Check out The Honest Cannabis Info Site (*www.thc.nl*). Regarding health, a **pharmacy** (*apotheek*) is the place to get a prescription filled; all are open Mon–Fri 8.30am–5.30pm. Outside this time there'll be a note of the nearest open pharmacy on the door. Duty doctors at the Centrale Doktorsdienst (☎0900/503 2042) offer general advice about medical symptoms; otherwise head for the casualty department of any **hospital** (*ziekenhuis*).

Emergency Numbers

Police, fire and ambulance ☎112.

AMSTERDAM

AMSTERDAM is a beguiling capital, a compact mix of the provincial and the cosmopolitan. It has a welcoming attitude towards visitors and a uniquely youthful orientation. For many, however, its world-class museums and galleries – notably the Rijksmuseum, with its collection of seventeenth-century Dutch paintings, and the Van Gogh Museum – are reason enough to visit.

Amsterdam was founded on a dam on the river Amstel in the thirteenth century. During the Reformation it rose in stature, taking trade away from Antwerp and becoming a haven for its religious refugees. Having shaken off the yoke of the Spanish, the city went from strength to strength in the seventeenth century, becoming the centre of a vast trading empire with colonies in Southeast Asia. Amsterdam accommodated its expansion with the cobweb of canals that gives the city its distinctive and elegant shape today. Come the eighteenth century, Amsterdam went into gentle decline, re-emerging as a fashionable focus for the alternative movements of the 1960s. Despite a backlash in the 1980s, the city still takes a uniquely progressive approach to social issues and culture, with a buzz of open-air summer events, intimate clubs and bars, and relaxed attitude to soft drugs.

Arrival, information and city transport

Schiphol **airport** (*www.schiphol.nl*) is connected by train with the main **Centraal Station** (every 15min; hourly at night). Centraal Station is at the hub of all **bus** and **tram** routes and just five minutes' walk from central Dam Square. International buses arrive at Amstel Station, ten minutes south of Centraal Station by metro. For **information**, the main VVV is outside Centraal Station, Stationsplein 10 (daily 9am–5pm; ☎0900/400 4040, *www.visitamsterdam.nl*); there's another branch inside the station (Mon–Sat 8am–8pm, Sun 9am–5pm), a smaller kiosk on the Leidseplein corner of Leidsestraat (daily 9am–5pm, Thurs–Sat closes 7pm), and an office in the airport (daily 7am–10pm). Any of these can sell you a map, book accommodation and provide answers to most enquiries, though summer queues can be a nightmare; they can also sell you an **Amsterdam Culture & Leisure Pass** (€29), which gives free or reduced entry to a selection of major attractions as well as free public transport for three days and discounts at some restaurants. The VVV's monthly listings guide, *Day to Day*, costs €1. *Infopocket Amsterdam*, written in four languages, costs €3 and contains photographs and practical information about the city.

The excellent network of **trams**, **buses** and the small **metro** (all daily 6/7am–midnight) isn't expensive. The GVB public transport office in front of Centraal Station (Mon–Fri 7am–9pm, Sat & Sun 8am–9pm; winter until 7pm; ☎0900/9292) has free route maps and an English guide to the ticketing system. As with the rest of the country, you use a *strippenkaart* – available from any GVB office, post offices, selected tobacconists, train stations and VVVs. Since you rarely need to travel outside the central zone, cancelling two strips is normally sufficient; this gives you an hour's travel (all trams display instructions in English for how to cancel strips). *Dagkaarten* (day tickets) cost €5 for one day, €8 for two, then €2 for each additional day. If caught without a ticket, you're liable for a €30 spot fine plus the journey fare. After midnight, **night buses** take over, running roughly hourly from Centraal Station to most parts of the city. **Taxis** are expensive, found in ranks on main city squares (Stationsplein, Dam Square, Leidseplein); to book one call ☎020/677 7777. **Bikes** can be rented from Centraal Station or from a number of firms around town (see Listings).

Accommodation

Hotels can be expensive, although the city's size means that you'll inevitably end up somewhere central. A viable alternative is to stay in one of the many **hostels** offering dorm beds and usually a few rooms. They're scattered all over the city, most densely in the red-light district along Warmoesstraat, which is five minutes' walk from Centraal Station, and not as seedy as it sounds. At peak periods throughout the year (April–August, but especially Easter) it's advisable to book ahead. The Amsterdam Reservation Centre (*www.amsterdamtourist.nl*) can book accommodation for a €9 fee; it's especially useful for last-minute bookings, but you may find that booking on the day means your cheapest options start at over €100.

Hostels

Bob's Youth Hostel, Nieuwezijds Voorburgwal 92 (☎020/623 0063). An old favourite of backpackers; lively and smoky, with small dorms, cheap meals and Internet access. Ten-minute walk from Centraal Station. ②.

Flying Pig Downtown, Nieuwendijk 100 (☎020/420 6822, *www.flyingpig.nl*). Clean, large and well run by ex-backpackers. Free kitchen facilities and Internet access, no curfew, all-night bar. Not for faint-hearted anti-smokers. Five-minute walk from Centraal Station. ③.

Flying Pig Palace Vondelpark, Vossiusstraat 46 (☎020/400 4187, *www.flyingpig.nl*). Tram #1/#2/#5 to Leidseplein, then walk. On the edge of the city's big park; clean and well maintained. Free kitchen facilities and Internet access, no curfew, good tourist information. Use their Safe service to store valuables. ③.

Hans Brinker, Kerkstraat 136 (☎020/622 0687, *www.hans-brinker.nl*). Well-established and raucously popular cheapie, though a little more upmarket than some. Good, basic and clean, and close to the Leidseplein buzz. Tram #1/#2/#5 to Prinsengracht. ③.

International Budget Hostel, Leidsegracht 76 (☎020/624 2784). Excellent budget option on a peaceful little canal in the heart of the city. Tram #1/#2/#5 to Prinsengracht. ③.

Kabul, Warmoesstraat 38 (☎020/623 7158). Huge, bustling hostel with multilingual staff, three minutes' walk from the station. Rooms sleep between one and 16 people. Immaculately clean. ③.

Meeting Point, Warmoesstraat 14 (☎020/627 7499). 24hr hostel. Breakfast not included. Two-minute walk from Centraal Station. ③.

The Shelter City, Barndesteeg 21 (☎020/625 3230, *www.shelter.nl*). Non-evangelical Christian hostel smack in the middle of the red-light district: single-sex dorms, lockers, midnight curfew (1am weekends). Sizeable breakfast included. Metro Nieuwmarkt. ②.

The Shelter Jordaan, Bloemstraat 179 (☎020/624 4717, *www.shelter.nl*). Another easy-going Christian hostel in the beautiful Jordaan district, west of the centre. About the cheapest beds in the city, in single-sex dorms. No smoking allowed anywhere inside the hostel. Tram #13/#17 to Marnixstraat. ②.

Stadsdoelen, Kloveniersburgwal 97 (☎020/624 6832, *www.njhc.org/stadsdoelen*). The more accessible of the two HI hostels, with clean semi-private dorm rooms. HI members have priority in high season. Tram #4/#9/#16/#24/#25 to Muntplein. ③.

Vondel Park, Zandpad 5 (☎020/589 8996, *www.njhc.org/vondelpark*). For facilities, the better of the two HI hostels, with bar, restaurant, TV lounge and kitchen; also well located on the edge of the park. Secure lockers and a lift. Tram #1/#2/#5 to Leidseplein, then walk. ③.

Hotels

Arena, 's-Gravesandestraat 51 (☎020/850 2400, *www.hotelarena.nl*). A little way out of the centre, but probably the best value in the city. On-site facilities include live music, tourist and cultural information, bike rental, a great bar and restaurant and even parking. Every room has its own bath or shower. Metro Weesperplein or tram #6/#7/#10 from Leidseplein to Korte 's-Gravesandestraat. ③.

Asterisk, Den Texstraat 16 (☎020/626 2396, *www.asteriskhotel.nl*). Good-value budget hotel on the edge of the centre, just across the canal from the Heineken Brewery. Tram #16/#24/#25 to Weteringcircuit. ⑤.

Bema, Concertgebouwplein 19b (☎020/679 1396, *www.hotel-bema.demon.nl*). Small place, kept very clean by the English-speaking manager. The rooms are not modern, but are full of character. Handier for concerts and museums than nightlife. Tram #2/#5 to Museumplein. ④.

Clemens, Raadhuisstraat 39 (☎020/624 6089, *www.clemenshotel.nl*). One of the many options on this hotel strip. Clean, neat and good value for money. Ask for a room at the back. Tram #13/#17 to Westermarkt. ④.

Euphemia, Fokke Simonszstraat 1 (☎020/622 9045, *www.euphemiahotel.com*). A likeable, laid-back atmosphere: rooms are big and basic, with free showers and TVs. Very reasonable prices, which means it's usually full. Tram #16/#24/#25 to Weteringcircuit. ④.

Keizersgracht, Keizersgracht 15 (☎020/625 1364). Terrific location on a major canal five minutes' walk from Centraal Station, with a good mix of small dorms, singles and doubles. Spotless. ③.

King, Leidsekade 85–86 (☎020/624 9603). Clean but very small rooms in a small hotel. Breakfast included. Minimum three nights during summer. Tram #1/#2/#5 to Leidseplein. ④.

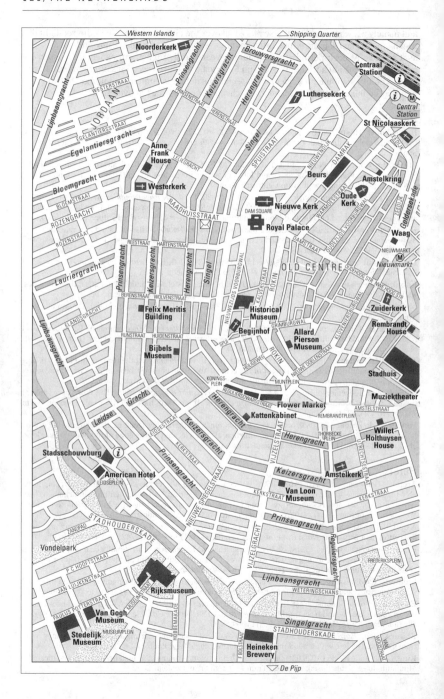

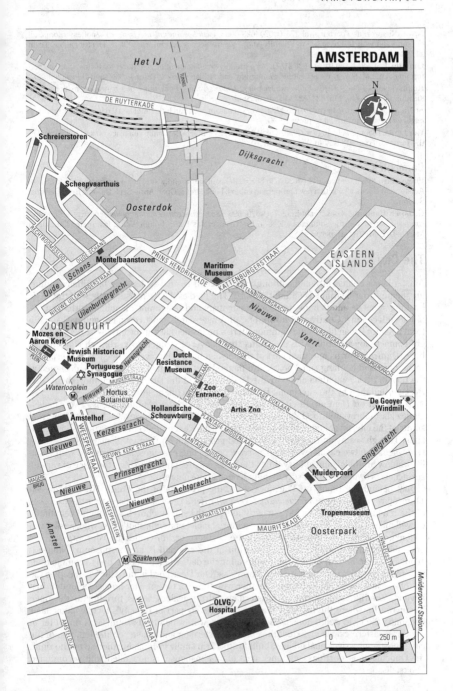

Nova, Nieuwezijds Voorburgwal 276 (☎020/623 0066, *www.bookings.nl/hotels/nova*). Spotless rooms, all en suite and with fridge and TV. Friendly staff, secure access and internal lift. Perfect location. Tram #1/#2/#5 to Spui. ⑧.

Quentin, Leidsekade 89 (☎020/626 2187). Very friendly small hotel, often a stopover for bands or artists performing at the Melkweg. Well regarded among gay and lesbian visitors. Tram #1/#2/#5 to Leidseplein. ④.

Rokin, Rokin 73 (☎020/626 7456, *www.bookings.nl/hotels/rokin*). Something of a bargain considering the location. Tram #4/#9/#16/#24/#25 to Dam or Spui. ⑤.

St Nicolaas, Spuistraat 1a (☎020/626 1384). Very pleasant, well-run little hotel housed in a former mattress factory (with a king-size lift to prove it). ⑥.

Van Onna, Bloemgracht 104 (☎020/626 5801). A quiet, comfortable, family-run place on a tranquil canal in the Jordaan. Tram #13/#17 to Westermarkt. ⑤.

Campsites

Vliegenbos, Meeuwenlaan 138 (☎020/636 8855). Relaxed and friendly site, just a ten-minute bus ride into Amsterdam North, also with a few four-person cabins; book ahead. Open April–Sept. Bus #32 from Centraal Station.

Gaasper Camping, Loosdrechtdreef 7 (☎020/696 7326, *www.gaaspercamping-amsterdam.nl*). "Family" campsite, way out in the southeast, close to the Gaasperplas Park, though with a fast metro link. Open March–Dec. Metro Gaasperplas.

The City

Amsterdam is a small city, and, although the concentric canal system can be initially confusing, finding your bearings is straightforward. The medieval core boasts the best of the city's bustling streetlife and is home to shops, many bars and restaurants, fanning south from the nineteenth-century **Centraal Station**, one of Amsterdam's most resonant landmarks and a focal point for urban life. Come summer there's no livelier part of the city, as street performers compete for attention with the trams that converge dangerously from all sides. From here, **Damrak** storms into the heart of the city, an unenticing avenue lined with overpriced restaurants and bobbing canal boats, and flanked on the left first by the **Beurs**, designed at the turn of the twentieth century by the leading light of the Dutch modern movement, H.P. Berlage, and then by the enormous **De Bijenkorf** department store.

To the left off Damrak, the infamous **red-light district**, stretching across two canals – Oudezijds (abbreviated to O.Z.) Voorburgwal and O.Z. Achterburgwal – is one of the real sights of the city, thronged in high season with visitors keen to discover just how shocking it all is. Though seamy and seedy, the legalized prostitution on flagrant display here is world-renowned. The two canals, with their narrow connecting passages, are thronged with neon-lit "window brothels", and at busy times the crass on-street haggling over the price of various sex acts is drowned out by a surprisingly festive atmosphere.

Just behind the Beurs off Warmoesstraat, the precincts of the **Oude Kerk** (Mon–Sat 11am–5pm, Sun 1–5pm; €3.60; *www.oudekerk.nl*) offer a reverential peace after the excesses of the red-light district; it's a bare, mostly fourteenth-century church with some beautifully carved misericords in the choir and the memorial tablet of Rembrandt's first wife, Saskia van Uylenburg. Nearby, the **Amstelkring**, at the northern end of Oudezijds Voorburgwal, was once the principal Catholic place of worship in the city and is now a museum (Mon–Sat 10am–5pm, Sun 1–5pm; €4.50) commemorating the days when Catholics had to confine their worship to the privacy of their homes. Known as "Our Dear Lord in the Attic", it occupies the loft of a wealthy merchant's house, together with those of two smaller houses behind it. Just beyond, **Zeedijk**, once haunt of Amsterdam's drug dealers, leads through to the open **Nieuwmarkt**, where the turreted **Waag** was originally part of the city's fortifications, later becoming the civic weigh-house. **Kloveniersburgwal**, which leads south, was the outer of the three eastern canals of sixteenth-century Amsterdam and boasts, on the left, one of the city's most impressive canal houses, built for the Trip family in 1662. Further up on the right, the Oudemanhuispoort passage, once part of an almshouse, is now filled with secondhand bookstalls.

At the southern end of Damrak, the **Dam** (or Dam Square), where the Amstel was first dammed, is the centre of the city, its tusk-like War Memorial serving as a meeting place for tourists. On the western side, the **Royal Palace** (June–Oct daily 11am–5pm; Nov–May opening hours variable; €4.30; *www.kon-paleisamsterdam.nl*) was originally built as the city hall in the mid-seventeenth century. It received its royal monicker in 1808 when Napoleon's brother Louis commandeered it as the one building fit for a king. He was forced to abdicate in 1810, leaving behind a sizeable amount of the Empire furniture. Vying for importance is the adjacent **Nieuwe Kerk** (open only during exhibitions; *www.nieuwekerk.nl*), a fifteenth-century structure rebuilt several times, which is now used only for exhibitions and state occasions. Inside rest numerous names from Dutch history, among them the seventeenth-century naval hero Admiral de Ruyter, who lies in an opulent tomb in the choir, and the poet Vondel, commemorated by a small urn near the entrance.

South of Dam Square, **Rokin** follows the old course of the Amstel River, lined with grandiose nineteenth-century mansions. Running parallel, **Kalverstraat** is a monotonous strip of clothes shops, halfway down which, at no. 92, a gateway forms the entrance to the former orphanage that's now the **Amsterdam Historical Museum** (Mon–Fri 10am–5pm, Sat & Sun 1–5pm; €6.10; *www.ahm.nl*), where artefacts, paintings and documents survey the city's development from the thirteenth century. Directly outside, the glassed-in Civic Guard Gallery draws passers-by with free glimpses of the large company portraits. Just around the corner, off Sint Luciensteeg, the **Begijnhof** is a small court of seventeenth-century buildings; the poor and elderly led a religious life here, celebrating Mass in their own, concealed, Catholic Church. The plain and unadorned English Reformed Church, which takes up one side of the Begijnhof, has pulpit panels designed by the young Piet Mondriaan. Close by, the **Spui** (pronounced *spow*) is a lively corner of town whose mixture of bookshops and packed bars centres around a cloying statue of a young boy known as *'t Lieverdje* (Little Darling). In the opposite direction, Kalverstraat comes to an end at **Muntplein** and the Munttoren – originally a mint and part of the city walls, topped with a spire by Hendrik de Keyser in 1620. Across the Singel canal is the fragrant daily **Flower Market**, while in the other direction Reguliersbreestraat turns left towards the loud restaurants of **Rembrandtplein**. To the south is Reguliersgracht, an appealing canal with seven distinctive steep bridges stretching in a perspective line from Thorbeckeplein.

The main canals and the Jordaan

Amsterdam's expansion in the seventeenth century was designed around three new canals, **Herengracht**, **Keizersgracht** and **Prinsengracht**, which formed a distinctive cobweb shape around the centre. Development was strictly controlled: even the richest burgher had to conform to a set of stylistic rules, and taxes were levied according to the width of the properties. The result was the tall, very narrow residences you see today, with individualism restricted to decorative gables and sometimes a gablestone to denote name and occupation. It's difficult to pick out any particular points to head for, since most of the canal houses have been turned into offices or hotels. Rather, the appeal lies in wandering along selected stretches admiring the gables; a uniquely Amsterdam experience is to wander along taking in the calm of the tree-lined waterways, while looking into people's windows (Amsterdammers tend not to bother with curtains, a habit which lends the city an open and homely atmosphere). For shops, bars and restaurants, you're better off exploring the crossing-streets which connect the canals.

Herengracht remains the grandest, especially between Leidsestraat and Vijzelstraat, a stretch known as the "Golden Curve". To see the interior of one of the canal houses you should head for the **Willet-Holthuysen House**, Herengracht 605 (daily 10/11am–5pm; €4.30; *www.ahm.nl*), splendidly decorated in Rococo style and containing Abraham Willet's collection of glass and ceramics and a well-equipped seventeenth-century kitchen. Perhaps more likeable, with a pleasantly down-at-heel interior of peeling stucco and shabby paintwork, is the **Van Loon House**, Keizersgracht 672 (Mon & Fri–Sun 11am–5pm; €4.50;

www.musvloon.box.nl), built in 1672 for the artist Ferdinand Bol. The Van Loon family bought the house in 1884, bringing with them a collection of family portraits and homely bits and pieces dating from between 1580 and 1949.

On the corner of **Keizersgracht** and Leidsestraat, the designer department store Metz & Co has a top-floor café with one of the best views of the city. **Leidsestraat** itself is a long, slender shopping street across the main canals that broadens at its southern end into **Leidseplein**, focus of Amsterdam's nightlife, with a concentration of bars and restaurants. On the far corner, the Stadsschouwburg is the city's prime performance space after the Muziektheater, while behind, the fairy-castle *American Hotel* has a bar whose carefully co-ordinated furnishings are a fine example of Art Nouveau.

The area immediately north of here, along **Prinsengracht**, is one of the city's loveliest neighbourhoods, focusing on the gracious tower of the **Westerkerk** (April–Sept Mon–Fri 11am–3pm; June–Aug also Sat same times; €1.40), designed by Hendrik de Keyser in 1631. The church has a small memorial to Rembrandt, who died in the neighbourhood, as well as guided tours to the top of the tower. Directly outside, a statue of Anne Frank, by the Dutch sculptor Marie Andriessen, signals the fact that the house where the young diarist lived is just a few steps away at Prinsengracht 263, the **Anne Frank House** (daily: April–Aug 9am–9pm; Sept–March 9am–7pm; closed Yom Kippur; €5.70; *www.annefrank.nl*). This is deservedly one of the most popular tourist attractions in town, so arrive before 9am and be prepared to queue. Anne Frank, her family and friends went into hiding from the Nazis in July 1942, staying in the annexe behind the house for two years until they were betrayed and taken away to labour camps, an experience which only Anne's father survived. Anne Frank's diary was among the few things left behind here, and was published in 1947, since when it has sold over thirteen million copies worldwide. The rooms the Franks lived in are left much as they were, even down to the movie-star pin-ups in Anne's bedroom and the marks on the wall recording the children's heights. A number of other rooms offer background detail on the war and the atrocities of Nazism, giving some up-to-date and pertinent examples of fascism in Europe.

Across Prinsengracht to the west, the **Jordaan** is a beguiling area of narrow canals, narrower streets and simpler, architecturally varied houses, originally home of artisans and religious refugees, and later the inner-city enclave of Amsterdam's industrial working class – which, in spite of widespread gentrification, it to some extent remains. With some of the city's best bars and restaurants, funky alternative clothes shops and good outdoor markets, especially those on the square outside the Noorderkerk (a fabric market on Mondays and a wonderful and very popular farmers' market on Saturdays), the Jordaan is a wonderful area to wander through. The country's hottest contemporary artists show work at the **Stedelijk Museum Bureau Amsterdam** gallery, Rozenstraat 59 (Tues–Sat 11am–5pm; *www.smba.nl*).

The Museum Quarter and south

Immediately south of Leidseplein begins the **Vondelpark**, the city's most enticing park, named after the seventeenth-century Dutch poet Joost van der Vondel and a regular forum for drama and other performance arts on summer weekends, when young Amsterdam flocks here to meet friends, laze by the lake and listen to music; in June, July and August there are free concerts every Sunday at 2pm. Southeast of the park is one of Amsterdam's better-heeled residential districts, with designer shops and delis along chic **P.C. Hooftstraat** and **Van Baerlestraat** and some of the city's major museums grouped around the grassy wedge of **Museumplein**.

The **Rijksmuseum**, Stadhouderskade 42 (daily 10am–5pm; €6.80; *www.rijksmuseum.nl*), is the one museum you shouldn't leave Amsterdam without visiting, with fine collections of medieval and Renaissance applied art, displays on Dutch history, a fine Asian collection and, most importantly, an array of seventeenth-century Dutch paintings that is far and away the best in the world. Most people head straight for one of the museum's great treasures, Rembrandt's *The Night Watch*, but there are many other, perhaps more interesting, examples of his work, not least the *Staalmeesters*, the late *Jewish Bride*, and some private and beautifully expressive works – a portrait of his first wife Saskia, a couple of his mother, a touching depiction of his son, Titus, and a late *Self-Portrait*, caught in mid-shrug as the Apostle Paul. There are also portraits by Frans Hals, landscapes by Jan van Goyen and Jacob van Ruisdael, the riotous scenes of Jan Steen and the peaceful interiors of Vermeer and Pieter de Hooch.

Just south, the **Vincent Van Gogh Museum**, Paulus Potterstraat 7 (daily 10am–6pm; €7; *www.vangoghmuseum.nl*), comprises the collection of the artist's art-dealer brother Theo, with drawings, notebooks and letters displayed on a rotating basis, and a collection arranged chronologically, from the early years in Holland and works like the dour *Potato Eaters*, to the brighter works he painted after moving to Paris and then Arles, where he produced vivid canvases like *The Yellow House* and the *Sunflowers* series. Later, more expressionistic works include the *Garden of St Paul's Hospital*, painted at the asylum in St-Rémy, and his final, tortured paintings, including *The Reaper* and *Wheatfield with Crows*.

Just along the street at Paulus Potterstraat 13 is the modern-art **Stedelijk Museum** (daily: April–Sept 10am–6pm; Oct–March 11am–5pm; €4.50; *www.stedelijk.nl*). Much of its wide-ranging permanent collection is on display in July and August, and parts of it year-round. There's normally a good showing on the first floor, starting off with drawings by Picasso, Matisse and their contemporaries, and moving on to paintings by the major Impressionists – Manet, Monet, Bonnard – and Post-Impressionists such as Ensor, Van Gogh and Cézanne. There's also work by Mondriaan and Malevich, a good stock of Marc Chagall's paintings, and a number of American Abstract Expressionists (Mark Rothko, Ellsworth Kelly and Barnett Newman). Two additional large-scale attractions are on the ground floor: Karel Appel's *Bar* in the foyer, installed for the opening of the Stedelijk in the 1950s, and the same artist's wild daubings in the museum's restaurant.

Further along Stadhouderskade from the Rijksmuseum, the **Heineken Brewery**, though no longer in production, runs tours of the characteristic red-copper brewery (Mon–Fri 9.30am & 11am, June to mid-Sept also 1pm & 2.30pm, July & Aug also Sat 11am, 1pm & 2.30pm; €1; over-18s only), providing a résumé of Heineken's history and the methods involved in the brewing process; afterwards you are given snacks and **free beer**. South of here is the neighbourhood known as **De Pijp** ("The Pipe") after its long, sombre canyons of brick tenements that went up in the nineteenth century as the city grew out of its canal-girded centre. This has always been one of the city's closest-knit communities, and one of its liveliest, with numerous inexpensive Surinamese and Turkish restaurants and a cheerful hub in the long slim thoroughfare of **Albert Cuypstraat**, whose general **market** is the largest in the city.

East of the centre

East of Rembrandtplein across the Amstel, the large, squat **Muziektheater** and **Town Hall** – dubbed the "Stopera" after the 1980s campaign to stop the construction of an opera house here – flank **Waterlooplein**, home to the city's excellent flea market. Behind, Jodenbreestraat was once the main street of the Jodenhoek, the city's **Jewish quarter** (emptied by the Nazis in the 1940s) and is the site of the **Rembrandt House** at no.4 (Mon-Sat 10am–5pm, Sun 1–5pm; €6.80; *www.rembrandthuis.nl*), which the painter bought at the height of his fame, living here for over twenty years. The interior was renovated in 1999 and displays a huge number of the artist's engravings. Close by, the most tangible mementoes of the Jewish community are shown in the **Portuguese Synagogue** (Mon–Fri & Sun 10am–4pm; closed Yom Kippur; €3.40), completed in 1675 and once the largest synagogue in the world. Across the way, the excellent, award-winning **Jewish Historical Museum** (daily 11am–5pm; closed Yom Kippur; €3.60; *www.jhm.nl*) is cleverly housed in a complex of Ashkenazi synagogues dating from the late seventeenth century and gives a broad and imaginative introduction to Jewish life and beliefs.

Down Muiderstraat from here, the prim **Hortus Botanicus**, Plantage Middenlaan 2 (Mon–Fri 9am–4/5pm, Sat & Sun 11am–4/5pm; €3.40), is a pocket-sized botanical garden whose 8000 plant species make a wonderfully relaxed break from the rest of central

Amsterdam; stop off for coffee and cakes in the orangery. Some 400m down Plantage Middenlaan, and entered off Plantage Kerklaan, is the **Zoo** (daily 9am–5/6pm; €12.70; *www.artis.nl*). Across the street from the zoo stands the eye-catching Plancius Building, which houses the **Dutch Resistance Museum**, Plantage Kerklaan 2 (Tues–Fri 10am–5pm, Sat & Sun noon–5pm; €3.60). Here a variety of exhibits depict the ways in which the Dutch people opposed Nazi oppression. A short walk northwest, the **Maritime Museum** on Kattenburgerplein (Tues–Sun 10am–5pm; €6.60; *www.scheepvaartmuseum.nl*), housed in a fortress-like seventeenth-century arsenal, has maps, navigational equipment and weapons, though the most impressive exhibits are the large models of sailing ships and men-of-war plus the replica of an old clipper outside in the harbour.

Eating and drinking

Amsterdam may not be the culinary capital of Europe, but there's a good supply of ethnic **restaurants**, especially Indonesian and Chinese, as well as *eetcafés* and bars which serve decent, well-priced food in a relaxed and unpretentious setting. We've also listed a handful of places to get just a snack (though you can do this easily enough in many bars), as well as the best of the city's so-called **coffeeshops**, where smoking dope is the primary pastime (all sell a range of hash and grass – ask to see "the menu"). Restaurants have been divided into **budget** (under €9), **inexpensive** (€9–14) and **moderate** (€14–18), denoting the average cost per person for a starter and main course without drinks.

Cafés and snacks

Café Esprit, Spui 10a. Swish modern café, with wonderful sandwiches and superb salads.

Gary's Muffins, Prinsengracht 454, near Leidseplein; also Reguliersdwarsstraat 53, near Koningsplein. The best muffins and bagels in town, with big cups of coffee (and half-price refills).

Greenwoods, Singel 103 near Dam Square. Small English-style tea shop, with a decent breakfast.

Maoz Falafel, Reguliersbreestraat 45, near Rembrandtplein. The best street-food in the city – falafel with bread and as much salad as you can eat for the grand sum of €3.

Mr Hot Potato, Leidsestraat 44. Baked potatoes – nothing fancy, but cheap.

The Pancake Bakery, Prinsengracht 191. A large selection of pancakes from €4.

Puccini, Staalstraat 17–21 near Waterlooplein. Dreamy cakes, pastries and chocolates, all handmade.

Studio 2, Singel 504. Pleasantly situated, airy tearoom with a delicious selection of rolls and sandwiches.

Villa Zeezicht, Torensteeg 3. Small place on the Singel canal, all in wood, with excellent sandwiches and some of the best apple-cake in the city.

Restaurants

Akbar, Korte Leidsedwarsstraat 33, near Leidseplein. Fabulous South Indian food, with a fine choice across the board. Plenty for vegetarians. Moderate.

De Blauwe Hollander, Leidsekruisstraat 28, near Leidseplein. Dutch food in generous quantities. Expect to share a table. Inexpensive.

Burger's Patio, 2e Tuindwarsstraat 12, Jordaan. Trendy but convivial Italian restaurant. Despite the name, not a burger in sight. Inexpensive.

Casa di David, Singel 426. Solid-value Italian with a long-standing reputation. Pizzas from wood-fired ovens and fresh handmade pasta. Moderate.

Duende, Lindengracht 62, Jordaan. Good Spanish bar with cheap tapas. Budget.

De Eetuin, 2e Tuindwarsstraat 10, Jordaan. Hefty portions of Dutch food. Inexpensive.

Golden Temple, Utrechtsestraat 126, near Frederiksplein. Laid-back nonsmoking vegetarian place with attentive service. Inexpensive.

Hoi Tin, Zeedijk 122, near Nieuwmarkt. One of the best places in the rather dodgy Chinatown, with an enormous menu (in English too) and some vegetarian dishes. Always busy. Moderate.

Kam Yin, Warmoesstraat 6. Excellent option for large portions of Chinese and Surinamese dishes. Budget.

Kilimanjaro, Rapenburgerplein 6. Small, friendly place serving North African specialities. Closed Mon. Moderate.

Keuken van 1870, Spuistraat 4. Former soup kitchen still serving Dutch meat-and-potato staples. Budget.

De Rozenboom, Rozenboomsteeg 6. Quaint little Dutch restaurant with good traditional food and a menu in English. Ideally situated, just off Spui. Inexpensive.

Shiva, Reguliersdwarsstraat 72. Outstanding Indian restaurant, with well-priced, expertly prepared food, including veggie. Inexpensive.

Tempo Doeloe, Utrechtsestraat 75, near Rembrandtplein. Reliable, quality Indonesian place. Moderate.

De Vliegende Schotel, Nieuwe Leliestraat 162, Jordaan. Perhaps the best of the city's vegetarian restaurants, serving delicious food in large portions. Budget.

Bars

Café Vertigo, Vondelpark 3. Attached to the Film Museum, a wonderful place to while away a sunny afternoon (or take refuge from the rain) with a spacious interior and a large terrace overlooking the park.

Last Waterhole, Oudezijds Armsteeg 12. Red-light district refuge, with a lively, warm atmosphere and a fun-loving house band playing until dawn.

De Drie Fleschjes, Gravenstraat 18, near Dam Square. Tasting house for spirits and liqueurs. No beer, and no seats either. Closes 8pm.

Durty Nelly's, Warmoesstraat 117. Irish pub in the heart of the red-light action, packed if there's weekend football.

De Engelbewaarder, Kloveniersburgwal 59. Once a meeting place of Amsterdam's bookish types, with live jazz on Sunday afternoons.

Flying Dutchman, Martelaarsgracht 13, near Centraal Station. Principal watering hole of British expats, and not a word of Dutch to be heard.

't IJ, Funenkade 7. Situated in the base of a windmill to the east of the centre, with exceptionally strong home brewed beers. Wed–Sun 3–8pm.

De Jaren, Nieuwe Doelenstraat 20–22, near Muntplein. Grand café overlooking the river – one of the best places to nurse the Sunday paper.

Koophandel, Bloemgracht 49, Jordaan. Empty before midnight, this is the early-hours bar you dreamt about, in an old warehouse on one of Amsterdam's most picturesque canals. Open until at least 3am.

Lokaal 't Loosje, Nieuwmarkt 32. Quiet old-style "brown café" that's been here for 200 years and looks its age.

Mulligans, Amstel 100, near Rembrandtplein. Best Irish pub in the city, with superb traditional music.

O'Donnells, Ferdinand Bolstraat 5. The best Guinness in town, just behind the Heineken Brewery.

Sound Garden, Marnixstraat 164, Jordaan. Grunge bar, packed with people and noise, with a canalside terrace to retreat to.

Tara, Rokin 89. Excellent Irish bar with regular live music.

De Tuin, 2e Tuindwarsstraat 13. The Jordaan has some marvellously unpretentious bars, and this is one of the best. Agreeably unkempt.

De Twee Zwaantjes, Prinsengracht 114. Tiny oddball Jordaan bar where locals sing along raucously to accordian music – you'll either love it or hate it.

Smoking coffeeshops

The Bulldog, Leidseplein 15 and a couple of other outlets. The oldest, biggest and noisiest, not at all the place for a thoughtful smoke.

Global Chillage, Kerkstraat 51. Celebrated slice of tie-dyed dope culture.

Grasshopper, Oudebrugsteeg 16 and other outlets. One of the more welcoming large coffeeshops.

Greenhouse Effect, Warmoesstraat 53. Better-than-average red-light district coffeeshop.

Dampkring, Handboogstraat 29. One of the best in town with nice decor and a refined menu, including top-notch Skunk.

Paradox, 1e Bloemdwarsstraat 2, Jordaan. Satisfies the munchies with outstanding natural food, including spectacular fresh-fruit concoctions. Closes 7pm.

Siberië, Brouwersgracht 11. Relaxed, long-standing place that's worth a visit whether you want to smoke or not.

Nightlife

Amsterdam is a gathering spot for fringe performances, and buzzes with places offering a wide and often inventive range of affordable entertainment. **Rock, jazz** and **Latin American** music are well represented in a number of small bars and clubs but the **club** scene is relatively tame: drinks prices are normally fifty percent or so more than what you pay in a bar, but entry prices are low – usually around €7 – and there's rarely any kind of door policy. Most places open around 10pm and close around 4am or slightly later. For more highbrow entertainment, the Concertgebouw assures Amsterdam a high ranking in the **classical music** stakes, and the city has also pulled itself up into the big leagues for **dance** and **opera**. The best source of information is the **Uitburo**, or **AUB**, in the Stadsschouwburg theatre on the corner of Marnixstraat and Leidseplein (daily 10am–6pm, Thurs until 9pm; ☎020/621 1211 or ☎0900/0191). They stock the free bimonthly *Pop & Jazz Uitlijst* and sell tickets for a small fee; you can also buy tickets for most events from the VVV. Saturday's *Het Parool* newspaper has good **listings**.

Rock and jazz venues

Akhnaton, Nieuwezijds Kolk 25, city centre. A "Centre for World Culture", specializing in African and Latin American music and dance parties.

Alto, Korte Leidsedwarsstraat 115, near Leidseplein. Legendary jazz bar, with free live music every night 9.30pm–3am. Big on atmosphere, not space.

Arena, 's-Gravesandestraat 51, near Oosterpark. Multimedia centre featuring live music every weekend, cultural events, a bar, coffeeshop and restaurant. Intimate hall features underground bands from around the world. €4–22.

Bimhuis, Oude Schans 73–77. Premier jazz venue. Big name concerts Thurs–Sat (around €10). Free workshop sessions Wed.

Casablanca, Zeedijk 26, red-light district. Live jazz every night.

Maloe Melo, Lijnbaansgracht 163, Jordaan. Dark low-ceilinged bar, with local bluesy acts.

Melkweg, Lijnbaansgracht 234a, near Leidseplein. Amsterdam's most famous entertainment venue, with a young hip clientele. Two halls feature a broad range of bands tending towards African music and lesser-knowns. Excellent offbeat disco sessions late on Fri & Sat. Also films, a tearoom selling dope, and a bar and restaurant. €7–17, plus €2.50 membership on the door. Closed Mon.

Paradiso, Weteringschans 6–8, near Leidseplein. A converted church featuring semi-big names and up-and-coming bands. €4–22, plus €2.50 membership on the door.

Winston Kingdom, Warmoesstraat 127, red-light district. Small renovated venue with spoken word, jazz-poetry, R&B and punk/noise nights. €5.

Clubs

Dansen bij Jansen, Handboogstraat 11, near Spui. Founded by – and for – students, and very popular; €2.50 weekends, €1 weekday discount with student ID.

Club More, Rozengracht 133, Amsterdam's finest dance club, where the queue gets longer every time. €11.50.

Club Vision, Olympisch Stadion 23. Relaxed club south of the city centre; a little left-field, playing non-commercial, futuristic house.

Escape, Rembrandtplein 11. Huge place packed at weekends, with several floors and top DJs every night. Wed–Sun, €11.50; Thurs €9.

iT, Amstelstraat 24, near Rembrandtplein. Large disco with popular and glamorous gay nights. Thurs & Sun are mixed gay/straight and attract a dressed-up, uninhibited crowd.

Mazzo, Rozengracht 114, Jordaan. Perhaps the city's hippest and most laid-back club, with a choice of music to appeal to all tastes. Nightly, around €7.

Multigroove, Hemkade 48, in the nearby town of Zaandam. Famous for its illegal parties in the 1980s and 1990s, but now featuring the ultimate in hard house, techno and trance. No public transport. €20.

Contemporary music, classical music and opera

Concertgebouw, Concertgebouwplein 2–6. One of the world's most dynamic orchestras, playing in one of the finest halls, just south of Museumplein. Free lunchtime concerts Sept–May. €11 and upwards.

Beurs van Berlage, Damrak 213, city centre. The splendid interior of the former stock exchange hosts a wide selection of music from the Dutch Philharmonic and Dutch Chamber Orchestras.

De IJsbreker, Weesperzijde 23. Varied programme of international modern, chamber and experimental music. €8–14. Also houses a pleasant riverside café/bar. Tram #3/#6/#7/#10.

Muziektheater, Amstel 3. Full opera programme. Tickets cost €10–50, and sell quickly. Free lunchtime concerts.
Stadsschouwburg, Leidseplein 26. Somewhat overshadowed by the Muziektheater, but still a significant stage for opera and dance. €9–18.

Film and theatre

Cinemas screen English-language movies in the original, subtitled in Dutch, and rarely show foreign-language films without English subtitles. Amsterdam's cinemas excel in beautiful Art Deco interiors; watch big Hollywood offerings at the lavish Tuschinski, Reguliersbreestraat 26, and check out the cult and classic flicks at The Movies, Haarlemmerdijk 161, and Kriterion, Roeterstraat 12. The Film Museum in Vondelpark shows all kinds of movies from all corners of the world, and has free open-air screenings on summer weekends. For film listings get hold of a *Week Agenda* from any cinema. The **theatre** company Toomler, Breitnerstraat 2, offers stand-up comedy in Dutch and English, while Boom Chicago, Leidseplein 12, is a hugely popular rapid-fire comedy troupe, performing nightly in English to crowds of tourists and locals.

Gay Amsterdam

Amsterdam has one of the biggest and best-established **gay** scenes in Europe: attitudes are tolerant and facilities unequalled, with a good selection of bookstores, clubs and bars catering to the needs of gay men – and, to a lesser extent, women. The nationwide gay and lesbian organization, COC, Rozenstraat 14 (☎020/626 3087), can provide on-the-spot **information**, and has a café and popular discos (men Fri, women Sat). For further advice on where to go contact the Gay & Lesbian Switchboard (daily 10am–10pm; ☎020/623 6565, *www.switchboard.nl*). There's a good concentration of **bars** around Rembrandtplein, along the Amstel and on Reguliersdwarsstraat. The *Amstel Taveerne*, Amstel 54, is perhaps the best established, at its most vivacious in summer when the guys spill out onto the street by the river; around the corner, *De Steeg*, Halvemaansteeg 10, is a tiny and similarly longtime favourite venue. *April*, Reguliersdwarsstraat 37, is a relaxed afternoon and evening hangout, with newspapers, coffee and cakes as well as booze. *Saarein*, Elandsstraat 119, once the best-known women-only/lesbian café, is now open to both sexes. Vrolijk, Paleisstraat 135, bills itself as "the largest gay and lesbian bookstore on the continent". Xantippe, Prinsengracht 290, has a wide range of books and resources by, for and about women.

Listings

Airlines Aer Lingus, Heiligeweg 14 (☎020/623 8620); British Airways, airport (☎020/601 5413); British Midland, airport (☎020/662 2211); easyJet (*www.easyjet.com*); KLM, airport (☎020/474 7747); Qantas, Stadhouderskade 6 (☎020/683 8081); Transavia, airport (☎020/406 0406).
Bike rental Cheapest from main train stations. Also try: Bike City, Bloemgracht 70 (☎020/626 3721); Damstraat, just off Damstraat (☎020/625 5029); or MacBike, Mr Visserplein 2 (☎020/620 0985) and Marnixstraat 220 (☎020/626 6964). All charge around €4.50 a day plus €100 deposit with ID.
Books Athenaeum, Spui 14–16; Esoro, Oudemanhuispoort 1; Scheltema Holkema Vermeulen, Koningsplein 20; Waterstones, Kalverstraat 152.
Car rental The international companies, which are all close to each other on Overtoom, can be undercut by local operators, such as Diks, van Ostadestraat 278 (☎020/662 3366), or Ouke Baas, van Ostadestraat 366 (☎020/679 4842).
Embassies and consulates Australia, Carnegielaan 4, The Hague (☎070/310 8200); Canada, Sophialaan 7, The Hague (☎070/311 1600); Ireland, Dr Kuyperstraat 9, The Hague (☎070/363 0993); New Zealand, Carnegielaan 10, The Hague (☎070/346 9324); UK, Koningslaan 44, Amsterdam (☎020/676 4343); USA, Museumplein 19, Amsterdam (☎020/664 5661, *www.usemb.nl*).
Exchange GWK, Centraal Station (open 24hr) and Leidseplein (daily 8am–11pm). Change Express, Leidsestraat 105, Damrak 17 and 86, and Kalverstraat 150 (all daily until midnight).

Internet Easyeverything, Reguliersbreestraat (24hr), is the largest Internet café in the world with 650 terminals. Another option is In De Waag, Nieuwmarkt 4.

Laundry The Clean Brothers, Kerkstraat 56 (daily 7am–9pm; €4 to wash and dry). Alternatives at Oudebrugsteeg 22, Warmoesstraat 30 and Oude Doelenstraat 12.

Left luggage Centraal Station (lockers €2 & €3 for 24hr).

Medical service 24hr Tourist Medical Service (☎020/592 3355).

Pharmacy There are no 24hr pharmacies, but every pharmacy has a sign giving the address of the nearest late-opening place.

Police Headquarters at Elandsgracht 117 (☎020/559 9111).

Post office Singel 250–256 (Mon–Fri 9am–6pm, Thurs until 8pm, Sat 10am–1.30pm).

Travel agents NBBS, Rokin 38 and Utrechtsestraat 48 (☎020/620 5071).

THE RANDSTAD TOWNS

The string of towns known as the **Randstad**, or "rim town", situated amid a typically Dutch landscape of flat fields cut by canals, form the country's most populated region and recall the seventeenth-century heyday of the provinces of North and South Holland, of which they are now a part. Much of the area is easily visited by means of day-trips from Amsterdam, but it's more rewarding – and not difficult – to make a proper tour. **Haarlem** is definitely worth an overnight stop, while to the south, the university centre of **Leiden** makes a pleasant detour before you reach the refined tranquillity of **The Hague** and the seedy lowlife of **Rotterdam**. Nearby **Delft** and **Gouda** repay visits too, the former with one of the best-preserved centres in the region.

Haarlem

Just over fifteen minutes from Amsterdam by train, **HAARLEM** is an easily absorbed city of around 150,000 people that sees itself as a cut above its neighbours and makes a good alternative base for exploring the province of North Holland, or even Amsterdam itself. The Frans Hals Museum, in the almshouse where the artist spent his last years, is worth an afternoon in itself, and there are numerous beaches within easy reach, as well as some of the best of the bulbfields.

Haarlem was one of the old Republic's most crucial centres, especially for the arts, and today retains an air of quiet affluence, with all the picturesque qualities of Amsterdam but little of the sleaze. The core of the city is **Grote Markt** and the adjoining Riviervischmarkt, flanked by the gabled, originally fourteenth-century **Stadhuis** and the impressive bulk of the **Grote Kerk of St Bavo** (Mon–Sat 10am–4pm; €1.30). Inside, the mighty Christian Müller organ of 1738, with its 5000 pipes and Baroque razzmatazz, is said to have been played by Handel and Mozart, while beneath, Xaverij's lovely group of draped marble figures represents Poetry and Music, offering thanks to the town patron for her generosity. In the choir there's a late-fifteenth-century painting traditionally (though dubiously) attributed to Geertgen tot Sint Jans, along with memorials to painters Pieter Saenredam and Frans Hals, both of whom are buried here. The town's main attraction is the **Frans Hals Museum**, Groot Heiligland 62 (Mon–Sat 11am–5pm, Sun noon–5pm; €4.50), a five-minute stroll from Grote Markt in the Oudemannhuis almshouse. It houses a good number of his lifelike seventeenth-century portraits, including (in the west wing) the "Civic Guard" portraits which established Hals' reputation. In the *Officers of the Militia Company of St George* (of which Hals was himself a member) he appears in the top left-hand corner, a rare self-portrait. His last, contemplative portraits include the *Governors of the St Elizabeth Gasthuis*, painted in 1641. Also on display are works by Gerard David, Jan Mostaert and the Haarlem Mannerists, including Carel van Mander, numerous scenes of Haarlem by Berckheyde and Saenredam, and landscapes by the Ruisdaels. Look out too for the recently restored and immaculate eighteenth-century doll's house, modelled on an Amsterdam merchant's house and one of only four of its type in the country. Hours of painstaking work were put into producing this tiny piece, at a cost reckoned at half-a-million euros.

Back at the Grote Markt, take a look at the Frans Hals Museum's annexe, **De Hallen** (Mon–Sat 11am–5pm, Sun noon–5pm; €3.40), an old meat-market building now filled with touring exhibitions and works by Haarlem-based Kees Verwey, Holland's oldest living painter, whose Impressionistic watercolours are much loved by senior Dutch aficionados. Just off the eastern side of Grote Markt, the **Teylers Museum**, Spaarne 16 (Tues–Sat 10am–5pm, Sun noon–5pm; €4.50; *www.teylersmuseum.nl*), is the oldest museum in the country, founded back in 1778 by wealthy local philanthropist Pieter Teyler van der Hulst. It should appeal to scientific and artistic tastes alike, containing everything from fossils, bones and crystals to weird early sci-fi technology and sketches and line drawings by Michelangelo, Raphael, Rembrandt and Claude. Look in on the rooms beyond, which are filled with work by eighteenth- and nineteenth-century Dutch painters, principally Breitner, Israëls, Weissenbruch and Wijbrand Hendriks, who was keeper of the art collection here.

Practicalities

Haarlem **train station**, connected to Amsterdam and to Leiden by four trains an hour, is on the north side of the city, about ten minutes' walk from the centre; **buses** stop right outside. The **VVV**, attached to the station (Mon–Fri 9.30am–5.30pm, Sat 10am–2pm; ☎0900/616 1600; *www.vvvzk.nl*), has maps and can book private rooms (③) for a small fee. Haarlem has a few reasonably priced and central **hotels**, such as *Carillon*, Grote Markt 27 (☎023/531 0591; ⑤); *Amadeus*, Grote Markt 10 (☎023/532 4530; ④); and *Joops Innercity Apartments*, Oude Groenmarkt 20 (☎023/532 2008; ④) and Lange Veerstraat 36 (☎023/512 5300; ④). There's an **HI hostel** at Jan Gijzenpad 3 (☎023/537 3793; ②; bus #2 from the station; takes 10min), and **campsites** among the dunes west of town, accessible on bus #81 from the station, including *Bloemendaal*, Zeeweg 72 in **BLOEMENDAAL-AAN-ZEE** (☎023/573 2178; April–Oct), and De Branding, Boulevard Barnaart 30 near **ZANDVOORT** (☎023/571 3035; April–Oct). Haarlem's own site, *De Liede*, is at Lieover 68 (☎023/533 2360; bus #2).

For **lunches**, *Café Mephisto*, Grote Markt 29, is open all day and serves Dutch food for €7–11, snacks for much less. *Café 1900*, Barteljorisstraat 10, is also a good place for lunch, serving drinks and snacks in a *fin-de-siècle* interior. In the evening, there's *Alfonso's* **restaurant**, Oude Groenmarkt 8, which does Tex-Mex meals for around €11; *Adagio*, Lange Veerstraat 17, which serves Italian meals for around €16; or the Indonesian *De Lachende Javaen* on Frankestraat, with *rijsttafels* from €18. *Ze Crack*, at the junction of Lange Veerstraat and Kleine Houtstraat, is a dim, smoky **bar** with good music and beer by the pint, or for a little traditional character, try the *proeflokaal* (a spirit-tasting room turned bar) *In den Uiver*, Riviervischmarkt 13.

Leiden and around

The home of the country's most prestigious university, **LEIDEN** has an academic air. The students give the town a certain energy, and Leiden's museums are varied and comprehensive enough to merit a visit in themselves, though the town's real charm lies in the peace and prettiness of its gabled streets and canals.

Leiden's most appealing quarter is that bordered by Witte Singel and Breestraat, focusing on Rapenburg, a peaceful area of narrow pedestrian streets and canals that is home to the city's best-known attraction, the **Rijksmuseum Van Oudheden**, Rapenburg 28 (Tues–Fri 10am–5pm, Sat & Sun noon–5pm; €3.20), the country's principal archeological museum. You can see one of its major exhibits for free in the front courtyard – the first-century AD Temple of Teffeh, a gift from the Egyptian government. Inside the museum are more Egyptian artefacts, along with Classical Greek and Roman sculpture and exhibits chronicling the archeology of the country through prehistoric, Roman and medieval times. Further along Rapenburg, at no. 73, the **Hortus Botanicus** (March–Oct daily 10am–6pm; Nov–April

Mon–Fri & Sun 10am–4pm; €3.60; *www.hortus.leidenuniv.nl*) are among the oldest botanical gardens in Europe, planted in 1587. Across Rapenburg, a network of narrow streets converges on the **Pieterskerk** (daily 1.30–4pm; free), deconsecrated these days but still bearing the tomb of John Robinson, leader of the Pilgrim Fathers, who lived in a house on the site of what is now the Jan Pesijn Hofje, at Kloksteeg 21.

East of here, **Breestraat** marks the edge of Leiden's commercial centre, behind which the two rivers converge at the busiest point in town, the site of a vigorous Wednesday and Saturday **market** which sprawls right over the sequence of bridges into the blandly pedestrian Haarlemmerstraat, the town's major shopping street. Close by, the **Burcht** (daily 10/11am–11pm; free) is a rather ordinary, graffiti-daubed shell of a fort perched on a mound, whose battlements you can clamber up for a view of Leiden's roofs and towers. The nearby **Hooglandsekerk** (mid-May to mid-Sept Mon 1–3.30pm, Tues–Sat 11am–3.30/4pm; free) is a light, lofty church with a central pillar that features an epitaph to Pieter van der Werff, the burgomaster at the time of a 1574 siege by the Spanish, who became a hero by offering his own body as food. His invitation was rejected, but – the story goes – it instilled new determination in the flagging citizens. Across Oude Rijn from here, the **Museum Boerhaave**, Lange Agnietenstraat 10 (Tues–Sat 10am–5pm, Sun noon–5pm; €3.40) is a brief but absorbing guide to medical developments over the last three centuries, with some gruesome surgical implements, pickled brains and the like. Five minutes' walk away, Leiden's municipal museum, in the old Cloth Hall, or **Lakenhal**, Oude Singel 28–32 (Tues–Fri 10am–5pm, Sat & Sun noon–5pm; €3.60) has mixed rooms of furniture, tiles, glass and ceramics and a collection of paintings centred on Lucas van Leyden's *Last Judgement* triptych, plus canvases by Jacob van Swanenburgh, the first teacher of the young Rembrandt, and by Rembrandt himself. Around the corner on Molenwerf, the **Molenmuseum de Valk**, 2e Binnenvestgracht 1 (Tues–Sat 10am–5pm, Sun 1–5pm; €2.30), is located in a restored grain mill, one of twenty that used to surround Leiden, with living quarters furnished in simple, period style and a slide show recounting the history of windmills. Between here and the station at Steenstraat 1, the **National Museum of Ethnology** (Rijksmuseum voor Volkenkunde; Tues–Sun 10am–5pm; €6), has extensive sections on Indonesia and the Dutch colonies. Near the station on Darwinweg, Leiden's newest museum, **Naturalis**, the Museum of Natural History (Tues–Sun noon–6pm; during school holidays daily 10am–6pm; €7.30; *www.naturalis.nl*), boasts two dinosaurs, a prehistoric horse and a whole host of exhibits from the animal, vegetable and mineral kingdoms.

Practicalities

Leiden's **train** and **bus stations** are both situated on the northwest edge of town, no more than ten minutes' walk from the centre. The **VVV**, a short walk from the stations at Stationsweg 2d (Mon–Fri 10am–6.30pm, Sat 10am–2pm; ☎0900/222 2333; *www.leiden.nl*), has a tourist guide and, for a €1 charge, can book private rooms (③). The cheapest central **accommodation** is *The Rose*, Beestenmarkt 14 (☎071/514 6630; ⑤). For a much better deal try *Pension Witte Singel*, Singel 80 (☎071/512 4592; ④) about fifteen minutes' walk from the station, or *Pension Schaefer*, Herensingel 1a (☎071/521 8104; ③), ten minutes' walk from the station. The closest **campsite** is *Koningshof* (☎071/402 6051) in **RIJNSBURG**, 6km north of Leiden (bus #40). For **lunch**, *M'n Broer*, by the Pieterskerk at Kloksteeg 7, has a reasonable Dutch menu, while *Barrera*, on Rapenburg, has good sandwiches. In the evening, *De Brasserie*, Lange Mare 38, has Dutch food; *Splinter* is a pleasant, reasonably priced vegetarian restaurant at Noordeinde 30; and the studenty *La Bota*, Herensteeg 11, by the Pieterskerk, has great-value food and beers. The Central Library, Nieuwstraat 4 (☎071/514 9943) has **Internet** access.

Around Leiden

Along with Haarlem to the north, Leiden is the best base for seeing something of the Dutch **bulbfields** which flourish here in spring. The view from the train can be sufficient in itself as the line cuts directly through the main growing areas, the fields divided into stark geometric blocks of pure colour. Should you want to get closer, make a bee-line for **LISSE**, home to the **Keukenhof Gardens** (late-March to late-May daily 8am–7.30pm; €9; *www.keukenhof.nl*), the largest flower gardens in the world. Some six million blooms are on show for their full flowering period, complemented, in case of harsh winters, by 5000 square metres of greenhouses. Special buses (#54) run daily to the Keukenhof from Leiden bus station twice an hour. You can also see the industry in action in **AALSMEER**, 23km north of Leiden, whose **flower auction**, held daily in a building approximately the size of 125 football pitches (Mon–Fri 7.30–11am; €4.50; *www.vba.nl*), trades roughly €1.5 billion of plants and flowers a year.

The Hague

With its urbane atmosphere, **THE HAGUE (Den Haag)** is different from any other Dutch city. Since the sixteenth century it's been the Netherlands' political capital and the focus of national institutions, and its older buildings are a rather subdued collection with little of Amsterdam's flamboyance. Diplomats and delegates from multinational businesses ensure that many of the city's hotels and restaurants are firmly in the expense-account category, and the nightlife is similarly packaged. But, away from this mediocrity, The Hague does have cheaper and livelier bars and restaurants, as well as some excellent museums.

Right in the centre, the **Binnenhof** is the home of the Dutch parliament. Count William II built a castle here in the thirteenth century, and the settlement that grew up around it became known as the "Count's Domain", or *'s Gravenhage* which served as the city's official name right up until the 1990s. The present complex is a rather mundane affair, the small **Hof Vijver** lake mirroring the symmetry of the facade; inside there's little to see except the **Ridderzaal**, a slender-turreted structure used for state occasions that can be viewed on regular guided tours from the information office at Binnenhof 8a (Mon–Sat 10am–3.45pm; €3.40). Immediately east, the **Royal Picture Gallery Mauritshuis**, Korte Vijverberg 8 (Tues–Sat 10am–5pm, Sun 11am–5pm; €6.80; *www.mauritshuis.nl*), located in a magnificent seventeenth-century mansion, is of more interest, famous for its extensive range of Flemish and Dutch paintings from the fifteenth to eighteenth centuries. Early works include paintings by Memling, Rogier van der Weyden and the Antwerp master, Quentin Matsys; there's also a number of Adriaen Brouwer's characteristically ribald canvases, work by Rubens, including a typically grand *Portrait of Isabella Brant*, his first wife, and the intriguing *Adam and Eve in Paradise* – a collaboration between Rubens, who painted the figures, and Jan Bruegel the Elder, who filled in the animals and landscape. In the same room are two examples of the work of Rubens' assistant, Van Dyck. There are also numerous works by Jan Steen, and several by Rembrandt, most notably the *Anatomy Lesson of Dr Tulp* from 1632, the artist's first commission in Amsterdam. West of the Binnenhof, the **Gevangenpoort**, Buitenhof 33, with its Prisoner's Gate Museum (Tues–Fri 10am–5pm, Sat & Sun noon–5pm; last tour 4pm; €3.60; *www.gevangenpoort.nl*), was originally part of the city fortifications. Used as a prison until the nineteenth century, it now contains an array of guillotine blades, racks and gibbets, with the old cells in a good state of preservation. Down the street at Buitenhof 35, the **Prince William V Gallery** (Tues–Sun 11am–4pm; €1.40, free with Mauritshuis ticket) has paintings by Rembrandt, Jordaens and Paulus Potter, but it's more interesting as a reconstruction of a typical eighteenth-century gallery, with paintings crammed on the walls from floor to ceiling.

Ten minutes' walk north along Noordeinde, the **Panorama Mesdag**, Zeestraat 65b (Mon–Sat 10am–5pm, Sun noon–5pm; €3.40; *www.panorama-mesdag.com*), was designed in the late nineteenth century by the local painter Hendrik Mesdag. It's a depiction of The Hague's neighbouring seaside resort of Scheveningen as it would have appeared in 1881, completed in four months with help from his wife and the young G.H. Breitner, and so naturalistic that it takes a few moments for the skills of lighting and perspective to become apparent. Five minutes away at Laan van Meerdervoort 7f, the house Mesdag bought as a home

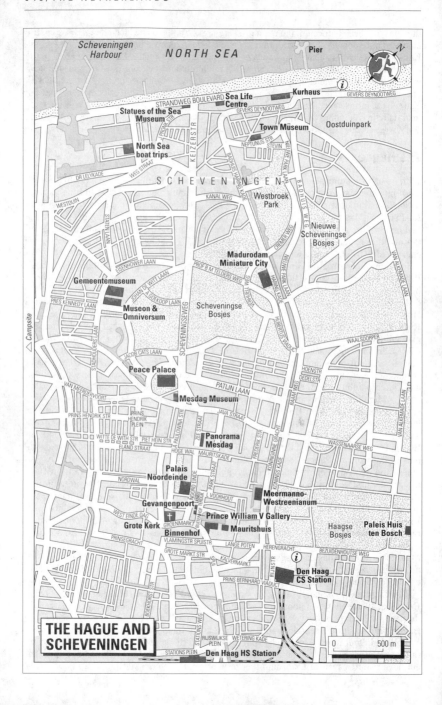

Scheveningen Harbour

NORTH SEA

Pier

i

STRANDWEG BOULEVARD

Sea Life Centre

Kurhaus

GEVERS DEYNOOTWEG

Statues of the Sea Museum

GEVERS DEYNOOTWEG

Town Museum

Oostduinpark

PRINA STR

KEIZERSTR

North Sea boat trips

NEPTUNUS STR

STEVIN

NIEUWE PARK LAAN

DR LELYKADE

WEG STRAAT

BADHUIS HARING KADE

S C H E V E N I N G E N

BADHUIS WEG

WESTDUIN

STATEN LAAN

KANAL WEG

Westbroek Park

Nieuwe Scheveningse Bosjes

VAN ALKEMADE LAAN

ORANJE BUITENS

△ Campsite

EISENHOWER LAAN

Gemeentemuseum

JOHAN DE WITT LAAN

A GOEKOOP LAAN

PROF B M TELDERS WEG

Madurodam Miniature City

HARING KADE

PRES KENNEDY LAAN

Museon & Omniversum

SCHEVENINGSEWEG

Scheveningse Bosjes

NIEUWE PARK LAAN

HUBERTUS VIADUCT

WAALSDORPER

STADHOUDERS LAAN

JACOB CATS LAAN

RAAM WEG

HOENSTR

DEDELSTR

VAN MEERDERVOORT

Peace Palace

PATIJN LAAN

VAN ALKEMADE LAAN

Mesdag Museum

JAVA STRAAT

WASSENAARSE WEG

PRINS HENDRIK STR

PRINS HENDRIK PLEIN

PAULOWNA STR

ZEE STRAAT

FREDERIK STR

KONINGINNE GRACHT

WITTE DE WITH STR

PIET HEIN STR

Panorama Mesdag

ELAND STRAAT

HOGE WAL

MAURITSKADE

KONINGS KADE

NORDWAL

Palais Noordeinde

NOORD EINDE

PARK STRAAT

VOORHOUT

Meermanno-Westreenianum

Gevangenpoort

WEST EINDE DAG

GROENMARKT

BUITENHOF

Prince William V Gallery

Grote Kerk

Binnenhof

Mauritshuis

Haagse Bosjes

Paleis Huis ten Bosch

PRINSEGRACHT

VLAMINGSTR SPUISTR

LANGE POTEN

HERENGRACHT

BEZUIDENHOUTSE WEG

GROTE MARKT STR

KALVERMARKT

RIJN STR

i

BLOKHURST STR

PRINS BERNHARD VIADUCT

Den Haag CS Station

THE HAGUE AND SCHEVENINGEN

STATIONS WEG

RIJSWIJKSE WETERING KADE

0   500 m

STATIONS PLEIN

Den Haag HS Station

and gallery today contains the **Mesdag Museum** (Mon–Fri 10am–5pm; €3.40), with a collection of Hague School paintings alongside works by Corot, Rousseau, Delacroix and Millet. Around the corner, framing Carnegieplein, the **Peace Palace** (guided tours: Mon–Fri 10am, 11am, 2pm & 3pm; June–Sept also 4pm; €2.30) is home to the Court of International Justice, with tapestries, urns, marble and stained glass on show inside – the donations of various world leaders. North, the **Gemeentemuseum**, Stadhouderslaan 41 (Tues–Sun 11am–5pm; €6.80; bus #4 from Centraal Station), is the most diverse of the city's museums, with outstanding collections of musical instruments and Islamic ceramics, and an array of modern art which traces the development of Dutch painting through the Romantic, Hague and Expressionist schools to the De Stijl movement – the museum has the world's largest collection of Mondriaan's paintings. Halfway between The Hague and Scheveningen is one of the city's best-known attractions, the moderately diverting **Madurodam Miniature City** (daily 9am–6/8/10pm; €10; *www.madurodam.nl*; tram #1/ #9), a scale model of a Dutch town.

Practicalities

The city has two **train stations** – "Den Haag HS" (short for Hollands Spoor) and about 1km to the north "Den Haag CS" (Centraal Station). Trains stop at one or the other and sometimes both; the latter is the more convenient, being next to the VVV (Mon–Sat 9am–5.30pm, July & Aug also Sun 10am–2pm; ☎0900/340 3505; *www.denhaag.com*). Accommodation can be quite expensive. The VVV has a small stock of private rooms (③), or there's a cluster of seedy but reasonably priced hotels just outside Den Haag HS station: the cheapest is *Aristo*, Stationsweg 164–166 (☎070/389 0847; ③), although you get a far better deal 4km north of the centre at the beach resort of **SCHEVENINGEN**, where hotels are more plentiful and a little cheaper; it's a short ride on tram #1/#7/#9 from Den Haag CS, or tram #8/#11 from Den Haag HS. In Scheveningen, try *Bali*, Badhuisweg 1 (☎070/350 2434; ⑤) or one of the group on the seafront road Zeekant that includes the comfortable *Aquarius*, Zeekant 107 (☎070/354 3543; ⑥). There are three **hostels** in Scheveningen: *Scheveningen*, Gevers Deynootweg 2 (☎070/354 7003; ③); *Marion*, Havenkade 3a (☎070/350 5050; ③); and pleasant *HI City Hostel*, Scheepmakerstraat 27 (☎070/315 7878, *www.njhc/denhaag*; ③). For **camping**, the best and largest site in the area, *Kijkduinpark*, Machiel Vrijenhoeklaan 450 (☎070/448 2271) lies just behind the beach at **KIJKDUIN** (bus #4 from CS or bus #26 from HS).

There are plenty of cheap places to **eat** around the town centre: *Greve*, Torenstraat 138, north of Grote Kerk, has snacks and full meals; *Pinelli*, Dagelikse Groenmarkt 31, serves pizzas; whilst Indonesian snacks are served at *Brasserie Surakarta*, Prinsestraat 13. There are several options on the streets around Denneweg and Frederikstraat, just north of Lange Voorhout, amongst them the popular vegetarian *De Dageraad*, Hooikade 4. In Scheveningen, the Haven harbour has some excellent places to eat fresh fish by the waterside: try the inexpensive *Bistro aan de Haven*, Lelykade 15, or the more upmarket *Ducdalf*, Lelykade 5. For **drinking**, aim for the studenty bar *Zwarte Ruiter* in the busy square south of the Hague's Grote Kerk. For **Internet** access try Internetcafé, Elandstraat 48 (☎070/363 6286).

Delft

DELFT, 2km inland from The Hague, has considerable charm, with its gabled red-roofed houses standing beside tree-lined canals. The pastel colours of the pavements, brickwork and bridges give the town a faded tranquillity – though one that is increasingly hard to find beneath the tourist onslaught during summer. The town is perhaps best known for **Delftware**, the clunky blue and white ceramics to which the town gave its name in the seventeenth century. If you've already slogged through the vast collection in Amsterdam's Rijksmuseum, it needs no introduction, but for those sufficiently interested, **De Porceleyne Fles**, Rotterdamseweg 196, a factory producing Delftware, is open for visits (Mon–Sat 9am–5pm, April–Oct also Sun 9.30am–5pm; €2.30), and the **Huis Lambert van Meerten**

Museum, Oude Delft 199 (Tues–Sat 10am–5pm, Sun 1–5pm; €2.30; *www.royaldelft.com*) has a large collection of Delft and other tiles.

Markt is the best place to start exploring, with the **Nieuwe Kerk** at one end (April–Oct Mon–Sat 9am–6pm, Sun noon–6pm; Nov–March Mon–Sat 11am–4pm, Sun noon–4pm; €1.80), under restoration and with a 103m tower (closes 30min earlier; €1.50) that gives a wonderful view of the town. The rather uninspiring interior contains the burial vaults of the Dutch royal family. Only the Mausoleum of William the Silent grabs your attention, a hotch-potch of styles concocted by Hendrik de Keyser, architect of the Renaissance **Stadhuis** opposite. South of here, **Wynhaven**, another old canal, leads to Hippolytusbuurt and the Gothic **Oude Kerk** (same hours as Nieuwe Kerk; €1.80), arguably the town's finest building. Simple and unbuttressed with an unhealthily leaning tower, it has an intricately carved pulpit dating from 1548, with figures emphasized in false perspective. Opposite is the former Convent of St Agatha, or **Prinsenhof** (Tues–Sat 10am–5pm, Sun 1–5pm; €2.30), housing Delft's municipal art collection (a good group of works including paintings by Aertsen and Honthorst), and restored in the style of the late sixteenth century when it served as William the Silent's base in his revolt against the Spanish. It was also the scene of his assassination; the mark of the bullets can still be seen on the walls. Finally, the **Royal Army and Weapon Museum** near the station (Mon–Fri 10am–5pm, Sat & Sun noon–5pm; €3.40) is worth a visit, with its good display of weaponry, uniforms and military accoutrements from the Spanish wars to the 1950s.

From the **train station**, it's a short walk into town and the **VVV** at Markt 83–85 (Mon–Fri 9am–5.30pm, Sat 9am–5pm; mid-April to Sept also Sun 10am–3pm; ☎015/212 6100, *www.vvvdelft.nl*), which can find you the best **accommodation** deals in the centre; try *Van Domburg*, Voldersgracht 24 (☎015/212 3029; ②). The **campsite**, *De Delftse Hout*, is at Kortftlaan 5 (☎015/213 0040; bus #64 from station). The cheapest **eating** is at a number of student mensas (term-time only) such as *De Koornbeurs* near the main square and *Jansbrug*, Kornmarkt 50–52. *Willem Van Oranje*, centrally located on Markt, has pancakes, *uitsmijters* (ham or cheese with eggs), and light meals for around €4.50 and three-course menus for €9. *Locus Publicus*, Brabantse Turfmarkt 67, is a popular local **bar**, serving a staggering array of beers as well as sandwiches. The library, Kruisstraat 71 (☎015/212 3450), has **Internet** access.

Rotterdam

Just beyond Delft lies **ROTTERDAM**, at the heart of a maze of rivers and artificial waterways which forms the seaward outlet of the rivers Rhine (Rijn in Dutch) and Maas. An important port as far back as the fourteenth century, it was one of the major cities of the Dutch Republic, and today, with the adjoining dockland area of **Europoort**, is the largest port in the world. The Luftwaffe bombed the town centre to pieces in 1940, and rebuilding has produced a sterile assembly of concrete and glass. However, the city has its moments, not least in one of the best and most overlooked galleries in the country, the Boymans-Van Beuningen Museum.

Southeast of the station, the **Lijnbaan** was Europe's first pedestrianized shopping precinct, completed in 1953. Beyond here lies some of the city centre's more fanciful modern architecture, and the seventeenth-century mansion at Korte Hoogstraat 31 that houses the **Schielandshuis Museum** (Tues–Fri 10am–5pm, Sat & Sun 11am–5pm; €2.70), featuring displays on the city's history. A couple of minutes south, the old city docks are enclosed by the Boompjes, a former sea dyke that's now a major motorway leading southwest to the **Euromast**, on a rather lonely park corner beside the Nieuwe Maas, originally just a drab, grey observation platform thrown up in 1960, but to which was later added the 185m-high **Spacetower** (daily: April–Sept 10am–7/10.30pm; Oct–March 10am–5pm; €7), which gives spectacular views. North of here, the **Boymans-Van Beuningen Museum**, Mathenesserlaan 18–20 (Tues–Sat 10am–5pm, Sun 11am–5pm; €5.70; *www.boijmans.rotterdam.nl*), is

Rotterdam's one great attraction, accessible from Centraal Station by tram #5 or walkable from Eendrachtsplein metro. It's an enormous museum, with a superb collection of work by the Surrealists Dalí, Magritte, Ernst and de Chirico. The Van der Vorm collection on the first floor contains work by Monet, Van Gogh, Picasso, Gauguin, Cézanne and Munch, and a series of small galleries alongside house paintings by most of the significant artists of the Barbizon and Hague Schools. Among the earlier canvases are several by Hieronymus Bosch, Pieter Bruegel the Elder's mysterious *Tower of Babel*, some Jan Steens, Gerrit Dou's *The Quack* and Rembrandt's intimate *Titus at his Desk*.

If nothing in the city centre can be called exactly picturesque, **Delfshaven** goes some way to make up for it. A good 45-minute walk southwest of Centraal Station – fifteen minutes by tram #6 or #9 – it was from here that the Pilgrims set sail for America in 1620, changing to the more reliable *Mayflower* in Plymouth. Delfshaven was only incorporated into Rotterdam in 1886 and managed to survive World War II virtually intact. It was long a neglected area, but the town council has recognized its tourist potential and has set about conserving and restoring the locality. The **Dubbelde Palmboom Museum**, Voorhaven 12 (Tues–Fri 10am–5pm, Sat & Sun 11am–5pm; €2.70), once a *jenever* distillery, is now a historical museum with a wide-ranging if unexceptional collection of objects pertaining to life in the Maas delta.

Practicalities

Rotterdam's large centre is bordered by its main rail terminal, **Centraal Station**, which serves as the hub of a useful **tram** and **metro** system, though it's a seamy, hostile place late at night. The main VVV office is a ten-minute walk away at Coolsingel 67 (Mon–Thurs 9.30am–6pm, Fri 9.30am–9pm, Sat 9.30am–5pm; April–Sept also Sun noon–5pm; ☎0900/403 4065; *www.vvv.rotterdam.nl*), where you can pick up free city transport maps and a comprehensive city brochure (€1.80). There are plenty of central, reasonably priced **hotels**. Southwest of the station is *Wilgenhof*, Heemraadssingel 92–94 (☎010/425 4892; ⑤; tram #1/#7 or bus #38/#45). Immediately north of the station, *Bienvenue*, Spoorsingel 24 (☎010/466 9394; ③), is excellent value. A five-minute walk from Wilhelminaplein metro, on the south bank of the Nieuwe Maas, is the stunning *New York*, Koninginnenhoofd 1 (☎010/439 0500; ③), occupying the building where trans-Atlantic cruise liners once docked; the place breathes atmosphere and also boasts an excellent restaurant. The **HI hostel**, *City Hostel Rotterdam*, is a 25-minute walk from the station, Rochussenstraat 107 (☎010/436 5763; ②; tram #4). The nearest **campsite**, *Stadscamping* (☎010/415 3440), is north of the station at Kanaalweg 84 (bus #33).

The cheapest sit-down **meal** in town is at *Eetcafé Streetlife*, Jonker Franslaan 237; *De Eend*, Mauritsweg 29 (Mon–Fri 4.30–7.30pm), is also inexpensive. Oude and Nieuwe Binnenweg support a number of good *eetcafés*, including *Rotown*, Nieuwe Binnenweg 19. *De Consul*, Westersingel 28, serves a variety of dishes at reasonable prices, and vegetarians should head for *Eetcafé BlaBla*, Piet Heynstraat 35 in Delfshaven. *Grand Café Dudok*, off Beursplein on Meent, is a good place to **drink**, and *Jazzcafe Dizzy*, 's-Gravendijkwal 127, has regular live music.

From the **Leuvenhaven** harbour, there are numerous **boat trips** through the harbour (year-round; 1hr 15min; €7.50), along the river delta (July & Aug; 2hr 15min; €12) and day-trips south to the Deltawerken (July & Aug; 7hr; €35; reserve in advance); contact Spido for details (☎010/275 9988; *www.spido.nl*).

Gouda

A pretty little place some 25km northeast of Rotterdam, **GOUDA** is almost everything you'd expect of a Dutch country town: a ring of quiet canals encircling ancient buildings and old quays. More surprisingly, its **Markt** is the largest in Holland – a reminder of the town's prominence as a centre of the medieval cloth trade, and later of its success in the manufacture of cheeses and clay pipes. The touristy **cheese market**, held here every Thursday morning (10am–12.30pm) in June, July and August, is a shadow of its former self – and mercilessly milked by the tour operators – but out of these times the Markt is worth visiting. Slapbang in the middle, the elegant Gothic **Stadhuis** dates from 1450; on the north side is the **Waag**, a tidy seventeenth-century building decorated with a detailed relief of cheese-weighing, with the remains of the old wooden scales inside; the two top floors (April–Oct Tues–Sun 1–5pm, Thurs 10am–5pm; €1.40) show an only marginally interesting display of cheesy matters. To the south, just off the square, the **St Janskerk** (April–Oct Mon–Sat 9am–5pm; Nov–March Mon–Sat 10am–4pm; €1.60) was built in the sixteenth century and is famous for its magnificent stained-glass windows, the best executed between 1555 and 1571 when the country was still Catholic. The post-Reformation windows, dating from 1572 to 1603, are more secular: the *Relief of Leiden*, for example, shows William the Silent retaking the town from the Spanish. By the side of the church, the flamboyant **Lazarus Gate** of 1609 was once part of the town's leper hospital until it was moved to form the back entrance to the Catharina Gasthuis, now the **Stedelijk Museum** (Mon–Sat 10am–5pm, Sun noon–5pm; €2.30), whose collection incorporates a fine selection of early religious art, notably a large triptych, *Life of Mary*, by Dirk Barendsz, and a characteristically austere *Annunciation* by the Bruges artist Pieter Pourbus. Other highlights include a spacious hall, Het Ruim, dominated by two group portraits by Ferdinand Bol, and a selection of Hague and Barbizon School canvases. Gouda's other museum, **De Moriaan** (Mon–Fri 10am–5pm, Sat 10am–12.30pm & 1.30–5.30pm, Sun noon–5pm; free with Stedelijk ticket), in an old merchant's house at Westhaven 29, has a mixed bag of exhibits, from clay pipes to ceramics and tiles.

Gouda's **train** and **bus stations** are north of the centre, ten minutes from the VVV, Markt 27 (Mon–Sat 9am–5pm; June–Aug also Sun noon–3pm; ☎0182/513666, *www.vvv .groenehart.nl*), which offers a limited supply of private rooms (③). The most reasonably priced **hotel** is *De Utrechtsche Dom*, fifteen minutes' walk from the train station at Geuzenstraat 6 (☎0182/528 833, *www.rsnet.nl/hotel*; ③); otherwise, try *H't Trefpunt*, Westhaven 46 (☎0182/512879; ④), or *De Keizerskroon*, Keizerstraat 11 (☎0182/528 096; ⑤). For **food**, there are literally hundreds of cafés catering to the swarms of summer day-trippers. You can eat cheaply at *'t Groot Stedelijk*, Markt 44, among other places; *'t Goudse Winkeltje*, Achter de Kerk 9a, has good pancakes; and you can get a decent Indonesian at *Warung Srikandi*, Lange Groenendaal 108. For a **drink**, find your way to the excellent *Eetcafé Vidocq*, Koster Gijzenstraat 8, or check out *Heeren Van Goude* on Zeugstraat, which is usually full of young people.

Utrecht

"I groaned with the idea of living all winter in so shocking a place", wrote Boswell in 1763, and **UTRECHT**, surrounded by shopping centres and industrial developments, still promises little as you approach. But the centre, with its distinctive sunken canals – whose brick cellar warehouses have been converted into chic cafés and restaurants – is one of the country's most pleasant.

The focal point is the **Dom Tower**, built between 1321 and 1382, which at over 110m is the highest church tower in the country, soaring to a delicate octagonal lantern added in 1380. A guided tour (Mon–Sat 10am–5pm, Sun noon–5pm; last entry 4pm; €3.40) takes you unnervingly close to the top, from where the gap between the tower and the Gothic **Dom Kerk** is most apparent. Only the eastern part of the great cathedral remains today, the nave having collapsed in 1674. It's worth peering inside (Mon–Fri 10/11am–4/5pm, Sat 10am–3.30pm, Sun 2–4pm; free) to get a sense of the hangar-like space the building once had and to wander through the Kloostergang, the fourteenth-century cloisters that link the cathedral to the chapterhouse, now part of the university. South of the church at Nieuwe Gracht 63, the national collection of ecclesiastical art, the **Catharijne Convent Museum** (Tues–Fri 10am–5pm, Sat & Sun 11am–5pm; €4.50; *www.catharijneconvent.nl*) has a wonderfully exhibited mass of paintings, manuscripts and church ornaments from the ninth century on, including work by Geertgen tot Sint Jans, Rembrandt, Hals and, best of all, a luminously beautiful *Virgin and Child* by Van Cleve. Further along, the **Centraal Museum**, Agnietenstraat 1 (Tues–Sun 11am–5pm; €6.80; *www.centraalmuseum.nl*) features a good collection of paintings by sixteenth- and seventeenth-century Utrecht artists, including the vividly individual portraits of Van Scorel's Jerusalem Brotherhood. The architecture of the 1920s *De Stijl* movement is best demonstrated by the **Rietveld-Schröder house** on Prins Hendriklaan (by appointment only; contact the Centraal Museum on ☎030/236 2310).

Practicalities

Train and **bus stations** both lead into the Hoog Catharijne shopping centre. The main VVV office is at Vredenburg 90 (Mon–Fri 9am–6pm, Sat 9am–5pm; ☎0900/414 1414; *www.tref.nl/utrecht/vvv*), a five-minute walk away. Of **hotels**, try *Ouwi*, FC Donderstraat 12 (☎030/271 6303; *www.bookings.nl*; ④), a fifteen-minute walk northeast of the centre; or *Parkhotel*, Tolsteegsingel 34 (☎030/251 6712; ③), a similar distance southeast of the station. There's a nice **HI hostel**, *Ridderhofstad "Rhijnauwen"*, in an old country manor house 6km out at Rhijnauwenselaan 14 in **BUNNIK** (☎030/656 1277; ②; bus #40/#41 from the station). The pleasant *Strowis* hostel, Boothstraat 8 (☎030/238 0280, *www.strowis.nl*; ④) is a more central option, a fifteen-minute walk from Centraal Station or a short ride on bus #3/#4/#8/#11 to the Janskerkhof stop, plus a two-minute walk. The well-equipped **campsite**, *De Berenkuil*, Ariënslaan 5 (☎030/271 3870) is served by bus #57. **Restaurants** are mainly situated along Oudegracht and the Lijnmarkt; the best is the moderately priced *Stadskasteel Oudaen* at no. 99, the oldest house in town, which serves beer from its own steam brewery downstairs. Also try *Milky*, a good vegetarian restaurant off the canal, Zakkerdragssteeg 22. A really cheap option is to go for a *dagschotel* at *Eetcafé De Baas*, Lijnmarkt 8, and there's the grand café *Stairway to Heaven*, Mariaplaats 11, with moderately priced meals and regular live music. *De Werfking*, Oude Gracht 123, has good vegetarian food. The city's best **bars** cluster around the junction of Oude Gracht and the Lijnmarkt; check out the lively *De Witte Ballons*, Lijnmarkt 10–12, or *Café Belgie* around the corner, Oude Gracht 196. The Central Library has Internet access.

BEYOND THE RANDSTAD

Outside the Randstad towns, the Netherlands is relatively unknown territory to visitors. In the north, the island of **Texel** has the country's most complete beach experience, with plenty of birdlife and the world's biggest catamaran races. In the northeast, the main draw is **Groningen**, a lively, cosmopolitan town with a buzzing streetlife – especially after dark – and a stunning museum and art gallery. To the south, the countryside grows steadily more rolling as you head towards Germany. The town of **Arnhem** is famous for its bridge, a key objective in the failed Allied attack of 1944; it also boasts one of the country's best modern art museums and is a good base for the nearby **Hoge Veluwe National Park**. Further south, in the provinces of North Brabant and Limburg, the landscape slowly fills out, rolling into a rougher countryside of farmland and forests and eventually into the hills around **Maastricht**, a city whose vibrant, pan-European air, is a world away from the clogs and canals of the north. The southwest, near the Belgian border across from Bruges and Antwerp, is a land apart, with the **Delta Expo** near Middelburg dramatically highlighting the country's long-standing tussle with the sea for supremacy.

The island of Texel

The largest of the islands of the Waddenzee framing the north coast of the country – and the easiest to get to (2hr from Amsterdam) – **Texel** (*tessel*) is a lush, green thumb of land 24km long by 9km wide, speckled with small villages and lined on its western side by large areas of dunes and extensive beaches. It's a diverse and pretty island, and is one of Europe's most important breeding-grounds for birds; crowds gather here during the summer, keen to follow the many walking routes and cycle paths (you can rent bikes easily from just about every hamlet on the island). **Ferries** from **DEN HELDER** on the mainland depart every hour (around €4.50; coming from Amsterdam, ask for an all-in discounted "Waddenbiljet"). From the dock, buses can shuttle you the 3km to Texel's tiny "capital", **DEN BURG**; one wander and you've seen it all. On the coast 3km southeast of Den Burg is **OUDESCHILD**, home to the **Beachcombers' Museum** (Juttersmuseum; Tues–Sat 10am–5pm; €3.60), a fascinating collection of marine junk picked up from offshore wrecks, while in the opposite direction is **DE KOOG**, halfway up the western coast, with a good sandy beach and the **EcoMare** nature centre, Ruyslaan 92 (daily 9am–5pm; €5.70), highlight of which is a refuge for lost birds and seals (feeding at 11am & 3pm); they also organize excursions to the Wad, the banks of sand and mud to the east of the island that are a regular gathering-place for seals. The northern tip of Texel is occupied by the solitary hamlet of **DE COCKSDORP**, its wedge of lonely little houses trailing along a slender inlet; ferries run from here to the neighbouring island of **Vlieland** (one-way €8; return €12.50), from where a different ferry shuttles back to the mainland at **HARLINGEN**, terminus of the train line.

Den Burg's **VVV** is at Emmalaan 66 (Mon–Fri 9am–6pm, Sat 9am–5pm; ☎0222/314741). The cheapest **hotel** is in Den Burg: *'t Koogerend*, Kogerstraat 94 (☎0222/313301; ②), while there's a **hostel**, *Panorama*, at Schanseweg 7 (☎0222/315441; ②). **Campers** are spoilt for choice: close to Den Burg is the small, well-run *De Koorn Aar*, Grensweg 388 (☎0222/312931; April–Oct); among the beachside dunes in De Koog is *Kogerstrand*, Badweg 33 (☎0222/317208; April–Oct); *Euroase Texel*, Bosrandweg 395 (☎0222/317290) also has bungalows on the beach; and there's *De Krim*, Roggeslootweg 6 in De Cocksdorp (☎0222/390111). The best **food** in Den Burg is *De Worsteltent*, Smitweg 6. In De Koog there are plenty of Mexican and Chinese restaurants, with *Het Pruttelhuus*, Dorpsstraat 170, a friendly local option, as well as *Café Sam-Sam* and *De Metro*, both on Dorpsstraat, for **drinking**.

Groningen

Nominally a fiefdom of the Bishops of Utrecht from 1040 until 1536, the northern city of **GRONINGEN** was once an important centre of trade. Heavily bombed in World War II, it is an architectural jumble with few notable sights, but its large, prestigious university gives it a cosmopolitan feel quite unexpected in this rustic part of the country. The centre of town is **Grote Markt**, a large open space that was badly damaged by wartime bombing and has been reconstructed with little imagination. At one corner is the **Martinikerk** (Easter–Nov Tues–Sat noon–5pm; €1.10), a beacon of architectural sanity in the surrounding shambles. Though the oldest parts of the church go back to 1180, most of it is mid-fifteenth-century Gothic. The vault paintings in the nave are beautifully restored, and the lofty choir holds two series of frescoes on the walled-up niches of the clerestory. Adjoining the church is the seventeenth-century tower **Martinitoren** (April–Sept daily 11am/noon–4.30pm; Oct–March Sat & Sun noon–4.30pm; €1.40). West along A-Kerkhof NZ from Grote Markt, the comprehensive **Noordelijk Scheepvaart Museum**, Brugstraat 24 (Tues–Sat 10am–5pm, Sun 1–5pm; €3.60), has displays on maritime trade with the Indies, the development of peat canals and a series of reconstructed nautical workshops. In the same building, the smaller **Niemeyer Tabaksmuseum** is devoted to tobacco smoking from 1600 to the present day. The city's biggest and best museum, the **Groninger Museum** (Tues–Sun 10am–5pm; €6.10; *www.groninger-museum.nl*) is housed in spectacular pavilions across from the train station. The west pavilion is given over to travelling exhibitions but also houses the permanent art collection, including Rubens' energetic *Adoration of the Magi* among a small selection of seventeenth-century works, Hague school paintings, and a number of late works by the

Expressionists of the Groningen De Ploeg group. Besides this, diaphanous drapes guide you through vitrines of Far Eastern ceramics and ivory.

Practicalities

Groningen's **bus** and **train stations** are on the south side of town, fifteen minutes' walk from the **VVV** at Ged Kattendiep 6 (Mon–Fri 9am–5.30pm, Sat 10am–5pm; ☎0900/202 3050; *www.groningen.nl*); they'll give you a short list of private rooms (②), though few are near the city centre. Otherwise, the cheapest **accommodation** is in the dorms of *Simplon Jongerenhotel*, north of the centre at Boterdiep 73 (☎050/313 5221; *www.xs4all.nl/~simplon*; ②). Three reasonably priced **hotels** are just south of the Grote Markt: *Friesland*, Kleine Pelsterstraat 4 (☎050/312 1307; ③); *Garni Groningen*, Damsterdiep 94 (☎050/313 5435; ④); and the likeable old *Weeva*, Gedempte Zuiderdiep 8 (☎050/312 9919; ⑤), with a decent restaurant. Bus #4 from the train station runs via Peizerweg on a ten-minute ride to the **campsite** *Stadspark* (☎050/525 1624; mid-March to mid-Oct).

For Groningen's cheapest **food**, head for *Roezemoes*, Gedempte Zuiderdiep 15. Best of the rest are concentrated around Poelestraat: *Bistango*, at no. 14, is a decent Tex-Mex with veggie specialities; the pizzeria *Costa Smeralda* next door is slightly cheaper; *'t Pakhuis*, around the corner at Peperstraat 8, has good Dutch snacks and a lively **bar** in an atmospheric building. On the south side of Grote Markt is a flank of outdoor **cafés**, best of which are the old-style brown café *Der Witz*, no. 47, and *Hooghoudt*, no. 42, which also contains a night café serving food until 4am at weekends. *De Smederij*, over the canal west of the centre at Tuinstraat 2, is an *eetcafé* with a great atmosphere; in the opposite direction at Akerstraat 24, you'll find high-quality, moderately priced fish and vegetarian food in *Brussels Lof*.

Thanks to its large student population, Groningen has good **nightlife**. For **live music** try *Vera*, in the basement at Oosterstraat 44; or *Troubadour*, Peperstraat 19. *De Spieghel*, Peperstraat 11, has live jazz most nights. Good **clubs** include *Index*, Poelestraat 53, and *Palace*, Gelkingestraat 1, which occasionally hosts live bands. There's an **Internet** café at Turfsingel 94.

Arnhem and around

Way south of Groningen, **ARNHEM** was once a wealthy resort, a watering-hole to which the merchants of Amsterdam and Rotterdam would flock to idle away their fortunes. Last century it became better known as the place where thousands of British and Polish troops died in the failed Allied airborne operation of September 1944, code-named "**Operation Market Garden**", which gutted the greater part of the city. What you see today is not especially enticing. But Arnhem is a lively town, with plenty going on, and a good centre for seeing the numerous attractions scattered around its forested outskirts. The best of the old town is the northwest part of the centre, around **Korenmarkt**, a small square which escaped much of the wartime destruction and has one or two good facades. The streets which lead off Korenmarkt are full of restaurants and bars, but otherwise Arnhem deteriorates as you walk southeast towards the **John Frostbrug** – the "Bridge Too Far" – named after the commander of the battalion that defended it for four days. It's just an ordinary bridge, but for Dutch and British alike it remains the symbol and focus of remembrance of the battle. At its north end, the characterless **Markt** is site of the sixteenth-century church of **St Eusabius** (Tues–Sat 10/11am–4/5pm, Sun noon–4/5pm; free), reconstructed in the 1960s after wartime bombing, when a new **tower** was added (same times; €2.30). To mark the fiftieth anniversary of Operation Market Garden a glassed-in viewing platform was added to the top of the church, from where you can look down on the fifteenth-century **Stadhuis** tucked in behind. In the opposite direction, fifteen minutes' walk west from the station along Utrechtsestraat, is the **Museum voor Moderne Kunst Arnhem**, Utrechtseweg 87 (Tues–Fri 10am–5pm, Sat & Sun 11am–5pm; €4.50). It's linked to the **Historisch Museum Het Burgerweehuis**, about ten minutes' walk away at Bovenbeekstraat 21 (same times); collections include numerous archeological finds from the surrounding area, a display of Chinese, Japanese and Delft ceramics, and a modest selection of paintings, with the emphasis on views of the landscape, villages and towns of Gelderland, and canvases by the so-called magic realists.

Immediately north of Arnhem, the **Nederlands Openluchtmuseum** (April–Oct daily 10am–5pm; €10.70; *www.openluchtmuseum.nl*; bus #3 towards Alteveer and, during July & Aug, special bus #13) is a huge collection of Dutch buildings assembled here from all over the country. Where possible, buildings have been placed in groups that resemble the traditional villages of the different regions of the Netherlands – from the farmsteads of Friesland to the peat colonies of Drenthe. There are about 120 buildings in all, including examples of farmhouses, bridges and every type of Dutch windmill, and several working craft shops demonstrating traditional skills. Other parts of the museum incorporate one of the most extensive regional costume exhibitions in the country and a modest herb garden. All in all, it's an imaginative attempt to re-create the rural Dutch way of life over the past two centuries, and the museum's own guidebook (around €3.60) explains everything with academic attention to detail.

Arnhem's **train station** is on the edge of the centre, next to the **bus** and trolleybus stations. Always check the destination of buses and trolleybuses, as several routes share one number. Nearby, the **VVV**, Willemsplein 8 (Mon 11am–5.30pm, Tues–Fri 9am–5.30pm, Sat 10am–4pm; ☎0900/202 4075; *www.vvvarnhem.nl*), operates an accommodation-booking service. Among the cheaper **hotels** in the centre are *Parkzicht*, Apeldoornsestraat 16 (☎026/442 0698, *www.bookings.nl*; ③), ten minutes' walk from the station; *Rembrandt*, Paterstraat 1 (☎026/442 0153; ③), the second right off Apeldoornsestraat; and the *Old Dutch*, Stationsplein 8 (☎026/442 0792; ④). Take bus #2 in the direction of Schaarsbergen out from the centre to reach *Pension Warnsborn*, Schelmseweg 1 (☎026/442 5994; ③). The **HI hostel**, *Alteveer*, 4km north at Diepenbrocklaan 27 (☎026/442 0114; ②), can be reached on trolleybus #3 (direction Alteveer). The nearest **campsite** is *Warnsborn* (☎026/442 3469), 6km northwest at Bakenbergseweg 257 (bus #31). For **eating**, *Pizzeria Da Leone* on Korenmarkt is a good, moderately priced place and there are plenty of cheap options on Jansplein near the post office; for more traditional Dutch fare try *Old Inn*, Stationsplein 40.

World War II memorials: Oosterbeek

The area around Arnhem is scattered with the graveyards of thousands of soldiers who died during Operation Market Garden, not least **OOSTERBEEK**, a prosperous suburb 6km west of Arnhem (4 trains hourly), where the **Airborne Cemetery** is a neat, symmetrical tribute to nearly two thousand paratroopers whose bodies were brought here from the surrounding fields. Ten minutes' walk south of the station (or bus #1 from Arnhem), the village proper has spruce lawns and walls dotted with details of the battle, as well as the **Airborne Museum** (Mon–Sat 11am–5pm, Sun noon–5pm; €2.70), in the former Hotel Hartenstein on Utrechtseweg, where the British forces were besieged by the Germans for a week before retreating across the river, their numbers depleted from 10,005 to 2163. With the use of an English commentary, photographs, dioramas and military artefacts, the museum gives an excellent outline of the battle.

The Hoge Veluwe National Park and Rijksmuseum Kröller-Müller

Spreading north from the Openluchtmuseum is the **Hoge Veluwe National Park** (daily: April–Oct 8/9am–sunset; Nov–March 9am–5.30pm; €3.60; plus €4 per car; *www.hogeveluwe.nl*), a pretty area of heath and woodland. Formerly the private estate of wealthy local couple Anton and Helene Kröller-Müller, it has three entrances – one near the village of **OTTERLO** on the northwest perimeter, another near **HOENDERLOO** on the northeast edge, and a third to the south at **RIJZENBURG**, near the village of Schaarsbergen, 6km from Arnhem. There are a number of ways to get to the park **by bus**; easiest is to take the regular museum special from outside Arnhem train station (April–Oct Tues–Sun, bus

#12; hourly; €3.60 return, plus €3.60 park admission; pay the driver) which runs direct to the **Visitors' Centre** (daily 10am–5pm), where you can find information on the park. This is one of the five places where you can pick up the **white bicycles** that are left out for everyone's use at no extra charge, and which are by far the best way of getting around within the park (the other sites are outside the Kröller-Müller museum and at the three entrances). In winter, either rent a bike at Arnhem station or take bus #107 to the Otterlo entrance, a 4km white-bike ride from the Visitors' Centre.

The main thing to see is the superb **Rijksmuseum Kröller-Müller** (Tues–Sun 10am–5pm; extra €9; *www.kmm.nl*), one of the country's finest museums. It holds a wide cross-section of modern European art from Impressionism to Cubism and beyond, housed in a purpose-built structure by the Belgian architect Van de Velde. There are paintings by Dutch artists such as Mondriaan and Charley Toorop and her father Jan, as well as work by Fernand Léger and other Cubist-era artists. But the collection's crowning glory is its array of works by **Vincent Van Gogh**, housed in a large room around a central courtyard and placed in context by accompanying contemporary pictures. There are early pieces, among them *Head of a Peasant with a Pipe*, rough unsentimental paintings of labourers from around his parents' home in Brabant; penetrating later self-portraits; examples from the *Sunflowers* series and the joyful *Haystacks in Provence* and *Bridge at Arles*; and later, more sombre creations from his last years, such as *Prisoners Exercising* from 1890. Outside, behind the main building, there's a **Sculpture Park** (April–Oct Tues–Sun 10am–4.30pm; free with museum ticket), spaciously laid out with works by Rodin, Giacometti, Jacob Epstein, Barbara Hepworth and, most notably, Jean Dubuffet's *Jardin d'Email*. Some 3km north of the Visitors' Centre is the **Jachtslot St Hubertus** (April–Oct daily 11am–4.30pm; free half-hourly guided tours), an impressive Art Deco hunting lodge built for the Kröller-Müllers by H.P. Berlage in 1920.

Maastricht

Situated in a thin finger of land that reaches down between Belgium and Germany, **MAAS-TRICHT** is one of the most delightful cities in the Netherlands, located firmly in the heart of Europe and quite different from the waterland centres of the north. A cosmopolitan place, where three languages happily coexist, it's also one of the oldest towns in the country. The first settlers here were Roman, when Maastricht became an important stop on the trade route between Cologne and the coast, and the later legacy of Charlemagne – whose capital was at nearby Aachen – is manifest in two of the best Romanesque churches in the Low Countries.

The busiest of Maastricht's many squares is **Markt**, at its most crowded during the Wednesday and Friday morning **market**. At the centre of the square, the 1664 **Stadhuis** (Mon–Fri 8.30am–12.30pm & 2–5.30pm; free), a typical slice of mid-seventeenth-century Dutch civic grandeur, was designed by Pieter Post. Just west, **Vrijthof** is a grander open space flanked by a line of café terraces on one side and on the other by **St Servaaskerk** (daily 10am–5pm; €1.80). Only the crypt remains of the original tenth-century church; the rest is mostly of medieval or later construction. On the northern side of the church, the fifteenth-century Gothic cloister leads into the treasury, which holds a large collection of liturgical accessories, including a bust reliquary of St Servaas, which is carried through the town in Easter processions. The second most prominent building on the square, next door, is Maastricht's main Protestant church, the fourteenth-century **St Janskerk** (Easter–Oct Mon–Sat 11am–4pm; free), the baptistry of the church of St Servaas when it was a cathedral and nowadays competing for attention with its high fifteenth-century Gothic **tower** (€1.10 donation). Inside are some medieval murals, but otherwise climbing the tower is the church's main appeal. Maastricht's other main church, the **Onze Lieve Vrouwe Basiliek**, is a short walk south of Vrijthof, down Bredestraat, in a small shady square crammed with café tables. Founded around 1000, its dark and eerily devotional interior, with a gorgeous galleried choir, is fronted by an unusual fortified west facade. Off the north aisle, the treasury (Easter to mid-

Sept Mon–Sat 11am–5pm, Sun 1–5pm; €1.60) holds the usual array of ecclesiastical odd-ments, most notably the tunic of St Lambert, a bishop of Maastricht who was murdered at Liège in 705.

Around the corner from the square, on Plankstraat, the **Museumkelder Derlon** (Sun noon–4pm; free), in the basement of the hotel of the same name, contains a few remnants of Roman Maastricht – the remains of a temple to Jupiter, a well and several layers of pavement, discovered during the building of the present hotel in the mid-1980s. On the other side of the square lies another of Maastricht's most appealing quarters, narrow streets winding out to the fast-flowing River Jeker, which weaves around the various houses and ancient mills and the best surviving part of the city walls, the **Helpoort** of 1229. Continuing south, the Casemates in the **Waldeck Park** (guided tours: July & Aug daily 12.30pm & 2pm; rest of year Sun 2pm; €2.70) are further evidence of Maastricht's once impressive fortifications, a system of galleries created through mining between 1575 and 1825 that were used in times of siege for surprise attacks on the enemy. Fifteen minutes' walk further south are more dank passageways, hollowed out of the soft sandstone or marl that makes up the flat-topped, 110m hill of **St Pietersberg**. Of two cave systems, the **Zonneberg** is probably the better, situated on the far side of the hill at Casino Slavante (guided tours: July & Aug daily 2.15pm; €2.70). There's some evidence of wartime occupation, plus what everyone claims is Napoleon's sig-nature on a graffiti-ridden wall.

Practicalities

The centre of Maastricht is on the west bank of the river. You're likely to arrive, however, on the east bank, in the district known as Wijk, home to the **train** and **bus stations** and many of the city's hotels. The **airport** is north of the city at Beek, served by bus #61 to Markt and the train station (every 30min; takes 20min). The **VVV** is in the centre at Kleine Straat 1, at the end of the main shopping street (Mon–Sat 9am–5/6pm; May–Oct also Sun 11am–3pm; ☎043/325 2121, *www.visitmaastricht.nl*); it has copies of *Uit In Maastricht* and a tourist guide which includes a decent map and a list of private rooms (③). There are several good central **hotels**, including *La Cloche*, Bredestraat 41 (☎043/321 2407, *www.lacloche.com*; ⑤), and *Anno 1604*, Kattenstraat 11 (☎043/325 0165; ③). Hotels conveniently located for the station and the city include the two-star *De Poshoorn*, Stationstraat 47 (☎043/321 7334; ⑤) and the one-star *Le Guide* at no. 17a (☎043/321 6176; ④); the *Botel Maastricht* (☎043/321 9023; ④) is moored on the river on Maasboulevard, not far from the Helpoort, and does an excellent breakfast. For **camping**, the large and well-equipped *De Dousberg* site (☎043/343 2171; April–Oct), is a ten-minute ride from the station on bus #11 (after 6.25pm, take bus #28 towards Pottenburg and ask the driver). The same bus also takes you to the **hostel** at Dousbergweg 4 (☎043/346 6777; ②), which has access to open-air and indoor swimming pools.

Eating is never a problem in Maastricht. At the bottom end of the price scale, the street to head for is Koestraat, which runs off Cortenstraat to the south of Onze Lieve Vrouweplein. Here you'll find the excellent and cheap Indonesian *De Branding* at no. 5; the low-cost pizze-ria *Alexandria* at no. 21; a good-value bakery around the corner; and the slightly upmarket *D'n Blind Genger*, no. 3, with a varied menu and a nice atmosphere. Also nearby, down towards the river on Graanmarkt, *Caribbean Embassy* is an *eetcafé* with reasonably priced Caribbean specialities and cheap snacks, and *Reitz*, Markt 75, is a Maastricht institution serv-ing huge cones of thick Belgian-style *frites*. The **bars** on the east side of Vrijthof are packed in summer; *In den Ouden Vogelstruys*, on the corner of Platielstraat, is one of the nicest. Away from Vrijthof, *De Bóbbel*, on Wolfstraat just off Onze Lieve Vrouweplein, is a bareboards bar, lively in the early evening; *Falstaff*, on St Amorsplein, down Platielstraat from Vrijthof, is younger and noisier, with good music and a wide range of beers. For **live music** all year round try *D'n Awwe Stiene*, Kesselskade 43 (Wed, Fri & Sat 10pm–5am; €6–16). **Internet** access is at the *Centre Céramique*, five minutes from the station (☎043/350 5600; *www .centreceramique.nl*), which also houses the European Centre of Journalism, a café and a reading-room.

The Delta Expo

The southwestern province of Zeeland comprises three main peninsulas formed by the delta of the Rijn, the Maas and the Schelde rivers. On February 1, 1953, a combination of an exceptionally high spring tide and powerful northwesterly winds drove the sea over the dykes to flood much of the province; 1855 people drowned, 47,000 homes and 500km of dykes were destroyed, and some of the country's most fertile agricultural land was ruined by salt water. The government's response was to launch the **Delta Project**, one of the world's largest engineering schemes, comprising a series of dams built across the estuaries of the area's many rivers. In 1968, work on the largest of these dams ran into opposition from environmental groups, campaigning to save the mud flats, and from local fisherfolk, who saw their oyster and mussel livelihoods vanishing should the dam permanently seal off the estuary. Compromise was reached in an ecologically sound, moveable **storm surge barrier** that would close only at extreme high tides, leaving the ecosystems of the saltwater mud flats untouched. The fascinating **Delta Expo** (April–Oct daily 10am–5.30pm; €10.20; Nov–March Wed–Sun 10am–5pm; €6.80) is housed on this monumentally impressive barrier, which is worth visiting not only to appreciate the engineering skill, but also to blow away your cobwebs by walking the bleak and windswept shores either side. In spring and summer, Expo admission includes a **boat-trip** for a closer look at the huge sluice gates. Inside, start with the excellent video presentation before taking in the hi-tech, well-presented exhibition itself.

Hourly **bus** #104 from Hof van Tange on the west side of the small town of **MIDDELBURG** runs to the Expo. Middelburg itself, capital of Zeeland, is a small, picturesque place. Its VVV is a short walk from the train station at Nieuweburg 40 (Mon–Sat 9.30am–5/5.30pm; April–Oct also Sun noon–4pm; ☎0118/659900; *www.vvvmiddelburg.nl*), and the best day to be here is Thursday for the lively **market**, where local women still wear traditional costume.

travel details

Trains

Amsterdam to: Arnhem (every 30min; 1hr 10min); Delta Expo (via Middelburg; hourly; 2hr 30min); Groningen (every 30min; 2hr 20min); Haarlem (every 10min; 15min); The Hague (every 15min; 45min); Leiden (every 15min; 35min); Maastricht (hourly; 2hr 30min); Rotterdam (every 30min; 1hr 10min); Schiphol Airport (every 15min; 20min); Texel (via Den Helder; every 30min; 1hr 15min); Utrecht (every 30min; 30min).

Arnhem to: Amsterdam (every 30min; 1hr 10min); Utrecht (every 10min; 35min).

Groningen to: Amsterdam (every 30min; 2hr 20min).

Delta Expo to: Amsterdam (hourly; 2hr 30min).

The Hague to: Delft (every 15min; 15min); Gouda (every 20min; 20min); Rotterdam (every 15min; 25min); Utrecht (every 20min; 40min).

Leiden to: Amsterdam (every 30min; 35min); The Hague (every 30min; 35min).

Maastricht to: Amsterdam (hourly; 2hr 30min).

Rotterdam to: Gouda (every 20min; 20min); Utrecht (every 20min; 45min).

Utrecht to: Arnhem (every 15min; 30min).

CHAPTER 20

NORWAY

Introduction

In many ways **Norway** is still a land of unknowns. Quiet for a thousand years since the Vikings stamped their mark on Europe, the country nowadays often seems more than just geographically distant. Beyond Oslo and the famous fjords the rest of the country might as well be blank for all many visitors know – and, in a manner of speaking, large parts of it are. Vast stretches in the north and east are sparsely populated, and it is possible to travel for hours without seeing a soul.

Despite this isolation, Norway has had a pervasive influence. Traditionally its inhabitants were explorers, from the Vikings to more recent figures like Amundsen, Nansen and Heyerdahl, while Norse language and traditions are common to many other isolated fishing communities, not least northwest Scotland and the Shetlands. At home, too, the Norwegian people have striven to escape the charge of national provincialism, touting the disproportionate number of acclaimed artists, writers and musicians (most notably Munch, Ibsen and Grieg) who have made their mark on the wider European scene. It's also a pleasing discovery that the great outdoors – great though it is – harbours some lively historical towns.

Beyond **Oslo**, one of the world's most prettily sited capitals, the major cities of interest are medieval **Trondheim**, **Bergen**, on the edge of the fjords, and hilly, northern **Tromsø**. None is exactly super-charged, but they are likeable, walkable cities, worth time for themselves as well as being on top of startlingly handsome countryside. The perennial draw is the **western fjords** – every bit as scenically stunning as they're cracked up to be. Dip into the region from Bergen or Åndalsnes, both accessible direct by train from Oslo, or take more time and appreciate the subtleties of the innumerable waterside towns and villages. Further north, the stunning Lofoten Islands are worth a trip for their calm atmosphere and sheer beauty. To the north of here, Norway grows increasingly barren, and the tourist trail focuses on the long journey to the North Cape, or **Nordkapp** – the northernmost accessible point of mainland Europe. The route leads through the province of **Finnmark**, a vast, eerily bleak wilderness where the Arctic tundra rolls as far as the eye can see, and one of the last strongholds of the Sami and their herds of reindeer, which you'll see right across the region.

Information and maps

Every town has a **tourist office**, usually with a stock of free maps, timetables and other bumph. Many book private rooms and hotel beds and some rent out bikes and change money. During the high season – June to August – they normally open daily for long hours, while in the shoulder season they mostly adopt shop hours; many close down altogether in winter. The best internationally available **map** of Norway is the *Hallwag International* 1:1,000,000, which comes complete with an index. If you're buying in Norway, the Statens Kartverk map is the best option; it also includes several city maps.

Money and banks

Norway has a reputation as one of the most expensive countries in Europe. In terms of consumables – from a cup of coffee to a roll of film – this is true, but certain major necessities – notably transport – are far more reasonably priced. Per day, £25/$40 represents an absolute minimum expenditure, £35–45/$55–70 being a more realistic amount. If you're a holder of an international student card it's always worth checking the position on discounts for transport and entrance to sights.

Norwegian **currency** is the **krone** (kr), which is divided into 100 øre. Coins in circulation are 50 øre, 1kr, 5kr, 10kr and 20kr; notes are for 50kr, 100kr, 200kr, 500kr and 1000kr. Banking hours are Mon–Fri 8.15am–3pm, and till 5pm on Thurs. In the summer (June–Aug), many banks close half an hour earlier. Most airports and some train stations have **exchange offices** open evenings and weekends, and some tourist offices also change money, though at less favourable rates than the banks and post offices. Credit or debit cards are by far the easiest way of having access to money in Norway. **ATM** machines are everywhere in larger cities, and you'll also find them in smaller towns throughout the country.

Communications

Norwegian communications are excellent, and things are made even easier by the fact that nearly all post and telephone staff speak good English. **Post office** opening hours are usually Mon–Fri 8/8.30am–4pm, Sat 8/9am–1pm. **Stamps** are available from post offices, kiosks and most bookstores. A general rule is that you can buy stamps at the same places that sell

NORWAY ON THE NET

www.tourist.no – official Norwegian Tourist Board site.
odin.dep.no/html/english – Norwegian government site with links to key information sources.

www.museumnett.no – comprehensive information on the country's museums and current exhibitions.

postcards; it costs 9kr to send a letter or postcard under 20g within Europe, 10kr to the rest of the world. Most **telephone boxes** take 1kr, 5kr, 10kr and 20kr coins, and there is a minimum 4kr charge. Coin-operated phones are gradually giving way to credit- and card-operated public telephones; cards come in denominations of 35kr (22 units), 98kr (65 units) and 210kr (150 units). The international access code is ☎00 47, directory enquiries ☎180 for Scandinavian countries and ☎181 otherwise, but note that these services are very expensive (10kr/min). To make an international collect call, dial ☎115. There are no area codes in Norway.

The Norwegians are into the **Internet** in a big way. Many hotels have Internet access, and you'll find at least a couple of Internet cafés in all the big cities. Most libraries have free Internet available for the public; you usually have to put your name on a list and then you'll get thirty minutes online for free.

Getting around

Norway's transport system is comprehensive and reliable. In the winter (especially in the north), services can be cut back severely, but no part of the country is isolated for long. A synopsis of all the main air, train, bus and ferry services is given in the free *NRI Guide to Transport and Accommodation* brochure, available in advance from the Norwegian Tourist Board. This general guide can be supplemented by detailed regional public transport timetables, available at all local tourist offices. Train schedules are detailed in the *NSB Togruter*, free at every station. In addition, *Nor-Way Bussekspress* co-ordinates and harmonizes long-distance bus services across the whole of the country.

■ Trains

Train services are operated by Norges Statsbaner (NSB) – Norwegian State Railways (☎815 00 888, *www.nsb.no*). Apart from a few branch lines, NSB work on four main routes. These link Oslo to Stockholm in the east, to Kristiansand and Stavanger in the southwest, to Bergen in the west and to Trondheim and on to Fauske and Bodø in the north.

The nature of the country makes most of the routes engineering feats of some magnitude and worth a trip in their own right – the tiny Flåm line and sweeping Rauma run to Åndalsnes are exciting examples, and the journey from Oslo to Bergen is an impressive six-and-a-half-hour cross-country ride, taking in forests, waterfalls, mountains, bleak uplands and plunging valleys. **InterRail** and **Eurail** passes are valid, as is the **ScanRail** pass, which covers train travel in all of Scandinavia including Finland. The ScanRail pass costs £125/US$200 (£95/$150 for under-26s) for five days of travel within two months; £169/$270 (£125/$200) for ten days within two months; and £195/$310 (£145/$230). Seniors (over 60) get a discount of around fifteen percent on the full price of the pass. The ScanRail and InterRail passes and, to a lesser extent, the Eurail pass also provide large discounts on many major ferry crossings and long-distance bus journeys. Rail passes are best purchased from travel agents before you go. NSB also have tickets at discounted rates for off-peak travel, pre-booked journeys and weekend excursions; details can be obtained from any major Norwegian train station. Fares are bearable – the popular Oslo-to-Bergen trip, for example, costs about 580kr one-way. Note that most express and all overnight trains require advance seat reservation (25kr for a seat) whether you have a rail pass or not. In high season it's wise to make a reservation anyway as trains can be packed. Sleepers are reasonably priced, starting at 150kr for a bed in a three-berth compartment. It's somewhat more expensive for more private facilities: 290kr for a two-berth compartment and 580kr for a single compartment; some trains also have ensuite compartments, they cost 740kr. Note that these prices are additional to the cost of the train-ticket.

■ Buses

You'll need to use **buses** principally in the western fjords and the far north, though there is also a network of long-distance **express buses** connecting major towns. **Tickets** aren't too expensive and are usually bought on board, although bus stations sell advance tickets too. Information on specific routes and timetables, is available from local tourist offices or from **Nor-Way Bussekspress**, Karl Johans Gate 2, N–0154 Oslo 1 (☎23 00 24 40, *www.nor-way.no*). Students and rail pass holders can get a fifty-percent discount on bus travel between the two rail termini of Fauske and Bodø and Narvik among several other bus routes. A long-distance bus, the **Nord-Norgeexpressen**, runs from Fauske and Bodø, the northernmost reach of the railway, to Nordkapp once or twice daily. The journey is divided up into four segments: Bodø/Fauske to Narvik, Narvik to Tromsø, Tromsø to Alta, and Alta to Nordkapp. If you have the stamina, you can change from one bus to the next at every stop except Tromsø, where you have to spend the night. If you're doing this much bus travel, you should invest in the *NOR-WAY BusPass*, which costs 1375kr for seven days and 2200kr for fourteen; you can buy it at major bus stations. Another good option for getting to and from Norway is the **Säfflebussen** which operate from Oslo–Stockholm and Oslo-Copenhagen at very competitive prices. Booking is essential (☎22 19 49 00, *www.safflebussen.se*).

■ Ferries

Travelling by **ferry** is one of the real pleasures of a trip to Norway. All along the west coast, and especially among the fjords, you'd be hard-pressed to find a journey of any length which doesn't include at least one car-ferry ride, though on the main ("E") roads many of the ferries have been replaced by tunnels. Ferry rates are fixed nationally on a sliding scale. The tariff is reasonable, with a fifteen-minute ferry ride costing 15kr for foot passengers, 80kr for a car and driver. Bus fares include the cost of any ferry journey made en route. Drivers should note that almost every ferry operates on a first-come, first-served basis. This presents few problems for most of the year, but in high summer, you should arrive one and a half to two hours before departure to be certain of a space. Some of the busier routes have a control kiosk, where you pay on arrival, but for the most part a sailor comes round to collect fares either on the quayside or on board.

There's also the *Hurtigrute* (literally "rapid route"), a **coastal ferry** service, whose several ships shuttle up and down the Norwegian coast linking Bergen with Kirkenes and stopping off at over thirty ports on the way. **Tickets** for short jumps are quite expensive, certainly compared with the bus fares, and the full eleven-day return cruise (including a cabin and meals) goes for anywhere between 8000kr and 23,000kr. However, prices are reduced outside May to August, when under-26s can buy a special **coastal pass** (*kystpass*), which costs 1750kr for 21 days' unlimited travel. Get it on board on your first

trip or at almost all travel agents at home or in Norway. Although it's a cruise ship you don't need to have a cabin: sleeping in the lounges or on deck is allowed. Note also that the older ships are the nicest and they mostly have showers you can use on the lower corridors, although they only have room for five or six vehicles, so car drivers should use the newer vessels. Bikes travel free. Each ship has a 24-hour cafeteria and first-rate restaurants.

■ Driving

By and large, Norwegian **roads** are excellent, although you'll need to take care on winding mountain passes and in the longer tunnels. However, venture off the main roads, especially in the north and in the mountains, and you'll need consummate driving skills. In winter, surfaces are often treacherous, many minor roads are closed and for certain parts of the network – like the E6 Arctic Highway – you need to be properly equipped for Arctic conditions. It's worth noting petrol prices are very high in Norway – around 10kr/ltr. EU **driving licences** are honoured in Norway, but other nationals will need an International Driver's Licence. If you're bringing your own car, you must have vehicle registration papers, adequate insurance, a first aid kit, a warning triangle and a Green Card. Vehicles should be driven on the right, with dipped headlights required at all times; there's a speed limit of 30kph in residential areas, 50kph in built up areas, 80kph on open roads and 90kph on motorways. Speed limits are rigorously enforced. Seat belts are compulsory for drivers and passengers, and drunken driving is severely punished. If you **break down** in a rental car, you'll get roadside assistance from the particular repair company the car firm has contracted. If you are taking your own vehicle, check with your home motoring organization that you have an appropriate insurance policy before you go. In Norway, one of the major breakdown companies is Norges Automobil-Forbund (NAF), whose 24hr **emergency number** is ☎810 00 505. **Car rental** is expensive: from around 3900kr a week with unlimited mileage.

Accommodation

Inevitably, hotel **accommodation** is one of the major expenses you will incur on a trip to Norway – but there are budget alternatives, principally private rooms arranged via the tourist office, hostels and camping.

ACCOMMODATION PRICE CODES

Throughout this guide, accommodation is coded on a scale of ① to ⑨, the code indicating the lowest price per person per night you could expect to pay in each establishment in high season. With hostels this is the nightly rate per person; with hotels, the price is arrived at by dividing the cost of the cheapest double room by two. The prices indicated by the codes are as follows:

① under £5/$8	④ £15–20/$24–32	⑦ £30–35/$48–56
② £5–10/$8–16	⑤ £20–25/$32–40	⑧ £35–40/$56–64
③ £10–15/$16–24	⑥ £25–30/$40–48	⑨ £40/$64 and over

■ Hostels

For many budget travellers as well as hikers, climbers and skiers, **hostels** provide the accommodation mainstay – there are about ninety in all, spread right across the country. The Norwegian hostelling association, Norske Vandrerhjem, Dronningensgate 26, Oslo (☎23 13 93 00, *www.vandrerhjem.no*), puts out a free booklet detailing addresses, opening dates and prices. Prices vary greatly – anything from 100kr to 180kr – although the more expensive ones nearly always include a first-rate breakfast. On average, reckon on paying 120kr a night for a bed, 50kr for breakfast and 80–100kr for a hot evening meal. Most hostels have a supply of doubles, often en suite, for around 250–450kr per night. Nonmembers can use the hostels but pay an extra 25kr a night. Between June and mid-September you should ring ahead to check on space. Most hostels close between 11am and 4pm, and there's often an 11pm/midnight curfew.

■ Campsites and cabins

Camping is another way of keeping accommodation costs down. There are hundreds of official sites throughout the country; the majority are situated with the motorist in mind and are of a high standard. Prices vary considerably, but on average expect to pay around 100kr per night for two people using a tent. The Norwegian Tourist Board detail around four hundred campsites in their free *Camping* brochure. Campsites also often have **cabins**, usually four-bedded affairs with kitchen facilities and sometimes a bathroom, for upwards of 300kr. **Camping rough**, as in Sweden, is a tradition enshrined in law known in Norway as *Lov om fri ferdsel*. You can camp anywhere in open areas as long as you are at least 150m away from houses or cabins or get permission from the owner of the land.

■ Hotels, pensions and private rooms

Hotels are generally out of the reckoning for travellers on a budget – the cheapest double room will set you back around 700kr a night. Still, there are bargains to be found, particularly during summer, when most hotels have discounts of between twenty and forty percent. Remember also that the price of a hotel room always includes breakfast. **Guest houses** (*pensjonater*) in the more touristy towns are slightly cheaper at about 500kr a double; breakfast is usually extra. Failing that, tourist offices in larger towns can sometimes fix you up with a **private room** in someone's house for around 300–350kr a double, though there's a booking fee (15–25kr) on top and the rooms are frequently way out of the centre.

Food and drink

Norwegian food can, at its best, be excellent: fish is plentiful, and carnivores can have a field day trying meats like reindeer steak or elk. But all this costs money, and those on a tight budget may have problems varying their diet. The same can be said of drinking: buying from the supermarkets and state off-licences, Vinmonopolet, is often the only way you'll afford a tipple: in a bar, a half-litre of beer will cost you around 40kr.

■ Food

Breakfast (*frokost*) – a self-service affair of bread, cheese, eggs, preserves, cold meat and fish, washed down with unlimited tea and coffee – is usually excellent at hostels, and memorable in hotels. Almost everywhere breakfast is included in the price of a room; where it isn't, reckon on an extra 50–70kr. **Picnic food** is the best stand-by during the day, although there are a number of **fast-food** alternatives. The indigenous Norwegian variety, served up at street stalls (*gatekjøkken*), consists mainly of rather unappetising hot dogs (*varm pølse*), pizza slices and chicken and chips. A much better choice, and often no more expensive, is simply to get a *smørbrød*, a huge open sandwich heaped with a variety of garnishes. You'll see them in any **café** or **bakery**. The Norwegians are very proud of their dairy products, with very good milk, cheese and yogurt. Good **coffee** is available everywhere and in cafeterias is usually half-price after the first cup. **Tea**, too, is ubiquitous, but usually served with lemon so if you want milk, ask for it.

The best deals for **sit-down food** are at lunchtime (*lunsj*), when self-service **kafeterias** offer a limited range of daily specials (*dagens rett*) – a fish or meat dish with vegetables or salad, often including a drink, sometimes bread, and occasionally coffee too, that costs around 70–90kr. Most department stores and large supermarkets have surprisingly good *kafeterias*; as do main railway stations but they tend to be rather overpriced. In the larger towns you'll also find more original cafés called *kaffistovas*, which serve high-quality Norwegian food at quite reasonable prices. **Restaurants**, serving dinner (*middag*) and classic Norwegian food, are out of the range of many budgets, but the seafood at the best of them is quite superb – main courses average 180–200kr. Again, the best deals are at lunchtime, when some restaurants put out a *koldtbord* (the Norwegian *smörgåsbord*), where, for a fixed price of around 100–150kr, you can get through as much as possible during the three or four hours it's served. There are also a sizeable number of urban **ethnic restaurants**, the most affordable of which are the pizza/pasta joints or Asian choices, and **café/bars** where a substantial main course and a couple of small beers will rush you about 180kr.

■ Drink

Norwegian alcohol prices are among the highest in Europe. **Beer** is lager-like and comes in three strengths: class I is light beer, class II is the beer you get in supermarkets and this is also most widely served in pubs, class III is the strongest beer and only available at Vinmonopolet (see below). If you are in Norway around Christmas, you should try some of the Christmas brews. Every year the different breweries are in fierce competition to win the coveted prizes organised by local and national newspapers. The drink is darker and fuller in taste and very popular with the locals.

Spirits are also way over the top in price. One local speciality worth trying at least once is *aquavit*, served ice-cold in little glasses and, at forty percent proof, real headache material. In bars and cafés a half-litre of beer costs about 40kr. In the smaller towns, bars (where they exist) tend to close down at around 11pm, but in the cities they are open until at least 1am and until 4am in many cases. Beer is sold in supermarkets and shops all over Norway and is about half the price you'd pay in a bar. Wines and spirits can only be purchased from the state controlled shops known as **Vinmonopolet**. Wine is not cheap, but it offers a reasonable alternative with good bottles of wine from 85kr. Vinmonopolet is also known to be one of the best winebuyers in Europe and has a wide selection in stock.

There's generally one in each small town, though there are more branches in the cities; opening hours are usually Mon–Wed 10am–4/5pm, Thurs 10am–5/6pm, Fri 9am–4/6pm, Sat 9am–1/3pm.

Opening hours and holidays

Shop **opening hours** are usually Mon–Wed & Fri 9am–5pm, Thurs 9am–6/8pm, Sat 9am–1/3pm. Almost everything including the supermarkets is closed on Sunday. Newspaper kiosks (*Narvesen*) and take-away food stalls are open every evening until 10 or 11pm. Most shops and businesses are **closed** on the following days: Jan 1; Maundy Thursday; Good Friday; Easter Sunday & Monday; May 1; Ascension Day (mid-May); May 17; Whit Sunday & Monday; Dec 25 & 26.

Emergencies

Like all the Scandinavian countries, Norway is in general a safe place to travel; the people are friendly and helpful, and petty crime has a relatively low profile. If you have to visit the **police** you'll usually find them fairly amiable and normally able to speak English. If you have something stolen, be sure to get a police report number – essential for any insurance claim. As for **health problems**, most good hotels as well as pharmacies and tourist offices have lists of local doctors and dentists. Norway is not in the EU, but is a member of the EEA and thus operates reciprocal health agreements with all EU countries. This means that EU citizens get free hospital treatment, providing they're carrying an E111 (from the UK) or similar documentation. Non-hospital treatment is not free, though EU citizens only pay part of the cost. These arrangements do not cover dental treatment or prescription charges. Prescriptions are taken to pharmacies (*apotek*) which – should they be closed – mostly carry a rota in the window advising of the nearest open pharmacy.

Emergency Numbers

Police ☎112; Ambulance ☎113; Fire ☎110.

OSLO

Despite tourist-office endeavours, **OSLO** retains a low profile among European cities, and even comparisons with other Scandinavian capitals are usually a little less than favourable. Inevitably, though, you'll pass through – the main train routes heading west to the fjords, north to the Arctic, south to the coast and east to Sweden are routed through the city – but take heart: Oslo is definitely worth seeing. The city has some of Europe's best museums, fields a street life that surprises most first-time visitors, and helps revive travellers weary of the austere northern wilderness.

Oslo is the oldest of the Scandinavian capital cities, founded, according to the Norse chronicler Snorre Sturlason, around 1048 by Harald Hardråde. Several decimating fires and 600 years later, Oslo upped sticks and shifted west to its present site, abandoning its old name in favour of Christiania – after the seventeenth-century Danish king Christian IV responsible for the move. The new city prospered and by the time of the break with Denmark (and union with Sweden) in 1814, Christiania – indeed Norway as a whole – was clamouring for independence, something it finally achieved in 1905, though the city didn't revert to its original name for another twenty years. Today's city centre is largely the work of the late nineteenth and early twentieth centuries, an era reflected in the wide streets, dignified parks and gardens, solid buildings and long, consciously classical vistas, which combine to lend it a self-satisfied, respectable air. Seeing the city takes – and deserves – time. Its half a million inhabitants have room to spare in a city whose vast boundaries encompass huge areas of woods, sand and water, and much of the time you're as likely to be swimming or trail-walking as strolling the city centre.

Arrival and information

International and domestic **trains** use Oslo Sentralstasjon, known as **Oslo S**, at the eastern end of the city centre. The central **bus terminal** (Bussterminalen) is connected to the Oslo S by a bridge on the northeast corner of the building. It handles most of the bus services within the city as well as those to and from the airport. Long-distance buses arrive and depart here too, but note that some services terminate on the south side of Oslo S at the bus stands beside Havnegata. For all bus enquiries, consult the **information** desk (Mon–Fri 7am–10pm, Sat 8am–5.30pm & Sun 8am–10pm). **Ferries** arrive at either the Vippetangen quays (Stena Line and DFDS), a fifteen-minute walk south of Oslo S, or at Hjortneskaia (Colorline), some 3km west of the city centre; take bus #56 to the centre – an infrequent service, though it's mostly linked to ferry arrival times – or, failing that, a taxi to Oslo S (100kr). Catamarans (*Hurtigbåt*) from Arendal, on the south coast, dock at the Palékaia, a five- to ten-minute walk south from Oslo S. Oslo's gleaming new **Gardermoen airport**, 45km north of the city, is linked to Oslo S by high-speed train and bus. The former is faster, the latter a tad cheaper. There is also a secondary airport at Torp, 100km southwest of Oslo by the city of Sandefjord. The best way to get to Oslo from Torp is by bus, 150kr return or 98kr single.

The main **tourist office** is in the Norwegian Information Centre down on the harbourfront at Brynjulf Bulls plass 1 (April, May & Sept Mon–Sat 9am–5pm; June–Aug daily 9am–7pm; Oct–March Mon–Fri 9am–4pm; ☎22 83 00 50, *www.oslopro.no*). They issue a free and detailed guide to the city, provide a monthly free listings booklet *What's On*, give away maps and help you find accommodation. They also sell the useful **Oslo Card**, which gives free admission to most of the museums, discounts in shops and restaurants and unlimited free travel on the transport system, including ferries. Valid for one, two or three days, it costs 180kr, 290kr and 390kr respectively.

City transport

The city's transport system is operated by AS Oslo Sporveier, whose **Trafikanten informa-tion office** is on Jernbanetorget, the pedestrianized square outside Oslo S (Mon–Fri 7am–8pm, Sat 8am–6pm). They have a useful free transit map and a free timetable booklet, *Rutebok for Oslo*, which details every transport schedule in the city. Most **buses** pass through Jernbanetorget; another common stop is outside the National Theatre (Nationaltheatret). Most buses stop running at around midnight, when **night buses** take over on certain routes. The **trams** are the preferred form of transportation for the people of Oslo. They run on eight lines, crossing the centre from east to west; major stops are Jernbanetorget, Nationaltheatret and Brugata. The underground Tunnelbanen (**T-bane**) has eight lines, all of which converge to share a common slice of track that crosses the city centre from Majorstuen in the west to Tøyen in the east, with Jernbanetorget, Stortinget and Nationaltheatret stations in between. From this central section, four lines run westbound (*Vest*) and four eastbound (*Øst*). Numerous **local ferries** cross the fjord to connect the city with its outlying districts and arch-ipelagos: to Bygdøy and the museums from the piers behind the Rådhus (May–Sept); for the inner Oslofjord islands from Vippetangen quay, behind Akershus Castle (bus #60 from Jernbanetorget).

A flat-fare **ticket** costs 20kr, a 24-hour **travel pass**, 45kr, the 8-journey Flexikort, 125kr, a seven-day pass, 150kr and a one-month pass, 580kr – all are available from Trafikanten (see above) and are valid on trams, buses and the T-bane. Taxis are expensive – around 100kr for up to a ten-minute, 5km ride; to get one ring Taxi2 (☎02 202) or Oslo Taxi (☎02 323).

Accommodation

Oslo has the range of hotels you would expect of a capital city, as well as private rooms and hostels. To appreciate the full flavour of the city, you're best off staying on or near the western reaches of Karl Johans gate, between the Stortinget and the Nationaltheatret, though the well-heeled area to the north and west of the Royal Palace is enjoyable too. Many of the least expen-sive lodgings are, however, to be found in the vicinity of Oslo S. It is always well worth calling ahead to check on space. You can cut the hassle and use the **accommodation service** pro-vided by the tourist office, the Norwegian Information Centre, Brynjulf Bulls plass 1, can give you full accommodation lists or make a reservation on your behalf for a nominal fee.

Hostels and private rooms

There are three official HI hostels in Oslo, each very popular and open to people of any age. Another good budget option is the private rooms booked by the tourist office for a cost of about 170kr for a single, 300kr a double; the supply of private rooms rarely dries up and they are something of a bargain, especially as many have self-catering facilities, but they do tend to be out of the city centre, and there's often a minimum two-night stay.

HOSTELS

Ekeberg Vandrerhjem, Kongsveien 82 (☎22 74 18 90). Small, simple HI hostel occupying part of a school complex 4km southeast of Oslo S. Take tram #19 or the less frequent #18 from the centre and it is 100m from the Holtet tram stop. June to mid-August. ③.

Oslo Haraldsheim Vandrerhjem, Haraldsheimveien 4, Grefsen (☎22 22 29 65). The best of the three HI youth hostels, 4km northeast of the centre, with 71 rooms, mostly in four-bed dorms, the majority en-suite. Advance booking necessary in the summer. Take tram #15 or #17 from Brugata to the Sinsenkrysset stop, from where it's a signposted ten-minute walk along a footpath. Open all year. ③.

Oslo Vandrerhjem Holtekilen, Michelets vei 55, 1320 Stabekk (☎67 51 80 40). Located 10km west of the city centre, this HI hostel has a dorm room (May–Sept only) and 1–4 bedded rooms plus kitchen and laun-dry facilities and a restaurant. From Bussterminalen, take bus #151 to the Kveldsroveien bus stop; the hos-tel is 100m away on the right. ③.

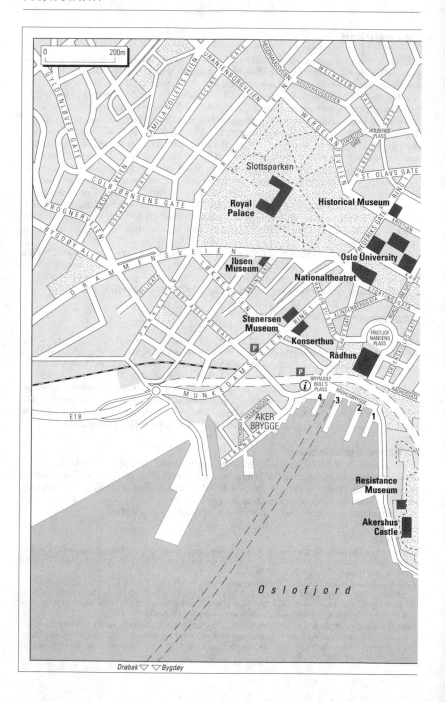

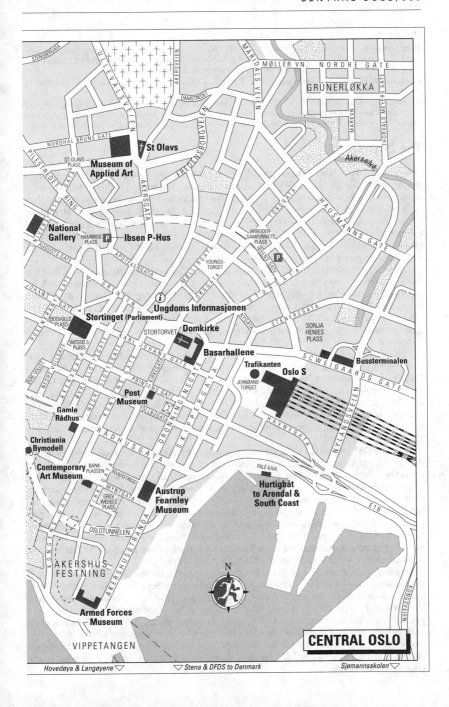

Hotels

Bondeheimen, Rosenkrantz gate 8 (☎23 21 41 00). One of Oslo's most delightful hotels, tastefully decorated with smooth polished pine everywhere you look. It's just two minutes' walk north of Karl Johans gate – and the buffet breakfast, included in the price, is excellent. ⑨.

Perminalen Hotell, Øvre Slottsgate 2 (☎23 09 30 81). Clean, basic and reasonably priced hotel/hostel close to the train station. ④.

Rainbow Norrøna, Grensen 19 (☎23 31 80 00). A pleasant hotel occupying an attractively modernized old apartment block right in the middle of town, about 200m north of the Stortinget. Comfortable rooms with modern furnishings. Excellent value, made even more attractive by summer and weekend discounts. ⑨.

The City

Oslo's main street, **Karl Johans gate**, leads west up the slope from Oslo S train station. It begins unpromisingly with a clutter of tacky shops and hang-around junkies, but steps away at the corner of Dronningens gate is the curious **Basarhallene**, a circular building of two tiers, whose brick cloisters once housed the city's food market. The adjacent **Domkirke** (daily 10am–4pm; free) dates from the late seventeenth century, though its heavyweight tower was remodelled in 1850; plain and dour from the outside, the cathedral's elegantly restored interior is in delightful contrast, its homely, low-ceilinged nave and transepts awash with maroon, green and gold paintwork.

Continuing along Karl Johans gate, it's a brief stroll up to the **Stortinget**, the parliament building, an imposing chunk of neo-Romanesque architecture that was completed in 1866. It's open to the public, but the obligatory guided tour (July to mid-Aug Mon–Sat 10am, 11.30am & 1pm; mid-Sept to June Sat only 11am & 12.30pm; free) shows little more than can be gleaned from the outside. In front of the parliament, a narrow **park-piazza** flanks Karl Johans gate; in summer it teems with promenading city folk, while in winter people flock to its flood-lit open-air skating rinks.

Lurking at the western end of the park is the neoclassical **Nationaltheatret**, built in 1899 and fronted by a stodgy statue of playwright Henrik Ibsen. Beyond, up the hill, is the **Royal Palace**, a monument to Norwegian openness; built between 1825 and 1848, when other monarchies were nervously counting their friends, it still stands without railings and walls and the grounds – **Slottsparken** – are open to the public. The daily changing of the guard (1.30pm) is a snappy affair, well worth a look. An equestrian statue of the king who built the palace, Karl XIV Johan, stands in front of the main facade inscribed with his motto, "The people's love is my reward".

Back on Karl Johans Gate, the nineteenth-century buildings of the **University** fit well in this monumental end of the city centre. Among them you will find Norway's largest and best collection of art at the **National Gallery**, Universitetsgata 13 (Mon, Wed & Fri 10am–6pm, Thurs 10am–8pm, Sat 10am–4pm, Sun 11am–4pm; free). An accessible collection, it may be short of internationally famous painters – with the notable exception of the Impressionists – but there is ample compensation in the museum's comprehensive display of Norwegian paintings. Highlights include some wonderfully romantic, nineteenth-century landscapes by the likes of Johan Christian Dahl and Thomas Fearnley, and two rooms devoted to Edvard Munch, featuring the original version of the famous *Scream* as well as *The Sick Child*, the first of an important series of depictions of Munch's dying sister.

Heading south from the University buildings, you can't miss the monolithic brickwork of the **Rådhus** (May–Aug Mon–Sat 9am–5pm, Sun noon–5pm; Sept–April Mon–Sat 9am–4pm, Sun noon–4pm; free), the massive City Hall, opened in 1950 to celebrate the city's 900th anniversary. Few people had a good word to say about the place when it was first built, but popular irritation has moved on to other, more modern targets, and the Rådhus has worn well, its twin towers a grandiose but somehow rather amiable statement of civic pride. The interior – best seen on one of the frequent free guided tours – celebrates all things Norwegian; the main hall or Rådhushallen is decorated with vast murals by several of the country's leading artists.

On the seaward side of the Rådhus is the central harbour, bordered to the west by the old, yellow **Oslo V railway station** – now the main tourist office – and Oslo's former shipyard, cleverly remodelled to hold the hi-tech shopping halls of the **Aker Brygge** development. In the opposite direction, running east from the Rådhus, is **Rådhusgata**, which leads to the city's other harbour, Vippetangen, the gridiron streets on either side of it a legacy of seventeenth-century Oslo – though sadly it's only the layout that survives. To the south of Rådhusgata is **Akershus Castle** (May to mid-Sept Mon–Sat 10am–4pm, Sun 12.30–6pm; late April & mid-Sept to Oct Sun only 12.30–4pm; 20kr; free guided tours Mon–Sat 11am, 1pm & 3pm, Sun 1pm & 3pm), the most significant memorial to medieval Oslo. Built on a rocky knoll overlooking the harbour around 1300, it was modernized in the seventeenth century by Christian IV. A visit to the castle takes in the royal chapel and mausoleum, but it's all rather bland. Very much more diverting is the **Resistance Museum**, beside the castle entrance (daily 10/11am–3/4pm; 20kr), where excellent displays detail the history of the war in Norway, from defeat and occupation through resistance to final victory. Surrounding the castle are the sprawling earth and stone ramparts and bastions of the **Akershus Festning** fortress, which date from the seventeenth century and which were designed to resist artillery bombardment – the part of the fortress adjoining the castle offers fine views over the central harbour.

The Bygdøy peninsula

The most enjoyable way to reach the leafy **Bygdøy peninsula**, southwest of the city centre, is by ferry, departing from behind the Rådhus (daily: May–Aug 9am–9pm every 40min; late April & Sept 9am–6pm every 40min) and returning to a similar schedule. They have two ports of call on the peninsula, stopping first at Dronningen pier, then at Bygdøynes pier. The two most popular attractions – the Viking Ships and the Norwegian Folk museums – are within easy walking distance of Dronningen pier; the other attractions are a stone's throw from Bygdøynes. If you decide to walk between the two, allow about fifteen minutes: the route is well signposted but dull. The alternative to the ferry is bus #30 (every 15min), which runs all year from Jernbanetorget and the National Theatre to the Viking Ships and Folk museums, and, when the ferry isn't running, to the other three museums as well.

The **Norwegian Folk Museum**, at Museumsveien 10 (Jan to mid-May & mid-Sept to Dec daily 11am–3/4pm; mid-May to mid-Sept daily 10am–5/6pm; 50kr), combines indoor collections of furniture, china and silverware with an open-air display of reassembled period farms, houses and other buildings. A few minutes' walk away, the **Viking Ships Museum** (daily: April & Oct 11am–4pm; May–Aug 9am–6pm; Sept 11am–5pm; Nov–March 11am–3pm; 30kr) occupies a large hall specially constructed to house a trio of ninth-century Viking ships, with viewing platforms to enable you to see inside the hulls. The three oak vessels were retrieved from ritual burial mounds in southern Norway towards the end of the last century, each embalmed in a subsoil of clay, which accounts for their excellent state of preservation. The star exhibit is the **Oseberg ship**, thought to be the burial ship of a Viking chieftain's wife. Its ornately carved prow and stern rise high above the hull, where thirty oar-holes indicate the size of the crew. Much of the treasure buried with the boat was retrieved as well, and this is on display at the back of the museum.

Down by Bygdøynes pier, the **Kon-Tiki Museum** (daily: April, May & Sept 10.30am–5pm; June to Aug 9.30am–5.45pm; Oct–March 10.30am–4pm; 30kr) displays the balsawood raft on which Thor Heyerdahl made his now legendary 1947 journey across the Pacific to prove that the first Polynesian settlers could have sailed from pre-Inca Peru. Over the road, in front of the **Fram Museum** (May–Sept daily 9/10am–4.45/6.45pm; Oct–April daily 10/11am–2.45/3.45/4.45pm; 25kr), is the *Gjøa*, the one-time sealing ship in which Roald Amundsen made the first complete sailing of the Northwest Passage in 1906. Another of Amundsen's ships, the polar vessel *Fram*, is displayed inside the museum and it was this vessel that carried him to within striking distance of the South Pole in 1911. Complete with most of its original fittings, the interior gives a superb insight into the life and times of these early Arctic explorers. Next door, the **Norwegian Maritime Museum** (Jan to mid-May & Oct–Dec Mon, Wed & Fri–Sun 10.30am–4pm, Tues & Thurs 10.30am–7pm; mid-May to Sept daily 10am–7pm; 30kr) is a sparkling new building housing a fairly pedestrian collection of maritime artefacts. You'll probably be more taken with the café, a handy vantage point overlooking the bay.

The Munch Museum

Also out of the centre but without question a major attraction, the **Munch Museum**, Tøyengata 53 (June to mid-Sept daily 10am–6pm; mid-Sept to May Tues–Sun 10am–4pm, Thurs & Sun till 6pm; 50kr), is reachable by T-bane: get off at Tøyen and it's a signposted five-minute walk. Born in 1863, Edvard Munch is Norway's most famous painter. His lithographs and woodcuts are shown in one half of the gallery, a dark catalogue of swirls and fog, and in the main gallery there are early paintings along with the great, signature works of the 1890s. Highlights include *Dagny Juel*, an emotive portrait of the Berlin socialite with whom both Munch and Strindberg were infatuated, and the haunting *Red Virginia Creeper*, a house being consumed by the plant – the museum also owns no less than fifty versions of *The Scream*. Later paintings reflect a renewed interest in nature and physical work, as in the *Workers on Their Way Home* and the light *Winter in Kragerø* and *Model by the Wicker Chair*, which reveals a happier, if rather idealized, attitude to his surroundings also evident in works such as *Spring Ploughing*.

Frogner Park: the Vigeland Sculpture Park

On the other side of the city and reachable on tram #12 and #15 from the centre (get off at Vigelandsparken), **Frogner Park** holds one of Oslo's most striking cultural targets in the **Vigeland Sculpture Park**, which commemorates another modern Norwegian artist of world renown, Gustav Vigeland. The open-air sculptures, which Vigeland started in 1924 and was still working on when he died in 1943, are simply fantastic. A long series of life-size figures frowning, fighting and posing lead up to the central fountain, an enormous bowl representing the burden of life, supported by straining, sinewy bronze Goliaths while, underneath, water tumbles out around clusters of playing and standing figures. The twenty-metre obelisk up on the stepped embankment behind, and the grouped granite sculptures around it, comprise the summation of the work, a writhing mass which depicts the cycle of life as Vigeland saw it. The park comes to life in summer when the city's inhabitants come out to play and enjoy the green space.

The islands of the inner Oslofjord

The archipelago of low-lying, lightly forested **islands** in the inner Oslofjord is the city's summer playground, and makes going to the beach an unusually viable option for a northern European capital. Jumping on a ferry, attractive enough in the heat of the day, is also one of the more pleasant forms of entertainment during the evenings, and although most of the islets are cluttered with summer homes, the least populated are favourite party venues for the city's preening youth. **Ferries** to the islands leave from the Vippetangen quay, at the foot of Akershusstranda – a twenty-minute walk, or a five-minute ride on bus #60, south from Jernbanetorget.

Conveniently, **Hovedøya** (ferry #92; mid-March to Sept 7.30am–7pm every 60–90min; Oct to mid-March 3 daily; 10min), the nearest island, is also the most interesting, its rolling hills incorporating both farmland and deciduous woods as well as the overgrown ruins of a twelfth-century Cistercian monastery. There are plenty of footpaths to wander, you can swim from the shingle beaches on the south shore, and there's a seasonal café opposite the monastery ruins. Camping is not permitted, however, as Hovedøya is a protected area – that's why there are no summer homes.

The pick of the other islands is wooded **Langøyene** (ferry #94; June–Aug 10am–6pm hourly; 30min), the most southerly of the archipelago and the one with the best beaches. The H-shaped island has a campsite, *Langøyene Camping* (☎22 36 37 98; June to mid-Aug), and at night the ferries are full of people armed with sleeping bags and bottles, on their way to join swimming parties.

Eating

As befits a capital city, Oslo boasts scores of **eating places**, the sheer variety ensuring there's something to suit almost every budget. Those carefully counting the kroner will find it easy to buy bread, fruit, snacks and sandwiches from stalls, shops and kiosks across the city centre, while fast-food joints offering hamburgers and hot dogs (*pølser*) are legion. Far more interesting are the city's cafés. These run the gamut from homely family places to student haunts and ultra-fashionable hangouts, but nearly all of them serve inexpensive lunches and sometimes bargain evening meals too. It's worth noting that quite a few of the cafés detailed below could equally be slotted into our "Pubs and Bars" section as the distinction between Oslo's cafés and bars is often very blurred. Regular **restaurants** are more expensive and frequently rather staid, but even here it's possible to find some excellent deals, especially if you stick to pizza and pasta in one of the many Italian places.

Markets, supermarkets and takeaway snacks

Markets are always good for fruit and vegetables, and Oslo's principal open-air market is on Youngstorget (Mon–Sat 7am–2pm), a brief stroll north of the Domkirke along Torggata. In the eastern part of the city, around Trondheimsveien and the areas of Grünerløkka or Grønland, Turkish- and Pakistani-run shops offer reasonably priced vegetables, bread, olives and feta cheese. The city centre is dotted with supermarkets; Rimi, the biggest name, has an outlet in Grensen, takeaway snacks are on sale from kiosks and fast-food outlets right across the city. For healthier snacks, numerous bakeries and cake shops sell a reasonable range of sandwiches.

Cafés and restaurants

Cafe Amsterdam, Universitetsgata 11. Done out in the style of a Dutch brown bar, this busy and agreeable café/bar serves an imaginative mixture of international dishes, all at moderate prices. Kitchen closes around 8pm; entrance on Kristian Augusts gate.

Celsius, Rådhusgata 19 at Øvre Slotts gate. Hidden behind an unlikely looking eighteenth-century gateway, this laid-back café/bar occupies one of Oslo's older buildings and offers delicious Mediterranean-inspired food at 130kr a dish. It's also a great place for a drink.

Ett Glass, Karl Johans gate 33, entrance round the corner on Rosenkrantz gate. Trendy, candlelit café/bar. An imaginative menu focusing on Mediterranean-influenced light meals and lunches provides some curious, often mouthwatering delights. Inexpensive.

Den Gode Cafe, Fredensborgveien. Reasonably priced snackfood like burritos, salads and really tasty burgers. Good coffee too. At night the place turns into a relaxed bar for drinking and chatting. Downstairs the *Bar Nede* opens at weekends with a chilled atmosphere and a cosy fireplace.

Kaffistova, Rosenkrantz gate 8. Part of the Bondeheimen hotel, this spick-and-span self-service café serves tasty, traditional Norwegian cooking at very fair prices. There's usually a vegetarian option, too.

Sult, Thv Meyers gate 26. On the "top" of Grünerløkka, this restaurant is one of the most popular in Oslo. Sult (the name means "hunger") serves innovative dishes using seasonal ingredients, at surprisingly low prices. The attached bar *Tørst* (meaning "thirst"), is a great place for a drink.

Tullins cafe, Tullins gate 2. Close to the National Gallery. This place looks unpretentious from the outside, but has an interesting interior. Serving light meals, snacks and coffee in the daytime and turning into a café/bar at night. Reasonably priced.

Vegeta Vertshus, Munkedamsveien 3b. Near the National Theatre, this unassuming vegetarian restaurant has a help-yourself buffet with fine salads, mixed vegetables and pizza. Small platefuls for 80kr.

Drinking

Downtown Oslo has a vibrant **bar** scene, a noisy, boisterous but generally good-tempered affair, at its most frenetic on summer weekends, when the city is crowded with visitors from all over Norway. The busiest mainstream bars are concentrated in the side streets near the Rådhus and down along the Aker Brygge, while other popular but less assertively heterosexual bars are clustered around Universitetsgata and on Rosenkrantz gate. Karl Johans gate also weighs in with a string of bars and in recent years nightlife has moved eastbound, Grünerløkka is now *the* place to go bar hopping and the area of Grønland also has a couple of hotspots.

Many of Oslo's bars stay open until well after midnight, until 3am or 4am in some cases. Drinks are uniformly expensive, and so, if you're after a big night out, it's a good idea to follow Norwegian custom and start with a few warm-up drinks at home.

Bars and pubs

Bar Boca, Thv Meyers gate 30. Very small Fifties-retro bar, with probably the best dry Martinis in Norway. The people here take great pride in the craft of drink making. Get here early.

Dattera til Hagen, Grønland 10. This colourful and trendy spot in the multicultural area of Grønland comes highly recommended. The daytime cafe becomes a lively bar in the evening, sometimes with a DJ on the small first floor dancefloor. Follow Brugata towards Grønland.

Mono, Pløens gate. Newly opened beerhaunt for students and the alternative crowd. Dark interior with old couches, velvet wallpaper and Sixties floor lamps. DJs play a good eclectic music selection.

Savoy Bar, Universitetsgata 11. With its stained-glass windows and wood-panelled walls, this small, intimate bar is an agreeably low-key spot to nurse a beer. Part of the Savoy hotel on the corner of Kristian Augusts gate. Daily 5pm–2am.

Nightlife

Tracking down **live music** is straightforward enough, both international and local acts. **Jazz** fans are well served, with several first-rate nightspots dotted round the city centre. Oslo's busiest **nightclubs** are on and around Karl Johans gate, although lately some good places have opened in the areas of Grønland and Grünerløkka. Entry will set you back in the region of 50–100kr – though drinks prices are the same as anywhere else. Nothing gets going much before 11pm; closing times are generally around 3–4am. For **entertainment listings** it's always worth checking *Natt & Dag*, a monthly Norwegian-language broadsheet available free from cafés, bars and shops.

Nightclubs, rock and jazz venues

BLÅ, Brenneri veien 9c. Down by the river Akerselven, this converted factory building holds one of the most exciting clubs in Oslo. Events range from jazz concerts to literature readings and club nights with high-profile national and international DJs. Outdoor cafe/pub in summer with tables along the riverside.

Cruise Kafé, Stranden 3, Aker Brygge. Small, modern bar that showcases live rock, rock 'n' roll and blues bands.

Herr Nilsen, C J Hambros plass 5. Very good spot for live jazz and blues with some of the best performers in Norway.

Jazid, Pilestredet 17. Popular choice for serious clubbers. DJs keep drum 'n' bass and other technobeats pumping until the early morning.

Nye Enka, Kirkegata. Popular pub on the ground floor, and disco on the first floor that attract both gay and hetero party people.

Rockerfeller Music Hall, Torggata 16. This venue in a former bathhouse accommodates up to 1500 people and is one of Oslo's major concert venues, hosting well-known and up-and-coming mostly rock or alternative bands. Opening times vary.

Listings

Airlines Braathens, at Oslo S (☎815 20 000); British Airways, Dronning Mauds gate 1–3 (☎800 33 142); SAS at Oslo S (☎810 03 300).

Bicycles For rental try Vestbanen, metres from the main tourist office, down at the central harbour; costs from around 180kr a day, refundable deposit around 1000kr. For routes and tours in and around Oslo try *www.freebike.no*.

Bookstores, Tanum bookstore (Mon–Fri 9am–7pm, Sat 9am–4pm) at Paleet in Karl Johanstreet has a good selection of English books and books on Norway. Bokkilden Interbok (Mon–Fri 10am–6pm, Sat 10am–3pm) in Akersgaten 34 has the best selection of local and international maps and travel guides.

Car rental Avis, Munkedamsveien 27 (☎23 23 92 00), and at the airport (☎64 81 06 60); Budget, Sonja Henie plass 4 and at the airport (☎800 30 210); Europcar, at the airport (☎64 81 05 60).

Embassies Canada, Wergelandveien 7 (☎22 99 53 00); UK, Thomas Heftyes gate 8 (☎23 13 27 00); USA, Drammensveien 18 (☎22 44 85 50). Australia and New Zealand use British embassy.

Exchange All banks and post offices exchange currency and cash travellers' cheques at comparable rates. Outside of normal banking and post office hours the best bets are the 24hr ATMs or the exchange office at Oslo S (Mon–Fri 7am–7pm, Sat & Sun 8am–5pm). There are also 24hr exchange facilities at the airport.

Ferries DFDS Seaways, Vippetangen Utstikker (quay) #2 (☎22 41 90 90); Stena Line, Jernbanetorget 2 (☎23 17 90 00); Color Line, Hjortneskaia (☎810 00 811).

Gay Oslo. Activities and events organized by LLH, St Olavs plass 2 (☎22 11 05 09, *llh@c2i.net*). In terms of nightlife lesbians should try Pottpurriet in Øvre Voll gate 13 and gay men, the London Pub in Rosenkrantz gate. Both places are quite lively after 11pm.

Hiking Den Norske Turistforening (DNT), Storgata 3 (Mon–Fri 10am–4pm, Thurs until 6pm, Sat 10am–2pm; ☎22 82 28 00), sells hiking maps and gives general advice and information on route planning. Join here to use their nationwide network of mountain huts; the subscription fee of around 360kr gives a year's membership.

Internet Akers Mik Internet café, Akersgaten 39. Most libraries have a free Internet service.

Laundry Mr Clean, Parkveien 6 at Welhavens gate (daily 7am–11pm).

Off-licences Vinmonopolet at Klingenberggata 4; and Møllergata 10–12.

Pharmacies There is a 24hr service at Jernbanetorgets Apotek, Jernbanetorget 4b, by Oslo S.

Post offices The main office is at Dronningens gate 15 at corner of Prinsens gate (Mon–Fri 8am–6pm, Sat 10am–3pm).

Travel agents KILROY travels, Nedre Slotts gate 23 (☎23 10 23 00).

SOUTHERN NORWAY

Southern Norway is an immediately appealing region – flatlands and fells fringed by a tempting coastal concentration of islands and long, if mostly rocky beaches. As such it's long been the Norwegians' principal domestic holiday choice, though everyone else tends to pass quickly through, which is fair enough if it's a choice between this region and the fjords. However, southern Norway may, of course, be your first view of the country, in which case it's worth spending at least some time at your point of arrival. International ferries put in to the western port of **Stavanger**, the region's major town, and **Kristiansand**, a lively resort. Both are pleasant centres in their own right, especially Stavanger with its pretty little old town.

Stavanger

STAVANGER is something of a survivor. While other Norwegian coastal towns have fallen foul of the precarious fortunes of fishing, Stavanger has grown into one of Norway's most dynamic economic powerhouses. Fish canning and its own merchant fleet brought initial prosperity, which shipbuilding and the oil industry have since sustained. It's a brash, breezy, international sort of place, with a sprinkling of interesting attractions and a good bar and restaurant scene, and well worth a day or so before moving on to the fjords or Oslo.

The old town, **Gamle Stavanger**, near the international ferry terminal, is of greatest appeal, a pristinely preserved area of wooden warehouses, narrow clapboard houses and cobbled streets that were once home for seamen and merchants. There's a good museum here, the **Canning Museum**, Øvre Strandgate 88 (mid-June to mid-Sept daily 11am–4pm; early June & late Sept Mon–Thurs 11am–4pm; rest of year Sun 11am–4pm; 40kr), located in a reconstructed sardine-canning factory; it gives a glimpse of the industry that saved Stavanger from decay in the late nineteenth century and smokes its own sardines on the first Sunday of every month and every Tuesday and Thursday from mid-June to mid-August – and very tasty they are too. Beside the harbour, on the main square, **Torget**, there's a bustling daily market, while the streets around **Skagen**, on the jut of land forming the eastern side of the harbour, make up the town's shopping area. It's a bright mix of spidery lanes, pedestrianized streets and white-timbered houses covering the area once occupied by medieval Stavanger. At the top stands the spiky **Valberg Tower**, a nineteenth-century firewatch, from where there are sweeping views over the city and its industry. The only relic of medieval Stavanger is the twelfth-century **Domkirke** (mid-May to mid-Sept Mon–Sat 11am–6pm & Sun 1–6pm; rest of year Wed–Sat 10am–3pm, Sundays only for service at 11am; free), on the fringes of Torget, whose pointed-hat towers signal a Romanesque structure that's suffered from several poorly conceived renovations. The church overlooks **Breiavatnet**, a pretty little lake right in the middle of the city. The Norwegian Petroleum Museum at Kjerringholmen is also worth a visit to understand the importance of the industry for Norway's recent history (June–Aug daily 10am–7pm; rest of year Mon–Sat 10am–4pm & Sun 10am–6pm; free).

Practicalities

International ferries arrive a short walk northwest of Torget, docking at the Strandkaien quay. **Express boats** from Bergen alight at the terminal on the northwest side of Skagen. The **airport** is 14km south of the city at Sola: a *flybussen* (40kr) runs into Stavanger, dropping you at the **bus and train station** on the south side of Breiavatnet. The **tourist office** on Rosenkildetorget 1 (June–Aug daily 9am–8pm; rest of year Mon–Fri 9am–4pm, Sat 9am–2pm; *www.visitstavanger.com*) have plenty of information, and they can also provide **private rooms**. If you decide to stay, there's plenty of choice. The cheapest option is the official HI **hostel**, *Mosvangen*, at Henrik Ibsens gate 21 (☎51 87 09 77; ③; mid-May to mid-Sept), a 3km walk southwest of the centre. A good choice among several **pensions** is the *Skagen Hotel og Gjestehus*, Skansegaten 7 (☎51 93 85 00; ⑤), which has newly redecorated rooms in an old wooden building on the east side of the harbour. All of the town's **hotels** offer summer discounts, including the *Comfort Hotel Grand*, Klubbgata 3 (☎51 89 58 00; ⑨), an excellent central choice with smart, modern rooms; and the delightful *Skagen Brygge*, Skagenkaien 30 (☎51 85 00 00; ⑨), a tastefully decorated modern place with enjoyable views over the harbour. For **camping**, the campsite next to the hostel (late May to early Sept) has cabins as well as caravan and tent pitches. For **food**, the *Café Sting*, by the tower on the Skagen at Valberget 3, dishes up some good, inexpensive fare – both Mediterranean and Norwegian dishes – and there's superb seafood at the pricey *Sjøhuset Skagen*, Skagenkaien 16.

The route to Bergen

If you're a train fanatic or already committed to a rail pass, you need to go to Oslo to travel on to Bergen. If not, you can get there more directly by bus and/or ferry. For speed, if not economy, the best bet is the **catamaran** (*Hurtigbåt*), which runs all year. This requires advance seat reservations (☎51 86 87 80) and costs around 590kr one way, though students and interrail-pass holders qualify for discounts of up to fifty percent off the ticket price. The trip takes four and a half hours. The bus trip takes about 6 hours and is only marginally less expensive.

Kristiansand

Founded by and named after King Christian IV, **KRISTIANSAND** is the closest thing to a seaside resort there is in Norway – a bright, energetic place which thrives on its ferry connections with Denmark and its popular beaches. There are also two reminders of its seventeenth-century origins: the quadrant street plan that Christian IV applied to the centre, and the squat **Christiansholm Fortress**, overlooking the colourful marina at the east harbour, which now hosts arts and crafts displays. Several excursions are on offer, the pick being the three-and-a-half-hour cruise along the fretted coastline to **Ny Hellesund**, the islet site of one of four hundred coastal defences built by the Germans – or more accurately their POWs – during their occupation. The excursion is on the *M/S Maarten* (late June to early Aug, 4 weekly; 150kr), which departs from the quay beside Vestre Strandgate, at the foot of Tollbodgaten. Kristiansand is also home to the annual five-day **Quart** music festival (*www.quart.no*) at the beginning of July. Recent years have seen international names like Moby, Beck and Nick Cave headlining. For tickets, contact Billettservice (☎815 33 133). Most concerts take place in Bendiksbukta, just outside the city, but there are also several events at clubs in the centre.

Train, **bus** and **ferry** terminals are all close to each other, by the west end of Vestre Strandgate, on the edge of the town grid. The **tourist office**, close by at Vestre Strandgate 32 (June–Aug Mon–Fri 8am–8pm, Sat 10am–8pm, Sun noon–8pm; rest of year Mon–Fri 8.30am–3.30pm), can provide a handy town map and has information on accessible beaches and islands. The rooms at the all-year **youth hostel**, on the edge of the centre at Skansen 8 (☎38 02 83 10; ③), are satisfactory, but the surroundings are a bit grim – the hostel adjoins a mini industrial estate. The *Roligheden* **campsite** (June to mid-Sept) is near the seashore, 3km east of the centre on Framnesveien: once across the bridge at the end of Dronningensgate, turn right along Marvikveien and then right again at the end of the road and the site is signposted. More upmarket is the *Villa Frobusdal*, also on the edge of the central grid at Frobusdalen 2 (☎38 07 05 15; ⑥). This excellent small hotel occupies an attractive old house, and the interior is packed with period furnishings and fittings.

BERGEN AND THE FJORDS

The fjords are the most familiar and alluring image of Norway: huge clefts in the landscape which occur along the west coast right up to the Russian border, though the fjord region is usually defined as lying between Stavanger and Ålesund. Wild, rugged and peaceful, these water-filled wedges are visually stunning; indeed, this part of the country elicits inordinate amounts of purple prose from tourist office handouts, and for once it's rarely overstated. In the summer, the fjords are, it's true, patrolled by a steady flotilla of cruise ships, and the hills heave with hikers, but the crowds are rarely oppressive and what little development there has been is seldom intrusive.

Bergen, Norway's second largest city, is a handy springboard for the western fjords, notably the **Flåm Valley** and its inspiring mountain railway, which trundles down to the Aurlandsfjord, a tiny arm of the mighty **Sognefjord**, Norway's longest and deepest. North of the Sognefjord, there is the smaller but less stimulating **Nordfjord**, though there's superb compensation in the **Jostedalsbreen** glacier which nudges the fjord from the east. The tiny S-shaped **Geirangerfjord**, further north again, is magnificent too – narrow, sheer and rugged – while the northernmost **Romsdalsfjord** and its many branches and inlets reach pinnacles of isolation in the **Trollstigen** mountain highway.

By rail, you can only reach Bergen in the south and Åndalsnes in the north. For everything in between – including the Sognefjord, Nordfjord and the Jostedalsbreen glacier – you're confined to **buses** and **ferries**. Consequently, although the buses and ferries virtually all connect up with each other, it means that there is no set way to approach the fjord region, and

although the much-modified medieval fortress, the Bergenhus, still commands the entrance to the harbour. The city centre divides into two distinct parts: the wharf area, **Bryggen**, adjacent to the fortress, once the working centre of the Hanseatic merchants and now the oldest part of Bergen; and the **modern centre**, which stretches inland from the head of the harbour and down along the Nordnes peninsula, taking the best of Bergen's museums and shops.

The obvious place to start a visit is the **Torget**, an appealing harbourside plaza that's home to a colourful fish market. From here, it's a short stroll round to the **Bryggen**, the principal historical and cultural target, where a string of distinctive wooden buildings line up along the wharf. These once housed the city's merchants and are now home to a string of shops, restaurants and bars. Although none of these structures was actually built by the Hanseatic Germans – most of the originals were destroyed by fire in 1702 – they carefully follow the original building line. Among them, the **Hanseatic Museum** (daily: June–Aug 9am–5pm; Sept–May 11am–2pm; 35kr) is the best preserved, an early eighteenth-century merchant's dwelling kitted out in late-Hansa style, complete with the possessions and documents of contemporary families. More than anything else, though, it's the gloomy warren-like layout of the place that impresses, as well as the all-pervading smell of fish. Good though this is, it's the **Bryggens Museum** (May–Aug daily 10am–5pm; Sept–April Mon–Fri 11am–3pm, Sat noon–3pm, Sun noon–4pm; 20kr), just along the harbourfront next to the *SAS Royal Hotel*, which is Bergen's showpiece, displaying all sorts of intriguing artefacts that were retrieved during the detailed archeological excavation of the Bryggen. A series of imaginative exhibitions attempts a complete reassembly of medieval life – from domestic implements, handicrafts and maritime objects through to trading items – set in context by a set of twelfth-century foundations that were unearthed during the first dig in the 1950s.

A few steps from the museum, **Øvregaten** has long marked the boundary of the Bryggen. By walking along its length you'll soon reach the terminal for the **Fløibanen**, the quaint funicular railway (every 30min: Mon–Fri 7.30am–11pm, Sat 8am–11pm, Sun 9am–11pm; May–Aug till midnight; 34kr return) that runs up to the top of 320m-high Mount Fløyen, from where there are panoramic views over the city.

In the other direction, back along the waterfront, lies the **Bergenhus**, a large and roughly star-shaped fortification now used mostly as a park; its stone and earth walls date from the nineteenth century, but enclose the remnants of earlier strongholds. Of the two medieval survivors (combined guided tours on the hour: mid-May to Aug daily 10am–4pm; rest of year Sun noon–3pm; 15kr), the first is the **Håkonshallen**, a dull reconstruction of the Gothic ceremonial hall built for King Håkon in the mid-thirteenth century. Rather better is the adjacent **Rosenkrantztårnet**, a tower whose thirteenth-century winding spiral staircases, medieval rooms and low rough corridors were enlarged in 1565 by the local lord, who used the place as a fortified residence.

About ten minutes' walk from the Bergenhus, in the modern centre, Bergen's four main **art museums** are on the south side of a pleasant, artificial lake. The pick of these is the **Rasmus Meyer Collection**, Rasmus Meyers Allé 3 (daily 11am–5pm, closed Mon mid-Sept to mid-May; 35kr), which holds an extensive collection of Norwegian painting, including many works by Edvard Munch.

Eating and drinking

Bergen has a good supply of first-rate restaurants, concentrated in the Bryggen, with seafood a particular speciality. Less expensive – and more fashionable – are the city's café/restaurants, which often double up as lively bars, mostly found to the southwest of Ole Bulls plass, the main pedestrianized square just a couple of minutes' walk from the head of the harbour. Cultural events are fairly thick on the ground during the summer, with the largest annual shindig, the Bergen International Festival and the NATTJAZZ, held for eleven days at the end of May.

CAFÉS, RESTAURANTS AND BARS

Bryggeloftet & Stuene, Bryggen 11. This restaurant may be slightly stuffy, but it serves the widest range of seafood in town – mouthwatering meals featuring every North Atlantic fish you've ever heard of, and some you probably haven't. Expensive.

Bryggen Tracteursted, Bryggen. Busy bar in one of the old wooden merchants' buildings on the Bryggen – the premises are its main appeal. Live music at weekends. Closed Sun.

Café Opera, Engen 24. White wooden building near Ole Bulls plass, bustling with a fashionable crew drinking beer and good coffee. Tasty, filling snacks including some good veggie options from as little as 45kr. Crowded clublike venue in the evening

Kafe Kippers, Kulturhuset USF, Georgernes verft. Ultra groovy café/bar in an imaginatively recycled old herring factory, with delicious, inexpensive food and a prime seashore location on the south side of the Nordnes peninsula; the terrace is the place to be on sunny summer days.

Smauet, Vaskerelvsmauet just off Ole Bulls Plass. Highly recommended restaurant which serves up a grand mix of exotic and traditional Norwegian food. A little pricey but well worth the extra money.

Zupperia, Nordahl Bruns gate 8. Trendy but fairly relaxed soup kitchen style café in the basement of the Museum of Applied Arts (Vestlanske Kunstindustrimuseum).

Listings

Airlines Braathens, at the airport (☎55 99 82 50); British Airways enquiries through Braathens; SAS, at the airport (☎55 11 43 00).

Bookstore Melvær Norli 7, Torgalmenning 7 (Mon–Fri 9am–8pm, Sat 9am–4pm), has a good selection of English literature as well as books about Norway, maps and travel guides.

Car rental All the major international car rental companies have offices in town, including Budget, off the Bryggen at Lodin Lepps gate 1 (☎55 90 26 15); and Avis, Lars Hilles gate 20b (☎55 32 01 30).

Consulate UK, Carl Konows gate 34 (☎55 94 47 05).

Ferries International: Fjord Line, Skoltegrunnskaien (☎815 33 500). Domestic (from the Strandkaiterminalen): HSD (☎55 23 87 80); Fylkesbaatane Reiseservice (☎55 32 40 15).

Hiking The DNT-affiliated Bergen Turlag, Tverrgaten 4–6 (Mon–Fri 10am–4pm, Thurs till 6pm), advises on hiking trails in the region, sells hiking maps and arranges guided weekend walks. A year's membership of DNT costs around 360kr.

Internet The library in Strømsgaten (next to the train station) has a free Internet service.

Medical emergencies Casualty (24-hour) at Vestre Strømkaien 19 (☎55 32 11 20).

Off licence Vinmonopolet, in the Bergen Storsenter shopping mall on Strømgaten.

Pharmacy Apoteket Nordstjernen, at the bus station (Mon–Sat 8am–midnight, Sun 9.30am–midnight).

Post office Olav Kyrres gate (Mon–Fri 8am–6pm, Sat 9am–3pm).

Travel agents Terra Nova Travel, Nygaten 3 (Mon–Fri 8.30am–4pm; ☎55 32 23 77).

Around Bergen

There is more to Bergen than the city centre, not least a number of sights just outside the city limits, most notably Edvard Grieg's old lakeside home, **Troldhaugen**. Further out, but still within day-tripping distance, are some of the fjords. If you're not journeying through the fjord region – the better option – you can get a taste by taking the train to Myrdal, at the head of the remarkable branch line down the valley to **Flåm** and the **Aurlandsfjord** – one of the most popular of all fjord trips. Pick up transport timetables from the tourist office or at the train station before you set out.

Troldhaugen

Troldhaugen (mid-April to Sept daily 9am–6pm; Oct–Nov & early April Mon–Fri 10am–2pm, Sat noon–4pm, Sun 10am–4pm; Jan–March Mon–Fri 10am–2pm, also Sun in Feb & March 10am–4pm; 40kr) was Edvard Grieg's home for the last 22 years of his life. To get there, take any **bus** leaving from platforms 19, 20 or 21 at Bergen's bus station and ask to be let off at the Hopsbroen stop. From the bus stop, follow the signs for a 1km walk to the entrance kiosk. A visit begins at the **museum** where Grieg's life and times are exhaustively chronicled. Close by, the **house** itself is a pleasant and unassuming villa built in 1885, and still much as Grieg left it, with a jumble of photos, manuscripts and period furniture; the obligatory guided tour is quite entertaining. Grieg didn't, in fact, compose much at home, but preferred to walk round to a tiny **hut** he had built just along the shore. The hut has survived, but today it stands beside a modern concert hall, the **Troldsalen**, where there are Grieg recitals from late June through to October: tickets, which include transport, are available from Bergen tourist office.

The train to Flåm

If you're short on time but want to sample a slice of fjord scenery, make the **train journey** east from Bergen, through Voss, along the main rail line as far as barren Myrdal, from where specially built trains squeak down a branch line that plummets 900m into the **Flåm valley**. The track took four years to lay and is one of the steepest anywhere in the world. If time's not too tight, you should consider taking the whole "Norway in a nutshell trip" which, as well as the magnificent train ride, includes a cruise on two of the narrowest "arms" of the Sognefjord from Flåm-Gudvangen and the spectacular bus ride from Gudvangen and back to Voss. This trip can be arranged both from Oslo and Bergen, tickets can be bought at any train station. One-way tickets from Oslo or Bergen cost 850kr and the trip takes around fourteen hours. Round trip tickets from Oslo cost 1140kr and take sixteen hours, from Bergen they cost 580kr and the trip takes twelve hours.

   FLÅM village, the train's destination, lies alongside meadows and orchards on the Aurlandsfjord, a matchstick-thin branch of the Sognefjord. It's a tiny village that can be packed on summer days with tourists who pour off the train, eat lunch and then zoom out by bus and ferry. However, out of season or in the early evening when the day-trippers have all moved on, Flåm can be a wonderfully restful place to spend the night. Hikers can get off the train at **Berekvam** station, the halfway point, and descend from there. If you decide **to stay** in Flåm, the trim *Fretheim Hotel* (☎57 63 22 00; ⑨) is located a couple of hundred metres from the station, whilst the more homely *Heimly Pensjonat* (☎57 63 23 00; ⑥) provides simple but adequate lodgings in a modern block about 450m east of the train station along the shore. Another option is the excellent *Flåm Camping* (☎57 63 21 21; ②; May–Sept), a combined **campsite** and **youth hostel** just a couple of hundred metres from the train station. The **tourist office** (May & Sept Mon–Fri 10.30am–6.30pm; June–Aug daily 8.30am–8.30pm; Oct–April Mon–Fri 8am–4pm) at the ferry dock, metres from the train station, has transport timetables as well as information on local hikes.

The Sognefjord

With the exception of Flåm, the southern shore of the **Sognefjord** remains sparsely populated and relatively inaccessible, whereas the north shore boasts a string of appealing places. Top-of-the-list **BALESTRAND** is the prettiest base (reachable by express boat from Bergen and Flåm), a tourist destination since the mid-nineteenth century when it was discovered by European travellers in search of cool, clear air and mountain scenery. These days the village is used as a touring centre for the immediate area, though farming remains the principal livelihood hereabouts. Buses arrive at the minuscule harbourfront, near which you'll find the **tourist office** (mid-June to mid-Aug Mon–Fri 7.30am–9pm, Sat 7.30am–6.30pm, Sun 8am–5.30pm; mid-Aug to mid-Sept Mon–Sat 7.30am–1pm & 3.30–5.30pm, Sun 8am–12.30pm & 4.30–5.30pm; late Sept Mon–Fri 9am–3pm). A hundred metres away, in the comfortable *Kringsjå Hotel*, the local **hostel** (☎57 69 13 03; ③; late June to late Aug) provides convenient lodgings, as does the charming *Midtnes Pensjonat* (☎57 69 11 33; ⑦), about 300m from the dock behind the spiky wooden church.

   There's not too much to see in Balestrand itself, but several lovely places are within easy striking distance, particularly the delightful village of **FJÆRLAND** which can be reached direct by passenger boat from June through to the middle of September. Formerly one of the most isolated spots on the Sognefjord, Fjærland is now connected to the road system, but it retains its old-fashioned atmosphere and appearance, its handsome clapboard buildings sited at the end of the wildly beautiful Fjærlandsfjord. Fjærland is also Norway's book town, and there are various literature events held here in the summer (*www.bokbyen.no* or *www.booktown.net*). You can rent a bike at Balestrand tourist office and cycle the 9km round the Sognefjord to **Dragsvik**; from here, car ferries shuttle across to **VANGSNES**, where Kaiser Wilhelm II, fascinated by Nordic mythology, erected a giant statue of the legendary Viking chief Fridtjof the Bold. Pressing on from Vangsnes, it's a further 12km south along the water's edge to the beautiful Hopperstad stave church on the edge of the hamlet of **VIK**. From Balestrand, it's also a straightforward affair to travel by bus to Stryn (see below), on the Nordfjord, the next fjord system to the north.

The Nordfjord and Jostedalsbreen glacier

Comprising several interconnected stretches of water, the **Nordfjord** does not have quite the lustre of its more famous neighbours. But the compensation is the **Jostedalsbreen glacier**, a 500-square-kilometre ice plateau whose lurking presence dominates the whole of the inner Nordfjord region, its 24 arms flowing down into the nearby valleys, giving the local rivers and glacial lakes their distinctive blue-green colouring. In 1991, the glacier was placed within the **Jostedalsbreen Nasjonalpark** in order to co-ordinate its conservation. The main benefit of this for tourists has been to provide guided glacier walks (June to early Sept) on its various arms, ranging from two-hour excursions to all-day, fully equipped hikes. Prices start at around 100kr, with a half-day trip weighing in at about 250kr. A variety of places take bookings for the guided glacier walks – including Stryn tourist office – and these are accepted up until about 6pm the evening beforehand. Equipment is provided, though you'll need good boots, warm clothes, gloves and hat, sunglasses, and food and drink. With your own vehicle, you can get within easy striking distance of the designated starting points for all the glacier walks. By bus it's a little trickier, but it's usually possible with a bit of preplanning. These starting points are also the places to head for if you just want to get close to the glacier without actually getting on it; two such routes are detailed below.

At the eastern end of the Nordfjord system, **STRYN** is the biggest town in the region and the most obvious target, though its modern centre is far from beguiling. Strynefjell is a natural stop for anyone interested in slalom skiing or snowboarding as the alpine centre on the glacier has good skiing conditions all year round. The town is also an important transport junction: buses stop beside the river, from where it's a five-minute walk east into the town centre, where the **tourist office** (June–Aug daily 9am–6/8pm) takes bookings for guided walks on the Jostedalsbreen. There's inexpensive **accommodation** in Stryn too, most conveniently at the fjordside *Walhalla Gjestgiveri* (☎57 87 10 72; ④), a delightfully unpretentious place down by the river, about 200m from the tourist office on Perhusvegen. The obvious alternative to Stryn is **LOEN** – just 11km southeast around the fjord along Hwy 60. The hamlet spreads ribbon-like along the low-lying, grassy foreshore within easy striking distance of an arm of the Jostedalsbreen glacier, and, like Stryn, it is on the main north–south bus route. It also has the big advantage of being home to one of Norway's more famous **hotels**, the *Alexandra* (☎57 87 50 00, *www.alexandra.no*; ⑨), a big and flashy modern block tucked in beneath the hills and fringed by carefully manicured gardens; the slightly less expensive motel-style *Hotel Loenfjord* (☎57 87 57 00; ⑨), across the road, has comfortable modern rooms. The *Alexandra* has all the **information** you'll need about visiting the nearest glacier nodule, the Kjenndalsbreen, to the southeast of Loen.

The Kjenndalsbreen and the Briksdalsbreen

With your own transport you can follow the single-track road from Loen for 17km up along a beautiful valley with the glacial Lovatnet lake down below. After about 10km, the road gets rougher and hairier as it worms its way on to the car park and café at the road's end. From here, it's a rocky 3km walk to the foot of the **Kjenndalsbreen**, whose blue and white folds of ice tumble down the rockface, split by fissures and undermined by a furious foaming river fed by plummeting waterfalls. This part of the glacier is popular with visitors, but it's not as big a target of day-tripping coaches as the Briksdalsbreen nodule further to the south. The 24km-long side road to the **Briksdalsbreen** car park begins at **OLDEN**, 7km south of Loen on Hwy 60. From the car park, the footpath leads up the valley for around 3km, passing waterfalls and weaving up the river on the way. Once there it's a simple matter to get close to the ice itself: there's a very flimsy rope barricade and a small warning sign – "Be careful!" Guided glacier walks begin at the souvenir/café area by the start of the track.

The Geirangerfjord

The **Geirangerfjord** is one of the region's smallest fjords, but also one of its most breath-taking. A convoluted branch of the Storfjord, it cuts well inland, marked by impressive water-falls and with a village at either end of its snake-like profile. You can reach the Geirangerfjord by bus or car from the north or south, but you'd do best to approach from the north if you can. From this direction, the journey begins in Åndalsnes from where Highway 63 wriggles over the mountains via the wonderful **Trollstigen Highway**, which climbs through some of the country's highest peaks before sweeping down to the Tafjord. From here, it's a quick ferry ride and dramatic journey along the Ørneveien, the Eagle's Highway, for a first view of the Geirangerfjord and the village that bears its name glinting in the distance. There is little as stunning anywhere in western Norway, and from mid-June to August it can all be seen on a twice-daily bus following this so-called "Golden Route".

GEIRANGER village enjoys a commanding position at one end of the sixteen-kilometre, S-shaped Geirangerfjord. However, it's hopelessly overdeveloped and your best bet, espe-cially in high season, is to pass straight through, taking the ferry on to the hamlet of **HELLE-SYLT**, an hour's boat ride away through the double bend of the fjord. There's nothing much to the place – it's primarily a stop-off on tourist itineraries – but by nightfall Hellesylt makes for a quiet and peaceful overnight stay. The ferry terminal is a few steps from the *Grand Hotel* (π70 26 51 00; ⑧), a local landmark since its construction in 1871, though patchily renovat-ed and enlarged – guests are put up in the modern annexe next door. The hotel's main com-petitor is the **hostel** (π70 26 51 28; ③; June–Aug), set on the hillside just above the village – just follow the signs. Alternatively, *Hellesylt Camping* (π70 26 51 88; summer only) occupies the shadeless field beside the fjord about 300m from the quay. Usefully, Hellesylt is also on the main Bergen to Loen, Stryn and Ålesund bus route; buses stop near the jetty.

The Romdalsfjord and around

Travelling north from Oslo by train, the line forks at Dombås – the Dovre line continuing northwards over the fells to Oppdal, and ultimately Trondheim, the Rauma line beginning a thrilling ninety-minute, roller-coaster rattle west down through the mountains to the **Romsdalsfjord**. Apart from the Sognefjord, reached from Bergen, the Romsdalsfjord is the only other Norwegian fjord accessible by train, which explains the number of backpackers wandering its principal town of **ÅNDALSNES**, many people's first – sometimes only – con-tact with fjord country. Despite a wonderful setting between lofty peaks and looking-glass water, the town is unexciting, but it does make a convenient base for further explorations. The pick of the local routes is the journey south to the Geirangerfjord, over the Trollstigen Highway (see above). From June to August, there are two buses a day from Åndalsnes to Geiranger, and three or four buses daily to another tempting destination, Ålesund (see oppo-site). Åndalsnes has an outstanding **hostel** (π71 22 13 82; ③; mid-May to mid-Sept), which occupies a group of charming wooden buildings in a rural setting 2km along the E136 towards Ålesund. Another very good option is the riverside *Åndalsnes Camping og Motell* (π71 22 16 29), with cabins (③), rowboats and bikes for rent, a 25-minute walk from the train station – take the first left after the river on the road out to the hostel. The **tourist office** at the train station (late June to late Aug Mon–Sat 10am–7pm, Sun 1–7pm; rest of year Mon–Fri

10am–3.30pm) has a free and comprehensive guide to local hikes as well as bus, boat and train timetables.

At the end of the E136, some 120km west of Åndalsnes, the fishing and ferry port of **ÅLESUND** is immediately – and obviously – different from any other Norwegian town. Instead of old clapboard houses and functional concrete and glass, there's a conglomeration of proud grey-and-white facades, lavishly decorated and topped with a forest of turrets and pinnacles. In 1904, a disastrous fire left 10,000 people homeless and the town centre destroyed. A hectic reconstruction programme saw almost the entire area rebuilt by 1907 in a style that borrowed heavily from the German Jugendstil movement. Kaiser Wilhelm II, who used to holiday hereabouts, gave assistance, and the architects ended up creating a strange but fetching hybrid of up-to-date foreign influences and folksy local elements, with dragons, faces, flowers and even a decorative pharaoh or two. The finest buildings are concentrated on the main street, Kongensgate, and around the slender, central harbour, the **Brosundet**.

Ålesund **bus station** is situated on the waterfront a few metres south of the Brosundet and across from the **tourist office** in the Rådhus (June–Aug Mon–Fri 8.30am–7pm, Sat 9am–5pm, Sun 11am–5pm; rest of year Mon–Fri 8.30am–4pm). The pick of the town's **hotels** are the *Comfort Home Hotel Bryggen*, an elegantly converted waterside warehouse at Apotekergata 1 (☎70 12 64 00; ⑨), and the similar *Brosundet Gjestehus* along the street at no. 5 (☎70 12 10 00, *www.brosundet.no*; ⑨). There's also a small and central **hostel** at Parkgata 14, at the top of Rådstuggata (☎70 11 58 30; ③; May–Sept). For **eating**, the *Sjøbua Fiskerestaurant*, Brunholmgata 1, is an expensive but first-rate seafood restaurant, which comes complete with its own lobster tank. A cheaper option is *Nilles Pizza* at Kirkegata 1. If it's sunny, everyone flocks to the terrace of the *Metz*, a café-restaurant overlooking the Brosundet.

NORTHERN NORWAY

The long, thin counties of **Trøndelag** and **Nordland** mark the transition from rural southern to blustery northern Norway. The main town of Trøndelag, appealing **Trondheim**, is easily accessible from Oslo by train, but north of here feels very far removed from the capital and travelling becomes more of a slog as the distances between places grow ever greater. In **Nordland** things get wilder still, though save the scenery there's little of delaying interest until you reach the surprisingly interesting steel town of **Mo-i-Rana**. Just north of here lies the **Arctic Circle**, beyond which the land becomes ever more spectacular, not least on the offshore chain of the **Lofoten Islands**, whose idyllic fishing villages (and cheap accommodation) richly merit a stop. Back on the mainland, **Narvik** was the scene of some of the fiercest fighting by the Allies and Norwegian resistance in World War II and is now a modern port handling vast quantities of iron ore amid some startling rocky surroundings. Further north still, the provinces of **Troms** and **Finnmark** are enticing too, but the travelling can be harder still, the specific attractions well distanced and – when you reach them – subtle in their appeal. It was from **Tromsø**, northern Norway's largest urban centre and a lively university town, that the king and his government proclaimed a "Free Norway" in 1940 before fleeing into exile in Britain. The appeal of Finnmark is less obvious: it was laid waste to during World War II, and it's now possible to drive for hours without coming across a building more than fifty years old. Most travellers head straight for **Nordkapp**, from where the Midnight Sun is visible between early May and the end of July.

The **train** network reaches as far north as Fauske and Bodø, buses making the link to Narvik, from where a separate rail line runs the few kilometres to the border and then south through Sweden. Further north, approaches are more limited, and access is either by the coastal boat (*Hurtigrute*) or bus. The Hurtigrute takes the best part of two days to circumnavigate the huge fjords between Tromsø and Kirkenes; bus transport throughout the summer (and some of the winter) is efficient and regular, using the windswept E6 Arctic Highway as far as Kirkenes, with the E69 branching off to Nordkapp on the way.

Trondheim

TRONDHEIM, an atmospheric city with much of its eighteenth-century centre still intact, has been an important Norwegian power base for centuries, its age-old importance guaranteed by the excellence of its harbour and its position at the head of a wide and fertile valley. The early Norse parliament, or Ting, met here, and the city was once a major pilgrimage centre. The city centre sits on a small triangle of land, a pocket-sized area where the main sights – bar the marvellous cathedral – have an amiable low-key quality about them. Trondheim also possesses a clutch of good restaurants and a string of busy bars.

The City

The colossal **Nidaros Domkirke**, Scandinavia's largest medieval building, gloriously restored following the ravages of the Reformation and several fires, remains the focal point of the city centre (May to mid-June & late Aug to mid-Sept Mon–Fri 9am–3pm, Sat 9am–2pm, Sun 1–4pm; mid-June to late Aug Mon–Fri 9am–6pm, Sat 9am–2pm, Sun 1–4pm; mid-Sept to April Mon–Fri noon–2.30pm, Sat 11.30am–2pm, Sun 1–3pm; 25kr). Taking Trondheim's former name (Nidaros means "mouth of the River Nid"), the cathedral is dedicated to King Olav, Norway's first Christian ruler, who was killed at the nearby battle of Stiklestad in 1030. After the battle, Olav's body was spirited away and buried here, his resting place marked by the erection of a chapel, which was altered and enlarged over the years to accommodate the growing bands of pilgrims, achieving cathedral status in 1152. Thereafter, it became the traditional burial place of Norwegian royalty and, since 1814, it has also been the place where Norwegian monarchs are crowned. The stonework of the early Gothic choir is especially fine, with the flying buttresses and pointed arches decorated with all manner of tiny heads and gargoyles. Inside, the gloomy half-light hides much of the lofty decorative work, but it is possible to examine the striking choir screen and font, both the work of the Norwegian sculptor Gustav Vigeland (1869–1943). If possible, visit in the early morning to avoid the tour-bus crowds.

Behind the Domkirke lies the heavily restored archbishop's palace, the **Erkebispegården**, a courtyard complex flanked by stone and brick wings of medieval provenance. The archbishops were kicked out during the Reformation and the palace was subsequently used as the city armoury. Some of the old weapons are now displayed in the west wing, which has been turned into the **Army and Resistance Museum** (June–Aug Mon–Fri 9am–3pm, Sat & Sun 11am–4pm; rest of year Sat & Sun 11am–4pm; free). Its most interesting section, on the top floor, recalls the German occupation during World War II, dealing honestly with the sensitive issue of collaboration. The south wing houses a lavish **ecclesiastical museum** (June–Aug Mon–Sat 10/11am–3/5pm, Sun noon–4/5pm; rest of year Tues–Sat 11am–3pm, Sun noon–4pm; 25kr, or free with cathedral ticket), largely devoted to a few dozen medieval sculptures stashed away when the cathedral was partly rebuilt at the end of the nineteenth century. A short walk north of the Domkirke, the **Museum of Decorative Arts**, Munkegata 5 (June–Aug Mon–Sat 10am–3/5pm, Sun noon–4/5pm; rest of year Wed–Sat 10am–3pm, Sun noon–4pm; 30kr), holds a splendid assortment of furniture, tapestries, glassware and silver; it also features a first-rate programme of temporary exhibitions.

Near at hand is **Torvet**, the main city square, a spacious open area anchored by a statue of Olav Tryggvason, perched on a stone pillar like some medieval Nelson; the statue is also a sundial. The broad and pleasant avenues of Trondheim's centre radiate out from here; they date from the late seventeenth century, when they doubled as fire breaks. They were originally flanked by long rows of wooden buildings, now mostly replaced by uninspiring modern structures. One conspicuous survivor is the **Stiftsgården** (June–Aug Mon–Sat 10am–3/5pm, Sun noon–5pm; guided tours every hour on the hour; 35kr), the yellow creation just north of

Torvet on Munkegata. Built in 1774–78 as the home of a provincial governor, it's now an official royal residence. A long series of period rooms with fanciful Italianate wall paintings reflect the genteel tastes of the early occupants, and the anecdotal guided tour raises a smile or two, but not perhaps 35kr wide.

Practicalities

Trondheim is the first major northbound stop of the Bergen–Kirkenes **coastal boat** (*Hurtigrute*), which docks about 600m behind and to the north of Sentralstasjon, the combined **bus and train terminal**. Sentralstasjon is situated just over the bridge from the town centre, which occupies a small island at the mouth of the River Nid. The **tourist office** is bang in the middle of town on the main square, the Torvet (mid-May to Aug Mon–Fri 8.30am–6/8/10pm, Sat & Sun 10am–4/6/8pm; Sept to mid-May Mon–Fri 9am–4pm; *www.taas.no*). They issue a very useful free city guide, change money and book **private rooms** for a fixed rate of 350kr for a double, plus a 30kr fee. There's a large **HI hostel** at Weidemannsvei 41 (☎73 87 44 50; ③), twenty minutes' hike east from the centre out over the romantic Bakkebru bridge; bus #63 runs out in that direction from Sentralstasjon. Another inexpensive choice is the *InterRail Centre*, Elgesetergate 1 (☎73 89 95 38; ②; late June to mid-Aug), providing basic bed and breakfast in the unusual round red house which serves as the student social building in the winter; it's a twenty-minute walk from Torvet or take bus #41, #42, #48, #49 or #52.

More convenient alternatives include *Pensjonat Jarlen*, Kongensgate 40 (☎73 51 32 18; ④), with frugal rooms at bargain prices; the *Rainbow Gildevangen*, Søndregate 22b (☎73 87 01 30; ⑤), a chain **hotel** with comfortable, modern rooms in an imposing old stone building, a short walk northeast of Torvet; and the *Rainbow Trondheim*, Kongensgate 15 (☎73 50 50 50; ⑤), a big and popular hotel offering well-maintained modern double rooms at reasonable rates. The city centre is best seen on foot, but if you're staying on the edge of town, take advantage of the brightly coloured **municipal bicycles** that are available from bike racks all over the centre; they are free, but you need 20kr to unlock them – as per a supermarket trolley.

For **eating**, the cafés and restaurants in the area of Bakklandet are a good choice, the groovy *Ni Muser*, Bispegata 9a, footsteps from the cathedral, is a relaxed and fashionable little café serving tasty snacks and meals based on a variety of European cuisines (daily 11am–midnight); the *Dromedar*, Nedre Bakklandet 3, is also fashionable, a café-bar offering tasty meals with a wholefood slant. *Credo*, Ørjaveita 4, has a very good restaurant serving innovative seasonal food on the ground floor, and a bar downstairs. The town has an active **nightlife**; the place to be right now is the Nedre Elvehavn area, especially the very popular venue/bar/café *Blæst* in Dokkgata 8, and several other café options.

The Arctic Circle and Bodø

North of Trondheim, it's a long haul up the coast to the next major places of interest: Bodø, which is the main ferry port for the Lofoten Islands, and the gritty but likeable town of Narvik, respectively 730km and 908km away. You can cover most of the ground by train, a rattling good journey with the scenery becoming wilder and bleaker the further north you go; it takes nine hours to reach Fauske, where the railway reaches its northern limit and turns west for the final 65km dash across to Bodø. On the way you cross the **Arctic Circle**, which, considering the amount of effort it takes to get there, is something of an anticlimax. The landscape, uninhabited for the most part, is undeniably bare and bleak, but the gleaming **Arctic Circle Centre** (daily: May & early Sept 10am–6pm; early to mid-June & Aug 9am–8pm; mid-June to July 8am–10pm) disfigures the scene – a giant lampshade of a building plonked by the E6 highway and stuffed with every sort of tourist bauble imaginable: from "Polarsirkelen" certificate to specially stamped postcards. Drivers will struggle to complete the journey from Trondheim to Bodø in one day and should consider resting up at **MO-I-RANA**, or simply "Mo", just south of the Arctic Circle. Formerly a grimy steel town, Mo has recently cleaned itself up and its leafy, spick-and-span centre holds a pretty nineteenth-century church with a dinky onion dome. Mo has a **hostel** (☎75 15 09 63; ③; mid-May to Aug) and an excellent **hotel**, the *Meyergården* (☎75 13 40 00; ⑧), an extremely comfortable establishment on Ole Tobias Olsensgate, about 300m from the train station. For the adventurous, there are two great options for cavewalking in Mo; one light tour to Grønligrotta and a more advanced one into Setergrotta. Information on these tours is available from the **tourist information** office (daily 9am–4pm, longer hours in summer) in Ole Tobias Olsens gate. FAUSKE is, along with Bodø, an important transport hub and one of the departure points of the Nord-Norgeekspressen bus service that complements the trains by carrying passengers as far as Nordkapp. These buses leave twice daily from beside Fauske train station, and tickets can be purchased from the driver or beforehand at any bus station. There's a fifty-percent discount for InterRail and Scanrail pass holders on the first step of the route, to Narvik, a gorgeous five-hour run past fjords and snowy peaks. In Fauske, Storgata – also a part of the E6 – accommodates the handful of shops that pass for a town centre. Although it's a much better option to stay in Bodø, there are a couple of useful accommodation options. At no. 82, you'll find the modern *Fauske Hotel* (☎75 60 20 00; ⑧), whose big breakfasts (from 7am; 60kr) are handy for travellers staying at the spartan youth **hostel** (☎75 64 67 06; ②), about 500m west of the hotel and signposted off Storgata. A third option is the *Lundhøgda campsite* (☎75 64 39 66; May–Oct). Advance booking advised.

An hour west of Fauske, **BODØ** is where the trains terminate. It's also a stop on the *Hurtigrute* coastal boat route and the main point of departure for the Lofoten Islands. Heavily bombed in World War II, the town is short of sights, but it manages a bright and cheerful air and is home to the **Norwegian Aviation Museum** (June–Aug Mon–Fri 10am–8pm, Sat 10am–5pm, Sun 10am–8pm; rest of year Tues–Fri 10am–4pm, Thurs till 7pm, Sat & Sun 11am–5pm; 70kr), which adopts an imaginative approach to the general history of Norwegian aviation and has two main sections: one devoted to the air force, the other to civilian aircraft. The coastal boat (*Hurtigrute*) and the southern Lofotens ferry (to Moskenes, Værøy and Røst) leave from the docks respectively 700m and 500m northeast of the train station, which is itself just 300m along Sjøgata from the **tourist office**, at Sjøgata 21 (June–Aug Mon–Fri 9am–8.30pm, Sat 10am–4pm & 6–8pm, Sun noon–4pm & 6–8pm; rest of year Mon–Fri 9am–4pm; *www.bodoe.com*). The **bus station** is a further 400m along Sjøgata. If you're heading further north, note that the same half-price bus deal for rail pass holders travelling from Fauske to Narvik operates from Bodø too. Close by the bus station, at the west end of Sjøgata, another dock handles the catamaran (*Hurtigbåt*) services to the Lofotens, notably to Svolvær and Stokmarknes.

Bodø offers plenty of choice in **accommodation**. The tourist office has a small supply of **private rooms** both in the town and its environs, with a fixed-rate tariff of 250–300kr per double, plus a 15kr booking fee (25kr outside town). Alternatively, the no-frills **youth hostel** is next door to the bus station at Sjøgata 55 (☎75 52 11 22; ②). Among several central hotels, the pick is the *Comfort Home Hotel Grand*, at Storgata 3 (☎75 54 61 00; ⑧), whose handsome public rooms boast elegant Art Deco flourishes. For **eating**, easily the best bet is the Pizzakjeller'n, in the basement of the *Radisson SAS Hotel Bodø*, Storgata 2, where an enormous pizza for two will set you back around 160kr.

The Lofoten Islands

Stretched out in a skeletal curve across the Norwegian Sea, the **Lofoten Islands** are perfect for a simple, uncluttered few days. For somewhere so far north the weather is exceptionally mild, and there's plentiful **accommodation** (*www.lofotenholidays.com*) in *rorbuer*, originally fishermen's shacks, but now usually well-equipped huts designed to accommodate from two to six people. These are rented out to tourists for around 600kr per night, though you can pay as little as 400kr and as much as 1000kr. In addition, the Lofotens have five hostels and plentiful campsites. The *Hurtigrute* **coastal boat** calls at two ports, Stamsund and Svolvær, while the southern Lofoten ferry leaves Bodø for Moskenes, Værøy and Røst. There are also passenger express **boats**, which work out slightly cheaper than the coastal boat, linking both Bodø and Narvik with Svolvær. By **bus** the main long-distance services from the mainland to the Lofotens are from Bodø to Svolvær via Fauske and from Narvik to Svolvær.

The islands

The main town on **Austvågøy**, the largest and northernmost island of the group, is **SVOLVÆR**, a rather disappointing place, although it is a hub of island bus routes and you may well arrive here. Pick up island-wide information and bus schedules at the **tourist office**, located beside the main town square by the harbour (late June to mid-Aug Mon–Sat 9am–4pm & 5–8pm, Sun 10am–9.30pm; reduced hours rest of year). One of the most pleasant **places to stay** in Svolvær is *Sjøhuscamping* (☎76 07 03 36; ④), by the seashore on Parkgata, five minutes' walk from the square, where the accommodation is in old boathouses and the price includes use of a well-equipped kitchen. Alternatively, the central *Hotel Havly* (☎76 06 90 00; ⑧) occupies a plain tower block and has perfectly adequate, en-suite rooms.

Reachable by bus from Svolvær, **HENNINGSVÆR**, 23km to the southwest, is a much more beguiling village, its cramped and twisting lanes of brightly painted wooden houses lining a postcard-pretty harbour. It's well worth an overnight stay, with some good value lodgings being the centrally located *Den Siste Viking* (☎76 07 49 11; ③).

However, it's the next large island to the southwest, **Vestvågøy**, which captivates many travellers to the Lofotens. This is due in no small part to the laid-back charm of **STAMSUND**, whose older buildings are strung along its rocky, fretted seashore. This is the first port of call for the coastal boat (*Hurtigrute*) as it heads north from Bodø, and is much the best place to stay on the island. Getting there by bus from Austvågøy is reasonably easy, too, with several buses making the trip daily, though you do have to change at Leknes, 16km away to the west. In Stamsund, the first place to head for is the friendly **hostel** (☎76 08 93 34; ②; closed late Oct to Dec), made up of several *rorbuer* perched over a pint-sized bay, about 1km down the road from the port and 200m from the Leknes bus stop. Fishing around here is first-class: the hostel rents out rowing boats and lines or you can go on an organized trip for just 150kr; afterwards, you can cook your catch on the hostel's wood-burning stoves. For touring the rest of Vestvågøy, the hostel rents out bikes (85kr a day).

By any standard the next two Lofoten islands, **Flakstadøya** and **Moskenesøya**, are extraordinarily beautiful. As the Lofotens taper towards their southerly conclusion, rearing peaks crimp a sea-shredded coastline studded with a string of fishing villages. Remarkably, the E10 travels along almost all of this dramatic shoreline, by way of tunnels and bridges, to **MOSKENES**, the ferry port midway between Bodø and the remote, southernmost bird islands of Værøy and Røst. Six kilometres further on, the E10 ends at the tersely named Å, one of the Lofotens' most delightful villages, its huddle of old buildings rambling over a foreshore that's wedged in tight between the grey-green mountains and the surging sea. If you want **to stay** in Å, the same family owns the assortment of smart *rorbuer* (③) that surround the dock, the adjacent **hostel** (①), the bar and the only restaurant, where the seafood is very good; accommodation reservations can be made on ☎76 09 11 21. **Local bus** #101 runs along the length of the E10 from Leknes to Å once or twice daily from late June to late August, less frequently the rest of the year. Buses do not, however, usually coincide with sailings to and from Moskenes. Consequently, if you're heading from the Moskenes ferry port to Å, you'll either have to walk – it's an easy 6km – or take a taxi (☎948 11 216, about 90kr).

Narvik

NARVIK was established less than a century ago as an ice-free port to handle the iron ore brought by train from northern Sweden, and the **iron ore docks** are still immediately conspicuous upon arrival, the rust-coloured machinery overwhelming the whole waterfront. There are guided tours of the iron ore terminal (1 daily; 30kr; times vary – ask at tourist office), interesting if only for the opportunity to spend ninety minutes amid such giant, ore-stained contraptions. Otherwise the town centre lacks appeal, with modern stone and concrete replacing the wooden buildings flattened during the last war. Nonetheless, try and devote an hour or so to the **Krigsminne Museum** (mid-June to Aug Mon–Sat 10am–10pm, Sun 11am–5pm; March to mid-June & Sept daily 10am–4pm; 30kr), in the main square close to the docks. Run by the Red Cross, it documents the wartime German saturation bombing and bitter sea and air battles for control of the ore supplies, in which hundreds of foreign servicemen died alongside the many locals.

The **train station** is at the north end of town and long-distance **buses** pull up outside. From here, it's a five- to ten-minute walk south along the main street to the main square, where the **tourist office** (mid-June to mid-Aug Mon–Fri 9am–7pm, Sat 10am–7pm, Sun noon–7pm; late Aug daily 11am–5pm; rest of year Mon–Fri 9am–4pm) issues free maps and has a wide range of leaflets on the region's attractions. The best place to **stay** is the *Briedablikk Gjestehus*, Tore Hundsgate 41 (☎76 94 14 18; ⑤), a well-tended guest house, a short, stiff walk from the tourist office at the top of Kinobakken. The nearest **campsite**, *Narvik Camping*, is along the E6 about 2km north of town and has cabins for rent (250kr).

On from Narvik

There's a choice of several routes on from Narvik. The **rail link**, cut through the mountains a century ago, runs east and then south into Sweden, reaching Kiruna in three and Stockholm in eighteen hours. It's a beautiful journey, but **bus** travellers, heading north on the *Nord-Norgeekspressen* to Tromsø and Alta, do no worse with a succession of switchback roads, lakeside forests, high peaks, gentle valleys and plunging, black-blue fjords. In summer, cut grass dries everywhere, stretched over wooden poles forming long lines on the hillsides like so much washing. Narvik is also connected to Svolvær, on the Lofotens, by bus and catamaran. Note that on all these buses and the catamaran InterRail and Scanrail pass holders get a fifty-percent discount.

Tromsø

TROMSØ was once known, rather preposterously, as the "Paris of the North", and though even the tourist office doesn't make any pretence to such grandiose titles now, the city still likes to think of itself as the capital of northern Norway. Certainly, as a base for this part of the country, it's hard to beat. It's a pleasant, small city set in magnificent landscape – dramatic mountains and sea and surrounded by almost bare wilderness. With two cathedrals, a clutch of reasonably interesting museums and an above-average (and affordable) nightlife, patronized by a high-profile student population. In the centre of town, the **Domkirke** (June–Aug Tues–Sun noon–4pm; free) reflects the town's nineteenth-century prosperity, the result of its barter trade with Russia. From the church, it's a short walk north along the harbourfront to the most diverting of the city's museums, the **Polar Museum** (daily: mid-May to mid-June 11am–6pm; mid-June to Aug 11am–8pm; rest of year 10am–3pm; 30kr), whose varied displays include skeletons retrieved from the permafrost of Svalbard and a detailed section on the daring deeds of the polar explorer Roald Amundsen. On the other side of the water, over the spindly Tromsø Bridge, the white and ultramodern **Arctic Cathedral** (May & mid-Aug to mid-Sept daily 4–6pm; June to mid-Aug Mon–Sat 10am–8pm, Sun 1–8pm; 15kr) is spectacularly original, made up of eleven immense triangular concrete sections representing the eleven Apostles left after the betrayal.

Practicalities

The coastal boat (*Hurtigrute*) docks in the centre of town at the foot of Kirkegata; buses arrive and leave from the adjacent car park. The **tourist office**, Destination Tromsø, is at Storgata 61, near the Domkirke (June to mid-Aug Mon–Fri 8.30am–6pm, Sat & Sun 10am–5pm; rest of year Mon–Fri 8.30am–4pm), and issues free town maps as well as having a small supply of **private rooms** at around 300kr per double per night (200kr single). The large and basic **hostel**, *Tromsø Vandrerhjem*, Gitta Jønsons vei 4 (☎77 68 53 19; ②; late June to late Aug), is located approximately 2km west of the quay, a steep twenty-minute walk up Fr. Langesgate. Alternatively, try one of two reasonable **guest houses**: *Skipperhuset Pensjonat*, Storgata 112 (☎77 68 16 60; ④), or *Kongsbakken*, on the hillside directly west of the city centre at Skolegata 24 (☎77 68 22 08; ④). The nearest **campsite**, *Tromsdalen Camping*, lies over the bridge on the mainland, about 1500m beyond the Arctic Cathedral. It has cabins and is open all year; several city buses go near there – ask at the bus station. Tromsø has a varied selection of **restaurants**, **cafés** and **pubs**. For excellent coffee, pastries and light snacks try *Kaffebønna*, Strandtorvet 1. *Aunegården*, at Sjøgata 29, has everything from coffee and tasty cake to traditional Norwegian dishes. The *Sjømatrestauranten Arctandria* and the adjacent *Biffhuset*, Strandtorget 1, have excellent food for around 200kr per person a main course, and a good, lively pub, *Skarven*. In the evening, *Blå Rock Café*, Strandgata 14, is a lively spot with a CD jukebox and weekend discos.

Honningsvåg and Nordkapp

Connected to the mainland by an ambitious combination of tunnels and bridges, bleak and treeless Magerøya is Norway's most northerly island. The only settlement of any size here is **HONNINGSVÅG**, a crusty fishing village that strings along the water's edge for a kilometre or two. Apart from the fish, Honningsvåg makes a steady income from accommodating the hundreds of tourists who flood north every summer intent on visiting the country's northernmost point, Nordkapp, just 34km away. Amongst several **hotels**, one of the more appealing is the *Rica Bryggen*, which occupies a plain but well-kept concrete high-rise down at the head of the harbour (☎78 47 28 88; ⑧). Much cheaper is the **campsite/cabin** complex 8km away on the road to Nordkapp (☎78 47 33 77; ②; May–Sept). Long-distance buses arrive in the centre of Honningsvåg and there's a limited bus service on to Nordkapp (late June to mid-Aug 2 daily except Sat; 50min). When the buses aren't running, the only option is a taxi (600kr) – though note that the road is closed throughout the winter and often in spring too. Travellers with the *Hurtigrute* **coastal boat**, which puts in at Honningsvåg, should note that there's a special coach which gets you to Nordkapp and back within the two-and-a-half-hour stop. If you need to eat in Honningsvåg, there are a couple of takeaway kiosks along Storgata and a very good seafood restaurant at the *Best Western Honningsvåg Brygge Hotel*.

NORDKAPP itself might be expected to be a bit of a disappointment. It is, after all, only a cliff, 307 metres high, with an arguable claim to being the northernmost point of Europe. But there is something exhilarating about this bleak, wind-battered promontory. Originally a Sami sacrificial site, it was actually named by the English explorer Richard Chancellor in 1553, but it was not until the late nineteenth century that a visit by King Oscar II opened the tourist floodgates. These days the headland is occupied by **North Cape Hall** (daily: early April to late May & early Sept to early Oct 2–5pm; late May to early June noon–1am; early June to early Aug 9am–2am; early Aug to late Aug 9am–midnight; late Aug to early Sept noon–5pm; 175kr), an extremely flashy complex that contains souvenir shops, cafés, restaurants and huge windows from where you can survey the surging ocean below. The complex also has a post office, where you can get your letters specially stamped. Tourists gather here in numbers to watch the Midnight Sun (from early May to the end of July).

travel details

Trains

Åndalsnes to: Dombås (2 daily; 1hr 30min); Oslo (2 daily; 6hr 30min).

Dombås to: Trondheim (3–4 daily; 2hr 30min).

Kristiansand to: Kongsberg (4–5 daily; 3hr 30min); Oslo (5 daily; 5hr).

Myrdal to: Flåm (June–Sept 11–12 daily; Oct–May 4 daily; 50min).

Oslo to: Åndalsnes (2–3 daily; 6hr 30min); Bergen (4–5 daily; 6hr 30min); Kristiansand (4–5 daily; 5hr); Røros (2–3 daily; 6hr); Stavanger (3 daily; 9hr); Trondheim (3–4 daily; 8hr 15min); Voss (4–5 daily; 5hr 40min).

Stavanger to: Kristiansand (3–4 daily; 3hr); Oslo (3 daily; 9hr).

Trondheim to: Bodø (2–3 daily; 10hr); Dombås (3–4 daily; 2hr 30min); Fauske (2–3 daily; 9hr 20min); Mo-i-Rana (2–3 daily; 7hr); Oslo (3–4 daily; 7hr); Røros (1–2 daily; 2hr 30min); Stockholm (2 daily; 12hr).

Buses

Ålesund to: Bergen (1–2 daily; 10hr); Hellesylt (1–2 daily except Sat; 2hr 40min); Molde (4–6 daily; 2hr 15min); Stryn (1–2 daily except Sat; 4hr); Trondheim (1–2 daily; 8hr 10min).

Alta to: Hammerfest (1–2 daily except Sat; 3hr); Honningsvåg (late June to mid-Aug 1–2 daily except Sat; 5hr); Kautokeino (1–2 daily except Sat; 2hr 30min); Tromsø (April to late Oct 1–2 daily; 7hr).

Åndalsnes to: Geiranger (mid-June to late Aug 2 daily; 3–4hr); Molde (3–7 daily; 1hr 30min); Ålesund (3–4 daily; 2hr 20min).

Balestrand to: Sogndal (2 daily; 1hr 10min).

Bergen to: Ålesund (1–2 daily; 10hr); Trondheim (1 daily; 14hr); Voss (4 daily; 1hr 45min).

Fauske to: Bodø (2–3 daily; 1hr 10min); Narvik (2 daily; 7hr).

Hammerfest to: Alta (1–2 daily except Sat; 3hr); Skaidi (1–2 daily except Sat; 1hr 15min).

Honningsvåg to: Nordkapp (late June to mid-Aug 2 daily except Sat; 50min).

Kautokeino to: Alta (1–2 daily except Sat; 2hr 30min).

Kongsberg to: Oslo (every hour between 5am and 2am; 2hr).

Narvik to: Alta (1 daily; 14hr); Tromsø (1–2 daily; 4hr 40min).

Oslo to: Bergen (4–5 daily; 10hr).

Stryn to: Bergen (2 daily; 7hr); Oslo (1 daily; 8hr 30min).

Tromsø to: Alta (April to late Oct 1–2 daily; 7hr); Narvik (2 daily; 7hr); Nordkapp (late June to mid-Aug 1 daily except Sat; 14hr).

Trondheim to: Ålesund (2–3 daily; 8hr); Bergen (2 daily; 14hr); Kristiansund (2–3 daily; 5hr); Stryn (2 daily; 7hr 20min).

Voss to: Bergen (4 daily; 1hr 45min); Sogndal (2 daily; 3hr).

Catamaran ferries

Arendal to: Oslo (July to mid-Aug 4 weekly; 6hr 45min).

Bergen to: Balestrand (1–2 daily; 4hr); Flåm (1–2 daily; 5hr 30min); Måløy (1–2 daily; 4hr 30min); Stavanger (2–5 daily; 4hr 30min).

Bodø to: Svolvær (1 daily except Sat; 5hr 30min).

Narvik to: Svolvær (1 daily except Sat; 4hr).

Stavanger to: Bergen (2–5 daily; 4hr 30min).

CHAPTER 21

POLAND

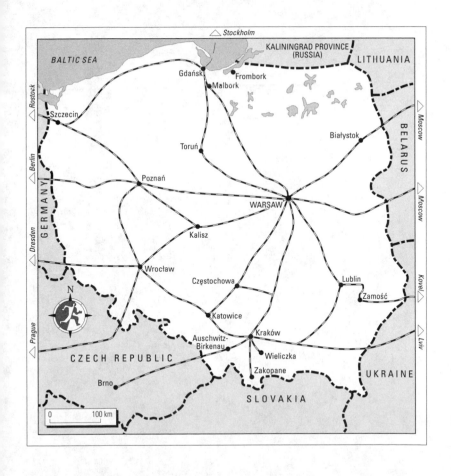

Introduction

Images of **Poland** flooded the world media throughout the 1980s. Strikes and riots at the Lenin Shipyards of Gdańsk were the harbingers of the disintegration of communism in Eastern Europe. The decade's end saw the establishment of a government led by the Solidarity trade union, followed by the victory of union leader Lech Wałęsa in Poland's first presidential election since the 1920s – thoughout to many people's surprise, he lost the presidency to "post-communist" Aleksander Kwasniewski in 1995, who remains president with a right-wing parliament.

The pattern was familiar enough through the Eastern bloc, but the rebirth of democratic Poland was a uniquely Catholic revolution. The **Church** has always been the principal defender of the nation's identity, and its physical presence is inescapable in Baroque buildings, roadside shrines and images of the national icon, the Black Madonna. Encounters with the **people** are at the core of any experience of the country. On trains and buses, in the streets or the village bar, you'll never be stuck for opportunities for contact: Polish hospitality is legendary. Tourism, like every other aspect of the Polish infrastructure, is currently in a state of flux, but it's never been easier to explore the country. Foreigners are no longer subject to currency restrictions and can travel as they please, if not always as smoothly as desired.

Unless you're driving to Poland, you're likely to begin your travels with one of the three major cities. Much of **Warsaw**, the capital, conforms to the stereotype of Eastern European greyness, but its historic centre, extensive parks and vibrant commercial life are diverting enough. **Kraków**, the ancient royal capital, is the real crowd puller, rivalling the Central European elegance of Prague and Vienna. The Hanseatic city of **Gdańsk** offers a dynamic brew of politics and commerce, while nearby **Sopot** features golden beaches. German influences abound in the north and southwest of the country, in Gdańsk itself, in the austere castles and fortified settlements along the River Wisła (Vistula) and in the divided province of Silesia. Yet, to the north of Silesia, quintessential-

ly Polish **Poznań** is revered as the cradle of the nation.

Poland has many regions of unspoilt natural beauty, none more popular than the alpine **Tatras**, the most exhilarating walking terrain in the country.

Information and maps

Tourist offices of the West European kind are a relatively new phenomenon in Poland, and the level of help you will get from them remains unpredictable. Most towns and cities now have a tourist office (known as IT or *informacja turystyczna*); sometimes these are run by the local municipality and are rather good; more often than not, however, they're privately run travel agencies which are using the label to lure in tourists in order to sell them tours and travel tickets. In addition, two long-established tourist organizations whose offices may also be of help are **PTTK**, who specialize in hiking tourism, and **Almatur**, a student-and-youth travel bureau which tends to have the best English speakers.

The easiest road **map** to follow is Bartholomew's *Europmap: Poland* (1:800,000), which is especially clear on rail lines. Once you're in the country, you'll find Empik stores (found on most high streets) are well stocked with maps of the regions and cities. Otherwise, city maps (*plan miasta*) are available cheaply in newspaper kiosks and bookshops. Most of these maps have tram and bus routes marked on them.

Money and banks

The Polish currency is the **złoty** (zł), which is divided into 100 groszy. Coins come in denominations of 1, 2, 5, 10, 20 and 50 groszy, and 1, 2 and 5 złoty; notes in denominations of 10, 20, 50, 100 and 200 złoty. There are about 4zł to the dollar and 5.5zł to the pound sterling.

There is no longer a significant difference between the **exchange rates** offered by the banks (usually open Mon–Fri 7.30am–5pm, Sat 7.30am–2pm) and those by the omnipresent exchange booths

---

POLAND ON THE NET

www.poland.pl – the official Web site
www.globopolis.com – information on Warsaw and Kraków
www.hotelsinpoland.com – comprehensive hotel information

www.gorski.com/poland.htm – skiing and snow-boarding in the Tatras
www.inyourpocket.com – independent travel guides to Warsaw, Kraków and Gdańsk

(kantors). Most kantors, however, will not change travellers' cheques. Hotels offer poor exchange rates. Major **credit cards** are accepted by most hotels and restaurants, and you can arrange a cash advance on most cards; an increasing number of shops take plastic, and there are **ATMs** in every city.

Communications

Post offices in Poland are identified by the name Urzad Pocztowy (Poczta for short). Theoretically, each city's head office has a **poste restante** facility: make sure that anyone addressing mail to you adds "No. 1" (denoting the head office) after the city's name. Head office opening hours are usually Mon–Sat 7/8am–8pm; branches usually close at 6pm or earlier. Outbound mail takes a few days; expect airmail delivery within three. Use the red post boxes.

A few of Poland's **pay phones** still accept jetons (tokens) but by far the best way to phone is to buy a **phone card**. Card phones are increasingly popular and less likely to be out of order. Cards can be purchased from post offices and newsagent kiosks in denominations of 25, 50, 75 and 100 units (7.5zł, 15zł, 22.5zł & 30zł) and can be used for international calls, but these are expensive.

You'll find at least one decent, central **Internet café** in the larger towns; an hour online costs 5–10zł.

Getting around

Poland has comprehensive and cheap public transport services, though they can often be overcrowded and excruciatingly slow.

■ Trains

The reasonably efficient Polish State Railways (PKP) runs three main types of **trains**: express services (*ekspresowy*), particularly the ones marked IC (intercity) or EC (Eurocity), are the ones to go for if you're travelling long distances, as they stop at the main cities only; seat reservations are compulsory and involve a small supplementary charge. So-called fast trains (*pośpieszny*) have far more stops, and reservations are optional. Normal services (*osobowy*) are best avoided: in rural areas they stop at every haystack.

Even a long cross-country haul will only set you back little more than £15/$22, but it's well worth paying the 50 percent extra to travel **first-class** or make a **reservation** (*miejscówka*), as sardine-like conditions are fairly common. Most long journeys are best done overnight; second-class sleepers are a bargain at around £10/$14 per person. **Buying tickets** in main stations can be a minor hassle though you will rarely have to queue for more than a few minutes. For journeys of over 100km, you can buy tickets at Orbis travel agencies (branches in all towns and cities). Tickets for international journeys can be bought at stations or Orbis offices – at the latter without queuing. First and second class **PolRail passes** for the whole network are available in Poland for periods of eight (£76/$114 first-class, £52/$78 second-class), fifteen (£85/$127, £60/$90) or 21 days (£100/$150, £68/$102). EuroDomino and European East InterRail passes are valid in Poland.

■ Buses

Intercity buses operated by **PKS**, the national bus company, can be slow and overcrowded; there are few long-haul routes and no overnight journeys. In rural areas, notably the mountain regions, there's greater choice and convenience, and on a rural journey the bus is often considerably faster than the train. Main bus stations are usually alongside the train station. The private company **Polski Express** (☎022/620 03 26, *www.polskiexpress.pl*) offers slightly pricier intercity journeys in rather more comfortable and quick buses – they're particularly useful if you're travelling on radial routes out from Warsaw, but are hard to find anywhere else. Seat numbers on most buses are allocated when you buy tickets, though many stations cannot allocate seats for services starting from another town – in such cases you have to buy a ticket from the driver. As with trains, Orbis offices are the best place to go if you want to book on an international route.

■ Driving and hitching

There are few multi-lane highways in Poland, and progress on the main traffic-clogged intercity routes is invariably slow. **Car rental** costs from around £40/$60 a day to £250/$400 a week (unlimited mileage). Many petrol stations in cities and on main international routes are open 24 hours a day, others from around 6am to 10pm. In rural areas stations can be a long way apart, so carry a fuel can. **Speed limits** are 60kph in built-up areas, 90kph on country roads, and 130kph on motorways.

Repairs are much less of problem than they used to be. There are authorized dealers for various Western makes of car, and **repair services** of a minor kind are the stock in trade of garages. If you break down call ☎9637.

Hitchhiking used to be a tradition when there were fewer cars on the road, but today it is not encouraged. The danger of robbery is high, and with public transport so cheap and omnipresent, it's not worth the risk.

Accommodation

Accommodation will almost certainly account for most of your costs in Poland, though there are now plenty of cheap alternatives to the heavily touted international hotels. Look out for weekend reductions in big-city hotels. In addition, there are exceptional deals to be had in several cities if you **book online** –*www.hotelspoland.com* is the best for bargain-hunting.

■ Hotels

Most Polish towns have at least one **budget hotel** offering spartan – but eminently habitable – rooms with WC and shower located in the hallway, usually costing less than £8/$12 per person. Hotels in this category often include 3- or 4-person rooms, which work out very cheaply indeed if you're travelling as a group. Establishments offering additional comforts such as ensuite shower, TV and a decent breakfast need not cost a great deal more (reckon on £10–18/$14–25 per person), although standards in these **mid-range places** can be unpredictable: some rooms boast wallpaper and fittings that haven't changed for decades, while others look like Scandinavian furniture showrooms. Hotels aiming at **international business standard** (especially those run by Orbis, the former state-run tourism dinosaur) are often overpriced for what they are – especially in Warsaw, where hotel prices across the board are higher than in many Western European capitals.

■ Hostels

Scattered throughout Poland are some 200 **hostels** (*schroniska młodzieżowe*). Many are only open at the height of summer and are liable to be booked solid, while most of the year-round hostels still conform to the hair-shirt ideals of the movement's founders with lockouts and curfews. Prices are rarely more than £4/$6 a head, though, and many hostels are located close to town centres. For a complete list, contact the Polish Youth Hostel Federation (PTSM) at ul Chocimska 28, Warsaw (Mon–Fri 8am–3.30pm; ☎022/498-128).

Alternatively you can ask in one of the tourist offices (especially Almatur) about summer accommodation in **university hostels**; charges (including breakfast) are around £3/$4.50 for ISIC card-holding students and £5–7/$7.50–12 for others (no age limit), depending on whether they wish to share a room. They are often the best bet in summer, being as cheap as hostels without the restrictions, although they tend to be located in the suburbs. A generous number of **refuges** (clearly marked on hiking maps) enable you to make long-distance treks. Accommodation is in basic dormitories, but costs are nominal and you can often get cheap, filling hot meals.

■ Private rooms

It's possible to get a **room in a private house** (*kwatery prywatne*) almost anywhere in the country. Those in the cities are often pretty shabby, although in mountain resorts they can be extremely comfortable. Several major cities have a **room-finding service**, usually known as the Biuro Zakwaterowania, and most tourist information offices will also help. Charges are usually £8/$12 per person, £12/$18 in Warsaw. You'll be given a choice of location and category; it makes sense not to register for too many nights until you know you'll like the place. Many houses in rural holiday areas hang out signs saying *Noclegi* (lodging) or *Pokoje* (rooms). It's up to you to bargain: £3/$4.50 is the least you can expect to pay. Individuals with rooms to let may approach you at train stations – this can be the way to a bargain, but carries all the usual risks of an unofficial deal.

ACCOMMODATION PRICE CODES

Throughout this guide, accommodation is coded on a scale of ① to ⑨, the code indicating the lowest price per person per night you could expect to pay in each establishment in high season. With hostels this is the nightly rate per person; with hotels, the price is arrived at by dividing the cost of the cheapest double room by two. The prices indicated by the codes are as follows:

① under £5/$8	④ £15–20/$24–32	⑦ £30–35/$48–56
② £5–10/$8–16	⑤ £20–25/$32–40	⑧ £35–40/$56–64
③ £10–15/$16–24	⑥ £25–30/$40–48	⑨ £40/$64 and over

■ Camping

There are some 400 **campsites** throughout the country; for a complete list see the *Campingi w Polsce* map, available from Empik and other bookshops. Apart from main holiday areas, they can be found in most cities: the ones on the outskirts are invariably linked by bus to the centre and often have the benefit of a peaceful location, all-day restaurant and swimming pool. Most open May–Sept only. Charges usually work out at less than £2/$3 a head, a bit more if you come by car. Many sites have chalets to rent which, though spartan, are good value at around £4/$6 per head. Camping rough, outside of the national parks, is fine so long as you're discreet.

Food and drink

Poles take their food seriously, providing meals of feast-like proportions for the most casual visitors. The cuisine is a complex mix of influences: Russian, German, Ukrainian, Lithuanian and Jewish traditions have all left their mark.

■ Food

Hotel **breakfasts** might include fried eggs with ham, mild frankfurters, a selection of cold meats and cheese, rolls and jam. If you need to find your own breakfast you could do worse than head for a **milk bar** (*bar mleczny*, usually open from early morning until 5–6pm), the traditional place for cheap but filling Polish snacks.

Traditional Polish **takeaway stands** usually sell *zapiekanki*, baguette-like pieces of bread topped with melted cheese. Hot-dog stalls dole out sub-frankfurter sausages in white rolls; in the tourist resorts there are stalls and shops selling chips (*frytki*) with sausage (*kiełbasa*) or chicken (*kurczak*), as well as a growing selection of Western-style takeaway joints. Some of these kiosk-type takeaways offer excellent food, increasingly adding Oriental cuisine to their repertoire, plus a plastic table or two in the street for consumption "on the premises".

Many **restaurants** close late, but the older tradition of closing at 9 or 10pm persists in some places so it's advisable to check the opening times before you go in. First on the menu in most places are **soups**, varying from delicate dishes to concoctions that are virtually meals in themselves. Best known is *barszcz*, a spicy beetroot broth that's ideally accompanied by a small pastry. In better restaurants, the **hors d'oeuvres** might include Jewish-style gefilte fish, jellied ham (*szynka w galerecie*), steak tartare

(*stek tatarski*), wild rabbit paté (*pasztet zajeca*), or hard-boiled eggs in mayonnaise, sometimes stuffed with vegetables (*jajka faszerowane*).

The basis of most **main courses** is fried or grilled meat, such as *kotlet schabowy* (a pork cutlet). Two inexpensive specialities you'll find everywhere are *bigos* (cabbage stewed with meat) and *pierogi*, dumplings stuffed with meat and mushrooms, or with cottage cheese, onion and spices (*pierogi ruskie*). Pancakes (*naleśniki*) often come as a main course, stuffed with cottage cheese (*ze serem*). Fried potato pancakes (*placki ziemniaczane*) are particularly good, served in sour cream or spicy paprika sauce.

Cakes, **pastries** and **other sweets** are an integral ingredient of most Poles' daily consumption, and the cake shops (*cukiernia*) – which you'll find even in small villages – are as good as any in Central Europe. *Sernik* (cheesecake) is a national favourite, as are *makowiec* (poppyseed cake), *drożdówka* (a sponge cake, often topped with plums), and *babka piaskowa* (marble cake).

■ Drink

Poles' capacity for **alcohol** has never been in doubt, and drinking is a national pursuit. All of the cities possess delightful cafés, and a growing number of Western-style bars and pubs. Most of the latter are open until at least midnight; usually longer at weekends.

Poles can't compete with their Czech neighbours in the production and consumption of **beer** (*piwo*), but there are a number of fairly drinkable and widely available Polish brands. It's with **vodka** (*wódka*) that Poles really get into their stride. Ideally it is served neat, well chilled, in measures of 25 or 50 grams and knocked back in one go, with a mineral water chaser. Best of the clear vodkas are *żytnia* and *Wyborowa*. Of the **flavoured varieties**, first on most people's list is *żubrówka*, infused with bison grass.

Opening hours and holidays

Most **shops** open on weekdays from around 10am to 6pm, except food stores which may open as early as 6am and stay open well into the evening. Many shops close on Saturday afternoons and all day Sunday. RUCH kiosks, where you buy newspapers and municipal transport tickets, generally open at about 6am. Increasing numbers of street traders do business well into the evening, and you can find shops in major cities (particularly the Empik stores) offering late-night opening throughout the week.

Museums and **historic monuments** almost invariably close one day per week, usually Monday. Entrance tends to cost very little, and is often free on one day of the week. **Public holidays** are: Jan 1; Easter Monday; May 1; May 3; Corpus Christi (May/June); Aug 15; Nov 1; Nov 11; Dec 25 & 26.

Emergencies

The biggest potential hassles are hotel room thefts, pickpocketing and car break-ins. Avoid leaving cars unattended overnight in city centres and beware of being mugged in the narrow corridors of trains. The **police** (*policja*) are courteous and helpful but may not speak English.

For serious **health problems** you'll be directed to a hospital (*szpital*), where conditions will probably be poor, but some are better than others. Paying for a stay in a private hospital may be forced on you by circumstances, but there are good public hospitals too (usually the teaching hospitals). If you are required to pay for treatment or medication, keep receipts for your insurance claim.

The usual **emergency numbers** (police ☎997, ambulance ☎999, fire ☎998) are of little use if you don't speak Polish. **Medicover** (☎022/622-1115; *www.medicover.com*) provides a network of medical centres in major cities with English-speaking staff and a 24-hour service. They will charge heavily, so use them only in real emergencies.

WARSAW

WARSAW, likely to be most visitors' first experience of Poland, makes an initial impression that is all too often negative. The years of communist rule have left no great aesthetic glories, and there's sometimes a hollowness to the faithful reconstructions of earlier eras. However, as throughout Poland, the pace of social change is tangible and fascinating, as the openings provided by the postcommunist order turn the streets into a continuous marketplace, while the postwar dearth of nightlife and entertainments has become a complaint of the past, as a plethora of new bars, restaurants and clubs establish themselves.

Warsaw became the capital of Poland in 1596, when **King Zygmunt III** moved his court here from Kraków. The city was badly damaged by the Swedes during the invasion of 1655 and was then extensively reconstructed by the **Saxon kings** in the late seventeenth century – the Saxon Gardens (Ogród Saski), right in the centre, date from this period. The **Partitions** abruptly terminated this golden age, as Warsaw was absorbed into Prussia in 1795. Napoleon's arrival in 1806 gave Varsovians brief hopes of liberation, but following the 1815 Congress of Vienna, the city was integrated into the Russian-controlled Congress **Kingdom of Poland**. It was only with the outbreak of World War I that Russian control began to crumble, and with the restoration of Polish independence in 1918, Warsaw reverted to its position as capital. Then, with the outbreak of World War II, came the progressive annihilation of the city. Hitler, infuriated by the **Warsaw Uprising**, ordered the elimination of Warsaw; by the end of the war 850,000 Varsovians – two-thirds of the city's 1939 population – were dead or missing. The task of rebuilding took ten years of ceaseless labour.

Arrival and information

Okęcie international airport is 8km southwest of the Old Town: avoid the rip-off taxi drivers and take bus #175 (#611 at night) into town, which passes the main **train station**, Warszawa Centralna, in the modern centre, before arriving in the Old Town some ten minutes' ride beyond. There's a 24-hour left-luggage office at Warszawa Centralna, as well as lockers where you can store luggage for up to ten days. The main **bus station**, Centralny Dworzec PKS, is located right next to the Warszawa Zachodnia suburban train station, 3km west of Centralna station. To get into town from here catch any eastbound train or bus #127, #508, #517 or #E5. Intercity buses operated by Polski Express arrive and depart from the bus stop on al Jana Pawła II, just outside the western entrance of Centralna train station.

The best source of general **information** is the IT office in the main hall of Centralna station, (daily 8am–8pm; ☎022/654 24 47), which can provide plenty of leaflets and maps, and book rooms in hotels and hostels for free. There's another IT office offering similar services on the Old Town's main square, Rynek Starego Miasta 28/42 (same times), as well as information booths at the airport arrivals hall and the main bus station. The lively English-language monthly *Warsaw Insider* (*www.warsawinsider.com*; 9zł), contains eating and drinking **listings**, and can be bought from information centres and at some hotels and bookstores. Less well distributed but stronger on detail is the pamphlet-shaped *Warsaw in Your Pocket* (*www.inyourpocket.com*; 6zł), which contains fuller reviews of hotels and hostels.

City transport

Warsaw is too big to get around without using public transport. **Buses** and **trams** are the main forms of transport, and both are still very cheap for foreigners. Regular bus and tram routes close down at about 11.15pm; from 11pm to 5am night buses leave every thirty minutes from behind the Palace of Culture. There is also a **metro** underground system running through the centre of town (as far as Ratusz station on Plac Bankowy), but it has only one line and doesn't take in many of the sights.

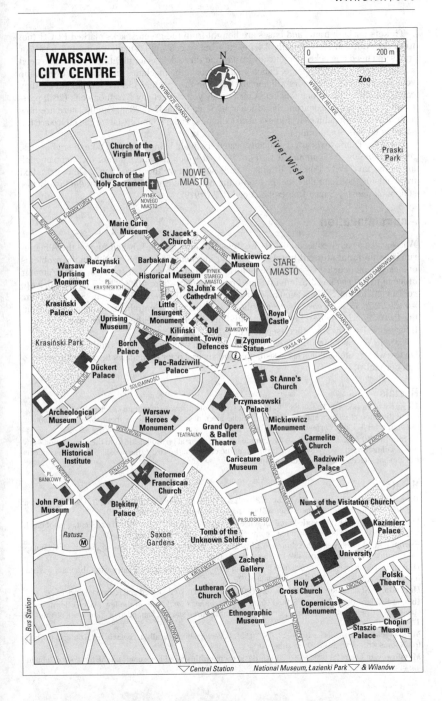

Tickets for both trams and buses are bought from the green shacks marked RUCH (not from drivers), and are currently 2.4zł each – but prices will certainly go up. For buses or trams you need one ticket per journey by day and three tickets for night buses. You also need a 2.4zł ticket for bulky luggage. Punch your tickets in the machines on board and every time you change tram – inspectors will fine you 120zł on the spot and 48zł for your luggage if they catch you without a validated ticket. Alternatively you can get day (7.2zł) or week (26zł) passes from some kiosks, or from the office at ul Senatorska 37 (7.30am–3pm). There are now automatic ticket machines in some central locations. Tickets (and costs) for the metro are the same as for buses and trams.

For Westerners, **taxis** are reasonably priced. To avoid being ripped off take the radio taxis, recognizable by the illuminated sign on the roof which has the name of the company, followed by "taxi" and a number (ordinary taxis simply have the word "taxi"). Don't get a taxi from outside the Centralna Station – go to the nearby ul Emilii Plater for a radio taxi. Better still, book one; try Super Taxi (☎9622) or MPT (☎919).

Accommodation

Warsaw has a paltry collection of **HI hostels**, although during July and August the Almatur-run **international student hotels** are another inexpensive possibility, without the problems of lockouts and curfews – ask at the Centralna Station information centre or at the Almatur office at ul Kopernika 23 (Mon–Fri 9am–7pm, Sat 10am–2pm; ☎022/826 35 12). For **private rooms** go to the Syrena agency at ul Kruczna 17 (Mon–Sat 9am–7pm, Sun 9am–5pm; ☎022/628 75 40, *www.syrena.hotel.pl*), about 300m from the Centralna Station just down from the *Grand Hotel*. The best bet for help with hotel bookings is either the Centralna Station or Informator Turystyczny office (see above).

Even in Warsaw, **camping** is extremely cheap and popular with Poles and foreigners alike. On the whole, site facilities are reasonable and several offer bungalows (around 20zł per person per night).

Hostels

Ul **Karolkowa 53a** (☎022/632 88 29). In the western Wola district – take tram #22 from Centralna station in the direction of Ochota and get off on al Solidarności, near the Wola department store; a good option. Lockout from 5–10pm; curfew 11pm. ②.

Ul **Smolna 30** (☎022/827 89 52). A five-minute bus ride along al Jerozolimskie from the main station – any bus heading towards Nowy Świat will drop you at the corner of the street. Barrack-like conditions but central location. Reception 4–9pm; curfew 11pm. ②.

Hotels

Dom Chłopa, pl Powstańców Warszawy 2 (☎022/625 15 45, *domchlopa@gromada.pl*). Used by a wider clientele than its name ("Farmers' House") suggests. Plush, central and well run. ⑨.

Dom Literatury, ul Krakowskie Przedmieście 87/89 (☎022/635 04 04). Cheap and excellent, but not much English spoken. This is basically a few rooms above a pub. Call and try your luck. ③.

Europejski, ul Krakowskie Przedmieście 13 (☎022/826 50 51, *www.orbis.pl*). One of the few Orbis hotels with character. Normally expensive but has special offers at weekends. ⑧.

Harctour, Niemcewicza 17 (☎022/659 00 11). Spartan but tolerable place 500m east of the main bus station. Rooms with shared facilities ③, en suites ⑤.

Harenda, ul Krakowskie Przedmieście 4/6 (☎022/826 00 71). Well located and reasonable prices. ⑥.

Ibis, al Solidarności 165 (☎022/520 30 00, *h2894@accor-hotel.com*). One of the few places offering good standards at genuinely mid-range prices. Comfortable three-star accommodation 2km west of the Old Town. ⑥.

Mazowiecki, ul Mazowiecka 10 (☎022/682 20 65). Careworn but basically acceptable hotel bang in the centre. Rooms with shared WC ④, en suites ⑤.

Metalowcy, ul Długa 29 (☎022/668 50 17). Basic rooms with shared bathrooms on the top floor of a building just west of the Old Town. ②.

Praski, al Solidarności 61 (☎022/818 49 89). Opposite a park and next to the wonderful *Le Cédre Lebanese* restaurant. In the outer edge of the Praga district of Warsaw over the river, which is not particularly safe, but the tram drops you right outside the hotel. ④.

Campsites

Camping Gromada, ul Żwirki i Wigury 32 (☎022/825 43 91). Best and most popular of the Warsaw campsites, on the way out to the airport – bus #188 or #175 will get you there. Besides tent space the site has a number of cheap bungalows (22zł).

Majawa, Boh. Bitwy Warszawskiej 1920r. 15/17 (☎022/823 37 48). Just south of the bus station – take bus #154. Less crowded than the Gromada site, with some bungalows at 70zł, and the usual small extra charges for linen, tents, electricity and car parking.

The City

Wending its way north towards Gdańsk and the Baltic Sea, the **Wisła** (Vistula) river divides Warsaw neatly in half, although almost everything you'll want to see in the city lies on its western bank. It's here that you'll find the central business and shopping district, **Śródmiescie**, grouped around Centralna station and the nearby Palace of Culture, with the more picturesque and tourist-friendly **Old Town** (Stare Miasto) just to the north. Opposite the Old Town on the east bank of the river lies the Praga suburb, consisting predominantly of residential districts.

The Old Town

The title "Old Town" – Stare Miasto – is in some respects a misnomer for the historic nucleus of Warsaw. Fifty-five years ago this compact network of streets and alleyways lay in rubble, only to be painstakingly reconstructed in the decade following World War II. **Plac Zamkowy** (Castle Square), on the south side of the Old Town, is the obvious place to start a tour. Here the first thing to catch your eye is the bronze **statue of Zygmunt III Waza**, the king who made Warsaw the capital.

On the east side of the square is the former **Royal Castle** (Zamek Królewski; *www.zamek-krolewski.art.pl*), once home of the royal family and seat of the Polish parliament, now the **Castle Museum** (Tues–Sat 10am–5pm, Sun 11am–5pm; 14zł). Though the structure is a replica, many of its furnishings are the originals, scooted into hiding during the first bombing raids. After the Chamber of Deputies, formerly the debating chamber of the parliament, the Grand Staircase leads to the most lavish section of the castle, the **Royal Apartments of King Stanisław August**. Through two smaller rooms you come to the magnificent **Canaletto Room**, with its views of Warsaw by Bernardo Bellotto, nephew of the famous Canaletto – whose name he appropriated to make his pictures sell better. Marvellous in their detail, these cityscapes provided important information for the architects rebuilding the city after the war. Next door is the richly decorated Royal Chapel, where an urn contains the heart – sacred to many Poles – of Tadeusz Kościuszko, swashbuckling leader of the 1794 insurrection and hero of the American War of Independence.

On Świćtojańska, north of the castle, stands **St John's Cathedral**, the oldest church in Warsaw, now regaining its old status after the communist era. A few yards away, the Old Town Square – **Rynek Starego Miasta** – is one of the most remarkable bits of postwar reconstruction anywhere in Europe. Flattened during the Warsaw Uprising, its three-storey merchants' houses have been rebuilt to their seventeenth- and eighteenth-century designs, multicoloured facades included. By day the Rynek teems with visitors, who are catered for by buskers, artists, cafés, moneychangers and *dorozki*, the traditional horse-drawn carts that clatter tourists round the Old Town for a sizeable fee. The **Warsaw Historical Museum** (Tues & Thurs 11am–6pm, Wed & Fri 10am–3.30pm, Sat & Sun 10.30am–4pm; 6zł, free Sun) takes up a large part of the north side; exhibitions here cover every aspect of Warsaw's life from its beginnings to the present day, with a particularly moving chronicle of everyday resistance to the Nazis. On the east side, the **Mickiewicz Museum** (Mon, Tues & Fri 10am–3pm, Wed & Thurs 11am–6pm, Sun 11am–5pm; 5zł, Thurs free) is a temple to the Romantic national poet.

From the Rynek, ul Nowomiejska leads to the sixteenth-century Barbakan, which used to guard the Nowomiejska Gate, the northern entrance to the city. The fortress is part of the old town defences, which run all the way around from Plac Zamkowy to the northeastern edge of the district.

The New Town and the Ghetto

Cross the ramparts from the Barbakan and you're into the **New Town** (Nowe Miasto) district, which despite its name dates from the early fifteenth century, but was formally joined to Warsaw only at the end of the eighteenth. **Ulica Freta**, the continuation of Nowomiejska, runs north through the heart of the district to the **Rynek Nowego Miasto**, once the commercial hub of the district, now a soothing change from the bustle of the Old Town. Tucked into the eastern corner is the **Church of the Holy Sacrament**, commissioned by Queen Maria Sobieska in memory of her husband Jan's victory over the Turks at Vienna in 1683; as you might expect, highlight of the sober interior is the Sobieski funeral chapel.

West from the square is the majestic **Krasiński Palace**, its facade bearing fine sculptures by Andreas Schlüter. Behind the palace are the gardens, now a public park, and beyond that the Ghetto area. In 1939 there were an estimated 380,000 Jews living in and around Warsaw – one-third of the total population. By May 1945, around 300 were left, and after the war Jewish Warsaw was replaced by the sprawling housing estates and tree-lined thoroughfares of the **Muranów** and **Mirów** districts, a little to the west of the city centre. However, a few traces of the Jewish presence in Warsaw do remain, and there's a small but increasingly visible Jewish community here. First stop on any itinerary of Jewish Warsaw is the **Nożyk Synagogue** on ul Twarda, the only one of the Ghetto's three synagogues still standing. Built in the early 1900s, it was gutted during the war, and reopened in 1983 after a complete restoration. Marooned in the middle of a drab square to the north of the Ghetto area, the imposing **Ghetto Heroes Monument** – unveiled in 1948 – was made from materials ordered by Hitler for a monument to the Reich's anticipated victory. Further evidence of Jewish Warsaw can be seen in the miraculously untouched street, **Próżna**, its original brickwork dotted with satellite dishes, which is now threatened with renovation – it's best viewed from the Palace of Culture.

Śródmieście

The area stretching from the Old Town down towards Łazienki Park – **Śródmieście** – is the increasingly fast-paced heart of Warsaw. Of all the thoroughfares bisecting central Warsaw from north to south, the most important is the one often known as the Royal Way, which runs almost uninterrupted from Plac Zamkowy to the palace of Wilanów. **Krakowskie Przedmieście**, the first part of the Royal Way, is lined with historic buildings.

Even in a city not lacking in Baroque churches, the **Church of the Nuns of the Visitation** stands out, with its columned, statue-topped facade; it's also one of the very few buildings in central Warsaw to have come through World War II unscathed. Its main claim to fame in Polish eyes is that Chopin used to play the church organ here. Most of the rest of Krakowskie Przedmieście is taken up by **Warsaw University**. On the main campus courtyard, the Library stands in front of the seventeenth-century **Kazimierz Palace**, once a royal summer residence, while across the street from the gates is the former **Czapski Palace**, now home of the Academy of Fine Arts. Just south is the Baroque **Holy Cross Church** (Kościół Świętego Krzyża), wrecked in a two-week battle during the Warsaw Uprising; photographs of the distinctive figure of Christ left standing among the ruins became poignant emblems of Warsaw's suffering. Another factor increases local affection for this church: on a pillar to the left side of the nave there's an urn containing Chopin's heart.

Biggest among Warsaw's palaces is the early-nineteenth-century **Staszic Palace**, now the headquarters of the Polish Academy of Sciences (not open to the public), which virtually blocks the end of Krakowskie Przedmieście. South from the Staszic, the main street becomes **Nowy Świat** (New World), an area first settled in the mid-seventeenth century. Moving down this wide boulevard, the palaces of the aristocracy give way to shops, offices and cafés. West along al Jerozolimskie is the **National Museum** (Tues, Wed & Fri 10am–4pm, Thurs noon–5pm, Sat & Sun 10am–5pm; 13zł, free Sat), an impressive compendium of art and archeology. The first floor has the ancient art while the European galleries on the upper floors display a wide range of paintings and sculptures – Caravaggio, Bellini, Brueghel and Rodin included. The remarkable display of Polish medieval altarpieces and religious sculpture includes some imaginative and exuberant wooden Madonnas, mainly from the Gdańsk region.

West of here lies the commercial heart of the city. **Marszałkowska**, the main north-south road cutting across Jerozolimskie, is lined with department stores and privately run boutiques and workshops selling everything from jewellery to car spares. Towering over everything is the Palace of Culture, a gift from Stalin that the Polish people could hardly refuse. Apart from a vast conference hall, the cavernous interior contains offices, shops, theatres, nightclubs, cinemas, swimming pools, and – the ultimate capitalistic revenge – a casino. Some locals maintain that the best view of Warsaw is from the thirtieth-floor platform – the only viewpoint from which one can't see the palace (daily 11am–5pm; 7zł).

Łazienki Park and Palace

Parks are one of Warsaw's distinctive and most attractive features. South of the commercial district, on the east side of al Ujazdowskie, is one of the best, the **Łazienki Park**. Once a hunting ground, the area was bought by King Stanisław August in the 1760s and turned into an English-style park with formal gardens. A few years later the slender Neoclassical **Łazienki Palace** (Tues–Sun 9.30am–3.30pm; 8zł) was built across the park lake: the best memorial to the country's last and most cultured monarch.

The oak-lined promenades and pathways leading from the park entrance to the palace are a favourite with both Varsovians and tourists. On summer Sunday lunchtimes, concerts and other events take place under the watchful eye of the ponderous **Chopin Monument**, just beyond the entrance. Nazi damage to the rooms themselves was not irreparable, and most of the lavish furnishings, paintings and sculptures survived the war intact, having been hidden during the occupation. The stuccoed **ballroom**, the biggest ground-floor room, is a fine example of Stanisław's classicist predilections, lined with a tasteful collection of busts and classical sculptures. As the adjoining picture galleries demonstrate, Stanisław was a discerning art collector. Upstairs are the king's private apartments, most of them entirely reconstructed since the war. The nearby **Myślewicki Palace** (9.30am–3pm; closed Tues; 4zł) houses more period interiors. The park itself stays open till dusk.

Wilanów

The grandest of Warsaw's palaces, **Wilanów** (Mon & Wed–Sun 9.30am–2.30pm; 15zł, free Thurs) makes an easy excursion from the city centre: take bus #122 south from anywhere along the main drag from the Old Town through Krakowskie Przedmieście and Nowy Świat to its terminus. Sometimes called the Polish Versailles, it was the brainchild of King Jan Sobieski, who purchased the existing manor house and estate in 1677 and spent nearly twenty years turning it into his ideal country residence. Among the sixty-odd rooms you'll find styles ranging from the lavish early Baroque of the apartments of Jan Sobieski and John III to the classical grace of the nineteenth-century Potocki museum rooms. Some find the cumulative pomp rather deadening – but if your interest hasn't flagged after the guided tour, there are a couple of other places of interest within the grounds. The gate on the left side beyond the main entrance opens onto the stately **palace gardens** (9.30am till sunset; closed Tues;

2zł), while to the right before you enter is the **Poster Museum** (Tues–Fri 10am–4pm, Sat & Sun 10am–5pm; 4zł), a mishmash of the inspired and the bizarre from an art form which has long had major currency in Poland.

Eating and drinking

Warsaw's **cafés** have long been favoured for get-togethers, clandestine political exchanges, stand-up rows or just passing the time. For basic snacks, **milk bars** (*bar mleczny*), street stalls (those on pl Konstytucji are open into the early hours) and fast-food joints provide a good fill for under £3/$5. There are quite a few perfectly good places to eat, and an increasing number of small, well-run private restaurants are now appearing. Bars, traditionally something of a low spot of Warsaw nightlife, are improving by leaps and bounds.

Cafés

Blikle, Nowy Świat 33. Fashionable café famous for its doughnuts (*paczki*). Good for breakfast. Open daily till 11pm.

Brama, ul Marszałkowska 8. Trendy if grungy hang-out with good snacks and no-smoking policy. Daily till 11pm.

Literacka, Krakowskie Przedmieście 87–9. Good location on the edge of the Old Town Square, with meals downstairs. Open 11am–midnight.

Nowy Świat Café, Nowy Świat 63. A good place to browse and relax. Fine coffee and English periodicals. Daily till 11pm.

Pożegnanie z Afryką, ul Freta 4/6. Good place for coffee-lovers as there's a variety on offer. Open 11am–9pm.

TriBeCa, ul Bracka 22. Wide range of teas and coffees, and a good line in sandwiches and cakes. Till 10pm.

Snack bars

Mata Hari, Nowy Świat 52. Vegetarian kiosk with a courtyard table outside and cheap, tasty fare. Mon–Sat 11am–7pm.

Pod Barbakanem, ul Mostowa 29. Deservedly popular New Town milk bar near the Barbakan, where you can sit outside and watch the crowds. Mon–Fri 8am–6pm, Sat & Sun 9am–5pm.

Uniwersytecki, Krakowskie Przedmieście 20. Milk bar much frequented by students; just up from the university gates. Mon–Fri 7am–8pm, Sat & Sun 9am–5pm.

Restaurants

Chianti, ul Foksal 17. A good range of well-prepared Italian dishes. Daily till 11pm.

Gessler, Rynek Starego Miasto 21a. Reasonably priced tourist haunt in the Old Town Square with meals for £10/$16. Head down into the labyrinthine cellars underneath rather than the upstairs area. Open 1pm–2am.

Grand Kredens, al Jerozolimskie 111. Stylish but informal place serving up modern European cuisine and steaks, near Warszawa Centralna train station. 11am–11pm.

Klub Aktora, al Ujazdowskie 45. Good, family-run Polish restaurant with bread baked on the premises. Mon–Sat 10am till last guest.

Le Cédre, al Solidarności 61. Wonderful Lebanese cuisine next to the Praski hotel. 11am–11pm.

Nove Miasto, New Town Square 13/15. Vegetarian restaurant with a good choice. Also serves fish. Open 10am–midnight.

Qchnia Artystyczna, al Ujazdowskie 6. Located in the Contemporary Art Centre near Łazienki Park, with a wonderful view from the terrace. Good vegetarian selection. Open noon to midnight.

Bars

Browar Soma, ul Foksal 19. Busy central bar with minimalist decor, a cool crowd, and live DJs spinning alternative dance discs. Till midnight.

Lolek, ul Rokitnicka 20, in Pole Mokotowskie. One of several watering-holes in the middle of a park bustling with Varsovians on summer nights. Barbecue-type food, beer and live music in and around an overgrown log cabin. One of the few places you can get to on the metro. Open till dawn.

Między Nami, ul Bracka 20. Relaxed gay-friendly café/bar with good salads and an excellent atmosphere. Open Sun–Thurs 10am–10pm, Fri & Sat 10am–midnight.

Modulor Café, pl Trzech Krzyży 8. Trendy new bar with a good menu. Open till midnight.

Muza, ul Chmielna 9. Spacious basement bar with fashionable clientele, groovy sounds and frequent live music. Till 4am.

Nora, ul Krakowskie Przedmieście 20/22. Popular bar; crowded and smoky, but being next to the university it's good for socializing with English-speaking Poles. Open until 10pm (11pm weekends).

Szpilka, pl Trzech Krzyży 18. Minimalist bar with abstract designs projected on the walls and decent food.

Nightlife

Good English-language tips on nightlife venues can be found in the monthly *Warsaw Insider* and the quarterly *Warsaw in Your Pocket* (see p.994). The Friday edition of the *Gazeta Wyborcza* newspaper offers the most complete listings – in Polish only. Regular Warsaw **festivals** include the excellent annual Jazz Jamboree in October, the biannual Warsaw Film Festival, the Festival of Contemporary Music held every September, and the five-yearly Chopin Piano Competition – always a launch pad for a major international career – the next is in 2005.

Clubs, discos and live music

Warsaw's nightlife scene has been feeling the economic pinch in recent years, and appearances by major bands are still a rarity. When big names do turn up, they generally play at the Gwardia Stadium in Praga. The **clubs** listed below all have something to recommend them in terms of decor, choice of music or atmosphere.

Harenda, ul Krakowskie Przedmieście 4/6. More a ranch than a club. Live music and good atmosphere with room to talk, dance or listen to music. Daily until 3am.

Labirynt, ul Smolna 12. Mainstream club not far from the main hostel and of huge dimensions. Bouncers are liable to fuss about dress code.

Piekarnia, ul Młocinska 11. Has the latest progressive dance music and prides itself on being at the forefront of musical fashion. Fri & Sat till 4am.

Proxima, ul Zwirki i Wigury 99a. Prime student club offering unsophisticated, hedonistic diet of chart music. Occasional live gigs. Mon–Sat till 3am.

Stodola, ul Batorego 10. Student club with different styles of music on different nights. Prime venue for alternative rock gigs. Till 4am.

Tam Tam, ul Foksal 18. Bar, café and club all in one. Soul on Fridays. Daily till 3am.

Listings

Airlines LOT, al Jerozolimskie 65/79 (☎022/630 50 07, *www.lot.pl*); British Airways, ul Krucza 49 (☎022/529 90 00).

Airport information ☎022/650 39 43.

Bus tickets International tickets from the main bus station (Dworzec PKS) or ring ☎022/9433. Orbis offices also arrange them. The privately run Polski Express, operating out of a kiosk behind Warszawa Centralna on al Jana Pawła (☎022/620 0330) operates a good intercity service.

Car rental Avis, at the airport (☎022/650 48 72, *www.avis.pl*); Hertz, ul Nowogrodzka 27 (☎022/621 02 39, *www.hertz.com*).

Embassies Australia, ul Nowogrodzka 11 (☎022/521 34 44, *www.australia.pl*); Britain, al Roż 1 (☎022/628 10 01, *www.britishembassy.pl*); Canada, al Jerozolimskie 123 (☎022/584 31 00); Ireland, ul Humanska 10 (☎022/849 66 33); Netherlands, ul Chocimska 6 (☎022/849 23 51); New Zealand, ul Migdalowa 4 (☎022/645 14 07); USA, al Ujazdowskie 29 (☎022/628 30 41, *www.usamb.pl*).

Exchange Orbis accept travellers' cheques but banks are the best option. Exchange offices (Kantors) change cash without commission, but will not handle travellers' cheques.

Gay Warsaw Information from Lambda, ul Czerniakowska 178/16 (Tues, Wed & Fri 6–9pm; ☎022/628 52 22, *lambdawa@polbox.com*). Check out the *Paradise* disco inside the tennis club at ul Wawelska 5 (Thurs–Sat), and *Klub M*, a gay-friendly bar at ul Walbrzyska 11. Check out Polish-language site *www.gej.net* for the latest information.

Internet access Casablanca, ul Krakowskie Przedmieście 4–6 (9.30am–2am; 10zł/hr); Empik Megastore, Marszałkowska 116/122 (Mon–Sat 9am–10pm, Sun 11am–7pm; 10zł/hr); W Sieci, ul Freta 49/51 (8.30am–11.30pm; 10zł/hr).

Laundry Alba, ul Chmielna 26.

Medical services English-speaking staff can be contacted at Medicover (☎022/622 11 15; 24hr).

Pharmacies All-night *apteka* can be found on the top floor of the Centralna Station in the main hall and at ul Wilcza 31.

Post offices At ul Świeokrzyska 31/33 (open 24hr) and in the main train station, behind the departures and arrivals board (Mon–Fri 8am–8pm, Sat 8am–2pm). Both have a 24-hour telephone service and the first a poste restante facility at window 12.

NORTHERN POLAND

Even in a country accustomed to shifts in its borders, northern Poland presents an unusually tortuous historical puzzle. Successively the domain of a Germanic crusading order, of the Hansa merchants and of the Prussians, it's only in the last forty years that the region has really become Polish. **Gdańsk**, **Sopot** and **Gdynia** – the Tri-City, as their conurbation is known – dominate the area from their coastal vantage point. Like Warsaw, historic Gdańsk was obliterated in World War II but now offers some reconstructed quarters, in addition to its contemporary political interest as the birthplace of Solidarity. The most enjoyable excursions from Gdańsk are to the medieval centres of **Malbork** and **Toruń**, or to **Frombork**, chief of many towns in the region associated with the astronomer Nicolaus Copernicus.

Gdańsk and around

For outsiders, **GDAŃSK** is perhaps the most familiar city in Poland. The home of Lech Wałęsa, the beginning of Solidarity and the former Lenin Shipyards, its images flashed across a decade of news bulletins in the 1980s. Expectations formed from the newsreels are fulfilled by the industrial landscape, and suggestions of latent discontent, radicalism and future strikes are all tangible, alongside evidence of new wealth and economic renewal. What is more surprising, at least for those with no great knowledge of Polish history, is the cultural complexity of the place. Prewar Gdańsk – or Danzig as it then was – was forged by years of Prussian and Hanseatic domination, and the reconstructed city centre looks not unlike Amsterdam.

The **Główne Miasto** (Main Town), the largest of the historic quarters, is the obvious starting point and is within easy walking distance of the train station. Entering it is like walking straight into a Hansa merchants' settlement, but the ancient appearance is deceptive: by May 1945 the fighting between German and Russian forces had reduced the core of Gdańsk to smouldering ruins, leaving the city's main monuments to be painstakingly rebuilt by postwar restorers. Huge stone gateways guard both entrances to **Ulica Długa**, the main thoroughfare. Start from the sixteenth gate at the top, **Brama Wyzynna**, which provides a brief respite from red brick, and then head in a straight line towards the canal. Topped by a golden statue of King Zygmunt August, which dominates the central skyline, the huge and well-proportioned tower of the **Town Hall** makes a powerful impact. "In all Poland there is no other, so Polish a town hall," observed one local writer, though the Dutch influences on the interior rooms might lead you to disagree. They now house the **Historical Museum** (Tues–Sat 10am–4pm, Sun 11am–4pm; 8zł), their lavish decorations almost upstaging the exhibits. Look out for the photographs of Gdańsk before and after the war which give a good indication of the extent of reconstruction.

Past the town hall, the street opens onto the wide expanses of **Długi Targ**, where the **Artus Court** (Dwór Artusa) stands out in a square filled with fine mansions. At the end of the street the archways of the **Green Gate** (Brama Zielona) open directly onto the waterfront. From the bridge over the Motława Canal you get a good view of the granaries on Spichlerze Island and to the left along the old harbour quay, now a tourist hangout and local promenade. Halfway down is the massive and largely original fifteenth-century **Gdańsk**

Crane, the biggest in medieval Europe (Tues–Sun 10am–4pm; 5zł). A few metres further on is the **Central Maritime Museum** (Centralne Museum Morskie; Tues–Fri 9.30am–4pm, Sat & Sun 10am–4pm; June–Sept same days until 6pm), where, for 8zł, you can buy a "carnet" of tickets entitling you to visit the exhibition of primitive boats and photographs illustrating the life of Polish writer Józef Teodor Konrad Korzeniowski, better known to the world as Joseph Conrad, on one side of the canal, then travel by ferry to the other side and explore an exhibition of Polish naval history and look over the large iron vessel moored nearby, the *Sołdek*.

All the streets back into the town from the waterfront are worth exploring, especially Mariacki, nowadays full of amber traders, which was used as the setting for the film of Gunther Grass's *The Tin Drum*. Next up from the Green Gate is ul Chlebnicka, which ends at the gigantic **St Mary's Church** (Kościół Mariacki), reputedly the biggest brick church in the world. Inside, the Chapel of 11,000 Virgins has a tortured Gothic crucifix, for which the artist apparently nailed his son-in-law to a cross as a model. Ulica Piwna, another street of high terraced houses west of the church entrance, ends at the monumental **Great Arsenal**, now a slightly tacky shopping mall, where a right turn takes you past St Nicholas' Church to the ul Podmłyńksa, the main route over the canal into the Old Town.

Dominating the waterside here is the seven-storey **Great Mill** (Wielki Młyn), the biggest mill in medieval Europe – even in the 1930s it was still grinding out 200 tons of flour a day. **St Catherine's Church** (Katarzynka), the former parish church of the Old Town, to the right of the crossway, is one of the nicest in the city. Fourteenth-century – and built in brick like almost all churches in the region – it has a well-preserved and luminous interior. The most interesting part of the district is west along the canal from the mill, centred on the **Old Town Hall** (Ratusz Staromiejski), on the corner of ul Bielanska and Korzenna, with the inevitable Irish pub underneath it. Looming large are the cranes of the famous **Gdańsk shipyards** (Stocznia Gdańska), the crucible of the political strife of the 1980s. Outside the gates looms the famous anchor-topped **monument** to the shipyard workers killed during the 1970s riots against price rises, while a range of stone tablets in the wall testify to Solidarity's subsequent long struggle.

Stare Przedmieście – the southern part of old Gdańsk – was the limit of the original town, as testified by the ring of seventeenth-century bastions running east from Plac Wałowy over the Motława. The main attraction today is the **National Art Museum** (Tues–Fri 9am–4pm, Sat & Sun 10am–4pm; 5zł; *www.muzeum.narodowe.gda.pl*), at Toruńska 1. There's enough local Gothic art and sculpture here to keep enthusiasts going all day, as well as a varied collection of fabrics, chests, gold and silverware. The museum's most famous possession is Hans Memling's colossal *Last Judgement* (1473), the painter's earliest known work.

Gdańsk itself isn't much of a seaside resort, but there's a vast stretch of sandy beach 15km north in **SOPOT**, Poland's liveliest coastal centre and an integral part of the vast Tri-City conurbation. Commuter trains run to and fro between Gdańsk and Sopot every twelve minutes during the day. Sopot's main artery, Bohaterów Monte Cassino, is packed with year-round bars and restaurants. It runs east from the train station towards the seaside gardens and the pier (*molo*), which affords excellent views of the coast.

Practicalities

Gdańsk's main **tourist office**, a couple of minutes northeast of the train station at ul Heweliusza 27 (Mon–Fri 8am–4pm; ☎058/301 43 55), is one of the more helpful in the country – a few minutes' walk beyond the huge high-rise *Hotel Hewelius*. The Almatur office, in the centre of town at Długi Targ 11/13 (Mon–Fri 10am–5pm, Sat 10am–2pm; ☎058/301 29 31), is also friendly, and employs several English-speakers; in summer they'll help you sort out accommodation in student hotels. Available from newsstands, the English-language booklet *Gdańsk in Your Pocket* is an invaluable source of hotel, restaurant and bar listings.

For **accommodation**, Gdańsk Tourist, in the mall opposite the train station at Podwale Grodzkie 8 (Mon–Fri 9am–6pm, Sat 10am–2pm; ☎058/301 26 34, *www.gt.com.pl*), offers private rooms (②) in the town centre. The nearest **hostel** to the centre is at ul Wałowa 21

(☎058/301 23 13; ②), a red-brick building with cramped dorms ten minutes' walk from the main station. Of the cheaper **hotels**, the very central *Dom Harcerza*, ul Za Murami 2/10 (☎58/301 49 36, *www.domharcerza.prv.pl*), has rooms to accommodate large numbers, dormitory style (①), and some frugal doubles (②); while *Załuek*, ul Ogarna 107/108 (☎58/301 41 69; ③), looks dowdy from the outside but offers clean rooms with shared bathrooms within. Right on the main street, *Jantar*, Długi Targ 19 (☎58/301 27 16), offers rooms with shower (④) or just with sink (③). Also in the centre, *Dom Aktora* at ul Straganiarska 55/6 (☎058/301 59 01; ⑤), has cosy en suites with TV. In Sopot, the *Pension Wanda*, 800m south of the pier at ul Poniatowskiego 7 (☎058/551 57 25; ④), offers comfy en suites; while *Chemik*, 1km further south at Bitwy pod Plowcami 61 (☎058/551 12 09; ③) is a frumpy concrete box which nevertheless harbours good-value rooms with TV. The most convenient campsite in Gdańsk is at ul Jelitkowska 23 (☎058/553 27 31; closed Oct–May), near the beach at Jelitkowo and a short walk from the terminus of trams #2, #6 or #8 from Gdańsk train station.

For cheap **meals**, you should check out the *Bar Neptun* at ul Długa 33, one of the city's classic milk bars (open till 6pm, closed Sun). The nearby *Karczma*, Długa 18, serves up traditional Polish food in rustic surroundings; while *Retman*, near the waterfront at ul Stagiewna 1, is a top-quality and not too pricey fish restaurant. *Towarzystwo Gastronomiczne*, underneath the Old Town Hall at Korzenna 33/35, doles out modern European cuisine to an arty clientele, and often features dancing at weekends. *Cocktail Bar Capri*, Długa 74, is the best place for coffee, cakes and ice cream. For **drinking**, *Piwnica Jameson Pub*, ul. Podgarbary 1, is good for a relaxed evening session; *Irish Pub*, ul Korzenna 33/35, attracts a hedonistic young crowd who are wont to hit the dancefloor at weekends. Best of the **clubbing** venues is the huge *Kazamaty*, 600m northwest of the centre at ul Doki 1.

In Sopot, *Greenway*, ul Powstańców Warszawy 2–6, is an excellent vegetarian restaurant; and *Zhong Hua*, al Wojska Polskiego 1, is one of the best Chinese eateries in the country. There are loads of pubs and bars on the main drag, ul Bohaterów Monte Cassino. Further afield, *Sfinks*, in the middle of the park off Powstańców Warszawy, is the wildest arty bar in Poland, and the nearby *Enzym*, ul Mamuszki 21, hosts a wide range of club nights.

You can also catch a **ferry** to Sweden from the Tri-City. PolFerries, ul. Przemysłowa 1 (☎058/343 18 87, *www.polferries.com.pl*) run a service from Gdańsk to Nynäshavn near Stockholm (June–Sept daily; Oct–May 3 weekly); while Stena Line, ul Kwiatkowskiego 60 (☎058/665 14 14, *www.stenaline.pl*), sail daily from Gdynia to Karlskrona.

Frombork

A little seaside town 98km east along the Baltic coast from Gdańsk, **FROMBORK** (*www.frombork.art.pl*) was the home town of Nicolaus Copernicus, the Renaissance astronomer whose ideas overturned the earth-centred model of the universe. Most of the research for his famous *De Revolutionibus* was carried out around this town, and it was here that he died and was buried in 1543. Today it's an out-of-the-way place, almost as peaceful as it must have been in Copernicus' day. The bus journey from Gdańsk takes between two and three hours. If there's no direct bus back, take one to Elblàg and change there.

The only part of Frombork to escape unscathed from the last war was the **Cathedral Hill**, which you'll find up from the old market square in the centre of town. A compact unit surrounded by high defensive walls, its main element is the Gothic **Cathedral** (Oct–April daily 9.30am–3.30pm; May–Sept 9.30am–5pm; 9zł for the whole complex of buildings), with its huge red-tiled and turreted roof. Inside, the lofty expanses of brick rise above a series of lavish altars – the high altar is a copy of the Wawel altarpiece in Kraków. It's kept locked until enough visitors arrive, so ask in the museum and a guide will let you in. To the west of the cathedral, the **Copernicus Tower** (May–Oct Mon–Sat 9.30am–5pm) is supposed to have been the great man's workshop and observatory. Doubting that the local authorities would have let him make use of a part of the town defences, others maintain that he's more likely to have studied at his home, just north of the cathedral complex. The **Radziejowska**

Tower, in the southwest corner of the walls, houses an assortment of Copernicus-related astronomical instruments and has an excellent view of the Wiślana lagoon. Further equipment and memorabilia are to be found in the **Copernicus Museum** across the tree-lined cathedral courtyard (May–Sept Tues–Sun 9am–4.30pm; Oct–April 9am–3.30pm). Among the exhibits are early editions of Copernicus' astronomical treatises, along with a collection of instruments, pictures and portraits.

For an overnight stay, the budget choice is a decent-quality PTTK **hostel** at ul Krasickiego 2, perfectly positioned next to the Cathedral Hill complex (☎055/243 72 52; ②), or the more comfortable *Rheticus*, ul Kopernika 10 (☎055/243 78 00; ③), a charming **pension** with neat modern en suites. The PTTK **campsite** at ul Braniewska 14 (☎055/243 73 68; closed mid-Sept to mid-June) is some way east from the centre on the Braniewo road. Among **places to eat** are the *Restauracja Akcent* at ul Rybacka 4 (open till 11pm) and the restaurant in the PTTK hostel (open 8am–10pm).

Malbork

Following the course of the Wisła south from Gdańsk takes you into the heart of the territory once ruled by the **Teutonic Knights**. From a string of fortresses overlooking the river, this religio-militaristic order controlled the medieval grain trade, and it was under their protection that merchants from the northern Hanseatic League cities established themselves on the Wisła. Their headquarters was at **MALBORK**, where the massive riverside fortress imparts a threatening atmosphere to an otherwise quiet and predominantly modern town. The train and bus stations are sited next to each other about ten minutes' walk south of the castle; Malbork is on the main Warsaw line, so there are plenty of trains from Gdańsk (30–40min) as well as a regular bus service.

You approach the **fortress** (Tues–Sun: May–Sept 9am–5pm; Oct–April 9am–2.30pm, 10zł) through the old outer castle, a zone of utility buildings which was never rebuilt after the war. Some parts of the complex are only viewed under supervision, so you may be forced to join a group. Passing over the moat and through the daunting main gate, you come to the **Middle Castle**, built following the Knights' decision to move their headquarters to Malbork in 1309. Spread out around an open courtyard, this part of the complex contains the Grand Master's palace, of which the **Main Refectory** is the highlight; begun in 1330, this huge vaulted chamber shows the growing influence of the Gothic cathedral architecture. Leading off from the **courtyard** are a host of dark, cavernous chambers. The largest ones contain collections of ceramics, glass, sculpture, paintings and, most importantly, a large display of Baltic amber, the trade in which formed the backbone of the order's fabulous wealth. From the Middle Castle a passage rises to the smaller courtyard of the **High Castle**, the oldest section of the fortress, harbouring the focus of the Knights' austere monasticism – the vast **Castle Church**.

There's a pricey but delightfully positioned **hotel** in the lower grounds of the castle itself, the Zamek (☎055/272 84 00, *www.hotelspoland.com/malbork/zamek*; ⑥), which also features an affordable restaurant.

Toruń

Poles are apt to wax lyrical on the glories of their ancient cities, and with **TORUŃ** – the biggest and most important of the Hanseatic trading centres along the Wisła – it is more than justified. Miraculously surviving the recurrent wars afflicting the region, the historic centre is one of the country's most evocative, bringing together a rich assembly of architectural styles. The principal stations are on opposite sides of the Old Town. Toruń Główny, the main train station, is 2km away south of the river; buses #22 and #27 (every 10min) run to pl Rapackiego, on the western edge of the Old Town. Make sure that you exit the station beyond platform 4 and not by the main hall, where only taxis wait. Buy tickets (*bilety*; 1.3zł) from the kiosk beside the bus stop. From the bus station on ul Dabrowskiego it is a short walk south to the centre.

The westerly Old Town area is the most obvious place to start looking around – and as usual it's the mansion-lined **Rynek**, in particular the **Town Hall**, that provides the focal point. Raised in the late fourteenth century on the site of earlier cloth halls and trading stalls, this is an austere, monumental statement of medieval civic pride. The **Town Museum** (Tues–Sun 10am–4pm, May–Sept until 6pm; 6zł), which now occupies much of the building, has a gorgeous collection of the stained glass for which the city was famed and some fine sculptures including the celebrated "Beautiful Madonnas". On the first floor, painting takes over, a small portrait of the most famous burgher, Copernicus, basking in the limelight of a Baroque gallery. The top floor houses an exhibition of modern art. Before leaving the town hall it's also worth climbing the tower for a view over the city and the winding course of the Wisła.

West of here, ul Kopernika and its dingy side streets are lined with crumbling Gothic mansions and granaries, evoking a blend of past glory and shabbier contemporary reality. Halfway down Kopernika at nos. 15/17 you'll find the **Copernicus Museum** (Tues–Sun 10am–4pm, May–Sept until 6pm; 5zł), installed in the high brick house where the great man was born and containing a studiously assembled collection of Copernicus artefacts and a half-hourly sound and light show of fifteenth-century Toruń. A planetarium next to the Copernicus University offers further evidence of the influence of the man who, as his statue in the main square says, "stopped the sun and moved the earth".

Following ul Przedzamcze north from the castle brings you onto ul Szeroka, the thoroughfare that links the Old and New Town districts. Although less grand than its mercantile neighbour, the **New Town** still boasts a number of illustrious commercial residences, most of them grouped around the **Rynek Nowomiejski**. The fourteenth-century **St James' Church**, located south of the market area of the Rynek, boasts the largest bell in Poland outside Kraków, the *Tuba Dei*. An unusual feature of this brick basilica is its flying buttresses – a common enough sight in Western Europe but rare in Poland. To the north of the square, ul Prosta leads onto Wały Sikorskego, a ring road which more or less marks the line of the old fortifications. Across it there's a small park, in the middle of which stands the former arsenal, now an **Ethnographic Museum** (Mon, Wed & Fri 9am–4pm; Tues, Thurs, Sat & Sun 10am–6pm; 8zł, free Mon) dealing with the customs and crafts of northern Poland, including an outdoor display of wooden buildings. After seeing the sights of the town, you shouldn't miss the opportunity of taking a walk along the riverfront just south of the centre, framed between the starkly impressive girders of Toruń's two bridges.

Practicalities

The main **tourist office** at Rynek Staromejski 1, in the town hall (Mon & Sat 9am–4pm, Tues–Fri 9am–6pm; May–Sept also Sun 9am–1pm; ☎056/621 09 31, *www.torun.com.pl*) provides an accommodation booking service. Of the **hotels**, the simple but clean PTTK *Dom Wycieczkowy*, north of the bus station at ul Legionów 24 (☎56/622 38 55), offers dorm beds (①) or basic doubles (②). The more central *Trzy Korony*, Rynek Staromiejski 21 (☎56/622 60 31) is an ageing but acceptable source of rooms with shared facilities (③) or en suites (④), although the en-suite rooms at the *Pod Orlem*, also in the Old Town at ul Mostowa 17 (☎056/622 50 24, *podorlem@hotel.torun.pl*; ④), are marginally comfier. The two **hostels** are both about 3km from the centre, at ul św Józefa 26 to the northwest (☎056/654 45 80), and ul Chobrego (at róg Mleczne intersection) to the northeast (☎056/655 82 36). The *Tramp* **campsite** at ul Kujawska 14 (☎056/654 71 87) is a short walk west of the train station, with bungalows (②) as well as general camping facilities and a restaurant.

Best of the cheap **places to eat** in town is the *Bar Mleczny*, just west of the Rynek on the corner of Rózana and Sw. Ducha, which offers filling soups and meaty snacks as well as excellent pancakes. *Browara*, ul Mostowa 17, offers a bewildering array of economical pizzas; while the next-door *U Sołtysa* (same address) serves up inexpensive Polish fare in folksy surroundings. For a few more złotys, the *Petite Fleur* hotel, Piekary 25, has an elegant cellar restaurant offering the best in Polish and European cuisine. Riverbank cafés provide numerous outdoor **drinking** opportunities on warm summer nights. Otherwise, best of the regular bars is *Pod Aniołem*, a roomy cellar nestling under the town hall which sometimes hosts DJs and dancing. *Guinness Pub*, on the eastern side of the Rynek, is a cosy little place in which to spend an evening, as is *Pod Krzywą Wieżą* ("Under the Leaning Tower"), a tremendous bar nestling in the Old Town battlements on ul Bankowa.

SOUTHERN POLAND

Southern Poland garners more visitors than any other region in the country, and its attractions are clear enough from just a glance at the map. The **Tatra Mountains**, which form the border with Slovakia, are Poland's grandest and most beautiful, snowcapped for much of the year and markedly alpine in feel. **Kraków** ranks with Prague and Vienna as one of the architectural gems of Central Europe, but its significance for Poles goes well beyond the aesthetic, for this was the country's ancient royal capital, and the Catholic Church has often looked to Kraków for guidance – Pope John Paul II was Archbishop of Kraków until his election in 1978. Equally important are Kraków's Jewish roots: until World War II, this was one of the great Jewish centres in Europe, a past whose fabric remains clear in the old ghetto area of Kazimierz, and whose culmination is starkly enshrined at the death camps of Auschwitz-Birkenau, west of the city. To the north, the major attraction is the pilgrim centre of **Częstochowa**, home of the Black Madonna, the country's principal religious symbol.

Kraków

KRAKÓW was the only major city in the country to come through World War II essentially undamaged, and its assembly of monuments has now been listed by UNESCO as one of the world's twelve most significant historic sites. The city's Old Town retains an atmosphere of *fin-de-siècle* stateliness, and its streets are a cavalcade of churches and aristocratic palaces. A longtime university centre, Kraków has a tangible buzz of arty youthfulness, and boasts a wealth of nightlife opportunities to match. Although swarming with visitors in summer, the city's dignified aura seems impervious to the commercialization of the tourist trade.

Arrival and information

Kraków Główny, the central **train station**, and the main bus station just opposite, are ten minutes walk northeast of the city's historic centre. Kraków is bisected by the **River Wisła**, though virtually everything of interest is concentrated on the north bank; the central area is compact enough to get around on foot – indeed parts are car-free. At the heart of things, enclosed by the **Planty** – a green belt following the course of the old ramparts – is the **Stare Miasto**, the Old Town, with its great central square, the **Rynek Główny**. Just south of the Stare Miasto, looming above the river bank, is **Wawel**, the royal castle hill, beyond which lies the old Jewish quarter of **Kazimierz**.

The city **tourist office** occupies a circular pavilion in the Planty midway between the stations and the Old Town at ul Szpitalna 25 (May–Sept Mon–Fri 8am–8pm, Sat & Sun 9am–5pm; Oct–April Mon–Fri 8am–4pm; ☎012/432 00 60, *www.krakow.pl*); they can give you information on accommodation possibilities but won't ring them up on your behalf. Staff at the regional tourist office, Rynek Gowny 1/3 (Mon–Fri 9am–6pm, Sat 9am–1pm; ☎421 77 06, *www.mcit.pol*), are well informed about the city and have a wealth of information on out-of-town sights. Just off the main square at ul Św. Jana 2 is the Centrum Informacji Kulturalnej (Cultural Information Centre; Mon–Fri 10am–7pm, Sat 11am–7pm; ☎012/421 77 87, *www.Krakow2000.pl*), which has **listings** of cultural events in a special monthly booklet called *Karnet*, and can advise on how to obtain tickets for these events. Finally, the English-language quarterly booklet *Kraków in Your Pocket*, available from bookshops and newsstands, is an invaluable companion to the ever-changing eating and nightlife scene.

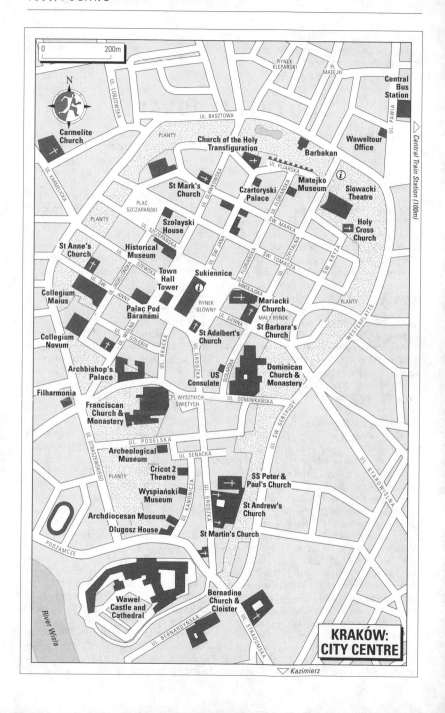

0   200m

N

RYNEK KLEPARSKI

PL MATEJKI

Central Bus Station

UL. LOBZOWSKA

UL. PAWIA

△ Central Train Station (100m)

UL. BASZTOWA

Carmelite Church

PLANTY

Church of the Holy Transfiguration

Wawaltour Office

UL. PIJARSKA

Barbakan

UL. KARMELICKA

St Mark's Church

UL. SŁAWKOWSKA

Czartoryski Palace

UL. FLORIAŃSKA

Matejko Museum

Słowacki Theatre

PLAC SZCZAPAŃSKI

SW. MARKA

Holy Cross Church

PLANTY

Szołayski House

UL. SZCZEPAŃSKA

UL. SW. JANA

St Anne's Church

Historical Museum

SZEWSKA

SW. TOMASZA

SW. SZPITALNA

UL. KRZYŻA

Collegium Maius

UL. SW. ANNY

UL. JAGIELLOŃSKA

Town Hall Tower

Sukiennice

RYNEK GŁÓWNY

MIKOŁAJSKA

Mariacki Church

MAŁY RYNEK

PLANTY

WESTERPLATTE

Pałac Pod Baranami

UL. WIŚLNA

UL. GOŁEBIA

UL. BRACKA

UL. SIENNA

St Adalbert's Church

St Barbara's Church

Collegium Novum

UL. GRODZKA

US Consulate

SOLARSKA

Dominican Church & Monastery

Archbishop's Palace

PL WYSZTKICH ŚWIĘTYCH

UL. DOMINIKAŃSKA

UL. SW. GERTRUDY

UL. STAROWIŚLNA

Filharmonia

Franciscan Church & Monastery

UL. STRASZEWSKIEGO

UL. POSELSKA

Archeological Museum

UL. SENACKA

PLANTY

Cricot 2 Theatre

Wyspiański Museum

UL. KANONICZA

UL. GRODZKA

SS Peter & Paul's Church

St Andrew's Church

Archdiocesan Museum

Długosz House

St Martin's Church

PODZAMCZE

River Wisła

Wawel Castle and Cathedral

Bernadine Church & Cloister

UL. BERNARDYŃSKA

UL. STRADOMSKA

KRAKÓW: CITY CENTRE

▽ Kazimierz

Accommodation

Kraków is turning into one of Europe's prime city-break destinations – so you should book hotels ahead in summer. If you can't do that, be prepared to try your luck with a **private room**, which run at around 40–50zł for a double, but may well be some way out from the centre; they can be booked at the main tourist office, which also deals with **student hotels**, available from late June to late September when the students are away – the cheapest is Bydgoska at ul Bydgoska 19 (☎01/423-7932; ①) at 15zł a night. For **hotel reservations**, the Dexter office in the cloth hall is your best bet (☎012/421 77 06), since they can obtain discounts. The most popular **campsite**, Krak Camping, ul Radzikowskiego 99 (☎012/637 21 22), is located in the northwest of the city; get there by buses #173 and #238, or trams #4, #12, #44.

HOSTELS

Piast, ul Piastowska 47 (☎637 49 33). Large university dormitory 3km west of the centre and popular with summer language students. Lots of regular student accommodation plus some higher-grade rooms with private bathroom. There's a cafeteria on site, plus it's the only place in Kraków with a laundry. Tram #4 from the train station to the Wawel stop followed by a 10-minute walk down Piastowska. ②.

Strawberry, ul Racławicka 9 (☎012/636 15 00). Summer-only hostel 2km northwest of the city centre, with small dorms (maximum four people). Look out for the shuttle service from the station, or take trams #4, #12 or #14. ①.

Ul Oleandry 4 (☎012/633 88 22). The main hostel, ten minutes walk west of the centre, is a gloomy grey place that still manages to get full up in summer. Noisy and with an early curfew, it's definitely a last resort. Tram #15 or #18 from the train station. ①.

Zaczek, al 3 Maja 5 (☎633 54 77). Well-placed students' hostel right in front of the main youth hostel (see above): easiest to get rooms during the summer months. Simple doubles with shared facilities ②, en suites ③.

HOTELS

Fortuna, ul Czapskich 5 (☎012/422 31 43, *www.hotel-fortuna.com.pl*). Smallish hotel with simply furnished en suites in easy walking distance west of the university district. ⑧.

Mistia, ul Szlak 73a (☎012/633 29 26, *www.mistia.org.pl*). Decent budget hotel ten minutes' walk north of the stations. Spartan but clean rooms. With shared facilities ④, en suite ⑤.

Monopol, Św. Gertrudy 6 (☎012/422 70 15). Gloomy but well-maintained place. With shared facilities ④, en suites ⑤.

Polonia, ul Basztowa 25 (☎012/422 12 33, *www.hotel-polonia.com.pl*). Best of the hotels close to the train station, although rooms come in various stages of modernization: from old-style rooms with facilities in the hallway to plush en suites. ③, ⑥.

Pollera, ul Szpitalna 30 (☎012/422-1044, *www.pollera.com.pl*). Charming hotel with Art Nouveau decor in a calm, central spot. ⑦.

Saski, ul Sławkowska 3 (☎012/421-4222, *www.hotelsaski.com.pl*). Central location, great ambience and a wonderful antique lift. Rooms with sink ④, en suites ⑥.

Wawel Tourist, ul Poselska 22 (☎012/422-6765, *www.wawel-tourist.com.pl*). Excellent Old Town location. Spartan but comfortable. ⑥.

The City

The **Rynek Główny** – the core of the Stare Miasto – was the largest square of medieval Europe: a huge expanse of flagstones, ringed by magnificent houses and towering spires. The dominant building on the square is the **Sukiennice**, rebuilt in the Renaissance and one of the most distinctive sights in the country: a vast cloth hall, topped by a sixteenth-century attic dripping with gargoyles. Its commercial traditions are perpetuated by a covered market, which bustles with tourists and street sellers at almost any time of year. The terrace cafés on either side of the hall are classic Kraków haunts, where locals idle away the afternoon over tea and *sernik*. The **Art Gallery** on the upper floor of the Sukiennice (Tues, Wed & Fri–Sun 10am–3.30pm, Thurs noon–6pm; 6zł, free Sun; entrance in the side of the Sukiennice opposite St Mary's Church) is worth a visit for its collection of works by nineteenth-century Polish artists.

To its south is the copper-domed **St Adalbert's** (Św. Wojchiecha), the oldest building in the square and the first church to be founded in Kraków. The tall tower nearby is all that remains of the fourteenth-century town hall; it's worth the climb for an excellent overview of the city.

On the east side is one of the finest Gothic structures in the country, the **Mariacki Church** (St Mary's), the taller of its towers topped by an amazing ensemble of spires, elaborated with a crown and helmet. Legend has it that during one of the Tatar raids, the watchman at the top of the tower saw the invaders approaching and took up his trumpet to raise the alarm; his warning was cut short by an arrow through the throat. Every hour on the hour a lone trumpeter plays the sombre *hejnał* melody, halting abruptly at the precise point the watchman was supposed to have been hit. Walking down the nave, you'll have to pick your way past devotees kneeling in front of the fifteenth-century Chapel of Our Lady of Częstochowa, with its copy of the venerated image of the Black Madonna. Focal point of the nave is the huge stone crucifix attributed to Veit Stoss, creator of the majestic high altar at the far east end. Carved between 1477 and 1489, this huge limewood polyptych is one of the finest examples of late-Gothic art. The outer sides of the folded polyptych feature reliefs of scenes from the lives of the Holy Family; at noon (Sundays and saints' days excluded) the altar is opened to reveal the inner panel of the Dormition of the Virgin, an amazing tableau of life-size figures.

NORTH OF THE RYNEK

Of the three streets leading north off the Rynek, **ul Floriańska** is the busiest and most striking, with fragments of medieval and Renaissance architecture among the myriad shops, cafés and restaurants. **Floriańska Gate**, at the end of the street, marks the edge of the Old Town proper. A square, robust fourteenth-century structure, it's part of a small section of fortifications saved when the old defensive walls were pulled down in the early nineteenth century. The strongest-looking defensive remnant is the **Barbakan** (daily 9am–12.45pm, 1.15–6pm; 4zł), just beyond Floriańska Gate. A bulbous, spiky fort, added in 1498, it's unusual in being based on Arab defensive architecture.

Back through Floriańska Gate, a right turn down the narrow ul Pijarska brings you to the corner of ul Św. Jana and back down to the main square. On the way, on the left, is the **Czartoryski Palace**, housing Kraków's finest art collection (Tues–Thurs, Sat & Sun 10am–3.30pm, Fri 10am–6pm; 6zł, free Sun). The ancient art section alone contains over a thousand exhibits, from sites in Mesopotamia, Etruria, Greece and Egypt. Another intriguing highlight is the collection of trophies from the Battle of Vienna (1683), which includes sumptuous Turkish carpets, scimitars and other Oriental finery. The picture galleries offer a rich display of art and sculpture ranging from thirteenth- to eighteenth-century works, the most famous being Rembrandt's brooding *Landscape Before a Storm* and Leonardo da Vinci's *Lady with an Ermine*.

THE UNIVERSITY DISTRICT

Head west from the Rynek on any of the three main thoroughfares – ul Szczepańska, ul Szewska or ul św Anny – and you're into the **university area**, whose heart is the Gothic Collegium Maius building, at the intersection of ul Św. Anny with ul Jagiellońska. Through the passageway from the street, you find yourself in a quiet, arcaded courtyard with a marble fountain playing in the centre: an ensemble that, during the early 1960s, was stripped of neo-Gothic accretions and restored to something approaching its original form. Now the **University Museum**, the Collegium is open to guided tours only (Mon–Sat 11am–5pm; 7zł), for which you need to book places at least a day in advance at ul Jagiellońska 15 (☎012/422 05 49). Inside, the ground-floor rooms retain the mathematical and geographical murals once used for teaching; the Alchemy Room, with its skulls and other wizards' accoutrements, was used according to legend by the fabled magician Doctor Faustus. Stairs up from the courtyard bring you to a set of elaborately decorated reception rooms and the treasury, where the most valued possession is the Jagiellonian globe, constructed around 1510, and featuring the earliest-known illustration of America.

WAWEL HILL

The traditional route used by Polish monarchs when entering the city took them through the Floriańska Gate, down ul Floriańska to the Rynek, then southwards down ul Grodzka to

Wawel Hill, where for over five hundred years the country's rulers lived and governed. The original **Cathedral** (May–Sept Mon–Sat 9am–5pm, Sun 12.15pm–5pm; Oct–April Mon–Sat 9am–3pm, Sun 12.15–3pm) was built here around the time King Bolesław the Brave established the Kraków bishopric in 1020, but the present brick-and-sandstone basilica is essentially Gothic. All bar four of Poland's forty-five monarchs are buried in the cathedral, and their tombs and side chapels are like a directory of the Central European architecture, art and sculpture of the last six centuries. Beginning from the right of the entrance, the **Gothic Holy Cross Chapel** (Kaplica Świętokrzyska) is the burial chamber of King Kazimierz IV Jagiełło (1447–92). Third chapel after this is the Baroque mausoleum of the seventeenth-century Waza dynasty, followed by the high spot of the whole cathedral, the opulent **Zygmuntowska chapel**, whose gilded cupola dominates the courtyard outside. The tomb of King Władysław the Short (1306–33), on the left-hand side of the altar, is the oldest in the cathedral, completed soon after his death; the coronation-robed figure lies on a white sandstone tomb edged with expressive mourning figures. An ascent of the **Zygmuntowska Tower** (same times as cathedral; 6zł – tickets from the office opposite the cathedral entrance) from the sacristy gives a far-reaching panorama over the city and close-up views of the five medieval bells. The largest, known as Zygmunt, is famed for its deep, sonorous tone, which local legends claim scatters rain clouds and brings out the sun.

The buildings on Wawel Hill are in the midst of a long-term renovation programme; work in the **Castle** (Tues & Fri 9.30am–4.30pm, Wed & Thurs 9.30am–3.30pm, Sat 9.30am–3pm, Sun 10am–3pm) is more extensive than in the cathedral but thankfully limited to the courtyard area so you should find everything open. The **Royal Treasury and Armoury** (Tues & Fri 9.30am–4.30pm, Wed & Thurs 9.30am–3.30pm, Sat 9.30am–3pm, Sun 10am–3pm; 12zł) is in the northeast corner of the castle (entrance on the ground floor). Much of the treasury's contents had been sold by the time of the Partitions to pay off marriage dowries and debts of state. The vaulted Gothic **Kazimierz Room** contains the finest items from a haphazard display of lesser royal possessions including the burial crown of Zygmunt August, while the prize exhibit in the next-door **Jadwiga and Jagiełło Room** is the solemnly displayed Szczerbiec, the thirteenth-century weapon used for centuries in the coronation of Polish monarchs. The **Lost Wawel** exhibition (Mon, Wed, Thur & Sat 9.30am–3pm, Fri 9.30am–4pm, Sun 10am–3pm; 6zł), beneath the old kitchens south of the cathedral, takes you past the excavated remains of the hill's most ancient buildings, including the foundations of the tenth-century **Rotunda of SS Felix and Adauctus**, the oldest-known church in Poland. Return to ground level via the **Dragon's Den** (daily 10am–5pm; 5zł), a spiral staircase leading to a rocky cavern which is perfect for cooling off in the heat of summer.

KAZIMIERZ

South from Wawel Hill lies the **Kazimierz** district, which in 1495 became the city's Jewish quarter. In tandem with Warsaw, where a **ghetto** was created around the same time, Kazimierz grew to become one of the main cultural centres of Polish Jewry, but in March 1941 the entire Jewish population of the city was crammed into a tiny ghetto over the river. After waves of deportations to the concentration camps, the ghetto was finally liquidated in March 1943, thus ending seven centuries of Jewish life in Kraków.

The tiny **Remu'h Synagogue** at ul Szeroka 40 (Mon–Fri 9am–4pm; 5zł), is one of two still functioning in the quarter. Built in 1557 on the site of an earlier wooden synagogue, it was ransacked by the Nazis – tombstones torn up by them have been collaged together to form a high, powerful Wailing Wall just inside the entrance. The grandest of all the Kazimierz synagogues was the **Old Synagogue** on ul Szeroka, completed in 1557 and thus the oldest surviving Jewish religious building in Poland. Since the war it's been carefully restored and turned into a **museum** of the history and culture of Kraków Jewry including a permanent exhibition of traditional art by Polish Jews (Wed, Thurs, Sat & Sun 9am–3.30pm, Fri 11am–6pm; closed first Sat and Sun of the month; 5zł). The museum provides an excellent English-language introduction to the basic beliefs and rituals of Judaism. Another excellent place to visit is the newly refurbished

Synagoga Izaaka (Isaac Synagogue) at ul Kupa 18, which has an exhibition of photographs and short silent films illustrating the life of Kazimierz Jews before the war and after the formation of the Jewish ghetto (Mon–Fri & Sun 9am–7pm; 6zł).

As the presence of several churches indicates, the western part of Kazimierz was where non-Jews tended to live. Despite its Baroque overlay, the interior of the Gothic **Corpus Christi** church, on the corner of ul Bożego Ciała, retains early features including stainedglass windows installed around 1420. The church looks onto Plac Wolnica, where the rebuilt town hall now houses the largest **Ethnographic Museum** in the country (Mon 10am–6pm, Wed–Fri 10am–3pm, Sat & Sun 10am–2pm; 4zł, free Sun). The collection focuses on Polish folk traditions, although there's also a selection of artefacts from Siberia, Africa, Latin America and various Slav countries.

Eating and drinking

The *cukiernia* dotted around the city centre provide delicious cakes to most Kraków cafés, and Kraków's tourist status has resulted in one of the best selections of **bars**, **cafés** and **restaurants** in Europe.

CAFÉS, MILK BARS AND SNACKS

Ariel Kawlarnia Artystyczna, ul Szeroka 17. Art café-restaurant in the Jewish quarter with live music. Open till 1am.

Bar Grodzki, ul Grodzka 47. Filling Polish standards (including excellent potato pancakes or *placki*) at reasonable prices. 9am–7pm.

Chimera, ul Św. Anny 3 off the main square. A subterranean labyrinth of atmospheric rooms with a garden area upstairs in summer. Offers cheap, filling, mainly veggie meals. Open 9am–10pm.

Jama Michalika, ul Floriańska 45. Historic artistic café, redolent of old-world Mitteleuropa. Occasional cabaret. Open 9am–10pm.

Kawiarnia u Literatów, Kanonicza 7. A courtyard-cum-garden retreat. Well worth finding. Open 9am–9pm.

Rózowy Słoń (Pink Elephant), ul Straszewskiego 24, ul Szpitalna 38 and ul Sienna 1. A chain of surrealist café/salad bars, the walls splayed with cartoons. Good for cheap fill-ups. Open till 9pm.

Pożegnanie z Afryką (Out of Africa), ul Św. Tomasza 21. Part of a chain dedicated to providing excellent coffee. Open 10am–10pm.

Singer Café, ul Estery 22. Café in the Kazimierz district, named after the sewing machines which make up the tables. Insists it's open till the last customer leaves (definitely till midnight).

RESTAURANTS

Arka Noego, (Noah's Ark), ul Szeroka 2. Kazimierz restaurant with Jewish and standard Polish fare, and occasional live music.

Balaton, ul Grodzka 37 (☎012/422 04 69). Plain decor but excellent food in this very busy Hungarian restaurant. Open 9am–10pm.

Bar Wegetaviański "Vega", ul Św. Gertrudy 7, next to *Hotel Monopol* (10am–9pm) and at ul Krupnicza 22 (9am–10pm). The best vegetarian options, with imaginative range of dishes and excellent salad bar.

Bombaj Tandoori, ul Mikołajska 11. Cosy little Indian place that does all the classics – including some vegetarian dishes – at reasonable prices. Noon–11pm.

Padva, ul Św. Anny 3. First-class Italian cuisine with emphasis on seafood. Open till midnight.

Staropolska, ul Sienna 2 (☎012/422 58 21). Traditional Polish fare with an emphasis on pork and poultry dishes. Booking essential in the evening. Open 11am–11pm.

Wierzynek, Rynek Główny 15 (☎012/422 103 5). This stately place is Kraków's most famous restaurant, with specialities like pheasant and lobster, plus vegetarian dishes. For Westerners, prices remain reasonable at around £20/$32 a head. Booking is essential. Open noon–11pm.

BARS

Numerous cafés, bars, and live-music venues are concentrated on and around the Rynek, or in the Kazimierz part of town just to the southeast.

Alchemia, ul Estery 5. Darkly atmospheric Kazimierz bar catering to a mixture of bohemian regulars, curious tourists, and permanently sozzled Cracovians. Till 4pm.

Black Gallery, ul Mikołajska 24. Cellar bar with industrial decor and lively crowd. Lovely garden courtyard at ground level. Till 2pm.

Dym, ul Św. Tomasza 13. Dim, smoky café/bar popular with arty types and hard-drinking locals. Till midnight.

Pod instytutem, ul Grodzka 49. Cellar-bar beneath the Italian Institute with a dancing area. Till 1am.

Pod Jemiola, ul Floriańska 20. Cramped and cosy bar with reggae or cutting-edge dance music on the sound system. Till 1am.

Surrestaurant Szuflada, ul Wiślna 5. Bar with food and surrealist decor – try the table with the zebra. Open noon–1am.

Entertainment

In addition to the information sources given on p.1007, you'll find the latest **cultural events** in *Miesiàc w Krakówie* (This Month in Kraków), which has some English and is clearly laid out. *Pod Jaszczurami* (Under the Lizards), Rynek Główny 7/8, is a student **club** with weekend discos, and frequent live music and literary readings. There are plenty of other **disco** options in the streets surrounding the square – *Music Bar 9*, ul Szewska 9, and *Jazz Rock Café*, ul Sławkowska 12, are hedonistic, techno-oriented bars with dance floors. There's live **jazz** at *U Muniaka*, ul Floriańska 3 (Thurs–Sat), and *Klub Indigo*, ul Floriańska 26 (check posters on the door for details) – the latter is also a relaxing drinking **pub**. Best of the dance-music DJs and live rock bands appear at *Miasto Krakoff,* just west of the centre at ul Lobzowska 3. *Klub Re*, ul Św. Kryza 4, also hosts occasional alternative, jazz and ethno concerts.

Listings

Airlines LOT, ul Basztowa 15 (☎012/422 42 15, *www.lot.com*); British Airways, ul Św. Tomasza 25 (☎012/422 86 21).

Car rental Avis, ul Lubicz 23 (☎012/629 61 08); Hertz, Hotel Cracovia, al F. Focha 1 (☎012/429 62 62).

Consulates UK, ul Św. Anny 9 (☎012/421 70 30); USA, ul Stolarska 9 (☎012/429 66 55).

Gay Kraków Hades, ul Starowiślna 60, is a nightclub open Fri & Sat.

Internet access Looz, ul Mikołajska 11 (*www.looz.com.pl*; 10am–midnight; 9zł/hr); and U Louisa, Rynek Główny13 (*www.louis.krakow.pl*; 11am–11pm; 9zł/hr).

Pharmacies All pharmacies have a list in their window of those currently open 24 hours in the neighbourhood. Apteka Grodzka, Grodzka 26 (Mon–Fri 8am–9pm, Sat 9am–4pm, Sun 10am–5pm) is conveniently central. In an emergency ring Medicover (☎012/430 00 34) for English-speaking assistance.

Post office Main office is at ul Wielopole 2 (Mon–Fri 7.30am–8.30pm, Sat 8am–2pm, Sun 9–11am), with 24-hour phone services and poste restante at window no. 1; the post office right opposite the station (Mon–Fri 7am–8pm) is also handy.

Taxis ☎919 for English-speakers; more reliable than cabs hailed from the street.

Train tickets Available from the Orbis office at Rynek Główny 41 and the train station.

Oświęcim: Auschwitz-Birkenau

In 1940, **OŚWIĘCIM**, an insignificant town 70km west of Kraków, became the site of the Oświęcim-Brzeźinka concentration camp, better known by its German name of **Auschwitz-Birkenau**. Of the many camps built by the Nazis in Poland and the other occupied countries during World War II, this was the largest and most horrific: something approaching two million people, 85–90 percent of them Jews, died here. If you want all the specifics on the camp, you can pick up a detailed guidebook or join a guided group, often led by former inmates. Children under 13 are not admitted.

To get to Auschwitz-Birkenau from Kraków, you can take either of the regular bus or train services to Oświęcim station. From there it's a short bus ride to the gates of Auschwitz. There's an hourly shuttle-bus service to Birkenau from the car park at Auschwitz; taxis are also available, otherwise it's a 3km walk.

Most of the Auschwitz camp buildings have been preserved as the **Museum of Martyrdom** (daily: summer 8am–7pm; winter 8am–3pm; free). The cinema is a sobering starting point: the film was taken by the Soviet troops who liberated the camp in May 1945 – harrowing images of the survivors and the dead confirming what really happened. The bulk of the camp consists of the prison cell blocks, the first section dedicated to "exhibits" found in the camp after liberation. Despite last-minute destruction of many of the storehouses used for the possessions of murdered inmates, there are rooms full of clothes and suitcases, toothbrushes, dentures, glasses, shoes, and a huge mound of women's hair – 154,322 pounds of it. Many of the camp barracks are given over to national memorials, moving testimonies to the sufferings of inmates of the different countries – Poles, Russians, Czechs, Slovaks, Norwegians, Turks, French, Italians. The prison blocks terminate by the gas chambers and the ovens where the bodies were incinerated. The **Birkenau camp** (same hours) is much less visited than Auschwitz, though it was here that the majority of captives lived and died. Killing was the main goal of Birkenau, most of it carried out in the huge gas chambers at the back of the camp, damaged but not destroyed by the fleeing Nazis in 1945. Most of the victims arrived in closed trains – cattle cars mostly – to be driven directly into the gas chambers; railway line, ramp, sidings – they are all still there, just as the Nazis abandoned them.

Częstochowa

Seen from a distance, **CZĘSTOCHOWA**, 100km from Kraków, shows the country at its worst. Its steelworks and textile factories unleash a noxious cocktail of multicoloured fumes, while the city centre is ringed by jerry-built concrete estates. Yet all this is overshadowed by the city's status, courtesy of the monastery of **Jasna Góra** (Bright Mountain), as one of the world's greatest places of pilgrimage. Its **Icon of the Black Madonna** has drawn the faithful here over the past six centuries, and reproductions of it adorn almost every church in the country. On the major Marian festivals – May 3, August 15, August 26, September 8 and December 8 – up to a million pilgrims converge here.

The special position that Jasna Góra and its icon hold in the hearts and minds of the majority of Poles is due to the tenuous position Poland has held on the map of Europe. Each of Poland's non-Catholic enemies – the Swedes, the Russians and the Germans – has laid siege to Jasna Góra, yet failed to destroy it, so adding to the icon's reputation as the guarantor of Poland's very existence.

Częstochowa Główny, the smart train station, feeds you into a main road with trams. Turn right and after 100m you meet a dead-straight, three-kilometre-long boulevard, aleja Najświętszej Marii Panny (abbreviated as al NMP). This avenue cuts through the heart of Częstochowa, terminating at the foot of Jasna Góra. Inevitably, the **Chapel of the Blessed Virgin** is the focal point of the complex – its walls covered in lockets, jewels and other votive offerings, as well as a pile of crutches and leg braces discarded by the healed. Much of the time, the Black Madonna is invisible behind a screen (usually visible Mon–Fri 6am–noon & 1pm–9pm Sat & Sun 6am–1pm & 2pm–9pm), each raising and lowering of which is accompanied by a solemn fanfare, but even when it's on view you don't get to see very much of the picture itself, as the figures are almost always decked out in jewelled crowns and robes, besides which there are always crowds of pilgrims or sightseers. According to tradition, the Black Madonna was painted by St Luke on a beam from the Holy Family's house in Nazareth, but tests have proved the icon cannot have been executed before the sixth century and is probably Italian in origin. At the southwestern end of the monastery is the **Arsenal** (daily 9am–5pm; voluntary donation), devoted to the military history of the complex. Alongside is the **600th Anniversary Museum** (same times), which tells the monastery's story. Exhibits include offerings from famous Poles, prominent among which is Lech Wałęsa's 1983 Nobel Peace Prize.

Tourist information is available at al NMP 65 (Mon–Fri 9am–5pm, Sat 9am–2pm; ☎034/3241 360). A day-trip from Kraków will suffice for most people, but those who wish to **stay** should be aware that the best hotel deals are in the streets east of the train station (use the ul Piłsudskiego exit to save yourself a long walk round): the *Polonia*, ul Piłsudskiego 9

(☎034/324 68 32; ③)) has reasonable en suites; while the nearby *Hotel Ha-Ga* at ul Katedralna 9 (☎034/324 61 73; ②) has some en suites with TV and some cheaper rooms with shared facilities. Just outside the grounds of the monastery itself you'll find *Hale Noclegowe* at ul.Klasztorna 1 (☎034/365 66 88; ①; closed Nov–March), offering simple dorm beds, and the slightly more salubrious Dom Pielgrzyma or Pilgrim House (☎034/324 70 11; dorm beds ③; en suite doubles ②), although both are run by nuns and feature night-time curfews. There's a **campsite** with bungalows (①–②) just behind the monastery at ul Oleńki 10/30 (☎034/324 74 95).

Zakopane and the Tatras

Ask Poles to define their country's natural attractions and they often come up with the following simple definition: the Lakes, the Sea and the Mountains. "The Mountains" consist of an almost unbroken chain of ridges extending the whole length of the southern border, of which the most spectacular and most revered are the **Tatras** – or Tatry as they're known in Polish. Eighty kilometres long, with peaks rising to 2500m, the Polish Tatras are actually a relatively small part of the range, most of which rises across the border in Slovakia. As the estimated 1.5 million annual tourists show, however, the Polish section has enough to keep most people happy: high peaks for the dedicated mountaineers, excellent trails for hikers, cable cars and creature comforts for day-trippers, and ski slopes in winter.

The major resort on the fringes of the mountains is **ZAKOPANE**, a town which has succumbed wholeheartedly to tourism. It's easily reached by train (3–4 hours) or bus (2 hours) from Kraków, and both stations are a ten-minute walk east of the main street, **ul Krupówki**. A bustling pedestrian precinct, this is the focus of the town, given over to a jumble of restaurants, cafés and souvenir shops. Uphill, the street merges into ul Zamoyskiego, which runs on out of town past the fashionable *fin-de-siècle* wooden villas of the outskirts towards the entrance to the Tatra National Park (4km away at Kuźnice; see below), while in the other direction it follows a rushing stream down towards Gulbałówka hill.

The well-signposted **tourist information centre**, housed in a wooden chalet just west of the stations at ul Kościuszki 17 (daily: July–Aug & Dec–March 8am–8pm; April–June & Sept–Nov 9am–5pm; ☎018/201 22 11, *promocja@um.zakopane.pl*), has maps and English speakers, and can book you into private rooms (①) or pensions (②), but will not make reservations in advance. Orbis at ul Krupówki 22 (Mon–Fri 9am–5pm, Sat 9am–3pm) helps with hotels, train and bus bookings, flights and local trips, while the PTTK office (Mon–Fri 8am–4pm, Sat 8am–2pm; ☎018/201 24 29), above the Snake disco at ul Krupówki 12, is your best source of information about the Tatra mountains (including, very importantly, precise information on the weather conditions). You can hire an English-speaking guide here for 240–340zł per person, depending on numbers and route, who will supervise challenging hikes involving chains for the steeper parts of the climb. Maps, guidebooks and details on mountain huts can also be obtained here or at the less central Tatra National Park Information Centre at ul Chałubińskiego 44 (daily 8am–4pm; ☎018/206 37 99, *kozica@tpn.zakopane.pl*).

For **accommodation** there's a **hostel** just north of the tourist office at ul Nowotarska 45 (☎018/206 62 03), offering multi-person dorms (①) or neat modern en-suite doubles (②). The more central *The Dom Turysty PTTK*, just off the main drag at ul Zaruskiego 5 (☎018/206 32 81, *domturysty@regle.zakopane.pl*) has a similar mixture of rooms, with dorms (②) and en-suite doubles (③). If you're in the market for a neat and cosy **bed-and-breakfast**, then you could do worse than the *Api-2*, north of the tourist office at Kamieniec 13a (☎018/206 29 31, *www.api.zakopane.top.pl*; ②). Mid-range, central **hotels** include *Gromada Gazda*, Zaruskiego 2 (☎018/201-5011, *gazda@zakopane.top.pl*; ④), and, for a little more but well worth it, the newly restored, timber-clad *Hotel Sabala* at ul Krupówki 11 (☎018/201 50 92, *www.sabala.zakopane.pl*; ⑥). For splendid views of the Tatras it's worth the walk south from the train and bus stations to the hillside *Antałówka*, ul Wierchowa 3 (☎018/201 32 71, *antalowka@polskietatry.pl*; ④), and the next-door *Panorama*, ul Wierchowa 6 (☎018/20150

81; ④), both large concrete places with serviceable en suites. *Pod Krokwià* **campsite** (☎018/201 22 56), located at the end of ul Żeromskiego on the south side of town, has bungalows (②) on offer too, while there is a smaller campsite at ul Za Strugiem 39 (☎018/201 45 66), to the west.

For a quick **snack**, there are plenty of cafés, milk bars, pizzerias and streetside *zapiekanki* merchants to choose from along ul Krupówki. **Restaurants** are plentiful too, with the *Hotel Sabala*, offering Mediterranean dishes, outside tables and indoor folk music, far outstripping the rest in quality and ambience. *Chata Zbojnicka*, 400m south of the train station on ul Jagiellońska, is a wooden hut with a log fire in the middle and authentic local dishes (including excellent roast lamb) on the menu. *Paparazzi Pub*, just off the main street at ul Galicy 8, is the most convivial place to **drink**. **Internet access** is at the Granet Internet Café, ul Krupówki 2 (daily 10am–8pm; 5zł/hr).

The Tatras

Most of the peaks in the **Tatras** are in the 2000–2500m range, but the unimpressive statistics belie their status and their appearance. For these are real mountains, as beautiful as any mountain landscape in northern Europe, the ascents taking you on boulder-strewn paths alongside woods and streams up to the ridges, where grand, windswept peaks rise in the brilliant alpine sunshine. Wildlife thrives here: the whole area was turned into a National Park in the 1950s and supports rare species, including lynx, golden eagles and brown bear – which you might even glimpse.

Most foreigners can cross the Slovak–Polish border provided they have a passport with them, and the new political climate means that exploration of the whole Tatra region is possible for the first time since the war. A decent **map** of the mountains is indispensable. The best is the *Tatrzański Park Narodowy* (1:30,000), which has all the paths accurately marked and colour-coded; available in English as *The Tatra National Park*, it marks not only hotels for overnight stays but also the distances of each section of pathway in red. **Staying** overnight in the eight PTTK-run huts dotted across the mountains is an experience in itself. **Food** is basic, but pricey for Poles, most of whom bring their own; the huts are an ideal place to meet people, preferably over a bottle of vodka. **Camping** isn't allowed in the National Park area; rock-climbing is, but only with a guide – ask at the PTTK for details. Check there for weather details too. The number for **mountain rescue** is ☎018/206 34 44.

The easiest way up to the peaks is by **cable car** from the hamlet of Kuźnice, a four-kilometre walk or bus journey south from Zakopane; get there before 8.30am to avoid queues. If you're here in winter for the skiing, you can rent gear for about 30zł a day from a number of outlets in town or in the car park below the cable car. The cable car ends near the summit of **Kasprowy Wierch** (1985m), where weather-beaten signs indicate the border. Many day-trippers simply walk back down to Kuźnice through the Hala Gàsienicowa. A rather longer alternative is to strike west to the cross-topped summit of Giewont (1909m) and head down to Kuźnice; this is fairly easy-going and quite feasible in a day if you start out early.

East of Kasprowy Wierch, the walking gets tougher. From Świnica (2300m), a strenuous ninety-minute walk, experienced hikers continue along the **Orla Perć** (Eagles' Path), a challenging, exposed ridge with spectacular views. The *Pięc Stawów* (Five Lakes) **hostel** (②), in the high valley of the same name, provides overnight shelter at the end. From the hostel you can hike back down Dolina Roztoki to **Łysa Polana**, a border crossing point in the valley, and take a bus back to Zakopane. An alternative is to continue a short distance east to the **Morskie Oko Lake** (1399m). Encircled by spectacular sheer cliff faces and alpine forest, this large glacial lake is one of the Tatras' big attractions, and an easy day-trip from Zakopane by bus – useful for those not up to or interested in the full cross-mountain hike. Six services a day (twenty in high summer) follow a scenic highland road to Polana Palenica (site of a big car park), from where it's a one-and-a-half hour walk by forest road to Morskie Oko itself. The lakeside PTTK **hostel** provides hearty food and a base for the ascent of **Rysy** (2499m), the highest peak in the Polish Tatras.

Zamość

The old towns and palaces of southeast Poland often have a Latin feel to them, and none more so than **ZAMOŚĆ**, 320km from Kraków. With its superb Renaissance centre, the town was the brainchild of the dynamic sixteenth-century chancellor Jan Zamoyski. Bernardo Morando of Padua, Zamoyski's architect, produced a planned town that was beautifully spacious and practical too: its defensive bastions protected Zamość through the seventeenth-century "Swedish Deluge" that flattened so many other Polish towns. The fortifications lasted until 1866, when the Russians ordered the liquidation of the fortress; parkland now covers much of the battlements. Somehow, the buildings of Zamość managed to get through World War II unscathed, although its people weren't spared: more than 8000 were executed by the Nazis, who also cleared out hundreds of neighbouring villages.

The **Rynek**, or Plac Mickiewicza, is a wide-open space of columned arcades, ringed by the decorative former homes of the Zamość mercantile bourgeoisie, and dominated from the north side by the elegant, spire-capped **Town Hall**. From the town hall, the vaulted arcade stretching east along ul Ormiańska features several mansions which today house the **Town Museum** (Tues–Sun 10am–4pm; 5zł); the focus is inevitably on the Zamoyskis and family memorabilia. The southern side of the square contains some of the oldest mansions, several designed by Morando himself, including the **Morando Tenement House** at no. 25, where the architect used to live. Immediately north of the Rynek lies the old Jewish quarter, centred on ul Zamenhofa and Rynek Solny. As in so many other eastern towns, Jews made up a significant portion of the population of Zamość – some 45 percent on the eve of World War II. The most impressive Jewish monument is the former Synagogue on the corner of Zamenhofa and Bazylianska, now a public library, a fine early-seventeenth-century structure built as part of Zamoyski's original town scheme.

Moving southwest of the Rynek, you'll see Morando's towering **Collegiate Church**, a powerful expression of the self-confidence of the Polish Counter-Reformation. West across the main road, ul Academicka, are two buildings that played a key role in the historic life of the town: the **Arsenal**, built by Morando in the 1580s, today houses a small military museum (Tues–Sun 10am–4pm; 5zł); and behind it, the massive **Zamoyski Palace**, which is a shadow of its former self, the original Morando-designed building having undergone substantial modification after the Zamoyskis abandoned it in the early nineteenth century.

North of the palace lies the grizzled red-brick form of the **Old Lublin Gate**, oldest of the surviving fortifications, now housing a basement bar frequented by alternative-leaning youth. A walk in the parkland stretching beyond the gate will provide a good view of the fortifications from the outside.

Practicalities

As Zamość is off the main communication lines, there are limited **public transport** options, with only one train and one express bus each from Warsaw and Kraków every day. If you miss these direct services, head for the regional city of Lublin, from where there are buses to Zamość every thirty minutes or so. The main **bus station** is over to the east of the town centre – tickets for the 2km ride to the town centre can be purchased from the MZK counter inside the bus station. The **train station** is 1km southwest of town along ul Akademicka. There's a helpful **tourist office** at Rynek 13, underneath the town hall (May–Sept Mon–Fri 8am–6pm, Sat 10am–4pm, Sun 10am–3pm; Oct–Nov Mon–Fri 10am–4pm; ☎084/639 22 92, *zoit@zamosc.um.gov.pl*), which has information on a meagre handful of private rooms (②), mostly in the suburbs. For **hotel accommodation**, the cheap and central *Marta*, ul Zamenhofa 11 (☎084/639 26 39) has a choice of dorm beds (①) or basic doubles (②); and the *Sportowy*, by the football stadium 500m west of the centre at ul Krolowej Jadwigi 8 (☎084/638 60 11), also has dorm beds (①) as well as roomy en suites (③). For more upmarket comforts head for the refurbished *Renesans*, just off the Rynek at ul Grecka 6 (☎084/639 20 01; ④); or the stylish Zamoyski, occupying a suite of historic buildings at ul S. Kołłataja 2/4/6, (☎084/639 28 86, *zamosc@orbis.pl*; ⑤).

The Rynek is lined with **café-restaurants** that move outdoors in summer. *Padwa*, Rynek 23, with a wonderful original ceiling, is a good place for a daytime coffee break as well as doing full meals. The *Ratuszowa*, strategically placed under the town hall at no. 13, has a quiet ambience: as well as decent cappuccinos and cakes they do the full range of Polish food. *Asia*, Staszica 10, specializes in cheap Chinese food – and pizzas. The *Piwnica Pod Rektorius*, Rynek 2, is the best of several basement beer **bars** around the main square; while *Green Pub*, Staszica 2, has a more suave, upmarket feel. *Jazz Club Kosz*, ul Zamenhofa 5, has occasional live jazz and blues, and is a cosy and intimate place for a drink on non-gig nights – find it through the courtyard at the back.

SILESIA AND WIELKOPOLSKA

In Poland it's known as Śląsk, in the Czech Republic as Sleszko, in Germany as Schlesien: all three countries hold part of the frequently disputed province that's called **Silesia** in English. Since 1945, Poland has held all of it except for a few of the westernmost tracts, a dominance gained as compensation for the Eastern Territories, which were incorporated into the USSR in 1939 as a result of the Nazi–Soviet pact, and never returned. Yet, although postwar Silesia has developed a strongly Polish character, people with family roots in the province are often bilingual and consider their prime loyalty to lie with Silesia rather than Poland. Heavy industry has blighted much of the region, especially in the huge **Katowice** conurbation, the largest unmodernized "black country" left in Europe. Similar problems, albeit on a smaller scale, also affect the province's chief city, **Wrocław**, holding back its potential to become a rival to Kraków, Prague and Budapest as one of Central Europe's most enticing cosmopolitan centres. North of Silesia, the region known as **Wielkopolska** formed the core of the original Polish nation, and its chief interest is supplied by the regional capital of **Poznań** – famed within Poland for the 1956 riots that marked the first major revolt against communism.

Wrocław

The special nature of **WROCŁAW** comes from the fact that it contains the soul of two great cities. One of these is the city that has long stood on this spot, Slav by origin but for centuries dominated by Germans and generally known as **Breslau**. The other is **Lwów** (now L'viv), capital of the Polish Ukraine, which was annexed by the Soviets in 1939. After the war, its displaced population was encouraged to take over the severely depopulated Breslau, which had been confiscated from Germany. The multinational influences which shaped the city are reflected in its architecture: several huge Germanic brick Gothic churches dominate the skyline, intermingled with Flemish-style Renaissance mansions, palaces and chapels of Viennese Baroque, and boldly utilitarian public buildings from the early years of this century, as well as the inevitable concrete boxes filling the gaps left by wartime destruction. The tranquillity of the parks, gardens and riverside walks offers an escape from the urban bustle.

The City

Wrocław's central area is delineated by the River Odra to the north and by the bow-shaped ul Podwale – the latter following the former defensive moat, whose ditch, now bordered by a shady park, still largely survives. At the centre of town is the vast space of the **Rynek**, given over mainly to museums, restaurants, cafés, travel agencies and bookshops. The magnificent Town Hall dates largely to the fifteenth century. The famous west face and the south facade are the real show stoppers, the latter with huge windows, filigree friezes of animals and foliage, and rich statuary. The town hall now serves as the **Historical Museum** (Wed–Sat 10am–4pm, Sun 10am–5pm; 6zł), although it's the largely unaltered interior which constitutes the main attraction: in the resplendent three-aisled Knights' Hall, the keystones of the vault feature character studies of all strata of society.

Of the mansions lining the main sides of the Rynek, those on the south and western sides are the most distinguished and colourful. At no. 6 is the House of the Golden Sun (Pod Złotym Słońcem), home of the **Museum of the Art of Medal Making** (Tues–Sun 10am–5pm; 3zł, free Wed); its shop sells examples of the craft, which must be the classiest souvenirs in town. Just off the northwest corner of the Rynek are two curious Baroque houses known as **Jaś i Małgosia**, linked by a gateway giving access to the close of **St Elizabeth**, the most impressive of Wrocław's churches. Since the mid-fifteenth century, its huge ninety-metre tower, which was under construction for 150 years, has been the city's most prominent landmark.

Southwest of the Rynek lies the maze-like former **Jewish quarter**, whose inhabitants fled or were driven from their tenements during the Third Reich. Immediately to the east of the Jewish quarter is a part of the city built in obvious imitation of the chilly classical grandeur of Berlin. Indeed, Carl Gotthard Langhans, designer of the Brandenburg Gate, had a hand in the monumental Royal Palace now housing the **Ethnographic Museum** (Tues–Wed & Fri–Sun 10am–4pm, Thurs 9am–4pm; 4zł, free Sat) in the southern wing, a good place to visit if you have kids in tow. Its main draw is a large collection of dolls decked out in what are deemed to be traditional dresses from all around the world. The lofty Gothic brick church of **St Dorothy** stayed in Catholic hands at the Reformation, and its whitewashed interior, littered with gigantic Baroque altars, forms an ornate contrast with other Wrocław churches, which still bear the hallmarks of four centuries of Protestant sobriety. One of the largest synagogues in Poland, the **Synagoga pod Białym Bocianem**, lies half-hidden through an archway at ul Włodkowica 9. Refurbishment began in 1996 with combined Polish and German financing, but reopening still looked some way off at the time of writing.

Further east, at the northern end of pl Dominikański, are the buildings of the **Dominican monastery**, centred on the thirteenth-century church of **St Adalbert** (Św. Wojciecha), which is embellished with fine brickwork and several lavish Gothic and Baroque chapels. A couple of blocks east stands the gargantuan former **Bernardine Monastery**; severely damaged during the war, the church and cloisters have been painstakingly reconstructed to house the **Museum of Architecture** (Tues, Thurs & Fri 10am–3.30pm, Wed & Sat 10am–4pm, Sun 10am–5pm; 2zł, free Wed), a fascinating record of the many historic buildings in the city which were destroyed in the war.

Wrocław's best-loved sight, the **Panorama of the Battle of Racławice** (Tues–Sun: May–Sept 9am–5.30pm; Oct–April 10am–3.30pm; shows every 30min; 15zł), is housed in a specially designed concrete rotunda in the shape of a crown in the park nearby. This painting, 120m long and 15m high, was commissioned in 1894 to celebrate the centenary of the Russian army's defeat by the people's militia of Tadeusz Kościuszko near the village of Racławice, between Kraków and Kielce. Not only is it Poland's most hi-tech tourist attraction, it's also one of the most popular, an icon second only in national affection to the Black Madonna. Make sure you ask to hear the English-language cassette, which explains all the details of the painting.

At the opposite end of the park is the ponderously Prussian neo-Renaissance home of the **National Museum** (Tues–Sun 10am–4pm, Thurs 9am–4pm; 6zł), which unites the collections of Breslau and Lwów. One of the most important sections, **medieval stone sculpture**, is housed on the ground floor. Here you can see the delicately linear carving of *The Dormition of the Virgin* from the portal of St Mary Magdalene. The other major highlight is the poignant early fourteenth-century *Tomb of Henryk the Righteous*, with its group of weeping mourners. On the first floor, the most eye-catching exhibits are the colossal statues of saints from St Mary Magdalene. The foreign paintings in the opposite wing include Cranach's *Eve*, originally part of a scene showing her temptation of Adam which was cut up and repainted as two portraits of a burgher couple in the seventeenth century.

North of the Rynek, the triangular-shaped university quarter, jam-packed with historic buildings, is bounded by two streets: ul Uniwersytecka to the south and ul Grodzka, which follows the Odra. Behind the fourteenth-century church of St Matthew spreads the colossal domed **Ossoliński Library**, built as a hospital at the end of the seventeenth century; one of the city's most impressive buildings, it has frequent exhibitions of items from its vast collection. However, the principal building of this district is the 171-metre-long **Collegium Maximum**, whose main assembly hall or **Aula Leopoldina**, upstairs at pl Uniwersytecki 1 (closed Wed 10am–3.30pm; 2.5zł), is one of the greatest secular interiors of the Baroque age, fusing architecture, painting, sculpture and ornament into one bravura whole.

From the Market Hall, the Piaskowski Bridge leads to the sandbank of **Wyspa Piasek** and the fourteenth-century hall church of **St Mary of the Sands** (Kościół NMP na Piasku), dull on the outside, majestically vaulted and surprisingly light inside. The two elegant little painted bridges of Most Młyński and Most Tumski, which look as though they should belong in an ornamental garden, connect Wyspa Piasek with **Ostrów Tumski**, the city's ecclesiastical heart.

Ulica Katedralny leads past several Baroque palaces (among which priests, monks and nuns are constantly scuttling) and a wall mural featuring the papal arms marking the papal visit of 1997 to the twin-towered **Cathedral of St John the Baptist**. Three chapels behind the high altar make a visit to the dank and gloomy interior worthwhile (restoration work permitting): St Elizabeth's Chapel, created by followers of Bernini; the Gothic Lady Chapel, with the masterly Renaissance funerary plaque of Bishop Jan Roth; and the Corpus Christi Chapel, a perfectly proportioned and subtly decorated Baroque gem.

Practicalities

The main **train station**, Wrocław Głowny – its Disneyland facade one of the city's sights, though its interior is seedy – faces the broad boulevard of ul Piłsudskiego, about fifteen minutes' walk south of the Rynek; the main **bus station** is at the back of the train station. The **tourist office** on the main square at Rynek 14 (Mon–Fri 9am–5pm, Sat 10am–2pm; ☎071/344 31 11) has a wealth of information and provides hotel listings, but doesn't book rooms.

A cluster of rather basic **hotels** can be found near the main train station – nearest of all is the *Hotel Piast* at ul Piłsudskiego 98 (☎071/343 00 33; rooms with shared facilities ②; en suites ③). Occupying the upper floors of the bus station, the *Podróznik*, ul Sucha 1–11 (☎071/373 28 45; ③) offers neat, if smallish, en suites. Between the stations and the Old Town, the *Savoy*, pl Kościuszki 19 (☎071/340 32 19; ③) offers acceptable en suites and fills up fast due to its attractive price – so ring in advance. Best deal in the town centre is the *Saigon*, ul Wita Stwosza 22/23 (☎071/344 28 81; ④), with cosy en suites above the Vietnamese restaurant of the same name. The most convenient **hostel** is 100m from the train station at ul Kołłataja 20, off ul Piłsudskiego (10am–5pm; lockout and 10pm curfew; ☎071/343 88 56; ①), although the new HI-affiliated hostel occupying one half of the *Hotel Tumski*, ten minutes north of the Old Town at Wyspa Słodowa 10 (☎71/322 60 99, *www.hotel-tumski.com.pl*; ①), offers better standards. There's a **campsite** on the east side of town near the Olympic Stadium at al Ignacego Padarewskiego 35 (☎071/348 46 51) – trams #9, #12, #17 and #32 run nearby. Information on summer student hostels (late June–Sept) is available at Almatur, ul Tadeusza Kościuszki 34 (Mon–Fri 10am–5pm, 6pm July; ☎071/343 41 35). These provide a single room for about 60zł and shared rooms for less. Anyone can stay there, though student holders of ISIC cards receive discounts.

Wrocław has a good selection of places to eat and drink, with the Rynek and nearby Plac Solny bubbling over with outdoor **cafés** and **restaurants** during the summer. *Vega*, Rynek-Ratusz 27a, is an excellent, inexpensive vegetarian haunt (Mon–Fri till 7pm, Sat & Sun till 5pm); while *Mis*, ul Kuźnicza 48 (Mon–Fri till 6pm, Sat till 5pm), is a student-packed canteen offering cheap Polish standards. *Lwów*, Rynek 4, is an atmospheric restaurant specializing in hearty meat dishes and pancakes; and *Spiż*, Rynek-Ratusz 2, is a restaurant-cum-superior-pub which brews its own beer. *Pod Kalamburem*, ul Kuźnicza 29a, boasts beautiful Jugendstil decor and some lethal cocktails; while the nearby *Kalogréodek*, ul Kuźnicza 29b, is an established student haunt with benches arranged around a little plaza. *Gumowa Róza*, Wita

Stwosza (entrance from the alley opposite the *Saigon* hotel) is a relaxed basement bar with a Bohemian edge.

The number of city-centre **clubbing** venues is on the increase, and many of the places round the Rynek feature dancing at the weekends. Also in the town centre, *Piec Nutek*, Podwale 37/38, concentrates on alternative tastes and features regular live gigs; and *Wagon*, located in the no-longer used Dworzec Świebodzki train station on the western fringes of the Old Town, organizes rave parties.

Poznań

Thanks to its position on the Paris–Berlin–Moscow rail line, and as the one place where all international trains stop between the German border and Warsaw, **POZNAŃ** is many visitors' first taste of Poland. In many ways it's the ideal introduction, as no other city is more closely identified with Polish nationhood. In the ninth century the Polonians founded a castle on an island in the River Warta, and in 968 Mieszko I made this one of the two main centres of his duchy and the seat of its first bishop. The settlement that developed here was given the name **Ostrów Tumski** (Cathedral Island), which it still retains. Nowadays it's a city of great diversity, its animated centre focused on one of Europe's most attractive squares, and with a dynamic business district to the west, whose trade fair is the most important in the country – it has a distinct influence on accommodation prices.

The City

For seven centuries the grandiose **Stary Rynek** has been the hub of life in Poznań, even if nowadays it has lost its position as the centre of political and economic power. The turreted Town Hall boasts a vivacious eastern facade, its lime-green pilasters framing a frieze of Polish monarchs. Inside lies the **Museum of the History of Poznań** (Mon & Tues 10am–4pm, Wed–Fri noon–6pm, Sat 9am–4pm, Sun 10am–3pm; 5.5zł) though this is less didactic than it sounds; the main reason for entering is to see the building itself. The stunner is the Renaissance **Great Hall** on the first floor, its coffered vault bearing polychrome bas-reliefs which embody the exemplary civic duties and virtues through scenes from the lives of Samson, King David and Hercules. Many a medieval and Renaissance interior lurks behind the Baroque facades of the **gabled houses** lining the outer sides of the Stary Rynek. Particularly fine are those on the eastern side, where no. 45 is the **Museum of Musical Instruments** (Tues & Sat 11am–5pm, Wed–Fri 10am–4pm, Sun 10am–3pm; 5.5zł, free Sat), the only collection of its kind in Poland.

Just to the west of the Stary Rynek at the end of ul Zamkowa stands a hill with remnants of the inner circle of the medieval walls. This particular section guarded the **Castle**, which was the seat of the rulers of Wielkopolska. Modified down the centuries, it was almost completely destroyed in 1945 but has been partly restored to house the **Museum of Applied Art** (Tues, Wed, Fri & Sat 10am–4pm, Sun 10am–3pm; 7zł, free Sat). This features an enjoyable enough collection from medieval times to the present day, while the Gothic cellars are used for changing displays of individual contemporary artists.

From here it's only a short walk to the vast elongated space of **Plac Wolności**, where the **National Museum**, at al Marcinkowskiego 9, houses one of the few important displays of old master paintings in Poland (Tues 10–6pm, Wed & Fri 9am–5pm, Thurs 10am–4pm, Sat 10am–5pm, Sun 11am–4pm; 7zł, free Fri). Dominating the gallery's small but choice Spanish section is the prize exhibit, Zurbarán's *Madonna of the Rosary*, while the extensive display of art from the Low Countries includes a regal *Adoration of the Magi* by Joos van Cleve.

To the south of the Stary Rynek is a complex of former Jesuit buildings, the finest Baroque architecture in the city. The **Parish Church** (Kościół Frany), completed just forty years before the expulsion of the Jesuits in 1773, boasts a magnificently sombre interior of fluted columns, gilded capitals, monumental sculptures, large altarpieces and rich stuccowork.

East of the Stary Rynek, the Bolesława Chrobrego bridge crosses to the holy island of **Ostrów Tumski**, a world away in spirit, if not in distance, from the hustle of the city. Only a small portion of the island is built upon, and a few priests and monks comprise its entire population; after 5pm the island is a ghost town. The first building you see is the late-Gothic **Psalteria**, characterized by its elaborate stepped gable. Immediately behind is an earlier brick structure, **St Mary's**, while behind that is the **Cathedral of SS Peter and Paul**. Most of this cathedral, Poland's oldest, was restored to its Gothic shape after wartime devastation, but a lack of documentary evidence for the eastern chapels meant that their successors had to be retained, as were the Baroque spires and the three lanterns around the ambulatory, which give a vaguely eastern touch. Inside, the **crypt** has been excavated, uncovering foundations of the pre-Romanesque and Romanesque cathedrals which stood on the site, as well as parts of the sarcophagi of the early Polish monarchs, Prince Mieszko I and King Bolesław the Brave. Their current resting place is the luscious Golden Chapel behind the altar, representing the diverse if dubious tastes of the 1830s.

Practicalities

The main **train station**, Poznań Główny, is 2km southwest of the historic quarter; tram #5 runs from the western exit (Dworzec Zachodnia) beyond platform 7 to the city centre. The **bus station** is five minutes' walk to the east of the train station along ul Towarowa. The city **tourist office**, next to the Empik store on the corner of Ratajczaka and 27 Grudnia (Mon–Fri 10am–7pm, Sat 10am–5pm; ☎061/9431), can book hotel and hostel rooms, and also sells *Iks*, a monthly **listings** guide with an English-language calendar of events. The Wielkopolska regional tourist office at Stary Rynek 59 (Mon–Fri 9am–5pm, Sat 10am–2pm; ☎061/852 61 56) has information on Poznań and the surrounding province. The **Eurostop office** at Aleksandra Fredry 7 (Mon–Fri 9am–6pm, Sat 10am–1pm; ☎061/852 03 44, *www.eurostop.com.pl*) incorporates Almatur and can therefore arrange accommodation in student hostels (vacated halls of residence) during the summer vacation (late June till mid-September).

Because of the trade fair, Poznań has plenty of **accommodation**, but hotel prices can double during fairs, which take place throughout the year, July and August excepted. One place that never increases its rates during fairs is the *PTTK Dom Turysty* at Rynek 91 (☎061/852 88 93, *www.domturysty-hotel.com.pl*), which has simple four-person dorms (①), doubles with shared facilities (②) and comfy en suites (③). Also representing reasonable value in the heart of the city are the friendly, if slightly musty *Wielkopolska* at ul Św. Martin 67 (☎061/852 76 31; rooms with shared facilities ④; en suites ⑤), and the nearby *Lech*, ul Św. Marcina 74 (☎061/85301 51, *www.hotel-lech.poznan.pl*; ④), which has comfy rooms with showers. Best-value mid-range place is the thoroughly modernized *Sport*, east of the bus station behind a sports arena at Chwiałkowskiego 34 (☎061/833 05 91, *www.posir.poznan.pl*; ④). There is a hostel 1.5km north of the bus and train stations, at ul Berwiniskiego 2/3 (☎061/866 36 80; ①). Private rooms (②) are available from the Globtour office in the train station (open 24hr; rooms available up until 10pm), or from the Biuro Zakwaterowania just outside the station's western exit at ul Głogowska 16 (Mon–Fri 8am–6pm, Sat 10am–2pm; ☎061/866 51 63, *www.przemyslaw.com.pl*). The nearest **campsite** is *Maltańska*, ul Krańcowa (☎061/876 62 03; tram #8 from the train station), set by a lake 2km east of the centre, although its fully equipped bungalows (⑤) are as expensive as a downtown hotel room.

There are plenty of **eating and drinking** possibilities in the main square, especially in summer, when café terraces spill out onto the cobbles. The heavily furnished *Stara Ratuszowa* at Stary Rynek 55, which stays open until 1am, offers pricey Polish specialities. *Piwnica Murna*, Murna 3, offers grilled meat dishes and decent salads in a candlelit brick cellar. For particularly good value, try one of the Italian pizzerias around or just off the main square, such as *Pizzeria di Trevi* at Wodna 7. *Bar Wegeterianski* at ul Wrocławska 21, off Stary Rynek to the south, is a healthy and cheap daytime snack bar. For coffee, cakes and ice cream try the mauve splendours of *Arezzo* at Stary Rynek 49. There are numerous evening drinking venues on and around the Rynek: *Pod Aniolem*, housed in a historic building at Wrocławska 8, is one of the more atmospheric. Ten minutes west of the Rynek at ul ŚW Marcina 80/82, *Blue Note* (*www.bluenote.info.poznan.pl*) is a jazz bar which hosts regular live gigs and club nights. **Internet access** is available at Klik, south of the Rynek on Jaskołca (daily 10am–11pm; 8zł/hr).

travel details

Trains

Częstochowa to: Kraków (4 daily; 2hr); Warsaw (1 daily; 3hr).

Gdańsk to: Częstochowa (3 daily; 6hr 30min); Kraków (1 daily; overnight); Poznań (5 daily; 3hr 30min–4hr); Toruń (4 daily; 3hr); Warsaw (13 daily; 4hr); Wrocław (5 daily; 6hr); Zakopane (1 daily; overnight).

Kraków to: Częstochowa (4 daily; 2hr); Gdańsk (5 daily; 7hr); Poznań (8 daily; 6hr); Warsaw (12 daily; 2hr 30min); Wrocław (14 daily; 4hr); Zakopane (14 daily; 3–4hr); Zamość (1 daily; 8hr).

Poznań to: Częstochowa (2 daily; 4hr 30min); Gdańsk (5 daily; 3hr 30min); Kraków (6 daily; 6hr); Toruń (5 daily; 2–3hr); Warsaw (16 daily; 3hr); Wrocław (20 daily; 2hr).

Toruń to: Częstochowa (1 daily; overnight); Gdańsk (4 daily; 3hr); Kraków (1 daily; overnight); Poznań (5 daily; 2hr); Warsaw (3 daily; 3hr); Wrocław (2 daily; 4hr 30min).

Warsaw to: Częstochowa (9 daily; 2hr 30min–3hr); Gdańsk (14 daily; 4hr 30min); Kraków (14 daily; 2hr 30min); Poznań (16 daily; 3hr); Toruń (3 daily; 3hr); Wrocław (9 daily; 5hr); Zakopane (4 daily; 6–9hr); Zamość (1 daily, via Lublin; 5hr).

Wrocław to: Częstochowa (2 daily; 2hr 30min); Gdańsk (4 daily; 5hr); Kraków (13 daily; 4hr–4hr 30min); Poznań (19 daily; 2hr); Toruń (2 daily; 4hr 30min); Warsaw (9 daily; 5hr).

Zakopane to: Kraków (14 daily; 3–4hr).

Zamość to: Warsaw (1 daily, via Lublin; 5hr).

Buses

For intercity routes look out for the more comfortable and faster Polski Express buses, only slightly pricier than the PKS state-run services detailed below:

Gdańsk to: Frombork (5 daily; 2hr 30min).

Kraków to: Zakopane (32 daily; 2hr 15min); Zamość (1 daily; 7hr).

Warsaw to: Toruń (3 daily); Zakopane (1 daily); Zamość (1 daily; 6hr 30min).

CHAPTER 22

PORTUGAL

- Tuy & Vigo
- 0 — 100 km
- Viana do Castelo
- Barcelos
- Braga
- Guimarães
- Bragança
- Amarante
- Vila Real
- Mirandela
- Oporto
- Tua
- Pocinho
- Salamanca
- Aveiro
- Viseu
- Figueira da Foz
- Coimbra
- Guarda
- ATLANTIC OCEAN
- Leiria
- Batalha
- Fátima
- Tomar
- Alcobaça
- Castelo de Vide
- To Madrid
- Óbidos
- Marvão
- SPAIN
- Mafra
- Sintra
- LISBON
- Évora
- Sines
- Odemira
- Portimão
- Silves
- Tavira
- Vila Real de Santo António
- Sevilla
- Sagres
- Lagos
- Faro
- Olhão
- Huelva
- N
- - - - - Bus link

Introduction

Portugal is around the size of Scotland with twice the population and has tremendous variety both geographically and in its ways of life and traditions. Along the coast around Lisbon, and on the well-developed Algarve in the south, there are highly sophisticated resorts, while the vibrant capital Lisbon has enough going on to please most city devotees. But in its rural areas this is still a conspicuously underdeveloped country, and there are plenty of opportunities to experience smaller towns and countryside regions that have changed little in the past century.

In terms of population, and of customs, differences between the **north and south** are particularly striking. Above a line more or less corresponding with the course of the River Tagus, the people are of predominantly Celtic and Germanic stock. It was here, at Guimarães, that the "Lusitanian" nation was born, in the wake of the Christian reconquest from the North African Moors. South of the Tagus, where the Moorish and Roman civilizations were most established, people tend to be darker-skinned and maintain more of a "Mediterranean" lifestyle. More recent events are woven into the pattern. The 1974 **revolution** came from the south – an area of vast estates, rich landowners and a dependent workforce – while the conservative backlash of the 1980s came from the north, with its powerful religious authorities and individual smallholders wary of change. More profoundly even than the revolution, **emigration** has altered people's attitudes and the appearance of the countryside. After Lisbon, the largest Portuguese community is in Paris, and there are migrant workers spread throughout France and Germany. Returning to Portugal, these emigrants have brought in modern ideas and challenged many traditional rural values.

The greatest of all Portuguese influences, however, is **the sea**. The Portuguese are very conscious of themselves as a seafaring race; mariners like Vasco da Gama led the way in the exploration of Africa and the Americas, and until less than thirty years ago Portugal remained a colonial power. The colonies brought African and South American strands to the country's culture: in the distinctive music of *fado*, sentimental songs heard in Lisbon and Coimbra, for example, or in the Moorish-influenced and Manueline architecture that abounds in coastal towns like Belém and Viana do Castelo.

Since Portugal is so compact, it's easy to take in something of each of its elements. Scenically, the most interesting parts of the country are in the north: the **Minho**, green, damp, and often startling in its rural customs; and the sensational gorge and valley of the **Douro**, followed along its course by the railway, off which antiquated branch lines edge into remote **Trás-os-Montes**. For contemporary interest, spend some time in both **Lisbon** and **Porto**, the only two cities of real size. And if it's monuments you're after, the centre of the country – above all, **Coimbra** and **Évora** – retain a faded grandeur. The **coast** is virtually continuous beach, and apart from the **Algarve** and a few pockets around Lisbon and Porto, resorts remain low-key and thoroughly Portuguese, with great stretches of deserted sands between them. Perhaps the loveliest are along the northern **Costa Verde**, around Viana do Castelo, or, for isolation, the wild beaches of **southern Alentejo**.

Information and maps

You'll find a tourist office, or **Turismo**, in almost every town of any size. Aside from the help they can give you in finding a room, they often have local maps and leaflets. Their hours are generally daily 9am–8pm. There is also a free English-speaking tourist help-line (freephone ☎0800 296 296; daily 9am–midnight). If you're doing any real exploration, or driving, it's worth investing in a good **road map**. The best are those put out by the Automóvel Clube de Portugal, the Spanish Plaza y Janes, and Michelin #437.

PORTUGAL ON THE NET

www.portugalvirtual.pt – cultural and tourist information covering all major towns.

www.portugal-insite.pt – 14 short tours of Portugal and good range of accommodation.

www.portugal-info.net – very comprehensive guide to everything from golf to rural tourism.

www.budgettravel.com/portugal.htm – good links to lots of tourist-related sites.

www.the-news.net/ – weekly English-language newspaper covering latest events in Portugal.

www.maisturismo.pt – general information on cultural events and tourism.

www.eurotrip.com – Excellent site for travel information.

Money and banks

Portugal is one of twelve European Union countries which have changed over to a single currency, the **euro** (€). Euro notes and coins are scheduled to be issued from the beginning of 2002, with Portugeuse escudos (esc or $) remaining in circulation during a transition period, at a fixed rate of 200.482 esc to 1 euro, until they are scrapped entirely at the end of February 2002. After this date you will still be able to exchange your escudos for euros in banks for at least a year. Euro notes are issued in **denominations** of 5, 10, 20, 50, 100, 200 and 500 euros, and coins in denominations of 1, 2, 5, 10, 20 and 50 cents and 1 and 2 euros.

All prices in this chapter are given in euros correct at the time of going to press. There will no doubt be some rounding off or, more probably, up of prices in the first few months after the introduction of the euro.

Portuguese **banks** are efficient, with perhaps the exception of some rural branches which can be painstakingly slow. You'll find at least one in all but the smallest towns. Banking **hours** are Mon–Fri 8.30am–3pm; in Lisbon and in some of the Algarve resorts they may be open in the evening to change money. ATMs are common throughout the country and offer a cheaper alternative to counter service in terms of commission. Commission on traveller's cheques can be high, so your best bet for cheap exchange is to use a credit or bank card at an ATM.

Communications

Post offices (*correios*) are normally open Mon–Fri 9am–6pm and Saturdays 9am–12pm. To buy **stamps**, queue at the counter marked *selos* at the post office, use the dispensing machines available in most post offices, or alternatively go anywhere that has the sign of the red horse on a white circle over a green background. For **poste restante** services, look for a counter marked *encomendas*. The Portuguese postal service is reasonably efficient: mail takes about 3 days to Europe and just under a week to the U.S.

International phone calls can be made direct from any telephone booth or post office in the country. Phone cards are available from post offices, kiosks or newsagents and vary in price depending on the latest offer. Cheap-rate international calls are between 8.00pm and 8.00am. The domestic operator number is ☎118; for international assistance – and collect calls – dial ☎098.

Internet cafés are common in most towns and cities and cost €4–5/hr. Most major post offices also now have Internet booths accessible by buying a card behind the counter.

Getting around

Distances are small in Portugal and you can get almost everywhere easily and efficiently by either train, bus or ferry. Although **trains** are usually cheaper, and some lines are highly scenic, it's often quicker to go by **bus** – especially on shorter or less obvious routes.

■ Trains

CP, the Portuguese railway company, operates all trains. About ninety percent are designated *Regional*, stop at most stations en route, and have first- and second-class cars. *Intercidades* are twice as fast and twice as expensive, and you should reserve a seat if using them. The fastest, most luxurious and priciest of all are the *Rápidos* (known as "*Alfa*"), which speed between Lisbon, Coimbra and Porto – sometimes they have only first-class seats. CP sells its own **rail passes** (valid on any train and in first class), but you'd have to do a lot of travelling to make them worthwhile. Both InterRail and Eurail passes are valid, although supplements equal to the difference from a standard fare must be paid to travel on *Intercidades* and *Rápidos*. A complete timetable of CP services can be bought at ticket offices (€2.50) or accessed via the Internet at *www.cp.pt*.

■ Buses

Buses can often be more flexible than trains and fares are usually competitive. The majority of buses used to be run by the Rodoviaria Nacional (RN), but the company has been broken up and privatized. Most of the former RN services leave from a town's central terminal. On a number of major routes (particularly Lisbon–Algarve) special **express coaches** can knock hours off the standard multiple-stop bus journeys.

■ Driving and hitching

Car rental rates in Portugal are high out of season (around €40–60/day) and it is well worth looking into prices before you leave as they can often work out cheaper. To rent a car you must be over 21 and have held a driving licence for over a year. Beware – Portugal has the highest **road fatality** rate in Europe;

most accidents occur on the infamous Lisbon–Oporto and Lisbon–Algarve motorways. August is especially lethal when Portuguese emigrant workers return home on holiday. If you **break down** you can get assistance from the Automóvel Clube de Portugal, which has reciprocal arrangements with most other automobile clubs. In the north, phone their Porto service (☎22 830 1127); in the south, phone Lisbon (☎21 942 9103). Both operate 24 hours a day.

Hitching should generally not be a good option, not only because of the country's high accident rate but it is often difficult to get a lift. It is definitely not recommended for women or solo travellers.

Cycling

Although there are few facilities and little respect from motorists, **cycling** is a popular sport in Portugal. Remember, however, that everywhere north of Lisbon is hilly and you'll find pedalling hard work in mountainous Beira Alta or across the burned plains of southern Alentejo. The railway system provides an efficient if expensive bicycle-carrying service; ask in advance as the service is not available on every train.

For **mountain biking** check out Bike Trails at *www.math.science.unitn.it/Bike/Countries/Portugal /–* the site contains a description of mountain biking in the country, a very detailed report on cycling in Portugal plus a 800km tour of the country.

Accommodation

In almost any town you should be able to find **accommodation** in a single room for under €25 and a double for under €50. Even in mid-season you shouldn't have many problems finding a bed, except in Lisbon and the Algarve.

■ Pensions and hotels

The main budget stand-bys are **pensions**, or **pensões** (*pensão* in the singular), which are graded from one to three stars. A three-star *pensão* is usually

about the same price as a one-star **hotel**, and sometimes the latter can even be cheaper: similarly, some one-star pensions are far nicer than those with two or three.

Additional categories include **pousadas**, run by the state and similar to the Spanish *paradores*. These are expensive, charging at least four-star hotel prices, but they are often converted from old monasteries or castles and well worth a visit even if you can't afford to stay. Reservations can be made through the central office in Lisbon (*Avenida Santa Joana a Princessa 10-A, Alvalade 17000*, ☎ 21 844 2000, *www.pousadas.pt*).

■ Youth Hostels

There are forty-one **youth hostels** (*Pousadas de Juventude*) in Portugal and, unlike in Spain, they do tend to stay open all year. The price for a dormitory bed is around €8–12 (£5–7/$8–11) a night (depending on season), a little extra if you need to rent sheets and blankets. Most have a curfew (usually midnight) and all demand a valid IYH card which costs €5 if you are under 26 and €15 if you are over.

■ Private rooms

In seaside resorts there are invariably rooms (*quartos* or *dormidas*) to let in **private houses**. These are sometimes advertised, sometimes just hawked by people at the bus and train stations. They're slightly cheaper than pension rooms – especially if you haggle, as expected in the main resorts. Tourist offices have lists.

■ Camping

Portugal has more than a hundred authorized **campsites**, most of them small, low-key and attractively located, and all of them remarkably inexpensive – it's rare that you'll end up paying more than €5 (£3/$5) a person. You can get a fairly complete map list from any Portuguese tourist office, or buy a detailed booklet, the *Roteiro Campista*, from bookshops or big

---

ACCOMMODATION PRICE CODES

Throughout this guide, accommodation is coded on a scale of ① to ⑨, the code indicating the lowest price per person per night you could expect to pay in each establishment in high season. With hostels this is the nightly rate per person; with hotels, the price is arrived at by dividing the cost of the cheapest double room by two. The prices indicated by the codes are as follows:

① under £5/$8 (€9)   ④ £15–20/$24–32 (€27–36)   ⑦ £30–35/$48–56 (€54–63)
② £5–10/$8–16 (€9–18)   ⑤ £20–25/$32–40 (€36–45)   ⑧ £35–40/$56–64 (€63–72)
③ £10–15/$16–24 (€18–27)   ⑥ £25–30/$40–48 (€45–54)   ⑨ £40/$64 (€72) and over

newsstands. Alternatively, for a full list of caravan and campsites, contact Federação Portuguesa de Campismo, Avenida Colonel Eduardo Galhardo 24D, (☎21 812 6890, *www.roteiro-campista.pt*).

Unofficial camping is banned in Portugal and beach areas are especially strict on this. Campsite thefts are a regular occurrence – but over most of the country the locals are extremely honest and you can leave equipment without worrying.

Food and drink

Portuguese food is excellent, cheap and served in quantity. Virtually all cafés, whatever their appearance, will serve you a basic meal, or at least a snack, for under €8 (£5/$7.50), and for a little more you have the run of most of the country's restaurants.

■ Food

Often you'll come across a whole range of dishes served at a **café** but it is usually **snacks and basic fare**. Favourites include *tosta mistas* (cheese and ham toasties), *prego* (steak sandwich), usually served with a fried egg; *bifoque* (steak, chips, fried egg); *rissóis* (deep-fried meat patties); *pasteis de bacalhau* (codfish cakes); and *sandes* (sandwiches). Sometimes, too, you'll see food displayed on café counters, particularly shellfish – if you see anything that looks appealing, just ask for *uma dose* (a portion). *Uma coisa destas* (one of those) can also be a useful phrase.

Restaurants usually offer a three-course *ementa turística* which is usually the most economical way to eat – restaurant servings tend to be so enormous that you can often have a substantial meal by ordering a *meia dose* (half portion), or one portion between two.

Regional differences aren't as marked as in Spain, but it's always worth taking stock of the *prato do dia* (dish of the day) and, if you're on the coast, going for **fish** and **seafood**. Typical Portuguese dishes include *sopa de marisco* (shellfish soup cooked and served with wine), *caldo verde* (finely shredded green kale leaves in broth) and *bacalhau* (dried cod, cooked in a myriad of different ways). *Caldeirada* is a fish stew with as many as nine kinds of fish, cooked with onions and tomatoes. Also typical is *carne de porco á Alentejana*, in which fried pork is covered with a clam, tomato and onion sauce or stewed with tomato and onions. **Meat** is usually excellent, and nearly all restaurants have pork, beef, lamb, goat and chicken dishes. Regional **cheeses** are well worth

experimenting, particularly goat and sheep cheese. **Puddings** include *arroz doce* (rice pudding), Madeira pudding and *nuvens* (egg custard). Portugal's **cakes** – *bolos* or *pastéis* – are often at their best in *casas de chá* (tearooms), though you'll also find them in cafés and in *pastelarias* (cake shops). Among the best are the Belém custard tarts (*pastéis de nata*), the Sintra cheesecakes (*queijadas de Sintra*), marzipan cakes from the Algarve, and the incredibly sweet egg-based *doces de ovos*.

■ Drink

In addition to food, all **cafés** serve alcohol – and they're much cheaper places to drink than bars, which tend to have slightly more cosmopolitan pretensions and prices. Portuguese **wines** (*tinto* for red, *branco* for white) are very inexpensive and of an amazing quality overall – even the standard *vinho da casa* that you get in the humblest of cafés. The fortified **port** (*vinho do Porto*) and **madeira** (*vinho da Madeira*) wines are by far the best known, and you should certainly aim to sample them both. Among **table wines**, the most popular regional names are Dão for red wines and Bucelas and Colares for white wines. Sparkling rosé wines are mostly produced for export; Mateus Rosé is one of the most famous. The light, slightly sparkling **vinhos verdes** – "green wines", in age not colour – are produced in the Minho, and are excellent and refreshing served chilled.

Portuguese **brandy** is available in two varieties, Macieiera and Constantino, and like local **gin** is ridiculously cheap; if you're asking for gin or any other spirits at a bar always specify you want "gin nacional", "vodka nacional", etc – it'll save you a fortune.

The two most common local **beers** (*cervejas*) are Sagres and Super Bock – both are served on tap and are very drinkable. You can order many other bottled foreign brands in most bars. Order *um fino* or *um imperial* if you want a small glass; *uma caneca* will get you a half-litre.

Opening hours and holidays

Shops generally open Mon–Sat between 9am–1pm and 3pm–6 or 7pm except for the large shopping centres which are popular in Portugal and stay open until 10pm or midnight. Larger supermarkets tend to stay open until 8pm. **Museums, churches and monuments** open from around 10am to 6pm; almost all museums and monuments, however, are closed on Mondays, and at Easter, when cultural life seems to cease completely.

The main **public holidays** are: Jan 1; Feb 12 (Carnival); Good Friday; April 25 (Revolution day); May 1 (Labour day); Corpus Christi; June 10 (Camões day) ; Jun 24 (St John's Day, Lisbon only); Aug 15 (Assumption); Oct 5 (Republic day); Nov 1 (All Saints); Dec 1 (Independence day); Dec 8 (Immaculate Conception day); Dec 25.

Emergencies

Portugal is a reasonably crime-free country although Lisbon and the larger tourist areas have recently seen significant increases in petty crime. Rented cars are always prey to thieves – leave them looking as empty as possible – and campsites in the Algarve are less reliable than elsewhere.

Violations of **drug trafficking laws** carry heavy sentences although possession of any kind of hard or soft drugs no longer constitutes a prisonable offence. Portuguese **police**, though relatively easy-going, carry guns and are not to be argued with.

For minor health complaints people generally go to a *farmácia* (**pharmacy**), which you'll find in almost any village; in larger towns there's usually one where English is spoken. They are normally open Mon–Fri 9am–1pm & 3–7pm, Sat 9am–1pm. A sign at each one will show the nearest 24hr pharmacy on duty. Pharmacists are highly trained and can dispense many drugs without a prescription. In the case of serious illness, you can get the address of an English-speaking doctor from a consular office or, with luck, from the local police or tourist office.

Emergency Numbers

All emergencies ☎112 – you will be given a choice between *policia*, *ambulância* or *bombeiros* (police, ambulance, fire brigade).

LISBON AND AROUND

These are few more immediately likeable capitals than **LISBON** (Lisboa). A lively and varied place, it remains in some ways curiously provincial, rooted as much in the 1920s as the 2000s. Pre-World War I wooden trams clank up outrageous gradients, past mosaic pavements and Art Nouveau cafés, and the medieval, village-like quarter of **Alfama** which hangs below the city's **São Jorge** castle. Modern Lisbon, with a population of just over 3 million, has kept an easy-going, human pace and scale, with little of the underlying violence of most cities and ports of its size. It also boasts a vibrant, cosmopolitan identity, with large communities of ex-colony Brazilians, Africans (from Angola, Mozambique and Cape Verde) and Asians (from Macao, Goa and East Timor). Many came over to work on two major urban development projects in the Nineties: the preparations for the **European City of Culture** in 1994 and the **Expo 98**. Lisbon invested heavily in these ventures and the rejuvenation of the city with new road, hotel, metro and bridge schemes. Disused dockland has been reclaimed and communication links improved with several showcase pieces of architecture and engineering like Santiago Calatrava's impressive Gare de Oriente and his sleek fourteen kilometre-long **Vasco de Gama** bridge which links Lisbon airport to a network of national motorways. The focus is still firmly on the future with Portugal's successful bid to stage the **European Football Championship** in 2004, an event which will again turn the world's attention on the Portuguese capital.

The **Great Earthquake** of 1755 (followed by a tidal wave and fire) destroyed most of the city's big buildings and twenty years of frantic reconstruction led to many impressive new palaces and churches and the street grid pattern spanning the seven hills of Lisbon. Several buildings from Portugal's golden age survived the quake – notably the **Torre de Belém**, the **Castelo de São Jorge** and the **Monastery of Jerónimos** at Belém. Many of the city's more modern sites also demand attention: the **Fundação Calouste Gulbenkian**, a museum and cultural complex with superb collections of ancient and modern art and the futuristic **Oceanarium** at the Parque das Nações, the largest of its kind in Europe. Half an hour south of Lisbon dunes stretch along the **Costa da Caparica** and twenty kilometres north you'll pass the coastal resorts of **Estoril** and **Cascais** before reaching the lush wooded heights and royal palaces of **Sintra** and the monastery of **Mafra**, one of the most extraordinary buildings in the country.

Arrival and information

From Portela **airport**, just twenty minutes' drive from the centre, local buses #44 and #45 (€1) run from the road outside the airport to Rossio and Cais do Sodré (train station for Cascais; ☎800 203 067). It's easier, but more expensive, to take the Aerobus (#91; every 20min 7am–9pm; €2.50), which leaves from right outside the Arrivals Hall and runs to Praça dos Restauradores, Rossio, Praça do Comércio and Cais do Sodré. **Taxis** into the centre of Lisbon should cost under €10 but it is always best to fix a price before you depart. **Long-distance trains** use the **Santa Apolónia station** (*www.eurotrip.com/rail/portugal.htm* for international train information), about fifteen minutes' walk from the waterfront Praça do Comércio, or a short ride on buses #9, #39, #46 or #90 to Rossio. **Local trains** from Sintra emerge at the heart of the city in the **Rossio station**, while **trains from the Algarve and south** terminate at **Barreiro**, on the far bank of the river, from where you catch a ferry (6am–2am; around €1.50 depending on destination) to the **Fluvial** station next to the Praça do Comércio. For **train timetables**, visit the information office on the ground floor of Rossio station (Mon–Sat 9am–7pm) or check out the Web site *www.cp.pt*, which is available in English. The new **main bus terminal** (24hr national bus information ☎707 22 33 44, *www.rede-expressos.pt* for timetables) is at **Arco do Cego** (metro Saldanha) and handles most international and domestic departures, including services to the Algarve and Madrid. The new terminal, **Gare do Oriente** (☎800 201 820), also has some international and domestic departures.

It could hardly be easier to get your bearings in the **Baixa**, the central city grid. At one end, opening onto the River Tagus, is the broad, arcaded **Praça do Comércio**; at the other stands Praça Dom Pedro IV, or the **Rossío**, merging with the **Praça da Figueira** and **Praça dos Restauradores**. These squares, filled with cafés, occasional street musicians, tourists and streetwise dealers, form the hub of Lisbon's daily activity. At night the focus shifts to the **Docas**, a new ultra-modern dockland area full of clubs and some of the capital's best restaurants and bars. A more time honoured but equally lively option is the **Bairro Alto**, high above and to the west of the Baixa, and best reached by funicular (Elevador da Glória) or the great street *elevador* (Elevador Santa Justa), built by Eiffel disciple Raul Mésnier de Ponsard. East of the Baixa, the **Castelo de São Jorge**, built by the Moors in 719 before becoming home to many of Portugal's kings, crowns the city's highest hill, with the **Alfama** district – the core of the medieval city – sprawled below.

The main **tourist office** is on the western side of Praça dos Restauradores in the Palácio da Foz (daily 9am–8pm; ☎21 346 6307, *www.icep.pt*); they can supply maps and accommodation lists and can assist with booking hire cars. There's also a tourist office at the airport (daily 6am–11pm; ☎21 844 6473), and there is a stylish, new tourism centre, **Lisboa Welcome Centre**, on the corner of Praça do Comércio and Rua do Arsenal (daily 9am–9pm; ☎21 031 2700, *www.alt-turismolisboa.pt*) that has the most up-to-date information. There are also several information kiosks (daily 10am–6pm) dotted around the city; in front of the Museu de Arte Popular in Belém, inside Santa Apolónia station, on Rua Augusta in Baixa, at the Parque Municipal de Campismo and at the Parque das Nações.

Finding your way around the Alfama and Bairro Alto district can be a problem as a lot of the streets are narrow and not marked on most maps. It's well worth investing in the *Falkplan* **map** sold in the newsagent next to the tourist office in Praça dos Restauradores; alternatively log on to *www.EUnet.pt/Lisboa* and print out a copy of their excellent city maps.

City transport

Getting around Lisbon presents few problems. Most places of interest are within easy walking distance – and transport connections are detailed in the text for those that aren't. The bus and tram networks operate from around 6am to midnight and the metro until 1am – pick up the useful public-transport map at any tourist office. **Trams**, the most enjoyable way of getting around, and **buses** (☎21 361 3000, *www.carris.pt*) are also a good bet – tickets for either are valid for two journeys (€0.90); alternatively, there are *Passe Turístico* bus/metro/*elevador* **passes**, valid for four days (€8.60) or seven days (€12.25), available from booths. The vastly improved **metro** (☎21 798 0600, *www.metrolisboa.pt*) now covers most of the city and it by far the fastest way of getting around; tickets cost €0.50 each, €4.25 for a block of ten or €1.35 for a day pass. The **Lisboa Card** gives unlimited travel on all the city's public transport, entry to 26 museums and discounts on a host of tourist-related activities. The cards cost €8.80 for 4 days, €12.45 for one week, €20.20 for one month and are available from any Carris kiosk or metro station. **Taxis** are beige (the older ones are black with a green roof) and have small green lights on top, indicating availability. All journeys are metered (starting at €1.50 plus €0.50 for each item of luggage carried), and a short hop should rarely cost more than €10. They can be found quite easily by day, especially around the main squares, but at night they're dearer (from €2) and more difficult to get hold of – if you're leaving a bar or club it's usually best to arrange for one by phone; try Rádio Táxis de Lisboa (☎21 811 9000) or Teletaxis (☎21 811 1100).

Ferries are particularly useful in the summer for short trips to reach various points on the other side of the Tagus river. These scenic trips typically cost between €0.50 and €1.75 and will save you waiting in long traffic jams when the masses descend on the beaches south of Lisbon. Most cross-Tagus ferries are operated by Transtejo (☎21 322 4000, *www.transtejo.pt*)

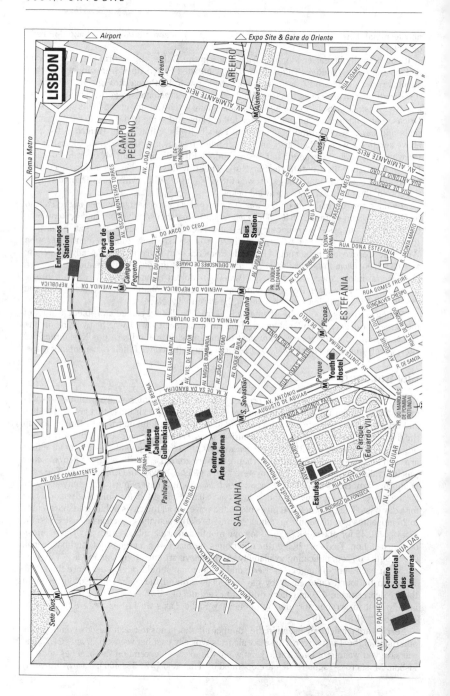

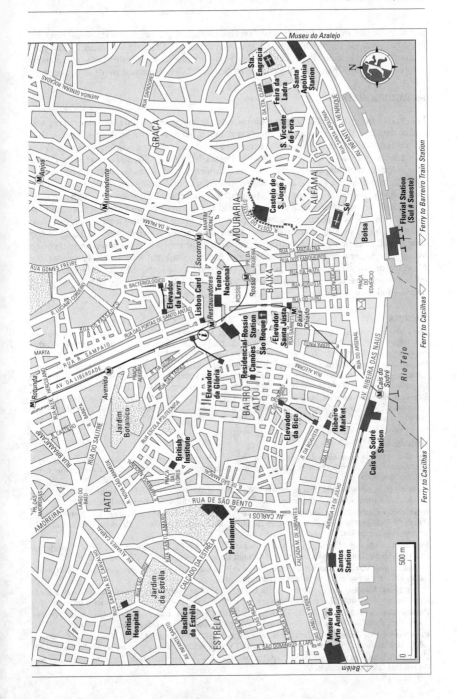

and arrive at Belém, Cais do Sodré and Terreiro do Paço. CP (Portuguese Railways) runs the ferry link from Barreiro (where the CP trains terminate) to Praça do Comércio; for rail travellers the fare is included in the ticket price. There are also 24-hour **water taxis**, operated by Taxitour (☎21 397 2783), which depart from a number of clearly marked points along the river.

Accommodation

Lisbon has scores of small, cheap **pensions**, often grouped one on top of the other in tall tenement blocks. The most obvious accommodation area is between Rossío station and Marquês de Pombal and in the streets and alleys between Praça dos Restauradores and Praça da Figueira – for budget choices, try Rua das Portas de Santo Antão and Rua da Glória. Bairro Alto is the most atmospheric part of the city in which to stay, though rooms can be hard to come by and noisy. At Easter, and in midsummer, room availability is stretched to the limit: many single rooms are "converted" to doubles and prices may start as high as €25. Fortunately, during most of the year you should have little difficulty finding a place, and for maybe a third less than the midsummer prices. For more expensive **hotels**, you can save yourself a lot of walking if you use the **24hr reservation service** (☎21 314 1562) at the Praça dos Restauradores tourist office or the airport; there is no commission charge. If you're looking for general backpacking information, free Internet and bargain places to stay try **Movijovem**, Avenida Duque d'Avila 137 (☎21 359 6000, *www.sej.pt*). Most of the pensions listed below are one- or two-star; **addresses**, written as 53-3°, for example, specify the street number followed by the floor.

Hostels

Casa da Juventude, Via da Moscavide 47–101 (☎21 892 0890/). Brand new hostel a twenty-minute bus/train journey out from the centre but right on the banks of the Tagus with the Expo Aquarium nearby. No curfew and all mod cons. Take Metro to Oriente. Dorms ②, doubles ④.

Pousada de Juventude da Catalazete, Estrada Marginal (☎21 443 0638). Overlooking the beach at Oeiras, 15km outside the city. Take any train from Cais do Sodré and follow signs from Oeiras station. It's small, so phone before setting out to be sure of getting a room. Reception open 6–11pm. Dorms ②, doubles ④.

Pousada de Juventude de Lisboa, Rua Andrade Corvo 46 (☎21 353 2696). Lisbon's main hostel, recently renovated, with good facilities and no curfew. Book in advance. One block south of the Picoas metro stop, or take buses #1, #21 or #36 from Restauradores or Rossío. Dorms ②, doubles ④.

Hotels

Pensão Arco da Bandeira, Rua dos Sapateiros 226-4°, Baixa (☎21 342 3478). Despite being opposite a peep-show club, this respectable *pensão* is highly recommended with six comfortable rooms, some overlooking Rossío. ④.

Casa de Hóspedes Atalaia, Rua da Atalaia 150-1°, Bairro Alto (☎21 346 4459). Tolerable at the price, but standards vary and you can find yourself uncomfortably remote from the shared bathrooms. ④.

Residential Camões, Trav. do Poço da Cidade 38-1° (☎21 346 7510). Brilliant location right in the heart of Bairro Alto, though invest in some earplugs for streetside rooms at weekends. Breakfast included in high season, English spoken. ⑤.

Pensão Coimbra e Madrid, Praça da Figueira 3-3°, Baixa (☎21 342 1760). Superb views, though the rooms are noisy. Decent proprietors, shabby though clean furnishings and a TV room, too. ④.

Pensão Dona Maria II, Rua Portas de Santo Antão 9-3°, Baixa (no phone). Large airy rooms (with washbasin) and nice views over Rossío, newly renovated. ④.

Hotel Duas Nações, Rua da Vitória 41, Baixa (☎21 346 0710, *hotel_duas_nacoes@hotmail.com*). Faded, nineteenth-century hotel. Rooms with bath are more attractive in every way, but cost quite a bit more. ⑤.

Pensão Duque, Calçada do Duque 53, Bairro Alto (☎21 346 3444, *pensao_duque@yahoo.com*). Near São Roque church, down the steps off the square. Basic rooms but recently redecorated – no en suites. ④.

Residencial Florescente, Rua das Portas de Santo Antão 99, Baixa (☎21 342 6609). One of the city's best-value establishments, with lots of rooms, some with TV, some without windows, so ask about alternatives. ⑤.

Pensão Galicia, Rua do Crucifixo 50-4°, Baixa (☎21 342 47 81). Cute little rooms, the best with sunny balconies, and fine Baixa location. ④.

Pensão Globo, Rua do Teixeira 37, Bairro Alto (☎21 346 2279). Up Trav. da Cara from Elevador da Glória and then right. Rooms are clean, management fine and the location superb. Shared shower and toilet at the top although there are some rooms with shower. ②.

Pensão Lafonense, Rua das Portas de Santo Antão 36-2°, Baixa (21 346 7122). With decor that makes you feel as if you're staying at your aged aunt's, this tiny *pensão* is homely and centrally located. ③.

Pensão Lar do Areeiro, Praça Dr. Francisco de Sá Carneiro 4-1° (☎21 849 3150). Respectable, old-fashioned place. All rooms with bath; those at the back are quieter; price includes breakfast. Metro Areeiro. ⑤.

Pensão Ninho das Águias, Costa do Castelo 74, Alfama (☎21 885 4070). On the northernmost point of the street looping around the castle, with a lovely garden terrace with spectacular views overlooking the city. Rooms are bright, white and light. ⑤.

Pensão Prata, Rua da Prata 71-3°, Baixa (☎21 346 8908). Small rooms, some with showers, up three extremely steep flights of stairs in a welcoming, family-run apartment. Book ahead. ③.

Pensão São João de Praça, Rua São João de Praça 97-2°, Alfama (☎21 886 2591). Clean, quiet and friendly place in a newly painted town house just below the cathedral. Front rooms have wrought-iron balconies. During high season half-board is compulsory. ⑤.

Campsites

There are several small and lively campsites on the beaches along the **Costa da Caparica**; and at just 30–50min from Lisbon, they can make a comfortable alternative to the city site. Alternatively head north past Cascais for surfer's Mecca **Guincho** for some of the best-sited campsites in Portugal.

Parque Municipal de Campismo (☎21 776 0061). Main city campsite, in the Parque Florestal Monsanto, about 6km west of the centre. The entrance is on Estrada da Circunvalação on the park's west side. Take bus #43 from Praça da Figueira.

Camping Obitur-Guincho Areia, Cascais (☎487 0450, *info@orbitur.pt*). With a supermarket as well as sports facilities and cabins to rent. From Cais do Sodré catch the train to Cascais or bus #405 or #415.

The City

The lower town – the **Baixa** – is very much the heart of the capital, housing many of the country's administrative departments, banks and business offices. Europe's first great example of Neoclassical design and urban planning, it remains an imposing quarter of rod-straight streets, cobbled underfoot and either streaming with traffic or turned over to pedestrians, street performers and pavement artists. Many of the streets in the Baixa grid maintain their crafts and businesses as devised by the autocratic Marquês de Pombal in his post-earthquake reconstruction: Rua da Prata (Silversmiths' Street), Rua dos Sapateiros (Cobblers' Street) and Rua do Ouro (Goldsmiths' Street) are all cases in point. Architecturally, the most interesting places in the Baixa are the squares – the Rossío and Praça do Comércio – and, on the periphery, the lanes leading east to the cathedral and west up towards Bairro Alto. This last area, known as **Chiado**, suffered much damage from a fire that swept across the Baixa in August 1988 but has been elegantly rebuilt by Portugal's premier architect Àlvaro Siza and remain the city's most affluent quarter, focused on the fashionable shops and the beautiful old tearooms of the **Rua Garrett**.

The **Rossío** is very much a focus for the city with its tree-lined avenues and new pedestrian areas as well as a handy Metro station, yet its main concession to grandeur is the **Teatro Nacional**, built along the north side in the 1840s. At the waterfront end of the Baixa, the **Praça do Comércio** was intended as the climax to Pombal's design; it's now pedestrianized and buzzing with some of Lisbon's best restaurants and cafés.

A couple of blocks east of the Praça do Comércio is the church of **Conceição Velha**, severely damaged by the earthquake but retaining its flamboyant Manueline doorway, an early example of this style which hints at the brilliance that emerged at Belém. The **Sé Cathedral** (Mon–Sat 9am–7pm) stands very stolidly above. Founded in 1150 to commemorate the city's reconquest from the Moors, it in fact occupies the site of the principal mosque of Moorish Lishbuna. Like so many of the country's cathedrals, it is Romanesque and extraordinarily restrained in both size and decoration. For admission to the thirteenth-century cloisters (Mon–Sat 10am–5pm) you must get a ticket (€0.50), as you must for the Baroque **sacristy** (€2.50) with its small museum of treasures – including the relics of St Vincent, allegedly brought to Lisbon in 1173 in a boat piloted by ravens.

From the Sé, Rua Augusto Rosa winds upward towards the Castelo, past sparse ruins of a Roman theatre and the **Miradouro de Santa Luzia**, where the conquest of Lisbon and the siege of the Castelo de São Jorge by the Crusaders in 1147 are depicted on the walls. At the entrance to the **Castelo São Jorge** (daily 9am–9pm; free) stands a triumphant statue of Afonso Henriques, conqueror of the Moors. Of the Moorish palace that once stood here only a much-restored shell remains – but the castle as a whole is an enjoyable place to spend a couple of hours, wandering amid the ramparts and towers and looking down upon the city. Crammed within the castle's outer walls is the tiny medieval quarter of **Santa Cruz**, once very much a village in itself though now littered with gift shops and restaurants.

The **Alfama** quarter, stumbling from the walls of the Castelo to the banks of the Tejo, is the oldest part of Lisbon. In Arab times this was the grandest part of the city, but with sub-sequent earthquakes the new Christian nobility moved out, leaving it to the fishing com-munity still here today. It is undergoing some commercialisation, thanks to its cobbled lanes and "character", but although the antique shops and restaurants may be moving in, the quar-ter retains a largely traditional life of its own. The **Feira da Ladra**, Lisbon's rambling **flea market**, fills the Campo de Santa Clara, at the edge of Alfama, every Tuesday and Saturday. While at the flea market, take a look inside **Santa Engrácia**, the loftiest and most tortuously built church in the city – begun in 1682, its vast dome was finally completed in 1966. Through the tiled cloisters of nearby **São Vicente de Fora** you can visit the old monastic refectory, since 1855 the pantheon of the Bragança dynasty. Here, in more or less complete (though unexciting) sequence, are the bodies of all Portuguese kings from João IV, who restored the monarchy in 1640, to Manuel II, who lost it and died in exile in England in 1932.

Mésnier's extraordinary funicular, **Elevador Santa Justa** just off the top end of Rua do Ouro on Rua de Santa Justa, is the most obvious approach to **Bairro Alto**. Alternatively, there are the two funicular-like trams – the Elevador da Glória from the Praça dos Restauradores (just up from the tourist office) or the Elevador da Bica from Rua de São Paulo/Rua da Moeda (both €0.80 one-way). The ruined Gothic arches of the **Convento do Carmo** hang almost directly above the exit of Mésnier's funicular. Once the largest church in the city, this was half-destroyed by the earthquake and is perhaps even more beautiful as a result; sadly it and the small archeological museum are both closed for restoration.

The Parque Eduardo VII and the Calouste Gulbenkian Museum

North of the Praça dos Restauradores are the city's principal gardens, the **Parque Eduardo VII**, most easily approached by metro to Rotunda. Though there are some pleasant cafés here, the park's big attractions are the **Estufas** (daily 9am–4.30/5.30pm; €1.10), huge and wonderful glasshouses filled with tropical plants, flamingo pools, and endless varieties of palms and cacti.

The **Museu Calouste Gulbenkian** (Tues–Sun 10am–5pm; €2.50), the great museum of Portugal, is ten minutes' walk north of the Parque Eduardo VII – take bus #16, #31 or #46 from the Rossío, or the metro to Palhavã or Praça de Espanha. Established by the Armenian oil magnate Calouste Gulbenkian, the Fundação Calouste Gulbenkian runs this amazing complex – featuring an orchestra, three concert halls and two galleries for temporary exhi-bitions – as well as financing work in all spheres of Portuguese cultural life, in even the small-est towns. This showpiece museum is divided into two distinct parts – the first devoted to Egyptian, Greco-Roman, Islamic and Oriental arts, the second to European, including paint-ings from all the major schools. Ghirlandaio's *Portrait of a Young Woman* is followed by out-standing portraits by Rubens and Rembrandt, while Fragonard ushers in an excellent show-ing of work from France, featuring Corot, Manet and Monet. There's also a stunning room full of Art Nouveau jewellery by René Lalique. Across the gardens, the separate **Centro de Arte Moderna** (Tues 2–6pm, Wed–Sun 10am–6pm; €2.50) has all the big names on the twentieth-century Portuguese scene.

Museu de Arte Antiga

The one other museum that stands up to Gulbenkian standards is the national art collection, the **Museu Nacional de Arte Antiga** (Tues 2–6pm, Wed–Sun 10am–6pm; €2.50, free Sun 10am–2pm), situated on the riverfront to the west of the city at Rua das Janelas Verdes 95 (trams #15 and #18 from Praça do Comércio or bus #51 from Rossío). Its core is formed by fifteenth- and sixteenth-century Portuguese works, the acknowledged masterpiece being Nuno Gonçalves' *St Vincent Altarpiece*, a brilliantly marshalled canvas depicting Lisbon's patron receiving homage from all ranks of its citizens. After Gonçalves and his contemporaries, the most interesting works are by Flemish and German artists (Cranach, Bosch – a fabulous *Temptation of St Anthony* – and Dürer), and miscellaneous gems by Raphael, Zurbarán and Rodin.

Belém and the Monastery of Jerónimos

Even before the Great Earthquake, the **Monastery of Jerónimos** (Mosteiro dos Jerónimos; Tues–Sun 10am–5pm; €2.50; tram #15 from Praça do Comércio or #14 from Praça da Figuera) at **Belém** was Lisbon's finest monument: since then, it has stood quite without comparison. It was from Belém in 1497 that Vasco da Gama set sail for India, and it was here, too, that he was welcomed home by Dom Manuel "the Fortunate". The monastery was funded by a levy on the fruits of his discovery – a five-percent tax on all spices other than pepper, cinnamon and cloves, whose import had become the sole preserve of the Crown. Begun in 1502, this is the most ambitious achievement of Manueline architecture. The main entrance to the church is a complex, shrine-like hierarchy of figures centred around Henry the Navigator. Vaulted throughout and fantastically embellished, the cloister is one of the most original and beautiful pieces of architecture in the country, holding Gothic forms and Renaisssance ornamentation in an exuberant balance.

The **Torre de Belém** (Tues–Sun 10am–5pm; €2.50, free Sun am), guarding the entrance to the port around five hundred metres from the monastery, is a multi-turreted whimsy built over the last five years of Dom Manuel's reign. Its architect had previously worked on Portuguese fortifications in Morocco, and a Moorish influence is very strong in the delicately arched windows and balconies. The interior is unremarkable except for a "whispering gallery". Back towards the monastery are a number of museums, of which the best is the **Museu de Arte Popular** (Tues–Sun 10am–12.30pm & 2–5pm; €1.50), a province-by-province display of Portugal's still very diverse folk arts, housed in a shed-like building on the waterfront. Almost adjacent is the vast concrete **Monument to the Discoveries** (Tues–Sun 9.30am–6pm; €1.60), erected in 1960 to commemorate the 500th anniversary of the death of Henry the Navigator; inside, a small exhibition space has changing displays on the city's history, and there are fine views of the Tejo from the top.

Eating

Lisbon has some of the best-value **cafés and restaurants** of any European city, serving large portions of food at sensible prices. **Seafood** is widely available – there's an entire central street, Rua das Portas de Santo Antão, as well as a whole enclave of restaurants across the River Tejo at Cacilhas, that specialize in it. Lisbon also has a rich vein of inexpensive **foreign restaurants** featuring food from the former colonies: Brazil, Mozambique, Angola and Goa. There are plenty of restaurants scattered around the Baixa, and check out the dockland area between Santa Apolónia and Alcântara where the capital's best eateries can now be found. **By night** head for the riverside Docas area or the Bairro Alto. Note that many restaurants are **closed on Sundays**, while on Saturday nights in midsummer you may need to book for the more popular places. Assume moderate **prices** at all the places listed below – no more than €17.50 per person – unless otherwise stated.

Most bars and cafés serve **snacks** and sandwiches; for listings of these, see the drinking section.

Restaurante Andorra, Rua das Portas de Santo Antão 82, Baixa. One of the less expensive fish restaurants on this street, with outdoor tables.

Bica do Sapato, Avenida Infant Dom Henrique, Armazem B, Santa Apolónia (☎21 881 0320). Very trendy sushi/fish diner owned by John Malkovich. Expensive.

Bota Alta, Trav. da Queimada 37, Bairro Alto. Old tavern restaurant that pulls in the punters for its large portions of traditional Portuguese food. Closed Sat lunch & Sun.

Brasuca, Rua João Pereira da Rosa 7, Bairro Alto (☎21 342 8542). A lively restaurant, set in an ageing mansion with great Brazilian food. Expensive. Closed Mon.

O Cantinho do Bem Estar, Rua do Norte 46, Bairro Alto. Inexpensive Alentejan restaurant that's as friendly and authentic as you can get. Closed Mon.

Carvoeiro, Rua Vieira Portuense 66–68. One of many inexpensive fish restaurants in this street. Outdoor tables.

Casa Faz Frio, Rua Dom Pedro V 96, Bairro Alto. A beautiful, very traditional restaurant, replete with tiles. Around €10 for a full meal and wine.

Cervejaria da Trindade, Rua Nova da Trindade 20. Wonderful, vaulted beer-hall restaurant. Expensive. Open till 2am.

Hell's Kitchen, Rua da Atalaia 176. Right at the top of the Bairro Alto and well worth finding for a menu of world foods that includes several vegetarian dishes.

Mestré André, Calçadinha de Santo Estêvão 4–6, Alfama. A fine neighbourhood tavern, with good grills (*churrasco*). Outdoor seating in summer. Closed Sun.

El Rei d'Frango, Caçada do Duque 5. Small and friendly *churrasqueira* near Rossío station serving filling *pratos* from €3.75–5. Open daily 9am–8.30pm.

Rei dos Frangos/Bom Jardim, Trav. de Santo Antão 7–11, Baixa. Excellent for spit-roast chicken – a whole one with fries for about €8.

A Severa, Rua dos Gavéas 57. Good, moderately priced late-night eating option (open till 3.30am). Closed Fri and Sun.

Sinal Vermelha, Rua das Gaveas 89, Bairro Alto (☎21 346 1252). Popular, trendy city haunt serving recommended Portuguese food. Expensive. Closed Sun.

O Sol, Calçada do Duque 21–23. Between Bairro Alto and Rossio, this tiny macrobiotic canteen serves a range of cheap dishes and fresh juices. Open noon–8pm. Closed Sun.

Solmar, Rua das Portas de Santo Antão 108, Baixa (☎21 342 3371). Noisy tourist trail seafood restaurant/beerhall, with fountain and marine mosaics. Moderate.

Os Tibetanos, Rua da Salitre 117, Rato. Lisbon's only true vegetarian restaurant run by Buddhists serving organic food. Open 10–noon or 4–7pm. Moderate.

Drinking and entertainment

Among the city's hundreds of bars and cafés, some of the older **cafés** and *pastelarias* (specializing in cakes) in particular are worth dropping in on at some stage during the day. For night-time drinking, the densest concentration of designer **bars and clubs** is found in **Bairro Alto** – Lisbon's traditional centre of nightlife, with its cramped streets sheltering bars, clubs, *fado* houses and restaurants. Much of the action has also now moved out to the **Docas** (Docklands) district, just to east of the 25 de Abril bridge (train to Alcântara Mar from Cais do Sodré or tram #15 or #18). Converted warehouses at the **Doca de Santo Amaro** are host to waterfront bars and cafés, while a little closer to the city centre the **Doca de Alcântara** has emerged over the last few years as the hangout for Lisbon's chic (buses #9, #28, #39 and #46). Late night clubbers should also try **Avenida 24 de Julho**, the avenue running west from Cais do Sodré to the more outlying **Alcântara** district. The electronic music scene has exploded in the last few years: head for Bairro Alto or the latest riverside venues at Santa Apólina or Alcântara. Clubs don't really get going until around 2am and are generally open until 6am. Admission fees are usually about €10 (often including one or two drinks), although some Lisbon clubs leave the cover charge to the doorman's discretion – anything from €5–20.

Tourist brochures tend to suggest that Lisbon entertainment begins and ends with **fado**, a form of music that developed in sailors' bars in Lisbon in the late eighteenth century. It is a mournful, romantic singing style somewhere between blues and flamenco and bemoans lost loves and better times (try Bairro Alto or Alfama expecting to pay over €15). Portuguese **jazz** can be good, **rock** can occasionally surprise, and if you check out the posters around Restauradores there's a good chance of catching **African music** from the former colonies. Entertainment **listings** are available in the *Agenda Cultural*, a free monthly booklet issued by Lisbon city council or in the Friday editions of the *Independente* or *Diario de Noticias* newspapers, which both have listings magazines.

Virtually all the city's **cinemas** show original-language films with Portuguese subtitles. Mainstream movies are on show at cinemas around Praça dos Restauradores and Avenida da Liberdade; and at the Amoreiras shopping complex (☎213 831 275), on Avenida Eng. Duarte Pacheco (bus #83 from Praça Marquês de Pombal), there are ten screens. The Instituto da Cinemateca Portuguesa (☎213 546 085, *www.cineworld.com/Lisbon/screen.html*; €2), Rua Barata Salgueiro 39 (Avenida metro), is the national film theatre – programmes are available at the main tourist office in Rossío. Lisbon's busy **theatre** season is from October to May.

Cafés

Antiga Casa dos Pasteis, Rua de Belém 90, Belém. Historic tiled café famous for its delicious custard tarts or *pastéis de nata*.

Café a Brasileira, Rua Garrett 120. The most famous of Rua Garrett's old-style coffee houses, open until 2am.

Café Nicola, Praça Dom Pedro IV 26. On the west side of Rossío, this grand old place is a good stop for breakfast.

Café Pastelaria Bernard, Rua Garrett 104. Superb cakes and an outdoor terrace on Chiado's most fashionable street.

Café Suiça, Praça Dom Pedro IV 96. Famous for cakes and pastries, so it can be tough getting an outdoor table.

Cerca Moura, Largo das Portas do Sol. Nice views – and suprisingly inexpensive – up in the Alfama.

Bars

Bar Artis, Rua Diário Notícias 95, Bairro Alto. Chill to mellow jazz with a good mix of locals and the odd visitor.

Cena de Copos, Rua da Barroca 103–105, Bairro Alto. The place to be if it's after midnight, you're under 25 and you're bursting with energy.

Instituto do Vinho do Oporto, Rua de São Pedro de Alcântara 45, Bairro Alto. Over 200 types and vintages of port, from €2.50 a glass upwards. Closed Sun.

Marquês Rock Club, Largo Marquês do Lavradio, Alfama. Dark rock bar with live music most nights. Thurs–Sat.

Pavilhão Chinês, Rua Dom Pedro V 89, Bairro Alto. Overly-decorated bar, completely lined with cabinets of bizarre artefacts. Daily till 2am. Very expensive.

República do Alcool, Rua do Diário de Notícias 3, Bairro Alto. Gay-friendly bar playing jazz and laid-back dance music.

A Tasca, Trav. da Quiemada 13–15, Bairro Alto. Cheerful and welcoming tequila bar.

Web C@fe, Ruo do Diário de Notícias 126, Bairro Alto. Drink and enjoy the cosmopolitan atmosphere and use the Internet. Open daily 4pm–2am; Internet €4/hr.

Clubs

Alcântara Mar, Rua Cozinha Económica 11, Alcântara. Big house/techno spot. Closed Mon & Tues.

Armazem F, Rua da Cintura, Armazem 56, Santos. Huge warehouse dancehall providing entertainment for the children of the upwardly mobile.

Doca de Santo, Doca de Santo Amaro, under Ponte 25 de Abril. Large palm-fringed club, one of the first and the most popular in this new area.

FL Café, Rua Atalaia 36, Bairro Alto. Lots of big-eyed folk getting down to house (and related hybrids) in this cosy and dark neon-lit club. Open Mon–Sat 11.30pm–4am. Sometimes charges an entrance fee (€5–10).

Kapital, Avda. 24 de Julho 68, opposite Santos station. Sweaty outmoded dance venue where you can have a laugh until 5am.

Kremlin, Escadinhas da Praia 5. One of the city's most snobbish nightspots, packed with flash young Lisboetas. Techno still rules. Closed Sun & Mon.

Lux, Avda. Dom Henrique, opposite Santa Apólina Station. Recently voted one of the best 35 clubs in the world. Top Portuguese DJs as well as big European names. Massive dancefloor and a chill-out area upstairs and a terrace overlooking the river. Closes 4am.

Metalúrgica, Avda. 24 de Julho 110. Cheaper than usual, dishes out happy pop and soul to a mixed crowd.

Plateau, Escadinhas da Praia 3, Avda. 24 de Julho. Gentler admission policy than most, with more of a rock orientation.

Trumps, Rua da Imprensa Nacional 104b, Rato, north of Bairro Alto. The biggest gay disco in Lisbon with a reasonably relaxed door policy. Closed Mon.

WIP, Elevador da Bica. Halfway down the hill, this bar has a host of different DJs covering mellow sounds from reggae/Afro through soul to drum'n'bass.

Fado

Adega do Ribatejo, Rua Diário de Notícias 23, Bairro Alto (☎21 346 8343). Popular with the locals and has a lower-than-usual minimum charge. Singers include a couple of professionals, the manager and even the cooks.

O Senhor Vinho, Rua do Meio a Lapa 18, Bairro Alto (☎21 397 7456). Famous Bairro Alto club sporting some of the best fado singers in Portugal.

A Severa, Rua das Gáveas 55, Bairro Alto (☎21 346 4006). A city institution featuring big *fado* names at big prices. Closed Thurs.

Other live music

Catacumbas, Rua da Rosa 154. Intimate club with live jazz on Thursdays. Closed Sun.

Coliseu dos Recreios, Rua das Portas de Santo Antão, Baixa (☎21 346 1997). Main indoor stadium venue for major visiting rock bands.

Hot Clube de Portugal, Praça da Alegría, off Avda. da Liberdade. Tiny basement jazz club which hosts local and visiting artists. Closed Mon.

Lontra, Rua de São Bento 157, Bairro Alto. Live African and Brazilian music weekends in this kicking bar.

Pê Sujo, Largo de São Martinho 6/7, Alfama (☎21 886 5629). Brazilian music venue that serves lethal *caipirinhas*, which regularly result in massive audience participation in table-banging samba sessions. Closed Mon.

Ritz Club, Rua da Glória 55, Baixa (☎21 342 5140). Lisbon's largest African club, one block west of Avda. da Liberdade, with a resident band, plus occasional big-name concerts. Closed Mon.

Listings

Airlines Air France, Avda. 5 de Outubro 206–3° (☎217 900 202); Alitalia, Praça de Marquês de Pombal 1–5° (☎213 536 141); British Airways, Avda. da Liberdade 36–2° (☎213 217 900); Iberia, Rua Rosa Araujo 2 (☎218 493 693); Swissair, Avda. da Liberdade 38–1° (☎213 226 000); TAP, Edifício Estação do Oriente, inside the Oriente station building, or Avda. Berlim (both ☎808 205 700).

American Express The local agent is Top Tours, Avda. Duque de Loulé 108 (☎213 155 877).

Banks Main branches are in the Baixa; Banco Borges & Irmão, Avda. da Liberdade 9a (open Mon–Fri until 7.30pm). There's a currency exchange office at the airport (open 24hr) and at Santa Apolónia station (daily 8.30am–4pm).

Bicycles Adrenalina Gravidade Zero (☎21 892 2300), at the north end of the Parque das Nações, rent out cycles for Esc750/hr; a passport or other ID must be left as a deposit.

Car rental Avis, Avda. Praia da Vitória 12c (☎213 561 176); Budget, Rua Castilho 167 (☎213 860 516); Europcar, Avda. António Augusto Aguiar 24 (☎21 353 5115); Hertz, Rua Castilho 72 (☎21 381 2430).

Embassies Australia, Avda. da Liberdade 244–4° (☎213 143 350); Canada, Avda. da Liberdade 198–200 (☎21 316 4600, *lsbon@dfait-maeci.gc.ca*); Ireland, Rua da Imprensa à Estrêla 1–4° (☎213 929 440); UK Consulate, Rua de São Bernardo 33 (☎213 924 000, *britembassy@mail.telepac.pt*); USA, Avda. das Forças Armadas (☎21 727 3300, *conslisbon@state.gov*).

Hospital British Hospital, Rua Saraiva de Carvalho 46 (☎213 955 067). For an ambulance call ☎112.

Internet Inside the Forum Telecom, Avda. Fontes Pereira de Melo 38 (Mon–Fri 9am–7pm; €2/hr; metro Picas); Web C@fe, Ruo do Diário de Notícias 126, Bairro Alto (daily 4pm–2am; €4/hr); Ciber Chiado, Centro Nacional de Cultura, Largo do Picadeiro 10, Chiado (Open 4pm–7.30 and 8.30–midnight. €3/hr); Café.com, Costa do Castelo 7, Castelo (Open daily 6pm–2am); Ciberbica, Rua Duques da Bragança 7 (Open Mon–Sat noon–2pm and 7pm–2am, closed Sun).

Laundry Lava Neve, Rua de Alegría 37, Bairro Alto; Lavandaria Saus Ana, in the Centro Comercial da Mouraria, Largo Martim Moniz (Mon–Sat 9.30am–1pm & 3–8pm).

Police 24-hour office at Rua Capelo 13 (☎213 461 144), west of the Baixa near the Teatro São Carlos. Report here if you need to make a claim on your travel insurance.

Post offices The main office is on Praça do Comércio (Mon–Fri 8.30am–6.30pm); more convenient is the office at Praça dos Restauradores 58 (daily 8am–10pm).

Sports For information on skates, paragliding, climbing, bungy-jumping, skimming, diving and sailing contact Adrenalina, R. Borja, 57-1º Esq. (☎21 60 42 07).

Telephones Next to the post office in Praça dos Restauradores; also at no. 65, on the corner of Rossío (daily 8am–11pm).

Travel Agencies Viagen Wasteels, Estação Cams F S Apolónia Gare International (☎218 866 577); Abreu, Avda. De Roma 66 (☎218 462 988).

Windsurfing Guincho (train to Cascais from Cais do Sodré then catch bus #405/415) is one of the best spots in the world for windsurfing, with the best conditions being in July and August. Check *Bar do Guincho* at the north end of the beach, it has a windsurf shop, lockers for storing equipment and an equipment rental service (see prices and latest APF windsurf calendar at *www.bardoguincho.pt*).

Around Lisbon

The long beaches of **Caparica** – which the quirks of the Tejo currents have largely spared from the pollution of Lisbon – and the architectural attractions of **Sintra** and **Mafra** can each be reached on a day-trip from Lisbon; but to do justice to Sintra you'll need to stay overnight.

Costa da Caparica and beyond

By car it takes something over an hour to reach **Costa da Caparica** from the capital, and it's here that most locals come if they want to swim or laze around on the sand. This is a thoroughly Portuguese resort, popular with surfers and crammed with restaurants and beach cafés, yet solitude is easy enough to find, thanks to the mini-railway (*transpraia*) that runs along the 8km of dunes in summer. The quickest and most enjoyable approach is to take a **ferry** from the Fluvial station by Praça do Comércio, or from Cais do Sodré, to **Cacilhas**, and then pick up the connecting bus from the dock where the boats come in. Alternatively, and more speedily, you can take the #52 or #53 **bus** direct to Caparica from the main Praça de Espanha terminal (metro Palhavã).

At **CAPARICA** buses either stop at a bus park by the beach, or at the station five minutes back from the sands. From the latter, walk up to the main road, turn right and keep walking until you reach Praça da Liberdade, the main square, where there's a **tourist office** (Mon–Sat 9.30am–1pm & 2.30–6pm, also Sun in summer; ☎212 900 071), market, cinema and banks. There aren't very many hotels in Caparica but buses run back to Lisbon/Cacilhas most of the day and night. **Campsites**, which range along the first few kilometres of the beach, are on the whole overcrowded and overpriced, but functional enough. There are dozens of good, relaxed, cheap fish and seafood places as well as beach bars along the main Rua dos Pescadores, which leads from the square to the beach. Try getting off at *transpraia* stop 12 to try the excellent food at the *Cabana do Pescador* restaurant.

Beyond Caparica along the coast between Setúbal and Sesimbra, you will find the **National Park of Arrábida**, set in a deep cove called Portinho da Arrábida, a nature-lover's paradise and one of the most attractive beach areas in Portugal. Designated a national park in 1976, the park's main feature is the impressive granite ridge of the Serra da Arrábida standing at 500m and offering spectacular views. Precariously perched on one of the hills in the Arrábida mountains is the **convent of Arrábida**, founded in 1542 by Franciscan friars; it is still a practising monastery. Guided tours are given by the monks, for more details contact ☎21 2180 520. If you're into **adventure sports** contact Arrábida Aventuras, Est. Barris, Apt. 39, in Palmela, on the northern edge of the park just above Setúbal (☎91 885 057, *arrabidaventura@mail.telepac.pt*). They organize a host of activities within the national park including hot-air ballooning (fixed flight with descent by slide or rappel), orienteering, and archery.

Sintra

SINTRA is one of Portugal's most spectacular sights and is one of the country's few UNESCO World Heritage sites. Sintra's extraordinary subtropical microclimate allows for an abundance of cool, deciduous woodland which attracted Moorish lords and the kings of Portugal here from Lisbon during the hot summer months. The layout of Sintra – an amalgamation of three villages – can be confusing, but the extraordinary **Palácio Nacional** (daily 10am–1pm & 2–5pm, closed Wed; €2.50), about twenty minutes' walk from the station, is an obvious landmark. The palace was probably in existence under the Moors, but takes its present form from the rebuilding commissioned by Dom João I and his successor, Dom Manuel, in the fourteenth and fifteenth centuries. Its style is a fusion of Gothic and the latter king's Manueline additions. The hourly tours are a bit of a trial unless you go early before the groups arrive, but the chapel and its adjoining chamber – its floor worn by the incessant pacing of the half-mad Afonso VI who was confined here for six years by his brother Pedro I – are well worth seeing.

The charms of Sintra, famously penned by Lord Byron, lie as much in its buildings as in its **walks and paths**; one of the best walks leads past the church of Santa Maria and up to the ruined ramparts of the **Moorish Castle** (daily 10am–8pm; free), from where the views are extraordinary. Beyond the castle, a steep ninety-minute walk from town, is the lower entrance to the immense **Pena Park**, at the top end of which rears the fabulous **Palácio de Pena** (Tues–Sun 10am–6.30pm; €2.50), a wild 1840s fantasy of domes, towers and a drawbridge that does not draw. The interior has been preserved exactly as left by the royal family on their flight from Portugal in 1910.

After the follies of Pena, a visit to Seteais and Monserrate comes as something of a relief. **Seteais**, just right of the Colares road, fifteen minutes' walk from town, is one of the most elegant palaces in Portugal, completed in the last years of the eighteenth century and entered through a majestic classical arch; it is now a luxurious hotel and restaurant. Beyond, the road leads past a series of beautiful private estates to **Monserrate** – about an hour's walk. It's difficult to do justice to the beauty of Monserrate, whose vast **gardens** (daily 9am–5/6pm; €1), filled with endless varieties of exotic trees and subtropical shrubs and plants, extend as far as the eye can see.

Finding **accommodation** at Sintra in summer can be a problem, though if you arrive early in the day you should end up with something. There are a fair number of pensions: best value is probably the *Adelaide*, Rua Guilherme Gomes Fernandes 11 (☎219 230 873; ③), midway between the train station and Sintra village; or try *Pensão Económica*, Patio de Olivença 6, handy for the train station (☎219 230 229; ②). The *Pensão Pielas* (☎219 241 691; ③), on Rua João de Deus 70–72 near the station, is not bad either and has a restaurant with budget menus. A bit further up the price scale try the Swiss-run *Casa Miradouro*, Rua Sotto Mayor 55 (☎219 235 900; ⑥) or the *Quinta Das Sequoias*, on the road to Monserrat (☎219 243 821; ⑦), a fairy-tale mansion that looks across beautiful woodland to the Pena Palace. Alternatively, some cheap private rooms (②–④) can be booked through the extremely helpful **tourist office** (Oct–May daily 9am–7pm, June–Sep open until 8pm; ☎219 231 157) in the centre, just off the central Praça da República. There's a **hostel** (☎219 241 210; ④; closed noon–6pm) at Santa Eufemia, in the hills above Sintra, 5km from town – take a local bus to São Pedro from outside the train station and walk from there (2km). The nearest **campsites** are well out of town: the most convenient are at the beach-villages of Praia das Maçãs, Praia Grande and Azenhas do Mar, all connected by bus. **Restaurants** are generally poor value, relying heavily on the tour parties. Try *Tulhas* behind the turismo or the two *Adega do Saloio* grillhouses, at the far end of the street.

Mafra

Connected by regular buses (timetables *www.cats.pt*) from Sintra train station and from Lisbon, **MAFRA** is dominated by one building: the vast, newly restored, pink marble **Palace-Convent** (daily except Tues 10am–5pm; €3), built in emulation of Madrid's El Escorial in

1717 by João V, the wealthiest and most extravagant of all Portuguese monarchs. The convent was initially intended for just thirteen Franciscan friars, but as more gold poured in from Brazil, João amplified it into the world's largest basilica, two royal wings and monastic quarters for 300 monks and 150 novices. The sheer magnitude of the building is what stands out: there are 5200 doorways, 2500 windows, and two bell towers each containing over 50 bells. The highlight is the magnificent Rococo library – with its chequered marble floor – rivalling that of Coimbra in both design and grandeur. The basilica, which can be seen outside the tour, is no less imposing, with the multicoloured marble designs of its floor mirrored in the ceiling decoration.

CENTRAL PORTUGAL

The **Estremadura** region has played a crucial role in each phase of the nation's history – and the monuments are there to prove it. A comparatively small area, it boasts quite extraordinary concentration of vivid architecture and engaging towns. **Alcobaça**, **Batalha**, **Óbidos** and **Tomar** – home to the most exciting buildings in Portugal – all lie within ninety minutes' bus ride of one another, as does the pilgrimage centre of **Fátima**. With its fertile rolling hills, Estremadura is second in beauty only to Minho, but the adjoining bull-breeding lands of **Ribatejo** (literally "banks-of-the-Tejo") fade into the dull expanses of northwestern Alentejo, and there's no great reason to cross the river unless you're pushing on to Évora or can catch up with one of the region's traditional festivals.

North of Estremadura, life on the fertile plain of the **Beira Litoral** has been conditioned over the centuries by the twin threats of floodwaters from Portugal's highest mountains and silting by the restless Atlantic. The highlight here is **Coimbra**, an ancient university town stacked high on the right bank of the Mondego. To the north is the little-explored **Mountain Beiras** region, historically the heart of ancient Lusitânia, where Viriatus the Iberian rebel made his last stand against the Romans. You'll see many signs of this patriotism in the fine old town of **Viseu**, where every other place of refreshment is the *Café Viriate* or the *Restaurante Lusitânia*. At an even higher altitude stands **Guarda**, pretty diminutive for somewhere of such renown, but nonetheless bristling with life, especially on market days.

Óbidos

ÓBIDOS is a small town of whitewashed houses draped in bougainvillea and encircled by lofty medieval walls. "The Wedding Town" was the traditional bridal gift of the kings of Portugal to their queens, a custom begun in 1282 by Dom Dinis. The town – a couple of hours from Lisbon by train – can hardly have changed in appearance since then: its cobbled streets and steep staircases wind up to the ramparts, from where you can gaze across a fable-like countryside of windmills and vineyards. The parish church, **Igreja de Santa Maria**, in the central Praça, was chosen for the wedding of the ten-year-old child-king Afonso V and his eight-year-old cousin, Isabel, in 1444. It dates mainly from the Renaissance, though the interior is lined with seventeenth-century blue *azulejos*, or painted tiles, in a homely manner typical of Portuguese churches. The retable in a side chapel on the right-hand side was painted by Josefa de Óbidos, one of the finest Portuguese painters – and one of the few women artists afforded any reputation by art historians. One corner of the triangular fortifications is occupied by a massively towered **Castle** built by Dom Dinis and now converted into a *pousada* (☎262 959 105; ⑨).

Other **hotels** in Óbidos also tend to be expensive. Your cheapest option is to consult the list of private houses offering **rooms** which is posted in the **tourist office**, on Rua Direita (Mon–Fri 9.30am–7pm, Sat & Sun 9.30am–1pm & 2–7pm; ☎262 959 231); there are comfortable rooms at Rua Direita 40 (☎262 959 188; ③). If you do feel like splashing out try the *Estalagem Do Convento*, Rua Dom Joao de Ornelas (☎262 959 217; ⑤), housed in an early-

19th-century convent, or the *Casa d'Óbidos* (☎258 835 065; ⑥), about 1km south of the town walls –built in 1889 it has beautiful gardens and an air of faded grandeur. It's worth staying around since, as is so often the case, the town reverts to its own life after the daytime tourists disperse. One of the better budget places to **eat** is the *Café 1 de Dezembro*, next to the church of São Pedro.

Leiria

With regular bus services to the three big sites of northern Estremadura – Alcobaça, Batalha and Fátima – **LEIRIA** makes a handy centre for excursions. The chief sight in Leiria itself is the **Castle** (Mon–Fri 9am–5.30/6.30pm, Sat & Sun 10am–5pm; €0.90), incorporating an elegant royal palace with a magnificent balcony high above the River Lis. At the heart of the old town, Praça Rodrigues Lobo is surrounded by beautiful buildings and arcades. The **tourist office** (daily: summer 10am–1pm & 3–7pm; winter 2–6pm; ☎244 814 748) and **bus station** are on opposite sides of a park overlooking the river in the modern city centre. The **train station** is about 4km out of town, with a connecting bus service. For **accommodation**, check the **pensions** such as *Pensão Berlinga*, Rua Miguel Bombarda 3D (☎244 823 846; ③), and restaurants (some offering rooms) around Praça Rodrigues Lobo and on narrow side streets such as Rua Mestre Aviz and Rua Miguel Bombarda. There's also a fancy **hostel** with a good atmosphere at Largo Cândido dos Reis 9 (☎244 831 868; doubles ③, dorms ②). As for **restaurants**, try the seafood at *Jardim*, by the tourist office, or real Portuguese cuisine – slightly more expensive, but worth it for the large portions – at *Montecarlo*, Rua Dr Correia Mateus 32–34.

Alcobaça

From the twelfth century until the middle of the nineteenth, the Cistercian **Abbey of Alcobaça** (9am–5/7pm; €2) was one of the greatest in the Christian world. Owning vast tracts of farmland, orchards and vineyards, it held jurisdiction over a dozen towns and three seaports until its ultimate dissolution in 1834. The monastery was originally founded by Dom Afonso Henriques in 1147 in celebration of the liberation of Santarém from the Moors, and is a truly vast complex – its main **Church** is the largest in Portugal. The exterior is disappointing, as the Gothic facade has been superseded by unexceptional Baroque additions. Inside, however, all later adornments have been swept away, restoring the narrow soaring aisles to their original vertical simplicity. The only exception to this magnificent Gothic purity is the frothy Manueline doorway to the sacristy, hidden behind the high altar.

The abbey's most precious treasures are the fourteenth-century **tombs of Dom Pedro and Dona Inês de Castro**, each occupying one of the transepts and sculpted with phenomenal wealth of detail to show the story of Pedro's love for Inês de Castro, the daughter of a Galician nobleman. Fearing Spanish influence over the Portuguese throne, Pedro's father, Afonso V, forbade their marriage. The ceremony nevertheless took place in secret, whereupon Afonso sanctioned his daughter-in-law's murder. When Pedro succeeded to the throne in 1357 he exhumed the corpse of his lover, forcing the entire royal circle to acknowledge her as queen by kissing her decomposing hand. The tombs – inscribed with the motto "Até o Fim do Mundo" (Until the End of the World) – have been placed foot to foot so that on the Day of Judgement the lovers may rise and immediately feast their eyes on one another.

The most amazing room in the building is the **kitchen**, with its cellars and gargantuan conical chimney, supported by eight trunk-like iron columns. A stream tapped from the River Alcôa still runs straight through the room: it was used not merely for cooking and washing but also to provide a constant supply of fresh fish. The **Sala dos Reis** (Kings' Room), off the beautiful **Cloisters of Silence**, displays statues of virtually every king of Portugal down to Dom José, who died in 1777. The rest of the abbey, including four cloisters, seven dormitories and endless corridors, is closed to the public.

Alcobaça's **tourist office** (daily 10am–6/7pm; ☎262 582 377) is opposite the abbey on Praça 25 de Abril. *Pensão Restaurante Corações Unidos* (☎262 582 142; ③), around the corner at Rua Frei António Brandão 39–45, has decent **rooms**. The *Quartos Alcôa* (☎262 582 727; ③), off the Praça da República, beside the abbey, is cheaper, but best of all is the *Residençial Mosteiro* (☎262 581 836; ③) on Avda. João de Deus 1. There's also a **campsite** (☎262 582 265), ten minutes north of the bus station along Avda. Manuel da Silva Carolino. Good-value places to **eat** include the touristy *Frie Bernado*, Rua D Pedro V, a huge place serving huge meals, and *Celeiro dos Frades*, or the monks' barn, atmospherically situated under the arches alongside the abbey.

Batalha

The **Mosteiro de Santa Maria da Vitória**, better known as the **Mosteiro de Batalha** (Battle Abbey; daily 9am–5/6pm; €2.50, free Sun am), is the finest building in Portugal, classified on the UNESCO's World Heritage list, and an enduring symbol of national pride. It was originally founded to commemorate the Battle of Aljubarrota (1385), which sealed Portugal's independence after decades of Spanish intrigue. It is possible to stay in the village around the abbey, but it's best to visit on a trip from Leiria (5 buses daily).

The honey-coloured abbey was transformed by Manueline additions in the late fifteenth and early sixteenth centuries, but the bulk was completed between 1388 and 1434 in a profusely ornate version of French Gothic. Within this flamboyant framework there are also strong elements of the English Perpendicular style, an influence explained by the **Capela do Fundador** (Founder's Chapel), directly to the right upon entering the church: beneath the octagonal lantern rests the tomb of Dom João I and Philippa of Lancaster, their hands clasped in the ultimate expression of harmonious relations between Portugal and England. The four younger sons of João and Philippa are buried along the south wall of the Capela do Fundador in a row of recessed arches. Second from the right is the **Tomb of Prince Henry the Navigator**, who guided the exploration of Madeira, the Azores and the African coast as far as Sierra Leone. Maritime exploration resumed under João II (1481–95) and accelerated with the accession of Manuel I (1495–1521), and the **Claustro Real** (Royal Cloister) dates from this period of burgeoning self-confidence, its intricate stone grilles being added by Diogo de Boitaca, architect of the cloisters at Belém and the prime genius of Manueline art. Off the east side, the early-fifteenth-century **Sala do Capítulo** (Chapter House) is remarkable for the unsupported span of its ceiling. The Church authorities were convinced that the whole chamber would come crashing down and only employed as labourers criminals already condemned to death.

The **Capelas Imperfeitas** (Unfinished Chapels) form a separate structure tacked on to the east end of the church and accessible only from outside the main complex. Dom Duarte, eldest son of João and Philippa, commissioned them in 1437 as a royal mausoleum but, as with the cloisters, the original design was transformed beyond all recognition by Dom Manuel's architects. It is unique among examples of Christian architecture in its evocation of the great shrines of Islam and Hinduism: perhaps it was inspired by the tales of Indian monuments that filtered back along the eastern trade routes.

Fátima

FÁTIMA is one of the most important centres of pilgrimage in the Catholic world, a status deriving from the six **Apparitions of the Virgin Mary**. On May 13 1917, three peasant children from the village were tending their parents' flock when, in a flash of lightning, they were confronted with "a lady brighter than the sun" sitting in the branches of a tree. The vision returned on the thirteenth day of the next five months, culminating in the so-called Miracle of the Sun on October 13, when a swirling ball of fire cured lifelong illnesses. To commemorate these extraordinary events a vast white **Basilica** and gigantic esplanade have been built, more than capable of holding the crowds of 100,000 who congregate here for the main **pilgrimages** on May 12 & 13 and October 12 & 13. In the church the tombs of two of the children, who died in the European flu epidemic of 1919–20, are the subject of constant attention. Hospices and convents have sprung up in the shadow of the basilica, and inevitably the fame of Fátima has resulted in its commercialization. **Pensions** and **restaurants** abound, but there's little reason to stay except during the big pilgrimages to witness the midnight processions. Regular **bus services** to Fátima from Tomar make a day-trip easy.

Tomar

TOMAR, 34km east of Fátima, is famous for the Convento de Cristo, an artistic *tour de force* which entwines the main military, religious and imperial strands in the history of Portugal. However, it's an attractive town in its own right – especially during the *Festas dos Tabuleiros*, in the first week of July, when the place goes wild – and you should aim to spend a couple of days here if you can.

Built on a simple grid plan, Tomar's old quarters preserve all their traditional charm, with whitewashed, terraced cottages lining narrow cobbled streets. On the central Praça da República stands an elegant seventeenth-century town hall, a ring of houses of the same period and the Manueline church of **São João Baptista**, remarkable for its octagonal belfry and elaborate doorway. Nearby, at Rua Joaquim Jacinto 73, you'll find an excellently preserved fourteenth-century **Synagogue**, now the **Museu Luso-Hebraicoa Abraham Zacuto** (daily 10am–7pm; free); in 1496 Dom Manuel ordered the expulsion or conversion of all Portuguese Jews, and the synagogue at Tomar was one of the few to survive.

The **Convento de Cristo** (Tues–Sun 9.15am–12.30pm & 2–6pm; winter pm only; €2.50) is set among pleasant gardens with splendid views, about a quarter of an hour's walk uphill from the centre of town. Founded in 1162 by Gualdim Pais, first Master of the Knights Templar, it was the headquarters of the Order. The heart of the complex remains the **Charola**, the temple from which the knights drew their moral conviction. It is a strange place, more suggestive of the occult than of Christianity; like almost every circular church, it is ultimately based on the Church of the Holy Sepulchre in Jerusalem, for whose protection the Knights Templar were originally founded. However, as the Moorish threat receded, the Knights became a challenge to the authority of European monarchs. In Spain this prompted a vicious witch-hunt and many of the Knights sought refuge in Portugal.

The highlight of the convent is the ornamentation of the windows on the main facade of its **Chapter House**, where maritime motifs form a memorial to the sailors who established the Portuguese empire. Later João III (1521–57) transformed the convent into a thoroughgoing monastic community, adding dormitories, kitchens and no fewer than four cloisters. The adjoining two-tiered **Great Cloisters** comprise one of the purest examples of the Renaissance style in Portugal.

Tomar has a pleasant all-year **campsite** (☎249 321 026) in town and a number of reasonable **pensions**, each with a **restaurant**: *Tomarense* (☎249 312 948; ③), near the bus station, and *Luz* (249 312 317; ④) and the very popular *Residencial União* (☎249 323 161; ④) in the centre of town, both at Rua Serpa Pinto.

Coimbra

COIMBRA was Portugal's capital from 1143 to 1255 and it ranks behind only the cities of Lisbon and Oporto in historic importance. Its university, founded in 1290 and finally established here in 1537 after a series of moves back and forth to Lisbon, was the only one existing in Portugal until the beginning of this century. For a provincial town it has remarkable riches, and it's an enjoyable place to be, too – lively when the students are in town, sleepy during the holidays. The best time of all to be here is in May, when the students celebrate the end of the academic year in the **Queima das Fitas**, tearing or burning their gowns and faculty ribbons. This is when you're most likely to hear the Coimbra *fado*, distinguished from the Lisbon version by its mournful pace and complex lyrics.

The city

Old Coimbra sits on a hill on the right bank of the River Mondego, with the university crowding its summit. The main buildings of the **Old University**, dating from the sixteenth century, are set around a courtyard dominated by a Baroque clocktower and a statue of João III looking remarkably like Henry VIII. The chapel is covered with *azulejos* – traditional glazed and painted tiles – and intricate decoration, but takes second spot to the **Library** (daily 9.30am–12.30pm & 2–5.30pm; €1.25), a Baroque fantasy presented to the faculty by João V in the early eighteenth century.

Below the university, a good first stop is the **Museu Machado de Castro** (Tues–Sun 9.30am–12.30pm & 2–5.15pm; €1.25), just down from the unprepossessing Sé Nova (New Cathedral). Named after an eighteenth-century sculptor, the museum is housed in the former archbishop's palace, which would be worth visiting in its own right even if it were empty. As it is, it's positively stuffed with sculpture, paintings, furniture and ceramics. The **Sé Velha** (Old Cathedral; daily 10am–noon & 2–7.30pm, closed Fri–Sun pm), halfway down the hill, is one of the most important Romanesque buildings in Portugal, little altered and seemingly unbowed by the years. Solid and square on the outside, it's also stolid and simple within, the decoration confined to a few giant conch shells and some unobtrusive *azulejos*. The Gothic tombs and low-arched **cloister** (€0.50) are equally restrained.

Restraint and simplicity certainly aren't the chief qualities of the **Igreja de Santa Cruz** (Mon–Sat 9am–noon & 2–5.45pm, Sun 4–6pm; €1.75 for cloister), at the bottom of the hill past the city gates. Although it was founded before the Old Cathedral, nothing remains that has not been substantially remodelled. In the early sixteenth century Coimbra was the site of a major sculptural school; the new tombs for Portugal's first kings, Afonso Henriques and Sancho I, and the elaborately carved pulpit, are among its very finest works. The Manueline theme is at its clearest in the airy arches of the Cloister of Silence, its walls decorated with bas-relief scenes from the life of Christ.

It was in Santa Cruz that Dom Pedro had his court pay homage to the corpse of Inês de Castro, which had lain in the now ruined **Convento de Santa Clara-a-Velha** across the river, alongside the convent's founder, Saint Queen Isabel. The tombs have long since been moved away, Inês's to Alcobaça (see p.1046) and Isabel's to the **Convento de Santa Clara-a-Nova** (Tues–Sun 8.30am–6pm; €0.50 for cloister), higher up the hill. Two features make the climb worthwhile: the silver tomb itself and the vast cloister financed by João V, whose devotion to nuns went beyond the bounds of spiritual comfort.

Practicalities

Most mainline **trains** stop at Coimbra B, 3km north of the city, from where there are frequent connecting services to Coimbra A, right at the heart of things. The main **bus station** is on Avenida Fernão de Magalhães, about fifteen minutes' walk from the centre – turn right out of the bus station and head down the main road. The **tourist office** (summer Mon–Fri 9am–6/7pm, Sat & Sun 10am–1pm & 2.30–5.30pm; winter daily 9am–6pm; ☎239 855 930, *www.turismo-centro.pt*) is opposite the bridge in the Largo da Portagem.

Near the station, the sleazy Rua da Sota and its side streets have a few **pensões** that aren't as bad as they look – try the *Pensão Vitória* at Rua da Sota 9 & 19 (☎239 824 049; ③), or the *Residencial Domus* at Rua Adelino Veiga 62 (☎239 828 584; ④). *Pensão Rivoli* (☎239 825 550; ④), nearby at Praça do Comércio 27, has good rooms, some with showers and the best with balconies overlooking the square. Alternatively, there are several options east of the university; beneath the aqueduct, at Rua Castro Matoso 8, *Antunes* (☎239 854 720; ④) offers good service. The **hostel**, above the park on Rua Henrique Seco 14 (☎239 822 955; doubles ③, dorms ②), is friendly and immaculately run – it's a twenty-minute walk from Coimbra A, or take bus #7, #8, #29 or #46. There's a reasonable all-year **campsite** at the municipal sports complex (☎239 701 497); to reach it, take bus #5 from Largo da Portagem or #7 from outside the tourist office.

There are plenty of inexpensive **places to eat** around the centre. For really basic fare, served up with loads of atmosphere, try the little dives tucked into the tiny alleys between the Largo da Portagem, Rua da Sota and Praça do Comércio. *Adega Paço do Conde* on Rua Paço do Conde is a cavernous, locally renowned *churrasqueira*, whilst *Viela*, at Rua das Azeiteiras 3 (closed Sat), serves enormous and reasonably priced portions that can easily be shared between two. Be sure, also, to try one of the traditional **coffee houses** along Rua Ferreira Borges – notably *Café Santa Cruz* – and Rua Visconde da Luz.

Viseu

From its high plateau, **VISEU** surveys the country around with the air of a feudal overlord, and indeed, this dignified little city is capital of all it can see. Its medieval heart has changed little, though the approach to it is now through the broad avenues of a prosperous provincial centre: parts of the walls survive and it's within their circuit, breached by two doughty gateways, that almost everything of interest lies. Surrounded by vineyards, orchards and pine-forests Viseu has been a northern crossroads since the time of the Romans, who chose its site for a military camp, the largest yet to be discovered in Portugal. Today, its main importance is as the centre of the Dão wine-growing region, where crispy white wines and some of Portugal's most popular full-bodied reds are produced.

At the city's highest point is the huge **Praça da Sé**, the paved square in front of the cathedral, best approached from the central Rossío through the Porta do Soar. Here, amid a line of granite buildings, stand the white Baroque facade of the **Igreja da Misericórdia** and the **Cathedral**, a weighty twin-towered Romanesque base on which a succession of generations have made their mark. Behind its twin-towered façade lies an elegantly simple Gothic interior featuring a two-storey cloister and fine *azulejo* glazed tiles in the north chapel. The sacristy boasts one of the finest ceilings in Portugal. Its Renaissance cloister is one of the most graceful in the country, while the rooms of its upper level, looking out over the tangled roofs of the oldest part of the town, house the cathedral's treasures, which include a twelfth-century Bible. The greatest treasure of Viseu, though, is the adjacent **Museu Grão Vasco** (Tues–Sun 9.30am–12.30pm & 2–5.30pm; €1.25). Vasco Fernandes – known always as *Grão Vasco*, the Great Vasco – was the key figure in a school of Flemish-influenced painters which flourished here in the first half of the sixteenth century. The centrepiece of the collection is his masterly *St Peter on his Throne*.

The **tourist office** up from the Rossío, just off Avda. 25 de Abril (Mon–Fri 9am–12.30pm & 2.30–6pm, Sat & Sun 10am–noon & 3–5.30pm; ☎232 420 950), is a good source of information for the region as a whole. **Accommodation** in Viseu is limited, but there are three decent places right in the centre: *Pensão Bela Vista*, Rua Alexandre Herculano 510, near the Turismo (☎232 422 026; ⑤); *Pensão Rossío Parque,* Praça da República 55 (☎232 42 20 85; ⑤); and *Residential Duque de Viseu*, Rua das Ameias 22, by the cathedral (☎232 421 286; ④). If you fancy a bit of luxury, try the *Quinta de São Caetano* (☎232 423 984; ⑦) on Rua Julio de Sousa Vieira de Matos, a romantic old manor house. There's a **campsite** (☎232 426 146) in the Parque do Fontelo, about ten minutes' walk east of the centre. Some of the best **food** in the province is to be had at *O Cortiço*, 45 Rua Augusto Hilário, where prices aren't too high but tables can be hard to get. **Moving on** from Viseu, which is a major stopover for routes north, there are regular buses to Lamego via Castro Daire, Guarda, Coimbra, Lisbon and Faro.

Guarda

GUARDA, at over 1000m, is the highest town in Portugal built on a plateau on the north-east flank of the Estrela mountains. It is chilly and windswept all year round and offers superb views. The city was founded in 1197 by Dom Sancho I to guard his borders against both

Moors and Spaniards, and though the castle and walls have all but disappeared, its arcaded streets and little squares can be distinctly picturesque. The **train station** is 3km north of the centre but there is, fortunately, a connecting bus that meets all the major trains; the **bus station** is about four hundred metres southeast of the cathedral, in the heart of the old town. Dour and grey, the castellated facade of the **Cathedral** looks like the gateway of a castle, but around the sides the exterior is lightened by flying buttresses, pinnacles and grimacing gargoyles. Inside it's surprisingly lofty, with twisted pillars and vaulting influenced by the Manueline style. The huge carved stone retable is by João de Rouão, a leading figure in the sixteenth-century resurgence of Portuguese sculpture at Coimbra. A short way east there are modern and imaginative displays of local archeology, art and sculpture in the **Museu de Guarda** (Tues–Sun 10am–12.30pm & 2–5.30pm; €1.25). Of the **Castle**, on a bleak little hill nearby, only the square keep survives, while the **walls** are recalled by just three surviving gates. The cobbled streets of the old town, though, are fascinating in themselves – the tangled area between the **Porta da Estrela** and **Porta do Rei**, north of the cathedral, has changed little in the past four hundred years.

There are two **tourist offices**: a central one on Praça Luis de Canões (Mon–Fri 9am–12.30pm & 2–5.30pm; ☎271 222 251), where you can pick up a town map: and a more helpful one next to the modern Câmara Municipal (Tues–Fri 9.30am–noon & 2–6pm, Sat closes 8pm; ☎271 221 817). **Places to stay** are fairly easy to come by if not especially cheap: try the attractive *Pensão Moreira*, Rua Mouzinho de Albuquerque 47 (☎271 214 131; ③), or cheerful rooms at the *Casa de Sé*, just off Praça Luis de Canões, on Rua Augusto Gil 17 (☎271 212 501; ④), off the central square. There is also a modern **hostel** on Av Alexandre Hercularo (☎271 224 482; ③, dorms ②), on the way to Guarda's **campsite**, open all year, in a park a short way from the castle; remember, though, that nights can be extremely cold. The **restaurants** between the Porta da Estrela and the church of São Vicente are cheap and cheerful.

NORTHERN PORTUGAL

The economic powerhouse of the north is **Oporto**, the country's second largest city and most industrious centre. It's an enticingly lively place, made especially attractive by the port-producing suburb of **Vila Nova de Gaia**, whose wines are supplied by the vineyards of the River Douro. The **Douro Valley**, a spectacular rocky gorge as it approaches the sea, is followed by a magnificent **rail route** whose branch lines run along some equally lovely valleys – along the River Tâmega to Amarante, along the Corgo to Vila Real, and along to Tua, from where there are bus connections to **Bragança**, capital of the isolated region of **Trás-os-Montes**. The Portuguese consider the northwest province of the **Minho** to be the most beautiful part of their country, and with its river valleys, wooded hills, trailing vines and wild coastline, the attractions are obvious. A small, thoroughly rural and conservative region, its towns are often outrageously picturesque and full of quiet charm. Monuments and museums are concentrated in **Braga** and **Guimarães**, while between them lie the extensive Celtic ruins of the **Citânia de Briteiros**, the most impressive archeological site in Portugal. **Viana do Castelo**, the main town of the Minho coast, is an enjoyably low-key resort with a wonderful beach.

Oporto

Capital of the north, **OPORTO (Pôrto)** is very different from Lisbon – unpretentious, inward-looking, unashamedly commercial. As the local saying goes: "Coimbra sings; Braga prays; Lisbon shows off; and Oporto works." The city's fascination lies very much in the life of the place, with its prosperous business core surrounded by smart suburbs and elegant villas, side by side with a heart of cramped streets and ancient alleys that has been declared a

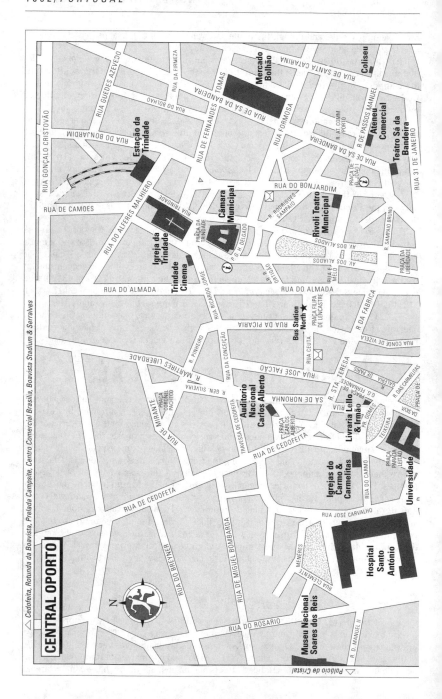

CENTRAL OPORTO

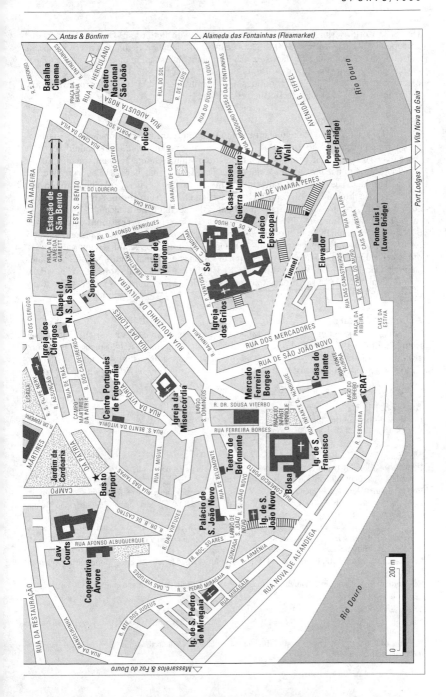

UNESCO World Heritage Classified Area. Together with Rotterdam, Oporto was declared **European City of Culture 2001**. The reality of the situation is that due to considerable delays, many events will take place in 2002. For further information on events, contact *Porto 2001*, Edifício Peninsula, Praça do Bom Sucesso 127-5° (☎22 605 9400, *www.porto2001.pt*). Meanwhile, daily life in the city continues to be inconvenienced by the major roadworks and construction sites that characterize the preparation.

Arrival and information

Most trains will drop you at the distant **Estação de Campanhã**; you should change here for a local train to central **São Bento** – it takes about five minutes and there should never be more than a twenty-minute wait. Certain trains from Minho (Guimarães) and the north coast (Póvoa de Varzim) use the smaller **Estação da Trindade**, from where it's a short walk down Rua da Trindade, past the town hall and into the centre. As a general rule, buses **from the south** come in around Rua Alexandre Herculano, and those **from the north** to the new bus station at Rua Dr Alfredo Magalhães 46, about 250m north of the Estação da Trindade. All major European airlines fly to Oporto's *Francisco Sá Carneiro* **international airport** (☎22 941 2534), 10 km north from the city centre. If you're coming in from the airport, the new Aerobus (7.45am–7.15pm every 30min; €3) stops at **Avenida dos Aliados** a few yards north of the central São Bento station. This is Oporto's main commercial centre, which culminates at Praça Dom João I, 43, site of the central post office and the main **tourist office** (daily 9am–7.00pm; ☎22 317 514). **Internet access** is available a few doors down at PortWeb (daily 9am–2am; €1.50/hr).

Accommodation

The **cheapest rooms** in town are on Ruas do Loureiro and Cimo do Vila, around the corner from São Bento. Be warned, though, that this is something of a red-light district. For more salubrious places, your best bet is to head for the areas west or east of Avenida dos Aliados; all the hotels listed below are to the west – with the exception of *Estoril*, which lies to the north.

HOSTEL

Pousada de Juventude, Rua Paulo Gama 552 (☎22 617 7257). Large and clean but lacking in atmosphere. Bus #35 from Largo Dos Loios. ④; dorms ②.

HOTELS

Pensão Residencial Duas Nações, Praça Guilherme Gomes Fernandes 59 (☎22 208 1616). Cheap and dependable, but often full; private bathroom included. ④.
Pensão Estoril, Rua de Cedofeita 193 (☎22 200 2751). Wonderful-value, well equipped en suite rooms. ④.
Pensão Oporto Chique, Rua Conde de Vizela 26 (☎22 208 0069). Reasonable and near São Bento. Breakfast included. ④.
Pensão Pão-de-Açucar, Rua do Almada 262 (☎22 200 2425). More expensive three-star with en suites. ⑦.
Pensão Universal, Avda. dos Aliados 38 (☎22 200 6758). Clean and in a perfect position, although it can be noisy. Breakfast included. ⑤.
Residencial Paris, Rua da Fábrica 27–29 (☎22 207 3140). A faded hotel with huge rooms; always popular. Breakfast included. ③.
Residencial Vera Cruz, Rua Ramalho Ortigão 14 (☎22 332 3296). Smartish and conveniently located. ④.

CAMPSITES

Marisol, Praia da Madalena (☎22 711 5942). Stunning location on the south side of the river; bus #57 from São Bento train station.
Prelada (☎22 831 2616). The closest of the campsites; take bus #56 or #87 from Cordoaria or the airport (both run until midnight).

The city

The stifled streets of the old town rarely permit any sort of overall view, so it's a good idea to climb the 250 steps to the Baroque **Igreja e Torre dos Clérigos** (daily 10am–noon & 2–5pm; tower €0.50) to get your bearings.

Not much goes on in the daytime at the waterfront since the big ships stopped calling here, but this is definitely the centre for nightlife. To the west, a statue of Oporto-born Henry the Navigator faces the glass-domed former **Stock Exchange** and the back of **São Francisco** (Mon–Sat 9am–5/6pm; April–Oct also Sun 10am–6pm; €2.50, including entry to museum), perhaps the most extraordinary church in Oporto. Outside it looks like an ordinary Gothic construction, but the interior has been transformed by an unbelievably ornate attack of eighteenth-century refurbishment. Don't miss the church's small **museum**, which consists largely of artefacts salvaged from the monastery that once stood nearby.

The **Museu Nacional Soares dos Reis** at Rua de Dom Manuel II (Tues 2–6pm, Wed–Sun 10am–12.30pm & 1.30–6pm; €2.50), over to the west behind the city hospital, was the first national museum in Portugal. Its collection includes glass, ceramics and a formidable array of eighteenth- and nineteenth-century paintings, as well as the late-nineteenth-century sculptures of Soares dos Reis – his *O Desterro* (The Exile) is probably the best-known work in Portugal. Follow the road past the museum, or take any bus from the Cordoaria stop except #6 and #18, and you'll come to the **Jardim do Palácio de Cristal**, a peaceful park dominated by a huge domed pavilion which now serves as an exhibition hall. In summer the park is home to a vast funfair. On the far side, across Rua Entre Quintas, stands the **Solar do Vinho do Porto** (Mon–Fri 10am–11.45pm, Sat 11am–10.45pm), where you can sample one of hundreds of varieties of **port** in air-conditioned splendour – a good prelude to visiting Vila Nova.

Vila Nove de Gaia

The only real reason to cross the river to Vila Nova de Gaia is to sample the many varieties of port it has to offer: the names of the various companies (Croft's, Taylor's, Sandeman, Graham's), spelled out in huge white letters across their roofs, dominate even the most distant view. You can walk to Gaia across the **Ponte Dom Luis**: the most direct route to the wine lodges is across the lower level from the Cais da Ribeira, but if you've a head for heights it's an amazing sensation to walk over the upper deck; otherwise, take bus #32, #57 or #91 from São Bento. Almost all the companies offer free **tasting** and tours of their factory. There's little pressure to buy anything – but do try the dry white ports, which are expensive and often unobtainable elsewhere. Check out *www.ivp.pt*, the official Web site of Portugal's Port Wine Institute.

Eating, drinking and nightlife

Oporto has a strong **café culture** which includes some elegant rivals to the fin-de-siècle places in Lisbon, while the **Cais da Ribeira** waterfront district offers a vibrant scene at night full of lively bars and clubs. Most of the city's big nightclubs are in the outlying **Matosinhos** district where you can dance to the latest techno until 2–3am. The city's culinary speciality is *Tripas á Modo* (tripe) and its citizens are affectionately referred to by the rest of the country as *tripeiros*. Don't let this put you off – there's always plenty of choice on the menu, and there are lots of places where you can eat cheaply. At the basic level, there are **workers' cafés** galore, all with wine on tap, and often with a set menu for the day. Prime areas are north and south of the Cordoaria, especially Rua do Almada and Rua de São Bento da Vitória. All are busy at midday and invariably close around 7.30pm and all of Sunday. There are also many good, cheap stand-bys around Praça da Batalha.

Restaurants

Café Majestic, Rua de Santa Catarina 112. Oporto's best loved café/restaurant with ornate surroundings and delicious breakfasts and teas. Closed Sun.

Café Restaurant Miradouro, Cais da Ribeira, on the arches by the entrance to the bridge. A popular local hangout with great salads and cheap meals.

Casa Filha da Mão Preta, Cais da Ribeira 39. Bustling restaurant with excellent views over the river. Dishes cost €9. Closed Sun.

Churrasqueira de Brasil, Campo dos Mártires da Pátria 136, near Torre dos Clerigos. Cheap workers' diner with a lively, friendly atmosphere, and serving ample portions.

Ginjal do Oporto, Rua do Bonjardim 724. Bargain local specialities in a no-frills setting.

Montecarlo, Rua Santa Catarina 17-2°. Looks like a 1930s tearoom, has views over the Praça da Batalha and serves good food. Closed Sun.

Adega do Olho, Rua Alfonso Martins Alho 6. Traditional cheap dive full of local character. Closed Sun.

Cafés and bars

Aniki-Bóbó, Rua da Fonte Taurinha 36. Upbeat late night acid jazz/house bar. Open till 4am. Closed Sun.

Bar da Praia do Ourigo, Esplanada do Castelo. Trendy tapas bar frequented by students, also serves good coffee on the beach. Open 9.30am–3am.

Labirinto, Rua Nossa Senhora da Fátima 334. A "bar-arcade", catering for a wide range of tastes, with exhibitions and live music. Open 9.30pm–3am.

Taberna da Ribeira, Praça da Ribeira. Prime riverside spot with outdoor tables. Open till 2am.

Clubs

Industria, Avenida Brasil 843. Like its Lisbon namesake attracts a mixed crowd out for a good time. Open Fri and Sat only.

River Café, Cançada João do Carmo 31. Pricey entrance fee and and strict dress code but worth it for the chilled, jazzy atmosphere. Open Wed–Sat.

Swing, Praçeta Enginheiro Amaro da Costa 766. Fun Seventies-revival disco. Smart dress code. Daily till 2am.

Tomate, Rua Manuel Pinto de Azevedo 15. Current hot spot in a warehouse atmosphere with visiting DJs playing drum'n'bass and trance. Closed Sun.

THE DOURO LINE

The valleys of **the Douro** and its tributaries are among the most spectacular landscapes in Portugal, and the Douro Valley itself, a narrow, winding gorge for the majority of its long route east to the Spanish border, is the most beautiful of all. The Douro **rail route**, which joins the river about 60km inland and then sticks to it across the country, is one of those journeys that needs no justification other than the trip itself. At present there are quite regular connections along the line as far as Peso da Régua, though you will most likely find yourself on a single carriage train; beyond Régua, there are less frequent connections to Tua and Pocinho.

Cete, half a dozen stations out of Oporto, is just a mile away from the village of **PAÇO DE SOUSA**, a former headquarters of the Benedictines in Portugal and a popular picnic spot for Oporto locals. If you're looking for a bed, it's not much further down the line to Penafiel station, connected by bus to the village itself. Split by main-road traffic, **PENAFIEL** is not that enticing a place, but it has a saving grace in its fabulous local *vinho verde* wine, served from massive barrels in the **adega** in the central Largo do Padré Américo. *Fado's* restaurant still has barrels but is quite smart – the owner will sing *fado* at weekends if you're lucky; above is the best and cheapest **hotel**, *Casa João da Lixa* (☎255 215 158; ②).

At Livração, about an hour from Oporto, the Tâmega line cuts off for Amarante in the mountains. Shortly after, the main line finally reaches the Douro and heads upstream until, at Mesão Frio, the valley broadens into the little plain commanded by **PESO DA RÉGUA,** the depot through which port wine must pass on its way from Pinhão – the centre of production – to Oporto. The tiny **tourist office** (summer daily 9am–12.30pm & 2–5.30pm; winter Mon–Fri only; ☎254 313 846), 1km from the train station, can inform you about visits to local cellars. Apart from these alcoholic diversions, there's not much to do except wander through the upper village and along the river. If you need to stay, the high-rise *Pensão Império* at Rua José Vasques Osório 8 (☎254 320 120; ④) offers good **accommodation**, breakfast and views, and *Pensão Borrajo* on Rua Dos Camilos near the post office, is basic but cheap (☎254 233 396; ③). There are plenty of **restaurants** along the main street.

Beyond Peso da Régua begin the terraced slopes where the **port vines** are grown: they look their best in August, with the grapes ripening, and in September when the harvest has begun. The country continues in this vein, craggy and beautiful, with the softer hills of the interior fading dark green into the distance, to Tua (junction for the Tua line) and Pocinho, where buses take over for routes east towards Miranda do Douro. From there it's a straightforward hitch in summer to Zamora in Spain.

Bragança

Trás-os-Montes – literally meaning "behind the mountains" – is a province tucked away into Portugal's most inland, northeast corner. Until the country's admission into the European Union in 1992, this glacial tabletop of granite boulders and rural communities was one of the most isolated pockets of the Continent. On a hillock above **BRAGANÇA**, the small and remote capital, stands a pristine circle of walls, enclosing a medieval village that rises to a massive keep and castle. Seemingly untouched by the centuries, this extraordinary **Citadel** – along with the fine local museum – is the principal reason for a visit to the town. The twelfth-century council chamber, the **Domus Municipalis**, stands in the heart of the citadel; very few Romanesque civic buildings have survived anywhere in Europe, and no other has this pentagonal form. Next to it is the church of **Santa Maria**, with its eighteenth-century barrel-vaulted, painted ceiling – a feature common to several churches in Bragança. Towering above these two is the **Castle**, which the Portuguese royal family rejected as a residence in favour of their vast estate in the Alentejo. At its side a curious pillory rises from the back of a pre-historic granite pig, or *porca*, thought to have been a fertility idol of a prehistoric cult. Celtic-inspired medieval tombstones rub shoulders with a menagerie of *porcas* in the gardens of **Museu do Abade de Baçal**, between the citadel and cathedral in Rua Abílio Beça (Tues–Fri 10am–5pm, Sat & Sun 10am–6pm; €1.25, free on Sun). Inside, a collection of sacred art and the watercolours of Alberto Souza are the highlights, along with displays of local costumes.

The **tourist office** (July–Sept Mon–Fri 9am–12.30pm & 2–7pm; Oct–June Mon–Fri 9am–12.30pm & 2–5pm; ☎273 381 273, *www.brangancanet.pt*) is on an extension of Avda. Cidade de Zamora, a couple of hundred metres north of the cathedral. The cheapest **pension** in town is the *Hospedaria Brigantina*, next to the post office on Rua Almirante Reis (☎273 324 321; ②); you'd be better advised to pay a little more and stay at *Residencial Poças*, Rua Combatentes da G. Guerra 200 (☎073 331 428; ②). The nearest **campsite** (☎273 351 535; May–Oct) is 6km out of town on the França road; a better option is the plush, private site (☎073 999 371; open all year) 8km down the Vinhais road, with good facilities and a pool. As for **restaurants**, two favourites are *Restaurante Poças*, next to the *Residencial*, serving big wholesome meals, and *Restaurante D Fernando*, Cidadela 197, inside the walled old town, which is surprisingly good value.

Crossing the border

From Bragança the most obvious route into Spain is via Quintanilha (34km), the nearest town to the **San Martin** border post. There are one or two direct buses daily, but any bus to Miranda do Douro will take you to a crossroads from where you can hitch the 12km to the border. You can stay here above the *Evaristo*, San Martin's only shop, restaurant and

pension. At 7am there's a bus to Zamora, connected to Madrid by road and rail. In Bragança there's also the possibility of reserving a seat on the Zamora–Valladolid–Madrid **express bus**, which passes through every Monday, Tuesday, Thursday and Friday (see timetable at *www.alsa.es/internacional*).

Braga and around

BRAGA, the tourist office pamphlet claims, is Portugal's answer to Rome. This clearly is going over the top – though it illustrates the city's ecclesiastical pretensions. Founded by the Romans in 279 BC, Braga was a bishopric before being occupied by the Moors. It was reconquered early in the eleventh century and by the end of the century its archbishops were pressing for recognition as "Primate of the Spains", a title they disputed with Toledo over the next six centuries. It is still Portugal's religious capital – the scene of spectacular **Easter celebrations** with torchlit processions and weirdly hooded penitents.

You won't be able to miss the **Archbishop's Palace**, a great fortress-like building, right at the centre of the old town. In medieval times it covered a tenth of the city and today easily accommodates the municipal library and various faculties of the university. Nearby is the **Sé**, which like the palace encompasses Gothic, Renaissance and Baroque styles. It was founded in 1070 and its south doorway is a survival from this earliest building; its most striking element, however, is the intricate ornamentation of the roofline, executed by João de Castilho, later the architect of Lisbon's Jerónimos Monastery. A guided tour of the interior (8.30am–6/6.30pm; free, museum and Capela dos Reis €1.50) takes you through three Gothic chapels, of which the outstanding specimen is the **Capela dos Reis** (King's Chapel), built to house the tombs of Henry of Burgundy and his wife Teresa, the cathedral's founders and the parents of Afonso Henriques, founder of the kingdom. Beyond the chapels is the cathedral **museum** – one of the richest collections in Portugal, but displayed like a junk shop.

The Art Deco **tourist office** (Mon–Fri 9am–7pm, Sat 9am–12.30pm & 2–5.30pm; ☎253 262 550) at the corner of Praça da Republica has copies of *Cultura Norte*, listing – in Portuguese – most events in the region. Two **hotels** offering excellent value are the *Residencial Inácio Filhos*, Rua Francisco Sanches 42 (☎253 263 849; ④), and the well-located *Grande Residencia Avenida*, Avda. da Liberdade 738 (☎253 262 955; ④). The *Casa Dos Lagos* (☎253 676 738; ⑤) is a lovely old farmhouse high up on the hill overlooking Braga on the road leading up to the Monte do Bom Jesus church. Braga's well-equipped **hostel** is at Rua Santa Margarida 6 (☎253 616 163; ④), off Avda. Central; the **campsite** (☎253 273 355) is a two-kilometre walk along the Guimarães road, but is very cheap and right next to the municipal swimming pool. *Churrasqueira Lareira do Conde*, on Praça Conde de Agrolongo, serves reasonably priced quality **food** in generous quantities, as does the *Restaurante Moçambicana* at Rua Andrade Corvo 8, one of several excellent cheap restaurants grouped around the Arco da Porta Nova. *Café Astória* (due to reopen soon after renovations), Praça da Republica, is by far the best of the old **coffee houses**, mahogany-panelled and with cut-glass windows. **Internet access** is available at Netstation, a new Internet café at the end of Rua de Santa Mareida, by Largo de Infias (€1.50/hr).

Bom Jesus

BOM JESUS, 3km outside Braga, is one of Portugal's best-known images, as much concept as building, a monumental place of pilgrimage created by Braga's archbishop in the first decades of the eighteenth century. It is a vast ornamental stairway of granite and white plaster cut into a densely wooded mount high above the city. There is no particular reason for its presence, no miracle or vision, yet it remains the object of devoted pilgrimage, penitents often climbing on their knees. **Buses** run from near the post office on Avda. da Liberdade in Braga to the foot of the stairway about every thirty minutes at weekends when half the city piles up there to picnic.

If you resist the temptation of the funicular and climb up the stairway, Bom Jesus' simple allegory unfolds. Each landing has a fountain: the first symbolizes the wounds of Christ, the next five the Senses, and the final three represent the Virtues. At each corner are chapels with mouldering wooden, larger-than-life tableaux of the life of Christ, leading to the Crucifixion at the altar of the church. Beyond are wooded gardens, grottoes and miniature boating pools, and several cheap, lively **restaurants** – filled on Saturdays with a constant stream of wedding parties.

Guimarães

Birthplace of Afonso Henriques and first capital of medieval Portucale, **GUIMARÃES** remains a lively and atmospheric university town. The town's chief attraction is the **Castelo** (Tues–Sun 10am–12.30pm & 2–5.30pm; free), whose square keep and seven towers are an enduring symbol of the emergent Portuguese nation. Built by Henry of Burgundy, it became the stronghold of his son, Afonso Henriques. From here the Reconquest began along with the creation of a kingdom which, within a century of Afonso's death, was to stretch to its present borders. Afonso is said to have been born in the keep, and was probably baptized in the font of the Romanesque chapel of **São Miguel** on the grassy slope below. The third building here, the **Paço dos Duques**, was once the palace of the dukes of Bragança, but under the Salazar dictatorship was "restored" as an official residence. Looking like a mock-Gothic Victorian folly, it now houses dull collections of portraits, furniture and porcelain.

The other two museums in Guimarães arc, in contrast, among the best outside Lisbon. The **Museu Alberto Sampaio**, ten minutes' walk south of the castle (Tues–Sun 10am–12.30pm & 2–5.30pm, July & Aug till 7pm; €1.50, free Sun am), is mostly the treasury of the adjoining Colegiada church and the monastery that used to be here. The highlight is a silver-gilt *Triptych of the Nativity*, said to have been found in the king of Castile's tent after the Portuguese victory at Aljubarrota. Like Batalha, the **Colegiada** itself was built in honour of a vow made by João I before that decisive battle. In front of it stands a Gothic canopy-shrine that marks the spot where Wamba, unwillingly elected king of the Visigoths, drove a pole into the ground swearing that he would not reign until it blossomed. Naturally it sprouted immediately. João, feeling this a useful precedent of divine favour, set out to meet the Castilians from this very point.

The finest church in town is **São Francisco**, a short distance east of the tourist office, with its huge eighteenth-century *azulejos*, or decorative tiles, of St Francis preaching to the fishes and its elegant Renaissance cloister and fountain.

Practicalities

Guimarães' **bus station** is fifteen minutes' walk west of town, near the football stadium; the **train station** is to the south. You'll pass one **tourist office** (Mon–Fri 9.30am–12.30pm & 2–6.30pm; ☎253 412 450, *www.cm-guimaraes.pt*) as you walk from here to the centre; the other office is in the centre of the old town in Praça de Santiago (same hours; summer also Sat 10am–1pm & 3–6pm, Sun 10am–1pm; ☎253 518 790). There is very little cheap **accommodation**: try *Casa dos Pombais*, Avda. de Londres 40 (☎253 412 917; ⑤), which has beautiful rooms overlooking attractive gardens, or the less expensive, but spartan *Casa dos Retiros*, Rua Francisco Agra 163 (☎253 511 515; ③ including breakfast). The town's **campsite** (☎253 515 912) is 6km away at Penha, a pilgrimage mount and chapel; take the São Roque bus (Mon–Sat 6am–10pm, Sun 6am–8pm; every 30min) from the main *turismo* and get off at "Costa"; or take the cable car from the end of Rua de Dr José Sanpaio (11am–6/7pm; €2.50 return). For **food**, *O Telheiro*, Rua Dom João I 39–41, above *Café Dom João*, serves great dishes in basic but bustling surroundings, and *Oriental* on Largo do Toural has budget, but very good regional specialities. *El Rei Dom Alfonso*, Praça de Santiago, is worth the moderate rise in price for its location in the heart of the old town.

SOUTHERN PORTUGAL

The huge, sparsely populated plains of the **Alentejo**, to the southeast of Lisbon, are overwhelmingly agricultural, dominated by vast cork plantations well suited to the low rainfall, sweltering heat and arid soil. This impoverished province is divided into vast estates which provide nearly half of the world's cork but only a sparse living for its rural inhabitants. Visitors to the Alentejo often head for **Évora**, the province's dominant and most historic city. But the **Portalegre** hills north of Évora and the Alentejo's **Costa Azul** are a breath of fresh air to the stifling plains of the inland landscape.

With its long, sandy beaches and picturesque rocky coves, the southern coastal region of the **Algarve** has attracted more tourist development than the rest of the country put together, turning much of the coast into a shabby concrete jungle. The coastline has two different characters. **West of Faro**, the lively capital of the Algarve, you'll find the classic postcard images of the province – a series of tiny bays and coves, broken up by weird rocky outcrops and fantastic grottoes, at their most exotic around the resort of **Lagos**. To the **east of Faro** you encounter the first of a series of sandy offshore islets, **the Ilhas**, which front the coastline for some 25 miles, and the lower-key resorts of **Olhão** and **Tavira**. Not only is this the quieter section of the coast but it has the bonus of much warmer water than further west. Throughout the Algarve **accommodation** can be a major problem in summer, with hotels block-booked by package companies and pensions filling up early in the day; private rooms or campsites help fill in the gaps, but if you're unlucky you might find yourself sleeping out for the odd night. If you fancy something a little less touristy, head inland where you'll find a more Portuguese way of life at **Silves**, the impressive former capital of the Moors.

Évora

ÉVORA is one of the most impressive cities in Portugal, its provincial atmosphere the perfect setting for a range of memorable and often intriguing monuments. The Romans were in occupation for four centuries and the Moors, who settled for just as long, have left their stamp in the tangle of narrow alleys which rise steeply among the whitewashed houses. Most of the monuments, however, date from the fourteenth to the sixteenth centuries, when, with royal encouragement, the city was one of the leading centres of Portuguese art and architecture.

Used as a slaughterhouse until 1870, the **Temple of Diana** in the central square is the best-preserved Roman temple in Portugal, its stark remains consisting of a small platform supporting more than a dozen granite columns with a marble entablature. Directly opposite, the former **Convento dos Lóios**, now converted into a luxuriant *pousada*, has been partly attributed to Francisco de Arruda, architect of the Tower of Belém in Lisbon. To the left of the *pousada* lies the church of the convent, dedicated to **São João Evangelista**. This is the private property of the ducal Cadaval family, who still occupy a wing or two of the adjacent ancestral palace. Wait outside and you should be admitted (Tues–Sun 10am–12.30pm & 2–5pm; €2.50) to see *azulejos* (decorative tiling), trick paintings and ossuary.

The **Cathedral**, or **Sé** (daily 9am–12.30pm & 2–5pm), was begun in 1186, about twenty years after the reconquest of Évora from the Moors, and the Romanesque solidity of its two huge square towers and battlemented roofline contrasts sharply with the pointed Gothic arches of the porch and central window. The interior is more straightforwardly Gothic, although the choir and high altar were remodelled in the eighteenth century. Adjacent, in the archbishop's palace, is the excellent **Museu de Évora** (Tues–Sun 10am–12.30pm & 2–5pm; €1.50), which houses important collections of fifteenth- and sixteenth-century Flemish and Portuguese paintings assembled from the city's churches and convents.

Perhaps the most memorable sight in Évora is the **Capela dos Ossos** (Chapel of Bones; 9am–1pm & 2.30–5.30/6.30pm; €1.50) in the church of **São Francisco**, close to the bus station. A gruesome reminder of mortality, the walls and pillars of this chilling chamber are entirely covered with the bones of more than 5000 monks; an inscription over the door reads, "Nós ossos que aqui estamos, Pelos vossos esperamos" (We bones here are waiting for your bones). Another interesting feature of this church is its large porch, which combines pointed, rounded and horseshoe arches in a manner typical of Manueline architecture. Appropriately enough, the restored **Palácio de Dom Manuel** – the king who gave his name to the style – lies no more than a minute's walk away, in the Jardim Público.

Practicalities
Both Évora's **bus station** and **train station** are about a kilometre out of the old town, though there are regular green buses from the former that run to **Praça do Giraldo**, centre of Évora's surprisingly lively social scene. Here you can find the **tourist office** (summer Mon–Fri 9am–7pm, Sat & Sun 9am–12.30pm & 2–5.30pm; winter daily 9am–12.30pm & 2–5.30pm; ☎266 702 671) and a couple of outdoor cafés. All the cheaper **places to stay** are within five minutes' walk, but Évora's tourist appeal pushes prices way over the norm. Best options are *Pensão Os Manuéis*, just west of the square at Rua do Raimundo 35 (☎266 702 861; ⑤); *Pensão Invicta*, Rua Romão Ramalho 37a, overlooking São Francisco (☎266 702 047; ③); and *Pensão Giraldo-Anexo* at Rua dos Mercadores 15 (☎266 702 833; ②). Évora's new **hostel** (☎267 444 848; ④, dorms ②) is just off Praça do Giraldo at Rua Miguel Bombarda 40. If you are looking for comfort try the converted sixteenth-century mansion *Solar Monfalim*, at Largo da Misericórdia 1 (☎266 750 000; ⑤). If you're stuck for a room, the tourist office will sometimes arrange accommodation in **private homes**. The **campsite** (☎266 705 190) is a couple of kilometres out of town on the Alcáçovas road; bus #5 goes there eight times daily from Praça do Giraldo (except Sun). **Restaurants** abound in the centre: for inexpensive food try *Adego do Neto*, Rua dos Mercadores 46 or the homely *O Portão*, on Rua do Cano alongside the aqueduct. For slightly more you could sample the outstanding Italian food at the enormously popular *Pane & Vino*, Patio do Salema (entrance on Rua Diogo Focardo). *Oficin@,* at Rua da Moeda 27, is an easy-going **bar** that also offers **Internet access** for €2.50/hr.

Castelo de Vide and Marvão

The upland district on the border with Spain is a bucolic landscape, with tree-clad mountain ranges and a series of gorgeous hilltop villages. Among these, the best targets are **Castelo de Vide** and **Marvão**, both with castles, and the former spa. Both villages are connected by daily bus to Portalegre (and so to Lisbon and Évora) twenty kilometres away, and by train to the nearby Marvão-Beirá station which is on the Lisbon-Madrid route. Not all trains stop, especially outside summer, so check before starting your journey.

Castelo de Vide
CASTELO DE VIDE covers the slopes around a fourteeth-century castle, its blindingly white cottages delineated in brilliant contrast to the greenery around. Arriving by bus, you'll be dropped outside the **tourist office** (daily: summer 9am–7pm; winter 9am–12.30pm & 2–5.30pm; ☎045 901 361) in the centre of town. From here the main road peters out into a narrow path, descending past a tranquil Renaissance fountain to the twisting alleyways of the **Judairia** – the old Jewish quarter. Amid the cottages with their Gothic doorways and windows, is a thirteenth-century **synagogue** (daily 9am–6pm), the oldest surviving one in Portugal. From the outside it doesn't look very different from the cottages, so you will probably need to ask for directions. On a hill above the Judaria, the **Castelo** (daily: summer 8am–6pm; winter 9am–12.30pm & 2–5.30pm; free) squats within the wider fortifications of the original medieval village. There's a surprising amount of **accommodation**: try the *Casa de Hóspedes Melanie*, Largo de Paço Novo 3 (☎245 901 632; ④), or for luxury and spectacular views the *Albergaria El Rei Dom Manuel* (☎045 909 150; ④) which also has a good restaurant. For delicious **snacks** try the pastries at the *Pasteleria Sol Nascente* at Rua de Olivena 31.

Marvão

Beautiful as Castelo de Vide is, **MARVÃO** surpasses it. The panoramas from its remote eyrie site are unrivalled and the atmosphere even quieter than a population of less than a thousand would suggest. No more a handful of houses – each as scrupulously whitewashed as the rest – lies outside the seventeenth-century walls. The thirteenth-century **castle** stands at the far end of the village, its walls blending into the sharp slopes of the serra. It's dauntingly impenetrable and was indeed captured only once, in 1833, when the attackers entered through a secret gate. The best time to visit is during the annual chestnut festival or **Festa da Castanha** held annually in the middle of November.

The **turismo**, on Rua Dr. Antônio Matos Magalhães (daily 9.30am–12.30pm & 2–5.30pm; ☎245 993 104) can help out with **accommodation** or try the *Pensão Dom Dinis* (☎245 993 235; ④) further along the same road. For **meals**, the *Restaurante Varanda do Alentejo* in Praça do Pelourinho is good and you can also eat and drink at the bars just off the square.

The Alentejo Coast

The coast south of Lisbon features towns and beaches as inviting as those of the Algarve. Admittedly, it's exposed to the winds and waves of the Atlantic, and the waters are colder, but it's fine for summer swimming and far quieter. Access is straightforward, with local bus services and the twice-daily Zambujeira Express from Lisbon, which takes you within easy range of the whole coastline and stops at the beaches of Vila Nova de Milfontes and Zambujeira do Mar.

Five buses a day run from Lisbon to Alcacer do Sal, from where there are reasonable connections south to **SANTIAGO DO CACÉM**, a pleasant little town overlooked by a castle. In turn, there are five buses a day (in summer) from Santiago to **Lagoa de Santo André** and the adjoining **Lagoa de Melides**, with two of the best beaches in the country. Each of these lagoons has its own small summer community entirely devoted to having a good time on the beach. The **campsites** at both places are of a high standard and there are masses of signs offering rooms, chalets and whole houses to let. Beyond the beach-cafés and ice-cream stalls miles and miles of sand stretch all the way to Comporta in the north and Sines in the south. The sea is enticing with high waves and good surf, but take local advice on water conditions, as the undertow can be fierce. If you want to base yourself at Santiago rather than at the beaches, there's no shortage of good **food and accommodation**. The *Restaurante Covas*, by the bus station at Rua Cidade de Setúbal 10 (☎269 822 675; ③), is recommended both for its **rooms** and for its outstanding meals. There are plenty of other places around town advertising rooms, and another great **restaurant** – *Praceta,* at Largo Zeca Afonso (behind the bus station).

On the southern half of the Alentejo coast, **ODEMIRA** is the main inland base. A quiet, unspoiled country town, it has an erratic bus service (8 daily) to the beach at Vila Nova de Milfontes and to Zambujeira do Mar (2 daily). Unless you're camping, you're unlikely to find anywhere to spend the night in these resorts from June to August, so it's not a bad idea to stay in Odemira and take day-trips to the seaside. The town has several restaurants and **pensions**, including *Casa Rita,* Largo do Poço Novo (☎283 322 531; ③), and *Residencial Idálio,* Rua Engl. Arantes Oliveira 28 (☎283 322 156; ②), just to the left when you come out of the bus station. Of the **restaurants**, try *O Tarro,* near the main road junction.

VILA NOVA DE MILFONTES lies on the estuary of the River Mira, whose sandy banks gradually expand and merge into the coastline. This is generally the most crowded and popular resort in the Alentejo, with lines of villas and hotels radiating from the centre of the old village. It's still a pretty place, though, with a handsome little castle and an ancient port, reputed to have harboured Hannibal and his Carthaginians during a storm. Recent development means finding reasonable **rooms** shouldn't be a problem, and there are a couple of large **campsites** to the north of the village: *Parque de Milfontes* (☎283 996 104) and the more modest *Campiférias* (☎283 996 409). At **ZAMBUJEIRA DO MAR**, south of Odemira and 7km west of the main road, a large cliff provides a dramatic backdrop to the beach, more than compensating for the winds. There's only a few small **pensions**, such as the *Mar-e-Sol* (☎283 961 171; ③), a few *dormidas* and a couple of bars, as well as a reasonable **campsite** open all year (☎283 961 172), about 1km from the cliffs. Lastly, the resort of **PORTO CÔVO**, although overdeveloped, has plentiful accommodation and beautiful, almost untouched beaches to the south.

Faro

FARO, a sleepy provincial town twenty years ago, now has all the facilities of a modern European town, with an attractive shopping area, some decent restaurants and a "real" Portuguese feel in contrast to many nearby resorts. Excellent **beaches**, too, are within easy reach, and in summer there's quite a nightlife scene, as thousands of travellers pass through on their way to and from the airport, 6km west of the town.

Sacked and burned by the Earl of Essex in 1596, and devastated by the Great Earthquake of 1755, the town has few historic buildings. By far the most curious sight is the Baroque **Igreja do Carmo** (Mon–Fri 10am–1pm & 3–5pm, Sat 10am–1pm; €2.50) near the central post office on Largo do Carmo. A door to the right of the altar leads to a macabre **Capela dos Ossos** (Chapel of Bones), its walls decorated with bones disinterred from the adjacent cemetery. This aside, the most interesting buildings are all in the old, semi-walled quarter on the south side of the harbour, centred around the majestic Largo da Sé and entered through the eighteenth-century town gate, the **Arco da Vila**. The Largo is flanked by the bishop's palace and the **Sé** itself (Mon–Fri 10am–5pm, Sun for Mass only), a miscellany of Gothic, Renaissance and Baroque styles, heavily remodelled after the Great Earthquake. More impressive is the nearby **Museu Arqueológico** (Mon–Fri 10am–6.30pm; €1.50), installed in a fine sixteenth-century convent. The most striking exhibit is a third-century Roman mosaic of Neptune and the four winds, unearthed near Faro train station.

Practicalities

Taxis from the **airport** to the centre should cost around €2.50; or take bus #16 (hourly 8am–8/9pm), a twenty-minute journey to town. The bus station is right in the centre, behind the *Hotel Eva*, across from the old town; the train station is a few minutes beyond, up the Avenida da República. There's a **tourist office** at the airport (daily 9am–midnight; ☎289 818 582); the main office is at Av. 5 de outubro (daily 9.30am–7pm; ☎289 800 400, *www.rtalgarve.pt*).

Pensões are concentrated just north of the harbour along Rua Infante D. Henrique and the noisy Rua Conselheiro Bivar, and around Praça Ferreira de Almeida on Rua Vasco da Gama, Rua Filipe Alistão and Rua do Alportel. Among the better places is the increasingly upmarket *Pensão Madalena* (☎289 805 806; ④) at Rua C. Bivar 109; *Casa de Hóspedes Adelaide* (☎289 802 383; ④), near the bus station at Rua Cruz das Mestras 7–9, is the best budget choice – during the summer they also open the roof as a dorm and charge around €5–6.25 per person. Also excellent value is the eccentric *Pensão Dandy*, F. Alistão 62 (☎289 824 791; ④), and *Pensão São Félipe*, Rua Infante Don Henrique 55a (☎289 824 182; ③). A slightly more expensive option is a stunning English-run 18th century farmhouse, Monte Do Casal, Cerro do Lobo (☎289 991 503; ⑥). The **campsite** (☎289 817 876) is at Praia de Faro, and is always packed in summer – phone ahead; take bus #16 from town. There are **restaurants** to meet most budgets: try the *Restaurant Dois Irmãos*, on Largo Terreiro do Bispo, or for something less expensive, cram in with locals at the *Churrasqueira Santo António*, close to the train station at Largo de Camões 23. The town's **nightlife** centres around Rua do Prior, a cobbled alley full of bars and discos; *3ʳᵈ Millenium* is one of the best discos. **Internet access** is available at Ciberlusa, Rua Conselheiro Bivar 40–42 (opposite McDonald's) for €5/hr.

Olhão

OLHÃO, 8km east of Faro, is the largest fishing port on the Algarve and an excellent base for visiting the sandbank islands (*ilhas*). **Train** and **bus** stations are near each other off the Avenida da República northeast of town. The **tourist office**, just off Rua do Comércio (daily 9.30am–12.30pm & 2–5.30/7pm, winter closed Tues; ☎289 713 936) will provide a town map and advice on rooms. For **accommodation**, try the highly rated *Pensão Bela Vista* (☎289 702 538; ③), left out of the tourist office then first left; or the *Pensão Boémia*, slightly further out of the centre at Rua da Cerca 20, off Rua 18 de Junho (☎289 714 513; ③). The nearest **campsite** (☎289 700 300) is at Marim, 3km east – buses hourly till 7pm from the main station. There are clusters of **restaurants** and **bars** around Rua do Comércio and along the seafront: *Taiti* at Rua Vasco da Gama 24 is reasonably good, as is *Santos* on Avda. 5 de Outubro 100.

Ferries leave for the **Ilhas of Armona** and **Culatra** from the jetty at the far end of Olhão's municipal gardens, five minutes from the market. The service to **ARMONA** (June–Sept 9–14 daily; Oct–May 4 daily; journey time 15min; €0.75 each way) drops you off at a long strip of holiday chalets and huts that stretches right across the island on either side of the main path. This is the only type of **accommodation** available here, and you'll be lucky to get one in summer; phone ahead to book (Orbitur ☎289 714 173). On the ocean side, the beach disappears into the distance and a short walk will take you to totally deserted stretches of sand and dune. The beach facing the mainland is smaller and tends to get very crowded in summer, but the water here is always warm. Boats to the more distant **Ilha of Culatra** are less frequent (4–7 daily; 35–45min; €1 each way) and call first at unattractive Culatra town, then at **FAROL**, an untidy village of holiday homes edged by beautiful beaches on the ocean side. Note that ferry services are drastically reduced outside July and August.

Tavira

TAVIRA is a clear winner if you are looking for an urban base on the eastern stretch. It's a good-looking little town with superb island beaches in easy reach, yet despite ever-increasing visitors it continues to make its living as a tuna-fishing port. **Buses** pull up at the new terminal by the river, a two-minute walk from the central square, the Praça da República; the **train station** is 1km from the centre of town, straight up the Rua da Liberdade. Boats cross from Quatro Águas (during winter dependent on the weather; €1 return), 2km east of town, to the eastern end of the **Ilha de Tavira**, which stretches west almost as far as Fuzeta, some 14km away. The beach is enormous, backed by dunes, and despite increasing development – a small chalet settlement, watersports, beach umbrellas and half a dozen bar/restaurants facing the sea – it's an enjoyable spot in which to hang out. Tavira has some of the best areas for **scuba diving** in Portugal, check out the diving school at Pedras Del Rei (☎281 793 495).

There's a **campsite** (☎281 323 505), a minute from the sands, but by far the best place **to stay** in Tavira is the *Residencial Lagoas*, north of the river at Rua Almirante Cândido dos Reis 24 (☎281 322 252; ③), with the bonus of the budget eatery, *Bica*, below. Alternatives include the rambling *Pensão do Castelo* (☎281 323 942; ③) in the main square, the *Residencial Mirante* at Rua da Liberdade 83 (☎281 322 255; ④ with breakfast) just up the main road (though it can be a bit noisy), and the lovely *Residencial Princesa do Gilão*, across the river on the quayside (☎281 325 171; ⑤), whose front rooms have balconies overlooking the river. If you want to get away from it all try the restored *Convento de Santo António* (☎258 835 065; ⑥). Founded in 1606, the Capochino convent has beautiful cloisters and views towards the sea over the salt pans. If these options fail to produce a bed, the **tourist office** just off the main Praça da República (daily 9.30am–5.30/7pm; ☎281 322 511) may be able to find you a **private room**. A succession of **bars and restaurants** line the gardens along the bank of the River Gilão, which flows through the centre of town. Probably the best of the restaurants here is the *Imperial*, which serves some of the finest seafood in the Algarve at fairly reasonable prices. Also good are *Anazu*, Rua Jacques Pessoa 13, a riverfront café which also has an **Internet** connection

(€4/hr), and the *Aquasul Restaurante*, Rua Dr Augusto Da Silva Carvalho 11–13, which serves fresh pizzas and cosmopolitan main dishes as well as **vegetarian** dishes on request. The *Arco*, at Rua Almirante Cândido dos Reis 67, is a friendly, laid-back, gay-friendly **bar**.

Silves

Capital of the Moorish kings of the al-Gharb (now Algarve), **SILVES** is still an imposing place and one of the few towns of inland Algarve that merits a detour. The **train station** – an easy approach from Lagos or Faro – lies 2km outside the town; there is a connecting bus, but it's worth walking, allowing the town and its fortress to appear slowly as you emerge from the wooded hills. Under the Moors, Silves was a place of grandeur and industry, described in contemporary accounts as being "of shining brightness" within its triple circuit of walls. In 1189 an army led by Sancho I put an end to this splendour, killing some 6000 Moors in the process. The castle is open to the public, but its ghastly past is lost amid well-tended jacaranda trees, oleander shrubs and flowerbeds. The impressively complete sandstone walls of the Moorish **fortress** (daily 9am–5/8pm; €1.75) retain their towers and elaborate communication system, but the inside is disappointing: apart from the great vaulted water cisterns that still serve the town, there's nothing left of the old citadel. Just below the fortress is Silves' **Cathedral** (daily 8.30am–6pm, Sun until 1pm), built on the site of the mosque in the thirteenth century. Much restored and rebuilt over the years, it contains the tombs of some of the Crusaders who died there. Flanked by two broad Gothic towers, it has a suitably defiant and military appearance, though the Great Earthquake of 1755 and centuries of impoverished restoration have left their mark inside.

The **tourist office**, in the heart of the town on Rua 25 de Abril (daily 9.30am–12.30pm & 2–5.30pm; ☎282 442 255), will help you find a **private room**. Recommended are those with Isabel Maria da Silva at Rua Cândido dos Reis 36 (☎282 442 667; ③), where you share the use of a kitchen and a little outdoor terrace. Another promising option is the *Residencial Sousa* **pension** at Rua Samora Barros 17 (☎282 442 502; ⑤).

Lagos

Once a quiet little town, **LAGOS** is now a thriving fishing port and market centre as well as being one of the most popular tourist destinations in the Algarve. Within walking distances of some superb beaches, the town is also an interesting historical centre. It was a favoured residence of Henry the Navigator, who used Lagos as a base for the new African trade – the richest of which was in slaves. Europe's first **slave market** was built here in 1441 in the arches of the **Customs House** which still stands in the Praça da República near the waterfront. In this same square is the **Church of Santa Maria**, from whose whimsical Manueline windows the youthful Dom Sebastião is said to have roused his troops before the ill-fated Moroccan expedition of 1578 – he was to perish at Alcácer-Quibir with almost the entire Portuguese nobility. He's commemorated in the centre of Lagos by a fantastically dreadful statue. On the waterfront and to the rear of the town are the remains of Lagos' once impregnable fortifications, devastated by the Great Earthquake. One rare and beautiful church which did survive for restoration was the **Igreja de Santo António**; decorated around 1715, its gilt and carved interior is wildly obsessive, every inch filled with a private fantasy of cherubic youths struggling with animals and fish.

To the **east** of Lagos is a splendid sweep of sand – **Meia Prais** – where there's space even at the height of summer, while the promontory **south** is fringed by extravagantly eroded cliff faces that shelter a series of tiny **cove beaches**. All are within easy walking distance of the old town, but the headland is now cut up by campsites, hotels, roads and a multitude of tracks, and the beaches all tend to be overcrowded. Of these **Praia de Dona Ana** is considered the most picturesque, though its crowds make the smaller coves of **Praia do Pinhão**, down a track just opposite the fire station, and **Praia Camilo**, a little further along, just as appealing.

Practicalities

The **train station** is across the river, fifteen minutes' walk from the centre via the new swing bridge in the marina; the **bus station** is a bit closer in, a block back from the main Avenida dos Descombrimentos. The **tourist office** is inconveniently located about fifteen minutes from the centre on the first main roundabout on the Portimão road (summer daily 9.30am–12.30pm & 2–5.30pm: winter closed Sat pm & Sun; ☎282 763 031). They can help find a room for you, but most economical are the **private rooms** (③) touted by little old ladies at the bus station – though the tourist office advise against it and always refer to them as "witches". Two of the more convenient and pleasant **pensions** are the *Pensão Caravela* at Rua 25 de Abril 16 (☎282 763 361; ④) and the *Residencial Mar Azul*, nearby at no. 13 (☎282 769 143; ⑤). There's a **hostel** at Rua de Lançarote de Freites 50, off the main Rua Cãndido dos Reis (☎282 761 970; ④, dorms ②), which also has **Internet** connection (€4/hr). Lagos has two **campsites**, close to each other on the main Sagres road – the *Campismo da Trindade* (☎282 763 893) and the larger and more attractive *Imulagos* (☎282 760 031). In season a regular bus service marked "D. Ana/Oporto de Mós" connects the bus station with both, and *Imulagos* provides its own free transport from the train station. On foot, follow the main road beyond the fort.

The centre of town is packed with **restaurants**. Some of the better ones are the cheap, good-quality fish and shellfish places by the market, where Rua das Portas de Portugal meets the main avenue. *O Cantinho Algarvio*, Rua Afonso d'Almeida 17, has a wide range of Algarve dishes at good prices; in the same street *Casa do Zé* is popular. For authentic *piri-piri* chicken try the tiny and inexpensive *O Franguinho* at Rua Luís de Azevedo 25. For a more expensive treat, *Dom Sebastião*, on the pedestrianized Rua 25 de Abril, is among the town's finest restaurants, where meals run to around €20. *Mullens bar*, Rua Cãndido dos Reis 86, serves meals until 10pm, plays jazz, salsa and soul on the sound system and stays open until 2am. *Hideaway*, Travessa 1º de Maio 9, just off Praça Luís Camões, is a cosily atmospheric bar, also open till 2am. *Eddies*, Rua 25 de Abril, is popular with the energetic and they also have an **Internet** connection during the day (€4/hr). For contemporary club sounds, try *Phoenix*, at Rua 5 de Outubro 11, or for something a bit funkier, *Reciclagem* on Rua Marreiros Neto; both stay open until 4am.

Lagos is the western terminus of the Algarve rail line, so for Sagres take one of the nine daily **buses**. Many of them call at the train station just after the arrival of the trains.

travel details

Trains

Lisbon to: Braga (2 daily; 4hr 40min); Coimbra (13 daily; 2hr–2hr 30min); Évora (1 daily; 3hr); Faro (2 daily; 5hr 30min–6hr); Guarda (5 daily; 6hr); Leiria (6 daily; 2–3hr); Óbidos (change at Cacém; 11 daily; 2hr); Oporto (10–13 daily; 3hr 30min–4hr); Sintra (every 15min; 50min); Tavira (4 daily; 6hr); Tomar (hourly; 2hr); Vilar Formoso (for Salamanca and Spain; 1 daily; 6hr 30min).

Coimbra to: Aveiro (hourly; 45min–1hr); Figueira da Foz (17 daily; 1hr–1hr 20min); Lisbon (15–16 daily; 2–3hr); Oporto (12 daily; 1hr 20min–2hr).

Figueira da Foz to: Leiria (3–6 daily; 1hr); Lisbon (2 daily; 3hr); Óbidos (6 daily; 2hr 30min).

Guarda to: Coimbra (6 daily; 3hr); Lisbon (5 daily; 6hr); Luso-Buçaco (5 daily; 2hr 30min); Salamanca, Spain (2 daily; 2hr 30min).

Lagos to: Faro (9 daily; 1hr 20min–2hr); Lisbon (5 daily; 5hr); Silves (6 daily; 30–40min); Vila Real de Santo António (for Spain; 5 daily; 3–4hr).

Oporto to: Aveiro (every 30min; 50min–1hr 30min); Barcelos (11 daily; 1hr 10min–1hr 40min); Braga (13–16 daily; 1hr–1hr 45min); Coimbra (15 daily; 2hr); Guimarães (hourly; 1hr 45min); Lisbon (14–15 daily; 3–4hr); Madrid (2 daily; 12hr); Peso da Régua (4–10 daily; 2hr 30min); Viana do Castelo (9 daily; 1hr 45min–2hr 30min); Vigo (Spain; 3 daily; 4hr 30min).

Peso da Régua to: Oporto (14–15 daily; 2hr 30min); Vila Real (5 daily; 1hr).

Buses

Lisbon to: Alcobaça (3 daily; 2hr); Coimbra (8 daily; 2hr 30min); Évora (5 daily; 2hr); Faro (5–10 daily; 4hr); Fátima (7 daily; 1hr 45min–2hr 15min); Guarda (1–4 daily; 5–6hr); Leiria (9 daily; 1hr–2hr 10min); Mafra (10 daily; 1hr); Oporto (hourly; 3hr); Tomar (2–4 daily; 2hr).

Braga to: Barcelos (hourly; 50min); Guimarães (every 30min; 45min); Oporto (hourly; 1hr); Viana do Castelo (4–10 daily; 1hr 40min).

Coimbra to: Fátima (4 daily; 1hr–1hr 20min); Guarda (4 daily; 2hr 40min); Lisbon (16 daily; 2hr 20min); Leiria (4 daily; 1hr); Luso/Bucaco (2–5 daily; 45min); Oporto (7–10 daily; 1hr 30min–2hr 45min); Tomar (2 daily; 2hr); Viseu (2–5 daily; 1hr 20min–2hr 20min).

Faro to: Évora (4 daily; 3hr 35min); Olhão (every 15min–1hr; 20min); Tavira (7–11 daily; 1hr); Lisbon (5–10 daily; 4hr 20min); Sevilla (2 daily; 5hr).

Leiria to: Alcobaça (4 daily; 50min); Batalha (5 daily; 15min); Coimbra (10 daily; 50min); Fátima (9 daily; 25min); Tomar (2 daily; 1hr 10min–2hr).

Oporto to: Braga (hourly; 1hr); Bragança (3 daily; 1hr 50min–3hr); Coimbra (8–10 daily; 1hr 30min); Guimarães (12 daily; 2hr); Viana do Castelo (12–14 daily; 2hr); Vila Real (9 daily; 2hr); Viseu (8 daily; 2hr).

Viseu to: Guarda (2–5 daily; 2hr 15min); Oporto (8 daily; 2hr); Peso da Régua (2–6 daily; 1hr 30min).

CHAPTER 23

ROMANIA

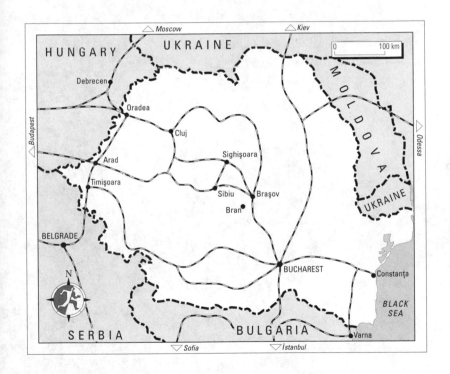

Introduction

No journey to Eastern Europe would be complete without paying a visit to **Romania**. The country has suffered somewhat from a poor public image over the last few years, but don't be deterred by this – travel in Romania is as rewarding as it is challenging. Outstanding landscapes, a huge diversity of wildlife and bizarre mix of cultures and people await those willing to seek them out. However, unless you visit on a package, it is one of the hardest countries of the former Eastern bloc to cope with. The regime of Nicolae Ceauşescu left the country on the verge of bankruptcy, and the semi-reformed economy that has since emerged seems to be characterized by hustle and sharp practice.

Romanians trace their ancestry back to the Romans, and it's not unfair to say that "Latin" traits prevail. The people are generally warm, spontaneous, anarchic, and appreciative of style and life's pleasures. In addition to ethnic Romanians, there are communities from half a dozen other races and cultures: Transylvanian Germans (Saxons) reside around the fortified towns and churches built to guard the mountain passes during the Middle Ages; so do some one and a half million Magyars, many of whom pursue a traditional lifestyle long since vanished in Hungary; and along the coast and in the Danube Delta there's a mixture of Ukrainians, Serbs, Bulgarians, Gypsies, Turks and Tatars.

The capital, **Bucharest** (Bucureşti), is, perhaps, daunting for the first-time visitor – its savage history is only too evident wherever you look – but parts of this once-beautiful city retain a certain voyeuristic appeal. More attractive by far – and easily accessible on Romania's public transport system – is **Transylvania**, a region steeped in history and legend, offering some of the most beautiful, yet unknown, mountain scenery in Europe.

Information and maps

Getting hold of **information** remains a nightmare in Romania. Western-style tourist information offices are virtually nonexistent and the state-owned ONT-Carpaţi is next to useless – a lot of the information provided here will be out of date. You're better off going to privately run tourist agencies, many of which have English-speaking staff.

Town and country **maps** (*harta*) are easier to come by. Most bookshops and street vendors selling magazines and books have up-to-date maps, though it remains best to buy them in your home country.

Money and Banks

Romania's currency, the **leu** (plural lei) comes in notes of 1000, 2000, 5000, 10,000, 50,000, 100,000 and 500,000 lei, with coins of 500 and 1000 lei. Many new plastic notes are entering circulation so when changing money it's best to ask for these. The leu has seen hyperinflation in recent years; exchange rates are volatile.

Exchanging money in most towns and cities should not be a problem, and is best done at private exchange bureaus rather than official tourist offices or banks, as they offer competitive rates. If you have torn or defaced Western banknotes, though, you'll have to change them at a bank. Whatever you do, don't change money on the streets – you'll be ripped off.

Romania still has a cash-oriented economy so take along a stash of **dollars**, preferably in small denominations. **Travellers' cheques** are seldom accepted and commission rates are sky-high. The only brand of travellers' cheque that guarantees a refund in the event of loss is American Express, whose agent is in Bucharest at B-dul Magheru 43. **Credit cards** are becoming increasingly accepted at hotels and some more upmarket shops and supermarkets. Finding an **ATM** (*Bancomat*) isn't difficult – just don't rely on it working.

For the Western tourist, **costs** in Romania are pretty low, though prices in Bucharest are naturally higher than elsewhere. Travel is generally cheap – your biggest expense will be for accommodation.

Communications

Post offices (*Poşta Româna*) in towns are open Mon–Fri 7am–8pm, Sat 8am–noon. **Stamps** (*timbru*) and prepaid envelopes (*plic*) can be bought here. Expect letters sent abroad to take seven days – postcards take longer.

Telephone calls can be made from the orange cardphones dotted around all towns and cities, all of which allow you to make international calls. **Phonecards** (either 50,000 or 100,000 lei) are available from post offices, and some metro stations in Bucharest. International calls can also be made via the operator (dial ☎971). If you can't find a cardphone, make your way to the post office in whichever town you're in. Call rates are cheaper between 11pm and 7am.

Internet access is available in virtually every town and city, but expect slow connection speeds.

Getting Around

Public transport in Romania is cheap and reliable, though both the trains and roads are poorly maintained. The country is relatively large so allow plenty of time for getting around.

■ Trains

Travelling by **train** is the best way of covering distances of over 100km on public transport, although unless you travel first class (*clasa unu*) or go on an *InterCity* train, you're likely to find it packed, so **seat reservations** (see below) are advisable. *InterCity* trains are the most expensive, clean and comfortable, with all the mod cons; they're closely followed by modern *Rapid* trains, which are almost as pricey but don't have the facilities. *Acelerats* are cheaper, slower and dirtier but offer more frequent stops and the *Personal* trains, which tend to be double-deckers, are excruciatingly slow, crowded and stop everywhere. Most overnight and international trains have **sleeping carriages** (*vagon de dormit*) and **couchettes** (*cuşet*) for a modest surcharge. On all trains, smoking is allowed only in the corridors and bear in mind that locals hate having the train windows open, even on hot days, as they see it as being unhealthy.

Rather than queue at the station, you're better off buying tickets and booking seats at the local **Agenţia SNCFR** up to 48 hours in advance – offices are generally open Mon–Fri 8am–7pm. If you buy your ticket at the station you can only do so up to one hour in advance. You can also buy return tickets for international journeys and various tourist routes to the mountains and the coast. InterRail passes are valid, Eurail are not.

■ Buses

Intercity and rural **bus** (*autobuz*) services should really only be used if a train does not serve your destination. Most routes offer only a few buses each day and some don't even run to a timetable. In the countryside, finding a bus stop often comes down to spotting people queuing randomly on the street, and on Sundays a lot of regions have no service at all. In towns, you'll also come across **trams and trolleybuses** (*tramvai* and *troleibuz*).

■ Driving and Hitching

Given the state of public transport, it may make sense to travel by **car**, although many roads are full of potholes and badly lit and local drivers somewhat anarchic. Petrol stations are sprouting up everywhere but it's wise to carry a full petrol canister in isolated regions such as the mountains and the far north of the country. You'll need an **International Driving Licence** and should have Green Card **insurance**, though temporary insurance is available at the borders. Foreign motorists belonging to organizations affiliated to the ACR (Romanian Automobile Club) receive free or cut-price technical **assistance**; and you can get motoring information from their head office in Bucharest at Str Tache Ionescu 27 (☎01/650 2595). For the ACR breakdown services phone the easy to remember ☎12345. **Car rental** is very pricey; local rates start at around £60/$90 a day with unlimited mileage. Major companies such as Hertz, Avis and Europcar have offices in all major cities.

Hitchhiking is legal on all roads with the exception of motorways (*Autostradă*). If you hitch you should offer some money but the driver is likely to refuse if you're foreign. When you successfully thumb down a car ask how much the driver wants ("*Cât costă pentru (destination)?*"; "*Opreşti aici.*" ("Stop here.") is also useful. Women are strongly advised not to hitch alone.

Accommodation

Though it will be your largest expense, **accommodation** is affordable in Romania. Beds can be booked through tourist offices, but you'll pay more than if you go directly to the place yourself. Finding a room in any resort in peak season is difficult, so you may want to consider booking ahead.

Apart from a growing number of four- and five-star hotels offering Western comforts (and prices), **hotel** standards tend to be fairly low. The cheaper hotels will cost between £4.50–8/$7–12 per night per per-

ACCOMMODATION PRICE CODES

Throughout this guide, accommodation is coded on a scale of ① to ⑨, the code indicating the lowest price per person per night you could expect to pay in each establishment in high season. With hostels this is the nightly rate per person; with hotels, the price is arrived at by dividing the cost of the cheapest double room by two. The prices indicated by the codes are as follows:

① under £5/$8	④ £15–20/$24–32	⑦ £30–35/$48–56
② £5–10/$8–16	⑤ £20–25/$32–40	⑧ £35–40/$56–64
③ £10–15/$16–24	⑥ £25–30/$40–48	⑨ £40/$64 and over

son, for a reasonably clean room and shared shower – check the availability of hot water; breakfast is normally an extra £1.50/$2. An alternative is to stay in a **private house** (*cazare la persoane particulare*), which may actually be the only option in smaller towns and villages. Usually you'll come across people offering accommodation at the train or bus stations; if approached ask them "*Cât costă pe noapte?*" ("How much per night?"). Private rooms tend to be cheaper than hotel rooms, and will be basic but comfortable. Expect to pay around £6/$10 per night.

Romania has a shortage of budget accommodation. Official hostels are scarce – the only ones are in Bucharest. Otherwise, university towns will have **student accommodation** (*caminul de studenţi*) from late June to August, which should cost around £1.50/$2 per night. There are around 150 **campsites** in the country, most of which offer very basic amenities. Expect to pay around £2.25/$3 per night for tent space, with little more than a tap and dirty loo. Some offer cabins for around £3/$4 per night.

Food and Drink

During the Ceauşescu years **food** became a precious commodity in what had been known as the breadbasket of Eastern Europe. Luckily, the situation is now far better. **Breakfast** (*micul dejun*) is typically a light meal, featuring rolls and butter (*chifle cu unt*) and an *omleta* – or long sausages (*patriciani*) – washed down with a large coffee (*cafea mare*) or tea (*ceai*). As for **snacks** – known as *gustări* – the most common are flaky pastries (*pateuri*) filled with cheese (*cu brânză*) or meat (*cu carne*), often dispensed through hatches in the walls of bakeries; sandwiches (*sandvici* or *tartină*); and a variety of spicy grilled sausages and meatballs such as *mici* and *chiftele*, which are normally sold by street vendors.

For **sit-down meals** it's best to go upmarket, since the choice of dishes in cheaper restaurants tends to be limited to grilled meats, French fries,

burgers and pizzas. The menus of most Romanian restaurants concentrate on grilled meats, or *friptura*. *Cotlet de porc* is the common pork chop, while *muşchi de vacă* denotes fillet of beef. Dishes usually arrive with a garnish of French fries, a minimalist side salad, and vegetables.

At smarter **restaurants** there's a fair likelihood of finding traditional Romanian dishes, which can be delicious. The best known of these is *sarmale* – pickled cabbage stuffed with rice, meat and herbs, usually served with sour cream. Stews (*tocană*) and other dishes often feature a sclerotic combination of meat and dairy products; ham and eggs (fried) are popular, as is *snitzel*. Most savoury dishes are topped with cheese.

Vegetarians in ordinary restaurants could try asking for *caşcaval pane* (hard cheese fried in breadcrumbs); *ghiveci* (mixed fried veg); *ardei umpluţii* (stuffed peppers) or vegetables and salads. When in doubt, stipulate something "*fără carne, vă rog*" (without meat, please), or enquire "*este cu carne?*" ("does it contain meat?").

Establishments called **cofetărie** serve coffee and cakes, and sometimes beer and ice cream. Coffee, whether *cafea naturală* (finely ground and cooked Turkish fashion), *filtru* (filtered), or *ness* (instant coffee) is usually drunk black and sweet; ask for it *cu lapte* or *fără zahăr* if you prefer it with milk or without sugar. The *cofetărie* is a good place to pick up daytime snacks: *cornuri* are croissants, *chifle* bread rolls, and *prăjituri* sweet buns. **Cakes** and **desserts** are sticky and sweet, as throughout the Balkans. Romanians enjoy pancakes (*clătite*) and pies (*plăcintă*) with various fillings; Turkish-influenced *baclava* and *cataif cu frisca*; and the traditional *dulceaţă*, or glass of jam.

Evening **drinking** takes place in outdoor beer gardens, more attractive *cramas* (beer cellars), restaurants (where boozers often outnumber the diners), and in a growing number of Western European-style cafés and bars. As an aperitif, or at any other time, people like to drink **ţuică**, a powerful plum brandy taken neat; in rural areas, it is homemade and often twice distilled to yield fearsomely strong *palincă*. Most **beer** (*bere*) is bottled, in the Germanic lager style. Romania's best **wines** are *Grasca* and *Feteasca Neagră* from the vineyards of Cotnari and Dealul Mare, and the sweet dessert wines of Murfatlar. Mineral water (*apă minerală*) and international **soft drinks**, such as Coke and Pepsi, are readily available.

Opening hours and holidays

Like so many things in Romania, **opening hours** are unreliable. You'll find most shops open Mon–Fri 9am–6pm, with some supermarkets open as late as 8pm. Museums and castles are open at similar times (though most are closed on Mon or Tues); **admission charges** are minimal and have therefore not been listed in the *Guide*. Most are open on Saturday morning, a few on Sunday morning. **National holidays** are: Jan 1 & 2; Easter Monday; May 1; Dec 1; and Dec 25 & 26.

Emergencies

Petty crime is on the increase in Romania; it's wise to pay attention to your belongings in crowded places and try not to flaunt the fact you are a tourist. Buses in Bucharest, in particular, are pickpockets' paradise. If your passport goes missing tell your embassy straight away, but you'll have to go to Bucharest to get a new one. Police stations can issue temporary emergency visas. You should also report thefts to the **police** (*Poliţa*) – but you'll most likely find them unhelpful and bureaucratic.

Make sure you have health insurance before going to Romania. In the event of a **health emergency**, dial the number given below. Bucharest's central emergency hospital is up to Western standards and Medicover, Calea Plevnei 96 (☎01/310-4066/310-4411), also offers Western-standard care, with English-speaking doctors; expect to pay £30-300/$40–400, depending on the problem. Bucharest is, at long last, starting to do something about its street **dog problem**, but you should still pay attention in the city's suburbs. If you are bitten go immediately to the hospital for jabs. Most cities have a well-stocked pharmacy (*farmacie*) and good dentist (*stomatologist*).

EMERGENCY NUMBERS
Police ☎955; Ambulance ☎961.

TRANSYLVANIA AND THE BANAT

The likeliest approach to Romania is by train from adjoining Hungary, from where two main rail routes take you through **Transylvania**. Whether you take the line via Arad, or the less popular one via Cluj, you should disembark before reaching Bucharest to see the best of the country. Thanks to Bram Stoker and Hammer films, Transylvania is famed abroad as the homeland of **Dracula**: a mountainous place where storms lash medieval hamlets, while wolves – or werewolves – howl from the woods. Happily, the fictitious image is accurate, up to a point. The scenery is dramatic, there are spooky Gothic citadels, and one Vlad (born in Sighişoara) did style himself Dracula and earned the grim nickname "The Impaler". But the Dracula image is just one element of Transylvania, whose 99,837 square kilometres take in caves, alpine meadows, dense forests sheltering bears and wild boars, and lowland valleys where buffalo cool off in the rivers.

The population is a jigsaw of Romanians, Magyars, Germans, Gypsies and others, formed over centuries of migration and colonization. The Trianon Treaty of 1920 placed Transylvania within the Romanian state, shifting the balance of power in favour of the Romanian majority, but the character of many towns still reflects past patterns of settlement and domination. **Cluj**, for example, is strongly Hungarian-influenced, but most striking of all are the *Stuhls* – the former seats of Saxon power – with their medieval streets, defensive towers and fortified churches. **Sighişoara**, the most picturesque, could almost be the Saxons' cenotaph: their culture has evaporated here, leaving only their citadels and churches, as it threatens to do in **Braşov** and **Sibiu**, and in the old German settlements roundabout. A similarly complex ethnic mix is found in **the Banat**, to the east of Transylvania proper and the westernmost region of Romania as a whole; the chief town here is **Timişoara**, crucible of the 1989 revolution.

Timişoara

TIMIŞOARA (*www.timisoara.ro*), 50km south of the rail junction at Arad, evolved around a Magyar fortress at the marshy confluence of the Timiş and Bega, and from the fourteenth century onwards functioned as the capital of the Banat. The Turks conquered the town in 1552, and ruled the surrounding terrain from here until 1716. The Habsburgs who ejected them proved relatively benign masters, and during the late nineteenth century the municipality rode a wave of progress, becoming one of the first towns in the world to have horse-drawn trams and the first in Europe to install electric street-lighting. This was also the period when Temeschwar (its German name) acquired many of its current features, including the **Bega Canal**, which cups the southern side of the historic centre and is flanked by a procession of stately **parks**.

Timişoara's fame abroad rests on its crucial role in the overthrow of the Ceauşescu regime. A local Hungarian priest, László Tökes, took a stand on the rights of his community, and when the police came to turf him out of his house on December 16, 1989, his parishioners barred their way. The five-day battle that ensued ended with the workers at the oil refinery forcing the troops to withdraw by threatening to blow the place sky-high. These events provided crucial inspiration for the people of Bucharest, so that Timişoara now regards itself as the guardian of the revolution – memorials around town mark the places where the democratic martyrs fell, and many streets have been renamed in their honour.

Approaching from the train station along B-dul Republicii, the town's architectural assets don't become evident until one enters the centre, with its carefully planned streets and squares. On Piaţa Huniade, just beyond the plush **Opera House**, you'll find the **Museum of the Banat** (Tues–Sun 10am–5pm) occupying the castle once extended by Iancu de Hunedoara. Warlords and rebels figure prominently in the large historical section, as does the great strike of 1920 in support of the Banat's union with Romania.

The central Piața Libertății boasts as fine a Baroque **Town Hall** as any municipality could wish for. Two blocks north of here, Piața Unirii's **Museum of Fine Arts**, displaying work by minor Italian, German and Flemish masters, is overshadowed by the monumental **Roman Catholic and Serbian Orthodox Cathedrals**. Built between 1736 and 1773, the former is a fine example of Viennese Baroque, designed by Fischer von Erlach; the latter is roughly contemporaneous and almost as impressive. The **Romanian Orthodox Cathedral** is located to the south of here, between the Opera House and the canal; completed in 1946, it blends neo-Byzantine and Moldavian architectural elements and exhibits a collection of icons (usually Wed–Sun 11am–3pm; ask at the bookstall inside the cathedral) in its basement.

In 1868, the municipality purchased the redundant citadel from the Habsburgs, and demolished all but two sections, the **Bastions**, to the east and west of Piața Unirii. Parts of each have been converted into wine bars, whilst to the east another section is occupied by an **Ethnographic Museum** (Tues–Sun 10am–5pm). Varied folk costumes and coloured charts illustrate the region's ethnic diversity effectively, but in an anodyne fashion – for example, there's no mention of the thousands of Serbs deported in 1951 when the Party turned hostile towards Tito's neighbouring Yugoslavia.

Practicalities

Timișoara's **train station**, Timișoara Nord, is a fifteen-minute walk east of the centre, along B-dul Republicii; the **bus station** is across the canal from the train station at Str Reșița 54. Finding a place to stay in Timișoara is becoming easier as increasingly more foreign investments and tourists come to the city. The *Banatul*, B-dul Republicii 5 (☎056/190130; ②), is central, renovated and clean; though the rooms are basic, they are en suite and all have their own TV. Another good place with an inappropriate name is the *Hotel Arizona*, Str Muzicescu 168 (☎056/185557 or 201221; ③), which has very clean, en suite rooms. *The Timișoara*, Str 9 Mai 2 (☎056/198854; ③), just behind the Opera House, has pretty plush en suite rooms with TVs. There's also a fairly basic but clean **campsite** on Aleea Pădurea Verde (☎056/208925), 4km east of town – take trolleybus #11 from the train station to the Strandul Tineretului terminus.

For good Romanian **food**, go to *Club XXI*, Piața Victoriei 2, which offers large, hearty meals and the best soups around. Staff wear all the traditional attire and are efficient and friendly. For a treat, try *The Maestro*, B-dul Janos 3 (☎056/293861), which serves high-quality local and international food in a great cellar, but at prices you may pay back home. In the evenings, hanging out in the studenty art-deco **bar**, *The Note*, Str Fagului 22, or the *Owen Roes Irish Pub*, Str Cetații 15, is well worth it for meeting a mixed local crowd. The canal-side *Jazz Club Pod 16*, on the banks of the Bega Canal just behind the Orthodox Cathedral, is great for summer evenings and offers **live music**. The *Java Coffeehouse*, Str Pacha 6 (☎056/132495; 10am–midnight; $1/hr), is a hip **Internet café**.

Cluj-Napoca

With its cupolas, Baroque outcroppings and weathered *fin-de-siècle* backstreets, downtown **CLUJ-NAPOCA** (*www.cjnet.ro*) looks like a Hungarian provincial capital – which in a sense it once was. In Hungary, and indeed within Transylvania itself, many people still regret the passing of Kolozsvár (the Hungarian name for the city), fondly recalled as a place that embodied the Magyar *belle époque*. Modern Cluj has scores of factories and over 300,000 inhabitants, but the city has retained something of the languor and raffish undercurrent that characterized it in the olden days – not to mention cultural fixtures like its opera and university.

The Town

In the centre of town is the Piața Unirii, a square dominated by the grand mid-fourteenth century **St Michael's Church**. Dwarfing the congregation in the bare nave, mighty pillars curve into vaulting like the canopy of a forest. St Michael's Gothic phase of construction ended three years before the death of the Hungarian king, Mátyás Corvinus (1440–90). He and his wife, Beatrix of Naples, had brought the culture of Renaissance Italy to the region, while his formidable "Black Army" kept the Kingdom of Hungary safe from lawlessness and invasion. Outside the church an imposing equestrian statue of the king accepts the homage of four dignitaries, with the crescent banner of the Turks trampled under hoof. Mátyás' birthplace was the small mansion at Str Matei Corvin 6, up a side street leading north off the square. It now houses the Fine Arts faculty of the university, although you can peek inside the courtyard. On the east side of the square, the **Art Museum** (Tues–Sun 10am–6pm) houses the superbly carved sixteenth-century Jimbor altar and paintings by Transylvanian artists. Many of the items were expropriated from Magyar aristocracy, in particular the Bánffy family, whose mansion this building once was.

Just to the north of the main square, at Str Daicovici 2, the **History Museum of Transylvania** (Wed–Sun 10am–4pm) is largely given over to charting the progress from the Neolithic and Bronze ages to the rise of the Dacian civilization, which peaked between the second century BC and the first AD. The Dacii were subdued by Roman legions, and the two races subsequently intermingled to form the ancestors of today's Romanians – or so the official version of Romanian history goes. An alternative theory, promulgated by those who insist on the Hungarian identity of this region, is that the Dacii died out completely, and that the Magyars took possession of a region that had no other legitimate claimants.

West of Piaţa Unirii, at Str Memorandumului 21, Cluj's **Ethnographic Museum** (Tues–Sun 9am–5pm) contains what is probably Romania's finest collection of carpets and folk costumes, demonstrating the country's various styles of weaving, from the dark herringbone patterns of the Padureni region to the bold yellow, black and red stripes of Maramureş – and an even greater variety of clothing and headgear. Southwest of Piaţa Unirii, at Str Republicii 42, you'll find probably the best **botanical gardens** in the country (daily 9am–8pm), including Japanese and rose gardens.

Practicalities

The **train station** is about 1.5km north of the centre, on Piaţa Gării; take a #3, #4 or #9 trolleybus to Piaţa Unirii, or make the twenty-minute walk there down Str Horea. There are two **bus stations**, one on Str Aurel Vlaicu on the eastern fringe of the city and one over the bridge next to the train station. The best value **hotel** is probably the dead central *Continental*, Str Napoca 1 (☎064/195405; ②), which has clean rooms with TVs. There's a beautifully kitsch restaurant downstairs. Another cheap and central option is the *Hotel Pax* at Piaţa Gării 1 (☎064/432927; ①), right outside the station. For some real luxury, try the *White House Villa*, Str Emil Racoviţa 22 (☎064/432277; ④), located in a nice old central building and providing large beds, TV and telephone in en-suite rooms. For a commanding view of the city, the modern *Hotel Transilvania*, Str Calaraşilor 1–3 (☎064/432071; ②), located on top of Cetaţuia Hill, is the place to be. The hotel has 250 state-owned but pleasant rooms, but is – as you might expect – a bit of a climb to reach. There's a **campsite** in the Făget hills to the southeast – supposedly the location of a lot of UFO sightings and supernatural phenomena; to get there, take bus #40A from behind the National Theatre.

There are many **restaurants** and **bars** around Piaţa Unirii and in the streets branching off. *Hubertus*, Str 21 Decembrie 22 (☎064/196743), serves up good local food, including game. *Matei Corvin*, Str Matei 3 (☎064/197496), offers typically Transylvanian specialities – or a menu of Romanian and Hungarian dishes to be less poetic. The *Gradina de Vară*, Str Iuliu Maniu 34, just off Piaţa Unirii, offers food and drinks in its courtyard along with classical music concerts. The trendy *Diesel*, Piaţa Unirii 17, offers live concerts and DJ nights in its basement. For a more studenty feel, go to the *Music Pub*, Str Horia 5, where you can also pick up a bite to eat. *Insomnia*, Str Iuliu Maniu 4, has a bohemian feel to it and is a good place to relax and have a drink for next to nothing.

Cluj is full of **Internet cafés**. Two of the best are Demo Internet, Str Memorandumului 6 (☎064/198679; 24hr; $1.25/hr), and the central Codec Internet, Piaţa Unirii, on the corner with Str Iuliu Maniu (☎064/193198; 9am–11pm; $1/hr).

Sibiu

"I rubbed my eyes in amazement", wrote Walter Starkie of **SIBIU** (*www.sibiunet.ro*) in 1929. "The town where I found myself did not seem to be in Transylvania . . . the narrow streets and old gabled houses made me think of Nuremberg." Nowadays the illusion is harder to sustain, but Sibiu's older quarters could still serve to illustrate the Brothers Grimm. Some people here speak German and cherish links with faraway Germany, calling Sibiu "Hermannstadt", the name given by the Transylvanian Saxons to this, their chief city. Like Braşov, Sibiu was founded by Germans invited by the Hungarian King Géza II to colonize strategic regions of Transylvania in 1143. Its inhabitants came to dominate trade in Transylvania and Wallachia, forming exclusive guilds under royal charter. The Turks dubbed Sibiu the "Red Town" on account of its red-brick defensive walls with their forty towers, built in the fifteenth century, and the bloodshed in attempting to breach them. Alas for the Saxons, their citadels were no protection against the tide of history, which eroded their influence after the eighteenth century. Within the last decade almost the entire Saxon community has left Romania.

To reach the centre from the main train and bus stations, cross the square and follow Str Gen. Magheru until you hit **Piaţa Mare**. Traditionally the hub of public life, it's surrounded by the premises of sixteenth- and seventeenth-century merchants, whose acumen and thrift were proverbial. On its western side stands the **Brukenthal Museum** (Tues–Sun 9am–5pm), one of the finest in Romania. Besides the best of local silverware, pottery and furniture, it has an evocative collection of works by Transylvanian painters. The city's **History Museum** (Tues–Sun 9am–5pm) is housed in the Old City Hall, just to the north, a building well worth a look even if you aren't interested in the contents.

On the north side of Piaţa Mare, the **Councillors' Tower** forms a phalanx with a Catholic church, largely blocking access to the Piaţa Mică, (Little Square). Just beyond, on Piaţa Huet, the **Evangelical Cathedral** (Mon–Fri 9am–1pm) – a massive hall-church raised during the fourteenth and fifteenth centuries – dominates its neighbours. The crypt contains the tomb of Mihnea the Bad, Dracula's son, who was stabbed to death outside in 1510.

Behind the cathedral, the **Passage of Stairs**, overshadowed by arches and the medieval citadel wall, descends into the lower town. Just to the east, Str Ocnei runs down through a kind of miniature urban canyon spanned by the elegant wrought-iron **Liars' Bridge** – so called because of the legend that no one can stand on it and tell a lie without the structure collapsing. Further to the east, on the far side of Piaţa Mică another ancient stairway leads down to Str Movilei, pock-marked with medieval windows, doorways and turrets. Down in the rambling lower town is the octagonal-based **Tanners' Tower** on Str Pulberăriei, part of the now-demolished Ocna Gate.

Sibiu also has an outstanding open-air museum, the **Muzeul Civilzaţiei Populare** on Calea Dumbrăvii, some 5km south of the centre; take trolleybus #T1 to the end of the line. The museum offers a fantastic insight into Romanian rural life, with authentic seventeenth-century houses and windmills, plus a traditional inn serving local food and drink.

Practicalities

The **train and bus stations** are next to each other on Piaţa 1 Dec 1918, 1km northeast of town; a ten-minute walk down Str General Magheru will take you into the main square. Sibiu has an excellent new **tourist office** bang in the centre of town at Str Nicolae Bălcescu 7 (✆ & fax 069/211110, *www.primsb.ro*). The best value **accommodation** is the popular and recently renovated *Împăratul Romanilor*, Str Bălcescu 4 (✆069/216500 or 092/416490; ③), which still has something of its original 1930s glamour. Those who like a little peace and quiet should head off to the well-equipped *Palace Dumbrava* at Pădurea Dumbrava 1, opposite the outdoor museum (✆069/422920 or 218086, fax 422222; ③). For considerably less outlay, and a more homely experience, contact Antrec Homestays (✆069/220179, fax 233803) who can fix you up with a nice room in a private house for $4–12.

Excellent local **food** is served up at *Mara*, Str Băcescu 21 (☎069/217025). The *Restaurant Gasthof Clara*, Str Râului 24 (☎069/222914, fax 224003), is also well worth trying; it offers both local and German dishes, as well as room to stay the night (③). Even though Sibiu seems to go to sleep at 9pm, there are a few places to hang out till the early hours. *Art Café*, Str Filarmonicii 2, is arty, cool, and a good place to meet the trendy local set. *The Cotton Club*, Str Ion Raţiu 9 (☎069/211516) is open till 5am, plays some better than average music and is ultra-trendy.

There's **Internet access** at Verena, Str Anton Pann 12 (☎069/233355; 24hr; $0.50/hr) and at Împăratul Romanilor, Str Bălcescu 4 (☎069/216500 or 416490; 24hr; $1/hr).

Sighişoara

A forbidding silhouette of battlements and needle spires looms over **SIGHIŞOARA** as the sun descends behind the hills of the Târnave Mare valley, and it seems fitting that this was the birthplace of **Vlad Ţepeş** – the man known to posterity as Dracula. Sighişoara makes the perfect introduction to Transylvania, especially as the Dacia, Traianus, Pannonia and Alutus international trains stop here during daylight, enabling travellers to break the long journey between Budapest and Bucharest.

The route from the train and bus stations to the centre passes close to the **Romanian Orthodox Cathedral**, its gleaming white, multifaceted facade a striking contrast to the dark interior, where blue and orange hues dominate the small panels of the iconostasis. Across the Târnave Mare river, the **Citadel** dominates the town from a rocky massif whose slopes support a jumble of ancient, leaning houses, their windows sited to cover the steps leading up from Piaţa Hermann Oberth to the main gateway. Above the gateway rises the mighty **Clock Tower** where, at the stroke of midnight, a wooden figure emerges from the belfry to mark the new day. The tower was founded in the fourteenth century when Sighişoara became a free town controlled by craft guilds – each of which had to finance the construction of a bastion and defend it during wartime – and rebuilt after earthquakes and fire in the 1670s. Sighişoara grew rich on the proceeds of trade with Moldavia and Wallachia, as attested by the regalia and strongboxes in the tower's **museum** (Tues–Sun 9am–3.30pm).

In 1431 or thereabouts, the child later known as **Dracula** was born in a two-storey house within the shadow of the clock tower at Str Muzeului 6. At the time his father – Vlad Dracul – was commander of the mountain passes into Wallachia, but the younger Vlad's privileged childhood ended eight years later, when he and his brother Radu were sent to Anatolia as hostages to the Turks. There Vlad observed the Turks' use of terror, which he would later turn against them, earning the nickname of "The Impaler". Nowadays, Vlad's birthplace is a tacky restaurant, while the **Museum of Armaments** next door (Tues–Sun 10am–3.30pm) has a small and poorly presented Dracula Exhibition. The emphasis is on his patriotic anti-Turkish deeds, while his subsequent reputation for cruelty is portrayed as the invention of hostile Saxon propagandists.

Churches are monuments to social identity here, as in many old Transylvanian towns. The Germans raised one opposite the clock tower; its stark, whitewashed interior is hung with colourful carpets, as in the Black Church at Braşov. Their other church, the **Bergkirche** (Church on the Hill), is approached by an impressive covered wooden stairway which ascends steeply from the far end of Str Şcolii. Ivy-grown and massively buttressed, the church has a roomy interior that seems austere despite the blue and canary yellow vaulting. However, it's unlikely you'll get inside for a while anyway, as the church is undergoing a massive renovation. Some lovely stone tombs near the entrance are a harbinger of the German cemetery, a melancholy, weed-choked mass of graves spilling over the hill beside the ruined citadel walls – nine of whose fourteen towers survive.

The **lower town** is less appealing than the Citadel, but there's a nice ambience around the shabby centre – consisting of Piaţa Hermann Oberth and Str 1 Decembrie – where townsfolk gather to consume grilled sausages and beer, conversing in Romanian, Magyar and antiquated German.

Practicalities

Sighişoara's **train station** is on the northern edge of the town, on Str Libertaţii, and the **bus station** is immediately to the east. **Hotels** are few and far between. The friendly and recently renovated *Pensiunea Turistică Hera*, Str Eminescu 62 (☎065/778850, fax 773191; ②), is spacious, cheap and clean; of for a little more expense, there's the picturesque *Poienţa*, Str D. Cantemir 24 (☎065/772739; ③), which has good views, nice rooms and a swimming pool, and all just a short walk from the centre. If you want a private room for the night, go to the Steaua Agenţie de Turism, Str 1 Decembrie 1918 12 (☎065/771072), which should be able to help. Expect to pay around $7–14 a night. The not-so-chic, but bearable *Hotel Chic*, Str Libertăţi 44 (☎065/775901; ②), is opposite the railway station, and handy if you arrive late on an international train.

When it comes to restaurants, there's plenty of choice in Sighişoara. *Rustic*, Str 1 Decembrie 1918, is anything but rustic, but offers fairly good local food; *Joker*, Str Tache Ionescu 19, offers hearty dishes at bargain prices; while *The Casa Vlad Dracul*, Piaţa Muzeului, is of interest primarily as Vlad Ţepeş' birthplace – the food here is limited and mediocre, but cheap.

The only **Internet café** is Kolping, Str Ilarie Chendi 3 (☎065/777664 or 094/785778, *www.kolping.ro*; 24hr; $0.75/hr).

Braşov and around

With an eye for trade and invasion routes, the medieval Saxons sited their largest settlements within a day's journey of Transylvania's mountain passes. **BRAŞOV** (*www.brasov.ro*), which they called Kronstadt, grew prosperous as a result, and for centuries the Saxons constituted an elite whose economic power long outlasted its feudal privileges. The Communist government, wanting to create its "own" skilled working class, brought thousands of Moldavian villagers to Braşov, where they were trained to work in the new factories and given modern housing during the 1960s. As a result, there are two parts to Braşov: the quasi-Gothic bit coiled beneath Mount Tâmpa and Mount Postăvaru, which looks great, and the surrounding sprawl of flats and factories, which doesn't. **Old Braşov** is worth at least a day's sightseeing, and the proximity of "Dracula's Castle" at Bran makes the city a worthy stopoff.

From the train station bus #4 lurches down to the central park beside B-dul Eroilor, which meets the eastern end of the pedestrianized Str Republicii, the hub of Braşov's social life and hosting a constant throng of strollers. At the top of Str Republicii, sturdy buildings line the main square – the Piaţa Sfatului – as if on parade, presenting their shopfronts to the fifteenth-century council house, which has now been relegated to the role of **History Museum** (Tues–Sun 10am–5pm). As can be guessed from the exhibits, Braşov used to be dominated by Saxon guilds, whose main hangout was the Merchants' Hall, built in the "Transylvanian Renaissance" style of the sixteenth century. Within sight of its terrace is the town's most famous landmark, the **Black Church** (Mon–Sat 10am–3.30pm), which stabs upwards like a series of daggers. An endearingly monstrous hall-church that took almost a century to complete (1385–1477), it is so called for its soot-blackened walls, the result of being torched by the Austrian army in 1689. Inside, by contrast, the church is startlingly white, with Oriental carpets hung in splashes of colour along the walls of the nave. In summer (June–Sept Tues, Thurs & Sat at 6pm), the church's 4000-pipe **Bucholz organ** is used for concerts.

When Turkish expansion became a threat in the fifteenth century, the inhabitants began to fortify Braşov, assigning the defence of each bastion or rampart to a particular guild. A length of fortress wall runs along the foot of Mount Tâmpa, beneath a maze of paths and a **cable car** running up to the summit. Of the original seven bastions the best preserved is that of the weavers, on Str Coşbuc. This complex of wooden galleries and bolt holes now contains the **Museum of the Bârsa Land Fortifications** (Tues–Sun 10am–4pm). Inside are models, pictures and weaponry recalling the bad old days when the surrounding region was repeatedly attacked by Tatars, Turks and, on a couple of occasions, by Dracula – who impaled hundreds of captives along the heights of St Jacob's Hill to terrorize the townsfolk.

Practicalities

Braşov's **train station** and principal **bus station** are northeast of the old town, 2km from the centre – take bus #4 into town. You're likely to be offered **private rooms** (①–②) outside the station; otherwise, there's excellent, inexpensive and central accommodation at the backpackers' favourite, *Hotel Aro Sport*, Str Sfântu Ioan 3 (☎068/142840; ①). *The Beke Guesthouse*, Str Cerbului 32 (no phone; ③), is cosy and professional and also very central. *Vila Silvania*, Str Căprioarei (☎068/415556; ②), is well located and has good views. Alternatively, there's the British-run and scrupulously clean *Centrul de Studii Hospice "Casa Speranţei"*, Str Piatra Mare 101 (☎068/151501 or 419780, *medipal@deuroconsult.ro*; ②), where a portion of rooms rates goes to help local cancer victims. Campers have the suburban *Dârste* **campsite**, Calea Bucureşti 285 (☎068/259080), on the road to Sinaia and Bucharest; it's best reached by taxi.

Finding a **place to eat** is no longer the hardship it was a few years ago. The area around Piaţa Sfatului and the old town is dotted with restaurants and cafés – all of which are affordable. If you're looking for good Romanian food, head straight to *Blue Corner*, Piaţa Enescu 13 (☎094/573338 or 092/381817), through the archway next to the Orthodox church in Piaţa Sfatului. Just a few metres away on Piaţa Enescu 11 is the newly opened *Bistro De L'Arte* (☎068/473994) – a German-run establishment serving up bistro dishes at slightly inflated prices. A great **place to drink** and have fun is at *Festival 39*, Str Mureşenilor 23, which is full of the strangest objects in town – from badly stuffed animals and fake plastic trophies, to what seems to be a communist-style Christmas tree. Alternatively, head a few doors up the street to *Saloon* at no. 11–13, which offers more seating and a wide range of drinks. The pleasantly cosy *Cabana*, Str Hirsher 1, is decked out like a mountain hut and is a great place to meet the locals.

Internet cafés are a-plenty in Braşov. Try the central and cheap Hercules, Piaţa Sfatului 7, (☎068/410164, *www.hercules.ro*; 24hr; \$0.75/hr). Nearby is Café Art, Str Republicii 40 (☎068/472535; 10am–midnight/2am; \$0.60/hr).

Dracula's Castle

Cosy little **BRAN**, a pleasant 28-kilometre journey by bus from Braşov, is situated at the foot of the stunning Bucegi mountains. What's now billed as **Dracula's Castle** (Tues–Sun 9am–5pm) has only tenuous associations with Vlad the Impaler – he may have attacked it in 1460 – but the hyperbole is forgivable as Bran really does look like a vampire count's residence. The castle was built in 1377 to safeguard what used to be the main route into Wallachia until the opening of the Predeal Pass, and it rises in tiers of towers and ramparts from amongst the woods, against a glorious mountain background. A warren of spiral stairs, nooks and secret chambers overhanging the courtyard, the interior is filled with elaborately carved four-poster beds, throne-like chairs and portraits of grim-faced boyars. Despite its medieval aspect, most of the interior dates from a conversion job early last century, the work of a crazed old architect commissioned by British-born Queen Marie of Romania. Marie called Bran a "pugnacious little fortress", but her alterations made it a welcoming abode, at odds with its forbidding exterior. Recent "restoration" has made it even more suburban, with patio windows and buckets of white paint. In the grounds are some old peasant buildings and the **Museum of the Bran Pass** (Tues–Sun 9am–5pm), displaying folk costumes, many of them from Marie's wardrobe. If you want a more authentically medieval experience, jump off the Braşov bus in the nearby village of Râsnov, where the castle on the hilltop at the edge of town has been restored with greater tact than that at Bran.

Buses to Bran go from Autogara 2 (opposite Bartolomeu church), 3km west of central Braşov at the junction of Str Lungă and Calea Făgăraşului; to get here, take bus #28 from Braşov's central park or bus #10 from the train station. Most people **staying at Bran** stay in the homes of locals. Either Geta, Str Bologa 355 (☎068/236692), or Ovi-Tours, Str Bologa 15 (☎068/420286), should be able to sort you out with something. Otherwise MotoRom, Str Tohăniţa 28 (☎068/471516 or 094/484500, *www.motorom.de*; ②), is a great, scenic and cheap place to stay. The last can also organize **adventure tours** into the mountains and rents out cross-country motorbikes and mountain bikes. **Eating** in Bran is sadly restricted to local shops or pizza joints.

BUCHAREST

BUCHAREST (Bucureşti) is an eye-opener for the first-time visitor. The reaction of most tourists is the urgent will to leave as soon as possible, but to do this would be missing the heart of Romania. Even though Bucharest does not really represent the rest of the country, it does have its charm and elegance – it's just that it does it in its own way. Add to which, it's a rapidly dynamic city, changing quickly. Old, grandiose tree-lined districts in the north still remain and show what the city was like in a bygone era. Head south and you'll come across unfinished projects from Ceauşescu's reign littering the landscape. Seeing the true scale of what a dictatorship can do with your own eyes is something you won't forget. Love it or hate it, Bucharest is a must-see.

Arrival, information and transport

If you are coming by plane you'll land at the surprisingly modern but small **Otopeni Airport**, 16km north of the city. It's best to ignore the hassling taxi drivers – you could easily find yourself paying $30–40 to the centre – and head for the #783 bus stop just outside to make the thirty-minute journey to the centre; note that, though you can buy your tickets on board the bus, some drivers have been known to pocket the money, so it's best to buy your ticket from the aluminium RATB kiosk just outside the entrance to the airport. Virtually all **trains** terminate at the Gara de Nord. The station has done much to improve its dodgy reputation of late, though it's still wise to keep a sharp eye on your belongings. Again, ignore offers of a taxi ride and head straight for the metro station and take a train into the centre (Piaţa Universitaţii is a good starting off point). The official **tourist agency** (ONT Carpaţi) has an office at B-dul Magheru 7 (Mon–Fri 8am–5pm, Sat & Sun 8am–1pm), and offers all you'd expect from the state-run institution. Head up B-dul N. Balcescu to make use of any one of a number of **exchange offices**.

    Public transport, although extraordinarily crowded, is efficient and cheap. The strangely lit but interesting metro system has four lines, but you'll probably only need to use two of these: line M1 (an almost circle line) and the more used M2 (north–south) complete with some swanky new trains. Above ground, you'll find a strange array of trams, buses and trolleybuses. Buy a ticket from the kiosks located near the bus stops and validate it in the machine onboard; travelling without a valid ticket can result in a $10 fine from one of the many plain-clothed inspectors. There is no nighttime transport, but thanks to a strict new mayor, the taxis tend to be fairly honest, and some drivers speak English; try Meridian (☎9444 or 9888), XXL (☎9791), Cobalcescu (☎9451) or Alfa (☎9488 or 9481). Make sure the driver has the meter running.

Accommodation

Places to stay for those on a tight budget do exist, just, but don't expect too much in the way of luxury – the hotels in the area around the Gara de Nord are your best bet, though this area can be less than salubrious, particularly at night. Due to lack of popularity, Bucharest no longer has a **campsite**, though it is possible to camp in the wilds of Băneasa forest – take bus #301 from Piaţa Romana to the end of the line.

Hostels

Villa Helga, Str Salcâmilor 2 (☎01/610-2214, *helga@rotravel.com*). A popular and friendly 34-bed youth hostel situated near the city centre. Facilities include a communal lounge with cable TV, a kitchen, showers and a free washing machine. Take trolleybus #79 or #86, or bus #133 from Gara de Nord. Get off two stops after Piaţa Romana. Noone from the *Villa Helga* meets trains at the Gara de Nord, so ignore anyone approaching you there and make your own way to the hostel instead. ①.

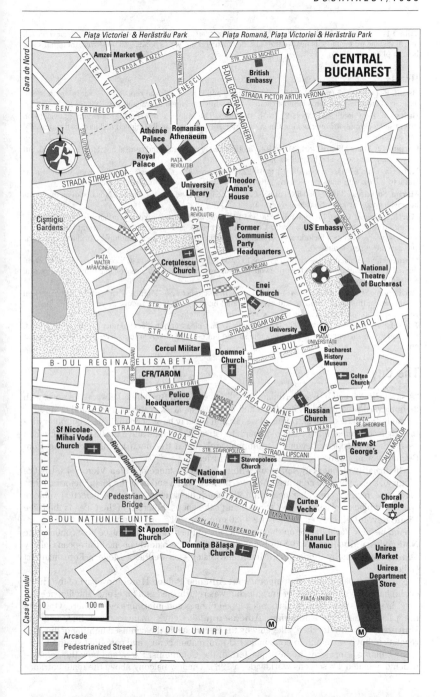

CENTRAL BUCHAREST

△ Piaţa Victoriei & Herăstrău Park   △ Piaţa Romană, Piaţa Victoriei & Herăstrău Park

Gara de Nord △

Amzei Market
STRADA P. AMZEI
STRADA ENESCU
STR. MENDELEEV
B-DUL GENERAL MAGHERU
STR. JULLES MICHELET
British Embassy
STRADA PICTOR ARTUR VERONA

STR. GEN. BERTHELOT
CALEA VICTORIEI
STR. LUTERANA

N

Athénée Palace
Romanian Athenaeum
Royal Palace
PIAŢA REVOLUŢIEI
STRADA C. A. ROSETTI
Theodor Aman's House
B-DUL N. BALCESCU
STRADA TOMA CARAGIU
STR. BATISTEI

STRADA ŞTIRBEI VODA
University Library
PIAŢA REVOLUŢIEI
STR. DR. C. IMPINENU
Former Communist Party Headquarters
US Embassy

Cişmigiu Gardens
PIAŢA WALTER MĂRĂCINEANU
Creţulescu Church
STR. CIMPINEANU
CALEA VICTORIEI
STRADA ACADEMIEI
Enei Church
National Theatre of Bucharest

STR. M. MILLO
STRADA EDGAR QUINET
University
PIAŢA UNIVERSITĂŢII
M
CAROL I

STR. C. MILLE
Cercul Militar
Doamnei Church
STRADA EDGAR QUINET
B-DUL
Bucharest History Museum

B-DUL REGINA ELISABETA
STR. BREZOIANU
CFR/TAROM
STRADA EFORIE
STR. ACADEMIEI
Colţea Church

STRADA LIPSCANI
Police Headquarters
PASAGIUL VILLACROSSE
STRADA DOAMNEI
Russian Church
B-DUL I.C. BRATIANU
PIAŢA SF. GHEORGHE

Sf Nicolae-Mihai Vodă Church
STRADA MIHAI VODA
River Dîmboviţa
SMIRDAN
SELARI
STR. BLANARI
STRADA LIPSCANI
New St George's
CALEA MOŞILOR

B-DUL LIBERTĂŢII
STR. STAVROPOLEOS
Stavropoleos Church
National History Museum
Pedestrian Bridge
STR. GABROVENI

Choral Temple

B-DUL NAŢIUNILE UNITE
STRADA IULIU MANIU
Curtea Veche

St Apostoli Church
SPLAIUL INDEPENDENTEI
Hanul Lur Manuc
Unirea Market

Domniţa Bălaşa Church
Unirea Department Store

Casa Poporului △

0   100 m
PIAŢA UNIRII

B-DUL UNIRII
M   M

Arcade
Pedestrianized Street

Villa 11, Str Institutul Medico Militar 11 (☎092/495900, *vila11bb@hotmail.com*). This friendly new hostel, offering standard facilities, is near to the Gara de Nord and not yet as popular as the *Helga*, though it's still best to phone ahead. ①.

Hotels

Banat, Piaţa Rosetti 5 (☎01/313-1057). Dead central and very cheap, the renovated *Banat* is worth trying out. Great en-suite bathrooms in most rooms – plus some apartments, available for $100 per night. ②.

Bulevard, B-dul Regina Elisabeta 21 (☎01/315-3300). The influence of French architecture is evident on this grand looking hotel overlooking Calea Victoriei. All rooms are well equipped and have bathrooms, TV and a phone. ⑤.

Carpaţi, Str Matei Milo 16 (☎01/315-0140). Another newly renovated and central hotel that has shared, but very clean, bathrooms and helpful staff. ②.

Helveţia, Piaţa Charles de Gaulle 13 (☎01/223-0566, *www.helvetia.netvision.net.it*). Lovely location near Herăstrau Park with massive beds and plush bathrooms. Completely modern and clean. ⑤.

Marna, Str Buzeşti 3 (☎01/650-6820 or 659-6733). Cheap hotel near to the Gara de Nord, with no mod-cons but clean enough rooms. Shared showers. ①.

Marriott Grand Calea 13 Septembrie 90 (☎01/403-0000). Offering luxury at a surprisingly affordable price, the *Grand* was originally built for Ceauşescu's cronies, and is centrally located right by the former leader's palace. Facilities include a shopping mall, sports centre and cinema multiplex, brilliant sports bar and a range of restaurants. ⑥.

Muntenia, Str Academiei 19–21 (☎01/313-6819 or 314-1782, *www.muntenia.dial.kappa.ro*). Looks nicer on the outside than inside, but for the price you get your own bathroom and a reasonable room, plus a central but slightly noisy location. ②.

Parliament, Str Izvor 106 (☎01/411-9990, *www.parliament-hotel.ro*). Popular with visiting politicians and businessmen, this small, intimate and personal hotel has Jacuzzis in the rooms as well as all the luxuries you'd expect in a place catering to an expense-account clientele. ④.

Triumf, Şosea Kiseleff 12 (☎01/222-3172). A massive but pleasant hotel located near the Arcul de Triumf. Pleasant green surroundings make up for the simple but clean rooms. All rooms have a TV, bathroom and phone. ②.

The City

"A savage hotch-potch" was Ferdinand Lasalle's verdict on Bucharest between the wars, with its boulevards and nightlife, its slums and beggars, its aristocratic mansions and crumbling Orthodox churches. The extremes of wealth and poverty have been mitigated, but otherwise the city has retained many of its old characteristics. Woodlands and a girdle of lakes freshen its northern outskirts, beyond a triumphal arch and a tree-lined avenue extending from Bucharest's main thoroughfare, the Calea Victoriei.

The majority of inner-city sights are within walking distance of **Calea Victoriei** (Street of Victory), a place of vivid contrasts. At its verdant northern end near the Piaţa Victoriei, it has touches of *ancien régime* elegance, but to the south the street becomes an eclectic jumble of apartment blocks, glass and steel facades and cake shops. Fulcrum of the Calea is the large **Piaţa Revoluţiei**, created during the 1930s on Carol II's orders to ensure a field of fire around his new Royal Palace on the western side of the square. The palace now contains the **National Art Museum** (Wed–Sun 10am–6pm), which has a newly opened European Gallery – including works by Rembrandt, Monet and Sisley – as well as a Modern Romanian Art Gallery.

North of the palace, the contemporaneous **Athénée Palace Hotel** (now part of the Hilton chain) has always been a hive of intrigue, but was refurbished as a hotel and "intelligence factory" in the 1950s, with bugged rooms, tapped phones and informers everywhere. Opposite the palace stand the **Romanian Athenaeum**, the city's main concert hall, and the **University Library**, torched, allegedly by the Securitate, in the confused fighting of the 1989 revolution, but now rebuilt to contain an EU information centre and café. Just south of here is the building – formerly the headquarters of the Communist Party, and now the Senate – which dominated TV screens worldwide in 1989. The low balcony above the main entrance is where Nicolae Ceauşescu made his last speech on December 21, to a disaffected and hostile crowd. Minutes into his speech the booing took over and the dictator's disbelief was broadcast to the nation just in time before the screens went blank. A few hours later, after much panicking, Ceauşescu and his wife Elena escaped by helicopter from the roof, only to fly to their eventual execution on Christmas Day.

Close by, the battered eighteenth-century **Creţulescu Church** fronts a tangle of streets wending west towards **Cişmigiu Gardens**, Bucharest's oldest park. The gardens originally belonged to a Turkish water inspector, and fittingly contain a serpentine lake upon which small rowing boats glide, rented by couples seeking solitude among the weeping willows. The residential area between Cişmigiu and the Gara de Nord has a real urban-village character, devout women genuflecting as they pass tiny street-corner churches while neighbours gossip outside dimly lit workshops.

Beyond the Creţulescu Church the Calea continues southwards past the police headquarters. Directly opposite is the elegant **Pasagiul Villacrosse** arcade, one of the few remnants of the Bucharest that used to be known as the "Paris of the Balkans". Beyond the junction with B-dul Regina Elisabeta, Bucharest's main east–west boulevard, the Calea crosses Stradă Lipscani, a shabby, shifty marketplace where you can probably buy anything if you know the people to ask. Nearing the river, the **National History Museum** (Tues–Sun 10am–4pm) looms up at no. 1. The permanent exhibitions on the ground and first floors are dull, but the downstairs vault holds superb gold and silverware left by Romania's pre-Christian inhabitants, the Dacians. To the east of here stands the small **Stavropoleos Church**, built in the 1720s, it has gorgeous, almost arabesque, mouldings and patterns decorating its facade, and a columned portico carved with delicate tracery. To the south of the church, a maze of streets and pleasantly decrepit houses surrounds the historical centre of Bucharest, where Vlad the Impaler built a citadel in the fifteenth century. The remains of the **Curtea Veche** (Old Court) are pretty modest: a few rooms, arches and shattered columns, and a cellar containing a **museum** (Tues–Sun 9am–5pm) where the skulls of boyars whom Vlad had decapitated are lovingly displayed.

A few doors along and opposite the Curtea Veche, an austere white building with barred windows conceals Bucharest's most famous hostelry, Manuc's Inn – **Hanul lui Manuc**. Originally a caravanserai founded by a wealthy Armenian, the building contains a restaurant and wine cellar. The inn's southern wall forms one side of **Piaţa Unirii** (Union Square) – which is where the old Bucharest makes way for the new.

The Centru Civic and Piaţa Universităţii

The most infamous district of Bucharest is the **Centru Civic** (Civic Centre) – Ceauşescu's huge urban project. After an earthquake in 1977 damaged much of the city, Ceauşescu decided to rebuild the entire southern portion of central Bucharest, which he deemed a slum, as a monument to Communism, modelling it on Pyong Yang in North Korea. By the early 1980s bulldozers had moved in to clear the way for high-rises and the Victory of Socialism Boulevard (now **Boulevard Unirii**), taking with them thousands of architecturally important houses, churches and monuments. One end of the road is now a banking district (near Piaţa Alba Iulia), surrounded by a mish-mash of skeletal buildings, while the other end is dominated by the **Casa Poporului** (Parliament Palace), the third largest building in the world, originally intended as Ceauşescu's adminstrative centre and now housing the Romanian Parliament. The structure took 100,000 workers five years to complete and has over 1100 rooms, a nuclear fallout shelter and a recently discovered private metro station. You can have a **guided tour** in English (daily 10am–4pm; $5) if you make your way around to the left-hand side of the building.

The Romanian government has initiated a project, named Bucharest 2000, to regenerate the Centru Civic. The project, working on designs thought up by an international team of architects and including renovation of the palace and addition of parks, is expected to take around fifteen years to realize – making it one of Europe's largest urban renewal projects ever.

Returning northwards from Piaţa Unirii along B-dul Brătianu, you'll see the *Hotel Intercontinental* towering above **Piaţa Universităţii**, a nexus for city life and traffic. This is where the students pitched their post-revolution City of Peace, an encampment broken up by the miners in June 1990. When the miners returned to Bucharest in 1991, this time in protest against the government rather than as its stormtroopers, they camped out here themselves before being rooted out by the police with the same violence they had earlier dispensed.

Just to the east rises the new **National Theatre**, a pet project of Elena Ceauşescu, resembling an Islamicized reworking of the Colosseum. Further to the west, **Bucharest University** occupies the first block on B-dul Carol I, its forecourt thronged with students and snack stands, while statues of illustrious pedagogues and statesmen gaze blindly at the crowds. The small, bulbous domes of the **Russian Church** appear through a gap in the domed buildings lining the southern side of the boulevard. Faced with yellow brick, Art Nouveau green tiling and pixie-faced nymphs, the church has a small interior, with frescoes so blackened with age and smoke that only the saintly haloes glow like golden horseshoes around Christ.

The northern districts

B-dul Brătianu quickly becomes B-dul Bălcescu, B-dul Magheru then, after passing Piaţa Romană, B-dul L. Catargiu; this route takes you back to Piaţa Victoriei. From here Şoseaua Kiseleff leads into the more pleasant, leafy suburbs. On the same street, at no. 3, the **Romanian Peasant Museum** (Tues–Sun 10am–6pm, *www.itcnet.ro/mtr/tar_e.htm*) is a must-see, giving a full insight into the country's varied traditions, with exhibits on everything from costume to religious icons. At the northern end of the Şoseaua is the **Arcul de Triumf**, commemorating Romania's participation on the side of the Allied victors in World War I. Just to the north of the arch is **Herăstrău Park** – the city's largest. Boating on the park's huge lake is popular; you can rent boats near the entrance to the park ($2.30/hr). Inside the park, just off the northern end of Şoseaua Kiseleff, is the **Village Museum** (Oct–March daily 9am–5pm; Aug–Sept Mon 9am–5pm, Tues–Sun 9am–8pm), boasting wooden houses, nearly 300 churches, farm buildings and windmills – all transported to Bucharest from various regions of the country.

Eating

Fast-food joints are ubiquitous in the capital but more traditional fresh **snacks**, such as *gogoşi* (Romanian doughnuts) and *covrigi* (similar to pretzels) are sold all over the city, and eaten on the move. You'll find a variety of international cuisines served in Bucharest's **restaurants** but, strangely, very few places serving actual Romanian food. Restaurants are on the whole affordable – a few still have the nasty habit of charging you by the weight of the food served (the menu shows the cost per 100 grams). Always check with the waiter first.

Restaurants

Barka Saffron, Str Av. Sănătescu 1, near Piaţa Domeni on B-dul Mihalache (☎01/224-1004). Trendy place serving excellent international food (with a menu that changes almost weekly). A little out the way, but worth the trip.

Byblos, Str N. Golescu 14–16 (☎01/313-2091). Beautiful restaurant in a beautifully quiet street in the heart of the city. The ambience is unique, the food and drinks are almost second to none in the city.

Casa Doina, Şos. Kiseleff 4 (☎01/222-3179). Probably the best restaurant for local dishes in Bucharest. The food is stunning, as are the wines from the vintage cellar. By local standards, it's very pricey, but it's still a lot cheaper than back home.

La Belle Epoque, Str Beller 6, just off Piaţa Dorobanţi (☎01/230-0770). Traditional Belgian dishes are on offer here, including sausages and mash, as well as Hoegaarden and Leffe beers.

La Mama, Str B. Văcărescu 3 (☎01/212-4086). Another good place for Romanian dishes, *La Mama* is cheap, very popular, and has great wines – so booking ahead is advisable.

Smarts, Str A. Donici 14. Located in a beautifully quiet tree-lined street, this quiet and friendly bar serves up various French food alongside the more usual local dishes. Nice bar downstairs.

Drinking and nightlife

This once docile city is now becoming a new hotspot for its nightlife and bars, and pretty much offers something for all tastes, with new places opening up almost every week. The most popular **nightclubs** are the horribly crowded *Club A*, Str Blanari 14, which caters for a studenty crowd; *Studio Martin*, B-dul Iancu de Hunedoara 41, which brings in the ravers with its international guest DJs and gay/drag friendly atmosphere; *Web Club*, B-dul Mihalache 12, which has an underground drum & bass crowd; and *Twice*, Str Sf. Vineri 4, which has to be Bucharest's biggest bar/club.

The recent change in legislation that previously outlawed "public displays of homosexuality" has seen a host of **gay bars and nightclubs** open up almost overnight. *Havana*, Str Tunari 67–69, and *Casablanca*, Sala Polivalenta in Tineretului park, both have weekly gay and lesbian nights. For more information, contact Accept, Str Lirei 10 (☎01/252-1637, *accept.ong.ro*).

For full **listings** of what's on in the city, get hold of the English language *Bucharest in your Pocket* for 30,000 lei; it's available at most hotels, some bars and restaurants and at *www .inyourpocket.com*.

Cafés and bars

High, Str Mihail Moxa 22. A hip English-owned bar-cum-disco set in a great old house playing plenty of cheesy 70s and 80s hits and serving up fancy cocktails.

Lăptăria lui Enache, 4th floor of the National Theatre, Piața Universității. Justifiably one of Bucharest's most popular bars. Live music at the weekends and access to a roof-terrace (*La Motor*) in summer. Cheap drinks and snacks and free art-house films during the week. Access is via the back entrance to the theatre near the Dominuszart shop.

MCM Café, B-dul Balcescu 3–5, underneath the Planet Diner. Fast becoming the focal point for listening to local bands and DJs, this place is run by a French-owned TV station. Drinks are cheap and the atmosphere is relaxed.

Newton Bar, Str J.L. Calderon 56. A bright, cheerful and friendly bar with a relaxed atmosphere. Perfect after a hard day's touring.

Terminus Pub, Str G. Enescu 5. An expat favourite and crowded most nights. Enter and go down the stairs into the cellar. Massive and pricey drinks list but well worth a visit. The *Terminus*'s far busier and pretentious brother, *Planters*, is just around the corner at Str Mendleev 10.

The Green Man, Str Puțul lui Zamfir 26. Probably the best of the English bars/pubs in the Piața Dorobanți area, with a slightly surreal but captivating atmosphere, and a good selection of beers.

Internet cafés

Brit C@fe, Calea Dorobanților 14 (☎01/210-0314). Chirpy Brit-run café has four computers, cheap sandwiches and tea. Located at the back of the British Council's courtyard. Mon–Fri 10am–9pm, Sat 10am–2pm. $1.25/hr.

FX, B-dul Magheru 8. Hi-tech 80s decor, very fast computers and a hip crowd. Open 10am–midnight. $1.50/hr.

Cyber C@fe, B-dul Dacia 77 (☎01/211-3836, *cyber@ifb.ro*). Located inside the French Institute, this café has great, inexpensive French dishes and beer on offer, as well as fairly fast computers. Open Mon–Fri 10am–8pm. $0.75.

Silence Café, Str Căderea Bastiliei 19 (☎01/659-4089). Good and fast in all terms. Also serves up good coffee and a few snacks. Open 24hr. $1.25.

Internet Café, Calea Victoriei 136 (☎01/650-4214, *icafe@icafe.ro*) & B-dul Carol 1 25 (☎01/313-1048, *icafe@icafe.ro*). Unoriginal name, but good and fast. Both open 24hr.

XES, Calea Victoriei 32–34 (no phone). Serves great coffee and snacks. Open 24hr. $0.75.

Listings

Airlines Aeroflot, Str Biserica Amzei 29 (☎01/615-0314); Air France, Str General Praporgescu 1–5, et. 1, ap. 1 (☎01/210-0934, *airfrance@pcnet.ro*); Austrian Airlines, B-dul Magheru 16–18 (☎01/3120-0545, *www.aua.com*); British Airways, B-dul Regina Elisabeta 3 (☎01/303-2222, *www.britishairways.ro*); Lufthansa, B-dul Magheru 18 (☎01/315-7575, *lufthansa@softnet.ro*); Swissair/Sabena, B-dul Magheru 18 (☎01/312-0238, *swissair@starnets.ro*); Tarom, Str Brezoianu 10 (☎01/314-2520/313-4295, *www.tarom.ro*), also at Splaiul Independenţei 17 (☎01/337-2037 or 337-0400).

Embassies & Consulates Australia (Consulate), Str. Dr. E Racota 16–18 ap. 1 (☎01/666-6923); Britain (Embassy), Str Jules Michelet 24 (☎01/312-0303); Canada (Embassy), Str N. Iorga 36 (☎01/650-6140); US, Str T. Arghezi 7 (☎01/312-4040).

Hospitals, Clinics & Dentists Medicover, Calea Plevnei 96 (☎01/310-4066 or 310-4411), also at Str Dr. Grozovici (☎01/212-2155). In an emergency make your way to the central Spitalul Clinic de Urgenţia, Calea Floreasca 8 (☎01/230-0106, for an ambulance ☎961). For a dentist, head to B.B. Clinic, Str G. Ionescu 4 (☎01/320-0151, *bbclinic@xnet.ro*), which charges Western prices, but does also provide a Western-standard service.

Post offices The main post office is at Str Matei Millo 10 (daily 7.30am–8pm, ☎01/315-8793).

Train tickets You can buy train tickets in advance, or on the day of travel if you don't mind queuing for what could be as much as thirty minutes. Seat reservations and ticket purchases can only be made at the station an hour or less before the train leaves, and note that you can only buy return tickets for international routes. International routes: Wasteels, in the Gara de Nord (8am–7pm; ☎01/222-7844, *www.wasteels.ro*). National routes: Agenţie de Voiaj SNCFR, Str. Ion Brezoianu 10 (☎01/313-2642; Mon–Fri 7.30am–7.30pm, Sat 8am–noon, closed Sun). Advance tickets can be purchased no earlier than 48 hours before the time of travel.

travel details

Trains

Bucharest to: Braşov (16–20 daily; 2hr 30min–4hr 45min); Cluj (6–8 daily; 8–11hr); Sibiu (6 daily; 4hr 45 min–9hr 30min); Sighişoara (10–12 daily; 4hr–7hr 30min); Timişoara (4–6 daily; 7–14hr).

Brauov to: Bucharest (16–20 daily; 2hr 30min–4hr 45min); Cluj (6–8 daily; 4hr–6hr 30min); Sibiu (9 daily; 2hr–4hr); Sighişoara (19–21 daily; 1hr 45min–3hr); Timişoara (1–2 daily; 8hr–10hr 30min).

Cluj to: Braşov (6–8 daily; 4hr–6hr 30min); Bucharest (6–8 daily; 8–11hr); Sibiu (2–3 daily; 3hr 30min–4hr); Sighişoara (6 daily; 3–4hr); Timişoara (4–6 daily; 5hr 30min–6hr 45min).

Sighişoara to: Braşov (19–21 daily; 1hr 45min–3hr); Cluj (6 daily; 3–4hr); Bucharest (10–12 daily; 4hr–7hr 30min); Sibiu (4 daily; 1hr 30min–3hr).

Timişoara to: Bucharest (4–6 daily; 7–14hr); Braşov (1–2 daily; 8hr–10hr 30min); Cluj (4–6 daily; 5hr 30min–6hr-45min).

Buses

Braşov to: Bran (7am–8pm every 30min ; 45 min).

CHAPTER 24

RUSSIA

Introduction

European **Russia** stretches from the borders of the states of Belarus and Ukraine to the Ural mountains, over 1000km east of Moscow; even without the rest of the Russian Federation, it constitutes by far the largest country in Europe. It was also, for many years, one of the hardest to visit. Today Russia is far more accessible, and although visas are still obligatory and accommodation often has to be booked in advance, independent travel is increasingly an option. Nonetheless, Moscow and St Petersburg remain the easiest places to visit, and these are covered below. For the adventurous, travel further afield can be booked through various agencies in Russia and abroad, and there are an increasing number of Web sites offering advice and travel services for the less standard routes.

Moscow and St Petersburg are mutually comple-mentary. **Moscow**, the capital, is hugely enthralling. It is not a beautiful city by any means, and is a somewhat chaotic place. However, Moscow's central core reflects Russia's long and fascinating history at the heart of a vast empire, whether in the relics of the Communist years, the Kremlin with its palaces and churches of the tsars, or in the wooden buildings still tucked away in back-streets, or in the massive building projects of the mayor, Yuriy Luzhkov, which have radically changed the face of the centre.

By contrast, Russia's second city, **St Petersburg**, is Europe at its most gracious, an attempt by the eighteenth-century tsar Peter the Great to re-create the best of Western European elegance in what was then a far-flung outpost. Its position in the delta of the River Neva is unparalleled, full of watery vistas of huge and faded palaces. St Petersburg has not been revamped anywhere near as much as Moscow, which many consider a good thing, and it preserves a unity and stability lacking in the capital.

You will not be bothered by the so-called Russian mafia in either city, but, as in any other big city, you should beware of petty crime.

Information and maps

Russia has few **tourist offices**. Most travellers use the information desks at hotels and hostels, but the best resources are English-language newspapers, such as the *Moscow Times* (daily) or *St Petersburg Times* (twice weekly), and free quarterly magazines available at leading hotels.

High-quality **maps** in English at very low prices are widely available from kiosks, street vendors and cen-tral department stores. Those maps most commonly found in the West are produced by Baedeker, Geocenter International and Falk, but often do not take account of streets which have reverted to their pre-Revolutionary names or of new metro lines.

Money and banks

The official **currency** of Russia is the ruble, which is divided into one hundred kopeks: there are 1, 5, 10 and 50 kopek coins, 1, 2 and 5 ruble coins, and notes to the value of 5, 10, 50, 100, 500 and 1000 rubles. Only notes and coins dated 1997 or after are valid.

Despite the end of soaring inflation, **prices** in this chapter are given in US dollars, a fairly stable mea-sure of real costs – but in practice they're charged and paid for in rubles. It is illegal to pay in foreign currency. The black market offers nothing but risks: always **change money** in an official bank or curren-cy exchange. Most **banks** are open Mon–Sat 10am–6/8pm, or later.

ATMs are now found in plenty, and using your **credit or debit card** to obtain cash from them is generally a safe way to get money in Russia. Some, however, have a very low cash limit per transaction, which may make your rubles expensive. You can also

---

RUSSIA ON THE NET

www.russia-tourism.com – for links to just about every sight you can think of, and several more besides.

www.infoservices.com – has Moscow and St Petersburg sections offering advice to travellers and lists of restaurants, cafés, hotels, etc.

www.themoscowtimes.com and *www.sptimesrussia .com* – the sites of Russia's two English-language newspapers, with all the latest news, ads and cultural events, as well as advice for travellers.

www.museum.ru – rarely updated, but good for gen-eral information on museums throughout Russia.

www.geographia.com/russia – original official site of the Russian National Tourist Office; a bit out of date but good on history and travel outside cities.

www.trans-siberian.co.uk – offers a range of adven-ture holidays in Russia, including trips on the world-famous railway.

obtain cash from most banks with a card (Visa, Mastercard and Cirrus are the most widely accepted; problems may occasionally occur with Diners and Amex). **Travellers' cheques** are time-consuming and expensive to use.

Be warned that Moscow is an expensive city, and the daily cost of life there is up to three times that of St Petersburg. In the provinces, life becomes ridiculously cheap.

Communications

Communications in Russia have improved greatly in recent years. Most **post offices** are open Mon–Sat 8am–7pm. All district post offices have **poste restante** (*do vostrébovaniya*) services. Both Moscow and St Petersburg have excellent express-letter post companies, such as Post International and Westpost, which despatch mail via Finland or the US for moderate sums.

Street phones are good for local and international calls. To use them you need a **phonecard** (available in 25, 50, 100, 200, 400 and 1000 units from newspaper kiosks and post offices). Moscow's public phones are less numerous and less efficient than those in St Petersburg. Phone booths in airports and major hotels aren't always run by the city phone network, and are much more expensive. You can buy cards for these phones on the spot or use your Amex or Visa card. By far the cheapest option in St Petersburg (with off-peak discounts) is the Telephone Service Card, usable from any tone-dial phone (available in 300, 600, 1200, 3000 and 6000 units). **Mobile phones** abound in both cities, and GSM users will have no trouble plugging in to the local system. **Email** and Internet access is offered cheaply in a number of Internet cafés.

Getting around

With an extensive and relatively efficient network of trains and (shaky) buses, you'll have few problems **getting around** the most populated parts of Russia. Regular Eurolines buses now connect major cities with the rest of Eastern and Western Europe.

■ Trains and buses

Buying **tickets** for long-distance and international trains is easy these days. Hundreds of agencies can help you avoid queues at train stations, for a minimal commission, and foreigners no longer pay more for tickets than Russians. A dozen trains leave

Moscow's Leningrad Station within an hour or so of midnight for the 8hr journey to St Petersburg, the most historic being the Red Arrow (#2). Many prefer the day train, the Aurora, which takes 6 hours, or the new evening train, in just 4 hours. All trains are generally safe and reliable, and cheap.

Most of Moscow's and St Petersburg's outlying sights are accessible from mainline stations (separate ticket office for suburban trains). Suburban buses and efficient minibuses from the end of a metro line often go straight to the tourist attraction. Fares are also low, although state-run buses are often packed.

■ Driving and hitching

Traffic in the cities is heavy and many Russian motorists show a reckless disregard for pedestrians and other cars. **Driving**, therefore, requires a fair degree of skill and nerve.

Unless otherwise specified, **speed limits** are 60kph in the city and 80kph on highways. Few **car rental** agencies offer cars without drivers, except for extremely high prices.

Many Russians **hitch**, especially after the public transport system closes down, when you'll see people flagging down anything that moves. If the driver finds the destination acceptable, he'll state a price, which may or may not be negotiable; if you're not happy, wait for another car. Russians will usually pay the ruble equivalent of a dollar or so to ride several kilometres; foreigners are likely to be charged more. Don't get into a vehicle which has more than one person in it, and never accept lifts from anyone who approaches you, particularly outside restaurants and nightclubs: instances of drunken foreigners being robbed in the back of cars have been known. Single women should stick to official taxis.

Accommodation

Anyone travelling on a tourist visa to Russia must (technically) have **accommodation** arranged before arrival, but this is increasingly easy to get round. Most hostels and all hotels can arrange the necessary visa support for you. Hostels can usually provide invitations of any length as long as you spend just one night there. Commercial (and thus more expensive) visas don't oblige you to prebook lodgings and are fairly easy to obtain. Try *www.Infinity.ru* or *www.visatorussia.com* – the latter also provides up to the minute info on visa

ACCOMMODATION PRICE CODES

Throughout this guide, accommodation is coded on a scale of ① to ⑨, the code indicating the lowest price per person per night you could expect to pay in each establishment in high season. With hostels this is the nightly rate per person; with hotels, the price is arrived at by dividing the cost of the cheapest double room by two. The prices indicated by the codes are as follows:

① under £5/$8	④ £15–20/$24–32	⑦ £30–35/$48–56
② £5–10/$8–16	⑤ £20–25/$32–40	⑧ £35–40/$56–64
③ £10–15/$16–24	⑥ £25–30/$40–48	⑨ £40/$64 and over

requirements, local embassies, etc. As **hotels** in Moscow and St Petersburg are expensive, anyone on a tight budget will almost certainly do better by opting for a **hostel or private accommodation**. Only St Petersburg has a decent **campsite**, albeit at some distance and prone to the unpredictable weather. On the Internet *http://all-hotels.ru/main.en* is the only hotel site to cover all grades, from the scrubbiest hostel to the smartest five-star joint. Note that cheaper hotels often have "improved" rooms which cost a few dollars more but have better bathroom facilities and newer furniture – it's always worth asking.

■ Hotels

Russia's **hotels** range from opulent citadels to seedy pits inhabited by wheeler-dealers, with numerous generally tolerable establishments in between. Two-star hotels tend to consist of 1950s low-rises with matchbox-sized rooms; three star hotels are typically 1960s and 1970s high-rises, equipped with several restaurants, bars and nightclubs; while four-star hotels tend to date from the 1980s and come closest to matching the standards (and prices) of their Western counterparts. Recent years have seen the appearance of central "family" hotels, with a very small number of clean, attractive rooms, but these are relatively expensive. Most hotels include **breakfast** in the price, but in cheaper places it's wise to check if there is a restaurant or only a bar.

Whatever class of accommodation you stay in, don't leave valuables in your room, put your money in the hotel safe, stash most other items in a locked suitcase under the bed, and lock the door before going to sleep.

■ Hostels and private accommodation

Hostels are definitely the best-value accommodation in Russia. They are safer and cleaner than most hotels offering similar rates, and can help with many of the problems that face budget travellers. **Reservations** should be made at least three to four weeks in advance. Note that there is no age restriction.

Private accommodation for tourists is catching on, and both Moscow and St Petersburg have agencies providing self-contained **apartments** or **bed and breakfast** in Russian households. The cost varies from $15 to $70 per person per night, depending on the location and whether you opt for B&B or full board.

Food and drink

Moscow and St Petersburg now abound in **cafés and restaurants**, offering everything from pizza to Indian, French and Chinese food. Many cater to the new rich or foreign businessmen, but cheap and middle-range establishments are plentiful, serving food with a local flavour. Credit cards are increasingly accepted, particularly in Moscow, but not in the cheaper establishments.

■ Food

Despite the increasing popularity of **fast food** and foreign cuisine, Russians remain loyal to their culinary heritage, above all to **zakuski** – small dishes consumed before a meal with vodka, as a snack or as a light meal in themselves. Herring is a firm favourite, as are gherkins, assorted cold meats and salads. Pancakes (*bliny*), served with caviar (*ikra*) are to be recommended; red caviar is very cheap and a worthy rival to the black.

Most Russians take **breakfast** (*zavtrak*) seriously, tucking into calorific pancakes or porridge (*kasha*), with curd cheese (*tvorog*) and sour cream (*smetana*). Hotels usually serve a "Continental" breakfast, probably just fried egg, bread, butter and jam; ritzier hotels provide a buffet. The main meal of the day is

lunch (*obed*), eaten between 1 and 4pm, while **supper** (*uzhin*) traditionally consists of just *zakuski* and tea. **Restaurants**, on the other hand, make much more of the evening meal, often staying open as late as 1am. **Menus** are usually written in Russian only, but an increasing number of places now offer a version in English (not always regularly updated). You can always ask what they recommend (*"shto-by vy porekomendovali?"*).

After the *zakuski*, the menu continues with **soup**. Cabbage soup (*shchi*), served with a generous dollop of sour cream, has been the principal Russian dish for the last thousand years. *Zelyonye shchi* – green (or sorrel) soup is a gourmet version of this. Beetroot soup, or *borshch*, originally from Ukraine, is equally ubiquitous, while *ukha*, fish soup, has become synonymous with pressing Russian hospitality. Russians don't regard even large meaty soups (*kharcho* or *solyanka*) as a main meal.

Main courses are overwhelmingly based on meat (*myaso*), usually beef, mutton or pork, sometimes accompanied by a mushroom, sour cream or cheese sauce. Meat also makes its way into *pelmeny*, a Russian version of ravioli. Most cafes now offer some alternatives however, and Georgian restaurants always have interesting **vegetarian** dishes, such as bean stew or stuffed aubergines. Marinated **fish** is a popular starter (try *selyodka pod shuboy*, herring "in a fur coat" of beetroot, carrot, egg and mayonnaise), while fresh fish – usually salmon, sturgeon or pike-perch – appears as a main course in all self-respecting eateries.

Pastries (*pirozhnoe*) are available from cake shops (*konditerskaya*). Savoury pies (*pirozhki*) are often also on sale – the best are filled with cabbage, curd cheese or rice; steer clear of the deep-fried ones at all times and of meat pies if buying from street vendors.

Desserts (*sladkoe*) are not a strong feature of Russian cuisine. Ice cream and jam pancakes (*blinchiki s varenyem*) are restaurant perennials (Russian ice cream is outstanding and is eaten even on the street when the temperature drops to -20°C). Caucasian restaurants may offer the flaky pastry and honey dessert *pakhlava*. There are many varieties of **cake** (*tort*), but all tend to have an excess of butter-cream.

■ Drink

Vodka (*vódka*) is still the national drink, normally served chilled and drunk neat in one gulp, followed by a mouthful of *zakuska*. Highly popular are flavoured vodkas such as Pertsovka (hot pepper vodka), Limonaya (lemon vodka), Okhotnichaya (hunter's vodka, with juniper berries, ginger and cloves) and Zubrovka (bison-grass vodka), although the hard drinker sticks to the straight stuff.

Beer (*pívo*) is increasingly threatening vodka's domination of the market. Russians drink beer in the morning to alleviate a hangover, or merely as a thirst quencher, and in recent years the country has begun to understand the term "lager lout". For specialists, the numerous local brands (in bottles and on tap) have an excellent fresh taste, with fewer preservatives than imports.

Wine (*vinó*) comes mostly from the vineyards of Moldavia, Georgia and the Crimea. Georgian dry and semi-sweet (such as Stalin's favourite, Khvanchkara) wines can be excellent, but Moldavian dry wine is more consistently reliable. The Crimea produces mainly fortified wines (*kheres* or sherry and Madeira) from Massandra.

Tea (*chay*) is traditionally brewed and stewed for hours, and topped up with boiling water from a samovar (cafes have discovered the convenience of teabags). Russians drink tea without milk; if you ask for milk it's likely to be UHT. **Coffee** (*kófe*) is readily available and often of excellent quality. Smaller cafes often offer Turkish coffee – served strong and black. Tea and coffee often have sugar already added unless you specifically ask for them without. **Juices and soft drinks** from the usual market leaders – Pepsi, Coca-Cola and Schweppes – are available, but Russians love the bitter *kvas* and carbonated *Baikal*. Local **mineral waters**, with or without gas, can be recommended.

Opening hours and holidays

Most **shops** open Mon–Sat 10am–7pm or later; few close for lunch. Department stores, bars and restaurants stay open on Sundays.

Opening hours for **museums** are 10am–5/6pm. They are invariably closed at least one day a week, and one further day in the month will be set aside as a "cleaning day". Note that ticket offices always close one hour before the museum itself. **Churches** tend to be accessible from 8am until the end of the evening service.

Russia's official **national holidays** have at last settled down, now that those associated purely with the former Soviet regime have gone, often to be replaced by traditional religious holidays. The current public holidays are: Jan 1; Jan 6/7 (Orthodox Christmas); March 8 (Women's Day); May 1 and 2;

May 9 (Victory Day); June 12; Nov 7. Russians also celebrate the unofficial Old New Year on 13/14 January – according to the Julian calendar.

Emergencies

Petty crime, which presents itself mostly as pickpocketing, is all that should worry you in Russia. Sensible precautions include making photocopies of your passport and visa, leaving passports and tickets in the hotel safe, and noting down travellers' cheque and credit card numbers. Do not carry large sums of money around with you and use a money belt if possible.

The **police** (*militsia*) can be recognized by their blue-grey uniforms; some may be armed. If you do have something **stolen**, report it to the *militsia*: try the phrase "*Menya obokrali*" ("I have been robbed").

It's unlikely that there'll be anyone who speaks English, and even less likely that your belongings will be retrieved, but you'll need a statement detailing what you've lost for your insurance claim.

Visitors to Russia are advised to get **booster-shots** for diphtheria, tetanus and polio. If you are on prescribed medication (particularly insulin), bring enough supplies for your stay, although high-street pharmacies (*aptéka*) offer many familiar medicines over the counter. Foreigners tend to rely for treatment on **private clinics**, which charge excessively high rates, so it's a good idea to take out insurance.

Emergency Numbers

Police ☎02; Ambulance ☎03; Fire ☎01.

MOSCOW

MOSCOW is all things to all people. For Westerners, the city may look European, but its unruly spirit seems closer to Central Asia. To Muscovites, however, Moscow is both a "Mother City" and a "big village", a tumultuous community which possesses an underlying collective instinct that shows itself in times of trouble. Home of one in fifteen Russians, it is huge, surreal and apocalyptic. Its beauty and ugliness are inseparable, its sentimentality the obverse of a brutality rooted in centuries of despotism, while private and cultural life in the city are as passionate as business and politics are cynical.

Moscow has been imbued with a sense of its own destiny since the fourteenth century, when the principality of Muscovy took the lead in the struggle against the Mongol-Tatars who had reduced the Kievan state to ruins. Under Ivan the Great and Ivan the Terrible – the "Gatherers of the Russian Lands" – its realm came to encompass everything from the White Sea to the Caspian, while after the fall of Constantinople to the Turks, Moscow assumed Byzantium's suzerainty over the Orthodox world. Despite the changes wrought by Peter the Great – not least the transfer of the capital to St Petersburg – Moscow kept its mystique and bided its time until the Bolsheviks made it the fountainhead of a new creed.

Since the fall of Communism, Muscovites have given themselves over largely to the "Wild Capitalism" that intoxicates the city, as Mayor Luzhkov puts into effect major building programmes which are changing the face of the city more radically than at any time since the Stalin era. The construction boom seemed to reach its height with the celebrations of the city's 850th anniversary in 1997, but intensive building activity continues throughout the centre.

Arrival and information

Arriving by **train** from London, Berlin or Warsaw, you'll end up at **Belarus Station** (Belorusskiy vokzal), about 1km northwest of the Garden Ring. Services from Budapest terminate at **Kiev Station** (Kievskiy vokzal), south of the Moskva River. If you're coming from St Petersburg, Finland or Estonia, your train will terminate at **Leningrad Station** (Leningradskiy vokzal). To get into the centre from any of these stations, your safest bet is to take the **metro**, as **taxis** tend to charge whatever they can get away with, which can be quite a hefty sum after the last bus has left.

The main **international airport** is at Sheremetevo-2, 28km northwest of the city centre. To avoid any hassle, or if you know you'll be arriving after dark, the *Travellers Guest House* (see "Accommodation" below) and most top hotels can arrange for you to be met at the airport. The fee ($40 plus) helps avoid haggling. If you have no booking, fight your way past the massed vultures at the exit to the official taxi stand, or the Taxi Blues stand, where the fee should be no more than $30. The alternative is to get into town by **public transport**, which involves a two-stage journey by bus and metro, and costs the ruble equivalent of under $1. There are frequent **express buses** into town from outside the arrivals terminal, most going either to Rechnoy vokzal or Planernaya metro.

If you need to pick up leaflets, maps and general **information** on what's going on in and around Moscow, you're best off going to the information desk of the *Metropol Hotel*, Teatralniy pr. 1/4 (☎095/927-6000). The *Travellers Guest House* also functions as an excellent information centre. Russian speakers would do best to buy the glossy bi-weekly *Afisha*, Moscow's equivalent of *Time Out*.

City transport

Although central Moscow is best explored on foot, the city is so big that you're bound to rely on its famous metro system to get around (check out its stunning interiors at *www.metro.ru*). The metro trains run daily from 6am to 1am, with services every two minutes during peak periods (8–10am & 5–7pm) and every three to five minutes at other times. You can buy travel cards valid for anything from one to sixty rides. The cost is minimal, at around 20 cents per ride. Providing you don't leave the metro, you can travel any distance, and change lines as many times as you like for the cost of one ride. Stations are marked with a large "M" and have separate doors for incoming and outgoing passengers. All signs and maps are in Russian, including "entrance" (*vkhód*), "exit" (*vykhod*) and "passage to another line" (*perekhód*).

Buses, trolleybuses and trams operate from 5.30am until about 11pm, although the odd one is occasionally seen at midnight. Buses and trolleybuses run through the centre of the city, trams usually in the outskirts. Bus stops are marked with yellow signs and trolleybus stops have blue and white signs suspended, like those for tram stops, from overhead cables. **Tickets** (*talony*) for buses, trolleybuses and trams are available from the driver of the vehicle (single tickets and batches of ten for around $1). Some buses and trams have conductors who sell and check tickets. In general, overground transport is inefficient in central Moscow and you're best off sticking with the metro.

The official **taxis** are yellow or grey Volgas, but others can come in all shapes and sizes. Taxi drivers often don't use their meters, so it's best to negotiate the fare before getting in to avoid any unpleasant surprises, especially as foreigners are likely to be charged more than the standard fare. Private cars will also stop if you stick your hand out and can be considerably cheaper than an official taxi with its meter off. They're generally safe, but for a woman travelling alone at night they should be avoided.

Accommodation

Independent travellers with a business visa will still find the accommodation situation in Moscow dispiriting. Most of the city's **hotels** are overpriced for what they offer, particularly those in the centre. Areas like Oktyabrskaya ploshchad, Leninskiy prospekt and the Sparrow Hills (Vorobyovie gory), located south and southwest of the Kremlin, offer a wider range of cheaper accommodation. If you need help finding somewhere to stay, you can reserve a room and pay for it on the spot at the hotel reservations desk at Sheremetevo-2 airport – pay for one night only in case you decide to move somewhere else.

A better option if you're on a very tight budget is to try a **hostel**, or **private accommodation**, which you can arrange in advance through the *Travellers Guest House* (see below) or the St Petersburg-based *HOFA* (☎812/275 19 92, *homestay@yahoo.com*).

Hostels

7th Floor, pr. Vernadskogo 88, korpus 1 (☎095/956 6038, *sev.floor@mtu-net.ru*); Yugo-Zapadnaya metro (30min ride from the centre). Very small B&B, with efficient and friendly staff. ⑦.

The Travellers Guest House, Bolshaya Pereyaslavskaya ul. 50 (☎095/971 40 59, *tgh@startravel.ru*); ten-minute walk from Prospekt Mira metro. Hidden away on the tenth floor, this American-run hostel is pleasant, clean and fairly central, with a laundry, café and bar. It also provides excellent tourist information and advice. ①.

Hotels

Izmailovo Complex – Delta, Izmailovskoe shosse 71 (☎095/166 4345); Izmailovskiy Park metro. Vast modern complex near park, offering rooms of all standards, from dead cheap to "luxury". ⑤.

Minsk Hotel, Tverskaya ul. 22 (☎095/299 13 49); Mayakovskaya or Pushkinskaya metro. Anonymous 1960s high-rise right in the centre, with a business centre and sauna. ⑤.

Moskva, Okhotniy ryad 2 (☎095/292 1100); Okhotniy ryad metro. OK so you won't be making friends with the other guests, but for location and view nothing beats this Stalin-era hotel. ⑨.

Pekin, ul. Bolshaya-Sadovaya 5/1 (☎095/209 2215); Mayakovskaya metro. Genuine period charm, plus a Chinese restaurant and a sauna. ⑨.

Rossiya Hotel, ul. Varvarka 6 (☎095/232 5200, *h-russia@col.ru*); Ploshchad Revolyutsii metro. Gigantic labyrinth with 3070 rooms and poor security, but it has a great location just off Red Square and is not too expensive. ⑨.

Tsentralnaya, Tverskaya ul. 10 (☎095/229 8957); Tverskaya, Pushkinskaya and Chekhovskaya metros. Extremely central, extremely characterful hotel, but with a shady clientele. No credit cards and no visa support. ④.

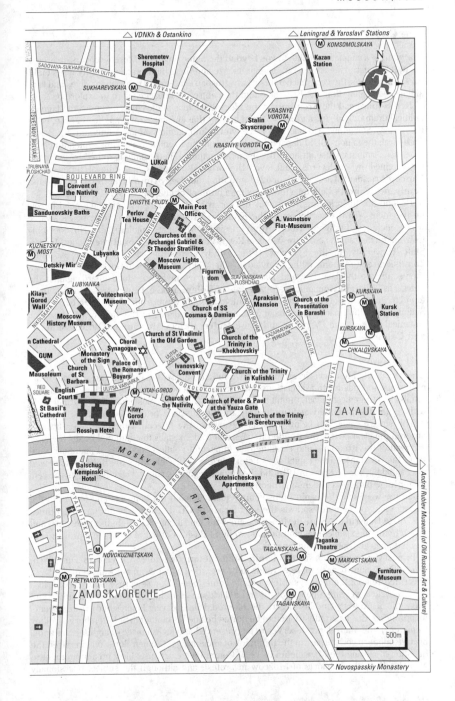

The City

Discounting a couple of satellite towns beyond the outer ring road, Moscow covers an area of about 900 square kilometres. Yet, despite its size and the inhuman scale of many of its buildings and avenues, the general layout is easily grasped – a series of concentric circles and radial lines, emanating from the Kremlin – and the centre is compact enough to explore on foot.

Red Square and the **Kremlin** are the historic nucleus of the city, a magnificent stage for political drama, signifying a great sweep of history that encompasses Ivan the Terrible, Peter the Great, Stalin and Gorbachev. Here you'll find Lenin's Mausoleum and St Basil's Cathedral, the famous GUM department store, and the Kremlin itself, whose splendid cathedrals and Armoury museum head the list of attractions. The Kremlin is ringed by two quarters defined by boulevards built over the original ramparts of medieval times, when Moscow's residential areas were divided into the inner **Beliy Gorod** and the humbler outer **Zemlyanoy Gorod** – both quarters housing a number of museums and art galleries.

Beyond this historic core Moscow is too sprawling to explore on foot: you'll need to rely on the metro. To the southwest of the Kremlin, **Krasnaya Presnya** describes a swathe which includes the White House (the Russian Parliament building); the Novodevichiy Convent further south across the Moskva River; Victory Park, to the southwest; and Moscow State University, in the Sparrow Hills. South across the river from the Kremlin, **Zamoskvoreche** is home of the Tretyakov Gallery of Russian art and Gorky Park, while further south are the Donskoy and Danilov monasteries that once stood guard against the Tatars, as well as the romantic ex-royal estate of **Kolomenskoe**. Fewer attractions are to be found to the north and east of the centre, but you should venture out to visit **VDNKh**, a huge Stalinist exhibition park with amazing statues and pavilions, in the vicinity of Moscow's Botanical Gardens and TV Tower, and to the **Andrei Rublev Museum of Old Russian Art and Culture**.

Red Square

Every visitor to Moscow is irresistibly drawn to Red Square, the historic and spiritual heart of the city, so loaded with associations and drama that it seems to embody all of Russia's triumphs and tragedies. In fact, the name Red Square (Krasnaya ploshchad) has nothing to do with communism, but derives from krasniy, the old Russian word for "beautiful".

The square came into being towards the end of the fifteenth century – after Ivan III ordered the clearance of the wooden houses and traders' stalls that huddled below the eastern wall of the Kremlin – and remained an important political and cultural landmark until Peter the Great moved the capital to St Petersburg in 1712. Only when the Bolsheviks moved the capital back to Moscow in 1918 did the square regain its political significance as the centre for huge parades and demonstrations.

On the west side the Lenin Mausoleum squats beneath the ramparts and towers of the Kremlin and on the other sprawls the long facade of **GUM** – what was during Soviet times the "State Department Store" (Mon–Sat 8am–9pm, Sun 11am–8pm) – built in 1890–93, and now a hymn to expensive fashion outlets, while St Basil's Cathedral erupts in a profusion of onion domes and spires at the far end.

In post-Communist Russia, the **Lenin Mausoleum** (Mavzoley V.I. Lenina; Tues, Wed, Thurs, Sat & Sun 10am–1pm; free) tends to be regarded either as an awkward reminder or a cherished relic of the old days. Most people come to see Lenin's corpse, softly spotlit in a crystal casket, wearing a polka-dot tie and a dark suit-cum-shroud, his body shrunken and waxy, his beard wispy and his fingers discoloured. While leaving Lenin's body *in situ* seems inappropriate (he apparently wished to be buried beside his mother in St Petersburg's Volkov Cemetery), the Mausoleum deserves to be preserved as a stylish piece of architecture and a bizarre, modern counterpart to the pyramids of ancient Egypt. When Boris Yeltsin raised the question of closing the Mausoleum in 1997, Communist extremists blew up a monument to Nicholas II on the outskirts of Moscow in protest, and although the subject occasionally comes up, emotions are always high and it is allowed to drop after a few weeks of hysteria. The famous goose-stepping guard which used to stand watch over the Mausoleum was removed – only to be reinstated, mainly for the tourists, at the more politically correct grave of the Unknown Soldier just round the corner.

The **Kremlin wall**, behind the Mausoleum – 19m high and 6.5m thick – contains a mass grave of Bolsheviks, who perished during the battle for Moscow in 1917, and the ashes of an array of luminaries, including writer Maxim Gorky and Yuriy Gagarin, the first man in space, and John Reed, the American communist who witnessed the Revolution (unmemorably played by Warren Beatty in the film *Reds*). Beyond lie the graves of a select group of Soviet leaders, each with its own bust: Chernenko, Andropov, a pompous Brezhnev and a benign-looking Stalin.

No description can do justice to **St Basil's Cathedral** (sobor Vasiliya Blazhennovo; Mon & Wed–Sun 10am–4.30pm; $5), silhouetted against the skyline where Red Square slopes down towards the Moskva River. Commissioned by Ivan the Terrible to celebrate his capture of the Tatar stronghold of Kazan in 1552, its popular title commemorates a "holy fool", St Basil the Blessed, who foretold the fire that swept Moscow in 1547, and was later buried in the Trinity Cathedral that then stood on this site. In modern times, this unique masterpiece was almost destroyed by Stalin, who resented the fact that it prevented his soldiers from leaving Red Square en masse.

At the other end of the square is the **State History Museum** (Istoricheskiy muzey; Mon & Wed–Sun 11am–7pm; $6), with only a tiny proportion of its varied collection of everything from archeological finds to Soviet badges and textiles on display. On the other side of it, just to the north of the square, is the supreme symbol of Moscow's exchange of communism for capitalism: in place of the empty space formerly used for displays of military hardware and demonstrations is Luzhkov's vast underground shopping centre, **Okhotniy ryad**, buried beneath a mass of fussy and tasteless landscaping.

The Kremlin

Brooding and glittering in the heart of Moscow, the Kremlin (daily except Thurs 10am–5pm) thrills and tantalizes whenever you see its towers stabbing the skyline, or its cathedrals and palaces arrayed above the Moskva River. Its name is synonymous with Russia's government, and in modern times assumed connotations of a Mecca for believers, and the seat of the Antichrist for foes of communism.

The founding of the Kremlin is attributed to Prince Yuriy Dolgorukiy, who erected a wooden fort above the confluence of the Moskva and Neglina rivers in about 1147 – although the site may have been inhabited as long ago as 500 BC. Despite raids by the Mongols and Tatars over the years, the Kremlin, under the building programme of Grand Duke Ivan III (1462–1505), grew to confirm Moscow's stature as the centre of Muscovy. However, as with Red Square, the Kremlin was also largely neglected during the reign of Peter the Great (1682–1725), when he spurned Moscow for St Petersburg – a situation that remained unchanged until 1918, when Lenin moved the seat of government back to Moscow.

One **ticket**, for a dollar or so, admits you to the Kremlin, while separate tickets for about $5 each are required to enter its cathedrals and the Patriarch's Palace. A ticket valid for all sights is available for around $20. While it's possible to see almost everything in one visit, a couple of visits are better if you have the time: one to see the inside and outside of the cathedrals, and another for touring the Armoury Palace, which can only be entered at set times. Visitors' movements within the Kremlin are strictly controlled, with white lines and whistle-tooting policemen marking the limits beyond which you can stroll (or even cross the road) – the following descriptions are structured to take account of these restrictions.

Roughly two-thirds of the Kremlin is off-limits to tourists – namely the trio of buildings in the northern half of the citadel, and the wooded Secret Garden sloping down towards the river. The accessible part begins around the corner from the Great Kremlin Palace (closed to the public, except for occasional ballet performances), from where the **Patriarch's Palace** heaves into view. The latter now houses a **Museum of Seventeenth-Century Life** and Applied Art, displaying ecclesiastical regalia, period furniture and domestic utensils. The exhibition concludes in the former Cathedral of the Twelve Apostles, which forms part of the same structure, also painted flesh-pink. Moving further along, the Tsar Cannon (Tsar-pushka), cast by Andrey Chokhov in 1586, is one of the largest cannons ever made and was intended to defend the Saviour Gate, but it has never been fired. Close by looms the earthbound Tsar Bell (Tsar-kolokol), the largest bell in the world, cast in 1655.

Beyond the Patriarch's Palace lies Cathedral Square (Sobornaya ploshchad), the historic heart of the Kremlin, surrounded by a superb array of buildings that give the square its name. Soaring above the square, the magnificent white Ivan the Great Bell Tower (Kolokolnya Ivana Velikovo) provides a focal point for the entire Kremlin, being the tallest structure within its walls. Opposite stands the oldest and most important of the Kremlin churches, the Cathedral of the Assumption (Uspenskiy sobor), which has symbolized Moscow's claim to be the protector of the seat of Russian Orthodoxy ever since the seat of the Church was transferred here from Vladimir in 1326. The cathedral was rebuilt in 1479 by the Bolognese architect Alberti Fioravanti, and its subsequent history reflects its role as Russia's premier church, used throughout tsarist times for coronations and solemn acts of state. Given the cathedral's exalted status, its exterior is remarkably plain, while the interior is spacious, light and echoing, its walls, roof and pillars entirely covered by icons, and frescoes applied onto a gilt undercoating. Tucked away beside the Cathedral of the Assumption is the lowly white Church of the Deposition of the Robe (tserkov Rizpolozheniya).

The last of the great churches to be erected on Cathedral Square, the Cathedral of the Archangel (Arkhangelskiy sobor), was built in 1505–08 as the burial place for the rulers of Muscovy. Unlike the vernacular Cathedral of the Assumption, its debt to the Italian Renaissance is obvious: four heavy square pillars take up much of the dimly lit interior, which is covered in frescoes. Around the walls and pillars cluster the tombs of Russia's rulers from Grand Duke Ivan I to Tsar Ivan V. Across from here glints the golden-domed Cathedral of the Annunciation (Blagoveshchenskiy sobor), which served as the private church of the grand dukes and tsars. Restored in 1562–64, the cathedral is lofty and narrow, with an interior that seems far more "Russian" than the other Kremlin cathedrals. It also houses some of the finest icons in Russia, with works by Theophanes the Greek and Andrei Rublev.

Situated between the Great Kremlin Palace and the Borovitskiy Gate, the Armoury Palace (Oruzheynaya palata; by ticket purchased in advance; $12, $6 for students) conceals a staggering array of treasures behind its Russo-Byzantine facade – among them the tsars' coronation robes, carriages, jewellery, dinner services and armour – whose splendour and curiosity value outweigh the trouble and expense involved in seeing them. The exhibits are labelled in Russian only. The palace also houses the State Diamond Fund (Almazniy Fond; 20min guided tours; tickets can occasionally be purchased at the Armoury counter for around $15), which contains the most valuable gems in Russia.

Those with the energy should also try viewing the Kremlin from different vantage points. The view from across the Moskva River is the finest in Moscow, with a glorious panorama of palaces and cathedrals arrayed above the wall that stretches from the Vodovzodnaya (Water-Drawing) Tower to the Moskva River Tower below Red Square. From high up on the Bolshoy Kamenniy bridge, you can even glimpse the Terem Palace, which is inaccessible to visitors. Lastly, you might consider walking right around the outside of the Kremlin walls, which total 2,235 metres in length.

The Beliy Gorod

The Beliy Gorod or "White Town" is the historic name of the residential district that encircled the Kremlin. Multi-domed churches cluster along ulitsa Varvarka, and around Kitaygorod east of the Kremlin: this was the very heart of the city during the sixteenth century, and even today it has a strongly medieval feel. Its main seventeenth-century thoroughfare, Tverskaya ulitsa, owes its present form to a massive reconstruction programme during the mid-1930s, and yet, despite the scale of some of its gargantuan buildings, the variety of older, often charming sidestreets gives the avenue a distinctive character.

There are countless museums and sights situated in the Beliy Gorod. For those interested in Russia's Communist past and turbulent politics, the **Museum of Contemporary Russian History**, at Tverskaya 21 (Muzey sovremennoy istorii Rossii; Mon–Thurs, Sat & Sun 10am–6pm; $3), formerly the Museum of the Revolution, organizes bold displays of propaganda posters, photographs and state gifts to Lenin and Stalin – fascinating even if you cannot read the Russian labelling.

South of Tverskaya, Moscow's **Pushkin Museum of Fine Arts**, at Volkhonka ul. 12 (Muzey izobrazitelnykh iskusstv imeni A.S. Pushkina; Tues–Sun 10am–7pm; $7), has a rich collection of European painting, from Italian High Renaissance works to Rembrandt and Poussin, and an outstanding display of Impressionists. It also has charming Egyptian portraits, and of course the magnificent gold of the lost city of Troy, removed from Germany at the end of World War II and still the subject of conflict between the two countries. Also fascinating are the hundreds of proudly displayed plaster casts of famous statues (Michelangelo's David, whole Gothic portals) made in the nineteenth century. More manageable in size than St Petersburg's Hermitage Museum, the Pushkin is still too big to do justice to in a single day.

Next door, the **Museum of Private Collections** (muzey Lichnykh Kollektsiy; Wed–Sun noon–7pm; $5) has a quirky display reflecting the individual tastes and limited resources of a score of collectors, most of whom gathered these works in the face of great difficulties during the Soviet period. The permanent exhibition begins on the **third floor**, with nineteenth-century Russian works by Wanderers such as Ilya Repin, while the **fourth floor** offers a feast of twentieth-century art, including two rooms devoted to Alexander Rodchenko and his wife Varvara Stepanova.

In 1994, Moscow's Mayor Luzhkov took the populist step of announcing the rebuilding of the **Cathedral of Christ the Redeemer** (khram Khrista Spasitelya) opposite the museums on Volkhonka. The vast original structure, built 1839–83, had been blown up by the Soviet government in 1934 and a swimming pool built on the site. Financed largely by donations and perceived as a symbol of Moscow's (and Russia's) revival, the rebuilding of the cathedral is now complete, monument to one man's overweening pride and ambition. Luzhkov appears smiling broadly in numerous photographs in the museum recording the history of the building, housed in the crypt (daily 10am–6pm; free).

The Zemlyanoy Gorod

In medieval times, the white-walled Beliy Gorod was encircled by a humbler Zemlyanoy Gorod or "Earth Town". Separated from the Beliy Gorod by the tree-lined "boulevard ring", this is one of the best-looking parts of Moscow, with Neoclassical and Art Nouveau mansions on every corner of the backstreets of the Patriarch's Ponds. Due south of here, the Arbat, which once stood for bohemian Moscow in the way that Carnaby Street represented swinging London, has a vibrant streetlife that was unique in Moscow during the 1980s and is still more tourist-friendly than anything else currently on offer.

Admirers of Bulgakov, Chekhov, Lermontov, Gorky, Pushkin or Alexei Tolstoy will find their former homes preserved as museums in and around the pretty, leafy backstreets of the **Patriarch's Ponds** (Patriarshiye prudy), the quarter to the southwest of Tverskaya. The Patriarch's Ponds are, in fact, one large pond, which forms the heart of a square surrounded by wrought-iron railings and mature trees and flanked by Art Nouveau mansions on every corner. At Bolshaya Sadovaya ul. 10, a plaque attests that Mikhail Bulgakov lived here from 1921 to 1924; his satirical fantasy *The Master and Margarita* is indelibly associated with this area in particular. To visit, go into the courtyard and look for entrance 6, on the left; the apartment (no. 50) is at the top of the stairs.

Anton Chekhov lived at Sadovaya-Kudrinskaya ul. 6, in what is now the **Chekhov House-Museum** (Tues, Thurs & Sat 11am–5pm, Wed & Fri 2–6pm; $4), while Maxim **Gorky's house-museum** (Mon & Thurs 10am–4.30pm, Tues, Wed & Fri noon–6pm;

closed last Thurs of each month; $4), on the corner of Povarskaya ulitsa and ulitsa Spiridonovka, is worth seeing purely for its amazing Art Nouveau decor, both inside and out.

Narrow and cobbled, with a tramline down the middle, the **Arbat** was the heart of a bohemian quarter where writers, actors and scientists frequented the same shops and cafés. Today, the Arbat retains some of these characteristics with its array of cafés and antique shops, and more recent fast-food outlets. The area tends to get busier once you get beyond the **Peace Wall** – a cute example of propaganda against Reagan's Star Wars. Portrait artists, buskers, and photographers offering a range of props from Gorby to Mickey Mouse are a few of the sights on offer, while the buildings bloom with bright colours and quirky details.

Krasnaya Presnya

The Krasnaya Presnya district just beyond ploshchad Vosstaniya is chiefly notable for the ex-parliament building known as the White House (Beliy dom), a marble-clad hulk known around the world for its starring role in two confrontations in the 1990s: the 1991 putsch against Gorbachev and the 1993 "October Events" when 200 deputies occupied the White House until they were stormed by Yeltsin's troops three weeks later. Since then, the building has been officially renamed the House of Government (Dom Pravitelstvo), and its present occupants have taken precautions against future trouble by erecting a concrete-slab fence around the perimeter. Demonstrations – such as the 1998 three-month camp-out by miners who had not received any pay for over six months – are limited to the humped bridge nearby.

Over the river, patriotic ardour finds an outlet at the unique, immense **Borodino Panorama** at Kutuzovskiy pr. 38 (Mon–Thurs, Sat & Sun 10am–6pm; $4), housing a painting 115m long and 15m high, with 3000 figures. This monument to the Battle of Borodino, fought against Napoleon in 1812, was completed in 1912, dismantled soon after the Revolution, then re-established here thirty years later. However, patriotism reaches a climax at the memorial complex to the Soviet victory in World War II, the sprawling **Victory Park** (Park Pobedy), on the far side of the highway. It's best to come here on Victory Day (May 9) – still a genuinely heartfelt celebration drawing thousands of veterans and their families.

Southeast of Victory Park, **Moscow State University** (or MGU, pronounced "em-gay-oo") occupies the largest of the city's seven Stalinist-Gothic skyscrapers, which dominates the plateau of the **Sparrow Hills** (Vorobyovie gory), overlooking the Moskva River. Besides the university, the attraction is quite simply the panoramic view of Moscow, with Luzhniki stadium and the Novodevichiy Convent in the foreground, the White House and the Kremlin in the middle distance, and six more Stalinist skyscrapers ranged across the city.

NOVODEVICHY CONVENT

Where the Moskva River begins its loop around the marshy tongue of Luzhniki, southwest of the Zemlyanoy Gorod, a cluster of shining domes above a fortified rampart proclaims the presence of the Novodevichiy Convent (Novodevichiy monastyr; daily 8am–7pm for worship), one of the loveliest monasteries in Moscow. Founded in 1524, Novodevichiy is undeniably rich in historical associations and a coherent architectural ensemble, with the added attraction of Moscow's most venerable cemetery attached to it. A museum (Mon & Wed–Sun 10am–5pm; $4) of icons and manuscripts is found in the grounds, while at the heart of the convent stands the white Cathedral of the Virgin of Smolensk (sobor Smolenskoy Bogomateri), with a superb interior. To get there take the metro out to Sportivnaya, taking the ulitsa 10-ti Letiya Oktyabrya exit; a ten-minute walk to the end of the road brings you within sight of the convent's towers and ramparts.

Beyond the convent's south wall lies the fascinating **Novodevichiy Cemetery** (Novodevicheskoe kladbishche; daily 10am–6pm), where many famous writers, artists and politicians are buried. During Soviet times, only burial in the Kremlin Wall was more prestigious. The highest concentration of famous dead is in the oldest part of the cemetery, starting with Nikolai Gogol, Anton Chekhov, Konstantin Stanislavsky, Mikhail Bulgakov, Dmitri Shostakovich and the Futurist poet Vladimir Mayakovsky, but Krushchev is also here – he died out of office, and was denied burial in the Kremlin wall.

Zamoskvoreche

South across the river from the Kremlin is Zamoskvoreche, which simply means "Across the Moskva River". This area is clearly defined by geography and history, dating back to medieval times and preserving a host of colourful churches and the mansions of civic-minded merchants. It is one of the most charming parts of the city, with a strongly residential feel, and can be easily traversed by one of the trams which run from Chistye prudy metro along the boulevards and then cut through the Zamoskvoreche.

Founded in 1892 by the financier Pavel Tretyakov, the well-renovated, airy, modern **Tretyakov Gallery** (Tues–Sun 10am–7.30pm; *www.tretyakov.ru*; $7), five minutes' walk from Tretyakovskaya metro, was designed by the Slav Romantic artist Viktor Vasnetsov, and displays an outstanding collection of Russian art before the Revolution.

Russian **icons** are magnificently displayed in rooms 56–61, on the second floor. Icons, which originally came to Russia from Byzantium, were valued for their religious and spiritual content rather than artistic merit, and pride of place is given to a series of icons by Andrei Rublev, Daniil Cherniy and Dionysius. The exhibition continues with works by graduates of the Academy, as well as those who were expelled – the Wanderers, who used their art to express social criticism. The Slav Romantics and Symbolists are well represented, and there is a vast room filled with the nightmare-like, fantastical works of Mikhail Vrubel. Twentieth-century and contemporary art is on show at the **New Tretyakov** opposite the entrance to Gorky Park, at Krymskiy val 10 (Tues–Sun 10am–7.30pm; $6). The display is dominated by the works of the likes of Tatlin, Chagall and Malevich.

Gorky Park is famous abroad from Martin Cruz Smith's classic thriller. Inaugurated in 1928, the Soviet Union's first "Park of Culture and Rest" was formed by uniting an exhibition zone near Krymskiy val with the vast gardens of the Golitsyn Hospital and the Neskuchniy Palace. The park's 300 acres now include funfairs, a large outdoor skating rink and lots of woodland (daily 10am–10pm; $1). The highlights are an American rollercoaster (scary but safe), a retired Soviet space shuttle, and a big wheel, which affords great views over Moscow.

South of Zamoskvoreche

About 3km southeast of Gorky Park is the Danilov Monastery (Danilovskiy monastyr; daily 7am–7pm); founded by Prince Daniil of Moscow in 1282, it claims to be the oldest monastery in Moscow. In 1988, it became the seat and official residence of the Russian Orthodox patriarch and the Holy Synod, although the patriarch is seldom in residence. As such it has a modern, businesslike air, which might disappoint some visitors, but it undeniably bespeaks the Orthodox Church's prestige and influence in the new Russia. To get there, catch the metro to Tulskaya Station and walk 200m along Danilovskiy val. No shorts or bare shoulders are allowed. The Danilov Cemetery (Danilovskoe kladbishche; daily 9am–7pm) is overgrown and archaic, but its funerary monuments are fine, owing to the numerous Orthodox metropolitans and nouveaux riches merchants buried here. To get there, alight at the 3-y Verkhniy Mikhailovskiy stop, before the bus turns off Roshchinskiy.

On the steep west bank of the Moskva River, 10km southeast of the Kremlin, **Kolomenskoe** (grounds: daily 9am–7pm; museum: Tues–Sun 10am–6pm; museum $8) grew from a village founded by refugees from Kolomna during the Mongol invasions of the thirteenth century to become a royal summer retreat. After the Revolution the cemetery was razed and the churches closed; then the village was destroyed by collectivization. Not until 1974 was the area declared a conservation zone, saving 400 hectares of ancient woodland from the factories and apartments that have advanced on all sides.

Though its legendary wooden palace no longer exists, Kolomenskoe still has one of the finest churches in the whole of Russia (services Sunday 8am), and vintage wooden structures such as Peter the Great's cabin, set amid hoary oaks above a great bend in the river. In summer, Muscovites flock here for the fresh air and to sunbathe, and kitsch – in the form of folk dancing and singing for tourists – reigns supreme. In winter, however, the eerie Church of the Ascension rises against a void of snow and mist with nobody around except kids sledging down the slopes. Despite its distance from the centre, getting there is easy: take the metro from Teatralnaya, near the Bolshoy Theatre, from where it's only four stops to Kolomenskaya, fifteen minutes' walk from the site itself.

Andronikov Monastery complex

The fourteenth-century **Andronikov Monastery** is situated on the steep east bank of the Yauza. Its most famous monk was the great icon painter Andrei Rublev who was canonized by the Russian Orthodox Church in 1989. In the centre of the monastery stands Moscow's oldest architectural monument, the **Church of the Saviour** (1420s) with wall paintings by Rublev himself (closed for restoration at the time of writing), and which now houses the **Andrei Rublev Museum of Old Russian Art and Culture** (Andronyevskaya pl. 10; Ploshchad Ilyicha metro; Mon, Tues & Thurs–Sun 11am–6pm; $4) containing icons and liturgical utensils. The most famous icons may be in the Tretyakov, but the atmosphere here is something else – you retire from the noise and bustle of the city and enter a peaceful, serene land. Even the fact that until the 1950s the church housed the archive of the Ministry of State Security could do nothing to destroy its romance. Rublev is buried in the grounds.

The VDNKh – the northern suburbs

The main reason for venturing this far north is the Exhibition of Economic Achievements – or the VDNKh ("Vay-den-ha"; grounds: daily 9am–8pm; pavilions: daily 10am–7pm) – a permanent trade-fair-cum-shopping-centre for Russian producers, which reflects the state of the national economy more faithfully than its founders intended. Its genesis was the All-Union Agricultural Exhibition of 1939, a display of the fruits of socialism and a showpiece of Stalinist monumental art. Scores of pavilions trumpeted the achievements of the Soviet republics and the planned economy. Today, imported cars have ousted Soviet products. Shoppers, lured by "Wild Capitalism" (dikiy kapitalizm) rather than the Five Year Plan, ignore the gilded fountains and the sows that once attested to the fecundity of Soviet livestock. Shorn of ideological pretensions, it has been renamed the **All-Russia Exhibition Centre** (VVTs) – but everyone still calls it VDNKh.

Near the main entrance to the VDNKh stands one of the best-ever Soviet monuments, the **Space Obelisk**, consisting of a rocket blasting nearly 100m into the sky on a stylized plume of energy clad in shining titanium. It was unveiled in 1964, three years after Gagarin orbited the earth, an unabashed expression of pride in this unique feat. On the other side of the entrance is the famous monument of the **Worker and Collective Farm Girl**, its colossal twin figures intended to embody Soviet industrial progress, though in fact they were handmade.

For a total contrast, head about 1km west towards the easily visible Ostankino TV tower, just north of which is **Ostankino Museum** (entry $5), an eighteenth-century wooden country estate so well preserved it justly claims to be unique in the whole of Europe. Its tiny palace theatre is one of just a few surviving eighteenth-century theatre buildings in the world and retains all its original stage machinery. An exquisite monument to the life of Russian nobles, and to the incredible skills of their serf artists, the museum works according to the weather: officially the hours are Wed–Sun 10am–5pm (mid-May to Sept), but due to the fragility of the whole it is also closed in extremely wet or humid conditions.

Eating and drinking

It's no problem finding good food and drink in Moscow these days. In fact, the problem is choosing where to go. For the homesick there are numerous American bars and steakhouses, plus American coffee bars. Nonetheless, the wide gap between the top and bottom ends of the market and the relative shortage of places in between means that good, affordable restaurants are often full in the evenings, so reserving in advance is advised. Most places have a member of staff with a rudimentary grasp of English, and many offer some kind of entertainment in the evening. Most cafés serve plentiful and excellent food, at much lower prices than full-blown restaurants, and seldom require bookings, making them a boon for budget travellers. Many middle-range and more expensive places now take a variety of credit cards.

In recent years a large number of small rock **clubs** and **bars** have opened up, offering great food at amazingly cheap prices. Ordinary Russians tend to buy alcohol in a shop and drink it at home, but there are more and more Western-style bars springing up all over the place.

In this list we have weighted the selection towards more traditional Russian eateries – after all, why come to Russia to eat Indian? – and the cheap but high-quality places. Caucasian food (Georgian, Armenian) is almost always good in Moscow, and the more Caucasians you see in there, the better the joint.

A full list of literally hundreds of worthy places can be found in the *Moscow Times* supplement, *The Beat*, updated weekly.

Cafés, bars and fast food

Amalteya, Stremyanny per. 28/1; Serpukhovksya metro. Choose from a vast range of *meze* in this cheap Turkish café, which has a singer in the evenings. Daily 11am–last client.

Dioscarius, Merzlyakovskiy per. 2; Arbatskaya metro. Georgian food and great variety of Georgian wine, right in the centre of town. No credit cards. Daily 11am–midnight.

Donna Clara, Malaya Bronnaya ul. 21/13; Mayakovskaya metro. Small café in the heart of literary Moscow, offering great window seats. Daily 10am–11.30pm.

Guriya, Komsomolskiy pr. 7/3; Park Kultury metro. Cheap and scrumptious Georgian food, if a little full of the foreign community. No credit cards. Daily 11am–11pm.

Kofe-In (Caffeine), Bolshaya Dmitrovka ul. 15; Teatralnaya metro. A few main meals, but mainly great coffee and desserts. No credit cards. Daily 9am–11pm.

Kot Begemot, Spiridonyevskiy per. 10A; Mayakovskaya metro. Food nearly as good as the location. No credit cards. Daily noon–midnight.

Krizis Zhanra, Prechistenskiy per. 22/4; Kropotninskaya metro. Ridiculously cheap and mellow bar with a variety of live music. Very popular, with live bands in the evening. Daily 11am–11pm. Concerts start 8pm.

Ogonyok, Krasnaya Presnaya ul. 36; 1905-goda metro. Russian food that doesn't limit itself to *pelmeni* and beetroot. No credit cards. Daily noon–11pm.

PiR O.G.I., Pyatnitskaya ul. 29l; Novokuznetskaya metro. Great food and beer, and you're bound to meet someone you know in here. No credit cards. 24 hours.

Project O.G.I., Potapovskiy per. 8/12; Chistiye prudy metro. Hip club, bar and restaurant with sessions for kids in the mornings. No credit cards. Daily 8am–6pm.

U Babushki (At Granny's), Bolshaya Ordynka ul. 42; Tretyakovskaya metro. Small, cosy, with homely food – just like its name implies. Daily noon–10.30pm.

U Nikitskikh Vorot, Bolshaya Nikitskaya ul. 23/9; Okhotny Ryad metro. Cheap Georgian food, in a comfortable bar (rather plain restaurant). No credit cards. Daily noon–midnight.

U Yuzefa, Dubininskaya ul 11/17; Paveletskaya metro. Jewish home cooking, old fashioned, with live music. No credit cards. Daily noon–11pm.

Yolki-Palki, Tverskaya ul. 18; Bolshaya Dmitrovka ul. 23/8; Klimentovskiy per. 14/1; Novyy Arbat ul. 11; etc. If you want to eat Russian/Ukrainian/Mongolian food at rock-bottom prices, join the queue at one of ten or so branches of this popular eatery. No credit cards. 11am–midnight.

Restaurants

Moosh, Oktyabrskaya ul. 2/4 (☎095/284 3670); Novoslobodskaya metro. Very cheap Armenian food, just behind the Red Army Park. Daily 10am–midnight.

Petrovich Club, Myasnitskaya ul. 24 (☎095/923 0082); Chistiye Prudy metro. Russian *nouvelle cuisine* and nostalgia for a Soviet childhood in the 1960s and 1970s. No credit cards. Daily 2pm–5am.

Praga, ul. Arbat 2 (☎095/290 61 71); Arbatskaya metro. Impossible to get into without a bribe during the Soviet period, ghastly dump in the early years of perestroika, the place lived on its reputation as a pre-Revolutionary palace of *haute cuisine* and high society. Now easily back in the running for quality, it should be visited if only for its place in Moscow's social history. Daily noon–midnight.

Raisky Dvor, Spiridonovka ul. 25 (☎095/290 13 41); Mayakovskaya metro. Russian and European food, inside Orwell's *Animal Farm*. Daily noon–6am.

Nightlife and entertainment

Moscow's **nightlife** has it all, and thankfully the days of disco dominance are gone, so there are plenty of small, intimate nightclubs and great **live music** of all genres.

Alongside the city's restaurants and clubs, there's a rich **cultural life** in Moscow. Classical music, opera and ballet are strongly represented with a busy schedule of concerts and performances throughout the year, sometimes held in the city's palaces, churches or – in summer – parks and gardens. Even if you don't speak Russian, puppetry and the circus transcend language barriers, while several cinemas show films in their original language. The **America Cinema** (*Radisson-Slavyanskaya Hotel*; ☎095/941 87 47; Kievskaya metro), and Dome Cinema, Olimpiiskiy pr. 18/1 (*Renaissance Hotel*; Prospekt Mira metro), show films in their original languages, and there's a discount for students. *The Moscow Times* has OK listings in English, but if you speak a little Russian buy *Afisha*, the equivalent of *Time Out*, which covers the full range of just about everything everywhere, from gigs to contemporary art exhibitions, to poetry readings.

Clubs and live music

Dom, Bolshoy Ovchinnikovskiy per. 24/4; Novokuznetskaya metro. For the hip "intellectual" crowd. Thurs–Sun 7.30–11pm.

Hungry Duck, 9 Pushechnaya ul.; Kuznetskiy Most metro. Renowned for its bad-taste raucous entertainments. Daily 8pm–6am.

Kitayskiy Lyotchik Dzhao Da, Lubyanskiy proezd 25; Kitay-gorod metro. Coolest place to be seen and hear the best bands on offer. No credit cards. 24 hours.

Luch, Monetchikovskiy per. 5/3; Paveletskaya metro. Rave, chemical, and some weird acts. Cover charge. Daily 10pm–4am.

Novie Vasyuki, Starokonyushenniy per. 2; Kropotkinskaya metro. Cellar club with a miniscule stage which draws some big names. No credit cards. 2pm to last customer.

Propaganda, Bolshoy Zlatoustinskiy per. 7; Kitay-gorod metro. Very young but dead cool, with some of the city's best DJs. No credit cards. Sun–Wed noon–12.30am; Thurs noon–3am, Fri 10pm–6am; Sat 3pm–6am.

Staraya ploshchad, Bolshoy Cherkasskiy per. 8; Kitay-gorod metro. Cellar club for the down-to-earth. No credit cards. Daily 6pm–6am.

Svalka, Profsoyuznaya ul. 27/1; Profsoyuznaya metro. This place has taken over from *Propaganda* for grunge, and has much better music. *Svalka* does, after all, mean "rubbish dump". Daily 7pm–6am.

Territoria, Tverskaya ul. 5/6; Okhotniy Ryad metro. Everyone seems to know each other here. Thurs–Sun 1pm–6am.

Opera and ballet

Bolshoy Theatre, Teatralnaya pl. 1 (☎095/292 99 86); Teatralnaya metro. Fighting hard in its rivalry with Petersburg's Mariinskiy, the competition is great for standards. The ballet and Russian opera is still stupendous, although Italian opera can be a bit off. Decent tickets cost $40 or more for foreigners. Performances Tues–Sun at 7pm, and a matinée on Sunday.

Helikon Opera, Bolshaya Nikitskaya ul. (☎095/290 0971); Pushkinskaya metro. Small theatre offering intimate, small-scale productions, including works by Handel and Bach.

Circuses

New Circus, pr. Vernadskovo 7 (☎095/930 28 15); Universitet metro. Moscow's Circus is one of the finest in the world, but still uses animal acts. Performances Wed–Fri 7pm, Sat & Sun 11.30am, 3pm & 7pm.

Yuriy Nikulin Circus, Tsvetnoy bul. 13 (☎095/200 06 68); Tsvetnoy bulvar metro. Clowns are their forte. Performances Thurs and Fri–Sun 7pm, matinées Sat & Sun 2.30pm.

Listings

Airlines Aeroflot, ul. Koroviy val 7 (☎095/156 8019); British Airways, 1-ya Tverskaya-Yamskaya 23 (☎095/363 2525, *www.britishairways.com/russia*). For flight information at Sheremetevo-2 call ☎095/956 4666.

American Express Sadovaya-Kudrinskaya ul. 21a (Mon–Fri 9am–5pm; ☎095/755 9024).

Bookshop Shakespeare & Company, 1-y Novokuznetskiy per. 5/7 (Mon–Sat 11am–7pm, Sun noon–6pm; ☎095/951 9360); Novokuznetskaya metro. English language books, new and secondhand.

Buses Eurolines desk on the second floor of the main building at Leningrad Station (☎095/975 3309).

Car rental These companies may have cars without drivers: A.M. Rent (☎095/952 9658, *www.amrent.ru*); Budget (☎095/578 7344, *budgetmoscow@col.ru*); Europcar (☎095/155 0170, *www.europcar.com*).

Embassies Australia, Kropotkinskiy per. 13 (Mon–Fri 9am–12.30pm & 1.30–5pm; ☎095/956 6070); Canada, Starokonyushenniy per. 23 (Mon–Fri 8.30am–5pm; ☎095/956 6666); Great Britain, Smolenskaya nab. 10 (Mon–Fri 9am–1pm & 2–4pm; ☎095/956 72 00); Ireland, Grokholskiy per. 5 (Mon–Fri 9.30am–1pm & 2.30–5.30pm; ☎095/937 5911); New Zealand, Povarskaya ul. 44 (Mon–Fri 10am–noon & 2–4pm; ☎095/956 3579); USA, Novinskiy bulvar 19/23 (Mon–Fri 9am–5pm; ☎095/728 5000).

Emergencies For medical assistance, American Medical Center, Grokholskiy per. 1 (☎095/933 7700, *www.amcenters.com*); European Medical Centre, 2-oy Tverskoy-Yamskoy per. 10 (☎095/787 7000, *www .emcmos.ru/eng*); both recognized by international insurance companies.

Exchange Official currency exchanges and ATMs all over the centre of Moscow.

Internet cafés Chevignon at Stoleshnikov per. 14 (☎095/733 9205; Teatralnaya metro); Internet Cafe, Novoslobodskaya ul. 16 (*www.cafe.image.ru*; Mendeleyevskaya metro); Internet Club, Kuznetskiy most 12 (☎095/250 6169; Kuznetskiy Most metro).

Laundry For laundry or dry cleaning try one of the many branches of California Cleaners – for instance at Petrovska 27 (Mon–Sat 10am–10pm; ☎095/200 6400) or Noviy Arbat 54 (daily 10am–8pm; ☎095/241 0761).

Left luggage Most train stations have lockers and/or a 24hr left-luggage office, but you would be tempting fate to use them.

Pharmacy Staryy Arbat, Arbatskaya ul. 25; Multifarma, Tursistkaya ul. 27; 24hr pharmacy at pr. Mira 71.

Post office Central Telegraph Office at Tverskaya ul. 7 (8am–10pm); the Main Post Office (*glávniy póchtamt*) is at Myasnitskaya ul. 26/2, 101000 (daily 8am–8pm), near Chistye Prudy metro. Express postal services via Courier Service, Bolshaya Sadovaya 10 (☎095/209 1735; Mayakovskaya metro); EMS Garant at the International Post Office, Varshavskoe shosse 37 (☎095/728 4151); PXPost, Zorge ul. 10 (☎095/956 2230).

Railway tickets. These can be bought cheaply at the stations or for a small commission from one of hundreds of agencies. Conveniently located in the centre is Intourtrans at Petrovka 15/13 (☎095/929 8855).

Student Travel Star Travel at Baltiyskaya ul. 9 (☎095/797 9555).

ST PETERSBURG

ST PETERSBURG, Petrograd, Leningrad and now again, St Petersburg – the city's succession of names mirrors Russia's turbulent history. Founded in 1703 as a "window on the West" by Peter the Great, St Petersburg was for two centuries the capital of the tsarist empire, synonymous with excess and magnificence. During World War I the city renounced its German-sounding name and became Petrograd, and as such was the cradle of the revolutions that overthrew tsarism and brought the Bolsheviks to power in 1917. As Leningrad it epitomized the Soviet Union's heroic sacrifices in the war, withstanding nine hundred days of Nazi siege. Finally, in 1991 – the year that Communism and the USSR collapsed – the change of name, back to St Petersburg, proved deeply symbolic of the country's democratic mood.

St Petersburg's sense of its own identity owes much to its origins and to the interweaving of myth and reality throughout its history. Created by the will of an autocrat, the imperial cap-

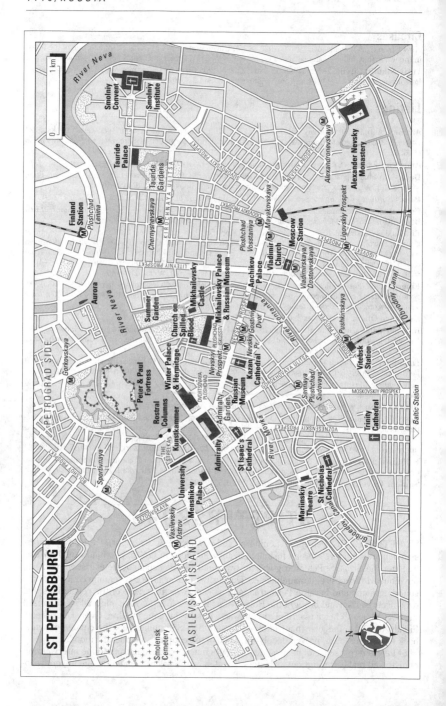

ital embodied both Peter the Great's rejection of Old Russia – represented by "Asiatic" Moscow, the former capital – and of his embrace of Europe. The city's architecture, administration and social life were all copied or imported.

Today, St Petersburg is beautiful yet drab, progressive yet stagnant, sophisticated and cerebral, industrial and maritime. Beggars and nouveaux riches rub shoulders on Nevskiy prospekt, yet after the enormous changes of recent years a sense of stability and relative well-being has at last arrived, reaching even beyond the historic centre to the sprawling outer ring of high-rise blocks.

Arrival and information

St Petersburg's **international airport**, Pulkovo-2 (☎812/104 3444), is 17km south of the city centre. Take one of the frequent minibuses or use the cheap **bus** service (#13), which runs every twenty minutes from the stop nearest the Arrivals building to Moskovskaya ploshchad, where you can change onto the **metro**; purchase your **ticket** (flat-fare) from the conductor. There are always plenty of taxis, both licensed and unofficial, but, either way, you'll pay over the odds: $12 is more than fair for a ride into the centre, but drivers often open the bidding at $40 or higher.

The first thing a visitor should do is pick up *St Petersburg: The Official City Guide*, an excellent full-colour quarterly freebie, or buy the pocket edition of the *Traveller's Yellow Pages*. The Friday edition of *The St Petersburg Times* and the monthly *Pulse* are both free and have good listings and reviews. All the hostels can provide everything from invitations and accommodation bookings to theatre tickets, restaurant advice and general help and advice should something go wrong. The **City Tourist Information Office** at Nevskiy pr. 41 (☎812/311 2843) is still near the bottom of a steep learning curve.

City transport

St Petersburgers walk, summer or winter. Around town, along canals, onto the islands, to and from work. Yet it is a big city, and sooner or later you're going to want to use its cheap and relatively efficient **public transport** system. Unlike Moscow, overground transport is more useful in the centre than the fast **metro** network (daily 6am to just after midnight). There is an overstretched network of **trams, buses** and **trolleybuses**, as well as very efficient commercial **minibuses**. For general information on public transport see the "City Transport" section of the Moscow account, much of which also applies to St Petersburg – note, however, that overground transport all has conductors, from whom one should purchase a ticket for a single ride only. Official **taxis** are more expensive than private cars, which are likely to stop if you stick out your arm and are generally safe during the day. As a guide, Nevskiy prospekt to the Peter and Paul Fortress is $2 to locals, though foreigners are likely to be charged more. One of the best ways to see St Petersburg May to October is by boat, whether a private motorboat, which can be picked up alongside any bridge on Nevskiy prospekt (from $35/hr), or one of the large tour boats with commentary by the Anichkov Bridge ($4). When the bridges go up (May to late-Oct) at 2am (until 5am) and you are stuck on the wrong island, the private boats sometimes run a very expensive ferry system.

Accommodation

As with Moscow, the **accommodation** situation in St Petersburg is far from ideal. If you're looking for a central location, within easy walking distance of the major sights, the choice of **hotels** is limited and prices high. Just a little further out, there are some pleasant and inexpensive options, but **hostels** offer the best alternative, being cheap, reasonably central and with decent facilities; note that there is no age restriction. *HOFA* (☎812/275 1992, *homestay @yahoo.com*) has long experience in helping find bed and breakfast for those on a tight budget, as well as offering onward tours around Russia and the CIS, also staying with (usually university) families. For several people over a short period it is sometimes cheaper to rent an **apartment**, notably in the off season; try Pulford Estates (☎812/325 6277, *www.pulford.com*).

Hostels

Herzen University Hostel, Kazanskaya ul. 6 (☎812/314 7472); Nevskiy Prospekt/Gostiniy Dvor metro. Great location, just behind the Kazan Cathedral off Nevskiy prospekt, with decent facilities, including a solarium and masseur. No visa support. ④.

Hostel Holiday, Mikhaylova ul. 1 (☎812/327 1070, *www.hostel.ru*); Ploshchad Lenina metro. Offers a full range of services, including visa support; some rooms overlook the River Neva. ③.

St Petersburg International Hostel, 3-ya Sovetskaya ul. 28 (☎812/329 8018, *www.ryh.ru*); Ploshchad Vosstaniya metro. Good facilities and helpful staff. Breakfast is included in the price; separate floors for men and women. In the summer months it's wise to book ahead. Visa support. ③.

Hotels

Mir, ul. Gastello 17 (☎812/108 5166); Moskovskaya metro. Clean and modest, although not exactly in the centre. No credit cards. ⑤.

Neva, Chaykovskovo ul. 17 (☎812/278 0500); Chernyshevskaya metro. Clean and old-fashioned, just a hop away from the Summer Garden and the Neva. No credit cards. ⑤.

Oktyabrskaya, Ligovskiy pr. 10 (☎812/277 63 30); Ploshchad Vosstaniya or Mayakovskaya metro. A gloomy, nineteenth-century warren overlooking Moscow Station; all rooms have satellite TV and bathroom, but best ask for an "upgraded room" – the plumbing is better. ⑥.

Rus, Artillereyskaya ul. 1 (☎812/279 5003); Chernyshevskaya metro. Modern Soviet-style hotel-cum-business centre a few minutes' walk from Liteyniy prospekt. ⑥.

Sovetskaya, Lermontovskiy pr. 43/1 (☎812/329 0181, *sovot@pop.convey.ru*); Tekhnologicheskiy Institut metro. Modern hotel offering excellent views up the River Fontanka. ⑥.

The City

Everything in St Petersburg is built on a grand scale, which makes mastering the public transport system a top priority. The city is split by the River Neva and its tributaries, with further sections delineated by the course of the canalized Moyka and Fontanka rivers, all of which conveniently divide St Petersburg into a series of islands, making it fairly easy to get your bearings.

St Petersburg's centre lies on the south bank of the **River Neva**, with the curving River Fontanka marking its southern boundary. The area within the **Fontanka** is riven by a series of wide avenues which fan out from the most obvious landmark on the south bank of the Neva, the Admiralty. Many of the city's greatest sights and monuments – the Winter Palace and the art collections of the Hermitage, the Russian Museum, the Mikhail Castle, the Summer Garden, and the St Isaac and Kazan cathedrals – are located in and around **Nevskiy prospekt**, the main avenue.

Across the River Neva, and connected by Dvortsoviy most (Palace Bridge), is **Vasilevskiy Island**, the largest of the city's islands. In an area known as the **Strelka**, located on the island's eastern tip, are some of St Petersburg's oldest institutions: the Academy of Sciences, the university and the former Stock Exchange, as well as some fascinating museums.

On the north side of the River Neva, opposite the Winter Palace, is the island known as the Petrograd Side, home to the **Peter and Paul Fortress**, whose construction is seen as marking the foundation of the city itself. As well as its strategic and military purpose, it also housed St Petersburg's first prison and cathedral.

Back on the mainland, east of the River Fontanka, the conventional sights are more dispersed and the distances that much greater. The two most popular destinations in this wedge of land, which was largely developed in the latter half of the nineteenth century, are the

Smolniy Complex, from where the Bolsheviks orchestrated the October Revolution, and, further south, the **Alexander Nevsky Monastery**.

Nevskiy prospekt

Nevskiy prospekt has been the backbone and heart of the city for the last two centuries. Built on an epic scale during the reign of Peter the Great, under the direction of the Frenchman Jean-Baptiste Le Blond, it manifests every style of architecture, from eighteenth-century Baroque to *fin-de-siècle* and is home to the city's most important sites.

Set back on the southern side of Nevskiy prospekt is the cream-coloured **Anichkov Palace** – now the Palace of Youth Creativity; access is limited to concerts and other cultural events. Further west along Nevskiy prospekt, near the Dom Knigi bookshop, former emporium of the Singer sewing-machine company, is **Kazan Cathedral** (Kazanskiy sobor; services 9am and 6pm daily), one of the grandest churches in the city, modelled on St Peter's in the Vatican. The cathedral was built to house the venerated icon, Our Lady of Kazan, reputed to have appeared miraculously overnight in Kazan in 1579, and transferred by Peter the Great to St Petersburg, where it resided until its disappearance in 1904. In Soviet times the cathedral housed the Museum of Religion and Atheism, but it has since been reconsecrated.

The Winter Palace

The **Winter Palace** (Zimniy dvorets), at the westernmost end of Nevskiy prospekt on the Neva embankment, is the finest example of Russian Baroque in St Petersburg, the largest, most opulent palace within the city.

As loaded with history as it is with gilt and stucco, the palace's two-hundred-metre-long facade features a riot of ornamentation in the fifty bays that now face Palace Square. Official residence of the tsars, not to mention the court and 1500 servants, the existing building was completed in 1762. Later, new buildings were added to the east: the **Small Hermitage** (Maliy Ermitazh), built as a private retreat for Catherine the Great, and the **Large Hermitage** (Bolshoy Ermitazh), further east. Beyond stands the **Hermitage Theatre** (Ermitazhniy teatr, 1775–84), Catherine the Great's private theatre, now used for concerts, ballet and conferences. The basement houses an exhibition documenting the remains of Peter the Great's original Winter Palace.

THE HERMITAGE

The **Hermitage** (Ermitazh; Tues–Sat 10.30am–6pm, Sun 10.30am–5pm; *www.hermitage museum.org*; $6) is one of the world's great art museums. Of awesome size and diversity, it embraces everything from ancient Scythian gold and Kyoto woodcuts to Cubism. It has been calculated that merely to glance at each of the 2.8 million objects it houses would take nine years and would entail walking a distance of more than 10km. In the magnificent state rooms of the Winter Palace itself the tsars once held court and the Provisional Government was arrested by the Bolsheviks.

The **Italian art** section has works by Leonardo, Botticelli, Michelangelo, Raphael, Titian, Veronese and Tiepolo; the **Dutch and Flemish art** collection features magnificent selections of paintings by Rembrandt, Rubens and Van Dyck; and there is an impressive collection of seventeenth- and eighteenth-century **French art**. After the state rooms and the Gold Collection, the most universally popular section of the Hermitage is that covering **modern European art** from the nineteenth and twentieth centuries, with a fine spread of Impressionist paintings and works by Matisse and Picasso. Look out, too, for the work of Rodin, Gauguin, Van Gogh, Henri Rousseau, Delacroix, Cézanne, Pissarro, Monet, Degas and Renoir. Paintings by Bonnard and Denis are on display in the museum annexe housed in the majestically curving General Staff Building on the other side of Palace Square, along with exhibits tracing the glory of Imperial Russia and its elite military forces.

North of Nevskiy prospekt

Before working your way up to the Summer Garden and Palace, make a short stop 600m north of Nevskiy prospekt, a short distance along the east side of the Moyka. Here a wide passageway at no. 12 leads to the garden-courtyard of **Pushkin's Apartment** (Mon & Wed–Sun 10.30am–5pm; closed last Fri of every month; $3), where the poet died after a duel. The most evocative room is Pushkin's study, containing a replica of his library of over 4500 books in fourteen languages.

To the east of the apartment stands the multicoloured, onion-domed **Church on Spilled Blood** (Khram "Spasa na krovi"; Mon–Tues & Thurs–Sun 11am–7pm; $7), begun in 1882 to commemorate Tsar Alexander II, who had been assassinated on the site the previous year. Designed in the style of St Basil's in Moscow, it is one of St Petersburg's most striking landmarks, quite unlike the rest of the city's architecture. Closed for twenty years, the church was fully restored and reopened in 1997.

East of the Church on Spilled Blood, the vast **Mikhail Palace** (Mikhaylovskiy dvorets), houses the Russian Museum. Designed by Rossi, its long facade epitomizes the Neoclassical architecture of Alexander I's reign. Little remains of Rossi's original interior, save the main staircase and the austere "White Room".

THE RUSSIAN MUSEUM

Along with the Tretyakov Gallery in Moscow, the **Russian Museum** (Russkiy muzey; Mon 10am–5pm, Wed–Sun 10am–6pm; $5) contains the finest collection of Russian art in the world. The museum, which celebrated its hundredth anniversary in 1998, also has three branch palaces with superb displays on selected themes.

The exhibition begins on the **upper floor** with icons and paintings from the fourteenth to nineteenth centuries, including works by Russia's greatest icon painter, the monk Andrei Rublev (c.1340–c.1430). The **lower floor** begins with a demonstration of how Russian art came of age in the late nineteenth century. Portraits by Ivan Kramskoy (1837–87) and Nikolai Ge (1831–94) are exhibited near the socialist conscious realism of Ilya Repin (1844–1930) and the vast historical canvases of Vasiliy Surikov (1846–1916). There is also a small display of traditional Russian folk art. From room 48 a corridor leads to the **Benois Wing**, which, apart from housing temporary exhibitions, presents the movements of the early twentieth century, from Symbolism to Analytical Art. There are also works by Mikhail Vrubel (1856–1910), whose impact on Russian art was comparable to that of Cézanne in the West, and the Suprematist Kazimir Malevich (1878–1935), but generally the display of Russian avant-garde art is disappointing, representing only a fraction of the museum's holdings. The Benois Wing also has its own entrance off Griboyedov Canal.

At the turn of the twentieth century, the east wing, stables and laundry of the palace were replaced by a Neoclassical annexe built to house the ethnographical collections of the Russian Museum. In 1934, this became an entirely separate **Museum of Ethnography** (Muzey etnografii; Tues–Sun 10am–6pm; closed last Fri of every month; $4), with displays of folk art, costumes, tools and reconstructed cottage and hut interiors of the peoples of the former USSR.

THE MIKHAIL CASTLE AND MARSOVO POLE

Moving north from the Museum of Ethnography, up Sadovaya ulitsa, you'll come across the idiosyncratic and heavily fortified **Mikhail Castle** (Mikhaylovskiy zamok; Mon 10am–5pm, Wed–Sun 10am–6pm; $5), begun by Paul I shortly after he came to the throne, to protect him from the assassination attempt he feared. To make way for it he had the wooden palace in which he had been born burnt to the ground, and commissioned Vasiliy Bazhenov to design the castle. In an atmosphere of almost pathological fear, Paul moved into the castle in February 1801, but was murdered in his bedroom there just three weeks later. Now a branch of the Russian Museum, the castle contains displays of portraiture and excellent temporary exhibitions. The **Mikhail Garden** next door (behind the Russian Museum) is much loved by young lovers, book-readers, football players and all true St Petersburgers for its truly relaxed atmosphere.

Between the River Moyka and the Neva embankment, **Marsovo pole** (the Field of Mars) is a pleasant park, heavy with the scent of lilac in spring. At its northwestern corner lies the costliest palace yet built in the city, the **Marble Palace** (Mramorniy dvorets; Mon 10am–5pm, Wed–Sun 10am–6pm; $5). Designed by Antonio Rinaldi for Catherine the Great's lover, Count Orlov, the palace is another annexe of the Russian Museum, this time showing works by foreign artists living in Russia in the eighteenth and nineteenth centuries and contemporary art.

THE SUMMER GARDEN AND PALACE

To the east of Marsovo pole is the **Summer Garden** (Letniy sad; daily: summer 8am–10pm; winter 11am–6pm; closed during very wet weather; weekdays free, summer weekends small admission fee), the city's most treasured public garden, commissioned by Peter the Great in 1704. The Frenchman, Le Blond, was to design a formal garden in the style of Versailles, with intricate parterres of flowers, shrubs and gravel, a glass conservatory, and numerous marble statues and fountains. However, after the disastrous flood of 1777, which wrecked the garden, Catherine the Great ordered its reconstruction in the less formal, less spectacular English style that survives today. In the northeastern corner of the Summer Garden, Domenico Trezzini began working on a **Summer Palace** (Letniy dvorets; May–Oct daily except Tues 11am–7pm; $5) for Peter the Great in 1710. A modest two-storey building of brick and stucco – one of the first such structures in the city – the new palace was only a small step up from Peter's first wooden cottage on the other side of the river.

Southwest of Nevskiy prospekt

The **Admiralty** (Admiralteystvo), standing at the western end of Nevskiy prospekt, is one of the world's most magnificent expressions of naval triumphalism, extending 407m (1300ft) along the waterfront, from Palace Square (Dvortsovaya ploshchad) to Decembrists' Square (ploshchad Dekabristov). Originally founded by Peter the Great in 1704 as a fortified ship-yard, with a primitive wooden tower and spire, the Admiralty gradually became purely administrative in function and a suitable building was erected in the early 1820s. Today, the key feature of the building is still its central tower (72.5m high), rising from an arched cube and culminating in a slender spire.

Largely obscuring the Admiralty, the wooded **Admiralty Garden** (Admiralteyskiy sad) leads towards Decembrists' Square. The square is named after a group of reformist officers who, in December 1825, marched three thousand soldiers into the square in an attempt to proclaim a constitutional monarchy. This revolt turned from farce to tragedy when Tsar Nicholas I ordered his loyalist troops to attack and crush the rebellion. From here, your eyes are inevitably drawn to Falconet's renowned statue of Peter the Great, known as the **Bronze Horseman** (Medniy vsadnik), which rears up towards the waterfront, and the newlyweds who come here to be photographed.

Looming majestically above the rooftops, **St Isaac's Cathedral** (Isaakievskiy sobor; daily except Wed 11am–7pm, colonnade till 5pm; $6, colonnade $4), just off ploshchad Dekabristov, is too massive to grasp at close quarters. Standing in its own square, the cathedral's gilded dome is one of the glories of St Petersburg's skyline, while its opulent interior is equally impressive, decorated with fourteen kinds of marble. The cathedral's height (101.5m) and rooftop statues are best appreciated by climbing the 262 steps up to its dome – the third largest cathedral dome in Europe, with enough gold leaf used to push the total cost of the cathedral to 23,256,000 rubles (six times that of the Winter Palace).

Few tourists can resist the **St Nicholas Cathedral** (Nikolskiy sobor), to the south of St Isaac's Cathedral and Theatre Square (Teatralnaya ploshchad). Traditionally known as the "Sailors' Church" after the naval officers who once prayed here, the cathedral is a lovely example of eighteenth-century Russian Baroque – painted ice blue with white Corinthian pilasters and aedicules, and crowned by five gilded onion domes. Its low, vaulted interior is festooned with icons, and during services (6pm) the cathedral resounds with the sonorous Orthodox liturgy, chanted and sung amid clouds of incense.

Vasilevskiy Island

Buffeted by storms from the Gulf of Finland, pear-shaped **Vasilevskiy Island** (Vasilevskiy ostrov) cleaves the River Neva into its Bolshaya and Malaya branches. The island forms a strategic wedge, whose eastern "spit", or **Strelka**, is as much a part of St Petersburg's waterfront as the Winter Palace or Admiralty.

Originally, Peter envisaged making the island the centre of his capital. Aleksander Menshikov, first governor of St Petersburg, was an early resident – the Menshikov Palace is the oldest building on the island – and Peter compelled other rich landowners and merchants to settle here. By 1726 the island had ten streets and over a thousand inhabitants, but wilderness still predominated and there were no bridges: the hazardous crossing by boat destroyed any hope of the island becoming the centre.

Although you can reach the Strelka by trolleybus (#1, #7 and #10), bus (#7) or numerous expresses (e.g. #47, #T128, #T129) from Nevskiy prospekt, it's better to walk across **Dvortsoviy most** (Palace Bridge), which offers fabulous views of both banks of the Neva (all richly illuminated at night). On the Strelka are the weird **Rostral Columns** and Classical **Stock Exchange** building (now housing the Naval Museum), an ensemble created at the beginning of the nineteenth century by Thomas de Thomon, who also designed the granite embankments and cobbled ramps leading down to the Neva – reminders that the city's port and commercial centre were once located here.

Facing Dvortsoviy most is the **Zoological Museum** (Zoologicheskiy muzey; daily except Fri 11am–6pm; $4). Founded in 1832, the museum has one of the finest collections of its kind in the world, with over one hundred thousand specimens, including a set of stuffed animals that once belonged to Peter the Great, while the most evocative display shows the discovery of a 44,000-year-old mammoth in the permafrost of Yakutia in 1903.

Even more alluring – or repulsive – is the former **Kunstkammer** next door, instantly recognizable by its tower and entered from an alley to the west. Founded by Peter in 1714, its name (meaning "art chamber" in German) dignified his fascination for curiosities and freaks. Peter offered rewards for "human monsters" and unknown birds and animals, with a premium for especially odd ones. Dead specimens had to be preserved in vinegar or vodka (which was reimbursed by the imperial pharmacy), while to attract visitors, each guest received a glass of vodka or a cup of coffee.

Within the Kunstkammer is the **Museum of Anthropology and Ethnography** (Muzey Antropologii i Etnografii; daily except Thurs 11am–6pm; closed last Wed of every month; $6), displaying everything from Balinese puppets to Inuit kayaks and including some fascinating dioramas of native village life. In the round hall between Africa and the Americas, a selection of Peter's pickled curios still excites wonder and disgust: Siamese twins, a two-faced man and a two-headed calf. Also shown are surgical and dental instruments, and teeth pulled by the tsar himself (a keen amateur dentist).

It's worth walking further along the embankment to admire the pastel-toned elegant ensemble of English Quay across the river and to visit the **Menshikov Palace** (Menshikovskiy dvorets; Tues–Sun 10.30am–5.30pm; $6), a gabled, yellow-and-white, early-eighteenth-century building, which is now a branch of the Hermitage, devoted to the life and culture of Peter the Great's time. It was the first – and finest – residential structure on Vasilevskiy Island, and though not as sumptuous as the later imperial palaces, it sports a fine Petrine-era decor. At the time it surpassed Peter's Summer Palace, though the tsar had no objections, preferring to entertain at the Menshikov Palace, which was furnished to suit his tastes. The entrance is below street level, past the main portico.

The Peter and Paul Fortress

Across the Neva from the Winter Palace, on a small island, stands the **Peter and Paul Fortress** (Petropavlovskaya krepost), begun in 1703 and built to secure Russia's hold on the Neva delta. Forced labourers toiled from dawn to dusk to construct the fortress in just seven months. The fortress is permanently open – with no admission charge – but its **cathedral** and **museums** (covering the history of the city and Russian life up to 1917) keep regular visiting hours (Mon, Tues & Thurs–Sun 11am–6pm; closed last Tues of every month) and require tickets (around $10 for all the museums).

The **Peter and Paul Cathedral** (Petropavlovskiy sobor) signals defiance from the heart of the fortress. The original wooden church commissioned by Peter on this site was replaced by a stone cathedral, completed by Trezzini in 1733, long after Peter had died. The facade of the cathedral looks Dutch, while the gilded spire was deliberately made higher than the Ivan the Great Bell Tower in the Kremlin – it remained the tallest structure (122m) in the city until the 1960s. Sited around the nave are the tombs of the Romanov monarchs from Peter the Great onwards – excluding Peter II, Ivan VI and Nicholas II. Nicholas and his family, whose bones were discovered in a mine shaft in the Urals in 1989, were finally buried in a chapel beside the cathedral in July 1998.

The fortress was also used as a prison from 1718, when Peter the Great's son Aleksey was tortured to death here. The **Prison Museum**, however, fails to convey the full horror of conditions in tsarist times. The accessible cells are stark and gloomy, but far worse ones existed within the ramparts, below the level of the river, where the perpetual damp and cold made tuberculosis inevitable. Prisoners were never allowed to see each other and rarely glimpsed their jailers. Some were denied visitors and reading material for decades; many went mad and several committed suicide. In a somewhat surreal move, some of the bastions on the river side now house a contemporary art centre, Pro Arte, where some of the latest shows of video, performance and conceptual art are held, as well as packed lectures by some of the brightest Russian and European critics and philosophers.

The Smolniy district

Nestling in the bend of the River Neva, northeast of Nevskiy prospekt, lies the quiet **Smolniy district**, whose sleepy streets lined with nineteenth-century apartment blocks belie the area's turbulent historic past. Lenin ran the Revolution from the Smolniy Institute and for the 74 years of Communist rule, the word "Smolniy" was synonymous with the Revolution and the Party.

The **Tauride Garden** (Tavricheskiy sad), at the end of Furshtadtskaya ulitsa, was designed by the English gardener, William Gould, in the eighteenth century but now also boasts a small antiquated fairground. On the north side of the park is the **Tauride Palace** (Tavricheskiy dvorets), built by Catherine the Great for her lover, Prince Potemkin, to celebrate his annexation of the Crimea (Tauris) to Russia. Completed in 1789, the palace is one of the city's earliest examples of austere Neoclassicism, but is sadly closed to the public, being used as headquarters for the Commonwealth of Independent States (the organization uniting the former Soviet republics).

Just east of the Tauride Palace, at the end of Shpalernaya ulitsa, it's impossible to ignore the glorious ice-blue cathedral towering on the eastern horizon, which is the focal point and architectural masterpiece of the **Smolniy Complex**. In the eighteenth century, Empress Elizabeth founded the **Smolniy Convent** (Smolniy monastyr) on the site. Rastrelli's grandiose Rococo plans – including a 140-metre-high bell tower, which would have been the tallest structure in the city – were never completed, and the building was only finished in 1835 by Stasov in a more restrained Neoclassical fashion. The cathedral's austere white interior (daily except Thurs 10am–5pm) is disappointingly severe and is used to host temporary exhibitions and concerts. The **Smolniy Institute**, now the Mayor's Office, was built 1806–08 to house the Institute for Young Noblewomen, but gained its notoriety after the Petrograd

Soviet moved here in August 1917, until the city's vulnerability in the Civil War impelled the government to move to Moscow in March 1918. It contains a **museum** (by appointment only; ☎812/276 1461), which includes Lenin's rooms.

Alexander Nevsky Monastery

Two kilometres south of the Smolniy, at the southeastern end of Nevskiy prospekt, lies the **Alexander Nevsky Monastery** (Aleksandro-Nevskaya lavra), founded in 1713 by Peter the Great. From 1797 it became one of only four monasteries in the Russian Empire to be given the title of *lavra*, the highest rank in Orthodox monasticism.

There are two main cemeteries within the monastery. The most famous names reside in the **Tikhvin Cemetery** (also known as Necropolis for Masters of the Arts), the more recent of the two, established in 1823: here lie Dostoyevsky, Rimsky-Korsakov, Tchaikovsky, Rubinstein and Glinka. Directly opposite is the much smaller **Lazarus Cemetery** (also known as Necropolis of the Eighteenth Century), established by Peter the Great, and the oldest in the city. There are fewer international celebrities, but it's just as interesting in terms of funereal art. You should be able to locate the tombs of the polymath Lomonosov and the architects Rossi and Quarenghi. **Tickets** are required for entry into the Tikhvin and Lazarus cemeteries (daily except Thurs: May–Oct 9.30am–7pm; Nov–April 9.30am–5.30pm; $4), but not for the monastery or the Trinity Cathedral, which are both open daily from dawn to dusk.

To reach the **monastery** itself (6am–8pm), continue along the walled path past Trezzini's **Church of the Annunciation**, the original burial place of Peter III, Catherine the Great's deposed husband (daily 11am–5pm; $2). Trezzini also drew up an ambitious design for the monastery's **Trinity Cathedral**, but failed to orientate it towards the east, as Orthodox custom required, so the plans were scrapped. The job was left to Ivan Starov, who completed a more modest building in a Neoclassical style which now sits awkwardly with the rest of the complex.

To escape the crowds in summer, head round the back of the cathedral to the **Nicholas Cemetery**, an overgrown graveyard where the monastery's scholars and priests are buried, as well as nobles and intellectuals. Recently it has become a "fashionable" burial place, partly since Galina Starovoitova, reformer and liberal politician, was buried here in 1998.

Eating and drinking

There is no longer any need to go to St Petersburg's top **restaurants** for good food these days: in recent years a growing number of more modestly priced, intimate establishments have opened up, serving good food and offering a better feel of local life than those aiming to imitate Western stereotypes and prices. The selection offered here are mentioned either for their convenient location or for outstanding food.

Cafés and bars

Green Crest, Vladimirskiy pr. 7; Vladimirskaya/Dostoevskaya metro. Salads, salads and more salads – good healthy eating. Daily 10am–10pm.

Idiot, nab. reki Moyki 82; trolleybus #5 or #22 from Nevskiy prospekt. Relaxed vegetarian bar with books and board games, stuffed with foreigners. Daily noon–midnight.

Kashtan, nab. reki Fontanki 46; Gostiniy Dvor metro. Tucked away in the yard behind the Foreign Languages Library and the British Council. Serves great soups. Daily noon–10pm.

Kavkaz-bar, Karavannaya ul. 18; Gostiniy Dvor metro. Heavenly Caucasian food, just off Nevskiy. More expensive restaurant attached. Daily 10am–midnight.

Krokodil, Galernaya ul. 181; trolleybus #5 or #22 from Nevskiy prospekt. Café for the in-crowd, with some performances. Original menu, all fresh food. Daily 1–11pm or until the last person leaves.

Layma, nab. kanala Griboedova 16; Gostiniy Dvor/Nevskiy Prospekt metro. Excellent fast food, including steaks and salads, plus beer; great for late, late suppers. Daily 24hr.

Minutka, Nevskiy pr. 20; Gostiniy Dvor/Nevskiy Prospekt metro. American-style sandwich and salad bar. Daily 10am–10pm.

Morozhenoe (Frogs' Pool), Nevskiy pr. 24; Gostiniy Dvor/Nevskiy Prospekt metro. Ice cream, snacks and alcohol, with a wondrous Stalinist interior at the back. Daily 10am–11pm.

Mukha Tsokotukha, Solyanoy per. 14; Chernyshevskaya metro. Armenian cuisine, transforms into a mellow jazz club in the evening. Daily noon–2am.

Russkie bliny, ul. Furmanova 13. Ornate, cosy, very popular and cheap lunchtime spot, off Liteyniy prospekt. Traditional Russian *bliny*, both savoury and sweet. Mon–Fri 11am–6pm.

Sadko's, Mikhaylovskaya ul. 1; Nevskiy Prospekt metro. Expat bistro bar with live music in the evenings. Daily 11am–1am.

Staroe Kafe, nab. reki Fontanki 108; Tekhnologicheskiy Institut metro. Tiny, cosy café with traditional Russian food. Daily noon–11pm.

Restaurants

Demyanova Ukha, Kronverkskiy pr. 53 (☎812/232 8090); Gorkovskaya metro. Serves fish and nothing else; reservations essential. Daily 11am–10pm.

Joy, nab. Kanala Griboedova 28/1 (☎812/312 1614); Nevskiy Prospekt metro. Inexpensive but tasty food, with views over the Griboedov canal. Daily noon–midnight.

Krunk, Solyanoy per. 14; Chernyshevskaya metro or a 5min walk from Summer Garden. Armenian food and a friendly atmosphere, opposite the Stieglitz Art School. Daily noon–midnight.

Patio Pizza, Nevskiy pr. 30 (☎812/271 3177); Gostiniy Dvor/Nevskiy Prospekt metro. Best salad bar in town. Daily noon–midnight.

Pirosmani, Bolshoy pr. 14 (☎812/235 6456); Sportivnaya metro. Heavenly food in this tiny re-creation of a Georgian hill village, complete with a "lake" and tables on "rafts". Daily noon–11pm.

Rioni, Shpalernaya ul. 24 (☎812/273 3261). Excellent Georgian food, tucked away up a side alley. Order lots of different *zakuski*! Daily 11am–11pm.

Nightlife and entertainment

Although St Petersburg has less **nightlife** than most of its Western counterparts, there is lots of potential for a wild night out. Of the permanent **clubs** and **discos**, some are just plain tacky, others have a brash and decadent appeal and feature themed nights, spectacular lights, casinos and raunchy floorshows, while others offer that spartan, underground atmosphere of warehouse clubs.

St Petersburg is increasingly attractive to foreign stars, but the chances of you catching anyone famous here are still minimal. For Russians, the city is associated with several home-grown legendary bands and is the most hip place in the country – a sort of Russian Manchester or Seattle.

Clubbing aside, St Petersburg has a wide variety of cultural events, such as **classical concerts**, **ballet** and **opera**: for ballet, it's best to avoid performances in the Hermitage Theatre or at the Mussorgsky Opera and Ballet Theatre, unless desperate, and stick to the Mariinskiy. English-language **films** can sometimes be seen at Avrora, Nevskiy pr. 60; Barrikada, Nevskiy pr. 15; and Crystal Palace, Nevskiy pr. 72. For details of what's happening, whatever your preference, check the listings in the free English-language papers – *The St Petersburg Times* (Friday edition) and *Pulse*.

Discos and nightclubs

Club 69, 2-ya Krasnoarmeyskaya ul. 6; Tekhnologicheskiy Institut metro. Gay club with occasional strippers, getting a little tired these days. Tues–Sun 10pm–6am.

Griboedov, Voronezhskaya ul. 2a; Ligovskiy Prospekt metro. Still the coolest of cool dance clubs in a bomb shelter. Daily 6pm–6am.

Fish Fabrique, Pushkinskaya ul. 10 (entrance from Ligovskiy pr.); Mayakovskovo metro. Café club at the heart of the city's famous artists' colony, one of the most happening places in town. Daily 3pm to last customer.

JFC Jazz Club, Shpalernaya ul. 33; Chernyshevskaya metro. Unstuffy venue with an exciting programme, tucked away in a courtyard. Daily 7–10pm.

Jimi Hendrix, Liteynyy pr. 33; Chernyshevskaya metro. Some of the bands are really bad, but most aren't – the food's good too. Noon–6am daily.

Mama, Malaya Monetnaya ul. 3B; Gorkovskaya metro. Fave techno location, with jungle music on Saturdays. Fri & Sat midnight–6am.

Moloko, Perekupnoy per. 12 (*www.moloko.piter.net*); Ploshchad Aleksandra Nevskovo metro. Mainly punk and grunge. Thurs–Sun 7pm–midnight.

Money Honey Saloon, Apraksin Dvor 14 (in yard); Gostiniy Dvor/Nevskiy Prospekt metro. Russian rockabilly, cheap beer, always packed; don't forget the leather jacket and quiff. Daily 11am–midnight.

Port, Antonenko ul. 2; Gostiniy Dvor/Nevskiy Prospekt metro. Two dance floors, gaming machines, lots of young young people with lots of money.

Opera and ballet

Mariinskiy Theatre, Teatralnaya pl. 1 (☎812/114 5264). Still known as The Kirov in the West. Look out for international ballet stars Faroukh Ruzimatov, Altynai Assymuratova and local girl Ulyana Lopatkina. Foreigners will pay $40 upwards for seats in the stalls but seats are available in the gods for $3. Performances at 7pm with Sunday (and occasionally Wednesday) matinees at noon. The theatre is increasingly making a name for itself as the home of excellent opera too.

Listings

Airlines Aeroflot/Pulkovo Airlines (☎812/315 0072); British Airways (☎812/329 25 65); Finnair (☎812/326 1870); Lufthansa (☎812/320 1000); SAS (☎812/325 3255).

American Express *Grand Hotel Europe*, Mikhaylovskaya ul. 1/7 (Mon–Fri 9am–5pm; ☎812/329 6061).

Bookshop Angliya, nab. reki Fontanki 40 (Mon–Fri 10am–7pm, Sat & Sun 11am–6pm; ☎812/279 8284).

Buses Eurolines desk at the Central Agency for Air Travel, Nevskiy pr. 7 (☎812/311 8004).

Consulates Britain, pl. Proletarskoy diktatury 5 (☎812/320 3200); Canada, Malodetskoselsky pr. 32 (☎812/325 8448); USA, Furshtadtskaya ul. 15 (☎812/275 1701).

Emergencies For medical assistance, try International Clinic, Dostoevskovo ul. 19/21 (☎812/320 3870, *www.icspb.com*); Euromed, Suvorovskiy pr. 60 (☎812/327 0301, *www.euromed.ru*); American Medical Service, Serpukhovskaya ul. 10 (24hr; ☎812/326 1730). All are recognized by international insurance companies.

Exchange All over town. Best ATM machine (24hr) at Sberbank, Dumskaya ul. 3. Bank transfers are widely available via Western Union.

Internet access Try Tertris Internet Cafe at Chernyakhovskovo 33 (☎812/325 4877) or Westpost at Nevskiy pr. 86.

Left luggage Most bus and train stations have lockers and/or a 24hr left-luggage office, but you would be tempting fate to use them.

Pharmacy Petropharm, at Nevskiy pr. 22 (24hr; other branches at no. 50, 66 & 83). Homeopathic pharmacies, Nevskiy pr. 50 and Svechnoy per. 7/11.

Post office Pochtamskaya ul. 9 (Mon–Sat 8am–8pm, Sun 8am–6pm), just off St Isaac's Square. Express letter post: Westpost, Nevskiy pr. 86 (Mon–Fri 9.30am–8pm, Sat noon–6pm; ☎812/327 3092); Post International, Nevskiy pr. 20 (Mon–Fri 10am–7pm, Sat noon–5pm; ☎812/318 4472). Letters can be sent abroad via Finnish post at the service desk of the *Grand Hotel Europe*.

Railway Tickets The Central Ticket Office is at Nab. kanala Griboedova 24; Nevskiy Prospekt metro. Foreigners use desks 1–3. To avoid queues try the Central Agency for Air Travel, Nevskiy pr. 7 (small commission payable).

Student Travel Sindbad Travel, 3-ya Sovetskaya ul. 28 (☎095/327 8384).

Telephones The main communications centre is at International Telephone and Telegraph Office, Bolshaya Morskaya ul. 3–5 (daily 9am–9pm).

Around St Petersburg

There are five imperial summer palaces set in rich parks just outside St Petersburg. In summer, most visitors opt for **Peterhof**, 29km west of the city, renowned for its fountains, while in winter **Pavlovsk** and **Tsarskoye Selo** are more striking. For a view of Old Russia, go to **Novgorod**, 190km south; this is the archetypal medieval Russian city. Both are easily accessible by public transport, and so each makes a perfect day-trip.

Peterhof

First of the great palatial ensembles to be founded outside St Petersburg, **Peterhof** embodies nearly three hundred years of tsarist self-aggrandisement. Its name means "Peter's Court" in German and its progenitor was Peter the Great, but the Grand Palace wasn't completed until the reign of Empress Elizabeth (1741–61).

Trains for Peterhof leave from Baltic Station (Baltiyskaya metro) every thirty minutes or so (there is a gap between 10am and noon at weekends) and cost around 25 cents each way, but in summer the best means of transport is **hydrofoil** (around $3 each way). These depart every ninety minutes (9.30am–5pm) from outside the Winter Palace, the last return boat leaving Peterhof at 6pm. Minibuses run from Avtovo metro station every ten minutes or so along the south bank of the Gulf of Finland, through small settlements and past decaying grand houses and estates; these cost 50 cents each way.

The yellow, white and gold **Great Palace** (Bolshoy dvorets; Tues–Sun 10.30am–5pm; closed last Tues of every month; $8) is far removed from that originally designed by Le Blond (1714–21), but despite later additions, there's a superb cohesion at work, a tribute both to the vision of the palace's creators and the skills of the craftsmen who rebuilt Peterhof from its ashes after World War II. The palace entrance is through the formal **Upper Garden**.

The **Lower Park** is where to find the fountains (late-May to late-Sept), from the Grand Cascade dropping down to the sea to joke fountains which spout water on (supposedly) unexpecting passers-by. To the east of the Grand Cascade, you'll find **Monplaisir** (May–Sept daily except Wed 10.30am–5pm, closed last Thurs of every month; Oct–April Sat & Sun 10.30am–4pm; $6), Peter the Great's favourite haunt; both homely and extravagant, it was designed by the tsar himself. Built around the same time was the **Marly Palace** (daily except Tues and the last Wed of every month: May–Sept 10am–5pm; Oct–April 10.30am–4pm; $3), more of a country house than a palace, which takes its name and inspiration from the hunting lodge of the French kings at Marly le Rois, which Peter the Great visited during his Grand Tour of Europe. Tickets for guided tours must be bought at the wooden hut nearby.

Finding Peterhof's Great Palace "unbearable", Empress Aleksandra Fyodorovna pressed Nicholas I to build a home suited to a cosier, bourgeois lifestyle: the resulting Neo-Gothic **Cottage Palace** (Kottedzh; May–Sept daily except Fri 10am–5pm, closed last Tues of every month; Oct–April Sat & Sun 10am–5pm; $6) is definitely worth the fifteen-minute walk through the overgrown park.

The best **lunch** in Peterhof (traditional and cheap) can be found at the tiny *Trapeza*, just outside the east entrance to the park and palace.

Tsarskoe Selo

Tsarskoe Selo ("Tsar's Village"; also known as Pushkin), 17km southeast of St Petersburg, was Catherine the Great's favourite summer residence, and today it draws locals and tourists alike for its vast blue-and-white, imperial, Baroque palace, set in a richly landscaped park.

The most convenient **transport** to the palace is provided by the minibuses which run from Moskovskiy prospekt outside Moskovskaya metro station every ten to twenty minutes and cost around 40 cents each way. Some go to Pushkin the town, several also run near the palace itself. Suburban trains run from Vitebsk Station (Vitebskiy vokzal) every fifteen to thirty minutes (there is a break between 10am and 11.45am); tickets are around 10 cents each way.

Catherine the Great hated the Baroque style and when she came to power she immediately set to building and remodelling the main **palace** (daily except Tues 10am–5pm; $5) to her own taste. It was she who installed in 1775 the famous **Amber Room**, a gift from Frederick I of Prussia to Peter the Great. Stolen by the Germans during the war, the amber panels have fascinated several generations of scholars and amateurs, who have produced varied conflicting theories as to whether they were destroyed or are still buried in some unknown location. Meanwhile, the Amber Room is being re-created by modern craftsmen in time for St Petersburg's 300th anniversary in 2003. Perhaps the highlights of the palace are the rooms designed by Catherine's beloved Scottish architect, Charles Cameron: the charming Neoclassical interiors of her private apartments, the rich interiors of the Agate Rooms (designed as a bathhouse and summer pavilion) and the supreme elegance of the Cameron Gallery, its light airy structure projecting out from the palace over the park. The **park** itself is dotted in the English manner with follies and monuments: from the Turkish bath resembling an Ottoman mosque to the Pyramid where Catherine buried her favourite dogs and the newly restored Chinese village (now containing elite apartments for the rich).

Pavlovsk

About 3km beyond Tsarskoe Selo you will come to **Pavlovsk** (same trains and minibuses as for Tsarskoe Selo), built on land which Catherine presented to her son Paul in 1777, to congratulate him on the birth of her grandson. The **Great Palace** (daily except Fri 10am–5pm; $5) is a monument to the taste and habits of Paul's wife Maria Fyodorovna, who collected works of fine and applied art, and who was herself a keen sculptor and carver of cameos. Light, airy, and feminine, the palace is renowned for its superb collection of eighteenth-century furniture and interior fittings. It dominates the hill above the dips and inclines of the landscape around the River Slavyanka. Pavlovsk **park** is perhaps the most beloved of all the parks around the city by inhabitants of St Petersburg, who walk here and feed the squirrels in summer, and ski through the grounds in winter.

The palace has a pleasant **café**, but for a truly kitsch experience, lunch at *Podvorie* at 16 Filtrovskoe shosse, just outside the park near the station (☎812/465 1399), a pseudo-medieval complex with a folk show (accepts payment by card).

Novgorod

Despite its name, **NOVGOROD** ("New Town") is one of Russia's oldest cities, founded, according to popular belief, by Prince Rurik in 862 AD. The easiest way to get there is by excursion **bus** from beside the portico on Nevskiy prospekt 33 (tickets from the kiosk beside Gostiniy Dvor for around $3–4), although the tours are in Russian only. More expensive tours in English are available through hotels. For information on all museums in Novgorod, look online at *www.novgorod-museum.ru*.

During its most prestigious and wealthy period – from the twelfth to the fifteenth century – Novgorod's republican-minded nobles bestowed a fantastic architectural legacy upon the town, including a Kremlin (a fortified inner city), Russia's oldest cathedral and numerous onion-domed stone churches. However, the foundation of St Petersburg in 1703 was a great blow to Novgorod's commercial prosperity, with the final straw coming in 1851, when the new rail line linking Moscow and St Petersburg bypassed the town entirely.

The impressive, nine-metre-high, red-brick walls of the **Kremlin** date from the fifteenth century, when they formed the inner ring of an entire series of fortifications. As many as eighteen churches and 150 houses were once crammed inside these walls, though much of the Kremlin now consists of open space. The Kremlin's main landmark is **St Sophia's Cathedral** (Sofiyskiy sobor), the city's earliest and largest cathedral by far, representing the peak of princely power in Novgorod and afterwards a symbol of great civic pride, its five bulbous domes clustered around a slightly raised, golden helmet dome. The cathedral now doubles as a working **church** and **museum** (daily 10am–6pm, closed last Tues of every month; there may be an entry charge). Inside, the well-preserved iconostasis is one of the oldest in Russia and includes works from the eleventh to seventeenth centuries.

The largest building in the Kremlin is an early-nineteenth-century mass of administrative offices; nowadays it is home to the **Museum of History, Architecture and Art** (daily except Tues 10am–6pm; closed last Thurs of every month; $3), and contains a fine collection of icons by the colourful Novgorod School, along with paintings, embroideries and early wooden sculpture.

From the riverbank on the east side of the Kremlin, there's a great view of the **Commercial Side** (Torgovaya storona), site of Novgorod's medieval market. All that remains now is a long section of the old seventeenth-century arcade. Immediately behind the arcade, where the palace of Yaroslav the Wise once stood, is a grassy area still known as **Yaroslav's Court** (Yaroslavovo dvorishche). Its most important surviving building is the **Cathedral of St Nicholas** (Nikolskiy sobor; daily except Tues 10am–6pm), built in 1113 in a Byzantine style that was a deliberate challenge to St Sophia's.

All that survives of the **Yuryev Monastery** (Yuryev monastyr), founded by Prince Vsevolod in 1117, is the majestic **Cathedral of St George** (Georgievskiy sobor), which was built by a "Master Peter", renowned as the first truly Russian architect, and which is one of the last great churches to be built by the Novgorod princes. Inside, some twelfth-century frescoes survive, but most date from the nineteenth century. The cathedral has been rapidly restored in recent years and the monastery revived – you should dress accordingly (covered head and no trousers for women). In the woods nearby is the Vitoslavitsy **Museum of Wooden Architecture** (daily except Wed: May to mid-Sept 10am–6pm; mid-Sept to April 10am–4pm; $5), an inspiring collection of timber constructions moved here from the surrounding area, including two churches and several peasant houses, with some of the buildings dating from the sixteenth century.

If you need somewhere to **stay**, try *Sadko*, Fyodorovskiy ruchey 16 (☎812/754 37; ⑤), a budget hotel on the Commercial Side. As far as **restaurants** go, everyone rightly goes to the *Detinets* (Mon 11am–4pm, Tues–Sun 11am–5pm & 7–11pm), in the Pokrov Tower of the Kremlin. It has a café downstairs and a relaxed restaurant upstairs, which has the occasional bit of live music in the evening; prices are low.

CHAPTER 25

SLOVAKIA

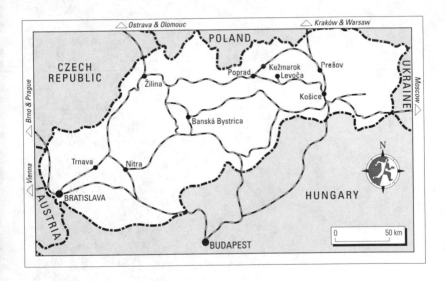

Introduction

The republic of **Slovakia** (Slovensko) – independent since 1993 – consists of the long, narrow strip of land which stretches from the fertile plains of the Danube basin up to the peaks of the High Tatras – perhaps Europe's most exhilarating mountain range outside of the Alps. The country's numerous mountains have long formed barriers to industrialization and modernization, and parts of the country remain surprisingly rural and unspoilt, some to the point of neglect.

There was only one independent Slovak state before 1993, when the country operated as a German protectorate during World War II – a period which remains a blot on the nation's **history**. Before 1918, current-day Slovakia was known as the region of Upper Hungary and lay under Magyar rule for roughly a millennium; Bratislava even became the Hungarian capital when the rest of Hungary was occupied by the Turks. However, in 1918, the Slovaks threw their lot in with their Slav neighbours, the Czechs, forming Czechoslovakia. This lasted 75 years until the country's "velvet divorce" took place in 1993. Although many Slovaks were ready to go it alone, it has to be said that others had major reservations about this, and none was given the chance to decide in a referendum. Political corruption, nationalism and slow-moving reforms put off overseas investors until a change of government in 1998, since when the country's economic prospects under Prime Minister Dzurinda have brightened and firm steps towards joining the European Union have begun.

For the first-time visitor, perhaps the most striking cultural difference from the Czechs is the Slovak attitude to religion. **Catholicism** is much stronger here than in the Czech Republic, and the churches are often full to overflowing on Sundays. The republic also has a much more diverse population, with over half a million ethnic **Hungarians** in the south, as well as thousands of Romanies (gypsies), who live a fairly miserable existence throughout the country, and several thousand Ruthenians (Rusyns) in the east. **Bratislava**, the capital, is potentially disappointing, especially for those who arrive expecting a Slovak Prague. Taken on its own terms, however, the city is a rewarding, lively place with a compact old town. **Poprad** provides the transport hub for the **High Tatras**, the most spectacular of Slovakia's many mountain ranges, and is also the starting point for exploring the intriguing medieval towns of the **Spiš** region, east Slovakia's architectural high point.

Further east still, **Prešov** is the cultural centre of the Ruthenian minority, while **Košice**, Slovakia's vibrant second city, boasts a fine Gothic cathedral, ethnic diversity and a lively independence from much of the rest of Slovakia.

Information and maps

As well as state-run **tourist offices** (*www.sacr.sk*) there's a chain of private AICES information points (*www.infoslovak.sk*; in Slovak only), which, in smaller towns, are often better. In summer they're generally open Mon–Fri 9am–6pm, Sat & Sun 9am–2pm; in winter they tend to be shut on Sundays and close an hour earlier on other days. Most tourist offices have English speakers.

All kinds of maps are available in the country. You can buy them, often very cheaply, from bookshops and some hotels – ask for a *plán mesta* or *orientačná mapa* (both town plans). Bookshops sell a huge range of Autoatlases, and a specific booklet, *Autokempingy*, produced by the Slovak tourist board, detailing routes, campsites, petrol stations, border crossings and even sites of historic interest. For hiking, the 1:100,000 *turistická mapa* series details the country's complex network of footpaths.

Money and banks

The **currency** in Slovakia is the Slovak crown or *Slovenská koruna* (abbreviated to Sk), which is divided into 100 *halier* (h). Coins come in the denominations 10h, 20h, 50h, 1Sk, 2Sk, 5Sk and 10Sk; notes as 20Sk, 50Sk, 100Sk, 500Sk, 1000Sk and 5000Sk. Although the Slovak crown is convertible, the amount you can take out of the country is limited, so check with customs if you plan to export large sums. Note that exchange rates continue to fluctuate.

Travellers' cheques in US dollars, Deutschmarks or Sterling are undoubtedly the safest way of carrying your money, though it's a good idea to keep at least some hard currency in **cash** for emergencies. Exchange offices (*zmenáren*) can be found in all major hotels, travel agencies and department stores. **Credit cards** are accepted in most hotels and restaurants and some shops, and you can also get cash on your plastic from the ATMs in both small towns and cities – EuroCard and MasterCard are most widely accepted.

Communications

Most **post offices** (*pošta*) are open Mon–Fri 8am–5pm and Sat 8am–noon – you can also buy stamps from some tobacconists (*tabák*) and street kiosks. Poste restante services are available in major towns, but remember to write *Pošta 1* (the main office), followed by the name of the town.

Cheap local calls can be made from any **phone**, but for international calls it's best to use a card phone, for which you need to buy a telephone card (*telefonná karta*) from a tobacconist or post office. **Internet cafés** have appeared in the larger cities; expect to pay 60–120Sk/hr.

Getting around

The most pleasant way of **getting around** Slovakia is by train – the system is not as extensive as some in the former Eastern bloc, but some of the journeys are beautifully scenic, albeit tortuous. Travelling by bus, however, is quicker and covers a more extensive network. In most cities the bus and train stations are neighbours, so you can easily check out both.

■ Trains

Slovak Railways, Železnice Slovenskej Republiky (ŽSR; *www.zsr.sk* – which includes the entire timetable in English), run two main types of trains: *rýchlik* trains are the faster ones, which stop only at major towns and charge a supplement, while *osobní*, or local trains, stop at every station and average about 30kph. **Tickets** (*lístok*) for domestic journeys can be bought at the station (*stanica*) before or on the day of departure. Fares are cheap – a second-class single from Bratislava to Košice currently costs around £9/$14, but prices are slowly increasing. SR run reasonably priced sleepers (*ležadlo*) to and from a number of places – make

sure you book as far in advance as possible and no later than six hours before departure. EuroDomino and InterRail passes are valid; Eurail passes require supplements.

■ Buses

Buses (*autobus*) are mostly run by the state bus company, Slovenská automobilová doprava (SAD; *www.sad.sk*). The usual practice is to buy your ticket from the driver – often the only option, since the ticket offices are often closed. If you can, it's a good idea to book your ticket in advance if you're travelling at the weekend or early in the morning on one of the main routes.

■ Driving

Since only around half the population own a vehicle and most of those are only used at the weekend, travelling by **car** in Slovakia is still a relaxing way to travel. **Speed limits** are 130kph on motorways, 90kph on other roads, and 50kph in all cities, towns and villages. To use the country's very small stretches of motorway, you need to buy a 400Sk windscreen sticker (*úhrada*) at the border or from a petrol station. There should be **no alcohol** at all in your bloodstream while driving or you could risk losing your license, high fines or even jail. **Fuel** is currently fairly cheap by European standards, but petrol stations are still not quite as widespread as in Western Europe and generally close by 6pm (though 24-hour ones can be found in the major towns and cities).

Car rental in Slovakia currently starts at around £260/$400 per week with international agencies, but local firms can be significantly cheaper. The multinationals have branches in Bratislava: Hertz are in the Hotel Fórum (☎07/5934 8155), while Avis are at Bajkalská 31 (☎07/5341 6111) and Europcar is at Pribinova 25 (☎07/5063 3895). For a cheaper deal you need to contact a local organization like Recar, Svätoplukova 1 (☎07/215 756 or 62 624).

Accommodation

The **accommodation** situation is much better than it used to be, though it remains the most expensive aspect of travelling in Slovakia. There is no real network of hostels, though a few are now affiliated to Hostelling International and others come under CKM, the student travel agency (*www.ckm.sk* – in Slovak only). If you're travelling in July or August and want to save yourself hassle, it's always a good idea to arrange accommodation as far in advance as possible.

■ Hotels and private rooms

Some **hotels** have double pricing, with higher rates for foreigners, but a basic room for £5/$7.50 per head is not hard to find in any city outside Bratislava, though probably with an extra £1/$1.50 for breakfast. While the old state hotels and spa complexes are slowly being refurbished, their rooms are usually box-like and overpriced; the new hotels and pensions that have opened up, particularly in the more heavily touristed areas, are often a better bet and far better value for money. **Private rooms** are a good option in many towns – keep your eyes peeled for signs saying *Zimmer Frei*. Prices start at around £4/$6 per person per night – only slightly below the cheaper hotel rates.

■ Hostels and campsites

Bratislava has a few private **hostels** which offer varying degrees of discomfort. Elsewhere, the student travel organization, CKM, or local tourist offices can give information on cheap **student accommodation** in the big university towns during July and August. In the High Tatras, in addition to panel-built spa accommodation, you can find a fair number of chalet-style **refuges** (*chata*) scattered about the hillsides. Some are little less than hotels and cost around £10/$15 a bed, less for the simpler, more isolated wooden shelters.

Campsites are plentiful all over Slovakia. Many of the sites feature simple **bungalows** (again, known as *chata*), often available for anything upwards of £5/$8 a bed. A fair number of sites remain open all year round, but about half don't open until May at the earliest, closing in mid- to late September. Even though prices are sometimes inflated for foreigners, costs are still reasonable.

Food and drink

Slovak food is no-nonsense, filling fare and pretty similar to Czech cuisine, although traces of Hungarian, Polish and Ukrainian influences can be found in different regions.

■ Food

The usual mid-morning Slovak snack at the **bufet** (stand-up canteen) is *párek*, perhaps the most ubiquitous **takeaway food** in Central Europe, a hot frankfurter, dipped in mustard or horseradish and served inside a white roll. The Slovak national dish is *bryndzové halušky* – gnocchi with a thick sheep's cheese sauce and crumbled grilled bacon, but Hungarian influences are strong here, too. Goulash is very popular (although a mild stew rather than the authentic spicy soup), as are *langoše* – deep-fried dough smothered in a variety of toppings.

Most menus start with **soup** (*polievka*), one of the country's culinary strong points and served at both midday and evening meals. **Main courses** are overwhelmingly based on pork or beef, but trout and carp are usually featured somewhere on the menu and you may find catfish or pike-perch if you're lucky, and occasionally lamb. Most main courses are served with delicious potatoes (*zemiaky*) – but fresh salads or green vegetables are still a rarity in local restaurants. In addition to *palačinky* (cold pancakes) filled with chocolate, fruit and cream, Slovak **desserts**

ACCOMMODATION PRICE CODES

Throughout this guide, accommodation is coded on a scale of ① to ⑨, the code indicating the lowest price per person per night you could expect to pay in each establishment in high season. With hostels this is the nightly rate per person; with hotels, the price is arrived at by dividing the cost of the cheapest double room by two. The prices indicated by the codes are as follows:

① under £5/$8	④ £15–20/$24–32	⑦ £30–35/$48–56
② £5–10/$8–16	⑤ £20–25/$32–40	⑧ £35–40/$56–64
③ £10–15/$16–24	⑥ £25–30/$40–48	⑨ £40/$64 and over

invariably feature apple or cottage-cheese strudel and ice cream.

In the last few years an increasing number of **restaurants** offering international cuisine have sprouted up, from the omnipresent fast-food joints and pizzerias to Bratislava's many Oriental eateries. Opening times have been extended too – though in outlying regions closing time will still be 9 or 10pm, the bigger cities have restaurants open till 11pm or later. Menus and prices are nearly always displayed outside.

Coffee (*káva*) is drunk black – espresso style in the big cities, but sometimes simply hot water poured over ground coffee in the smaller towns and villages (described rather hopefully as "Turkish" or *turecká*). The **cake shop** (*cukráreň*) is an important part of the country's social life, particularly on Sunday mornings when it's often the only place that's open in town. Whatever the season, Slovaks love to have their daily fix of **ice cream** (*zmrzlina*), available at *cukráreň* or dispensed from little window kiosks in the sides of buildings.

■ Drink

The vineyards in the south of Slovakia produce some pretty good medium-quality white **wines**, which share characteristics with their Hungarian and Austrian neighbours. The home production of brandies is a national pastime, resulting sometimes in almost terminally strong brews. The most famous is *slivovice*, a plum **brandy**, originally from the border hills between the Czech and Slovak Republics, but now available just about everywhere.

After more than seventy years of close association with the Czechs, the Slovaks have also learnt to love draught **beer**, but the *pivnica*, where most heavy drinking goes on, is still less common in Slovakia than in the Czech Republic. Slovaks tend to head instead for restaurants or **wine bars** (*vináreň*), which usually have slightly later opening hours and often double as nightclubs.

Opening hours and holidays

Opening hours for shops in Slovakia are Mon–Fri 9am–6pm, Sat 8am–noon, with some shops and most supermarkets staying open later. Smaller shops close for lunch for an hour or so sometime between noon and 2pm. Most shops are closed on Sunday, but supermarkets and out-of-town hypermarkets are open all day in large towns and cities.

The basic opening hours for **castles** and **monasteries** are Tues–Sun 9am–5pm, though last admission will be half an hour before closing. In April and October, opening hours are often restricted to weekends and holidays. From the end of October to the beginning of April, most castles are closed. When visiting a sight, always ask for an *anglický text*, an often unintentionally hilarious English resumé. In Bratislava the main **museums** open Tues–Fri 10am–5pm, Sat & Sun 11am–6pm, though there are exceptions. In winter, many museums close half an hour earlier than the times quoted in this guide. **Entrance tickets** for all sights never cost more than £1/$1.50 – hence no prices are quoted in the text.

Public holidays include Jan 1 (Independence Day); Jan 6 (Epiphany); Easter Monday; May 1 (Labour Day); July 5 (SS Cyril and Methodius day); Aug 29 (Slovak National Uprising); Sept 1 (Constitution Day); Sept 15 (Our Lady of Sorrows); Nov 1 (All Saints' Day); and Dec 24, 25 & 26.

Emergencies

There are two types of **police** (*polícia*): the state police, who wear the standard khaki uniforms that are a hangover from communist days, and the local municipal or *mestská polícia*, who wear a variety of natty outfits depending on the fashion-consciousness of the local council. For tourists, theft from cars and hotel rooms is the biggest worry – the best way to protect yourself against such disasters is to take out travel insurance. If you are unlucky enough to have something stolen, report it immediately to the nearest police station in order to get a statement detailing what you've lost for your insurance claim. Everyone is obliged to carry some form of ID and you should carry your **passport** with you at all times, though realistically you're extremely unlikely to get stopped unless you're driving.

Minor ailments can be easily dealt with by the **pharmacist** (*lekáreň*), but language is likely to be a major problem. If it's a repeat prescription you want, take any empty bottles or remaining pills along with you. If the pharmacy can't help, they'll be able to direct you to a **hospital** or *nemocnica*. If you do have to pay for any medication, keep the receipts for claiming on your insurance once you're home.

Emergency Numbers
Police ☎158; Ambulance/First Aid ☎155; Fire ☎150.

BRATISLAVA

BRATISLAVA has two distinct sides: the old quarter is an attractive slice of Habsburg Baroque, while the rest of the city has the brash and butchered feel of the average East European metropolis. More buildings have been destroyed here since the war than were bombed out during it, the whole Jewish quarter having been bulldozed to make way for a colossal suspension bridge and highway. Yet, even though the multicultural atmosphere of the prewar days has gone, there is a certain Central European cosmopolitanism here, at the meeting of three nations – boosted by a thriving café culture.

Arrival and information

Bratislava has an **airport** (letisko Štefánik; ☎07/4857 3353), but at present there are very few direct flights to or from the rest of Europe, other than the likes of Moscow and Prague, plus the odd domestic flight to Košice and Poprad. From the airport take bus #61 to the main train station, or else catch the ASA bus, which runs a shuttle service to and from the ASA office on Štúrova, timed to coincide with the flight schedule. Part of the reason for Bratislava airport's underuse is the proximity of Vienna's Schwechat airport, from which there's a regular bus service that drops passengers at the main bus station in Bratislava (see below).

A short distance north of the city centre is Bratislava's spruced-up main **train station** or *Hlavná stanica*, where most international or long-distance trains pull in. Once you've arrived, go down to the tram terminus below and, having bought your ticket from one of the machines on the platform, hop on tram #1 into town. Some trains, particularly those heading for destinations within west Slovakia, pass through Bratislava's Nové Mesto station, linked to the centre by tram #6 and to the main train station by an irregular train connection. **Buses** usually arrive at the main bus station, or *Autobusová stanica*, on Mlynské nivy, fifteen minutes' walk east of the city centre. Trolleybus #210 will take you across town to the main train station; #211 goes past *Hotel Fórum* on Hodžovo námestie. Bratislava's **tourist office**, BIS, is at Klobučnícka 2 (Mon–Fri 8am–7pm, Sat 9am–2pm; ☎07/5443 4370; *www.isnet.sk/bis*): it's good for general queries and getting hold of a map and the monthly listings magazine, *Kam v Bratislave*; it also books accommodation for a 50Sk fee. There's an additional, smaller office in the main train station.

For news and current affairs, plus a few **listings**, one publication worth getting is the weekly *Slovak Spectator* (*www.slovakspectator.sk*; 30Sk).

City transport

The best way to see Bratislava is to walk – in fact it's the only way to see the pedestrianized old town, or staré mesto, where most of the sights are concentrated. However, if you're staying outside the city centre or visiting the suburbs, you'll need to make use of the city's inexpensive and comprehensive **transport system**. Buy your ticket (12Sk to the centre of town) beforehand (from newsagents, kiosks, hotel lobbies or ticket machines), validate it as soon as you get on, and use a fresh ticket each time you change; if you're going to use the system a lot go to the small booth on the left outside the main entrance of the train station, near the bus departure points, which sells one-day (70Sk) and two-day (130Sk) passes. **Night buses** congregate at námestie SNP, every quarter to the hour.

Accommodation

Bratislava's proximity to Vienna, and its capital city status, mean that **hotels** are more expensive than anywhere else in the country. This makes **private rooms** the most popular option for most budget travellers – BIS can arrange such accommodation for you for a 50Sk fee (☎07/5443 4370) as can SATUR (☎07/5441 0133), who charge no fee.

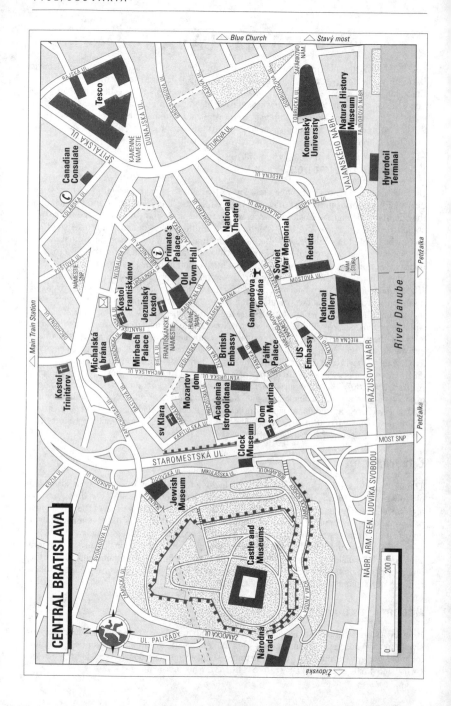

Hostels, student halls and camping

Bernolák, Bernolákova 1 (☎07/5249 7723). The liveliest and cheapest hostel in the city, and only a short tram ride northeast of the centre; tram #7 or #11 from Kamenné námestie. Open July & Aug. ①.

Družba, Botanická 25 (☎07/6542 0065). One block of student rooms specifically given over as tourist accommodation, with use of student facilities. Situated to the west of town, near the botanical gardens; tram #1 from the train station. Open year-round. ①–②.

Mladá garda, Racianská 103 (☎07/4425 3065, *www.mlada-garda.sk*). The student dorm of the Technical University. Open July & Aug. ①.

Zlaté piesky (☎07/4425 7373). Two campsites with cabins and a range of sports activities, 8km northeast of the city centre, near the unlovely swimming lake of the same name. To get there, take tram #4 from the main train station or tram #4 from Kamenné námestie. Open May to mid-Oct. 75Sk per person.

Hotels and pensions

Arcus, Moskovská 5 (☎07/5557 2522). Wonderful little pension not far from the bus station and connected to the centre by tram #4, #6 or #14 (nearest stop Odborárske námestie). ③.

Chez David, Zámocká 13 (☎07/5441 3824). Swish kosher pension right by the castle and the old Jewish quarter, with a kosher restaurant attached. ⑤.

Club Slovan hotel, Odbojárov 3 (☎07/4425 6369). Cheap hotel 3km northeast of the centre, but easily reached by tram #2 from the main train station, and by tram #4 or #6 from Kamenné námestie. ②.

Gracia, Rázusovo nábrežie (☎07/5443 2132). Rather elderly "Botel" on the Danube, right in the centre of town. ③.

Gremium, Gorkého 11 (☎07/541 30 653). This is the only decent, if basic, inexpensive option in the old town, so book ahead if possible. ②.

Rybársky cech, Žižkova 1 (☎07/5441 8334, *rybarskycech@ba.pubnet.sk*). Simple but pleasant pension on the busy road below the castle. ③.

The City

Trams from the main train station offload their shoppers and sightseers behind the *Hotel Fórum* in Obchodná – literally Shop Street – which descends into Hurbanovo námestie, a busy junction on the northern edge of the old town (staré mesto). Here you'll find the hefty mass of the **Kostol trinitárov**, one of the city's finest churches, its exuberant trompe l'oeil frescoes creating a magnificent false cupola.

Opposite the church, a footbridge passes under a tower of the city's last remaining double gateway. Below is a small section of what used to be the city moat, now a garden belonging to the Baroque apothecary called *U červeného raka*, on your left between the towers, which now houses a **Pharmaceutical Museum** (Farmaceutická expozícia; Tues–Fri 10am–5pm, Sat & Sun 11am–6pm), displaying everything from seventeenth-century drug grinders to reconstructed period pharmacies. The second and taller of the towers is the **Michalská brána** (Mon & Wed–Sun 10am–5pm), an evocative and impressive entrance to the old town and now a weapons museum; the rooftop view from the top of the tower is superb.

Michalská and Ventúrska, which run into each other, have both been beautifully restored and are lined with some of Bratislava's finest Baroque palaces. There are usually plenty of students milling about amongst the shoppers, as the main university library is on this thoroughfare. The palaces of the Austro-Hungarian aristocracy continue into Panská, starting with the **Pálffy Palace**, at Panská 19, today an **art gallery** (Tues–Sun 10am–5/6pm), housing a patchy collection of Slovak paintings from the nineteenth and twentieth centuries.

A little northeast of here are the adjoining main squares of the old town – **Hlavné námestie** and **Františkánske námestie** – on the east side of which is the **Old Town Hall** (Stará radnica; Tues–Fri 10am–6pm, Sat & Sun 11am–6pm), a lively hotchpotch of Gothic, Renaissance and nineteenth-century styles containing the Municipal Museum – worth visiting if only for the medieval torture exhibition in the basement dungeons. The Counter-Reformation, which gripped the parts of Hungary not under Turkish occupation, issues forth from the square's **Jesuit Church** (Jezuitský kostol), whose best feature is its richly gilded pulpit. Diagonally opposite is the **Mirbach Palace** (Tues–Sun 10am–5pm), arguably the finest of Bratislava's Rococo buildings, preserving much of its original stucco decor.

Round the back of the Old Town Hall, with the stillness of a provincial Italian piazza during siesta, is the **Primaciálne námestie**, dominated by the Neoclassical **Primate's Palace** (Tues–Sun 10am–5pm), whose pediment frieze is topped by a cast-iron cardinal's hat. The palace's main claim to fame is its Hall of Mirrors, where Napoleon and the Austrian emperor signed the Peace of Pressburg (as Bratislava was then called) in 1805. You can now visit this, and several other rooms hung with portraits of the Habsburgs and seventeenth-century English tapestries, found by chance during the building's renovation.

Despite its proximity to Vienna and Budapest, the city has produced only one composer of note, **Johann Nepomuk Hummel** (1778–1837). The composer's birthplace, a cute apricot-coloured cottage hidden away behind two fashionable shops on Klobučnícka, is now a **museum** (Tues–Sun 11am–5pm). Beyond, at the top end of Stúrova, is **Kamenné námestie**, overlooked by a giant Tesco supermarket, in front of which the whole city seems to wind up after work, to grab a beer or takeaway from one of the many stand-up stalls, then jabber away the early evening before catching the bus or tram home.

From the Cathedral to the Castle

On the west side of the staré mesto, the most insensitive of Bratislava's postwar developments took place. After the annihilation of the city's Jewish population by the Nazis, the communist authorities tore down virtually the whole of the Jewish quarter in order to build the brutal showpiece bridge, the SNP Bridge, or most SNP (see below). The traffic which now tears along Staromestská has seriously undermined the foundations of the Gothic **Cathedral of St Martin** (Dóm sv Martina; Mon–Fri 10–11.45am & 2–4.45pm, Sat 10am–noon & 2–4.45pm, Sun 2–4.45pm), coronation church of the kings and queens of Hungary for over 250 years, whose ill-proportioned steeple is topped by a tiny gilded Hungarian crown.

As you pass under the approach road for the new bridge, you'll notice the **Clock Museum** at Židovská 1 (Múzeum hodin; Mon & Wed–Sun 10am–5pm), with a display of brilliantly kitsch Baroque and Empire clocks. To pay tribute to the large prewar Slovak Jewish population, largely decimated in concentration camps, there is a **Jewish Museum** at Židovská 17 (Múzeum židovskej kultúry; Mon–Fri & Sun 11am–5pm), with a display of Judaica and a brief history of Slovak Jews.

The **Castle**, or *Hrad*, is an unwelcoming giant box built in the fifteenth century by Emperor Sigismund and burnt down by its own drunken soldiers in 1811. It houses the half of the uneven collections of the **Slovak National Museum** (Slovenské národné múzeum; Tues–Fri 9am–5pm, Sat & Sun 10am–6pm) that they couldn't squeeze into the main building on the waterfront, as well as the **Historical Museum** (Tues–Sun 9am–5pm), which features Slovak trades, handicrafts and folk art, and the **Music Museum** (Tues–Sun 10am–4pm) which contains traditional Slovak instruments. The most interesting section so far is the **Treasures of the Far Past of Slovakia**, but most punters will probably get more out of the incredible view from outside the castle gates south across the Danube plain to the Petržalka housing estate, where a third of the city's population lives. The castle courtyard is open until 8pm in summer; until 6pm for the rest of the year.

Along the waterfront

Despite the fast dual carriageway of the embankment, it is just about possible to enjoy a stroll along the banks of the (far from blue) **River Danube** – *Dunaj* in Slovak. In addition to a terminal for boats to Budapest and Vienna, there's a ferry (summer Sat & Sun) across the river, an alternative to crossing by either of the two bridges, the larger of which is the infamous **Bridge of the Slovak National Uprising** or **most SNP**. Its one support column leans at an alarming angle, topped by a saucer-like penthouse café reminiscent of the *Starship Enterprise*. The view from the café is superlative, though it's pricey.

While you're in the waterfront district, the **Slovak National Gallery** (Slovenská národná galéria; Tues–Sun 10am–6pm) is worth exploring. There are two entrances: the one on the embankment lets you into the main building, a converted naval barracks, while the one on Stúrovo námestie gives access to the Esterházy Palace wing – inside, both parts connect on the upper floor. The permanent collection in the main building is an exhaustive rundown of Slovak art from Gothic times to the late nineteenth century, while the Esterházy Palace houses sixteenth- to eighteenth-century paintings of dubious merit. You're better off heading straight for the fascinating top-floor display of twentieth-century applied arts, architecture and design.

Further along the quayside, past the rather tatty **Natural History Museum** (Tues–Sun 9am–5pm) and hidden away behind Safárikovo námestie, is Ödön Lechner's sky-blue Art Nouveau **Blue Church** (Modrý kostol) at Bezručova 2, a lost monument to this once-Hungarian city, abandoned in the Slovak capital. This masterpiece of Budapest-style Art Nouveau is decorated, inside and out, with the richness of a central European cream cake, and dedicated to St Elizabeth, the city's one and only famous saint, born in Bratislava in 1207.

Eating and drinking

The choice of places to eat in Bratislava has improved enormously over the last few years, as have standards, which in some cases are as high as anywhere else in Europe. The most memorable aspect of the whole experience is often the ambience, and exploring the atmospheric streets of the old town by night is all part of the fun. In addition, you can also be fairly sure that, away from the places catering for those on expenses, prices remain uniformly low.

Cafés, bars and pubs

The Dubliner, Sedlárska 6. Every European capital, it seems, has to have an Irish pub, and this, the most popular expat hangout in town, is a no-holds-barred evocation, complete with miniature cobbled street.

Gremium, Gorkého 11. Smoky, spacious café downstairs, with pool and more seats up in the balcony. There's a more formal restaurant on the first floor, too. Occasional live music.

Kaffee Mayer, Hlavné námestie 4. A resurrected turn-of-the-century café that emulates its Viennese-style ancestor – very popular with the city's older cake-and-coffee fans.

KGB, Obchodná 52 (*www.angelfire.com/sk/kgb*). Friendly, late-opening cellar pub full of communist memorabilia and portraits. Some food.

Korzo, Rybné námestie. Tables outside overlooking the SNP Bridge, or inside with the morning papers – a good place for breakfast.

Restaurants

Arkádia, Zámocké schody (☎07/5443 5650). Swish restaurant serving great Slovak cuisine in an old Renaissance building on the way up to the castle. Pricey and reservations necessary.

Chez David, Zámocká 13. A moderately priced kosher restaurant. Closed Sat.

Crepa, Zamočnícka 3. French crêpes for takeaway or sit-down make a good fast-food snack.

Leberfinger, Viedenská cesta 257. Good Slovak food in this restaurant on the south bank of the Danube, with pleasant murals on the walls.

Mekong, Palackého 18. Swish Thai restaurant with, strangely, Italianate decor. Fantastic food though.

Rybársky cech, Žižkova 1. Popular and reliable fish restaurant down by the waterfront below the castle.

Slovenská Reštaurácia, Hviezdoslavovo nám. Excellent source of traditional Slovak cuisine in a relaxed atmosphere. Live piano music.

Sushi Bar Tokyo, Panská 27. Japanese restaurant with Slovakia's only sushi bar in the heart of the old town. Pricey but good, fresh food.

U Liszta, Klariská 1. Good place for trying out Slovak cuisine at reasonable prices. The courtyard at the back is great in summer.

Nightlife and entertainment

Bratislava's most established **nightlife** is heavily biased towards high culture, with **opera** and **ballet** at the Slovak National Theatre (Slovenské národné divadlo or SND) and orchestral concerts at the Reduta, as well as the varied programme put on at the modern Dom odborov complex (tram #4 or #6 from Kamenné námestie). Tickets for the first two are available from the box office at Palackého 2 (Mon, Tues, Thurs & Fri 1–7pm, Wed 8am–2pm), and for the Dom odborov from a box office inside the building from 3pm. The excellent Arena theatre, Viedenska cesta 10 (*www.milan-sladek.sk*), specializes in **mime** – you can find it easily by crossing the river via the Starý most. Many theatres close down in July and August. The city hosts a couple of large-scale **festivals**, starting with its own spring music festival in April.

The longest-serving nightspot is the *Charlie centrum*, Spitálska 4, the entrance is one block east of the *Hotel Kyjev* on Rajská. Inside there's a multiscreen art-house **cinema**, and a late-night bar/disco in the basement. **Clubs** include the *Cirkus Barok*, a floating bar and nightclub on the Danube with dancing in the basement, while a grungy club at Vysoká 14 called *Kráter* attracts a young crowd. *Hysteria*, Odbojárov 9, behind the ice hockey stadium (tram #4 or #6 from Kamenné námestie), is worth the trek for its Tex-Mex food, pool and regular live music.

Listings

Airlines British Airways, Stefankova 22 (☎07/5245 0000); Tatra Air Slovakia, M.R. Štefanik Airport (☎07/4329 2306).

Embassies Canada, Mišikova 28D (☎07/5244 2175); Great Britain, Panská 16 (☎07/5441 0541); USA, Hviezdoslavovo námestie 4 (☎07/5443 3338).

Internet access Internet Café, Múzejna 6, at the back of the National Museum; Internet club, Jesenského 7.

Pharmacy 24hr emergency service from Mýtná 5, Palackého 10 & nám. SNP 20.

Police The "foreigners' police" (*cudzinecká polícia*) are at Sasinkova 23 (☎0961/011111).

Post office The main post office is at námestie SNP 35 (Mon–Fri 7am–8pm, Sat 7am–6pm, Sun 9am–2pm).

Telephone There's a 24hr telephone exchange at Kolárska 12.

THE MOUNTAIN REGIONS

The great virtue of Slovakia is its mountains, particularly the **High Tatras**, which, in their short span, reach alpine heights and have a bleak, stunning beauty. By far the republic's most popular destination, they are, in fact, the least typical of Slovakia's mountains, which are predominantly densely forested, round-topped limestone ranges. In the heart of the mountains is **Banská Bystrica**, one of the many towns in the region originally settled by German miners, and still redolent of those times. Generally, though, the towns in the valley bottoms have been fairly solidly industrialized, and are only good as bases for exploring the surrounding countryside. Railways, where they do exist, make for some of the most scenic train journeys in the country.

Banská Bystrica

Lying at the very heart of Slovakia's mountain ranges, the old medieval German mining town of **BANSKÁ BYSTRICA** (Neusohl) is a useful introduction to the area. Connected to the outlying districts by some of the country's most precipitous railways, it's also a handsome historic town in its own right – once you've made it through the tangled suburbs of the burgeoning cement and logging industries.

Námestie SNP, the old medieval marketplace, is still the centre of life in Banská Bystrica. The black obelisk of the Soviet war memorial and a revolving fountain, enthusiastically chucking water over a pile of mossy rocks, form the square's centrepiece. One or two of the burgher houses bear closer inspection, particularly the **Venetian House** (Benického dom) at no. 16, with its slender first-floor arcaded loggia. The sgraffitoed building opposite is now an art gallery. Just a few doors down is the most imposing building on the square, the honey-coloured Thurzo Palace at no. 4, decorated like a piece of embroidery and sporting cute oval portholes, and now housing the **town museum** (Mon–Fri 8am–noon & 1–4pm, Sun 9am–noon & 1–4pm), with a small selection of folk art and period furniture.

At the top end of the square, beyond the leaning clock tower, there's an interesting ensemble of buildings which is all that's left of the old castle. The first building in view is the last remaining **barbican**, curving snugly round a Baroque tower. Next door, the former **town hall** or *radnica* (Tues–Fri 9am–5pm, Sat & Sun 10am–4pm), a boxy little Renaissance structure, is now the town's main art gallery, which puts on temporary exhibitions from its extensive catalogue of twentieth-century Slovak art. Behind it is the rouge-red church of **Panna Mária**, which dates back to the thirteenth century; the north side chapel contains the town's greatest art treasure, a carved late-Gothic altarpiece by Master Pavol of Levoča.

A short distance southeast of námestie SNP on Kapitulská, 200m south of the clock tower, is the **SNP Museum** at no. 23 (Tues–Sun: May–Sept 8am–6pm; Oct–April 9am–4pm), looking something like an intergalactic mushroom chopped in half and dating from 1969. The museum deals as best it can with the complex issues raised by the Slovak National Uprising (SNP) against the Nazis (and the Slovak puppet regime), which began on August 29, 1944, in Banská Bystrica and which was eventually crushed by the Germans two months later, just a month or so before the town's liberation. Outside on the grass you'll notice an exhibition of tanks, an armoured train and guns from the uprising amid the bushes and the town's last two surviving medieval bastions.

Practicalities

Banská Bystrica's **bus terminus** and the main **train station** are in the modern part of town, ten minutes' walk east of the centre. A second, smaller train station, Banská Bystrica Mesto, is just a five-minute walk due south of the centre. **Tourist offices** at nám. Š. Moyzesa 26 (Mon–Fri 8.30am–5pm, Sat 9am–1pm; ☎088/415 5085) and at nám. SNP 13 (☎088/413 8765, *www.isternet.sk/pkobb*) can help with **accommodation**. The cheapest options are the *Milvar*, a five-minute walk to the west of town at Školská 9 (☎088/413 8765; ①), and the *Národný Dom*, at Národná ulica 11 (☎088/412 3737; ②). A pricier option is the renovated *Hotel Arcade* at nám. SNP 5 (☎088/430 2111; ④). There's a **campsite** 1km west of the main square at Tajovského cesta, just by the road to Tajov (☎088/419 732; open all year). **Eating options** include a cheap and filling plate of *bryndzové halušky* at the *Slovenská pivnica* at Lazovná 18 (closed Sun); *Zlatý Bažant* at nám. SNP 11 also has well-priced Slovak fare.

The High Tatras

Rising like a giant granite reef above the patchwork Poprad plain, the **High Tatras** are for many people the main reason for venturing this far into Slovakia. Even after all the tourist-board hype, they are still an inspirational sight. A wilderness, however, they are not; all summer, visitors are shoulder to shoulder in the necklace of resorts which sit at the foot of the mountains. But once you're above the tree line, surrounded by bare primeval scree slopes and icy blue tarns, nothing can take away the exhilaration or the breathtaking views.

The mainline train station for the Tatras is Poprad-Tatry in **Poprad** (the main bus station is outside, across the road and to the right). From the high-level platform here, cute red tram-like trains trundle across the fields, linking Poprad with the string of resorts and spas halfway up the Tatras and lying within the **Tatra National Park** or **TANAP**. They range from taste-less new hotels and cosier half-timbered lodges to spectacular turreted edifices from the nineteenth century set in eminently civilized spa gardens and pine woods – but it's the mountains to which they give access that make them worth visiting. Perhaps the best to head for is **Starý Smokovec**, the central resort.

Poprad

POPRAD is an unprepossessing town on the plain. With its great swathe of off-white high-rise housing encircling a small old centre, it is best viewed as a stop-over on the way to the mountains proper. Unbeautiful but practical hotels include the towering *Hotel Garni* at Karpatska 11 námestie (☎092/7763 877; ①–②) and the boxy *Domov Mladeže*, by the train station (☎092/7763 414; ①) – you're probably better off at one of the not much more expensive, but a lot more comfortable hotels in the mountains (see below). The excellent **tourist office** at nám. sv Egídia 2950/114 (Mon–Fri 8.30am–5pm, Sat 9am–1pm; ☎092/772 1700, *www.tatradata.sk*), five minutes' walk south of the train station, can book you into **private rooms** in the Tatras. The office is just opposite the *Domenico* **café**, which offers a good range of cakes.

Camping in the High Tatras

Accommodation should be your first priority in the mountains, since finding a place can be difficult. The cheapest option is **camping**, though all the sites are outside the boundaries of the national park and therefore a long hike from the nearest peaks. By far the best one is *Eurocamp FICC* (☎0969/4467 741; year-round), with bungalows, a restaurant and café, hot showers and many other facilities.

Starý Smokovec – and Tatra hikes

The best base for accommodation in the Tatras is the scattered settlement of **STARÝ SMOKOVEC**, whose nucleus is the stretch of lawn between the half-timbered supermarket and the sandy-yellow *Grand Hotel*. The new *Hotel Smokovec* (☎0969/4425 191/3; *smokovec@tanap.sk;* ②), in particular, offers rooms overlooking the valley at bargain prices. T-Ski (daily 9am–6pm), by the funicular railway (60Sk) behind the *Grand*, is a good source of **information**; they also rent out **skis** in winter and **mountain bikes** in summer. You can rent mountain bikes from Tatrasport Adam a Andreas, in a wooden chalet at the end of the main drag (350Sk per day). Climbers and hikers wanting information should go to Horská služba, the 24-hour mountain rescue service, close to the train station, or should check out *www.tanap.sk*. The self-service buffet just beneath the funicular offers cheap but filling snacks. To book into one of the mountain **refuges** (*chata*), you could visit Slovakoturist in the neighbouring resort of Horný Smokovec, a couple of minutes' walk to the east.

If the weather's reasonably good, the most straightforward and rewarding climb is to follow the blue-marked path that leads from behind the *Grand Hotel* to the summit of **Slavkovský štít** (2452m), a return journey of nine hours. Alternatively, there's also a narrow-gauge funicular, again starting from behind the *Grand* (every 30min), which climbs 250m to **HREBIENOK** (45min on foot), one of the lesser ski resorts on the edge of the pine forest. The smart wooden *Bilíkova chata* (☎0969/442 2439; ②–③) is a five-minute walk from the top of the funicular – even if you don't stay there you should stop for a drink on the balcony. Beyond the *chata*, the path continues through the wood, joining two others, from Tatranská Lesná and Tatranská Lomnica respectively, before passing the gushing waterfalls of the **Studenovodské vodopády**.

Just past the waterfall, a whole variety of trekking possibilities opens up. The right-hand fork takes you up the **Malá Studená dolina** and then zigzags above the tree line to the *Téryho chata*, set in a lunar landscape by the shores of the **Päť Spišských ples**. Following the spectacular trail over the Prieane sedlo to *Zbojnicka chata*, you can return via the **Vejká studená dolina** – an eight-hour round trip from Hrebienok. Another possibility is to take the left-hand fork to the *Zbojnicka chata*, and continue to Zamruznuté pleso, which sits in the shadow of **Východná Vysoká** (2428m); only a thirty-minute hike from the lake, this peak dishes out the best view of **Gerlachovský stít** – the highest peak in the Tatras and a symbol of Slovak nationhood – that a non-climber can get.

EAST SLOVAKIA

Stretching from the High Tatras east to the Ukrainian border, the landscape of **East Slovakia** is decidedly different from the rest of the country. Ethnically, this is probably the most diverse region in the country, with different groups coexisting even within a single valley. The majority of the country's Romanies live here, mostly on the edge of Slovak villages, in shanty towns of almost medieval squalor. In the ribbon-villages of the north and east, the Rusyn minority struggle to preserve their culture and religion, while along the southern border there are large numbers of Hungarians. After spending time in the rural backwaters, **Košice**, Slovakia's second largest city, can be a welcome though somewhat startling return to city life. Gradually realizing its potential as a diverse and vibrant cosmopolitan centre, it certainly contains enough of interest for at least a day's stopover.

The Spiš region

The land that stretches northeast up the Poprad Valley to the Polish border and east along the River Hornád towards Prešov is known as the **Spiš** (Zips) region, for centuries a semi-autonomous province within the Hungarian kingdom. After the devastation of the mid-thirteenth-century Tatar invasions, the Hungarian Crown encouraged Saxon families to repopulate the area. The wealthy settlers built some wonderful Gothic churches, and later enriched almost every town and village with the distinctive touch of the Renaissance. Today, with only a few of its ethnic Germans and Hungarians remaining, the Spiš shares the low-living standards of the rest of East Slovakia. But the region's architectural richness offers a glimmer of hope in the growth of tourism – indeed in towns like Levoča you can often hardly move for the tour buses.

Kežmarok

Just 14km up the road from Poprad, **KEŽMAROK** (Käsmark) is one of the easiest Spiš towns to visit from the High Tatras. It's an odd place, combining the distinctive traits of a Teutonic town with the dozy feel of an oversized Slovak village. Kežmarok is dominated by the giant, gaudy **Lutheran Church** (May–Oct daily 10am–noon & 2–4pm; Nov–April Tues & Fri 10am–noon), built by Theophil Hansen, the Danish architect responsible for much of late-nineteenth-century Vienna, and funded by the town's merchants. It's a seemingly random fusion of styles – Renaissance campanile, Moorish dome, Classical dimensions, all dressed up in grey-green and rouge rendering. Next door is an even more remarkable **wooden Lutheran Church** (daily 9am–noon & 2–5pm), a work of great carpentry that's capable of seating almost 1500 people.

The old town itself is little more than two long leafy streets which fork off from the important-looking central town hall. The town's Catholic church, **sv Kríž**, is tucked away in the tangle of dusty back alleys between the two prongs, once surrounded by its own line of fortifications. It is now protected by a Renaissance belfry whose uppermost battlements burst into sgraffito life in the best Spiš tradition. The **Castle** or **zámok** (entry every hour Tues–Sun 9am–4pm), at the end of the right-hand fork, is impressively fortified and decorated with Renaissance crenellations, but the interior doesn't really justify signing up for the compulsory hour-long guided tour. A better idea is to head for the **town museum**, back along the street at Hradné námestie 55 (Tues–Sat 9am–noon & 1–5pm), which contains, among other things, the personal effects of Countess Hedviga Mária Szirmayova-Badányiova.

The **tourist office**, opposite the town hall at Hlavné námestie 46 (Mon–Fri 8.30am–5pm, Sat 9am–2pm; May–Sept also Sun 9am–2pm), can help with **accommodation**. The best place to stay is the pleasant *Hotel Club*, on ulica MUDr Alexandra (☎0968/4524 0512; ③), though the *Penzion Regent*, 63 Starý Trh (☎0968/452 4258; ②), a ten-minute walk from the train station at the foot of the castle gates, provides some stiff competition. For budget travellers the *Štart* (☎0968/4522 916; ③), which lies in the woods to the north of the castle, is good value. The *Castellan Club* tucked into the side of the castle provides a watering-hole late at night.

Levoča

Twenty-five kilometres east of Poprad across the broad sweep of Spiš countryside, the ravishingly beautiful walled town of **LEVOČA** (Leutschau), set on a slight incline, makes a wonderfully medieval impression, and is very much a Gothic and Renaissance haven. The Euclidian efficiency with which the old town is laid out means you'll inevitably end up at the main square, **námestie Majstra Pavla**. To the north is the square's least distinguished but most important building, the municipal weigh-house; a law of 1321 obliged every merchant passing through the region to hole up at Levoča for fourteen days, pay various taxes and allow the locals first refusal on their goods.

Of the three freestanding buildings on the main square paid for with these riches, it's the Catholic church of **sv Jakub** that has the most valuable booty; the church is only opened for tour parties at a charge of 40Sk, though you can usually tag onto whatever group is struggling to get in or out. Every nook and cranny is crammed with religious art, the star attraction being the magnificent sixteenth-century wooden **altarpiece** by Master Pavol of Levoča, which, at 18.6m, is reputedly the tallest of its kind in the world. A small **museum** (Tues–Sun 9am–5pm) dedicated to Master Pavol stands opposite the church on the eastern side of the square. South of the church is the **town hall** or *radnica* (Tues–Sun 9am–5pm), built in a sturdy Renaissance style. On the first floor, there's a museum on the Spiš region, and some fine examples of Spiš handicrafts on the top floor. The third building in the centre of the square is the oddly squat **Lutheran Church**, built in an uncompromisingly Neoclassical style.

You can get to Levoča by train from Poprad, but you must change at Spišská Nová Ves – much easier to take a bus from either Poprad, Prešov or Košice. The **train** and **bus stations** are southeast of the old town. Outside the annual pilgrimage in early July, **accommodation** shouldn't be hard to find; the helpful **tourist office** (Mon–Fri 9am–5pm, Sat & Sun 9am–1.30pm; ☎0966/451 3763, *www.levoca.sk*) in the northwest corner of the square can book private rooms. Best choice is the decidedly comfortable *Hotel Barbakan* at Košická 15 (☎0966/451 4310; ③), which includes a buffet breakfast in the price and rents out bikes. Alternatively, there's the *Penzion pri Košickej bráne* (☎0966/451 2879; ③) and the *Hotel Arkada* (☎0966/4512 255, *arkada@stonline.sk*; ③), both on the main square; the **campsite** (☎0966/2701; open year-round) is a three-kilometre walk north of Levoča. Authentic Slovak pub **food** can be had from *U Janusa*, Klástorská 22, and from the atmospheric *U troch apoštolov*, above a butcher's, on the east side of the main square, while more upmarket fare can be sampled at the *Restaurácia Biela Pani* on the south side. There's a self-service vegetarian restaurant, *Vegeterián*, at Uholná 3, northwest of the main square, and the *Pizzeria Bella Fonte* is on the next street (follow the signpost).

Spišský hrad

The road east from Levoča takes you to the edge of Spiš territory, clearly defined by the Branisko ridge which blocks the way to Prešov. Even if you're not going any further east, you should at least take the bus as far as **SPIŠSKÉ PODHRADIE**, for arguably the most spectacular sight in the whole country – the **Spišský hrad** (May–Oct Tues–Sun 9am–6pm). This pile of chalk-white ruins, strung out on a bleak green hill, is irresistibly photogenic and finds its way into almost every tourist hand-out in the country. The ruins themselves don't quite live up to expectations, though the view from the top is pretty good. The *Penzíon Podzámok* at Podzámková 28 (☎0966/454 1755; ②) has superb views up to the castle.

Prešov

Capital of the Slovak Šariš region and a cultural centre for the Rusyn (Ruthenian) minority, **PREŠOV** has a split personality indicative of its long and chequered ethnic history. Over the past decade, it has been treated to a wonderful face-lift, and although there's not much of interest beyond its main square, it's a refreshingly youthful and vibrant town, partly due to its university.

The lozenge-shaped main square, **Hlavná ulica**, is flanked by creamy, pastel-coloured, almost edible eighteenth-century facades. At the square's southern tip is the **Greek-Catholic Cathedral**, a wonderful Rococo affair with a fabulously huge iconostasis. Further along, on the same side of the square, is Prešov's **town hall** or *radnica*, from whose unsuitably small balcony Béla Kun's Hungarian Red Army declared the short-lived Slovak Socialist Republic in 1919. Further north along the square, the **town museum**, situated in the dog-tooth-gabled Rákociho dom at no. 86 (Tues–Fri 8am–noon & 12.30–4pm, Sat & Sun 11am–3pm), offers a thorough retelling of the history of the Šariš region.

Prešov's Catholic and Protestant churches vie with each other at the widest point of the square. The fourteenth-century Catholic church of **sv Mikuláš** has the edge, not least for its modern Moravian stained-glass windows and its sumptuous Baroque altarpiece. Behind sv Mikulás, the much plainer **Lutheran Church**, built in the mid-seventeenth century, bears witness to the strength of religious reformism in the outer reaches of Hungary at a time when the rest of the Habsburgs' lands were suffering the full force of the Counter-Reformation.

Lastly, the town's ornate turn-of-the-century **synagogue** in the northwest corner of the old town – access from Svermova – has been turned into a small **museum of Judaica** (Múzeum Expozícia Judaík; Tues & Wed 11am–4pm, Thurs 3–6pm, Fri 10am–1pm, Sun 1–5pm), with an exhibition on Judaism and Prešov's Jews, 6000 of whom perished in the Holocaust.

The **bus** and **train stations** are situated opposite one another about 1km south of the main square; the best buses and trolleybuses into town are those which stop at Na Hlavnej. The best budget **accommodation** is to be had at the *Sen*, Vajanského 65 (☎091/7733 170; ①), two blocks east of the main square; otherwise there's the *Senator*, at Hlavná 67 (☎091/7731 186; *mssh@vadium.sk*; ④), or the super-cheap *Studentský domov TU* at Budovatelská 31 (☎091/7723 241; ①). The **restaurant** *Leonardo* at Hlavná 144, the north end of the main square, offers Slovak and Italian alternatives, and there's a pleasant Irish **pub** at Slovenská 39.

Košice

Slovak towns often never amount to much more than their one long main square, and even **KOŠICE**, Slovakia's second largest city, is no exception. Rather like Bratislava, Košice was, until relatively recently, a modest little town on the edge of the Hungarian plain. Then, in the 1950s, the communists established a giant steel works on the outskirts of the city. Forty years on, it has a population of over 250,000, a number of worthwhile museums, the best cathedral in the republic, and a lively cosmopolitanism that can be quite reassuring after a week or so in the Slovak back-of-beyond. Just 21km north of the Hungarian border, Košice also acts as a magnet for the Hungarian community – to whom the city is known as Kassa – and the terminally underemployed Romanies of the surrounding region, lending it a diversity and vibrancy absent from small-town Slovakia, and only recently viewed as contributing positively to the town.

The old town

Almost everything of interest is situated on Košice's long pedestrianized main square, which is called **Hlavná ulica** at its northern and southern extremities, **Hlavné námestie** to the north of the cathedral, and **námestie slobody** to the south of the cathedral. Lined with handsome

Baroque and Neoclassical palaces, it's dominated by the city's unorthodox Gothic **Cathedral of St Elizabeth**, its charcoal-coloured stone recently sandblasted back to its original honeyed hue. Begun in 1378, it's an unusual building from the outside, with striped roof tiles and two contorted towers. Inside, imposing Gothic furnishings add an impressive touch to an otherwise plain nave, the main gilded altar depicting scenes from the life of the cathedral's patron saint.

On the busy north side of the cathedral, the fourteenth-century **Urbanova veža** (Tues–Sat 9am–5pm, Sun 9am–1pm), standing on its own set of mini-arcades, has recently been converted into an upmarket café. The public park and fountains beyond are a favourite spot for hanging out and make an appropriately graceful approach to the city's grand Austro-Hungarian **theatre**.

The peculiar **Vojtecha Löfflera Museum**, at Alžbetina 20 (Tues–Sat 10am–6pm, Sun 1–5pm), west off the main square, features the work and private collections of Košice's most prominent communist-sanctioned sculptor. Another unusual attraction is the **Mikluš Prison** (Miklušova väznica; Tues–Sat 9am–5pm; May–Sept also Mon 9am–5pm & Sun 9am–1pm), east off the square down Univerzitna, whose original dimly lit dungeons and claustrophobic cells graphically transport you into its history as the city prison and torture chamber. At the northern tip of the main square, námestie Maratónu mieru is flanked to the east and west by the bulky nineteenth-century **East Slovak Museum** (Východoslovenské múzeum; Tues–Sat 9am–5pm, Sun 10am–1pm). The western building is worth visiting for its basement collection of fifteenth- to seventeenth-century **gold coins** – 2920 in all – minted at Kremnica but stashed away by city burghers and discovered by accident in 1935. Hidden round the back of the museum is a wooden Orthodox Church, brought here from Carpatho-Ruthenia (now in Ukraine).

Practicalities

The **train** and **bus stations** are opposite each other, ten minutes' walk east of the old town. There are two **tourist offices**, one at Hlavná 8 on the main square (Mon–Fri 8am–6pm, Sat & Sun 9am–1pm, ☎095/186, *www.pangea.sk*), which also has an **Internet** facility (20Sk per 15min), and a second, small kiosk round the corner in the Dargov Mall (Mon–Fri 10am–noon & 1–6pm, Sat 9am–1pm; ☎095/16186). Both can help with finding **accommodation**, including private rooms. The best budget accommodation is provided by the *Hotel Metropole* at Šturova 32 (☎095/625 5948; ①), 200m west of the southern tip of the square, with a pleasant garden area featuring live music in summer. Slightly pricier are the welcoming *Penzión pri radnici*, Bačíkova 18 (☎095/6227 824; ③), and the *Hotel Alessandria* at Jiskrova 3 (☎095/622 5903; ③–④). The nearest **campsite** (☎095/58309; year-round) is 5km south of the city centre and also rents out bungalows; take a tram or bus #31 to the flyover, then get off and walk the remaining 500m west along Alejová, the road to Ružnava (maps of the transport system inside tram and bus shelters mark the spot as *Autokemping*).

If you're looking for somewhere to **eat**, there's *Pizza Venezia*, at Mlynská 20, en route from the stations, and *Ajvega*, Orlia 10, one block east of the main square, a bizarre place doing soya versions of standard Slovak dishes upstairs and Mexican food downstairs, while *Caravelia* at no. 4 on the same street has a range of fish specialities. The *Gallery Club*, Hlavná 27, and the next door *Kaviareň Slávia* cafés are well worth a try for coffee, cakes and ices. For splashing out on Slovak cuisine try the *Zlatá Hus* (Golden Goose) at Hlavná 78 (☎095/622 6472). The city has plenty of options for **drinking**: *Music Bar Diesel* at Hlavná 92 has frequent live music and a good atmosphere.

The city's Slovak State Philharmonic Orchestra plays regular **concerts** at the *Dom umenia* at Moyzesova 66 and inside the cathedral itself, and a wide range of classical plays and opera is on offer at the main theatre at Hlavná 58 (☎095/622 1231-2, *www. sdke.box.sk*). Košice has a **Hungarian theatre**, Thália, at Timonovova 3 (☎095/622 5866), and also boasts Slovakia's one and only **Romany theatre**, Romathan, which puts on a whole range of events from concerts to plays, at Štefánikova 4 (☎095/622 4980). Košice's **nightlife** revolves around the main square (more a long boulevard). For late-night dancing the *Jumbo Centrum* at Masarykova 2 is a popular haunt for young Košicans (Wed, Fri & Sat) with an adjoining restaurant, cinema and café.

travel details

Trains

Bratislava to: Banská Bystrica (2 daily; 4hr–4hr 30min); Poprad-Tatry (6 daily; 4hr–5hr 30min); Prešov (1 daily; 7hr); Košice (6 daily; 5hr–6hr 15min).

Poprad-Tatry to: Starý Smokovec (2 hourly in high season, hourly in low season; 45min); Kežmarok (12 daily; 30min); Prešov (2 daily; 1hr 30min); Košice (12 daily; 1hr 30min).

Buses

Levoča to: Spišské Podhradie (up to 15 daily; 30min).

Poprad to: Levoča (up to 15 daily; 30min–1hr 30min); Spišské Podhradie (up to 12 daily; 30–45min); Prešov (up to 20 daily; 2hr).

CHAPTER 26

SLOVENIA

Introduction

The northernmost republic of what was once Yugoslavia, **Slovenia** currently appears the most stable, prosperous and welcoming of all Europe's erstwhile communist countries. It was always the richest and most westernized of the Yugoslav federation, and apart from the Ten-Day War which brought it independence in 1991, it has avoided the strife which has plagued the republics to the south. For centuries, Slovenia was administered by German-speaking overlords and was, until 1918, part of the Austro-Hungarian empire. The Slovenes absorbed the culture of their captors during this period while managing to retain a strong sense of ethnic identity through the Slav-rooted Slovene language, a close relation of Czech, Serbo-Croat and Slovak.

Slovenia's landscape is as varied as it is beautiful: along the Austrian border the **Julian Alps** provide stunning mountain scenery, most accessibly at **Lake Bled** and **Lake Bohinj**; further south, the brittle karst scenery is riddled with spectacular caves like those at **Postojna**. Slovenia's capital, **Ljubljana**, is easily the best of the cities, a vital, youthful place, manageably small and cluttered with Baroque and Habsburg buildings, while the short stretch of Slovenian coast, along the northern edge of the Istrian peninsula, is punctuated by a couple of towns that were among the most attractive resorts of the former Yugoslavia – **Piran** and **Portorož** – not to mention the port of **Koper**, with its appealingly ancient centre. Despite its relative isolation in the eastern part of the country, the attractively preserved town of **Ptuj** is also well worth a visit.

Information and maps

There is an excellent network of local authority-run **tourist information centres** in most towns and well-touristed places. As well as providing local information and maps, many centres supply information on other parts of the country, and some also act as an agency for private rooms. Elsewhere, travel agencies (Globtour, Slovenijaturist and Kompas are the biggest-selling chains) can be a useful source of information, although they understandably concentrate on selling you tours and changing your money. A high standard of English is spoken pretty much everywhere.

There's a good 1:300,000 **map** of Slovenia published by Freytag & Berndt. Excellent small-scale hiking maps are published by the Slovene Alpine Association (Planinska zveza Slovenije; Dvoržakova ulica 9; ☎01/231-2553, *www.pzs.si*) and are widely available in bookshops in Slovenia.

Money and banks

Slovenia's unit of **currency** is the tolar, which is divided into 100 (virtually worthless) stotini. Coins come in denominations of 50 stotini and 1, 2, 5 and 10 tolars; and there are notes of 10, 20, 50, 100, 200, 500, 1000, 5000 and 10,000 tolars. Prices are usually followed by the initials SIT. The exchange rate is currently approximately 350SIT to £1, and 240SIT to $1.

Banks (*hanka*) are generally open Mon-Fri 8.30am–12.30pm & 2–5pm and Sat 8.30am–11/12pm. Money can also be changed in tourist offices, post offices, travel agencies and exchange bureaux (*menjalnica*), all of which have more flexible hours. Travellers' cheques and credit cards are widely accepted; and you can use credit cards to get cash advances from ATMs and in the bigger banks.

Prices for accommodation and tours are sometimes given in Deutschmarks – although payment is usually made in tolars.

Communications

Most **post offices** (*pošta*) are open Mon–Fri 8am–6pm and Sat 8am–noon. In big towns and resorts, some offices are open longer on Saturdays and for a few hours on Sundays too. Stamps (*znamke*) can also be bought at newsstands.

Public **phone** boxes use cards (*telekartice*) which come in denominations of 700SIT, 1000SIT, 1700SIT and 3500SIT; you can buy these from post offices, newspaper kiosks and tobacco shops. When making long-distance and international calls it's usually eas-

---

SLOVENIA ON THE NET

www.matkurja.com – comprehensive site

www.slovenia-tourism.si – official tourist board

www.ijs.si/slo/ljubljana – sights in the capital

www.bled.si – useful site on Slovenia's premier attraction.

ier to go to the post office, where you're assigned to a cabin and given the bill afterwards.

For a country that has readily embraced the **Internet**, access is quite poor, even in the capital, and it will be a struggle to find access in other places. Expect to pay around 400SIT/hr.

Getting around

Traversing Slovenia by any kind of public transport is relatively easy and usually very scenic. Generally speaking, trains provide the fastest means of travelling on the main routes linking the capital with Maribor and Koper, or with Austria and Italy. Everywhere else, buses are far more convenient.

■ Trains and buses

Slovene railways (Slovenske železnice) run a smooth and efficient service. **Trains** (*vlaki*) are divided into *potniški* (slow ones which stop at every halt) and *IC* (intercity trains which are faster and slightly more expensive). Some of the latter, colloquially known as *zeleni vlaki* (green trains), are designated on timetables by the initials ICZV, and are express services on which prior seat reservations (*rezervacije*) are obligatory. Timetable leaflets (*vozni red*) are sometimes available although most timetables have explanations in English. *Odhodi* are departures, *prihodi* arrivals. Both Eurail and InterRail passes are valid.

Slovenia's **bus** network consists of an array of small local companies, but their services are well coordinated. Big towns such as Ljubljana, Maribor and Koper have big bus stations with computerized booking facilities where you can buy your tickets hours (if not days) in advance – recommended if you're travelling between Ljubljana and the coast at the height of summer. Elsewhere, simply pile onto the bus and pay the driver or conductor. You'll be charged extra for cumbersome items of baggage, like a backpack, which must be stored in the hold.

■ Driving and hitching

The road system is both comprehensive and of reasonable quality. Stretches of the main Ljubljana–Koper, Ljubljana–Maribor and Ljubljana–Jesenice routes are classed as motorways (*avtoceste*) and large stretches of them have been converted to dual carriageway (tolls are levied on these routes); elsewhere main roads soon get clogged up with summer traffic. **Speed limits** on Slovene roads are 50kph in built-up areas, 90kph on normal roads, 100kph on highways and 130kph on motorways. If you break down, the Slovene Automobile Club (AMZS) has a 24hr emergency service (☎987), and there are technical centres in all the larger towns. **Car rental** charges are about £50/$75 a day for a standard mid-range vehicle with unlimited mileage.

Hitching is pretty common on the main Ljubljana–Maribor, Ljubljana–Koper and Bled–Bohinj routes, although you should be prepared to wait a long time for a lift, and remember that hitching is forbidden on anything classified as a motorway (recognizable by the green road signs). Elsewhere in the country, prospects for hitching vary from one region to another.

Accommodation

While tourist **accommodation** is universally clean and good quality, it doesn't come much cheaper than in neighbouring Italy or Austria unless you opt for a private room.

■ Hotels, guest houses and private rooms

Apart from a couple of fin-de-siècle establishments in Ljubljana, Slovene **hotels** tend to be high-rise concrete affairs providing modern comforts but little atmosphere. They are classified according to the international five-star system, with three-star places (usually offering rooms with en-suite facili-

---

ACCOMMODATION PRICE CODES

Throughout this guide, accommodation is coded on a scale of ① to ⑨, the code indicating the lowest price per person per night you could expect to pay in each establishment in high season. With hostels this is the nightly rate per person; with hotels, the price is arrived at by dividing the cost of the cheapest double room by two. The prices indicated by the codes are as follows:

① under £5/$8 (€9)	④ £15–20/$24–32 (€27–36)	⑦ £30–35/$48–56 (€54–63)
② £5–10/$8–16 (€9–18)	⑤ £20–25/$32–40 (€36–45)	⑧ £35–40/$56–64 (€63–72)
③ £10–15/$16–24 (€18–27)	⑥ £25–30/$40–48 (€45–54)	⑨ £40/$64 (€72) and over

ties and TV) making up the bulk of the hotel stock. Cheaper two-star places are occasionally available, but anything lower than this is very rare. Expect to pay £30/$45 a double upwards for two-star hotels, £40/$60 a double upwards for three-star. In recent years there's been a growth in the number of family-run **pensions** in rural Slovenia, especially in the alpine regions, offering the same facilities as hotels (and rated according to the same star system), but usually with a cosier atmosphere and a lower price. Outside alpine resorts, however, *pensions* tend to be well away from town centres and are therefore hard to find unless you have your own transport.

Private rooms (*zasebne sobe*) are available throughout Slovenia, with bookings administered by tourist information centres in places like Ljubljana, or by travel agents like Slovenijaturist or Kompas elsewhere. Private rooms are pretty good value at about £14–20/$21–30 a double, although stays of three nights or under are invariably subject to a thirty-percent surcharge. The more expensive private rooms will have en-suite bathrooms, perhaps even a TV. Self-catering **apartments** (*apartmaji*) are also plentiful in the mountains and on the coast, with per-person rates working out the same as, or sometimes cheaper than, private rooms if there are more than two people travelling together.

■ Hostels and campsites

Hostels are thin on the ground in Slovenia and the only year-round one is at Bled, although there's a modest scattering of student hostels (*dijaški dom*) which open their doors to non-students over the summer and at weekends at other times of year. Beds in all hostels are in short supply, and advance booking is advised. Expect to pay about £8–12/$12–18 per person per night.

Campsites are plentiful in the mountains and on the coast and tend to be large-scale, well-organized affairs with plentiful facilities, restaurants and shops. Two people travelling with a tent can expect to pay £8–10/$12–15; add another £2/$3 for a vehicle. Camping rough without permission is punishable by a spot fine.

Serious hikers planning an assault on the peaks of Slovenia's Julian Alps could make use of **mountain huts** (*planinske koče*). The ones on the way up Mount Triglav are little less than hotels; elsewhere they are much more basic. You'll need to book in advance or arrive early. Details can be obtained from the Planinska zveza Slovenije, Dvoržakova 9, Ljubljana (☎01/231-2553), or from tourist information centres once you arrive.

Food and drink

Slovene cuisine draws on Austrian, Italian and Balkan influences. There's a native Slovene tradition, too, based on age-old peasant recipes, although this is gradually losing out as restaurants and cafés become increasingly international.

■ Food

Slovenia's well-stocked supermarkets and *delikatesa* are good places to stock up on **sandwich and picnic ingredients**, like local cheese (*sir*) and salami (*salama*). Buy fresh fruit and vegetables (*sadje in zelenjava*) from outdoor markets or roadside stalls, and bread (*kruh*) from a *pekarna* (bakery).

For **breakfast and quick snacks**, *okrepčevalnice* (snack bars) and street kiosks dole out *burek*, a flaky pastry filled with cheese (*sirov burek*) or meat (*burek z mcsom*). Sausages (*klobase*) come in various forms, most commonly hot dogs, *hrenovke* (Slovene frankfurters), or *kranjska klobasa* (big spicy sausages of local provenance).

Menus in a Slovene *restavracija* (restaurant) or *gostilna* (inn) are dominated by roast meats (*pečenka*) and schnitzels (*zrezek*), mostly pork (*svinjina*) and veal (*teletina*). The Slovenes are unsqueamish about offal: liver (*jetra*) and grilled or fried brains (*možgani*) are popular standbys in cheaper restaurants. Goulash (*golaž*) is found almost everywhere; *segedin* is goulash with lashings of sauerkraut. Two traditional Slovene dishes are *žlikrofi*, ravioli filled with potato, onion and bacon; and *žganci*, once the staple diet of rural Slovenes, a buckwheat or maize porridge often served with sauerkraut. *Ocvrti sir* (cheese fried in breadcrumbs) is one of the few dishes that will appease vegetarians. On the coast you'll find plenty of fish (*riba*), mussels (*žkoljke*) and squid (*kalamari*). Italian pasta dishes appear on most restaurant menus, and no Slovene high street is without at least one pizzeria.

Typical desserts include several solid Central European favourites: strudel, filled with apple or rhubarb; *žtruklji*, dumplings with fruit filling; *potica*, a doughy roll filled with nuts and honey; and *prekmurska gibanica*, a delicious local cheesecake.

■ Drink

Daytime drinking takes place in small café/bars, or in a *kavarna*, where a range of cakes, pastries and ice cream is usually on offer. Coffee (*kava*) is usually served black unless specified otherwise – ask for *mleko* (milk) or *smetana* (cream) – and often drunk alongside a glass of mineral water (*mineralna voda*). Tea (*čaj*) is usually served black. Familiar nonalcoholic drinks (*brezalkoholne pijače*) such as Coca-Cola, Pepsi and Sprite are all fairly ubiquitous.

Evening drinking usually goes on in small European-style bars or the more traditional *pivnica* (beer hall) or *vinarna* (wine cellar). Slovene beer (*pivo*) is of the Pilsner type and is usually excellent (*Lažko Zlatorog* is regarded as the best), although most breweries also produce *temno pivo* (literally "dark beer"), a Guinness-like stout. The local wine (*vino*) is either *črno* (red) or *belo* (white) and has an international reputation: dry whites like *Lazki rizling* and *Ljutomerčan* are regularly found on Western supermarket shelves; the less common and more refined *Šipon* and *Haložan* are worth seeking out. Best of the reds are the light *Cviček* and the dark, dry *Kraški teran*. Favourite aperitifs include *slivovka* (plum brandy), *vilijemovka* (pear brandy), the fiery *sadjevec*, a brandy made from various fruits, and the gin-like juniper-based *brinovec*.

Opening hours and holidays

Most **shops** open Mon–Fri 8am–7pm and Sat 8am–1pm, with an increasing number opening up on Sundays. Some shops outside major centres may take lengthy lunch breaks. Museum times differ from place to place, but they're usually closed on Mondays.

All shops and banks will be closed on the following **public holidays**: Jan 1 and 2; Feb 8 (Day of Slovene Culture); Easter Monday; April 27 (Resistance Day); May 1 and 2; June 25 (Day of Slovene Statehood); Aug 15 (Assumption); Oct 31 (Reformation Day); Nov 1 (All Saints'); and Dec 25 & 26.

Emergencies

Slovenia's crime rate is low and you're unlikely to have much contact with Slovene **police** (*policija*); if you do, they're generally easy-going and helpful, but unlikely to speak English. As far as health is concerned, citizens of the EU are entitled to free health care. **Pharmacies** (*lekarna*) tend to follow normal shopping hours, and a rota system covers night-time and weekend opening; details are posted in the window of each pharmacy.

Emergency Numbers

Police ☎113; Ambulance and Fire ☎112.

LJUBLJANA AND AROUND

LJUBLJANA curls under its castle-topped hill, an old centre marooned in the shapeless modernity that stretches out across the plain, a vital and self-consciously growing capital. At first glance it seems Austrian, a few strands of Vienna pulled out of place, typically exuberant and refined; but really Ljubljana is Slovenian through and through, with outside influences absorbed and tinkered with over the years. The city's sights are only part of the picture; first and foremost Ljubljana is a place to meet people and to get involved in the nightlife – the buildings just provide the backdrop.

Arrival, information and city transport

Your likely point of arrival (and drop-off point for buses from Brnik airport, 23km north of the city), is the main **train and bus station**, on Trg osvobodilne fronte, ten minutes' walk north of the centre. The main **Tourist Information Office (TIC)** is in the old town on Stritarjeva next to the Triple Bridge (June–Sept Mon–Fri 8am–8pm, Sat & Sun 10am–6pm; Oct–May Mon–Fri 8am–6pm, Sat & Sun 10am–6pm; ☎01/306-1215, *www.ljubljana.si*). In addition there is an information desk at the train station (June–Sept daily 8am–9pm; Oct–May Mon–Fri 10am–5.30pm; ☎01/433-9475). Both offices hand out maps and book rooms. Ljubljana's **buses** are cheap, frequent and usually overcrowded. You can pay in cash by depositing notes in a box next to the driver (a single journey currently costs a flat fare of 210SIT) or by using the slightly cheaper tokens (*žetoni*; 150SIT) bought in advance from post offices and most newspaper kiosks.

Accommodation

Finding cheap accommodation in Ljubljana is tough. Inexpensive **hotels** are in short supply and the **HI hostel** (*Dijaški Dom Tabor*), 1km southeast of the train station at Vidovdanska 7 (☎01/232-1060, *www2.arnes.si/~ssljddta1s*; ②), is open between June and August only.

The TIC has a limited stock of central **private rooms** (③), and will also book rooms in **student hostels** (open July & Aug only; ②–③). The main venue for these is usually the *Študentsko Naselje* (Student Village) at cesta 27 Aprila 31 (☎01/423-2122; bus #14 or a 20-min walk), in a suburb to the west of town. It's important that you check at the TIC first, as venues change regularly.

Five kilometres north of the centre, the **campsite** at Ježica (☎01/568-3913) can be reached by taking bus #8 north along Dunajska cesta. It's situated in a pleasant recreation area and has a few bungalows (③).

Hotels

Bellevue, Pod gozdom 12 (☎01/433-4049, *super.li@siol.net*). Very small, and with few amenities, but occupying an attractive old building above Tivoli Park with a breathtaking view across Ljubljana. ③.

BIT Center, Litijska 57 (☎01/548-0055, *www.bit-center.net*). Modern, functional rooms in this sports centre 2km east of the centre; 50-percent discount on use of sporting facilities and free use of pool in summer. Buses # 5, #9 and #13 from the centre. ③.

Lipa, Celovška 264 (☎01/519-2125, *aa-lipa@siol.net*). Comfortable and affordable pension, but not ideally located: it's in a medium-rise building 5km northwest of the centre, beside a busy main road. Buses #1, #15, #16 from the centre. ④.

M Hotel, Derčeva 4 (☎01/513-7000, *www.m-hotel.si*). An uninspiring but acceptable modern hotel, newly refurbished, 2.5km northwest of the city centre off Celovška cesta. ⑤.

Pri Mrak-u, Rimska 4 (☎01/421-9600, *www.daj-dam.si*). Smallish downtown *pension*, with comfortable en-suite rooms. 10-percent discount for stays of more than 3 nights. ⑤.

Park, Tabor 9 (☎01/433-1306). High-rise located amidst a jumble of apartment buildings a few blocks east of the station with shabby, bare rooms; some with en-suite facilities. ③.

Turist, Dalmatinova 15 (☎01/234-9130, *www.hotelturist.si*). Reasonable downtown hotel with a mix of older, bland rooms and modern, refurbished rooms; all rooms en suite. ⑤.

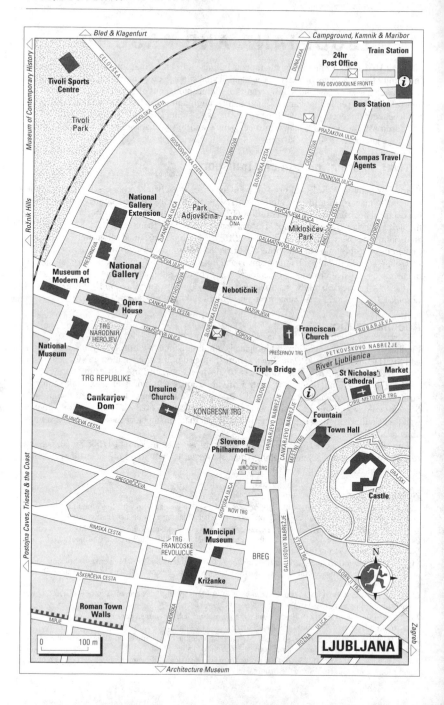

△ Bled & Klagenfurt △ Campground, Kamnik & Maribor

Museum of Contemporary History

CELOVŠKA

Tivoli Sports
Centre

Tivoli
Park

TIVOLSKA CESTA

Rožnik Hills

GOSPOSVETSKA CESTA

KERSNIKOVA

DUNAJSKA

24hr
Post Office

Train Station

ⓘ

TRG OSVOBODILNE FRONTE

Bus Station

PRAŽAKOVA ULICA

CIGALETOVA

SLOVENSKA CESTA

Kompas Travel
Agents

TRDINOVA ULICA

National
Gallery
Extension

ŽUPANČIČEVA ULICA

Park
Adjovščina

ADJOVŠ-
ČINA

TAVČARJEVA ULICA

MIKLOŠIČEVA CESTA

KOLODVORSKA

Miklošičev
Park

DALMATINOVA ULICA

KIDRIČEVA ULICA

Museum of
Modern Art

PREŠERNOVA

National
Gallery

BEETHOVNOVA

CANKARJEVA CESTA

Nebotičnik

NAZORJEVA

PREČNA

Opera
House

SLOVENSKA CESTA

TRUBARJEVA

TRG
NARODNIH
HEROJEV

TOMŠIČEVA ULICA

ČOPOVA

Franciscan
Church

†

PETKOVŠKOVO NABREŽJE

PREŠERNOV TRG

National
Museum

TRG REPUBLIKE

River Ljubljanica

Cankarjev
Dom

Ursuline
Church

†

ERJAVČEVA CESTA

KONGRESNI TRG

WOLFOVA

Triple Bridge

HRIBARJEVO NABREŽJE

CANKARJEVO NABREŽJE

St Nicholas'
Cathedral

†

Market

CIRIL METODOV TRG

ⓘ

Fountain

●

MESTNI TRG

Town Hall

Slovene
Philharmonic

JURČIČEV TRG

GREGORČIČEVA

GOSPOSKA ULICA

NOVI TRG

GALLUSOVO NABREŽJE

STARI TRG

GRAJSKI

Castle

RIMSKA CESTA

TRG
FRANCOSKE
REVOLUCIJE

Municipal
Museum

BREG

N

AŠKERČEVA CESTA

Križanke

GORNJI TRG

Postojna Caves, Trieste & the Coast

Roman Town
Walls

MIRJE

KAMNISKA

ROŽNA ULICA

Zagreb

0 100 m

LJUBLJANA

▽ Architecture Museum

The City

Ljubljana's main point of reference is Slovenska cesta, a busy north–south thoroughfare that slices the city down the middle. Most of the sights are within easy walking distance from here, with the Old Town straddling the River Ljubljanica to the south and east with its castle and cathedral, and the nineteenth-century quarter to the west, where the principal museums and galleries are to be found.

The Old Town

From the bus and train stations, head south down Miklošičeva for ten minutes and you're on **Prešernov trg**, the hub around which everything in Ljubljana's **Old Town** revolves. Overlooking everything, the seventeenth-century **Franciscan Church** (daily 6.45am–12.30pm & 3–8pm) blushes a sandy red above the bustling square and the River Ljubljanica: in its tired-feeling interior the old wall paintings look like faded photographs, and even Francesco Robba's Baroque high altar seems a little weary. Robba, an Italian architect and sculptor, was brought in to remodel the city in its eighteenth-century heyday.

Across the Tromostovje, or Triple Bridge, a **fountain**, also by Robba, symbolizes the meeting of the rivers Sava, Krka and Ljubljanica (he stole the idea from Bernini's fountain in Rome), and the whole stretch down from Prešernov trg west of the river is decaying Baroque grandeur. East of the river along Gallusovo Nabrežje most of the houses are ramshackle and medieval, occasionally slicked up as clothes shops and stores but mainly high, dark and crumbling.

Opposite Robba's fountain is the **Town Hall** (Magistrat) on Mestni trg – an undistinguished Baroque building around a courtyard. A little east of here **St Nicholas' Cathedral** (Stolna Cerkev Sv Nikolaja) on Ciril-Metodov trg is the most sumptuous and overblown of Ljubljana's Baroque statements, all whimsical ostentation and elaborate embellishment, its sheer size inducing hushed reverence as you enter. Designed by Andrea Pozzo (also architect of Dubrovnik's Jesuit Church), this is the best preserved of the city's ecclesiastical buildings. Just to the west of the cathedral buildings you can't fail to miss the **general market** (Mon–Sat) on Vodnikov trg, a brash free-for-all along the riverside, where everyone competes to sell their particular produce.

Opposite the market, Študentovska winds up the thickly wooded hillside to the **Castle**, visible from all over town and currently being restored to the glory it had when protecting Ljubljana's defensive position in earlier times – what's left today dates mainly from a sixteenth-century rebuilding. Climb the **clock tower** (10am–dusk; 300SIT) for a superlative view of the crowded Old Town below, the urban sprawl of high-rises beyond and the Kamniške Alps to the north. The best time to visit is towards sunset, when the haze across the plains burns red and gold, suffusing the town in luxurious light.

Central Ljubljana and beyond

Back on the western side of the river, the broad slash of **Slovenska cesta** forms the commercial heart of Ljubljana. Dominated by nineteenth- and twentieth-century shops and offices, it's a place to do business rather than sightsee – save perhaps for its only real landmark, **Nebotičnik**: a gaudily painted twelve-storey response to the American Art Deco skyscrapers of the 1930s.

Continuing south along Slovenska cesta, the park-like expanse of Kongresni trg slopes away from the early-eighteenth-century **Ursuline Church** (Uršulinska Cerkev), whose looming Baroque coffee-cake exterior is one of the city's most imposing: should you manage to gain entry there's another florid high altar by Robba. Lower down, by the side of the main university building, Vegova Ulica leads southwards from Kongresni trg towards Trg francoske revolucije, passing on the way the chequered pink, green and grey brickwork of the University Library. This was designed in the late 1930s by **Jože Plečnik** (1872–1957), the architect who more than any other determined the appearance of present-day Ljubljana. The whole atmosphere around the River Ljubljanica, including the riverbanks and several bridges, is the result of rebuilding work by Plečnik. His legacy, in the shape of Neoclassical columns, pillars and miniature brick pyramids scattered all over the city, is impossible to avoid.

One such oddity is the **Illyrian Monument** on Trg francoske revolucije, erected in 1930 in belated recognition of Napoleon's short-lived attempt to create a fiefdom of the same name centred on Ljubljana. Virtually next door is the seventeenth-century monastery complex of **Križanke**: originally the seat of a thirteenth-century order of Teutonic Knights, its delightful colonnaded courtyard was restored by Plečnik to form a permanent venue for the Ljubljana *Summer Festival*, see p.1157. Across Gosposka, at no. 15, the seventeenth-century Turjak Palace contains the **Municipal Museum**, which is currently closed while it undergoes a major transformation (due to open in 2003). In the meantime pop over to the Cultural Information Centre, 50 metres away, where you can view a small exhibition illustrating the extensive work in progress.

Beyond Trg francoske revolucije there's little of importance to see, except for a remaining stretch of the town's **Roman Walls** (again rearranged by Plečnik) on Mirje, and, a little further on, Plečnik's old house – now an **Architectural Museum** (Tues & Thurs 10am–2pm; 600SIT) at Karunova 4, where you can wander around Plečnik's ascetic living quarters.

West of Slovenska: museums and Tivoli Park

West of Slovenska, Cankarjeva heads down towards a neatly ordered corner of town that contains the city's most important **museums**. The **National Museum** (Narodni muzej; Tues–Sun 10am–6pm, Thurs until 8pm; 500SIT; *www.narmuz-lj.si*) at Muzejska 1 contains numerous dim halls of archeological objects, most famous of which is the **Vačka Situla**, a locally found Iron Age cauldron decorated with scenes of ritual feasting. The museum's natural history section is notable only for having the one complete mammoth skeleton found in Europe. The **National Gallery** (Tues–Sun 10am–6pm; 500SIT, free Sat pm; *www.ng-slo.si*) at Cankarjeva 20 is housed in the former Narodni Dom, built in the 1890s to accommodate Slovene cultural institutions in defiance of the Habsburgs. The gallery is rich in local medieval Gothic work, although most visitors gravitate towards the halls devoted to the Slovene Impressionists Rihard Jakopič, Ivan Grohar, Matija Jama and Matej Sternen. Their movement had considerable importance for the development of the Slovene national consciousness, extolling the virtues of rural Slovene peasantry and elevating them to the status of a subject fit for art. There's more Gothic stuff, as well as high-profile temporary exhibitions, in a new **extension** to the gallery (same times & prices) one block to the north at Puharjeva 9.

Back on the Cankarjeva, the **Museum of Modern Art** at no. 15 (Moderna galerija; Tues–Sat 10am–6/7pm, Sun 10am–1pm; 500SIT) carries on where the National Gallery left off, showing how the Slovene Impressionists developed more experimental styles in the early years of the twentieth century. The rest of the collection is pretty uninspiring save for inter-war works by the Kralj brothers and paintings from the 1980s by Irwin – a group of artists whose mixing of Slovene folkloric imagery with totalitarian symbols earned them considerable notoriety.

Beyond the art galleries, Cankarjeva leads you past an unobtrusive twentieth-century Serbian Orthodox church to **Tivoli Park**, an expanse of lawns and tree-lined walkways backed by dense woodland. Most of Ljubljana's recreational and sporting facilities can be found in the sports centre at the northern end of the park. A villa above the centre contains the most enjoyable of Ljubljana's museums, the **Museum of Modern History** (Tues–Sun 10am–6pm; 400SIT, free first Sun of the month) with dioramas, imaginative lighting, video screens and period music combining to produce an evocative journey through twentieth-century Slovene history.

To the south and west of the park, a succession of pathways winds up into the **Rožnik Hills** – a beautiful, tranquil region of woodland no more than ten minutes from the city centre. There are a number of tracks leading to the not-too-distant summit of Cankarjev Vrh, where you'll find the **Rožnik Inn**, site of a memorial room dedicated to the turn-of-the-twentieth-century novelist **Ivan Cankar** (summer only 10am–2pm) who died here after one of his customary bouts of heavy drinking. The area comes to life on the night of April 30/May 1, when bonfires are lit near the summit and thousands of locals assemble for a mass outdoor party.

Eating

As befits its sophisticated, cosmopolitan image, Ljubljana is able to boast a tight concentration of **restaurants**, most of which offer excellent value for money. There is a handful of good fish restaurants and many offering traditional Slovene variations, and because of Ljubljana's proximity to Italy, Austria, Hungary and the Adriatic coast, the range is impressive.

Snacks and lunches

For **snacks**, the numerous *burek* kiosks near the station, along with the stands you'll come across throughout town which sell hot dogs and the local *gorenjska* sausages, are the quickest and cheapest choice for on-your-feet eating. You should also try the numerous stalls selling **fish** snacks in the riverside arcade beside the market. The quality of Ljubljana's **delicatessens** makes them a good option for putting together picnics from locally produced cheeses, sausages and hams, washed down with a bottle of decent Slovene wine. Telephone numbers are given for those places where it's wise to book in advance.

Restaurants

As, Čopova (entry Knafljev prehod) (☎01/425-8822). Superb fish restaurant between Slovenska and the Triple Bridge. Not cheap, but tell them your budget and they will cook a meal to fit it. Also has a café/bar upstairs. Daily 9am–2am.

Casa del Papa, Celovška 54a (☎01/434-3158). International food in rooms decorated on an Ernest Hemingway theme (there's a Key West room, a Cuba room and so on). Daily 11am–2am.

Čerin, Trubarjeva 52. Chic pizzeria with salad bar and good-value lunchtime menus. Daily 10am–11pm.

Figovec, Gosposvetska 1. Charmingly old-fashioned downtown restaurant specializing in pony steaks (sic), horsemeat goulash, and a wide range of traditional Slovene standards as well. Mon–Fri 8am–11pm, Sat & Sun 11am–5pm.

Lovec, Trg mladinskih delovnih brigad 1. One of the more characterful places in which to eat medium-priced Slovene standards, five minutes' west of Trg francoske revolucije. Good range of pizzas too. Mon–Sat 8am–midnight, Sun 10am–10pm.

Meson don Felipe, Streliška 22. Lively tapas bar and restaurant ten minutes east of the cathedral. Daily noon–midnight.

Mexico 1867, Medvedova 18. Brilliantly designed and highly authentic Mexican restaurant with inventive menu (including vegetarian options) and comprehensive drinks list (including cocktails). Mon–Sat 11am–midnight.

Pizza Napoli, Prečna 1. Enormous, reasonably authentic and very cheap pizzas in a buzzing meeting place.

Pizzeria Foculus, Gregorčičeva 3. Extensive range of affordable pizzas in lively surroundings, including several vegetarian options and a generous salad buffet. Daily 10am–midnight.

Prima Donna, Čopova (entry Knafljev prehod) (☎01/421-9310). Lavishly decorated restaurant specializing in mid-priced Mediterranean food. Mon–Sat noon–midnight. American-themed bar upstairs open until 3am.

Rio, Slovenska 28. Massive beer garden in a cobbled courtyard serving inexpensive grills and stews. Daily 10am–11.30pm.

Šestica, Slovenska 40. Traditional place on the main street with elegant vine-trellised interior. Slovene, meat-heavy menu. Closed Sun.

Vinoteka, Dunajska 18. Good for Slovene specialities and fresh fish. Located beneath a circular pavilion in the Ljubljana fair grounds. Excellent wine list. Mon–Fri 10am–midnight, Sat 4pm–midnight.

Drinking and nightlife

On summer evenings the **cafés and bars** of Ljubljana's Old Town spill out onto the streets with the hectic atmosphere of a mass open-air bar. A wander up and down the banks of the River Ljubljanica and along Stari trg and Mestni trg will yield an interesting locale every fifty yards or so.

Some bars and clubs double up as venues for home-grown rock bands and occasional foreign groups. Otherwise, the bigger acts play in the main hall of the Tivoli sports centre in Tivoli Park. Other gig **venues** are KUD France Preseren at Karunova 14, the Cankarjev Dom Congress Centre on Trg republike, or the open-air stage at Križanke, Trg francoske revolucije. The free English-language *Ljubljana Life* magazine (*www.ljubljanalife.com*), available from the tourist office, has excellent – indeed essential – bar and club listings.

Cafés and bars

Čajna Hiša, Stari trg 3. Bijou café serving the best teas in town, excellent sandwiches and cakes and decent breakfasts. Mon–Sat 9am–11pm

Gajo Jazz Club, Beethovnova 8. Refined late-night café with regular live jazz. See *www.jazzclubgajo.com* for programme.

Café Gaudi, Nazorjeva 10. Delightful interior and seductive range of coffees makes this a terrific place for a coffee stop. Mon–Sat 8am–10pm, Sun 2–10pm.

Hound Dog, *M Hotel*, Derčeva. Animated basement bar with regular live (rock) music. A fifteen-minute walk northeast of the centre.

Kratochwill, Kolodvorska 14. Bar with a Czech beer-hall atmosphere which brews its own ale. Try the *mešano pivo* (a mixture of stout and lager).

Maček, corner of Krojačka and Cankarjevo nabrežje. Stylish café with large outdoor terrace. The place to be seen on Ljubljana's riverfront, and consequently crammed. Happy hour between 4–7pm. Daily 9am–3am.

Nostalgia, Stari trg 9. Café with 1950s decor and a wide range of tasty sandwiches.

Orto Bar, Grablovičeva 1. Stylish media haunt east of the train station with decor reminiscent of the interior of a submarine. Frequent live-rock evenings.

Patrick's, Prečna 6. Cosy basement pub with Irish decor and well-kept beers.

Petite Café, Trg francoske revolucije 4. Atmospheric place, ideal for a coffee and croissant as well as for an evening drinking session. Mon–Sat 8am–11pm, Sun noon–9pm.

Propaganda, Grablovičeva 1. Techno and jungle-oriented bar with dance floor. East of the train station, near the *Orto*.

Pr'skelet, Ključavničarska 5. Devilishly original bar – it's full of skeletons – in the old town. Daily 9am–1am.

Ragamuffin, Krojaška 4. In an alleyway just behind *Maček* (see above). Small, reggae-oriented café/bar, good for a daytime chill-out or more boisterous evening drink. Mon–Thu 9am–midnight, Fri & Sat 11am–1pm, Sun 11am–11pm.

Samsara, Atmospheric ice-cream garden by the Triple Bridge, with accompanying live (usually jazz) music.

Sax Pub, Eipprova cesta 7. Gaudily decorated youth hangout of many years' standing, occupying a leafy riverside site.

True-bar, Trubarjeva 23. Trendy, youthful hangout with loud hip-hop and techno music. Daily 9am–1am.

Clubs and discos

Central, Dalmatinova 15. Mainstream techno and retro club in the centre of town. Tues–Sat.

Papillon, Nazorjeva 4. Commercial disco with mainstream techno at weekends and themed retro nights on weekdays. Tues–Sat.

K4, Kersnikova 4. Mecca of Ljubljana's alternative scene, offering different styles of music on different nights – including at least one gay night (currently Sunday). Good place to check out live bands and alternative happenings.

Metelkova, Metelkova cesta. Old barracks just east of the train station which now functions as an alternative cultural centre. Club nights, gigs and happenings.

Classical music, opera and ballet

For a relatively small city, Ljubljana offers a surprisingly rich diet of classical culture. The Cankarjev Dom, Prešernova 10 (ticket office Mon–Fri 10am–2pm & 4.30–8pm, Sat 10am–1pm and one hour before each performance; ☎01/241-7299), is the scene of major orchestral and theatrical events, as well as occasional folk and jazz concerts. Ljubljana's energetic **symphony orchestra**, the Slovenska Filharmonija, performs at Kongresni trg 9 (☎01/241-0800), while the republic's **opera and ballet** companies are housed in the Slovene National Theatre (Slovensko Narodno Gledališče), a sumptuous nineteenth-century Neoclassical building at Zupančičeva 1 (ticket office Mon–Fri 2–5pm, Sat 6–7pm and one hour before each performance; ☎01/425-4840, *www.sngdrama-lj.si*). Two big music festivals take place throughout July and August: the Ljubljana **Summer Festival** features orchestral concerts by international artists at Križanke (festival box office 11am–1pm & 6–7pm and one hour before each performance; ☎061/252-6544), while **Summer in Old Ljubljana** concentrates on chamber music in a number of venues scattered throughout the Old Town. **Druga Godba** (again centred on Križanke) is a **world music** festival which attracts big international names in the second week of June. The monthly *Where To? Events* pamphlet, published in English and available free from the TIC, has complete listings of concerts and events.

Listings

Airline offices Adria, Gosposvetska 6 (☎01/231-3312, *www.adria.si*); Lufthansa, Gosposvetska 6 (☎01/434-7246, *www.lufthansa.com*); Swissair, World Trade Centre, Dunajska 156 (☎01/569-1010).

Airport information ☎04/202-2700.

American Express Trubarjeva 50 (Mon–Fri 8am–8pm; ☎01/431-9020).

Books Both MK, Slovenska 29 and DZS, Slovenska 55 have a wide selection of English-language paperbacks. Kod in Kam, Trg francoske revolucije, has a range of maps.

Car rental Avis, Aufarjeva 2 (☎01/430-8010, *www.avis-alpe.si*); Budget, *Holiday Inn Hotel*, Miklošičeva 3 (☎01/421-7340, *www.budget-slovenia.com*); Kompas Hertz, Miklošičeva 11 (☎01/361-3112, *www.hertz.si*).

Embassies and consulates Australia, Trg republike 3 (☎01/425-4252); Britain, Trg republike 3 (☎01/200-3910); Canada, Miklošičeva 19 (☎01/430-3570); USA, Prešernova 31 (☎01/200-5500).

Exchange The post office at Trg osvobodilne fronte has a desk which is open 24hrs.

Hospital Bohoričeva 4 (☎01/232-3060).

Internet access Čerin, Trubarjeva 52 (Mon–Fri 9am–7pm; free); Library, Vilharjev podhod (☎01/291-2326).

Laundry Chemo-express, Wolfova 12 (service washes only; Mon–Fri 7am–6pm; ☎01/251-4404).

Left Luggage Train station (24hr).

Library British Council, Cankarjevo nabrežje 27 (Mon–Thurs 9am–8pm, Fri 9am–3pm; ☎01/200-0130, *www.britishcouncil.si*). English-language newspapers and books and Internet access.

Pharmacies Lekarna Miklošič, Miklošičeva 24 (☎01/231 4558), has a 24hr service.

Police For accidents and emergencies go to Trdinova 10 (☎01/432-0341).

Post office Main office at Slovenska 32 (Mon–Fri 7am–8pm, Sat 7am–1pm); 24-hour service for all facilities at Trg osvobodilne fronte, next to the train station.

Taxis To book, call ☎9700-9.

Telephones At the main post office.

Travel agents Atlas, Mestni trg 8 (☎01/252-2711); Globtour, Slovenska 52 (☎01/231-1164); Kompas, Miklošičeva 11 (☎01/432-1053).

THE REST OF THE COUNTRY

Emphatically not to be missed while you're in Ljubljana is a visit to the **Postojna Caves** – easily managed either as a day-trip from the capital or en route south to Slovene Istria, to Croatia or to Italy. A lower-key alternative to the cave stopoff is **Lipica**, where the celebrated white Lipizzaner horses are bred, or **Predjamski Grad**, near Postojna, an atmospherically sombre castle high above a cave entrance in the midst of a dramatic landscape.

Close to the borders with Italy and Croatia, the towns of **Slovene Istria** have long been popular tourist resorts, although through all the crowds, concrete and tourist settlements, the region has managed to retain some charm and identity. The basis of this is Italian, coming from the 400 years of Venetian rule that preceded the region's incorporation into the Austro-Hungarian Empire, and eventually into the Yugoslav federation. There's still a fair-sized Italian community here although many of the Italian speakers left Istria after World War II, afraid of what might happen once the communists took control. Even so, Slovene Istria remains one of the most Italianate parts of the entire region: there's a steady flow of traffic to and fro across the border, Italian is fairly widely spoken, and road signs are in Italian as well as Slovene. Along the coast, diminutive towns like **Piran**, with their cobbled piazzas, shuttered houses and back alleys laden with laundry, are almost overwhelmingly pretty. **Koper**, too, is worth a look, more port than resort and a good base for exploring northern Istria.

To the northwest of Ljubljana, and within easy reach of the capital, are the **mountain lakes** of **Bled** and **Bohinj**, Slovenia's number-one tourist attraction. The **Soča valley**, on the western side of the Slovene alps, is much less touristed, although small towns like **Kobarid** and **Bovec** are excellent bases from which to indulge in rafting and walking. East of Ljubljana on the main route to Hungary, **Ptuj** is Slovenia's oldest town and one of its most attractive.

Postojna

POSTOJNA is on the main rail route south 65km from Ljubljana, but as the walk to the caves from Postojna train station is further than from the bus stop, most people go by one of the regular buses. Once in the town, signs direct you to the **caves** and their suitably cavernous entrance (daily: May–Sept 9am–6pm tours hourly; Oct–April 10am–4pm tours every 2 hours; last tour leaves 1hr before closing; 2200SIT, *www.postojna-cave.com*); inside a railway whizzes you helter-skelter through 2km of preliminary systems before the guided tour starts. It's little use trying to describe the vast and fantastic jungles of rock formations; the point is to see them for yourself – breathtaking stuff. Postojna's caves are about four million years old and provide a chilly home for *Proteus anguineus*, a weird creature that looks like a cross between a bloated sperm and a prawn. Actually it's a sort of salamander, one of whose odd capabilities is to give birth to live young in temperatures above 16°F (-10°C) and to lay eggs if it's colder. They live their seventy-year lives down here in total darkness and hence are blind – and no doubt very confused at being put on display to inquisitive tourists.

Accommodation in private rooms (②–③) is arranged by Kompas in the town centre at Titov trg 2a (Mon–Fri 8am–7pm, Sat 9am–1pm; ☎05/726-4281, *info@kompas-postojna.si*). They can also supply information on the town and the caves. There's a **campsite**, the *Pivka Jama* (☎05/726-5382), 4km beyond the cave entrance and not served by public transport, which also has four-person apartments and bungalows for about £12/$18 per person. There are only two **hotels** in town, both of which are very drab; the *Kras*, in the town centre at Tržaška 1 (☎05/726-4071; ④); and *Jama* (☎05/728-2400; ④), by the caves. *Pizzeria Minutka*, at Ljubljankska 14, is a pleasant alternative to the cluster of tourist eateries by the caves.

Predjamski Grad

The other site you're steered to near Postojna is **PREDJAMSKI GRAD** (May–Sept 9am–6pm; Oct–April 10am–4pm; 900SIT), 7km from Postojna and well signposted from the caves. It's walkable if you're in the mood or you can book a taxi through Kompas; otherwise it's only accessible with your own transport or on an organized trip. Pushed up high against a cave entrance in the midst of karst landscape, the sixteenth-century castle is damp and melancholy, unimproved by a museum holding a lacklustre collection of odds and ends from this and an earlier castle that stood nearby. The previous castle was the home of one **Erazem**, a colourful brigand knight of the fifteenth century who spent his days waylaying the merchant caravans that passed through the region. Sheriff of Nottingham to his Robin Hood was the governor of Trieste, who laid exasperated siege to the castle for over a year. Secure in his defensive position and supplied by a secret passage to the outside world, Erazem taunted the governor by tossing fresh cherries and the occasional roast ox over the wall to show he was far from beaten. Such hubris couldn't go unnoticed, and Erazem finally met with one of the more ignominious deaths on record: he was blown to bits by a cannonball while sitting on the castle loo. There are **guided tours** of the cave below the castle (daily May–Sept 11am, 1pm, 3pm & 5pm; 700SIT, 1200SIT joint ticket with castle).

Lipica

After Postojna, Slovenia's most emblematic tourist draw is probably **LIPICA**. 7km west of the drab railway-junction town of Divača near the Italian border, Lipica gave its name to the **Lipizzaner** horses that are associated with the Spanish Riding School of Vienna. There are three hundred horses here, the results of fastidious breeding that can be dated back to 1580, when the Austrian Archduke Charles established the farm in order to add Spanish and Arab blood to the Lipizzaner strain that was first used by the Romans for chariot races. Tours are given round the **stud farm** (April–Oct 9/10am–5/6pm; Nov–Mar 11am–3pm; 1100SIT; *www.k-lipica.si*), and the horses give the elegant displays for which they're famous (May–Sept Tues, Fri & Sun at 3pm; Oct & April Fri & Sun at 3pm; 1500SIT). If you've any horse-riding ability, it's also possible to go on rides around the region – a wonderfully relaxing way to explore the area. Public **transport** is meagre: a few buses run from Divača weekday mornings, but you have little time to look around before catching the last bus back. Alternatives include spending a night here in one of the (expensive) hotels, or joining a weekend excursion run by the big high-street travel agents in Ljubljana or Portorož. One day tours combining Postojna and Lipica currently cost around £35/$50 per person. There are two good, but pricey **hotels** in the stable complex, the *Klub* and *Maestoso* (both ☎05/739-1580; ⑨).

Koper and around

Arriving on Slovenia's coast, **KOPER**, or Capodistria in Italian, is the first town you reach, a prosperous place sited on what was originally a small island. From the main road it's an unalluring spectacle, dominated by tower blocks, cranes and industrial estates. But within this surge of development, Koper is a rickety old Venetian town, crowded with a dense lattice of narrow streets.

All of Koper's paved alleys lead to **Titov trg**, the fulcrum of the old city, flanked by a Venetian **Loggia**, dating from 1463 and now a café. At the opposite end is the **Praetor's Palace**, Koper's most enduring symbol, with its battlements, balconies, busts and coats of arms like the stage backdrop for a Renaissance drama. Built originally in the thirteenth century, and added to and adapted 200 years later (the battlements were actually added in 1664 and only ever served a decorative purpose), this was the seat of the mayor and Venetian governor, evidenced by the facade's Lion of St Mark. Also on the square, Koper's **Cathedral** (daily 7am–noon & 3–7pm) is a mixture of architectural styles, its facade blending a Venetian Gothic lower storey with an upper level completed a hundred years later in Renaissance fashion. Dedicated to St Nazarius, patron saint of the town, the interior is large and imposing, and holds a *Madonna and the Saints* by Vittore Carpaccio, hung to the right of the main altar as you face it. Heading downhill from the square along Kidričeva brings you to the **Civic Museum** (Tues–Sat 9am–1pm; July & Aug also 6–8pm; 350SIT) which holds more paintings, including works by Correggio, together with archeological fragments, ancient maps and the like.

Practicalities

Koper's **bus** and **train stations** are located next door to each other, twenty minutes' walk from the town centre, or a short ride on one of the frequent Koper–Piran buses. These drop you just outside the city centre, inside which only residents are allowed to drive. Koper's **tourist office**, on the seafront at Ukmarjev trg 7 (June–Sept daily 9am–8pm; rest of year

Mon–Fri 9am–5pm, Sat 8am–1pm; ☎05/663-2010), has plentiful **private rooms** (②), as does nearby Kompas, Pristanička 17 (daily 8am–8pm; ☎05/627-1581, *info@kompas-koper.si*). The best of the more inexpensive **hotels** is the newly renovated *Žusterna*, on the seafront 2km west of town at Istrska 67 (☎05/628-4385; ④), served by Koper–Piran buses or a thirty-minute walk along the seafront path from the centre. Conveniently located midway between the stations and town is the bright, modern *Hotel Vodišek*, Kolodvorska 2 (☎05/639-2468, *www.hotel-vodisek.com*; ⑤). There's a **hostel** (☎05/627-3250; ②) just east of the old town at Cankarjeva 5, although it's only likely to have room in July and August. Several **snack bars and restaurants** are clustered around the harbour area: *Skipper*, near the marina at Kopališko Nabrežje 3, has a wide range of seafood; while the next-door *Školjka* has good pizzas. In the centre of town, *Cantina Istriana Slavček*, Županičeva 39, has cheap grills and seafood. For **drinking**, the liveliest place is *Carpaccio Pub*, on the square of the same name; alternatively try one of the numerous bars that line Kidričeva ulica, or on Titov trg itself; a drink on the *Loggia Caffe's* terrace will allow you to do a spot of people-watching. There are also regular gigs at MKC, a youth cultural centre at Gregorčičeva 4. *Ambasada Gavioli*, 5km west of town in Izola, is the coast's best **club**, attracting DJs from all over Europe.

Portorož

Heading west from Koper the road veers right soon after Izola onto a long, tapering peninsula that projects like a lizard's tail north into the Adriatic. **PORTOROŽ** ("Port of Roses") appears almost without warning, a sprawling resort that by the end of the nineteenth century was already known for its mild climate and the health-inducing properties of its salty mud baths. Maladied middle-aged Austrians flocked here by the thousand to be smothered with murky balm dredged up from the nearby salt pans. Up went the *Palace Hotel*, in came the opportunists – and so began Portorož, a town entirely devoted to the satisfaction of its visitors. After World War II, the transition from health to package resort wasn't hard to make, and it's now one of the most developed stretches of coast in all Istria, a vibrant strip of hotels and (largely concrete) beaches. Combining Portorož's modernity with the charm of Piran (a short bus ride or forty-minute walk away; see below) is the key to enjoying this brash, consumption-oriented place. The very helpful **tourist office** is on the main coastal strip, Obala Maršala Tita, just down from the bus terminal (July & Aug 9am–1.30pm & 3–9.30pm; rest of year 10am–5pm; ☎05/674-0231, *www.portoroz.si*). **Private rooms** (②) are available from either Maona (☎05/674-0363, *www.maona.si*) or Maestral (☎05/677-9280, *www.maestral.si*), both on Obala Maršala Tita. This is also the place to choose from any number of places to eat.

Piran

PIRAN, at the very tip of the peninsula 4km from Portorož's bus station, couldn't be more different. There are tourists here too, lots of them, thronging the main square, packing the ranks of restaurants, milling around the souvenir-stacked harbour. But few actually stay (most are in fact from Portorož's hotel complexes), and the town preserves tangible remnants of atmosphere in its sloping web of arched alleys and little Italianate squares.

The centre of town, a couple of hundred metres around the harbour from where the buses stop, is **Tartinijev trg**, named after the eighteenth-century Italian violinist and composer Giuseppe Tartini, who was born in a house on the square and is remembered by a bronze statue in the centre. With its striking oval-shaped interior, it's one of the loveliest squares on this coast, fringed by a mix of Venetian palaces and a portentous Austrian town hall. Just off the square there's a small **Aquarium** (daily 10am–noon & 2–7pm; 350SIT), with a rather sad set of tanks full of local marine life. Opposite, across the bay of the harbour, the **Maritime Museum** (July & Aug Tues–Sun 9am–noon & 6–9pm; rest of year Tues–Sun 9am–noon & 3–6pm; 300SIT) pays further homage to Tartini with a copy of his violin and assorted genuine memorabilia, along with an interesting display on Piran's salt industry and a scatter of paintings that includes native ex-votive works by Piran sailors and a ropey portrait of the local authorities by Tintoretto. Follow Ulica IX Korpusa uphill from the square to the barnlike Baroque **Church of Sv Jurij**, which crowns a commanding spot on the far side of Piran's peninsula. The campanile is visible from just about everywhere in the town and may seem familiar – it's a replica of the one in St Mark's Square in Venice. Five minutes' walk further up, the town's formidable sixteenth-century **walls** stagger across the hill, the remaining towers providing excellent views of the town below.

Practicalities

The **tourist office** on Tartinijev trg (July & Aug daily 9am–1.30pm & 3–9.30pm; rest of year Mon–Fri 9am–4pm, Sat 10am–2pm; ☎05/673-0220) is helpful and sells maps. **Rooms** can be booked through Maona, between the bus station and the square at Cankarjevo nabrežje 7 (Mon–Sat 9am–7pm, Sun 9am–1pm; ☎05/673-4520). The cheapest place to stay is the **hostel** *Val*, in the old town at Gregorčičeva 38 (☎05/673-2555; ③); its excellent facilities are complemented by a delightful restaurant; the stylish *Tartini*, Tartinijev trg 15 (☎05/671-1000; ⑤) is the priciest option but it boasts its own swimming pool. For **eating**, the main square offers a couple of good possibilities; *Batana*, on Kidričevo Nabrežje, is a stylish pizzeria with pleasant terrace, and *Mario*, up a flight of steps from Tartinijev trg, has good-value fish and meat dishes in uncomplicated surroundings. Numerous more expensive seafood restaurants line Piran's seafront, of which *Pavel* and *Tri Vdove* are probably the best. *Kavana Galerija Tartini*, on Tartinijev trg, is the most relaxing place for a daytime or evening **drink**. Liveliest of the **bars** is *Da Noi*, a cellar-like space tucked between restaurants on the seafront.

Bled and Bohinj

Fifty kilometres northwest of Ljubljana, towards Austria and at the eastern end of the Julian Alps, are the **mountain lakes** of **Bled** and **Bohinj**, Slovenia's number one tourist attraction. While Bled, surrounded by Olympian mountains and oozing charm, lives up to expectations it's also chock-full with tourists, which can't help but temper its delights. Bohinj, in contrast, is less visited, more beautiful and much cheaper – and, should you want to explore the imposing and exhilarating mountains around Mt Triglav, at 2864m Slovenia's highest peak, this is the place to go. If you're interested in serious **hiking**, good maps are essential: your best bets are the 1:50,000 *Triglav National Park*, the 1:25,000 *Mount Triglav*, and the 1:25,000 *Bled and environs* – all published by the Slovene alpine association. Pick them up in Ljubljana bookshops or from the tourist offices in Bled and Ribčev Laz.

Buses are the easiest way to reach both Bled and Bohinj (hourly from Ljubljana; 1hr 15min to Bled, 2hr to Bohinj). **Rail** access to the region is either via the main northbound line from Ljubljana, which calls at Bled-Lesce 3km southeast of Bled itself (and linked to Bled by a regular bus), or a branch line which leaves the main Ljubljana–Villach route at Jesenice and crosses the mountains towards Italy and the coast, calling at Bled-Jezero and Bohinjska Bistrica on the way. The trip from Jesenice, chugging steadily through the mountains and karst, is as impressive as you'd imagine. Train buffs should note that a **steam train**, the museum train or *muzejni vlak*, is laid on in summer months, at considerable additional expense.

Bled

There's no denying that the lake resort of **BLED** has all the right ingredients to make up a memorable visit – a placid mirror lake with a romantic island, a fairy-tale castle high on a bluff, leafy lakeside lanes and a backdrop of snow-tipped mountains. As such it's worth a day of anyone's time, and one advantage of the tourist trade is that everything is efficiently packaged. In summer the lake, fed by warm-water springs that take the water temperature up to

76° F, forms the setting for a whole host of water sports – major rowing contests are held here throughout summer – and in winter the surface becomes a giant skating rink.

Paths run uphill from Bled's bus station to **Bled Castle** (daily: April–Oct 8am–7pm; Nov–Mar 9am–4pm; 600SIT) – now a pricey restaurant with a fine view and a very ordinary museum, its only surprise a small sixteenth-century chapel.

During the day a constant relay of stretched gondolas leaves from below the *Park Hotel*, the bathing resort below the castle and Mlino, towards the western end of the lake, ferrying tourists back and forth to Bled's picturesque **island** (1700SIT return). With an early start (and by renting your own rowing boat or canoe from the same places as the gondolas) you can beat them to it. Crowning the island, the Baroque-decorated **Church of Sv Marika Božja** is the last in a line of churches on a spot that's long held religious significance: under the present building are remains of early graves and, below the north chapel, a pre-Roman temple. In summer months it's feasible to swim from the western end of the lake to the island, but remember to bring some light clothes in a watertight bag if you want to get into the church. During winter, under the snug muffle of alpine snow, you can walk or skate across.

The main attraction in the outlying hills is the **Vintgar Gorge** (mid-May to September daily 8am–7pm; SIT400), 5km north of town, an impressive defile accessed by a wooden walk-way. To get there, head northwest out of Bled on the Vintgar road (just up from the bus station), turning right on the outskirts of town towards the villages of Gmajna and Zasip. Head uphill through Zasip to the hilltop chapel of Sv Katarina (where you can savour an excellent view back towards the lake), before picking up a path through the forest to the gorge entrance. If that's too taxing, then a daily bus runs from *Hotel Jelovica* to the gorge between mid-June and September.

The helpful **tourist office**, down behind the *Park Hotel* at Cesta svobode 15 (July & Aug daily 8am–10pm, June & Sept Mon–Sat 8am–8pm; rest of year Mon–Sat 9am–5pm, Sun 9am–2pm; ☎04/574-1122, *www.bled.si*) hands out maps and brochures although **private rooms** are available through Kompas, in the shopping centre at Ljubljanska 4 (Mon–Sat 8am–7pm, Sun 8am–noon & 4–7pm; ☎04/574-1515, *www.kompas-bled.si*), or Globtour further up at no. 7 (Mon–Fri 8am–7pm, Sat & Sun 8am–noon & 4–7pm; ☎04/574-1821).

There's an outstanding **HI hostel** (☎04/574-5250, *mlino@siol.net*; ③) just above the bus station at Grajska 17, and some reasonable **pensions** – the smallish *Pletna* at Cesta svobode 37 (☎04/574-3702; ③); the *Mlino*, further along at no. 45 (☎04/574-1404; ③); and the *Alp*, 2km west of town along the lakeside road at Cankarjeva 20a (☎04/534-1616; ④). The nearest **campsite**, *Zaka* (☎04/575-2000) is beautifully placed, sheltered at the western end of the lake amid the pines and with its own stretch of beach; catch a bus towards Bohinj and ask to be set down near the access road.

One downside of the all-embracing tourist industry around here is that there are few cheap places **to eat** – the best places to look are in the hillside area between Bled's bus station and castle. *Gostilna Pri Planincu*, Grajska 8, offers solid Slovene home cooking, while *Pizzeria Portobello* on Rikljeva is probably the best of the Italian places. For a treat, the high-ly regarded *Okarina*, Rikljeva 9, offers traditional Slovene meals for around 5000–6000SIT per person.

Lake Bohinj

It's 30km from Bled to Lake Bohinj and buses run hourly through the **Sava Bohinjka Valley** – dense, verdant and often laden with mist and low cloud. In appearance and character **Lake Bohinj** is utterly different from Bled: the lake crooks a narrow finger under the wild mountains, woods slope gently down to the water, and a lazy stillness hangs over all – in comparison to Bled it feels almost uninhabited.

BOHINJSKA BISTRICA, 4km before Lake Bohinj on the Bled–Bohinj bus route, has little except a few rooms. **RIBČEV LAZ** (often referred to as Jezero on bus timetables, after the name of a local hotel), at the eastern end of the lake, is where most facilities are based, including the **tourist office** (July & Aug Mon–Sat 7am–8pm, Sun 8am–6pm; rest of year

Mon–Sat 8am–6pm, Sun 9am–3pm; ☎04/574-6010, *www.bohinj.si*), which offers rooms (②) and apartments around Ribčev Laz and in the idyllic village of **STARA FUŽINA** 1km north. The main attraction in Ribčev Laz is the **Church of Sv Janez** (June–Sept daily 9am–noon & 4–7pm), a solid-looking structure whose nave and frescoes date back to the fourteenth century. Beyond the church, a road leads to Stara Fužina, a traditional Slovene alpine village filled with the timber hay-drying barns (*kozolci*) which are particular to the region. There's a **museum of highland pasture life** (Planšarski muzej; Tues–Sun: summer 11am–7pm; winter 10am–noon & 4–6pm; 300SIT) housed in a former dairy in the centre of the village. The key to the museum is kept in the *Okrepčevalnica Planešar* immediately opposite, a snack bar selling local cheeses (including *mohant*, a sharp cream cheese made by only a few local households). **Walking trails** lead north from both sides of the lake, or northwards onto the eastern shoulders of the Triglav range. One route leads north from Stara Fužina into the Voje valley, passing through the dramatic **Mostrica Canyon**, a popular local beauty spot.

Five kilometres from Ribčev Laz at the western end of the lake is the hamlet of **UKANC**, although the area is more popularly referred to as Zlatorog, after the local hotel. There are several **private rooms** (②) and apartments here, which you can book through the tourist office in Ribčev Laz. The **campsite** (☎04/572-3483), just east of the bus stop, occupies an idyllic lakeside position.

An easy walk back east takes you to the **cable car** (*žičnica*; daily 7.30am–6pm, every 30min; closed Nov; 1500SIT return) at the foot of **Mt Vogel** (1540m). If the Alps look dramatic from the lakeside, from Vogel's summit they're breathtaking. As the cable car briskly climbs the 1000-metre drop, the panorama is gradually revealed, with Mount Triglav forming the crest of a line of pale red mountains, more like a clenched claw than the three-headed god after which it's named.

An hour's walk north from Zlatorog are the photogenic **Savica Waterfalls** (Slap Savice; mid–April to Oct 9am–5pm; 300SIT). The falls themselves mark the start of one of the most popular hiking routes up Mount Triglav, which zigzags up the mountain wall to the north before bearing northwest into the **Valley of the Seven Lakes** – an area strewn with eerie boulders and hardy firs – before continuing to the summit of Triglav itself. Although steep in parts, it's not a hike of great technical difficulty, although good maps and careful planning are required. The Seven Lakes can be treated as a day-long hiking expedition from Bohinj, but the assault on Triglav itself requires at least one night in a mountain hut. The tourist office in Ribčev Laz will supply details and book you a place, although huts on Triglav are only open from late June to late September – the upper stretches of the mountain shouldn't be tackled outside these times.

Finally, if you're around Bohinj in September, the return of the cattle from the higher alpine pastures is celebrated in the mass booze-up called the **Kravji Bal** or "Cow Dance" (held on the second or third weekend of the month in Ukanc).

The Soča valley

On the other, less-touristed side of the mountains from Bohinj, the river Soča cuts through the western spur of the Julian alps, running parallel with Slovenia's border with Italy. During World War I, the Soča (Isonzo in Italian) marked the front line between the Italian and Austro-Hungarian armies, and three years of bitter warfare on the surrounding peaks rivalled the Western Front in terms of futile offensives and wasted lives. Memorial chapels and abandoned fortifications abound, located incongruously amidst awesome alpine scenery. However there's more to the Soča valley than military history: it's also a major centre for activity-based tourism, with the foaming river itself providing the ideal venue for **rafting** and **kayaking** throughout the spring and summer. Main tourist centres are **Kobarid** and **Bovec**, both small towns with a range of **walking** possibilities right on the doorstep. The 1:50,000 *Posočje* **map** covers trails in the region: pick it up in Ljubljana if you can, as not all local shops have it.

Although both places are served by four daily buses from Ljubljana, transport connections with the rest of Slovenia are patchy. Approaching the Soča valley from the Bled-Bohinj area involves catching one of six daily trains from Bled-Jezero or Bohinjska Bistrica to **Most na Soči**, where 5 buses daily run onwards up the valley. Getting here from the coast entails catching buses working the Koper-Sežana-Nova Gorica-Tolmin-Kobarid route (minimum journey time of 4hr depending on connections), although you might have to change at each stage of the journey.

Kobarid

It was at the little alpine town of **KOBARID** (Caporetto in Italian) that German and Austrian troops finally broke through Italian lines in 1917, almost knocking Italy out of the war in the process. Ernest Hemingway, then a volunteer ambulance driver on the Italian side, took part in the chaotic retreat that followed – an experience which resurfaced in his novel *A Farewell to Arms*. A processional way leads up from Kobarid's main square to a monumental, three-tiered **Italian War Memorial** (Italijanska Kostnica) officially opened by Benito Mussolini in 1938, and a fitting place from which to enjoy views of the surrounding alps and ponder Kobarid's violent past. Back in town, the **Kobarid museum** at Gregorčičeva 10 (Kobariški muzej; summer Mon–Fri 9am–6pm, Sat & Sun 9am–7pm; winter daily 10am–5pm; 500SIT), presents a thoughtful and balanced record of the war with a gripping collection of photographs. Continue past the museum, head downhill and take the Drežnica road across the river Soča to pick up trails to the **Kozjak waterfall** (Slap Kozjak; 50min), less impressive for its height than for the cavern-like space which it has carved out of the surrounding rock. Numerous paths branch off from here into the wooded hills, passing trench systems dug by the Italians during the war. The *Kobarid Historical Walk* brochure, available from the museum, maps out a few potential itineraries.

Kobarid's **tourist office** is housed in the museum (same times; ☎05/389-9200, *www.kobarid.si*), and has a limited number of **private rooms** (②) in Kobarid and surrounding villages. The chic rooms at the *Hvala* **hotel** on the main square (☎05/389-9300, *www.topli-val.si*; ⑤) are remarkably good value for the level of comfort on offer. There's also a **campsite**, the *Koren* (☎05/388-5312), about 500m out of town on the way towards the Kozjak waterfall. As for **eating**, there's nowhere cheap in town save for *Pizzeria pri Vitku*, hidden away in a residential district (take the road south out of town and follow the signs). The *Topli Val*, attached to the *Hotel Hvala* (see above), is one of the best restaurants in the country and specializes in fish (including Soča trout); and with meals costing from around £20/$30 per person it's well worth a splash-out.

Details of local firms offering **rafting** trips can be picked up from the tourist office or the reception area of the *Hotel Hvala*. One of the biggest is Alpin Action in Trnovo ob Soči, 6km north of town (☎05/388-5022). Expect to pay £20/$30 to £30/$45 per trip.

Bovec

Twenty-five kilometres up the valley from Kobarid, the village of **BOVEC** straggles between imperious mountain ridges. A useful base for the Soča Valley, it has more in the way of accommodation than Kobarid because of its status as a winter ski resort. It's also the location of most of the rafting and adventure sport companies, and is the departure point for any number of alpine walks. The quickest route up into the mountains is provided by the **gondola** (*gondolna žičnica*; daily July, Aug & Dec–May; 2200SIT return) at the southern entrance to the village, which ascends to the pasture-cloaked Mt Kanin over to the west. The **tourist office** is in the Bovec Community Centre at Trg golobarskih žrtev 8 (July & Aug daily 9am–8pm; rest of year Mon–Fri 9am–5pm, Sat & Sun 9am–2pm; ☎05/384-1919, *www.bovec.si*). Private **rooms** (②) and apartments are available from either *Gotour*, at Trg golobarskih žrtev 50 (Mon–Sat 9–5pm; ☎05/389-6366, *www.gotourbovec.com*), or *Avrigo*, at no. 47 (Mon–Sat 8am–6pm; ☎05/384-1150). The nearest **campsite** is *Polovnik*, Ledina 8

(☎05/388-6069); follow the road north out of the village and it's signed to the right after 500m. There are plenty of places to eat and drink on and around the main square, although the atmosphere in all of them ranges from the boisterous to the deathly depending on how many tourists are in town. Stari Kovač, down from the main square on Rupa 3, has a long list of inexpensive pizzas alongside the usual schnitzels. Soča Rafting, up the road from the tourist office in the Sports Centre (☎05/389-6200, *www.arctur.si/soca_rafting*), is the biggest of many companies grouped around the main square offering **rafting** trips (with prices working out much the same as in Kobarid; see above). It also organizes kayaking and canyoning and rents out mountain bikes.

Ptuj and around

One hundred and twenty kilometres northeast of Ljubljana, **PTUJ** is the oldest town in Slovenia and about the most attractive as well, rising up from the Drava Valley in a flutter of red roofs and topped by a friendly looking castle. But the best thing is its streets, with scaled-down mansions standing shoulder to shoulder on scaled-down boulevards, medieval fantasies crumbling next to Baroque extravagances. Out of the windows hang plants and the locals; watching the world go by is a major occupation here.

Ptuj is on the main rail line from Ljubljana to Budapest (the Venice–Ljubljana–Budapest express passes through here once a day in both directions), and can also be reached by bus from Slovenia's second-largest city **Maribor**, which is on the Ljubljana-Vienna line. On arriving at Maribor, turn left outside the train station and head downhill – the bus station is on the other side of the crossroads.

The Town

Ptuj's main street, Prešernova cesta, snakes along the base of the castle-topped hill. At its eastern end is the **Priory Church of St George** (open mornings only), a building of twelfth-century origin that holds a statue of its patron nonchalantly killing a rather homely dragon. Nearby, its rather unambitious **tower** started life in the sixteenth century as a bell tower, became city watchtower in the seventeenth century and was retired in the eighteenth, when it was given an onion bulb spire for decoration. Roman tombstones have been embedded in its lower reaches, but a more noticeable leftover of Roman times is the **tablet** that stands below like an oversize tooth, actually a funeral monument to a Roman mayor. It's just possible to make out its carvings of Orpheus entertaining assembled fauna.

From here Prešernova cesta leads to the **Archeological Museum** (daily: May–mid-Oct 9am–6pm; also July & Aug Sat & Sun open until 8pm; mid-Oct–Nov 9am–5pm; 600SIT) housed in what was once a Dominican monastery, a mustardy building gutted in the eighteenth century and now hung with spidery decoration, and worth a look for the carvings and statuary around its likeably dishevelled cloisters.

A path opposite the monastery winds up to the **Castle** (daily: 9am–5/6pm; also July & Aug Sat & Sun open until 8pm; 600SIT; guided tours upon request, 750SIT). There's been a castle of sorts here for as long as there's been a town, since Ptuj was the only bridging point across the Drava for miles around, holding the defences against the tribes of the north. An agglomeration of styles from the fourteenth to the eighteenth centuries, the castle was home to a succession of noble families who made it rich in the town. Most prominent were the Herbersteins, Austro–Slovene aristocrats who made their fortune in the Habsburg Empire's sixteenth- and seventeenth-century wars against the Turks. Their portraits hang on the walls of the castle's **museum**, a collection mixed in theme and quality, containing period rooms with original tapestries and wallpaper on the first floor.

At Shrovetide (late Feb/early March) Ptuj is venue to one of the oldest and most unusual customs in Slovenia. The *Kurenti* **processions** are a sort of fertility rite and celebration of the dead confused together: participants wear sinister masks of sheepskin and feathers with a coloured beak for a nose and white beads for teeth, and possibly represent ancestral spirits. So dressed, the *Kurenti* move in hopping procession from house to house, scaring off evil spirits with the din from the cowbells tied to their costumes. At the head of the procession is the Devil, wrapped in a net to symbolize his capture: behind the *Kurenti*, the *Orači* ("the ploughers") pull a small wooden plough, scattering sand around to represent the sowing of seed, and housewives smash clay pots at their feet in the hope that this will bring health and luck to their households.

Practicalities

Ptuj's **train station** is 500m northeast of the centre on Osojnikova cesta, the **bus station** 100m nearer town on the same road. From both points, walk down Osojnikova to its junction with ul. Heroja Lacka: a right turn here lands you straight in the centre. The **tourist office** in the clocktower outside the church (Mon–Fri 9am–5pm, Sat 8am–4pm, Sun 10am–3pm; ☎02/779-6011, *www.poetovio-vivat.si*) has **private rooms** in the town itself and in local farmhouses (②–③). There are two moderately priced **hotels**, the central *Mitra*, Prešernova 6 (☎02/774-2101, *www.zerak.com/hotelmira*; ④); and the *Poetovio*, near the bus station at Trstenjakova 13 (☎02/779-8201; ③). The well-regimented Terme Ptuj **campsite**, Pot v Toplice 9 (☎02/782-7821), lies among fields 2km east of town.

For **eating**, *Slonček*, Prešernova 19, is a convenient pizzeria in the centre of town, while *Kitajski Vrt*, down by the riverfront on Dravska, serves Chinese food in lively surroundings. *Ribič*, also on Dravska, is an excellent but expensive fish restaurant with a riverside terrace. If you can't stretch to that, *Amadeus*, at Prešernova 36, serves more affordable Slovene standards. *Café Bo* and *Café Orfei* on Prešernova are both good places to enjoy an evening **drink**; if you fancy a more vigorous bout of drinking head for *Kult Bar*, just off Prešernova.

travel details

Trains

Bohinjska Bistrica to: Most na Soai (6 daily; 45min).

Ljubljana to: Divača (hourly; 1hr 30min); Koper (5 daily; 2hr 30min); Maribor (hourly; 2hr 20min–3hr 20min); Postojna (hourly; 1hr); Ptuj (7 daily; 2hr 30min).

Buses

Ljubljana to: Bled (hourly; 1hr 15min); Bohinj (hourly; 2hr); Bovec (4 daily; 4hr 45min); Divača (10 daily; 1hr 30min); Kobarid (4 daily; 4hr); Koper (11 daily; 2hr); Maribor (10 daily; 3hr 45min); Piran (9 daily; 2hr 40min); Portorož (9 daily; 2hr 30 min); Postojna (hourly; 1hr); Ptuj (1 daily; 4hr).

Kobarid to: Bovec (5 daily; 40min); Ljubljana (3 daily; 4hr); Nova Gorica (3 daily; 1hr 15min).

Koper to: Bled (1 daily; 3hr 30min); Piran (every 20min; 40min); Portorož (every 20min; 30min); Trieste (Mon–Sat hourly; 1hr).

Maribor to: Ptuj (every 30min; 40min).

CHAPTER 27

SPAIN

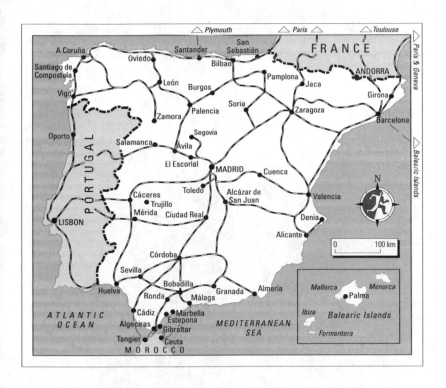

Introduction

Spain might appear from the tourist brochures to be no more than a clichéd whirl of bullfights and crowded beaches, castles and Moorish palaces. Travel for any length of time, however, and the sheer variety of this huge country, which in the north can look like Ireland and in the south like Morocco, cannot fail to impress. The separate kingdoms which made up the original Spanish nation remain very much in evidence, in a diversity of language, culture and artistic traditions.

The sheer pace of change in the wake of the forty-year dictatorship of Franco is one of the country's most stimulating aspects. Early in the 1990s, Spain enjoyed the fastest economic growth in Europe, and for the first time in centuries, there is now a feeling of political stability. Spanish culture has been allowed off the leash, and virtually every aspect of life has been radically transformed. 1992, Spaniards believe, was the year which restored them to their rightful place among Europe's leading nations: Barcelona hosted the Olympics, Seville the World Fair, and Madrid was official "Cultural Capital of Europe" – all 500 years after Columbus arrived in the Americas.

In the **cities** there is always something happening – in clubs, on the streets, in fashion, in politics – and even in the most out-of-the-way places there's nightlife, music and entertainment, not to mention the more traditional fiestas. In the **countryside** you can still find villages that have been decaying steadily since Columbus set sail: rural areas are more and more depopulated as the young head for the cities. Yet for the visitor the landscape retains its fascination; even local variations can be so extreme that a journey of just a few hours can take you through scenes of total contrast. Spain is as mountainous a nation as any in Europe and the sierras have always formed formidable barriers to centralization.

It's almost impossible to summarize Spain as a single country. **Catalunya** is vibrant and go-ahead; **Galicia** a verdant rural idyll; the **Basque** country grappling with postindustrial depression and its own identity; **Castile** and the south still, somehow, quintessentially "Spanish". There are definite highlights to Spanish travel: the three great cities of **Barcelona**, **Madrid** and **Sevilla**; the Moorish monuments of **Andalucía** and the Christian ones of **Old Castile**; beach-life in **Ibiza** or on the more deserted sands around **Cádiz** and in the north; and, for some of the best trekking in Europe, the **Pyrenees** and the Asturian **Picos de Europa**.

Information and maps

The **Spanish National Tourist Office** (*Información* or *Iniciativo de turismo*) has a branch in virtually every major town, giving away a variable array of maps, accommodation lists and leaflets – in the busiest towns they often run out. Offices are often supplemented by provincial or municipal **Turismos**, which vary in quality. Both types of office are usually open Mon–Fri 9am–1pm & 4–7pm, Sat 9am–1pm.

Among the best **road maps** are those published by Editorial Almax. Good alternatives are the 1:800,000 map produced by RV (Reise- und Verkehrsverlag, Stuttgart) and packaged in Spain by Plaza & Janes, and the less detailed offerings from Michelin, Firestone or Rand McNally. Serious **trekkers** should look for topographical maps issued by the IGN (Instituto Geográfico Nacional) and the SGE (Servicio Geográfico del Ejército), although in the northern mountain areas, Editorial Alpina is more practical.

Money and banks

Spain is one of twelve European Union countries which have changed over to a single currency, the **euro** (€). Euro notes and coins are scheduled to be issued from the beginning of 2002, with Spanish pesetas (ptas) remaining in circulation during a transition period, at a fixed rate of 1666.386 ptas to 1 euro, until they are scrapped entirely at the end of February 2002. After this date you will still be able to exchange your pesetas for euros in banks for at least a year. Euro notes are issued in **denominations** of 5, 10, 20, 50, 100, 200 and 500 euros, and coins in denominations of 1, 2, 5, 10, 20 and 50 cents and 1 and 2 euros.

SPAIN ON THE NET

www.gospain.org – has almost every Spain-related link; especially good for fiesta listings.

www.icom.org/vlmp/spain.html – a comprehensive list of all Spain's museums and art galleries.

www.paginas-amarillas.es – Spain's Yellow Pages online, and very useful it is too.

www.spainalive.com – loads of information on the country, including an excellent what's on section.

Banks and *cajas de ahorro* (equivalent to a building society or savings and loan) have branches in all but the smallest towns. **Hours** are Mon–Fri 8.30am–2pm in summer, plus Sat 9am–1pm in winter. Outside these times it's usually possible to change cash at larger hotels (generally bad rates, but low commission), with travel agents in the cities and big resorts, and at most El Corte Inglés department stores, which have surprisingly reasonable rates. In tourist areas you'll also find **casas de cambio**, with more convenient hours, but worse exchange rates. ATMs are widespread throughout Spain and accept both credit cards and ordinary bankcards with the Cirrus or Plus symbols. They are more convenient to use than travellers' cheques, and can be just as cheap, with withdrawal fees of around two percent.

For a Western European country, Spain is a relatively cheap place to visit. Public transport is subsidized and food and accommodation, in general, are reasonably priced. If you are eligible, it's always worth asking for student or senior citizen reductions as many tourist sites offer discounts.

Communications

You can have your letters sent **poste restante** to any Spanish post office: they should be addressed to "Lista de Correos" followed by the name of the town and province. **American Express** in Madrid and Barcelona will hold mail for a month for cardholders. **Post offices** (*correos*) are open Mon–Fri 8.30am–2pm & Sat 9am–noon, though big branches in large cities have longer hours. Queues can be long, but stamps are also sold at tobacconists (*estancos*).

All Spanish regional prefixes are now an integral part of **telephone numbers**. For example, in Madrid the two-digit prefix is 91 and it is necessary to dial these digits even when calling from within the city. However, on business cards and other publicity these preliminary digits may not appear, and people don't always include them when giving out a number.

You can make **international phone calls** direct from almost any phone box, and from booths in phone centres (*locutorios publicos*) or Telefónica offices, where you pay afterwards. The various brands of discount long-distance cards for domestic and overseas calls are the cheapest and most convenient option. Most phone boxes accept all denominations of coins as well as cards (available from tobacconists). The **operator** number is 1003 for domestic calls, 025 for international information.

The **Internet** has made great inroads into Spanish life and access is widely available at Internet cafés, some computer shops and many phone centres. Prices vary; in cities hourly rates can be as little as €1.80 rising to around €6 in some smaller towns.

Getting around

Most of Spain is well covered by both bus and rail networks and for journeys between major towns there's often little to choose between the two in cost or speed. On shorter or minor routes buses tend to be quicker and will normally take you closer to your destination. Car rental is worth considering, with costs among the lowest in Europe especially if booked from outside the country.

■ Trains

RENFE, the Spanish rail company (*www.renfe.es*), operates a horrendously complicated variety of **train** services. It is divided into three sections. *Cercanías* (red) are local trains in and around the major cities. *Regionales* (orange) are equivalent to buses in speed and cost, and run between cities – *regional exprés* and *delta* trains can cover longer distances. *Largo recorrido* express trains (some variation on grey) have a bewildering number of names. In ascending order of speed and luxury, they are known as *Diurno*, *Intercity (IC)*, *Estrella (*)*, *Talgo*, *Talgo Pendular*, *Talgo 200 (T200)*, and *Trenhotel*. Anything above Intercity can cost upwards of twice as much as standard second class. There is also a growing number of private super-high-speed trains from Madrid, such as *AVE* to Sevilla and *EuroMed* to Alicante. These are white, look like aeroplanes, and for those who can afford it have cut travelling times drastically.

A good way to avoid the queues is to buy tickets at travel agents which display the RENFE sign – they have a sophisticated computer system which can also make seat reservations (€3), obligatory on *largo recorrido* trains; the cost is the same as at the station. Most larger towns also have a RENFE office in the centre, or you can use the new centralized 24-hour telephone reservation service on ☎902 24 02 02.

InterRail and Eurail **passes** are valid on all RENFE trains and also on *EuroMed* but supplements are charged on the fastest trains, as well as a reservation fee of €1.80–3. Within Spain itself there are two passes available. The **Tarjeta Turística** is valid for three to ten days' unlimited rail travel in a two-month period; a second-class pass costs approximately €155 for three days, €210 for five days and

€360 for ten days. The other pass available is the **RENFE Tarjeta Explorerail** (under 30s with ISIC card), accepted on all trains, though a supplement of €3 is payable on *EuroMed* on top of the reservation fee; second-class passes are available for seven days (€114), fifteen days (€138) or thirty days (€180).

■ Buses

Unless you're travelling on a rail pass, **buses** will probably meet most of your transport needs; many smaller villages are accessible only by bus, almost always leaving from the capital of their province. Service varies in quality, but buses are often faster than trains and are usually as reliable and comfortable, with prices pretty standard at around €6 per 100km. Many towns still have no main station, and buses may leave from a variety of places. All public transport, and the bus service especially, is drastically reduced on **Sundays and holidays** – it's best to avoid travelling to out-of-the-way places on these days.

■ Driving, hitching and cycling

You obviously have much more freedom if you have your **own car**. Major roads are generally good, and traffic, while a little hectic in the cities, is usually well behaved. Speed limits are 60kph in built-up areas, 120kph on highways and 90–100kph on other roads. The national **breakdown service**, Ayuda en Carretera, is run by the Guardia Civil. Roadside phones on major routes are connected to the local police station, which will arrange assistance. On minor routes, contact the nearest police station via the operator.

You'll find a choice of **car rental** firms in all major towns, with the biggest ones represented at the airports and in town centres. These all charge about the same, upwards of £150/US\$240 a week, but you can usually get a deal from local operators (Atesa is the main Spanish company). It's a lot cheaper to arrange it before you arrive though.

Hitching in Spain is not a reliable means of long-distance travel. The road down the east coast is notoriously difficult, and trying to get out of either Madrid or Barcelona can prove a nightmare, but thumbing on back roads can be surprisingly productive.

The Spanish are great aficionados of **cycling**, and outside of the hottest months, this is another excellent option for independant rural travel. Still, care should be taken, particularly on busy roads – on average two cyclists are killed per week.

Accommodation

Simple, reasonably priced rooms are widely available in Spain, and in almost any town you'll be able to get a double for around €18, a single for €7.20. Only in major resorts and a handful of tourist cities need you pay more. In Spain, unlike most countries, you don't seem to pay extra for a central location, though you do tend to get a comparatively bad deal if you're travelling on your own as there are few single rooms. It's always worth bargaining over room prices and, although they're officially regulated, this doesn't necessarily mean much. In high season you're unlikely to have much luck, but at quiet times you may get quite a discount. For groups, most places have rooms with three or four beds at not a great deal more than the double room price.

■ Hotel-type accommodation

The one thing all travellers need to master is the elaborate variety of types and places to stay. Cheapest of all, but increasingly rare, are **fondas** (identifiable by a square blue sign with a white F on it), closely followed by **casas de huéspedes** (CH on a similar sign), **pensiones** (P) and, less commonly, **hospedajes**. Distinctions between all of these are rather blurred, but in general you might find food served at both *fondas* and *pensiones* (some of which

---

ACCOMMODATION PRICE CODES

Throughout this guide, accommodation is coded on a scale of ① to ⑨, the code indicating the lowest price per person per night you could expect to pay in each establishment in high season. With hostels this is the nightly rate per person; with hotels, the price is arrived at by dividing the cost of the cheapest double room by two. The prices indicated by the codes are as follows:

① under £5/\$8 (€9)	④ £15–20/\$24–32 (€27–36)	⑦ £30–35/\$48–56 (€54–63)
② £5–10/\$8–16 (€9–18)	⑤ £20–25/\$32–40 (€36–45)	⑧ £35–40/\$56–64 (€63–72)
③ £10–15/\$16–24 (€18–27)	⑥ £25–30/\$40–48 (€45–54)	⑨ £40/\$64 (€72) and over

may offer rooms only on a meals-inclusive basis). *Casas de huéspedes* – literally "guest houses" – were traditionally for longer stays, and to some extent they still are.

Slightly more expensive than all these, but far more common, are **hostales** (marked Hs) and **hostal-residencias** (HsR). These are categorized from one to three stars, but prices vary enormously according to location. Most *hostales* offer good functional rooms, usually with private shower, and, for doubles at least, they can be excellent value.

Moving up the scale you finally reach **hoteles** (H), again star-graded by the authorities. One-star hotels cost no more than three-star *hostales* – sometimes they're actually cheaper – but at three stars you pay a lot more, at four or five you're in the luxury class with prices to match. Near the top end of this scale there are also state-run **paradores**: beautiful places, often converted from castles, monasteries and other minor Spanish monuments.

Tourist offices always have lists of places to stay, but often miss the cheaper deals. You can also buy the *Guía de Hoteles* (€7.80), which includes some *hostales*.

■ Private rooms and hostels

Outside all of these categories you will sometimes see **camas** (beds) and **habitaciones** (rooms) advertised in private houses or above bars, often with the phrase "*camas y comidas*" (beds and meals) – these can be the cheapest of all options. **Hostels** (*Albergues Juveniles*), on the other hand, are rarely very practical, except in northern Spain where it can be difficult for solo travellers to find any other bed in summer. Few stay open all year, and in towns they are often inconveniently located. They tend to have curfews, are often block-reserved by school groups, and demand production of an HI card (though this is generally available on the spot). At between €6 and €12 a person, you can easily pay more than for sharing a cheap double room in a *fonda* or *casa de huéspedes*. It is sometimes possible to stay at Spanish **monasteries**, which may let empty cells for around €3 a person, but if you want to be sure of a reception it's best to approach the local tourist office first, and phone ahead. Throughout the country there are *agroturismo* and *casa rural* programmes that offer excellent cheap accommodation in rural areas, usually in beautifully preserved and well-maintained private houses. Full lists are available from the relevant tourist offices.

■ Camping

There are over 350 authorized **campsites** in Spain, mostly on the coast and holiday areas. They usually work out at about €3 per person plus the same again for a tent and a similar amount for each car or caravan. If you plan to camp extensively pick up the free *Mapa de Campings* from the National Tourist Board, the more complete *Guía de Campings* (€6) or look on the Internet at *www.vayacamping.net*. **Camping rough** is generally not a good idea, although exact laws vary from province to province. It is definitely unwise to set up a tent anywhere near a tourist beach or campsite though and can result in a hefty fine. Wherever you decide to pitch up, check at the local *Ayuntamiento* (Town Hall) before you start hammering in the pegs.

Food and Drink

There are two ways to eat in Spain: you can go to a *restaurante* or *comedor* (dining room) and have a full meal, or you can have a succession of tapas (small snacks) or *raciones* (larger ones) at one or more bars.

■ Food

For **breakfast** you're probably best off in a bar or café, though some *hostales* and *fondas* will serve the "Continental" basics. Traditionally, it's *churros con chocolate* – long tubular doughnuts with thick drinking chocolate – but most places also serve *tostadas* (toasted bread) with oil (*con aceite*) or butter and jam (*con mantequilla y mermelada*), or more substantial egg dishes. Cold *tortilla* (omelette) also makes an excellent breakfast. **Coffee and pastries** (*bollería*) or doughnuts are available at most cafés, too, though for a wider selection of cakes you should head for one of the many excellent *pastelerías* or *confiterías*.

One of the advantages of eating in **bars** is being able to experiment. **Tapas** are small portions, three or four small chunks of fish or meat, or a dollop of salad, which traditionally used to be served up free with a drink. These days you usually have to pay for anything more than a few olives, but a single helping rarely costs more than €1.20–2.40. In the Basque Country and Navarra bars often have on offer a mouthwatering selection of *pinchos* – meat, fish or just about anything else on a cocktail stick – on the bar. **Raciones** are simply bigger plates of the same for €3–6, and can be enough in themselves for a light meal. *Tascas, bodegas, cervecerías* and *tabernas* are all types of bar where you'll find tapas and *raciones.* Most have separate prices depending on whether you eat at the bar or at a table (up to fifty percent more expensive – more if you sit out on a terrace).

For main meals, **comedores** are the places to seek out if your main criteria are price and quantity, although they're increasingly hard to find as the tradition is on the way out. Sometimes they're attached to a bar, *pensión* or *fonda*, but as often as not they're virtually unmarked. Since they're essentially workers' cafés they tend to serve more substantial meals at lunchtime and may be closed in the evening. When you find one you'll pay €5–8 for a *menú del día* or *cubierto*, a three-course meal (usually) with wine.

Replacing *comedores* are **cafeterías**. These can be good value, especially the self-service places, but their emphasis is more northern European, and their light snack-meals tend to be dull. Food often comes as a *plato combinado* – literally a combined plate – something like egg and fries or *calamares* and salad, often with bread and a drink included. This usually costs €3.50–6. *Cafeterías* often serve a *menú del día* as well. You may prefer to get your *plato combinado* at a bar, which in small towns with no *comedores* may be the only way to eat inexpensively.

Moving up the scale there are **restaurantes** (graded by one to five forks) and **marisquerías**, the latter serving exclusively fish and seafood. Cheaper *restaurantes* are often not much different in price to *comedores*. A fixed-price *cubierto*, *menú del día* or *menú de la casa* (all of which mean the same) is often the best value here: two or three courses plus wine and bread for €4.80–9. Above two forks, however, prices can escalate rapidly.

Fish and seafood form the basis of a vast variety of tapas and are fresh and excellent even hundreds of miles from the sea. Fish stews (*zarzuelas*) and rice-based paellas (which also contain meat, usually rabbit or chicken) are often memorable. **Meat** is most often grilled and served with a few fried potatoes and salad, or cured and served as a starter or in sandwiches. *Jamón Serrano*, the Spanish version of Parma ham, is superb. **Vegetarians** have a fairly hard time of it in Spain, although an increasing number of vegetarian restaurants are springing up in the larger cities. A mixed salad often comes with tuna and egg and promising sounding beans and lentil dishes are usually cooked with bacon. Try to establish the contents beforehand. Even in the smallest bar there's always something to eat, but you may get weary of eggs and omelettes, and vegans usually have to content themselves with salad and bread.

■ Drink

Wine, either *tinto* (red), *blanco* (white) or *rosado/clarete* (rosé), is the invariable accompaniment to every meal and is extremely cheap. The most common bottled variety is Valdepeñas, from New Castile; Rioja, from the area around Logroño, is better but more expensive. Other good wines include Penedes and Bach from Catalunya, Ribera del Duero from Castilla and Mendizabal, a wonderful, light Rioja rosé.

The classic Andalucian wine is **sherry** – *Vino de Jerez*. This is served chilled and, like everything Spanish, comes in a perplexing variety of forms: *fino* or *Jerez seco* (dry sherry), *amontillado* (medium), or *oloroso* or *Jerez dulce* (sweet). **Cerveza**, lager-type beer, is generally pretty good, though more expensive than wine. Local brands, such as Cruzcampo in Sevilla or Alhambra in Granada, are often better than the national ones. Equally refreshing, though often deceptively strong, is **sangría**, a wine-and-fruit punch which you'll come across at fiestas and in tourist bars. *Sidra*, a dry farmhouse cider, is most typical in the Basque Country and Asturias.

In mid-afternoon – or even at breakfast – many Spaniards take a *copa* of **liqueur** with their coffee, or else tip a brandy into the coffee, calling the concoction *carajillo*. The best are *anís* (like Pernod) or *coñac*, excellent local brandy with a distinct vanilla flavour. Most **spirits** are ordered by brand name, since there are generally cheaper Spanish equivalents for standard imports. Specify *nacional* to avoid getting an expensive foreign brand and be prepared for huge measures.

Coffee – served in cafés, *heladerías* (ice-cream parlours) and bars – is invariably espresso, slightly bitter and served black, unless you specify *cortado* (with a drop of milk), *con leche* (a more generous dollop) or *americano* (weaker black coffee). **Tea** is also available at most bars, although Spaniards tend to drink it black. If you want milk, ask afterwards: ordering *té con leche* might well get you a glass of milk with a teabag floating on top. There is also usually a choice of herb teas, such as *tila* (lime blossom), *menta* (mint) and *manzanilla* (camomile)

Opening hours and holidays

Almost everything in Spain – shops, museums, churches, tourist offices – closes for a **siesta** of at least two hours in the hottest part of the day. There's a lot of variation, and certain **shops** now stay open all day, but basic summer working hours are Mon–Sat 9.30am–1.30pm & 5–8pm. **Museums**, with few exceptions, take a break between 1 and 4pm, and are closed Sunday afternoon and all day Monday. The really important **churches**, including most cathedrals, operate similarly; others open only for worship in the early morning and/or the evening.

There are twelve national **holidays** and scores of local ones. The national ones are: Jan 1; Jan 6; Maundy Thursday; Good Friday; Easter Sunday; May 1; Aug 15; Oct 12; Nov 1; Dec 6; Dec 8; Dec 25. Certain Comunidades (regions) also observe Easter Monday; Corpus Christi (early or mid-June); June 24; and July 25.

Emergencies

Though their role has been cut back since the days when they operated as Franco's right hand, the paramilitary **Guardia Civil** (green uniforms and patent-leather hats or green kepis) still police some rural areas, borders and most highways. In Catalunya, some of their reponsibilities have devolved to the **Mossos d'Esquadra**, and in the Basque country, to the **Ertzaintza**. In cities you'll find the **Policía Nacional** (talk to them if you get robbed), and the **Policía Municipal** (for traffic infractions), and there is a **Patrulla Rural** in some outlying areas.

A common source of trouble is **petty theft**, which has risen to almost epidemic proportions in cities like Sevilla and Barcelona. If you take precautions, such as not leaving bags on tables, and wearing them across the shoulder, you've little to worry about, though fiestas seem to be a particularly dangerous time.

For minor **health** complaints it's easiest to go to a *farmacia*, which you'll find in almost any town. In more serious cases you can head directly to *Urgencias* at the nearest hospital, or get the address of an English-speaking doctor from the nearest relevant consulate, or from a *farmacia*, the local police or tourist office.

Emergency Numbers

All emergencies ☎112, Ambulance ☎ 081

HAMISH BROWN

The walls, Essaouira, Morocco

FRANCESCA YORKE

Amsterdam, Netherlands

GREG EVANS

The Old Town square, Warsaw, Poland

CHRIS COE/AXIOM

Fjords, West Coast, Norway

J. PHILLIPS/TRAVEL INK

PETER WILSON

The summit of Giewont, Tatra mountains, Poland

Cais da Ribeira, Porto, Portugal

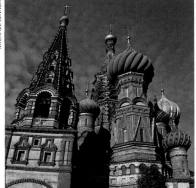

St Basil's Cathedral, Moscow, Russia

Old town, Stockholm, Sweden

Mosaic lizard, Parc Güell, Barcelona, Spain

Masquers at a festival in Portugal

Sevilla house front, Spain

House in Transylvania, Romania   Iztuzu Beach, Dalyan, Turkey

View from Gornergrat, above Zermatt, Switzerland

MADRID

MADRID became Spain's capital simply through its geographical position at the centre of Iberia. When Philip II moved the seat of government here in 1561 his aim was to create a symbol of the unification and centralization of the country. The city has few natural advantages – it is 300km from the sea on a 650-metre-high plateau, freezing in winter, burning in summer – and only the determination of successive rulers to promote a strong central capital ensured its success. Today, it is a vast, predominantly modern city, with a population of some five million and growing. Pretty it isn't, but the streets at the heart of the city are a pleasant surprise, with odd pockets of medieval buildings and narrow atmospheric alleys. There may be few sights of great architectural interest, but the monarchs did acquire outstanding picture collections, which formed the basis of the Prado museum. This has long ensured Madrid a place on the European art-tour, and the more so since the 1990s arrival of the Reina Sofía and Thyssen-Bornemisza galleries, state-of-the-art homes to fabulous arrays of modern Spanish painting (including Picasso's *Guernica*) and European and American masters.

Galleries and sights aside, though, the capital has enough going for it in its own city life and style to ensure a diverting stay. As you get to grips with the place you soon realize that it's the inhabitants – the Madrileños – that are the capital's key attraction: hanging out in the traditional cafés and *chocolaterías* or the summer *terrazas*, packing the lanes of the Sunday Rastro flea market, or playing hard and very, very late in a thousand bars, clubs, discos and *tascas*. Whatever Barcelona or San Sebastián might claim, the Madrid scene, immortalized in the movies of Pedro Almodóvar, remains the most vibrant and fun in the country.

Arrival and information

Barajas airport is 16km out of town and connected with the centre by metro (€0.80) or a bus service to Plaza de Colon (☎91 431 6192 for information; €2.40). Taxis from the airport cost about €13.60 unless you get caught in rush-hour traffic. Trains from the north and from Portugal arrive at the **Estación de Chamartín**, rather isolated in the north of the city. A metro line connects it with the centre and a suburban train line runs to the much more central **Estación de Atocha** – for travel to and from the south, east, west, and Andalucía. Many local trains, or *cercanías*, use the **Estación de Príncipe Pío**, more widely known as **Estación del Norte**, below the central Plaza de España. **Bus terminals** are scattered throughout the city, but the largest – used by all international services – is the **Estación Sur** (metro Méndez Álvaro) on c/Méndez Álvaro, south of Atocha station.

Despite being the capital, Madrid's **tourist offices** are uniformily unprofessional and unhelpful. Branches can be found at c/Duque de Medinaceli 2, near the Prado (Mon–Fri 9am–7pm, Sat 9am–1pm; ☎91 429 4951); the airport (Mon–Fri 8am–8pm, Sat 9am–1pm; ☎91 305 8656); and in Chamartín station (Mon–Fri 8am–8pm, Sat 9am–1pm; ☎91 315 9976). There's also a busy municipal tourist office at Plaza Mayor 3 (Mon–Sat 10am–8pm, Sun 10am–3pm; ☎91 588 16 36). All supply free leaflets and maps of Madrid and – if you're lucky – other Spanish cities; the best and most detailed city map is, in fact, the bus map, also free. There's also a tourist information phone-line (☎901 300 600) and Web site (*www.munimadrid.es*).

For details of **what's on**, check out the weekly *Guía del Ocio* (available from newsstands) or the listings in the daily *El Pais* or *El Mundo* newspapers (both have entertainments supplements on Fri & Sat). The free tourist office handout, *In Madrid*, is also quite useful but best of all is the excellent free monthly *En Madrid*, also available at tourist offices and in many bars.

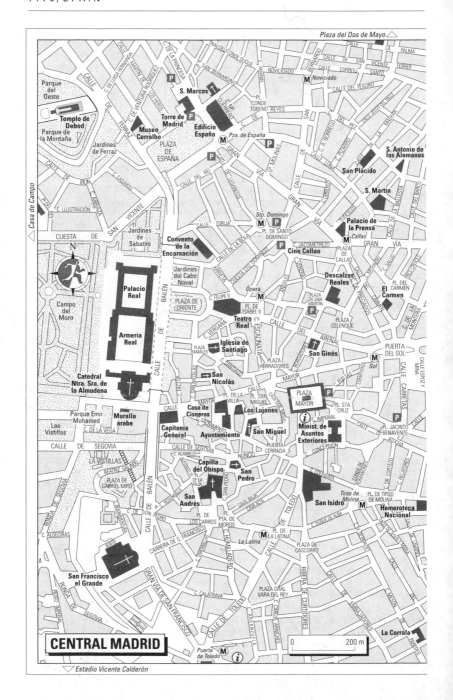

CENTRAL MADRID

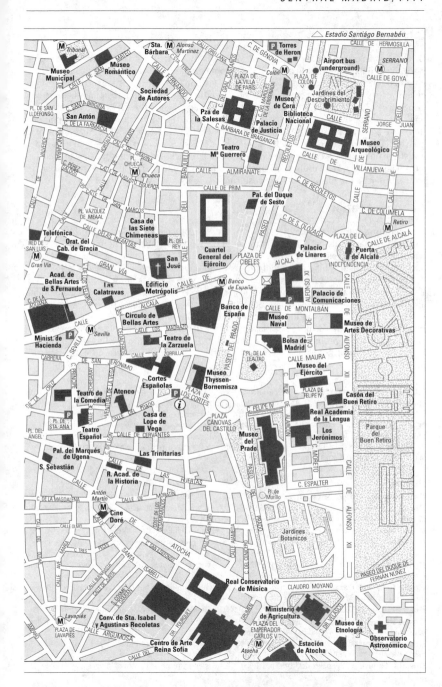

City transport

By far the easiest way of getting around Madrid is by **metro**, and the system serves most places you're likely to want to get to. It runs from 6am until 1.30am with a flat fare of €0.90, or €4.50 for the metrobus ten-ride ticket, valid for both bus and metro. You can get a free colour map of the system at any station. The urban **bus network** is more comprehensive but also more complicated. There's a transport information stand in the Plaza de Cibeles, whose advice you should trust before that of any handout. Buses run from 6am to 11.30pm, but there are also several nightbus lines around the central area (every 30min midnight–3am, hourly 3–6am, from Plaza de Cibeles and Puerta del Sol). **Taxis** – white cars with a diagonal red stripe on the side – can be hailed if their green light is showing; they are easy to find and surprisingly cheap. **Hop-on hop-off bus** companies (including Madrid Vision ☎91 767 1743) have stops at all the major sights and cost from €9.50 for a daily adult ticket.

Accommodation

An **accommodation service**, Brújula, has offices at Atocha (daily 8am–10pm; ☎91 539 11 73) and Chamartín (daily 7.15am–11pm; ☎91 315 7894) train stations. The service covers the whole of Spain and costs from €2.40. You shouldn't really need it, however; once you start to look there's an astonishing amount of cheap accommodation available in the old town.

Much of the cheapest accommodation is to be found in the area immediately **around the Estación de Atocha**, though the places closest to the station are rather grim and at night the area can feel somewhat threatening. Better to head up c/Atocha towards the centre, where you'll find better pickings in the streets surrounding the buzzing **Plaza Santa Ana**. Prices rise as you get up towards the Plaza Mayor and Puerta del Sol, but even here there are affordable options. Other promising areas are along the **Gran Vía**, where the huge old buildings hide a vast array of hotels and *hostales* at all prices, and north of here up **c/Fuencarral** towards Malasaña.

Hostels

Hostel Richard Schirmann, in the Casa del Campo (☎91 463 5699). Way out in the park west of the centre, but friendly, comfortable, clean and cheap, with an enjoyably noisy bar. Metro El Lago is roughly 1km away – consider taking a taxi rather than walk after dark as the area is a notorious red-light district. ①.
Hostel Santa Cruz de Marcenado, c/Santa Cruz de Marcenado 28 (☎91 547 4532). North of the Plaza de España near the Palacio Liria; reasonably pleasant, modern and quiet. Curfew 1.30am. Often full, so arrive early morning if possible. Metro Argüelles. ①.

Hotels

Hostal Aguilar, Carrera San Jerónimo 32 (☎91 429 3661). Just one in a building packed with possibilities. ③.
Hostal Alcázar Regis, Gran Vía 61 (☎91 547 9317). Near the Plaza de España, deservedly popular and often full. Others in the same building. ③.
Hostal Alonso, c/Espoz y Mina 17 (☎91 531 5679). Very cheap, if a little shabby; family-run, great location. ②.
Hostal Aranzazu, c/Doctor Mata 1–3 (☎91 522 5976). Centrally located near Atocha and well equipped with mini-bar. ③.
Hostal Armesto, c/San Agustín 6 (☎91 429 9031). Small, very pleasant *hostal*, well positioned for the Santa Ana area and the art galleries. ③.
Hostal Cruz Sol, Plaza Santa Cruz 6 (☎91 532 7197). Slightly run-down, but in excellent, quiet position at other side of Plaza Mayor. Some very cheap doubles. ③.
Hostal Lisboa, c/Ventura de la Vega 17 (☎91 429 9894). Good 3-star *hostal*, central but not too hectic. ③.
Hostal Plaza D'Ort, Plaza del Angel 13 (☎91 429 9041, *info@plazadort.com*). Well-equipped *hostal* with one self-catering apartment; a good option for groups. ③.
Hostal Carreras, c/del Príncipe 18 (☎91 522 0036). Comfortable place in elegant old building off Plaza Santa Ana; several others share the same building. ③.
Hostal Ribadavia, c/Fuencarral 25 (☎91 531 1058). Clean, friendly place, with others in the same building. ②.

Hostal Riosol, c/Mayor 5 (☎91 532 3142). Just off Puerta del Sol towards Plaza Mayor. A few cheaper rooms without bath. ②.

Hostal San Antonio, c/León 13 (☎91 429 5137). Clean, comfortable, and in a quiet street between Atocha and Santa Ana. ②.

Hostal Sud-Americana, Paseo del Prado 12 (☎91 429 2564). Almost opposite the Prado; though standards vary, there are some excellent rooms here. Closed Aug. ②.

Hostal Victoria II, c/Carretas 3 (☎91 522 1549). Cheap rooms with satellite TV and video. Air-conditioned. ③.

Campsites

Osuna, Avenida de Logroño (☎91 741 0510), out near the airport. Friendly, with good facilities, reasonable prices and plenty of shade, but the ground is rock-hard and, being so close to the airport, it's extremely noisy. Metro to Canillejas, then bus #105.

The City

The central **Puerta del Sol**, with its bustling crowds and traffic, is an excellent starting point for viewing the city. This is officially the centre of the capital and of the nation: a stone slab in the pavement outside the main building on the south side marks **Kilometre Zero**, from where six of Spain's National Routes begin, while beneath the streets, three of the city's ten metro lines converge. On the north side, at the bottom of c/del Carmen, is a statue of a bear pawing a *madroño* bush; this is both the emblem of the city and a favourite meeting place.

Immediately north of Sol, c/de Preciados and c/del Carmen head towards the Gran Vía; both have been pedestrianized and constitute the most popular **shopping** area in Madrid. West, c/del Arenal heads directly towards the Opera and Royal Palace, but there's more interest along c/Mayor, one of Madrid's oldest and most important thoroughfares, which runs southwest through the heart of the medieval city, also to end close to the Royal Palace.

Plaza de la Villa and Plaza Mayor

About two-thirds of the way along c/Mayor is the **Plaza de la Villa**, almost a casebook of Spanish architectural development. The oldest survivor here is the **Torre de los Lujanes**, a fifteenth-century building in Mudéjar style; next in age is the **Casa de Cisneros**, built by a nephew of Cardinal Cisneros in sixteenth-century Plateresque style; and to complete the picture the **Ayuntamiento** (tours Mon at 5pm; free) was begun in the seventeenth century, but later remodelled in Baroque mode. Baroque is taken a stage further around the corner in c/San Justo, where the church of **San Miguel** shows the unbridled imagination of the eighteenth-century Italian architects who designed it.

Walking straight from the Puerta del Sol to the Plaza de la Villa, you could easily miss altogether the **Plaza Mayor**, the most important architectural and historical landmark in Madrid. This almost perfectly preserved, extremely beautiful, seventeenth-century arcaded square, set back from the street, was planned by Philip II and Juan Herrera (architect of El Escorial; see p.1190) as the public meeting place of the new capital: *autos-da-fé* (trials of faith) were held by the Inquisition here, kings were crowned, festivals and demonstrations passed through, bulls were fought and gossip spread. The more important of these events would be watched by royalty from the be-frescoed **Casa Panadería**, named after the bakery which it replaced. Along with its popular but pricey cafés, the plaza still performs several public functions today. In summer it becomes an outdoor theatre and music stage; in the autumn there's a book fair; and just before Christmas it becomes a bazaar for festive decorations and religious regalia. The warren of streets surrounding the Plaza Mayor are well worth exploring and are a treasure trove of quality tapas bars and restaurants.

The Palacio Real

Calle del Arenal ends at the Plaza Isabel II opposite the **Teatro Real** or Opera House, which is separated from the Palacio Real by the newly renovated **Plaza de Oriente**. In the centre of the square is a superb statue of Felipe IV on horseback; it was based on designs by Velázquez, and Galileo is said to have helped with the calculations to make it balance.

The chief attraction of the area is the grandiose **Palacio Real**, or Royal Palace (Mon–Sat 9.30am–5pm, Sun 9am–2pm; €5.90 or €6.80 guided, free Wed for EU citizens). Built after the earlier Muslim Alcazar burned down on Christmas Day 1734, this was the principal royal residence until Alfonso XIII went into exile in 1931. The present royal family inhabits a more modest residence on the western outskirts of the city, using the Palacio Real only on state occasions. The building scores high on statistics: it claims more rooms than any other European palace; a **library** with one of the biggest collections of books, manuscripts, maps and musical scores in the world; an **armoury** with an unrivalled and often bizarre collection of weapons dating back to the fifteenth century; and an original **pharmacy**, a curious mixture of alchemist's den and early laboratory, its walls lined with jars labelled for various remedies.

It is no longer compulsory to follow a guided tour, so you can take your own time to contemplate the extraordinary opulence of the place: acres of Flemish and Spanish tapestries, endless Rococo decoration, bejewelled clocks and pompous portraits of the monarchs. In the **Sala del Trono** (Throne Room) there's a magnificent frescoed ceiling by Tiepolo representing the glory of Spain – an extraordinary achievement for an artist by then in his seventies.

Facing the Palacio Real, to the south, across the shadeless Plaza Armeria, is Madrid's brand new **Catedral** (daily 9am–9pm; free). This was planned centuries ago and worked upon for decades but only opened for business in 1993 with an inauguration by Pope John Paul II, whose statue stands at the entrance. Its Neoclassical bulk is as undistinguished inside as out, though the boutique-like Opus Dei chapel has, at least, novelty value.

The Gran Vía

North from the palace, c/Bailén runs into the **Plaza de España**, home to a couple of ageing skyscrapers, for long the city's tallest. These look down on an elaborate monument to Cervantes in the middle of the square, which in turn overlooks the bewildered bronze figures of Don Quixote and Sancho Panza. From here head off along **Gran Vía**, once the capital's major thoroughfare, which effectively divides the old city to the south from the newer parts. Permanently crowded with shoppers and sightseers, this Gran Vía is appropriately named, with splendidly quirky Art Nouveau and Art Deco facades fronting its banks, offices and apartments, and huge hand-painted posters on the cinemas. At its far end, by the magnificent cylindrical **Edificio Metropolis**, the street joins with c/Alcalá on the approach to Plaza de la Cibeles. Just across the junction is the majestic old **Círculo de las Bellas Artes**, a contemporary art exhibition space with a rather formal-looking but very trendy bar/café (entry charge of €0.60 for non members during exhibitions).

On an entirely different plane, the **Monasterio de las Descalzas Reales** (Tues–Thurs & Sat 10.30am–12.45pm & 4–5.45pm, Fri 10.30am–12.45pm, Sun 11am–1.45pm; €4.20, free Wed), one of the hidden treasures of the city, lies just south of the Gran Vía on the Plaza de las Descalzas. This convent was founded by Juana de Austria, daughter of Carlos V, sister of Philip II and, at nineteen, already the widow of Prince Don Juan of Portugal. In her wake came a succession of titled ladies (the name means the Convent of the Barefoot Royals) who brought fame and, above all, fortune. The place is unbelievably rich and also quite beautiful, the tranquillity within its thick walls making an extraordinary contrast to the frenzied commercialism all around. A whistle-stop guided tour takes you through the cloisters and up a ridiculously fancy stairway to a series of chambers packed with art and treasures of every kind.

Santa Ana and Huertas

Although there are few sights here, the area east of the Puerta del Sol, a rough triangle bordered to the east by the Paseo del Prado, on the north by c/Alcalá, and to the south by c/Atocha, is likely to claim more of your time than any conventional tourist attraction, due to its concentration of superb bars and restaurants. This area developed in the nineteenth century and has a strong literary past: there are streets named after **Cervantes** and **Lope de Vega** (where one lived and the other died), the Atheneum club is here, as is the Círculo de las Bellas Artes (see "The Gran Vía", above) and the Teatro Español. The Cortes, Spain's parliament, also sits here.

The **Paseo del Prado** is part of one of the city's great avenues, running from Atocha station (opposite which is the Centro Reina Sofía), past the Prado and Thyssen galleries, to the **Plaza de la Cibeles**, named after a fountain and statue of the goddess Cibeles awash in a sea of traffic in the middle. Dominating this square is Madrid's fabulously ornate central post office, the **Palacio de Comunicaciones**. To the north of Cibeles, the *paseo* continues, with name-changes first to **Recoletos** and then **Castellana**, past the major shopping and business areas. In summer, the centre of Paseo de Castellana becomes an almost continuous line of *terrazas*, or pavement café/bars, where Madrid's sleepless society comes to talk, drink and be seen from midnight to dawn.

The Prado

The **Museo del Prado** (Tues–Sat 9am–7pm, Sun 9am–2pm; €3, free Sat after 2.30pm and Sun; admission can be gained with the little-advertised "Paseo del Arte" voucher, which includes entrance to all three of the great art museums, costs €7.50, and is valid for a year – available at any of the participating museums) has been one of Europe's key art galleries ever since it was opened to the public in 1819. It houses the finest works collected by Spanish royalty – for the most part avid, discerning and wealthy buyers – as well as standout items from other Spanish sources: over three thousand paintings in all, including the world's finest collections of Goya, Velázquez and Bosch. Although all the major works are still on display, ongoing restoration work means that many paintings are being temporarily rehung elsewhere in the gallery, so pick up a leaflet at the entrance to find any changes to the plan described here.

Even in a full day you couldn't hope to do justice to everything in the Prado, and it's much more enjoyable to make short visits with a clear idea of what you want to see. Perhaps the best approach to the museum is through the Puerta de Goya, the side entrance on c/Felipe IV. In the first rooms on the ground floor are early Spanish paintings, mostly religious subjects, then in a series of rooms to your left the early **Flemish masters** are displayed. The great triptychs of **Hieronymus Bosch** – the early *Hay Wain*, the middle-period *Garden of Earthly Delights* and the late *Adoration of the Magi* – are familiar from countless reproductions but infinitely more chilling in the original, and there's much more of his work here, along with that of **Pieter Bruegel the Elder**, Rogier van der Weyden, Memling, Bouts, Gerard David and Massys. The few German paintings are dominated by four Dürers.

The long, central downstairs gallery houses the **early Spanish collection**, and a dazzling array of portraits and religious paintings by the Cretan-born **El Greco**, among them his mystic and hallucinatory *Crucifixion* and *Adoration of the Shepherds*. Beyond this is the beginning of the Prado's Italian treasures: the superb **Titian** portraits of Charles V and Philip II, as well as works by Tintoretto, Bassano, Caravaggio and Veronese. Upstairs are Goya's unmissable **Black Paintings** – best seen after visiting the rest of his work on the top floor – and, to the left of the Puerta de Goya entrance, the Italian paintings include a series of panels by Botticelli illustrating a story from the Decameron. The museum's collection of over 160 works of **later Flemish and Dutch art** has been imaginatively rehoused in a new suite of twelve rooms off the main gallery on the first floor. Rubens is extensively represented – by the beautifully restored *Three Graces* among others – as are Van Dyck and Jan Brueghel.

Continuing on the **first floor** you come to the great Spanish painters, where the outstanding presence is **Velázquez** – among the collection are intimate portraits of the family of Felipe IV, most famously his masterpiece *Las Meninas*. Adjacent are important works by Zurbarán and Murillo. The **top floor** of the building is devoted almost entirely to **Francisco**

de Goya, whose many portraits of his patron, Charles IV, are remarkable for their lack of any attempt at flattery while those of Queen María Luisa, whom he despised, are downright ugly. He was an enormously versatile artist: contrast the voluptuous *Majas* with the horrors depicted in *The Second of May* and *The Third of May*, on-the-spot portrayals of the rebellion against Napoleon and the subsequent reprisals.

The Thyssen-Bornemisza collection

The **Colección Thyssen-Bornemisza** (Tues–Sun 10am–7pm; €4.80) occupies the old Palacio de Villahermosa, diagonally opposite the Prado, at the end of the Carrera de San Jerónimo. This prestigious site played a large part in Spain's acquisition – for a knock-down $300,000,000 in June 1993 – of what was perhaps the world's greatest private art trove. The seven-hundred-odd paintings accumulated by the Swiss steel family create a very enjoyable collection of important works from every major period and movement: **medieval** to **seventeenth century** on the top floor, **Rococo** and **Neoclassicism** to **Fauves** and **Expressionists** on the first floor, and **Surrealists**, **Pop Art** and the **Avant-Garde** on ground level. How the Thyssens got hold of classic works by everyone from Duccio and Holbein, through El Greco and Caravaggio, to Schiele and Rothko, takes your breath away. Surprises include a strong showing of nineteenth-century Americans, some very early and very late Van Goghs, and side-by-side hangings of parallel Cubist studies by Picasso, Braque and Mondrian. The museum has a handy **bar and cafeteria** in the basement and allows re-entry, so long as you get your hand stamped at the exit desk.

Centro de Arte Reina Sofía

Luckily, the Centro de Arte Reina Sofía (Mon–Sat 10am–9pm, Sun 10am–2.30pm; €3, free Sat after 2.30pm and Sun), facing Atocha station at the end of Paseo del Prado, keeps different opening hours and days from its neighbours. For this permanent collection of modern Spanish art, and leading exhibition space, is another essential stop on the Madrid art scene. The museum, a massive former convent and hospital, is a kind of Madrid response to the Pompidou centre in Paris. Transparent lifts shuttle visitors up the outside of the building, whose levels feature a cinema, excellent art book and design shops, a print, music and photographic library, restaurant, bar and café, as well as the exhibition halls (top floor) and the collection of twentieth-century art (second floor).

It is for **Picasso's Guernica** that most visitors come to the Reina Sofía, and rightly so. Superbly displayed, along with its preliminary studies, this icon of twentieth-century Spanish art and politics – a response to the fascist bombing of the Basque town of Guernica in the Spanish Civil War – carries a shock that defies all familiarity. The painting is on the 2nd floor in Room 6, midway around. The post-*Guernica* halls are devoted to **Dalí** and Surrealism, while the final rooms are devoted to early-twentieth-century Spanish artists including **Miró**. The fourth floor displays post-World War II figurative art, mapping the beginning of abstraction through to Pop and avant-garde.

The Rastro

The area south of the Plaza Mayor and c/Atocha has traditionally been a tough, working-class district. In many places the old houses survive, huddled together in narrow streets, but the character of **La Latina** and **Lavapiés** has changed in recent years as their inhabitants, and the districts themselves, become increasingly popular with a younger and more fashionable crowd. Part of the reason for this rise in status must be the **Rastro** (metro La Latina), which is as much part of Madrid's weekend ritual as a Mass or a *paseo*. This gargantuan, thriving, thieving shambles of a **street market** sprawls south from metro La Latina to the Ronda de Toledo, especially along c/Ribera de Curtidores. Through it, crowds flood between 10am and 3pm every Sunday and holidays too. Don't expect to find fabulous bargains; the serious antiques trade has mostly moved off the streets and into the shops. It's definitely worth a visit, though, if only to see the locals out in their thousands and to drop into traditional bars for tapas. Keep a tight grip on your bags, pockets, cameras and jewellery. Afterwards head over to the bars and *terrazas* around Puerta de Moros where half of Madrid congregates for an *aperitivo* and to while away the afternoon.

Retiro and other parks

When you get tired of sightseeing, Madrid's many parks provide great places to escape to for a few hours. The most central and most popular is the **Parque del Buen Retiro** behind the Prado, a stunning mix of formal gardens and wider spaces. Originally the grounds of a royal retreat (*retiro* in Spanish), it has been public property for more than a hundred years – the palace itself burned down in the eighteenth century. In its 330 acres you can jog, row a boat, picnic, have your fortune told, and above all promenade – on Sunday afternoon half of Madrid turns out for the *paseo*. Travelling art exhibitions are frequently housed in the beautiful **Palacio de Velázquez** and the nearby **Palacio de Cristal** (times and prices vary according to exhibition). The nearby **Jardines Botanicos** (daily 10am–sunset; €1.50, students €0.70; metro Atocha), whose entrance faces the southern end of the Prado, are also delightful.

North of Gran Vía: Chueca, Malasaña and beyond

The chief reason to explore the quarters **north of Gran Vía** is for restaurants and nightlife. Although the late-late-nightclubs and discos are scattered around the city, and some even a few kilometres out from the centre, it is in **Chueca** and **Malasaña** that you'll find by far the heaviest concentration of bars and clubs downtown. Heading up in this direction by day, you might stop off at the **Museo Municipal**, c/Fuencarral 78 (Tues–Fri 9.30am–8pm, Sat & Sun 10am–2pm; €1.80; metro Tribunal). Better known for its superb Churrigueresque facade than its contents, this eighteenth-century building houses exhibits tracing the development of Madrid from prehistoric times, with some fascinating scale models of the city as it used to be.

Malasaña, centred on the Plaza Dos de Mayo, was the focus of the *movida Madrileña*, the "happening scene" of the late 1970s and early 1980s after the death of Franco. Then it was the mecca of the young: bars appeared behind every doorway, drugs were sold openly in the streets, and there was an extraordinary atmosphere of new-found freedom. To some extent it still is, although its a grungy studenty scene in the evening, but the shops and restaurants now reflect increasingly upmarket tastes. **Chueca**, especially around Plaza Chueca, has gone through a similar transformation and is now the centre of Gay Madrid, crammed with bars, clubs and boutiques. From here, as you walk east towards the expensive shopping areas around the Paseo Recoletos, are some of the city's most enticing streets. Offbeat restaurants, small private art galleries, and odd corner shops are to be found here in abundance and c/Almirante has some of the city's most expensive designer clothes shops too.

Salamanca, across the Paseo Recoletos from Chueca, is full of traditional apartments and expensive shops. A stroll up **c/Serrano** will take you past many of these and past a trio of museums and galleries. At no. 13 is the dusty and chaotic **Museo Arqueológico** (Tues–Sat 9.30am–6.30/8.30pm, Sun 9.30am–2.30pm; €3, students €1.50, free Sat pm & Sun; metro Colón), which contains the celebrated Celto-Iberian bust known as *La Dama de Elche*, the slightly later *Dama de Baza*, and a wonderfully rich hoard of Visigothic treasures found at Toledo. In the gardens you can visit a replica of the Altamira Caves complete with convincing copies of their prehistoric wall paintings. At no. 60 is the Fundación La Caixa, a superb exhibition space maintained by the Barcelona savings bank (ask at tourist office for details of exhibitions), and finally, at no. 122, is the **Museo Lazaro Galdiano** (Tues–Sun 10am–2pm; €3, students €1.50, Sat free; metro Rubén Darío), the pick of Madrid's smaller museums. This originally private collection, donated to the state by José Galdiano, spreads over the four floors of his former home, its jumble of artworks including paintings by Bosch, Rembrandt, Velázquez, El Greco and Goya.

Not far to the west of here, across the Paseo de la Castellana, is one of the hidden treasures of Madrid, the **Museo Sorolla**, c/General Martínez Campos 37 (Tues–Sat 10am–3pm, Sun 10am–2pm; €2.40, students €1.20, free Sun; metro Rubén Darío/Iglesia), a large collection of work by the painter Joaquín Sorolla (1863–1923), displayed in his old home and studio. The ground floor has been kept largely intact, re-creating the atmosphere of the artist's living and working areas, while upstairs is a gallery displaying a variety of his striking impressionistic work.

Eating and drinking

Madrid is a superb place to eat and, above all, drink: there can be few places in the world which rival the area around **Puerta del Sol** in either quantity or variety of outlets, from bars with spectacular seafood displays to old-time canteens offering cheap three-course *menús del día*, from *haute* Spanish (or French, or Moroccan) cuisine to drinkers' dive bars and traditional *chocolate con churros* cafés. And the feasts continue in all directions, especially towards **Plaza Santa Ana** and along **c/de las Huertas** to Atocha, but also south in the neighbourhood haunts of **La Latina** and **Lavapiés**, and north in the gary *barrio* **Chueca** and the grungier district **Malasaña**.

In summer, all areas of the city spring forth *terrazas* – pavement café/bars – where coffees are taken by day and drinks pretty much all night. The prime area is **Paseo Castellana**, where many of the top discos encamp (and charge accordingly). Smaller scenes are in Plaza de **Chueca**, Paseo **Rosales** del Pintor along the Parque del Oeste, the more relaxed and pleasant **c/Argumosa** in Lavapies/Atocha, **Puerta de Moros** in La Latina and **Las Vistillas**, on the south side of the viaduct on c/Bailén, due south of the royal palace.

Tapas bars

El Abuelo, c/Nuñez de Arce 5, Huertas. Excellent selection of tapas and *raciones*. Another branch on c/de la Victoria is a stand-up bar serving just 4 delicious prawn dishes.

Casa Alberto, c/de las Huertas 18. One of the most traditional Huertas bars: very friendly, lots of tables and huge portions. Also a restaurant at the back.

Almendro 13, c/del Almendro 13. Fashionable wood-panelled bar that serves great *fino* and innovative tapas.

El Anciano Rey de los Vinos, c/Bailén. Wine and sherry in the traditional manner straight from the barrel.

Las Bravas, c/Espoz y Mina, Huertas. The original premises of this Madrid insitution which now has branches throughout the city; sample their famous *patatas bravas* standing at the bar under glaring neon lights.

Café Comercial, Glorieta de Bilbao. Traditional café and meeting place to linger over coffee, *coñac* and cakes.

Café Gijón, Paseo de Recoletos 21, north of Plaza de Cibeles. Traditional nineteenth-century café, tremendously atmospheric. Lunchtime *menú* and pricey summer terrace.

La Mallorquina, c/Mayor, right on Puerta del Sol. Good for breakfast or snacks – try one of their *napolitanas* (filled croissants).

Mejillonera El Pasaje, Pasaje Matheu, off c/Vitoria, near Sol. One of many places filling this narrow street with outdoor tables – this one specializes in mussels served in every way conceivable.

Café Melo's, c/Ave María 44. Excellent-value Galician place serving huge portions. A Lavapiés institution.

Museo del Jamón, Carrera San Jerónimo 6, Puerta del Sol end. Extraordinary place where hundreds of hams hang from the ceiling, and you can sample the different (expensive) varieties over a glass or two; also has full meals and the best breakfast deal in town for €1.50. Numerous branches.

Café de Oriente, Plaza de Oriente. Rich kids' haunt with expensive food, but a lovely old café with a small summer *terraza* looking over to the Palacio Real.

Casa Rúa, c/Ciudad Rodrigo 3, just off Plaza Mayor. Stand-up seafood tapas bar, popular with a young crowd.

Viña P, Plaza de Santa Ana 3. Friendly bar, decked out in bullfighting mementos, serving a great range of tapas.

Mainly-for-drinking bars

Cervecería Alemána, Plaza Santa Ana. One of Hemingway's favourite haunts and consequently full of Americans; good traditional atmosphere none the less.

Bodega Ángel Sierra, Plaza Chueca. Great old bar right on the square, just the place for an apéritif.

Casa Antonio, c/de Latoneros near the Plaza Mayor. Specializing in sherries and fine wines, a great place for an apéritif.

Los Gabrieles, c/Echegaray 17. One of the most spectacular tiled bars in Madrid, with fabulous nineteenth-century drinking scenes on the glazed ceramic tileworks (or *azulejos*), including a great version of Velázquez's *Los Borrachos* (The Drunkards).

La Luna, Amor de Diós 13, off Huertas. A perennially popular dive. Daily from 10pm till late.

Star's Dance Café, c/Marqués de Valdeiglesias 5. Hip, happening gay/mixed bar with funky basement grooves at weekends. Closed Sun.

La Venencia, c/Echegaray 7. Marvellous old wooden bar, serving only sherry and the most basic of tapas – cheese and pressed tuna. A must.

Viva Madrid, c/Manuel Gonzalez. More splendid tiles and a young, lively crowd. Quite pricey.

O'Neill's Irish Pub, c/Principe 12. Typical Irish pub serving pub grub. One of a number springing up around the city.

Restaurants

Artemisa, c/Ventura de la Vega 4. Decent low-priced vegetarian restaurant.

Casa Alberto, c/Huertas 18. Small traditional taberna where you can eat at the bar or a small dining room at the back.

Casa Ciriaco, c/Mayor 84. Good, traditional restaurant, not too expensive for the area.

Casa Eduardo, Cava San Miguel, next to the market behind Plaza Mayor. Outdoor tables, Galician specialties and very cheap set *menú*.

Champagnería Gala, c/Moratin 22. Excellent value *menú* in this colourful paella restaurant with a lovely conservatory patio at the back.

Creperie Ma Bretagne, c/San Vicente Ferrer. Tiny place with good pancakes, open until after midnight.

El Estragón, Plaza de la Paja 10. Good vegetarian tapas and an economical *menú del día* in an attractive plaza.

Elqui, c/Buenavista 18. One of Madrid's best vegetarian restaurants. Self-service with excellent lunchtime *menú*.

La Farfala, c/Santa María 17. Relaxed, inexpensive place for Argentinian pizzas and grilled steaks. Open daily 10pm–3am.

Fernández, c/Palma 6. Simple, inexpensive restaurant, always packed with locals and adventurous low-budget travellers.

El Gambón, c/Barbieri 1, Chueca. Excellent African food: more expensive than many of its neighbours, but worth it.

Gula Gula, c/Infante 5 and Gran Vía 1. Extremely popular and very kitsch restaurants with unbeatable vegetarian salad bar. The Gran Vía branch is very popular for hen nights.

Casa Mingo, Paseo de la Florida, next to chapel of San Antonio de la Florida. Asturian place where you eat roast chicken washed down with cider. Good value and great fun, especially on Sunday afternoons.

Mushashi, c/Conchas 4. Taking advantage of Madrid's role as the second biggest fish market in the world, this basic, friendly restaurant serves very tasty sushi at reasonable prices.

Sabatini, c/Bailén 15, opposite Jardines Sabatini. Outdoor tables looking towards the Palacio Real in summer; the food's significantly less expensive than you might expect.

La Trucha, c/Manuel Fernández y González, between Echegaray and c/del Principe, Huertas. Not the cheapest, but good meals in a very Madrileño atmosphere.

Viuda de Vacas, c/Cava Alta 23. Good value no-frills Castilian restaurant in an area packed with great bars.

Nightlife

The **bars, clubs and discos** of **Malasaña**, and **Huertas** around Plaza Santa Ana or a little further south in **Lavapiés**, could easily occupy your whole stay in Madrid, with the many clubs starting around 1am and staying open until well beyond dawn. The names and styles change constantly but even where a place has closed down a new alternative usually opens up at the same address. To supplement our listings, check out the English-language magazine *En Madrid*, or the quarterly *Madrid Concept* for *terrazas* (open-air terrace bars), *bares de noche* (nightclubs), *discotecas* and *actuaciones* (where you'll often find live music).

Music concerts – classical, flamenco, salsa, jazz and rock – are advertised on posters around Sol and are also listed in the *Guia del Ocio* and in the newspaper *El Pais*. In July and especially in August there's not too much happening inside, but the city council sponsors a "Veranos de la Villa" programme of concerts and free cinema in some attractive outside venues. If you find that you've somehow stayed out all night and feel in need of early morning sustenance, a final station on the clubbers' circuit is to take *chocolate con churros* at the *Chocolatería San Gines* (Tues–Sun 10am–7pm) on c/de Coloreros, just off c/Mayor.

Discos, music bars and clubs

Discos and music bars can be found all over the city. Of the big **nightclubs**, *Pacha*, c/Barcelo 11, is the eternal survivor – it's exceptionally cool during the week, less so at weekends when the out-of-towners take over. Other good clubs include *El Sol* on c/Jardines 3 (metro Gran Vía) for house, soul and acid jazz, plus live music; *Torero* on c/de la Cruz 26 (near Huertas, metro Sevilla; no trainers) for house/Latino; *Kathmandú*, c/Señores de Luzón 3 (metro Sol), for funk and acid jazz; *La Via Lactea*, c/Velarde 18 (Malasaña, metro Tribunal), for indie and grunge; *Soma* c/Leganitos 25 (metro Plaza España), for Goa trance; and *Morocco*, c/Marqués de Leganes 7 (metro Santo Domingo), for funk and disco.

For diving in and out of clubs, however, as Madrileños like to do, the student area of **Malasaña**, focused around Plaza Dos de Mayo, holds most promise and the music in the clubs is more of a grunge scene. A key street to start off explorations is c/San Vicente Ferrer, where *Maravillas* at no. 35 sometimes has live music, while *La Habana* at Atocha no. 107 has a great mix of salsa and reggae. For more of a chance to talk, try *Café Manuela* on c/San Vicente Ferrer, or the pubs in the Plaza Dos de Mayo: *El Arco–Café Mahon, El Sol de Mayo* and *Pepe Botella*. **Chueca** is more exclusively (but not entirely) **gay** – c/Pelayo is a good point to start from, with the quarter's most eclectic bar, *Torito*, at no. 4 and several gay bars, including *New Leather* at no. 42 and *LL* at no. 11. Finally, the-up-and coming **Lavapiés/Anton Martín** area, south of Sol, is a popular bar and club locale: try *La Ventura* at c/Olmo 31 for some of Madrid's top *electronica* DJs or *Kappa* on c/del Olmo 26 which attracts a mixed crowd in stylish atmosphere.

Live music

The music scene in Madrid, sets the pattern for the rest of the country, and the best rock **bands** either come from Madrid or make their name here. For young local groups try *Al Lab'oratorio*, c/Colón 14. Bigger rock concerts are usually held in one of the football stadiums or at *La Riviera* on Paseo Bajo de la Virgen del Puerto. A good array of **jazz bars** includes the topnotch *Café Central*, Plaza del Ángel 10, near Sol, *Clamores* in c/Albuquerque 14, and *Populart* at c/de las Huertas 22. **South American** music is on offer at various venues, especially during summer festivals; the best year-round club is the *Café del Mercado* in the Mercado Puerta de Toledo, which puts on live salsa more or less every night. **Flamenco** can also be heard at its best in the summer festivals, especially at the *noches de flamenco* in the beautiful courtyard of the old barracks on c/de Conde Duque. Promising year-round venues include *Caracol*, c/Bernardino Obregón 18; *Café de Chinitas*, c/Torija 7; *La Soleá*, Cava Baja 34; *Casa Patas*, Cañizares 10; and Wednesdays at *Suristán*, c/de la Cruz 7, which is the place to head for modern flamenco and live performances of all types of **world music** most nights.

Film and theatre

Cinema-going is a huge pastime in Madrid, reflected in the queues outside the huge-capacity cinemas on Gran Vía. The Spanish routinely dub foreign movies, but a few cinemas specialize in original-language screenings. These include the Alphaville, Renoir and Lumière at c/Martín de los Heros 14 and 12, near Plaza de España, the tiny California at c/Andrés Mellado 47 (metro Moncloa) and the six-screen Multicinés Ideal at c/Doctor Cortezo 6, near

Sol. A programme of classic films is shown at the lovely Art-Deco Filmoteca at c/Santa Isabel 3, which has a pleasant bar and, in summer, an outdoor *cine-terraza*.

Classical Spanish **theatre** performances can be seen at the Teatro Español, Plaza Santa Ana, and more modern works in the Centro Cultural de la Villa, Plaza de Colón, and in the beautiful Círculo de Bellas Artes, Marqués de Casa Riera 2. Cultural events in English are held from time to time at the **British Institute**, c/Almagro 5 (☎91 337 3500; metro Alonso Martínez), which can also be a useful point for contacts.

Listings

Airlines Almost all have their offices along the Gran Vía, on c/de la Princesa, its continuation beyond the Plaza de España, or in the Torre de Madrid on the Plaza. Exceptions are Iberia, c/Goya 29 (☎91 587 8100), British Airways, c/Serrano 60 5° (☎91 577 6959), EasyJet (☎902 29 9992), and Virgin Express (☎91 662 5261).

American Express Plaza de las Cortes 2 (Mon–Fri 9am–5.30pm, Sat 9am–noon; helpline ☎91 572 0303).

Books There's a good stock of English titles at Booksellers S.A., c/José Abascal 48 (metro Iglesias or Ríos Rosas) and a larger selection at Fnac on c/Preciados 28 and the Casa del Libro on Gran Vía 29.

Bullfights Madrid's Plaza de Toros – Las Ventas – hosts some of the year's most prestigious events, especially during the May/June San Isidro festivities. Tickets are available at the box office (except for big events) from around €11.80.

Car rental Atesa (☎902 100 101), Budget (☎901 20 1212), Europcar (☎90 210 5030), Hertz (☎91 372 9300) and Auto Chamartín (☎91 405 45 99) all have offices at the airport and/or the main train stations.

Embassies Australia, Plaza Descubridor Diego de Ordás 3 (☎91 441 900); Britain, Fernando el Santo 16 (☎91 700 8200); Canada, Nuñez de Balboa 35 (☎91 431 4558); Ireland, Paseo de la Castellana 46 (☎91 577 1787); New Zealand, Plaza de la Lealtad 2 (☎91 523 0226); USA, c/Serrano 75 (☎91 577 4000).

Exchange Round the clock at the airport. Branches of El Corte Inglés department store all have exchange offices with long hours and highly competitive rates and commissions. Banco Central for American Express travellers' cheques.

Football Real Madrid's colossal Estadio Santiago Bernebeu (metro Bernebeu) allows access to the glittering trophy room for €3 on non-match days and is well worth the trip if only to see the European Cup. Atletico Madrid's Estadio Vicente Calderon (metro Piramides) is smaller but easier on the eye. Access is free on non-match days. Both stadia boast a host of attractions including shops, gymnasia and bars.

Hospitals El Clínico, Plaza de Cristo Rey (☎91 330 3747); Ciudad Sanitaria La Paz, Avenida Castillana #261. For an ambulance, call ☎061 or ☎112 (emergencies).

Internet access Amiweb Cyber, Gran Vía 80 (Mon–Sun 10/11am–12pm, €1.50/hr); Cellnet Mundo, c/Mayor 4 (Mon–Sun 10.30am–8.30/9.30pm, €1.50/hr).

Laundry c/Barco 26 (metro Gran Vía); c/Donoso Cortés 17 (metro Quevedo); c/Hermosilla 121 (metro Goya); c/Jerónima Llornte 47 (metro Estrecha).

Lost/stolen credit cards Visa & Mastercard (☎91 362 6200); Amex (☎91 572 0303).

Left luggage At Estación Sur de Autobuses, c/Méndez Álvaro; Auto-Res; Continental Auto stations; and the airport bus terminal beneath Plaza Colón. Lockers at Atocha and Chamartín stations.

Post office Palacio de Comunicaciones in the Plaza de las Cibeles (Mon–Fri 8.30am–9.30pm, Sat 9.30am–9.30pm, Sun 8.30am–2pm) for stamps, telegrams, poste restante and registered delivery.

Telephones Telefónica, Gran Vía 30 (daily 9am–11.30pm).

Travel agencies Viajes TIVE, c/Fernando el Católico 88 (☎91 543 7412; metro Moncloa), for discount airfares, rail passes and bus tickets; Viajes Zeppelin, Plaza Santo Domingo 2 (metro Santo Domingo; ☎ 91 542 5154), for excellent deals on flights and holidays.

AROUND MADRID

Circling the capital are some of Spain's most fascinating cities, all an easy day-trip from Madrid, or otherwise a convenient stopoff on the main routes out. From Toledo you can turn south to Andalucía or strike west towards Extremadura. To the northwest the roads lead past El Escorial, from where a bus runs to Franco's tomb at El Valle de los Caídos, and through the dramatic scenery of the Sierra de Guadarrama, with Madrid's weekend ski resorts, to

Ávila and Segovia. From Ávila it's just a short way on to Salamanca, or there are beautiful routes down through the Sierra de Gredos into Extremadura. From Segovia the routes north to Valladolid, Burgos and beyond await. To the east there's less of interest, but Alcalá de Henares and Guadalajara can both offer a worthwhile break on the journey into Aragón and Catalunya.

Toledo

Capital of medieval Spain until 1560, **TOLEDO** remains the seat of the Catholic primate and a city redolent of past glories. Set in a desolate landscape, Toledo sits on a rocky mound isolated on three sides by a looping gorge of the Río Tajo (Tagus). Every available inch of this outcrop has been built on: houses, synagogues, churches and mosques are heaped upon one another in a haphazard spiral which the cobbled lanes infiltrate as best they can. Despite the extraordinary number of day-trippers, and the intense summer heat, Toledo is one of the most extravagant of Spanish experiences. The sightseeing crowds are in any case easy enough to avoid; simply slip into the backstreets or stay the night, for by 6pm the tour buses will have all gone home.

Arrival and accommodation

Toledo's train station is some way out on the Paseo de la Rosa, a beautiful twenty-minute walk or a bus ride (#5 or #6) to the central Plaza Zocódover. The **bus station** is on Avenida de Castilla la Mancha in the modern, lower part of the city; buses run frequently to the same Plaza. Buses to Toledo run from Madrid's Estación del Sur and cost €3.60 one way. The last bus to Madrid leaves Toledo at 10pm. The main **tourist office** (Mon–Sat 9am–6/7pm, Sun 9am–3pm; ☎925 22 08 43), outside the walls opposite the Puerta de Bisagra, has full lists of places to stay, maps, and an information board outside; there's also a useful office in the Plaza Ayuntamiento (Mon–Fri 10.30am–2.30pm & 4.30–7pm, closed Mon afternoon).

If your first concern is **accommodation**, head directly for the old town. In summer rooms can be very hard to find, so it's worth arriving early; you may be picked up by a guide who'll earn commission for taking you to a particular place but should at least know where there's space. Among the more central cheap establishments are *Pensión Lumbreras*, Juan Labrador 9 (☎925 22 15 71; ②); *Pension Segovia*, Recoletos 2 (☎925 21 1124; ③); and the *Hostal las Armas* on the corner of Plaza Zocódover at c/Armas 7 (☎925 22 1668; ②; closed Nov–March). Moving up a notch, you could try the comfortable new *Hostal Madrid*, c/Marqués de Mendigorría 14 (☎925 22 1114; ②), or the *Hostal Nuevo Labrador* at Juan Labrador 10 (☎925 22 2620; ③). The **hostel** is on the outskirts of town in a wing of the Castillo San Servando (☎925 22 4554; ②). The nearest **campsite**, *El Circo Romano* (☎925 22 0442), is a ten-minute walk from the Puerta de Bisagra along Avda. Carlos III, and enjoys great views of the city.

The City

Right at the heart of the city sits the **Cathedral** (daily 10.30am–noon & 4–6/7pm; €4.80 museum 10.30am–6pm Sun 2–6pm). A robust Gothic construction which took over 250 years (1227–1493) to complete, its rich internal decoration includes masterpieces of the Gothic, Renaissance and Baroque periods. The exterior is best appreciated from outside the city, from where the hundred-metre spire and the weighty buttressing can be seen to advantage. The main entrance is at present through the **Puerta Llana** on the southern side of the main body of the cathedral, opposite the ticket office. At the heart of the church, blocking the nave, is the Choir, or **Coro** (closed Sun morning), with two tiers of magnificently carved wooden stalls. Directly opposite stands the gargantuan altarpiece of the **Capilla Mayor**, one of the triumphs of Gothic art, overflowing with intricate detail; it contains a synopsis of the entire New Testament, culminating in a Calvary at the summit. Directly behind the main altar is perhaps the most extraordinary piece of fantasy in the cathedral, the **Transparente**. Wonderfully

Baroque, with marble cherubs sitting on fluffy marble clouds, it's especially magnificent when the sun reaches through the hole punched in the roof specifically for that purpose. Over twenty chapels are dotted around the walls, all of them of interest. In the **Capilla Mozárabe** Mass is still celebrated daily according to the ancient Visigothic rites; if you want to look inside, get there at 9.30am, when the Mass is celebrated. You should also see the Capilla de San Juan, housing the riches of the cathedral **Treasury**; the **Sacristía**, with the cathedral's finest paintings, including works by El Greco, Velázquez and Goya; and the **New Museums**, with more work from El Greco, who was born in Crete but settled in Toledo in about 1577.

Toledo is physically dominated by the bluff, imposing **Alcázar** (Tues–Sun 9.30am–2.30pm; €1.20), to the east of the cathedral. There has probably always been a **fortress** in this commanding location, though it has been burned and bombarded so often that almost nothing is original. The most recent destruction was in 1936, during one of the most symbolic episodes of the Civil War, when some six hundred barricaded Nationalists held out for over two months against everything the Republicans could throw at them, until finally relieved by one of Franco's armies. Franco's regime completely rebuilt the fortress as a monument to the glorification of its defenders.

An excellent collection of El Grecos can be seen to the north of here in the **Museo de Santa Cruz** (Tues–Sat 10am–6.30pm, Sun 10am–2pm; €1.20, free Sat pm and Sunday am), a superlative Renaissance building which also boasts outstanding works by Goya and Ribera, a huge collection of ancient carpets and faded tapestries, sculpture and a small archeological collection. The **Museo de Arte Visigótico** (Tues–Sat 10am–2pm & 4–6.30pm, Sun 10am–2pm; €0.60), in the Mudéjar church of **San Román**, a short way northwest of the cathedral, is also well worth a visit. The building, a delightful combination of Moorish and Christian elements, perhaps even outshines the Visigothic jewellery and other artefacts contained within.

The masterpiece of El Greco, *The Burial of the Count of Orgaz*, is housed in an annexe to the nearby church of **Santo Tomé** (daily 10am–5.45/6.45pm; €1.20). From Santo Tomé the c/de San Juan de Dios leads down to the old Jewish quarter and to the **Casa del Greco** (Tues–Sat 10am–2pm & 4–6pm, Sun 10am–2pm; €2.40, free Sat pm and Sun am), which wasn't where the artist actually lived, but is a construction of a typical Toledan home of the period. Although the house is presently under restoration, you can still see many of his paintings as well as other works of art from the fifteenth to seventeenth centuries. Almost next door, on c/Reyes Católicos, is the synagogue of **El Tránsito**, built along Moorish lines by Samuel Levi in 1366. Nowadays it houses a small **Sephardic Museum** (Tues–Sat 10am–2pm & 4–6pm, Sun 10am–2pm; €2.40, free Sat pm and Sun am), tracing the distinct traditions and development of Jewish culture in Spain. The only other surviving synagogue, **Santa María la Blanca** (10am–2pm & 3.30–6/7pm; €1.20), is a short way down the same street. Like El Tránsito, which it predates by over a century, it has been both church and synagogue, though it looks more like a mosque.

Continuing down c/Reyes Católicos, you come to the superb church of **San Juan de los Reyes** (daily 10am–1.45pm & 3.30–5.45/6.45pm; €1.20), with its magnificent double-storey cloister. If you leave the city here by the **Puerta de Cambrón** you can follow the Paseo de Recaredo, which runs alongside a stretch of Moorish walls towards the **Hospital de Tavera** (10am–1.30pm & 3.30–6pm; €3), a Renaissance palace with beautiful twin patios, which houses a number of fine paintings. Heading back to town, you can pass through the main city gate, the **Nueva Puerta de Bisagra**, marooned in a constant swirl of traffic. The main road bears to the left, but on foot you can climb towards the centre of town by a series of stepped alleyways, past the intriguing Mudéjar church of **Santiago del Arrabal** and the tiny mosque of **Santo Cristo de la Luz**. Built in the tenth century on the foundations of a Visigothic church, this is one of the oldest Moorish monuments surviving in Spain. Only the nave, however, with its nine different cupolas, is the original Arab construction.

Eating, drinking and entertainment

Food is relatively expensive and not always very good quality in Toledo, but at least it's easy to find. *La Bisagra*, c/Arrabal 14, just uphill from the Puerta Bisagra, and *Arrabal*, opposite, are touristy but reasonably priced; similar tourist places surround the Plaza Magdalena, southwest of Zocódover. One of the best here is *Bar Ludeña* at Plaza Magdalena 10, with a cheap set *menú* and the local speciality, *carcamusa* (a meat stew in spicy tomato sauce). Northeast from Zocódover, c/Santa Fe has several outdoor cafés popular with young people in the evenings, including *Yogui's*. Less obvious places, all with good-value lunchtime *menús*, include the well-hidden *Posada del Estudiante*, c/de San Pedro 2 behind the cathedral; *Restaurante Palacios*, c/Alfonso X El Sabio 3; *Bar Mesón El Greco* on c/de Bodegones 10; and *Bar La Ria*, a fish restaurant and *sidrería*, also on c/de Bodegones. At night there's not a whole lot of action, but there are a couple of late **bars** worth a look along c/de la Sillería and c/de los Alfileritos: try *La Abadía* which caters for an older crowd. *Broadway Jazz Club* on Plaza Marrón and the popular *Black & Blue* just off c/Santa Fe usually offer **live music**. For **discos**, try the music-bars along c/de Gerardo Lobo or the excellent *Venta de Alma*, housed in an old farmhouse across the Puente de San Martín on the Carretera de Piedrabuena.

El Escorial and El Valle de Los Caídos

Northwest of Madrid extends the line of mountains formed by the Sierra de Guadarrama and the Sierra de Gredos, snowcapped and forbidding even in summer. Beyond them lie Ávila and Segovia, but on the near side, in the foothills of the Guadarrama, are **SAN LORENZO DEL ESCORIAL**, a pretty village, although a little hard on the legs, and the bleak monastery of **El Escorial** (Real Monasterio del Escorial; Tues–Sun 10am–5/6pm; €6, Wed free for EU citizens). Enormous and overbearing, its severe grandeur can be impressive, but all too often it's just depressing. Planned by Philip II as a monastery and mausoleum, it was the centre of his web of letters, a place from which he boasted he could "rule the world with two inches of paper".

Visits used to be deeply regulated, with guided tours to each section, but recently they've become more relaxed and you can use your ticket to enter, in whatever sequence you like, the basilica, sacristy, chapter houses, library and royal apartments. The outlying **Casita del Príncipe** (aka de Abajo) and **Casita del Infante** (aka de Arriba) charge separate admission. To avoid the worst of the crowds don't come on a Wednesday, and try visiting just before lunch, or pick that time for the royal apartments, which are the focus of all the bus tours. A good starting place is the **west gateway**, facing the mountains, and through the traditional main entrance. It leads into the **Patio de los Reyes**, where to the left is a school, to the right the monastery, both of them still in use, and straight ahead the **church**. In here, notice above all the flat vault of the *coro* above your head as you enter, apparently entirely without support, and the white marble Christ carved by Benvenuto Cellini. This is one of the few things permanently illuminated in the cold, dark interior, but put some money in the slot to light up the main altarpiece and the whole aspect of the church is brightened.

Back outside and around to the left are the **Sacristía** and the **Salas Capitulares** (Chapterhouses) which contain many of the monastery's religious treasures, including paintings by Titian, Velázquez and Ribera. Beside the sacristy a staircase leads down to the **Panteón de los Reyes**, the final resting place of virtually all Spanish monarchs since Charles V. Just above the entry is the *Pudrería*, a separate room in which the bodies rot for twenty years or so before the cleaned-up skeletons are moved. Their many children are laid in the **Panteón de los Infantes**. Nearby are the **Library**, with probably the most valuable collection of books in Spain, and the so-called **New Museums**, where much of the Escorial's art collection – works by Bosch, Gerard David, Dürer, Titian, Zurbarán and many others – is kept in an elegant suite of rooms.

Finally, there's the **Palace** itself, including the spartan quarters inhabited by Philip II. Later, less ascetic monarchs enlarged and richly decorated the palace apartments, but Philip's simple rooms, with the chair that supported his gouty leg and the deathbed from which he could look down into the church where Mass was constantly celebrated, remain the most fascinating. Adding a splash of colour and considerably less morose than the rest of the complex is the **Jardín de los Frailes** (same hours) which offers spectacular views of the surrounding countryside.

Nine kilometres north of El Escorial is **El Valle de los Caídos** (The Valley of the Fallen; Tues–Sun: April–Sept 9.30am–7pm; Oct–March 10am–6pm; €4.40, free Wed for EU citizens). This is an equally megalomaniacal yet far more chilling monument than El Escorial: an underground basilica hewn under Franco's orders, allegedly as a monument to the Civil War dead of both sides, though in reality it's a memorial to the *Generalísimo* and his regime. The dictator himself lies buried behind the high altar, while the only other named tomb is that of his guru, the Falangist leader José Antonio Primo de Rivera, who was shot dead by Republicans at the beginning of the war. The "other side" is present only in the fact that the complex was built by the Republican army's survivors – political prisoners on quarrying duty. Above the complex is a vast **cross**, reputedly the largest in the world, and visible for miles around. From the entrance to the basilica a shaky **funicular** (Tues–Sun: April–Sept 11am–1.30pm & 4–6.30pm; Oct–March 11am–1.30pm & 3–5.30pm; €2.10) ascends to its base, offering superlative views over the Sierra de Guadarrama and of the giant, grotesque figures propping up the cross. (Closed at the time of writing.)

Practicalities

Trains run all day every day from Madrid to El Escorial, though **buses** (every 30–60min, €2.60) are faster, slightly cheaper and take you right to the monastery. If you arrive by train get immediately on the local bus (€0.90) which shuttles up to the centre of town; it leaves promptly and it's a long uphill walk if you miss it. From El Escorial the local bus run by Herranz makes the **day-trip** from the bus station to El Valle de los Caídos (Tues–Sun; departs 3.15pm returns 5.30pm; €7 including entry).

Though usually visited on a day-trip, El Escorial does offer **accommodation**, which is useful if you're making a trip to El Valle de los Caídos; cheap *hostales* include *Pensión El Retiro*, c/Aulencia 24 (☎91 890 0946; ②) and *Hostal Vasco*, Plaza Santiago (☎91 890 16 19; ②). There's also a **campsite** (☎91 890 2412) 2km out on the road to Segovia and a **youth hostel** (☎91 890 5924; ②), usually crowded with school groups, at c/Residencia 14.

Eating is expensive everywhere, but try the bar just inside the gate. Otherwise, there are several inexpensive eateries along c/Juan de Toledo, off Plaza Virgen de Gracia, and up the hill on c/Pozas. The **tourist office** is near the monastery at c/Grimaldi 2 (Mon–Thurs 11am–6pm, Fri–Sun 10am–7pm; ☎91 890 5313).

Ávila

Two things distinguish **ÁVILA**: its medieval walls and Saint Teresa, who was born here and whose spirit still dominates the city. It's the **walls** (daily 10am–6pm; €1.20; access from steps just inside Puerta del Alcázar) which first impress, especially if you approach the city with the evening sun highlighting their golden tone and the details of the 88 towers around the ramparts. Modern life takes place almost exclusively in the new developments outside the fortifications, but restoration is slowly bringing life back to the old town.

The legacy of **Santa Teresa**, who was born here to a noble family in 1515, is expressed in the many convents and churches with which she was associated. By the age of seven she was already deeply religious, running away with her brother in the hope of being martyred by the Moors. The spot where they were recaptured and brought back, **Los Cuatro Postes**, 1.5km along the Salamanca road, is a fine vantage point from which to admire the walls. She went on to reform the Carmelite order, found many convents of her own and become one of the most important figures of the Counter-Reformation. Perhaps the most interesting of the monuments associated with the saint is the **Convento de San José** (daily 9am–1pm & 3.30–7.30pm; €0.60), the first one she founded, in 1562. Its **museum** contains relics and memorabilia, including assorted personal possessions and the coffin in which she once slept. The **Convento de Santa Teresa**, or Casa Natal (daily 9am–1pm & 3.30–7.30pm; free), built over the saint's birthplace, is less interesting, although the reliquary beside the gift shop contains not only her rosary beads, but one of the fingers she used to count them with. The third major point of pilgrimage is the **Monasterio de la Encarnación** (daily 9.30am–1.30pm & 3.30/4–6/7pm; €1.20), where she spent 27 years as a nun. The rooms are labelled with the various things she did in each of them, and everything she touched and looked at or could have used is on display.

The most beautiful churches in Ávila – the cathedral, San Vicente and the convent of Santo Tomás – are less directly associated with its most famous resident. The **Cathedral** (Mon–Fri 10am–1.30pm & 3.30–5.30pm, Sat & Sun 12–5pm; €1.80) was started in the twelfth century but has never been finished; the earliest parts were as much fortress as church, and the apse forms an integral part of the city walls. Inside, the succeeding changes of style are immediately apparent: the old parts are Romanesque in design and made of a strange red-and-white mottled stone, but then there's an abrupt break and the rest of the main structure is pure white and Gothic. The basilica of **San Vicente** (daily 10am–1.30pm & 4–6.30pm; €1.20) displays a similar mixture of styles: its twelfth-century doorways, and the portico that protects them, are magnificent examples of Romanesque art, while the church itself reflects later trends. St Vincent was martyred here, and his tomb depicts a series of gruesome deaths.

El Real Monasterio de Santo Tomás (daily 10am–1pm & 4–7/8pm; cloisters €0.60, museum €1.20, closed mid-Oct to 25 Dec and 1–6 Feb) is a Dominican monastery founded in 1482, but greatly expanded over the following decade by Ferdinand and Isabella, whose summer palace it became. On every surface is carved the yoke-and-arrows motif of the Reyes Católicos, surrounded by pomegranates, symbol of the newly conquered kingdom of Granada. Inside are three exceptional cloisters, the largest of which contains an **Oriental collection**, an incongruous display accumulated by the monks over centuries of missionary work in the Orient. In the **Church** is the elaborate tomb of Prince Juan, Ferdinand and Isabella's only son, whose early death opened the way for Charles V's succession. Notorious inquisitor Torquemada is buried in the sacristy. Santo Tomás is quite a walk (downhill) from the south part of town – you can get back up by the #1 bus, whose circular route takes in much of the old city.

Practicalities

Up to seventeen **trains** make the journey each day from Madrid via El Escorial to Ávila, with onward connections to Salamanca, León and Valladolid. The **train station** is at the bottom of Avda. José Antonio, to the east below the new part of town. **Buses** to and from Madrid and Segovia use a terminal on the Avda. de Madrid. The **tourist office** (daily 9/10am–2pm & 4/5–7pm; ☎920 21 13 87, *www.avila.net*) is in the Plaza de la Catedral, directly opposite the cathedral entrance.

Cheap rooms are easy enough to come by, though many of them are around the train station or at the end of Avda. José Antonio, which is neither the most central nor most pleasant place to be based. Nearer the centre, *Pension Santa Ana*, c/Alfonso de Montalvo 2 (☎920 22 00 63; ②), is a good-value place near the church of the same name. Within the walls, places are likely to be more expensive, but the *Hostal Continental* at Plaza de la Catedral 4 (☎920 21 15 02; ③) and *Hostal el Rastro* at Plaza del Rastro 1 (☎920 21 12 18; ③) are pleasant and not too exorbitant. *Hostal Bellas*, c/Caballeros 19 (☎920 21 29 10; ⑤), is excellent value, especially out of season.

For cheap **meals** you're best off in the heart of the old town around the unfinished Plaza de la Victoria or, again, down by the train station. Two places off this plaza are *Cafeteria Baviera*, c/Vallespin 10, for a cheap set *menú*, and the *Bar El Rincón*, Plaza Zurraquín 4, for a more expensive but generous three-course deal. The *Cafeteria Maspalomas*, opposite the bus station, offers cheap, simple food. Other places are *Mesón del Rastro*, Plaza del Rastro 1, with a good, reasonably priced restaurant, and *La Posada de la Fruta*, Plaza de Pedro Dávila 8, with an attractive, sunny courtyard to drink in. There are excellent **bars** in c/García Villareal at the western edge of the old town, though c/de Vallespin is the centre of the action at weekends.

Segovia

For such a small city, **SEGOVIA** has a remarkable number of outstanding architectural monuments. Most celebrated are the Roman aqueduct, the cathedral and the fairy-tale Alcázar, but the less obvious attractions – the cluster of ancient churches and the many mansions found in the lanes of the old town, all in a warm, honey-coloured stone – are what really make it worth visiting. In winter, at over 1000m, it can be very cold here.

The **Cathedral** (daily 9am–6.30/7.30pm) was the last major Gothic building in Spain, probably the last anywhere. Accordingly it takes that style to its logical extreme, with pinnacles and flying buttresses tacked on at every conceivable point. Though impressive for its size alone, the interior is surprisingly bare, and spoiled by a great green marble *coro* at its very centre. The treasures are almost all confined to the **museum** which opens off the cloisters (€1.80).

Down beside the cathedral, c/de Daoiz leads past a line of souvenir shops to the church of San Andrés and on to a small park in front of the **Alcázar** (daily 10am–6/7pm; €3, concessions €2.10, free Tues to EU citizens). It's an extraordinary fantasy of a castle which, with its narrow towers and many turrets, looks like something out of Disneyland. And indeed it is a sham – originally built in the fourteenth and fifteenth centuries but almost completely destroyed by a fire in 1862, it was rebuilt as a deliberately hyperbolic parody of the original. Still, it should be visited, if only for the magnificent panoramas from the tower.

The **Aqueduct**, over 800m long and at its highest point towering some 30m above the Plaza de Azoguejo, stands up without a drop of mortar or cement. No one knows exactly when it was built, but it was probably around the end of the first century AD under the emperor Trajan. If you climb the stairs beside the aqueduct you can get a view looking down over it from a surviving fragment of the city walls – though frankly it's more impressive from a distance.

Segovia is an excellent city for walking, with some fine views and beautiful churches to be enjoyed just outside the boundaries. Perhaps the most interesting of all the ancient churches here is **Vera Cruz** (Tues–Sun 10.30am–1.30pm & 3.30–6/7pm; €1.20 closed November), a remarkable twelve-sided building in the valley facing the Alcázar. It was built by the Knights Templar in the early thirteenth century on the pattern of the church of the Holy Sepulchre in Jerusalem, and once housed part of the True Cross. Inside, the nave is circular, its heart occupied by a strange two-storeyed chamber – again twelve-sided – in which the knights, as part of their initiation, stood vigil over the cross. Climb the tower for a highly photogenic vista of the city. While you're over here you could also visit the prodigiously walled **Convento de los Carmelitas** (daily 10am–1.30pm & 4–7/8pm, closed Mon morning; free), with the gaudy mausoleum of its founder-saint, and the rather damp, ramshackle **Monasterio del Parral** (Mon–Sun 10am–11.30am/12.30pm & 4.30–6.30pm; free).

Practicalities

You can get to Segovia by **train** or **bus** (€5.10) from Madrid; there are onward connections by bus to Ávila and Valladolid, and by train to Valladolid. The **train station** is some distance out of town; take any bus (every 15min) marked Puente Hierro/Estación Renfe to the central Plaza Mayor. This main square, right by the cathedral and surrounded by pricey cafés, is the place to start looking for **somewhere to stay**. There are two cheap *fondas* – *Cubo* (☎921 46 03 18; ③) and *Aragón* (☎921 46 09 14; ②) – on different floors of the same building at Plaza

Mayor 4; *Hostal Juan Bravo*, on c/Juan Bravo 12 (☎921 46 34 13; ②), has lots of big comfortable rooms, while there are other cheap possibilities in the streets behind the plaza or near the aqueduct. There's a **youth hostel** (☎921 42 00 27; ②) on Paseo Conde de Sepulveda near the train station and a **campsite**, *Camping Acueducto* (April–Sept), a couple of kilometres out on the road to La Granja.

The **regional tourist office** (Mon–Sat 9am–8pm, Sun 10am–2pm; ☎921 46 29 14) is in the Plaza Azoguejo next to the aqueduct. The Calle de la Infanta Isabella, which opens off the Plaza Mayor beside the **local tourist office** (Mon–Fri 10am 2pm & 5–8pm, Sat 10am–2pm, Sun 10am–2pm; ☎921 46 03 34) is packed with noisy **bars** and cheap **places to eat**. Segovia's culinary speciality is roast suckling pig (*cochinillo asado*) and you'll see the little pink creatures hanging in the windows of restaurants. But it's very expensive unless you're in a large group, and to many tastes overrated. *Mesón del Campesino*, on c/Infanta Isabel 14, is one of the best restaurants, with decent value *menús*. *Mesón de Cándido*, on Plaza del Azonguejo next to the aqueduct, is much more expensive but well worth it, especially for its *cochinillo asado*. Other recommended places include *José María* at c/Cronista Lecea 11, *Santa Bárbara* at c/Ezequiel González 32, *Narízotas* in Plaza de San Martin, and the *Cocina de San Millán* at c/San Millán 3.

EXTREMADURA

The harsh environment of **Extremadura**, west of Madrid, was the cradle of the *conquistadores*, men who opened up a new world for the Spanish Empire. Remote before and forgotten since, Extremadura enjoyed a brief golden age when the heroes returned with their gold to live in a flourish of splendour. **Trujillo**, the birthplace of Pizarro, and **Cáceres** both preserve entire towns built with conquistador wealth, the streets crowded with the ornate mansions of returning empire builders, and there is also **Mérida**, the most completely preserved Roman city in Spain.

Trujillo

TRUJILLO, about three hours' bus ride southeast of the capital, is the first place you're likely to want to stop on the main road from Madrid to Extremadura and Portugal. At its heart – on a rise dominating the surrounding plains – is a walled town virtually untouched since the sixteenth century, redolent above all of the exploits of the conquerors of the Americas; Francisco Pizarro was born here, as were many of his tiny band who defeated the Incas with such extraordinary cruelty.

From the bus station work your way uphill through the narrow streets to the Plaza Mayor, where a statue of the town's most famous son bars the way to the monuments on the hill behind. In the southwest corner is the **Palacio de la Conquista** (closed for lengthy restoration), perhaps the grandest of Trujillo's mansions, and just one of many built by the Pizarro clan. Diagonally opposite is the bulky church of **San Martín** with the tomb, among others, of Francisco de Orellana, the first explorer of the Amazon, and his family. From here you can begin to climb into the walled town – where much restoration work is going on as people move into and do up the old houses – and towards the Moorish castle at its highest point.

From the plaza, c/de Ballesteros leads up to the walls, past the domed **Torre Del Alfiler** with its coats of arms and storks' nests, and through the gateway known as the Arco de Santiago. Here, to the left, is **Santa María Mayor** (daily 10am–2pm & 4–7/8pm; €1.20), the most interesting of the town's many churches. Of the many remaining mansions, or *solares*, the **Palacio de Orellana-Pizarro** (daily 10am–2pm & 4–7/8pm; voluntary contribution) is perhaps the most interesting. The **Castle** itself is now virtually in open countryside; for the last hundred metres of the climb you see nothing but the occasional broken-down remnant of a wall clambered over by sheep and dogs. The fortress, its original Moorish towers much reinforced by later defenders, has recently been restored. Below the castle, the **Casa Museo Pizarro** commemorates the conquistador's life and exploits in Peru, but is a dull, overpriced affair (daily 10am–2pm & 4–7/8pm; €1.20).

Plaza Mayor is the site of the **tourist office** (daily 10am–2pm & 4–7/7.30pm; (☎927 32 26 77, *www.ayto-trujillo.com*) and a couple of **hostales**. *La Cadena* at no. 8 (☎927 32 14 63; ③) and *Nuria* at no. 17 (☎927 32 09 07; ③) offer a degree of luxury while on c/Domingo de Ramos, *Pensión Boni*, at no. 11 (☎927 32 16 04; ②), and Pensión Casa Roque, at no. 30 (☎927 32 23 13; ②), are both clean, well-run budget choices. Just out of town off the road to Cáceres, is another good value upmarket option in the old fashioned *Hostal Restaurante Trujillo*, c/Fco Pizarro 4–6 (☎927 32 22 74, *www.arrakis.es/-hstruji/hostal.htm*; ③). There are plenty of **places to eat** in the Plaza Mayor: perhaps the best value is *La Troya*, with its gargantuan *menús*. The *Pizarro* is a rather more fancy restaurant, while the café/bar *El Escudo* on Plaza Santiago has excellent tapas and *raciones*. Otherwise, for budget-eating, all the *pensiones* along c/General Mola have reasonably priced *menús* on offer – the cheapest being at the *Emilia*.

Cáceres

CÁCERES is in many ways remarkably like Trujillo: its centre is an almost perfectly preserved medieval town adorned with mansions built on the proceeds of American exploration, and every available tower and spire crowned by a clutch of storks' nests. Cáceres has perhaps been over-restored, and it can be very commercial, but on the other hand it's a much larger and livelier place than Trujillo, a rapidly growing provincial capital which is also home to the University of Extremadura.

Even with a map you'll probably get lost among the winding alleys of the old town, so as a preliminary orientation try standing in the Plaza Mayor opposite the tourist office. To your left is the **Torre del Bujaco** – whose foundations date back to Roman times – with a chapel next to it and steps leading up to the low **Arco de la Estrella**, piercing the walls. To the right is the **Torre del Horno**, one of the best-preserved Moorish mud-brick structures surviving in Spain. A staircase leads up to another gateway, and beyond this is the most intact stretch of the ancient walls with several more of the original towers. Though basically Moorish in construction, the walls have been added to, altered and built against ever since. Around the other side of the old town, one Roman gateway, the **Arco del Cristo**, can still be seen.

Inside the walls, almost every building is magnificent – look out in particular for the family crests adorning many of the mansions. Through the Estrella gate, the **Casa de Toledo-Montezuma** with its domed tower is immediately to the left. To this house a follower of Cortés brought back one of the New World's more exotic prizes – a daughter of the Aztec emperor as his bride. Directly ahead is the **Plaza Santa María** with an impressive group of buildings around a refreshingly unencumbered Gothic church. The church of **San Mateo**, on the site of the ancient mosque at the town's highest point, is another Gothic structure with several attractive chapels. In the Casa de las Valetas, on Plaza San Mateo, is the **Museo Provincial** (Tues–Sat 9.30am–2.30pm, Sun 10.15am–2.30pm; €1.80, free to EU citizens), worth visiting as much for the chance to see inside one of the finer mansions as for its well-displayed local collection. Its highlight is the cistern of the original Moorish Alcázar with fine rooms of wonderful horseshoe arches. The same ticket admits you to the **Fine Arts** section in the Casa de los Caballos behind it, where the work is all religious in inspiration; the same building also has two floors dedicated to contemporary art and sculpture, with work by Miró and Picasso as well as younger, up-and-coming artists.

Practicalities

The train station and the **bus station** face each other across the Carretera Sevilla, some way out; bus #1 runs from here (every 15min) to Plaza de San Juan, a square near the centre, with signs leading on towards the Plaza Mayor and the **tourist office** (Mon–Fri 9.30am–2pm & 4–6.30/7.30pm; Sat & Sun 9.30am–2pm; ☎927 24 63 47, *www.turismoextremadura.com*).

The best **places to stay** are all in its immediate vicinity – try the basic, but clean, convenient and friendly *Pensión Carretero* at no. 23 (☎927 24 74 82; ②) or the good-value *Pensión Márquez* (☎927 24 49 60; ②), just off the plaza at c/Gabriel y Galán 2. Right on Plaza Mayor, the cheapest **meals** are served at *El Puchero*, though the food is nothing special; the slightly more expensive *El Pato* is probably worth the extra. *El Figón*, in Plaza San Juan just off c/Pintores, is another step up in class and cost. There are a couple of good areas for **bar-hopping**: try c/de Pizarro, just outside the walls on the west side of the old town, or just north, the Plaza Mayor.

Mérida

Former capital of the Roman province of Lusitania, **MÉRIDA** contains one of the most remarkable assemblages of Roman monuments to be found anywhere: scattered in the midst of the modern city are remains of everything from engineering works to domestic villas. With the aid of a map and a little imagination, it's not hard to reconstruct the Roman city within the not especially attractive modern town. A **combined ticket**, costing €4.80, gains access to all the main sites (daily 9.30am–1.45pm & 4/5–6.15/7.15pm) except the museum.

Start your tour by the magnificent **Puente Romano**, the Roman bridge across the islet-strewn Guadiana – sixty arches long, though seven in the middle were replaced in the fifteenth century. It is defended by an enormous, plain **Alcazaba**, built by the Moors to replace a Roman construction. The interior is a rather barren archeological site, though you can descend into the impressive cistern. Nearby is the sixteenth-century **Plaza de España**, the heart of the modern town, while on c/Romero Leal Sagasta east of here is the so-called **Templo de Diana**, currently the object of an overzealous restoration project. In the other direction you'll find the **Arco Trajano**, an unadorned triumphal arch 15m high and 9m across.

By far the most important site, however, is that containing the **Teatro Romano and Anfiteatro**. The theatre, a present to the city from Agrippa around 15 BC, is one of the best preserved anywhere, and one of the most beautiful monuments of the entire Roman world. The stage is in a particularly good state of repair, while many of the seats have been rebuilt to offer more comfort to the audiences of the annual July season of classical plays. The adjacent amphitheatre is a slightly later and much plainer construction which in its day could accommodate as many as fifteen thousand people – almost half Mérida's population today.

Just across from these buildings is the vast, red-brick bulk of the **Museo Nacional de Arte Romano** (Tues–Sat 10am–2pm & 4/5–6/7pm, Sun 10am–2pm; €2.40, free Sat pm and Sun am), a magnificent museum by the architect Rafael Moneo, which does full justice to its high-class collection, including portrait statues of Augustus, Tiberius and Drusus, and some glorious mosaics. One of two Roman villas in Mérida, the **Casa Romana Anfiteatro** (combined ticket for €2.40) lies immediately below the museum. The other, the **Mitreo**, is situated in the shadow of the Plaza de Toros. Both have good mosaics – especially the Casa Romana. The remaining monuments are further out, near the rail lines. In the midst of vegetable gardens a good portion survives of the **Acueducto de los Milagros**. Its tall arches of granite with brick courses brought water to the city in its earliest days from the reservoir at Proserpina, 5km away.

Practicalities

Mérida is a lively place for its size, and the whole area between the train station and the Plaza de España is full of **bars and restaurants**. Inexpensive food in the town is hard to come by – *Restaurante Briz*, just off the main plaza at Félix Valverde Lillo 5, has about the best-value *menú*, while for tapas, *Casa Benito* at c/San Francisco 3 is atmospheric and friendly. **Budget accommodation** isn't plentiful either. Best bet is the popular *Pensión El Arco*, c/Cervantes 16 (☎924 31 83 21; ②), near the Arco Trajaro. Otherwise *Hostal Nueva España*, Avda. Extremadura 6 (☎924 31 33 56; ②) and *Hostal Salud*, c/Vespasiano 41 (☎924 31 22 59, *hsalud@bluenet.com*; ③) are both good value. There's an all-year **campsite** (☎924 30 34 53) not far out of town towards Lisbon, on the Madrid-Lisbon highway, or a much more attractive site at Proserpina (☎924 12 30 55; May–Sept), some 5km north, where you can swim in the reservoir. The **tourist office** is at the entrance to the Roman theatre site (Mon–Fri 9am–1.45pm & 4/5–6.30/7.30pm, Sat & Sun 9.30am–2pm; ☎924 31 53 53, *www.turismoextramadura.com*) on Paseo José Saenz de Burnaga.

ANDALUCÍA

Above all else – and there is plenty – it is the great Moorish monuments that vie for your attention in **Andalucía**. The Moors, a mixed race of Berbers and Arabs who crossed into Spain from North Africa, occupied al-Andalus for over seven centuries. Their first forces landed at Tarifa in 711 AD and within a decade they had conquered virtually the whole of Spain; their last kingdom, Granada, fell to the Christian Reconquest in 1492. Between these dates they developed the most sophisticated civilization of the Middle Ages, centred in turn on the three major cities of **Córdoba**, **Sevilla** and **Granada**. Each one preserves extraordinarily brilliant and beautiful monuments, of which the most perfect is Granada's **Alhambra palace**.

On the coast it's easy to despair. Extending to either side of **Málaga** is the **Costa del Sol**, Europe's most developed resort area, with its beaches hidden behind a remorseless curtain of concrete hotels and apartment complexes. However, there is life beyond the Costa del Sol, especially the beaches of the Costa de la Luz towards Cádiz on the Atlantic coast, and those around Almería in the southeast corner of Spain.

Inland, and in the cities away from the tourist gaze, this is still an undeveloped, often extremely poor part of the country. For all its poverty, however, Andalucía is also Spain at its most exuberant: the home of flamenco and the bullfight, and other traditional exotic images. These are best absorbed at one of the hundreds of annual **ferias** and **romerías**. The best of them include the giant April Fair in Sevilla, the pilgrimage to El Rocío near Huelva in late May, and the Easter celebrations throughout the region but especially in Málaga and Sevilla. Check out the accurate regularly updated Web site – *www.andalucia.com* – to find out what's going on where.

Córdoba

CÓRDOBA is a minor provincial capital, prosperous in a modest sort of way. Once, however, it was the largest city of Roman Spain, and for three centuries it formed the heart of the great medieval caliphate of the Moors. For visitors, its main attraction comes down to a single building, the **Mezquita** – the grandest and most beautiful mosque ever constructed by the Moors. This stands right in the centre of the city, surrounded by the labyrinthine Jewish and Moorish quarters, and is a building of extraordinary mystical and aesthetic power. The Mezquita apart, Córdoba is an engaging, atmospheric city, easily explored and with some excellent budget accommodation.

Arrival and accommodation
Close to the **train station and bus terminal**, the broad Avda. del Gran Capitán leads down to the old quarters and the Mezquita. Apart from the Málaga service, the buses will be quicker, unless you can afford the surcharge for the fast train to Sevilla.

The **tourist office** at the Palacio de Congresos y Exposiciones at c/Torrijos 10, alongside the Mezquita (Mon–Fri 9.30am–7/8pm, Sat 10am–7/8pm, Sun 10am–2pm; ☎957 47 12 35, *www.ayuncordoba.es*) has free maps to help you negotiate the narrow, wandering streets of the Judería. Watch out for the tiled street signs: elegant as they are, they look exactly the same as the plaques on bars and houses. The best **places to stay** are concentrated in the narrow maze of streets northeast of the Mezquita, many with beautiful tiled courtyards and greenery. One of the most atmospheric is *Hostal Deanes*, at c/

Deanes 6 (☎ 957 29 37 44; ②). Calle Rey Heredia also has some good places, such as *Pension Rey Heredia* at no. 26 (☎957 47 41 82; ②). Less savoury, but likely to have room, are the cheap, run-down *fondas* in the wonderfully ramshackle Plaza de la Corredera: *Hostal Plaza Corredera* (☎957 47 05 81; ②), at the corner of the plaza and c/Rodríguez Marin, is clean and friendly, with great views over the plaza from some rooms. A more upmarket choice is the **hotel** or adjacent *Hostal Maestre*, at c/Romero Barros 4 & 6, both of which are good value, though the hotel is swankier with a pretty central courtyard and original artwork on the walls (☎957 47 24 10; ④, ③). Córdoba's main **campsite,** *Campamento Municipal* (☎957 28 21 65), is located 2km north on the road to Villaviciosa; take bus #10 or #11.

The City

Córdoba's domination of Moorish Spain began thirty years after the conquest, in 756, when the city was placed under **Abd ar-Rahman I**, who established control over all but the north of Spain. It was he who commenced the building of the Great Mosque – **La Mezquita** in Spanish – which was enlarged by **Abd ar-Rahman II** (822–52). In the tenth century **Abd ar-Rahman III** (912–67) re-established order after a period of internal strife and settled Córdoba firmly at the head of a caliphate that took in much of Spain and North Africa. His son **al-Hakam II** virtually doubled the mosque's extent, demolishing the south wall to add fourteen extra rows of columns, and employing Byzantine craftsmen to construct a new *mihrab* (prayer niche); this remains complete and is perhaps the most beautiful example of all Moorish religious architecture. The final enlargement, under the chamberlain-usurper **al-Mansur** (977–1002), involved adding seven rows of columns to the whole east side. This spoiled the symmetry of the mosque, depriving the *mihrab* of its central position, but it meant there was a bay for every day of the year.

The **Mezquita** (Mon–Sat 10am–7.30pm; Sun morning for worship & 2–7.30pm; €6) is approached through the **Patio de los Naranjos**, a classic Islamic court which preserves both its orange trees and the fountains for ritual purification before prayer. Originally all nineteen naves of the mosque were open to this court, so that the rows of interior columns appeared as an extension of the trees. Inside, nearly a thousand twin-layered red and white pillars combine to mesmeric effect, the harmony culminating only at the foot of the exquisite **Mihrab**, incorrectly facing due south and not aligned to Mecca and the focus for prayer.

Originally the whole design of the mosque would have directed worshippers naturally towards the *mihrab*. Today, though, you almost stumble upon it, for in the centre of the mosque squats a vulgar Renaissance **choir**. To the left of the choir stands an earlier and happier Christian addition – the Mudéjar **Capilla de Villaviciosa**, built by Moorish craftsmen in 1371. Beside it are the dome and pillars of the earlier *mihrab*, constructed under Abd ar-Rahman II.

After the Mezquita, the rest of Córdoba can only be anticlimactic, though there are plenty of pleasant strolls to be had. The **river** with its great **Arab waterwheels** and its **bridge** built on Roman foundations is perhaps the most attractive area. Down behind the **Episcopal Palace** you can visit the **Alcázar de los Reyes Cristianos** (Tues–Sat 10am–2pm & 4.30/5.30–6.30/7.30pm, Sun 9.30am–3pm; €1.80, free Fri), a fortified palace built by Ferdinand and Isabella and later occupied by the Inquisition; the gardens are more enjoyable than the interior.

North of the Mezquita lies the **Judería**, Córdoba's old Jewish quarter, a fascinating network of lanes that are more atmospheric and less commercialized than Sevilla's. Near the heart of the quarter, at c/Maimonides 18, is a tiny **synagogue** (Tues–Sat 10.30am–1.30pm & 3.30–5.30pm, Sun 10am–1.30pm; €0.30, free to EU citizens), one of only three in Spain that survived the Jewish expulsion of 1492 – the other two are in Toledo. Nearby is a rather bogus **Zoco** – an Arab *souk* turned into a crafts arcade – and, adjoining this, the small but fabulously kitschy **Museo Municipal Taurino** (Tues–Sat 10am–2pm & 5.30–7.30pm, Sun 9.30am–2.30pm; €3, free Fri).

East of the Judería, the **Museo Arqueológico** (Tues 3–8pm, Wed–Sat 9am–8pm, Sun 9am–3pm; €1.50, EU citizens free) occupies a small Renaissance mansion in which Roman foundations were discovered during conversion: these have been incorporated into an imaginative and enjoyable display. A couple of blocks below, back towards the river, you'll come upon the **Plaza del Potro**, a fine old square named after the colt (*potro*) which adorns its fountain. This, as local guides proudly point out, is mentioned in *Don Quixote*, and indeed Cervantes himself is reputed to have stayed at the inn opposite, the **Mesón del Potro**. On the other side of the square is the **Museo de Bellas Artes** (Tues 3–8pm, Wed–Sat 9am–8pm, Sun 9am–3pm; €1.50, free to EU citizens) with paintings by Ribera, Valdés Leal and Zurbarán.

Eating and drinking

Bars and **restaurants** are on the whole reasonably priced – you need only to avoid the touristy places round the Mezquita. Loads of alternatives can be found not too far away in the Judería and in the old quarters off to the east, above the Paseo de la Ribera: one of the best (and most expensive) in the former is *El Churrasco* at c/Romero 16; more reasonable is *El Extremeño* at Plaza Agrupacíon de Cofradias, just north of the Mesquita. *Taberna Salinas*, c/Tundidores 3 off the Plaza Corredera, is also excellent. The cheapest place to eat is *Bocadi*, Conde Cárdenas, 7, which serves sandwiches from €0.60. For **Internet** access, head for Excalibur Café Internet, at c/Enrique Barrios 9 (daily 11–2am; €1.80/hr) or Enred at c/Sacramento 36 (daily 11am–2pm & 6–10pm; €3/hr).

There's lots of choice for **drinking** and tapas, try *Sociedad Plateros* at c/Deanes 5. The local barrelled **wine** is mainly *Montilla* or *Moriles* – both are magnificent, vaguely resembling mellow, dry sherries. Near the synagogue, *Bodega Guzmán* on c/Judíos 7 is loaded with Andalusian atmosphere, and for a night on the tiles try *Milenium* on c/Alfaros 33. **Flamenco** performances take place at *La Buleria*, c/Pedro López 3, from 10.30pm every night; it costs €1.20 (including one drink) but is poor fare compared to what you can see in Sevilla or Granada.

Sevilla

SEVILLA is the great city of the Spanish south, intensely hot in summer and with an abiding reputation for theatricality and intensity. It has three important monuments – the **Giralda tower**, the **Cathedral** and the **Alcázar** – and an illustrious history, but it's the living self of this city of Carmen, Don Juan and Figaro that remains the great attraction. It is expressed on a phenomenally grand scale at the city's two great festivals – **Semana Santa**, during the week before Easter, and the **April Feria**, which lasts a week at the end of the month. Sevilla is also Spain's second most important centre for **bullfighting**, after Madrid.

Sevilla was the site of the **Expo 92** world fair but, despite all the attendant benefits, it remains poor: petty crime is a big problem, especially in the form of bag-snatching and breaking into cars. On a more positive note, while the architectural legacy and infrastructure from this Expo are not a patch on Sevilla's 1929 effort, the hi-tech new bridges and few remaining pavilions add an upbeat modern dimension to the city. The soul of Sevilla lies in its historic town centre, however, where minarets jostle for space among cupolas and palms, against a latticework of narrow streets, patios and plazas.

Arrival and information

The San Justa **train station** is a fair way out of the centre on Avda. Kansas City, which is also the airport road; buses #70 and #32 connect it to the El Prado de San Sebastián bus station. There is an hourly bus service (6.15am–9.30pm; €2.10) connecting the **airport** to the town. The main **bus station** is at the Plaza de Armas beside the river by the Puente del Cachorro, but buses for destinations within Andalucía (plus Barcelona) leave from the more central terminal at Plaza de San Sebastián. Bus #C4 connects the two terminals. The **tourist office** is at Avda. de la Constitución 21 (Mon–Sat 9am–7pm, Sun 10am–2pm; ☎95 422 14 04, *www.ayunt_sevilla.es*).

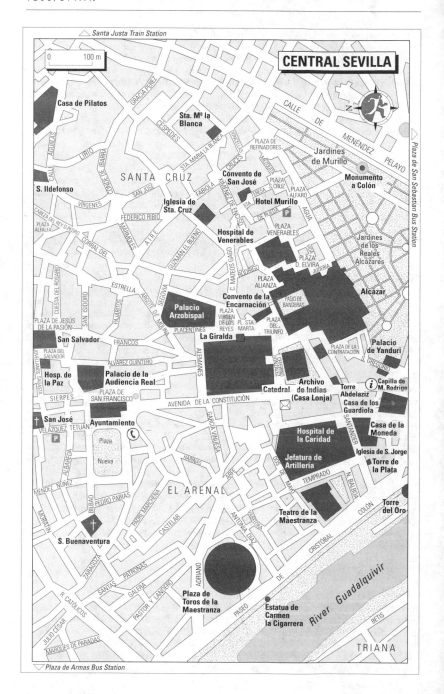

△ Santa Justa Train Station

CENTRAL SEVILLA

0   100 m

Casa de Pilatos

Sta. Mª la Blanca

CALLE   DE   MENÉNDEZ   PELAYO

GRACIA PEREZ

CESPEDES

PLAZA DE REFINADORES

Jardines de Murillo

SANTA CRUZ

S. Ildefonso

Convento de San José

Monumento a Colón

Iglesia de Sta. Cruz

Hotel Murillo

Jardines de los Reales Alcázares

Hospital de Venerables

PLAZA VENERABLES

PLAZA D. ELVIRA

Alcázar

Convento de la Encarnación

PATIO DE BANDERAS

PLAZA ALIANZA

Palacio Arzobispal

PLAZA VIRGEN DE LOS REYES

PL. STA. MARTA

PLAZA DEL TRIUNFO

Palacio de Yanduri

San Salvador

La Giralda

PLAZA DE LA CONTRATACIÓN

Capilla de M. Rodrige

Hosp. de la Paz

Palacio de la Audiencia Real

Archivo de Indias (Casa Lonja)

Catedral

Torre Abdelaziz

Casa de los Guardiola

San José

Ayuntamiento

AVENIDA DE LA CONSTITUCIÓN

Casa de la Moneda

Plaza Nueva

Hospital de la Caridad

Iglesia de S. Jorge

Torre de la Plata

Jefatura de Artillería

EL ARENAL

Teatro de la Maestranza

Torre del Oro

S. Buenaventura

Plaza de Toros de la Maestranza

Estatua de Carmen la Cigarrera

River Guadalquivir

TRIANA

▽ Plaza de Armas Bus Station

Plaza de San Sebastian Bus Station

Accommodation

The most attractive **area to stay** in town is undoubtedly the maze-like **Barrio Santa Cruz**, near the cathedral, although this is generally reflected in the prices you have to pay. Rooms are relatively expensive everywhere, in fact, and almost impossible to find during the big festivals. If you can't find anything in the Barrio, try on its periphery or slightly further out beyond the Plaza Nueva, over towards the river and the Plaza de Armas bus stations. The prices below will double during Easter week and the April fair.

HOSTELS AND HOTELS

Pensión Alcázar, c/Deán Miranda 12 (☎95 422 84 57). Tiny place in a tiny street beside the Alcázar, good value if they have space. ③.

Hostal Buen Dormir, c/Farnesio 8 (☎95 421 74 92). Friendly spot in a street with several possibilities; check the room. ②.

Hostal Bienvenido, c/Archeros 14 (☎95 441 36 55). Another fairly modest place; small rooms but nice roof terrace, with several other likely places nearby. ②.

Hostal Capitol, Zaragoza 66 (☎95 421 24 41). Just off Plaza Nueva – a range of rooms and prices, so look first. ③.

Hostal Goya, c/Mateos Gago 31 (☎95 421 11 70). Bit pricier than some but excellent location with a range of rooms. ③.

Hostal Lis, c/Escarpín 10 (☎95 421 30 88). A good bet just north of Plaza de la Encarnación. ③.

Hostal Monreal, c/Rodrigo Caro 8 (☎95 421 41 66). Plenty of rooms in this very central, newly converted town house. ③.

Hostal Pérez Montilla, Plaza Curtidores 13 (☎95 442 18 54, *amadil2000@hotmail.com*). Comfortable place with many facilities, including air-conditioning. ④.

Hotel Murillo, Lope de Rueda 9 (☎ 95 421 60 95). Wonderful hotel with a lobby stuffed with antiques and oddities, next to the gardens of the Alcázar. ③.

Albergue Juvenil Sevilla, c/Isaac Peral 2 (☎95 461 31 50). Refurbished youth hostel some way out in the university district; can get crowded. Take bus #34 from Puerta de Jerez or Plaza Nueva. ②.

Hotel Simón, c/García de Vinuesa 19 (☎95 422 66 60). Well-restored mansion with excellent position across from the cathedral. Can be a bargain out of season. ⑤.

CAMPSITES

Camping Sevilla (☎95 451 43 79). Right by the airport. Relatively cheap place with a pool. A site bus shuttles in and out daily except Sun from the Avenida Portugal, Plaza de España, or bus #70 will drop you at a petrol station 1km away.

Club de Campo (☎95 472 02 50). About 9km out in Dos Hermanas, a pleasant shady site with a pool. Take one of the half-hourly buses that leave from the Prado de San Sebastián bus station or the train to Utrera; both stop at the village.

The City

Sevilla was one of the earliest **Moorish conquests** (in 712) and, as part of the Caliphate of Córdoba, became the second city of al-Andalus. When the caliphate broke up in the early eleventh century it was the most powerful of the independent states to emerge, and under the Almohad dynasty became the capital of the last real Moorish empire in Spain from 1170 until 1212. The Almohads rebuilt the Alcázar, enlarged the principal **mosque** and erected a new and brilliant minaret – the **Giralda** – topped with four copper spheres that could be seen from miles round. This minaret was used by the Moors both for calling the faithful to prayer and as an observatory, and was so venerated that they wanted to destroy it before the Christian conquest of the city. Instead the Giralda became the bell tower of the Christian **Cathedral**, and continues to dominate the skyline. You can ascend to the bell chamber for a remarkable view of the city and of the Gothic details of the cathedral's buttresses and statuary. But most impressive of all is the tower's inner construction, a series of 35 gentle ramps wide enough to allow two mounted guards to pass.

Originally the mosque was reconsecrated as the cathedral. But in 1402 the cathedral chapter dreamt up plans for a new monument to Christian glory: "a building on so magnificent a scale that posterity will believe we were mad". From the old structure only the Giralda (Mon–Sat 11am–5pm, free Sun; €4.20 including entrance to cathedral) and the mosque's courtyard, the **Patio de los Naranjos**, were spared. The cathedral was completed in just over a century and is the largest Gothic church in the world by cubic capacity. The nave rises to 42m, and even the side chapels seem tall enough to contain an ordinary church while the total area covers 11,520 square metres. In the centre of the church, an impressive choir opens onto the Capilla Mayor, dominated by a vast Gothic **retable** composed of 45 carved scenes from the life of Christ. The lifetime's work of a single craftsman, Pierre Dancart, this is the supreme masterpiece of the cathedral – the largest altarpiece in the world and one of the finest examples of Gothic woodcarving. You can also visit the domed Renaissance **Capilla Real**, built on the site of the original royal burial chapel, the **Sala Capitular**, with paintings by Murillo, and the grandiose **Sacristía Mayor**, which houses the treasury.

Rulers of Sevilla have occupied the site of the **Alcázar** (Tues–Sat 9.30am–6/8pm, Sun 9.30am–2.30/6pm; €4.20) from the time of the Romans. Under the Almohads, the complex was turned into an enormous citadel, forming the heart of the town's fortifications. Parts of the walls survive, but the palace was rebuilt in the Christian period by **Pedro the Cruel** (1350–69), employing workmen from Granada and utilizing fragments of earlier Moorish buildings. His works, some of the best surviving examples of **Mudéjar architecture**, form the nucleus of the Alcázar today. Later additions include a wing in which early expeditions to the Americas were planned, and the huge Renaissance apartments of Charles V. Don't miss the beautiful and rambling **Alcázar gardens**, the confused but enticing product of several eras.

Just ten minutes' walk to the east of the cathedral, the **Plaza de España** and adjoining **María Luisa Park**, laid out in 1929 for an abortive "Fair of the Americas", are an ideal place to spend the middle part of the day. En route you pass by the **Fábrica de Tabacos**, the old tobacco factory that was the setting for Bizet's *Carmen*. Nowadays it's part of the university. Towards the end of the María Luisa Park, the grandest surviving pavilions from the fair (which was scuppered by the Wall Street Crash) have been adapted as museums. The furthest contains the city's **archeology** collections (Tues 3–8pm, Wed–Sat 9am–8pm, Sun 9am–2pm; €1.50, free to EU citizens), and opposite is the **Popular Arts Museum** (Tues 3–8pm, Wed–Sat 9am–8pm, Sun 9am–2.30pm; €1.50, free to EU citizens), with interesting displays relating to the April *feria*.

Down by the **Río Guadalquivir** the main landmark is the twelve-sided **Torre del Oro**, built in 1220 as part of the Alcázar fortifications. The tower later stored the gold brought back to Sevilla from the Americas – hence its name – and now houses a small **naval museum** (Tues–Fri 10am–2pm, Sat–Sun 11am–2pm; €0.60). One block away is the **Hospital de la Caridad** (Mon–Sat 9am–1.30pm & 3.30–6.30pm; €2.40) founded in 1676 by Don Miguel de Manara, the inspiration for Byron's Don Juan, who repented his youthful excesses and set up this hospital for the relief of the dying and destitute. There are some magnificent paintings by Murillo and Valdés Leal inside. There's more art further along at the **Museo de Bellas Artes** on Plaza del Museo (Tues 3–8pm, Wed–Sat 9am–8pm, Sun 9am–2pm; €1.50, free to EU citizens), housed in a beautiful former convent. Outstanding are the paintings by Zurbarán of Carthusian monks at supper and El Greco's portrait of his son.

Triana and La Cartuja

Across the river lies the **Triana** barrio that was once home to the city's gypsy community and is still a lively and atmospheric place. At Triana's northern edge lies **La Cartuja** (Tues–Sat 10am–8pm, Sun 10am–3pm; €1.80, free Tues for EU citizens), a fourteenth-century former Carthusian monastery expensively restored as part of the Expo 92 world fair. Part of the complex is now given over to the **Museo del Arte Contemporáneo** (Tues–Sat 10am–8pm, Sun 10am–3pm; €1.80, free Tues for EU citizens), which, in addition to work by *Andaluz* artists, frequently stages important exhibitions by international artists.

The remnants of much of the **Expo 92 site** itself have been incorporated into the **Isla Mágica** (daily May–Sept and most weekends in March, April, Oct & Nov 11am–10pm; €22, half-day €13.80), an amusement park based on sixteenth-century Spain, with water and rollercoaster rides, shows and period street animations.

Eating, drinking and nightlife

Sevilla is a tremendously atmospheric place, and the city is packed with lively bars. Remember, though, that it can also be expensive, particularly in the Barrio Santa Cruz. If you want to **eat** well and cheaply you'll generally have to steer clear of the sights, but there are exceptions: c/Sta María La Blanca has several reasonable restaurants – notably the *Alta Mira* – as does c/Mateus Gago opposite La Giralda – try the *Alcazaba*. Other promising central areas are down towards the bullring and north of here towards the Plaza del Duque de la Victoria, where you'll find cheap *comidas* at places on c/San Eloy, c/Canalejas and c/Antonia Días where *Cafeteria Serranito* is one of the more interesting. *Habanita* is a pleasant **vegetarian** Cuban restaurant on c/Golfo just off c/Pérez Galdos in the Alfalfa area.

For straight drinking and occasional **tapas** you can be much less selective. There are **bars** all over town – a high concentration of them with barrelled sherries from nearby Jerez and Sanlúcar (the locals drink the cold, dry *fino* with their tapas, especially shrimp). In the centre of **Santa Cruz** one of the liveliest places is *Las Teresas* in c/Ximénez de Enciso (expensive tapas), but perhaps the best tapas bar in the city, with just about every imaginable snack, is the *Bar Modesto* at c/Cano y Cuento 5, up at the north corner of the quarter by Avda. Menéndez Pelayo. The innocuous-looking *Bodeguita* at c/Arfe 5, south of Plaza Nueva, is also worth searching out and less expensive, while *Bar Giralda* at c/Mateus Gago is also excellent, as is the *Bodega Santa Cuiz* on c/Rodrigo Caro just off Mateus Gago. The Alfalfa area just north of the cathedral is a lively, young area with loud **music** in many of the bars: *Bar Nao* and *Sopa de Ganso* in c/Pérez Galdos are both worth a look. The other main area for nightlife, popular with the substantial foreign student population, is just across the river on c/Betis.

Flamenco – or more accurately *Sevillanas* – music and dance are offered at dozens of places in the city, some of them extremely tacky and expensive. Unless you've heard otherwise, avoid the fixed "shows", or *tablaos*, and stick to bars – an excellent bar, highly recommended, which often has spontaneous *Sevillanas* is *La Carbonería* at c/Levías 18, slightly to the northeast of the Iglesia de Santa Cruz.

Listings

American Express In the *Hotel Inglaterra* on Plaza Nueva 7 (☎95 421 16 17).

Bookshop Libreria Beta, Avda. de la Constitucíon 27 has a good selection of English books.

Bullfighting The season starts with the April *feria* and continues until October with most corridas being held on Sunday evenings. Tickets can be bought from the *taquilla* (booking office) at the Maestranza bullring, Paseo de Colon 12, prices from €18.

Car rental Most agents are along the c/Almirante de Lobo or the airport, although one of the cheapest operators, Atesa, is at c/Secoya 2 (☎95 451 47 35).

Consulates Australia, Federico Rubio 14 (☎95 422 09 71); Canada, Avda. de la Constitución 30 (☎944 22 95 43); Ireland, Plaza de Santa Cruz 6 (☎95 421 63 61); UK, Plaza Nueva 8 (☎95 422 88 74); USA, Paseo de las Delicias 7 (☎95 423 18 85).

Hospital There are English-speaking doctors at the Hospital Universitario, Avda. Dr. Fedriani 3 (☎95 455 74 00).

Internet access Undernet Ciber Café, Galeria Comercial Corona, Pages del Corro 182 (Daily 11–3am; €1.80/hr; Torredeoro.Net, c/Núñez de Balboa 3, just off Paseo de Colón. Operates on a coin-operated system (Daily 8.30–1am €0.60/20mins).

Laundry c/Castelar 2 (Mon–Fri 9.30am–1.30pm & 5–8.30pm; 2hr service wash €0.60).

Police Plaza de la Gavidia (☎95 422 88 40).

Post office Avda. de la Constitución 32, by the cathedral; poste restante stays open Mon–Fri 8.30am–8.30pm, Sat 9.30am–2pm.

Train tickets RENFE office at c/Zaragoza 29, off Plaza Nueva (Mon–Fri 9.30am–2pm & 5–8pm; ☎95 422 26 93).

Cádiz and around

CÁDIZ is among the oldest settlements in Spain, founded about 1100 BC by the Phoenicians and one of the country's principal ports ever since. Its greatest period, however, was the eighteenth century, when it enjoyed a virtual monopoly on the Spanish-American trade in gold and silver. Inner Cádiz, built on a peninsula-island, remains much as it must have looked in those days, with its grand open squares, sailors' alleyways and high, turreted houses. Crumbling from the effect of the sea air on its soft limestone, it has a tremendous atmosphere – slightly seedy, definitely in decline, but still full of mystique.

Arriving by **train** you'll find yourself on the periphery of the old town, close to the Plaza de San Juan de Dios, busiest of the many squares and home of the main **tourist office** (Mon–Fri 9am–2pm & 4–6pm; ☎956 24 10 01, *www.cadizayto.es*) and booth nearby that's open at weekends. By **bus** you'll be a few blocks further north, along the water. With its blind alleys, cafés and backstreets, Cádiz is fascinating to wander around. To understand the city's layout, climb the **Torre Tavira** (daily 10am–6/8pm; €3), tallest of the 160 lookout towers in the city, with an excellent camera obscura. Some specific sites to check out are the **Museo de Cádiz** at Plaza de Mina 5 (Tues 2.30pm–8pm, Wed–Sat 9am–8pm, Sun 9am–2pm; €1.50, free on Sun and for EU citizens), just across from the cathedrals. The huge **Catedral Nueva** (Tues–Sat 10am–1pm) is an unusually successful blend of High Baroque and Neoclassical, decorated entirely in stone and with perfect proportions, while the "Old" Cathedral, **Santa Cruz**, is worth a look mainly for an interior studded with coin-in-the-slot votive candles. The oval, eighteenth-century chapel of **Santa Cueva** (Mon–Fri 10am–1pm; free) has eight magnificent arches decorated with frescoes by Goya.

Plaza de San Juan de Dios, protruding across the neck of the peninsula from the port, has several **cafés** and cheap **restaurants**. *La Caleta*, whose interior is built like the bow of a ship, is particularly good – though for something cheaper try the other side of the plaza. There's plenty of budget **accommodation** in the dense network of alleyways around the square. *El Isleña* is on the square itself at number 12 (☎ 956 28 70 64; ②) and is a reasonable place to stay. For something more salubrious, *Hostal Bahía*, c/ Plocia 5 (☎956 25 90 61; ③) is a well-priced option with air-conditioning, TVs and balconies in most rooms. More beds can be found a couple of blocks away, on or just off c/Marquez de Cádiz. The best bet is *Pension Fontani*, c/Flamenco 5 ((956 282 704; ②), but *Hostal España*, c/Marquez de Cádiz 9 (☎956 28 55 00; ③), is also good. There is a fairly smart **youth hostel** on c/Diego Arias, 1 (☎956 22 19 39; ②) and an **Internet Café**, CiberCádiz on Plaza Ingeniero La Cierva (Daily 5pm–midnight; €3/hr (☎956 28 24 59).

Cádiz has two daily **ferries to Tangier** (7am & 7pm; 1hr; €19.20); tickets are available at the maritime station.

Jerez de la Frontera

JEREZ DE LA FRONTERA, inland towards Sevilla, is the home and heartland of sherry and also, less known but equally important, of Spanish brandy. It seems a tempting place to stop, arrayed as it is round the scores of wine **bodegas**. But you're unlikely to want to make more than a quick visit (and tasting) between buses; the town itself is hardly distinctive unless you happen to arrive during one of the two big **festivals** – the May Horse Fair, or the celebration of the vintage towards the end of September.

The **tours of the sherry and brandy processes**, however, can be interesting, if not intoxicating, and provided you don't arrive in August, when most of the industry closes down (check with the tourist office to see which bodegas stay open), there are many firms and bodegas to choose from. Many of the firms were founded by British Catholic refugees who even now form a kind of Anglo-Andalusian aristocracy. One bodega that does stay open all summer is also one of the most central: next to the ruins of the Moorish Alcázar on Manuel Maria González is **González Byass** (hourly tours 11am–6pm; Mon–Fri €2.70, Sat & Sun €3.30).

Most of the other bodegas are on the outskirts of town; pick up a plan of them from the **tourist office** (Mon–Fri 9am–2pm & 4–7pm; ☎956 33 11 50, *www.jerez.com*) at c/Larga 39. The **train** and **bus stations** are close to each other, eight blocks east of the González bodega and the central Plaza de los Reyes Católicos. For **accommodation**, head for c/Higueras, off c/Medina (left out of the bus station and 3 blocks along) or c/Morenos, off the parallel c/Arcos. Enjoy classic Jerez architecture at the excellent and central *El Ancla* on Plaza del Mamelón (☎956 21 23 19; ③) or cheaper options include *Las Palomas* (☎956 34 37 73; ②) on Higueras, or *Hostal Sanvi*, c/Morenos 10 (☎956 34 56 24; ③). There's also a **hostel** at Avda. Carrero Blanco 30 (☎956 14 39 01; ②).

Algeciras

The main reason to visit **ALGECIRAS**, along the coast from Cádiz, is for the **ferry to Morocco** – and the number of people passing through guarantees plenty of inexpensive rooms. If you have trouble finding space, pick up a plan and check out the list in the **tourist office** on c/Juan de la Cierva ((☎956 57 26 36, *www.ayto-algeciras.es*), towards the river and rail line from the port. The port/harbour area also has plenty of **places to eat**, though they tend to be overpriced – try *Casa Maria* in the centre on c/Emilio Castelar.

There are six daily **crossings to Tangier** (7am–1.30pm; €21) and to the Spanish presidio of **Ceuta** (7am–8.30pm; €12; fewer crossings at weekends) – both take about an hour and a half. **Tickets** are available at scores of travel agents along the waterside and on most approach roads. Wait till Tangier – or if you're going via Ceuta, Tetouan – before buying any Moroccan currency. Local **buses** connect La Línea – the frontier town for Gibraltar – and Algeciras (every 30min), and there are equally regular direct services between Algeciras and Gibraltar.

Gibraltar

The interest of **GIBRALTAR** is essentially its novelty: the genuine appeal of the strange, looming physical presence of its rock, and the increasingly dubious one of its preservation as one of Britain's last colonies. It's a curious place to visit, not least to witness the bizarre mix of English squaddie town and Costa del Sol harbour being visited by coachloads of tourists. Beware that the **currency** used here is the Gibraltar pound (the same value as the British pound, but different notes and coins).

Town and rock have a necessarily simple layout. **Main Street** (La Calle Real) runs for most of the town's length a couple of blocks back from the port; from the frontier it's a short bus ride or about a fifteen-minute walk. From near the end of Main Street, you can hop on a **cable car** (Mon–Sat 9.30am–6pm; £7 return, including the Upper Rock Nature Reserve, Apes' Den and St Michael's Cave, £5 omitting the nature reserve), which will carry you up to the summit of Gibraltar. From the top you can look over to the Rif Mountains and down to the town and nearby beaches. From Apes' Den it's an easy walk south along Queens Road to **St Michael's Cave**, an immense natural cavern often used as a venue for concerts. Although you can be lazy and take the cable car both ways, you might instead walk up via Willis Rd to visit the **Tower of Homage**. Dating from the fourteenth century, this is the most visible survival from the old **Moorish Castle**. Further up you'll find the **Great Siege Tunnels**, blasted out of the rock during the Great Siege of 1779–82 in order to point guns down at the Spanish lines. To walk down, take the **Mediterranean Steps** – a very steep descent most of the way down the east side, turning the southern corner of the Rock. You'll pass through the Jews' Gate and into Engineer Rd. From here, return to town through the Alameda Gardens and the **Trafalgar Cemetery**. This grand tour takes a half to a full day and shows you almost all there is to see: all sites on it are open Monday to Saturday from 10am to 5pm in summer; except the cemetery which, naturally, never closes.

Practicalities

The main **tourist office** (Mon–Fri 9am–5.30pm, (☎9567 749 50, *tourism@gibraltar.gi*) is on the Piazza, and there are also offices at the airport and the customs building on the border. If you have a car, don't attempt to bring it to Gibraltar – the queues at the border are nearly always atrocious, and parking is a nightmare.

Shortage of space also means that **accommodation** is at a premium. The only remotely cheap beds are at the *Toc H Hostel* at 36a Line Wall Rd (☎9567 734 31; ②), which is invariably full and irredeemably seedy. Not cheap, but certainly not seedy, is the *Cannon Hotel*, 9 Cannon Lane, off Main St (☎9567 517 11; ⑦) which is very comfortable with all mod cons. **Camping** is strictly forbidden, but there is a new and central **hostel**, *Emile*, at Montagu Bastion on Line wall Rd (☎9567 511 06; ③, breakfast included). **Food and drink** are fairly expensive by Spanish standards, though pub snacks or fish and chips are reliable standbys. Main St is crowded with touristy places, among which *Mr Smith's Fish and Chip Shop*, opposite the Convent, is worth a try. Elsewhere, try the *Penny Farthing* on King St, *Corks Wine Bar* in Irish Town, the *Market Café* in the public market, or the more Spanish *Splendid Bar* in George's Lane. **Pubs** all tend to mimic traditional English styles (and prices), the difference being that they are often open into the wee hours. Places on Main St tend to be rowdy at night – full of squaddies and visiting sailors.

A functional attraction of Gibraltar is its role as a **port for Morocco**. There are daily ferries to Tangier at 8.30am and 2pm (1hr; around £30 return). Tickets are sold in scores of travel agent shops around Gibraltar.

THE COSTA DEL SOL

Perhaps the outstanding feature of the **Costa del Sol** is its ease of access. Hundreds of charter flights arrive here every week, and it's often possible to get an absurdly cheap ticket from London. **Málaga airport** is positioned midway between Málaga, the main city on the coast, and Torremolinos, its most grotesque resort. You can get to either town cheaply and easily by taking the electric rail line (every 30min) along the coast between Málaga and Fuengirola. Granada, Córdoba and Sevilla are all within easy reach of Málaga; so too are Ronda and the white villages (*pueblos blancos*). In some ways then, this coast's enormous popularity isn't surprising: what is surprising is that the **beaches** are generally grit-grey rather than golden and the sea is none too clean.

Málaga

MÁLAGA is the second city of the south, after Sevilla, and also one of the poorest. Yet though the clusters of high-rises look pretty grim as you approach, it can be a surprisingly attractive place. Around the old fishing villages of El Palo and Pedregalejo, now absorbed into the suburbs, are a series of small beaches and an avenue, or *paseo*, lined with some of the best fish and seafood cafés in the province. Overlooking the town and port are the Moorish citadels of the **Alcazaba** (Mon & Wed–Sun 9.30am–6/7pm; free) - where a **Roman amphitheatre** is currently under excavation - and the **Gibralfaro castle** (daily 9am–6/8pm; free), just fifteen minutes' walk from the train or bus stations, and visible from most central points. The palace near the top of the hill was the residence of the Arab emirs of Málaga, who briefly ruled an independent kingdom from here.

These monuments aside, Málaga is famed for its **fried fish** and sweet **Malaga wine**, enjoyed at a vast choice of tapas bars and restaurants. One of the most atmospheric spit 'n sawdust style **bodegas** is *Antigua Casa de Guardia,* Alameda Principal 18, reputed to be the oldest bar in town, where you can sample both with wine served straight from the barrel.

You'll find many fish restaurants around the Alameda, but for the very best you need to head out to the suburbs of Pedregalejo and El Palo, served by bus #11 (from the Paseo del Parque). On the seafront *paseo* at **Pedregalejo**, almost any of the cafés and restaurants will serve terrific fish, though you'll have to watch the price – *Marisqueria Godoy*, on c/Almeria, isn't too steep. The city's also a great place for **bars**, with the area between Plaza de la Merced and Plaza de los Martires buzzing till late at the weekend. There are plenty of reasonably priced **rooms** if you want to stay in Málaga, especially in the grids of streets north and south of the Alameda. A couple to try are the *Hostal La Palma*, c/Martínez 7 (☎95 222 67 72; ②), and the *Hostal Castilla*, c/Córdoba 7 (☎95 221 86 35; ②). The closest **campsite** (☎95 238 26 02) is at Torremolinos on Ctra. National; take the Málaga-Torremolinos bus from the main RENFE station in the centre of town.

Buses #3 (from c/Cuarteles) and #18 (from Paseo de los Tilos) connect the centre to the main **train and bus stations**, which are very close to each other. The main **tourist office** is at Pasaje de Parque 1 (summer daily 9.30am–3pm & 5–8pm; winter Mon–Fri 8.30am–3pm & 4.30–7pm, Sat 9.30am–1.30pm; ☎952 60 44 10, *info@malagaturismo.com*), supplemented by two kiosks (one at the bus station and the other on the Puente de Tetuan) and yellow-jacketed information officers who roam the main tourist drags (daily 11am–7pm). Arriving at the **airport**, catch the electric train to the main train station, or continue another stop to *Málaga Centro - Alameda* for the city centre.

Along the coast

It's estimated that three hundred thousand foreigners live on the **Costa del Sol**, the richest and fastest-growing resort area in the Mediterranean. Approached in the right kind of spirit it's possible to have fun in **TORREMOLINOS**, a resort so over-the-top it's magnificent, and with furious competition keeping prices down. The concrete is a little less in evidence at **Carihuela**, 15 minutes' walk west of Torremolinos Station, where *Hostal Pedro*, Paseo Maritimo La Carihuela 67 (☎95 238 54 79; ②) is a good **place to stay,** together with *Hostal Flor Blanco* (☎95 238 220 71; ②) a few doors away at number 71. A good time costs more in chic **MARBELLA**, where there are bars and nightclubs galore alongside a surprisingly well-preserved old village and some wonderfully conspicuous consumption. But if you've come to Spain to be in Spain, put on the shades and stay on the bus at least until you reach **ESTEPONA** – it may be somewhat drab, but at least it's restrained, and there's space to breathe. The long dark-pebbled beach has been enlivened a little by a promenade studded with flowers and palms, and, away from the seafront, the old town is very pretty, with cobbled alleyways and two delightful plazas. There's a **campsite** here, and a number of **hostales**, such as the *Hostal Vista al Mar*, c/Real 154 (☎95 280 32 47; ②), which has an excellent bar round the corner specializing in seafood **tapas**.

Ronda

Andalucía is dotted with small, brilliantly whitewashed settlements known as the **Pueblos Blancos** or "white villages", most often straggling up hillsides towards a castle or towered church. The most spectacular lie in a roughly triangular area between Málaga, Algeciras and Sevilla, at whose centre is the startling town of **RONDA**, connected by a marvellous rail line to Algeciras. Built on an isolated ridge of the sierra, and ringed by dark, angular mountains, Ronda is split in half by a gaping river gorge that drops sheer for 130m. Still more spectacular, the gorge is spanned by a stupendous eighteenth-century arched **bridge**, while tall white-washed houses lean from its precipitous edges. The town itself is fascinating to wander around and has sacrificed surprisingly little of its character to the flow of day-trippers from the Costa.

Crossing the eighteenth-century **Puente Nuevo** from the Plaza de España takes you from the modern **Mercadillo** quarter to the old Moorish town, the **Ciudad**, centred around the church of **Santa María la Mayor**, originally the mosque. Turning off the main street to the left takes you steeply down to the old bridges – the **Puente Viejo** of 1616 and the Roman single-span "**Puente Arabe**". Nearby, on the southeast bank of the river, are the distinctive **Baños Árabes** (Tues 9.30am–1.30pm & 4–7/8pm, Wed–Sat 9.30am–3.30pm; free). Crossing the old bridge takes you back to the modern town via the **Jardin de la Mina**, which ascends the gorge in a series of stepped terraces with superb views of the river, new bridge and remarkable stairway of the **Casa del Rey Moro** (daily 10am–7pm; €3.60), an early eighteenth-century mansion built on Moorish foundations whose 365 steps were cut by Christian slaves in the fourteenth century and were intended to guarantee a water supply in times of siege. Near the centre of the Ciudad stands the splendid Renaissance **Palacio del Marqués de Salvatierra** which is temporarily closed for renovation. Behind the church, is the **Palacio de Mondragón** (Mon–Fri 10am–6/7pm, Sat & Sun 10am–3pm; €1.50), probably the palace of the Moorish kings and now home to the **Museo Municipal** – a steep path descends to the river from here. The principal gate of the town, through which the Christian conquerors passed, stands at the entrance to the suburb of San Francisco, beside the ruins of the **Alcázar**, destroyed by the French in 1809. Back in Mercadillo quarter is the **bullring** (daily 10am–7/8pm; €2.40 including museum) – one of the most prestigious in Spain – and the beautiful clifftop *paseo*, facing the open valley and the dramatic mountains of the Serrenía de Ronda.

Practicalities

The **tourist office** is on Plaza de España (Mon–Fri 9am–7pm, Sat & Sun 10am–2pm; ☎95 287 12 72, *www.ronda.net)*. All the **places to stay** are in the Mercadillo quarter. Cheap and very close to the bridge near the Plaza de España is the *Hotel Virgen del Rocío* on c/Nueva (☎95 287 74 25; ②). Various options can be found going up c/Lorenzo Borrego, off the Plaza del Socorro, including the cheap *Hostal Ronda Sol* (☎95 287 44 97; ②) at c/Cristo 11; and the 2-star *Hostal Virgen de los Reyes* (☎95 287 11 40; ③). There are three **campsites** at the ends of town; the best is *El Sur* (☎95 287 59 39), 1.5km down the Algeciras road.

As for **eating**, most of the bargain options are grouped round the far end of the Plaza del Socorro as you leave it on c/Almendra. *El Brillante* on c/Sevilla is friendly and cheap as is *Pizzeria Michel Angelo* on c/Lorenzo Borrego. At the weekend, Ronda's **nightlife** kicks off along c/Niño and around.

Granada

If you see only one town in Spain it should be **GRANADA**. For here, extraordinarily well preserved and in a tremendous natural setting, stands the **Alhambra** – the spectacular and serene climax of Moorish art in Spain. Granada was established as an independent kingdom in 1238 by **Ibn Ahmar**, a prince of the Arab Nasrid tribe which had been driven south from Zaragoza. By a series of shrewd manoeuvres, the Moors of Granada maintained their autonomy for two and a half centuries, but by 1490 only the city itself remained in Muslim hands. **Boabdil**, the last Moorish king, appealed in vain for help from his fellow Muslims in Morocco, Egypt and Turkey, and in the following year Ferdinand and Isabella marched on Granada with an army said to total 150,000 troops. For seven months, through the winter of 1491, they laid siege to the city. On January 2 1492, Boabdil surrendered: the Christian Reconquest of Spain was complete.

Arrival and information

Virtually everything of interest in Granada – including the hills of **Alhambra** (to the east) and **Sacromonte** (to the north) – is within easy walking distance of the centre. The only times you'll need a bus are when arriving and leaving, since bus and train stations are both some way out. The **train station** is a kilometre or so out on the Avda. de Andaluces, and is connected to the centre by buses #4, #9 and #11. The main **bus station**, on the Carretera de Jaén, is a bit further out; bus #3 runs into town. If you **fly** in, there's a bus (4–7 daily; 7.55am–5.55pm; €3) connecting the airport with both ends of Gran Vía de Colón. Details and timetables of all buses, trains, and much else besides, are posted on the walls of the **tourist**

office on c/Mariana Pineda off c/Reyes Católicos (Mon–Sat 9am–7pm, Sun 10am–2pm; ☎958 22 59 90). The provincial tourist office is in Plaza Mariana Pineda (☎958 24 71 28, *www.turismodegranada.orh*).

Accommodation

The **Gran Vía** is Granada's main street, cutting through the middle of town. It forms a "T" at its end with **c/Reyes Católicos**, which runs east to the **Plaza Nueva** and west to the **Puerta Real**, the city's two main squares. Finding a **place to stay** in this area is easy except at the very height of season (Semana Santa is impossible). Try the streets to either side of the Gran Vía, at the back of the Plaza Nueva, around the Puerta Real and Plaza del Carmen (particularly c/de Navas), the Plaza de la Trinidad in the university area, or along the Cuesta de Gomérez, which leads up from the Plaza Nueva towards the Alhambra.

HOTELS AND HOSTELS

Hostal Atenas, Gran Vía de Colón 38 (☎958 27 87 50, *hatenas@moebius.es*). Large place, so worth a try, though rooms vary in quality. ②.

Hostal Britz, Cuesta de Gomérez 1 (☎958 22 36 52). Noisy, but otherwise very comfortable and well placed. Some rooms with bath. ②.

Pension Doña Lupe, Avda. del Generalife, Alhambra (☎958 22 14 73). On the road leading up to the cemetery, this is the cheapest option up here. It also has a summertime terrace offering fantastic views and dorm beds for around €12 per person. Book ahead if possible. ③.

Casa de Huéspedes González, c/Buensuceso 51 (☎958 26 03 51). At the end of the street, a five-minute walk west of Plaza Trinidad. Perfectly good rooms and very good value. ②.

Hotel La Perla, Plaza Bib-Rambla 4 (☎958 26 67 12). Great situation on bustling plaza with fourth floor terrace for sunning and views.②.

Hostal Lisboa, Plaza del Carmen 27 (☎958 22 14 13). Noisy at the front, but clean and comfortable. ②.

Hostal Mario, Cardenal Mendoza 15 (☎958 20 14 27). A friendly and economical choice, closer to the train station than most. ②.

Hostal Marquez, c/Fabrica Vieja 8 (☎958 27 50 13). Friendly, cheap, clean and just west of the cathedral. ②.

Hostal Navarro-Ramos, Cuesta de Gomérez 21 (☎958 25 05 55). Small rooms, small balconies, bargain prices but showers are extra. ②.

Hostal Olimpia, Alvaro de Bazán 6, off Gran Vía de Colón, opposite Banco de Jeréz (☎958 27 82 38). Central, good-value place run by nice people. ②.

Youth Hostel, Avda. Ramón y Cajal 2 (☎902 51 00 00). Handy for the train station (from RENFE, turn left onto c/del Halcón, then first left across the railway line), with lots of facilities including a pool, but institutional and unfriendly. ②.

CAMPSITES

Camping Reina Isabel, Laurel de la Raina 15 (☎958 59 00 41). Near the town of Zubia; take the bus from Paseo de Salon (half-hourly).

Camping Sierra Nevada, Avda. de Madrid 107 (☎958 15 00 62). The closest site to the centre and probably the best too; easily reached on bus #3 from the Gran Vía de Colón. March–Oct.

The City

There are three distinct groups of buildings on the **Alhambra** hill: the **Palacios Reales** (Royal Palace), the palace gardens of the **Generalife**, and the **Alcazaba**. The latter was all that existed when Ibn Ahmar made Granada his capital, but from its reddish walls the hilltop had already taken its name: *al-Hamra* in Arabic means literally "the red". Ibn Ahmar rebuilt the Alcazaba and added to it the huge circuit of walls and towers. Within the walls he began a palace, which he supplied with running water by diverting the River Darro; water is an integral part of the Alhambra and this engineering feat was Ibn Ahmar's greatest contribution. The palace was essentially the product of his fourteenth-century successors, particularly Mohammed V. After their conquest of the city, Ferdinand and Isabella lived for a while in the Alhambra. They restored some rooms and converted the mosque but left the palace struc-

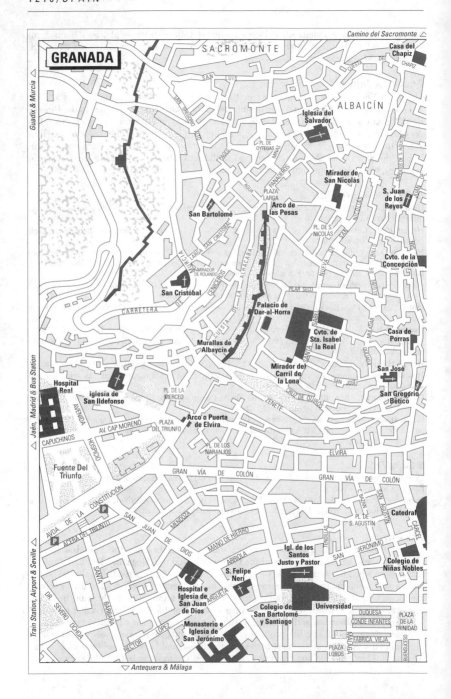

GRANADA

△ Camino del Sacromonte

SACROMONTE

Casa del
Chapiz

ALBAICÍN

Iglesia del
Salvador

Mirador de
San Nicolás

S. Juan
de los
Reyes

San Bartolomé

Arco de
las Pesas

PLAZA
LARGA

PL. DE
OYTEGAS

San Cristóbal

MIRADOR
DE ROLANDO

Cvto. de la
Concepción

PILAR SECO

Palacio de
Dar-al-Horra

Casa de
Porras

Cvto. de
Sta. Isabel
la Real

CARRETERA

Murallas de
Albaycín

Mirador del
Carril de
la Lona

San José

San Gregorio
Bético

Hospital
Real

Iglesia de
San Ildefonso

CRUZ DE QUIROS

Arco o Puerta
de Elvira

PLAZA
DEL TRIUNFO

PL. DE LA
MERCED

AV. CAP MORENO

CAPUCHINOS

PL. DE LOS
NARANJOS

ELVIRA

Fuente Del
Triunfo

GRAN VÍA DE COLÓN

GRAN VÍA DE COLÓN

PL. DE
S. AGUSTÍN

Catedral

SAN JUAN DE DIOS

Igl. de los
Santos
Justo y Pastor

Colegio de
Niñas Nobles

S. Felipe
Neri

Hospital e
Iglesia de
San Juan
de Dios

Colegio de
San Bartolomé
y Santiago

Universidad

DUQUESA
CONDE INFANTES

PLAZA
DE LA
TRINIDAD

Monasterio e
Iglesia de
San Jerónimo

FÁBRICA VIEJA

PLAZA
LOBOS

▽ Antequera & Málaga

◁ Guadix & Murcia

◁ Jaén, Madrid & Bus Station

◁ Train Station, Airport & Seville

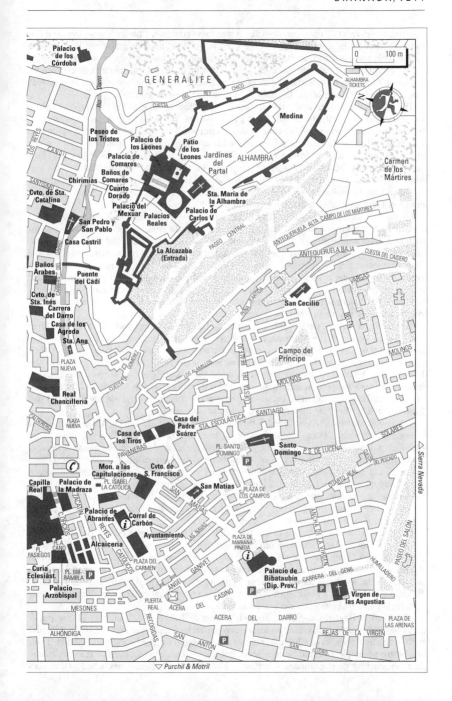

ture unaltered. As at Córdoba and Sevilla, it was their grandson Charles V who wreaked the most destruction: he demolished a whole wing to build yet another grandiose Renaissance palace. This and the Alhambra itself were simply ignored by his successors, and by the eighteenth century the Royal Palace was in use as a prison. In 1812 it was taken and occupied by Napoleon's forces, who looted and damaged whole sections of the palace, and on their retreat from the city tried (but fortunately failed) to blow up the entire complex.

The standard approach to the **Alhambra** (daily 8.30am–8/5pm; €6) is along the Cuest de Gomérez, the road that climbs uphill from Plaza Nueva. You need to arrive early or, ideally, book in advance; during holiday time and midsummer, it is essential to reserve otherwise you may well arrive to find the tickets are sold out. Buy your ticket from the booth at the entrance (times as above); from any Banco BBV in Spain, including the one in town at Plaza Isabel la Católica (Mon–Sat 9am–2pm); by phone on (☎902 22 44 60; payment by Visa and Mastercard with an extra €1 fee); or online at *www.alhambratickets.com*. Tickets usually specify a time for visiting the Palacio Nazaries, if you get the choice opt for later in the day between 4 and 8pm, after most tour groups have left.

Ideally you should start your visit with the earliest, most ruined, part of the fortress – the **Alcazaba**. At the summit of the Alcazaba is the **Torre de la Vela**, named after a huge bell on its turret, from where there's a fine overview of the whole area. It's in the **Casa Real**, however, that the real wonders start: the first being that the place itself has survived, since it was built from wood, brick and adobe, and was designed not to last but to be renewed and redecorated by succeeding rulers. Its buildings show a brilliant use of light and space but they are principally a vehicle for ornamental stucco decoration, in rhythmic repetitions of supreme beauty. Arabic inscriptions feature prominently: some are poetic eulogies of the buildings and rulers, but most are taken from the Koran.

The palace is in three parts, each arrayed round an interior court and with a specific function. The sultans used the **Mexuar**, the first series of rooms, for business and judicial purposes, and this is as far as most people would have penetrated. In the **Serallo**, beyond, they received embassies and distinguished guests: here is the royal throne room, known as the **Hall of the Ambassadors**, the largest room of the palace. The last section, the **Harem**, formed their private living quarters and would have been entered by no one but their family or servants. These are the most beautiful rooms of the palace, and include the **Court of the Lions**, which has become the archetypal image of Granada.

The usual exit from the Casa Real is through the courtyard of **Charles V's palace** – now housing a museum (Tues–Sat 9am–2.30pm; free) – where bullfights were once held. Although wilfully out of place here, the palace is a distinguished piece of Renaissance design, stamping an imperialist authority over the gardens of the **Generalife**. Paradise is described in the Koran as a shaded, leafy garden refreshed by running water where the "fortunate ones" may take their rest under tall canopies. It is an image which perfectly describes the Generalife, the gardens and summer palace of the sultans. Its name means literally "garden of the architect" and the grounds consist of a luxuriantly imaginative series of patios, enclosed gardens and walkways.

From just below the entrance to the Generalife the **Cuesta del Rey Chico** winds down towards the River Darro and the old Arab quarter of the Albaicín. Here the little-visited **Baños Árabes** (Tues–Sat 10am–2pm; free) at 31 Corredera del Darro are marvellous, and the plaza in front of the church of **San Nicolás** offers probably the best view of the Alhambra in town. To the southwest of the Albaicín, opposite the Capilla Real, is the strangely painted **Palacio de Madraza**, a fourteenth-century Islamic college that retains part of its old prayer hall, including a magnificently decorated *mihrab*.

The **Capilla Real** (Mon–Sat 10.30am–1/1.30pm & 3.30/4–6.30/7pm, Sun 11am–1pm & 3.30/4–6.30/7pm; €1.80) is itself an impressive building, flamboyant late Gothic in style and built in the first decades of Christian rule as a mausoleum for Ferdinand and Isabella. Their tombs are as simple as could be imagined, but above them is a fabulously elaborate monument erected by their grandson Charles V. For all its stark Renaissance bulk, Granada's

Cathedral, adjoining the Capilla Real and entered from the door beside it (Mon–Sat 10.45am–1.30pm & 4–6.30pm, Sun 4–7pm; €1.80), is a disappointment. It was begun in 1521, just as the chapel was finished, but left uncompleted well into the eighteenth century, and still lacks a tower.

Eating, drinking and nightlife

You don't come to Granada for the food, and it's certainly not one of the gastronomic centres of Spain. On the other hand, like so many Spanish cities, the centre has plenty of animated bars serving good, cheap **food** and staying open late. The open-air places on Plaza Nueva are great to while away some time, but pricey if you eat. Better-value dining, and numerous late-night bars, can be found in "Little Morocco", the warren of streets between here and the Gran Vía: good-value choices include the *Nueva Bodega* at c/Cetti Merién 3, the lively *Gargantua* at Placeta Sillería 7 (near c/Reyes Católicos), and *Cafetería-Restaurante La Riviera* at c/Cetti Merién 5. If you're wandering around the Albaicin, check out the Moroccan-owned *El Acebreche* at Placeta de San Miguel el Bajo 6, which specializes in organic and veggie food. Another nucleus of reasonable eateries is the area around Plaza del Carmen (near the *Ayuntamiento*) and along c/Navas leading away from it.

Moroccan-style teashops known as **teterías** are increasingly popular, particularly with students, and serve a wide choice of herb teas (*infusiones*), accompanied by traditional Arab pastries. There are several **Internet** cafés, including Avalon Informatica, c/Santiago Lozano 17 (daily 10.30am–9.45pm; €1.50/hr) and the Red Isis Café, Verónica de la Magdalena 1 (daily 10am–midnight; €1.50/hr).

One of the most atmospheric **bars** in the centre is *Bodegas Castañeda*, on the corner of c/Elvira and c/Almireceros. Popular with locals, serving excellent unusual **tapas** is the bustling *La Gran Taberna* at 12 Plaza Nueva on the way up to the Alhambra. The best area for drinking through the early hours is around the university, on c/Gran Capitán and c/Pedro Antonio de Alarcón. In term time, students also gather in **pubs** near the bus station around the Campo del Príncipe, a square on the southern slopes of the Alhambra, where you'll often find great tapas. At the weekend, the best **disco** in town is *El Camborio* inside the caves at the end of Camino del Sacramento.

Granada is also one of the best places in Spain to hear **flamenco**, though finding the real thing can be difficult. There are numerous – and mostly lame – *espectaculares* for the tourists around Sacromonto, but you're better off searching the bars around Plaza Larga, west of the Iglesia del Salvador, where the gypsies play spontaneously.

ALMERÍA PROVINCE

The **province of Almería** is a strange corner of Spain. Inland it has an almost lunar landscape of desert, sandstone cones and dried-up riverbeds. On the coast it's still largely unspoiled; lack of water and roads frustrated development in the 1960s and 1970s and it is only now beginning to take off. A number of good beaches are accessible by bus, and they are worth considering during what would be the "off-season" elsewhere, since Almería's summers start well before Easter and last into November. In midsummer it frequently touches 38°C in the shade, and all year round there's an intense, almost luminous, sunlight. This and the weird scenery have made Almería one of the most popular film locations in Europe – much of *Lawrence of Arabia* was shot here, along with scores of spaghetti westerns.

Almería city

ALMERÍA itself is a pleasant modern city, spread at the foot of a stark grey mountain at whose summit is a tremendous **Alcazaba** (summer daily 10am–2pm & 5.30–8.30pm; winter 9am–1.30pm & 3.30–6.30pm; €1.50, free to EU citizens). From here there's a superb view of the coast, of Almería's cave quarter – the Barrio de la Chanca on a low hill to the left – and of the city's strange fortified **Cathedral** (Mon–Fri 10am–5pm, Sat 10am–1pm, Sun for mass only; €1.80). There's little else to do in town, and your time is probably best devoted to strolling between the cafés, bars and *terrazas* on the main Paseo de Almería, which runs from the central Puerta de Purchena down towards the harbour, and taking day-trips out to the beaches. The city's own **beach**, southeast of the centre beyond the rail lines, is long but dismal.

Best for **accommodation** is the area between the bus and train stations and the centre. Possibilities include *Hostal Nixar*, c/Antonio Vico 24 (☎ 950 23 72 55; ②) or *Hostal Maribel*, Avda. Lorca 153 (☎950 23 51 73; ②); the nearest **campsite** is on the coast at La Garrofa, 5km west, reached by buses to Aguadulce and Roquetas de Mar (where there's another, giant site). The **tourist office** (Mon–Fri 9am–7pm, Sat & Sun 10am–2pm; ☎950 27 43 55, *www.almeriaturismo_orh*) is towards the train station, on c/Hermanos Muchado 4, at the south end of the Avda. Frederico García Lorca. The most centrally placed **Internet** café is *Abarkon* on c/Marcos 19 (Daily 9.30am–2pm & 5–8.30pm; €3hr (☎954 99 00 96).

The beaches

Almería's best **beaches** lie on its eastern coast, on the strip between Carboneras and La Garrucha, centred on the town of Mojácar. This is some way up the coast and to get there you'll have to travel through some of Almería's distinctive desert scenery. There are two possible routes: via Níjar to Carboneras, or via Tabernas and Sorbas to Mojácar. **MOJÁCAR** – Almería's chief resort – lies a couple of kilometres back from the sea, a striking town of white cubist houses wrapped round a harsh outcrop of rock. There's plenty of development here, and prices can seem inflated, but it's still pleasant. There's a handful of small **hostales** in town, but you're probably best off down at the beach where there's a cheap **campsite**, lots of fine beach bars, rooms to let and several *hostales* on Paseo Mediterraneo – try the *Bahia* (☎950 47 80 10; ③) or the *Puntazo* (☎950 47 82 29; ④), for which it's often necessary to book ahead. The **beach** itself is excellent and the water warm and brilliantly clear.

OLD CASTILE

The foundations of modern Spain were laid in the kingdom of **Castile**. A land of frontier fortresses – the *castillos* from which it takes its name – it became the most powerful and centralizing force of the Reconquest, extending its domination through military gains and marriage alliances. The monarchs of this triumphant and expansionist age were enthusiastic patrons of the arts, endowing their cities with superlative monuments above which, quite literally, tower the great Gothic cathedrals of **Salamanca**, **León** and **Burgos**. The most impressive of the castles are at **Coca**, **Gormaz** and **Berlanga de Duero**, and there's also a wealth of Romanesque churches spread along the **Pilgrim Route to Santiago** which cuts across the top of the province.

Over the past decades these and the other historic cities of Old Castile have grown to dominate the region more than ever. Although its soil is fertile, the harsh extremes of land and climate don't encourage rural settlement, and the vast central plateau is given over almost entirely to grain. The sporadic and depopulated villages are rarely of interest – travel consists of getting quickly from one grand town to the next.

Salamanca

SALAMANCA is probably the most graceful city in Spain. It is home to what was for four centuries one of the most prestigious universities in the world, and it has kept the unmistakable atmosphere of a seat of learning. It's still a small place, untouched by the piles of suburban concrete which blight so many of its contemporaries, and given a gorgeous harmony by the golden sandstone from which almost the entire city seems to be constructed. The architectural hoard is endless: two cathedrals, one Gothic, the other Romanesque, vie for attention with Renaissance palaces; the Plaza Mayor is the finest in Spain; and the surviving university buildings are tremendous.

Two great architectural styles were developed, and see their finest expression, in Salamanca. **Churrigueresque**, a particularly florid form of Baroque, takes its name from José Churriguera (1665–1723), the dominant member of a prodigiously creative family. **Plateresque** came earlier, a decorative technique of shallow relief and intricate detail named after its alleged resemblance to the art of the silversmith (*platero*).

The City

If on arrival you'd like to get a picture-perfect overall view of Salamanca, go to the extreme south of the city and cross its oldest surviving monument, the much-restored **Puente Romano** (Roman Bridge), some 400m long and itself worth seeing. Otherwise make for the grand **Plaza Mayor**, its bare central expanse completely enclosed by one continuous four-storey building decorated with iron balconies and medallion portraits. Nowhere is the Churrigueras' inspired variation of Baroque so refined as here, where the restrained elegance of the designs is heightened by the changing strength and angle of the sun. From the south side, Rua Mayor leads to the vast Baroque church of **La Clerecía**, seat of the Pontifical University (open for visits only one hour before Mass, which takes place Mon–Fri 1.30, Sat 7.30pm, Sun 12.30pm), and the celebrated **Casa de las Conchas**, or House of Shells (Mon–Fri 9am–9pm, Sat 9am–2pm & 4–7pm, Sun 10am–2pm & 4–7pm; free), so called because its facades are decorated with rows of carved scallop shells, symbol of the pilgrimage to Santiago.

From the Casa de las Conchas, c/Libreros leads to the **Patio de las Escuelas** and the Renaissance entrance to the **University** (Mon–Sat 9.30am–1.30pm & 4–7/8pm, Sun 10am–1pm; €1.80, free Mon morning). The ultimate achievement of Plateresque art, this reflects the tremendous reputation of Salamanca in the early sixteenth century, when it was one of Europe's greatest universities. Today it's socially prestigious, but academically no great shakes. It does, however, run a highly successful summer language school – nowhere in Spain will you see so many young Americans.

As a further declaration of Salamanca's prestige, and in a glorious last-minute assertion of Gothic, the **Catedral Nueva** (daily: summer 9am–2pm & 4–8pm; winter 10am–1pm & 4–6pm; free) was begun in 1512. It was built within a few yards of the university and acted as a buttress for the Old Cathedral which was in danger of collapsing. The main Gothic-Plateresque facade is contemporary with that of the university and equally dazzling in its wealth of ornamental detail. Alberto Churriguera and his brother Joaquín both worked here – the former on the choir stalls, the latter on the dome. Entry to the **Catedral Vieja** (same times; €1.80) is through the first chapel on the right. Tiny by comparison and stylistically entirely different, its most striking feature is the huge fifteenth-century retable. In the chapterhouse there's a small **museum** with a fine collection of works by Fernando Gallego, Salamanca's most famous painter.

Another faultless example of Plateresque art, the **Convento de San Esteban** (daily: 9am–1/1.30pm & 4–6/8pm; €1.20), is a short walk down c/del Tostado from the Plaza de Anaya at the side of the Catedral Nueva. Its golden facade is divided into three horizontal sections and covered in a veritable tapestry of sculpture, while the east end of the church is occupied by a huge Baroque retable by José Churriguera himself. The monastery's cloisters, through which you enter, are magnificent too, but the most beautiful cloisters in the city stand across the road in the **Convento de las Dueñas** (daily 10.30am–1pm & 4.30–7pm; €1.20). Built on an irregular pentagonal plan in the Renaissance-Plateresque style, it has upper-storey capitals wildly carved with human heads and skulls. You should also see the **Convento de Las Claras** (Mon–Fri 9.30am–1.40pm & 4–6.40pm, Sat & Sun 9am–2.40pm; €1.20), outwardly plain but with interior features in virtually every important Spanish style.

Most of the remaining interest lies in the western part of the city. If you follow c/de la Compañía from the Casa de las Conchas, you pass the Plaza San Benito, which has some fine houses, and come to the Plaza Agustinas. Buildings to look out for here include the large sixteenth-century **Palacio de Monterrey**, the seventeenth-century Augustinian monastery of **La Purísima** (Fri & Sat noon–1pm & 5–7pm; free), opposite, and another interesting convent, **Convento Las Ursulas** (daily 11am–1pm & 4.30–6pm; €0.60), behind the Palacio. Facing the east wall of its church is the impressive facade of the **Casa de las Muertes**, and along c/de Fonseca is the magnificent Plateresque palace known as the **Colegio de los Irlandeses**.

Practicalities

The **bus** and **train stations** are on opposite sides of the city, each about fifteen minutes' walk from the centre. The municipal **tourist office** is at the edge of Plaza Mayor 14 (daily 9/10am–2pm & 4.30–6.30pm; ☎923 21 83 42), and the regional office at Casa de las Conchas (Mon–Fri 9am–2pm & 5–7pm, Sat & Sun 10am–2pm & 4–7pm; ☎923 26 85 71). Prices for **accommodation** are reasonable, but it can be hard to find in high season – especially at fiesta time in September. Touts tend to be out in force at the RENFE station during the summer. On the way into town from here, there are a few choices around Plaza de España – try the *Hostal Internacional*, Avda. de Mirat 15 (☎923 26 27 99; ②). Otherwise, the Plaza Mayor is the most obvious place to head for – in the small streets surrounding it you'll find scores of small *fondas* and *hostales*, most of a high standard: *Pensión Estefania*, at c/Jesus 3 (☎923 21 73 72; ②), is particularly good. A new **Youth Hostel** (☎923 26 91 41; ③), on c/Escoto 13–15 just off the Plaza Mayor, has 6-bed dorms and excellent facilities. There are several campsites nearby, the least expensive being *Don Quijote* (☎923 20 90 52) at Cabrerizos, about 4km out but served by bus #2 from Gran Vía.

The **cafés** in Plaza Mayor are expensive but worth the extra for the surroundings. Close by in Plaza del Mercado (by the **market**, itself a good source of provisions), there's a row of lively tapas bars, while the university area has loads of good-value bars and restaurants catering to student budgets. Good-value food places include *Rio Tormes*, Plaza Corrillo 20, Mandala, near the university entrance on c/de Serranos 9, and *El Bardo*, c/Compañía 8, both of which sell vegetarian food and the latter alcohol. About the cheapest *menús del día* are at *Cerveceria O'Pazo*, Plaza de la Constitución, and at places along the streets around the market and towards the bus station. Late-night bars abound in the Gran Vía area; among the most popular are *El Corrillo*, in c/Melendez, for jazz, *O'Neill's*, c/Zamora with students, and *El Callejón* at Gran Vía 68, for folk. *El Sabor*, c/San Justo, has good Latin music, while *El Moderno* at c/España 65 is lively and plays Spanish disco tunes. The most popular clubs include *El Cum Laude*, off Plaza Mayor, which attracts mainly teenagers at weekends; *El Country*, on c/Juan de Almeida; *Potemkin*, off Gran Vía, which is open until sunrise, and *El Puerto de Chus*, on Plaza de San Julián.

Burgos

BURGOS has always been a military town. For some five centuries of the Middle Ages the city was the capital of Old Castile: in the eleventh century it was the home of El Cid; in the thirteenth century of Fernando III, who began the city's famous Gothic cathedral. One of the greatest in all Spain, the cathedral seems somehow to share the forceful solemnity and severity of Burgos' history. More recently Burgos was a Francoite stronghold – his temporary capital during the Civil War and strongly loyal to the end, with an abiding reputation for conservatism.

The City

Orientation in Burgos could not be simpler, since wherever you are the **Cathedral** (daily 9.30am–11.45pm & 4–7pm) makes its presence felt. The cathedral is so large and varied that it's hard to appreciate as a whole, but its profile of spires and pinnacles is magnificent from almost any angle. It is currently being restored, however, so some wings are obscured by scaffolding. Inside, you're immediately struck by the size and number of side chapels, the greatest of which, the Capilla del Condestable, is almost a cathedral in itself. The most curious, though, is the Capilla del Santo Cristo (first right) which contains the *Cristo de Burgos*, a cloyingly realistic image of Christ endowed with real human hair and nails and covered with the withered hide of a water buffalo, still popularly believed to be human skin. To get into some of these smaller chapels you'll have to buy a treasury ticket (€3.60), which also admits you to the cloisters, the diocesan museum inside them, and the choir at the heart of the cathedral, which affords the best view into the dome.

Overlooking the plaza in front of the cathedral stands the fifteenth-century church of **San Nicolás**. Unassuming from the outside, it has an altarpiece within by Francisco de Colonia, which is as rich as anything in the city. At the side of San Nicolás, c/Pozo Seco ascends to the early Gothic church of **San Esteban**, now the **Museo del Retablo** (summer Tues–Sat 10.30am–2pm & 4.30–7pm, Sun 10.30am–2pm; winter Sat 10.30am–2pm & 4.30–7pm, Sun 10.30am–2pm; €1.20), which houses a fine collection of icons and altarpieces. Beyond San Esteban lies the ruined castle with a fine view of the city and the surrounding countryside.

On the outskirts is the Cistercian **Monasterio de las Huelgas** (summer Tues–Sat 10.30am–1.15pm & 3.30–5.45pm, Sun 10.30am–2.15pm; winter Tues–Sat 11am–1.15pm & 4–5.15pm, Sun 10.30am–2.15pm; €4.80 includes guided tour, Wed free) on the "new side" of the river, about twenty minutes' walk from the city centre: cross the bridge, turn right and follow the signs along the riverbank. Founded in 1187, the convent grew to extraordinary wealth and power, and is remarkable for its wealth of Mudéjar craftsmanship. Priceless embroidery, jewellery and weaponry are exhibited in a small museum, but the highlight is the Mudéjar-Gothic cloister, adorned with eight-pointed stars and rare peacock designs – a bird holy to the Moors.

Practicalities

The **bus station** is south of the Puente de Santa María at c/Miranda 4; the **train station** a short walk away at the bottom of Avda. Conde Guadalhorce. The main **tourist office** (Mon–Fri 9am–2pm & 5–7pm, Sat & Sun 10am–2pm & 5–8pm; ☎947 20 31 25) is at Plaza de Alonso Martínez 7, around the side of the cathedral and a short walk up c/Lain Calvo.

For **rooms**, the best areas to try are around the tourist office and c/San Juan, or near the bus station: *Pensión Peña*, c/La Puebla 18 (☎947 20 63 23; ②) is near the former; next to the latter is the more expensive, but delightful *Pensión Ansa*, c/Miranda 9-1° (☎947 20 47 67; ②). *Hostal Manjón*, c/Conde Jordana 1-7° (☎947 20 86 89; ②), is a clean and comfortable option near to the river at the end of c/San Lesmes. There's a **youth hostel** (☎947 22 03 62; ②; July–Sept; reservation essential) about 2km out of town on Avda. de General Vigón, and a good **campsite**, *Fuentes Blancas* (☎947 48 60 16; April–Sept), 45 minutes' walk out on the Cartuja road, or bus #27 (4 daily) from Plaza España. There are several tapas **bars** and a swarm of **nightclubs** around c/Huerto del Rey behind the cathedral: *Mesón Astorga* and *Mesón El Cardenal* are both good for tapas. More formal restaurants include the *Rincón de España* between the river and the cathedral, the cheapish *Don Diego*, immediately behind the cathedral on c/Porcelos, or the economic friendly *Bar Restaurante Ibañez*, c/Calatravas 3, behind the bus station.

León

The stained glass in the cathedral of **LEÓN** and the Romanesque wall paintings in its Royal Pantheon are reason enough for many people to visit the city, but León is also – unusually for this part of the country – as attractive and enjoyable in its modern quarters as it is in those areas that remain from its heyday. In 914, as the Reconquest edged its way south from Asturias, the Christian capital moved to León. Despite being sacked by al-Mansur in 996, the new capital and its territories grew rapidly: in 1035 the county of Castile matured into a fully fledged kingdom, and for the next two centuries León and Castile jointly spearheaded the war against the Moors until by the thirteenth century Castile had come to dominate her mother kingdom.

León's **Cathedral** (daily 8.30am–1.30pm & 4.30–7.30/8pm) dates from the city's final years of greatness. It is said to be a miracle that it's still standing: it has the largest proportion of window to stone of any Gothic cathedral. The kaleidoscopic stained-glass **windows** present one of the most magical and harmonious spectacles in Spain, and the colours used – reds, golds and yellows – could only be Spanish. The glass screen added to the choir this century to give a clear view up to the altar enhances the sensation of light with its bewildering refractions. Outside, the west facade, dominated by a massive rose window, is also magnificent.

The other great attraction is the church of **San Isidoro** and the Royal Pantheon of the early kings of León and Castile. Ferdinand I, who united the two kingdoms in 1037, commissioned the complex as a shrine for the bones of Saint Isidore, which lie in a reliquary on the high altar, and a mausoleum for himself and his successors. The **Pantéon** (Mon–Sat 10am–1.30pm & 4–6.30pm, Sun 10am–1.30pm; €2.40), a pair of small crypt-like chambers, is in front of the west facade. One of the earliest Romanesque buildings in Spain (1054–63), it was decorated towards the end of the twelfth century with some of the most imaginative and impressive paintings of Romanesque art. They are extraordinarily well preserved and their biblical and everyday themes are perfectly adapted to the architecture of the vaults. Eleven kings and twelve queens were laid to rest here, but the chapel was desecrated during the Peninsular War and their tombs command little attention in such a marvellous setting.

Also worth seeing is the opulent **Monasterio de San Marcos**, built in 1168 for the Knights of Santiago, one of several chivalric orders founded in the twelfth century to protect pilgrims on their way to Santiago and lead the Reconquest. In the sixteenth century the monastery was rebuilt as a palatial headquarters for the order, its massive facade lavishly embellished with Plateresque designs. Fittingly, it has been converted into a *parador*, where the guests enjoy the luxury of a magnificent church of their own, the **Iglesia San Marcos**. The church can be visited by non-patrons too; its sacristy houses a small **museum** (Tues–Sat 10am–2pm & 4.30/5–8/8.30pm, Sun 4.30/5–8/8.30pm; €1.20) of beautiful and priceless exhibits, grouped in a room separated from the lobby of the hotel by a thick pane of glass.

Practicalities

The **train and bus stations** are both just south of the river; the train station at the end of Avenida de Palencia, the bridge across into town, and the bus station on Paseo Ingeniero Saenz de Miera – from here, turn left onto Paseo Ingeniero Miera to reach the bridge. From the roundabout, just across the river at Glorieta Guzmán El Bueno, you can see straight down the Avenida de Ordoño II and across the Plaza de Santo Domingo to the cathedral. Directly opposite the cathedral's west facade stands the friendly **tourist office** (Mon–Fri 9am–2pm & 5–7pm, Sat & Sun 10am–2pm & 5–8pm; ☎987 23 70 82, *www.jcyl.es/turismo*).

There are plenty of **places to stay**, particularly on the main roads leading off the Glorieta, Avda. de Roma and Avda. Ordoño II: try the *Pensión Oviedo*, Avda. de Roma 26 (☎987 22 22 36; ②); the *Hostal Central,* Avda. Ordoño II 27-3° (☎987 25 18 06; ②); or the *Pensión Suarez*, right next to the cathedral on c/Ancha 7-2° (☎987 25 42 88; ②). There's a **hostel** with a pool at c/de la Corredera 4 (☎987 20 34 14; ①; July & Aug); follow Avda. de Independencia from Plaza de Santo Domingo. The city **campsite** (☎987 68 02 33) is 5km out on the Valladolid road – unfortunately there's no bus.

For sheer enjoyment, the best time of year to be in León is for the **fiesta** of St Peter in the last week of June. The rest of the year, the liveliest places tend to be the **bars and restaurants** in the small square of San Martín, behind Plaza Mayor, and the dark narrow streets which surround it. You'll find good food at the *Restaurante Fornos*, c/Cid 8, or *Mesón Leones Racimo de Oro*, Caño Badillo 2 (closed Tues), and inexpensive and filling platos at *Mesón Alhambra*, c/Roa de la Vega, just south of Plaza Calvo. A short walk from the cathedral lies the *Dickens Tavern* c/Pablo Florez 2, a strange mix of traditional Irish and Spanish culture, offering a friendly atmosphere and good food.

THE NORTH COAST

Spain's **Atlantic coast** is very different from the popular image of the country, with a rocky, indented coastline full of cove beaches and fjord-like *rías*. It's an immensely beautiful region – mountainous, green and thickly forested. It rains often, and much of the time the countryside is shrouded in a fine mist. But the summers, if you don't mind the occasional shower, are a glorious escape from the unrelenting heat of the south.

In the east, butting against France, is **Euskadi** – the **Basque Country** – which, despite some of the heaviest industrialization on the peninsula, remains remarkably unspoiled: neat and quiet inland, rugged and enclosed along the coast, with easy, efficient transport everywhere. **San Sebastián** is the big draw on the coast, a major resort with superb but crowded beaches, but there are any number of lesser-known, equally attractive coastal villages all the way to **Bilbao** and beyond. Note that the Basque **language**, which bears almost no relation to Spanish, is very widespread (we've given the alternative Basque names where popularly used) and the most obvious sign of Spain's strongest separatist movement.

To the west lies **Cantabria**, centred on the port of **Santander**, with more good beaches and superb trekking in the mountains of the **Picos de Europa**. The mountains extend into **Asturias**, the one part of Spain never to be conquered by the Moors. It remains today an idiosyncratic principality standing slightly apart from the rest of the nation. Its high, remote valleys are mining country, providing the raw materials for the heavy industry of the three cities: **Gijón, Avilés** and **Oviedo**.

In the far west, **Galicia** looks like Ireland, and there are further parallels in its climate, culture and – despite its fertile appearance – its history of famine and poverty. While right-wing Galicia may not share the radical traditions of the Basque country or of industrial Asturias it does treasure its independence, and Gallego is still spoken by around 85 percent of the population – again, we've given Gallego place names in parentheses. For travellers, the obvious highlight is **Santiago de Compostela**, the greatest goal for pilgrims in medieval Europe.

Once you leave the Basque country, communications in this region are generally slow. If you're not in a great hurry, you may want to make use of the independent **FEVE rail line** (rail passes are not valid). The rail line begins at Bilbao and follows the coast, with inland branches to Oviedo and León, all the way to El Ferrol in Galicia. Despite recent major repairs and upgrading, it's still slow, but it's a terrific journey, skirting beaches, crossing rivers and snaking through a succession of limestone gorges.

San Sebastián

The undisputed queen of the Basque resorts, **SAN SEBASTIÁN** (Donostia), just half an hour down the coast from Irún, is a picturesque – though expensive – town with excellent beaches. Along with Santander, it has always been the most fashionable place to escape the heat of the southern summers, and in July and August it's always packed. Though it tries hard to be chic, San Sebastián is still too much of a family resort to compete with the South of France. Set around the deep, still bay of La Concha and enclosed by rolling low hills, it's beautifully situated; the old town sits on the eastern promontory, its back to the wooded slopes of Monte Urgull, while newer development has spread inland along the banks of the River Urumea and around the edge of the bay to the foot of Monte Igüeldo.

The **old quarter** is the centre of interest – cramped and noisy streets where crowds congregate in the evenings to wander among the small bars and shops or sample the shellfish from the traders down by the fishing harbour. Prices tend to reflect the popularity of the area, especially in the waterside restaurants, but it's no hardship to survive on the delicious tapas which are laid out in all but the fanciest bars – check the prices first, as it's quite easy to run up a sizeable bill: around €1.20 per *pincho* is now the norm. Here too are the town's chief sights: the gaudy Baroque facade of the church of **Santa María**, and the more elegantly restrained sixteenth-century **San Vicente**. The centre of the old part is the Plaza de la Constitución, known locally as "La Consti"; the numbers on the balconies of the buildings around the square refer to the days when it was used as a bullring. Just behind San Vicente, the excellent **Museo de San Telmo** (Tues–Sat 10.30am–1.30pm & 4–8pm, Sun 10.30am–2pm; free) is a fascinating jumble of Basque folklore, funerary relics and assorted artworks. At the end of the harbour is the expensive **Aquarium** (daily 10am–8/10pm; €6.50), featuring an undersea viewing tunnel and a disappointing naval museum. Behind this, **Monte Urgull** is crisscrossed by winding footpaths to the top. From the mammoth figure of Christ on its summit there are great views out to sea and back across the bay to the town, weather permitting. Still better views across the bay can be had from the top of **Monte Igüeldo**; take bus #16 or walk around the bay to its base, from where a funicular (daily: July–Sept 10am–10pm; Oct–March 11am–6pm; April–June 11am–8pm, closed Wed; €1.30 return) will carry you to the summit, the home of a **funfair**.

There are three **beaches** in San Sebastián: Playa de la Concha, Playa de Ondaretta and Playa de la Zurriola. **La Concha** is the most central and the most celebrated, a wide crescent of yellow sand stretching round the bay from the town. Despite the almost impenetrable mass of flesh here during most of the summer, this is the best of the beaches. Out in La Concha bay is a small island, **Isla de Santa Clara**, which makes a good spot for picnics; a boat leaves from the port every thirty minutes in the summer from 10am to 8pm (€1.20). **Ondaretta**, considered the best beach for swimming and never quite as packed as La Concha, is a continuation of the same strand beyond the rocky outcrop which supports the **Palacio Miramar** (gardens open 9/10am–sunset; free), once a summer home of Spain's royal family. The atmosphere here is rather more staid – it's known as *La Diplomática* for the number of Madrid's "best" families who vacation here. Though it's far less crowded, don't risk the **Playa de Zurriola**; swimming is extremely dangerous due to strong currents, and, despite recent efforts to clean it up, the water isn't too clean either.

South of the city centre lies the futuristic **Miramon** science museum (Tues–Sun 10/11am–7/8pm, €4.20), which takes a fresh look at scientific concepts. With a planetarium and exhibition rooms it will be of interest to frustrated scientists. Take bus #28 from the Boulevard.

Practicalities

National **buses** use the terminal at Plaza Pío XII (the ticket office is round the corner on c/Hiribidea), twenty minutes' walk inland along the river, while regional ones go from the Plaza de Guipúzcoa. The main-line **train station** is across the River Urumea on the Paseo de Francia, although local lines to Hendaye and Bilbao have their terminus on c/Easo (rail passes not valid). The **tourist office**, on c/Reina Regente beside the Puente Kursaal in the old town (summer Mon–Sat 8am–8pm, Sun 10am–1pm; winter Mon–Sat 9am–1.30pm & 3.30–7pm, Sun 10am–1.30pm; ☎943 48 11 66, *www.paisvasco.com/donostia*), is very helpful in finding a place to stay and providing accommodation, although for a greater selection of pamphlets there is a useful Basque Government tourist office at Paseo de los Fuieros 1, just off Avda. de la Libertad (Mon–Sat 9am–1pm & 3.30–6.30pm, Sun 9.30am–1.30pm, closed Sat pm and Sun am in winter).

Accommodation, though plentiful, is not cheap and can be very hard to come by in season and at weekends. In the old town, look around La Consti and c/San Jerónimo; in the central district there's better value around the cathedral, especially Calles Easo, San Martín and San Bartolomé; or on the other side of the river try behind the Plaza de Cataluña, where you'll also find excellent tapas bars. Places to try in the old part include *Pensión San Jerómino*, c/San Jerómino 25-2° (☎943 42 08 30; ③); *Pensión Urgull*, c/Esterlines 10-3° (☎943 43 00 47; ③); *and Pensión Aussie*, c/San Jerónimo 23-2° (☎943 42 28 74; ③). Around the cathedral, try the *Pensión Artea*, c/San Bartolomé 33-1° (☎943 45 51 00; ③); *Pensión La Perla*, c/Loyola 10-1° (☎943 42 81 23; ③); *Pensión Añorga*, c/Easo 12-1° (☎943 46 79 45; ③); *Pensión San Martín*, c/San Martín 10-1° (☎943 42 87 14; ④); or *Eder II*, Alameda del Boulevard 16-2° (☎943 42 64

49; ④). San Sebastián's **campsite** (☎943 21 45 02) is excellent, but it's a long way from the centre on the landward side of Monte Igüeldo, reached by bus #16 from the Alameda del Boulevard. The **hostel** (☎943 31 02 68; ②), known as "La Sirena", is located on Paseo de Igüeldo, just a few minutes' walk back from the end of Ondarreta Beach, but away from the centre.

If you're in the mood for some spectacularly expensive **food**, San Sebastián has some of the best restaurants in the country. Luckily for the more impecunious, help is at hand in the good-value, delicious *pintxos* which are set out in all but the fanciest of bars, or try the fixed *menú* at places near the cathedral such as *Bodegón Ardandegi*, c/Reyes Católicos 7; the highly recommended *La Barranquesa*, c/Larramendi 21; or, in the old quarter, *Morgan Jatetxea* on c/Narrika Kalea. Alternatively, order some well-priced *raciones* at either *Gaztelu*, c/31 de Agosto 22, or *Bar Beti-Ja*, both on c/Narrika, in the old town.

In the evenings you'll find no shortage of action, with **clubs** and **bars** wherever the tourists congregate. The fanciest are along the promenade by the beach, Paseo de la Concha, where you'll pay €12–18 entrance; the cheaper places are mostly in the old town where people normally start the evening off – later everyone heads to the area along c/Reyes Católicos behind the cathedral or c/San Bartolomé for the young crowd. For late nights, head for *Etxekalte* at 11 c/de Mar, overlooking the port and beach, where a funky clientele groove to choice jazz, urban soul and even some trip-hop (free entry). Throughout the summer, too, there are constant **festivals**, many involving Basque sports such as the annual rowing races between the villages along the coast. The International Jazz Festival (*www.basquetravel.com/jazz*), at different locations throughout the town in the third week of July, invariably attracts top performers as well as hordes of people on their way home from the fiesta in Pamplona.

Bilbao

Although traditionally an industrial city, **BILBAO** (Bilbo) is embracing the new millennium with confidence and plenty of civic swagger. A state-of-the-art metro (designed by Lord Norman Foster) is up and running; the awesome new Guggenheim Museum by Frank O. Gehry is a major draw; a unified transport terminus is planned and there are various bids to further develop the riverfront with university buildings and public parks connected by footpaths, dramatic bridges and a tramway. Coupled with a vibrant atmosphere and some of the best cafés, restaurants and bars in Euskadi, Bilbao's gleaming new buildings and verdant parks are slowly reinventing this city.

The **Casco Viejo**, the old quarter on the east bank of the river, is still a main point of interest for the beautiful **Teatro Arriaga**, the elegantly arcaded **Plaza Nueva**, the Gothic **Catedral de Santiago** (closed at time of writing; contact tourist office for details) and, slightly to the northeast, the interesting **Basque Museum** on c/Cruz (Tues–Sat 10.30am–1.30pm & 4–7pm, Sun 10.30am–1.30pm; €1.80, Thurs free).

It is along the Río Nervión that a whole number of exciting new buildings have appeared. A good route through leads from the Casco Viejo down the river past the imposing Zubizuri bridge to the billowing curves of the **Guggenheim Museum** (Tues–Sun 10am–8pm; €7.10). Inside, the Guggenheim is divided into two parts: the permanent collection is housed in more traditional (rectangular) galleries, and descends in chronological order from the Picassos and Surrealists on the third floor to the Pop and contemporary artists at ground level; temporary exhibitions and individual artists' collections are displayed in the huge sculptured spaces nearer the river. Further along the river from the Guggenheim, on the edge of the Parque de Doña Casilda de Hurriza, is the **Museo de Bellas Artes** (Tues–Sat 10am–8pm, Sun 10am–2pm; €3.60, Wed free), which houses works by Goya and El Greco and has played host to some acclaimed temporary exhibitions.

Football fans shouldn't miss the chance to venture a little further east to one of the shrines of Spanish football, **El Estadio San Mamés**. Known as "La Catedral", it is home to Atletico

Bilbao and is famed for its atmosphere and discerning spectators. Tickets for home matches are available at the stadium (☎94 424 08 77).

Practicalities

Arriving in Bilbao, the **train station** is conveniently located just over the river from the Casco Viejo, while most **buses** arrive some way out of the centre at San Mamés – from here you can catch the metro to the centre. Buses from Burgos, Barcelona and Madrid arrive on c/Autonomía, a twenty-minute walk via Plaza de Zabálburu from the old town. The **tourist office** (Mon–Fri 9am–2pm & 4–7.30pm, Sat 9am–2pm, Sun 10am–2pm; ☎94 479 57 60, *www.bilbao.net*) is just north of the Teatro Arriaga on Paseo del Arenal; there's another branch just outside the Guggenheim (Tues–Sat 11am–2pm & 4–6pm, Sun 11am–2pm). The best **places to stay** are almost all in the Casco Viejo – especially along and around the streets leading off c/Bidebarrieta, which leads from Plaza Arriaga to the cathedral. Prices have risen substantially since the opening of the Guggenheim, but good possibilities are *the Hostal Gurea*, c/Bidebarrieta 14 (☎94 416 32 99; ②); *Hostal La Estrella*, c/María Muñoz 6, off Plaza Miguel Unamuno (☎94 416 40 66; ③); the superb *Pensión Ladero*, c/Lotería 1 (☎94 415 09 32; ②); *Pensión Serantes*, c/Somera 14 (944 15 15 57; ②); and *Hostal Roquefer*, c/Lotería 2 (☎94 415 07 55; ③). For a medium-range hotel, the *Hotel Arriaga*, c/Ribera 3 (☎94 479 00 01; ④) is a friendly and convenient option next to the Teatro. Booking ahead is advised during the summer and at weekends.

Eating and drinking are also best in the Casco Viejo, although there are few regular restaurants – this is one of those cities where the most enjoyable way to eat is to move from bar to bar, snacking on tapas: Plaza Nueva has numerous options. For breakfast try the excellent *Café Boulevard* on Paseo del Arenal, and for a mid-afternoon coffee you can't beat the Arabic-style *Café Iruña* across the river at c/Jardines de Albia 5. If you do fancy a sit-down meal, try the highly recommended Basque restaurant *Bar Rio-Oja*, c/Perro 4, just west of the cathedral. Bilbao can be very lively indeed at **night** – and totally wild during the August fiesta, "La Semana Grande", which usually begins on the first Saturday after August 15, with scores of open-air bars, live music and impromptu dancing in an incredible atmosphere. Head for the streets around c/Licenciado Poza and c/Ledesma.

Santander and around

Long a favourite summer resort of Madrileños, **SANTANDER** has a French feel – an elegant, reserved resort in a similar vein to San Sebastián. Some people find it a clean, restful base for a short stay; for others it is dull and snobbish. On a brief visit, the balance is tipped in its favour by its excellent (and no longer polluted) beaches, and the sheer style of its setting. The narrow **Bahía de Santander** is dramatic, with the city and port on one side in clear view of open countryside and high mountains on the other; a great first view of Spain if you're arriving on the **ferry** from Plymouth.

Santander was severely damaged by fire in 1941, and what's left of the city divides into two parts: the **town and port**, which are still quite a tangle, having been reconstructed on the old grid around the cathedral; and the beach suburb of **El Sardinero**, a twenty-minute walk (or bus #1, #3, #4, #7 or #9) from the centre, more if you follow the coast around the wooded headland of **La Magdalena**. There are few real sights to distract you: the **Cathedral** (daily 10am–1pm & 4–7.30pm, Sat & Sun till 8.45pm; free), with its Gothic crypt, is of passing interest; the pick of the museums is the **Museo Provincial de Prehistoria y Arqueología**, c/Casimiro Sainz (Tues–Sat 9/10am–1pm & 4–7/8.45pm, Sun 8am–2pm & 4.30–9pm; free), where finds from the province's numerous prehistorically inhabited caves are exhibited. The chief pleasures lie on the **beaches**. The first of these, **Playa de la Magdalena**, begins on the near side of the headland. The beautiful yellow strand, sheltered by cliffs and flanked by a summer windsurfing school, is deservedly popular, as is **El Sardinero** itself. If you find both beaches too crowded for your taste, there are long stretches of dunes across the bay at

Somo (which has windsurfing boards for rent and a summer campsite) and **Pedreña**; to get to them, jump on a *lancha*, a cheap taxi-ferry (€2.50 return) which leaves every fifteen minutes from the central dock.

Practicalities

The RENFE and FEVE **train stations** are side by side, just off the waterside; the **bus station** is directly across the Plaza Porticada. There are three **tourist offices**: the best is in the Jardines de la Pereda (summer daily 9am–2pm & 4–9pm; winter Mon–Fri 9.30am–1.30pm & 4–7pm, Sat 10am–1pm; ☎942 20 30 00, *www.congresos-santander.org*); another is in the ferry terminal (Mon–Fri 9am–1pm & 4–7pm); and the third is in front of the casino at El Sardinero (same hours). Good places to start looking for **rooms** are c/de Rodríguez in front of the station – *San Miguel* at no. 9 (☎942 22 03 63; ③) is an option – and Avda. de los Castros, which runs all the way across the northeastern side of town, where you'll find many budget options – *La Soledad* at no. 17 (☎942 27 09 36; ②) is recommended. There are some very popular cheapish places by the beach, on the Avda. de los Castros at Sardinero, including the *Botín* on c/Isabel Segundo 1 (☎942 21 00 94; ②), and a **campsite** (☎942 39 15 30) a short walk further down the coast on Cabo Mayor which also rents bungalows (⑦). **Food** options are plentiful along c/San Simón and c/Río de la Pila, above Plaza de Velarde, as well as around the main square and station. If you're after seafood, wander down to the fishing port (*barrio pesquero*), to the east of the ferry port and stations; there's no shortage of places along the c/Marqués de la Ensanada, but check prices before ordering – *Casa José* on nearby c/Mocejón is more reasonably priced than most.

Oviedo and around

The principal reason for visiting **OVIEDO** is to see three small churches. They are perhaps the most remarkable in Spain, built in a unique style during the first half of the ninth century, a period of almost total isolation for the tiny Asturian kingdom, which was then the only part of Spain under Christian rule. Oviedo, the modern capital of Asturias, became the centre of this outpost in 810. Here King Alfonso II built a chapel, the Cámara Santa, to house the holy relics rescued from Toledo when it fell to the Moors. Remodelled in the twelfth century, this now forms the inner sanctuary of the **Cathedral** (Mon–Fri 10am–1pm & 4–7pm, Sat 10am–1pm & 4–6pm; €1.20, €2.40 including museum, free Thurs), a fine Gothic structure at the heart of the modern city. Around the cathedral, enclosed by scattered sections of the medieval town walls, is what remains of **old Oviedo**: a compact, attractive quarter in what is a fairly bleak industrial city. Some of the **palaces** – not least the archbishop's, opposite the cathedral – are worth a look, though none are open to visitors. Of interest, too, is the **Archeological Museum**, immediately behind the cathedral in the former convent of San Vicente (Tues–Sat 10am–1.30pm & 4–6pm, Sun 11am–1pm; free), which displays various pieces of sculpture from the three "Asturian-Visigoth" churches.

The nearest of these churches, **Santullano**, lies ten minutes' walk to the northeast of the centre along c/de Gijón, right next to a busy main road. Built around 830, it's considerably larger and more spacious than the other Asturian churches, with an unusual "secret chamber" built into the outer wall. It is kept locked but the keys are available at the priest's house to the left; there are original frescoes inside, executed in similar style to Roman villas. The most impressive of the churches is **Santa María del Naranco** (Tues–Sat 9.30am–1pm & 3–7pm, Sun–Mon 9.30am–1pm; €1.50, Mon free), majestically located on a wooded slope 3km above the city. It's a 45-minute walk from the centre along a beautiful marked route, or thirty minutes from the station. This perfectly harmonious little building was designed not as a church but as a royal palace or hunting lodge: the present structure was just the main hall. A couple of hundred metres beyond Santa María is the palace chapel, **San Miguel de Lillo** (same hours and prices as Santa María), built with soft golden sandstone and red tiles. This is generally assumed to be by the same architect as Santa María, though its design, the Byzantine cross-in-square, is quite different.

Practicalities

Central Oviedo is easy enough to find your way around, but transport can be confusing. Most **buses** use the underground station in the Plaza General Primo de Rivera, but it's worth checking departures with the **tourist office** (Mon–Fri 9am–2pm & 4–6.30pm; ☎98 521 33 85) in the cathedral square, or at the municipal branch on the corner of Campo de San Francisco (Mon–Fri 10.30am–2pm & 4.30–7.30pm, Sat–Sun 11am–2pm). For trains, there are two FEVE **stations** in addition to the regular RENFE one serving León. The FEVE Asturias, next to the RENFE, is for the line to Santander; the so-called FEVE Basque, oddly enough, serves stations west to El Ferrol. They're fifteen minutes apart, so don't try to make too tight a connection.

Accommodation is plentiful, with many **hostales** on c/de Uría alongside San Francisco park, including *Pension La Armania*, c/Nuevo de Mayo 14 (☎98 522 03 01; ②). Other promising areas are c/Jovellanos north of the cathedral – the *Pomar* (☎98 522 27 91; ②) is friendly – and c/9 de Mayo or c/de Caveda near the main train stations. For **food**, try any number of good restaurants at c/Gascona or *La Gran Taverna* next to the cathedral. And lastly, whether you stay or not, don't leave without ordering at least one glass of Asturian *sidra* (cider) – if only for bewilderment's sake. Onlookers will show you the correct drinking protocol, and if the cloudy nectar is to your taste there is a new **cider museum** in Nava on the road to Santander (summer Tues–Sat noon–2pm & 4–8pm, Sun noon–2pm & 6–9pm; winter Tues–Fri 11am–2pm & 4–7pm, Sat 11am–3pm, Sun 11am–2pm; €1.80).

Santiago de Compostela

SANTIAGO DE COMPOSTELA, built in a warm golden granite, is one of the most beautiful of all Spanish cities. The medieval city has been declared a national monument in its entirety, and remains a remarkably integrated whole, all the better for being almost completely pedestrianized. The **pilgrimage** to Santiago captured the imagination of medieval Christian Europe on an unprecedented scale. At the height of its popularity, in the eleventh and twelfth centuries, the city was receiving over half a million pilgrims each year. People of all classes came to visit the supposed shrine of Saint James the Apostle (Santiago to the Spanish), making this the third-holiest site in Christendom, after Jerusalem and Rome. The atmosphere of the place is much as it must have been in the days of the pilgrims, though tourists are now as likely to be attracted by art and history as by religion. But Santiago is by no means a dead city – it's the seat of Galicia's regional government and there's a large student population too. It's also a manageable size – you can wander fifteen minutes out of town and reach open countryside.

The City

All roads to Santiago lead to the **Cathedral** (daily 7.30am–9pm), whose sheer grandeur you first appreciate upon venturing into the vast expanse of the Plaza de Obradoiro. Directly ahead stands a fantastic Baroque pyramid of granite, flanked by immense bell towers and everywhere adorned with statues of St James in his familiar pilgrim guise with staff, broad hat and scallop-shell badge. This **Obradoiro facade** was built in the mid-eighteenth century by an obscure Santiago-born architect, Fernando Casas y Novoa, and no other work of Spanish Baroque can compare with it.

The main body of the cathedral is Romanesque, rebuilt in the eleventh and twelfth centuries after a devastating raid by the Moors. The building's highlight is the **Pórtico de Gloria**, the original west front, which now stands inside the cathedral behind the Obradoiro. This was both the culmination of all Romanesque sculpture and a precursor of the new Gothic realism, with a host of wonderfully carved figures. St James sits on the central column, beneath Christ and just above eye level; the pilgrims would give thanks at journey's end by praying with the fingers of one hand pressed into the roots of the *Tree of Jesse* below the saint. So many millions have performed this act of supplication that five deep and shiny holes have been worn into the solid marble. On the other side of the pillar, kneeling at the foot, is the sculptor himself, Maestro Mateo. Pilgrims would touch the statue's head with their foreheads to absorb his wisdom.

The spiritual climax of the pilgrimage was the approach to the **High Altar**. This remains a peculiar experience: you climb steps behind the altar, embrace the Most Sacred Image of Santiago, kiss his bejewelled cape, and are handed, by way of certification, a document in Latin called a *Compostela*. The altar is an exuberant creation of eighteenth-century Churrigueresque, but the statue has stood there for seven centuries and the procedure is quite unchanged. You'll notice an elaborate pulley system in front of the altar. This is for moving the immense incense-burner which, operated by eight priests, is swung in a vast ceiling-to-ceiling arc across the transept. It is stunning to watch, but takes place only during certain services such as Friday and Saturday Mass at noon – check with the tourist office.

You can visit the treasury, cloisters, archeological museum and the beautiful crypt (summer Mon–Sat 10am–1.30pm & 4–7.30pm, Sun 10/10.30am–1.30pm; winter 11am–1pm & 4–6pm, Sun 11am–1.30pm; €3). The late Gothic **cloisters** in particular are well worth seeing: from the plain, mosque-like courtyard you get a wonderful view of the riotous mixture of the exterior, crawling with pagodas, domes, obelisks, battlements, scallop shells and cornucopias.

The north side of the cathedral is occupied by the **Palace of Archbishop Gelmírez** (Easter–Sept only Mon–Sat 10am–1.30pm & 4.30–7.30pm; €1.20). Gelmírez was one of the seminal figures in Santiago's development: he rebuilt the cathedral in the twelfth century, raised the see to an archbishopric, and most importantly made the place extremely rich. In his palace, suitably luxuriant, are a vaulted kitchen and some fine Romanesque chambers.

Further afield, the main interest lies in the multifarious monasteries and convents. The enormous Benedictine **San Martín** stands close to the cathedral, the vast altarpiece in its church depicting its patron riding alongside St James. Nearby is **San Francisco**, reputedly founded by the saint himself during his pilgrimage to Santiago. In the north of the city are Baroque **Santa Clara**, with a unique curving facade, and a little beyond it, **Santo Domingo**. This last is perhaps the most interesting of the buildings, featuring a magnificent seventeenth-century triple stairway, each spiral leading to different storeys of a single tower, and a fascinating museum of Gallego crafts and traditions, the **Museo do Pobo Gallego** (Mon–Sat 10am–1pm & 4–7pm; free).

Practicalities

Arriving at the **bus station** you are 1km or so north of the town centre; bus #10 will take you in to the Plaza de Galicia at the southern edge of the old city. The **train station** is a walkable distance south of this plaza along c/del Horreo. The **tourist office** is at Rúa do Vilar 43 (Mon–Fri 10am–2pm & 4–7pm, Sat 11am–2pm & 5–7pm, Sun 11am–2pm; ☎981 58 40 81, *www.turgalicia.es*), and can provide complete lists of accommodation and facilities. There is online access at the **Internet** shop at c/Rúa Nova 50 (€1.20/hr).

You should have no difficulty finding an inexpensive **room** in Santiago, though note that *pensiones* here are often called *hospedajes*. The biggest concentration of places is on the three parallel streets leading down from the cathedral: Rúa Nueva, Rúa do Vilar and c/del Franco. *Hospedaje Santa Cruz*, Rúa do Vilar 42 (☎981 58 23 62; ②), has very friendly English-speaking owners; *Hostal Residencia La Estela*, Avda. Rajoy 1 (☎981 58 27 96; ③), just off Plaza Obradoiro, has rooms overlooking the front of the cathedral; and *Hostal Barbantes*, c/del Franco 1 (☎981 58 10 77; ②) has a lively bar and restaurant. Another very cheap place is *Hospedaje Viño* on Plaza Mazarelos 7 (☎981 58 51 85; ①) – the indomitable owner also has dozens of other rooms scattered around town. The **campsite**, *Camping As Cancelas*, two and half kilometres north of the cathedral (☎981 58 02 66), is excellent; take the airport bus or city bus #9.

Thanks, perhaps, to the students, there are plenty of cheap places to eat here, along with excellent bars; it's also the best place in Galicia to hear local Breton-style music, played on *gaitas* (bagpipes). An excellent student eatery is the *Casa Manolo* at Rúa Traviesa 27, while c/del Franco is full of bars with reliable tapas such as *Tacita de Juan*. *Bodegón de Xulio* here is a really good seafood restaurant, though if you really want to push the boat out try *O Dezseis* at San Pedro 28. For **drinking** you're spoilt for choice in Santiago; good starting points are the laid-back *A Casa das Crechas* at Via Sacra 3 and the arty *Bar Atlantico* or alternative *Bar Tolo*, both on Fonte de San Miguel. For **dancing**, the area around Praza Roja has a host of brash bars as well as the town's three meat-market discos, the best of which is *Ruta 66*.

THE PYRENEES

With the singular exception of **Pamplona** at the time of its bull-running fiesta, the area around the Spanish Pyrenees is little visited – most people who come here at all travel straight through. In doing so they miss out on some of the most wonderful scenery in Spain, and some of the country's most attractive trekking. You'll also be struck by the slower pace of life, especially in **Navarra** (in the west, a partly Basque region) and **Aragón** (in the centre) – the Catalan Pyrenees, along with **Andorra**, are more developed. There are few cities here – Pamplona itself and **Zaragoza**, with its fine Moorish architecture, are the only large centres – but there are plenty of attractive small towns and of course the mountains themselves, with several beautiful **national parks** as a focus for exploration.

Pamplona

PAMPLONA (Iruña) has been the capital of Navarra since the ninth century, and long before that was a powerful fortress town defending the northern approaches to Spain. Even now it has something of the appearance of a garrison city, with its hefty walls and elaborate pentagonal citadel. There's plenty to look at – the elaborately restored **Cathedral** with its magnificent cloister and interesting **Museo Diocesano** (summer Mon–Fri 10am–7pm, Sat 10am–1.30pm; winter Mon–Sat 10am–1.30pm & 4–7pm; €3), the colossal **city walls** and **citadel**, the display of regional archeology, history and art in the **Museo de Navarra** (Tues–Sat 10am–2pm & 5–7pm, Thurs until 9pm for special exhibitions, Sun 11am–2pm; €1.80), and much more. But ninety percent of visitors come here for just one thing: the thrilling week of the **Fiesta of San Fermín**. From midday on July 6 until midnight on July 14 the city gives itself up to riotous nonstop celebration.

The centre of the festivities is the **encierro**, or running of the bulls – in which the animals decisively have the upper hand. Six bulls are released each morning at eight to run from their corral near the Plaza San Domingo to the bullring. In front, around and occasionally under them run the hundreds of locals and tourists who are foolish or drunk enough to test their daring against the horns. It was Hemingway's *The Sun Also Rises* that really put "Los San Fermines" on the map, and the area in front of the Plaza de Toros has been renamed Plaza Hemingway by a grateful council. To watch the *encierro* it's essential to arrive early – crowds have already formed an hour before it starts. The best **vantage points** are near the starting point or on the wall leading to the bullring. The event divides into two parts: there's the actual running of the bulls; and then after the bulls have been through the streets, bullocks with padded horns are let loose on the crowd in the bullring. If you watch the actual running, you won't be able to get into the bullring, so go on two separate mornings to see both. **Bullfights** take place daily at 6.30pm, with the bulls that ran that morning; tickets are expensive (€12–74 from the Plaza de Toros one day before the show) and are fiendishly difficult to get hold of. At the end of the week (midnight on July 14) there's a mournful candlelit procession, the **Pobre De Mi**, at which the festivities are officially wound up for another year.

Practicalities

The **train station** is a long way from the old part of town, but bus #9 runs every twenty minutes to the end of Paseo de Sarasate, a few minutes' walk from the central Plaza del Castillo – there is a RENFE ticket office at c/Estella 8. The **bus station** is more central, on c/Conde Oliveto in front of the citadel, while the **tourist office** (summer Mon–Sat 10am–2pm & 4–7pm, Sun 10am–2pm; winter Mon–Fri 10am–2pm & 4–7pm, Sat 10am–2pm; ☎948 20 65 40, *www.cfnavarra.es/turismonavarra*) is on Plaza de San Francisco. During San Fermín, there is also an information bus on Plaza del Castillo, and the main office is open from 10am–5pm.

You'll find a cluster of cheap **hostales** on noisy c/San Nicolás and its continuation c/San Gregorio, off Plaza del Castillo. Rooms are in short supply during summer, and at fiesta time you've virtually no chance of a place on spec. Prices are fairly similar, but good ones to try include *Hostal Otano*, c/San Nicolás 5 (☎948 22 50 95; ③); and *Hostal Bearán*, c/San Nicolás 25 (☎948 22 34 28; ③). Most at least double their prices during the fiesta. Otherwise, try nearer the cathedral – *Santa Cecilia*, c/Navarrería 17 (☎948 22 22 30; ②) is good. There's a **campsite**, *Ezcaba* (☎948 33 03 15), 7km out of town on the road to France; again it fills several days before the fiesta. Bus #4 runs to the campsite but there are only four daily departures – hitching there isn't too hard if you miss them.

The best **bars** are on and around c/San Nicolás but there are also a number of grungy latenight dives on Calderia S. Augustín on the other side of the square. **Food** is expensive in Pamplona and you'll be hard pressed to find a *menú del día* for less than €7 – about the cheapest is *Catachu*, c/Indatxikia 16, parallel to Paseo de Sarasate. Alternatively, try the streets around c/Mayor, in particular *Bar la Cepa* or *Bar Poliki* on c/San Lorenzo and Bar la Campana on c/de la Campana, all of which offer a combination of *bocadillos* and good *menús*. C/San Nicolás also has several reasonable restaurants including *Dom Luis* and the vegetarian *Sarasate*. *Café Roch* on c/de las Comedias is great for tapas or, to get away from the crowds, go to the elegant *Meson del Caballo Blanco* on c/Redin up above the ramparts behind the cathedral – you can order cheap *raciones* upstairs. The elegant *Café Iruña*, on Plaza del Castillo, is the place to sit over a leisurely coffee as you take in the action.

Zaragoza

ZARAGOZA is the capital of Aragón, and easily its largest and liveliest city, with over half the province's one million people and the majority of its industry. There are some excellent bars and restaurants tucked in among its remarkable monuments, and it's also a handy transport centre, with good connections into the Pyrenees and east towards Barcelona. If you're in town during Semana Santa – the week before Easter – you can watch some spectacular processions.

The most imposing of the city's churches, majestically fronting the Río Ebro, is the **Basilica de Nuestra Señora del Pilar** (daily 5.45am–9.30pm, earlier in winter), one of Zaragoza's two cathedrals. It takes its name from the column which the Virgin is said to have brought from Jerusalem during her lifetime to found the first Marian chapel in Christendom. Topped by a diminutive image of the Virgin, the pillar forms the centrepiece in the Holy Chapel and is the focal point for pilgrims, who line up to kiss an exposed section encased in a silver sheath. The cathedral also has a couple of small museums, a few minor dome frescoes by Goya, and a curious display of two unexploded bombs dropped on the cathedral during the Civil War, but stylistically the building itself is something of an outsized Baroque shed. In terms of beauty it can't compare with the nearby Gothic-Mudéjar old cathedral, **La Seo** (Tues–Fri 10am–2pm & 4–7pm, Sat–Sun 10am–12/1pm & 4/5pm–6/7pm), at the far end of the pigeon-thronged Plaza del Pilar. The city has recently been bringing to light its **Roman past** in three underground excavations: the Forum and River port (just off the Plaza del Pilar) and the Roman Baths (Tues–Sat 10am–noon & 5–8pm, Sun 10am–2pm; €2.40 each museum or combined ticket available from the Forum €3.60). You can also see the remains of the amphitheatre in c/Veronica.

The highlight of Zaragoza, which you should see even if you plan to do no more than change trains or buses here, is the city's only surviving legacy from Moorish times. From the tenth to the eleventh century Zaragoza was the centre of an independent dynasty, the Beni Kasim. Their palace, the newly restored **Aljafería** (Tues–Wed & Fri–Sat 10am–2pm & 4/4.30–6.30/8pm, Sun 10am–2pm, closed Thurs; €1.80), was built in the heyday of their rule in the mid-eleventh century, and thus predates the Alhambra in Granada as well as Sevilla's Alcázar. Much was added after the Reconquest, when the palace was adapted and used by the kings of Aragón. From the original design the foremost relic is a tiny and beautiful mosque adjacent to the ticket office. Further on is an intricately decorated court, the Patio de Santa Isabella. Crossing from here, the Grand Staircase (added in 1492) leads to a succession of mainly fourteenth-century rooms, remarkable chiefly for their carved ceilings. There are guided tours on the half-hour.

If you're interested in chasing the Moorish influence further, four **Mudéjar towers** survive in Zaragoza, the finest of which is the square tower of the church of **Santa María Magdalena**.

Practicalities

Points of arrival in Zaragoza are rather scattered. From the **train station** (*Estación Portillo*), walk the short c/General Mayandia, turn right onto Paseo María Agustín and take bus #22 to Plaza España – or walk it in about 20 minutes. There are various **bus terminals**; most long-distance services leave from the Agreda terminal at Paseo María Agustín 7 (right from the train station), although destinations for León and the north coast leave from the Plaza del Portillo, just north of the train station. For closer destinations (such as Pamplona or Tarazona) check with one of the city's three **tourist offices**. The main office is in the Plaza del Pilar (☎976 20 12 00, *www.turismozaragoza.com*) with another at the Torreón de la Zuda – part of the city fortifications overlooking the river – and the third at the train station; all are open daily from 10am to 8pm.

There are **rooms** – and some cheap **restaurants** – close to the train station, along c/Madre Sacramento, parallel to Paseo María Agustín. *Fonda Miramar*, c/Capitán Casado 17 (☎976 28 10 94; ②) is better than most. However, there's more atmosphere, better accommodation possibilities and most of the city's nightlife crowded into an area known as **El Tubo**, between c/de Alfonso I and c/Don Jaime I, close to the Plaza del Pilar. There are upwards of a dozen cheap *fondas* and *pensiones* here, rarely full: try particularly the ultra-cheap *Fonda Satue*, Espoz y Mina 4 (☎976 39 07 09; ①) or along c/Estébares. Other recommended lodgings include *Hostal Cumbre*, Avda de Cataluña 24 (☎976 29 11 48; ③) and *Hotel Las Torres*, Plaza del Pilar 11 (☎976 39 42 50; ④), right next to the tourist office where all rooms have baths. You can **camp** at the large, barren *Camping Casablanca* (April to mid-Oct), on Paseo del Canal, 2km west of the city. Take bus #36 or #24 from the train station or Plaza de España. For **food** in El Tubo, try *Casa Lac* on c/Mártiries, supposedly the oldest restaurant in Spain, which is atmospheric and not too costly.

Jaca and around

Heading towards the Pyrenees from Zaragoza, **JACA** is the northernmost town of any size in Aragón and an obvious staging post. It's also a place of considerable interest – an early capital of the kingdom of Aragón that lay astride one of the main medieval pilgrim routes to Santiago. Accordingly, a magnificent **Cathedral** (daily 9am–1.30pm & 4–8pm), the first in Spain to be built in the Romanesque style, dominates the centre of town from its position at the north edge of the old quarter. It remains impressive despite much internal remodelling over the centuries, and there's a powerful added attraction in its **Museo Diocesano** (summer daily 10am–2pm & 4–8pm; winter Tues–Sun 11am–1.30pm & 4–6.30pm; €1.80), which should not be missed. The dark cloisters are home to a collection of beautiful twelfth- to fifteenth-century frescoes, gathered from village churches in the area and from higher up in the Pyrenees.

Although barely 800m up, Jaca ranks as a Pyrenean resort, becoming crowded in August; even at other times of the year accommodation prices tend to be pushed up by the ski and cross-border trade. But Jaca is foremost an army town, with a mass of conscripts attending the local mountain warfare academy. The military connection is nothing new: the **Ciudadela**, a sixteenth-century fort built to the stellar ground plan in vogue at the time, still offers good views of surrounding peaks. You can visit the interior (daily 11am–noon/12.30pm & 4/5–5/6.30pm; €1.80 including guided tour), but it's hardly worth it, as the outside, with slumbering deer in the dry moat, is by far the most interesting part.

Arriving in Jaca by **train**, you'll find yourself more than a kilometre's walk out of town; move quickly and take the city bus which connects with most trains. Returning, the bus leaves twenty minutes before train departures from the small square at the end of c/Mayor, just down from the Ciudadela. The more central **bus station** is on Avda. Jacetania, 200m northwest of the cathedral. The **tourist office** (Mon–Fri 9am–1.30/2pm & 4.30–7/8pm, summer Sat 10am–1.30pm & 5–9pm, Sun 10am–1.30pm) – worth a browse for its noticeboards offering all sorts of sport- and mountaineering-related services – is on Avda. Regimiento Galicia, just downhill from the bus stop and Ciudadela.

All of Jaca's budget **accommodation** can be found on the northeast edge of the old town, with two good, quiet choices being *Hostal París* by the cathedral, Plaza de San Pedro 5 (☎974 36 10 20; ②), and a bit closer to the action *Hostal Residencia El Abeto*, c/Bellido 15 (☎974 36 16 42; ③). There's also a **youth hostel** (☎974 36 05 36; ①) on Avda. Pcrimetral, next to the ice rink at the southern end of town, and two **campsites** – the closer but more basic *Victoria* (☎974 36 03 23) is 1km west of town on the Pamplona road, the wooded *Peña Oroel* (☎974 36 02 15) is 3km down the Sabiñanigo road. Good-value **eating** is found in the same part of the old district: carnivores will appreciate *La Fragua*, at c/Gil Berges 4 (closed Wed), while *La Cadiera* on c/Domingo Midal and *La Campanilla* on c/Escuelas Pias 8 both offer cheap but filling set *menús*.

The Aragonese Pyrenees

If you're not a keen trekker or skier, then the foothill villages of **ANSÓ** and **HECHO** (often spelt without the 'h') set in their beautiful namesake valleys are perhaps your best single target in the **Aragonese Pyrenees**: they're noted for their distinctive, imposing architecture, and are accessible by a 6.30pm bus (Mon–Sat) from Jaca, returning 6am from Ansó, 6.45am from Hecho. Hecho, to the east, is more visited and inevitably more expensive for **accommodation and food**: try *Casa Blasquico*, Plaza de la Fuente (☎974 37 50 07; ③), and the *comedor* at the *Fonda Lo Foratón* respectively. There's also a delightful campsite, *Valle de Hecho* (☎974 37 53 61). In the westerly valley, less-frequented Ansó offers several reasonable places to stay and eat, including *Hostal Aisa* (☎974 37 00 09; ③) on Plaza Domingo Miral.

As a worthwhile target for a winter visit to alpine Aragón the adjacent ski resorts of **ASTÚN-CANDANCHU**, north of Jaca, are easily reached by bus. Hostales are uniformly pricey; if your budget is limited and/or you're primarily interested in nordic skiing, then either of the two year-round *albergues*, the highly rated *El Aguila* (☎974 37 32 91; ②) or *Valle de Aragón* (☎974 37 32 22; ③), should suit you nicely. Between Jaca and the slopes lies **CAN-FRANC**, the final stop on the rail line up from Zaragoza since the French discontinued the onward section of track in a fit of pique over the success of the Spanish ski resorts. There are trains from Jaca (2 daily), or use the same buses as for Candanchú (5–6 daily). The small village is rather forlorn now, and you wouldn't come especially to see it, but you can **stay** at *Hotel Ara* at c/Fernando el Católico 1 (☎974 37 30 28; ②), and eat at the other end of the street at *Casa Flores*.

For a summertime walking visit, there's no better taster for the Aragonese Pyrenees than the **Parque Nacional de Ordesa**, centred on a vast, trough-like valley flanked by impossingly striated limestone palisades. On Monday to Saturday a 10.15am bus from Jaca serves Sabiñanigo, from where there's a bus at 11am (plus an evening service at 6.30pm in high season) to Torla, the best base for the park; the return **bus** leaves Torla at 3.30pm. Approaching

Sabiñanigo by bus or train from Zaragoza, you'll need departures before 8.30am and 7.15am respectively to make the connection.

TORLA itself, formerly a sleepy, stone-built village, has, since the 1980s, been over-whelmed in its role as gateway to the park; the older corners though are still visually attractive. Don't hope for a **room** or refuge bed from late July to late August, however, without reserving well in advance – even the two **campsites**, *San Antón* (☎974 48 60 63) and *Valle de Bujaruelo* (☎974 48 63 48), 2km and 3km north, can often fill up. At other times of the year you can usually find space at the central *Hotel Ballarín*, c/Capuvita 11 (☎974 48 61 55; ③); *Hotel Villa de Torla*, Plaza Nueva 1 (☎974 48 61 56; ③); or the 43-bunk *Refugio Lucien Briet* (☎974 48 62 21; ①, half-board ②). Both the *Fonda* and the *Bar Brecha*, which manages the *albergue*, serve good-value **meals**.

Vehicle entrance to the **park** itself lies 5km by road beyond Torla, but trekkers should opt instead for the lovely hour-and-a-half trail-walk on the far side of the river, well marked as part of the Pyrenean GR (long-distance path) system and once actually in Ordesa. Further **treks** can be as gentle or as strenuous as you like, the most popular outing being the all-day trip to the **Circo de Soaso** waterfalls.

Several valleys east of Torla and Ordesa and cradled between the two highest summits in the Pyrenees, **BENASQUE** serves as another favourite jump-off point for mountain rambles. There is a twice-daily bus service from Jaca at 8am and 3pm (change at Barbastro), and a marginally better chance of finding a **bed** during high season. *Fonda Barrabes*, c/Mayor 5 (☎974 55 16 54; ②), is the budget standby; try also the unmarked *Hostal Valero* (③), managed by the pricier *Hotel Aneto* next door on c/Anciles (☎974 55 10 61; ④). Best meals, strangely, are above the *Disco Ñaka* near the church, venerable focus of the very attractive backstreets.

CATALUNYA

With its own language, culture and, to a degree, government, **Catalunya** (Cataluña in Castilian Spanish, traditionally Catalonia in English) has a unique identity. **Barcelona**, the capital, is very much the main event. One of the most vibrant and exciting cities in Europe, it is the kind of place where you end up staying far longer than planned. Inland, the monastery of **Montserrat**, Catalunya's main "sight," is perched on one of the most unusual rock formations in Spain, and there are provincial cities too – **Tarragona**, **Girona** and **Lleida** – of considerable charm and historic interest. Sadly, large tracts of the coastline are a disaster, with much of the **Costa Brava** in particular a turgid sprawl of concrete. There are parts of the northernmost stretch, from **Cadaqués** to **Port Bou** on the French border, which have managed to retain some attraction but on the whole if it's beaches you're after you'd do better to keep going south – or take a ferry from Barcelona for the Balearics. As for the **Catalan Pyrenees**, they are more developed than their western neighbours, but access to the mountains is easier. Since the use of the Catalan language is so widespread, we've used Catalan spellings, with Castilian equivalents in parentheses.

Barcelona

BARCELONA, the self-confident and progressive capital of Catalunya, is a tremendous place to be. Though it boasts outstanding Gothic and Art Nouveau buildings, and some great museums – most notably those dedicated to Picasso, Miró and Catalan art – it is above all a place where there's enjoyment simply in walking the streets, stopping in at bars and cafés, soaking up the atmosphere. A thriving port and the most prosperous commercial centre in Spain, it has a sophistication and cultural dynamism way ahead of the rest of the country. In part this reflects the city's proximity to France, whose influence is apparent in the elegant boulevards and imaginative cooking. But Barcelona has also evolved an individual and eclectic cultural identity, most perfectly and eccentrically expressed in the architecture of Antoni Gaudí. The planning for the 1992 Olympics led to a new wave of civic pride, culminating in gleaming, renovated monuments and some spectacular modern buildings too. There are, however, darker sides to this prosperity and confidence: there is a great deal of poverty and a considerable drug problem, which means that the **petty crime** rate is very high. It's not unusual for tourists to feel threatened in the seedier areas flanking the Ramblas. It's wise to take a few precautions: leave passports and tickets locked up in your hotel, don't be too conspicuous with expensive cameras and, if attacked, don't offer any resistance. Be especially careful at Estació de Sants and in the old city where gangs of pickpockets and bag-snatchers target tourists.

Arrival and information

The **airport**, 12km southwest of the city, is linked by a train service (daily every 30min 6am–10.08pm; Mon–Sat €2) to the main **Estació de Sants**, from where you can take the metro to the city centre (line #3 to Liceu for the Ramblas). Many trains from the airport also run on to **Plaça de Catalunya**, a more direct way of reaching the Barri Gòtic. Alternatively, there's the efficient **Airbus** (every 15min 5.30/6am–midnight; €3), which departs from outside the terminals on a circular route and runs into the centre via Plaça d'Espanya, Gran Vía and Plaça de Catalunya. A **taxi** will cost around €15 to Estació de Sants, €18 to somewhere more central.

Estació de Sants is the city's main **train station**, for national and some international arrivals – from here metro line #3 takes you directly to the Ramblas. The **Estació de França**, next to the Parc de la Ciutadella, is the terminal for long-distance Spanish and European express and intercity trains. Leaving França you can take the metro (line #4) from nearby Barceloneta, or simply walk for five minutes into the Barri Gòtic, up Vía Laietana and into c/Jaume. The main **bus terminal** is the **Estació del Nord** (three blocks north of the Parc de la Ciutadella; metro Arc de Triomf). If, by chance, you don't arrive here, you'll be dropped at a central point within easy reach of a metro station. Arriving by **ferry** from the Balearics, you'll dock at the Estació Marítima at the bottom of the Ramblas on Moll de Barcelona.

The **tourist offices** in Barcelona are very well organized: any of them will give you free, large-scale **maps** of the city and transport networks. The best office is beneath the Plaça de Catalunya (daily 9am–9pm; ☎906 30 12 82). Other offices are at the airport (Mon–Sat 9.30am–8pm, Sun 9.30am–3pm); Estació de Sants (summer daily 8am–8pm; winter Mon–Fri 8am–8pm, Sat & Sun 8am–2pm); and Passeig de Gràcia 107 for information on Catalunya (Mon–Sat 9am–7pm, Sat 10am–2pm). There's also a 24-hour, English-speaking **information service** (call ☎010) as well as "Red Jacket" street information officers (daily 10am–8pm) who you'll find around the Barri Gòtic, the Ramblas and Passeig de Gràcia.

City transport

The quickest way of getting around is by the modern and efficient **metro**; stations are marked by a red diamond sign. The metro starts at 5am (6am on Sun) and shuts down at 11pm – just when most people in Barcelona are thinking of going out. It's extended to 2am on Friday, Saturday, and the evening before a holiday, and to midnight on Sunday. **Bus** routes (4.30am–10.30pm) are far more complicated, but every bus stop displays a comprehensive route map. There's a flat **fare** on both metro and buses of €1; if you're staying a couple of days or more it's better to buy a ticket strip or **targeta** from metro station ticket offices, which gives you ten journeys at a discounted price. The T-10 costs €5.30 and covers the metro, buses, and some regional train lines within the city (passes are also available for outlying zones), while a one-day T-Dia costs €4.80. A limited number of yellow **night buses** run from 10.30/11.30pm to 3.30/4.30am, most starting or passing through Plaça de Catalunya; they cost a little more than daytime services. The two routes of the **bus turístic** link Barcelona's major sights, at which you can hop off and on. Tickets are available at tourist offices or on the bus itself (adults: 1 day €13.20, 2 days €16.80) and include a booklet of discount coupons for museums, shops and restaurants.

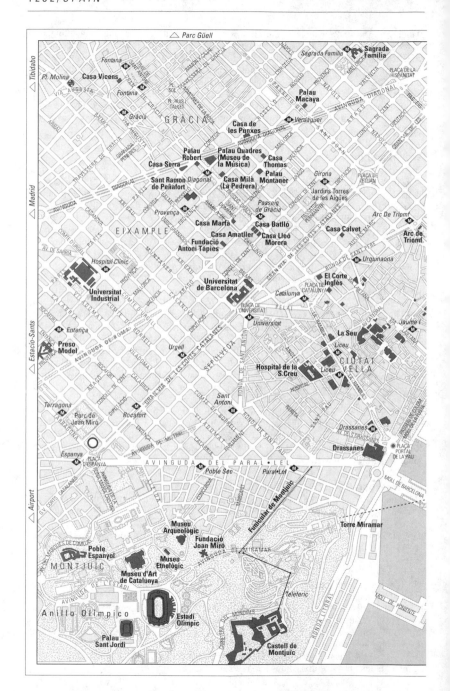

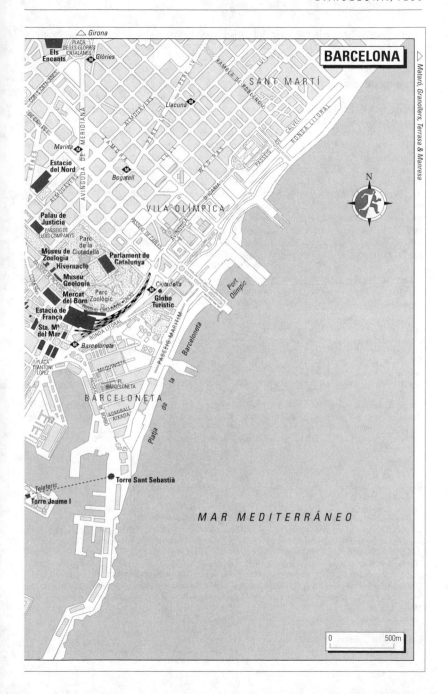

Black and yellow **taxis** (with a green roof-light lit when available for hire) are inexpensive, plentiful and very useful late at night. There's a minimum charge of €1.80, and after that it's around €0.70 per kilometre, depending on the time of day. Most journeys will cost less than €6.

Accommodation

Accommodation in Barcelona is among the most expensive in Spain and unless you stay in a hostel, you'll be hard pushed to find a room for under €18 for a double. The tourist offices dish out lists of **hotels** and **hostales**, but these are hardly necessary as a walk through the streets of the old town reveals heavy concentrations of places to stay and it's easy to stroll around comparing rooms. Most of the **cheapest accommodation** is to be found in the side streets off and around the Ramblas, a convenient and atmospheric area in which to base yourself. The further down towards the port you get, the less salubrious and noisier the surroundings: as a general rule, anything above c/Escudellers tends to be all right. Perhaps the best hunting ground for cheap rooms is between the Ramblas and the Plaça de Sant Jaume, in the area bordered by c/Escudellers and c/de la Boqueria near Plaça Reial. Bookings are no longer done by The tourist office do not help with accommodation reservations but you can use Barcelona Online (☎93 24 73 131, *www.barcelona-on-line.es/reserves/index.htm*). Be warned that finding a bed in the city can be a nightmare almost all year round. Visitors are strongly advised to book at least the first two nights of accommodation as far ahead as possible.

There are several official and not-so-official **hostels** in Barcelona, where accommodation is in multi-bedded dorm rooms. Prices are around €12 each in a private hostel, more in an HI hostel. There are hundreds of **campsites** on the coast in either direction, but none less than 11km from the city; we've detailed the easiest to access, out towards the airport.

HOSTELS

Hedy Holiday Hostal, c/Buenaventura Muñoz 4 (☎93 30 05 785). Just off Ciutadella, this brand new 50-place private youth hostel has dorm accommodation with good facilities and a great bar. No membership is necessary. Curfew 2am–7am. ③.

Hostal de Joves, Passeig de Pujades 29 (☎93 30 03 104). An HI hostel right by the Parc de la Ciutadella and handy for the Nord bus terminal and Estació de França. Open 7–10am and 3pm–midnight. Breakfast included. ①.

Alberg Palau, c/Palau 6 (☎93 41 25 080). Central, friendly and secure. Curfew 3am. Breakfast included. ②.

Gothic Point, c/ Vigatans 5,7,9 (☎93 26 87 808). Lively place with big dorms and good facilities. Very popular with younger travellers and, hence, noisy. Open 24hr; breakfast included. ③.

Albergue Mare de Déu de Montserrat, Passeig Mare de Déu del Coll 41–51, metro Vallcarca (☎93 21 05 151). A beautiful HI hostel a little more than half an hour from the city centre. Open 24hr. ②.

HOTELS

Residencia Australia, Ronda Universitat 11 (☎93 31 74 177). Just off Plaça Catalunya and very popular; book in advance. ⑤.

Hostal Canaletes, Ramblas 133 (☎93 30 15 660). Near Plaça de Catalunya (and at the top of a building containing other *pensiones*); fair rooms, though hot and noisy in summer. ④.

Hostal-Pensión El Cantón, c/Nou de Sant Francesc 40 (☎93 31 73 019). On a tiny street parallel to the Ramblas, this recently renovated hotel has much to offer: good-sized rooms and apartments, with fridges, disabled access and very friendly staff. ④.

Hostal Levante, Baixada Sant Miquel 2 (☎93 31 79 565). Just off the Plaça de Sant Miquel, behind the Ajuntament, this quiet, friendly place has decent, plain rooms in a well-kept building. ④.

Hostal Marítima, Ramblas 4 (☎93 30 23 152). Next to the Wax Museum, this backpackers' favourite offers basic doubles and triples with and without showers. Also has baggage storage and washing facilities. ④.

Hotel Oriente, Ramblas 45 (☎93 30 22 558). Stylish 3-star hotel on the Ramblas; attractive *fin-de-siècle* decor and modern rooms with bath are worth the splurge. ⑨.

Hostal Opera, c/de Sant Pau 20 (☎93 31 88 201). Close enough to the Ramblas to make you overlook the rather unkempt rooms. Cheaper rooms without shower too. ④.

Hostal Rembrandt, c/Portaferrissa 23 (☎93 31 81 011). Spotless rooms with shower and balcony, cheaper rooms without. ⑦.

Hotel La Terrassa, c/Junta del Comerç 11 (☎93 30 25 174). Clean backpackers' favourite, with plain singles, doubles and triples, some en suite and a pleasant terrace. Night staff can be a bit cranky. ④.

CAMPSITES

Cala-Gogo, El Prat de Llobregat (☎93 37 94 600). A mammoth, all mod-cons camp-city out near the airport. Open mid-March to mid-Oct, bus #65 from Plaça d'Espanya or 30 min southwest on foot.

Masnou, Canetra N-11 (☎93 55 51 503). About 200m from Masnou station, take the train (12 min) from Sants or Plaça de Catalunya. Smaller and more peaceful than Cala-Gogo, it has good facilities (including laundry and a shop).

The City

Scattered as Barcelona's main sights may be, the greatest concentration of interest is around the **old town** (*la ciutat vella*). These cramped streets above the harbour are easily manageable, and far more enjoyable, on foot. Start, as everyone else does, with the Ramblas.

AROUND THE RAMBLAS

It is a telling comment on Barcelona's character that one can recommend a single street (or strictly streets) – **the Ramblas** – as a highlight. The heart of Barcelona's life and self-image, the Ramblas are littered with cafés, shops, restaurants and newspaper stands, a focal point for locals as much as for tourists. Heading down from the Plaça de Catalunya, you gradually leave the opulent facades of the banks and department stores for a seedier area towards the port where the Ramblas cut right through the heart of the notorious red-light district, with side streets at the harbour end packed with dimly lit clubs, bars and sex shops. It's much less threatening than it once was, however: the Olympic clean-up and the transformation of the Port Vell area has meant new hip bars and clubs now rub shoulders with sleazy old ones.

On your way down there are plenty of interesting buildings, some of them open for visits: don't miss the glorious **La Boqueria**, the city's main food market (Mon–Sat 8am–8pm), a splendid gallery of sights and smells with several excellent snack bars and a restaurant at the back selling market-fresh dishes. Almost adjacent is the majestic **Liceu**, Barcelona's celebrated opera house now renovated after it went up in smoke in January 1994 – tickets cost as little as €3 with students receiving a 30-percent discount within two hours of a performance. More or less opposite is the famous *Café de l'Òpera*, an opulent high-society meeting place – though not as expensive as you might imagine. A few minutes' walk north of here is the stunning **Museu d'Art Contemporani** (Mon & Wed–Fri 11am–7.30pm, Sat 10am–8pm, Sun 10am–3pm; €4.70, Wed €2.30) with exciting, evolving displays by international and national artists.

A little way down from the Liceu, hidden behind an archway just off the Ramblas and easy to miss, lies the elegant nineteenth-century **Plaça Reial**. Decorated with tall palm trees and iron lamps (designed by the young Gaudí), it's the haunt of crusties, Catalan eccentrics, the odd drunk and hundreds of alfresco diners and drinkers.

Gaudí's magnificent **Palau Güell** (Mon–Sat 10am–1.30pm & 4–6.30pm; €2.40) stands just off the Ramblas, towards the bottom, at c/Nou de la Rambla 3. Much of Gaudí's early career was spent constructing elaborate follies for wealthy patrons, the most important of whom was Don Eusebio Güell, a shipowner and industrialist. In 1885 he commissioned this mansion, an essential stop, where Gaudí's feel for different materials and textures is astounding. Wrought iron supports blend magnificently with granite, marble, ceramics, woodwork and stained and etched glass. Don't miss the roof.

Right at the harbour end of the Ramblas, Columbus stands pointing out to sea from the top of a tall, grandiose column, the **Monument a Colom** (summer daily 9am–8.30pm; winter Mon–Sat 10am–1.30pm & 3.30–6.30pm, Sun 10am–6.30pm; €1.50). Risk the lift to his head (it fell down in 1976) for a fine view of the city. Opposite, to the west side of the Ramblas, are the Drassanes, medieval shipyards originating from the thirteenth century. The impressive stone-vaulted buildings are home to a fine **Museu Marítim** (daily 10am–7pm, €4.80), whose star exhibit is a sixteenth-century Royal Galley.

THE BARRI GÒTIC

A remarkable concentration of beautiful medieval Gothic buildings, just a couple of blocks off the Ramblas, the **Barri Gòtic** forms the very heart of the old city. What you see now dates principally from the fourteenth and fifteenth centuries, when Catalunya reached the height of its commercial prosperity. The quarter is centred on the **Plaça de Sant Jaume**, on one side of which stands the restored town hall, the **Ajuntament**. Across the square rises the **Palau de la Generalitat**, home of the Catalan government (only open April 23; massive queues); restored during the sixteenth century in Renaissance style, it has a beautiful cloister on the first floor with superb coffered ceilings. Just behind the square **La Seu**, Barcelona's cathedral (daily 8am–1.30pm & 4/5–7.30pm), is one of the great Gothic buildings of Spain. Modern lighting shows off the soaring airiness of the interior superbly. Outside, the magnificent **cloisters** (9.30am–1pm & 4–7pm) look over a lush tropical garden with soaring palm trees and white geese, and open into, among other things, the small **cathedral museum** (daily 11am–1pm; €0.60). Nearby, next to the Palau Episcopal and at various points in and near Vía Laietana, you can see some of the city's remaining **Roman walls**.

The cathedral and its associated buildings aside, the most concentrated batch of historic monuments in the Barri Gòtic is the grouping around the nearby **Plaça del Rei**. Barcelona's finest Roman remains were uncovered beneath the **Palau Reial** (the former palace of the counts of Barcelona) which now houses the **Museu d'Història de la Ciutat** (summer daily 10am–8pm; winter Tues–Sat 10am–2pm & 4–8pm, Sun 10am–2pm; Tues–Fri; €4.20, free Wed pm). Underground, both Roman and Visigothic remains have been preserved where they were discovered during works in the 1930s. The museum also gives access to the beautiful fourteenth-century **Capella Reial de Santa Àgata** with its tall single nave and unusual stained glass, and to an extension of the royal palace known as the **Saló de Tinell**, a fine spacious example of fourteenth-century secular Gothic architecture. It was on the steps leading from the Saló de Tinell into the Plaça del Rei that Ferdinand and Isabella stood to receive Columbus on his return from the Americas. The **Museu Marès** (Tues & Thurs 10am–5pm, Wed, Fri & Sat 10am–7pm, Sun & hols 10am–2pm; €2.40, free first Sun of month) occupies another wing of the palace, behind the *plaça*. The bulk of the museum consists of a fine collection of religious sculpture, including a vast number of wooden crucifixes from the twelfth to the fifteenth century. The upper floors house the **Museu Sentimental** of local nineteenth-century sculptor Federico Marès, an impressive but rather tedious jumble gathered during fifty years of travel. After the museum, have a drink in its calm courtyard bar.

For a quick respite from the city centre, nip into the greenery and relative peace of **Parc de la Ciutadella**, which is within easy walking distance of the Barri Gòtic. Its attractions include a lake, Gaudí's monumental fountain and the city zoo (daily 10am–5/7pm; €9.40), and you'll also find the meeting place of the Catalan parliament.

PICASSO AND THE CARRER DE MONTCADA

Heading east from the Plaça de Sant Jaume, you'll cross Vía Laietana and reach the Carrer de Montcada, crowded with beautifully restored old buildings. One of these houses the **Museu Picasso** (Tues–Sat 10am–8pm, Sun 10am–3pm; €4.40, free first Sun of month), one of the most important collections of Picasso's work in the world and the only one of any significance in his native country, although it's a rather selective collection and contains none of his best-known work. Continue down the street and you'll come out opposite the great basilica of **Santa María del Mar** (daily 9am–1.30pm & 4.30–8pm; Sun choral Mass at 1pm), built on what was the seashore in the fourteenth century. Its soaring lines were the symbol of Catalan supremacy in Mediterranean commerce and it is still much dearer to the heart of the average local than the cathedral. The stained glass is especially beautiful.

PORT VELL AND VILLA OLYMPICA

The whole **Port Vell** area has been revitalized, notably with the construction of the harbourside *passeig* and the vast new Maremagnum complex reached from near the Monument a Colom via a dramatic wooden walkway. The city planners' desire to refocus attention on the sea has provided an upmarket shopping mall, an excellent aquarium, a cinema, an IMAX theatre and a multitude of cheesy bars and overpriced restaurants all grouped together in the old harbour area with fine views back to the old city, the marina and Montjuïc.

Looping back towards the city towards Plaça d'Antoni López is the new **Museu d'Historia de Catalunya** (Tues, Thurs–Sat 10am–7pm, Wed 10am–8pm, Sun 10am–2.30pm; €3), housed in the Palau de Mar, a historic old dock building.There are great views from the restaurant terrace, but the museum itself is little more than a publicly-funded PR exercise. It lies on the fringe of the **Barceloneta district**, home to Barcelona's cleaned up beaches and seafood restaurants. *Telefèrics* (cable cars) run from here to Montjuïc via Port Vell (10am–6pm; €6 one way). Walk 1km east along the beach and you'll find Port Olímpic with its myriad bars and restaurants. At night the tables are stacked up, dance floors emerge and the area hosts one of the city's most vibrant dance scenes. Dozens of bars pump out a pulsating mix of salsa, house and techno to an uptown clientele.

ANTONI GAUDÍ AND THE SAGRADA FAMÍLIA

Besides modern art, Barcelona offers – above all through the work of **Antoni Gaudí** (1852–1926) – some of the most fantastic and exciting modern architecture to be found anywhere in the world. Without doubt his most famous creation is the incomplete **Temple Expiatiori de la Sagrada Família** (daily 9am–6/8pm; €4.80, lift to top of the pinnacles €1.20; metro Sagrada Família), a good way northeast of the Plaça de Catalunya. Amid great controversy, work to complete the cathedral has begun, turning the interior into a giant building site, but it's fascinating to watch Gaudí's last known plans being slowly realized. The size alone is startling, with eight spires rising to over 100m. For Gaudí these were metaphors for the Twelve Apostles; he planned to build four more above the main facade and to add a 180-metre tower topped with a gallery over the transept, itself to be surrounded by four smaller towers symbolizing the Evangelists. Take the lift, or climb up one of the towers, and you can enjoy a dizzy view down over the whole complex and clamber still further round the walls and into the towers.

Inside the Temple a small **Gaudí museum** traces the career of the architect and the history of the building. The tourist offices also issue a handy leaflet describing all his works, with a map of their locations. Above all, check out the **Parc Güell** (daily 10am–6/9pm; free), his most ambitious project apart from the Sagrada Família. This almost hallucinatory experience, with giant decorative lizards and a vast Hall of Columns, contains another small **museum** (daily 10am–6/8pm; €2.40) with some of the furniture Gaudí designed. To get there, take the metro to Lesseps or bus #24 from the Plaça de Catalunya to Travesera de Dalt, from where it's a half-kilometre walk to the main gates on c/d'Olot.

MONTJUÏC

The hill of **Montjuïc** has far more varied attractions – five museums, the "Spanish Village", the Olympic arena and a castle with grand views of the city. The most obvious way to approach is to take a bus or metro to the Plaça d'Espanya and walk from there up the imposing Avda de la Reina María Cristina, past the 1929 International Fair buildings and the rows of fountains. If you'd rather start with the castle, take the **funicular railway** (every 10min 10.45am–8pm; summer daily; winter weekends only; €2.30 return) which runs from Parallel metro station to the start of the cable car (summer only), which in turn leads to the castle. And lastly there is bus #50 that runs along Gran Vía and up to Parc Montjuïc.

If you tackle the stiff climb from the Plaça d'Espanya you'll arrive at the **Palau Nacional**, centrepiece of Barcelona's 1929 International Fair and now home to one of Spain's great museums, the **Museu Nacional d'Art de Catalunya** (Tues–Sat 10am–7pm, Sun 10am–2.30pm; €4.80, 1st Thurs of the month free), with its enormous collection. The Gothic collection is fascinating, but it's the Romanesque section that is the more remarkable, perhaps the best collection of its kind in the world: 35 rooms of eleventh- and twelfth-century frescoes, meticulously removed from a series of small Pyrenean churches and beautifully displayed. There is also a substantial collection of Baroque and Renaissance works. The **Museu d'Art Modern** (Mon & Wed–Sat 10am–7pm, Sun 10am–2.30pm; €3, free first Thurs of month) displays a collection that ranges from the eighteenth century to the 1980s, but it is in the process of being shifted to the MNAC; during the move some of the collection remains open to visitors.

Barcelona's important **Museu Arqueològic** (Tues–Sat 9.30am–7pm, Sun & hols 10am–2.30pm; €2.40), containing exhibits mostly from the Roman period, but also Carthaginian and Etruscan relics, stands to the east of the Palau Nacional, lower down the hill. Nearby is the **Fundació Joan Miró** (Tues–Sat 10am–7pm, Thurs closes 9.30pm, Sun & hols 10.30am–2.30pm; €4.80), the most adventurous of Barcelona's art museums, devoted to one of the greatest Catalan artists. A beautiful white building houses a permanent collection of paintings, graphics, tapestries and sculptures donated by Miró himself and covering the period from 1914 to 1978.

A short walk over to the other side of the Palau Nacional will bring you to the **Poble Espanyol** or "Spanish Village" (Mon 9am–8pm, Tues–Thurs 9am–2am, Fri & Sat 9am–4am, Sun 9am–midnight; €5.90), consisting of replicas of famous or characteristic buildings from all over Spain, and with a lively club scene at night. Prices, especially for products of the "genuine Spanish workshops" (and in the bars), are exorbitant. Just down the road, the reconstruction of the **Mies van der Rohe Pavilion** for the 1929 Exhibition (daily 10am–6/8pm; €2.40) is a far greater treat.

From the Poble Espanyol, the main road climbs around the hill to what was the principal **Olympic arena** in 1992, passing some dazzling new buildings – the Picornell swimming pools and the Japanese-designed Palau Sant Jordi. These are overshadowed only by the Olympic Stadium itself, the **Estadi Olimpic** (May–Oct 10am–6pm; free), built originally for the 1929 Exhibition and completely refitted to accommodate the 1992 opening and closing ceremonies. The new Olympic museum, the **Galeria Olímpica**, on Passeig Olimpic (Tues–Sat 10am–2pm & 4–6/7pm, Sun 10am–2pm; €2.40), is a hands-on affair covering the staging of the Games in the city. Far above this complex of museums and sports arenas, and offering magnificent views across the city, stands the eighteenth-century **Castell de Montjuïc**, built on seventeenth-century ruins.

TIBIDABO

If the views from the Castell de Montjuïc are good, those from the top of **Mount Tibidabo** – which forms the northwestern boundary of the city – are legendary. On one of those mythical clear days you can see across to Montserrat and the Pyrenees, and out to sea even as far as Mallorca. The name is taken from the Temptations of Christ in the wilderness, when Satan led him to a high place and offered him everything that could be seen: *Haec omnia tibi dabo si cadens adoraberis me* ("All these things will I give thee, if thou wilt fall down and worship me") and all around there are pleasant walks through the woods. To get there, take the Ferrocarriles Catalanes rail line from Plaça de Catalunya to Avda. Tibidabo; from there the Tramvia Blau (tram) connects with the funicular rail line to the top (Mon–Fri 7.15am–9.45pm; €2.40 return; Sat & Sun 10am–10pm; winter weekends only).

MONESTIR DE PEDRALBES

On the outskirts of the city, about fifteen minutes' walk from the metro at Palau Reial is the Gothic **Monestir de Pedralbes** (Tues–Sun 10am–2pm; €1.80, joint ticket with Collecció Thyssen-Bornemisza €3; #22 bus from Passeig de Gràcia). The monastery gives a vivid impression of monastic life, but perhaps more engaging is the superb collection of fourteenth- to eighteenth-century religious paintings here that form part of the Thyssen-Bornemisza art collection, the remainder of which is displayed in Madrid.

Eating, drinking and nightlife

There's a huge variety of **food** available in Barcelona and even low-budget travellers can do well for themselves. Be aware that a lot of places close on Sundays and throughout August, and that the *menú del día* is rarely available in the evening. If you want to buy picnic material the covered **market** (Mercat Sant Josep/La Boqueria) off the Ramblas is the place to go. A couple of **supermarkets** to know about are Centro Comercial Simago, Ramblas 113 (food department in the basement); and Drugstore, Passeig de Gràcia 71, which is open all night.

Amusing yourself in Barcelona is unlikely to be a problem. There are hundreds of excellent **bars** and **cafés** in the city centre to start your evening, including the lively tapas places in the Barri Gòtic. Around the Museu Picasso is a particularly good area: the Passeig del Born, the square at the end of c/Montcada behind Santa María del Mar, is crowded with popular bars. Gràcia, north of the centre, is the most studenty area in Barcelona and ideal for low-key, lateish drinking, especially on the numerous little squares around the main Plaça del Sol, itself bordered by café terraces. Barcelona's **nightlife** is some of Europe's most exciting. It keeps going all night too, the music bars closing at 3am, the discos at 4 to 5am, and (for the seriously dissipated) some clubs open between 5am and 9am at weekends. Among the more expensive, trendier places, *bars modernos* are still in fashion, hi-tech theme palaces concentrated mainly in the Eixample, or in the rich kids' stamping ground bordered by c/Ganduxer, Avda. Diagonal and Vía Augusta, west of Gràcia. Drinks are expensive, the music echoes the often elaborate decorations, and the "in" places change rapidly, with new ones starting up all the time. Currently, the waterfront Port Olímpic area seems to be in favour, although weekdays out of summer are dead. **Clubbing** can be more expensive still; in the most exclusive places even a beer is going to cost you roughly ten times what it costs in the bar next door.

For **listings** of almost anything you could want in the way of entertainment and culture, buy a copy of the weekly *Guía del Ocio* (€0.75) from any newsstand. There's a thriving **gay scene** in Barcelona: *SexTienda*, at c/Rauric 11 (very near Plaça Reial), supplies free maps of gay Barcelona with a list of bars, clubs and contacts.

TAPAS BARS

Bar Mundial, Plaça de Sant Agustí el Vell 1, Barri Gòtic. This unpretentious, family-owned bar has been a neighbourhood highlight for more than 70 years; famous for its seafood.

Jai-Ca, c/Ginebra 13, Barceloneta. Small, cornerside bar with some of the best tapas in Barceloneta.

Euskal Etxea, Placeta Montcada 1–3, Barri Gòtic. A Basque restaurant specializing in mouthwatering tapas, which are served around 12.30pm and 7.30pm

El Xampanyet, c/de Montcada 22, Barri Gòtic. Terrific blue-tiled champagne bar with fine seafood tapas, *cava* by the glass and local *sidra*. Closed Mon, Sun night & Aug.

RESTAURANTS

Amaya, Rambla Santa Mónica 20–24. Busy, smoke-filled tapas bar on one side, mid-range (around €18) restaurant on the other. Serves Basque specialities.

El Raco d'En Joan, c/Nou de la Rambla 44, Barri Xines. Friendly, family-run *comedor* with a €5.50 *menú del día*.

El Cangrejo Loco ("The Crazy Crab"), Moll del Gregal 29, Port Olímpic. As its name suggests, serves Mediterranean/seafood cuisine (around €18) with lively drinking and a new takeaway hatch where you can try the *mariscos* without breaking the bank.

Los Caracoles, c/Escudellers 14, Barri Gòtic (☎93 30 23 185). Barcelona landmark restaurant whose name means "snails", the house speciality, along with the spit-roast chicken on display outside. Around €21 per head for a big meal; reservations advised.

Comme-Bio & Comme-Bio II, Via Layetana, Barrio Gòtic & Gran Vía 603 (corner Rambla de Catalunya), Eixample; metro Catalunya. Sibling vegetarian restaurants that double as health-food stores. A €6.50 *menú del día* (Mon–Fri lunch only), otherwise €12–15 a head to fill up on Catalan dishes, pizzas and salads.

El Convent, c/Jerusalem 3, Barri Xines. Long-standing favourite restaurant, with an extensive Catalan *menú*. You can eat well for around €15. Closed Sun.

España, c/Sant Pau 9–11, Barri Xines. Eat fine food in *modernista* splendour in a building designed by Domenèch i Montaner. The *menú del día* is good value, but not available at night when a full meal costs upwards of €18 a head.

El Gallo Kiriko, c/Avinyo 19, Barri Gòtic. Filling, reasonable Pakistani curries plus Pakistani TV in what looks like a bathroom – for as little as €3.60 with rice.

Illa de Gràcia, c/Sant Domènec 19. Gràcia; metro Fontana. Bright vegetarian restaurant serving decent salads, pasta, rice dishes, omelettes and crepes – all around €4.80.

El Jardín, in El Mercadillo off Portaferrisa. Eclectic, healthy food in a delightful garden setting.

Llar del Filador, c/ Cortines 13, Barri Gòtic (☎93 31 92 690). Tucked away in a dark lane in the Ribera, this renovated workshop is the place to enjoy meat, cheese and dessert fondues in a subdued and romantic atmosphere (about €12 per person). Open evenings 7.30pm–1.30am and lunch by reservation

Perú, Passeig de Bourbó 10, Barceloneta. Barcelona's best seafood is served in Barceloneta. This is one of the few there that has a *menú del día*, good value at around €12.

Pitarra, c/d'Avinyó 56, Barri Gòtic. A Catalan cookery in operation since 1890, lined with paintings and serving good, reasonably priced food. Closed Sun.

Pollo Rico, c/Sant Pau 31, Barri Xines. Spit-roasted chicken, fries and a glass of *cava* for under €4.20 make this one of the area's most popular budget spots. Closed Wed.

Set Portes (Las Siete Puertas), Passeig d'Isabel II 14, Barri Gòtic (☎93 31 93 033). Wood-panelled classic where the decor has barely changed in 150 years. Elegant but not exclusive, though you'll need to book ahead. The seafood is excellent, particularly the dark paella. From €24 a head.

El Tastavins, c/Ramon y Cajals 12 (☎93 21 36 031); Gria; metro Fontana. Publishing empresario and Gràcia legend Salvador Montserrat's latest venture. Food of exceptional quality and good prices. Choose from a wide range of Catalan specialties at about €12 for a meal.

CAFÉS AND BARS

Café de l'Òpera, Ramblas 74. Elegant *fin-de-siècle* café/bar with fine coffee and a range of cakes and snacks. Open daily until 2.30/3am.

Café del Sol, Plaça del Sol 29, Gràcia. Trendy hangout, just one of several similar places in this square.

Cocktel, Passeig del Born 18. A tiny bar with eclectic popular music. The cocktail list is exhaustive and they're always ready to whip up a new creation on the spur of the moment. Open Tues–Sun 6pm–3am.

Horchatería Fillol, Plaça de la Universitat 5, Eixample. *Horchata* as well as enormous milkshakes and other delights. Breakfast of coffee and croissant for €1.35.

Mi Bar, c/Guilleries 6. Gràcia; metro Fontana. Favourite neighbourhood bar for Gràcia's alternative music set. Bar tender/DJ Felipe spins a mix of everything from punk to flamenco, but with a heavy accent on alternative. Tues–Sat 11pm–3am.

London Bar, c/Nou de la Rambla 34, Barri Xines. Laid-back 1920s bar with live music daily – mainly jazz and blues – with cabaret after midnight on Thurs & Sun.

Parnasse, c/Gignás 21. Laid-back and friendly atmosphere in this weirdly hip bar. Listen to jazz, and drink modestly priced single-malt whiskies or the legendary absinthe, *à la française*. Open Tues–Sat 6pm–3am.

Téxtil Café, c/Montcada, 12. In the atmospheric medieval courtyard of the textile museum, with braziers in winter, although fairly pricey drinks keep out the art students.

Els Quatre Gats, c/Montsió 5, Barri Gòtic. *Modernista*-designed haunt of Picasso and his contemporaries, still an interesting and arty place for a drink and nibble. Closed Sun lunch.

DESIGNER BARS AND CLUBS

Apolo, c/Nou de la Rambla 113, Barri Xines. Trip-hop and techno for a gay/straight crowd, old-town location; from 11pm until 6am.

La Fira, c/Provença 171, Eixample; metro Provença. A museum-bar with seats in *fin-de-siècle* fairground rides, plus a bar under a circus awning. Open until 4.30am, Sun until 1am.

KGB, c/Alegre de Dalt 55, Gràcia. Pop sounds becoming hardcore later. Occasional live acts. Open until 5am.

Mirablau, Plaza Doctor Andreu. Cocktail bar and popular disco in dramatic location at the foot of the cable car to Mt Tibidabo, with fantastic views. Open until 5am.

Moog, Arc del Teatre 3, Barri Xines. Techno temple. Regular appearances from top UK and Euro DJs. Best on Sun & Wed, open 11pm–5am.

Nick Havanna, c/Rosselló 208, Eixample; metro Diagonal. One of the most futuristic bars in town, enormous, yet packed to the gills at weekends. Open 8pm–4/5am.

Otto Zutz, c/Lincoln 15, Gràcia. A 3-storey warehouse converted into a nocturnal shop window of every-thing that's for sale or rent in Barcelona. With the right rags and face you're in for free. The club starts at 2am; it's a bar before that. One of the best during the week. Closed Sun & Mon.

Paradís, c/Paradís 4. Reggae, African and Latin sounds in the Barri Gòtic.

Torres de Avila, Avda. Marqués de Comillas 25, Poble Espanyol, Montjuïc. The city's newest and most fantastic bar yet – see it to believe it. Attracts an international crowd. Open Thurs–Sat 11pm–5am.

Universal Bar, c/Mariano Cubí 182, Gràcia; metro Fontana. Postmodern bar, long one of the trendiest. Open until 4.30am.

Up & Down, c/Numancia 179. More chic than trendy, but very much in vogue after refit. Open from mid-night.

Yabba Dabba Club, c/Avenir 63, Gràcia. Haunt of the spiky-haired crowd, with Gothic decor including candelabras and a sculpted torso protruding from the wall. Open until 3am, closed Sun.

Listings

Airlines Air France, Pg. de Gràcia 56 (☎901 11 22 66); British Airways, Pg. de Gràcia 16 (☎902 13 21 32); EasyJet (☎902 29 99 92); Iberia, Plaça d'Espanya (☎902 40 05 00); TWA, Consell de Cent 360 (☎932 158 486).

American Express c/Rosellón 269, off Pg. de Gràcia 101 (Mon–Fri 9.30–6pm, Sat 10am–noon; ☎93 21 70 070; 24hr helpline ☎93 21 55 342).

Books in English Itaca, Rambla de Catalunya 81, Salas, c/Jaume-I 5; The Book Store, c/la Granja 13; and from newspaper stands down the Ramblas.

Car rental Most rental agencies are represented at the airport. In town, contact Eurodollar-Atesa, c/Muntaner 45 (☎93 32 30 701); Avis, c/Casanovas 209 (☎93 20 99 533); Hertz, c/Tuset 10 (☎93 21 78 076); Ital-Budget, Avda. Josep Tarradellas 35 (☎934 10 25 08).

Consulates Australia, Gran Vía Carles III 98 (☎93 33 09 496); Canada, c/Elisenda de Pinós 10 (☎93 20 42 700); Ireland, Gran Vía Carles III 94 (☎93 49 15 021); New Zealand, Trav. de Grácia 64 (☎93 20 90 399); UK, Avda. Diagonal 477 (☎93 41 99 044); USA, Passeig de la Reina Elisenda 23 (☎93 28 02 227).

Exchange Most banks are located in Plaça de Catalunya and Pg. de Gràcia. Money can also be changed at the airport (daily 7.30am–10.45pm); Estacío de Sants (daily 8am–10pm, Sun closes 9pm); Víajes Marsans, Ramblas 134 (Mon–Fri 9am–1.30pm & 4–7.30pm); and at Casas de Cambio throughout the centre.

Ferries Tickets for Balearic ferries from Transmediterránea, at the Estació Maritima (☎93 44 32 532; 7hr) or Buquebus (☎90 24 14 242; 7hr). Book in advance July & Aug.

Hospitals Hospital de la Creu Roja, c/Dos de Maig 301 (☎93 43 31 551); Hospital Clínic I Provincial, c/Villarocl 170 (☎93 45 46 000). For emergency doctors or ambulance dial ☎061.

Left luggage Lockers at Sants station (5am–11pm; €2.40–3.60 per day); Estació Marítima (9am–1pm & 4–11pm; €1.80–3); Estació de França (6am–11.30pm; €2.40–3.60); Estació del Nord (24hr; €3.60); and Airport (24hr; €3.60).

Police Turisme Attention, Las Ramblas 43 (daily 7am–midnight; ☎93 30 19 060 or ☎092 for emergencies).

Post office Correus, Plaça Antoni Lòpez at the bottom of Vía Laietana (Mon–Fri 8am–9pm, Sat 8am–2pm, Sun 9am–1pm); poste restante at Window 17 (Mon–Fri 9am–9pm, Sat 9am–2pm).

Telephones Telefónica at Sants station (daily 8am–10.30pm, Sun opens 9am; also has a fax machine), and at Las Ramblas 88 Local 46 (daily 10am–11pm).

Travel agencies TIVE at Gran Vía 1, between the Ramblas and Plaça de la Universitat; Usit Unlimited Rda. Universitat 16 (☎93 41 20 104); other general travel firms can be found around the Gran Vía, Pg. de Gràcia, Vía Laietana and the Ramblas.

Montserrat

The extraordinary mountain of **Montserrat**, with its weirdly shaped crags of rock, its monastery and its ruined hermitage caves, stands just 40km northwest of Barcelona, off the road to Lleida, and is an ideal natural sanctuary from the city heat in summer. This saw-toothed outcrop is one of the most spectacular of all Spain's natural sights, and legends hang easily upon it. St Peter is said to have deposited a carving of the Virgin by St Luke in one of the mountain caves, fifty years after the birth of Christ; another tale claims this as the spot where Parsifal discovered the Holy Grail. Inevitably it's no longer remote, but the place itself is still magical and you can avoid the crowds by striking out along well-marked paths to deserted hermitages. Another option is to stay the night, since the crowds disperse by early evening.

It is the **Black Virgin** (La Moreneta), the icon supposedly hidden by St Peter, which is responsible for the monastery's existence: over 150 churches were dedicated to her in Italy alone, as were the first chapels of Mexico, Chile and Peru – even a Caribbean island bears her name. According to the story it was lost after being hidden during the Moorish invasion and reappeared here in 880: in the first of its miracles, it could not be moved. The chapel built to house it was the predecessor of the present monastic structures, about three-quarters of the way up the mountain.

The **monastery** itself is of no particular architectural interest, except in its monstrous bulk. Only the sixteenth-century **Basilica** is open to the public, where you can catch the boys' choir singing the famous "Salve Regina" (daily 1pm). La Moreneta, blackened by the smoke of countless candles, stands above the high altar, reached from behind, up a stairway. Near the entrance to the basilica is a **museum** (older section open Tues–Sun 10.30am–2pm; newer section open daily 3–6pm; €3) containing paintings by Caravaggio and El Greco. The **walks** around the woods and mountainside of Montserrat are a greater attraction, with tracks to caves and hermitages in every direction. You can also take funicular rail lines to the hermitages of **Sant Joan** and **Sant Jeronimo**, near the summit of the mountain at 1300m.

Practicalities

The most thrilling approach is by train and cable car, about an hour and a half from Barcelona. The Ferrocarriles Catalanes **trains** leave from beneath the Plaça de Espanya (hourly 8.36am–3.36pm; closed mid-Feb to mid-March), connecting at Montserrat Aeri with a cable car for an exhilarating ride. The last train back is at 6.36pm. Combined tickets, bought at Plaça de Espanya, cost €17.50. There are also **tours** from Barcelona, leaving at 9am from Plaça de Espanya and returning at 5pm – tickets (€30, including all travel, breakfast, lunch and museum entrance) are available from any travel agent or tourist office.

There's a **campsite** up by the funicular rail lines and a **hotel** which should be booked in advance: the *Hostal-Residencia El Monasterio* (☎938 35 02 01; ⑤). The **bar** in the square outside the monastery gates serves sandwiches, and there are a couple of high-priced **restaurants** and gift shops too.

THE CATALAN PYRENEES

The Catalan Pyrenees, every bit as spectacular as their Aragonese neighbours, have been exploited for far longer. While this has resulted in numerous less-than-aesthetic ski resorts and hydroelectric projects, it also means good public transport to the villages and a well-developed tourism infrastructure. In the less frequented corners, such as the westerly **Parc Nacional**, the scenery is the equal of any in Europe, while even the touristy train ride up to **Núria** to the east rarely fails to impress. The principality of **Andorra**, between these two attractions, has considerably less going for it, though **La Seu d'Urgell**, on the approach from the south, is a bit more worthwhile.

The Parc Nacional and around

After Ordesa, the most popular target of trekkers in the Pyrenees is the **Parc Nacional de Sant Maurici and Aigües Tortes**, covering nearly 200 square kilometres of forest, lakes and cirques, presided over by 3000-metre snow-capped peaks. For the less adventurous, there are lower-altitude track walks through fine scenery and visits to several villages around the park. Initial access is from Pobla de Segur, reached by 7.30am or 2.30pm bus or morning train from Barcelona (change at Lleida), or by the 4.30pm bus from Lleida (weekdays only). The other access town is Pont de Suert – buses leave from Lleida daily at 9am and 5pm.

The two main "base" villages are Boí and Espot, west and east of the park boundaries respectively, with Capdella to the south a less busy alternative; all are set in their own gorgeous valleys. **BOÍ** is 21km from Pont de Suert on the main road up to the Viella tunnel, served by daily morning bus from Pobla via Pont de Suert. In the town itself, the tiny old quarter is dwarfed by modern construction, and tourism facilities are expensive. Exceptions include a few nameless *habitaciones* (③) for **accommodation** in the old quarter, or try *Hostal Fondevila* (☎973 69 60 11; ⑥); *Casa Higinio*, 200m up the road to Taüll, is a good place to **eat**. If you draw a blank here, the more handsome neighbouring village of **TAÜLL**, 3km uphill and east, has a good *pension, Sant Climent*, c/Les Feixes 8 (☎973 69 60 52; ④), several possibilities in its *cases de pagès* (rural home-stays; ②) and an attractive **campsite** (☎973 69 61 74). Although further from the park entrance, Taüll also boasts the Romanesque **Church of Sant Clement**, one of several in the area. **ESPOT** lies only 7km off the main road between Pobla and the overrated Vall d'Aran (see below), but there's no bus service, and failing a lift, you'll face a steep two-hour climb. Once there, the place is appealing enough, with *Hotel Roya* (☎973 62 40 40; ⑧) providing the least expensive **accommodation**. One of the three local **campsites**, *Solan* (☎973 62 40 68), also has a few cheap rooms to let (②). **Restaurants** are generally expensive, but best of these is *L'Isard*. **CAPDELLA** is served by buses at 7am and 4.30pm from Pobla (weekdays only), and boasts two **hostales**, both of which provide **meals**: *Leo* (☎973 66 31 38; ②) and *Montseny* (☎973 66 30 79; ③).

Within the park itself, camping is forbidden and accommodation is limited to four **mountain refuges** (②), but there are as many more or nearly as impressive alpine areas just outside the park boundaries. Trails or cross-country routes are, not surprisingly, well marked, and you rarely have to walk more than four hours between the huts.

North of the park, the long, narrow **Vall d'Aran** was once a sort of Pyrenean Shangri-La, where summer hay-reapers picturesquely wielded scythes against a backdrop of stone-built villages with pointy-steepled churches, but the giant Baqueira-Beret ski complex, phalanxes of holiday condos and swarms of French trippers have put paid to that. It's now easily the most expensive corner of Catalunya outside of Barcelona, and only worth passing through on your way to or from Aigües Tortes.

Near the top of the valley, **SALARDÚ** will be your most likely target, the meeting point of two walking routes serving the national park. There are several reasonable places to **stay**, among which the *Pension Montaña*, c/Major (☎973 64 41 08; ③), can be singled out. **VIELLA**, 9km west and much lower, is the capital of the region and cross point for the two bus routes from Pobla: one (summer only) via Baqueira-Beret and Salardú, the other (all year) through the namesake tunnel. It's not a particularly memorable town, but if you're forced by the bus schedules to **stay**, try the *Pension Busquets*, c/Major 9 (☎973 64 02 38; ③), and the *Pensión Puig*, north of the main drag at c/Camí Reiau 6 (☎973 64 00 31; ③).

Andorra and La Seu

As recently as 1960, **ANDORRA** was virtually cut off from the rest of the world, a semi-autonomous principality conceived late in the thirteenth century to resolve a quarrel between the counts of Foix in France and the bishops of La Seu. There are still no planes or trains, but any quaintness has been banished by Andorra's current role as a drive-in, duty-free supermarket: the main highway through the tiny country is clogged with French and Spanish tourists after the cheap electronic and sports gear, the (not especially) cheap booze in the restaurants and a tankful of discounted petrol. Andorra has no currency of its own, so both francs and pesetas are accepted. The capital, **ANDORRA LA VELLA**, must once have been an attractive town, but it's now a seething mass of cars, touristy restaurants (six-language *menús* a speciality) and shopfronts. For travellers, the bazaar ethic makes this a foolproof spot to cheaply replace lost or worn-out trekking or skiing items – otherwise you're best off moving on.

The twice-daily bus from Barcelona to Andorra (6am & 3pm; 5hr; continues to France) stops in **LA SEU D'URGELL**, 18km south, from where there is also a more frequent local service to Andorra. Named after its imposing twelfth-century cathedral, La Seu is a fairly sleepy place. The **Cathedral** itself, at the end of c/Major, has been restored over the years but retains some graceful interior decoration and an exceptional cloister with droll column capitals; the **Cloister**, along with the adjacent **Museu Diocesano**, has controlled admission (Oct–May Mon–Fri noon–1pm, Sat & Sun 11am–1pm; June–Sept Mon–Sat 10am–1pm & 4–7pm, Sun 10am–1pm). The **tourist office** (summer Mon–Fri 9am–9pm, Sat & Sun 10am–2pm & 4–8pm; winter Mon–Sat 10am–2 & 4–7pm, Sun 10am–2pm; ☎973 36 01 56) is on Plaça dels Oms near the **Town Hall** and there is another branch at the Parc del Segre complex (Mon–Sat 9am–2pm & 3–7pm, Sun 10am–2pm). The **bus station** is on Avda. Joan Garriga Masso, just north of the old quarter. This offers a rather limited number of inexpensive places to **stay**: closest to the terminal are *Hotel Avenida* at Avda. Pau Claris 24 (☎973 35 01 04; ⑥) or head towards the centre where you'll find *Pensió palomares* (☎973 35 02 19; ③). The nearest **campsite** is *En Valira* (☎973 35 10 35), just out of town on the Lleida road at Avda. del Valira 10. **Eating** is best at *Cal Pacho*, c/del Font 11.

Núria and beyond

For a beautiful but easy way to see the Pyrenees, look no further than the *Ferrocarril Cremallera* (**rack-and-pinion rail line**) up to the cirque and shrine at **NÚRIA**. After a leisurely start from Ribes de Freser (see below), the tiny two-carriage train lurches up into the mountains, following a river between great crags. Occasionally it stops, the track only inches away from a terrifying drop, a sheer rock face soaring way above you. Once through a final tunnel, the train emerges alongside a small lake (dry in summer), at the other side of which is the one giant building that constitutes Núria. A severe stone structure, it combines church, café, hotel and ski centre all in one; behind it is an official **campsite**.

The *Hotel Vall de Núria* (☎972 73 20 00; ⑨, half-board) is expensive in summer, but the price plummets in winter; there are also several dorm-style **refuges** around, though they are often full of groups, in which case you'll have to use the campsite or the **hostel**, *Pic de l'Aliga* (☎972 73 20 48; ②, including breakfast), at the end of the cable car. You'll need good equipment, even in summer, since it gets cold at night. As for **food**, you can buy hot snacks or breakfast at the *Bar Finestrelles*; there's a self-service place for midday or evening meals; and the hotel dining room is another modestly priced possibility.

Moving on, the privately owned Núria train (hourly; €13.20 return; rail passes not valid, *www.valldenuria.com/valldenuria/cas/crem.htm*) runs all year, from Ribes-Enllaç, via the towns of Ribes de Freser and Queralbs, where there are also places to stay. Trains from Barcelona connect with the Cremallera train at Ribes-Enllaç (Barcelona–Núria return summer/weekends €19.40). Mainline trains continue to Puigcerdà, right on the **French frontier**, astride the only surviving rail link over the Pyrenees to France. Four trains a day currently leave for La Tour de Carol, 3km over the border, but if you miss them it's easy enough to walk a slightly shorter distance east to Bourg-Madame, the actual border town. PUIGCERDÀ is a lot cheaper than anywhere in France, should schedules compel an **overnight stay**: try the *Hostal La Muntanya*, c/Coronel Molera 1 (☎972 88 02 02; ⑤), or *Pensión Sala*, c/Alfons Primero 17 (☎972 88 01 04; ⑤) – both include breakfast in the price. **Restaurant** prices are slightly inflated by the cross-border trade, but good bets include *La Cantonada*, c/Major 46 (beyond the bell tower), and *Bar-Restaurant Kennedy*, c/Espanya 33.

The Costa Brava

The **Costa Brava** (Rugged Coast), stretching from **Blanes** to the French border, with its wooded coves, high cliffs, pretty beaches and deep blue water, was once the most beautiful part of the Spanish coast. Today, although the natural beauty cannot be entirely disguised, it's an almost total disaster, with a density of concrete tourist developments greater even than the Costa del Sol. The southern part, including the monstrous resort of **Lloret de Mar**, is the worst: further up the main road runs inland and coastal development is relatively low-key. Added attractions here are the ancient Greek site of **Empuries**, and Dalí's birthplace **Figueres**.

Buses in the region are almost all operated by the *SARFA* company, with an office in every town. Although they are reasonably efficient in the summer months, it can be frustrating either trying to get to some of the smaller coastal villages or simply attempting to stick to the coast. A car or bike solves all your problems; otherwise it's worth considering using Figueres or, better, Girona as a base for lateral trips to the coast – both are big bus termini. There is also an expensive private **boat service** (*Cruceros*) which runs in the summer from Lloret de Mar to Palamos, calling chiefly at Blanes, Lloret, Tossa, Sant Feliu and Platja d'Aro. It's worth taking at least once, since the rugged coastline makes for an extremely beautiful ride.

Tossa de Mar

Leaving Barcelona, there's really nowhere to tempt you to stop before **TOSSA DE MAR**. Out of season it's a really attractive place to spend some time, and even in high summer, arriving at Tossa by boat is one of the Costa Brava's highlights, the medieval walls and turrets pale and shimmering on the hill above the modern town. The walls themselves still surround an **old quarter**, all cobbled streets and flower boxes, offering terrific views over beach and bay, and there are a couple of good beaches. If you're going to stay, pick up a free map and accommodation lists from the **tourist office** (summer Mon–Sat 9am–9pm, Sun 10am–1pm; winter Mon–Fri 10am–1pm, Sat 10am–1pm; ☎972 34 01 08, *oftossa@ddgi es*), in the same building as the **bus station**, and then head straight down the road in front of you and turn right at the roundabout for "downtown" and beaches. There is cheapish **accommodation** to be had in the maze of tiny streets around the church and below the old city walls – try *Pensión Moré*, c/Sant Elmo 9 (☎972 34 03 39; ③) – and there are a couple of **campsites** within half an hour's walk of the centre. **Eating and drinking** is not cheap in Tossa – this is package-tourist land – but there are some good deals around, as well as endless "Full English Breakfast" bargains. For something of higher quality, try the upmarket seafood place, *Sa Palma*, overlooking the bay at c/Sant Ramon de Penyafort 11 (☎972 34 20 51).

Palafrugell and Empuries

Tossa is something of an aberration. The coast immediately to the north is thoroughly spoiled, with another immense concentration of cement in the area around La Platja d'Aro. **PALAFRUGELL**, an old town at its liveliest during the morning market, is little to get excited about either, but it has been overlooked by most tourists and hence remains pleasant even if there's little to see. It's also a convenient and relatively cheap place to base yourself if you're aiming for the delightful coastline a few kilometres away: pine-covered slopes and some quiet little coves with scintillatingly turquoise waters. The *Pensión Familiar*, c/Sant Sebastian 23 (☎972 30 52 43; ④), just off the central square, is the cheapest **accommodation** in Palafrugell, very clean and attached to an excellent *bar/comedor*. Such is the popularity of the nearby **beaches** that in summer a virtual shuttle service runs from the **bus station** to Calella and then on to Llafranc every thirty minutes. You might as well get off at Calella – a beautiful fishing port with tiny, crowded beaches – since Llafranc is only a twenty-minute walk away and you can get a return bus from there. Other, less frequent services run to the even lovelier Tamariu (a 90min walk from Calella, with a campsite (☎972 62 04 22) and to Begur.

From Palafrugell you're within striking distance of **EMPURIES**, one of the most interesting archeological sites in Spain. It started life in 550 BC as Greek *Emporion* (literally "Trading Station") and for three centuries conducted a vigorous trade throughout the Mediterranean. Later a splendid Roman city with an amphitheatre, fine villas and a broad marketplace grew up above the old Greek town. The Romans were replaced in turn by the Visigoths, who built several basilicas and made it the seat of a bishopric. The **site** (daily 10am–6/8pm; €2.40) lies behind a sandy bay about 2km north of L'Escala. The remains of the original Greek colony occupy the lower ground, where remains of temples, the town gate, agora and several streets can easily be made out, along with a mass of house foundations (some with mosaics) and the ruins of the Visigoth basilicas. A small **museum** stands above with audiovisuals, and beyond it stretches the vast but only partly excavated Roman town.

There are buses to **L'ESCALA** from Palafrugell (2–3 daily), Girona (3 daily) and Figueres (5 daily), arriving and leaving from the SARFA company's office just down the road from the combined tourist office/post office at the top of town. L'Escala usually has **rooms** available but it's an expensive and unattractive place, where you're still a fair walk from the ruins and the good beaches. You could instead **camp** out on the beaches and in the woods around the archeological site, where there's little development apart from the one-star *Ampurias* (☎972 77 02 07; ⑤, half-board; June–Sept only) and a few villas. Alternatively there's a **hostel**, *L'Escala*, c/Les Coves 41 (☎972 77 12 00; ②), with **camping**, right on the beach by the ruins, though this is often full.

Figueres

The northernmost resorts of the Costa Brava are reached via **FIGUERES**, a provincial Catalan town with a lively Rambla and plenty of cheap food and accommodation. The place would pass almost unnoticed, however, were it not for the most visited museum in Spain after the Prado: the **Museu Dalí** (July–Sept daily 9am–7.15pm; €7.20; Oct–June Tues–Sun 10.30am–6pm; €6). Dalí was born in Figueres and, on January 23 1989, died there; his embalmed body now lies in a glass case inside the museum. Installed by the artist in a building as surreal as the exhibits, the Museu Dalí is a treat, appealing to everyone's innate love of fantasy, absurdity and participation.

To make your way into the middle of town, simply follow the "Museu Dalí" signs from the **train station**. For a comfortable **room** try the *Pensión Bartis*, c/Méndez Núñez 2 (☎972 50 14 73; ③). There's a good all-year **hostel** (☎972 50 12 13; ②) at c/Anicet de Pages 2, off the Plaça del Sol; the town **campsite**, *Pous* (☎972 67 54 96), is on the way to the castle. There's a gaggle of cheap tourist **restaurants** in the narrow streets around the Dalí museum and, although a little more expensive, some nice pavement cafés lining the Rambla. The **tourist office** (summer Mon–Sat 8.30am–9pm; winter Mon–Fri 8.30am–3pm; ☎972 50 31 55) is in front of the post office building by the Plaça del Sol, and dishes out timetables for all onward transport.

Girona

The ancient walled town of **GIRONA** stands on a fortress-like hill, high above the Riu Onyar. It's a fine place, full of interest and oddly devoid of tourists considering that the town's airport serves most of the Costa Brava's resorts. Much of the pleasure of being in Girona is simply wandering around. The streets are narrow and medieval, the churches are cool and fascinating, while above the river high rows of houses lean precipitously on the banks. A combined €4.80 ticket from the tourist office gives entry to all of the following sights.

Centrepoint of the old town is the **Cathedral** (daily 10am–6pm), a mighty Gothic building approached by a magnificent seventeenth-century flight of Baroque steps. Inside it is equally awesome, just one tremendous single-naved vault with a span of 22m, the largest in the world. This emphasis on width and height is a feature of Catalan Gothic with its "hall churches", of which, unsurprisingly, Girona's is the perfect example. Buy a ticket to visit the superb cloisters, the sacristy and the **Museu Capitular** (Mon–Sat 10am–2pm & 4–6/7pm, Sun 10am–2pm, closed Tues in winter; €3), with an excellent small collection of religious art. If you find the collection interesting, the **Museu d'Art** (Tues–Sat 10am–6/7pm, Sun 10am–2pm; €1.80) contains further examples; it's housed alongside in the Episcopal Palace.

The well-preserved **Banys Arabs** (summer Mon–Sat 10am–7pm, Sun 10am–2pm; winter Tues–Sat 10am–2pm; €1.50), built by Moorish craftsmen in the thirteenth century, long after the Moors' occupation of Girona had ended, are also well worth a look, as is the surviving portion of the **Jewish quarter**, *El Call*. This was centred on c/de la Força, off which a steep alley leads up to the **Centre Bonastruc Ça Porta** (Mon–Fri 10am–6/8pm, Sun10am–3pm; €1.80), a little complex of rooms, staircases and adjoining buildings restored in an attempt to give expression to the cultural and social life of Catalunya's Jews in medieval times – though no synagogue remains.

Practicalities

If you're using **Girona airport**, 13km from the city centre, bear in mind that there's no bus service from the town and a taxi will be pretty expensive (easily €12); most charters coming from England are linked directly by bus with the Costa Brava. The large **bus station** (behind the **train station**) is well connected with most of Catalunya. From here it's a ten-minute walk up to the river and the Pont de Pedra, just over which is the **tourist office**, on the left at Rambla de Llibertat 1 (Mon–Fri 8am–8pm, Sat 8am–2pm & 4–8pm, Sun 9am–2pm; ☎972 22 65 75). There's a second information office at the train station (July & Aug only Mon–Sat 8am–1pm & 3–8pm).

There's plenty of cheap **accommodation** in Girona, with all the best places to stay found in the old town. The *Pension Viladomat*, c/Ciutadans 5 (☎972 20 31 76; ⑤), is centrally located and good value; the *Bellmirall* is near the cathedral, at c/Bellmirall 3 (☎972 20 40 09; ⑥). For cheaper rooms, the *Fonda Barnet*, c/Santa Clara 16 (☎972 20 00 03; ③), just to the left before you cross the Pont de Pedra, is a bit grubby but has some rooms overlooking the river. There's a modern **hostel**, very central at c/dels Ciutadans 9, off Plaça del Vi (☎972 21 80 03; ②), though it has limited spaces during term-time.

There are lots of **restaurants** in the town, though few that aren't quite pricey; *El Museu de Vi* at Cort Reial 4 is fairly reasonable and typically Catalan; *L'Arcada*, underneath the arches at Rambla de Llibertat 38, is a nice bar/restaurant and has the best pizzas in town, and there are also some good *menús* to be had on the terraces on Plaza Independencia – the least expensive being *Lloret*.

VALENCIA AND THE EAST COAST

The area known as the **Levante** (the East) is a bizarre mixture of ancient and modern, of beauty and beastliness. The rich *huerta* of **Valencia** is said to be the most fertile slab of land in Europe, crowded with orange, lemon and peach groves, and with rice fields still irrigated by systems devised by the Moors. Yet **Murcia**, to the south, could hardly provide a more severe contrast, with some of the driest land in Europe, some of it virtually a desert. Despite a few fine beaches, much of the region's **coast** – with the exception of the coastline from Jávea to Altea – is marred by the southbound highway, the industrial development which has sprouted all around it, and of course the heavy overdevelopment of villas and vacation homes.

Valencia

VALENCIA, the third largest city in Spain, may not approach the vitality of Barcelona or the cultural variety of Madrid, but it does at least have a lively night scene, and its clothes and furniture designers are renowned throughout Spain. As a whole the city is sprawling and confused, marred by unthinking modernization, but there are some exquisite corners away from the crowds, a few really fine buildings and a couple of excellent museums. Probably the most attractive features are the relaxed pavement café scene around the Plaza San Jaime and the colourful markets – Central Market, Mercado Colon and Ruzafa Market. The most interesting area for wandering is undoubtedly the mazelike **Barrio del Carmen**, the oldest part of town, roughly between c/de Caballeros and the Río Turia around the Puerta de Serranos. Among Valencia's renowned **fiestas** is Las Fallas de San José (March 12–19) when dozens of giant wooden caricatures are displayed and then ceremoniously burned amidst a riot of fireworks that explode on the final night of the festival.

Arrival and information

Valencia's **train station** is reasonably central: Avda. Marqués de Sotelo leads from opposite the entrance towards the main Plaza del Ayuntamiento, beyond which lie the old parts of the city. The **bus station** is further out, at Avda. Menéndez Pidal 13, on the far bank of the dried-up river from the centre. From here it's easier to take local bus #8 into the centre; allow twenty minutes if you decide to walk. The **Balearic ferry terminal** is connected to the Ayuntamiento by bus #4.

The **Plaza del Ayuntamiento** is home to the **post office** as well as the municipal **tourist office** (Mon–Fri 8.30am–2.15pm & 4.15–6.15pm, Sat 9.15am–12.45pm; ☎963 51 04 17). The regional tourist office is at c/de la Paz (Mon–Fri 10am–6pm, Sat 10am–2pm), and there's a third inside the train station (Mon–Fri 9am–6.30pm).

Accommodation

Most of the cheaper **places to stay** are very near the train station, in c/Bailén and c/Pelayo, which run parallel to the tracks off c/Játiva. This area, however, is pretty sleazy; you may feel more comfortable spending more in the centre, or much further out near the beach. Budget accommodation can be found at the basic but friendly *Hostal-Residencia Lyon*, c/Xátiva 10 (☎963 517 247; ③); the *Pensión Paris*, c/Salvia 12 (☎963 52 67 66; ③); the excellently sited and very popular *El Rincón*, c/Carda 11, near Plaza del Mercado (☎963 91 60 83; ④); and the nearby *Hospedería del Pilar*, Plaza del Mercad 19 (☎963 91 66 00; ④). More upmarket, the *Hotel Alkázar*, c/Mosén Femades 11 (☎963 52 95 75; ④), is a dependable and well-cared-for town-centre establishment, near the post office, while the *Hotel La Pepica*, Paseo de Neptuno 2, near the beach (☎963 71 11; ③), offers good-value rooms with bath, and an excellent restaurant. There are two **hostels**, the less attractive one halfway to the port on Avda. del Puerto 69 (☎963 61 74 59; ②; July & Aug; midnight curfew); the scruffier but more sociable one at c/Egenia Viñes 24 (☎963 56 42 88; ②, 50-percent reduction to RG readers; no curfew), right by the southern end of Malvarossa beach at the end of bus line #32. The most convenient **campsite** is the all-year *Devesa Gardens* (☎961 61 11 36), 7km out on the Nazaret-Oliva road by La Albufera; take the hourly bus from Plaza de los Torros.

The City

The distinctive feature of Valencian architecture is its wealth of elaborate Baroque facades – you'll see them on almost every old building in town, but none so extraordinary or rich as the **Palacio del Marqués de Dos Aguas**, a short walk north of the train station. Hipólito Rovira, who designed its amazing alabaster doorway, died insane in 1740, which should come as no surprise to anyone who's seen it. Inside is the **Museo Nacional de Cerámica** (Mon–Sat 10am–2pm & 4–8pm, Sun 10am–2pm; €2.40, free Sat pm & Sun), with a vast collection of ceramics from all over Spain. In the same decorative vein is the church of **San Juan de la Cruz** next door. Nearby, in the Plaza Patriarca, is the Neoclassical former university – with its beautiful cloisters and a series of classical concerts in July – and the beautiful Renaissance **Colegio del Patriarca**, whose small **art museum** (daily 11am–1.30pm; €0.60) includes excellent works by El Greco, Morales and Ribalta.

It's not far from here, up c/de la Paz, to the **Plaza Zaragoza** and Valencia's **Cathedral**. The plaza is dominated by two octagonal towers, the florid spire of the church of Santa Catalina and the **Miguelete**, the unfinished bell-tower of the cathedral. You can make the long climb up to its roof (daily 10am–1pm & 5–7/8pm; €0.60) for a fantastic view over the city with its many blue-domed churches. The cathedral's most attractive feature is the lantern above the crossing, its windows glazed with sheets of alabaster; there's also a **museum** (Mon–Sat: March–Nov 10am–1pm & 4.30–8pm, till 7pm June–Sept; Dec–Feb mornings only; €1.20) whose exhibits include a gold and agate cup (the Santo Cáliz) said to be the one used by Christ at the Last Supper – the Holy Grail itself.

A side exit leads from the cathedral to the **Plaza de la Virgen**, where you'll find the Archbishop's Palace and the tiny chapel of **Nuestra Señora de los Desamparados**. Here, thousands of candles constantly burn in front of the image of the Virgin, patron of Valencia. Five minutes' walk away, is the enormous **Mercado Central**, a huge iron and glass structure housing one of the biggest markets in Europe, full of amazing local fruit, fish and vegetables; it closes around 2pm every day. Other museums worth visiting include **IVAM**, the modern art museum on c/Guillém de Castro 118 (Tues–Sun 10am–7pm; €2.10, free Sun), and the **Museo de Bellas Artes** on c/San Pío V (Mon–Sat 9am–2.15pm & 4–7.30pm, Sun 10am–7.30pm; free).

Also worth a look are the town's defences, including the fourteenth-century **Torres de Serranos** (Tues–Sat 9am–1.45pm & 4.30–7.45pm, Sun 9am–1.45pm; free), an impressive gateway defending the entrance to the town across the Río Turia with panoramic views from the top. The river itself, diverted after serious flooding in 1956, which damaged much of the old part of the city, is no more than a trickle now, and a huge park has been landscaped in the riverbed; the park has been grassed and planted, and includes a sports stadium, football pitches and even a huge Gulliver to climb on. Near here stands the **Palau de la Música**, a futuristic glass-structure venue for concerts, and the site of the **City of Arts and Sciences**, an ambitious project for an Expo-style group of pavilions including more concert halls, a science museum, and a giant oceanographic theme park. Currently, only the futuristic-looking Hemisféric is completed, containing a planetarium, laser display and inevitable IMAX theatre (daily 10am–11.30pm; €6). Ask at the tourist office for further information as work is ongoing, and although it was due to be completed by the end of 1999, it may be a while yet.

Eating, drinking and nightlife

Food in the **restaurants** in Valencia can be poor, especially considering that this is the home of paella. Decent mid-range possibilities include *El Generalife* behind the cathedral on Plaza de la Virgen, where the superb fixed *menú* costs €7.80; *La Utielana*, Plaza Picadero de los Aguas, with good roast lamb, though you may have to wait for a table; and *Bar Cánovas*, Plaza Cánovas Castillo, one of the city's best tapas bars, which also serves meals including a €5.40 *menú*.

For bistros and cheap restaurants the best area is Barrio del Carmen around c/Caballeros. A traditional place to go for *mejillones* (mussels) is the *Bar Pilar* on the corner of c/Moro Zeit, on Plaza del Espart off c/Caballeros. A good **vegetarian** option is *La Lluna*, San Ramón 23. For paella, go to either Malvarossa's *La Pepica* on Paseo Neptuno, or – best of all – go out of town on the El Saler bus down the south-coast road to the villages of El Palmar or El Perellonet.

If you don't know where to go, Valencia can seem dead at night: the action is widely dispersed, with many locations across the Turia. To get back late at night you'll have to walk or take a taxi. In summer everyone is in the **bars** lining the Malvarrosa Beach, including *Genaro* and *Tropical*, large bar/discos on c/Eugenio Vines (the beach road). To get there, take bus #1, #2 from the bus station or #19 from Plaza del Ayuntamiento. The best of the **nightlife** is around the central Barrio del Carmen (c/Caballeros and c/Quart); *Café del Temps*, c/Obispo Jerónimo 4, is one of the more interesting bars here, while the *Radio City Bar*, c/Santa Teresa 19, is larger and has a mainly young ex-pat clientele. Another area is above the Gran Vía de Fernando el Católico, along c/Juan Llorens and c/Calixto, where the *Café Carioca* and *Café La Havana*, at c/Juan Llorens 52 and 41, are currently in favour. The new university area, around Avda. Blasco Ibáñez, is also popular: try the *Metro*, *El Asesino*, or *Hipódromo* for salsa, or the bars on Plaza Xuquer, just off Blasco Ibáñez – though these are all fairly disparate. A more upmarket zone is the Plaza Cánovas del Castillo and the side streets off it, full of *pubs* (music bars) where people go to see and be seen. Most **gay bars and discos**, like *Venial*, are around or in the c/Quart, though others like *North Dakota*, just off c/de la Paz on Plaza Margarita Valldaura are more central – pick up the map produced by the Collectiu Lambada de Gais i Lesbianes, available free at most venues or their offices at c/Salvador Giner 9 (Mon–Sat 5–10pm; *www.arrakis/-lambada*).

Many of the **discos** are in the university area – they include the perennially popular *Warthol*, Blasco Ibañez 113, or more hardcore club music next door at *Acción*. Otherwise, most of the big techno discos – such as *The Face, Heaven* and *Puzzle* – are out of town and you'll need your own transport. For more details about **what's on**, buy one of the two weekly listings guides, *Qué y Dónde* and *Turia* – though neither of them are exhaustive.

Listings

Airlines Iberia, c/de la Paz 14 (☎963 52 06 77) or their telephone information line (☎902 40 05 00).

Airport Manises, 8km away (☎961 59 85 15); bus #15 from bus station (5am–11.40pm; 2–6 hourly).

Balearic ferries Information and tickets from Trasmediterránea, Avda. Manuel Soto 15 (☎902 45 46 45, *www. trasmediterranea.es*), or from any of the half-dozen travel agents on Plaza del Ayuntamiento. Note that if you are going to Ibiza outside of the summer months, it's far better to go from Denia, with more services that take 10 hours less and cost only a little more.

Car rental Best value is probably Cuñauto Car Hire, c/Burriana 51 (☎963 74 85 61). Otherwise, there's Avis at the airport and at c/Isabel la Católica 17 (☎963 51 07 34), Hertz at the airport and c/Segorbe 7 (☎963 41 50 36), Atesa at the airport and c/Joaquín Costa 57 (☎963 95 36 05), and many more.

Consulates USA, c/Romagosa 1 (☎963 51 69 73); UK Consulate in Alicante (☎965 21 60 22).

Exchange Main branches of most banks are around the Plaza del Ayuntamiento or along c/Játiva 24. Outside banking hours, try: Caja de Ahorros, c/Játiva 14, to the left as you come out of the train station; or Nuevo Centro, near the bus station (both Mon–Sat 9am–8pm). The División Internacional, at Banco de Valencia, c/Colon 20, currently charges the lowest commission.

Hospitals General hospital on Avda. Cid, at the Tres Cruces junction (☎963 86 29 00).

Internet access An hour of Internet daily can be had for free on the fifth floor of the Centro Cultural Bancaja, Plaza de Teuán (Mon–Fri 9am–2pm & 4–9pm, Sat 9am–2pm) on production of your passport. Otherwise try Confederation, near the train station at c/Ribera 8 (daily 11am–11pm; €3/hr, minimum 1hr).

Left luggage Self-store lockers at RENFE; 24hr access; €1.80–3.60/day.

Police Headquarters at Gran Vía Ramón y Cajal 40 (☎963 53 95 39).

Post office Plaza del Ayuntamiento 24 (Mon–Fri 8.30am–8.30pm, Sat 9.30am–2pm).

Telephones Pasaje Rex 7, off Avda. Marques de Sotelo (Mon–Fri 9am–2.30pm & 4–8.30pm, Sat 9.30am–2pm) or inside the RENFE station (daily 10am–10pm).

Taxis ☎963 70 33 33 or ☎963 57 13 13.

The Costa Blanca

South of Valencia stretches the **Costa Blanca**, a long strip of country with, between Gandía and Benidorm, some of the best beaches on this coast. Much of it, though, suffers from the worst excesses of package tourism and in the summer it's hard to get a room anywhere – in August virtually impossible. Campers have it somewhat easier – there are hundreds of campsites – but driving can be a nightmare unless you stick to the dull highway. **Gandía** is the first of the big resorts, and one of the best bets for a room, since the quiet and provincial old town lies a few kilometres inland. Oliva, 8km south, is a much lower-key development. Again the village is set back from the coast and although the main road charges through its centre, it's relatively unspoiled and there are a number of *hostales* and *fondas*.

DENIA is a far bigger place, a sizeable town even without its summer visitors, and less appealing. You might though be tempted to take the daily **boat to Palma de Mallorca** or **Ibiza**. A rattling narrow-gauge rail line (FGV) runs hourly down the coast from Alicante. Beneath the wooded capes beyond, bypassed by the main road, stretch probably the most beautiful beaches on this coastline, centred on Javea – but you'll need a car to get to any of them, and even if you have a vehicle there's barely a cheap room to be found.

Back on the main road again, **ALTEA** is set on a small hill overlooking this whole stretch of coastline. Restrained tourist development is centred on the seafront, and being so close to Benidorm it does receive some overspill. In character, however, it's a world apart. The old village up the hill is picturesquely attractive with its white houses, blue-domed church and profuse blossoms.

Beyond Altea there's nothing between you and the crowded beaches at **BENIDORM**. If you want hordes of British and Scandinavian sunseekers, scores of "English" pubs, at least seventy discos, and bacon and eggs for breakfast, this is the place to come. The beach – nearly 6km of it, regularly topped up with imported Moroccan sand – is undeniably impressive, backed by a Manhattan skyline. Surprisingly, except in August, you can usually find a room in Benidorm, though it takes a lot of walking. The cheaper places are all near the centre and away from the sea, but out of season many of the giant hotels and apartment buildings slash their prices dramatically. Check with the **tourist office** (Mon–Sat 10am–2pm & 4–8pm, till 9pm July–Sept; ☎965 86 81 89, *www.benidorm.org*), at the bottom of Avda. Martínez Alejos, near the old village.

Alicante

Locals describe **ALICANTE** as *la millor terra del mond* and while that's a gross exaggeration it is at least a living city, thoroughly Spanish, and a definite relief after some of the places you may have been passing through. There are good beaches nearby, too, a lively nightlife in season and plenty of cheap places to stay and to eat. Wide esplanades such as the Rambla de Méndez Núñez and Avda. Alfonso Sabio give the town an elegant air, and around the Plaza de Luceros and along the seafront *paseo* you can relax in style at terrace cafés – paying a bit extra for the palm-tree setting, of course. The most interesting area is around the Ayuntamiento, where, among the bustle of small-scale commerce, you'll see plenty of evidence of Alicante's large Algerian community – the links with Algeria have always been strong, and boats depart from here for Oran twice a week.

The rambling **Castillo de Santa Bárbara** on the bare rock behind the town beach is Alicante's only real "sight" – with a tremendous view from the top. It's best approached from the seaward side where a lift shaft has been cut straight up through the hill to get you to the top; the lift is directly opposite Meeting Point 5 on the other side of the road from Playa Postiguet. For the best local **beaches** head for San Juan de Alicante, 6km out, reached either by half-hourly bus from the Plaza del Mar or the FGV rail line. Still better, take a trip to the **island of Tabarca** to the south – boats leave from Puerto on the Explanada de España daily in summer, weather permitting.

Practicalities

The main **train station** is on Avda. Salamanca, but trains on the private FGV line to Benidorm and Denia leave from the small station at the far end of the Playa del Postiguet. The **bus station** for local and international services is in c/Portugal. The **airport**, 12km west, is connected with the centre by a special service which stops at the central Avda. Rambla Mendez Nuñez 23. This is where you'll find the very helpful regional **tourist office** at no. 23 (Mon–Fri 10am–7/8pm, Sat 10am–2pm & 3–7/8pm; ☎965 20 00 00), with additional municipal offices at the bus station and the airport.

Except in August you should have little problem finding a **room**, with the bulk of the possibilities concentrated at the lower end of the old town, above the Explanada de España and around the Plaza Gabriel – especially on c/San Fernando, c/San Francisco, c/Jorge Juan and c/Castaño. Places to try include the beautiful *Les Monges*, c/Las Monjas 2 (☎965 21 50 46; ③), *Hostal Residencia Portugal*, c/Portugal 26 (☎965 92 92 44; ③), and the no-frills *Habitaciones La Orensana*, c/San Fernando 10 (☎965 20 78 20; ②). There are cheaper places on c/San Francisco, but they are all pretty seedy and not advisable for lone women. There are several **campsites**, including *El Molino* at Playa de San Juan to the north (connected by FGV train and bus #21) and *La Marina*, south of town in woods on a good beach and connected by Costa Azul buses.

Cheap **restaurants** are clustered around the Ayuntamiento, including a couple of places where you can eat couscous on c/Miguel Soler. Over on the other side of town c/San Francisco, leading off a square near the bottom end of the Rambla, has a group of cheap restaurants with seats outside. For tapas try the atmospheric *Mesón de Labradores*, near the cathedral at c/Labradores 19. For **bars** and the best **nightlife**, head into the Barrio Santa Cruz, whose narrow streets lie roughly between the cathedral, Plaza Carmen and Plaza San Cristóbal. An excellent starting point is *Desden*, c/Labradores 22, which plays jazz in the afternoon and house, dance and funk through the night till 4am.

THE BALEARIC ISLANDS

The four chief **Balearic islands** – Ibiza, Formentera, Mallorca and Menorca – maintain a character distinct from the mainland and from each other. **Ibiza**, firmly established among Europe's trendiest resorts, has an intense, outrageous street life and a floating summer population that seems to include every club-going Spaniard from Sevilla to Barcelona. It can be fun, if this sounds your idea of island activity, and above all if you're gay – Ibiza is a very tolerant place. **Formentera**, small and a little desolate, is something of a beach-annexe to Ibiza, though it struggles to present its own alternative image of reclusive artists and "in the know" tourists. **Mallorca**, the largest and best-known Balearic, also battles with its image, popularly reckoned as little more than sun, booze and beach parties. In reality you'll find all the clichés, most of them crammed into the mega-resorts of the Bay of Palma, but there's certainly much else besides: mountains, lively fishing ports, some beautiful coves and the Balearics' one real city, **Palma**. Mallorca is in fact the one island in the group you might come to other than for beaches and nightlife, with scope to explore, walk and travel about. And last, to the east, there is windswept **Menorca** – more conservative in its development, more modest in its clientele and, after the others, a little dull.

Ferries from mainland Spain (and Marseille) are severely overpriced considering the distances involved; likewise, monopolies keep rates high for inter-island ferries, and for journeys like Ibiza–Mallorca or even Mallorca–Menorca it can be cheaper to fly. The catch here is that in mid-season flights are often booked out: the solution is to get up before dawn, head for the airport and get yourself on a waiting list for the first flight.

Expense and overdemand can be crippling in other areas too. As "holiday islands", each with a buoyant international tourist trade, the Balearics charge considerably above mainland prices for rooms – which from mid-June to mid-September are in very short supply. If you go at these times, and you're not into camping, it's sensible to try to fix up some kind of reservation in advance. Something you may want to do, and which will alleviate accommodation problems to some extent, is to rent transport: cars (also in short supply in season) can be driven off and slept in, and a moped will get you and a sleeping bag to some tempting and acceptable spots, although there is a risk of a fine unless you're discreet.

Ibiza

IBIZA (*Eivissa* in Catalan) is an island of excess. Beautiful and indented with scores of barely accessible cove beaches, it's nevertheless the islanders and their visitors who make it special. However outrageous you may want to be (and outrageousness is the norm), the locals have seen it all before. By day thousands of Nivea-smeared tourists spread themselves across the nudist beaches, preparing for the nightly flounce through bars and clubs. For years it was *the* European hippy escape, but nowadays is as synonymous with the European club scene as with its 1960s denizens, who keep coming back.

Ibiza Town

In physical, as well as atmospheric terms, **IBIZA TOWN** is the most attractive place on the island. Most people stay in rented apartments or small *pensiones* which means fewer hotels to ruin the skyline and no package incursions. Approach by sea and you'll get the full frontal effect of the old town's walls rising like a natural extension of the rocky cliffs which protect the port. Within the walls, the ancient quarter is topped by a sturdy **Cathedral**, whose illuminated clock shines out across the harbour throughout the night.

The capital is a simple enough place to find your way around. From the **ferry terminal**, the old streets of the Sa Peña quarter lead straight ahead towards the walls of the ancient city – D'Alt Vila. A waterside walk will take you from here – past bars and restaurants which at night give front-row viewing for the fashion display – round to the harbour wall from where the entire bay can be surveyed. Continue past the port and you'll be in the new town, below the old to the west. If you fly in you'll arrive at the **airport** about 6km out; there's a regular bus from here between 7.30am and 10.30pm, or you can take a taxi for around €12. In the airport there's an efficient tourist office (May–Sept daily 10am–midnight) which can provide maps and lists of accommodation as well as details on vehicle rental.

The principal **tourist office** on the harbourfront on Passeig des Moll (Mon–Fri 9.30am–1.30pm & 5–7pm, Sat 10.30am–1pm; ☎971 30 19 00, *www.visitbalears.com*) can offer more extensive lists of **hotels** and **hostales** for the whole island, as well as details of apartments for stays of a week or more – not cheap, but abundant and usually pleasant. Most of the cheaper hotels are in the area around the tourist office and a short walk away around Paseo Vara del Rey. Even if you stay a kilometre or so east of town in Talamanca, or on the other side of the port in Figueretas, you're not that far removed from the action. A couple of starter possibilities are *Hostal Sol y Brisa*, Avda. Bartolomeu Vicente Ramón 15 (☎971 31 08 18; ③), near the port in the street parallel to Vara de Rey, which has many others, including *Hostal Montesol* at no. 31 (☎971 31 01 61; ③); and next to other options, there's a choice of rooms at *Hostal La Marina*, in front of the ferry at the port (☎971 31 01 72; ②).

Daylight hours are usually spent on the **beaches** at Las Salinas or Es Cabellet (both a short bus ride away) or the nearer but not as nice Figueretas. At night, before the discos open their doors, the shops stay open until 11pm to provide entertaining window-shopping on the way to supper. Most of the cheaper places **to eat** are in the Sa Peña quarter. One of the best bets is smoky *C'an Costa* at c/Cruz 19; along the road on the corner, *La Victoria*, c/Rimbau 1, is another popular and long-established eatery. Down by the waterside, or up in the walled town, you'll be paying a lot more, though *La Brasa*, c/Congresso Agricola 3 is not astronomical for the standard and setting.

The bulk of the **bars** in which to begin your night out are in the area around the port, though many are incredibly posey and overpriced even during happy hour – avoid anywhere that employs PR people to entice you in and you'll be all right. One place that's out of the centre – but definitely worth checking out – is *Grial*, (☎971 31 46 39), a fifteen-minute walk out on Avda. 8 de Agosto, which is friendly, reasonably priced, has art exhibitions, plays great music and is actually frequented by locals. There are a few gay bars along c/D'Enmig, among them *Teatro* and *JJ's*, but the most crowded ones are found up by the city walls – *Incognito's* and *Angelo's* are neighbours nestling by the Portal de las Tablas. As for **clubs**, even if you haven't heard of *Pacha* or the gay *Amnesia*, you'll certainly be made aware of them during your wanderings round the port in the evening. None of them really get going much before midnight, and the dancing goes on until dawn. The season lasts from June to September, with the best time to party being the first and last two weeks. Be prepared to spend a lot of money if you go to any club, with entrance fees of €30–75 and astronomical bar prices – even a glass of water will set you back about €6. For the free full-moon beach-parties, try asking around in the hippy markets in Es Canar, Las Dalias or Santa Eularía. **Internet cafés** on the island include Centro Internet Elvissa, Ignacio Wallis 39 (daily 10am–11pm; €5/hr) and E-Station, Avda Fleming 1, San Antonio (daily 11am–midnight; €5/hr).

Around the island

Nowhere else can compare to the capital, certainly not the second city, San Antonio Abad, which is a highly avoidable package-resort nightmare, though can be quite pleasant off-season. **SANTA EULALIA**, the only other real town, retains a certain charm in its hilltop church looking down over the sprawling old town and modern seafront, while close by the persistent can find a number of relatively empty beaches. The same holds true for most of the rest of the coast – plenty of golden sands but a good deal of effort required to reach them. The one major exception is the northern bay of **Portinatx**, connected by a relatively major road and, despite hotel development, with a number of clean, not overly populated beaches. **Inland** there's little of anything – a few villages and holiday homes that are exceedingly pretty to drive through but offer little if you stop.

There is a good **bus** service between Ibiza Town, San Antonio Abad, Santa Eulalia, Portinatx and a few of the larger beaches, but hiring a vehicle will widen your options no end. It should prove particularly useful on Ibiza for finding accommodation – as difficult here as on any of the other islands and even more expensive. You may well be reduced to one of the five **campsites**. Only one of these – *Cala Llonga* (☎971 33 21 18) on the road to Playa d'en Bossa – is at all near the capital; the tourist office can provide details of the others.

Formentera

Just three nautical miles south of Ibiza, **FORMENTERA** (population 6200) is the smallest of the inhabited Balearics and is almost completely barren, the few crops having to be protected, as on Menorca, against the lashing of winter winds. Most of the island is covered in wild rosemary, and crawling with thousands of brilliant green lizards. Its income is derived from tourism (especially German and British), taking advantage of some of Spain's longest, whitest and least-crowded beaches. The shortage of fresh water, fortunately, continues to keep away the crowds and for the most part visitors are seeking escape with little in the way of sophistication. It is, however, becoming more popular, and is certainly not the paradise it once was.

The crossing from Ibiza is short, but strong currents ensure that it's slow – between thirty minutes to an hour – and rough. Fares are about €15 (€27 on the hydrofoil) and there are usually rival sailings to choose from: check the return times before deciding. Boats dock at the tiny but functional harbour of **LA SABINA**, where the two waterside streets are lined with places offering cars, mopeds or bicycles for rent, interspersed with the odd bar and café. This is the place to get yourself mobile, but if possible phone ahead, certainly if you want a car – try Moto Rent La Sabina (☎971 32 22 75), Moto Rent Pujol (☎971 32 24 88) or Autos Isla Blanca (☎971 32 25 59). Check with the **tourist office** (Mon–Fri 10am–2pm & 5–7pm; ☎971 32 20 57, *www.illadeformentera*) by the harbour if you need help with this, or with island accommodation. The capital, **SAN FRANCISCO JAVIER**, is just a couple of kilometres away, easily reached on foot or by local bus or taxi. As well as the whitewashed fortified church – now stripped of its defensive cannon – this metropolis has several restaurants and cafés, at least three banks, four bars, a hotel, supermarkets, a pharmacist, a doctor and a *Telefónica* for international calls. An open-air market adds a touch of interest.

Formentera's main road continues from San Francisco to the island's easternmost point at La Mola. Along it, or just off it, are concentrated almost all of the island's habitation and most of the beaches. The next largest town, **SAN FERNANDO** – with a bar, a church and an *hostal* or two – serves the beach of Es Pujols where the package-tour industry, such as it is, is concentrated. Despite relative crowding, it's a beautiful coast with clear water and pure white sand dunes backed by low pines. Playa Mitjorn, on the south side of this narrow stretch of the island, is an enormous expanse of sand broken only by the occasional bar or hotel. Formentera's strict regulations on new building mean that this area remains relatively undeveloped: rather soulless, but definitely the place to go for total isolation, and the main area for nude sunbathing.

Practicalities

Most people treat Formentera as a day-trip from Ibiza, and if you want to be one of the few who **stay** you may have difficulty finding anywhere not given over entirely to agency reservations. Among the better deals are *Hostal La Sabina* (☎971 32 22 79; ④), just outside La Sabina; *Casa Rafal* in San Francisco Javier (☎971 32 22 05; ②, with breakfast); *Hostal Pepe* (☎971 32 80 33; ②) in San Fernando; *Hostal Bar Los Rosales* (☎971 32 81 23; ⑤); and *Tahiti* (May–Sept; ☎971 32 81 22; ③, with breakfast;) on Playa Pujols. There's a basic **bus** service from La Sabina but journeys rarely keep to timetables, and they connect only the towns, leaving you long, hot walks to the beaches. **Taxis** are cheap, with ranks at La Sabina, San Francisco and Es Pujols.

There aren't many cheap places to **eat** on the island. All the *hostales* mentioned above serve food – particularly good value at *Casa Rafal* – or you can get your own supplies from the supermarket in San Francisco. Es Pujols has the most restaurants, generally speaking, and there are plenty of beach bars, although the food is geared for tourists, so tends to be bland and overpriced.

Mallorca

MALLORCA, perhaps more than anywhere in Spain, has a split identity. So much so, in fact, that there's a long-standing joke here about a fifth Balearic island, "*Majorca*", a popular sort of place that pulls in an estimated three million tourists a year. There are sections of coast where high-rise hotels and shopping centres are continuous, wedged beside and upon one another and broken only by a dual carriageway down to more of the same. But the spread of development, even after 25 years, is surprisingly limited: "Majorca" occupies only the Bay of Palma, a forty-kilometre strip flanking the island capital. Beyond, to the north and east, things are very different. Not only are there good cove beaches, but there's a really startling variety and physical beauty to the land itself, which makes the island many people's favourite in the group.

Palma

You may arrive by boat from Menorca at Puerto de Alcúdia in the north of the island, but the odds are you'll find yourself in **PALMA DE MALLORCA**, the capital and the only real "city" in the Balearics. Palma is in some ways like a mainland Spanish city – lively, solid and industrious – though it is immediately set apart by its insular, Mediterranean aura. The port is by far the largest in the Balearics, the evening *paseo* the most ingrained, and, in the evenings at least, you feel the city has only passing relevance to the tourist enclaves around its bay. Arriving by sea, it is also beautiful and impressive, with the grand limestone bulk of the cathedral towering above the old town and the remnants of medieval walls.

The **ferry** port is some 3.5km west of the centre of Palma, connected to the centre by bus #1; Palma **airport**, 9km east of the city, is served by bus #25 (every 30min) to the Plaza de España. Finding your way around is fairly straightforward once you're in the centre. Around the Cathedral is the Portela quarter, "Old" Palma, a cluster of alleyways and lanes that become more spacious and ordered as you move towards the zigzag of avenues built beside or in place of the city walls. Cutting up from the sea, beside the cathedral, is Paseo Borne, garden promenade as well as boulevard, and way up the hill to the northeast lies the Plaza Mayor, target for most of the day-tripping tourists.

There are hundreds of *pensiones* and hotels, and your first move in the summer should be to pick up the official lists of these from the **tourist office** at Plaça de la Reina 2 (daily 9am–8pm; (☎971 71 22 16, *www.visitbalears.com*). They can also supply maps, bus schedules and leaflets. Best initial areas to look for **accommodation** are around the Passeig Mallorca, on c/Apuntadores or c/San Felio running west from Paseo Borne (cheaper), and on c/San Jaime at the top of the Paseo Borne (mid-range). Specific recommendations are probably futile in summer, but some to try are the British-run *Hostal Borne*, c/San Jaime 3 (☎971 71 29 42, *hborne@bitel.es*; ⑦ with breakfast), very popular, with a courtyard café; *Hostal Ritzi*, c/Apuntadores 6 (☎971 71 46 10; ②); and *Hostal Pons*, c/VI 8, in an old Palma house (☎971 72 26 58; ②). There's also a **hostel** at c/Costa Brava 13 in El Arenal (☎971 260 892; ②), but it's well out of town and invariably booked en masse by school groups; take bus #15 from Plaza de España or Plaza de Reina. There are several **Internet** cafés in central Palma, including CyberCentral, Calle Soledad 4 (Mon–Sat 9am–10pm & Sun noon–8pm; €5) and Internet Mallorca Cybercafe, c/Olmos 50a (Mon–Sat 10am–9pm; €3).

Eating in Palma can be cheaper than anywhere in the Balearics. There are plenty of touristy *menús del día* along Avda. d'Antoni Maura and Passeig des Borns for around €6–9, but better fare is available nearby in the Barrio de Llotje between c/Apuntados and the seafront. Here you'll find several lower-priced, low-key restaurants including *Vecchio Giovani*, c/San Juan 3, which does an excellent €6.60 local-style *menú* as well as fine Italian fare. Paella fans should head for *S'Arrosseria*, at Passeig Marítim 13, which also has a veggie option. Good fish dishes can be found at *Caballito de Mar* at Paseo Sagrada 5, and quality international cuisine at *Mediterraneo 1930* at Paseo Maritimo 33 – though expect a hefty bill from either.

The town's **nightlife** generally starts within the Barrio de Llotja, moving on at around 3am to the seafront Avda. Gabriel Roca. This can be ludicrously expensive, but there's a fair selection of discos – both straight and gay – amid the souvenir shops and hamburger bars. Many of these are free to get in, though they make up for it behind the bar.

Around the island

When you feel you've exhausted the city's possibilities move across to Sóller, Deiá, Puerto Pollensa, Puerto de Alcúdia or one of the small resorts around Porto Cristo on the southeast coast. **Accommodation** is reasonable at each of these towns, though in July or August it'll be almost impossible to find. **Camping** is an alternative but not particularly provided for – there's only one "official" campsite (at Platja Brava) and a scattering of private ones registered with the Palma tourist office. Mallorca's **bus service** is reasonably good and there are even a couple of **train lines** – one, a beautiful ride up through the mountains from Palma to Sóller, is an attraction in itself. Transport of your own, though, is a strong advantage – the Palma tourist office can again advise on rental.

Menorca

Second largest of the Balearics, **MENORCA** is littered with stone reminders of its prehistoric past: rock mounds known as *talayots*, megalithic *taulas* (huge stones topped with another to form a T, around 4m high) and *navetas*, stone slab constructions shaped like an inverted loaf tin. These, and the incessant wind, are the island's most characteristic features. There's not much in the way of excitement, but if you're looking for peace and for some beautiful, relatively isolated beaches head for the sheltered Cala Turqueta on the southwest coast or more windswept Cala Pregonda near Fornells on the north. Menorca is probably your best Balearic bet.

The island is boomerang-shaped, stretching from Mahón (*Maó*) in the east to the smaller, pretty port of Ciudadela (*Ciutadella* in Catalan), in the west. Menorca's **airport** is 5km out of Mahón and is served only by taxi (around €6.60). **Bus** routes are limited, adhering mostly to the main central road between Mahón and Ciudadela occasionally branching off to the major coastal towns. You'll need your own vehicle to get to any of the more attractive beaches. There are one or two points to remember, though. To reach any of the emptier sands you'll probably have to drive down a track fit only for four-wheel drive – and the wind, which can be very helpful when it's blowing behind you, is distinctly uncomfortable if you're trying to ride into it on a moped. Bear in mind too that petrol stations are few and far between. After 10pm and on Sundays and fiestas, only a few pumps are open; take note of the rota posted outside and keep a full tank.

Accommodation is at a premium, with little of anything outside the bigger coastal towns. Once you find something reasonable, stay there. There's just one fairly pricey **campsite** (☎971 15 45 46), at Cala Santa Galdana on the coast south of Ferrerías.

Mahón

If you arrive by ferry from Barcelona or Palma you'll sail into the vast natural harbour of **MAHÓN**, the island capital. It's a quiet, respectable little town: the people are restrained and polite, and the architecture is a strange hybrid of classical Georgian bay-windowed town houses and tall, gloomy Spanish apartment buildings shading the narrow streets. Four adjacent squares form a hub close to the docks. The **Plaza España** is reached by a twisting flight of steps from the pier and offers great views right across the port and bay; there's a fish market here in the early mornings. Immediately behind is the **Plaza Carmen**, with a simple Carmelite church whose cloisters have been adapted to house a small museum. Wander on from here up c/Virgen del Carmen and take any of the streets to the left to reach one of the oldest and most atmospheric parts of town, overlooking the port from on high. In the other direction from Plaza España lie the **Plaza de la Conquista**, with the town's main church, and the Plaza de la Constitución.

Mahón's main square is actually the Plaza Explanada, some way above all these along c/Hanover and c/Dr Orfila. The main **tourist office** (Mon–Fri 9am–8pm & 1.30pm–5/8pm, Sat 9.30am–1pm; ☎971 36 37 90, *www.visitbalears.com*) is here and it's also home to a bunch of overfed pigeons and a military barracks. Otherwise the only excitement is on Sunday, when crowds converge on its bars and ice-cream parlours, and street entertainers play to the strolling multitudes. The port area is considerably more interesting, and you can walk the entire length of the quayside from the Xoriguer gin distillery (free samples in the shop) to the suburb of Villacarlos, passing through Cala Figuera and Castelfons – a relaxed stroll past any number of small restaurants and bars.

Mahón is the best bet for **accommodation** on the island, and most options are all fairly central. The best place to start looking is around Plaza Reial: try the American/Scottish-owned *Hostal Orsi* at c/Infanta 19 (☎971 36 47 51; ③) or *Hostal La Isla* at c/Santa Catalina 4 (☎971 36 64 92; ③). Mahón has a place in culinary history as the birthplace of mayonnaise (*mahonesa*), and you should have no problem finding somewhere to eat. The majority of **restaurants** are down by the port. For local food try *Ca'n Sintes*, off Plaça Princep at c/Camí de's Castell 203–205, or the pricier *Cafeteria Consey* on Plaça Explanada.

travel details

Trains

Madrid to: Algeciras (2 daily; 5hr 50min–10hr 30min); Alicante (10 daily; 3hr 45min); Almería (2 daily; 7–8hr 45min); Ávila (29 daily; 1hr 20min); Barcelona (8 daily; 6hr 30min); Bilbao (2–3 daily; 6hr 30min); Burgos (6 daily; 4hr 30min); Cáceres (5 daily; 4hr 30min); Cádiz (2 daily; 5hr); Córdoba (28 daily; 1hr 40min–4hr 45min; plus 9–14 AVEs daily; 1hr); Girona (1 daily; 10hr); Granada (2 daily; 6–8hr); Jaca (1 daily; 6hr 50min); Lisbon (1 daily; 9hr 30min); León (7 daily; 4hr); Málaga (6 daily; 4hr–7hr); Merida (4–5 daily; 4hr 20min–7hr 30min); Oviedo (2–3 daily; 6hr–7hr 30min); Pamplona (2 daily; 4hr 50min); Paris (1 daily; 13hr 30min); Salamanca (3 daily; 2hr 35min–3hr 15min); San Sebastián (3 daily; 6hr 30min–8hr 10min); Santander (2–3 daily; 5hr 35min); Santiago (2 daily; 7hr 50min–8hr 30min); Segovia (7–9 daily; 2hr); Sevilla (14 daily; 3hr 30min; plus 9–16 AVEs daily; 2hr 30min); Toledo (7–9 daily' 1hr 15min–1hr 30min); Valencia (11 daily; 3hr 30min); Vigo (2 daily; 8–9hr); Zaragoza (13 daily; 3–4hr).

Algeciras to: Córdoba (2 daily; 2hr 50min); Granada (1 daily; 4hr); Ronda (6 daily; 1hr 40min).

Barcelona to: Bilbao (2 daily; 9hr–10hr 20min); Figueres (hourly; 1hr 30min–2hr); Geneva (4–7 weekly; 9hr); Girona (hourly; 1hr 10min–1hr 30min); Lleida (19 daily; 2hr 20min–4hr 20min); Milan (3–7 weekly; 12hr 20min); Paris (1 daily; 12hr 10min); Puigcerdà (6 daily; 3hr); Valencia (14 daily; 2hr 50min–5hr); Zaragoza (15 daily; 3hr 35min–4hr 25min).

Bilbao to: Barcelona (2 daily, 1 Sat; 8hr 50 min–10hr 20min); León (1 daily; 4hr 35min); Madrid (2 daily; 5hr 30min–8hr 50min); San Sebastián (every 30min; 2hr 30min); Santander (4 daily; 2hr).

Burgos to: Bilbao (5 daily; 3hr); Madrid (5 daily; 4hr); San Sebastián (6 daily; 3hr 30min).

Córdoba to: Madrid (28 daily; 1hr 40min–4hr 45min); Malaga (10 daily; 2hr 10min); Sevilla (4–6 daily; 1hr–1hr 30min).

Granada to: Madrid (2 daily; 5hr 50min); Ronda (1 daily; 4hr 20min); Valencia (1–2 daily; 8hr 20min).

León to: Avila (7 daily; 2hr 45min–3hr 30min); Barcelona (3–4 daily; 9hr 30min–11hr 40min); Burgos (5 daily; 1hr 40min); Madrid (7 daily; 4hr 15min); Oviedo (5 daily; 2hr); Salamanca (6 daily; 3–5hr); San Sebastián (1 daily; 5hr); Santiago (1 daily; 5hr 40min); Valladolid (9 daily; 1hr 45min–2hr).

Málaga to: Córdoba (10 daily; 2hr 30min–3hr 30min); Madrid (9 daily; 4hr 10min–7hr); Ronda (1 daily; 2hr); Sevilla (6 daily; 3hr).

Salamanca to: Ávila (5 daily; 1hr 10min–1hr 40min); Burgos (3 daily; 2hr 30min); Madrid (3 daily; 2hr 30min); Valladolid (6 daily; 1hr 45min–2hr).

San Sebastián to: Bilbao (9 daily; 2hr 30min–3hr); Burgos (6 daily; 2hr 45min–3hr 30min); Madrid (3 daily; 8hr 30min–9hr 45min); Pamplona (1–2 daily; 1hr 45min–2hr); Salamanca (2 daily; 6hr); Valencia (1 weekly on Fri; 10hr); Zaragoza (1–2 daily; 4hr–5hr 10min).

Santiago to: La Coruña (19 daily; 1hr–1hr 30min); León (1 daily; 6hr); Madrid (2 daily; 7hr 20min–9hr 10min).

Zaragoza to: Barcelona (14–16 daily; 2hr 55min–5hr 55min); Canfranc (2 daily; 3hr 30min); Huesca (3–5 daily; 1hr 15min); Jaca (3 daily; 3hr 10min); Lleida (9–11 daily; 1hr 30min–2hr 30min); Madrid (13 daily; 2hr 50min–4hr 20min); Pamplona (5 daily; 1hr 45min–2hr 40min).

Buses

Madrid to: Alicante (5 daily; 5hr 15min); Almería (3 daily; 7hr); Ávila (8 daily; 2hr); Barcelona (7 daily; 7hr 30min); Bilbao (11 daily; 4hr 45min); Burgos (8 daily; 3hr 30min); Cáceres (8–10 daily; 4hr); Cádiz (6 daily; 7hr); Córdoba (6 daily; 4hr 30min); Granada (9 daily; 6hr); Lagós (1 Wed and Sun; 10hr 30min); León (11 daily; 4hr); Lisbon (1 daily; 7hr); Málaga (7 daily; 7hr); Merida (8 daily; 4hr 10min); Oviedo (12 daily; 5hr 30min); Pamplona (4 daily; 6hr); Salamanca (21 daily; 3hr); San Sebastián (9 daily; 6hr); Santander (8 daily; 6hr); Santiago (1 daily; 9hr); Sevilla (11 daily; 6hr); Toledo (every 30min; 1hr); Trujillo (9 daily; 3hr 15min); Valencia (11 daily; 4–5hr); Valencia (13 daily; 4hr).

Alicante to: Almería (2 daily; 7hr); Barcelona (7 daily; 8hr); Granada (5 daily; 5hr); Madrid (9 daily; 8hr); Málaga (5 daily; 8hr); Valencia (hourly; 4hr).

Barcelona to: Alicante (7 daily; 8hr); Andorra (3 daily; 5hr); Girona (3–7 daily; 1hr 30min); Madrid (15 daily; 7hr 30min); Seu d'Urgell (4 daily; 5hr); Tarragona (hourly; 1hr 30min); Valencia (14–17 daily; 4hr 15min–5hr); the Vall d'Aran (1 daily; 6hr 30min); Zaragoza (22–25 daily; 3hr 30min–5hr).

Burgos to: Bilbao (4 daily; 2hr); León (1 daily; 2hr 30min); Madrid (8 daily; 3hr 30min); San Sebastián (6 daily; 3hr); Santander (3 daily; 3hr).

Córdoba to: Granada (7 daily; 3hr); Madrid (4 daily; 4hr 30min); Malaga (5 daily; 3hr–3hr 30min); Sevilla (10 daily–2hr 30min).

Figueres to: Barcelona (3–6 daily; 2hr 15min); Cadaqués (3 daily; 1hr); L'Escala (5 daily; 45min); Girona (4–8 daily; 1hr); Palafrugell (4 daily; 1hr 30min).

Granada to: Alicante (3 daily; 5hr); Almería (4–6 daily; 2–3hr); Cádiz (2 daily; 6hr); Córdoba (7 daily; 3hr); Madrid (6–9 daily; 6hr); Sevilla (7–9 daily; 4hr 30min); Valencia (3 daily; 7hr).

León to: Madrid (11 daily; 4hr); Oviedo (8 daily; 1hr 30min); Salamanca (2 daily; 2hr); Santander (1 daily; 5hr); Valladolid (8 daily; 2hr).

Málaga to: Algeciras (10 daily; 3hr); Córdoba (5 daily; 3hr); Granada (14 daily; 2hr); Osuna (2 daily; 3hr); Ronda (6 daily; 3hr); Sevilla (11 daily; 3hr); Torremolinos (every 30min; 30min).

Oviedo to: León (8 daily; 1hr 30min); Madrid (12 daily; 5hr 30min).

Salamanca to: Ávila (4 daily; 1hr 30min–2hr); León (2 daily; 2hr); Madrid (15 daily; 2hr 30min–3hr); Mérida (5 daily; 4hr 30min); Santander (2 daily; 5hr); Sevilla (5 daily; 8hr), Valladolid (6 daily; 1hr 30min).

San Sebastian to: Bilbao (1–2 hourly; 1hr 10min); Burgos (6 daily; 3hr); Madrid (8 daily; 6hr 30min); Pamplona (13 daily; 2hr).

Santander to: Bilbao (18+ daily; 1hr 30min); Burgos (3 daily; 3hr); Madrid (6 daily; 6hr); Oviedo (4 daily; 3hr 30min); Pamplona (2 daily; 3hr 45min).

Santiago to: Bilbao (3 daily; 11–12hr); Madrid (4 daily; 8–9hr); Porto (2 weekly; 3hr); Vigo (hourly; 1hr 30min).

Sevilla to: Cádiz (11 daily; 2hr); Córdoba (10 daily; 2hr 30min); Granada (9 daily; 3hr 30min–4hr 30min); Lagós (4 weekly; 9hr); Madrid (11 daily; 8hr).

Valencia to: Alicante (hourly; 4hr); Barcelona (14–17 daily; 4hr 15min–5hr); Cuenca (3 daily; 4hr); Madrid (13 daily; 4hr); Sevilla (3 daily; 11hr).

Zaragoza to: Barcelona (15 daily, more at weekends; 3hr 30min–5hr); Huesca (Mon–Sat 18, Sun 7 daily; 1hr); Lleida (5 daily 1 Sun; 2hr 30min); Madrid (15 daily; 3hr 30min); Pamplona (7–8 daily; 2hr–2hr 45min).

Ferries

Barcelona to: Ibiza (4–6 weekly; 9hr 30min); Mahón (3–8 weekly; 9hr); Palma (2–4 daily; 8hr 30min).

Bilbao: Portsmouth, Britain (2 weekly; 24hr).

Denía: Ibiza (1 daily; 4hr); San Antonio, Ibiza (4–7 daily; 4hr)

Ibiza to: Formentera (6–9 daily; 40min–1hr 30min); Palma (1–3 weekly; 6hr 30min); Valencia (1 weekly, July–Sept 6 weekly; 9hr).

Palma to: Ibiza (1–3 weekly; 6hr 30min); Mahón (1 weekly; 6hr 30min).

Santander to: Plymouth, Britain (2 weekly; 24hr).

Valencia to: Ibiza (1 weekly, July–Sept 6 weekly; 7hr); Palma (6–13 weekly; 9hr).

CHAPTER 28

SWEDEN

Introduction

Sweden is a large, geographically varied and strangely little-known country whose sense of space is one of its best features. Away from the relatively densely populated south, travelling without seeing a soul is not uncommon. The **south and southwest** of the country are gently undulating, picturesque holiday lands, long-disputed Danish territory, and fringed with some of Europe's finest beaches. The west coast harbours a host of historic ports – **Gothenburg**, **Helsingborg** and **Malmö**, which is now linked by bridge to Copenhagen – while off the **southeast** coast, the Baltic islands of **Öland** and **Gotland** are the country's most hyped resorts, supporting a lazy beach-life to match that of the best southern European spots but without the hotel blocks and crowds.

Stockholm, the capital, is the country's supreme attraction, a bundle of islands housing monumental architecture, fine museums and the country's most active culture and nightlife. The two university towns, **Lund** and **Uppsala**, demand a visit too, while, moving northwards, **Gävle** and **Gällivare** both make justified demands on your time. This area, **central and northern** Sweden, is the country of tourist brochures: great swathes of forest, inexhaustible lakes – around 96,000 – and some of the best wilderness hiking in Europe. Two train routes link it with the south. The eastern run, close to the **Bothnian coast**, passes old wood-built towns and planned new ones, and ferry ports for connections to Finland. In the centre, the trains of the **Inlandsbanan** strike off through lakelands and mountains, clearing reindeer off the track as they go. The routes meet in Sweden's **far north** – home of the Sami, the oldest indigenous Scandinavian people.

Information and maps

Almost all towns in Sweden have a **tourist office**, giving out maps, timetables and other bumf, and usually booking private rooms, renting bikes and changing money. Some also sell discount cards during the summer which give reductions on local travel, museum entry and other freebies. They're normally open long hours daily in high season, shorter hours during the rest of the summer, and Monday to Friday in winter. The best general **map** of Sweden is the Motormännens *Sveriges Atlas*.

Money and banks

Swedish **currency** is the krona (plural kronor), made up of 100 öre. It comes in coins of 50öre, 1kr, 5kr and 10kr; and notes of 20kr, 50kr, 100kr, 500kr, 1000kr and 10,000kr. You can change money in **banks** all over Sweden, which are open Mon–Fri 9.30am–3pm, Thurs also 4–5.30pm. Outside normal banking hours you can change money in exchange offices at airports and ferry terminals, and in post offices (look for the "Växel" sign), as well as at Forex exchange offices, which usually offer the best rates – expect to pay a minimum 20kr commission or 15kr per travellers' cheque. Bankomat machines give cash advances and accept most credit cards – check with your bank before you go.

Communications

Post and phones in Sweden are good, and as most people speak at least some English you won't go far wrong in the post or telephone office. **Post offices** open Mon–Fri 9am–6pm, Sat 10am–1pm. You can buy stamps at post offices, and at most newspaper kiosks, tobacconists and hotels.

For international **telephone calls** you can dial direct from public phones. These take 1kr and 5kr coins (minimum charge 2kr), but card phones (*Telefonkort*) are more common; cards are available from newsagents and kiosks. It is also possible to use credit cards in many payphones, marked with the "CCC" sign. All operators speak English (domestic directory enquiries ☎ 118118, international ☎118119).

Getting around

Sweden's internal transport system is quick and efficient and runs through all weathers. Services are often reduced in the winter (especially on northern bus routes), but it's unlikely you'll ever get stranded. In summer, when everyone is on holiday, trains and buses are packed: on long journeys it's a good idea to make reservations. All train, bus and ferry schedules are contained within the giant and confusing **Rikstidtabellen** (80kr), or pick up specific route information from train station offices, most of whom will happily print out all your options for you.

Trains

Swedish State Railways (**SJ** – Statens Järnvägar; up-to-date timetable information from *www.sj.se* or call free in Sweden ☎020/75 75 75) have an extensive network, running right into the north of the country above the Arctic Circle and on into Norway. **Tickets** are expensive but happily it's almost never necessary to pay the full rate. InterRail and Eurail **passes** are valid, as is the ScanRail pass (see "Getting around" in Denmark chapter, p.326).

To ensure a seat, you might want to make a **reservation**; on some trains – indicated by an "R" or "IC" in the timetable – this costs 30kr; on the high-speed X2000 trains and most national routes reservations are mandatory, though the fee is included in the price. If you are using a travel pass, you must reserve seats separately before the journey (50kr). Kustpilen trains (bookable through SJ) run between Karlskrona and Copenhagen via Malmö. Interrail passes are valid and reservations are not mandatory. One booklet worth picking up is the quarterly *SJ Tågtider* **timetable** from any train station, an accurate and comprehensive list of the most useful train services in the country, except for those of the Inlandsbanan up to northern Sweden and the Pågatågen private rail line in the south (InterRail valid on both). The Inlandsbanan is only open during the summer.

For all train travel north of the line between Sundsvall and Ostersund, it is necessary to book tickets through **Tågkompaniet** (☎020/44 41 11). They will also book SJ tickets, but SJ will not book Tagkompaniet.

Buses

Complementing the rail system are **long-distance buses** (*Expressbussar*), operated by Swebus (*www.swebus.se*) and Svenska Buss between large towns and to and from Stockholm. Services tend to be cheaper and slower than the equivalent train ride. In the north, buses are more frequent since they are used to carry mail to isolated regions. Several companies operate daily services, and fares are broadly similar. You can pick up a comprehensive **timetable** at any *Expressbuss* terminal, which will normally be adjacent to the train station.

Ferries

Unlike Norway and Finland, there are few domestic **ferry** services in Sweden. The various archipelagos on the southeast coast are served by small ferries, the most comprehensive network being within the Stockholm archipelago, for which you can buy an island-hopping boat pass. The other major link is between the Baltic island of **Gotland** and the mainland at Nynäshamn and Oskarshamn, very popular routes in summer for which you should really book ahead.

Driving and hitching

Driving presents few problems since roads are good and generally reliable. The only real dangers are the reindeer and elk which wander onto roads in the north. To drive, you need a full licence and the vehicle registration document. Speed limits are 110kph on motorways, 90kph and 70kph on other roads, 50kph in built-up areas. It's compulsory to use dipped headlights during daylight hours. Swedish drink-driving laws are among the toughest in Europe and random breath-tests the norm. For **emergency assistance** on the road call ☎020/24 10 00.

Car rental can be less pricey than imagined, particularly if you book directly at a company's Swedish office. Most rental companies have special weekend tourist rates – from around 500kr. Otherwise, expect to pay from 1750kr a week, with unlimited mileage.

Despite the amount of holiday traffic and the number of young Swedes with cars, **hitching** is rarely worth the effort as lifts are so few and far between. Shorter hops are a little easier to find, especially when travelling along the coasts and in the north. If you do try it though, always use a sign.

Accommodation

Finding somewhere cheap to sleep is not too much hassle. There's an excellent network of HI hostels and campsites, while in the cities private rooms and bed and breakfast places are a common alternative to hotels.

Hotels and private rooms

Hotels come cheaper than you'd think, especially in Stockholm and the bigger cities during the summer, when many Swedes are out of the country. The rest of the year, rooms at weekends are much cheaper than midweek: on average, for a room with TV and bathroom you can expect to pay from 500kr a double. Nearly all hotels include breakfast in the price, which

ACCOMMODATION PRICE CODES

Throughout this guide, accommodation is coded on a scale of ① to ⑨, the code indicating the lowest price per person per night you could expect to pay in each establishment in high season. With hostels this is the nightly rate per person; with hotels, the price is arrived at by dividing the cost of the cheapest double room by two. The prices indicated by the codes are as follows:

① under £5/$8
② £5–10/$8–16
③ £10–15/$16–24

④ £15–20/$24–32
⑤ £20–25/$32–40
⑥ £25–30/$40–48

⑦ £30–35/$48–56
⑧ £35–40/$56–64
⑨ £40/$64 and over

can be a useful bonus. **Package deals** operating in Malmö, Stockholm and Gothenburg get you a hotel bed for one night, breakfast and the relevant city discount card from around 370–450kr per person. These schemes are generally valid from mid-June to mid-August and at weekends throughout the year. Further details are available in the free booklet *Hotels in Sweden*, available from the National Tourist Board and larger tourist offices, which also lists every hotel in the country. A further option is a **private room**, booked through tourist offices for 100–150kr per person, with access to showers and sometimes a kitchen.

■ Hostels

The biggest choice lies with the country's huge chain of **hostels**, operated by the Svenska Turistföreningen (STF), PO Box 25, 10120, Stockholm (☎08/463 21 00, *www.stfturist.se*). There are 280 hostels in the country, usually with single and double rooms too. Virtually all have well-equipped self-catering kitchens and serve a buffet breakfast. Prices are low (120–150kr); non-HI/YHA members pay an extra 40kr a night. The STF publish a comprehensive handbook for 95kr, available from hostels, tourist offices and large bookshops. There are also an increasingly large number of non STF-affiliated hostels, mostly run by SVIF (☎0413/55 34 50, *info@grottbyn.com*), appearing all over the country. Always ring ahead in the summer, and bear in mind that hostels usually close between 10am and 5pm, sometimes with curfews around midnight.

■ Campsites and cabins

Practically every town and village has at least one **campsite**, generally of a high standard. Pitching a tent costs from 90kr for two people sharing in July and August, a little less during the rest of the year, though all costs are considerably higher near the big cities. Most sites are open June to September, some throughout the year, and most are approved and classified by the Swedish Tourist Board; a comprehensive listings book, *Camping Sverige*, is available at larger sites and

most Swedish bookshops. The Swedish National Tourist Board also puts out a short free list. Note that at most sites you'll need a camping card (49kr from your first stop, or visit *www.camping.se*) and that camping gas is tricky to get hold of in Sweden. Many campsites also boast **cabins**, usually decked out with bunk beds and kitchen equipment but not sheets. They're an excellent alternative to camping for a group or couple; cabins go for around 250–350kr for a four-bedded affair. It's wise to ring ahead to secure one. It's also possible to **camp rough** throughout the country, without asking permission, provided you stay a reasonable distance away from other dwellings.

Food and drink

Eating and drinking is nothing like as expensive as it used to be in Sweden, though filling up at breakfast and lunch is still much better value than eating out at restaurants in the evening. At its best, Swedish food is excellent, largely meat-, fish- and potato-based, but varied and generally tasty and filling. Specialities include the northern Swedish delicacies – reindeer and elk meat, and wild berries – and herring in many different guises.

■ Food

Breakfast (*frukost*) is invariably a help-yourself buffet – served in most hostels and some restaurants for around 50kr–70kr, and free in hotels – consisting of juice, cereals, bread, boiled eggs, jams, salami, tea and coffee on even the most limited tables. Something to watch out for is the jug of *filmjölk* next to the ordinary milk, a thicker, sour milk for pouring on cereals. **Coffee** in Sweden is usually of the filter variety and can be bitter. It's often free after the first cup. **Tea** is weak as a rule but costs around the same – 10–15kr. For **snacks** and lighter meals the choice expands. A *Gatukök* (street kitchen) or *Korvstånd* (hot-dog stall) will serve a selection of hot dogs, burgers, chips and the like for around 30kr. **Burger bars** are just about everywhere now and a hefty burger and chips meal will set you back a shade over 50kr: the local Clockburger is cheaper than McDonald's and Burger King, but all are generally the source of the cheapest (and weakest) coffee in town. If you can afford a little extra, it's far better to hit the coffee shops (*konditori*), which always display a range of freshly baked pastries and cakes. They're not particularly cheap (coffee and cake for 20–35kr), but are generally good, also serving *smörgåsar*, open **sandwiches** piled high with an elaborate variety of toppings for 30–40kr a time.

Eating in a **restaurant** is cheapest at lunchtime, when most places offer something called the *Dagens Rätt* at 50–60kr, often the only affordable way to sample real Swedish cooking. Served between 11am and 2pm, it consists of a main dish with bread and salad, sometimes a drink, and coffee. Other cheapish places for lunch are **cafeterias**, usually self-service with cheaper snacks and hot meals; large department stores and train stations are good places to look. More expensive but good for a blowout are restaurants and hotels that put out the *smörgåsbord* at lunchtime for 150–200kr, where you help yourself to unlimited portions of herring, smoked and fresh salmon, hot and cold meats, eggs, potatoes, salad, cheese and fruit. A variation on the buffet theme is the *Sillbricka*, a specialist buffet for around the same price where the dishes are all based on cured and marinated herring.

If you don't eat the set lunch, meals in restaurants, especially at **dinner** (*middag*), can be expensive: 150–200kr for a three-course affair, plus 30–50kr for a beer and at least 100kr for a bottle of house plonk. Pizzerias and Chinese restaurants offer better value. Large pizzas cost 40–60kr, usually with free salad and bread, and the price is generally the same at lunch and dinner. Chinese restaurants nearly always offer a set lunch for around 50kr, though they're pricier in the evening. Also widespread are Middle Eastern kebab takeaways and cafés, where you'll get something fairly substantial in pitta bread for around 30kr.

■ Drink

Drinking is still pricey, though in Stockholm it's no more than most European capitals now. The cheapest choice is probably **beer**, which costs 35–45kr for 400ml of lager-type drink – a *sto stark*. Unless you specify, it will be *starköl*, the strongest Class III beer, or the slightly weaker *mellanöl*; *folköl* is the Class II and cheaper and weaker brew; cheapest (around half the price) is *lättöl*, a Class I concoction that is virtually nonalcoholic. Classes I and II are available in supermarkets; Class III is only on sale in state-licensed liquor stores (*Systembolaget*), where it's

around a third of the price you'll pay in a bar. Pripps and Spendrups are the two main brands. A glass of **wine** in a bar or restaurant costs around 30–40kr, while you can buy a whole bottle for a little more in a state off-licence. For experimental drinking, **aquavit** is a good bet, served ice-cold in tiny shots and washed down with beer. There are various different "flavours", too, with spices and herbs added.

You'll find **bars** in all towns and cities and most villages, though they're not the focus of the social scene. In Stockholm and the larger cities the move is towards brasserie-type places; elsewhere there are more down-to-earth drinking dens, where the clientele is normally male and drunk. Wherever you drink, you'll find that things close down around 11pm or midnight, though not in Gothenburg and Stockholm, where you can keep drinking into the small hours. The shops are open Mon–Fri 9am–6pm, the minimum age for being served is 20, and you may need to show ID.

Opening hours and holidays

Shops are open Mon–Fri 9am–6pm, Sat 9am–1/4pm. Some larger department stores stay open until 8/10pm, and open Sun noon–4pm. Banks, offices and shops close on the following days and may close early on the preceding day: Jan 1; Jan 6; Good Friday; Easter Sunday & Monday; May 1; Ascension (mid-May); Whit Sunday & Monday; Midsummer's Eve & Day; All Saint's Day (the Sat between Oct 31 & Nov 6); Dec 24, 25, 26 & 31.

Emergencies

You're unlikely to encounter too many problems with **crime** in Sweden, and thus will have little need to contact the police. If you do, you'll find them courteous and generally able to speak English. In case of **health problems**, there is no GP system and you should instead go direct to a hospital with your passport, where for 140kr you'll receive treatment; if you have to stay in hospital it will cost you an additional 80kr per day. If you need medicine, take your prescription to a **pharmacist** – *Apotek* in Swedish – which will be open shop hours, although Stockholm has a 24-hour pharmacy. Larger towns operate a rota system of late opening, with the address of the nearest late-opener posted on the door of each pharmacy.

Emergency Numbers

All emergencies ☎112.

STOCKHOLM AND AROUND

STOCKHOLM comes lauded as Sweden's most beautiful city, and apart from some sad central squares of concrete developments and a tangled road junction or two, it lives up to it – it's delightful, not least as a contrast to the apparently endless lakes and forests of the rest of the country. It's also a remarkably disparate capital, one whose tracts of water and range of monumental buildings give it an ageing, lived-in feel and an atmosphere quite at odds with its status as Sweden's most contemporary, forward-looking city.

Built on fourteen small islands, Stockholm was a natural site for the fortifications, erected by one Birger Jarl in 1255, that grew into the current city. In the sixteenth century, the city fell to King Gustav Vasa, a century later becoming the centre of the Swedish trading empire that covered present-day Scandinavia. Following the waning of Swedish power it entered something of a quiet period, only rising to prominence again in the nineteenth century when industrialization sowed the seeds of the Swedish economic miracle.

Arrival and information

By **train**, you arrive at **Central Station**, a cavernous structure on Vasagatan in Norrmalm. All branches of the Tunnelbana, Stockholm's underground system, meet at T-Centralen, the station directly below Central Station. **Cityterminalen**, adjacent, handles all the **bus** services, both domestic and international, including the airport bus. Viking Line **ferries** arrive at **Tegelvikshamnen** in Södermalm, in the south of the city, a thirty-minute walk from the modern centre, or connected by bus to Slussen and then by Tunnelbana to T-Centralen. Birka Cruises services dock in Södermalm, too, just up the quayside at Stadsgården. The Silja Line terminal is in the northeastern reaches of the city, a short walk from Gärdet or Ropsten, from where you can take the Tunnelbana. **Arlanda airport** is 45km north of Stockholm; buses run every ten minutes to Cityterminalen (6.40am–11pm; journey time 40min; 70kr), and high speed trains leave every fifteen minutes from **Arlanda Express Station** beneath the airport for the city's Central Station (5am–midnight; journey time 20min; 140kr).

You should be able to pick up a map of the city at most points of arrival, but it's worth making your way to one of the **tourist centres**, which hand out fistfuls of free information and sell decent maps for 15kr. The **main office** (Mon–Fri 8/9am–6pm, Sat & Sun 9am–3/5pm; ☎08/789 24 90, *www.stockholmtown.com*) is on Hamngatan in Norrmalm, on the ground floor of Sverigehuset, and sells the invaluable **Stockholm Card** (220kr for 24hr, 380kr for 48hr, 540kr for 72hr), which gives unlimited travel on city transport (except on direct buses to the airport or on the connecting night bus to the Nynäshamn ferry terminal), free museum entry to most museums and free sightseeing boat tours. The office also rents out the digital pocket guide, *Citikey*, for 69kr per day (with a 3000kr returnable deposit), and stocks free copies of *What's On*, which lists forthcoming events. There is now also a summer tourist office at central station, open slightly longer hours than the main tourist office (June–Aug 8am–7/8pm).

City transport

The best way to explore Stockholm's initially confusing centre is to **walk** – it takes about 25 minutes to cross central Stockholm on foot – but to reach the more distant sights you'll have to use some form of **transport**. Storstockholms Lokaltrafik (SL) operates a comprehensive system of buses and trains (underground and local) reaching well out of the city centre. The **SL-Center** information office (Mon–Sat 6.30am–11.15pm, Sun 7am–11.15pm), inside T-Centralen station at Sergels Torg, doles out timetables and sells a useful transport map

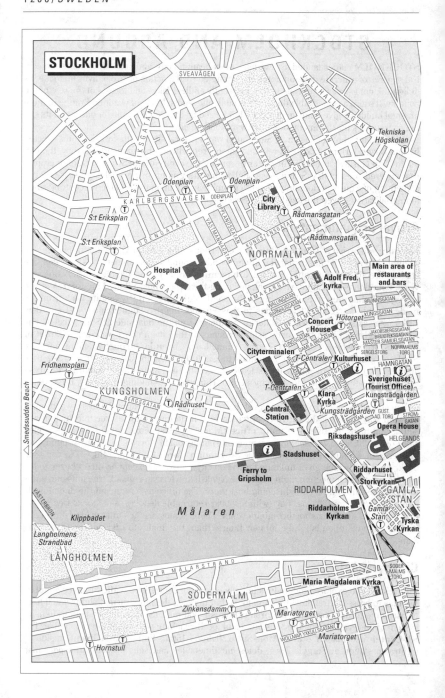

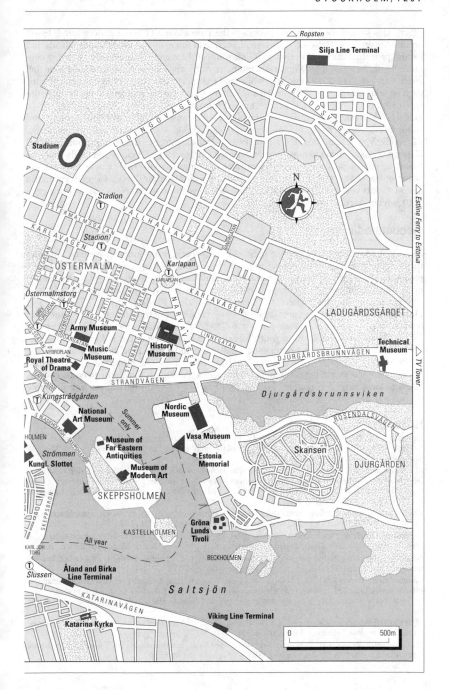

(35kr). Quickest of the transport systems is the **Tunnelbana** (T-bana) underground, based on three main lines. **Buses** can be less direct due to the nature of Stockholm's islands and central pedestrianization. **Ferries** also link some of the central islands: Djurgården is connected with Nybroplan in Norrmalm (summer only) and Skeppsbron in Gamla Stan (all year). Ferry trips cost 20kr one way, while land transport costs 16kr within one zone, 8kr for each additional zone – so you're normally better off investing in a **pass**. Do not confuse the Stockholm Card with the much more limited **tourist card** valid for 24 hours (70kr) or 72 hours (135kr), which gives unlimited travel on public transport within Stockholm county and some free island ferry trips. The three-day card includes some museum discounts too. Alternatively, you can buy a strip of twenty transferable SL **ticket coupons** (*Rabbat Kuponger*, 110kr), using two per person for each journey. Buy SL tickets and cards from the tourist office and SL offices inside T-Centralen or Central Station. **Taxis** can be hailed in the street, or booked on ☎08/15 00 00. If you ring, it will cost 28kr for the taxi to get to you; a trip across the city centre costs 100–150kr, more in the evenings and at weekends (women get a 5–10 percent discount at weekends).

Accommodation

There's plenty of **accommodation** in Stockholm, especially for budget travellers, but don't turn up late in summer and expect to get a cheap bed. Booking your first night's accommodation in advance is always a good idea, either through the Sverigehuset tourist centre or by phoning direct. The cheapest choices, on the whole, are found to the north of Cityterminalen, in the streets to the west of Adolf Fredriks Kyrka. There's also **Hotellcentralen**, a booking service on the lower level of Central Station (daily: June–Aug 8am–8pm; rest of year daily 9am–6pm; ☎08/789 24 25, *hotels@stoinfo.se*), which charges a fee of 50kr per room, 20kr for a youth hostel if you go in person, but is free over the telephone. Hotellcentralen also brokers special deals, including the Stockholm Package (from 455kr to 700kr per person for a better hotel), available mid-June to mid-Aug and at weekends, which gets you a hotel room, breakfast and a Stockholm Card. For **private rooms**, contact Hotelltjänst, Vasagatan 15–17 (☎08/10 44 67), who can fix you up with a double room for around 300kr per person.

HI Hostels

Brygghusest, Norrtullsgatan 12 (☎08/31 24 24, *youth.hostel.brygghuset@snfr.se*). Situated near Odenplan T-bana this converted brewery is one of the more tranquil in Stockholm. Closed mid-Sept to May. ②.

af Chapman, Skeppsholmen (☎08/463 22 66, *www.stfchapman.com*). Official hostel on a ship moored at Skeppsholmen. Without a reservation, the chances of a space in summer are negligible, although queueing from around 7am has been known to yield a bed. Full of facilities, it is now linked to the HI's growing worldwide computer-booking system. ③.

City Backpackers, Upplandsgatan 2A, Norra Bantorget (☎08/20 69 20, *www.citybackpackers.se*). Curfewless non-STF hostel with four-bed rooms and cheaper eight-bed dorms. ③.

Columbus Hotell & Vandrarhem, Tjärhovsgatan 11, Södermalm (☎08/644 17 17, *www.columbus.se*). A friendly, non-STF hostel with cheap beds, housed in a former brewery. T-bana Medborgarplatsen. ⑤.

Gustav af Klint, Stadsgårdskajen 153, Södermalm (☎08/640 40 77). Singles, doubles and four-bedded cabins in this floating hotel-hostel, which tends to be very noisy. ⑤.

Långholmen, Kronohäktet, Långholmen (☎08/668 05 10, *www.langholmen.com*). Stockholm's grandest official hostel, in an old prison on Långholmen island, with ordinary doubles in summer as well as hostel beds. Some rooms have TVs, phones and showers. T-bana to Hornstull. Turn left and follow the signs. ⑤.

M/S Rygerfjord, Söder Mälarstrand-Kaj 12 (☎08/84 08 30, *www.rygerfjord.se*). Homely hostel-ship moored on Södermalm close to Slussen T-bana station. ③.

Zinkensdamm, Zinkens väg 20, Södermalm (☎08/616 81 00, *www.zinkensdamm.se*). T-bana Zinkensdamm. Huge official hostel with kitchen facilities. Nicely situated by the water. ③.

Hotels and pensions

Anno 1647, Mariagränd 3 (☎08/442 16 80, *www.swedenhotels.se*). Near Slussen, a handy location for the old town. Not recommended for people with disabilities. ⑦.

Birger Jarl, Tulegatan 8 (☎08 674 1800, *www.birgerjarl.se*). This renovated dull '70s block is now a sensationally interior-designed contemporary hotel. Very comfortable and well situated in Norrmalm. T-bana Radmansgatan; ⑨.

Gustav Vasa, Västmannagatan 61 (☎08/34 38 01, *www.hotel.wineasy.se\gustav.vasa*). Early twentieth century place and not a bad location, in the northern part of Norrmalm. T-bana Odenplan. ⑦.

Lady Hamilton, Storkyrkobrinken 5 (☎08/23 46 80, *www.lady-hamilton.se*) and its brother hotel, the **Lord Nelson**, nearby on Vasterlanggatan 22 (☎08/23 23 90, *www.lord-nelson.se*), are beautifully situated in the old town, and perfect if you want to splash out. Both ⑨.

Stockholm, Norrmalmstorg 1 (☎08/440 57 60, *www.hotelstockholm.aos.se*). Very central, situated in the top floor of an ugly office block, but with fantastic views over the water. T-bana östermalmstorg or Kungstrádgürden. ⑧.

Tre smü rum, Högbergsgatan 81 (☎08/641 23 71, *www.tresmarum.se*). T-bana Mariatorget. Seven bright modern non-smoking rooms in the heart of Söder. No en-suites. ⑤.

Campsites

Ängby (☎08/37 04 20). West of the city on Lake Mälaren and near the beach. T-bana line #18 or #19 to Ängbyplan, then a 300-metre walk. Open all year, but must be booked in advance between Sept and April.

Bredäng (☎08/97 70 71). Pricey place with a hostel and restaurant on site. Ten kilometres southwest of the centre and also by Lake Mälaren. Take T-bana line #13 and #15 to Bredäng from where it's a 700-metre walk. Closed Nov–March.

Flaten (☎08/773 01 00). One-star place 15km southeast of city in a rural setting near a lake. Bus #401 from Slussen. Closed Oct–April.

Klubbensborg (☎08/646 12 55). In a peaceful location on a small peninsula on Lake Mälaren, with a hostel, café and bakery on site. T-bana line #13 and #18 to Mälarhojden and then a ten-minute walk. Closed Oct–May.

Solvalla City Camping, Sundbybergkopplet (☎08/627 03 80). Eight kilometres from the city on a gravel site. Take T-bana to Rissne.

The City

The **Stadshuset**, Hantverkargatan 1 (guided tours: mid-May to Sept daily 10am, noon & 2pm; rest of year 10am & noon; 50kr; T-Centralen), at the water's edge near Central Station, and in particular its gently-tapering 106-metre high red-brick **tower** (May–Sept daily 10am–4.30pm; 15kr), has the best fix on the city's layout. The building itself, a flagship of the National Romantic movement in the 1910s and 1920s, draws heavily on Swedish materials and themes, exemplified in the cavernous Blue Room, where the Nobel prize-givings are held, and the Golden Room, where a précis of Swedish history covers the walls in a gilt mosaic.

Gamla Stan

Three islands – Riddarholmen, Staden and Helgeandsholmen – make up **Gamla Stan** or **Old Stockholm**, a clutter of seventeenth- and eighteenth-century Renaissance buildings, hairline medieval alleys and tall, dark houses whose intricate doorways still bear the arms of the wealthy merchants who once dwelled within. On Helgeandsholmen, the **Riksdagshuset** is the Swedish parliament building, which can be visited on guided tours starting from the glassed-in rear (May–Aug Mon–Fri noon & 1.30pm; free). Being Sweden rather than Westminster, the members' seating is arranged in nonadversarial rows by constituency, not by party. In front of the Riksdagshuset, accessible by a set of steps leading down from Norrbro, the **Medeltidsmuseum** (Sept–June Tues & Thurs–Sun; 40kr; T-Gamla Stan) is the best city-related historical collection in Stockholm. Ruins of medieval tunnels and walls were discovered during excavations under the parliament building, and they've been incorporated into a walk-through underground exhibition. There are reconstructed houses, models and pictures, boats and street scenes.

Over a second set of bridges is the most distinctive monumental building in Stockholm, the **Kungliga Slottet** (Royal Palace; T-Gamla Stan), a beautiful Renaissance successor to the original castle of Stockholm. Finished in 1760, it's a striking achievement, outside sombre, inside a magnificent Baroque and Rococo swirl. The **Apartments** (May to mid-Aug daily 10am–4pm; rest of year Tues–Sun noon–3pm; 50kr) form a relentlessly linear collection of furniture and tapestries; the **Treasury** (same times as apartments; 50kr) has ranks of jewel-studded crowns, the oldest that of Karl X (1650). Also worth catching is **Livrustkammaren**, the Royal Armoury (same times as apartments; 60kr), less to do with weapons than with ceremony – suits of armour, costumes and horse-drawn coaches from the sixteenth century onwards, most notably the stuffed horse and mud-spattered garments of King Gustav II Adolf, who died in the Battle of Lützen in 1632. For those with the energy, the **Gustav III's Antikmuseum** (guided tours: mid-May to Aug Tues–Sun nooon, 1pm, 2pm & 3pm; 50kr) contains parts of the older castle, its ruins underneath the present building and an extensive collection of antique sculptures.

Beyond the palace lies Gamla Stan proper, where the streets suddenly narrow and darken. The first major building is the **Storkyrkan** (mid-May to mid-Sept 9am–6pm; mid-Sept to mid-May 9am–4pm; 10kr, free in winter), a rectangular brick church consecrated in 1306, which is technically Stockholm's cathedral – the monarchs of Sweden are married and crowned here. The Baroque interior is marvellous, with an animated fifteenth-century sculpture of *St George and the Dragon*, and – perhaps more impressive – the royal pews, more like golden billowing thrones, and a monumental black and silver altarpiece. **Stortorget**, Gamla Stan's main square, is handsomely proportioned and crowded with eighteenth-century buildings. The surrounding narrow streets house a succession of arts and craft shops, restaurants and discreet fast-food outlets, clogged by summer buskers and evening strollers. Just off Västerlånggatan, on Tyska Brinken, the **Tyska kyrkan**, or "German Church" (Sat & Sun noon–4pm), which belonged to Stockholm's medieval German merchants, is a copper-topped red-brick church that was also richly fashioned in the Baroque period.

Keep right on as far as the handsome Baroque **Riddarhuset** (Mon–Fri 11.30am–12.30pm; 40kr), in whose Great Hall the Swedish aristocracy met during the seventeenth-century Parliament of the Four Estates. Their coats of arms – around 2500 of them – are splattered across the walls. Take a look downstairs, too, in the Chancery, which stocks heraldic bone china by the shelf-load and racks of fancy signet rings. From here it's a matter of seconds across the bridge onto **Riddarholmen** ("Island of the Knights"), and to **Riddarholms Kyrkan** (mid-May to Aug daily 10am–4pm; 20kr), originally a Franciscan monastery and long the burial place of Swedish royalty. You'll find the unfortunate Gustav II Adolf in the green marble sarcophagus.

Skeppsholmen

Off Gamla Stan's eastern reaches, but not connected by bridge from the old town, the island of **Skeppsholmen** is home to an eclectic clutch of museums. Among them is the small but intriguing **Moderna Muséet** (Tues–Thurs 11am–8pm, Fri–Sun 11am–6pm; 75kr; T-Kungsträdgården then bus #65), which houses one of the best collections of modern art in Europe, with work by many of the twentieth century's greatest artists: from Matisse, Picasso, Dalí and Man Ray to Francis Bacon, Warhol and Lichtenstein. A steep climb up the nearby hill, to the northern tip of the island, leads to the **Östasiatiska Muséet** (Tues noon–8pm, Wed–Sun noon–5pm; 50kr; T-Kungsträdgården), whose Eastern antiquities display incredible craftsmanship – fifth-century Chinese tomb figures, delicate jade amulets, an awesome assembly of sixth-century Buddhas, Indian watercolours and gleaming bronze Krishnas.

By the bridge to the island is the waterfront **National Art Museum** (Tues 11am–8pm, Wed–Sun 11am–5pm; 75kr; T-Kungsträdgården), another impressive collection of applied art – beds slept in by kings, cabinets used by queens, plates eaten off by nobles, alongside Art Nouveau coffee pots and vases and examples of Swedish furniture design. Upstairs there is a plethora of European sculpture, mesmerizing sixteenth- and seventeenth-century Russian

Orthodox icons, and, among a quality selection of paintings, Rembrandt's *Conspiracy of Claudius Civilis*, one of his largest works; there are also minor works by other, later masters, notably Renoir. The gallery explores the development of the Swedish "oppositionists", who were inspired by the French Impressionists; the works of Carl Frederick Hill and Ernst Josephson's *Portrait of a Journalist* are particularly striking.

Norrmalm and Östermalm

Modern Stockholm lies immediately to the north of Gamla Stan. It's split into two distinct sections: the central **Norrmalm** and the classier, residential streets of **Östermalm** to the east – though there's not much apart from a couple of specialist museums to draw you here. On the waterfront, at the foot of Norrbro, is **Gustav Adolfs Torg**, more a traffic island than a square, with the eighteenth-century **Opera House** its proudest and most notable building. It was at a masked ball here in 1792 that King Gustav III was shot by one Captain Ankarström; you'll find Gustav's ball costume, as well as the assassin's pistols and mask, displayed in the palace armoury in Gamla Stan. Gustav's statue marks the centre of the square, where, apart from the views, the only affordable entertainment is to rent a fishing rod and try and land a fish in the **Strömmen**, which flows through the centre of the city – a right Stockholmers have enjoyed since the seventeenth century.

Just off the square, at Fredsgatan 2, the **Medelhavsmuseet** is devoted to Mediterranean and Near Eastern antiquities (Tues 11am–8pm, Wed–Fri 11am–4pm, Sat & Sun 11am–5pm; 50kr; T-Kungsträdgården), with an enormous display showing just about every aspect of Egyptian life up to the Christian era. The huge Cypriot collections – the largest outside the island itself – depict life through a period spanning 6000 years. North of here Klarabergsgatan leads to the **Klara Kyrka** (Mon–Fri 10am–6pm, Sat 10am–7pm, Sun 8.30am–6pm), typical of Stockholm's hidden churches, hemmed in by buildings on all sides and with a light and flowery eighteenth-century painted interior and an impressive golden pulpit. Back towards the water, Norrmalm's eastern boundary is marked by **Kungsträdgården**, the most fashionable and central of the city's numerous parks – once a royal kitchen garden and now Stockholm's main meeting place, especially in summer when there's almost always something going on.

On the opposite side of Norrmalm in Östermalm is the **Historiska Muséet** (Tues–Sun 11am–5pm, open late on Thurs in winter; 60kr; T-Karlaplan). Ground-floor highlights include a Stone Age household and a mass of Viking weapons, coins and boats, while upstairs there's a worthy collection of medieval church art and architecture, evocatively housed in massive vaulted rooms, including some rare reassembled bits of stave churches uncovered on the Baltic island of Gotland.

Djurgården

Djurgården is Stockholm's nearest large expanse of park. A royal hunting ground throughout the sixteenth to eighteenth centuries, it is actually two distinct park areas separated by the water of Djurgårdsbrunnsviken, which freezes over in winter to provide some central skating. You could walk to the park from Central Station, but it's quite a hike: take the bus instead – #44 from Karlaplan or #47 from Nybroplan – or in summer, the ferry from Nybroplan, or year round from Slussen on Skeppsbron (Mon–Fri 7.40am–7pm, Sat & Sun 9am–7pm; every 15min).

From the northeast of the park are excellent views from 155-metre-high **Kaknäs TV tower** (daily: May–Aug 9am–10pm; rest of year 10am–9pm; 25kr), Scandinavia's tallest building. South over Djurgårdsbron are numerous museums. Palatial **Nordiska Museet** (Tues–Sun 10am–9pm; 60kr) is a good attempt to represent Swedish cultural history in an accessible fashion, with a particularly good Sami section. On the ground floor of the cathedral-like interior is Carl Milles' statue of Gustav Vasa, the sixteenth-century king who drove out the Danes. Close by, the **Vasa Muséet** (daily: mid-June to mid-Aug 9.30am–7pm; rest of year 10am–5pm, until 8pm on Wed; 60kr) is an essential stop, displaying the *Vasa* warship which sank in Stockholm harbour after just twenty minutes of its maiden voyage in 1628. Preserved in mud for over 333 years, the ship was raised along with 12,000 objects in 1961, and now forms the centrepiece of a startling, purpose-built hall on the water's edge. Walkways bring you nose to nose with the cannon hatches and restored decorative relief, exhibition halls display the retrieved bits and pieces, while films and videos explain the social and political life of the period – all with excellent English notes and regular English-language **guided tours**.

Södermalm and Långholmen

It's worth venturing beyond Slussen's traffic interchange for the heights of **Södermalm**'s crags, an area largely neglected by most visitors to the city. The perched buildings are vaguely forbidding, but get beyond the speeding main roads skirting the island and a lively and surprisingly green area unfolds – one that's still, at heart, emphatically working-class. By bus, take the #48 from Norrmalm getting off at Bondegatan or #53 from Tegelbacken to Folkungagatan, or use the T-bana and get off at either Slussen or Medborgarplatsen (on Götagatan). Walking, you reach the island over a double bridge from Gamla Stan, to the south of which is the rewarding **Stadsmuseet** (Tues–Sun 11am–5pm, Thurs until 7/9pm; 40kr), hidden in a basement courtyard, which houses a set of collections relating to the city's history as a sea port and industrial centre. Nearby, take a look at the **Katarina kyrka**, rebuilt in Renaissance style in the eighteenth century. On this site the victims of the so-called "Stockholm Blood Bath" were buried in 1520, the betrayed nobility of Sweden who had opposed King Christian II's Danish invasion and were burned as heretics outside the city walls.

Whether you stop in Södermalm or not, the buses and T-bana trains come this way for the island of **Långholmen**, just off its western side. There's a popular **beach** here, which gets packed in the summer, a chance to swim and plenty of shady walks through the island's trees, as well as the city's best **hostel** (see p.1268). You don't have to come through Södermalm to reach Långholmen – though if you do, get off the T-bana at Hornstull and follow the signs.

Eating and drinking

The Hötorgshallen in Hötorget is a cheap and varied indoor market, useful for those planning on **self-catering** and awash with small cafés and ethnic snacks. Outside is an excellent daily fruit and vegetable market too. The three main areas for decent **eating**, day or night, are Norrmalm, Gamla Stan and Södermalm. It's most expensive to eat in the old town, but set lunch deals make even that very affordable. Drinking in **bars** is expensive, though less so in Stockholm, where there's healthy competition, than elsewhere in Sweden. Wherever there's live music you'll pay a cover charge of 30–50kr, as well as 10kr to leave your coat at the cloakroom. There's a fairly fine line between cafés, restaurants and bars in Stockholm, many offering music and entertainment in the evening and food during the day. Stockholm boasts an ever-increasing number of stylish **cafés**, perfect for coffee, cake and people-watching, either during the day or in the evening.

Cafés and restaurants

Babs Kök & Bar, Birger Jarlsgatan 37. Lively, young and laid-back atmosphere at this quirky restaurant/bar. Interesting eats such as duck terrine with pear and raisin. Mostly meat dishes. Mains around 120kr.

Blå Lotus, Katrina Bangata 21. The hangout of the alternative crowd – always has an intellectual buzz.

Café Art, Västerlånggatan 60–62, Gamla Stan. A fifteenth-century cellar-café with sandwiches, good coffee and cakes and art for sale.

Café Tic Tac, Central Station. Good substantial food at reasonable prices, with salad and seafood snacks from 50kr. Connected to Asian Station, a fair value, tasty Asian buffet in dull surroundings.

Chokladcoppen, Stortorget 18, Gamla Stan. A fabulous café specializing in rich chocolate tart and overlooking the grand old square. Coffee served in badly designed handless cups. Open daily 9am–11pm.

Cinnamon, Verkstadgatan 7, Södermalm, two blocks from Hornstull T-bana. Relaxed café with cheese rolls, cakes and chatty, dog-walking locals. A good morning-time café.

Collage, Smålandsgatan 2, Norrmalm. An American diner to look at, you can fill up here on huge portions from the short meat and fish menu. Delicious options such as Africana pork with bananas, peanuts and mandarins. Cheap, light meals around 85kr.

Cosmic Café, Wollmar Yxkullsgatan 5B, Södermalm, opposite Mariatorget T-bana. A tiny, fun, wholefood vegetarian café with very good-value salads, pastas and great fresh fruit milkshakes. Veg lasagne 55kr.

Creperie Fyra Knop, Svartensgatan 4. Excellent value crepes served in this dark, evocative restaurant which is fashionably tatty and plays the likes of Leonard Cohen.

Hannas Café, Hornsgatan 156, Södermalm. Small, gay-friendly café serving cheap coffee on this interesting shopping street. Also hosts regular art exhibitions. Open daily 10am–7pm.

Hermitage, Stora Nygatan 11. Excellent, filling vegetarian place with delicious fresh salads and breads. Lunches for 50kr, dinners for 60kr until 7.30pm.

Jerusalem Kebab, Gåsgränd 2. Tucked away in a cobbled street in Gamla Stan of Västerlånggatan, this tiny Israeli-style place serves kebabs in pita for just 20kr, falafel for 30kr and filling lunches for 50kr.

Kaffegillet, Trångsund 4, Gamla Stan. Fourteenth-century cellar-restaurant with traditional Swedish food. Lunches around the 50kr mark.

Lasse i Parken, Högalidsgatan 56, Södermalm. Beautiful daytime café in an eighteenth-century house with a pleasant garden. Summer daily 11am–5pm. T-bana Hornstull.

Samborombon, Stora Nygatan 28, Gamla Stan. Argentinian restaurant serving steaks with excellent homemade sauce, as well as South American wines.

String Café, Nytorgsgatan 38, Södermalm. Ultra laid-back retro café full of young studenty types who love the mirror. Lots of big, cheapish coffees with muffins, brownies and the like for 15–30kr.

Bars, brasseries and pubs

Brasserie Vau de Ville, Hamngatan 17, Kungsträdgården, Norrmalm. Popular brasserie with snacks and drinks, as well as a regular menu.

Fenix, Götgatan 40, Södermalm. Trendy and lively American-style bar. Good selection of beers and cheapish food.

Gråmunken, Västerlånggatan 18, Gamla Stan. Cosy café with live jazz several nights a week.

Hannas Krog, Skånegatan 80. A restaurant with a basement bar that's been the living room of Nineties Swedish pop music. *Hannas Deli* opposite is more relaxed and has *Bar K* in the basement.

Indigo, Götgatan 14, Södermalm, near exit to Slussen T-bana. Psychedelic flock wallpaper, great lighting and wacky furnishings are an intriguing setting for this relaxed bar. Serves cheap light meals.

Kristina, Västerlånggatan 68, Gamla Stan. Café by day (with a 50kr lunch); happy hour 4–8pm when beer is only 30kr, and live jazz after 8pm.

Mushrooms, Nybroplan 6. Always full to bursting with loud happy beer-drinkers. A youthful venue.

O'Learys, Götgatan 11, Södermalm. A good bar/restaurant for watching sport on the widescreen TV.

Sloppy's, Hamngatan 2. A popular bar and nightclub open until 5am; serves food from around 39kr. Becomes gay disco *Propaganda* on Sat.

Söders Hjärta, Bellmansgatan 22, Södermalm. Swanky restaurant with a less intimidating and friendly bar on the mezzanine floor.

Nightlife

There's plenty to keep you occupied at night in Stockholm and the city's tag of being prohibitively expensive is less and less true. As well as the weekend, Wednesday night is an active time, with usually plenty going on and queues at the more popular places. At specifically **live music venues** you'll pay 60–100kr entrance. For up-to-date **what's on information**, check *På Stan*, the Friday supplement of the *Dagens Nyheter* newspaper, or the latest issue of *Stockholm This Week*, free from the tourist centre. Popular venues in the summer are Kungsträdgården and Skansen, where there's always something going on.

Live music

Engelen, Kornhamnstorg 59, Gamla Stan. Jazz, rock and blues nightly until 3am.

Fasching, Kungsgatan 63, Norrmalm. Stockholm's premier jazz venue, with local acts and big names.

Kaos, Stora Nygatan 21, Gamla Stan. Good live music from 9pm nightly; rock bands on Fridays and Saturdays in the cellar and reasonable late-night food.

Nalen, Regeringsgatan 74. The place to go for boogie, R & B, swing and rock & roll bands playing regularly.

Stampen, Stora Nygatan 5, Gamla Stan. Long-established and rowdy jazz club.

Tre Backar, Tegnérgatan 12–14, Norrmalm; T-bana Rådmansgatan. Good, cheap pub with a live cellar venue. Music every night; open until midnight (closed Sun).

Discos and clubs

Collage, Smålandsgatan 2, Norrmalm. Upstairs from the restaurant is a lively bar and dance floor with a lively, noisy young crowd packing the place. Black jack is also played. Open Wed–Sat until 3am.

Gossip, Sveavägen 36; T-bana Hötorget. On two floors with lots of dark corners.

La Isla, Fridhemsplan. Latin platters into the small hours, as well as salsa dancing. Underground in the Fridhemsplan T-bana station complex.

Sture Compagniet, Sturegatan 4, Norrmalm. Terrific light show with house and techno sounds blaring on three floors of bars.

Gay Stockholm

Although Stockholm's **gay scene** is still disappointingly small, considering the general tolerance of alternative lifestyles afforded in the city, the action is by no means as limited as it once was. The city's main gay centre is *TipTop* at Sveavägen 57 (☎08/736 02 12; T-bana Rådmansgatan), which has a bar and bookshop, counselling and meeting facilities, as well as a club, restaurant and bar. On the floor above are the national offices of Sweden's gay rights group RFSL (*www.rfsl.se*), which has an excellent free paper, *Kom Ut*. Also pick up the widely available *QX* paper from gay venues. The best gay **bars** – almost all are very male-oriented – are *Häktet*, Hornsgatan 82 (Wed & Fri only; Zinkensdamm T-bana), a real haven, and best for women on Wednesdays; *Regnbågsrummet*, Sturecompagniet, Stureplan (Fri & Sat 10pm–5am), currently the hippest spot hence long queues; *Stargayte*, Södrariddarholmshammen 19, Gamla Stan (Sat 9pm–3am) with three bars and two dance floors with the widest age range of party animals; *Patricia*, Stadsgårdskajen, with drag shows and comedy on what was the Queen Mother's royal yacht (gay on Sun only; 50kr; Slussen T-bana); and *TipTop* (see above), which is particularly popular on Friday and Saturday. For Lesbians, there is *Bitch Girl Club*, Kolingsborg, Slussen, every other Friday in summer and Saturday rest of year.

Listings

Airlines British Airways, Hamngatan 11 (☎08/679 78 00); Delta, Kungsgatan 18 (☎08/796 96 00); Finnair, Norrmalmstorg 1 (☎08/679 93 90); KLM, Arlanda Airport (☎08/590 799 10); Lufthansa, Norrmalmstorg 1 (☎08/614 15 50); SAS, Stureplan 8 (international ☎020/72 75 55, domestic ☎020/72 70 00); Air New Zealand, Kungsbron 1G (☎08/21 91 80); Qantas, Kungsgatan 64 (☎08/24 25 02); United, Kungsgatan 3 (☎08/678 15 70).

American Express Birger Jarlsgatan 1 (Mon–Fri 9am–5pm, Sat 10am–1pm; ☎08/679 78 80).

Car rental Avis, Vasagatan 10b (☎020/78 82 00); Budget, Sveavägen 115 (☎020/ 78 77 87); Europcar/InterRent, Arlanda airport (☎08/593 609 40); Hertz, Arlanda airport (☎020/ 21 12 11).

Doctor Medical Care Information, ☎08/411 71 77.

Embassies Australia, Sergels Torg 12 (☎08/613 29 00); Britain, Skarpögatan 6–8 (☎08/671 90 00); Canada, Tegelbakken 4 (☎08/453 30 00); Ireland, Östermalmsgatan 97 (☎08/661 80 05); Netherlands, Götgatan 16a (☎08/24 71 80); USA, Strandvägen 101 (☎08/783 53 00).

Exchange At Arlanda airport (daily 7am–10pm); Forex offices at Central Station (daily 7am–9pm), Cityterminalen (Mon–Fri 8am–9pm, Sat 8am–4pm) and Sverigehuset (Mon–Fri 8am–6pm, Sat & Sun 9/10am–3pm).

Ferries Tickets for Finland from Silja Line, Kungsgatan 2 at Stureplan (☎08/22 21 40); Viking Line, Central Station (☎08/452 40 00); Birka Cruises, Södermalmstorg 2 (☎08/714 55 20).

Internet access Choose from *Internet Café*, 3rd floor, Pub department store, 63 Drottningatan; *Café Access*, Kulturhuset, Sergels torg; *Internet aswellas Coffee*, Tegnergatan 33; and *NK IT-Center*, Hamngatan 18–20.

Left luggage On the lower level at Central Station (daily 7am–11.30pm; 40kr); there are safe lockers, too, all over Central Station (15–25kr).

Pharmacy 24-hour service from C.W. Scheele, Klarabergsgatan 64 (☎08/454 81 30).

Police Stations are in Central Station and Brunkebergs torg 1–5. For the 24-hour station, go to Bryggargatan 19 or Torkel Knutssonsgatan 20 (☎08/40 10 00).

Post office Drottninggatan 53 (Mon–Fri 9.30am–6pm, Sat 10am–2pm). Also in Central Station (Mon–Fri 7am–10pm, Sat 10am–7pm).

Travel agency Kilroy Travels, Kungsgatan 4 (☎08/23 45 15).

Millesgarden and Drottningholm

Just a short way to the northeast of the city centre, on the mainly residential island of **Lindingö**, the **Millesgården** (May–Sept daily 10am–5pm; Oct–April Tues–Sun noon–4pm; 80kr) is the outdoor sculpture garden of Carl Milles (1875–1955), one of Sweden's greatest sculptors. Arranged on a number of garden terraces carved from the steep cliffs, this is one of the most enticing visual attractions within easy reach of central Stockholm – to get there, take the T-bana to Ropsten and then go on by train one stop to Torvikstorg before walking down Herserudsvägen. Milles' animated, Classical figures perch precariously on pillars, overlooking the distant harbour, while the sculptor's former home contains his staggeringly rich collection of Greek and Roman antiquities.

Try also to visit the harmonious royal palace of **Drottningholm** (May–Aug daily 10am–4.30pm; Sept daily noon–3.30pm; guided tours noon, 1pm & 2pm; 50kr), beautifully located on the shores of leafy Lovön island, 11km west of the centre. It's a lovely fifty-minute boat trip there (85kr return); ferries leave every thirty minutes from Stadshusbron to coincide with the opening times. You could also take the T-bana to Brommaplan and then bus #177, #301–323, #336 or #338 from there – a less thrilling ride, but free with the Stockholm Card. Modelled in a thoroughly French style, Drottningholm is perhaps the greatest achievement of the architects Tessin – father and son – and was begun in 1662 on the orders of King Karl X's widow, Eleonora. Good English notes are available to help you sort out the riot of Rococo decoration. Though it's an expensive extra, try not to miss the **Court Theatre** (tours May–Sept daily noon–4.30pm; 50kr) in the grounds, which dates from 1766. The original backdrops and stage machinery are still in place, complete with a display of the eighteenth-century special effects – wind and thunder machines, trapdoors and simulated lightning. If you've time to spare, the extensive palace grounds also yield the **Chinese Pavilion** (May–Aug daily 11am–4.30pm; 50kr), an eighteenth-century royal summer house and World Heritage Site.

Uppsala and around

Forty minutes train ride north of Stockholm, **UPPSALA** is regarded as the historical and religious centre of the country. It's a tranquil daytime alternative to the capital, with a delightful river-cut centre, not to mention an active student-geared nightlife. At the centre of the medieval town, a ten-minute walk from the train station, is the great **Domkyrkan** (daily 8am–6pm; free), Scandinavia's largest cathedral. The echoing interior remains impressive, particularly the French Gothic ambulatory, sided by tiny chapels, one of which contains a lively set of restored fourteenth-century wall paintings that tell the legend of St Erik, Sweden's patron saint, while another contains his relics. Poke around and you'll also find the tombs of Reformation rebel monarch Gustav Vasa and his son Johan III, and that of the great botanist Carl Von Linné (self styled as Carolus Linnaeus), who lived in Uppsala.

Opposite the cathedral is the **Gustavianum** (mid-May to mid-Sept daily 11am–4pm, Thurs till 9pm; mid-Sept to mid-May Wed–Sun 11am–4pm; 40kr), built in 1625 as part of the university, and much touted for its tidily preserved anatomical theatre. The same building houses a couple of small collections of Egyptian, Classical and Nordic antiquities and the **Uppsala University Museum**, which contains the glorious Augsburg Art Cabinet, an ebony treasure chest presented to Gustav II Adolf. The current **University building** (Mon–Fri 8am–4pm) is the imposing nineteenth-century Renaissance edifice over the way, among whose alumni are Anders Celsius, inventor of the temperature scale. No one will mind if you stroll in for a quick look at the extensive collection of portraits and the imposing central hall. A little way beyond is the **Carolina Rediviva** (mid-May to mid-Sept Mon–Fri 9am–8pm, Sat 10am–4pm, Sun 11am–4pm; rest of year closed Sun; 10kr in summer, free rest of year), one of Scandinavia's largest libraries, with a collection of rare letters and other paraphernalia, including a beautiful sixth-century silver Bible and Mozart's manuscript for *The Magic Flute*. The **Castle** (summer daily 11am–4pm, also Wed 7–9pm; 40kr) has recently been made open to the public – a 1702 fire that destroyed three-quarters of the city did away with all but one side and two towers of this opulent palace. Now you can wander around the excavations and peruse the waxworks in authentic costumes. There are also guided tours in English of the opulent **State Apartments** (mid-June to mid-Aug daily 1pm & 3pm; 40kr).

Practicalities

Uppsala's **train** and **bus stations** are adjacent to each other, not far from the **tourist office** (Mon–Fri 10am–6pm, Sat 10am–3pm; July also Sun noon–4pm; ☎018/27 48 00, *www.res.till.uppland.nu*), Fyris Torg 8, which hands out an English guide to the town with a map inside. The beautifully sited official HI **hostel** is 6km south at Sunnerstavägen 24 (☎018/32 42 20; ②; open all year) – take bus #20, #25 or #50 from Dragarbrunnsgatan, two blocks west of the train station.

A central **hotel** is *Basic*, Kungsgatan 27 (☎018/480 50 00, *www.basichotel.com*; ⑥), with simple, bright and clean rooms and weekend reductions. For **camping**, *Sunnersta Camping* (☎018/27 60 84) is at a site 7km out by Lake Mälaren at Graneberg, which also has two- to four-berth cabins for 250–400kr a night; take bus #20, #22 or #50 from the centre. It's difficult to beat **lunch** at *Sten Sture & Co.*, a large wooden house immediately below the castle off Nedre Slottsgatan, with a good range of meat-based dishes during the day and live bands in the evening. The best **cafés** are *Ofvandahls*, Sysslomansgatan 3–5, a student classic, but only fun for smokers, and *Güntherska*, Östra Ågatan 31, another favourite and strictly non-smoking. Also popular is the *Café Katalin* at Östra Station, behind the train station, which holds sporadic jazz nights. The best café of all, though, is *Wayne's Coffee*, Smedgränd 4, with vast windows looking out onto the street. There's a wide range of really good **restaurants**, such as *Svenssons krog/bakficka*, Sysslomansgatan 15, which is the best place for fish dishes and traditional Swedish fare, and there are also cheaper pasta options. During the summer, the most popular option is an outdoor café and of these, the first to try is *Svenssons åkanten* on St. Eriks Torg right by the river.

Gamla Uppsala

Five kilometres north of town three huge **barrows**, atmospheric royal burial mounds dating back to the sixth century, mark the original site of Uppsala, **GAMLA UPPSALA** – reached on frequent buses #2, #20 and #24 (#54 on Sun) from Dragarbrunnsgatan. This was a pagan settlement and a place of ancient sacrificial rites: every ninth year a festival demanded the death of nine men, hanged from a nearby tree until their corpses rotted. There is now a worthwhile **Historical Visitor Centre** (mid-May to mid-Aug daily 10am–5pm, early May & late Aug till 4pm, rest of year Sat & Sun noon–3pm only; *gamlauppsala@raa.se*; 50kr) with exhibitions illustrating the origin of local myths from Roman times and Uppsala's era of greatness until the thirteenth century. The pagan temple where this took place is marked by the Christian **Gamla Uppsala Kyrka** (Mon–Fri 8.30am till dusk, Sat & Sun 10am till dusk), built when the Swedish kings first took baptism in the new faith. Look in for the faded wall paintings and the tomb of Celsius.

SOUTHERN SWEDEN

Southern Sweden is a nest of coastal provinces, extensive lake and forest regions, gracefully ageing cities and superb beaches. Much of the area, especially the southwest coast, is the target of Swedish holiday-makers, with a wealth of campsites and cycle tracks yet retaining a sense of space and tranquility as well as plenty of historical and cultural high points. The grandest coastal city is **Gothenburg**, Sweden's charming second city and well deserving of far more exploration beyond its gargantuan shipyards than the traditional post-ferry exodus allows.

South of here, **Helsingborg**, a stone's throw from Denmark, and **Malmö**, still solidly sixteenth century at its centre, are both worth a day or two each for their charismatic charms, and **Lund**, a medieval cathedral and university town, is a convenient and enjoyable point between the two. To the east, the historic fortress town of **Kalmar** is a less obvious target than the south coast resorts, but repays a stop on the southern routes to and from Stockholm. Close by, the island of **Gotland** has long been a domestic tourist haven for its climate, beaches and stunning medieval Hanseatic capital, **Visby**, and is easy and inexpensive to reach by ferry from Nynäshamn, south of Stockholm, and Oskarshamn, further south still.

Gothenburg

Although **GOTHENBURG** is Scandinavia's largest port, shipbuilding has long since taken a back seat to ferry arrivals – those from Newcastle alongside the dock-strewn river, and those from Denmark right in the centre of the port and shipyards. Beyond the shipyards, Gothenburg is the prettiest of Sweden's cities, with broad avenues split and ringed by an elegant seventeenth-century, Dutch-designed canal system.

Arrival and information

You're likely to arrive in Gothenburg by **ferry**. DFDS ferries from England now dock at Frihamnen, opposite the Opera House. Trams #2 and #5 will trundle you from here to the centre in around ten minutes (16kr). Other arrival points are strung out along the docks. Stena Line ferries from Frederikshavn in Denmark dock within twenty minutes' walk of the centre, the Kiel ferries another ten minutes away (3km from the centre in all). Trams #3 and #9 run past both to the centre. Seacat and Stena Line both have offices in Nordstan Shopping Centre (see below), and all DFDS tickets can be bought at the Seacat Offices. **Trains** arrive at Central Station on Drottningtorget. **Buses** from all destinations use Nils Ericsonsplatsen bus terminal. The **airport** is 25km east of the city, linked with the centre by buses running every fifteen minutes from Gate 21 in Nils Ericsonsplatsen or Korsvägen just outside Liseberg Amusement Park to the south of the centre (30min; 45kr).

Gothenburg has two **tourist offices**: a kiosk in Nordstan, the shopping centre next to Central Station (Mon–Fri 9.30am–6pm, Sat 10am–4pm, Sun noon–3pm), and a main office on the canal front at Kungsportsplatsen 2 (May Mon–Fri 9am–6pm, Sat & Sun 10am–2pm; June to late Aug daily 9am–6/8pm; *www.gbg-co.se*). Both have free maps and a room-booking service (60kr fee). They also sell the **Gothenburg Card**, giving unlimited bus and tram travel, free or half-price museum entry and other concessions, including a free boat trip to Elfsborgs fortress and free entry to the Lisebergs amusement park, though not the rides there. The card is valid for 24 hours and costs 95kr. Gothenburg is perhaps the most immediately attractive Swedish city around which to **walk**, though you may well use the **public transport** system of trams and buses. Each city journey costs 16kr for adults, though it's cheaper to buy a ten-trip Rabattkort for 120kr. Tickets can be bought from the driver, but are cheaper from *Tidpunkten* and *pressbyran* kiosks around the city. Fare dodging now incurs an instant 600kr fine, and ticket inspectors are on the increase. Just get on and punch "2" for city rides and

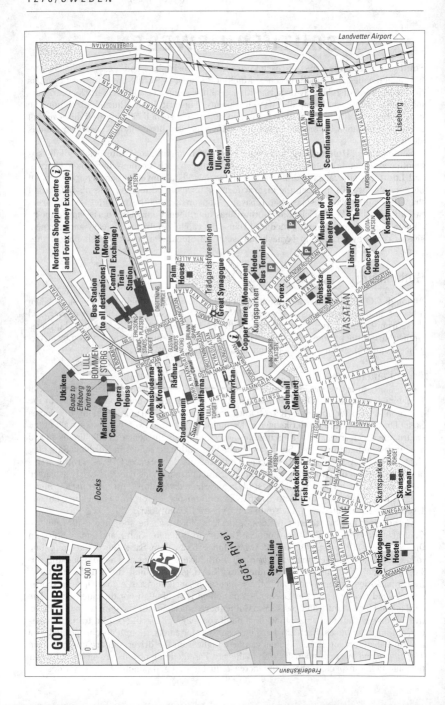

Landvetter Airport

GOTHENBURG

Museum of Ethnography

Liseberg

Gamla Ullevi Stadium

Museum of Scandinavium

Nordstan Shopping Centre ⓘ and Forex (Money Exchange)

Forex — (Money Exchange)

Lorensburg Theatre

Konstmuseet

Central Train Station

Trädgårdsföreningen

Museum of Theatre History

Bus Station (to all destinations)

Palm House

Library

Concert House

Great Synagogue

Heden Bus Terminal

Röhsska Museum

VASATAN

Forex

Copper Mare (Monument)

Kungsparken

Bus Station

ⓘ

Utkiken

Boats to Elfsborg Fortress

LILLE BOMMEN

Kronhusbodarna & Kronhuset

Rådhus

Domkyrkan

Saluhall (Market)

Maritima Centrum

Opera House

Stadmuseum

Antikhallarna

HAGA

Stena Line Terminal

Feskekörkan ('Fish Church')

Skansparken

Docks

Stenpiren

Skansen Kronan

Slottskogens Youth Hostel

Göta River

N

500 m

0

Frederikshavn

"BYTE" if you are continuing on another bus or tram. **Night time** bus/tram tickets are double the daytime rates. **Taxi** rides (☎031/65 00 00) within the city centre cost around 70kr, and there are 20-percent discounts for women travelling at night, but check with the driver first.

Accommodation

Of the **hostels**, the most central and best appointed is the excellent *Slottskogen*, Vegagatan 21 (☎031/42 65 20, *www.slottsskogenvh.se*; ③), two minutes' walk from Linnégatan – take tram #1 or #2 to Olivedahlsgatan. Another fine option, and well placed for ferries to Denmark, is *Stigbergssliden*, Stigbergssliden 10 (☎031/24 16 20, *www.hostel-gothenburg.com;* ②; with disabled access, basins in all rooms and buffet breakfast at 45kr). Closest to the Stena Line ferry terminal from Denmark is *Masthuggsterrassen*, Masthuggsterrassen 8 (☎031/42 48 20, *www.svif.se*; ②), which is served by trams #3 or #4. If you want something a little more peaceful try *Kvibergs*, Kvibergsvägen 5 (☎031/43 50 55, *www.vandrarhem.com*; ②), housed in an old barracks building and close to Gothenberg's largest weekend fleamarket – take tram #6 or #7 to Kviberg. If it's vital to stay right in the middle of things, take advantage of the tourist office's special **hotel deal**, called the **Gothenburg package** (from 420kr per person), which gets you a room in a central hotel, with breakfast and a free Gothenburg Card. The package operates every weekend from early June to August, though some hotels extend this limit. If this is beyond your budget, the tourist office can book **private rooms** for around 175kr a head. Alternatively, try the *Allén* **hotel**, Parkgatan 10 (☎031/10 14 50, *hotel.allen@telia.com*; ⑤), near the Heden bus terminal; or the friendliest option, the *Lilton*, Föreningsgatan 9 (☎031/82 88 08, *www.hotellilton.se*; ③), in a charming old house tucked away close to the Haga area and offering a homely atmosphere. For character and great location, the 1907 sailing ship *Barken Viking*, Gullbergskajen (☎031/63 58 00, *barken.viking@liseberg.se*; ⑤), is moored outside the Opera House on the river and is very comfortable. All provide price reductions at weekends.

The all-year *Kärralunds* **campsite** (140kr per pitch; *www.liseberg.se*) is 4km out (tram #5 to Welandergatan) and has four-bed cabins from 615kr and an attached **hostel** (☎031/84 02 00; ②). For beaches, the two campsites at Askim, 12km out, are better – notably *Askim Strand* (☎031/28 62 61; closed late-Aug to early May), which has four-bed cabins for 630kr in July and August, 520kr outside this time. Catch the Blå Express (5am–midnight; every 15min; 25min) from the bus terminal.

The City

King Gustav II Adolf, looking for western trade, founded Gothenburg in the early seventeenth century as a response to the high tolls charged by the Danes for using the narrow sound between the two countries. As a Calvinist and businessman, Gustav much admired Dutch merchants, inviting them to trade and live in Gothenburg, and it's their influence that shaped the city, parts of which have an oddly Dutch feel. The area defined by the central canal represents what's left of old Gothenburg, centring on **Gustav Adolfs Torg**, a windswept square flanked by the nineteenth-century **Börshuset** (Exchange Building), and the fine **Rådhus**, originally built in 1672. Around the corner, the **Kronhuset**, off Kronhusgatan, built in 1643, is a typical seventeenth-century Dutch construction, and looks like the backdrop to a Vermeer. The cobbled courtyard outside is flanked by the mid-eighteenth-century **Kronhusbodarna** (Mon–Fri 11am–4pm, Sat 11am–2pm), now togged up as period craft shops selling sweets and souvenirs.

The **Stadsmuseum**, Norra Hamngatan 12 (daily 10am–5pm; 40kr, ticket valid for a year), housed in the eighteenth-century headquarters of the East India Company, has been restored and now incorporates a rich collection of archeological, cultural and industrial exhibits. Close by, the **Maritima Centrum** (daily: March–May & Sept–Nov 10am–4pm; June & Aug 10am–6pm; July 10am–9pm; 50kr) allows you to clamber aboard a destroyer and submarine moored at the quayside. It is worth coming down here just to look at the shipyards beyond, like a rusting Meccano set put into sharp perspective by the striking **Opera House** (daily noon–6pm; guided tours July Tues & Wed noon–3pm; ☎031/10 82 03; tickets from 50kr), a graceful and imaginative ship-like structure.

Crossing the canal from Kungsportsplatsen and running all the way up to Götaplatsen, Kungsportsavenyn is Gothenburg's showiest thoroughfare. Known simply as **Avenyn**, this wide strip was once flanked by private houses fronted by gardens and is now lined with over-priced, posey yet popular pavement restaurants and brasseries. About halfway down, the excellent **Röhsska Museum of Arts and Crafts** at Vasagatan 37–39 (May–Aug Mon–Fri noon–4pm, Sat & Sun noon–5pm; Sept–April Tues noon–9pm, Wed–Fri noon–4pm, Sat & Sun noon–5pm; 40kr), celebrates Swedish design through the ages, among other things. At the top end, **Götaplatsen** is the modern cultural centre of Gothenburg, home to a concert hall, theatre and **Art Museum** (May–Aug Mon–Fri 11am–4pm, Sat & Sun 11am–5pm; Sept–April Tues–Fri 11am–4pm, Wed till 9pm, Sat & Sun 11am–5pm; 40kr), whose enormous collections include a good selection of Impressionist paintings, Pop Art and – most impressively – superb Swedish work in the Furstenburg galleries on the sixth floor. Just a few minutes' walk to the west from Avenyn, the old working-class district of **Haga** is now a picturesque area of gen-trified chic with plenty of daytime cafés and boutiques, while **Linnégatan**, a few steps further, is a more charismatic and cosmopolitan version of Avenyn with the most diverse places to eat, drink and stroll. Just five minutes' walk southeast of Götaplatsen, on the edge of the cen-tre, is **Liseberg**, a surprisingly aesthetic amusement park (late April to June & late Aug daily 3–11pm; July to mid-Aug daily noon–11pm; Sept Sat 1–11pm, Sun noon–8pm; 45kr) with some high-profile rides and acres of gardens, restaurants and fast food. In the opposite direc-tion, great views of the harbour and surrounding area can be had from the excursion boats that run from Lilla Bommen to the **Nya Elfsborg Fortress** (early May to mid-Aug daily 9.30am–3pm; 70kr, including guided tour of fortress), a seventeenth-century island defence guarding the harbour entrance, whose surviving buildings have been turned into a museum and café.

Eating and drinking

There's no shortage of places to **eat** in Gothenburg, and the city's range of ethnic restaurants is particularly good, reflecting its trading past. For **picnic food**, Saluhallen, the indoor mar-ket in Kungstorget (Mon–Thurs 9am–6pm, Fri 8am–6.30pm, Sat 8am–3pm), is tempting beyond words, and houses the two cheapest snack bars in town. In Linne, *Saluhall Briggen*, Tredje Långgatan, is smaller but brimming with mouthwatering fish, cheeses and cheap cafés. Many of the most glitzy places to **eat** flank Avenyn, though they are generally samey, packed and overpriced; less obvious and more interesting, and usually cheaper, places can be found in the streets clustered on Haga Nygatan with the cheapest, filling lunches at *Café Kringlan*, Haga Nygatan 13, while further west off Linnégatan is a range of good eateries and cafés. For **sit-down food**, the best cafés for value and friendly, laid-back atmosphere are *Café Engelen* and *Tintin Café*, just a few steps from each other on Engelbrecktsgatan just off Avenyn – both are open round the clock. For **vegetarian** and vegan meals, the classic place is *Solrosen*, Kaponjärgatan 4a in Haga district (Mon–Fri 11.30am–1am, Sat 2pm–1am), which turns into a lively drinking venue at night. A lovely choice is *Cyrano*, Prinsgatan 7 (☎031/14 31 10), an authentic Provençal bistro with a laid-back atmosphere (Mon–Fri 11am–11pm, Sat 2–11pm, Sun 2–9pm). At lunch time, try *Fröken Olssens Kafe*, Östra Latmgatan 14, which serves huge sandwiches and terrific cakes. On Avenyn, head for *Junggrens Café* at no. 37. It's a Gothenburg institution and the only reasonably priced place on the avenue.

There's an excellent choice of places to **drink**, some staying open well into the small hours. Avenyn is the focal point of much of night-time Gothenburg. At the junction of Avenyn and Kristinelundsgatan, *Java Café*, at Vasagatan 23, is a studenty coffee house with a Parisian feel. It opens for breakfast (30kr), is a great Sunday-morning hang-out and stays open till 11.30pm at weekends. *Napoleon* at Vasagatan 11 has a lovely, mellow interior and is set in a fabulous old house with exterior wall paintings (Mon–Thurs 10am–midnight, Fri & Sat till 3am). *Greta's*, Drottninggatan 35 (5pm–1am), is a stylish yet casual bar/restaurant (though now a little more frenetic on Fri & Sat) which is very popular as a **gay** venue and also serves good food. There's live music at the *Auld Dubliner* at Ostra Hamngatan 50b, which claims to have been established in 1870 and serves Guinness and whisky. *Nefertiti*, Hvitfeldtsplatsen 6, is one of the best places to see live jazz and world **music**. The city's large student community means lots of local **live bands**. The best place to hear them is at *Kompaniet*, Kungsgatan, which has a bar on the top floor and dancing downstairs.

Listings

Car rental Avis, at Central Station (☎031/80 57 80); Europcar, Stampgatan 22d (☎031/80 53 90) and at the airport (☎031 94 71 00); Hertz, Central Station (☎031/80 37 30) and at the airport (☎031/94 60 20).

Exchange Forex exchange office inside Central Station (daily 7am–9pm), at Avenyn 22 (Mon–Fri 8am–7pm, Sat 9am–5pm (Nordstan shopping centre (9am–7pm), and Kungportsplatsen (Mon–Fri 8am–7pm, Sat 10am–5pm).

Ferries DFDS (☎031/65 06 50, *www.dfdsseaways.se*); Stena Line (☎031/704 00 00, *www2.stenaline.se*).

Pharmacy Apoteket Vasen, Götagatan 10, in the Nordstan shopping centre, is open till 10pm daily (☎031/80 44 10).

Police Ernst Fontells Plats (☎031/700 20 00).

Post office Main office in Nordstan (daily 10am–6pm).

Travel agent Kilroy Travels, Berzeliigatan 5 (☎031/20 08 60).

Helsingborg

At **HELSINGBORG** only a narrow sound separates Sweden from Denmark; indeed, Helsingborg was Danish for most of the Middle Ages, with a castle controlling the southern regions of what is now Sweden. The town's enormously important strategic position meant that it bore the brunt of repeated attacks and rebellions, the Swedes conquering the town on six separate occasions, only to lose it back to the Danes each time. Finally, in 1710, a terrible battle saw off the Danes for the last time, and the battered town lay dormant for almost two hundred years, depopulated and abandoned. Only in the nineteenth century, when the harbour was expanded and the railway constructed, did Helsingborg find new prosperity. Today, the dramatically redeveloped harbour area has breathed new life into this likeable, relaxed town which is well worth a day's stay for its bars, cafés and cosily buzzing atmosphere.

Directly south of the the North Harbour café-bars, the strikingly designed **Henry Dunker Cultural House**, named after the city's foremost industrialist benefactor, is due to open in 2002 and aims to provide a full vision of the city's history in context and will also house a theatre and concert hall (ask at the tourist office). East from Hamntorget and the harbours, the massive, neo-Gothic **Rådhus** marks the bottom of **Stortorget**, the long thin square sloping up to the lower battlements of what's left of Helsingborg's castle, the **kärnan** or keep (daily: April, May & Sept 9am–4pm; June–Aug 10am–7pm; Oct–March 10am–2pm; 15kr), a fourteenth-century brick tower, the only survivor from the original fortress. The views from the top are worth the entrance fee although you don't miss much from the lower (free) battlements. Off Stortorget, **Norra Storgatan** contains Helsingborg's oldest buildings, attractive seventeenth- and eighteenth-century merchants' houses with quiet courtyards.

Apart from the Sundbussarna passenger ferry to Helsingør, which pulls up across an arm of the docks, all **ferries**, **trains** and **buses** arrive at Knutpunkten, the harbourside **central terminal**. It's just a couple of minutes' walk from here up Stortorget towards Kärnen to the **tourist office** at Södra Storgatan 1 (June–Aug Mon–Fri 9am–8pm, Sat & Sun 9am–5pm; Sept–May Mon–Fri 9am–6pm, Sat 10am–2pm; ☎042/10 43 50, *www.visit.helsingborg.se*), which has free city maps and books **private rooms** at 125kr per person (plus 75kr fee). Otherwise, the cheapest of the central **hotels** is *Linnea*, Prästgatan 4 (☎042/21 46 60; ④), which drops prices in summer and at weekends. The *Villa Thalassa* **youth hostel** (☎042/21 03 84; ③; bus #7, or #44 after 7pm) is 4km north along Drottninggatan. For **camping**, try the waterfront site at Kustgatan Råå, 5km southeast; bus #1A or #1B from outside the Rådhus.

You shouldn't have any difficulty finding somewhere to eat. Lovely daytime **cafés** include the classic *Fahlmans* on Stortorget – try their apple meringue pie – and the charismatic *Ebba's Fik*, Bruksgatan 20, which is all decked out with authentic 1950s memorabilia. There are plenty of harbour-front bars, though the best laid-back style café is the gay-run *K & Co*, Nedre Långwinkelsgatan 9, for great muffins, cakes and ciabattas. The cheapest **restaurant** is the unglamorous *Graffitti* on the first floor at Knutpunkten.

There are several good **clubs**, including Sweden's biggest jazz club, *Jazz Klubben*, Nedre Långvinkelsgatan 22 (Wed, Fri & Sat), and the noisy, popular *Tivoli* club, Hamntorget 11, where you can get down to the very latest sounds for a 60kr entrance.

Lund

Just forty minutes south of Helsingborg and fifteen minutes from Malmö, **LUND** is the most obvious target for a trip, a beautiful university town with a picturesque medieval centre and a unique buzz thanks to the student population. This does mean, though, that the life drains out of the place during the summer when the students are on vacation. Its weather-beaten **Domkyrkan** (Mon–Fri 8am–6pm, Sat 9.30am–5pm, Sun 9.30am–6pm), consecrated in 1145, is considered by many to be Scandinavia's finest medieval building. Its plain interior culminates in a delicate, semicircular apse with a gleaming fifteenth-century altarpiece and a mosaic of Christ surrounded by angels – although what draws most attention is a fourteenth-century astronomical clock, revealing an ecclesiastical Punch and Judy show daily at noon and 3pm. Below the apse is a crypt, supported by vividly sculpted pillars and littered with elaborately carved tombstones.

Outside the cathedral, **Kyrkogatan**, lined with staunch, solid, nineteenth-century civic buildings, leads into the main square, **Stortorget**, off which **Kattesund** is home to a glassed-in set of excavated medieval walls. Adjacent is the **Drottens Kyrkoruin** (Tues–Fri & Sun noon–4pm, Sat 10am–2pm; 10kr), the remains of a medieval church in the basement of another modern building, but the real interest is in the powerful atmosphere of the old streets behind the Domkyrkan. **Kiliansgatan**, directly behind the cathedral's apse, is a delightful cobbled street, whose fine houses sport tiny courtyards and gardens. In this web of streets, **Kulturen** (mid-April to Sept daily 11am–5pm, rest of year Tues–Sun noon–4pm; 50kr, under 18s free) is a village in itself of indoor and open-air collections of southern Swedish art, silverware, ceramics, musical instruments, etc. Worth a visit at Finngatan 2 is **Skissernas Museum** (Museum of Sketches; Tues–Sat noon–4pm, Sun 1–5pm; 30kr special exhibitions, otherwise free) – though renovations may involve temporary closure. Inside the museum is an amazing collection of models, maquettes and sketches of internationally renowned works from Chagall to Matisse, Picasso to Henry Moore. Finish off your meanderings with a visit to the **Botaniska Trädgård** (daily 6am–8pm) just beyond, an extensive botanical garden with some shaded pathways.

Trains arrive on the western edge of town, an easy walk from the centre. The **tourist office** is opposite the Domkyrkan at Kyrkogatan 11, and is well signposted from the train station (June–Aug Mon–Fri 10am–6pm, Sat & Sun 10am–2pm; rest of year Mon–Fri 10am–5pm, May & Sept also Sat 10am–2pm; ☎046/ 35 50 40, *turistbyran@lund.se*). **Internet access** is available at Nine (daily noon–1am; 55kr/hour; ☎046/15 90 50), Paradisgatan 1, and at the city library, St. Petri Kyrkogata 6 (☎046/35 59 90; free). Lund makes an appealing alternative stopover to Malmö or Helsingborg by virtue of private rooms which the tourist office can book for 175kr plus a 50kr booking fee. Its unusual **hostel**, Tåget, Vävaregatan 22 (☎046/14 28 20; ②), packs you into three-tiered sleeping compartments of six 1940s carriages parked on a branch line behind the train station; turn right and follow the signs. The *Ahlström*, Skomakaregatan 3 (☎046/211 01 74; ⑤; closed June–Aug), is a central **hotel**. Another good value option is *Hotel Överliggaren*, Bytaregatan 14 (☎046/15 72 30; ⑤). There are plenty of cheap places to **eat**. *Café Ariman*, attached to the Nordic Law

Department on Kungsgatan, has been updated, but maintains its shabby, left-wing coffee house appeal with good, cheap light food; while *Conditori Lundagård* on Kyrkogatan is the classic student café. *Fellini*, opposite the train station, is a popular Italian eatery, while *Spot*, Klostergatan 14, does excellent meals during the day with gorgeous salads – upstairs is a more wallet-taxing European restaurant. *Tegners*, next to the student union, serves really fine food at student prices. Lund's most popular meeting place is the *Stortorget* on Stortorget with a bar, restaurant and club. The best **club** is *Palladium*, Stora Södergatan 13, just south of Stortorget – it has a soul night on Thursdays, minimum age 20. *Mejeriet*, at the end of Stora Södergatan, has a good art house **cinema** (☎046/14 38 13) and a concert hall with a busy and varied programme.

Malmö

The third largest city in Sweden, **MALMÖ**, won back for Sweden from Denmark by Karl X in the seventeenth century, was a handsome city then and is now, with a cobbled medieval core that has a lived-in, workaday feel worlds apart from the museum-piece quality of most other Swedish town centres. With the opening in 2000 of the **Øresund Link**, a sensational seventeen-kilometre-long road and rail bridge, Malmö really is the Swedish gateway from continental Europe, and after years in the doldrums after the failure of much of its industry, it is enjoying a revival, and is as lively and up-beat as ever for travellers wanting to find a cosmopolitan Swedish city outside the capital.

Arrival, information and accommodation

Trains arrive at Central Station, including the local Pågatåg services (to and from Helsingborg, Lund and Ystad; rail passes valid). The train station also has showers (20kr) and beds (5.30am–11pm; 15kr per hour) or you can use both for 25kr. The main **bus terminal** is outside Central Station, in Centralplan, though buses from Stockholm, Helsingborg and Gothenburg arrive at Slussplan, east of Central Station, at the end of Norra Vallgatan. A one-way ticket across the Oresund bridge costs 70kr by train, or 275kr for a car load (payment is at a toll station on the Swedish side). Passenger-only **ferries and catamarans** from Copenhagen dock at various terminals along Skeppsbron. The one remaining ferry company making the trip is Flygbåtarna (☎040/10 39 30; 60kr one way).

The **tourist office** is inside the station (June–Aug Mon–Fri 9am–8pm, Sat & Sun 9am–5pm; Sept–May Mon–Fri 9am–5pm, Sat 10am–2pm; ☎040/34 12 00, *imalmo.turism@malmo.se/ www.malmo.se/turist*). It stocks the handy *Malmö This Month* and sells the **Malmö Card**, which gives free museum entry, free travel on city buses, free car parking in public places and discounts on restaurants and certain shops; it costs 150kr for 24 hours and is also available for 48 hours (275kr) and 72 hours (400kr). The tourist office also sells a good-value round-trip (Oresund rundt) ticket (199kr or 249kr depending on extent of trip; *www.skanetrafiken.skane.se*), valid for two days for the train to Lund and Helsingborg, the crossing to Helsingør, travel on to Copenhagen (museum discounts in Copenhagen and Malmö) and then return by catamaran to Malmö. For **Internet** use, head for *Surfer's Paradise*, Amiralsgatan 14 (Mon–Fri 10am–midnight, Sat & Sun noon–midnight; 40kr/hour), *Cyber Space*, Engelbrektsgatan 13a (daily 10am–10pm; 44kr/hour), or the library at Regementsgatan 3 (Mon–Thurs 10am–7pm, Fri till 6pm, Sat noon–4pm; free for 30min).

Malmö is one of the easier places in the south to find good, cheap **accommodation**. The tourist office sells the useful **Malmö Package**, providing a double room in a central **hotel**, breakfast and Malmö Card, for 410kr per person. Of the many hotels within the scheme, one comfortable option is the *Ibis Hotel Malmö City*, Citadellvägen 4 (☎040/23 96 05; ④), which is far more pleasant than its drab 1950s office-block facade would suggest. For a beautiful hotel with much-reduced summer prices, try the small but pleasant *Hotel Tunneln*, Adelgatan

4 (☎040/10 16 20; ⑨). There is now just one HI **hostel**, the inconveniently placed *STF Vandrarhem*, Backvägen 18 (☎040/822 20; ②; closed Christmas), 5km out – take bus #21A from Central Station. A better bet is *Bosse's Gäst och Företagsvåningar*, Södra Förstadsgatan 110B (☎040/32 62 50; ③), a comfortable **B&B**, twenty minutes' walk south from the station or bus #17 to Södervarn, with family rooms for 500kr. The nearest **campsite** is *Sibbarps Camping* (☎040/34 26 50) on Strandgatan; bus #82 from Central Station.

The City

Few places in Sweden are more enjoyable – or more conducive to a leisurely stroll – than Malmö, with its canals, parks, and largely pedestrianized streets and squares. Most of the medieval centre was taken apart in the early sixteenth century to make way for **Stortorget**, a vast market square. It's as impressive today as it must have been when it first appeared, flanked on one side by the **Rådhus**, built in 1546 and covered with statuary and spiky accoutrements; there are tours of the well-preserved interior (check with the tourist office for times). **Södergatan**, Malmö's main pedestrianized shopping street, runs south from here towards the canal. Behind the Rådhus stands the **St Petri Kyrka** (Mon–Fri 8am–6pm, Sat 10am–6pm, Sun 10am–6pm), a fine Gothic church with an impressively decorative pulpit and a four-tiered altarpiece. **Lilla Torget** is everyone's favourite part of the city, a late-sixteenth-century spin-off from an overcrowded Stortorget, usually full and doing a roaring trade from jewellery stalls and summer buskers. The southern side of the square is formed by a row of mid-nineteenth-century brick and timber warehouses, unremarkable given the other preserved buildings around, except that they contain the **Form Design Centre** (Tues–Fri 11am–5pm, Sat 10am–4pm; free), a kind of yuppies' Habitat museum. The shops around here sell books, antiques and gifts, though the best place to drop into is the nearby **Saluhallen**, an excellent indoor market. Further west still lie the **Kungsparken** and the **Malmöhus** (daily 10am/noon–4pm; 40kr), a low fortified castle defended by a wide moat, two circular keeps and grassy ramparts, raised by Danish king Christian III in 1536. For a time a prison (Bothwell, third husband of Mary, Queen of Scots, was the most notable inmate), the castle and its outbuildings now constitute a series of exhibitions including Malmö's main **museum**, and collections covering areas including natural history, science, maritime history, military life and city-related art, unfortunately with no information in English. There's a café inside, too, and the grounds, peppered with small lakes and an old windmill, are good for a stroll.

Eating, drinking and nightlife

The Saluhall on Landbygatan by Lilla Torget stocks a marvellous array of picnic supplies. For **lunch**, a delightful option is the quirky *Café Siesta*, Ostindiefararegatan – turn right at the western end of Landbygatan off Lilla Torget – a fun café serving filling sandwiches and homemade apple cake. Alternatively, try *Pelles Cafe*, Tegelgårdsgatan 5, whose very friendly staff serve generous, cheap baguettes in a quaint, period house. *Bageri Café* at Saluhall (Mon–Fri 8am–6pm, Sat 10am–4pm) is excellent for filled baguettes and health foods, while *Café Horisont*, Davidshallgatan 9, just south of the centre, is a very likeable no-smoking eco-café serving lots of salads, muffins and homemade cakes. *Spot* restaurant, Stora Nygatan 33, is a chic Italian and very good for cheese, fish and meat, but now only open weekdays from 9am to 6pm and Saturday from 10am to 5pm. A charming **restaurant** is *QD*, Erik Dahlbergsgatan 3 (☎040/12 83 71), an intimate place with an intriguing menu including vegetables in coconut and delicious meat dishes which aren't over-priced. For **drinking**, Lilla Torget swarms with bustling venues through the evening. *Gustav Adolf*, Gustav Adolfs Torg, is popular at weekends. The best place for occasional **live music** is *Matssons Musikpub*, Göran Olsgatan 1, behind the Rådhus. A twenty-minute walk south from the docks is Möllevångens Torget, where *Nyhavn* is one of the more appealing of the bar-pubs that are springing up all across the south city's trendy immigrant quarter. The best **gay club** is the long-established and friendly *Fyran* (Fri & Sat 11pm–3am; 70kr) at Snapperupsgatan 4.

Ystad

An hour by train from Malmö, **YSTAD** sits at the end of a ride through rolling farmland. The train station is by the docks, a murky area that gives no hint of the cosy little town to come. In the nineteenth century, the town's inhabitants made a mint from smuggling, a profitable occupation in the days of Napoleon's Continental Blockade. Quite apart from coming to see the crumbling medieval market town, you might well be leaving Sweden from here: ferries depart for the Danish island of Bornholm and for Poland.

The narrow, cobbled streets wind up to **Stortorget**, a well-proportioned square, at the back of which sits the grand **Sta Maria Kyrka**, a church which has been added to continually since its original foundation in the fourteenth century. The red-brick interior displays heavy, decorative tablets lining the aisle walls and enclosed wooden pews – the end-pieces sculpted with flowers and emblems. The green box-pews at either side of the entrance were reserved for women who hadn't yet been received back into the church after childbirth. From the church, take a walk down **Lilla Västergatan**, the main street in Ystad in the seventeenth and eighteenth centuries, with neat pastel-coloured houses. At no. 28 you'll find Galleri Z, which looks like a furniture store, but upstairs has a superb gallery of contemporary art exhibitions. Walk back through Stortorget and it's not far down to the old **Greyfriars Monastery** and museum (Mon–Fri 10am–5pm, Sat & Sun noon–4pm; 20kr), a thirteenth-century survivor in a pleasant setting which contains the usual local cultural and historical collections.

From the **train station**, cross the tracks to St Knuts Torg, where you'll find the **tourist office** (May to mid-June Mon–Fri 9am–7pm, Sat 11am–2pm, Sun 11am–6pm; mid-June to mid-Aug Mon–Fri 9am–7pm, Sat 10am–7pm, Sun 11am–6pm; mid-Aug to April Mon–Fri 9am–5pm; ☎0411/776 81, *turistinfo@ystad.se*). The square is also where **buses** from Lund, Malmö and Kristianstad will drop you. There are several **hotels** in town, the most charming being *Sekelgården*, Stora Västergatan 9, a family-run former tannery dating from 1793 with a great courtyard (☎0411/739 00; ⑥). The **hostel** (☎0411/665 66; ②) has one branch inside the central station and another 2km away at Sandskogen, where there's also a **campsite** (closed mid-Sept to April), with cabins for rent (①) – take bus #572 or #304. For light **food**, *The English Book Café*, Gäsegränd, down a tiny cobbled street off Stora Östergatan, is an evocative spot for homemade scones in an eighteenth-century courtyard, though this charming place may be closing down (check with the tourist office), while *Kaffestugan Backahasten*, at Tvattorget, is the place to head for deeply filled sandwiches and light lunches to eat outside, surrounded by ducklings in the heart of the town. For **dinner**, try the popular *Lotta's* (Mon–Sat 6pm–1am), which serves the best fish and meat dishes in central Stortorget.

Kalmar

Bright **KALMAR** had much to do with Sweden's medieval development. It was the scene of the first meeting of the *Riksdag* called by failing king Magnus Eriksson in the mid-fourteenth century, and played host to the formation of the Kalmar Union, the 1397 agreement uniting Sweden, Norway and Denmark – a history manifest in the surviving castle, **Kalmar Slott** (April–Sept 10am–4/6pm; Oct–March 11am–4pm; 60kr), beautifully set on a tiny island a few minutes' walk away from the bus and train stations. Defended by a range of steep embankments and gun emplacements, the fourteenth-century buildings survived eleven sieges virtually unscathed, a record not respected by King Johan III who rebuilt the structure in the late sixteenth century. The castle is now a storybook confection, with turrets, ramparts, moat and drawbridge. The spruce interior repays a long dawdle; highlights include the intricately panelled Lozenge Hall and a dark dungeon.

If the castle seems to defend nothing in particular it's because the town was shifted to Kvarnholmen, an island to the north, in the mid-seventeenth century following a fire. This is modern Kalmar, a graceful, straightforward grid settlement which centres on the Baroque

Domkyrkan (daily 10am–6pm) on Stortorget. Time is best spent wandering the streets around **Lilla Torget**: there's not a great deal left – some seventeenth-century buildings and city walls – but what remains is authentic and atmospheric enough. The one place really worth making a beeline for is the **Kronan Exhibition**, the main attraction of the **Länsmuseum**, Skeppsbrogatan (daily: mid-June to mid-Aug 10am–6pm; rest of year 10am–4pm; 50kr). The *Kronan* was one of the three biggest ships in the world – twice the size of the *Vasa* (see p.1271) – when it went down after an explosion in the gunpowder magazine in 1676, lying undisturbed until 1980. There's an inventive walk-through reconstruction of the gun decks and admiral's cabin, as well as a swag of gold coins, clothing, sculpture, jewellery and weapons – in fact, a complete picture of seventeenth-century maritime life and a remarkable insight into a society at the height of its political powers.

The **tourist office** at Larmgatan 6 (early June & late Aug daily 9am–9pm; mid-June to mid-Aug daily 9am–8pm; rest of year Mon–Fri 9am–5pm; ☎0480/153 50, *info@turistbyra.kalmar.se*), 100m from the **train station** and bus **terminal**, doles out a decent map of Kalmar and arranges **private rooms** from around 300kr a double or 190kr for a single. Or stay at the **youth hostel** at Rappegatan 1c (☎0480/129 28; ③), 1500m away on Ängo, the next island north. The *Sjöfartsklubben* on Skeppsbrogatan (a seaman's mission but open to all) has doubles for 270kr and cheaper dorm accommodation, while there's a **campsite** on Stensö island, 3km from the centre, with a few cheap cabins. For **food**, most places centre around Larmtorget, where you can get a tasty and filling lunch for around 50kr. For an atmospheric café, try the elegant *Kullzenska Caféet*, upstairs at Kaggensgatan 26. The hippest eaterie though is *T & T*, Unionsgatan 20, where you can down delicious and unusual pizzas and a good range of wines (Mon–Thurs 11am–midnight, Fri & Sat noon–1am, Sun noon–midnight).

Gotland

The rumours about good times on **Gotland** are rife. You'll hear that the short summer season really motors like nowhere else in Sweden, and it's hot and fun. Largely, these rumours are true: the island has a youthful feel as young, mobile Stockholmers desert the capital for a boisterous summer on its beaches. But it's not all just brochure fodder. The island was an important trading post during Viking times, and later a powerbase of the Hanseatic League. The capital Visby became one of the great cities of medieval Europe, and no other part of Scandinavia has such a concentration of unspoilt medieval country churches.

Numerous **ferries** to Gotland, operated by Destination Gotland, run from Nynäshamn and Oskarshamn, but are packed in summer, so try to plan ahead. The main operator is Destination Gotland (☎0498/20 10 20; Stockholm office ☎08/20 10 20, *www.destinationgotland.se*). Otherwise, Gotland City at Kungsgatan 57 in Stockholm (☎08/406 15 00, *www.gotlandcity.se*) can provide plenty of information and sell advance tickets. One-way **fares** cost 145kr to 465kr June to mid-August, and students are entitled to a discount from 60kr to 170kr. Under-26s may find flying a competitive option, with return fares from 200kr if you just turn up at the airport, but if you're over 26 this shoots up to 890kr to 1795kr return.

Visby

Undoubtedly the finest approach to **VISBY** is by ship, seeing the old trading centre as it should be seen. The magnificent three-kilometre city **wall** was built around the end of the thirteenth century to isolate the city's foreign traders from the islanders. The old Hanseatic **harbour** at Almedalen is now a public park and nothing is much more than a few minutes' walk from here. Close by, pretty **Packhusplan**, the oldest square in the city, is bisected by curving Strandgatan which runs south to the fragmentary ruins of **Visborg Castle**, overlooking the harbour. Built in the fifteenth century by Erik of Pomerania, it was blown up by the Danes in the seventeenth century. In the opposite direction, Strandgatan runs towards the sea and the lush **Botanical Gardens**, just beyond which is the **Jungfrutornet** (Maiden's

Tower) where a local goldsmith's daughter was walled up alive, reputedly for betraying the city to the Danes. Strandgatan is the best place to view the merchants' houses looming over the narrow streets, and is also home to the **Gotlands Fornsal Museum** at no. 14 (May to mid-Sept daily 10am–5pm; rest of year Tues–Sun noon–4pm; 50kr), which, along with the usual Viking and medieval relics, claims the largest collection of painted windows in Scandinavia. The museum also tells the tale of the slaughter of thousands of Swedes by the Danes in 1361 – an event remembered by **Valdemar's Cross**, a few hundred metres east of Söderport, where excavations earlier this century revealed a mass grave. The strikingly towered **Domkyrkan**, a short walk west of the museum (daily 8am–5pm), was built between 1190 and 1225, just before the great age of Gothic church building on the island. Used both as warehouse and treasury, it's been heavily restored and about the only original fixture left is the thirteenth-century sandstone font.

Ferries serving Visby dock just outside the city walls; turn left and keep walking for the centre. On the way you'll see the **tourist office** (Oct–April Mon–Fri 8am–4pm; May to early June & late Aug Mon–Fri 8am–5pm, Sat & Sun 10am–4pm, mid June to mid Aug Mon–Fri 7am–7pm, Sat & Sun 7am–6pm; Sept Mon–Fri 8am–5pm, Sat & Sun 11am–2pm; ☎0498/20 17 00, *info@gtf.i.se*) at Hamngatan 4 just within the city walls. It sells the excellent *Turistkarta Gotland* (30kr), describing all points of interest. Alternatively, a short way to the right along the harbour is **Gotlandsresor** at Färjeledon 3 (☎0498/20 12 60, *info@gotlandsresor.se*), which has a room-booking service. For getting around the island it's best to rent a **bike** and there are plenty of places to do this, all charging 50kr to 70kr a day. For the best advice on travel throughout the island, local historian Peter Doolk (☎0498/48 03 33) is a mine of information. **Accommodation** does fill up quickly during the summer, and pre-booking is advisable. The tourist office can book **private rooms** in town from 210kr a head, but are unwilling to do so unless hotels are all full, while of the several **hostels**, the most convenient is *Fängelset Sjumastarn* (☎0498/20 60 50; ②), just opposite the ferry terminal and based in an old prison. For a cheapish **hotel**, *Donnerplats*, Donnersplats 6 (☎0498/21 03 73; ②), has apartments for around 950kr for three people. *Gotlands Ice Hockey Federation Youth Hostel* (☎0498/24 82 02) charges 175kr per person, but is 3km from the centre; ask the bus driver to drop you at Isall (Ice-hall). Gotland is a great place for **camping**; *Nordenstrands* is the closest site, 1km outside the city walls and open from May to September – follow the cycle path that runs through the Botanical Gardens along the seafront. For **eating**, Adelsgatan is lined with cafés and snack bars and has a couple of cheap kebab takeaways. Best place for sit-down **drinking** is the hugely popular bar/restaurant *Muntkälleren*, Lilla Torggränd, though queues can be long.

CENTRAL AND NORTHERN SWEDEN

In many ways, the long wedge of land that comprises **central and northern Sweden** – from the northern shores of Lake Vänern to the Norwegian border – encompasses all that is most popular and typical of the country. Rural and underpopulated, this is Sweden as seen in the brochures – lakes, holiday cottages, forests and reindeer. Essentially the region divides into two. On the eastern side, Sweden's coast forms one edge of the **Gulf of Bothnia**. With its jumble of erstwhile fishing towns and squeaky-clean contemporary urban planning, this corridor of land is quite unlike the rest of the country – worth stopping off in if you're travelling north or have just arrived from Finland by ferry. Though the weather isn't as reliable as further south, you are guaranteed clean beaches, crystal-clear waters and fine hiking. To the west, folklorish **Dalarna** county is the most picturesque region, with sweeping green countryside and inhabitants who maintain a cultural heritage (echoed in contemporary handicrafts and traditions) that goes back to the Middle Ages. This is *the* place to spend midsummer, particularly Midsummer's Night when the whole region erupts in a frenzy of celebration. The **Inlandsbanan**, the great Inland Railway, cuts right through this area from Lake Siljan though the shimmering, modern lakeside town of **Östersund** to **Gällivare** above the

Arctic Circle. An enthralling 1300-kilometre, two-day ride, it ranks with the best European train journeys.

Gävle

It's only two hours north by train from Stockholm to **GÄVLE**, principal city of the county of Gästrikland and communications hub for the west and north. Gävle's charter was granted in 1446, but the town was almost completely redesigned after a fire in 1869. Its large squares, broad avenues and proud monumental buildings, centring on the roomy **Stortorget**, reflect its late-nineteenth-century success as an export centre for timber and metal. The place to head for is the one surviving part of the old town, **Gamla Gefle**, an area of wooden cottages and narrow cobbled streets on the other side of the river from Stortorget. **Länsmuséet Gävleborg**, on the riverfront at Södra Strandgatan 20 (Tues–Sun noon–4pm, Wed till 9pm; 25kr, free for students and under-20s), has work by many Swedish artists from 1600 to the present including local naive painter Johan Erik Olson. The **Joe Hill-Gården** at Nedre Bergsgatan 28 (June–Aug daily 11am–3pm; other times by appointment; ☎026/61 34 25; free) is the birthplace museum of US labour organizer Joe Hill. Born Johan Emanuel Hägglund in 1879, he emigrated in 1902, rallying comrades to the International Workers of the World with his songs and speeches until he was framed for murder and executed in 1915. The most piquant items are Hill's last testament and the telegram announcing his execution.

The **train** and **bus station** are at the east end of the city, only a few minutes from the centre or Gamle Gefle. The **tourist office** is opposite the train station at Drottninggatan 37 (June–Aug Mon–Fri 9am–6pm, Sat 9am–2pm, Sun 11am–4pm; *www.gavle.se*), with maps and information about furnished **apartments** in central Gävle, from 345kr a night per person, though the weekly rate works out cheaper. Of the two **hostels**, the best placed by far is in the old town at Södra Rådmansgatan 1 (☎026/62 17 45; ②); if this is full, try the other at Bönavägen 118 in Engeltofta, 6km northeast of town (☎026/961 60; ②), or try for a summer price at the central **hotels** such as the *Aveny*, Södra Kungsgatan 31 (☎026/61 55 90; ⑦). As a rule, places round Nygatan and Stortorget are good for basic daily **lunch**: for a change, *Bali Garden*, Nygatan 37, is Indonesian with meat dishes at under 90kr, while the *Roma* next door does takeaway pizzas from around 50kr.

Sundsvall

Known as the "Stone City", **SUNDSVALL** is immediately and obviously different. Once home to a rapidly expanding nineteenth-century sawmill industry, the whole city burned down in 1888 and a new centre built completely of stone emerged within ten years. The result is a living document of early-twentieth-century urban architecture, designed by architects who were engaged in rebuilding Stockholm's residential areas at the same time. This was achieved at a price, however: the workers who built 573 residential buildings in four years became the victims of their own success, and were shifted from their old homes in the centre and moved to a poorly serviced suburb.

The materials are limestone and brick, the style simple and the size often overwhelming. The **Esplanaden**, a wide central avenue, cuts the grid in two, itself crossed by **Storgatan**, the widest street. The area around **Stortorget** is still the roomy commercial centre that was envisaged. Behind the mock-Baroque exterior of the **Sundsvall Museum** (Mon–Thurs 10am–7pm, Fri 10am–6pm, Sat & Sun 11am–4pm; June–Aug 20kr, rest of year free), four late-nineteenth-century warehouses have been developed into a cultural complex called Kulturmagasinet (Culture Warehouse), devoted to art exhibits and city history. The **Gustav Adolfs Kyrkan** (daily 11am–2/4pm) – a soaring red-brick structure whose interior looks like a large Lego set – marks one end of the new town. To get the best perspective on the city's plan, climb to the heights of **Gaffelbyn** and the **Norra Bergets Hantyerks Och Friluttsmuseum** (June–Aug Mon–Fri 9am–4pm, Sat & Sun 11am–3pm; Sept–May Mon–Fri

9am–4pm; free; *skvadern@telia.com*), an open-air crafts museum down Storgatan and over the main bridge.

From the **train station** the centre is five minutes' walk away, with the **tourist office** in the main Stortorget (Mon–Fri 10am–6pm, Sat 10am–2pm; summer also Sun 10am–2pm; ☎060/61 04 50, *info@sundsvallturism.com*). There is also a small summer tourist office in the harbour with free car parking. The **bus station** is at the bottom of Esplanaden. The **hostel** (☎060/61 21 19 from 4 to 6pm; ②) at Norra Berget has recently been renovated at last, but takes about half an hour to walk to from the centre. The tourist office will help book accommodation for a 20kr fee, but does not book private rooms; otherwise *Svea Hotel*, Rådhusgatan 11 (☎060/61 16 05; ⑤), has doubles. For **eating**, Storgatan is lined with restaurants, most offering daily lunch menus, or *Spezia*, Sjögatan 6, has bargain pizzas for around 45kr.

Dalarna

It's fruitless to dwell too much on the agreed beauty of **Dalarna**. It holds a special, misty-eyed place in the Swedish heart and should certainly be seen, though not to the exclusion of points further north. And despite its charms, you may soon tire of the prominent folksy image: one small lakeside town looks pretty much like another, as do the ubiquitous handicrafts and souvenirs. Dalarna actually spreads further north and west than most brochures ever acknowledge. They, like most tourists, prefer to concentrate on the area immediately surrounding Lake Siljan – which on the whole isn't a bad idea. Most of the towns are connected by rail, and there are ferries across the lake at Mora and Leksand; you also don't need to worry unduly about accommodation, of which there is plenty. North of Orsa, the county becomes more mountainous and less populous.

Lake Siljan is what draws many tourists to Sweden, its gentle surroundings, traditions and local handicrafts weaving a subtle spell. There's a lush feel to much of the region, the vegetation enriched by the lake, which adds a pleasing dimension to what are, essentially, small, low-profile towns and villages. If you've only got time to see part of the lake, **MORA** is as good a place as any, and a starting point for the Inlandsbanan rail route (see p.1290). At the northwestern corner of Lake Siljan, the little town is more or less a showcase for the work of Anders Zorn, the Swedish painter who lived in Mora and whose work is exhibited in the **Zorn Museum**, Vasagatan 36 (mid-June to mid-Sept Mon–Sat 9am–5pm, Sun 11am–5pm; rest of year Mon–Sat noon–5pm, Sun 1–5pm; 35kr), along with his small but well-chosen personal collection. Zorn's oils reflect a passion for Dalarna's pastoral lifestyle, but it's his earlier watercolours of southern Europe and North Africa that really stand out. It's also possible to see his former home and studio, **Zorngården** (Mon–Sat 10am–4pm, Sun 11am–4pm; guided tours in English every 30min; 45kr). The **tourist office** (mid-June to mid-Aug Mon–Fri 9am–8pm, Sat & Sun 10am–5pm; rest of year Mon–Fri 9am–5pm, Sat 10am–1pm; ☎0250/56 76 00, *mora@stab.se*) is at the central Mora Strand station, and the **hostel** at Fredsgatan 6 (☎0250/381 96, *105rum@telia.com*; ②).

At **RÄTTVIK**, on the eastern bulge of the lake, there's an introductory spread of museums and craft exhibitions, the **Gammelgård**, 2km from town, with reconstructed buildings, period furniture and traditional costumes. The **tourist office** is at the train station (mid-June to mid-Aug Mon–Fri 9am–8pm, Sat & Sun 10am–7pm; rest of year Mon–Fri 9am–5pm, Sat 10am–1pm; *rattvik@stab.se*). The traditional pine log-built **hostel** is on Centralgatan (☎0248/105 66; ②); and there's a **campsite** (☎0248/516 91) with its own pool, on the lakeside just 200m from the station.

LEKSAND is perhaps the most popular and traditional of the Dalarna villages and certainly worth making the effort to reach at midsummer, when the festivals recall age-old maypole dances, the celebrations culminating in the **church boat races**, an aquatic procession of decorated longboats which the locals once rowed to church every Sunday. The **tourist office** in the train station building (mid-June to mid-Aug Mon–Fri 9am–8pm, Sat & Sun 10am–5pm; rest of year Mon–Fri 9am–5pm, Sat 10am–1pm; ☎0247/803 00, *leksand@stab.se)* has lots of information on the area as does the **hostel** (☎0247/152 50; ①), 2km south of the centre at Parkgården. **Bikes** can be rented from Stamnäs Diverse (☎0247/330 15; 60–100kr/day, 350kr/week).

Nearby **FALUN** was prosperous in the seventeenth and eighteenth centuries due to its **copper mines** (May–Aug daily 10am–4.30pm; Sept to mid-Nov, March & April Sat & Sun 12.30–4.30pm; 80kr). Two-thirds of the world's copper ore was mined here, and Falun acquired buildings and a proud layout in line with its status as Sweden's second largest town. An unnerving element of eighteenth-century mining was the omnipresence of copper vitriol fumes, a strong preservative. One case records the body of a young man found in the mines in 1719, who died 49 years previously in an accident; his corpse was so well preserved that his erstwhile fiancée, by then an old woman, recognized him immediately. Falun's **tourist office** is in Trotzgatan (Mon–Fri 9am–7pm, Sat 9am–6pm, Sun 10am–5pm; shorter hours in winter; ☎023/830 50, *turist@welcom.falun.se*); from the train or bus stations, take the underpass and then head towards the shops. A reasonable **hotel** is *Hotel Winn*, Bergskolegränd 7 (☎023/636 00; *info@winnfalun.softwarehotels.se*; ⑤). There's also a **hostel** (☎023/105 60; ②; bus #701) 4km away at Haraldsbro and a **campsite** at the National Ski Stadium at Lugnet.

The Inlandsbanan

The **Inlandsbanan** (Inland Railway; ☎020/53 53 53, *www.inlandsbanan.se*), linking central Sweden with Gällivare 1300km further north, is the most charismatic of Scandinavian rail routes, the trip everyone wants to make. Long under threat of closure, the line has now been privatized and looks like surviving for the moment, but only operates between late June and early August. InterRail pass holders under the age of 26 travel for free while those over 26 pay full fare. With a Scanrail Pass there is a 25 percent discount on individual journeys, but you do get a 25 percent discount off an Inland Railway Card which otherwise costs 700kr and which offers unlimited travel on the line for fourteen days. The full fare, travelling second class from Mora to Östersund, a six-hour trip, costs from 209kr depending on the time of year, plus a 50kr seat reservation. Cunning timetabling on the single daily service allows unlimited breaks on your journey but enforces a stop at Östersund whichever way you travel. A number of packages can be booked directly through the Inlandsbanan (*swedenbooking@gtsab.se*), including accommodation and a guide in English. These packages range from 3260kr to 4100kr depending on distance travelled.

Mora to Östersund

The Inlandsbanan begins in Mora, making its first stop at **ORSA**, fifteen minutes up the line, where the nearby **Grönklitt bear park** (mid-May to late June & late Aug to mid-Sept Mon–Fri 10am–3pm; late June to mid-Aug 10am–6pm; mid-Sept to mid-Oct open Sat & Sun 10am–3pm; 75kr) provides the best chance to see the bears that roam the countryside. The **hostel** at the park (☎0250/462 00; ①) has fine facilities.

Several hours north of here, the line's halfway point is marked by **ÖSTERSUND**. It's a welcoming place, and its **Storsjön** – or Great Lake – gives it a holiday atmosphere unusual this far north. In summer, you can make a tour of the lake on a **steamboat cruise**, stopping off on the small island of Verön (June & mid- to late Aug Wed, Fri & Sun at 11am; late June, July & first two weeks of Aug also Tues at 1.30pm, 4pm, 6pm & 7.30pm, Wed at 9pm, Thurs at 3.30pm, Fri at 6.30pm & Sat at 1.30pm, 3.30pm & 5pm; 95kr; also Fri at 6.30pm in high summer; 295kr, including dinner in the castle). Otherwise, the main thing to do in town is to visit **Jamtli** (late June to mid-Aug daily 11am–5pm; 90kr), an impressive open-air museum fifteen minutes' walk north from the centre along Rådhusgatan, full of volunteers milling around in traditional country costume. They live here throughout the summer and everyone is encouraged to join in – baking, tree felling, grass cutting. For kids it's ideal, and you'd have to be pretty hard-bitten not to enjoy the enthusiastic atmosphere. Historical re-enactments are performed from late June to mid-August. On the way in, the **Länsmuseum** (late June to mid-

Aug daily 11am–5pm; rest of year closed Mon; entry covered by the Jamtli ticket) shows off the county collections, a rambling houseful of local exhibits that includes monster-catching gear from the last century. Back in the centre, the town slopes steeply down to the water, and it's tiring work strolling the pedestrianized streets that run around Stortorget. Apart from the **Stadmuseum** (late June to early Aug daily noon–4pm; rest of year for special exhibitions only; free), a crowded two hundred years of history in a house the size of a shoebox, there's not a vast amount in the way of sights. The **harbour** is a better bet, from where you can take the bridge over the lake to **Frösön** island, site of the original Viking settlement here.

The **tourist office** is at Rådhusgatan 44 (Mon–Fri 9am–5/7/9pm; June also Sat & Sun 9am–3pm; July to early Aug also Sat 9am–9pm, Sun 9am–7pm; ☎063/14 40 01, *www.ostersund.se/turist*) and sells the *Östersundskortet* (mid-May to mid-Aug; 120kr), giving free access to the town's sights, half-price round trip bus journey (normally 90kr) and half-price on the steamboat cruise for nine days. For a central **hotel**, try either *Hotell Aston*, Köpmansgatan 40 (☎063/ 51 08 51; ④), or the *Hotell Linden*, close to the train station at Storgatan 64 (☎063/51 73 35; ⑤). During the Storsjöyran festival week (26 & 29 July) rooms are very hard to come by so it's worth booking early. The STF **hostel** in Östersund (☎063/13 91 00; ②) is a ten-minute walk from the train station at Södra Gröngatan 36 in the town centre. More atmospheric is the **hostel** at Jamtli (☎063/10 59 84; ②; take bus #2 to the end of the line) – although slightly more expensive, staying there saves on entrance fees to the museum. **Campers** can stay at either *Östersunds Camping*, 2km down Rådhusgatan (☎063/14 46 15), or on Frösön island at *Frösö Camping* (☎063/14 46 15; early June to early Aug; bus #3 or #4 from the centre). For **food**, try the young and trendy *Brunkullans* restaurant with its outdoor garden at Postgränd 5, or the daily specials at the Australian *Captain Cook*, Hamngatan 9 – cheaper than *Brunkullans*, with live entertainment on Wednesdays, and very popular for **drinking** too.

Storuman, Sorsele, Arvidsjaur and the Arctic Circle

Travelling on the Inlandsbanan, you may well spend the night at **STORUMAN**, five hours north of Östersund and ten hours from Gällivare. The **tourist office** (mid-June to mid-Aug Mon–Fri 9am–8pm, Sat & Sun 11am–5pm; rest of year Mon–Fri 9am–5pm; ☎0951/105 00, *entrelappland@swipnet.se*) is just to the right of the train station, and will give you details of the excellent mountain hiking to be had around the town. There's a **hostel** in the same building as the tourist office (☎0951/777 00; ②). **SORSELE** is the next major stop on the Inlandsbanan, a pint-sized town that became a cause célèbre among conservationists in Sweden, pushing the government to abandon its plans to regulate the flow of the River Vindel here by building a hydroelectric station. It remains wild, untouched and seething with rapids, with a **campsite** on the river bank. There's also a **hostel** (☎0952/100 10; ②), a small place open from mid-June to August. **ARVIDSJAUR** contains Sweden's oldest surviving Sami village, dating from the late eighteenth century, a huddle of houses that was once the centre of a great winter market. They were not meant to be permanent homes, but rather a meeting place during festivals, and the last weekend in August is still taken up by a great celebratory shindig. There's a cosy private **hostel** at Västra Skolgatan 9 (☎0960/124 13; ②), and *Camp Gielas*, beside one of the lakes 1km south of the station, has cabins from 375kr. A couple of hours north of Arvidsjaur the Inlandsbanan finally crosses the **Arctic Circle**, signalled by a bout of whistle-blowing as the train pulls up. Painted white rocks curve away over the hilly ground, a crude but popular representation of the Circle.

Jokkmokk

In the midst of remote, densely forested, marshy country, **JOKKMOKK** is a welcome oasis. Once wintertime Sami quarters, the town is today a renowned handicraft centre, with a Sami high school keeping the language and culture alive. The **ájtte Museum** (mid-June to Aug daily 9am–6pm; rest of year Mon–Fri 10am–4pm, Sat & Sun noon–4pm; Oct–April closed Sat; 40kr) on Kyrkegatan is the place to see some of the intricate work. Have a glance, too, at the so-called **Lapp Kyrka**, in which corpses were interned in wall vaults during winter, waiting for the thaw when the Sami could go out and dig graves – the temperatures in this part of Sweden plunge below -35°C in winter. The great **winter market** still survives, now nearly 400 years old, held on the first Thursday, Friday and Saturday of each February, when 30,000 people gather in town. It's the best time to be in Jokkmokk, and staying means booking accommodation a good six months in advance. A smaller, less traditional autumn fair at the end of August is an easier though poorer option. The **tourist office** is at Stortorget 4 (mid-June to mid-Aug daily 9am–7pm; during winter market Thurs–Sun 8am–6pm; rest of year Thurs–Sat 8.30am–4pm; ☎0971 121 40, *www.jokkmokk.se/turism*). In summer there should be no problem getting a place at the HI **hostel** at Åsgatan 20 (☎0971/559 77; ①); just follow the signs from the station. The **campsite** is 3km east on route 97.

Gällivare

GÄLLIVARE is one of Europe's most important sources of iron ore, while Europe's largest open-cast copper mine sears the landscape 20km to the south, its gargantuan bucket-shovels and dump trucks just dots 250m down. The tourist office ferries trips to the **iron ore mines** (mid-June to Aug Mon–Fri 9.30am & 1.30pm; 160kr) and **copper mine** (June–Aug Mon–Fri 2pm; 160kr). Astounding statistics – 300 tonnes of high explosives are used for each blast – pepper the tour, which also takes in **Kåkstan**, a rebuilt shantytown on the site of the original iron ore mine; and you stop long enough to sample local delicacies like reindeer, salmon and lingonberry juice, all for 75kr at *Café Endast för Nyktra*. There's not much to Gällivare itself. Little remains of the seventeenth-century Sami village, and the river and surrounding mountains are really the nicest feature of the town. You can walk up to **Björnfällän**, a four-kilometre hike on a well-marked path – the views are magnificent. Buses make the journey (160kr return) to the summit 3km north beyond Björnfällan to see the Midnight Sun daily between mid-June and mid-July. Buses leave from the train station at 11pm, returning at 1am.

The **tourist office** is at Storgatan 16 (June to mid-Aug Mon–Fri 9am–8pm, Sat & Sun 10am–6pm; rest of year Mon–Fri 9am–4pm; ☎0970/166 60, *www.gellivare.se*). Its long summer hours are aimed at late Inlandsbanan arrivals, and the office has a café downstairs and a museum upstairs dealing with Sami history. The **youth hostel** (☎0970/143 80; ②) is at Barnhemsvägen 2, behind the train station, and offers accommodation in small two-person cabins (no bed linen provided), though there are a few three and four bed cabins too. There's also a small private hostel, *Lapphärbärget* (☎0970/125 34; ②), next to the Lappkyrkan by the river, and a **hotel**, the *Dundret*, Per Högströmsgatan 1 (☎0970/145 60; ⑤), close to the station. The **campsite** (☎ 0970 100 10) is by the river; for **snacks** or an evening coffee and cakes by the river, make for the *Strand Kaféet* near the campsite at Malmbergsvägen 2, beside some relocated vernacular buildings and a few captive reindeer.

travel details

Trains

Stockholm to: Gällivare (2 daily; 16hr); Gävle (hourly; 1hr 20min); Gothenburg (21 daily; 3hr 10min by X2000, 4hr 30min InterCity); Helsingborg (14 daily; 5hr by X2000, 6hr 30min InterCity); Kalmar, change at Alvesta (8 Mon–Sat, 3 Sun; 6hr); Lund (6 daily; 4hr 40min); Malmö (11 daily; 4hr 30 min by X2000); Mora (11 daily; 3hr 30min by X2000); Narvik (2 daily; 20hr); Östersund (6 daily; 6hr); Sundsvall (9 daily; 3hr 30min by X2000); Uppsala (half hourly; 40min).

Gällivare to: Narvik (2 daily; 4hr 40min).

Gothenburg to: Copenhagen (2–3 daily; 4hr 20min); Helsingborg (6–9 daily; 2hr 40min); Kalmar (3–5 daily; 4hr 40min); Lund (6–9 daily; 3hr 30min); Malmö (8–12 daily; 3hr by X2000, 3hr 45min InterCity); Oslo (4 daily; 4hr 40min).

Malmö to: Helsingborg (at least hourly; 50min); Lund (at least hourly; 15min); Ystad (Mon–Fri hourly, Sat & Sun 4–6 daily; 50min).

Sundsvall to: Gävle (8 daily; 2hr 30min); Östersund (5 daily; 2hr 15min).

Uppsala to: Gävle (hourly; 40 min); Mora (11 daily; 2hr 15min by X2000).

Buses

Stockholm to: Gävle (3 Fri, 1 Sat, 4 Sun; 2hr 20min); Gothenburg (2–5 daily; 4hr 30min, or 7hr 20min via Jönköping); Helsingborg (1 daily, 2 Fri & Sun; 8hr); Kalmar (2–5 daily; 6hr 30min); Malmö (1 Fri, 1 Sun; 10hr 20min); Nynäshamn (3 daily; 1hr); Oskarshamn (2–5 daily; 4hr 30min); Oslo (1 Fri, 1 Sun; 9hr); Sundsvall (3 Fri, 1 Sat, 4 Sun; 6hr); Uppsala (3 Fri, 1 Sat, 4 Sun; 1hr).

Gothenburg to: Gävle (1–2 daily; 10hr); Kalmar (1 Fri, 1 Sun; 6hr 30min); Malmö (3 Fri, 3 Sun; 4hr 40min); Oslo (3–4 daily; 4hr 50min); Uppsala (1 Fri, 1 Sun; 8hr).

Ferries

Nynäshamn to: Visby (mid-June to mid-Aug 3 daily; 5hr by day, 6hr by night).

Oskarshamn to: Visby (mid-June to mid-Aug 1 daily; 4hr by day, 6hr by night).

International ferries

Stockholm to: Helsinki (Helsingsfors), Finland (2 daily; 15hr); Tallinn (summer 1 daily plus 1 every 2 days; 15hr); Turku (Åbo), Finland (4 daily; 13hr).

Gothenburg to: Frederikshavn (4–8 daily; 3hr 15min); Harwich (April–Oct 4 weekly; 24hr); Newcastle (mid-June to mid-Aug 1 weekly; 24hr); Kiel (1 daily; 14hr).

Helsingborg to: Helsingor (3 hourly; 25min).

Malmö to: Copenhagen (every 30min; 40min).

Trelleborg to: Rostock (3 daily; 6hr); Travämunde (2 daily; 7–9hr).

CHAPTER 29

SWITZERLAND
AND LIECHTENSTEIN

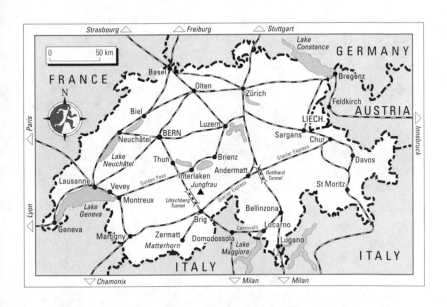

Introduction

Switzerland is one of Europe's most visited countries, but one of its least understood. Pass through for a day or two, as most people do, and you'll get the quaint stereotype of Switzerland that the locals deem suitable for public consumption – the Alpine idyll of cheese and chocolate, Heidi and the Matterhorn. Stay longer though and another Switzerland will emerge, the one which the Swiss inhabit, and one which can be an infinitely more rewarding place to explore. Sights are breathtaking, transport links are excellent, costs are no higher than in Britain or Germany, and the locals are unfailingly courteous. Almost everyone speaks some English along with at least one of the official Swiss languages (German, French, Italian, or, in the southeast, Romansh).

Notoriously placid these days, Switzerland nonetheless spent the first five hundred years of its existence rent by conflict, and fought a civil war as recently as 1847. The Swiss Confederation (abbreviated in Latin to **"CH"**) dates back to 1291, when Alpine peasants formed an alliance to defend themselves against the Hapsburgs. By the early 1500s, the Confederation had grown into a military superpower feared throughout Europe. It was only with the Reformation that the Swiss began to earn their reputation for neutrality, a reputation which served them well right through into the boom years after World War II. In the 1990s, the country's image was tainted, as exposés uncovered Swiss banks' dubious wartime collusion with the Nazis. Public soul-searching in the aftermath of the scandal is heralding Switzerland's first tentative steps towards ending its dogged isolation and joining the EU and the UN.

As for **where to go**, Switzerland invented tourism: the country's breathtaking scenery has drawn travellers since the early 1800s. The most visited Alpine area is the central **Bernese Oberland**, which has the highest concentration of picturesque peaks and mountainside villages, although the loftiest Alps are further south, where the small but crowded resort of **Zermatt** provides access to the country's most distinctive mountain, the Toblerone-peaked **Matterhorn**. In the southeastern corner of the country, wild, thickly forested mountain slopes provide the setting for the world-famous resorts of **St Moritz** and **Davos**. Of the northern German-speaking cities, **Zürich** has a wealth of sightseeing and nightlife possibilities and provides easy access to the tiny independent principality of **Liechtenstein** overlooking the Rhine. **Basel** and especially the capital **Bern** are quieter, each with an attractive historic core, while **Luzern** is in an appealing setting close to lakes and mountains. In the French-speaking west, the cities lining the northern shore of Lake Geneva – notably **Geneva** itself, and **Lausanne** – make up the heart of **Suisse-Romande**. South of the Alps, sunny, Italian-speaking **Ticino** can seem a world apart from the rest of the country, particularly the palm-fringed lakeside resorts of **Lugano** and **Locarno**, with their Mediterranean, riviera atmosphere.

Information and maps

Almost all towns have a **tourist office** (*Verkehrsverein* or *Tourismus*; *Office du Tourisme*; *Ente Turistico*), invariably located beside or opposite the train station and always extremely useful. Most staff speak English and are scrupulously helpful, but opening hours in smaller towns allow for a long lunch and can be limited at weekends and in the off-season. All of them have lists of local accommodation and transport information, and provide local and regional **maps**. The Federal Office of Topography (*www.swisstopo.ch*) has excellent 1:50,000 and 1:25,000 walkers' maps.

Money and banks

The currency of Switzerland and Liechtenstein is the **Swiss franc** (Schweizer Franken, francs suisses, franchi svizzeri; Sfr). Each franc is divided into 100 Rappen (Rp), centimes or centisimi (c). There are coins of 5c, 10c, 20c, 50c, Sfr1, Sfr2 and Sfr5, and notes of Sfr10, Sfr20, Sfr50, Sfr100, Sfr200 and Sfr1000. Train stations are the best places for **changing money**; almost all have a commission-free change counter that is open long hours. You can also change money at banks, which are usually open Mon–Fri 8.30am–4.30pm (small-town branches often close noon–2pm). Some city and tourist resort banks open Sat 9am–4pm, although times vary. Post offices

---

give a similar exchange rate to banks, and **ATMs** are everywhere.

Communications

Post offices tend to open Mon–Fri 7.30am–noon & 1.30–6.30pm, Sat 8–11am, although watch out for regional variations and restricted hours in smaller branches. It costs Sfr1.10 to send a postcard to Europe, Sfr1.80 worldwide. **Public phones** are operated by Swisscom; a few still accept coins, but the majority take only phonecards (*taxcards*), available from post offices, newsagents and vending machines in Sfr5, Sfr10 and Sfr20 denominations. Phones that take phonecards also accept credit cards. Many news kiosks and train stations also sell good-value cards from other companies (such as diAx) for calling internationally. The expensive operator is on ☎111 (domestic) and ☎1141 (international); directory enquiries is on ☎1159. You can use Swisscom phonecards in Liechtenstein.

For **Internet access**, there are cybercafés in all towns (Sfr8–13/hr), and you'll also find access at some hostels, main train stations and for free at the airports. You can send a short **email** from the screens in all phonebooths for Sfr0.90, but you can't pick up any email this way. The same screens let you send an SMS **text message** to any mobile phone for Sfr0.90.

Getting around

The efficiency of the massively comprehensive Swiss **public transport** system remains one of the wonders of the modern world. Services depart on the dot, and train timetables are well integrated with those of the postbus system, which operates on rural routes not covered by trains.

■ Trains and buses

Travelling through Switzerland by **train** is invariably comfortable, hassle-free and extremely scenic, with many mountain routes an attraction in their own right. The main network, run by SBB CFF FFS (Schweizerische Bundesbahnen, Chemins de Fer Fédéraux, Ferrovie Federali Svizzere), covers much of the country, but many routes, especially Alpine lines, are operated by the smaller companies which pioneered them a century or more ago.

Main stations keep a public copy of the national **timetable**, which covers all rail, bus, boat and cable-car services. The national enquiry number is ☎0900/300 300, and *www.rail.ch* has complete information.

InterRail (also EuroDomino) and Eurail pass-holders get free travel on SBB and most smaller lines, but only patchy discounts on boats, cable cars and mountain railways (specified in the text as **IR** for InterRail and **ER** for Eurail), and no discounts on buses or city trams. The **Swiss Pass** (**SP**), available from Swiss tourist offices at home or main stations in Switzerland, allows free travel on virtually all trains, buses and boats, as well as on most city tram and bus networks; discounts apply on cable cars, mountain railways and bike rental. A Swiss Pass for 4/8 consecutive days costs Sfr230/320, with discounts for two or more people travelling together. The **Swiss Flexi-pass** gives 3/4/5 days' travel in a month with the same benefits as the Swiss Pass for Sfr220/260/300. The **Swiss Half-Fare Card** (Sfr95) gets fifty percent off all trains, buses, boats and most city trams for a month. If you plan to concentrate on one region, check out the relevant tourist office's **regional pass**, typically giving five days' travel in fifteen with discounts for the other ten days. If you're under 25, you can pay Sfr249 for a **Track 7** card which gives a year's travel nationwide after 7pm plus half-price travel before 7pm.

Buses take over where train track runs out. These are generally yellow **postbuses** (*www.post.ch*), which invariably depart from train station forecourts. They're free to holders of all Swiss passes (although certain Alpine routes command a Sfr5–10 supplement, along with advance seat reservation), but full-price to Eurailers and InterRailers.

■ Boats

All of Switzerland's bigger lakes are crossed by **ferry services** of one sort or another. Most run only dur-

---

THE SWISS MUSEUM PASSPORT

If you are thinking of doing some sightseeing in Switzerland, the **Swiss Museum Passport** gives free entry to some 250 museums, galleries and castles around the country for a month. It costs Sfr30 (students Sfr25) from tourist offices or member museums, and can easily pay for itself in a weekend of gallery-hopping. Consult *www.museums.ch/pass* for more.

ing the summer season (June–Sept), and duplicate routes which can be covered more cheaply and quickly by rail. But if you have the time, cruising through the Alpine foothills to Interlaken or between villages on the Lake Geneva shoreline beats the equivalent train journeys hands down.

■ Driving, hitching and cycling

Switzerland's **road network** is comprehensive and well planned, and although the mountainous terrain can make for some circuitous routes there is, of course, the compensation of impressively scenic mountain drives. **Speed limits** are 50kph in built-up areas, 80kph on main roads and 120kph on motorways. To drive on motorways (signposted in green) you must pay Sfr40 for a *vignette* or tax disc, which is valid for a year and available from Swiss tourist offices abroad, at every border-post and most petrol stations. It's easy, though, to stick to main roads (signposted in blue), which are fast and free. The Touring Club Suisse (*www.tcs.ch*) operates a 24-hour breakdown service on ☎140. **Car rental** costs upwards of Sfr130/day for unlimited kilometrage, or about Sfr750/week. Most firms require the driver to be over 21.

Hitching is feasible on the main routes linking the cities of the north and east, or on a through-trip to the south, but the really scenic bits of Switzerland are so widely scattered that it's usually difficult to get a direct ride. The risks attached to hitching are the same as in any country.

Given the nature of the landscape, **cycling** is not the easiest way of exploring the country, but the scenery often more than compensates for the extra effort required. It's a popular Swiss pursuit, especially along valley floors and around lakes; there are nine national long-distance cycle routes, and bike-lanes abound in cities. Tourist offices can give you a map showing routes. You can **rent** a brand-new country- or mountain-bike at over 130 train stations nationwide for Sfr27 per day, Sfr21 if you hold a Swiss travel pass, less for a half-day. For an extra Sfr7 you can pick the bike up at one station and drop it off at another (this charge is waived on rentals of two days or more). It's always a good idea to reserve a few days ahead at any train station or online (*www.rent-a-bike.ch*). The city councils of Zurich, Geneva and Bern also operate free or cut-price bike-rental schemes (ask at tourist offices), and some HI hostels rent bikes for Sfr15/day. You can take a bike on regional/InterCity trains for Sfr6/12, but many people take the sweat-free option of going by train into the high Alps, then renting a bike at the top station and freewheeling the whole way down again.

■ Adventure sports

With its landscape of mountains, glaciers, deep gorges and fast-flowing rivers, Switzerland is ideal territory for **adventure sports**. Dozens of companies based in all the main resorts operate thrill-making schemes galore, mostly in summer only (typical prices are in brackets): canyoning (half-day Sfr100), river-rafting (the same), bungee-jumping (from 100m Sfr80; 150m Sfr150; 180m Sfr220), zorbing (where you're strapped inside a giant plastic sphere and rolled down a mountainside; Sfr50), house-running (where you hook a rope round yourself and run full-tilt down the side of a tall building; Sfr70), flying fox (where you glide down a vertical cliff on a rope; Sfr75), and more. Hang-gliding (Sfr130), paragliding (Sfr170) and skydiving from 4000m (Sfr400) can all be done alone or in tandem with an instructor. Two main centres for adventure sports are Interlaken and Luzern; you generally book at the company's office in advance, then get bussed out to their preferred site in the mountains and back into town afterwards. Local tourist offices always have full information.

Accommodation

Accommodation is expensive, but nearly always excellent. Tourist offices can generally book rooms for free in their area, and they normally have a dis-

---

ACCOMMODATION PRICE CODES

Throughout this guide, accommodation is coded on a scale of ① to ⑨, the code indicating the lowest price per person per night you could expect to pay in each establishment in high season. With hostels this is the nightly rate per person; with hotels, the price is arrived at by dividing the cost of the cheapest double room by two. The prices indicated by the codes are as follows:

① under £5/$8	④ £15–20/$24–32	⑦ £30–35/$48–56
② £5–10/$8–16	⑤ £20–25/$32–40	⑧ £35–40/$56–64)
③ £10–15/$16–24	⑥ £25–30/$40–48	⑨ £40/$64 and over

play-board on the street with details of the region's hotels, often with a courtesy phone. In many cases you'll find these boards at train stations. When you check in, you should always ask for a **guest card** (*Gästekarte, carte des visiteurs, tessera di soggiorno*): these can give substantial discounts on local attractions and transport.

■ Hotels

Just about every Swiss settlement above hamlet-size offers a choice of **hotels**, where accommodation is of a uniformly high standard, and not excessively expensive. Consult the Swiss Hotel Association at *www.swisshotels.ch* for a list of approved establishments, and occasional offers. A good low-price chain is E&G Budget Hotels (*www.rooms.ch*), who have 150 places around the country, mostly in towns. In general, double rooms with a shared shower and toilet start at about Sfr85; only hostels offer cheaper doubles, and a more usual hotel average is Sfr110. En-suite hotel rooms cost from around Sfr135.

■ Hostels and campsites

If you're travelling on a budget, a **hostel** (*Jugendherberge; Auberge de Jeunesse; Albergo/Ostello per la Gioventù*) is likely to be your accommodation of choice; Switzerland has an extensive network, with most places offering very good value. You should definitely book ahead between June and September. **HI hostels** (*www.youthhostel.ch*) are of a universally high standard and feature a good proportion of double rooms as well as small dorms. Prices range from Sfr19 to Sfr40; the average is Sfr25 for a dorm bed including breakfast and bedding. Non-HI members pay Sfr5 extra. Note that under-25s are given priority and that there's usually a three-night maximum stay during summer in the towns. Meals, where available, are around Sfr10. A rival group known as **Swiss Backpackers** (*www.backpacker.ch*) has lively hostels that are less institutional, often in prime locations in the town and city centres, and are priced to compete; they're specified in the text as "**SB**" hostels. Their excellent *Swiss Backpacker Newspaper*, packed with information, is widely available. Outside the towns and cities, **Naturfreunde** hostels are a good budget option, located in wilder rural areas well off any beaten tracks (*www.naturfreunde.ch*).

The typical Swiss **campsite** is clean and well equipped, although the higher the altitude the more limited the opening times; many close altogether outside the summer season (June–Sept). Prices tend to be around Sfr8 per person plus Sfr8–12 per pitch and per vehicle. Many sites require an international camping carnet. Camping outside official sites is against the law. For those hiking in the mountains there's a network of Swiss Alpine Club **huts**, where dorm beds cost around Sfr30 per night (*www.sac-cas.ch*).

Food and drink

Food and drink can inflict a fairly massive hole in your budget if you're not careful. Prices are high across the board, although by combining a judicious choice of eateries with forays into picnicking and self-catering you can manage fine on a tight budget without any compromise on nutrition.

■ Food

Dairy products – cheese, milk, cream, butter and/or yoghurt – find their way into most Swiss dishes. All but a handful of places offer **vegetarian** set menus, but veggies should be aware that most restaurants default onto standard meat-based dishes: fresh salads may come layered with cold meats. Co-operative-run diners, many located in squats in the major cities, offer budget vegetarian and vegan meals as standard.

Burgers, pizza slices, kebabs and falafels are universal **snack** standbys. You'll also find various different kinds of sausage (*Wurst, saucisse, salsiccia*) served as chargrilled fast food; the most popular are pork *Bratwürste*. **Cheese fondue** – a pot of fragrant wine-laced molten cheese into which you dip cubes of bread or potato – is the national dish. It's usually priced as a two-person (or more) deal, or as an all-you-can-eat deal, dubbed *à discrétion* or *à gogo*. Another speciality is *raclette*, where piquant molten cheese is spread on a plate and scooped up with bread or potato. Lakeside resorts nationwide offer fresh trout and perch. A Swiss-German staple is **Rösti**, grated potatoes fried to a golden-brown hash and often topped with cheese, chopped ham or a fried egg. *Älpler Magrone* is macaroni cheese with extra onion, bacon, potatoes and cream. *Käseschnitten* is toasted cheese. In and around Bern, you'll find *Berneteller* or *Bernerplatte*, a hefty pile of cold and hot meats with sauerkraut; Zurich has *Gschnetzlets*, diced veal in a creamy mushroom sauce; Luzern has *Chögalipaschtetli*, a large puff-pastry shell also filled with creamy diced veal. Ticinese eateries specialize in home made gnocchi, risotto and polenta.

The line between a **café** and a **restaurant** is blurred: either can do you a meal, although usually at set times (mostly noon–2pm & 6–10pm), with only snacks available in between. The key to avoiding expense in these places is to make lunch your main meal, and always to plump for the dish of the day (*Tagesmenu, Tagesteller, Tageshit, plat/assiette du jour, piatto del giorno*) – often substantial, quality nosh for Sfr15 or less. The same meal in the evening, or choosing *à la carte* anytime, can cost double, although beerhalls in the German-speaking cities often serve hearty inexpensive evening meals, and pizza-pasta joints and simple diners can fill your stomach for Sfr15–20. Chain department stores in town centres nationwide invariably have surprisingly good **self-service diners** attached, where pick-and-choose meals can amount to just Sfr13; Manora (aka Placette or Inova) is usually best, followed by Migros, EPA and Coop. Most of these places let you pay Sfr6/10 for a small/large plate, with no limit on the quantity of fresh salad or hot daily special you can pile onto it, and some offer a twenty-percent discount to students. Migros is also the biggest chain of **supermarkets**, while Aperto are small deli-style outlets with long opening hours located at main train stations. Watch out for *sinalco* or *alkohol-frei* restaurants, as well as the widespread lack of smoking restrictions.

■ Drink

Cafés are open from breakfast until about midnight/1am and often sell alcohol; **bars** and pubs tend to open their doors for late-afternoon and evening business only. Daytime places for tea and cakes are dubbed **tearooms**. Other than pubs, drinking venues vary according to region. A cosy *Bierstube* or *Stübli* – replete with wood-beams and Swiss kitsch decor – is the evening meeting-place of choice throughout German-speaking Switzerland, while in Romandie and Ticino pavement cafés are more common. Table service is ubiquitous, except at the English or Irish pubs gracing most towns. Local **beers** vary between regions and are invariably excellent, costing Sfr3–4 for a third of a litre. A beer-lemonade shandy is a *panaché*. Even the simplest bars and restaurants have **wine**, most affordably as *Offene Wein, vin ouvert, vino aperto*, a handful of house reds and whites chalked up on a board and sold by the decilitre (small glass Sfr3–5). Premier Swiss wines are the Valais whites (Fendant) and reds (Dôle). Also look out for local spirits/liquors (*Schnapps, eau-de-vie, aquavite*), including cherry *Kirsch*, aromatic pear *Williamine*, and excellent Ticinese *grappa*.

Opening hours and holidays

Shop **opening hours** are customarily Mon–Fri 9am–noon & 2–6.30pm, Sat 8.30am–noon, although it's becoming more common in the cities to ignore the lunch break and stay open on Saturday until 4pm; the flipside is that many places take Monday morning off. Most shops now have one day of late-opening, often Thursday until 9pm; those in the subterranean malls at train stations are open daily, and close later. Most big-city stations also have 24-hour vending machines dispensing loaves of bread, cheese and cartons of milk. Museums and attractions are often open on Sundays, but virtually all are closed on Mondays.

Almost everything is closed on the following **public holidays**: Jan 1; Good Friday & Easter Monday (March 29 & 31); Ascension Day (May 9); Whit Monday (May 18); Dec 25 & 26. In Switzerland, shops and banks tend to close for all or part of Swiss National Day (Aug 1) and on a range of local holidays as well. As well as the above, Liechtenstein keeps May 1 as a public holiday, and Aug 15 as the national holiday.

Emergencies

Compared to most Europeans, the Swiss are scrupulously law-abiding, rendering even the minimal **police** presence superfluous. Regarding **health problems**, the E111 is valid in Liechtenstein but not in Switzerland, so you must have private insurance. Virtually every hospital (*Spital, hôpital, ospedale*) has some kind of 24-hour service, although you will have to pay hefty medical bills upfront and claim expenses back later; make sure you keep full receipts and doctors' reports. Every district has a rota system whereby one local **pharmacy** (*Apotheke, pharmacie, farmacia*) stays open outside normal shopping hours. Each pharmacy will have a sign in the window telling you where the nearest open one is. Local newspapers also have details.

Emergency Numbers
Police ☎117; Fire ☎118; Ambulance ☎144.

SUISSE-ROMANDE

French-speaking Switzerland, or **Suisse-Romande**, occupies the western third of the country, comprising the shores of Lake Geneva and the hills and lakes leading north almost to Basel. The ambience here is thoroughly Gallic: historical animosity between Calvinist Geneva and Catholic France has nowadays given way to a yearning on the part of most francophone Swiss to abandon their bumpkin compatriots in the east and embrace the EU. The short train-ride from the Swiss-German cities of the Mittelland crosses more than just a linguistic boundary – it seems to span a whole continent of attitude.

Geneva, at the southwestern tip of **Lake Geneva** (Lac Léman in French) was once a haven for free-thinkers from all over Europe; now it's a city of diplomats and big business. Halfway around the lake, **Lausanne** is full of young people, an energetic, funky town acclaimed as the skateboarding capital of Europe. Further east, the lakeshore is lined with vineyards and opulent villas – **Montreux** is particularly chic – although you can still taste the unspoilt paradise, evoked by the stunning medieval **Château de Chillon**, which drew Byron and the Romantic poets and which inspired Mary Shelley to write *Frankenstein*. Mont Blanc, Western Europe's highest mountain (4807m), is visible from Geneva city centre, while Montreux and neighbouring **Vevey** have breathtaking views across the water to the French Alps. On a sunny day, the train ride around the vineyard-rich northern shore is memorably scenic, but taking advantage of the lake's excellent **boat** service (IR no discount; ER & SP free; *www.cgn.ch*) will help bring home the full grandeur of the setting.

Geneva

The Puritanism of **GENEVA** (Genève in French) is inextricably linked with the city's struggle for independence. Long ruled by the dukes of Savoy, who regarded the local bishopric as their private property, sixteenth-century Genevans saw the Reformation in neighbouring Switzerland as a useful aid in their struggle to rid themselves of Savoyard influence. By the time the city's independence was won in 1602, its religious zeal had painted it as the "Protestant Rome". What continues to be known today as the Republic and Canton of Geneva remained outside the Swiss Confederation until 1815 (the Catholic cantons opposed its entry), and acquired a reputation for joylessness which it still struggles to shake off. Today, it's a working city that remains sharply focused on its prominent role in international diplomacy and big business. Time and effort are needed to penetrate the facade of money and power.

Arrival, information and accommodation

The main **train station**, Gare de Cornavin, lies at the head of Rue du Mont-Blanc in the city centre. Expresses from Paris and Lyon arrive in a separate French section (passport control), but local French trains from Annecy/Chamonix terminate at Gare des Eaux-Vives on the east side of town (tram #12 or #16 into the centre). From the **airport**, 5km northwest, trains and bus #10 run regularly into the city. The international **bus station** is on Place Dorcière in the centre. The **tourist office** is in the main post office at 18 Rue du Mont-Blanc (Mon–Sat 9am–6pm; ☎022/909 70 00, *www.geneva-tourism.ch*); pick up the weekly **listings** magazine *Genève Agenda*, and the excellent *Info-Jeunes* brochure, geared towards budget travellers. There's also an information office on the Pont de la Machine (Mon noon–6pm, Tues–Fri 9am–6pm, Sat 10am–5pm; ☎022/311 99 70, *www.ville-ge.ch*), and a CAR info-bus parked at the Mont-Blanc exit of the train station (mid-June to early Sept daily 9am–11pm; ☎022/731 46 47). There are dozens of city **tours**, including self-guided strolls by Walkman (deposit Sfr50), guided walks (Sfr12; mostly June–Oct), and scenic boat trips (lake cruises from Sfr11; downriver journey Sfr22). Local **trams** and **buses** cost Sfr2.20 (1hr) or Sfr5 (24hr).

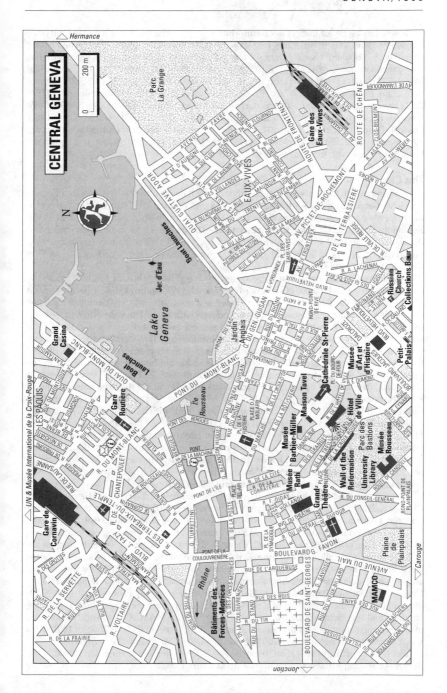

Geneva has plenty of budget **accommodation** – ask at the tourist office about cut-price multi-night deals. Their brochure *Info-Jeunes* lists 21 **hostels**, eight of them women-only, including the popular *Home St-Pierre*, 4 Cour St-Pierre (beside the cathedral), which now has one dorm for men (☎022/310 37 07; ③). The bustling HI hostel, 30 Rue Rothschild (☎022/732 62 60, *www.yh-geneva.ch*; ③), is spotless, as is the SB *City Hostel*, 2 Rue Ferrier (☎022/901 15 00, *www.cityhostel.ch*; ③). *Cité Universitaire*, 46 Avenue Miremont (☎022/839 22 22, *www.unige.ch/cite-uni*; ③), has dorms and cut-price rooms. Of cheaper **hotels**, *De la Cloche*, 6 Rue de la Cloche (☎022/732 94 81, *www.smpage.ch/cloche*; ⑤), and *St Victor*, 1 Rue François-LeFort (☎022/346 17 18; ⑤), are quiet and characterful. Best **campsite** is *Camping d'Hermance* (☎022/751 14 83; closed Oct–March; bus #E), 14km northeast, just before the French frontier – with free lake access.

The City

Genevans orientate their city around the Rhône, which flows from the lake west into France. The **Rive Gauche**, on the south bank, takes in a grid of waterfront streets which comprise the main shopping and business districts and the adjacent high ground of the Old Town. Behind the grand hotels lining the northern **Rive Droite** waterfront is the main station and the cosmopolitan (and sometimes sleazy) Les Pâquis district, filled with cheap restaurants. Further north are the offices of the dozens of international organizations headquartered in Geneva, including the UN.

On the Rive Gauche, beyond the ornamental flowerbeds of the **Jardin Anglais**, erupts the roaring 140-metre-high plume of Geneva's trademark **Jet d'Eau**. Immediately beside Pont du Mont-Blanc, **Île de Rousseau** bears a seated statue of the eighteenth-century Genevan philosopher Jean-Jacques Rousseau. Three blocks downriver, the **Pont de l'Île** boasts a thirteenth-century tower, from where Rue de la Monnaie leads up to the main thoroughfare of the Old Town, the cobbled, steeply ascending **Grande Rue**. Here, among the secondhand bookshops and galleries, you'll find the atmospheric seventeenth-century **Hôtel de Ville** and the arcaded **armoury**, backed by a lovely terrace with the longest wooden bench in the world (126m). A few steps north is **Maison Tavel**, 6 Rue Puits-St-Pierre (Tues–Sun 10am–5pm; free; *mah.ville-ge.ch*), an old patrician house containing the town museum and an impressive model of Geneva circa 1850. A block away is the huge late-Romanesque **Cathedral** (Mon–Sat 9/10am–5/7pm, Sun 11am–5/7pm), with an incongruous eighteenth-century portal and a plain, soaring interior. The frescoes of the internal Chapelle des Maccabées, with their intricate floral patterns and lute-strumming angels, are modern versions of the faded fifteenth-century originals now in Geneva's main museum. Round the corner is the hub of the Old Town, **Place du Bourg-de-Four**, a picturesque split-level square perched on the hillside and ringed by cafés. Alleys wind down from here to the university park and its austere **Wall of the Reformation** (1909–17) alongside busy Place Neuve.

A few metres east of the Old Town is the gigantic **Musée d'Art et d'Histoire**, 2 Rue Charles Galland (Tues–Sun 10am–5pm; free; *mah.ville-ge.ch*). Upstairs are three stunning sculptures – a graceful *Venus and Adonis* by Canova and two powerful pieces by Rodin. The fine-art collection is crowned by Konrad Witz's famous altarpiece, made for the cathedral in 1444, showing Christ and the fishermen transposed onto Lake Geneva. Other highlights are by local artist Félix Vallotton; Cézanne, Renoir and Modigliani; and some striking blue Swiss landscapes by Bern-born Symbolist Ferdinand Hodler. The basement holds the massive archeological collection, including Egyptian mummies and Greek and Roman statuary. Nearby is the astonishing **Collections Baur**, 8 Rue Munier-Romilly (Tues–Sun 2–6pm; Sfr5), the country's premier collection of East Asian art, featuring luminescent yellow Yongzhang ceramics and spectacular porcelain and jade. Make time for **MAMCO**, a top-quality museum of modern and contemporary art housed in an old factory west of the Old Town at 10 Rue des Vieux-Grenadiers (Tues noon–9pm, Wed–Sun noon–6pm; Sfr9; *mamco-ge.tripod.com*).

About 1km north of the station, opposite the UN complex on Avenue de la Paix, is the thought-provoking **Musée International de la Croix-Rouge** (Red Cross Museum; Mon &

Wed–Sun 10am–5pm; Sfr10; *www.micr.ch*; bus #8 or #F to Appia), which documents the origins, growth and achievements of the organization without resorting to self-congratulation. Carefully chosen audiovisual material combines with quietly dramatic exhibits – such as the 34 footprints in a tiny cell-space where a Red Cross delegate found 17 people crammed together – to leave a powerful impression.

Twenty minutes south of the centre by tram #12 lies the late-Baroque suburb of **CAROUGE**, built by the king of Sardinia in the eighteenth century as a separate town. Its low Italianate houses and leafy lanes are now largely occupied by fashion designers and small galleries, and the area's reputation as an outpost of tolerance and hedonism beyond Geneva's jurisdiction lives on in its numerous cafés and music bars. Carouge hosts a colourful **market** on Wednesdays and Saturdays; the flea market at Plainpalais, near Geneva's Old Town, is also worth a browse.

Eating, drinking and nightlife

Central Geneva has plenty of cafés and bars offering lunchtime *plats du jour*, as well as inexpensive evening **food**. The smoky upstairs bar in the L'Usine squat, a young people's cultural centre on Place des Volontaires, offers meals for Sfr10; *Le Zofage*, 6 Rue des Voisins, is a university cafeteria open to non-students; and *Manora*, 4 Rue de Cornavin, is a high-quality self-service restaurant with plentiful vegetarian selections and meals from Sfr12. *Café Gallay*, 42 Boulevard St Georges, is a friendly neighbourhood café/bar; *Al-Amir*, 12 Rue des Alpes, does excellent Lebanese kebabs and falafel (from Sfr7); budget veggies are equally well served at *Hang-Zhou*, 19 Rue de la Couluvrenière (Chinese) and *Jeck's*, 14 Rue de Neuchâtel (Thai) – both offer Sfr15 lunches. *Au Petit Chalet*, 17 Rue de Berne, is the least pretentious place for Swiss cuisine; *Spaghetti Factory*, 13 Rue de la Fontaine, for Italian. As for **drinking**, Place du Bourg-de-Four's pavement cafés are packed during the day. In the Old Town, *Flanagan's*, 4 Rue de Cheval Blanc, is an Irish pub with live music (Thurs–Sat). In Carouge *Le Chat Noir*, 13 Rue Vautier, is a bar and cellar venue dedicated to live performance (nightly until 4am); close by are the traditional *Café des Amis*, 23 Rue Ancienne, and boisterous *La Marchand de Sable*, 4 Rue Vautier. Sleek, postmodern *Le 2e Bureau*, 9 Rue du Stand, thumps with deep beats, and the nearby *Café Mozart* waterfront wine bar, 4 Quai des Forces Motrices, hosts some live jazz. Tiny, kitschy *La Bretelle*, 15 Rue des Étuves, features great drag cabaret.

Listings

Books Elm Books, 5 Rue Versonnex, for new; Bookworm, 5 Rue Sismondi, for secondhand. L'Inédite, 15 Rue St-Joseph in Carouge, is a women's bookshop.

Consulates Australia, 56 Rue Moillebeau (☎022/918 29 00); Canada, 1 Chemin du Pré-de-la-Bichette (☎022/919 92 00); New Zealand, 28a Chemin du Petit-Saconnex (☎022/734 95 30); UK, 37 Rue de Vermont (☎022/918 24 00); USA, 29 Route de Pré-Bois (☎022/798 16 15).

Hospital Hôpital Cantonal, 24 Rue Micheli-du-Crest (☎022/372 33 11).

Internet access Café Video ROM, 19 Rue des Alpes; Charly's, 7 Rue de Fribourg.

Laundry Lavseul, 29 Rue de Monthoux (daily 7am–midnight).

Post office 18 Rue du Mont-Blanc (Mon–Fri 7.30am–6pm, Sat 8–11am).

Lausanne

Geneva's neighbour **LAUSANNE** is interesting, attractive, worldly and well aware of how to have a good time – in short, Switzerland's sexiest city. Tiered above the lake on a succession of south-facing terraces, with the Old Town at the top, the train station and commercial districts in the middle, and the one-time fishing village of **Ouchy**, now prime territory for waterfront café-lounging and strolling, at the bottom, it has incredibly steep hills which may do your legs in after a while. If so, copy the locals and catch a bus into the Joret forests above the city, and then blade or **skateboard** your way down to Ouchy: aficionados have been clocked doing 90kph through the streets this way, and when the sun shines, every public space hisses with the spinning of tiny wheels (there's also a huge indoor skatepark at 36 Avenue de Sévelin). Intrepid Lausannois have even been known to ski down to Ouchy after days of heavy snow. Switzerland's biggest university aids the youthful spirit, and a wealth of international student programmes feeds an unusually diverse, multi-ethnic makeup.

To get to the central **Place St François** from the train station, either walk up the steep Rue du Petit-Chêne, or take the metro to Flon; from the metro platforms, lifts shuttle you up to the level of the giant **Grand Pont**, surfing between Place Bel-Air on the left and St François on the right. Glitzy **Rue de Bourg** entices shoppers uphill from St François; beside it, Rue St François drops down into the valley and up the other side to the cobbled **Place de la Palud**, an ancient, fountained square flanked by the arcades of the Renaissance town hall. From here the medieval **Escaliers du Marché** lead up to the **Cathedral** (daily 8am–7pm), a fine Romanesque-Gothic jumble, its clean lines only peripherally adorned with memorials and fifteenth-century frescoes. Opposite, in the former bishop's palace, is the **Musée Historique** (Tues–Sun 11am–6pm, Thurs until 8pm; Sfr4, students free), which houses a model of old Lausanne – invaluable for grasping the city's confusing topography – plus enlightening English commentary. Further up, behind the cathedral, you'll find the fourteenth-century **château**, now occupied by cantonal government offices. Lausanne suffered from many medieval fires, and is the last city in Europe to keep alive the tradition of the night-watch: every night, on the hour (10pm–2am), a sonorous-voiced civil servant calls out from the cathedral tower *"C'est le guet; il a sonné l'heure"* ("This is the nightwatch; the hour has struck"), assuring the lovers and assorted drunks below that all is well.

West of the cathedral hill is **Place de la Riponne**, an arid expanse of concrete dominated by the splendidly ostentatious Palais de Rumine, housing the university library and various museums. Save your francs for the outstanding **Collection de l'Art Brut**, 11 Avenue des Bergières (Tues–Sun 11am–1pm & 2–6pm; Sfr6; *www.artbrut.ch*), ten minutes' walk north-west of Riponne on Avenue Vinet, or bus #2 or #3 to Jomini. This unique gallery is filled with the work of "outsider" artists – ordinary people who discovered their talents late in life, the mentally ill, long-term prisoners, lone obsessives, and so on. Relating the potted biographies of each artist (often heart-rendingly sad) to the work they produced (often passionate and brilliant) is sobering, but the art also stands alone for its quality.

In a park on the Ouchy waterfront sits Lausanne's flagship **Olympic Museum** (daily 9am–6pm, Thurs until 8pm; Oct–April closed Mon; Sfr14; *www.museum.olympic.org*), a vacuous and expensive place that trumpets the Olympic ideal by means of snippets of archive footage, stirring music and Carl Lewis's old running shoes. Bypass it for the **Musée de l'Elysée**, an outstanding museum of photography in the same park (Tues–Sun 10am–6pm, Thurs until 9pm; Sfr5; *www.elysee.ch*).

Practicalities

The **tourist office** (☎021/613 73 73, *www.lausanne-tourisme.ch*) has branches in the train station (daily 9am–7pm), and beside Ouchy metro station (daily: April–Sept 9am–8pm; Oct–March 9am–6pm). City **transport** costs Sfr2.20 (1hr) or Sfr6.50 (24hr). A two-day Lausanne Card (Sfr15) gives free transport, reduced museum entry, and discounts on meals at *Manora*. The well-run **HI hostel**, *Jeunotel*, is at 36 Chemin du Bois-de-Vaux (☎021/626 02 22, *www.jeunotel.ch*; ③); bus #2 direction Bourdonnette to Bois de Vaux). *La Croisée*, 15 Avenue Marc-Dufour (☎021/321 09 09; ③), has rooms and dorms. The *Lausanne Guesthouse* opened in 2001 at 4 Chemin des Epinettes (☎021/601 80 00; ③). Of the **hotels**, *Pension Old Inn*, 11 Avenue de la Gare (☎021/323 62 21; ④), is friendly and pleasant, while *Hotel du Raisin*, 19 Place de la Palud (☎021/312 27 56; ⑤), is better placed. The lakeside **campsite** *Vidy* (☎021/624 20 31, *www.campinglausannevidy.ch*; closed Oct–April) is close to *Jeunotel*.

The self-service *Manora* **restaurant**, 17 Place St François, has a wide range of excellent cheap food; just down from it, *Ma Jong* does freshly wok-fried meals for Sfr14; the atmospheric *Café de l'Évêché*, below the cathedral at 4 Rue Curtat, is also affordable, fondue sharing the menu with horse steaks. *Café Romand*, Place St François (under *Pizza Hut*) is a heart-warming place for beer, coffee or Swiss belt-busters; *Laxmi*, 5 Escaliers du Marché, has excellent Indian/veggie food; and *Au Couscous*, 2 Rue Enning, does Arabic/veggie. *Le Bleu Lézard*, 10 Rue Enning, is a chic and lively café/bar, while *La Bossette*, way up above Place du Nord, is calmer and cosier. **Bars** and **nightlife** abound. The first place to look is Le Flon, a low-lying warehouse district bounded by Bel-Air, Grand Pont and the metro. Hereabouts you'll find genteel *Lecaféthéâtre*, featuring live *chansons*; the infamous *MAD (Moulin à Danse)*, a cutting-edge dance club with adjoining theatre, art galleries and alternative-style café; and *D!* and *Le Loft*, both equally happening clubs. Otherwise, around Place du Tunnel are funky *Au Château*, serving flavourful home-brewed beers; *VO Le Jazz Café*; and *Kerrigan's*, a hilltop Irish pub on Rue de la Barre. The *Captain Cook*, 2 Rue Enning, shows English football on TV. Ouchy's waterfront hosts regular free music events all summer, and people come down here to do a spot of café sunbathing, or blade-cruising (rent blades or skates from beside Ouchy metro). Lausanne's big party is the **Festival de la Cité** held in early July (*www.lausanne.ch*), featuring music, dance, drama and mime on several open-air stages in the Old Town. Also check out May's **Atlantis Festival**, devoted to electronic music and dance, the **International Circus Festival** every January, and the prestigious, big-name **Paleo Rock Festival** in late July (*www.paleo.ch*).

Vevey and Montreux

East of Lausanne, trains meander through steep vineyards to **VEVEY**, a small market town looking over to the French Alps across the lake. Vevey's charm centres on the huge lakeside **Grande Place**, a few minutes' walk southeast of the station – known also as **Place du Marché** and packed with market stalls (Tues & Sat) – and the narrow streets which lead off into the old town to the east. Vevey's excellent fine-art museum, **Musée Jenisch** on Rue de la Gare (Tues–Sun: March–Oct 11am–5.30pm; Nov–Feb 2–5.30pm; Sfr10), has Europe's largest collection of Rembrandt lithographs, as well as graphic works by Dürer, Corot, Le Corbusier and others. Uphill from the big green building west of the centre (Nestlé's world HQ) is **CORSIER**, location of the grave of Charlie Chaplin, who moved here from the US in the 1950s to escape McCarthyism; there's a statue of "The Tramp" just east of Place du Marché. To head on to Montreux and Chillon, ditch the train in favour of bus #1, which plies the coast road every 10min. If you have time, walk the floral lakeside path at least as far as the town of **LA TOUR-DE-PEILZ**, which is dominated by a whitewashed thirteenth-century castle now hosting the hands-on **Museum of Games** (Tues–Sun 2–6pm; Sfr6; *www.msj.ch*).

MONTREUX, 6km east of Vevey, is a snooty place, full of money and not particularly exciting, but it enjoys spectacular views of the Dents-du-Midi peaks opposite and hosts a colourful Friday market. The whole town is protected from chill northerly winds by a wall of mountains and so basks in its own microclimate, nurturing lakeside palm trees and exotic flowers. The zigzagging streets and hillside terraces of the old quarter above the train station provide marginally more interest than the thronging honky-tonk of the Grand-Rue below (head 100m left out of the station and cut down the stairs between buildings), although you should make time for the touching statue of one-time resident **Freddie Mercury** silently serenading the swans on the lakefront beside the vast covered market.

The climax of a journey around Lake Geneva is the stunning thirteenth-century **Château de Chillon** (daily: April–Sept 9am–7pm; Oct–March 9.30/10am–5/6pm; last entry 1hr before closing; Sfr7.50; *www.chillon.ch*), one of the best-preserved medieval castles in Europe. Whether you opt for the 45-minute shoreline walk east from Montreux, bus #1 from Vevey or Montreux, a local train, a bike, or best of all a lake steamer, your first glimpse of the castle is unforgettable – an elegant, turreted pile jutting out into the water, framed by trees and craggy mountains. At the gate you'll get a follow-the-numbers pamphlet, which starts you off in the dungeons where the dukes of Savoy imprisoned François Bonivard, a Genevan priest, from 1530 to 1536 (he was manacled to the fifth pillar along); Lord Byron, after a sailing trip here with Shelley in 1816, was so affected by the story that he spent the next day in his Ouchy hotel room writing the poem *The Prisoner of Chillon*. Byron's signature, scratched on the dungeon's third pillar, probably isn't genuine, but has been absorbed into the legend nonetheless. As you look out onto the lake, it's sobering to realize how sheer the rock is that Chillon's built on: just below the castle walls yawns 165m of cold water, enough to swallow the Eiffel Tower without a trace. Upstairs you'll find more wonders: gloriously grand knights' halls, secret twisting passages between lavish bedchambers, Gothic windows with dreamy views and a frescoed chapel.

Practicalities

Tourist offices are on Grande Place in Vevey (July–Sept daily 8.30/10am–7pm; Oct–June Mon–Fri 8.30am–noon & 1.30–6pm; ☎021/922 20 20, *www.montreux-vevey.com*); and beside the ferry landing-stage in Montreux (June–Aug daily 9am–7pm; Sept–May Mon–Sat 9am–noon & 1.30–6pm, Sun 9am–noon; ☎021/962 84 36). The excellent brochure *On The Trail of Hemingway* pinpoints a welter of sites in the area with famous-name associations. The pristine *Riviera Lodge* SB **hostel**, 5 Grande Place in Vevey (☎021/923 80 40, *www.rivieralodge.ch*; ②), is friendlier, cheaper and easier to get to than the HI hostel at 8 Passage de l'Auberge beside Territet station just east of Montreux (☎021/963 49 34, *www.youthhostel.ch*; ③). The best budget **hotels** are in Vevey: central *Des Négociants*, 27 Rue du Conseil (☎021/922 70 11, *www .hotelnegociants.ch*; ⑤); or rustic *De La Place* at 5 Place du Temple in Corsier (☎021/921 12 87; ⑤; bus #11). In Montreux, aim for *Hôtel Elite*, 25 Avenue du Casino (☎021/966 03 03; ④). You can **camp** east of Vevey at lakeside *La Maladaire* (☎021/944 31 37).

Vevey has a self-service *Manora* **restaurant** in the St Antoine mall outside the station, and plenty of pavement cafés in the centre, such as *Close-Up*, 8 Rue du Lac; the food at *Hôtel des Négociants* is good. Cyberworld, 4 Rue du Torrent in Vevey, has Internet access. Montreux has plenty of eateries outside the station on Avenue des Alpes, including some with lakeview terraces, as well as the oriental-fantasy *Palais Hoggar*, 14 Quai du Casino, which serves Arabic specialities (meals start from Sfr25) and Moroccan mint tea to accompany the lake sunset. The star-studded **Montreux Jazz Festival** in July features world-famous artists from REM to B.B. King; get tickets (Sfr40–100) from *www.montreuxjazz.com* well in advance, or just join the street parties and free entertainment all over town. Vevey holds a **Street Artists' Festival** in late August, jugglers, acrobats and mime artists performing on the lakeside.

Above Montreux

A scenic narrow-gauge train line climbs through the hills behind Montreux on the flagship **Golden Pass** route, which is well worth incorporating into an eastward journey (ER, IR & SP free; reservations in the special panoramic carriages cost Sfr4–8; *www.goldenpass.ch*). The memorable route switchbacks up to a series of tunnels beneath the prominent Dent de Jaman peak before meandering on a single track through lush, quiet and beautiful countryside to the exclusive Alpine resort of **Gstaad**, and then on to **Zweisimmen**, from where connections continue to Spiez, Bern, Interlaken and Luzern.

Expo 02

From May 15 to October 20, 2002, four small lakeside towns north of Lausanne will host the **Swiss National Expo 02**, planned as a showcase for cutting-edge interpretations of the culture and outlook of the country in the new millennium. It will be focused on five "arteplages", huge, futuristic-looking, ecologically sound, floating exhibition sites and performance venues, designed by leading architects on grandiose themes such as "nature and artificiality" or "power and freedom". Four arteplages will be moored (at **Neuchâtel** and **Yverdon**, at either end of Lake Neuchâtel, and at the bilingual towns of **Murten/Morat** and **Biel/Bienne**, each on their own neighbouring lake), and one will be mobile, trundling between the three connected lakes, all of them hosting exhibits that will run in conjunction with dozens of on-land shows and events. At the time of writing, it's still impossible to say exactly what you'll be faced with on the day, or whether the whole thing will be worth your hard-earned francs or not. Check online for the latest news (*www.expo.02.ch*). A three-day ticket, bought in advance and valid for all five arteplages, costs Sfr99 (Sfr120 after May 14); or you can buy a day-ticket for one arteplage for Sfr48, or an evening ticket for Sfr10. Included in the panoply of planned tourist services – cafés, restaurants, reception centres, and so on – are modular hotels offering basic accommodation.

THE NORTHERN CITIES

Northern Switzerland, much of it known as the Schweizer Mittelland – the populated countryside between the Jura to the north and the high Alps to the south – is a region of gentle hills, lakes and some high peaks, though ones by no means as grandiose as the heights further south. There's a wealth of cultural and historical interest in the German-speaking cities of **Zürich**, **Basel**, **Luzern** and the federal capital, **Bern**. Wherever you base yourself, the mountains are never more than a couple of hours away by train.

Zürich

Not so long ago, **ZÜRICH** was famed for being the most icily calm, cleanest city in Europe. Apocryphal stories abound from the 1970s of tourists setting out to find a cigarette butt or a food wrapper discarded on the streets and drawing a blank every time. Since then, Zürich has reinvented itself. This most beautiful of cities, astride a river and turned towards a crystal-clear lake and distant snowy peaks, has plenty to recommend it. Now you can people-watch on crowded, multi-ethnic streets, drink, dance or hang out at bars and clubs as hip and varied as those in more celebrated European cities, and feel a lived-in urban buzz that contradicts the Swiss stereotype. The steep, cobbled alleys of the Old Town are perfect for exploratory wanderings, and with an engaging café culture and a wealth of nightlife, you could easily spend days here.

Arrival and accommodation

The main point of arrival is the giant **Hauptbahnhof** (HB) in the city centre, served by trains from all over Europe and every quarter-hour from the **airport**, 11km northeast. The international **bus station** is 50m north of the station on Sihlquai. The **tourist office** on the station concourse (Mon–Fri 8.30am–7/8.30pm, Sat & Sun 8.30/9am–6.30pm; ☎01/215 40 00, *www.zurichtourism.ch*) sells maps and transport tickets, books rooms for free, and offers guided tours on foot (Sfr18) or inline skates (Sfr20) as well as river and lake cruises (from Sfr13). Pick up the useful **listings** booklet *Zürich News* (*www.zuerich.ch*).

You can cover most sights by walking, but the **public transport** system is easy to use. The most important hubs are the city squares of Bahnhofplatz and, on the east side of the river, Central and Bellevue. Buy tickets from machines at every stop: choose between the green button (Sfr7.20; valid for 24hr); blue button (Sfr3.60; 1hr); or yellow button (Sfr2.10; a short one-way hop). All tickets are valid on trams, buses, some boats and local city trains (not to/from the airport). The tourist office sells Welcome 24 and 48 tickets (Sfr10.80/25), valid for 24/48hr citywide, including the airport.

Hostels pack the Niederdorf district, on the east bank of the river, including the excellent SB *City Backpacker*, Niederdorfstrasse 5 (☎01/251 90 15, *www.backpacker.ch*; ③), and *Martahaus*, Zähringerstrasse 36 (☎01/251 45 50, *www.martahaus.ch*; ④), which also has a women-only annexe. The institutional HI hostel *Jugendherberge*, Mutschellenstrasse 114 (☎01/482 35 44, *www.youthhostel.ch*; ③), is way south; take tram #7 to Morgental, from where it's a five-minute walk. Niederdorf's good-value budget **hotels** include comfy, colourful and

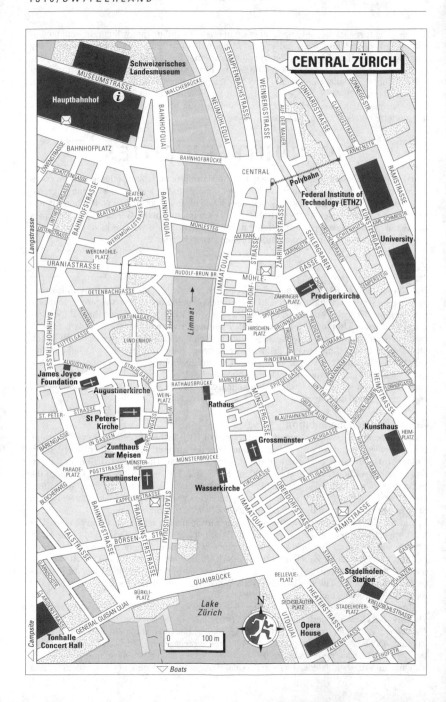

CENTRAL ZÜRICH

Schweizerisches Landesmuseum
MUSEUMSTRASSE
Hauptbahnhof
BAHNHOFPLATZ
CENTRAL
Polybahn
Federal Institute of Technology (ETHZ)
University
MÜHLESTEG
AM RANK
RUDOLF-BRUN BR
MÜHLE-
Predigerkirche
Limmat
James Joyce Foundation
Augustinerkirche
Rathaus
St Peters-Kirche
Zunfthaus zur Meisen
Grossmünster
Kunsthaus
Fraumünster
Wasserkirche
MÜNSTERBRÜCKE
Stadelhofen Station
QUAIBRÜCKE
BELLEVUE-PLATZ
Lake Zürich
N
Opera House
Tonhalle Concert Hall
0   100 m

◁ Langstrasse
◁ Campsite
▽ Boats

laid-back *Otter*, Oberdorfstrasse 7 (☎01/251 22 07, *www.wueste.ch*; ⑤), the plainer *Splendid*, Rosengasse 5 (☎01/252 58 50; ④), and *Villette*, Kruggasse 4 (☎01/251 23 35; ⑤). *Rothaus*, Sihlhallenstrasse 1 (☎01/241 24 51; ④), is on the hip Langstrasse – its clean, spacious rooms are a bargain, if you can overlook the neighbourhood's red-light tendencies. **Campers** should head for lakeside *Seebucht*, Seestrasse 559 (☎01/482 16 12, *www.camping-zurich.ch*; closed Nov–April; bus #161 or #165 from Bürkliplatz to Stadtgrenze).

The City

From Central, the narrow pedestrian-only streets of the medieval **Niederdorf** district stretch south along the east bank of the River Limmat, tranquil during the day and bustling after dark. The waterfront is lined with fine Baroque *Zunfthäuser* (guildhalls), arcaded lower storeys fronting the quayside, their extravagantly decorated dining-rooms now mostly upmarket restaurants. One block in is **Niederdorfstrasse**, initially tacky, but offering plenty of opportunities to explore atmospheric cobbled side-alleys and secluded courtyards: Spiegelgasse 14 was Lenin's digs in 1917 (pre-Revolution), and a pub at Spiegelgasse 1 – long since renovated – housed the original *Cabaret Voltaire*, birthplace of the Dada art movement. Just south is Zürich's trademark **Grossmünster** (Mon–Sat 9/10am–4/6pm), where Huldrych Zwingli, father of Swiss Protestantism, began preaching in 1519. Its exterior is largely fifteenth-century, while its twin towers were topped with distinctive octagonal domes three hundred years later. The interior is austere but for the intensely coloured choir windows by Augusto Giacometti and the Romanesque crypt which contains an oversized fifteenth-century statue of Charlemagne, popularly associated with the foundation of the church in the ninth century. As you leave, a door on the right gives into the atmospheric **cloister**. Alleys behind the church lead up the hill to Switzerland's best gallery, the **Kunsthaus** (Tues–Thurs 10am–9pm, Fri–Sun 10am–5pm; Sfr6, free on Sun; *www .kunsthaus.ch*). Some fascinating late-Gothic paintings, a roomful of Venetian masters and fine Flemish work are fleshed out by Swiss artists, among them Füssli, whose macabre fantasies contrast with the restrained classicism of his compatriot Angelika Kauffmann. The collection of twentieth-century art is stunning: works by Miró, Dalí and De Chirico head a wonderful Surrealist overview; Picasso, Chagall, Klee and Kandinsky all have rooms to themselves; there are two of Monet's most beautiful waterlily canvases, plenty of Warhols, an array of Giacometti's sculpture, and the largest Munch collection outside Scandinavia.

The **west bank** is the site of most business and commercial activity. Leading south from the station, **Bahnhofstrasse** is one of the most prestigious shopping streets in Europe, an enduring symbol of Zürich's wealth and a stark counterpoint to the quaintness of the Niederdorf alleys. This is the gateway into the modern city, and is where all of Zürich strolls, whether to browse at the inexpensive department stores that crowd the first third of the street, or to sign away Sfr25,000 on a Rolex watch or a Vuitton bag at the understated superchic boutiques further south. Two-thirds of the way down is **Paradeplatz**, a tram-packed little square offering some of the best people-watching in the city, and where most of Switzerland's banks are headquartered: Bahnhofstrasse, if not paved with gold, is at least founded on the stuff, with ingots piled high in well-protected vaults beneath the pavement. The narrow lanes between Bahnhofstrasse and the river lead up to the **Lindenhof** courtyard, site of a Roman fortress and customs post. James Joyce wrote *Ulysses* in Zürich (1915–19), and the Joyce Foundation, nearby at Augustinergasse 9, can point you to his various hangouts, and his grave. Steps away is the **Peterskirche** (Mon–Fri 8am–6pm, Sat 8am–4pm), renowned for the enormous sixteenth-century clock face – the largest in Europe – adorning its medieval tower and a simple interior that's more like a ballroom than a church. Immediately south rises the slender-spired Gothic **Fraumünster** (Mon–Sat 9/10am–4/6pm), which began life as a convent in 853; its spectacular stained glass by Marc Chagall is unmissable.

The **Schweizerisches Landesmuseum** (Swiss National Museum; Tues–Sun 10.30am–5pm; Sfr5; *www.musee-suisse.ch*) is just north of the train station, an eccentric nineteenth-century mock castle. The ground floor is packed with medieval religious art, including a panorama of the city of Zürich painted around 1500 which shows the grisly end of the city's patron saints, Felix and Regula, Christian Romans who deserted, were chased to Zürich, decapitated, put on a wheel and boiled. Upstairs, an extensive military history section serves as a reminder of the warlike past of the Swiss.

Eating, drinking and nightlife

Zürich offers a wealth of places to **eat cheaply**, with *Manora*, Bahnhofstrasse 75, offering best value. The train station, in addition to the good-value *Nordsee* seafood bar opposite the tourist office, hides *Suan Long* on the lower shopping-level, which does filling stir-fries for Sfr13–15 (stand-up only). *Mensa Polyterrasse*, on Künstlergasse at the university, is a student cafeteria open to all. A wander through Niederdorf will turn up dozens of falafel, sausage, noodle and french-fry stalls, plus beer halls serving up daily specials for about Sfr13; *Schlauch*, upstairs at Münstergasse 20, serves health food in a quiet atmosphere; *Zähringer*, on Zähringerplatz, is a co-operative-run café/bar with an alternative-minded clientele; *Pinte Vaudoise*, Kruggasse 4, serves what's been voted the best fondue in Zürich; *Bodega Española*, Münstergasse 15, is an unmissable, deeply atmospheric tapas bar and paella restaurant; and frothy *Café Schober*, Napfgasse 4, could bring out the little old lady in anyone – don't leave Zürich without sampling their **hot chocolate**. On the west bank, *Hiltl*, Sihlstrasse 28, is a top-quality buffet vegetarian, with budget prices for takeaway. Of Niederdorf's innumerable **bars**, *Pigalle*, Marktgasse 14, is a popular hangout; *Wüste*, Oberdorfstrasse 7, is mellow and comfortable; *Babalu*, Schmidgasse 6, chic and black-lit. Lenin once watched the world go by from the big-windowed *Odeon*, Limmatquai 2; and legend has it that if you can swing up and wriggle your way through the gap between beam and ceiling at the *Oepfelchammer*, Rindermarkt 12, then your beers are on the house. *Rheinfelder Bierhalle*, Niederdorfstrasse 76, is choice of the hearty beer halls. On the west bank, *James Joyce*, Pelikanstrasse 8, comprises an original nineteenth-century bar interior, transported here piece by piece from Dublin; and *Nelson*, Beatengasse 11, and *Noble Dubliner*, Talstrasse 82, are English-style pubs. *Barfüsser*, Spitalgasse 14, is Europe's longest-running gay bar, and *Venus*, Badenerstrasse 219, is women-only.

Supplementing its lively **music** venues, Zürich's **club** scene has skyrocketed recently, and you'll find dance floors heaving. The deeply hip quarter around Langstrasse, west of the centre, is full of DJ-bars, and the industrial quarter to the northwest is where the best underground clubs hide themselves; check flyers on Langstrasse or at Zap Records, Zähringerstrasse 47. *Rote Fabrik*, Seestrasse 395 (*www.rotefabrik.ch*), is a former squat venue with live bands and big-name DJs (as well as excellent cheap food); *Abart*, Manessestrasse 170, has good live music; *Casa Bar*, Münstergasse 20, and *Moods*, Sihlamtstrasse 5, focus on jazz; *Dynamo*, Wasserwerkstrasse 21, hosts alternative, punkish bands and dance nights; *Labyrinth*, Pfingstweidstrasse 70, plays house (mixed gay/straight); and *Oxa*, Andreasstrasse 70, is famous for its after-hours parties (Sat & Sun 5–11am). Early August sees the **Street Parade** (*www.street-parade.ch*), a hedonistic weekend of techno street-dancing second only to Berlin's Love Parade. **Listings** are in *ZüriTipp*, Friday supplement to *Tages Anzeiger* newspaper.

Listings

Books Stäheli, Bahnhofstrasse 70; Travel Bookshop, Rindermarkt 20.

Consulates UK, Minervastrasse 117 (✆01/383 65 60).

Internet access Cybergate at *Stars* bistro in the station (*www.cybergate.ch*); *Café Urania* in the Uraniastrasse car park.

Laundry Mühlegasse 11, Niederdorf.

Medical facilities Permanence Medical Centre, Bahnhofplatz 15 (24hr emergency; ✆01/215 44 44). Pharmacy Bellevue is at Theaterstrasse 14 (daily 24hr).

Post office Kasernenstrasse, beside the station (Mon–Fri 6.30am–10.30pm, Sat 6.30am–8pm, Sun 11am–10.30pm); within the main station; and offices around the centre.

The Rhine falls

An excellent fine-weather excursion is to the **Rhine falls** (*www.rheinfall.ch*), Europe's largest waterfalls, which tumble 3km west of the northern Swiss town of **SCHAFFHAUSEN**. They are truly magnificent, not so much for their height (a mere 23m) as for their impressive breadth (150m) and the sheer drama of the place, with spray rising in a cloud of rainbows above the forested banks. The turreted castle **Schloss Laufen** on the south bank completes the spectacle. Be here on August 1, Switzerland's national day, for a famous fireworks display. Zürich's 9-Uhr-Tagespass (valid Mon–Fri after 9am, Sat & Sun all day; Sfr20; press *141 on the ticket machines) covers all city transport as well as the train-ride north to Schloss Laufen station (change at Winterthur). Damp steps lead down from the castle souvenir shop (Sfr1) to platforms at the water's edge, where the falls roar inches from your nose. In summer, the best views are from daredevil boats, which scurry about in the spray (Sfr5–7).

Basel (Bâle)

With both a gigantic river-port on the Rhine – Switzerland's only outlet to the sea – and the research headquarters of several pharmaceutical multinationals, **BASEL** (Bâle in French), nurtures a reputation as Switzerland's wealthiest city. Its medieval past is endowed with some of the greatest minds of European history, including Erasmus, Zwingli, and later Nietzsche and Hesse, and its long-standing patronage of the arts has resulted in a panoply of first-rate museums and galleries. However, it's almost as if Baslers lost the plot when it came to defining their city for today. You might expect it, situated exactly where Switzerland, Germany and France touch noses, to hum with pan-European energy, but the close proximity of foreign languages and cultures has introverted the city rather than energized it: Basel's a curiously measured place, where equilibrium is everything. You won't find anyone shouting about the new Europe here; in fact, you're unlikely to find anyone shouting about anything at all. Even the city's massive carnival is a rigorously organized set-piece.

The City

Basel's old town lies to the north of the main **train station**. It revolves around the photogenic main square **Barfüsserplatz**, ringed by higgledy-piggledy medieval buildings, where the city's cultural pre-eminence in the fifteenth and sixteenth centuries is amply demonstrated in the bare-footed Franciscans' splendid Barfüsserkirche, which is now home to the **Historisches Museum** (Mon & Wed–Sun 10am–5pm; Sfr5, free on first Sun of month; *www.historischesmuseumbasel.ch*); don't miss the sumptuous medieval tapestries, hidden behind protective blinds. Shop-lined Gerbergasse and Freiestrasse run north from the square to Marktplatz, which boasts the elaborate scarlet facade of the **Rathaus** (Town Hall), the central section of which is sixteenth-century. Just beyond Marktplatz is **Schifflände**, site of the main tourist office and from where **boats** depart regularly on journeys up and down the Rhine (*www.bpg.ch*). Alongside is the **Mittlere Brücke**, which for many centuries was the only bridge across the Rhine between its source and the sea. The working-class quarter across the river, known as Kleinbasel, was traditionally the object of scorn for the cosmopolitan merchants of the city centre: their **Lällekönig** bust still faces down the bridge, sticking out its tongue at the Kleinbaslers.

From Barfüsserplatz, Steinenberg climbs south past the **Kunsthalle** (Tues–Sun 11am–5pm, Wed until 8.30pm; Sfr9; *www.kunsthallebasel.ch*), with quality contemporary art shows, to a junction; head left to the superb Greek and Etruscan pottery and Egyptian antiquities in the **Antikenmuseum**, St Alban-Graben 5 (Tues–Sun 10am–5pm; Sfr5, free on first Sun of month; *www.antikenmuseumbasel.ch*). Opposite is the absorbing **Kunstmuseum**, St Alban-Graben 16 (Tues–Sun 10am–5pm; Sfr7, joint admission with Museum für Gegenwartskunst; free on first Sun of month; *www.kunstmuseumbasel.ch*). Its dazzling array of twentieth-century art, including paintings by Léger, Chagall, Munch, Braque and the

Impressionists, is surpassed by a medieval collection featuring roomfuls of works by the prolific Holbein family. Down to the river, then right, is the **Museum für Gegenwartskunst** (Contemporary Art; Tues–Sun 11am–5pm; Sfr7, joint admission with Kunstmuseum; *www.mgkbasel.ch*), St Alban-Rheinweg 60, with installations by Frank Stella and Joseph Beuys sharing space with video art. A walk away on the north bank, in Solitude Park, is the beautifully designed **Museum Jean Tinguely** (Wed–Sun 11am–7pm; Sfr7; *www.tinguely.ch*), dedicated to one of Switzerland's best-loved artists. Tinguely's Monty-Pythonesque moving mechanical sculptures made of scrap are endearing and quite unique, and though most are imbued with an irreverent sense of humour, some, such as the *Mengele-Dance of Death*, are darkly apocalyptic. A Tinguely fountain spits and burbles outside the Kunsthalle.

Sixteenth-century Rittergasse leads from the Kunstmuseum up to the impressive red sandstone **Münster** overlooking the Rhine (Easter–Oct Mon–Sat 10am–4/5pm, Sun 1–5pm; Oct–Easter Mon–Sat 11am–4pm, Sun 2–4pm). Medieval stone carving above the main portal shows the cathedral's founder, Emperor Heinrich II, holding a model of the church; beside him is a Foolish Virgin. Inside, in the north aisle, is the tomb of the Renaissance humanist Erasmus, who lived in Basel from 1521 until his death in 1536. The ninth-century remains of an earlier cathedral can be seen in the crypt, and the large adjoining **cloisters** are memorably atmospheric.

Basel's finest gallery is **Fondation Beyeler** (daily 10am–6pm, Wed until 8pm; Sfr12; *www.beyeler.com*; tram #6 to Riehen Dorf from Barfüsserplatz), sympathetically designed by Renzo Piano, architect of Paris's Pompidou Centre. A small but exceptionally high-quality collection features some of the best works by Picasso, Giacometti, Rothko, Rodin, Bacon, Miró and others. Sink into a huge white sofa opposite a giant Monet, where piped Debussy (daily at 1pm) fuels dreamy contemplation of the waterlilies.

Practicalities

Basel has two **train stations** straddling three countries. Basel SBB is the main one, most of it in Switzerland, although the section entitled Bâle SNCF is in French territory, receiving trains from Paris and Strasbourg (passport control); trams #1 and #8 shuttle to Barfüsserplatz. Some trains from Germany terminate at Basel Badischer Bahnhof (Basel Bad. for short), in a German enclave on the north side of the river (passport control); tram #6 runs to Barfüsserplatz. The **tourist office** (☎061/268 68 68, *www.baseltourismus.ch*) has branches at SBB station (Mon–Fri 8.30am–6/7pm, Sat 8.30am–noon; June–Sept also Sat 1.30–6pm & Sun 10am–2pm), and in the centre at Schifflände 5 (Mon–Fri 8.30am–6pm, Sat 10am–4pm). Booking a room through them costs Sfr10. Basel thrives on conference business, so accommodation prices drop at weekends. Ask for a Mobility Card giving **free city transport** when you check in. The pleasant riverside **HI hostel** is at St Alban-Kirchrain 10 (☎061/272 05 72, *www.youthhostel.ch*; ③), and **hotels** include *Stadthof*, in the old town at Gerbergasse 84 (☎061/261 87 11, *www.stadthof.ch*; ⑤), and friendlier *Hecht am Rhein*, Rheingasse 8 in Kleinbasel (☎061/691 22 20; ⑤). You can **camp** at *Waldhort*, Heideweg 16, Reinach (☎061/711 64 29).

Plenty of cafés and beer halls on and around Marktplatz and Barfüsserplatz offer cheap **food**: *Mr Wong*, Steinenvorstadt 3, piles your dish high for Sfr12; *Zum Roten Engel*, Andreasplatz, is a pleasant vegetarian café; *Pfalz*, Münsterberg 11, has fresh juices and a salad buffet; arty literati meet at the Kunsthalle's terrace-café; and *Zum Isaak* is a tranquil tea-drinkers' café on Münsterplatz. Kleinbasel offers more conviviality for less money: friendly *Parterre*, Klybeckstrasse 1, has excellent food, as does adjacent *Kaserne* (with shady outdoor tables); and graffiti-daubed *Hirscheneck*, Lindenberg 23, has menus for under Sfr15 – all these places often serve for **drinking** too. For bars, the excellent *Fischerstube* beer hall and microbrewery is steps away from *Hirscheneck* at Rheingasse 45; while the convivial bar at *Kaserne* mutates on Tuesdays into Basel's premier gay/lesbian meeting-point. *Atlantis*, Klosterberg 10, also features regular music and dance, and *Bird's Eye*, Kohlenberg 20, is a jazz club. Basel's February **carnival** is famous, the masked parades and musical festivities beginning at 4am on the Monday after Mardi Gras and lasting for 72 more-or-less-continuous hours (*www.fasnacht.ch*).

Luzern and Lake Luzern

An hour south of Basel and Zürich is beautiful **LUZERN** (Lucerne in French), offering captivating mountain views, lake cruises and a picturesque medieval quarter. The giant Mount Pilatus (see below) rears up behind the town, which is split by the River Reuss, flowing rapidly out of the northwestern end of the oddly shaped **Vierwaldstättersee** ("Lake of the Four Forest Cantons" or plain Lake Luzern). In the Middle Ages, the communities dotted around the lake guarded the northern approaches to the Gotthard Pass, the main route between northern and southern Europe. When Habsburg overlords tried to encroach on their privileges, the communities formed an alliance in 1291 at the lakeside **Rütli Meadow** which was to prove the beginning of the Swiss Confederation. Luzern, as the principal market town for the region, was drawn into the bond shortly after. About this time in Altdorf, just around the lake, **William Tell** shot the apple from his son's head; the Tell legend lies at the core of Swiss national identity, and the semi-mystical Vierwaldstättersee is the spiritual as well as the geographical centre of the country.

Luzern was (and is) the main town of the region, and evidence of its medieval prosperity is manifest in the frescoed facades of its charming Old Town and the two surviving covered wooden bridges spanning the river, both formerly part of the city's fortifications and both boasting unique triangular paintings fixed to their roof-beams. In 1993, fire almost destroyed the fourteenth-century **Kapellbrücke**, a dog-leg angled around the squat mid-river **Wasserturm**; it was reconstructed with facsimiles of the roof-paintings (although a few charred originals remain) – check out no. 31's William Tell. The **Spreuerbrücke** downstream is also worth a look for its macabre "Dance of Death" paintings. The north bank is home to a compact cluster of medieval houses, with Mühlenplatz, Weinmarkt, Hirschenplatz and Kornmarkt forming an ensemble of cobbled, fountained squares ringed by colourful facades. Next to the Renaissance town hall on Kornmarkt is the **Picasso Museum** in Am Rhyn-Haus, Furrengasse 21, containing a small fine-art collection supplemented by hundreds of intimate photographs of the artist's later years (daily: April–Oct 10am–6pm; Nov–March 11am–1pm & 2–4pm; Sfr6). A few minutes west along riverside St Karliquai brings you to the **Nölliturm**, a fortified gate marking the southwestern extent of a lengthy stretch of the surviving fourteenth-century town walls. Pass through the gate and head right up the hill to gain access to the **battlements** (Easter–Sept daily 8am–7pm) and their impressive views. Northeast of the Old Town is Löwenplatz, overlooked by a circular building holding the **Bourbaki Panorama**, a 10x110m painting depicting the Franco-Prussian War of 1870–71, newly revamped with audio effects (daily 9am–6pm; Sfr6; *www.panorama-luzern.ch*). Just north of the square is the moving **Löwendenkmal** (Lion Memorial), a dying beast hewn out of a cliff-face to commemorate the seven hundred Swiss mercenaries killed by French revolutionaries in 1792 for defending Louis XVI. Adjacent is the **Gletschergarten** (daily 9/10am–5/6pm; Nov–Feb closed Mon; Sfr9; *www.gletschergarten.ch*), a set of geological potholes demonstrating Luzern's prehistoric subglacial existence which are completely upstaged by a nightmarish century-old **Mirror Maze** in the same complex.

A big reason to visit Luzern is the **Verkehrshaus**, 2km east of the centre at Lidostrasse 5 (daily 9/10am–5/6pm; Sfr21, discounts with rail passes; *www.verkehrshaus.org*) – take bus #6 or #8 from the station, or have a pleasant walk along the lakeside. The museum, inadequately translated as the "Transport Museum", is a vast complex that could keep you amused all day. It's packed with loads of hands-on technology including videophones and fully equipped TV and radio studios, various original space capsules, railway locomotives (including a walk-through account of the digging of the Gotthard tunnel beneath the Alps, dramatized with slides and soundtrack), aeroplanes, cable cars and more. An incongruous highlight is an excellent museum housing the whimsical and attractive works of the little-known Swiss artist

Hans Erni. Adjoining the complex is an **IMAX cinema**, with shows throughout the day (Sfr16; joint admission with museum Sfr31; *www.imax.ch*). The newest attraction is a tethered helium balloon known as the **Hiflyer**, which can lift thirty people up to a height of about 150m (daily 11am–5pm; Sfr20; *www.hiflyer.ch*).

Practicalities

Luzern's **train station** is on the south bank, where the lake narrows into the river, across from the Kapellbrücke and beside a stunning Convention Centre designed by French architect Jean Nouvel. The **tourist office** is on platform 3 (April–Oct daily 8.30/9am–7.30/8.30pm; Nov–March Mon–Sat 8.30/9am–6pm, Sun 9am–1pm; ☎041/227 17 17, *www.luzern.org*). Luzern's **HI hostel** is northwest of town by Lake Rotsee, Sedelstrasse 12 (☎041/420 88 00, *www.youthhostel.ch*; ③; bus #18 to Jugendherberge); friendly SB *Backpackers*, Alpenquai 42 (☎041/360 04 20, *www.backpacker.ch*; ③; bus #6/7/8 to Weinbergli, then cut left), and central *Tourist Hotel*, St Karliquai 12 (☎041/410 24 74, *www.touristhotel.ch*; ④), also have dorms. Of the **hotels**, *Löwengraben*, in the Old Town at Löwengraben 18 (☎041/417 12 12, *www.loewengraben.ch*; ⑤; dorms ③) was Luzern's prison from 1862 to 1998: now you can bed down in the comfortably refurbished cells. *Lido* **camp-site**, Lidostrasse 8 (☎041/370 21 46), also has dorms (③). When you check in, ask for a stamped **visitors' card**, which grants plenty of discounts around town (including a bargain three-day bus pass from the tourist office for Sfr8). Luzern's main **adventure sports** operator is Outventure (☎041/611 14 41, *www.outventure.ch*), offering canyoning, bungee-jumping and more.

Eating and **drinking** venues crowd the waterfront and the Old Town squares. *Manora* has a rooftop terrace at Weggisgasse 11; shabby *Bahnhof Buffet* on the top floor of the station charges bargain prices for gourmet dishes prepared by *Au Premier* adjacent. *Hofgarten*, Stadthofstrasse 14, has excellent veggie food; relaxed *Parterre*, Mythenstrasse 7, offers Internet access. Top **bars** include the buzzing *Jazz Kantine*, Grabenstrasse 8, with DJs and live bands downstairs; *Wärchhof*, Werkhofstrasse 11, with Sfr5 meals, music galore and women-only nights (Mon); chic *Löwengraben* (see above); and frenetic *Schüür*, Tribschenstrasse 1, with excellent music and cheap weekday lunches. Luzern's infamously raucous six-day February **carnival**, ending on Mardi Gras night, is the biggest and best in Switzerland, a constant round of drinking, dancing and partying.

Lake Luzern

You shouldn't leave Luzern without taking a trip on the **lake**, Switzerland's most beautiful and dramatic by far, the thickly wooded slopes rising sheer from the water, bays and peninsulas giving constantly changing views. A dense web of boat routings is run by SGV (☎041/367 67 67, *www.lakelucerne.ch*; IR half-price; ER & SP free), and the regional tourist office also has more details (☎041/418 40 80, *www.centralswitzerland.ch*). Of the lakeside towns, **VITZNAU** is the base-station of the oldest rack-railway in the world, serving the majestic **Mount Rigi** (IR no discount, ER & SP 25 percent discount; *www.rigi.ch*); and **KEHRSITEN** has a funicular up to **Bürgenstock**, from where a twenty-minute clifftop walk brings you to Europe's fastest outdoor lift, swishing you in seconds to the Hammetschwand summit. From **ALP-NACHSTAD**, the steepest rack-railway in the world climbs to the top of **Mount Pilatus** (IR half-price; SP/ER 30/35 percent discount; *www.pilatus.com*). Taking a leisurely boat ride to the far point of the lake at **FLÜELEN** (3hr) connects with mainline trains running west to Luzern and Basel, north to Zürich and south to Lugano and Milan.

Bern

Of all Swiss cities, **BERN** is most immediately charming. Founded in 1191 by the powerful local Zähringen dynasty, it began life as a fortress town peopled by knights. The growth of the Swiss Confederation in subsequent centuries owed much to the conquests of the warlike

Bernese. Crammed onto a steep-sided peninsula in a crook of the fast-flowing River Aare, the city's quiet, cobbled lanes, lined with sandstone arcaded buildings, have changed barely at all in over five hundred years. The hills all around, and the steep banks of the river, are still liberally wooded. It's sometimes hard to remember that this quiet, attractive town of just 130,000 people is the nation's capital.

The City

Bern's old centre – designated a UN World Heritage Site for the preservation of its medieval street plan – is best explored from the focal east–west **Spitalgasse**. As it leads away from the train station, Spitalgasse becomes Marktgasse, Kramgasse, and then Gerechtigkeitsgasse, but all the way down is lined with seventeenth- and eighteenth-century houses, fountains and arcaded shops. Some 200m east of the station, the street crosses **Bärenplatz**, scene of much outdoor daytime drinking and a lively Saturday morning market, to the right of which is the **Bundeshaus** or Federal Parliament Building, a domed neo-Renaissance edifice. Beyond Bärenplatz, Marktgasse continues under the oft-rebuilt **Käfigturm** (prisoners' tower), a thirteenth-century town gate. Further along is an eleventh-century gate which was subsequently converted into the **Zytglogge** – a distinctively top-heavy clocktower adorned with brightly coloured figures that judder into movement four minutes before each hour. (To the left, in Kornhausplatz, is the most famous of Bern's many ornate fountains, the horrific **Kindlifresserbrunnen**, depicting an ogre devouring a struggling baby.) Further east along the main street, the **Albert Einstein House**, Kramgasse 49 (Feb–Nov Tues–Fri 1–5pm, Sat noon–4pm; Sfr2; *www.einstein-bern.ch*), preserves the study occupied by the famous physicist for two years from 1903. Münstergasse, one block south, leads to the fifteenth-century Gothic **Münster** (Tues–Sat 10am–4/5pm, Sun 11am–5pm; Nov–Easter Sun closes 2pm), noted for the magnificently gilded high-relief *Last Judgement* above the main entrance and the elegant buttressed terrace on its south side. Its 254-stepped **tower** (closes 30min earlier; Sfr3), the tallest in Switzerland, offers terrific views of the city and distant mountains. At the eastern end of the centre, the Nydeggbrücke crosses the river to the **Bärengraben** (daily 8/9am–4/6pm), Bern's famed bear-pits, which have housed generations of morose shaggies since the early sixteenth century. Legend has it that the town's founder Berchtold V of Zähringen named Bern after killing one of the beasts during a hunt; the bear has remained a symbol of the town ever since.

Bern's magical **Kunstmuseum**, near the station at Hodlerstrasse 8 (Tues 10am–9pm, Wed–Sun 10am–5pm; Sfr7; *www.kunstmuseumbern.ch*), is especially strong on twentieth-century art, with plenty of works by Matisse, Kandinsky, Braque and Picasso, whole rooms devoted to Paul Klee, who was born in Bern and who returned here from Germany after the rise of Nazism, and a good selection of contemporary art as well. More museums are grouped around **Helvetiaplatz**, south of the river: the **Alpine Museum** houses detailed and interesting displays exploring mountain culture (Mon 2–5pm, Tues–Sun 10am–5pm; Sfr7; *www.alpinesmuseum.ch*); the **Kunsthalle** gallery shows good contemporary art (Tues 10am–7pm, Wed–Sun 10am–5pm; Sfr6; *www.kunsthallebern.ch*); and the engaging **Museum für Kommunikation** explores information exchange from smoke-signals to the Internet (Tues–Sun 10am–5pm; Sfr5; *www.mfk.ch*). You could also spend hours in the fascinating seven-floored **Bernisches Historisches Museum** (Tues–Sun 10am–5pm, Wed until 8pm; Sfr5; *www.bhm.ch*); check out the "Dance of Death" sequence in the basement, and their fine late-medieval Flemish tapestries and weaponry.

Practicalities

Bern's main **train station** is at the western end of the old centre; cross Bahnhofplatz and turn left to reach Spitalgasse. The **tourist office** is in the station (June–Sept daily 9am–8.30pm; Oct–May Mon–Sat 9am–6.30pm, Sun 10am–5pm; ☎031/328 12 12, *www.bernetourism.ch*), plus a desk at the Bärengraben (daily 9/10am–4/6pm). The riverside **HI hostel**, Weihergasse 4 (☎031/311 63 16, *www.jugibern.ch*; ③), is below the Bundeshaus; the quality SB *Landhaus*, Altenbergstrasse 4 (☎031/331 41 66, *www.backpacker.ch*; ③), and *Glocke*, very central at Rathausgasse 75 (☎031/311 37 71; ③), both have dorms and rooms. *Eichholz* **campsite**, Strandweg 49 (☎031/961 26 02; closed Oct–March), is a fifteen-minute tram ride (#9) towards Wabern. For **eating**, *Manora*, just off Bahnhofplatz, has filling cheap food, and the popular *Reitschule*, a dilapidated squat-cum-arts centre beside the tracks northeast of the station, offers a Sfr5 meal daily along with its cheap beer and liberal dope-smoking policy. Cosy *Brasserie Lorraine*, Quartiergasse 17, has a top Sunday brunch; *Café Bubenberg Vegi*, Bubenbergplatz 8 upstairs, quality veggie menus for Sfr15; *Anker* tavern, Kornhausplatz 16, serves fondue and *Rösti*; and the old Toblerone factory at Länggassstrasse 49a (bus #12), now absorbed by the university, has a lively student café at the back. There's no shortage of good **café/bars**, including plenty ringing Bärenplatz; *Café des Pyrénées*, a jovial hangout on Kornhausplatz for artists, alcoholics and others with loud voices; *Drei Eidgenossen*, Rathausgasse 69; traditional *Klötzlikeller*, Gerechtigkeitsgasse 62; or the colourful *Art'Café*, Gurtengasse 3. The *Reitschule* (see above) and *Dampfzentrale*, Marzilistrasse 47, are the two premier venues for **live music** and dance; *U1*, Junkerngasse 1, is a DJ-bar in an old-town cellar; *ISC*, Neubrückstrasse 10, is a student gig venue. **Listings** are in *Berner Woche*, the Thursday supplement to *Der Bund* newspaper, free from many cinemas; the free fortnightly *Bern aktuell* has information and some listings. Bern hosts a carnival in February, a major jazz festival in May and a huge open-air rock event in July.

Listings

Books Stauffacher, Neuengasse 25, is one of Switzerland's best bookstores.
Embassies Canada, Kirchenfeldstrasse 88 (☎031/357 32 00); Ireland, Kirchenfeldstrasse 68 (☎031/352 14 42); Britain, Thunstrasse 50 (☎031/359 77 00); USA, Jubiläumsstrasse 93 (☎031/357 70 11).
Internet access Jäggi Books, Loeb department store basement, opposite the station.
Medical facilities Inselspital University Hospital, Freiburgstrasse (☎031/632 21 11). Pharmacy Hörning is in the station (daily 6.30am–10pm).
Post office Schanzenstrasse, behind the station (Mon–Fri 7.30am–6.30pm, Sat 8am–noon).

ALPINE SWITZERLAND

South of Bern and Luzern lies the grand Alpine heart of Switzerland, a massively impressive region of classic Swiss scenery – high peaks, sheer valleys and cool lakes – that makes for great hiking and gentle walking, not to mention world-class winter sports. The **Bernese Oberland** is the most accessible and touristed area, but beyond this first great wall of peaks is another even more daunting range in which the **Matterhorn**, marking the Italian border, is star attraction, offering skiing all summer long. The wild summits and remote valleys in the southeastern corner of Switzerland shelter the world-famous mountain resorts of **Davos** and **St Moritz**.

Note that very little happens in the low seasons of April–May and October–November – shops and hotels may be shut, cable cars may be closed for renovations, and smaller resorts may be virtually deserted.

The Bernese Oberland

Most spectacular of the Alpine regions, the **Bernese Oberland** (*www.berneroberland.com*) is best known for a grand triple-peaked ridge – the Eiger, Mönch and Jungfrau (Ogre, Monk and Virgin), which crests 4000m. The excursion that is endlessly touted hereabouts is the rack-railway up to the **Jungfraujoch**, the highest train station in Europe at 3454m. The cable-car ride up to the **Schilthorn** (2970m) gets second billing, and is rejected by most visitors, but is in fact quicker, cheaper, offers a more scenic ride up, and has better mountain-top views. (Local cable-TV broadcasts continuous live pictures from both summits, to help plan a trip.) Most beautiful of the region's countryside is the **Lauterbrunnen valley**, overlooked by the resorts of **Wengen** and **Mürren** which provide excellent winter skiing and summer hiking, as does **Grindelwald**, in its own valley slightly east. **Interlaken** is the main transport hub for the region, but the sheer volume of tourist traffic passing through the town can make it a less-than-restful place to stay. Tourist offices can provide details of the region's numerous **mountain huts** (generally open June–Sept), which exist to offer hikers a bed and simple comforts in the wilds of nature. **Ski passes** cost Sfr40/52 for a half-/full day in a single sector; or Sfr109 for a two-day universal pass (under-19s get a twenty percent discount).

Interlaken

INTERLAKEN isn't much more than its long main street, **Höheweg**, with a train station at each end. It has little to amuse the trippers passing through on their way to the mountains, save for the cafés and hotel bars lining Höheweg and some great **views** towards the Jungfrau massif, perfectly framed between two hills and best savoured from Höhematte, a central grassy rectangle of parkland. The town lies on a neck of land between two of Switzerland's most attractive **lakes**, and the best way to arrive is by boat.

Interlaken Ost station is the terminus of mainline trains and the departure point for branch lines into the mountains (see below); boats also dock here from Brienz, on the Luzern rail line. Trains from the Bern/Zürich direction pass first through **Interlaken West** (docking point for Thunersee boats), and this station is nearer to the **tourist office**, which sits beneath the town's tallest building at Höheweg 37 (Mon–Fri 8am–noon & 2–6pm, also June–Sept Sat 8am–5pm, Oct–May Sat 8am–noon; July & Aug also Sun 5–7pm; ☎033/822 21 21, *www.interlakentourism.ch*). Beware that accommodation fills up very quickly in the summer and winter high seasons; there are hotel lists and courtesy phones at both stations. Interlaken's **HI hostel** is 2km east, at Aareweg 21 in Bönigen (☎033/822 43 53, *www.youthhostel.ch*; ③; bus #1); you'd do better joining the backpacker crowd at the excellent SB *Balmer's Herberge*, fifteen minutes south of town at Hauptstrasse 23, Matten (☎033/822 19 61, *www.balmers.com*; ②). There are quieter hostels in town, led by the quality SB *Backpackers Villa Sonnenhof*, Alpenstrasse 16 (☎033/826 71 71, *www.villa.ch*; ③), which also has **Internet** access; also try *Alp Lodge*, Marktgasse 59 (☎033/822 47 48, *www.alplodge.ch*; ③), or the SB *Happy Inn*, Rosenstrasse 17 (☎033/822 32 25, *www.happy-inn.com*; ②). The nearest **campsite** is *Sackgut* behind Ost station (☎033/822 44 34; closed Nov–April). Of the dozens of **hotels**, *Alphorn*, Rugenaustrasse 8 (☎033/822 30 51, *www.hotel-alphorn.ch*; ⑤) is a charming, well-run little place. For budget **food**, visit *Migros* restaurant opposite West station (currently undergoing rebuilding work); *PizPaz* on Centralstrasse for pasta, pizza and fish dishes; or *El Azteca*, Jungfraustrasse 30, offering Mexican set-meals from Sfr14. *Café Runft* opposite West station is a tearoom, snackerie and **bar** open until 3am; *Positiv Einfach*, Centralstrasse 11, is a small but hip music bar; and *Balmer's* hostel has cheap beer. In **adventure sports**, Alpin Raft (☎033/823 41 00, *www.alpinraft.ch*) is the local leader, running loads of activities every day from skydiving to horse trekking.

Lauterbrunnen and Wengen

It's hard to overstate just how stunning the **Lauterbrunnen valley** is. An immense U-shaped cleft with bluffs on either side rising 1000m sheer, doused by some 72 waterfalls, it is utterly spectacular. The **Staubbach falls**, the highest in Switzerland at nearly 300m, tumble just beyond the village of **LAUTERBRUNNEN** at the valley entrance. The **tourist office** is opposite Lauterbrunnen's station (Mon–Fri 8am–6pm, Sat 9am–5pm; July & Aug also Sun 10am–3pm; ☎033/855 20 08; with Internet access. Down by the tracks is *Valley Hostel* (☎033/855 20 08; ③); *Matratzenlager Stocki* just over the river has dorms in a converted farmhouse (☎033/855 17 54; ②; closed Nov & Dec). Among cheaper **hotels** are *Horner* at the far end of the village (☎033/855 16 73, *www.hornerpub.ch*; ⑤); and *Bahnhof* beside the station (☎033/855 17 23, *www.bahnhof-hotel.ch*; ⑤). There are two **campsites**: *Jungfrau* (☎033/856 20 10, *www.camping-jungfrau.ch*) and the quieter *Schützenbach*

(☎033/855 12 68), both with dorms and rooms (②). From Lauterbrunnen, a bus or a scenic half-hour walk 3km along the valley floor takes you to the spectacular **Trümmelbach falls** (daily: July & Aug 8am–6pm; Sept–June 9am–5pm; Sfr10), a series of thunderous waterfalls – the runoff from the high mountain glaciers – which have carved corkscrew channels within the valley walls. The same bus continues 1.5km to **STECHELBERG** at the end of the road, where you'll find a *Naturfreundehaus* (☎033/855 12 02; ②).

Trains bound for the Jungfraujoch (see below) grind up from Lauterbrunnen to **WENGEN**, a scenic little car-free resort perched way above the valley floor on a shelf of tranquil southwest-facing meadow, which stays lively with skiers well into April. Once the snows have receded, it sits amidst ideal hiking country. The village is overlooked by the mighty Jungfrau and, with such a lofty outlook, enjoys unrivalled valley sunsets. You'll find the **tourist office** on the main street, just up from the train station (Mon–Fri 8am–noon & 2–6pm, Sat 8.30–11.30am; July–Sept & Dec–April also Sat & Sun 4–6pm; ☎033/855 14 14, *www .wengen-muerren.ch*). Several **hotels** have dorms: best is Christian-run *Bergheim* (☎033/855 27 55, *www.jungfraublick.com*; ③), part of *Hotel Jungfraublick*. The popular SB *Hot Chili Peppers* (☎033/855 50 20, *www.backpacker.ch*; ③) has dorms and rooms, while smoke-free *Edelweiss* (☎033/855 23 88, *edelweiss@vch.ch*; ⑥) overlooks the valley. Every January, Wengen hosts World Cup downhill and slalom ski races on the Lauberhorn, which are great to watch (Sfr20), but which can book the village, and the valley, out. Further up on the train line is **KLEINE SCHEIDEGG**, whose station has comfortable dorms and rooms (☎033/855 11 51; ③). The scenic 1hr 30min hike from Kleine Scheidegg to **Männlichen** (*www.maennlichen.ch*), perched on a ridge, is particularly lovely (1hr 30min); from Männlichen a cable car runs down to Wengen on one side, or an amazing half-hour gondola ride whisks you in the other direction to Grindelwald-Grund (ER & IR no discount; SP 25 percent discount).

Mürren and the Schilthorn

From just before Stechelberg, Schilthornbahn cable cars (see below) leap the valley's west wall to reach the quiet hamlet of **GIMMELWALD**, with the popular self-catering *Mountain Hostel* (☎033/855 17 04, *www.gimmelwald-news.ch*; ②), then rise further to **MÜRREN**, another endearing car-free village which has managed to retain its atmosphere of isolation (in the off season at least). Mürren is also accessible from directly opposite Lauterbrunnen station via the BLM Bergbahn – a steep funicular to Grütschalp and a spectacular little cliff-edge **train** from there (IR no discount; ER 25-percent discount; SP free). Whichever way you arrive, it's worth it for the views. From Mürren, the valley floor is 800m straight down, and the panorama of peaks filling the sky is dazzling. The sports centre houses the **tourist office** (Mon–Fri 9am–noon & 1–6.30pm, Thurs until 8.30pm; July–Sept & Dec–April also Sat & Sun 1–5.30pm; ☎033/856 86 86, *www.wengen-muerren.ch*). For **accommodation**, *Eiger* (☎033/855 35 35; ③) is outside the train station, while at the other end of the village, near the cable-car station, is *Regina* (☎033/855 42 42; ④). The cable car continues from Mürren on a breathtaking 20min ride up to the 2970m summit of the **SCHILTHORN** (*www.schilthorn.ch*), where you can enjoy exceptional panoramic views and sip cocktails in the revolving *Piz Gloria* summit restaurant, featured in the James Bond film *On Her Majesty's Secret Service*.

Schilthornbahn **prices**, compared to the Jungfraujoch ride, are a bargain. From Stechelberg, a round-trip is Sfr89, from Mürren Sfr60 (IR no discount; ER 25 percent discount; SP free to Mürren, then 25 percent discount). Make the trip before 9am, after 3.30pm, or any time in May or October, and these drop to Sfr67/45 (discounts still apply). If you stay overnight in Mürren, ask your hotel for a free voucher to exchange for breakfast in the Schilthorn's panoramic restaurant.

Grindelwald

Valley-floor trains from Interlaken Ost also run to the more popular and visited holiday centre of **GRINDELWALD** in its own broad valley further east, nestling under the craggy trio of the Wetterhorn, Mettenberg and Eiger. Numerous trails around **Pfingstegg** and especially **First** – both at the end of gondola lines from Grindelwald – provide excellent hiking, and the icy caverns of the Oberer Gletscher are a ninety-minute walk, plus 890 stairs, away (May–Oct daily 9am–6pm; Sfr5). The **tourist office** (Mon–Fri 8am–6/7pm, Sat 8am–5pm; July & Aug also Sun 9–11am & 3–5pm; ☎033/854 12 12, *www.grindelwald.ch*) is near the station, alongside the region's main **Bergsteigerzentrum** (Mountaineering Centre; ☎033/853 12 00), which offers easy guided ascents (Sfr77 to the 2928-metre Schwarzhorn), canyon jumps (Sfr95), glacier abseils (Sfr45), and more. Grindelwald is famous **paragliding** country, and Tandem Flights (☎033/853 55 53, *www.paragliding-grindelwald.ch*) offers accompanied jumps from Sfr150. A bus from opposite *Hotel Bernerhof*, or a steep fifteen-minute walk, will get you to Terrassenweg, a quiet lane running above the village, where there's an excellent **HI hostel** (☎033/853 10 09, *www.youthhostel.ch*; ③) and a *Naturfreundehaus* (☎033/853 13 33; ③). SB *Mountain Hostel* (☎033/853 39 00, *www.mountainhostel.ch*; ③) is on the valley floor beside Grindelwald-Grund station. (Trains from Grindelwald pass through Grund on their way up to Kleine Scheidegg.) **Camp** at *Aspen* (☎033/853 11 24, *aspen@grindelwald.ch*; closed Nov–Feb).

The nearby **Grosse Scheidegg** pass is closed to private cars, but you can cross it on any of several two-, three- and four-pass summer tours by postbus, which take in spectacular scenery on some of the highest roads in Europe around the major Alpine pass-routes of the Grimsel, Furka and Susten. Consult the tourist office or postbus office (☎033/828 88 28, *www.post.ch*) for reservations. Regular buses ply over the Grosse Scheidegg to **MEIRIN-GEN**, from where trains depart to Luzern and Interlaken.

The Jungfraujoch

Switzerland's most popular (and expensive) mountain railway trundles through lush countryside south from Interlaken before coiling spectacularly up across mountain pastures, breaking the treeline and tunnelling clean through the Eiger to emerge at the **JUNGFRAU-JOCH** (3454m), an icy, windswept col just beneath the Jungfrau summit with the awesome Aletsch glacier, longest in the Alps, for company. The journey up is scenic in parts, but very long (two-and-a-half hours from Interlaken, with most of the final hour climbing in a pitch-dark tunnel), and the top station, inevitably, is a tourist circus of ice sculptures, husky sleigh rides, glacier walks, a short ski run, restaurants and a post office, all invariably overflowing with tour-groups. Nonetheless, on a clear day and with time to spare, it's worth the expense. Panoramic views from the Sphinx Terrace (3571m) to Germany's Black Forest in one direction and across a gleaming wasteland to the Italian Alps in the other are heart-thumping – as is the thin air.

There are two **routes** to the top. Trains head southwest from Interlaken Ost along the valley floor to Lauterbrunnen, from where you pick up the mountain line which climbs through Wengen; trains also head southeast from Interlaken Ost to Grindelwald, where you change for the climb, arriving from the other direction. All trains terminate at Kleine Scheidegg, where you must change for the final pull to Jungfraujoch; the popular practice is to go up one way and down the other (*www.jungfraubahn.ch*). The adult round-trip **fare** from Interlaken is a budget-crunching Sfr162 (IR no discount; ER 25 percent discount; SP free to Wengen or Grindelwald then 25 percent discount). The best deal is the discounted **Good Morning ticket**, valid if you travel up on the first train of the day (6.35am from Interlaken), and leave the summit by noon (Nov–April: first or second train plus later departure permitted); this costs Sfr125 from Interlaken (ER Sfr110; SP Sfr98), Sfr109 from Lauterbrunnen or Grindelwald, Sfr97 from Wengen, or Sfr62 from Kleine Scheidegg. **Walking** some sections of the journey, up or down, is perfectly feasible in summer, and can save a lot of money. Excellent transport networks and vista-rich footpaths linking all intermediate points mean that with judicious use of a hiking map and train timetable you can see and do a great deal in a day and still get back to Interlaken, or even Bern or Zürich, by bedtime.

Zermatt and the Matterhorn

The shark's-tooth **Matterhorn** (4478m) is the most famous of Switzerland's peaks, and no other natural or human structure in the whole country is so immediately recognizable: in most people's minds, the Matterhorn stands for Switzerland like the Eiffel Tower stands for France. One reason it's so famous is that it stands alone, its impossibly pointy shape sticking up from an otherwise uncrowded horizon above **ZERMATT** village; another is that the quintessential Swiss chocolate, Toblerone, is modelled on it. The only way to reach Zermatt is on the spectacular narrow-gauge BVZ train line (ER no discount, IR half-price for under-26s only, SP free), accessed from mainline junctions at **Brig** and **Visp**. BVZ trains depart on tracks laid in the road outside both stations. The most celebrated way to arrive is on the long east–west St Moritz-to-Zermatt **Glacier Express** which takes in some of Switzerland's finest scenery in a day-long journey by panoramic train (reserve at any train station; ER & SP free; IR half-price; small supplement payable on the Disentis–Brig section; *www.glacierexpress.ch*). Coming from Zürich, head for Göschenen, where you switch onto the narrow-gauge FO Furka-Oberalp line through Andermatt to Brig (ER & SP free; IR half-price).

Zermatt's main street throngs year-round with an odd mixture of professional climbers, tour-groups, backpackers and fur-clad socialites. Electric minibuses ferry people between the train station at the northern end of the village and the cable-car terminus 1km south. In the village, the **Alpine Museum** (May–Oct daily 10am–noon & 4–6pm; Nov–April Mon–Fri & Sun 4.30–6.30pm; Sfr5), commemorates the tragic first ascent of the Matterhorn, led by Edward Whymper in 1865: one of his party slipped on the way down, sending four people to their deaths. They, and many more Matterhorn hopefuls, are commemorated in the town's burgeoning cemetery. Opposite the station, GGB Gornergrat-Bahn trains (ER no discount, SP 25 percent discount, IR half-price) climb above the village, giving spectacular Matterhorn views (sit on the right) all the way up to the **Gornergrat**, a vantage point with a magnificent Alpine panorama including Switzerland's highest peak, the Dufourspitze (4634m). In summer, GGB trains leave Zermatt once-weekly at dawn to arrive in time for a breathtaking Alpine sunrise. At the south end of Zermatt village a cable car heads up via Furi to the **Schwarzsee** (2583m), the most popular point from which to view the peak and, in summer, the trailhead for a zigzag walk (2hr) to the Berghaus Matterhorn inn (3260m), right below the mountain. All Zermatt's cable cars and trains bring you to trailheads and spectacular views, and lifts to **Trockener Steg** give access to 21km of ski runs and a snowboard half-pipe that are open all **summer** long (day-pass Sfr60).

Practicalities

There's a hotel list and courtesy phone in the station; otherwise consult the helpful **tourist office** nearby (June–Sept & Dec–April Mon–Sat 8.30am–6/7pm, Sun 9.30am–noon & 4–7pm; rest of year Mon–Fri 8.30am–noon & 1.30–6pm, Sat 8.30am–noon; ☎027/967 01 81, *www.zermatt.ch*). The **mountain guides** office (☎027/966 24 60) organizes tours and climbs. The excellent **HI hostel** is on the east side of the village (☎027/967 23 20, *www.youthhostel.ch*; ④); nearby is the SB *Matterhorn Hostel* (☎027/968 19 19, *www.matterhornhostel.com*; ③) and a *Naturfreundehaus* (☎027/967 27 88; ④). *Camping Zermatt* (☎027/967 54 14; closed Oct–May) is north of the station. Of the many **hotels**, *Mischabel*, down by the river, is quiet and characterful (☎027/967 11 31; ⑤), while youthful *Post*, in the centre, is livelier (☎027/967 19 32, *www.postzermatt.com*; ⑥) and offers Internet access. Plenty of mountain inns and huts bring you closer to the elements, including at Schwarzsee (☎027/967 22 63; dorms ⑦) and the *Berghaus Matterhorn* (☎027/967 22 64; dorms ⑥; closed Oct–June); these price codes include half-board. There are plenty of places to **eat** all along Zermatt's main drag: *Hotel Post* has budget pizza/pasta, while the popular *North Wall* après-ski bar, on the other side of the river, also has pizzas and cheap beer. Pleasant *Café du Pont*, just past the church, serves affordable fondues and other snacks.

Davos and St Moritz

Switzerland's largest canton, in the southeast corner of the country, is officially trilingual, known as **Graubünden** in German (*www.graubuenden.ch*), *Grigioni* in Italian and *Grischun* in Romansh, the last of these a direct descendant of Latin which has survived locked away in the mountains since the Roman legions departed 1500 years ago and is now first language of some 70,000 people. (You may also come across the canton's French name of *Grisons*, though there are no French-speaking communities.) The name Graubünden, which translates as "The Grey Leagues", stems from a 1471 pact of commoners which overthrew the rule of the region's bishop-princes. Since then, Bündners have been free, and they relish the fact more than most other Swiss: it took until 1803 for them to join the Confederation, and even today they vote unequivocally against joining the EU. The folded landscape of deep, isolated valleys and thick pine forests makes this the wildest and loneliest part of the country, despite the presence of renowned mountain resorts such as **St Moritz** and **Davos**. The cantonal capital **Chur** is on a fast train link from Zürich, but all other trains in Graubünden are run by the local Rhätische Bahn (ER, IR & SP free; *www.rhb.ch*).

Davos

Twinned with Aspen, Colorado, **DAVOS** isn't so much a resort as a full-blown town, way up at 1560m. Its two halves, Davos-Platz and Davos-Dorf, are strung along a 4km ribbon of low-key development: Platz (to the west) is where most hotels and amenities are; Dorf (to the east) is where locals take refuge; and between the two is the giant Congress Centre, where every January political and business leaders of the World Economic Forum meet to discuss global cashflow, regularly sparking anticapitalist demos in the process. Davos is most famous for its toothpaste-fresh air and its consistently excellent snow cover, and has recently gained new life (and hipness) with the seal of approval of Switzerland's snowboarding cognoscenti. In summer, hotel prices plummet and the town becomes the hub of some beautiful walking trails. There are many routes up the slopes on both sides of the valley. The **Parsennbahn** funicular (*www.parsenn.ch*) heads from near Dorf station up the **Weissfluh**, the mountain which dominates the resort, terminating at the Wcissfluhjoch, a col below the summit; from here, a cable car runs to the top, or the invigorating walk down takes a couple of hours. The **Schatzalpbahn** runs from behind the tourist office up into fragrant woods, where you'll find the **Alpinum** flower garden in summer (May–Sept daily 9am–5pm; Sfr3) and an excellent, free 2.5km toboggan run in winter. Focus of winter snowboarding is the **Jakobshorn** (*www.fun-mountain.ch*), rising south of Platz station, with good slopes and a half-pipe, plus long, scenic summer walking trails. There are dozens of easier walks, especially in the meadows and woods around the small **Davosersee** lake, a short distance east of Dorf, or you could **rent bikes** from Dorf station or a handful of sports shops around town. A huge open-air **ice rink** forms in winter in the large, central Sportzentrum. Some 2km east of Platz along the main street, Promenade, is the **Kirchner Museum** (Christmas–Easter & July–Sept Tues–Sun 10am–noon & 2–6pm; rest of year Tues–Sun 2–6pm; Sfr8), displaying vibrant works by the German Expressionist painter Ernst Ludwig Kirchner.

Trains stop at both Davos-Dorf and Davos-Platz, although postbuses direct from Chur can be faster. There are **tourist offices** opposite Dorf station and at Promenade 67 in Platz (both Mon–Fri 8.30am–6pm, Sat 8.30am–4/5pm; Dec–March also Sun 10am–noon; ☎081/415 21 21, *www.davos.ch*). A Guest Card gives free use of buses and trains between Platz and Dorf, and along 15km of the valley floor; this makes it easy to reach the **HI hostel** *Höhwald*, overlooking Davosersee (☎081/416 14 84, *www.youthhostel.ch*; ②; bus #6/11 to Seebühl). The *Sportzentrum* beside the stadium has dorms (☎081/415 36 36; ④), while the riverside *Färich* **campsite** (☎081/416 10 43) is ten minutes' walk from Dorf towards the Flüelapass.

St Moritz

Plopped down amidst the quiet villages of the wild and beautiful Engadine Valley that runs for 100km along the south side of the Alps, brassy **ST MORITZ** is the prime winter retreat of the international jet set, who over the years have created a mini-Manhattan of Vuitton and Armani in this stunningly romantic setting of forest, lake and mountains; when the tourist office trumpets St Moritz's "champagne climate", they don't necessarily mean the sparkling sunshine (although there's an amazing 322 days of that a year on average). The town spans two villages, St Moritz-Bad on the lake and St Moritz-Dorf on the hillside 2km above, linked by the main Via dal Bagn. Dorf is the upmarket one, while Bad – site of a Roman spa – is more down-to-earth. The area boasts legendary bob and toboggan courses, including the death-defying 1.2km **Cresta Run** (five rides Sfr450; book on ☎081/833 46 09, *www.cresta-run.com*). You can rent wooden sleds (Sfr4/hr or Sfr10/day) for the famous winter **Preda–Bergün toboggan run** (daily 10am–5pm; *www.berguen.ch*), starting from Preda train station and taking a zigzag 5km route down through the scenic Albula valley to Bergün, where trains cart you back to the beginning; the course is floodlit six nights a week (Tues–Sun 7–11.30pm). Another toboggan run, also with rental, drops from the **Muottas Muragl** viewpoint above St Moritz down into the valley. On the hillside west of Dorf, a curious domed church-like building holds the excellent **Giovanni Segantini Museum** (June–Oct & Dec–April Tues–Sun 10am–noon & 3–6pm; Sfr7), displaying the mystically beautiful work of this largely self-taught artist, acclaimed as the definitive painter of Alpine life.

Via Serlas winds up from the **train station** below Dorf to a central square, from where the **tourist office** is 100m east at Via Maistra 12 (Mon–Sat 9am–6pm; Christmas–March also Sun 4–6pm; ☎081/837 33 33, *www.stmoritz.ch*). The **HI hostel** *Stille*, Via Surpunt 60 (☎081/833 39 69, *www.youthhostel.ch*; ④), is a twenty-minute walk around the lake (or bus stop Sonne), alongside a separate *Stille* **hotel** (☎081/833 69 48, *www.hotelstille.ch*; ⑤; closed Nov–May) and near the *Olympiaschanze* **campsite** (☎081/833 40 90; closed Oct–May). *Hotel Bellaval* (☎081/833 32 45; ⑤) is beside Dorf station. Most **restaurants** are ridiculously expensive; affordable ones include *Boccalino* pizzeria, Via dal Bagn 6, but with this kind of scenery all around, you might prefer to picnic. Your best bet for a **drink** is *Bobby's Pub*, Via dal Bagn 52.

You need to reserve at the station a day ahead for the stunningly scenic four-hour **Palm Express** postbus journey to Lugano (June–Oct daily, otherwise Fri–Sun only). This takes you west over the Maloja Pass into the gorgeous Val Bregaglia, then along the shoreline of Italy's Lake Como (passport needed) before crossing back into Switzerland for the final stretch alongside Lake Lugano.

TICINO

The Italian-speaking canton of **Ticino** (*Tessin* in German and French; *www.tourism-ticino.ch*) occupies the balmy, lake-laced southern foothills of the Alps. It's radically different from the rest of the country in almost every way: culture, food, architecture, attitude and driving style owe more to Milan than Zürich, and the glamour of the place – its lushly wooded hills, azure lakes and date palms – often seems to blind outsiders with romance. The German Swiss in particular fall head over heels for the Latin paradise on their doorstep: it takes just three hours from the grey streets of suburban Zürich to the fragrant subtropical gardens of Lugano, and you'll find throughout the canton that printed information tends to be in Italian and German, sidelining English. Switzerland has controlled the area since the early 1500s, when it moved to secure the southern approaches of the St Gotthard Pass against the dukes of Milan. It's a cruel irony that the determinedly patriotic Ticinesi now suffer the country's highest unemployment rates, even while the region's service industries thrive, staffed by Italian guest-workers and paid for by thousands of Swiss-German tourists and second-home-owners.

The main attractions are the lakeside resorts of **Locarno** and **Lugano**, where mountain scenery merges with the subtropical flora encouraged by the warm climate. The area is also known for its old churches, many containing medieval frescoes and most featuring huge external murals of St Christopher, patron saint of travellers. Unless you approach from Italy, there's only one train line in – through the 16km **Gotthard Tunnel**. The track's spiralling contortions on the approach climb south of Lake Luzern are famous: trains pass the onion-domed church at Wassen three times, first far above you, then on a level, and finally far below, before entering blackness at Göschenen and emerging at Airolo for the descent to Ticino's capital, **Bellinzona**.

Bellinzona

Guarding the southern approaches to the San Gottardo and San Bernardino passes, **BELLINZONA** is the junction-point through which most traffic flows without stopping, but it's worth spending some quiet time here before the bustle of the lakes. High on the town's central rock, and accessible by lift from behind Piazza del Sole, is **Castelgrande** (Tues–Sun 9am–midnight; *www.castelgrande.ch*), most impressive of Bellinzona's three medieval castles. Steps wind down from here to the elegant Renaissance buildings of **Piazza Collegiata**, dominated by a lavish church and surrounded by atmospheric old-town alleys; Piazza Nosetto is just south, as is peaceful Piazza Indipendenza. On the eastern side of Collegiata, a path rises to **Castello di Montebello** (Tues–Sun 8am–6pm), with great views, from where a stiff 15-minute climb further up will bring you to **Castello di Sasso Corbaro** (April–Oct Tues–Sun 8am–6pm), with a particularly welcome vine-shaded restaurant and a spectacular rampart panorama. All three castles house missable historical museums.

The **train station** is ten minutes north of the centre. The **tourist office** under the arcades just off Piazza Nosetto (Mon–Fri 8am–6.30pm, Sat 9am–5pm; Oct–March Sat closes noon; ☎091/825 21 31, *www.bellinzona.ch*) has lots of material and can provide some excellent walking suggestions. The riverside *Molinazzo* **campsite** (☎091/829 11 18; closed Oct–March) is well north of town. Of the **hotels**, rooms above the *Tsui-Fok* Chinese restaurant, Via Nocca 20 (☎091/825 13 32; ④) and the *San Giovanni* diner, Via San Giovanni 7 (☎091/825 19 19; ⑤) are most affordable. Cheap **food** is available at *Inova*, Ticino's version of *Manora*, in the Innovazione store on Viale Stazione. Castelgrande houses the *Grotto San Michele* (a *grotto* is a Ticinese tavern for local wine and cheap home-cooking), where you can eat on the panoramic terrace for Sfr14–20. Pavement **café/bars** abound, especially around Via Codeborgo.

On a journey north or south, it's worth getting off the train at little **GIORNICO**, about 30km north of Bellinzona. It was here in 1478 that a Swiss force numbering six hundred defeated a 10,000-strong Milanese army, thereby linking Ticino's future to Switzerland instead of Italy. Giornico is lovely, a typical Ticinese village built on both sides of the tumbling river, with picturesque cobbled alleys, the fine Romanesque church of San Nicolao and a photogenic hump-backed bridge. There are also a couple of terrific *grotti*, both of them serving excellent home-cooked food; the shaded *Grotto dei Due Ponti* occupies a fairytale mid-river island, but food at the less attractive *Grotto Pergola*, south of San Nicolao, is even better.

Locarno

Mainline trains speed south to Lugano and Milan, while a branch line heads west to Lake Maggiore and its principal Swiss resort, **LOCARNO**, overrun with the rich and wannabe-famous on summer weekends yet still managing to retain its Mediterranean, shades-and-*gelati* cool. The focus of town is **Piazza Grande**; a busy arcaded square just off the palm-fringed lakefront. Most interest lies in the narrow streets of the characterful Old Town, ranged on gently rising ground behind Piazza Grande; wandering through the alleys with an ice cream is the best way to blend in with local life. From the west end of the piazza, lanes run up to Via

Cittadella and the richly Baroque **Chiesa Nuova**, with a sumptuously stuccoed ceiling. Via Borghese, one street further up, brings you to the huge and rather sombre church of **Sant'Antonio**, next to which is the **Casa Rusca** gallery (Tues–Sun 10am–noon & 2–5pm; Sfr5) focusing on twentieth-century Swiss artist Jean Arp. Alleys lead south downhill to the tall fourteenth-century church of **San Francesco**, with faded Baroque frescoes, and further down to the thirteenth-century **Castello Visconteo**, housing an archeological museum (April–Oct Tues–Sun 10am–noon & 2–5pm; Sfr5), especially strong on beautiful Roman glass. Most striking of all, though, is the church of **Madonna del Sasso** (daily 6.30am–7pm), an impressive ochre vision floating above the town founded in 1480. The walk up (or down) through a wooded ravine and past decaying shrines, is glorious; or take the funicular from just west of the station to Ticino's greatest photo-opportunity, looking down on the church and lake. From the top, a cable car runs further up to **Cardada** on the ridge (*www.cardada.ch*), where there are more walking routes and a chairlift whisking you up to the spectacular views at Cimetta. East of Locarno is **Valle Verzasca**, where deathwish freaks can re-enact the opening scene of the James Bond film *Goldeneye*, by bungeeing a world-record 220m off the **Verzasca Dam** (Sfr260; book on ☎01/950 33 88, *www.trekking.ch*; closed Nov–March).

Practicalities

Locarno's **train station** is 150m northeast of Piazza Grande. Between the two is the landing stage on the lake; summer boats run to nearby Swiss lakeside resorts such as Ascona, and way south to Italian ones such as Stresa (IR, ER & SP no discount; *www.navlaghi.it*). The **tourist office** is in the Casino complex opposite the landing stage (Mon–Fri 9am–6pm; March–Oct also Sat 10am–4pm, Sun 10am–2pm; ☎091/751 03 33, *www.maggiore.ch*). Both the modern **HI hostel** *Ostello Palagiovani*, Via Varenna 18 (☎091/756 15 00, *www.youthhostel.ch*; ③; bus #31/#36 to Cinque Vie) and central *Città Vecchia*, Via Torretta 13 (☎091/751 45 54, *www.cittavecchia.ch*; ③; closed Nov–Feb) have dorms and rooms; *Ostello Giaciglio*, Via Rusca 7 (☎091/751 30 64; ③) has dorms only. The pricey *Delta* **campsite** (☎091/751 60 81) is fifteen minutes south along the lakeshore. There's a self-service *Inova* beside the station and Piazza Grande is full of cafés and pizzerias buzzing from morning until after midnight, although **eating** and **drinking** is more atmospheric in the Old Town alleys. *Cittadella* (see above) serves affordable pizzas; friendly *Bar del Pozzo* is on Piazza Sant'Antonio; *Cantina Canetti* off Piazza Grande has live accordion on weekend nights; *Simba*, Lungolago 3a, is a popular DJ bar. Music festivals devoted to country, blues, funk and jazz follow hot on each other's heels during June and July, while early August's excellent **Locarno International Film Festival** (*www.pardo.ch*) is stealing a march on Cannes for movie quality and star-appeal; catch nightly offerings on Europe's largest movie screen (26x14m), set up in Piazza Grande.

The Centovalli railway

Locarno is the eastern terminus of the dramatic **Centovalli railway** (ER, IR & SP free; *www.centovalli.ch*), well worth putting aside half a day for. Clanky little trains run from beneath Locarno's station west into the impressive Centovalli – so named for its "hundred" side-valleys – most of the time sidewinding above ravine-like depths; sit on the left for the best views. After the border at **Camedo** (passport needed), trains roll on through rustic villages amid spectacular scenery before easing down into the Italian town of **DOMODOSSOLA**. Swiss express trains from here run west to Brig (for Zermatt), Geneva and Bern; Italian ones head south to Milan.

Lugano

With its compact cluster of Italianate piazzas and extensive tree-lined promenades, **LUGANO** is the most alluring of Ticino's lake resorts, less touristic than Locarno but with, if anything, double the chic. Centre of town is **Piazza di Riforma**, a huge café-lined square perfect for eyeballing passers-by over a cappuccino, while Lugano's exceptionally beautiful lake is metres away, as are the characterful steep lanes of the old town. Through the maze northwest of Riforma, Via Cattedrale dog-legs up to **Cattedrale San Lorenzo**, characterized by a fine Renaissance portal, fragments of interior frescoes, and spectacular views from its terrace. Also from Riforma, narrow Via Nassa – rivalling Zürich's Bahnhofstrasse for big-name designer glitz – heads southwest to the medieval church of **Santa Maria degli Angioli**, containing a stunning wall-sized fresco of the Crucifixion. A little further south is the **Museo d'Arte Moderna**, Riva Caccia 5 (Tues–Sun 9am–7pm; Sfr10), with world-class exhibitions; and a little further still is the modestly named district of **PARADISO**, from where a funicular rises to **San Salvatore**, a rugged rock pinnacle offering fine views of the lake and surrounding countryside (*www.montesansalvatore.ch*). East from Riforma along the shore on foot or with bus #1, you'll come to the gates of **Villa Favorita** (Easter–Oct Fri–Sun 10am–5pm; Sfr10), home to part of the great Thyssen-Bornemisza art collection. On display is a high-quality selection of modernist works by European and American painters, many of them relative unknowns but all the more eye-opening for that – but the setting is as impressive as the art: the villa can only be approached on foot via a long cypress-lined path through lavishly beautiful waterside gardens, a dreamy wander worth the entrance fee by itself. The slopes of **Monte Brè** behind are home to most of Lugano's many millionaires, while a funicular rises from the adjacent district of **CASSARATE** to the summit, with bracing walks and views (*www.montebre.ch*). The best of the lake is behind (south of) San Salvatore on the Ceresio peninsula, accessed by boats or postbuses. Here you'll find tiny **MONTAGNOLA**, where the writer Hermann Hesse lived for 43 years; his first house, Casa Camuzzi, is now a small museum (March–Oct Tues–Sun 10am–12.30pm & 2–6.30pm; Nov–Feb Sat & Sun same times; Sfr5; *tcp.ch/cultura*), with an excellent 45-minute English film on Hesse's life in Ticino. Jewel of the lake, however, is **MORCOTE** on the gorgeous southern tip of the peninsula. Tranquil stepped lanes lead up to its photogenic church of Santa Maria del Sasso, with striking interior frescoes and a grand vista. Several walks explore the lush woodlands, including a trail back to San Salvatore (2hr 30min).

Practicalities

Lugano's **train station** overlooks the town from the west, linked to the centre by a short funicular or by steps down to Via Cattedrale. The **tourist office** is in Palazzo Civico, between Riforma and the lake (Mon–Fri 9am–5.30/6.30pm; April–Oct also Sat 9am–5pm, Sun 10am–2pm; ☎091/913 32 32, *www.lugano-tourism.ch*). **Boats** around the lake (IR & ER no discount, SP free) depart from opposite the tourist office. One of Switzerland's best-value **HI hostels** (complete with swimming pool) is at Via Cantonale 13, Savosa (☎091/966 27 28, *www.youthhostel.ch*; ②; closed Nov–March; bus #5 to Crocifisso from the stop 200m left out of the train station); another HI hostel is at Figino, southwest of town (☎091/995 11 51; ②; closed Nov–March; postbus from Riforma to Casoro). The SB *Montarina*, behind the station at Via Montarina 1 (☎091/966 72 72, *www.montarina.ch*; ③), also has dorms. Affordable **hotels** include *Ginevra*, Via Ginevra 7 (☎091/923 61 70; ④). *Molinazzo* (☎091/605 17 57) is one of several lakeside **campsites** in Agno, a short train ride west. Lugano is blessed with fine espresso, served at *La Cafferia Cattedrale*, Via Cattedrale 6, and reasonably priced **eateries** on all the central squares: Piazza Cioccaro, the lower terminus of the funicular, is home to a big *Inova* and *Sayonara* (for pasta not sushi), while *La Tinèra*, off Via dei Gorini, behind Riforma, has tasty Ticinese chicken stews and *Hotel Pestalozzi* (see above) has a good vegetarian restaurant. Although the many bars and cafés around Riforma are packed with evening **drinkers**, hip Luganesi tuck themselves away elsewhere: off Via Vegezzi, east of the post office, pumping *La Salsita* doubles as cool drinking-den and Mexican eatery, while in the unlikely warren of the Quartiere Maghetti nearby is *Etnic* (closed Sat eve & Sun), with superb inexpensive Mediterranean-style food, beer, cocktails and a cosy studentish atmosphere.

If you're going south to **Milan**, ask at Lugano station for a free city-transport pass with your train ticket. Heading north, reserve at the train station a day ahead for the scenic four-hour **Palm Express** postbus journey (June–Oct daily, otherwise Fri–Sun only), which follows the shoreline of Lake Como northeast to Chiavenna (passport needed), then heads into the spectacular Val Bregaglia and over the Maloja Pass to the famous Swiss resort of **St Moritz**.

LIECHTENSTEIN

Only slightly larger than Manhattan island, **Liechtenstein** is the world's fourth-smallest country. It's a quiet, unassuming place, ruled over by His Serene Highness Prince Hans Adam II, and has made a mint from nursing some Sfr90 billion in its numbered bank accounts, a living that has inevitably laid it open to accusations of dubious practice. Money-laundering aside, the main reason to visit is inevitably the novelty value. You have to feel sorry for little **VADUZ**, labouring under the weight of being capital of a historical oddity: the tiny town bulges with glass-plated banks and squadrons of whistle-stop visitors aimless with anticlimax. Central hub is the post office, where all buses stop, midway between the two parallel main streets, Äulestrasse and pedestrianized Städtle. Facing it is the sleek new **Kunstmuseum** (Tues–Sun 10am–5pm, Thurs until 8pm; Sfr5; *www.kunstmuseum.li*), holding the world-famous private **art** collection inherited – and added to – by the prince, which includes exquisite works by Rubens, Rembrandt and others. Perched picturesquely on the forested hillside above the town is the prince's restored sixteenth-century **castle** (no public access). If you have some time to spare, catch bus #10 to Liechtenstein's sole mountain resort of **MALBUN**, a small, blissfully quiet retreat up at 1602m.

Practicalities

Bus #1 shuttles over the Rhine to Vaduz from **Sargans** train station on the Zürich–Chur line (no border controls). Postbuses from Vaduz serve all points in Liechtenstein as well as **Feldkirch** just across the border in Austria (passport needed), from where trains run on to Bregenz, Innsbruck and Vienna. All Swiss transport passes are valid on Liechtenstein buses; normal fares are Sfr2–4.

The Vaduz **tourist office**, Städtle 37 (Mon–Fri 8am–noon & 1.30–5.30pm; April–Oct also Sat 10am–noon & 1–4pm; May–Sept also Sun same times; ☎232 14 43, *www.fuerstlichemomente.li*), has good information and will bang a stamp into your passport as a memento (Sfr2). There's an **HI hostel** at Untere Rüttigasse 6, beside Mühleholz bus stop in **SCHAAN**, 2km north of Vaduz (☎232 50 22; ③; closed Dec–Feb). The best-value **hotel** is friendly *Uf der Säga* (☎392 43 77; ⑤), in the countryside near **TRIESEN**, 5km south of Vaduz, alongside *Mittagspitz* **campsite** (☎392 36 77). At **STEG**, near Malbun, *Sücka* doubles as a working farm and guest house, with dorms (☎263 25 79; ③). For **food** in Vaduz, *Cesare*, Städtle 15 (closed Sat & Sun), offers good Italian *menus* for Sfr20; while gourmet stand-up deli *Eredi Florini*, Herrengasse 9 (closed Sun), has delicious point-and-choose meals (Sfr12–20).

travel details

TRAINS

Basel to: Bern (hourly; 1hr); Geneva (hourly; 2hr 50min); Interlaken West & Ost (hourly; 2hr 10min); Lausanne (hourly; 2hr 30min); Lugano (hourly; 3hr 50min); Luzern (hourly; 1hr 5min); Zürich (every 30min; 1hr).

Bellinzona to: Locarno (every 30min; 20min); Lugano (every 30min; 25min); Luzern (hourly; 2hr 35min); Zürich (hourly; 2hr 45min).

Bern to: Basel (hourly; 1hr); Brig (hourly; 1hr 40min); Geneva (every 30min; 1hr 45min); Interlaken West & Ost (hourly; 45min); Lausanne (every 30min; 1hr 10min); Luzern (every 2hr; 1hr 20min); Zürich (every 30min; 1hr 10min).

Brig to: Bern (hourly; 1hr 40min); Lausanne (twice hourly; 1hr 45min); Zermatt (hourly; 1hr 20min).

Davos to: Chur (hourly; 1hr 35min); St Moritz (hourly; 1hr 35min).

Geneva to: Basel (hourly; 2hr 50min); Bern (hourly; 1hr 45min); Brig (twice hourly; 2hr 20min); Lausanne (3 hourly; 35min); Montreux (hourly; 1hr 5min); Vevey (hourly; 1hr); Zürich (every 30min; 3hr).

Grindelwald to: Interlaken Ost (hourly; 20min); Jungfraujoch (every 30min; 1hr 30min – change at Kleine Scheidegg).

Interlaken Ost to: Bern (hourly; 50min); Grindelwald (hourly; 40min); Jungfraujoch (hourly; 2hr 30min – change at Grindelwald or Lauterbrunnen, then Kleine Scheidegg); Lauterbrunnen (hourly; 20min); Luzern (hourly; 1hr 55min); Wengen (hourly; 40min – change at Lauterbrunnen); Zürich (hourly; 2hr 15min).

Interlaken West to: Bern (hourly; 45min); Zürich (hourly; 2hr 10min).

Kleine Scheidegg to: Grindelwald (every 30min; 35min); Jungfraujoch (every 30min; 50min); Lauterbrunnen (every 30min; 1hr); Wengen (every 30min; 30min).

Lausanne to: Basel (hourly; 2hr 30min); Bern (every 30min; 1hr 10min); Brig (every 30min; 1hr 40min); Geneva (3 hourly; 35min); Montreux (every 20min; 25min); Vevey (every 20min; 15min); Zürich (every 30min; 2hr 30min).

Lauterbrunnen to: Interlaken Ost (hourly; 20min); Jungfraujoch (every 20min; 1hr 40min – change at Kleine Scheidegg); Wengen (every 20min; 15min).

Locarno to: Bellinzona (every 30min; 20min); Domodossola, Italy (hourly; 1hr 45min).

Lugano to: Bellinzona (twice hourly; 30min); Luzern (hourly; 2hr 50min); Milan, Italy (hourly; 1hr 30min); Zürich (hourly; 3hr 10min).

Luzern to: Basel (hourly; 1hr 15min); Bern (every 2hr; 1hr 20min); Brienz (hourly; 1hr 35min); Interlaken Ost (hourly; 1hr 55min); Lugano (hourly; 2hr 50min); Zürich (every 30min; 45min).

Montreux to: Brig (twice hourly; 1hr 20min); Geneva (twice hourly; 1hr 20min); Interlaken (every 2hr; 3hr – change at Zweisimmen & Spiez); Lausanne (every 20min; 25min); Vevey (3 hourly; 10min).

St Moritz to: Chur (hourly; 2hr).

Vevey to: Brig (twice hourly; 1hr 30min); Geneva (twice hourly; 1hr 10min); Lausanne (every 20min; 15min); Montreux (3 hourly; 10min).

Wengen to: Jungfraujoch (every 30min; 1hr 25min – change at Kleine Scheidegg); Lauterbrunnen (every 20min; 15min).

Zürich to: Basel (every 30min; 1hr); Bern (every 30min; 1hr 10min); Chur (hourly; 1hr 35min); Geneva (every 30min; 3hr); Interlaken Ost (hourly; 2hr 15min); Lausanne (every 30min; 2hr 30min); Lugano (hourly; 3hr 10min); Luzern (hourly; 50min); Sargans (hourly; 1hr 10min).

BUSES

Lugano to: St Moritz (twice daily; 4hr).

Sargans to: Vaduz (every 20min; 30min).

Vaduz to: Malbun (hourly; 30min).

BOATS

(May–Sept summary; very few boats run in winter)

Geneva to: Lausanne (3 daily; 3hr 30min); Montreux (3 daily; 5hr); Vevey (3 daily; 4hr 30min).

Interlaken Ost to: Brienz (hourly; 1hr 20min).

Lausanne to: Evian, France (hourly; 40min); Geneva (3 daily; 3hr 30min); Montreux (5 daily; 1hr 30min); Vevey (5 daily; 1hr).

Luzern to: Alpnachstad (6 daily; 1hr 40min); Flüelen (8 daily; 2hr 50min); Kehrsiten (hourly; 35min); Vitznau (hourly; 1hr).

CHAPTER 30

TURKEY

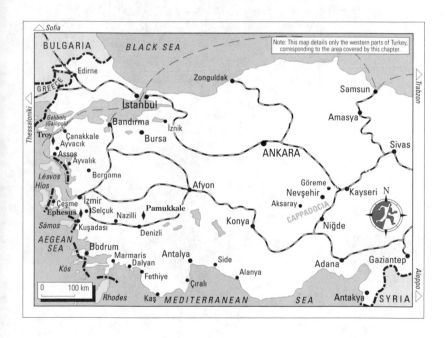

Note: This map details only the western parts of Turkey, corresponding to the area covered by this chapter.

Introduction

Turkey is a country with a multiple identity, poised uneasily between East and West. The only NATO member in the Middle East region, the country has recently been accepted as a candidate for membership of the EU. Yet although in many respects Western, Turkey retains its frustrating differences, and its contradictions: mosques coexist with churches, and remnants of the Roman Empire crumble alongside ancient Hittite and Neolithic sites. Politically, modern Turkey was a bold experiment, founded on the remaining Anatolian kernel of the Ottoman Empire and almost entirely the creation of a single man, **Mustafa Kemal Atatürk**. An explicitly secular republic, though one in which almost all of the inhabitants are at least nominally Muslim, it's a vast country and incorporates large disparities in levels of development. But it's an immensely rewarding place to travel, not least because of the people, whose reputation for friendliness and hospitality is richly deserved.

Western Turkey is the most visited and economically developed part of the country. **İstanbul**, straddling the Bosphorus straits and the Marmara coast, is a heady mix of the Oriental and state-of-the-art modern. It's the country's cultural and commercial centre and also visibly the old imperial capital, and would take months of exploration to truly do it justice. Flanking İstanbul on opposite sides of the **Sea of Marmara** are the two earlier Ottoman capitals, **Bursa** and **Edirne**, and the former Byzantine capital of **İznik**, with, just beyond, the World War I battlefields of the **Dardanelles**.

Moving south, on the **Aegean Coast** small country towns like **Ayvalık** are swathed in olive groves, while the area is littered with ancient sites like **Assos, Bergama** and **Ephesus**, which have been a magnet for travellers since the eighteenth century. Beyond the functional but not unattractive city of **İzmir**, the Aegean coast is Turkey at its most developed, with large numbers of visitors drawn to resorts like **Çeşme, Bodrum** and **Marmaris**, beyond which the Mediterranean coast begins. There are remnants of the Lycians at **Xanthos**, and more resorts in **Kaş** and **Fethiye**, along the aptly named "Turquoise Coast".

On the Mediterranean coast, **Antalya** is one of Turkey's fastest-growing cities, a sprawling place that is the best starting-point on the stretch towards the Syrian border, featuring extensive sands and archeological sites – most notably at **Perge** and **Aspendos** – until castle-topped **Alanya**, where the tourist numbers begin to diminish. It's worth heading inland from here for the spectacular attractions of **Cappadocia**, with its famous rock churches, subterranean cities and landscape studded with "fairy chimneys", as well as the Selçuk architecture and dervish associations of **Konya**. Further north, **Ankara**, Turkey's capital, is a planned city whose contrived Western feel gives some indication of the priorities of the modern Turkish Republic.

Information and maps

Most Turkish towns of any size will have a **tourist office**, *Turizm Danışma Bürosu*, generally open Mon–Fri 8.30am–12.30pm & 1.30–5.30pm, with extended evening and weekend hours in big resorts and cities, and during the peak summer season. Staff outside the larger cities and resorts may not speak English, but they often have surprisingly good brochures and maps, and should at least be able to help you with accommodation.

The best available **maps** are produced by Geo Centre/RV ("Turkey West" and "Turkey East"), sold separately as sheets or together in book form at most major resorts. City tourist offices normally stock reasonable **street plans**. The *A–Z Atlas of İstanbul* (pub. Asya) is a worthwhile investment if you're spending time in the city.

Money and banks

Turkish **currency** is the lira, abbreviated as TL. There are coins of 50,000 (written on the coin as "50 bin") and 100,000, and notes of 250,000, 500,000, 1,000,000, 5,000,000 and 10,000,000. Bear in mind that the 5,000,000 note looks very similar to the old 100,000 one, and it's not unknown for visitors to be fooled into accepting the worthless lower denomination. **Rates** for foreign currency are always better

---

TURKEY ON THE NET

inside Turkey, and because of the TL's constant deval-
uation you should change money only as you need it.
Many pensions and hotels, particularly in the popular
destinations, will quote prices in **US dollars** as well
as TL and you can pay in both.

Banks are open mainly Mon–Fri 8.30am–noon &
1.30–5pm, although some, notably Garanti Bankasi,
open at lunchtimes and on Saturdays. Most charge a
commission of about US$2.50 for travellers' cheques.
Between April and October many coastal resorts
between Çanakkale and Alanya have weekend and
evening hours at specific *nöbetçi* banks; a list is posted in the window or door of each branch. You can
also use the **exchange booths** run by banks in
coastal resorts, airports and ferry docks, though
some charge a small commission. Easiest option is a
private exchange office, which will offer competitive
rates and charge no commission. Almost all bank
branches have **ATMs** which accept Cirrus and Plus,
but it's wise to use them during banking hours in case
your card is swallowed; avoid stand-alone ATMs for
the same reason. **Post offices** in sizeable towns
also sometimes change currency and travellers'
cheques, for a one-percent commission.

Communications

The Turkish **postal service** is run by the **PTT**, with
most post offices open Mon–Sat 8am–5pm; main
branches are open until 7 or 8pm and on Sundays.
Post boxes are clearly labelled with categories of
destination – *yurtdışı* means overseas.

The PTT is the best place to make **phone calls**.
Post offices sell phonecards (30, 60 and 100 units)
and *jetons* (tokens), and have both types of phone, as
well as metered phones. Some main PTTs have 24-
hour phone services. However, Turk Telekom is currently being privatized so it's unclear how long the
PTT will continue to offer these services. A new generation of payphones accepting credit cards has
appeared, as have numerous private **phone shops**
(Köntürlü telefon) offering metered calls at dubious,
unofficial rates. Call ☎118 for **directory** enquiries,
☎115 for the international **operator**. There are three
GSM **mobile-phone** companies, all of which sell
pre-paid SIM cards for around $20. Top-up cards are
widely available.

Internet access is excellent in Turkey, with cybercafés in most towns charging $0.50–1.50/hr depend-
ing on location and the mode of access (dial-up or
leased-line).

Getting around

Public transport in Turkey is easy and inexpensive.
The train system is limited and slow, but makes a fun
change from the myriad private buses used by most
Turks. Short stretches are best covered by *dolmuş* –
a name referring either to shared taxis in towns or to
minibuses that link rural villages.

■ Buses and dolmuşes

Long-distance bus is the best way of getting
around. There is no national bus company; most
routes are covered by several competing firms, which
will all have ticket booths at the **otogars** (bus stations) from which they operate, as well as offices in
the relevant town centres. **Terminal** is the name
given to a new bus station in a town that already has
an *otogar*. (In bigger cities, the better bus companies
will run a minibus transfer service between their central offices and the *otogar* or *terminal* – useful if the
latter is some way out of town.) There's no such thing
as a comprehensive timetable. Better companies will
have a seasonal schedule of sorts but even these are
subject to weekly or even daily changes and it's best
to shop around to find the most convenient **departure time**; bigger companies tend to make fewer
stops enroute, which means their quoted journey time
is more accurate. Bus companies in smaller *otogars*
employ touts to drum up trade, but larger *otogars* are
mercifully free of them. **Fares** vary only slightly
between the best and scruffiest companies: as a
broad example, expect to pay about $3 per 100km on
the better buses. Top companies such as Ulusoy,
Pamukkale, Kamil Koç and Varan are worth the bit
extra in comfort, service and safety. From October to
April (ie outside the main tourist season), the bigger
companies may stop running buses altogether along
routes that are popular with summer visitors, in which
case you may have to make do with slower, more
uncomfortable local minibus services; in extreme
cases you may not find any transport at all.

For short hops you're most likely to use a **dolmuş**,
a car or minibus that follows a set route, picking up
and dropping off along the way; sometimes the destination will be posted on a sign at the kerbside, and
sometimes also within the *dolmuş* itself, though
you'll generally have to ask. On busy urban routes it's
better to take the *dolmuş* from the start of its run;
otherwise, hail it like a taxi to stop it in the street.
Fares are very low; passengers traditionally make up
change between themselves and pass the total up to
the driver, a system less haphazard than it sounds.

■ Trains

Turkey's **train network**, run by the TCDD, is patchy. The most useful services are the expresses between İstanbul and Ankara, and other long-distance links from İstanbul or Ankara to main provincial cities such as Edirne, Konya, Eskişehir, Denizli and İzmir. Most routes are slow, tortuous and wonderfully scenic. Sleeper cabins are available on overnight services at very reasonable rates. Reservations for most journeys can be made in İstanbul, İzmir or Ankara, though they're only really necessary at weekends or on national holidays. Basic prices are about the same per kilometre as the buses; students with an ISIC card get a twenty-percent discount. **InterRail** is valid, **Eurail** isn't.

■ Driving, hitching and taxis

Given the excellent bus services, you don't need to **drive** in Turkey, but doing so can let you see more of the country more quickly. Roads are usually adequate, although often dangerously narrow. Drive on the right, and give priority to the right, even on roundabouts. Speed limits are 50kph in towns, 100kph on main roads and highways. Foreigners are rarely stopped by the police at the frequent checkpoints, but if you are you'll be required to show your driving licence and proof of ownership (or car-rental papers) and may be given an on-the-spot fine for not wearing a seatbelt or for speeding. You have to pay a hefty supplement to Green Card **insurance** for it to be valid in Turkey. In the event of **breakdown** or other problems the Turkish motoring organization TTOK (☎0212/282 8140 or 269 0875) can provide advice and put you in touch with approved repair centres. **Car rental** is expensive, from $500 a week with unlimited mileage. Local chains tend to be a lot cheaper, and are responsive to bargaining, particularly in the bigger cities/resorts. Comprehensive insurance is rare; if you have an accident make sure you get a police report or you'll be held responsible for repairs.

Hitching is an option where public transport is scarce or unavailable, and lifts tend to be frequent and friendly. You may be expected to share a glass of tea with the driver upon arrival. It is polite to offer a little money, though it will almost always be refused.

If you're travelling in a small group of three or four people, it can be quicker and often not much more expensive to negotiate a price with a taxi. This is a very good idea if you want to see a couple of places in a day, and may work out cheaper than the equivalent bus or *dolmuş* fares.

■ Ferries

Nearly all Turkey's **ferries** are run by the Türkiye Denizcilik İşletmesi (Turkish Maritime Lines or TDİ), who operate everything from inner-city shuttles and inter-island lines to international routings. Overnight services are popular, and you should buy tickets well in advance through authorized TDİ agents. There are five classes of cabin on long-haul ferries, where it's also possible to reserve a "Pullman" reclining seat, but if you leave booking to the last minute you won't even get one of these. Sleeping on deck is viable – but you need a seat booking before you'll be allowed on board. **Fares** are reasonable; for example, a third-class double cabin from İstanbul to İzmir costs about $60 per person, with a car costing roughly the same. Students aged 28 or under get a thirty-percent discount with an ISIC card.

■ Planes

The domestic **air** network is fairly comprehensive, with full-fare prices roughly five times that of ground transport. Still, the size of the country may mean that, on a short visit, you resort to a plane at least once to make the most of your stay. The state-run THY is the main operator, flying between most big cities; the only alternative currently is Onur Air, offering limited summer services from İstanbul to Antalya and Bodrum.

Accommodation

Finding **accommodation** is generally no problem, except in high season at the busier coastal resorts and larger towns. The economic crisis of early 2001 has left prices distinctly low by northern European standards, although it remains to be seen how long this will last.

■ Hotels and pensions

Many Turkish **hotels** are graded by the tourism ministry on a scale of one to five stars. Ungraded establishments, which can be either hotels or **pensions** *(pansiyons)* – there's effectively no difference – are licensed by municipalities, and may be as good as equivalent graded ones. A double room in a one-star hotel costs $15–30 in season, with breakfast sometimes included. The most basic ungraded places may offer spartan rooms, with or without toilet, washbasin and/or shower, for as low as $12 per person. A new type of "bijou" hotel/pension, often in historic buildings, offers high levels of comfort, sometimes at surprisingly reasonable prices.

There's also a well-established breed of "**backpacker**" hotels/pensions. In the coastal resorts and other tourist targets, touts acting for these places meet every incoming bus, *dolmuş* and ferry. Rooms tend to be sparse but clean, roughly $10–20 for an ensuite double ($10–15 without facilities) or $5–10 for a dorm bed. If a place is open during the low season (Nov–April), you may find prices dropping to half the summer rates; however, most resort-based places close in winter. It would be wise to call them or the local tourist office in advance to check what is open.

■ Hostels and campsites

Turkey has a small chain of **hostels** under the banner "Turkish YHA", but of these only one is actually HI-affiliated (the *Interyouth* hostel in İstanbul). That said, hostels differ little in price and facilities from the backpacker-oriented hotels and pensions outlined above.

Campsites are common on the coast and in national parks but rare elsewhere. Charges per person run from a couple of dollars for the most basic places to $10 in a well-appointed site at a major resort in season, plus $3–4 per tent. You may also be charged anything from $5 to $20 for your vehicle. Campsites often rent out tents or provide chalet accommodation for $10–20. Camping rough is not illegal, but hardly anybody does it except when trekking in the mountains. The tourism ministry produces an excellent **map and guide** for recommended campsites, which is generally available from tourist offices.

Food and drink

At its finest, Turkish **food** is one of the world's great cuisines, yet prices are on the whole affordable. Unadventurous travellers are prone to get stuck in a kebab rut, but everyone apart from the most dedicated vegetarians should find enough variety to keep budget meals interesting.

■ Food

These days the Turkish **breakfast** (*kahvaltı*) served at hotels and *pansiyons* is usually an open buffet, offering bread or toast along with butter, cheese, jam, honey and olives. There's usually unlimited quantities of tea, but coffee is generally extra. Many workers start the morning with a *börek* or a *poça*, pastries filled with meat, cheese or potato that are sold at a tiny *büfe* (stall/café) or at street carts. Others made do with a simple *simit* (sesame-seed bread ring). The traditional eastern Anatolian breakfast is a bowl of *mercimek çorba* (lentil soup) served with lemon and chilli powder.

Later in the day, vendors hawk *lahmacun*, small "pizzas" with meat-based toppings, and, in coastal cities, *midye tava* (deep-fried mussels). Another option is *pide*, or Turkish pizza – flat bread with various toppings – served at a *pideci* or *pide salonu*. Another snack speciality is *mantı*, meat-filled ravioli drenched in yoghurt and oil.

A **restaurant** (*lokanta*) serves more substantial hot dishes in rich tomato sauces, while a *kebapcı* specializes in grilled or roast kebabs. Most budget-priced restaurants are alcohol-free; some places marked *içkili* (licensed) may be more expensive. A useful exception is a *meyhane* (tavern), which usually serves *meze* – an extensive array of cold appetizers – as well as grilled kebabs and fish as the focus for a full evening's eating and drinking.

Prices vary widely according to the type of establishment: from $3 a head at a simple *lokanta*, or $10–20 at regular resort *restaurants*, up to $50–100 a head at flashier places. Many don't have **menus**; you'll need to ascertain the prices of most main courses beforehand. **Meze**, or appetizers, come in all shapes and sizes, the commonest being *dolma* (usually peppers stuffed with rice), *patlıcan salata* (aubergine in tomato sauce), and *acılı* (a mixture of tomato paste, onion, chilli and parsley), as well as seafood salads and pickled fish. **Main courses** served in *lokantas* include a number of vegetable dishes such as green beans or baked beans in tomato sauces, though they're invariably prepared with lamb- or chicken-based stock. **Meat** dishes include several variations on the kebab *(kebap)*, for example *İskender kebap* (slices of meat on *pide*, with spicy tomato sauce, yoghurt and salad), *köfte* (meatballs), *şış* (grilled meat chunks) or *çöp şiş* (small bits of lamb). **Fish and seafood** are good, if usually pricey, and sold by weight more often than by item. Budget mainstays include fresh-ly grilled *sardalya* (sardines), *palamut* (bonito), *ıskumru* (mackerel), *kalkan* (turbot) and *kefal* (grey mullet).

Finally, those with a **sweet** tooth will find every imaginable concoction at a *pastane* (sweet-shop): best are the honey-soaked *baklava*, and a variety of milk puddings, most commonly *sütlaç* (rice pud-ding), which is consistently available in ordinary restaurants too. Other sweets include *aşure* (Noah's pudding), a sort of rosewater jelly laced with pulses, raisins and nuts, and the best known Turkish sweet, *lokum* or "Turkish Delight" – solidi-fied sugar and pectin, flavoured with rosewater and sometimes pistachios, and sprinkled with pow-dered sugar.

■ Drink

Tea *(çay)* is the Turkish national drink, served in tiny tulip-shaped glasses, with sugar on the side but no milk. **Turkish coffee** *(kahve)* is also common, served in tiny cups; don't drink the last mouthful (it's the grounds). Instant coffee is thankfully losing ground to fresh filter coffee in trendier cafés. **Fruit juices** *(meyva suyu)* can be excellent but are usually sweet-ened. Mineral water, either still *(su)* or fizzy *(maden suyu)*, is found at the tableside in most restaurants. *Meşrubat* is the generic term for all carbonated **soft drinks**. You'll also come across *ayran*, watered-down yoghurt.

Alcoholic drinks *(içkiler)* are available without restriction in resorts and in most other places, though you may have some thirsty moments in smaller inte-rior towns in the east. The main locally brewed brands of **beer** *(bira)* are Efes Pilsen, Tuborg and, as a likely newcomer this year, Carlsberg; imported beers are available, but at a horrendous mark-up. Turkish **wine** *(şarap)* varies alarmingly in quality; the commonest labels are Kavaklıdere and Doluca, which both offer a variety of vintages. The national aperitif is anis-flavoured **rakı** – stronger than Greek ouzo. It's usually drunk with ice and topped up with water.

Opening hours and holidays

Ordinary **shops** are open from around 9am until 7 or 8pm, possibly with a day off on Sunday, depending on the owner. **Museums** are generally open from 8 or 8.30am until 5 or 6pm, closed on Monday and often at lunchtime (usually 12.30–1.30pm). **Archeological sites** have more variable opening hours, but are generally open daily from just after sunrise until just before sunset. **Mosques** in busy areas stay open all the time; others open only for *namaz*, or Muslim prayer, five times a day. It's a cour-tesy for both men and women to cover their legs before entering a mosque – shorts are considered offensive – and for women to cover their heads. You should always take off your shoes at the door.

The two **religious holidays** are the Şeker Bayram (Sugar Holiday), which marks the end of the Muslim fasting month of Ramadan (Dec 17–19, 2001; Dec 6–8, 2002), and Kurban Bayram (the Feast of the Sacrifice) which falls about six weeks later (Feb 22–25, 2002; March 5–8, 2003). Confusingly, if either fall midweek the government may choose to extend the holiday period to as much as nine days – announcing it only a couple of weeks beforehand. In main tourist destinations, museums generally stay open but in smaller towns they may close. Many shops and restaurants also close as their owners return to their home towns for the holiday. (Note that the first morning of Kurban Bayram sees the public slaughter and dismemberment of a phenomenal number of sheep, cows and goats – not a sight for the faint-hearted.) Four **secular holidays** involve the closure of banks and public offices: Jan 1; May 19 (Atatürk's birthday); Aug 30 (victory over the Greeks in 1922); and Oct 29 (proclamation of the republic). At 9.05am on Nov 10 (anniversary of Atatürk's death), sirens sound all over the country and you will be expected to stop whatever you're doing and maintain a minute's respectful silence.

Emergencies

Despite exaggerated reports of football-related vio-lence, you're unlikely to encounter any **trouble** in Turkey, save for passport-related crime (see box over-leaf). Violent street crime is uncommon, theft is rare and the authorities usually treat tourists with cour-tesy. Keep your wits about you and an eye on your belongings and you shouldn't have any problems. The **police** come in a variety of subdivisions; all wear dark blue uniforms with baseball caps, and have their

In recent years it's become clear that there's a thriving trade in **stolen British passports** in Turkey, and it would appear that British Asians are at particular risk of being robbed; several people have even gone missing, and there's been at least one murder. You should exercise caution, particularly in İstanbul, and particularly if you're travelling alone.

division – *trafik*, *narkotik*, etc – clearly marked. Confusingly, the *Belediye Zabitas*, a sort of trading standards police, also wear dark blue, while in rural areas, you'll find the camouflage-clad *Jandarma*, a division of the regular army.

For **minor health complaints** head for the nearest *eczane* (pharmacy), where you'll be able to obtain cheap remedies for ailments like diarrhoea, sunburn and flu, though you may find it difficult to find exact equivalents to any home prescriptions. Night-duty pharmacists are known as **nöbet(ci)**; a list of the current rota is posted in every pharmacy's front window. For more **serious ailments**, your consulate or the tourist office may be able to provide you with the address of an English-speaking doctor. Otherwise it's best to go direct to a hospital *(klinik)* – either public *(Devlet Hastane* or *SSK Hastanesi)*, or private *(Özel Hastane)*. Private hospitals are far preferable in terms of cleanliness and standard of care, and since all foreigners must pay for medical attention, you might as well get the best available.

Emergency Numbers

Police ☎155; Ambulance ☎112; Fire ☎110.

İSTANBUL

Arriving in **İSTANBUL** can come as a shock. Most visitors head for the old city in and around **Sultanahmet**, where though you're still technically in Europe, there are immediate differences: back streets teem with traders pushing handcarts, stevedores carrying burdens twice their size, and omnipresent shoeshine boys. Men still monopolize the public bars and teahouses, while many women cover their heads, averting their gaze. Yet this is merely one aspect of modern İstanbul; only a couple of kilometres to the north you'll find the former European quarter of **Beyoğlu**, with its trendy bars and cutting-edge dance clubs, while north again are the pavement cafés and restaurants of **Ortaköy** and the swish Bosphorus suburbs of Arnavutköy, Bebek and Etiler. These days the city has a social and cultural diversity to match any of its Western counterparts.

İstanbul is the only city in the world to have played capital to consecutive Christian and Islamic empires, and retains features of both, often in congested proximity. **Byzantium**, as the city was formerly known, was an important trading centre, but only gained real power in the fourth century AD, when Constantine chose it as the new capital of the **Roman Empire**. Later, as **Constantinople**, the city became increasingly dissociated from Rome, adopting the Greek language and Christianity and becoming, effectively, the capital of an independent empire. In 1203 the city was sacked by the Crusaders, and when the Byzantines, led by Michael VIII Palaeologus, regained control in 1261, many of the major buildings had fallen into disrepair, with the empire itself greatly diminished in size. As the Byzantines declined, the **Ottoman Empire** prospered, and in 1453 the city was captured by Mehmet the Conqueror, who shortly after began rebuilding works. In the following century, the victory was reinforced by the great military achievements of Selim the Grim and by the reign of Süleyman the Magnificent, whose conquests helped fund the greatest of all Ottoman architects, Mimar Sinan. By the nineteenth century, however, the glory days of Ottoman domination were firmly over. Defeat in World War I was followed by the **War of Independence**, after which Atatürk created a new capital in Ankara – although İstanbul retained its importance as a centre of trade and commerce. In **recent years**, the population of the city has reached twelve million, a fifth of the country's total, and is still on the rise, adding further to the cacophony and congestion.

The city is divided in two by the **Bosphorus**, which runs between the Black Sea and the Sea of Marmara, dividing Europe from Asia. At right angles to it, the inlet of the **Golden Horn** cuts the European side in two. The old centre of Sultanahmet, occupying the tip of the peninsula south of the Golden Horn, is home to the city's main sightseeing attractions: the cathedral of **Aya Sofya**, **Topkapı Palace** and the **Blue Mosque**, and as such many people find that they spend all their time here. Annoying hustlers mean first impressions can be negative – but thankfully omnipresent tourist police have done much to clear out the worst, and will respond quickly to any problems you may have. Further west near the explorable **city walls** lies the **Kariye Camii**, which contains the city's finest surviving Byzantine mosaics and frescoes. Across the Golden Horn to the north, the **Galata Tower** offers superb panoramic views over the city.

Arrival and information

İstanbul's **airport**, 24km west, has two connected terminals, international and domestic. Buses run to Taksim Square northeast of Beyoğlu ($4) stopping at Aksaray, from where trams run to Sultanahmet ($0.40). Taxis taking the direct route along the seafront road (Sahil Yolu) cost $12–15 – make sure they use the meter. Construction work on the airport metro station is due to be completed in 2002, when it will give a direct link to the centre. There are two main **train stations**: trains from Europe terminate at **Sirkeci**, linked to Sultanahmet by a short tram ride; trains from Asia end at **Haydarpaşa** on the east bank of the Bosphorus,

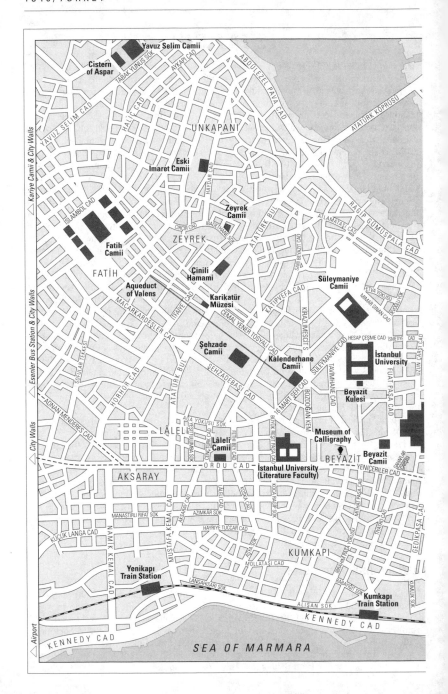

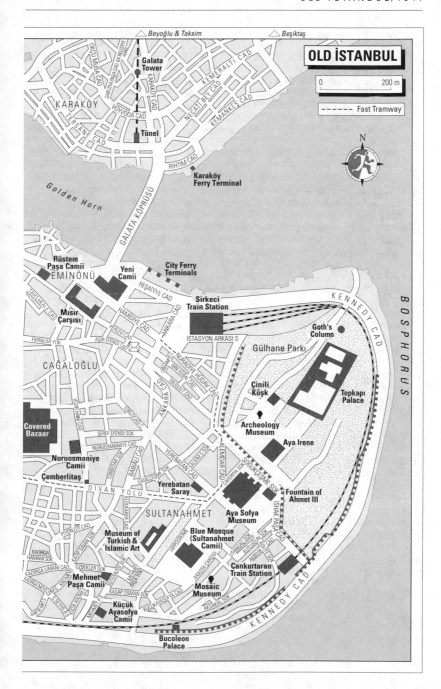

from where you can get a **ferry** to Karaköy and a bus from there to Sultanahmet. From İstanbul's **otogar** (bus station) at Esenler, around 15km northwest, the better bus companies run courtesy minibuses to various points of the city including Taksim, although if you're heading for Sultanahmet it might be quicker to take the **metro** (actually an express tramway) to Aksaray, where you can change to the Eminönü-bound tram line which passes through Sultanahmet and Sirkeci. Most buses arrive at the Esenler *otogar*, including European and Asian services, although some also stop at the Harem bus station on the Asian side, from where there are regular *dolmuşes* to Haydarpaşa station.

The most central **tourist office** is in Sultanahmet near the Hippodrome on Divanyolu Caddesi (daily 9am–5pm, sometimes later; ☎0212/518 8754); with other branches at the airport and the two train stations. They usually have a good range of brochures and maps and can help with accommodation.

City transport

The **public transport system** is improving, with a new line connecting Taksim and the northern suburbs and work under way to extend the single-line **metro** out as far as the airport. Single-journey metro tickets cost $0.40 from a counter (*gişe*) at station entrances. There are two kinds of **buses** serving the same routes, both of which come in a confusing array of colours. The first is a private service, Halk Otobus, for which you pay the conductor on entry ($0.40). More common are the municipality buses (marked IETT), for which you have to buy tickets ($0.40) in advance from bus stations, newspaper kiosks or fast-food booths, or at a small mark-up from touts; some longer routes, usually served by double-deckers, require two advance tickets (look for the sign *iki bilet geçerlidir*). Tickets should be deposited next to the driver on boarding. There are route maps at main bus stops. The European side has two **tram** lines, one running from Eminönü through Sultanahmet to Topkapı and outlying suburbs, the other running along İstiklâl Caddesi from Beyoğlu to Taksim using antique trams; buy tickets ($0.40) from a booth before you enter the platform. There's also a **municipal train** network, consisting of two lines running along the Marmara shore – west from Sirkeci station on the European side, and east from Haydarpaşa on the Asian. Journeys cost the same as for buses; on the European side you buy a token to let you through the turnstile onto the platform, while on the Asian side you buy a ticket. There are also **dolmuşes** or shared taxis (usually specially designed minibuses). They have their point of departure and destination displayed somewhere about the windscreen, and you can get on and off wherever you want en route: flag them down as you would a taxi. **Ferries** run between Eminönü and Karaköy on the European side, and Üsküdar, Kadiköy and Haydarpaşa in Asia; dockside kiosks sell a small *jeton* ($1) for the journey.

Accommodation

Finding **accommodation** in İstanbul is rarely a problem, but it's best to phone ahead to avoid a lot of trudging from one full *pansiyon* to the next; in high season anything up to a week's advance booking is advisable. Some of the city's nicest small hotels and *pansiyons* are situated in **Sultanahmet**, right at the heart of the city, particularly around Yerebatan Caddesi and the backstreets between the Blue Mosque and the sea. Prices here vary enormously and it's worth shopping around for a good deal; most hotels include breakfast in the price and some offer air-con and cable TV, while some hostels offer inclusive deals and even free Internet access. Failing that, **Taksim** is also a convenient base from which to sightsee, and comes into its own at night, when it becomes the centre of cultural and culinary activity.

To get to Taksim from Sultanahmet, take bus #14, which runs via Karaköy. From Eminönü and Aksaray, any number of buses pass through either Karaköy or Taksim, or both.

Sultanahmet

Alp Guesthouse, Adliye Sok 4, Sultanahmet (☎0212/517 9570, *alpguesthouse@turk.net*). Very friendly place with clean and pleasant, if slightly pricey, rooms. Breakfast on the roof terrace included. ④.

Antique, Küçük Ayasoyfa Cad, Oğul Sok 17 (☎0212/516 4936, *www.hotelantique.com*). Quiet, comfortable hotel – the top rooms have excellent sea views. ③.

Atlantis, Divanyolu Cad, Biçki Yurdu Sok 12 (☎0212/520 2620, *www.atlantishotel.net*). New, conveniently situated hotel, offering good-value ensuite rooms with satellite TV and minibar. Includes breakfast. ②.

Buhara, Küçük Ayasoyfa Cad, Yeğen Sok 11 (☎0212/517 3427). Pleasant hotel with outstanding views from its rooftop terrace. ②.

Ema, Yerebatan Cad, Salkım Söğüt Sok 18 (☎0212/511 7166). Functional quiet double rooms, most with showers. ②.

Fehmi Bey, Uçler Sok 15 (☎0212/638 9083). Friendly bijou hotel with period furniture, ensuite rooms with TV, air-con and breakfast included. ⑤.

Hanedan, Akbıyık Cad, Adliye Sok 3 (☎0212/516 4869). Uninspiring but clean and central, with good views from the rooftop café. ②.

Interyouth Hostel, Caferiye Sok 6/1 (☎0212/513 6150, *www.yucelthostel.com*). Large, well-managed HI hostel next to Aya Sofya, with Internet access. Dorms ①, rooms ②.

Istanbul Hostel, Kutlugün Sok 35 (☎0212/516 9380, *www.istanbul-hostel.com*). Friendly hostel, also with Internet access. Dorms ①, spartan doubles ②.

Mavi Guesthouse, İshak Paşa Cad, Kutlugün Sok 3 (☎0212/516 5878, *www.maviguesthouse.com*). Backpacker-friendly place just round the corner from the *Alp*. Dorms and terrace space ①, rooms ②.

Merih, Alemdar Cad 24 (☎0212/526 9708, *merihotel@superonline.com*). Accommodating hostel style hotel just down from Aya Sofya; front rooms can be noisy. Dorms ①, rooms ②.

Orient International Youth Hostel, Akbıyık Cad 13 (☎0212/517 9493, *www.hostels.com/orienthostel*). Long-established hostel with Internet. Dorms ①, rooms ②.

Side Hotel and Pansiyon, Utangaç Sok 20 (☎0212/517 6590, *www.sidehotel.com*). Welcoming staff, with clean rooms and excellent sea views from the terrace. ②.

Star Guest House, Yeni Akbıyık Cad 10 (☎0212/638 2302). Friendly place with neat rooms. ①.

Taksim and Beyoğlu

Büyük Londra Oteli, Meşrutiyet Cad 117, Tepebaşi (☎0212/249 1025). Italian-built more than a century ago and full of character, with spacious, well-furnished rooms. Bargaining has been known to halve the price. ⑥.

Dünya, Meşrutiyet Cad 79, Tepebaşi (☎0212/244 0940). Run-down and seedy, but with clean, bargain ensuite rooms. ①.

Gezi, Mete Cad 42 (☎0212/251 7430). Classy and well-run, with Bosphorus views from the restaurant and some of the rooms. ⑤.

Plaza, Aslanyatağa Sok 19–21, Sıraselviler Cad, Taksim (☎0212/274 1313). Quiet backwater with large but basic ensuite doubles with TV and marvellous Bosphorus views. ③.

Campsite

Londra Camping, Londra Asfaltı, beyond Ataköy (☎0212/560 4200). Pretty grim location on the E5 motorway next to a lorry park. $2 per person. From the airport, 10min by taxi ($5); from Taksim Square, a 16km ride on bus #73T.

The City

The old imperial centre of İstanbul stretches from the **Sultanahmet** district northwest to the Süleymaniye mosque complex, the covered bazaar and the remains of the city walls. To the north, across the Galata Bridge, the old Levantine areas of **Galata** and **Pera** are home to one of the city's most famous landmarks, the Galata tower. Close by is the entrance to the **Tünel**, an underground funicular railway running from Karaköy up to the start of İstiklâl Caddesi, home to many of the city's restaurants and much of the nightlife, and on to **Taksim Square**, the heart of modern İstanbul.

Aya Sofya

Perhaps the single most compelling sight in Sultanahmet is the former Byzantine cathedral of **Aya Sofya**, the massive domed structure commissioned in the sixth century by the Emperor Justinian. It was converted to a mosque in 1453, after which the minarets were added. In 1934 it became a **museum** (Tues–Sun 9.15am–4.30pm; $4). For centuries this was the largest enclosed space in the world, and the interior – filled with shafts of light from the high windows around the dome – is still profoundly impressive.

Scaffolding for a massive **restoration** programme currently obscures part of the dome's interior, but nevertheless helps bring home the scale of the place. Inside there are a few features left over from its time as a mosque – a *mihrab* (niche indicating the direction of Mecca), a *mimber* (pulpit) and the enormous wooden plaques which bear sacred names of God, the prophet Muhammad and the first four caliphs – but the most interesting elements are the Byzantine ones. Between the four great piers that hold up the dome, columns of green marble support the galleries; the smaller columns above are a deep red. The balconies, pediments and capitals are of white marble, the latter a riot of interlacing leaf carvings, many bearing the monograms of Justinian and his wife Theodora. Upstairs in the western gallery a large circle of green Thessalian marble marks the position of the throne of the empress.

There are also remains of abstract and figurative **mosaics**. One, beyond a pair of false marble doors in the south gallery, depicts Christ, the Virgin and John the Baptist; another, on the east wall of the gallery, shows Christ flanked by an emperor and empress believed to be Constantine IX Monomachus and the Empress Zoë. One of the most beautiful of all the mosaics can be seen downstairs in the Vestibule of Warriors; dated to the last quarter of the tenth century, it shows Virgin and Child flanked by the emperors Justinian, offering a model of the church, and Constantine, offering a model of the city. Outside, more scaffolding heralds the removal of ugly cement cladding to expose the original brickwork.

The Topkapı Palace

Immediately to the north of Aya Sofya, the **Topkapı Palace** (daily 9am–5pm; $4) is the other unmissable sight in the area. Shortage of funds and ongoing restoration work means parts of the museum and some less important palace rooms are often closed, but this is unlikely to spoil your visit – there's still plenty of interest on view. Built between 1459 and 1465, the palace consists of a collection of buildings arranged around a series of courtyards and was the centre of the Ottoman Empire for nearly four centuries until the removal of the retinue to Dolmabahçe in 1853. The first courtyard, as service area of the palace, was always open to the general public and is today home to the ticket office. The second courtyard is the site of the now beautifully restored **Divan**, with the Imperial Council Hall and the couch which gave the institution its name. The **Divan tower**, visible from many vantage points all over the city, was rebuilt in 1825 by Mahmut II. Next door is the **Inner Treasury** (currently closed), a six-domed hall that holds an exhibition of arms and armour. Across the courtyard are the **palace kitchens**, with their magnificent rows of chimneys. The furthest rooms house a fascinating array of utensils, while others display a collection of some fine porcelain and silverware – an ever-changing display continually replenished from the Topkapı collection.

Around the corner is the **Harem**, which, consisting of over 400 rooms, is well worth the obligatory guided tour (every 30min 9.30am–noon & 1–4pm; $2; buy your ticket at least 15min in advance). The only men that were allowed to enter the harem were black eunuchs and the imperial guardsmen, who were only employed at certain hours and even then blinkered. Many rooms have never been opened to the public and are awaiting restoration, but the tour takes in a good part of the complex, including the **Hünkar Sofası** (Imperial Hall) where the sultan entertained his visitors, and the bedchamber of Murat III – a masterwork of the architect Sinan – covered in sixteenth-century İznik tiles and kitted out with a marble fountain and bronze fireplace.

Back in the main body of the palace, in the third courtyard, the **throne room**, mainly dating from the reign of Selim I, was where the sultan awaited the outcome of sessions of the

Divan in order to give his assent or otherwise to their proposals. The room, sadly, is also currently closed but can be viewed through the wide windows. Nearby, the **Pavilion of the Conqueror** houses the Topkapı treasury, filled with excesses like the Topkapı Dagger, decorated with three enormous emeralds, and the Spoonmaker's Diamond, the fifth-largest in the world. Across the courtyard from the treasury, the **Pavilion of the Holy Mantle** houses the holy relics brought home by Selim the Grim after his conquest of Egypt in 1517, including a footprint, hair and a tooth of the prophet Muhammad as well as his mantle and standard. Next door, the **Privy Chamber** holds a collection of portraits of sultans (currently closed). Beyond, the fourth courtyard consists of gardens graced with pavilions such as the **circumcision room** decorated with sixteenth-century İznik tiles and the **Baghdad Pavilion**, decorated with tiles and ivory inlaid ceilings, that was built to celebrate Murat IV's Baghdad campaign of 1640. The sumptuously decorated **Mecidiye Köşkü** – the last building to be erected at Topkapı – commands the best view of any of the Topkapı pavilions and was recently re-opened as an annex to the Konyalı Restaurant.

Just north of Topkapı, **Gülhane Parkı**, once the palace gardens, now houses the **Archeological Museum** (Tues–Sun 9am–4pm; $3). Sadly many of the galleries are closed, including that housing the spectacular jewellery uncovered at Troy, but it's still worth the admission to see the collection of sarcophagi. The adjacent **Çinili Köşk** is the oldest secular building in İstanbul, constructed in 1472 as a kind of grandstand from which the sultan could watch sporting activities, now a **Museum of Ceramics** (Tues–Sun 9.30am–5pm; $4), housing a small but superb collection of İznik ware and Seljuk tiles. Nearby, the **Museum of the Ancient Orient** (Wed–Sun 9.30am–5pm; $4) contains a small but dazzling collection of Anatolian, Egyptian and Mesopotamian artefacts.

The Blue Mosque and around

South of Aya Sofya, the **Hippodrome** arena was constructed by Septimus Severus in 200 AD. At its southern end is the **Egyptian Obelisk**, commissioned to commemorate the campaigns of Thutmos III in Egypt during the sixteenth century BC. Originally 60m tall, only the upper third survived shipment from Egypt in the fourth century. The scenes carved on the base record its erection in Constantinople under the direction of Theodosius I. Nearby, the **Serpentine Column** comes from the Temple of Apollo at Delphi and was brought here by Constantine.

With its six minarets, the **Sultanahmet Camii**, or **Blue Mosque**, on the Hippodrome's southeast side, is both impressive and instantly recognizable – though inside it's rather clumsy, its four "elephant foot" pillars obscuring parts of the building and dwarfing the dome they support. The main attraction is the twenty thousand-odd blue tiles which give the mosque its name. Fine examples of late-sixteenth-century İznik ware, they include flower and tree panels as well as more abstract designs. Outside the precinct wall is the **tomb of Sultan Ahmet** (daily 8.30am–5pm), where the sultan is buried along with his wife and three of his sons; like the mosque, it's tiled with seventeenth-century İznik tiles. Behind the mosque is the **Vakıf carpet museum** (Tues–Sat 9am–4pm; $2) which houses antique carpets and kilims from all over Turkey.

On the west side of the Hippodrome, the former palace of İbrahim Paşa, completed in 1524 for the grand vizier of Süleyman the Magnificent, is a fitting home for the **Museum of Turkish and Islamic Art** (Tues–Sun 9am–4.30pm; $2), a well-planned museum containing what is probably the best-exhibited collection of Islamic artefacts in the world, with examples of Selçuk, Mamluk and Ottoman Turkish art. İbrahim Paşa's magnificent audience hall is devoted to a collection of Turkish carpets; on the ground floor, in rooms off the central courtyard, is an exhibition of the folk art of the Yörük tribes of Anatolia.

To the north, on the corner of Yerebatan Caddesi, the **Yerebatan Saray** or "Sunken Palace" (daily: summer 9am–5.30pm; winter 9am–4.30pm; $4) is one of several underground cisterns which riddle the foundations of the city, but the only one to have been properly excavated. Probably built by Constantine and enlarged by Justinian, the cistern supplied water to the Great

Palace of the Byzantine emperors. Raised pathways allow you to walk through the cistern's forest of columns, and gaze upon the monumental Medusa heads which support two of them. In the opposite direction from Sultan Ahmet, the **Mosaic Museum** (Tues–Sun 9.15am–4.30pm; $1), on Torun Sokak behind the Blue Mosque, displays some of the magnificent mosaics which once decorated the floors of the Great Palace. This vast complex once stretched from the Hippodrome down to the sea walls, where you can still see the great marble-framed windows of the **Bucoleon**, a pavilion looking out on to what was once the emperors' private harbour.

The Covered Bazaar and the Sülemaniye Camii

West of Sultanahmet, continue along the run-down and busy **Divan Yolu** to the **Column of Constantine (Cemberlitaş)**, erected in 330 AD to mark the city's dedication as capital of the Roman Empire. Off the main street to the right lies the district of **BEYAZIT**, the **Kapalı Çarşı**, or Covered Bazaar (Mon–Sat 8.30am–7pm; *www.kapali-carsi.com*), a huge web of passageways housing over four thousand shops. It has long since spilled out of the covered area, sprawling into the streets which lead down to the Golden Horn. Now that the foundation which runs it has banned traders from hassling tourists, it's a wonderful place to wander through. There are carpet shops everywhere catering for all budgets, shops selling leather goods around Kurkçular Kapı and Perdahçılar Cad, and gold jewellery on Kuyumcular Cad. When you need a break, the swish *Fes Café* on Halıcılar Cad is a comfortable place to swig coffee and gloat over hard-won booty.

West of the bazaar, peek into the **Beyazit Camii**, completed in 1506 and the oldest surviving imperial mosque in the city, with a beautiful, sombre courtyard full of richly coloured marble. The interior of the mosque is a perfect square of exactly the same proportions as the courtyard, its plan basically a simplified version of Aya Sofya, with beautiful sixteenth-century carvings.

Beyond the Covered Bazaar, in a pleasant area of shady courtyards behind the university, stands one of the finest of all the Ottoman mosque complexes, the **Süleymaniye Camii**, built in the 1550s by Mimar Sinan in honour of his most illustrious patron, Süleyman the Magnificent, and arguably his greatest achievement. The dome of the light and spacious mosque collapsed during the earthquake of 1766, and further damage was done in the nineteenth century by the Fossati brothers, whose attempt at Ottoman Baroque redecoration jars with the simplicity of the building. But the original stained glass of İbrahim the Mad remains, above a simply graceful marble pulpit, along with a few İznik tiles – a first cautious use of tiling by Sinan. Outside, the **cemetery** (Wed–Sun 9.30am–6.30pm; winter closes 4.30pm) holds the tombs of Süleyman the Magnificent and of Roxelana, his powerful wife. Süleyman's tomb is particularly impressive, with doors inlaid with ebony and ivory, silver and jade and a peristyle supported by four antique columns leading through to the huge turban-like tomb of the sultan. The rest of the complex is made up of the famous **Süleymaniye library**, established by Süleyman in an effort to bring together collections of books scattered throughout the city, and the **Tomb of Mimar Sinan**, a simple tomb except for a magnificent carved turban, a measure of the architect's high rank.

Eminönü

The area sloping down to the river behind the bazaar is known as **EMİNÖNÜ**, adjacent to which lies **SİRKECİ**, home to the main **train station** and ferry docks. Close by, on the waterfront, is the last of İstanbul's imperial mosques to be built in the Classical era, **Yeni Camii**. A large, grey edifice, it's one of the least impressive of the city centre's mosques, partly owing to the heavy layer of soot which covers its walls and windows. Next door, the **Mısır Çarşısı** (Egyptian Bazaar), also known as the Spice Bazaar, sells everything from saffron to aphrodisiacs. A short walk west, the **Rüstem Paşa Camii** is one of the most attractive of İstanbul's smaller mosques, built for Süleyman the Magnificent's grand vizier, Rüstem Paşa. Designed by Sinan on a particularly awkward site, above a tangle of streets that seems to offer no room for such a building, it is barely detectable as you wander about in the streets below. But it's a successful, dramatic structure, with tiles that are among the most profuse in Turkey, from the finest period of İznik tile production.

On the waterfront, the most prominent landmark is the **Galata Bridge**, a modern two-tier structure which provides access to Galata (and 1.5km beyond, Taksim) on the opposite side of the Golden Horn.

West to the city walls

West of Beyazit, İstanbul becomes tattier and more intimate, almost like a collection of villages intersected by major roads. These areas contain some of the city's most compelling sites, including the magnificent Byzantine mosaics and frescoes in the **Kariye Camii** and the great **Land Walls** that barred the peninsula to attackers for 800 years, and there are several other sites worth visiting on the way.

On the far side of the **Aqueduct of Valens** – part of a fourth-century water system that remained in use right up to the end of the nineteenth century – is **Şehzade Camii**, the Mosque of the Sultan's Son. Commissioned in 1543 on the death of Şehzade Mehmet, the 21-year-old heir of Süleyman the Magnificent, it was the first major building of Mimar Sinan. Across Atatürk Bulvarı, the aqueduct continues into **ZEYREK**, an attractively rundown area notable for its steep, cobbled streets and ramshackle wooden houses. At the top of the hill stands **Zeyrek Camii**, the twelfth-century Byzantine monastery church of Christ Pantocrator, which served as a mausoleum for the Comneni dynasty before being converted to a mosque. The building is now in a sadly dilapidated condition, and some areas are closed off due to crumbling masonry. Beyond Zeyrek, **FATİH** ("the Conqueror") is a fundamentalist area, where you'll notice that more women cover themselves. In the centre of the district, the **Fatih Camii** on İslambol Caddesi was begun in 1463 just ten years after the conquest of Constantinople, although much of it was rebuilt after an eighteenth-century earthquake.

Twenty minutes' walk north of here, **Yavuz Selim Camii**, on Yavuz Selim Caddesi, holds a commanding position over the surrounding suburbs. It was begun in the reign of Selim the Grim, after whom it is named, and the bleak exterior seems a fitting memorial to a man with such a reputation for cruelty. Once inside, though, it's one of the most attractive of all the imperial mosques – a simple, restrained building, its long pendentives alternating with tall arches to support the great shallow dome. The **Tomb of Selim the Grim** next-door (Wed–Sun 9.30am–4.30pm; free) has lost its original interior decoration, but retains two beautiful tiled panels on either side of the door.

About 25 minutes' walk northwest of the Selim mosque is one of the city's most compelling sights, **Kariye Camii** (9.30am–6pm; closed Wed; $5). It can also be reached by taking the metro to Topkapı (a western district, not the city-centre palace) and walking north beside the city walls as far as the Edirnekapa gate, from where it's signposted. This is the former church of St Saviour in Chora, built in the early twelfth century on the site of a building which pre-dated the walls, hence the name ("in chora" means "in the country"). The building contains a series of superbly preserved fourteenth-century frescoes and mosaics that are among the most evocative of all the city's Byzantine treasures. Most prominent of the mosaics are those in the narthex, the largest of which are a Christ Pantocrator and another showing the builder of the church, Metochites, offering a model of the building to a seated Christ. The frescoes in the burial chapel are equally eloquent, the most spectacular being the Resurrection, a dramatic representation of Christ trampling the gates of hell underfoot and forcibly dragging Adam and Eve from their tombs.

THE WALLS

Over 6km long, İstanbul's western **Land Walls** are among the most fascinating Byzantine remains in Turkey. Raised by the Emperor Theodosius II, they are the result of a hasty rebuilding to repel Attila the Hun's forces in 447 AD; an ancient edict was brought into effect whereby all citizens, regardless of rank, were required to help, and sixteen thousand men finished the project in just two months. They originally consisted of an inner wall, 5m thick and

12m high, plus an outer wall of 2m by 8m, and a 20-metre-wide moat. Most of the outer wall and its 96 towers are still standing, and although long sections have been rebuilt rather taste-lessly and closed off, untouched sections can still be examined in detail if you're willing to clamber in the dirt and brick dust. Most of the squatters who lived around the western dis-tricts of Topkapı and Edirnekapı have been moved on as a road development has engulfed the area, but do pay attention to your personal security here, especially in the evening.

To reach the walls, plenty of **buses** run from Eminönü and Sultanahmet, including bus #80 to Yedikule, #84 to Topkapı and #86 to Edirnekapı, and the **tram** line runs west from Aksaray to the Topkapı gate. However, the best way is to take the scenic **train** ride along the coast from Eminönü to **YEDİKULE**, a district lying at the southern end of the walls in the attractive for-mer Greek quarter of Samatya (apparent from the number of Orthodox churches). It also has a few reasonable restaurants and cafés where you can stop before setting off on your explo-ration of the walls. The **Ottoman fortress of Yedikule**, off Yedikule Caddesi, encompasses one of the best-preserved sections of wall, including the legendary **Golden Gate**. The Gate, flanked by two marble towers, was constructed on this site by Theodosius I in 390, before the walls themselves. It was bricked up in the declining years of the empire, but the shape of the three arches is still visible on both sides of the wall. It takes a degree of imagination, howev-er, to invest the structure with the glamour and dignity it once possessed. The other five towers of the Yedikule fortifications were added by Mehmet the Conqueror, and with their twelve-metre-high curtain walls form an enclave which can be seen today, including two prison towers covered with inscriptions carved into the walls by prisoners. The fortress is open as a **museum** (Mon, Tues & Thurs–Sun 9.30am–6.30pm; $1), in which the most interesting exhib-it is a section of graffiti left by European inhabitants prior to their brutal demise.

Across the Golden Horn: Galata and Beyoğlu

Across the Galata Bridge from the old centre, the separate township of **GALATA** (*www.gala-ta.net*) has its own fascinating history, concurrent with that of Constantinople itself. By the fifth century the area already had city walls, soon after which Tiberius built a fortress on this side of the Horn – part of which remains as the Yeraltı Camii on Kemankeş Cad – in order to close the water to enemy shipping. In 1261 Galata became a Genoese trading colony, and during the early centuries of Ottoman rule it functioned as the capital's "European" quarter, home to non-Muslim Jewish, Greek and Armenian minorities, as well as European merchants and diplomats. Overcrowding during the subsequent centuries saw the Europeans gradually spread from Galata along the hilltop into **Pera**, which, by the early twentieth century, was known by its cur-rent name, **BEYOĞLU**, boasting fashionable music halls, cinemas and restaurants. After the exodus of much of the Greek population from Beyoğlu in the 1960s the area began to lose its cosmopolitan flavour, becoming home to brothels, pick-up joints and sex cinemas, but over the last decade it has undergone a remarkable metamorphosis and now plays host to dozens of trendy café-bars, restaurants and clubs coexisting alongside the fast-disappearing sleaze.

The **Galata Tower** (daily 9am–6.30pm; $2), built in 1348, is the area's most obvious land-mark, and one of the first places to head for on a sightseeing tour, since its viewing galleries, reached by means of a modern lift, offer the best panoramas of the city. Up towards **İstiklâl Caddesi**, Beyoğlu's main boulevard, an unassuming doorway leads to the courtyard of the **Galata Mevlevihane** (Mon & Wed–Sun 9.30am–4.30pm; $1), a former monastery and cere-monial hall of the "Whirling Dervishes" and now a museum of the Mevlevi sect, which was banned by Atatürk along with other Sufi organizations because of its political affiliations. Exhibits include instruments and dervish costumes, and the building itself has been beauti-fully restored to late eighteenth-century splendour. Staged dervish ceremonies take place in December and on specific summer evenings (check inside or call ☎0212/245 4141 for details). The best way to continue along from the bottom of İstiklâl Caddesi, formerly La Grande Rue de Pera, is to hop on the antique tram which trundles along its 1200-metre length to **Taksim Square**, taking in the sumptuous *fin-de-siècle* architecture. The **Military Museum** (Wed–Sun 9am–5pm; $1), about 1.5km north along Cumhuriyet Caddesi, is worth visiting mainly for the Mehter band who play traditional Ottoman music (3–4pm). The wide assortment of Ottoman armour and weaponry, along with various campaign memorabilia including the tent used by campaigning sultans, should appeal to military buffs.

North along the Bosphorus shore

Beyond Taksim, along the European shore of the Bosphorus, the most obvious place to head for is **BEŞİKTAŞ** (best reached from Eminönü by bus #43k, #43r or #51e; or from Taksim by bus #30b and frequent *dolmuşes*), where the huge, sumptuous **Dolmabahçe Palace** (Tues, Wed & Fri–Sun 9am–4pm; guided tours only: $5 short tour, $8 complete tour) was built in the mid-nineteenth century to replace Topkapı as the imperial residence of the Ottoman sultans. To the contemporary eye it's not so much magnificent as a grossly excessive display of ostentatious wealth, suggesting that good taste suffered along with the fortunes of the Ottoman Empire. But it retains an Oriental feel in the organization of its rooms, divided into *selâmlık* and harem by the enormous throne room – where the ceremonies were watched by women of the harem through grilles. The four-tonne chandelier in the throne room, one of the largest ever made, was a present from Queen Victoria.

Back towards the ferry landing, the **Maritime Museum** (Wed–Sun 9am–noon & 1–5pm; $1) is one of the city's most interesting, with a collection divided between two buildings, one facing the water housing seagoing craft, and the other, on Cezayir Caddesi, devoted to the maritime history of the Ottoman Empire and the Turkish Republic. A quarter-hour walk north along the coast road is the **Yıldız Parkı** (daily 9am–11pm), a vast wooded area dotted with lakes and gardens which formed the grounds of Yıldız Palace, to the north. The most important surviving building is **Yıldız Şale** (Tues, Wed & Fri–Sun 9.30am–5pm; $3) which resembles a Swiss chalet and was built for the first visit of Kaiser Wilhelm II in 1889. **Yıldız Palace** itself (Tues–Sun 9.30am–4.30pm; $3) is entered from Beşiktaş' other main road, Barbaros Bulvar, and consists of a collection of structures in old Ottoman and Art Nouveau styles – a total contrast to Dolmabahçe. Most of the pavillions date from the reign of Abdül Aziz, but it was Abdül Hamid – a reforming sultan whose downfall was brought about by his intense paranoia – who transformed Yıldız into a small city and power base.

Eating

The historical centre around Sultanahmet is increasingly well-served by decent **restaurants**, although there's always been a higher concentration of eateries around Taksim and Beyoğlu; the Balık Pazar, behind the Çiçek Pasajı off İstiklâl Caddesi, is a great area for *meze*, kebabs and fish, while Çiçek Pasajı itself offers similar fare but is now somewhat overpriced and touristy. **Snack** options – which abound in all areas – vary from the dubious fish sandwiches served off boats by fishermen in Kadıköy, Karaköy and Eminönü, to *kokoreç* (skeins of sheep's innards) sold from booths in less salubrious areas.

Afacan, İstiklâl Cad 331, Beyoğlu. Very reasonably priced lunch stop with an excellent take on Turkish home cooking and some of the best stews in town. There's a second branch in the building next to İstiklâl Cad's only mosque.

Alem, Nevizade Sok, Balık Pazarı, Beyoğlu. Newish place serving *meze*, fish and kebabs, with a huge upstairs dining room. Popular with the younger crowd.

Boncuk, Nevizade Sok, Balık Pazarı, Beyoğlu. Old, traditional restaurant, still serving some of the best food on this street despite the ever-growing competition.

Çatı, İstiklâl Cad, A. Apaydın Sok 20, Baro Han, floor 7, Beyoğlu (☎0212/251 0000). Open for 22 years and still popular among İstanbul's intelligentsia. Mixed Turkish and international cuisine plus assorted live music. Good views of the city lights. Closed Sun.

Cennet, Divan Yolu Cad 90. Serves only two dishes: *Gözleme* (fried pastries with various fillings) and *Mantı* (Turkish ravioli), consumed from cushions on the floor to a backdrop of traditional decor, accompanied by live music. Immense fun and reasonably priced.

Darüzziyafe, Şifahane Cad 33. Reasonably priced Ottoman cuisine in a Sinan-designed annexe to his masterpiece mosque. Live traditional music most evenings.

Degustasyon, Balık Pazar, Beyoğlu. Run by Turkey's only TV chef and offering unusual variations of Turkish dishes. Boasts an adjacent wine bar.

Doy Doy, Şifa Hamamı Sok 13, off Küçükayasofya Cad at the Hippodrome end. Newly re-decorated but still offers good, cheap kebabs, *pide* and stews.

Dubb Indian Restaurant, İncili Çavuş Sok 10, Sultanahmet. Offers a reasonable but vaguely Turkish take on Indian standards in neatly restored Ottoman house.

Hacı Abdullah, Sakızağa Cad 19, Beyoğlu. A legend among locals, offering stunning home cooking at very reasonable prices. Packed at weekends. No alcohol.

İlhamenin Yeri, Osmanzade Sok 6, Ortaköy. Last of the real *meyhanes* in this former quiet fishing village turned night-time haunt. Excellent *meze*, kebabs and fish.

Kör Agop (Blind Hagop), Ördekli Bakkal Cad 7–9, Kumkapı. Third-generation Armenian-owned joint in this block of fish restaurants. One of the oldest in town, still offering great fish dishes, *meze* and salads.

Nature and Peace, Büyükparmakkapı Cad 21, İstikal Cad, Beyoğlu. Vegetarian place three blocks away from Taksim, offering lentil köfte and other veggie favourites.

Nizam Pide, branches on Büyükparmakkapı Sok and Kalyoncu Kulluğu Sok, Beyoğlu. Two branches serving excellent *pide*, beans and rice. Cheap and very popular, especially after the bars close.

Padaliza, at the entrance to Cebeci Han in the Kapalı Çarşı. Fairly new but easily the best eating establishment in the bazaar, offering reasonably priced Ottoman specialities.

Rumeli Café, Ticarethane Sok 8, Divan Yolu Cad. Chic establishment offering fish, pasta and very interesting takes on Ottoman cuisine.

Şehzade Mehmet Efendi, Şehzade Camii, Şehzadebaşı Cad. Wonderfully atmospheric restaurant located in the *medrese* of the Şehzade mosque. Excellent value *pide*, kebabs and stews, and exemplary service.

Türkistan Aşevi, Tavukhane Sokağı 36. Behind the Blue Mosque, a conventional Ottoman house specializing in central Asian cuisine with a good set menu. You'll be asked to take off your shoes.

Yeni İskele, İskele Sok 17, Yeniköy. Lively Bosphorus fish restaurant with less common specialities such as fishcakes and stuffed squid.

Nightlife

Traditional İstanbul **nightlife** used to centre around restaurants and *gazinos* – clubs where *meze* is served, accompanied by singers and Oriental dancers. These days, Western-style bars and clubs – the latter invariably trendy and expensive – have all but taken over, packed with younger revellers, although traditional music is making something of a comeback, with some laid-back bar-restaurants serving food accompanied by an ever-changing crowd of musicians. Locations tend to centre around Taksim and its nearby suburbs, and along the Bosphorus, particularly the district of Ortaköy, just beyond Beşiktaş.

Bars

Baraka, 2nd floor, Ezine Apt, Balo Sok, İstiklâl Cad, Beyoğlu. Noisy hang-out with cheap beer and good music.

Cheers Bar, Akbıyık Cad 20. Loud music, cheap beer and a backpackerish clientele.

Gizli Bahçe, Nevizade Sok 27, İstiklâl Cad, Beyoğlu. Cutting-edge dance music in this bar housed in a dilapidated Ottoman town house. Very young crowd, and deliciously illicit atmosphere.

Hayal Kahvesi, Büyükparmakkapı Sok 19, İstiklâl Cad, Beyoğlu. Upmarket café/bar with live jazz and blues.

Line Bar, Büyükparmakkapı Sok 14. Hi-tech rock venue with live music every night. Unusually affordable drinks. Closes 2am.

Madrid Bar, İpek Sok 20, Beyoğlu. Cheap bar popular with students and impecunious expats alike. Beer $1.

Pano Şaraphanesi, Hamalbaşı Cad 26, opposite the British Consulate, Beyoğlu. Greek wine bar 120 years old, reborn as a unique tapas-bar-like drinking den also offering a wide variety of Turkish and international cuisine. Packed at weekends.

Sal Bar, Büyükparmakkapı Sok 18a, Beyoğlu. Traditional Turkish music and beer. Try also *Ekin* and *Barabar* on the same street.

Clubs and discos

Babylon, Şeybender Sok 3, Asmalımescit, Tünel (*www.babylon-ist.com*). Purpose-built club and venue with regular stints by foreign bands and DJs alike. Expensive but occasionally has special offers.

Milk, Akarsu Sok 5, İstiklâl Cad, Beyoğlu. Hi-tech dance venue sometimes calling itself *Magma*. Weekends until 4am.

Mojo, İstiklâl Cad, Akarsu Sok 5, Beyoğlu. Trendy basement dive with live bands most nights. Closes 4am.

People, Muallin Nacı Cad, Kuruçeşme, Ortaköy. Outdoor dance club overlooking the Bosphorus – popular but pricey. June–Sept.

Roxy, Aslanyatağı Sok 113, Siraselviler Cad, Taksim. DJs and regular live bands in a pricey, yuppy-oriented bar/disco.

Shaft, Osmancık Sok 13, Serasker Cad, Kadıköy. Live blues and jazz club on the Asian shore.

Switch, Muammer Karaca Çıkmazı, İstiklal Cad, Beyoğlu. Underground dance club with local and foreign DJs.

Listings

Airlines Aeroflot, Mete Cad 30, Taksim (☎0212/243 4725); British Airways, Cumhuriyet Cad 10 (☎0212/234 1300); Olympic Airways, Cumhuriyet Cad 171a (☎0212/247 3701); THY Turkish Airlines, Cumhuriyet Cad 199–201, Harbiye (☎0212/663 6363).

Banks The Garanti Bankası in Sultanahmet stays open through lunchtime, and the Akbank at the airport is open 24hr. However, you'll get the best rates to change money from the Döviz offices throughout the city.

Boats Ferry journeys north along the Bosphorus are one of the city's highlights. There are special sightseeing boats throughout the year from Eminönü ($6 for the 2hr journey to Anadolu Kavağı). Ordinary ferries on the same routes are reasonably frequent. Last return boat from Anadolu Kavağı in summer is at 5pm, after which you must resort to a bus or *dolmuş*.

Books Galeri Kayseri, Divanyolu Cad 58, Sultanahmet; Pandora, Büyükparmakkapı Sok 3, İstiklâl Cad; Robinson Crusoe, İstiklâl Cad 389; and Homer, Yeni Çarsı Cad 28, Beyoğlu.

Buses The better bus companies are: Pamukkale (☎0212/658 2222), Varan (☎0212/658 0277), Ulusoy (☎0212/658 3000) and Kâmil Koç (☎0212/658 2010).

Car rental Avis, airport (☎0212/663 0646) and *Hilton Hotel*, Cumhuriyet Cad, Harbiye (☎0212/241 7896); Budget, airport (☎0212/663 0858) and Cumhuriyet Cad 19, Taksim (☎0212/253 9200); Europcar, airport (☎0212/663 0746) and Cumhuriyet Cad 47/2, Taksim (☎0212/238 0084); Hertz, Küçükbayar Sok, Harbiye (☎0212/234 4300).

Consulates Australia, Tepecik Yolu 58, Etiler (☎0212/257 7050); Canada, Buyukdere Cad 107/3 Begun Han, Gayrettepe (☎0212/272 5174); Ireland, Cumhuriyet Cad 26a, Elmadağ (☎0212/246 6025); Netherlands, İstiklâl Cad 393, Galatasaray, Beyoğlu (☎0212/251 5030); UK, Meşrutiyet Cad 34, Tepebazı, Beyoğlu (☎0212/293 7546); USA, Meşrutiyet Cad 104–108, Tepebaşı, Beyoğlu (☎0212/251 3602).

Hospitals American Hospital, Güzelbahçe Sok 20, Nişantaşı (☎0212/231 4050); International Hospital, İstanbul Cad 82, Yeşilköy (☎0212/663 3000).

Internet Internet Café, Divan Yolu, İncili Çavuş Sok 31 (2nd floor); Net Café at no. 37 on the same street (also 2nd floor); Blue Internet Café, Yerbatan Cad 54. Single women should head for Yağmur, Şeyh Bender Sok 18, Tünel, Beyoğlu.

Laundry Active, Dr Eminpasa Sok 14, off Divan Yolu; the Hobby, Caferiya Sok 6/1, Sultanahmet.

Left luggage Left-luggage offices *(Emanet)* are in both Sirkeci and Haydarpaşa train stations.

Police The tourist police are at Yerebatan Cad, Sultanahmet (☎0212/527 4503).

Post office Main office is on Yeni Posthane Cad, Sirkeci (daily 9am–5.30pm; stamps 8am–8pm).

Train stations Haydarpaşa (☎0212/336 0475); Sirkeci (☎0212/527 0051).

Travel agents For plane and bus tickets try Marco Polo, Divan Yolu Cad 54/11, Sultanahmet (☎0212/519 2804), or Imperial, Divan Yolu Cad 30, Sultanahmet (☎0212/513 9430).

Turkish baths The most central, and most frequented by tourists, are the 400-year-old Çemberlitaş Hamam on Divan Yolu, and Cağaoğlu Hamam, Hilali Ahmed Cad 34 (daily: men 7am–10pm, women 8am–8pm). Expect to pay between $10 and $30. Outside the main tourist areas *hamams* are much cheaper; the 500-year-old Tophane Hamam on the Bosphorus at Tophane costs only $3 (daily 7am–10pm).

AROUND THE SEA OF MARMARA

Despite their proximity to İstanbul, the shores and hinterland of the **Sea of Marmara** are relatively neglected by foreign travellers. This is not altogether surprising: here Turkey is, at first glance anyway, at its least exotic. But this may well be your first view of the country and the area is not entirely without charm or interest. The border town of **Edirne**, at the end of the Roman and Byzantine Via Egnatia, later the medieval route to the Ottoman parts of Europe, was once the Ottoman capital and is home to some of the finest early Ottoman architecture. To the east the quaint country town of **İznik** was briefly the Byzantine capital and boats extensive ruins, while nearby **Bursa** – on many routes towards the Aegean coast – was the first Ottoman capital and aside from many fine buildings has an exquisite city centre. Many visitors also stop off at the extensive World War I battlefields and cemeteries of the **Gelibolu peninsula** (Gallipoli), using either the north Marmara port of **Gelibolu** as a base, or, more commonly, **Çanakkale** – from where it's also easy to visit the ruins of ancient Troy a little further south.

Edirne

EDİRNE, a former Ottoman capital, boasts an impressive number of elegant monuments and makes for an easily digestible introduction to Turkey, on the borders with both Greece and Bulgaria. It's a lively city, albeit somewhat seedy thanks to vast numbers of truck drivers and assorted East European traders who pass through.

The main sights of Edirne are best seen on foot; allow a full day as there are myriad lesser monuments and old houses well worthy of a detour. The best starting point is the **Eski Camii** bang in the centre, the oldest mosque in town and a boxy structure begun in 1403 that is a more elaborate version of Bursa's Ulu Camii. Recently completed restoration work has revealed the splendour of the calligraphy for which the mosque is justly famous. Just across the way, the **Bedesten** was Edirne's first covered market, though the plastic goods it now touts are no match for the building. Nearby, the **Semiz Ali Paşa Çarşısı** is the other main bazaar, begun by Sinan in 1568 at the behest of Semiz Ali, one of the most able of the Ottoman grand viziers. A short way north of here is the bizarrely beautiful **Üç Şerefeli Camii**, dating from 1447; its name means "three-balconied", derived from the presence of three galleries for the muezzin on the tallest of the four idiosyncratic **minarets**. Restoration work on the *medrese* is expected to be completed by mid-2002. A little way west, the masterly **Selimiye Camii** was designed by the eighty-year-old Sinan in 1569 at the command of Selim II. Its four slender minarets also have three balconies, and at 71m are among the tallest in the world; the interior is most impressive, its dome planned to surpass that of Aya Sofya in İstanbul – which, at 31.5m in diameter, it manages by a few centimetres. Next door, the **Museum of Turkish and Islamic Arts** (Tues–Sun 9am–1pm & 2.30–6.30pm; $1) houses assorted wooden, ceramic and martial knick-knacks from the province, plus a portrait gallery of champions of oiled-wrestling (a speciality of Edirne). The main **Archeological Museum** (Tues–Sun 9am–noon & 2.30–6.30pm; $1), just east of the mosque, contains an assortment of Greco-Roman fragments, some Neolithic finds and an ethnographic section that focuses on local crafts. Ten minutes further on, down the slope and up Mimar Sinan Caddesi, the **Muradiye Camii** was built as a sanctuary for Mevlevi dervishes by Murat II in 1435, its interior distinguished by some of the best İznik tiles outside Bursa.

Practicalities

From elsewhere in Turkey, you'll most likely arrive around 4km southeast of the centre at Edirne's new **bus station**, known as *Yeni Terminal*, from where there are frequent *dolmuşes* ($0.50) and less frequent free city buses to the town centre. The **train station** is 3km southeast of the centre. There are two **tourist offices**, both on Talat Paşa Cad; the main one is about 500m west towards the Gazi Mihal bridge at no. 76a, and an annexe is up near Hürriyet Meydanı by the traffic signals (both daily 8am–5.30pm; ☎0284/213 9208).

Edirne's few genuinely budget **hotels** are either grim dosshouses or are booked solid by truck drivers. The *Rüştem Paşa Kervanseray*, just off the main Hürriyet Meydanı on İki Kapılı Han Cad (☎0284/225 2195, *k.saray@netone.com*; ⑤), offers overpriced rooms in a restored Ottoman caravanserai, but the complex also unfortunately houses a dubious nightclub; bargaining is recommended. Cheapest place is the seedy but otherwise friendly *Aksaraylı Hotel*,

Alipaşa Ortakapı Cad 10 (☎0284/212 6035; ③), a dilapidated old house where most rooms come with bathroom and TV. It's worth paying the extra for the relative comfort of *Şaban Açıkgöz*, Çilingirler Cad 9 (☎0284/213 0313; ②), which has nicer en-suite rooms with TV; or *Efe*, 13 Maarif Cad (☎0284/213 6166, *www.efehotel.com*; ③), which offers the same plus air-conditioning. The only nearby **campsite** is *Fifi Mocamp* (☎0284/226 0101), 8km along the road to İstanbul, which also has en-suite motel rooms (②).

Restaurants in Edirne mainly cater for pass-through trade and do little to encourage return custom. Look out for the tiny *ciğerci* shops serving the city speciality, deep-fried liver. The lower end of Saraçlar Cad offers some reasonable options: the licensed *Café London* offers a daily special plus Western fast-food and sandwiches, and is also the only place in town to get a decent filter coffee; *Urfa-Gaziantep Kepapcisi* at no. 33 has good-value kebab fare and an upstairs dining room for women; *Balkan Piliç* at no. 14 offers various chicken options; and all along the street you'll find stalls packed with every kind of Turkish pudding and sweet. Avoid the intimidating **Internet** station in *Rüştem Paşa Kervansaray* and head instead for *Eska Internet Café*, along from the Kervansaray at İlk Kapalıhan Cad 5.

Crossing the Greek and Bulgarian borders

The closest crossing into **Greece** from Edirne is 7km away at **PAZARKULE**, separated from the Greek frontier post at Kastaniés by a kilometre-wide no-man's-land. At the time of writing the crossing is open daily 6am–noon, but you should definitely check the latest situation with the Edirne tourist office before departing. A **taxi** from Edirne to the border (or vice versa) should cost $9. **KARAAĞAÇ**, the nearest village, is served by red **city buses** running every 20min from behind the Edirne Belediye building, and **dolmuşes** from behind the *Kervanseray*. From Karaağaç you can catch a bus marked "Yunanistan" to Kastaniés in Greece. At present it's permitted to walk from Karaağaç across the border but once on the Greek side, you'll have to take a taxi ($5). On the Greek side, between 8am and 1pm there are three trains, and about as many buses, for the three-hour run down to Alexandhroúpoli, the first major Greek city, with a couple more services later in the day.

The **Bulgarian** border at **KAPIKULE**, on the E5/100 motorway 18km northwest of Edirne, is open around the clock. International trains stop at Edirne en route to Bulgaria; oth erwise the frontier can be reached by *dolmuş* from behind the Edirne *Kervanseray* (daily every 20min 6.30am–9pm). You can walk across the border, but then the only public transport is a taxi to Svilengrad train station ($10), from where there are five trains a day to Plovdiv.

Çanakkale and around

Though celebrated for its setting on the Dardanelles, **ÇANAKKALE** has little to detain you. However, it is the best base for visiting the **Gelibolu** (Gallipoli) sites and the sparse ruins of **Troy**. Almost everything of interest in Çanakkale is within walking distance of the **ferry docks**, close to the start of the main Demircioğlu Caddesi. The nearby **tourist office** (daily 8am–8pm; winter closes 5pm; ☎0286/217 1187) is worth a stop if only for their free map of the Gallipoli battlefields. The **bus station** is out on the coastal highway Atatürk Caddesi, a 15-minute walk from the waterfront; if you're arriving on the bus from İstanbul, get off at the ferry rather than going out to the bus station. In the town, the **Çimenlik Park** (daily 9am–8pm), southwest of the bazaar, houses a replica of the minelayer Nusrat, which stymied the Allied fleet by re-mining zones at night that the French and British had swept clean by day; it is festooned inside with rather forgettable newspaper clippings of the era. The **Naval Museum** nearby (daily 9am–noon & 1.30–5pm; $1) is more worthwhile, featuring photos and military paraphernalia, including Atatürk's pocket watch which stopped a shell fragment at Gelibolu and saved his life. Some 2km south of the centre, the **Archeological Museum** (daily 8am–noon & 1–5pm; $1) is accessible by any *dolmuş* along Atatürk Caddesi labelled "Kepez" or "Güzelyalı" and has exhibits from all over the area, including exquisite gold jew-ellery from nearby tombs.

Except for a crowded couple of weeks during mid-August during the Çanakkale/Troy Festival, or on ANZAC Day (April 25) when the town is inundated with Antipodeans, you'll have little trouble finding budget **accommodation**. *Anzac House*, Cumhuriyet Meydanı 61 (☎0286/213 5969, *www.anzachouse.com*; ②), has small but neat rooms and Internet access, as well as dorm beds (①). The clean and airy, newly renovated *Yellow Rose*, Yeni Sok 5 (☎0286/217 3343, *www.yellowrose.4mg.com*; ①), in the street behind *Kervanseray*, is a good option with some en-suite rooms, Internet access and dorms (①). The eccentric, dilapidated *Kervanseray* round the corner at Fetvahane Sok 13 (☎0286/217 8192; ①) is a quiet place in an old mansion. More upmarket, the *Anafartalar*, overlooking the ferry landing (☎0286/217 4454; ③), offers en-suite doubles with TV and fabulous views over the straits, breakfast included. There are several **campsites** – at Güzelyalı, Dardanos and Kepez – all accessible by minibus from the minibus garage. The expansion of the local university has led to a broadening of Çannakale's **restaurant** and café options. On the quayside south of the ferry jetty, the long-established *Entellektüel* isn't cheap but offers great fish and scenic views. One street back from the water, *Dadaşım*, 17 Yalı Cad, offers a good range of kebabs and stews, while one street further inland, the female-run *Köy Ev*, 15 Fetvahane Sok, offers a taste of real Turkish home cooking. Nearby on Cumhuriyet Cad, *Taş Firin* does a brisk trade in *lahmacun* and *pide*-style fast food. For **drinking**, there is a burgeoning café and bar scene on Yalı Cad and Fetvahane Sok, with the latter boasting the current top spot, *Depo*. The *TNT* bar on Saat Kule Meydanı is popular with the Anzac crowd. There are also numerous **Internet** café options in this area, with Efe Internet Café overlooking the water.

The Gelibolu peninsula (Gallipoli)

Though endowed with some fine scenery and beaches, the slender **Gelibolu peninsula (Gallipoli)**, which forms the northwest side of the **Dardanelles**, is mainly known for its grim military history. In April 1915 it was the site of a plan, devised by Winston Churchill, to land Allied troops, many of them Australian and New Zealand units, with a view to their linking up to neutralize the Turkish shore batteries controlling the Dardanelles. It was a harebrained scheme and it failed miserably, with massive casualties. Nevertheless, this was the first time Australian and New Zealand soldiers had seen action under their own commanders, and the six months they were dug in here has subsequently been seen as the respective countries' "coming of age" as sovereign states; the date of the first landings, April 25, is celebrated as **ANZAC Day**.

Two companies currently offer **tours** of the Gallipoli battlefields, both of them based in Çanakkale and both offering English-speaking guides: Hassle Free Tours, which is owned by *Anzac House Pension*, and the *Yellow Rose Pension*. Any other outfit offering tours – even those in İstanbul – is almost certainly an agent for one of these two. Prices are around $20 per person: for a group of four or five, renting a car and doing it yourself would work out cheaper.

The **World War I battlefields** and **Allied cemeteries** scattered along the Gelibolu peninsula are by turns moving and numbing in the sheer multiplicity of graves, memorials and obelisks. It's difficult to imagine the bare desolation of 1915 in the lush landscape of much of the area, but the final 20km have been designated a **national park**, and some effort has been made by the Turkish authorities to signpost road junctions and sites. The open-air sites have no admission fees or restricted hours, but since there's little public transport through the area you should take a **tour** unless you have your own vehicle. The first stop on most tours is the **Kabatepe Orientation Centre and Museum** (daily 8am–6pm; $1), 6km along, beyond which are the **Beach, Shrapnel Valley** and **Shell Green** cemeteries, followed by **Anzac Cove** and **Arıburnu**, site of the bungled ANZAC landing and ringed by more graves. Looking inland, you'll see the murderous badlands that gave the defenders such an advantage. Beyond Arıburnu, a left fork leads towards the beaches and salt lake at **Cape Suvla**, today renamed Kemikli Burnu; most tourists bear right for Büyük Anafartalar village and **Çonkbayırı hill**, where there's a massive New Zealand memorial and a Turkish memorial describing Atatürk's words and deeds. The spot where the Turkish leader's pocket watch stopped a fragment of shrapnel is highlighted, as is the grave of a Turkish soldier discovered in 1990 when the trenches were reconstructed. Working your way back down towards the visitors' centre, you pass **The Nek, Walker's Ridge** and **Quinn's Post**, where the trenches of the opposing forces lay within a few metres of each other: the modern road corresponds to no-man's-land. From here the single, perilous supply line ran down-valley to the present location of **Beach Cemetery**.

GELİBOLU PRACTICALITIES

The peninsula's principal town, **GELİBOLU** – an inviting place with a colourful fishing harbour ringed by cafés and restaurants – is a good alternative base from which to visit the battle sites. The **ferry** jetty is right at the inner harbour entrance; the new **bus terminal** is on the coast road 1km east of the town centre. There's a good range of excellent value **accommodation**. *Hotel Yılmaz*, Liman Caddesi 6 (☎0286/566 1256; ①), is the general backpacker stopover, but if you want to avoid the crowds the friendly *Hotel Oya*, Miralay Şeflik Aker Cad 7 (☎0286/566 0392; ①), has very clean ensuite rooms with TV. There's a municipal **campsite** on the beach to the west of town. Most people opt to take **tours** of the World War I sites from Çanakkale, but you can do it (more expensively) from Gelibolu town through *Hotel Yılmaz*, an agent for Hassle Free Tours (see opposite), for about $30 per person. Waterfront **restaurants** include the *İmren*, the *İlhan* and the *Yelkenci*, all of which are licensed and offer several variations on the local speciality, sardines.

Troy

Although by no means the most spectacular archeological site in Turkey, **TROY** (Truva) is probably the most celebrated, thanks to its key role in Homer's *Iliad*. The ruins of the ancient city, just west of the main road around 20km south of Çanakkale, are on a much smaller scale than other sites, consisting mainly of defensive walls, a small theatre and the remains of a temple. Many visitors come away disappointed, but it's worth remembering that the settlement dates back to the late Bronze Age, making Troy far older than most other Classical cities. It was generally thought to have existed in legend only until 1871, when a German businessman, Heinrich Schliemann, excavated the site. Schliemann's work actually caused a certain amount of damage, and he removed many of his discoveries to Germany without permission, but his digging uncovered nine layers of remains, representing distinct and consecutive city developments spanning four millennia. The oldest, Troy I, dates back to about 3600 BC and was followed by four similar settlements. Troy VI is known to have been destroyed by an earthquake in about 1275 BC, while Troy VII shows signs of having been destroyed by fire about 25 years later, around the time historians generally estimate the Trojan War to have taken place. Troy VIII, which thrived from 700 to 300 BC, was a Greek city, while the final layer of development, Troy IX, was built between 300 BC and 300 AD, during the heyday of the Roman Empire.

Çanakkale is the most sensible base for seeing Troy. Despite what pension owners and tour operators will tell you, frequent *dolmuşes* ($1) run from Çanakkale's minibus station direct to the site, whereas an "organized" tour will set you back $10–12 per person. You'll find a cluster of shops and overpriced **eateries** by the *dolmuş* stop, and the nearby village of **TEVFİKİYE** has a couple of rather feeble pensions.

The **site** (daily 8am–7pm; winter closes 5pm; $4) is signalled by the ticket office opposite the bus drop-off point, from where a road leads to a giant wooden horse. Just beyond is the ruined city itself, a craggy outcrop overlooking the plain, which stretches about 8km to the sea. It's a fantastic view, and despite the sparseness of the remains, as you stand on what's left of the ramparts and look out across the plain it's not too difficult to imagine a besieging army camped out below. Walking around the site, the **walls** of Troy VI are the most obvious feature, curving around in a crescent from the entrance; there are also more definite and visible remains from Troys VIII and IX, including a council chamber and a small theatre a little way north.

İznik

Tucked away at the eastern end of the lake which bears its name, the sleepy little town of İZNİK boasts extensive, well-preserved ruins. Originally the ancient Greek city of Nicaea, as a Christian centre it later gave its name to the Nicene Creed which affirmed the divinity of Christ. When İstanbul fell to the Crusaders in 1204, Nicaea became the Byzantine capital. Under the Ottomans, the city became a centre for ceramic production, an art which has been recently revived. Orientation is easy thanks to the Hellenistic grid street-plan, and you're free to wander the length of the Byzantine city walls which enclose almost everything of interest. The **tourist office** is in the centre of town, Kılıçaslan Cad 130 (Mon–Fri 8.30am–noon & 1–5.30pm; ☎0224/757 1933), opposite the **Aya Sofya Museum** (daily 9am–noon & 1–6.30pm; the remains of a Byzantine church originally founded by Justinian. To the northeast lie the **Hacı Özbek Camii** – the earliest-known Ottoman mosque, built in 1333 – and the later **Yeşil Camii** (Green Mosque), so named for the green tiles decorating its minaret. Across the park sprawls the fourteenth-century **Nilüfer Hatun İmareti**, a religious hostel which nowadays houses İznik's **Archeological Museum** (daily 9.30am–noon & 1–6.30pm; $1), displaying artefacts from nearby Neolithic settlements and some fabulous examples of Ottoman İznik ceramics. In the mid-1990s, the **İznik Foundation** (*www.iznik.com*) restarted local ceramic production using original materials and techniques; their factory (free tours daily 9am–7pm) is signposted as *İznik Vakfı* on Halı Saha Arkası, beyond the remains of the **Roman amphitheatre** outside the walls to the southwest.

Buses arrive at İznik's tiny *otogar*, southeast of the centre, from where everything is within walking distance. In summer, what accommodation there is tends to fill up so you should reserve in advance. The English-speaking *Kaynarca Pansiyon*, Gündem Sok 1 (☎0224/757 1723; ①) is backpacker-friendly and provides a useful map; there's satellite TV in every room and an attached **Internet** café. With views over the lake are the *Çamlık Motel* (☎0224/757 1631; ②), with en-suite doubles, and *Cem Pansiyon* (☎0224/757 1687; ①), with rooms ensuite and not. **Eating** isn't great. The fish restaurants on the coast road Sahil Yolu include the *Sahil Restaurant*, which can manage grills and has a good range of *meze*. There's a row of cheap restaurants behind Aya Sofya, including the funky old *Konat Barbeku Izgara*, which has good stews and *pide*. The *Tutku Bar* on Sahil Yolu has a big-screen TV showing local football games.

Bursa

Draped along the leafy lower slopes of Uludağ, which towers more than 2000m above, BURSA – first capital of the Ottoman Empire and the burial place of several sultans – does more justice to its setting than any other Turkish city besides İstanbul. Gathered here are some of the finest early Ottoman monuments in Turkey, in a tidy and appealing city centre.

Flanked by the busy Atatürk Cad, the compact **Koza Parkı**, with its fountains, benches, crowds and cafés, is the real heart of Bursa. On the far side looms the **Ulu Camii**, built between 1396 and 1399 by Yıldırım Beyazit I from the proceeds of booty won from the Crusaders at Nicopolis on the Danube. Before the battle Yıldırım had vowed to construct twenty mosques if victorious; the present building of twenty domes was his rather free interpretation of this promise. The interior is dominated by a huge *şadırvan* pool for ritual ablutions in the centre, whose skylight was once open to the elements, and an intricate walnut *mimber* (pulpit) pieced together, it's claimed, without nails or glue. Close by is Bursa's covered market, the **Bedesten**, given over to the sale of jewellery and precious metals, and the **Koza Hanı**, flanking the park, still entirely occupied by silk and brocade merchants. Across the river to the east, the **Yeşil Camii** (Green Mosque; daily 8am–8.30pm) is easily the most spectacular of Bursa's imperial mosques – though never completed, as you can see from the entrance. The hundreds of tiles inside give the mosque its name. Tucked above the foyer, and usually closed to visitors, the imperial loge is the most extravagantly decorated chamber of all, the work attributed to a certain Al-Majnun ("The Mad One"). The nearby hexagonal **Yeşil Türbe** (daily 8am–noon & 1–7pm; free) contains the sarcophagus of Çelebi Mehmet I and assorted offspring. The immediate environs of the mosque are a busy tangle of cafés and souvenir shops. The *medrese,* the largest surviving dependency of the mosque, now houses Bursa's **Museum of Turkish and Islamic Art** (Tues–Sun 8.30am–noon & 1–5pm; $1.50), with İznik ware, Çanakkale ceramics, glass items and a mock-up of an Ottoman circumcision chamber.

West from the centre of town, the **Hisar** ("citadel") district was Bursa's original nucleus. A warren of narrow lanes wind up through dilapidated Ottoman houses to the remaining ramparts, while a skeleton of new walkways clinging to the rock face offer fabulous views. The best-preserved dwellings are a little way west in medieval **Muradiye**, where the **Muradiye Külliyesi** mosque and *medrese* complex was begun in 1424 by Murat II. This is the last imperial foundation in Bursa, although it's most famous for its **tombs**, set in lovingly tended gardens. Best of these commemorate Şehzade Ahmet and his brother Şehinşah, both murdered in 1513 by their cousin Selim the Grim to preclude any succession disputes, covered with İznik tiles, which contrast sharply with the adjacent austerity of Murat II's tomb, where Roman columns inside and a wooden awning are the only superfluities: in accordance with his wishes, both the coffin and the dome were originally open to the sky "so that the rain of heaven might wash my face like any pauper's". From Muradiye it's a short walk down to Çekirge Caddesi and the southeast gate of the **Kültür Parkı** (daily 9.30am–12.30pm & 1.30–6.30pm; $0.10) where there's a popular tea garden, a small boating lake and three pricey restaurants. At the far end there's also an **Archeological Museum** (Tues–Sun 8am–noon & 1–5pm; $1), whose exhibits include metal jewellery from all over Anatolia, a collection of Roman glass items, and Byzantine and Roman bronzes. Just beyond the Kültür Parkı, the **Yeni Kaplıca** (daily 9am–11pm; $2), accessible via a steep driveway, are the nearest of Bursa's baths, a faded reminder of the days when the town was patronized as a spa.

Practicalities

Bursa's new **bus terminal** is 5km north on the main road to İstanbul, from where bus #90a (every 15min) runs to Koza Parkı in a subterranean mall, at one corner of which is Bursa's **tourist office** (Mon–Fri 8.30am–5.30pm; ☎0224/220 1848). Avoid the few grim **hotels** around the old bus station, now the main *dolmuş* garage: better hotels lie in the centre and the leafy spa suburb of **ÇEKİRGE**, a *dolmuş* ride to the north. In the centre, *Hotel Dikmen*, Maksem Cad 78 (☎0224/224 1840; ③), is clean and friendly; on Heykel Gümüşçeken Cad, the female-run *Çeşmeli* at no. 6 (☎0224/224 1512; ②) has great views from the upper rooms, while the brand-new *Hotel Efehan* at no. 34 (☎0224/225 2260, *www.efehan.com.tr,* ②) offers extremely comfortable rooms complete with TV. In Çekirge, the *Demirci Otel,* Hammamlar Cad 33 (☎0224/236 5104; ②), is functional and unpretentious, as is the *Özha Yat Hotel* over the road at no. 31 (☎0224/236 5105; ①). Both have their own *hamams.*

Restaurants are not Bursa's strong point. The rather touristy *Hunkar Kebap* next to the *Yeşil Camii* offers good kebabs with fabulous views over the valley. In the central Heykel district, *Kebapcı İskender,* Unlu Cad 7, claims to have been founded in 1867 and is one of a number of restaurants on Unlu Cad offering Bursa's speciality, *İskender kebap*; others include *Adanur Hacibey* and *Yilmaz İşhani Girizi.* Close to the tourist office at Belediye Cad 15, the more elegant *Çiçek Izgara* offers a decent take on many Ottoman dishes. In the evening, head for the old fish market on Sakarya Caddesi at the foot of the citadel: the street is dominated by lively fish restaurants, of which *Arap Şükrü,* at no. 6, is reasonably priced and not quite so male-dominated as the rest. This street also boasts a number of reasonable **bars**, including *Barantico, Cevriye* and, tucked down an adjacent side street, *Kuytu.* There are plenty of **Internet** cafés: try Ernet, Bozkurt Cad 3/C, or Elite Internet Café just behind the Yeşil Turbe.

THE AEGEAN COAST

The **Aegean coast** is, in many ways, Turkey's most enticing destination for visitors, home to some of the best of its classical antiquities and the most appealing resorts. The north shore is a quiet, rocky region, well endowed with Hellenistic remains but with few sandy beaches – and so is spared the tourist excesses of the south. Tiny **Assos** with its ancient ruins is one of the gems of the coast. **Ayvalık**, the north's longest-established resort, makes an excellent place to stop for a few days, with good beaches and easy access to **Bergama** a little inland, with its unmissable ruins. Further south, the city of **İzmir** is for most travellers an obstacle on the way to more compelling destinations, but it is not without charm and serves as a base for day-trips to adjacent sights and beaches. The territory to the south is home to the best concentration of classical, Hellenistic and Roman ruins, notably **Ephesus**, usually first on everyone's list of dutiful pilgrimages, and the remains inland at **Aphrodisias** and **Hierapolis** – although the latter is more often visited for the pools and rock formations of adjacent **Pamukkale**. The **coast** itself is better down here, too, and although the larger resorts, including **Kuşadası** and **Marmaris**, are beginning to be lost to the developers, **Bodrum** and **Çeşme** still have a certain amount of charm.

Assos

ASSOS, 70km south of Çanakkale, is a tiny stone village built on a hill around the ruins of the ancient town, founded in the sixth century BC and once home to Aristotle. The ruins (daily 8.30am–7pm; winter closes 5pm; $1) are for the most part blissfully untouristed; the **Temple of Athena** has had its Doric columns re-erected, and there are fabulous views from here to the Greek island of Lésvos 10km offshore, while downhill lie the recently unearthed **theatre** and **necropolis**.

The only transport is a minibus from **AYVACIK**, 25km to the north, which passes through both the upper village of Assos and its twin settlement downhill around the fishing harbour; it runs according to demand, so out of season you may have a long wait. On summer weekends, **rooms** may be hard to find and prices double or triple those midweek. Pensions in the upper village are all in restored stone houses and include the delightful *Timur Pansiyon* (☎0286/721 7449, *www.hitit.co.uk/timur*, ①), which offers waterless doubles, and *Dolunay* (☎0286/721 7172; ②), which has ensuite doubles; both include breakfast. Down on the shore are several beautiful but expensive stone-built hotels, which can generally be bargained down in midweek and also offer half-board; longest-running is the seriously plush *Hotel Assos* (☎0286/721 7107; ⑧) right on the harbour, but the unlikely named *Dr No Pansiyon* (☎0286/721 7076; ①) which has waterless and ensuite doubles is more affordable. Further along the shore are several small **campsites** including *Çatır* (☎0286/721 7048) which also has several shacks for rent (②).

Ayvalık and around

AYVALIK, 2km west of the main coast road, is a small fishing port that also makes a living from olive-oil production and low-key tourism; it makes a nice base for beach lounging and ruin-spotting at **Bergama**, 70km southeast. Refounded during the 1400s on ancient ruins, Ayvalık suffered two serious earthquakes last century, though the most devastating effect on the town occurred when its mainly Greek inhabitants were kicked out during the exchange of populations that followed the Greek–Turkish war of 1920–22. There's not a great deal to see, though its tangle of central streets, lined with terraces of sumptuous Greek houses and clattering with speeding horsecarts, is worth a wander, and there are some decent beaches in the surrounding area.

The centre is focused on the small square İskele Meydanı 1.5km south of the main **bus station**. Buses from the south will drop you off near the centre on Atatürk Cad, but some buses from the north don't make the detour into the town, in which case it may be easier to pick up a connecting service at Edremit, 40km north. Confusingly, and despite what ticket-sellers in Edremit's bus station may tell you, few buses to Ayvalık actually enter the town's *otogar*, stopping instead 50m away on the adjacent main road. The **tourist office** (summer Mon–Fri 8am–noon & 1–6pm, Sat 9am–noon & 2–6pm; winter Mon–Fri 8am–noon & 1–5pm; ☎0266/312 2122) is about fifteen minutes' walk south of the town centre on the main coast road, but you're more likely to use the information kiosk on the seafront (June–Sept). There's a wealth of **pensions** in Ayvalık's old houses, the best by far being the beautiful *Taksiyarhis* (☎0266/312 1494, *info@taksiyarhis.com*; ②), behind the Taksiyarhis church, signposted inland and uphill from the seafront. Alternatives are *Yalı* (☎0266/312 2423; ②), housed in a beautiful old seafront mansion, and, also signposted from the seafront, *Chez Beliz*, Fethiye Mahallesi, Marezal Çakmak Cad 28 (☎0266/312 4897; ②; May–Sept). **Eating** possibilities include *Osmanlı Mutfağı* on Talatpaşa Cad, which offers well-priced superior Turkish dishes; *Kardeşler Pide Salonu*, opposite the PTT on İnönü Cad, with a good choice of kebabs; and *Öz Canlı Balık* on the seafront, specializing in fish and *meze*. There's a clutch of **drinking** dens between the main street Edremit Caddesi and the parallel İnönü Caddesi, plus *Circus Bar*, on Gümrük Sok. **Internet** access is at *Star Internet*, 39 Atatürk Cad, five minutes' walk south of the tourist office.

You can buy tickets for **ferries** to the Greek island of **Lésvos** ($40 one-way, $50 open return) at Jale Tour, Gümrük Cad 24 (boats June–Sept Mon–Sat; ☎0266/312 2740), and Yeni İstanbulTur next to the *Aziz Arslan Otel* (boats June–Sept 3 weekly; ☎0266/312 6123). Bear in mind, though, that if you arrived on the Greek boat, you may only be permitted to travel back on the same vessel.

Around Ayvalık

About 6km south, **SARIMSAKLI** (literally "Garlic Beach") is a resort development accessible by *dolmuş* or municipal bus. Across the bay from Ayvalık, the island of **CUNDA** (aka **Alibey**) is also a good day-trip destination, with a couple of stretches of beach on its west and north edges and some excellent harbourside fish restaurants in a quaint old Greek villlage. The best way to get here in summer is by **boat**, though at other times you'll have to rely on the roughly hourly bus service from Atatürk Square or a taxi across the causeway connecting Cunda to the mainland. **Accommodation** on Cunda includes *Artur Motel* on the square (☎0266/327 1014; ②), *Atün Pansiyon* (☎0266/327 1554; ①) or the family-run *Altay Pansiyon* further inland (☎0266/327 1024; ②). There's a number of **campsites** including *Ada* about 4km southwest (☎0266/327 1211). Fish **restaurants** crowd the waterside, including at the *Artur*, while the *Dinosaur Bar* stages live music.

Bergama

Frequently touted as a day-trip from Ayvalık, **BERGAMA** is the site of the Hellenistic – and later Roman – city of Pergamon, ruled for several centuries by a powerful local dynasty. Excavations were completed here in 1886, but unfortunately much of what was found has since been carted off to Germany. However, the acropolis of Eumenes II remains a major attraction, and there are a host of lesser sights and an old quarter of chaotic charm.

The old town lies at the foot of the acropolis, about ten minutes' walk from the bus station. Its foremost attraction is the **Kızıl Avlu** or "Red Basilica" (daily 8.30am–5.30pm; $2), a huge edifice on the river not far from the acropolis, originally built as a temple to the Egyptian god Osiris and converted to a basilica by the early Christians, when it was one of the Seven Churches of Asia Minor addressed by St John in the Book of Revelation. Crumbling but still impressive, it houses a mosque in one of its towers. The area around the basilica is a jumble of ramshackle buildings, carpet and antique shops, mosques and maze-like streets. South along the main street is the **Archeological Museum** (Tues–Sun 8.30am–6pm; $2), which has a large collection of locally unearthed booty, including a statue of Hadrian from the

Asclepion (see below), and busts of Zeus and Socrates along with a model of the Zeus altar, complete with the reliefs that are now in Berlin. Bergama has a particularly good **hamam**, the *Haci Hekim*, Bankalar Cad 32: $5 gets you a bath, $9 the full works.

The **Acropolis** (daily 9am–5/7pm; $4), the ancient city of the kings of Pergamon, is set on top of a rocky bluff towering over modern Bergama. Taking a short cut through the old town still means an uphill walk of around half-an-hour. By taxi, the ride costs $10 or more; a taxi-tour around all Bergama's sights costs about $15–20. The first main attraction on the acropolis is the huge horseshoe-shaped **Altar of Zeus**, built during the reign of Eumenes II to commemorate his father's victory over the Gauls, and formerly decorated with reliefs depicting the battle between the giants and the gods. Even today its former splendour is apparent, though it has been much diminished by the removal of the reliefs to Berlin. North of the Zeus altar lie the sparse remains of a **Temple of Athena**, above which loom the restored columns of the **Temple of Trajan**, where the deified Roman emperor and his successor Hadrian were revered in the imperial era. From the Temple of Athena a narrow staircase leads down to the theatre, the most spectacular part of the ruined acropolis, capable of seating ten thousand spectators, and a **Temple of Dionysos**, just off-stage to the northwest. Lower down the hill and less well-marked – but just as impressive – are the remains of the **Gymnasium** where the city's children were educated.

Bergama's other significant archeological site is the **Asclepion** (daily 8.30am–6.30pm; $4), a Greco-Roman medical centre which can be reached on foot from the road beginning at the Kurşunlu Camii in the modern town. Much of what can be seen today was built during the first- and second-century heyday of the centre, when its function was similar to that of the nineteenth-century spa. The main features are a **Propylon** or monumental entrance gate, built during the third century AD, and a circular **Temple of Asclepios**, dating from 150 AD and modelled on the Pantheon in Rome. At the western end of the northern colonnade is a **theatre** seating 3500, while at the centre of the open area a **sacred fountain** still gushes mildly radioactive drinking water, near to which an underground passage leads to the two-storey circular **Temple of Telesphorus**.

Practicalities

Bergama's **bus station** is on the main road about 500m from the town centre, and within 15 minutes' walk of most accommodation. The **tourist office** (daily 8.30am–5.30pm; ☎0232/633 1862) is further along the same road. Beware that Bergama's taxi-drivers are a cunning lot, and will blithely insist your choice of pension has closed before whisking you somewhere else entirely. Many of the budget **hotels** are located in the old town; *Athena*, Barbaros Mahallı, İmam Çıkmazı 5 (☎0232/633 3420, *www.athenapension.8m.com*; ①), has elegant waterless rooms in a nineteenth-century mansion, plus ensuite rooms in a newer annexe; over the bridge, the family-run *Nike Pansiyon* (☎0232/633 3901, *fikretnike@yahoo.com*; ①) has clean rooms around a tidy garden with shared bathrooms; *Pergamon Pansiyon* (☎0232/632 3492; ①) occupies an atmospheric 150-year-old stone house in the town centre; *Bobligen*, Zafer Mah, Cad 2 (☎0232/633 2153; ①), is a clean and well-run option on the way to the Asclepion. If you're on a day-trip from Ayvalık don't feel obliged to eat at the restaurant stop: cheaper and better options abound. The **restaurant** in the *Pergamon Pansiyon*'s courtyard has excellent home cooking; *Sağlam*, Hükümet Meydanı 29, has a good range of traditional Turkish food and a shady courtyard. There's a number of outdoor **drinking** places opposite the museum.

İzmir

Turkey's third city and its second port after İstanbul, **İZMİR** – ancient Smyrna – is home to nearly three million people. It was the Ottoman Empire's window to the West and the primary port for the shipping of goods brought from Asia, granted to Greece under an indefinite mandate after World War I. But by September 1922 Greek attempts to extend their area of control had failed, the army beaten back by Atatürk's "free" Turkish forces; the ensuing struggle was bitter and resulted in seventy percent of the city burning to the ground. Today's İzmir has been built pretty much from scratch, its central boulevards wide and tree-lined, and is nowadays booming and cosmopolitan – partly due to its role as headquarters of NATO Southeast. Its mild climate is offset by its location, straddling a heavily polluted 50km-long gulf fed by several streams and flanked by mountains on all sides. Despite an illustrious history, much of the city is relentlessly modern. **Orientation** can be confusing – many streets are unmarked – but most points of interest lie near each other and walking is the most enjoyable way of exploring. For **city buses**, buy tickets in advance ($0.40) from white kiosks near most stops, and deposit them in the container when boarding. A cross-town **taxi** ride shouldn't cost more than about $2.

The City

İzmir cannot be said to have a single centre, although **Konak**, the busy park, bus terminal and shopping centre on the waterfront, is where visitors spend most time. It's marked by the ornate **Saat Kulesi** (clock tower), the city's official symbol, and the **Konak Camii**, distinguished by its facade of enamelled tiles. Southwest of here, the **Archeological Museum** (Tues–Sun 9am–5pm; $3) features an excellent collection of finds from all over İzmir province, including the showcased bronze statuette of a runner and a large Roman mosaic, a graceful Hellenistic statuette of Eros clenching a veil in his teeth and a stunning collection of terracotta sarcophagi. Opposite it is the **Ethnographic Museum** (Tues–Sun 9am–5pm; $1.50), a more enjoyable and certainly more interesting collection, with reconstructions of local mansions and the first Ottoman pharmacy in the area, a nuptial chamber, a sitting room and circumcision recovery suite, along with vast quantities of household utensils and Ottoman weaponry.

Immediately east of Konak, İzmir's **bazaar** warrants a stroll, although you're highly likely to get lost. The main drag, Anafartalar Caddesi, is lined with clothing, jewellery and shoe shops; Fevzipaşa Bulvarı and the alleys just south are strong on leather garments. Worth seeking out is the handsome vaulted **Kızılara Gazi Kervanseray** on 871 Sok, which houses antique and carpet shops. East, across Gaziosmanpaşa Bulvarı, the **Agora** (daily 9am–5pm; $1), commercial centre of the classical city, dates back to the early second century BC, although what you see now is a later construction, financed during the reign of the Roman emperor, Marcus Aurelius. Above this is the unmissable **Kadifekale** (Velvet Castle), an irregularly shaped fortress dating from Byzantine and Ottoman times that gives great views over the city from its pine-shaded tea garden. The less energetic can take a red-and-white city bus #33 from Konak, but it's worth trying the walk up from the Agora, threading through once-elegant narrow streets past dilapidated pre-1922 houses.

Practicalities

Ferries anchor at the **Alsancak terminal**, 2km north of the centre, where there's also a Turkish Maritime Lines office selling onward boat tickets (☎0232/464 7835); a taxi into town costs $2 or you could walk 250m south and pick up bus #2 (blue-and-white) or bus #12 (red-and-white) from Alsancak train station. Intercity **trains** pull in at **Basmane station**, 1km from the seafront at the eastern end of Fevzipaşa Bulvarı (left-luggage daily 8am–7pm; $2 per piece). From the **airport**, there's an hourly shuttle train to Alsancak train station, as well as Havaş buses (14 daily) to the main THY office at the central *Büyük Efes Hotel*. The **bus station** is way out on the east side of the city (left-luggage daily 7am–midnight; $2 per piece), from where buses #50, #51 and #54 run to Basmane and Konak. Buses to and from destinations on the Çeşme peninsula depart from the separate Uçkuyular bus station, accessible by bus #12 and #169 from Konak. There's a **tourist office** in the airport arrivals hall (☎0232/274 2214), another in Konak Meydanı near the seafront (☎0232/483 5117), and a third adjacent to the *Büyük Efes Hotel* at Akdeniz Mah. 1344 Sok 2 (daily 8am–7pm; ☎0232/445 7390).

The main areas for budget **hotels** are Çankaya, Akinci and Altınordu, immediately west and southwest of Basmane train station, around Fevzipaşa Bulvarı and Anafartalar Caddesi. In Akinci, *Hikmet Otel,* 945 Sok 25 (☎0232/484 2672; ①), has rooms ensuite and not; *Nil Otel,* Fevzipaşa Bul 155 (☎0232/483 5228; ①) has all ensuite rooms with TV, though the ones at the front may be noisy. In Çankaya, *Oba,* 1369 Sok 27 (☎0232/483 5474; ①), is worth trying, as is *Güzel İzmir,* 1368 Sok 8 (☎0232/483 5069; ①), which has small ensuite rooms.

Not surprising given its size, İzmir boasts seemingly inexhaustible **restaurant** options. Avoid the clutch of obvious eateries within sight of Basmane station: there are more decent places in the bazaar area, although most of them close by early evening; *Ömür,* Anafartalar Cad 794, is cheap and friendly, serving ready-prepared dishes but no alcohol; *Bolulu Hasan Usta,* 853 Sok 13/B, does the best pudding and ice cream in town – but nothing else. The best eating options by far are in Alsancak on the Birinci Kordon, and on and around the pedestrianized Kıbrıs Şehit Caddesi. Typical are *La Sera,* Birinci Kordon 190a, with kebabs, fish and desserts plus live music evenings; and *Café Reci* on 398 Sok, serving salads, crêpes and ice cream. More upmarket is the pricey *Kemal'ın Yeri,* 1453 Sok 20/A, which is famous for its seafood, while for the budget-conscious the *Kurçiçeği* at 75 Kıbrıs Şehit Caddesi boasts that it's open 25 hours a day and offers 21 types of *pide*. Best-value **bar** is the long-standing *Eko* on the corner of Pilevne Bul and Cumhuriyet Cad, which also serves kebabs and chips. Further along on 1482 Sok *Kahve Bahane* and *Kaos* are brisk, inexpensive student hangouts housed in a row of dilapidated old Greek merchants' houses. There are several **Internet** cafés around Alsancak, including Chat Internet Café, 1453 Sok 14a.

Çeşme

A once-attractive town of old Greek houses wrapped around a castle, **ÇEŞME** these days is little more than İzmir on holiday, and a convenient stopover on the way to the Greek island of Híos. The town's two main streets are **İnkilap Caddesi**, the main bazaar thoroughfare, and its continuation Çarşı Caddesi, which saunters south along the waterfront. The **sights** comprise the town's thirteenth-century Genoese **castle** (daily 8.30am–noon & 1–5.30pm; $1), with a museum containing finds from the nearby site of Erythrae, and the **Kervanseray**, a few paces south, dating from the reign of Süleyman the Magnificent but now a somewhat dubious luxury hotel.

Coming by **ferry** from Híos (Chios in Turkish), you arrive at the small jetty in front of the castle. By **bus** from İzmir you'll probably arrive at the *otogar* 1km south, although some services meet the top of İnkilap Cad. **Dolmuşes** to Dalyan leave from the roundabout at the northeast of İnkilap Cad; those to other nearby attractions depart from next to the harbourside **tourist office** (daily 8.30/9am–noon & 1–5/5.30pm; ☎0232/712 6653). In summer there are many options for **accommodation**, with a clutch of pensions on the right-hand side of the castle as it faces the sea. The efficient *Avrupalı* (☎0232/712 7039; ①) has a picturesque garden and well-appointed rooms including suites with kitchenettes, while *Özge* (☎0232/712 7021; ①) is immaculately kept and comfortable. A bit further along and away from the harbour past the local **hamam** is the friendly, clean and basic *Aras Apartments* (☎0232/712 7375; ①), which offers rooms with balconies in and out of season. Down in the flatlands, the *Alim Pansiyon,* Müftü Sok 3 (☎0232/712 8319; ①), has simple ensuites, while in the opposite direction, a ten-minute walk beyond the harbour is the pleasant two-star *Kerman Otel* (☎0232/712 7112, *kerman2001@anet.com.tr*; ②), overlooking the beach. Among Çeşme's better **restaurants** are the *Rıhtım* and *Marina*, both overlooking the fishing harbour; *Körfez,* on the marina, is possibly the most elegant, serving up excellent charcoal-grilled fish at a price. Best-value is the nearby *Kordon Pide* next to the post office. *Rumeli Pastanesi* at İnkilap Cad 44 serves some of the best ice-cream on the Aegean, and specializes in desserts and jams made from the sap of gum trees. *Lezzet Aş Evi* at no. 14 offers good basic *lokanta* fare. **Internet** access is at Emre Internet Café, Kutludal Sok 11.

You can buy tickets for the **ferry to Híos** ($30 one-way, $40 open return, plus $70–90 for a car) from Ertürk (☎0232/712 6768, *www.erturk.com*) or Karavan (☎0232/712 7230, *ikucur@superonline.com*), both in front of the tourist office. Schedules change according to demand, from as low as one a week in winter to twice daily in high season. There are no taxes departing Çeşme, but roughly $20 in tax coming from Híos. Tickets for the weekly **ferry to Brindisi** in Italy can be had from Tamer (☎0232/712 7932) and Maskot (☎0232/712 7654).

Kuşadası

KUŞADASI (*www.kusadasi.net*) is Turkey's most bloated resort, a brash coastal playground which extends along several kilometres of seafront. In just three decades its population has swelled from 6000 to around 50,000, though far fewer stay year-round. The town is many people's introduction to the country: efficient ferry services link it with the Greek islands of Sámos and Míkonos, plus the resort is an obligatory port of call for Aegean cruise ships, which disgorge vast numbers in summer – who delight the local souvenir merchants after a visit to the ruins of Ephesus just inland.

Liman Caddesi runs from the ferry port up to **Atatürk Bulvarı**, the main harbour esplanade, from which pedestrianized **Barbaros Hayrettin Bulvarı** ascends the hill. To the left of here, the **Kale** district, huddled inside the town walls, is the old and most appealing part of town, with a namesake mosque and some fine traditional houses. Kuşadası's most famous **beach**, the **Kadınlar Denizi** (Ladies' Beach), around 3km southwest of town, is a popular strand, usually too crowded for its own good in season. **Güvercin Island**, closer to the centre, is mostly landscaped terraces, dotted with tea gardens and snack bars, but the swimming is rocky. For the closest decent sand, head 500m further south to the small beach north of **Yılancı Burnu**, or 7km north of town to **Tusan** beach; both are served by all Kuşadası–Selçuk *dolmuşes*, as well as more frequent ones labelled *Şehir İçi*. Much the best beach in the area is **Pamucak**, at the mouth of the Kücük Menderes River 15km north, an exposed, 4km stretch of sand that is as yet little developed; it's served by regular *dolmuşes* from both Kuşadası and Selçuk in season.

Practicalities

Ferries arrive at Liman Cad, right by the **tourist office** (daily 8am–5.30pm; winter closed Sat & Sun; ☎0256/614 1103), which has exhaustive lists of accommodation. The combined **dolmuş** and long-distance **bus station** is around 2km out, past the end of Kahramanlar Cad on the ring road to Söke, while the *dolmuş* stop is closer to the centre on Adnan Menderes Bulvara.

There are plenty of **places to stay**, though you'll need to exercise caution; the collapse in tourism in 1999 saw many hotels and pensions, especially those in areas favoured by backpackers, open their doors to East European prostitutes and their unsavoury minders. Most of the good pensions, as well as some to be avoided, are just south of the core of the town, uphill from Barbaros Hayrettin Bulvarı. *Sezgin Hotel*, Zafer Sok 15 (☎0256/614 4225, *sezgin@ispro.net.tr*, ①), has comfortable ensuite rooms and **Internet** access, while lively and friendly *Sammy's Palace*, Kıbrıs Cad 14 (☎0256/612 2588, *www.hotelsammyspalace.com*; ②), is firmly on the ANZAC network. *Golden Bed*, Aslanlar Cad, Uğurlu Çıkmazı 4 (☎0256/614 8708; ②), is similarly friendly and has ensuite rooms. Behind the tourist office at Buyral Sok 4 is *Hotel Liman* (☎0256/614 7770, *hasandegirmenci@superonline.com*; ②), which has air-conditioned rooms with sea views and some dorm space on the roof. For **campers**, the *Turyat* out at Tusan beach is well-appointed but expensive; *Önder* and *Yat,* both behind the yacht marina, are marginally cheaper, well-kept and popular.

Eating out is unlikely to be memorable, with few options between the overpriced tourist traps and more basic establishments. *Konyalı*, Saglik Cad 40, is a standard kebab place popular with locals and open 24hr. *Öz Urfa*, in the Kale district on Cephane Sok, has excellent-value *lahmacun* and *pide*; while the *Avlu*, also on Cephane Sok, has a wide range of kebab and steam-tray food and a cosy outdoor courtyard. *Kapı*, Cephane Sok 20, offers reasonable kebabs and *meze* with live traditional *fasil* music. If you want to eat by the water without emptying your entire wallet, try *Ada Restaurant-Plaj-Café*, on Güvercin Adası. The *She* **bar** is on the corner of Bahar and Sakarya Sokaks, with half-a-dozen more along nearby Kışla Sok. Rather more downmarket are the dozen-plus "Irish" and "English" pubs along an inland alley officially renamed Barlar Sok (Pub Lane).

Ferries to Samos are, as ever, subject to predicted demand; there are no scheduled services in winter and up to three boats a day in high summer. Diana on Kıbrıs Cad (✆0256/614 3859) runs up to two boats daily in summer; the morning Turkish boat is handled by Azim, on Liman Cad Yayla Pasajı (✆0256/614 1553). Fares are $30 single, $35 day return and $55 open return. Add $70–130 if you want to take a car. The Minoan Lines **ferries to Greece and Italy** are handled by Karavan, Kıbrıs Cad 2/1 (✆0256/614 1279).

Selçuk and around

SELÇUK has been catapulted into the limelight of first-division tourism by its proximity to the ruins of **Ephesus**, and a number of other attractions within the city limits and around. The flavour of tourism here, though, is different from that at nearby Kuşadası, its inland location and ecclesiastical connections making it a haven for a disparate mix of backpackers and Bible-belters from every corner of the globe. Furthermore the beaches in and around Kuşadası are easily accessible from here on a short *dolmuş* ride.

The **hill of Ayasoluk** (daily 8am–6.30pm; $2), the traditional burial place of St John the Evangelist, who died here around 100 AD, boasts the remains of a basilica built by Justinian that was one of the largest Byzantine churches in existence; various colonnades and walls have been re-erected, giving a hint of the building's magnificence. The tomb of the evangelist is marked by a slab at the former site of the altar; beside the nave is the baptistry, where religious tourists pose in the act of dunking as friends' cameras click. The virtually empty **castle**, 200m past the church, is closed. Just behind the tourist office, the **Archeological Museum** (daily 8.30am–noon & 1–5pm; $5) has galleries of finds from Ephesus, including the famous Artemis room, with two renditions of the goddess studded with multiple testicles (not breasts, as is commonly believed) and tiny figurines of real and mythical beasts, honouring her role as mistress of animals. Beyond the museum, 600m along the road toward Ephesus, are the scanty remains of the **Artemision** or sanctuary of Artemis, a massive Hellenistic structure that was considered one of the Seven Wonders of the Ancient World, though this is hard to believe today. Within sight of here, the fourteenth-century **İsa Bey Camii** is the most distinguished of various Selçuk monuments.

At the base of the castle hill, a pedestrian precinct leads east to the **train station**. Following the main highway a bit further south brings you to the **bus** and **dolmuş** terminal, opposite which is the **tourist office** (daily 8.30am–noon and 1–5pm; winter closed Sat & Sun). The majority of pensions and hotels will organize a free lift from the bus station if you call them on arrival, and many will arrange free lifts to Ephesus and some other local sights. Bear in mind that **hotel** touts in Selçuk can be aggressive, employing a gamut of tricks, including heavy pressure to buy something from a conveniently attached shop. The *Barım*, 1034 Sok 34 (✆0232/892 6923; ①), an eccentric rambling old house, is reasonable, while the large *Artemis Guest House "Jimmy's Place"*, 1012 Sok 2 (✆0232/892 1982, *www.artemisguesthouse.com*; ①), has ensuite doubles (some with nice views), **Internet** access and veggie food, as well as offering lots of advice and help with getting around. *Otel Ürkmez*, Namık Kemal Cad 20 (✆0232/892 6312, *urkmez35@hotmail.com*; ②), near the *hamam*, has ensuite facilities throughout and a roof terrace. More upmarket is the beautifully furnished, female-run *Nilya*, Atatürk Mah 1051 Sok 7 (✆0232/892 9081; ④), which offers beautiful views over the Artemision. Selçuk's **campsite**, *Garden*, lies just beyond the Isa Bey Camii and is well rated; alternatively, there's the *Blue Moon/Develi*, 9km west at Pamucak Beach, served by Selçuk–Kuşadası *dolmuşes*. Best of the **restaurants** are in the pedestrianized grid of streets in the centre of town. *Köşk pide* on Zigberg Cad, and *Ephesus* on Namik Kemal Cad, are worth a try, as is the licensed *Old House* restaurant on Deniz Topel Cad. The **hamam**, next to the main police station, offers a cheap introduction to good Turkish scrub and massage: expect to pay about $9 for the full treatment (plus a small tip for the masseur).

Around Selçuk

Some 8km southwest of Selçuk lies **Meryemana** (daily dawn–dusk; $3), a tiny Greek chapel where some Orthodox theologians believe the Virgin Mary passed her last years, having travelled to the region with St John the Evangelist, who is buried on Ayasoluk hill. Evidence of Mary's residence is somewhat circumstantial but that doesn't stop coach tours to Ephesus making the detour. The chapel's appeal is all spiritual, with regular Catholic masses (summer daily 7.15am, Sun also 10.30am).

ŞIRINCE, to the south and served by hourly minibuses from Selçuk, is a 600-year-old Greek stone village where, against the odds, the winemaking tradition has been continued by Muslim Turks who settled here in the 1920s. Numerous local vintages are on offer in the village's many shops. There are several **accommodation** options, including the beautifully restored village houses which make up *Şirince Evler* (☎0232/898 3209; ⑨). Some 12km along the road from Selçuk to Aydin, **ÇAMLIK** is the site of Turkey's **Open-Air Rail Museum** (daily 8am–8pm; $1; *www.tcdd3bolge.gov.tr/muze.htm*) which boasts 29 steam locomotives and a host of other rolling stock, mostly pre-World War I; the oldest dates back to 1887. You don't have to be a trainspotter to enjoy clambering into the cabs and operating the hand wound turntable.

Efes (Ephesus)

With the exception of Pompeii and some hard-to-reach ruins in Libya and Albania, **EPHESUS** is the largest and best-preserved ancient city around the Mediterranean. Not surprisingly, the ruins are mobbed in summer, although with a little planning and initiative it's possible to tour the site in relative peace. Certainly, it's a place you should not miss, though you may come away disappointed at the commercialization and the extent of the off-limits areas. You'll need three or four partly shady hours, and a water bottle.

Originally situated close to a temple devoted to the goddess Artemis, Ephesus' location by a fine harbour was the secret of its success in ancient times, eventually making it the wealthy capital of Roman Asia, ornamented with magnificent public buildings by a succession of emperors. Later, after Christianity took root, St John the Evangelist arrived here, and St Paul spent the years 51 to 53 AD in the city. During the Byzantine era the city went into decline, owing to the abandoning of Artemis worship, Arab raids, and (worst of all) the final silting up of the harbour, leading the population to siphon off to the nearby hill crowned by the tomb and church of St John, future nucleus of the town of Selçuk.

Approaching from Kuşadası, get the *dolmuş* to drop you at the *Tusan Motel* junction, 1km from the gate. From Selçuk, it's a 3km walk. In the centre of the **site** (daily 8am–6.30pm; winter closes 4.30pm; $6) is the **Arcadian Way**, which was once lined with hundreds of shops and illuminated at night. These days it's generally closed in summer, since grass presents a fire risk. The nearby **theatre** has been partly restored to allow its use for open-air concerts and occasional summer festivals; it's worth the climb to the top for the views over the surrounding countryside. From the theatre, the **Marble Street** heads south, passing the main **agora**, and a **Temple of Serapis** where the city's Egyptian merchants would have worshipped. About halfway along is a footprint, a female head and a heart etched into the rock – an alleged signpost for a **brothel** – at the junction with the Street of the Curetes, the other main street. Inside are some fine floor mosaics denoting the four seasons.

Across the intersection looms the **Library of Celsus**, erected by the consul Gaius Julius Aquila between 110 and 135 AD as a memorial to his father Celsus Polemaeanus, entombed under the west wall. The elegant, two-storey facade was fitted with niches for statues of the four personified intellectual virtues, today filled with copies (the originals are in Vienna). Just uphill from here, a **Byzantine fountain** looks across the Street of the Curetes to the **public latrines**, a favourite with visitors owing to the graphic obviousness of their function. Continuing along the same side of the street, you'll come to the so-called **Temple of Hadrian**, actually donated in 118 AD by a wealthy citizen in honour of Hadrian, Artemis and the city in general. Behind sprawl the **Baths of Scholastica,** so named after a fifth-century Byzantine woman whose headless statue adorns the entrance and who restored the complex, which was actually four hundred years older. On the far side of the street from the Hadrian shrine lies a huge pattern **mosaic**, which once fronted a series of shops. Nearby, a sign points to the **terraced houses** (an extra $6), housed under a hi-tech steel and glass structure to protect the amazingly well-preserved mosaics and murals of what were the houses of two very rich families. Further up Curetes, you pass the **Temple of Domitian**, the lower floor of which houses a mildly interesting **Museum of Inscriptions** (currently closed), on the way to the large, overgrown **upper agora**, fringed by a colonnade to the north, and a restored *odeion* and *prytaneum* or civic office.

Bodrum

In the eyes of its devotees, **BODRUM** (*www.bodrum-info.org*) – ancient Halicarnassos – with its whitewashed houses and subtropical gardens, is the most attractive Turkish resort, a quality outfit in comparison to its upstart Aegean rivals. And it is a pleasant town in most senses, despite having no real beach, although development has proceeded apace over the last couple of decades, spreading beyond the town boundaries into the until recently little-disturbed peninsula. The centrepiece of Bodrum is the **Castle of St Peter** (daily 8.30am–6pm; $5), built by the Knights of St John over a Selçuk fortress between 1437 and 1522. The castle was subsequently neglected until the nineteenth century, when the chapel was converted to a mosque and had a *hamam* installed, though the place was not properly refurbished until the 1960s, when it was turned into a museum. Inside, there are bits of ancient masonry incorporated into the walls, coats of arms, and a chapel housing a local Bronze Age and Mycenean collection. The various towers house a **Museum of Underwater Archeology** which includes coin and jewellery rooms, classical and Hellenistic statuary and Byzantine relics retrieved from two wrecks, alongside a diorama explaining salvage techniques. The **Carian princess hall** (daily 10am–noon & 2–4pm; $2 extra) displays the skeleton and sarcophagus of a fourth-century BC Carian noblewoman unearthed in 1989. There is also the **Glass Wreck Hall** (daily 10–11am & 2–4pm; $2 extra) containing the wreck and cargo of an ancient Byzantine ship, which sank at Serce near Marmaris.

Immediately north of the castle lies the **bazaar**, most of which is pedestrianized along the main thoroughfares of Kale Caddesi and Dr Alim Bey Caddesi and given over to souvenir stores and the like. From here, stroll up Türkkuyusu Caddesi and turn left to the town's other main sight, the **Mausoleum** (daily 8.30am–6pm; $3). This is the burial place of Mausolus, who ruled Halicarnassos in the fourth century BC, greatly increasing its power and wealth. His tomb, completed by Artemisia II, his sister and wife, was regarded as one of the Seven Wonders of the Ancient World, giving rise to the word "mausoleum". Decorated with friezes, it stood nearly 60m high, though its present condition is disappointing, with little left besides the precinct wall, assorted column fragments and some subterranean vaults – the bulk of it being in London's British Museum. By way of contrast, the ancient amphitheatre, just above the main highway to the north, has been almost over-zealously restored and is used during the September festival. Begun by Mausolus, it was modified in the Roman era and originally seated thirteen thousand, though it has a present capacity of about half that.

Dolmuşes from Bodrum's main bus station head to nearby **AKYARLAR**, which offers the combination of the best sandy beach around and some quiet *pansiyons* and restaurants, as well as one of only two campsites on the Bodrum peninsula.

Practicalities

Ferries dock at the jetty west of the castle, quite close to the **tourist office** on İskele Meydanı (daily 8.30am–5.30pm; winter closed Sat & Sun). The **bus station** is 500m up Cevat Şakir Cad, which divides the town roughly in two. Some of the best **accommodation** is southeast of the bus station in Kumbahçe. *Emiko Pansiyon*, Atatürk Cad, Uslu Sok 11 (☎0252/316 5560, *emiko@turk.net*; ③), has a pleasant courtyard, a friendly Japanese owner and quiet ensuite rooms. *Durak*, Rasthane Sok 8 (☎0252/316 1564; ③), has clean, tidy ensuite rooms, some with balconies, as does the friendly *Uğur*, just across the road at no. 13 (☎0252/316 2106; ③). West of the bus station, *Melis*, Türkkuyusu Cad 50 (☎0252/316 0560; ③), has ensuite rooms and attractive courtyards. The nearby *Dönen* (☎0252/316 4017; ②) is a quiet family-run operation with a garden and ample parking.

You don't come to Bodrum to ease your budget, and **eating out** is no exception. Best of the budget places are the *Zetaş Ocakbaşı* and the *Kaş Buhara Et Lokantası*, both on Atatürk Cad, which offer good *pide* and meat dishes and are frequented by local artists. *Gemibaşi*, opposite the yacht harbour, on the corner of Firkayten Sok and Neyzen Tevfik, is good for a no-nonsense meat meal. The Karadeniz cake shop on Dr Alim Bey Cad does wonderful fruit and cream cakes. The same street boasts many of the town's fast-changing **bars**, which currently include the *Robin Hood* and the *White House*. There are also a number of good bars along Neyzen Tevfik Cad. For **clubs**, the *Halikarnas* disco at the east end of Cumhuriyet Cad is the most famous on the Aegean, while the *M&M Marine Club* is reputedly the biggest floating disco in the world; it sets sail at 2am when the onshore establishments close. **Internet** access is at Palmiye Internet Café, opposite the Marina.

Tickets for the **ferry to Kos** are best booked through the two main agents, beside each other at the ferry dock: Bodrum Express Lines (☎0252/316 1087) handles hydrofoils ($20 one-way; $30 return), and Bodrum Ferryboat Association (☎0252/316 0882) handles ferries ($12 one-way; $15 day return; $25 open return) as well as domestic services to Datça. You must pay a port tax of $10 on arrival in Greece if you're not returning the same day.

Marmaris and around

MARMARIS (*www.marmaris-online.com*) rivals Kuşadası as the largest and most developed Aegean resort. Its huge marina and proximity to Dalaman airport mean that tourists pour in more or less nonstop during the warmer months. According to legend, the place was named when Süleyman the Magnificent, not finding the castle here to his liking, was heard to mutter *"Mimar as"* ("Hang the architect") – a command which should perhaps still apply to the designers of the seemingly endless high-rises. Ulusal Egemenlik Bulvarı cuts Marmaris in half, and the maze of narrow streets east of it is home to most things of interest, though little is left of the sleepy fishing village that Marmaris was a mere two decades ago. The bazaar is now little more than an area of covered streets, and only the **Kaleiçi** district, the warren of streets at the base of the tiny castle, offers a pleasant wander. The **castle museum** (Tues–Sun 8am–noon & 1–5.30pm; $1) has a worthwhile archeology and ethnography collection.

A new bus station has recently opened about 1.5km south of the town centre, from where you can pick up a *dolmuş* to take you to the town centre, or it's a $3 taxi-ride. Many of the bus companies also offer a free transfer minibus to their offices in the centre. The **ferry** dock abuts İskele Meydanı, on one side of which stands the very helpful **tourist office** (summer daily 8.30am–7.30pm; winter Mon–Fri 8.30am–noon & 1–5.30pm), which dispenses town plans and **accommodation** details. The development of package tourism has ensured that hotels here are expensive and welcoming *pansiyons* few and far between – but the tourist office is tuned in to the needs of backpackers and can help out. The cheapest option is the *Interyouth Hostel* at Tepe Mahallesi 42, Sok 45, in the bazaar close to the Atatürk statue (☎0252/412 3687, *interyouth@turk.net*; ③), with around 180 beds in single, double and dormitory rooms, a lively rooftop café, and facilities including **Internet** access and a competitively priced travel service. Behind the huge Tansaş shopping centre is the *Nadir* (☎0252/412 1167; ③) which has both en-suite *pansiyon* rooms and hotel rooms complete with air-conditioning and TV. Another good budget pension is the *Yeşim*, west of the centre towards Uzunyalı beach at Atatürk Cad 60, Sok 3 (☎0252/412 3001; ③), a well-maintained place offering en-suite rooms. More upmarket is the great-value *Marina Motel* (☎0252/412 6598; *www.turquaz-guide.net*; ②), which has clean en-suite rooms and a breakfast terrace.

Getting a decent **meal** at a reasonable price is a challenge, although the fabulous *Kırçiçeği* on Kübilay Alpagün Cad behind the bazaar offers excellent traditional Turkish food at reasonable prices. Among the several options in the bazaar area close to the PTT, *Marmaris* and *Liman* are both acceptable and are frequented by the locals. To the west, Uzunyali harbours various pizza joints and a reasonable Turkish restaurant, *Turhan*, at Uzunyali 26. For **drinking**, *Panorama*, up on the castle hill, offers great views, and the nearby Hacı Mustafa Sokaği (aka "Bar Street") contains a wealth of other drinking venues, such as *Davy Jones' Locker* and *Casablanca*. Lin Net, 38 Atatürk Cad opposite the Atatürk statue, has **Internet** access.

Ferries to Rhodes ($35 one-way or day-return; $50 open return; sometimes less in high season) run daily in high season, dropping to one a week in winter. Agents include Yeşil Marmaris, Barbaros Cad 13 (☎0252/412 2290), and Engin Turizm, 3rd floor, G. Mustafa Cad 16 (☎0252/412 6944). There's a once-weekly **car ferry** (cars $150 one-way).

Datça

Although a little staid, **DATÇA**, 30km west of Marmaris, is a great deal calmer than Bodrum or Marmaris. It's essentially the shore annexe of inland **Reşadiye** village, but, thanks to visiting yachtspeople and package operators, has outgrown its parent. The single main street, crammed with carpet shops, meanders between two sheltered bays separated by a hillock and then a narrow isthmus. There's little to do other than swim and sunbathe. The **east beach**, part sand, part cement quay with cafés, is quieter but the cleanliness is suspect. The west beach, mixed pebble and sand, is acceptable and gets better the further you get from the yachts. The nearest good beaches are at Özil (15km), Aktur (30km) and Perili Köşk (15km) on the road to Marmaris.

Datça's new **otogar** is around 1.5km from the centre, connected by service bus or *dolmuş*. **Ferries to Bodrum**, operated by the Bodrum Ferryboat Service (mid-June to mid-Sept), run from Körmen Limanı 9km north, connected by a short bus ride, with tickets available from the ferryboat office next to the mosque. The **tourist office** is on the main road near the PTT (daily: summer 8.30am–7pm; winter 8am–5pm; ☎0252/712 3163). A good **place to stay** is the hillock separating the two bays, where the *Huzur* (☎0252/712 3052; ③) is the most modern, while *Tunç* (☎0252/712 3036; ③) near the centre of town offers clean, pleasant en-suite rooms. Also near the centre and the beach is *Mandalina* (☎0252/712 4995; ③), with comfortable, newish en-suite rooms. Most **restaurants** offer local fish plus kebabs: *Küçük Ev* and *Kaptanın Yeri*, overlooking the harbour, are recommended, as is *Dütdibi* on the east beach, offering *pide*. Best budget option is the *06 Aspava*, inland from the main drag, which does stews and *pide*. The west harbour is the place to look for music **bars** and pubs, of which *Mırmır* is currently the favourite.

Denizli, Pamukkale and Hierapolis

Devastated by earthquakes in 1710 and 1899, **DENİZLİ**, 50km east of Nazilli, is a gritty agricultural town of around 200,000 inhabitants. It has little appeal itself, but you may well pass through, especially if you're heading on to Pamukkale, to which there are regular buses and *dolmuşes*. Best **accommodation** is *Denizli Pension*, 1993 Sok 14 (☎0258/261 8738; ③), which has friendly staff, a free pick-up from the bus station and free lifts to Pamukkale.

The rock formations of **PAMUKKALE** (literally "Cotton Castle"), 10km or so north, are perhaps the most-visited attraction in this part of Turkey, a series of white terraces saturated with dissolved calcium bicarbonate, bubbling up from the feet of the Çal Dağı Mountains beyond. As the water surges over the edge of the plateau and cools, carbon dioxide is given off and calcium carbonate precipitated as hard chalk or travertine. The spring emerges in what was once the exact middle of the ancient city of **Hierapolis**, the ruins of which would merit a stop even if they weren't coupled with the natural phenomenon. Uncontrolled hotel development in the 1980s caused much of the travertine to turn from white to yellow and even to brown. An official rescue campaign saw all but two hotels demolished, returning the terraces to their pristine whiteness, now enhanced by nighttime illumination. Most budget accommodation is now down in the village of **PAMUKKALE KÖYÜ**, with larger resort places along the main roads further out.

The **travertine terraces** (daily 24hr; $4) are deservedly the first item on most visitors' agenda, but you should bear in mind the fragility of this natural phenomenon. Nowadays most of the pools are very shallow and closed off, with tourists confined to walking on specially marked routes, though this is, thankfully, having a positive effect, as the travertines slowly return to their former grandeur. Up on the plateau is what is spuriously billed as the **sacred pool** of the ancients, which, with mineral water bubbling up from its bottom at 35°C, is open for bathing (daily 8am–8pm; $4). In reality though it's little more than a few big lumps of carved marble submerged in a concrete pool, these days popular mainly with east European coach parties.

The **archeological zone** of Hierapolis lies west of Pamukkale Köyü, via a narrow road winding up past the *Turism Motel*. Its main features include a **temple of Apollo** and the adjacent **Plutonium** – the latter a cavern emitting a toxic mixture of sulphur dioxide and carbon dioxide, capable of killing man and beast alike. There's also a restored **Roman theatre** just east of here, dating from the second century AD and in exceptionally good shape, with most of the stage buildings and their elaborate reliefs intact. Arguably the most interesting part of the city, though, is the colonnaded street which once extended for almost 1km from a gate 400m southeast of the sacred pool, terminating in monumental portals a few paces outside the walls – only the most northerly of which, a triple arch flanked by towers and dedicated to the Emperor Domitian in 84 AD, still stands. Just south of the arch is the elaborate tomb of Flavius Zeuxis – the first of more than a thousand tombs constituting the necropolis, the largest in Asia Minor, extending for nearly 2km along the road. There's also a **museum** (Tues–Sun 8am–noon & 1–6.30pm; $4), housed in the restored, second-century baths, whose disappointing collection consists of statuary, sarcophagi, masonry fragments and smaller knick-knacks recovered during excavations.

Practicalities

With over forty pensions, there's no shortage of **accommodation** in Pamukkale Köyü, and touts at the bus stand can be particularly aggressive. Most will pick you up from Denizli, have a pool of some description and offer rates for full board. One of the best and friendliest is the air-conditioned *Koray* (☎0258/272 2222; ②), which has a pleasant garden and buffet meals. The *Meltem Guest House* (☎0258/272 3134; ②) and *Meltem Motel Backpacker's Inn* (☎0258/272 2413, *meltemmotel@superonline.com.tr*; ①) both have en-suite doubles and Internet access, plus various other mod cons. Up the hill the family-owned *Kervanseray* (☎0258/272 2209; ①) also has a number of decent en-suite doubles and Internet access. **Eating out** is not likely to be memorable; most of the handful of restaurants are attached to hotels such as the *Mustafa*, which offers vegetarian dishes cooked to order, and you'd probably do best eating at your *pansiyon*. Otherwise, there's little other than *pide*.

Aphrodisias

Situated on a high plateau around 100km inland, **APHRODISIAS** is one of the more isolated of Turkey's major archeological sites. It was one of the earliest occupied centres in Anatolia, but remained a shrine for many centuries, and only really grew into a major cultural centre in the second century BC. It was renowned in particular for its school of sculpture, benefiting from nearby quarries of high-grade marble, examples of which adorned every corner of the empire.

A loop path around the site (daily 8am–5.30pm; $4) passes all of the major monuments, beginning with the virtually intact **theatre**, founded in the first century BC but extensively modified by the Romans three centuries later. Further on you pass the **double agora**, two squares ringed by Ionic and Corinthian stoas, and the fine **baths of Hadrian**, well-preserved right down to the floor tiles and the odd mosaic. North of the baths, several columns sprout from a multi-roomed structure commonly known as the **bishop's palace**, east of which is the appealing Roman **odeon**, with nine rows of seats. Perhaps the most impressive feature of the site is, however, the 30,000-seat **stadium**, a little way north, one of the largest and best preserved in Anatolia. The **museum** (daily 8am–5.30pm; $3) consists almost entirely of sculpture recovered from the ruins, including statuary related to the cult of Aphrodite, a joyous satyr carrying the child Dionysus in his arms, and a quasi-satirical portrait of Flavius Palmatus, Byzantine governor of Asia.

The nearest sizeable town is **KARACASU**, 13km west, connected by frequent **dolmuş** to **NAZİLLİ**, 50km northwest. If you're staying in Pamukkale, it's tempting to try and devise a loop to Aphrodisias via Nazilli, and then back to Pamukkale the other way, through Tavas, but you must get to Tavas in time for the last *dolmuş* back to Denizli, and thence to Pamukkale, which is difficult. Whatever happens, try to avoid getting stranded at Aphrodisias or Karacasu. **GEYRE**, 600m from Aphrodisias on the main Karacasu–Tavas highway, has the *Chez Mestan* **campsite/pension** (✆0256/448 8046; ①).

THE MEDITERRANEAN COAST

The first stretch of Turkey's **Mediterranean Coast**, dominated by the Arkdağ and Bey mountain ranges of the Taurus chain and known as the "**Turquoise Coast**", is perhaps its most popular, famed for its pine-studded shore, minor ruins and beautiful scenery. Most of this is connected by Highway 400, which winds precipitously above the sea from Marmaris to Antalya. In the west of the region, **Dalyan** is renowned for its beach – a breeding ground of loggerhead turtles – as well as being a characterful small resort. West, **Fethiye**, along with the nearby lagoon of **Ölüdeniz**, is a full-blown regional centre, and gives good access to some of the pick of the region's Lycian ruins, the best of which – **Xanthos** and **Patara** – are close to one of the coast's nicest beaches. The region's second major resort, **Kaş**, smaller than Fethiye but no less popular, is a good base for scenery which becomes increasingly spectacular until you reach the site of **Olympos**, close to another fine beach. Further along, past the port and major city of **Antalya**, the landscape becomes less dramatic but is home to yet more impressive ruins, notably those of the old Pamphylian cities of **Perge** and **Aspendos**. **Side**, too, has its share of antiquities, although it's better known as a tourist resort, as is the former pirate refuge of **Alanya**, set on a spectacular headland topped by a stunning Selçuk citadel. Beyond here you're entering the relatively undiscovered reaches of eastern Turkey.

Dalyan

DALYAN (*www.dalyan.net*), 7km off Highway 400, is one of the calmer resorts along this stretch of coast, and a good base for surrounding attractions. Life here centres on the Dalyan River, which flows past the village: the one drawback in the summer months is mosquitoes, especially along the riverbank, for which the area has been notorious since antiquity. Go armed with a good repellent, and drop into any good pharmacy to buy an *esemymat*, a machine that you plug into the electricity supply to kill the critters. There are a string of pleasant **pensions** on the riverbank, one of the nicest being *Midas* (✆0252/284 2195; ②), at the far end, or the newly refurbished *Lindos* (✆0252/284 2005, *lindos@superonline.com*; ②), next door, also has a couple of cabin rooms right on the water; other good options are *Aktaş* (☎0252/284 2042; ②), or its friendly neighbour, *Miletos* (☎0252/284 2532; ①), both of which include breakfast in the room price. **Restaurants** are fairly undistinguished; the riverfront *Denizatı* and *Caretta* are typical – and pricey. There's better home cooking at *Dostlar Sofrası*, below *Altay Pansiyon*, where you'll come away replete for less than $3.

İstuzu Beach, a twenty-minute ride by regular boat service from Dalyan, is the breeding ground of the loggerhead turtle (May–Oct: no admission at night). During the day the beach is open to the public, and is a good place to swim and sunbathe, although you should be careful of disturbing the turtle eggs and nests, which are easily disrupted. You can also visit the nearby ruins of the Greek city of **Kaunos**; it's a river-boat crossing ($1), followed by a twenty-minute walk.

Fethiye and around

FETHİYE (*www.fethiye.net*) is well-situated for access to some of the region's ancient sites, many of which date from the time when this area was the independent kingdom of Lycia. The best beaches, around the Ölüdeniz Lagoon, are now much too crowded for comfort, but unlike Kaş, which is confined by its sheer rock backdrop, Fethiye is still a real market town and has been able to spread to accommodate increased tourist traffic.

Fethiye occupies the location of the Lycian city of **Telmessos**, little of which remains other than the impressive ancient **theatre**, which was only unearthed in 1992, and a number of Lycian rock tombs on the hillside above the bus station. Most notable is the Amyntas Tomb, carved in close imitation of the facade of a temple. You can also visit the remains of the medieval fortress, on the hillside behind the harbour area of town. In the centre of town, off Atatürk Caddesi, the small **museum** (Tues–Sun 10am–6.30pm; $1.50) has some fascinating exhibits from local sites and a good ethnographic section. The most interesting piece is the stele found at the Letoön, dating from 358 BC, which was important in translating the Lycian language.

One of the most dramatic sights in the area is the ghost village of **KAYA KÖYÜ** (Levissi), 7km out of town, served by *dolmuşes* from behind the PTT. The village was abandoned in 1923, when its Anatolian Greek population were relocated, along with more than a million others, to a country which had never been their homeland, and whose language many of them couldn't speak. All you see now is a hillside covered with more than 2000 ruined cottages and an attractive **basilica**, to the right of the main path 200m up the hill from the road, one of three churches here – but the general state of neglect only serves to highlight the plight of the former inhabitants. There are plans to make an international "peace and friendship" conference centre here, but ordinary travellers must still stay at a couple of *pansiyons* at the edge of Kaya.

Ölüdeniz is about two hours on foot from Kaya Köyü – through the village, over the hill and down to the lagoon – although it is also served by frequent *dolmuşes* from Fethiye. The warm waters of the lagoon make for pleasant swimming if you don't mind paying the small entrance fee, although the crowds can reach saturation level in high season – in which case the nearby, more prosaic beaches of Belceğiz and Kidrak are better bets. Ölüdeniz is also the starting point for the **Lycian Way**, Turkey's only marked trekking route which starts from near the Montana Holiday Village on the Fethiye–Ölüdeniz road and winds along the coast almost as far as Antalya.

Practicalities

Fethiye's **bus station** is about 2km east of the centre; *dolmuşes* to Ölüdeniz, Çalış beach and Kaya village arrive and leave from the old *otogar*, east of the central market. The **tourist office** is close to the theatre, near the harbour at İskele Meydanı 1 (daily: summer 8.30am–7pm; winter 8am–5pm; ☎0252/612 1975). There are two main concentrations of **hotels** – in the downtown area and in the suburb of Karagözler overlooking the marina to the west (there are direct *dolmuşes* to Karagözler from the bus station). Downtown, the *Ülgen Pansiyon* (☎0252/614 3491; ①), up the stairs beyond Paspatir Cad, has simple ensuites. Southeast of the centre and handiest for the bus station is *Sinderella*, Merdivenli Geçit 3 (☎0252/614 2288; ①). In quieter Karagözler, *Savaşci* (☎0252/614 4108; ②) is a long hike up above the marina but boasts great views, while *Pınara*, Fevzi Çakmak Cad 39 (☎0252/614 2151; ①), is slightly noisier but friendly. Just behind it and before you reach the *Savaşci* is *Ideal* (☎0252/614 1981; ①), similarly friendly and popular with backpackers, with a great terrace. Along from the *Ideal* on Ordu Cad is the *Duygu Pansiyon* (☎0252/614 3563; ②). All these include breakfast in the room price. For **camping**, one of the best sites is the *Ölüdeniz*, which has its own beach and restaurant; it's just past the official entrance to Ölüdeniz Lagoon on the left.

Some of Fethiye's best **food** is at *Paşa Kebap* on Çarşi Cad, while *Sedir*, Tütün Sok 3, offers excellent, reasonably priced *pide* and home-cooked stews. Also reasonable is *Pizza 74* opposite the marina, and *Birlik Lokanta* opposite the PTT on Atatürk Cad, which offers traditional Turkish cooking and ice cream. Outdoor seafront cafés provide ample **drinking** opportunities, while the hillside above the tourist office offers the garish *Yasmin*, specializing in live Turkish music; the *Music Factory* and *Car Cemetery Bar*, both on Paspartu Sok, vie for being the hottest joint in town. **Internet** access is at Line Bilgisayer, Yalı Sok 5b.

Around Fethiye: the Lycian sites

East of Fethiye lies the heartland of ancient Lycia, home to a number of archeological sites, all within easy reach of Fethiye. The closest is the **LETOÖN**, accessible by taking a *dolmuş* from Fethiye to **Kumluova**, the site lying 4km off the main highway. The Letoön was the official sanctuary of the Lycian Federation, and the extensive **ruins** bear witness to its importance (admission $1.50 when warden present). The low ruins of three **temples** occupy the centre of the site, the westernmost of which bears a dedication to Leto. The central temple, dating from the fourth century BC, is identified by a dedication to Artemis, while the easternmost temple has a floor mosaic of a lyre, bow and quiver, suggesting a dedication to Artemis and Apollo, who were apparently the region's most revered deities. Beyond the temple to the southwest is a **nymphaeum** with statue niches, though it's now permanently flooded. There is also a large, well-preserved **theatre** on the right, entered through a vaulted passage.

On the other side of the valley, the remains of the hilltop city of **XANTHOS** are perhaps the most fascinating of the Lycian sites, though sadly the most important relic discovered at the site, the fourth-century Nereid Monument, is now in the British Museum in London. However, there is still enough to see here to reward a lengthy visit. Buses between Fethiye and **Patara** drop you off in Kanak, from where it's a ten-minute walk up to the **ruins** (daily 7am–7.30pm; $2). West of the car park are the acropolis and agora and a Roman theatre, beside which are two Lycian tombs – the so-called **Harpy Tomb**, a cement cast of the original decorated with pairs of bird-woman figures carrying children in their arms, and a Lycian-type **sarcophagus** standing on a pillar tomb, thought to date from the third century BC. Northeast of the agora looms a structure known popularly as the Xanthian obelisk – in fact the remains of a pillar tomb covered on all four sides by the longest-known Lycian inscription, running to 250 lines and including twelve lines of Greek verse. The nearby Roman theatre is pretty complete, only missing the upper seats which were incorporated into the Byzantine city wall.

PATARA

PATARA *(www.patara.org)*, a little way south and reachable by regular *dolmuş* from Fethiye and Kaş in season (otherwise, Fethiye–Kaş buses will drop you 4km north of the site) was the principal port of Lycia, famed for its oracle of Apollo and as the birthplace of St Nicholas. Two kilometres from the modern village of **Gelemiş**, the **site** (daily: summer 7.30am–7pm; winter 8am–5pm; $4; ticket valid for a week) is marked by a triple-arched Roman gateway, which is reasonably intact and adjacent to some recently excavated tombs. Also on view are some well-preserved baths and a small temple lodged in a course of boundary wall. To the south, 1km from the beach, is a theatre, the *cavea* of which is now half full of sand – although the stage building is partly intact. Nowadays Patara is best known for its white sand **beach**, served by *dolmuş* from Gelemiş. It can get a bit crowded in season, but the walk along the dunes towards the river mouth, 7km northwest, turns up more than enough solitary spots. If you are planning to visit Patara or Gelemiş out of season it's best to call ahead, as most facilities close down for winter.

Mosquitoes are a constant problem in Patara and all good **pensions** equip their rooms with nets; check before committing yourself. Accommodation can fill up quickly, so you'd do best to reserve at the better places. Best budget option is the family-run *Flower* (✆0242/843 5164; ①) at the entrance to the village, which has excellent en-suite rooms with balconies and home-cooking. They will also pick you up from the main road for free, and from Dalaman Airport for petrol money. Just behind this is the reasonable *Rose* (✆0242/843 5173; ①), with basic, clean, en-suite rooms with balconies. They also offer the same pick-up deals, and, unusually, stay open in winter. Another choice is the Otlu brothers' long-running *Golden Pansiyon* (✆0242/843 5162; ②) at the crossroads, which has been joined by their posher, and well-positioned *Patara View Point Hotel* (✆0242/843 5184, *www.pataraviewpoint.com*; ③) on the ridge east of the main crossroads, which has a pool and **Internet** access. Another good option in the centre of the village is the *St Nicolas Pansiyon* (✆0242/843 5154, *stnicolaspansion@hotmail.com*; ②). **Eating** possibilities aren't scintillating, with names and themes changing often; the *Golden Pansiyon's* diner often has trout, as do several others, best of which is the *Sofra*. The two cafés down at the beach feature *mantı*, meat ravioli in yoghurt.

Kaş and around

KAŞ, 41km east of Patara, is beautifully situated, nestled in a curving bay against a backdrop of vertical, 500m-high cliffs. However, what was a quaint fishing village as recently as the early 1980s has grown to become a tourist metropolis. There's no beach to speak of, but there's plenty to see in the countryside around, and the town does get lively at night. It's also the site of ancient **Antiphellos**, the ruins of which litter the streets of the modern town, as well as covering the peninsula to the west. Most interesting of these is the **lion tomb**, a towering structure that had two burial chambers, at the top of Uzun Çarşı. Some 500m from the main square, along Hastane Caddesi, a small, almost complete Hellenistic **theatre** looks out to sea; on a nearby hilltop stands a unique rock-cut **Doric tomb**, also almost completely intact.

From the **bus station** it's a five-minute walk downhill to the waterfront. The **tourist office** at Cumhuriyet Meydanı 5 (summer daily 8am–7pm; winter Mon–Fri 8am–5pm; ✆0242/836 1238) has lists of **hotel** and **pension** prices. Cheapest options can be found west of the centre along Hastane Cad. *Yalı*, Hastane Cad 11 (✆0242/836 1132; ②), has ensuite rooms and sea views plus a shared kitchen, as does the next door *Andifli* (✆0242/836 1042; ②) which includes breakfast. Further along, the *Gülşen*, Hastane Cad 23 (✆0242/836 1171; ①), has rooms and a few sea-facing balconies. The *Karakedi Korsan* hotel up the hill to the north at Yeni Camii Sok 7 (✆0242/836 1887; ②) features a roof terrace overlooking the amphitheatre, plus a pool and **Internet** access. There are two nearby **campsites**: the tidy *Olympos* (✆0242/836 2252) is about 2km from the centre on the Kalkan road, while *Kaş Camping* (✆0242/836 1050), is 1km west of town on Hastane Caddesi, and has its own seaside diving platform, restaurant and bar.

Cheapest **restaurant** is the unlicensed *Mevlana*, Elmalı Cad, offering simple kebab dishes. Otherwise *Smiley's*, at 11 Gursoy Sok, also offers good simple Turkish fare, as does *Oba*, behind the main post office – though at a price. *Chez Evy*, in the backstreets east of the waterfront at Terzi Sok 2, serves up an enticing blend of Turkish and French cuisine. The current crop of **bars** includes the *Red Post*, round the corner from *Chez Evy*, and the *Déjà Vu*, east of the harbour, which has live music. For **Internet** access, *Magicomm* and *Net House* are beside the post office.

East of Kaş: Demre, Myra and Andriake

A winding 45-minute drive beyond Kaş lies the river delta town of **DEMRE** (officially **Kale**), a rather scruffy citrus- and tomato-growing town afforded more attention by tour parties than it can really deal with. However, it is worth visiting for its **Church of St Nicholas** (daily 9am–7pm; $5) on Müze Caddesi. The saint's sarcophagus, left of the entrance, is not considered the genuine article, after relic hunters stole some of the saint's bones from the real one, which allegedly now lies under the floor (the bones are at last due to be sent back from Italy). The remains of the ancient Lycian city of **Myra** (daily 9am–7pm; $1), 2km north of the centre, make up one of the most beautiful Lycian sites, consisting mainly of a large theatre and some of the best examples of house-style rock tombs to be seen in Lycia. And the site of the ancient city's port, **Andriake**, now known as Çayağzı, 2km west of Demre, is also worth a visit, itself close to a minimally developed sandy **beach**; however, there are no minibuses, so you'll need to get a taxi. The substantial remains of the so-called **Hadrian's granary** are the most prominent feature of the site, built between 119 and 139 AD by the Emperor Hadrian and consisting of eight rooms constructed of well-fitting blocks, the outer walls still standing to their original height on the far bank of the stream running parallel to the road to the beach. Above the main gate are busts of Hadrian and a woman who is thought to be the Empress Sabina.

It's best to treat Demre as a day-trip from Kaş, as decent **pensions** are few and far between. Best is the family-run *Kent* (☎0242/871 2042; ①), 2km north of the centre on the road to Myra. The closest **campsite** is the *Ocakbaşi*, at Andriake.

Olympos and Çıralı

Around 50km east of Demre is another Lycian city, **OLYMPOS**, an idyllic site (free access), located on a beautiful sandy bay and the banks of a largely dry river. Close to the beach are some recently excavated tombs with a quay wall, as well as a warehouse; to the east on the same side lie the walls of a Byzantine church; while further back, in the undergrowth, there is a theatre, most of whose seats have gone. On the north side of the river are more striking ruins, namely a well-preserved marble temple entrance. Beyond is a Byzantine bath-house with mosaic floors, and a Byzantine canal which would have carried water to the heart of the city.

A pleasant 1.5km walk away is the village of **ÇIRALI**. About an hour's well-marked stroll above the village's citrus groves flickers the dramatic **Chimaera**, a series of eternal flames issuing from cracks in the bare rock – you can put them out, but they will always reignite, since eleven percent of the gas mix issuing from deep underground is flammable methane. The fire has been burning since antiquity, and inspired the Lycians to worship the god Hephaestos (or Vulcan to the Romans) here. The mountain was also associated with a fire-breathing monster, also known as the Chimaera, with a lion's head, a goat's rear and a snake for a tail.

There are no banks in Olympos or Çıralı, so make sure you have enough cash before arriving. There are one or two **minibuses** a day from Antalya to Çıralı in season; otherwise you'll have to hitch or take a taxi ($10) from the main road. To get directly to Olympos, catch any Kaş–Antalya bus to the Olympos minibus stop on the main highway 8km up from the shore; there are minibuses down every 1–2 hours in season starting at around 7am. Çıralı now boasts around forty **pensions** ranging from the fairly basic to the frankly luxurious, all hidden in the citrus groves behind the beach – but the area is a National Park and nesting turtles mean that camping on the beach and night access is forbidden. A reasonably priced option is *Blue and White* (☎0242/825 7006, *bluewhite@tr.net*; ②) which offers spotless air-conditioned en-suite lodges; *Yavuz* (☎0242/825 7021; ②) is a moderately priced two-storey motel tucked inside a grove of poplars, all rooms ensuite. *Olympos Lodge* (☎0242/825 7171, *www.olymposlodge.com*; ⑨), offering a small taste of heaven with half-board, is located in a paradisal garden overlooking the beach. Back along the beach and ranged along the road behind the ruins are a group of backpacker "tree-house" camps, including *Kadir* (☎0242/892 1250, *www.olympostreehouse.com*; ③) and *Bayram's* (☎0242/892 1243, *www.bayrams.com*; ①); these offer a variety of huts and **Internet** access, but both can get fairly rowdy. The handful of beach **restaurants**, such as the *Orange*, the *Kadir* and the *Azur*, are simple and uninspiring; you'd do better eating in your hotel.

Antalya

Turkey's fastest growing city, **ANTALYA** (*www.antalyaonline.net*) is also the one metropolis besides İstanbul that is also a major destination. Blessed with an ideal climate and a stunning setting, Antalya has seen its annual tourist influx grow to almost match its permanent population, which now stands at just under half-a-million. Despite the grim appearance of its concrete sprawl, it's an agreeable place, although the main area of interest for visitors is confined to the relatively small old quarter; its beaches don't rate much consideration. The city also makes a good base for visiting the nearby ancient sites of Perge and Aspendos.

The intersection of Cumhuriyet Caddesi and Sarampol is the most obvious place to begin a tour of Antalya, dominated by the **Yivli Minare** or "Fluted Minaret", erected in the thirteenth century and today something of a symbol of the city. Downhill from here is the **old harbour**, recently restored and site of the evening promenade. North is the disappointing bazaar, while south, beyond the Saat Kalesi, lies **Kaleiçi** or the old town, currently succumbing to tweeness as every house is redone as a carpet shop, café or pension. On the far side, on Atatürk Caddesi, the triple-arched **Hadrian's Gate** recalls a visit by the emperor in 130 AD, while Hesapçı Sokak leads south past the **Kesik Minare** (Broken Minaret) to a number of tea gardens and the **Hıdırlık Kulesi**, of indisputable Roman vintage but ambiguous function – it could have been a lighthouse, bastion or tomb. The one thing you shouldn't miss is the **Archeological Museum** (Tues–Sun: summer 9am–6.30pm; winter 8am–5pm; $5), one of the top five archeological collections in the country; it's on the western edge of town at the far end of Kenan Evren Bulvarı, easily reachable by a tram which departs from the clock tower in Kaleiçi. Highlights include an array of Bronze Age urn burials from near Elmalı, and finds from an unusually southerly Phrygian tumulus. There's also second-century statuary from Perge, an adjoining sarcophagus wing with an almost undamaged coffer depicting the life of Hercules, a number of mosaics and a reliquary containing some purported bones of St Nicholas, not to mention an ethnography section with ceramics, household implements, weapons and embroidery and a small but well-thought-out children's section.

Practicalities

Antalya's main **bus station** is 8km north of town, although regular *dolmuşes* run from here to a terminal at the top of Kazım Özalp Cad, still known by its old name of Sarampol, which runs for just under 1km down to the Saat Kulesi on the fringe of the old town. A **taxi** from the *otogar* to the old town costs around $12. About 5km west of the centre is the **ferry dock**, also connected by *dolmuş*. The **airport** is around 10km northeast; Havaş buses into town depart from the domestic terminal, five minutes' walk from the international terminal, while city-centre-bound *dolmuşes* pass nearby. The main **tourist office**, a fifteen-minute walk west from the clock tower on Cumhuriyet Cad (daily 8am–7pm; winter closes 6pm; ☎0242/241 1747), provides free city maps but otherwise only very basic information.

Most travellers **stay** in the atmospheric old town, where almost every other building is a *pansiyon*, although there's also a nucleus of **hotels** between the bus station and the bazaar. *Sabah Pansiyon*, Hesapçı Sok 60/A (☎0242/247 5345; ①), is clean, well-run and the owner speaks English; book ahead in season. Near the Hadarlak Kulesi, the ageing *Hadrianus*, Zeytin Sok 4/A (☎0242/244 0030; ②) has a wonderful garden, but the rooms are musty.

There are unparalleled rooftop sea views from *Keskin 1*, Hadarlak Sok 35 (☎0242/244 0135; ③), and the family-run *Senem,* Zeytingeçidi Sok 9 (☎0242/247 1752; ②). *Keskin 2*, Hadarlak Sok 37 (☎0242/242 3941; ②), has no views but a nice orange garden in which to breakfast. The *Adler*, Barbaros Mahalle Civelek Sok 16 (☎0242/241 7818; ③), is one of the cheapest but most characterful of the old town pensions, with no en-suite rooms. Best of all is the *Antique Pansiyon*, Tuzcular Mah, Paşa Camii Sok 28 (☎0242/242 4615, *antique@ixir.com*; ②), housed in an old Ottoman building and boasting **Internet** access as well as an English-speaking owner. *Bambus* **camping** (☎0242/322 5557), 3km south of town on the Lara road, is expensive but has its own rocky cove for swimming.

Many Kaleiçi *pansiyons* have their own **restaurant**, and you may prefer to eat in rather than attempt to explore the limited and overpriced options. For elegant dining, *Antique Pansiyon's* evening menu is particularly good but you'll have to book in advance. Otherwise, the licensed *Parlak*, just off Sarampol Cad, mainly serves delicious grilled chicken – something of a local speciality – while the *Sim*, Kaledibi Sok 7, offers reasonably priced home cooking. Cumhuriyet Cad is the location of a number of eating-places with terraces offering excellent views of the harbour that are good for leisurely breakfasts. Southwest of the junction of Cumhuriyet Cad and Atatürk Bulvarı is the covered pedestrian precinct, Eski Sebzeciler İçi Sokak, which has recently been modernized and lost some of its atmosphere, but still has a small number of restaurants serving the local speciality *tandır kebap* (mutton roasted in a clay pot). The *Gaziantep* eatery, at the edge of the bazaar through the *pasaj* at İsmet Paşa Cad 3, is excellent. Two other quality choices are *Karadeniz Pideci* on Recep Peker Cad, which offers a good take on standard *pide* fare and *Ol Gunegliler,* just north of the clock tower, serving southeastern specialities. **Nightlife** is mostly located around the harbour and single men – even tourists – may well be refused admission. The popular *Café İskele* has tables grouped around a fountain, while the nearby *Cece* often has live music and *Club 29*, an expensive disco, boasts a terrace with pool and a restaurant. A little inland in the Kale district, *İçi Karatayhan Pansiyon* boasts the reasonably priced and laid back Gizli Bahçe bar. Further out, the *Olympos* disco, beside *Falez Hotel* near the archeological museum, is a popular late-night dance venue. There's an **Internet** café on Recep Peker Sok near Hadrian's Gate.

East of Antalya

East of Antalya lies an area known in ancient times as **Pamphylia**, a remote region that was home to four great cities – Perge, Sillyon, Aspendos and Side. **PERGE** is about 15km east of Antalya, reachable by taking a *dolmuş* to the village of Aksu on the main eastbound road, from where it's a fifteen-minute walk to the site (daily: summer 8.30am–7pm; winter 8am–5pm; $6, stadium free). Perge was founded around 1000 BC and is an enticing spot nowadays, the ruins expansive and impressive. Just beyond the site entrance, the **theatre** (closed) was originally constructed by the Greeks but substantially altered by the Romans in the second century AD; built into the side of a hill, it could accommodate 14,000 people on 42 seating levels. Northeast of here is Perge's massive horseshoe-shaped **stadium**, the largest in Asia Minor and excellently preserved. East of the stadium is the city proper, marked by a cluster of souvenir and soft drinks stands. Just in front of the outer gates is the **tomb of Plancia Magna**, a benefactress of the city, whose name appears later on a number of inscriptions. Inside is a **Byzantine basilica**, beyond which lies the fourth-century AD **agora**; southwest are some **Roman baths**, a couple of whose pools have been exposed. At the northwest corner of the agora is Perge's **Hellenistic Gate**, with its two mighty circular towers, the only building to have survived from the period. Behind, there's a 300m-long colonnaded street, with a water channel running down the middle and shells of shops on either side.

ASPENDOS (daily: summer 7.30am–7.30pm; winter 8am–5.30pm; $7) lies off the main road close to the villages of Serik and Belkis, accessible from Antalya by regular *dolmuş* during summer. The principal feature is the well-preserved **theatre**, built in the second century AD to a Roman design, with an elaborate stage behind which the scenery could be lowered. The stage, auditorium and arcade above are all intact, and what you see today is pretty much what the spectators saw during the theatre's heyday – a state of preservation due in part to Atatürk, who after a visit declared that it should be preserved and used for performances rather than as a museum – although during the Selçuk period it saw use as a *kervanseray*, and restoration work from that period (plasterwork decorated with red zigzags) is visible over the stage.

Side

About 25km east of Aspendos, **SİDE**, a ruined Hellenistic port and one-time trysting place of Antony and Cleopatra, was perhaps the foremost of the Pamphylian cities. The ruins of the ancient port just about survive; over the last ten years or so, the development of myriad theme-hotel complexes has obliterated areas of real archeological interest. The **beaches** are superb, but if you're more interested in the ruins, try and visit out of season.

Fortunately, the buildings and monuments that remain are still impressive. The **city walls** are particularly well preserved, with a number of towers still in place, and the **agora** is today fringed with the stumps of many remaining columns. Opposite the agora is the site of the former **Roman baths**, now restored to house a **museum** (Tues–Sun 9am–noon & 1.30–5pm; $5) with a cross-section of locally unearthed objects – mainly Roman statuary, reliefs and sarcophagi. South of here, a still-intact monumental gateway serves as an entrance to the modern resort and to Side's 15,000-seat **theatre**, the largest in Pamphylia, and supported by arched vaults rather than built into a hillside, unlike those at Perge and Aspendos. At the back of the theatre, reached via the agora, is a row of ancient toilets, complete with niches for statues facing the cubicles. To the **west** of town, the beach stretches for about 10km, lined by hotels and beach clubs, though the crowds can be heavy during high season. To the **east** the sands are emptier and stretch all the way to Alanya, though there's less in the way of facilities.

Buses from Antalya most often drop off at **MANAVGAT**, 10km east of Side; **dolmuşes** from the street behind Manavgat's *otogar* will take you to Side's new **otogar**, which is around 1km from the central waterfront, close to the monumental gateway. From here you can either walk, take a taxi or a tractor-drawn "tourist train" into the centre. Travelling on from Side, the best bus connections are from Manavgat.

Side's **tourist office** (summer daily 8am–6pm; winter Mon–Fri 9am–5pm; ☎0242/753 1265) is out of town, 300m from the *otogar*, but offers nothing other than a feeble map. **Accommodation** possibilities are endless, although Side is thronging with north European package tourists from mid-March onwards and *pansiyon* prices are relatively steep. Most options are in the warren of alleys east of the main street. *Morning Star* (☎0242/753 1134; ①) is friendly and has en-suite rooms, upper-floor ones with balconies; *Evin* (☎0242/753 1074; ①) has clean, bright rooms near the agora, beside the friendly *Yıldırım Pansiyon* (☎0242/753 3209; ①), with a shaded courtyard and pool table; while *Hanimeli Pansiyon* (☎0242/753 1789; ②) on Turgut Reis Sok offers en-suite doubles. For **camping**, there are a number of sites along the western beach, beginning about 500m from the theatre. There's no shortage of places to **eat and drink**: pricey *Charlies Restaurant* off Liman Cad offers locally caught fish and kebabs and nice views over the harbour; the better-value *Aphrodite* offers a variety of fish dishes including excellent swordfish. The *Apollonik*, just west of the temple of Apollo, is an atmospheric **bar**, while *Pasakoy Bar* on Liman Cad is notable as a masterpiece of kitsch. Further east, *Stones Bar* and *Barracuda* are louder and offer fine views out onto the Mediterranean. Side Internet Café is near the harbour.

Alanya

Until fifteen years ago, **ALANYA** was a sleepy coastal town with no more than a handful of flyblown hotels. Now it's one of the Mediterranean coast's major resorts, a booming place that has fortunately managed to hold on to much of its character and is much less crowded than Side, even in midsummer.

Most of old Alanya lies on the great rocky promontory that juts out into the sea, dominating the modern town, the bulk of which is occupied by the **castle** – an hour's winding climb or a short ride on an hourly bus from the tourist office. At the end of the road is the **İç Kale**, or inner fortress (daily 8am–sunset; $5), built in 1226 and virtually intact, with the shell of a Byzantine **church**, decorated with fading frescoes, in the centre. In the northwestern corner of the fortress, a platform gives fine views of the western beaches and the mountains, though this originally served as a springboard from which prisoners were thrown to their deaths on the rocks below. On the opposite side of the promontory, the **Kızılkule** ("Red Tower") is a 35m-high defensive tower that today houses a pedestrian **Ethnographic Museum** (daily 8am–noon & 1.30–5.30pm; $4), and has a roof terrace that overlooks the town's eastern harbour. Back down at sea-level, apart from the hotels and restaurants, modern Alanya has little to offer. On the western side of the promontory, the **Alanya Museum** (daily 9am–noon & 1.30–6.30pm; $1) is filled with local archeological finds and ethnological ephemera, though the best thing about it is the garden, a former Ottoman graveyard. Nearby, the **Damlataş** or "Cave of Dripping Stones" (daily 6–10am for asthma sufferers; daily 10am–sunset for others; $1.50), is a stalactite- and stalagmite-filled cavern with a moist, warm atmosphere said to ease asthma; it's accessible from behind the *Damlataş* restaurant.

Alanya's **beaches**, though not particularly clean, are at least extensive, stretching 3km west and 8km east. Finer sand and fewer crowds can be found 23km away on the road to Side at **İncekum** (meaning "fine sand"), still a beautiful spot despite recent bouts of hotel building.

Practicalities

Alanya's **bus station** is a twenty-minute walk from the centre, but if you come in by local bus from Side or Manavgat you'll probably arrive at the *dolmuş* terminal, five minutes north of the centre. The **tourist office** is at Çarşı Mahallesi, Kalearkası (daily 8.30am–5.30pm; ☎0242/513 1240), opposite the town museum. As in Side, **accommodation** soon fills up and prices can be high, although there's a concentration of *pansiyons* in the grid of streets between the bus station and the seafront. *Oba*, Meteoroloji Sok 8 (☎0242/513 2675; ②), is a good budget choice, as is *Üstün Pansiyon* on the same street (☎0242/513 2262; ③). Nearer the centre, behind Damlataş Cad, *Pension Best*, Alaaddinoğlu Sok 23 (☎0242/513 0446; ①), has immaculately clean rooms and apartments and a very helpful host. Two other central alternatives are *Hotel Günaydın*, Kültür Cad 26 (☎0242/513 1943; ①), and *Pansiyon Alanya*, Nergis Sok 4 (☎0242/513 1897; ①). **Campers** can head to the Forestry Authority-run *Orman Kamp*, 30km to the west, or *Perle*, 15km to the east. For **food**, the small streets running between Gazipaşa Cad and Hükümet Cad have lots of cheap *pide* and kebab places. Immediately north of here, *Burak*, Müftüler Cad, Kalgadam Sok 7, and *Buhara* and *Gülistan* on Kuyular Önü Sok offer excellent steam-tray and grilled food at very reasonable prices. *Kale*, overlooking the harbour, offers good food and views, at a price. My Donose Chatroom is one of a number of **Internet** cafés on İskele Caddesi.

CENTRAL TURKEY

When the first Turkish nomads arrived in **Anatolia** during the tenth and eleventh centuries, the landscape must have been strongly reminiscent of their Central Asian homeland. The terrain that so pleased the tent-dwelling herdsmen of a thousand years ago, however, has few attractions for modern visitors: monotonous, rolling vistas of stone-strewn grassland, dotted with rocky outcrops, hospitable only to sheep. In winter it can be numbingly cold, while in summer, temperatures can rise to unbearable levels.

It seems appropriate that the heart of original Turkish settlement should be home to the political and social centre of modern Turkey – **Ankara**, a modern European-style capital, symbol of Atatürk's dream of a secular Turkish republic. The south-central part of the country draws more visitors, not least for **Cappadocia** in the far east of the region, where water and wind have created a land of fantastic forms from the soft tufa rock, including forests of cones, table mountains and canyon-like valleys, all further hewn by civilizations that have found the area sympathetic to their needs. Further south still, **Konya** is best known as the birthplace of the mystical Sufi Muslim sect and is a good place to stop over between Cappadocia and the coast.

Ankara

Modern **ANKARA** is really two cities, a double identity that is due to the breakneck pace at which it has developed since being declared capital of the Turkish Republic in 1923. Until then Ankara – known as Angora – had been a small provincial city, famous chiefly for the production of soft goat's wool. This city still exists, in and around the old citadel that was the site of the original settlement. The other Ankara is the modern metropolis that has grown up around a carefully planned attempt to create a seat of government worthy of a modern, Western-looking state. It's worth visiting just to see how successful this has been, although there's not much else to the place, and the museums and handful of other sights need only detain you for a day or two at most.

Arrival, information and accommodation

Ankara's Esenboğa **airport** is 33km north of town. Havaş buses into the centre ($3) are timetabled to coincide with arriving Turkish Airlines flights; a taxi could set you back $30. The imposing new **otogar** lies around 8km to the southeast; some bus companies run service minibuses to the centre, otherwise take the **Ankaray** rapid transit system ($0.50), which will take you to Kızılay, in the heart of modern Ankara. To catch a *dolmuş* from the *otogar* to Ulus, where most of the budget hotels are located, follow the signs to the Ankaray station and ascend to street level. Otherwise you can change from the Ankaray onto the city's other underground system, the **metro**, at Kızılay and take this to Ulus. The main **train station** is at the corner of Talat Paşa Cad and Cumhuriyet Bulvarı, from where frequent buses run to Kızılay and Ulus.

City transport is no problem, with plenty of **buses** running the length of the main Atatürk Bulvarı. Buy bus tickets in advance from kiosks next to the main bus stops (it's a good idea to stock up on tickets, as in some areas of the city there are no kiosks). Ankara has two linked underground train systems: the metro runs from Kızılay northbound through Ulus, and the Ankaray cuts east to west with an interchange at Kızılay; tickets are interchangable between the two systems. There's a **tourist office** at Gazi Mustafa Kemal Bulvarı 121, just outside Maletepe station on the Ankaray (summer Mon–Fri 9am–6.30pm, Sat & Sun 10am–5pm; winter Mon–Fri 9am–5pm, Sat 9am–3pm; ☎0312/231 5572), but they can offer nothing other than a map.

Most of the cheaper **hotels** are in the streets east of Atatürk Bulvarı between Ulus and Opera Meydanı; there are a few more upmarket places north of Ulus, on and around Çankırı Cad, and clusters of options along Gazi Mustafa Kemal Bulvarı in Maltepe and on Atatürk Bulvarı south of Kızılay, with prices increasing as you move south.

Angora House, Kalekapısı, Kaleiçi (☎0312/309 8380). Pricey but beautiful renovated house in the old castle. The hosts are attentive and the rooms sumptuous. ⑨.

Buhara, Sanayi Cad 13, Ulus (☎0312/310 7999). One of the better choices in Ulus, with en-suites with TV. ②.

Devran, Opera Meydanı, Ulus (☎0312/311 0485). Small, clean en-suite rooms. ①.

Ergen, Karanfil Sok 48, Kızılay (☎0312/417 5906). Not a budget choice but very comfortable, with TV, aircon and all rooms en-suite. ③.

Güleryüz, Sanayi Cad 37, Ulus (☎0312/310 4910). Comfortable, but slightly shabby and distinctly over-priced. All rooms ensuite with TV. ③.

Mithat, İtfaiye Meydanı, Tavus Sok 2, Ulus (☎0312/311 5410, *www.otelmithat.com.tr*). Professionally run, offering single and double rooms with bathrooms and TV. ③.

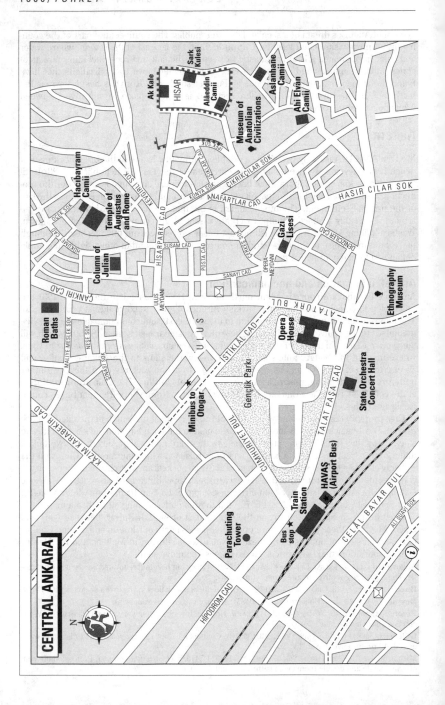

CENTRAL ANKARA

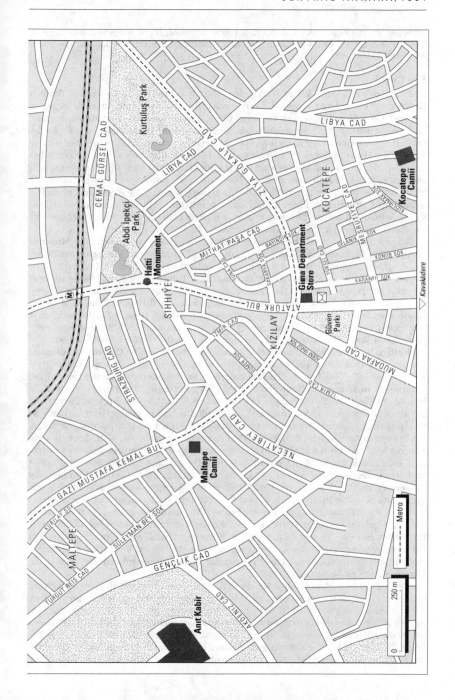

Olimpiyat, Rüzgarlı Eşdost Sok 1, Ulus (☎0312/324 3088). Reasonably priced with good en-suite rooms. ②.
Yeni Yavuz, Anafartalar Cad, Konya Sok 6, Ulus (☎0312/324 3255). Clean, presentable rooms with or without en-suite facilities. ①.

The City

Finding your way around Ankara is fairly easy. The city is bisected north–south by **Atatürk Bulvarı**, and everything you need is in easy reach of this broad and busy street. At the northern end, **Ulus Meydanı** (known simply as Ulus), a large square and an important traffic intersection marked by a huge equestrian Atatürk statue, is the best jumping-off point for the old part of the city, a village of narrow cobbled streets and ramshackle wooden houses centring on the **Hisar**, Ankara's old fortress and citadel. It was the Gauls who built the first fortifications on this site, but most of what can be seen today dates from Byzantine times, with substantial Selçuk and Ottoman additions. There are tremendous views of the rest of the city from inside, as well as an unexceptional twelfth-century mosque, the **Alâeddin Camii**. The **Aslanhane Camii** and **Ali Elvan Camii** bazaar areas to the south are more impressive, built by the Selçuks during the thirteenth century, with beautifully carved ceilings supported by wooden columns and intricately carved *mihrabs*.

Follow Kadife Sokak from here towards the modern city and you come to **the Museum of Anatolian Civilizations** (Tues–Sun 8.30am–5pm; $5), which boasts an incomparable collection of archeological objects housed in a restored Ottoman *bedesten*, or covered market, but offers frustratingly little in the way of explanation. Hittite carving and relief work form the most compelling section of the museum, mostly taken from Carchemish, near the present Syrian border. There are also Neolithic finds from Çatal Höyük, 52km southeast of Konya, the site of one of Anatolia's oldest settlements and widely regarded as the world's first "city"; early Bronze Age stag figures, pottery and vessels unearthed at Kültepe, near Kayseri; examples of Urartian metalwork; and Phrygian finds from the royal tombs at Gordion.

North of Ulus Meydanı is what's left of Roman Ankara, namely the **Column of Julian** on Hükümet Meydanı, erected in honour of a visit to Ankara by Julian the Apostate, who reigned briefly from 361 AD. Close by, the **Hacıbayram Camii** was erected on the ruins of the **Temple of Augustus and Rome**, built by the Phrygians during the second century BC in honour of Cybele. Today the remains of the temple wall on the square next to the mosque are about all that's left. The Hacıbayram Camii itself was built in 1400 by Hacı Bayram Veli, the founder of an order of dervishes, whose tomb in front is a popular place of pilgrimage. South down Atatürk Bulvarı, the **Gençlik Parkı** was built on the orders of Atatürk to provide a recreational spot for the hard-working citizens of his model metropolis; it features an artificial lake, funfair, cafés and an **Opera House** near the entrance (Atatürk developed a taste for opera while serving in Sofia in 1905). Further down Atatürk Bulvarı, the **Ethnography Museum** (closed for restoration at the time of writing) boasts rooms used as an office by the great man, as well as the usual collection of folk costumes and Ottoman art and artefacts.

Across the main west–east rail line lies **Sıhhıye Meydanı** and the real heart of modern Ankara, which focuses on the large square of **Kızılay**, the main transport hub of the city. A few streets east rise the four minarets of the **Kocatepe Camii**, a modern mosque built in Ottoman-style that ranks as one of the biggest in the world. Beyond lies Turkey's parliament building, a strip of embassies and the **Presidential Palace**, whose grounds are home to the **Çankaya Atatürk Museum**.

Northeast of here, **Anıt Kabir** is the site of Atatürk's mausoleum (daily 9am–5pm; winter closes 4pm; bus #265 from Ulus and near Tandoğan Ankaray station), at the end of a long colonnaded avenue lined by Hittite lions. A twentieth-century reworking of a Hellenistic temple, it's almost bare inside except for the forty-tonne sarcophagus and the guards who keep an eye on visitors to make sure they evince an appropriate degree of respect. Outside, on the left of the courtyard, is the sarcophagus of **İsmet İnönü**, Atatürk's friend and prime minister, who succeeded him as president of the republic. At the southeastern end of the courtyard is a **museum** (Sun 1.30–4.30pm) containing various pieces of Atatürk memorabilia, including a number of Lincoln limousines which served as his official transport.

Eating and drinking

There are some **bars and cafés** in the more affluent parts of town towards the southern end of Atatürk Bulvarı. A good starting point would also be Sakarya Cad in Kızılay where there are a number of decent watering holes in the neighbouring streets. Two worthwhile options are *Café Seven*, Reşit Galip Cad 57/A in Gaziosmanpaşa, a café/bar student hangout with live music in the evening and some snack food; and *London Pub*, 40 Arjantin Cad, Kavaklıdere, popular with richer students and professionals, and packed at the weekends.

Standard *pide* and kebab places can be found on just about every street in Ankara and there's an abundance of good sweet and cake shops, though really good **restaurants** are surprisingly rare. Ulus, particularly along Çankırı Cad, is a good place to look for cheap lunchtime venues, although most night-time eating and drinking takes place in the modern centre around Kızılay where a grid of streets comprising Sakarya, Selanik and Bayindir Soks harbours a range of possibilities, or further south in the well-heeled district of Kavaklıdere.

Altin Şiş, Karanfil Sok 17, Kızılay. A reasonably priced kebab place which does good puddings.

Çiçek Lokantası, Çankırı Cad 12A, Kavaklidere. One of Ankara's mainstays serving traditional dishes in regal splendour, albeit at a price.

Gaziantepli Fethi Bey Kebab, Sanaycilar Cad 35, Ulus. Good variations on standard southeastern specialities.

Hisar Kule, on the left inside the entrance to the Kule (☎0312/309 7898). One of several old-citadel restaurants in restored houses. Wonderful views from the terrace. Book ahead for evenings.

Hünkar kebap, Selanik Sok 16, Kızılay. Excellent place to savour *İskender kebap* dishes.

Kebabıstan, Karanfil Sok/Yüksel Cad, Kızılay. Plush kebab restaurant, offering all kinds of kebab including excellent mushroom *şiş*.

Körfez Lokantası, Bayındır Sok 24. Arguably the best restaurant in town, always packed, and serving good-sized portions of excellent, moderately priced Turkish food.

Samsun & Bafra, Selanik Cad 6, Kızılay. Great *pide* and friendly staff at the heart of the Kızılay restaurant quarter.

Listings

Airlines British Airways, Atatürk Bul 237/29 (☎0312/467 5557); THY, Atatürk Bul 231A (☎0312/419 2800).

Buses Most bus companies have offices on Gazi Mustafa Kemal Bulvarı, Ziya Gökalp Cad, İzmir Cad and Menekşe Sok, where you can buy tickets in advance.

Car rental Avis, Tunus Cad 68/2, Kavaklıdere (☎0312/467 2313); Europcar, Akay Yokuşu 25c, Bakanlıkar (☎0312/418 3430); Hertz, Atatürk Bul. 138B, Kavaklıdere (☎0312/468 1029).

Cinema Foreign language films are usually shown in the original language with Turkish subtitles. Most cinemas show mainstream releases with regularly changing programmes; try the six-screen Metropol, Selanik Cad 76, Kızılay.

Discos *Graffiti* and *Complex*, both on Farabi Sok, Çankaya.

Embassies Australia, Nenehatun Cad 83, Gaziosmanpaşa (☎0312/446 1180); Canada, Nenehatun Cad 75, Gaziosmanpaşa (☎0312/459 9200); Netherlands, Üğür Mumcu Cad 16, Gaziosmanpaşa (☎0312/446 0470); UK, Şehit Ersan Cad 46/A, Çankaya (☎0312/455 3344); USA, Atatürk Bulvarı 110, Kavaklıdere (☎0312/455 5555).

Exchange Most banks will change money for a 1–2 percent commission. Otherwise, try the many exchange *(döviz)* offices or the main PTT, open 24hr.

Hamams Karacabey Hamami, Talat Paşa Bulvarı 101 (men 6.30am–11pm; women 8am–7pm), dates back to 1441 AD. Prices start from around $5.

Hospital The Hacettepe University Medical faculty, just west of Hasırcılar Sok in Sıhhıye (☎0312/311 9393), normally has an English-speaking doctor available.

Internet Internet Evi, third floor Altın Çarşısı, Ziya Gökalp Cad.

Left luggage At the bus station and at the train station. Both charge $2 per piece.

Opera The Opera House at Opera Meydanı is usually less than $5 for lively and well-attended performances of works like *Madame Butterfly* and *La Bohème*.

PTT Main PTT is the Merkez Postahane, on Atatürk Bulvarı, Kızılay, just up from the Opera House in Ulus. *Poste restante* is at PTT, Eşref Bitlis Cad.

Cappadocia

A land created by the complex interaction of natural and human forces over vast spans of time, **Cappadocia** (*www.cappadocia.net*), around 150km southeast of Ankara, is initially a disturbing place, the great expanses of bizarrely eroded volcanic rock giving an impression of barrenness. It's in fact an exceedingly fertile region, and one whose weird formations of soft, dusty rock have been adapted over millennia by many varying cultures, from Hittites to later Christians hiding away from Arab marauders. There are more than a thousand rock-churches in Cappadocia, dating from the earliest days of Christianity to the thirteenth century, and some caves are still inhabited; the fields are still fertilized with guano collected in rock-cut pigeon houses; and pottery is still made from the clay of the Kızılırmak River. It's a popular area with tourists, and getting more so, but the crowds are largely confined to a few areas. Cappadocia's **airport** is near Tuzkoy, twenty minutes from Göreme.

The **best-known sites** are located within the triangle delimited by the roads connecting Nevşehir, Avanos and Ürgüp. Within this region is the greater part of the valleys of "**fairy chimneys**", which are formed when patches of hard lava have settled on top of the soft greyish bedrock (composed of compacted volcanic ash); the areas topped by lava chunks resist erosion, eventually forming 50m-high cones which dot the landscape. Also here are the rock-cut churches of the **Göreme** open-air museum, with their amazing selection of frescoes, and the **Zelve** monastery, a complex of troglodyte dwellings and churches hewn out of the rock. Nevşehir itself isn't much of a town, but it's an important travel centre, and while **Ürgüp** makes perhaps a more attractive base from which to tour the surrounding valleys, it isn't as well served by public transport. Outside the triangle to the south are the underground cities of **Derinkuyu** and **Kaymaklı**, fascinating warrens attesting to the ingenuity of the ancient inhabitants.

Nevşehir

Though said to be Turkey's richest town, **NEVŞEHİR**, at the very heart of Cappadocia, can hardly be accused of ostentatious wealth. It is the regional transport hub: frequent bus services all over Cappadocia run from here, and you'll probably find yourself detouring through when travelling between other apparently neighbouring towns.

The **Ottoman castle** at the heart of the old city, southwest of the modern centre, is a good landmark. The new city below is divided by two main streets, **Atatürk Bulvarı**, on which are situated most of the hotels and restaurants, and **Lale Caddesi**, turning into Gülzehir Caddesi to the north, where you'll find the main *dolmuş* station. The remains of the citadel are no big deal in themselves but the views are good. On the side of the hill, the impressive eighteenth-century **Damat İbrahim Paşa Camii** is set in a large precinct surrounded by narrow streets, and has a cool, dark interior enhanced by small decorative details. Opposite, the **Damat İbrahim Paşa Hamamı** (daily 6am–midnight; women only Wed 10am–4pm; men only at other times; $5) is also in good working order and well run. The **Nevşehir Museum**, on Yeni Kayseri Caddesi (Tues–Sun 8.30am–6pm; winter closes 5pm; $1), is worth the visit for a collection that includes three terracotta sarcophagi dating from the third to the fourth century AD, finds from the Phrygian and Byzantine periods, and Turkish carpets, kilims and looms.

The **tourist office** on Atatürk Bulvarı, on the right as you head downhill towards Ürgüp (summer daily 9am–5.30pm; winter Mon–Fri 9am–5pm; ☎0384/213 3659), will arm you with a hotel price list and a map. There's also a private information office near the bus station, run by a tour company. Local *dolmuşes* and those for the underground cities leave from the bus station. Several companies run **organized tours** of the area; try Agami on Lale Cad (☎0384/212 7854), or Rock City, Ürgüp Cad 39 (☎0384/212 0600, *www.rockcitytours.com*).
Pensions in Nevşehir are neither as cheap nor as good as elsewhere in Cappadocia. *Hotel Şems* (☎0384/213 3597; ①), on Atatürk Bulvarı next to the *Aspava Restaurant*, is comfortable and friendly. A step up, *Orsan*, Atatürk Bulvarı (☎0384/213 2115; ②), is comfortable and has

a swimming pool. Just opposite the *Orsan* on Yeni Kayseri Cad is the friendly and clean *Hotel Seven Brothers* (☎0384/213 4979; ②). The nicest of the **campsites** in the region, the *Koru Mocamp*, is signposted off to the right as you turn from Nevşehir into Üçhisar. For **food**, the *Aspava Restaurant*, Atatürk Bulvarı 29, serves well-prepared dishes, and the *Sölen*, just before *Hotel Şems* on Atatürk Bulvarı, has a good choice of *meze* and kebabs. The *Park-Bostan*, in gardens just off Atatürk Bulvarı, is more pricey but licensed. *Uzay Internet* is on Atatürk Bulvarı opposite the *Göreme Hotel*.

Derinkuyu and Kaymaklı

Among the most extraordinary phenomena of the Cappadocia region are the remains of a number of **underground settlements**, some of them large enough to have accommodated up to 30,000 people. The cities are thought to date back to Hittite times, though the complexes were later enlarged by Christian communities who created missionary schools, churches and wine cellars. A total of forty such settlements, from villages to vast cities, have been discovered, but only a few are open to the public.

The most thoroughly excavated is in the village of **DERİNKUYU** (daily: winter 8am–5.30pm; summer dawn–dusk; $4), 29km from Nevşehir and accessible by *dolmuş*. The city is well lit and the original ventilation system still functions remarkably well, but some of the passages are small and cramped. The size of this rock-cut warren is difficult to comprehend even on a thorough exploration, since only part of what has been excavated is open, and even this is thought to comprise only a quarter of the original city. The area consists of a total of eight floors reaching to a depth of 55m. What you'll see includes – on the first two floors – stables, wine presses and a dining hall or schoolroom with two long, rock-cut tables; living quarters, churches, armouries and tunnels on the third and fourth floors; and a cruciform church, a meeting hall, a dungeon and a grave on the lower levels.

Some 9km north of Derinkuyu on the Nevşehir–Niğde highway you'll have passed **KAYMAKLI** (daily 8am–6pm; Oct–Feb closes 5pm; $4). Smaller and less popular than Derinkuyu, only five of its underground levels have been excavated to date. The layout is very similar, networks of streets with small living spaces leading off into underground plazas with various functions, the more obvious of which are stables, smoke-blackened kitchens, storage spaces and wine presses.

Göreme and around

The small town of **GÖREME** is of central importance to Cappadocian tourism, principally because it is the best-known of the few remaining Cappadocian villages whose rock-cut houses and "fairy chimneys" are still inhabited. However, in the last few years these ancient living quarters have slowly been destroyed by development and tourism, which has led to a "Save Göreme" campaign to try to get the government to act in order to preserve the unique geology that has provided homes to the indigenous population for hundreds of years. It is still possible to get away from what is now essentially a holiday village, though, and the tufa landscapes are just a short stroll away. Göreme also makes a good base from which to explore the nearby attractions and sites. When approaching Göreme from elsewhere in Turkey, bear in mind that only two **bus companies** – Göreme and Nevtour – actually travel here direct. Other firms may sell you a ticket to Göreme, but will actually drop you off in Nevşehir, from where you'll have to continue your journey by local bus or *dolmuş* (the last of which leaves Nevşehir at about 6pm).

There are two **churches** in the hills above, the **Durmuş Kadir Kilisesi**, clearly visible across the vineyard next to a cave-house with rock-cut steps, and the double-domed **Karşıbucak Yusuf Koç Kilisesi**, which houses frescoes in very good condition. About 2km outside the village, the **Göreme Open-Air Museum** (daily 8am–6pm; winter closes 5pm; $5), up a steep hill on the road to Ürgüp, is the best known and most visited of all the monastic settlements in the Cappadocia region, the site of over thirty churches, mainly dating from the ninth to the end of the eleventh century and containing some of the best of all the frescoes in Cappadocia. Most are barely discernible from the outside, apart from a few small holes serving as windows or air shafts. But inside, the churches re-create many of the features of Byzantine buildings, with domes, barrel-vaulted ceilings and cruciform plans supported by mock pillars, capitals and pendentives. The best-preserved church is the **Tokalı Kilise** (Church with the Buckle), located away from the others on the opposite side of the road about 50m back towards the village. It's two churches, in fact, both frescoed, an **Old Church**, dating from the 920s, and a **New Church**, whose frescoes represent some of the finest examples of tenth-century Byzantine art. The best known of the churches in the main complex are the three columned churches, the **Elmalı Kilise** (Church of the Apple), the **Karanlık Kilise** (Dark Church; $10 extra) whose frescoes have recently been restored, and the **Çarıklı Kilise** (Church of the Sandals) – eleventh-century churches heavily influenced by Byzantine forms and painted with superb skill. Look, too, at the church of **St Barbara**, named after the depiction of the saint on the north wall, although most famous for the strange insect figure, the significance of which can only be guessed at.

Practicalities

At the time of writing there is no official **tourist office** in Göreme, although numerous private tour operators offer information; bear in mind that they're unlikely to be objective and may be taking commission for recommending accommodation. Cheapest of the **pensions** is probably the *Tuna Caves* (☎0384/271 2681; ②; April–Oct) which has cave rooms/dorms and a pleasant terrace, while the *Blue Moon*, just east of the *otogar* (☎0384/271 2433; ①), features immaculate ensuite rooms. Friendliest is the *Paradise* (☎0384/271 2248, *mbozlak @hotmail.com*; ①), which has constant hot water, some cave rooms and a cave bar, and the *Peri Pansiyon* (☎0384/271 2136, *peripansiyon@yahoo.com*; ②), unique and pretty with its high-rise chimneys – both towards the Open-Air Museum – and *L'Elysee Pension* (☎0384/271 2244, *elyseegoreme@yahoo.tr*; ②) which has clean simple rooms. For luxury try *Göreme House* (☎0384/271 2668; ②), just up a cobbled road behind the mosque, which has excellent ensuite rooms, central heating and a fantastic terrace. This place can be a real bargain in winter and some rooms even have jacuzzis. There are several **campsites** on the fringes of Göreme. The best are *Panorama*, 1km out on the Üçhısar road, and *Dilek*, on the *Ürgüp* road near the *Peri Pansiyon*, which is more sheltered and has a nice little restaurant. Both have swimming pools. There are a number of tour operators, bike, moped and car rental agencies at the bus station. There's **Internet** access at the *Neşe Café* next to the *Sedef*.

There is also plenty of accommodation in **ÜRGÜP**, a pretty old town with its own cave dwellings 5km east of Göreme. In some ways, this can make a more sophisticated alternative to Göreme as it has managed to accommodate tourism much better and still allows access to the more traditional aspects of Turkish life. Ürgüp's informative **tourist office** (summer daily 8.30am–7pm; winter Mon–Fri 8am–5pm; ☎0384/341 4059) on the main shopping street, Kayseri Cad, maintains an up-to-date price list of **hotels and pensions**. They also keep information on where current tour bargains may be had. There are several decent accommodation options on the way in from Nevşehir: the *Asia Minor* (☎0384/341 4645; ③), with its courtyard, is one of Ürgüp's most attractive buildings; the *Otel Melis*, out of the centre on the Nevşehir road (☎0384/341 2495, *rdvw@hotmail.com*; ③), has a variety of pleasant en-suite rooms ranged around a swimming pool; the *Sun Pansiyon*, behind the *hamam* on İstiklâl Cad (☎0384/341 4493; ②), has a few cave rooms reputed to be a thousand years old; and the *Yıldız Hotel*, just past the police station on the Kayseri road (☎0384/341 4610; ②), has basic, spacious en-suite rooms. There are numerous **tour operators** in Ürgüp; try Magic Valley, next to the bus station at Güllüce Cad 7 (☎0384/341 2145). *Kaya Bar* on Cumhuriyet Meydanı doubles as an **Internet** café.

Eating in Göreme can prove expensive, as almost everywhere caters only for tourists. *Hotel Ataman* harbours the best **restaurant**, serving everything from local specialities to French soufflés; the *Ottoman House* is another place to sample traditional cuisine. Among the handful of overpriced restaurants on the main road, *Sultan* serves vegetarian food and pasta while *Sedef* is more lively. Ürgüp's best restaurant is the *Şömine* in the central square, Cumhuriyet Meydanı (above the taxi rank on Suat Hayrı Ürgüplu Cad), serving well-prepared Turkish specialities. Another excellent and very affordable choice is the *Kervan* courtyard restaurant, serving quality Turkish home cooking. On Cumhuriyet Meydanı, *Kardeşler 2* offers an excellent vegetarian *güveç* (casserole). Cheaper options include the *Kardeşler Pide Salonu*, Dumlupınar Cad 13, which serves good *pide*, and the neighbouring *Kent*, with excellent *saç kavurma* (fried beef).

Around Göreme: Zelve

The deserted **monastery complex** in the three valleys of **ZELVE** (daily 8am–5.30pm; $4), a few kilometres north of Göreme off the Avanos–Çavuşin road, is accessible by an hourly *dolmuş* from Göreme. The churches here date back to before the ninth century, but until 1952 the valley was inhabited by troglodyte Turkish Muslims, who hacked their dwellings out of the tufa rock face. On the left-hand side of the first valley, about halfway up, are the remains of a small Ottoman mosque, the prayer hall and *mihrab* of which are partly hewn from the rock, and a large number of chapels and medieval oratories are scattered up and down the valleys, many of them decorated with carved crosses. A thorough exploration really requires a torch: some of the rooms are entered by means of precarious steps, others by swinging up through holes in the floors, and, on occasion, massive leaps to a lower floor – good fun if you're reasonably energetic and have a head for heights.

Konya

Roughly midway between Antalya and Nevşehir, **KONYA** is a place of pilgrimage for the entire Muslim world – the home of Celalledin Rumi or the **Mevlâna** ("Our Master"), the mystic who founded the Mevlevi or "Whirling Dervish" sect, and the centre of Sufic mystical practice and teaching. It was also something of a capital during the Selçuk era, many of the buildings from which are still standing, along with examples of their highly distinctive crafts and applied arts which are on display in Konya's museums. In recent years, Konya has developed a reputation as a hotbed of fundamentalism, though this now appears to be on the decline. As a result, although initially not a very appealing city of over half-a-million people, it's well worth a stop, especially if you're making your way down to the coast from Cappadocia.

The City

The **Mevlâna Müzesi** (Mon 10am–5pm, Tues–Sun 9am–5pm; $2) is among Turkey's more rewarding sights, housed in the first lodge (*tekke*) of the Mevlevi dervish sect, at the eastern end of Mevlâna Bulvarı, and easily recognizable by its distinctive fluted turquoise dome. The *tekke* served as a place of teaching, meditation and ceremonial dance from shortly after Rumi's death in 1273 until 1925, when Atatürk banned all Sufic orders. The main building of the museum holds the mausoleum containing the tombs of the Mevlâna, his father and other notables – as with mosques, shoes must be left at the door, women must cover their heads, and whether you're male or female, if you're wearing shorts you'll be given a skirt-like affair to cover your legs. It is permitted to take photographs of the **mausoleum**, but remember to be respectful; for some it is an extremely holy and venerated site. In the adjoining room, the original **semahane** (or ceremonial hall) exhibits include some of the musical instruments of the first dervishes, the original illuminated *Mathnawi* – the poetical work of the Mevlâna – and silk and woollen carpets, including one 500-year-old silk carpet from Selçuk Persia that is supposedly the finest ever woven. The latticed gallery above was for women spectators, a modification introduced by the followers of the Mevlâna after his death. In the adjoining room, a casket containing hairs from the beard of the Prophet Muhammad is displayed alongside illuminated medieval Korans. A separate building houses an exhibition of dervish memorabilia and some bizarre waxwork figures.

At the opposite end of Mevlâna Caddesi (later Alâeddin Caddesi, once west of Aziziye Caddesi) from the Mevlâna Müzesi, the **Alâeddin Parkı** is a nice place to stroll. This is the site of the original Selçuk acropolis and the source of finds dating back to 7000 BC, most of which are now in the museum in Ankara. At the foot of the hill to the north are the scant remains of a Selçuk palace, although you'd do better to head straight for the imposing **Alâeddin mosque** (daily 9.30am–5.30pm) begun in 1130 and completed in 1221, with an odd facade graced with bits of masonry from an earlier construction. Recently restored, the interior has distinctly Selçuk features like a network of wooden beams, and the remains of eight Selçuk sultans are enshrined in the courtyard. The nearby **Karatay Medrese** on Alâeddin Bulvarı (daily 9am–noon & 1.30–5.30pm; $1.50) is another important Selçuk monument, built in 1251 and combining elements such as Arabic striped stonework and Greek Corinthian columns with a structure which is distinctly Selçuk, its tall doorway surmounted by a pointed stalactite arch. Inside, the symmetrical design of the dome of stars forms a perfect backdrop for the **Selçuk ceramics** on display, which are covered with striking images of birds, animals and even angels. Behind its fine Selçuk portal the **İnce Minare Medrese**, below the park on Alâeddin Bulvarı, is also now a museum, featuring stone and woodcarving, with exhibits from the palace on the present site of the Alâeddin Parkı, but is currently closed for restoration. The other museum worthy of note is the **Museum of Archeology** (Tues–Sun 8am–noon & 1.30–5.30pm; $1) in the south of the city, containing the only pre-Selçuk remains in the city, including a few Hittite artefacts and three well-preserved Roman sarcophagi from Pamphylia.

Practicalities

Konya's new **bus station** is 10km out of town, from where the Konak *dolmuş* connects with the town centre; the **train station** is around 2km out of the centre at the far end of İstasyon Cad, connected to the centre by regular *dolmuşes*. The **tourist office** is at Mevlâna Cad 21 (Mon–Fri 8am–5.30pm; ☎0332/351 1074). Konya's better **hotels** are on or just north of Mevlâna Cad. The recently renovated *Otel Tur*, Esarizade Sok 13 (☎0332/351 9825; ②), is quiet, comfortable and friendly; the *Yeni Köşk*, Kadılar Sok 28 (☎0332/352 0671; ②), has clean rooms with en-suite facilities and is probably the best of the cheapish options; and the *Otel Çeşme* at Akifpaşa Sok 21, off İstanbul Cad (☎0322/351 2426; ①), has rooms with baths which can be bargained down except in December, during the annual Mevlâna festival, when many hotels fill up. It's worth also keeping in mind the reasonable *Bella Hotel*, Aziziye Cad 19 (☎0322/351 4070; ②). As for **eating**, the *Şifa Lokantası*, Mevlâna Cad 29, is popular and very reasonably priced and the nearby *Sema* offers reasonable kebab options. The *Tilsum Restaurant*, west of the centre on Meram Cad, serves excellent kebabs but closes early. The *Köşk* next to the Mevlâna museum serves local Konya kebab specialities and has live music. Express Internet is at 21 Alâeddin Bulvarı, and Online Internet at İnceminare Sok 81c.

travel details

Trains

Ankara to: İzmir (2 daily; 14hr).

İstanbul to: Ankara (5 daily; 8hr); Edirne (1 daily; 6hr 30min); Denizli (1 daily; 14hr 30min); İzmir (2 daily; 11hr); Konya (3 daily; 14hr).

İzmir to: Selçuk (6 daily; 2hr).

Buses and Dolmuşes.

Ankara to: Antalya (12 daily; 10hr); Bodrum (10 daily; 12hr); Bursa (hourly; 7hr); İstanbul (every 30min; 6hr); İzmir (hourly; 9hr); Konya (14 daily; 3hr 30min); Nevşehir (12 daily; 4hr 30min).

Antalya to: Alanya (hourly; 2hr); Antakya (1 daily; 12hr); Denizli (6 daily; 5hr 30min); Fethiye, by inland

route (3 daily; 4hr); İzmir (6 daily; 9hr 30min); Kaş (7 daily; 4hr 30min); Konya (6 daily; 6hr 30min); Side (3 per hour; 1hr 15min).

Ayvalık to: Bergama (8 daily; 1hr); Bursa (10 daily; 4hr 30min); Çanakkale (hourly; 3hr); İzmir (hourly; 2hr 30min).

Bergama to: Ayvalık (8 daily; 1hr); İzmir (12 daily; 2hr).

Bodrum to: Ankara (several daily; 13hr); Fethiye (6 daily; 4hr 30min); Marmaris (8 daily; 3hr 15min).

Bursa to: Ankara (hourly; 7hr); Çanakkale (hourly; 6hr); İstanbul (hourly; 5hr); İzmir (15 daily; 7hr).

Çanakkale to: Ayvalık (hourly; 3hr); Bursa (16 daily; 6hr); İzmir (hourly; 5hr 30min).

Datça to: Ankara (3 daily; 15hr); Marmaris (13 daily; 2hr 15min).

Denizli to: Antalya (8 daily; 5hr 30min); Bodrum (2–3 daily; 4hr 30min); Konya (several daily; 7hr 15min); Marmaris (6 daily; 4hr).

Edirne to: Çanakkale (2 daily; 4hr 30min); İstanbul (hourly; 3hr).

Fethiye to: Ankara (2 daily; 12hr); Antalya (8 daily; 4hr); Bodrum (6 daily; 5hr); Denizli (5 daily; 4hr); İzmir (every 30min; 7hr); Kaş (15 daily; 2hr 30min); Marmaris (10 daily; 3hr); Patara (10 daily; 1hr 30min).

Kuşadası to: Bodrum (3 daily; 3hr); Pamukkale (12 daily; 3hr 30min).

İstanbul to: Alanya (hourly; 14hr); Ankara (every 30min; 6hr); Antalya (4 daily; 12hr); Ayvalık (4 daily; 9hr); Bodrum (4 daily; 12hr); Bursa (hourly; 5hr); Çanakkale (hourly; 5hr 30min); Datça (1 daily; 17hr); Denizli (hourly; 15hr); Fethiye (hourly; 15hr); İzmir (hourly; 10hr); Göreme (5 daily; 12hr 30min); Kuşadası (3 daily; 11hr); Marmaris (4 daily; 13hr); Nevşehir (3 daily; 12hr); Side (1 daily; 13hr); Ürgüp (5 daily; 12hr 30min); Konya (7 daily; 11hr).

İzmir to: Ankara (8 daily; 9hr); Antalya (8 daily; 8hr 30min); Ayvalık (every 30min; 2hr 30min); Bergama (hourly; 2hr); Bodrum (hourly; 4hr); Bursa (6 daily; 7hr); Çanakkale (4 daily; 5hr 30min); Çeşme (every 15–20min; 1hr 30min); Datça (hourly; 7hr); Denizli (hourly; 4hr); Fethiye (12–18 daily; 7hr); Kuşadası (every 30min; 1hr 40min); Marmaris (hourly; 5hr); Selçuk (every 20min; 1hr 20min).

Kaş to: Antalya (6 daily; 5hr); Bodrum (3 daily; 7hr); Fethiye (8 daily; 2hr 30min); Marmaris (4 daily; 4hr 30min); Pamukkale (2 daily; 10hr); Patara (10 daily; 1hr).

Marmaris to: Ankara (14 daily; 13hr); Bodrum (8 daily; 3hr 15min); Dalaman (hourly; 1hr 30min); Denizli (6 daily; 4hr); Fethiye (10 daily; 3hr).

Nevşehir to: Antalya (1 daily; 11hr); İzmir (1 daily; 12hr); Konya (4 daily; 3hr); Marmaris (1 daily; 14hr).

Selçuk to: Bodrum (hourly; 3hr); İzmir (hourly; 1hr); Kuşadası (every 30min; 40min).

Domestic Ferries

Çanakkale to: Eceabat (hourly; 20min).

Datça to: Bodrum (April–Oct 2 daily; 2hr).

Gelibolu to: Lapseki (15 daily; 20min).

İzmir to: İstanbul (1 weekly; 19hr).

Kilitbahir to: Çanakkale (hourly; 10min).

INDEX

España
THE ROUGH GUIDE TO
Andalucía
Spain
THE ROUGH GUIDE TO
Spai
Mark Ellingham and
THE ROUGH GUIDE TO
Barcelona
THE ROUGH GUIDE TO
Mallorca
Madrid
MINI ROUGH GUIDE
Simon Baskett
THE MINI ROUGH GUIDE TO
Tenerife
Christian Williams

The ideas expressed in this code were developed by and for independent travellers.

Learn About The Country You're Visiting
Start enjoying your travels before you leave by tapping into as many sources of information as you can.

The Cost Of Your Holiday
Think about where your money goes - be fair and realistic about how cheaply you travel. Try and put money into local peoples' hands; drink local beer or fruit juice rather than imported brands and stay in locally owned accommodation. Haggle with humour and not aggressively. Pay what something is worth to you and remember how wealthy you are compared to local people.

Embrace The Local Culture
Open your mind to new cultures and traditions. Think carefully about what's appropriate in terms of your clothes and the way you behave. You'll earn respect and be more readily welcomed by local people. Respect local laws and attitudes towards drugs and alcohol that vary in different countries and communities. Think about the impact you could have on them.

Exploring The World – The Travellers' Code
Being sensitive to these ideas means getting more out of your travels - and giving more back to the people you meet and the places you visit.

Minimise Your Environmental Impact
Think about what happens to your rubbish - take biodegradable products and a water filter bottle. Be sensitive to limited resources like water, fuel and electricity. Help preserve local wildlife and habitats by respecting rules and regulations, such as sticking to footpaths and not standing on coral.

Don't Rely On Guidebooks
Use your guidebook as a starting point, not the only source of information. Talk to locals, then discover your own adventure!

Be Discreet With Photography
Don't treat people as part of the landscape, they may not want their picture taken. Ask first and respect their wishes.

Tourism Concern works with people the world over to promote tourism that benefits their communities, but we can only carry on our work with the support of people like you. For membership details or to find out how to make your travels work for local people and the environment,
visit our website

TourismConcern
Campaigning for Ethical and Fairly Traded Tourism

www.tourismconcern.org.uk

Will you have enough stories to tell your grandchildren?

Yahoo! Travel

DO YOU YAHOO!?

Lost cash.

One travel adventure you can live without.

Travel smart.
Carry American Express® Travelers Cheques.
They're safer than cash.

Whether you're surfing Baja, backpacking Europe, or just getting away for the weekend, American Express Travelers Cheques are the way to go. They're accepted virtually everywhere around the world — at hotels, stores, and restaurants. Simply sign the Cheques and use them as you would cash.

American Express Travelers Cheques never expire. And if they're lost or stolen, they can be replaced quickly — usually within 24 hours. Pick them up at any participating American Express Travel Service location, bank, credit union, or AAA office.

American Express Travelers Cheques.
Don't leave home without them.®

Travelers Cheques